THE ULTIMATE RED SOX COMPANION

Edited by
Gary Gillette and Pete Palmer

Matt Silverman, managing editor

Greg Spira, Doug White, and Stuart Shea, associate editors

MAPLE STREET PRESS

HINGHAM, MASSACHUSETTS

Maple Street Press LLC is in no way affiliated with Major League Baseball, or any minor league affiliates. The opinions expressed in this book are those of the author and not necessarily those of Maple Street Press.

Cover design: Garrett Cullen

Front Cover photos, left to right: Photo File/MLB Photos via Getty Images, Al Martin/MLB Photos via Getty Images, JOHN MOTTERN/ AFP/Getty Images

Interior design: Scribe, Inc.

Gary Gillette and Pete Palmer. *The Ultimate Red Sox Companion*

ISBN: 978-1-934186-02-2

Library of Congress Control Number: 2007928646

Maple Street Press LLC
11 Leavitt Street
Hingham, MA 02043
www.maplestreetpress.com

Printed in Canada
07 7 6 5 4 3 2 First Edition

*This book is respectfully dedicated to the fans of Red Sox Nation,
whose consuming passion for their team for more than a century has
helped make the National Pastime the greatest game in the world.*

◖◗ ◖◗ ◖◗

ACKNOWLEDGEMENTS

The editors acknowledge help or inspiration from the following good folks, all of whom contributed to this work in some important way: Dave Bird, Sean Forman, Jim Golen, Richard Johnson, Sean Lahman, Rod Nelson, Bill Nowlin, David Pietrusza, Todd Radom, Tom Ruane, Matt Spengler, Glenn Stout, Frank Williams, and Kimon Zachary.

We also tip our Sox caps to Ned Martin, Sherm Feller, and Pumpsie Green—gone but not forgotten.

Jointly and severally, the editors pledge allegiance to the sometimes unsung spice of our lives—namely Vicki Gillette, Debbie Silverman, Beth Palmer, Anita White, and Cecilia Garibay. Without their constant support, our books might not get done and our lives might not be worth living.

Finally, the editors express their gratitude to Maple Street Press publisher Jim Walsh for his vision and patience. As the publishing industry has consolidated tremendously in recent years, the role of independent publishers has become critical in producing high-quality work.

FOREWORD

The Ultimate Red Sox Companion is just what its title promises—a definitive historical document, a treasure trove of memories, a keepsake for the die-hahds. All the names are here, all the stats, all the greatest games, as listed by the authors. There's even a chapter on the team's radio history.

Gary Gillette and Pete Palmer, authors of the *ESPN Baseball Encyclopedia*, show their well-established love for the game and trademark attention to detail. So, find a comfy chair, open the book and savor the history. The Nation is more than a collection of fans; it's a collective state of mind. A state of mind captured magically in this book.

Ken Rosenthal
Senior Baseball Writer, FOXSports.com
May 2007

INTRODUCTION

To everything/turn, turn, turn
There is a season/turn, turn, turn

—Pete Seeger, lyrics for *Turn! Turn! Turn!*
(based on the Book of Ecclesiastes)

Welcome to the new *Ultimate Red Sox Companion*. As longtime Boston fans can and will tell anyone in the vicinity, there has been a season for literally *everything* for the loyal members of Red Sox Nation.

The *Companion* was modeled after our successful *ESPN Baseball Encyclopedia*, published by Barnes & Noble Publishing/Sterling since 2004. We have tried to put together as complete a history of the Red Sox as possible at an affordable price, packing as much information as we could into 416 pages.

The Lineup. Leading off is, naturally enough, a section covering the history of the Red Sox, followed by rundowns of the 50 greatest games in franchise history and then biographies of the greatest BoSox. It covers every era, the great moments and the tragic, in the always exhilarating New England saga that is the Red Sox.

The heart of the order and the core of any baseball encyclopedia, of course, are the player registers. Our batter and pitcher registers include year-by-year statistics for every player who has appeared in a regular-season game in a Boston uniform since the club's inception in 1901. If a player spent a large portion of his career in Boston, we also show his year-by-year stats with other clubs.

Along with sections such as All-Stars, coaches, managers, single-season and career leaders, plus complete rosters for every season, this book features an in-depth postseason section with composite boxes for each series for both the Red Sox and their opponents, as well as the

American League standings and league leaders for every year since 1901. Rounding out the *Ultimate Red Sox Companion* lineup is a variety of special features that are either unique or are not included in other baseball encyclopedias:

- All Red Sox owners and GMs with their won-lost records;
- Boston radio and TV broadcasters for each season;
- A complete list of Red Sox minor league farm clubs;
- All players picked in the amateur draft by the Red Sox since 1965;
- A selection of the best and worst trades and free agent signings in Boston history;
- A complete list of trades, player sales, and free agent signings by the Sox;
- A comprehensive section on awards won and honors bestowed on Red Sox players;
- Great performances by Boston heroes over the years; and
- A look at the history of that beloved and enduring institution, Fenway Park.

Because an encyclopedia is first and foremost a historical record, this book was written and edited from a neutral standpoint. So readers looking for BoSox-centric material will find plenty of it between these covers, but those looking for overt hometown bias will be disappointed.

If the other 29 teams had a fan base that was as literate, as passionate, and as involved as Boston's, our National Game would be a hell of a lot stronger. Nevertheless, despite Pete Seeger's mellifluous assertion that there is a time for peace, I swear it really is too late for pacific relations between Red Sox Nation and the Yankees' Empire.

Standards

One of the most precious aspects of the history of our National Pastime is its well-documented history and its treasure-trove of statistics. And a critical factor in keeping baseball fans fascinated with that long history is the incredibly high standards of accuracy present in most of that documentation and in most of those statistics.

We go to enormous lengths to ensure that our scholarship is the best in the field, constantly working on filling in gaps in our knowledge. And we benefit from being active participants in a generous community of like-minded historians and researchers—many of them members of the Society for American Baseball Research (*www.SABR.org*).

Accuracy

Despite the widespread belief that historical baseball statistics were graven in stone and handed down from the top of Mount Macmillan, the more prosaic truth is that all databases covering well more than a century are going to have errors in them. We try to be realistic about this, recognizing the limits of our knowledge while not ignoring opportunities to vet our data.

If you want to see a detailed discussion about how baseball statistics are researched and why they can change over time, please check out the introduction of the *ESPN Baseball Encyclopedia*.

Every statistic and piece of information in this book is accurate to the best of our knowledge. We understand, however, that we are not infallible and that mistakes unfortunately creep into all reference works. If you find a mistake, including omissions of relevant information, please don't hesitate to contact us.

Feedback

If you have any questions, comments, or suggestions—including criticism—for us, you can find a feedback form on the Maple Street Press web site at www.*Maple Street Press.com/feedback*.

—*Gary Gillette*

TABLE OF CONTENTS

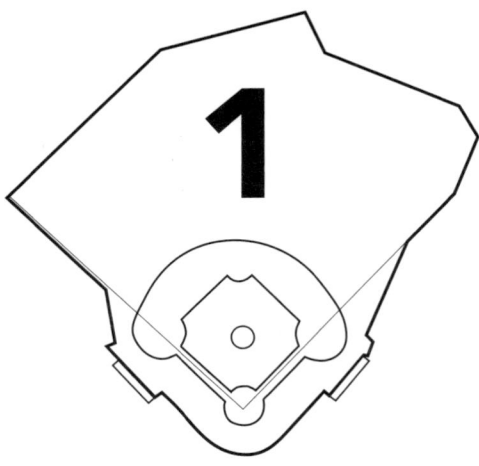

HISTORY OF THE RED SOX

Though many cities, states, and regions assert to being hotbeds of professional baseball, no place can supersede the claim to the game made by Boston, Massachusetts, New England. In 1871, the first year of the first professional league in baseball history, the Boston Red Stockings scored 401 runs, the most of any club in the inaugural year of the National Association. While these Red Stockings became the Boston Braves, who later moved to Milwaukee and then Atlanta, Boston has retained a professional club for each of the 135 years since.

Boston's American League team has, with rare exception, never been second fiddle in its hometown. From the fledgling league's beginning in 1901, the American League nine has always captured the fancy of the Boston sporting fan. Local wags tried to attach a variety of nicknames to the club in its early years—Americans, Somersets, Pilgrims, Puritans, Plymouth Rocks, and Speedboys—but none of them stuck, so for consistency's sake, this book shall refer to the club as the Red Sox, as everyone has known them since 1907. The Red Sox are so ingrained in the regional culture from New Haven, Connecticut, to New Sweden, Maine, it is hard to imagine Boston without its beloved Sox.

Yet Ban Johnson's intention heading into 1901 wasn't to have a team in Boston; he eyed Buffalo instead. The National League's snubbing of the AL president at a meeting that winter, along with the NL's support of a third major league, the American Association, made Johnson follow through on his plans to go head-to-head with the senior circuit in its Boston stronghold. Wealthy

Ohio coal dealer Charles Somers provided financial backing for Johnson's bold venture in Boston and a number of other cities, including Cleveland, Chicago, and Philadelphia.

The club that came to be known as the Red Sox, New England's heart and soul, lost their first game, 10–6, to the Baltimore Orioles, who would move to New York after the following season and become their arch-nemesis, the Yankees. Win Kellum, a rookie, lost that first game on April 26, 1901; he started just five more times for Boston. When the club arrived at Huntington Avenue Grounds for its first home game on May 8, a reported 11,500 came to see Cy Young beat the Athletics, 12–4. The NL Braves, playing nearby at South End Grounds and charging 50 cents to the 25 cents asked by the Red Sox, drew only about 2,000. The Sox doubled the attendance of the NL club that first year and had the best home winning percentage of any team in either league at .710 (49–20). The Red Sox finished second to the White Sox for the first pennant, but they'd delivered a knockout punch to their local competition. Pennants would follow.

Cy Young won 93 games his first three seasons with the club, leading the league each season. Young brought legitimacy to the franchise and the league from the start. He'd already won 300 games in the National League before he hopped to the upstart league for $3,500 in 1901. Young was considered old at 34. In 1903 he achieved a singular feat by winning three 1–0 games in eight days. (The first win put Boston in first place to stay, and he drove in the only run of the third game.) He led

the league in shutouts, innings, and wins, and was the choice to start the first game of the World Series. Young lost that historic start in Boston, but he beat the Pirates twice and Bill Dinneen won three times as the first modern world championship went to Boston.

The 1904 team is often forgotten because it had the misfortune of being the only American League club for 90 years to have the league's best record and not get the chance to play for a World Series title. It was a hard-fought pennant and satisfying at that, won on the last day of the year against the pitcher with the most wins in a season of anyone in league history, and it happened, best of all, in New York. Jimmy Collins, Boston's manager and third baseman, had a team with a half-game lead heading into a unique five-game series with New York to end the season: Friday in New York, a Saturday doubleheader back in Boston, and—since no games were played Sunday—two more to finish the season on Monday. Boston lost the first game but came back the next day to sweep behind Dinneen and Young. If New York swept the doubleheader Monday, however, they'd still take the pennant. The Highlanders (sounds much less menacing than Yankees, doesn't it?) pitched Jack Chesbro, who'd won his 41st game of the season Friday before being hammered Saturday. Chesbro uncorked one of his fabled spitballs over the catcher's head to bring in the go-ahead run in the first game of the deciding twinbill. New York City still got the last laugh as the Giants decided not to play a World Series against the upstart American League.

There were no more pennants for the Red Sox this decade. The club went through three different owners in its first three years, Cy Young retired (eventually), and the team had its first losing season (105 losses in '06). By 1912 the Red Sox had moved into a home that would become melded into the psyche of New Englanders for more than four generations...in good times and in bad.

An Era of Greatness

General Charles H. Taylor, publisher of the *Boston Globe*, and son, John Irving, had bought the team from Milwaukee attorney Henry Killilea in 1904. The Taylors located talent and kept it in Boston. Tris Speaker, a raw cow-puncher from Texas, went begging for a team to take him; the Red Sox played him a few games in 1908, and ancient Cy Young, a master with the fungo bat, hit him balls by the hundreds. Speaker learned how to anticipate where each ball was going to go before it was hit, honing a technique and a style that made him the greatest center fielder of his day. He won the center field job in 1909 and became the franchise's first superstar hitter. Joe Wood, an 18-year-old smoke-throwing kid who grew up in western mining towns, signed for $7,000 in 1908. He learned how to handle the big leagues with the help of Speaker, his roommate.

Ban Johnson took an indirect hand at running the Red Sox himself, with hand-picked ownership that took control in 1911. Former ballplayer Jimmy McAleer and AL secretary Robert McRoy bought 50 percent of the team from the Taylors; John Taylor remained as vice president. The Red Sox had played a dozen seasons at Huntington Avenue Grounds and had some remarkable moments—the first World Series and Cy Young throwing the American League's first perfect game in 1904 topping the list—but the club wanted to accommodate more people and allow them to enjoy the game without smoke billowing in from the train yard nearby and protecting them from fire, which had razed several wooden ballparks in the first decade of the century. Even then, open land in Boston wasn't plentiful, but a piece of reclaimed swampland was available about a mile from the Huntington Avenue Grounds. Over the winter of 1912 this constricted plot transformed from swamp to fabled ballpark that was completed in time for Opening Day at a cost of $650,000. And then it rained. For two days. Boston's new park wound up opening the same day as the rebuilt stadium in Detroit (later called Tiger Stadium). The 11-inning Red Sox victory over New York had to fight for space in Taylor's paper with the sinking of the Titanic. Fenway Park—thus called for the area's marshes, or fens—was open for business.

Fenway Park always had a tall fence in left field because of an adjoining street and railroad tracks just beyond it. The original 25-foot wall was covered with billboards and faced a cliff, Duffy's Cliff. The cliff was actually an incline caused by the low field and the height of Landsdowne Street behind it. The area was manned and mastered by Red Sox left fielder Duffy Lewis, part of the "Million Dollar Outfield." By 1912 the Red Sox had Lewis in left, Speaker in center, and Harry Hooper, another superb fielder, in right. While the million bucks may have been an exaggeration—given the era and the fact that they were later sold off for a windfall of $70,000 plus several dispensable players—the trio's value on the field was immeasurable. They constituted three of the first four hitters in the lineup, with second baseman Sam Yerkes batting second, and the trio accumulated 90 steals, batted .303 (Speaker carried the load at .383), knocked 160 extra-base hits, and scored 319 of Boston's 800 runs. Wood, now known as Smoky Joe, did the rest. He won 34 times, including 16 in a row to tie Walter Johnson's record—beating the Big Train in a legendary showdown—as the Red Sox set a still-unparalleled team mark with 105 wins and a .691 winning percentage.

In what can fairly be called the most exciting World Series ever won by the Red Sox—or just about anyone

else—Boston and the New York Giants went toe to toe for eight games. The extra game was played because of a tie in Game 2, the most electrifying game of the Series...until Game 8. Wood started three times in the Series and entered Game 8 in relief after pinch hitter Olaf Henriksen singled in the tying run. Hugh Bedient was actually Boston's most effective pitcher in the Series, beating Christy Mathewson in Game 5 while posting an ERA of 1.00 in 18 innings, but he was wisely lifted for Henriksen when the Sox had a chance to tie the do-or-die game. The Giants scored off Wood in the 10th, but pinch hitter Clyde Engle's fly ball was dropped by Giants center fielder Fred Snodgrass leading off the bottom of the inning. Snodgrass followed his infamous "muff" by robbing the next batter, Hooper, with a spectacular catch, as Engle took third. After a walk to Yerkes, Mathewson got Speaker to pop up. Three Giants watched the ball drop in foul territory and Speaker followed with a single to tie the game. Larry Gardner's long fly brought in the winning run. Matty was brilliant in his last World Series, but he lost twice. (Maybe it would have been different if he'd been in his prime, like he'd been in 1904 when the Giants decided they'd rather not play Boston, or any AL team, in the World Series.)

Jake Stahl, who'd been a little-used rookie for Boston in their last championship year in 1903, had been working at a bank when Ban Johnson talked him into returning to play and manage the Red Sox in 1912. He delivered all right, batting .301 after a year away from the game and winning a thrilling world championship. Still, club president Jimmy McAleer had several run-ins with Stahl and fired him in 1913 with the Red Sox in fourth place. McAleer was that way. He'd also rubbed Boston's Royal Rooters the wrong way with his ticket pricing and seat allotment during the World Series, which may be one reason for the half-full house for the dramatic Game 8 in 1912. McAleer, who'd known Ban Johnson since the league's early days and had helped raid players from the National League, was forced out by Johnson after the 1913 season.

While the change in ownership seemed somewhat disruptive for the Red Sox, things were actually setting up for a remarkable championship run. Hotelier Joe Lannin bought the club and stumbled on the greatest player in the game's history because 17 fans showed up for a minor league game in Baltimore. Jack Dunn, owner of the International League Orioles, had signed 19-year-old George Herman Ruth out of a nearby reform school. He'd even gotten a new nickname when Orioles veterans chastised the southpaw as one of Dunn's babes. But because the new major league, the Federal League, also debuted that year in Baltimore, Dunn's Orioles lost money hand over fist and he was forced to sell his top players. Dunn offered Ruth to

Connie Mack in Philadelphia—Cincinnati had its chance to acquire the young southpaw, too—but Lannin put down $25,000 and got the Babe. Ruth debuted with the club on July 11 and got the win when Duffy Lewis batted for him and came around to score the go-ahead run. Ruth won just once more that year, but he won 18 games in his first full season to help Boston claim the 1915 pennant.

Catcher Bill Carrigan, who'd been named manager to replace Stahl in 1913, had so much success with his staff that his pitchers were one through four in winning percentage in 1915: Wood (.750), Ernie Shore (.704), Rube Foster (.704), and Ruth (.692). Babe appeared just once in the World Series as a pinch hitter, but Foster, Shore, and Dutch Leonard started and completed every game and held the Phillies to a .182 average. The Red Sox won in five games.

It was the last appearance in a Boston uniform for Tris Speaker. A salary dispute led to Speaker and his .337 career average being sent to Cleveland, where he turned into an even better hitter. In 1916, however, the Red Sox were still so loaded that they plugged journeyman Tilly Walker into the middle of their lower-priced but still very effective outfield and won another pennant. Boston's fielding was the best in the game and the pitching wasn't far behind. Ruth had his best season—as a pitcher—winning 23 times in 41 starts with 9 shutouts and a 1.75 ERA, all tops in the league. Ruth threw a record 14 innings in his first World Series start and Ernie Shore beat Brooklyn twice. Boston rolled again in five games, and for the second straight October the Red Sox celebrated at Braves Field, where they'd set up shop in the World Series for a bigger gate. The next defection was Carrigan, who left the team to be with his growing family in his native Maine. He eventually returned to manage the club long after the ship had sailed in the 1920s.

Second baseman Jack Barry, purchased from the Philadelphia Athletics' White Elephant Sale in 1915, replaced Carrigan as manager in 1917. He managed the Red Sox to a 90-win season in his only year at the helm—Barry would later coach alma mater Holy Cross for 39 years—but Boston was a distant second to the '17 White Sox. Barry entered the military after the season in World War I.

Ed Barrow was chosen as the replacement after getting a strong recommendation from Ban Johnson. Hooper suggested that Barrow try Ruth in the outfield when he wasn't pitching. That idea worked out pretty well. Ruth tied for the lead with 11 homers and slugged a league-best .555 in the shortened 140-game season. Ruth won 13 games on the mound during the season, plus twice more in the World Series. He dominated the Cubs, running his consecutive scoreless streak in the World Series to 29 ⅔. Carl Mays also won twice as both

clubs struggled for offense. Boston scored nine runs in the six games and won the world championship with a .186 average. That title would have to last for a while.

The Red Sox, the first team to win a World Series, now had five world championships. Four other American League foes—the New York Yankees, St. Louis Browns (now Baltimore Orioles), Washington Senators (now Minnesota Twins), and Detroit Tigers—hadn't won any. That all these franchises would win multiple World Series before the Red Sox finally reached No. 6 is part of the unique nature of Red Sox fandom. And it is proof that baseball can be a cruel game indeed.

A Musical Death

Show business entrepreneur Harry Frazee purchased the Red Sox in 1916 and won two world championships in his first three seasons as owner. While the team slid to sixth in 1919, Boston still had the greatest slugger in the game, the same man who'd been the top left-handed pitcher in the game when Frazee bought the team. Despite his Broadway background, Frazee couldn't tell he had the biggest hit ever on his hands.

Ruth was as hard to deal with as the most petulant star in any musical. He'd been suspended for punching an umpire after walking the first batter in a 1917 game (Ernie Shore came in and retired every batter he faced in the most bizarre combined no-hitter on record). Ruth bristled against management and was once challenged to a fight by manager Ed Barrow (Babe backed down). Ruth's nightlife urges and excesses were already legend; he wanted more money to fuel them. His $10,000 salary from Frazee was half what Ruth thought he was worth now that he'd just set the major league mark with 29 home runs in a park that didn't favor left-handed sluggers. Ruth threatened to sit out the season if he didn't get what he wanted. At the same time, Frazee was pressed by the club's former owner, Joe Lannin, to pay a large portion of the purchase price the two had arranged in 1916. Frazee was friends with Yankees part owner Colonel T.L. Huston. Good news for Frazee's credit; bad news for Boston's credibility.

Ruth went to New York in a complex purchase for $100,000, nearly twice what Lannin had gotten for Speaker in 1915. Through the terms of the deal the Red Sox earned nearly $10,000 more, plus the Yankees helped Frazee secure a $300,000 loan...meaning that the Yankees essentially held a mortgage on Fenway Park! Further, these cordial relations between the clubs led to Waite Hoyt, Everett Scott, Joe Bush, Sad Sam Jones, Joe Dugan, George Pipgras, and Herb Pennock, among others, going from Boston to New York. Frazee

also let Ed Barrow leave to run the Yankees. Barrow proceeded to strip more parts from Boston, culminating in Red Ruffing going to New York in 1930 for Cedric Durst and $50,000.

The 1920s were the lost decade in Boston. The Red Sox did not win more than 75 games for 13 seasons. The club had three straight 100-loss seasons from 1925 to 1927, finishing last six straight years. Nine times in 11 years the club finished at the bottom of the American League. Predictably, Fenway was empty during this time and Bob Quinn, who organized $1.5 million to get Frazee out of the baseball business in 1923, was soon deep in debt. There was no way the team could make money given its situation. They would need someone willing to sink his pockets into the club and not expect to make a dime for a significant period. Enter Tom Yawkey.

Yawkey had been adopted by an immensely wealthy uncle after his father died. Eddie Collins, a coach with the Philadelphia Athletics at the time and an alumnus of Yawkey's prep school in Tarrytown, New York, casually mentioned the dire straits of the Red Sox one day during a hunting excursion. Yawkey, just coming into his inheritance at age 30, bagged the club for $1 million. He hired Collins to help him run the club and started spending.

Yawkey bought George Pipgras, who'd been sold by Frazee to the Yankees before his rookie year, and young infielder Billy Werber from New York for $100,000. It was a start. Yawkey bought Lefty Grove for $125,000, and plunked down smaller sums for shortstop Lyn Lary, pitcher Wes Ferrell, and outfielders Bing Miller and Doc Cramer. Along the way he got the manager he wanted in Joe Cronin, prying Washington owner Calvin Griffith's son-in-law away from the Senators for Lary and $225,000. While the sum was exorbitant, Cronin had already won a pennant at age 26 and was a power-hitting shortstop to boot. The 1935 Red Sox had their first winning season in 17 years during Cronin's initial year at the helm in Boston. That winter Yawkey got Cronin some protection in the lineup by bringing in the most feared right-handed hitter in the league: Jimmie Foxx. Despite excellent production from Grove and Foxx, the Red Sox actually slid back to sixth place. Yawkey resolved to put his vast resources toward the farm system.

The Yankees, meanwhile, surpassed Boston's record of five world championships in 1937. By this time most of the players they'd bought wholesale from the Red Sox in the 1920s were mostly retired and had been replaced by players uncovered by scouts. The Red Sox followed a similar trail. Boston looked west to its future and found it in Washington state (Johnny Pesky and Earl Johnson) and California (Bobby Doerr, Dom DiMaggio, and Ted Williams), with stops along the way in Texas (Tex Hughson) and Alabama (Jim Tabor).

With Jimmie Foxx piling up a club-record 175 RBIs and winning the 1938 MVP, the Red Sox had their highest finish in 20 years. Second place was still 9 ½ games behind the Yankees, but with talent nurturing in the minors—and an owner with no intention of selling it off—the fans started taking notice. The Red Sox drew the largest crowds since Fenway had opened and the most people to see the team play in three decades. The ballpark they came to was as state of the art as Fenway would ever get. Yawkey had refurbished the park in 1934 and made the entire place steel and concrete enforced two decades after it had gone up. He had the 37-foot high, 240-foot long fence built from 30,000 pounds of iron, and sank it 22 feet into the ground. Left field, former site of "Duffy's Cliff" was on the level, or at least closer to it. All they needed was a left fielder worthy of this grand stage.

Teddy Ballgame

Ted Williams actually did not play left field until his second year with the Red Sox. He burst on the scene at 19 and batted .327 with 31 home runs and league-high 145 RBIs. He walked 107 times, the first of 11 season hitting three digits in free passes. When he moved from right field to left, right field changed as well. The club moved the fence in 23 feet, exchanging the bullpens from foul territory to home run territory. Williams hit eight fewer home runs than he had as a rookie, but he would not hit fewer than those 23 home runs over a full season until 1959.

Bill Terry had batted .400 for the Giants in 1930, but no American Leaguer had reached that number since Harry Heilmann's .403 for the Tigers in 1923. Williams pursued the number all season with a sense of purpose even as the Yankees and Joe DiMaggio—he of the 56-game hitting streak that summer—pulled away to win the pennant with ease. The final day of the season Williams stood at .3996 and manager Joe Cronin offered for the Kid to sit out the season-ending doubleheader at Philadelphia's Shibe Park; that way he would go on the books with a rounded-up .400. With his John Wayne bravado, Williams played both games and went 6-for-8. Following his stated goal that he wanted to go down as "the greatest hitter who ever lived," Teddy Ballgame's .406 was the first and perhaps most lasting achievement to back up this boast.

Williams won the Triple Crown the next season as the Red Sox won 93 times, the club's highest win total since 1915. The progress of the past decade was put on hold as Williams and most every other star left to fight in World War II. The Red Sox were fortunate that all returned safe and sound. While some teams had All-Stars worn down by time and grueling battle conditions in Europe and the Pacific, the Red Sox returned ready to play ball and were the best team in baseball that summer.

Boston dominated the 1946 season, including the first All-Star Game at Fenway Park. Williams drove in five runs, scored four times, and hit two home runs, including his famous blast off Rip Sewell's "eephus" pitch. He hit another fabled home run, a 500-foot blast to right field that crushed a fan's straw hat (the seat is still painted red). The Red Sox were the only team to win in triple digits that year, their 104 victories just missed the 1912 franchise mark. Unlike the 1912 club, though, these Red Sox did not have someone watching over them and making sure that everything bounced their way in the last inning.

Williams, who led the league in runs, total bases, walks, on-base percentage, slugging, and was second in the league with a .343 average, batted just .200 against the Cardinals in the World Series. Dave "Boo" Ferriss, a 25-win pitcher, was knocked out in the fifth inning of Game 7. Dom DiMaggio's double tied the game in the top of the eighth, but Harry Walker's hit in the bottom of the inning brought in Enos Slaughter with the go-ahead run for St. Louis. Shortstop Johnny Pesky's brilliant season was forever marred by the press box aficionados' decree that his hesitation on the throw home cost Boston the Series. To add to the angst, the Red Sox got the first two runners on in the bottom of the inning yet could not push across the tying run.

The next year the Red Sox installed lights and created the Green Monster. Tom Yawkey removed the signs plastered on the left-field wall and painted it a green that drew every eye—and there were a record 1.47 million sets of eyes at Fenway that summer—to the ballpark's most obtrusive feature and its most obvious talent. Williams won the Triple Crown for the second time in three seasons (not counting the 1943–45 seasons spent in the service), and just as remarkable was that he again lost the MVP to a Yankee despite a superior year. DiMaggio, who'd beaten out Williams when he'd hit .406 in '41, won the '47 trophy by a single vote. Williams' difficulties with the Boston press didn't help in the post-season awards. He finished in the top 10 in the MVP voting 12 times, and though he won the trophy in '46 and '49, he did not win it the two times he won the Triple Crown. Williams and Rogers Hornsby remain the only players in major league history to win the Triple Crown twice.

With Joe Cronin promoted to the general manager's chair, former Yankees manager Joe McCarthy replaced him in the dugout. He had a .609 winning percentage in his two-plus years in Boston, but he didn't have much luck. The Red Sox battled the Yankees and Indians all

summer for the 1948 pennant. While Cleveland lost two of its last three games, the Red Sox swept a two-game series against the Yankees (what they would have given for that the next year). That set up the first one-game playoff in baseball history. McCarthy chose journeyman Denny Galehouse, 8–7 during the year, to pitch at Fenway. Cleveland's Lou Boudreau chose rookie workhorse Gene Bearden, looking for his 20th win that day. He got it. Boudreau hit two home runs to win the pennant and the Indians went on to beat another Boston club, the Braves, for the world championship.

The summer of '49 was even more frustrating. The Red Sox were the best-hitting team in the game, and had 25-game winner Mel Parnell plus 23-game winner Ellis Kinder. Boston held a one-game heading into the final two games of the year at Yankee Stadium with both pitchers rested and ready...and both lost. Boston was lousy on the road all season, going just 35–42 away from Boston as opposed to 61–16 at Fenway.

The promise of the 1940s faded in the 1950s as the club's youth grayed. The new decade belonged to the Yankees and their deeper farm system. New York won the pennant 9 out of 10 seasons; the Red Sox had some solid years but just couldn't keep up. Ted Williams was recalled to active duty as a Marine pilot in Korea. Sent off amid fanfare and melancholy during the 1952 season, his jet was shot down after a bombing mission. He crash-landed safely and escaped with only minor injuries. He returned to the major leagues exhausted in 1953, but just to show he was still the Thumper, he batted .407 with 13 home runs and .901 slugging in just 91 at bats. He hit .328 or better each of the next five seasons, becoming the oldest player to win a batting title in 1957 at age 38. He didn't miss .400 by much, finishing at .388 with an OBP of .528 plus .731 slugging. Mickey Mantle, who'd taken DiMaggio's place in center field at Yankee Stadium, finished ahead of Williams for the MVP.

Williams won the batting title for the sixth and last time in 1958, beating out teammate Pete Runnels in the final weekend of the season. (With a perfect left-handed swing for dinging balls off the Green Monster, Runnels would win batting titles in 1960 and 1962.) Shortstop Jackie Jensen won the 1958 MVP with a league-high 122 RBIs. Despite all the hitting talent, Boston still finished a distant third.

The Red Sox finally joined the rest of baseball and integrated in 1959. After turning a blind eye to numerous outstanding African American ballplayers, including Willie Mays, the Red Sox debuted utlityman Pumpsie Green on July 21, 1959, 13 months after the second-to-last club, the Tigers, had added an African American to their major league roster, and 12 years after Jackie Robinson had broken the color barrier in Brooklyn. This shameful record speaks for itself, but it should be noted that Green debuted after Joe Cronin left the organization to become American League president. While many said racism pervaded from management to the stands, Ted Williams was later the first to publicly call for African Americans to be welcomed into the Hall of Fame during his induction speech in Cooperstown.

The 1960 season was clearly the end of the line for Williams as a player. Several years earlier he thought about quitting because of injuries and incidents at Fenway—spitting and throwing a bat in the stands among the most notorious—but he put off retirement and was better off for it. A fan in Baltimore, Ed Mifflin, explained to Williams where he might end up on the all-time list if he played a while longer. Thanks to his resurgence after age 35, Williams met those numbers. He hit his 500th home run in Cleveland on June 18, 1960, joining Babe Ruth, Jimmie Foxx, and Mel Ott in that once-exclusive club. His last home run, however, was probably his most famous.

The club had a ceremony for Williams the day of his final game, September 28, 1960. He made his peace with Boston, saying the city had "the greatest fans in America," but he still had sharp words for the local press. His career ended in storybook style with a home run off Jack Fischer his last time up. He didn't tip his cap despite repeated ovations from the 10,454 at Fenway. John Updike's brilliant and adoring writeup, "Hub Fans Bid Kid Adieu," inspired yet more adulation of the Splendid Splinter. The Yankees were interested in bringing Williams back at age 42 just to pinch hit, but he turned them down. He'd already gone out his way.

"To Dream the Impossible Dream"

The Red Sox struggled in the 1960s, devoid of an identity now that Ted Williams had gone fishing for good. Even with the increase from 154 to 162 games, the Red Sox did not exceed 76 wins between 1959 and 1966. Eight different men took turns managing the club, including Johnny Pesky and Pinky Higgins. Local boy Tony Conigliaro was pure joy while the more polished Long Island product Carl Yastrzemski was all success through hard work. Joy met work in 1967, with tragedy on both ends.

General manager Dick O'Connell had assembled a talented young team in 1967. Yaz was the oldest regular at 27 and Dick Williams, 38, was a rookie manager taking over a club that had finished ninth the previous two years. Boston had improved to the middle of the pack by July 14 when they reeled off a 10-game winning streak, including a 6–0 road trip to Baltimore and Cleveland that vaulted them within a half-game of the White Sox. And there they stayed for the rest of the season as the

teams bunched up and pummeled each other in one of the tightest races in league history.

Although Tony C. was lost for the year when struck in the face by a pitch in a devastating moment at Fenway in August, the Red Sox filled in with several players in right field. Dick Williams constantly tinkered with the order except for one spot: Yaz at number three. He tore through American League pitching on his way to the second Triple Crown in the AL in as many years, but Yaz remains the last to achieve the feat to date in the major leagues. Besides his 44 homers, 121 RBIs, and .326 average during a down period for offense, Yaz also led the league in runs, hits, total bases, on-base percentage, and slugging.

Heading into the last weekend of the year, the Red Sox trailed by one game to Minnesota, with two games against the Twins at Fenway. Minnesota had beaten Boston 11 of 16 times, but the teams were even in the standings after Jose Santiago's win on Saturday. Sunday's starter Jim Lonborg was the league's best pitcher, and perhaps worst hitter, but his bunt ignited a rally in the sixth that started a decisive five-run inning. Yaz singled in the tying runs and finished the Twins set 7-for-8 with 6 RBIs. Lonborg was carried off the field by scores of fans in an incredible scene and the dream continued in the World Series. Lonborg threw a one-hitter in Game 2 (his no-hitter was broken up in the eighth), pitched superbly to win Game 5 in St. Louis, and then started the deciding game two days later. Bob Gibson was better and the dream ended.

Yaz batted .400 in the World Series, but the rest of the Sox hit .193. Yaz and 22-game winner Lonborg were the overwhelming choices for MVP and Cy Young, the only time two Red Sox have won the two awards in the same year. Lonborg missed much of the following year because of a ski accident and Yastrzemski's average dropped 25 points, yet he still won the batting title. His .301 average in "the Year of the Pitcher" was the lowest ever for a batting champion, but he spared the league the indignity of having someone win the batting title at .290 (the average of runner-up Danny Cater in Oakland). Ken Harrelson had a fine season with 35 home runs and 109 RBIs, as the Sox batted just .236 and still finished third in the league in hitting.

The mound was lowered and the league split in two in 1969, but the dominance of the Orioles transformed winning records in Boston into four third-place and two second-place finishes from 1969 to 1974. Their best chance was 1972, the one year in that period that the Orioles slipped. The first baseball strike lopped off a week or so worth of games; the Tigers played 156 games and the Red Sox 155. Boston came into Detroit for the final three games of the season holding a half-game lead. The Tigers won the first two and clinched the division title; a win the last day of the year left Eddie Kasko's club a half-game out and wondering what might have been if they'd played an even number of games. It spoiled a wonderful rookie year by Carlton Fisk, who batted .293 with 22 home runs to become the first unanimous American League Rookie of the Year.

In 1974, under rookie manager Darrell Johnson, the Red Sox had their best month in August and held a five-game lead over the Yankees and an eight-game bulge over the Orioles. The Red Sox fell flat, losing 18 of 29 games in September and watching the O's streak past for another division crown. One consolation for the brutal finish was that the Red Sox got to see a couple of young ball players make their debuts.

Slugging in the Seventies

Rookies Fred Lynn and Jim Rice, soon dubbed the "Gold Dust Twins," spent most of the 1975 season batting four and five in the Red Sox order, pulverizing AL pitching. The rookie ringers were much needed since Fisk missed much of the season, Tony Conigliaro's last comeback try ended sadly, and Rico Petrocelli, the slugging shortstop during the "Impossible Dream" and now the third baseman, had his least productive year in a decade. The players weren't in love with the manager, but won in spite of him. The pitching staff got 54 wins out of starters Rick Wise, Luis Tiant, and Bill Lee, while swingmen Rogelio Moret and Reggie Cleveland won 14 and 13, respectively.

A 10-RBI game for Lynn in June was followed by a 10-game winning streak in July as Boston built up a 6 ½-game cushion. The Red Sox were able to maintain the lead, but in the closing weeks of the season they lost Rice, the second-most dangerous hitter in the league that year to Lynn, the first player to ever win both Rookie of the Year and MVP in the same year. Carl Yastrzemski shifted back to left field in the postseason. And what a postseason it was.

Yaz led the hit parade against the Oakland A's, the three-time defending world champions who suddenly looked like they hadn't been to the postseason since 1967. The Red Sox swept the A's in three and looked awfully good for the first 53 outs of the World Series. After Luis Tiant shut out the Reds to open the Series, the Red Sox were one out away from taking a two-game lead when Dick Drago couldn't hold a ninth-inning lead for Bill Lee. The Reds took two of three in Cincinnati and held the World Series lead when the teams returned to Fenway for one of the greatest games in history. Tiant, whose twists and turns on the mound captivated the country, wasn't as sharp as in his first two wins and it looked like Cincinnati's night. But Bernie Carbo's three-run home run was topped by an acrobatic catch and

double play in right field by Dwight Evans in the 11th, and both were trumped by Carlton Fisk's home run off the foul pole, complete with manic waving. It was hard to believe it all happened in one night. After Lee's blooper pitch was blasted by Tony Perez to break up a shutout and Joe Morgan's blooper in the ninth snapped a tie in Game 7, it was just as hard to believe the season was over.

The Red Sox had arrived, though, even if their hangover from the World Series lasted all of 1976. The season is best remembered for a May fight in the first Red Sox game at refurbished Yankee Stadium. Lou Piniella decked Fisk after a play at the plate and Bill Lee was knocked out for the season after ending up at the bottom of the scrum pile. Owner Tom Yawkey died in July after a battle with leukemia. Nine days later, and just four games after serving as AL manager of the All-Star Game, Darrell Johnson was fired. Don Zimmer took his place.

Boston signed reliever Bill Campbell at the first free-agent draft while most other teams were still figuring out how this novel system worked. A month later Boston traded Cecil Cooper, just starting to come into his own, to Milwaukee for George Scott and Bernie Carbo, both of whom they'd previously traded to the Brewers. During the year it was a pitcher they'd traded to the Yankees in 1972, Sparky Lyle, who became the first reliever to win the AL Cy Young Award and helped make the difference in a tight race between the Yankees, Orioles, and Sox.

The 1977 Red Sox produced one of the best lineups in club history as Fenway seemed suddenly smaller whenever the Red Sox had bats in their hands. Five players had at least 26 home runs and four drove in 102 RBIs or more for the '77 "Crunch Bunch." Third baseman Butch Hobson, with 30 home runs and 112 RBIs, spent most of the year batting eighth. Bernie Carbo and Dwight Evans, sharing time in the outfield, amassed 29 home runs between them. The Red Sox hit a club-record 213 home runs during the year, including 8 in a July 4 game against Toronto as Fred Lynn, Jim Rice, Carl Yastrzemski, and Scott all homered in the eighth to overcome a one-run deficit. Two million fans entered Fenway for the first time.

Despite the offensive explosion at Fenway, the Red Sox upgraded at second base in 1978 as Jerry Remy replaced Denny Doyle. As always, more pitching was needed. They signed Mike Torrez and landed Dennis Eckersley just before the 1978 season. Jim Rice, who'd been tossing out monster numbers since his debut, put up the gaudiest bunch yet: league-leading 46 home runs, 139 RBIs, 15 triples, 406 total bases, and .600 slugging. The wins piled up, too.

Boston reached 30 games over .500 in June. On July 19 the 62–28 Red Sox led by 9 games over Milwaukee, 12 ½ over Baltimore, and 14 over the Yankees. Then the nightmare began. The Red Sox lost 9 of 10 while the Yankees switched managers, from Billy Martin to Bob Lemon, and took off. The Red Sox went into Yankee Stadium and swept two games in the beginning of August to push the lead to 8 ½. From there, the clubs went in different paths. The Yankees went 23–7 and the Red Sox 19–13 until the start of a four-game early September series at Fenway Park. With Boston up by four games heading in, the Yankees pummeled the Red Sox, outscoring them by a margin of 42–9 in the "Boston Massacre." After a win against Baltimore, the Red Sox lost five more in a row. It was at that moment that the Red Sox showed their true mettle.

Suddenly trailing by 3 ½ games, Eckersley ended the slide and beat the Yankees in the last game between the teams on the schedule. Boston won 12 of its last 14, including the last 8 games. New York went 9–5, losing the last day of the season to Cleveland while Luis Tiant shut out Toronto in what turned out to be his final start for the franchise. For the first time since 1948, a one-game playoff was needed to decide first place. That game had also been at Fenway and that game had also gone awry.

A season that featured the greatest race between the Yankees and Red Sox culminated with the greatest game played between the two teams in the 20th century. Ron Guidry—at 24–3 coming in—was touched for two early runs, Bucky Dent's pop fly home run off Torrez gave the Yankees the lead in the seventh, Lou Piniella's blind stab at Jerry Remy's single was the most significant defensive play, and Rich Gossage preserved it with almost three innings of hard work as Carl Yastrzemski popped up with two on to end the final threat.

The Red Sox ran their record string to 16 consecutive winning seasons before dropping to sixth place at 78–84 under Ralph Houk in 1983. In that time many favorite faces said farewell to the Fenway stage. Luis Tiant, Carlton Fisk, and Bill Campbell left as free agents. Rick Burleson, Butch Hobson, and Fred Lynn were traded to the Angels in two separate deals. Bill Lee, George Scott, and Dick Drago were sent away as well. Mike Torrez, ironically, lasted the longest of this group, traded in 1983 to the Mets. Yaz finally called it quits in '83 after setting numerous franchise longevity records and becoming the first player in Boston history to reach 3,000 hits. A new era was about to start at Fenway and the fans who poured into the place, who'd been raised on the "Impossible Dream," the '75 Sox, and the four-letter word D-E-N-T, were ready for something different.

Rocket Power

The Red Sox built carefully. Wade Boggs emerged from the minor leagues as a hitting machine. He won five

batting titles in six years, clanging enough doubles off the Green Monster with his inside-out, left-handed swing to shame Pete Runnels, Fred Lynn, and Earl Webb, who'd set the standing major league mark with 67 doubles in 1931 (many of those two-baggers banged off the original wall). Second baseman Marty Barrett, a first-round pick, and undrafted catcher Rich Gedman came up through the system and showed prowess with the bat and glove. The outfield was familiar: Rice and Evans in the corner spots and Tony Armas, the 1984 home run champion, in between. The first baseman was steady Bill Buckner, a former batting champ, who'd come from the Cubs for the seemingly over-the-hill Dennis Eckersley in 1984.

The pitching staff had made real strides with first-round picks Roger Clemens and Bruce Hurst, plus 16th-round find Oil Can Boyd, who was both durable on the field and quotable in the locker room. General manager Lou Gorman, hired from the Mets, acquired Tom Seaver, and brought in an apprentice for longtime Sox reliever Bob Stanley: Calvin Schiraldi. Schiraldi, Clemens' teammate at the University of Texas, came from the Mets in return for Bob Ojeda, who had fallen from favor in Boston's clubhouse. Gorman traded with the Yankees to get former MVP Don Baylor. And as the Red Sox maintained their division lead, Gorman's August deal with Seattle steadied the infield with Spike Owen and bolstered the outfield with Dave Henderson.

The idea that it was a special year came early when Clemens set a major league mark with 20 strikeouts against Seattle on April 29. From there the Red Sox went 26–7 and had a 4 ½-game lead on the Yankees at the start of June. The Red Sox cruised most of the way from there as Clemens dominated on the mound (24–4, 2.48 ERA, holding opponents to a .195 average), while Boggs won the batting title and led the league in walks. Boston doubled clubs to death—their 320 two-baggers were more than anyone else in the Majors—and their pitchers issued the fewest walks in the game. Yet they quickly got into trouble against California.

The Angels won three of the first four games in the ALCS. Three runs in the ninth tied Game 4 and then they won in the 11th inning. Mike Witt, who'd gone the distance in beating the Red Sox in the opener, held a 4–1 lead in the ninth inning in Game 5. A two-run home run by Baylor made it a one-run game and Witt was replaced with John Lucas, who hit Rich Gedman. In came worn-out Donnie Moore, who surrendered a two-run blast to Henderson for the lead. The Angels tied it in the bottom of the inning, but they were unable to push across the clinching run despite loading the bases with one out. Henderson broke the tie with a sacrifice fly two innings later. Boston pounded the Angels in the final two games at Fenway, denying Gene Mauch his last chance for a pennant.

The Red Sox won twice at Shea Stadium in the World Series, returning to Fenway looking to hammer the Mets further. Although New York took the next two, Bruce Hurst won for the second time in the Series to put the Red Sox a win away heading back to Shea. Game 6 went back and forth and featured everything from a parachutist landing on the field during the game to a controversy over whether Clemens asked John McNamara to remove him with the lead. The Mets tied the game in the eighth, but in the 10th Dave Henderson's again stunned the home crowd with a homer and the Red Sox added another run to lead, 5–3. Schiraldi got the first two outs in the bottom of the inning but never got the third. A Bob Stanley wild pitch tied the game and Mookie Wilson's grounder eluded Bill Buckner. The Mets came from behind to win Game 7 as well. Marty Barrett, who batted .400 in 60 postseason at bats (.433 in the World Series), struck out to end it.

The Red Sox dropped to fifth the next year, as if to hide, but reappeared in 1988. Buoyed by a change in command from John McNamara to Joe Morgan, the Red Sox caught fire in mid-summer and reeled off 20 straight wins at Fenway Park. Boston held off the Tigers and won the division by a single game (perhaps a little payback for 1972). Dennis Eckersley, reborn as a closer in Oakland, shut the door on "Morgan Magic" pretty quickly in the ALCS as the Athletics swept. Another surge late in the 1990 season helped the Red Sox win a nip-and-tuck division race. The ALCS went the same way against the same foe, only this time Clemens was ejected from the fourth and final game of the sweep for cursing from the stretch position at the umpire.

The Curse of the Bambino, a 1991 book by *Boston Globe* writer Dan Shaughnessy, turned the repeated misfortunes of one baseball club into something that could constantly be rolled into a convenient explanation based on coincidence. (George Vescey had put the elements together in a newspaper column in 1986; he later apologized.) The Red Sox hadn't won since Babe Ruth was sold to the Yankees after the 1919 season. Holding players and the team to something that happened seven decades earlier—and heaping all the misfortunes on the club onto the ample but undeserving shoulders of Ruth—seemed silly enough, but many people bought into it. And untold millions were spent in mojo-reversing agents by the fans over the next 13 (oooohhh!) years as the ball club tried to win so they could forever flush this baseball hokum. More of a burden on the extended misfortune of the club should have been placed on the ownership situation than any rationalized curse.

The failure to integrate, the coddling of players past their prime, and too many people shuffling from manager to executive to drinking buddy helped stifle the

club through the Ted Williams years and into the early years of Carl Yastrzemski. When Tom Yawkey died in 1976, the club went into the Yawkey Trust, controlled by widow Jean Yawkey. She maintained control despite the assumptions and attempts of others. Executive Haywood Sullivan, whose best season as a Red Sox catcher was hitting .161 in 1960, and John Harrington, Mrs. Yawkey's executor, battled for control after her death in 1992. The two bickered over ownership until Sullivan sold out in 1993. Boston's muddled, complicated, and onerous ownership problems did not end until the team was finally sold a decade after Jean Yawkey's death and 26 years after Tom Yawkey's passing.

Up and Down

The 1990s saw both success and frustration at Fenway. Promising minor league infielder Jeff Bagwell was traded for reliever Larry Andersen, who pitched all of 15 games for Boston and was hammered in the 1990 play-off sweep. Joe Morgan was fired the next year despite four winning seasons and two division titles without a lot to work with. Pawtucket manager Butch Hobson took Morgan's place and threw away more games with his questionable managing than he had with his scatter-shot arm as the team's third baseman in the 1970s. His mishandling of players and personal problems led to Boston's first last-place finish in 60 years. Nonetheless, the fans kept coming as baseball's popularity and a growing interest in Boston's tradition-steeped home peaked. The club drew two million fans for eight consecutive years until the games ended on August 11, 1994. It took a crippling strike, of all things, for the Red Sox to actually turn around the team on the field.

While other cities took years to recover from the strike, Boston was more forgiving. Maybe it was because their uniforms still said, "Red Sox," and maybe it was because they won. While the club played to empty stadiums on the road, Fenway was consistently packed, one of only three AL cities to surpass two million in attendance in 1995. The Red Sox took two of three at Fenway from the Yankees in mid-May to move into first place. With castoffs Tim Wakefield, Erik Hanson, and Jose Canseco mixing well with holdovers Mike Greenwell, Tim Naehring, and John Valentin, manager Kevin Kennedy's club tore through the division. A 12-game winning streak in August sealed the deal. Mo Vaughn batted .300, knocked in 126, and took home the MVP despite superior seasons by Cleveland's Albert Belle and Seattle's Edgar Martinez. The postseason was over in a blink, but a 15-inning Division Series opening game loss on a home run by former Red Sox All-Star Tony Pena made the Indians' sweep sting.

Boston's recent success had come without a huge contribution from Roger Clemens. The Rocket had won three Cy Youngs, plus his 1986 AL MVP, but he hadn't won more than 11 games since 1992. With his hefty contract up after 1996, there were questions aplenty whether he would come back to Boston or try his luck elsewhere. His final win as a Red Sox was a 20-strikeout performance at Tiger Stadium. He lost his last start to the Yankees, leaving him tied for the club lead in career wins at 192 with the man whose name had trailed his since that first 20-K game: Cy Young. When Clemens shocked everyone and signed with Toronto, the Red Sox issued a statement that they "had hoped to keep him in Boston during the twilight of his career." That twilight turned out to last a long, long time.

The Red Sox found their new ace in another Canadian city: Montreal. Unlike Boston, Expos fans gave up on their team after the strike wiped out the division crown they'd sewed up in 1994. Montreal couldn't afford Pedro Martinez, who'd just turned 26. The Red Sox sent prospects Carl Pavano and Tony Armas Jr., a bargain at any exchange rate, in return for a pitcher who'd just fanned 305 with a 1.90 ERA. Clemens won successive Cy Youngs for the Blue Jays, with Martinez placing second in 1998, but Pedro won the award the next two years. In a time of ridiculous offensive numbers, Martinez pitched like someone from the dead ball era. His 313 strikeouts in 1999 were a new franchise record and his 1.74 ERA in 2000 was 3.18 lower than the league average. He was also in the middle of the '99 All-Star spectacle at Fenway. Players crowded around the frail yet hearty Ted Williams as he briefly held court before throwing out the game's first pitch. With grown men still wiping away tears in the stands, at home, and on the field, Martinez wiped out the National League, fanning five of the six batters he faced.

Martinez had ended the club's 13-game postseason losing streak that stretched back to Game 6 of the 1986 World Series by earning Boston's only win in the 1998 Division Series loss to Cleveland. Pedro and the Red Sox would repay a long overdue debt to the Indians in the final three games of the 1999 Division Series.

Cleveland seemed poised to end Boston's postseason aspirations for the third time in five seasons when the Red Sox turned the series around in Game 3 at Fenway Park. A record 23–7 postseason rout the next night tied the series as John Valentin, who drove in 12 runs in the ALDS, suddenly transformed into Babe Ruth. Martinez entered the final game of the series in the fourth inning and did not allow a hit as Boston took the ALDS. The Red Sox had finally beaten their postseason foe; now all they had to do to reach the World Series was beat their archrival in the House That Ruth Built.

Fighting the Evil Empire at Warp Speed

If it's possible, the addition of the wild card increased the intensity of the Yankees-Red Sox rivalry by adding the luster of the postseason. It's like seven one-game playoffs with the media crush locked on stun and plenty of hatred between fans in different jerseys to go around. The only thing that hasn't been marketed in the rivalry is an antacid with the team logos. Maybe next year.

In the first postseason meeting between the clubs, the Yankees took control. New York scored late to win the first two games of the 1999 ALCS at Yankee Stadium. The first installment of the postseason rivalry at Fenway featured Clemens and Martinez. Boston fans howled as the Rocket was shelled early while Pedro fanned 12 and allowed just 2 hits in a 13–1 laugher. The Yankees still took the pennant at Fenway; not an unfamiliar sight, but not a pleasant one, either.

The Red Sox, admitting to a lineup problem, changed dramatically by adding Manny Ramirez at $20 million annually over eight years in 2001. Ramirez, one of the most productive—and flighty—players in the game, fit right into the cleanup slot. The only problem was an absence of anyone to hit in front of or behind him. Nomar Garciaparra, the two-time batting champion and third-place hitter, missed all but 21 games, while Dante Bichette, at the end of the line at age 37, found Boston a long, long way from Colorado. With John Valentin, Jason Varitek, and Pedro Martinez also missing significant time with injuries, the club was in trouble. Manager Jimy Williams' departure mirrored the Joe Morgan situation of a decade earlier: an unnecessary firing despite a superior record. The Red Sox were 12 games over .500 and 5 games out when Williams was axed on August 15. By season's end the Joe Kerrigan-led club was 3 games over .500 and 13 out.

The Red Sox were sold that winter for $700 million to financier John Henry, owner of the Marlins, and a group that included Hollywood producer Tom Werner, the New York Times Co., and former U.S. Senator George Mitchell. For the first time since 1933, the Yawkey name was not involved in any way in the ownership decisions for the club.

The new ownership wasn't afraid to bump heads. First, they stopped maligning Fenway—perhaps realizing the ballpark might be a reason the team sold so many darned tickets—and made improvements to keep the oldest stadium in baseball going (at least for the time being). Dan Duquette, already hated by many for not keeping Clemens (among other perceived sins), was dismissed as GM and Mike Port took his place temporarily;

Grady Little replaced Kerrigan. The new regime's first season had some giddy moments, like Derek Lowe throwing the first no-hitter at Fenway since 1965 and becoming the first pitcher in history to go from 20 saves to 20 wins in successive years. Yet while the Red Sox were the second-best team in baseball in terms of batting average and runs, Boston placed 10 ½ games behind the Yankees. When New York signed Cuban defector Jose Contreras from under Boston's nose on December 27, Red Sox president Larry Lucchino told the *New York Times*, "The evil empire extends its tentacles even into Latin America." The gloves were off.

Billy Beane wouldn't leave Oakland, so the Red Sox boldly hired the youngest general manager in history: Brookline native Theo Epstein, 28. Unwanted in Minnesota, David Ortiz arrived in Boston and slid into the lineup as the protection Manny Ramirez always needed but never got. Kevin Millar, on his way to Japan, got a U.S. reprieve when the Red Sox worked out a deal. With Johnny Damon at the top of the order and batting champ Bill Mueller near the bottom, the Red Sox led the league in batting average, on-base percentage, slugging, and runs. With a staff that didn't allow a lot of baserunners and missed more bats than any AL team, Boston secured the wild card. Facing the top pitching team in the league, the Athletics, the Red Sox lost the first two games in Oakland. Then, as they'd done in 1999 against the Indians, Boston won the last three games to become the first team to pull off that trick twice.

Waiting for them was the Yankees, just like 1999. The Red Sox were better prepared this time and were able to "cowboy up" as Millar often said. The ALCS was a donnybrook, literally. Martinez and Clemens threw inside in Game 3 and former Boston manager Don Zimmer, now an ancient yet hotheaded Yankees coach, bit the Fenway grass when he took a run at Pedro. Tim Wakefield beat the Yankees twice and the bullpen pitched in to beat New York in Game 6. The next night, though, it was Little's reluctance to go to his pen that helped the Yankees tie the game against a tiring Martinez in the eighth. With Wakefield on in relief, Aaron Boone homered in the 11th to give the Yankees the pennant. One more difficult chapter in a Stephen King horror novel that seemed to have no end...but the denouement was closer than anyone in Red Sox Nation (even Stephen King) could have dared hope.

Theo Epstein spent Thanksgiving in Arizona and brought back Curt Schilling, giving Boston its most formidable four-man staff in decades. Schilling's former manager in Philadelphia, Terry Francona, took over for his Little-appreciated predecessor. That winter the Red Sox spent weeks trying to figure every which way to get Alex Rodriguez's massive contract to fit into Fenway (with Ramirez going to Texas). It didn't

happen and A-Rod wound up in the Bronx, Manny stayed in Boston, and everyone lived happily ever after.

A contentious scene at Fenway in July led to Jason Varitek slugging A-Rod during another Yankees-Red Sox brawl. From that evening on, with Bill Mueller's home run beating Mariano Rivera in the ninth, the Red Sox had the best record in baseball. A week later, Nomar Garciaparra was traded and the Red Sox came out on the other side a better team, one that easily won the wild card and swept the Angels in the Division Series. Now all they had to worry about was the Yankees. Again.

The 2004 ALCS was a tale of two series: one hideous, one glorious. The moral of the tale was redemption. The 19–8 thumping they absorbed at Fenway in Game 3 was the most runs allowed in LCS history and it put them on the verge of being swept. The sweep seemed assured with Mariano Rivera on the mound in the ninth inning the next night, but a stolen base by Dave Roberts and a single by Bill Mueller tied the game. David Ortiz, whose homer ended the Division Series against the Angels, sent everyone home in the 12th. Another late rally the next night tied the game and Ortiz won it again…this time with a single in the 14th. Schilling wore his heart on his sock in Game 6 and two reversed calls by the umpires enabled the Sox to tie the series. As if realizing it was too much to take, the script deviated there and there was little drama in Game 7. The Red Sox hammered the Yankees early, allowing fans to relish the final innings in the place that had haunted them since it was built in 1923, the same year Babe Ruth led the Yankees to their first world championship.

The only question remaining was whether the Red Sox would fizzle in the World Series after so much buildup. That they were facing the Cardinals, who had historically dealt them cruel blows in the 1946 and 1967 World Series, seemed enough to vex the delirious fans. But what did the players, these self-claimed shaggy "idiots" know of history and such? They came out slugging. And once the Red Sox finished off the sloppy opening game, thanks to a late home run off the foul pole by Mark Bellhorn, Boston cruised from there. Boston's pitching stifled St. Louis as Schilling, Martinez, and Lowe were all spectacular. Lowe's third clinching win in the postseason elicited a celebration 86 years in the making.

A sentimental fan base toasted departed friends and relatives who hadn't lived to see this day. Children of all ages were fully aware of the importance of the moment. The Red Sox were treated like the returning heroes that they were. Estimates of up to 3.2 million fans came to the victory parade in Boston. While the numbers were disputed, if the parade had snaked through every New England state up to the Canadian border, there would not have been too many gaps in the line. It had been drummed into Red Sox Nation from day one: You don't see something like this every year.

The next year they didn't. Pedro Martinez left for New York (the Mets), as did spare part Doug Mientkiewicz, whose grip on the last out did not relent until the threat of a lawsuit made the Red Sox and their former employee talk about proper custody for the ball that ended 86 years of regional angst. The Yankees and Red Sox battled until the final weekend of the '05 season. The Yankees won the battle, but the Red Sox took the wild card, and neither team made it past the Division Series. By 2006 the glow from '04 had faded and the AL East once more came down to the two rivals. It ended with a five-game sweep in August by the Yankees at Fenway Park that closed up Red Sox Nation early. Toronto even snuck past Boston and pushed the Red Sox to third, the first time since 1997 the team hadn't placed second to the Yankees. Fans still logged in to countless web sites—Curt Schilling, too—and there was always the *Faith Rewarded* DVD of 2004 to pop in over the winter.

In November 2006 the Red Sox submitted a record $51.1 million bid to the Seibu Lions for Japanese pitching sensation Daisuke Matsuzaka. The 26-year-old righty signed a six-year, $52 million deal with Boston shortly before Christmas and the imposed 30-day deadline in the posting system. Even with the posting fee figured in, it was still a far more reasonable deal than most clubs were able to ink with proven domestic arms. Dice-K mania swept Boston and every other park he was scheduled to pitch in, expanding Red Sox Nation to the other side of the globe.

The Red Sox are more beloved now than they have ever been, if that is possible. Every pitch in every game is scrutinized, agonized, and overanalyzed in the celebration that is Red Sox Nation. In Boston, Burlington, Bar Harbor, and places all over the globe where the relocated and reborn watch their Red Sox, followers are firmly in touch with the Olde Towne Team's past, rooted—and rooting—in the present, and dreaming of a better future.

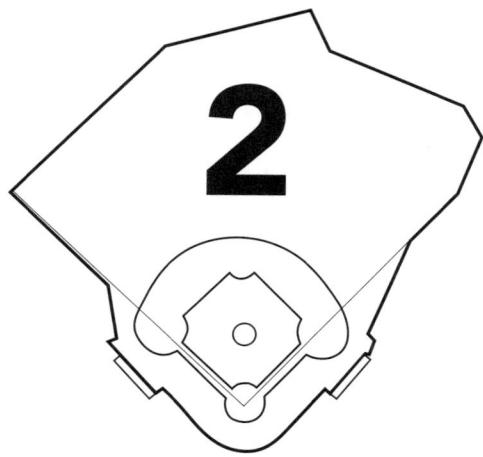

GREATEST GAMES IN RED SOX HISTORY

1. October 21, 1975

Red Sox 7, Reds 6: Game 6 of the 1975 World Series is the game against which any future Game 6—and any future World Series *game*—will be judged against. Three days of rain makes the anticipation even greater. Yet when Fred Lynn hits a three-run home run in the first and Reds starter Gary Nolan is knocked out in the third inning, it looks like the Red Sox might win the game in a romp. The Reds use eight pitchers, including Rawly Eastwick, who allows an epic three-run homer to Bernie Carbo, and culminating with Pat Darcy, who surrenders Carlton Fisk's famous foul-pole drive, complete with hand signals. In between, Dwight Evans makes one of the greatest catch and throws in Series history.

2. October 17, 2004

Red Sox 6, Yankees 4: Trailing three games to none and down by a run in the ninth inning, pinch runner Dave Roberts steals second and then scores on Bill Mueller's single up the middle of Mariano Rivera. David Ortiz gives the Red Sox the win with a home run off Paul Quantrill in the 12th inning. It sparks the greatest comeback ever in a major league postseason series.

3. October 16, 1912

Red Sox 3, Giants 2: Fred Merkle singles in the go-ahead run in the top of the 10th inning to give the New York Giants a 2-1 lead in deciding Game 8 of the World Series. Christy Mathewson, who went 11 innings without a decision because of five New York errors in Game 2, has an even worse fate in the finale. Sure-handed center fielder Fred Snodgrass drops a flyball and then a catchable foul popup drops among three players. Given another chance, Tris Speaker singles in the tying run and Larry Gardner hits a sacrifice fly that brings in the winning run. Smoky Joe Wood, winner of 34 games during the season, gets his third victory of the Series.

4. October 20, 2004

Red Sox 10, Yankees 3: The smug chants of "1918" are about to become extinct at the "House That Ruth Built (After the Red Sox Sold Him)." The Yankees, who came from behind to beat Boston in Game 7 of the 2003 ALCS, held a three games to none lead in '04, but the Red Sox won the next three to force a seventh game. After David Ortiz homers in the first inning of Game 7, Johnny Damon knocks a grand slam in the second and connects for a two-run blast two innings later. The Red Sox are the first team to rally from three games down in baseball postseason history.

5. October 27, 2004

Red Sox 3, Cardinals 0: Boston ends 86 years of waiting with a decisive sweep of St. Louis. It's a fitting terminus since the Red Sox twice lost seven-game World Series to the Cardinals in 1946 and 1967. With a full lunar eclipse overhead, Johnny Damon leads off with a home run. Trot Nixon has three doubles in the game and brings in the other two runs in the third inning. Derek Lowe, pitching his final game for the Red Sox, gets his third clinching victory of the 2004 postseason. Keith Foulke snares Edgar Renteria's grounder and throws to Doug Mientkiewicz, who will require legal action to pry the ball from his grasp. The Red Sox are world champions for the first time since 1918. There is indeed joy in Mudville.

6. September 28, 1941

Athletics 7, Red Sox 1: Ted Williams goes 6-for-8 on the final day of the season to finish at .406. He goes 2-for-3 in the nightcap of a season-ending doubleheader after a 4-for-5 performance in a 12–11 first-game win. Manager Joe Cronin offered to sit Williams for the twinbill because his .3995 would be rounded up to an even .400. Williams brashly grabs a bat and plays every inning. He remains the last major leaguer to top the mark.

7. October 12, 1986

Red Sox 7, Angels 6: Dave Henderson turns into a god. With the Red Sox down by three runs in the ninth inning, Don Baylor homers for the Red Sox off Mike Witt. Witt gets the second out of the inning, but southpaw Gary Lucas comes in to face Rich Gedman, whom he drills. With Donnie Moore on the hill, Henderson homers to give Boston the lead. The Angels tie the game in the bottom of the ninth, but the Red Sox escape a bases-loaded, one-out jam. The Red Sox win in 11 innings on Henderson's sacrifice fly. The Red Sox make mincemeat out of the Angels the next two games.

8. October 2, 1978

Yankees 5, Red Sox 4: The game would not even be necessary today in the wild card era, but this one-game playoff game for a division title meant everything. Bucky Dent's pop fly catches the net over the Green Monster and shatters Boston's dreams of finally beating the Yankees in a do-or-die struggle. Dent earns a new middle name throughout New England and Don Zimmer and Mike Torrez are forever held in contempt by followers of the Olde Town Team.

9. September 28, 1960

Red Sox 5, Orioles 4: Exactly 19 years after his famous final day in 1941 where he refused to sit on .400 and went out and hit .406, Ted Williams homers in his final major league at bat. He homers into the right field bullpen off Baltimore's Jack Fisher, amid the frenzy of 10,454 fans, including author John Updike, who immortalizes "the Kid" with his story, "Hub Fans Bid Kid Adieu." Williams refuses to tip his cap, even after he is replaced in left field during the next inning. His 521 homers puts him third on the all-time home run list of the day, behind only Babe Ruth and Williams teammate Jimmie Foxx.

10. October 25, 1986

Mets 6, Red Sox 5: In one of the most difficult games for Red Sox fans to forget, a slow groundball provides lasting pain after the team had been a pitch away from an elusive world championship moments earlier. Three times the Red Sox have the lead in Game 6; three times the Mets tie it. The last time is in the bottom of the 10th

on a wild pitch by Bob Stanley. Mookie Wilson then hits a grounder that rolls between Bill Buckner's legs and the Mets win the game. They'll win the Series with another comeback two days later.

11. April 29, 1986

Red Sox 3, Mariners 1: Roger Clemens fans 20 Mariners to set the all-time record for a nine-inning game. Four M's whiff three or more times, including Ken Phelps, who finally puts a bat on the ball to ground out to end the game. Clemens is 4–0 and will win 20 more games to earn league MVP and Cy Young.

12. September 11, 1918

Red Sox 2, Cubs 1: Les Mann hits a grounder to second baseman Dave Shean, who throws to Stuffy McInnis and the Red Sox win the 1918 World Series. Carl Mays pitches a three-hitter against the Cubs in Game 6 at Fenway Park. Five of the first 15 World Series belong to the Red Sox, but it will be 2004—and four bitter Series defeats—until they win another.

13. October 15, 1946

Cardinals 4, Red Sox 3: The Red Sox rally from a 3–1 deficit in the eighth inning of Game 7 as Dom DiMaggio doubles off the wall to tie the game. Enos Slaughter, on first with two down in the bottom of the eighth, never stops running on Harry Walker's shot. Generations of Red Sox fans will argue that a second's hesitation on the relay by Johnny Pesky costs them a shot at the runner, but Slaughter just beats the throw to the plate. Reliever Bob Klinger allows the deciding hit in his only appearance of the Series. Harry Brecheen wins his third game, allowing two hits to start the ninth, but he retires the next three batters. Ted Williams bats .200 and drives in one run in his only World Series.

14. October 9, 1916

Red Sox 2, Robins 1: Boston's Babe Ruth and Brooklyn's Sherry Smith, both pitching in their first World Series games, lock horns in the two longest outings in postseason history. Hi Myers of the Robins hits an inside-the-park home run in the first inning at cavernous Braves Field, where the Red Sox are playing because it holds more fans. Ruth drives in the tying score in the third inning and allows no runs over his next 29 2/3 World Series innings. Pinch hitter Del Gainer finally breaks the tie in the 14th to end the longest World Series game by innings (that mark won't be matched until 2005), although the game lasts just 2:32.

15. October 1, 1967

Red Sox 5, Twins 3: The Red Sox win one of the tightest American League races in history, clinching on the season's final weekend. A five-run Boston sixth helps Jim

Lonborg beat Dean Chance in a battle of 20-game winners. Carl Yastrzemski clinches the Triple Crown with a 4-for-4 performance.

16. October 24, 2004
Red Sox 6, Cardinals 2: "The Bloody Sock Game, Part II." A wall of stitches holds Curt Schilling's ruptured tendon sheath on his right ankle together. TV cameras focus on the few inches of sock visible next to his red stirrup. It's bloody, all right. The Cardinals, meanwhile, score just once in six innings against the wounded Schilling and the Red Sox go up two games to none. Schilling won't have to pitch again nor will the Red Sox need to return to Fenway as they will sweep in St. Louis for their first world championship since 1918. The "Bloody Sock" makes it to the Hall of Fame.

17. October 1, 1903
Pirates 7, Americans 3: At Huntington Avenue Grounds, Boston's Cy Young throws the first pitch in the "modern" World Series. Tommy Leach triples for the first World Series hit. He comes around to score on a Honus Wagner hit and the Pirates score four times and go on to win. Boston and Young will come back and stun observers by winning the best-of-nine Series in eight games. Pittsburgh's Deacon Philippe and Bill Dinneen each win three games, the only time pitchers from two different teams win that many games in the same Series.

18. July 13, 1999
AL 4, NL 1: All-Stars from both leagues and from the All-Century Team surround 80-year-old Ted Williams in an impromptu tribute at "the Kid's" home park. When the game starts, the admiration switches to the mound, where Pedro Martinez whiffs the first four batters and throws so hard that he winds up on the disabled list a few days later. Still, Pedro is the game's MVP and he'll still be the overwhelming choice for Cy Young. (He'll just miss winning the league MVP as well in a controversial vote.)

19. April 20, 1912
Red Sox 7, Highlanders 6: The opening of Fenway Park is delayed two days by rain and spirits are dampened early as the Highlanders, forerunners of the Yankees, take a 5–1 lead. Boston, which already swept the Highlanders in New York to open what will be a 105-win season, rallies to tie the game at Fenway. Sam Yerkes, 5-for-6 on the day, scores the winning run on a hit by Tris Speaker in the 11th. The grand opening of Fenway is pushed off the front page by news of the sinking of the Titanic.

20. October 10, 1904
Americans 3, Highlanders 2: A rivalry is born, even though the names have changed. The neck-and-neck struggle for the pennant between the Boston Americans and New York Highlanders comes down to a season-ending doubleheader in New York. The game is tied in the top of the ninth when Jack Chesbro's spitball sails over the catcher's head to bring in the winning run. Some view Chesbro as a goat despite winning an American league-record 41 games. New York takes the meaningless second game. There is no World Series because the New York Giants refuse to play.

21. September 12, 1979
Red Sox 9, Yankees 2: Carl Yastrzemski's single against Jim Beattie is his 3,000th career hit. Yaz becomes the first American League player to collect both 3,000 hits and 400 home runs. Henry Aaron and Willie Mays had done it in the National League. The game is delayed 15 minutes for a speech and both teams congratulate him. Jim Dwyer pinch runs and scores the game's final run.

22. October 11, 1999
Red Sox 12, Indians 8: A night after Boston's postseason record 23–7 rout at Fenway, both teams keep hitting. Pedro Martinez tosses six innings of no-hit relief and Troy O'Leary's second home run of the game—a three-run shot in the seventh, following a grand slam in the third—gives the Red Sox the lead. Boston had not won a postseason series since 1986, including losses to the Indians in both the 1995 and '98 Division Series (plus a one-game playoff in '48). Rallying from a two-game deficit, Boston wins the '99 ALDS with a 6.02 ERA; Cleveland's ERA is 9.63.

23. May 5, 1904
Americans 3, Athletics 0: Cy Young throws the first perfect game in American League history. He is also the first to pitch a no-hitter in each league, having done so for the Cleveland Spiders in 1897. Young retires another future Hall of Famer, and fellow pitcher, Rube Waddell, for the last out. The game is over in 85 minutes at Huntington Avenue Grounds before an appreciative crowd of 10,267.

24. September 18, 1996
Red Sox 5, Tigers 0: Roger Clemens strikes again. The Rocket ties his own 10-year-old record with 20 strikeouts in a 5–0 shutout at Tiger Stadium. Detroit, which had lost its 100th game the previous night, manages five hits off Clemens. Just as he did in his 1986 20K night, he walks none. After getting his 19th strikeout in the eighth, the next four batters put the ball in play, but he fans Travis Fryman for the last out. It is the last victory in a Red Sox uniform for Clemens.

25. September 10, 1999
Red Sox 3, Yankees 1: In perhaps his signature performance for the Red Sox, Pedro Martinez fans 17 Yankees

and walks none at Yankee Stadium. The only hit he allows is a home run to Chili Davis, whom he strikes out his next two times up. He'll capture the pitching Triple Crown at 23–4 with a 2.07 ERA and 313 strikeouts, 100 more K's than innings pitched.

26. June 23, 1917
Red Sox 4, Washington 0 at Fenway Park: Babe Ruth never finishes a no-hitter during his short but remarkable pitching career, but he does start one—as well as a small-scale brawl. In perhaps the strangest beginning to a no-hitter in history, Ruth walks Washington leadoff man Eddie Foster to start the first game of a doubleheader at Fenway Park. He is livid at umpire Brick Owens and punches the ump after the base on balls. He is ejected and Ernie Shore comes out of the dugout with little time to warm up. Foster is thrown out stealing on Shore's first pitch and he retires the next 26 batters. Shore is credited with the fourth perfect game ever pitched, although that distinction will be removed by Major League Baseball more than seven decades later because of the leadoff walk. And Ruth? He would get a 10-day suspension. He'll lead the AL with 35 complete games, failing to complete just two starts other than this one.

27. October 12, 1916
Red Sox 4, Robins 1: The Red Sox win their fourth world championship, and their second at Braves Field. (More than 90 years later, the Red Sox have still clinched as many world championships at Braves Field as they have at Fenway.) Ernie Shore tosses a three-hitter against Brooklyn, inducing Mike Mowrey to pop up to shortstop Everett Scott for the final out. Brooklyn's 26-year-old Casey Stengel leads all regulars with a .364 average.

28. October 16, 2003
Yankees 6, Red Sox 5: Boston is five outs away from a pennant at Yankee Stadium. With a 5–2 lead into the bottom of the eighth inning and Pedro Martinez on the mound in Game 7 of the ALCS, manager Grady Little leaves Martinez in and he allows a game-tying double to Jorge Posada. Aaron Boone—like Bucky Dent before him—earns a new nickname in New England when he homers off Tim Wakefield in the 11th inning. Little will be fired and replaced by Terry Francona.

29. October 13, 1915
Red Sox 5, Phillies 4: The Red Sox win their fourth straight game, including two at October home Braves Field, to beat Philadelphia for the title. Owner Bill Baker's decision to put in temporary bleachers in center field at the Baker Bowl costs more than just a few extra admissions. Harry Hooper's second bounce home run of the game into those seats breaks a 4–4 tie in the ninth inning of Game 5. The Phillies had led, 4–2, until Duffy

Lewis launched a two-run home run in the eighth to tie the game. It is Boston's third world championship.

30. September 9, 1918
Red Sox 3, Cubs 2: Babe Ruth finally allows a run after 29 2/3 scoreless innings in the World Series. The left-handed ace will never again be a full-time pitcher after 1918 and he shows where his future lies with a long triple for the first two runs of Game 4. He will be the only Red Sox player with more than one RBI in the Series. After Ruth allows two Cubs runs to tie the game in the top of the eighth, Boston scores the go-ahead run in the bottom of the inning on an error on a bunt. Boston's 3–2 win is the highest scoring game of this Series played a month early because of World War I. Bullet Joe Bush saves it for the Babe. Ruth's career World Series numbers are 3–0, 31 innings, 0.87 ERA.

31. July 25, 1941
Red Sox 10, Indians 6: Lefty Grove, 41, tosses all nine innings in 90-degree heat to earn his 300th win. It is the last win of his career, although he will start six more games. He retires after the season with the fifth-most wins in history.

32. October 18, 2004
After going five hours the night before, Game 5 of the ALCS goes later still. Yet once again, "Big Papi," David Ortiz knocks in the winning run. The 14-inning marathon features another Red Sox comeback, this time in the eighth inning on an Ortiz home run and a Jason Varitek sacrifice fly. The Red Sox survive three passed balls in the 13th by Varitek trying to catch Tim Wakefield's knuckleball, and win when Ortiz singles in Johnny Damon an inning later. The momentum continues into New York, where the Red Sox will finally exorcise some old ghosts in the Bronx.

33. October 11, 2003
Yankees 4, Red Sox 3: Pedro Martinez and Roger Clemens go at it in Game 3 of the ALCS, but a more unlikely spar between Zim and Pedro is the defining moment. Don Zimmer, the 72-year-old coach, charges out at Martinez during an exchange between benches; Pedro brushes him aside and onto the ground. Yankees right fielder Karim Garcia later hops the wall during a bullpen fracas with a Boston groundskeeper. Mariano Rivera preserves New York's bizarre win. The strange series will go to the wire with Boston tripped up in the end.

34. October 19, 2004
Red Sox 4, Yankees 2: Curt Schilling pitches seven strong innings in Game 6 of the ALCS despite a ruptured ankle tendon that leaves blood on his sock. Schilling's replacement, Bronson Arroyo, has the ball swatted away

by Alex Rodriguez on a play at first base in the eighth. As happened earlier with Mark Bellhorn's home run, the umpires confer and change the call. A run comes off the scoreboard and the Yankees—once up three games to none in the series—are fit to be tied.

35. October 4, 1948

Indians 8, Red Sox 3: A Boston win and a Detroit loss on the final day sets up the first tie in American League history. With one game for the pennant, the Red Sox go with journeyman Denny Galehouse and are pounded in the first-ever one-game playoff as Lou Boudreau homers twice. Ken Keltner's three-run homer is the big blast.

36. July 9, 1946

AL 12, NL 0: After a year off from All-Star competition because of World War II travel restrictions, the American League—and Ted Williams, who hadn't played in one since 1942 because of military service—returned with a vengeance. Williams hits two home runs, including the first-ever home run hit off Rip Sewell's "eephus" pitch. He ties the All-Star mark by reaching base five times, with four hits and a walk.

37. October 5, 2003

Red Sox 5, A's 4: A day after Trot Nixon won Game 3 with an 11th-inning home run, David Ortiz brings in the tying and go-ahead runs with a two-out, eighth-inning double. Scott Williamson gets the win for the second straight day as the Division Series is tied. The Red Sox will complete the comeback by taking Game 5 in Oakland.

38. October 22, 1975

Red Sox 4, Reds 3: The low after the high of Game 6. Boston takes a 3–0 lead into the sixth, holds a 3–2 lead in the seventh, and clings to a tie in the ninth, but Joe Morgan's bloop single adds to a long line of heartbreaking hits for the post-Ruth Red Sox. It is the fifth one-run game of the Series, the fourth decided in the ninth inning or later. Carl Yastrzemski's popup in the ninth off Will McEnaney gives the Reds their first world championship since 1940.

39. August 18, 1967

In the midst of Boston's "Impossible Dream" season, tragedy strikes at Fenway Park. Jack Hamilton's fastball hits Tony Conigliaro in the left eye, fracturing his cheekbone, dislocating his jaw, and damaging his retina. Tony C., beloved native of Swampscott, Massachusetts, and the youngest player to lead the league in home runs at age 20 in 1965, will miss the rest of the '67 season and all of '68, but in '69 he will hit 20 home runs and win AL Comeback Player of the Year Award. Those numbers will improve to 36 homers and 116 RBIs. Following a trade to the Angels, his vision will worsen and he'll be forced to retire, although he tries one last time to come back with the Red Sox in 1975. He dies at age 45 in 1990.

40. October 23, 2004

Red Sox 11, Cardinals 9: The first World Series game at Fenway since 1986 is a seesaw affair. The Red Sox go up 4–0 and 7–2 in the early innings, but the Cardinals rally. Two muffed flyballs by Manny Ramirez in left field in the top of the eighth ties the game, but Mark Bellhorn hits the "Pesky Pole" in the bottom of the inning and the Red Sox hold on to win.

41. October 11, 1975

Red Sox 6, Reds 0: The opening game of the World Series is scoreless until the seventh inning when Boston explodes for six runs against three Reds pitchers. Luis Tiant makes the first of his three starts and tosses a five-hit shutout.

42. October 5, 1967

Red Sox 5, Cardinals 0: Jim Lonborg, coming off a brilliant season to pitch Boston to a pennant, is even better in the World Series. After Carl Yastrzemski hits his second home run of Game 2, a three-run job in the home seventh, Lonborg takes the mound in the eighth with a no-hitter intact. Julian Javier breaks it up with a double to the left-field corner with two outs. Lonborg's one-hitter is the fourth in World Series history. He will pitch a three-hitter in Game 5 but come up short on two day's rest in the deciding game.

43. September 3, 1912

Red Sox 1, Senators 0: A "challenge match" is set up between Washington's Walter Johnson and Boston's Smoky Joe Wood at first-year Fenway Park. Johnson, whose AL-record 16-game losing streak ended a week earlier, is held back in the rotation to face Wood, whose schedule is moved up so he can pursue his 14th consecutive win. Johnson's only trouble comes on back-to-back doubles by future Hall of Famers Tris Speaker and Duffy Lewis in the sixth. Wood wins, 1–0, and will go on to tie Johnson's 16 straight wins before he loses to Detroit on September 20. It is one of 26 career games Johnson loses by a 1–0 score, compared with 38 games he wins by that same tally. Wood will win 34 games in 1912 to surpass Cy Young's top total in Beantown.

44. July 24, 2004

Red Sox 11, Yankees 10: Bill Mueller ends a classic Yankees–Red Sox donnybrook with a two-run home run against Mariano Rivera in the bottom of the ninth. Jason Varitek and Alex Rodriguez go at it around home plate as four players are ejected. It seems to spark the Red Sox, who trail 9–4 in the sixth inning; they go on to finish the season 46–20 to take the wild card.

45. July 15, 1988

Red Sox 7, Royals 4: With John McNamara fired, the team in fourth place, and nine games back, low-key coach Joe Morgan takes over as manager as the Red Sox consider several bigger names. Boston sweeps the Royals in a doubleheader to start his managerial career. They then reel off 10 more in a row. Boston will win 24 straight at Fenway through August 13, with five of those victories on McNamara's account. But "Morgan Magic" takes over the Boston and "Walpole Joe" is anointed full-time skipper as the Red Sox play nearly .600 ball and squeak past the Tigers by a game for the AL East crown.

46. October 15, 1986

Red Sox 8, Angels 1: Roger Clemens and the Red Sox finish off the Angels. Calvin Schiraldi gets the final out to bring Boston its first pennant since 1975. Dwight Evans and Jim Rice are the only holdovers from that year's team.

47. October 2, 1949

Yankees 5, Red Sox 3: The Red Sox need to win one of the final two games of the year to take the pennant, but Boston goes home empty-handed. After blowing a four-run lead in the opener on Saturday, New York breaks open a 1–0 game with four runs in the eighth in the Sunday game. Vic Raschi holds off the Red Sox rally in the ninth inning. The Yankees have their 16th pennant since Babe Ruth headed south.

48. October 9, 1912

Red Sox 6, Giants 6: The most notable tie in World Series history goes Boston's way. The Red Sox blow a 4–2 lead in the eighth inning at Fenway Park. Buck Herzog's two-run double brings in the tying and go-ahead runs (Boston catcher Bill Carrigan's had dropped Herzog's foul pop). Boston ties it in the bottom of the inning against Christy Mathewson when a grounder goes through shortstop Art Fletcher's legs. After New York takes a lead in the 10th, the Red Sox tie it after Giants catcher Art Wilson, who just entered the game, drops a throw that would have nailed Tris Speaker. Fred Snodgrass and Beals Becker are both thrown out stealing by Carrigan in the top of the 11th and the game is called by darkness in the bottom of the inning.

49. September 28, 1990

Red Sox 7, Blue Jays 6: With the Red Sox and Blue Jays tied for first place, Toronto takes the lead on a two-run homer in the top of the ninth. The Red Sox rally in the home ninth and tie the game on a single by Mike Greenwell. Jeff Stone, who entered the game as pinch runner and hasn't batted all season, comes up with the bases loaded and one out in the ninth against Toronto closer Tom Henke. Stone singles in the winning run. The Red Sox will clinch the division title on the final day of the season on a sprawling catch by right fielder Tom Brunansky.

50. October 8, 2004

Red Sox 8, Angels 6: After Vladimir Guerrero caps a five-run seventh inning with a game-tying grand slam in Game 3 of the Division Series, David Ortiz breaks the tie with a homer to sweep the Angels. Ironically, if Mark Bellhorn had gotten down a sacrifice, the Angels could have pitched around Ortiz.

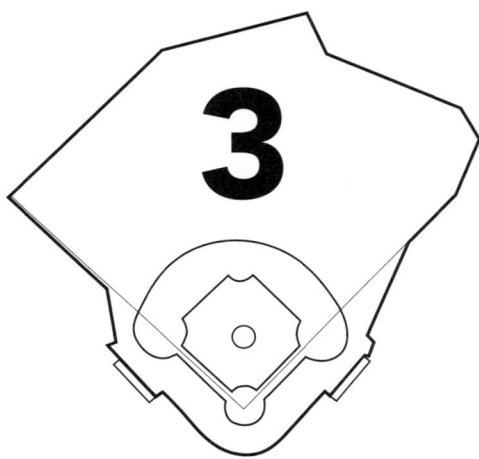

BIOGRAPHIES OF THE GREATEST RED SOX

Almost 1,600 players and managers have suited up for the Boston Red Sox since they first took the field in 1901. So how does one go about picking the greatest performers in a Red Sox uniform (plus Ed Barrow wore a suit)? It's a careful procedure and one done with all due respect to representatives of the team's glory days as well as the days of the also-rans. And being careful not to overlook players the club gave up on too soon and those who spent more than two decades wearing the Red Sox uniform.

A total of 34 people associated with the Red Sox have been voted into the National Baseball Hall of Fame, but almost half of that total landed with the club late in their careers and spent most of their time in Boston polishing up already impressive Cooperstown credentials. Then there are others who may never get their own plaque in the Hall of Fame but whose contributions to the Red Sox were significant enough to merit putting their story along with the game's immortals.

These types of lists by their very nature invariably leave a handful of readers feeling that an idol of their youth has been ignored and replaced by some Johnny-come-lately or that someone they've never heard of has taken the spot of a current favorite. Like the manager who can only pick so many players in spring training to bring north each year, the final cuts are always the most agonizing. Yet any way you look at, the lineup has plenty of power and the ball club is built to go the distance.

Ed Barrow	Dennis Eckersley	Duffy Lewis	Dick Radatz	Luis Tiant
Wade Boggs	Dwight Evans	Jim Lonborg	Manny Ramirez	Jason Varitek
Roger Clemens	Carlton Fisk	Fred Lynn	Jim Rice	Mo Vaughn
Jimmy Collins	Jimmie Foxx	Pedro Martinez	Red Ruffing	Tim Wakefield
Tony Conigliaro	Nomar Garciaparra	David Ortiz	Babe Ruth	Ted Williams
Joe Cronin	Lefty Grove	Herb Pennock	Curt Schilling	Smoky Joe Wood
Dom DiMaggio	Harry Hooper	Johnny Pesky	Tris Speaker	Carl Yastrzemski
Bobby Doerr	Jackie Jensen	Rico Petrocelli	Bob Stanley	Cy Young

Ed Barrow

Ed Barrow never played the game professionally, but he did just about everything else. He was a newspaperman, a partner with concessionaire Harry M. Stevens, a night baseball pioneer, a manager of teams in four states and Canada, the International League president, and finally, ate age 50, settled in to start his Hall of Fame career in the major leagues. With manager Jack Barry off to war in France, owner Harry Frazee—at the urging of AL president Ban Johnson—brought Barrow from the International League to run the Red Sox.

Barrow had briefly managed the Tigers 15 seasons earlier, but this time he took over a championship-caliber team...and took them to a championship. Even during a watered-down, war-shortened year, this was not a juggernaut offensive club. Only one team batted lower than the Red Sox, and Boston had Babe Ruth. Barrow, listening to outfielder Harry Hooper, tried the ace southpaw in the outfield and at first base. Ruth tied for the league lead with 11 homers and also poked 11 triples in 317 at bats, nearly as many times up as he'd received in the previous four seasons as a pitcher. Ruth helped the Red Sox win the World Series with his arm and his bat. The next year Barrow got Ruth 122 more at bats, and the slugger rewarded his faith by hitting a record 29 home runs. Ruth would shatter that record many times over, but alas, not in Boston.

While Barrow tried to talk Frazee out of the sale, it came to pass. Frazee erred yet again by letting Barrow go run the Yankees at the end of the 1920 season. He picked budding stars from the Red Sox and watched them blossom in the Bronx as the Yankees won 14 pennants and 10 world championships with Barrow calling the shots. He died in 1953, the same year he was inducted into the Hall of Fame.

Wade Boggs

Wade Boggs certainly wasn't your typical corner slugger. That didn't make him any less of a great player or a less-deserving member of the Hall of Fame. He consistently hit for a high average and was on base more than any American Leaguer for eight straight years, scoring 100 times seven years running.

Boggs had a swing made for Fenway Park. His inside-out cut was perfect for taking any pitch from the middle of the plate out to left field, where it invariably careened off the Green Monster. He was among the top three in doubles seven times. Twice he hit better than .400 for the season at home (.418 in 1985 and .411 in 1987), and he batted .380 or better at Fenway three other years, including .397 in 1983.

For his career, Boggs hit 52 points better at home than on the road (.354 to .302), and had a nearly 100-point home advantage in slugging. If not for his high hit total, a modern player who hit .302 yet slugged only .395 would have been a reach to make the Hall of Fame, as Boggs did in 2005, but it's not fair to diminish his career because he simply took advantage of a home park ideally suited to his abilities. It was a good fit from the start.

His batting average reached .380 in mid-September of his rookie year in 1982 before a 2-for-36 slump, including a 1-for-21 slide at home, pushed him down to .349. It was still the highest batting average for a rookie

in American League history. He didn't have enough at bats to qualify for the batting title, but he'd take care of that soon enough.

Boggs won the first of his five AL batting crowns in 1983, and led the league in on-base percentage six times between 1983 and 1989. He was an All-Star 12 straight years starting in 1985. He was even good for the poultry industry; his eating chicken every day before games was just one of his many well-known superstitions. The only stain on his career, other than, according to Red Sox fans, spending five years with the Yankees, was a long-term adulterous affair that became very public in 1989. He batted .330 that season and led the league in on-base percentage, but his average dipped to .302 the next year. After batting just .259 in 1992, it was obvious his time in Boston was up.

He won a World Series crown with the Yankees in 1996 and gained his only two Gold Gloves at third base while in New York. He finished his career with two years in Tampa, where he'd first played Little League baseball as a child. His 3,000th career hit, collected the day after Tony Gwynn reached the milestone for San Diego in 1999, remains the most noteworthy event in Devil Rays history.

Roger Clemens

Roger Clemens was easy to love in Boston. When he left he proved just as easy to hate. When Clemens one day stops pitching—and becomes eligible for the Hall of Fame—he likely will be inducted into Cooperstown as a Red Sox.

Clemens made his major league debut with Boston less than a year after signing as a first-round pick out of the University of Texas. He showed promise his first two years, but no one could have expected what happened to him in 1986. He won his first 14 decisions, none more spectacularly than April 29, when he struck out a major league record 20 Mariners. He finished with the best record in baseball at 24–4, plus a win in the first of his 11 All-Star games, and he led the league in innings, strike-outs, shutouts, and fewest hits per game to capture the AL MVP and his first Cy Young Award. He started three times in the ALCS and twice in the World Series, leaving with the lead in Game 6 only to watch the agonizing finish from the dugout.

Clemens captured two more Cy Youngs with Boston as well as two more 20-win seasons, three straight ERA crowns (1989–91), and leading the league lead in strikeouts three times. His last strikeout title in Boston came in 1996, when he equaled his own record by fanning 20 Tigers in what turned out to be his last win for the club. His 192 victories for the Red Sox tied

him for the franchise lead with Cy Young, the man whose award the Rocket has won a record seven times. Two of those awards came immediately after choosing free agency and Toronto (1997–98), becoming the first American Leaguer to win successive pitching Triple Crowns since Lefty Grove (1930–31).

Traded to the Yankees at his request, he won another Cy Young (2000) and picked up his 300th career win and 4,000th strikeout in the same game in 2003. He announced his retirement that year, receiving a standing ovation at Fenway Park along the way. A few months later, however, he returned to pitch for his hometown Astros. He was reborn once more in the National League, winning his last Cy Young at the age of 42. A year later he had the lowest ERA of his remarkable career at 1.87 and helped Houston win its first pennant.

Jimmy Collins

Jimmy Collins spent the vast majority of his career in Boston, though only half of it was with the Red Sox. He spent most of his first six seasons with the Boston's National League team, known as the Beaneaters, and jumped to the American League when it started in 1901. He was the franchise's first manager and third baseman.

Collins hit .332 in 1901 and led Boston to a second-place finish in the AL's first season. He batted .322 the next year, as Boston finished third, but age was taking its toll on his body. His averaged dropped to .296 in 1903, though he led the league in fielding and guided the Red Sox to a win over Pittsburgh in the inaugural World Series. Boston won the AL pennant again the next year, though his average continued to fall, this time all the way down to .271. There was no World Series as the New York Giants refused to participate.

Boston dropped to fourth in 1905 and when the club started poorly the next year, on its way to 105 losses, Collins was replaced as skipper. He remained with the club, however, until he was dealt to the Athletics in June 1906. A poor final season at age 38 pulled his career average below .300.

Aside from being a good hitter and manager, Collins is credited with revolutionizing the way third baseman played the field. He was one of the first third sackers to play several steps away from the bag, toward the shortstop, to cut off balls hit in the hole. Collins also changed the way third baseman played the bunt, charging hard toward the plate and throwing underhand and off balance to first. One story had him throwing out four straight bunters in his first big league game at third, after coming in from center field in the middle of the game. Because of his combination of abilities, Collins was named to the Hall of Fame in 1945 by the Veterans Committee.

Tony Conigliaro

Tony Conigliaro's seemingly unlimited potential came crashing down with one pitch in the best year his hometown had seen since he was in diapers. The Swampscott High School star played at Fenway Park at 19, homered in his first game, and clubbed 24 home runs as a rookie. The next year he became, at 20, the youngest home run champ in American League history. In 1967 the Red Sox rose from the depths to compete with the best teams in the league. The Fenway faithful adored Tony C. He'd recently hit his 100th career home run at age 22 as he stepped in against Jack Hamilton of the Angels on August 18. The pitch hit Conigliaro in the face; even old-school manager Dick Williams couldn't watch as his player writhed in pain. The Red Sox won the pennant, but Tony C. did not play again for two years.

By then the Red Sox had another Conigliaro in the outfield. Younger brother, Billy, Boston's first pick in 1965, hit 18 home runs at age 22. Tony showed him up by hitting 20 and winning Comeback Player of the Year. Tony hit 36 the next year and drove in 116 runs, both career highs. Then the Red Sox broke up the act. Tony was traded to the Angels (Hamilton had since retired) for two players named Tatum and young infielder Doug Griffin. Tony C.'s eye problems made for a miserable season in Anaheim and he retired. Billy's star faded, too, and he was traded to Milwaukee.

Tony C. made a comeback with the Red Sox in 1975. It was an almost entirely new club—a real contender—but it was not the same. Tony C. hit the last two home runs of his career and was released in September. Tragedy continued to dog him. Conigliaro suffered a heart attack in 1982, requiring constant care until his death at 45 in 1990. That year the Red Sox initiated an award in his honor to a major league player who best displays the qualities and determination of Tony C.

Joe Cronin

Joe Cronin, a slick-fielding shortstop when he first came up with the Pirates, managed the Red Sox to more victories and for more years—1,071 over 13 seasons—than anyone in franchise history. Yet Cronin won only one pennant in Boston despite a remarkable collection of talent. Cronin was player/manager for most of those years, having served in the same capacity with the Senators, where in 1933 as a 26-year-old first-time skipper he won that club's last pennant before it relocated to Minnesota (a decision he later signed off on as league president).

Cronin, the son-in-law of Washington owner Clark Griffith, did not come cheaply. In the middle of the Depression, he cost Boston $225,000—plus shortstop

Lyn Lary—to take over the club in 1935. Cronin was still a feared hitter, batting .300 or higher in four of his seven seasons as the everyday shortstop, including a .325 season with a league-high 51 doubles in 1938. Defensively, though, he had lost his range. Despite his defensive lapses, he never moved himself to another position. With Cronin at shortstop, the Red Sox traded hotshot minor leaguer Pee Wee Reese to Brooklyn in 1939. Cronin eventually stopped playing regularly at age 35 in 1942.

Even when he was hitting, Cronin wasn't a popular manager with most of his players. Some felt the Red Sox would have won more pennants with another man at the helm. He irritated his pitchers by calling all the pitches from the dugout. After 11 years at the helm, with his best players having gone and returned from World War II, the Red Sox finally won a pennant in 1946. Boston fell to the Cardinals when Enos Slaughter beat Johnny Pesky's relay throw home in the bottom of the eighth inning of the seventh game.

Cronin managed the club just one more season, a third-place finish in 1947, before being named the club's general manager. Cronin's performance in that role was even more suspect. Boston finished second in each of his first two years as GM, and never finished higher than third until he left to become AL president in 1959. Under his watch, the Red Sox lavished large bonuses on several players who didn't pan out, and they were also the last team to integrate. The first African American in a Red Sox uniform, Pumpsie Green, debuted several months after Cronin left the franchise, more than 12 years after Jackie Robinson first played with the Brooklyn Dodgers. Coincidence? Despite several glowing recommendations from scouts practically begging him to make a deal, Cronin repeatedly passed on signing Willie Mays for only $5,000.

Cronin served as AL president until 1973. The club retired his uniform number 4 shortly before his death in 1984. He was elected to the Hall of Fame in 1956.

Dom DiMaggio

"He's better than his brother Joe, Dominic DiMaggio," was the refrain sung at Fenway Park in the 1940s. It wasn't true, but it was heartfelt. Dom DiMaggio wore glasses and was 5 inches and 25 pounds smaller than his famous older brother on the Yankees. Dom *was* better than his brother, Vince, who played for six National League teams during the same period. Dom was essential to Boston's mainly futile cause of trying to knock off Joe's Yankees.

Dom DiMaggio got on base so that Ted Williams, who was better than Dom's brother Joe, could knock him in. Six times Dom scored 100 or more runs, leading the league in both 1950 and 1951. Dom's best season

was 1946, Boston's first pennant since 1918. Returning from World War II after missing three years, he batted .316 and placed ninth in the MVP balloting behind Williams (teammates Bobby Doerr, Johnny Pesky, and Dave "Boo" Ferriss were also in the top 10; Joe DiMaggio was 19th). Dom had a better season in 1948, scoring 127 times, driving in a career-best 87 runs, lacing 40 doubles, and producing his only 100-walk season. In 1949 he set the franchise record by hitting in 34 straight games. (Those DiMaggio genes!) Dom's best year of all, though, was 1950 when he set career highs in runs (131), hits (193), triples (11), and batting average (.328), while leading the lead-footed American League with 15 steals.

He excelled in center field, setting an AL record of 503 putouts in 1948 that stood for 39 years. In one of the biggest moments in Red Sox history, though, DiMaggio wasn't there. He turned his ankle going to second on his game-tying double in the eighth-inning of Game 7 of the 1946 World Series. His replacement, Leon Culberson, was a notch below DiMaggio in speed and arm strength; just a second might have made the difference on Enos Slaughter's decisive "Mad Dash" for the Cardinals. Dom played until 1953, the last DiMaggio standing in the major leagues.

Bobby Doerr

A reliable hitter and outstanding fielder, Bobby Doerr anchored second base for Boston for 14 seasons and was a key part of the only Red Sox team to win a pennant between 1918 and 1967.

After a rookie campaign that saw him bat only .224 in 55 games, Doerr batted .282 or higher for each of the next seven seasons. He had limited power, though he taught himself to pull the ball and take advantage of Fenway Park's short left-field porch. In many ways, Doerr was a right-handed version of Wade Boggs, because his career numbers reflect a man who hit much better while playing at home. He hit about 45 percent fewer home runs on the road than he did at home, and batted 55 points better in his career at Fenway (.315 to .261).

Doerr was one of the AL's top players in 1944, when he hit .325 and led the league in slugging, though he was one of the few All-Stars still playing in the big leagues that late in World War II. Doerr had chronic back troubles, and he wasn't able to serve in the military until 1945.

He continued his fine play after the war, driving in 116 and helping the Red Sox to their first pennant since the year he was born. The 28-year-old Doerr finished third in the MVP voting that year, behind teammate Ted Williams and Detroit's Hal Newhouser. Doerr was even better in 1948, as the Red Sox were locked in an epic pennant race with the Indians and Yankees. Doerr

clubbed a career-best 27 home runs, drove in 111, and went nearly three months without making an error. The Red Sox lost the first one-game playoff in history to Cleveland despite a two-run homer by Doerr.

He was an above average hitter every season from 1939 to the end of his career in 1951, when his back forced him to retire. He had an adjusted OPS greater than 100 each of his last 12 seasons. A nine-time All-Star who played every game in his career at second base, Doerr made it to the Hall of Fame in 1986 as a selection of the Veterans Committee.

Dennis Eckersley

In the mid-1970s the Red Sox were desperate for another starting pitcher. Hard-throwing 23-year-old Dennis Eckersley, who'd pitched a no-hitter for Cleveland the previous year, came to Boston for four players, including Rick Wise, just before the 1978 season. Eck's wife was so pleased she asked for a divorce. His career benefited, as the Red Sox were stacked with power hitters. His 20th win that year came the last Saturday of the season as the Red Sox tried to catch the Yankees, who'd rallied from 14 games back to take the division lead. Eck didn't pitch again as New York won the one-game playoff on Mike Torrez's turn in the rotation.

After 17 wins the next year, his totals dropped each season and his ERA went up. The 1982 season was the exception. Eck started the All-Star Game, but he gave up the decisive home run that night and finished the year on the downside at 13–13. Yet Eckersley wasn't just ineffective; he was an alcoholic. The situation worsened when he was traded to the Cubs for Bill Buckner in 1984. He helped them reach the postseason for the first time since 1945, but he was hit hard in the potential NLCS clincher and Chicago lost in a manner only slightly less gut wrenching than 1978 was in Boston.

Eck eventually entered a treatment center in Rhode Island, although he didn't tell the Cubs, who were so eager to be rid of him they paid part of his salary to Oakland to take him. Tony La Russa turned him into a reliever and 386 saves, three pennants (two against Boston in the ALCS), a world championship, an AL MVP, and a Cy Young later, he was rightly considered one of the greatest closers of all time.

He spent one last season in Boston as a set-up man in 1998. Baseball's oldest player at 43—the same as the uniform number he'd worn since first joining the Red Sox in '78—Eck earned his 390th career save and helped Boston reach the postseason 20 years after he first thought it would happen. He was elected to the Hall of Fame in 2004.

Dwight Evans

Dwight Evans was a slow starter, but a big finisher. He came to the Red Sox in 1973 as a bona fide prospect whose bat, glove, and arm made scouts drool. While fielding wasn't a problem, hitting was. He lost playing time to hard-hitting bench players like Bernie Carbo, but the Red Sox were a better team with Dewey in right field.

Carbo tied legendary Game 6 of the 1975 World Series with a pinch-hit home run, but Evans' spectacular catch of Joe Morgan's deep drive in the 11th inning—which he turned into a double play—kept the game tied so Carlton Fisk could become a hero. Other teams took notice. Fewer clubs tested his right arm and he won his first of eight Gold Gloves the next year. His hitting still lagged until hitting coach Walt Hriniak got him to stick to one stance and stop shooting for the Green Monster on every pitch. He led the league in home runs and walks in strike-shortened 1981, placing third in the American League MVP voting. The next year he played all 162 games, scored 122 runs, walked 112 times, had the first of three 30-homer seasons, and led the league with a .402 on-base percentage. From that point on he drove in 100 runs four times and twice won the Silver Slugger.

Evans was the only holdover from the 1975 World Series to play in 1986 (Jim Rice was hurt in the '75 postseason). Evans knew what he was doing. He hit two home runs and drove in nine runs in the agonizing seven-game loss to the Mets. Evans continued playing every day, but he slowed down and spent time at first base and designated hitter in addition to his right field duties. In 1990 he played only as a DH and after the year the Red Sox bought out his contract. He played one final year with the Orioles.

Carlton Fisk

Despite playing two fewer seasons in Boston than he did in Chicago, Carlton Fisk will always be recalled in a Red Sox uniform, if for no other reason than for the timeless shot of him waving his home run fair in the bottom of the 12th inning in Game 6 of the 1975 World Series.

Fisk exploded on the scene in 1972, clubbing 22 home runs, batting .293, and winning what would be his only Gold Glove. The New Hampshire native was the first unanimous selection in the Rookie of the Year voting, garnering all 24 votes. The next three years weren't so productive. "Pudge" mysteriously dropped 30 pounds during the 1973 season, blew out his knee in 1974, and broke his forearm in 1975.

He spent 119 days on the disabled list that year, but he returned to guide Boston's pitching staff to its first AL East title. He batted .417 in an ALCS sweep of Oakland

that ended three straight world championships for the A's. His most visible moment of the first five games of the World Series was throwing a ball into center field on a controversial 10th-inning bunt in Cincinnati. That was forgotten with one swing in Game 6. NBC's cameras caught Fisk hopping up and down on his way down the first-base line, desperately heaving his arms toward fair territory. It is perhaps the signature shot in the history of televised baseball, but it happened by accident. The camera operator stationed in the bottom of the Green Monster was startled by a rat and didn't follow the flight of the ball. The prolonged shot of Fisk proved so dramatic it changed the way all sports were covered by television. Fisk's reaction for the ages made it seem impossible the Red Sox could lose the World Series. They did the next night with Fisk waiting on deck in a bitter one-run loss.

The 11-time All-Star played 18 more seasons until age 45. He switched Sox in 1980, famously exchanging his number 27 from the Red Sox for number 72 with the White Sox. Both numbers were eventually retired. He set career highs with 37 homers and 107 RBIs for the 1985 White Sox.

Fisk caught 2,226 games, the most ever by a backstop. He held the record for most home runs by a catcher when his playing days were done (he still owns the AL mark with 376). His acerbic temperament was legend during his feud with Yankees catcher Thurman Munson in the 1970s, but his constant complaining led to his release by the White Sox in 1993 only days after breaking Bob Boone's record for catching longevity. He was voted to the Hall of Fame in 2000 on his second year on the ballot.

Jimmie Foxx

His penchant for hitting mammoth home runs was the reason they called him "the Beast." He broke a seat in the far reaches of left field in Yankee Stadium with one blast, he was the first man to hit a ball over the left-field upper deck in Chicago's Comiskey Park, and he retired with the second-highest career home run total in baseball history.

Foxx began his career in Philadelphia with the Athletics, and won back-to-back MVP awards in 1932–33, claiming the Triple Crown in the latter season and coming within just a couple of hits of winning it in the other one. (Four times he won at least two legs of the Triple Crown.) The Red Sox acquired "Double X" when Philadelphia's Connie Mack tried to cut his salary by 25 percent the year *after* he won the Triple Crown. Naturally, Foxx was irate and asked to be traded, and the Athletics finally did—for $150,000 and two players—in the off-season before the 1936 campaign.

Foxx was not as consistently good with Boston as he'd been in Philadelphia, though he had one more monster year remaining in his bat. Foxx was again named league MVP in 1938 after hitting .349 with 50 homers and driving in 175, still the fourth-highest RBI total ever. He was second in the MVP voting the next season, when he hit .360 with 36 homers. The Red Sox finished second both years, though never seriously contending with the Yankees for either pennant.

Even though he was only in his early 30s, his hard-drinking ways took a toll on his body. Foxx was a regular for only two more years before he was waived to the Cubs in the middle of 1942. He sat out most of the next two seasons, then returned for one final hurrah in Philadelphia in1945, this time with the Phillies. On his last legs, the slugger even pitched nine times (with a 1–0 mark and 1.59 ERA) for the worst team in baseball. Foxx was elected to the Hall of Fame in 1951.

Nomar Garciaparra

Nomar Garciaparra was one of the most popular as well as one of the best Red Sox players of the post-strike era. Fans called out "Nomah" in every flavor of New England accent whenever he strode to the plate, famously fidgeting with his batting gloves until it seemed he might pass out from lack of blood flow. Garciaparra hit .300 or better in each of his seven full seasons for the Red Sox, winning two batting titles, and his .323 career average with Boston was the highest since Wade Boggs moved south in 1992. Garciaparra's .372 average in 2000, his second consecutive batting title, exceeded any season by Boggs and was the best by any Sox hitter since Ted Williams' .388 in 1957.

A natural athlete—Garciaparra was recruited by UCLA for soccer and by Arkansas as a kicker, among other suitors—he was the first freshman to make the U.S. Olympic baseball team. Drafted in the first round in 1994 out of Georgia Tech, Garciaparra's arrival in the big leagues necessitated the move of Fenway favorite John Valentin from short to third base. Garciaparra made it worth everyone's while when he set an AL rookie record with a 30-game hitting streak and became the first Boston Rookie of the Year since Fred Lynn in 1975. Garciaparra also earned the first of five All-Star berths for the Red Sox despite a surfeit of outstanding shortstops in the league.

Garciaparra added a lot of muscle to his lean frame in the late 1990s. He missed most of the 2001 season after wrist surgery to fix an unusual ruptured tendon and never really regained his peak hitting form of 1998–2000. Though still very popular, the glare of the Boston spotlight seemed to wear on Nomar, and he ultimately

turned down a lucrative contract extension after hard negotiations with the club. Suffering through an injury-marred first half in 2004 and playing very poor defense at short, Garciaparra was traded to the Cubs in a four-team, seven-player deal at the trading deadline. Thus the longtime New England idol ended up missing Boston's first world championship since 1918 by a few months. Despite moving across the diamond and across the country to play first base for his hometown Dodgers, Garciaparra's place as one of the great Red Sox short-stops remains secure.

Lefty Grove

Lefty Grove, one of the best pitchers in baseball history, came to the Red Sox in 1934 when Philadelphia Athletics owner Connie Mack broke up the team that had won three straight pennants between 1929 and 1931. Robert Moses Grove cost new owner Tom Yawkey $125,000. For a franchise begging for respectability, it was a deal that had to be made.

Grove's time in Boston didn't start out well, however. The flame-throwing lefty, who had won 108 games the previous four seasons, blew out his arm in spring training and was never the same. He struggled with arm pain all through '34, though he figured out by the end of the season his arm hurt less if he threw his curve. That discovery allowed Grove to throw more than 200 innings each of the next three years, averaging 18 wins during that span. He also led the league in ERA in 1935 and 1936, as well as in 1938–39, though he barely threw enough innings in the latter two seasons to qualify for the title.

Even though he was much better with Mack's Athletics—his 1931 campaign, going 31–4 with an ERA almost 2 ½ runs below the league average during a hit-ter-dominated period, stands as one of the all-time great seasons—Grove was good enough to record 105 wins with the Red Sox. His last was his 300th on July 25, 1941, fittingly against the Athletics.

All told, Grove led the AL in wins four times, strike-outs seven times, and twice won the pitching Triple Crown, though those feats occurred before he reached Boston. He also topped the AL in ERA an amazing nine seasons. Grove was voted to the Hall of Fame in 1947.

Harry Hooper

Harry Hooper played right field in what some baseball historians call the greatest outfield ever assembled. Teaming with Tris Speaker in center and Duffy Lewis in left, the Million Dollar Outfield combined to set the stan-dard for outfield excellence in the early days of the American League. Yet Hooper was the only one of the trio who was around for all four World Series titles the Red Sox won between 1912 and 1918.

While he wasn't the kind of hitter Speaker was, Hooper was consistently above average. In fact, he posted an adjusted OPS total better than the league average in 15 of his 17 seasons. That, combined with his stellar play in right field, allowed him to be one of the top players in the game. He also broke many of Speaker's franchise marks and still holds the club record for steals (300) and triples (130).

Hooper was at his best in the World Series. He bat-ted .293 over the four World Series, including two home runs—both on bounces—in Game 5 to clinch the 1915 Series against the Phillies. Hooper's worst World Series produced a .200 average against the Cubs in 1918, but that came when the teams combined to bat was just .198. The 1918 regular season, shortened because of World War I, was one of Hooper's best. He batted .289 with 26 doubles and 13 triples, posting a .391 on-base percentage.

Hooper had another stellar year in 1920, batting .312 with 30 doubles, 17 triples, and a slugging percentage among the best in the league. On the surface it appears to be better than his 1918 campaign, but after normaliz-ing the totals to account for the increased offense throughout baseball that year, it was slightly below '18.

Unfortunately, Boston's ownership was in the busi-ness just then of selling off its best players. Babe Ruth went to the Yankees after 1919, and Hooper went to the White Sox after 1920. Hooper had five more good sea-sons in Chicago, retiring after the 1925 campaign.

Hooper made it to the Hall of Fame in 1971, joining former outfield mate Speaker, plus Ruth, via the Veterans Committee.

Jackie Jensen

Jackie Jensen may be best remembered today for quit-ting baseball a year after winning an MVP award because of a professed fear of flying, but he was a feared bat in the Boston lineup in the late 1950s.

Known as "the Golden Boy" as a fullback at the University of California, he ran for a 67-yard touchdown in his last college game: the 1949 Rose Bowl. The San Francisco native began his professional baseball career that spring in the Pacific Coast League, choosing the local, high-paying Oakland Oaks over the major leagues. The Yankees purchased Jensen along with Billy Martin after former Oakland manager Casey Stengel won his first world championship in New York. Jensen's postseason moment literally lasted a moment. The rookie pinch ran with two outs in the eighth inning of Game 3 of the 1950 World Series and was back sitting in

the dugout before he knew what happened. Traded first to Washington and then to Boston, he would never come close to the postseason again.

Because of his fear of flying, GM Joe Cronin had to give Jensen $1,000 just to get him to report to Boston. The club was glad to have him. Jensen led the American League in RBIs three times in a four-year span with the Red Sox, certainly helped out by having Ted Williams constantly on base in front of him. After career highs with 35 home runs, 122 RBIs, and 99 walks (one more than Williams), Jensen was named AL MVP in 1958. He followed that with a solid 1959, but he retired after the season to spend time with his wife, Olympic diving medallist Zoe Ann Olson, and his family. Though Jensen returned after a year, an airport panic episode forced him to briefly leave the team. He struggled through an ugly season in 1961 after Williams retired, then quit for good, dying in 1982. Boston baseball writers still give an award in his name annually to the Red Sox player with the most effort and desire: the Jackie Jensen Spirit Award.

Duffy Lewis

Before there was the Green Monster, there was "Duffy's Cliff." This 5-foot incline in the early years of Fenway Park was named for Duffy Lewis, a strong-armed left-handed ballplayer good enough to be part of "the Million Dollar Outfield."

With Lewis in left, Tris Speaker in center, and Harry Hooper in right, the Red Sox won world championships in 1912 and 1915. Speaker was traded because of a salary dispute, but Lewis and Hooper—with Tilly Walker roaming between them—won again in 1916. Lewis missed the 1918 world championship while serving in the military in World War I. He returned in 1919 to find himself a Yankee. He played in the same outfield in New York as his former ace pitcher in Boston, Babe Ruth. He'd been the first to pinch-hit for Ruth, batting for the Babe in his debut in 1914.

Lewis batted .289 over eight seasons in Boston and drove in 629 runs, better marks than Hooper or Larry Gardner, the third baseman on those three championship clubs. Lewis was at his best in the World Series, batting .444 against the Phillies in 1915 and tying Game 5 with a two-run homer in the eighth. He hit .353 the next year against Brooklyn. Lewis lived to be 91, experienced the leveling of his Cliff, its replacement with the Green Monster, and his pal Babe's last home run in 1935 as traveling secretary for the Boston Braves.

Jim Lonborg

Jim Lonborg and Carl Yastrzemski were the poster boys for Boston's "Impossible Dream" of 1967. While Yaz went on to have a long and storied career, Lonborg was the Cinderella character who lost the glass slipper after the clock struck midnight in Game 7 of the World Series. Except Lonborg didn't drop a shoe; he blew out his knee.

Lonborg's ill-fated ski trip after the '67 season led to the contract language barring future generations of ballplayers from hitting the slopes, but that season remains a landmark season in club history. His 246 strikeouts were the most in Boston since Smoky Joe Wood in 1912, and no Red Sox pitcher had started as many as 39 games since 1923. He won 22 times, though none was as important as the final game of the year.

With the Red Sox needing to win to take their first pennant since 1946, Lonborg pitched a beauty and started the game-winning rally with a bunt single. When he finished off the Twins, Lonborg was carried off the field by adoring fans. He was brilliant on three day's rest in his first World Series start, carrying a no-hitter into the eighth and finishing with a one-hit shutout. He beat Steve Carlton in Game 5 in St. Louis, with only a ninth-inning home run by Roger Maris spoiling his second straight shutout bid. He matched with Bob Gibson in Game 7 on two days rest, but this time Lonborg was spent. The Cardinals romped and the dream was over.

Lonborg was the first Red Sox pitcher to win the Cy Young Award (1967 was the inaugural year the award was given in each league), but in the four season after the injury he went just 27–29. He was sent to Milwaukee after the 1971 season in a nine-player swap that netted Boston Tommy Harper. Lonborg was traded to Philadelphia the next year and he helped the Phillies dominate the National League East. The Stanford grad retired in 1979 and became a dentist.

Fred Lynn

Although the rest of his career never quite matched his banner first season, Fred Lynn was a Boston legend. The Yankees wanted him first. New York drafted him out of high school, but he opted for the University of Southern California on a football scholarship under John McKay. He starred in Rod Dedeaux's legendary baseball program, winning a national championship all three years at USC. The Red Sox took him in the second round in 1973, picking just ahead of the Dodgers, who had their eyes on the local kid. Lynn and Jim Rice helped Pawtucket win a minor league championship and then they set their sights on Boston.

Lynn made jaws drop at Fenway Park even before '75. He batted .419 in 15 games at the end of '74. By Opening Day he was in center field; by June he had the game of his career in Detroit, hitting three home runs— and just missing a fourth—while knocking in 10 runs.

He drove the Red Sox to their first AL East crown, leading the league in slugging, runs, and doubles, while placing second in batting and third in RBIs. He was not only the first player to win a league MVP and Rookie of the Year the same season, he won both awards handily (Rice was second in ROY balloting and third in MVP). Lynn's flashy fielding made the Gold Glove a foregone conclusion as well. Ichiro Suzuki would match Lynn's award trifecta in 2001, but Ichiro had already been a star in Japan, and his team missed the World Series.

Lynn was the original star of Game 6 of the 1975 World Series. His three-run homer in the first inning put Boston on the way to what seemed like an easy night, and his collision with the wall in the fifth made hearts stop (and padding go up in 1976). He played every inning of the Series, batting .280. Lynn's national exposure as a rookie led him to nine straight All-Star Games. He hit the first grand slam home run in All-Star history in 1983, earning the game's MVP. By then, however, he was an Angel.

After battling injuries, Lynn won a batting title for the Red Sox in 1979—adding career highs with 39 homers, 122 RBIs, and a .423 on-base percentage—but he left something behind when he was sent to California in a blockbuster trade in 1981. His stroke was perfect for Fenway, batting .347 with a .420 on-base average and a .601 slugging average in his career there. He never reached another World Series, although his .611 batting average for the Angels in the 1982 ALCS made him the first player on the losing side to be MVP in an LCS. Lynn also played in Baltimore, Detroit, and San Diego, but in the memory of fans he's tumbling on the grass at Fenway, losing his hat, and raising his glove to show he got it.

Pedro Martinez

When picking the greatest Red Sox pitcher of all-time, the mind can go in many directions. Roger Clemens, Babe Ruth, and Cy Young are all Boston legends, but who's going to argue with Pedro?

Pedro Martinez debuted professionally at 16 in the Dominican Summer League in 1988. Dodgers manager Tommy Lasorda didn't think the slightly-built younger brother of ace Ramon Martinez was durable enough. After using Pedro as a reliever in 1993, the Dodgers traded him to the Expos for Delino DeShields. Pedro started 117 of 118 games as an Expo, and in 1997 he ended the six-year monopoly the Braves and/or Greg Maddux had on the NL Cy Young Award. Then financially strapped Montreal waved au revoir.

Landed for Carl Pavano and Tony Armas, Pedro rewarded Boston by going 19–7 with a 2.89 ERA and just 5.89 hits per game. It was the only year in four Pedro didn't win a Cy Young, losing to Clemens in Toronto. The next year Pedro was even better. He captured the pitching Triple Crown: 23–4 with a 2.07 ERA and 313 strikeouts, the most K's in franchise history; his 13.2 strikeouts per game was better than any pitcher in the 20th century.

Pedro won the '99 Cy Young unanimously and would have won the MVP over Ivan Rodriguez if he hadn't been left off a writer's ballot. Five National Leaguers struck out against him in the All-Star Game at Fenway and in September he fanned 17 in a 1-hitter at Yankee Stadium. He followed that with two memorable performances in that year's postseason: six innings of hitless relief in Game 5 of the Division Series to beat Cleveland, and a sparkling ALCS outing against the Yankees while Clemens was shelled and then booed out of Fenway.

The next year Pedro's ERA dropped to 1.74, almost 2 runs lower than runner-up Clemens, and more than 3 runs better than the league average. It was the lowest mark in the American League since Ron Guidry in 1978. Pedro's 5.31 hits per game had only been touched by Nolan Ryan since Luis Tiant in 1968. This Pedro was something.

Though fun-loving, he was all business on the field. He pushed Don Zimmer into the ground in a bizarre melee in the 2003 ALCS, and he stayed in as long as Grady Little let him in Game 7 of that series, much to the detriment of Red Sox Nation. The next year his star had been passed by Curt Schilling, but Pedro endured calls of "Who's Your Daddy?" at Yankee Stadium to pitch an inning the night Boston finally beat New York for the pennant. His gem in Game 3 of the World Series set up the sweep that ended a championship drought dating back to the Babe. That was his last game with the Red Sox.

Management balked at giving him a four-year contract, but the Mets, in need of the kind of splash only Pedro can offer, took a $53 million chance. He was excellent yet frail in his return to the National League. Pedro missed the end of his stellar 2005 season and was injured for much of '06, including the postseason. It's harder to win without Pedro.

David Ortiz

What were the Twins thinking? They had a 27-year-old hitter coming off his most productive season and they didn't offer him a contract. Minnesota general manager Terry Ryan thought the 20 home runs, 75 RBIs, and .500 slugging—career highs for the Dominican DH at the time—were replaceable on his division champion club. What the American League quickly learned is that you don't replace David Ortiz.

Ortiz signed with the Red Sox for $300,000 more than he'd gotten in Minnesota and Boston took off. In 2003 he set new standards in every category and finished in the top five in the MVP for the first of four straight seasons. How he didn't win one brings to mind another question: What were the voters thinking?

Ortiz offered Manny Ramirez ample protection and the lineup hummed. In 2003 Boston increased its runs by 102, leading the majors in that category as well as hits, doubles, batting, on-base percentage, and slugging. Ortiz showed a flair for the dramatic with a two-run double to plate the tying and go-ahead runs in the eighth inning of Game 4 of the Division Series. He homered twice in the ALCS against the Yankees. It was the next October, however, that belonged to "Big Papi."

After the Red Sox squandered a lead in Game 3 of the Division Series, Ortiz sent fans rushing into the streets with a series-clinching home run in the 10th inning. When the Red Sox were on the verge of being swept by the hated Yankees in the ALCS, his 12th-inning homer provided hope. He singled in the winning run the next night in the 14th inning. The Red Sox rallied to win the pennant with Big Papi producing 3 homers, 11 RBIs, and a .387 batting average to earn series MVP. He hit .308 in the World Series as an 86-year-old monkey lifted off Boston's back.

Ortiz continued to provide oohs and ahs, driving in 148 runs in 2005 and barely missing the AL MVP to Alex Rodriguez. He launched a league-high 54 homers to break Jimmie Foxx's 67-year-old club record and claim his second straight RBI crown in 2006. And he's not done yet, folks.

Herb Pennock

Going 11–4 in his first full year in the big leagues didn't convince Connie Mack that Herb Pennock could pitch, and winning 58 games over four seasons for a string of second-division clubs likewise didn't make the Red Sox realize what they had, either. In the end, it was the Yankees who took advantage of the mistakes of other clubs to add another key piece to their developing dynasty.

Pennock had trouble getting a chance at starting because he didn't throw hard and had control problems early in his career. He appeared in only 14 games over his first year and a half with the Sox, then missed out on Boston's 1918 World Series triumph because he was serving in the military during World War I. Although the Sox wouldn't be a .500 team again until 1934, Pennock went 16–8 and 16–13 the next two seasons as he cemented himself as a valued starting pitcher. His record dropped to 12–14 in 1921 and 10–17 in 1922, though the blame for the Red Sox finishing dead last, 33 games behind the Yankees, can hardly be put on Pennock, as his adjusted ERA was 12 percent better than league average in '21 and just one percent below average in '22.

Boston's front office was in the midst of making a series of terrible baseball decisions, and management made another doozy by dealing Pennock to the Yankees. While that move doesn't rival the selling of Babe Ruth a few years earlier, Pennock won 115 games—and four pennants and three World Series titles—over the next six seasons.

Pennock spent 11 years pitching in the Bronx before returning to Boston in 1934 for one final season with the Red Sox, pitching out of the bullpen. He was elected to the Hall of Fame in 1948 by the baseball writers.

Johnny Pesky

Johnny Pesky's Boston legacy is remarkable, and yet he has never been able to shake the perceived momentary pause on a relay throw from backup outfielder Leon Culberson in the eighth inning of Game 7 of the 1946 World Series. Would he have gotten Enos Slaughter at the plate? Would the Red Sox have gone on to win? No one knows, but Pesky's life has been far more than a moment of waiting.

Born John Michael Paveskovich to Croatian immigrants in Portland, Oregon, he worked at the Pacific Coast League home of the Portland Beavers as a youth. He signed with the Red Sox in 1940 for less money than the Cardinals offered because his parents trusted scout Earl Johnson. The decision provided decades of paid enjoyment.

In 1946 Pesky improved on his stellar rookie numbers of four years earlier, setting career highs in hits, doubles, RBIs, and batting (.335) for the pennant-winning Sox. He led the American League in hits three times and was solid right through 1951, playing both shortstop and third base. The arrival of manager Lou Boudreau hastened Pesky's departure in 1952. He finished his career in Detroit and Washington before becoming a minor league manager. He made his way back to Fenway Park to manage in 1963–64, and he later spent a decade as a Red Sox coach, even filling in as manager for five games in 1980. He made countless appearances on behalf of the club and could often be spied hitting fungoes or watching games from the bench.

Announcer and former teammate Mel Parnell is credited with first calling the 302-foot right-field foul pole, "Pesky's Pole," because he jokingly pointed out that all of the little left-handed hitter's 6 career Fenway homers (he hit just 17 in all) seemed to barely land in fair territory. The pole was officially designated in his name on his 87th birthday in 2006.

Rico Petrocelli

For someone watching the Red Sox for the first time in 1975, it was hard to imagine veteran third baseman Rico Petrocelli as a shortstop, but that's where he started out and that's where he helped forge the "Impossible Dream." At a time when few players did much hitting—least of all middle infielders—he hit 17 home runs as a 24-year-old shortstop for the surprise 1967 AL pennant winners. He homered twice in Game 6 of the World Series at Fenway to force a seventh game and had one of Boston's three hits against Bob Gibson in the deciding game.

Brooklyn-born Americo Peter Petrocelli had his signature year in 1969. He homered 40 times—still a record for a Red Sox shortstop—and knocked in 97 runs. He set career highs in several categories with his .297 average, which was 30 points better than any of his other dozen seasons. Petrocelli made the All-Star team for the second time in three years and was seventh in voting for AL MVP. He hit 29 home runs and drove in 103 runs in 1970 as the Red Sox, concerned about his diminished range, tried him at third base for the first time. He shifted over to the position full-time when shortstop Luis Aparicio arrived in 1971.

Though he hit a key home run in Game 2 of the 1975 ALCS and batted .308 against the Reds in the 1975 World Series, Petrocelli was on the way out. He was replaced by Butch Hobson during 1976 and released the following spring. Petrocelli then became a minor league coach and manager, taking Class AAA Pawtucket to the playoffs in 1992 after replacing Hobson, who had been promoted to manage Boston, but he left after a year to spend more time with his family.

Dick Radatz

Dick Radatz's famous nickname said it all about his meteoric career. Originally nicknamed "Moose" for his imposing 6-foot, 5-inch, 235-pound frame, he was later dubbed "the Monster" for multiple reasons: his devastating fastball, his perplexing off-speed and breaking pitches, and the left-field wall at his home park in Fenway. With absolutely dominant performances in the first three years of his career, Radatz defined a new prototype for what were called "firemen" or "relief aces." (The term *closer* wasn't used back then.) While there had previously been ace relievers reliant on overpowering fastballs, the best relievers in the 1950s and early 1960s ran the gamut from hard throwers to junkball pitchers.

Radatz played college ball at Michigan State, graduating in 1959 before being signed by Boston. He was converted to relief in the high minors a year before his stunning rookie season in 1962, when he led the AL with 62 appearances and 24 saves. The save did not become an official statistic until 1969, but his unofficial single-season Boston total wasn't topped until 1977 and his career mark of 104 lasted well into the 1980s. His Red Sox record for relief wins in a season (16) still stands.

Radatz fanned 144 hitters in 124 ⅔ innings as a rookie, following that with 162 punchouts in 132 ⅓ innings in 1963 and 181 K's in 157 innings in 1964. The lethal right-hander saved 25 games, second in the AL, in 1963. He saved a league-leading, club-record 29 games in 1964. In that three-year stretch, Radatz also won 40 games while losing only 21.

In the 1963 All-Star Game, Radatz wowed the crowd in Cleveland by striking out five NL hitters—including Willie Mays, Willie McCovey, and Duke Snider—in two innings. In 1964 Radatz fanned five more NL All-Stars—including Billy Williams and Hank Aaron—in 2 ⅔ innings, though he ultimately lost the game on a two-out home run by Johnny Callison in the bottom of the ninth.

In 1965 the wheels started to come off the Radatz express, however, as his ERA jumped from 2.17 (1962–64) to 3.91. Mysterious control problems were supposedly responsible, and Radatz was traded to Cleveland during the 1966 season. "The Monster" never regained his previous form; he retired after the 1969 season and died in 2005.

Manny Ramirez

Left field has been in good hands since the Green Monster was erected at Fenway Park more than seven decades ago: Ted Williams, Carl Yastrzemski, Jim Rice, and now Manny Ramirez. Yaz was the only one who actually seemed to understand the wall and studied its caroms. Rice and Williams appeared to always be concentrating on their next at bat. Manny...he's thinking about something out there, right?

Manny was a little flaky during his tenure with the Indians, but he batted .313 and hit 236 home runs in Cleveland (through 2006 he had almost the same numbers—.316 and 234—for Boston). His eight-year, $160 million contract with the Red Sox was the second biggest in history at the time, coming two days after Alex Rodriguez's $252 million deal. As for his flakiness—from having half the PawSox scour the field for his lost $15,000 earring during a 2002 rehab assignment to missing a 2003 game yet going to a bar with Yankee Enrique Wilson to his numerous requests to be traded only to rescind them and declare his love for the club—the man has a phrase that sums it all up: "Manny being Manny."

What team wouldn't be patient with a hitter who averaged .314 with 42 homers and 135 RBIs for his

career? And while Teddy Ballgame and Yaz are in the Hall of Fame, with Jim Rice hoping one day to follow, Manny has something they were unable to achieve in a cumulative 48 seasons in Boston: a world championship. It started pretty ugly, too, as Manny botched two eighth-inning balls at Fenway in Game 1 of the 2004 World Series. It turned out just fine as the Red Sox won the game and Manny wound up the MVP of the first Boston world championship since 1918. He batted .412 in the sweep of St. Louis, reaching base in half his plate appearances.

Manny grew up playing baseball incessantly in the Dominican Republic. At 13 he joined his parents—his father a cab diver, his mother a seamstress—in New York. Years of tireless work on his swing, not to mention 430-foot shots at George Washington High, made him Cleveland's 1991 first-round draft choice. His 165 RBIs for the Indians in 1999 were the most in the major leagues since Jimmie Foxx drove in 175 for the Red Sox in 1938.

With Boston Manny has won a batting title in 2002, a home run crown in '04, and was three-time leader in slugging and on-base percentage (including '06 when he started just eight times after the five-game August debacle with the Yankees). He has been named to play in 10 All-Star Games, but has shown up for only 7, much to Bud Selig's consternation. Though Manny's numbers look like he stepped right out of the power-laden 1930s, he's certainly a now player and Red Sox fans have learned to embrace Manny and the now.

Jim Rice

At a time when offense was a little harder to come by, it wasn't hard for Jim Rice. He was one of the most dominating hitters from the late 1970s to the middle of the 1980s. Something always seemed to dampen the brilliant luster of his career.

He was not an Opening Day starter in 1975 and didn't get the full-time job until Boston legend Tony Conigliaro's last-ditch comeback failed. Despite a brilliant inaugural season, he was overshadowed by teammate Fred Lynn, who won the Rookie of the Year and AL MVP while Rice took second and third, respectively. Carlton Fisk's home run in Game 6 of that year's World Series clearly helped his later enshrinement in the Hall of Fame, but Rice missed the postseason after being hit in the wrist in September. Although he won the AL MVP in 1978, Rice's monster season (121 runs, 213 hits, 46 home runs, 139 RBIs, 315 average, 600 slugging, and the only player since 1951 to lead the league in homers and triples) was overshadowed by Boston's ill-fated battle with the Yankees. In the famous one-game playoff he singled in a run for a 2–0 lead in the sixth, one inning before Bucky

Dent's crushing home run. Rice's long fly in the ninth moved Rick Burleson to third, but it would have tied the game if not for Lou Piniella's blind snag of Jerry Remy's hit to sunny right field one batter earlier.

In 1979 Rice batted a career-best .325 while coming close to his numbers the previous year in most categories. After two off years, Rice returned as one of the top run producers in the game from 1983 to 1986. He made the last of his eight All-Star appearances in '86 and batted .324, drove in 110, and reached base just 10 fewer times than in his great '78 campaign. Rice made the World Series for the only time and batted .333. In the crushing Game 6 loss to the Mets, Rice had to hold at third on a two-out double in the first inning and was thrown out at the plate by the weak-armed Mookie Wilson in the seventh. His only other postseason appearance was an ALCS sweep by Oakland in 1988.

So why no Hall of Fame? Rice had problems with the press. His first year on the ballot coincided with Mike Schmidt's and Rice had trouble catching up; he's since gotten as high as 60 of the 75 percent needed. His career dropped off quickly after knee surgery in 1987 and his average fell just under .300. Yet look at who's in Cooperstown and Rice is more deserving than many. His total Red Sox hits (2,452), home runs (382), and RBIs (1,451) trail only two other pretty good left fielders: Carl Yastrzemski and Ted Williams.

Red Ruffing

Red Ruffing was one of the most unlikely Hall of Fame pitchers in history. After parts of seven unsuccessful seasons with the Red Sox, he went to the Yankees and became one of the biggest winners in the game.

Ruffing first appeared with the Red Sox in 1924 at age 19, even though he had a losing record for the two minor league teams he'd been with previously. The Red Sox were brutal back then, so they gave Ruffing a shot. He started 67 games over the next three years despite walking more batters than he struck out and compiled a 20–46 record. In 1928 he had the most losses in the AL with a 10–25 record, but he also led the league in complete games and batters faced, with an ERA a quarter-run below the league average. The next year he was the league's top loser again, although he was not as durable and was hit harder.

Of course, even today instead of an outcry, there would be sighs of relief from the fans if their team dumped a guy who was 39–96 and had walked more batters than he'd fanned for his career.

Red flags should have gone off in the Red Sox front office when the powerful Yankees were willing to pay $50,000 for him and throw in outfielder Cedric Durst,

who never played again after 1930. Smart organizations don't trade for table scraps; instead they raid the weaker clubs for undervalued players. So the Yankees acquired Ruffing and turned him into an instant winner. He was 0–3 with a 6.38 ERA before the trade on May 6, 1930, but Ruffing went 15–5 the rest of the way for the Yankees. New York was in the midst of a three-year rebuilding plan after winning six pennants in eight years during the 1920s. (Their rebuilding plan was obviously far different than Boston's, which saw the Red Sox finish last nine times between 1922 and 1932.)

Ruffing won at least 14 games in 12 of his first 13 years in the Bronx. He won 20 or more from 1936–39, with the Yankees claiming the World Series crown each year. Ruffing came out of retirement to pitch during World War II, finally quitting for good at age 42 in 1947. The Veterans Committee chose Ruffing for the Hall of Fame in 1967, one more immortal who got away from the Red Sox during that era.

Babe Ruth

The "Curse of the Bambino" is legend in baseball circles. Three Red Sox World Series crowns in four seasons with Ruth turned into 85 years of futility for the franchise after he left. But somewhat forgotten in all of Ruth's home runs is the fact that the portly left-hander quickly became one of the top pitchers in the American League upon arriving in Beantown.

George Herman Ruth, 19, was brought to spring training for the minor-league Baltimore Orioles by owner Jack Dunn in 1914; the slim, raw youth was quickly dubbed "Babe." By season's end he was in Boston. He won 18 games in his first full season with the Red Sox in 1915. He was the best pitcher in the league a year later, topping the AL with a 1.75 ERA and nine shutouts. The Red Sox beat Brooklyn in five games in the World Series, with Ruth playing no small part. He was the winning pitcher in Boston's 2–1 marathon victory in Game 2. He allowed a run in the first inning, drove in the tying run, and pitched 14 innings. It was the longest World Series outing in history and also started a 29 2/3 scoreless innings streak he added to during two more Boston World Series victories.

Ruth was at his finest on the mound in 1917, going 24–13 with a 2.01 ERA. He was first in the AL in complete games, second in wins and innings, third in opponent batting average, and fifth in strikeouts. Despite his consistently outstanding pitching, Ruth's bat was beginning to get even more attention. He batted .325 and slugged .472 that year, his last as a full-time pitcher.

After Boston manager Ed Barrow was talked into making the move, Ruth split time between the hill and the outfield in 1918. He went 13–7 with a 2.22 ERA (and winning twice in Boston's six-game World Series win over the Cubs) while clubbing 11 homers for a share of the lead league, batting .300, slugging .555, and compiling a .411 on-base percentage. The rest, as they say, is history. Ruth played 116 games in the field the next year, pitching just 17 times, and forever altering the face of the game with his legendary swats. His 29 home runs became the single-season record, and he also led the AL in runs, RBIs, slugging, and on-base percentage.

Following his sale to the Yankees by Boston's impatient and impetuous owner Harry Frazee shortly after Christmas 1919, Boston became a second-division club and the downtrodden Yankees transformed into the best team in the game. (Several other one-way transactions between Boston and New York helped, too.) Ruth hit 659 home runs for the Yankees, becoming the greatest player in baseball history, as well as the most popular. He played his final season in Boston in 1935, as a member of the lowly Braves. He quit by Memorial Day, still a legend, but never becoming a manager as he craved. Ruth was a member of the inaugural Hall of Fame class of 1936.

Curt Schilling

Curt Schilling does not appear among the top 50 Red Sox pitchers in most categories, although his pronouncement that he plans to pitch until 2008 may change that. Schilling's bravado, backbone, and bloody sock can't be measured in numbers.

Boston general manager Theo Epstein moved into the Schilling household around Thanksgiving 2003. As the clock ticked on a deal deadline, Epstein used every number and every argument he could to convince a 37-year-old pitcher with 16 years experience in Baltimore, Houston, Philadelphia, and Arizona that he should come to Boston. While certainly known for his talking, Schilling listened; the idea of being part of a team that meant everything to an entire region of the country and possibly altering its fortune was something the history buff couldn't pass up. The fans immediately embraced him, and he embraced back, going so far as to leave e-mail pronouncements on web sites.

When it came time to put up or shut up, he came through. Schilling had his third 20-win season in four years in '04, and had the league's lowest strikeouts to walk ratio; most veteran National League pitchers coming to the American League had the exact opposite experience.

Injured during Game 1 of the ALCS, Schilling's right ankle had to be stitched together to pitch Game 6 at Yankee Stadium. He was brilliant, with a little blood showing through his sock, and the Red Sox evened the

series and won the pennant the next night. He woke the day of Game 2 of the World Series unable to walk, but an extra stitch by team doctor William Morgan helped Schilling go six solid innings and the Red Sox went on to a sweep St. Louis.

While Schilling probably won't have the numbers to get to the Hall of Fame—200 wins, 3,000 strikeouts, and a stellar postseason record notwithstanding—his bloody sock is in Cooperstown. His role in getting the club its long coveted world championship will, however, forever remain part of Red Sox lore.

Tris Speaker

Tris Speaker's time in Boston was relatively short. He played for the Red Sox only seven full seasons, but he was one of the key players on two World Series winners. Speaker almost didn't play for Boston at all. He basically had to beg for a job, especially after hitting only .158 and .224 in part-time duty in his first two years with the club. But once he started hitting, Spoke didn't stop until he amassed 3,514 hits, a .345 average, and a still-standing record of 792 doubles. And he was one of the finest center fielders in history.

Speaker became a Boston regular in 1909, with the first of 18 seasons hitting .300 or better. He won the MVP award in 1912 when he hit .383, stole 52 bases, and clubbed 10 home runs, tying him with Frank "Home Run" Baker for the lead league. The Red Sox won the pennant that year and claimed an epic World Series title over the New York Giants. Speaker played a pivotal role. He collected the game-tying hit during a two-run rally in the bottom of the 10th inning in the eighth game of the Series (Game 2 ended in a tie after Speaker circled the bases, again in the bottom of the 10th).

He was a top performer in 1915, again helping the Red Sox to a World Series crown. It was his final year in Boston, however. A salary dispute led to a trade to Cleveland, where he spent 11 years, the last seven as player/manager. He led the Tribe to their first World Series title in 1920, batting .388 with 50 doubles. He finished his career amid controversy over the alleged fixing of a game against Detroit back in 1919. Ty Cobb and Speaker were cleared, but both clubs released the player/managers. Spoke spent single seasons with the Senators and Athletics. He was elected to the Hall of Fame in 1937, one of the first eight players enshrined.

Bob Stanley

Bob Stanley pitched for the Red Sox for 13 years, and he pitched pretty well—yet the memories of his career in Red Sox Nation will always be defined by one pitch.

"Steamer" Stanley was far from the prototypical closer. The tall, workman-like right-hander depended on inducing groundouts via a sinker instead of blowing enemy hitters away with a blazing fastball, and his out pitch was a deceptive palm ball. Making his debut with Boston at the start of the 1977 season, Stanley worked both in the rotation as well as out of the bullpen for four years before becoming a full-time reliever. In 1978 he went 15–2, with a career-low 2.46 ERA; Ron Guidry barely nudged past Stanley's .882 winning percentage for the league lead.

After a terrific season in middle relief in 1982, saving 14 and winning 12—his fifth straight year with 10 or more wins—Stanley was promoted to closer. In an era of 60–80 inning workloads for closers, Stanley's career years in 1982 and 1983 are hard to believe now. He finished second in the AL in ERA at 3.10 in 1982, with 48 relief appearances covering 168 1/3 innings. Stanley actually compiled a slightly better Adjusted ERA (40 percent better than league-average) than the ERA leader, Rick Sutcliffe. Stanley followed that bravura performance by making the 1983 All-Star team while posting 33 saves (his career-high) with an ERA of 2.85 (AERA of 154), though he also blew 14 saves—a problem that would plague him thereafter.

Though he pitched creditably for another six seasons and set virtually every Red Sox record for relievers, Stanley met his Waterloo with his infamous wild pitch in Game 6 of the 1986 World Series. The fact that virtually every inside pitch like that one (i.e., that isn't in the dirt, behind the hitter, or over the head of the catcher) is routinely called a passed ball doesn't even rate as an historical footnote.

Luis Tiant

The Legend of El Tiante says that Luis Tiant suddenly appeared in the 1975 World Series mowing down the Big Red Machine. In truth, Tiant came from a solid baseball pedigree and was a star in the major leagues when many of the participants in the '75 Series were still in high school.

Tiant was the son of Luis Eleuterio Tiant, a great Cuban pitcher kept out of the major leagues because of his color. The younger Tiant signed with the Mexico City Tigers against his father's wishes. The Indians purchased his contract and he eventually made his way to Cleveland. Tiant had a penchant for shutouts, throwing 10 in his first 61 starts. While 1968 was "the Year of the Pitcher" and the year Denny McLain won 31 games, Tiant threw four consecutive shutouts in May (he had nine for the season), and started over McLain in the All-Star Game. Tiant's 1.60 ERA was the lowest in the

American League since the dead ball era. The next year the mound was lowered and his ERA increased by two runs a game. He went from a 21-game winner to 20-game loser.

After a trade to the Twins, he was released by both Minnesota and Atlanta over a 45-day span. The Red Sox picked him up in May 1971; Tiant went 1–7. Pitching-thin Boston brought him back the next year and he rewarded them with his versatility as both a starter and reliever. Tiant went 15–6, led the AL with a 1.91 ERA, and earned Comeback Player of the Year. He won 20 games each of the next two seasons. Tiant won 18 in 1975, but it was his 4 starts in October that forever made his image.

Facing the three-time defending world champion A's in Game 1 of the ALCS, Tiant stymied Oakland on three hits. The Red Sox went on to a sweep. A week later in Game 1 of the World Series, Tiant was in his whirling, wheeling glory against the 108-win Reds. Tiant mowed down Cincinnati while announcer Joe Garagiola spun stories of his cigar-chomping, fun-loving nature and the reunion with his parents after 14 years apart. When Tiant singled to start a six-run rally in what had been a scoreless duel, he was a full-fledged national star. He followed that shutout with a 163-pitch, complete-game effort to even the Series in Cincinnati.

Three days of rain enabled him to start Game 6 in Boston. He wasn't at his best, blowing a 3–0 lead, but he lasted into the eighth. Bernie Carbo was a hero for the moment with his game-tying homer and Carlton Fisk became a hero for all-time with his game-winning blast and body English. Boston won all three of Tiant's starts; a little more rain and maybe it could have been four.

Tiant had his fourth 20-win season—and third with Boston—while lowering his ERA by a run in 1976. His last win for the Red Sox was a two-hitter on the last day of the season to force the one-game playoff with the Yankees. The next spring, he was playing in New York, signing as a free agent and doing Yankee Franks ads on TV: "It's great to be with a wiener." He bounced around with the Pirates and Angels, finishing with 229 wins. In 2002 he returned to the Boston fold as pitching coach for the Red Sox farm club the Lowell Spinners.

Jason Varitek

When a team is about to acquire a known name and only giving up prospects in return, beware. Red Sox fans know too well the trade that sent minor leaguer Jeff Bagwell to Houston for veteran reliever Larry Andersen in 1990. Seven years later it worked the other way. Reliever Heathcliff Slocumb went from Boston to Seattle for a young pitcher and a catcher: Derek Lowe and Jason Varitek.

Slocumb? He just made Lou Piniella even angrier at his bullpen. Lowe saved 85 games and won 70 for Boston, not counting his clinching victories in each postseason series in 2004. As for Varitek, he's already passed Carlton Fisk on the club's all-time list for games caught and should surpass most of Pudge's Red Sox records. Even with his four-year contract signed after 2004, the only question is whether Varitek will remain with the club his entire career like previous captains Jim Rice and Carl Yastrzemski.

Varitek not only keeps the pitching staff grounded, the switch hitter is an integral part of the lineup as well. His loss for much of the 2006 season was felt on a daily basis as the team struggled. Varitek has been through the wars, batting .321 and driving in seven runs in the stirring 2004 ALCS comeback, the touchstone of the modern Red Sox fan. While Fisk has his iconic moment of waving his homer fair in 1975, Varitek's legacy is already secure with two images: slugging Alex Rodriguez as the Red Sox turned the 2004 season around and jumping into Keith Foulke's arms as Boston finally won its all after 86 years.

Mo Vaughn

Mo Vaughn was the type of sincere leader that Red Sox fans have long been attached to. Large and thoughtful from a young age, the son of two teachers obliterated the competition in his hometown of Norwalk, Connecticut; earned a scholarship to Trinity Pawling Prep; and dominated in college. At Seton Hall University, Vaughn hit a school-record 28 home runs as a freshman, making the most of ample opportunities to drive in future big leaguers Craig Biggio and John Valentin. A first-round pick in 1989—three years after his cousin Greg Vaughn was drafted—Maurice Samuel Vaughn quickly made his way to the majors. He took over at first base full-time following an injury to Carlos Quintana in 1992, persevering despite some early setbacks.

His patience paid off in 1993 when he batted .297 with 29 home runs and 101 RBIs. The next year he broke .300 for the first time, and he did not fall below that mark in his last five seasons in Boston. Vaughn struck out often, had a less than adequate glove, and grew even less mobile as his size increased, but the popular slugger lashed dangerous line drives all over Fenway Park.

The 1995 season was his best. With MLB coming back from a crippling strike and even the loyal Boston fans in a cantankerous mood, Vaughn was the linchpin of a team full of veterans whose careers had stalled. Vaughn led the Red Sox to a division title, hitting 39 home runs and tying for the league lead with 126 RBIs in the shortened season—somehow stealing 11 bases as well. Friendly, charitable, and a hitter pitchers truly

feared, Vaughn wound up getting the most votes for AL MVP, even if the despised Albert Belle and quiet Edgar Martinez had far better seasons.

Vaughn homered 44 times and knocked in 143 runs the next season. In 1998 he just missed winning the batting title on the final day, and a bitter dispute with GM Dan Duquette led to Vaughn leaving after the season to join the Angels. He continued to put up good numbers his first two years in Anaheim, but a ruptured tendon in his left arm cost him the 2001 season. The New York Mets traded for the much bigger, much less productive Vaughn in 2002. His career ended in New York because of a chronic knee injury.

Tim Wakefield

Tim Wakefield has been pitching for so long that he has totaled up more losses than Cy Young did for the Red Sox. Wakefield has started more games than Young in Boston, trailing only Roger Clemens in that category. The durable knuckleballer stands in third place all-time for strikeouts, innings, and wins—a long way from the 192 victories shared by Young and Clemens, but ahead of legendary names in Red Sox history like Pedro Martinez, Luis Tiant, and Smoky Joe Wood.

Wakefield has been hammered, disparaged, and demoted to the bullpen; he's also won one of the most important games in franchise history (the 14-inning Game 5 in the 2004 ALCS) and lost one that cost the pennant (the 11-inning Game 7 of the 2003 ALCS). He has given up more home runs in a Red Sox uniform than Clemens, Wood, and Young combined, and will soon own the walks record as well. He is so difficult to catch that the Red Sox desperately reacquired backup catcher Doug Mirabelli in 2006 because no one in the organization could handle his signature pitch.

Wakefield was drafted as a power-hitting infielder, but his school-record 40 home runs at Florida Tech didn't translate into much power in Pittsburgh's minor league system. Thus, the failing prospect took his sideline knuckler to the mound and made his major league debut just before his 25th birthday, a relative spring chicken for late-blooming knuckleballers. Wakefield went 8-1 for the Pirates to help them win the NL East title in 1992, then twice twirled complete-game wins against the Braves in the NLCS. Failing to repeat this success in 1993, Wakefield spent a brutal year in the minors before the Red Sox scooped him up quickly after Pittsburgh cut him in April 1995.

Wakefield instantly became Boston's ace. He went 16-8 with a 2.75 ERA, winning Comeback Player of the Year, finishing third in the Cy Young Award voting, and helping the Red Sox take the 1995 AL East title.

As often seems the case with knuckleballers, hard times follow good, yet Wakefield has persevered. He was sensational in 1998, going 17-8 as Boston reached the postseason again. The Red Sox have stuck with him partly due to a lack of a better alternative but mostly because of his durability and versatility. He has started at least 15 games for Boston every year and has also pitched 25 or more times in relief in four of the last 12 seasons. He has 22 career saves, including 15 picked up while filling in for injured Tom Gordon in 1999 to help the Red Sox take the wild card. In 2004, with the Red Sox staff in need of rest after rallying to beat the Yankees for the pennant, Wakefield started the first World Series game in Boston in 18 years. He wasn't great, but he was ready when the bell rang, and the Red Sox won it all in the end.

Ted Williams

The greatest hitter who ever lived? Of all the hitters who have ever played major league baseball, the consensus seems to be that if it's not Ted Williams, it's pretty close.

The case for the Splendid Splinter has been made many times. He's the last player to hit better than .400, he won the Triple Crown twice, captured six batting titles, was named to 17 All-Star teams, and left the game in 1960 with a home run his last time up. He was first in runs six times (including five straight seasons), home runs and RBIs four times each, walks eight times (including six straight years), slugging eight times, and on-base percentage an even dozen times. He finished with a lifetime .344 batting average (tied for sixth-best all-time), 1,798 runs (15th), 2,654 hits (64th), 521 home runs (tied for 15th), 1,839 RBIs (13th), and only Barry Bonds, Rickey Henderson, and Babe Ruth have surpassed his 2,021 walks.

Unlike most other great hitters, Williams missed five prime seasons while serving as a Marine pilot during both World War II and Korea. He survived being shot down during a combat mission in Korea in 1953. The loss of so much time, much of it during his prime, doesn't paint a true picture of what the Kid *could* have done in the record book. To compensate for his lost at bats, his totals for the two years prior to and following each tour of duty have been averaged and added, for the respectful number of seasons missed, to his career marks (subtracting, of course, the small numbers he accumulated in 1952 and 1953). When that is done, the numbers show 568 more runs, 766 more hits, 150 more homers, 531 more RBIs, and 663 more walks. If added to his already impressive career marks, Williams would be first all-time in runs, RBIs, and walks, fourth all-time in home runs (behind Hank Aaron, Bonds, and Ruth), and

tied for sixth with Honus Wagner in hits (behind Pete Rose, Ty Cobb, Aaron, Stan Musial, and Tris Speaker).

Williams won two MVP awards, in 1946 and 1949, finished second in the voting four other times, and third once, which normally would be impressive totals for any player. He would have, without a doubt, won more had he not feuded so famously with the media, especially the Boston press. Williams finished second to Joe DiMaggio in the MVP voting in 1941 and 1947. Joltin' Joe was also one of the all-time greats and his 56-game hitting streak in '41 trumped the Kid's .406. In '47, though, Williams was clearly the best player in the league, winning the Triple Crown and also topping the AL in runs, walks, slugging, and on-base percentage. His adjusted OPS that year was 199, compared to 154 for DiMaggio, meaning Williams was a 45 percent better hitter that year than the Yankee Clipper, yet DiMaggio got eight first place votes and Williams only three. Williams finished second by one point because a Boston writer was so irritated with Williams that he didn't include the slugger in any of the 10 spots he was required to fill.

Getting into the Hall of Fame was much simpler. He went in on the first ballot in 1966 (DiMaggio had gone in on the third try in 1955). Williams' exceptional eye made him a superlative hitter as well as a coveted pilot in the Marines. He managed in Washington, winning Manager of the Year as a rookie skipper in 1969, the only man to bring the expansion Senators home with a winning record. He had much less luck when the team moved to Texas. He spent several springs working with Red Sox hitters in Florida, but preferred to be fishing.

A long-running sore point to some was Boston's winning only one pennant in his 19 years with the club, losing a seven-game World Series to the Cardinals in 1946 with Williams batting .200. Boston's lack of postseason appearances in that period can hardly be placed at the foot of the greatest hitter who ever lived. He wouldn't swing at that.

Smoky Joe Wood

No Red Sox pitcher since Cy Young—not the Babe, El Tiante, the Rocket, or even Pedro—has ever had a season like Smoky Joe Wood's 1912. Washington's Walter Johnson, no slouch himself in terms of speed, set the record straight that summer: "Listen, my friend, no man alive can throw harder than Smoky Joe Wood."

The year that Fenway Park opened, Wood started 38 games, completed 35, won 34 (breaking Cy Young's 1901 club record), had 10 shutouts, and pitched 5 games in relief. It came to 344 innings. His 258 strikeouts stood as a franchise record until Roger Clemens broke it in

1988, but no American League pitcher has ever surpassed his winning streak that year.

Johnson had won 16 straight for the Senators earlier in the year and Wood immediately threatened the record. Manager and first baseman Jake Stahl moved Wood up a day to face Johnson on September 6. He beat the Senators, 1–0, and went on to tie Johnson's mark. Wood started three times in the World Series against the Giants, winning twice, but the 22-year-old righty's nerves got to him with a chance to clinch in Game 7; he was lifted after one horrendous inning. Lucky for him there was a Game 8. (A game had ended in a tie because of darkness.) Wood relieved Hugh Bedient in a tie game in the eighth inning against Christy Mathewson. Wood allowed a run in the 10th, but a dropped fly ball by surehanded Fred Snodgrass ("Snodgrass' Muff") and an untouched pop foul helped Boston beat New York for the world championship in the bottom of the inning.

Wood was never the same pitcher. He broke his thumb in 1913, which led to shoulder trouble. He won the ERA title in his final year as a pitcher with a 1.49 mark in 1915. He quit for a year but returned...as an outfielder. Former Boston roommate Tris Speaker, now player/manager in Cleveland, bought him from the Red Sox for $15,000. (He'd once hit .290 as a pitcher, another impressive number from 1912.) The World War I player shortage gave Wood an opportunity and he hit .296. He surpassed that number three of five years in Cleveland until he took a job as coach at Yale. He stayed there 20 seasons.

Carl Yastrzemski

Carl Yastrzemski did nearly everything well, including putting up with the pressure of being the man who replaced Ted Williams. Yastrzemski, as hard for pitchers to get out as his name is to spell, captured the hearts of generations of New Englanders during his 23 seasons at Fenway Park.

Yet Yaz wasn't an instant success. He batted below .250 at the All-Star break as a rookie in 1961—the year after Williams retired—but Yaz wouldn't be as bad as those first three months for a long, long time. He hit nearly .290 the rest of the way in '61 and was one of the best players in the league in '63, leading the American League in batting, on-base percentage, hits, doubles, and walks.

His best season was 1967, not coincidentally the ballclub's best season since 1950 and its first pennant-winner in 21 years. He won the Triple Crown, the last player to do so. For good measure, he also led the AL in runs, hits, on-base percentage, and slugging percentage. Boston needed everything it could get from Yaz as

the Red Sox eked out a pennant over the Tigers and Twins, both of whom finished just one game back, with the White Sox just three out. September was his finest month, batting .391 with 9 home runs and 24 RBIs, and when the Red Sox clinched the final day of the season he went 4-for-4 and knocked in the tying runs in the decisive sixth inning. He even won a Gold Glove, one of seven he was awarded for conquering the Green Monster in left field. Although Boston lost in seven games in the World Series to the Cardinals, Yaz batted .500 in the Series and hit two home runs in Game 2.

Yaz demonstrated that he could hit in any conditions in 1968. In the "Year of the Pitcher," with the American League's first 30-game winners since 1931 in Denny McLain and the league batting just .230 overall, Yaz was the only AL player to top .300. His .301 remains the lowest average ever for a batting champion. It was his third batting title in eight seasons, though it was also his last.

Yaz had only one more outstanding year left in his bat, 1970, when he hit .329 and topped AL hitters in on-base and slugging. He remained a respected player and feared hitter for another decade. He was an All-Star 15 consecutive seasons from 1965–1979, was named to the game 18 times in all, and earned MVP in the 1970 contest.

Injuries sent him to the disabled list for the first time in his career in 1972. He became essentially a full-time first baseman and later a designated hitter, although he returned to left field in the 1975 postseason. Yaz batted .455 as the Red Sox brought down the Oakland A's dynasty in the ALCS and hit .310 in the World Series against Cincinnati's Big Red Machine. Yaz made the final out against the Reds at Fenway, just as he would do in the heartrending one-game playoff against the Yankees in 1978.

He appeared in more games than any player in AL history and was second all-time to Pete Rose in that category. Yaz was the first AL player with at least 400 home runs and 3,000 hits. He was elected to the Hall of Fame in 1989 after being named on 95 percent of the ballots, at the time the seventh-highest total in history.

Cy Young

Cy Young's presence on Boston's hill helped give the American League instant credibility as a bona fide "major league" during its early years. Already a superstar hurler with the National League's Cleveland Spiders and St. Louis Cardinals (then called the Browns or Perfectos), Young defected to the fledgling AL when it began play in 1901. Although his $3,000 salary was 25 percent more than he made in St. Louis, it was a relative bargain for Boston ownership. Young was 33–10 that year, with a 1.62 ERA, nearly two runs below the league average, and he also led the league in strikeouts, among other categories. As NL escapee Napoleon Lajoie did with the bat for the Philadelphia Athletics, Young thoroughly dominated the Triple Crown pitching categories. Young had seven more wins than Baltimore's Joe McGinnity, 31 more strikeouts than Chicago's Roy Patterson, and an ERA 80 points lower than Chicago's Nixey Callahan.

Young was nearly as dominant the next two years, leading the AL in wins and innings pitched both seasons. He was second in the league in ERA in 1903, the year Boston claimed its first world championship. Young was the losing pitcher in the first "modern" World Series game, but he came back to win Games 5 and 7 as Boston claimed four of the final six contests against Pittsburgh in a best-of-nine format.

He was 26–16 with a 1.97 ERA in 1904, when he was 37 years old, and threw the American League's first perfect game. The endless wear and tear on his arm, however, finally caught up with him. Young lost more games than he won each of the next two years and would have only one more dominating year left in his career, which finally ended in 1911 at age 43 in Boston with the Braves after two seasons in Cleveland.

Young owns—and likely will forever own—most career pitching records for longevity: wins (511), losses (316), games started (815), complete games (749), and innings pitched (7,356). A pitcher would have to win 25 games a year for 20 seasons just to reach 500 wins. And that is seemingly the easiest of Young's records to reach. To equal his career innings, a pitcher would need to average 368 frames per season for 20 years. To top his mark for complete games, he'd have to start and finish 38 games a year for 20 campaigns. Denton True Young—known as Cyclone, the story goes, for his speedy delivery as a youth—remains a man whose legend lives on. The annual award in his name for best pitcher (given since 1956) keeps his name on people's tongues nearly a century after his final pitch.

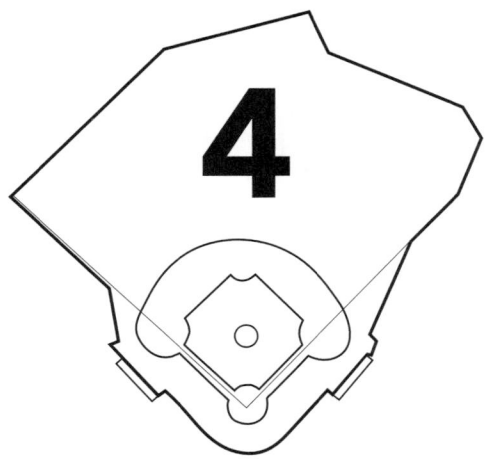

RED SOX BATTERS

At least since the disastrous sale of the record-setting pitcher-slugger George Herman Ruth, the Boston American League club has primarily been known for its hitting. To be sure, superstar pitchers like Lefty Grove, Pedro Martinez, and Roger Clemens have trod the sod at Fenway to the lusty cheers of tens of thousands, and strong-willed stars with strong arms like Jim Lonborg and Luis Tiant have taken their bows on the stage.

Yet New England's team has been defined by its hitters for most of the last century—mostly its sluggers. Too few now remember that Babe Ruth led the AL in home runs twice in a Boston uniform, though his 11 round-trippers in 1918 and 29 four-baggers in 1919 no longer seem so impressive.

The roll of Boston's hometown heroes who terrorized enemy pitchers with their lumber is as impressive as it is long:

- Jimmy Collins: the future Hall of Famer hit .332 with 64 extra-base hits for the first Red Sox team in 1901;
- Tris Speaker: "The Grey Eagle" holds the all-time ML record with 792 doubles and is fifth all-time with 222 triples;
- Harry Hooper: elected to the Hall of Fame for his defense, his offensive prowess is disguised by the Deadball Era conditions;
- Jimmie Foxx: the feared "Double X" right-handed power hitter of the pre-war years;
- Joe Cronin and Bobby Doerr, slugging middle infielders and Hall of Famers;
- Ted Williams: a/k/a "Teddy Ballgame," many believe he was the best hitter who ever lived; his fearsome ability with a bat gave rise to many wondrous

nicknames aside from "Teddy Ballgame," among them "The Splendid Splinter," "The Kid," and "The Thumper." After his career, Williams extended his legend when he wrote the best book on hitting ever published, *The Science of Hitting*. That classic work has been continuously in-print since its publication in 1970.

- Carl Yastrzemski: the beloved "Yaz" forged his own legend after replacing a legend;
- Tony Conigliaro: the idol tragically cut down in his prime;
- Rico Petrocelli and Nomar Garciaparra: fan favorites and dangerous hitters;
- Jim Rice and Dwight Evans: anchoring the corners of the Boston outfield for so many years;
- Carlton Fisk and Jason Varitek: team leaders and rugged receivers with dangerous bats;
- Fred Lynn and Reggie Smith: slugging center fielders;
- Wade Boggs: his line-drive bat won five AL batting titles in Boston;
- Mo Vaughn: the popular MVP whose many moon shots delighted the crowds;
- Manny Ramirez and David Ortiz: the twin titans of the twenty-first century Sox' lineup, fondly known to all simply as "Manny" and "Big Papi"; and
- A passel of other sluggers of less renown who all had their moments in the sun, including Bob Johnson, Vern Stephens, Walt Dropo, Jackie Jensen, Frank Malzone, Butch Hobson, Tony Armas, Mike Greenwell, Ellis Burks, and John Valentin.

The batter register offers a mix of traditional statistics and analytical statistics for perusal. Traditional stats like

at-bats, runs, home runs, runs batted in, and batting average percentage are familiar to every kid that ever read the back of a bubblegum card. Analytical stats like OPS (On-Base Plus Slugging), Adjusted OPS, and Batter-Fielder Wins offer the opportunity to evaluate a player in the context of his ballpark, his league, and his era—as well as making reasonable cross-era comparisons possible.

Biographical Information

The biographical information for each player in the register answers questions about a player's life aside from his statistics. When he was born, how long he lived, how tall he was, was he ever a manager, etc., can all be found there. The biographical line goes beyond the statistics to fill in a more complete picture of each player.

Every player in this register has, at a minimum, a last name and a debut date. If a Hispanic player also has a matronymic name, it is placed in parentheses—for example, David Ortiz (Arias). Commonly used nicknames are included in the biographical line unless the player was called by his nickname instead of his given name during his career (e.g., Higgins, Pinky).

Birth and death information is:

- *Bmm. dd. yyyy* showing date and place of birth.
- *Dmm. dd. yyyy* showing date and place of death.

The way a player bats from is shown as *BR* (bats right), *BL* (bats left), or *BB* (bats both for switch-hitters). The way a player throws is shown as *TR* (throws right) or *TL* (throws left). In the extremely rare cases when a pitcher threw both right and left in his career, *TB* (throws both) is used and the season is included in parentheses. Likewise, if a player changed to or from switch-hitting during his career, that change is presented in parentheses.

Height is shown in feet (') and inches (") followed by weight in pounds. If a player's listed weight varied, the upper and lower limits of his major league weights are shown.

Debut dates are shown with a *d*—note the lower-case letter so as not to be confused with the abbreviation for death—followed by the date the player made his first major league appearance. The debut year is the first year he played and is not repeated in the bio line.

Other designations for players whose career, family, or duty proved noteworthy.

- *Mil* indicates wartime military service in the army, navy, air force, or marines;
- *Mer* indicates wartime merchant marine service;
- *Def* indicates wartime defense plant work.

Seasons missed—including partial seasons—are listed after the abbreviations for duty. Since the founding of the Red Sox in 1901, four wars involving the U.S. have caused some major leaguers to miss playing time during the big-league careers due to military duty (years below include post-war service):

- World War I, 1917–19;
- World War II, 1941–46;
- Korean War, 1951–59; and
- Vietnam War, 1962–72.

Players who were also major league coaches, managers, or umpires are indicated by the following abbreviations:

- *C*: Coach
- *M*: Manager
- *U*: Umpire

Players inducted into the Baseball Hall of Fame in Cooperstown are identified by *HF*, followed by the year of induction.

If the player had a close family member in the major leagues, the relative's relationship is shown by the codes below. The relative's first name is given; the last name is included only if different than the player's.

- *b*: brother
- *twb*: twin brother
- *f*: father
- *s*: son
- *gf*: grandfather
- *gs*: grandson
- *ggf*: great grandfather
- *ggs*: great grandson

Defensive games at the three outfield positions (*LF-CF-RF*) are included at the end of the biographical data if there is not enough room to place it in the career line.

▲ at the end of a player's bio information (e.g., Babe Ruth or Smoky Joe Wood) indicates that the player is also listed in the pitcher register. A player whose primary position was not pitcher must have pitched at least 9 innings to appear in the Pitching Register.

Statistical Information

Symbols in the first two columns:

† before the team name means he participated in Postseason Play that year;

★ after team name means he participated in All-Star game;

☆ after team name means he was selected to All-Star team but did not play;

✳ after team name means he was selected to All-Star team but replaced due to injury;

The columns that appear in the player register after **Year**:

TM: Team. Each team is identified by a three-letter code that is usually the first three letters of the city, state, or area where the team is located.

L: League. The leagues in this book include the National League (N), the American League (A), the Federal League (F), and the American Association (AA).

G: Games. The number of games is boldfaced if the player appeared in every one of his team's games in a given year.

AB: At Bats

R: Runs

H: Hits

2B: Doubles

3B: Triples

HR: Home Runs

RBI: Runs Batted In

BB: Bases on Balls. Walks.

IB: Intentional Base on Balls. These have been counted as a distinct category since 1955

HBP: Hit-by-Pitch.

SO: Strikeouts. Strikeouts are not available for most players before 1913

AVG: Batting Average. Hits divided by at bats.

OBP: On-Base Percentage. The official current definition of OBP is (Hits plus Bases on Balls plus Hit-by-Pitches) divided by (At Bats plus Bases on Balls plus Hit-by-Pitches plus Sacrifice Flies). This volume

uses that definition from 1954 on, but sacrifice fly data is not available in previous years, so it is not used in calculating the statistic in earlier years.

SLG: Slugging Percentage. Total bases divided by at bats.

OPS: On-Base plus Slugging. The sum of on-base percentage and slugging percentage.

AOPS: Adjusted On-Base plus Slugging. On-base percentage and slugging average are added and normalized for the context of the offensive level of the league and the player's home park(s) and then converted to a scale in which 0 represents the league average.

SB: Stolen Bases

CS: Caught Stealing. This data has only been recorded for all major league players since 1951, though the totals for all Red Sox are available from 1920 on.

SB: Stolen Base Percentage

G/Pos: Games at Position. Positions are listed left to right by decreasing number of games. There are several different variations in this category.

A * before the position indicates that the player fielded the position in the large majority (100 games per year) of his team's games during that season or for at least 1,000 games during his career

/: Any positions listed after the slash indicate that the player appeared there in fewer than 10 games that season or in fewer than 100 games during his career.

Positions are shown with one-letter abbreviations:

P: Pitcher
1: First Base
2: Second Base
3: Third Base
S: Shortstop

O: Outfield
D: Designated Hitter.

Positions are followed by a dash and the number of games the player played at that position during the season or career. The positions are separated by commas except when there is a slash. If the player spent only one game at that position, the one-letter abbreviation is used without a dash or number. If the player spent only one game at multiple positions, no comma is placed between the abbreviations for those positions.

Outfield is officially counted as only position, but if the player spent time playing at least two of the three outfield positions, a breakdown of the games in left, center, and right is presented in that order, separated by dashes, in parentheses. If the outfielder only played one outfield position, that position will be identified (**LF**, **CF**, or **RF**) after the number of outfield games played. If a breakdown of the games in left, center, and right is needed in the career line, but there is not enough room, that information will be added to the end of the biographical data and the primary outfield position played will be identified by **L**, **C**, or **R** following the number of games played in the outfield.

DL: Disabled List. *The number of days spent on the disabled list in each year since the DL was instituted in 1941.* This does *not* include time spent on the DL before or after the season; this explains why some players will have DL stints shorter than the 15-day minimum. If a player spent the entire season on the disabled list, the information is given in brackets in his biographical line because there is no line for that year in the player's statistics.

BFW: Batter-Fielder Wins. The sum of a player's batting wins, base-stealing wins, and fielding wins, indicating how many games the player won or lost for his team compared to an average player.

When there is incomplete or missing data (such as years in which CS or SO weren't officially kept), a player's career total is underlined if it represents only a partial figure.

Year	Tm Lg	G	AB	R	H	2B	3B	HR	RBI	BB	IB	HP	SO	AVG	OBP	SLG	OPS	AOPS	SB	CS	SB%	Games at Position	DL	BFW
ABAD, ANDY Fausto Andres B8.25.1972 Palm Beach FL BL/TL/6'1"/(184–210) [BosA93 16/443] d9.10 Col Middle Georgia JC																								
2001	Oak A	1	1	0	0	0	0	0	0	0	0	0	0	.000	.000	.000	.000	-199	0	0	0	/1	0	0.0
2003	Bos A	9	17	1	2	0	0	0	0	2	0	0	5	.118	.211	.118	.329	-110	0	1	0	1b7/rf	0	-0.5
2006	Cin N	5	3	0	0	0	0	0	0	2	0	0	0	.000	.400	.000	.400	-85	0	0	0	/H	0	-0.1
Total	3	15	21	1	2	0	0	0	0	4	0	0	5	.095	.240	.095	.335	-107	0	1	0	1b8/rf	0	-0.6
ADAIR, JERRY Kenneth Jerry B12.17.1936 Sand Springs OK D5.31.1987 Tulsa OK BR/TR/6'0"/(175–185) d9.2 C4 Col Oklahoma St.																								
1967	†Bos A	89	316	41	92	13	1	3	26	13	0	2	35	.291	.321	.367	.688	-4	1	4	20	3b35,S30,2b23	0	-0.7
1968	Bos A	74	208	18	45	1	0	2	12	9	2	1	28	.216	.252	.250	.502	-50	0	0	0	S46,2b12,3b7/1	0	-1.6
Total	13	1165	4019	378	1022	163	19	57	366	208	31	17	499	.254	.292	.347	.639	-20	29	29	50	2b810,S310,3b46/1	0	-4.6
Team	2	163	524	59	137	14	1	5	38	22	2	3	63	.261	.294	.321	.615	-22	1	4	20	S76,3b42,2b35/1	0	-2.3
/150	2	150	482	54	126	13	1	5	35	20	2	3	58	.261	.294	.321	.615	-22	1	4	20	S70,3b39,2b32/1	0	-2.1
AGBAYANI, BENNY Benny Peter B12.28.1971 Honolulu HI BR/TR/6'0"/225 [NYN93 30/836] d6.17 Col Hawaii Pacific																								
2002	Bos A	13	37	5	11	1	0	0	8	6	1	0	5	.297	.395	.324	.719	-7	0	0	0	O13(11/1/3)	0	0.0
Total	5	383	1091	145	299	57	6	39	156	139	7	15	246	.274	.362	.445	.807	+9	16	16	50	O333(282/9/66),D4	59	-0.5
AGGANIS, HARRY Harry "The Golden Greek" B4.20.1929 Lynn MA D6.27.1955 Cambridge MA BL/TL/6'2"/200 d4.13 Col Boston U.																								
1954	Bos A	132	434	54	109	13	8	11	57	47		0	57	.251	.321	.394	.715	-14	6	3	67	1b119	0	-1.0
1955	Bos A	25	83	11	26	10	1	0	10	10	0	0	10	.313	.383	.458	.841	+16	2	0	100	1b20	0	0.1
Total	2	157	517	65	135	23	9	11	67	57	0	0	67	.261	.331	.404	.735	-9	8	3	73	1b139	0	-0.9
/150	2	150	494	62	129	22	9	11	64	54	0	0	64	.261	.331	.404	.735	-9	8	3	73	1b133	0	-0.9
AGNEW, SAM Samuel Lester "Slam" B4.12.1887 Farmington MO D7.19.1951 Sonoma CA BR/TR/5'11"/185 d4.10																								
1913	StL A	105	307	27	64	9	5	2	24	20		7	49	.208	.272	.290	.562	-34	11			C103		0.0
1914	StL A	115	311	22	66	5	4	0	16	24		5	63	.212	.279	.254	.533	-37	10	8	56	C115		-0.7
1915	StL A	104	295	18	60	4	2	0	19	12		5	36	.203	.247	.231	.478	-55	5	2	71	C102		-1.3
1916	Bos A	40	67	4	14	2	1	0	7	6		2	4	.209	.293	.269	.562	-31	0			C38		0.5
1917	Bos A	85	260	17	54	6	2	0	16	19		2	30	.208	.267	.246	.513	-43	2			C85		-1.2
1918	†Bos A	72	199	11	33	8	0	0	6	11		3	26	.166	.221	.206	.427	-71	0			C72		-0.4
1919	Was A	42	98	6	23	7	0	0	10	10		1	8	.235	.312	.306	.618	-26	1			C36		0.6
Total	7	563	1537	105	314	41	14	2	98	102		25	216	.204	.265	.253	.518	-44	29	10	100	C551		-2.5
Team	3	197	526	32	101	16	3	0	29	36		7	60	.192	.253	.234	.487	-52	2			C195		-1.1
/150	2	150	401	24	77	12	2	0	22	27		5	46	.192	.253	.234	.487	-52	2			C148		-0.8
ALCANTARA, ISRAEL Israel (Cristosomo) B5.6.1973 Bani, D.R. BR/TR/6'2"/(180–210) d6.25																								
2000	Bos A	21	45	9	13	1	0	4	7	3	0	0	7	.289	.333	.578	.911	+21	0	0	0	O7(1/0/7),1b5,D8	18	0.0
2001	Bos A	14	38	3	10	1	0	0	3	3	0	0	13	.263	.317	.289	.606	-39	1	0	100	O8(6/0/2),1b4/D	0	-0.3
2002	Mil N	16	32	3	8	1	0	2	5	0	0	0	6	.250	.250	.469	.719	-16	0	1	0	O7(2/0/5),1b2	0	-0.3
Total	3	51	115	15	31	3	0	6	15	6	0	0	26	.270	.306	.452	.758	-8	1	1	50	O22(9/0/14),1b11,D9	18	-0.6
Team	2	35	83	12	23	2	0	4	10	6	0	0	20	.277	.326	.446	.772	-7	1	0	100	O15(7/0/9),1b9,D9	18	-0.3
ALEXANDER, DALE David Dale "Moose" B4.26.1903 Greeneville TN D3.2.1979 Greeneville TN BR/TR/6'3"/210 d4.16 Col Milligan																								
1932	Bos A	101	376	58	140	27	3	8	56	55		1	19	.372	.454	.524	.978	+57	4	5	44	1b101		2.4
1933	Bos A	94	313	40	88	14	1	5	40	25		1	22	.281	.336	.380	.716	-10	0	1	0	1b79		-0.8
Total	5	662	2450	369	811	164	30	61	459	248		6	197	.331	.394	.497	.891	+28	20	28	42	1b617,O4L		3.5
Team	2	195	689	98	228	41	4	13	96	80		2	41	.331	.402	.459	.861	+28	4	6	40	1b180		1.6
/150	2	150	530	75	175	32	3	10	74	62		2	32	.331	.402	.459	.861	+28	3	5	38	1b138		1.2
ALEXANDER, MANNY Manuel De Jesus (b Manuel De Jesus (Alexander)) B3.20.1971 San Pedro de Macoris, D.R. BR/TR/5'10"/(150–180) d9.18 OF(4/0/2) [DL 1994 Bal A 29]																								
2000	Bos A	101	194	30	41	4	3	4	19	13	0	0	41	.211	.261	.325	.586	-54	2	0	100	3b63,S20,2b7,D2	2	-1.4
Total	11	594	1271	166	293	50	12	15	115	86	7	7	276	.231	.282	.324	.606	-44	37	10	79	S205,2b190,3b131,O6L,D6/1P	77	-8.1
/150	1	150	288	45	61	6	4	6	28	19	0	0	61	.211	.261	.325	.586	-54	3	0	100	3b94,S30,2b10,D3	3	-2.1
ALICEA, LUIS Luis Rene (De Jesus) B7.29.1965 Santurce, PR BB/TR/5'9"/(165–177) [StLN86 1/23] d4.23 OF(10/0/1)																								
1995	†Bos A	132	419	64	113	20	3	6	44	63	0	7	61	.270	.367	.375	.742	-7	13	10	57	2b132	0	1.7
Total	13	1341	3971	551	1031	189	53	47	422	500	26	48	624	.260	.346	.369	.715	-12	81	50	62	2b999,3b109,D72,O10L,S8,1b2	51	-1.7
/150	1	150	476	73	128	23	3	7	50	72	0	8	69	.270	.367	.375	.742	-7	15	11	58	2b150	0	1.9
ALLENSON, GARY Gary Martin B2.4.1955 Culver City CA BR/TR/5'11"/(185–193) [BosA76 9/214] d4.8 C6 Col Arizona St.																								
1979	Bos A	108	241	27	49	10	2	3	22	20	0	1	42	.203	.264	.299	.563	-50	1	1	50	C104,3b3	0	-1.1
1980	Bos A	36	70	9	25	6	0	0	10	13	0	0	11	.357	.452	.443	.895	+40	2	2	50	C24,3b5,D6	0	0.7
1981	Bos A	47	139	23	31	8	0	5	25	23	0	1	33	.223	.335	.388	.723	+2	0	0	0	C47	25	0.1
1982	Bos A	92	264	25	54	11	0	6	33	38	1	1	39	.205	.306	.314	.620	-33	0	3	0	C91	0	-0.2
1983	Bos A	84	230	19	53	11	0	3	30	27	0	2	43	.230	.311	.317	.628	-30	0	1	0	C84	0	-0.8
1984	Bos A	35	83	9	19	2	0	2	8	9	2	0	14	.229	.304	.325	.629	-29	0	0	0	C35	0	-0.8
1985	Tor A	14	34	2	4	1	0	0	3	0	0	0	10	.118	.118	.147	.265	-127	0	0	0	C14	0	-0.8
Total	7	416	1061	114	235	49	2	19	131	130	3	5	192	.221	.307	.325	.632	-29	3	7	30	C399,3b8,D6	25	-2.9
Team	6	402	1027	112	231	48	2	19	128	130	3	5	182	.225	.312	.331	.643	-26	3	7	30	C385,3b8,D6	25	-2.1
/150	2	150	383	42	86	18	1	7	48	49	1	2	68	.225	.312	.331	.643	-26	1	3	25	C144,3b3,D2	9	-0.8
ALMADA, MEL Baldomero Melo (Quiros) B2.7.1913 Huatabampo, Sonora, Mexico D8.13.1988 Caborca, Sonora, Mexico BL/TL/6'0"/170 d9.8																								
1933	Bos A	14	44	11	15	0	0	1	3	11		0	3	.341	.473	.409	.882	+37	3	1	75	O13(7/6/0)		0.3
1934	Bos A	23	90	7	21	2	1	0	10	6		0	8	.233	.281	.278	.559	-58	3	2	60	O23(0/16/7)		-0.7
1935	Bos A	151	607	85	176	27	9	3	59	55		1	34	.290	.350	.379	.729	-17	20	9	69	O149(0/126/25),1b3		-1.9
1936	Bos A	96	320	40	81	16	4	1	21	24		0	15	.253	.305	.338	.643	-45	2	4	33	O81(11/3/69)		-2.5
1937	Bos A	32	110	17	26	6	2	1	9	15		0	6	.236	.328	.355	.683	-31	0	1	0	O27(4/2/21),1b4		-1.0
1937	Was A	100	433	74	134	21	4	4	33	38		0	21	.309	.365	.404	.769	-2	12	4	75	O100(0/97/3)		0.6
1937	Year	132	543	91	160	27	6	5	42	53		0	27	.295	.357	.394	.751	-9	12	5	71	O127(4/99/24),1b4		-0.4
1938	Was A	47	197	24	48	7	4	1	15	8		1	16	.244	.277	.335	.612	-44	4	1	80	O47C		-1.3
1938	StL A	102	436	77	149	22	2	3	37	38		3	22	.342	.398	.422	.820	+6	9	5	64	O101C		0.0
1938	Year	149	633	101	197	29	6	4	52	46		4	38	.311	.362	.395	.757	-8	13	6	68	O148C		-1.3
1939	StL A	42	134	17	32	2	1	1	7	10		0	8	.239	.292	.291	.583	-52	1	0	100	O34(3/31/0)		-1.2
1939	Bro N	39	112	11	24	4	0	0	3	9		0	17	.214	.273	.250	.523	-60	2			O32C		-0.9
1939	Major	81	246	28	56	6	1	1	10	19	0	0	25	.228	.283	.272	.555	+34	3	0				-2.1
Total	7	646	2483	363	706	107	27	15	197	214		5	150	.284	.342	.367	.709	-21	56	27	100	O607(25/461/125),1b7		-8.6
Team	5	316	1171	160	319	51	16	6	102	111		1	66	.272	.336	.359	.695	-27	28	17	62	O293(10/105/102),1b7		-5.8
/150	2	150	556	76	151	24	8	3	48	53		0	31	.272	.336	.359	.695	-27	13	8	62	O139(5/50/48),1b3		-2.8
ALVARADO, LUIS Luis Cesar (Martinez) B1.15.1949 Lajas, PR D3.20.2001 Lajas, PR BR/TR/5'9"/(162–170) d9.13																								
1968	Bos A	11	46	3	6	2	0	0	1	1	0	1	11	.130	.167	.174	.341	-97	0	0	0	S11	0	-1.1
1969	Bos A	6	5	0	0	0	0	0	0	0	0	0	2	.000	.000	.000	.000	-196	0	1	0	S5	0	-0.1
1970	Bos A	59	183	19	41	11	0	1	10	9	2	0	30	.224	.258	.301	.559	-49	1	2	33	3b29,S27	0	-1.1
Total	9	463	1160	116	248	43	4	5	84	49	10	3	160	.214	.247	.271	.518	-53	11	10	52	S241,2b141,3b44,D4	0	-7.6
Team	3	76	234	22	47	13	0	1	11	10	2	1	43	.201	.235	.269	.504	-61	1	3	25	S43,3b29	0	-2.3
ANDERSON, BRADY Brady Kevin B1.18.1964 Silver Spring MD BL/TL/6'1"/(185–202) [BosA85 10/257] d4.4 Col California–Irvine																								
1988	Bos A	41	148	14	34	5	3	0	12	15	0	4	35	.230	.315	.304	.619	-28	4	2	67	O41(0/17/25)	0	-0.6
Total	15	1834	6499	1062	1661	338	67	210	761	960	59	154	1190	.256	.362	.425	.787	+8	315	100	76	O1691(688/927/139),D76	92	5.7
ANDRES, ERNIE Ernest Henry "Junie" B1.11.1918 Jeffersonville IN BR/TR/6'1"/200 d4.16 Col Indiana																								
1946	Bos A	15	41	0	4	2	0	0	1	3		0	5	.098	.159	.146	.305	-114	0	0	0	3b15	0	-0.6
ANDREW, KIM Kim Darrell B11.14.1953 Glendale CA BR/TR/5'10"/160 d4.16 Col Los Angeles Valley (CA) JC																								
1975	Bos A	2	2	0	1	0	0	0	0	0	0	0	0	.500	.500	.500	1.000	+69	0	0	0	2b2	0	0.0
ANDREWS, SHANE Darrell Shane B8.28.1971 Dallas TX BR/TR/6'1"/(215–220) [MonN90 1/11] d4.26																								
2002	Bos A	7	13	2	1	1	0	0	0	1	0	1	3	.077	.200	.154	.354	-104	0	0	0	3b4,1b2/lfD	0	-0.1
Total	7	569	1704	196	375	76	4	86	263	191	17	7	515	.220	.298	.421	.719	-14	7	10	41	3b502,1b56,D2/lf	273	-0.5

Year	Tm Lg	G	AB	R	H	2B	3B	HR	RBI	BB	IB	HP	SO	AVG	OBP	SLG	OPS	AOPS	SB	CS	SB%	Games at Position	DL	BFW
ANDREWS, MIKE Michael Jay B7.9.1943 Los Angeles CA BR/TR/6'3"/(185–195) d9.18 b–Rob																								
1966	Bos A	5	18	1	3	0	0	0	0	0	0	0	2	.167	.167	.167	.334	-104	0	0	0	2b5	0	0.0
1967	†Bos A	142	494	79	130	20	0	8	40	62	4	2	72	.263	.346	.352	.698	-1	7	7	50	2b139,S6	0	1.1
1968	Bos A	147	536	77	145	22	1	7	45	81	1	3	57	.271	.368	.354	.722	+13	3	8	27	2b139,S4/3	0	3.3
1969	Bos A★	121	464	79	136	26	2	15	59	71	0	5	53	.293	.390	.455	.845	+30	1	1	50	2b120	0	3.0
1970	Bos A	151	589	91	149	28	1	17	65	81	0	3	63	.253	.344	.390	.734	-4	2	1	67	2b148	0	-2.2
1971	Chi A	109	330	45	93	16	0	12	47	67	1	1	36	.282	.400	.439	.839	+35	3	5	38	2b76,1b25	0	2.2
1972	Chi A	148	505	58	111	18	0	7	50	70	3	2	78	.220	.313	.297	.610	-18	2	2	50	2b145,1b5	0	-1.0
1973	Chi A	52	159	10	32	9	0	0	10	23	3	0	28	.201	.302	.258	.560	-43	0	1	0	D30,1b9,2b6,3b5	0	-1.1
1973	†Oak A	18	21	1	4	1	0	0	0	3	0	0	1	.190	.292	.238	.530	-47	0	0	0	2b9,D2	0	-0.1
1973	Year	70	180	11	36	10	0	0	10	26	3	0	29	.200	.301	.256	.557	-43	0	1	0	D32,2b15,1b9,3b5	0	-1.2
Total	8	893	3116	441	803	140	4	66	316	458	12	16	390	.258	.353	.369	.722	+4	18	25	42	2b787,1b39,D32,S10,3b6	0	5.2
Team	5	566	2101	327	563	96	4	47	209	295	5	13	247	.268	.360	.385	.745	+8	13	17	43	2b551,S10/3	0	5.2
/150	1	150	557	87	149	25	1	12	55	78	1	3	65	.268	.360	.385	.745	+8	3	5	38	2b146,S3/3	0	1.4
APARICIO, LUIS Luis Ernesto (Montiel) B4.29.1934 Maracaibo, Zulia, Venez. BR/TR/5'9"/(155–160) d4.17 HF1984																								
1971	Bos A★	125	491	56	114	23	0	4	45	35	0	2	43	.232	.284	.303	.587	-38	6	4	60	S121	0	-3.0
1972	Bos A✱	110	436	47	112	26	3	3	39	26	0	2	28	.257	.299	.351	.650	-12	3	3	50	S109	40	-0.4
1973	Bos A	132	499	56	135	17	1	0	49	43	1	0	33	.271	.324	.309	.633	-24	13	1	93	S132	0	-1.0
Total	18	2599	10230	1335	2677	394	92	83	791	736	22	27	742	.262	.311	.343	.654	-18	506	136	79	S2581	40	15.6
Team	3	367	1426	159	361	66	4	7	133	104	1	4	104	.253	.303	.320	.623	-25	22	8	73	S362	40	-4.4
/150	1	150	583	65	148	27	2	3	54	43	0	2	43	.253	.303	.320	.623	-25	9	3	75	S148	16	-1.8
ARMAS, TONY Antonio Rafael (Machado) B7.2.1953 Anzoategui, Venezuela BR/TR/6'1"/(182–224) d9.6 b–Marcos s–Tony																								
1976	Pit N	4	6	0	2	0	0	0	1	0	0	0	2	.333	.333	.333	.666	-12	0	0	0	O2(1/1/0)	0	0.0
1977	Oak A	118	363	26	87	8	2	13	53	20	2	0	99	.240	.274	.380	.654	-21	1	2	33	O112(3/84/30)/S	27	-0.6
1978	Oak A	91	239	17	51	6	1	2	13	10	2	2	62	.213	.250	.272	.522	-51	1	2	33	O85(2/40/47),D3	35	-1.2
1979	Oak A	80	278	29	69	9	3	11	34	16	2	1	67	.248	.290	.421	.711	-6	1	0	100	O80(12/17/53)	51	-0.1
1980	Oak A	158	628	87	175	18	8	35	109	29	4	2	128	.279	.310	.500	.810	+26	5	3	63	O158(0/10/152)	0	1.9
1981	†Oak A★	**109**	440	51	115	24	3	**22**	76	19	6	2	115	.261	.294	.480	.774	+24	5	1	83	O109(0/2/108)	0	1.0
1982	Oak A	138	536	58	125	19	2	28	89	33	5	1	128	.233	.275	.433	.708	-5	2	2	50	O135(0/5/133)/D	15	-0.9
1983	Bos A	145	574	77	125	23	2	36	107	29	0	2	131	.218	.254	.453	.707	-15	0	1	0	O116C,D27	0	-1.8
1984	Bos A☆	157	639	107	171	29	5	**43**	**123**	32	9	1	156	.268	.300	.531	.831	+20	1	3	25	O126(0/126/1),D31	0	0.1
1985	Bos A	103	385	50	102	17	5	23	64	18	4	2	90	.265	.298	.514	.812	+13	0	0	0	O79(16/69/2),D19	29	-0.3
1986	†Bos A	121	425	40	112	21	4	11	58	24	1	2	77	.264	.305	.409	.714	-8	0	3	0	O117(9/108/19)/D	15	-1.4
1987	Cal A	28	81	8	16	3	1	3	9	1	0	0	11	.198	.205	.370	.575	-50	1	0	100	O27(2/0/26)	0	-0.9
1988	Cal A	120	368	42	100	20	2	13	49	22	0	0	87	.272	.311	.443	.754	+12	1	3	25	O113(74/36/10),D5	0	-0.2
1989	Cal A	60	202	22	52	7	1	11	30	7	2	0	48	.257	.280	.465	.745	+9	0	0	0	O47(5/1/42),1b2,D6	69	0.0
Total	14	1432	5164	614	1302	204	39	251	815	260	37	15	1201	.252	.287	.453	.740	+2	18	20	47	O1306(124/615/623),D93,1b2/S	241	-4.4
Team	4	526	2023	274	510	90	16	113	352	103	14	7	454	.252	.288	.480	.768	+3	1	7	13	O438(8/263/147),D78	44	-3.4
/150	1	150	577	78	145	26	5	32	100	29	4	2	129	.252	.288	.480	.768	+3	0	2	0	O125(2/75/42),D22	13	-1.0
ARMBRUSTER, CHARLIE Charles Anthony B8.30.1880 Cincinnati OH D10.7.1964 Grants Pass OR BR/TR/5'9"/180 d7.17																								
1905	Bos A	35	91	13	18	4	0	0	6	18		1		.198	.336	.242	.578	-17	3			C35		-0.1
1906	Bos A	72	201	9	29	6	1	0	6	25		1		.144	.242	.184	.426	-66	2			C66/1		-1.3
1907	Bos A	23	60	2	6	1	0	0	0	8		0		.100	.206	.117	.323	-97	1			C21		-0.3
1907	Chi A	1	3	0	0	0	0	0	0	1		0		.000	.250	.000	.250	-120	0			/C		0.0
1907	Year	24	63	2	6	1	0	0	0	9		0		.095	.208	.111	.319	-98	1			C22		-0.3
Total	3	131	355	24	53	11	1	0	12	52		2		.149	.262	.186	.448	-58	6			C123/1		-1.7
Team	3	130	352	24	53	11	1	0	12	51		2	0	.151	.262	.188	.450	-58	6			C122/1		-1.7
/150	3	150	406	28	61	13	1	0	14	59		2	0	.151	.262	.188	.450	-58	7			C141/1		-2.0
ASBJORNSON, CASPER Robert Anthony (Name Changed To Asby) B6.19.1909 Concord MA D1.21.1970 Williamsport PA BR/TR/6'1"/196 d9.17																								
1928	Bos A	6	16	0	3	1	0	0	1	1		0	1	.188	.235	.250	.485	-72	0	0	0	C6		-0.3
1929	Bos A	17	29	1	3	0	0	0	0	1		0	6	.103	.133	.103	.236	-139	0	0	0	C15		-0.7
Total	4	97	221	19	52	10	1	1	27	9		2	45	.235	.272	.303	.575	-44	0	0	0	C68		-1.6
Team	2	23	45	1	6	1	0	0	1	2		0	7	.133	.170	.156	.326	-115	0	0	0	C21		-1.0
ASHLEY, BILLY Billy Manual B7.11.1970 Trenton MI BR/TR/6'7"/(220–242) [LAN88 3/62] d9.1																								
1998	Bos A	13	24	3	7	3	0	3	7	2	0	0	11	.292	.346	.792	1.138	+80	0	0	0	1b2,O2L,D5	17	0.3
Total	7	281	618	56	144	23	1	28	84	63	5	4	236	.233	.307	.409	.716	-6	0	0	0	O184(158/0/26),D5,1b2	39	-1.9
ASPROMONTE, KEN Kenneth Joseph B9.22.1931 Brooklyn NY BR/TR/6'0"/180 d9.2 M3 b–Bob																								
1957	Bos A	24	78	9	21	5	0	0	4	17	0	0	10	.269	.396	.333	.729	-3	0	1	0	2b24	0	-0.3
1958	Bos A	6	16	0	2	0	0	0	0	3	0	0	1	.125	.263	.125	.388	-90	0	0	0	2b6	0	-0.5
Total	7	475	1483	171	369	69	3	19	124	179	4	6	149	.249	.330	.338	.668	-18	7	5	58	2b342,3b56,S13,1b3/lf	0	-1.7
Team	2	30	94	9	23	5	0	0	4	20	0	0	11	.245	.374	.298	.672	-17	0	1	0	2b30	0	-0.8
AULDS, LESLIE Leycester Doyle "Tex" B12.28.1920 Farmerville LA D10.13.1999 Hondo TX BR/TR/6'2"/185 d5.25																								
1947	Bos A	3	4	0	1	0	0	0	0	0		0	1	.250	.250	.250	.500	-63	0	0	0	C3	0	0.0
AVILA, BOBBY Roberto Francisco (Gonzalez) B4.2.1924 Veracruz, Veracruz, Mexico D10.26.2004 Veracruz, Veracruz, Mexico BR/TR/5'10"/(171–175) d4.30																								
1959	Bos A	22	45	7	11	0	0	3	6	6	0	0	11	.244	.333	.444	.777	+7	0	0	0	2b11	0	-0.3
Total	11	1300	4620	725	1296	185	35	80	467	561	3	14	399	.281	.359	.388	.747	+4	78	52	60	2b1168,3b50,O10(1/0/9),S9	0	6.8
AVILES, RAMON Ramon Antonio (Miranda) B1.22.1952 Manati, PR BR/TR/5'9"/155 d7.10																								
1977	Bos A	1	0	0	0	0	0	0	0	0	0	0	0	+	+	+	.000	-100	0	0	0	/2	0	0.0
Total	4	117	190	21	51	9	0	2	24	21	3	1	22	.268	.341	.347	.688	-12	0	0	0	2b63,S34,3b13	0	-1.1
AZCUE, JOE Jose Joaquin (Lopez) B8.18.1939 Cienfuegos, Cuba BR/TR/6'0"/(195–200) d8.3																								
1969	Bos A	19	51	7	11	2	0	0	3	4	1	0	5	.216	.273	.255	.528	-54	0	0	0	C19	0	0.0
Total	11	909	2828	201	712	94	9	50	304	207	45	17	344	.252	.304	.344	.648	-15	5	12	29	C868	36	2.5
BAERGA, CARLOS Carlos Obed (Ortiz) B11.4.1968 Santurce, PR BB/TR/5'11"/(165–220) d4.14																								
2002	Bos A	73	182	17	52	11	0	2	19	7	1	2	20	.286	.316	.379	.695	-17	6	0	100	D32,2b17/3	24	-0.2
Total	14	1630	5439	731	1583	279	17	134	774	291	41	73	580	.291	.332	.423	.755	+0	59	24	71	2b1063,3b199,1b54,D50,S50	63	5.6
BAILEY, GENE Arthur Eugene B11.25.1893 Pearsall TX D11.14.1973 Houston TX BR/TR/5'8"/160 d9.10 Mil 1918																								
1920	Bos A	46	135	14	31	2	0	0	5	9		1	15	.230	.283	.244	.527	-58	2	7	22	O40(9/16/15)		-1.6
Total	5	213	634	95	156	16	7	2	52	63		7	61	.246	.321	.303	.624	-31	13	15	100	O172(43/91/42),1b5		-4.1
BAILEY, BOB Robert Sherwood B10.13.1942 Long Beach CA BR/TR/6'0"/(175–188) d9.14 OF(399/2/3)																								
1977	Bos A	2	2	0	0	0	0	0	0	0	0	0	1	.000	.000	.000	.000	-190	0	0	0	/H	0	-0.1
1978	Bos A	43	94	12	18	3	0	4	9	19	0	1	19	.191	.328	.351	.679	-16	2	1	67	D34/3lf	0	-0.2
Total	17	1931	6082	772	1564	234	43	189	773	852	67	17	1126	.257	.347	.403	.750	+10	85	83	51	3b1194,O399L,1b138,D34,S7	49	4.4
Team	2	45	96	12	18	3	0	4	9	19	0	1	20	.188	.322	.344	.666	-19	2	1	67	D34/3lf	0	-0.3
BAKER, FLOYD Floyd Wilson B10.10.1916 Luray VA D11.17.2004 Youngstown OH BL/TR/5'9"/160 d5.4 C4																								
1953	Bos A	81	172	22	47	4	2	0	24	24		1	10	.273	.365	.320	.685	-18	0	2	0	3b37,2b16	0	-0.4
1954	Bos A	21	20	1	4	2	0	0	3	0		0	1	.200	.200	.300	.500	-68	0	0	0	3b7/2	0	-0.2
Total	13	874	2280	285	573	76	13	1	196	382	0	6	165	.251	.360	.297	.657	-18	23	25	48	3b510,2b143,S41,O2L	0	-1.1
Team	2	102	192	23	51	6	2	0	27	24		1	11	.266	.350	.318	.668	-23	0	2	0	3b44,2b17	0	-0.6
/150	3	150	282	34	75	9	3	0	40	35		1	16	.266	.350	.318	.668	-23	0	3	0	3b65,2b25	0	-0.9
BAKER, JACK Jack Edward B5.4.1950 Birmingham AL BR/TR/6'5"/225 [BosA71 26/604] d9.11 Col Auburn																								
1976	Bos A	12	23	1	3	0	0	1	2	1	0	0	5	.130	.160	.261	.421	-79	0	0	0	1b8/D	0	-0.4
1977	Bos A	2	3	0	0	0	0	0	0	0	0	0	1	.000	.000	.000	.000	-190	0	0	0	/1	0	-0.1
Total	2	14	26	1	3	0	0	1	2	1	0	0	6	.115	.143	.231	.374	-92	0	0	0	1b9/D	0	-0.5

Year	Tm Lg	G	AB	R	H	2B	3B	HR	RBI	BB	IB	HP	SO	AVG	OBP	SLG	OPS	AOPS	SB	CS	SB%	Games at Position	DL	BFW
BAKER, TRACE Trace Lee B11.7.1891 Pendleton OR D3.14.1975 Placerville CA BR/TR/6'1"/180 d6.19 Col Washington																								
1911	Bos A	1	0	0	0	0	0	0	0	0		0		+	+	+	.000	-100	0			/1		0.0
BALL, NEAL Cornelius B4.22.1881 Grand Haven MI D10.15.1957 Bridgeport CT BR/TR/5'7"/145 d9.12																								
1912	†Bos A	18	45	10	9	2	0	0	6	3		0		.200	.250	.244	.494	-60	5			2b17		-0.6
1913	Bos A	23	58	9	10	2	0	0	4	9		1	13	.172	.294	.207	.501	-54	3			2b10,S7/3		-0.6
Total	7	502	1613	163	404	56	17	4	151	99		4	13	.250	.295	.314	.609	-17	92			S271,2b179,3b21,O6(0/5/1)		-5.7
Team	2	41	103	19	19	4	0	0	10	12		1	13	.184	.276	.223	.499	-56	8			2b27,S7/3		-1.2
BARBARE, WALTER Walter Lawrence "Dinty" B8.11.1891 Greenville SC D10.28.1965 Greenville SC BR/TR/6'0"/162 d9.17																								
1918	Bos A	13	29	2	5	3	0	0	2	0		0	1	.172	.172	.276	.448	-64	1			3b11/S		-0.5
Total	8	500	1777	173	462	52	21	1	156	88		6	121	.260	.297	.315	.612	-29	37	16	100	3b230,S157,2b66,1b15		-6.8
BARD, JOSH Joshua David B3.30.1978 Ithaca NY BB/TR/6'3"/(205–215) [ColN99 3/100] d8.23 Col Texas Tech																								
2006	Bos A	7	18	2	5	1	0	0	0	3	0	0	3	.278	.381	.333	.714	-15	0	0	0	C7	0	-0.2
Total	5	256	744	75	201	44	1	22	101	68	2	1	119	.270	.329	.421	.750	-3	1	2	33	C227/D	92	2.3
BARNA, BABE Herbert Paul B3.2.1915 Clarksburg WV D5.18.1972 Charleston WV BL/TR/6'2"/210 d9.16 Col West Virginia																								
1943	Bos A	30	112	19	19	4	1	2	10	15		0	24	.170	.268	.277	.545	-42	2	1	67	O29L	0	-1.1
Total	5	207	664	88	154	22	9	12	96	76		0	98	.232	.311	.346	.657	-12	9	1	100	O175(163/0/12)/1	0	-3.3
BARRETT, JIMMY James Erigena B3.28.1875 Athol MA D10.24.1921 Detroit MI BL/TR/5'7"/170 d9.13																								
1907	Bos A	106	390	52	95	11	6	1	28	38		2		.244	.314	.310	.624	+0	3			O99(96/3/0)		-0.6
1908	Bos A	3	8	0	1	0	0	0	1	1		0		.125	.222	.125	.347	-87	0			O2C		-0.1
Total	10	866	3306	580	962	83	47	16	255	440		29		.291	.379	.359	.738	+17	143			O855(99/707/49)		7.8
Team	2	109	398	52	96	11	6	1	29	39		2	0	.241	.312	.307	.619	-2	3			O101(96/3/0)		-0.7
/150	3	150	548	72	132	15	8	1	40	54		3	0	.241	.312	.307	.619	-2	4			O139(132/4/0)		-1.0
BARRETT, MARTY Martin Glenn B6.23.1958 Arcadia CA BR/TR/5'10"/(170–176) [BosA79 S1/1] d9.6 b–Tom Col Arizona St.																								
1982	Bos A	8	18	0	1	0	0	0	0	0	0	0	1	.056	.056	.056	.112	-165	0	0	0	2b7	0	0.0
1983	Bos A	33	44	7	10	1	1	0	2	3	0	0	1	.227	.271	.295	.566	-47	0	0	0	2b23,D5	0	-0.6
1984	Bos A	139	475	56	144	23	3	3	45	42	2	1	25	.303	.358	.383	.741	+1	5	3	63	2b136	0	1.0
1985	Bos A	156	534	59	142	26	0	5	56	56	3	2	50	.266	.336	.343	.679	-17	7	5	58	2b155	0	1.4
1986	†Bos A	158	625	94	179	39	4	4	60	65	0	1	31	.286	.353	.381	.734	+0	15	7	68	2b158	0	0.8
1987	Bos A	137	559	72	164	23	0	3	43	51	0	1	38	.293	.351	.351	.702	-15	15	2	88	2b137	16	3.0
1988	†Bos A	150	612	83	173	28	1	1	65	40	1	7	35	.283	.330	.337	.667	-16	7	3	70	2b150	0	-0.2
1989	Bos A	86	336	31	86	18	0	1	27	32	0	2	12	.256	.320	.318	.638	-23	4	1	80	2b80,D4	61	-0.7
1990	†Bos A	62	159	15	36	4	0	0	13	15	1	1	13	.226	.294	.252	.546	-48	4	0	100	2b60/3D	0	-1.0
1991	SD N	12	16	1	3	1	0	1	3	0	0	1	3	.188	.235	.438	.673	-18	0	0	0	2b2,3b2	33	0.1
Total	10	941	3378	418	938	163	9	18	314	304	7	16	209	.278	.337	.347	.684	-14	57	21	73	2b908,D10,3b3	110	3.8
Team	9	929	3362	417	935	162	9	17	311	304	7	15	206	.278	.338	.347	.685	-14	57	21	73	2b906,D10/3	77	3.7
/150	1	150	543	67	151	26	1	3	50	49	1	2	33	.278	.338	.347	.685	-14	9	3	75	2b146,D2/3	12	0.6
BARRETT, BOB Robert Schley "Jumbo" B1.27.1899 Atlanta GA D1.18.1982 Atlanta GA BR/TR/5'11"/175 d4.30																								
1929	Bos A	68	126	15	34	10	0	0	19	10		0	6	.270	.324	.349	.673	-25	3	1	75	3b34,1b4,2b2/lf		0.2
Total	5	239	650	57	169	23	5	10	86	32		1	61	.260	.296	.357	.653	-28	6	3	100	3b144,2b31,1b14/lf		-2.5
BARRETT, TOM Thomas Loren B4.2.1960 San Fernando CA BB/TR/5'9"/170 [NYA82 26/667] d7.2 b–Marty Col Arizona [DL 1990 Phi N 178]																								
1992	Bos A	4	3	1	0	0	0	0	0	2	0	0	0	.000	.400	.000	.400	-81	0	0	0	2b2	0	-0.1
Total	3	54	84	9	17	1	0	0	4	10	0	1	15	.202	.295	.214	.509	-53	0	0	0	2b21	178	-0.2
BARRETT, BILL William Joseph "Whispering Bill" B5.28.1900 Cambridge MA D1.26.1951 Cambridge MA BR/TR/6'0"/175 d5.13 OF(74/28/400)																								
1929	Bos A	111	370	57	100	23	4	3	35	51		3	38	.270	.363	.378	.741	-7	11	8	58	O109(1/10/101)/3		-0.3
1930	Bos A	6	18	3	3	1	0	0	1	1		0	3	.167	.211	.222	.433	-90	0	0	0	O5R		-0.3
Total	9	718	2395	318	690	151	30	23	328	209		8	239	.288	.347	.405	.752	-3	80	51	61	O496R,S89,2b66,3b16,P4,1b3		-4.3
Team	2	117	388	60	103	24	4	3	36	52		3	41	.265	.357	.371	.728	-11	11	8	58	O114(1/10/101)/3		-0.6
/150	3	150	497	77	132	31	5	4	46	67		4	53	.265	.357	.371	.728	-11	14	10	58	O146(1/13/129)/3		-0.8
BARRY, JACK John Joseph B4.26.1887 Meriden CT D4.23.1961 Shrewsbury MA BR/TR/5'9"/158 d7.13 Mil 1918 M1 Col Holy Cross																								
1915	†Bos A	78	248	30	65	13	2	0	26	24		6	11	.262	.342	.331	.673	+4	0			2b78		-0.1
1916	Bos A	94	330	28	67	6	1	0	20	17		**17**	24	.203	.277	.227	.504	-48	8			2b94		-1.9
1917	Bos A	116	388	45	83	9	0	2	30	47		4	27	.214	.305	.253	.558	-29	12			2b116,M		-1.7
1919	Bos A	31	108	13	26	5	1	0	2	5		3	5	.241	.293	.306	.599	-28	2			2b31		-0.9
Total	11	1223	4146	532	1009	142	38	10	429	396		76	142	.243	.321	.303	.624	-12	153	18	100	S877,2b339,3b3		-9.9
Team	4	319	1074	116	241	33	4	2	78	93		30	67	.224	.304	.268	.572	-27	22			2b319/M		-4.6
/150	2	150	505	55	113	16	2	1	37	44		14	32	.224	.304	.268	.572	-27	10			2b150/M		-2.2
BATTS, MATT Matthew Daniel B10.16.1921 San Antonio TX BR/TR/5'11"/(200–214) d9.10 Col Baylor																								
1947	Bos A	7	16	3	8	1	0	1	5	1		0	1	.500	.529	.750	1.279	+136	0	0	0	C6	0	0.3
1948	Bos A	46	118	13	37	12	0	1	24	15		0	9	.314	.391	.441	.832	+15	0	0	0	C41	0	0.4
1949	Bos A	60	157	23	38	9	1	3	31	25		1	22	.242	.350	.369	.719	-16	1	0	100	C50	0	0.0
1950	Bos A	75	238	27	65	15	3	4	34	18		1	19	.273	.327	.412	.739	-20	0	0	0	C73	0	-0.3
1951	Bos A	11	29	1	4	1	0	0	2	1		0	2	.138	.167	.172	.339	-108	0	0	0	C11	0	-0.4
1951	StL A	79	248	26	75	17	1	5	31	21		0	21	.302	.357	.440	.797	+11	2	0	100	C64	0	-0.1
1951	Year	90	277	27	79	18	1	5	33	22		0	23	.285	.338	.412	.750	-2	2	0	100	C75	0	-0.5
1952	Det A	56	173	11	41	4	1	3	13	14		1	22	.237	.298	.324	.622	-28	1	0	100	C55	33	-0.2
1953	Det A	116	374	38	104	24	3	6	42	24		0	36	.278	.322	.406	.728	-3	2	3	40	C103	0	-1.4
1954	Det A	12	21	1	6	1	0	0	5	2		0	4	.286	.333	.333	.666	-11	0	0	0	C8	0	0.1
1954	Chi A	55	158	16	36	7	1	3	19	17		0	15	.228	.299	.342	.641	-26	0	1	0	C42	0	0.1
1954	Year	67	179	17	42	8	1	3	24	19		0	19	.235	.303	.341	.644	-24	0	1	0	C50	0	0.2
1955	Cin N	26	71	4	18	4	1	0	13	4	0	0	11	.254	.286	.338	.624	-37	0	0	0	C21	0	-0.3
1956	Cin N	3	2	0	0	0	0	0	0	1	0	0	1	.000	.333	.000	.333	-100	0	0	0	/H	0	0.0
Total	10	546	1605	163	432	95	11	26	219	143	0	3	163	.269	.329	.391	.720	-11	6	4	60	C474	33	-1.8
Team	5	199	558	67	152	38	4	9	96	60		2	53	.272	.345	.403	.748	-11	1	0	100	C181	0	0.0
/150	4	150	421	51	115	29	3	7	72	45		2	40	.272	.345	.403	.748	-11	1	0	100	C136	0	0.0
BAYLOR, DON Don Edward B6.28.1949 Austin TX BR/TR/6'1"/(190–210) [BalA67 2/39] d9.18 M9/C7																								
1986	†Bos A	160	585	93	139	23	1	31	94	62	8	**35**	111	.238	.344	.439	.783	+11	3	5	38	D143,1b13,O3L	0	0.2
1987	Bos A	108	339	64	81	8	0	16	57	40	3	24	47	.239	.355	.404	.759	-1	5	2	71	D97	0	-0.1
Total	19	2292	8198	1236	2135	366	28	338	1276	805	91	267	1069	.260	.342	.436	.778	+18	285	120	70	D1285,O822(623/37/195),1b148	46	10.2
Team	2	268	924	157	220	31	1	47	151	102	11	59	158	.238	.348	.426	.774	+7	8	7	53	D240,1b13,O3L	0	0.1
/150	1	150	517	88	123	17	1	26	85	57	6	33	88	.238	.348	.426	.774	+7	4	4	50	D134,1b7,O2L	0	0.1
BELL, JUAN Juan (Mathey) B3.29.1968 San Pedro de Macoris, D.R. BR/TR (BB 1995)/5'11"/(157–176) d9.6 b–George																								
1995	Bos A	17	26	7	4	2	0	1	2	2	0	0	10	.154	.207	.346	.553	-58	0	0	0	S6,2b5/3	0	-0.3
Total	7	329	836	107	177	30	6	10	71	84	5	3	189	.212	.284	.298	.582	-40	16	7	70	2b156,S133,D11,3b4,O4(1/1/2)	0	-3.7
BELLHORN, MARK Mark Christian B8.23.1974 Boston MA BB/TR/6'1"/(190–209) [OakA95 2/35] d6.10 Col Auburn OF(1/3/4)																								
2004	†Bos A	138	523	93	138	37	3	17	82	88	1	5	177	.264	.373	.444	.817	+6	6	1	86	2b124,3b16/S	18	1.0
2005	Bos A	85	283	41	61	20	0	7	28	49	1	0	109	.216	.328	.360	.688	-19	3	0	100	2b83/S	32	0.2
Total	9	718	2093	322	483	113	13	69	245	342	6	17	718	.231	.342	.396	.738	-9	30	13	70	2b349,3b219,1b41,S31,D11,O8R	72	-0.6
Team	2	223	806	134	199	57	3	24	110	137	2	5	286	.247	.357	.414	.771	-3	9	1	90	2b207,3b16,S2	50	1.2
/150	1	150	542	90	134	38	2	16	74	92	1	3	192	.247	.357	.414	.771	-3	6	1	86	2b139,3b11/S	34	0.8
BELTRE, ESTEBAN Esteban (Valera) B12.26.1967 Ingenio Quisquella, D.R. BR/TR/5'10"/(155–172) d9.3																								
1996	Bos A	27	62	6	16	2	0	0	6	4	0	0	14	.258	.299	.290	.589	-50	1	0	100	3b13,2b8,S6/D	0	-0.7
Total	5	186	401	46	95	17	0	1	35	28	0	0	73	.237	.285	.287	.572	-49	5	5	50	S134,2b24,3b19,D5	0	-3.5

Year	Tm Lg	G	AB	R	H	2B	3B	HR	RBI	BB	IB	HP	SO	AVG	OBP	SLG	OPS	AOPS	SB	CS	SB%	Games at Position	DL	BFW
BENIQUEZ, JUAN Juan Jose (Torres) B5.13.1950 San Sebastian, PR BR/TR/5'11"/(148–175) d9.4 OF(295/735/184)																								
1971	Bos A	16	57	8	17	2	0	0	4	3	0	0	4	.298	.333	.333	.666	-17	3	1	75	S15	0	-0.8
1972	Bos A	33	99	10	24	4	1	1	8	7	0	0	11	.242	.287	.333	.620	-19	2	0	100	S27	0	0.3
1974	Bos A	106	389	60	104	14	3	5	33	25	2	1	61	.267	.313	.357	.670	-14	19	11	63	O97(7/91/0),D4	25	-1.2
1975	†Bos A	78	254	43	74	14	4	2	17	25	1	2	26	.291	.358	.402	.760	+6	7	10	41	O44(31/13/2),D20,3b14	16	-0.1
Total	17	1500	4651	610	1274	190	30	79	476	349	11	31	551	.274	.327	.379	.706	-5	104	76	58	O1155C,D111,1b68,3b49,S43/2	270	-10.5
Team	4	233	799	121	219	34	8	8	62	60	3	3	102	.274	.326	.367	.693	-8	31	22	58	O141(38/104/0),S42,D24,3b14	41	-1.8
/150	3	150	514	78	141	22	5	5	40	39	2	2	66	.274	.326	.367	.693	-8	20	14	59	O91(24/67/0),S27,D15,3b9	26	-1.2
BENJAMIN, MIKE Michael Paul B11.22.1965 Euclid OH BR/TR/6'0"/(169–195) [SFN87 3/74] d7.7 Col Arizona St. [DL 2001 Pit N 190]																								
1997	Bos A	49	116	12	27	9	1	0	7	4	0	1	27	.233	.262	.328	.590	-48	2	3	40	3b19,S16,2b5,1b4/PD	0	-0.4
1998	†Bos A	124	349	46	95	23	0	4	39	15	1	6	73	.272	.312	.372	.684	-24	3	0	100	2b87,S20,3b11,1b10,D2	0	-0.3
Total	13	818	1926	227	442	109	15	24	169	106	19	25	429	.229	.277	.339	.616	-39	44	14	76	S375,3b199,2b184,1b16,D3/rfP	395	1.8
Team	2	173	465	58	122	32	1	4	46	19	1	7	100	.262	.300	.361	.661	-30	5	3	63	2b92,S36,3b30,1b14,D3/P	0	-0.7
/150	2	150	403	50	106	28	1	3	40	16	1	6	87	.262	.300	.361	.661	-30	4	3	57	2b80,S31,3b26,1b12,D3/P	0	-0.6
BENZINGER, TODD Todd Eric B2.11.1963 Dayton KY BB/TR/6'1"/(185–195) [BosA81 4/96] d6.21																								
1987	Bos A	73	223	36	62	11	1	8	43	22	3	2	41	.278	.344	.444	.788	+5	5	4	56	O61(14/5/47),1b2	0	0.7
1988	†Bos A	120	405	47	103	28	1	13	70	22	4	1	80	.254	.293	.425	.718	-5	2	3	40	1b85,O48(5/0/43)/D	19	-1.4
Total	9	924	2856	316	733	135	18	66	376	181	35	14	552	.257	.301	.386	.687	-12	21	29	42	1b622,O192(69/5/123),D2/3	19	-13.5
Team	2	193	628	83	165	39	2	21	113	44	7	3	121	.263	.312	.432	.744	-1	7	7	50	O109(19/5/90),1b87/D	19	-0.7
/150	2	150	488	65	128	30	2	16	88	34	5	2	94	.263	.312	.432	.744	-1	5	5	50	O85(15/4/70),1b68/D	15	-0.5
BERBERET, LOU Louis Joseph B11.20.1929 Long Beach CA D4.6.2004 Las Vegas NV BL/TR/5'11"/(200–212) d9.17 Col Santa Clara																								
1958	Bos A	57	167	11	35	5	3	2	18	31	1	1	32	.210	.337	.311	.648	-26	0	2	0	C49	0	-0.4
Total	7	448	1224	118	281	34	10	31	153	200	20	7	195	.230	.337	.350	.687	-14	2	3	40	C367	0	-1.4
BERG, MOE Morris B3.2.1902 New York NY D5.29.1972 Belleville NJ BR/TR/6'1"/185 d6.27 C2 Col Princeton																								
1935	Bos A	38	98	13	28	5	0	2	12	5		0	3	.286	.320	.398	.718	-21	0	0	0	C37		0.1
1936	Bos A	39	125	9	30	4	1	0	19	2		2	6	.240	.264	.288	.552	-66	0	0	0	C39		-0.2
1937	Bos A	47	141	13	36	3	1	0	20	5		0	4	.255	.281	.291	.572	-57	0	0	0	C47		-0.8
1938	Bos A	10	12	0	4	0	0	0	0	0		0	1	.333	.333	.333	.666	-36	0	0	0	C7/1		0.0
1939	Bos A	14	33	3	9	1	0	1	5	2		0	3	.273	.314	.394	.708	-23	0	0	0	C13		0.1
Total	15	663	1813	150	441	71	6	6	206	78		9	117	.243	.278	.299	.577	-51	12	5	71	C529,S84,2b14,3b4/1		-7.8
Team	5	148	409	38	107	13	2	3	56	14		2	17	.262	.289	.325	.614	-48	0	0	0	C143/1		-0.8
/150	5	150	415	39	108	13	2	3	57	14		2	17	.262	.289	.325	.614	-48	0	0	0	C145/1		-0.8
BERGER, BOZE Louis William B5.13.1910 Baltimore MD D11.3.1992 Bethesda MD BR/TR/6'2"/180 d8.17 Col Maryland																								
1939	Bos A	20	30	4	9	2	0	0	2	1		0	10	.300	.323	.367	.690	-27	0	0	0	S10,3b5,2b2		0.0
Total	6	343	1144	146	270	51	8	13	97	94		3	226	.236	.296	.329	.625	-43	12	7	63	2b173,S84,3b62,1b10		-4.9
BERRY, CHARLIE Charles Francis B10.18.1902 Phillipsburg NJ D9.6.1972 Evanston IL BR/TR/6'0"/185 d6.15 C5/U21 f–Charlie Col Lafayette																								
1925	Phi A	10	14	1	3	1	0	0	3	0		0	2	.214	.214	.286	.500	-76	0	0	0	C4		-0.2
1928	Bos A	80	177	18	46	7	3	1	19	21		1	19	.260	.342	.350	.692	-16	1	1	50	C63		-0.9
1929	Bos A	77	207	19	50	11	4	1	21	15		3	29	.242	.302	.348	.650	-31	2	6	25	C72		-0.5
1930	Bos A	88	256	31	74	9	6	6	35	16		0	22	.289	.331	.441	.772	-2	2	0	100	C85		1.0
1931	Bos A	111	357	41	101	16	2	6	49	29		0	38	.283	.337	.389	.726	-4	4	0	100	C102		0.4
1932	Bos A	10	32	0	6	3	0	0	6	3		0	2	.188	.257	.281	.538	-60	0	0	0	C10		-0.3
1932	Chi A	72	226	33	69	15	6	4	31	21		0	23	.305	.364	.478	.842	+24	3	0	100	C70		1.0
1932	Year	82	258	33	75	18	6	4	37	24		0	25	.291	.351	.453	.804	+14	3	0	100	C80		0.7
1933	Chi A	86	271	25	69	8	3	2	28	17		1	16	.255	.301	.328	.629	-30	0	0	0	C83		-1.7
1934	Phi A	99	269	14	72	10	2	0	34	22		0	23	.268	.323	.320	.643	-31	1	0	100	C99		-0.9
1935	Phi A	62	190	14	48	7	3	3	29	10		0	20	.253	.290	.368	.658	-30	0	0	0	C56		-0.8
1936	Phi A	13	17	0	1	1	0	0	1	6		0	2	.059	.304	.118	.422	-92	0	0	0	C12		-0.2
1938	Phi A	1	2	0	0	0	0	0	0	0		0	0	.000	.000	.000	.000	-199	0	0	0	/C		0.0
Total	11	709	2018	196	539	88	29	23	256	160		5	196	.267	.322	.374	.696	-17	13	7	65	C657		-3.1
Team	5	366	1029	109	277	46	15	14	130	84		4	110	.269	.327	.384	.711	-13	9	7	56	C332		-0.3
/150	2	150	422	45	114	19	6	6	53	34		2	45	.269	.327	.384	.711	-13	4	3	57	C136		-0.1
BERRY, SEAN Sean Robert B3.22.1966 Santa Monica CA BR/TR/5'11"/(200–210) [KCA86*S1/9] d9.17 C1 Col UCLA																								
2000	Bos A	1	4	0	0	0	0	0	0	0	0	0	2	.000	.000	.000	.000	-197	0	0	0	/3	0	-0.2
Total	11	860	2413	310	657	153	10	81	369	206	19	32	438	.272	.334	.445	.779	+4	47	24	66	3b629,1b67,D4	30	-0.0
BERRYHILL, DAMON Damon Scott B12.3.1963 South Laguna CA BB/TR/6'0"/(205–210) [ChiN84*1/4] d9.5 Col Orange Coast (CA) JC																								
1994	Bos A	82	255	30	67	17	2	6	34	19	0	0	59	.263	.312	.416	.728	-18	0	1	0	C67,D6	0	-0.4
Total	10	683	2030	175	488	106	6	47	257	139	23	6	409	.240	.288	.368	.656	-23	3	6	33	C590,D6,1b2	289	-5.3
BEVAN, HAL Harold Joseph B11.15.1930 New Orleans LA D10.5.1968 New Orleans LA BR/TR/6'2"/198 d4.24																								
1952	Bos A	1	1	0	0	0	0	0	0	0		0	0	.000	.000	.000	.000	-193	0	0	0	/3	0	0.0
Total	3	15	24	2	7	0	0	1	5	0	0	0	3	.292	.292	.417	.709	-11	2	0	100	3b8	106	0.0
BICHETTE, DANTE Alphonse Dante B11.18.1963 W.Palm Beach FL BR/TR/6'3"/(212–238) [CalA84 17/424] d9.5 Col Palm Beach (FL) CC																								
2000	Bos A	30	114	13	33	5	0	7	14	8	0	0	22	.289	.336	.518	.854	+9	0	0	0	D30	0	-0.1
2001	Bos A	107	391	45	112	30	1	12	49	20	1	3	76	.286	.325	.460	.785	+4	2	2	50	O53(37/0/16),D46	0	-0.4
Total	14	1704	6381	934	1906	401	27	274	1141	355	32	41	1078	.299	.336	.499	.835	+4	152	73	68	O1552(649/56/907),D89/3	0	-3.0
Team	2	137	505	58	145	35	1	19	63	28	1	3	98	.287	.328	.473	.801	+5	2	2	50	D76,O53(37/0/16)	0	-0.5
/150	2	150	553	64	159	38	1	21	69	31	1	3	107	.287	.328	.473	.801	+5	2	2	50	D83,O58(41/0/18)	0	-0.5
BIGELOW, ELLIOT Elliot Allardice "Babe","Gilly" B10.13.1897 Tarpon Springs FL D8.13.1933 Tampa FL BL/TL/5'11"/185 d4.18																								
1929	Bos A	100	211	23	60	16	0	1	26	23		1	18	.284	.357	.374	.731	-9	1	4	20	O59(2/2/55)		-0.8
/150	2	150	317	35	90	24	0	2	39	35		2	27	.284	.357	.374	.731	-9	2	6	25	O89(3/3/83)		-1.2
BISCHOFF, JOHN John George "Smiley" B10.28.1894 Granite City IL D12.28.1981 Granite City IL BR/TR/5'7"/165 d4.18																								
1925	Chi A	7	11	1	1	0	0	0	0	1		0	5	.091	.167	.091	.258	-135	0	0	0	C4		-0.2
1925	Bos A	41	133	13	37	9	1	1	16	6		0	11	.278	.309	.383	.692	-25	1	2	33	C40		-0.7
1925	Year	48	144	14	38	9	1	1	16	7		0	16	.264	.298	.361	.659	-33	1	2	33	C44		-0.9
1926	Bos A	59	127	6	33	11	2	0	19	15		1	16	.260	.343	.378	.721	-9	1	3	25	C46		-0.4
Total	2	107	271	20	71	20	3	1	35	22		1	32	.262	.320	.369	.689	-22	2	5	29	C90		-1.3
Team	2	100	260	19	70	20	3	1	35	21		1	27	.269	.326	.381	.707	-17	2	5	29	C86		-1.1
/150	3	150	390	29	105	30	5	2	53	32		2	41	.269	.326	.381	.707	-17	3	8	27	C129		-1.6
BISHOP, MAX Max Frederick "Tilly","Camera Eye" B9.5.1899 Waynesboro PA D2.24.1962 Waynesboro PA BL/TR/5'8.5"/165 d4.15 Col CC of Baltimore (MD)																								
1934	Bos A	97	253	65	66	13	1	1	22	82		2	22	.261	.445	.332	.777	-4	3	2	60	2b57,1b15		0.9
1935	Bos A	60	122	19	28	3	1	1	14	28		1	14	.230	.377	.295	.672	-29	0	2	0	2b34,1b11,S2		-0.6
Total	12	1338	4494	966	1216	236	35	41	379	1156		31	452	.271	.423	.366	.789	+2	40	51	44	2b1230,1b26,S2		10.9
Team	2	157	375	84	94	16	2	2	36	110		3	36	.251	.424	.320	.744	-12	3	4	43	2b91,1b26,S2		0.3
/150	2	150	358	80	90	15	2	2	34	105		3	34	.251	.424	.320	.744	-12	3	4	43	2b87,1b25,S2		0.3
BLACKWELL, TIM Timothy P B8.19.1952 San Diego CA BB/TR/5'11"/(170–185) [BosA70 13/311] d7.3																								
1974	Bos A	44	122	9	30	1	1	0	8	10	1	1	21	.246	.308	.270	.578	-37	1	1	50	C44	0	-0.8
1975	Bos A	59	132	15	26	3	2	0	6	19	0	1	13	.197	.303	.250	.553	-47	0	0	0	C57,D2	0	-0.5
Total	10	426	1044	91	238	40	11	6	80	154	14	4	183	.228	.328	.305	.633	-27	3	3	50	C414,D2	0	-1.9
Team	2	103	254	24	56	4	3	0	14	29	1	2	34	.220	.305	.260	.565	-42	1	1	50	C101,D2	0	-1.3
/150	3	150	370	35	82	6	4	0	20	42	1	3	50	.220	.305	.260	.565	-42	1	1	50	C147,D3	0	-1.9
BLOSSER, GREG Gregory Brent B6.26.1971 Manatee FL BL/TL/6'3"/205 [BosA89 1/16] d9.5																								
1993	Bos A	17	28	1	2	1	0	0	1	2	0	0	7	.071	.133	.107	.240	-132	1	0	100	O9L/D	0	-0.5
1994	Bos A	5	11	2	1	0	0	0	1	4	0	0	4	.091	.333	.091	.424	-84	0	0	0	O3(1/0/2)/D	0	-0.1
Total	2	22	39	3	3	1	0	0	2	6	0	0	11	.077	.200	.103	.303	-116	1	0	100	O12(10/0/2),D2	0	-0.6

Year	Tm Lg	G	AB	R	H	2B	3B	HR	RBI	BB	IB	HP	SO	AVG	OBP	SLG	OPS	AOPS	SB	CS	SB%	Games at Position	DL	BFW
BLUHM, RED Harvey Fred B6.27.1894 Cleveland OH D5.7.1952 Flint MI BR/TR/5'11"/165 d7.3																								
1918	Bos A	1	1	0	0	0	0	0	0	0		0	0	.000	.000	.000	.000	-199	0			/H		0.0
BOGGS, WADE Wade Anthony B6.15.1958 Omaha NE BL/TR/6'2"/(185–197) [BosA76 7/166] d4.10 C1 HF2005																								
1982	Bos A	104	338	51	118	14	1	5	44	35	4	0	21	.349	.406	.441	.847	+26	1	0	100	1b49,3b44/lfD	0	2.9
1983	Bos A	153	582	100	210	44	7	5	74	92	2	1	36	**.361**	**.444**	.486	.930	+46	3	3	50	3b153	0	4.4
1984	Bos A	158	625	109	203	31	4	6	55	89	6	0	44	.325	.407	.416	.823	+23	3	2	60	3b156,D2	0	4.4
1985	Bos A★	161	653	107	**240**	42	3	8	78	96	5	4	61	**.368**	**.450**	.478	.928	+48	2	1	67	3b161	0	5.6
1986	†Bos A★	149	580	107	207	47	2	8	71	**105**	14	0	44	**.357**	**.453**	.486	.939	+55	0	4	0	3b149	0	**5.4**
1987	Bos A★	147	551	108	200	40	6	24	89	105	**19**	2	48	**.363**	**.461**	.588	1.049	+72	1	3	25	3b145/1D	0	**6.5**
1988	†Bos A★	155	584	**128**	214	**45**	6	5	58	**125**	**18**	3	34	**.366**	**.476**	.490	.966	+65	2	3	40	3b151,D3	0	**6.4**
1989	Bos A★	156	621	**113**	205	**51**	7	3	54	107	**19**	7	51	.330	**.430**	.449	.879	+40	2	6	25	3b152,D3	0	4.3
1990	†Bos A★	155	619	89	187	44	5	6	63	87	**19**	1	68	.302	.386	.418	.804	+20	0	0	0	3b152,D3	0	0.6
1991	Bos A★	144	546	93	181	42	2	8	51	89	**25**	0	32	.332	.421	.460	.881	+37	1	2	33	3b140	0	3.8
1992	Bos A★	143	514	62	133	22	4	7	50	74	**19**	4	31	.259	.353	.358	.711	-6	1	3	25	3b117,D21	0	-0.4
1993	NY A★	143	560	83	169	26	1	2	59	74	4	0	49	.302	.378	.363	.741	+4	0	1	0	3b134,D8	0	2.8
1994	NY A★	97	366	61	125	19	1	11	55	61	3	1	29	.342	.433	.489	.922	+43	2	1	67	3b93,1b4	0	3.3
1995	†NY A★	126	460	76	149	22	4	5	63	74	5	0	50	.324	.412	.422	.834	+20	1	1	50	3b117,1b9	0	1.5
1996	†NY A★	132	501	80	156	29	2	2	41	67	7	0	32	.311	.389	.389	.778	-1	1	2	33	3b123,D4	0	-0.1
1997	†NY A	104	353	55	103	23	1	4	28	48	3	0	38	.292	.373	.397	.770	+3	0	1	0	3b76,D19/P	0	0.4
1998	TB A	123	435	51	122	23	4	7	52	46	6	0	54	.280	.348	.400	.748	-8	3	2	60	3b78,D33	21	-0.5
1999	TB A	90	292	40	88	14	1	2	29	38	2	0	23	.301	.377	.377	.754	-7	1	0	100	3b74,1b4/PD	46	-0.8
Total	18	2440	9180	1513	3010	578	61	118	1014	1412	18	23	745	.328	.415	.443	.858	+29	24	35	41	3b2215,D107,1b67,P2/lf	67	50.5
Team	11	1625	6213	1067	2098	422	47	85	687	1004	31	22	470	.338	.428	.462	.890	+40	16	27	37	3b1520,1b50,D34/lf	0	43.9
/150	1	150	574	98	194	39	4	8	63	93	3	2	43	.338	.428	.462	.890	+40	1	2	33	3b140,1b5,D3/OfL	0	4.1
BOLLING, MILT Milton Joseph B8.9.1930 Mississippi City MS BR/TR/6'1"/(180–185) d9.10 b–Frank																								
1952	Bos A	11	36	4	8	1	0	1	3	3		0	5	.222	.282	.333	.615	-34	0	1	0	S11	0	0.2
1953	Bos A	109	323	30	85	12	1	5	28	23		3	41	.263	.318	.353	.671	-23	1	4	20	S109	0	0.1
1954	Bos A	113	370	42	92	20	3	6	36	47		4	55	.249	.337	.368	.705	-16	2	4	33	S107,3b5	0	1.1
1955	Bos A	6	5	0	1	0	0	0	0	0	0	0	1	.200	.200	.200	.400	-93	0	0	0	S2	63	-0.1
1956	Bos A	45	118	19	25	3	2	3	8	18	1	1	20	.212	.319	.347	.666	-32	0	1	0	S26,3b11/2	0	-0.9
1957	Bos A	1	1	0	0	0	0	0	0	0	0	0	0	.000	.000	.000	.000	-195	0	0	0	/H	0	0.0
1957	Was A	91	277	29	63	12	1	4	19	18	0	2	59	.227	.277	.321	.598	-36	2	2	50	2b53,S37/3	0	-0.5
1957	Year	92	278	29	63	12	1	4	19	18	0	2	59	.227	.276	.320	.596	-36	2	2	50	2b53,S37/3	0	-0.5
1958	Det A	24	31	3	6	2	0	0	0	5	0	0	7	.194	.306	.258	.564	-47	0	0	0	S13/23	0	-0.1
Total	7	400	1161	127	280	50	7	19	94	114	1	10	188	.241	.313	.345	.658	-26	5	12	29	S305,2b55,3b18	63	-0.2
Team	6	285	853	95	211	36	6	15	75	91	1	8	122	.247	.324	.356	.680	-22	3	10	23	S255,3b16/2	63	0.4
/150	3	150	449	50	111	19	3	8	39	48	1	4	64	.247	.324	.356	.680	-22	2	5	29	S134,3b8/2	33	0.2
BOONE, IKE Isaac Morgan B2.17.1897 Samantha AL D8.1.1958 Northport AL BL/TR/6'0"/195 d4.22 b–Dan Col Alabama																								
1922	NY N	2	2	0	1	0	0	0	0	0		0	1	.500	.500	.500	1.000	+57	0	0	0	/H		0.0
1923	Bos A	5	15	1	4	0	1	0	2	1		0	0	.267	.313	.400	.713	-14	0	1	0	O4C		-0.1
1924	Bos A	128	487	72	164	31	4	13	98	54		1	32	.337	.404	.497	.901	+31	2	2	50	O124R		0.3
1925	Bos A	133	476	79	157	34	5	9	68	60		1	19	.330	.406	.479	.885	+24	1	4	20	O118R		0.0
1927	Chi A	29	53	10	12	4	0	1	11	3		0	4	.226	.268	.358	.626	-37	0	0	0	O11(1/0/10)		-0.4
1930	Bro N	40	101	13	30	9	1	3	13	14		0	8	.297	.383	.495	.878	+11	0			O27L		0.0
1931	Bro N	6	5	0	1	0	0	0	0	1		0	1	.200	.333	.200	.533	-53	0			/H		0.0
1932	Bro N	13	21	2	3	1	0	0	2	5		0	2	.143	.308	.190	.498	-62	0			O8(2/0/6)		-0.1
Total	8	356	1160	177	372	79	11	26	194	138		2	67	.321	.394	.475	.869	+21	3	7	100	O292(30/4/258)		-0.3
Team	3	266	978	152	325	65	10	22	168	115		2	51	.332	.404	.487	.891	+27	3	7	30	O246C		0.2
/150	2	150	552	86	183	37	6	12	95	65		1	29	.332	.404	.487	.891	+27	2	4	33	O139C		0.1
BOONE, RAY Raymond Otis "Ike" B7.27.1923 San Diego CA D10.17.2004 San Diego CA BR/TR/6'1"/(185–190) d9.3 s–Bob gs–Bret gs–Aaron																								
1960	Bos A	34	78	6	16	1	0	1	11	11	0	0	15	.205	.300	.256	.556	-49	0	0	0	1b22	0	-0.7
Total	13	1373	4589	645	1260	162	46	151	737	608	20	27	463	.275	.361	.429	.790	+15	21	19	52	3b510,S464,1b285/2	0	7.7
BOUDREAU, LOU Louis B7.17.1917 Harvey IL D8.20.2001 Olympia Fields IL BR/TR/5'11"/185 d9.9 M16 HF1970 Col Illinois																								
1951	Bos A	82	273	37	73	18	1	5	47	30		6	12	.267	.353	.396	.749	-7	1	0	100	S52,3b15,1b2	0	0.2
1952	Bos A	4	2	1	0	0	0	0	2	0		0	0	.000	.000	.000	.000	-193	0	0	0	/S3M	0	-0.1
Total	15	1646	6029	861	1779	385	66	68	789	796		34	309	.295	.380	.415	.795	+21	51	50	50	S1539,3b57,1b16,2b3,C3	0	43.6
Team	2	86	275	38	73	18	1	5	49	30		6	12	.265	.350	.393	.743	-8	1	0	100	S53,3b16,1b2/M	0	0.1
BOWEN, SAM Samuel Thomas B9.18.1952 Brunswick GA BR/TR/5'9"/167 [BosA74 7/164] d8.25 Col Valdosta St.																								
1977	Bos A	3	2	0	0	0	0	0	0	0	0	0	2	.000	.000	.000	.000	-190	0	0	0	O3(2/1/0)	0	0.0
1978	Bos A	6	7	3	1	0	0	1	1	1	0	0	2	.143	.250	.571	.821	+13	0	0	0	O4(1/3/0)	0	-0.1
1980	Bos A	7	13	0	2	0	0	0	0	2	0	0	3	.154	.267	.154	.421	-83	1	0	100	O6(1/4/1)	0	0.0
Total	3	16	22	3	3	0	0	1	1	3	0	0	7	.136	.240	.273	.513	-62	1	0	100	O13(4/8/1)	0	-0.1
BRADLEY, HUGH Hugh Frederick "Corns" B5.23.1885 Grafton MA D1.26.1949 Worcester MA BR/TR/5'10"/175 d4.25 Col Holy Cross																								
1910	Bos A	32	83	8	14	6	2	0	7	5		0		.169	.216	.289	.505	-43	2			1b21,C3/rf		-0.7
1911	Bos A	12	41	9	13	2	0	1	4	2		1		.317	.364	.439	.803	+25	1			1b12		0.1
1912	Bos A	40	137	16	26	11	1	1	19	15		1		.190	.275	.307	.582	-37	3			1b40		-0.7
Total	5	277	913	84	238	46	12	2	117	59		12	44	.261	.314	.344	.658	-16	23			1b225,O23R,C4		-4.0
Team	3	84	261	33	53	19	3	2	30	22		2	0	.203	.270	.322	.592	-29	6			1b73,C3/rf		-1.3
BRADY, CLIFF Clifford Francis B3.6.1897 St.Louis MO D9.25.1974 Belleville IL BR/TR/5'5.5"/140 d8.8																								
1920	Bos A	53	180	16	41	5	1	0	12	13		1	12	.228	.284	.267	.551	-52	0	1	0	2b53		-0.2
BRAGG, DARREN Darren William B9.7.1969 Waterbury CT BL/TR/5'9"/180 [SeaA91 22/578] d4.12 Col Georgia Tech																								
1994	Sea A	8	19	4	3	1	0	0	2	2	1	0	5	.158	.238	.211	.449	-83	0	0	0	O3L,D3	0	-0.3
1995	Sea A	52	145	20	34	5	1	3	12	18	1	4	37	.234	.331	.345	.676	-23	9	0	100	O47(32/0/17),D2	0	0.1
1996	Sea A	69	195	36	53	12	1	7	25	33	4	2	35	.272	.376	.451	.827	+9	8	5	62	O63(48/5/16)	0	0.6
1996	Bos A	58	222	38	56	14	1	3	22	36	2	2	39	.252	.357	.365	.722	-17	6	4	60	O58(7/47/29)	0	-0.3
1996	Year	127	417	74	109	26	2	10	47	69	6	4	74	.261	.366	.405	.771	-5	14	9	61	O121(55/52/45)	0	0.3
1997	Bos A	153	513	65	132	35	2	9	57	61	5	3	102	.257	.337	.386	.723	-13	10	6	63	O150(1/118/41)/3	0	-0.3
1998	†Bos A	129	409	51	114	29	3	8	57	42	0	6	99	.279	.351	.423	.774	-1	5	3	63	O124(7/12/112),D4	0	-0.7
1999	StL N	93	273	38	71	12	1	6	26	44	1	3	67	.260	.369	.377	.746	-12	3	0	100	O88(22/43/33)	62	-0.4
2000	Col N	71	149	16	33	7	1	3	21	17	1	0	41	.221	.296	.342	.638	-50	4	1	80	O43(34/0/9)	0	-1.4
2001	NY N	18	57	4	15	6	0	0	5	4	0	1	23	.263	.323	.368	.691	-16	3	2	60	O16(8/2/10)	0	-0.3
2001	NY A	5	4	1	1	1	0	0	0	0	0	0	1	.250	.250	.500	.750	-10	0	0	0	O3R	0	0.0
2001	Major	23	61	5	16	7	0	0	5	4	0	1	24	.262	.318	.377	.695	-68	3	2	60		0	-0.3
2002	†Atl N	109	212	34	57	15	2	3	15	24	0	2	52	.269	.347	.401	.748	-3	5	2	71	O63(12/18/36),D3	0	-0.3
2003	†Atl N	104	162	21	39	5	1	0	9	13	1	2	38	.241	.305	.284	.589	-45	2	1	67	O78(29/21/35)	0	-1.6
2004	SD N	9	7	2	1	0	0	0	0	2	0	0	2	.143	.333	.143	.476	-69	0	0	0	/H	0	-0.1
2004	Cin N	38	94	11	18	3	1	4	9	8	1	0	29	.191	.255	.372	.627	-39	1	0	100	O26(2/14/11)	0	-0.3
2004	Year	47	101	13	19	3	1	4	9	10	1	0	31	.188	.261	.356	.617	-41	1	0	100	O26(2/14/11)	0	-0.4
Total	11	916	2461	341	627	145	14	46	260	304	17	25	570	.255	.340	.381	.721	-16	56	24	70	O762(205/280/352),D12/3	62	-5.3
Team	3	340	1144	154	302	78	6	20	136	139	7	11	240	.264	.346	.395	.741	-10	21	13	62	O332(8/177/34),D4/3	0	-1.3
/150	1	150	505	68	133	34	3	9	60	61	3	5	106	.264	.346	.395	.741	-10	9	6	60	O146(4/78/15),D2/3	0	-0.6
BRATSCHI, FRED Frederick Oscar "Fritz" B1.16.1892 Alliance OH D1.10.1962 Massillon OH BR/TR/5'10"/170 d7.24																								
1921	Chi A	16	28	0	8	1	0	0	3	0		0	2	.286	.286	.321	.607	-45	0	0	0	O5(1/0/4)		-0.1
1926	Bos A	72	167	12	46	10	1	0	19	14		1	15	.275	.335	.347	.682	-19	0	1	0	O37(29/0/8)		-1.2

Year	Tm Lg	G	AB	R	H	2B	3B	HR	RBI	BB	IB	HP	SO	AVG	OBP	SLG	OPS	AOPS	SB	CS	SB%	Games at Position	DL	BFW
1927	Bos A	1	1	0	0	0	0	0	0	0		0	0	.000	.000	.000	.000	-199	0	0	0	/H		0.0
Total	3	89	196	12	54	11	1	0	22	14		1	17	.276	.327	.342	.669	-24	0	1	0	O42(30/0/12)		-1.3
Team	2	73	168	12	46	10	1	0	19	14		1	15	.274	.333	.345	.678	-20	0	1	0	O37(29/0/8)		-1.2
BRESSOUD, EDDIE Edward Francis B5.2.1932 Los Angeles CA BR/TR/6'1"/(175–185) d6.14																								
1956	NY N	49	163	15	37	4	2	0	9	12	1	1	20	.227	.284	.276	.560	-48	1	0	100	S48	0	-1.6
1957	NY N	49	127	11	34	2	2	5	10	4	1	2	19	.268	.299	.433	.732	-6	0	1	0	S33,3b12	0	-0.5
1958	SF N	66	137	19	36	5	3	0	8	14	1	0	22	.263	.331	.343	.674	-19	0	1	0	2b57,3b6,S4	0	-0.8
1959	SF N	104	315	36	79	17	2	9	26	28	6	0	55	.251	.311	.403	.714	-9	0	0	0	S92/123	0	-0.6
1960	SF N	116	386	37	87	19	6	9	43	35	12	2	72	.225	.290	.376	.666	-13	1	2	33	S115	0	0.3
1961	SF N	59	114	14	24	6	0	3	11	11	4	0	23	.211	.276	.342	.618	-34	1	1	50	S34,3b3/2	0	-1.3
1962	Bos A	153	599	79	166	40	9	14	68	46	4	2	118	.277	.329	.444	.773	+3	2	3	40	S153	0	3.7
1963	Bos A	140	497	61	129	23	6	20	60	52	2	2	93	.260	.329	.451	.780	+13	1	1	50	S137	0	0.8
1964	Bos A☆	158	566	86	166	41	3	15	55	72	4	1	99	.293	.372	.456	.828	+23	1	1	50	S158	0	2.7
1965	Bos A	107	296	29	67	11	1	8	25	29	4	1	77	.226	.297	.351	.648	-21	0	1	0	S86,3b2/lf	0	-0.2
1966	NY N	133	405	48	91	15	5	10	49	47	4	1	107	.225	.304	.360	.664	-13	2	2	50	S94,3b32,1b9,2b7	0	1.0
1967	†StL N	52	67	8	9	1	1	1	1	9	1	0	18	.134	.237	.224	.461	-67	0	0	0	S48/3	0	-1.5
Total	12	1186	3672	443	925	184	40	94	365	359	44	12	723	.252	.319	.401	.720	-4	9	13	41	S1002,2b66,3b57,1b10/lf	0	2.0
Team	4	558	1958	255	528	115	19	57	208	199	14	6	387	.270	.337	.435	.772	+8	4	6	40	S534,3b2/lf	0	7.0
/150	1	150	526	69	142	31	5	15	56	53	4	2	104	.270	.337	.435	.772	+8	1	2	33	S144/3OfL	0	1.9
BROGNA, RICO Rico Joseph B4.18.1970 Turners Falls MA BL/TL/6'2"/(200–205) [DetA88 1/26] d8.8																								
2000	Bos A	43	56	8	11	3	0	1	8	3	0	0	13	.196	.237	.304	.541	-65	0	0	0	1b37,D2	0	-0.8
Total	9	848	2958	379	795	176	13	106	458	227	29	7	655	.269	.320	.445	.765	-3	32	16	67	1b817,D4	172	-5.3
BROHAMER, JACK John Anthony B2.26.1950 Maywood CA BL/TR (BB 1972p)/5'10"/(165–170) [CleA67 34/638] d4.18																								
1978	Bos A	81	244	34	57	14	1	1	25	25	1	0	13	.234	.300	.311	.611	-33	1	3	25	3b30,D25,2b23	0	-1.8
1979	Bos A	64	192	25	51	7	1	1	11	15	1	0	15	.266	.316	.328	.644	-29	0	3	0	2b36,3b22	17	-0.8
1980	Bos A	21	57	5	18	2	0	1	6	4	0	0	3	.316	.361	.404	.765	+3	0	0	0	3b13,2b4,D3	0	-0.1
Total	9	805	2500	262	613	91	12	30	227	222	22	8	178	.245	.306	.327	.633	-21	9	17	35	2b639,3b105,D30	78	-2.1
Team	3	166	493	64	126	23	2	3	42	44	2	0	31	.256	.313	.329	.642	-27	1	6	14	3b65,2b63,D28	17	-2.7
/150	3	150	445	58	114	21	2	3	38	40	2	0	28	.256	.313	.329	.642	-27	1	5	17	3b59,2b57,D25	15	-2.4
BROWN, ADRIAN Adrian Demond B2.7.1974 McComb MS BB/TR (BR 2002p)/6'0"/(175–200) [PitN92 48/1351] d5.16																								
2003	†Bos A	9	15	2	3	0	0	0	1	1	0	0	4	.200	.250	.200	.450	-80	2	0	100	O9(3/6/0)	0	-0.2
Total	9	447	1134	166	293	44	8	11	86	109	3	6	161	.258	.325	.340	.665	-28	45	15	75	O380(24/256/106)	230	-5.1
BROWN, KEVIN Kevin Lee B4.21.1973 Valparaiso IN BR/TR/6'2"/(200–224) [TexA94 2/56] d9.12 Col Southern Indiana																								
2002	Bos A	2	1	0	0	0	0	0	0	0	0	0	0	.000	.000	.000	.000	-198	0	0	0	C2	0	0.0
Total	7	85	189	30	48	12	2	7	31	14	0	4	59	.254	.311	.450	.761	-4	0	0	0	C83/D	17	0.2
BRUMLEY, MIKE Anthony Michael B4.9.1963 Oklahoma City OK BB/TR/5'10"/(165–175) [BosA83 2/33] d6.16 f–Mike Col Texas																								
1991	Bos A	63	118	16	25	5	0	0	5	10	0	0	22	.212	.273	.254	.527	-56	2	0	100	S31,3b17,2b7,O4C,D2	0	0.1
1992	Bos A	2	1	0	0	0	0	0	0	0	0	0	0	.000	.000	.000	.000	-193	0	0	0	/H	0	0.0
Total	8	295	635	78	131	17	8	3	38	46	1	2	136	.206	.261	.272	.533	-53	20	6	77	S159,2b42,3b37,O17(9/6/3),D11/1	35	-4.4
Team	2	65	119	16	25	5	0	0	5	10	0	0	22	.210	.271	.252	.523	-57	2	0	100	S31,3b17,2b7,O4C,D2	0	0.1
BRUNANSKY, TOM Thomas Andrew B8.20.1960 Covina CA BR/TR/6'4"/(205–220) [CalA78 1/14] d4.9																								
1990	†Bos A	129	461	61	123	24	5	15	71	54	7	3	105	.267	.342	.438	.780	+13	5	10	33	O121(0/1/121),D7	0	0.6
1991	Bos A	142	459	54	105	24	1	16	70	49	2	3	72	.229	.303	.390	.693	-13	1	2	33	O137(0/1/136)/D	0	-1.3
1992	Bos A	138	458	47	122	31	3	15	74	66	2	0	96	.266	.354	.445	.799	+15	2	5	29	O92R,1b28,D17	0	0.5
1994	Bos A	48	177	22	42	10	1	10	34	23	1	0	48	.237	.319	.475	.794	-2	0	2	0	O42(14/0/33),1b5,D3	0	-0.6
Total	14	1800	6289	804	1543	306	33	271	919	770	43	30	1187	.245	.327	.434	.761	+5	69	70	50	O1679(88/81/1569),D61,1b36	60	-1.0
Team	4	457	1555	184	392	89	10	56	249	192	12	6	321	.252	.332	.430	.762	+4	8	19	30	O392(0/35/290),1b33,D28	0	-0.8
/150	1	150	510	60	129	29	3	18	82	63	4	2	105	.252	.332	.430	.762	+4	3	6	33	O129(0/11/95),1b11,D9	0	-0.3
BUCHER, JIM James Quinter B3.24.1911 Manassas VA D10.21.2004 Elizabethtown PA BL/TR/5'11"/170 d4.18																								
1944	Bos A	80	277	39	76	9	2	4	31	19		2	13	.274	.326	.365	.691	-2	3	3	50	3b44,2b21	0	-0.4
1945	Bos A	52	151	19	34	4	3	0	11	7		1	13	.225	.264	.291	.555	-40	1	3	25	3b32,2b2	0	-0.9
Total	7	554	1792	242	474	66	19	17	193	91		6	113	.265	.302	.351	.653	-22	19	6	100	3b204,2b179,O73(32/1/40)	0	-7.6
Team	2	132	428	58	110	13	5	4	42	26		3	26	.257	.304	.339	.643	-15	4	6	40	3b76,2b23	0	-1.3
/150	2	150	486	66	125	15	6	5	48	30		3	30	.257	.304	.339	.643	-15	5	7	42	3b86,2b26	0	-1.5
BUCKNER, BILL William Joseph B12.14.1949 Vallejo CA BL/TL/6'0"/(182–195) [LAN68 2/25] d9.21 C2																								
1984	Bos A	114	439	51	122	21	2	11	67	24	5	5	38	.278	.321	.410	.731	-4	2	2	50	1b113	0	-0.4
1985	Bos A	162	673	89	201	46	3	16	110	30	5	2	36	.299	.325	.447	.772	+6	18	4	82	1b162	0	2.2
1986	†Bos A	153	629	73	168	39	2	18	102	40	9	4	25	.267	.311	.421	.732	-2	6	4	60	1b138,D15	0	0.7
1987	Bos A	75	286	23	78	6	1	2	42	13	1	0	19	.273	.299	.322	.621	-36	1	3	25	1b74	16	-1.7
1990	Bos A	22	43	4	8	0	0	1	3	3	2	0	2	.186	.234	.256	.490	-63	0	0	0	1b15	0	-0.5
Total	22	2517	9397	1077	2715	498	49	174	1208	450	11	42	453	.289	.321	.408	.729	-1	183	73	71	1b1555,O644(493/0/168),D126	65	-4.7
Team	5	526	2070	240	577	112	8	48	324	110	22	11	120	.279	.314	.410	.724	-6	27	13	68	1b502,D15	16	0.3
/150	1	150	590	68	165	32	2	14	92	31	6	3	34	.279	.314	.410	.724	-6	8	4	67	1b143,D4	5	0.1
BUDDIN, DON Donald Thomas B5.5.1934 Turbeville SC BR/TR/5'11"/178 d4.17																								
1956	Bos A	114	377	49	90	24	0	5	37	65	1	4	62	.239	.352	.342	.694	-24	2	0	100	S113	0	0.6
1958	Bos A	136	497	74	118	25	2	12	43	82	1	4	106	.237	.349	.368	.717	-8	0	4	0	S136	0	2.6
1959	Bos A	151	485	75	117	24	1	10	53	92	0	5	99	.241	.366	.357	.723	-5	6	1	86	S150	0	0.7
1960	Bos A	124	428	62	105	21	5	6	36	62	5	1	59	.245	.338	.360	.698	-13	4	2	67	S124	0	0.2
1961	Bos A	115	339	58	89	22	3	6	42	72	7	2	45	.263	.394	.398	.792	+10	2	1	67	S109	0	1.6
1962	Hou N	40	80	10	13	4	1	2	10	17	2	1	17	.162	.316	.313	.629	-25	0	0	0	S27,3b9	0	-0.1
1962	Det A	31	83	14	19	3	0	0	4	20	0	1	16	.229	.385	.265	.650	-24	1	0	100	S19,2b5,3b2	0	-0.2
1962	Major	71	163	24	32	7	1	2	14	37	2	2	33	.196	.351	.288	.640	+1	1	0	100		0	-0.3
Total	6	711	2289	342	551	123	12	41	225	410	16	18	404	.241	.358	.359	.717	-10	15	8	65	S678,3b11,2b5	0	5.4
Team	5	640	2126	318	519	116	11	39	211	373	14	16	371	.244	.358	.364	.722	-8	14	8	64	S632	0	5.7
/150	1	150	498	75	122	27	3	9	49	87	3	4	87	.244	.358	.364	.722	-8	3	2	60	S148	0	1.3
BUFORD, DAMON Damon Jackson B6.12.1970 Baltimore MD BR/TR/5'10"/(170–180) [BalA90 10/283] d5.4 f–Don Col USC																								
1998	†Bos A	86	216	37	61	14	4	10	42	22	1	1	43	.282	.349	.523	.872	+21	5	5	50	O67C,D15/23	31	0.4
1999	†Bos A	91	297	39	72	15	2	6	38	21	0	2	74	.242	.294	.367	.661	-34	9	2	82	O84(5/82/0),D5	17	-1.2
Total	9	699	1853	280	448	86	9	54	218	173	4	20	430	.242	.311	.385	.696	-23	56	35	62	O624(52/519/62),D41/32	48	-6.6
Team	2	177	513	76	133	29	6	16	80	43	1	3	117	.259	.317	.433	.750	-10	14	7	67	O151(5/149/82),D20/23	48	-0.8
/150	2	150	435	64	113	25	5	14	68	36	1	3	99	.259	.317	.433	.750	-10	12	6	67	O128(4/126/69),D17/23	41	-0.7
BURDA, BOB Edward Robert B7.16.1938 St.Louis MO BL/TL/5'11"/(175–180) d8.25 Col Illinois																								
1972	Bos A	45	73	4	12	1	0	2	9	8	3	0	11	.164	.241	.260	.501	-52	0	0	0	1b15/lf	0	-0.7
Total	7	388	634	53	142	21	0	13	78	70	11	5	65	.224	.302	.319	.621	-26	2	1	67	1b106,O97(12/0/86)	0	-3.8
BURKETT, JESSE Jesse Cail "Crab" B12.4.1868 Wheeling WV D5.27.1953 Worcester MA BL/TL/5'8"/155 d4.22 C1 HF1946▲																								
1905	Bos A	148	573	78	147	12	13	4	47	67		4		.257	.339	.344	.683	+15	13			O148L		0.1
Total	16	2067	8426	1720	2850	320	182	75	952	1029		75	231	.338	.415	.446	.861	+40	389			O2054(1936/7/115),P23/3S2		27.9
/150	1	150	581	79	149	12	13	4	48	68		4	0	.257	.339	.344	.683	+15	13			O150L		0.1
BURKHART, MORGAN Morgan B1.29.1972 St.Louis MO BB/TL/5'11"/(220–225) d6.27 Col Central Missouri																								
2000	Bos A	25	73	16	21	3	0	4	18	17	1	4	25	.288	.442	.493	.935	+34	0	0	0	D19,1b5/lf	0	0.3
2001	Bos A	11	33	3	6	1	0	1	4	1	0	0	11	.182	.206	.303	.509	-68	0	0	0	1b5,D6	0	-0.4
2003	KC A	6	15	1	3	0	0	0	1	1	0	0	2	.200	.250	.200	.450	-80	0	0	0	1b2,D2	0	-0.2
Total	3	42	121	20	30	4	0	5	23	19	1	4	38	.248	.366	.405	.771	-4	0	0	0	D27,1b12/lf	0	-0.3
Team	2	36	106	19	27	4	0	5	22	18	1	4	36	.255	.380	.434	.814	+7	0	0	0	D25,1b10/lf	0	-0.1

Year	Tm Lg	G	AB	R	H	2B	3B	HR	RBI	BB	IB	HP	SO	AVG	OBP	SLG	OPS	AOPS	SB	CS	SB%	Games at Position	DL	BFW
BURKS, ELLIS Ellis Rena B9.11.1964 Vicksburg MS BR/TR/6'2"/(175–209) [BosA83*1/20] d4.30 Col Ranger (TX) JC																								
1987	Bos A	133	558	94	152	30	2	20	59	41	0	2	98	.272	.324	.441	.765	-3	27	6	82	O132C/D	0	0.7
1988	†Bos A	144	540	93	159	37	5	18	92	62	1	3	89	.294	.367	.481	.848	+31	25	9	74	O142C,D2	8	2.7
1989	Bos A	97	399	73	121	19	6	12	61	36	2	5	52	.303	.365	.471	.836	+27	21	5	81	O95C/D	47	1.6
1990	†Bos A✱	152	588	89	174	33	8	21	89	48	4	1	82	.296	.349	.486	.835	+25	9	11	45	O143C,D6	0	0.6
1991	Bos A	130	474	56	119	33	3	14	56	39	2	6	81	.251	.314	.422	.736	-3	6	11	35	O126C,D2	0	-1.5
1992	Bos A	66	235	35	60	8	3	8	30	25	2	1	48	.255	.327	.417	.744	+0	5	2	71	O63C/D	102	-1.1
1993	†Chi A	146	499	75	137	24	4	17	74	60	2	4	97	.275	.352	.441	.793	+15	6	9	40	O146(0/21/132)	0	0.3
1994	Col N	42	149	33	48	8	3	13	24	16	3	0	39	.322	.388	.678	1.066	+46	3	1	75	O39C	74	0.7
1995	†Col N	103	278	41	74	10	6	14	49	39	0	2	72	.266	.359	.496	.855	-4	7	3	70	O80(23/65/1)	10	0.0
1996	Col N★	156	613	**142**	211	45	8	40	128	61	2	6	114	.344	.408	**.639**	1.047	+39	32	6	84	O152(129/32/0)	0	3.3
1997	Col N	119	424	91	123	19	2	32	82	47	0	3	75	.290	.363	.571	.934	+14	7	2	78	O112(66/89/0)	31	0.3
1998	Col N	100	357	54	102	22	5	16	54	39	0	2	80	.286	.355	.510	.865	+3	3	7	30	O98(45/78/0)	0	-0.5
1998	SF N	42	147	22	45	6	1	5	22	19	1	3	31	.306	.387	.463	.850	+32	8	1	89	O41(0/36/10)	0	0.6
1998	Year	142	504	76	147	28	6	21	76	58	1	5	111	.292	.365	.496	.861	+10	11	8	58	O139(45/114/10)	0	0.1
1999	SF N	120	390	73	110	19	0	31	96	69	2	6	86	.282	.394	.569	.963	+51	7	5	58	O107R,D3	17	2.5
2000	†SF N	122	393	74	135	21	5	24	96	56	5	1	49	.344	.419	.606	1.025	+68	5	1	83	O108R,D2	14	3.7
2001	†Cle A	124	439	83	123	29	1	28	74	62	2	5	85	.280	.369	.542	.911	+33	5	1	83	D102,O20(18/0/2)	16	1.5
2002	Cle A	138	518	92	156	28	0	32	91	44	3	6	108	.301	.362	.541	.903	+33	2	3	40	D127,O6L	0	1.5
2003	Cle A	55	198	27	52	11	1	6	28	27	2	3	46	.263	.360	.419	.779	+5	1	1	50	D51,O2L	113	0.0
2004	Bos A	11	33	6	6	0	0	1	1	3	0	1	8	.182	.270	.273	.543	-60	2	0	100	D9	150	-0.3
Total	18	2000	7232	1253	2107	402	63	352	1206	793	33	60	1340	.291	.363	.510	.873	+23	181	84	68	O1612(289/1062/360),D307	582	16.6
Team	7	733	2827	446	791	160	27	94	388	254	11	19	458	.280	.341	.455	.796	+13	95	44	68	O701C,D22	307	2.7
/150	1	150	579	91	162	33	6	19	79	52	2	4	94	.280	.341	.455	.796	+13	19	9	68	O143C,D5	63	0.6
BURLESON, RICK Richard Paul "Rooster" B4.29.1951 Lynwood CA BR/TR/5'10"/160 [BosA70*S1/5] d5.4 C5 [DL 1985 Cal A 182]																								
1974	Bos A	114	384	36	109	22	0	4	44	21	0	2	34	.284	.320	.372	.692	-7	3	3	50	S88,2b31,3b2	0	0.6
1975	†Bos A	158	580	66	146	25	1	6	62	45	1	3	44	.252	.305	.329	.634	-26	8	5	62	S158	0	0.1
1976	Bos A	152	540	75	157	27	1	7	42	60	2	5	37	.291	.365	.383	.748	+7	14	9	61	S152	0	2.9
1977	Bos A★	154	663	80	194	36	7	3	52	47	1	2	69	.293	.338	.382	.720	-13	13	12	52	S154	0	2.4
1978	Bos A✱	145	626	75	155	32	5	5	49	40	2	4	71	.248	.295	.339	.634	-29	8	8	50	S144	14	1.0
1979	Bos A★	153	627	93	174	32	5	5	60	35	0	3	54	.278	.315	.368	.683	-20	9	5	64	S153	0	2.8
1980	Bos A	155	644	89	179	29	2	8	51	62	0	2	51	.278	.341	.366	.707	-10	12	13	48	S155	0	3.7
1981	Cal A★	109	430	53	126	17	1	5	33	42	2	3	38	.293	.357	.372	.729	+10	4	6	40	S109	0	4.5
1982	Cal A	11	45	4	7	1	0	0	2	6	2	0	3	.156	.255	.178	.433	-79	0	0	0	S11	169	0.1
1983	Cal A	33	119	22	34	7	0	0	11	12	0	0	12	.286	.348	.345	.693	-7	0	2	0	S31	102	0.3
1984	Cal A	7	4	2	0	0	0	0	0	0	0	0	2	.000	.000	.000	.000	-199	0	0	0	/H	152	-0.1
1986	†Cal A	93	271	35	77	14	0	5	29	33	1	1	32	.284	.363	.391	.754	+7	1	3	25	D38,S37,2b6,3b4	0	0.0
1987	Bal A	62	206	26	43	14	1	2	14	17	0	3	30	.209	.279	.316	.595	-41	0	2	0	2b55,D7	0	-1.5
Total	13	1346	5139	656	1401	256	23	50	449	420	11	28	477	.273	.328	.361	.689	-13	72	68	51	S1192,2b92,D45,3b6	619	16.8
Team	7	1031	4064	514	1114	203	21	38	360	310	6	21	360	.274	.326	.362	.688	-15	67	55	55	S1004,2b31,3b2	14	13.5
/150	1	150	591	75	162	30	3	6	52	45	1	3	52	.274	.326	.362	.688	-15	10	8	56	S146,2b5/3	2	2.0
BURNS, GEORGE George Henry "Tioga George" B1.31.1893 Niles OH D1.7.1978 Kirkland WA BR/TR/6'1.5"/180 d4.14																								
1922	Bos A	147	558	71	171	32	5	12	73	20		9	28	.306	.341	.446	.787	+4	8	2	80	1b140		-0.7
1923	Bos A	146	551	91	181	47	5	7	82	45		7	33	.328	.386	.470	.856	+24	9	7	56	1b146		0.8
Total	16	1866	6573	901	2018	444	72	72	951	363		110	433	.307	.354	.429	.783	+12	154	63	100	1b1671,O50(1/0/49)		2.2
Team	2	293	1109	162	352	79	10	19	155	65		16	61	.317	.364	.458	.822	+14	17	9	65	1b286		0.1
/150	1	150	568	83	180	40	5	10	79	33		8	31	.317	.364	.458	.822	+14	9	5	64	1b146		0.1
BUSBY, JIM James Franklin B1.8.1927 Kenedy TX D7.8.1996 Augusta GA BR/TR/6'1"/175 d4.23 C18 Col TCU																								
1959	Bos A	61	102	16	23	8	0	1	5	5	0	1	18	.225	.266	.333	.599	-39	0	1	0	O34(8/25/1)	0	-0.8
1960	Bos A	1	0	0	0	0	0	0	0	0	0	0	0	+	+	+	.000	-100	0	0	0	/lf	0	0.0
Total	13	1352	4250	541	1113	162	35	48	438	310	4	23	439	.262	.314	.350	.664	-18	97	48	67	O1280(12/1267/3)/C3	0	-11.7
Team	2	62	102	16	23	8	0	1	5	5	0	1	18	.225	.266	.333	.599	-39	0	1	0	O35(8/25/1)	0	-0.8
BYRD, JIM James Edward B10.3.1968 Wewahitchka FL BR/TR/6'1"/185 [BosA87 8/214] d5.31 Col Seminole St. (OK) JC																								
1993	Bos A	2	0	0	0	0	0	0	0	0	0	0	0	+	+	+	.000	-100	0	0	0	/R	0	0.0
CABRERA, ORLANDO Orlando Luis B11.2.1974 Cartagena, Colombia BR/TR/5'10"/(150–190) d9.3 b–Jolbert																								
2004	†Bos A	58	228	33	67	19	1	6	31	11	0	1	23	.294	.320	.465	.785	-2	4	1	80	S57	0	-0.2
Total	10	1256	4663	605	1254	306	27	89	541	333	24	20	429	.269	.317	.403	.720	-14	145	35	81	S1211,2b33	105	6.4
CADY, HICK Forrest Leroy (b Forrest Leroy Bergland) B1.26.1886 Bishop Hill IL D3.3.1946 Cedar Rapids IA BR/TR/6'2"/179 d4.26																								
1912	†Bos A	47	135	19	35	13	2	0	9	10		3		.259	.324	.385	.709	-2	0			C43,1b4		1.2
1913	Bos A	40	96	10	24	5	2	0	6	5		1	14	.250	.294	.344	.638	-16	1			C39		0.4
1914	Bos A	61	159	14	41	6	1	0	8	12		0	22	.258	.310	.308	.618	-14	2	1	67	C58		0.4
1915	†Bos A	78	205	25	57	10	2	0	17	19		1	25	.278	.342	.346	.688	+9	0	2	0	C77		1.2
1916	†Bos A	78	162	5	31	6	3	0	13	15		1	16	.191	.264	.265	.529	-41	0			C63,1b3		-1.1
1917	Bos A	17	46	4	7	1	1	0	2	1		0	6	.152	.170	.217	.387	-82	0			C14		-0.4
1919	Phi N	34	98	6	21	6	0	1	19	4		1	8	.214	.252	.306	.558	-37	1			C29		-0.9
Total	7	355	901	83	216	47	11	1	74	66		7	91	.240	.297	.320	.617	-18	4	3	100	C323,1b7		0.8
Team	6	321	803	77	195	41	11	0	55	62		6	83	.243	.302	.321	.623	-15	3	3	100	C294,1b7		1.7
/150	3	150	375	36	91	19	5	0	26	29		3	39	.243	.302	.321	.623	-15	1	1	100	C137,1b3		0.8
CALDERON, IVAN Ivan (Perez) B3.19.1962 Fajardo, PR D12.27.2003 Loiza, PR BR/TR/6'1"/(160–221) d8.10																								
1993	Bos A	73	213	25	47	8	2	1	19	21	1	1	28	.221	.291	.291	.582	-46	4	2	67	O47(9/2/39),D19	19	-1.5
Total	10	924	3312	470	901	200	25	104	444	306	30	13	556	.272	.333	.442	.775	+13	97	49	66	O755(378/11/383),D103,1b34	249	2.2
CALDWELL, RAY Raymond Benjamin "Rube","Sum" B4.26.1888 Corydon PA D8.17.1967 Salamanca NY BL/TR/6'2"/190 d9.9▲																								
1919	Bos A	33	48	5	13	1	1	0	4	0		0	9	.271	.271	.333	.604	-27	0			P18,O2L		-0.1
Total	12	590	1164	138	289	46	8	8	114	78		3	158	.248	.297	.322	.619	-22	23	6	100	P343,O46(11/18/15),1b6		-1.2
CAMILLI, DOLPH Adolph Louis B4.23.1907 San Francisco CA D10.21.1997 San Mateo CA BL/TL/5'10"/185 d9.9 s–Doug																								
1945	Bos A	63	198	24	42	5	2	2	19	35		0	38	.212	.330	.288	.618	-22	2	0	100	1b54	0	-0.5
Total	12	1490	5353	936	1482	261	86	239	950	947		28	961	.277	.388	.492	.880	+34	60	0	100	1b1476	0	13.4
CAMPBELL, PAUL Paul McLaughlin B9.1.1917 Paw Creek NC D6.22.2006 Charlotte NC BL/TL/5'10"/185 d4.15 Mil 1943–45																								
1941	Bos A	1	0	0	0	0	0	0	0	0		0	0	+	+	+	.000	-100	0	0	0	/R	0	0.0
1942	Bos A	26	15	4	1	0	0	0	0	1		0	5	.067	.125	.067	.192	-144	1	0	100	O4C	0	-0.3
1946	†Bos A	28	26	3	3	1	0	0	0	2		0	7	.115	.179	.154	.333	-106	0	0	0	1b5	0	-0.4
Total	6	204	380	61	97	17	5	4	41	28		1	54	.255	.308	.358	.666	-24	4	3	57	1b106,O4C	0	-1.8
Team	3	55	41	7	4	1	0	0	0	3		0	12	.098	.159	.122	.281	-120	1	0	100	1b5,O4C	0	-0.7
CANSECO, JOSE Jose (Capas) B7.2.1964 Havana, Cuba BR/TR/6'4"/(195–240) [OakA82 15/392] d9.2 twb–Ozzie																								
1995	†Bos A	102	396	64	121	25	1	24	81	42	4	7	93	.306	.378	.556	.934	+36	4	0	100	D101/rf	36	1.5
1996	Bos A	96	360	68	104	22	1	28	82	63	3	6	82	.289	.400	.589	.989	+44	3	1	75	D84,O11(10/0/2)	68	1.9
Total	17	1887	7057	1186	1877	340	14	462	1407	906	63	84	1942	.266	.353	.515	.868	+32	200	88	69	O1011(356/1/679),D834/P	483	23.3
Team	2	198	756	132	225	47	2	52	163	105	7	13	175	.298	.389	.571	.960	+40	7	1	88	D185,O12(0/2/3)	104	3.4
/150	2	150	573	100	170	36	2	39	123	80	5	10	133	.298	.389	.571	.960	+40	5	1	83	D140,O9(0/2/2)	79	2.6
CARBO, BERNIE Bernardo B8.5.1947 Detroit MI BL/TR/6'0"/(175–185) [CinN65 1/16] d9.2																								
1969	Cin N	4	3	0	0	0	0	0	0	0	0	0	2	.000	.000	.000	.000	-195	0	0	0	/H	0	-0.1
1970	†Cin N	125	365	54	113	19	3	21	63	94	9	4	77	.310	.454	.551	1.005	+67	10	4	71	O119(118/0/1)	0	3.4
1971	Cin N	106	310	33	68	20	1	5	20	54	4	2	56	.219	.338	.339	.677	-7	2	1	67	O90L	0	-0.5
1972	Cin N	19	21	2	3	0	0	0	0	6	1	1	3	.143	.357	.143	.500	-51	0	0	0	O4R	0	-0.1

Year	Tm Lg	G	AB	R	H	2B	3B	HR	RBI	BB	IB	HP	SO	AVG	OBP	SLG	OPS	AOPS	SB	CS	SB%	Games at Position	DL	BFW
1972	StL N	99	302	42	78	13	1	7	34	57	9	5	56	.258	.381	.377	.758	+18	0	1	0	O92R/3	0	1.3
1972	Year	118	323	44	81	13	1	7	34	63	10	6	59	.251	.380	.362	.742	+14	0	1	0	O96R/3	0	1.2
1973	StL N	111	308	42	88	18	0	8	40	58	7	1	52	.286	.397	.422	.819	+27	2	0	100	O94(2/0/93)	0	1.4
1974	Bos A	117	338	40	84	20	0	12	61	58	7	4	90	.249	.364	.414	.778	+16	4	3	57	O87(33/0/56),D15	0	0.5
1975	†Bos A	107	319	64	82	21	3	15	50	83	5	1	69	.257	.409	.483	.892	+40	2	4	33	O85(38/0/47),D13	0	1.7
1976	Bos A	17	55	5	13	4	0	2	6	8	1	0	17	.236	.333	.418	.751	+7	1	0	100	D15/lf	0	0.0
1976	Mil A	69	183	20	43	7	0	3	15	33	3	0	55	.235	.352	.322	.674	+0	1	2	33	O33(4/0/29),D24	0	0.5
1976	Year	86	238	25	56	11	0	5	21	41	4	0	72	.235	.348	.345	.693	+2	2	2	50	D39,O34(5/0/29)	0	0.5
1977	Bos A	86	228	36	66	6	1	15	34	47	3	0	72	.289	.409	.522	.931	+37	1	2	33	O67(8/0/59),D7	0	1.2
1978	Bos A	17	46	7	12	3	0	1	6	8	0	0	8	.261	.370	.391	.761	+4	1	1	50	O9(1/0/8),D8	0	0.1
1978	Cle A	60	174	21	50	8	0	4	16	20	1	1	31	.287	.362	.402	.764	+16	1	0	100	D49,O4R	0	0.2
1978	Year	77	220	28	62	11	0	5	22	28	1	1	39	.282	.364	.400	.764	+13	2	1	67	D57,O13(1/0/12)	0	0.3
1979	StL N	52	64	6	18	1	0	3	12	10	0	0	22	.281	.368	.438	.806	+20	1	0	100	O17(4/0/13)	0	0.0
1980	StL N	14	11	0	2	0	0	0	0	1	0	0	0	.182	.250	.182	.432	-79	0	0	0	/H	0	-0.2
1980	Pit N	7	6	0	2	0	0	0	1	1	0	0	1	.333	.429	.333	.762	+11	0	0	0	/H	0	0.0
1980	Year	21	17	0	4	0	0	0	1	2	0	0	1	.235	.316	.235	.551	-46	0	0	0	0		-0.2
Total	12	1010	2733	372	722	140	9	96	358	538	50	19	611	.264	.387	.427	.814	+25	26	18	59	O702(299/0/406),D131/3	0	9.4
Team	5	344	986	152	257	54	4	45	157	204	16	5	256	.261	.388	.460	.848	+28	9	10	47	O249(80/0/103),D58	0	3.5
/150	2	150	430	66	112	24	2	20	68	89	7	2	112	.261	.388	.460	.848	+28	4	4	50	O109(35/0/45),D25	0	1.5
CAREY, TOM Thomas Francis Aloysius "Scoops" B10.11.1906 Hoboken NJ D2.21.1970 Rochester NY BR/TR/5'8.5"/170 d7.19 Mil 1943–45 C2																								
1939	Bos A	54	161	17	39	6	2	0	20	3		2	9	.242	.265	.304	.569	-56	0	0	0	2b35,S10		-0.6
1940	Bos A	43	62	4	20	4	0	0	7	2		0	1	.323	.344	.387	.731	-14	0	0	0	S20,2b4,3b4		0.3
1941	Bos A	25	21	7	4	0	0	0	2	0		0	2	.190	.190	.190	.380	-99	0	0	0	2b9,S8/3	0	-0.1
1942	Bos A	1	1	0	1	0	0	0	1	0		0	0	1.000	1.000	1.000	2.000	+348	0	0	0	/2	0	0.0
1946	Bos A	3	5	0	1	0	0	0	0	0		0	1	.200	.200	.200	.400	-89	0	0	0	2b3	0	0.0
Total	8	466	1521	169	418	79	13	2	169	66		6	75	.275	.308	.348	.656	-37	3	5	38	2b343,S83,3b6	0	-5.6
Team	5	126	250	28	65	10	2	0	30	5		2	13	.260	.280	.316	.596	-48	0	0	0	2b52,S38,3b5	0	-0.4
/150	6	150	298	33	77	12	2	0	36	6		2	15	.260	.280	.316	.596	-48	0	0	0	2b62,S45,3b6	0	-0.5
CARLISLE, WALTER Walter "Rosy" B7.6.1881 Yorkshire, England D5.27.1945 Los Angeles CA BB/TR/5'9"/154 d5.8																								
1908	Bos A	3	10	0	1	0	0	0	0	1		0		.100	.182	.100	.282	-108	1			O3L		-0.1
CARLSTROM, SWEDE Albin Oscar B10.26.1886 Elizabeth NJ D4.28.1935 Elizabeth NJ BR/TR/6'0"/167 d9.12																								
1911	Bos A	2	6	0	1	0	0	0	0	0		0		.167	.167	.167	.334	-107	0			S2		0.0
CARLYLE, CLEO Hiram Cleo B9.7.1902 Fairburn GA D11.12.1967 Los Angeles CA BL/TR/6'0"/170 d5.16 b–Roy																								
1927	Bos A	95	278	31	65	12	8	1	28	36		1	40	.234	.324	.345	.669	-25	4	4	50	O83(30/3/50)		-1.8
CARLYLE, ROY Roy Edward "Dizzy" B12.10.1900 Buford GA D11.22.1956 Norcross GA BL/TR/6'2.5"/195 d4.16 b–Cleo Col Oglethorpe																								
1925	Was A	1	1	0	0	0	0	0	0	0		0	1	.000	.000	.000	.000	-199	0	0	0	/H		0.0
1925	Bos A	93	276	36	90	20	3	7	49	16		1	28	.326	.365	.496	.861	+17	1	1	50	O67(43/0/24)		-0.4
1925	Year	94	277	36	90	20	3	7	49	16		1	29	.325	.364	.495	.859	+16	1	1	50	O67(43/0/24)		-0.4
1926	Bos A	45	165	22	47	6	2	2	16	4		2	18	.285	.310	.382	.692	-18	0	0	0	O38R		-1.3
1926	NY A	35	62	3	20	5	1	0	11	4		1	9	.323	.373	.435	.808	+12	0	0	0	O15R		0.0
1926	Year	80	227	25	67	11	3	2	27	8		3	27	.295	.328	.396	.724	-9	0	0	0	O53R		-1.3
Total	2	174	504	61	157	31	6	9	76	24		4	56	.312	.348	.450	.798	+5	1	1	50	O120(43/0/77)		-1.7
Team	2	138	441	58	137	26	5	9	65	20		3	46	.311	.345	.454	.799	+4	1	1	50	O105(43/0/24)		-1.7
/150	2	150	479	63	149	28	5	10	71	22		3	50	.311	.345	.454	.799	+4	1	1	50	O114(47/0/26)		-1.8
CARRIGAN, BILL William Francis "Rough" B10.22.1883 Lewiston ME D7.8.1969 Lewiston ME BR/TR/5'9"/175 d7.7 M7 Col Holy Cross																								
1906	Bos A	37	109	5	23	0	0	0	10	5		1		.211	.252	.211	.463	-55	3			C35		-0.8
1908	Bos A	57	149	13	35	5	2	0	14	3		1		.235	.255	.295	.550	-23	1			C47,1b3		0.5
1909	Bos A	94	280	25	83	13	2	1	36	17		2		.296	.341	.368	.709	+21	2			C77,1b8		1.9
1910	Bos A	114	342	36	85	11	1	3	53	23		6		.249	.307	.313	.620	-8	10			C110		-1.0
1911	Bos A	72	232	29	67	6	1	1	30	26		5		.289	.373	.336	.709	-1	5			C62,1b6		0.6
1912	†Bos A	87	266	34	70	7	1	0	24	38		2		.263	.359	.297	.656	-16	7			C87		-0.1
1913	Bos A	87	256	17	62	15	5	0	28	27		2	26	.242	.319	.340	.659	-9	6			C82,M		-0.3
1914	Bos A	82	178	18	45	5	1	1	22	40		2	18	.253	.395	.309	.704	+12	1	2	33	C78,M		2.1
1915	†Bos A	46	95	10	19	3	0	0	7	16		1	12	.200	.321	.232	.553	-32	0			C44,M		0.8
1916	†Bos A	33	63	7	17	2	1	0	11	11		0	3	.270	.378	.333	.711	+13	2			C27,M		0.9
Total	10	709	1970	194	506	67	14	6	235	206		22	59	.257	.334	.314	.648	-6	37	2	100	C649,1b17		4.6
/150	2	150	417	41	107	14	3	1	50	44		5	0	.257	.334	.314	.648	-6	8	0	100	C137,1b4	0	1.0
CATER, DANNY Danny Anderson B2.25.1940 Austin TX BR/TR/5'11.5"/(170–198) d4.14 OF(293/2/16)																								
1972	Bos A	92	317	32	75	17	1	8	39	15	2	2	33	.237	.270	.372	.642	-14	0	1	0	1b90	0	-0.9
1973	Bos A	63	195	30	61	12	0	1	24	10	1	1	22	.313	.348	.390	.738	+2	0	0	0	1b37,3b21,D3	0	-0.1
1974	Bos A	56	126	14	31	5	0	5	20	10	1	2	13	.246	.309	.405	.714	-2	1	0	100	1b23,D14	0	-0.2
Total	12	1289	4451	491	1229	191	29	66	519	254	33	22	406	.276	.316	.377	.693	+1	26	30	46	1b731,O308L,3b225,D17,2b5	40	-9.2
Team	3	211	638	76	167	34	1	14	83	35	4	5	68	.262	.301	.384	.685	-7	1	1	50	1b150,3b21,D17	0	-1.2
/150	2	150	454	54	119	24	1	10	59	25	3	4	48	.262	.301	.384	.685	-7	1	1	50	1b107,3b15,D12	0	-0.9
CEPEDA, ORLANDO Orlando Manuel (Penne) "Baby Bull","Cha Cha" B9.17.1937 Ponce, PR BR/TR/6'2"/(200–210) d4.15 C1 HF1999																								
1973	Bos A	142	550	51	159	25	0	20	86	50	13	3	81	.289	.350	.444	.794	+16	0	2	0	D142	0	0.7
Total	17	2124	7927	1131	2351	417	27	379	1365	588	15	102	1169	.297	.350	.499	.849	+33	142	80	64	1b1683,O231(214/0/18),D168,3b4	224	18.4
/150	1	150	581	54	168	26	0	21	91	53	14	3	86	.289	.350	.444	.794	+16	0	2	0	D150	0	0.7
CERONE, RICK Richard Aldo B5.19.1954 Newark NJ BR/TR/5'11"/(184–195) [CleA75 1/7] d8.17 Col Seton Hall																								
1988	Bos A	84	264	31	71	13	1	3	27	20	0	3	32	.269	.326	.360	.686	-12	0	0	0	C83/D	0	-0.2
1989	Bos A	102	296	28	72	16	1	4	48	34	1	2	40	.243	.320	.345	.665	-16	0	0	0	C97/rfD	0	-0.3
Total	18	1329	4069	393	998	190	15	59	436	320	9	24	450	.245	.301	.343	.644	-22	6	22	21	C1279,D11,1b2,P2/2rf3	237	-7.1
Team	2	186	560	59	143	29	2	7	75	54	1	5	72	.255	.323	.352	.675	-14	0	0	0	C180,D2/rf	0	-0.5
/150	2	150	452	48	115	23	2	6	60	44	1	4	58	.255	.323	.352	.675	-14	0	0	0	C145,D2/rf	0	-0.4
CHADBOURNE, CHET Chester James "Pop" B10.28.1884 Parkman ME D6.21.1943 Los Angeles CA BL/TR/5'9"/170 d9.17																								
1906	Bos A	11	43	7	13	1	0	0	3	3		0		.302	.348	.326	.674	+11	1			2b11/S		0.3
1907	Bos A	10	38	0	11	0	0	0	1	7		0		.289	.400	.289	.689	+21	1			O10L		0.1
Total	5	347	1353	183	345	41	18	2	82	146		12	83	.255	.333	.316	.649	-14	78			O335(161/174/0),2b11/S		-6.2
Team	2	21	81	7	24	1	0	0	4	10		0	0	.296	.374	.309	.683	+16	2			2b11,O10L/S		0.4
CHAMBERLAIN, WES Wesley Polk B4.13.1966 Chicago IL BR/TR/6'2"/(210–230) [PitN87 4/86] d8.31 Col Jackson St.																								
1994	Bos A	51	164	13	42	9	1	4	20	12	2	0	38	.256	.307	.396	.703	-24	0	2	0	O34R,D12	0	-0.6
1995	Bos A	19	42	4	5	1	0	1	1	3	0	0	11	.119	.178	.214	.392	-99	1	0	100	O12R,D5	0	-0.6
Total	6	385	1263	144	322	72	6	43	167	77	7	4	249	.255	.299	.424	.723	-5	20	7	74	O321(133/0/193),D17	81	-1.5
Team	2	70	206	17	47	10	1	5	21	15	2	0	49	.228	.281	.359	.640	-39	1	2	33	O46R,D17	0	-1.2
CHAPLIN, ED Bert Edgar (b Bert Edgar Chapman) B9.25.1893 Pelzer SC D8.15.1978 Sanford FL BL/TR/5'7"/158 d9.4 Col South Carolina																								
1920	Bos A	4	5	2	1	1	0	0	1	4		0	1	.200	.556	.400	.956	+63	0	0	0	C2		0.1
1921	Bos A	3	2	0	0	0	0	0	0	0		0	1	.000	.000	.000	.000	-199	0	0	0	/C		-0.1
1922	Bos A	28	69	8	13	1	1	0	6	9		0	9	.188	.282	.232	.514	-65	2	1	67	C21		-0.7
Total	3	35	76	10	14	2	1	0	7	13		0	11	.184	.303	.237	.540	-57	2	1	67	C24		-0.7
CHAPMAN, BEN William Benjamin B12.25.1908 Nashville TN D7.7.1993 Hoover AL BR/TR/6'0"/190 d4.15 M4/C1 OF(404/583/541)▲																								
1937	Bos A	113	423	76	130	23	11	7	57	57		1	35	.307	.391	.463	.854	+10	27	12	69	O112(2/10/100)/S		0.6
1938	Bos A	127	480	92	163	40	8	6	80	65		0	33	.340	.418	.494	.912	+22	13	6	68	O126(1/0/125)/3		1.6
Total	15	1717	6478	1144	1958	407	107	90	977	824		26	556	.302	.383	.440	.823	+15	287	13	100	O1495C,3b96,2b56,P25/S	0	14.5
Team	2	240	903	168	293	63	19	13	137	122		1	68	.324	.405	.480	.885	+16	40	18	69	O238(3/10/225)/3S		2.2
/150	1	150	564	105	183	39	12	8	86	76		1	43	.324	.405	.480	.885	+16	25	11	69	O149(2/6/141)/3S		1.4

Year	Tm Lg	G	AB	R	H	2B	3B	HR	RBI	BB	IB	HP	SO	AVG	OBP	SLG	OPS	AOPS	SB	CS	SB%	Games at Position	DL	BFW
CHRISTOPHER, JOE Joseph O'Neal B12.13.1935 Frederiksted, V.I. BR/TR/5'10"/(175–182) d5.26																								
1966	Bos A	12	13	1	1	0	0	0	0	2	0	0	4	.077	.200	.077	.277	-115	0	0	0	O2L	0	-0.2
Total	8	638	1667	224	434	68	17	29	173	157	8	19	277	.260	.329	.374	.703	-4	29	19	60	O479(152/54/277)	0	-4.8
CHRISTOPHER, LOYD Loyd Eugene B12.31.1919 Richmond CA D9.5.1991 Richmond CA BR/TR/6'2"/190 d4.20 b–Russ																								
1945	Bos A	8	14	4	4	0	0	0	4	3		0	2	.286	.412	.286	.698	+1	0	0	0	O3C	0	0.0
1945	Chi N	1	0	0	0	0	0	0	0	0		0	0	+	+	+	.000	-100	0			/lf	0	0.0
1945	Major	9	14	4	4	0	0	0	4	3	0	0	2	.286	.412	.286	.697	-83	0	0			0	0.0
1947	Chi A	7	23	1	5	0	1	0	0	2		0	4	.217	.280	.304	.584	-35	0	1	0	O7L	0	-0.1
Total	2	16	37	5	9	0	1	0	4	5		0	6	.243	.333	.297	.630	-20	0	1	0	O11(8/3/0)	0	-0.1
CICERO, JOE Joseph Francis "Dode" B11.18.1910 Atlantic City NJ D3.30.1983 Clearwater FL BR/TR/5'8"/167 d9.20																								
1929	Bos A	10	32	6	10	2	2	0	4	0		0	2	.313	.313	.500	.813	+8	0	0	0	O7(1/6/0)		-0.1
1930	Bos A	18	30	5	5	1	2	0	4	1		0	5	.167	.194	.333	.527	-68	0	0	0	O5(1/0/4),3b2		-0.3
1945	Phi A	12	19	3	3	0	0	0	0	1		1	6	.158	.238	.158	.396	-84	0	0	0	O7(1/0/6)	0	-0.3
Total	3	40	81	14	18	3	4	0	8	2		1	13	.222	.250	.358	.608	-40	0	0	0	O19(3/6/10),3b2	0	-0.7
Team	2	28	62	11	15	3	4	0	8	1		0	7	.242	.254	.419	.673	-29	0	0	0	O12(2/6/4),3b2		-0.4
CISSELL, BILL Chalmer William B1.3.1904 Perryville MO D3.15.1949 Chicago IL BR/TR/5'11"/170 d4.11																								
1934	Bos A	102	416	71	111	13	4	4	44	28		1	23	.267	.315	.346	.661	-34	11	4	73	2b96,S7,3b2		-1.7
Total	9	956	3707	516	990	173	43	29	423	212		10	250	.267	.308	.360	.668	-27	113	63	100	2b483,S439,3b34		-9.6
/150	1	150	612	104	163	19	6	6	65	41		1	34	.267	.315	.346	.661	-34	16	6	73	2b141,S10,3b3		-2.5
CLARK, TONY Anthony Christopher B6.15.1972 Newton KS BB/TR/6'7"/(205–250) [DetA90 1/2] d9.3																								
2002	Bos A	90	275	25	57	12	1	3	29	21	0	1	57	.207	.265	.291	.556	-53	0	0	0	1b85,D2	0	-2.3
Total	12	1302	4094	579	1087	219	10	227	738	464	51	20	1071	.266	.341	.490	.831	+12	6	9	40	1b1081,D92/lf	144	-2.6
CLARK, DANNY Daniel Curran B1.18.1894 Meridian MS D5.23.1937 Meridian MS BL/TR/5'9"/167 d4.12																								
1922	Det A	83	185	31	54	11	3	3	26	15		0	11	.292	.345	.432	.777	+5	1	0	100	2b38,O5R/3		-0.1
1924	Bos A	104	325	36	90	23	3	2	54	51		2	19	.277	.378	.385	.763	-3	4	7	36	3b94		0.4
1927	StL N	58	72	8	17	2	2	0	13	8		0	7	.236	.313	.319	.632	-33	0			O9R		-0.4
Total	3	245	582	75	161	36	8	5	93	74		2	37	.277	.360	.392	.752	-4	5	7	100	3b95,2b38,O14R		-0.1
/150	1	150	469	52	130	33	4	3	78	74		3	27	.277	.378	.385	.763	-3	6	10	38	3b136		0.6
CLARK, JACK Jack Anthony B11.10.1955 New Brighton PA BR/TR/6'2"/(170–210) [SFN73 13/294] d9.12 C3 OF(11/23/1014)																								
1991	Bos A	140	481	75	120	18	1	28	87	96	3	3	133	.249	.374	.466	.840	+25	0	2	0	D135	0	1.4
1992	Bos A	81	257	32	54	11	0	5	33	56	3	2	87	.210	.350	.311	.661	-18	1	1	50	D64,1b13	0	-0.7
Total	18	1994	6847	1118	1826	332	39	340	1180	1262	12	24	1441	.267	.379	.476	.855	+37	77	61	56	O1039R,1b580,D311,3b4	246	29.6
Team	2	221	738	107	174	29	1	33	120	152	6	5	220	.236	.365	.412	.777	+10	1	3	25	D199,1b13	0	0.7
/150	1	150	501	73	118	20	1	22	81	103	4	3	149	.236	.365	.412	.777	+10	1	2	33	D135,1b9	0	0.5
CLARK, PHIL Phillip Benjamin B5.6.1968 Crockett TX BR/TR/6'0"/(180–205) [DetA86 1/18] d5.27 b–Jerald																								
1996	Bos A	3	3	0	0	0	0	0	0	0	0	0	1	.000	.000	.000	.000	-198	0	0	0	/13D	0	-0.1
Total	5	264	543	62	150	30	0	17	65	27	5	9	76	.276	.317	.425	.742	-3	4	4	50	O100(52/0/50),1b51,C16,D8,3b7	0	-0.2
CLINTON, LOU Luciean Louis B10.13.1937 Ponca City OK D12.6.1997 Wichita KS BR/TR/6'1"/(185–195) d4.22																								
1960	Bos A	96	298	37	68	17	5	6	37	20	1	3	66	.228	.278	.379	.657	-25	4	3	57	O89R	0	-1.3
1961	Bos A	17	51	4	13	2	1	0	3	2	0	0	10	.255	.283	.333	.616	-37	0	0	0	O13R	0	-0.1
1962	Bos A	114	398	63	117	24	10	18	75	34	3	1	79	.294	.349	.540	.889	+32	2	1	67	O103R	0	1.0
1963	Bos A	148	560	71	130	23	7	22	77	49	6	1	118	.232	.294	.416	.710	-6	0	0	0	O146R	0	-1.0
1964	Bos A	37	120	15	31	4	3	3	6	9	1	0	33	.258	.310	.417	.727	-5	1	0	100	O35R	0	0.2
1964	LA A	91	306	30	76	18	0	9	38	31	0	1	40	.248	.317	.395	.712	+8	3	0	100	O86R	0	-0.1
1964	Year	128	426	45	107	22	3	12	44	40	1	1	73	.251	.315	.401	.716	+4	4	0	100	O121R	0	0.1
1965	Cal A	89	222	29	54	12	3	1	8	23	1	1	37	.243	.316	.338	.654	-12	2	3	40	O73(1/0/72)	0	-0.8
1965	KC A	1	1	0	0	0	0	0	0	0	0	0	0	.000	.000	.000	.000	-199	0	0	0	/rf	0	0.0
1965	Cle A	12	34	2	6	1	0	1	2	3	0	0	7	.176	.243	.294	.537	-49	0	0	0	O9(9/1/1)	0	-0.3
1965	Year	102	257	31	60	13	3	2	10	26	1	1	44	.233	.305	.331	.636	-17	2	3	40	O83(10/1/74)	0	-1.1
1966	NY A	80	159	18	35	10	2	5	21	16	1	0	27	.220	.288	.403	.691	+1	0	0	0	O63(5/1/57)	0	-0.4
1967	NY A	6	4	1	2	1	0	0	2	1	1	0	1	.500	.600	.750	1.350	+208	0	0	0	/lf	0	0.1
Total	8	691	2153	270	532	112	31	65	269	188	14	7	418	.247	.308	.418	.726	-1	12	7	63	O619(16/2/603)	0	-2.7
Team	5	412	1427	190	359	70	26	49	198	114	11	5	306	.252	.307	.440	.747	+0	7	4	64	O386R	0	-1.2
/150	2	150	520	69	131	25	9	18	72	42	4	2	111	.252	.307	.440	.747	+0	3	1	75	O141R	0	-0.4
COCHRAN, GEORGE George Leslie B2.12.1889 Rusk TX D5.21.1960 Harbor City CA TR d7.29																								
1918	Bos A	24	60	7	7	0	0	0	3	10		2	6	.117	.264	.117	.381	-85	3			3b22/S		-0.7
COFFEY, JACK John Francis B1.28.1887 New York NY D2.14.1966 Bronx NY BR/TR/5'11"/178 d6.23 Col Fordham																								
1918	Bos A	15	44	5	7	1	0	1	2	3		0	2	.159	.213	.250	.463	-60	2			3b14/2		-0.2
Total	2	110	368	33	69	5	6	1	26	22		4	8	.188	.241	.242	.483	-52	6			S73,2b23,3b14		-3.2
COLE, ALEX Alexander B8.17.1965 Fayetteville NC BL/TL/6'0"/(170–184) [StLN85*2/43] d7.27 Col Manatee (FL) CC																								
1996	Bos A	24	72	13	16	5	1	0	7	8	0	0	11	.222	.296	.319	.615	-44	5	3	63	O24C	0	-0.6
Total	7	573	1760	286	493	58	26	5	117	217	8	7	296	.280	.360	.351	.711	-10	148	59	71	O483(42/390/54),D14	133	-1.4
COLEMAN, DAVE David Lee B10.26.1950 Dayton OH BR/TR/6'3"/195 [BosA69 18/419] d4.13																								
1977	Bos A	11	12	1	0	0	0	0	0	1	0	0	3	.000	.077	.000	.077	-169	0	0	0	O9(3/5/1)	0	-0.4
COLEMAN, MICHAEL Michael Donnell B8.16.1975 Nashville TN BR/TR/5'11"/(180–225) [BosA94 18/495] d9.1 [DL 2000 Bos A 96, 2002 Bos A 25]																								
1997	Bos A	8	24	2	4	1	0	0	2	0	0	0	11	.167	.167	.208	.375	-103	1	0	100	O7C	0	-0.4
1999	Bos A	2	5	1	1	0	0	0	0	1	0	0	0	.200	.333	.200	.533	-61	0	0	0	O2(1/1/0)	0	-0.1
2001	NY A	12	38	5	8	0	0	1	7	0	0	0	15	.211	.205	.289	.494	-70	0	1	0	O9(1/7/3),D3	0	-0.6
Total	3	22	67	8	13	1	0	1	9	1	0	0	26	.194	.203	.254	.457	-81	1	1	50	O18(2/15/3),D3	121	-1.1
Team	2	10	29	3	5	1	0	0	2	1	0	0	11	.172	.200	.207	.407	-95	1	0	100	O9(1/8/1)	121	-0.5
COLLIER, LOU Louis Keith B8.21.1973 Chicago IL BR/TR/5'10"/(180–191) [PitN92 31/875] d6.28 Col Triton (IL) JC																								
2003	Bos A	4	1	0	0	0	0	0	0	0	0	0	0	.000	.000	.000	.000	-196	0	1	0	3b2,O2(1/1/0)	0	-0.1
Total	8	315	713	89	172	33	7	8	78	75	7	9	160	.241	.317	.341	.658	-28	12	6	67	S156,O60(38/22/2),3b28,2b6/D	16	-2.6
COLLINS, JIMMY James Joseph B1.16.1870 Buffalo NY D3.6.1943 Buffalo NY BR/TR/5'9"/178 d4.19 M6 HF1945																								
1895	Bos N	11	38	10	8	3	0	1	8	4		1	4	.211	.302	.368	.670	-33	0			O10R		-0.3
1895	Lou N	96	373	65	104	17	5	6	49	33		9	16	.279	.352	.399	.751	+0	12			3b77,O18(0/7/11),2b2/S		1.7
1895	Year	107	411	75	112	20	5	7	57	37		10	20	.273	.347	.397	.744	-4	12			3b77,O28(0/7/21),2b2/S		1.4
1896	Bos N	84	304	48	90	10	9	1	46	30		8	12	.296	.374	.398	.772	-2	10			3b80,S4		1.4
1897	†Bos N	134	529	103	183	28	13	6	132	41		7		.346	.400	.482	.882	+25	14			3b134		3.3
1898	Bos N	**152**	597	107	196	35	5	**15**	111	40		7		.328	.377	.479	.856	+38	12			3b152		3.9
1899	Bos N	151	599	98	166	28	11	5	92	40		12		.277	.335	.386	.721	-11	12			3b151		0.8
1900	Bos N	**142**	586	104	178	25	5	6	95	34		10		.304	.352	.394	.746	-6	23			3b141/S		0.6
1901	Bos A	**138**	564	108	187	42	16	6	94	34		5		.332	.375	.495	.870	+42	19			3b138,M		4.2
1902	Bos A	108	429	71	138	21	10	6	61	24		2		.322	.360	.459	.819	+23	18			3b107,M		2.1
1903	†Bos A	130	540	88	160	33	17	5	72	24		2		.296	.329	.448	.777	+25	23			3b130,M		2.9
1904	Bos A	156	631	85	171	33	13	3	67	27		5		.271	.306	.379	.685	+10	19			3b156,M		1.7
1905	Bos A	131	508	66	140	26	5	4	65	37		4		.276	.330	.370	.700	+20	18			3b131,M		2.2
1906	Bos A	37	142	17	39	8	4	1	16	4		0		.275	.295	.408	.703	+20	1			3b32,M		0.5
1907	Bos A	41	158	13	46	8	0	0	10	10		0		.291	.333	.342	.675	+16	4			3b41		-0.2
1907	Phi A	99	364	38	99	21	0	0	35	24		8		.272	.331	.330	.661	+8	4			3b98		0.5
1907	Year	140	522	51	145	29	0	0	45	34		8		.278	.332	.333	.665	+10	8			3b139		0.3
1908	Phi A	115	433	34	94	14	3	0	30	20		4		.217	.258	.263	.521	-35	5			3b115		-2.3
Total	14	1725	6795	1055	1999	352	116	65	983	426		84	32	.294	.343	.409	.752	+12	194			3b1683,O28(0/7/21),S6,2b2		23.0

Year	Tm Lg	G	AB	R	H	2B	3B	HR	RBI	BB	IB	HP	SO	AVG	OBP	SLG	OPS	AOPS	SB	CS	SB%	Games at Position	DL	BFW
Team	7	741	2972	448	881	171	65	25	385	160		18	0	.296	.336	.423	.759	+23	102			3b735,M6		13.4
/150	1	150	602	91	178	35	13	5	78	32		4	0	.296	.336	.423	.759	+23	21			3b149/M		2.7
COLLINS, SHANO John Francis B12.4.1885 Charlestown MA D9.10.1955 Newton MA BR/TR/6'0"/185 d4.21 M2 gs–Bob Gallagher																								
1921	Bos A	141	542	63	155	29	12	4	69	18		4	38	.286	.314	.406	.720	-15	15	8	65	O139(1/44/94),1b3		-1.9
1922	Bos A	135	472	33	128	24	7	1	52	7		5	30	.271	.289	.358	.647	-32	7	9	44	O117(11/45/63)/1		-3.7
1923	Bos A	97	342	41	79	10	5	0	18	11		5	29	.231	.265	.289	.554	-54	7	8	47	O89(0/57/32)		-3.4
1924	Bos A	89	240	37	70	17	5	0	28	18		3	17	.292	.349	.404	.753	-6	4	6	40	O56(18/11/27),1b12		-1.5
1925	Bos A	2	3	1	1	0	0	0	1	0		0	0	.333	.333	.333	.666	-30	0	0	0	/cf		0.0
Total	16	1799	6390	747	1687	310	133	22	709	331		57	405	.264	.306	.364	.670	-10	226	83	100	O1343(133/292/918),1b368,2b3		-18.7
Team	5	464	1599	175	433	80	29	5	168	54		17	114	.271	.302	.366	.668	-27	33	31	52	O402(12/157/103),1b16		-10.5
/150	2	150	517	57	140	26	9	2	54	17		5	37	.271	.302	.366	.668	-27	11	10	52	O130(4/51/33),1b5		-3.4
COMBS, MERL Merrill Russell B12.11.1919 Los Angeles CA D7.7.1981 Riverside CA BL/TR/6'0"/172 d9.12 C2 Col USC																								
1947	Bos A	17	68	8	15	1	0	1	6	9		2	9	.221	.329	.279	.608	-35	0	0	0	3b17	0	0.0
1949	Bos A	14	24	5	5	1	0	0	1	9		0	0	.208	.424	.250	.674	-25	0	0	0	3b9/S	0	-0.1
1950	Bos A	1	0	0	0	0	0	0	0	1		0	0	+	1.000	+	1.000	+58	0	0	0	/H	0	0.0
Total	5	140	361	45	73	6	1	2	25	57		2	43	.202	.314	.241	.555	-48	0	1	0	S96,3b26,2b3	0	-0.7
Team	3	32	92	13	20	2	0	1	7	19		2	9	.217	.363	.272	.635	-31	0	0	0	3b26/S	0	-0.1
CONGALTON, BUNK William Millar B1.24.1875 Guelph ON, Can. D8.19.1937 Cleveland OH BL/TL/5'11"/190 d4.17																								
1902	Chi N	47	188	16	45	3	0	1	27	7		0		.239	.267	.271	.538	-32	4			O47(0/5/43)		-1.0
1905	Cle A	12	47	4	17	0	0	0	5	2		0		.362	.388	.362	.750	+36	3			O12R		0.0
1906	Cle A	117	419	51	134	13	5	3	50	24		3		.320	.361	.396	.757	+39	12			O114(21/1/93)		0.4
1907	Cle A	9	22	2	4	0	0	0	2	4		0		.182	.308	.182	.490	-44	0			O6R		-0.1
1907	Bos A	124	496	44	142	11	8	2	47	20		3		.286	.318	.353	.671	+15	13			O123R		-0.3
1907	Year	133	518	46	146	11	8	2	49	24		3		.282	.317	.346	.663	+12	13			O129R		-0.4
Total	4	309	1172	117	342	27	13	6	131	57		6		.292	.328	.352	.680	+16	32			O302(21/6/277)		-1.0
/150	1	150	600	53	172	13	10	2	57	24		4	0	.286	.318	.353	.671	+15	16			O149R		-0.4
CONIGLIARO, TONY Anthony Richard B1.7.1945 Revere MA D2.24.1990 Salem MA BR/TR/6'3"/(185–205) d4.16 b–Billy [DL 1968 Bos A 175]																								
1964	Bos A	111	404	69	117	21	2	24	52	35	1	5	78	.290	.354	.530	.884	+35	2	4	33	O106(81/25/2)	37	1.4
1965	Bos A	138	521	82	140	21	5	**32**	82	51	6	5	116	.269	.338	.512	.850	+31	4	2	67	O137(0/2/135)	0	2.1
1966	Bos A	150	558	77	148	26	7	28	93	52	8	5	112	.265	.330	.487	.817	+20	0	2	0	O146R	0	-0.1
1967	Bos A★	95	349	59	100	11	5	20	67	27	2	5	58	.287	.341	.519	.860	+41	4	6	40	O95R	40	1.3
1969	Bos A	141	506	57	129	21	3	20	82	48	6	4	111	.255	.321	.427	.748	+4	2	4	33	O137R	0	-1.9
1970	Bos A	146	560	89	149	20	1	36	116	43	4	8	93	.266	.324	.498	.822	+17	4	2	67	O146R	0	0.0
1971	Cal A	74	266	23	59	18	0	4	15	23	1	1	52	.222	.285	.335	.620	-19	3	3	50	O72R	80	-0.7
1975	Bos A	21	57	8	7	1	0	2	9	8	0	0	9	.123	.221	.246	.467	-68	1	0	100	D15	0	-0.6
Total	8	876	3221	464	849	139	23	166	516	287	28	33	629	.264	.327	.476	.803	+18	20	23	47	O839(81/27/733),D15	332	1.5
Team	7	802	2955	441	790	121	23	162	501	264	27	32	577	.267	.331	.488	.819	+21	17	20	46	O767(81/27/138),D15	252	2.2
/150	1	150	553	82	148	23	4	30	94	49	5	6	108	.267	.331	.488	.819	+21	3	4	43	O143(15/5/26),D3	47	0.4
CONIGLIARO, BILLY William Michael B8.15.1947 Revere MA BR/TR/6'0"/(180–190) [BosA65 1/5] d4.11 b–Tony																								
1969	Bos A	32	80	14	23	6	2	4	7	9	0	1	23	.287	.367	.563	.930	+50	1	1	50	O24(3/18/6)	0	-0.1
1970	Bos A	114	398	59	108	16	3	18	58	35	0	7	73	.271	.339	.462	.801	+12	3	7	30	O108(77/25/20)	0	0.0
1971	Bos A	101	351	42	92	26	1	11	33	25	4	0	68	.262	.310	.436	.746	+2	3	2	60	O100(1/79/20)	0	-0.4
1972	Mil A	52	191	22	44	6	2	7	16	8	0	0	54	.230	.261	.393	.654	-6	1	0	100	O50(2/6/45)	0	0.0
1973	†Oak A	48	110	5	22	2	2	0	14	9	1	0	26	.200	.252	.255	.507	-52	1	0	100	O40(21/18/3)/2	59	-0.7
Total	5	347	1130	142	289	56	10	40	128	86	5	8	244	.256	.311	.429	.740	+3	9	10	47	O322(104/146/94)/2	59	-1.2
Team	3	247	829	115	223	48	6	33	98	69	4	8	164	.269	.330	.461	.791	+12	7	10	41	O232(80/122/85)	0	-0.5
/150	2	150	503	70	135	29	4	20	60	42	2	5	100	.269	.330	.461	.791	+12	4	6	40	O141(49/74/52)	0	-0.3
CONNOLLY, ED Edward Joseph Sr. B7.17.1908 Brooklyn NY D11.12.1963 Pittsfield MA BR/TR/5'8.5"/180 d9.20 s–Ed																								
1929	Bos A	5	8	0	0	0	0	0	0	0		0	2	.000	.000	.000	.000	-199	0	0	0	C5		-0.3
1930	Bos A	27	48	1	9	2	0	0	7	4		0	3	.188	.250	.229	.479	-77	0	0	0	C26		-0.4
1931	Bos A	42	93	3	7	1	0	0	3	5		1	18	.075	.131	.086	.217	-144	0	0	0	C41		-1.8
1932	Bos A	75	222	9	50	8	4	0	21	20		0	27	.225	.289	.297	.586	-46	0	1	0	C75		-1.3
Total	4	149	371	13	66	11	4	0	31	29		1	50	.178	.239	.229	.468	-77	0	1	0	C147		-3.8
/150	4	150	373	13	66	11	4	0	31	29		1	50	.178	.239	.229	.468	-77	0	1	0	C148	0	-3.8
CONNOLLY, JOE Joseph H. "Coaster Joe" B6.27.1894 San Francisco CA D3.30.1960 San Francisco CA BR/TR/6'0"/170 d10.1																								
1924	Bos A	14	10	1	1	0	0	0	1	2		0	2	.100	.250	.100	.350	-107	0	0	0	O3R		-0.2
Total	4	80	168	32	45	12	2	3	32	21		0	18	.268	.349	.417	.766	+0	2	2	50	O55(3/15/37)		-0.6
CONNOLLY, BUD Mervin Thomas "Mike" B5.25.1901 San Francisco CA D6.12.1964 Berkeley CA BR/TR/5'8"/154 d5.3																								
1925	Bos A	43	107	12	28	7	1	0	21	23		0	9	.262	.392	.346	.738	-12	0	3	0	S34,3b2		-0.2
CONROY, BILL William Gordon B2.26.1915 Bloomington IL D11.13.1997 Citrus Heights CA BR/TR/6'0"/185 d9.21 Mil 1945 Col Illinois Wesleyan																								
1935	Phi A	1	4	0	1	1	0	0	0	1		0	0	.250	.400	.500	.900	+33	0	0	0	/C		0.0
1936	Phi A	1	2	0	1	0	0	0	0	0		0	1	.500	.500	.500	1.000	+51	0	0	0	/C		0.0
1937	Phi A	26	60	4	12	1	1	0	3	7		0	9	.200	.284	.250	.534	-64	1	0	100	C18/1		-0.5
1942	Bos A	83	250	22	50	4	2	4	20	40		2	47	.200	.315	.280	.595	-34	2	0	100	C83	0	-0.6
1943	Bos A	39	89	13	16	5	0	1	6	18		3	19	.180	.336	.270	.606	-23	0	0	0	C38	0	0.1
1944	Bos A	19	47	6	10	2	0	0	4	11		0	9	.213	.362	.255	.617	-21	0	0	0	C19	0	0.0
Total	6	169	452	45	90	13	3	5	33	77		5	85	.199	.322	.274	.596	-34	3	0	100	C160/1	0	-1.0
Team	3	141	386	41	76	11	2	5	30	69		5	75	.197	.326	.275	.601	-30	2	0	100	C140	0	-0.5
/150	3	150	411	44	81	12	2	5	32	73		5	80	.197	.326	.275	.601	-30	2	0	100	C149	0	-0.5
CONSOLO, BILLY William Angelo B8.18.1934 Cleveland OH BR/TR/5'11"/180 d4.20 C15																								
1953	Bos A	47	65	9	14	2	1	1	6	2		0	23	.215	.239	.323	.562	-52	1	2	33	3b16,2b11	0	0.0
1954	Bos A	91	242	23	55	7	1	1	11	33		2	69	.227	.324	.277	.601	-41	2	1	67	S50,3b18,2b12	0	-1.0
1955	Bos A	8	18	4	4	0	0	0	0	5	0	0	4	.222	.391	.222	.613	-37	0	0	0	2b4	0	-0.3
1956	Bos A	48	11	13	2	0	0	0	1	3	0	0	5	.182	.357	.182	.539	-59	0	0	0	2b25	0	0.3
1957	Bos A	68	196	26	53	6	1	4	19	23	0	0	48	.270	.345	.372	.717	-9	1	3	25	S42,2b16,3b2	0	0.7
1958	Bos A	46	72	13	9	2	1	0	5	6	0	0	14	.125	.192	.181	.373	-97	0	0	0	2b13,S11/3	0	-1.1
1959	Bos A	10	14	3	3	1	0	0	0	2	0	0	5	.214	.313	.286	.599	-37	0	0	0	S2	0	-0.2
1959	Was A	79	202	25	43	5	3	0	10	36	0	0	54	.213	.332	.267	.599	-33	1	0	100	S75,2b4	0	1.3
1959	Year	89	216	28	46	6	3	0	10	38	0	0	59	.213	.331	.269	.600	-34	1	0	100	S77,2b4	0	1.1
1960	Was A	100	174	23	36	4	2	3	15	25	1	1	29	.207	.310	.305	.615	-32	1	1	50	S82,2b12,3b2	0	-1.3
1961	Min A	11	5	1	0	0	0	0	0	0	0	0	1	.000	.000	.000	.000	-195	0	0	0	2b3,S3/3	0	-0.3
1962	Phi N	13	5	3	2	0	0	0	0	0	0	0	1	.400	.400	.400	.800	+19	0	0	0	/3	0	0.0
1962	LA A	28	20	4	2	0	0	0	0	3	0	0	11	.100	.217	.100	.317	-112	2	0	100	3b20,S4/2	0	-0.2
1962	KC A	54	154	11	37	4	2	0	16	23	2	0	33	.240	.337	.292	.629	-32	1	3	25	S48	0	-0.7
1962	Year	82	174	15	39	4	2	0	16	26	2	0	44	.224	.323	.270	.593	-39	3	3	50	S52,3b20/2	0	-0.9
1962	Major	95	179	18	41	4	2	0	16	26	2	0	45	.229	1.327	.274	1.601	-29	3	3	50		0	-0.9
Total	10	603	1178	158	260	31	11	9	83	161	3	3	297	.221	.315	.289	.604	-37	9	10	47	S317,2b101,3b61	0	-2.8
Team	7	318	618	91	140	18	4	6	42	74	0	2	168	.227	.310	.298	.608	-38	4	6	40	S105,2b81,3b37	0	-1.6
/150	3	150	292	43	66	8	2	3	20	35	0	1	79	.227	.310	.298	.608	-38	2	3	40	S50,2b38,3b17	0	-0.8
COOKE, DUSTY Allen Lindsey B6.23.1907 Swepsonville NC D11.21.1987 Raleigh NC BL/TR/6'1"/205 d4.15 M1/C5																								
1930	NY A	92	216	43	55	12	3	6	29	32		1	61	.255	.353	.421	.774	+0	4	6	40	O73(21/28/24)		-0.3
1931	NY A	27	39	10	13	1	0	1	6	8		0	11	.333	.447	.436	.883	+41	4	1	80	O11(7/0/6)		0.3
1932	NY A	3	0	1	0	0	0	0	0	1		0	0	+	1.000	+	1.000	+91	0	0	0	/H		0.0
1933	Bos A	119	454	86	133	35	10	5	54	67		2	71	.293	.386	.447	.833	+21	7	5	58	O118(47/70/30)		0.6

Year	Tm Lg	G	AB	R	H	2B	3B	HR	RBI	BB	IB	HP	SO	AVG	OBP	SLG	OPS	AOPS	SB	CS	SB%	Games at Position	DL	BFW
1934	Bos A	74	168	34	41	8	5	1	26	36		0	25	.244	.377	.369	.746	-13	7	2	78	O44(9/14/21)		-0.5
1935	Bos A	100	294	51	90	18	6	3	34	46		0	24	.306	.400	.439	.839	+9	6	8	43	O82(7/35/44)		-0.1
1936	Bos A	111	341	58	93	20	3	6	47	72		1	48	.273	.401	.402	.803	-7	4	3	57	O91(24/1/67)		-0.7
1938	Cin N	82	233	41	64	15	1	2	33	28		1	36	.275	.355	.373	.728	+3	0			O51(46/0/7)		0.0
Total	8	608	1745	324	489	109	28	24	229	290		5	276	.280	.384	.416	.800	+6	32	25	100	O470(161/148/199)		-0.7
Team	4	404	1257	229	357	81	24	15	161	221		3	168	.284	.392	.422	.814	+6	24	18	57	O335(56/120/162)		-0.7
/150	1	150	467	85	133	30	9	6	60	82		1	62	.284	.392	.422	.814	+6	9	7	56	O124(21/45/60)		-0.3
COONEY, JIMMY James Edward "Scoops" B8.24.1894 Cranston RI D8.7.1991 Warwick RI BR/TR/5'11"/160 d9.22 Mil 1918 f–Jimmy b–Johnny																								
1917	Bos A	11	36	4	8	1	0	0	3	6		0	2	.222	.333	.250	.583	-21	0			2b10/S		0.3
Total	7	448	1575	181	413	64	16	2	150	76		4	58	.262	.298	.327	.625	-33	30	13	100	S400,2b31,3b7/lf		0.0
COOPER, CECIL Cecil Celester B12.20.1949 Brenham TX BL/TL/6'2"/(165–190) [BosA68 6/128] d9.8 C3																								
1971	Bos A	14	42	9	13	4	1	0	3	5	1	1	4	.310	.388	.452	.840	+30	1	0	100	1b11	0	0.0
1972	Bos A	12	17	0	4	1	0	0	2	2	1	0	5	.235	.316	.294	.610	-22	0	0	0	1b3	0	-0.1
1973	Bos A	30	101	12	24	2	0	3	11	7	1	0	12	.238	.284	.347	.631	-27	1	2	33	1b29	0	-0.7
1974	Bos A	121	414	55	114	24	1	8	43	32	3	1	74	.275	.327	.396	.723	+1	2	5	29	1b74,D41	0	-1.0
1975	†Bos A	106	305	49	95	17	6	14	44	19	6	3	33	.311	.355	.544	.899	+40	1	4	20	D54,1b35	0	1.2
1976	Bos A	123	451	66	127	22	6	15	78	16	6	1	62	.282	.304	.457	.761	+9	7	1	88	1b66,D53	0	-0.5
Total	17	1896	7349	1012	2192	415	47	241	1125	448	79	17	911	.298	.337	.466	.803	+21	89	49	64	1b1475,D373	56	8.3
Team	6	406	1330	191	377	70	14	40	181	81	18	6	190	.283	.324	.447	.771	+11	12	12	50	1b218,D148	0	-1.1
/150	2	150	491	71	139	26	5	15	67	30	7	2	70	.283	.324	.447	.771	+11	4	4	50	1b81,D55	0	-0.4
COOPER, SCOTT Scott Kendrick B10.13.1967 St.Louis MO BL/TR/6'3"/(200–215) [BosA86 3/69] d9.5																								
1990	Bos A	2	1	0	0	0	0	0	0	0	0	0	1	.000	.000	.000	.000	-195	0	0	0	/H	0	0.0
1991	Bos A	14	35	6	16	4	2	0	7	2	0	0	2	.457	.486	.686	1.172	+109	0	0	0	3b13	0	0.6
1992	Bos A	123	337	34	93	21	0	5	33	37	0	0	33	.276	.346	.383	.729	-3	1	1	50	1b62,3b47/2SD	0	0.2
1993	Bos A★	156	526	67	147	29	3	9	63	58	15	5	81	.279	.355	.397	.752	-4	5	2	71	3b154,1b2/S	0	-1.1
1994	Bos A★	104	369	49	104	16	4	13	53	30	2	1	65	.282	.333	.453	.786	-3	0	3	0	3b104	8	0.6
1995	StL N	118	374	29	86	18	2	3	40	49	3	3	85	.230	.321	.313	.634	-32	0	3	0	3b110	0	-0.8
1997	KC A	75	159	12	32	6	1	3	15	17	0	2	32	.201	.283	.308	.591	-46	1	1	50	3b39,1b8,D5	40	-1.3
Total	7	592	1801	197	478	94	12	33	211	193	20	11	299	.265	.337	.386	.723	-11	7	10	41	3b467,1b72,D7,S2/2	48	-1.8
Team	5	399	1268	156	360	70	9	27	156	127	17	6	182	.284	.349	.417	.766	-1	6	6	50	3b318,1b64,S2/2D	8	0.3
/150	2	150	477	59	135	26	3	10	59	48	6	2	68	.284	.349	.417	.766	-1	2	2	50	3b120,1b24/S2D	3	0.1
CORA, ALEX Jose Alexander B10.18.1975 Caguas, PR BL/TR/6'0"/(180–200) [LAN96 3/88] d6.7 b–Joey Col Miami																								
2005	†Bos A	47	104	14	28	3	2	2	16	6	0	1	12	.269	.310	.394	.704	-16	1	2	33	2b35,S11,3b5	0	0.1
2006	Bos A	96	235	31	56	7	2	1	18	19	1	6	29	.238	.312	.298	.610	-42	6	2	75	S63,2b18,3b11,D2	0	-0.3
Total	9	876	2446	259	596	99	27	31	215	178	28	63	320	.244	.310	.344	.654	-28	31	15	67	S436,2b403,3b16,D2/lf	83	-1.1
Team	2	143	339	45	84	10	4	3	34	25	1	7	41	.248	.311	.327	.638	-34	7	4	64	S74,2b53,3b16,D2	0	-0.2
/150	2	150	356	47	88	10	4	3	36	26	1	7	43	.248	.311	.327	.638	-34	7	4	64	S78,2b56,3b17,D2	0	-0.2
CORDERO, WIL Wilfredo (Nieva) B10.3.1971 Mayaguez, PR BR/TR/6'2"/(185–230) d7.24 OF(400/0/17)																								
1996	Bos A	59	198	29	57	14	0	3	37	11	4	2	31	.288	.330	.404	.734	-17	2	1	67	2b37,D13/1	83	-0.5
1997	Bos A	140	570	82	160	26	3	18	72	31	7	4	122	.281	.320	.432	.752	-8	1	3	25	O137L/2D	0	-1.8
Total	14	1247	4311	587	1178	261	19	122	566	325	35	57	775	.273	.330	.428	.758	-6	49	19	72	O413L,S383,1b265,D58,2b47,3b2	369	-12.9
Team	2	199	768	111	217	40	3	21	109	42	11	6	153	.283	.323	.424	.747	-10	3	4	43	O137L,2b38,D14/1	83	-2.3
/150	2	150	579	84	164	30	2	16	82	32	8	5	115	.283	.323	.424	.747	-10	2	3	40	O103L,2b29,D11/1	63	-1.7
CORRELL, VIC Victor Crosby B2.5.1946 Washington DC BR/TR/5'10"/(175–185) [CleA67 9/171] d10.4 Col Georgia Southern																								
1972	Bos A	1	4	1	2	0	0	0	1	0	0	0	1	.500	.500	.500	1.000	+87	0	0	0	/C	0	0.1
Total	8	410	1132	124	259	60	4	29	125	128	19	8	220	.229	.310	.366	.676	-16	2	8	20	C380	145	-2.7
COUGHTRY, MARLAN James Marlan B9.11.1934 Hollywood CA BL/TR/6'1"/170 d9.2 Col Long Beach (CA) City																								
1960	Bos A	15	19	3	3	0	0	0	0	5	0	0	8	.158	.333	.158	.491	-64	0	0	0	2b13/3	0	-0.2
1962	LA A	11	22	0	4	0	0	0	2	0	0	0	6	.182	.182	.182	.364	-102	0	0	0	3b5,2b2	0	-0.1
1962	KC A	6	11	1	2	0	0	0	1	4	0	0	3	.182	.400	.182	.582	-40	0	0	0	3b3	0	0.1
1962	Cle A	3	2	1	1	0	0	0	1	1	0	0	1	.500	.667	.500	1.167	+126	0	0	0	/H	0	0.1
1962	Year	20	35	2	7	0	0	0	4	5	0	0	10	.200	.300	.200	.500	-62	0	0	0	3b8,2b2	0	0.1
Total	2	35	54	5	10	0	0	0	4	10	0	0	18	.185	.313	.185	.498	-63	0	0	0	2b15,3b9	0	-0.1
COX, TED William Ted B1.24.1955 Oklahoma City OK BR/TR/6'3"/(190–205) [BosA73 1/17] d9.18																								
1977	Bos A	13	58	11	21	3	1	1	6	3	0	0	6	.362	.393	.500	.893	+27	0	0	0	D13	0	0.2
Total	5	272	771	65	189	29	1	10	79	57	5	3	98	.245	.298	.324	.622	-29	3	6	33	3b166,O54(49/0/5),D27,1b8,2b4/S	0	-5.3
CRAMER, DOC Roger Maxwell "Flit" B7.22.1905 Beach Haven NJ D9.9.1990 Manahawkin NJ BL/TR/6'2"/185 d9.18 C4																								
1936	Bos A	154	643	99	188	31	7	0	41	49		5	20	.292	.347	.362	.709	-29	4	6	40	O154C		-2.1
1937	Bos A☆	133	560	90	171	22	11	0	51	35		4	14	.305	.351	.384	.735	-18	8	6	57	O133C		-1.7
1938	Bos A★	148	658	116	198	36	8	0	71	51		3	19	.301	.354	.380	.734	-20	4	9	31	O148C/P		-1.9
1939	Bos A★	137	589	110	183	30	6	0	56	36		2	17	.311	.352	.382	.734	-15	3	3	50	O135C		-2.1
1940	Bos A☆	150	661	94	**200**	27	12	1	51	36		1	29	.303	.340	.384	.724	-16	3	5	38	O149(16/96/37)		-2.9
Total	20	2239	9140	1357	2705	396	109	37	842	572		41	345	.296	.340	.375	.715	-13	62	73	46	O2142(25/2031/87)/PS	0	-29.6
Team	5	722	3111	509	940	146	44	1	270	207		15	99	.302	.349	.378	.727	-20	22	29	43	O719(16/666/96)/P		-10.7
/150	1	150	646	106	195	30	9	0	56	43		3	21	.302	.349	.378	.727	-20	5	6	45	O149(3/138/20)/P		-2.2
CRAVATH, GAVY Clifford Carlton "Cactus" B3.23.1881 Poway CA D5.23.1963 Laguna Beach CA BR/TR/5'10.5"/186 d4.18 M2/C1																								
1908	Bos A	94	277	43	71	10	11	1	34	38		4		.256	.354	.383	.737	+36	6			O77(62/0/15),1b5		0.8
Total	11	1220	3951	575	1134	232	83	119	719	561		28	514	.287	.380	.478	.858	+49	89	20	100	O1090(108/40/947),1b5		18.4
CREEDEN, PAT Patrick Francis "Whoops" B5.23.1906 Newburyport MA D4.20.1992 Brockton MA BL/TR/5'8"/175 d4.14 Col Boston College																								
1931	Bos A	5	8	0	0	0	0	0	0	1		0	3	.000	.111	.000	.111	-173	0	0	0	2b2		-0.2
CRESPO, CESAR Cesar Antonio (Claudio) B5.23.1979 Rio Piedras, PR BB/TR/5'11"/170 [NYN97 3/90] d5.29 b–Felipe																								
2001	SD N	55	153	27	32	6	0	4	12	25	0	0	50	.209	.320	.327	.647	-27	6	2	75	2b34,O18(6/11/2),3b2/S	0	-0.9
2002	SD N	25	29	5	5	2	0	0	0	3	0	0	6	.172	.250	.241	.491	-67	3	2	60	O7(6/1/1),2b4,3b4/S	0	-0.4
2004	Bos A	52	79	6	13	2	1	0	2	0	0	0	20	.165	.165	.215	.380	-102	2	0	100	S27,O19(10/7/2),2b11	0	-1.0
Total	3	132	261	38	50	10	1	4	14	28	0	0	76	.192	.270	.284	.554	-54	11	4	73	2b49,O44(22/19/5),S29,3b6	0	-2.3
CRIGER, LOU Louis B2.3.1872 Elkhart IN D5.14.1934 Tucson AZ BR/TR/5'10"/165 d9.21																								
1896	Cle N	2	5	0	0	0	0	0	0	1		0	0	.000	.167	.000	.167	-151	1			/C		0.0
1897	Cle N	39	138	15	31	4	1	0	22	23		1		.225	.340	.268	.608	-42	5			C37,1b2		-0.3
1898	Cle N	84	287	43	80	13	4	1	32	40		5		.279	.377	.362	.739	+13	2			C82		2.9
1899	StL N	77	258	39	66	4	5	2	44	28		2		.256	.333	.333	.666	-19	14			C75		0.6
1900	StL N	80	288	31	78	8	6	2	38	4		2		.271	.286	.361	.647	-22	5			C75/3		0.0
1901	Bos A	76	268	26	62	6	3	0	24	11		3		.231	.270	.276	.546	-48	7			C68,1b8		0.7
1902	Bos A	83	266	32	68	16	6	0	28	27		0		.256	.324	.361	.685	-13	7			C80/lf		1.7
1903	†Bos A	96	317	41	61	7	10	3	31	26		1		.192	.256	.306	.562	-35	5			C96		1.8
1904	Bos A	98	299	34	63	10	5	2	34	27		3		.211	.283	.298	.581	-21	1			C95		2.3
1905	Bos A	109	313	33	62	6	7	1	36	54		3		.198	.322	.272	.594	-12	5			C109		1.7
1906	Bos A	7	17	0	3	1	0	0	1	1		0		.176	.222	.235	.457	-57	1			C6		0.2
1907	Bos A	75	226	12	41	4	0	0	14	19		2		.181	.251	.199	.450	-56	2			C75		-0.3
1908	Bos A	84	237	12	45	4	2	0	25	13		0		.190	.232	.224	.456	-53	1			C84		0.7
1909	StL A	74	212	15	36	1	1	0	9	25		1		.170	.261	.184	.445	-56	2			C73		0.0
1910	NY A	27	69	3	13	2	0	0	4	10		0		.188	.291	.217	.508	-44	0			C27		-0.1
1912	StL A	1	2	1	0	0	0	0	0	0		0		.000	.000	.000	.000	-199	0			/C		0.0
Total	16	1012	3202	337	709	86	50	11	342	309		23	0	.221	.295	.290	.585	-28	58			C984,1b10/lf3		11.9
Team	8	628	1943	190	405	54	33	6	193	178		12	0	.208	.279	.279	.558	-32	29			C613,1b8/lf		8.8
/150	2	150	464	45	97	13	8	1	46	43		3	0	.208	.279	.279	.558	-32	7			C146,1b2/OfL		2.1

Year	Tm Lg	G	AB	R	H	2B	3B	HR	RBI	BB	IB	HP	SO	AVG	OBP	SLG	OPS	AOPS	SB	CS	SB%	Games at Position	DL	BFW
CRISP, COCO Covelli Loyce B11.1.1979 Los Angeles CA BB/TR/6'0"/(180–185) [StLN99 7/222] d8.15 Col Los Angeles Pierce (CA) JC																								
2006	Bos A	105	413	58	109	22	2	8	36	31	1	1	67	.264	.317	.385	.702	-21	22	4	85	O103C	49	-1.2
Total	5	520	2039	293	576	112	16	43	212	145	7	1	287	.282	.329	.416	.745	-4	76	33	70	O498(216/291/0),D13	64	-2.2
/150	1	150	590	83	156	31	3	11	51	44	1	1	96	.264	.317	.385	.702	-21	31	6	84	O147C	70	-1.7
CRONIN, JOE Joseph Edward B10.12.1906 San Francisco CA D9.7.1984 Barnstable MA BR/TR/5'11.5"/180 d4.29 M15 HF1956																								
1926	Pit N	38	83	9	22	2	2	0	11	6		0	15	.265	.315	.337	.652	-28	0			2b27,S7		0.2
1927	Pit N	12	22	2	5	1	0	0	3	2		0	3	.227	.292	.273	.565	-52	0			2b7,S4/1		-0.4
1928	Was A	63	227	23	55	10	4	0	25	22		0	27	.242	.309	.322	.631	-34	4	0	100	S63		0.4
1929	Was A	145	494	72	139	29	8	8	61	85		1	37	.281	.388	.421	.809	+7	5	9	36	S143/2		2.6
1930	Was A	**154**	587	127	203	41	9	13	126	72		5	36	.346	.422	.513	.935	+35	17	10	63	S154		6.9
1931	Was A	**156**	611	103	187	44	13	12	126	81		4	52	.306	.391	.480	.871	+27	10	9	53	S155		4.5
1932	Was A	143	557	95	177	43	**18**	6	116	66		3	45	.318	.393	.492	.885	+29	7	5	58	S141		3.8
1933	†Was A★	152	602	89	186	**45**	11	5	118	87		2	49	.309	.398	.445	.843	+24	5	4	56	S152,M		3.9
1934	Was A★	127	504	68	143	30	9	7	101	53		1	28	.284	.353	.421	.774	+3	8	0	100	S127,M		2.4
1935	Bos A★	144	556	70	164	37	14	9	95	63		3	40	.295	.370	.460	.830	+6	3	3	50	S139,1b2,M		-0.1
1936	Bos A	81	295	36	83	22	4	2	43	32		1	21	.281	.354	.403	.757	-18	1	3	25	S60,3b21,M		-0.8
1937	Bos A★	148	570	102	175	40	4	18	110	84		6	73	.307	.402	.486	.888	+18	5	3	63	S148,M		1.2
1938	Bos A★	143	530	98	172	**51**	5	17	94	91		5	60	.325	.428	.536	.964	+34	7	5	58	S142,M		4.4
1939	Bos A★	143	520	97	160	33	3	19	107	87		0	48	.308	.407	.492	.899	+24	6	6	50	S142,M		3.2
1940	Bos A	149	548	104	156	35	6	24	111	83		1	65	.285	.380	.502	.882	+22	7	5	58	S146,3b2,M		2.7
1941	Bos A★	143	518	98	161	38	8	16	95	82		1	55	.311	.406	.508	.914	+37	1	4	20	S119,3b22/lfM	0	3.5
1942	Bos A	45	79	7	24	3	0	4	24	15		0	21	.304	.415	.494	.909	+50	0	1	0	3b11,1b5/SM	0	0.5
1943	Bos A	59	77	8	24	4	0	5	29	11		0	4	.312	.398	.558	.956	+76	0	0	0	3b10,M	0	0.8
1944	Bos A	76	191	24	46	7	0	5	28	34		1	19	.241	.358	.356	.714	+6	1	4	20	1b49,M	0	-0.3
1945	Bos A	3	8	1	3	0	0	0	1	3		0	2	.375	.545	.375	.920	+65	0	0	0	3b3,M	67	0.2
Total	20	2124	7579	1233	2285	515	118	170	1424	1059		34	700	.301	.390	.468	.858	+19	87	71	100	S1843,3b69,1b57,2b35/lf	67	39.6
Team	11	1134	3892	645	1168	270	44	119	737	585		18	408	.300	.394	.484	.878	+21	31	34	48	S897,3b69,1b56,M11/lf	67	15.3
/150	1	150	515	85	154	36	6	16	97	77		2	54	.300	.394	.484	.878	+21	4	4	50	S119,3b9,1b7/MOfL	9	2.0
CRUZ, JOSE Jose Luis B4.19.1974 Arroyo, PR BB/TR/6'0"/(190–210) [SeaA95 1/3] d5.31 f–Jose Col Rice																								
2005	Bos A	4	12	0	3	1	0	0	0	1	0	0	4	.250	.308	.333	.641	-32	0	0	0	O4R	0	-0.2
Total	10	1259	4419	670	1101	239	33	198	602	616	37	5	1073	.249	.339	.453	.792	+3	107	38	74	O1227(229/592/434),D2	95	-0.6
CULBERSON, LEON Delbert Leon "Lee" B8.6.1919 Halls GA D9.17.1989 Rome GA BR/TR/5'11"/180 d5.16																								
1943	Bos A	81	312	36	85	16	6	3	34	31		0	35	.272	.338	.391	.729	+11	14	0	100	O79(28/51/0)	0	0.6
1944	Bos A	75	282	41	67	11	5	2	21	20		0	20	.238	.288	.333	.621	-22	6	4	60	O72C	0	-1.2
1945	Bos A	97	331	26	91	21	6	6	45	20		0	37	.275	.316	.429	.745	+13	4	3	57	O91(1/89/1)	0	0.4
1946	†Bos A	59	179	34	56	10	1	3	18	16		0	19	.313	.369	.430	.799	+16	3	2	60	O49(6/18/26),3b4	0	-0.1
1947	Bos A	47	84	10	20	1	0	0	11	12		3	10	.238	.354	.250	.604	-35	1	1	50	O25(5/4/16),3b4	0	-0.5
1948	Was A	12	29	1	5	0	0	0	2	8		0	5	.172	.351	.172	.523	-57	0	0	0	O11C	0	-0.3
Total	6	371	1217	148	324	59	18	14	131	107		3	126	.266	.327	.379	.706	+0	28	10	74	O327(40/245/43),3b8	0	-1.1
Team	5	359	1188	147	319	59	18	14	129	99		3	121	.269	.326	.384	.710	+1	28	10	74	O316(37/78/0),3b8	0	-0.8
/150	2	150	496	61	133	25	8	6	54	41		1	51	.269	.326	.384	.710	+1	12	4	75	O132(15/33/0),3b3	0	-0.3
CUMMINGS, MIDRE Midre Almeric B10.14.1971 St.Croix, V.I. BL/TR/6'0"/(190–225) [MinA90 1/29] d9.10																								
1998	†Bos A	67	120	20	34	8	0	5	15	17	0	2	19	.283	.381	.475	.856	+18	3	3	50	D29,O17R	40	0.0
2000	Bos A	21	25	1	7	0	0	0	2	6	0	0	3	.280	.419	.280	.699	-20	0	0	0	O4(0/1/3)/D	0	-0.1
Total	11	460	1113	136	286	60	8	22	124	94	4	9	200	.257	.318	.385	.703	-20	9	6	60	O249(59/95/101),D62	40	-3.7
Team	2	88	145	21	41	8	0	5	17	23	0	2	22	.283	.388	.441	.829	+11	3	3	50	D30,O21(0/1/17)	40	-0.1
CUYLER, MILT Milton B10.7.1968 Macon GA BB/TR/5'10"/(175–185) [DetA86 2/46] d9.6																								
1996	Bos A	50	110	19	22	1	2	2	12	13	0	3	19	.200	.299	.300	.599	-48	7	3	70	O45(0/30/22),D2	109	-0.6
Total	8	490	1386	227	329	47	23	10	119	121	0	16	273	.237	.305	.326	.631	-29	77	26	75	O466(48/398/33),D7	296	-5.5
DAHLGREN, BABE Ellsworth Tenney B6.15.1912 San Francisco CA D9.4.1996 Arcadia CA BR/TR/6'0"/190 d4.16 C1																								
1935	Bos A	149	525	77	138	27	7	9	63	56		3	67	.263	.337	.392	.729	-17	6	5	55	1b149		-3.3
1936	Bos A	16	57	6	16	3	1	1	7	7		0	1	.281	.359	.421	.780	-13	2	1	67	1b16		-0.3
Total	12	1137	4045	470	1056	174	37	82	569	390		22	401	.261	.329	.383	.712	-8	18	11	100	1b1030,3b48,S25/C	0	-16.1
Team	2	165	582	83	154	30	8	10	70	63		3	68	.265	.339	.395	.734	-17	8	6	57	1b165		-3.6
/150	2	150	529	75	140	27	7	9	64	57		3	62	.265	.339	.395	.734	-17	7	5	58	1b150		-3.3
DALEY, PETE Peter Harvey B1.14.1930 Grass Valley CA BR/TR/6'0"/195 d5.3																								
1955	Bos A	17	50	4	11	2	1	0	5	3	0	0	6	.220	.264	.300	.564	-53	0	0	0	C14	0	-0.2
1956	Bos A	59	187	22	50	11	3	5	29	18	5	2	30	.267	.338	.439	.777	-8	1	0	100	C57	0	-0.5
1957	Bos A	78	191	17	43	10	0	3	25	16	4	1	31	.225	.288	.325	.613	-36	0	0	0	C77	0	-0.5
1958	Bos A	27	56	10	18	2	1	2	8	7	1	0	11	.321	.397	.500	.897	+36	0	0	0	C27	0	0.4
1959	Bos A	65	169	9	38	7	0	1	11	13	1	0	31	.225	.279	.284	.563	-47	1	1	50	C58	0	-0.2
1960	KC A	73	228	19	60	10	2	5	25	16	1	0	41	.263	.311	.390	.701	-12	0	0	0	C61/lf	0	-0.7
1961	Was A	72	203	12	39	7	1	2	17	14	3	0	37	.192	.244	.266	.510	-63	0	1	0	C72	0	-1.6
Total	7	391	1084	93	259	49	8	18	120	87	15	3	187	.239	.297	.349	.646	-29	2	2	50	C366/lf	0	-3.3
Team	5	246	653	62	160	32	5	11	78	57	11	3	109	.245	.308	.360	.668	-26	2	1	67	C233	0	-1.0
/150	3	150	398	38	98	20	3	7	48	35	7	2	66	.245	.308	.360	.668	-26	1	1	50	C142	0	-0.6
DALLESSANDRO, DOM Nicholas Dominic "Dim Dom" B10.3.1913 Reading PA D4.29.1988 Indianapolis IN BL/TL/5'6"/168 d4.24 Mil 1945																								
1937	Bos A	68	147	18	34	7	1	0	11	27		0	16	.231	.351	.293	.644	-39	2	1	67	O35(30/1/4)		-1.1
Total	8	746	1945	242	520	110	23	22	303	310		3	150	.267	.369	.381	.750	+12	16	1	100	O505(370/125/12)	0	0.4
DAMON, JOHNNY Johnny David B11.5.1973 Fort Riley KS BL/TL/6'2"/(175–190) [KCA92 1/35] d8.12																								
1995	KC A	47	188	32	53	11	5	3	23	12	0	1	22	.282	.324	.441	.765	-4	7	0	100	O47(0/44/4)	0	-0.4
1996	KC A	145	517	61	140	22	5	6	50	31	3	3	64	.271	.313	.368	.681	-28	25	5	83	O144(0/89/63)/D	0	-2.0
1997	KC A	146	472	70	130	12	8	8	48	42	2	3	70	.275	.338	.386	.724	-14	16	10	62	O136(48/65/47),D5	0	-0.8
1998	KC A	**161**	642	104	178	30	10	18	66	58	4	4	84	.277	.339	.439	.778	-3	26	12	68	O158(14/130/24)	0	-0.4
1999	KC A	145	583	101	179	39	9	14	77	67	5	3	50	.307	.379	.477	.856	+13	36	6	86	O140(132/8/3),D4	0	1.2
2000	KC A	159	655	**136**	214	42	10	16	88	65	4	1	60	.327	.382	.495	.877	+15	**46**	9	84	O133(67/69/0),D25	0	2.0
2001	†Oak A	155	644	108	165	34	4	9	49	61	1	5	70	.256	.324	.363	.687	-19	27	12	69	O154(67/86/5)	0	-2.2
2002	Bos A★	154	623	118	178	34	**11**	14	63	65	5	6	70	.286	.356	.443	.799	+10	31	6	84	O151C/D	0	1.0
2003	†Bos A	145	608	103	166	32	6	12	67	68	4	2	74	.273	.345	.405	.750	-6	30	6	83	O144C/D	0	0.0
2004	†Bos A	150	621	123	189	35	6	20	94	76	1	2	71	.304	.380	.477	.857	+15	19	8	70	O148C/D	0	1.4
2005	†Bos A★	148	624	117	197	35	6	10	75	53	3	2	69	.316	.366	.439	.805	+10	18	1	95	O147C/D	0	1.9
2006	†NY A	149	593	115	169	35	5	24	80	67	1	4	85	.285	.359	.482	.841	+16	25	10	71	O131C,D16/1	0	1.0
Total	12	1704	6770	1188	1958	361	85	154	780	665	33	36	789	.289	.353	.436	.789	+1	306	85	78	O1633(328/1212/146),D55/1	0	2.7
Team	4	597	2476	461	730	136	29	56	299	262	13	12	284	.295	.362	.441	.803	+7	98	21	82	O590C,D4	0	4.3
/150	1	150	622	116	183	34	7	14	75	66	3	3	71	.295	.362	.441	.803	+7	25	5	83	O148C/D	0	1.1
DANZIG, BABE Harold Paul B4.30.1887 Binghamton NY D7.14.1931 San Francisco CA BR/TR/6'2"/205 d4.12																								
1909	Bos A	6	13	0	2	0	0	0	0	2		1		.154	.313	.154	.467	-53	0			1b3		-0.2
DARWIN, BOBBY Arthur Bobby Lee B2.16.1943 Los Angeles CA BR/TR/6'2"/(190–200) d9.30																								
1976	Bos A	43	106	9	19	5	2	3	13	2	0	3	35	.179	.216	.349	.565	-43	1	0	100	O17(3/0/14),D16	0	-0.7
1977	Bos A	4	9	1	2	1	0	0	1	0	0	0	4	.222	.222	.333	.555	-56	0	0	0	/rfD	0	-0.1
Total	9	646	2224	250	559	76	16	83	328	160	13	37	577	.251	.311	.412	.723	+3	15	9	63	O538(37/87/417),D48,P4	34	-4.3
Team	2	47	115	10	21	6	2	3	14	2	0	3	39	.183	.217	.348	.565	-44	1	0	100	O18(3/0/14),D17	0	-0.8
DAUBACH, BRIAN Brian Michael B2.11.1972 Belleville IL BL/TR/6'1"/(201–230) [NYN90 17/469] d9.10																								
1998	Fla N	10	15	0	3	1	0	0	3	1	0	1	5	.200	.294	.267	.561	-48	0	0	0	1b4	0	-0.2

Year	Tm Lg	G	AB	R	H	2B	3B	HR	RBI	BB	IB	HP	SO	AVG	OBP	SLG	OPS	AOPS	SB	CS	SB%	Games at Position	DL	BFW
1999	†Bos A	110	381	61	112	33	3	21	73	36	0	3	92	.294	.360	.562	.922	+26	0	1	0	1b61,D43,O2L/3	0	0.6
2000	Bos A	142	495	55	123	32	2	21	76	44	2	6	130	.248	.315	.448	.763	-11	1	1	50	1b83,D41,O8(7/0/1)/3	0	-1.6
2001	Bos A	122	407	54	107	28	3	22	71	53	7	5	108	.263	.350	.509	.859	+24	1	0	100	1b106,O14(6/0/8)	17	0.5
2002	Bos A	137	444	62	118	24	2	20	78	51	4	7	126	.266	.348	.464	.812	+12	2	1	67	1b60,O48(35/0/13),D28	0	-0.3
2003	Chi A	95	183	26	42	11	0	6	21	34	1	1	54	.230	.352	.388	.740	-8	1	0	100	1b45,D14,O12(3/0/9)	0	-0.6
2004	Bos A	30	75	9	17	8	0	2	8	10	0	1	21	.227	.326	.413	.739	-14	0	0	0	1b14,O7(6/0/1)	0	-0.2
2005	NY N	15	25	4	3	2	0	1	3	7	1	1	5	.120	.324	.320	.644	-26	0	0	0	1b6,D2	0	-0.1
Total	8	661	2025	271	525	139	10	93	333	236	15	25	541	.259	.341	.476	.817	+7	5	3	63	1b379,D128,O91(59/0/32),3b2	17	-1.9
Team	5	541	1802	241	477	125	10	86	306	194	13	22	477	.265	.341	.488	.829	+10	4	3	57	1b324,D112,O79(14/9/9),3b2	17	-1.0
/150	1	150	500	67	132	35	3	24	85	54	4	6	132	.265	.341	.488	.829	+10	1	1	50	1b90,D31,O22(4/2/2)/3	5	-0.3
DAUGHTERS, BOB Robert Francis "Red" B8.5.1914 Cincinnati OH D8.22.1988 Southbury CT BR/TR/6'2"/185 d4.24 Col Holy Cross																								
1937	Bos A	1	0	1	0	0	0	0	0	0		0	0	+	+	+	.000	-100	0	0	0	/R		0.0
DAWSON, ANDRE Andre Nolan B7.10.1954 Miami FL BR/TR/6'3"/(180–197) [MonN75 11/250] d9.11 Col Florida A&M																								
1993	Bos A	121	461	44	126	29	1	13	67	17	4	13	49	.273	.313	.425	.738	-8	2	1	67	D97,O20R	19	-1.2
1994	Bos A	75	292	34	70	18	0	16	48	9	3	4	53	.240	.271	.466	.737	-18	2	2	50	D74	31	-1.3
Total	21	2627	9927	1373	2774	503	98	438	1591	589	14	111	1509	.279	.323	.482	.805	+18	314	109	74	O2323(39/1027/1284),D171	219	17.2
Team	2	196	753	78	196	47	1	29	115	26	7	17	102	.260	.297	.441	.738	-12	4	3	57	D171,O20R	50	-2.5
/150	2	150	576	60	150	36	1	22	88	20	5	13	78	.260	.297	.441	.738	-12	3	2	60	D131,O15R	38	-1.9
DEER, ROB Robert George B9.29.1960 Orange CA BR/TR/6'3"/(210–230) [SFN78 4/85] d9.4																								
1993	Bos A	38	143	18	28	6	1	7	16	20	0	2	49	.196	.303	.399	.702	-18	2	0	100	O36R,D2	0	-0.2
Total	11	1155	3881	578	853	148	13	230	600	575	27	32	1409	.220	.324	.442	.766	+8	43	31	58	O1053(186/5/871),1b47,D21	99	2.2
DEININGER, PEP Otto Charles B10.10.1877 Wasseralfingen, Germany D9.25.1950 Boston MA BL/TL/5'8.5"/180 d4.26▲																								
1902	Bos A	2	6	0	2	1	1	0	0	0		0		.333	.333	.833	1.166	+110	0			P2		0.0
Total	3	58	175	22	46	10	1	0	16	11		1		.263	.310	.331	.641	-3	5			O46(1/39/6),P2/2		-0.5
DELGADO, ALEX Alexander B1.11.1971 Palmerejo, Zulia, Venez. BR/TR/6'0"/160 d4.4																								
1996	Bos A	26	20	5	5	0	0	0	1	3	0	0	3	.250	.348	.250	.598	-46	0	0	0	C14,O6(5/0/2),3b4/12	0	-0.2
DEMETER, DON Donald Lee B6.25.1935 Oklahoma City OK BR/TR/6'4"/(189–190) d9.18																								
1966	Bos A	73	226	31	66	13	1	9	29	5	1	1	42	.292	.305	.478	.783	+11	1	0	100	O57(0/55/3),1b2	0	-0.2
1967	Bos A	20	43	7	12	5	0	1	4	3	0	0	11	.279	.326	.465	.791	+22	0	0	0	O12(3/1/9)/3	0	0.2
Total	11	1109	3443	467	912	147	17	163	563	180	31	42	658	.265	.307	.459	.766	+8	22	25	47	O802(143/592/92),3b150,1b112	0	-2.0
Team	2	93	269	38	78	18	1	10	33	8	1	1	53	.290	.309	.476	.785	+13	1	0	100	O69(3/56/12),1b2/3	0	0.0
DENTE, SAM Samuel Joseph "Blackie" B4.26.1922 Harrison NJ D4.21.2002 Montclair NJ BR/TR/5'11"/(172–175) d7.10																								
1947	Bos A	46	168	14	39	4	2	0	11	19		0	15	.232	.310	.280	.590	-40	0	1	0	3b46	0	-1.2
Total	9	745	2320	205	585	78	16	4	214	167	1	4	96	.252	.303	.305	.608	-38	9	9	50	S563,3b88,2b56,O6(4/0/2),1b2	0	-10.2
DERRICK, MIKE James Michael B9.19.1943 Columbia SC BL/TR/6'0"/190 d4.9																								
1970	Bos A	24	33	3	7	1	0	0	5	0	0	0	11	.212	.206	.242	.448	-77	0	1	0	O2L/1	0	-0.4
DESAUTELS, GENE Eugene Abraham "Red" B6.13.1907 Worcester MA D11.5.1994 Flint MI BR/TR/5'11"/170 d6.22 Mil 1944–45 Col Holy Cross																								
1930	Det A	42	126	13	24	4	2	0	9	7		1	9	.190	.239	.254	.493	-75	2	0	100	C42		-0.8
1931	Det A	3	11	1	1	0	0	0	1	0		0	1	.091	.091	.091	.182	-150	0	0	0	C3		-0.3
1932	Det A	28	72	8	17	2	0	0	2	13		1	11	.236	.360	.264	.624	-38	0	0	0	C24		0.0
1933	Det A	30	42	5	6	1	0	0	4	4		1	6	.143	.234	.167	.401	-92	0	0	0	C30		-0.4
1937	Bos A	96	305	33	74	10	3	0	27	36		1	26	.243	.325	.295	.620	-45	1	2	33	C94		-1.1
1938	Bos A	108	333	47	97	16	2	2	48	57		1	31	.291	.396	.369	.765	-11	1	1	50	C108		0.7
1939	Bos A	76	226	26	55	14	0	0	21	33		0	13	.243	.340	.305	.645	-36	3	1	75	C73		0.0
1940	Bos A	71	222	19	50	7	1	0	17	32		2	13	.225	.328	.266	.594	-46	0	1	0	C70		-1.6
1941	Cle A	66	189	20	38	5	1	1	17	14		1	12	.201	.260	.254	.514	-62	1	0	100	C66	0	-0.8
1942	Cle A	62	162	14	40	5	0	0	9	12		1	13	.247	.303	.278	.581	-32	1	0	100	C61	71	-0.9
1943	Cle A	68	185	14	38	6	1	0	19	11		0	16	.205	.250	.249	.499	-51	2	0	100	C66	0	-0.7
1945	Cle A	10	9	1	1	0	0	0	0	1		0	1	.111	.200	.111	.311	-109	0	0	0	C10	0	-0.1
1946	Phi A	52	130	10	28	3	1	0	13	12		0	16	.215	.282	.254	.536	-49	1	1	50	C52	0	-0.4
Total	13	712	2012	211	469	73	11	3	187	232		9	168	.233	.315	.285	.600	-43	12	6	67	C699	71	-6.4
Team	4	351	1086	125	276	47	6	2	113	158		4	83	.254	.351	.314	.665	-33	5	5	50	C345		-2.0
/150	2	150	464	53	118	20	3	1	48	68		2	35	.254	.351	.314	.665	-33	2	2	50	C147		-0.9
DEVINE, MICKEY William Patrick B5.9.1892 Albany NY D10.1.1937 Albany NY BR/TR/5'10"/165 d8.2																								
1920	Bos A	8	12	1	2	0	0	0	0	1		0	2	.167	.231	.167	.398	-93	1	0	100	C5		-0.1
Total	3	33	53	7	12	4	0	0	4	3		0	6	.226	.268	.302	.570	-49	1	0	100	C19/3		-0.2
DEVORMER, AL Albert E. B8.19.1891 Grand Rapids MI D8.29.1966 Grand Rapids MI BR/TR/6'0.5"/175 d8.4																								
1918	Chi A	8	19	2	5	2	0	0	0	0		0	4	.263	.263	.368	.631	-10	1			C6/rf		-0.1
1921	†NY A	22	49	6	17	4	0	0	7	2		0	4	.347	.373	.429	.802	+2	2	0	100	C17		0.1
1922	NY A	24	59	8	12	4	1	0	11	1		0	6	.203	.217	.305	.522	-66	0	0	0	C17/1		-0.6
1923	Bos A	74	209	20	54	7	3	0	18	6		1	21	.258	.282	.321	.603	-42	3	0	100	C55,1b2		-1.0
1927	NY N	68	141	14	35	3	1	2	21	11		2	11	.248	.312	.326	.638	-29	1			C54,1b3		-0.7
Total	5	196	477	50	123	20	5	2	57	20		3	46	.258	.292	.333	.625	-35	7	0	100	C149,1b6/rf		-2.3
DIAZ, BO Baudilio Jose (Seijas) B3.23.1953 Cua, Miranda, Venezuela D11.23.1990 Caracas, Distrito Capital, Venez. BR/TR/5'11"/(190–205) d9.6																								
1977	Bos A	2	1	0	0	0	0	0	0	0	0	0	1	.000	.000	.000	.000	-190	0	0	0	C2	0	0.0
Total	13	993	3274	327	834	162	5	87	452	198	22	13	429	.255	.297	.387	.684	-13	9	17	35	C965,D3	336	0.3
DIAZ, JUAN Juan Carlos B2.19.1974 San Jose de las Lajas, Cuba BR/TR/6'2"/228 d6.12																								
2002	Bos A	4	7	2	2	1	0	1	2	1	0	0	2	.286	.375	.857	1.232	+110	0	0	0	/1D	0	0.1
DICKEY, GEORGE George Willard "Skeets" B7.10.1915 Kensett AR D6.16.1976 DeWitt AR BB/TR/6'2"/180 d9.21 Mil 1943–45 b–Bill																								
1935	Bos A	5	11	1	0	0	0	0	1	1		0	3	.000	.083	.000	.083	-172	0	0	0	C4		-0.3
1936	Bos A	10	23	0	1	1	0	0	0	2		0	3	.043	.120	.087	.207	-146	0	0	0	C10		-0.4
Total	6	226	494	36	101	12	0	4	54	63		0	62	.204	.294	.253	.547	-47	4	4	50	C170	0	-2.5
Team	2	15	34	1	1	1	0	0	1	3		0	6	.029	.108	.059	.167	-154	0	0	0	C14		-0.7
DIDIER, BOB Robert Daniel B2.16.1949 Hattiesburg MS BB/TR/6'0"/(180–190) d4.7 C5																								
1974	Bos A	5	14	0	1	0	0	0	1	2	2	0	1	.071	.176	.071	.247	-122	0	0	0	C5	0	-0.3
Total	6	247	751	56	172	25	4	0	51	59	16	2	72	.229	.286	.273	.559	-46	2	3	40	C244	0	-4.5
DILLARD, STEVE Stephen Bradley B2.8.1951 Memphis TN BR/TR/6'1"/(170–180) [BosA72 2/40] d9.28 Col U. of Mississippi																								
1975	Bos A	1	5	2	2	0	0	0	0	0	0	0	0	.400	.400	.400	.800	+17	1	0	100	/2	0	0.1
1976	Bos A	57	167	22	46	14	0	1	15	17	1	0	20	.275	.341	.377	.718	-1	6	4	60	3b18,2b17,S12,D7	0	-0.5
1977	Bos A	66	141	22	34	7	0	1	13	7	0	0	13	.241	.270	.312	.582	-46	4	3	57	2b45,S9,D6	0	-0.7
Total	8	438	1013	148	246	50	6	13	102	76	7	2	147	.243	.295	.343	.638	-28	15	12	56	2b250,3b85,S25,D17	0	-2.7
Team	3	124	313	46	82	21	0	2	28	24	1	0	33	.262	.310	.348	.658	-20	11	7	61	2b62,S21,3b18,D13	0	-1.1
/150	4	150	379	56	99	25	0	2	34	29	1	0	40	.262	.310	.348	.658	-20	13	8	62	2b75,S25,3b22,D16	0	-1.3
DIMAGGIO, DOM Dominic Paul "The Little Professor" B2.12.1917 San Francisco CA BR/TR/5'9"/(160–168) d4.16 Mil 1943–45 b–Joe b–Vince																								
1940	Bos A	108	418	81	126	32	6	8	46	41		2	46	.301	.367	.464	.831	+9	7	6	54	O94(11/59/26)		0.7
1941	Bos A★	144	584	117	165	37	6	8	58	90		**7**	57	.283	.385	.408	.793	+7	13	6	68	O144C	0	1.0
1942	Bos A☆	151	622	110	178	36	8	14	48	70		6	52	.286	.364	.437	.801	+21	16	10	62	O151C	0	2.7
1946	†Bos A★	142	534	85	169	24	7	7	73	66		1	58	.316	.393	.427	.820	+22	10	6	63	O142C	0	1.7
1947	Bos A	136	513	75	145	21	5	8	71	74		3	62	.283	.376	.390	.766	+5	10	6	63	O134C	0	1.8
1948	Bos A	**155**	648	127	185	40	4	9	87	101		2	58	.285	.383	.401	.784	+4	10	2	83	O155C	0	1.2
1949	Bos A★	145	605	126	186	34	5	8	60	96		2	55	.307	.404	.420	.824	+10	9	7	56	O144C	0	1.3
1950	Bos A★	141	588	**131**	193	30	**11**	7	70	82		4	68	.328	.414	.452	.866	+11	**15**	4	79	O140C	0	1.3
1951	Bos A★	146	639	**113**	189	34	4	12	72	73		2	53	.296	.370	.418	.788	+3	4	7	36	O146C	0	-1.0

Year	Tm Lg	G	AB	R	H	2B	3B	HR	RBI	BB	IB	HP	SO	AVG	OBP	SLG	OPS	AOPS	SB	CS	SB%	Games at Position	DL	BFW
1952	Bos A★	128	486	81	143	20	1	6	33	57		2	61	.294	.371	.377	.748	+0	6	8	43	O123C	0	-0.6
1953	Bos A	3	3	0	1	0	0	0	0	0		0	1	.333	.333	.333	.666	-24	0	0	0	/H	0	0.0
Total	11	1399	5640	1046	1680	308	57	87	618	750		31	571	.298	.383	.419	.802	+9	100	62	62	O1373(11/1338/26)	0	10.1
/150	1	150	605	112	180	33	6	9	66	80		3	61	.298	.383	.419	.802	+9	11	7	61	O15(1/143/3)	0	1.1
DIPIETRO, BOB Robert Louis Paul B9.1.1927 San Francisco CA BR/TR/5'11"/185 d9.23 Col San Jose St.																								
1951	Bos A	4	11	0	1	0	0	0	0	1		0	1	.091	.167	.091	.258	-126	0	0	0	O3R	0	-0.2
DODSON, PAT Patrick Neal B10.11.1959 Santa Monica CA BL/TL/6'4"/(210–220) [BosA80 6/154] d9.5 Col UCLA																								
1986	Bos A	9	12	3	5	2	0	1	3	3	0	0	3	.417	.533	.833	1.366	+163	0	0	0	1b7	0	0.2
1987	Bos A	26	42	4	7	3	0	2	6	8	1	0	13	.167	.288	.381	.669	-23	0	0	0	1b21/D	0	-0.4
1988	Bos A	17	45	5	8	3	1	1	1	6	0	0	17	.178	.275	.356	.631	-28	0	0	0	1b17	0	-0.1
Total	3	52	99	12	20	8	1	4	10	17	1	0	33	.202	.314	.424	.738	-3	0	0	0	1b45/D	0	-0.3
DOERR, BOBBY Robert Pershing B4.7.1918 Los Angeles CA BR/TR/5'11"/175 d4.20 Mil 1944–45 C8 HF1986																								
1937	Bos A	55	147	22	33	5	1	2	14	18		1	25	.224	.313	.313	.626	-44	2	4	33	2b47		-0.6
1938	Bos A	145	509	70	147	26	7	5	80	59		0	39	.289	.363	.397	.760	-14	5	10	33	2b145		0.4
1939	Bos A	127	525	75	167	28	2	12	73	38		1	32	.318	.365	.448	.813	+3	1	10	9	2b126		3.0
1940	Bos A	151	595	87	173	37	10	22	105	57		0	53	.291	.353	.497	.850	+13	10	5	67	2b151		3.1
1941	Bos A★	132	500	74	141	28	4	16	93	43		0	43	.282	.339	.450	.789	+5	1	3	25	2b132	0	0.8
1942	Bos A☆	144	545	71	158	35	5	15	102	67		1	55	.290	.369	.455	.824	+27	4	4	50	2b142	0	4.1
1943	Bos A★	**155**	604	78	163	32	3	16	75	62		1	59	.270	.339	.412	.751	+17	8	8	50	2b155	0	3.2
1944	Bos A★	125	468	95	152	30	10	15	81	58		0	31	.325	.399	**.528**	.927	+66	5	2	71	2b125	0	5.1
1946	†Bos A★	151	583	95	158	34	9	18	116	66		1	67	.271	.346	.453	.799	+15	5	6	45	2b151	0	4.8
1947	Bos A★	146	561	79	145	23	10	17	95	59		0	47	.258	.329	.426	.755	+1	3	3	50	2b146	0	3.3
1948	Bos A★	140	527	94	150	23	6	27	111	83		4	49	.285	.386	.505	.891	+29	3	2	60	2b138	0	3.7
1949	Bos A	139	541	91	167	30	9	18	109	75		0	33	.309	.393	.497	.890	+26	2	2	50	2b139	0	5.1
1950	Bos A★	149	586	103	172	29	**11**	27	120	67		1	42	.294	.367	.519	.886	+14	3	4	43	2b149	0	2.4
1951	Bos A★	106	402	60	116	21	2	13	73	57		1	33	.289	.378	.448	.826	+12	2	1	67	2b106	0	1.9
Total	14	1865	7093	1094	2042	381	89	223	1247	809		11	608	.288	.362	.461	.823	+14	54	64	46	2b1852	0	40.3
/150	1	150	570	88	164	31	7	18	100	65		1	49	.288	.362	.461	.823	+14	4	5	44	2b15	0	3.2
DOMINIQUE, ANDY Andrew John B10.30.1975 Tarzana CA BR/TR/6'0"/220 [PhiN97 26/776] d5.25 Col Nevada–Reno																								
2004	Bos A	7	11	0	2	0	0	0	1	0	0	0	3	.182	.182	.182	.364	-105	0	0	0	1b5/C	0	-0.2
2005	Tor A	2	2	0	0	0	0	0	0	0	0	1	0	.000	.333	.000	.333	-100	0	0	0	/C	0	-0.1
Total	2	9	13	0	2	0	0	0	1	0	0	1	3	.154	.214	.154	.368	-101	0	0	0	1b5,C2	0	-0.3
DONAHUE, JOHN John Frederick "Jiggs" B4.19.1894 Roxbury MA D10.3.1949 Boston MA BB/TR/5'8"/170 d9.25																								
1923	Bos A	10	36	5	10	4	0	0	1	4		0	5	.278	.350	.389	.739	-6	0	1	0	O9R		0.1
DONAHUE, PAT Patrick William B11.8.1884 Springfield OH D1.31.1966 Springfield OH BR/TR/6'0"/175 d5.29 b–Jiggs																								
1908	Bos A	35	86	8	17	2	0	1	6	9		2		.198	.289	.256	.545	-25	0			C32,1b3		0.2
1909	Bos A	65	177	14	42	4	1	2	25	17		1		.237	.308	.305	.613	-8	2			C58		0.4
1910	Bos A	2	4	0	0	0	0	0	0	0		0		.000	.000	.000	.000	-198	0			/C		-0.1
1910	Phi A	14	34	2	5	0	0	0	4	3		1		.147	.237	.147	.384	-79	1			C13		0.1
1910	Cle A	2	6	0	1	0	0	0	0	0		0		.167	.167	.167	.334	-96	0			C2/1		-0.1
1910	Phi A	1	1	0	0	0	0	0	0	0		0		.000	.000	.000	.000	-199	0			/C		0.0
1910	Year	19	45	2	6	0	0	0	4	3		1		.133	.204	.133	.337	-94	1			C17/1		-0.1
Total	3	119	308	24	65	6	1	3	35	29		4		.211	.287	.266	.553	-25	3			C107,1b4		0.5
Team	3	102	267	22	59	6	1	3	31	26		3	0	.221	.297	.285	.582	-16	2			C91,1b3		0.5
/150	4	150	393	32	87	9	1	4	46	38		4	0	.221	.297	.285	.582	-16	3			C134,1b4		0.7
DONNELS, CHRIS Chris Barton B4.21.1966 Los Angeles CA BL/TR/6'0"/185 [NYN87 1/24] d5.7 Col Loyola Marymount																								
1995	Bos A	40	91	13	23	2	2	2	11	9	0	0	18	.253	.317	.385	.702	-20	0	0	0	3b27,1b8,2b3	0	-0.3
Total	8	450	798	83	186	36	5	17	86	103	7	1	165	.233	.319	.355	.674	-18	5	1	83	3b163,1b62,2b22,O6L/P	94	-2.4
DORAN, TOM Thomas J. "Long Tom" B12.2.1880 Westchester Co. NY D6.22.1910 New York NY BL/TR/5'11"/152 d4.19																								
1904	Bos A	12	32	1	4	0	1	0	0	4		1		.125	.243	.188	.431	-65	1			C11		-0.5
1905	Bos A	3	3	0	0	0	0	0	0	0		0		.000	.000	.000	.000	-199	0			/C		0.0
1906	Bos A	2	3	1	0	0	0	0	0	0		0		.000	.000	.000	.000	-199	0			C2		-0.1
Total	3	51	132	10	19	3	1	0	4	12		4		.144	.236	.182	.418	-67	3			C46		-1.6
Team	3	17	38	2	4	0	1	0	0	4		1	0	.105	.209	.158	.367	-84	1			C14		-0.6
DOUGHERTY, PATSY Patrick Henry B10.27.1876 Andover NY D4.30.1940 Bolivar NY BL/TR/6'2"/190 d4.19																								
1902	Bos A	108	438	77	150	12	6	0	34	42		6		.342	.407	.397	.804	+20	20			O102L/3		-0.1
1903	†Bos A	139	590	**107**	**195**	19	12	4	59	33		6		.331	.372	.424	.796	+31	35			O139L		1.8
1904	Bos A	49	195	33	53	5	4	0	4	25		0		.272	.355	.338	.693	+13	10			O49L		0.1
Total	10	1233	4558	678	1294	138	78	17	413	378		54		.284	.346	.360	.706	+17	261			O1181L,3b2		-4.8
Team	3	296	1223	217	398	36	22	4	97	100		12	0	.325	.382	.401	.783	+24	65			O290L/3		1.8
/150	2	150	620	110	202	18	11	2	49	51		6	0	.325	.382	.401	.783	+24	33			O147L/3		0.9
DOWD, TOMMY Thomas Jefferson "Buttermilk Tommy" B4.20.1869 Holyoke MA D7.2.1933 Holyoke MA BR/TR/5'8"/173 d4.8 M2 Col Brown OF(284/331/350)																								
1901	Bos A	**138**	594	104	159	18	7	3	52	38		3		.268	.315	.337	.652	-18	33			O137L,1b2/3		-1.9
Total	10	1321	5514	903	1493	163	88	24	501	370		22	200	.271	.319	.345	.664	-18	368			O961R,2b328,3b37,S6,1b2		-23.9
/150	1	150	646	113	173	20	8	3	57	41		3	0	.268	.315	.337	.652	-18	36			O149L,1b2/3		-2.1
DOYLE, DANNY Howard James B1.24.1917 McLoud OK D12.14.2004 Stillwater OK BB/TR/6'1"/195 d9.14 Mil 1944–45 Col Oklahoma St.																								
1943	Bos A	13	43	2	9	1	0	0	6	7		0	9	.209	.320	.233	.553	-38	0	1	0	C13	0	-0.4
DOYLE, DENNY Robert Dennis B1.17.1944 Glasgow KY BL/TR/5'9"/(170–174) d4.7 b–Brian Col Morehead St.																								
1970	Phi N	112	413	43	86	10	7	2	16	33	3	0	64	.208	.266	.281	.547	-52	6	5	55	2b103	0	-4.4
1971	Phi N	95	342	34	79	12	1	3	24	19	0	5	31	.231	.280	.298	.578	-36	4	2	67	2b91	15	-0.2
1972	Phi N	123	442	33	110	14	2	1	26	31	2	0	33	.249	.295	.296	.591	-32	6	7	46	2b119	0	-2.5
1973	Phi N	116	370	45	101	9	3	3	26	31	8	0	32	.273	.327	.338	.665	-17	1	3	25	2b114	0	0.0
1974	Cal A	147	511	47	133	19	2	1	34	25	2	1	49	.260	.295	.311	.606	-21	6	7	46	2b146,S2	0	1.1
1975	Cal A	8	15	0	1	0	0	0	0	1	0	0	1	.067	.125	.067	.192	-148	0	0	0	2b6/3	0	-0.2
1975	†Bos A	89	310	50	96	21	2	4	36	14	0	1	11	.310	.339	.429	.768	+8	5	7	42	2b84,3b6,S2	0	-1.6
1975	Year	97	325	50	97	21	2	4	36	15	0	1	12	.298	.329	.412	.741	+2	5	7	42	2b90,3b7,S2	0	-1.8
1976	Bos A	117	432	51	108	15	5	0	26	22	0	0	39	.250	.285	.308	.593	-34	8	5	62	2b112	0	-2.7
1977	Bos A	137	455	54	109	13	6	2	49	29	3	4	50	.240	.289	.308	.597	-43	2	4	33	2b137	0	-2.8
Total	8	944	3290	357	823	113	28	16	237	205	18	11	310	.250	.295	.316	.611	-30	38	40	49	2b912,3b7,S4	15	-13.3
Team	3	343	1197	155	313	49	13	6	111	65	3	5	100	.261	.301	.339	.640	-27	15	16	48	2b333,3b6,S2	0	-7.1
/150	1	150	523	68	137	21	6	3	49	28	1	2	44	.261	.301	.339	.640	-27	7	7	50	2b146,3b3/S	0	-3.1
DROPO, WALT Walter "Moose" B1.30.1923 Moosup CT BR/TR/6'5"/(220–225) d4.19 Col Connecticut																								
1949	Bos A	11	41	3	6	2	0	0	1	3		0	7	.146	.205	.195	.400	-94	0	0	0	1b11	0	-0.7
1950	Bos A★	136	559	101	180	28	8	34	**144**	45		5	75	.322	.378	.583	.961	+30	0	0	0	1b134	0	1.3
1951	Bos A	99	360	37	86	14	0	11	57	38		0	52	.239	.312	.369	.681	-24	0	0	0	1b93	0	-1.6
1952	Bos A	37	132	13	35	7	1	6	27	11		2	22	.265	.331	.470	.801	+12	0	0	0	1b35	0	0.0
Total	13	1288	4124	478	1113	168	22	152	704	328	12	24	582	.270	.326	.432	.758	+0	5	6	45	1b1174,3b3	0	-7.1
Team	4	283	1092	154	307	51	9	51	229	97		7	156	.281	.344	.484	.828	+5	0	0	0	1b273	0	-1.0
/150	2	150	579	82	163	27	5	27	121	51		4	83	.281	.344	.484	.828	+5	0	0	0	1b145	0	-0.5
DUFFY, FRANK Frank Thomas B10.14.1946 Oakland CA BR/TR/6'1"/180 [CinN67 S1/6] d9.4 Col Stanford																								
1978	Bos A	64	104	12	27	5	0	0	4	6	0	1	11	.260	.306	.308	.614	-34	1	1	50	3b22,S21,2b12,D6	0	-0.5
1979	Bos A	6	3	0	0	0	0	0	0	0	0	0	1	.000	.000	.000	.000	-195	0	0	0	2b3/1	0	-0.1
Total	10	915	2665	248	619	104	14	26	240	171	7	8	342	.232	.279	.311	.590	-32	49	30	62	S839,3b23,2b16,D6/1	25	-0.6
Team	2	70	107	12	27	5	0	0	4	6	0	1	12	.252	.298	.299	.597	-38	1	1	50	3b22,S21,2b15,D6/1	0	-0.6

Year	Tm Lg	G	AB	R	H	2B	3B	HR	RBI	BB	IB	HP	SO	AVG	OBP	SLG	OPS	AOPS	SB	CS	SB%	Games at Position	DL	BFW
DUGAN, JOE	Joseph Anthony "Jumping Joe" B5.12.1897 Mahanoy City PA D7.7.1982 Norwood MA BR/TR/5'11"/160 d7.5 Col Holy Cross																							
1922	Bos A	84	341	45	98	22	3	3	38	9		1	28	.287	.308	.396	.704	-17	2	3	40	3b64,S21		-1.2
Total	14	1447	5410	665	1516	277	46	42	571	250		42	419	.280	.317	.372	.689	-18	37	28	100	3b1048,S281,2b76,O2L		-16.2
DURST, CEDRIC	Cedric Montgomery B8.23.1896 Austin TX D2.16.1971 San Diego CA BL/TL/5'11"/160 d5.30																							
1930	Bos A	102	302	29	74	19	5	1	24	17		2	24	.245	.290	.351	.641	-36	3	1	75	O75(46/0/29)		-2.3
Total	7	481	1103	145	269	39	17	15	122	75		3	100	.244	.294	.351	.645	-33	7	11	39	O295(134/68/93),1b18		-7.3
/150	1	150	444	43	109	28	7	1	35	25		3	35	.245	.290	.351	.641	-36	4	1	80	O110(68/0/43)		-3.4
DWYER, JIM	James Edward "Pig Pen" B1.3.1950 Evergreen Park IL BL/TL/5'10"/(165–195) [StLN71 11/253] d6.10 Col Southern Illinois																							
1979	Bos A	76	113	19	30	7	0	2	14	17	1	1	9	.265	.361	.381	.742	-4	3	1	75	1b25,O19(6/1/12),D4	0	0.0
1980	Bos A	93	260	41	74	11	1	9	38	28	5	2	23	.285	.357	.438	.795	+11	3	2	60	O65(11/29/27),D12,1b9	0	0.2
Total	18	1328	2761	409	719	115	17	77	349	402	34	12	402	.260	.353	.398	.751	+7	26	15	63	O634(250/75/329),D226,1b75	91	0.7
Team	2	169	373	60	104	18	1	11	52	45	6	3	32	.279	.358	.421	.779	+6	6	3	67	O84(17/30/12),1b34,D16	0	0.2
/150	2	150	331	53	92	16	1	10	46	40	5	3	28	.279	.358	.421	.779	+6	5	3	63	O75(15/27/11),1b30,D14	0	0.2
EASLER, MIKE	Michael Anthony B11.29.1950 Cleveland OH BL/TR/6'1"/(190–196) [HouN69 14/312] d9.5 C6																							
1984	Bos A	156	601	87	188	31	5	27	91	58	4	4	134	.313	.376	.516	.892	+37	1	1	50	D126,1b29	0	2.8
1985	Bos A	155	568	71	149	29	4	16	74	53	1	3	129	.262	.325	.412	.737	-3	0	1	0	D130,O20(18/0/2)	0	-0.9
Total	14	1151	3677	465	1078	189	25	118	522	321	46	17	696	.293	.349	.454	.803	+17	20	26	43	O538(479/0/82),D433,1b29	37	4.5
Team	2	311	1169	158	337	60	9	43	165	111	5	7	263	.288	.351	.465	.816	+18	1	2	33	D256,1b29,O20(18/0/2)	0	1.9
/150	1	150	564	76	163	29	4	21	80	54	2	3	127	.288	.351	.465	.816	+18	0	1	0	D123,1b14,O10(9/0/1)	0	0.9
EGGERT, ELMER	Elmer Albert "Mose" B1.29.1902 Rochester NY D4.9.1971 Rochester NY BR/TR/5'9"/160 d4.27																							
1927	Bos A	5	3	0	0	0	0	0	0	1		0	1	.000	.250	.000	.250	-131	0	0	0	/2		-0.1
EIBEL, HACK	Henry Hack B12.6.1893 Brooklyn NY D10.16.1945 Macon GA BL/TL/5'11"/220 d6.13▲																							
1912	Cle A	1	3	0	0	0	0	0	0	0		0		.000	.000	.000	.000	-197	0			/rf		-0.1
1920	Bos A	29	43	4	8	2	0	0	6	3		0	6	.186	.239	.233	.472	-74	1	1	50	O5(3/0/2),P3/1		-0.5
Total	2	30	46	4	8	2	0	0	6	3		0	6	.174	.224	.217	.441	-81	1	1	100	O6(3/0/3),P3/1		-0.6
ENGLE, CLYDE	Arthur Clyde "Hack" B3.19.1884 Dayton OH D12.26.1939 Boston MA BR/TR/5'10"/190 d4.12 OF(142/111/26)																							
1909	NY A	135	492	66	137	20	5	3	71	47		5		.278	.347	.358	.705	+22	18			O134(119/16/0)		2.3
1910	NY A	5	13	0	3	0	0	0	0	2		0		.231	.333	.231	.564	-27	1			O3L		-0.1
1910	Bos A	106	363	59	96	18	7	2	38	31		2		.264	.326	.369	.695	+15	12			3b51,2b27,O15(0/13/2),S7		0.6
1910	Year	111	376	59	99	18	7	2	38	33		2		.263	.326	.364	.690	+13	13			3b51,2b27,O18(3/13/2),S7		0.5
1911	Bos A	146	514	58	139	13	3	2	48	51		6		.270	.343	.319	.662	-14	24			1b65,3b51,2b13,O10(3/7/0)		-1.0
1912	†Bos A	58	171	32	40	5	3	0	18	28		2		.234	.348	.298	.646	-19	12			1b25,2b15,3b11,S2/rf		-1.0
1913	Bos A	143	498	75	144	17	12	2	50	53		5	41	.289	.363	.384	.747	+16	28			1b133,O2(0/1/1)		-0.1
1914	Bos A	59	134	14	26	2	0	0	9	14		1	11	.194	.275	.209	.484	-54	4	9	31	1b29,2b5,3b3/rf		-1.8
1914	Buf F	32	110	12	28	4	1	0	12	11		1	18	.255	.328	.309	.637	-27	5			3b23,O9(3/0/7)		-1.1
1914	Major	91	244	26	54	6	1	0	21	25	0	2	29	.221	.299	.254	.553	+32	9	9				-2.9
1915	Buf F	141	501	56	131	22	8	3	71	34		3	43	.261	.312	.355	.667	-14	24			O100(14/74/13),2b21,3b17/1		-3.3
1916	Cle A	11	26	1	4	0	0	0	1	0		0	6	.154	.154	.154	.308	-107	0			3b7,1b2/rf		-0.6
Total	8	836	2822	373	748	101	39	12	318	271		25	119	.265	.335	.341	.676	-3	128	9	100	O276L,1b255,3b163,2b81,S9		-6.1
Team	5	512	1680	238	445	55	25	6	163	177		16	52	.265	.341	.338	.679	-3	80	9	100	1b252,3b116,2b60,O29(3/21/3),S9		-3.3
/150	1	150	492	70	130	16	7	2	48	52		5	15	.265	.341	.338	.679	-3	23	3	100	1b74,3b34,2b18,O8(1/6/1),S3		-1.0
ESASKY, NICK	Nicholas Andrew B2.24.1960 Hialeah FL BR/TR/6'3"/(200–215) [CinN78 1/17] d6.19 [DL 1991 Atl N 182, 1992 Atl N 85]																							
1989	Bos A	154	564	79	156	26	5	30	108	66	9	3	117	.277	.355	.500	.855	+30	1	2	33	1b153/lf	0	1.1
Total	8	810	2703	336	677	120	21	122	427	314	23	15	712	.250	.329	.446	.775	+10	18	14	56	1b478,3b230,O98L	530	-4.5
/150	1	150	549	77	152	25	5	29	105	64	9	3	114	.277	.355	.500	.855	+30	1	2	33	1b149/lf	0	1.1
EVANS, AL	Alfred Hubert B9.28.1916 Kenly NC D4.6.1979 Wilson NC BR/TR/5'11"/190 d9.13 Mil 1943–44																							
1951	Bos A	12	24	1	3	1	0	0	2	4		0	2	.125	.250	.167	.417	-87	0	0	0	C10	0	-0.2
Total	12	704	2053	188	514	70	23	13	211	243		7	206	.250	.332	.326	.658	-18	14	9	61	C647	0	-6.8
EVANS, DWIGHT	Dwight Michael "Dewey" B11.3.1951 Santa Monica CA BR/TR/6'2"/(180–208) [BosA69 5/107] d9.16 C2																							
1972	Bos A	18	57	2	15	3	1	1	6	7	0	0	13	.263	.344	.404	.748	+15	0	0	0	O17(16/0/1)	0	0.1
1973	Bos A	119	282	46	63	13	1	10	32	40	2	1	52	.223	.320	.383	.703	-8	5	0	100	O113(17/2/95),D2	0	-0.7
1974	Bos A	133	463	60	130	19	8	10	70	38	2	2	77	.281	.335	.421	.756	+10	4	4	50	O122(1/3/120),D7	0	1.1
1975	†Bos A	128	412	61	113	24	6	13	56	47	3	4	60	.274	.353	.456	.809	+18	3	4	43	O115R,D7	0	2.3
1976	Bos A	146	501	61	121	34	5	17	62	57	4	6	92	.242	.324	.431	.755	+8	6	7	46	O145(0/8/140)/D	0	0.5
1977	Bos A	73	230	39	66	9	2	14	36	28	0	0	58	.287	.363	.526	.889	+25	4	2	67	O63(0/14/54),D6	44	0.5
1978	Bos A★	147	497	75	123	24	2	24	63	65	2	2	119	.247	.336	.449	.785	+8	8	5	62	O142(0/3/140),D4	0	-0.1
1979	Bos A	152	489	69	134	24	1	21	58	69	7	1	76	.274	.364	.456	.820	+14	6	9	40	O149R	0	0.5
1980	Bos A	148	463	72	123	37	5	18	60	64	6	5	98	.266	.358	.484	.842	+23	3	1	75	O144(0/1/144),D2	0	0.7
1981	Bos A★	**108**	412	84	122	19	4	**22**	71	**85**	1	1	85	.296	.415	.522	.937	+59	3	2	60	O108(1/0/107)	0	3.6
1982	Bos A	**162**	609	122	178	37	7	32	98	112	1	1	125	.292	**.402**	.534	.936	+46	3	2	60	O161R/D	0	3.2
1983	Bos A	126	470	74	112	19	4	22	58	70	5	2	97	.238	.338	.436	.774	+4	3	0	100	O99R,D21	19	-0.1
1984	Bos A	**162**	630	**121**	186	37	8	32	104	96	2	4	115	.295	.388	.532	.920	+45	3	1	75	O161R/D	0	2.9
1985	Bos A	159	617	110	162	29	1	29	78	**114**	4	5	105	.263	.378	.454	.832	+22	7	2	78	O152R,D7	0	1.2
1986	†Bos A	152	529	86	137	33	2	26	97	97	4	6	117	.259	.376	.476	.852	+30	3	3	50	O149R/D	0	1.8
1987	Bos A★	154	541	109	165	37	2	34	123	**106**	6	3	98	.305	.417	.569	.986	+55	4	6	40	1b79,O77R,D4	0	2.8
1988	†Bos A	149	559	96	164	31	7	21	111	76	3	1	99	.293	.375	.487	.862	+34	5	1	83	O85(0/1/84),1b64,D6	0	1.6
1989	Bos A	146	520	82	148	27	3	20	100	99	1	3	84	.285	.397	.463	.860	+35	3	3	50	O77R,D69	0	2.3
1990	†Bos A	123	445	66	111	18	3	13	63	67	5	4	73	.249	.349	.391	.740	+3	3	4	43	D122	16	-0.2
1991	Bal A	101	270	35	73	9	1	6	38	54	2	2	54	.270	.393	.378	.771	+19	2	3	40	O67R,D21	27	0.7
Total	20	2606	8996	1470	2446	483	73	385	1384	1391	60	53	1697	.272	.370	.470	.840	+25	78	59	57	O2146(35/32/2092),D282,1b143	106	24.7
Team	19	2505	8726	1435	2373	474	72	379	1346	1337	58	51	1643	.272	.369	.473	.842	+26	76	56	58	O2079(81/115/115),D261,1b143	79	24.0
/150	1	150	523	86	142	28	4	23	81	80	3	3	98	.272	.369	.473	.842	+26	5	3	63	O124(5/7/7),D16,1b9	5	1.4
EVERETT, CARL	Carl Edward B6.3.1971 Tampa FL BB/TR/6'0"/(181–220) [NYA90 1/10] d7.1																							
2000	Bos A★	137	496	82	149	32	4	34	108	52	5	8	113	.300	.373	.587	.960	+35	11	4	73	O126C,D5	0	2.2
2001	Bos A	102	409	61	105	24	4	14	58	27	3	13	104	.257	.323	.438	.761	-2	9	2	82	O93(0/84/9),D7	36	-0.9
Total	14	1405	4809	707	1304	258	26	202	792	442	39	87	1021	.271	.341	.462	.803	+7	107	54	66	O1028(121/675/304),D267	184	1.3
Team	2	239	905	143	254	56	8	48	166	79	8	21	217	.281	.351	.519	.870	+18	20	6	77	O219C,D12	36	1.3
/150	1	150	568	90	159	35	5	30	104	50	5	13	136	.281	.351	.519	.870	+18	13	4	76	O137C,D8	23	0.8
EVERS, HOOT	Walter Arthur B2.8.1921 St.Louis MO D1.25.1991 Houston TX BR/TR/6'2"/185 d9.16 Mil 1943–45 C1 Col Illinois																							
1952	Bos A	106	401	53	105	17	4	14	59	29		4	55	.262	.318	.429	.747	-1	5	2	71	O105(90/12/20)	0	-0.8
1953	Bos A	99	300	39	72	10	1	11	31	23		3	41	.240	.301	.390	.691	-19	2	1	67	O93(78/16/0)	0	-1.6
1954	Bos A	6	8	1	0	0	0	0	0	0		0	2	.000	.000	.000	.000	-190	0	0	0	/lf	0	-0.2
Total	12	1142	3801	556	1055	187	41	98	565	415	0	27	420	.278	.353	.426	.779	+6	45	36	56	O1051(503/486/97)	0	-2.6
Team	3	211	709	93	177	27	5	25	90	52		7	98	.250	.307	.408	.715	-11	7	3	70	O199(168/28/20)	0	-2.6
/150	2	150	504	66	126	19	4	18	64	37		5	70	.250	.307	.408	.715	-11	5	2	71	O141(119/20/14)	0	-1.8
EZZELL, HOMER	Homer Estell B2.28.1896 Victoria TX D8.3.1976 San Antonio TX BR/TR/5'10"/158 d4.22																							
1923	StL A	88	279	31	68	6	0	0	14	15		2	20	.244	.287	.265	.552	-56	4	3	57	3b73,2b8		-1.5
1924	Bos A	90	277	35	75	8	4	0	32	14		2	21	.271	.311	.329	.640	-35	12	5	71	3b64,S21/C		-0.1
1925	Bos A	58	186	40	53	6	4	0	15	19		0	18	.285	.351	.360	.711	-19	9	7	56	3b47,2b9		-0.9
Total	3	236	742	106	196	20	8	0	61	48		4	59	.264	.312	.313	.625	-39	25	15	63	3b184,S21,2b17/C		-2.5
Team	2	148	463	75	128	14	8	0	47	33		2	39	.276	.327	.341	.668	-28	21	12	64	3b111,S21,2b9/C		-1.0
/150	2	150	469	76	130	14	8	0	48	33		2	40	.276	.327	.341	.668	-28	21	12	64	3b113,S21,2b9/C		-1.0
FANZONE, CARMEN	Carmen Ronald B8.30.1943 Detroit MI BR/TR/6'0"/200 d7.21 Col Central Michigan																							
1970	Bos A	10	15	0	3	1	0	0	3	2	0	1	2	.200	.316	.267	.583	-37	0	0	0	3b5	0	-0.1
Total	5	237	588	66	132	27	0	20	94	74	8	6	119	.224	.313	.372	.685	-14	3	6	33	3b104,1b54,2b23,O14(13/0/1)/S	0	-1.6

Year	Tm Lg	G	AB	R	H	2B	3B	HR	RBI	BB	IB	HP	SO	AVG	OBP	SLG	OPS	AOPS	SB	CS	SB%	Games at Position	DL	BFW
FARRELL, DUKE Charles Andrew B8.31.1866 Oakdale MA D2.15.1925 Boston MA BB/TR/6'1"/208 d4.21 C6 OF(48/22/39)																								
1903	†Bos A	17	52	5	21	5	1	0	8	5		1		.404	.466	.538	1.004	+90	1			C17		0.9
1904	Bos A	68	198	11	42	9	2	0	15	15		4		.212	.281	.278	.559	-27	1			C56		-0.1
1905	Bos A	7	21	2	6	1	0	0	2	1		0		.286	.318	.333	.651	+5	0			C7		0.2
Total	18	1565	5682	829	1572	211	123	52	916	480		50	246	.277	.338	.385	.723	+0	150			C1004,3b290,O109L,1b106,S13		9.8
Team	3	92	271	18	69	15	3	0	25	21		5	0	.255	.320	.332	.652	-2	2			C80		1.0
FARRELL, DOC Edward Stephen B12.26.1901 Johnson City NY D12.20.1966 Livingston NJ BR/TR/5'8"/160 d6.15 Col Penn																								
1935	Bos A	4	7	1	2	1	0	0	1	1		0	0	.286	.375	.429	.804	+1	0	0	0	2b4		0.0
Total	9	591	1799	181	467	63	8	10	213	109		10	120	.260	.306	.320	.626	-34	14	1	100	S376,2b118,3b56,1b3		-8.5
FERRELL, RICK Richard Benjamin B10.12.1905 Durham NC D7.27.1995 Bloomfield Hills MI BR/TR/5'10"/160 d4.19 C8 HF1984 b–Wes Col Guilford																								
1933	Bos A★	118	421	50	125	19	4	3	72	58		2	19	.297	.385	.382	.767	+5	2	2	50	C116		1.4
1934	Bos A☆	132	437	50	130	29	4	1	48	66		0	20	.297	.390	.389	.779	-5	0	0	0	C128		1.1
1935	Bos A☆	133	458	54	138	34	4	3	61	65		0	15	.301	.388	.413	.801	+0	5	8	38	C131		2.1
1936	Bos A★	121	410	59	128	27	5	8	55	65		0	17	.312	.406	.461	.867	+8	0	1	0	C121		2.0
1937	Bos A	18	65	8	20	2	0	1	4	15		0	4	.308	.438	.385	.823	+5	0	0	0	C18		0.3
Total	18	1884	6028	687	1692	324	45	28	734	931		10	277	.281	.378	.363	.741	-5	29	35	45	C1806	0	11.5
Team	5	522	1791	221	541	111	17	16	240	269		2	75	.302	.394	.410	.804	+2	7	11	39	C514		6.9
/150	1	150	515	64	155	32	5	5	69	77		1	22	.302	.394	.410	.804	+2	2	3	40	C148		2.0
FERRELL, WES Wesley Cheek B2.2.1908 Greensboro NC D12.9.1976 Sarasota FL BR/TR/6'2"/195 d9.9 b–Rick▲																								
1927	Cle A	1	0	0	0	0	0	0	0	0		0	0	+	+	+	.000	-100	0	0	0	/P		0.0
1928	Cle A	2	4	0	1	0	1	0	0	0		0	0	.250	.250	.750	1.000	+52	0	0	0	P2		0.0
1929	Cle A	47	93	12	22	5	3	1	12	6		0	28	.237	.283	.387	.670	-32	1	0	100	P43		0.0
1930	Cle A	53	118	19	35	8	3	0	14	12		0	15	.297	.362	.415	.777	-7	0	0	0	P43		0.0
1931	Cle A	48	116	24	37	6	1	9	30	10		0	21	.319	.373	.621	.994	+49	0	0	0	P40		0.0
1932	Cle A	55	128	14	31	5	2	2	18	6		0	21	.242	.276	.359	.635	-41	0	0	0	P38		0.0
1933	Cle A☆	61	140	26	38	7	0	7	26	20		0	22	.271	.363	.471	.834	+14	0	0	0	P28,O13L		0.1
1934	Bos A	34	78	12	22	4	0	4	17	7		0	15	.282	.341	.487	.828	+4	1	0	100	P26		0.0
1935	Bos A	75	150	25	52	5	1	7	32	21		0	16	.347	.427	.533	.960	+38	0	0	0	P41		0.0
1936	Bos A	61	135	20	36	6	1	5	24	14		0	10	.267	.336	.437	.773	-16	0	0	0	P39		0.0
1937	Bos A	18	33	7	12	2	0	1	9	7		0	3	.364	.475	.515	.990	+44	0	0	0	P12		0.0
1937	Was A☆	53	106	7	27	5	0	0	16	9		0	18	.255	.313	.302	.615	-42	0	0	0	P25		0.0
1937	Year	71	139	14	39	7	0	1	25	16		0	21	.281	.355	.353	.708	-19	0	0	0	P37		0.0
1938	Was A	26	49	6	11	2	0	1	6	15		0	7	.224	.406	.327	.733	-8	0	0	0	P23		0.0
1938	NY A	5	12	1	2	1	0	0	1	1		0	4	.167	.231	.250	.481	-80	0	0	0	P5		0.0
1938	Year	31	61	7	13	3	0	1	7	16		0	11	.213	.377	.311	.688	-21	0	0	0	P28		0.0
1939	NY A	3	8	0	1	1	0	0	1	0		0	2	.125	.125	.250	.375	-106	0	0	0	P3		0.0
1940	Bro N	2	2	0	0	0	0	0	0	0		0	2	.000	.000	.000	.000	-194	0			/P		0.0
1941	Bos N	4	4	2	2	0	0	1	2	1		0	1	.500	.600	1.250	1.850	+330	0			P4	0	0.0
Total	15	548	1176	175	329	57	12	38	208	129		0	185	.280	.351	.446	.797	-1	2	0	100	P374,O13L	0	0.1
Team	4	188	396	64	122	17	2	17	82	49		0	44	.308	.384	.490	.874	+14	1	0	100	P118		0.0
/150	3	150	316	51	97	14	2	14	65	39		0	35	.308	.384	.490	.874	+14	1	0	100	P94		0.0
FERRIS, HOBE Albert Sayles B12.7.1877 Providence RI D3.18.1938 Detroit MI BR/TR/5'8"/162 d4.26																								
1901	Bos A	**138**	523	68	131	16	15	2	63	23		6		.250	.290	.350	.640	-22	13			2b138/S		-0.8
1902	Bos A	134	499	57	122	16	14	8	63	21		1		.244	.276	.381	.657	-21	11			2b134		0.7
1903	†Bos A	**141**	525	69	132	19	7	9	66	25		1		.251	.287	.366	.653	-10	11			2b139,S2		0.8
1904	Bos A	156	563	50	120	23	10	3	63	23		1		.213	.245	.306	.551	-30	7			2b156		-2.2
1905	Bos A	142	523	51	115	24	16	6	59	23		0		.220	.253	.361	.614	-7	11			2b142		0.9
1906	Bos A	130	495	47	121	25	13	2	44	10		2		.244	.262	.360	.622	-6	8			2b126,3b4		0.3
1907	Bos A	150	561	41	135	25	2	4	60	10		0		.241	.254	.314	.568	-18	11			2b150		-0.6
1908	StL A	148	555	54	150	26	7	2	74	14		2		.270	.291	.353	.644	+8	6			3b148		2.3
1909	StL A	148	556	36	120	18	5	4	58	12		0		.216	.232	.288	.520	-31	11			3b114,2b34		-1.5
Total	9	1287	4800	473	1146	192	89	40	550	161		13		.239	.265	.341	.606	-16	89			2b1019,3b266,S3		-0.1
Team	7	991	3689	383	876	148	77	34	418	135		11	0	.237	.266	.347	.613	-17	72			2b985,3b4,S3		-0.9
/150	1	150	558	58	133	22	12	5	63	20		2	0	.237	.266	.347	.613	-17	11			2b149/3S		-0.1
FEWSTER, CHICK Wilson Lloyd B11.10.1895 Baltimore MD D4.16.1945 Baltimore MD BR/TR/5'11"/160 d9.19																								
1922	Bos A	23	83	8	24	4	1	0	9	6		1	10	.289	.344	.361	.705	-15	8	3	73	3b23		0.2
1923	Bos A	90	284	32	67	10	1	0	15	39		3	35	.236	.334	.278	.612	-38	7	14	33	2b49,S37,3b3		-2.3
Total	11	644	1963	282	506	91	12	6	167	240		25	264	.258	.346	.326	.672	-23	57	47	100	2b366,O123(42/52/30),S67,3b43		-9.9
Team	2	113	367	40	91	14	2	0	24	45		4	45	.248	.337	.297	.634	-33	15	17	47	2b49,S37,3b26		-2.1
/150	3	150	487	53	121	19	3	0	32	60		5	60	.248	.337	.297	.634	-33	20	23	47	2b65,S49,3b35		-2.8
FINNEY, LOU Louis Klopsche B8.13.1910 Buffalo AL D4.22.1966 Lafayette AL BL/TR/6'0"/180 d9.12 Def 1943–45 b–Hal																								
1931	Phi A	9	24	7	9	0	1	0	3	6		1	1	.375	.516	.458	.974	+49	0	0	0	O8R		0.3
1933	Phi A	74	240	26	64	12	2	3	32	13		1	17	.267	.307	.371	.678	-22	1	3	25	O63(17/1/46)		-1.0
1934	Phi A	92	272	32	76	11	4	1	28	14		0	17	.279	.315	.360	.675	-23	4	3	57	O54(12/4/40),1b15		-1.4
1935	Phi A	109	410	45	112	11	6	0	31	18		2	18	.273	.307	.329	.636	-35	7	2	78	O76(5/0/72),1b18		-2.8
1936	Phi A	151	653	100	197	26	10	1	41	47		3	22	.302	.351	.377	.728	-19	7	9	44	1b78,O73(22/21/32)		-3.4
1937	Phi A	92	379	53	95	14	9	1	20	20		0	16	.251	.288	.343	.631	-41	2	5	29	1b50,O39(2/37/0)/2		-3.4
1938	Phi A	122	454	61	125	21	12	10	48	39		0	25	.275	.333	.441	.774	-6	5	8	38	1b64,O46(19/21/6)		-2.0
1939	Phi A	9	22	1	3	0	0	0	1	2		0	0	.136	.208	.136	.344	-110	0	0	0	O4(0/3/1)		-0.4
1939	Bos A	95	249	43	81	18	3	1	46	24		0	11	.325	.385	.434	.819	+5	2	5	29	1b32,O24(3/16/5)		-0.7
1939	Year	104	271	44	84	18	3	1	47	26		0	11	.310	.370	.410	.780	-4	2	5	29	1b32,O28(3/19/6)		-1.1
1940	Bos A★	130	534	73	171	31	15	5	73	33		0	13	.320	.360	.463	.823	+7	5	2	71	O69R,1b51		-0.5
1941	Bos A	127	497	83	143	24	10	4	53	38		1	17	.288	.340	.400	.740	-7	2	5	29	O92(1/0/91),1b24	0	-1.9
1942	Bos A	113	397	58	113	16	7	3	61	29		1	11	.285	.335	.383	.718	-2	3	3	50	O95(3/1/92),1b2	0	-1.0
1944	Bos A	68	251	37	72	11	2	0	32	23		0	7	.287	.347	.347	.694	+0	1	0	100	1b59,O2(1/0/1)	0	-0.8
1945	Bos A	2	2	0	0	0	0	0	0	0		0	1	.000	.000	.000	.000	-198	0	0	0	/H	0	-0.1
1945	StL A	57	213	24	59	8	4	2	22	21		1	6	.277	.345	.380	.725	+5	0	0	0	O36(24/0/13),1b22/3	0	-0.2
1945	Year	59	215	24	59	8	4	2	22	21		1	7	.274	.342	.377	.719	+3	0	0	0	O36(24/0/13),1b22/3	0	-0.3
1946	StL A	16	30	0	9	0	0	0	3	2		0	4	.300	.344	.300	.644	-23	0	0	0	O7(4/0/3)	0	-0.1
1947	Phi N	4	4	0	0	0	0	0	0	0		0	0	.000	.000	.000	.000	-199	0			/H	0	-0.1
Total	15	1270	4631	643	1329	203	85	31	494	329		10	186	.287	.336	.388	.724	-12	39	45	100	O688(113/104/479),1b415/32	0	-19.5
Team	6	535	1930	294	580	100	37	13	265	147		2	60	.301	.351	.411	.762	+0	13	15	46	O282(4/200/189),1b168	0	-5.0
/150	2	150	541	82	163	28	10	4	74	41		1	17	.301	.351	.411	.762	+0	4	4	50	O79(1/56/53),1b47	0	-1.4
FIORE, MIKE Michael Gary Joseph B10.11.1944 Brooklyn NY BL/TL/6'0"/(180–185) d9.21																								
1968	Bal A	6	17	2	1	0	0	0	0	4	0	1	4	.059	.273	.059	.332	-95	0	0	0	1b5/lf	0	-0.3
1969	KC A	107	339	53	93	14	1	12	35	84	4	2	63	.274	.420	.428	.848	+36	4	4	50	1b91,O13(3/8/2)	0	2.7
1970	KC A	25	72	6	13	2	0	0	4	13	0	0	24	.181	.306	.208	.514	-56	1	1	50	1b20	0	-0.6
1970	Bos A	41	50	5	7	0	0	0	4	8	1	0	4	.140	.254	.140	.394	-88	0	0	0	1b17,O2(1/0/1)	0	-0.7
1970	Year	66	122	11	20	2	0	0	8	21	1	0	28	.164	.285	.180	.465	-70	1	1	50	1b37,O2(1/0/1)	0	-1.3
1971	Bos A	51	62	9	11	2	0	1	6	12	1	0	14	.177	.311	.258	.569	-42	0	3	0	1b12	0	-0.5
1972	StL N	17	10	0	1	0	0	0	1	2	0	0	3	.100	.250	.100	.350	-97	0	0	0	1b6/rf	0	-0.2
1972	SD N	7	6	0	0	0	0	0	0	1	1	0	3	.000	.143	.000	.143	-161	0	0	0	/H	0	-0.1
1972	Year	24	16	0	1	0	0	0	1	3	1	0	6	.063	.211	.063	.274	-120	0	0	0	1b6/rf	0	-0.3
Total	5	254	556	75	126	18	1	13	50	124	7	3	115	.227	.369	.333	.702	-4	5	8	38	1b151,O17(5/8/4)	0	0.3
Team	2	92	112	14	18	2	0	1	10	20	2	0	18	.161	.286	.205	.491	-62	0	3	0	1b29,O2(1/0/1)	0	-1.2

Year	Tm Lg	G	AB	R	H	2B	3B	HR	RBI	BB	IB	HP	SO	AVG	OBP	SLG	OPS	AOPS	SB	CS	SB%	Games at Position	DL	BFW
FISK, CARLTON Carlton Ernest "Pudge" B12.26.1947 Bellows Falls VT BR/TR/6'2"/(200–235) [BosA67*1/4] d9.18 HF2000 Col New Hampshire																								
1969	Bos A	2	5	0	0	0	0	0	0	0	0	0	2	.000	.000	.000	.000	-196	0	0	0	/C	0	-0.3
1971	Bos A	14	48	7	15	2	1	2	6	1	0	0	10	.313	.327	.521	.848	+27	0	0	0	C14	0	0.1
1972	Bos A★	131	457	74	134	28	**9**	22	61	52	6	4	83	.293	.370	.538	.908	+59	5	2	71	C131	0	5.1
1973	Bos A★	135	508	65	125	21	0	26	71	37	2	10	99	.246	.309	.441	.750	+3	7	2	78	C131,D3	0	1.9
1974	Bos A✱	52	187	36	56	12	1	11	26	24	2	2	23	.299	.383	.551	.934	+56	5	1	83	C50,D2	119	2.3
1975	†Bos A	79	263	47	87	14	4	10	52	27	4	2	32	.331	.395	.529	.924	+47	4	3	57	C71,D6	77	2.4
1976	Bos A★	134	487	76	124	17	5	17	58	56	3	6	71	.255	.336	.415	.751	+7	12	5	71	C133/D	0	3.3
1977	Bos A★	152	536	106	169	26	3	26	102	75	3	9	85	.315	.402	.521	.923	+36	7	6	54	C151	0	4.6
1978	Bos A★	157	571	94	162	39	5	20	88	71	6	7	83	.284	.366	.475	.841	+23	7	2	78	C154/lfD	0	3.9
1979	Bos A	91	320	49	87	23	2	10	42	10	0	6	38	.272	.304	.450	.754	-4	3	0	100	D42,C39/lf	37	-0.6
1980	Bos A★	131	478	73	138	25	3	18	62	36	6	**13**	62	.289	.353	.467	.820	+17	11	5	69	C115,O5L,1b3,3b3,D5	0	1.2
1981	Chi A★	96	338	44	89	12	0	7	45	38	3	12	37	.263	.354	.361	.715	+9	3	2	60	C92/13lf	0	1.3
1982	Chi A★	135	476	66	127	17	3	14	65	46	7	6	60	.267	.336	.403	.739	+2	17	2	89	C133,1b2	0	1.5
1983	†Chi A	138	488	85	141	26	4	26	86	46	3	6	88	.289	.355	.518	.873	+32	9	6	60	C133,D2	0	3.1
1984	Chi A	102	359	54	83	20	1	21	43	26	4	5	60	.231	.289	.468	.757	+1	6	0	100	C90,D5	22	-0.2
1985	Chi A★	153	543	85	129	23	1	37	107	52	12	17	81	.238	.320	.488	.808	+13	17	9	65	C130,D28	0	2.1
1986	Chi A	125	457	42	101	11	0	14	63	22	2	6	92	.221	.263	.337	.600	-39	2	4	33	C71,O31L,D22	0	-1.8
1987	Chi A	135	454	68	116	22	1	23	71	39	8	8	72	.256	.321	.460	.781	+2	1	4	20	C122,1b9,O2L,D7	0	1.5
1988	Chi A	76	253	37	70	8	1	19	50	37	9	5	40	.277	.377	.542	.919	+55	0	0	0	C74	78	2.2
1989	Chi A	103	375	47	110	25	2	13	68	36	8	3	60	.293	.356	.475	.831	+36	1	0	100	C90,D13	51	1.7
1990	Chi A	137	452	65	129	21	0	18	65	61	8	7	73	.285	.378	.451	.829	+34	7	2	78	C116,D14	0	4.1
1991	Chi A★	134	460	42	111	25	0	18	74	32	4	7	86	.241	.299	.413	.712	-3	1	2	33	C106,D13,1b12	0	0.9
1992	Chi A	62	188	12	43	4	1	3	21	23	5	1	38	.229	.313	.309	.622	-24	3	0	100	C54,D2	59	-0.4
1993	Chi A	25	53	2	10	0	0	1	4	2	0	1	11	.189	.228	.245	.473	-71	0	1	0	C25	0	-1.1
Total	24	2499	8756	1276	2356	421	47	376	1330	849	10	143	1386	.269	.341	.457	.798	+16	128	58	69	C2226,D166,O41L,1b27,3b4	443	38.8
Team	11	1078	3860	627	1097	207	33	162	568	389	32	59	588	.284	.356	.481	.837	+25	61	26	70	C989,D60,O7L,1b3,3b3	233	23.9
/150	2	150	537	87	153	29	5	23	79	54	4	8	82	.284	.356	.481	.837	+25	8	4	67	C138,D8/OfL13	32	3.3
FITZGERALD, HOWIE Howard Chumney "Lefty" B5.16.1902 Eagle Lake TX D2.27.1959 Matthews TX BL/TL/5'11.5"/163 d9.17 Col Texas																								
1922	Chi N	10	24	3	8	1	0	0	4	3		0	2	.333	.407	.375	.782	+1	1	0	100	O6R		-0.1
1924	Chi N	7	19	1	3	0	0	0	2	0		0	2	.158	.158	.158	.316	-115	0	0	0	O5(0/1/4)		-0.4
1926	Bos A	31	97	11	25	2	0	0	8	5		0	7	.258	.294	.278	.572	-48	1	4	20	O23(21/0/2)		-1.3
Total	3	48	140	15	36	3	0	0	14	8		0	11	.257	.297	.279	.576	-48	2	4	33	O34(21/1/12)		-1.8
FLAGSTEAD, IRA Ira James "Pete" B9.22.1893 Montague MI D3.13.1940 Olympia WA BR/TR/5'9"/165 d7.20 Mil 1918																								
1917	Det A	4	4	0	0	0	0	0	0	0		0	1	.000	.000	.000	.000	-199	0			O2R		-0.1
1919	Det A	97	287	43	95	22	3	5	41	35		7	39	.331	.416	.481	.897	+55	6			O83R		2.0
1920	Det A	110	311	40	73	13	5	3	35	37		1	27	.235	.318	.338	.656	-24	3	4	43	O82(1/6/75)		-1.3
1921	Det A	85	259	40	79	16	2	0	31	21		6	21	.305	.371	.382	.753	-7	8	4	67	S55,O12(6/2/5),2b8/3		-0.3
1922	Det A	44	91	21	28	5	3	3	8	14		2	16	.308	.411	.527	.938	+48	0	1	0	O32(8/9/15)		0.5
1923	Det A	1	1	0	0	0	0	0	0	0		0	0	.000	.000	.000	.000	-199	0	0	0	/H		0.0
1923	Bos A	109	382	55	119	23	4	8	53	37		5	26	.312	.380	.455	.835	+19	7	10	41	O102(0/3/99)/S		1.3
1923	Year	110	383	55	119	23	4	8	53	37		5	26	.311	.379	.454	.833	+18	7	10	41	O102(0/3/99)/S		1.3
1924	Bos A	149	560	106	172	35	7	5	43	77		11	41	.307	.401	.421	.822	+12	10	13	43	O144(0/143/1)		-0.4
1925	Bos A	148	572	84	160	38	2	6	61	63		5	30	.280	.356	.385	.741	-12	5	6	45	O144C		-0.2
1926	Bos A	98	415	65	124	31	7	3	31	36		6	22	.299	.363	.429	.792	+10	4	6	40	O98C		0.2
1927	Bos A	131	466	63	133	26	8	4	69	57		9	25	.285	.374	.401	.775	+3	12	2	86	O129(0/128/1)		0.4
1928	Bos A	140	510	84	148	41	4	1	39	60		1	23	.290	.366	.392	.758	+1	12	9	57	O135C		-0.1
1929	Bos A	14	36	9	11	2	0	0	3	5		0	1	.306	.390	.361	.751	-3	1	3	25	O13(13/1/0)		-0.2
1929	Was A	18	39	5	7	1	0	0	9	4		0	5	.179	.256	.205	.461	-80	1	0	100	O11(1/10/0)		-0.2
1929	Year	32	75	14	18	3	0	0	12	9		0	6	.240	.321	.280	.601	-43	2	3	40	O24(14/11/0)		-0.4
1929	Pit N	26	50	8	14	2	1	0	6	4		0	2	.280	.333	.360	.693	-30	1			O9(6/1/2)		-0.3
1929	Major	58	125	22	32	5	1	0	18	13	0	0	8	.256	.326	.312	.638	-54	3	3				-0.7
1930	Pit N	44	156	21	39	7	4	2	21	17		0	9	.250	.324	.385	.709	-30	1			O40(21/15/5)		-1.0
Total	13	1218	4139	644	1202	262	50	40	450	467		53	288	.290	.370	.407	.777	+3	71	58	100	O1036(56/695/288),S56,2b8/3		0.3
Team	7	789	2941	466	867	196	32	27	299	335		37	168	.295	.374	.411	.785	+4	51	49	51	O765(128/149/100)/S		1.0
/150	1	150	559	89	165	37	6	5	57	64		7	32	.295	.374	.411	.785	+4	10	9	53	O145(24/28/19)/S		0.2
FLAHERTY, JOHN John Timothy B10.21.1967 New York NY BR/TR/6'1"/(195–205) [BosA88 25/641] d4.12 Col George Washington																								
1992	Bos A	35	66	3	13	2	0	0	2	3	0	0	7	.197	.229	.227	.456	-73	0	0	0	C34	0	-1.2
1993	Bos A	13	25	3	3	2	0	0	2	2	0	1	6	.120	.214	.200	.414	-89	0	0	0	C13	0	-0.5
Total	14	1047	3372	319	849	176	3	80	395	175	15	19	514	.252	.290	.377	.667	-27	10	19	34	C1032,D2/1	25	-13.2
Team	2	48	91	6	16	4	0	0	4	5	0	1	13	.176	.224	.220	.444	-78	0	0	0	C47	0	-1.7
FLAIR, AL Albert Dell "Broadway" B7.24.1916 New Orleans LA D7.26.1988 New Orleans LA BL/TL/6'4"/195 d9.6 Mil 1942–45 Col Louisiana St.																								
1941	Bos A	10	30	3	6	2	1	0	2	1		0	1	.200	.226	.333	.559	-55	1	1	50	1b8	0	-0.3
FLETCHER, SCOTT Scott Brian B7.30.1958 Fort Walton Beach FL BR/TR/5'11"/(150–173) [ChiN79 S1/6] d4.25 Col Georgia Southern																								
1993	Bos A	121	480	81	137	31	5	5	45	37	1	5	35	.285	.341	.402	.743	-7	16	3	84	2b116,S2/3D	15	1.6
1994	Bos A	63	185	31	42	9	1	3	11	16	1	2	14	.227	.296	.335	.631	-41	8	1	89	2b53,D4	29	0.3
Total	15	1612	5258	688	1376	243	38	34	510	514	13	57	541	.262	.332	.342	.674	-16	99	58	63	S839,2b729,3b84,D11/1	80	6.4
Team	2	184	665	112	179	40	6	8	56	53	2	7	49	.269	.328	.383	.711	-17	24	4	86	2b169,D5,S2/3	44	1.9
/150	2	150	542	91	146	33	5	7	46	43	2	6	40	.269	.328	.383	.711	-17	20	3	87	2b138,D4,S2/3	36	1.5
FLOYD, CLIFF Cornelius Clifford B12.5.1972 Chicago IL BL/TL/6'4"/(220–250) [MonN91 1/14] d9.18																								
2002	Bos A	47	171	30	54	21	0	7	18	15	0	2	28	.316	.374	.561	.935	+43	4	0	100	O26(21/0/6),D19	0	0.8
Total	14	1423	4775	752	1331	317	22	213	781	537	80	81	952	.279	.359	.488	.847	+21	147	43	77	O1173(1067/28/89),1b116,D40	455	11.9
FONVILLE, CHAD Chad Everette B3.5.1971 Jacksonville NC BB/TR/5'6"/155 [SFN92 11/299] d4.28 Col Louisburg (NC) JC																								
1999	Bos A	3	2	1	0	0	0	0	0	2	0	0	0	.000	.500	.000	.500	-59	1	0	100	2b2	0	0.1
Total	4	226	546	80	133	10	2	0	31	45	2	1	77	.244	.302	.269	.571	-44	30	10	75	2b68,S60,O49(30/22/0),3b2/D	0	-3.6
FOSTER, EDDIE Edward Cunningham "Kid" B2.13.1887 Chicago IL D1.15.1937 Washington DC BR/TR/5'6.5"/145 d4.14																								
1920	Bos A	117	386	48	100	17	6	0	41	42		3	17	.259	.336	.334	.670	-18	10	4	71	3b88,2b21		0.2
1921	Bos A	120	412	51	117	18	6	0	35	57		0	15	.284	.371	.357	.728	-11	13	7	65	3b94,2b22		-0.8
1922	Bos A	48	109	11	23	3	0	0	3	9		1	10	.211	.277	.239	.516	-64	1	1	50	3b28,S3		-1.6
Total	13	1500	5652	732	1490	191	71	6	451	528		25	255	.264	.329	.326	.655	-11	195	53	100	3b1161,2b269,S25		-9.2
Team	3	285	907	110	240	38	12	0	79	108		4	42	.265	.345	.333	.678	-20	24	12	67	3b210,2b43,S3		-2.2
/150	2	150	477	58	126	20	6	0	42	57		2	22	.265	.345	.333	.678	-20	13	6	68	3b111,2b23,S2		-1.2
FOTHERGILL, BOB Robert Roy "Fats" B8.16.1897 Massillon OH D3.20.1938 Detroit MI BR/TR/5'10.5"/230 d4.18																								
1933	Bos A	28	32	1	11	1	0	0	5	2		0	4	.344	.382	.375	.757	+2	0	0	0	O4(1/0/3)		0.0
Total	12	1106	3269	453	1064	225	52	36	582	202		20	177	.325	.368	.459	.827	+15	42	52	45	O832(594/65/175)		-2.7
FOWLER, BOOB Joseph Chester "Gink" B11.11.1900 Waco TX D10.8.1988 Dallas TX BL/TR/5'11.5"/180 d5.6 Col TCU																								
1926	Bos A	2	8	1	1	0	0	0	1	0		0	0	.125	.125	.125	.250	-136	0	0	0	3b2		-0.2
Total	4	78	175	30	57	7	2	1	18	6		0	19	.326	.348	.406	.754	+2	3	2	60	S42,3b4,2b4		-0.3
FOX, PETE Ervin B3.8.1909 Evansville IN D7.5.1966 Detroit MI BR/TR/5'11"/165 d4.12																								
1941	Bos A	73	268	38	81	12	7	0	31	21		2	32	.302	.357	.399	.756	-3	9	2	82	O62(8/5/49)	0	-0.4
1942	Bos A	77	256	42	67	15	5	3	42	20		3	28	.262	.323	.395	.718	-2	8	7	53	O71(7/0/64)	0	-1.1
1943	Bos A	127	489	54	141	24	4	2	44	34		2	40	.288	.337	.366	.703	+4	22	8	73	O125(3/0/122)	0	-0.9
1944	Bos A☆	121	496	70	156	37	6	1	64	27		3	34	.315	.354	.419	.773	+22	10	5	67	O119R	0	0.5
1945	Bos A	66	208	21	51	4	1	0	20	11		4	18	.245	.296	.274	.570	-36	2	2	50	O57R	0	-1.8

Year	Tm Lg	G	AB	R	H	2B	3B	HR	RBI	BB	IB	HP	SO	AVG	OBP	SLG	OPS	AOPS	SB	CS	SB%	Games at Position	DL	BFW
Total	13	1461	5636	895	1678	314	75	65	694	392		33	471	.298	.347	.415	.762	-2	158	81	66	O1368(37/166/1170)	0	-11.0
Team	5	464	1717	225	496	92	23	6	201	113		14	152	.289	.338	.380	.718	+2	51	24	68	O434(18/5/126)	0	-3.7
/150	2	150	555	73	160	30	7	2	65	37		5	49	.289	.338	.380	.718	+2	16	8	67	O140(6/2/41)	0	-1.2
FOXX, JIMMIE James Emory "Beast","Double X" B10.22.1907 Sudlersville MD D7.21.1967 Miami FL BR/TR/6'0"/195 d5.1 C1 HF1951 OF(12/0/9)▲																								
1925	Phi A	10	9	2	6	1	0	0	0	0		0	1	.667	.667	.778	1.445	+149	0	0	0	/C		0.2
1926	Phi A	26	32	8	10	2	1	0	5	1		0	6	.313	.333	.438	.771	-5	1	0	100	C12,O3R		0.1
1927	Phi A	61	130	23	42	6	5	3	20	14		1	11	.323	.393	.515	.908	+27	2	1	67	1b32,C5		0.2
1928	Phi A	118	400	85	131	29	10	13	79	60		1	43	.327	.416	.548	.964	+47	3	9	25	3b60,1b30,C19		2.8
1929	†Phi A	149	517	123	183	23	9	33	118	103		2	70	.354	**.463**	.625	1.088	+71	9	7	56	1b142,3b8		4.3
1930	†Phi A	153	562	127	188	33	13	37	156	93		0	66	.335	.429	.637	1.066	+59	7	7	50	1b153		3.5
1931	†Phi A	139	515	93	150	32	10	30	120	73		1	84	.291	.380	.567	.947	+38	4	3	57	1b112,3b26/lf		1.3
1932	Phi A	**154**	585	**151**	213	33	9	**58**	**169**	116		0	96	.364	.469	**.749**	1.218	+103	3	7	30	1b141,3b13		**6.7**
1933	Phi A☆	149	573	125	204	37	9	**48**	**163**	96		1	93	**.356**	.449	**.703**	1.152	+99	2	2	50	1b149/S		**6.9**
1934	Phi A★	150	539	120	180	28	6	44	130	**111**		1	75	.334	.449	.653	1.102	+88	11	2	85	1b140,3b9		6.1
1935	Phi A★	147	535	118	185	33	7	**36**	115	114		0	99	.346	.461	**.636**	1.097	+82	6	4	60	1b121,C26,3b2		**5.9**
1936	Bos A★	**155**	585	130	198	32	8	41	143	105		1	119	.338	.440	.631	1.071	+53	13	4	76	1b139,O16(11/0/5)/3		3.3
1937	Bos A★	150	569	111	162	24	6	36	127	99		1	96	.285	.392	.538	.930	+27	10	8	56	1b150/C		1.8
1938	Bos A★	149	565	139	197	33	9	50	**175**	**119**		0	76	**.349**	**.462**	**.704**	1.166	+80	5	4	56	1b149		**5.8**
1939	Bos A☆	124	467	130	168	31	10	**35**	105	89		2	72	.360	**.464**	**.694**	1.158	+85	4	3	57	1b123/P		5.2
1940	Bos A★	144	515	106	153	30	4	36	119	101		0	87	.297	.412	.581	.993	+48	4	7	36	1b95,C42/3		3.0
1941	Bos A★	135	487	87	146	27	8	19	105	93		0	103	.300	.412	.505	.917	+38	2	5	29	1b124,3b5/rf	0	2.3
1942	Bos A	30	100	18	27	4	0	5	14	18		2	15	.270	.392	.460	.852	+34	0	0	0	1b27	0	0.9
1942	Chi N	70	205	25	42	8	0	3	19	22		0	55	.205	.282	.288	.570	-31	1			1b52/C	0	-1.8
1942	Major	100	305	43	69	12	0	8	33	40	0	2	70	.226	.320	.344	.664	+56	1	0			0	-0.9
1944	Chi N	15	20	0	1	1	0	0	2	2		0	5	.050	.136	.100	.236	-133	0			3b2/C	0	-0.2
1945	Phi N	89	224	30	60	11	1	7	38	23		0	39	.268	.336	.420	.756	+12	0			1b40,3b14,P9	0	0.0
Total	20	2317	8134	1751	2646	458	125	534	1922	1452		13	1311	.325	.428	.609	1.037	+61	87	73	100	1b1919,3b141,C108,O21L,P10/S	0	58.3
Team	7	887	3288	721	1051	181	45	222	788	624		6	568	.320	.429	.605	1.034	+54	38	31	55	1b807,C43,O17(11/0/5),3b7/P	0	22.3
/150	1	150	556	122	178	31	8	38	133	106		1	96	.320	.429	.605	1.034	+54	6	5	55	1b136,C7,O3(2/0/1)/3P	0	3.8
FOY, JOE Joseph Anthony B2.21.1943 New York NY D10.12.1989 Bronx NY BR/TR/6'0"/(210–215) d4.13																								
1966	Bos A	151	554	97	145	23	8	15	63	91	2	2	80	.262	.364	.413	.777	+12	2	5	29	3b139,S13	0	1.6
1967	†Bos A	130	446	70	112	22	4	16	49	46	1	3	87	.251	.325	.426	.751	+11	8	6	57	3b118/rf	0	-0.6
1968	Bos A	150	515	65	116	18	2	10	60	84	5	4	91	.225	.336	.326	.662	-4	26	8	76	3b147,O3L	0	0.6
1969	KC A	145	519	72	136	19	2	11	71	74	4	5	75	.262	.354	.370	.724	+3	37	15	71	3b113,1b16,O16(2/13/1),S5,2b3	0	-0.6
1970	NY N	99	322	39	76	12	0	6	37	68	5	4	58	.236	.373	.329	.702	-11	22	13	63	3b97	0	-0.2
1971	Was A	41	128	12	30	8	0	0	11	27	0	0	14	.234	.363	.297	.660	-6	4	1	80	3b37,2b3/S	0	0.5
Total	6	716	2484	355	615	102	16	58	291	390	17	18	405	.248	.351	.372	.723	+3	99	48	67	3b651,O20(5/13/2),S19,1b16,2b6	0	1.3
Team	3	431	1515	232	373	63	14	41	172	221	8	9	258	.246	.343	.387	.730	+6	36	19	65	3b404,S13,rf	0	1.6
/150	1	150	527	81	130	22	5	14	60	77	3	3	90	.246	.343	.387	.730	+6	13	7	65	3b141,S5/OfL	0	0.6
FREEMAN, JOHN John Edward B1.24.1901 Boston MA D4.14.1958 Washington DC BR/TR/5'8"/160 d6.17 Col Holy Cross																								
1927	Bos A	4	2	0	0	0	0	0	0	0		0	0	.000	.000	.000	.000	-199	0	0	0	O3(1/2/0)		-0.1
FREEMAN, BUCK John Frank B10.30.1871 Catasauqua PA D6.25.1949 Wilkes-Barre PA BL/TL/5'9"/169 d6.27▲																								
1891	Was AA	5	18	1	4	1	0	0	1	2		0	2	.222	.300	.278	.578	-31	0			P5		0.0
1898	Was N	29	107	19	39	2	3	3	21	7		4		.364	.424	.523	.947	+71	2			O29R		0.9
1899	Was N	**155**	588	107	187	19	25	**25**	122	23		18		.318	.362	.563	.925	+54	21			O155R,P2		1.7
1900	Bos N	117	418	58	126	19	13	6	65	25		10		.301	.355	.452	.807	+9	10			O91(16/3/72),1b19		-0.7
1901	Bos A	129	490	88	166	23	15	12	114	44		6		.339	.400	.520	.920	+57	17			1b128/2rf		2.7
1902	Bos A	**138**	564	75	174	38	19	11	**121**	32		6		.309	.352	.502	.854	+31	17			O138R		1.2
1903	†Bos A	**141**	567	74	163	39	20	**13**	**104**	30		4		.287	.328	.496	.824	+37	5			O141R		1.0
1904	Bos A	**157**	597	64	167	20	**19**	7	84	32		12		.280	.329	.412	.741	+26	7			O157R		0.2
1905	Bos A	130	455	59	109	20	8	3	49	46		5		.240	.316	.338	.654	+6	8			1b66,O57(0/1/56),3b2		-1.1
1906	Bos A	121	392	42	98	18	9	1	30	28		1		.250	.302	.349	.651	+4	5			O65(0/3/62),1b43,3b4		0.2
1907	Bos A	4	12	1	2	0	0	1	2	3		0		.167	.333	.417	.750	+40	0			O3R		0.0
Total	11	1126	4208	588	1235	199	131	82	713	272		66	2	.293	.346	.462	.808	+31	92			O837(16/7/814),1b256,P7,3b6/2		6.1
Team	7	820	3077	403	879	158	90	48	504	215		34	0	.286	.339	.442	.781	+28	59			O562(0/11/12),1b237,3b6/2		4.2
/150	1	150	563	74	161	29	16	9	92	39		6	0	.286	.339	.442	.781	+28	11			O103(0/2/2),1b43/32		0.8
FRENCH, CHARLIE Charles Calvin B10.12.1883 Indianapolis IN D3.30.1962 Indianapolis IN BL/TR/5'6"/140 d5.23																								
1909	Bos A	51	167	15	42	3	1	0	13	15		3		.251	.324	.281	.605	-10	8			2b28,S23		-0.7
1910	Bos A	9	40	4	8	1	0	0	3	1		0		.200	.220	.225	.445	-62	0			2b8		-0.4
1910	Chi A	45	170	17	28	1	1	0	4	10		3		.165	.224	.182	.406	-71	5			2b28,O16R		-2.7
1910	Year	54	210	21	36	2	1	0	7	11		3		.171	.223	.190	.413	-69	5			2b36,O16R		-3.1
Total	2	105	377	36	78	5	2	0	20	26		6		.207	.269	.231	.500	-42	13			2b64,S23,O16R		-3.8
Team	2	60	207	19	50	4	1	0	16	16		3	0	.242	.305	.271	.576	-19	8			2b36,S23		-1.1
FRIBERG, BERNIE Bernard Albert (b Gustaf Bernhard Friberg) B8.18.1899 Manchester NH D12.8.1958 Lynn MA BR/TR/5'11"/178 d8.20 OF(84/52/62)																								
1933	Bos A	17	41	5	13	3	0	0	9	6		0	1	.317	.404	.390	.794	+12	0	0	0	2b6,3b5,S2		0.2
Total	14	1299	4169	544	1170	181	44	38	471	471		16	498	.281	.356	.373	.729	-13	51	60	100	3b479,2b434,O195L,S123,1b21/CP		0.3
FRIEND, OWEN Owen Lacey "Red" B3.21.1927 Granite City IL BR/TR/6'1"/(175–180) d10.2 Mil 1951–52 C1																								
1955	Bos A	14	42	3	11	3	0	0	2	4	0	0	11	.262	.326	.333	.659	-29	0	0	0	S14/2	0	0.0
Total	5	208	598	69	136	24	2	13	76	55	0	2	109	.227	.295	.339	.634	-37	2	2	50	2b141,3b27,S26	0	-2.2
FRYE, JEFF Jeffrey Dustin B8.31.1966 Oakland CA BR/TR/5'9"/(160–170) [TexA88 30/765] d7.9 Col Southeastern Oklahoma OF(9/8/18) [DL 1993 Tex A 182, 1998 Bos A 181]																								
1992	Tex A	67	199	24	51	9	1	1	12	16	0	3	27	.256	.320	.327	.647	-16	1	3	25	2b67	0	-0.1
1994	Tex A	57	205	37	67	20	3	0	18	29	0	1	23	.327	.408	.454	.862	+22	6	1	86	2b54/3D	15	0.5
1995	Tex A	90	313	38	87	15	2	4	29	24	0	5	45	.278	.335	.377	.712	-17	3	3	50	2b83	30	0.2
1996	Bos A	105	419	74	120	27	2	4	41	54	0	5	57	.286	.372	.389	.761	-8	18	4	82	2b100,O5(2/1/2),S3/D	0	1.7
1997	Bos A	127	404	56	126	36	2	3	51	27	1	2	44	.312	.352	.433	.785	+3	19	8	70	2b80,3b18,O13(5/5/3),D11,S3/1	0	1.5
1999	Bos A	41	114	14	32	3	0	1	12	14	1	1	11	.281	.362	.333	.695	-23	2	2	50	2b26,3b7,S2,D2	77	-0.8
2000	Bos A	69	239	35	69	13	0	1	13	28	0	1	38	.289	.364	.356	.720	-18	1	3	25	2b52,O15(1/2/13),3b3,D3	0	-0.9
2000	Col N	37	87	14	31	6	0	0	3	8	0	1	16	.356	.412	.425	.837	-8	4	0	100	2b27/3	0	0.3
2000	Major	106	326	49	100	19	0	1	16	36	0	2	54	.307	2.379	.374	2.753	+77	5	3	63		0	-0.6
2001	Tor A	74	175	24	43	6	1	2	15	12	0	3	18	.246	.305	.326	.631	-35	2	1	67	2b47,3b27,S2/lf	8	-0.4
Total	8	667	2155	316	626	135	11	16	194	212	2	22	279	.290	.357	.386	.743	-9	56	25	69	2b536,3b57,O34R,D18,S10/1	493	2.0
Team	4	342	1176	179	347	79	4	9	117	123	2	9	150	.295	.363	.392	.755	-8	40	17	70	2b258,O33(8/8/6),3b28,D17,S8/1	258	1.5
/150	2	150	516	79	152	35	2	4	51	54	1	4	66	.295	.363	.392	.755	-8	18	7	72	2b113,O14(4/4/3),3b12,D7,S4/1	113	0.7
FULLER, FRANK Frank Edward "Rabbit" B1.1.1893 Detroit MI D10.29.1965 Warren MI BB/TR/5'7"/150 d4.14																								
1923	Bos A	6	21	3	5	0	0	0	0	1		0	1	.238	.273	.238	.511	-65	1	1	50	2b6		-0.2
Total	3	40	63	11	11	0	0	0	3	11		0	12	.175	.297	.175	.472	-65	6	4	100	2b23,S2		-0.9
GAETTI, GARY Gary Joseph B8.19.1958 Centralia IL BR/TR/6'0"/(180–205) [MinA79 S1/11] d9.20 C3 Col Northwest Missouri OF(13/0/1)																								
2000	Bos A	5	10	0	0	0	0	0	1	0	0	0	3	.000	.000	.000	.000	-197	0	0	0	D5	0	-0.3
Total	20	2507	8951	1130	2280	443	39	360	1341	634	57	96	1602	.255	.308	.434	.742	-4	96	65	60	3b2282,1b138,D48,O14L,S14,P3,2b2	64	1.8
GAFFKE, FABIAN Fabian Sebastian B8.5.1913 Milwaukee WI D2.8.1992 Milwaukee WI BR/TR/5'10"/185 d9.9																								
1936	Bos A	15	55	5	7	2	0	1	3	4		1	5	.127	.200	.218	.418	-97	0	0	0	O15(5/0/10)		-0.9
1937	Bos A	54	184	32	53	10	4	6	34	15		0	25	.288	.342	.484	.826	+2	1	2	33	O50(16/1/33)		-0.5
1938	Bos A	15	10	2	1	0	0	0	1	3		0	2	.100	.308	.100	.408	-94	0	0	0	O2R/C		-0.1
1939	Bos A	1	1	0	0	0	0	0	1	0		0	0	.000	.000	.000	.000	-196	0	0	0	/H		0.0

Year	Tm Lg	G	AB	R	H	2B	3B	HR	RBI	BB	IB	HP	SO	AVG	OBP	SLG	OPS	AOPS	SB	CS	SB%	Games at Position	DL	BFW
1941	Cle A	4	4	0	1	0	0	0	0	2		0	2	.250	.500	.250	.750	+9	0	0	0	O2C	0	0.0
1942	Cle A	40	67	4	11	2	0	0	3	6		1	13	.164	.243	.194	.437	-75	1	0	100	O16(5/1/10)	0	-0.8
Total	6	129	321	43	73	14	4	7	42	30		2	47	.227	.297	.361	.658	-33	2	2	50	O85(26/4/55)/C	0	-2.3
Team	4	85	250	39	61	12	4	7	39	22		1	32	.244	.308	.408	.716	-25	1	2	33	O67(21/1/13)/C		-1.5
GAGLIANO, PHIL Philip Joseph B12.27.1941 Memphis TN BR/TR/6'1"/(179–188) d4.16 b–Ralph OF(34/0/31)																								
1971	Bos A	47	68	11	22	5	0	0	13	11	0	0	5	.324	.412	.397	.809	+23	0	0	0	O11(7/0/4),2b7,3b4	0	0.0
1972	Bos A	52	82	9	21	4	1	0	10	10	0	0	13	.256	.333	.329	.662	-7	1	0	100	O12L,3b5,2b4,1b2	0	0.1
Total	12	702	1411	150	336	50	7	14	159	163	7	4	184	.238	.316	.313	.629	-23	5	4	56	2b172,3b130,O63L,1b30,S2	0	-5.4
Team	2	99	150	20	43	9	1	0	23	21	0	0	18	.287	.370	.360	.730	+7	1	0	100	O23(7/0/4),2b11,3b9,1b2	0	0.1
GAINER, DEL Dellos Clinton "Sheriff" B11.10.1886 Montrose WV D1.29.1947 Elkins WV BR/TR/6'0"/180 d10.2 Mil 1918																								
1909	Det A	2	5	0	1	0	0	0	0	0		0		.200	.200	.200	.400	-75	0			1b2		-0.1
1911	Det A	70	248	32	75	11	4	2	25	20		5		.302	.366	.403	.769	+9	10			1b69		-0.2
1912	Det A	52	179	28	43	5	6	0	20	18		3		.240	.320	.335	.655	-10	15			1b50/cf		-0.7
1913	Det A	105	363	47	97	16	8	2	25	30		6	45	.267	.333	.372	.705	+8	10			1b103		-0.5
1914	Det A	1	0	0	0	0	0	0	0	0		0	0	+	+	+	.000	-100	0			/1		0.0
1914	Bos A	38	84	11	20	9	2	2	13	8		1	14	.238	.312	.464	.776	+33	2	2	50	1b18,2b11/cf		0.1
1914	Year	39	84	11	20	9	2	2	13	8		1	14	.238	.312	.464	.776	+33	2	2	50	1b19,2b11/cf		0.1
1915	†Bos A	82	200	30	59	5	8	1	29	21		3	31	.295	.371	.415	.786	+39	7	2	78	1b56,O6(0/5/1)		1.1
1916	†Bos A	56	142	14	36	6	0	3	18	10		0	24	.254	.303	.359	.662	-2	5			1b48,2b2		-0.1
1917	Bos A	52	172	28	53	10	2	2	19	15		3	21	.308	.374	.424	.798	+45	1			1b50		0.8
1919	Bos A	47	118	9	28	6	2	0	13	13		1	15	.237	.318	.322	.640	-15	5			1b21,O18L		-0.4
1922	StL N	43	97	19	26	7	4	2	23	14		0	6	.268	.360	.485	.845	+22	0	2	0	1b26,O10(6/4/0)		0.1
Total	10	548	1608	218	438	75	36	14	185	149		22	156	.272	.342	.390	.732	+13	55	6	100	1b444,O36(24/11/1),2b13		0.1
Team	5	275	716	92	196	36	14	8	92	67		8	105	.274	.343	.397	.740	+23	20	4	100	1b193,Ocf,2b13		1.5
/150	3	150	391	50	107	20	8	4	50	37		4	57	.274	.343	.397	.740	+23	11	2	100	1b105,Ocf,2b7		0.8
GALLAGHER, BOB Robert Collins B7.7.1948 Newton MA BL/TL/6'3"/185 [LAN68 17/377] d5.17 gf–Shano Collins Col Stanford																								
1972	Bos A	7	5	0	0	0	0	0	0	0	0	0	3	.000	.000	.000	.000	-194	0	0	0	/H	0	-0.1
Total	4	213	255	34	56	6	1	2	13	16	2	1	56	.220	.266	.275	.541	-48	1	1	50	O120(30/17/74),1b5	0	-1.8
GALVIN, JIM James Joseph B8.11.1907 Somerville MA D9.30.1969 Marietta GA BR/TR/5'11.5"/180 d9.27																								
1930	Bos A	2	2	0	0	0	0	0	0	0		0	0	.000	.000	.000	.000	-199	0	0	0	/H		-0.1
GARBARK, BOB Robert Michael B11.13.1909 Houston TX D8.15.1990 Meadville PA BR/TR/5'11"/178 d9.3 b–Mike																								
1934	Cle A	5	11	1	0	0	0	0	0	1		0	3	.000	.083	.000	.083	-176	0	0	0	C5		-0.4
1935	Cle A	6	18	4	6	1	0	0	4	5		0	1	.333	.478	.389	.867	+24	0	0	0	C6		0.2
1937	Chi N	1	1	0	0	0	0	0	0	0		0	0	.000	.000	.000	.000	-196	0			/H		0.0
1938	Chi N	23	54	2	14	0	0	0	5	1		0	0	.259	.273	.259	.532	-54	0			C20/1		-0.3
1939	Chi N	24	21	1	3	0	0	0	0	0		0	3	.143	.143	.143	.286	-123	0			C21		-0.3
1944	Phi A	18	23	2	6	2	0	0	2	1		0	0	.261	.292	.348	.640	-17	0	0	0	C15	0	-0.1
1945	Bos A	68	199	21	52	6	0	0	17	18		2	10	.261	.329	.291	.620	-21	0	1	0	C67	0	-0.4
Total	7	145	327	31	81	9	0	0	28	26		2	17	.248	.307	.275	.582	-36	0	1	0	C134/1	0	-1.3
GARCIAPARRA, NOMAR Anthony Nomar B7.23.1973 Whittier CA BR/TR/6'0"/(167–190) [BosA94 1/12] d8.31 Col Georgia Tech																								
1996	Bos A	24	87	11	21	2	3	4	16	4	0	0	14	.241	.272	.471	.743	-18	5	0	100	S22/2D	0	-0.4
1997	Bos A★	153	684	122	**209**	44	**11**	30	98	35	2	6	92	.306	.342	.534	.876	+22	22	9	71	S153	0	3.4
1998	†Bos A	143	604	111	195	37	8	35	122	33	1	8	62	.323	.362	.584	.946	+39	12	6	67	S143	19	3.0
1999	†Bos A★	135	532	103	190	42	4	27	104	51	7	8	39	**.357**	.418	.603	1.021	+52	14	3	82	S134	0	4.7
2000	Bos A★	140	529	104	197	51	3	21	96	61	**20**	2	50	**.372**	.434	.599	1.033	+55	5	2	71	S136/D	14	5.0
2001	Bos A	21	83	13	24	3	0	4	8	7	0	1	9	.289	.352	.470	.822	+14	0	1	0	S21	161	0.4
2002	Bos A★	156	635	101	197	**56**	5	24	120	41	4	6	63	.310	.352	.528	.880	+29	5	2	71	S154	0	5.4
2003	†Bos A★	156	658	120	198	37	13	28	105	39	1	11	61	.301	.345	.524	.869	+21	19	5	79	S156	0	3.7
2004	Bos A	38	156	24	50	7	3	5	21	8	2	4	16	.321	.367	.500	.867	+16	2	0	100	S37/D	66	-0.1
2004	Chi N	43	165	28	49	14	0	4	20	16	0	2	14	.297	.364	.455	.819	+7	2	1	67	S42	0	0.0
2004	Major	81	321	52	99	21	3	9	41	24	2	6	30	.308	2.368	.477	2.844	+75	4	1	80		66	-0.1
2005	Chi N	62	230	28	65	12	0	9	30	12	0	2	24	.283	.320	.452	.772	-3	0	0	0	3b34,S26	106	-0.4
2006	†LA N☆	122	469	82	142	31	2	20	93	42	9	8	30	.303	.367	.505	.872	+21	3	0	100	1b118	29	0.1
Total	11	1193	4832	847	1537	336	52	211	833	349	46	58	474	.318	.367	.540	.907	+29	89	29	75	S1024,1b118,3b34,D3/2	395	24.8
Team	9	966	3968	709	1281	279	50	178	690	279	17	46	406	.323	.370	.553	.923	+33	84	28	75	S956,D3/2	260	25.1
/150	1	150	616	110	199	43	8	28	107	43	3	7	63	.323	.370	.553	.923	+33	13	4	76	S148/D2	40	3.9
GARDNER, BILLY William Frederick "Shotgun" B7.19.1927 Waterford CT BR/TR/6'0"/(170–180) d4.22 M6/C5																								
1962	Bos A	53	199	22	54	9	2	0	12	10	0	1	39	.271	.310	.337	.647	-28	0	1	0	2b38,3b7,S4	0	-1.1
1963	Bos A	36	84	4	16	2	1	0	1	4	1	1	19	.190	.236	.238	.474	-68	0	0	0	2b21,3b2	0	-0.3
Total	10	1034	3544	356	841	159	18	41	271	246	18	33	439	.237	.292	.327	.619	-30	19	22	46	2b839,S108,3b92	0	-10.2
Team	2	89	283	26	70	11	3	0	13	14	1	2	58	.247	.288	.307	.595	-40	0	1	0	2b59,3b9,S4	0	-1.4
GARDNER, LARRY William Lawrence B5.13.1886 Enosburg Falls VT D3.11.1976 St.George VT BL/TR/5'8"/165 d6.25 Col Vermont																								
1908	Bos A	3	10	0	3	1	0	0	1	0		0		.300	.300	.400	.700	+24	0			3b3		-0.2
1909	Bos A	19	37	7	11	1	2	0	5	4		1		.297	.381	.432	.813	+53	1			3b8,S5		0.0
1910	Bos A	113	413	56	117	12	10	2	36	41		4		.283	.354	.375	.729	+25	8			2b113		0.4
1911	Bos A	138	492	80	140	17	8	4	44	64		5		.285	.373	.376	.749	+10	27			3b72,2b62		3.3
1912	†Bos A	143	517	88	163	24	18	3	86	56		1		.315	.383	.449	.832	+31	25			3b143		2.2
1913	Bos A	131	473	64	133	17	10	0	63	47		1	34	.281	.347	.359	.706	+4	18			3b130		-0.9
1914	Bos A	155	553	50	143	23	19	3	68	35		0	39	.259	.303	.385	.688	+7	16	23	41	3b153		-0.1
1915	†Bos A	127	430	51	111	14	6	1	55	39		5	24	.258	.327	.326	.653	-2	11	12	48	3b127		-0.7
1916	†Bos A	148	493	47	152	19	7	2	62	48		2	27	.308	.372	.387	.759	+28	12			3b147		0.9
1917	Bos A	146	501	53	133	23	7	1	61	54		3	37	.265	.341	.345	.686	+10	16			3b146		0.5
1918	Phi A	127	463	50	132	22	6	1	52	43		0	22	.285	.346	.365	.711	+13	9			3b127		2.6
1919	Cle A	**139**	524	67	157	29	7	2	79	39		3	29	.300	.352	.393	.745	+3	7			3b139		0.1
1920	†Cle A	**154**	597	72	185	31	11	3	118	53		1	25	.310	.367	.414	.781	+3	3	20	13	3b154		0.0
1921	Cle A	153	586	101	187	32	14	3	120	65		4	16	.319	.391	.437	.828	+9	3	3	50	3b152		1.8
1922	Cle A	137	470	74	134	31	3	2	68	49		2	21	.285	.355	.377	.732	-10	9	8	53	3b128		-0.4
1923	Cle A	52	79	4	20	5	1	0	12	12		0	7	.253	.352	.342	.694	-17	0	1	0	3b19		0.2
1924	Cle A	38	50	3	10	0	0	0	4	5		0	1	.200	.273	.200	.473	-77	0	1	0	3b8,2b6		-0.8
Total	17	1923	6688	867	1931	301	129	27	934	654		32	282	.289	.355	.384	.739	+9	165	68	100	3b1656,2b181,S5		8.9
Team	10	1123	3919	496	1106	151	87	16	481	388		22	161	.282	.350	.377	.727	+15	134	35	100	3b929,2b175,S5		5.4
/150	1	150	523	66	148	20	12	2	64	52		3	22	.282	.350	.377	.727	+15	18	5	100	3b124,2b23/S		0.7
GARRISON, FORD Robert Ford "Rocky","Snapper" B8.29.1915 Greenville SC D6.6.2001 Largo FL BR/TR/5'10.5"/180 d4.22 Mil 1945 C1																								
1943	Bos A	36	129	13	36	5	1	1	11	5		0	14	.279	.306	.357	.663	-8	0	1	0	O32(26/6/0)	0	-0.5
1944	Bos A	13	49	5	12	3	0	0	2	6		0	4	.245	.327	.306	.633	-18	0	0	0	O12R	0	-0.2
Total	4	185	687	80	180	22	3	6	56	37		2	67	.262	.302	.329	.631	-19	11	5	69	O176(134/6/36)	0	-2.8
Team	2	49	178	18	48	8	1	1	13	11		0	18	.270	.312	.343	.655	-11	0	1	0	O44(26/6/0)	0	-0.7
GASTON, ALEX Alexander Nathaniel B3.12.1893 New York NY D2.8.1979 Marina Del Ray CA BR/TR/5'9"/170 d9.26 b–Milt																								
1920	NY N	4	10	2	1	0	0	0	1	1		0	2	.100	.182	.100	.282	-118	0	0	0	C3		-0.2
1921	NY N	20	22	1	5	1	1	0	3	1		0	9	.227	.261	.364	.625	-37	0	0	0	C11		-0.1
1922	NY N	16	26	1	5	0	0	0	1	0		0	3	.192	.192	.192	.384	-101	1	0	100	C13		-0.3
1923	NY N	22	39	3	8	2	0	1	5	0		1	6	.205	.225	.333	.558	-54	0	0	0	C21		-0.2
1926	Bos A	98	301	37	67	5	3	0	21	21		4	28	.223	.282	.259	.541	-57	3	0	100	C98		-3.4
1929	Bos A	55	116	14	26	5	2	2	9	6		0	8	.224	.262	.353	.615	-42	1	0	100	C49		-0.5
Total	6	215	514	58	112	13	6	3	40	29		5	56	.218	.266	.284	.550	-55	5	0	100	C195		-4.7

Year	Tm Lg	G	AB	R	H	2B	3B	HR	RBI	BB	IB	HP	SO	AVG	OBP	SLG	OPS	AOPS	SB	CS	SB%	Games at Position	DL	BFW
Team	2	153	417	51	93	10	5	2	30	27		4	36	.223	.277	.285	.562	-53	4	0	100	C147		-3.9
/150	2	150	409	50	91	10	5	2	29	26		4	35	.223	.277	.285	.562	-53	4	0	100	C144		-3.8
GEDMAN, RICH Richard Leo B9.26.1959 Worcester MA BL/TR/6'0"/(205–222) d9.7																								
1980	Bos A	9	24	2	5	0	0	0	1	0	0	0	5	.208	.208	.208	.416	-86	0	0	0	C2,D4	0	-0.3
1981	Bos A	62	205	22	59	15	0	5	26	9	1	1	31	.288	.317	.434	.751	+9	0	0	0	C59	0	-0.2
1982	Bos A	92	289	30	72	17	2	4	26	10	2	2	37	.249	.279	.363	.642	-29	0	1	0	C86	0	-1.6
1983	Bos A	81	204	21	60	16	1	2	18	15	6	1	37	.294	.345	.412	.757	+0	0	1	0	C68	0	-0.2
1984	Bos A	133	449	54	121	26	4	24	72	29	8	1	72	.269	.312	.506	.818	+17	0	0	0	C125	0	1.0
1985	Bos A★	144	498	66	147	30	5	18	80	50	11	3	79	.295	.362	.484	.846	+24	2	0	100	C139	0	3.5
1986	†Bos A★	135	462	49	119	29	0	16	65	37	13	4	61	.258	.315	.424	.739	-1	1	0	100	C134	0	2.3
1987	Bos A	52	151	11	31	8	0	1	13	10	2	0	24	.205	.250	.278	.528	-60	0	0	0	C51	82	-1.0
1988	†Bos A	95	299	33	69	14	0	9	39	18	2	3	49	.231	.279	.368	.647	-23	0	0	0	C93/D	24	-0.1
1989	Bos A	93	260	24	55	9	0	4	16	23	1	0	47	.212	.273	.292	.565	-44	0	1	0	C91	0	-1.9
1990	Bos A	10	15	3	3	0	0	0	0	5	0	1	6	.200	.429	.200	.629	-23	0	0	0	C9	0	-0.2
1990	Hou N	40	104	4	21	7	0	1	10	15	6	0	24	.202	.300	.298	.598	-32	0	0	0	C39	0	0.1
1990	Major	50	119	7	24	7	0	1	10	20	6	1	30	.202	1.321	.286	1.607	-33	0	0	0		0	-0.1
1991	StL N	46	94	7	10	1	0	3	8	4	0	0	15	.106	.140	.213	.353	-101	0	1	0	C43	0	-0.6
1992	StL N	41	105	5	23	4	0	1	8	11	1	0	22	.219	.291	.286	.577	-34	0	0	0	C40	0	0.2
Total	13	1033	3159	331	795	176	12	88	382	236	53	16	509	.252	.304	.399	.703	-10	3	4	43	C979,D5	106	1.0
Team	11	906	2856	315	741	164	12	83	356	206	46	16	448	.259	.311	.412	.723	-6	3	3	50	C857,D5	106	1.3
/150	2	150	473	52	123	27	2	14	59	34	8	3	74	.259	.311	.412	.723	-6	0	0	0	C142/D	18	0.2
GEIGER, GARY Gary Merle B4.4.1937 Sand Ridge IL D4.24.1996 Murphysboro IL BL/TR/6'0"/(162–170) d4.15																								
1958	Cle A	91	195	28	45	3	1	1	6	27	0	3	43	.231	.330	.272	.602	-30	2	2	50	O53(1/44/8),3b2/P	0	-0.5
1959	Bos A	120	335	45	82	10	4	11	48	21	0	0	55	.245	.289	.397	.686	-17	9	3	75	O95(46/61/1)	0	-1.5
1960	Bos A	77	245	32	74	13	3	9	33	23	0	3	38	.302	.369	.490	.859	+26	2	2	50	O66(5/7/59)	67	1.1
1961	Bos A	140	499	82	116	21	6	18	64	87	4	4	91	.232	.349	.407	.756	-1	16	4	80	O137C	0	0.2
1962	Bos A	131	466	67	116	18	4	16	54	67	3	2	66	.249	.344	.408	.752	-1	18	11	62	O129C	0	-0.4
1963	Bos A	121	399	67	105	13	5	16	44	36	2	3	63	.263	.327	.441	.768	+10	9	4	69	O95(2/89/4),1b6	0	1.0
1964	Bos A	5	13	3	5	0	1	0	1	2	0	0	2	.385	.467	.538	1.005	+70	0	0	0	O4(0/1/3)	0	0.1
1965	Bos A	24	45	5	9	3	0	1	2	13	1	0	10	.200	.379	.333	.712	-2	3	0	100	O16(5/10/1)	94	0.1
1966	Atl N	78	126	23	33	5	3	4	10	21	1	1	29	.262	.367	.444	.811	+24	0	1	0	O49(5/33/15)	0	0.2
1967	Atl N	69	117	17	19	1	1	1	5	20	0	0	35	.162	.285	.214	.499	-55	1	1	50	O38(6/26/7)	0	-1.2
1969	Hou N	93	125	19	28	4	1	0	16	24	2	1	34	.224	.351	.272	.623	-22	2	1	67	O65(47/5/14)	0	-0.3
1970	Hou N	5	4	0	1	0	0	0	0	0	0	0	0	.250	.250	.250	.500	-64	0	0	0	O2R	0	0.0
Total	12	954	2569	388	633	91	29	77	283	341	13	17	466	.246	.337	.394	.731	-2	62	29	68	O749(117/542/114),1b6,3b2/P	161	-1.2
Team	7	618	2002	301	507	78	23	71	246	249	10	12	325	.253	.338	.422	.760	+2	57	24	70	O542(64/87/69),1b6	161	0.6
/150	2	150	486	73	123	19	6	17	60	60	2	3	79	.253	.338	.422	.760	+2	14	6	70	O132(16/21/17)/1	39	0.1
GELBERT, CHARLIE Charles Magnus B1.26.1906 Scranton PA D1.13.1967 Easton PA BR/TR/5'11"/170 d4.16 Col Lebanon Valley																								
1940	Bos A	30	91	9	18	2	0	0	8	8		0	16	.198	.263	.220	.483	-75	0	0	0	3b29/S		-0.6
Total	9	876	2869	398	766	169	43	17	350	290		7	245	.267	.336	.374	.710	-18	34	0	100	S680,3b147,2b22,P2		1.0
GERBER, WALLY Walter "Spooks" B8.18.1891 Columbus OH D6.19.1951 Columbus OH BR/TR/5'10"/152 d9.23 Mil 1918																								
1928	Bos A	104	300	21	64	6	1	0	28	32		0	31	.213	.289	.240	.529	-59	6	1	86	S103		1.2
1929	Bos A	61	91	6	15	3	1	0	5	8		0	12	.165	.232	.220	.452	-83	1	0	100	S30,2b22		-0.4
Total	15	1522	5099	558	1309	172	46	7	476	465		33	357	.257	.323	.313	.636	-33	43	47	100	S1447,2b26,3b24		-8.1
Team	2	165	391	27	79	9	2	0	33	40		0	43	.202	.276	.235	.511	-65	7	1	88	S133,2b22		0.8
/150	2	150	355	25	72	8	2	0	30	36		0	39	.202	.276	.235	.511	-65	6	1	86	S121,2b20		0.7
GERNERT, DICK Richard Edward B9.28.1928 Reading PA BR/TR/6'3"/(205–210) d4.16 C2 Col Temple																								
1952	Bos A	102	367	58	89	20	2	19	67	35		5	83	.243	.317	.463	.780	+7	4	1	80	1b99	0	-0.2
1953	Bos A	139	494	73	125	15	1	21	71	88		5	82	.253	.371	.415	.786	+6	0	7	0	1b136	0	-0.6
1954	Bos A	14	23	2	6	2	0	0	1	6		0	4	.261	.414	.348	.762	-1	0	0	0	1b6	0	-0.1
1955	Bos A	7	20	6	4	2	0	0	1	1	0	0	5	.200	.238	.300	.538	-60	0	0	0	1b5	0	-0.2
1956	Bos A	106	306	53	89	11	0	16	68	56	1	2	57	.291	.399	.484	.883	+19	1	0	100	O50L,1b37	0	0.9
1957	Bos A	99	316	45	75	13	3	14	58	39	3	3	62	.237	.324	.430	.754	-1	1	1	50	1b71,O16L	0	-0.6
1958	Bos A	122	431	59	102	19	1	20	69	59	4	2	78	.237	.330	.425	.755	+0	2	0	100	1b114	0	0.2
1959	Bos A	117	298	41	78	14	1	11	42	52	3	0	49	.262	.369	.426	.795	+13	1	2	33	1b75,O25(21/0/7)	0	0.8
1960	Chi N	52	96	8	24	3	0	0	11	10	0	0	19	.250	.321	.281	.602	-33	1	0	100	1b18,O5L	0	-0.2
1960	Det A	21	50	6	15	4	0	1	5	4	0	0	5	.300	.352	.440	.792	+10	0	0	0	1b13,O6L	0	-0.1
1960	Major	73	146	14	39	7	0	1	16	14	0	0	24	.267	.331	.336	.667	-26	1	0	100		0	-0.3
1961	Det A	6	5	1	1	0	0	1	1	1	0	0	2	.200	.333	.800	1.133	+87	0	0	0	/H	0	0.1
1961	†Cin N	40	63	4	19	1	0	0	7	7	1	0	9	.302	.361	.317	.678	-16	0	0	0	1b21	0	0.1
1961	Major	46	68	5	20	1	0	1	8	8	1	0	11	.294	2.368	.353	2.721	-74	0	0	0		0	0.2
1962	Hou N	10	24	1	5	0	0	0	1	5	0	0	7	.208	.345	.208	.553	-43	0	0	0	1b9	0	-0.3
Total	11	835	2493	357	632	104	8	103	402	363	12	17	462	.254	.351	.426	.777	+4	10	11	48	1b604,O102(98/0/7)	0	-0.2
Team	8	706	2255	337	568	96	8	101	377	336	11	17	420	.252	.352	.436	.788	+6	9	11	45	1b543,O91L	0	0.2
/150	2	150	479	72	121	20	2	21	80	71	2	4	89	.252	.352	.436	.788	+6	2	2	50	1b115,O19L	0	0.0
GESSLER, DOC Henry Homer "Brownie" B12.23.1880 Greensburg PA D12.24.1924 Greensburg PA BL/TL/5'10"/180 d4.23 M1 Col Ohio U.																								
1908	Bos A	128	435	55	134	13	14	3	63	51		11		.308	**.394**	.423	.817	+61	19			O126R		2.4
1909	Bos A	111	396	57	115	24	1	0	46	31		8		.290	.354	.356	.710	+22	16			O109R		0.9
Total	8	880	2969	370	831	127	50	14	363	333		92		.280	.370	.370	.740	+28	142			O713(17/94/602),1b120/2		8.3
Team	2	239	831	112	249	37	15	3	109	82		19	0	.300	.376	.391	.767	+43	35			O235R		3.3
/150	1	150	522	70	156	23	9	2	68	51		12	0	.300	.376	.391	.767	+43	22			O147R		2.1
GEYGAN, CHAPPIE James Edward B6.3.1903 Ironton OH D3.15.1966 Columbus OH BR/TR/5'11"/170 d7.16																								
1924	Bos A	33	82	7	21	5	2	0	4	4		2	16	.256	.307	.366	.673	-27	0	2	0	S32		0.0
1925	Bos A	3	11	0	2	0	0	0	0	0		0	2	.182	.182	.182	.364	-108	0	0	0	S3		-0.3
1926	Bos A	4	10	0	3	0	0	0	0	1		0	1	.300	.364	.300	.664	-23	0	0	0	3b3		-0.1
Total	3	40	103	7	26	5	2	0	4	5		2	19	.252	.300	.340	.640	-35	0	2	0	S35,3b3		-0.4
GIAMBI, JEREMY Jeremy Dean B9.30.1974 San Jose CA BL/TL/6'0"/(185–218) [KCA96 6/169] d9.1 b–Jason Col Cal St.–Fullerton																								
2003	Bos A	50	127	15	25	5	0	5	15	26	0	2	42	.197	.342	.354	.696	-19	1	0	100	D30,O11(9/0/2)	83	-0.4
Total	6	510	1417	219	372	75	3	52	209	251	10	16	356	.263	.377	.430	.807	+10	1	3	25	O187(82/0/106),D176,1b72	163	-1.1
GIANNINI, JOE Joseph Francis B9.8.1888 Drytown CA D9.26.1942 San Francisco CA BL/TR/5'8"/155 d8.7 Col San Francisco																								
1911	Bos A	1	2	0	1	1	0	0	0	0		0		.500	.500	1.000	1.500	+217	0			/S		0.0
GIBSON, RUSS John Russell B5.6.1939 Fall River MA BR/TR/6'1"/195 d4.14																								
1967	†Bos A	49	138	8	28	7	0	1	15	12	3	0	31	.203	.263	.275	.538	-44	0	0	0	C48	0	-0.9
1968	Bos A	76	231	15	52	11	1	3	20	8	1	0	38	.225	.247	.320	.567	-32	1	2	33	C74/1	22	-1.0
1969	Bos A	85	287	21	72	9	1	3	27	15	1	1	25	.251	.289	.321	.610	-32	1	1	50	C83	0	-1.7
1970	SF N	24	69	3	16	6	0	0	6	7	1	0	12	.232	.303	.319	.622	-33	0	0	0	C23	0	-0.4
1971	SF N	25	57	2	11	1	1	1	7	2	0	0	13	.193	.220	.298	.518	-54	0	0	0	C22	0	-0.7
1972	SF N	5	12	0	2	0	1	0	3	0	0	0	4	.167	.167	.333	.500	-62	0	0	0	C5	0	-0.3
Total	6	264	794	49	181	34	4	8	78	44	6	1	123	.228	.267	.311	.578	-36	2	3	40	C255/1	22	-5.0
Team	3	210	656	44	152	27	2	7	62	35	5	1	94	.232	.269	.311	.580	-35	2	3	40	C205/1	22	-3.6
/150	2	150	469	31	109	19	1	5	44	25	4	1	67	.232	.269	.311	.580	-35	1	2	33	C146/1	16	-2.6
GILBERT, ANDY Andrew B7.18.1914 Bradenville PA D8.29.1992 Davis CA BR/TR/6'0"/203 d9.14 Mil 1943–45 C4																								
1942	Bos A	6	11	0	1	0	0	0	1	1		0	3	.091	.167	.091	.258	-126	0	0	0	O5C	0	-0.2
1946	Bos A	2	1	1	0	0	0	0	0	0		0	0	.000	.000	.000	.000	-195	0	0	0	/cf	0	0.0
Total	2	8	12	1	1	0	0	0	1	1		0	3	.083	.154	.083	.237	-131	0	0	0	O6C	0	-0.2

Year	Tm Lg	G	AB	R	H	2B	3B	HR	RBI	BB	IB	HP	SO	AVG	OBP	SLG	OPS	AOPS	SB	CS	SB%	Games at Position	DL	BFW
GILE, DON Donald Loren "Bear" B4.19.1935 Modesto CA BR/TR/6'6"/(220–225) d9.25 Col Arizona																								
1959	Bos A	3	10	1	2	1	0	0	1	0	0	1	2	.200	.250	.300	.550	-45	0	0	0	C3	0	0.0
1960	Bos A	29	51	6	9	1	1	1	4	1	0	0	13	.176	.189	.294	.483	-71	0	0	0	C15,1b11	0	-0.8
1961	Bos A	8	18	2	5	0	0	1	1	1	0	0	5	.278	.316	.444	.760	-2	0	0	0	1b6/C	0	-0.1
1962	Bos A	18	41	3	2	0	0	1	3	3	0	1	15	.049	.133	.122	.255	-130	0	0	0	1b14	0	-1.0
Total	4	58	120	12	18	2	1	3	9	5	0	2	35	.150	.194	.258	.452	-79	0	0	0	1b31,C19	0	-1.9
GILHOOLEY, FRANK Frank Patrick "Flash" B6.10.1892 Toledo OH D7.11.1959 Toledo OH BL/TR/5'8"/155 d9.18 Col St. Johns																								
1919	Bos A	48	112	14	27	4	0	0	1	12		0	8	.241	.315	.277	.592	-29	2			O33(30/2/1)		-0.6
Total	9	312	1068	142	289	30	10	2	58	140		4	80	.271	.357	.323	.680	+2	37			O285(30/19/236)		-1.0
GILKEY, BERNARD Otis Bernard B9.24.1966 St.Louis MO BR/TR/6'0"/(170–200) d9.4																								
2000	Bos A	36	91	11	21	5	1	1	9	10	0	3	12	.231	.327	.341	.668	-32	0	0	0	O22(7/0/16),D8	0	-0.4
Total	12	1239	4061	606	1115	244	24	118	546	466	21	42	708	.275	.352	.434	.786	+10	115	71	62	O1076(997/3/87),D11,1b3	95	7.3
GILLIS, GRANT Grant B1.24.1901 Grove Hill AL D2.4.1981 Thomasville AL BR/TR/5'10"/165 d9.19 Col Alabama																								
1927	Was A	10	36	8	8	3	1	0	2	2		0	0	.222	.263	.361	.624	-39	0	0	0	S10		-0.2
1928	Was A	24	87	13	22	5	1	0	10	4		3	5	.253	.309	.333	.642	-31	0	1	0	S16,2b5,3b3		-0.9
1929	Bos A	28	73	5	18	4	0	0	11	6		0	8	.247	.304	.301	.605	-42	0	1	0	2b25		-0.7
Total	3	62	196	26	48	12	2	0	23	12		3	13	.245	.299	.327	.626	-37	0	2	0	2b30,S26,3b3		-1.8
GINSBERG, JOE Myron Nathan B10.11.1926 New York NY BL/TR/5'11"/(178–182) d9.15																								
1961	Bos A	19	24	1	6	0	0	0	5	0	0	0	2	.250	.250	.250	.500	-67	0	0	0	C6	0	-0.4
Total	13	695	1716	168	414	59	8	20	182	226	9	14	135	.241	.332	.320	.652	-21	7	5	58	C574	0	-4.4
GLEASON, HARRY Harry Gilbert B3.28.1875 Camden NJ D10.21.1961 Camden NJ BR/TR/5'6"/160 d9.27 b–Kid																								
1901	Bos A	1	1	0	1	0	0	0	0	0		0		1.000	1.000	1.000	2.000	+364	1			/3		0.1
1902	Bos A	71	240	30	54	5	5	2	25	10		3		.225	.265	.313	.578	-42	6			3b35,O23(8/15/0),2b4		-1.7
1903	Bos A	6	13	3	2	1	0	0	2	0		0		.154	.154	.231	.385	-87	0			3b2		-0.2
Total	5	274	944	88	206	24	11	3	90	48		10		.218	.263	.276	.539	-33	31			3b202,O24(8/16/0),S20,2b16		-6.0
Team	3	78	254	33	57	6	5	2	27	10		3	0	.224	.262	.311	.573	-43	7			3b37,O23(8/15/0),2b4		-1.8
GLENN, JOE Joseph Charles "Gabby" (b Joseph Charles Gurzensky) B11.19.1908 Dickson City PA D5.6.1985 Tunkhannock PA BR/TR/5'11"/175 d9.15																								
1940	Bos A	22	47	3	6	1	0	0	4	5		0	7	.128	.212	.149	.361	-105	0	0	0	C19		-0.8
Total	8	248	718	77	181	34	5	5	89	81		2	91	.252	.330	.334	.664	-31	6	5	55	C235		-3.0
GODWIN, JOHN John Henry "Bunny" B3.10.1877 E.Liverpool OH D5.5.1956 E.Liverpool OH BR/TR/6'0"/190 d8.14																								
1905	Bos A	15	43	4	14	1	0	0	10	3		3		.326	.408	.349	.757	+39	3			O7(5/2/0),2b5		0.2
1906	Bos A	66	193	11	36	2	1	0	15	6		1		.187	.215	.207	.422	-68	6			3b27,S14,O10(0/1/9),2b3/1		-1.5
Total	2	81	236	15	50	3	1	0	25	9		4		.212	.253	.233	.486	-47	9			3b27,O17(5/3/9),S14,2b8/1		-1.3
GOGGIN, CHUCK Charles Francis B7.7.1945 Pompano Beach FL BB/TR/5'11"/175 d9.8 Col Broward (FL) CC																								
1974	Bos A	2	1	0	0	0	0	0	0	0	0	0	1	.000	.000	.000	.000	-193	0	0	0	2b2	19	0.0
Total	3	72	99	19	29	5	0	0	7	10	0	0	21	.293	.355	.343	.698	-11	0	1	0	2b22,O6(5/0/1),S5,C2	19	-0.7
GONZALEZ, ALEX Alexander B2.15.1977 Cagua, Aragua, Venez. BR/TR/6'0"/(170–200) d8.25																								
2006	Bos A	111	388	48	99	24	2	9	50	22	1	5	67	.255	.299	.397	.696	-22	1	0	100	S111	15	-0.6
Total	9	1007	3609	411	887	207	25	90	425	192	40	56	739	.246	.292	.392	.684	-22	24	17	59	S991	183	-4.5
/150	1	150	524	65	134	32	3	12	68	30	1	7	91	.255	.299	.397	.696	-22	1	0	100	S150	20	-0.8
GONZALEZ, EUSEBIO Eusebio Miguel (Lopez) "Papo" B7.13.1892 Havana, Cuba D2.14.1976 Havana, Cuba BR/TR/5'10"/165 d7.26																								
1918	Bos A	3	5	2	2	0	1	0	0	1		1	1	.400	.571	.800	1.371	+219	0			S2/3		0.1
GOOCH, JOHNNY John Beverley B11.9.1897 Smyrna TN D5.15.1975 Nashville TN BB/TR/5'11"/175 d9.9 C3																								
1933	Bos A	37	77	6	14	1	1	0	2	11		0	7	.182	.284	.221	.505	-64	0	0	0	C26		-0.4
Total	11	805	2363	227	662	98	29	7	293	206		15	141	.280	.342	.355	.697	-21	11	5	100	C758		-1.1
GOODMAN, BILLY William Dale B3.22.1926 Concord NC D10.1.1984 Sarasota FL BL/TR/5'11"/(158–165) d4.19 C3 OF(68/0/43)																								
1947	Bos A	12	11	1	2	0	0	0	1	1		0	2	.182	.250	.182	.432	-80	0	0	0	/rf	0	-0.1
1948	Bos A	127	445	65	138	27	2	1	66	74		5	44	.310	.414	.387	.801	+8	5	3	63	1b117,2b2,3b2	0	0.3
1949	Bos A★	122	443	54	132	23	3	0	56	58		2	21	.298	.382	.363	.745	-9	2	0	100	1b117	0	-0.7
1950	Bos A	110	424	91	150	25	3	4	68	52		2	25	**.354**	.427	.455	.882	+15	2	4	33	O45L,3b27,1b21,2b5/S	0	0.5
1951	Bos A	141	546	92	162	34	4	0	50	79		2	37	.297	.388	.374	.762	-3	7	4	64	1b62,2b44,O38(2/0/36)/3	0	-0.1
1952	Bos A	138	513	79	157	27	3	4	56	48		4	23	.306	.370	.394	.764	+4	8	2	80	2b103,1b23,3b5,O4L	0	3.4
1953	Bos A★	128	514	73	161	33	5	2	41	57		2	11	.313	.384	.409	.793	+8	1	4	20	2b112,1b20	0	1.3
1954	Bos A	127	489	71	148	25	4	1	36	51		2	15	.303	.370	.376	.746	-5	3	3	50	2b72,1b27,O13L,3b12	0	0.7
1955	Bos A	149	599	100	176	31	2	0	52	99	1	3	44	.294	.394	.352	.746	-6	5	5	50	2b143,1b5/rf	0	-1.0
1956	Bos A	105	399	61	117	22	8	2	38	40	1	0	22	.293	.356	.404	.760	-10	0	3	0	2b95	0	-0.8
1957	Bos A	18	16	1	1	1	0	0	0	2	0	0	1	.063	.167	.125	.292	-118	0	0	0	/H	0	-0.3
1957	Bal A	73	263	36	81	10	3	3	33	21	1	3	18	.308	.362	.403	.765	+17	0	2	0	3b54,O9(4/0/5),1b8,2b5,S5	0	0.1
1957	Year	91	279	37	82	11	3	3	33	23	1	3	19	.294	.351	.387	.738	+6	0	2	0	3b54,O9(4/0/5),1b8,2b5,S5	0	-0.2
1958	Chi A	116	425	41	127	15	5	0	40	37	1	2	21	.299	.355	.358	.713	+0	1	0	100	3b111,1b3/2S	0	-0.4
1959	†Chi A	104	268	21	67	14	1	1	28	19	0	2	20	.250	.304	.321	.625	-27	3	0	100	3b74,2b3	0	-0.5
1960	Chi A	30	77	5	18	4	0	0	6	12	1	0	8	.234	.337	.286	.623	-29	0	0	0	3b20,2b7	0	0.2
1961	Chi A	41	51	4	13	4	0	1	10	7	0	0	6	.255	.339	.392	.731	-2	0	0	0	3b7,1b2/2	0	0.0
1962	Hou N	82	161	12	41	4	1	0	10	12	2	0	11	.255	.306	.292	.598	-34	0	0	0	2b31,3b17/1	0	-1.1
Total	16	1623	5644	807	1691	299	44	19	591	669	7	29	329	.300	.376	.378	.754	-2	37	30	55	2b624,1b406,3b330,O111L,S7	0	1.5
Team	11	1177	4399	688	1344	248	34	14	464	561	2	22	245	.306	.386	.387	.773	-1	33	28	54	2b576,1b392,O1rf,3b47/S	0	3.2
/150	1	150	561	88	171	32	4	2	59	71	0	3	31	.306	.386	.387	.773	-1	4	4	50	2b73,1b50,O13L,3b6/S	0	0.4
GOSGER, JIM James Charles B11.6.1942 Port Huron MI BL/TL/5'11"/(178–185) d5.4 Col St. Clair Co. (MI) CC																								
1963	Bos A	19	16	3	1	0	0	0	0	3	0	0	5	.063	.211	.063	.274	-119	0	0	0	O4(0/2/2)	0	-0.3
1965	Bos A	81	324	45	83	15	4	9	35	29	1	2	61	.256	.318	.410	.728	+0	3	1	75	O81(0/61/22)	0	0.2
1966	Bos A	40	126	16	32	4	0	5	17	15	0	0	20	.254	.333	.405	.738	+1	0	1	0	O32(0/29/4)	0	-0.4
Total	10	705	1815	197	411	67	16	30	177	217	25	6	316	.226	.309	.331	.640	-17	25	18	58	O555(216/291/83),1b25	30	-5.4
Team	3	140	466	64	116	19	4	14	52	47	1	2	86	.249	.319	.397	.716	-4	3	2	60	O117(0/65/4)	0	-0.5
/150	3	150	499	69	124	20	4	15	56	50	1	2	92	.249	.319	.397	.716	-4	3	2	60	O125(0/70/4)	0	-0.5
GRAFFANINO, TONY Anthony Joseph B6.6.1972 Amityville NY BR/TR/6'1"/(175–195) [AtlN90 10/264] d4.19																								
2005	†Bos A	51	188	39	60	12	1	4	20	9	1	2	23	.319	.355	.457	.812	+10	4	1	80	2b51	0	0.3
Total	11	888	2556	407	688	136	21	49	272	250	6	25	437	.269	.338	.396	.734	-10	53	24	69	2b517,3b156,S106,1b42,D16,O3L	126	3.8
GRAHAM, SKINNY Arthur William B8.12.1909 Somerville MA D7.10.1967 Cambridge MA BL/TR/5'7"/162 d9.14																								
1934	Bos A	13	47	7	11	2	1	0	3	6		0	13	.234	.321	.319	.640	-39	2	2	50	O13(0/4/9)		-0.4
1935	Bos A	8	10	1	3	0	0	0	1	1		0	3	.300	.364	.300	.664	-31	1	0	100	O2R		0.0
Total	2	21	57	8	14	2	1	0	4	7		0	16	.246	.328	.316	.644	-38	3	2	60	O15(0/4/11)		-0.4
GRAHAM, CHARLIE Charles Henry B4.24.1878 Santa Clara CA D8.29.1948 San Francisco CA BR/TR/6'0"/190 d4.16 Col Santa Clara																								
1906	Bos A	30	90	10	21	1	0	1	12	10		3		.233	.330	.278	.608	-9	1			C27		0.5
GRAHAM, LEE Lee Willard B9.22.1959 Summerfield FL BL/TL/5'10"/170 [BosA77 26/641] d9.3																								
1983	Bos A	5	6	2	0	0	0	0	1	0	0	0	0	.000	.000	.000	.000	-193	0	1	0	O3(0/2/1)	0	-0.1
GREBECK, CRAIG Craig Allen B12.29.1964 Johnstown PA BR/TR/5'7"/(148–160) d4.13 Col Cal St.–Dominguez Hills																								
2001	Bos A	23	41	1	2	1	0	0	2	2	0	0	9	.049	.093	.073	.166	-155	0	0	0	S23	143	-1.1
Total	12	752	1988	239	518	116	8	19	187	228	2	19	274	.261	.340	.356	.696	-14	4	11	27	2b299,S281,3b152,D13,O5(4/0/1)	388	-0.2
GREEN, PUMPSIE Elijah Jerry B10.27.1933 Oakland CA BB/TR/6'0"/175 d7.21																								
1959	Bos A	50	172	30	40	6	3	1	10	29	0	2	22	.233	.350	.320	.670	-19	4	2	67	2b45/S	0	0.5
1960	Bos A	133	260	36	63	10	3	3	21	44	2	1	47	.242	.350	.338	.688	-15	3	4	43	2b69,S41	0	-1.3
1961	Bos A	88	219	33	57	12	3	6	27	42	3	0	32	.260	.376	.425	.801	+12	4	2	67	S57,2b7	38	0.8

Year	Tm Lg	G	AB	R	H	2B	3B	HR	RBI	BB	IB	HP	SO	AVG	OBP	SLG	OPS	AOPS	SB	CS	SB%	Games at Position	DL	BFW
1962	Bos A	56	91	12	21	2	1	2	11	11	0	0	18	.231	.308	.341	.649	-26	1	0	100	2b18,S5	0	-0.8
1963	NY N	17	54	8	15	1	2	1	5	12	0	0	13	.278	.409	.426	.835	+39	0	2	0	3b16	0	0.4
Total	5	344	796	119	196	31	12	13	74	138	5	3	132	.246	.357	.364	.721	-6	12	10	55	2b139,S104,3b16	38	-0.4
Team	4	327	742	111	181	30	10	12	69	126	5	3	119	.244	.353	.360	.713	-9	12	8	60	2b139,S104	38	-0.8
/150	2	150	340	51	83	14	5	6	32	58	2	1	55	.244	.353	.360	.713	-9	6	4	60	2b64,S48	17	-0.4
GREEN, LENNY Leonard Charles B1.6.1933 Detroit MI BL/TL/5'11"/(161–177) d8.25																								
1965	Bos A	119	373	69	103	24	6	7	24	48	0	3	43	.276	.361	.429	.790	+17	8	2	80	O95(12/86/0)	0	0.9
1966	Bos A	85	133	18	32	6	0	1	12	15	1	2	19	.241	.325	.308	.633	-24	0	1	0	O27(4/23/0)	0	-0.5
Total	12	1136	2956	461	788	138	27	47	253	368	12	29	260	.267	.351	.379	.730	-1	78	41	66	O883(331/683/44)	0	-2.2
Team	2	204	506	87	135	30	6	8	36	63	1	5	62	.267	.351	.397	.748	+6	8	3	73	O122(16/109/0)	0	0.4
/150	1	150	372	64	99	22	4	6	26	46	1	4	46	.267	.351	.397	.748	+6	6	2	75	O90(12/80/0)	0	0.3
GREENWELL, MIKE Michael Lewis B7.18.1963 Louisville KY BL/TR/6'0"/(170–205) [BosA82 3/72] d9.5 C1																								
1985	Bos A	17	31	7	10	1	0	4	8	3	1	0	4	.323	.382	.742	1.124	+91	1	0	100	O17(16/0/3)	0	0.2
1986	†Bos A	31	35	4	11	2	0	0	4	5	0	0	7	.314	.400	.371	.771	+11	0	0	0	O15(8/0/7),D3	0	0.3
1987	Bos A	125	412	71	135	31	6	19	89	35	1	6	40	.328	.386	.570	.956	+46	5	4	56	O91(64/0/28),D15/C	0	2.2
1988	†Bos A★	158	590	86	192	39	8	22	119	87	**18**	9	38	.325	.416	.531	.947	+57	16	8	67	O147(143/0/8),D11	0	4.7
1989	Bos A★	145	578	87	178	36	0	14	95	56	15	3	44	.308	.370	.443	.813	+21	13	5	72	O139L,D5	15	0.5
1990	†Bos A	159	610	71	181	30	6	14	73	65	12	4	43	.297	.367	.434	.801	+18	8	7	53	O159L	0	0.6
1991	Bos A	147	544	76	163	26	6	9	83	43	6	3	35	.300	.350	.419	.769	+7	15	5	75	O143L/D	0	0.2
1992	Bos A	49	180	16	42	2	0	2	18	18	1	2	19	.233	.307	.278	.585	-39	2	3	40	O41L,D6	120	-1.3
1993	Bos A	146	540	77	170	38	6	13	72	54	12	4	46	.315	.379	.480	.859	+22	5	4	56	O134L,D10	15	1.0
1994	Bos A	95	327	60	88	25	1	11	45	38	6	4	26	.269	.348	.453	.801	+1	2	2	50	O84L,D6	8	-0.2
1995	†Bos A	120	481	67	143	25	4	15	76	38	4	2	35	.297	.349	.459	.808	+6	9	5	64	O118L,D2	21	-0.8
1996	Bos A	77	295	35	87	20	1	7	44	18	3	2	27	.295	.336	.441	.777	-6	4	0	100	O76(75/1/1)	82	-0.2
Total	12	1269	4623	657	1400	275	38	130	726	460	79	39	364	.303	.368	.463	.831	+19	80	43	65	O1164(1124/1/47),D59/C	261	7.2
/150	1	150	546	78	165	33	4	15	86	54	9	5	43	.303	.368	.463	.831	+19	9	5	64	O14(133/0/6),D7/C	31	0.9
GRIFFIN, DOUG Douglas Lee B6.4.1947 South Gate CA BR/TR/6'0"/(150–170) [AnaA65 14/538] d9.11																								
1970	Cal A	18	55	2	7	1	0	0	4	6	1	0	5	.127	.213	.145	.358	-99	0	0	0	2b11,3b8	0	-0.9
1971	Bos A	125	483	51	118	23	2	3	27	31	3	2	45	.244	.291	.319	.610	-32	11	5	69	2b124	27	-0.5
1972	Bos A	129	470	43	122	12	1	2	35	45	6	2	48	.260	.325	.302	.627	-17	9	2	82	2b129	23	-0.2
1973	Bos A	113	396	43	101	14	5	1	33	21	0	3	42	.255	.293	.323	.616	-30	7	5	58	2b113	50	-1.5
1974	Bos A	93	312	35	83	12	4	0	33	28	3	2	21	.266	.329	.330	.659	-15	2	8	20	2b91/S	62	-1.6
1975	†Bos A	100	287	21	69	6	0	1	29	18	0	2	29	.240	.288	.272	.560	-45	2	2	50	2b99/S	0	-2.7
1976	Bos A	49	127	14	24	2	0	0	4	9	0	1	14	.189	.248	.205	.453	-70	2	1	67	2b44,D2	0	-2.2
1977	Bos A	5	6	0	0	0	0	0	0	0	0	0	0	.000	.000	.000	.000	-190	0	0	0	2b3	0	-0.2
Total	8	632	2136	209	524	70	12	7	165	158	13	12	204	.245	.299	.299	.598	-32	33	23	59	2b614,3b8,D2,S2	162	-9.8
Team	7	614	2081	207	517	69	12	7	161	152	12	12	199	.248	.301	.303	.604	-30	33	23	59	2b603,S2,D2	162	-8.9
/150	2	150	508	51	126	17	3	2	39	37	3	3	49	.248	.301	.303	.604	-30	8	6	57	2b147/SD	40	-2.2
GRIMES, RAY Oscar Ray Sr. B9.11.1893 Bergholz OH D5.25.1953 Minerva OH BR/TR/5'11"/168 d9.24 twb–Roy s–Oscar																								
1920	Bos A	1	4	1	1	0	0	0	0	1		0	0	.250	.400	.250	.650	-22	0	0	0	/1		0.0
Total	6	433	1537	269	505	101	25	27	263	204		17	133	.329	.413	.480	.893	+32	21	17	100	1b426		3.5
GRIMSHAW, MYRON Myron Frederick B11.30.1875 St.Johnsville NY D12.11.1936 Canajoharie NY BB/TR/6'1"/173 d4.25																								
1905	Bos A	85	285	39	68	8	2	4	35	21		1		.239	.293	.323	.616	-6	4			1b74		-1.0
1906	Bos A	110	428	46	124	16	12	0	48	23		4		.290	.332	.383	.715	+24	5			1b110		0.7
1907	Bos A	64	181	19	37	7	2	0	33	16		1		.204	.273	.265	.538	-28	6			1b20,O18(1/0/17),S2		-1.1
Total	3	259	894	104	229	31	16	4	116	60		6		.256	.307	.340	.647	+4	15			1b204,O18(1/0/17),S2		-1.4
/150	2	150	518	60	133	18	9	2	67	35		3	0	.256	.307	.340	.647	+4	9			1b118,O10(1/0/10)/S	0	-0.8
GROSS, TURKEY Ewell B2.21.1896 Mesquite TX D1.11.1936 Dallas TX BR/TR/6'0"/165 d4.14																								
1925	Bos A	9	32	2	3	0	1	0	2	2		1	2	.094	.171	.156	.327	-116	0	0	0	S9		-0.4
GUBANICH, CREIGHTON Creighton Wade B3.27.1972 Belleville NJ BR/TR/6'3"/200 [OakA90 6/181] d4.16																								
1999	Bos A	18	47	4	13	2	1	1	11	3	0	2	13	.277	.346	.426	.772	-8	0	0	0	C14/3D	0	-0.3
GUERRA, MIKE Fermin (Romero) B10.11.1912 Havana, Cuba D10.9.1992 Miami Beach FL BR/TR/5'9"/162 d9.19																								
1951	Bos A	10	32	1	5	0	0	0	2	6		0	5	.156	.289	.156	.445	-79	1	0	100	C10	0	-0.3
Total	9	565	1581	168	382	42	14	9	168	131		1	123	.242	.300	.303	.603	-35	25	12	68	C482/lf	0	-7.2
GUERRERO, MARIO Mario Miguel (Abud) B9.28.1949 Santo Domingo, D.R. BR/TR/5'10"/(154–155) d4.8																								
1973	Bos A	66	219	19	51	5	2	0	11	10	0	2	21	.233	.272	.274	.546	-49	2	2	50	S46,2b24	0	-0.9
1974	Bos A	93	284	18	70	6	2	0	23	13	0	2	22	.246	.282	.282	.564	-41	3	1	75	S93	0	-0.9
Total	8	697	2251	166	578	79	12	7	170	84	8	16	152	.257	.285	.312	.597	-31	8	12	40	S576,2b77,D26	36	-10.7
Team	2	159	503	37	121	11	4	0	34	23	0	4	43	.241	.278	.278	.556	-44	5	3	63	S139,2b24	0	-1.8
/150	2	150	475	35	114	10	4	0	32	22	0	4	41	.241	.278	.278	.556	-44	5	3	63	S131,2b23	0	-1.7
GUINDON, BOBBY Robert Joseph B9.4.1943 Brookline MA BL/TL/6'2"/185 d9.19																								
1964	Bos A	5	8	0	1	1	0	0	0	1	0	0	4	.125	.222	.250	.472	-70	0	0	0	/1lf	0	-0.1
GUNNING, HY Hyland B8.6.1888 Maplewood NJ D3.28.1975 Togus ME BL/TR/6'1.5"/189 d8.8 Col Princeton																								
1911	Bos A	4	9	0	1	0	0	0	2	2		0		.111	.273	.111	.384	-91	0			1b4		-0.2
GUTIERREZ, JACKIE Joaquin Fernando B6.27.1960 Cartagena, Colombia BR/TR/5'11"/(145–180) d9.6																								
1983	Bos A	5	10	2	3	0	0	0	0	1	0	0	1	.300	.364	.300	.664	-21	0	1	0	S4	0	-0.1
1984	Bos A	151	449	55	118	12	3	2	29	15	0	0	49	.263	.284	.316	.600	-37	12	5	71	S150	0	-3.4
1985	Bos A	103	275	33	60	5	2	2	21	12	0	0	37	.218	.250	.273	.523	-58	10	2	83	S99	0	-1.6
1986	Bal A	61	145	8	27	3	0	0	4	3	0	1	27	.186	.207	.207	.414	-86	3	1	75	2b53,3b6/D	74	-2.0
1987	Bal A	3	1	0	0	0	0	0	0	0	0	0	0	.000	.000	.000	.000	-199	0	0	0	/23	0	-0.1
1988	Phi N	33	77	8	19	4	0	0	9	2	0	0	9	.247	.259	.299	.558	-40	0	0	0	S22,3b13	0	-0.6
Total	6	356	957	106	227	24	5	4	63	33	0	1	123	.237	.261	.285	.546	-50	25	9	74	S275,2b54,3b20/D	74	-7.8
Team	3	259	734	90	181	17	5	4	50	28	0	0	87	.247	.272	.300	.572	-45	22	8	73	S253	0	-5.1
/150	2	150	425	52	105	10	3	2	29	16	0	0	50	.247	.272	.300	.572	-45	13	5	72	S147	0	-3.0
GUTIERREZ, RICKY Ricardo B5.23.1970 Miami FL BR/TR/6'1"/(175–195) [BalA88 1/28] d4.13																								
2004	Bos A	21	40	6	11	1	0	0	3	2	0	0	6	.275	.310	.300	.610	-43	1	0	100	2b14,S6	0	-0.1
Total	12	1119	3632	471	967	141	25	38	357	364	20	48	586	.266	.338	.350	.688	-18	50	30	63	S878,2b152,3b44,O5(3/0/2)/D	361	-5.6
GUTTERIDGE, DON Donald Joseph B6.19.1912 Pittsburg KS BR/TR/5'10.5"/165 d9.7 M2/C14 Col Pittsburg St. (KS)																								
1946	†Bos A	22	47	8	11	3	0	1	6	2		0	7	.234	.265	.362	.627	-30	0	0	0	2b9,3b8	0	-0.3
1947	Bos A	54	131	20	22	2	0	2	5	17		0	13	.168	.264	.229	.493	-65	3	1	75	2b20,3b19	0	-1.3
Total	12	1151	4202	586	1075	200	64	39	391	309		5	444	.256	.308	.362	.670	-16	95	37	100	2b580,3b412,S78,O14L	0	-14.4
Team	2	76	178	28	33	5	0	3	11	19		0	20	.185	.264	.264	.528	-56	3	1	75	2b29,3b27	0	-1.6
HALE, ODELL Arvel Odell "Bad News" B8.10.1908 Hosston LA D6.9.1980 El Dorado AR BR/TR/5'10"/175 d8.1																								
1941	Bos A	12	24	5	5	2	0	1	1	3		0	4	.208	.296	.417	.713	-15	0	0	0	3b6/2	0	-0.3
Total	10	1062	3701	551	1071	240	51	73	573	353		3	315	.289	.352	.441	.793	+0	57	45	100	2b518,3b439/S	0	7.0
HALEY, RAY Raymond Timothy "Pat" B1.23.1891 Danbury IA D10.8.1973 Bradenton FL BR/TR/5'11"/180 d4.21 Mil 1918–19 Col Western Illinois																								
1915	Bos A	5	7	2	1	1	0	0	0	1		0	0	.143	.250	.286	.536	-38	0			C4		0.0
1916	Bos A	1	1	0	0	0	0	0	0	0		0	1	.000	.000	.000	.000	-199	0			/H		0.0
Total	3	81	214	17	53	8	1	0	15	11		2	32	.248	.291	.294	.585	-20	2			C71		-0.7
Team	2	6	8	2	1	1	0	0	0	1		0	1	.125	.222	.250	.472	-56	0			C4		0.0
HANCOCK, GARRY Ronald Garry B1.23.1954 Tampa FL BL/TL/6'0"/(175–190) [CleA76*S1/17] d7.16 Col South Carolina																								
1978	Bos A	38	80	10	18	3	0	0	4	1	0	0	12	.225	.232	.262	.494	-64	0	0	0	O19(4/5/10),D13	0	-0.5
1980	Bos A	46	115	9	33	6	0	4	19	3	0	0	11	.287	.300	.443	.743	-3	0	3	0	O27(6/20/1),D12	0	-0.4

Year	Tm Lg	G	AB	R	H	2B	3B	HR	RBI	BB	IB	HP	SO	AVG	OBP	SLG	OPS	AOPS	SB	CS	SB%	Games at Position	DL	BFW
1981	Bos A	26	45	4	7	3	0	0	3	2	1	0	4	.156	.191	.222	.413	-82	0	0	0	O8(0/5/3),D4	0	-0.4
1982	Bos A	11	14	3	0	0	0	0	0	1	0	0	1	.000	.067	.000	.067	-175	0	0	0	O7R	0	-0.4
1983	Oak A	101	256	29	70	7	3	8	30	5	4	1	13	.273	.289	.418	.707	-3	2	0	100	O67(26/1/40),1b27,D9	0	-0.6
1984	Oak A	51	60	2	13	2	0	0	8	0	0	0	1	.217	.217	.250	.467	-69	0	0	0	O18(9/2/9),1b4/PD	31	-0.6
Total	6	273	570	57	141	21	3	12	64	12	5	1	42	.247	.262	.358	.620	-30	2	3	40	O146(45/33/70),D43,1b31/P	31	-2.9
Team	4	121	254	26	58	12	0	4	26	7	1	0	28	.228	.246	.323	.569	-46	0	3	0	O61(10/30/14),D29	0	-1.7
/150	5	150	315	32	72	15	0	5	32	9	1	0	35	.228	.246	.323	.569	-46	0	4	0	O76(12/37/17),D36	0	-2.1
HANEY, FRED Fred Girard "Pudge" B4.25.1898 Albuquerque NM D11.9.1977 Beverly Hills CA BR/TR/5'6"/170 d4.18 M10/C1																								
1926	Bos A	138	462	47	102	15	7	0	52	74		1	28	.221	.330	.284	.614	-37	13	6	68	3b137		-0.7
1927	Bos A	47	116	23	32	4	1	3	12	25		0	14	.276	.404	.405	.809	+13	4	1	80	3b34/cf		0.3
Total	7	622	1977	338	544	66	21	8	228	282		10	123	.275	.368	.342	.710	-13	51	25	100	3b450,2b72,S22,1b11/cf		0.9
Team	2	185	578	70	134	19	8	3	64	99		1	42	.232	.346	.308	.654	-27	17	7	71	3b171/cf		-0.4
/150	2	150	469	57	109	15	6	2	52	80		1	34	.232	.346	.308	.654	-27	14	6	70	3b139/cf		-0.3
HARDY, CARROLL Carroll William B5.18.1933 Sturgis SD BR/TR/6'0"/185 d4.15 Col Colorado																								
1958	Cle A	27	49	10	10	3	0	1	6	6	0	1	14	.204	.298	.327	.625	-25	1	2	33	O17(0/16/1)	30	-0.1
1959	Cle A	32	53	12	11	1	0	0	2	3	0	0	7	.208	.250	.226	.476	-67	1	1	50	O15(1/14/0)	0	-0.3
1960	Cle A	29	18	7	2	1	0	0	1	2	0	0	2	.111	.200	.167	.367	-100	0	0	0	O17(4/9/5)	0	-0.3
1960	Bos A	73	145	26	34	5	2	2	15	17	0	0	40	.234	.313	.338	.651	-26	3	2	60	O59(44/8/14)	0	-0.5
1960	Year	102	163	33	36	6	2	2	16	19	0	0	42	.221	.301	.319	.620	-33	3	2	60	O76(48/17/19)	0	-0.8
1961	Bos A	85	281	46	74	20	2	3	36	26	0	2	53	.263	.330	.381	.711	-13	4	2	67	O76(20/38/21)	0	-0.8
1962	Bos A	115	362	52	78	13	5	8	36	54	1	2	68	.215	.318	.345	.663	-23	3	7	30	O105(3/45/64)	0	-1.8
1963	Hou N	15	44	5	10	3	0	0	3	3	0	0	7	.227	.277	.295	.572	-31	1	0	100	O10L	0	-0.2
1964	Hou N	46	157	13	29	1	1	2	12	8	0	2	30	.185	.232	.242	.474	-64	0	0	0	O41(5/33/4)	0	-1.3
1967	Min A	11	8	1	3	0	0	1	2	1	0	0	1	.375	.444	.750	1.194	+129	0	0	0	O4(1/0/3)	0	0.1
Total	8	433	1117	172	251	47	10	17	113	120	1	7	222	.225	.302	.330	.632	-28	13	14	48	O344(88/163/112)	30	-5.2
Team	3	273	788	124	186	38	9	13	87	97	1	4	161	.236	.321	.357	.678	-20	10	11	48	O240(64/91/22)	0	-3.1
/150	2	150	433	68	102	21	5	7	48	53	1	2	88	.236	.321	.357	.678	-20	5	6	45	O132(35/50/12)	0	-1.7
HARPER, TOMMY Tommy B10.14.1940 Oak Grove LA BR/TR/5'10"/(160–168) d4.9 C18 Col San Francisco St. OF(683/258/348)																								
1972	Bos A	144	556	92	141	29	2	14	49	67	1	9	104	.254	.341	.388	.729	+11	25	7	78	O144C	0	0.4
1973	Bos A	147	566	92	159	23	3	17	71	61	2	1	93	.281	.351	.422	.773	+10	**54**	14	79	O143(139/5/0)/D	0	0.8
1974	Bos A	118	443	66	105	15	3	5	24	46	2	3	65	.237	.312	.318	.630	-23	28	12	70	O61L,D51	0	-2.0
Total	15	1810	6269	972	1609	256	36	146	567	753	30	35	1080	.257	.338	.379	.717	+0	408	116	78	O1227L,3b270,D139,2b85,1b36	59	1.4
Team	3	409	1565	250	405	67	8	36	144	174	5	13	262	.259	.336	.381	.717	+1	107	33	76	O348(139/149/5),D52	0	-0.8
/150	1	150	574	92	149	25	3	13	53	64	2	5	96	.259	.336	.381	.717	+1	39	12	76	O128(51/55/2),D19	0	-0.3
HARRELL, BILLY William B7.18.1928 Norristown PA BR/TR/6'1.5"/180 d9.2 Negro Lg 1951 Col Siena																								
1961	Bos A	37	37	10	6	2	0	0	1	1	0	0	8	.162	.184	.216	.400	-94	1	0	100	3b10,S7,1b3	0	-0.3
Total	4	173	342	54	79	7	1	8	26	23	2	2	54	.231	.283	.327	.610	-32	17	3	85	S77,3b62,2b8,1b3/rf	0	-1.8
HARRELSON, KEN Kenneth Smith "Hawk" B9.4.1941 Woodruff SC BR/TR/6'2"/(185–195) d6.9																								
1967	†Bos A	23	80	9	16	4	1	3	14	5	2	0	12	.200	.247	.387	.634	-21	1	1	50	O23R/1	0	-0.7
1968	Bos A★	150	535	79	147	17	4	35	**109**	69	9	2	90	.275	.356	.518	.874	+54	2	6	25	O132R,1b19	0	3.1
1969	Bos A	10	46	6	10	1	0	3	8	4	0	0	6	.217	.275	.435	.710	-7	0	1	0	1b10	0	-0.1
Total	9	900	2941	374	703	94	14	131	421	382	33	6	577	.239	.325	.414	.739	+9	53	30	64	1b469,O365(70/0/296)	148	-1.8
Team	3	183	661	94	173	22	5	41	131	78	11	2	108	.262	.338	.496	.834	+41	3	8	27	O155R,1b30	0	2.3
/150	2	150	542	77	142	18	4	34	107	64	9	2	89	.262	.338	.496	.834	+41	2	7	22	O127R,1b25	0	1.9
HARRIS, JOE Joseph "Moon" B5.20.1891 Plum Borough PA D12.10.1959 Renton PA BR/TR/5'9"/170 d6.9 Mil 1918																								
1914	NY A	2	1	0	0	0	0	0	0	3		1	1	.000	.800	.000	.800	+43	0			/1lf		0.1
1917	Cle A	112	369	40	112	22	4	0	65	55		3	32	.304	.398	.385	.783	+29	11			1b95,O5R,3b2		2.5
1919	Cle A	62	184	30	69	16	1	1	46	33		1	21	.375	.472	.489	.961	+60	2			1b46,S4		2.0
1922	Bos A	119	408	53	129	30	9	6	54	30		1	15	.316	.364	.478	.842	+19	2	6	25	O83(71/0/12),1b21		0.6
1923	Bos A	142	483	82	162	28	11	13	76	52		5	27	.335	.406	.520	.926	+42	7	3	70	O132L,1b9		1.7
1924	Bos A	133	491	82	148	36	9	3	77	81		5	25	.301	.406	.430	.836	+15	6	1	86	1b128,O3L		1.2
1925	Bos A	8	19	4	3	0	1	1	2	5		0	5	.158	.333	.421	.754	-10	0	0	0	1b6		-0.1
1925	†Was A	100	300	60	97	21	9	12	59	51		5	28	.323	.430	.573	1.003	+56	6	3	67	1b58,O41(16/0/25)		2.3
1925	Year	108	319	64	100	21	10	13	61	56		5	33	.313	.424	.564	.988	+52	6	3	67	1b64,O41(16/0/25)		2.2
1926	Was A	92	257	43	79	13	9	5	55	37		5	9	.307	.405	.486	.891	+35	2	3	40	1b36,O35(3/0/32)		0.8
1927	†Pit N	129	411	57	134	27	9	5	73	48		4	19	.326	.402	.472	.874	+25	0			1b116,O3L		1.0
1928	Pit N	16	23	2	9	2	1	0	2	4		1	2	.391	.500	.565	1.065	+71	0			1b6		0.4
1928	Bro N	55	89	8	21	6	1	1	8	14		0	4	.236	.340	.360	.700	-16	0			O16(6/0/10)		-0.3
1928	Year	71	112	10	30	8	2	1	10	18		1	6	.268	.374	.402	.776	+3	0			O16(6/0/10),1b6		0.1
Total	10	970	3035	461	963	201	64	47	517	413		31	188	.317	.404	.472	.876	+31	36	16	100	1b522,O319(235/0/84),S4,3b2		12.2
Team	4	402	1401	221	442	94	30	23	209	168		11	72	.315	.393	.475	.868	+25	15	10	60	O218(71/0/12),1b164		3.4
/150	1	150	523	82	165	35	11	9	78	63		4	27	.315	.393	.475	.868	+25	6	4	60	O81(26/0/4),1b61		1.3
HARRIS, WILLIE William Charles B6.22.1978 Cairo GA BL/TR/5'9"/(170–175) [BalA99 24/727] d9.2 Col Kennesaw St.																								
2006	Bos A	47	45	17	7	2	0	0	1	4	0	2	11	.156	.250	.200	.450	-80	6	3	67	O36(11/24/1)/2	0	-0.5
Total	6	369	899	138	214	27	4	5	53	87	0	4	171	.238	.306	.294	.600	-43	55	15	79	2b175,O141(12/128/1),D11,S5	25	-3.0
HARTLEY, GROVER Grover Allen "Slick" B7.2.1888 Osgood IN D10.19.1964 Daytona Beach FL BR/TR/5'11"/175 d5.13 C10																								
1927	Bos A	103	244	23	67	11	0	1	31	22		1	14	.275	.337	.332	.669	-24	1	0	100	C86		-1.7
Total	14	569	1319	135	353	60	11	3	144	127		15	97	.268	.339	.337	.676	-15	29	1	100	C435,1b19,2b13,3b4,O2C/S		-2.4
/150	1	150	355	33	98	16	0	1	45	32		1	20	.275	.337	.332	.669	-24	1	0	100	C125		-2.5
HASELMAN, BILL William Joseph B5.25.1966 Long Branch NJ BR/TR/6'3"/(205–223) [TexA87 1/23] d9.3 C2 Col UCLA [DL 1992 Tex A 28]																								
1990	Tex A	7	13	0	2	0	0	0	3	1	0	0	5	.154	.214	.154	.368	-95	0	0	0	/CD	0	-0.1
1992	Sea A	8	19	1	5	0	0	0	0	0	0	0	7	.263	.263	.263	.526	-53	0	0	0	C5,O2L	0	-0.2
1993	Sea A	58	137	21	35	8	0	5	16	12	0	1	19	.255	.316	.423	.739	-4	2	1	67	C49,O2R,D4	0	-0.1
1994	Sea A	38	83	11	16	7	1	1	8	3	0	1	11	.193	.230	.337	.567	-57	1	0	100	C33,O2R,D3	0	-0.8
1995	†Bos A	64	152	22	37	6	1	5	23	17	0	2	30	.243	.322	.395	.717	-16	0	2	0	C48,D11/13	0	0.2
1996	Bos A	77	237	33	65	13	1	8	34	19	3	1	52	.274	.331	.439	.770	-9	4	2	67	C69,1b2,D2	0	0.9
1997	Bos A	67	212	22	50	15	0	6	26	15	2	2	44	.236	.290	.392	.682	-25	0	2	0	C66	39	-0.8
1998	Tex A	40	105	11	33	6	0	6	17	3	0	0	17	.314	.327	.543	.870	+16	0	0	0	C36,D2	0	0.2
1999	Det A	48	143	13	39	8	0	4	14	10	1	0	26	.273	.320	.413	.733	-16	2	0	100	C39,D9	0	-0.2
2000	Tex A	62	193	23	53	18	0	6	26	15	0	1	36	.275	.329	.461	.790	-4	0	1	0	C62	0	0.2
2001	Tex A	47	130	12	37	6	0	3	25	8	0	1	27	.285	.331	.400	.731	-11	0	1	0	C47	82	-0.5
2002	Tex A	69	179	16	44	7	0	3	18	11	1	2	25	.246	.297	.335	.632	-34	0	0	0	C67,D2	0	-1.5
2003	Bos A	4	3	0	0	0	0	0	0	0	0	0	1	.000	.000	.000	.000	-196	0	0	0	C2,D2	0	-0.1
Total	13	589	1606	185	416	94	3	47	210	114	7	11	300	.259	.311	.409	.720	-17	9	9	50	C524,D38,O6(2/0/4),1b3/3	149	-2.8
Team	4	212	604	77	152	34	2	19	83	51	5	5	127	.252	.313	.409	.722	-17	4	6	40	C185,D15,1b3/3	39	0.2
/150	3	150	427	54	108	24	1	13	59	36	4	4	90	.252	.313	.409	.722	-17	3	4	43	C131,D11,1b2/3	28	0.1
HATCHER, BILLY William Augustus B10.4.1960 Williams AZ BR/TR/5'9"/(175–190) [ChiN81*6/131] d9.10 C8 Col Yavapai (AZ) JC																								
1992	Bos A	75	315	37	75	16	2	1	23	17	1	3	41	.238	.283	.311	.594	-38	4	6	40	O75(63/13/0)	0	-2.4
1993	Bos A	136	508	71	146	24	3	9	57	28	4	11	46	.287	.336	.400	.736	-8	14	7	67	O130(0/129/2),2b2	0	-1.5
1994	Bos A	44	164	24	40	9	1	1	18	11	0	1	14	.244	.292	.329	.621	-42	4	5	44	O43R/D	0	-1.2
Total	12	1233	4339	586	1146	210	30	54	399	267	23	55	476	.264	.312	.364	.676	-15	218	87	71	O1143(583/553/87),D2,2b2	62	-10.5
Team	3	255	987	132	261	49	6	11	98	56	5	15	101	.264	.312	.360	.672	-23	22	18	55	O248(63/142/2),2b2/D	0	-5.1
/150	2	150	581	78	154	29	4	6	58	33	3	9	59	.264	.312	.360	.672	-23	13	11	54	O146(37/84/1)/2D	0	-3.0

Year	Tm Lg	G	AB	R	H	2B	3B	HR	RBI	BB	IB	HP	SO	AVG	OBP	SLG	OPS	AOPS	SB	CS	SB%	Games at Position	DL	BFW
HATFIELD, FRED Fred James B3.18.1925 Lanett AL D5.22.1998 Tallahassee FL BL/TR/6'1"/(171–176) d8.31 C2																								
1950	Bos A	10	12	3	3	0	0	0	2	3		0	1	.250	.400	.250	.650	-37	0	0	0	3b3	0	0.1
1951	Bos A	80	163	23	28	4	2	2	14	22		1	27	.172	.274	.258	.532	-60	1	0	100	3b49	0	0.0
1952	Bos A	19	25	6	8	1	1	1	3	4		1	2	.320	.433	.560	.993	+62	0	3	0	3b17	0	0.3
Total	9	722	2039	259	493	67	10	25	165	248	10	33	247	.242	.332	.321	.653	-22	15	14	52	3b408,2b179,S27	0	-2.3
Team	3	109	200	32	39	5	3	3	19	29		2	30	.195	.303	.295	.598	-43	1	3	25	3b69	0	0.4
/150	4	150	275	44	54	7	4	4	26	40		3	41	.195	.303	.295	.598	-43	1	4	20	3b95	0	0.6
HATTEBERG, SCOTT Scott Allen B12.14.1969 Salem OR BL/TR/6'1"/(192–210) [BosA91 1/43] d9.8 Col Washington St.																								
1995	Bos A	2	2	1	1	0	0	0	0	0	0	0	0	.500	.500	.500	1.000	+56	0	0	0	C2	0	0.1
1996	Bos A	10	11	3	2	1	0	0	0	3	0	0	2	.182	.357	.273	.630	-39	0	0	0	C10	0	0.0
1997	Bos A	114	350	46	97	23	1	10	44	40	2	2	70	.277	.354	.434	.788	+2	0	1	0	C106/D	0	-0.5
1998	†Bos A	112	359	46	99	23	1	12	43	43	3	5	58	.276	.359	.446	.805	+6	0	0	0	C108	0	1.8
1999	†Bos A	30	80	12	22	5	0	1	11	18	0	1	14	.275	.410	.375	.785	+0	0	0	0	C23,D6	112	0.3
2000	Bos A	92	230	21	61	15	0	8	36	38	3	0	39	.265	.367	.435	.802	+0	0	1	0	C48,D20/3	0	-0.4
2001	Bos A	94	278	34	68	19	0	3	25	33	0	4	26	.245	.332	.345	.677	-21	1	1	50	C72,D8	0	-2.5
2002	†Oak A	136	492	58	138	22	4	15	61	68	1	6	56	.280	.374	.433	.807	+15	0	0	0	1b91,D42	0	1.2
2003	†Oak A	147	541	63	137	34	0	12	61	66	0	9	53	.253	.342	.383	.725	-9	0	1	0	1b128,D15	0	-1.5
2004	Oak A	152	550	87	156	30	0	15	82	72	5	5	48	.284	.367	.420	.787	+7	0	0	0	1b148,D2	0	-0.6
2005	Oak A	134	464	52	119	19	0	7	59	51	4	4	54	.256	.334	.343	.677	-18	0	1	0	D79,1b53	0	-1.8
2006	Cin N	141	456	62	132	28	0	13	51	74	3	3	41	.289	.389	.436	.825	+6	2	2	50	1b131	0	-0.6
Total	12	1164	3813	485	1032	219	6	96	473	506	21	39	461	.271	.360	.407	.767	-1	3	7	30	1b551,C369,D173/3	112	-4.5
Team	7	454	1310	163	350	86	2	34	159	175	8	12	209	.267	.357	.414	.771	-3	1	3	25	C369,D35/3	112	-1.2
/150	2	150	433	54	116	28	1	11	53	58	3	4	69	.267	.357	.414	.771	-3	0	1	0	C122,D12/3	37	-0.4
HATTON, GRADY Grady Edgebert B10.7.1922 Beaumont TX BL/TR/5'9"/175 d4.16 M3/C3 Col Texas																								
1954	Bos A	99	302	40	85	12	3	5	33	58		2	25	.281	.399	.391	.790	+6	1	1	50	3b93/1S	0	1.1
1955	Bos A	126	380	48	93	11	4	4	49	76	3	0	28	.245	.367	.326	.693	-19	0	1	0	3b111/2	0	-0.4
1956	Bos A	5	5	0	2	0	0	0	2	0	0	0	0	.400	.400	.400	.800	+0	0	0	0	/H	0	0.0
Total	12	1312	4206	562	1068	166	33	91	533	646	5	13	430	.254	.354	.374	.728	-4	42	9	100	3b956,2b196,1b14,O5L,S4	0	-3.1
Team	3	230	687	88	180	23	7	9	84	134	3	2	53	.262	.382	.355	.737	-8	1	2	33	3b204/12S	0	0.7
/150	2	150	448	57	117	15	5	6	55	87	2	1	35	.262	.382	.355	.737	-8	1	1	50	3b133/12S	0	0.5
HAYDEN, JACK John Francis B10.21.1880 Bryn Mawr PA D8.3.1942 Haverford PA BL/TL/5'9"/170 d4.26 Col Villanova																								
1901	Phi A	51	211	35	56	6	4	0	17	18		0		.265	.323	.332	.655	-22	4			O50(30/4/16)		-1.2
1906	Bos A	85	322	22	80	6	4	1	14	17		3		.248	.292	.301	.593	-14	6			O85R		-1.4
1908	Chi N	11	45	3	9	2	0	0	2	1		0		.200	.217	.244	.461	-55	1			O11R		-0.5
Total	3	147	578	60	145	14	8	1	33	36		3		.251	.298	.308	.606	-20	11			O146(30/4/112)		-3.1
HAYES, FRANKIE Franklin Witman "Blimp" B10.13.1914 Jamesburg NJ D6.22.1955 Point Pleasant NJ BR/TR/6'0"/185 d9.21																								
1947	Bos A	5	13	0	2	0	0	0	1	0		0	1	.154	.154	.154	.308	-113	0	0	0	C4	0	-0.2
Total	14	1364	4493	545	1164	213	32	119	628	564		13	627	.259	.343	.400	.743	+0	30	20	60	C1311,1b4	0	-3.2
HEARNE, ED Edmund B9.17.1887 Ventura CA D9.8.1952 Los Angeles CA BR/TR/5'9"/160 d6.9																								
1910	Bos A	2	2	0	0	0	0	0	0	0		0		.000	.000	.000	.000	-198	0			S2		0.0
HEEP, DANNY Daniel William B7.3.1957 San Antonio TX BL/TL/5'11"/(176–185) [HouN78 2/37] d8.31 Col St. Marys (TX)																								
1989	Bos A	113	320	36	96	17	0	5	49	29	4	1	26	.300	.356	.400	.756	+7	0	1	0	O75(17/0/59),1b19,D9	0	-0.4
1990	†Bos A	41	69	3	12	1	1	0	8	7	0	1	14	.174	.256	.217	.473	-67	0	0	0	O14(1/0/13),1b5/PD	66	-0.5
Total	13	883	1961	208	503	96	6	30	229	220	25	9	242	.257	.330	.357	.687	-6	12	14	46	O429(181/26/232),1b131,D15,P2	81	-4.6
Team	2	154	389	39	108	18	1	5	57	36	4	2	40	.278	.338	.368	.706	-6	0	1	0	O89(18/0/72),1b24,D10/P	66	-0.9
/150	2	150	379	38	105	18	1	5	56	35	4	2	39	.278	.338	.368	.706	-6	0	1	0	O87(18/0/70),1b23,D10/P	64	-0.9
HEISE, BOB Robert Lowell B5.12.1947 San Antonio TX BR/TR/6'0"/(165–175) d9.12 Col Solano (CA) CC																								
1975	Bos A	63	126	12	27	3	0	0	21	4	0	2	6	.214	.246	.238	.484	-64	0	0	0	3b45,2b14,S4/1	0	-0.9
1976	Bos A	32	56	5	15	2	0	0	5	1	0	1	2	.268	.293	.304	.597	-33	0	1	0	3b22,S9/2	26	-0.3
Total	11	499	1144	104	283	43	3	1	86	47	3	6	77	.247	.280	.293	.573	-37	3	7	30	S174,2b154,3b135,1b6,D2/lf	26	-4.9
Team	2	95	182	17	42	5	0	0	26	5	0	3	8	.231	.260	.258	.518	-55	0	1	0	3b67,2b15,S13/1	26	-1.2
HELMS, TOMMY Tommy Vann B5.5.1941 Charlotte NC BR/TR/5'10"/(165–175) d9.23 M2/C9																								
1977	Bos A	21	59	5	16	2	0	1	5	4	1	1	4	.271	.328	.356	.684	-22	0	0	0	D13,3b2/2	0	-0.4
Total	14	1435	4997	414	1342	223	21	34	477	231	60	15	301	.269	.300	.342	.642	-21	33	40	45	2b1129,3b143,S74,D13	44	-2.9
HEMPHILL, CHARLIE Charles Judson "Eagle Eye" B4.20.1876 Greenville MI D6.22.1953 Detroit MI BL/TL/5'9"/160 d6.27 b-Frank																								
1901	Bos A	136	545	71	142	10	10	3	62	39		2		.261	.312	.332	.644	-20	11			O136(0/2/134)		-2.4
Total	11	1242	4541	580	1230	117	68	22	421	435		17		.271	.337	.341	.678	+6	207			O1175(45/607/525),2b3		-6.2
/150	1	150	601	78	157	11	11	3	68	43		2	0	.261	.312	.332	.644	-20	12			O150(0/2/148)		-2.6
HENDERSON, DAVE David Lee B7.21.1958 Merced CA BR/TR/6'2"/(210–220) [SeaA77 1/26] d4.9																								
1986	†Bos A	36	51	8	10	3	0	1	3	2	0	0	15	.196	.226	.314	.540	-55	1	0	100	O32C	0	-0.1
1987	Bos A	75	184	30	43	10	0	8	25	22	0	0	48	.234	.313	.418	.731	-10	1	1	50	O64(5/29/30)/D	0	-0.7
Total	14	1538	5130	710	1324	286	17	197	708	465	19	22	1105	.258	.320	.436	.756	+8	50	38	57	O1388(36/1157/229),D99/2	244	5.1
Team	2	111	235	38	53	13	0	9	28	24	0	0	63	.226	.295	.396	.691	-19	2	1	67	O96(5/61/29)/D	0	-0.8
/150	3	150	318	51	72	18	0	12	38	32	0	0	85	.226	.295	.396	.691	-19	3	1	75	O130(7/82/39)/D	0	-1.1
HENDERSON, RICKEY Rickey Henley B12.25.1958 Chicago IL BR/TL/5'10"/(180–195) [OakA76 4/96] d6.24																								
2002	Bos A	72	179	40	40	6	1	5	16	38	0	4	47	.223	.369	.352	.721	-8	8	2	80	O54(49/4/1),D5	0	-0.2
Total	25	3081	10961	2295	3055	510	66	297	1115	2190	61	98	1694	.279	.401	.419	.820	+27	1406	335	81	O2826(2421/448/27),D149	176	70.2
HENDRYX, TIM Timothy Green B1.31.1891 LeRoy IL D8.14.1957 Corpus Christi TX BR/TR/5'9"/170 d9.4																								
1911	Cle A	4	7	0	2	0	0	0	0	0		0		.286	.286	.286	.572	-41	0			3b3		0.0
1912	Cle A	23	70	9	17	2	4	1	14	8		1		.243	.329	.429	.758	+13	3			O22C		-0.2
1915	NY A	13	40	4	8	2	0	0	1	4		1	2	.200	.289	.250	.539	-39	0	3	0	O12C		-0.3
1916	NY A	15	62	10	18	7	1	0	5	8		1	6	.290	.380	.435	.815	+42	4			O15R		0.2
1917	NY A	125	393	43	98	14	7	5	44	62		5	45	.249	.359	.359	.718	+18	6			O107(0/30/77)		0.6
1918	StL A	88	219	22	61	14	3	0	33	37		2	35	.279	.388	.370	.758	+33	5			O65(28/20/18)		0.5
1920	Bos A	99	363	54	119	21	5	0	73	42		2	27	.328	.400	.413	.813	+21	7	9	44	O98C		-0.8
1921	Bos A	49	137	10	33	8	2	0	22	24		2	13	.241	.362	.328	.690	-21	1	1	50	O41(2/2/37)		-0.8
Total	8	416	1291	152	356	68	22	6	192	185		14	128	.276	.372	.376	.748	+15	26	13	100	O360(30/184/147),3b3		-0.8
Team	2	148	500	64	152	29	7	0	95	66		4	40	.304	.389	.390	.779	+9	8	10	44	O139(2/100/0)		-1.6
/150	2	150	507	65	154	29	7	0	96	67		4	41	.304	.389	.390	.779	+9	8	10	44	O141(2/101/0)		-1.6
HENRIKSEN, OLAF Olaf "Swede" B4.26.1888 Kirkerup, Denmark D10.17.1962 Norwood MA BL/TL/5'7.5"/158 d8.11																								
1911	Bos A	27	93	17	34	2	1	0	8	14		0		.366	.449	.409	.858	+41	4			O25(5/0/20)		0.5
1912	†Bos A	44	56	20	18	3	1	0	8	14		0		.321	.457	.411	.868	+42	0			O11(0/1/10)		0.2
1913	Bos A	31	40	8	15	1	0	0	2	7		0	5	.375	.468	.400	.868	+51	3			O7(6/1/0)		0.3
1914	Bos A	63	95	16	25	2	1	1	5	22		1	12	.263	.407	.337	.744	+24	5	4	56	O29(8/11/10)		0.2
1915	†Bos A	73	92	9	18	2	2	0	13	18		1	7	.196	.333	.261	.594	-20	1	5	17	O25(9/4/12)		-0.3
1916	†Bos A	68	99	13	20	2	2	0	11	19		0	15	.202	.331	.263	.594	-22	2			O31(14/7/9)		-0.3
1917	Bos A	15	12	1	1	0	0	0	1	3		0	4	.083	.267	.083	.350	-93	0			/H		-0.1
Total	7	321	487	84	131	12	7	1	48	97		2	43	.269	.392	.329	.721	+12	15	9	100	O128(42/24/61)		0.5
/150	3	150	228	39	61	6	3	0	22	45		1	0	.269	.392	.329	.721	+12	7	0	100	O60(20/11/29)	0	0.2
HERRERA, MIKE Ramon B12.19.1897 Havana, Cuba D2.3.1978 Havana, Cuba BR/TR/5'6"/147 d9.22																								
1925	Bos A	10	39	2	15	0	0	0	8	2		0	2	.385	.415	.385	.800	+4	1	0	100	2b10		0.3
1926	Bos A	74	237	20	61	14	1	0	19	15		1	13	.257	.304	.325	.629	-34	0	5	0	2b48,3b16,S4		-0.5
Total	2	84	276	22	76	14	1	0	27	17		1	15	.275	.320	.333	.653	-28	1	5	17	2b58,3b16,S4		-0.2

Year	Tm Lg	G	AB	R	H	2B	3B	HR	RBI	BB	IB	HP	SO	AVG	OBP	SLG	OPS	AOPS	SB	CS	SB%	Games at Position	DL	BFW
HEVING, JOHNNIE John Aloysius B4.29.1896 Covington KY D12.24.1968 Salisbury NC BR/TR/6'0"/175 d9.24 b–Joe																								
1920	StL A	1	1	0	0	0	0	0	0	0		0	0	.000	.000	.000	.000	-197	0	0	0	/H		0.0
1924	Bos A	45	109	15	31	5	1	0	11	10		0	7	.284	.345	.349	.694	-21	0	0	0	C29		0.0
1925	Bos A	45	119	14	20	7	0	0	6	12		0	7	.168	.244	.227	.471	-80	0	1	0	C34		-1.2
1928	Bos A	82	158	11	41	7	2	0	11	11		0	10	.259	.308	.329	.637	-31	1	1	50	C62		-1.0
1929	Bos A	76	188	26	60	4	3	0	23	8		2	7	.319	.354	.372	.726	-11	1	2	33	C55		0.4
1930	Bos A	75	220	15	61	5	3	0	17	11		0	14	.277	.312	.327	.639	-35	2	0	100	C71		-0.7
1931	†Phi A	42	113	8	27	3	2	1	12	6		0	8	.239	.277	.327	.604	-45	0	0	0	C40		-0.3
1932	Phi A	33	77	14	21	6	1	0	10	7		0	6	.273	.333	.377	.710	-19	0	0	0	C28		-0.1
Total	8	399	985	103	261	37	12	1	90	65		2	59	.265	.312	.330	.642	-34	4	4	50	C319		-2.9
Team	5	323	794	81	213	28	9	0	68	52		2	45	.268	.315	.326	.641	-34	4	4	50	C251		-2.5
/150	2	150	369	38	99	13	4	0	32	24		1	21	.268	.315	.326	.641	-34	2	2	50	C117		-1.2
HICKMAN, CHARLIE Charles Taylor "Cheerful Charlie","Piano Legs" B3.4.1876 Taylortown (Dunkard Twp.) PA D4.19.1934 Morgantown WV BR/TR/5'9"/180 d9.8 Col West Virginia OF(46/3/242)▲																								
1902	Bos A	28	108	13	32	5	2	3	16	3		4		.296	.339	.463	.802	+18	1			O27L		-0.1
Total	12	1081	3982	478	1176	217	91	59	614	153		58		.295	.331	.440	.771	+33	72			1b394,O290R,2b152,3b140,P30,S23		10.7
HIGGINS, PINKY Michael Franklin "Mike" B5.27.1909 Red Oak TX D3.21.1969 Dallas TX BR/TR/6'1"/185 d6.25 Mil 1945 M8 Col Texas																								
1937	Bos A	153	570	88	172	33	5	9	106	76		1	51	.302	.385	.425	.810	+0	2	6	25	3b152		-1.4
1938	Bos A	139	524	77	159	29	5	5	106	71		1	55	.303	.388	.406	.794	-5	10	9	53	3b138		-0.8
1946	†Bos A	64	200	18	55	11	1	2	28	24		1	24	.275	.356	.370	.726	-3	0	2	0	3b59	0	-0.1
Total	14	1802	6636	930	1941	374	51	140	1075	800		22	590	.292	.370	.428	.798	+6	61	59	51	3b1768,2b2/S	0	-1.2
Team	3	356	1294	183	386	73	11	16	240	171		3	130	.298	.382	.409	.791	-2	12	17	41	3b349	0	-2.3
/150	1	150	545	77	163	31	5	7	101	72		1	55	.298	.382	.409	.791	-2	5	7	42	3b147	0	-1.0
HILLENBRAND, SHEA Shea Matthew B7.27.1975 Mesa AZ BR/TR/6'1"/(200–210) [BosA96 10/301] d4.2 Col Mesa (AZ) CC [DL 1999 Bos A 34]																								
2001	Bos A	139	468	52	123	20	2	12	49	13	3	7	61	.263	.291	.391	.682	-22	3	4	43	3b129,1b6/D	0	-1.9
2002	Bos A★	156	634	94	186	43	4	18	83	25	4	12	95	.293	.330	.459	.789	+6	4	2	67	3b156	0	0.9
2003	Bos A	49	185	20	56	17	0	3	38	7	1	4	26	.303	.335	.443	.778	+1	1	0	100	3b29,1b28,D2	0	-0.2
2003	Ari N	85	330	40	88	18	1	17	59	17	3	2	44	.267	.302	.482	.784	-6	0	0	0	1b56,3b34	20	-1.4
2003	Major	134	515	60	144	35	1	20	97	24	4	6	70	.280	9.319	.468	9.787	+170	1	0	100		20	-1.6
2004	Ari N	148	562	68	174	36	3	15	80	24	2	12	49	.310	.348	.464	.812	+2	2	0	100	1b131,3b17	0	-1.4
2005	Tor A★	152	594	91	173	36	2	18	82	26	2	**22**	79	.291	.343	.449	.792	+4	5	1	83	1b67,3b54,D33	0	-0.7
2006	Tor A	81	296	40	89	15	1	12	39	14	2	6	40	.301	.342	.480	.822	+6	1	2	33	D44,1b19,3b17	0	-0.7
2006	SF N	60	234	33	58	12	0	9	29	7	0	3	40	.248	.275	.415	.690	-26	0	0	0	1b58,3b8	0	-1.5
2006	Major	141	530	73	147	27	1	21	68	21	2	9	80	.277	6.316	.451	6.767	+186	1	2	33		0	-2.2
Total	6	870	3303	438	947	197	13	104	459	133	17	68	434	.287	.325	.449	.774	-3	16	9	64	3b444,1b365,D80	54	-6.9
Team	3	344	1287	166	365	80	6	33	170	45	8	23	182	.284	.317	.432	.749	-5	8	6	57	3b314,1b34,D3	34	-1.2
/150	1	150	561	72	159	35	3	14	74	20	3	10	79	.284	.317	.432	.749	-5	3	3	50	3b137,1b15/D	15	-0.5
HILLER, HOB Harvey Max B5.12.1893 E.Mauch Chunk PA D12.27.1956 Lehighton PA BR/TR/5'8"/162 d4.22																								
1920	Bos A	17	29	4	5	1	1	0	2	2		0	5	.172	.226	.276	.502	-66	0	3	0	3b6,S5,2b2/rf		-0.3
1921	Bos A	1	1	0	0	0	0	0	0	0		0	0	.000	.000	.000	.000	-199	0	0	0	/H		0.0
Total	2	18	30	4	5	1	1	0	2	2		0	5	.167	.219	.267	.486	-71	0	3	0	3b6,S5,2b2/rf		-0.3
HINKLE, GORDIE Daniel Gordon B4.3.1905 Toronto OH D3.19.1972 Houston TX BR/TR/6'0"/185 d4.19																								
1934	Bos A	27	75	7	13	6	1	0	9	7		0	23	.173	.244	.280	.524	-67	0	0	0	C26		-0.3
HINSKE, ERIC Eric Scott B8.5.1977 Menasha WI BL/TR/6'2"/(225–235) [ChiN98 17/496] d4.1 Col Arkansas																								
2006	Bos A	31	80	8	23	8	0	1	5	8	0	0	30	.287	.352	.425	.777	-2	1	1	50	O15(5/0/10),1b12,D2	0	-0.2
Total	5	686	2339	361	607	154	12	79	318	271	14	15	551	.260	.337	.437	.774	-2	47	17	73	3b435,1b116,D65,O45(6/0/40)	31	-3.2
HINSON, PAUL James Paul B5.9.1904 Vanleer TN D9.23.1960 Muskogee OK BR/TR/5'10"/150 d4.19																								
1928	Bos A	3	0	1	0	0	0	0	0	0		0	0	+	+	+	.000	-100	0	0	0	/R		0.0
HITCHCOCK, BILLY William Clyde B7.31.1916 Inverness AL D4.9.2006 Opelika AL BR/TR/6'1.5"/(180–185) d4.14 Mil 1943–45 M5/C7 b–Jim Col Auburn																								
1948	Bos A	49	124	15	37	3	2	1	20	7		1	9	.298	.341	.379	.720	-13	0	0	0	2b15,3b15	0	0.1
1949	Bos A	55	147	22	30	6	1	0	9	17		1	11	.204	.291	.259	.550	-57	2	3	40	1b29,2b8	0	-1.8
Total	9	703	2249	231	547	67	22	5	257	206		10	230	.243	.310	.299	.609	-35	15	11	58	3b240,2b201,S142,1b48	0	-10.4
Team	2	104	271	37	67	9	3	1	29	24		2	20	.247	.313	.314	.627	-37	2	3	40	1b29,2b23,3b15	0	-1.7
/150	3	150	391	53	97	13	4	1	42	35		3	29	.247	.313	.314	.627	-37	3	4	43	1b42,2b33,3b22	0	-2.5
HOBLITZEL, DICK Richard Carleton "Doc" (b Hoblitzell) B10.26.1888 Waverly WV D11.14.1962 Parkersburg WV BL/TL/6'0"/172 d9.5 Mil 1918–20 Col Pittsburgh																								
1908	Cin N	32	114	8	29	3	2	0	8	7		2		.254	.309	.316	.625	+2	2			1b32		0.1
1909	Cin N	142	517	59	159	23	11	4	67	44		2		.308	.364	.418	.782	+44	17			1b142		2.1
1910	Cin N	155	611	85	170	24	13	4	70	47		2	32	.278	.332	.380	.712	+12	28			1b148,2b7		-0.3
1911	Cin N	158	622	81	180	19	13	11	91	42		8	44	.289	.342	.415	.757	+16	32			1b158		0.7
1912	Cin N	148	558	73	164	32	12	2	85	48		2	28	.294	.352	.405	.757	+10	23			1b147		0.5
1913	Cin N	137	502	59	143	23	7	3	62	35		2	26	.285	.334	.376	.710	+3	18	12	60	1b134		-0.7
1914	Cin N	78	248	31	52	8	7	0	26	26		1	26	.210	.287	.298	.585	-28	7			1b75		-1.7
1914	Bos A	69	229	31	73	10	3	0	33	19		6	21	.319	.386	.389	.775	+33	12	12	50	1b68		0.1
1914	Major	147	477	62	125	18	10	0	59	45	0	7	47	.262	.335	.342	.676	+161	19	12	61			-1.6
1915	†Bos A	124	399	54	113	15	12	2	61	38		4	26	.283	.351	.396	.747	+28	9	14	39	1b117		0.6
1916	†Bos A	130	417	57	108	17	1	0	39	47		3	28	.259	.338	.305	.643	-7	10			1b126		-0.7
1917	Bos A	120	420	49	108	19	7	1	47	46		4	22	.257	.336	.343	.679	+8	12			1b118		-0.7
1918	Bos A	25	69	4	11	1	0	0	4	8		2	3	.159	.266	.174	.440	-67	3			1b19		-0.5
Total	11	1318	4706	591	1310	194	88	27	593	407		38	256	.278	.341	.374	.715	+11	173	38	100	1b1284,2b7		-0.5
Team	5	468	1534	195	413	62	23	3	184	158		19	100	.269	.345	.346	.691	+9	46	26	100	1b448		-1.2
/150	2	150	492	63	132	20	7	1	59	51		6	32	.269	.345	.346	.691	+9	15	8	100	1b144		-0.4
HOBSON, BUTCH Clell Lavern B8.17.1951 Tuscaloosa AL BR/TR/6'1"/(190–193) [BosA73 8/185] d9.7 M3 Col Alabama																								
1975	Bos A	2	4	0	1	0	0	0	0	0	0	0	2	.250	.250	.250	.500	-62	0	0	0	/3	0	0.0
1976	Bos A	76	269	34	63	7	5	8	34	15	1	0	62	.234	.272	.387	.659	-17	0	1	0	3b76	0	-1.5
1977	Bos A	159	593	77	157	33	5	30	112	27	4	4	162	.265	.300	.489	.789	+0	5	4	56	3b159	0	-2.3
1978	Bos A	147	512	65	128	26	2	17	80	50	3	0	122	.250	.312	.408	.720	-7	1	0	100	3b133,D14	0	-1.5
1979	Bos A	146	528	74	138	26	7	28	93	30	2	0	78	.261	.298	.496	.794	+5	3	2	60	3b142/2	0	-1.8
1980	Bos A	93	324	35	74	6	0	11	39	25	2	0	69	.228	.281	.349	.630	-31	1	1	50	3b57,D36	30	-1.6
1981	Cal A	85	268	27	63	7	4	4	36	35	0	1	60	.235	.321	.336	.657	-10	1	1	50	3b83,D2	0	-1.1
1982	NY A	30	58	2	10	2	0	0	3	1	0	0	14	.172	.183	.207	.390	-92	0	0	0	D15,1b11	19	-0.9
Total	8	738	2556	314	634	107	23	98	397	183	12	5	569	.248	.297	.423	.720	-9	11	9	55	3b651,D67,1b11/2	49	-10.7
Team	6	623	2230	285	561	98	19	94	358	147	12	4	495	.252	.296	.439	.735	-7	10	8	56	3b567,D50/2	30	-8.7
/150	1	150	537	69	135	24	5	23	86	35	3	1	119	.252	.296	.439	.735	-7	2	2	50	3b137,D12/2	7	-2.1
HODAPP, JOHNNY Urban John B9.26.1905 Cincinnati OH D6.14.1980 Cincinnati OH BR/TR/6'0"/185 d8.19																								
1933	Bos A	115	413	55	129	27	5	3	54	33		1	14	.312	.365	.424	.789	+9	1	1	50	2b101,1b10		1.1
Total	9	791	2826	378	880	169	34	28	429	163		5	136	.311	.350	.425	.775	-2	18	20	47	2b460,3b212,O31(29/0/2),1b27		4.3
/150	1	150	539	72	168	35	7	4	70	43		1	18	.312	.365	.424	.789	+9	1	1	50	2b132,1b13		1.4
HODERLEIN, MEL Melvin Anthony B6.26.1923 Mt.Carmel OH D5.21.2001 Mt.Carmel OH BB/TR/5'10"/185 d8.16																								
1951	Bos A	9	14	1	5	1	1	0	1	6		0	2	.357	.550	.571	1.121	+85	0	1	0	2b3,3b3	0	0.2
Total	4	118	294	22	74	10	3	0	24	31		2	37	.252	.327	.306	.633	-22	2	1	67	2b77,S8,3b3	0	-1.3
HOEY, JACK John Bernard B11.10.1881 Watertown MA D11.14.1947 Waterbury CT BL/TL/5'9"/185 d6.27 Col Holy Cross																								
1906	Bos A	94	361	27	88	8	4	0	24	14		1		.244	.274	.288	.562	-24	10			O94L		-2.6
1907	Bos A	39	96	7	21	2	1	0	8	1		0		.219	.227	.260	.487	-44	2			O21(17/4/0)		-1.1
1908	Bos A	13	43	5	7	0	0	0	3	0		0		.163	.163	.163	.326	-94	1			O11R		-0.5

Year	Tm Lg	G	AB	R	H	2B	3B	HR	RBI	BB	IB	HP	SO	AVG	OBP	SLG	OPS	AOPS	SB	CS	SB%	Games at Position	DL	BFW
Total	3	146	500	39	116	10	5	0	35	15		1		.232	.256	.272	.528	-34	13			O126(111/4/11)		-4.2
/150	3	150	514	40	119	10	5	0	36	15		1	0	.232	.256	.272	.528	-34	13			O129(114/4/11)	0	-4.3
HOFFMAN, GLENN Glenn Edward B7.7.1958 Orange CA BR/TR/6'2"/(180–190) [BosA76 2/46] d4.12 M1/C8 b–Trevor																								
1980	Bos A	114	312	37	89	15	4	4	42	19	2	2	41	.285	.326	.397	.723	-7	2	4	33	3b110,S5,2b2	0	-0.8
1981	Bos A	78	242	28	56	10	0	1	20	12	0	1	25	.231	.271	.285	.556	-43	0	1	0	S78/3	0	-0.4
1982	Bos A	150	469	53	98	23	2	7	49	30	5	5	69	.209	.262	.311	.573	-46	0	4	0	S150	0	-0.1
1983	Bos A	143	473	56	123	24	1	4	41	30	1	2	76	.260	.306	.340	.646	-28	1	1	50	S143	0	-0.9
1984	Bos A	64	74	8	14	4	0	0	4	5	0	0	10	.189	.241	.243	.484	-67	0	1	0	S56,3b4,2b2	0	-0.8
1985	Bos A	96	279	40	77	17	2	6	34	25	0	5	40	.276	.343	.416	.759	+3	2	2	50	S93,2b3,3b3	27	1.4
1986	Bos A	12	23	1	5	2	0	0	1	2	0	0	3	.217	.269	.304	.573	-41	0	0	0	S11/3	76	-0.3
1987	Bos A	21	55	5	11	3	0	0	6	3	0	2	9	.200	.267	.255	.522	-62	0	0	0	S16,3b3,2b2	0	-0.1
1987	LA N	40	132	10	29	5	0	0	10	7	1	2	23	.220	.270	.258	.528	-58	0	1	0	S40	0	-0.9
1987	Major	61	187	15	40	8	0	0	16	10	1	4	32	.214	.269	.257	.525	+3	0	1	0		0	-1.0
1989	Cal A	48	104	9	22	3	0	1	3	3	0	1	13	.212	.241	.269	.510	-56	0	2	0	S23,3b18,2b4/1D	0	-0.8
Total	9	766	2163	247	524	106	9	23	210	136	9	20	309	.242	.291	.331	.622	-32	5	16	24	S615,3b140,2b13/D1	103	-3.7
Team	8	678	1927	228	473	98	9	22	197	126	8	17	273	.245	.296	.340	.636	-29	5	13	28	S552,3b122,2b9	103	-2.0
/150	2	150	426	50	105	22	2	5	44	28	2	4	60	.245	.296	.340	.636	-29	1	3	25	S122,3b27,2b2	23	-0.4
HOFMANN, FRED Fred "Bootnose" B6.10.1894 St.Louis MO D11.19.1964 St.Helena CA BR/TR/5'11.5"/175 d9.26 C13																								
1919	NY A	1	1	0	0	0	0	0	0	0		0	0	.000	.000	.000	.000	-199	0			/C		0.0
1920	NY A	15	24	3	7	0	0	0	1	1		1	2	.292	.346	.292	.638	-32	0	0	0	C14		-0.3
1921	NY A	23	62	7	11	1	1	1	5	5		1	13	.177	.250	.274	.524	-67	0	0	0	C18/1		-0.6
1922	NY A	37	91	13	27	5	3	2	10	9		0	12	.297	.360	.484	.844	+16	0	0	0	C29		0.1
1923	†NY A	72	238	24	69	10	4	3	26	18		4	27	.290	.350	.403	.753	-4	2	1	67	C70		0.0
1924	NY A	62	166	17	29	6	1	1	11	12		2	15	.175	.239	.241	.480	-76	2	1	67	C54		-1.4
1925	NY A	3	2	0	0	0	0	0	0	0		0	0	.000	.000	.000	.000	-199	0	0	0	/C		-0.1
1927	Bos A	87	217	20	59	19	1	0	24	21		2	26	.272	.342	.369	.711	-14	2	0	100	C81		-0.8
1928	Bos A	78	199	14	45	8	1	0	16	11		1	25	.226	.270	.276	.546	-55	0	1	0	C71		-1.3
Total	9	378	1000	98	247	49	11	7	93	77		11	120	.247	.308	.339	.647	-32	6	3	100	C339/1		-4.4
Team	2	165	416	34	104	27	2	0	40	32		3	51	.250	.308	.325	.633	-33	2	1	67	C152		-2.1
/150	2	150	378	31	95	25	2	0	36	29		3	46	.250	.308	.325	.633	-33	2	1	67	C138		-1.9
HOLLINS, DAVE David Michael B5.25.1966 Buffalo NY BB/TR/6'1"/(195–232) [SDN87 6/146] d4.12 Col South Carolina																								
1995	Bos A	5	13	2	2	0	0	0	1	4	0	0	7	.154	.353	.154	.507	-63	0	0	0	O2R,D3	54	-0.1
Total	12	983	3346	578	870	166	17	112	482	464	28	66	687	.260	.358	.420	.778	+6	47	27	64	3b778,1b96,D33,O3R/S	410	-4.1
HOLM, BILLY William Frederick Henry B7.21.1912 Chicago IL D7.27.1977 East Chicago IN BR/TR/5'10.5"/168 d9.24																								
1943	Chi N	7	15	0	1	0	0	0	0	2		0	4	.067	.176	.067	.243	-129	0			C7	0	-0.2
1944	Chi N	54	132	10	18	2	0	0	6	16		1	19	.136	.235	.152	.387	-90	1			C50	0	-1.6
1945	Bos A	58	135	12	25	2	1	0	9	23		3	17	.185	.317	.215	.532	-46	1	1	50	C57	0	-0.8
Total	3	119	282	22	44	4	1	0	15	41		4	40	.156	.272	.177	.449	-70	2	1	100	C114	0	-2.6
HOOPER, HARRY Harry Bartholomew B8.24.1887 Bell Station CA D12.18.1974 Santa Cruz CA BL/TR/5'10"/168 d4.16 HF1971 Col St. Marys (CA)																								
1909	Bos A	81	255	29	72	3	4	0	12	16		5		.282	.337	.325	.662	+7	15			O74(62/4/8)		0.3
1910	Bos A	155	584	81	156	9	10	2	27	62		8		.267	.346	.327	.673	+8	40			O155(9/4/142)		0.9
1911	Bos A	130	524	93	163	20	6	4	45	73		4		.311	.399	.395	.794	+23	38			O130R		1.8
1912	†Bos A	147	590	98	143	20	12	2	53	66		7		.242	.326	.327	.653	-17	29			O147R		-2.0
1913	Bos A	148	586	100	169	29	12	4	40	60		5	51	.288	.359	.399	.758	+19	26			O147(1/9/137)/P		1.4
1914	Bos A	142	530	85	137	23	15	1	41	58		4	47	.258	.336	.364	.700	+10	19	14	58	O140(0/1/139)		0.9
1915	†Bos A	149	566	90	133	20	13	2	51	89		3	36	.235	.342	.327	.669	+3	22	20	52	O149R		0.3
1916	†Bos A	151	575	75	156	20	11	1	37	80		1	35	.271	.361	.350	.711	+13	27	11	71	O151R		1.1
1917	Bos A	151	559	89	143	21	11	3	45	80		6	40	.256	.355	.349	.704	+16	21			O151R		0.1
1918	†Bos A	**126**	474	81	137	26	13	1	44	75		4	25	.289	.391	.405	.796	+42	24			O126R		2.2
1919	Bos A	128	491	76	131	25	6	3	49	79		5	28	.267	.374	.360	.734	+13	23			O128R		1.2
1920	Bos A	139	536	91	167	30	17	7	53	88		2	27	.312	.411	.470	.881	+39	16	18	47	O139(2/0/137)		2.7
1921	Chi A	108	419	74	137	26	5	8	58	55		1	21	.327	.406	.470	.876	+25	13	7	65	O108R		0.6
1922	Chi A	152	602	111	183	35	8	11	80	68		5	33	.304	.379	.444	.823	+14	16	12	57	O149R		0.5
1923	Chi A	145	576	87	166	32	4	10	65	68		7	22	.288	.370	.410	.780	+6	18	18	50	O143R		-1.3
1924	Chi A	130	476	107	156	27	8	10	62	65		4	26	.328	.413	.481	.894	+34	16	13	55	O123R		2.4
1925	Chi A	127	442	62	117	23	5	6	55	54		5	21	.265	.351	.380	.731	-10	12	8	60	O124R		-1.1
Total	17	2309	8785	1429	2466	389	160	75	817	1136		76	412	.281	.368	.387	.755	+14	375	12	100	O2284(74/18/2192)/P		12.0
Team	12	1647	6270	988	1707	246	130	30	497	826		54	289	.272	.362	.367	.729	+15	300	63	100	O1637(79/18/174)/P		10.9
/150	1	150	571	90	155	22	12	3	45	75		5	26	.272	.362	.367	.729	+15	27	6	100	O149(7/2/16)/P		1.0
HORN, SAM Samuel Lee B11.2.1963 Dallas TX BL/TL/6'5"/(215–250) [BosA82 1/16] d7.25																								
1987	Bos A	46	158	31	44	7	0	14	34	17	0	2	55	.278	.356	.589	.945	+40	0	1	0	D40	0	0.7
1988	Bos A	24	61	4	9	0	0	2	8	11	3	0	20	.148	.274	.246	.520	-54	0	0	0	D16	0	-0.5
1989	Bos A	33	54	1	8	2	0	0	4	8	1	0	16	.148	.258	.185	.443	-75	0	0	0	D14,1b2	50	-0.6
Total	8	389	1040	132	250	49	1	62	179	132	11	7	323	.240	.328	.468	.796	+18	0	1	0	D293,1b12	71	1.3
Team	3	103	273	36	61	9	0	16	46	36	4	2	91	.223	.317	.432	.749	-5	0	1	0	D70,1b2	50	-0.4
/150	4	150	398	52	89	13	0	23	67	52	6	3	133	.223	.317	.432	.749	-5	0	1	0	D102,1b3	73	-0.6
HORTON, TONY Anthony Darrin B12.6.1944 Santa Monica CA BR/TR/6'3"/(195–210) d7.31																								
1964	Bos A	36	126	9	28	5	0	1	8	3	0	0	20	.222	.238	.286	.524	-56	0	0	0	O24L,1b8	0	-1.1
1965	Bos A	60	163	23	48	8	1	7	23	18	1	0	36	.294	.361	.485	.846	+31	0	2	0	1b44	0	0.2
1966	Bos A	6	22	0	3	0	0	0	2	0	0	0	5	.136	.136	.136	.272	-119	0	0	0	1b6	0	-0.3
1967	Bos A	21	39	2	12	3	0	0	9	0	0	0	5	.308	.300	.385	.685	-4	0	0	0	1b6	0	-0.2
Total	7	636	2228	251	597	102	15	76	297	140	17	13	319	.268	.313	.430	.743	+9	12	8	60	1b555,O24L	0	-2.9
Team	4	123	350	34	91	16	1	8	42	21	1	0	66	.260	.299	.380	.679	-12	0	2	0	1b64,O24L	0	-1.4
/150	5	150	427	41	111	20	1	10	51	26	1	0	80	.260	.299	.380	.679	-12	0	2	0	1b78,O29L	0	-1.7
HOSEY, DWAYNE Dwayne Samuel B3.11.1967 Sharon PA BB/TR/5'10"/175 [ChiA87 13/323] d9.1 Col Pasadena (CA) City																								
1995	†Bos A	24	68	20	23	8	1	3	7	8	0	0	16	.338	.408	.618	1.026	+57	6	0	100	O21(2/19/1)/D	0	0.7
1996	Bos A	28	78	13	17	2	2	1	3	7	0	0	17	.218	.282	.333	.615	-46	6	3	67	O26(7/20/0),D2	0	-0.3
Total	2	52	146	33	40	10	3	4	10	15	0	0	33	.274	.342	.466	.808	+2	12	3	80	O47(9/39/1),D3	0	0.4
HOUSIE, WAYNE Wayne Tyrone B5.20.1965 Hampton VA BB/TR/5'9"/165 [DetA86*8/199] d9.17 Col Riverside (CA) CC																								
1991	Bos A	11	8	2	2	1	0	0	0	1	0	0	3	.250	.333	.375	.708	-9	1	0	100	O4C,D2	0	0.0
1993	NY N	18	16	2	3	1	0	0	1	1	0	0	1	.188	.235	.250	.485	-70	0	0	0	O2R	0	-0.2
Total	2	29	24	4	5	2	0	0	1	2	0	0	4	.208	.269	.292	.561	-49	1	0	100	O6(0/4/2),D2	0	-0.2
HOWARD, ELSTON Elston Gene B2.23.1929 St.Louis MO D12.14.1980 New York NY BR/TR/6'2"/(196–208) d4.14 C11 Negro Lg 1948–50																								
1967	†Bos A	42	116	9	17	3	0	1	11	9	3	1	24	.147	.211	.198	.409	-79	0	0	0	C41	0	-0.7
1968	Bos A	71	203	22	49	4	0	5	18	22	7	1	45	.241	.317	.335	.652	-7	1	1	50	C68	0	-0.5
Total	14	1605	5363	619	1471	218	50	167	762	373	82	26	786	.274	.322	.427	.749	+8	9	14	39	C1138,O265(230/0/40),1b85	32	11.1
Team	2	113	319	31	66	7	0	6	29	31	10	2	69	.207	.279	.285	.564	-33	1	1	50	C109	0	-1.2
/150	3	150	423	41	88	9	0	8	38	41	13	3	92	.207	.279	.285	.564	-33	1	1	50	C145	0	-1.6
HOWARD, PAUL Paul Joseph "Del" B5.20.1884 Boston MA D8.29.1968 Miami FL BR/TR/5'8"/170 d9.16																								
1909	Bos A	6	15	2	3	1	0	0	2	3		1		.200	.368	.267	.635	-1	0			O6(4/0/2)		0.0
HUCKABY, KEN Kenneth Paul B1.27.1971 San Leandro CA BR/TR/6'1"/(200–210) [LAN91 22/585] d10.6 Col San Joaquin Delta (CA) JC																								
2006	Bos A	8	5	0	1	0	0	0	1	0	0	0	0	.200	.200	.200	.400	-96	0	0	0	C8	0	-0.2
Total	6	161	427	42	95	14	1	3	31	19	1	0	78	.222	.256	.281	.537	-59	0	0	0	C160	0	-2.9

Year	Tm Lg	G	AB	R	H	2B	3B	HR	RBI	BB	IB	HP	SO	AVG	OBP	SLG	OPS	AOPS	SB	CS	SB%	Games at Position	DL	BFW
HUGHES, TERRY Terry Wayne B5.13.1949 Spartanburg SC BR/TR/6'1"/185 [ChiN67 1/2] d9.2																								
1970	Chi N	2	3	0	1	0	0	0	0	0	0	0	0	.333	.333	.333	.666	-29	0	0	0	/3rf	0	-0.1
1973	StL N	11	14	1	3	1	0	0	1	1	0	0	4	.214	.267	.286	.553	-47	0	0	0	3b5/1	0	-0.1
1974	Bos A	41	69	5	14	2	0	1	6	6	0	2	18	.203	.282	.275	.557	-42	0	0	0	3b36/D	0	-0.5
Total	3	54	86	6	18	3	0	1	7	7	0	2	22	.209	.281	.279	.560	-42	0	0	0	3b42/D1rf	0	-0.7
HUNTER, BUDDY Harold James B8.9.1947 Omaha NE BR/TR/5'10"/170 [BosA69 3/61] d7.1 Col Nebraska																								
1971	Bos A	8	9	2	2	1	0	0	0	2	0	0	1	.222	.364	.333	.697	-8	0	0	0	2b6	0	-0.1
1973	Bos A	13	7	3	3	1	0	0	2	3	0	1	1	.429	.636	.571	1.207	+128	0	0	0	3b3,2b2/D	0	0.3
1975	Bos A	1	1	0	0	0	0	0	0	0	0	0	0	.000	.000	.000	.000	-192	0	0	0	/2	0	0.0
Total	3	22	17	5	5	2	0	0	2	5	0	1	2	.294	.478	.412	.890	+44	0	0	0	2b9,3b3/D	0	0.2
HUNTER, HERB Herbert Harrison B12.25.1895 Boston MA D7.25.1970 Orlando FL BL/TR/6'0.5"/165 d4.29																								
1920	Bos A	4	12	2	1	0	0	0	0	1		0	1	.083	.154	.083	.237	-138	0	0	0	O4(3/1/0)		-0.3
Total	4	39	49	8	8	0	0	1	4	2		0	6	.163	.196	.224	.420	-76	0	3	0	3b8,O4(3/1/0),1b3/2		-0.7
HUSKEY, BUTCH Robert Leon B11.10.1971 Anadarko OK BR/TR/6'3"/244 [NYN89 7/190] d9.8																								
1999	†Bos A	45	124	18	33	6	0	7	28	7	1	0	20	.266	.305	.484	.789	-6	0	0	0	D37,O4(2/0/2),3b2	0	-0.4
Total	7	642	2078	259	555	98	4	86	336	164	15	4	384	.267	.318	.442	.760	-3	21	17	55	O331(78/0/264),1b124,D88,3b64	55	-4.1
HYZDU, ADAM Adam Davis B12.6.1971 San Jose CA BR/TR/6'2"/220 [SFN90 1/15] d9.8																								
2004	Bos A	17	10	3	3	2	0	1	2	1	0	0	2	.300	.364	.800	1.164	+80	0	0	0	O14(11/0/4),D2	0	0.1
2005	†Bos A	12	16	1	4	1	0	0	0	2	0	0	3	.250	.333	.313	.646	-30	0	0	0	O12(3/5/5)	0	-0.1
Total	7	221	358	54	82	18	0	19	61	41	0	3	98	.229	.310	.439	.749	-8	1	1	50	O155(47/65/56),1b5,D2	0	-0.8
Team	2	29	26	4	7	3	0	1	2	3	0	0	5	.269	.345	.500	.845	+12	0	0	0	O26(14/5/9),D2	0	0.0
JACKSON, DAMIAN Damian Jacques B8.16.1973 Los Angeles CA BR/TR/5'11"/(160–185) [CleA91 44/1148] d9.12 Col Laney (CA) JC OF(75/59/20)																								
2003	†Bos A	109	161	34	42	7	0	1	13	8	0	0	28	.261	.294	.323	.617	-39	16	8	67	2b38,O38(13/13/12),S18,3b3,1b2,D9	0	-0.8
Total	11	827	2209	332	536	121	17	32	198	245	11	24	517	.243	.323	.356	.679	-21	133	39	77	2b325,S284,O152L,3b19,D16,1b2	71	-1.4
/150	1	150	222	47	58	10	0	1	18	11	0	0	39	.261	.294	.323	.617	-39	22	11	67	2b52,O52(18/18/17),S25,D12,3b4,1b3	0	-1.1
JACKSON, RON Ronald Harris B10.22.1933 Kalamazoo MI BR/TR/6'7"/(225–230) d6.15 Col Western Michigan																								
1960	Bos A	10	31	1	7	2	0	0	0	1	0	0	6	.226	.250	.290	.540	-56	0	0	0	1b9	0	-0.3
Total	7	196	474	54	116	18	1	17	52	45	4	5	119	.245	.315	.395	.710	-8	6	1	86	1b148	0	-1.9
JACOBSON, BABY DOLL William Chester B8.16.1890 Cable IL D1.16.1977 Orion IL BR/TR/6'3"/215 d4.14 Mil 1918																								
1926	Bos A	98	394	44	120	36	1	6	69	22		2	22	.305	.344	.447	.791	+9	4	1	80	O98(6/57/36)		-1.0
1927	Bos A	45	155	11	38	9	3	0	24	5		2	12	.245	.278	.342	.620	-39	1	0	100	O39L		-1.2
Total	11	1472	5507	787	1714	328	94	83	819	355		39	410	.311	.357	.450	.807	+11	86	54	100	O1378(88/1098/194),1b47		-1.5
Team	2	143	549	55	158	45	4	6	93	27		4	34	.288	.325	.417	.742	-4	5	1	83	O137(6/57/36)		-2.2
/150	2	150	576	58	166	47	4	6	98	28		4	36	.288	.325	.417	.742	-4	5	1	83	O144(6/60/38)		-2.3
JAMES, CHRIS Donald Chris B10.4.1962 Rusk TX BR/TR/6'1"/(190–202) d4.23 Col Blinn (TX) JC OF(322/51/229)																								
1995	Bos A	16	24	2	4	1	0	0	1	1	0	0	4	.167	.200	.208	.408	-94	0	0	0	O8(4/0/4),D6	15	-0.3
Total	10	946	3040	343	794	145	24	90	386	193	14	21	490	.261	.307	.413	.720	-2	27	17	61	O568L,D204,3b48,1b15	243	-4.3
JANVRIN, HAL Harold Chandler "Childe Harold" B8.27.1892 Haverhill MA D3.1.1962 Boston MA BR/TR/5'11.5"/168 d7.9 Mil 1918 OF(17/4/1)																								
1911	Bos A	9	27	2	4	1	0	0	1	3		1		.148	.258	.185	.443	-75	0			3b5,1b4		-0.5
1913	Bos A	87	276	18	57	5	1	3	25	23		2	27	.207	.272	.264	.536	-44	17			S48,3b19,2b8,1b6		-2.4
1914	Bos A	145	492	65	117	18	6	1	51	38		3	50	.238	.296	.305	.601	-19	29	20	59	2b59,1b57,S20,3b6		-3.4
1915	†Bos A	99	316	41	85	9	1	0	37	14		8	27	.269	.317	.304	.621	-12	8	14	36	S64,3b20,2b8		-2.2
1916	†Bos A	117	310	32	69	11	4	0	26	32		2	32	.223	.299	.284	.583	-25	6			S59,2b39,1b4,3b4		-2.0
1917	Bos A	55	127	21	25	3	0	0	8	11		1	13	.197	.266	.220	.486	-51	2			2b38,S10/1		-0.8
1919	Was A	61	208	17	37	4	1	1	13	19		2	17	.178	.253	.221	.474	-66	8			2b56,S2		-4.3
1919	StL N	7	14	1	3	1	0	0	1	2		0	2	.214	.313	.286	.599	-14	0			2b2/S3		-0.1
1919	Major	68	222	18	40	5	1	1	14	21	0	2	19	.180	.257	.225	.482	-24	8	0				-4.4
1920	StL N	87	270	33	74	8	4	1	28	17		0	19	.274	.317	.344	.661	-7	5	6	45	S27,1b25,O20(16/4/0),2b6		-0.5
1921	StL N	18	32	5	9	1	0	0	5	1		0	0	.281	.303	.313	.616	-35	1	0	100	1b9/2		-0.2
1921	Bro N	44	92	8	18	4	0	0	14	7		0	6	.196	.253	.239	.492	-70	3	1	75	S17,2b10,1b8,3b5/rf		-1.2
1921	Year	62	124	13	27	5	0	0	19	8		0	6	.218	.265	.258	.523	-62	4	1	80	1b17,S17,2b11,3b5/rf		-1.4
1922	Bro N	30	57	7	17	3	1	0	1	4		0	4	.298	.344	.386	.730	-11	0	0	0	2b15,S4,3b2/1lf		-0.3
Total	10	759	2221	250	515	68	18	6	210	171		19	197	.232	.292	.287	.579	-30	79	41	100	S252,2b242,1b115,3b62,O22L		-17.9
Team	6	512	1548	179	357	47	12	4	148	121		17	149	.231	.293	.284	.577	-27	62	34	100	S201,2b152,1b72,3b54		-11.3
/150	2	150	454	52	105	14	4	1	43	35		5	44	.231	.293	.284	.577	-27	18	10	100	S59,2b45,1b21,3b16		-3.3
JEFFERSON, REGGIE Reginald Jirod B9.25.1968 Tallahassee FL BL/TL (BB 1991–93)/6'4"/(210–215) [CinN86 3/72] d5.18																								
1991	Cin N	5	7	1	1	0	0	1	1	1	0	0	2	.143	.250	.571	.821	+19	0	0	0	1b2	0	0.0
1991	Cle A	26	101	10	20	3	0	2	12	3	0	0	22	.198	.219	.287	.506	-61	0	0	0	1b26	16	-0.8
1991	Major	31	108	11	21	3	0	3	13	4	0	0	24	.194	1.223	.306	1.529	-68	0	0	0		16	-0.8
1992	Cle A	24	89	8	30	6	2	1	6	1	0	1	17	.337	.352	.483	.835	+33	0	0	0	1b15,D7	89	0.3
1993	Cle A	113	366	35	91	11	2	10	34	28	7	5	78	.249	.310	.372	.682	-18	1	3	25	D88,1b15	0	-1.7
1994	Sea A	63	162	24	53	11	0	8	32	17	5	1	32	.327	.392	.543	.935	+35	0	0	0	D32,1b13,O2L	20	0.7
1995	†Bos A	46	121	21	35	8	0	5	26	9	1	0	24	.289	.333	.479	.812	+7	0	0	0	D32,1b7,O2L	71	0.0
1996	Bos A	122	386	67	134	30	4	19	74	25	5	3	89	.347	.388	.593	.981	+42	0	0	0	D49,O45L,1b16	0	1.7
1997	Bos A	136	489	74	156	33	1	13	67	24	5	7	93	.319	.358	.470	.828	+12	1	2	33	D119,1b12	0	0.0
1998	Bos A	62	196	24	60	16	1	8	31	21	2	1	40	.306	.374	.520	.894	+27	0	0	0	D48,1b7	75	0.5
1999	Bos A	83	206	21	57	13	1	5	17	17	0	2	54	.277	.338	.422	.760	-11	0	0	0	D58,1b2	11	-0.6
Total	9	680	2123	285	637	131	11	72	300	146	25	20	451	.300	.349	.474	.823	+11	2	5	29	D433,1b115,O49L	282	0.1
Team	5	449	1398	207	442	100	7	50	215	96	13	13	300	.316	.363	.505	.868	+19	1	2	33	D306,O47L,1b44	157	1.6
/150	2	150	467	69	148	33	2	17	72	32	4	4	100	.316	.363	.505	.868	+19	0	1	0	D102,Olf,1b15	52	0.5
JENKINS, TOM Thomas Griffith "Tut" B4.10.1898 Camden AL D5.3.1979 Weymouth MA BL/TR/6'1.5"/174 d9.15																								
1925	Bos A	15	64	9	19	2	1	0	5	3		1	4	.297	.338	.359	.697	-23	0	0	0	O15L		-0.5
1926	Bos A	21	50	3	9	1	1	0	6	3		0	7	.180	.226	.240	.466	-78	0	0	0	O13(12/1/0)		-0.8
Total	6	171	459	42	119	14	6	3	44	28		1	53	.259	.303	.336	.639	-36	1	3	25	O109(32/2/75)		-3.5
Team	2	36	114	12	28	3	2	0	11	6		1	11	.246	.289	.307	.596	-47	0	0	0	O28(27/1/1)		-1.3
JENSEN, JACKIE Jack Eugene B3.9.1927 San Francisco CA D7.14.1982 Charlottesville VA BR/TR/5'11"/190 d4.18 Col California																								
1950	†NY A	45	70	13	12	2	2	1	5	7		0	8	.171	.247	.300	.547	-59	4	0	100	O23(17/0/7)	0	-0.7
1951	NY A	56	168	30	50	8	1	8	25	18		1	18	.298	.369	.500	.869	+38	8	2	80	O48(21/27/1)	0	0.9
1952	NY A	7	19	3	2	1	1	0	2	4		0	4	.105	.261	.263	.524	-51	1	0	100	O5C	0	-0.2
1952	Was A★	144	570	80	163	29	5	10	80	63		3	40	.286	.360	.407	.767	+17	17	6	74	O143(0/7/142)	0	1.4
1952	Year	151	589	83	165	30	6	10	82	67		3	44	.280	.357	.402	.759	+15	18	6	75	O148(0/12/142)	0	1.2
1953	Was A	147	552	87	147	32	8	10	84	73		5	51	.266	.357	.408	.765	+9	18	8	69	O146(0/1/145)	0	-0.5
1954	Bos A	152	580	92	160	25	7	25	117	79		2	52	.276	.359	.472	.831	+15	**22**	7	76	O151(8/106/44)	0	-0.3
1955	Bos A★	152	574	95	158	27	6	26	**116**	89	8	3	63	.275	.369	.479	.848	+18	16	7	70	O150R	0	0.6
1956	Bos A	151	578	80	182	23	**11**	20	97	89	5	1	43	.315	.405	.497	.902	+23	11	3	79	O151R	0	1.1
1957	Bos A	145	544	82	153	29	2	23	103	75	3	2	66	.281	.367	.469	.836	+21	8	5	62	O144(4/0/143)	0	1.3
1958	Bos A★	154	548	83	157	31	0	35	**122**	99	7	3	65	.286	.396	.535	.931	+44	9	4	69	O153(2/0/153)	0	3.1
1959	Bos A	148	535	101	148	31	0	28	**112**	88	3	0	67	.277	.372	.492	.864	+31	20	5	80	O146(0/7/142)	0	3.3
1961	Bos A	137	498	64	131	21	2	13	66	66	2	3	69	.263	.350	.392	.742	-4	9	8	53	O131(2/0/129)	0	-0.4
Total	11	1438	5236	810	1463	259	45	199	929	750	28	23	546	.279	.369	.460	.829	+19	143	55	72	O1391(54/153/1207)	0	9.6
Team	7	1039	3857	597	1089	187	28	170	733	585	28	14	425	.282	.375	.478	.853	+22	95	39	71	O1026(12/113/188)	0	8.7
/150	1	150	557	86	157	27	4	25	106	84	4	2	61	.282	.375	.478	.853	+22	14	6	70	O148(2/16/27)	0	1.3
JENSEN, MARCUS Marcus Christian B12.14.1972 Oakland CA BB/TR/6'4"/(195–204) [SFN90 1/33] d4.14																								
2001	Bos A	1	4	0	1	0	0	0	0	0	0	0	1	.250	.250	.250	.500	-68	0	0	0	/C	0	0.1
Total	7	145	343	33	63	16	1	6	29	50	4	0	106	.184	.287	.289	.576	-52	0	1	0	C134/D	0	-2.2

Year	Tm Lg	G	AB	R	H	2B	3B	HR	RBI	BB	IB	HP	SO	AVG	OBP	SLG	OPS	AOPS	SB	CS	SB%	Games at Position	DL	BFW
JOHNS, KEITH Robert Keith B7.19.1971 Callahan FL BR/TR/6'1"/175 [StLN92 6/167] d5.23 Col U. of Mississippi																								
1998	Bos A	2	0	0	0	0	0	0	0	1	0	0	0	+	1.000	+	1.000	+87	0	0	0	/2D	0	0.1
JOHNSON, DERON Deron Roger B7.17.1938 San Diego CA D4.23.1992 Poway CA BR/TR/6'2"/(200–209) d9.20 C13 OF(216/1/32)																								
1974	Bos A	11	25	0	3	0	0	0	2	0	0	0	6	.120	.115	.120	.235	-129	0	0	0	D8	0	-0.5
1975	Bos A	3	10	2	6	0	0	1	3	2	0	0	0	.600	.667	.900	1.567	+213	0	0	0	1b2/D	0	0.2
1976	Bos A	15	38	3	5	1	1	0	0	5	1	0	11	.132	.233	.211	.444	-73	0	0	0	1b5,D9	0	-0.5
Total	16	1765	5941	706	1447	247	33	245	923	585	54	20	1318	.244	.311	.420	.731	+2	11	18	38	1b880,3b332,D287,O249L	31	-13.4
Team	3	29	73	5	14	1	1	1	5	7	1	0	17	.192	.259	.274	.533	-48	0	0	0	D18,1b7	0	-0.8
JOHNSON, BOB Robert Lee "Indian Bob" B11.26.1905 Pryor OK D7.6.1982 Tacoma WA BR/TR/6'0"/180 d4.12 b–Roy OF(1592/162/24)																								
1944	Bos A★	144	525	106	170	40	8	17	106	95		4	67	.324	**.431**	.528	.959	+75	2	7	22	O142L	0	5.3
1945	Bos A✷	143	529	71	148	27	7	12	74	63		1	56	.280	.358	.425	.783	+24	5	3	63	O140(140/1/0)	0	1.2
Total	13	1863	6920	1239	2051	396	95	288	1283	1075		24	851	.296	.393	.506	.899	+39	96	64	60	O1769L,1b39,2b28,3b20	0	35.7
Team	2	287	1054	177	318	67	15	29	180	158		5	123	.302	.396	.476	.872	+50	7	10	41	O282(282/1/1)	0	6.5
/150	1	150	551	93	166	35	8	15	94	83		3	64	.302	.396	.476	.872	+50	4	5	44	O147(147/1/1)	0	3.4
JOHNSON, ROY Roy Cleveland B2.23.1903 Pryor OK D9.10.1973 Tacoma WA BL/TR/5'9"/175 d4.18 b–Bob																								
1929	Det A	148	640	128	201	**45**	14	10	69	67		0	60	.314	.379	.475	.854	+18	20	16	56	O146(91/37/23)		1.1
1930	Det A	125	462	84	127	30	13	2	35	40		0	46	.275	.333	.409	.742	-15	17	10	63	O118(7/2/110)		-1.4
1931	Det A	151	621	107	173	37	**19**	8	55	72		2	51	.279	.355	.438	.793	+4	33	21	61	O150(0/5/148)		0.4
1932	Det A	49	195	33	49	14	2	3	22	20		1	26	.251	.324	.390	.714	-19	7	2	78	O48R		-0.8
1932	Bos A	94	349	70	104	24	4	11	47	44		1	41	.298	.378	.484	.862	+25	13	4	76	O85(14/16/56)		0.2
1932	Year	143	544	103	153	38	6	14	69	64		2	67	.281	.359	.450	.809	+9	20	6	77	O133(14/16/104)		-0.6
1933	Bos A	133	483	88	151	30	7	10	95	55		4	36	.313	.387	.466	.853	+26	13	10	57	O125(26/10/95)		1.1
1934	Bos A	143	569	85	182	43	10	7	119	54		0	36	.320	.379	.467	.846	+9	11	5	69	O137L		-0.4
1935	Bos A	145	553	70	174	33	9	3	66	74		3	34	.315	.398	.423	.821	+5	11	12	48	O142L		0.0
1936	†NY A	63	147	21	39	8	2	1	19	21		1	14	.265	.361	.367	.728	-17	3	1	75	O33(28/0/3)		-0.5
1937	NY A	12	51	5	15	3	0	0	6	3		0	2	.294	.333	.353	.686	-27	1	0	100	O12L		-0.4
1937	Bos N	85	260	24	72	8	3	3	22	38		0	29	.277	.369	.365	.734	+10	5			O63L/3		0.0
1937	Major	97	311	29	87	11	3	3	28	41	0	0	31	.280	.364	.363	.727	+101	6	0				-0.4
1938	Bos N	7	29	2	5	0	0	0	1	1		0	5	.172	.200	.172	.372	-96	1			O7L		-0.7
Total	10	1155	4359	717	1292	275	83	58	556	489		12	380	.296	.369	.437	.806	+7	135	81	100	O1066(527/70/483)/3		-1.4
Team	4	515	1954	313	611	130	30	31	327	227		8	147	.313	.386	.458	.844	+15	48	31	61	O489(40/26/151)		0.9
/150	1	150	569	91	178	38	9	9	95	66		2	43	.313	.386	.458	.844	+15	14	9	61	O142(12/8/44)		0.3
JOLLEY, SMEAD Smead Powell "Guinea","Smudge" B1.14.1902 Wesson AR D11.17.1991 Alameda CA BL/TR/6'3.5"/210 d4.17																								
1930	Chi A	152	616	76	193	38	12	16	114	28		3	52	.313	.346	.492	.838	+14	3	1	75	O151(68/0/83)		-0.1
1931	Chi A	54	110	5	33	11	0	3	28	7		2	4	.300	.353	.482	.835	+25	0	0	0	O23(8/0/15)		0.0
1932	Chi A	12	42	3	15	3	0	0	7	3		1	0	.357	.413	.429	.842	+27	1	0	100	O11(7/0/4)		0.1
1932	Bos A	137	531	57	164	27	5	18	99	27		2	29	.309	.345	.480	.825	+15	0	5	0	O126(120/0/6),C5		-0.3
1932	Year	149	573	60	179	30	5	18	106	30		3	29	.312	.350	.476	.826	+16	1	5	17	O137(127/0/10),C5		-0.2
1933	Bos A	118	411	47	116	32	4	9	65	24		2	20	.282	.325	.445	.770	+3	1	1	50	O102(87/0/15)		-0.5
Total	4	473	1710	188	521	111	21	46	313	89		10	105	.305	.343	.475	.818	+12	5	7	42	O413(290/0/123),C5		-0.8
Team	2	255	942	104	280	59	9	27	164	51		4	49	.297	.336	.465	.801	+10	1	6	14	O228(207/0/21),C5		-0.8
/150	1	150	554	61	165	35	5	16	96	30		2	29	.297	.336	.465	.801	+10	1	4	20	O134(122/0/12),C3		-0.5
JONES, CHARLIE Charles Claude "Casey" B6.2.1876 Butler PA D4.2.1947 Two Harbors MN BR/TR/6'1"/165 d5.2 Col Grove City																								
1901	Bos A	10	41	6	6	2	0	0	6	1		0		.146	.167	.195	.362	-100	2			O10(0/8/2)		-0.7
Total	6	483	1799	217	420	56	28	5	144	93		13		.233	.276	.304	.580	-13	100			O468(12/443/12),2b6,1b4,S2		-3.7
JONES, DALTON James Dalton B12.10.1943 McComb MS BL/TR/6'1"/(177–185) d4.17 OF(12/0/8)																								
1964	Bos A	118	374	37	86	16	4	6	39	22	2	1	38	.230	.274	.342	.616	-33	6	3	67	2b85/S3	0	-1.8
1965	Bos A	112	367	41	99	13	5	5	37	28	0	2	45	.270	.325	.373	.698	-8	8	1	89	3b81,2b8	0	-0.2
1966	Bos A	115	252	26	59	11	5	4	23	22	4	3	27	.234	.303	.365	.668	-17	1	2	33	2b70,3b3	0	-1.3
1967	†Bos A	89	159	18	46	6	2	3	25	11	3	0	23	.289	.333	.409	.742	+10	0	1	0	3b30,2b19/1	0	-0.1
1968	Bos A	111	354	38	83	13	0	5	29	17	0	1	53	.234	.271	.314	.585	-28	1	1	50	1b56,2b26,3b8	0	-2.8
1969	Bos A	111	336	50	74	18	3	3	33	39	3	2	36	.220	.303	.318	.621	-29	1	1	50	1b81,3b9/2	0	-2.2
1970	Det A	89	191	29	42	7	0	6	21	33	4	1	33	.220	.333	.351	.684	-11	1	1	50	2b35,3b18,1b10	0	-0.5
1971	Det A	83	138	15	35	5	0	5	11	9	1	1	21	.254	.304	.399	.703	-6	1	3	25	O16(10/0/8),3b13,1b3/2	0	-0.9
1972	Det A	7	7	0	0	0	0	0	0	0	0	0	2	.000	.000	.000	.000	-197	0	0	0	/H	0	-0.2
1972	Tex A	72	151	14	24	2	0	4	19	10	1	0	31	.159	.207	.252	.459	-61	1	0	100	3b23,2b17,1b7,O2L	0	-1.8
1972	Year	79	158	14	24	2	0	4	19	10	1	0	33	.152	.199	.241	.440	-68	1	0	100	3b23,2b17,1b7,O2L	0	-2.0
Total	9	907	2329	268	548	91	19	41	237	191	18	11	309	.235	.295	.343	.638	-21	20	13	61	2b262,3b186,1b158,O18L/S	0	-11.8
Team	6	656	1842	210	447	77	19	26	186	139	12	9	222	.243	.298	.347	.645	-20	17	9	65	2b209,1b138,3b132/S	0	-8.4
/150	1	150	421	48	102	18	4	6	43	32	3	2	51	.243	.298	.347	.645	-20	4	2	67	2b48,1b32,3b30/S	0	-1.9
JONES, JAKE James Murrell B11.23.1920 Epps LA D12.13.2000 Delhi LA BR/TR/6'3"/197 d9.20 Mil 1942–45																								
1941	Chi A	3	11	0	0	0	0	0	0	0		0	4	.000	.000	.000	.000	-199	0	0	0	1b3	0	-0.4
1942	Chi A	7	20	2	3	1	0	0	0	2		0	2	.150	.227	.200	.427	-79	1	0	100	1b5	0	-0.3
1946	Chi A	24	79	10	21	5	1	3	13	2		0	13	.266	.284	.468	.752	+12	0	0	0	1b20	0	-0.4
1947	Chi A	45	171	15	41	7	1	3	20	13		1	25	.240	.297	.345	.642	-19	1	0	100	1b43	0	-0.7
1947	Bos A	109	404	50	95	14	3	16	76	41		3	60	.235	.310	.403	.713	-9	5	4	56	1b109	0	-1.4
1947	Year	154	575	65	136	21	4	19	96	54		4	85	.237	.306	.386	.692	-12	6	4	60	1b152	0	-2.1
1948	Bos A	36	105	3	21	4	0	1	8	11		0	26	.200	.276	.267	.543	-57	1	0	100	1b31	0	-0.8
Total	5	224	790	80	181	31	5	23	117	69		4	130	.229	.294	.368	.662	-20	8	4	67	1b211	0	-4.0
Team	2	145	509	53	116	18	3	17	84	52		3	86	.228	.303	.375	.678	-19	6	4	60	1b140	0	-2.2
/150	2	150	527	55	120	19	3	18	87	54		3	89	.228	.303	.375	.678	-19	6	4	60	1b145	0	-2.3
JOOST, EDDIE Edwin David B6.5.1916 San Francisco CA BR/TR/6'0"/175 d9.11 Def 1944 M1																								
1955	Bos A	55	119	15	23	2	0	5	17	17	2	1	21	.193	.299	.336	.635	-35	0	0	0	S20,2b17,3b2	0	-0.3
Total	17	1574	5606	874	1339	238	35	134	601	1043	2	33	827	.239	.361	.366	.727	-1	61	31	100	S1299,2b166,3b95,1b2	0	8.3
JOSEPHSON, DUANE Duane Charles B6.3.1942 New Hampton IA D1.30.1997 New Hampton IA BR/TR/6'0"/(185–195) d9.15 Col Northern Iowa [DL 1973 Bos A 9]																								
1971	Bos A	91	306	38	75	14	1	10	39	22	4	0	35	.245	.294	.395	.689	-12	2	0	100	C87	0	-0.3
1972	Bos A	26	82	11	22	4	1	1	7	4	0	1	11	.268	.310	.378	.688	-2	0	2	0	1b16,C6	64	-0.7
Total	8	470	1505	147	388	58	12	23	164	92	8	11	174	.258	.303	.358	.661	-11	4	10	29	C420,1b16	180	-1.2
Team	2	117	388	49	97	18	2	11	46	26	4	1	46	.250	.297	.392	.689	-10	2	2	50	C93,1b16	73	-1.0
/150	3	150	497	63	124	23	3	14	59	33	5	1	59	.250	.297	.392	.689	-10	3	3	50	C119,1b21	94	-1.3
JUDGE, JOE Joseph Ignatius B5.25.1894 Brooklyn NY D3.11.1963 Washington DC BL/TL/5'8.5"/155 d9.20 C2																								
1933	Bos A	35	108	20	32	8	1	0	22	13		0	4	.296	.372	.389	.761	+3	2	1	67	1b29		-0.2
1934	Bos A	10	15	3	5	2	0	0	2	2		0	1	.333	.412	.467	.879	+18	0	0	0	1b2		0.0
Total	20	2171	7898	1184	2352	433	159	71	1034	965		51	478	.298	.378	.420	.798	+15	213	92	100	1b2084,O2R		8.1
Team	2	45	123	23	37	10	1	0	24	15		0	5	.301	.377	.398	.775	+5	2	1	67	1b31		-0.2
JURAK, ED Edward James B10.24.1957 Los Angeles CA BR/TR/6'2"/(165–187) [BosA75 3/63] d6.30																								
1982	Bos A	12	21	3	7	0	0	0	7	2	0	0	4	.333	.375	.333	.708	-4	0	0	0	3b11/cf	0	0.1
1983	Bos A	75	159	19	44	8	4	0	18	18	1	1	25	.277	.350	.377	.727	-6	1	2	33	S38,1b19,3b12/2D	0	0.4
1984	Bos A	47	66	6	16	3	1	1	7	12	0	0	12	.242	.359	.364	.723	-4	0	2	0	1b19,2b14,3b9,S2	0	0.1
1985	Bos A	26	13	4	3	0	0	0	0	1	0	0	3	.231	.286	.231	.517	-58	0	0	0	3b7,S3/1lfD	0	0.0
1988	Oak A	3	1	1	0	0	0	0	0	0	0	0	0	.000	.000	.000	.000	-199	0	0	0	/3D	0	0.0
1989	SF N	30	42	2	10	0	0	0	1	5	0	0	5	.238	.319	.238	.557	-37	0	0	0	S6,3b5,2b4,O2(1/0/1)/1	0	-0.3
Total	6	193	302	35	80	11	5	1	33	38	1	1	49	.265	.346	.344	.690	-12	1	4	20	S49,3b45,1b40,2b19,D8,O4(2/1/1)	0	0.3
Team	4	160	259	32	70	11	5	1	32	33	1	1	44	.270	.351	.363	.714	-8	1	4	20	S43,1b39,3b39,2b15,O2(1/1/0),D2	0	0.6
/150	4	150	243	30	66	10	5	1	30	31	1	1	41	.270	.351	.363	.714	-8	1	4	20	S40,1b37,3b37,2b14,O2(1/1/0),D2	0	0.6

Year	Tm Lg	G	AB	R	H	2B	3B	HR	RBI	BB	IB	HP	SO	AVG	OBP	SLG	OPS	AOPS	SB	CS	SB%	Games at Position	DL	BFW
KAPLER, GABE Gabriel Stefan B8.31.1975 Hollywood CA BR/TR/6'2"/(190–210) [DetA95 57/1488] d9.20 Col Moorpark (CA) JC																								
1998	Det A	7	25	3	5	0	1	0	0	1	0	0	4	.200	.231	.280	.511	-68	2	0	100	O6R/D	0	-0.3
1999	Det A	130	416	60	102	22	4	18	49	42	0	2	74	.245	.315	.447	.762	-9	11	5	69	O128(0/114/32),D2	0	-0.8
2000	Tex A	116	444	59	134	32	1	14	66	42	2	0	57	.302	.360	.473	.833	+8	8	4	67	O116(0/84/40)	36	0.7
2001	Tex A	134	483	77	129	29	1	17	72	61	2	3	70	.267	.348	.437	.785	+3	23	6	79	O133C/D	21	0.8
2002	Tex A	72	196	25	51	12	1	0	17	8	0	0	30	.260	.285	.332	.617	-37	5	2	71	O64(31/23/18)/1D	22	-0.7
2002	Col N	40	119	12	37	4	3	2	17	8	0	1	23	.311	.359	.445	.804	-3	6	2	75	O38(15/1/23)	0	0.1
2002	Major	112	315	37	88	16	4	2	34	16	0	1	53	.279	3.316	.375	3.691	+58	11	4	73		22	-0.6
2003	Col N	39	67	10	15	2	0	0	4	8	1	0	18	.224	.307	.254	.561	-57	2	0	100	O29(15/2/13)	0	-0.4
2003	†Bos A	68	158	29	46	11	1	4	23	14	0	0	23	.291	.349	.449	.798	+4	4	2	67	O61(25/8/30)/1	0	-0.2
2003	Major	107	225	39	61	13	1	4	27	22	1	0	41	.271	.336	.391	.727	+44	6	2	75		0	-0.6
2004	†Bos A	136	290	51	79	14	1	6	33	15	0	2	49	.272	.311	.390	.701	-23	5	4	56	O127(18/17/101),D2	0	-1.4
2005	Bos A	36	97	15	24	7	0	1	9	3	0	2	15	.247	.282	.351	.633	-35	1	0	100	O36(8/12/22)	15	-0.5
2006	Bos A	72	130	21	33	7	0	2	12	14	0	3	15	.254	.340	.354	.694	-22	1	1	50	O68(21/14/37)	0	-0.3
Total	9	850	2425	362	655	140	13	64	302	216	5	13	378	.270	.331	.418	.749	-10	68	26	72	O806(133/408/322),D7,1b2	94	-3.0
Team	4	312	675	116	182	39	2	13	77	46	0	7	102	.270	.321	.391	.712	-18	11	7	61	O292(43/51/45),D2/1	15	-2.4
/150	2	150	325	56	88	19	1	6	37	22	0	3	49	.270	.321	.391	.712	-18	5	3	63	O140(21/25/22)/D1	7	-1.2
KAROW, MARTY Martin Gregory (b Martin Gregory Karowsky) B7.18.1904 Braddock PA D4.27.1986 Bryan TX BR/TR/5'10.5"/170 d6.21 Col Ohio St.																								
1927	Bos A	6	10	0	2	1	0	0	0	0		0	2	.200	.200	.300	.500	-71	0	0	0	S3,3b2		0.0
KASKO, EDDIE Edward Michael B6.27.1932 Linden NJ BR/TR/6'0"/(180–183) d4.18 M4																								
1966	Bos A	58	136	11	29	7	0	1	12	15	0	0	19	.213	.291	.287	.578	-39	1	0	100	S20,3b10,2b8	27	0.3
Total	10	1077	3546	411	935	146	13	22	261	265	33	20	353	.264	.317	.331	.648	-24	31	31	50	S544,3b426,2b63	85	-6.1
KELL, GEORGE George Clyde B8.23.1922 Swifton AR BR/TR/5'9"/175 d9.28 HF1983 b–Skeeter Col Arkansas St.																								
1952	Bos A∗	75	276	41	88	15	2	6	40	31		1	10	.319	.390	.453	.843	+24	0	1	0	3b73	0	0.5
1953	Bos A★	134	460	68	141	41	2	12	73	52		5	22	.307	.383	.483	.866	+26	5	2	71	3b124,O7L	0	0.6
1954	Bos A	26	93	15	24	3	0	0	10	15		0	3	.258	.361	.290	.651	-28	0	0	0	3b25	0	-0.6
Total	15	1795	6702	881	2054	385	50	78	870	621	7	36	287	.306	.367	.414	.781	+11	51	36	59	3b1692,1b85,O10(10/0/1)/2	0	8.5
Team	3	235	829	124	253	59	4	18	123	98		6	35	.305	.383	.451	.834	+19	5	3	63	3b222,O7L	0	0.5
/150	2	150	529	79	161	38	3	11	79	63		4	22	.305	.383	.451	.834	+19	3	2	60	3b142,O4L	0	0.3
KELLETT, RED Donald Stafford B7.15.1909 Brooklyn NY D11.3.1970 Ft.Lauderdale FL BR/TR/6'0"/185 d7.2 Col Penn																								
1934	Bos A	9	9	0	0	0	0	0	0	1		0	5	.000	.100	.000	.100	-168	0	0	0	S4,2b2/3		-0.2
KELTNER, KEN Kenneth Frederick "Butch" B10.31.1916 Milwaukee WI D12.12.1991 New Berlin WI BR/TR/6'0"/190 d10.2 Mil 1945																								
1950	Bos A	13	28	2	9	2	0	0	2	3		0	6	.321	.387	.393	.780	-9	0	0	0	3b8/1	0	-0.1
Total	13	1526	5683	737	1570	308	69	163	852	514		13	480	.276	.338	.441	.779	+13	39	33	54	3b1500/1	0	12.7
KENDALL, FRED Fred Lyn B1.31.1949 Torrance CA BR/TR/6'1"/(185–190) [CinN67 4/68] d9.8 C7 s–Jason																								
1978	Bos A	20	41	3	8	1	0	0	4	1	0	0	2	.195	.205	.220	.425	-80	0	0	0	1b13,C5/D	0	-0.5
Total	12	877	2576	170	603	86	11	31	244	189	29	6	240	.234	.285	.312	.597	-28	5	5	50	C795,1b19,D2/3lf	0	-15.0
KENNEDY, JOHN John Edward B5.29.1941 Chicago IL BR/TR/6'0"/185 d9.5 Mil 1968																								
1970	Bos A	43	129	15	33	7	1	4	17	6	1	1	14	.256	.292	.419	.711	-12	0	0	0	3b33,2b2	0	0.1
1971	Bos A	74	272	41	75	12	5	5	22	14	0	4	42	.276	.320	.412	.732	-1	1	1	50	2b37,S33,3b5	0	-1.1
1972	Bos A	71	212	22	52	11	1	2	22	18	4	3	40	.245	.311	.335	.646	-12	0	1	0	2b32,S27,3b11	0	-0.6
1973	Bos A	67	155	17	28	9	1	1	16	12	0	2	45	.181	.246	.271	.517	-56	0	0	0	2b31,3b24,D9	0	-1.1
1974	Bos A	10	15	3	2	0	0	1	1	1	0	0	6	.133	.188	.333	.521	-56	0	0	0	2b6,3b4	0	-0.3
Total	12	856	2110	237	475	77	17	32	185	142	10	25	461	.225	.281	.323	.604	-30	14	10	58	3b455,S226,2b143,D9/1	65	-10.6
Team	5	265	783	98	190	39	8	13	78	51	5	10	147	.243	.295	.363	.658	-18	1	2	33	2b108,3b77,S60,D9	0	-3.0
/150	3	150	443	55	108	22	5	7	44	29	3	6	83	.243	.295	.363	.658	-18	1	1	50	2b61,3b44,S34,D5	0	-1.7
KEOUGH, MARTY Richard Martin B4.14.1934 Oakland CA BL/TL/6'0"/(180–181) d4.21 b–Joe s–Matt																								
1956	Bos A	3	2	1	0	0	0	0	1	1	0	0	0	.000	.333	.000	.333	-105	0	0	0	/H	0	0.0
1957	Bos A	9	17	1	1	0	0	0	0	4	0	0	3	.059	.238	.059	.297	-114	0	0	0	O7(0/2/5)	0	-0.2
1958	Bos A	68	118	21	26	3	3	1	9	7	0	0	29	.220	.262	.322	.584	-43	1	1	50	O25(1/21/3),1b2	0	-1.3
1959	Bos A	96	251	40	61	13	5	7	27	26	0	3	40	.243	.320	.418	.738	-3	3	1	75	O69C,1b3	0	-0.2
1960	Bos A	38	105	15	26	6	1	1	9	8	1	0	8	.248	.296	.352	.648	-27	2	2	50	O29(1/28/0)	0	-0.5
Total	11	841	1796	256	434	71	23	43	176	164	11	17	318	.242	.309	.379	.688	-14	26	19	58	O464(127/203/148),1b130	0	-6.0
Team	5	214	493	78	114	22	9	9	46	46	1	3	80	.231	.299	.367	.666	-22	6	4	60	O130(2/52/5),1b5	0	-2.2
/150	4	150	346	55	80	15	6	6	32	32	1	2	56	.231	.299	.367	.666	-22	4	3	57	O91(1/36/4),1b4	0	-1.5
KLAUS, BILLY William Joseph B12.9.1928 Spring Grove IL BL/TR/5'10"/(160–165) d4.16 b–Bobby																								
1952	Bos N	7	4	3	0	0	0	0	0	1		0	1	.000	.200	.000	.200	-142	0	0	0	S4	0	-0.2
1953	Mil N	2	2	1	0	0	0	0	1	0		0	0	.000	.000	.000	.000	-199	0	0	0	/H	0	-0.1
1955	Bos A	135	541	83	153	26	2	7	60	60	0	0	44	.283	.351	.377	.728	-11	6	0	100	S126,3b8	0	0.1
1956	Bos A	135	520	91	141	29	5	7	59	90	0	1	43	.271	.378	.387	.765	-8	1	0	100	3b106,S26	0	0.1
1957	Bos A	127	477	76	120	18	4	10	42	55	0	0	53	.252	.326	.369	.695	-15	2	0	100	S118	0	2.3
1958	Bos A	61	88	5	14	4	0	1	7	5	0	0	16	.159	.204	.239	.443	-80	0	0	0	S27	0	-1.5
1959	Bal A	104	321	33	80	11	0	3	25	51	1	0	38	.249	.350	.312	.662	-14	2	4	33	S59,3b49/2	0	-0.4
1960	Bal A	46	43	8	9	2	0	1	6	9	0	0	9	.209	.346	.326	.672	-16	0	0	0	2b30,S12,3b2	0	0.2
1961	Was A	91	251	26	57	8	2	7	30	30	3	2	34	.227	.311	.359	.670	-19	2	2	50	3b51,S18/2lf	0	-0.7
1962	Phi N	102	248	30	51	8	2	4	20	29	3	1	43	.206	.290	.302	.592	-39	1	1	50	3b53,S30,2b11	0	-1.0
1963	Phi N	11	18	1	1	0	0	0	0	1	0	0	4	.056	.105	.056	.161	-153	0	0	0	S5,3b3	0	-0.5
Total	11	821	2513	357	626	106	15	40	250	331	7	4	285	.249	.335	.351	.686	-18	14	7	67	S425,3b272,2b43/lf	0	-1.7
Team	4	458	1626	255	428	77	11	25	168	210	0	1	156	.263	.345	.370	.715	-15	9	0	100	S297,3b114	0	1.0
/150	1	150	533	84	140	25	4	8	55	69	0	0	51	.263	.345	.370	.715	-15	3	0	100	S97,3b37	0	0.3
KLEINOW, RED John Peter B7.20.1877 Milwaukee WI D10.9.1929 New York NY BR/TR/5'10"/165 d5.3 Col St. Edwards																								
1910	Bos A	50	147	9	22	1	0	1	8	20		0		.150	.251	.177	.428	-66	3			C49		-0.5
1911	Bos A	8	14	0	3	0	0	0	0	2		0		.214	.313	.214	.527	-52	1			C8		0.0
Total	8	584	1665	146	354	45	20	3	135	153		8	1	.213	.282	.269	.551	-29	42			C558,1b5,2b2,3b2/rf		-2.6
Team	2	58	161	9	25	1	0	1	8	22		0	0	.155	.257	.180	.437	-65	4			C57		-0.5
KNIGHT, JOHN John Wesley "Schoolboy" B10.6.1885 Philadelphia PA D12.19.1965 Walnut Creek CA BR/TR/6'2.5"/180 d4.14 Col Penn																								
1907	Bos A	98	360	31	78	9	3	2	29	19		0		.217	.256	.275	.531	-30	8			3b92,2b4		-0.8
Total	8	767	2664	301	636	96	24	14	270	211		24	27	.239	.300	.309	.609	-16	86			S316,3b211,1b124,2b104/rf		-7.4
KOSCO, ANDY Andrew John B10.5.1941 Youngstown OH BR/TR/6'3"/(200–210) d8.13																								
1972	Bos A	17	47	5	10	2	1	3	6	2	0	1	9	.213	.260	.489	.749	+13	0	0	0	O12L	0	0.0
Total	10	658	1963	204	464	75	8	73	267	99	18	6	350	.236	.273	.394	.667	-8	5	8	38	O453(136/14/312),1b69,3b20	40	-7.4
KRONER, JOHN John Harold B11.13.1908 St.Louis MO D8.26.1968 St.Louis MO BR/TR/6'0"/185 d9.29																								
1935	Bos A	2	4	1	1	0	0	0	0	1		0	1	.250	.400	.250	.650	-33	0	0	0	3b2		0.0
1936	Bos A	84	298	40	87	17	8	4	62	26		0	24	.292	.349	.443	.792	-11	2	3	40	2b38,3b28,S18/rf		-0.6
1937	Cle A	86	283	29	67	14	1	2	26	22		0	25	.237	.292	.314	.606	-48	1	1	50	2b64,3b11		-1.3
1938	Cle A	51	117	13	29	16	0	1	17	19		0	6	.248	.353	.410	.763	-8	0	1	0	2b31,1b7,3b3/S		0.6
Total	4	223	702	83	184	47	9	7	105	68		0	56	.262	.327	.385	.712	-25	3	5	38	2b133,3b44,S19,1b7/rf		-1.3
Team	2	86	302	41	88	17	8	4	62	27		0	25	.291	.350	.440	.790	-11	2	3	40	2b38,3b30,S18/rf		-0.6
KRUG, MARTY Martin John B9.10.1888 Koblenz, Germany D6.27.1966 Glendale CA BR/TR/5'9"/165 d5.29																								
1912	Bos A	20	39	6	12	2	1	0	7	5		0		.308	.386	.410	.796	+22	2			S11,2b4		0.0
Total	2	147	489	73	136	25	5	4	67	48		3	43	.278	.346	.374	.720	-15	9	9	100	3b104,2b27,S12		-1.1
KUTCHER, RANDY Randy Scott B4.20.1960 Anchorage AK BR/TR/5'11"/175 [SFN79 4/96] d6.19 OF(26/78/52)																								
1986	SF N	71	186	28	44	9	1	7	16	11	0	0	41	.237	.279	.409	.688	-8	6	5	55	O51(7/44/1),S13,3b4,2b3	0	-0.6

Year	Tm Lg	G	AB	R	H	2B	3B	HR	RBI	BB	IB	HP	SO	AVG	OBP	SLG	OPS	AOPS	SB	CS	SB%	Games at Position	DL	BFW
1987	SF N	14	16	7	3	1	1	0	1	1	0	0	5	.188	.235	.375	.610	-39	1	0	100	O6(1/4/1),2b2,3b2/S	0	0.0
1988	Bos A	19	12	2	2	1	0	0	0	0	0	0	2	.167	.167	.250	.417	-86	0	1	0	O7(5/0/2),3b2,D7	0	-0.1
1989	Bos A	77	160	28	36	10	3	2	18	11	0	0	46	.225	.273	.363	.636	-27	3	0	100	O57(11/21/25),3b6/CD	15	-0.6
1990	†Bos A	63	74	18	17	4	1	1	5	13	0	0	18	.230	.345	.351	.696	-10	3	3	50	O34(2/9/23),3b11,2b5,D5	0	0.2
Total	5	244	448	83	102	25	6	10	40	36	0	0	112	.228	.285	.377	.662	-18	13	9	59	O155C,3b25,D18,S14,2b10/C	15	-1.1
Team	3	159	246	48	55	15	4	3	23	24	0	0	66	.224	.292	.354	.646	-24	6	4	60	O98(21/21/23),3b19,D13,2b5/C	15	-0.5
/150	3	150	232	45	52	14	4	3	22	23	0	0	62	.224	.292	.354	.646	-24	6	4	60	O92(20/20/22),3b18,D12,2b5/C	14	-0.5
LACHANCE, CANDY George Joseph B2.14.1870 Putnam CT D8.18.1932 Waterville CT BB/TR/6'1"/183 d8.15																								
1893	Bro N	11	35	1	6	1	0	0	6	2		1	12	.171	.237	.200	.437	-83	0			C6,O5(4/0/1)		-0.7
1894	Bro N	69	261	48	83	13	8	5	52	16		1	32	.318	.360	.487	.847	+10	20			1b56,C11,O3R		-0.3
1895	Bro N	128	541	102	170	23	9	8	111	29		8	48	.314	.358	.434	.792	+13	37			1b126,O3R		0.2
1896	Bro N	89	348	60	99	10	13	7	58	23		1	32	.284	.331	.448	.779	+10	17			1b89		-0.1
1897	Bro N	126	520	86	160	28	16	4	90	15		5		.308	.333	.446	.779	+11	26			1b126		0.0
1898	Bro N	136	526	62	130	23	7	5	65	31		8		.247	.299	.346	.645	-15	23			1b74,S48,O13(11/2/0)		-2.5
1899	Bal N	125	472	65	145	23	10	1	75	21		10		.307	.350	.405	.755	+1	31			1b125		-0.7
1901	Cle A	133	548	81	166	22	9	1	75	7		2		.303	.314	.381	.695	-4	11			1b133		-0.9
1902	Bos A	**138**	541	60	151	13	4	6	56	18		5		.279	.309	.351	.660	-20	8			1b138		-2.9
1903	†Bos A	**141**	522	60	134	22	6	1	53	28		7		.257	.303	.328	.631	-15	12			1b141		-2.5
1904	Bos A	**157**	573	55	130	19	5	1	47	23		7		.227	.265	.283	.548	-31	7			1b157		-4.2
1905	Bos A	12	41	1	6	1	0	0	5	6		0		.146	.255	.171	.426	-64	0			1b12		-0.4
Total	12	1265	4928	681	1380	198	87	39	693	219		55	124	.280	.318	.379	.697	-7	192			1b1177,S48,O24(15/2/7),C17		-15.0
Team	4	448	1677	176	421	55	15	8	161	75		19	0	.251	.291	.316	.607	-23	27			1b448		-10.0
/150	1	150	561	59	141	18	5	3	54	25		6	0	.251	.291	.316	.607	-23	9			1b150		-3.3
LAFOREST, TY Byron Joseph (b Biron Joseph La Forest) B4.18.1917 Edmundston NB, Can. D5.5.1947 Arlington MA BR/TR/5'9"/165 d8.4																								
1945	Bos A	52	204	25	51	7	4	2	16	10		0	35	.250	.285	.353	.638	-17	4	4	50	3b45,O5(3/0/2)	0	-0.2
LAFRANCOIS, ROGER Roger Victor B8.2.1956 Norwich CT BL/TR/6'2"/202 [BosA77 8/195] d5.27 Col Oklahoma																								
1982	Bos A	8	10	1	4	1	0	0	1	0	0	0	0	.400	.400	.500	.900	+37	0	0	0	C8	0	0.1
LAHOUD, JOE Joseph Michael B4.14.1947 Danbury CT BL/TL/6'0"/(188–198) d4.10 Col New Haven																								
1968	Bos A	29	78	5	15	1	0	1	6	16	0	0	16	.192	.330	.244	.574	-29	0	2	0	O25(3/1/22)	0	-0.8
1969	Bos A	101	218	32	41	5	0	9	21	40	0	1	43	.188	.317	.335	.652	-21	2	1	67	O66(24/12/33)/1	0	-1.2
1970	Bos A	17	49	6	12	1	0	2	5	7	1	0	6	.245	.339	.388	.727	-6	0	0	0	O13(9/0/5)	0	0.1
1971	Bos A	107	256	39	55	9	3	14	32	40	3	4	45	.215	.330	.438	.768	+8	2	2	50	O69(7/0/63)	0	0.2
Total	11	791	1925	239	429	68	12	65	218	309	21	16	339	.223	.334	.372	.706	+3	20	20	50	O492(198/14/296),D116/1	39	-1.4
Team	4	254	601	82	123	16	3	26	64	103	4	5	110	.205	.326	.371	.697	-9	4	5	44	O173(27/13/28)/1	0	-1.7
/150	2	150	355	48	73	9	2	15	38	61	2	3	65	.205	.326	.371	.697	-9	2	3	40	O102(16/8/17)/1	0	-1.0
LAKE, EDDIE Edward Erving "Sparky" B3.18.1916 Antioch CA D6.7.1995 Castro Valley CA BR/TR/5'7"/160 d9.26▲																								
1943	Bos A	75	216	26	43	10	0	3	16	47		1	35	.199	.345	.287	.632	-16	3	6	33	S63	0	0.5
1944	Bos A	57	126	21	26	5	0	0	8	23		0	22	.206	.329	.246	.575	-34	5	2	71	S41,P6,2b3/3	0	-0.3
1945	Bos A	133	473	81	132	27	1	11	51	106		1	37	.279	**.412**	.410	.822	+36	9	7	56	S130/2	0	6.5
Total	11	835	2595	442	599	105	9	39	193	546		8	312	.231	.366	.323	.689	-9	52	45	100	S609,2b90,3b52,P6	0	-0.5
Team	3	265	815	128	201	42	1	14	75	176		2	94	.247	.382	.352	.734	+12	17	15	53	S234,P6,2b4/3	0	6.7
/150	2	150	461	72	114	24	1	8	42	100		1	53	.247	.382	.352	.734	+12	10	8	56	S132,P3,2b2/3	0	3.8
LAMAR, BILL William Harmong "Good Time Bill" B3.21.1897 Rockville MD D5.24.1970 Rockport MA BL/TR/6'1"/185 d9.19 Mil 1918																								
1919	Bos A	48	148	18	43	5	1	0	14	5		0	9	.291	.314	.338	.652	-12	3			O36(6/29/1)		-0.7
Total	9	550	2040	303	633	114	23	19	245	86		2	78	.310	.339	.417	.756	-6	25	27	100	O494(425/58/11)/1		-8.0
LANCELLOTTI, RICK Richard Anthony B7.5.1956 Providence RI BL/TL/6'3"/(195–210) [PitN77 11/278] d8.27 Col Rowan																								
1990	Bos A	4	8	0	0	0	0	0	1	0	0	0	3	.000	.000	.000	.000	-195	0	0	0	1b2	0	-0.2
Total	3	36	65	4	11	2	0	2	11	2	0	0	18	.169	.191	.292	.483	-65	0	0	0	1b10,O4(2/0/2)	0	-0.8
LANDIS, JIM James Henry B3.9.1934 Fresno CA BR/TR/6'1"/(170–180) d4.16 Col Contra Costa (CA) JC																								
1967	Bos A	5	7	1	1	0	0	1	1	1	0	0	3	.143	.250	.571	.821	+26	0	0	0	O5R	0	0.0
Total	11	1346	4288	625	1061	169	50	93	467	588	22	59	767	.247	.344	.375	.719	+0	139	51	73	O1265(63/1132/87)	0	-0.6
LANGFORD, SAM Elton B5.21.1900 Briggs TX D7.31.1993 Plainview TX BL/TR/6'0"/180 d4.13																								
1926	Bos A	1	1	1	0	0	0	0	0	0		0	0	.000	.000	.000	.000	-199	0	0	0	/H		0.0
Total	3	131	495	61	136	22	8	5	57	26		4	42	.275	.316	.382	.698	-19	3	9	25	O127(33/94/1)		-3.2
LANSFORD, CARNEY Carney Ray B2.7.1957 San Jose CA BR/TR/6'2"/195 [CalA75 3/49] d4.8 C3 b–Jody																								
1981	Bos A	102	399	61	134	23	3	4	52	34	3	2	28	**.336**	.389	.439	.828	+30	15	10	60	3b86,D16	0	1.3
1982	Bos A	128	482	65	145	28	4	11	63	46	2	2	48	.301	.359	.444	.803	+14	9	4	69	3b114,D13	27	-0.6
Total	15	1862	7158	1007	2074	332	40	151	874	553	45	64	719	.290	.343	.411	.754	+11	224	104	68	3b1720,1b124,D49,S4,2b2	296	-9.1
Team	2	230	881	126	279	51	7	15	115	80	5	4	76	.317	.372	.442	.814	+21	24	14	63	3b200,D29	27	0.7
/150	1	150	575	82	182	33	5	10	75	52	3	3	50	.317	.372	.442	.814	+21	16	9	64	3b130,D19	18	0.5
LANSING, MIKE Michael Thomas B4.3.1968 Rawlins WY BR/TR/6'0"/(180–195) [Mial90 5/155] d4.7 Col Wichita St.																								
2000	Bos A	49	139	10	27	4	0	0	13	7	1	0	26	.194	.230	.223	.453	-84	0	0	0	2b49/3	0	-2.1
2001	Bos A	106	352	45	88	23	0	8	34	22	1	1	50	.250	.294	.384	.678	-23	3	3	50	S76,2b31	28	-1.0
Total	9	1110	4150	554	1124	254	17	84	440	299	17	37	570	.271	.324	.401	.725	-17	119	38	76	2b893,S143,3b110	179	-1.9
Team	2	155	491	55	115	27	0	8	47	29	2	1	76	.234	.276	.338	.614	-40	3	3	50	2b80,S76/3	28	-3.1
/150	2	150	475	53	111	26	0	8	45	28	2	1	74	.234	.276	.338	.614	-40	3	3	50	2b77,S74/3	27	-3.0
LAPORTE, FRANK Frank Breyfogle "Pot" B2.6.1880 Uhrichsville OH D9.25.1939 Newcomerstown OH BR/TR/5'8"/175 d9.29																								
1908	Bos A	62	156	14	37	1	3	0	15	12		1		.237	.296	.282	.578	-14	3			2b27,3b12,O5(0/2/3)		0.4
Total	11	1194	4212	501	1185	198	78	16	560	288		27	85	.281	.331	.377	.708	+7	101			2b731,3b254,O147(39/16/92)/1		-0.3
LARY, LYN Lynford Hobart "Broadway" B1.28.1906 Armona CA D1.9.1973 Downey CA BR/TR/6'0"/165 d5.11																								
1934	Bos A	129	419	58	101	20	4	2	54	66		0	51	.241	.344	.322	.666	-32	12	5	71	S129		-1.4
Total	12	1302	4603	805	1239	247	56	38	526	705		25	470	.269	.369	.372	.741	-10	162	49	100	S1138,3b95,1b9,2b5,O2L		5.8
/150	1	150	487	67	117	23	5	2	63	77		0	59	.241	.344	.322	.666	-32	14	6	70	S150		-1.6
LAZOR, JOHNNY John Paul B9.9.1912 Taylor WA D12.9.2002 Renton WA BL/TR/5'9.5"/180 d4.22																								
1943	Bos A	83	208	21	47	10	2	0	13	21		0	25	.226	.297	.293	.590	-28	5	6	45	O63(51/7/8)	0	-1.0
1944	Bos A	16	24	0	2	1	0	0	0	1		0	0	.083	.120	.125	.245	-130	0	0	0	O6(1/0/5)/C	0	-0.4
1945	Bos A	101	335	35	104	19	2	5	45	18		0	17	.310	.346	.424	.770	+20	3	2	60	O81(12/0/73)	0	-0.5
1946	Bos A	23	29	1	4	0	0	1	4	2		0	11	.138	.194	.241	.435	-80	0	0	0	O7(3/0/4)	0	-0.4
Total	4	223	596	57	157	30	4	6	62	42		0	53	.263	.312	.357	.669	-8	8	8	50	O157(67/7/90)/C	0	-2.3
/150	3	150	401	38	106	20	3	4	42	28		0	36	.263	.312	.357	.669	-8	5	5	50	O106(45/5/61)/C	0	-1.5
LEE, DUD Ernest Holford (aka Ernest Dudley in 1920-21) B8.22.1899 Denver CO D1.7.1971 Denver CO BL/TR/5'9"/150 d10.3																								
1920	StL A	1	2	2	2	0	0	0	1	0		0	0	1.000	1.000	1.000	2.000	+318	1	0	100	/S		0.0
1921	StL A	72	180	18	30	4	2	0	11	14		2	34	.167	.235	.211	.446	-86	1	1	50	S31,2b30,3b3		-2.0
1924	Bos A	94	288	36	73	9	4	0	29	40		3	17	.253	.350	.313	.663	-28	8	4	67	S90		-0.7
1925	Bos A	84	255	22	57	7	3	0	19	34		0	19	.224	.315	.275	.590	-49	2	3	40	S84		0.1
1926	Bos A	2	7	2	1	0	0	0	0	0		1	0	.143	.250	.143	.393	-96	0	0	0	S2		-0.1
Total	5	253	732	80	163	20	9	0	60	88		6	70	.223	.311	.275	.586	-50	12	8	60	S208,2b30,3b3		-2.7
Team	3	180	550	60	131	16	7	0	48	74		4	36	.238	.333	.293	.626	-39	10	7	59	S176		-0.7
/150	3	150	458	50	109	13	6	0	40	62		3	30	.238	.333	.293	.626	-39	8	6	57	S147		-0.6
LEFEBVRE, BILL Wilfred Henry "Lefty" B11.11.1915 Natick RI BL/TL/5'11.5"/180 d6.10 Mil 1945 Col Holy Cross▲																								
1938	Bos A	1	1	1	1	0	0	1	1	0		0	0	1.000	1.000	4.000	5.000	+948	0	0	0	/P		0.0
1939	Bos A	7	10	3	3	0	0	0	1	2		0	2	.300	.417	.300	.717	-17	0	0	0	P5		0.0
Total	4	75	87	8	24	5	2	1	11	15		0	11	.276	.382	.414	.796	+29	0	0	0	P36,1b2	0	0.0
Team	2	8	11	4	4	0	0	1	2	2		0	2	.364	.462	.636	1.098	+57	0	0	0	P5		0.0

Year	Tm Lg	G	AB	R	H	2B	3B	HR	RBI	BB	IB	HP	SO	AVG	OBP	SLG	OPS	AOPS	SB	CS	SB%	Games at Position	DL	BFW
LEGETT, LOU Louis Alfred "Doc" B6.1.1901 New Orleans LA D3.6.1988 New Orleans LA BR/TR/5'10"/166 d5.8																								
1929	Bos N	39	81	7	13	2	0	0	6	3		0	18	.160	.190	.185	.375	-107	2			C28		-1.3
1933	Bos A	8	5	1	1	1	0	0	1	0		0	0	.200	.200	.400	.600	-44	0	0	0	C2		0.0
1934	Bos A	19	38	4	11	0	0	0	1	2		0	4	.289	.325	.289	.614	-44	0	0	0	C17		-0.2
1935	Bos A	2	0	1	0	0	0	0	0	0		0	0	+	+	+	.000	-100	0	0	0	/R		0.0
Total	4	68	124	13	25	3	0	0	8	5		0	22	.202	.233	.226	.459	-84	2	0	100	C47		-1.5
Team	3	29	43	6	12	1	0	0	2	2		0	4	.279	.311	.302	.613	-44	0	0	0	C19		-0.2
LEHNER, PAUL Paul Eugene "Peanuts","Gulliver" B7.1.1920 Dolomite AL D12.27.1967 Birmingham AL BL/TL/5'9"/165 d9.10																								
1952	Bos A	3	3	0	2	0	0	0	2	2		0	0	.667	.800	.667	1.467	+188	0	0	0	O2R	0	0.1
Total	7	540	1768	175	455	80	21	22	197	127		4	118	.257	.309	.364	.673	-22	6	11	35	O432(110/297/37),1b20	0	-9.1
LEIBOLD, NEMO Harry Loran B2.17.1892 Butler IN D2.4.1977 Detroit MI BL/TR/5'6.5"/157 d4.12																								
1921	Bos A	123	467	88	143	26	6	0	31	41		1	27	.306	.363	.388	.751	-6	13	7	65	O117(0/107/10)		-0.9
1922	Bos A	81	271	42	70	8	1	1	18	41		2	14	.258	.360	.306	.666	-24	1	6	14	O71(1/66/4)		-1.1
1923	Bos A	12	18	1	2	0	0	0	0	1		0	2	.111	.158	.111	.269	-128	0	1	0	O10C		-0.4
Total	13	1268	4167	638	1109	145	49	3	284	571		16	335	.266	.357	.327	.684	-9	136	60	100	O1120(144/593/381)/3		-5.8
Team	3	216	756	131	215	34	7	1	49	83		3	43	.284	.357	.352	.709	-15	14	14	50	O198(1/173/14)		-2.4
/150	2	150	525	91	149	24	5	1	34	58		2	30	.284	.357	.352	.709	-15	10	10	50	O138(1/120/10)		-1.7
LEMKE, MARK Mark Alan B8.13.1965 Utica NY BB/TR/5'9"/167 [AtlN83 27/677] d9.17																								
1998	Bos A	31	91	10	17	4	0	0	7	6	0	0	15	.187	.232	.231	.463	-78	0	1	0	2b31	125	-1.6
Total	11	1069	3230	349	795	125	15	32	270	348	48	0	341	.246	.317	.324	.641	-29	11	19	37	2b965,3b73/S	253	-3.9
LENHARDT, DON Donald Eugene "Footsie" B10.4.1922 Alton IL BR/TR/6'3"/190 d4.18 C4 Col Illinois																								
1952	Bos A	30	105	18	31	4	0	7	24	15		0	18	.295	.383	.533	.916	+42	0	1	0	O27L	0	0.2
1954	Bos A	44	66	5	18	4	0	3	17	3		1	9	.273	.310	.470	.780	+1	0	0	0	O13L/3	0	-0.1
Total	5	481	1481	192	401	64	9	61	239	214		6	235	.271	.365	.450	.815	+14	6	7	46	O297(291/1/5),1b93,3b17	0	-0.7
Team	2	74	171	23	49	8	0	10	41	18		1	27	.287	.356	.509	.865	+27	0	1	0	O40L/3	0	0.1
LEPCIO, TED Thaddeus Stanley B7.28.1930 Utica NY BR/TR/5'10"/(175–180) d4.15 Col Seton Hall																								
1952	Bos A	84	274	34	72	17	2	5	26	24		3	41	.263	.329	.394	.723	-7	3	3	50	2b57,3b25/S	0	0.8
1953	Bos A	66	161	17	38	4	2	4	11	17		1	24	.236	.313	.360	.673	-23	0	0	0	2b34,S20,3b11	0	0.8
1954	Bos A	116	398	42	102	19	4	8	45	42		3	62	.256	.328	.384	.712	-14	3	4	43	2b80,3b24,S14	0	0.7
1955	Bos A	51	134	19	31	9	0	6	15	12	0	4	36	.231	.313	.433	.746	-9	1	1	50	3b45	0	0.1
1956	Bos A	83	284	34	74	10	0	15	51	30	1	3	77	.261	.335	.454	.789	-4	1	3	25	2b57,3b22	0	0.3
1957	Bos A	79	232	24	56	10	2	9	37	29	1	1	61	.241	.328	.418	.746	-3	0	0	0	2b68	0	0.9
1958	Bos A	50	136	10	27	3	0	6	14	12	1	1	47	.199	.268	.353	.621	-35	0	1	0	2b40	0	-0.6
1959	Bos A	3	3	1	1	1	0	0	1	0	0	0	2	.333	.333	.667	1.000	+60	0	0	0	/2	0	0.0
1959	Det A	76	215	25	60	8	0	7	24	17	2	0	49	.279	.332	.414	.746	-2	2	0	100	S35,2b24,3b11	0	0.1
1959	Year	79	218	26	61	9	0	7	25	17	2	0	51	.280	.332	.417	.749	-1	2	0	100	S35,2b25,3b11	0	0.1
1960	Phi N	69	141	16	32	7	0	2	8	17	1	2	41	.227	.315	.319	.634	-25	0	3	0	3b50,S14,2b5	0	-1.4
1961	Chi A	5	2	0	0	0	0	0	0	1	1	0	0	.000	.333	.000	.333	-102	0	0	0	/3	0	-0.1
1961	Min A	47	112	11	19	3	1	7	19	8	0	1	31	.170	.230	.402	.632	-38	1	0	100	3b35,2b22,S6	0	-0.6
1961	Year	52	114	11	19	3	1	7	19	9	1	1	31	.167	.232	.395	.627	-38	1	0	100	3b36,2b22,S6	0	-0.7
Total	10	729	2092	233	512	91	11	69	251	209	7	19	471	.245	.318	.398	.716	-13	11	15	42	2b388,3b224,S90	0	1.0
Team	8	532	1622	181	401	73	10	53	200	166	3	16	350	.247	.322	.403	.725	-12	8	12	40	2b337,3b127,S35	0	3.0
/150	2	150	457	51	113	21	3	15	56	47	1	5	99	.247	.322	.403	.725	-12	2	3	40	2b95,3b36,S10	0	0.8
LERCHEN, DUTCH Bertram Roe B4.4.1889 Detroit MI D1.7.1962 Detroit MI BR/TR/5'8"/160 d8.14																								
1910	Bos A	6	15	1	0	0	0	0	0	1		0		.000	.063	.000	.063	-178	0			S6		-0.6
LEWIS, DARREN Darren Joel B8.28.1967 Berkeley CA BR/TR/6'0"/(175–195) [OakA88 18/463] d8.21 Col California																								
1990	Oak A	25	35	4	8	0	0	0	1	7	0	1	4	.229	.372	.229	.601	-26	2	0	100	O23(3/16/5),D2	0	0.0
1991	SF N	72	222	41	55	5	3	1	15	36	0	2	30	.248	.358	.311	.669	-8	13	7	65	O68C	0	0.1
1992	SF N	100	320	38	74	8	1	1	18	29	0	1	46	.231	.295	.272	.567	-35	28	8	78	O94C	0	-1.3
1993	SF N	136	522	84	132	17	7	2	48	30	0	7	40	.253	.302	.324	.626	-30	46	15	75	O131C	15	-1.5
1994	SF N	114	451	70	116	15	**9**	4	29	53	0	4	50	.257	.340	.357	.697	-15	30	13	70	O113C	0	-0.9
1995	SF N	74	309	47	78	10	3	1	16	17	0	6	37	.252	.303	.314	.617	-35	21	7	75	O73C	0	-1.1
1995	†Cin N	58	163	19	40	3	0	0	8	17	0	2	20	.245	.324	.264	.588	-43	11	11	50	O57C	0	-0.7
1995	Year	132	472	66	118	13	3	1	24	34	0	8	57	.250	.311	.297	.608	-38	32	18	64	O130C	0	-1.8
1996	Chi A	141	337	55	77	12	2	4	53	45	1	3	40	.228	.321	.312	.633	-35	21	5	81	O138(1/137/0)	0	-1.8
1997	Chi A	81	77	15	18	1	0	0	5	11	0	0	14	.234	.330	.247	.577	-45	11	4	73	O64C,D6	0	0.0
1997	LA N	26	77	7	23	3	1	1	10	6	0	0	17	.299	.349	.403	.752	+3	3	2	60	O25(23/2/1)	0	0.1
1997	Major	107	154	22	41	4	1	1	15	17	0	0	31	.266	.339	.325	.664	-15	14	6	70		0	0.1
1998	†Bos A	155	585	95	157	25	3	8	63	70	0	8	94	.268	.352	.362	.714	-15	29	12	71	O152(4/109/55)/D	0	-0.7
1999	†Bos A	135	470	63	113	14	6	2	40	45	0	5	52	.240	.311	.309	.620	-42	16	10	62	O130(0/88/51),D2	0	-2.9
2000	Bos A	97	270	44	65	12	0	2	17	22	0	3	34	.241	.305	.307	.612	-46	10	5	67	O89(18/41/37),D5	14	-2.2
2001	Bos A	82	164	18	46	9	1	1	12	8	0	3	25	.280	.326	.366	.692	-18	5	5	50	O69(27/21/29),D6	0	-0.3
2002	Chi N	58	79	7	19	3	1	0	7	7	0	3	11	.241	.326	.304	.630	-33	1	3	25	O47(22/18/9)	0	-0.2
Total	13	1354	4081	607	1021	137	37	27	342	403	1	48	514	.250	.323	.322	.645	-28	247	107	70	O1273(98/1032/187),D22	29	-13.4
Team	4	469	1489	220	381	60	10	13	132	145	0	19	205	.256	.328	.336	.664	-29	60	32	65	O440(19/259/172),D14	14	-6.1
/150	1	150	476	70	122	19	3	4	42	46	0	6	66	.256	.328	.336	.664	-29	19	10	66	O141(6/83/55),D4	4	-2.0
LEWIS, DUFFY George Edward B4.18.1888 San Francisco CA D6.17.1979 Salem NH BR/TR/5'10.5"/165 d4.16 Mil 1918 C5 Col St. Marys (CA)																								
1910	Bos A	151	541	64	153	29	7	8	68	32		4		.283	.328	.407	.735	+27	10			O149L		1.9
1911	Bos A	130	469	64	144	32	4	7	86	25		10		.307	.355	.437	.792	+22	11			O125L		1.2
1912	†Bos A	**154**	581	85	165	36	9	6	109	52		3		.284	.346	.408	.754	+10	9			O154L		0.6
1913	Bos A	149	551	54	164	31	12	0	90	30		2	55	.298	.336	.397	.733	+12	12			O142L/P3		1.1
1914	Bos A	146	510	53	142	37	9	2	79	57		5	41	.278	.357	.398	.755	+27	22	31	42	O142L		0.3
1915	†Bos A	152	557	69	162	31	7	2	76	45		4	63	.291	.348	.382	.730	+22	14	7	67	O152L		0.2
1916	†Bos A	152	563	56	151	29	5	1	56	33		4	56	.268	.313	.343	.656	-3	16			O151(136/15/0)		-1.6
1917	Bos A	150	553	55	167	29	9	1	65	29		5	54	.302	.342	.392	.734	+25	8			O150L		1.4
1919	NY A	**141**	559	67	152	23	4	7	89	17		0	42	.272	.293	.365	.658	-16	8			O141L		-3.1
1920	NY A	107	365	34	99	8	1	4	61	24		2	32	.271	.320	.332	.652	-30	2	8	20	O99(98/0/1)		-2.3
1921	Was A	27	102	11	19	4	1	0	14	8		1	10	.186	.252	.245	.497	-71	1	1	50	O27(26/0/1)		-1.4
Total	11	1459	5351	612	1518	289	68	38	793	352		40	353	.284	.333	.384	.717	+8	113	47	100	O1432(1415/15/2)/3P		-1.7
Team	8	1184	4325	500	1248	254	62	27	629	303		37	269	.289	.340	.395	.735	+18	102	38	100	O1165(1000/1/1)/P3		5.1
/150	1	150	548	63	158	32	8	3	80	38		5	34	.289	.340	.395	.735	+18	13	5	100	O148L/P3		0.6
LEWIS, JACK John David B2.14.1884 Pittsburgh PA D2.25.1956 Steubenville OH BR/TR/5'8"/158 d9.16																								
1911	Bos A	18	59	7	16	0	0	0	6	7		2		.271	.368	.271	.639	-20	2			2b18		-0.1
Total	3	217	684	63	169	20	10	1	80	32		9	77	.247	.290	.310	.600	-34	18			2b178,S12,O6R,1b5/3		-4.1
LEYRITZ, JIM James Joseph B12.27.1963 Lakewood OH BR/TR/6'0"/(190–220) d6.8 Col Kentucky OF(25/0/30)																								
1998	Bos A	52	129	17	37	6	0	8	24	21	1	2	34	.287	.385	.519	.904	+32	0	0	0	D39/C1	0	0.5
Total	11	903	2527	325	667	107	2	90	387	337	16	65	581	.264	.362	.415	.777	+6	7	7	50	C308,D195,1b149,3b105,O54R,2b3	37	0.3
LICKERT, JOHN John Wilbur B4.4.1960 Pittsburgh PA BR/TR/5'11"/175 [BosA78 13/336] d9.19																								
1981	Bos A	1	0	0	0	0	0	0	0	0	0	0	0	+	+	+	.000	-100	0	0	0	/C	0	0.0
LIPON, JOHNNY John Joseph "Skids" B11.10.1922 Martins Ferry OH D8.17.1998 Houston TX BR/TR/6'0"/(170–175) d8.16 Mil 1943–45 M1/C4																								
1952	Bos A	79	234	25	48	8	1	0	18	32		0	20	.205	.301	.248	.549	-50	1	1	50	S69,3b7	0	0.1
1953	Bos A	60	145	18	31	7	0	0	13	14		0	16	.214	.283	.262	.545	-54	1	0	100	S58	0	-0.5
Total	9	758	2661	351	690	95	24	10	266	347		7	152	.259	.346	.324	.670	-23	28	25	53	S717,3b15,2b2	0	-3.4
Team	2	139	379	43	79	15	1	0	31	46		0	36	.208	.294	.253	.547	-51	2	1	67	S127,3b7	0	-0.4
/150	2	150	409	46	85	16	1	0	33	50		0	39	.208	.294	.253	.547	-51	2	1	67	S137,3b8	0	-0.4

Year	Tm Lg	G	AB	R	H	2B	3B	HR	RBI	BB	IB	HP	SO	AVG	OBP	SLG	OPS	AOPS	SB	CS	SB%	Games at Position	DL	BFW
LITTON, GREG Jon Gregory B7.13.1964 New Orleans LA BR/TR/6'0"/(175–190) [SFN84*1/10] d5.2 Col Pensacola (FL) JC OF(42/0/50)																								
1994	Bos A	11	21	2	2	0	0	0	1	0	0	0	5	.095	.091	.095	.186	-148	0	0	0	2b4,1b3,3b2/D	0	-0.4
Total	6	374	809	78	195	43	5	13	97	58	2	4	167	.241	.293	.355	.648	-19	1	6	14	2b100,O91R,3b69,1b39,S33,D13,C3/P	29	-2.3
LOCK, DON Don Wilson B7.27.1936 Wichita KS BR/TR/6'2"/(195–205) d7.17 Col Wichita St.																								
1969	Bos A	53	58	8	13	1	0	1	2	11	0	0	21	.224	.348	.293	.641	-23	0	1	0	O28(15/9/4),1b4	0	-0.3
Total	8	921	2695	359	642	92	12	122	373	373	19	15	776	.238	.331	.417	.748	+11	30	29	51	O831(102/684/70),1b4	0	3.7
LOCKWOOD, SKIP Claude Edward B8.17.1946 Boston MA BR/TR/6'0"/(180–200) d4.23▲																								
1980	Bos A	24	0	0	0	0	0	0	0	0	0	0	0	+	+	+	.000	-100	0	0	0	P24	0	0.0
Total	13	468	260	15	40	4	0	3	11	18	0	2	66	.154	.214	.204	.418	-81	0	2	0	P420,3b7	103	-0.3
LOEPP, GEORGE George Herbert B9.11.1901 Detroit MI D9.4.1967 Los Angeles CA BR/TR/5'11"/170 d8.29																								
1928	Bos A	15	51	6	9	3	1	0	3	5		0	12	.176	.250	.275	.525	-62	0	0	0	O14(1/10/6)		-0.5
Total	2	65	185	29	46	10	2	0	17	25		3	21	.249	.347	.324	.671	-27	0	4	0	O62(13/44/9)		-1.0
LOFTON, JAMES James O'Neal B3.6.1974 Los Angeles CA BB/TR/5'10"/170 [CinN93 13/372] d9.19 Col Los Angeles (CA) City																								
2001	Bos A	8	26	1	5	1	0	0	1	1	0	0	4	.192	.214	.231	.445	-80	2	1	67	S7	0	-0.4
LOMASNEY, STEVE Steven James B8.29.1977 Melrose MA BR/TR/6'0"/195 [BosA95 5/130] d10.3																								
1999	Bos A	1	2	0	0	0	0	0	0	0	0	0	2	.000	.000	.000	.000	-197	0	0	0	/C	0	0.1
LONERGAN, WALTER Walter E. B9.22.1885 Boston MA D1.23.1958 Lexington MA BR/TR/5'7"/156 d8.17																								
1911	Bos A	10	26	2	7	0	0	0	1	1		0		.269	.296	.269	.565	-41	1			2b7/S3		-0.2
LOPEZ, JAVY Javier (Torres) B11.5.1970 Ponce, PR BR/TR/6'3"/(185–230) d9.18																								
2006	Bos A	18	63	6	12	5	0	0	4	2	0	0	16	.190	.215	.270	.485	-76	0	0	0	C17	0	-1.0
Total	15	1503	5319	674	1527	267	19	260	864	357	43	66	969	.287	.337	.491	.828	+12	8	19	30	C1351,D110/1	202	21.1
LORD, HARRY Harry Donald B3.8.1882 Porter ME D8.9.1948 Westbrook ME BL/TR/5'10.5"/165 d9.25 M1 Col Bates																								
1907	Bos A	10	38	4	6	1	0	0	3	1		0		.158	.179	.184	.363	-84	1			3b10		-0.4
1908	Bos A	145	560	61	145	15	6	2	37	22		8		.259	.297	.318	.615	-3	23			3b144		-0.9
1909	Bos A	136	534	89	168	12	7	0	31	20		8		.315	.349	.363	.712	+22	36			3b134		0.7
1910	Bos A	77	288	25	72	5	5	1	32	14		4		.250	.294	.313	.607	-12	17			3b70/S		-0.9
1910	Chi A	44	165	26	49	6	3	0	10	14		0		.297	.352	.370	.722	+32	17			3b44		0.2
1910	Year	121	453	51	121	11	8	1	42	28		4		.267	.315	.333	.648	+3	34			3b114/S		-0.7
1911	Chi A	141	561	103	180	18	18	3	61	32		6		.321	.364	.433	.797	+26	43			3b138		0.1
1912	Chi A	151	570	81	152	19	12	5	54	52		5		.267	.333	.368	.701	+4	30			3b106,O45(32/4/9)		-2.2
1913	Chi A	150	547	62	144	18	12	1	42	45		7	39	.263	.327	.346	.673	-2	24			3b150		-3.0
1914	Chi A	21	69	8	13	1	1	1	3	5		0	3	.188	.243	.275	.518	-43	2	2	50	3b19/lf		-0.7
1915	Buf F	97	359	50	97	12	6	1	21	21		0	15	.270	.311	.345	.656	-17	15			3b92/rfM		-2.2
Total	9	972	3691	509	1026	107	70	14	294	226		38	57	.278	.326	.356	.682	+4	208	2	100	3b907,O47(33/4/10)/S		-9.3
Team	4	368	1420	179	391	33	18	3	103	57		20	0	.275	.313	.330	.643	+2	77			3b358/S		-1.5
/150	2	150	579	73	159	13	7	1	42	23		8	0	.275	.313	.330	.643	+2	31			3b146/S		-0.6
LORETTA, MARK Mark David B8.14.1971 Santa Monica CA BR/TR/6'0"/(175–190) [MilA93 7/207] d9.4 Col Northwestern																								
2006	Bos A★	155	635	75	181	33	0	5	59	49	1	12	63	.285	.345	.361	.706	-18	4	1	80	2b138,1b11,D6	0	-0.7
Total	12	1385	4910	670	1466	263	20	68	525	462	17	65	513	.299	.363	.402	.765	+0	45	32	58	2b731,S328,1b171,3b171,D13/Plf	183	3.8
/150	1	150	615	73	175	32	0	5	57	47	1	12	61	.285	.345	.361	.706	-18	4	1	80	2b134,1b11,D6	0	-0.7
LOWELL, MIKE Michael Averett B2.24.1974 San Juan, PR BR/TR/6'4"/(193–212) [NYA95 20/562] d9.13 Col Florida International																								
2006	Bos A	153	573	79	163	47	1	20	80	47	5	4	61	.284	.339	.475	.814	+6	2	2	50	3b153	0	2.5
Total	9	1142	4142	557	1132	288	4	163	658	401	33	43	590	.273	.339	.463	.802	+10	23	9	72	3b1099,2b8,D5	97	8.8
/150	1	150	562	77	160	46	1	20	78	46	5	4	60	.284	.339	.475	.814	+6	2	2	50	3b150	0	2.5
LUCAS, JOHNNY John Charles "Buster" B2.10.1903 Glen Carbon IL D10.31.1970 Maryville IL BR/TL/5'10"/186 d4.15																								
1931	Bos A	3	2	0	0	0	0	0	0	0		0	1	.000	.000	.000	.000	-199	0	0	0	O2(1/1/0)		-0.1
1932	Bos A	1	1	0	0	0	0	0	0	0		0	0	.000	.000	.000	.000	-199	0	0	0	/H		0.0
Total	2	4	3	0	0	0	0	0	0	0		0	1	.000	.000	.000	.000	-199	0	0	0	O2(1/1/0)		-0.1
LUPIEN, TONY Ulysses John B4.23.1917 Chelmsford MA D7.9.2004 Norwich VT BL/TL/5'10.5"/185 d9.12 Mil 1945 Col Harvard																								
1940	Bos A	10	19	5	9	3	2	0	4	1		0	1	.474	.500	.842	1.342	+132	0	0	0	1b8		0.3
1942	Bos A	128	463	63	130	25	7	3	70	50		0	20	.281	.351	.384	.735	+3	10	12	45	1b121	0	-1.8
1943	Bos A	154	608	65	155	21	9	4	47	54		1	23	.255	.317	.339	.656	-10	16	9	64	1b153	0	-1.5
1944	Phi N	153	597	82	169	23	9	5	52	56		2	29	.283	.347	.377	.724	+7	18			1b151	0	-0.1
1945	Phi N	15	54	1	17	1	0	0	3	6		0	0	.315	.383	.333	.716	+3	2			1b15	0	0.2
1948	Chi A	**154**	617	69	152	19	3	6	54	74		0	38	.246	.327	.316	.643	-26	11	7	61	1b154	0	-3.2
Total	6	614	2358	285	632	92	30	18	230	241		3	111	.268	.337	.355	.692	-6	57	28	100	1b602	0	-6.1
Team	3	292	1090	133	294	49	18	7	121	105		1	44	.270	.335	.367	.702	-2	26	21	55	1b282	0	-3.0
/150	2	150	560	68	151	25	9	4	62	54		1	23	.270	.335	.367	.702	-2	13	11	54	1b145	0	-1.5
LYNCH, WALT Walter Edward "Jabber" B4.15.1897 Buffalo NY D12.21.1976 Daytona Beach FL TR/6'0"/176 d7.8 Col Niagara																								
1922	Bos A	3	2	1	1	0	0	0	0	0		0	0	.500	.500	.500	1.000	+63	0	0	0	C3		0.0
LYNN, FRED Fredric Michael B2.3.1952 Chicago IL BL/TL/6'1"/(185–191) [BosA73 2/41] d9.5 Col USC																								
1974	Bos A	15	43	5	18	2	2	2	10	6	2	1	6	.419	.490	.698	1.188	+126	0	0	0	O12(6/4/2)/D	0	0.6
1975	†Bos A★	145	528	**103**	175	**47**	7	21	105	62	10	3	90	.331	.401	**.566**	.967	+59	10	5	67	O144C	0	4.1
1976	Bos A★	132	507	76	159	32	8	10	65	48	2	1	67	.314	.367	.467	.834	+30	14	9	61	O128(0/127/1),D5	0	2.1
1977	Bos A★	129	497	81	129	29	5	18	76	51	2	3	63	.260	.327	.447	.774	-1	2	3	40	O125C/D	30	-0.4
1978	Bos A★	150	541	75	161	33	3	22	82	75	11	1	50	.298	.380	.492	.872	+31	3	6	33	O149C	0	1.6
1979	Bos A★	147	531	116	177	42	1	39	122	82	4	4	79	**.333**	**.423**	**.637**	1.060	+73	2	2	50	O143C/D	0	5.3
1980	Bos A★	110	415	67	125	32	3	12	61	58	3	0	39	.301	.383	.480	.863	+29	12	0	100	O110C	0	2.3
1981	Cal A★	76	256	28	56	8	1	5	31	38	4	3	42	.219	.322	.316	.638	-15	1	2	33	O69C	0	-0.8
1982	†Cal A★	138	472	89	141	38	1	21	86	58	4	3	72	.299	.374	.517	.891	+42	7	8	47	O133C	0	1.7
1983	Cal A★	117	437	56	119	20	3	22	74	55	10	2	83	.272	.352	.483	.835	+29	2	2	50	O113C,D2	0	0.5
1984	Cal A	142	517	84	140	28	4	23	79	77	8	2	97	.271	.366	.474	.840	+31	2	2	50	O140(0/62/112)	0	1.8
1985	Bal A	124	448	59	118	12	1	23	68	53	6	1	100	.263	.339	.449	.788	+17	7	3	70	O123C	0	0.4
1986	Bal A	112	397	67	114	13	1	23	67	53	1	2	59	.287	.371	.499	.870	+36	2	2	50	O107C/D	16	0.9
1987	Bal A	111	396	49	100	24	0	23	60	39	6	1	72	.253	.320	.487	.807	+13	3	7	30	O101C,D8	15	-0.3
1988	Bal A	87	301	37	76	13	1	18	37	28	1	0	66	.252	.312	.482	.794	+23	2	2	50	O83(0/64/21),D2	28	0.6
1988	Det A	27	90	9	20	1	0	7	19	5	0	1	16	.222	.265	.467	.732	+6	0	0	0	O22(19/3/0),D3	0	0.0
1988	Year	114	391	46	96	14	1	25	56	33	1	1	82	.246	.302	.478	.780	+19	2	2	50	O105(19/67/21),D5	0	0.6
1989	Det A	117	353	44	85	11	1	11	46	47	1	1	71	.241	.328	.371	.699	+0	1	1	50	O68L,D46	15	-0.3
1990	SD N	90	196	18	47	3	1	6	23	22	2	1	44	.240	.315	.357	.672	-15	2	0	100	O55(42/6/8)	0	-0.9
Total	17	1969	6925	1063	1960	388	43	306	1111	857	77	30	1116	.283	.360	.484	.844	+28	72	54	57	O1825(135/1584/144),D70	104	19.2
Team	7	828	3062	523	944	217	29	124	521	382	34	13	394	.308	.382	.520	.902	+39	43	25	63	O811(6/275/129),D8	30	15.6
/150	1	150	555	95	171	39	5	22	94	69	6	2	71	.308	.382	.520	.902	+39	8	5	62	O147(1/50/23)/D	5	2.8
LYONS, STEVE Stephen John B6.3.1960 Tacoma WA BL/TR/6'3"/(190–195) [BosA81 1/19] d4.15 Col Oregon St. OF(59/237/43)																								
1985	Bos A	133	371	52	98	14	3	5	30	32	0	1	64	.264	.322	.358	.680	-17	12	9	57	O114(2/111/2)/3SD	0	-1.6
1986	Bos A	59	124	20	31	7	2	1	14	12	2	0	23	.250	.312	.363	.675	-16	2	3	40	O55C	0	-0.2
1986	Chi A	42	123	10	25	2	1	0	6	7	0	1	24	.203	.248	.236	.484	-67	2	3	40	O35(22/6/7),3b3/1D	0	-1.3
1986	Year	101	247	30	56	9	3	1	20	19	2	1	47	.227	.280	.300	.580	-42	4	6	40	O90(22/61/7),3b3/1D	0	-1.5
1987	Chi A	76	193	26	54	11	1	1	19	12	0	0	37	.280	.320	.363	.683	-21	3	1	75	3b51,O15(6/8/2)/2D	0	0.0
1988	Chi A	146	472	59	127	28	3	5	45	32	1	1	59	.269	.313	.373	.686	-8	1	2	33	3b128,O14(0/8/6),2b4,C2/1	0	0.3
1989	Chi A	140	443	51	117	21	3	2	50	35	3	1	68	.264	.317	.339	.656	-13	9	6	60	2b70,1b40,3b28,O20(10/1/9),S3/CD	0	-0.6
1990	Chi A	94	146	22	28	6	1	1	11	10	1	1	41	.192	.245	.267	.512	-55	1	0	100	1b61,2b15,O7(2/3/3),3b5/SDP	0	-1.3
1991	Bos A	87	212	15	51	10	1	4	17	11	2	0	35	.241	.277	.354	.631	-30	10	3	77	O45(8/36/3),2b16,3b12,1b2/SDP	0	-0.6

Year	Tm Lg	G	AB	R	H	2B	3B	HR	RBI	BB	IB	HP	SO	AVG	OBP	SLG	OPS	AOPS	SB	CS	SB%	Games at Position	DL	BFW
1992	Atl N	11	14	0	1	0	1	0	1	0	0	0	4	.071	.071	.214	.285	-121	0	0	0	O6(2/0/4),2b2	0	-0.3
1992	Mon N	16	13	2	3	0	0	0	1	1	0	0	3	.231	.286	.231	.517	-52	1	2	33	O8(7/1/0)/1	0	-0.1
1992	Year	27	27	2	4	0	1	0	2	1	0	0	7	.148	.179	.222	.401	-87	1	2	33	O14(9/1/4),2b2/1	0	-0.4
1992	Bos A	21	28	3	7	0	1	0	2	2	0	0	1	.250	.300	.321	.621	-31	0	1	0	1b8,O5(0/2/3)/2D	0	-0.1
1992	Major	48	55	5	11	0	2	0	4	3	0	0	8	.200	.241	.273	.514	-75	1	3	25		0	-0.5
1993	Bos A	28	23	4	3	1	0	0	0	2	0	0	5	.130	.200	.174	.374	-99	1	2	33	O10(0/6/4),2b9/C13D	0	-0.3
Total	9	853	2162	264	545	100	17	19	196	156	9	5	364	.252	.301	.340	.641	-23	42	32	57	O334C,3b229,2b118,1b115,D24,S6,C4,P2	0	-6.1
Team	5	328	758	94	190	32	7	10	63	59	4	1	128	.251	.303	.351	.654	-23	25	18	58	O229(11/120/2),2b26,3b14,1b11,D4,S2/PC	0	-2.8
/150	2	150	347	43	87	15	3	5	29	27	2	0	59	.251	.303	.351	.654	-23	11	8	58	O105(5/55/1),2b12,3b6,1b5,D2/SPC	0	-1.3
MACFARLANE, MIKE Michael Andrew B4.12.1964 Stockton CA BR/TR/6'1"/(200–210) [KCA85 4/97] d7.23 Col Santa Clara																								
1995	†Bos A	115	364	45	82	18	1	15	51	38	0	14	78	.225	.319	.404	.723	-15	2	1	67	C111,D3	0	0.1
Total	13	1164	3602	458	906	221	17	129	514	295	17	97	700	.252	.322	.430	.752	-2	12	16	43	C1058,D47	108	4.0
/150	1	150	475	59	107	23	1	20	67	50	0	18	102	.225	.319	.404	.723	-15	3	1	75	C145,D4	0	0.1
MACHADO, ALEJANDRO Alejandro Jose B4.26.1982 Caracas, Distrito Capital, Venezuela BB/TR/6'0"/185 d9.2																								
2005	†Bos A	10	5	4	1	1	0	0	0	1	0	0	1	.200	.333	.400	.733	-10	0	0	0	O6(2/3/1),2b3/SD	0	-0.1
MACK, SHANE Shane Lee B12.7.1963 Los Angeles CA BR/TR/6'0"/(185–190) [SDN84 1/11] d5.25 b–Quinn Col UCLA [DL 1989 SD N 31]																								
1997	Bos A	60	130	13	41	7	0	3	17	9	1	3	24	.315	.368	.438	.806	+9	2	1	67	O45(3/43/0),D5	25	-0.2
Total	9	923	2857	436	853	155	28	80	398	256	6	51	509	.299	.364	.456	.820	+19	90	43	68	O830(393/358/149),D35	160	8.2
MADDEN, BUNNY Thomas Francis B9.14.1882 Boston MA D1.20.1954 Cambridge MA BR/TR/5'10"/190 d6.3 Col Villanova																								
1909	Bos A	10	17	0	4	0	0	0	1	0		0		.235	.235	.235	.470	-52	0			C7		0.0
1910	Bos A	14	35	4	13	3	0	0	4	3		1		.371	.436	.457	.893	+75	0			C12		0.2
1911	Bos A	4	15	2	3	0	0	0	2	2		0		.200	.294	.200	.494	-61	0			C4		-0.2
1911	Phi N	28	76	4	21	1	1	0	4	0		0	13	.276	.276	.316	.592	-35	0			C22		-0.3
1911	Major	32	91	6	24	1	1	0	6	2	0	0	13	.264	.280	.297	.576	-46	0	0				-0.5
Total	3	56	143	10	41	4	1	0	11	5		1	13	.287	.315	.329	.644	-13	0			C45		-0.3
Team	3	28	67	6	20	3	0	0	7	5		1	0	.299	.356	.343	.699	+14	0			C23		0.0
MAHONEY, JIM James Thomas "Moe" B5.26.1934 Englewood NJ BR/TR/6'0"/(170–175) d7.28 C7																								
1959	Bos A	31	23	10	3	0	0	1	4	3	0	0	7	.130	.231	.261	.492	-67	0	0	0	S30	0	0.1
Total	4	120	210	32	48	4	1	4	15	11	2	0	47	.229	.266	.314	.580	-43	1	2	33	S89,2b10/3	0	0.0
MALAVE, JOSE Jose Francisco B5.31.1971 Cumana, Sucre, Venez. BR/TR/6'2"/212 d5.23																								
1996	Bos A	41	102	12	24	3	0	4	17	2	0	1	25	.235	.257	.382	.639	-42	0	0	0	O38(8/0/30)	19	-1.0
1997	Bos A	4	4	0	0	0	0	0	0	0	0	0	2	.000	.000	.000	.000	-198	0	0	0	O4L	0	-0.1
Total	2	45	106	12	24	3	0	4	17	2	0	1	27	.226	.248	.368	.616	-48	0	0	0	O42(12/0/30)	19	-1.1
MALLETT, JERRY Gerald Gordon B9.18.1935 Bonne Terre MO BR/TR/6'5"/205 d9.19 Col Baylor																								
1959	Bos A	4	15	1	4	0	0	0	1	1	0	0	3	.267	.313	.267	.580	-42	0	0	0	O4C	0	0.1
MALZONE, FRANK Frank James B2.28.1930 Bronx NY BR/TR/5'10"/(180–185) d9.17																								
1955	Bos A	6	20	2	7	1	0	0	1	1	0	0	3	.350	.381	.400	.781	+1	0	0	0	3b4	0	0.2
1956	Bos A	27	103	15	17	3	1	2	11	9	0	0	8	.165	.230	.272	.502	-71	1	0	100	3b26	0	-0.9
1957	Bos A★	153	634	82	185	31	5	15	103	31	1	1	41	.292	.323	.427	.750	-2	2	1	67	3b153	0	1.8
1958	Bos A★	**155**	627	76	185	30	2	15	87	33	3	4	53	.295	.333	.421	.754	+0	1	3	25	3b155	0	1.5
1959	Bos A★	**154**	604	90	169	34	2	19	92	42	6	1	58	.280	.323	.437	.760	+3	6	0	100	3b154	0	1.2
1960	Bos A★	152	595	60	161	30	2	14	79	36	4	4	42	.271	.313	.398	.711	-11	2	3	40	3b151	0	0.1
1961	Bos A	151	590	74	157	21	4	14	87	44	3	1	49	.266	.314	.386	.700	-15	1	3	25	3b149	0	-1.4
1962	Bos A	156	619	74	175	20	3	21	95	35	2	0	43	.283	.319	.426	.745	-4	0	1	0	3b156	0	0.1
1963	Bos A★	151	580	66	169	25	2	15	71	31	5	3	45	.291	.327	.419	.746	+5	0	2	0	3b148	0	0.5
1964	Bos A☆	148	537	62	142	19	0	13	56	37	1	2	43	.264	.312	.372	.684	-14	0	0	0	3b143	0	-0.5
1965	Bos A	106	364	40	87	20	0	3	34	28	0	1	38	.239	.293	.319	.612	-30	1	1	50	3b96	0	-1.6
1966	Cal A	82	155	6	32	5	0	2	12	10	1	0	11	.206	.253	.277	.530	-46	0	0	0	3b35	0	-1.0
Total	12	1441	5428	647	1486	239	21	133	728	337	26	17	434	.274	.315	.399	.714	-9	14	14	50	3b1370	0	-0.0
Team	11	1359	5273	641	1454	234	21	131	716	327	25	17	423	.276	.317	.403	.720	-8	14	14	50	3b1335	0	1.0
/150	1	150	582	71	160	26	2	14	79	36	3	2	47	.276	.317	.403	.720	-8	2	2	50	3b147	0	0.1
MANTILLA, FELIX Felix (Lamela) B7.29.1934 Isabela, PR BR/TR/6'0"/160 d6.21 OF(74/76/10) [DL 1967 Chi N 81]																								
1956	Mil N	35	53	9	15	1	1	0	3	1	0	1	8	.283	.309	.340	.649	-21	0	1	0	S15,3b3	0	0.4
1957	†Mil N	71	182	28	43	9	1	4	21	14	2	2	34	.236	.296	.363	.659	-18	2	0	100	S35,2b13,3b7/cf	0	0.0
1958	†Mil N	85	226	37	50	5	1	7	19	20	2	0	20	.221	.282	.345	.627	-28	2	0	100	O43(12/33/0),2b21,S5,3b2	0	-1.8
1959	Mil N	103	251	26	54	5	0	3	19	16	1	2	31	.215	.266	.271	.537	-52	6	1	86	2b60,S23,3b9,O7C	0	-1.7
1960	Mil N	63	148	21	38	7	0	3	11	7	1	1	16	.257	.291	.365	.656	-14	3	1	75	2b26,S25,O8(3/5/0)	0	-1.0
1961	Mil N	45	93	13	20	3	0	1	5	10	0	1	16	.215	.298	.280	.578	-42	1	1	50	S19,2b10,O10(2/6/2),3b6	0	-0.8
1962	NY N	141	466	54	128	17	4	11	59	37	0	5	51	.275	.330	.399	.729	-6	3	1	75	3b95,S25,2b14	0	-0.8
1963	Bos A	66	178	27	56	8	0	6	15	20	1	0	14	.315	.384	.461	.845	+31	2	1	67	S27,O11C,2b5	0	0.9
1964	Bos A	133	425	69	123	20	1	30	64	41	1	4	46	.289	.357	.553	.910	+42	0	1	0	O48(36/5/8),2b45,3b7,S6	0	2.3
1965	Bos A★	150	534	60	147	17	2	18	92	79	5	8	84	.275	.374	.416	.790	+18	7	3	70	2b123,O27(20/8/0),1b2	0	0.2
1966	Hou N	77	151	16	33	5	0	6	22	11	0	2	32	.219	.279	.371	.650	-15	1	0	100	1b14,3b14,2b9/lf	25	-0.8
Total	11	969	2707	360	707	97	10	89	330	256	13	26	352	.261	.329	.403	.732	+0	27	10	73	2b326,S180,O156C,3b143,1b16	106	-3.1
Team	3	349	1137	156	326	45	3	54	171	140	7	12	144	.287	.369	.474	.843	+29	9	5	64	2b173,O86(36/16/5),S33,3b7,1b2	0	3.4
/150	1	150	489	67	140	19	1	23	73	60	3	5	62	.287	.369	.474	.843	+29	4	2	67	2b74,O37(15/7/2),S14,3b3/1	0	1.5
MANTO, JEFF Jeffrey Paul B8.23.1964 Bristol PA BR/TR/6'3"/210 [CalA85 14/355] d6.7 C1 Col Temple																								
1996	Bos A	10	30	5	8	3	1	2	4	3	0	1	6	.267	.353	.633	.986	+40	0	0	0	2b4,S4	32	0.6
1996	Bos A	12	18	3	2	0	0	0	2	5	0	0	6	.111	.304	.111	.415	-89	0	0	0	3b10/1	0	0.0
Total	9	289	713	97	164	35	2	31	97	97	1	9	182	.230	.329	.415	.744	-7	3	6	33	3b165,1b72,D21,2b5,S5,C5,O4L	49	-2.0
Team	2	22	48	8	10	3	1	2	6	8	0	1	12	.208	.333	.438	.771	-12	0	0	0	3b10,2b4,S4/1	32	0.6
MANUSH, HEINIE Henry Emmett B7.20.1901 Tuscumbia AL D5.12.1971 Sarasota FL BL/TL/6'1"/200 d4.20 C2 HF1964 b–Frank																								
1936	Bos A	82	313	43	91	15	5	0	45	17		1	11	.291	.329	.371	.700	-31	1	3	25	O72L		-2.2
Total	17	2008	7654	1287	2524	491	160	110	1183	506		70	345	.330	.377	.479	.856	+21	113	59	100	O1845(1379/309/159)/1		4.5
MARQUARDT, OLLIE Albert Ludwig B9.22.1902 Toledo OH D2.7.1968 Port Clinton OH BR/TR/5'9"/156 d4.14																								
1931	Bos A	17	39	4	7	1	0	0	2	3		0	4	.179	.238	.205	.443	-82	0	1	0	2b13/S3		-0.6
MARSHALL, MIKE Michael Allen B1.12.1960 Libertyville IL BR/TR/6'5"/(215–220) [LAN78 6/151] d9.7																								
1990	†Bos A	30	112	10	32	6	1	4	12	4	0	1	26	.286	.316	.464	.780	+10	0	0	0	D14,1b8,O8R	0	0.0
1991	Bos A	22	62	4	18	4	0	1	7	0	0	0	19	.290	.290	.403	.693	-15	0	0	0	1b5,O4(1/0/3),D7	16	-0.4
Total	11	1035	3593	433	971	173	8	148	530	247	33	37	810	.270	.321	.446	.767	+14	26	33	44	O777(123/0/657),1b180,D22,3b3	164	-3.0
Team	2	52	174	14	50	10	1	5	19	4	0	1	45	.287	.307	.443	.750	+1	0	0	0	D21,1b13,O12(1/0/8)	16	-0.4
MARSHALL, BILL William Henry B2.14.1911 Dorchester MA D5.5.1977 Sacramento CA BR/TR/5'8.5"/156 d6.20																								
1931	Bos A	1	0	1	0	0	0	0	0	0		0	0	+	+	+	.000	-100	0	0	0	/R		0.0
Total	2	7	8	1	1	0	0	0	0	0		0	2	.125	.125	.125	.250	-134	0	0	0	2b2		-0.1
MARTIN, BABE Boris Michael (b Boris Michael Martinovich) B3.28.1920 Seattle WA BR/TR/5'11.5"/194 d9.25																								
1948	Bos A	4	4	0	2	0	0	0	0	0		0	1	.500	.500	.500	1.000	+58	0	0	0	/C	0	0.0
1949	Bos A	2	2	0	0	0	0	0	0	0		0	0	.000	.000	.000	.000	-193	0	0	0	/C	0	-0.1
Total	6	69	206	13	44	6	2	2	18	13		0	27	.214	.260	.291	.551	-44	0	1	0	O49(44/0/6),1b6,C5	0	-1.1
Team	2	6	6	0	2	0	0	0	0	0		0	1	.333	.333	.333	.666	-26	0	0	0	/C	0	-0.1
MARTINEZ, SANDY Angel Sandy (Martinez) B10.3.1970 Villa Mella, D.R. BL/TR/6'2"/(200–215) d6.24																								
2004	Bos A	3	4	0	0	0	0	0	0	0	0	2	.000	.000	.000	.000	-194	0	0	0	C3		0	-0.2
Total	8	218	564	39	130	32	4	6	51	37	0	6	147	.230	.284	.333	.617	-42	1	0	100	C198	231	-1.5

Year	Tm Lg	G	AB	R	H	2B	3B	HR	RBI	BB	IB	HP	SO	AVG	OBP	SLG	OPS	AOPS	SB	CS	SB%	Games at Position	DL	BFW
MARZANO, JOHN John Robert B2.14.1963 Philadelphia PA BR/TR/5'11"/(185–197) [BosA84 1/14] d7.31 Col Temple																								
1987	Bos A	52	168	20	41	11	0	5	24	7	0	3	41	.244	.283	.399	.682	-23	0	1	0	C52	0	0.0
1988	Bos A	10	29	3	4	1	0	0	1	1	0	0	3	.138	.167	.172	.339	-105	0	0	0	C10	0	0.0
1989	Bos A	7	18	5	8	3	0	1	3	0	0	0	2	.444	.421	.778	1.199	+124	0	0	0	C7	0	0.2
1990	Bos A	32	83	8	20	4	0	0	6	5	0	0	10	.241	.281	.289	.570	-42	0	1	0	C32	0	-0.1
1991	Bos A	49	114	10	30	8	0	0	9	1	0	1	16	.263	.271	.333	.604	-36	0	0	0	C48	0	-0.6
1992	Bos A	19	50	4	4	2	1	0	1	2	0	1	12	.080	.132	.160	.292	-117	0	0	0	C18/D	111	-0.9
1995	Tex A	2	6	1	2	0	0	0	0	0	0	0	0	.333	.333	.333	.666	-28	0	0	0	C2	0	0.0
1996	Sea A	41	106	8	26	6	0	0	6	7	0	4	15	.245	.316	.302	.618	-43	0	0	0	C39	0	-0.6
1997	Sea A	39	87	7	25	3	0	1	10	7	0	0	15	.287	.340	.356	.696	-18	0	0	0	C37/D	0	-0.3
1998	Sea A	50	133	13	31	7	1	4	12	9	1	9	24	.233	.325	.391	.716	-16	0	0	0	C48/D	0	0.4
Total	10	301	794	79	191	45	2	11	72	39	1	18	138	.241	.289	.344	.633	-33	0	2	0	C293,D3	111	-1.9
Team	6	169	462	50	107	29	1	6	44	16	0	5	84	.232	.262	.338	.600	-40	0	2	0	C167/D	111	-1.4
/150	5	150	410	44	95	26	1	5	39	14	0	4	75	.232	.262	.338	.600	-40	0	2	0	C148/D	99	-1.2
MATCHICK, TOM John Thomas B9.7.1943 Hazleton PA BL/TR/6'0"/175 d9.2																								
1970	Bos A	10	14	2	1	0	0	0	0	2	0	0	2	.071	.188	.071	.259	-124	0	1	0	3b2/2S	0	-0.3
Total	6	292	826	63	178	21	6	4	64	39	8	5	148	.215	.254	.270	.524	-51	6	6	50	S110,3b74,2b72,1b8	21	-4.9
MAUCH, GENE Gene William "Skip" B11.18.1925 Salina KS D8.8.2005 Rancho Mirage CA BR/TR/5'10"/(165–175) d4.18 Mil 1944–45 M26/C1																								
1956	Bos A	7	25	4	8	0	0	0	1	3	0	0	3	.320	.393	.320	.713	-20	0	0	0	2b6	0	-0.1
1957	Bos A	65	222	23	60	10	3	2	28	22	0	1	26	.270	.335	.369	.704	-12	1	0	100	2b58	0	-0.3
Total	9	304	737	93	176	25	7	5	62	104	0	2	82	.239	.333	.312	.645	-25	6	0	100	2b158,S65,3b17	0	-1.8
Team	2	72	247	27	68	10	3	2	29	25	0	1	29	.275	.341	.364	.705	-13	1	0	100	2b64	0	-0.4
MAXWELL, CHARLIE Charles Richard "Smokey" B4.8.1927 Lawton MI BL/TL/5'11"/(185–190) d9.20 Col Western Michigan																								
1950	Bos A	3	8	1	0	0	0	0	0	1		0	3	.000	.111	.000	.111	-163	0	0	0	O2R	0	-0.2
1951	Bos A	49	80	8	15	1	0	3	12	9		0	18	.188	.270	.313	.583	-48	0	1	0	O13(5/0/8)	0	-0.8
1952	Bos A	8	15	0	1	1	0	0	0	3		0	11	.067	.222	.133	.355	-100	0	0	0	1b3,O3(0/1/2)	0	-0.1
1954	Bos A	74	104	9	26	4	1	0	5	12		0	21	.250	.328	.308	.636	-33	3	0	100	O27(21/3/6)	0	-0.5
Total	14	1133	3245	478	856	110	26	148	532	484	31	22	545	.264	.360	.451	.811	+16	18	7	72	O834(783/4/55),1b43	0	5.1
Team	4	134	207	18	42	6	1	3	17	25		0	53	.203	.289	.285	.574	-49	3	1	75	O45(6/5/7),1b3	0	-1.6
/150	4	150	232	20	47	7	1	3	19	28		0	59	.203	.289	.285	.574	-49	3	1	75	O50(7/6/8),1b3	0	-1.8
MAYER, WALLY Walter A. B7.8.1890 Cincinnati OH D11.18.1951 Minnetonka MN BR/TR/5'11"/168 d9.28 Mil 1918																								
1917	Bos A	4	12	2	2	0	0	0	0	5		0	2	.167	.412	.167	.579	-22	0			C4		0.2
1918	Bos A	26	49	7	11	4	0	0	5	7		0	7	.224	.321	.306	.627	-9	0			C23		0.1
Total	7	132	274	22	53	14	3	0	20	42		1	51	.193	.303	.266	.569	-32	1	3	100	C112/3		0.7
Team	2	30	61	9	13	4	0	0	5	12		0	9	.213	.342	.279	.621	-12	0			C27		0.3
MAYNARD, CHICK Le Roy Evans B11.2.1896 Turners Falls MA D1.31.1957 Bangor ME BL/TR/5'9"/150 d6.27 Col Dartmouth																								
1922	Bos A	12	24	1	3	0	0	0	0	3		0	2	.125	.222	.125	.347	-108	0	1	0	S12		-0.6
MCAULIFFE, DICK Richard John B11.29.1939 Hartford CT BL/TR/5'11"/(175–176) d9.17																								
1974	Bos A	100	272	32	57	13	1	5	24	39	5	1	40	.210	.310	.320	.630	-24	2	0	100	2b53,3b40,S3,D3	0	-1.0
1975	Bos A	7	15	0	2	0	0	0	1	1	0	0	2	.133	.188	.133	.321	-107	0	0	0	3b7	0	-0.5
Total	16	1763	6185	888	1530	231	71	197	697	882	59	33	974	.247	.343	.403	.746	+8	63	59	52	2b971,S666,3b146,D4	124	12.4
Team	2	107	287	32	59	13	1	5	25	40	5	1	42	.206	.304	.310	.614	-28	2	0	100	2b53,3b47,S3,D3	0	-1.5
/150	3	150	402	45	83	18	1	7	35	56	7	1	59	.206	.304	.310	.614	-28	3	0	100	2b74,3b66,S4,D4	0	-2.1
MCBRIDE, TOM Thomas Raymond B11.2.1914 Bonham TX D12.26.2001 Wichita Falls TX BR/TR/6'0"/190 d4.23																								
1943	Bos A	26	96	11	23	3	1	0	7	7		0	3	.240	.291	.292	.583	-30	2	0	100	O24(0/21/3)	0	-0.5
1944	Bos A	71	216	29	53	7	3	0	24	8		1	13	.245	.276	.306	.582	-33	4	0	100	O57(23/14/22),1b5	0	-0.9
1945	Bos A	100	344	38	105	11	7	1	47	26		0	17	.305	.354	.387	.741	+12	2	2	50	O81(15/50/22),1b11	0	0.2
1946	†Bos A	61	153	21	46	5	2	0	19	9		0	6	.301	.340	.359	.699	-10	0	1	0	O43(10/2/32)	0	-0.6
1947	Bos A	2	5	0	1	0	0	0	0	0		0	0	.200	.200	.200	.400	-89	0	0	0	/rf	0	0.0
1947	Was A	56	166	19	45	4	2	0	15	15		0	9	.271	.331	.319	.650	-16	3	1	75	O51(43/4/5)/3	0	-0.7
1947	Year	58	171	19	46	4	2	0	15	15		0	9	.269	.328	.316	.644	-19	3	1	75	O52(43/4/6)/3	0	-0.7
1948	Was A	92	206	22	53	9	1	1	29	28		0	15	.257	.346	.325	.671	-19	2	2	50	O55(25/0/30)	0	-0.2
Total	6	408	1186	140	326	39	16	2	141	93		1	63	.275	.328	.340	.668	-12	13	6	68	O312(116/91/115),1b16/3	0	-2.7
Team	5	260	814	99	228	26	13	1	97	50		1	39	.280	.323	.348	.671	-9	8	3	73	O206(23/72/40),1b16	0	-1.8
/150	3	150	470	57	132	15	8	1	56	29		1	23	.280	.323	.348	.671	-9	5	2	71	O119(13/42/23),1b9	0	-1.0
MCCANN, EMMETT Robert Emmett B3.4.1902 Philadelphia PA D4.15.1937 Philadelphia PA BR/TR/5'11"/150 d4.19																								
1926	Bos A	6	3	0	0	0	0	0	0	1		0	1	.000	.250	.000	.250	-132	0	0	0	/S3		-0.1
Total	3	71	194	19	44	6	1	0	18	8		1	8	.227	.261	.268	.529	-64	2	2	50	S44,3b10,2b2/1		-1.8
MCCARTY, DAVID David Andrew B11.23.1969 Houston TX BR/TL/6'5"/(207–215) [MinA91 1/3] d5.17 Col Stanford																								
2003	†Bos A	16	27	4	11	3	0	1	6	2	0	0	7	.407	.448	.630	1.078	+73	0	0	0	O8(7/0/1),1b5/D	0	0.2
2004	Bos A	91	151	24	39	8	1	4	17	14	0	2	40	.258	.327	.404	.731	-15	1	0	100	1b67,O17(10/0/7),P3,D3	19	-0.3
2005	Bos A	13	4	2	2	0	0	0	2	2	0	0	0	.500	.667	.500	1.167	+109	0	0	0	1b12/lf	0	0.1
Total	11	632	1493	182	362	68	8	36	175	126	3	14	367	.242	.305	.371	.676	-26	9	9	50	1b368,O177(103/2/80),D22,P3/S	40	-6.7
Team	3	120	182	30	52	11	1	5	25	18	0	2	47	.286	.355	.440	.795	+1	1	0	100	1b84,O26(17/0/1),D4,P3	19	-0.0
/150	4	150	228	38	65	14	1	6	31	23	0	3	59	.286	.355	.440	.795	+1	1	0	100	1b105,O33(21/0/1),D5,P4	24	-0.0
MCCARVER, TIM James Timothy B10.16.1941 Memphis TN BL/TR/6'1"/(185–201) d9.10																								
1974	Bos A	11	28	3	7	1	0	0	1	4	2	0	1	.250	.344	.286	.630	-23	1	0	100	C8,D2	0	0.1
1975	Bos A	12	21	1	8	2	1	0	3	1	1	0	3	.381	.409	.571	.980	+61	0	0	0	C7/1	0	0.2
Total	21	1909	5529	590	1501	242	57	97	645	548	11	30	422	.271	.337	.388	.725	+2	61	49	55	C1387,1b103,O15(15/0/1),3b6,D2	122	10.2
Team	2	23	49	4	15	3	1	0	4	5	3	0	4	.306	.370	.408	.778	+11	1	0	100	C15,D2/1	0	0.3
MCCONNELL, AMBY Ambrose Moses B4.29.1883 N.Pownal VT D5.20.1942 Utica NY BL/TR/5'7"/150 d4.17 Col Beloit																								
1908	Bos A	140	502	77	140	10	6	2	43	38		11		.279	.343	.335	.678	+17	31			2b126,S3		-0.5
1909	Bos A	121	453	61	108	7	8	0	36	34		6		.238	.300	.289	.589	-16	26			2b121		0.4
1910	Bos A	11	35	6	6	0	0	0	1	5		2		.171	.310	.171	.481	-50	4			2b10		-0.3
1910	Chi A	33	120	13	33	2	3	0	5	7		1		.275	.320	.342	.662	+12	4			2b32		0.1
1910	Year	44	155	19	39	2	3	0	6	12		3		.252	.318	.303	.621	-3	8			2b42		-0.2
1911	Chi A	104	396	45	111	11	5	1	34	23		7		.280	.331	.341	.672	-10	7			2b103		-0.4
Total	4	409	1506	202	398	30	22	3	119	107		27		.264	.324	.319	.643	-2	72			2b392,S3		-0.7
Team	3	272	990	144	254	17	14	2	80	77		19	0	.257	.322	.308	.630	-1	61			2b257,S3		-0.4
/150	2	150	546	79	140	9	8	1	44	42		10	0	.257	.322	.308	.630	-1	34			2b142,S2		-0.2
MCDERMOTT, MICKEY Maurice Joseph "Maury" B8.29.1929 Poughkeepsie NY D8.7.2003 Phoenix AZ BL/TL/6'2"/(170–190) d4.24 C1▲																								
1948	Bos A	7	8	2	3	1	0	0	0	0		0	0	.375	.375	.500	.875	+25	0	0	0	P7	0	0.0
1949	Bos A	12	33	3	7	3	0	0	6	3		0	6	.212	.278	.303	.581	-50	0	0	0	P12	0	0.0
1950	Bos A	39	44	11	16	5	0	0	12	9		0	3	.364	.472	.477	.949	+31	0	0	0	P38	0	0.0
1951	Bos A	43	66	8	18	1	1	1	6	3		1	14	.273	.314	.364	.678	-24	0	1	0	P34	0	0.0
1952	Bos A	36	62	10	14	1	1	1	7	4		0	11	.226	.273	.323	.596	-40	0	0	0	P30	0	0.0
1953	Bos A	45	93	9	28	8	0	1	13	2		0	13	.301	.316	.419	.735	-8	0	1	0	P32	0	0.0
1954	Was A	54	95	7	19	3	0	0	4	7		0	12	.200	.255	.232	.487	-64	0	0	0	P30	0	0.0
1955	Was A	70	95	10	25	4	0	1	10	6	0	1	16	.263	.311	.337	.648	-21	1	0	100	P31	0	0.0
1956	†NY A	46	52	4	11	0	0	1	4	8	0	0	13	.212	.317	.269	.586	-42	0	0	0	P23	0	0.0
1957	KC A	58	49	6	12	1	0	4	7	9	2	0	16	.245	.362	.510	.872	+33	0	0	0	P29,1b2	0	0.0
1958	Det A	4	3	0	1	0	0	0	1	0	0	0	2	.333	.333	.333	.666	-22	0	0	0	P2	0	0.0
1961	StL N	22	14	1	1	1	0	0	3	0	0	0	4	.071	.071	.143	.214	-141	0	0	0	P19	0	0.0
1961	KC A	7	5	0	1	1	0	0	1	1	0	0	2	.200	.333	.400	.733	-7	0	0	0	P4	0	0.0

Year	Tm Lg	G	AB	R	H	2B	3B	HR	RBI	BB	IB	HP	SO	AVG	OBP	SLG	OPS	AOPS	SB	CS	SB%	Games at Position	DL	BFW
1961	Major	29	19	1	2	2	0	0	4	1	0	0	6	.105	.150	.211	.361	-100	0	0	0		0	0.0
Total	12	443	619	71	156	29	2	9	74	52	2	2	112	.252	.312	.349	.661	-24	1	2	33	P291,1b2	0	0.0
Team	6	182	306	43	86	19	2	3	44	21		1	47	.281	.329	.386	.715	-15	0	2	0	P153	0	0.0
/150	5	150	252	35	71	16	2	2	36	17		1	39	.281	.329	.386	.715	-15	0	2	0	P126	0	0.0
MCFARLAND, ED Edward William B8.3.1874 Cleveland OH D11.28.1959 Cleveland OH BR/TR/5'10"/180 d7.7																								
1908	Bos A	19	48	5	10	2	1	0	4	1		0		.208	.224	.292	.516	-34	0			C13		0.3
Total	14	894	3007	398	826	146	49	13	383	254		18	19	.275	.335	.369	.704	+4	65			C830,O10(3/5/2),1b5,3b3/2		10.3
MCGAH, EDDIE Edward Joseph B9.30.1921 Oakland CA D9.30.2002 Oakland CA BR/TR/6'0"/183 d4.26																								
1946	Bos A	15	37	2	8	1	1	0	1	7		0	7	.216	.341	.297	.638	-25	0	0	0	C14	0	-0.2
1947	Bos A	9	14	1	0	0	0	0	2	3		0	0	.000	.176	.000	.176	-145	0	0	0	C7	0	-0.1
Total	2	24	51	3	8	1	1	0	3	10		0	7	.157	.295	.216	.511	-59	0	0	0	C21	0	-0.3
MCGEE, WILLIE Willie Dean B11.2.1958 San Francisco CA BB/TR/6'1"/(160–195) [NYA77*S1/15] d5.10 Col Diablo Valley (CA) JC																								
1995	†Bos A	67	200	32	57	11	3	2	15	9	0	0	41	.285	.311	.400	.711	-18	5	2	71	O64(3/27/47)	0	-0.4
Total	18	2201	7649	1010	2254	350	94	79	856	448	58	15	1238	.295	.333	.396	.729	+0	352	121	74	O1979(146/1351/535),1b10,D7/S	244	-4.7
MCGOVERN, ART Arthur John B2.27.1882 St.John NB, Can. D11.14.1915 Danvers MA BR/TR/5'10"/160 d4.21																								
1905	Bos A	15	44	1	5	1	0	0	1	4		1		.114	.204	.136	.340	-91	0			C15		-0.6
MCGUIRE, DEACON James Thomas B11.18.1863 Youngstown OH D10.31.1936 Duck Lake MI BR/TR/6'1"/185 d6.21 M6/C6																								
1907	Bos A	6	4	1	3	0	0	1	1	0		0		.750	.750	1.500	2.250	+520	0			/HM		0.2
1908	Bos A	1	1	0	0	0	0	0	0	0		0		.000	.000	.000	.000	-197	0			/HM		0.0
Total	26	1782	6295	770	1750	300	79	45	840	515		84	215	.278	.341	.372	.713	+1	118			C1612,1b94,O33(4/4/25),3b5,S4/P		4.8
Team	2	7	5	1	3	0	0	1	1	0		0	0	.600	.600	1.200	1.800	+377	0			/HM		0.2
MCHALE, JIM James Bernard "J.B." B12.17.1875 Miners Mills PA D6.17.1959 Los Angeles CA BR/TR/5'11"/165 d4.14 Col St. Marys (CA)																								
1908	Bos A	21	67	9	15	2	2	0	7	4		1		.224	.278	.313	.591	-10	4			O19(1/18/0)		-0.3
MCINNIS, STUFFY John Phalen "Jack" B9.19.1890 Gloucester MA D2.16.1960 Ipswich MA BR/TR/5'9.5"/162 d4.12 Mil 1918 M1																								
1918	†Bos A	117	423	40	115	11	5	0	56	19		2	10	.272	.306	.322	.628	-9	10			1b94,3b23		-0.4
1919	Bos A	120	440	32	134	12	5	1	58	23		1	11	.305	.341	.361	.702	+3	8			1b118		0.0
1920	Bos A	148	559	50	166	21	3	2	71	18		2	19	.297	.321	.356	.677	-17	6	11	35	1b148		-2.3
1921	Bos A	152	584	72	179	31	10	0	76	21		4	9	.307	.335	.394	.729	-12	2	4	33	1b152		-1.8
Total	19	2128	7822	872	2405	312	101	20	1062	380		38	189	.307	.343	.381	.724	+6	172	59	100	1b1995,S55,3b27,2b5/lf		-3.3
Team	4	537	2006	194	594	75	23	3	261	81		9	49	.296	.326	.361	.687	-9	26	15	100	1b512,3b23		-4.5
/150	1	150	560	54	166	21	6	1	73	23		3	14	.296	.326	.361	.687	-9	7	4	100	1b143,3b6		-1.3
MCKEEL, WALT Walt Thomas B1.17.1972 Wilson NC BR/TR/6'2"/200 [BosA90 3/91] d9.14																								
1996	Bos A	1	0	0	0	0	0	0	0	0	0	0	0	+	+	+	.000	-100	0	0	0	/C	0	0.0
1997	Bos A	5	3	0	0	0	0	0	0	0	0	0	1	.000	.000	.000	.000	-198	0	0	0	C4/1	0	-0.1
2002	Col N	5	13	1	4	0	0	0	0	0	0	0	3	.308	.308	.308	.616	-45	0	0	0	C5	0	-0.2
Total	3	11	16	1	4	0	0	0	0	0	0	0	4	.250	.250	.250	.500	-71	0	0	0	C10/1	0	-0.3
Team	2	6	3	0	0	0	0	0	0	0	0	0	1	.000	.000	.000	.000	-198	0	0	0	C4/1	0	-0.1
MCLEAN, LARRY John Bannerman B7.18.1881 Fredericton NB, Can. D3.24.1921 Boston MA BR/TR/6'5"/228 d4.26																								
1901	Bos A	9	19	4	4	1	0	0	2	0		0		.211	.211	.263	.474	-69	1			1b5		-0.1
Total	13	862	2647	183	694	90	26	6	298	136		9	79	.262	.301	.323	.624	-14	20			C761,1b37		1.1
MCMANUS, MARTY Martin Joseph B3.14.1900 Chicago IL D2.18.1966 St.Louis MO BR/TR/5'10.5"/160 d9.26 M2																								
1931	Bos A	17	62	8	18	4	0	1	9	8		0	1	.290	.371	.403	.774	+10	1	1	50	3b11,2b7		0.7
1932	Bos A	93	302	39	71	19	4	5	24	36		0	30	.235	.317	.374	.691	-20	1	2	33	2b49,3b30,S2/1M		-0.4
1933	Bos A	106	366	51	104	30	4	3	36	49		0	21	.284	.369	.413	.782	+8	3	0	100	3b76,2b26,1b4,M		0.8
Total	15	1831	6660	1008	1926	401	88	120	996	675		30	558	.289	.357	.430	.787	+1	126	91	100	2b927,3b725,1b92,S56/rf		9.7
Team	3	216	730	98	193	53	8	9	69	93		0	52	.264	.348	.396	.744	-3	5	3	63	3b117,2b82,1b5,S2,M2		1.1
/150	2	150	507	68	134	37	6	6	48	65		0	36	.264	.348	.396	.744	-3	3	2	60	3b81,2b57,1b3/SM		0.8
MCMILLAN, NORM Norman Alexis "Bub" B10.5.1895 Latta SC D9.28.1969 Marion SC BR/TR/6'0"/175 d4.12 Col Clemson OF(0/15/12)																								
1923	Bos A	131	459	37	116	24	5	0	42	28		2	44	.253	.299	.327	.626	-36	13	5	72	3b67,2b34,S28		-1.2
Total	5	413	1356	157	353	74	16	6	147	95		10	133	.260	.313	.352	.665	-31	36	10	100	3b229,2b90,S35,O26C,1b2		-3.8
/150	1	150	526	42	133	27	6	0	48	32		2	50	.253	.299	.327	.626	-36	15	6	71	3b77,2b39,S32		-1.4
MCNAIR, ERIC Donald Eric "Boob" B4.12.1909 Meridian MS D3.11.1949 Meridian MS BR/TR/5'8.5"/160 d9.20																								
1936	Bos A	128	494	68	141	36	2	4	74	27		5	34	.285	.329	.391	.720	-27	3	3	50	S84,2b35,3b11		-2.1
1937	Bos A	126	455	60	133	29	4	12	76	30		3	33	.292	.340	.453	.793	-6	10	7	59	2b106,S9,3b4/1		-0.4
1938	Bos A	46	96	9	15	1	1	0	7	3		0	6	.156	.182	.188	.370	-107	0	1	0	S15,2b14,3b3		-1.3
Total	14	1251	4519	592	1240	229	29	82	633	261		25	328	.274	.318	.392	.710	-20	59	54	52	S669,2b288,3b220,1b3/rf	0	-15.2
Team	3	300	1045	137	289	66	7	16	157	60		8	73	.277	.321	.399	.720	-25	13	11	54	2b155,S108,3b18/1		-3.8
/150	2	150	523	69	145	33	4	8	79	30		4	37	.277	.321	.399	.720	-25	7	6	54	2b78,S54,3b9/1		-1.9
MCNALLY, MIKE Michael Joseph "Minooka Mike" B9.13.1893 Minooka PA D5.29.1965 Bethlehem PA BR/TR/5'11"/150 d4.21 Mil 1918																								
1915	Bos A	23	53	7	8	0	1	0	0	3		0	7	.151	.196	.189	.385	-84	0	2	0	3b18,2b5		-0.8
1916	†Bos A	87	135	28	23	0	0	0	9	10		0	19	.170	.228	.170	.398	-80	9			2b35,3b14,S7/cf		-1.2
1917	Bos A	42	50	9	15	1	0	0	2	6		0	3	.300	.375	.320	.695	+13	3			3b14,S9,2b6		0.5
1919	Bos A	33	42	10	11	4	0	0	6	1		0	2	.262	.279	.357	.636	-17	4			S11,3b11,2b3		0.5
1920	Bos A	93	312	42	80	5	1	0	23	31		1	24	.256	.326	.279	.605	-36	13	10	57	2b76,S8,1b6		-2.2
1921	†NY A	71	215	36	56	4	2	1	24	14		0	15	.260	.306	.312	.618	-44	5	6	45	3b49,2b16		0.1
1922	†NY A	52	143	20	36	2	2	0	18	16		1	14	.252	.331	.294	.625	-37	3	0	100	3b34,2b9,S4/1		-0.7
1923	NY A	30	38	5	8	0	0	0	1	3		0	4	.211	.268	.211	.479	-73	2	0	100	S13,3b7,2b5		-0.4
1924	NY A	49	69	11	17	0	0	0	2	7		0	5	.246	.316	.246	.562	-54	1	1	50	2b25,3b13,S6		0.0
1925	Was A	12	21	1	3	0	0	0	0	1		0	4	.143	.182	.143	.325	-117	0	0	0	3b7,S2/2		-0.4
Total	10	492	1078	169	257	16	6	1	85	92		2	97	.238	.299	.267	.566	-46	40	19	100	2b181,3b167,S60,1b7/cf		-4.6
Team	5	278	592	96	137	10	2	0	40	51		1	55	.231	.293	.255	.548	-45	29	12	100	2b125,3b57,S35,1b6/cf		-3.2
/150	3	150	319	52	74	5	1	0	22	28		1	30	.231	.293	.255	.548	-45	16	6	100	2b67,3b31,S19,1b3/cf		-1.7
MCNEELY, JEFF Jeffrey Lavern B10.18.1969 Monroe NC BR/TR/6'2"/200 [BosA89 2/53] d9.5 Col Spartanburg Methodist (SC) JC																								
1993	Bos A	21	37	10	11	1	1	0	1	7	0	0	9	.297	.409	.378	.787	+6	6	0	100	O13C,D3	0	0.0
MCNEIL, NORM Norman Francis B10.22.1892 Chicago IL D4.11.1942 Buffalo NY BR/TR/5'11"/180 d6.21																								
1919	Bos A	5	9	0	3	0	0	0	1	1		0	0	.333	.400	.333	.733	+13	0			C5		-0.1
MCWILLIAMS, BILL William Henry B11.28.1910 Dubuque IA D1.21.1997 Garland TX BR/TR/6'0"/185 d7.8 Col Iowa																								
1931	Bos A	2	2	0	0	0	0	0	0	0		0	1	.000	.000	.000	.000	-199	0	0	0	/H		-0.1
MEJIAS, ROMAN Roman (Gomez) B8.9.1930 Abreus, Cuba BR/TR/6'0"/(175–180) d4.13																								
1963	Bos A	111	357	43	81	18	0	11	39	14	2	3	36	.227	.260	.370	.630	-28	4	1	80	O86(7/65/15)	0	-1.9
1964	Bos A	62	101	14	24	3	1	2	4	7	1	1	16	.238	.294	.347	.641	-26	0	0	0	O37(14/13/11)	0	-0.4
Total	9	627	1768	212	449	57	12	54	202	89	13	17	238	.254	.294	.391	.685	-14	22	12	65	O495(117/118/270)	0	-6.1
Team	2	173	458	57	105	21	1	13	43	21	3	4	52	.229	.267	.365	.632	-28	4	1	80	O123(21/78/16)	0	-2.3
/150	2	150	397	49	91	18	1	11	37	18	3	3	45	.229	.267	.365	.632	-28	3	1	75	O107(18/68/14)	0	-2.0
MELE, SAM Sabath Anthony B1.21.1922 Astoria NY BR/TR/6'1"/187 d4.15 M7/C3 Col NYU																								
1947	Bos A	123	453	71	137	14	8	12	73	37		1	35	.302	.356	.448	.804	+14	0	3	0	O116(3/29/87)/1	0	0.1
1948	Bos A	66	180	25	42	12	1	2	25	13		2	21	.233	.292	.344	.636	-34	1	1	50	O55(3/0/52)	0	-1.1
1949	Bos A	18	46	1	9	1	1	0	7	7		0	14	.196	.302	.261	.563	-54	2	0	100	O11R	0	-0.4
1954	Bos A	42	132	22	42	6	0	7	23	12		2	12	.318	.378	.523	.901	+32	0	1	0	1b22,O13(3/0/13)	0	0.2
1955	Bos A	14	31	1	4	2	0	0	1	0	0	0	7	.129	.125	.194	.319	-113	1	0	100	O7(6/0/1)	0	-0.3
Total	10	1046	3437	406	916	168	39	80	544	311	0	10	342	.267	.328	.408	.736	-3	15	14	52	O840(90/101/674),1b79	0	-7.6
Team	5	263	842	120	234	35	10	21	129	69	0	5	89	.278	.335	.418	.753	-2	4	5	44	O202(30/29/139),1b23	0	-1.5
/150	3	150	480	68	133	20	6	12	74	39	0	3	51	.278	.335	.418	.753	-2	2	3	40	O115(17/17/79),1b13	0	-0.9

Year	Tm Lg	G	AB	R	H	2B	3B	HR	RBI	BB	IB	HP	SO	AVG	OBP	SLG	OPS	AOPS	SB	CS	SB%	Games at Position	DL	BFW
MELILLO, SKI Oscar Donald "Spinach" B8.4.1899 Chicago IL D11.14.1963 Chicago IL BR/TR/5'8"/150 d4.18 M1/C13																								
1935	Bos A	106	400	45	104	13	2	1	39	38		2	22	.260	.327	.310	.637	-39	3	2	60	2b105		0.1
1936	Bos A	98	327	39	74	12	4	0	32	28		0	16	.226	.287	.287	.574	-60	0	0	0	2b93		-3.0
1937	Bos A	26	56	8	14	2	0	0	6	5		0	4	.250	.311	.286	.597	-50	0	1	0	2b19,S2,3b2		-0.6
Total	12	1377	5063	590	1316	210	64	22	548	327		12	306	.260	.306	.340	.646	-36	69	65	51	2b1316,3b32,S2		-7.2
Team	3	230	783	92	192	27	6	1	77	71		2	42	.245	.310	.299	.609	-48	3	3	50	2b217,3b2,S2		-3.5
/150	2	150	511	60	125	18	4	1	50	46		1	27	.245	.310	.299	.609	-48	2	2	50	2b142/3S		-2.3
MELVIN, BOB Robert Paul B10.28.1961 Palo Alto CA BR/TR/6'4"/(205–210) [DetA81*S1/2] d5.25 M4/C4 Col California																								
1993	Bos A	77	176	13	39	7	0	3	23	7	0	1	44	.222	.251	.313	.564	-51	0	0	0	C76/1	15	-1.3
Total	10	692	1955	174	456	85	6	35	212	98	10	1	396	.233	.268	.337	.605	-32	4	13	24	C627,D24,1b11/3	74	-7.7
MENOSKY, MIKE Michael William "Leaping Mike" B10.16.1894 Glen Campbell PA D4.11.1983 Detroit MI BL/TR/5'10"/163 d4.18 Mil 1918 Col Indiana (PA)																								
1914	Pit F	68	140	26	37	4	1	2	9	16		3	30	.264	.352	.350	.702	-8	5			O41(6/3/32)		-0.5
1915	Pit F	17	21	3	2	0	0	0	1	2		1	0	.095	.208	.095	.303	-113	2			O9(6/1/2)		-0.4
1916	Was A	11	37	5	6	1	1	0	3	1		0	10	.162	.184	.243	.427	-71	1			O9(1/8/0)		-0.3
1917	Was A	114	322	46	83	12	10	1	34	45		6	55	.258	.359	.366	.725	+23	22			O94(93/0/1)		1.8
1919	Was A	116	342	62	98	15	3	6	39	44		7	46	.287	.379	.401	.780	+20	13			O103(87/15/1)		0.7
1920	Bos A	141	532	80	158	24	9	3	64	65		9	52	.297	.383	.393	.776	+10	23	19	55	O141L		-0.2
1921	Bos A	133	477	77	143	18	5	3	45	60		9	45	.300	.388	.377	.765	-1	12	6	67	O133L		-1.1
1922	Bos A	126	406	61	115	16	5	3	32	40		5	33	.283	.355	.369	.724	-10	9	5	64	O103(74/4/26)		-0.8
1923	Bos A	84	188	22	43	8	4	0	25	22		0	19	.229	.310	.314	.624	-36	3	6	33	O49(28/18/3)		-1.1
Total	9	810	2465	382	685	98	38	18	252	295		40	290	.278	.364	.370	.734	+0	90	36	100	O682(569/49/65)		-1.9
Team	4	484	1603	240	459	66	23	9	166	187		23	149	.286	.369	.373	.742	-4	47	36	57	O426(348/7/3)		-3.2
/150	1	150	497	74	142	20	7	3	51	58		7	46	.286	.369	.373	.742	-4	15	11	58	O132(108/2/1)		-1.0
MERCED, ORLANDO Orlando Luis (Villanueva) B11.2.1966 Hato Rey, PR BL/TR (BB 1990–92)/5'11"/(170–195) d6.27																								
1998	Bos A	9	9	0	0	0	0	0	2	2	0	0	3	.000	.167	.000	.167	-146	0	0	0	/rfD	0	-0.2
Total	13	1391	3998	564	1108	229	28	103	585	487	53	12	661	.277	.355	.426	.781	+6	57	29	66	O700(93/0/617),1b418,D20,3b5/C	154	1.3
MERCHANT, ANDY James Anderson B8.30.1950 Mobile AL BL/TR/5'11"/190 [BosA72 10/232] d9.28 Col Auburn																								
1975	Bos A	1	4	1	2	0	0	0	0	1	0	0	0	.500	.600	.500	1.100	+97	0	0	0	/C	0	0.0
1976	Bos A	2	2	0	0	0	0	0	0	0	0	0	2	.000	.000	.000	.000	-190	0	0	0	/C	0	0.0
Total	2	3	6	1	2	0	0	0	0	1	0	0	2	.333	.429	.333	.762	+10	0	0	0	C2	0	0.0
MERLONI, LOU Louis William B4.6.1971 Framingham MA BR/TR/5'10"/(194–200) [BosA93 10/275] d5.10 Col Providence OF(9/0/1)																								
1998	Bos A	39	96	10	27	6	0	1	15	7	1	2	20	.281	.343	.375	.718	-15	1	0	100	2b32,3b5/S	75	-0.2
1999	†Bos A	43	126	18	32	7	0	1	13	8	0	2	16	.254	.307	.333	.640	-38	0	0	0	S24,3b9,2b8/1lfD	0	-0.3
2000	Bos A	40	128	10	41	11	2	0	18	4	1	1	22	.320	.341	.438	.779	-6	1	0	100	3b40	0	-0.1
2001	Bos A	52	146	21	39	10	0	3	13	6	0	3	31	.267	.306	.397	.703	-16	2	1	67	S45,2b5/3	15	0.1
2002	Bos A	84	194	28	48	12	2	4	18	20	0	5	35	.247	.332	.392	.724	-10	1	2	33	2b66,3b8,S5,1b3,O2(1/0/1)	0	0.4
2003	SD N	65	151	20	41	7	2	1	17	22	2	1	33	.272	.362	.364	.726	+1	2	3	40	3b25,S23,2b10,1b2,O2L	26	0.3
2003	Bos A	15	30	4	7	1	0	0	1	4	0	0	8	.233	.324	.267	.591	-44	0	0	0	2b7,3b7/lf	0	0.0
2003	Major	80	181	24	48	8	2	1	18	26	2	1	41	.265	3.361	.348	3.709	+24	2	3	40		26	0.3
2004	Cle A	71	190	25	55	12	1	4	28	14	1	3	41	.289	.343	.426	.769	+4	1	2	33	1b42,3b10,2b7,O4L,D3	23	-0.3
2005	LA A	5	5	1	0	0	0	0	1	1	0	0	2	.000	.143	.000	.143	-151	0	0	0	3b4/1	154	0.0
2006	Cle A	9	19	1	4	1	0	0	1	2	0	0	5	.211	.286	.263	.549	-55	1	0	100	2b3,3b3,S3	0	-0.4
Total	9	423	1085	138	294	67	7	14	125	88	5	17	213	.271	.332	.384	.716	-13	9	8	53	2b138,3b112,S101,1b49,O10L,D6	293	-0.5
Team	6	273	720	91	194	47	4	9	78	49	2	13	132	.269	.325	.383	.708	-18	5	3	63	2b118,S75,3b70,1b4,O4L/D	90	-0.1
/150	3	150	396	50	107	26	2	5	43	27	1	7	73	.269	.325	.383	.708	-18	3	2	60	2b65,S41,3b38,1b2,lf/D	49	-0.1
MERSON, JACK John Warren B1.17.1922 Elkridge MD D4.28.2000 Elkridge MD BR/TR/5'11"/175 d9.14																								
1953	Bos A	1	4	0	0	0	0	0	0	0		0	0	.000	.000	.000	.000	-195	0	0	0	/2	0	-0.1
Total	3	125	452	47	116	22	4	6	52	23		1	45	.257	.294	.363	.657	-22	1	1	50	2b95,3b27	0	-0.8
METKOVICH, CATFISH George Michael B10.8.1920 Angels Camp CA D5.17.1995 Costa Mesa CA BL/TL/6'1"/185 d7.16																								
1943	Bos A	78	321	34	79	14	4	5	27	19		3	38	.246	.294	.361	.655	-10	1	3	25	O76(0/54/25),1b2	0	-1.4
1944	Bos A	134	549	94	152	28	8	9	59	31		3	57	.277	.319	.406	.725	+8	13	4	76	O82(0/81/3),1b50	0	-0.1
1945	Bos A	138	539	65	140	26	3	5	62	51		6	70	.260	.331	.347	.678	-6	19	6	76	1b97,O42(0/29/14)	0	-1.2
1946	†Bos A	86	281	42	69	15	2	4	25	36		1	39	.246	.333	.356	.689	-12	8	3	73	O81(6/2/73)	0	-1.3
1947	Cle A	126	473	68	120	22	7	5	40	32		1	51	.254	.302	.362	.664	-14	5	3	63	O119(0/119/2)/1	0	-1.8
1949	Chi A	93	338	50	80	9	4	5	45	41		1	24	.237	.321	.331	.652	-25	5	4	56	O87(9/79/1)	0	-2.4
1951	Pit N	120	423	51	124	21	3	3	40	28		1	23	.293	.338	.378	.716	-10	3	2	60	O69(3/66/0),1b37	0	-1.1
1952	Pit N	125	373	41	101	18	3	7	41	32		4	29	.271	.335	.391	.726	-2	5	2	71	1b72,O33(5/21/8)	0	-1.0
1953	Pit N	26	41	5	6	0	1	1	7	6		0	3	.146	.255	.268	.523	-63	0	0	0	1b5,O4(0/3/1)	0	-0.5
1953	Chi N	61	124	19	29	9	0	2	12	16		1	10	.234	.326	.355	.681	-24	2	1	67	O38(10/11/18),1b7	0	-0.6
1953	Year	87	165	24	35	9	1	3	19	22		1	13	.212	.309	.333	.642	-34	2	1	67	O42(10/14/19),1b12	0	-1.1
1954	Mil N	68	123	7	34	5	1	1	15	15		1	15	.276	.352	.358	.710	-6	0	0	0	1b18,O13R	0	0.0
Total	10	1055	3585	476	934	167	36	47	373	307		22	359	.261	.322	.367	.689	-9	61	28	69	O644(33/465/158),1b289	0	-11.4
Team	4	436	1690	235	440	83	17	23	173	137		13	204	.260	.321	.370	.691	-3	41	16	72	O281(0/166/115),1b149	0	-4.0
/150	1	150	581	81	151	29	6	8	60	47		4	70	.260	.321	.370	.691	-3	14	6	70	O97(0/57/40),1b51	0	-1.4
MIENTKIEWICZ, DOUG Douglas Andrew B6.19.1974 Toledo OH BL/TR/6'2"/(193–205) [MinA95 5/128] d9.18 Col Florida St.																								
2004	†Bos A	49	107	13	23	6	1	1	10	10	0	1	18	.215	.286	.318	.604	-46	0	1	0	1b47/2	0	-0.8
Total	9	870	2843	359	768	189	9	59	348	377	31	35	415	.270	.359	.405	.764	-2	14	15	48	1b848,O3R,D3,2b2/3	128	-9.7
MILES, DEE Wilson Daniel B2.15.1909 Kellerman AL D11.2.1976 Birmingham AL BL/TR/6'0"/175 d7.7																								
1943	Bos A	45	121	9	26	2	2	0	10	3		0	3	.215	.234	.264	.498	-55	0	2	0	O25(1/24/0)	0	-1.2
Total	7	503	1467	175	411	53	24	2	143	50		5	74	.280	.306	.353	.659	-24	15	16	48	O323(52/110/165)	0	-7.3
MILLAR, KEVIN Kevin Charles B9.24.1971 Los Angeles CA BR/TR/6'1"/(185–215) d4.11 Col Lamar																								
1998	Fla N	2	2	1	1	0	0	0	0	1	0	0	0	.500	.667	.500	1.167	+127	0	0	0	3b2	161	0.1
1999	Fla N	105	351	48	100	17	4	9	67	40	2	7	64	.285	.362	.433	.795	+8	1	0	100	1b94/3lf	0	-0.6
2000	Fla N	123	259	36	67	14	3	14	42	36	0	8	47	.259	.364	.498	.862	+22	0	0	0	1b34,O18(17/0/1),3b13,D6	0	1.1
2001	Fla N	144	449	62	141	39	5	20	85	39	2	5	70	.314	.374	.557	.931	+41	0	0	0	O86(27/0/66),1b15,3b10,D6	0	1.5
2002	Fla N	126	438	58	134	41	0	16	57	40	0	5	74	.306	.366	.509	.875	+34	0	2	0	O108(89/0/22),1b2,3b2,D6	29	1.8
2003	†Bos A	148	544	83	150	30	1	25	96	60	5	5	108	.276	.348	.472	.820	+10	3	2	60	1b101,O31(19/0/12),D19	0	0.4
2004	†Bos A	150	508	74	151	36	0	18	74	57	0	**17**	91	.297	.383	.474	.857	+16	1	1	50	O74(20/0/55),1b69,D8	0	1.0
2005	†Bos A	134	449	57	122	28	1	9	50	54	0	8	74	.272	.355	.399	.754	-2	0	1	0	1b110,O34(20/0/14)	0	0.0
2006	Bal A	132	430	64	117	26	0	15	64	59	3	12	74	.272	.374	.437	.811	+13	1	1	50	1b98,D30	0	0.5
Total	9	1064	3430	483	983	231	14	126	535	386	12	67	602	.287	.366	.472	.838	+17	6	7	46	1b523,O352(193/0/170),D75,3b28	190	5.8
Team	3	432	1501	214	423	94	2	52	220	171	5	30	273	.282	.362	.451	.813	+8	4	4	50	1b280,O139(59/0/81),D27	0	1.4
/150	1	150	521	74	147	33	1	18	76	59	2	10	95	.282	.362	.451	.813	+8	1	1	50	1b97,O48(20/0/28),D9	0	0.5
MILLER, CORKY Abraham Philip B3.18.1976 Yucaipa CA BR/TR/6'1"/(225–245) d9.4 Col Nevada–Reno																								
2006	Bos A	1	4	0	0	0	0	0	0	0	0	0	1	.000	.000	.000	.000	-198	0	0	0	/C	0	-0.1
Total	6	89	248	20	47	12	0	6	26	24	2	11	58	.190	.285	.310	.595	-44	1	0	100	C83/D	0	-0.0
MILLER, BING Edmund John B8.30.1894 Vinton IA D5.7.1966 Philadelphia PA BR/TR/6'0"/185 d4.16 C17 b-Ralph																								
1935	Bos A	78	138	18	42	8	1	3	26	10		1	8	.304	.356	.442	.798	-1	0	1	0	O29(1/0/28)		-0.2
1936	Bos A	30	47	9	14	2	1	1	6	5		1	5	.298	.377	.447	.824	-3	0	0	0	O13(7/0/7)		-0.1
Total	16	1820	6212	946	1934	389	96	116	990	383		80	340	.311	.359	.461	.820	+8	127	83	60	O1601(380/242/997),1b26		-4.8
Team	2	108	185	27	56	10	2	4	32	15		2	13	.303	.361	.443	.804	-2	0	1	0	O42(8/0/35)		-0.3
/150	3	150	257	38	78	14	3	6	44	21		3	18	.303	.361	.443	.804	-2	0	1	0	O58(11/0/49)		-0.4
MILLER, ELMER Elmer B7.28.1890 Sandusky OH D11.28.1944 Beloit WI BR/TR/6'0"/175 d4.26																								
1922	Bos A	44	147	16	28	2	3	4	16	5		1	10	.190	.222	.327	.549	-58	3	1	75	O35(2/33/0)		-1.6
Total	7	413	1414	170	343	43	20	16	151	113		18	140	.243	.307	.335	.642	-20	31	6	100	O395(67/268/60)		-6.6

Year	Tm Lg	G	AB	R	H	2B	3B	HR	RBI	BB	IB	HP	SO	AVG	OBP	SLG	OPS	AOPS	SB	CS	SB%	Games at Position	DL	BFW
MILLER, HACK Laurence H. B1.1.1894 New York NY D9.16.1971 Oakland CA BR/TR/5'9"/195 d9.22																								
1918	†Bos A	12	29	2	8	2	0	0	4	0		0	4	.276	.276	.345	.621	-11	0			O10(9/1/0)		-0.2
Total	6	349	1200	164	387	65	11	38	205	64		8	103	.322	.361	.490	.851	+20	10	9	100	O311(306/3/3)		0.0
MILLER, OTTO Otis Louis B2.2.1901 Belleville IL D7.26.1959 Belleville IL BR/TR/5'10.5"/168 d4.17																								
1927	StL A	51	76	8	17	5	0	0	8	8		1	5	.224	.306	.289	.595	-47	0	1	0	S35,3b11		-0.5
1930	Bos A	112	370	49	106	22	5	0	40	26		0	21	.286	.333	.373	.706	-18	2	4	33	3b83,2b15		-0.7
1931	Bos A	107	389	38	106	12	1	0	43	15		1	20	.272	.301	.308	.609	-36	1	1	50	3b75,2b25		-1.4
1932	Bos A	2	2	0	0	0	0	0	0	0		0	0	.000	.000	.000	.000	-199	0	0	0	/H		-0.1
Total	4	272	837	95	229	39	6	0	91	49		2	46	.274	.315	.335	.650	-29	3	6	33	3b169,2b40,S35		-2.7
Team	3	221	761	87	212	34	6	0	83	41		1	41	.279	.316	.339	.655	-28	3	5	38	3b158,2b40		-2.2
/150	2	150	517	59	144	23	4	0	56	28		1	28	.279	.316	.339	.655	-28	2	3	40	3b107,2b27		-1.5
MILLER, RICK Richard Alan B4.19.1948 Grand Rapids MI BL/TL/6'0"/(175–185) [BosA69 2/37] d9.4 Col Michigan St.																								
1971	Bos A	15	33	9	11	5	0	1	7	8	0	0	8	.333	.452	.576	1.028	+80	0	2	0	O14(4/4/6)	0	0.5
1972	Bos A	89	98	13	21	4	1	3	15	11	0	0	27	.214	.291	.367	.658	-10	0	2	0	O75(24/47/4)	0	0.2
1973	Bos A	143	441	65	115	17	7	6	43	51	2	3	59	.261	.339	.372	.711	-5	12	7	63	O137(15/71/61)	0	-0.8
1974	Bos A	114	280	41	73	8	1	5	22	37	2	0	47	.261	.347	.350	.697	-6	13	2	87	O105(21/77/7)	0	0.8
1975	†Bos A	77	108	21	21	2	1	0	15	21	6	0	20	.194	.326	.231	.557	-45	3	2	60	O65(25/15/26)	0	-0.2
1976	Bos A	105	269	40	76	15	3	0	27	34	2	0	47	.283	.359	.361	.720	+1	11	10	52	O82(17/37/32),D4	0	0.7
1977	Bos A	86	189	34	48	9	3	0	24	22	1	3	30	.254	.341	.333	.674	-24	11	5	69	O79(2/29/48)/D	27	-0.9
1978	Cal A	132	475	66	125	25	4	1	37	54	1	4	70	.263	.341	.339	.680	-5	3	13	19	O129(0/93/36)	0	0.1
1979	†Cal A	120	427	60	125	15	5	2	28	50	1	1	69	.293	.367	.365	.732	+2	5	4	56	O117C,D2	37	0.9
1980	Cal A	129	412	52	113	14	3	2	38	48	4	1	71	.274	.349	.337	.686	-9	7	3	70	O118(0/98/24)	0	0.2
1981	Bos A	97	316	38	92	17	2	2	33	28	1	1	36	.291	.349	.377	.726	+3	3	5	38	O95C	0	-0.9
1982	Bos A	135	409	50	104	13	2	4	38	40	2	2	41	.254	.323	.325	.648	-26	5	6	45	O127C	0	-2.6
1983	Bos A	104	262	41	75	10	2	2	21	28	1	1	30	.286	.356	.363	.719	-8	3	3	50	O66(6/22/40),1b2,D2	0	-0.5
1984	Bos A	95	123	17	32	5	1	0	12	17	0	0	22	.260	.348	.317	.665	-18	1	1	50	O31(0/21/10),1b8	0	-0.4
1985	Bos A	41	45	5	15	2	0	0	9	5	0	0	6	.333	.392	.378	.770	+10	1	0	100	O8(4/1/3),D4	29	0.1
Total	15	1482	3887	552	1046	161	35	28	369	454	23	16	583	.269	.346	.350	.696	-8	78	65	55	O1248(118/854/297),D13,1b10	93	-2.8
Team	12	1101	2573	374	683	107	23	23	266	302	17	10	373	.265	.343	.352	.695	-10	63	45	58	O884(66/420/177),D11,1b10	56	-4.0
/150	2	150	351	51	93	15	3	3	36	41	2	1	51	.265	.343	.352	.695	-10	9	6	60	O120(9/57/24)/D1	8	-0.5
MILLS, BUSTER Colonel Buster "Bus" B9.16.1908 Ranger TX D12.1.1991 Arlington TX BR/TR/5'11.5"/195 d4.18 Mil 1943–45 M1/C7 Col Oklahoma																								
1937	Bos A	123	505	85	149	25	8	7	58	46		6	41	.295	.361	.418	.779	-8	11	8	58	O120(107/10/5)		-1.7
Total	7	415	1379	200	396	62	19	14	163	131		15	137	.287	.355	.390	.745	-9	23	21	100	O341(255/76/12)	0	-3.5
/150	1	150	616	104	182	30	10	9	71	56		7	50	.295	.361	.418	.779	-8	13	10	57	O146(130/12/6)		-2.1
MIRABELLI, DOUG Douglas Anthony B10.18.1970 Kingman AZ BR/TR/6'1"/(210–228) [SFN92 5/131] d8.27 Col Wichita St.																								
1996	SF N	9	18	2	4	1	0	0	1	3	0	0	4	.222	.333	.278	.611	-35	0	0	0	C8	0	-0.2
1997	SF N	6	7	0	1	0	0	0	0	1	0	0	3	.143	.250	.143	.393	-94	0	0	0	C6	0	-0.1
1998	SF N	10	17	2	4	2	0	1	4	2	0	0	6	.235	.316	.529	.845	+23	0	0	0	C10	0	0.1
1999	SF N	33	87	10	22	6	0	1	10	9	1	1	25	.253	.327	.356	.683	-21	0	0	0	C30	0	-0.3
2000	†SF N	82	230	23	53	10	2	6	28	36	2	2	57	.230	.337	.370	.707	-16	1	0	100	C80	0	-1.0
2001	Tex A	23	49	4	5	2	0	2	3	10	0	0	21	.102	.254	.265	.519	-64	0	0	0	C23/D	0	-0.3
2001	Bos A	54	141	16	38	8	0	9	26	17	2	4	36	.270	.360	.518	.878	+29	0	0	0	C52/D	0	0.8
2001	Year	77	190	20	43	10	0	11	29	27	2	4	57	.226	.332	.453	.785	+4	0	0	0	C75,D2	0	0.5
2002	Bos A	57	151	17	34	7	0	7	25	17	0	3	33	.225	.312	.411	.723	-10	0	0	0	C50,D4	0	0.0
2003	†Bos A	62	163	23	42	13	0	6	18	11	0	1	36	.258	.307	.448	.755	-8	0	0	0	C55,1b2,D4	0	-0.1
2004	†Bos A	59	160	27	45	12	0	9	32	19	0	3	46	.281	.368	.525	.893	+22	0	0	0	C53,D4	0	0.1
2005	†Bos A	50	136	16	31	7	0	6	18	14	0	2	48	.228	.309	.412	.721	-14	2	0	100	C43,D5	24	0.1
2006	SD N	14	22	1	4	1	0	0	0	4	0	0	5	.182	.308	.227	.535	-57	0	0	0	C9	0	-0.2
2006	Bos A	59	161	12	31	6	0	6	25	11	0	4	54	.193	.261	.342	.603	-47	0	0	0	C57,D2	0	-1.5
2006	Major	73	183	13	35	7	0	6	25	15	0	4	59	.191	.267	.328	.595	+9	0	0	0		0	-1.7
Total	11	518	1342	153	314	75	2	53	190	154	5	20	374	.234	.320	.411	.731	-11	3	0	100	C476,D21,1b2	24	-2.6
Team	6	341	912	111	221	53	0	43	144	89	2	17	253	.242	.320	.442	.762	-5	2	0	100	C310,D20,1b2	24	-0.6
/150	3	150	401	49	97	23	0	19	63	39	1	7	111	.242	.320	.442	.762	-5	1	0	100	C136,D9/1	11	-0.3
MITCHELL, FRED Frederick Francis (b Frederick Francis Yapp) B6.5.1878 Cambridge MA D10.13.1970 Newton MA BR/TR/5'9.5"/185 d4.27 M7/C3 OF(1/2/0)▲																								
1901	Bos A	20	44	5	7	0	2	0	4	2		0		.159	.196	.250	.446	-77	0			P17,2b2/S		-0.1
1902	Bos A	1	1	0	0	0	0	0	0	0		0		.000	.000	.000	.000	-197	0			/P		0.0
Total	7	202	572	55	120	16	7	0	52	22		5	2	.210	.245	.262	.507	-48	8			P97,C62,1b16,3b6,O3C,S2,2b2		-1.8
Team	2	21	45	5	7	0	2	0	4	2		0	0	.156	.191	.244	.435	-80	0			P18,2b2/S		-0.1
MITCHELL, JOHNNY John Franklin B8.9.1894 Detroit MI D11.4.1965 Birmingham MI BB/TR/5'8"/155 d5.21																								
1921	NY A	13	42	4	11	1	0	0	2	4		0	4	.262	.326	.286	.612	-44	1	0	100	S7,2b5		-0.6
1922	NY A	4	4	1	0	0	0	0	0	0		0	1	.000	.000	.000	.000	-198	0	0	0	S4		-0.1
1922	Bos A	59	203	20	51	4	1	1	8	16		4	17	.251	.318	.296	.614	-39	1	2	33	S58		-0.8
1922	Year	63	207	21	51	4	1	1	8	16		4	18	.246	.313	.290	.603	-42	1	2	33	S62		-0.9
1923	Bos A	92	347	40	78	15	4	0	19	34		1	18	.225	.296	.291	.587	-45	7	11	39	S87,2b5		-1.2
1924	Bro N	64	243	42	64	10	0	1	16	37		0	22	.263	.361	.317	.678	-14	3	1	75	S64		0.5
1925	Bro N	97	336	45	84	8	3	0	18	28		0	19	.250	.308	.292	.600	-45	2	0	100	S90		-1.4
Total	5	329	1175	152	288	38	8	2	63	119		5	81	.245	.317	.296	.613	-38	14	14	50	S310,2b10		-3.6
Team	2	151	550	60	129	19	5	1	27	50		5	35	.235	.304	.293	.597	-43	8	13	38	S145,2b5		-2.0
/150	2	150	546	60	128	19	5	1	27	50		5	35	.235	.304	.293	.597	-43	8	13	38	S144,2b5		-2.0
MITCHELL, KEITH Keith Alexander B8.6.1969 San Diego CA BR/TR/5'10"/(180–195) [AtlN87 4/90] d7.23																								
1998	Bos A	23	33	4	9	2	0	0	6	7	1	0	5	.273	.400	.333	.733	-8	1	0	100	D12,O10(4/0/6)	0	-0.2
Total	4	128	242	38	63	5	0	8	29	34	1	1	42	.260	.353	.380	.733	-9	4	1	80	O87(57/5/29),D18	41	-1.0
MITCHELL, KEVIN Kevin Darnell B1.13.1962 San Diego CA BR/TR/5'11"/(210–244) d9.4 OF(756/6/53) [DL 1993 SF N 24]																								
1996	Bos A	27	92	9	28	4	0	2	13	11	0	1	14	.304	.385	.413	.798	+0	0	0	0	O21(1/0/21),D4	63	-0.3
Total	13	1223	4134	630	1173	224	25	234	760	491	87	27	719	.284	.360	.520	.880	+42	30	31	49	O807L,3b235,D69,S25,1b9	203	20.3
MOHR, DUSTAN Dustan Kyle B6.19.1976 Hattiesburg MS BR/TR/6'0"/(210–215) [CleA97 9/291] d8.29 Col Alabama																								
2006	Bos A	21	40	5	7	1	0	2	3	3	0	0	20	.175	.233	.350	.583	-53	0	0	0	O20(7/13/5)	0	-0.3
Total	6	497	1351	202	338	78	6	48	154	141	8	12	387	.250	.325	.423	.748	-10	13	11	54	O433(131/41/301),D12	23	-1.6
MONCEWICZ, FREDDIE Frederick Alfred B9.1.1903 Brockton MA D4.23.1969 Brockton MA BR/TR/5'8.5"/175 d6.19 Col Boston College																								
1928	Bos A	3	1	0	0	0	0	0	0	0		0	1	.000	.000	.000	.000	-199	0	0	0	S2		0.0
MONTGOMERY, BOB Robert Edward B4.16.1944 Nashville TN BR/TR/6'1"/(195–210) d9.6																								
1970	Bos A	22	78	8	14	2	0	1	4	6	0	1	20	.179	.244	.244	.488	-66	0	0	0	C22	0	-0.6
1971	Bos A	67	205	19	49	11	2	2	24	16	4	3	43	.239	.300	.341	.641	-23	1	0	100	C66	0	-0.9
1972	Bos A	24	77	7	22	1	0	2	7	3	0	0	17	.286	.309	.377	.686	-1	0	0	0	C22	0	-0.2
1973	Bos A	34	128	18	41	6	2	7	25	7	0	0	36	.320	.353	.563	.916	+46	0	0	0	C33	0	0.8
1974	Bos A	88	254	26	64	10	0	4	38	13	1	1	50	.252	.287	.339	.626	-25	3	0	100	C79,D5	0	-0.8
1975	†Bos A	62	195	16	44	10	1	2	26	4	0	1	37	.226	.241	.318	.559	-46	1	1	50	C53,1b6,D3	0	-1.8
1976	Bos A	31	93	10	23	3	1	3	13	5	1	0	20	.247	.283	.398	.681	-12	0	1	0	C30/D	0	-0.4
1977	Bos A	17	40	6	12	2	0	2	7	4	0	1	9	.300	.370	.500	.870	+23	0	0	0	C15	0	-0.1
1978	Bos A	10	29	2	7	1	1	0	5	2	0	0	12	.241	.290	.345	.635	-29	0	0	0	C10	0	-0.1
1979	Bos A	32	86	13	30	4	1	0	7	4	1	0	24	.349	.374	.419	.793	+9	1	0	100	C31	62	-0.2
Total	10	387	1185	125	306	50	8	23	156	64	7	7	268	.258	.296	.372	.668	-17	6	2	75	C361,D9,1b6	62	-4.3
/150	4	150	459	48	119	19	3	9	60	25	3	3	104	.258	.296	.372	.668	-17	2	1	67	C140,D3,1b2	24	-1.7

Year	Tm Lg	G	AB	R	H	2B	3B	HR	RBI	BB	IB	HP	SO	AVG	OBP	SLG	OPS	AOPS	SB	CS	SB%	Games at Position	DL	BFW
MOORE, BILL William Henry "Willie" B12.12.1903 Kansas City MO D5.24.1972 Kansas City MO BL/TR/5'11"/170 d9.7																								
1926	Bos A	5	18	2	3	0	0	0	0	0		0	2	.167	.167	.167	.334	-113	0	0	0	C5		-0.3
1927	Bos A	44	69	7	15	2	0	0	4	13		0	8	.217	.341	.246	.587	-44	0	0	0	C42		-0.4
Total	2	49	87	9	18	2	0	0	4	13		0	10	.207	.310	.230	.540	-57	0	0	0	C47		-0.7
MORGAN, ED Edward Carre B5.22.1904 Cairo IL D4.9.1980 New Orleans LA BR/TR/6'0.5"/180 d4.11 Col Tulane																								
1934	Bos A	138	528	95	141	28	4	3	79	81		2	46	.267	.367	.352	.719	-20	7	1	88	1b137		-2.9
Total	7	771	2810	512	879	186	45	52	473	385		10	252	.313	.398	.467	.865	+17	36	25	59	1b593,O121(1/18/102),3b18		0.3
/150	1	150	574	103	153	30	4	3	86	88		2	50	.267	.367	.352	.719	-20	8	1	89	1b149		-3.2
MORGAN, RED James Edward B10.6.1883 Neola IA D3.25.1981 New York NY BR/TR/5'10.5"/180 d6.20 Col Georgetown																								
1906	Bos A	88	307	20	66	6	3	1	21	16		7		.215	.270	.264	.534	-33	7			3b88		-2.3
MORTON, GUY Guy Jr. "Moose" B11.4.1930 Tuscaloosa AL BR/TR/6'2"/200 d9.17 f-Guy Col Alabama																								
1954	Bos A	1	1	0	0	0	0	0	0	0		0	1	.000	.000	.000	.000	-190	0	0	0	/H	0	0.0
MOSES, JERRY Gerald Braheen B8.9.1946 Yazoo City MS BR/TR/6'3"/(205–215) d5.9																								
1965	Bos A	4	4	1	1	0	0	1	1	0	0	0	2	.250	.250	1.000	1.250	+124	0	0	0	/H	0	0.1
1968	Bos A	6	18	2	6	0	0	2	4	1	0	0	4	.333	.368	.667	1.035	+96	0	1	0	C6	0	0.0
1969	Bos A	53	135	13	41	9	1	4	17	5	1	1	23	.304	.326	.474	.800	+18	0	1	0	C36	0	-0.3
1970	Bos A☆	92	315	26	83	18	1	6	35	21	9	2	45	.263	.313	.384	.697	-14	1	1	50	C88/lf	0	0.4
1971	Cal A	69	181	12	41	8	2	4	15	10	4	0	34	.227	.266	.359	.625	-18	0	0	0	C63/rf	0	-0.2
1972	Cle A	52	141	9	31	3	0	4	14	11	3	3	29	.220	.290	.326	.616	-20	0	0	0	C39,1b3	0	-0.3
1973	NY A	21	59	5	15	2	0	0	3	2	0	0	6	.254	.270	.288	.558	-39	0	0	0	C17/D	0	0.2
1974	Det A	74	198	19	47	6	3	4	19	11	2	2	38	.237	.282	.359	.641	-19	0	1	0	C74	23	-0.4
1975	SD N	13	19	1	3	2	0	0	1	2	0	0	3	.158	.238	.263	.501	-58	0	0	0	C5	0	-0.3
1975	Chi A	2	2	1	1	0	1	0	0	0	0	0	0	.500	.500	1.500	2.000	+342	0	0	0	/1D	0	0.1
1975	Major	15	21	2	4	2	1	0	1	2	0	0	3	.190	.261	.381	.642	-96	0	0	0		0	-0.2
Total	9	386	1072	89	269	48	8	25	109	63	19	8	184	.251	.295	.381	.676	-11	1	4	20	C328,1b4,D2,O2(1/0/1)	23	-0.7
Team	4	155	472	42	131	27	2	13	57	27	10	3	74	.278	.318	.426	.744	+0	1	3	25	C130/lf	0	0.2
/150	4	150	457	41	127	26	2	13	55	26	10	3	72	.278	.318	.426	.744	+0	1	3	25	C126/lf	0	0.2
MOSES, WALLY Wallace B10.8.1910 Uvalda GA D10.10.1990 Vidalia GA BL/TL/5'10"/160 d4.17 C16																								
1946	†Bos A	48	175	23	36	11	3	2	17	14		1	15	.206	.268	.337	.605	-35	2	4	33	O44(0/2/43)	0	-1.3
1947	Bos A	90	255	32	70	18	2	2	27	27		0	16	.275	.344	.384	.728	-5	3	0	100	O58R	0	-0.7
1948	Bos A	78	189	26	49	12	1	2	29	21		2	19	.259	.340	.365	.705	-17	5	0	100	O45R	0	-0.4
Total	17	2012	7356	1124	2138	435	110	89	679	821		21	457	.291	.364	.416	.780	+9	174	81	68	O1792(10/204/1587)	0	4.7
Team	3	216	619	81	155	41	6	6	73	62		3	50	.250	.322	.365	.687	-17	10	4	71	O147(0/2/43)	0	-2.4
/150	2	150	430	56	108	28	4	4	51	43		2	35	.250	.322	.365	.687	-17	7	3	70	O102(0/1/30)	0	-1.7
MOSKIMAN, DOC William Bankhead B12.20.1879 Oakland CA D1.11.1953 San Leandro CA BR/TR/6'0"/170 d8.23																								
1910	Bos A	5	9	1	1	0	0	0	1	2		0		.111	.273	.111	.384	-80	0			1b2/rf		-0.1
MOSS, LES John Lester B5.14.1925 Tulsa OK BR/TR/5'11"/(188–205) d9.10 M2/C13																								
1951	Bos A	71	202	18	40	6	0	3	26	25		1	34	.198	.289	.272	.561	-52	0	0	0	C69	0	-1.3
Total	13	824	2234	210	552	75	4	63	276	282	3	6	316	.247	.333	.369	.702	-14	1	5	17	C720	0	-5.9
MUELLER, BILL William Richard B3.17.1971 Maryland Heights MO BB/TR/5'10"/(170–180) [SFN93 15/414] d4.18 Col Missouri St.																								
1996	SF N	55	200	31	66	15	1	0	19	24	0	1	26	.330	.401	.415	.816	+19	0	0	0	3b45,2b8	0	0.6
1997	†SF N	128	390	51	114	26	3	7	44	48	1	3	71	.292	.369	.428	.797	+12	4	3	57	3b122	17	1.3
1998	SF N	145	534	93	157	27	0	9	59	79	1	1	83	.294	.383	.395	.778	+12	3	3	50	3b137,2b10	0	1.5
1999	SF N	116	414	61	120	24	0	2	36	65	1	3	52	.290	.388	.362	.750	-2	4	2	67	3b108,2b3	41	0.0
2000	†SF N	153	560	97	150	29	4	10	55	52	0	6	62	.268	.333	.387	.720	-12	4	2	67	3b145,2b2	0	-1.2
2001	Chi N	70	210	38	62	12	1	6	23	37	3	3	19	.295	.403	.448	.851	+25	1	1	50	3b64/2	91	1.0
2002	Chi N	103	353	51	94	19	4	7	37	51	2	0	41	.266	.355	.402	.757	+0	0	0	0	3b101	36	0.2
2002	SF N	8	13	0	2	0	0	0	1	1	0	0	1	.154	.214	.154	.368	-101	0	0	0	3b3	0	-0.2
2002	Year	111	366	51	96	19	4	7	38	52	2	0	42	.262	.350	.393	.743	-3	0	0	0	3b104	0	0.0
2003	†Bos A	146	524	85	171	45	5	19	85	59	2	7	77	**.326**	.398	.540	.938	+40	1	4	20	3b135,2b10/SD	0	3.1
2004	†Bos A	110	399	75	113	27	1	12	57	51	1	4	56	.283	.365	.446	.811	+5	2	2	50	3b96,2b14	43	0.3
2005	†Bos A	150	519	69	153	34	3	10	62	59	3	6	74	.295	.369	.430	.799	+8	0	0	0	3b142,2b5	0	0.6
2006	LA N	32	107	12	27	7	0	3	15	17	3	1	9	.252	.357	.402	.759	-5	1	1	50	3b30	143	0.0
Total	11	1216	4223	663	1229	265	22	85	493	543	17	35	571	.291	.373	.425	.798	+9	20	18	53	3b1128,2b53,D3/S	371	7.2
Team	3	406	1442	229	437	106	9	41	204	169	6	17	207	.303	.378	.474	.852	+19	3	6	33	3b373,2b29/SD	43	4.0
/150	1	150	533	85	161	39	3	15	75	62	2	6	76	.303	.378	.474	.852	+19	1	2	33	3b138,2b11/SD	16	1.5
MULLEAVY, GREG Gregory Thomas "Moe" B9.25.1905 Detroit MI D2.1.1980 Arcadia CA BR/TR/5'9"/167 d7.4 C7																								
1933	Bos A	1	0	1	0	0	0	0	0	0		0	0	+	+	+	.000	-100	0	0	0	/R		0.0
Total	3	79	292	28	76	14	5	0	28	20		0	23	.260	.308	.342	.650	-33	5	2	71	S73/2		-1.3
MULLER, FREDDIE Frederick William B12.21.1907 Newark CA D10.20.1976 Davis CA BR/TR/5'10"/170 d7.8																								
1933	Bos A	15	48	6	9	1	1	0	3	5		0	5	.188	.264	.250	.514	-63	1	0	100	2b14		-0.6
1934	Bos A	2	1	1	0	0	0	0	0	1		0	0	.000	.500	.000	.500	-64	0	0	0	/23		-0.1
Total	2	17	49	7	9	1	1	0	3	6		0	5	.184	.273	.245	.518	-62	1	0	100	2b15/3		-0.7
MUNDY, BILL William Edward B6.28.1889 Salineville OH D9.23.1958 Kalamazoo MI BL/TL/5'10"/154 d8.17																								
1913	Bos A	16	47	4	12	0	0	0	4	4		0	12	.255	.314	.255	.569	-35	0			1b14		-0.5
MURPHY, DAVID David Matthew B10.18.1981 Houston TX BL/TL/6'4"/190 [BosA03 1/17] d9.2 Col Baylor																								
2006	Bos A	20	22	4	5	1	0	1	2	4	0	0	4	.227	.346	.409	.755	-8	0	0	0	O16(6/8/2)/D	0	-0.1
MUSER, TONY Anthony Joseph B8.1.1947 Van Nuys CA BL/TL/6'2"/(175–200) d9.14 M6/C14 Col San Diego Mesa (CA) JC																								
1969	Bos A	2	9	0	1	0	0	0	1	1	0	0	1	.111	.200	.111	.311	-111	0	0	0	1b2	0	-0.1
Total	9	663	1268	123	329	41	9	7	117	95	10	1	138	.259	.309	.323	.632	-18	14	13	52	1b505,D37,O26(15/10/1)	0	-6.4
MYER, BUDDY Charles Solomon B3.16.1904 Ellisville MS D10.31.1974 Baton Rouge LA BL/TR/5'10.5"/163 d9.26 Col Mississippi St.																								
1927	Bos A	133	469	59	135	22	11	2	47	48		4	15	.288	.359	.394	.753	-3	9	5	64	S101,3b14,O10L/2		1.4
1928	Bos A	147	536	78	168	26	6	1	44	53		4	28	.313	.379	.390	.769	+4	**30**	16	65	3b144		2.0
Total	17	1923	7038	1174	2131	353	130	38	850	965		33	428	.303	.389	.406	.795	+8	157	109	59	2b1340,S238,3b219,O13(12/0/1)	0	14.3
Team	2	280	1005	137	303	48	17	3	91	101		8	43	.301	.370	.392	.762	+1	39	21	65	3b158,S101,O10L/2		3.4
/150	1	150	538	73	162	26	9	2	49	54		4	23	.301	.370	.392	.762	+1	21	11	66	3b85,S54,O5L/2		1.8
MYERS, HAP Ralph Edward B4.8.1887 San Francisco CA D6.30.1967 San Francisco CA BR/TR/6'3"/175 d4.16 Col California																								
1910	Bos A	3	6	0	2	0	0	0	0	0		0		.333	.333	.333	.666	+6	0			O2R		0.1
1911	Bos A	13	38	3	14	2	0	0	0	4		0		.368	.429	.421	.850	+39	4			1b12		0.1
Total	5	377	1251	203	335	42	7	4	116	119		13	130	.268	.338	.322	.660	-15	132	18	100	1b353,O2R		-2.9
Team	2	16	44	3	16	2	0	0	0	4		0	0	.364	.417	.409	.826	+35	4			1b12,O2R		0.2
NAEHRING, TIM Timothy James B2.1.1967 Cincinnati OH BR/TR/6'2"/(190–205) [BosA88 8/199] d7.15 Col Miami–Ohio [DL 1998 Bos A 181]																								
1990	Bos A	24	85	10	23	6	0	2	12	8	1	0	15	.271	.333	.412	.745	+2	0	0	0	S19,3b5/2	49	0.3
1991	Bos A	20	55	1	6	1	0	0	3	6	0	0	15	.109	.197	.127	.324	-108	0	0	0	S17,3b2/2	142	-0.7
1992	Bos A	72	186	12	43	8	0	3	14	18	0	3	31	.231	.308	.323	.631	-28	0	0	0	S30,2b23,3b10/lfD	40	0.7
1993	Bos A	39	127	14	42	10	0	1	17	10	0	0	26	.331	.377	.433	.810	+11	1	0	100	2b15,D10,3b9,S4	88	0.0
1994	Bos A	80	297	41	82	18	1	7	42	30	1	4	56	.276	.349	.414	.763	-8	1	3	25	2b49,3b11,1b8,S8,D7	29	0.3
1995	†Bos A	126	433	61	133	27	2	10	57	77	5	4	66	.307	.415	.448	.863	+21	0	2	0	3b124/D	0	2.3
1996	Bos A	116	430	77	124	16	0	17	65	49	4	4	63	.288	.363	.444	.807	+2	2	1	67	3b116/2	18	0.9
1997	Bos A	70	259	38	74	18	1	9	40	38	0	1	40	.286	.375	.467	.842	+17	1	1	50	3b68/D	97	-0.1
Total	8	547	1872	254	527	104	4	49	250	236	11	16	312	.282	.365	.420	.785	+2	5	7	42	3b345,2b90,S78,D23,1b8/lf	644	3.7
/150	2	150	513	70	145	29	1	13	69	65	3	4	86	.282	.365	.420	.785	+2	1	2	33	3b95,2b25,S21,D6,1b2/OfL	226	1.0

Year	Tm Lg	G	AB	R	H	2B	3B	HR	RBI	BB	IB	HP	SO	AVG	OBP	SLG	OPS	AOPS	SB	CS	SB%	Games at Position	DL	BFW
NARLESKI, BILL William Edward "Cap" B3.9.1900 Perth Amboy NJ D6.20.1964 Laurel Springs NJ BR/TR/5'9"/160 d4.18 s–Ray																								
1929	Bos A	96	260	30	72	16	1	0	25	21		1	22	.277	.333	.346	.679	-23	4	4	50	S51,2b29,3b7		-1.2
1930	Bos A	39	98	11	23	9	0	0	7	7		3	5	.235	.306	.327	.633	-37	0	0	0	S19,3b14,2b5		-0.8
Total	2	135	358	41	95	25	1	0	32	28		4	27	.265	.326	.341	.667	-27	4	4	50	S70,2b34,3b21		-2.0
/150	2	150	398	46	106	28	1	0	36	31		4	30	.265	.326	.341	.667	-27	4	4	50	S78,2b38,3b23	0	-2.2
NEITZKE, ERNIE Ernest Fredrich B11.13.1894 Toledo OH D4.27.1977 Sylvania OH BR/TR/5'10"/180 d6.2																								
1921	Bos A	11	25	3	6	0	0	0	2	4		0	4	.240	.345	.240	.585	-47	0	0	0	O8(4/1/3),P2		-0.2
NELSON, BRY Bryant Lawrence B1.27.1974 Crossett AR BB/TR/5'10"/205 [HouN93 44/1230] d5.14 Col Texarkana (TX) JC																								
2002	Bos A	25	34	6	9	3	0	0	2	4	0	0	1	.265	.342	.353	.695	-16	1	1	50	2b11,O11(7/2/2)/D	0	0.0
NEWMAN, JEFF Jeffrey Lynn B9.11.1948 Fort Worth TX BR/TR/6'2"/(210–218) [CleA70 26/608] d6.30 M1/C11 Col TCU																								
1983	Bos A	59	132	11	25	4	0	3	7	10	1	2	31	.189	.255	.288	.543	-54	0	1	0	C51,D6	0	-0.9
1984	Bos A	24	63	5	14	2	0	1	3	5	0	0	16	.222	.275	.302	.577	-42	0	0	0	C24	0	-0.2
Total	9	735	2123	189	475	85	4	63	233	116	16	6	369	.224	.264	.357	.621	-27	7	12	37	C513,1b175,D25,3b10/2P	15	-9.7
Team	2	83	195	16	39	6	0	4	10	15	1	2	47	.200	.262	.292	.554	-50	0	1	0	C75,D6	0	-1.1
NEWSOME, SKEETER Lamar Ashby B10.18.1910 Phenix City AL D8.31.1989 Columbus GA BR/TR/5'9"/170 d4.19																								
1935	Phi A	59	145	18	30	7	1	1	10	5		0	9	.207	.233	.290	.523	-65	2	1	67	S24,2b13,3b4/rf		-1.0
1936	Phi A	127	471	41	106	15	2	0	46	25		1	27	.225	.266	.265	.531	-68	13	4	76	S123,2b2/3lf		-2.8
1937	Phi A	122	438	53	111	22	1	1	30	37		0	22	.253	.312	.315	.627	-41	11	5	69	S122		-0.8
1938	Phi A	17	48	7	13	4	0	0	7	1		0	4	.271	.286	.354	.640	-39	1	1	50	S15		-0.1
1939	Phi A	99	248	22	55	9	1	0	17	19		0	12	.222	.277	.266	.543	-60	5	7	42	S93,2b2		-1.7
1941	Bos A	93	227	28	51	6	0	2	17	22		1	11	.225	.296	.278	.574	-49	10	4	71	S69,2b23	0	-0.2
1942	Bos A	29	95	7	26	6	0	0	9	9		0	5	.274	.337	.337	.674	-13	2	1	67	3b12,2b10,S7	0	0.1
1943	Bos A	114	449	48	119	21	2	1	22	21		2	21	.265	.301	.327	.628	-18	5	6	45	S98,3b15	0	0.5
1944	Bos A	136	472	41	114	26	3	0	41	33		0	21	.242	.291	.309	.600	-28	4	3	57	S126,2b8/3	0	0.2
1945	Bos A	125	438	45	127	30	1	1	48	20		1	15	.290	.322	.370	.692	-2	6	3	67	2b82,S33,3b11	0	2.3
1946	Phi N	112	375	35	87	10	2	1	23	30		0	23	.232	.289	.277	.566	-37	4			S107,2b3,3b2	0	-2.4
1947	Phi N	95	310	36	71	8	2	2	22	24		0	24	.229	.284	.287	.571	-46	4			S85,2b6,3b3	0	-1.3
Total	12	1128	3716	381	910	164	15	9	292	246		5	194	.245	.293	.304	.597	-38	67	35	100	S902,2b149,3b49,O2(1/0/1)	0	-7.2
Team	5	497	1681	169	437	89	6	4	137	105		4	73	.260	.305	.327	.632	-21	27	17	61	S333,2b123,3b39	0	2.9
/150	2	150	507	51	132	27	2	1	41	32		1	22	.260	.305	.327	.632	-21	8	5	62	S101,2b37,3b12	0	0.9
NIARHOS, GUS Constantine Gregory B12.6.1920 Birmingham AL D12.29.2004 Harrisonburg VA BR/TR/6'0"/165 d6.9 C3																								
1952	Bos A	29	58	4	6	0	0	0	4	12		1	9	.103	.268	.103	.371	-94	0	0	0	C25	0	-0.2
1953	Bos A	16	35	6	7	1	1	0	2	4		1	4	.200	.300	.286	.586	-44	0	1	0	C16	0	0.0
Total	9	315	691	114	174	26	5	1	59	153	0	4	56	.252	.390	.308	.698	-11	6	7	46	C287	42	3.7
Team	2	45	93	10	13	1	1	0	6	16		2	13	.140	.279	.172	.451	-76	0	1	0	C41	0	-0.2
NICHOLS, REID Thomas Reid B8.5.1958 Ocala FL BR/TR/5'11"/(165–175) [BosA76 12/286] d9.16 C1																								
1980	Bos A	12	36	5	8	0	1	0	3	3	0	0	8	.222	.282	.278	.560	-49	0	1	0	O9C/D	0	-0.4
1981	Bos A	39	48	13	9	0	1	0	3	2	0	0	6	.188	.216	.229	.445	-72	0	1	0	O27(1/25/1)/3D	0	-0.6
1982	Bos A	92	245	35	74	16	1	7	33	14	1	1	28	.302	.341	.461	.802	+11	5	3	63	O82(30/57/2),D4	16	0.6
1983	Bos A	100	274	35	78	22	1	6	22	26	2	3	36	.285	.352	.438	.790	+8	7	5	58	O72(11/32/30),D18/S	0	0.2
1984	Bos A	74	124	14	28	5	1	1	14	12	1	3	18	.226	.307	.306	.613	-32	2	1	67	O48(17/26/4)/D	0	-0.6
1985	Bos A	21	32	3	6	1	0	1	3	2	0	1	4	.188	.250	.313	.563	-47	1	0	100	O10(2/7/1),2b3,D4	0	-0.3
1985	Chi A	51	118	20	35	7	1	1	15	15	1	0	13	.297	.373	.398	.771	+7	5	5	50	O48(25/27/8)/D	0	-0.1
1985	Year	72	150	23	41	8	1	2	18	17	1	1	17	.273	.347	.380	.727	-4	6	5	55	O58(27/34/9),D5,2b3	0	-0.4
1986	Chi A	74	136	9	31	4	0	2	18	11	0	0	23	.228	.282	.301	.583	-42	5	4	56	O53(31/14/11),2b2,D3	22	-0.8
1987	Mon N	77	147	22	39	8	2	4	20	14	1	1	13	.265	.329	.429	.758	-4	2	1	67	O59(7/50/5),3b3	0	0.2
Total	8	540	1160	156	308	63	8	22	131	99	6	9	149	.266	.326	.391	.717	-9	27	21	56	O408(124/247/62),D39,2b5,3b4/S	38	-1.8
Team	6	338	759	105	203	44	5	15	78	59	4	8	100	.267	.325	.398	.723	-8	15	11	58	O248(59/68/59),D29,2b3/3S	16	-1.1
/150	3	150	337	47	90	20	2	7	35	26	2	4	44	.267	.325	.398	.723	-8	7	5	58	O110(26/30/26),D13/23S	7	-0.5
NIEMIEC, AL Alfred Joseph B5.18.1911 Meriden CT D10.29.1995 Kirkland WA BR/TR/5'11"/158 d9.19 Col Holy Cross																								
1934	Bos A	9	32	2	7	0	0	0	3	3		0	4	.219	.286	.219	.505	-70	0	0	0	2b9		0.0
Total	2	78	235	24	47	3	2	1	23	29		1	20	.200	.291	.243	.534	-66	2	2	50	2b61,S5		-1.2
NILES, HARRY Herbert Clyde B9.10.1880 Buchanan MI D4.18.1953 Sturgis MI BR/TR/5'8"/175 d4.24																								
1908	Bos A	18	33	4	8	0	0	1	3	6		1		.242	.375	.333	.708	+27	3			2b8,S2		0.1
1909	Bos A	145	546	65	134	12	5	1	38	39		13		.245	.311	.291	.602	-12	27			O117(77/12/28),3b13,S9,2b5		-1.7
1910	Bos A	18	57	6	12	3	0	1	3	4		0		.211	.262	.316	.578	-21	1			O15(4/0/11)		-0.2
Total	5	608	2270	279	561	58	24	12	152	163		30		.247	.306	.310	.616	-5	107			O298(95/19/184),2b214,3b52,S18		-4.5
Team	3	181	636	75	154	15	5	3	44	49		14	0	.242	.310	.296	.606	-11	31			O132(81/12/39),2b13,3b13,S11		-1.8
/150	2	150	527	62	128	12	4	2	36	41		12	0	.242	.310	.296	.606	-11	26			O109(67/10/32),2b11,3b11,S9		-1.5
NIXON, TROT Christopher Trotman B4.11.1974 Durham NC BL/TL/6'2"/(196–210) [BosA93 1/7] d9.21																								
1996	Bos A	2	4	2	2	1	0	0	0	0	0	0	1	.500	.500	.750	1.250	+107	1	0	100	O2R	0	0.1
1998	†Bos A	13	27	3	7	1	0	0	0	1	0	0	3	.259	.286	.296	.582	-49	0	0	0	O7(1/0/6),D2	0	-0.1
1999	†Bos A	124	381	67	103	22	5	15	52	53	1	3	75	.270	.357	.472	.829	+8	3	1	75	O121R	0	-0.7
2000	Bos A	123	427	66	118	27	8	12	60	63	2	2	85	.276	.368	.461	.829	+6	8	1	89	O118(0/6/115)/D	30	0.2
2001	Bos A	148	535	100	150	31	4	27	88	79	1	7	113	.280	.376	.505	.881	+30	7	4	64	O145(0/70/83)/D	0	1.6
2002	Bos A	152	532	81	136	36	3	24	94	65	2	5	109	.256	.338	.470	.808	+11	4	2	67	O152(0/13/145)	0	0.1
2003	†Bos A	134	441	81	135	24	6	28	87	65	4	3	96	.306	.396	.578	.974	+47	4	2	67	O130(0/1/129)	0	2.0
2004	†Bos A	48	149	24	47	9	1	6	23	15	1	1	24	.315	.377	.510	.887	+22	0	0	0	O40R,D3	117	0.1
2005	†Bos A	124	408	64	112	29	1	13	67	53	3	3	59	.275	.357	.446	.803	+9	2	1	67	O118R,D2	27	0.9
2006	Bos A	114	381	59	102	24	0	8	52	60	1	7	56	.268	.373	.394	.767	-2	0	2	0	O110R	34	-0.2
Total	10	982	3285	547	912	204	28	133	523	454	15	31	621	.278	.366	.478	.844	+16	29	13	69	O943(1/90/869),D9	208	4.0
/150	2	150	502	84	139	31	4	20	80	69	2	5	95	.278	.366	.478	.844	+16	4	2	67	O144(0/14/133)/D	32	0.6
NIXON, OTIS Otis Junior B1.9.1959 Columbus Co. NC BB/TR/6'2"/180 [NYA79 S1/3] d9.9 b–Donell Col Louisburg (NC) JC																								
1994	Bos A	103	398	60	109	15	1	0	25	55	1	0	65	.274	.360	.317	.677	-26	42	10	81	O103C	0	-0.8
Total	17	1709	5115	878	1379	142	27	11	318	585	10	5	694	.270	.343	.314	.657	-24	620	186	77	O1527(357/1136/72),D19/S	79	-8.2
/150	1	150	580	87	159	22	1	0	36	80	1	0	95	.274	.360	.317	.677	-26	61	15	80	O150C	0	-1.2
NIXON, RUSS Russell Eugene B2.19.1935 Cleves OH BL/TR/6'1"/(190–200) d4.20 M5/C12																								
1957	Cle A	62	185	15	52	7	1	2	18	12	7	0	12	.281	.323	.362	.685	-12	0	1	0	C57	0	-0.5
1958	Cle A	113	376	42	113	17	4	9	46	13	4	0	38	.301	.322	.439	.761	+11	0	3	0	C101	0	0.0
1959	Cle A	82	258	23	62	10	3	1	29	15	1	0	28	.240	.277	.314	.591	-34	0	0	0	C74	0	-1.4
1960	Cle A	25	82	6	20	5	0	1	6	6	2	2	6	.244	.308	.341	.649	-21	0	1	0	C25	0	0.0
1960	Bos A	80	272	24	81	17	3	5	33	13	3	0	23	.298	.329	.438	.767	+2	0	1	0	C74	0	-0.6
1960	Year	105	354	30	101	22	3	6	39	19	5	2	29	.285	.324	.415	.739	-3	0	2	0	C99	0	-0.6
1961	Bos A	87	242	24	70	12	2	1	19	13	1	2	19	.289	.327	.368	.695	-16	0	1	0	C66	0	-0.7
1962	Bos A	65	151	11	42	7	2	1	19	8	3	0	14	.278	.313	.371	.684	-19	0	0	0	C38	31	-0.6
1963	Bos A	98	287	27	77	18	1	5	30	22	5	4	32	.268	.327	.390	.717	-2	0	0	0	C76	0	-0.1
1964	Bos A	81	163	10	38	7	0	1	20	14	3	2	29	.233	.297	.294	.591	-36	0	0	0	C45	0	-1.0
1965	Bos A	59	137	11	37	5	1	0	11	6	2	0	23	.270	.295	.321	.616	-28	0	0	0	C38	0	-1.2
1966	Min A	51	96	5	25	2	1	0	7	7	3	1	13	.260	.314	.302	.616	-26	0	0	0	C32	0	-0.7
1967	Min A	74	170	16	40	6	1	1	22	18	3	0	29	.235	.304	.300	.604	-26	0	0	0	C69	0	-0.6
1968	Bos A	29	85	1	13	2	0	0	6	7	1	0	13	.153	.217	.176	.393	-81	0	0	0	C27	0	-1.3
Total	12	906	2504	215	670	115	19	27	266	154	38	11	279	.268	.310	.361	.671	-16	0	7	0	C722	31	-8.7
Team	7	499	1337	108	358	68	9	13	138	83	18	8	153	.268	.312	.361	.673	-18	0	2	0	C364	31	-5.5
/150	2	150	402	32	108	20	3	4	41	25	5	2	46	.268	.312	.361	.673	-18	0	1	0	C109	9	-1.7

RED SOX BATTERS

Year	Tm Lg	G	AB	R	H	2B	3B	HR	RBI	BB	IB	HP	SO	AVG	OBP	SLG	OPS	AOPS	SB	CS	SB%	Games at Position	DL	BFW
NONNENKAMP, RED Leo William B7.7.1910 St.Louis MO D12.3.2000 Little Rock AR BL/TL/5'11"/165 d9.6																								
1933	Pit N	1	1	0	0	0	0	0	0	0		0	1	.000	.000	.000	.000	-199	0			/H		0.0
1938	Bos A	87	180	37	51	4	1	0	18	21		0	13	.283	.358	.317	.675	-33	6	1	86	O39(5/5/29),1b5		-0.7
1939	Bos A	58	75	12	18	2	1	0	5	12		0	6	.240	.345	.293	.638	-38	0	1	0	O15(7/4/4)		-0.5
1940	Bos A	9	7	0	0	0	0	0	1	0		1	4	.000	.125	.000	.125	-162	0	0	0	/H		-0.2
Total	4	155	263	49	69	6	2	0	24	33		1	24	.262	.347	.300	.647	-38	6	2	100	O54(12/9/33),1b5		-1.4
Team	3	154	262	49	69	6	2	0	24	33		1	23	.263	.348	.302	.650	-38	6	2	75	O54(12/9/33),1b5		-1.4
/150	3	150	255	48	67	6	2	0	23	32		1	22	.263	.348	.302	.650	-38	6	2	75	O53(12/9/32),1b5		-1.4
NUNAMAKER, LES Leslie Grant B1.25.1889 Aurora NE D11.14.1938 Hastings NE BR/TR/6'2"/190 d4.28																								
1911	Bos A	62	183	18	47	4	3	0	19	12		0		.257	.303	.311	.614	-28	1			C59		0.1
1912	Bos A	35	103	15	26	5	2	0	6	6		3		.252	.313	.340	.653	-18	2			C35		-0.1
1913	Bos A	29	65	9	14	5	2	0	9	8		1	8	.215	.311	.354	.665	-8	2			C27		0.3
1914	Bos A	5	5	0	1	0	0	0	0	1		0	0	.200	.333	.200	.533	-39	0			C3/1		0.0
Total	12	716	1990	194	533	75	30	2	216	176		14	150	.268	.332	.339	.671	-5	36	12	100	C614,1b15/rf		3.8
Team	4	131	356	42	88	14	7	0	34	27		4	8	.247	.307	.326	.633	-21	5			C124/1		0.3
/150	5	150	408	48	101	16	8	0	39	31		5	9	.247	.307	.326	.633	-21	6			C142/1		0.3
NUNNALLY, JON Jonathan Keith B11.9.1971 Pelham NC BL/TR/5'10"/190 [CleA92 3/70] d4.26 Col Miami–Dade Kendall (FL) CC																								
1999	Bos A	10	14	4	4	1	0	0	1	0	0	0	6	.286	.286	.357	.643	-39	0	0	0	O2(1/0/1),D3	0	-0.1
Total	6	364	885	162	218	47	12	42	125	146	10	5	239	.246	.354	.469	.823	+11	19	12	61	O311(70/88/193),D11	0	1.6
O'BERRY, MIKE Preston Michael B4.20.1954 Birmingham AL BR/TR/6'2"/(190–195) [BosA75 22/516] d4.8 Col South Alabama																								
1979	Bos A	43	59	8	10	1	0	1	4	5	0	1	16	.169	.242	.237	.479	-71	0	0	0	C43	0	-0.8
Total	7	197	376	38	72	10	1	3	27	43	0	1	77	.191	.274	.247	.521	-54	1	0	100	C196/3	0	-2.8
O'BRIEN, JACK John Joseph B2.5.1873 Watervliet NY D6.10.1933 Watervliet NY BL/TR/6'1"/165 d4.14																								
1903	†Bos A	96	338	44	71	14	4	3	38	21		3		.210	.262	.302	.564	-35	10			O71(2/68/1),3b11,2b4/S		-2.5
Total	3	326	1226	171	317	39	14	9	133	77		11		.259	.308	.335	.643	-18	42			O295(165/68/62),3b16,2b4/S		-4.8
O'BRIEN, SYD Sydney Lloyd B2.18.1944 Compton CA BR/TR/6'1"/(185–195) d4.15 Col Long Beach (CA) City																								
1969	Bos A	100	263	47	64	10	5	9	29	15	0	1	37	.243	.287	.422	.709	-8	2	3	40	3b53,S15,2b12	0	-0.4
Total	4	378	1052	135	242	35	8	24	100	60	5	4	155	.230	.273	.347	.620	-27	5	9	36	3b144,S76,2b72,1b2/rf	0	-4.7
/150	2	150	395	71	96	15	8	14	44	23	0	2	56	.243	.287	.422	.709	-8	3	5	38	3b80,S23,2b18	0	-0.6
O'BRIEN, TOMMY Thomas Edward "Obie" B12.19.1918 Anniston AL D11.5.1978 Anniston AL BR/TR/5'11"/195 d4.24																								
1949	Bos A	49	125	24	28	5	0	3	10	21		0	12	.224	.336	.336	.672	-27	1	0	100	O32(0/8/25)	0	-0.7
1950	Bos A	9	31	0	4	1	0	0	3	3		0	5	.129	.206	.161	.367	-105	0	0	0	O9(3/4/2)	0	-0.5
Total	5	293	714	110	198	30	14	8	78	70		2	66	.277	.344	.392	.736	+0	2	0	100	O185(49/12/125),3b10	0	-1.3
Team	2	58	156	24	32	6	0	3	13	24		0	17	.205	.311	.301	.612	-42	1	0	100	O41(3/12/27)	0	-1.2
O'DOUL, LEFTY Francis Joseph B3.4.1897 San Francisco CA D12.7.1969 San Francisco CA BL/TL/6'0"/180 d4.29▲																								
1923	Bos A	36	35	2	5	0	0	0	4	2		0	3	.143	.189	.143	.332	-112	0	0	0	P23/rf		0.0
Total	11	970	3264	624	1140	175	41	113	542	333		23	122	.349	.413	.532	.945	+42	36	0	100	O804(744/1/59),P34		12.6
OFFERMAN, JOSE Jose Antonio (Dono) B11.8.1968 San Pedro de Macoris, D.R. BB/TR/6'0"/(160–200) d8.19 OF(5/1/3)																								
1999	†Bos A★	149	586	107	172	37	**11**	8	69	96	5	2	79	.294	.391	.435	.826	+8	18	12	60	2b128,D17,1b8	0	-0.7
2000	Bos A	116	451	73	115	14	3	9	41	70	0	1	70	.255	.354	.359	.713	-20	0	8	0	2b80,1b38,D9	32	-0.8
2001	Bos A	128	524	76	140	23	3	9	49	61	2	1	97	.267	.342	.374	.716	-11	5	2	71	2b91,1b43	0	-0.3
2002	Bos A	72	237	39	55	10	0	4	27	33	0	1	29	.232	.325	.325	.650	-27	8	5	62	1b41,D24,O2R	0	-1.1
Total	15	1651	5681	840	1551	252	72	57	537	772	34	18	914	.273	.360	.373	.733	-7	172	100	63	S607,2b595,1b259,D100,O9L	93	-2.5
Team	4	465	1798	295	482	84	17	30	186	260	7	5	275	.268	.359	.384	.743	-9	31	27	53	2b299,1b130,D50,O2R	32	-2.9
/150	1	150	580	95	155	27	5	10	60	84	2	2	89	.268	.359	.384	.743	-9	10	9	53	2b96,1b42,D16/rf	10	-0.9
OGLIVIE, BEN Benjamin Ambrosio (Palmer) B2.11.1949 Colon, Pan BL/TL/6'2"/(160–170) [BosA68 11/248] d9.4 C1																								
1971	Bos A	14	38	2	10	3	0	0	4	0	0	0	5	.263	.263	.342	.605	-35	0	0	0	O11(10/0/1)	0	-0.1
1972	Bos A	94	253	27	61	10	2	8	30	18	2	1	61	.241	.293	.391	.684	-3	1	1	50	O65(32/0/33)	0	-0.8
1973	Bos A	58	147	16	32	9	1	2	9	9	2	2	32	.218	.269	.333	.602	-34	1	1	50	O32(4/0/28),D13	0	-0.9
Total	16	1754	5913	784	1615	277	33	235	901	560	10	35	852	.273	.336	.450	.786	+18	87	70	55	O1439(1098/15/357),D127,1b44	0	7.3
Team	3	166	438	45	103	22	3	10	43	27	4	3	98	.235	.282	.368	.650	-16	2	2	50	O108(42/0/6),D13	0	-1.8
/150	3	150	396	41	93	20	3	9	39	24	4	3	89	.235	.282	.368	.650	-16	2	2	50	O98(38/0/5),D12	0	-1.6
OKRIE, LEN Leonard Joseph B7.16.1923 Detroit MI BR/TR/6'0"/185 d6.16 C5 f–Frank																								
1952	Bos A	1	1	0	0	0	0	0	0	0		0	1	.000	.000	.000	.000	-193	0	0	0	/C	0	0.0
Total	4	42	78	3	17	1	1	0	3	9		1	16	.218	.307	.256	.563	-49	0	0	0	C40	0	-0.2
O'LEARY, TROY Troy Franklin B8.4.1969 Compton CA BL/TL/6'0"/(175–200) [MilA87 13/331] d5.9																								
1993	Mil A	19	41	3	12	3	0	0	3	5	0	0	9	.293	.370	.366	.736	-1	0	0	0	O19(15/0/5)	0	0.1
1994	Mil A	27	66	9	18	1	1	2	7	5	0	1	12	.273	.329	.409	.738	-14	1	1	50	O21(13/0/10)/D	0	-0.1
1995	Bos A	112	399	60	123	31	6	10	49	29	4	1	64	.308	.355	.491	.846	+14	5	3	63	O105(16/13/91),D3	0	0.2
1996	Bos A	149	497	68	129	28	5	15	81	47	3	4	80	.260	.327	.427	.754	-13	3	2	60	O146(66/17/110)	0	-2.2
1997	Bos A	146	499	65	154	32	4	15	80	39	7	2	70	.309	.358	.479	.837	+14	0	5	0	O142(24/0/119)/D	0	0.0
1998	†Bos A	156	611	95	165	36	8	23	83	36	2	5	108	.270	.314	.468	.782	-2	2	2	50	O155L	0	-0.8
1999	†Bos A	157	596	84	167	36	4	28	103	56	5	4	91	.280	.343	.495	.838	+8	1	2	33	O157(157/0/2)	0	0.0
2000	Bos A	138	513	68	134	30	4	13	70	44	2	2	76	.261	.320	.411	.731	-18	0	2	0	O137L	14	-2.4
2001	Bos A	104	341	50	82	16	6	13	50	25	2	5	73	.240	.298	.437	.735	-9	1	3	25	O89(52/0/41),D4	0	-1.1
2002	Mon N	97	273	27	78	12	2	3	37	34	5	3	47	.286	.371	.377	.748	-7	1	2	33	O70(69/0/1),D3	0	-0.5
2003	†Chi N	93	174	18	38	9	0	5	28	14	1	1	31	.218	.275	.356	.631	-37	3	0	100	O51(28/0/24)	0	-1.1
Total	11	1198	4010	547	1100	234	40	127	591	334	31	28	661	.274	.332	.448	.780	-3	17	22	44	O1092(732/30/403),D12	14	-7.9
Team	7	962	3456	490	954	209	37	117	516	276	25	23	562	.276	.331	.459	.790	-1	12	19	39	O931(96/30/115),D8	14	-6.3
/150	1	150	539	76	149	33	6	18	80	43	4	4	88	.276	.331	.459	.790	-1	2	3	40	O145(15/5/18)/D	2	-1.0
OLERUD, JOHN John Garrett B8.5.1968 Seattle WA BL/TL/6'5"/(205–225) [TorA89 3/79] d9.3 Col Washington St.																								
2005	†Bos A	87	173	18	50	7	0	7	37	16	2	0	20	.289	.344	.451	.795	+6	0	0	0	1b80	16	0.1
Total	17	2234	7592	1139	2239	500	13	255	1230	1275	15	88	1016	.295	.398	.465	.863	+29	11	14	44	1b2053,D133	16	24.4
OLIVER, GENE Eugene George B3.22.1935 Moline IL BR/TR/6'2"/(210–225) d6.6 Col Northwestern																								
1968	Bos A	16	35	2	5	0	0	0	1	4	1	1	12	.143	.250	.143	.393	-80	0	0	0	C10/rf	0	-0.4
Total	10	786	2216	268	546	111	5	93	320	215	22	15	420	.246	.315	.427	.742	+3	24	21	53	C381,1b201,O91(87/0/6)	63	0.4
OLIVER, JOE Joseph Melton B7.24.1965 Memphis TN BR/TR/6'3"/(210–220) [CinN83 2/41] d7.15																								
2001	Bos A	5	12	1	3	1	0	0	1	1	0	0	3	.250	.308	.333	.641	-31	0	0	0	C5	0	-0.2
Total	13	1076	3367	320	831	174	3	102	476	248	52	15	637	.247	.299	.391	.690	-18	13	13	50	C1033,1b25,D7,O4(2/0/2)	154	-2.6
OLIVER, TOM Thomas Noble "Rebel" B1.15.1903 Montgomery AL D2.26.1988 Montgomery AL BR/TR/6'0"/168 d4.14 C4																								
1930	Bos A	**154**	646	86	189	34	2	0	46	42		3	25	.293	.339	.351	.690	-22	6	6	50	O154C		-2.0
1931	Bos A	148	586	52	162	35	5	0	70	25		1	17	.276	.307	.353	.660	-23	4	6	40	O148C		-1.9
1932	Bos A	122	455	39	120	23	3	0	37	25		2	12	.264	.305	.327	.632	-34	1	6	14	O116C		-2.4
1933	Bos A	90	244	25	63	9	1	0	23	13		0	7	.258	.296	.303	.599	-40	1	1	50	O86C		-0.8
Total	4	514	1931	202	534	101	11	0	176	105		6	61	.277	.316	.340	.656	-27	12	19	39	O504C		-7.1
/150	1	150	564	59	156	29	3	0	51	31		2	18	.277	.316	.340	.656	-27	4	6	40	O147C	0	-2.1
OLSON, KARL Karl Arthur "Ole" B7.6.1930 Kentfield CA BR/TR/6'3"/205 d6.30 Mil 1952–54																								
1951	Bos A	5	10	0	1	0	0	0	0	0		0	3	.100	.100	.100	.200	-142	0	0	0	O5(2/0/3)	0	-0.2
1953	Bos A	25	57	5	7	2	0	1	6	1		0	9	.123	.138	.211	.349	-107	0	0	0	O24(23/2/0)	0	-1.0
1954	Bos A	101	227	25	59	12	2	1	20	12		0	23	.260	.293	.344	.637	-32	2	1	67	O78(29/36/16)	0	-1.1
1955	Bos A	26	48	7	12	1	2	0	1	1	0	0	10	.250	.265	.354	.619	-40	0	0	0	O21(11/8/5)	0	-0.3
1956	Was A	106	313	34	77	10	2	4	22	28	1	1	41	.246	.305	.329	.634	-31	1	1	50	O101(16/84/3)	0	-2.3
1957	Was A	8	12	2	2	0	0	0	0	1	0	0	2	.167	.231	.167	.398	-90	0	0	0	O6(2/4/0)	0	-0.1

Year	Tm Lg	G	AB	R	H	2B	3B	HR	RBI	BB	IB	HP	SO	AVG	OBP	SLG	OPS	AOPS	SB	CS	SB%	Games at Position	DL	BFW
1957	Det A	8	14	1	2	0	0	0	1	0	0	0	6	.143	.143	.143	.286	-121	0	0	0	O5(4/1/0)	0	-0.3
1957	Year	16	26	3	4	0	0	0	1	1	0	0	8	.154	.185	.154	.339	-106	0	0	0	O11(6/5/0)	0	-0.4
Total	6	279	681	74	160	25	6	6	50	43	1	1	94	.235	.278	.316	.594	-43	3	2	60	O240(87/135/27)	0	-5.3
Team	4	157	342	37	79	15	4	2	27	14	0	0	45	.231	.259	.316	.575	-48	2	1	67	O128(33/10/11)	0	-2.6
/150	4	150	327	35	75	14	4	2	26	13	0	0	43	.231	.259	.316	.575	-48	2	1	67	O122(32/10/11)	0	-2.5
OLSON, MARV Marvin Clement "Sparky" B5.28.1907 Gayville SD D2.5.1998 Tyndall SD BR/TR/5'7"/160 d9.13 Col Luther																								
1931	Bos A	15	53	8	10	1	0	0	5	9		0	3	.189	.306	.208	.514	-60	0	0	0	2b15		-0.3
1932	Bos A	115	403	58	100	14	6	0	25	61		0	26	.248	.347	.313	.660	-26	1	5	17	2b106/3		-1.8
1933	Bos A	3	1	1	0	0	0	0	0	0		0	1	.000	.000	.000	.000	-199	0	0	0	/2		0.0
Total	3	133	457	67	110	15	6	0	30	70		0	30	.241	.342	.300	.642	-30	1	5	17	2b122/3		-2.1
/150	3	150	515	76	124	17	7	0	34	79		0	34	.241	.342	.300	.642	-30	1	6	14	2b138/3	0	-2.4
O'NEILL, STEVE Stephen Francis B7.6.1891 Minooka PA D1.26.1962 Cleveland OH BR/TR/5'10"/165 d9.18 M14/C4 b–Jim b–Jack b–Mike																								
1924	Bos A	106	307	29	73	15	1	0	38	63		2	23	.238	.371	.293	.664	-27	0	2	0	C92		-0.4
Total	17	1590	4795	448	1259	248	34	13	537	592		43	383	.263	.349	.337	.686	-12	30	23	100	C1532/1		8.6
/150	1	150	434	41	103	21	1	0	54	89		3	33	.238	.371	.293	.664	-27	0	3	0	C130		-0.6
O'NEILL, BILL William John B1.22.1880 St.John NB, Can. D7.20.1920 Woodhaven NY BB/TR/5'11"/175 d5.7																								
1904	Bos A	17	51	7	10	1	0	0	5	2		0		.196	.226	.216	.442	-62	0			O9(8/1/0),S2		-0.7
Total	2	206	746	77	181	15	2	2	42	46		7		.243	.293	.276	.569	-19	41			O195(22/87/87),2b3,S2		-4.3
ORME, GEORGE George William B9.16.1891 Lebanon IN D3.16.1962 Indianapolis IN BR/TR/5'10"/160 d9.14																								
1920	Bos A	4	6	4	2	0	0	0	1	3		0	0	.333	.556	.333	.889	+46	0	0	0	O3(0/1/2)		0.1
O'ROURKE, FRANK James Francis "Blackie" B11.28.1894 Hamilton ON, Can. D5.14.1986 Chatham NJ BR/TR/5'10.5"/165 d6.12																								
1922	Bos A	67	216	28	57	14	3	1	17	20		3	28	.264	.335	.370	.705	-16	6	6	50	S49,3b20		-1.0
Total	14	1131	4069	547	1032	196	42	15	430	314		53	377	.254	.315	.333	.648	-32	100	59	100	3b598,S289,2b220,1b7/O		-13.4
ORTIZ, DAVID David Americo (Arias) "Big Papi" B11.18.1975 Santo Domingo, D.R. BL/TL/6'4"/(190–230) d9.2																								
1997	Min A	15	49	10	16	3	0	1	6	2	0	0	19	.327	.353	.449	.802	+6	0	0	0	1b11/D	0	0.1
1998	Min A	86	278	47	77	20	0	9	46	39	3	5	72	.277	.371	.446	.817	+10	1	0	100	1b70,D10	60	-0.1
1999	Min A	10	20	1	0	0	0	0	0	5	0	0	12	.000	.200	.000	.200	-141	0	0	0	/1D	0	-0.4
2000	Min A	130	415	59	117	36	1	10	63	57	2	0	81	.282	.364	.446	.810	-2	1	0	100	D88,1b27	0	-0.6
2001	Min A	89	303	46	71	17	1	18	48	40	8	1	68	.234	.324	.475	.799	+2	1	0	100	D80,1b8	77	-0.5
2002	†Min A	125	412	52	112	32	1	20	75	43	0	3	87	.272	.339	.500	.839	+17	1	2	33	D95,1b15	23	0.3
2003	†Bos A	128	448	79	129	39	2	31	101	58	8	1	83	.288	.369	.592	.961	+42	0	0	0	D74,1b45	0	1.9
2004	†Bos A★	150	582	94	175	47	3	41	139	75	8	4	133	.301	.380	.603	.983	+43	0	0	0	D115,1b34	0	2.7
2005	†Bos A★	159	601	119	180	40	1	47	**148**	102	9	1	124	.300	.397	.604	1.001	+56	1	0	100	D148,1b10	0	4.2
2006	Bos A★	151	558	115	160	29	2	**54**	**137**	**119**	23	4	117	.287	.413	.636	1.049	+63	1	0	100	D138,1b10	0	4.5
Total	10	1043	3666	622	1037	263	11	231	763	540	61	19	796	.283	.374	.550	.924	+33	6	2	75	D754,1b231	160	12.1
Team	4	588	2189	407	644	155	8	173	525	354	48	10	457	.294	.391	.609	1.000	+52	2	0	100	D475,1b99	0	13.3
/150	1	150	558	104	164	40	2	44	134	90	12	3	117	.294	.391	.609	1.000	+52	1	0	100	D121,1b25	0	3.4
ORTIZ, LUIS Luis Alberto (Galarza) B5.25.1970 Santo Domingo, D.R. BR/TR/6'0"/195 [BosA91 8/226] d8.31 Col Union (TN)																								
1993	Bos A	9	12	0	3	0	0	0	1	0	0	0	2	.250	.250	.250	.500	-67	0	0	0	3b5,D3	0	-0.2
1994	Bos A	7	18	3	3	2	0	0	6	1	0	0	5	.167	.182	.278	.460	-77	0	0	0	D6	0	-0.2
Total	4	60	145	14	33	7	3	2	26	7	0	0	26	.228	.256	.359	.615	-42	0	1	0	3b40,D13	0	-1.7
Team	2	16	30	3	6	2	0	0	7	1	0	0	7	.200	.206	.267	.473	-73	0	0	0	D9,3b5	0	-0.4
OSTDIEK, HARRY Henry Girard B4.12.1881 Ottumwa IA D5.6.1956 Minneapolis MN BR/TR/5'11"/185 d9.10																								
1908	Bos A	1	3	0	0	0	0	0	0	0		0		.000	.000	.000	.000	-197	0			/C		-0.1
Total	2	8	21	1	3	0	1	0	3	3		1		.143	.280	.238	.518	-35	1			C8		-0.1
OSTROWSKI, JOHNNY John Thaddeus B10.17.1917 Chicago IL D11.13.1992 Chicago IL BR/TR/5'10.5"/170 d9.24																								
1948	Bos A	1	1	0	0	0	0	0	0	0		0	1	.000	.000	.000	.000	-195	0	0	0	/H	0	0.0
Total	7	216	561	73	131	20	9	14	74	68		4	125	.234	.321	.376	.697	-11	7	3	100	O108(87/9/15),3b66/2	0	-1.8
OWEN, MICKEY Arnold Malcolm B4.4.1916 Nixa MO D7.13.2005 Mount Vernon MO BR/TR/5'10"/190 d5.2 Mil 1945 C2																								
1954	Bos A	32	68	6	16	3	0	1	11	9		0	6	.235	.309	.324	.633	-30	0	1	0	C30	0	-0.3
Total	13	1209	3649	338	929	163	21	14	378	326		13	181	.255	.318	.322	.640	-24	36	1	100	C1175,3b3/2S	0	-4.6
OWEN, MARV Marvin James "Freck" B3.22.1906 Agnew CA D6.22.1991 Mountain View CA BR/TR/6'1"/175 d4.16 Col Santa Clara																								
1940	Bos A	20	57	4	12	0	0	0	6	8		0	4	.211	.308	.211	.519	-64	0	0	0	3b9,1b8		-0.4
Total	9	1011	3782	473	1040	167	44	31	497	338		27	283	.275	.339	.367	.706	-20	30	30	50	3b921,1b37,S37,2b4		-11.3
OWEN, SPIKE Spike Dee B4.19.1961 Cleburne TX BB/TR/5'10"/(160–170) [SeaA82 1/6] d6.25 b–Dave Col Texas																								
1986	†Bos A	42	126	21	23	2	1	1	10	17	0	1	9	.183	.283	.238	.521	-56	3	1	75	S42	0	-0.6
1987	Bos A	132	437	50	113	17	7	2	48	53	2	1	43	.259	.337	.343	.680	-20	11	8	58	S130	0	-1.1
1988	†Bos A	89	257	40	64	14	1	5	18	27	0	2	27	.249	.324	.370	.694	-10	0	1	0	S76,D7	0	0.0
Total	13	1544	4930	587	1211	215	59	46	439	569	57	15	519	.246	.324	.341	.665	-17	82	62	57	S1373,3b99,2b17,D11,1b4	73	5.9
Team	3	263	820	111	200	33	9	8	76	97	2	4	79	.244	.324	.335	.659	-23	14	10	58	S248,D7	0	-1.7
/150	2	150	468	63	114	19	5	5	43	55	1	2	45	.244	.324	.335	.659	-23	8	6	57	S141,D4	0	-1.0
OWENS, FRANK Frank Walter "Yip" B1.26.1886 Toronto ON, Can. D7.2.1958 Minneapolis MN BR/TR/6'0"/170 d9.11																								
1905	Bos A	1	2	0	0	0	0	0	0	0		0		.000	.000	.000	.000	-199	0			/C		-0.1
Total	4	222	694	59	170	25	11	5	65	34		4	50	.245	.284	.334	.618	-23	9			C215		-3.6
PAGLIARONI, JIM James Vincent "Pag" B12.8.1937 Dearborn MI BR/TR/6'4"/(200–210) d8.13 Mil 1956–57																								
1955	Bos A	1	0	0	0	0	0	0	1	0	0	0	0	+	.000	+	.000	-100	0	0	0	/C	0	0.0
1960	Bos A	28	62	7	19	5	2	2	9	13	0	1	11	.306	.434	.548	.982	+58	0	0	0	C18	0	0.7
1961	Bos A	120	376	50	91	17	0	16	58	55	0	4	74	.242	.342	.415	.757	+0	1	1	50	C108	0	0.4
1962	Bos A	90	260	39	67	14	0	11	37	36	0	5	55	.258	.359	.438	.797	+10	2	1	67	C73	0	0.7
Total	11	849	2465	269	622	98	7	90	326	330	39	25	494	.252	.344	.407	.751	+9	4	7	36	C767,1b2/rf	99	5.3
Team	4	239	698	96	177	36	2	29	105	104	0	10	140	.254	.357	.436	.793	+9	3	2	60	C199	0	1.8
/150	3	150	438	60	111	23	1	18	66	65	0	6	88	.254	.357	.436	.793	+9	2	1	67	C125	0	1.1
PANKOVITS, JIM James Franklin B8.6.1955 Pennington Gap VA BR/TR/5'10"/(174–175) [HouN76 4/73] d5.27 Col South Carolina OF(28/0/20)																								
1990	Bos A	2	0	0	0	0	0	0	0	0	0	0	0	+	+	+	.000	-100	0	0	0	2b2	0	-0.1
Total	6	318	567	62	142	25	2	9	55	44	3	3	115	.250	.307	.349	.656	-14	8	3	73	2b104,O47L,3b16,S5,1b2/C	41	-1.1
PAPI, STAN Stanley Gerard B2.4.1951 Fresno CA BR/TR/6'0"/(165–180) [HouN69 2/26] d4.11																								
1979	Bos A	50	117	9	22	8	0	1	6	5	0	0	20	.188	.221	.282	.503	-67	0	0	0	2b26,S21/D	47	-0.2
1980	Bos A	1	0	0	0	0	0	0	0	0	0	0	0	+	+	+	.000	-100	0	0	0	/3	0	0.0
Total	6	225	523	49	114	26	6	7	51	24	1	2	99	.218	.253	.331	.584	-41	2	0	100	3b69,2b65,S57,D4,1b2/lf	47	-3.1
Team	2	51	117	9	22	8	0	1	6	5	0	0	20	.188	.221	.282	.503	-67	0	0	0	2b26,S21/3D	47	-0.2
PARENT, FREDDY Frederick Alfred B11.25.1875 Biddeford ME D11.2.1972 Sanford ME BR/TR/5'7"/154 d7.14																								
1899	StL N	2	8	0	1	0	0	0	1	0		0		.125	.125	.125	.250	-131	0			2b2		-0.2
1901	Bos A	**138**	517	87	158	23	9	4	59	41		9		.306	.367	.408	.775	+17	16			S138		1.4
1902	Bos A	**138**	567	91	156	31	8	3	62	24		4		.275	.309	.374	.683	-14	16			S138		-0.7
1903	†Bos A	139	560	83	170	31	17	4	80	13		6		.304	.326	.441	.767	+22	24			S139		2.6
1904	Bos A	155	591	85	172	22	9	6	77	28		6		.291	.330	.389	.719	+20	20			S155		0.9
1905	Bos A	**153**	602	55	141	16	5	0	33	47		6		.234	.296	.277	.573	-19	25			S153		-2.0
1906	Bos A	149	600	67	141	14	10	1	49	31		4		.235	.277	.297	.574	-20	16			S143,2b6		-1.7
1907	Bos A	114	409	51	113	19	5	1	26	22		5		.276	.321	.355	.676	+16	12			O47(26/13/9),S43,3b7,2b5		0.6
1908	Chi A	119	391	28	81	7	5	0	35	50		2		.207	.300	.251	.551	-19	9			S118		-0.1
1909	Chi A	136	472	61	123	10	5	0	30	46		7		.261	.335	.303	.638	+6	32			S98,O38(7/30/1)/2		2.3
1910	Chi A	81	258	23	46	6	1	1	16	29		2		.178	.266	.221	.487	-45	14			O62(1/59/2),2b11,S4/3		-2.0
1911	Chi A	3	9	2	4	1	0	0	3	2		0		.444	.545	.556	1.101	+114	0			2b3		0.2

Year	Tm Lg	G	AB	R	H	2B	3B	HR	RBI	BB	IB	HP	SO	AVG	OBP	SLG	OPS	AOPS	SB	CS	SB%	Games at Position	DL	BFW
Total	12	1327	4984	633	1306	180	74	20	471	333		51		.262	.315	.340	.655	-1	184			S1129,O147(34/102/12),2b28,3b8		1.3
Team	7	986	3846	519	1051	156	63	19	386	206		40	0	.273	.317	.361	.678	+2	129			S909,O47(26/13/9),2b11,3b7		1.1
/150	1	150	585	79	160	24	10	3	59	31		6	0	.273	.317	.361	.678	+2	20			S138,O7(4/2/1),2b2/3		0.2
PARRISH, LARRY	Larry Alton B11.10.1953 Winter Haven FL BR/TR/6'3"/(190–215) d9.6 M2/C2 Col Seminole (FL) CC OF(3/0/405)																							
1988	†Bos A	52	158	10	41	5	0	7	26	8	0	1	32	.259	.298	.424	.722	-4	0	1	0	1b36,D14	0	-0.2
Total	15	1891	6792	850	1789	360	33	256	992	529	79	42	1359	.263	.318	.439	.757	+6	30	36	45	3b1021,O407R,D401,1b36/S2	114	-10.7
PARTEE, ROY	Roy Robert B9.7.1917 Los Angeles CA D12.27.2000 Eureka CA BR/TR/5'10"/180 d4.23 Mil 1945																							
1943	Bos A	96	299	30	84	14	2	0	31	39		2	33	.281	.368	.341	.709	+6	0	0	0	C91	0	0.5
1944	Bos A	89	280	18	68	12	0	2	41	37		1	29	.243	.333	.307	.640	-15	0	1	0	C85	0	-0.3
1946	†Bos A	40	111	13	35	5	2	0	9	13		0	14	.315	.387	.396	.783	+13	0	0	0	C38	0	0.0
1947	Bos A	60	169	14	39	2	0	0	16	18		0	23	.231	.305	.243	.548	-50	0	0	0	C54	0	-0.9
1948	StL A	82	231	14	47	8	1	0	17	25		1	21	.203	.284	.247	.531	-59	2	2	50	C76	0	-2.0
Total	5	367	1090	89	273	41	5	2	114	132		4	120	.250	.334	.303	.637	-22	2	3	40	C344	0	-2.7
Team	4	285	859	75	226	33	4	2	97	107		3	99	.263	.347	.318	.665	-11	0	1	0	C268	0	-0.7
/150	2	150	452	39	119	17	2	1	51	56		2	52	.263	.347	.318	.665	-11	0	1	0	C141	0	-0.4
PASCHAL, BEN	Benjamin Edwin B10.13.1895 Enterprise AL D11.10.1974 Charlotte NC BR/TR/5'11"/185 d8.16																							
1920	Bos A	9	28	5	10	0	0	0	5	5		0	2	.357	.455	.357	.812	+22	1	0	100	O7R		0.1
Total	8	364	787	143	243	47	11	24	138	72		3	93	.309	.369	.488	.857	+23	24	19	100	O223(67/44/114)		1.1
PATTERSON, HANK	Henry Joseph Colquit B7.17.1907 San Francisco CA D9.30.1970 Los Angeles CA BR/TR/5'11.5"/170 d9.5 C1																							
1932	Bos A	1	1	0	0	0	0	0	0	0		0	0	.000	.000	.000	.000	-199	0	0	0	/C		0.0
PAVLETICH, DON	Donald Stephen B7.13.1938 Milwaukee WI BR/TR/5'11"/(190–214) d4.20 Mil 1957–58																							
1970	Bos A	32	65	4	9	1	1	0	6	10	0	0	15	.138	.250	.185	.435	-79	1	0	100	1b16,C10	0	-1.1
1971	Bos A	14	27	5	7	1	0	1	3	5	0	0	5	.259	.375	.407	.782	+13	0	0	0	C8	0	0.0
Total	12	536	1373	163	349	73	8	46	193	148	26	8	237	.254	.328	.420	.748	+3	5	2	71	C291,1b159/3	31	-1.7
Team	2	46	92	9	16	2	1	1	9	15	0	0	20	.174	.287	.250	.537	-51	1	0	100	C18,1b16	0	-1.1
PAYTON, JAY	Jason Lee B11.22.1972 Zanesville OH BR/TR/5'10"/185 [NYN94 S1/29] d9.1 Col Georgia Tech																							
2005	Bos A	55	133	24	35	7	0	5	21	10	0	0	14	.263	.313	.429	.742	-9	0	0	0	O53(13/16/31)	0	-0.1
Total	9	981	3347	469	952	158	22	105	422	210	9	28	404	.284	.330	.439	.769	-2	33	29	53	O938(329/569/82),D5	113	-1.7
PEACOCK, JOHNNY	John Gaston B1.10.1910 Fremont NC D10.17.1981 Wilson NC BL/TR/5'11"/165 d9.23 Col North Carolina																							
1937	Bos A	9	32	3	10	2	1	0	6	1		0	0	.313	.333	.438	.771	-11	0	0	0	C9		0.1
1938	Bos A	72	195	29	59	7	1	1	39	17		0	4	.303	.358	.364	.722	-22	4	1	80	C57/1lf		-0.8
1939	Bos A	92	274	33	76	11	4	0	36	29		0	11	.277	.347	.347	.694	-25	1	1	50	C84		-1.0
1940	Bos A	63	131	20	37	4	1	0	13	23		0	10	.282	.390	.328	.718	-15	1	1	50	C48		-0.6
1941	Bos A	79	261	28	74	20	1	0	27	21		1	3	.284	.339	.368	.707	-15	2	1	67	C70	0	-0.2
1942	Bos A	88	286	17	76	7	3	0	25	21		0	11	.266	.316	.311	.627	-26	1	1	50	C82	0	-0.8
1943	Bos A	48	114	7	23	3	1	0	7	10		0	9	.202	.266	.246	.512	-51	1	1	50	C32	0	-0.8
1944	Bos A	4	4	0	0	0	0	0	0	0		0	0	.000	.000	.000	.000	-199	0	0	0	C2	0	-0.1
1944	Phi N	83	253	21	57	9	3	0	21	31		0	15	.225	.310	.285	.595	-30	1			C73/2	0	-0.5
1944	Major	87	257	21	57	9	3	0	21	31	0	0	15	.222	.306	.280	.586	-772	1	0			0	-0.6
1945	Phi N	33	74	6	15	6	0	0	6	6		0	0	.203	.262	.284	.546	-47	1			C23	0	-0.7
1945	Bro N	48	110	11	28	5	1	0	14	24		0	10	.255	.388	.318	.706	-2	2			C38	0	0.3
1945	Year	81	184	17	43	11	1	0	20	30		0	10	.234	.341	.304	.645	-18	3			C61	0	-0.4
Total	9	619	1734	175	455	74	16	1	194	183		1	73	.262	.333	.325	.658	-24	14	6	100	C518/2lf1	0	-5.1
Team	8	455	1297	137	355	54	12	1	153	122		1	48	.274	.337	.336	.673	-24	10	6	63	C384/1lf	0	-4.2
/150	3	150	428	45	117	18	4	0	50	40		0	16	.274	.337	.336	.673	-24	3	2	60	C127/1OfL	0	-1.4
PEDROIA, DUSTIN	Dustin Luis B8.17.1983 Woodland CA BR/TR/5'9"/180 [BosA04 2/65] d8.22 Col Arizona St.																							
2006	Bos A	31	89	5	17	4	0	2	7	7	0	1	7	.191	.258	.303	.561	-56	0	1	0	2b27,S6	0	0.1
PELLAGRINI, EDDIE	Edward Charles B3.13.1918 Boston MA D10.11.2006 Weymouth MA BR/TR/5'9"/(160–165) d4.22 Col Boston College																							
1946	Bos A	22	71	7	15	3	1	2	4	3		1	18	.211	.253	.366	.619	-32	1	0	100	3b14,S9	0	-0.6
1947	Bos A	74	231	29	47	8	1	4	19	23		2	35	.203	.281	.299	.580	-43	2	2	50	3b42,S26	0	-2.0
Total	8	563	1423	167	321	42	13	20	133	128		13	201	.226	.295	.316	.611	-38	13	7	65	S222,2b113,3b106,1b8	0	-5.9
Team	2	96	302	36	62	11	2	6	23	26		3	53	.205	.275	.315	.590	-41	3	2	60	3b56,S35	0	-2.6
PEMBERTON, RUDY	Rudy Hector (Perez) B12.17.1969 San Pedro de Macoris, D.R. BR/TR/6'1"/185 d4.26																							
1995	Det A	12	30	3	9	3	1	0	3	1	0	1	5	.300	.344	.467	.811	+8	0	0	0	O8(6/0/2),D3	0	0.0
1996	Bos A	13	41	11	21	8	0	1	10	2	0	2	4	.512	.556	.780	1.336	+129	3	1	75	O13(1/0/12)	0	0.5
1997	Bos A	27	63	8	15	2	0	2	10	4	0	3	13	.238	.314	.365	.679	-25	0	0	0	O23R	0	-0.3
Total	3	52	134	22	45	13	1	3	23	7	0	6	22	.336	.395	.515	.910	+30	3	1	75	O44(7/0/37),D3	0	0.2
Team	2	40	104	19	36	10	0	3	20	6	0	5	17	.346	.409	.529	.938	+35	3	1	75	O36(1/0/12)	0	0.2
PENA, TONY	Antonio Francisco (Padilla) B6.4.1957 Monte Cristi, D.R. BR/TR/6'0"/(175–190) d9.1 M4/C2 b–Ramon s–Tony																							
1990	†Bos A	143	491	62	129	19	1	7	56	43	3	1	71	.263	.322	.348	.670	-16	8	6	57	C142/1	0	0.8
1991	Bos A	141	464	45	107	23	2	5	48	37	1	4	53	.231	.291	.321	.612	-34	8	3	73	C140	0	-0.1
1992	Bos A	133	410	39	99	21	1	1	38	24	0	1	61	.241	.284	.305	.589	-39	3	2	60	C132	0	0.5
1993	Bos A	126	304	20	55	11	0	4	19	25	0	2	46	.181	.246	.257	.503	-66	1	3	25	C125/D	0	-0.2
Total	18	1988	6489	667	1687	298	27	107	708	455	72	23	846	.260	.309	.364	.673	-17	80	63	56	C1950,1b13,O3R/3D	58	13.1
Team	4	543	1669	166	390	74	4	17	161	129	4	8	231	.234	.290	.313	.603	-36	20	14	59	C539/1D	0	1.0
/150	1	150	461	46	108	20	1	5	44	36	1	2	64	.234	.290	.313	.603	-36	6	4	60	C149/1D	0	0.3
PENA, CARLOS	Carlos Felipe B5.17.1978 Santo Domingo, D.R. BL/TL/6'2"/(210–215) [TexA98 1/10] d9.5 Col Northeastern																							
2006	Bos A	18	33	3	9	2	0	1	3	4	0	0	10	.273	.351	.424	.775	-3	0	0	0	1b17/lf	0	-0.1
Total	6	507	1685	229	410	75	15	86	243	209	5	16	502	.243	.331	.459	.790	+9	13	9	59	1b460,D33/lf	25	-1.9
PENA, WILY MO	Wily Modesto B1.23.1982 Laguna Salada, D.R. BR/TR/6'3"/(215–245) d9.10 [DL 2000 NY A 80]																							
2006	Bos A	84	276	36	83	15	2	11	42	20	0	3	90	.301	.349	.489	.838	+13	0	1	0	O76(18/27/39),D5	52	0.3
Total	5	386	1106	144	289	48	4	62	176	74	3	15	378	.261	.315	.480	.795	+4	10	6	63	O301(40/124/155),D5/3	192	-0.5
PEREZ, TONY	Atanasio (Rigal) B5.14.1942 Ciego de Avila, Cuba BR/TR/6'2"/(175–215) d7.26 M2/C6 HF2000 s–Eduardo																							
1980	Bos A	151	585	73	161	31	3	25	105	41	11	1	93	.275	.320	.467	.787	+8	1	0	100	1b137,D13	0	-0.8
1981	Bos A	84	306	35	77	11	3	9	39	27	0	0	66	.252	.310	.395	.705	-4	0	0	0	1b56,D23	0	-0.8
1982	Bos A	69	196	18	51	14	2	6	31	19	3	0	48	.260	.326	.444	.770	+3	0	1	0	D46,1b2	0	-0.1
Total	23	2777	9778	1272	2732	505	79	379	1652	925	15	43	1867	.279	.341	.463	.804	+21	49	33	60	1b1778,3b760,D82/2	0	10.0
Team	3	304	1087	126	289	56	8	40	175	87	14	1	207	.266	.318	.443	.761	+4	1	1	50	1b195,D82	0	-1.7
/150	1	150	536	62	143	28	4	20	86	43	7	0	102	.266	.318	.443	.761	+4	0	0	0	1b96,D40	0	-0.8
PERRIN, JOHN	John Stephenson B2.4.1898 Escanaba MI D6.24.1969 Detroit MI BL/TR/5'9"/160 d7.11 Col Michigan																							
1921	Bos A	4	13	3	3	0	0	0	1	0		0	3	.231	.231	.231	.462	-81	0	0	0	O4R		-0.2
PESKY, JOHNNY	John Michael (b John Michael Paveskovich) B9.27.1919 Portland OR BL/TR/5'9"/(165–168) d4.14 Mil 1943–45 M3/C13																							
1942	Bos A	147	620	105	**205**	29	9	2	51	42		2	36	.331	.375	.416	.791	+18	12	7	63	S147	0	4.5
1946	†Bos A★	153	621	115	**208**	43	4	2	55	65		3	29	.335	.401	.427	.828	+24	9	8	53	S153	0	4.6
1947	Bos A	155	638	106	**207**	27	8	0	39	72		0	22	.324	.393	.392	.785	+10	12	9	57	S133,3b22	0	0.9
1948	Bos A	143	565	124	159	26	6	3	55	99		6	32	.281	.394	.365	.759	-2	3	5	38	3b141	0	0.8
1949	Bos A	148	604	111	185	27	7	2	69	100		4	19	.306	.408	.384	.792	+3	8	4	67	3b148	0	2.5
1950	Bos A	127	490	112	153	22	6	1	49	104		5	31	.312	.437	.388	.825	+3	2	1	67	3b116,S8	0	2.3
1951	Bos A	131	480	93	150	20	6	3	41	84		2	15	.313	.417	.398	.815	+10	2	2	50	S106,3b11,2b5	0	2.0
1952	Bos A	25	67	10	10	2	0	0	2	15		1	5	.149	.313	.179	.492	-64	0	3	0	3b19,S2	0	-1.1
1952	Det A	69	177	26	45	4	0	1	9	41		0	11	.254	.394	.294	.688	-7	1	2	33	S41,2b22,3b3	0	0.1
1952	Year	94	244	36	55	6	0	1	11	56		1	16	.225	.372	.262	.634	-23	1	5	17	S43,3b22,2b22	0	-1.0
1953	Det A	103	308	43	90	22	1	2	24	27		2	10	.292	.353	.390	.743	+2	3	7	30	2b73	0	-0.2

Year	Tm Lg	G	AB	R	H	2B	3B	HR	RBI	BB	IB	HP	SO	AVG	OBP	SLG	OPS	AOPS	SB	CS	SB%	Games at Position	DL	BFW
1954	Det A	20	17	5	3	0	0	1	1	3		0	1	.176	.300	.353	.653	-20	0	0	0	/H	0	-0.1
1954	Was A	49	158	17	40	4	3	0	9	10		0	7	.253	.296	.316	.612	-28	1	1	50	2b37/S	0	-0.8
1954	Year	69	175	22	43	4	3	1	10	13		0	8	.246	.296	.320	.616	-28	1	1	50	2b37/S	0	-0.9
Total	10	1270	4745	867	1455	226	50	17	404	662		25	218	.307	.394	.386	.780	+6	53	49	52	S591,3b460,2b137	0	15.5
Team	8	1029	4085	776	1277	196	46	13	361	581		23	189	.313	.401	.393	.794	+8	48	39	55	S549,3b457,2b5	0	16.5
/150	1	150	595	113	186	29	7	2	53	85		3	28	.313	.401	.393	.794	+8	7	6	54	S80,3b67/2	0	2.4
PETAGINE, ROBERTO Roberto Antonio (Guerra) B6.7.1971 Nueva Esparta, Venezuela BL/TL/6'1"/(170–172) d4.4																								
2005	Bos A	18	32	4	9	2	0	1	9	4	0	0	5	.281	.361	.438	.799	+7	0	0	0	1b10,O2L,D3	0	0.0
Total	7	242	366	48	83	17	1	12	54	63	3	4	103	.227	.345	.377	.722	-7	1	2	33	1b133,O20(5/0/16),D3	0	-0.6
PETERSON, BOB Robert Andrew B6.16.1884 Philadelphia PA D11.27.1962 Evesham Twp. NJ BR/TR/6'1"/160 d4.18																								
1906	Bos A	39	118	10	24	1	1	1	9	11		1		.203	.277	.254	.531	-33	1			C30,2b3,1b2/lf		-1.2
1907	Bos A	4	13	1	1	0	0	0	0	0		0		.077	.077	.077	.154	-151	0			C4		-0.2
Total	2	43	131	11	25	1	1	1	9	11		1		.191	.259	.237	.496	-44	1			C34,2b3,1b2/lf		-1.4
PETROCELLI, RICO Americo Peter B6.27.1943 Brooklyn NY BR/TR/6'0"/(175–185) d9.21																								
1963	Bos A	1	4	0	1	1	0	0	1	0	0	0	1	.250	.250	.500	.750	+1	0	0	0	/S	0	0.0
1965	Bos A	103	323	38	75	15	2	13	33	36	4	1	71	.232	.309	.412	.721	-2	0	2	0	S93	0	1.6
1966	Bos A	139	522	58	124	20	1	18	59	41	2	3	99	.238	.295	.383	.678	-15	1	1	50	S127,3b5	18	0.6
1967	†Bos A★	142	491	53	127	24	2	17	66	49	9	5	93	.259	.330	.420	.750	+12	2	4	33	S141	0	2.6
1968	Bos A	123	406	41	95	17	2	12	46	31	2	4	73	.234	.292	.374	.666	-4	0	1	0	S117/1	0	2.1
1969	Bos A★	154	535	92	159	32	2	40	97	98	13	1	68	.297	.403	.589	.992	+68	3	5	38	S153/3	0	**7.6**
1970	Bos A	157	583	82	152	31	3	29	103	67	6	2	82	.261	.334	.473	.807	+14	1	1	50	S141,3b18	0	2.7
1971	Bos A	158	553	82	139	24	4	28	89	91	5	2	108	.251	.354	.461	.815	+22	2	0	100	3b156	0	1.7
1972	Bos A	147	521	62	125	15	2	15	75	78	9	2	91	.240	.339	.363	.702	+3	0	1	0	3b146	0	1.0
1973	Bos A	100	356	44	87	13	1	13	45	47	3	1	64	.244	.333	.396	.729	-1	0	0	0	3b99	29	0.6
1974	Bos A	129	454	53	121	23	1	15	76	48	4	2	74	.267	.336	.421	.757	+10	1	0	100	3b116,D9	0	-0.7
1975	†Bos A	115	402	31	96	15	1	7	59	41	1	3	66	.239	.310	.333	.643	-23	0	2	0	3b113/D	15	-2.7
1976	Bos A	85	240	17	51	7	1	3	24	34	3	0	36	.213	.307	.287	.594	-32	0	5	0	3b73,2b5/1SD	0	-1.5
Total	13	1553	5390	653	1352	237	22	210	773	661	61	26	926	.251	.332	.420	.752	+8	10	22	31	S774,3b727,D14,2b5,1b2	62	15.6
/150	1	150	521	63	131	23	2	20	75	64	6	3	89	.251	.332	.420	.752	+8	1	2	33	S75,3b70/D21	6	1.5
PHILLEY, DAVE David Earl B5.16.1920 Paris TX BB/TR/6'0"/(185–195) d9.6 Mil 1943–45																								
1962	Bos A	38	42	3	6	2	0	0	4	5	0	1	3	.143	.250	.190	.440	-80	0	0	0	O4R	0	-0.5
Total	18	1904	6296	789	1700	276	72	84	729	594	14	17	551	.270	.334	.377	.711	-9	101	63	62	O1454(204/590/714),1b125,3b21	0	-14.9
PICINICH, VAL Valentine John B9.8.1896 New York NY D12.5.1942 Nobleboro ME BR/TR/5'9"/165 d7.25 Mil 1918 C1																								
1923	Bos A	87	268	33	74	21	1	2	31	46		2	32	.276	.386	.384	.770	+3	3	5	38	C81		0.5
1924	Bos A	69	161	25	44	6	3	1	24	29		3	19	.273	.394	.366	.760	-3	5	1	83	C52		0.1
1925	Bos A	90	251	31	64	21	0	1	25	33		1	21	.255	.344	.351	.695	-23	2	0	100	C74,1b2		-1.1
Total	18	1037	2877	298	743	166	26	26	298	314		11	382	.258	.334	.361	.695	-14	31	9	100	C935,1b2		-1.5
Team	3	246	680	89	182	48	4	4	80	108		6	72	.268	.373	.368	.741	-8	10	6	63	C207,1b2		-0.5
/150	2	150	415	54	111	29	2	2	49	66		4	44	.268	.373	.368	.741	-8	6	4	60	C126/1		-0.3
PICKERING, CALVIN Calvin Elroy B9.29.1976 St.Thomas, V.I. BL/TL/6'5"/(260–295) [BalA95 35/976] d9.12 [DL 2002 Bos A 183]																								
2001	Bos A	17	50	4	14	1	0	3	7	8	0	0	13	.280	.379	.480	.859	+24	0	0	0	1b12,D2	0	0.0
Total	5	95	264	37	59	10	1	14	45	43	1	0	91	.223	.329	.428	.757	-3	1	0	100	D46,1b33	183	-0.9
PICKERING, URBANE Urbane Henry "Pick" B6.3.1899 Hoxie KS D5.13.1970 Modesto CA BR/TR/5'10"/180 d4.18																								
1931	Bos A	103	341	48	86	13	4	9	52	33		0	53	.252	.318	.393	.711	-9	3	4	43	3b74,2b16		-0.4
1932	Bos A	132	457	47	119	28	5	2	40	39		1	71	.260	.320	.357	.677	-23	3	4	43	3b126/C		-1.6
Total	2	235	798	95	205	41	9	11	92	72		1	124	.257	.319	.372	.691	-17	6	8	43	3b200,2b16/C		-2.0
/150	1	150	509	61	131	26	6	7	59	46		1	79	.257	.319	.372	.691	-17	4	5	44	3b128,2b10/C	0	-1.3
PIERSALL, JIM James Anthony B11.14.1929 Waterbury CT BR/TR/6'0"/(175–190) d9.7 C1																								
1950	Bos A	6	7	4	2	0	0	0	0	4		0	0	.286	.545	.286	.831	+7	0	0	0	O2C	0	0.1
1952	Bos A	56	161	28	43	8	0	1	16	28		1	26	.267	.379	.335	.714	-7	3	3	50	S30,O22(0/1/21)/3	0	-0.2
1953	Bos A	151	585	76	159	21	9	3	52	41		9	52	.272	.329	.354	.683	-20	11	10	52	O151(1/2/150)	0	-1.3
1954	Bos A★	133	474	77	135	24	2	8	38	36		3	42	.285	.338	.395	.733	-10	5	1	83	O126(0/30/96)	0	-1.3
1955	Bos A	149	515	68	146	25	5	13	62	67	7	2	52	.283	.364	.427	.791	+4	6	1	86	O147C	0	-0.2
1956	Bos A★	**155**	601	91	176	**40**	6	14	87	58	2	1	48	.293	.350	.449	.799	-1	7	7	50	O155C	0	-0.2
1957	Bos A	151	609	103	159	27	5	19	63	62	1	4	54	.261	.331	.415	.746	-2	14	6	70	O151C	0	-0.6
1958	Bos A	130	417	55	99	13	5	8	48	42	2	0	43	.237	.303	.350	.653	-25	12	2	86	O125C	0	-1.5
1959	Cle A	100	317	42	78	13	2	4	30	25	1	2	31	.246	.303	.338	.641	-21	6	3	67	O91C/3	0	-1.2
1960	Cle A	138	486	70	137	12	4	18	66	24	3	0	38	.282	.313	.434	.747	+4	18	5	78	O134(8/127/2)	0	0.4
1961	Cle A	121	484	81	156	26	7	6	40	43	1	2	46	.322	.378	.442	.820	+22	8	2	80	O120C	0	2.0
1962	Was A	135	471	38	115	20	4	4	31	39	3	0	53	.244	.301	.329	.630	-30	12	7	63	O132C	0	-2.4
1963	Was A	29	94	9	23	1	0	1	5	6	0	0	11	.245	.284	.287	.571	-37	4	0	100	O25C	0	-0.5
1963	NY N	40	124	13	24	4	1	1	10	10	1	0	14	.194	.250	.266	.516	-51	1	2	33	O38C	0	-1.2
1963	LA A	20	52	4	16	1	0	0	4	5	0	0	5	.308	.368	.327	.695	+3	0	1	0	O18(1/12/5)	0	-0.3
1963	Major	89	270	26	63	6	1	2	19	21	1	0	30	.233	4.289	.285	4.574	-13	5	3	63		0	-2.0
1964	LA A	87	255	28	80	11	0	2	13	16	1	0	32	.314	.353	.380	.733	+16	5	3	63	O72(48/32/0)	0	0.0
1965	Cal A	53	112	10	30	5	2	2	12	5	1	1	15	.268	.305	.402	.707	+1	2	2	50	O41(29/10/4)	55	-0.1
1966	Cal A	75	123	14	26	5	0	0	14	13	0	0	19	.211	.283	.252	.535	-42	1	2	33	O63(25/14/27)	0	-1.0
1967	Cal A	5	3	0	0	0	0	0	0	0	0	0	2	.000	.000	.000	.000	-199	0	0	0	/lf	0	-0.1
Total	17	1734	5890	811	1604	256	52	104	591	524	23	25	583	.272	.332	.386	.718	-8	115	57	67	O1614(113/1214/305),S30,3b2	55	-9.6
Team	8	931	3369	502	919	158	32	66	366	338	12	20	317	.273	.340	.397	.737	-8	58	30	66	O879(2/18/11),S30/3	0	-5.2
/150	1	150	543	81	148	25	5	11	59	54	2	3	51	.273	.340	.397	.737	-8	9	5	64	O142(0/3/2),S5/3	0	-0.8
PIRKL, GREG Gregory Daniel B8.7.1970 Long Beach CA BR/TR/6'5"/(225–240) [SeaA88 2/44] d8.13																								
1996	Bos A	2	2	0	0	0	0	0	0	0	0	0	1	.000	.000	.000	.000	-198	0	0	0	/H	0	-0.1
Total	4	45	116	12	26	4	0	8	16	2	1	1	27	.224	.242	.466	.708	-23	0	0	0	1b20,D16	71	-0.7
PITTINGER, PINKY Clarke Alonzo B2.24.1899 Hudson MI D11.4.1977 Ft.Lauderdale FL BR/TR/5'10"/160 d4.15 Col Ohio St.																								
1921	Bos A	40	91	6	18	1	0	0	5	4		0	13	.198	.232	.209	.441	-87	3	2	60	O27(19/4/4),3b3,S2/2		-1.0
1922	Bos A	66	186	16	48	3	0	0	7	9		2	10	.258	.299	.274	.573	-49	2	5	29	3b33,S29		-1.2
1923	Bos A	60	177	15	38	5	0	0	15	5		0	10	.215	.236	.243	.479	-74	3	1	75	2b42,S10,3b3		-2.5
1925	Chi N	59	173	21	54	7	2	0	15	12		2	7	.312	.364	.376	.740	-12	5	4	56	S24,3b24		0.2
1927	Cin N	31	84	17	23	5	0	1	10	2		0	5	.274	.291	.369	.660	-22	4			2b20,S9,3b2		-0.1
1928	Cin N	40	38	12	9	0	1	0	4	0		0	1	.237	.237	.289	.526	-63	2			S12,2b4,3b4		0.1
1929	Cin N	77	210	31	62	11	0	0	27	5		2	4	.295	.318	.348	.666	-32	8			S50,3b8,2b4		-0.3
Total	7	373	959	118	252	32	3	1	83	37		6	50	.263	.294	.306	.600	-45	27	12	100	S136,3b77,2b71,O27(19/4/4)		-4.8
Team	3	166	454	37	104	9	0	0	27	18		2	33	.229	.262	.249	.511	-66	8	8	50	2b43,S41,3b39,O27(19/4/4)		-4.7
/150	3	150	410	33	94	8	0	0	24	16		2	30	.229	.262	.249	.511	-66	7	7	50	2b39,S37,3b35,O24(17/4/4)		-4.2
PLANTIER, PHIL Phillip Alan B1.27.1969 Manchester NH BL/TR/5'11"/(175–205) [BosA87 11/292] d8.21																								
1990	Bos A	14	15	1	2	1	0	0	3	4	0	1	6	.133	.333	.200	.533	-45	0	0	0	/lfD	0	-0.1
1991	Bos A	53	148	27	49	7	1	11	35	23	2	1	38	.331	.420	.615	1.035	+74	1	0	100	O40(16/0/27),D5	0	1.6
1992	Bos A	108	349	46	86	19	0	7	30	44	8	2	83	.246	.332	.361	.693	-12	2	3	40	O76(13/0/63),D23	0	-0.7
Total	8	610	1883	260	457	90	3	91	292	237	27	23	476	.243	.332	.439	.771	+3	13	15	46	O504(382/1/126),D33	153	0.4
Team	3	175	512	74	137	27	1	18	68	71	10	4	127	.268	.358	.430	.788	+12	3	3	50	O116(1/2/2),D29	0	0.8
/150	3	150	439	63	117	23	1	15	58	61	9	3	109	.268	.358	.430	.788	+12	3	3	50	O99(1/2/2),D25	0	0.7
PLEWS, HERB Herbert Eugene B6.14.1928 Helena MT BL/TR/5'11"/(160–165) d4.18 Col Illinois																								
1959	Bos A	13	12	0	1	1	0	0	0	0	0	0	4	.083	.083	.167	.250	-132	0	0	0	2b2	0	-0.1
Total	4	346	1017	125	266	42	17	4	82	74	5	4	133	.262	.312	.348	.660	-20	3	9	25	2b217,3b49,S9	0	-3.1

Year	Tm Lg	G	AB	R	H	2B	3B	HR	RBI	BB	IB	HP	SO	AVG	OBP	SLG	OPS	AOPS	SB	CS	SB%	Games at Position	DL	BFW
POLLY, NICK Nicholas (b Nicholas Joseph Polachanin) B4.18.1917 Chicago IL D1.17.1993 Chicago IL BR/TR/5'11"/190 d9.11																								
1945	Bos A	4	7	0	1	0	0	0	1	0		0	1	.143	.143	.143	.286	-117	0	0	0	3b2	0	-0.1
Total	2	14	25	2	5	0	0	0	3	0		0	2	.200	.200	.200	.400	-89	0	0	0	3b9	0	-0.2
POND, RALPH Ralph Benjamin B5.4.1890 Eau Claire WI D9.8.1947 Cleveland OH TR/5'9"/? d6.8 Col Maine																								
1910	Bos A	1	4	0	1	0	0	0	0	0		0		.250	.250	.250	.500	-45	1			/cf		-0.1
POQUETTE, TOM Thomas Arthur B10.30.1951 Eau Claire WI BL/TR/5'10"/175 [KCA70 4/81] d9.1 C2 [DL 1980 Bos A 180]																								
1979	Bos A	63	154	14	51	9	0	2	23	8	1	3	7	.331	.365	.429	.794	+10	2	2	50	O43(3/30/11),D4	0	-0.3
1981	Bos A	3	2	0	0	0	0	0	0	0	0	0	0	.000	.000	.000	.000	-194	0	0	0	O2L	0	-0.1
Total	7	452	1226	127	329	62	18	10	136	81	7	15	82	.268	.317	.373	.690	-8	13	13	50	O373(241/39/105),D7	215	-3.3
Team	2	66	156	14	51	9	0	2	23	8	1	3	7	.327	.360	.423	.783	+8	2	2	50	O45(3/30/11),D4	180	-0.4
PORTER, DICK Richard Twilley "Wiggles","Twitches" B12.30.1901 Princess Anne MD D9.24.1974 Philadelphia PA BL/TR/5'10"/170 d4.16																								
1934	Bos A	80	265	30	80	13	6	0	56	21		1	15	.302	.355	.396	.751	-13	5	2	71	O65(1/0/64)		-1.3
Total	6	675	2515	426	774	159	37	11	282	268		7	186	.308	.376	.414	.790	-1	23	27	46	O599(12/0/589),2b21		-6.7
POULSEN, KEN Ken Sterling B8.4.1947 Van Nuys CA BL/TR/6'1"/190 [BosA65 3/45] d7.3																								
1967	Bos A	5	5	0	1	1	0	0	0	0	0	0	2	.200	.200	.400	.600	-32	0	0	0	3b2/S	0	0.0
POZO, ARQUIMEDEZ Arquimedez (Ortiz) B8.24.1973 Santo Domingo, D.R. BR/TR/5'10"/160 d9.12																								
1995	Sea A	1	1	0	0	0	0	0	0	0	0	0	0	.000	.000	.000	.000	-199	0	0	0	/2	0	0.0
1996	Bos A	21	58	4	10	3	1	1	11	2	0	1	10	.172	.210	.310	.520	-70	1	0	100	2b10,3b10	0	-0.5
1997	Bos A	4	15	0	4	1	0	0	3	0	0	0	5	.267	.250	.333	.583	-46	0	0	0	3b4	0	0.2
Total	3	26	74	4	14	4	1	1	14	2	0	1	15	.189	.215	.311	.526	-67	1	0	100	3b14,2b11	0	-0.3
Team	2	25	73	4	14	4	1	1	14	2	0	1	15	.192	.218	.315	.533	-65	1	0	100	3b14,2b10	0	-0.3
PRATT, DEL Derrill Burnham B1.10.1888 Walhalla SC D9.30.1977 Texas City TX BR/TR/5'11"/175 d4.11 Col Alabama OF(3/3/8)																								
1921	Bos A	135	521	80	169	36	10	5	102	44		1	10	.324	.378	.461	.839	+16	8	10	44	2b134		1.4
1922	Bos A	**154**	607	73	183	44	7	6	86	53		4	20	.301	.361	.427	.788	+6	7	10	41	2b154		-0.6
Total	13	1836	6826	856	1996	392	117	43	968	513		37	360	.292	.345	.403	.748	+12	247	10	100	2b1688,1b79,S22,3b17,O14R		22.5
Team	2	289	1128	153	352	80	17	11	188	97		5	30	.312	.369	.442	.811	+11	15	20	43	2b288		0.8
/150	1	150	585	79	183	42	9	6	98	50		3	16	.312	.369	.442	.811	+11	8	10	44	2b149		0.4
PRATT, LARRY Lester John B10.8.1887 Gibson City IL D1.8.1969 Peoria IL BR/TR/6'0"/183 d9.19																								
1914	Bos A	5	4	0	0	0	0	0	0	0		0	4	.000	.000	.000	.000	-199	0			C5		0.0
Total	2	30	57	7	11	3	0	1	2	5		0	23	.193	.258	.298	.556	-42	4			C25		-0.4
PRIDE, CURTIS Curtis John B12.17.1968 Washington DC BL/TR/6'0"/(195–210) [NYN86 10/258] d9.14																								
1997	Bos A	2	2	1	1	0	0	1	1	0	0	0	1	.500	.500	2.000	2.500	+401	0	0	0	/H	0	0.1
2000	Bos A	9	20	4	5	1	0	0	0	1	0	0	7	.250	.286	.300	.586	-53	0	0	0	O9(7/2/0)/D	0	-0.1
Total	11	421	796	132	199	39	12	20	82	85	2	7	211	.250	.327	.405	.732	-12	29	14	67	O205(167/6/37),D68	143	-2.0
Team	2	11	22	5	6	1	0	1	1	1	0	0	8	.273	.304	.455	.759	-14	0	0	0	O9(7/2/0)/D	0	0.0
PROTHRO, DOC James Thompson B7.16.1893 Memphis TN D10.14.1971 Memphis TN BR/TR/5'10.5"/170 d9.26 M3																								
1920	Was A	6	13	2	5	0	0	0	2	0		0	4	.385	.385	.385	.770	+7	0	0	0	S2,3b2		0.0
1923	Was A	6	8	2	2	0	1	0	3	1		0	3	.250	.333	.500	.833	+24	0	0	0	3b6		0.2
1924	Was A	46	159	17	53	11	5	0	24	15		1	11	.333	.394	.465	.859	+25	4	4	50	3b45		-0.1
1925	Bos A	119	415	44	130	23	3	0	51	52		0	21	.313	.390	.383	.773	-3	9	11	45	3b108,S3		0.3
1926	Cin N	3	5	1	1	0	1	0	1	1		0	1	.200	.333	.600	.933	+51	0			3b2		0.0
Total	5	180	600	66	191	34	10	0	81	69		1	40	.318	.390	.408	.798	+5	13	15	100	3b163,S5		0.4
/150	1	150	523	55	164	29	4	0	64	66		0	26	.313	.390	.383	.773	-3	11	14	44	3b136,S4		0.4
PURTELL, BILLY William Patrick B1.6.1886 Columbus OH D3.17.1962 Bradenton FL BR/TR/5'9"/170 d4.16																								
1910	Bos A	49	168	15	35	1	2	1	15	18		1		.208	.289	.256	.545	-31	2			3b41,S8		-1.0
1911	Bos A	27	82	5	23	5	3	0	7	1		1		.280	.298	.415	.713	-1	1			3b15,2b3,S3/cf		-0.1
Total	5	335	1124	82	255	26	11	2	104	63		11	7	.227	.275	.275	.550	-27	24	2	100	3b270,2b36,S13/cf		-3.7
Team	2	76	250	20	58	6	5	1	22	19		2	0	.232	.292	.308	.600	-22	3			3b56,S11,2b3/cf		-1.1
PYTLAK, FRANKIE Frank Anthony B7.30.1908 Buffalo NY D5.8.1977 Buffalo NY BR/TR/5'7.5"/160 d4.22 Mil 1942–45																								
1941	Bos A	106	336	36	91	23	1	2	39	28		1	19	.271	.329	.363	.692	-19	5	7	42	C91	0	-0.4
1945	Bos A	9	17	1	2	0	0	0	0	3		0	0	.118	.250	.118	.368	-92	0	0	0	C6	0	-0.1
1946	Bos A	4	14	1	2	0	0	0	1	0		0	0	.143	.143	.143	.286	-119	0	0	0	C4	0	-0.1
Total	12	795	2399	316	677	100	36	7	272	247		24	97	.282	.355	.363	.718	-16	56	29	66	C699/rf	0	0.4
Team	3	119	367	38	95	23	1	2	40	31		1	19	.259	.318	.343	.661	-26	5	7	42	C101	0	-0.6
/150	4	150	463	48	120	29	1	3	50	39		1	24	.259	.318	.343	.661	-26	6	9	40	C127	0	-0.8
QUINONES, REY Rey Francisco (Santiago) B11.11.1963 Rio Piedras, PR BR/TR/5'11"/185 d5.17																								
1986	Bos A	62	190	26	45	12	1	2	15	19	0	3	26	.237	.315	.342	.657	-21	3	2	60	S62	0	-0.7
Total	4	451	1533	173	373	75	6	29	159	89	3	11	240	.243	.287	.357	.644	-26	5	11	31	S444,D4	9	-4.2
QUINTANA, CARLOS Carlos Narcis (Hernandez) B8.26.1965 Estado Miranda, Venezuela BR/TR/6'2"/(195–220) d9.16 [DL 1992 Bos A 182]																								
1988	Bos A	5	6	1	2	0	0	0	2	2	0	0	3	.333	.500	.333	.833	+32	0	0	0	O3R/D	0	0.0
1989	Bos A	34	77	6	16	5	0	0	6	7	0	0	12	.208	.274	.273	.547	-49	0	0	0	O21(4/1/17)/1D	15	-0.7
1990	†Bos A	149	512	56	147	28	0	7	67	52	0	2	74	.287	.354	.383	.737	+1	1	2	33	1b148,O3R	0	0.5
1991	Bos A	149	478	69	141	21	1	11	71	61	2	2	66	.295	.375	.412	.787	+12	1	0	100	1b138,O13(1/0/12)/D	0	0.9
1993	Bos A	101	303	31	74	5	0	1	19	31	2	2	52	.244	.317	.271	.588	-44	1	0	100	1b53,O51(1/0/50)	0	-2.4
Total	5	438	1376	163	380	59	1	19	165	153	4	6	207	.276	.350	.362	.712	-8	3	2	60	1b340,O91(6/1/85),D9	197	-1.7
/150	2	150	471	56	130	20	0	7	57	52	1	2	71	.276	.350	.362	.712	-8	1	1	50	1b116,O31(2/0/29),D3	130	-0.6
RADER, DAVE David Martin B12.26.1948 Claremore OK BL/TR/5'11"/(160–176) [SFN67 1/18] d9.5																								
1980	Bos A	50	137	14	45	11	0	3	17	14	1	0	12	.328	.388	.474	.862	+29	1	1	50	C34,D9	0	0.8
Total	10	846	2405	254	619	107	12	30	235	245	64	11	180	.257	.326	.349	.675	-14	8	4	67	C771,D9	0	-5.3
RAMIREZ, HANLEY Hanley B12.23.1983 Samana, D.R. BR/TR/6'3"/195 d9.20																								
2005	Bos A	2	2	0	0	0	0	0	0	0	0	0	2	.000	.000	.000	.000	-196	0	0	0	S2	0	-0.1
Total	2	160	635	119	185	46	11	17	59	56	0	4	130	.291	.352	.479	.831	+16	51	15	77	S156	0	3.2
RAMIREZ, MANNY Manuel Aristides (Onelcida) B5.30.1972 Santo Domingo, D.R. BR/TR/6'0"/(190–215) [CleA91 1/13] d9.2																								
1993	Cle A	22	53	5	9	1	0	2	5	2	0	0	8	.170	.200	.302	.502	-67	0	0	0	D20/rf	0	-0.6
1994	Cle A	91	290	51	78	22	0	17	60	42	4	0	72	.269	.357	.521	.878	+23	4	2	67	O84R,D5	0	0.5
1995	†Cle A★	137	484	85	149	26	1	31	107	75	6	5	112	.308	.402	.558	.960	+45	6	6	50	O131R,D5	0	1.5
1996	†Cle A	152	550	94	170	45	3	33	112	85	8	3	104	.309	.399	.582	.981	+45	8	5	62	O149R,D3	0	3.1
1997	†Cle A	150	561	99	184	40	0	26	88	79	5	7	115	.328	.415	.538	.953	+42	2	3	40	O146R,D4	0	2.4
1998	†Cle A★	150	571	108	168	35	2	45	145	76	6	6	121	.294	.377	.599	.976	+45	5	3	63	O148R,D2	0	2.4
1999	†Cle A★	147	522	131	174	34	3	44	**165**	96	9	13	131	.333	.442	**.663**	1.105	+70	2	4	33	O146R,D2	0	4.4
2000	Cle A✷	118	439	92	154	34	2	38	122	86	9	3	117	.351	.457	**.697**	1.154	+81	1	1	50	O93R,D25	43	4.1
2001	Bos A★	142	529	93	162	33	2	41	125	81	**25**	8	147	.306	.405	.609	1.014	+62	0	1	0	D87,O55L	0	3.8
2002	Bos A★	120	436	84	152	31	0	33	107	73	14	8	85	**.349**	**.450**	.647	1.097	+84	0	0	0	O68(64/0/7),D51	42	4.6
2003	†Bos A✷	154	569	117	185	36	1	37	104	97	**28**	8	94	.325	**.427**	.587	1.014	+58	3	1	75	O128L,D26	0	4.1
2004	†Bos A★	152	568	108	175	44	0	**43**	130	82	15	6	124	.308	.397	**.613**	1.010	+50	2	4	33	O132L,D19	0	2.5
2005	†Bos A★	152	554	112	162	30	1	45	144	80	9	10	119	.292	.388	.594	.982	+51	1	0	100	O149L,D2	0	3.5
2006	Bos A✷	130	449	79	144	27	1	35	102	100	16	1	102	.321	**.439**	.619	1.058	+68	0	1	0	O123L,D5	0	3.2
Total	14	1817	6575	1258	2066	438	16	470	1516	1054	15	78	1451	.314	.411	.600	1.011	+55	34	31	52	O1553(651/0/904),D256	85	39.5
Team	6	850	3105	593	980	201	5	234	712	513	54	41	671	.316	.416	.610	1.026	+61	6	7	46	O655L,D190	42	21.7
/150	1	150	548	105	173	35	1	41	126	91	10	7	118	.316	.416	.610	1.026	+61	1	1	50	O116L,D34	7	3.8
REDER, JOHNNY John Anthony B9.24.1909 Lublin, Poland D4.12.1990 Fall River MA BR/TR/6'0"/184 d4.16																								
1932	Bos A	17	37	4	5	1	0	0	3	6		0	6	.135	.256	.162	.418	-89	0	0	0	1b10/3		-0.5

Year	Tm Lg	G	AB	R	H	2B	3B	HR	RBI	BB	IB	HP	SO	AVG	OBP	SLG	OPS	AOPS	SB	CS	SB%	Games at Position	DL	BFW
REED, JODY Jody Eric B7.26.1962 Tampa FL BR/TR/5'9"/(160–170) [BosA84 8/198] d9.12 Col Florida St.																								
1987	Bos A	9	30	4	9	1	1	0	8	4	0	0	0	.300	.382	.400	.782	+5	1	1	50	S4,2b2/3	0	0.3
1988	†Bos A	109	338	60	99	23	1	1	28	45	1	4	21	.293	.380	.376	.756	+8	1	3	25	S94,2b11,3b4/D	0	2.0
1989	Bos A	146	524	76	151	42	2	3	40	73	0	4	44	.288	.376	.393	.769	+11	4	5	44	S77,2b70,3b4/rfD	0	2.1
1990	†Bos A	155	598	70	173	**45**	0	5	51	75	4	4	65	.289	.371	.390	.761	+8	4	4	50	2b119,S50/D	0	2.3
1991	Bos A	153	618	87	175	42	2	5	60	60	2	4	53	.283	.349	.382	.731	-3	6	5	55	2b152,S6	0	1.4
1992	Bos A	143	550	64	136	27	1	3	40	62	2	0	44	.247	.321	.316	.637	-26	7	8	47	2b142/D	0	1.6
1993	LA N	132	445	48	123	21	2	2	31	38	10	1	40	.276	.333	.346	.679	-13	1	3	25	2b132	29	0.8
1994	Mil A	108	399	48	108	22	0	2	37	57	1	2	34	.271	.362	.341	.703	-21	5	4	56	2b106	0	0.2
1995	SD N	131	445	58	114	18	1	4	40	59	1	5	38	.256	.348	.328	.676	-18	6	4	60	2b130,S5	0	1.4
1996	†SD N	146	495	45	121	20	0	2	49	59	8	3	53	.244	.325	.297	.622	-31	2	5	29	2b145	0	-1.9
1997	Det A	52	112	6	22	2	0	0	8	10	0	3	15	.196	.278	.214	.492	-68	3	2	60	2b41,D5	0	-0.2
Total	11	1284	4554	566	1231	263	10	27	392	542	29	30	407	.270	.349	.350	.699	-10	40	44	48	2b1050,S236,D9,3b9/rf	29	10.0
Team	6	715	2658	361	743	180	7	17	227	319	9	16	227	.280	.358	.372	.730	-1	23	26	47	2b496,S231,3b9,D4/rf	0	9.7
/150	1	150	558	76	156	38	1	4	48	67	2	3	48	.280	.358	.372	.730	-1	5	5	50	2b104,S48,3b2/DOfL	0	2.0
REESE, POKEY Calvin B6.10.1973 Columbia SC BR/TR/5'11"/(180–190) [CinN91 1/20] d4.1 [DL 1996 Cin N 13, 2005 Sea A 183]																								
2004	†Bos A	96	244	32	54	7	2	3	29	17	1	0	60	.221	.271	.303	.574	-53	6	2	75	S71,2b30	49	0.8
Total	8	856	2833	366	704	128	17	44	271	226	21	23	531	.248	.307	.352	.659	-32	144	26	85	2b521,S293,3b40	457	1.2
REEVES, BOBBY Robert Edwin "Gunner" B6.24.1904 Hill City TN D6.4.1993 Chattanooga TN BR/TR/5'11"/170 d6.9 Col Georgia Tech																								
1926	Was A	20	49	4	11	0	1	0	7	6		1	9	.224	.321	.265	.586	-44	1	1	50	3b16/2S		-0.3
1927	Was A	112	380	37	97	11	5	1	39	21		1	53	.255	.296	.318	.614	-40	3	1	75	S96,3b12,2b2		-2.2
1928	Was A	102	353	44	107	16	8	3	42	24		2	47	.303	.351	.419	.770	+2	4	8	33	S66,2b22,3b8/rf		0.0
1929	Bos A	140	460	66	114	19	2	2	28	60		**7**	57	.248	.343	.311	.654	-29	7	8	47	3b131,2b2,S2/1		-0.6
1930	Bos A	92	272	41	59	7	4	2	18	50		3	36	.217	.345	.294	.639	-34	6	2	75	3b62,S15,2b11		-0.6
1931	Bos A	36	84	11	14	2	2	0	1	14		1	16	.167	.293	.238	.531	-57	0	1	0	2b29/P		-1.2
Total	6	502	1598	203	402	55	22	8	135	175		15	218	.252	.331	.329	.660	-27	21	21	50	3b229,S180,2b67/P1rf		-4.9
Team	3	268	816	118	187	28	8	4	47	124		11	109	.229	.338	.298	.636	-34	13	11	54	3b193,2b42,S17/P1		-2.4
/150	2	150	457	66	105	16	4	2	26	69		6	61	.229	.338	.298	.636	-34	7	6	54	3b108,2b24,S10/P1		-1.3
REGAN, BILL William Wright B1.23.1899 Pittsburgh PA D6.11.1968 Pittsburgh PA BR/TR/5'10"/155 d6.2																								
1926	Bos A	108	403	40	106	21	3	4	34	23		4	37	.263	.309	.360	.669	-23	6	3	67	2b106		0.3
1927	Bos A	129	468	43	128	37	10	2	66	26		2	51	.274	.315	.408	.723	-12	10	10	50	2b121		-0.8
1928	Bos A	138	511	53	135	30	6	7	75	21		2	40	.264	.296	.387	.683	-20	9	6	60	2b137/rf		0.1
1929	Bos A	104	371	38	107	27	7	1	54	22		0	38	.288	.328	.407	.735	-10	7	5	58	2b91,3b10/1		-1.6
1930	Bos A	134	507	54	135	35	10	3	53	25		2	60	.266	.303	.393	.696	-22	4	2	67	2b127,3b2		-2.2
1931	Pit N	28	104	8	21	8	0	1	10	5		0	19	.202	.239	.308	.547	-54	2			2b28		-1.0
Total	6	641	2364	236	632	158	36	18	292	122		10	245	.267	.306	.387	.693	-19	38	26	100	2b610,3b12/1rf		-5.2
Team	5	613	2260	228	611	150	36	17	282	117		10	226	.270	.309	.391	.700	-18	36	26	58	2b582,3b12/1rf		-4.2
/150	1	150	553	56	150	37	9	4	69	29		2	55	.270	.309	.391	.700	-18	9	6	60	2b142,3b3/1OfL		-1.0
REHG, WALLY Walter Phillip B8.31.1888 Summerfield IL D4.5.1946 Burbank CA BR/TR/5'8"/160 d4.14 Mil 1918																								
1912	Pit N	8	9	1	0	0	0	0	0	0		0	1	.000	.000	.000	.000	-199	0			O2(0/1/1)		-0.3
1913	Bos A	30	101	13	28	3	2	0	9	2		0	7	.277	.291	.347	.638	-16	4			O26(8/3/15)		-0.5
1914	Bos A	88	151	14	33	4	2	0	11	18		1	11	.219	.306	.272	.578	-26	5	8	38	O43(16/0/28)		-0.8
1915	Bos A	5	5	2	1	0	0	0	0	0		0	1	.200	.200	.200	.400	-80	1			/rf		0.0
1917	Bos N	87	341	48	92	12	6	1	31	24		1	32	.270	.320	.349	.669	+11	13			O86R		-0.6
1918	Bos N	40	133	6	32	5	1	1	12	5		0	14	.241	.268	.316	.584	-19	3			O38(30/1/7)		-0.2
1919	Cin N	5	12	1	2	0	0	0	3	1		0	0	.167	.231	.167	.398	-79	0			O5(0/1/3)		-0.1
Total	7	263	752	85	188	24	11	2	66	50		2	66	.250	.299	.319	.618	-10	26	8	100	O201(54/6/141)		-2.5
Team	3	123	257	29	62	7	4	0	20	20		1	19	.241	.299	.300	.599	-23	10	8	100	O70(24/3/17)		-1.3
/150	4	150	373	35	76	9	5	0	24	24		1	23	.241	.299	.300	.599	-23	12	10	100	O85(29/4/21)		-1.6
REICHLE, DICK Richard Wendell B11.23.1896 Lincoln IL D6.13.1967 Richmond Heights MO BL/TR/6'0"/185 d9.19 Col Illinois																								
1922	Bos A	6	24	3	6	1	0	0	0	0		1	2	.250	.280	.292	.572	-50	0	0	0	O6C		-0.2
1923	Bos A	122	361	40	93	17	3	1	39	22		8	34	.258	.315	.330	.645	-31	3	6	33	O93(3/87/4),1b2		-2.3
Total	2	128	385	43	99	18	3	1	39	22		9	36	.257	.313	.327	.640	-32	3	6	33	O99(3/93/4),1b2		-2.5
/150	2	150	451	50	116	21	4	1	46	26		11	42	.257	.313	.327	.640	-32	4	7	36	O116(4/109/5),1b2	0	-2.9
REMY, JERRY Gerald Peter B11.8.1952 Fall River MA BL/TR/5'9"/(155–165) [AnaA71*A8/130] d4.7 [DL 1985 Bos A 182]																								
1975	Cal A	147	569	82	147	17	5	1	46	45	1	0	55	.258	.311	.311	.622	-18	34	21	62	2b147	0	1.1
1976	Cal A	143	502	64	132	14	3	0	28	38	1	0	43	.263	.313	.303	.616	-13	35	16	69	2b133,D5	0	2.2
1977	Cal A	154	575	74	145	19	10	4	44	59	2	2	59	.252	.322	.341	.663	-16	41	17	71	2b152/3	0	-0.4
1978	Bos A☆	148	583	87	162	24	6	2	44	40	0	0	55	.278	.321	.350	.671	-19	30	13	70	2b140/SD	0	-0.4
1979	Bos A	80	306	49	91	11	2	0	29	26	1	0	25	.297	.350	.346	.696	-15	14	9	61	2b76	52	-1.9
1980	Bos A	63	230	24	72	7	2	0	9	10	0	0	14	.313	.339	.361	.700	-12	14	6	70	2b60/rf	83	-0.2
1981	Bos A	88	358	55	110	9	1	0	31	36	2	0	30	.307	.368	.338	.706	-1	9	2	82	2b87	0	-0.4
1982	Bos A	155	636	89	178	22	3	0	47	55	1	2	77	.280	.337	.324	.661	-22	16	9	64	2b154	0	-2.5
1983	Bos A	146	592	73	163	16	5	0	43	40	2	0	35	.275	.320	.319	.639	-28	11	3	79	2b144	11	-3.1
1984	Bos A	30	104	8	26	1	1	0	8	7	0	0	11	.250	.297	.279	.576	-42	4	3	57	2b24	135	-0.6
Total	10	1154	4455	605	1226	140	38	7	329	356	10	4	404	.275	.327	.328	.655	-18	208	99	68	2b1117,D9/rfS3	463	-6.2
Team	7	710	2809	385	802	90	20	2	211	214	6	2	247	.286	.334	.334	.668	-19	98	45	69	2b685/SrfD	463	-9.1
/150	1	150	593	81	169	19	4	0	45	45	1	0	52	.286	.334	.334	.668	-19	21	10	68	2b145/SOfLD	98	-1.9
RENNA, BILL William Beneditto "Big Bill" B10.14.1924 Hanford CA BR/TR/6'3"/(218–230) d4.14 Col Santa Clara																								
1958	Bos A	39	56	5	15	5	0	4	18	6	1	0	14	.268	.339	.571	.910	+36	0	0	0	O11L	0	0.2
1959	Bos A	14	22	2	2	0	0	0	2	5	0	0	9	.091	.259	.091	.350	-100	0	0	0	O7L	0	-0.4
Total	6	370	918	123	219	36	10	28	119	99	1	6	166	.239	.315	.391	.706	-9	2	7	22	O277(81/6/192)	0	-2.3
Team	2	53	78	7	17	5	0	4	20	11	1	0	23	.218	.315	.436	.751	-5	0	0	0	O18L	0	-0.2
RENTERIA, EDGAR Edgar Enrique B8.7.1976 Barranquilla, Colombia BR/TR/6'1"/(172–200) d5.10																								
2005	†Bos A	153	623	100	172	36	4	8	70	55	0	3	100	.276	.335	.385	.720	-12	9	4	69	S153	0	-1.2
Total	11	1598	6143	934	1770	340	23	105	705	551	33	28	864	.288	.346	.402	.748	-6	263	99	73	S1578,D2/1	32	1.7
/150	1	150	611	98	169	35	4	8	69	54	0	3	98	.276	.335	.385	.720	-12	9	4	69	S150	0	-1.2
REPULSKI, RIP Eldon John B10.4.1928 Sauk Rapids MN D2.10.1993 Waite Park MN BR/TR/6'0"/(195–201) d4.14 Col St. Cloud St.																								
1960	Bos A	73	136	14	33	6	1	3	20	10	0	0	25	.243	.289	.368	.657	-25	0	0	0	O33L	0	-0.7
1961	Bos A	15	25	2	7	1	0	0	1	1	0	0	5	.280	.308	.320	.628	-34	0	2	0	O4L	0	-0.3
Total	9	928	3088	407	830	153	23	106	416	207	9	33	433	.269	.319	.436	.755	-2	25	29	46	O802(488/169/156)	0	-9.0
Team	2	88	161	16	40	7	1	3	21	11	0	0	30	.248	.291	.360	.651	-26	0	2	0	O37L	0	-1.0
REYNOLDS, CARL Carl Nettles B2.1.1903 Larue TX D5.29.1978 Houston TX BR/TR/6'0"/194 d9.1 Col Southwestern (TX)																								
1934	Bos A	113	413	61	125	26	9	4	86	27		3	28	.303	.350	.438	.788	-5	5	3	63	O100(2/66/33)		-0.8
1935	Bos A	78	244	33	66	13	4	6	35	24		0	20	.270	.336	.430	.766	-9	4	1	80	O64(3/1/60)		-0.3
Total	13	1222	4495	672	1357	247	107	80	699	260		42	308	.302	.346	.458	.804	+7	112	40	100	O1112(281/301/574)		-2.2
Team	2	191	657	94	191	39	13	10	121	51		3	48	.291	.345	.435	.780	-7	9	4	69	O164(5/67/93)		-1.1
/150	2	150	516	74	150	31	10	8	95	40		2	38	.291	.345	.435	.780	-7	7	3	70	O129(4/53/73)		-0.9
RHODES, KARL Karl Derrick "Tuffy" B8.21.1968 Cincinnati OH BL/TL/5'11"/(170–195) [HouN86 3/68] d8.7																								
1995	Bos A	10	25	2	2	1	0	0	1	3	0	0	4	.080	.179	.120	.299	-120	0	0	0	O9C	0	-0.5
Total	6	225	590	74	132	29	3	13	44	74	7	2	121	.224	.310	.349	.659	-22	14	7	67	O189(53/101/53)	0	-1.9
RHYNE, HAL Harold J. B3.30.1899 Paso Robles CA D1.7.1971 Orangevale CA BR/TR/5'8.5"/163 d4.18																								
1926	Pit N	109	366	46	92	14	3	2	39	35		6	21	.251	.327	.322	.649	-29	1			2b66,S44/3		-0.3
1927	†Pit N	62	168	21	46	5	0	0	17	14		0	9	.274	.330	.304	.634	-34	0			2b45,3b10,S7		-1.3

Year	Tm Lg	G	AB	R	H	2B	3B	HR	RBI	BB	IB	HP	SO	AVG	OBP	SLG	OPS	AOPS	SB	CS	SB%	Games at Position	DL	BFW
1929	Bos A	120	346	41	87	24	5	0	38	25		4	14	.251	.309	.350	.659	-29	4	1	80	S113/3rf		-0.5
1930	Bos A	107	296	34	60	8	5	0	23	25		2	19	.203	.269	.264	.533	-63	1	4	20	S107		-1.6
1931	Bos A	147	565	75	154	34	3	0	51	57		2	41	.273	.341	.343	.684	-15	3	3	50	S147		1.6
1932	Bos A	71	207	26	47	12	5	0	14	23		2	14	.227	.310	.333	.643	-31	3	2	60	S55,3b4/2		-0.1
1933	Chi A	39	83	9	22	1	1	0	10	5		1	9	.265	.315	.301	.616	-33	1	1	50	2b19,3b13,S2		-0.2
Total	7	655	2031	252	508	98	22	2	192	184		17	127	.250	.318	.323	.641	-31	13	11	100	S475,2b131,3b29/rf		-2.4
Team	4	445	1414	176	348	78	18	0	126	130		10	88	.246	.314	.327	.641	-31	11	10	52	S422,3b5/2rf		-0.6
/150	1	150	477	59	117	26	6	0	42	44		3	30	.246	.314	.327	.641	-31	4	3	57	S142,3b2/2OfL		-0.2
RICE, JIM James Edward B3.8.1953 Anderson SC BR/TR/6'2"/(200–217) [BosA71 1/15] d8.19 C7																								
1974	Bos A	24	67	6	18	2	1	1	13	4	0	1	12	.269	.307	.373	.680	-8	0	0	0	D16,O3L	0	-0.2
1975	Bos A	144	564	92	174	29	4	22	102	36	7	4	122	.309	.350	.491	.841	+26	10	5	67	O90L,D54	0	0.8
1976	Bos A	153	581	75	164	25	8	25	85	28	2	4	123	.282	.315	.482	.797	+19	8	5	62	O98L,D54	0	0.1
1977	Bos A★	160	644	104	206	29	15	**39**	114	53	10	8	120	.320	.376	**.593**	.969	+44	5	4	56	D116,O44(19/0/27)	0	3.0
1978	Bos A★	**163**	677	121	**213**	25	**15**	**46**	**139**	58	7	5	126	.315	.370	**.600**	.970	+53	7	5	58	O114(101/1/15),D49	0	4.2
1979	Bos A★	158	619	117	201	39	6	39	130	57	4	4	97	.325	.381	.596	.977	+52	9	4	69	O125(124/0/1),D33	0	3.1
1980	Bos A✱	124	504	81	148	22	6	24	86	30	5	4	87	.294	.336	.504	.840	+21	8	3	73	O109L,D15	35	0.7
1981	Bos A	**108**	451	51	128	18	1	17	62	34	3	3	76	.284	.333	.441	.774	+15	2	2	50	O108L	0	0.1
1982	Bos A	145	573	86	177	24	5	24	97	55	6	7	98	.309	.375	.494	.869	+29	0	1	0	O145L	0	1.0
1983	Bos A★	155	626	90	191	34	1	**39**	**126**	52	10	6	102	.305	.361	.550	.911	+37	0	2	0	O151L,D4	0	3.3
1984	Bos A★	159	657	98	184	25	7	28	122	44	8	1	102	.280	.323	.467	.790	+11	4	0	100	O157L,D2	0	0.5
1985	Bos A★	140	546	85	159	20	3	27	103	51	5	2	75	.291	.349	.487	.836	+22	2	0	100	O130L,D7	0	0.3
1986	†Bos A★	157	618	98	200	39	2	20	110	62	5	4	78	.324	.384	.490	.874	+37	0	1	0	O156L/D	0	3.3
1987	Bos A	108	404	66	112	14	0	13	62	45	3	7	77	.277	.357	.408	.765	+0	1	1	50	O94L,D12	0	-0.3
1988	†Bos A	135	485	57	128	18	3	15	72	48	2	3	89	.264	.330	.406	.736	+2	1	1	50	D112,O19L	0	-0.5
1989	Bos A	56	209	22	49	10	2	3	28	13	0	1	39	.234	.276	.344	.620	-29	1	0	100	D55	82	-1.0
Total	16	2089	8225	1249	2452	373	79	382	1451	670	77	64	1423	.298	.352	.502	.854	+26	58	34	63	O1543(1504/1/43),D530	117	18.4
/150	1	150	591	90	176	27	6	27	104	48	6	5	102	.298	.352	.502	.854	+26	4	2	67	D38,O11(108/0/3)	8	1.3
RICHARDSON, JEFF Jeffrey Scott B8.26.1965 Grand Island NE BR/TR/6'2"/(175–180) [CinN86 7/176] d7.14 Col Louisiana Tech																								
1993	Bos A	15	24	3	5	2	0	0	2	1	0	0	3	.208	.240	.292	.532	-60	0	0	0	2b8,S5/3D	127	0.2
Total	3	74	153	13	27	6	0	2	13	11	0	1	29	.176	.235	.255	.490	-62	1	0	100	S46,3b12,2b8,D2	127	-1.9
RICHTER, AL Allen Gordon B2.7.1927 Norfolk VA BR/TR/5'11"/(165–175) d9.23																								
1951	Bos A	5	11	1	1	0	0	0	0	3		0	0	.091	.286	.091	.377	-95	0	0	0	S3	0	0.0
1953	Bos A	1	0	0	0	0	0	0	0	0		0	0	+	+	+	.000	-100	0	0	0	/S	0	0.0
Total	2	6	11	1	1	0	0	0	0	3		0	0	.091	.286	.091	.377	-95	0	0	0	S4	0	0.0
RIGGERT, JOE Joseph Aloysius B12.11.1886 Janesville WI D12.10.1973 Kansas City MO BR/TR/5'9.5"/170 d5.12																								
1911	Bos A	50	146	19	31	4	4	2	13	12		4		.212	.290	.336	.626	-25	5			O39(21/11/6)		-1.0
Total	3	174	558	68	134	18	14	8	44	46		6	64	.240	.305	.366	.671	-2	20			O150(31/91/28)		-1.7
RIGNEY, TOPPER Emory Elmo B1.7.1897 Groveton TX D6.6.1972 San Antonio TX BR/TR/5'9"/150 d4.12 Col Texas A&M																								
1926	Bos A	148	525	71	142	32	6	4	53	108		0	31	.270	.395	.377	.772	+5	6	8	43	S146		4.3
1927	Bos A	8	18	0	2	1	0	0	0	1		0	2	.111	.158	.167	.325	-116	0	0		3b4/S		-0.4
Total	6	694	2326	324	669	113	39	13	315	377		5	176	.288	.388	.387	.775	+4	44	36	55	S660,3b14		8.4
Team	2	156	543	71	144	33	6	4	53	109		0	33	.265	.388	.370	.758	+1	6	8	43	S147,3b4		3.9
/150	2	150	522	68	138	32	6	4	51	105		0	32	.265	.388	.370	.758	+1	6	8	43	S141,3b4		3.8
RILES, ERNEST Ernest B10.2.1960 Cairo GA BL/TR/6'1"/180 [MilA81*S3/63] d5.14 Col Middle Georgia JC OF(2/0/3)																								
1993	Bos A	94	143	15	27	8	0	5	20	20	3	2	40	.189	.292	.350	.642	-31	1	3	25	2b20,D15,3b11/1	0	-0.6
Total	9	919	2504	309	637	92	20	48	284	244	15	9	409	.254	.319	.365	.684	-11	20	28	42	S362,3b301,2b88,D21,1b10,O5R	83	-6.1
RISING, POP Percival Sumner B1.2.1872 Industry PA D1.28.1938 Rochester PA TR d8.10																								
1905	Bos A	11	29	2	3	1	1	0	2	2		0		.103	.161	.207	.368	-84	0			O6R/3		-0.3
RIVERA, LUIS Luis Antonio (Pedraza) B1.3.1964 Cidra, PR BR/TR/5'9"/(165–175) d8.3 C1																								
1986	Mon N	55	166	20	34	11	1	0	13	17	0	2	33	.205	.285	.283	.568	-42	1	1	50	S55	0	-1.5
1987	Mon N	18	32	0	5	2	0	0	1	1	0	0	8	.156	.182	.219	.401	-95	0	0	0	S15	0	-0.4
1988	Mon N	123	371	35	83	17	3	4	30	24	4	1	69	.224	.271	.318	.589	-34	3	4	43	S116	0	-1.2
1989	Bos A	93	323	35	83	17	1	5	29	20	1	1	60	.257	.301	.362	.663	-19	2	3	40	S90/2D	0	-1.0
1990	†Bos A	118	346	38	78	20	0	7	45	25	0	1	58	.225	.279	.344	.623	-30	4	3	57	S112,2b3/3	0	-0.1
1991	Bos A	129	414	64	107	22	3	8	40	35	0	3	86	.258	.318	.384	.702	-11	4	4	50	S129	0	1.0
1992	Bos A	102	288	17	62	11	1	0	29	26	0	3	56	.215	.287	.260	.547	-49	4	3	57	S93/23lfD	0	0.0
1993	Bos A	62	130	13	27	8	1	1	7	11	0	1	36	.208	.273	.308	.581	-47	1	2	33	2b27,S27,3b2,D7	42	-1.1
1994	NY N	32	43	11	12	2	1	3	5	4	0	2	14	.279	.367	.581	.948	+44	0	1	0	S11,2b5	0	0.6
1997	Hou N	7	13	2	3	0	1	0	3	1	0	0	6	.231	.286	.385	.671	-24	0	0	0	S6/2	0	-0.2
1998	KC A	42	89	14	22	4	0	0	7	7	0	0	17	.247	.302	.292	.594	-47	1	1	50	S30,2b6,3b6	0	-0.1
Total	11	781	2215	249	516	114	12	28	209	171	5	14	443	.233	.291	.333	.624	-30	20	22	48	S684,2b44,3b10,D10/lf	42	-4.0
Team	5	504	1501	167	357	78	6	21	150	117	1	9	296	.238	.295	.340	.635	-28	15	15	50	S451,2b32,D9,3b4/lf	42	-1.2
/150	1	150	447	50	106	23	2	6	45	35	0	3	88	.238	.295	.340	.635	-28	4	4	50	S134,2b10,D3/3OfL	13	-0.4
ROBERTS, DAVE David Ray B5.31.1972 Okinawa, Japan BL/TL/5'10"/(172–180) [DetA94 28/781] d8.7 Col UCLA																								
2004	†Bos A	45	86	19	22	10	0	2	14	10	0	1	17	.256	.330	.442	.772	-4	5	2	71	O38(18/16/14)/D	0	0.0
Total	8	666	2204	358	594	76	42	21	181	245	6	16	278	.270	.344	.371	.715	-11	207	50	81	O627(207/422/17),D3	177	-1.7
ROBIDOUX, BILLY JO William Joseph B1.13.1964 Ware MA BL/TR/6'1"/200 [MilA82 6/157] d9.11																								
1990	Bos A	27	44	3	8	4	0	1	4	6	1	1	14	.182	.288	.341	.629	-27	0	0	0	1b11,D4	62	-0.3
Total	6	173	468	43	98	21	0	5	43	71	6	1	106	.209	.313	.286	.599	-35	1	2	33	1b115,D26,O12L	134	-2.8
ROBINSON, AARON Aaron Andrew B6.23.1915 Lancaster SC D3.9.1966 Lancaster SC BL/TR/6'2"/205 d5.6 Mil 1943–45																								
1951	Bos A	26	74	9	15	1	1	2	7	17		0	10	.203	.352	.324	.676	-24	0	0	0	C25	0	-0.1
Total	8	610	1839	208	478	74	11	61	272	337		3	194	.260	.375	.412	.787	+12	0	6	0	C577	0	4.9
ROBINSON, FLOYD Floyd Andrew B5.9.1936 Prescott AR BL/TR/5'9"/(170–175) d8.10																								
1968	Bos A	23	24	1	3	0	0	0	2	3	0	1	4	.125	.250	.125	.375	-85	1	0	100	O10(5/0/5)	0	-0.4
Total	9	1011	3284	458	929	140	36	67	426	408	33	27	282	.283	.365	.409	.774	+18	42	21	67	O886(242/5/723)	42	0.7
RODGERS, BILL Wilbur Kincaid "Rawmeat Bill" B4.18.1887 Pleasant Ridge OH D12.24.1978 Goliad TX BL/TR/5'9.5"/170 d4.15																								
1915	Bos A	11	6	2	0	0	0	0	0	3		0	2	.000	.333	.000	.333	-100	0			2b6		0.0
Total	2	102	268	30	65	15	4	0	19	22		7	40	.243	.316	.328	.644	-7	11	8	100	2b75,S7/rf3		0.3
RODRIGUEZ, CARLOS Carlos (Marquez) B11.1.1967 Mexico City, Distrito Federal, Mexico BB/TR/5'9"/160 d6.16																								
1991	NY A	15	37	1	7	0	0	0	2	1	0	0	2	.189	.211	.189	.400	-89	0	0	0	S11,2b3	0	-0.3
1994	Bos A	57	174	15	50	14	1	1	13	11	0	0	13	.287	.330	.397	.727	-18	1	0	100	S32,2b20,3b4	0	-0.1
1995	Bos A	13	30	5	10	2	0	0	5	2	0	1	2	.333	.394	.400	.794	+4	0	0	0	2b7,S6/3	0	0.1
Total	3	85	241	21	67	16	1	1	20	14	0	1	17	.278	.320	.365	.685	-25	1	0	100	S49,2b30,3b5	0	-0.3
Team	2	70	204	20	60	16	1	1	18	13	0	1	15	.294	.339	.397	.736	-15	1	0	100	S38,2b27,3b5	0	0.0
RODRIGUEZ, TONY Luis Antonio B8.15.1970 Rio Piedras, PR BR/TR/5'11"/178 [BosA91 10/278] d7.6 Col Charleston (WV)																								
1996	Bos A	27	67	7	16	1	0	1	9	4	0	1	8	.239	.292	.299	.591	-51	0	0	0	S21,3b5	0	-0.2
RODRIGUEZ, STEVE Steven James B11.29.1970 Las Vegas NV BR/TR/5'8"/170 [BosA92 5/142] d4.30 Col Pepperdine																								
1995	Bos A	6	8	1	1	0	0	0	0	1	0	0	1	.125	.222	.125	.347	-106	1	0	100	S4/2D	0	-0.2
ROGELL, BILLY William George B11.24.1904 Springfield IL D8.9.2003 Sterling Heights MI BB/TR/5'10.5"/163 d4.14																								
1925	Bos A	58	169	12	33	5	1	0	17	11		0	17	.195	.244	.237	.481	-78	0	3	0	2b49,S6		-1.3
1927	Bos A	82	207	35	55	14	6	2	28	24		0	28	.266	.342	.420	.762	-1	3	1	75	3b53,2b2,O2(1/0/1)		0.8
1928	Bos A	102	296	33	69	10	4	0	29	22		4	47	.233	.295	.294	.589	-44	2	6	25	S67,2b22,O6(1/2/3),3b3		-1.6
Total	14	1482	5149	755	1375	256	75	42	609	649		21	416	.267	.351	.370	.721	-16	82	62	100	S1235,3b104,2b78,O9(3/2/4)		5.3

Year	Tm Lg	G	AB	R	H	2B	3B	HR	RBI	BB	IB	HP	SO	AVG	OBP	SLG	OPS	AOPS	SB	CS	SB%	Games at Position	DL	BFW
Team	3	242	672	80	157	29	11	2	74	57		4	92	.234	.297	.318	.615	-39	5	10	33	2b73,S73,3b56,O8(2/2/4)		-2.1
/150	2	150	417	50	97	18	7	1	46	35		2	57	.234	.297	.318	.615	-39	3	6	33	2b45,S45,3b35,O5(1/1/2)		-1.3
ROLLINGS, RED William Russell B3.21.1904 Mobile AL D12.31.1964 Mobile AL BL/TR/5'11"/167 d4.17																								
1927	Bos A	82	184	19	49	4	1	0	9	12		4	10	.266	.325	.299	.624	-36	3	1	75	3b44,1b10,2b2		-1.0
1928	Bos A	50	48	7	11	3	1	0	9	6		0	8	.229	.315	.333	.648	-28	0	0	0	1b5,2b4,O4(2/0/2)/3		-0.4
1930	Bos N	52	123	10	29	6	0	0	10	9		0	5	.236	.288	.285	.573	-60	2			3b28,2b10		-0.9
Total	3	184	355	36	89	13	2	0	28	27		4	23	.251	.311	.299	.610	-43	5	1	100	3b73,2b16,1b15,O4(2/0/2)		-2.3
Team	2	132	232	26	60	7	2	0	18	18		4	18	.259	.323	.306	.629	-34	3	1	75	3b45,1b15,2b6,O4(2/0/2)		-1.4
/150	2	150	264	30	68	8	2	0	20	20		5	20	.259	.323	.306	.629	-34	3	1	75	3b51,1b17,2b7,O5(2/0/2)		-1.6
ROMERO, MANDY Armando B10.29.1967 Miami FL BB/TR/5'11"/(180–190) [PitN88 19/486] d7.15 Col Brevard (FL) CC																								
1998	Bos A	12	13	2	3	1	0	0	1	3	0	0	3	.231	.375	.308	.683	-21	0	0	0	C4,D3	0	0.1
Total	3	42	77	12	16	2	0	2	5	6	0	2	25	.208	.282	.312	.594	-43	1	0	100	C31,D3	0	-0.0
ROMERO, ED Edgardo Ralph (Rivera) B12.9.1957 Santurce, PR BR/TR/5'11"/(150–180) d7.16 OF(17/1/14)																								
1977	Mil A	10	25	4	7	1	0	0	2	4	0	0	3	.280	.379	.320	.699	-7	0	0	0	S10	0	-0.2
1980	Mil A	42	104	20	27	7	0	1	10	9	0	0	11	.260	.319	.356	.675	-13	2	0	100	S22,2b15,3b3	0	-0.1
1981	†Mil A	44	91	6	18	3	0	1	10	4	0	0	9	.198	.227	.264	.491	-56	0	2	0	S22,2b18,3b3	0	0.0
1982	Mil A	52	144	18	36	8	0	1	7	8	0	0	16	.250	.289	.326	.615	-28	0	0	0	2b39,S10,3b2/lf	0	-0.5
1983	Mil A	59	145	17	46	7	0	1	18	8	0	0	8	.317	.348	.386	.734	+11	1	0	100	S22,O15(14/0/1),3b5,2b3,D5	0	-0.7
1984	Mil A	116	357	36	90	12	0	1	31	29	2	1	25	.252	.307	.294	.601	-29	3	3	50	3b59,S39,2b11,1b4/rfD	0	-0.5
1985	Mil A	88	251	24	63	11	1	0	21	26	0	0	20	.251	.321	.303	.624	-28	1	1	50	S43,2b31,O14(2/0/12)/3	0	0.2
1986	†Bos A	100	233	41	49	11	0	2	23	18	0	2	16	.210	.270	.283	.553	-49	2	0	100	S75,3b18,2b4/cf	0	-1.8
1987	Bos A	88	235	23	64	5	0	0	14	18	0	0	22	.272	.322	.294	.616	-36	0	2	0	2b29,S24,3b24,1b8	0	-1.0
1988	†Bos A	31	75	3	18	3	0	0	5	3	0	1	8	.240	.272	.280	.552	-46	0	0	0	3b15,S8,2b5/1D	45	-0.6
1989	Bos A	46	113	14	24	4	0	0	6	7	1	1	7	.212	.260	.248	.508	-58	0	2	0	2b22,3b14,S10,D2	0	-0.2
1989	Atl N	7	19	1	5	1	0	1	1	0	0	0	0	.263	.263	.474	.737	+4	0	0	0	2b4,S2/3	0	0.4
1989	Mil A	15	50	3	10	3	0	0	3	0	0	0	10	.200	.200	.260	.460	-71	0	0	0	2b11,3b4/S	0	-0.8
1989	Major	68	182	18	39	8	0	1	10	7	1	1	17	.214	2.247	.275	2.522	-51	0	2	0		0	-0.6
1990	Det A	32	70	8	16	3	0	0	4	6	1	0	4	.229	.286	.271	.557	-43	0	0	0	3b27,D3	0	-0.4
Total	12	730	1912	218	473	79	1	8	155	140	4	5	159	.247	.298	.302	.600	-33	9	10	47	S288,2b192,3b176,O32L,1b13,D13	45	-6.2
Team	4	265	656	81	155	23	0	2	48	46	1	4	53	.236	.287	.280	.567	-46	2	4	33	S117,3b71,2b60,1b9,D3/cf	45	-3.6
/150	2	150	371	46	88	13	0	1	27	26	1	2	30	.236	.287	.280	.567	-46	1	2	33	S66,3b40,2b34,1b5,D2/cf	25	-2.0
ROMINE, KEVIN Kevin Andrew B5.23.1961 Exeter NH BR/TR/5'11"/(171–204) [BosA82 1/29] d9.5 Col Arizona St.																								
1985	Bos A	24	28	3	6	2	0	0	1	1	0	0	4	.214	.241	.286	.527	-58	1	0	100	O23(12/1/12)/D	0	-0.2
1986	Bos A	35	35	6	9	2	0	0	2	3	0	0	9	.257	.316	.314	.630	-28	2	0	100	O33(0/28/5)	0	0.1
1987	Bos A	9	24	5	7	2	0	0	2	2	0	0	6	.292	.346	.375	.721	-11	0	0	0	O7(1/4/3),D2	0	0.0
1988	†Bos A	57	78	17	15	2	1	1	6	7	0	0	15	.192	.259	.282	.541	-51	2	0	100	O45(5/9/38),D5	0	-0.9
1989	Bos A	92	274	30	75	13	0	1	23	21	1	2	53	.274	.327	.332	.659	-18	1	1	50	O89(9/48/32),D2	0	-0.7
1990	Bos A	70	136	21	37	7	0	2	14	12	0	1	27	.272	.331	.368	.699	-8	4	0	100	O64(16/18/30)/D	0	-0.5
1991	Bos A	44	55	7	9	2	0	1	7	3	0	0	10	.164	.207	.255	.462	-75	1	1	50	O23(10/4/10),D14	0	-0.8
Total	7	331	630	89	158	30	1	5	55	49	1	3	124	.251	.306	.325	.631	-27	11	2	85	O284(53/112/130),D25	0	-3.0
/150	3	150	285	40	72	14	0	2	25	22	0	1	56	.251	.306	.325	.631	-27	5	1	83	O129(24/51/59),D11	0	-1.4
ROSAR, BUDDY Warren Vincent B7.3.1914 Buffalo NY D3.13.1994 Rochester NY BR/TR/5'9"/190 d4.29 Def 1944–45																								
1950	Bos A	27	84	13	25	2	0	1	12	7		0	4	.298	.352	.357	.709	-25	0	0	0	C25	0	-0.3
1951	Bos A	58	170	11	39	7	0	1	13	19		0	14	.229	.307	.288	.595	-44	0	0	0	C56	0	-0.7
Total	13	988	3198	335	836	147	15	18	367	315		10	161	.261	.330	.334	.664	-16	17	18	49	C934	0	2.4
Team	2	85	254	24	64	9	0	2	25	26		0	18	.252	.321	.311	.632	-38	0	0	0	C81	0	-1.0
ROSENTHAL, SI Simon B11.13.1903 Boston MA D4.7.1969 Boston MA BL/TL/5'9"/165 d9.8																								
1925	Bos A	19	72	6	19	5	2	0	8	7		0	3	.264	.329	.389	.718	-18	1	0	100	O17(7/0/10)		-0.4
1926	Bos A	104	285	34	76	12	3	4	34	19		2	18	.267	.317	.372	.689	-18	4	1	80	O67(48/0/19)		-2.3
Total	2	123	357	40	95	17	5	4	42	26		2	21	.266	.319	.375	.694	-18	5	1	83	O84(55/0/29)		-2.7
/150	2	150	435	49	116	21	6	5	51	32		2	26	.266	.319	.375	.694	-18	6	1	86	O102(67/0/35)	0	-3.3
ROTH, BRAGGO Robert Frank B8.28.1892 Burlington WI D9.11.1936 Chicago IL BR/TR/5'7.5"/170 d9.1 b–Frank																								
1919	Bos A	63	227	32	58	9	4	0	23	24		4	32	.256	.337	.330	.667	-7	9			O58(1/57/0)		-1.1
Total	8	811	2831	427	804	138	73	30	422	335		35	389	.284	.367	.416	.783	+22	190	41	100	O727(42/135/550),3b35		1.4
ROTHROCK, JACK John Huston B3.14.1905 Long Beach CA D2.2.1980 San Bernardino CA BB/TR/5'11.5"/165 d7.28 OF(138/194/311)																								
1925	Bos A	22	55	6	19	3	3	0	7	3		0	7	.345	.379	.509	.888	+24	0	0	0	S22		0.0
1926	Bos A	15	17	3	5	1	0	0	2	3		0	1	.294	.400	.353	.753	+1	0	0	0	S2		-0.1
1927	Bos A	117	428	61	111	24	8	1	36	24		2	46	.259	.302	.360	.662	-27	5	5	50	S40,2b36,3b20,1b13		-1.0
1928	Bos A	117	344	52	92	9	4	3	22	33		1	40	.267	.333	.343	.676	-21	12	6	67	O53(26/12/19),3b17,1b16,S13,2b2/PC		-2.0
1929	Bos A	143	473	70	142	19	7	6	59	43		2	47	.300	.361	.408	.769	+0	24	13	65	O128(0/126/2)		-0.2
1930	Bos A	45	65	4	18	3	1	0	4	2		0	9	.277	.299	.354	.653	-33	0	2	0	O9(1/0/8)/3		-0.4
1931	Bos A	133	475	81	132	32	3	4	42	47		0	48	.278	.343	.383	.726	-4	13	7	65	O79(75/2/2),2b23,1b8,3b2/S		-0.8
1932	Bos A	12	48	3	10	1	0	0	0	5		0	5	.208	.283	.229	.512	-65	3	0	100	O12L		-0.4
1932	Chi A	39	64	8	12	2	1	0	6	5		0	9	.188	.246	.250	.496	-69	1	0	100	O19(12/1/6),3b8/1		-0.9
1932	Year	51	112	11	22	3	1	0	6	10		0	14	.196	.262	.241	.503	-67	4	0	100	O31(24/1/6),3b8/1		-1.3
1934	†StL N	**154**	647	106	184	35	3	11	72	49		1	56	.284	.336	.399	.735	-10	10			O154(5/0/149)/2		-1.5
1935	StL N	129	502	76	137	18	5	3	56	57		0	29	.273	.347	.347	.694	-16	7			O127(1/1/125)		-2.0
1937	Phi A	88	232	28	62	15	0	0	21	28		0	15	.267	.346	.332	.678	-27	1	0	100	O58(6/52/0)/2		-1.1
Total	11	1014	3350	498	924	162	35	28	327	299		6	312	.276	.336	.370	.706	-15	76	33	100	O639R,S78,2b63,3b48,1b38/CP		-10.4
Team	8	604	1905	280	529	92	26	14	172	160		5	203	.278	.335	.375	.710	-13	57	33	63	O281(26/140/31),S78,2b61,3b40,1b37/PC		-4.9
/150	2	150	473	70	131	23	6	3	43	40		1	50	.278	.335	.375	.710	-13	14	8	64	O70(6/35/8),S19,2b15,3b10,1b9/PC		-1.2
ROWLAND, RICH Richard Garnet B2.25.1964 Cloverdale CA BR/TR/6'1"/(210–215) [DetA88 17/447] d9.7 Col Mendocino (CA) CC																								
1990	Det A	7	19	3	3	1	0	0	0	2	1	0	4	.158	.238	.211	.449	-74	0	0	0	C5,D2	0	-0.2
1991	Det A	4	4	0	1	0	0	0	1	1	0	0	2	.250	.333	.250	.583	-18	0	0	0	C2/D	0	0.1
1992	Det A	6	14	2	3	0	0	0	0	3	0	0	3	.214	.353	.214	.567	-39	0	0	0	C3/13D	0	-0.2
1993	Det A	21	46	2	10	3	0	0	4	5	0	0	16	.217	.294	.283	.577	-44	0	0	0	C17,D3	0	0.0
1994	Bos A	46	118	14	27	3	0	9	20	11	0	0	35	.229	.295	.483	.778	-8	0	0	0	C39/1D	0	-0.4
1995	Bos A	14	29	1	5	1	0	0	1	0	0	0	11	.172	.172	.207	.379	-102	0	0	0	C11,D3	0	-0.3
Total	6	98	230	22	49	8	0	9	26	22	1	0	71	.213	.281	.365	.646	-33	0	0	0	C77,D15,1b2/3	0	-1.0
Team	2	60	147	15	32	4	0	9	21	11	0	0	46	.218	.272	.429	.701	-25	0	0	0	C50,D4/1	0	-0.7
ROYER, STAN Stanley Dean B8.31.1967 Olney IL BR/TR/6'3"/(195–221) [OakA88 1/16] d9.11 Col Eastern Illinois																								
1994	Bos A	4	9	0	1	0	0	0	1	0	0	0	3	.111	.111	.111	.222	-141	0	0	0	3b3/1	0	-0.2
Total	4	89	164	14	41	10	0	4	21	4	0	0	41	.250	.266	.384	.650	-27	0	1	0	3b28,1b18	0	-1.0
RUDI, JOE Joseph Oden B9.7.1946 Modesto CA BR/TR/6'2"/200 d4.11 C2 [DL 1983 Oak A 182]																								
1981	Bos A	49	122	14	22	3	0	6	24	8	1	2	29	.180	.239	.352	.591	-35	0	0	0	D21,1b5/rf	0	-0.8
Total	16	1547	5556	684	1468	287	39	179	810	369	59	35	870	.264	.311	.427	.738	+12	25	15	63	O1195(1160/2/47),1b249,D51/3	418	-3.1
RUEL, MUDDY Herold Dominic B2.20.1896 St.Louis MO D11.13.1963 Palo Alto CA BR/TR/5'9"/150 d5.29 Mil 1918 M1/C14																								
1921	Bos A	113	358	41	99	21	1	1	45	41		1	15	.277	.352	.349	.701	-18	2	7	22	C109		-0.5
1922	Bos A	116	361	34	92	15	1	0	28	41		1	26	.255	.333	.302	.635	-33	4	2	67	C112		-1.0
1931	Bos A	33	83	6	25	5	0	0	6	9		0	6	.301	.370	.361	.731	-2	0	0	0	C30		0.2
Total	19	1468	4514	494	1242	187	29	4	534	606		29	238	.275	.365	.332	.697	-16	61	60	100	C1410,1b3		7.0
Team	3	262	802	81	216	41	2	1	79	91		2	47	.269	.345	.329	.674	-23	6	9	40	C251		-1.3
/150	2	150	459	46	124	23	1	1	45	52		1	27	.269	.345	.329	.674	-23	3	5	38	C144		-0.7

Year	Tm Lg	G	AB	R	H	2B	3B	HR	RBI	BB	IB	HP	SO	AVG	OBP	SLG	OPS	AOPS	SB	CS	SB%	Games at Position	DL	BFW
RUFFING, RED Charles Herbert B5.3.1905 Granville IL D2.17.1986 Mayfield Hts. OH BR/TR/6'1.5"/205 d5.31 Mil 1943–44 C1 HF1967▲																								
1924	Bos A	8	7	0	1	0	1	0	0	0		0	1	.143	.143	.429	.572	-56	0	0	0	P8		0.0
1925	Bos A	37	79	6	17	4	2	0	11	1		1	22	.215	.235	.316	.551	-61	0	0	0	P37		0.0
1926	Bos A	37	51	8	10	1	0	1	5	2		0	12	.196	.226	.275	.501	-69	0	1	0	P37		0.0
1927	Bos A	29	55	5	14	3	1	0	4	0		1	6	.255	.268	.345	.613	-41	0	0	0	P26		0.0
1928	Bos A	60	121	12	38	13	1	2	19	3		0	12	.314	.331	.488	.819	+15	0	0	0	P42		0.0
1929	Bos A	60	114	9	35	9	0	2	17	2		1	13	.307	.325	.439	.764	-3	0	0	0	P35,O2L		-0.1
1930	Bos A	6	11	2	3	2	0	0	1	0		0	1	.273	.273	.455	.728	-16	0	0	0	P4		0.0
Total	22	882	1937	207	521	98	13	36	273	97		6	266	.269	.306	.389	.695	-19	1	1	50	P624,O3(2/0/1)	138	-0.2
Team	7	237	438	42	118	32	5	5	57	8		3	67	.269	.287	.400	.687	-22	0	1	0	P189,O2L		-0.1
/150	4	150	277	27	75	20	3	3	36	5		2	42	.269	.287	.400	.687	-22	0	1	0	P120/lf		-0.1
RUNNELS, PETE James Edward (b James Edward Runnells) B1.28.1928 Lufkin TX D5.20.1991 Pasadena TX BL/TR/6'0"/170 d7.1 M1/C2																								
1951	Was A	78	273	31	76	12	2	0	25	31		1	24	.278	.354	.337	.691	-11	0	3	0	S73	0	-1.5
1952	Was A	152	555	70	158	18	3	1	64	72		1	55	.285	.368	.333	.701	-1	0	10	0	S147/2	0	-0.5
1953	Was A	137	486	64	125	15	5	2	50	64		3	36	.257	.347	.321	.668	-17	3	4	43	S121,2b11	0	-2.1
1954	Was A	139	488	75	131	17	15	3	56	78		0	60	.268	.368	.383	.751	+12	2	3	40	S107,2b27/lf	0	0.3
1955	Was A	134	503	66	143	16	4	2	49	55	2	1	51	.284	.353	.344	.697	-6	3	9	25	2b132,S2	0	0.7
1956	Was A	147	578	72	179	29	9	8	76	58	2	2	64	.310	.372	.433	.805	+13	5	5	50	1b81,2b69,S3	0	1.3
1957	Was A	134	473	53	109	18	4	2	35	55	5	2	51	.230	.310	.298	.608	-31	2	3	40	1b72,3b32,2b23	0	-2.3
1958	Bos A	147	568	103	183	32	5	8	59	87	0	6	49	.322	.416	.438	.854	+27	1	2	33	2b106,1b42	0	4.1
1959	Bos A★	147	560	95	176	33	6	6	57	95	1	1	48	.314	.415	.427	.842	+26	6	5	55	2b101,1b44,S9	0	**3.9**
1960	Bos A★	143	528	80	169	29	2	2	35	71	2	2	51	**.320**	.401	.394	.795	+12	5	2	71	2b129,1b57,3b3	0	3.5
1961	Bos A	143	360	49	114	20	3	3	38	46	2	3	32	.317	.396	.414	.810	+15	5	1	83	1b113,3b11,2b7/S	0	0.6
1962	Bos A★	152	562	80	183	33	5	10	60	79	11	3	57	**.326**	.408	.456	.864	+29	3	4	43	1b151	0	1.3
1963	Hou N	124	388	35	98	9	1	2	23	45	2	3	42	.253	.332	.296	.628	-11	2	0	100	1b70,2b36,3b3	0	-1.8
1964	Hou N	22	51	3	10	1	0	0	3	8	1	0	7	.196	.305	.216	.521	-47	0	0	0	1b14	0	-0.6
Total	14	1799	6373	876	1854	282	64	49	630	844	28	28	627	.291	.375	.378	.753	+6	37	51	42	1b644,2b642,S463,3b49/lf	0	6.9
Team	5	732	2578	407	825	147	21	29	249	378	16	15	237	.320	.408	.427	.835	+23	20	14	59	1b407,2b343,3b14,S10	0	13.4
/150	1	150	528	83	169	30	4	6	51	77	3	3	49	.320	.408	.427	.835	+23	4	3	57	1b83,2b70,3b3,S2	0	2.7
RUSSELL, RIP Glen David B1.26.1915 Los Angeles CA D9.26.1976 Los Alamitos CA BR/TR/6'1"/180 d5.5																								
1946	†Bos A	80	274	22	57	10	1	6	35	13		1	30	.208	.247	.318	.565	-46	1	1	50	3b70,2b3	0	-2.0
1947	Bos A	26	52	8	8	1	0	1	3	8		0	7	.154	.267	.231	.498	-64	0	0	0	3b13	0	-0.4
Total	6	425	1402	133	344	52	8	29	192	83		2	142	.245	.289	.356	.645	-23	4	1	100	1b234,3b96,2b27,O3L	0	-9.1
Team	2	106	326	30	65	11	1	7	38	21		1	37	.199	.251	.304	.555	-49	1	1	50	3b83,2b3	0	-2.4
/150	3	150	461	42	92	16	1	10	54	30		1	52	.199	.251	.304	.555	-49	1	1	50	3b117,2b4	0	-3.4
RUTH, BABE George Herman "The Bambino","The Sultan of Swat" B2.6.1895 Baltimore MD D8.16.1948 New York NY BL/TL/6'2"/215 d7.11 C1 HF1936▲																								
1914	Bos A	5	10	1	2	1	0	0	2	0		0	4	.200	.200	.300	.500	-50	0			P4		0.0
1915	†Bos A	42	92	16	29	10	1	4	21	9		0	23	.315	.376	.576	.952	+91	0			P32		0.0
1916	†Bos A	67	136	18	37	5	3	3	15	10		0	23	.272	.322	.419	.741	+22	0			P44		0.0
1917	Bos A	52	123	14	40	6	3	2	12	12		0	18	.325	.385	.472	.857	+63	0			P41		0.0
1918	†Bos A	95	317	50	95	26	11	**11**	66	58		2	58	.300	.411	**.555**	.966	+95	6			O59(47/12/0),P20,1b13		2.7
1919	Bos A	130	432	**103**	139	34	12	**29**	**114**	101		6	58	.322	**.456**	**.657**	1.113	+124	7			O111L,P17,1b5		**7.3**
Total	22	2503	8399	2174	2873	506	136	714	2213	2062		43	1330	.342	.474	.690	1.164	+109	123	11	100	O2241(1057/64/1131),P163,1b32		112.0
Team	6	391	1110	202	342	82	30	49	230	190		8	184	.308	.413	.568	.981	+94	13			O170(47/12/0),P158,1b18		10.0
/150	2	150	426	77	131	31	12	19	88	73		3	71	.308	.413	.568	.981	+94	5			O65(18/5/0),P61,1b7		3.8
RYAN, JACK John Francis B5.5.1905 West Mineral KS D9.2.1967 Rochester MN BR/TR/6'0"/185 d6.18																								
1929	Bos A	2	3	0	0	0	0	0	0	0		0	0	.000	.000	.000	.000	-199	0	0	0	O2(1/0/1)		-0.1
RYAN, MIKE Michael James B11.25.1941 Haverhill MA BR/TR/6'2"/(200–215) d10.3 C16																								
1964	Bos A	1	3	0	1	0	0	0	2	1	1	0	0	.333	.500	.333	.833	+31	0	0	0	/C	0	0.0
1965	Bos A	33	107	7	17	0	1	3	9	5	1	0	19	.159	.193	.262	.455	-73	0	0	0	C33	0	-1.2
1966	Bos A	116	369	27	79	15	3	2	32	29	3	0	68	.214	.271	.287	.558	-45	1	0	100	C114	0	-2.2
1967	†Bos A	79	226	21	45	4	2	2	27	26	5	1	42	.199	.282	.261	.543	-42	2	0	100	C79	0	-0.5
1968	Phi N	96	296	12	53	6	1	1	15	15	3	0	59	.179	.218	.216	.434	-69	0	3	0	C96	0	-2.8
1969	Phi N	133	446	41	91	17	2	12	44	30	4	2	66	.204	.256	.332	.588	-35	1	1	50	C132	0	-1.4
1970	Phi N	46	134	14	24	8	0	2	11	16	3	0	24	.179	.265	.284	.549	-51	0	0	0	C46	98	-1.9
1971	Phi N	43	134	9	22	5	1	3	6	10	1	0	32	.164	.222	.284	.506	-58	0	0	0	C43	0	-0.2
1972	Phi N	46	106	6	19	4	0	2	10	10	2	1	25	.179	.254	.274	.528	-51	0	0	0	C46	0	-0.2
1973	Phi N	28	69	7	16	1	2	1	5	6	0	0	19	.232	.289	.348	.637	-25	0	0	0	C27	0	-0.2
1974	Pit N	15	30	2	3	0	0	0	0	4	0	0	16	.100	.206	.100	.306	-113	0	0	0	C15	28	-0.3
Total	11	636	1920	146	370	60	12	28	161	152	23	4	370	.193	.252	.280	.532	-49	4	4	50	C632	126	-10.9
Team	4	229	705	55	142	19	6	7	70	61	10	1	129	.201	.264	.275	.539	-48	3	0	100	C226	0	-3.9
/150	3	150	462	36	93	12	4	5	46	40	7	1	84	.201	.264	.275	.539	-48	2	0	100	C148	0	-2.6
RYE, GENE Eugene Rudolph "Half-Pint" (b Eugene Rudolph Mercantelli) B11.15.1906 Chicago IL D1.21.1980 Park Ridge IL BL/TR/5'6"/165 d4.22																								
1931	Bos A	17	39	3	7	0	0	0	1	2		0	5	.179	.220	.179	.399	-94	0	0	0	O10L		-0.6
SADLER, DONNIE Donnie Lamont B6.17.1975 Clifton TX BR/TR/5'6"/(165–175) [BosA94 11/299] d4.1 OF(50/64/26)																								
1998	†Bos A	58	124	21	28	4	4	3	15	6	0	3	28	.226	.276	.395	.671	-29	4	0	100	2b50,S4,D4	0	-0.8
1999	†Bos A	49	107	18	30	5	1	0	4	5	0	0	20	.280	.313	.346	.659	-34	2	1	67	S14,2b10,3b9,O8(1/6/1),D3	0	-0.9
2000	Bos A	49	99	14	22	5	0	1	10	5	0	1	18	.222	.262	.303	.565	-57	3	1	75	S19,O17(3/13/1),2b12,3b3,D2	0	-0.6
2001	Cin N	39	84	9	17	3	0	1	3	9	0	0	20	.202	.280	.274	.554	-58	3	3	50	2b15,S12,O8(6/2/2)/D	0	-0.8
2001	KC A	54	101	19	13	3	0	0	2	9	0	2	17	.129	.212	.158	.370	-100	4	1	80	O16(5/4/7),3b15,2b13,S6	0	0.1
2001	Major	93	185	28	30	6	0	1	5	18	0	2	37	.162	1.244	.211	1.455	-7	7	4	64		0	-0.7
2002	KC A	35	68	10	13	1	1	0	5	4	0	0	12	.191	.233	.235	.468	-77	3	1	75	O15(11/0/4),3b11,2b4,S4,D3	24	-1.0
2002	Tex A	38	30	6	3	1	0	0	2	3	0	2	7	.100	.229	.133	.362	-100	2	2	50	O18(2/14/3),S12,3b4,2b2/D	0	-0.3
2002	Year	73	98	16	16	2	1	0	7	7	0	2	19	.163	.231	.204	.435	-83	5	3	63	O33(13/14/7),S16,3b15,2b6,D4	0	-1.3
2003	Tex A	77	131	27	26	5	2	1	5	13	0	2	34	.198	.277	.290	.567	-52	4	3	57	O41(19/22/7),3b23,S19/2	0	-1.0
2004	Ari N	18	23	1	3	2	0	0	0	1	0	0	7	.130	.167	.217	.384	-102	0	0	0	O6(3/3/1),S3,2b2,3b2	0	-0.5
Total	7	417	767	125	155	29	8	6	46	55	0	10	163	.202	.262	.284	.546	-60	25	12	68	O129C,2b109,S93,3b67,D14	24	-5.8
Team	3	156	330	53	80	14	5	4	29	16	0	4	66	.242	.283	.352	.635	-39	9	2	82	2b72,S37,O25(4/19/1),3b12,D9	0	-2.3
/150	3	150	317	51	77	13	5	4	28	15	0	4	63	.242	.283	.352	.635	-39	9	2	82	2b69,S36,O24(4/18/1),3b12,D9	0	-2.2
SADOWSKI, ED Edward Roman B1.19.1931 Pittsburgh PA D11.6.1993 Garden Grove CA BR/TR/5'11"/175 d4.20 b–Bob b–Ted																								
1960	Bos A	38	93	10	20	2	0	3	8	8	2	1	13	.215	.284	.333	.617	-36	0	0	0	C36	30	0.1
Total	5	217	495	55	100	20	1	12	39	39	8	1	94	.202	.261	.319	.580	-44	5	4	56	C181	30	-0.9
SANCHEZ, FREDDY Frederick Philip B12.21.1977 Hollywood CA BR/TR/5'11"/(185–190) d9.10 Col Oklahoma City																								
2002	Bos A	12	16	3	3	0	0	0	2	2	0	0	3	.188	.278	.188	.466	-73	0	0	0	2b5,S5	0	-0.2
2003	Bos A	20	34	6	8	2	0	0	2	0	0	0	8	.235	.235	.294	.529	-63	0	0	0	3b7,S6,2b3	0	0.0
Total	5	330	1104	150	346	81	6	11	126	60	7	12	102	.313	.352	.428	.780	+0	5	4	56	3b172,2b92,S54	96	3.8
Team	2	32	50	9	11	2	0	0	4	2	0	0	11	.220	.250	.260	.510	-66	0	0	0	S11,2b8,3b7	0	-0.2
SANCHEZ, REY Rey Francisco (Guadalupe) B10.5.1967 Rio Piedras, PR BR/TR/5'9"/(165–175) [TexA86 13/319] d9.8																								
2002	Bos A	107	357	46	102	12	3	1	38	17	1	2	31	.286	.318	.345	.663	-24	2	2	50	2b100,S10	37	-0.3
Total	15	1490	4850	549	1317	193	32	15	389	229	29	40	508	.272	.308	.334	.642	-32	55	32	63	S984,2b480,3b19,D2	290	3.5
/150	1	150	500	64	143	17	4	1	53	24	1	3	43	.286	.318	.345	.663	-24	3	3	50	2b140,S14	52	-0.4
SANTOS, ANGEL Angel Ramon B8.14.1979 Rio Piedras, PR BB/TR/5'11"/185 [BosA97 4/131] d9.8																								
2001	Bos A	9	16	2	2	1	0	0	1	2	0	0	7	.125	.211	.188	.399	-90	0	0	0	2b6	0	-0.3
Total	2	41	92	11	19	4	1	3	7	5	0	0	25	.207	.245	.370	.615	-40	1	1	50	2b34,3b4	0	-0.5

Year	Tm Lg	G	AB	R	H	2B	3B	HR	RBI	BB	IB	HP	SO	AVG	OBP	SLG	OPS	AOPS	SB	CS	SB%	Games at Position	DL	BFW
SATRIANO, TOM Thomas Victor Nicholas B8.28.1940 Pittsburgh PA BL/TR/6'1"/(185–195) d7.23 Col USC																								
1969	Bos A	47	127	9	24	2	0	0	11	22	7	2	12	.189	.310	.205	.515	-53	0	0	0	C44	0	-0.7
1970	Bos A	59	165	21	39	9	1	3	13	21	3	1	23	.236	.326	.358	.684	-17	0	0	0	C51	0	0.0
Total	10	674	1623	130	365	53	5	21	157	214	27	6	225	.225	.316	.303	.619	-21	7	8	47	C321,3b168,1b83,2b58,S3	0	-4.1
Team	2	106	292	30	63	11	1	3	24	43	10	3	35	.216	.319	.291	.610	-33	0	0	0	C95	0	-0.7
/150	3	150	413	42	89	16	1	4	34	61	14	4	50	.216	.319	.291	.610	-33	0	0	0	C134	0	-1.0
SAX, DAVE David John B9.22.1958 Sacramento CA BR/TR/6'0"/(175–185) d9.1 b–Steve																								
1982	LA N	2	2	0	0	0	0	0	0	0	0	0	0	.000	.000	.000	.000	-199	0	0	0	/lf	0	0.0
1983	LA N	7	8	0	0	0	0	0	1	0	0	0	0	.000	.000	.000	.000	-199	0	0	0	C4	0	-0.3
1985	Bos A	22	36	2	11	3	0	0	6	3	0	0	3	.306	.350	.389	.739	+0	0	1	0	C16,O4(2/0/2)	0	-0.3
1986	Bos A	4	11	1	5	1	0	1	1	0	0	0	1	.455	.455	.818	1.273	+136	0	0	0	C2/1	0	0.2
1987	Bos A	2	3	0	0	0	0	0	0	0	0	0	1	.000	.000	.000	.000	-197	0	0	0	C2	0	0.0
Total	5	37	60	3	16	4	0	1	8	3	0	0	5	.267	.297	.383	.680	-16	0	1	0	C24,O5(3/0/2)/1	0	-0.4
Team	3	28	50	3	16	4	0	1	7	3	0	0	5	.320	.352	.460	.812	+17	0	1	0	C20,O4(2/0/2)/1	0	-0.1
SCARRITT, RUSS Stephen Russell Mallory B1.14.1903 Pensacola FL D12.4.1994 Pensacola FL BL/TR/5'10.5"/165 d4.18 Col Florida																								
1929	Bos A	151	540	69	159	26	17	1	71	34		1	38	.294	.337	.411	.748	-6	13	11	54	O145(134/1/10)		-2.0
1930	Bos A	113	447	48	129	17	8	2	48	12		3	49	.289	.312	.376	.688	-24	4	7	36	O110L		-2.6
1931	Bos A	10	39	2	6	1	0	0	1	2		0	2	.154	.195	.179	.374	-101	0	0	0	O9L		-0.6
1932	Phi N	11	11	0	2	0	0	0	0	1		0	2	.182	.250	.182	.432	-84	0			/lf		-0.1
Total	4	285	1037	119	296	44	25	3	120	49		4	91	.285	.320	.385	.705	-18	17	18	100	O265(254/1/10)		-5.3
Team	3	274	1026	119	294	44	25	3	120	48		4	89	.287	.321	.387	.708	-17	17	18	49	O264(134/1/10)		-5.2
/150	2	150	562	65	161	24	14	2	66	26		2	49	.287	.321	.387	.708	-17	9	10	47	O145(73/1/5)		-2.8
SCHANG, WALLY Walter Henry B8.22.1889 S.Wales NY D3.6.1965 St.Louis MO BB/TR/5'10"/180 d5.9 C3 b–Bobby																								
1918	†Bos A	88	225	36	55	7	1	0	20	46		2	35	.244	.377	.284	.661	+1	4			C57,O16(14/2/0),3b5/S		0.0
1919	Bos A	113	330	43	101	16	3	0	55	71		5	42	.306	.436	.373	.809	+36	15			C103		3.1
1920	Bos A	122	387	58	118	30	7	4	51	64		7	37	.305	.413	.450	.863	+34	7	7	50	C73,O40(0/39/1)		1.8
Total	19	1842	5307	769	1506	264	90	59	710	849		107	573	.284	.393	.401	.794	+17	121	49	100	C1435,O167(97/65/5),3b60/S		20.4
Team	3	323	942	137	274	53	11	4	126	181		14	114	.291	.412	.383	.795	+27	26	7	100	C233,O56(14/41/1),3b5/S		4.9
/150	1	150	437	64	127	25	5	2	59	84		7	53	.291	.412	.383	.795	+27	12	3	100	C108,O26(7/19/0),3b2/S		2.3
SCHERBARTH, BOB Robert Elmer B1.18.1926 Milwaukee WI BR/TR/6'0"/180 d4.23																								
1950	Bos A	1	0	0	0	0	0	0	0	0		0	0	+	+	+	.000	-100	0	0	0	/C	0	0.0
SCHILLING, CHUCK Charles Thomas B10.25.1937 Brooklyn NY BR/TR/5'11"/(165–170) d4.11 Col Manhattan																								
1961	Bos A	158	646	87	167	25	2	5	62	78	0	2	77	.259	.340	.327	.667	-23	7	6	54	2b158	0	0.9
1962	Bos A	119	413	48	95	17	1	7	35	29	5	4	48	.230	.286	.327	.613	-37	1	0	100	2b118	30	-0.5
1963	Bos A	146	576	63	135	25	0	8	33	41	0	5	72	.234	.291	.319	.610	-31	3	2	60	2b143	0	-2.5
1964	Bos A	47	163	18	32	6	0	0	7	15	0	0	22	.196	.263	.233	.496	-62	0	1	0	2b42	0	-1.2
1965	Bos A	71	171	14	41	3	2	3	9	13	0	0	17	.240	.292	.333	.625	-27	0	1	0	2b41	0	0.7
Total	5	541	1969	230	470	76	5	23	146	176	5	11	236	.239	.304	.317	.621	-32	11	10	52	2b502	30	-2.6
/150	1	150	546	64	130	21	1	6	40	49	1	3	65	.239	.304	.317	.621	-32	3	3	50	2b139	8	-0.7
SCHLESINGER, RUDY William Cordes B11.5.1941 Cincinnati OH BR/TR/6'2"/175 d5.4 Col Cincinnati																								
1965	Bos A	1	1	0	0	0	0	0	0	0	0	0	0	.000	.000	.000	.000	-194	0	0	0	/H	0	0.0
SCHMEES, GEORGE George Edward "Rocky" B9.6.1924 Cincinnati OH D10.30.1998 San Jose CA BL/TL/6'0"/195 d4.15																								
1952	StL A	34	61	9	8	1	1	0	3	2		0	18	.131	.159	.180	.339	-106	0	0	0	O19(9/2/8),1b2	0	-0.9
1952	Bos A	42	64	8	13	3	0	0	3	10		0	11	.203	.311	.250	.561	-47	0	1	0	O29(0/18/11),P2,1b2	0	-0.5
1952	Year	76	125	17	21	4	1	0	6	12		0	29	.168	.241	.216	.457	-74	0	1	0	O48(9/20/19),1b4,P2	0	-1.4
SCHMIDT, DAVE David Frederick B12.22.1956 Mesa AZ BR/TR/6'1"/205 [BosA75 2/39] d4.28																								
1981	Bos A	15	42	6	10	1	0	2	3	7	0	0	17	.238	.347	.405	.752	+9	0	0	0	C15	0	-0.2
SCHOFIELD, DICK John Richard "Ducky" B1.7.1935 Springfield IL BB/TR/5'9"/(155–170) d7.3 s–Dick gs–Jayson Werth																								
1969	Bos A	94	226	30	58	9	3	2	20	29	1	4	44	.257	.349	.350	.699	-8	0	2	0	2b37,S11,3b9,O5(3/0/2)	0	0.6
1970	Bos A	76	139	16	26	1	2	1	14	21	2	1	26	.187	.294	.245	.539	-52	0	1	0	2b15,3b15,S3	0	-1.1
Total	19	1321	3083	394	699	113	20	21	211	390	18	26	526	.227	.317	.297	.614	-27	12	29	29	S660,2b159,3b95,O11(5/0/7)	0	0.7
Team	2	170	365	46	84	10	5	3	34	50	3	5	70	.230	.328	.310	.638	-25	0	3	0	2b52,3b24,S14,O5(3/0/2)	0	-0.5
/150	2	150	322	41	74	9	4	3	30	44	3	4	62	.230	.328	.310	.638	-25	0	3	0	2b46,3b21,S12,O4(3/0/2)	0	-0.4
SCHRECKENGOST, OSSEE Ossee Freeman (aka Ossee Schreck) (b Schrecongost) B4.11.1875 New Bethlehem PA D7.9.1914 Philadelphia PA BR/TR/5'10"/180 d9.8																								
1901	Bos A	86	280	37	85	13	5	0	38	19		4		.304	.356	.386	.742	+8	6			C72,1b4		1.3
Total	11	895	3057	304	829	136	31	9	338	102		12		.271	.297	.345	.642	-10	52			C751,1b99,O3(0/1/2)/2S		8.1
SCOTT, GEORGE George Charles "Boomer" B3.23.1944 Greenville MS BR/TR/6'2"/(205–225) d4.12																								
1966	Bos A★	**162**	601	73	147	18	7	27	90	65	13	8	152	.245	.324	.433	.757	+5	4	0	100	1b158,3b5	0	-0.7
1967	†Bos A	159	565	74	171	21	7	19	82	63	10	4	119	.303	.373	.465	.838	+36	10	8	56	1b152,3b2	0	1.0
1968	Bos A	124	350	23	60	14	0	3	25	26	3	5	88	.171	.236	.237	.473	-58	3	5	38	1b112,3b6	0	-3.7
1969	Bos A	152	549	63	139	14	5	16	52	61	12	4	74	.253	.331	.384	.715	-5	4	3	57	3b109,1b53	0	-1.7
1970	Bos A	127	480	50	142	24	5	16	63	44	5	2	95	.296	.355	.467	.822	+18	4	11	27	3b68,1b59	30	-0.6
1971	Bos A	146	537	72	141	16	4	24	78	41	5	5	102	.263	.317	.441	.758	+6	0	3	0	1b143	0	-1.8
1972	Mil A	152	578	71	154	24	4	20	88	43	4	4	130	.266	.321	.426	.747	+23	16	4	80	1b139,3b23	0	0.3
1973	Mil A	158	604	98	185	30	4	24	107	61	6	2	94	.306	.370	.488	.858	+42	9	5	64	1b157/D	0	2.5
1974	Mil A	158	604	74	170	36	2	17	82	59	5	3	90	.281	.345	.432	.777	+24	9	9	50	1b148,D9	0	1.4
1975	Mil A★	158	617	86	176	26	4	**36**	**109**	51	7	3	97	.285	.341	.515	.856	+39	6	5	55	1b144,D12,3b5	0	1.9
1976	Mil A	156	606	73	166	21	5	18	77	53	6	5	118	.274	.334	.414	.748	+21	0	1	0	1b155	0	0.1
1977	Bos A★	157	584	103	157	26	5	33	95	57	4	6	112	.269	.337	.500	.837	+13	1	1	50	1b157	0	-0.4
1978	Bos A	120	412	51	96	16	4	12	54	44	3	0	86	.233	.305	.379	.684	-17	1	1	50	1b113,D7	0	-2.9
1979	Bos A	45	156	18	35	9	1	4	23	17	1	0	22	.224	.299	.372	.671	-24	0	0	0	1b41	0	-1.1
1979	KC A	44	146	19	39	8	2	1	20	12	1	2	32	.267	.329	.370	.699	-13	1	1	50	1b41/3D	0	-0.7
1979	NY A	16	44	9	14	3	1	1	6	2	0	0	7	.318	.340	.500	.840	+28	1	0	100	D15/1	0	0.1
1979	Year	105	346	46	88	20	4	6	49	31	2	2	61	.254	.317	.387	.704	-13	2	1	67	1b83,D17/3	0	-1.7
Total	14	2034	7433	957	1992	306	60	271	1051	699	85	53	1418	.268	.333	.435	.768	+13	69	57	55	1b1773,3b219,D46	30	-6.3
Team	9	1192	4234	527	1088	158	38	154	562	418	56	34	850	.257	.326	.421	.747	+2	27	32	46	1b988,3b190,D7	30	-11.9
/150	1	150	533	66	137	20	5	19	71	53	7	4	107	.257	.326	.421	.747	+2	3	4	43	1b124,3b24/D	4	-1.5
SCOTT, EVERETT Lewis Everett "Deacon" B11.19.1892 Bluffton IN D11.2.1960 Fort Wayne IN BR/TR/5'8"/148 d4.14																								
1914	Bos A	144	539	66	129	15	6	2	37	32		3	43	.239	.286	.301	.587	-24	9	14	39	S143		-2.4
1915	†Bos A	100	359	25	72	11	0	0	28	17		0	21	.201	.237	.231	.468	-59	4	7	36	S100		-2.3
1916	†Bos A	123	366	37	85	19	2	0	27	23		3	24	.232	.283	.295	.578	-27	8			S121/23		0.0
1917	Bos A	**157**	528	40	127	24	7	0	50	20		0	46	.241	.268	.313	.581	-22	12			S157		0.3
1918	†Bos A	**126**	443	40	98	11	5	0	43	12		0	16	.221	.242	.269	.511	-45	11			S126		0.2
1919	Bos A	**138**	507	41	141	19	0	0	38	19		1	26	.278	.306	.316	.622	-21	8			S138		0.4
1920	Bos A	**154**	569	41	153	21	12	4	61	21		4	15	.269	.300	.369	.669	-20	4	11	27	S154		0.1
1921	Bos A	**154**	576	65	151	21	9	1	62	27		0	21	.262	.295	.335	.630	-38	5	9	36	S154		1.9
1922	†NY A	**154**	557	64	150	23	5	3	45	23		5	22	.269	.304	.345	.649	-33	2	3	40	S154		0.5
1923	†NY A	**152**	533	48	131	16	4	6	60	13		2	19	.246	.266	.325	.591	-46	1	3	25	S152		-3.6
1924	NY A	**153**	548	56	137	12	6	4	64	21		0	15	.250	.278	.316	.594	-47	3	7	30	S153		-1.6
1925	NY A	22	60	3	13	0	0	0	4	2		0	2	.217	.242	.217	.459	-83	0	1	0	S18		-0.4
1925	Was A	33	103	10	28	6	1	0	18	4		0	4	.272	.299	.350	.649	-35	1	2	33	S30,3b2		-0.4
1925	Year	55	163	13	41	6	1	0	22	6		0	6	.252	.278	.301	.579	-52	1	3	25	S48,3b2		-0.8
1926	Chi A	40	143	15	36	10	1	0	13	9		0	8	.252	.296	.336	.632	-33	1	3	25	S39		0.0
1926	Cin N	4	6	1	4	0	0	0	1	0		0	0	.667	.667	.667	1.334	+167	0			S4		0.1

Year	Tm Lg	G	AB	R	H	2B	3B	HR	RBI	BB	IB	HP	SO	AVG	OBP	SLG	OPS	AOPS	SB	CS	SB%	Games at Position	DL	BFW
1926	Major	44	149	16	40	10	1	0	14	9	0	0	8	.268	.310	.349	.659	-65	1	3				0.1
Total	13	1654	5837	552	1455	208	58	20	551	243		18	282	.249	.281	.315	.596	-35	69	60	100	S1643,3b3/2		-7.2
Team	8	1096	3887	355	956	141	41	7	346	171		11	212	.246	.280	.309	.589	-31	61	41	100	S1093/23		-1.8
/150	1	150	532	49	131	19	6	1	47	23		2	29	.246	.280	.309	.589	-31	8	6	100	S150/23		-0.2
SEEDS, BOB Ira Robert "Suitcase Bob" B2.24.1907 Ringgold TX D10.28.1993 Erick OK BR/TR/6'0"/180 d4.19																								
1933	Bos A	82	230	26	56	13	4	0	23	21		1	20	.243	.310	.335	.645	-29	1	3	25	1b41,O32(17/0/16)		-1.4
1934	Bos A	8	6	0	1	0	0	0	1	0		0	1	.167	.167	.167	.334	-113	0	0	0	/rf		-0.1
Total	9	615	1937	268	537	77	21	28	233	160		10	190	.277	.336	.382	.718	-11	14	15	100	O472(194/160/131),1b43,3b3		-7.2
Team	2	90	236	26	57	13	4	0	24	21		1	21	.242	.306	.331	.637	-31	1	3	25	1b41,O33(17/0/16)		-1.5
SELBACH, KIP Albert Karl B3.24.1872 Columbus OH D2.17.1956 Columbus OH BR/TR/5'7"/190 d4.24																								
1904	Bos A	98	376	50	97	19	8	0	30	48		3		.258	.347	.351	.698	+14	10			O98L		0.4
1905	Bos A	121	418	54	103	16	6	4	47	67		3		.246	.355	.342	.697	+20	12			O112(0/20/92)		0.2
1906	Bos A	60	228	15	48	9	2	0	23	18		3		.211	.277	.268	.545	-29	7			O58L		-1.1
Total	13	1612	6165	1066	1807	301	149	44	779	785		42	76	.293	.377	.412	.789	+21	334			O1570(1356/66/148),S26,2b5/3		13.9
Team	3	279	1022	119	248	44	16	4	100	133		9	0	.243	.335	.329	.664	+7	29			O268(98/20/20)		-0.5
/150	2	150	549	64	133	24	9	2	54	72		5	0	.243	.335	.329	.664	+7	16			O144(53/11/11)		-0.3
SELBY, BILL William Frank B6.11.1970 Monroeville AL BL/TR/5'9"/(190–195) [BosA92 13/366] d4.19 Col Southern Mississippi																								
1996	Bos A	40	95	12	26	4	0	3	6	9	1	0	11	.274	.337	.411	.748	-14	1	1	50	2b14,3b14,O6L	0	-0.7
Total	5	198	431	45	96	20	3	11	48	33	4	2	71	.223	.279	.360	.639	-37	1	2	33	3b69,2b48,O35(24/0/11),D8,1b3	0	-3.0
SHANER, WALLY Walter Dedaker "Skinny" B5.24.1900 Lynchburg VA D11.13.1992 Las Vegas NV BR/TR/6'2"/195 d5.4 Col VPI																								
1923	Cle A	3	4	1	1	0	0	0	0	1		0	1	.250	.400	.250	.650	-26	0	0	0	O2L/3		0.0
1926	Bos A	69	191	20	54	12	2	0	21	17		2	13	.283	.348	.366	.714	-11	1	0	100	O48L		-0.9
1927	Bos A	122	406	54	111	33	6	3	49	21		1	35	.273	.311	.406	.717	-13	11	4	73	O108(85/25/10)/1		-1.6
1929	Cin N	13	28	5	9	0	0	1	4	4		0	5	.321	.406	.429	.835	+12	1			1b8,O2L		-0.1
Total	4	207	629	80	175	45	8	4	74	43		3	54	.278	.327	.394	.721	-11	13	4	100	O160(137/25/10),1b9/3		-2.6
Team	2	191	597	74	165	45	8	3	70	38		3	48	.276	.323	.394	.717	-12	12	4	75	O156(133/2/2)/1		-2.5
/150	2	150	469	58	130	35	6	2	55	30		2	38	.276	.323	.394	.717	-12	9	3	75	O123(104/2/2)/1		-2.0
SHANKS, HOWIE Howard Samuel "Hank" B7.21.1890 Chicago IL D7.30.1941 Monaca PA BR/TR/5'11"/170 d5.9 C5 OF(603/55/44)																								
1923	Bos A	131	464	38	118	19	5	3	57	19		1	37	.254	.285	.336	.621	-37	6	6	50	3b83,2b38,O6(4/1/1)/S		-3.3
1924	Bos A	72	193	22	50	16	3	0	25	21		0	12	.259	.332	.373	.705	-19	1	0	100	S41,3b22,O4R,1b2,2b2		0.5
Total	14	1665	5699	604	1440	211	96	25	620	415		37	443	.253	.308	.337	.645	-18	185	64	100	O702L,3b485,S235,2b159,1b25		-16.6
Team	2	203	657	60	168	35	8	3	82	40		1	49	.256	.299	.347	.646	-31	7	6	54	3b105,S42,2b40,O10(4/1/1),1b2		-2.8
/150	1	150	485	44	124	26	6	2	61	30		1	36	.256	.299	.347	.646	-31	5	4	56	3b78,S31,2b30,O7(3/1/1)/1		-2.1
SHANNON, RED Maurice Joseph B2.11.1897 Jersey City NJ D4.12.1970 Jersey City NJ BB/TR/5'11"/170 d10.7 twb–Joe Col Seton Hall																								
1919	Bos A	80	290	36	75	11	7	0	17	17		6	42	.259	.313	.345	.658	-10	7			2b79		-0.5
Total	7	310	1070	124	277	38	22	0	91	109		12	178	.259	.334	.336	.670	-11	21	6	100	2b159,S123,3b15		-2.0
SHAW, AL Alfred Louis "Shoddy" B5.22.1873 Burslem, England D3.25.1958 Uhrichsville OH BR/TR/5'8"/170 d6.8																								
1901	Det A	55	171	20	46	7	0	1	23	10		3		.269	.321	.327	.648	-24	2			C42,1b9,3b2/S		-0.1
1907	Bos A	76	198	10	38	1	3	0	7	18		3		.192	.269	.227	.496	-41	4			C73/1		1.0
1908	Chi A	32	49	0	4	1	0	0	2	2		0		.082	.118	.102	.220	-129	0			C29		-0.6
1909	Bos N	18	41	1	4	0	0	0	0	5		1		.098	.213	.098	.311	-103	0			C14		-0.2
Total	4	181	459	31	92	9	3	1	32	35		7		.200	.267	.240	.507	-47	6			C158,1b10,3b2/S		0.1
SHEA, MERV Mervyn John B9.5.1900 San Francisco CA D1.27.1953 Sacramento CA BR/TR/5'11"/175 d4.23 C8																								
1933	Bos A	16	56	1	8	3	0	0	8	4		0	7	.143	.200	.196	.396	-95	0	0	0	C16		-0.7
Total	11	439	1197	105	263	39	7	5	115	189		1	145	.220	.327	.277	.604	-42	8	3	100	C407	0	-3.8
SHEAFFER, DANNY Danny Todd B8.2.1961 Jacksonville FL BR/TR/6'0"/(185–202) [BosA81*1/20] d4.9 Col Clemson OF(20/2/9)																								
1987	Bos A	25	66	5	8	1	0	1	5	0	0	0	14	.121	.119	.182	.301	-121	0	0	0	C25	0	-1.5
Total	7	389	946	87	219	38	5	13	110	60	2	5	122	.232	.278	.323	.601	-44	6	8	43	C243,3b51,O29L,1b18,2b3,D3	0	-4.2
SHEAN, DAVE David William B7.9.1883 Arlington MA D5.22.1963 Boston MA BR/TR/5'11"/175 d9.10 Col Fordham																								
1918	†Bos A	115	425	58	112	16	3	0	34	40		3	25	.264	.331	.315	.646	-3	11			2b115		-0.4
1919	Bos A	29	100	4	14	0	0	0	8	5		1	7	.140	.189	.140	.329	-107	1			2b29		-1.2
Total	9	630	2167	225	495	59	23	6	166	155		13	133	.228	.284	.285	.569	-30	66			2b554,S38,1b11,O3C/3		-1.9
Team	2	144	525	62	126	16	3	0	42	45		4	32	.240	.305	.282	.587	-22	12			2b144		-1.6
/150	2	150	547	65	131	17	3	0	44	47		4	33	.240	.305	.282	.587	-22	13			2b150		-1.7
SHEETS, ANDY Andrew Mark B11.19.1971 Baton Rouge LA BR/TR/6'2"/180 [SeaA92 4/110] d4.22 Col Louisiana St.																								
2000	Bos A	12	21	1	2	0	0	0	1	0	0	0	3	.095	.095	.095	.190	-150	0	0	0	S10/1D	0	-0.3
Total	7	356	960	118	207	38	3	19	113	76	3	2	275	.216	.271	.321	.592	-45	16	7	70	S201,2b75,3b74,1b3,D2	0	-6.4
SHERIDAN, NEILL Neill Rawlins "Wild Horse" B11.20.1921 Sacramento CA BR/TR/6'1.5"/195 d9.19 Col San Francisco																								
1948	Bos A	2	1	0	0	0	0	0	0	0		0	1	.000	.000	.000	.000	-195	0	0	0	/H	0	0.0
SHOFNER, STRICK Frank Strickland B7.23.1919 Crawford TX D10.10.1998 Crawford TX BL/TR/5'10.5"/187 d4.19																								
1947	Bos A	5	13	1	2	0	1	0	0	0		0	3	.154	.154	.308	.462	-75	0	0	0	3b4	0	-0.1
SHOPPACH, KELLY Kelly Brian B4.29.1980 Fort Worth TX BR/TR/6'1"/210 [BosA01 2/48] d5.28 Col Baylor																								
2005	Bos A	9	15	1	0	0	0	0	0	0	0	1	7	.000	.063	.000	.063	-178	0	0	0	C7,D2	0	-0.6
Total	2	50	125	8	27	6	0	3	16	8	0	1	52	.216	.269	.336	.605	-43	0	0	0	C47,D2	0	-0.2
SHORTEN, CHICK Charles Henry B4.19.1892 Scranton PA D10.23.1965 Scranton PA BL/TL/6'0"/175 d9.22 Mil 1918																								
1915	Bos A	6	14	1	3	1	0	0	0	0		0	2	.214	.214	.286	.500	-49	0			O5(0/4/1)		-0.1
1916	†Bos A	53	112	14	33	2	1	0	11	10		0	8	.295	.352	.330	.682	+5	1			O33(13/19/1)		-0.4
1917	Bos A	69	168	12	30	4	2	0	16	10		1	10	.179	.229	.226	.455	-61	2			O43(16/20/7)		-2.0
Total	8	527	1345	161	370	51	20	3	134	110		1	68	.275	.330	.349	.679	-13	12	8	100	O352(47/144/162)		-6.2
Team	3	128	294	27	66	7	3	0	27	20		1	20	.224	.276	.269	.545	-35	3			O81(13/30/27)		-2.5
/150	4	150	345	32	77	8	4	0	32	23		1	23	.224	.276	.269	.545	-35	4			O95(15/35/32)		-2.9
SHUMPERT, TERRY Terrance Darnell B8.16.1966 Paducah KY BR/TR/5'11"/(185–200) [KCA87 2/41] d5.1 Col Kentucky OF(84/9/15)																								
1995	Bos A	21	47	6	11	3	0	0	3	4	0	0	13	.234	.294	.298	.592	-47	3	1	75	2b8,3b5,S3/D	0	0.0
Total	14	854	1969	295	497	109	26	49	223	166	5	24	369	.252	.315	.409	.724	-20	85	29	75	2b467,O108L,3b94,D25,S23,1b6	248	-5.9
SIEBERN, NORM Norman Leroy B7.26.1933 St.Louis MO BL/TR/6'3"/(200–205) d6.15																								
1967	†Bos A	33	44	2	9	0	2	0	7	6	1	0	8	.205	.300	.295	.595	-29	0	0	0	1b13/lf	0	-0.2
1968	Bos A	27	30	0	2	0	0	0	0	0	0	0	5	.067	.067	.067	.134	-156	0	0	0	1b2,O2(1/0/1)	0	-0.7
Total	12	1406	4481	662	1217	206	38	132	636	708	47	10	748	.272	.369	.423	.792	+17	18	25	42	1b827,O420(402/16/11)	0	5.8
Team	2	60	74	2	11	0	2	0	7	6	1	0	13	.149	.213	.203	.416	-77	0	0	0	1b15,O3L	0	-0.9
SIMMONS, AL Aloysius Harry "Bucketfoot Al" (b Aloys Szymanski) B5.22.1902 Milwaukee WI D5.26.1956 Milwaukee WI BR/TR/5'11"/190 d4.15 C11 HF1953																								
1943	Bos A	40	133	9	27	5	0	1	12	8		0	21	.203	.248	.263	.511	-51	0	1	0	O33L	0	-1.3
Total	20	2215	8759	1507	2927	539	149	307	1827	615		30	737	.334	.380	.535	.915	+32	88	65	100	O2142(1377/771/1)/1	0	23.0
SIZEMORE, TED Theodore Crawford B4.15.1945 Gadsden AL BR/TR/5'10"/(155–170) [LAN66 15/299] d4.7 Col Michigan																								
1979	Bos A	26	88	12	23	7	0	1	6	4	0	1	5	.261	.301	.375	.676	-23	1	0	100	2b26,C2	0	0.6
1980	Bos A	9	23	1	5	1	0	0	0	0	0	0	0	.217	.217	.261	.478	-71	0	0	0	2b8	0	-0.2
Total	12	1411	5011	577	1311	188	21	23	430	469	60	20	350	.262	.325	.321	.646	-21	59	46	56	2b1288,S88,O26(16/0/10),3b7,C4	116	3.4
Team	2	35	111	13	28	8	0	1	6	4	0	1	5	.252	.284	.351	.635	-33	1	0	100	2b34,C2	0	0.4
SKINNER, CAMP Elisha Harrison B6.25.1897 Douglasville GA D8.4.1944 Douglasville GA BL/TR/5'11"/165 d5.2																								
1923	Bos A	7	13	1	3	2	0	0	1	0		0	0	.231	.231	.385	.616	-40	0	0	0	O2C		-0.1
Total	2	34	46	2	9	2	0	0	3	0		1	4	.196	.213	.239	.452	-82	1	0	100	O6(1/5/0)		-0.6
SLATTERY, JACK John Thomas B1.6.1878 S.Boston MA D7.17.1949 Boston MA BR/TR/6'2"/191 d9.28 M1/C2 Col Fordham																								
1901	Bos A	1	3	1	1	0	0	0	1	1		0		.333	.500	.333	.833	+37	0			/C		0.1
Total	4	103	288	14	61	5	2	0	27	6		3		.212	.236	.243	.479	-53	3			C65,1b18		-2.1

Year	Tm Lg	G	AB	R	H	2B	3B	HR	RBI	BB	IB	HP	SO	AVG	OBP	SLG	OPS	AOPS	SB	CS	SB%	Games at Position	DL	BFW
SMALL, CHARLIE	Charles Albert B10.24.1905 Auburn ME D1.14.1953 Auburn ME BL/TR/5'11"/180 d7.7 Col Bates																							
1930	Bos A	25	18	1	3	1	0	0	0	2		0	5	.167	.250	.222	.472	-78	1	0	100	/cf		-0.2
SMITH, ALECK	Alexander Benjamin "Broadway Aleck" B1871 New York NY D7.9.1919 New York NY TR d4.23 OF(35/13/10)																							
1903	Bos A	11	33	4	10	1	0	0	4	0		0		.303	.303	.333	.636	-14	0			C10		0.1
Total	9	287	955	107	252	30	11	1	130	26		6		.264	.288	.321	.609	-31	37			C187,O57L,1b18,3b10,2b5		-5.4
SMITH, AL	Alphonse Eugene "Fuzzy" B2.7.1928 Kirkwood MO D1.3.2002 Hammond IN BR/TR/6'0"/(189–196) d7.10 Negro Lg 1946–48																							
1964	Bos A	29	51	10	11	4	0	2	7	13	0	1	10	.216	.385	.412	.797	+16	0	0	0	3b10,O8(2/0/6)	0	0.2
Total	12	1517	5357	843	1458	258	46	164	676	674	30	63	768	.272	.358	.429	.787	+13	67	43	61	O1118(399/87/679),3b378,S9,2b2	0	-0.9
SMITH, REGGIE	Carl Reginald B4.2.1945 Shreveport LA BB/TR/6'0"/(170–195) d9.18 Mil 1963 C5 OF(3/808/874)																							
1966	Bos A	6	26	1	4	1	0	0	0	0	0	0	5	.154	.154	.192	.346	-101	0	0	0	O6C	0	-0.4
1967	†Bos A	158	565	78	139	24	6	15	61	57	11	1	95	.246	.315	.389	.704	-1	16	6	73	O144C,2b6	0	0.1
1968	Bos A	155	558	78	148	**37**	5	15	69	64	13	4	77	.265	.342	.430	.772	+26	22	18	55	O155C	0	1.7
1969	Bos A★	143	543	87	168	29	7	25	93	54	7	1	67	.309	.368	.527	.895	+42	7	13	35	O139(3/136/0)	0	1.9
1970	Bos A	147	580	109	176	32	7	22	74	51	1	4	60	.303	.361	.497	.858	+26	10	7	59	O145C	0	2.4
1971	Bos A	159	618	85	175	**33**	2	30	96	63	4	5	82	.283	.352	.489	.841	+27	11	3	79	O159(0/87/74)	0	2.6
1972	Bos A★	131	467	75	126	25	4	21	74	68	12	4	63	.270	.365	.475	.840	+41	15	4	79	O129(0/4/125)	0	2.3
1973	Bos A	115	423	79	128	23	2	21	69	68	7	1	49	.303	.398	.515	.913	+47	3	2	60	O104C/1D	0	3.0
1974	StL N★	143	517	79	160	26	9	23	100	71	10	1	70	.309	.389	.528	.917	+56	4	3	57	O132R/1	0	3.4
1975	StL N★	135	477	67	144	26	3	19	76	63	9	3	59	.302	.382	.488	.870	+36	9	7	56	O69(0/1/68),1b66/3	0	1.1
1976	StL N	47	170	20	37	7	1	8	23	14	2	1	28	.218	.281	.412	.693	-7	1	2	33	1b17,O16(0/3/13),3b13	0	0.2
1976	LA N	65	225	35	63	8	4	10	26	18	4	1	42	.280	.335	.484	.819	+32	2	0	100	O58(0/1/57)/3	0	0.7
1976	Year	112	395	55	100	15	5	18	49	32	6	2	70	.253	.312	.453	.765	+15	3	2	60	O74(0/4/70),1b17,3b14	0	0.9
1977	†LA N★	148	488	104	150	27	4	32	87	104	11	3	76	.307	**.427**	.576	1.003	+67	7	5	58	O140(0/9/138)	0	3.7
1978	†LA N★	128	447	82	132	27	2	29	93	70	8	1	90	.295	.382	.559	.941	+63	12	5	71	O126(0/1/126)	0	3.0
1979	LA N	68	234	41	64	13	1	10	32	31	3	2	50	.274	.359	.466	.825	+27	6	5	55	O62(0/5/59)	42	1.4
1980	LA N★	92	311	47	100	13	0	15	55	41	1	1	63	.322	.392	.508	.900	+57	5	6	45	O84(0/7/82)	42	2.7
1981	†LA N	41	35	5	7	1	0	1	8	7	3	0	8	.200	.318	.314	.632	-12	0	0	0	1b2	0	0.0
1982	SF N	106	349	51	99	11	0	18	56	46	9	0	46	.284	.364	.470	.834	+34	7	0	100	1b99	15	1.7
Total	17	1987	7033	1123	2020	363	57	314	1092	890	11	33	1030	.287	.366	.489	.855	+36	137	86	61	O1668R,1b186,3b15,D8,2b6	99	31.5
Team	8	1014	3780	592	1064	204	33	149	536	425	55	20	498	.281	.355	.471	.826	+28	84	53	61	O981(0/40/21),2b6/1D	0	13.6
/150	1	150	559	88	157	30	5	22	79	63	8	3	74	.281	.355	.471	.826	+28	12	8	60	O145(0/6/3)/21D	0	2.0
SMITH, ELMER	Elmer John B9.21.1892 Sandusky OH D8.3.1984 Columbia KY BL/TR/5'10"/165 d9.20 Mil 1918																							
1922	Bos A	73	231	43	66	13	6	6	32	25		1	21	.286	.358	.472	.830	+16	0	3	0	O58(0/1/57)		0.2
Total	10	1012	3195	469	881	181	62	70	541	319		16	359	.276	.344	.437	.781	+12	54	27	100	O870(123/16/732)		-1.7
SMITH, GEORGE	George Cornelius B7.7.1937 St.Petersburg FL D6.15.1987 St.Petersburg FL BR/TR/5'10"/168 d8.4 Col Michigan St.																							
1963	Det A	52	171	16	37	8	2	0	17	18	1	2	34	.216	.298	.287	.585	-37	4	0	100	2b52	0	0.4
1964	Det A	5	7	1	2	0	0	0	2	1	0	0	4	.286	.375	.286	.661	-14	1	0	100	2b3	0	0.0
1965	Det A	32	53	6	5	0	0	1	1	3	0	0	18	.094	.143	.151	.294	-116	0	0	0	2b22,S3,3b3	0	-1.0
1966	Bos A	128	403	41	86	19	4	8	37	37	6	3	86	.213	.283	.340	.623	-29	4	0	100	2b109,S19	0	-0.2
Total	4	217	634	64	130	27	6	9	57	59	7	5	142	.205	.277	.309	.586	-38	9	0	100	2b186,S22,3b3	0	-0.8
/150	1	150	472	48	101	22	5	9	43	43	7	4	101	.213	.283	.340	.623	-29	5	0	100	2b128,S22	0	-0.2
SMITH, JOHN	John Marshall B9.27.1906 Washington DC D5.9.1982 Silver Spring MD BB/TR/6'1"/180 d9.17																							
1931	Bos A	4	15	2	2	0	0	0	1	2		0	1	.133	.235	.133	.368	-101	1	0	100	1b4		-0.3
SMITH, PADDY	Lawrence Patrick B5.16.1894 Pelham NY D12.2.1990 New Rochelle NY BL/TR/6'0"/195 d7.6 Col Fordham																							
1920	Bos A	2	2	0	0	0	0	0	0	0		0	1	.000	.000	.000	.000	-199	0	0	0	/C		-0.1
SNELL, WALLY	Walter Henry "Doc" B5.19.1889 W.Bridgewater MA D7.23.1980 Providence RI BR/TR/5'10"/170 d8.1 Col Brown																							
1913	Bos A	6	12	1	3	0	0	0	0	0		0	1	.250	.250	.250	.500	-55	1			C2		-0.1
SNOPEK, CHRIS	Christopher Charles B9.20.1970 Cynthiana KY BR/TR/6'1"/185 [ChiA92 6/176] d7.31 Col U. of Mississippi																							
1998	Bos A	8	12	2	2	0	0	0	2	2	0	0	5	.167	.286	.167	.453	-79	0	0	0	2b3,3b3,D2	0	-0.2
Total	4	215	607	76	142	27	1	13	66	49	0	3	108	.234	.293	.346	.639	-33	7	3	70	3b132,S55,2b15,D6/rf1	0	-4.0
SNOW, J.T.	Jack Thomas B2.26.1968 Long Beach CA BL/TL (BB 1992–98)/6'2"/(202–210) [NYA89 5/129] d9.20 Col Arizona																							
2006	Bos A	38	44	5	9	0	0	0	4	8	0	1	8	.205	.340	.205	.545	-55	0	0	0	1b26/D	0	-0.4
Total	15	1715	5641	798	1509	293	19	189	877	760	61	64	1142	.268	.357	.427	.784	+5	20	23	47	1b1656,D2	118	-6.8
SNYDER, EARL	Earl Clifford B5.6.1976 New Britain CT BR/TR/6'0"/(200–207) [NYN98 36/1084] d4.28 Col Hartford																							
2004	Bos A	1	4	0	1	0	0	0	0	0	0	0	1	.250	.250	.250	.500	-71	0	0	0	/3	0	0.0
Total	2	19	59	5	12	2	0	1	4	6	0	0	22	.203	.277	.288	.565	-51	0	0	0	1b12,3b3/D	0	-0.5
SOLTERS, MOOSE	Julius Joseph (b Julius Joseph Soltesz) B3.22.1906 Pittsburgh PA D9.28.1975 Pittsburgh PA BR/TR/6'0"/190 d4.17																							
1934	Bos A	101	365	61	109	25	4	7	58	18		1	50	.299	.333	.447	.780	-7	9	4	69	O89(6/57/26)		-0.9
1935	Bos A	24	79	15	19	6	1	0	8	2		1	7	.241	.268	.342	.610	-47	1	1	50	O21(10/0/11)		-0.5
Total	9	938	3421	503	990	213	42	83	599	221		9	377	.289	.334	.449	.783	-4	42	23	65	O825(687/76/67)	0	-4.6
Team	2	125	444	76	128	31	5	7	66	20		2	57	.288	.322	.428	.750	-14	10	5	67	O110(16/57/37)		-1.4
/150	2	150	533	91	154	37	6	8	79	24		2	68	.288	.322	.428	.750	-14	12	6	67	O132(19/68/44)		-1.7
SPEAKER, TRIS	Tristram E "The Grey Eagle" B4.4.1888 Hubbard TX D12.8.1958 Lake Whitney TX BL/TL/5'11.5"/193 d9.12 M8 HF1937 Col Texas Wesleyan																							
1907	Bos A	7	19	0	3	0	0	0	1	1		0		.158	.200	.158	.358	-86	0			O4R		-0.1
1908	Bos A	31	116	12	26	2	2	0	9	4		2		.224	.262	.276	.538	-27	3			O31(1/30/0)		-0.1
1909	Bos A	143	544	73	168	26	13	7	77	38		7		.309	.362	.443	.805	+51	35			O142C		4.6
1910	Bos A	141	538	92	183	20	14	7	65	52		6		.340	.404	.468	.872	+69	35			O140C		4.8
1911	Bos A	141	500	88	167	34	13	8	70	59		13		.334	.418	.502	.920	+58	25			O138C		3.3
1912	†Bos A	153	580	136	222	**53**	12	**10**	90	82		6		.383	**.464**	.567	1.031	+85	52			O153C		**7.2**
1913	Bos A	141	520	94	189	35	22	3	71	65		7	22	.363	.441	.533	.974	+80	46			O139C		6.5
1914	Bos A	158	571	101	**193**	**46**	18	4	90	77		7	25	.338	.423	.503	.926	+78	42	29	59	O156C/P1		**7.3**
1915	†Bos A	150	547	108	176	25	12	0	69	81		7	14	.322	.416	.411	.827	+52	29	25	54	O150C		3.6
1916	Cle A	151	546	102	**211**	**41**	8	2	79	82		4	20	**.386**	**.470**	**.502**	.972	+81	35	27	56	O151C		**5.7**
1917	Cle A	142	523	90	184	42	11	2	60	67		7	14	.352	.432	.486	.918	+68	30			O142C		4.1
1918	Cle A	127	471	73	150	**33**	11	0	61	64		3	9	.318	.403	.435	.838	+40	27			O127C		2.7
1919	Cle A	134	494	83	146	38	12	2	63	73		8	12	.296	.395	.433	.828	+25	19			O134C,M		2.6
1920	†Cle A	150	552	137	214	**50**	11	8	107	97		5	13	.388	.483	.562	1.045	+71	10	13	43	O148C,M		5.4
1921	Cle A	132	506	107	183	**52**	14	3	75	68		2	12	.362	.439	.538	.977	+46	2	4	33	O128C,M		3.8
1922	Cle A	131	426	85	161	**48**	8	11	71	77		1	11	.378	**.474**	.606	1.080	+78	8	3	73	O109C,M		5.1
1923	Cle A	150	574	133	218	**59**	11	17	130	93		4	15	.380	.469	.610	1.079	+83	8	9	47	O150C,M		6.5
1924	Cle A	135	486	94	167	36	9	9	65	72		4	13	.344	.432	.510	.942	+41	5	7	42	O128(0/127/1),M		2.5
1925	Cle A	117	429	79	167	35	5	12	87	70		4	12	.389	**.479**	.578	1.057	+66	5	2	71	O109C,M		**4.3**
1926	Cle A	150	539	96	164	52	8	7	86	94		0	15	.304	.408	.469	.877	+27	6	1	86	O149C,M		2.4
1927	Was A	141	523	71	171	43	6	2	73	55		4	8	.327	.395	.444	.839	+19	9	8	53	O120(0/119/1),1b17		0.7
1928	Phi A	64	191	28	51	22	2	3	30	10		2	5	.267	.310	.450	.760	-5	5	1	83	O50(1/49/0)		-0.2
Total	22	2789	10195	1882	3514	792	222	117	1529	1381		103	220	.345	.428	.500	.928	+56	436	12	100	O2698(2/2690/6),1b18/P		82.7
Team	9	1065	3935	704	1327	241	106	39	542	459		55	61	.337	.414	.482	.896	+65	267	54	100	O1053(1/11/7)/P1		37.1
/150	1	150	554	99	187	34	15	5	76	65		8	9	.337	.414	.482	.896	+65	38	8	100	O148(0/2/1)/P1		5.2
SPENCE, STAN	Stanley Orville B3.20.1915 S.Portsmouth KY D1.9.1983 Kinston NC BL/TL/5'10.5"/180 d6.8 Mil 1945																							
1940	Bos A	51	68	5	19	2	1	2	13	4		0	9	.279	.319	.426	.745	-12	0	1	0	O15(6/0/9)		-0.3
1941	Bos A	86	203	22	47	10	3	2	28	18		3	14	.232	.304	.340	.644	-32	1	0	100	O52(27/10/16)/1	0	-0.8
1948	Bos A	114	391	71	92	17	4	12	61	82		0	33	.235	.368	.391	.759	-3	0	2	0	O92(24/0/70),1b14	0	-0.8
1949	Bos A	7	20	3	3	1	0	0	1	6		0	1	.150	.346	.200	.546	-57	0	0	0	O5(0/2/3)	0	-0.1

Year	Tm Lg	G	AB	R	H	2B	3B	HR	RBI	BB	IB	HP	SO	AVG	OBP	SLG	OPS	AOPS	SB	CS	SB%	Games at Position	DL	BFW
Total	9	1112	3871	541	1090	196	60	95	575	520		19	248	.282	.369	.437	.806	+26	21	23	48	O990(90/801/104),1b19	0	12.9
Team	4	258	682	101	161	30	8	16	103	110		3	57	.236	.345	.374	.719	-14	1	3	25	O164(35/83/92),1b15	0	-2.0
/150	2	150	397	59	94	17	5	9	60	64		2	33	.236	.345	.374	.719	-14	1	2	33	O95(20/48/53),1b9	0	-1.2
SPENCER, TUBBY Edward Russell B1.26.1884 Oil City PA D2.1.1945 San Francisco CA BR/TR/5'10"/215 d7.23																								
1909	Bos A	28	74	6	12	1	0	0	9	6		0		.162	.225	.176	.401	-74	2			C26		-0.6
Total	9	449	1326	106	298	43	10	3	133	87		17	46	.225	.281	.279	.560	-24	13			C405/1		-3.9
SPOGNARDI, ANDY Andrea Ettore B10.18.1908 Boston MA D1.1.2000 Dedham MA BR/TR/5'9.5"/160 d9.2 Col Boston College																								
1932	Bos A	17	34	9	10	1	0	0	1	6		0	6	.294	.400	.324	.724	-8	0	0	0	2b9,S3,3b2		0.3
SPRAGUE, ED Edward Nelson Jr. B7.25.1967 Castro Valley CA BR/TR/6'2"/(205–215) [TorA88 1/25] d5.7 f-Ed Col Stanford OF(14/0/2)																								
2000	Bos A	33	111	11	24	4	0	2	9	12	0	0	18	.216	.293	.306	.599	-49	0	0	0	3b30,1b3/D	0	-0.8
Total	11	1203	4095	506	1010	225	12	152	558	358	21	91	833	.247	.318	.419	.737	-10	6	12	33	3b1019,1b77,D34,C18,O16L/2	63	-12.4
STAHL, CHICK Charles Sylvester B1.10.1873 Avilla IN D3.28.1907 W.Baden IN BL/TL/5'10"/160 d4.19 M1																								
1897	†Bos N	114	469	112	166	30	13	4	97	38		3		.354	.406	.499	.905	+30	18			O111(1/0/110)		0.8
1898	Bos N	125	467	72	144	21	8	3	52	46		4		.308	.375	.407	.782	+18	6			O125(8/0/118)		0.2
1899	Bos N	148	576	122	202	23	19	7	52	72		4		.351	.426	.493	.919	+38	33			O148(1/1/146)/P		2.4
1900	Bos N	136	553	88	163	23	16	5	82	34		0		.295	.336	.421	.757	-4	27			O135(64/1/71)		-1.0
1901	Bos A	131	515	105	156	20	16	6	72	54		7		.303	.377	.439	.816	+28	29			O131(0/130/1)		0.8
1902	Bos A	127	508	92	164	22	11	2	58	37		5		.323	.375	.421	.796	+17	24			O125C		0.0
1903	†Bos A	77	299	60	82	12	6	2	44	28		1		.274	.338	.375	.713	+8	10			O74C		-0.3
1904	Bos A	**157**	587	83	170	27	**19**	3	67	64		7		.290	.366	.416	.782	+39	11			O157C		0.2
1905	Bos A	134	500	61	129	17	4	0	47	50		5		.258	.332	.308	.640	+2	18			O134C		-1.1
1906	Bos A	**155**	595	63	170	24	6	4	51	47		8		.286	.346	.366	.712	+23	13			O155C,M		1.8
Total	10	1304	5069	858	1546	219	118	36	622	470		44		.305	.369	.416	.785	+21	189			O1295(74/777/446)/P		3.8
Team	6	781	3004	464	871	122	62	17	339	280		33	0	.290	.357	.389	.746	+21	105			O776(0/131/1)/M		1.4
/150	1	150	577	89	167	23	12	3	65	54		6	0	.290	.357	.389	.746	+21	20			O149C/M		0.3
STAHL, JAKE Garland B4.13.1879 Elkhart IL D9.18.1922 Monrovia CA BR/TR/6'2"/195 d4.20 M4 Col Illinois																								
1903	Bos A	40	92	14	22	3	5	2	8	4		2		.239	.286	.446	.732	+11	1			C28/If		0.3
1904	Was A	142	520	54	136	29	12	3	50	21		15		.262	.309	.381	.690	+19	25			1b119,O23C		1.3
1905	Was A	141	501	66	125	22	12	5	66	28		**17**		.250	.311	.371	.682	+21	41			1b140,M		1.1
1906	Was A	137	482	38	107	9	8	0	51	21		8		.222	.266	.274	.540	-27	30			1b136,M		-2.3
1908	NY A	75	274	34	70	18	5	2	42	11		8		.255	.304	.380	.684	+20	17			O68(64/4/0),1b6		0.7
1908	Bos A	78	262	29	64	9	11	0	23	20		15		.244	.333	.363	.696	+23	13			1b78		0.4
1908	Year	153	536	63	134	27	16	2	65	31		**23**		.250	.319	.371	.690	+22	30			1b84,O68(64/4/0)		1.1
1909	Bos A	127	435	62	128	19	12	6	60	43		15		.294	.377	.434	.811	+53	16			1b126		1.5
1910	Bos A	144	531	68	144	19	16	**10**	77	42		8		.271	.334	.424	.758	+34	22			1b142		0.9
1912	†Bos A	95	326	40	98	21	6	3	60	31		6		.301	.372	.429	.801	+23	13			1b92,M		0.6
1913	Bos A	2	2	0	0	0	0	0	0	0		0	1	.000	.000	.000	.000	-198	0			/HM		-0.1
Total	9	981	3425	405	894	149	87	31	437	221		94	1	.261	.323	.382	.705	+20	178			1b839,O92(65/27/0),C28		4.4
Team	6	486	1648	213	456	71	50	21	228	140		46	1	.277	.350	.419	.769	+34	65			1b438,C28/IfM		3.6
/150	2	150	509	66	141	22	15	6	70	43		14	0	.277	.350	.419	.769	+34	20			1b135,C9/OfLM		1.1
STAIRS, MATT Matthew Wade B2.27.1968 St.John NB, Can. BL/TR/5'9"/(175–217) d5.29																								
1995	†Bos A	39	88	8	23	7	1	1	17	4	0	1	14	.261	.298	.398	.696	-22	0	1	0	O23(17/0/6),D2	0	-0.8
Total	14	1416	4243	633	1125	243	11	220	751	588	40	47	881	.265	.358	.483	.841	+18	25	22	53	O671(166/2/511),D338,1b242/2	55	3.7
STANDAERT, JERRY Jerome John B11.2.1901 Chicago IL D8.4.1964 Chicago IL BR/TR/5'10"/168 d4.16																								
1929	Bos A	19	18	1	3	2	0	0	4	3		0	2	.167	.286	.278	.564	-53	0	0	0	1b10		-0.1
Total	3	86	132	14	42	10	2	0	18	8		1	10	.318	.362	.424	.786	+11	0	0	0	2b21,3b14,1b10,S6		-0.4
STANLEY, MIKE Robert Michael B6.25.1963 Ft.Lauderdale FL BR/TR/6'1"/(185–205) [TexA85 16/395] d6.24 C1 Col Florida																								
1996	Bos A	121	397	73	107	20	1	24	69	69	3	5	62	.270	.383	.506	.889	+20	2	0	100	C105,D10	0	-0.7
1997	Bos A	97	260	45	78	17	0	13	53	39	0	6	50	.300	.394	.515	.909	+35	0	1	0	D53,1b31,C15	0	0.7
1998	†Bos A	47	156	25	45	12	0	7	32	26	2	2	43	.288	.388	.500	.888	+28	1	0	100	D34,1b13	0	0.4
1999	†Bos A	136	427	59	120	22	0	19	72	70	3	11	94	.281	.393	.466	.859	+15	0	0	0	1b111,D20	0	0.1
2000	Bos A	58	185	22	41	5	0	10	28	30	0	0	44	.222	.327	.411	.738	-16	0	0	0	1b39,D18	20	-0.5
Total	15	1467	4222	625	1138	220	7	187	702	652	25	48	929	.270	.370	.458	.828	+17	13	4	76	C751,D321,1b301,3b26,O4L	71	2.8
Team	5	459	1425	224	391	76	1	73	254	234	8	24	293	.274	.382	.483	.865	+17	3	1	75	1b194,D135,C120	20	0.0
/150	2	150	466	73	128	25	0	24	83	76	3	8	96	.274	.382	.483	.865	+17	1	0	100	1b63,D44,C39	7	0.0
STANSBURY, JACK John James B12.6.1885 Phillipsburg NJ D12.26.1970 Easton PA BR/TR/5'9"/165 d6.30																								
1918	Bos A	20	47	3	6	1	0	0	2	6		1	3	.128	.241	.149	.390	-82	0			3b18,O2C		-0.2
STAPLETON, DAVE David Leslie B1.16.1954 Fairhope AL BR/TR/6'1"/(170–185) [BosA75 10/231] d5.30 Col South Alabama OF(5/0/2)																								
1980	Bos A	106	449	61	144	33	5	7	45	13	1	1	32	.321	.338	.463	.801	+12	3	2	60	2b94,1b8,O6(4/0/2),3b2,D3	0	2.2
1981	Bos A	93	355	45	101	17	1	10	42	21	1	1	22	.285	.325	.423	.748	+7	0	4	0	S33,3b25,2b23,1b12,D3	0	-0.2
1982	Bos A	150	538	66	142	28	1	14	65	31	5	3	40	.264	.305	.398	.703	-13	2	4	33	1b106,S27,2b9,3b5/IfD	0	-1.0
1983	Bos A	151	542	54	134	31	1	10	66	40	2	2	44	.247	.297	.363	.660	-24	1	1	50	1b145,2b5	0	-2.7
1984	Bos A	13	39	4	9	2	0	0	1	3	1	0	3	.231	.286	.282	.568	-45	0	0	0	1b10/D	0	-0.2
1985	Bos A	30	66	4	15	6	0	0	2	4	0	0	11	.227	.271	.318	.589	-42	0	0	0	2b14,1b8,D5	22	-0.4
1986	†Bos A	39	39	4	5	1	0	0	3	2	0	0	10	.128	.171	.154	.325	-111	0	0	0	1b29,2b6,3b2	0	-0.7
Total	7	582	2028	238	550	118	8	41	224	114	10	7	162	.271	.310	.398	.708	-10	6	11	35	1b318,2b151,S60,3b34,D16,O7L	22	-3.0
/150	2	150	523	61	142	30	2	11	58	29	3	2	42	.271	.310	.398	.708	-10	2	3	40	1b82,2b39,S15,3b9,D4,O2L	6	-0.8
STATZ, JIGGER Arnold John B10.20.1897 Waukegan IL D3.16.1988 Corona Del Mar CA BR/TR (BB 1922p)/5'7.5"/150 d7.30 Col Holy Cross																								
1920	Bos A	2	3	0	0	0	0	0	0	0		0	0	.000	.000	.000	.000	-199	0	0	0	O2R		-0.1
Total	8	683	2585	376	737	114	31	17	215	194		9	211	.285	.337	.373	.710	-13	77	46	100	O638(8/618/12),2b8		-5.3
STEINER, BEN Benjamin Saunders B7.28.1921 Alexandria VA D10.27.1988 Venice FL BL/TR/5'11"/165 d4.17																								
1945	Bos A	78	304	39	78	8	3	3	20	31		1	29	.257	.327	.332	.659	-11	10	6	63	2b77	0	-0.2
1946	Bos A	3	4	1	1	0	0	0	0	0		0	0	.250	.250	.250	.500	-62	0	0	0	/3	0	-0.1
1947	Det A	1	0	1	0	0	0	0	0	0		0	0	+	+	+	.000	-100	0	0	0	/R	0	0.0
Total	3	82	308	41	79	8	3	3	20	31		1	29	.256	.326	.331	.657	-11	10	6	63	2b77/3	0	-0.3
Team	2	81	308	40	79	8	3	3	20	31		1	29	.256	.326	.331	.657	-12	10	6	63	2b77/3	0	-0.3
STEINER, RED James Harry B1.7.1915 Los Angeles CA D11.16.2001 Gardena CA BL/TR/6'0"/185 d5.11																								
1945	Cle A	12	20	0	3	0	0	0	2	1		0	4	.150	.190	.150	.340	-101	0	0	0	C4	0	-0.2
1945	Bos A	26	59	6	12	1	0	0	4	14		0	2	.203	.356	.220	.576	-33	0	0	0	C24	0	-0.3
1945	Year	38	79	6	15	1	0	0	6	15		0	6	.190	.319	.203	.522	-48	0	0	0	C28	0	-0.5
STENHOUSE, MIKE Michael Steven B5.29.1958 Pueblo CO BL/TR/6'1"/195 [MonN80*S1/4] d10.3 f-Dave Col Harvard																								
1986	Bos A	21	21	1	2	1	0	0	1	12	0	0	5	.095	.424	.143	.567	-38	0	0	0	O4(2/0/2),1b3	0	0.0
Total	5	207	416	40	79	15	0	9	40	71	5	1	66	.190	.308	.291	.599	-33	1	0	100	O77(43/0/37),1b30,D27	0	-2.3
STEPHENS, GENE Glen Eugene B1.20.1933 Gravette AR BL/TR/6'3.5"/(175–185) d4.16																								
1952	Bos A	21	53	10	12	5	0	0	5	3		0	8	.226	.268	.321	.589	-41	4	2	67	O13(2/0/11)	0	-0.3
1953	Bos A	78	221	30	45	6	2	3	18	29		2	56	.204	.302	.290	.592	-43	3	3	50	O72(71/0/3)	0	-2.0
1955	Bos A	109	157	25	46	9	4	3	18	20	0	2	34	.293	.374	.459	.833	+14	0	0	0	O75(71/4/0)	0	0.4
1956	Bos A	104	63	22	17	2	0	1	7	12	0	0	12	.270	.387	.349	.736	-15	0	1	0	O71(69/2/2)	0	0.1
1957	Bos A	120	173	25	46	6	4	3	26	26	1	0	20	.266	.353	.399	.752	+2	0	2	0	O90(75/6/11)	0	-0.6
1958	Bos A	134	270	38	59	10	1	9	25	22	1	1	46	.219	.279	.363	.642	-29	1	2	33	O110(92/26/3)	0	-1.6
1959	Bos A	92	270	34	75	13	1	3	39	29	0	4	33	.278	.353	.367	.720	-5	5	2	71	O85(62/17/7)	42	0.0
1960	Bos A	35	109	9	25	4	0	2	11	14	0	0	22	.229	.312	.321	.633	-29	5	1	83	O31(21/4/8)	0	-0.6
1960	Bal A	84	193	38	46	11	0	5	11	25	0	1	25	.238	.327	.373	.700	-9	4	2	67	O77(36/19/42)	0	0.1

Year	Tm Lg	G	AB	R	H	2B	3B	HR	RBI	BB	IB	HP	SO	AVG	OBP	SLG	OPS	AOPS	SB	CS	SB%	Games at Position	DL	BFW
1960	Year	119	302	47	71	15	0	7	22	39	0	1	47	.235	.322	.354	.676	-17	9	3	75	O108(57/23/50)	0	-0.5
1961	Bal A	32	58	4	11	2	0	0	2	14	0	0	7	.190	.347	.224	.571	-42	1	1	50	O30(27/5/5)	0	-0.4
1961	KC A	62	183	22	38	6	1	4	26	16	0	2	27	.208	.279	.317	.596	-42	3	2	60	O54(6/28/25)	0	-0.9
1961	Year	94	241	26	49	8	1	4	28	30	0	2	34	.203	.297	.295	.592	-41	4	3	57	O84(33/33/30)	0	-1.3
1962	KC A	5	4	0	0	0	0	0	0	1	0	0	1	.000	.200	.000	.200	-139	0	0	0	/H	127	-0.1
1963	Chi A	6	18	5	7	0	0	1	2	1	0	0	3	.389	.421	.556	.977	+74	0	0	0	O5(2/0/3)	0	0.2
1964	Chi A	82	141	21	33	4	2	3	17	21	3	2	28	.234	.335	.355	.690	-3	1	2	33	O59(32/25/6)	0	0.1
Total	12	964	1913	283	460	78	15	37	207	233	5	14	322	.240	.325	.355	.680	-18	27	20	57	O772(566/136/126)	169	-5.6
Team	8	693	1316	193	325	55	12	24	149	155	2	9	231	.247	.327	.362	.689	-17	18	13	58	O547(295/39/44)	42	-4.6
/150	2	150	285	42	70	12	3	5	32	34	0	2	50	.247	.327	.362	.689	-17	4	3	57	O118(64/8/10)	9	-1.0
STEPHENS, VERN Vernon Decatur "Junior","Buster" B10.23.1920 McAlister NM D11.4.1968 Long Beach CA BR/TR/5'10"/(178–185) d9.13 Col Long Beach (CA) City																								
1941	StL A	3	2	0	1	0	0	0	0	0		0	0	.500	.500	.500	1.000	+60	0	0	0	/S	0	0.0
1942	StL A	145	575	84	169	26	6	14	92	41		0	53	.294	.341	.433	.774	+15	1	3	25	S144	0	0.6
1943	StL A★	137	512	75	148	27	3	22	91	54		0	73	.289	.357	.482	.839	+42	3	2	60	S123,O11(9/0/3)	0	1.3
1944	†StL A★	145	559	91	164	32	1	20	**109**	62		1	54	.293	.365	.462	.827	+28	2	2	50	S143	0	2.8
1945	StL A✱	149	571	90	165	27	3	**24**	89	55		1	70	.289	.352	.473	.825	+32	2	1	67	S144,3b4	0	1.6
1946	StL A★	115	450	67	138	19	4	14	64	35		0	49	.307	.357	.460	.817	+21	0	1	0	S112	0	1.7
1947	StL A	150	562	74	157	18	4	15	83	70		0	61	.279	.359	.406	.765	+10	8	4	67	S149	0	3.1
1948	Bos A★	**155**	635	114	171	25	8	29	137	77		2	56	.269	.350	.471	.821	+12	1	0	100	S155	0	2.5
1949	Bos A★	**155**	610	113	177	31	2	39	**159**	101		0	73	.290	.391	.539	.930	+35	2	2	50	S155	0	3.9
1950	Bos A☆	149	628	125	185	34	6	30	**144**	65		0	43	.295	.361	.511	.872	+10	1	0	100	S146	0	1.6
1951	Bos A★	109	377	62	113	21	2	17	78	38		0	33	.300	.364	.501	.865	+20	1	2	33	3b89,S2	0	2.0
1952	Bos A	92	295	35	75	13	2	7	44	39		1	31	.254	.343	.383	.726	-5	2	2	50	S53,3b29	0	0.5
1953	Chi A	44	129	14	24	6	0	1	14	13		0	18	.186	.261	.256	.517	-61	2	0	100	3b38,S3	0	-1.1
1953	StL A	46	165	16	53	8	0	4	17	18		0	24	.321	.388	.442	.830	+21	0	0	0	3b46	0	0.3
1953	Year	90	294	30	77	14	0	5	31	31		0	42	.262	.332	.361	.693	-15	2	0	100	3b84,S3	0	-0.8
1954	Bal A	101	365	31	104	17	1	8	46	17		0	36	.285	.311	.403	.714	+4	0	3	0	3b96	0	-0.3
1955	Bal A	3	6	0	1	0	0	0	0	0	0	1	0	.167	.286	.167	.453	-74	0	0	0	3b2	0	-0.1
1955	Chi A	22	56	10	14	3	0	3	7	7	0	0	11	.250	.328	.464	.792	+10	0	0	0	3b18	0	0.3
1955	Year	25	62	10	15	3	0	3	7	7	0	1	11	.242	.324	.435	.759	+2	0	0	0	3b20	0	0.2
Total	15	1720	6497	1001	1859	307	42	247	1174	692	0	6	685	.286	.355	.460	.815	+18	25	22	53	S1330,3b322,O11(9/0/3)	0	20.7
Team	5	660	2545	449	721	124	20	122	562	320		3	236	.283	.364	.492	.856	+16	7	6	54	S511,3b118	0	10.5
/150	1	150	578	102	164	28	5	28	128	73		1	54	.283	.364	.492	.856	+16	2	1	67	S116,3b27	0	2.4
STERN, ADAM Adam James B2.12.1980 London ON, Can. BL/TR/5'11"/180 [AtlN01 3/105] d7.7 Col Nebraska																								
2005	Bos A	36	15	4	2	0	0	1	2	0	0	1	4	.133	.188	.333	.521	-67	1	1	50	O21(2/6/13)	110	-0.2
2006	Bos A	10	20	3	3	1	0	0	4	0	0	1	4	.150	.190	.200	.390	-99	1	0	100	O10(2/8/0)	35	-0.1
Total	2	46	35	7	5	1	0	1	6	0	0	2	8	.143	.189	.257	.446	-85	2	1	67	O31(4/14/13)	145	-0.3
STOKES, AL Albert John (b Albert John Stocek) B1.1.1900 Chicago IL D12.19.1986 Grantham NH BR/TR/5'9"/175 d5.10																								
1925	Bos A	17	52	7	11	0	1	0	1	4		0	8	.212	.268	.250	.518	-68	0	0	0	C17		-0.3
1926	Bos A	30	86	7	14	3	3	0	6	8		0	28	.163	.234	.267	.501	-68	0	0	0	C29		-1.3
Total	2	47	138	14	25	3	4	0	7	12		0	36	.181	.247	.261	.508	-68	0	0	0	C46		-1.6
STONE, GEORGE George Robert B9.3.1876 Lost Nation IA D1.3.1945 Clinton IA BL/TL/5'9"/175 d4.20																								
1903	Bos A	2	2	0	0	0	0	0	0	0		0		.000	.000	.000	.000	-195	0			/H		0.0
Total	7	848	3271	426	984	106	68	23	268	282		22		.301	.360	.396	.756	+45	132			O837(813/1/23)		12.4
STONE, JEFF Jeffrey Glen B12.26.1960 Kennett MO BL/TR/6'0"/(175–180) d9.9																								
1989	Bos A	18	15	3	3	0	0	0	1	1	1	0	2	.200	.235	.200	.435	-73	1	0	100	O11(0/4/7),D3	0	-0.1
1990	Bos A	10	2	1	1	0	0	0	1	0	0	0	1	.500	.500	.500	1.000	+72	0	1	0	D2	0	0.0
Total	8	372	941	129	261	23	18	11	72	60	1	11	186	.277	.327	.375	.702	-8	75	20	79	O234(191/36/12),D21	108	-2.0
Team	2	28	17	4	4	0	0	0	2	1	1	0	3	.235	.263	.235	.498	-57	1	1	50	O11(0/4/7),D5	0	-0.1
STORIE, HOWIE Howard Edward "Sponge" B5.15.1911 Pittsfield MA D7.27.1968 Pittsfield MA BR/TR/5'10"/175 d9.7																								
1931	Bos A	6	17	2	2	0	0	0	0	3		0	2	.118	.250	.118	.368	-101	0	0	0	C6		-0.2
1932	Bos A	6	8	0	3	0	0	0	0	0		0	0	.375	.375	.375	.750	-2	0	0	0	C5		0.0
Total	2	12	25	2	5	0	0	0	0	3		0	2	.200	.286	.200	.486	-69	0	0	0	C11		-0.2
STRINGER, LOU Louis Bernard B5.13.1917 Grand Rapids MI BR/TR/5'11"/173 d4.15 Mil 1943–45																								
1948	Bos A	4	11	1	1	0	0	1	1	0		0	3	.091	.091	.364	.455	-83	0	0	0	2b2	0	0.0
1949	Bos A	35	41	10	11	4	0	1	6	5		0	10	.268	.348	.439	.787	+0	0	0	0	2b9	0	0.3
1950	Bos A	24	17	7	5	1	0	0	2	0		0	4	.294	.294	.353	.647	-41	1	0	100	3b3/2S	0	0.0
Total	6	409	1196	148	290	49	10	19	122	121		1	192	.242	.313	.348	.661	-10	7	0	100	2b324,S9,3b5	0	2.1
Team	3	63	69	18	17	5	0	2	9	5		0	17	.246	.297	.406	.703	-22	1	0	100	2b12,3b3/S	0	0.3
STRUNK, AMOS Amos Aaron B1.22.1889 Philadelphia PA D7.22.1979 Llanerch PA BL/TL/5'11.5"/175 d9.24																								
1918	†Bos A	114	413	50	106	18	9	0	35	36		0	13	.257	.316	.344	.660	+1	20			O113(1/112/0)		-1.6
1919	Bos A	48	184	27	50	11	3	0	17	13		1	13	.272	.323	.364	.687	-2	3			O48C		-0.9
Total	17	1512	4999	696	1418	213	96	15	530	573		12	331	.284	.359	.374	.733	+12	185	86	100	O1327(143/955/228),1b37		-0.8
Team	2	162	597	77	156	29	12	0	52	49		1	26	.261	.318	.350	.668	+0	23			O161(1/112/0)		-2.5
/150	2	150	553	71	144	27	11	0	48	45		1	24	.261	.318	.350	.668	+0	21			O149(1/104/0)		-2.3
STUART, DICK Richard Lee "Dr. Strangeglove" B11.7.1932 San Francisco CA D12.15.2002 Redwood City CA BR/TR/6'4"/(200–215) d7.10																								
1963	Bos A	157	612	81	160	25	4	42	**118**	44	2	1	144	.261	.312	.521	.833	+25	0	0	0	1b155	0	1.5
1964	Bos A	156	603	73	168	27	1	33	114	37	7	3	130	.279	.320	.491	.811	+17	0	0	0	1b155	0	0.3
Total	10	1112	3997	506	1055	157	30	228	743	301	34	22	957	.264	.316	.489	.805	+17	2	7	22	1b1024,O2L/3	17	2.7
Team	2	313	1215	154	328	52	5	75	232	81	9	4	274	.270	.316	.506	.822	+21	0	0	0	1b310	0	1.8
/150	1	150	582	74	157	25	2	36	111	39	4	2	131	.270	.316	.506	.822	+21	0	0	0	1b149	0	0.9
STUMPF, GEORGE George Frederick B12.15.1910 New Orleans LA D3.6.1993 Metairie LA BL/TL/5'8"/155 d9.19																								
1931	Bos A	7	28	2	7	1	1	0	4	1		0	2	.250	.276	.357	.633	-31	0	0	0	O7(6/2/0)		-0.2
1932	Bos A	79	169	18	34	2	2	1	18	18		0	21	.201	.278	.254	.532	-60	1	1	50	O51(17/2/32)		-1.9
1933	Bos A	22	41	8	14	3	0	0	5	4		0	2	.341	.400	.415	.815	+17	4	0	100	O15(3/8/4)		0.2
1936	Chi A	10	22	3	6	1	0	0	5	2		0	1	.273	.333	.318	.651	-41	0	0	0	O4L		-0.1
Total	4	118	260	31	61	7	3	1	32	25		0	26	.235	.302	.296	.598	-43	5	1	83	O77(30/12/36)		-2.0
Team	3	108	238	28	55	6	3	1	27	23		0	25	.231	.299	.294	.593	-44	5	1	83	O73(23/12/8)		-1.9
/150	4	150	331	39	76	8	4	1	38	32		0	35	.231	.299	.294	.593	-44	7	1	88	O101(32/17/11)		-2.6
STYNES, CHRIS Christopher Desmond B1.19.1973 Queens NY BR/TR/5'10"/(175–205) [TorA91 3/94] d5.19 OF(134/2/22)																								
2001	Bos A	96	361	52	101	19	2	8	33	20	0	3	56	.280	.322	.410	.732	-9	4	5	44	3b46,2b43,O3L	46	-0.8
Total	10	828	2326	351	640	118	9	51	265	191	9	22	308	.275	.335	.399	.734	-13	49	16	75	3b388,2b167,O152L,D5,S2	46	-4.5
SULLIVAN, DENNY Dennis William B9.28.1882 Hillsboro WI D6.2.1956 W.Los Angeles CA BL/TR/5'10"/? d4.22																								
1905	Was A	3	11	0	0	0	0	0	0	1		0		.000	.083	.000	.083	-176	0			O3R		-0.3
1907	Bos A	144	551	73	135	18	0	1	26	44		12		.245	.315	.283	.598	-8	16			O143C		-1.2
1908	Bos A	101	355	33	85	7	8	0	25	14		4		.239	.276	.304	.580	-14	4			O97(0/92/5)		-0.8
1908	Cle A	4	6	0	0	0	0	0	0	0		0		.000	.000	.000	.000	-199	0			O2(1/0/1)		-0.2
1908	Year	105	361	33	85	7	8	0	25	14		4		.235	.272	.299	.571	-17	4			O99(1/92/6)		-1.0
1909	Cle A	3	2	0	1	0	0	0	0	0		0		.500	.500	.500	1.000	+107	0			O2R		0.0
Total	4	255	925	106	221	25	8	1	51	59		16		.239	.296	.286	.582	-13	20			O247(1/235/11)		-2.5
Team	2	245	906	106	220	25	8	1	51	58		16	0	.243	.300	.291	.591	-10	20			O240C		-2.0
/150	1	150	555	65	135	15	5	1	31	36		10	0	.243	.300	.291	.591	-10	12			O147C		-1.2
SULLIVAN, HAYWOOD Haywood Cooper B12.15.1930 Donalsonville GA D2.12.2003 Fort Myers FL BR/TR/6'4"/(210–215) d9.20 M1 s–Marc Col Florida [DL 1958 Bos A 168]																								
1955	Bos A	2	6	1	0	0	0	0	0	0	0	0	1	.000	.000	.000	.000	-192	0	0	0	C2	0	-0.1

Year	Tm Lg	G	AB	R	H	2B	3B	HR	RBI	BB	IB	HP	SO	AVG	OBP	SLG	OPS	AOPS	SB	CS	SB%	Games at Position	DL	BFW
1957	Bos A	2	1	0	0	0	0	0	0	0	0	0	0	.000	.000	.000	.000	-195	0	0	0	/C	0	0.0
1959	Bos A	4	2	0	0	0	0	0	0	1	0	0	1	.000	.333	.000	.333	-100	0	0	0	C2	0	0.0
1960	Bos A	52	124	9	20	1	0	3	10	16	2	0	24	.161	.255	.242	.497	-65	0	0	0	C50	0	-0.7
Total	7	312	851	94	192	30	5	13	87	109	9	1	140	.226	.312	.318	.630	-31	2	0	100	C274,1b17,O5(2/0/3)	168	-3.0
Team	4	60	133	10	20	1	0	3	10	17	2	0	26	.150	.245	.226	.471	-72	0	0	0	C55	168	-0.8
SULLIVAN, MARC Marc Cooper B7.25.1958 Quincy MA BR/TR/6'4"/(198–213) [BosA79 2/52] d10.1 f–Haywood Col Florida																								
1982	Bos A	2	6	0	2	0	0	0	0	0	0	0	2	.333	.333	.333	.666	-21	0	0	0	C2	0	0.1
1984	Bos A	2	6	1	3	0	0	0	1	1	0	0	0	.500	.571	.500	1.071	+90	0	0	0	C2	0	0.2
1985	Bos A	32	69	10	12	2	0	2	3	6	0	0	15	.174	.240	.290	.530	-58	0	0	0	C32	46	-0.6
1986	Bos A	41	119	15	23	4	0	1	14	7	0	4	32	.193	.260	.252	.512	-60	0	0	0	C41	0	-1.5
1987	Bos A	60	160	11	27	5	0	2	10	4	0	2	43	.169	.198	.237	.435	-85	0	0	0	C60	0	-2.0
Total	5	137	360	37	67	11	0	5	28	18	0	6	92	.186	.236	.258	.494	-67	0	0	0	C137	46	-3.8
/150	5	150	394	41	73	12	0	5	31	20	0	7	101	.186	.236	.258	.494	-67	0	0	0	C150	50	-4.2
SUMNER, CARL Carl Ringdahl "Lefty" B9.28.1908 Cambridge MA D2.8.1999 Chatham MA BL/TL/5'8"/170 d7.28																								
1928	Bos A	16	29	6	8	1	1	0	3	5		0	6	.276	.382	.379	.761	+3	0	0	0	O10(5/4/1)		-0.1
SWANSON, BILL William Andrew B10.12.1888 New York NY D10.14.1954 New York NY BB/TR/5'6"/156 d9.2																								
1914	Bos A	11	20	0	4	2	0	0	0	3		0	4	.200	.304	.300	.604	-18	0	1	0	2b6,3b3/S		-0.4
SWEENEY, BILL William Joseph B12.29.1904 Cleveland OH D4.18.1957 San Diego CA BR/TR/5'11"/180 d4.13 C2																								
1928	Det A	89	309	47	78	15	5	0	19	15		0	28	.252	.287	.333	.620	-38	12	8	60	1b75,O3L		-1.9
1930	Bos A	88	243	32	75	13	0	4	30	9		0	15	.309	.333	.412	.745	-9	5	3	63	1b56/3		-0.7
1931	Bos A	131	498	48	147	30	3	1	58	20		0	30	.295	.322	.373	.695	-13	5	12	29	1b124		-1.6
Total	3	308	1050	127	300	58	8	5	107	44		0	73	.286	.314	.370	.684	-20	22	23	49	1b255,O3L/3		-4.2
Team	2	219	741	80	222	43	3	5	88	29		0	45	.300	.326	.386	.712	-12	10	15	40	1b180/3		-2.3
/150	1	150	508	55	152	29	2	3	60	20		0	31	.300	.326	.386	.712	-12	7	10	41	1b123/3		-1.6
TABOR, JIM James Reubin "Rawhide" B11.5.1916 New Hope AL D8.22.1953 Sacramento CA BR/TR/6'2"/175 d8.2 Mil 1944–45 Col Alabama																								
1938	Bos A	19	57	8	18	3	2	1	8	1		0	6	.316	.328	.491	.819	-2	0	1	0	3b11,S2		-0.1
1939	Bos A	149	577	76	167	33	8	14	95	40		1	54	.289	.337	.447	.784	-5	16	10	62	3b148		0.3
1940	Bos A	120	459	73	131	28	6	21	81	42		0	58	.285	.345	.510	.855	+14	14	10	58	3b120		1.4
1941	Bos A	126	498	65	139	29	3	16	101	36		0	48	.279	.328	.446	.774	+0	17	9	65	3b125	0	0.4
1942	Bos A	139	508	56	128	18	2	12	75	37		0	47	.252	.303	.366	.669	-15	6	13	32	3b138	0	-1.9
1943	Bos A	137	537	57	130	26	3	13	85	43		1	54	.242	.299	.374	.673	-5	7	7	50	3b133,O2L	0	-1.3
1944	Bos A	116	438	58	125	25	3	13	72	31		1	38	.285	.334	.445	.779	+23	4	4	50	3b114	0	1.7
1946	Phi N	124	463	53	124	15	2	10	50	36		1	51	.268	.322	.374	.696	+0	3			3b124	0	-0.5
1947	Phi N	75	251	27	59	14	0	4	31	20		2	21	.235	.297	.339	.636	-29	2			3b67	0	-2.3
Total	9	1005	3788	473	1021	191	29	104	598	286		6	377	.270	.322	.418	.740	-1	69	54	100	3b980,O2L,S2	0	-2.3
Team	7	806	3074	393	838	162	27	90	517	230		3	305	.273	.324	.431	.755	+1	64	54	54	3b789,S2,O2L	0	0.5
/150	1	150	572	73	156	30	5	17	96	43		1	57	.273	.324	.431	.755	+1	12	10	55	3b147/SO2L	0	0.1
TAITT, DOUG Douglas John "Poco" B8.3.1902 Bay City MI D12.12.1970 Portland OR BL/TR/6'0"/176 d4.10																								
1928	Bos A	143	482	51	144	28	14	3	61	36		2	32	.299	.350	.434	.784	+7	13	6	68	O139(9/0/130)/P		-0.1
1929	Bos A	26	65	6	18	4	0	0	6	8		1	5	.277	.365	.338	.703	-16	0	1	0	O21(11/0/11)		-0.1
1929	Chi A	47	124	11	21	7	0	0	12	8		0	13	.169	.220	.226	.446	-85	0	0	0	O30R		-1.6
1929	Year	73	189	17	39	11	0	0	18	16		1	18	.206	.272	.265	.537	-61	0	1	0	O51(11/0/41)		-1.7
1931	Phi N	38	151	13	34	4	2	1	15	4		0	14	.225	.245	.298	.543	-58	0			O38L		-1.1
1932	Phi N	4	2	0	0	0	0	0	1	2		0	0	.000	.500	.000	.500	-57	0			/H		0.0
Total	4	258	824	81	217	43	16	4	95	58		3	64	.263	.314	.369	.683	-21	13	7	100	O228(58/0/171)/P		-2.9
Team	2	169	547	57	162	32	14	3	67	44		3	37	.296	.352	.422	.774	+4	13	7	65	O160(20/0/141)/P		-0.2
/150	2	150	486	51	144	28	12	3	59	39		3	33	.296	.352	.422	.774	+4	12	6	67	O142(18/0/125)/P		-0.2
TANNEHILL, JESSE Jesse Niles "Powder" B7.14.1874 Dayton KY D9.22.1956 Dayton KY BB/TL (BL 1903)/5'8"/150 d6.17 C1 b–Lee▲																								
1904	Bos A	45	122	14	24	2	6	0	6	9		0		.197	.252	.311	.563	-27	1			P33,O2L		0.1
1905	Bos A	37	93	11	21	2	0	1	12	16		0		.226	.339	.280	.619	-4	1			P37		0.0
1906	Bos A	31	79	12	22	2	2	0	4	6		0		.278	.329	.354	.683	+14	1			P27		0.0
1907	Bos A	21	51	2	10	3	1	0	6	2		1		.196	.241	.294	.535	-29	0			P18		0.0
1908	Bos A	1	2	0	1	0	0	0	0	0		0		.500	.500	.500	1.000	+119	0			/P		0.0
Total	15	507	1414	190	361	55	23	5	142	105		8	3	.255	.310	.337	.647	-11	19			P359,O87(28/32/27)		-0.2
Team	5	135	347	39	78	9	9	1	28	33		1	0	.225	.294	.311	.605	-11	3			P116,O2L		0.1
/150	6	150	386	43	87	10	10	1	31	37		1	0	.225	.294	.311	.605	-11	3			P129,O2L		0.1
TARBERT, ARLIE Wilbur Arlington B9.10.1904 Cleveland OH D11.27.1946 Cleveland OH BR/TR/6'0"/160 d6.18 Col Ohio St.																								
1927	Bos A	33	69	5	13	1	0	0	5	3		3	12	.188	.253	.203	.456	-80	0	0	0	O27(10/3/14)		-0.9
1928	Bos A	6	17	1	3	1	0	0	2	1		0	1	.176	.222	.235	.457	-79	1	0	100	O6R		-0.2
Total	2	39	86	6	16	2	0	0	7	4		3	13	.186	.247	.209	.456	-80	1	0	100	O33(10/3/20)		-1.1
TARTABULL, JOSE Jose Milages (Guzman) B11.27.1938 Cienfuegos, Cuba BL/TL/5'11"/(160–165) d4.10 s–Danny																								
1962	KC A	107	310	49	86	6	5	0	22	20	0	1	19	.277	.321	.329	.650	-27	19	5	79	O85(1/85/0)	0	-0.9
1963	KC A	79	242	27	58	8	5	1	19	17	0	0	17	.240	.290	.326	.616	-32	16	1	94	O71(1/70/0)	0	-1.4
1964	KC A	104	100	9	20	2	0	0	3	5	0	0	12	.200	.238	.220	.458	-72	4	0	100	O59(44/13/5)	0	-0.9
1965	KC A	68	218	28	68	11	4	1	19	18	0	0	20	.312	.361	.413	.774	+22	11	5	69	O54(26/27/8)	0	1.3
1966	KC A	37	127	13	30	2	3	0	4	11	0	0	13	.236	.297	.299	.596	-26	8	1	89	O32(1/32/0)	0	-0.7
1966	Bos A	68	195	28	54	7	4	0	11	6	0	0	11	.277	.297	.354	.651	-21	11	3	79	O47C	0	-1.1
1966	Year	105	322	41	84	9	7	0	15	17	0	0	24	.261	.297	.332	.629	-23	19	4	83	O79(1/79/0)	0	-1.8
1967	†Bos A	115	247	36	55	1	2	0	10	23	0	0	26	.223	.287	.243	.530	-46	6	6	50	O83(12/19/55)	0	-2.4
1968	Bos A	72	139	24	39	6	0	0	6	6	0	0	5	.281	.306	.324	.630	-13	2	3	40	O43(12/11/20)	25	-0.4
1969	Oak A	75	266	28	71	11	1	0	11	9	0	0	11	.267	.290	.316	.606	-28	3	4	43	O63(28/36/0)	0	-1.6
1970	Oak A	24	13	5	3	2	0	0	2	0	0	0	2	.231	.231	.385	.616	-31	1	0	100	O6(4/2/0)	0	-0.1
Total	9	749	1857	247	484	56	24	2	107	115	0	1	136	.261	.303	.320	.623	-26	81	28	74	O543(129/342/88)	25	-8.2
Team	3	255	581	88	148	14	6	0	27	35	0	0	42	.255	.295	.299	.594	-30	19	12	61	O173(12/59/1)	25	-3.9
/150	2	150	342	52	87	8	4	0	16	21	0	0	25	.255	.295	.299	.594	-30	11	7	61	O102(7/35/1)	15	-2.3
TARVER, LA SCHELLE La Schelle B1.30.1959 Modesto CA BL/TL/5'11"/165 d7.12 Col Cal St.–Sacramento																								
1986	Bos A	13	25	3	3	0	0	0	1	1	0	0	4	.120	.154	.120	.274	-124	0	1	0	O9(3/7/0)	0	-0.5
TASBY, WILLIE Willie B1.8.1933 Shreveport LA BR/TR/5'11"/(175–183) d9.9																								
1960	Bos A	105	385	68	108	17	1	7	37	51	0	5	54	.281	.371	.384	.755	+1	3	1	75	O102C	0	-0.5
Total	6	583	1868	246	467	61	10	46	174	201	7	16	327	.250	.327	.367	.694	-11	12	20	38	O543(65/460/48)/23	0	-7.5
/150	1	150	550	97	154	24	1	10	53	73	0	7	77	.281	.371	.384	.755	+1	4	1	80	O146C	0	-0.7
TATE, BENNIE Henry Bennett B12.3.1901 Whitwell TN D10.27.1973 W.Frankfort IL BL/TR/5'8"/165 d4.29																								
1932	Bos A	81	273	21	67	12	5	2	26	20		0	6	.245	.297	.348	.645	-32	0	1	0	C76		-1.5
Total	10	566	1560	144	435	68	16	4	173	118		1	51	.279	.330	.351	.681	-22	5	16	100	C468		-4.0
TATUM, JIM James Ray B10.9.1967 Grossmont CA BR/TR/6'2"/200 [SDN85 3/76] d9.18																								
1996	Bos A	2	8	1	1	0	0	0	0	0	0	0	2	.125	.125	.125	.250	-136	0	0	0	3b2	0	-0.2
Total	5	173	201	16	39	7	3	3	29	10	0	1	58	.194	.229	.303	.532	-63	0	0	0	1b21,3b17,O9(8/0/1),C5/D	0	-2.3
TAVAREZ, JESUS Jesus Rafael (Alcantaras) B3.26.1971 Santo Domingo, D.R. BB/TR/6'0"/170 d5.23																								
1997	Bos A	42	69	12	12	3	1	0	9	4	0	0	9	.174	.216	.246	.462	-79	0	0	0	O35(4/29/4),D2	0	-0.8
Total	5	228	423	63	101	12	3	3	33	30	1	1	62	.239	.289	.303	.592	-44	13	8	62	O180(34/113/60),D2	16	-2.7
TEBBETTS, BIRDIE George Robert B11.10.1912 Burlington VT D3.24.1999 Manatee FL BR/TR/5'11.5"/(170–190) d9.16 Mil 1943–45 M11 Col Providence																								
1936	Det A	10	33	7	10	1	2	1	4	5		0	3	.303	.395	.545	.940	+29	0	0	0	C10		0.2
1937	Det A	50	162	15	31	4	3	2	16	10		0	13	.191	.238	.290	.528	-68	0	0	0	C48		-1.9

Year	Tm Lg	G	AB	R	H	2B	3B	HR	RBI	BB	IB	HP	SO	AVG	OBP	SLG	OPS	AOPS	SB	CS	SB%	Games at Position	DL	BFW
1938	Det A	53	143	16	42	6	2	1	25	12		0	13	.294	.348	.385	.733	-21	1	2	33	C53		-0.4
1939	Det A	106	341	37	89	22	2	4	53	25		2	20	.261	.315	.372	.687	-30	2	1	67	C100		0.1
1940	†Det A	111	379	46	112	24	4	4	46	35		1	14	.296	.357	.412	.769	-10	4	5	44	C107		1.5
1941	Det A☆	110	359	28	102	19	4	2	47	38		1	29	.284	.354	.376	.730	-15	1	2	33	C98	0	0.4
1942	Det A★	99	308	24	76	11	0	1	27	39		2	17	.247	.335	.292	.627	-29	4	0	100	C97	0	0.3
1946	Det A	87	280	20	68	11	2	1	34	28		0	23	.243	.312	.307	.619	-31	1	3	25	C87	0	-0.8
1947	Det A	20	53	1	5	1	0	0	2	3		0	3	.094	.143	.113	.256	-127	0	1	0	C20	0	-0.4
1947	Bos A	90	291	22	87	10	0	1	28	21		0	30	.299	.346	.344	.690	-14	2	4	33	C89	0	-0.3
1947	Year	110	344	23	92	11	0	1	30	24		0	33	.267	.315	.308	.623	-31	2	5	29	C109	0	-0.7
1948	Bos A★	128	446	54	125	26	2	5	68	62		2	32	.280	.371	.381	.752	-5	5	2	71	C126	0	-0.1
1949	Bos A★	122	403	42	109	14	0	5	48	62		1	22	.270	.369	.342	.711	-17	8	1	89	C118	0	-0.2
1950	Bos A	79	268	33	83	10	1	8	45	29		0	26	.310	.377	.444	.821	+0	1	1	50	C74	0	0.0
1951	Cle A	55	137	8	36	6	0	2	18	8		1	7	.263	.308	.350	.658	-18	0	0	0	C44	0	-0.1
1952	Cle A	42	101	4	25	4	0	1	8	12		2	9	.248	.339	.317	.656	-11	0	1	0	C37	0	-0.2
Total	14	1162	3704	357	1000	169	22	38	469	389		12	261	.270	.341	.358	.699	-19	29	23	56	C1108	0	-1.9
Team	4	419	1408	151	404	60	3	19	189	174		3	110	.287	.367	.374	.741	-9	16	8	67	C407	0	-0.6
/150	1	150	504	54	145	21	1	7	68	62		1	39	.287	.367	.374	.741	-9	6	3	67	C146	0	-0.2
THOMAS, PINCH Chester David B1.24.1888 Camp Point IL D12.24.1953 Modesto CA BL/TR/5'9.5"/173 d4.24																								
1912	Bos A	13	30	0	6	0	0	0	5	2		0		.200	.250	.200	.450	-72	1			C8		-0.1
1913	Bos A	38	91	6	26	1	2	1	15	2		1	11	.286	.309	.374	.683	-3	1			C31		0.1
1914	Bos A	66	130	9	25	1	0	0	5	18		0	17	.192	.291	.200	.491	-52	1			C64/1		-0.2
1915	†Bos A	86	203	21	48	4	4	0	21	13		1	20	.236	.286	.296	.582	-24	3	2	60	C82		0.5
1916	†Bos A	99	216	21	57	10	1	1	21	33		1	13	.264	.364	.333	.697	+9	4			C90		1.1
1917	Bos A	83	202	24	48	7	0	0	24	27		2	9	.238	.333	.272	.605	-14	2			C77		0.9
1918	Cle A	32	73	2	18	0	1	0	5	6		0	6	.247	.304	.274	.578	-32	0			C24		0.0
1919	Cle A	34	46	2	5	0	0	0	2	4		0	3	.109	.180	.109	.289	-117	0			C21		-0.7
1920	†Cle A	9	9	2	3	1	0	0	0	3		0	1	.333	.500	.444	.944	+47	0	0	0	C7		0.2
1921	Cle A	21	35	1	9	3	0	0	4	10		0	2	.257	.422	.343	.765	-4	0	0	0	C19		-0.3
Total	10	481	1035	88	245	27	8	2	102	118		5	82	.237	.318	.284	.602	-22	12	2	100	C423/1		1.5
Team	6	385	872	81	210	23	7	2	91	95		5	70	.241	.319	.290	.609	-17	12	2	100	C352/1		2.3
/150	2	150	340	32	82	9	3	1	35	37		2	27	.241	.319	.290	.609	-17	5	1	100	C137/1		0.9
THOMAS, FRED Frederick Harvey "Tommy" B12.19.1892 Milwaukee WI D1.15.1986 Rice Lake WI BR/TR/5'10"/160 d4.22 Mil 1918																								
1918	†Bos A	44	144	19	37	2	1	1	11	15		1	20	.257	.331	.306	.637	-6	4			3b41/S		0.3
Total	3	247	859	88	193	19	14	4	45	84		5	90	.225	.297	.293	.590	-35	24	5	100	3b228,S13		-3.3
THOMAS, GEORGE George Edward B11.29.1937 Minneapolis MN BR/TR/6'3.5"/190 d9.11 C1 Col Minnesota OF(136/170/186)																								
1966	Bos A	69	173	25	41	4	0	5	20	23	1	2	33	.237	.332	.347	.679	-13	1	0	100	O48(10/25/15),3b6,C2,1b2	0	-0.2
1967	†Bos A	65	89	10	19	2	0	1	6	3	0	2	23	.213	.255	.270	.525	-49	0	1	0	O43(20/3/20),1b3/C	23	-0.9
1968	Bos A	12	10	3	2	0	0	1	1	1	0	0	3	.200	.273	.500	.773	+23	1	0	100	O9(5/2/2)	0	0.1
1969	Bos A	29	51	9	18	3	1	0	8	3	0	1	11	.353	.400	.451	.851	+31	0	0	0	O12(8/1/3),1b10/C3	69	0.1
1970	Bos A	38	99	13	34	8	0	2	13	11	0	2	12	.343	.420	.485	.905	+39	0	0	0	O26(25/0/1),3b6	0	0.1
1971	Bos A	9	13	0	1	0	0	0	1	1	0	0	4	.077	.143	.077	.220	-134	0	0	0	O5(3/0/2)	0	-0.4
Total	13	685	1688	203	430	71	9	46	202	138	4	18	343	.255	.316	.389	.705	-8	13	12	52	O481R,3b64,1b20,C4,2b2/S	92	-5.9
Team	6	222	435	60	115	17	1	9	49	42	1	7	86	.264	.338	.370	.708	-6	2	1	67	O143(33/30/39),1b15,3b13,C4	92	-1.2
/150	4	150	294	41	78	11	1	6	33	28	1	5	58	.264	.338	.370	.708	-6	1	1	50	O97(22/20/26),1b10,3b9,C3	62	-0.8
THOMAS, LEE James Leroy B2.5.1936 Peoria IL BL/TR/6'2"/(187–198) d4.22 C2																								
1964	Bos A	107	401	44	103	19	2	13	42	34	4	4	29	.257	.319	.411	.730	-3	2	1	67	O107R/1	0	-0.8
1965	Bos A	151	521	74	141	27	4	22	75	72	8	3	42	.271	.361	.464	.825	+26	6	2	75	1b127,O20(14/0/6)	0	1.5
Total	8	1027	3324	405	847	111	22	106	428	332	35	32	397	.255	.327	.397	.724	-1	25	11	69	O485(83/20/392),1b425	0	-7.3
Team	2	258	922	118	244	46	6	35	117	106	12	7	71	.265	.343	.441	.784	+14	8	3	73	1b128,O127(14/0/107)	0	0.7
/150	1	150	536	69	142	27	3	20	68	62	7	4	41	.265	.343	.441	.784	+14	5	2	71	1b74,O74(8/0/62)	0	0.4
THOMSON, BOBBY Robert Brown "The Staten Island Scot" B10.25.1923 Glasgow, Scotland BR/TR/6'2"/(185–190) d9.9																								
1960	Bos A	40	114	12	30	3	1	5	20	11	0	0	15	.263	.323	.439	.762	+2	0	1	0	O27(12/13/2)/1	0	-0.1
Total	15	1779	6305	903	1705	267	74	264	1026	559	23	34	804	.270	.332	.462	.794	+11	38	20	100	O1506(511/982/59),3b184,2b9/1	91	-0.3
THONEY, JACK John "Bullet Jack" (b John Thoeny) B12.8.1879 Ft.Thomas KY D10.24.1948 Covington KY BR/TR/5'10"/175 d4.26																								
1902	Cle A	28	105	14	30	7	1	0	11	9		0		.286	.342	.371	.713	+2	4			2b14,S11,O2R		-1.0
1902	Bal A	3	11	1	0	0	0	0	0	1		0		.000	.083	.000	.083	-172	1			3b3		-0.4
1902	Year	31	116	15	30	7	1	0	11	10		0		.259	.317	.336	.653	-16	5			2b14,S11,3b3,O2R		-1.4
1903	Cle A	32	122	10	25	3	0	1	9	2		0		.205	.218	.254	.472	-58	7			O24(0/23/1),2b5,3b2		-1.1
1904	Was A	17	70	6	21	3	0	0	6	1		0		.300	.310	.343	.653	+8	2			O17(0/8/9)		0.0
1904	NY A	36	128	17	24	4	2	0	12	8		1		.188	.241	.250	.491	-47	9			3b26,O10C		-1.0
1904	Year	53	198	23	45	7	2	0	18	9		1		.227	.264	.283	.547	-29	11			O27(0/18/9),3b26		-1.0
1908	Bos A	109	416	58	106	5	9	2	30	13		3		.255	.282	.325	.607	-6	16			O101(87/11/3)		-0.8
1909	Bos A	13	40	1	5	1	0	0	3	2		0		.125	.167	.150	.317	-100	2			O10L		-0.6
1911	Bos A	26	20	5	5	0	0	0	2	0		0		.250	.250	.250	.500	-60	1			/H		-0.2
Total	6	264	912	112	216	23	12	3	73	36		4		.237	.269	.298	.567	-25	42			O164(97/52/15),3b31,2b19,S11		-5.1
Team	3	148	476	64	116	6	9	2	35	15		3	0	.244	.271	.307	.578	-16	19			O111(87/11/3)		-1.6
/150	3	150	482	65	118	6	9	2	35	15		3	0	.244	.271	.307	.578	-16	19			O113(88/11/3)		-1.6
THRONEBERRY, FAYE Maynard Faye B6.22.1931 Fisherville TN D4.26.1999 Memphis TN BL/TR/6'0"/(185–199) d4.15 Mil 1953–54 b–Marv																								
1952	Bos A	98	310	38	80	11	3	5	23	33		1	67	.258	.331	.361	.692	-14	16	7	70	O86(11/4/71)	0	-0.7
1955	Bos A	60	144	20	37	7	3	6	27	14	1	1	31	.257	.323	.472	.795	+4	0	0	0	O34(32/0/3)	0	-0.2
1956	Bos A	24	50	6	11	2	0	1	3	3	0	0	16	.220	.264	.320	.584	-52	0	0	0	O13(8/2/3)	56	-0.6
1957	Bos A	1	1	0	0	0	0	0	0	0	0	0	1	.000	.000	.000	.000	-195	0	0	0	/H	0	0.0
1957	Was A	68	195	21	36	8	2	2	12	17	0	1	37	.185	.252	.277	.529	-55	0	1	0	O58(14/48/2)	0	-2.2
1957	Year	69	196	21	36	8	2	2	12	17	0	1	38	.184	.251	.276	.527	-55	0	1	0	O58(14/48/2)	0	-2.2
1958	Was A	44	87	12	16	1	1	4	7	4	0	3	28	.184	.245	.356	.601	-36	0	1	0	O26(5/13/8)	0	-0.8
1959	Was A	117	327	36	82	11	2	10	42	33	3	3	61	.251	.322	.388	.710	-5	6	4	60	O86(16/1/71)	0	-0.8
1960	Was A	85	157	18	39	7	1	1	23	18	3	1	33	.248	.326	.325	.651	-22	1	1	50	O34(12/7/17)	0	-0.8
1961	LA A	24	31	1	6	1	0	0	0	5	0	0	10	.194	.306	.226	.532	-60	0	0	0	O5(3/0/2)	0	-0.2
Total	8	521	1302	152	307	48	12	29	137	127	7	10	284	.236	.307	.358	.665	-21	23	14	62	O342(101/75/177)	56	-6.3
Team	4	183	505	64	128	20	6	12	53	50	1	2	115	.253	.322	.388	.710	-13	16	7	70	O133(43/6/77)	56	-1.5
/150	3	150	414	52	105	16	5	10	43	41	1	2	94	.253	.322	.388	.710	-13	13	6	68	O109(35/5/63)	46	-1.2
TILLMAN, BOB John Robert B3.24.1937 Nashville TN D6.23.2000 Gallatin TN BR/TR/6'4"/(200–210) d4.15 Col Middle Tennessee																								
1962	Bos A	81	249	28	57	6	4	14	38	19	0	1	65	.229	.283	.454	.737	-7	0	0	0	C66	0	-0.8
1963	Bos A	96	307	24	69	10	2	8	32	34	8	1	64	.225	.304	.349	.653	-20	0	0	0	C95	0	-1.1
1964	Bos A	131	425	43	118	18	1	17	61	49	11	0	74	.278	.352	.445	.797	+14	0	0	0	C131	0	0.8
1965	Bos A	111	368	20	79	10	3	6	35	40	3	0	69	.215	.288	.307	.595	-34	0	0	0	C106	0	-1.9
1966	Bos A	78	204	12	47	8	0	3	24	22	3	0	35	.230	.303	.314	.617	-29	0	0	0	C72	0	-1.3
1967	Bos A	30	64	4	12	1	0	1	4	3	0	0	18	.188	.224	.250	.474	-63	0	0	0	C26	0	-0.7
1967	NY A	22	63	5	16	1	0	2	9	7	1	0	17	.254	.324	.365	.689	+9	0	0	0	C15	0	-0.1
1967	Year	52	127	9	28	2	0	3	13	10	1	0	35	.220	.275	.307	.582	-30	0	0	0	C41	0	-0.8
1968	Atl N	86	236	16	52	4	0	5	20	16	2	3	55	.220	.278	.301	.579	-26	1	0	100	C75	0	-1.4
1969	†Atl N	69	190	18	37	5	0	12	29	18	1	0	47	.195	.263	.411	.674	-14	0	0	0	C69	0	-1.1
1970	Atl N	71	223	19	53	5	0	11	30	20	4	0	66	.238	.299	.408	.707	-17	0	0	0	C70	0	-0.8
Total	9	775	2329	189	540	68	10	79	282	228	33	5	510	.232	.300	.371	.671	-15	1	0	100	C725	0	-8.4
Team	6	527	1617	131	382	53	10	49	194	167	25	2	325	.236	.307	.372	.679	-15	0	0	0	C496	0	-5.0
/150	2	150	460	37	109	15	3	14	55	48	7	1	93	.236	.307	.372	.679	-15	0	0	0	C141	0	-1.4

Year	Tm Lg	G	AB	R	H	2B	3B	HR	RBI	BB	IB	HP	SO	AVG	OBP	SLG	OPS	AOPS	SB	CS	SB%	Games at Position	DL	BFW
TINSLEY, LEE Lee Owen B3.4.1969 Shelbyville KY BB/TR/5'10"/(185–198) [OakA87 1/11] d4.6 C1																								
1993	Sea A	11	19	2	3	1	0	1	2	2	0	0	9	.158	.238	.368	.606	-41	0	0	0	O6(5/1/1),D2	0	-0.1
1994	Bos A	78	144	27	32	4	0	2	14	19	1	1	36	.222	.315	.292	.607	-44	13	0	100	O60(27/26/11),D10	0	-0.6
1995	†Bos A	100	341	61	97	17	1	7	41	39	1	1	74	.284	.359	.402	.761	-5	18	8	69	O97C	36	0.0
1996	Phi N	31	52	1	7	0	0	0	2	4	0	0	22	.135	.196	.135	.331	-111	2	4	33	O22(18/7/0)	16	-1.0
1996	Bos A	92	192	28	47	6	1	3	14	13	0	2	56	.245	.298	.333	.631	-41	6	8	43	O83(4/79/0)	0	-1.1
1996	Major	123	244	29	54	6	1	3	16	17	0	2	78	.221	1.278	.291	1.569	+142	8	12	40		16	-2.1
1997	Sea A	49	122	12	24	6	2	0	6	11	0	0	34	.197	.263	.279	.542	-58	2	0	100	O41(34/6/2),D5	107	-1.0
Total	5	361	870	131	210	34	4	13	79	88	2	4	231	.241	.313	.334	.647	-34	41	20	67	O309(88/216/14),D17	159	-3.8
Team	3	270	677	116	176	27	2	12	69	71	2	4	166	.260	.332	.359	.691	-23	37	16	70	O240(27/26/11),D10	36	-1.7
/150	2	150	376	64	98	15	1	7	38	39	1	2	92	.260	.332	.359	.691	-23	21	9	70	O133(15/14/6),D6	20	-0.9
TOBIN, JOHNNY John Patrick "Jackie" B1.8.1921 Oakland CA D1.18.1982 Oakland CA BL/TR/6'0"/165 d4.20 b–Jim Col St. Marys (CA)																								
1945	Bos A	84	278	25	70	6	2	0	21	26		2	24	.252	.320	.288	.608	-25	2	6	25	3b72,2b5/cf	0	-0.2
TOBIN, JACK John Thomas B5.4.1892 St.Louis MO D12.10.1969 St.Louis MO BL/TL/5'8"/142 d4.16 C3																								
1926	Bos A	51	209	26	57	9	0	1	14	16		0	3	.273	.324	.330	.654	-27	6	5	55	O51(1/0/51)		-1.6
1927	Bos A	111	374	52	116	18	3	2	40	36		0	9	.310	.371	.390	.761	+0	5	4	56	O93(5/0/89)		-1.0
Total	13	1619	6174	936	1906	294	99	64	581	508		29	267	.309	.364	.420	.784	+6	147	62	100	O1491(220/137/1139),1b3		-10.1
Team	2	162	583	78	173	27	3	3	54	52		0	12	.297	.354	.369	.723	-10	11	9	55	O144(6/0/140)		-2.6
/150	2	150	540	72	160	25	3	3	50	48		0	11	.297	.354	.369	.723	-10	10	8	56	O133(6/0/130)		-2.4
TODT, PHIL Philip Julius "Hook" B8.9.1901 St.Louis MO D11.15.1973 St.Louis MO BL/TL/6'0"/175 d4.25																								
1924	Bos A	52	103	17	27	8	2	1	14	6		1	9	.262	.309	.408	.717	-16	0	1	0	1b18,O4(0/2/2)		-0.5
1925	Bos A	141	544	62	151	29	13	11	75	44		10	29	.278	.343	.439	.782	-3	3	2	60	1b140		-1.1
1926	Bos A	**154**	599	56	153	19	12	7	69	40		4	38	.255	.306	.362	.668	-24	3	2	60	1b154		-2.4
1927	Bos A	140	516	55	122	22	6	6	52	28		3	23	.236	.280	.337	.617	-39	6	2	75	1b139		-3.1
1928	Bos A	144	539	61	136	31	8	12	73	26		3	47	.252	.290	.406	.696	-17	6	5	55	1b144		-2.3
1929	Bos A	153	534	49	140	38	10	4	64	31		2	28	.262	.305	.393	.698	-20	6	7	46	1b153		-2.5
1930	Bos A	111	383	49	103	22	5	11	62	24		0	33	.269	.312	.439	.751	-8	4	1	80	1b104		-1.0
1931	†Phi A	62	197	23	48	14	2	5	44	8		0	22	.244	.273	.411	.684	-27	1	1	50	1b52		-1.6
Total	8	957	3415	372	880	183	58	57	453	207		23	229	.258	.305	.395	.700	-19	29	21	58	1b904,O4(0/2/2)		-14.5
Team	7	895	3218	349	832	169	56	52	409	199		23	207	.259	.306	.394	.700	-19	28	20	58	1b852,O4(0/2/2)		-12.9
/150	1	150	539	58	139	28	9	9	69	33		4	35	.259	.306	.394	.700	-19	5	3	63	1b143/O/L		-2.2
TOMBERLIN, ANDY Andy Lee B11.7.1966 Monroe NC BL/TL/5'11"/(180–185) d8.12																								
1994	Bos A	18	36	1	7	0	1	1	1	6	0	0	12	.194	.310	.333	.643	-37	1	0	100	O11(5/0/6)/PD	47	-0.2
Total	6	192	305	40	71	6	2	11	38	26	1	5	103	.233	.304	.374	.678	-23	6	1	86	O84(30/18/37),D29/1P	220	-1.5
TONNEMAN, TONY Charles Richard B9.10.1881 Chicago IL D8.4.1951 Prescott AZ BR/TR/5'10.5"/175 d9.19																								
1911	Bos A	2	5	0	1	1	0	0	3	1		0		.200	.333	.400	.733	+5	0			C2		0.0
TRUESDALE, FRANK Frank Day B3.31.1884 St.Louis MO D8.27.1943 Albuquerque NM BB/TR/5'8"/145 d4.27																								
1918	Bos A	15	36	6	10	1	0	0	2	4		0	5	.278	.350	.306	.656	-1	1			2b10		-0.1
Total	4	216	668	68	147	12	2	1	40	91		5	40	.220	.318	.249	.567	-22	41	11	100	2b199,3b4		-1.4
UMPHLETT, TOM Thomas Mullen B5.12.1930 Scotland Neck NC BR/TR/6'2"/(180–185) d4.16																								
1953	Bos A	137	495	53	140	27	5	3	59	34		2	30	.283	.331	.376	.707	-14	4	2	67	O136C	0	-1.7
1954	Was A	114	342	21	75	8	3	1	33	17		0	42	.219	.255	.269	.524	-54	1	2	33	O101(12/4/86)	0	-3.0
1955	Was A	110	323	34	70	10	0	2	19	24	0	0	35	.217	.271	.266	.537	-53	2	1	67	O103(18/62/23)	0	-2.5
Total	3	361	1160	108	285	45	8	6	111	75	0	2	107	.246	.292	.314	.606	-35	7	5	58	O340(30/202/109)	0	-7.2
/150	1	150	542	58	153	30	5	3	65	37		2	33	.283	.331	.376	.707	-14	4	2	67	O149C	0	-1.9
UNGLAUB, BOB Robert Alexander B7.31.1881 Baltimore MD D11.29.1916 Baltimore MD BR/TR/5'11"/178 d4.15 M1 Col Maryland																								
1904	NY A	6	19	2	4	0	0	0	2	0		0		.211	.211	.211	.422	-68	0			3b4/S		-0.3
1904	Bos A	9	13	1	2	1	0	0	2	1		0		.154	.214	.231	.445	-61	0			2b3,3b2/S		-0.4
1904	Year	15	32	3	6	1	0	0	4	1		0		.188	.212	.219	.431	-65	0			3b6,2b3,S2		-0.7
1905	Bos A	43	121	18	27	5	1	0	11	6		0		.223	.260	.281	.541	-29	2			3b21,2b7,1b2		-0.5
1907	Bos A	139	544	49	138	17	13	1	62	23		0		.254	.284	.338	.622	-1	14			1b139,M		-0.8
1908	Bos A	72	266	23	70	11	3	1	25	7		2		.263	.287	.338	.625	+0	6			1b72		-0.1
1908	Was A	72	276	23	85	10	5	0	29	8		0		.308	.327	.380	.707	+42	8			3b39,2b27,1b4		2.0
1908	Year	144	542	46	155	21	8	1	54	15		2		.286	.308	.360	.668	+20	14			1b76,3b39,2b27		1.9
1909	Was A	130	480	43	127	14	9	3	41	22		3		.265	.301	.350	.651	+11	15			1b57,O42(8/0/34),2b25,3b4		0.3
1910	Was A	124	431	29	101	9	4	0	44	21		0		.234	.270	.274	.544	-26	21			1b124		-1.2
Total	6	595	2150	188	554	67	35	5	216	88		5		.258	.288	.328	.616	-1	66			1b398,3b70,2b62,O42(8/0/34),S2		-1.0
Team	4	263	944	91	237	34	17	2	100	37		2	0	.251	.281	.329	.610	-5	22			1b213,3b23,2b10/SM		-1.8
/150	2	150	538	52	135	19	10	1	57	21		1	0	.251	.281	.329	.610	-5	13			1b121,3b13,2b6/SM		-1.0
VACHE, TEX Ernest Lewis B11.17.1888 Santa Monica CA D6.11.1953 Los Angeles CA BR/TR/6'1"/200 d4.16																								
1925	Bos A	110	252	41	79	15	7	3	48	21		7	33	.313	.382	.464	.846	+14	2	2	50	O53(52/0/1)		-0.6
/150	1	150	344	56	108	20	10	4	65	29		10	45	.313	.382	.464	.846	+14	3	3	50	O72(71/0/1)		-0.8
VALDEZ, JULIO Julio Julian (b Julio Julian Castillo (Valdez) B6.3.1956 San Cristobal, D.R. BB/TR (BR 1980)/6'2"/160 d9.2																								
1980	Bos A	8	19	4	5	1	0	1	4	0	0	1	5	.263	.300	.474	.774	+3	2	0	100	S8	0	0.5
1981	Bos A	17	23	1	5	0	0	0	3	0	0	0	2	.217	.208	.217	.425	-76	0	1	0	S17	0	-0.1
1982	Bos A	28	20	3	5	1	0	0	1	0	0	0	7	.250	.250	.300	.550	-53	1	0	100	S22,D3	0	0.1
1983	Bos A	12	25	3	3	0	0	0	0	1	0	1	4	.120	.185	.120	.305	-113	0	0	0	2b9,S2/D	0	-0.7
Total	4	65	87	11	18	2	0	1	8	1	0	2	18	.207	.231	.264	.495	-64	3	1	75	S49,2b9,D4	0	-0.2
VALENTIN, JOHN John William B2.18.1967 Mineola NY BR/TR/6'0"/(170–185) [BosA88 5/121] d7.27 Col Seton Hall																								
1992	Bos A	58	185	21	51	13	0	5	25	20	0	2	17	.276	.351	.427	.778	+9	1	0	100	S58	0	1.3
1993	Bos A	144	468	50	130	40	3	11	66	49	2	2	77	.278	.346	.447	.793	+5	3	4	43	S144	15	2.9
1994	Bos A	84	301	53	95	26	2	9	49	42	1	3	38	.316	.400	.505	.905	+27	3	1	75	S83/D	33	2.2
1995	†Bos A	135	520	108	155	37	2	27	102	81	2	10	67	.298	.399	.533	.932	+37	20	5	80	S135	0	4.6
1996	Bos A	131	527	84	156	29	3	13	59	63	0	7	59	.296	.374	.436	.810	+3	9	10	47	S118,3b12/D	15	1.7
1997	Bos A	143	575	95	176	**47**	5	18	77	58	5	5	66	.306	.372	.499	.871	+23	7	4	64	2b79,3b64	0	4.0
1998	†Bos A	153	588	113	145	44	1	23	73	77	3	9	82	.247	.340	.442	.782	+0	4	5	44	3b153/2	0	1.8
1999	†Bos A	113	450	58	114	27	1	12	70	40	2	4	68	.253	.315	.398	.713	-21	0	1	0	3b111,D2	38	-0.2
2000	Bos A	10	35	6	9	1	0	2	2	2	0	0	5	.257	.297	.457	.754	-15	0	1	0	3b10	161	-0.4
2001	Bos A	20	60	8	12	2	0	1	5	9	0	1	8	.200	.314	.283	.597	-41	0	0	0	S18,3b3	161	-0.3
2002	NY N	114	208	18	50	15	0	3	30	22	0	10	37	.240	.339	.356	.695	-11	0	0	0	S24,1b22,3b18,2b3,D2	17	-0.4
Total	11	1105	3917	614	1093	281	17	124	558	463	15	53	524	.279	.360	.454	.814	+8	47	31	60	S580,3b371,2b83,1b22,D6	440	17.2
Team	10	991	3709	596	1043	266	17	121	528	441	15	43	487	.281	.361	.460	.821	+9	47	31	60	S556,3b353,2b80,D4	423	17.6
/150	2	150	561	90	158	40	3	18	80	67	2	7	74	.281	.361	.460	.821	+9	7	5	58	S84,3b53,2b12/D	64	2.7
VALLE, DAVE David B10.30.1960 Bayside NY BR/TR/6'2"/(200–220) [SeaA78 2/32] d9.7																								
1994	Bos A	30	76	6	12	2	1	1	5	9	1	1	18	.158	.256	.250	.506	-70	0	1	0	C28,1b2	0	-1.0
Total	13	970	2775	314	658	121	12	77	350	258	11	63	413	.237	.314	.373	.687	-15	5	7	42	C902,1b24,D20/rf	239	2.1
VAN CAMP, AL Albert Joseph B9.7.1903 Moline IL D2.2.1981 Davenport IA BR/TR/5'11.5"/175 d9.11																								
1928	Cle A	5	17	0	4	1	0	0	2	0		0	1	.235	.235	.294	.529	-62	1	0	100	1b5		-0.2
1931	Bos A	101	324	34	89	15	4	0	33	20		1	24	.275	.319	.346	.665	-21	3	2	60	O59(58/3/2),1b25		-1.6
1932	Bos A	34	103	10	23	4	2	0	6	4		0	17	.223	.252	.301	.553	-56	0	0	0	1b25		-1.0
Total	3	140	444	44	116	20	6	0	41	24		1	42	.261	.301	.333	.634	-31	4	2	67	O59(58/3/2),1b55		-2.8
Team	2	135	427	44	112	19	6	0	39	24		1	41	.262	.303	.335	.638	-29	3	2	60	O59(58/3/2),1b50		-2.6
/150	2	150	474	49	124	21	7	0	43	27		1	46	.262	.303	.335	.638	-29	3	2	60	O66(64/3/2),1b56		-2.9

Year	Tm Lg	G	AB	R	H	2B	3B	HR	RBI	BB	IB	HP	SO	AVG	OBP	SLG	OPS	AOPS	SB	CS	SB%	Games at Position	DL	BFW
VARITEK, JASON Jason Andrew B4.11.1972 Rochester MN BB/TR/6'2"/(210–230) [SeaA94 1/14] d9.24 Col Georgia Tech																								
1997	Bos A	1	1	0	1	0	0	0	0	0	0	0	0	1.000	1.000	1.000	2.000	+315	0	0	0	/C	0	0.0
1998	†Bos A	86	221	31	56	13	0	7	33	17	1	2	45	.253	.309	.407	.716	-17	2	2	50	C75,D3	0	-0.3
1999	†Bos A	144	483	70	130	39	2	20	76	46	2	2	85	.269	.330	.482	.812	+2	1	2	33	C140,D2	0	1.7
2000	Bos A	139	448	55	111	31	1	10	65	60	3	6	84	.248	.342	.388	.730	-17	1	1	50	C128/D	0	-0.2
2001	Bos A	51	174	19	51	11	1	7	25	21	3	1	35	.293	.371	.489	.860	+24	0	0	0	C50	122	1.9
2002	Bos A	132	467	58	124	27	1	10	61	41	3	7	95	.266	.332	.392	.724	-9	4	3	57	C127/D	0	1.3
2003	†Bos A☆	142	451	63	123	31	1	25	85	51	8	7	106	.273	.351	.512	.863	+20	3	2	60	C137,D4	0	1.5
2004	†Bos A	137	463	67	137	30	1	18	73	62	9	10	126	.296	.390	.482	.872	+18	10	3	77	C130/D	0	3.2
2005	†Bos A★	133	470	70	132	30	1	22	70	62	3	3	117	.281	.366	.489	.855	+20	2	0	100	C130	0	1.8
2006	Bos A	103	365	46	87	19	2	12	55	46	7	2	87	.238	.325	.400	.725	-15	1	2	33	C99	33	-0.5
Total	10	1068	3543	479	952	231	10	131	543	406	39	40	780	.269	.348	.450	.798	+3	24	15	62	C1017,D12	155	10.4
/150	1	150	498	67	134	32	1	18	76	57	5	6	110	.269	.348	.450	.798	+3	3	2	60	C14,D2	22	1.5
VAUGHN, MO Maurice Samuel B12.15.1967 Norwalk CT BL/TR/6'1"/(225–268) [BosA89 1/23] d6.27 Col Seton Hall [DL 2001 Ana A 190, 2004 NY N 183]																								
1991	Bos A	74	219	21	57	12	0	4	32	26	2	2	43	.260	.339	.370	.709	-8	2	1	67	1b49,D16	0	-0.6
1992	Bos A	113	355	42	83	16	2	13	57	47	7	3	67	.234	.326	.400	.726	-4	3	3	50	1b85,D20	0	-1.0
1993	Bos A	152	539	86	160	34	1	29	101	79	23	8	130	.297	.390	.525	.915	+36	4	3	57	1b131,D19	0	0.6
1994	Bos A	111	394	65	122	25	1	26	82	57	**20**	10	112	.310	.408	.576	.984	+44	4	4	50	1b106/D	0	1.1
1995	†Bos A★	140	550	98	165	28	3	39	**126**	68	17	14	150	.300	.388	.575	.963	+43	11	4	73	1b138,D2	0	1.9
1996	Bos A★	161	635	118	207	29	1	44	143	95	19	14	154	.326	.420	.583	1.003	+49	2	0	100	1b146,D15	0	2.3
1997	Bos A	141	527	91	166	24	0	35	96	86	17	12	154	.315	.420	.560	.980	+50	2	2	50	1b131,D9	23	2.3
1998	†Bos A✱	154	609	107	205	31	2	40	115	61	13	8	144	.337	.402	.591	.993	+51	0	0	0	1b142,D12	0	2.7
1999	Ana A	139	524	63	147	20	0	33	108	54	7	11	127	.281	.358	.508	.866	+18	0	0	0	1b72,D67	15	0.2
2000	Ana A	161	614	93	167	31	0	36	117	79	11	14	181	.272	.365	.498	.863	+13	2	0	100	1b147,D14	0	-1.2
2002	NY N	139	487	67	126	18	0	26	72	59	6	10	145	.259	.349	.456	.805	+17	0	1	0	1b134	15	-1.5
2003	NY N	27	79	10	15	2	0	3	15	14	2	2	22	.190	.323	.329	.652	-25	0	0	0	1b24	149	-0.7
Total	12	1512	5532	861	1620	270	10	328	1064	725	14	108	1429	.293	.383	.523	.906	+31	30	18	63	1b1305,D175	575	6.1
Team	8	1046	3828	628	1165	199	10	230	752	519	98	71	954	.304	.394	.542	.936	+38	28	17	62	1b928,D94	23	9.3
/150	1	150	549	90	167	29	1	33	108	74	14	10	137	.304	.394	.542	.936	+38	4	2	67	1b133,D13	3	1.3
VAZQUEZ, RAMON Ramon Luis B8.21.1976 Aibonito, PR BL/TR/5'11"/170 [SeaA95 27/734] d9.7 Col Indian Hills (IA) CC																								
2005	Bos A	27	61	6	12	2	0	0	4	3	0	0	14	.197	.234	.230	.464	-77	0	0	0	S12,3b8,2b4/D	0	-1.0
Total	6	386	1147	141	293	48	11	7	92	119	7	3	229	.255	.324	.335	.659	-20	18	6	75	S202,2b119,3b57,1b3/D	67	-3.1
VEACH, BOBBY Robert Hayes B6.29.1888 St.Charles KY D8.7.1945 Detroit MI BL/TR/5'11"/160 d9.6																								
1924	Bos A	142	519	77	153	35	9	5	99	47		5	18	.295	.359	.426	.785	+2	5	5	50	O130L		-1.3
1925	Bos A	1	5	0	1	0	0	0	2	1		0	1	.200	.333	.200	.533	-62	0	0	0	/lf		-0.1
Total	14	1821	6656	953	2063	393	147	64	1166	571		59	**367**	.310	.370	.442	.812	+27	195	**84**	100	O1740(1671/14/65)/P		17.9
Team	2	143	524	77	154	35	9	5	101	48		5	19	.294	.359	.424	.783	+1	5	5	50	O131L		-1.4
/150	2	150	550	81	162	37	9	5	106	50		5	20	.294	.359	.424	.783	+1	5	5	50	O137L		-1.5
VERAS, WILTON Wilton Andres B1.19.1978 Monte Cristi, D.R. BR/TR/6'2"/198 d7.1																								
1999	Bos A	36	118	14	34	5	1	2	13	5	0	2	14	.288	.323	.398	.721	-19	0	2	0	3b35	0	-0.4
2000	Bos A	49	164	21	40	7	1	0	14	7	0	2	20	.244	.278	.299	.577	-54	0	0	0	3b49	0	-0.9
Total	2	85	282	35	74	12	2	2	27	12	0	4	34	.262	.297	.340	.637	-39	0	2	0	3b84	0	-1.3
VERNON, MICKEY James Barton B4.22.1918 Marcus Hook PA BL/TL/6'2"/(175–184) d7.8 Mil 1944–45 M3/C6 Col Villanova																								
1956	Bos A★	119	403	67	125	28	4	15	84	57	6	7	40	.310	.403	.511	.914	+25	1	0	100	1b108	0	0.6
1957	Bos A	102	270	36	65	18	1	7	38	41	2	5	35	.241	.350	.393	.743	-3	0	0	0	1b70	0	0.0
Total	20	2409	8731	1196	2495	490	120	172	1311	955	**22**	49	869	.286	.359	.428	.787	+16	137	90	60	1b2237,O4(2/0/2)	0	3.7
Team	2	221	673	103	190	46	5	22	122	98	8	12	75	.282	.382	.464	.846	+14	1	0	100	1b178	0	0.6
/150	1	150	457	70	129	31	3	15	83	67	5	8	51	.282	.382	.464	.846	+14	1	0	100	1b121	0	0.4
VICK, SAMMY Samuel Bruce B4.12.1895 Batesville MS D8.17.1986 Memphis TN BR/TR/5'10.5"/163 d9.20 Mil 1918 Col Millsaps																								
1921	Bos A	44	77	5	20	3	1	0	9	1		0	10	.260	.269	.325	.594	-48	0	1	0	O14R		-0.7
Total	5	213	641	90	159	28	11	2	50	51		2	91	.248	.305	.335	.640	-24	12	**2**	100	O158(4/1/153)		-4.0
VITT, OSSIE Oscar Joseph B1.4.1890 San Francisco CA D1.31.1963 Oakland CA BR/TR/5'10"/150 d4.11 M3																								
1919	Bos A	133	469	64	114	10	3	0	40	44		1	11	.243	.309	.277	.586	-31	9			3b133		0.3
1920	Bos A	87	296	50	65	10	4	1	28	43		1	10	.220	.321	.291	.612	-35	5	4	56	3b64,2b21		-1.3
1921	Bos A	78	232	29	44	11	1	0	13	45		0	13	.190	.321	.246	.567	-52	1	2	33	3b71,O3L,1b2		-1.5
Total	10	1065	3760	560	894	106	48	4	295	455		12	**131**	.238	.322	.295	.617	-20	114	**32**	100	3b833,2b161,O38(31/6/1),S3,1b2		-2.4
Team	3	298	997	143	223	31	8	1	81	132		2	34	.224	.315	.274	.589	-37	15	**6**	100	3b268,2b21,O3L,1b2		-2.5
/150	2	150	502	72	112	16	4	1	41	66		1	17	.224	.315	.274	.589	-37	8	**3**	100	3b135,2b11,O2L/1		-1.3
VOLLMER, CLYDE Clyde Frederick "Dutch the Clutch" B9.24.1921 Cincinnati OH D10.2.2006 Florence KY BR/TR/6'1"/190 d5.31 Mil 1943–45																								
1942	Cin N	12	43	2	4	0	0	1	4	1		0	5	.093	.114	.163	.277	-120	0			O11(10/1/0)	0	-0.8
1946	Cin N	9	22	1	4	0	0	0	1	1		0	3	.182	.217	.182	.399	-86	2			O7(5/3/1)	0	-0.4
1947	Cin N	78	155	19	34	10	0	1	13	9		1	18	.219	.267	.303	.570	-49	0			O66(8/58/0)	0	-0.8
1948	Cin N	7	9	0	1	0	0	0	0	1		0	1	.111	.200	.111	.311	-114	0			O2(0/1/1)	0	-0.2
1948	Was A	1	5	1	2	0	0	0	0	0		0	1	.400	.400	.400	.800	+16	0	0	0	/cf	0	0.0
1948	Major	8	14	1	3	0	0	0	0	1	0	0	2	.214	.267	.214	.481	-96	0	0	0		0	-0.2
1949	Was A	129	443	58	112	17	1	14	59	53		2	62	.253	.335	.391	.726	-6	1	2	33	O114(0/99/15)	0	-0.8
1950	Was A	6	14	4	4	0	0	0	1	2		0	3	.286	.375	.286	.661	-25	1	0	100	O3L	0	0.0
1950	Bos A	57	169	35	48	10	0	7	37	21		0	35	.284	.363	.467	.830	+2	1	0	100	O39(17/11/11)	0	-0.3
1950	Year	63	183	39	52	10	0	7	38	23		0	38	.284	.364	.454	.818	+0	2	0	100	O42(20/11/11)	0	-0.3
1951	Bos A	115	386	66	97	9	2	22	85	55		1	66	.251	.346	.456	.802	+5	0	0	0	O106(2/8/97)	0	-0.5
1952	Bos A	90	250	35	66	12	4	11	50	39		3	47	.264	.370	.476	.846	+24	2	2	50	O70(43/9/21)	0	0.5
1953	Bos A	1	0	0	0	0	0	0	0	1		0	0	+	1.000	+	1.000	+80	0	0	0	/H	0	0.0
1953	Was A	118	408	54	106	15	3	11	74	48		3	59	.260	.342	.392	.734	+0	0	2	0	O106(104/0/2)	0	-0.5
1953	Year	119	408	54	106	15	3	11	74	49		3	59	.260	.343	.392	.735	+1	0	2	0	O106(104/0/2)	0	-0.5
1954	Was A	62	117	8	30	4	0	2	15	12		1	28	.256	.331	.342	.673	-11	0	0	0	O26(5/0/21)	0	-0.4
Total	10	685	2021	283	508	77	10	69	339	243		11	328	.251	.335	.402	.737	-5	7	**6**	100	O551(197/191/169)	0	-4.2
Team	4	263	805	136	211	31	6	40	172	116		4	148	.262	.358	.465	.823	+10	3	2	60	O215(19/28/129)	0	-0.3
/150	2	150	459	78	120	18	3	23	98	66		2	84	.262	.358	.465	.823	+10	2	1	67	O123(11/16/74)	0	-0.2
VOSMIK, JOE Joseph Franklin B4.4.1910 Cleveland OH D1.27.1962 Cleveland OH BR/TR/6'0"/185 d9.13																								
1938	Bos A	146	621	121	**201**	37	6	9	86	59		2	26	.324	.384	.446	.830	+3	0	3	0	O146(146/1/0)		-0.2
1939	Bos A	145	554	89	153	29	6	7	84	66		3	33	.276	.356	.388	.744	-13	4	3	57	O144L		-2.2
Total	13	1414	5472	818	1682	335	92	65	874	514		21	272	.307	.369	.438	.807	+4	23	**24**	100	O1370(1283/15/75)	0	-2.3
Team	2	291	1175	210	354	66	12	16	170	125		5	59	.301	.371	.419	.790	-5	4	6	40	O290(146/1/0)		-2.4
/150	1	150	606	108	182	34	6	8	88	64		3	30	.301	.371	.419	.790	-5	2	3	40	O149(75/1/0)		-1.2
WAGNER, HEINIE Charles F. B9.23.1880 New York NY D3.20.1943 New Rochelle NY BR/TR/5'9"/183 d7.1 M1/C7																								
1902	NY N	17	56	4	12	1	0	0	2	0		0		.214	.214	.232	.446	-62	3			S17		-0.8
1906	Bos A	9	32	1	9	0	0	0	4	1		0		.281	.303	.281	.584	-17	2			2b9		0.1
1907	Bos A	111	385	29	82	10	4	2	21	31		2		.213	.275	.275	.550	-24	20			S109/23		-1.4
1908	Bos A	153	526	62	130	11	5	1	46	27		3		.247	.288	.293	.581	-14	20			S153		3.2
1909	Bos A	124	430	53	110	16	7	1	49	35		3		.256	.316	.333	.649	+3	18			S123/2		1.7
1910	Bos A	142	491	61	134	26	7	1	52	44		2		.273	.335	.360	.695	+15	26			S140		0.0
1911	Bos A	80	261	34	67	13	8	1	38	29		4		.257	.340	.379	.719	+1	15			2b40,S32		-0.3
1912	†Bos A	144	504	75	138	25	6	2	68	62		4		.274	.358	.359	.717	+0	21			S144		-0.1
1913	Bos A	110	365	43	83	14	8	2	34	40		7	29	.227	.316	.326	.642	-14	9			S103,2b5/3		0.0

Year	Tm Lg	G	AB	R	H	2B	3B	HR	RBI	BB	IB	HP	SO	AVG	OBP	SLG	OPS	AOPS	SB	CS	SB%	Games at Position	DL	BFW
1915	Bos A	84	267	38	64	11	2	0	29	37		3	34	.240	.339	.296	.635	-7	8	4	67	2b79/3lf		-1.6
1916	Bos A	6	8	2	4	1	0	0	0	3		0	0	.500	.636	.625	1.261	+178	2			3b4/2S		0.4
1918	Bos A	3	8	0	1	0	0	0	0	1		0	0	.125	.222	.125	.347	-95	0			2b2/3		-0.1
Total	12	983	3333	402	834	128	47	10	343	310		28	63	.250	.319	.326	.645	-5	144	4	100	S822,2b138,3b8/lf		1.1
Team	11	966	3277	398	822	127	47	10	341	310		28	63	.251	.321	.327	.648	-4	141	4	100	S805,2b138,3b8/lf		1.9
/150	2	150	509	62	128	20	7	2	53	48		4	10	.251	.321	.327	.648	-4	22	1	100	S125,2b21/3OfL		0.3
WAGNER, HAL Harold Edward B7.2.1915 E.Riverton NJ D8.7.1979 Riverside NJ BL/TR/6'0"/165 d10.3 Mil 1944–45 Col Duke																								
1944	Bos A	66	223	21	74	13	4	1	38	29		4	14	.332	.418	.439	.857	+47	1	1	50	C64	0	1.8
1946	†Bos A★	117	370	39	85	12	2	6	52	69		2	32	.230	.354	.322	.676	-15	3	1	75	C116	0	-0.4
1947	Bos A	21	65	5	15	3	0	0	6	9		0	5	.231	.324	.277	.601	-37	0	0	0	C21	0	-0.3
Total	12	672	1849	179	458	90	12	15	228	253		15	152	.248	.343	.334	.677	-13	10	6	100	C626	0	-1.8
Team	3	204	658	65	174	28	6	7	96	107		6	51	.264	.372	.357	.729	+3	4	2	67	C201	0	1.1
/150	2	150	484	48	128	21	4	5	71	79		4	38	.264	.372	.357	.729	+3	3	1	75	C148	0	0.8
WALKER, TILLY Clarence William B9.4.1887 Telford TN D9.20.1959 Unicoi TN BR/TR/5'11"/165 d6.10 Col Washington College																								
1916	†Bos A	128	467	68	124	29	11	3	46	23		2	45	.266	.303	.394	.697	+9	14			O128(3/125/0)		-1.3
1917	Bos A	106	337	41	83	18	7	2	37	25		1	38	.246	.300	.359	.659	+2	6			O96C		-0.4
Total	13	1421	5067	696	1423	244	71	118	679	416		31	504	.281	.339	.427	.766	+15	129	47	100	O1348(726/578/44)/2		1.7
Team	2	234	804	109	207	47	18	5	83	48		3	83	.257	.302	.379	.681	+6	20			O224(3/125/0)		-1.7
/150	1	150	515	70	133	30	12	3	53	31		2	53	.257	.302	.379	.681	+6	13			O144(2/80/0)		-1.1
WALKER, CHICO Cleotha B11.25.1958 Jackson MS BB/TR/5'9"/(160–185) [BosA76 22/525] d9.2																								
1980	Bos A	19	57	3	12	0	0	1	5	6	1	1	10	.211	.292	.263	.555	-48	3	2	60	2b11,D7	0	-0.5
1981	Bos A	6	17	3	6	0	0	0	2	1	0	0	2	.353	.389	.353	.742	+8	0	2	0	2b5	0	-0.3
1983	Bos A	4	5	2	2	0	2	0	1	0	0	0	0	.400	.400	1.200	1.600	+198	0	0	0	O3L	0	0.2
1984	Bos A	3	2	0	0	0	0	0	1	0	0	0	1	.000	.000	.000	.000	-195	0	0	0	/2	0	-0.1
Total	11	526	1217	150	299	37	7	17	116	109	7	1	212	.246	.305	.329	.634	-25	67	19	78	O174(87/66/42),3b122,2b74,D7	0	-5.3
Team	4	32	81	8	20	0	2	1	9	7	1	1	13	.247	.311	.333	.644	-26	3	4	43	2b17,D7,O3L	0	-0.7
WALKER, TODD Todd Arthur B5.25.1973 Bakersfield CA BL/TR/6'0"/(170–185) [MinA94 1/8] d8.30 Col Louisiana St.																								
2003	†Bos A	144	587	92	166	38	4	13	85	48	0	1	54	.283	.333	.428	.761	-4	1	1	50	2b139,D2	0	-0.4
Total	11	1270	4506	642	1303	283	30	107	541	419	34	16	567	.289	.349	.437	.786	-2	66	37	64	2b1007,3b83,1b49,D49/lfS	44	-4.5
/150	1	150	611	96	173	40	4	14	89	50	0	1	56	.283	.333	.428	.761	-4	1	1	50	2b145,D2	0	-0.4
WALSH, JIMMY James Charles B9.22.1885 Kallila, Ireland D7.3.1962 Syracuse NY BL/TR/5'10.5"/170 d8.26 Mil 1918																								
1916	†Bos A	14	17	5	3	1	0	0	2	4		0	2	.176	.333	.235	.568	-29	3	2	60	O6(1/3/2),3b2		-0.1
1917	Bos A	57	185	25	49	6	3	0	12	25		0	14	.265	.352	.330	.682	+9	6			O47(2/43/2)		-0.2
Total	6	541	1771	235	410	71	31	6	150	249		11	204	.232	.330	.317	.647	-4	92	49	100	O492(163/170/166),3b7,1b5/S		-3.2
Team	2	71	202	30	52	7	3	0	14	29		0	16	.257	.351	.322	.673	+6	9	2	100	O53(3/46/2),3b2		-0.3
WALTERS, ROXY Alfred John B11.5.1892 San Francisco CA D6.3.1956 Alameda CA BR/TR/5'8.5"/160 d9.16																								
1915	NY A	2	3	0	1	0	0	0	0	0		0	0	.333	.333	.333	.666	+0	0			C2		0.1
1916	NY A	66	203	13	54	9	3	0	23	14		2	42	.266	.320	.340	.660	-4	2			C65		1.8
1917	NY A	61	171	16	45	2	0	0	14	9		1	22	.263	.304	.275	.579	-24	2			C57		0.9
1918	NY A	64	191	18	38	5	1	0	12	9		1	18	.199	.239	.236	.475	-58	3			C50,O9R		-1.4
1919	Bos A	48	135	7	26	2	0	0	9	7		5	15	.193	.259	.207	.466	-67	1			C47		-0.6
1920	Bos A	88	258	25	51	11	1	0	28	30		9	21	.198	.303	.248	.551	-51	2	2	50	C85,1b2		-0.8
1921	Bos A	54	169	17	34	4	1	0	14	10		2	11	.201	.254	.237	.491	-73	3	0	100	C54		-0.4
1922	Bos A	38	98	4	19	2	0	0	6	6		0	8	.194	.240	.214	.454	-81	0	0	0	C36		-0.7
1923	Bos A	40	104	9	26	4	0	0	5	2		0	6	.250	.264	.288	.552	-55	0	2	0	C36/2		-0.4
1924	Cle A	32	74	10	19	2	0	0	5	10		0	6	.257	.345	.284	.629	-37	0	1	0	C25,2b7		0.0
1925	Cle A	5	20	0	4	0	0	0	0	0		0	2	.200	.200	.200	.400	-98	0	0	0	C5		-0.2
Total	11	498	1426	119	317	41	6	0	116	97		20	151	.222	.281	.259	.540	-49	13	5	100	C462,O9R,2b8,1b2		-1.7
Team	5	268	764	62	156	23	2	0	62	55		16	61	.204	.272	.240	.512	-63	6	4	100	C258,1b2/2		-2.9
/150	3	150	428	35	87	13	1	0	35	31		9	34	.204	.272	.240	.512	-63	3	2	100	C144/12		-1.6
WALTERS, FRED Fred James "Whale" B9.4.1912 Laurel MS D2.1.1980 Laurel MS BR/TR/6'1"/210 d4.17 Col Mississippi St.																								
1945	Bos A	40	93	2	16	2	0	0	5	10		0	9	.172	.252	.194	.446	-71	1	1	50	C38	0	-0.4
WALTERS, BUCKY William Henry B4.19.1909 Philadelphia PA D4.20.1991 Abington PA BR/TR/6'1"/180 d9.18 M2/C8▲																								
1933	Bos A	52	195	27	50	8	3	4	28	19		1	24	.256	.326	.390	.716	-10	1	1	50	3b43,2b7		-0.1
1934	Bos A	23	88	10	19	4	4	4	18	3		0	12	.216	.242	.489	.731	-21	0	0	0	3b23		0.0
Total	19	715	1966	227	477	99	16	23	234	114		5	303	.243	.286	.344	.630	-31	12	1	100	P428,3b184,2b16,O6L	60	-1.9
Team	2	75	283	37	69	12	7	8	46	22		1	36	.244	.301	.420	.721	-13	1	1	50	3b66,2b7		-0.1
WAMBSGANSS, BILL William Adolph B3.19.1894 Cleveland OH D12.8.1985 Lakewood OH BR/TR/5'11"/175 d8.4 Mil 1918																								
1924	Bos A	156	636	93	174	41	5	0	49	54		4	33	.274	.334	.354	.688	-23	14	8	64	2b156		-0.3
1925	Bos A	111	360	50	83	12	4	1	41	52		1	21	.231	.329	.294	.623	-41	3	5	38	2b103,1b6		-1.1
Total	13	1491	5241	710	1359	215	59	7	520	490		47	357	.259	.328	.327	.655	-22	140	74	100	2b1205,S175,3b46,1b9		-9.8
Team	2	267	996	143	257	53	9	1	90	106		5	54	.258	.332	.332	.664	-30	17	13	57	2b259,1b6		-1.4
/150	1	150	560	80	144	30	5	1	51	60		3	30	.258	.332	.332	.664	-30	10	7	59	2b146,1b3		-0.8
WANNINGER, PEE-WEE Paul Louis B12.12.1902 Birmingham AL D3.7.1981 N.Augusta SC BL/TR/5'7"/150 d4.22																								
1927	Bos A	18	60	4	12	0	0	0	1	6		1	2	.200	.284	.200	.484	-72	2	4	33	S15		-0.6
Total	2	163	556	53	130	15	8	1	31	23		1	43	.234	.266	.295	.561	-55	5	9	100	S154,3b3/2		-3.6
WARNER, JOHN John Joseph B8.15.1872 New York NY D12.21.1943 Far Rockaway NY BL/TR/5'11"/165 d4.23																								
1902	Bos A	65	222	19	52	5	7	0	12	13		3		.234	.286	.320	.606	-34	0			C64		0.3
Total	14	1074	3497	348	870	81	35	6	303	181		91	33	.249	.303	.297	.600	-27	83			C1033,1b8/rf2		3.1
WARSTLER, RABBIT Harold Burton B9.13.1903 N.Canton OH D5.31.1964 N.Canton OH BR/TR/5'7.5"/150 d7.24																								
1930	Bos A	54	162	16	30	2	3	1	13	20		0	21	.185	.275	.253	.528	-64	0	2	0	S54		-1.2
1931	Bos A	66	181	20	44	5	3	0	10	15		2	27	.243	.308	.304	.612	-35	2	3	40	2b42,S19/3		-0.7
1932	Bos A	115	388	26	82	15	5	0	34	22		3	43	.211	.259	.276	.535	-60	9	6	60	S107		-0.5
1933	Bos A	92	322	44	70	13	1	1	17	42		0	36	.217	.308	.273	.581	-45	2	4	33	S87		-1.5
Total	11	1205	4088	431	935	133	36	11	332	405		11	414	.229	.300	.287	.587	-41	42	22	100	S705,2b442,3b26		-12.7
Team	4	327	1053	106	226	35	12	2	74	99		5	127	.215	.285	.276	.561	-52	13	15	46	S267,2b42/3		-3.9
/150	2	150	483	49	104	16	6	1	34	45		2	58	.215	.285	.276	.561	-52	6	7	46	S122,2b19/3		-1.8
WATSON, BOB Robert Jose "Bull" B4.10.1946 Los Angeles CA BR/TR/6'2"/(200–218) d9.9 C3																								
1979	Bos A	84	312	48	105	19	4	13	53	29	7	5	33	.337	.401	.548	.949	+45	3	2	60	1b58,D26	0	1.7
Total	19	1832	6185	802	1826	307	41	184	989	653	98	48	796	.295	.364	.447	.811	+30	27	28	49	1b1088,O570(570/0/1),D54,C10	99	11.9
WATWOOD, JOHNNY John Clifford "Lefty" B8.17.1905 Alexander City AL D3.1.1980 Goodwater AL BL/TL/6'1"/186 d4.16 Col Auburn																								
1932	Bos A	95	266	26	66	11	0	0	30	20		0	11	.248	.301	.289	.590	-45	7	4	64	O46(7/25/14),1b18		-2.1
1933	Bos A	13	30	2	4	0	0	0	2	3		0	3	.133	.212	.133	.345	-107	0	0	0	O9(5/0/4)		-0.5
Total	6	469	1423	192	403	66	16	5	158	154		6	103	.283	.356	.363	.719	-11	27	17	100	O299(22/191/90),1b86		-3.1
Team	2	108	296	28	70	11	0	0	32	23		0	14	.236	.292	.274	.566	-51	7	4	64	O55(12/25/18),1b18		-2.6
/150	3	150	411	39	97	15	0	0	44	32		0	19	.236	.292	.274	.566	-51	10	6	63	O76(17/35/25),1b25		-3.6
WEBB, EARL William Earl B9.17.1897 Bon Air TN D5.23.1965 Jamestown TN BL/TR/6'1"/185 d8.13																								
1925	NY N	4	3	0	0	0	0	0	0	1		0	1	.000	.250	.000	.250	-131	0	0	0	/H		-0.1
1927	Chi N	102	332	58	100	18	4	14	52	48		1	31	.301	.391	.506	.897	+38	3			O86(8/0/78)		1.2
1928	Chi N	62	140	22	35	7	3	3	23	14		0	17	.250	.318	.407	.725	-10	0			O31R		-0.4
1930	Bos A	127	449	61	145	30	6	16	66	44		1	56	.323	.385	.523	.908	+33	2	1	67	O116R		0.7
1931	Bos A	151	589	96	196	**67**	3	14	103	70		0	51	.333	.404	.528	.932	+51	2	2	50	O151R		3.0
1932	Bos A	52	192	23	54	9	1	5	27	25		0	15	.281	.364	.417	.781	+5	0	0	0	O50R,1b2		-0.2

Year	Tm Lg	G	AB	R	H	2B	3B	HR	RBI	BB	IB	HP	SO	AVG	OBP	SLG	OPS	AOPS	SB	CS	SB%	Games at Position	DL	BFW
1932	Det A	88	338	49	97	19	8	3	51	39		0	18	.287	.361	.417	.778	-3	1	1	50	O85R		-0.6
1932	Year	140	530	72	151	28	9	8	78	64		0	33	.285	.362	.417	.779	+0	1	1	50	O135R,1b2		-0.8
1933	Det A	6	11	1	3	0	0	0	3	3		0	0	.273	.429	.273	.702	-13	0	0	0	O2R		0.0
1933	Chi A	58	107	16	31	5	0	1	8	16		0	13	.290	.382	.364	.746	+3	0	0	0	O16(5/0/11),1b10		-0.2
1933	Year	64	118	17	34	5	0	1	11	19		0	13	.288	.387	.356	.743	+1	0	0	0	O18(5/0/13),1b10		-0.2
Total	7	650	2161	326	661	155	25	56	333	260		2	202	.306	.381	.478	.859	+25	8	4	100	O537(13/0/524),1b12		3.4
Team	3	330	1230	180	395	106	10	35	196	139		1	122	.321	.391	.509	.900	+37	4	3	57	O317R,1b2		3.5
/150	1	150	559	82	180	48	5	16	89	63		0	55	.321	.391	.509	.900	+37	2	1	67	O144R/1		1.6
WEBSTER, LENNY Leonard Irell B2.10.1965 New Orleans LA BR/TR/5'9"/(185–202) [MinA85 21/535] d9.1 Col Grambling St.																								
1999	Bos A	6	14	0	0	0	0	0	1	2	0	1	2	.000	.176	.000	.176	-148	0	0	0	C6	0	-0.3
Total	12	587	1450	157	368	73	2	33	176	140	5	12	209	.254	.324	.375	.699	-16	1	3	25	C528,D9	95	-3.4
WEBSTER, RAY Raymond George B11.15.1937 Grass Valley CA BR/TR/6'0"/(160–175) d4.17																								
1960	Bos A	7	3	1	0	0	0	0	1	1	0	0	2	.000	.200	.000	.200	-125	0	0	0	/2	0	0.0
Total	2	47	77	11	15	2	1	2	11	6	0	0	7	.195	.250	.325	.575	-41	1	0	100	2b25,3b4	0	-0.6
WEDGE, ERIC Eric Michael B1.27.1968 Fort Wayne IN BR/TR/6'3"/(215–224) [BosA89 3/83] d10.5 M4 Col Wichita St.																								
1991	Bos A	1	1	0	1	0	0	0	0	0	0	0	0	1.000	1.000	1.000	2.000	+331	0	0	0	/D	0	0.0
1992	Bos A	27	68	11	17	2	0	5	11	13	0	0	18	.250	.370	.500	.870	+32	0	0	0	D20,C5	0	0.2
1993	Col N	9	11	2	2	0	0	0	1	0	0	0	4	.182	.182	.182	.364	-102	0	0	0	/C	111	-0.1
1994	Bos A	2	6	0	0	0	0	0	0	1	0	0	3	.000	.143	.000	.143	-156	0	0	0	D2	0	-0.2
Total	4	39	86	13	20	2	0	5	12	14	0	0	25	.233	.340	.430	.770	+3	0	0	0	D23,C6	111	-0.1
Team	3	30	75	11	18	2	0	5	11	14	0	0	21	.240	.360	.467	.827	+21	0	0	0	D22,C5	0	0.0
WELCH, FRANK Frank Tiguer "Bugger" B8.10.1897 Birmingham AL D7.25.1957 Birmingham AL BR/TR/5'9"/175 d9.9																								
1927	Bos A	15	28	2	5	2	0	0	4	5		0	1	.179	.303	.250	.553	-54	0	2	0	O6R		-0.1
Total	9	738	2310	310	634	100	31	41	295	250		20	225	.274	.350	.398	.748	-8	18	28	100	O623(35/203/390)		-7.6
WELCH, HERB Herbert M. "Dutch" B10.19.1898 RoEllen TN D4.13.1967 Memphis TN BL/TR/5'6"/154 d9.15																								
1925	Bos A	13	38	2	11	0	1	0	2	0		0	6	.289	.289	.342	.631	-40	0	0	0	S13		0.1
WERBER, BILLY William Murray B6.20.1908 Berwyn MD BR/TR/5'10"/170 d6.25 Col Duke																								
1930	NY A	4	14	5	4	0	0	0	2	3		0	1	.286	.412	.286	.698	-16	0	0	0	S3/3		0.0
1933	NY A	3	2	0	0	0	0	0	0	0		0	0	.000	.000	.000	.000	-199	0	0	0	/3		-0.1
1933	Bos A	108	425	64	110	30	6	3	39	33		0	39	.259	.312	.379	.691	-17	15	5	75	S71,3b38,2b2		-1.7
1933	Year	111	427	64	110	30	6	3	39	33		0	39	.258	.311	.377	.688	-18	15	5	75	S71,3b39,2b2		-1.8
1934	Bos A	152	623	129	200	41	10	11	67	77		1	37	.321	.397	.472	.869	+15	**40**	15	73	3b130,S22		3.9
1935	Bos A	124	462	84	118	30	3	14	61	69		4	41	.255	.357	.424	.781	-5	**29**	7	81	3b123		1.8
1936	Bos A	145	535	89	147	29	6	10	67	89		4	37	.275	.382	.407	.789	-10	23	13	64	3b101,O45(38/0/7)/2		-1.5
1937	Phi A	128	493	85	144	31	4	7	70	74		1	39	.292	.386	.414	.800	+3	**35**	13	73	3b125,O3(1/2/0)		1.5
1938	Phi A	134	499	92	129	22	7	11	69	93		2	37	.259	.377	.397	.774	-4	19	15	56	3b134		0.6
1939	†Cin N	147	599	**115**	173	35	5	5	57	91		6	46	.289	.388	.389	.777	+9	15			3b147		2.7
1940	†Cin N	143	584	105	162	35	5	12	48	68		8	40	.277	.361	.416	.777	+13	16			3b143		2.3
1941	Cin N	109	418	56	100	9	2	4	46	53		2	24	.239	.328	.299	.627	-23	14			3b107	0	0.2
1942	NY N	98	370	51	76	9	2	1	13	51		4	22	.205	.308	.249	.557	-36	9			3b93	0	0.0
Total	11	1295	5024	875	1363	271	50	78	539	701		32	363	.271	.364	.392	.756	-3	215	68	100	3b1143,S96,O48(39/2/7),2b3	0	9.7
Team	4	529	2045	366	575	130	25	38	234	268		9	154	.281	.367	.425	.792	-3	107	40	73	3b392,S93,O45(38/0/7),2b3		2.5
/150	1	150	580	104	163	37	7	11	66	76		3	44	.281	.367	.425	.792	-3	30	11	73	3b111,S26,O13(11/0/2)/2		0.7
WERTZ, VIC Victor Woodrow B2.9.1925 York PA D7.7.1983 Detroit MI BL/TR/6'0"/(186–203) d4.15																								
1959	Bos A	94	247	38	68	13	0	7	49	22	5	2	32	.275	.337	.413	.750	+1	0	0	0	1b64	0	0.0
1960	Bos A	131	443	45	125	22	0	19	103	37	4	1	54	.282	.335	.460	.795	+10	0	2	0	1b117	0	0.2
1961	Bos A	99	317	33	83	16	2	11	60	38	3	2	43	.262	.339	.429	.768	+3	0	0	0	1b86	0	0.1
Total	17	1862	6099	867	1692	289	42	266	1178	828	33	27	842	.277	.364	.469	.833	+21	9	19	32	O889(105/4/783),1b715	98	11.2
Team	3	324	1007	116	276	51	2	37	212	97	12	5	129	.274	.337	.439	.776	+6	0	2	0	1b267	0	0.3
/150	1	150	466	54	128	24	1	17	98	45	6	2	60	.274	.337	.439	.776	+6	0	1	0	1b124	0	0.1
WHITE, SAMMY Samuel Charles B7.7.1927 Wenatchee WA D9.4.1991 Princeville HI BR/TR/6'3"/195 d9.26 Col Washington																								
1951	Bos A	4	11	0	2	0	0	0	0	0		0	3	.182	.182	.182	.364	-101	0	0	0	C4	0	-0.1
1952	Bos A	115	381	35	107	20	2	10	49	16		0	43	.281	.310	.423	.733	-5	2	3	40	C110	0	0.4
1953	Bos A☆	136	476	59	130	34	2	13	64	29		2	48	.273	.318	.435	.753	-4	3	2	60	C131	0	1.3
1954	Bos A	137	493	46	139	25	2	14	75	21		0	50	.282	.307	.426	.733	-10	1	3	25	C133	0	0.2
1955	Bos A	143	544	65	142	30	4	11	64	44	4	7	58	.261	.323	.392	.715	-16	1	2	33	C143	0	-0.7
1956	Bos A	114	392	28	96	15	2	5	44	35	7	0	40	.245	.304	.332	.636	-39	2	1	67	C114	0	-1.3
1957	Bos A	111	340	24	73	10	1	3	31	25	6	0	38	.215	.267	.276	.543	-54	0	1	0	C111	0	-2.3
1958	Bos A	102	328	25	85	15	3	6	35	21	4	1	37	.259	.305	.378	.683	-19	1	1	50	C102	0	-0.6
1959	Bos A	119	377	34	107	13	4	1	42	23	6	1	39	.284	.324	.347	.671	-19	4	2	67	C119	0	-0.2
1961	Mil N	21	63	1	14	1	0	1	5	2	0	0	9	.222	.242	.286	.528	-57	0	0	0	C20	0	-0.2
1962	Phi N	41	97	7	21	4	0	2	12	2	0	1	16	.216	.238	.320	.558	-50	0	0	0	C40	0	-0.6
Total	11	1043	3502	324	916	167	20	66	421	218	27	12	381	.262	.305	.377	.682	-21	14	15	48	C1027	0	-4.1
Team	9	981	3342	316	881	162	20	63	404	214	27	11	356	.264	.308	.381	.689	-20	14	15	48	C967	0	-3.3
/150	1	150	511	48	135	25	3	10	62	33	4	2	54	.264	.308	.381	.689	-20	2	2	50	C148	0	-0.5
WHITEMAN, GEORGE George "Lucky" B12.23.1882 Peoria IL D2.10.1947 Houston TX BR/TR/5'7"/160 d9.13																								
1907	Bos A	4	12	0	2	0	0	0	1	0		0		.167	.167	.167	.334	-94	0			O2L		-0.2
1913	NY A	11	32	8	11	3	1	0	2	7		0	2	.344	.462	.500	.962	+81	2			O11(4/4/3)		0.3
1918	†Bos A	71	214	24	57	14	0	1	28	20		2	9	.266	.335	.346	.681	+7	9			O69(65/0/4)		-0.6
Total	3	86	258	32	70	17	1	1	31	27		2	11	.271	.345	.357	.702	+13	11			O82(71/4/7)		-0.5
Team	2	75	226	24	59	14	0	1	29	20		2	9	.261	.327	.336	.663	+2	9			O71L		-0.8
WHITEN, MARK Mark Anthony B11.25.1966 Pensacola FL BB/TR/6'3"/(210–235) [TorA86*5/130] d7.12 Col Pensacola (FL) JC																								
1995	Bos A	32	108	13	20	3	0	1	10	8	0	0	23	.185	.239	.241	.480	-75	1	0	100	O31R/D	18	-1.1
Total	11	940	3104	465	804	129	20	105	423	378	42	17	712	.259	.341	.415	.756	+1	78	40	66	O867(131/67/696),D19/P	114	0.7
WHITT, ERNIE Leo Ernest B6.13.1952 Detroit MI BL/TR/6'2"/(200–205) [BosA72 15/352] d9.12 C2 Col Macomb (MI) CC																								
1976	Bos A	8	18	4	4	2	0	1	3	2	0	0	2	.222	.300	.500	.800	+18	0	0	0	C8	0	0.0
Total	15	1328	3774	447	938	176	15	134	534	436	43	4	491	.249	.324	.410	.734	-2	22	26	46	C1246,D11	128	11.3
WILBER, DEL Delbert Quentin "Babe" B2.24.1919 Lincoln Park MI D7.18.2002 St.Petersburg FL BR/TR/6'3"/200 d4.21 M1/C4																								
1946	StL N	4	4	0	0	0	0	0	0	1		0	0	.000	.200	.000	.200	-139	0			C4	0	0.0
1947	StL N	51	99	7	23	8	1	0	12	5		0	13	.232	.269	.333	.602	-43	0			C34	0	-0.5
1948	StL N	27	58	5	11	2	0	0	10	4		0	9	.190	.242	.224	.466	-75	0			C26	0	-0.7
1949	StL N	2	4	0	1	0	0	0	0	0		0	0	.250	.250	.250	.500	-67	0			C2	0	0.0
1951	Phi N	84	245	30	68	7	3	8	34	17		0	26	.278	.324	.429	.753	+2	0	1	0	C73	0	0.5
1952	Phi N	2	2	0	0	0	0	0	0	0		0	1	.000	.000	.000	.000	-199	0	0	0	/H	0	-0.1
1952	Bos A	47	135	7	36	10	1	3	23	7		1	20	.267	.308	.422	.730	-6	1	0	100	C39	0	0.3
1952	Major	49	137	7	36	10	1	3	23	7	0	1	21	.263	.303	.416	.720	-2749	1	0	100		0	0.2
1953	Bos A	58	112	16	27	6	1	7	29	6		1	21	.241	.286	.500	.786	+3	0	0	0	C28,1b2	0	-0.1
1954	Bos A	24	61	2	8	2	1	1	7	4		0	6	.131	.179	.246	.425	-85	0	0	0	C18	0	-1.0
Total	8	299	720	67	174	35	7	19	115	44		2	96	.242	.286	.389	.675	-21	1	1	100	C224,1b2	0	-1.6
Team	3	129	308	25	71	18	3	11	59	17		2	47	.231	.274	.416	.690	-18	1	0	100	C85,1b2	0	-0.8
/150	3	150	358	29	83	21	3	13	69	20		2	55	.231	.274	.416	.690	-18	1	0	100	C99,1b2	0	-0.9
WILHOIT, JOE Joseph William B12.20.1885 Hiawatha KS D9.25.1930 Santa Barbara CA BL/TR/6'2"/175 d4.12 Col DePaul																								
1919	Bos A	6	18	7	6	0	0	0	2	5		0	2	.333	.478	.333	.811	+38	1			O5R		0.0
Total	4	283	782	93	201	23	9	3	73	75		1	82	.257	.323	.321	.644	+1	28			O234(5/37/190)/1		-1.0

Year	Tm Lg	G	AB	R	H	2B	3B	HR	RBI	BB	IB	HP	SO	AVG	OBP	SLG	OPS	AOPS	SB	CS	SB%	Games at Position	DL	BFW
WILLIAMS, RIP Alva Mitchel "Buff" B1.31.1882 Carthage IL D7.23.1933 Keokuk IA BR/TR/6'0.5"/187 d4.12																								
1911	Bos A	95	284	36	68	8	5	0	31	24		7		.239	.314	.303	.617	-27	9			1b57,C38		-0.9
Total	7	497	1186	111	314	51	23	2	145	95		17	80	.265	.328	.352	.680	-3	27	5	100	C212,1b144,O6(0/1/5),3b2		1.1
WILLIAMS, DANA Dana Lamont B3.20.1963 Weirton WV BR/TR/5'10"/170 d6.19 Col Enterprise St. (AL) JC																								
1989	Bos A	8	5	1	1	1	0	0	0	0	0	1	1	.200	.333	.400	.733	-1	0	0	0	/lfD	0	0.1
WILLIAMS, DIB Edwin Dibrell B1.19.1910 Greenbrier AR D4.2.1992 Searcy AR BR/TR/5'11.5"/175 d4.27 Col Hendrix																								
1935	Bos A	75	251	26	63	12	0	3	25	24		1	23	.251	.319	.335	.654	-35	2	0	100	3b30,2b29,S15/1		-1.1
Total	6	475	1574	198	421	74	12	29	201	133		7	140	.267	.327	.385	.712	-18	7	3	70	2b215,S195,3b31,1b3/lf		-2.6
WILLIAMS, DENNY Evon Daniel B12.13.1896 Portland OR D3.23.1929 San Clemente CA BL/TR/5'8.5"/150 d4.15																								
1921	Cin N	10	7	0	0	0	0	0	0	0		0	2	.000	.000	.000	.000	-199	0	1	0	/lf		-0.2
1924	Bos A	25	85	17	31	3	0	0	4	10		1	5	.365	.438	.400	.838	+17	3	3	50	O19L		0.0
1925	Bos A	69	218	28	50	1	3	0	13	17		0	11	.229	.285	.261	.546	-61	2	6	25	O52(42/11/0)		-2.7
1928	Bos A	16	18	1	4	0	0	0	1	1		0	1	.222	.263	.222	.485	-71	0	0	0	O6(0/5/1)		-0.2
Total	4	120	328	46	85	4	3	0	18	28		1	19	.259	.319	.290	.609	-44	5	10	33	O78(62/16/1)		-3.1
Team	3	110	321	46	85	4	3	0	18	28		1	17	.265	.326	.296	.622	-40	5	9	36	O77(61/2/2)		-2.9
/150	4	150	438	63	116	5	4	0	25	38		1	23	.265	.326	.296	.622	-40	7	12	37	O105(83/3/3)		-4.0
WILLIAMS, KEN Kenneth Roy B6.28.1890 Grants Pass OR D1.22.1959 Grants Pass OR BL/TR/6'0"/170 d7.14 Mil 1918																								
1928	Bos A	133	462	59	140	25	1	8	67	37		1	15	.303	.356	.413	.769	+4	4	9	31	O127L		-1.2
1929	Bos A	74	139	21	48	14	2	3	21	15		0	7	.345	.409	.540	.949	+46	1	5	17	O39(0/30/10),1b2		0.7
Total	14	1397	4862	860	1552	285	77	196	913	566		28	287	.319	.393	.530	.923	+36	154	10	100	O1298(1132/158/10),1b2/2		17.5
Team	2	207	601	80	188	39	3	11	88	52		1	22	.313	.369	.443	.812	+14	5	14	26	O166(127/30/0),1b2		-0.5
/150	1	150	436	58	136	28	2	8	64	38		1	16	.313	.369	.443	.812	+14	4	10	29	O120(92/22/0)/1		-0.4
WILLIAMS, DICK Richard Hirschfeld B5.7.1929 St.Louis MO BR/TR/6'0"/190 d6.10 M21/C1 OF(283/156/64)																								
1963	Bos A	79	136	15	35	8	0	2	12	15	0	0	25	.257	.329	.360	.689	-9	0	0	0	3b17,1b11,O7L	0	-0.4
1964	Bos A	61	69	10	11	2	0	5	11	7	0	1	10	.159	.247	.406	.653	-26	0	0	0	1b21,3b13,O5(4/1/0)	0	0.0
Total	13	1023	2959	358	768	157	12	70	331	227	12	12	392	.260	.312	.392	.704	-8	12	21	36	O456L,3b257,1b188,2b20	0	-6.8
Team	2	140	205	25	46	10	0	7	23	22	0	1	35	.224	.301	.376	.677	-15	0	0	0	1b32,3b30,O12(11/1/1)	0	-0.4
/150	2	150	220	27	49	11	0	8	25	24	0	1	38	.224	.301	.376	.677	-15	0	0	0	1b34,3b32,O13(12/1/1)	0	-0.4
WILLIAMS, TED Theodore Samuel "The Kid", "The Thumper","The Splendid Splinter" B8.30.1918 San Diego CA D7.5.2002 Inverness FL BL/TR/6'3"/(190–205) d4.20 Mil 1943–45, 1952–53 M4 HF1966																								
1939	Bos A	149	565	131	185	44	11	31	**145**	107		2	64	.327	.436	.609	1.045	+58	2	1	67	O149R		4.1
1940	Bos A★	144	561	**134**	193	43	14	23	113	96		3	54	.344	**.442**	.594	1.036	+59	4	4	50	O143(128/0/16)/P		4.0
1941	Bos A★	143	456	**135**	185	33	3	**37**	120	**147**		3	27	**.406**	**.553**	**.735**	1.288	+132	2	4	33	O133(130/0/4)	0	**8.5**
1942	Bos A★	150	522	**141**	186	34	5	**36**	**137**	**145**		4	51	**.356**	**.499**	**.648**	1.147	+114	3	2	60	O150L	0	**8.5**
1946	†Bos A★	150	514	**142**	176	37	8	38	123	**156**		2	44	.342	**.497**	**.667**	1.164	+111	0	0	0	O150L	0	**8.1**
1947	Bos A★	156	528	**125**	181	40	9	**32**	**114**	**162**		2	47	**.343**	**.499**	**.634**	1.133	+99	0	1	0	O156L	0	**7.2**
1948	Bos A★	137	509	124	188	**44**	3	25	127	**126**		3	41	**.369**	**.497**	**.615**	1.112	+85	4	0	100	O134L	0	5.9
1949	Bos A★	**155**	566	**150**	194	**39**	3	**43**	**159**	**162**		2	48	.343	**.490**	**.650**	1.140	+87	1	1	50	O155L	0	**6.4**
1950	Bos A★	89	334	82	106	24	1	28	97	82		0	21	.317	.452	.647	1.099	+63	3	0	100	O86L	0	2.2
1951	Bos A★	148	531	109	169	28	4	30	126	**144**		0	45	.318	**.464**	**.556**	1.020	+59	1	1	50	O147L	0	4.1
1952	Bos A	6	10	2	4	0	1	1	3	2		0	2	.400	.500	.900	1.400	+164	0	0	0	O2L	0	0.2
1953	Bos A✱	37	91	17	37	6	0	13	34	19		0	10	.407	.509	.901	1.410	+161	0	1	0	O26L	0	1.7
1954	Bos A★	117	386	93	133	23	1	29	89	**136**		1	32	.345	**.513**	.635	1.148	+93	0	0	0	O115L	0	**5.1**
1955	Bos A★	98	320	77	114	21	3	28	83	91	**17**	2	24	.356	.496	.703	1.199	+103	2	0	100	O93L	0	4.3
1956	Bos A★	136	400	71	138	28	2	24	82	102	**11**	1	39	.345	**.479**	.605	1.084	+64	0	0	0	O110L	0	2.9
1957	Bos A★	132	420	96	163	28	1	38	87	119	**33**	5	43	**.388**	**.526**	**.731**	1.257	+127	0	1	0	O125L	0	7.3
1958	Bos A★	129	411	81	135	23	2	26	85	98	12	4	49	**.328**	**.458**	.584	1.042	+74	1	0	100	O114L	0	2.8
1959	Bos A★	103	272	32	69	15	0	10	43	52	6	2	27	.254	.372	.419	.791	+13	0	0	0	O76L	0	-0.2
1960	Bos A★	113	310	56	98	15	0	29	72	75	7	3	41	.316	.451	.645	1.096	+87	1	1	50	O87L	0	3.4
Total	19	2292	7706	1798	2654	525	71	521	1839	2021	86	39	709	.344	.482	.634	1.116	+86	24	17	59	O2151(1984/0/169)/P	0	86.5
/150	1	150	504	118	174	34	5	34	120	132	0	3	46	.344	.482	.634	1.116	+86	2	1	67	O14(130/0/11)/P	0	5.7
WILSON, ARCHIE Archie Clifton B11.25.1923 Los Angeles CA BR/TR/6'0"/175 d9.18 Col USC																								
1951	NY A	4	4	0	0	0	0	0	0	0		1	0	.000	.200	.000	.200	-144	0	0	0	O2R	0	-0.1
1952	NY A	3	2	0	1	0	0	0	1	0		0	0	.500	.500	.500	1.000	+90	0	0	0	/H	0	0.0
1952	Was A	26	96	8	20	2	3	0	14	5		1	11	.208	.255	.292	.547	-46	0	0	0	O24(14/10/0)	0	-0.9
1952	Bos A	18	38	1	10	3	0	0	2	2		0	3	.263	.300	.342	.642	-27	0	0	0	O13(2/2/9)	0	-0.2
1952	Year	47	136	9	31	5	3	0	17	7		1	14	.228	.271	.309	.580	-39	0	0	0	O37(16/12/9)	0	-1.1
Total	2	51	140	9	31	5	3	0	17	7		2	14	.221	.268	.300	.568	-42	0	0	0	O39(16/12/11)	0	-1.2
WILSON, SQUANTO George Francis B3.29.1889 Old Town ME D3.26.1967 Winthrop ME BB/TR/5'9.5"/170 d10.2 Col Bowdoin																								
1914	Bos A	1	0	0	0	0	0	0	0	0		0	0	+	+	+	.000	-100	0			/1		0.0
Total	2	6	16	2	3	0	0	0	0	2		0	0	.188	.278	.188	.466	-71	0			C5/1		-0.2
WILSON, GARY James Garrett B1.12.1879 Baltimore MD D5.1.1969 Randallstown MD BR/TR/5'7"/168 d9.27																								
1902	Bos A	2	8	0	1	0	0	0	1	0		0		.125	.125	.125	.250	-130	0			2b2		-0.2
WILSON, LES Lester Wilbur "Tug" B7.17.1885 St.Louis MI D4.4.1969 Edmonds WA BL/TR/5'11"/170 d7.15																								
1911	Bos A	5	7	0	0	0	0	0	0	2		0		.000	.222	.000	.222	-136	0			O3(2/0/1)		-0.1
WINNINGHAM, HERM Herman Son B12.1.1961 Orangeburg SC BL/TR/5'11"/(170–190) [NYN81*S1/9] d9.1 Col Georgia Perimeter JC																								
1992	Bos A	105	234	27	55	8	1	1	14	10	0	0	53	.235	.266	.291	.557	-48	6	5	55	O67(36/32/0),D6	0	-1.7
Total	9	868	1888	212	452	69	26	19	147	157	17	0	417	.239	.296	.334	.630	-27	105	53	66	O677(106/547/32),D6/S	34	-8.4
/150	1	150	334	39	79	11	1	1	20	14	0	0	76	.235	.266	.291	.557	-48	9	7	56	O96(51/46/0),D9	0	-2.4
WINSETT, TOM John Thomas "Long Tom" B11.24.1909 McKenzie TN D7.20.1987 Memphis TN BL/TR/6'2"/190 d4.20 Col Bethel																								
1930	Bos A	1	1	0	0	0	0	0	0	0		0	1	.000	.000	.000	.000	-199	0	0	0	/H		0.0
1931	Bos A	64	76	6	15	1	0	1	7	4		1	21	.197	.247	.250	.497	-67	0	0	0	O8L		-0.7
1933	Bos A	6	12	1	1	0	0	0	0	1		0	6	.083	.154	.083	.237	-136	0	0	0	O4(2/0/2)		-0.3
Total	7	230	566	60	134	25	5	8	76	69		5	113	.237	.325	.341	.666	-21	3	0	100	O145(136/1/8)/P		-2.1
Team	3	71	89	7	16	1	0	1	7	5		1	28	.180	.232	.225	.457	-78	0	0	0	O12L		-1.0
WOLFE, LARRY Laurence Marcy B3.2.1953 Melbourne FL BR/TR/5'11"/170 [MinA73 9/203] d9.16 Col Sacramento (CA) City																								
1977	Min A	8	25	3	6	1	0	0	6	1	1	0	0	.240	.269	.280	.549	-49	0	0	0	3b8	0	-0.1
1978	Min A	88	235	25	55	10	1	3	25	36	0	0	27	.234	.332	.323	.655	-16	0	1	0	3b81,S7	0	-0.4
1979	Bos A	47	78	12	19	4	0	3	15	17	0	1	21	.244	.378	.410	.788	+9	0	0	0	2b27,3b9,S2/C1D	0	0.5
1980	Bos A	18	23	3	3	1	0	1	4	0	0	0	5	.130	.125	.304	.429	-85	0	0	0	3b14,D4	0	-0.4
Total	4	161	361	43	83	16	1	7	50	54	1	1	53	.230	.327	.338	.665	-16	0	1	0	3b112,2b27,S9,D5/1C	0	-0.4
Team	2	65	101	15	22	5	0	4	19	17	0	1	26	.218	.328	.386	.714	-9	0	0	0	2b27,3b23,D5,S2/C1	0	0.1
WOLTER, HARRY Harry Meiggs B7.11.1884 Monterey CA D7.6.1970 Palo Alto CA BL/TR/5'10"/175 d5.14 Col Santa Clara▲																								
1909	Bos A	54	121	14	29	2	4	2	10	9		0		.240	.292	.372	.664	+7	2			1b17,P11,O9R		-0.2
Total	7	588	1907	286	514	69	42	12	167	268		17	90	.270	.365	.369	.734	+14	95			O491(5/126/362),1b22,P15		1.0
WOOD, JOE Joe "Smoky Joe" (b Howard Ellsworth Wood) B10.25.1889 Kansas City MO D7.27.1985 West Haven CT BR/TR/5'11"/180 d8.24 s–Joe▲																								
1908	Bos A	6	7	1	0	0	0	0	0	0		0		.000	.000	.000	.000	-197	0			P6		0.0
1909	Bos A	24	55	4	9	0	1	0	3	2		1		.164	.207	.200	.407	-72	0			P24		0.0
1910	Bos A	35	69	9	18	2	1	1	5	5		0		.261	.311	.362	.673	+8	0			P35		0.0
1911	Bos A	44	88	15	23	4	2	2	11	10		1		.261	.343	.420	.763	+14	1			P44		0.0
1912	†Bos A	43	124	16	36	13	1	1	13	11		0		.290	.348	.435	.783	+18	0			P43		0.0
1913	Bos A	25	56	10	15	5	0	0	10	4		0	7	.268	.317	.357	.674	-5	1			P23		0.0
1914	Bos A	21	43	2	6	1	0	0	1	3		1	14	.140	.213	.163	.376	-87	1			P18		0.0

Year	Tm Lg	G	AB	R	H	2B	3B	HR	RBI	BB	IB	HP	SO	AVG	OBP	SLG	OPS	AOPS	SB	CS	SB%	Games at Position	DL	BFW
1915	Bos A	29	54	6	14	1	1	1	7	5		0	10	.259	.322	.370	.692	+11	1	1	50	P25		0.0
Total	14	697	1952	266	553	118	31	23	325	208		16	189	.283	.357	.411	.768	+10	23	3	100	O419(106/31/295),P225,2b19,1b4		0.7
Team	8	227	496	63	121	26	6	5	50	40		3	31	.244	.304	.351	.655	-9	4	1	100	P218		0.0
/150	5	150	328	42	80	17	4	3	33	26		2	20	.244	.304	.351	.655	-9	3	1	100	P144		0.0
WOOD, KEN	Kenneth Lanier B7.1.1924 Lincolnton NC BR/TR/6'0"/(200–205) d4.28																							
1952	Bos A	15	20	0	2	0	0	0	0	3		0	4	.100	.217	.100	.317	-109	0	0	0	O13(1/0/12)	0	-0.4
Total	6	342	995	110	223	52	7	34	143	102		2	141	.224	.298	.393	.691	-19	1	7	13	O278(100/7/176)	0	-3.6
WOOTEN, SHAWN	William Shawn B7.24.1972 Glendora CA BR/TR/5'10"/(205–230) [DetA93 18/501] d8.19 Col Mt. San Antonio (CA) JC																							
2005	Bos A	1	1	0	0	0	0	0	0	0	0	0	0	.000	.000	.000	.000	-196	0	0	0	/C	0	0.0
Total	6	267	669	66	182	28	1	18	86	37	6	7	120	.272	.314	.398	.712	-12	4	4	50	1b83,D81,C51,3b23	102	-2.8
WRIGHT, TOM	Thomas Everette B9.22.1923 Shelby NC BL/TR/5'11.5"/180 d9.15																							
1948	Bos A	3	2	1	1	0	1	0	0	0		0	0	.500	.500	1.500	2.000	+300	0	0	0	/H	0	0.1
1949	Bos A	5	4	1	1	1	0	0	1	1		0	1	.250	.400	.500	.900	+28	0	0	0	/H	0	0.0
1950	Bos A	54	107	17	34	7	0	0	20	6		1	18	.318	.360	.383	.743	-18	0	0	0	O24(5/0/19)	0	-0.4
1951	Bos A	28	63	8	14	1	1	1	9	11		1	8	.222	.347	.317	.664	-27	0	0	0	O18(1/0/17)	0	-0.5
Total	9	341	685	75	175	28	11	6	99	76	0	7	123	.255	.336	.355	.691	-15	2	1	67	O170(71/0/101)	0	-2.6
Team	4	90	176	27	50	9	2	1	30	18		2	27	.284	.357	.375	.732	-17	0	0	0	O42(6/0/36)	0	-0.8
YASTRZEMSKI, CARL	Carl Michael "Yaz" B8.22.1939 Southampton NY BL/TR/5'11"/(170–185) d4.11 HF1989 Col Notre Dame OF(1917/159/7)																							
1961	Bos A	148	583	71	155	31	6	11	80	50	3	3	96	.266	.324	.396	.720	-10	6	5	55	O147L	0	-2.2
1962	Bos A	**160**	646	99	191	43	6	19	94	66	7	3	82	.296	.363	.469	.832	+18	7	4	64	O160L	0	1.7
1963	Bos A★	151	570	91	**183**	**40**	3	14	68	**95**	6	1	72	**.321**	**.418**	.475	.893	+45	8	5	62	O151(151/1/0)	0	**4.2**
1964	Bos A	151	567	77	164	29	9	15	67	75	6	2	90	.289	.374	.451	.825	+22	6	5	55	O148(18/131/0),3b2	0	3.5
1965	Bos A✷	133	494	78	154	**45**	3	20	72	70	8	1	58	.312	**.395**	**.536**	.931	+54	7	6	54	O130(125/7/1)	0	3.5
1966	Bos A☆	160	594	81	165	**39**	2	16	80	84	10	1	60	.278	.368	.431	.799	+17	8	9	47	O158(157/1/0)	0	1.7
1967	†Bos A★	161	579	**112**	**189**	31	4	**44**	**121**	91	11	4	69	**.326**	**.418**	**.622**	1.040	+89	10	8	56	O161(161/1/0)	0	**6.9**
1968	Bos A★	157	539	90	162	32	2	23	74	**119**	13	2	90	**.301**	**.426**	.495	.921	+69	13	6	68	O155(154/1/0),1b3	0	**6.3**
1969	Bos A★	**162**	603	96	154	28	2	40	111	101	9	1	91	.255	.362	.507	.869	+35	15	7	68	O143(140/3/0),1b22	0	2.7
1970	Bos A★	161	566	**125**	186	29	0	40	102	128	12	1	66	.329	**.452**	**.592**	1.044	+74	23	13	64	1b94,O69(67/3/0)	0	5.5
1971	Bos A★	148	508	75	129	21	2	15	70	106	12	1	60	.254	.381	.392	.773	+12	8	7	53	O146L	0	1.6
1972	Bos A★	125	455	70	120	18	2	12	68	67	3	4	44	.264	.357	.391	.748	+17	5	4	56	O83L,1b42	30	1.1
1973	Bos A✷	152	540	82	160	25	4	19	95	105	13	0	58	.296	.407	.463	.870	+37	9	7	56	1b107,3b31,O14L	0	1.8
1974	Bos A★	148	515	**93**	155	25	2	15	79	104	16	3	48	.301	.414	.445	.859	+39	12	7	63	1b84,O63L,D4	0	1.5
1975	†Bos A★	149	543	91	146	30	1	14	60	87	12	2	67	.269	.371	.405	.776	+10	8	4	67	1b140,O8L,D2	0	-0.1
1976	Bos A★	155	546	71	146	23	2	21	102	80	6	1	67	.267	.357	.432	.789	+18	5	6	45	1b94,O51L,D10	0	-0.7
1977	Bos A★	150	558	99	165	27	3	28	102	73	6	1	40	.296	.372	.505	.877	+24	11	1	92	O140(138/0/2),1b7,D6	0	2.6
1978	Bos A✷	144	523	70	145	21	2	17	81	76	8	3	44	.277	.367	.423	.790	+11	4	5	44	O71(63/8/0),1b50,D27	0	0.5
1979	Bos A★	147	518	69	140	28	1	21	87	62	8	2	46	.270	.346	.450	.796	+8	3	3	50	D56,1b51,O36L	0	0.3
1980	Bos A	105	364	49	100	21	1	15	50	44	5	0	38	.275	.350	.462	.812	+15	0	2	0	D49,O39(34/1/4),1b16	0	0.1
1981	Bos A	91	338	36	83	14	1	7	53	49	4	0	28	.246	.338	.355	.693	-5	0	1	0	D48,1b39	0	-0.2
1982	Bos A★	131	459	53	126	22	1	16	72	59	1	2	50	.275	.358	.431	.789	+9	0	1	0	D102,1b14,O2C	0	0.4
1983	Bos A★	119	380	38	101	24	0	10	56	54	11	2	29	.266	.359	.408	.767	+3	0	0	0	D107,1b2/lf	0	0.0
Total	23	3308	11988	1816	3419	646	59	452	1844	1845	19	40	1393	.285	.379	.462	.841	+28	168	116	59	O2076L,1b765,D411,3b33	30	42.7
/150	1	150	544	82	155	29	3	20	84	84	0	2	63	.285	.379	.462	.841	+28	8	5	62	1b35,D19,O9L/3	1	1.9
YERKES, STEVE	Stephen Douglas B5.15.1888 Hatboro PA D1.31.1971 Lansdale PA BR/TR/5'9"/165 d9.29 Col Penn																							
1909	Bos A	5	7	0	2	0	0	0	0	0		0		.286	.286	.286	.572	-21	0			S2		-0.1
1911	Bos A	142	502	70	140	24	3	1	57	52		6		.279	.354	.345	.699	-4	14			S116,2b14,3b11		-0.6
1912	†Bos A	131	523	73	132	22	6	0	42	41		4		.252	.312	.317	.629	-24	4			2b131		-3.0
1913	Bos A	137	483	67	129	29	6	1	48	50		2	32	.267	.338	.358	.696	+1	11			2b129		-1.8
1914	Bos A	92	293	23	64	17	2	1	23	14		2	23	.218	.259	.300	.559	-32	5	6	45	2b91		-1.4
1914	Pit F	39	142	18	48	9	5	1	25	11		0	13	.338	.386	.493	.879	+39	2			S39		1.5
1914	Major	131	435	41	112	26	7	2	48	25	0	2	36	.257	.301	.363	.664	+104	7	6				0.1
1915	Pit F	121	434	44	125	17	8	1	49	30		2	27	.288	.337	.371	.708	+0	17			2b114,S8		-0.6
1916	Chi N	44	137	12	36	6	2	1	10	9		0	7	.263	.308	.358	.666	-6	1			2b41		-0.2
Total	7	711	2521	307	676	124	32	6	254	207		16	102	.268	.328	.350	.678	-7	54	6	100	2b520,S165,3b11		-6.2
Team	5	507	1808	233	467	92	17	3	170	157		14	55	.258	.323	.333	.656	-13	34	6	100	2b365,S118,3b11		-6.9
/150	1	150	535	69	138	27	5	1	50	46		4	16	.258	.323	.333	.656	-13	10	2	100	2b108,S35,3b3		-2.0
YORK, RUDY	Preston Rudolph B8.17.1913 Ragland AL D2.5.1970 Rome GA BR/TR/6'1"/209 d8.22 M1/C4																							
1946	†Bos A★	154	579	78	160	30	6	17	119	86		1	93	.276	.371	.437	.808	+18	3	2	60	1b154	0	1.7
1947	Bos A	48	184	16	39	7	0	6	27	22		0	32	.212	.296	.348	.644	-27	0	0	0	1b48	0	-0.7
Total	13	1603	5891	876	1621	291	52	277	1152	792		12	867	.275	.362	.483	.845	+21	38	26	59	1b1263,C239,3b41,O14L	0	13.3
Team	2	202	763	94	199	37	6	23	146	108		1	125	.261	.353	.415	.768	+7	3	2	60	1b202	0	1.0
/150	1	150	567	70	148	27	4	17	108	80		1	93	.261	.353	.415	.768	+7	2	1	67	1b150	0	0.7
YOUKILIS, KEVIN	Kevin Edmund B3.15.1979 Cincinnati OH BR/TR/6'1"/220 [BosA01 8/243] d5.15 Col Cincinnati																							
2004	†Bos A	72	208	38	54	11	0	7	35	33	0	4	45	.260	.367	.413	.780	-2	0	1	0	3b65,D2	16	0.5
2005	Bos A	44	79	11	22	7	0	1	9	14	0	2	19	.278	.400	.405	.805	+11	0	1	0	3b24,1b9,2b2	0	-0.1
2006	Bos A	147	569	100	159	42	2	13	72	91	0	9	120	.279	.381	.429	.810	+9	5	2	71	1b127,O18L,3b16	0	0.6
Total	3	263	856	149	235	60	2	21	116	138	0	15	184	.275	.379	.423	.802	+6	5	4	56	1b136,3b105,O18L,2b2,D2	16	1.0
/150	2	150	488	85	134	34	1	12	66	79	0	9	105	.275	.379	.423	.802	+6	3	2	60	1b78,3b60,O10L/2D	9	0.6
ZARILLA, AL	Allen Lee "Zeke" B5.1.1919 Los Angeles CA D8.28.1996 Honolulu HI BL/TR/5'11"/180 d6.30 Mil 1945 C1																							
1949	Bos A	124	474	68	133	32	4	9	71	48		4	51	.281	.352	.422	.774	-3	4	4	50	O122(2/2/119)	0	-1.2
1950	Bos A	130	471	92	153	32	10	9	74	76		4	47	.325	.423	.493	.916	+22	2	3	40	O128R	0	0.9
1952	Bos A	21	60	9	11	0	1	2	8	7		0	8	.183	.269	.317	.586	-42	2	0	100	O19(0/6/14)	0	-0.3
1953	Bos A	57	67	11	13	2	0	0	4	14		0	13	.194	.333	.224	.557	-50	0	1	0	O18(3/7/9)	0	-0.5
Total	10	1120	3535	507	975	186	43	61	456	415		30	382	.276	.357	.405	.762	+2	33	33	50	O978(229/131/660)	0	-5.0
Team	4	332	1072	180	310	66	15	20	157	145		8	119	.289	.378	.435	.813	+3	8	8	50	O287(8/25/142)	0	-1.1
/150	2	150	484	81	140	30	7	9	71	66		4	54	.289	.378	.435	.813	+3	4	4	50	O130(4/11/64)	0	-0.5
ZAUCHIN, NORM	Norbert Henry B11.17.1929 Royal Oak MI D1.31.1999 Birmingham AL BR/TR/6'4.5"/(220–225) d9.23 Mil 1952–53																							
1951	Bos A	5	12	0	2	1	0	0	0	0		0	4	.167	.167	.250	.417	-89	0	1	0	1b4	0	-0.2
1955	Bos A	130	477	65	114	10	0	27	93	69	1	3	105	.239	.335	.430	.765	-3	3	0	100	1b126	0	-1.0
1956	Bos A	44	84	12	18	2	0	2	11	14	0	1	22	.214	.333	.310	.643	-37	0	0	0	1b31	0	-0.7
1957	Bos A	52	91	11	24	3	0	3	14	9	0	2	13	.264	.343	.396	.739	-4	0	0	0	1b36	0	-0.2
1958	Was A	96	303	35	69	8	2	15	37	38	1	1	68	.228	.310	.416	.726	+1	0	0	0	1b91	0	-0.4
1959	Was A	19	71	11	15	4	0	3	4	7	0	1	14	.211	.291	.394	.685	-13	2	0	100	1b19	0	-0.5
Total	6	346	1038	134	242	28	2	50	159	137	2	8	226	.233	.324	.408	.732	-7	5	1	83	1b307	0	-3.0
Team	4	231	664	88	158	16	0	32	118	92	1	6	144	.238	.333	.407	.740	-9	3	1	75	1b197	0	-2.1
/150	3	150	431	57	103	10	0	21	77	60	1	4	94	.238	.333	.407	.740	-9	2	1	67	1b128	0	-1.4
ZUPCIC, BOB	Robert B8.18.1966 Pittsburgh PA BR/TR/6'4"/(220–225) [BosA87 1/32] d9.7 Col Oral Roberts																							
1991	Bos A	18	25	3	4	0	0	1	3	1	0	0	6	.160	.192	.280	.472	-73	0	0	0	O16(3/7/6)	0	-0.4
1992	Bos A	124	392	46	108	19	1	3	43	25	1	4	60	.276	.322	.352	.674	-16	2	2	50	O114(32/68/22),D5	0	-1.0
1993	Bos A	141	286	40	69	24	2	2	26	27	2	2	54	.241	.308	.360	.668	-25	5	2	71	O122(48/37/54),D5	0	-1.2
1994	Bos A	4	4	0	0	0	0	0	0	0	0	0	1	.000	.000	.000	.000	-196	0	1	0	O2L/D	0	-0.2
1994	Chi A	32	88	10	18	4	1	1	8	4	0	0	16	.205	.237	.307	.544	-60	0	0	0	O28(15/0/14),3b2/1	0	-0.8
1994	Year	36	92	10	18	4	1	1	8	4	0	0	17	.196	.227	.293	.520	-66	0	1	0	O30(17/0/14),3b2/D1	0	-1.0
Total	4	319	795	99	199	47	4	7	80	57	3	6	137	.250	.303	.346	.649	-27	7	5	58	O282(100/112/96),D11,3b2/1	0	-3.6
Team	4	287	707	89	181	43	3	6	72	53	3	6	121	.256	.310	.351	.661	-23	7	5	58	O254(42/129/128),D11	0	-2.8
/150	2	150	370	47	95	22	2	3	38	28	2	3	63	.256	.310	.351	.661	-23	4	3	57	O133(22/67/67),D6	0	-1.5

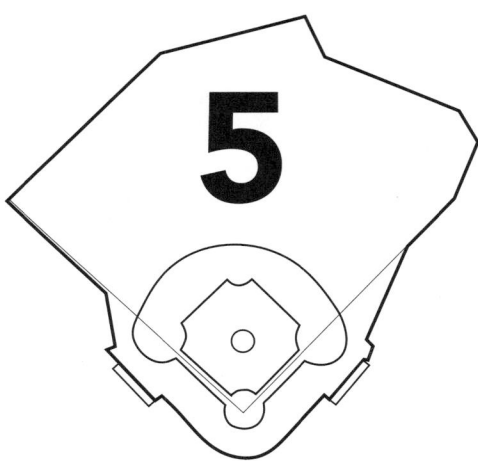

RED SOX PITCHERS

While the Red Sox may lay claim to the greatest hitter who ever lived, they are not so far off in the pitching department. Ted Williams, of course, boasted as a young man that he wanted to be known as "the greatest hitter who ever lived" and he wasn't shy in piling up the numbers to prove it, even if war and injury decreased his cumulative totals. Cy Young had no such problems. He began pitching in the major leagues at age 23 and threw 22 seasons in the major leagues. Young pitched eight years for the Red Sox, winning 20 games six times and leading the American League in victories the first three years of the new league's existence. His ERA for the club was a precise 2.00 with 275 complete games out of 297 starts. Roger Clemens tied Young's club mark with 192 wins. Tim Wakefield surpassed Young's 112 losses.

Cy Young is the starting point for any discussion on Red Sox pitching greats. Even if his exploits are forgotten because they happened a century ago and were accrued during a time when pitchers worked far more often and didn't come out of the game without a good reason, Cy Young's name is always brought up when great modern pitchers are discussed. The award given annually to the best pitcher in each league keeps Cy forever young. Roger Clemens and Pedro Martinez have collected a total of five Cy Young Awards wearing Red Sox uniforms (and 10 all in all). Jim Lonborg was the first Red Sox pitcher honored with the award. Yet even with his wondrous 1967 season, Lonborg won just 68 games for the Red Sox...or 21 fewer than Babe Ruth.

Ruth, who certainly features prominently into that greatest hitter debate with the Splendid Splinter, was a pitching progeny with the Red Sox before he was converted into an everyday slugger because of his otherworldly prowess with the bat. Ruth debuted as a Red Sox pitcher at age 19 and if he had remained on the mound, who knows what pitching records he might have set? But that's a specious argument. Cy Young's career marks—511 wins, 815 starts, 749 complete games, and 7,356 innings (not to mention his less desirable marks for losses, hits, and earned runs)—have been etched in stone since he retired in 1911. Neither Ruth nor anyone else ever had a legitimate shot at those records. Ruth found major league hitting marks much easier to shatter.

While hitting a baseball is a singular skill, throwing a baseball so a professional can't hit it—or hit it well—requires equally remarkable talent. The pitchers in this section possess or possessed this talent (some have much more of it than others). While all-time greats who made their names with other clubs have cameo appearances in this section—such as Tom Seaver, Juan Marichal, Fergie Jenkins, and Jack Chesbro—names that mean so much to Red Sox fans over their long history come through as the pages turn: Bill Campbell, Bill Dinneen, Joe Dobson, Dennis Eckersley, Dave Ferriss, Rube Foster, Lefty Grove, Bruce Hurst, Ellis Kinder, Bill Lee, Dutch Leonard, Derek Lowe, Bill Monbouquette, Mel Parnell, Curt Schilling, Ernie Shore, Luis Tiant, and Joe Wood. There will invariably be names whose existence in this register will be surprising to a few readers: "Jamie Moyer?" There will be names that may make a handful of fans shout with joy at the memory of a singular moment: "Keith Foulke!" And there will invariably be

names that elicit the gnashing of teeth at first sight...no example provided at the request of the Witness Protection Bureau.

This Register also chronicles the changes in pitching since 1901. That Cy Young had nearly twice as many complete games in 1902 as Pedro Martinez did in his Boston career speaks more about the evolution of the game than about the talent of the two men. Likewise, some of the numbers herein provide insight to compare the likes of Cy and Pedro in the context of the eras they dominated.

Biographical Information

As evidenced by the name, this section is for pitchers. The separate Batter Register only includes a small number of pitchers. (Don't fear, Babe Ruth is in both.) In order for a pitcher to appear in the Batter Register, he must have at least once had a season in which he played at least 10 games at a position other than pitcher. Or he must have at least 150 more career games played than games pitched. In order for a batter to appear in the Pitcher Register, he must have at least 9 career innings pitched (plus more games at a position other than pitcher).

Pitchers are listed by last name. If a Latin American pitcher has a matronymic name, it is in parentheses, as in Santiago, Jose Rafael (Alfonso). Commonly used nicknames are also included in the biographical line; if a pitcher was primarily known by his nickname throughout his career, it will be listed as part of his name, as in Hughson, Tex. Other features and abbreviations follow.

B4.2.1937 Detroit, MI is the date of birth and birthplace for Dick "The Monster" Radatz.

D3.16.2005 Easton, MA is the date and place of his death.

The arm a pitcher threw with is expressed *TR* (throws right) and *TL* (throws left). The side of the plate he bats from is listed *BR* (bats right), *BL* (bats left) and *BB* (bats both sides). *TB* is used for a pitcher who throws with both hands during a game. The only pitcher to do so since 1901 was Greg Harris, a one-time Red Sox right-hander who threw with both hands in a game for Montreal at the end of his career in 1995.

Height is shown by feet followed by inches. Weight is given in pounds. Most pitchers since 1950 have a weight range listed, as opposed to a single weight. When weight is given in most sources, it refers to only a single weight for a player's entire career, often using the weight he played at in his first year or two. As is the case with most pitchers, such as Bruce Hurst (185–220), there is often a difference between waistlines from first career pitch to last. (Who among us weighs the exact same as 15 years earlier?) Research in this area by the editors—information before 1950 is harder to come by—assures that these figures are accurate, if not necessarily flattering in every case.

Pitchers selected in the annual amateur/first-year player drafts since 1965 have draft information included in their bio lines. Complete draft information is shown in square brackets in the biographical lines for everyone selected in the draft since 1965 using a format of [Team/League/Year/Round/Pick Number]. Using Ray Jarvis, the first pitcher from Boston's first draft to make it to the major leagues, as an example, it reads: [BosA65 11/370]. The 1965 Red Sox 11th-round draft pick was the 370th player taken in the first draft. In recent years "sandwich picks" at the end of the first three rounds, given by teams as compensation for losing a free agent, are considered here to be part of that round. Casey Fossum, for example, was taken in the 48th pick in 1999, but he is still considered a first-round pick despite the high number [BosA99 1/48].

Debuts are marked *d*—note the lower-case letter so as not to be confused with the abbreviation for death—followed by the date the pitcher made his first major league appearance. The debut year is the first year listed in his entry in the register, so it is not repeated in the biographical line.

Besides the basic pieces of information for pitchers available on the biographical line, there are a few other designations for players whose career, family, or duty proved noteworthy.

Mil indicates military service in the army, navy, air force, or marines;
Mer indicates merchant marine;
Def indicates defense plant work.

The seasons missed—including partial seasons—are listed after the abbreviations for duty. Since the founding of the Red Sox in 1901, four wars involving the U.S. have caused some major leaguers to miss time for military duty (dates include post-war service):

World War I, 1917–19
World War II, 1941–46
Korean War, 1951–59
Vietnam War, 1962–72

If the pitcher spent time as a coach, manager, or umpire, this is indicated by the following abbreviations:

C: Coach
M: Manager
U: Umpire

A select few pitchers have reached the Hall of Fame, indicated by *HF* and followed by the year of induction.

If the pitcher had a close family member in the major leagues, the relative's relationship is identified by the codes listed below. The relative's first name is given; the last name is included if it is different than the pitcher's.

b: brother
twb: twin brother
f: father
s: son
gf: grandfather
gs: grandson
ggf: great grandfather
ggs: great grandson

For pitchers who attended college, this information is on the biographical line following the abbreviation *Col*. Ray Collins, for example, one of the earliest Red Sox players to have gone to college, attended the University of Vermont in the early 1900s. His school information is listed as: Col Vermont.

▲ included at the end of the biographical information means the pitcher is also listed in the Batter Register.

Statistical Information

Every pitcher who appeared in a game for the Red Sox is included in the Pitcher Register. Every year they pitched for the Red Sox is listed here, but the year-by-year annual statistics for other teams are only displayed if they pitched more than one third of their career games for the Red Sox. Career statistics for all pitchers who lasted more than one year in the major leagues are listed under *Total*. If they pitched more than one year for the Red Sox and pitched for other teams as well, their career Red Sox statistics are tallied under *Team*. Below that, some pitchers will have a line that reads */180I* or */60G*.

A */180I* line is added to the pitcher's entry if he averaged more than 3 innings per outing and accumulated 120 innings with the team.

These lines feature pro-rated statistics that represent a starting pitcher's seasonal average if he were to pitch 180 innings. This seasonal average, among other things, allows pitchers to be compared more easily.

A */60G* line is added to the pitcher's entry if he averaged less than 3 innings per outing and accumulated 40 games with the team. These lines feature pro-rated statistics that represent a reliever's seasonal average if he were to pitch 60 games. This season average provides an easier comparison for relievers.

Symbols included in this section indicate the following:

† before the team name means the pitcher participated in the postseason play that season;

★ after the team name means that the pitcher participated in the All-Star Game;

☆ after the team name means that the pitcher participated in the All-Star Game but did not play;

✳ after the team name means that the pitcher was chosen for the All-Star Game but was replaced due to injury.

Boldface statistics in any category indicates that the pitcher was the league leader or shared the honor.

The columns that appear in the Pitcher Register after **Year**:

TM: Team Each team is identified with a three-letter. This book provides a list of codes for clubs in the major leagues from 1892 forward.

LG: League The leagues mentioned in this book include the American League (A), the National League (N), and the Federal League, which existed in 1914–15.

W: Wins

L: Losses

PCT: Winning Percentage. This is derived by dividing wins by (wins plus losses).

G: Games

GS: Games Started

CG: Complete Games

ShO: Shutouts. Requires that one pitcher get every out in a game without allowing a run to score, earned or unearned, and with no relief help.

QS: Quality Starts. A pitcher is considered to have made a quality start if he throws at least the first six innings of a game and allows three runs or less. It is available for starting pitchers from 1957 forward.

SV: Saves. In 1969 this became an official statistic. Saves are calculated based on its official definition of the time. Saves before 1969 are based on the number of winning games a relief pitcher finished for his team without getting a win.

BS: Blown Saves. Since 1969 this is the number of times a pitcher entered a game in a save situation and allowed the opposing team to tie the game or take the lead. It is not calculated for pitchers before 1969.

QR Quality Relief. This is based on a reliever allowing less than one run for every two innings pitched and taking into account inherited runners. Information is available since 1957.

IP: Innings Pitched. Exact innings pitched, including thirds of an inning. One third of an inning is expressed as .1. Two thirds is expressed as .2.

H: Hits Allowed

R: Runs. This includes unearned runs.

HR: Home Runs Allowed

HB: Hit Batsmen

BB: Bases on balls. Bases on balls (commonly called walks) allowed by a pitcher.

IB: Intentional Walks Allowed. Walking an opponent on purpose was the first counted as its own category in 1955.

SO: Strikeouts

ERA: Earned Run Average. This is calculated by dividing earned runs by innings and multiplying by 9.

AERA: Adjusted Earned Run Average. AERA is calculated by normalizing ERA for the context of the level of the league and pitcher's home park. The number is converted to a scale where 20 is average and –20 is batting practice.

OAV Opponents Batting Average

OOB Opponents On-Base Percentage

Sup: Run Support. This is calculated by dividing the total number of runs scored by the pitcher's team during his starts by pitchers total Games Started. The product is normalized for the offensive level of the league and the pitcher's home park and converted to a scale where 20 is average and –20 should be grounds for suing for lack of support.

DL: Disabled List. This shows the number of days spent on the disabled list for each year indicated since the DL was instituted in 1941. This column does not include time spent on the DL before or after the season, but this carryover explains why some players will have DL stints shorter than the 15-day minimum. If a pitcher spent the entire season on the disabled list, the information is given in brackets in his biographical line with the team and time indicated. Don Aase, for instance, has the 182 days he spent on the disabled list without throwing a pitch for the 1983 California Angels listed: [DL 1983 Cal A 182].

PW: Pitcher Wins. This adds the pitcher's adjusted pitching wins, batting wins, and fielding wins to calculate how many wins the pitcher added to or subtracted from his team compared to what the average pitcher would have done.

Year	Tm Lg	W	L	Pct	G	GS	CG	ShO	QS	SV	BS	QR	IP	H	R	HR	HB	BB	IB	SO	ERA	AERA	OAV	OOB	Sup	DL	PW
AASE, DON Donald William B9.8.1954 Orange CA BR/TR/6'3"/(185–222) [BosA72 6/136] d7.26 [DL 1983 Cal A 182]																											
1977	Bos A	6	2	.750	13	13	4	2	9	0	0	0	92.1	85	36	6	1	19	1	49	3.12	+44	.244	.283	-20	0	1.0
Total	13	66	60	.524	448	91	22	5	44	82	29	253	1109.1	1085	503	89	7	457	45	641	3.80	+4	.259	.331	+4	569	4.5
ADAMS, BOB Robert Burdette B7.24.1901 Holyoke MA D10.17.1996 Lemoyne PA BR/TR/5'11"/168 d9.22 Col Lehigh																											
1925	Bos A	0	0	+	2	0	0	0		0			5.2	10	5	1	0	3		1	7.94	-43	.417	.481			0.0
ADAMS, TERRY Terry Wayne B3.6.1973 Mobile AL BR/TR/6'3"/(205–225) [ChiN91 4/111] d8.10																											
2004	Bos A	2	0	1.000	19	0	0	0	0	0	0	9	27	35	19	6	1	6	1	21	6.00	-19	.321	.353		0	-0.2
Total	11	51	62	.451	574	41	0	0	21	42	30	372	869.1	890	448	63	17	380	33	691	4.17	+2	.266	.342	+0	63	0.1
ADKINS, DOC Merle Theron B8.5.1872 Troy WI D2.21.1934 Durham NC BR/TR/5'10.5"/220 d6.24 Col Beloit																											
1902	Bos A	1	1	.500	4	2	1	0		0			20	30	20	2	0	7		3	4.05	-12	.345	.394	-30		-0.3
1903	NY A	0	0	+	2	1	0	0		1			7	10	8	0	1	5		0	7.71	-60	.333	.444	+83		-0.2
Total	2	1	1	.500	6	3	1	0		1			27	40	28	2	1	12		3	5.00	-31	.342	.408	+4		-0.5
AGUILERA, RICK Richard Warren B12.31.1961 San Gabriel CA BR/TR/6'5"/(193–210) [NYN83 3/58] d6.12 Col Brigham Young																											
1995	†Bos A	2	2	.500	30	0	0	0	0	20	1	24	30.1	26	9	4	0	7	0	23	2.67	+82	.228	.268		0	1.5
Total	16	86	81	.515	732	89	10	0	49	318	77	488	1291.1	1233	568	138	36	351	42	1030	3.57	+18	.251	.303	+6	319	17.3
ALMONTE, HECTOR Hector Radhames (Moreta) B10.17.1975 Santo Domingo, D.R. BR/TR/6'2"/190 d7.26																											
2003	Bos A	0	1	.000	7	0	0	0	0	0	0	5	7.2	9	7	1	0	7	1	6	8.22	-43	.310	.421		0	-0.3
Total	2	1	4	.200	50	0	0	0	0	0	1	29	51.2	63	36	6	2	30	5	40	6.27	-29	.307	.396		0	-0.6
ALTROCK, NICK Nicholas B9.15.1876 Cincinnati OH D1.20.1965 Washington DC BB/TL/5'10"/197 d7.14 C42																											
1902	Bos A	0	2	.000	3	2	1	0		1			18	19	13	0	1	7		5	2.00	+79	.271	.346	-30		0.0
1903	Bos A	0	1	.000	1	1	1	0		0			8	13	10	0	0	4		3	9.00	-66	.361	.425	-29		-0.3
Total	16	83	75	.525	218	161	128	16		7			1514	1455	600	16	22	272		425	2.67	-5	.255	.291	+8		1.5
Team	2	0	3	.000	4	3	2	0		1			26	32	23	0	1	11		8	4.15	-18	.302	.373	-30		-0.3
ALVAREZ, ABE Abraham B10.17.1982 Los Angeles CA BL/TL/6'2"/190 [BosA02 2/49] d7.22 Col Cal St.–Long Beach																											
2004	Bos A	0	1	.000	1	1	0	0	0	0	0	0	5	8	5	2	0	5	0	2	9.00	-46	.400	.520	-43	0	-0.3
2005	Bos A	0	0	+	2	0	0	0	0	0	0	1	2.1	6	4	1	0	0	0	1	15.43	-71	.462	.462		0	-0.1
2006	Bos A	0	0	+	1	0	0	0	0	0	0	0	3	5	4	2	0	2	0	2	12.00	-61	.385	.467		13	-0.1
Total	3	0	1	.000	4	1	0	0	0	0	0	1	10.1	19	13	5	0	7	0	5	11.32	-58	.413	.491	-43	13	-0.5
ANDERSEN, LARRY Larry Eugene B5.6.1953 Portland OR BR/TR/6'3"/(180–205) [CleA71 7/155] d9.5																											
1990	†Bos A	0	0	+	15	0	0	0	0	1	3	11	22	18	3	0	1	3	0	25	1.23	+234	.220	.256		0	0.3
Total	17	40	39	.506	699	1	0	0	0	49	41	507	995.1	932	402	58	17	311	64	758	3.15	+20	.249	.306	+6	238	7.9
ANDERSON, JIMMY James Drew B1.22.1976 Portsmouth VA BL/TL/6'1"/(190–215) [PitN94 9/242] d7.4																											
2004	Bos A	0	0	+	5	0	0	0	0	0	0	2	6	10	4	0	0	3	0	3	6.00	-19	.400	.464		0	0.0
Total	6	25	47	.347	122	96	3	0	41	1	0	15	574.2	672	371	58	26	240	24	241	5.42	-18	.295	.366	-9	0	-6.7
ANDERSON, FRED John Frederick B12.11.1885 Calahaln NC D11.8.1957 Winston–Salem NC BR/TR/6'2"/180 d9.25 Mil 1918 Col Maryland																											
1909	Bos A	0	0	+	1	1	0	0		0			8	3	3	0	0	1		5	1.13	+122	.115	.148	+13		0.0
1913	Bos A	0	6	.000	10	8	4	0		0			57.1	84	51	0	1	21		32	5.97	-51	.353	.408	+4		-1.9
Total	7	53	57	.482	178	114	62	11		8			986.1	912	415	22	15	247		514	2.86	-5	.248	.298	-1		-4.2
Team	2	0	6	.000	11	9	4	0		0			65.1	87	54	0	1	22		37	5.37	-46	.330	.383	+5		-1.9
ANDREWS, IVY Ivy Paul "Poison" B5.6.1907 Dora AL D11.24.1970 Birmingham AL BR/TR/6'1"/200 d8.15																											
1932	Bos A	8	6	.571	25	19	8	0		0			141.2	144	76	4	2	53		30	3.81	+18	.262	.329	-4		0.4
1933	Bos A	7	13	.350	34	17	5	0		1			140	157	96	8	1	61		37	4.95	-12	.279	.350	-13		-1.4
Total	8	50	59	.459	249	108	43	2		8			1041	1151	562	59	4	342		257	4.14	+15	.279	.335	-11		4.4
Team	2	15	19	.441	59	36	13	0		1			281.2	301	172	12	3	114		67	4.38	+1	.270	.340	-8		-1.0
/180I	1	10	12	.441	38	23	8	0		1			180	192	110	8	2	73		43	4.38	+1	.270	.340	-8		-0.6
APONTE, LUIS Luis Eduardo (Yuripe) B6.14.1953 ElTigre, Anzoategui, Venez. BR/TR/6'0"/(165–185) d9.4																											
1980	Bos A	0	0	+	4	0	0	0	0	0	0	4	7	6	1	0	0	2	1	1	1.29	+232	.250	.308		0	0.1
1981	Bos A	1	0	1.000	7	0	0	0	0	1	0	7	15.2	11	1	0	0	3	0	11	0.57	+582	.208	.250		0	0.5
1982	Bos A	2	2	.500	40	0	0	0	0	3	0	32	85	78	31	5	0	25	3	44	3.18	+37	.246	.299		0	0.6
1983	Bos A	5	4	.556	34	0	0	0	0	3	1	19	62	74	28	7	2	23	3	32	3.63	+21	.301	.364		0	0.7
1984	Cle A	1	0	1.000	25	0	0	0	0	0	0	17	50.1	53	25	5	1	15	0	25	4.11	+0	.269	.322		0	0.0
Total	5	9	6	.600	110	0	0	0	0	7	1	79	220	222	86	17	3	68	7	113	3.27	+31	.265	.321		0	1.9
Team	4	8	6	.571	85	0	0	0	0	7	1	62	169.2	169	61	12	2	53	7	88	3.02	+43	.264	.321			1.9
/60G	3	6	4	.571	60	0	0	0	0	5	1	44	119.2	119	43	8	1	37	5	62	3.03	+43	.264	.321			1.3
APPLETON, PETE Peter William "Jake" (aka Jablonowski in 1927-33) B5.20.1904 Terryville CT D1.18.1974 Trenton NJ BR/TR/5'11"/180 d9.14 Mil 1943–45 Col Michigan																											
1932	Bos A	0	3	.000	11	3	0	0		0			46	49	35	2	2	26		15	4.11	+9	.265	.362	-49		0.0
Total	14	57	66	.463	341	73	34	6		26			1141	1187	667	76	26	486		420	4.30	+4	.268	.343	-16	0	2.9
ARELLANES, FRANK Frank Julian B1.28.1882 Santa Cruz CA D12.13.1918 San Jose CA BR/TR/6'0"/180 d7.28 Col Santa Clara																											
1908	Bos A	4	3	.571	11	8	6	1		0			79	60	26	1	3	18		33	1.82	+35	.205	.259	-3		0.3
1909	Bos A	16	12	.571	45	28	17	1		**8**			230.2	192	80	3	5	43		82	2.18	+14	.229	.270	+14		0.8
1910	Bos A	4	7	.364	18	13	2	0		0			100	106	41	1	3	24		33	2.88	-11	.283	.332	-7		-0.2
Total	3	24	22	.522	74	49	25	2		8			409.2	358	147	5	11	85		148	2.28	+10	.238	.283	+5		0.9
/180I	1	11	10	.522	33	22	11	1	0	4	0	0	180	157	65	2	5	37		65	2.28	+10	.238	.283	-54		0.4
ARROJO, ROLANDO Luis Rolando B7.18.1968 Santa Clara, Cuba BR/TR/6'4"/(215–220) d4.1																											
1998	TB A★	14	12	.538	32	32	2	2	17	0	0	0	202	195	84	21	19	65	2	152	3.56	+35	.256	.329	-16	7	3.3
1999	TB A	7	12	.368	24	24	2	0	10	0	0	0	140.2	162	84	23	14	60	2	107	5.18	-4	.296	.378	-16	51	0.1
2000	Col N	5	9	.357	19	19	0	0	7	0	0	0	101.1	120	77	14	12	46	6	80	6.04	-4	.299	.381	-14	14	-0.5
2000	Bos A	5	2	.714	13	13	0	0	5	0	0	0	71.1	67	41	10	4	22	0	44	5.05	-1	.245	.310	+8	0	0.1
2000	Major	10	11	.476	32	32	0	0	12	0	0	0	172	187	118	24	16	68	6	124	5.63	-3	.277	.353	-5	14	-0.4
2001	Bos A	5	4	.556	41	9	0	0	6	5	2	19	103.1	88	44	8	12	35	4	78	3.48	+27	.230	.313	+4	20	1.0
2002	Bos A	4	3	.571	29	8	0	0	3	1	3	12	81.1	83	47	7	6	27	1	51	4.98	-10	.269	.337	-22	58	-0.3
Total	5	40	42	.488	158	105	4	2	48	6	5	31	700	715	377	83	67	255	15	512	4.55	+8	.267	.344	-10	150	3.7
Team	3	14	9	.609	83	30	0	0	14	6	5	31	256	238	132	25	22	84	5	173	4.39	+5	.247	.320	-1	78	0.8
/180I	2	10	6	.609	58	21	0	0	10	4	4	22	180	167	93	18	15	59	4	122	4.39	+5	.247	.320	-1	55	0.6
ARROYO, BRONSON Bronson Anthony B2.24.1977 Key West FL BR/TR/6'5"/(180–190) [PitN95 3/69] d6.12																											
2000	Pit N	2	6	.250	20	12	0	0	3	0	0	4	71.2	88	61	10	4	36	6	50	6.40	-28	.302	.384	+9	0	-1.5
2001	Pit N	5	7	.417	24	13	1	0	2	0	0	7	88.1	99	54	12	4	34	6	39	5.09	-12	.289	.355	-3	0	-0.8
2002	Pit N	2	1	.667	9	4	0	0	0	0	0	4	27	30	14	1	0	15	3	22	4.00	+5	.283	.369	-6	0	0.0
2003	†Bos A	0	0	+	6	0	0	0	0	1	0	4	17.1	10	5	0	1	4	2	14	2.08	+124	.164	.227		0	0.2
2004	†Bos A	10	9	.526	32	29	0	0	16	0	0	2	178.2	171	99	17	20	47	3	142	4.03	+21	.249	.314	+5	0	1.1
2005	†Bos A	14	10	.583	35	32	0	0	20	0	0	2	205.1	213	116	22	14	54	3	100	4.51	+1	.266	.322	+7	0	-0.3
2006	Cin N★	14	11	.560	35	**35**	3	1	23	0	0	0	**240.2**	222	98	31	5	64	7	184	3.29	+43	.243	.296	-12	0	3.5
Total	7	47	44	.516	161	125	4	1	64	1	0	23	829	833	447	93	48	254	30	551	4.21	+11	.260	.322	+0	0	2.2
Team	3	24	19	.558	73	61	0	0	36	1	0	8	401.1	394	220	39	35	105	8	256	4.19	+12	.254	.315	+6		1.0
/180I	1	11	9	.558	33	27	0	0	16	0	0	4	180	177	99	17	16	47	4	115	4.19	+12	.254	.315	+6		0.4
ASTACIO, PEDRO Pedro Julio (Pura) B11.28.1969 Hato Mayor, D.R. BR/TR/6'2"/(174–210) d7.3																											
2004	Bos A	0	0	+	5	1	0	0	0	0	0	2	8.2	13	10	2	0	5	0	6	10.38	-53	.342	.419	+33	0	-0.2
Total	15	129	124	.510	392	343	31	12	191	0	1	33	2196.2	2292	1213	291	111	726	54	1664	4.67	-3	.271	.334	-2	305	-3.6
ATKINS, JAMES James Curtis B3.10.1921 Birmingham AL BL/TR/6'3"/205 d9.29																											
1950	Bos A	0	0	+	1	0	0	0		0			4.2	4	2	1	1	4		0	3.86	+27	.235	.409		0	0.0
1952	Bos A	0	1	.000	3	1	0	0		0			10.1	11	6	0	0	7		2	3.48	+13	.275	.383	-56	0	0.1
Total	2	0	1	.000	4	1	0	0		0			15	15	8	1	1	11		2	3.60	+18	.263	.391	-56	0	0.1

Year	Tm Lg	W	L	Pct	G	GS	CG	ShO	QS	SV	BS	QR	IP	H	R	HR	HB	BB	IB	SO	ERA	AERA	OAV	OOB	Sup	DL	PW
AUKER, ELDEN Elden Le Roy "Submarine" B9.21.1910 Norcatur KS D8.4.2006 Vero Beach FL BR/TR/6'2"/194 d8.10 Col Kansas St.																											
1939	Bos A	9	10	.474	31	25	6	1		0			151	183	108	13	1	61		43	5.36	-12	.294	.358	+14		-1.0
Total	10	130	101	.563	333	261	126	14		2			1963.1	2230	1106	129	36	706		594	4.42	+1	.285	.347	+10	0	1.7
/180I	1	11	12	.474	37	30	7	1		0			180	218	129	15	1	73		51	5.36	-12	.294	.358	+36		-1.2
AVERY, STEVE Steven Thomas B4.14.1970 Trenton MI BL/TL/6'4"/(180–205) [AtlN88 1/3] d6.13																											
1997	Bos A	6	7	.462	22	18	0	0	6	0	0	2	96.2	127	76	15	2	49	0	51	6.42	-28	.320	.394	+24	62	-2.0
1998	Bos A	10	7	.588	34	23	0	0	10	0	1	5	123.2	128	74	14	4	64	0	57	5.02	-6	.269	.361	+15	0	-0.2
Total	11	96	83	.536	297	261	14	6	131	0	2	19	1554.2	1529	800	148	26	569	27	980	4.19	+0	.259	.325	+7	184	1.0
Team	2	16	14	.533	56	41	0	0	16	0	1	7	220.1	255	150	29	6	113	0	108	5.64	-17	.292	.376	+19	62	-2.2
/180I	2	13	11	.533	46	33	0	0	13	0	1	6	180	208	123	24	5	92	0	88	5.64	-17	.292	.376	+19	51	-1.8
BADER, LORE Lore Verne "King" B4.27.1888 Bader IL D6.2.1973 LeRoy KS BL/TR/6'0"/175 d9.30 C1																											
1912	NY N	2	0	1.000	2	1	1	0		0			10	9	2	0	1	6		3	0.90	+276	.250	.372	-13		0.5
1917	Bos A	2	0	1.000	15	1	0	0		1			38.1	48	15	1	1	18		14	2.35	+10	.306	.381	-16		0.1
1918	Bos A	1	3	.250	5	4	2	1		0			27	26	13	1	3	12		10	3.33	-19	.271	.369	-58		-0.4
Total	3	5	3	.625	22	6	3	1		1			75.1	83	30	2	5	36		27	2.51	+9	.287	.376	-42		0.2
Team	2	3	3	.500	20	5	2	1		1			65.1	74	28	2	4	30		24	2.76	-5	.292	.376	-50		-0.3
BAGBY, JIM James Charles Jacob Jr. B9.8.1916 Cleveland OH D9.2.1988 Marietta GA BR/TR/6'2"/170 d4.18 Def 1944 f–Jim																											
1938	Bos A	15	11	.577	43	25	10	1		2			198.2	218	110	9	3	90		73	4.21	+17	.283	.360	+19		1.6
1939	Bos A	5	5	.500	21	11	3	0		0			80	119	66	7	2	36		35	7.09	-33	.347	.412	+17		-1.5
1940	Bos A	10	16	.385	36	21	6	1		2			182.2	217	104	15	1	83		57	4.73	-5	.296	.368	-7		-0.5
1941	Cle A	9	15	.375	33	27	12	0		2			200.2	214	104	10	6	76		53	4.04	-2	.273	.341	-10	0	-0.1
1942	Cle A☆	17	9	.654	38	**35**	16	4		1			270.2	267	105	19	1	64		54	2.96	+17	.258	.302	+9	0	1.5
1943	Cle A☆	17	14	.548	36	**33**	16	3		1			**273**	248	112	15	3	80		70	3.10	+0	.240	.296	+2	0	0.6
1944	Cle A	4	5	.444	13	10	2	0		0			79	101	48	2	4	34		12	4.33	-24	.312	.384	+4	0	-1.0
1945	Cle A	8	11	.421	25	19	11	3		1			159.1	171	70	3	2	59		38	3.73	-13	.279	.344	+1	0	-0.2
1946	†Bos A	7	6	.538	21	11	6	1		0			106.2	117	55	4	1	49		16	3.71	-1	.279	.356	-13	0	-0.5
1947	Pit N	5	4	.556	37	6	2	0		0			115.2	143	75	14	5	37		23	4.67	-10	.304	.361	+36	0	-0.4
Total	10	97	96	.503	303	198	84	13		9			1666.1	1815	849	98	28	608		431	3.96	-3	.278	.342	+4	0	-0.5
Team	4	37	38	.493	121	68	25	3		4			568	671	335	35	7	258		181	4.69	-3	.296	.370	+5		-0.9
/180I	1	12	12	.493	38	22	8	1		1			180	213	106	11	2	82		57	4.69	-3	.296	.370	+5		-0.3
BAILEY, CORY Phillip Cory B1.24.1971 Marion IL BR/TR/6'1"/(195–210) [BosA91 15/408] d9.1 Col Southeastern Illinois JC																											
1993	Bos A	0	1	.000	11	0	0	0	0	0	0	6	15.2	12	7	0	0	12	3	11	3.45	+34	.231	.369		0	0.1
1994	Bos A	0	1	.000	5	0	0	0	0	0	1	3	4.1	10	6	2	0	3	1	4	12.46	-60	.476	.542		0	-0.6
Total	8	9	10	.474	172	0	0	0	0	1	9	120	207	208	99	13	3	116	17	150	3.96	+18	.269	.364		0	1.1
Team	2	0	2	.000	16	0	0	0	0	0	1	9	20	22	13	2	0	15	4	15	5.40	-13	.301	.416			-0.5
BAKER, AL Albert Jones B2.28.1906 Batesville MS D11.6.1982 Kenedy TX BR/TR/5'11"/170 d8.20																											
1938	Bos A	0	0	+	3	0	0	0		0			7.2	13	8	2	1	2		2	9.39	-47	.371	.421			-0.2
BANKHEAD, SCOTT Michael Scott B7.31.1963 Raleigh NC BR/TR/5'10"/(175–185) [KCA84 1/16] d5.25 Col North Carolina																											
1993	Bos A	2	1	.667	40	0	0	0	0	0	2	24	64.1	59	28	7	0	29	3	47	3.50	+33	.250	.327		0	0.3
1994	Bos A	3	2	.600	27	0	0	0	0	0	0	20	37.2	34	21	5	0	12	3	25	4.54	+11	.239	.295		53	0.2
Total	10	57	48	.543	267	110	7	3	56	1	6	103	901	876	451	111	15	289	26	614	4.18	+3	.254	.311	-8	368	1.1
Team	2	5	3	.625	67	0	0	0	0	0	2	44	102	93	49	12	0	41	6	72	3.88	+23	.246	.315		53	0.5
/60G	2	4	3	.625	60	0	0	0	0	0	2	39	91.1	83	44	11	0	37	5	64	3.88	+23	.246	.315		47	0.4
BANKS, WILLIE Willie Anthony B2.27.1969 Jersey City NJ BR/TR/6'1"/(190–202) [MinA87 1/3] d7.31																											
2001	Bos A	0	0	+	5	0	0	0	0	0	0	5	10.2	5	4	0	0	4	0	10	0.84	+426	.132	.214		0	0.1
2002	Bos A	2	1	.667	29	0	0	0	0	1	0	20	39	32	15	5	3	14	0	26	3.23	+39	.222	.302		0	0.4
Total	9	33	39	.458	181	84	1	1	33	2	3	59	610.1	632	370	65	15	302	16	428	4.75	-10	.268	.353	-10	0	-4.0
Team	2	2	1	.667	34	0	0	0	0	1	0	25	49.2	37	19	5	3	18	0	36	2.72	+64	.203	.284			0.5
BARBERICH, FRANK Frank Frederick B2.3.1882 Newtown NY D5.1.1965 Ocala FL BB/TR/5'10.5"/175 d9.17																											
1907	Bos N	1	1	.500	2	2	1	0		0			12.1	19	10	0	0	5		1	5.84	-56	.358	.414	+67		-0.6
1910	Bos A	0	0	+	2	0	0	0		0			5	7	6	0	0	2		0	7.20	-65	.350	.409			-0.1
Total	2	1	1	.500	4	2	1	0		0			17.1	26	16	0	0	7		1	6.23	-59	.356	.412	+67		-0.7
BARK, BRIAN Brian Stuart B8.26.1968 Baltimore MD BL/TL/5'9"/170 [AtlN90 12/318] d7.6 Col North Carolina St.																											
1995	Bos A	0	0	+	3	0	0	0	0	0	0	3	2.1	2	0	0	0	1	0	0	0.00	-100	.286	.375		0	0.1
BARKLEY, BRIAN Brian Edward B12.8.1975 Conroe TX BL/TL/6'2"/180 [BosA94 5/131] d5.28 gf–Red Col Okaloosa–Walton (FL) CC [DL 1999 Bos A 73]																											
1998	Bos A	0	0	+	6	0	0	0	0	0	0	2	11	16	13	2	1	9	1	2	9.82	-52	.340	.441		0	-0.3
BARR, STEVE Steven Charles B9.8.1951 St.Louis MO BL/TL/6'4"/200 [BosA69 7/155] d10.1																											
1974	Bos A	1	0	1.000	1	1	1	0	1	0	0	0	9	7	4	0	0	6	0	3	4.00	-4	.212	.333	+60	0	0.0
1975	Bos A	0	1	.000	3	2	0	0	0	0	0	1	7	11	9	1	0	7	0	2	2.57	+58	.367	.474	+8	0	-0.2
Total	3	3	7	.300	24	13	4	0	5	0	0	5	83.2	88	64	11	0	57	1	32	5.16	-29	.272	.379	+17	23	-1.9
Team	2	1	1	.500	4	3	1	0	1	0	0	1	16	18	13	1	0	13	0	5	3.38	+17	.286	.403	+25		-0.2
BARRETT, FRANK Francis Joseph "Red" B7.1.1913 Ft.Lauderdale FL D3.6.1998 Leesburg FL BR/TR/6'2"/173 d10.1 Col St. Leo																											
1939	StL N	0	1	.000	1	0	0	0		0			1.2	1	1	0	0	1		3	5.40	-24	.167	.286			0.0
1944	Bos A	8	7	.533	38	2	0	0		8			90.1	93	45	5	1	42		40	3.69	-8	.271	.352	+60	0	-0.8
1945	Bos A	4	3	.571	37	0	0	0		3			86	77	30	0	0	29		35	2.62	+30	.249	.314		0	0.6
1946	Bos N	2	4	.333	23	0	0	0		1			35.1	35	21	2	1	17		12	5.09	-33	.252	.338		0	-0.9
1950	Pit N	1	2	.333	5	0	0	0		0			4.1	5	3	1	0	1		0	4.15	+6	.357	.400		0	0.0
Total	5	15	17	.469	104	2	0	0		12			217.2	211	100	8	2	90		90	3.51	-2	.260	.336	+60	0	-1.1
Team	2	12	10	.545	75	2	0	0		11			176.1	170	75	5	1	71		75	3.16	+8	.261	.334	+60		-0.2
/60G	2	10	8	.545	60	2	0	0		9			141	136	60	4	1	57		60	3.17	+8	.261	.334	+60		-0.2
BARRY, ED Edward "Jumbo" B10.2.1882 Madison WI D6.19.1920 Montague MA BR/TL/6'3"/185 d8.21																											
1905	Bos A	1	2	.333	7	5	2	0		0			40.2	38	19	2	4	15		18	2.88	-6	.248	.331	+31		-0.2
1906	Bos A	0	3	.000	3	3	3	0		0			21	23	22	2	3	5		10	6.00	-54	.280	.344	-56		-1.0
1907	Bos A	0	1	.000	2	2	1	0		0			17.1	13	6	1	1	5		6	2.08	+24	.210	.279	-48		0.0
Total	3	1	6	.143	12	10	6	0		0			79	74	47	5	8	25		34	3.53	-24	.249	.324	-11		-1.2
BAUMANN, FRANK Frank Matt "The Beau" B7.1.1933 St.Louis MO BL/TL/6'1"/(200–210) d7.31																											
1955	Bos A	2	1	.667	7	5	0	0		0			34	38	28	2	1	17	0	27	5.82	-26	.281	.361	+8	0	-0.5
1956	Bos A	2	1	.667	7	1	0	0		0			24.2	22	11	3	0	14	0	18	3.28	+41	.234	.333	+131	0	0.4
1957	Bos A	1	0	1.000	4	1	0	0	9	0		13	12	13	5	1	1	3	0	7	3.75	+6	.277	.333	-33	0	0.1
1958	Bos A	2	2	.500	10	7	2	0	9	0		13	52.1	56	27	4	4	27	2	31	4.47	-10	.276	.370	-23	0	0.0
1959	Bos A	6	4	.600	26	10	2	0	9	1		14	95.2	96	47	11	1	55	3	48	4.05	+0	.259	.356	+4	0	0.1
Total	11	45	38	.542	244	78	19	4	55	13		125	797.1	856	406	70	12	300	32	384	4.11	-5	.276	.340	+13	31	-0.6
Team	5	13	8	.619	54	24	4	0	27	1		40	218.2	225	118	21	7	116	5	131	4.32	-4	.265	.357	+1		0.1
/180I	4	11	7	.619	44	20	3	0	22	1		33	180	185	97	17	6	95	4	108	4.32	-4	.265	.357	+1		0.1
BAYNE, BILL William Lear "Beverly" B4.18.1899 Pittsburgh PA D5.22.1981 St.Louis MO BL/TL/5'9"/160 d9.20																											
1929	Bos A	5	5	.500	27	6	2	0		0			84.1	111	72	9	8	29		26	6.72	-36	.326	.392	-37		-1.8
1930	Bos A	0	0	+	1	0	0	0		0			4	5	2	1	0	1		1	4.50	+2	.294	.333			0.0
Total	9	31	32	.492	199	55	21	2		8			662	711	409	37	50	297		259	4.84	-13	.283	.370	-1		-2.5
Team	2	5	5	.500	28	6	2	0		0			88.1	116	74	10	8	30		27	6.62	-35	.325	.389	-37		-1.8
BECK, ROD Rodney Roy B8.3.1968 Burbank CA BR/TR/6'1"/(215–236) [OakA86 13/327] d5.6																											
1999	†Bos A	0	1	.000	12	0	0	0	0	3	1	11	14	9	3	0	1	5	0	12	1.93	+158	.184	.273		0	0.5
2000	Bos A	3	0	1.000	34	0	0	0	0	0	3	24	40.2	34	15	2	2	12	1	35	3.10	+62	.222	.287		94	0.5
2001	Bos A	6	4	.600	68	0	0	0	0	6	5	45	80.2	77	42	15	3	28	6	63	3.90	+14	.252	.319		0	0.4

Year	Tm Lg	W	L	Pct	G	GS	CG	ShO	QS	SV	BS	QR	IP	H	R	HR	HB	BB	IB	SO	ERA	AERA	OAV	OOB	Sup	DL	PW
Total	13	38	45	.458	704	0	0	0	0	286	55	523	768	703	308	97	20	191	33	644	3.30	+24	.242	.291		183	10.4
Team	3	9	5	.643	114	0	0	0	0	9	9	80	135.1	120	60	17	6	45	7	110	3.46	+35	.236	.305		94	1.4
/60G	2	5	3	.643	60	0	0	0	0	5	5	42	71.1	63	32	9	3	24	4	58	3.45	+35	.236	.305		49	0.7
BECKETT, JOSH Joshua Patrick B5.15.1980 Spring TX BR/TR/6'4"/(190–220) [FlaN99 1/2] d9.4																											
2006	Bos A	16	11	.593	33	33	0	0	20	0	0	0	204.2	191	120	36	10	74	1	158	5.01	-7	.245	.317	+2	0	-0.6
Total	6	57	45	.559	139	136	3	2	80	0	0	3	813.2	720	386	91	27	297	12	765	3.85	+9	.237	.309	+8	219	3.9
/180I	1	14	10	.593	29	29	0	0	18	0		0	180	168	106	32	9	65	1	139	5.01	-7	.245	.317	-10		-0.5
BEDIENT, HUGH Hugh Carpenter B10.23.1889 Gerry NY D7.21.1965 Jamestown NY BR/TR/6'0"/185 d4.26																											
1912	†Bos A	20	9	.690	41	28	19	0		2			231	206	93	6	3	55		122	2.92	+16	.240	.288	+2		1.7
1913	Bos A	15	14	.517	43	28	15	1		5			259	255	104	0	6	67		122	2.78	+6	.263	.314	-20		0.2
1914	Bos A	8	12	.400	42	16	7	1		2			177.1	187	97	4	5	45		70	3.60	-25	.281	.331	+29		-2.3
1915	Buf F	16	18	.471	53	30	16	2		**10**			269.1	284	131	5	3	69		106	3.17	-12	.274	.321	-8		-2.7
Total	4	59	53	.527	179	102	57	4		19			936.2	932	425	15	17	236		420	3.08	-4	.264	.313	-2		-3.1
Team	3	43	35	.551	126	72	41	2		9			667.1	648	294	10	14	167		314	3.05	-1	.260	.310	-1		-0.4
/180I	1	12	9	.551	34	19	11	1		2			180	175	79	3	4	45		85	3.05	-1	.260	.310	-1		-0.1
BELINDA, STAN Stanley Peter B8.6.1966 Huntingdon PA BR/TR/6'3"/(187–215) [PitN86 10/238] d9.8 Col Allegany (MD) CC																											
1995	†Bos A	8	1	.889	63	0	0	0	0	10	4	46	69.2	51	25	5	4	28	3	57	3.10	+57	.205	.291		11	1.8
1996	Bos A	2	1	.667	31	0	0	0	0	2	2	20	28.2	31	22	3	4	20	1	18	6.59	-23	.272	.399		113	-0.4
Total	12	41	37	.526	585	0	0	0	0	79	37	411	685.1	590	336	85	34	285	43	622	4.15	+3	.233	.315		290	3.2
Team	2	10	2	.833	94	0	0	0	0	12	6	66	98.1	82	47	8	8	48	4	75	4.12	+20	.226	.326		124	1.4
/60G	1	6	1	.833	60	0	0	0	0	8	4	42	62.2	52	30	5	5	31	3	48	4.13	+20	.226	.326		79	0.9
BELL, GARY Gary B11.17.1936 San Antonio TX BR/TR/6'1"/(195–198) d6.1 Col San Antonio (TX) JC																											
1967	†Bos A	12	8	.600	29	24	8	0	16	3		4	165.1	143	70	16	4	47	3	115	3.16	+10	.231	.288	+15	0	0.6
1968	Bos A☆	11	11	.500	35	27	9	3	19	1		6	199.1	177	82	7	5	68	6	103	3.12	+1	.239	.306	+1	0	0.2
Total	12	121	117	.508	519	233	71	9	163	51	0	231	2015	1794	932	207	54	842	64	1378	3.68	-2	.239	.318	+1	0	-1.4
Team	2	23	19	.548	64	51	17	3	35	4		10	364.2	320	152	23	9	115	9	218	3.13	+5	.235	.298	+8		0.8
/180I	1	11	9	.548	32	25	8	1	17	2		5	180	158	75	11	4	57	4	108	3.13	+5	.235	.298	+8		0.4
BENNETT, DENNIS Dennis John B10.5.1939 Oakland CA BL/TL/6'5"/(185–205) d5.12 b–Dave Col Shasta (CA) JC																											
1962	Phi N	9	9	.500	31	24	7	2	12	3		6	174.2	144	78	17	6	68	3	149	3.81	+2	.224	.302	-2	0	0.2
1963	Phi N	9	5	.643	23	16	6	1	12	1		5	119.1	102	44	12	4	33	5	82	2.64	+22	.231	.287	+23	74	1.1
1964	Phi N	12	14	.462	41	32	7	2	17	1		5	208	222	92	23	5	58	8	125	3.68	-6	.280	.331	-16	0	0.0
1965	Bos A	5	7	.417	34	18	3	0	6	0		9	141.2	152	76	15	6	53	6	85	4.38	-15	.279	.346	-2	0	-0.5
1966	Bos A	3	3	.500	16	13	0	0	7	0		2	75	75	30	9	1	23	2	47	3.24	+17	.261	.316	-18	80	0.4
1967	Bos A	4	3	.571	13	11	4	1	6	0		1	69.2	72	32	12	2	22	2	34	3.88	-10	.268	.327	+41	0	-0.2
1967	NY N	1	1	.500	8	6	0	0	2	0		1	26.1	37	15	4	1	7	1	14	5.13	-34	.336	.378	-9	0	-0.3
1967	Major	5	4	.556	21	17	4	1	8	0		2	95	109	47	16	3	29	3	48	4.22	-17	.288	.341	+23	0	-0.5
1968	Cal A	0	5	.000	16	7	1	0	3	1		6	48.1	46	22	6	4	17	0	36	3.54	-18	.250	.324	-53	0	-0.5
Total	7	43	47	.478	182	127	28	6	65	6		35	863	850	389	98	29	281	27	572	3.69	-4	.260	.322	-3	154	0.2
Team	3	12	13	.480	63	42	7	1	19	0		12	286.1	299	138	36	9	98	10	166	3.96	-7	.272	.334	+4	80	-0.3
/180I	2	8	8	.480	40	26	4	1	12	0		8	180	188	87	23	6	62	6	104	3.96	-7	.272	.334	+4	50	-0.2
BENNETT, FRANK Francis Allen "Chip" B10.27.1904 Mardela Springs MD D3.18.1966 Wilmington DE BR/TR/5'10.5"/163 d9.17																											
1927	Bos A	0	1	.000	4	1	0	0		0			12.1	15	4	0	0	6		1	2.92	+45	.333	.412	-60		0.1
1928	Bos A	0	0	+	1	0	0	0		0			1	1	0	0	0	0		0	0.00	-100	.250	.250			0.0
Total	2	0	1	.000	5	1	0	0		0			13.1	16	4	0	0	6		1	2.70	+56	.327	.400	-60		0.1
BENTON, AL John Alton B3.18.1911 Noble OK D4.14.1968 Lynwood CA BR/TR/6'4"/215 d4.18 Mil 1943–44																											
1952	Bos A	4	3	.571	24	0	0	0		6			37.2	37	11	1	0	17		20	2.39	+65	.268	.348		0	1.2
Total	14	98	88	.527	455	167	58	10		66			1688.1	1672	831	106	15	733		697	3.66	+15	.259	.336	-6	0	6.5
BEVILLE, BEN Clarence Benjamin B8.28.1877 Colusa CA D1.5.1937 Yountville CA BR/TR/5'9"/190 d5.24																											
1901	Bos A	0	2	.000	2	2	1	0		0			9	8	7	0	1	9		1	4.00	-12	.235	.409	-71		-0.1
BILLINGHAM, JACK John Eugene B2.21.1943 Orlando FL BR/TR/6'4"/(185–215) d4.11																											
1980	Bos A	1	3	.250	7	4	0	0	0	0	0	0	24.1	45	30	6	4	12	0	4	11.10	-62	.413	.484	-27	0	-2.1
Total	13	145	113	.562	476	305	74	27	173	15	9	114	2231.1	2272	1069	176	98	750	97	1141	3.83	-6	.268	.333	+17	0	-9.9
BIRD, DOUG James Douglas B3.5.1950 Corona CA BR/TR/6'4"/(180–195) [KCA69 S3/60] d4.29 Col Mt. San Antonio (CA) JC																											
1983	Bos A	1	4	.200	22	6	0	0	2	1	0	9	67.2	91	52	14	2	16	4	33	6.65	-34	.324	.360	-24	0	-1.0
Total	11	73	60	.549	432	100	8	3	48	60	29	217	1213.2	1273	590	122	22	296	56	680	3.99	-4	.272	.315	-1	21	0.0
BLACK, DAVE David B4.19.1892 Chicago IL D10.27.1936 Pittsburgh PA BL/TR/6'2"/175 d5.2																											
1923	Bos A	0	0	+	2	0	0	0		0			1	2	0	0	0	0		0	0.00	-100	.500	.500			0.0
Total	3	8	10	.444	43	15	4	0		0			181.1	166	83	7	8	52		72	3.18	-18	.256	.319	+25		-1.0
BLETHEN, CLARENCE Clarence Waldo "Climax" B7.11.1893 Dover–Foxcroft ME D4.11.1973 Frederick MD BL/TR/5'11"/165 d9.17 Col Maine																											
1923	Bos A	0	0	+	5	0	0	0		0			17.2	29	15	0	0	7		2	7.13	-42	.382	.434			-0.4
1929	Bro N	0	0	+	2	0	0	0		0			2	4	2	0	0	3		0	9.00	-49	.444	.583			0.0
Total	2	0	0	+	7	0	0	0		0			19.2	33	17	0	0	10		2	7.32	-43	.388	.453			-0.4
BODDICKER, MIKE Michael James B8.23.1957 Cedar Rapids IA BR/TR/5'11"/(172–190) [BalA78 6/152] d10.4 Col Iowa																											
1988	†Bos A	7	3	.700	15	14	1	1	11	0	0	1	89	85	30	3	3	26	1	56	2.63	+57	.257	.313	+21	0	1.6
1989	Bos A	15	11	.577	34	34	3	2	15	0	0	0	211.2	217	101	19	10	71	4	145	4.00	+3	.267	.330	+4	0	0.6
1990	†Bos A	17	8	.680	34	34	4	0	23	0	0	0	228	225	92	16	10	69	6	143	3.36	+22	.258	.319	+11	0	2.0
Total	14	134	116	.536	342	309	63	16	172	3	0	20	2123.2	2082	992	188	87	721	39	1330	3.80	+8	.257	.323	-1	132	9.9
Team	3	39	22	.639	83	82	8	3	49	0	0	1	528.2	527	223	38	23	166	11	344	3.49	+18	.261	.323	+10		4.2
/180I	1	13	7	.639	28	28	3	1	17	0	0	0	180	179	76	13	8	57	4	117	3.49	+18	.261	.323	+10		1.4
BOERNER, LARRY Lawrence Hyer B1.21.1905 Staunton VA D10.16.1969 Staunton VA BR/TR/6'4.5"/175 d6.30 Col McDaniel																											
1932	Bos A	0	4	.000	21	5	0	0		0			61	71	41	2	3	37		19	5.02	-10	.302	.404	-39		-0.4
BOLIN, BOBBY Bobby Donald B1.29.1939 Hickory Grove SC BR/TR/6'4"/(200–212) d4.18																											
1970	Bos A	2	0	1.000	6	0	0	0	0	2	0	6	8	2	0	0	1	5	2	8	0.00	-100	.080	.250		0	0.7
1971	Bos A	5	3	.625	52	0	0	0	0	6	3	30	69.2	74	34	7	0	24	4	51	4.26	-13	.273	.329		0	-0.4
1972	Bos A	0	1	.000	21	0	0	0	0	5	1	11	30.2	24	11	3	1	11	1	27	2.93	+10	.209	.283		0	0.1
1973	Bos A	3	4	.429	39	0	0	0	0	15	5	27	53.1	45	16	5	1	13	2	31	2.70	+49	.232	.282		0	1.6
Total	13	88	75	.540	495	164	32	10	90	50	9	228	1576	1364	687	164	60	597	71	1175	3.40	+3	.231	.306	+3	15	3.3
Team	4	10	8	.556	118	0	0	0	0	28	9	74	161.2	145	61	15	3	53	9	117	3.28	+14	.240	.302			2.0
/60G	2	5	4	.556	60	0	0	0	0	14	5	38	82.1	74	31	8	2	27	5	59	3.28	+14	.240	.302			1.0
BOLTON, TOM Thomas Edward B5.6.1962 Nashville TN BL/TL/6'3"/(175–185) [BosA80 20/518] d5.17																											
1987	Bos A	1	0	1.000	29	0	0	0	0	0	0	15	61.2	83	33	5	2	27	2	49	4.38	+4	.329	.394		0	0.1
1988	Bos A	1	3	.250	28	0	0	0	0	1	0	15	30.1	35	17	1	0	14	1	21	4.75	-13	.285	.355		0	-0.2
1989	Bos A	0	4	.000	4	4	0	0	1	0	0	0	17.1	21	18	1	0	10	1	9	8.31	-50	.292	.373	-67	0	-1.3
1990	†Bos A	10	5	.667	21	16	3	0	11	0	0	4	119.2	111	46	6	3	47	3	65	3.38	+21	.251	.323	-3	0	1.3
1991	Bos A	8	9	.471	25	19	0	0	6	0	0	5	110	136	72	16	1	51	2	64	5.24	-17	.308	.378	-13	22	-1.5
1992	Bos A	1	2	.333	21	1	0	0	0	0	0	14	29	34	11	0	2	14	1	23	3.41	+25	.286	.370	-79	0	0.3
1992	Cin N	3	3	.500	16	8	0	0	1	0	0	3	46.1	52	28	9	2	23	2	27	5.24	-31	.284	.368	+13	0	-1.0
1992	Major	4	5	.444	37	9	0	0	1	0	0	17	75	86	39	9	4	37	3	50	4.54	-9	.285	.369	+3	0	-0.7
1993	Det A	6	6	.500	43	8	0	0	4	0	0	18	102.2	113	57	5	7	45	10	66	4.47	-3	.282	.363	+27	0	-0.1
1994	Bal A	1	2	.333	22	0	0	0	0	0	0	14	23.1	29	15	3	0	13	1	12	5.40	-6	.309	.389		0	-0.1
Total	8	31	34	.477	209	56	3	0	23	1	0	88	540.1	614	297	46	17	244	23	336	4.56	-7	.289	.364	-8	22	-2.5
Team	6	21	23	.477	128	40	3	0	18	1	0	53	368	420	197	29	8	163	10	231	4.45	-4	.290	.361	-16	22	-1.3
/60G	3	10	11	.477	60	19	1	0	8	0	0	25	172.2	197	92	14	4	76	5	108	4.45	-4	.290	.361	-16	10	-0.6

Year	Tm Lg	W	L	Pct	G	GS	CG	ShO	QS	SV	BS	QR	IP	H	R	HR	HB	BB	IB	SO	ERA	AERA	OAV	OOB	Sup	DL	PW
BORLAND, TOM Thomas Bruce "Spike" B2.14.1933 ElDorado KS BL/TL/6'3"/175 d5.15 Col Oklahoma St.																											
1960	Bos A	0	4	.000	26	4	0	0	0	3		13	51	67	40	4	0	23	4	32	6.53	-38	.322	.388	+25	0	-1.2
1961	Bos A	0	0	+	1	0	0	0	0	0		0	1	3	2	0	0	0	0	0	18.00	-77	.500	.500		0	-0.1
Total	2	0	4	.000	27	4	0	0	0	3		13	52	70	42	4	0	23	4	32	6.75	-40	.327	.391	+25	0	-1.3
BORLAND, TOBY Toby Shawn B5.29.1969 Ruston LA BR/TR/6'6"/(186–215) [PhiN87 27/702] d5.27																											
1997	Bos A	0	0	+	3	0	0	0	0	0	0	1	3.1	6	5	1	2	7	0	1	13.50	-66	.400	.625		0	-0.1
Total	9	11	9	.550	207	0	0	0	0	8	8	143	269.2	263	144	23	18	146	19	211	4.17	+2	.254	.354		161	-0.6
BOWERS, STEW Stewart Cole "Doc" B2.26.1915 New Freedom PA D12.14.2005 Havertown PA BB/TR/6'0"/170 d8.5 Col Gettysburg																											
1935	Bos A	2	1	.667	10	2	1	0		0			23.2	26	14	1	0	17		5	3.42	+39	.283	.394	-54		0.2
1936	Bos A	0	0	+	5	0	0	0		0			5.2	10	7	1	0	2		0	9.53	-44	.370	.414			-0.1
Total	2	2	1	.667	15	2	1	0		0			29.1	36	21	2	0	19		5	4.60	+6	.303	.399	-54		0.1
BOWMAN, JOE Joseph Emil B6.17.1910 Kansas City KS D11.22.1990 Kansas City MO BL/TR/6'2"/190 d4.18																											
1944	Bos A	12	8	.600	26	24	10	1		0			168.1	175	95	14	2	64		53	4.81	-29	.269	.336	+38	0	-2.3
1945	Bos A	0	2	.000	3	3	0	0		0			11.2	18	12	1	0	9		0	9.26	-63	.360	.458	-8	0	-0.9
Total	11	77	96	.445	298	184	74	5		11			1465.2	1656	837	102	41	484		502	4.40	-11	.282	.341	+8	0	-6.1
Team	2	12	10	.545	29	27	10	1		0			180	193	107	15	2	73		53	5.10	-33	.275	.345	+33		-3.2
/180I	2	12	10	.545	29	27	10	1		0			180	193	107	15	2	73		53	5.10	-33	.275	.345	+33		-3.2
BOWSFIELD, TED Edward Oliver B1.10.1935 Vernon BC, Can. BR/TL/6'1"/190 d7.20																											
1958	Bos A	4	2	.667	16	10	2	0	4	0		6	65.2	58	32	3	1	36	1	38	3.84	+4	.233	.331	+21	0	0.0
1959	Bos A	0	1	.000	5	2	0	0	4	0		6	9	16	15	2	0	9	0	4	15.00	-73	.390	.500	+52	0	-0.9
1960	Bos A	1	2	.333	17	2	0	0	1	2		10	21	20	12	1	1	13	0	18	5.14	-21	.260	.366	+63	0	-0.2
Total	7	37	39	.487	215	86	12	4	41	6		90	662.1	699	369	63	12	259	14	326	4.35	-7	.270	.336	-1	0	-3.3
Team	3	5	5	.500	38	14	2	0	9	2		22	95.2	94	59	6	2	58	1	60	5.17	-22	.256	.358	+31		-1.1
BOYD, OIL CAN Dennis Ray B10.6.1959 Meridian MS BR/TR/6'1"/(144–160) [BosA80 16/414] d9.13 Col Jackson St.																											
1982	Bos A	0	1	.000	3	1	0	0	0	0	1	0	8.1	11	5	2	0	2	0	2	5.40	-19	.314	.351	-79	0	-0.1
1983	Bos A	4	8	.333	15	13	5	0	9	0	0	1	98.2	103	46	9	1	23	0	43	3.28	+34	.269	.308	-19	0	0.9
1984	Bos A	12	12	.500	29	26	10	3	15	0	0	0	197.2	207	109	18	1	53	5	134	4.37	-4	.269	.314	+8	0	-0.3
1985	Bos A	15	13	.536	35	35	13	3	22	0	0	0	272.1	273	117	26	4	67	3	154	3.70	+17	.261	.306	+7	0	2.1
1986	†Bos A	16	10	.615	30	30	10	0	19	0	0	0	214.1	222	99	32	2	45	1	129	3.78	+11	.265	.302	+19	0	1.2
1987	Bos A	1	3	.250	7	7	0	0	1	0	0	0	36.2	47	31	6	2	9	1	12	5.89	-22	.315	.356	+8	143	-0.6
1988	Bos A	9	7	.563	23	23	1	0	12	0	0	0	129.2	147	82	25	2	41	2	71	5.34	-23	.289	.341	+12	57	-1.7
1989	Bos A	3	2	.600	10	10	0	0	3	0	0	0	59	57	31	8	0	19	0	26	4.42	-7	.253	.309	+28	122	-0.1
1990	Mon N	10	6	.625	31	31	3	3	22	0	0	0	190.2	164	64	19	3	52	10	113	2.93	+26	.233	.287	+10	0	0.9
1991	Mon N	6	8	.429	19	19	1	1	10	0	0	0	120.1	115	49	9	0	40	2	82	3.52	+4	.256	.314	-6	0	0.2
1991	Tex A	2	7	.222	12	12	0	0	3	0	0	0	62	81	47	12	0	17	1	33	6.68	-39	.314	.356	-32	0	-2.0
1991	Major	8	15	.348	31	31	1	1	13	0	0	0	182	196	96	21	0	57	3	115	4.59	-11	.277	.329	-16	0	-1.8
Total	10	78	77	.503	214	207	43	10	116	0	1	1	1389.2	1427	680	166	15	368	25	799	4.04	+2	.266	.313	+5	322	0.5
Team	8	60	56	.517	152	145	39	6	81	0	1	1	1016.2	1067	520	126	12	259	12	571	4.15	+2	.270	.314	+9	322	1.4
/180I	1	11	10	.517	27	26	7	1	14	0	0	0	180	189	92	22	2	46	2	101	4.15	+2	.270	.314	+9	57	0.2
BRADFORD, CHAD Chadwick Lee B9.14.1974 Jackson MS BR/TR/6'5"/205 [ChiA96 13/377] d8.1 Col Southern Mississippi [DL 2005 Oak A 86]																											
2005	†Bos A	2	1	.667	31	0	0	0	0	0	1	19	23.1	29	10	1	3	4	1	10	3.86	+18	.312	.356		0	0.2
Total	9	27	18	.600	395	0	0	0	0	9	16	286	381.1	369	161	23	21	104	29	261	3.40	+34	.255	.312		101	5.0
BRADLEY, HERB Herbert Theodore B1.3.1903 Agenda KS D10.16.1959 Clay Center KS BR/TR/6'0"/170 d5.9 Col Kansas																											
1927	Bos A	1	1	.500	6	2	2	0		0			23	16	9	0	2	7		6	3.13	+35	.198	.278	-31		0.3
1928	Bos A	0	3	.000	15	5	1	1		0			47.1	64	41	2	2	16		14	7.23	-43	.339	.396	-26		-0.8
1929	Bos A	0	0	+	3	0	0	0		0			4	7	3	1	0	2		0	6.75	-37	.438	.500			0.0
Total	3	1	4	.200	24	7	3	1		0			74.1	87	53	3	4	25		20	5.93	-30	.304	.368	-28		-0.5
BRADY, KING James Ward B5.28.1881 Elmer NJ D8.21.1947 Albany NY BR/TR/6'0"/190 d9.21																											
1908	Bos A	1	0	1.000	1	1	1	1		0			9	8	0	0	0	0		3	0.00	-100	.242	.242	+11		0.3
Total	5	3	2	.600	8	5	4	1		0			49.2	64	21	0	0	10		20	3.08	-11	.306	.338	+5		0.0
BRANDENBURG, MARK Mark Clay B7.14.1970 Houston TX BR/TR/6'0"/180 [TexA92 26/734] d7.20 Col Texas Tech [DL 1998 Tex A 181]																											
1995	Tex A	0	1	.000	11	0	0	0	0	0	0	5	27.1	36	18	5	1	7	1	21	5.93	-18	.316	.358		0	-0.1
1996	Tex A	1	3	.250	26	0	0	0	0	0	1	18	47.2	48	22	3	2	25	1	37	3.21	+64	.262	.354		0	0.6
1996	Bos A	4	2	.667	29	0	0	0	0	0	1	21	28.1	28	13	5	1	8	1	29	3.81	+34	.250	.301		0	0.8
1996	Year	5	5	.500	55	0	0	0	0	0	2	39	76	76	35	8	3	33	2	66	3.43	+51	.258	.334		0	1.4
1997	Bos A	0	2	.000	31	0	0	0	0	0	0	20	41	49	25	3	2	16	3	34	5.49	-15	.299	.364		62	-0.1
Total	3	5	8	.385	97	0	0	0	0	0	2	64	144.1	161	78	16	6	56	6	121	4.49	+11	.281	.347		243	1.2
Team	2	4	4	.500	60	0	0	0	0	0	1	41	69.1	77	38	8	3	24	4	63	4.80	+1	.279	.339		62	0.7
/60G	2	4	4	.500	60	0	0	0	0	0	1	41	69.1	77	38	8	3	24	4	63	4.80	+1	.279	.339		62	0.7
BRANDON, BUCKY Darrell G B7.8.1940 Nacogdoches TX BR/TR/6'2"/200 d4.19																											
1966	Bos A	8	8	.500	40	17	5	2	12	2		16	157.2	129	70	13	4	70	3	101	3.31	+15	.222	.309	-2	0	0.8
1967	Bos A	5	11	.313	39	19	2	0	8	3		15	157.2	147	86	21	7	59	7	96	4.17	-16	.245	.318	-4	0	-1.2
1968	Bos A	0	0	+	8	0	0	0	0	0		3	12.2	19	11	1	1	9	0	10	6.39	-51	.333	.433		0	-0.3
1969	Sea A	0	1	.000	8	1	0	0	0	0	0	4	15	15	15	4	2	16	1	10	8.40	-57	.250	.423	+70	0	-0.5
1969	Min A	0	0	+	3	0	0	0	0	0	0	2	3.1	5	3	1	0	3	2	1	2.70	+35	.357	.471		0	0.0
1969	Year	0	1	.000	11	1	0	0	0	0	0	6	18.1	20	18	5	2	19	3	11	7.36	-51	.270	.432	+70	0	-0.5
1971	Phi N	6	6	.500	52	0	0	0	0	4	4	31	83	81	42	5	0	47	9	44	3.90	-9	.264	.357		0	-0.6
1972	Phi N	7	7	.500	42	6	0	0	3	2	2	29	104.1	106	49	9	6	46	8	67	3.45	+5	.268	.352	-2	0	-0.2
1973	Phi N	2	4	.333	36	0	0	0	0	2	0	26	56.1	54	35	5	3	25	7	25	5.43	-30	.261	.343		0	-0.9
Total	7	28	37	.431	228	43	7	2	23	13	6	126	590	556	311	59	23	275	37	354	4.04	-10	.250	.337	-1	0	-2.9
Team	3	13	19	.406	87	36	7	2	20	5		34	328	295	167	35	12	138	10	207	3.84	-6	.238	.319	-3		-0.7
/180I	2	7	10	.406	48	20	4	1	11	3		19	180	162	92	19	7	76	5	114	3.84	-6	.238	.319	-3		-0.4
BRESLOW, CRAIG Craig Andrew B8.8.1980 New Haven CT BL/TL/6'1"/180 [MilN02 26/769] d7.23 Col Yale																											
2005	SD N	0	0	+	14	0	0	0	0	0	0	12	16.1	15	6	1	1	13	0	14	2.20	+78	.238	.372		0	0.1
2006	Bos A	0	2	.000	13	0	0	0	0	0	0	7	12	12	5	0	1	6	1	12	3.75	+25	.261	.345		0	0.2
Total	2	0	2	.000	27	0	0	0	0	0	0	19	28.1	27	11	1	2	19	1	26	2.86	+48	.248	.361		0	0.3
BRETT, KEN Kenneth Alven B9.18.1948 Brooklyn NY D11.18.2003 Spokane WA BL/TL/5'11"/(180–195) [BosA66 1/4] d9.27 b–George																											
1967	†Bos A	0	0	+	1	0	0	0	0	0		1	2	3	1	0	0	0	0	2	4.50	-23	.375	.375		0	0.0
1969	Bos A	2	3	.400	8	8	0	0	4	0	0	0	39.1	41	24	6	3	22	1	23	5.26	-27	.275	.377	+1	0	-0.4
1970	Bos A	8	9	.471	41	14	1	0	8	2	0	18	139.1	118	71	17	3	79	6	155	4.07	-2	.223	.327	+1	0	0.6
1971	Bos A	0	3	.000	29	2	0	0	0	1	0	20	59	57	38	7	1	35	6	57	5.34	-30	.253	.356	-64	0	-0.5
Total	14	83	85	.494	349	184	51	8	107	11	3	111	1526.1	1490	734	127	23	562	62	807	3.93	-6	.257	.323	+7	54	0.5
Team	4	10	15	.400	79	24	1	0	12	3	0	39	239.2	219	134	30	7	136	13	237	4.58	-15	.240	.343	-4		-0.3
/180I	3	8	11	.400	59	18	1	0	9	2	0	29	180	164	101	23	5	102	10	178	4.58	-15	.240	.343	-4		-0.2
BREWER, TOM Thomas Austin B9.3.1931 Wadesboro NC BR/TR/6'1"/175 d4.18 Col Elon																											
1954	Bos A	10	9	.526	33	23	7	0		0			162.2	152	90	15	7	95		69	4.65	-12	.249	.355	+23	0	-0.5
1955	Bos A	11	10	.524	31	28	9	2		0			192.2	198	101	21	8	87	3	91	4.20	+2	.263	.344	+21	0	0.2
1956	Bos A★	19	9	.679	32	32	15	4		0			244.1	200	103	14	5	112	6	127	3.50	+32	.220	.307	-2	0	3.9
1957	Bos A	16	13	.552	32	32	15	2	61	0		4	238.1	225	113	24	7	93	9	128	3.85	+3	.250	.324	+19	0	0.6
1958	Bos A	12	12	.500	33	32	10	1	60	0		4	227.1	227	122	21	8	93	2	124	3.72	+8	.259	.333	+11	0	0.3
1959	Bos A	10	12	.455	36	32	11	3	60	2		4	215.1	219	96	14	2	88	5	121	3.76	+8	.265	.336	+3	0	0.6
1960	Bos A	10	15	.400	34	29	8	1	13	1		3	186.2	220	115	13	6	72	5	60	4.82	-16	.301	.364	-8	0	-1.9
1961	Bos A	3	2	.600	10	9	0	0	3	0		1	42	37	21	4	0	29	0	13	3.43	+22	.242	.357	-15	90	0.4
Total	8	91	82	.526	241	217	75	13	197	3		16	1509.1	1478	761	126	43	669	30	733	4.00	+4	.257	.337	+8	90	3.6
/180I	1	11	10	.526	29	26	9	2	0	0	0	0	180	176	91	15	5	80	0	87	4.00	+4	.257	.337	-87	11	0.4

Year	Tm Lg	W	L	Pct	G	GS	CG	ShO	QS	SV	BS	QR	IP	H	R	HR	HB	BB	IB	SO	ERA	AERA	OAV	OOB	Sup	DL	PW
BRICKNER, RALPH Ralph Harold "Brick" B5.2.1925 Cincinnati OH D5.9.1994 Port Jefferson NY BR/TR/6'3.5"/215 d5.4 Col Indiana																											
1952	Bos A	3	1	.750	14	1	0	0		1			33	32	8	1	0	11		9	2.18	+81	.264	.326	-56	0	0.8
BRILLHEART, JIM James Benson B9.28.1903 Dublin VA D9.2.1972 Radford VA BR/TL/5'11"/170 d4.17 Col Roanoke																											
1931	Bos A	0	0	+	11	1	0	0		0			19.2	27	16	2	0	15		7	5.49	-22	.325	.429	-21		0.0
Total	4	8	9	.471	86	23	7	0		1			286	314	156	10	13	137		98	4.19	-7	.290	.376	+17		-1.2
BRODOWSKI, DICK Richard Stanley B7.26.1932 Bayonne NJ BR/TR/6'2"/(190–195) d6.15 Mil 1953–54																											
1952	Bos A	5	5	.500	20	12	4	0		0			114.2	111	66	12	3	50		42	4.40	-10	.252	.333	+24	0	-0.4
1955	Bos A	1	0	1.000	16	0	0	0		0			32	36	25	5	1	25	2	10	5.63	-24	.295	.416		0	0.0
1956	Was A	0	3	.000	7	3	1	0		0			17.2	31	18	5	0	12	0	8	9.17	-53	.397	.473	-52	0	-1.2
1957	Was A	0	1	.000	6	0	0	0	0	0		2	11.1	12	15	2	1	10	0	4	11.12	-65	.261	.404		0	-0.7
1958	Cle A	1	0	1.000	5	0	0	0	0	0		20	10	3	0	0	0	6	0	12	0.00	-100	.100	.250		0	0.4
1959	Cle A	2	2	.500	18	0	0	0	0	5		18	30	19	13	3	3	21	1	9	1.80	+105	.181	.328		0	0.6
Total	6	9	11	.450	72	15	5	0	0	5		40	215.2	212	137	27	8	124	3	85	4.76	-16	.258	.359	+9	0	-1.3
Team	2	6	5	.545	36	12	4	0		0			146.2	147	91	17	4	75	2	52	4.66	-14	.262	.353	+24		-0.4
/180I	2	7	6	.545	44	15	5	0		0			180	180	112	21	5	92	2	64	4.66	-14	.262	.353	+24		-0.5
BROWN, HAL Hector Harold "Skinny" B12.11.1924 Greensboro NC BR/TR/6'2"/(181–185) d4.19 C1 Col North Carolina																											
1953	Bos A	11	6	.647	30	25	6	1		0			166.1	177	94	16	0	57		62	4.65	-10	.269	.327	-11	0	-0.1
1954	Bos A	1	8	.111	40	5	1	0		0			118	126	64	6	3	41		66	4.12	+0	.269	.329	-18	0	-0.1
1955	Bos A	1	0	1.000	2	0	0	0		0			4	2	1	0	0	2	0	2	2.25	+91	.143	.250		0	0.2
Total	14	85	92	.480	358	211	47	13	159	11		70	1680	1677	781	173	14	389	27	710	3.81	-2	.260	.302	-12	45	0.6
Team	3	13	14	.481	72	30	7	1		0			288.1	305	159	22	3	100	0	130	4.40	-5	.268	.327	-12		0.0
/180I	2	8	9	.481	45	19	4	1		0			180	190	99	14	2	62	0	81	4.40	-5	.268	.327	-12		0.0
BROWN, JAMIE Jamie Monroe B3.31.1977 Meridian MS BR/TR/6'2"/200 [CleA96 21/633] d5.20 Col Meridian (MS) CC [DL 2000 Cle A 27]																											
2004	Bos A	0	0	+	4	0	0	0	0	0	0	3	7.2	15	7	1	0	4	0	6	5.87	-17	.417	.463		0	-0.1
BROWN, LLOYD Lloyd Andrew "Gimpy" B12.25.1904 Beeville TX D1.14.1974 Opa–Locka FL BL/TL/5'9"/170 d7.17																											
1933	Bos A	8	11	.421	33	21	9	2		1			163.1	180	93	4	0	64		37	4.02	+9	.281	.347	-15		1.2
Total	12	91	105	.464	404	181	77	10		21			1693	1899	937	83	22	590		510	4.20	+5	.288	.348	-12		5.2
/180I	1	9	12	.421	36	23	10	2		1			180	198	102	4	0	71		41	4.02	+9	.281	.347	-6		1.3
BROWN, MACE Mace Stanley B5.21.1909 North English IA D3.24.2002 Greensboro NC BR/TR/6'1"/190 d5.21 Mil 1944–45 C1 Col Iowa																											
1942	Bos A	9	3	.750	34	0	0	0		6			60.1	56	27	4	0	28		20	3.43	+9	.255	.339		0	0.3
1943	Bos A	6	6	.500	**49**	0	0	0		9			93.1	71	26	2	0	51		40	2.12	+56	.222	.329		0	1.6
1946	†Bos A	3	1	.750	18	0	0	0		1			26.1	26	7	2	0	16		10	2.05	+79	.268	.372		0	0.7
Total	10	76	57	.571	387	55	18	2		48			1075.1	1125	502	44	7	388		435	3.46	+10	.271	.335	+10	0	3.8
Team	3	18	10	.643	101	0	0	0		16			180	153	60	8	0	95		70	2.55	+37	.240	.339			2.6
/60G	2	11	6	.643	60	0	0	0		10			107	91	36	5	0	56		42	2.55	+37	.240	.339			1.5
BROWN, MIKE Michael Gary B3.4.1959 Camden Co. NJ BR/TR/6'2"/(195–205) [BosA80 2/48] d9.16 C1 Col Clemson																											
1982	Bos A	1	0	1.000	3	0	0	0	0	0	0	3	6	7	0	0	0	1	0	4	0.00	-100	.304	.333		0	0.4
1983	Bos A	6	6	.500	19	18	3	1	9	0	0	1	104	110	62	12	2	43	1	35	4.67	-6	.276	.345	+34	22	-0.4
1984	Bos A	1	8	.111	15	11	0	0	1	0	0	1	67	104	63	9	3	19	1	32	6.85	-39	.347	.388	-24	0	-2.3
1985	Bos A	0	0	+	2	1	0	0	0	0	0	0	3.1	9	8	0	0	3	0	3	21.60	-80	.500	.545	+26	0	-0.3
1986	Bos A	4	4	.500	15	10	0	0	4	0	0	2	57.1	72	35	10	1	25	1	32	5.34	-21	.316	.381	-16	0	-0.7
1986	Sea A	0	2	.000	6	2	0	0	1	0	0	2	15.2	19	14	4	0	11	0	9	7.47	-43	.302	.405	-100	0	-0.6
1986	Year	4	6	.400	21	12	0	0	5	0	0	4	73	91	49	14	1	36	1	41	5.79	-27	.313	.387	-30	0	-1.3
1987	Sea A	0	0	+	1	0	0	0	0	0	0	0	0.1	3	2	0	0	0	0	0	54.00	-91	.750	.750		0	-0.1
Total	6	12	20	.375	61	42	3	1	15	0	0	9	253.2	324	184	35	6	102	3	115	5.75	-25	.313	.374	+1	22	-4.0
Team	5	12	18	.400	54	40	3	1	14	0	0	7	237.2	302	168	31	6	91	3	106	5.57	-23	.312	.370	+5	22	-3.3
/180I	4	9	14	.400	41	30	2	1	11	0	0	5	180	229	127	23	5	69	2	80	5.57	-23	.312	.370	+5	17	-2.5
BULLINGER, KIRK Kirk Matthew B10.28.1969 New Orleans LA BR/TR/6'2"/170 [StLN92 32/895] d8.30 b–Jim Col Southeastern Louisiana																											
1999	Bos A	0	0	+	4	0	0	0	0	0	0	4	2	2	1	0	0	2	0	0	4.50	+11	.286	.444		0	0.0
Total	5	2	0	1.000	49	0	0	0	0	1	2	31	51	63	39	8	1	13	2	22	6.53	-33	.296	.336		69	-0.8
BURCHELL, FRED Frederick Duff B7.14.1879 Perth Amboy NJ D11.20.1951 Jordan NY BR/TL/5'11"/175 d4.17																											
1903	Phi N	0	3	.000	6	3	2	0		0			44	48	28	0	2	14		12	2.86	+14	.293	.356	-93		-0.1
1907	Bos A	0	1	.000	2	1	0	0		0			10	8	5	0	1	2		6	2.70	-5	.222	.282	+31		-0.1
1908	Bos A	10	8	.556	31	19	9	0		0			179.2	161	84	2	11	65		94	2.96	-17	.247	.326	+33		-0.9
1909	Bos A	3	3	.500	10	5	1	0		0			52	51	22	1	2	11		12	2.94	-15	.271	.318	+2		-0.2
Total	4	13	15	.464	49	28	12	0		0			285.2	268	139	3	16	92		124	2.93	-11	.258	.328	+8		-1.3
Team	3	13	12	.520	43	25	10	0		0			241.2	220	111	3	14	78		112	2.94	-16	.251	.323	+27		-1.2
/180I	2	10	9	.520	32	19	7	0		0			180	164	83	2	10	58		83	2.94	-16	.251	.323	+27		-0.9
BURGMEIER, TOM Thomas Henry B8.2.1943 St.Paul MN BL/TL/5'11"/(180–187) d4.10 C4																											
1978	Bos A	2	1	.667	35	1	0	0	0	4	2	22	61.1	74	33	7	3	23	1	24	4.40	-6	.302	.368	-13	0	0.0
1979	Bos A	3	2	.600	44	0	0	0	0	4	3	27	88.2	89	32	8	4	16	4	60	2.74	+63	.263	.302		0	0.9
1980	Bos A☆	5	4	.556	62	0	0	0	0	24	2	47	99	87	30	3	2	20	3	54	2.00	+113	.241	.283		0	3.1
1981	Bos A	4	5	.444	32	0	0	0	0	6	1	22	59.2	61	23	5	4	17	4	35	2.87	+37	.268	.329		0	1.1
1982	Bos A	7	0	1.000	40	0	0	0	0	2	2	32	102.1	98	30	6	2	22	7	44	2.29	+91	.259	.300		0	1.6
Total	17	79	55	.590	745	3	0	0	0	102	34	506	1258.2	1231	521	94	32	384	55	584	3.23	+18	.261	.318	-30	97	11.5
Team	5	21	12	.636	213	1	0	0	0	40	10	150	411	409	148	29	15	98	19	217	2.72	+57	.264	.312	-13		6.7
/60G	1	6	3	.636	60	0	0	0	0	11	3	42	115.2	115	42	8	4	28	5	61	2.72	+57	.264	.312			1.9
BURKETT, JOHN John David B11.28.1964 New Brighton PA BR/TR/6'2"/(175–215) [SFN83 6/148] d9.15																											
2002	Bos A	13	8	.619	29	29	1	1	15	0	0	0	173	199	93	25	8	50	5	124	4.53	-1	.287	.340	+21	20	-0.1
2003	†Bos A	12	9	.571	32	30	1	0	15	0	0	1	181.2	202	108	20	9	47	1	107	5.15	-10	.281	.330	+9	0	-0.7
Total	15	166	136	.550	445	423	21	6	221	1	1	16	2648.1	2866	1374	257	90	700	59	1766	4.31	-1	.277	.326	+4	64	-2.8
Team	2	25	17	.595	61	59	2	1	30	0	0	1	354.2	401	201	45	17	97	6	231	4.85	-6	.284	.335	+15	20	-0.8
/180I	1	13	9	.595	31	30	1	1	15	0	0	1	180	204	102	23	9	49	3	117	4.85	-6	.284	.335	+15	10	-0.4
BURNS, MIKE Michael John B7.14.1978 Westminster CA BR/TR/6'0"/(205–210) [HouN00 30/907] d5.13 Col Cal St.–Los Angeles																											
2006	Bos A	0	0	+	7	0	0	0	0	0	0	4	7.2	10	4	0	0	1	1	7	4.70	+0	.323	.324		0	0.0
Total	2	0	0	+	45	0	0	0	0	0	0	27	52	69	35	8	7	12	3	36	5.88	-25	.318	.370		0	-0.3
BURTON, JIM Jim Scott B10.27.1949 Royal Oak MI BR/TL/6'3"/195 [BosA71 D1/5] d6.10 Col Michigan																											
1975	†Bos A	1	2	.333	29	4	0	0	1	1	1	19	53	58	30	6	0	19	2	39	2.89	+41	.276	.333	-13	0	0.1
1977	Bos A	0	0	+	1	0	0	0	0	0	0	1	2.2	2	0	0	0	1	0	3	0.00	-100	.200	.273		0	0.1
Total	2	1	2	.333	30	4	0	0	1	1	1	20	55.2	60	30	6	0	20	2	42	2.75	+49	.273	.331	-13	0	0.2
BUSH, JOE Leslie Ambrose "Bullet Joe" B11.27.1892 Brainerd MN D11.1.1974 Ft.Lauderdale FL BR/TR/5'9"/173 d9.30																											
1918	†Bos A	15	15	.500	36	31	26	7		2			272.2	241	88	3	3	91		125	2.11	+27	.242	.307	-20		2.8
1919	Bos A	0	0	+	3	2	0	0		0			9	11	5	0	0	4		3	5.00	-40	.324	.395	+95		0.0
1920	Bos A	15	15	.500	35	32	18	0		1			243.2	287	138	3	10	94		88	4.25	-14	.300	.369	-5		-1.6
1921	Bos A	16	9	.640	37	32	21	3		1			254.1	244	111	10	6	93		96	3.50	+21	.260	.330	+7		2.8
Total	17	196	184	.516	489	370	225	35		19			3087.1	2992	1441	96	63	1263		1319	3.51	-1	.260	.336	-2		6.7
Team	4	46	39	.541	111	97	65	10		4			779.2	783	342	16	19	282		312	3.27	+7	.268	.336	-4		4.0
/180I	1	11	9	.541	26	22	15	2		1			180	181	79	4	4	65		72	3.27	+7	.268	.336	-4		0.9
BUSHELMAN, JACK John Francis B8.29.1885 Cincinnati OH D10.26.1955 Roanoke VA BR/TR/6'2"/175 d10.5 Col Cincinnati																											
1909	Cin N	0	1	.000	1	1	1	0		0			7	7	7	1	0	4		3	2.57	+1	.241	.333	+8		-0.2
1911	Bos A	0	1	.000	3	1	1	0		0			12	8	9	0	1	10		5	3.00	+9	.186	.352	-78		-0.1
1912	Bos A	1	0	1.000	3	0	0	0		0			7.2	9	4	0	0	5		5	4.70	-28	.310	.412			-0.1
Total	3	1	2	.333	7	2	2	0		0			26.2	24	20	1	1	19		13	3.38	-7	.238	.364	-43		-0.4
Team	2	1	1	.500	6	1	1	0		0			19.2	17	13	0	1	15		10	3.66	-9	.236	.375	-78		-0.2

Year	Tm Lg	W	L	Pct	G	GS	CG	ShO	QS	SV	BS	QR	IP	H	R	HR	HB	BB	IB	SO	ERA	AERA	OAV	OOB	Sup	DL	PW
BUSHEY, FRANK Francis Clyde B8.1.1906 Wheaton KS D3.18.1972 Topeka KS BR/TR/6'0"/180 d9.17																											
1927	Bos A	0	0	+	1	0	0	0		0			1.1	2	1	0	0	2		0	6.75	-37	.500	.667			0.0
1930	Bos A	0	1	.000	11	0	0	0		0			30	34	22	1	2	15		4	6.30	-27	.306	.398			-0.3
Total	2	0	1	.000	12	0	0	0		0			31.1	36	23	1	2	17		4	6.32	-27	.313	.410			-0.3
BUTLAND, BILL Wilburn Rue B3.22.1918 Terre Haute IN D9.19.1997 Terre Haute IN BR/TR/6'5"/185 d5.29 Mil 1943–45																											
1940	Bos A	1	2	.333	3	3	1	0		0			21	27	13	0	0	10		5	5.57	-19	.307	.378	-41		-0.3
1942	Bos A	7	1	.875	23	10	6	2		1			111.1	85	35	8	3	33		46	2.51	+49	.206	.270	+26	0	1.0
1946	Bos A	1	0	1.000	5	2	0	0		0			16.1	23	20	3	0	13		10	11.02	-67	.343	.450	+64	0	-0.6
1947	Bos A	0	0	+	1	0	0	0		0			2	3	1	0	0	0		1	4.50	-14	.333	.333		0	0.0
Total	4	9	3	.750	32	15	7	2		1			150.2	138	69	11	3	56		62	3.88	-1	.240	.310	+17	0	0.1
/180I	5	11	4	.750	38	18	8	2	0	1	0	0	180	165	82	13	4	67		74	3.88	-1	.240	.310	+40		0.1
BYERLY, BUD Eldred William B10.26.1920 Webster Groves MO BR/TR/6'2.5"/185 d9.26																											
1958	Bos A	1	2	.333	18	0	0	0	0	0		12	30.1	31	12	1	1	7	3	16	1.78	+125	.272	.312		0	0.4
Total	11	22	22	.500	237	17	4	0	0	14		109	491.2	519	242	34	9	167	14	209	3.70	+5	.273	.333	+12	0	0.5
CALDWELL, EARL Earl Welton "Teach" B4.9.1905 Sparks TX D9.15.1981 Mission TX BR/TR/6'1"/178 d9.8																											
1948	Bos A	1	1	.500	8	0	0	0		0			9	11	14	2	1	11		5	13.00	-66	.333	.511		0	-1.5
Total	8	33	43	.434	200	49	18	5		25			587.2	656	347	44	25	259		202	4.69	-8	.284	.363	-13	0	-1.2
CALDWELL, RAY Raymond Benjamin "Rube","Sum" B4.26.1888 Corydon PA D8.17.1967 Salamanca NY BL/TR/6'2"/190 d9.9▲																											
1919	Bos A	7	4	.636	18	12	6	1		0			86.1	92	49	1	3	31		23	3.96	-24	.279	.346	+15		-1.1
Total	12	134	120	.528	343	259	184	21		8			2242	2089	972	59	63	738		1006	3.22	-1	.253	.319	+5		6.1
CAMPBELL, BILL William Richard B8.9.1948 Highland Park MI BR/TR/6'3"/(190–200) d7.14 C1 Col Mt. San Antonio (CA) JC																											
1977	Bos A★	13	9	.591	69	0	0	0	0	**31**	11	52	140	112	48	13	5	60	10	114	2.96	+52	.224	.311		0	**4.5**
1978	Bos A	7	5	.583	29	0	0	0	0	4	11	17	50.2	62	25	3	0	17	3	47	3.91	+5	.308	.362		0	0.3
1979	Bos A	3	4	.429	41	0	0	0	0	9	8	26	54.2	55	28	5	1	23	6	25	4.28	+4	.262	.338		0	0.3
1980	Bos A	4	0	1.000	23	0	0	0	0	0	0	14	41.1	44	26	1	0	22	0	17	4.79	-11	.284	.367		72	-0.3
1981	Bos A	1	1	.500	30	0	0	0	0	7	0	21	48.1	45	23	5	0	20	4	37	3.17	+24	.245	.316		0	0.2
Total	15	83	68	.550	700	9	2	1	3	126	72	480	1229.1	1139	550	82	20	495	10	864	3.54	+10	.248	.321	+34	104	9.3
Team	5	28	19	.596	192	0	0	0	0	51	30	130	335	318	150	27	6	142	23	240	3.57	+21	.254	.331		72	5.0
/60G	2	9	6	.596	60	0	0	0	0	16	9	41	104.2	99	47	8	2	44	7	75	3.57	+21	.254	.331		23	1.6
CARRASCO, HECTOR Hector (Pacheco) B10.22.1969 San Pedro de Macoris, D.R. BR/TR/6'2"/(175–220) d4.4																											
2000	Bos A	1	1	.500	8	1	0	0	0	0	1	3	6.2	15	8	2	1	5	1	7	9.45	-47	.469	.553	-63	0	-0.6
Total	11	42	49	.462	618	9	0	0	3	19	23	407	794	748	377	61	32	364	32	629	3.88	+17	.250	.334	-36	101	5.1
CARROLL, ED Edgar Fleischer B7.27.1907 Baltimore MD D10.13.1984 Rossville MD BR/TR/6'3"/185 d5.1																											
1929	Bos A	1	0	1.000	24	2	0	0		0			67.1	77	46	6	4	20		13	5.61	-24	.291	.349	-1		-0.6
CASALE, JERRY Jerry Joseph B9.27.1933 Brooklyn NY BR/TR/6'2"/(200–205) d9.14																											
1958	Bos A	0	0	+	2	0	0	0	12	0		4	3	1	0	0	0	2	0	3	0.00	-100	.111	.273		0	0.1
1959	Bos A	13	8	.619	31	26	9	3	12	0		4	179.2	162	89	20	5	89	3	93	4.31	-6	.238	.329	+10	0	-0.2
1960	Bos A	2	9	.182	29	14	1	0	3	0		10	96.1	113	78	14	1	67	5	54	6.17	-34	.294	.394	-13	0	-2.1
1961	LA A	1	5	.167	13	7	0	0	1	1		4	42.2	52	34	9	1	25	0	35	6.54	-31	.297	.386	-44	0	-0.7
1961	Det A	0	0	+	3	1	0	0	0	0		1	12	15	8	3	0	3	0	6	5.25	-22	.313	.353	+8	0	-0.1
1961	Year	1	5	.167	16	8	0	0	1	1		5	54.2	67	42	12	1	28	0	41	6.26	-29	.300	.379	-37	0	-0.8
1962	Det A	1	2	.333	18	1	0	0	0	0		12	36.2	33	19	5	0	18	1	16	4.66	-13	.236	.321	-12	0	-0.2
Total	5	17	24	.415	96	49	10	3	28	1		35	370.1	376	228	51	7	204	9	207	5.08	-19	.262	.354	-5	0	-3.2
Team	3	15	17	.469	62	40	10	3	27	0		18	279	276	167	34	6	158	8	150	4.90	-17	.257	.353	+2		-2.2
/180I	2	10	11	.469	40	26	6	2	17	0		12	180	178	108	22	4	102	5	97	4.90	-17	.257	.353	+2		-1.4
CASCARELLA, JOE Joseph Thomas "Crooning Joe" B6.28.1907 Philadelphia PA D5.22.2002 Baltimore MD BR/TR/5'10.5"/175 d4.17																											
1935	Bos A	0	3	.000	6	4	0	0		0			17	25	17	3	0	11		9	6.88	-31	.329	.414	-22		-0.7
1936	Bos A	0	2	.000	10	1	0	0		0			20.2	27	16	0	0	9		7	6.97	-24	.329	.396	+165		-0.3
Total	5	27	48	.360	143	54	20	3		8			540.2	602	329	25	10	267		192	4.84	-9	.287	.370	-7		-4.3
Team	2	0	5	.000	16	5	0	0		0			37.2	52	33	3	0	20		16	6.93	-27	.329	.404	+15		-1.0
CASSIDY, SCOTT Scott Robert B10.3.1975 Syracuse NY BR/TR/6'2"/(175–180) d4.1 Col LeMoyne (NY)																											
2005	Bos A	0	0	+	1	0	0	0	0	0	0	0	0.2	4	3	0	0	0	0	0	40.50	-89	.667	.667		0	-0.1
Total	3	8	9	.471	111	0	0	0	0	0	9	76	121.2	110	73	23	8	54	5	109	4.88	-10	.247	.335		0	0.1
CASTILLO, CARLOS Carlos B4.21.1975 Boston MA BR/TR/6'2"/(240–250) [ChiA94 3/89] d4.2																											
2001	Bos A	0	0	+	2	0	0	0	0	0	0	1	3	3	2	1	0	0	0	0	6.00	-26	.273	.250		0	0.0
Total	4	10	7	.588	111	6	0	0	1	1	2	64	210.2	210	124	37	6	82	5	130	5.04	-9	.258	.326	+11	0	-0.6
CASTILLO, FRANK Frank Anthony B4.1.1969 ElPaso TX BR/TR/6'1"/(180–200) [ChiN87 6/140] d6.27																											
2001	Bos A	10	9	.526	26	26	0	0	9	0	0	0	136.2	138	72	14	5	35	2	89	4.21	+5	.260	.308	-5	40	0.3
2002	Bos A	6	15	.286	36	23	0	0	11	1	1	10	163.1	174	101	19	7	58	6	112	5.07	-12	.274	.337	-18	0	-1.2
2004	Bos A	0	0	+	2	0	0	0	0	0	0	2	1	1	0	0	0	1	0	0	0.00	-100	.333	.500		0	0.0
Total	13	82	104	.441	297	268	10	3	125	2	1	24	1595.1	1660	878	190	59	506	32	1101	4.56	-5	.268	.327	-6	155	-5.1
Team	3	16	24	.400	64	49	0	0	20	1	1	12	301	313	173	33	12	94	8	201	4.66	-4	.268	.325	-11	40	-0.9
/180I	2	10	14	.400	38	29	0	0	12	1	1	7	180	187	103	20	7	56	5	120	4.66	-4	.268	.325	-11	24	-0.5
CECIL, REX Rex Rolston B10.8.1916 Lindsay OK D10.30.1966 Long Beach CA BL/TR/6'3"/195 d8.13																											
1944	Bos A	4	5	.444	11	9	4	0		0			61	72	44	5	1	33		33	5.16	-34	.286	.371	+12	0	-1.6
1945	Bos A	2	5	.286	7	7	1	0		0			45	46	37	4	0	27		30	5.20	-34	.261	.360	+14	0	-1.5
Total	2	6	10	.375	18	16	5	0		0			106	118	81	9	1	60		63	5.18	-34	.276	.366	+13	0	-3.1
CHAKALES, BOB Robert Edward "Chick" B8.10.1927 Asheville NC BR/TR/6'1"/(180–185) d4.21																											
1957	Bos A	0	2	.000	18	0	0	0	0	3		9	32	53	30	5	1	11	0	16	8.16	-51	.379	.425		0	-1.0
Total	7	15	25	.375	171	23	3	1	0	10		11	420.1	445	246	31	7	225	12	187	4.54	-15	.277	.366	+2	0	-2.8
CHANEY, ESTY Esty Clyon B1.29.1891 Hadley PA D2.5.1952 Cleveland OH BR/TR/5'11"/170 d8.2																											
1913	Bos A	0	0	+	1	0	0	0		0			1	1	1	0	0	2		0	9.00	-67	.200	.429			0.0
1914	Bro F	0	0	+	1	0	0	0		0			4	7	3	0	0	2		1	6.75	-57	.389	.450			-0.1
Total	2	0	0	+	2	0	0	0		0			5	8	4	0	0	4		1	7.20	-60	.348	.444			-0.1
CHARTON, PETE Frank Lane B12.21.1942 Jackson TN BL/TR/6'2"/190 d4.19 Col Baylor																											
1964	Bos A	0	2	.000	25	5	0	0	3	0		11	65	67	39	12	1	24	1	37	5.26	-27	.275	.342	-45	0	-0.4
CHASE, KEN Kendall Fay "Lefty" B10.6.1913 Oneonta NY D1.16.1985 Oneonta NY BL/TL/6'2"/210 d4.23																											
1942	Bos A	5	1	.833	13	10	4	0		0			80.1	82	37	5	0	41		34	3.81	-2	.263	.348	+54	0	0.0
1943	Bos A	0	4	.000	7	5	0	0		0			27.1	36	25	0	0	30		9	6.91	-52	.316	.458	-34	0	-1.5
Total	8	53	84	.387	188	160	62	4		1			1165	1188	647	55	15	694		582	4.27	-3	.265	.365	-14	0	-3.0
Team	2	5	5	.500	20	15	4	0		0			107.2	118	62	5	0	71		43	4.60	-21	.277	.380	+25		-1.5
CHECH, CHARLIE Charles William B4.27.1878 Madison WI D1.31.1938 Los Angeles CA BR/TR/5'11.5"/190 d4.14 Col Wisconsin–Madison																											
1909	Bos A	7	5	.583	17	13	6	1		0			106.2	107	51	3	5	27		40	2.95	-15	.260	.314	+15		-1.0
Total	4	33	30	.524	94	63	45	6		3			606	602	273	10	29	162		187	2.52	+13	.263	.320	+3		1.2
CHECO, ROBINSON Robinson (Perez) B9.9.1971 Santo Domingo, D.R. BR/TR/6'1"/185 d9.16																											
1997	Bos A	1	1	.500	5	2	0	0	1	0	0	3	13.1	12	5	0	0	3	0	14	3.38	+38	.235	.278	-51	42	0.3
1998	Bos A	0	2	.000	2	2	0	0	0	0	0	0	7.2	11	8	3	0	5	0	5	9.39	-50	.379	.471	-11	0	-0.6
1999	LA N	2	2	.500	9	2	0	0	0	0	0	2	15.2	24	20	5	0	13	1	11	10.34	-58	.333	.435	+37	45	-1.9
Total	3	3	5	.375	16	6	0	0	1	0	0	5	36.2	47	33	8	0	21	1	30	7.61	-40	.309	.393	-9	87	-2.2
Team	2	1	3	.250	7	4	0	0	1	0	0	3	21	23	13	3	0	8	0	19	5.57	-16	.287	.352	-31	42	-0.3
CHEN, BRUCE Bruce Kastulo B6.19.1977 Panama City, Pan BL/TL/6'2"/(150–215) d9.7																											
2003	Bos A	0	1	.000	5	2	0	0	0	0	0	2	12.1	12	8	4	0	2	0	12	5.11	-9	.255	.280	+29	0	-0.1
Total	9	35	37	.486	237	112	2	0	45	0	0	82	797	797	448	151	19	308	21	635	4.60	-4	.260	.328	+2	0	-1.7

Year	Tm Lg	W	L	Pct	G	GS	CG	ShO	QS	SV	BS	QR	IP	H	R	HR	HB	BB	IB	SO	ERA	AERA	OAV	OOB	Sup	DL	PW
CHESBRO, JACK John Dwight "Happy Jack" B6.5.1874 N.Adams MA D11.6.1931 Conway MA BR/TR/5'9"/180 d7.12 C1 HF1946																											
1909	Bos A	0	1	.000	1	1	0	0		0			6	7	4	1	0	4		3	4.50	-44	.318	.423	+41		-0.2
Total	11	198	132	.600	392	332	260	35		5			2896.2	2647	1206	39	113	690		1265	2.68	+11	.244	.297	+4		11.0
CHITTUM, NELSON Nelson Boyd B3.25.1933 Harrisonburg VA BR/TR/6'1"/180 d8.17 Col Elizabethtown																											
1958	StL N	0	1	.000	13	2	0	0	0	0		7	29.1	31	21	5	1	7	0	13	6.44	-36	.265	.310	+41	0	-0.3
1959	Bos A	3	0	1.000	21	0	0	0	0	0		16	30.1	29	9	0	0	11	2	12	1.19	+242	.266	.333		0	0.7
1960	Bos A	0	0	+	6	0	0	0	0	0		4	8.1	8	4	0	0	6	1	5	4.32	-6	.242	.359		0	0.0
Total	3	3	1	.750	40	2	0	0	0	0		27	68	68	34	5	1	24	3	30	3.84	+6	.263	.326	+41	0	0.4
Team	2	3	0	1.000	27	0	0	0	0	0		20	38.2	37	13	0	0	17	3	17	1.86	+118	.261	.340			0.7
CHO, JIN HO Jin Ho B8.16.1975 Jun Ju City, South Korea BR/TR/6'0"/(207–220) d7.4 [DL 2000 Bos A 24]																											
1998	Bos A	0	3	.000	4	4	0	0	1	0	0	0	18.2	28	17	4	1	3	0	15	8.20	-42	.341	.368	-7	0	-0.8
1999	Bos A	2	3	.400	9	7	0	0	2	0	0	1	39.1	45	26	7	2	8	0	16	5.72	-13	.287	.324	-28	0	-0.3
Total	2	2	6	.250	13	11	0	0	3	0	0	1	58	73	43	11	3	11	0	31	6.52	-25	.305	.339	-20	24	-1.1
CICOTTE, EDDIE Edward Victor "Knuckles" B6.19.1884 Springwells MI D5.5.1969 Detroit MI BB/TR/5'9"/175 d9.3																											
1908	Bos A	11	12	.478	39	24	17	2		2			207.1	198	77	0	11	59		95	2.43	+1	.256	.318	+9		0.5
1909	Bos A	14	5	.737	27	17	10	1		1			162.1	117	63	3	1	56		82	1.94	+29	.207	.280	+34		0.9
1910	Bos A	15	11	.577	36	30	20	3		0			250	213	94	4	13	86		104	2.74	-7	.233	.308	+16		0.1
1911	Bos A	11	15	.423	35	25	16	1		0			220	236	121	2	4	73		106	2.82	+16	.282	.342	-1		0.5
1912	Bos A	1	3	.250	9	6	2	0		0			46	58	34	0	1	15		20	5.67	-40	.319	.374	+37		-0.7
Total	14	209	148	.585	502	361	249	35		24			3226	2897	1161	32	52	827		1374	2.38	+23	.245	.297	+8		24.3
Team	5	52	46	.531	146	102	65	7		3			885.2	822	389	9	30	289		407	2.69	+2	.251	.318	+14		1.3
/180I	1	11	9	.531	30	21	13	1		1			180	167	79	2	6	59		83	2.69	+2	.251	.318	+14		0.3
CISCO, GALEN Galen Bernard B3.7.1936 St.Marys OH BR/TR/5'11"/(200–215) d6.11 C28 Col Ohio St.																											
1961	Bos A	2	4	.333	17	8	0	0	2	0		4	52.1	67	40	5	0	28	0	26	6.71	-38	.325	.397	-28	0	-1.2
1962	Bos A	4	7	.364	23	9	1	0	2	0		10	83	95	66	11	3	50	1	43	6.72	-39	.292	.387	-23	0	-2.4
1967	Bos A	0	1	.000	11	0	0	0	0	1		8	22.1	21	10	4	0	8	0	8	3.63	-4	.266	.326		0	-0.1
Total	7	25	56	.309	192	78	9	3	36	2	0	75	659	681	370	68	20	281	10	325	4.56	-19	.271	.346	-20	0	-6.3
Team	3	6	12	.333	51	17	1	0	4	1		22	157.2	183	116	20	3	86	1	77	6.28	-35	.300	.383	-25		-3.7
/180I	3	7	14	.333	58	19	1	0	5	1		25	180	209	132	23	3	98	1	88	6.28	-35	.300	.383	-25		-4.2
CLARK, OTEY William Otis B5.22.1915 Boscobel WI BR/TR/6'1.5"/190 d4.17																											
1945	Bos A	4	4	.500	12	9	4	1		0			82	86	33	6	1	19		20	3.07	+11	.268	.311	-25	0	0.1
CLEAR, MARK Mark Alan B5.27.1956 Los Angeles CA BR/TR/6'4"/(200–215) [PhiN74 8/171] d4.4																											
1979	†Cal A★	11	5	.688	52	0	0	0	0	14	7	34	109	87	48	6	3	68	5	98	3.63	+12	.219	.333		0	0.9
1980	Cal A	11	11	.500	58	0	0	0	0	9	6	41	106.1	82	51	2	5	65	9	105	3.30	+20	.216	.336		0	0.8
1981	Bos A	8	3	.727	34	0	0	0	0	9	5	23	76.2	69	36	11	2	51	2	82	4.11	-5	.239	.357		0	0.0
1982	Bos A☆	14	9	.609	55	0	0	0	0	14	9	39	105	92	39	11	7	61	6	109	3.00	+45	.238	.348		0	3.0
1983	Bos A	4	5	.444	48	0	0	0	0	4	1	27	96	101	71	10	3	68	5	81	6.28	-30	.273	.385		0	-1.6
1984	Bos A	8	3	.727	47	0	0	0	0	8	2	34	67	47	38	2	2	70	3	76	4.03	+4	.198	.378		0	-0.1
1985	Bos A	1	3	.250	41	0	0	0	0	3	3	25	55.2	45	26	1	5	50	10	55	3.72	+16	.225	.389		0	0.3
1986	Mil A	5	5	.500	59	0	0	0	0	16	3	45	73.2	53	23	4	1	36	2	85	2.20	+98	.201	.295		0	2.6
1987	Mil A	8	5	.615	58	1	0	0	0	6	3	41	78.1	70	46	9	5	55	3	81	4.48	+3	.239	.363	-1	0	0.0
1988	Mil A	1	0	1.000	25	0	0	0	0	0	0	17	29	23	12	4	0	21	0	26	2.79	+43	.215	.338		63	0.1
1990	Cal A	0	0	+	4	0	0	0	0	0	0	3	7.2	5	7	0	2	9	0	6	5.87	-35	.200	.421		0	-0.1
Total	11	71	49	.592	481	1	0	0	0	83	39	329	804.1	674	397	60	35	554	45	804	3.85	+10	.228	.353	-1	63	5.9
Team	5	35	23	.603	225	0	0	0	0	38	20	148	400.1	354	210	35	19	300	26	403	4.27	+0	.239	.370			1.6
/60G	1	9	6	.603	60	0	0	0	0	10	5	39	106.2	94	56	9	5	80	7	107	4.28	+0	.239	.370			0.4
CLEMENS, ROGER William Roger "Rocket" B8.4.1962 Dayton OH BR/TR/6'4"/(205–235) [BosA83 1/19] d5.15 Col Texas																											
1984	Bos A	9	4	.692	21	20	5	1	8	0	0	1	133.1	146	67	13	2	29	3	126	4.32	-3	.271	.309	+32	0	0.1
1985	Bos A	7	5	.583	15	15	3	1	7	0	0	0	98.1	83	38	5	3	37	0	74	3.29	+31	.228	.303	-14	73	1.3
1986	†Bos A★	**24**	4	**.857**	33	33	10	1	25	0	0	0	254	179	77	21	4	67	0	238	**2.48**	+69	**.195**	**.252**	+32	0	5.1
1987	Bos A	**20**	9	**.690**	36	36	**18**	0	26	0	0	0	281.2	248	100	19	9	83	4	256	2.97	+54	.235	.295	+11	0	**4.5**
1988	†Bos A★	18	12	.600	35	35	**14**	0	28	0	0	0	264	217	93	17	6	62	4	**291**	2.93	+41	.220	.270	-3	0	3.7
1989	Bos A	17	11	.607	35	35	8	3	24	0	0	0	253.1	215	101	20	8	93	5	230	3.13	+32	.231	.305	+0	0	2.7
1990	†Bos A☆	21	6	.778	31	31	7	0	27	0	0	0	228.1	193	59	7	7	54	3	209	**1.93**	+112	.228	.278	-6	0	**6.2**
1991	Bos A★	18	10	.643	35	**35**	13	0	26	0	0	0	**271.1**	219	93	15	5	65	12	**241**	**2.62**	+65	.221	.270	-5	0	**4.7**
1992	Bos A★	18	11	.621	32	32	11	0	24	0	0	0	246.2	203	80	11	9	62	5	208	**2.41**	+77	.224	.278	-14	0	**5.3**
1993	Bos A	11	14	.440	29	29	2	1	14	0	0	0	191.2	175	99	17	11	67	4	160	4.46	+4	.244	.315	-36	27	0.8
1994	Bos A	9	7	.563	24	24	3	1	19	0	0	0	170.2	124	62	15	4	71	1	168	2.85	+77	**.203**	.288	-29	0	3.2
1995	†Bos A	10	5	.667	23	23	0	0	13	0	0	0	140	141	70	15	14	60	0	132	4.18	+16	.259	.346	+8	38	1.1
1996	Bos A	10	13	.435	34	34	6	2	23	0	0	0	242.2	216	106	19	4	106	2	**257**	3.63	+40	.237	.317	-20	0	3.3
1997	Tor A★	**21**	7	.750	34	34	**9**	0	26	0	0	0	**264**	204	65	9	12	68	1	**292**	**2.05**	+124	.213	**.273**	-9	0	**7.9**
1998	Tor A★	**20**	6	.769	33	33	5	3	25	0	0	0	234.2	169	78	11	7	88	0	**271**	**2.65**	+76	**.197**	.277	-9	0	**5.2**
1999	†NY A	14	10	.583	30	30	1	1	16	0	0	0	187.2	185	101	20	9	90	0	163	4.60	+3	.261	.350	-12	23	0.6
2000	†NY A	13	8	.619	32	32	1	0	21	0	0	0	204.1	184	96	26	10	84	0	188	3.70	+29	.236	.317	-5	16	2.1
2001	†NY A★	20	3	**.870**	33	33	0	0	21	0	0	0	220.1	205	94	19	5	72	1	213	3.51	+26	.246	.309	+23	0	2.2
2002	†NY A	13	6	.684	29	29	0	0	16	0	0	0	180	172	94	18	7	63	6	192	4.35	+0	.250	.317	+16	25	0.2
2003	†NY A★	17	9	.654	33	33	1	1	21	0	0	0	211.2	199	99	24	5	58	1	190	3.91	+12	.247	.299	+7	0	1.4
2004	†Hou N★	18	4	**.818**	33	33	0	0	23	0	0	0	214.1	169	76	15	6	79	5	218	2.98	+47	.217	.292	+0	0	3.1
2005	†Hou N★	13	8	.619	32	32	1	0	26	0	0	0	211.1	151	51	11	3	62	5	185	**1.87**	+125	**.198**	.261	-24	0	5.7
2006	Hou N	7	6	.538	19	19	0	0	12	0	0	0	113.1	89	34	7	4	29	1	102	2.30	+96	.216	.274	-19	0	2.8
Total	23	348	178	.662	691	690	118	46	471	0	0	1	4817.2	4086	1833	354	154	1549	63	4604	3.10	+44	.228	.294	-3	202	73.2
Team	13	192	111	.634	383	382	100	10	264	0	0	1	2776	2359	1045	194	86	856	43	2590	3.06	+45	.229	.291	-3	138	42.0
/180I	1	12	7	.634	25	25	6	1	17	0	0	0	180	153	68	13	6	56	3	168	3.06	+45	.229	.291	-3	9	2.7
CLEMENT, MATT Matthew Paul B8.12.1974 McCandless Twp. PA BR/TR/6'3"/(180–210) [SDN93 3/86] d9.6																											
2005	†Bos A★	13	6	.684	32	32	1	0	19	0	0	0	191	192	102	18	16	68	1	146	4.57	-1	.260	.333	+20	0	0.0
2006	Bos A	5	5	.500	12	12	0	0	4	0	0	0	65.1	77	50	8	6	38	0	43	6.61	-29	.291	.392	+14	109	-1.6
Total	9	87	86	.503	238	236	6	3	122	0	0	1	1412.2	1326	762	144	94	650	23	1217	4.47	-3	.248	.338	+2	109	-3.9
Team	2	18	11	.621	44	44	1	0	23	0		0	256.1	269	152	26	22	106	1	189	5.09	-10	.268	.349	+18	109	-1.6
/180I	1	13	8	.621	31	31	1	0	16	0		0	180	189	107	18	15	74	1	133	5.09	-10	.268	.349	+18	77	-1.1
CLEMONS, LANCE Lance Levis B7.6.1947 Philadelphia PA BL/TL/6'2"/205 [KCA68 7/156] d8.12 Col West Chester																											
1974	Bos A	1	0	1.000	6	0	0	0	0	0	0	4	6.1	8	8	1	1	4	3	1	9.95	-61	.296	.406		0	-0.6
Total	3	2	1	.667	19	4	0	0	1	0	0	8	35.2	42	31	4	3	21	3	23	6.06	-42	.284	.382	+2	0	-1.3
CLEVELAND, REGGIE Reginald Leslie B5.23.1948 Swift Current SK, Can. BR/TR/6'1"/(185–205) d10.1																											
1969	StL N	0	0	+	1	1	0	0	0	0	0	0	4	7	4	0	0	1	0	3	9.00	-60	.368	.400	+48	0	-0.1
1970	StL N	0	4	.000	16	1	0	0	0	0	0	7	26	31	27	3	0	18	6	22	7.62	-46	.298	.392	+52	0	-1.4
1971	StL N	12	12	.500	34	34	10	2	18	0	0	0	222	238	107	20	6	53	12	148	4.01	-9	.271	.315	+0	0	-0.9
1972	StL N	14	15	.483	33	33	11	3	18	0	0	0	230.2	229	120	21	5	60	12	153	3.94	-13	.258	.306	+2	0	-1.7
1973	StL N	14	10	.583	32	32	6	3	23	0	0	0	224	211	88	13	4	61	12	122	3.01	+22	.246	.298	+1	0	1.9
1974	Bos A	12	14	.462	41	27	10	0	14	0	0	10	221.1	234	121	25	9	69	5	103	4.31	-11	.271	.329	+15	0	-1.3
1975	†Bos A	13	9	.591	31	20	3	1	12	0	1	5	170.2	173	90	19	3	52	1	78	4.43	-8	.263	.317	+4	0	-0.6
1976	Bos A	10	9	.526	41	14	3	0	9	2	2	16	170	159	73	3	4	61	4	76	3.07	+27	.246	.314	-18	0	1.3
1977	Bos A	11	8	.579	36	27	9	1	13	2	1	7	190.1	211	97	20	4	43	2	85	4.26	+5	.281	.320	+8	0	0.3
1978	Bos A	0	1	.000	1	0	0	0	0	0	0	1	0.1	1	1	0	0	0	0	0	0.00	-100	.333	.333		0	-0.1
1978	Tex A	5	7	.417	53	0	0	0	0	12	7	38	75.2	65	33	5	3	23	6	46	3.09	+21	.236	.295		0	0.8

Year	Tm Lg	W	L	Pct	G	GS	CG	ShO	QS	SV	BS	QR	IP	H	R	HR	HB	BB	IB	SO	ERA	AERA	OAV	OOB	Sup	DL	PW
1978	Year	5	8	.385	54	0	0	0	0	12	7	39	76	66	34	5	3	23	6	46	3.08	+22	.237	.296		0	0.7
1979	Mil A	1	5	.167	29	1	0	0	0	4	2	13	55	77	44	9	0	23	4	22	6.71	-37	.344	.394	+29	0	-1.6
1980	Mil A	11	9	.550	45	13	5	2	6	4	2	22	154.1	150	73	9	5	49	2	54	3.73	+5	.254	.312	+9	0	0.3
1981	Mil A	2	3	.400	35	0	0	0	0	1	0	21	64.2	57	41	5	1	30	2	18	5.15	-33	.239	.326		0	-1.1
Total	13	105	106	.498	428	203	57	12	113	25	15	140	1809	1843	919	152	44	543	68	930	4.01	-4	.264	.318	+4	0	-4.2
Team	5	46	41	.529	150	88	25	2	48	4	4	39	752.2	778	382	67	20	225	12	342	4.04	+1	.266	.321	+5		-0.4
/180I	1	11	10	.529	36	21	6	0	11	1	1	9	180	186	91	16	5	54	3	82	4.04	+1	.266	.321	+5		-0.1
CLEVENGER, TEX Truman Eugene B7.9.1932 Visalia CA BR/TR/6'1"/(180–185) d4.18 Col Cal St.–Fresno																											
1954	Bos A	2	4	.333	23	8	1	0		0			67.2	67	42	9	2	29		43	4.79	-14	.262	.337	-30	0	-0.4
Total	8	36	37	.493	307	40	6	2	45	30		352	694.2	706	370	61	14	298	30	361	4.18	-6	.265	.339	-22	0	-1.6
CLOWERS, BILL William Perry B8.14.1898 San Marcos TX D1.13.1978 Sweeny TX BL/TL/5'11"/175 d7.20																											
1926	Bos A	0	0	+	2	0	0	0		0			1.2	2	1	0	0	0		0	0.00	-100	.333	.333			0.0
COLLINS, RIP Harry Warren B2.26.1896 Weatherford TX D5.27.1968 Bryan TX BR/TR (BB 1920–23)/6'1"/205 d4.19 Col Texas A&M																											
1922	Bos A	14	11	.560	32	29	15	3		0			210.2	219	101	4	10	103		69	3.76	+9	.274	.364	-14		0.6
Total	11	108	82	.568	311	219	84	15		5			1712.1	1795	926	73	81	674		569	3.99	+6	.275	.351	+5		2.3
/180I	1	12	9	.560	27	25	13	3		0			180	187	86	3	9	88		59	3.76	+9	.274	.364	-27		0.5
COLLINS, RAY Ray Williston B2.11.1887 Colchester VT D1.9.1970 Burlington VT BL/TL/6'1"/185 d7.19 Col Vermont																											
1909	Bos A	4	3	.571	12	8	4	2		0			73.2	70	29	2	0	18		31	2.81	-11	.269	.317	+20		-0.1
1910	Bos A	13	11	.542	35	26	18	4		1			244.2	205	73	1	1	41		109	1.62	+58	.229	.264	-10		1.9
1911	Bos A	11	12	.478	31	24	14	0		1			194.2	184	81	1	4	44		86	2.40	+36	.256	.302	-24		2.0
1912	†Bos A	13	8	.619	27	24	17	4		0			199.1	192	65	4	2	42		82	2.53	+35	.256	.297	+18		2.1
1913	Bos A	19	8	.704	30	30	19	3		0			246.2	242	88	3	2	37		88	2.63	+12	.264	.294	+8		1.3
1914	Bos A	20	13	.606	39	30	16	6		0			272.1	252	95	3	0	56		72	2.51	+7	.258	.298	-9		0.7
1915	Bos A	4	7	.364	25	9	2	0		2			104.2	101	62	1	1	31		43	4.30	-35	.261	.317	+22		-1.4
Total	7	84	62	.575	199	151	90	19		4			1336	1246	493	15	10	269		511	2.51	+15	.254	.294	+0		6.5
/180I	1	11	8	.575	27	20	12	3	0	1	0	0	180	168	66	2	1	36		69	2.51	+15	.254	.294	-87		0.9
COMSTOCK, RALPH Ralph Remick "Commy" B11.24.1890 Sylvania OH D9.13.1966 Toledo OH BR/TR/5'10"/168 d8.26																											
1915	Bos A	1	0	1.000	3	0	0	0		0			9	10	3	2	0	2		1	2.00	+39	.294	.333			0.1
Total	3	11	14	.440	40	22	10	0		4			203	222	116	4	4	39		100	3.72	-24	.284	.322	-6		-2.5
CONE, DAVID David Brian B1.2.1963 Kansas City MO BL/TR/6'1"/(180–200) [KCA81 3/74] d6.8																											
2001	Bos A	9	7	.563	25	25	0	0	10	0	0	0	135.2	148	74	17	10	57	4	115	4.31	+3	.275	.351	-4	43	0.0
Total	17	194	126	.606	450	419	56	22	268	1	0	19	2898.2	2504	1222	258	106	1137	42	2668	3.46	+20	.232	.309	+3	310	23.2
/180I	1	12	9	.563	33	33	0	0	13	0		0	180	196	98	23	13	76	5	153	4.31	+3	.275	.351	+27	57	0.0
CONLEY, GENE Donald Eugene B11.10.1930 Muskogee OK BR/TR/6'8"/(220–227) d4.17 Col Washington St.																											
1961	Bos A	11	14	.440	33	30	6	2	13	1		2	199.2	229	116	33	3	65	2	113	4.91	-15	.287	.343	-6	0	-1.0
1962	Bos A	15	14	.517	34	33	9	2	19	1		1	241.2	238	116	28	5	68	5	134	3.95	+5	.256	.308	-2	0	1.0
1963	Bos A	3	4	.429	9	9	0	0	2	0		0	40.2	51	31	4	1	21	0	14	6.64	-43	.305	.386	+28	66	-1.7
Total	11	91	96	.487	276	214	69	13	89	9		64	1588.2	1606	767	162	31	511	42	888	3.82	+1	.264	.322	+1	135	0.2
Team	3	29	32	.475	76	72	15	4	34	2		3	482	518	263	65	9	154	7	261	4.57	-10	.273	.330	+0	66	-1.7
/180I	1	11	12	.475	28	27	6	1	13	1		1	180	193	98	24	3	58	3	97	4.57	-10	.273	.330	+0	25	-0.6
CONNOLLY, ED Edward Joseph Jr. B12.3.1939 Brooklyn NY D7.1.1998 New Canaan CT BL/TL/6'1"/(188–190) d4.19 f–Ed Col Massachusetts																											
1964	Bos A	4	11	.267	27	15	1	1	5	0		5	80.2	80	50	3	6	64	2	73	4.91	-21	.261	.395	-43	0	-1.6
1967	Cle A	2	1	.667	15	4	0	0	2	0		6	49.1	63	46	6	1	34	2	45	7.48	-56	.315	.414	+33	0	-1.3
Total	2	6	12	.333	42	19	1	1	7	0		11	130	143	96	9	7	98	4	118	5.88	-38	.282	.402	-27	0	-2.9
COOPER, GUY Guy Evans "Rebel" B1.28.1893 Rome GA D8.2.1951 Santa Monica CA BB/TR/6'1"/185 d5.2																											
1914	NY A	0	0	+	1	0	0	0		0			3	3	3	0	0	2		3	9.00	-69	.273	.385			-0.1
1914	Bos A	1	0	1.000	9	1	0	0		0			22	23	15	1	3	9		5	5.32	-49	.299	.393	+144		-0.4
1914	Year	1	0	1.000	10	1	0	0		0			25	26	18	1	3	11		8	5.76	-53	.295	.392	+143		-0.5
1915	Bos A	0	0	+	1	0	0	0		0			2	0	0	0	0	2		0	0.00	-100	.000	.286			0.0
Total	2	1	0	1.000	11	1	0	0		0			27	26	18	1	3	13		8	5.33	-49	.280	.385	+142		-0.5
Team	2	1	0	1.000	10	1	0	0		0			24	23	15	1	3	11		5	4.88	-45	.299	.385	+144		-0.4
COREY, BRYAN Bryan Scott B10.21.1973 Thousand Oaks CA BR/TR/6'1"/(170–180) [DetA93 12/333] d5.13 Col Los Angeles Pierce (CA) JC																											
1998	Ari N	0	0	+	3	0	0	0	0	0	0	1	4	6	4	1	1	2	0	1	9.00	-52	.375	.474		0	-0.1
2002	LA N	0	0	+	1	0	0	0	0	0	0	1	1	0	0	0	0	0	0	0	0.00	-100	.000	.000		15	0.0
2006	Tex A	1	1	.500	16	0	0	0	0	0	0	12	17.1	15	5	0	0	8	0	13	2.60	+80	.231	.311		0	0.4
2006	Bos A	1	0	1.000	16	0	0	0	0	0	0	11	21.2	20	11	1	2	7	0	15	4.57	+2	.250	.319		0	0.0
2006	Year	2	1	.667	32	0	0	0	0	0	0	23	39	35	16	1	2	15	0	28	3.69	+27	.241	.315		0	0.4
Total	3	2	1	.667	36	0	0	0	0	0	0	25	44	41	20	2	3	17	0	29	4.09	+13	.250	.326		15	0.3
CORMIER, RHEAL Rheal Paul B4.23.1967 Moncton NB, Can. BL/TL/5'10"/(185–200) [StLN88 6/158] d8.15 Col CC of Rhode Island																											
1995	†Bos A	7	5	.583	48	12	0	0	4	0	2	29	115	131	60	12	3	31	2	69	4.07	+19	.294	.342	-3	0	0.8
1999	†Bos A	2	0	1.000	60	0	0	0	0	0	3	43	63.1	61	34	4	5	18	2	39	3.69	+35	.246	.307		0	0.3
2000	Bos A	3	3	.500	64	0	0	0	0	0	2	41	68.1	74	40	7	0	17	2	43	4.61	+9	.275	.316		0	0.2
Total	15	71	64	.526	677	108	7	1	51	2	31	409	1218.2	1244	601	120	50	316	37	759	4.02	+5	.265	.316	-8	325	1.7
Team	3	12	8	.600	172	12	0	0	4	0	7	113	246.2	266	134	23	8	66	6	151	4.12	+20	.276	.326	-3		1.3
/60G	1	4	3	.600	60	4	0	0	1	0	2	39	86	93	47	8	3	23	2	53	4.13	+20	.276	.326	-3		0.5
CORSI, JIM James Bernard B9.9.1961 Newton MA BR/TR/6'1"/(210–230) [NYA82 25/642] d6.28 Col St. Leo [DL 1990 Oak A 178]																											
1988	Oak A	0	1	.000	11	1	0	0	0	0	0	8	21.1	20	10	1	0	6	1	10	3.80	+0	.260	.302	+68	0	0.0
1989	Oak A	1	2	.333	22	0	0	0	0	0	0	16	38.1	26	8	2	1	10	0	21	1.88	+97	.194	.252		0	0.6
1991	Hou N	0	5	.000	47	0	0	0	0	0	3	34	77.2	76	37	6	0	23	5	53	3.71	-5	.259	.310		0	-0.1
1992	†Oak A	4	2	.667	32	0	0	0	0	0	0	23	44	44	12	2	0	18	2	19	1.43	+164	.273	.343		0	1.3
1993	Fla N	0	2	.000	15	0	0	0	0	0	0	8	20.1	28	15	1	0	10	3	7	6.64	-34	.337	.404		115	-0.4
1995	Oak A	2	4	.333	38	0	0	0	0	2	2	30	45	31	14	2	2	26	1	26	2.20	+106	.203	.324		47	1.4
1996	Oak A	6	0	1.000	56	0	0	0	0	3	3	41	73.2	71	33	6	3	34	4	43	4.03	+23	.269	.356		21	0.7
1997	Bos A	5	3	.625	52	0	0	0	0	2	7	39	57.2	56	26	1	4	21	7	40	3.43	+36	.255	.327		29	0.9
1998	†Bos A	3	2	.600	59	0	0	0	0	0	3	44	66	58	23	6	1	23	2	49	2.59	+82	.235	.301		19	1.0
1999	Bos A	1	2	.333	23	0	0	0	0	0	3	13	24	25	15	4	2	19	3	14	5.25	-5	.284	.418		0	0.0
1999	Bal A	0	1	.000	13	0	0	0	0	0	1	10	13.1	15	4	2	0	1	0	8	2.70	+74	.294	.308		15	0.2
1999	Year	1	3	.250	36	0	0	0	0	0	4	23	37.1	40	19	6	2	20	3	22	4.34	+13	.288	.383		0	0.2
Total	10	22	24	.478	368	1	0	0	0	7	22	266	481.1	450	197	33	13	191	28	290	3.25	+33	.254	.328	+68	424	5.6
Team	3	9	7	.563	134	0	0	0	0	2	13	96	147.2	139	64	11	7	63	12	103	3.35	+41	.250	.332		48	1.9
/60G	1	4	3	.563	60	0	0	0	0	1	6	43	66	62	29	5	3	28	5	46	3.36	+41	.250	.332		21	0.9
COUMBE, FRITZ Frederick Nicholas B12.13.1889 Antrim PA D3.21.1978 Paradise CA BL/TL/6'0"/152 d4.22																											
1914	Bos A	1	2	.333	17	5	1	0		1			62.1	49	20	0	0	16		17	1.44	+86	.222	.274	-3		0.3
Total	8	38	38	.500	193	70	30	4		13			761.1	773	335	10	13	217		212	2.80	+8	.277	.332	-2		2.0
CRAWFORD, PAXTON Paxton Keith B8.4.1977 Little Rock AR BR/TR/6'3"/205 [BosA95 9/242] d7.1 [DL 2002 Bos A 82]																											
2000	Bos A	2	1	.667	7	4	0	0	2	0	0	2	29	25	15	0	2	13	2	17	3.41	+47	.240	.325	-25	0	0.3
2001	Bos A	3	0	1.000	8	7	0	0	4	0	0	1	36	40	19	3	2	13	0	25	4.75	-7	.276	.342	+43	0	0.0
Total	2	5	1	.833	15	11	0	0	6	0	0	3	65	65	34	3	4	26	2	42	4.15	+13	.261	.335	+15	82	0.3
CRAWFORD, STEVE Steven Ray B4.29.1958 Pryor OK BR/TR/6'5"/(220–240) d9.2																											
1980	Bos A	2	0	1.000	6	4	2	0	2	0	0	2	32.1	41	14	3	0	8	2	10	3.62	+18	.306	.345	+42	0	0.1
1981	Bos A	0	5	.000	14	11	0	0	3	0	0	3	57.2	69	38	10	3	18	0	29	4.99	-22	.301	.354	+6	0	-0.6
1982	Bos A	1	0	1.000	5	0	0	0	0	0	0	5	9	14	3	0	0	0	0	2	2.00	+118	.341	.341		129	0.2
1984	Bos A	5	0	1.000	35	0	0	0	0	1	3	25	62	69	31	6	1	21	5	21	3.34	+26	.286	.341		0	0.3

Year	Tm Lg	W	L	Pct	G	GS	CG	ShO	QS	SV	BS	QR	IP	H	R	HR	HB	BB	IB	SO	ERA	AERA	OAV	OOB	Sup	DL	PW
1985	Bos A	6	5	.545	44	1	0	0	1	12	4	23	91	103	47	5	0	28	8	58	3.76	+15	.289	.338	+5	30	0.4
1986	†Bos A	0	2	.000	40	0	0	0	0	4	4	27	57.1	69	29	5	0	19	7	32	3.92	+7	.308	.359		45	0.1
1987	Bos A	5	4	.556	29	0	0	0	0	0	0	16	72.2	91	48	13	2	32	2	43	5.33	-14	.314	.386		15	-0.7
1989	KC A	3	1	.750	25	0	0	0	0	0	1	19	54	48	19	2	3	19	3	33	2.83	+37	.242	.317		0	0.5
1990	KC A	5	4	.556	46	0	0	0	0	1	1	32	80	79	38	7	3	23	3	54	4.16	-7	.254	.310		29	0.0
1991	KC A	3	2	.600	33	0	0	0	0	1	0	20	46.2	60	31	3	1	18	5	38	5.98	-31	.311	.367		72	-0.8
Total	10	30	23	.566	277	16	2	0	6	19	13	172	562.2	643	298	54	13	186	35	320	4.17	+0	.290	.346	+13	320	-0.5
Team	7	19	16	.543	173	16	2	0	6	17	11	101	382	456	210	42	6	126	24	195	4.15	+3	.301	.354	+15	219	-0.2
/60G	2	7	6	.543	60	6	1	0	2	6	4	35	132.1	158	73	15	2	44	8	68	4.15	+3	.301	.354	+15	76	-0.1
CREMINS, BOB Robert Anthony "Lefty","Crooked Arm" B2.15.1906 Pelham Manor NY D3.27.2004 Pelham NY BL/TL/5'11"/178 d8.17																											
1927	Bos A	0	0	+	4	0	0	0		0			5.1	5	4	0	0	3		0	5.06	-17	.250	.348			0.0
CROUCH, ZACH Zachary Quinn B10.26.1965 Folsom CA BL/TL/6'3"/190 [BosA84 13/328] d6.4																											
1988	Bos A	0	0	+	3	0	0	0	0	0	0	1	1.1	4	1	0	0	2	0	0	6.75	-39	.571	.667		0	0.0
CROUSHORE, RICH Richard Steven B8.7.1970 Lakehurst NJ BR/TR/6'4"/210 d5.18 Col James Madison [DL 2001 NY N 17]																											
2000	Bos A	0	1	.000	5	0	0	0	0	0	0	3	4.2	4	3	0	1	5	1	3	5.79	-13	.250	.435		0	0.0
Total	3	5	11	.313	111	0	0	0	0	11	10	73	142	131	87	16	9	83	8	149	4.88	-7	.240	.347		17	-0.5
CULP, RAY Raymond Leonard B8.6.1941 Elgin TX BR/TR/6'0"/(197–200) d4.10																											
1963	Phi N★	14	11	.560	34	30	10	5	19	0		4	203.1	148	76	15	6	102	8	176	2.97	+9	.206	.308	+6	0	0.8
1964	Phi N	8	7	.533	30	19	3	1	11	0		4	135	139	77	15	5	56	4	96	4.13	-16	.263	.337	+12	0	-1.4
1965	Phi N	14	10	.583	33	30	11	2	17	0		1	204.1	188	89	14	12	78	9	134	3.22	+8	.243	.321	+14	0	0.1
1966	Phi N	7	4	.636	34	12	1	0	6	1		16	110.2	106	66	19	7	53	4	100	5.04	-29	.246	.337	+0	0	-1.8
1967	Chi N	8	11	.421	30	22	4	1	12	0		3	152.2	138	69	22	2	59	4	111	3.89	-9	.239	.309	+15	0	-0.7
1968	Bos A	16	6	.727	35	30	11	6	20	0		5	216.1	166	79	18	9	82	8	190	2.91	+8	.210	.291	+9	0	0.4
1969	Bos A★	17	8	.680	32	32	9	2	18	0	0	0	227	195	103	25	6	79	6	172	3.81	+0	.231	.299	+24	0	0.4
1970	Bos A	17	14	.548	33	33	15	1	24	0	0	0	251.1	211	104	22	11	91	8	197	3.04	+31	.224	.299	+4	0	2.2
1971	Bos A	14	16	.467	35	35	12	3	19	0	0	0	242.1	236	108	21	5	67	4	151	3.60	+3	.253	.305	-15	0	-0.1
1972	Bos A	5	8	.385	16	16	4	1	10	0	0	0	105	104	60	8	3	53	3	52	4.46	-27	.260	.347	+28	48	-1.6
1973	Bos A	2	6	.250	10	9	0	0	4	0	0	0	50.1	46	32	9	4	32	0	32	4.47	-10	.247	.366	-24	31	-0.6
Total	11	122	101	.547	322	268	80	22	160	1	0	33	1898.1	1677	863	188	70	752	58	1411	3.58	+0	.235	.313	+7	79	-2.3
Team	6	71	58	.550	161	155	51	13	95	0	0	5	1092.1	958	486	103	38	404	29	794	3.50	+4	.234	.307	+6	79	0.7
/180I	1	12	10	.550	27	26	8	2	16	0	0	1	180	158	80	17	6	67	5	131	3.50	+4	.234	.307	+6	13	0.1
CUPPY, NIG George Joseph (b George Koppe) B7.3.1869 Logansport IN D7.27.1922 Elkhart IN BR/TR/5'7"/160 d4.16																											
1901	Bos A	4	6	.400	13	11	9	0		0			93.1	111	58	1	2	14		22	4.15	-15	.292	.321	+6		-0.5
Total	10	162	98	.623	302	262	224	9		5			2283	2520	1346	62	69	609		504	3.48	+27	.275	.325	-2		20.4
CURRY, STEVE Stephen Thomas B9.13.1965 Winter Park FL BR/TR/6'6"/217 [BosA84 7/172] d7.10 Col Manatee (FL) CC																											
1988	Bos A	0	1	.000	3	3	0	0	0	0	0	0	11	15	10	0	0	14	2	4	8.18	-50	.357	.500	+33	0	-0.3
CURTIS, JOHN John Duffield B3.9.1948 Newton MA BL/TL/6'2"/(175–190) [BosA68 S1/10] d8.13 Col Clemson																											
1970	Bos A	0	0	+	1	0	0	0	0	0	0	0	2.1	4	4	1	0	1	0	1	11.57	-66	.333	.385		0	-0.1
1971	Bos A	2	2	.500	5	3	1	0	3	0	1	2	26	30	9	3	0	6	1	19	3.12	+20	.291	.330	-36	0	0.2
1972	Bos A	11	8	.579	26	21	8	3	11	0	0	2	154.1	161	69	8	0	50	6	106	3.73	-13	.271	.327	+0	0	-1.0
1973	Bos A	13	13	.500	35	30	10	4	16	0	0	4	221.1	225	103	24	2	83	10	101	3.58	+13	.264	.330	-9	0	0.9
Total	15	89	97	.478	438	199	42	14	107	11	10	153	1641	1695	810	140	13	669	92	825	3.96	-8	.270	.339	-3	82	-5.8
Team	4	26	23	.531	67	54	19	7	30	0	1	8	404	420	185	36	2	140	17	227	3.65	+1	.269	.329	-7		0.0
/180I	2	12	10	.531	30	24	8	3	13	0	0	4	180	187	82	16	1	62	8	101	3.65	+1	.269	.329	-7		0.0
DARWIN, DANNY Daniel Wayne B10.25.1955 Bonham TX BR/TR/6'3"/(185–202) d9.8 b–Jeff Col Grayson Co. (TX) JC																											
1991	Bos A	3	6	.333	12	12	0	0	5	0	0	0	68	71	39	15	4	15	1	42	5.16	-16	.263	.309	-26	123	-0.5
1992	Bos A	9	9	.500	51	15	2	0	10	3	3	22	161.1	159	76	11	5	53	9	124	3.96	+7	.257	.319	-21	0	0.7
1993	Bos A	15	11	.577	34	34	2	1	24	0	0	0	229.1	196	93	31	3	49	8	130	3.26	+42	.230	**.272**	-13	0	3.5
1994	Bos A	7	5	.583	13	13	0	0	5	0	0	0	75.2	101	54	13	1	24	6	54	6.30	-20	.317	.361	+19	57	-1.1
Total	21	171	182	.484	716	371	53	9	207	32	25	237	3016.2	2951	1431	321	81	874	10	1942	3.84	+6	.256	.310	-5	230	9.2
Team	4	34	31	.523	110	74	4	1	44	3	3	22	534.1	527	262	70	13	141	24	350	4.14	+10	.256	.305	-11	180	2.6
/180I	1	11	10	.523	37	25	1	0	15	1	1	7	180	178	88	24	4	47	8	118	4.14	+10	.256	.305	-11	61	0.9
DEAL, COT Ellis Fergason B1.23.1923 Arapaho OK BB/TR (BL 1947–48)/5'10.5"/185 d9.11 C15																											
1947	Bos A	0	1	.000	5	2	0	0		0			12.2	20	13	0	0	7		6	9.24	-58	.364	.435	+25	0	-0.4
1948	Bos A	1	0	1.000	4	0	0	0		0			4	3	0	0	0	3		2	0.00	-100	.200	.333		0	0.4
Total	4	3	4	.429	45	2	0	0		1			89.1	111	74	14	4	48		34	6.55	-37	.307	.390	+25	0	-1.1
Team	2	1	1	.500	9	2	0	0		0			16.2	23	13	0	0	10		8	7.02	-43	.329	.412	+25		0.0
DEININGER, PEP Otto Charles B10.10.1877 Wasseralfingen, Germany D9.25.1950 Boston MA BL/TL/5'8.5"/180 d4.26▲																											
1902	Bos A	0	0	+	2	1	0	0		0			12	19	16	3	2	9		2	9.75	-63	.358	.469	+1		-0.2
DELCARMEN, MANNY Manuel B2.16.1982 Boston MA BR/TR/6'2"/190 [BosA00 2/62] d7.26																											
2005	Bos A	0	0	+	10	0	0	0	0	0	0	8	9	8	3	0	1	7	0	9	3.00	+51	.242	.390		0	0.1
2006	Bos A	2	0	1.000	50	0	0	0	0	0	4	35	53.1	68	32	2	2	17	2	45	5.06	-8	.309	.363		0	-0.1
Total	2	2	0	1.000	60	0	0	0	0	0	4	43	62.1	76	35	2	3	24	2	54	4.76	-2	.300	.367		0	0.0
/60G	2	2	0	1.000	60	0	0	0	0	0	4	43	62.1	76	35	2	3	24	2	54	4.76	-2	.300	.367			0.0
DELOCK, IKE Ivan Martin B11.11.1929 Highland Park MI BR/TR/5'11"/(175–178) d4.17																											
1952	Bos A	4	9	.308	39	7	1	1		5			95	88	50	9	2	50		46	4.26	-8	.245	.341	-11	0	-0.5
1953	Bos A	3	1	.750	23	1	0	0		1			48.2	60	27	2	2	20		22	4.44	-5	.308	.378	-58	0	-0.2
1955	Bos A	9	7	.563	29	18	6	0		3			143.2	136	67	17	4	61	2	88	3.76	+14	.247	.325	-9	0	0.8
1956	Bos A	13	7	.650	48	8	1	0		9			128.1	122	65	12	5	80	3	105	4.21	+10	.252	.359	-33	0	0.9
1957	Bos A	9	8	.529	49	2	0	0	22	11		54	94	80	40	11	3	45	7	62	3.83	+4	.230	.322	-66	0	0.6
1958	Bos A	14	8	.636	31	19	9	1	22	2		52	160	155	66	13	0	56	6	82	3.37	+19	.252	.314	-10	0	1.1
1959	Bos A	11	6	.647	28	17	4	0	22	0		52	134.1	120	53	12	2	62	1	55	2.95	+38	.236	.318	+16	0	1.2
1960	Bos A	9	10	.474	24	23	3	1	11	0		1	129.1	145	77	21	4	52	3	49	4.73	-15	.283	.353	+4	0	-1.6
1961	Bos A	6	9	.400	28	28	3	1	7	0		0	156	185	110	24	2	52	2	80	4.90	-15	.293	.346	+11	0	-1.7
1962	Bos A	4	5	.444	17	13	4	2	7	0		2	86.1	89	39	10	0	24	2	49	3.75	+10	.268	.315	-27	39	0.2
1963	Bos A	1	2	.333	6	6	1	0	2	0		0	32	31	18	4	0	12	0	23	4.50	-16	.246	.309	-2	0	-0.4
1963	Bal A	1	3	.250	7	5	0	0	0	0		2	30.1	25	17	7	0	16	1	11	5.04	-31	.236	.336	-44	0	-0.7
1963	Year	2	5	.286	13	11	1	0	2	0		2	62.1	56	35	11	0	28	1	34	4.76	-24	.241	.322	-20	0	-1.1
Total	11	84	75	.528	329	147	32	6	93	31		163	1238	1236	629	142	24	530	27	672	4.03	+2	.259	.335	-6	39	-0.3
Team	11	83	72	.535	322	142	32	6	93	31		161	1207.2	1211	612	135	24	514	26	661	4.01	+3	.260	.334	-4	39	0.4
/180I	2	12	11	.535	48	21	5	1	14	5		24	180	180	91	20	4	77	4	99	4.01	+3	.260	.334	-4	6	0.1
DENMAN, BRIAN Brian John B2.12.1956 Minneapolis MN BR/TR/6'4"/205 [BosA78*S1/13] d8.22 Col Minnesota																											
1982	Bos A	3	4	.429	9	9	2	1	3	0	0	0	49	55	32	6	0	9	3	9	4.78	-9	.282	.312	-5	0	-0.5
DEUTSCH, MEL Melvin Elliott B7.26.1915 Caldwell TX D11.18.2001 Austin TX BR/TR/6'4"/215 d4.21 Col Texas																											
1946	Bos A	0	0	+	3	0	0	0		0			6.1	7	5	1	0	3		2	5.68	-36	.280	.357		0	-0.1
DEVINEY, HAL Harold John B4.11.1893 Newton MA D1.4.1933 Westwood MA BR/TR d7.30																											
1920	Bos A	0	0	+	1	0	0	0		0			3	7	5	0	0	2		0	15.00	-76	.500	.563			0.0
DICKMAN, EMERSON George Emerson B11.12.1914 Buffalo NY D4.27.1981 New York NY BR/TR/6'2"/175 d6.27 Mil 1941–42 Col Washington and Lee																											
1936	Bos A	0	0	+	1	0	0	0		0			1	2	2	0	0	1		2	9.00	-41	.400	.500			0.0
1938	Bos A	5	5	.500	32	11	3	1		0			104	117	74	9	4	54		22	5.28	-7	.288	.377	+4		-0.1
1939	Bos A	8	3	.727	48	1	0	0		5			113.2	126	70	10	3	43		46	4.43	+7	.282	.349	+217		-0.1
1940	Bos A	8	6	.571	35	9	2	0		3			100	121	74	15	4	38		40	6.03	-25	.291	.356	+9		-2.1
1941	Bos A	1	1	.500	9	3	1	0		0			31	37	23	4	0	17		16	6.39	-35	.301	.386	+38	0	-0.5

Year	Tm Lg	W	L	Pct	G	GS	CG	ShO	QS	SV	BS	QR	IP	H	R	HR	HB	BB	IB	SO	ERA	AERA	OAV	OOB	Sup	DL	PW
Total	5	22	15	.595	125	24	6	1		8			349.2	403	243	38	11	153		126	5.33	-12	.288	.363	+18	0	-2.8
/60G	2	11	7	.595	60	12	3	0	0	4	0	0	168	193	117	18	5	73		60	5.32	-12	.288	.363	-43		-1.3
DINARDO, LENNY	Leonard Edward B9.19.1979 Miami FL BL/TL/6'4"/(190–195) [NYN01 3/102] d4.23 Col Stetson																										
2004	Bos A	0	0	+	22	0	0	0	0	0	0	14	27.2	34	17	1	2	12	1	21	4.23	+15	.298	.372		106	0.0
2005	Bos A	0	1	.000	8	1	0	0	1	0	0	6	14.2	13	6	1	0	5	1	15	1.84	+147	.236	.295	-39	0	0.2
2006	Bos A	1	2	.333	13	6	0	0	0	0	0	3	39	61	35	6	1	20	1	17	7.85	-40	.363	.432	+28	101	-0.8
Total	3	1	3	.250	43	7	0	0	1	0	0	23	81.1	108	58	8	3	37	3	53	5.53	-15	.320	.389	+16	207	-0.6
/60G	4	1	4	.250	60	10	0	0	1	0	0	32	113.1	151	81	11	4	52	4	74	5.54	-15	.320	.389	+62	289	-0.8
DINNEEN, BILL	William Henry "Big Bill" B4.5.1876 Syracuse NY D1.13.1955 Syracuse NY BR/TR/6'1"/190 d4.22 U29																										
1898	Was N	9	16	.360	29	27	22	0		0			218.1	238	140	6	16	88		83	4.00	-8	.275	.353	-11		-1.2
1899	Was N	14	20	.412	37	35	30	0		0			291	350	191	6	11	106		91	3.93	+0	.297	.361	-6		0.1
1900	Bos N	20	14	.588	40	37	33	1		0			320.2	304	161	11	9	105		107	3.12	+33	.250	.314	-2		**3.1**
1901	Bos N	15	18	.455	37	34	31	0		0			309.1	295	136	8	6	77		141	2.94	+23	.250	.299	-30		2.1
1902	Bos A	21	21	.500	42	42	39	2		0			371.1	348	155	9	8	99		136	2.93	+22	.248	.302	-5		2.3
1903	†Bos A	21	13	.618	37	34	32	6		**2**			299	255	98	6	4	66		148	2.26	+34	.230	.276	+3		2.9
1904	Bos A	23	14	.622	37	37	37	5		0			335.2	283	115	8	2	63		153	2.20	+22	.230	.268	+5		1.7
1905	Bos A	12	14	.462	31	29	23	2		1			243.2	235	117	7	7	50		97	3.73	-28	.255	.299	+0		-2.6
1906	Bos A	8	19	.296	28	27	22	1		0			218.2	209	101	4	1	52		60	2.92	-6	.255	.300	-33		-1.0
1907	Bos A	0	4	.000	5	5	3	0		0			32.2	42	25	5	2	8		8	5.23	-51	.313	.361	-37		-1.1
1907	StL A	7	10	.412	24	16	15	2		4			155.1	153	67	3	5	33		38	2.43	+3	.260	.305	-3		-0.2
1907	Year	7	14	.333	29	21	18	2		**4**			188	195	92	8	7	41		46	2.92	-14	.270	.315	-11		-1.3
1908	StL A	14	7	.667	27	16	11	2		0			167	133	52	2	4	53		39	2.10	+14	.231	.300	-11		0.8
1909	StL A	6	7	.462	17	13	8	3		0			112	112	53	3	1	29		26	3.46	-30	.267	.316	-10		-1.1
Total	12	170	177	.490	391	352	306	24		7			3074.2	2957	1411	78	76	829		1127	3.01	+7	.254	.308	-8		5.8
Team	6	85	85	.500	180	174	156	16		3			1501	1372	611	39	24	338		602	2.81	+6	.244	.290	-6		2.2
/180I	1	10	10	.500	22	21	19	2		0			180	165	73	5	3	41		72	2.81	+6	.244	.290	-6		0.3
DOBENS, RAY	Raymond Joseph "Lefty" B7.28.1906 Nashua NH D4.21.1980 Stuart FL BL/TL/5'8"/175 d7.7 Col Holy Cross																										
1929	Bos A	0	0	+	11	1	0	0		0			28.1	32	12	0	1	9		4	3.81	+12	.302	.362	+97		0.1
DOBSON, JOE	Joseph Gordon "Burrhead" B1.20.1917 Durant OK D6.23.1994 Jacksonville FL BR/TR/6'2"/(190–197) d4.26 Mil 1944–45																										
1939	Cle A	2	3	.400	35	3	0	0		1			78	87	56	3	1	51		27	5.88	-25	.290	.395	-13		-0.9
1940	Cle A	3	7	.300	40	7	2	1		3			100	101	60	8	0	48		57	4.95	-15	.268	.351	-29		-0.7
1941	Bos A	12	5	.706	27	18	7	1		0			134.1	136	70	8	2	67		69	4.49	-7	.262	.349	+19	0	-0.2
1942	Bos A	11	9	.550	30	23	10	3		0			182.2	155	73	9	2	68		72	3.30	+13	.231	.303	-8	0	1.0
1943	Bos A	7	11	.389	25	20	9	3		0			164.1	144	63	4	0	57		63	3.12	+6	.239	.305	-2	0	-0.1
1946	†Bos A	13	7	.650	32	24	9	1		0			166.2	148	72	11	1	68		91	3.24	+13	.234	.309	+19	0	0.5
1947	Bos A	18	8	.692	33	31	15	1		1			228.2	203	84	15	1	73		110	2.95	+32	.238	**.299**	+10	0	2.6
1948	Bos A☆	16	10	.615	38	32	16	5		2			245.1	237	115	14	1	92		116	3.56	+23	.253	.320	+24	0	1.8
1949	Bos A	14	12	.538	33	27	12	2		2			212.2	219	103	12	2	97		87	3.85	+13	.269	.348	-6	0	0.9
1950	Bos A	15	10	.600	39	27	12	1		4			206.2	217	103	15	0	81		81	4.18	+17	.275	.343	+15	0	1.9
1951	Chi A	7	6	.538	28	21	6	0		3			146.2	136	68	17	0	51		67	3.62	+11	.248	.312	+31	0	0.0
1952	Chi A	14	10	.583	29	25	11	3		1			200.2	164	66	11	0	60		101	2.51	+45	.222	.280	-10	0	2.7
1953	Chi A	5	5	.500	23	15	3	1		1			100.2	96	46	10	0	37		50	3.67	+10	.249	.314	-15	0	0.1
1954	Bos A	0	0	+	2	0	0	0		0			2.2	5	2	0	0	1		1	6.75	-39	.385	.429		0	0.0
Total	14	137	103	.571	414	273	112	22		18			2170	2048	981	137	10	851		992	3.62	+12	.250	.322	+7	0	9.6
Team	9	106	72	.596	259	202	90	17		9			1544	1464	685	88	9	604		690	3.57	+15	.251	.322	+9		8.4
/180I	1	12	8	.596	30	24	10	2		1			180	171	80	10	1	70		80	3.57	+15	.251	.322	+9		1.0
DODGE, SAM	Samuel Edward B12.19.1889 Neath PA D4.5.1966 Utica NY BR/TR/6'1"/170 d9.24																										
1921	Bos A	0	0	+	1	0	0	0		0			1	1	1	0	0	1		0	9.00	-53	.500	.667			0.0
1922	Bos A	0	0	+	3	0	0	0		0			6	11	6	0	0	3		3	4.50	-9	.379	.438			-0.1
Total	2	0	0	+	4	0	0	0		0			7	12	7	0	0	4		3	5.14	-20	.387	.457			-0.1
DOHERTY, JOHN	John Harold B6.11.1967 New York NY BR/TR/6'4"/(200–215) [DetA89 19/499] d4.8 Col Concordia (NY)																										
1996	Bos A	0	0	+	3	0	0	0	0	0	0	1	6.1	8	10	1	1	4	0	3	5.68	-10	.276	.382		0	-0.1
Total	5	32	31	.508	148	61	5	2	28	9	4	53	521.1	613	316	47	19	140	28	177	4.87	-8	.296	.344	+12	67	-2.2
DONOHUE, PETE	Peter Joseph B11.5.1900 Athens TX D2.23.1988 Ft.Worth TX BR/TR/6'2"/185 d7.1 Col TCU																										
1932	Bos A	0	1	.000	4	2	0	0		0			12.2	18	11	2	0	6		1	7.82	-43	.340	.407	-34		-0.3
Total	12	134	118	.532	344	267	137	16		12			2112.1	2439	1082	68	46	422		571	3.87	+3	.293	.330	+0		5.6
DOPSON, JOHN	John Robert B7.14.1963 Baltimore MD BL/TR/6'4"/(205–235) [MonN82 2/45] d9.4																										
1985	Mon N	0	2	.000	4	3	0	0	1	0	0	0	13	25	17	4	0	4	0	4	11.08	-69	.379	.414	-49	0	-1.3
1988	Mon N	3	11	.214	26	26	1	0	19	0	0	0	168.2	150	69	15	1	58	3	101	3.04	+20	.235	.299	-20	0	0.3
1989	Bos A	12	8	.600	29	28	2	0	16	0	0	1	169.1	166	84	14	2	69	0	95	3.99	+3	.257	.328	+2	26	0.4
1990	Bos A	0	0	+	4	4	0	0	0	0	0	0	17.2	13	7	2	0	9	0	9	2.04	+101	.200	.293	-6	151	0.2
1991	Bos A	0	0	+	1	0	0	0	0	0	0	0	1	2	2	0	0	1	0	0	18.00	-76	.500	.500		148	-0.1
1992	Bos A	7	11	.389	25	25	0	0	11	0	0	0	141.1	159	78	17	2	38	2	55	4.08	+4	.287	.334	-20	41	0.1
1993	Bos A	7	11	.389	34	28	1	1	9	0	0	2	155.2	170	93	16	2	59	12	89	4.97	-7	.281	.343	-2	0	-0.3
1994	Cal A	1	4	.200	21	5	0	0	1	1	1	8	58.2	67	41	6	3	26	3	33	6.14	-20	.288	.365	-29	50	-0.5
Total	8	30	47	.390	144	119	4	1	57	1	1	11	725.1	752	391	74	10	264	20	386	4.27	-2	.268	.331	-11	416	-1.2
Team	5	26	30	.464	93	85	3	1	36	0	0	3	485	510	264	49	6	176	14	248	4.29	+1	.272	.334	-6	366	0.3
/180I	2	10	11	.464	35	32	1	0	13	0	0	1	180	189	98	18	2	65	5	92	4.29	+1	.272	.334	-6	136	0.1
DORISH, HARRY	Harry "Fritz" B7.13.1921 Swoyersville PA D12.31.2000 Wilkes–Barre PA BR/TR/5'11"/206 d4.15 C5																										
1947	Bos A	7	8	.467	41	9	2	0		2			136	149	80	6	1	54		50	4.70	-17	.283	.351	-6	0	-1.3
1948	Bos A	0	1	.000	9	0	0	0		0			14.1	18	13	1	0	6		5	5.65	-22	.281	.343		0	-0.2
1949	Bos A	0	0	+	5	0	0	0		0			7.2	7	2	1	0	1		5	2.35	+86	.241	.267		0	0.1
1956	Bos A	0	2	.000	15	0	0	0		0			22.2	23	10	1	0	10	1	11	3.57	+29	.277	.351		0	0.3
Total	10	45	43	.511	323	40	13	2		44			834.1	850	406	58	19	301	4	332	3.83	+6	.267	.333	-5	0	2.8
Team	4	7	11	.389	70	9	2	0		2			180.2	197	105	9	1	71	1	71	4.53	-11	.280	.347	-6		-1.1
/60G	3	6	9	.389	60	8	2	0		2			155	169	90	8	1	61	1	61	4.53	-11	.280	.347	-6		-0.9
DORSEY, JIM	James Edward B8.2.1955 Oak Park IL BR/TR/6'2"/(190–200) [AnaA75*2/26] d9.2 Col Los Angeles Valley (CA) JC																										
1980	Cal A	1	2	.333	4	4	0	0	0	0	0	0	15.2	25	16	2	1	8	0	8	9.19	-57	.368	.436	-4	0	-1.2
1984	Bos A	0	0	+	2	0	0	0	0	0	0	1	2.2	6	3	0	0	2	0	4	10.13	-58	.462	.533		0	-0.1
1985	Bos A	0	1	.000	2	1	0	0	0	0	0	0	5.1	12	12	2	0	10	1	2	20.25	-79	.444	.595	-37	0	-1.1
Total	3	1	3	.250	8	5	0	0	0	0	0	1	23.2	43	31	4	1	20	1	14	11.79	-66	.398	.492	-12	0	-2.4
Team	2	0	1	.000	4	1	0	0	0	0	0	1	8	18	15	2	0	12	1	6	16.88	-75	.450	.577	-37		-1.2
DRAGO, DICK	Richard Anthony B6.25.1945 Toledo OH BR/TR/6'1"/(186–200) d4.11 Col Detroit Mercy																										
1969	KC A	11	13	.458	41	26	10	2	15	1	0	10	200.2	190	95	19	2	65	6	108	3.77	-2	.248	.306	-26	0	-0.4
1970	KC A	9	15	.375	35	34	7	1	21	0	0	1	240	239	110	20	7	72	5	127	3.75	+0	.266	.322	-12	0	-0.5
1971	KC A	17	11	.607	35	34	15	4	24	0	0	0	241.1	251	84	14	9	46	1	109	2.98	+15	.276	.315	-5	0	1.8
1972	KC A	12	17	.414	34	33	11	2	24	0	0	1	239.1	230	88	22	6	51	4	135	3.01	+1	.254	.297	-18	0	-0.3
1973	KC A	12	14	.462	37	33	10	1	18	0	0	2	212.2	252	116	16	7	76	10	98	4.23	-3	.300	.360	+5	0	-0.5
1974	Bos A	7	10	.412	33	18	8	0	12	3	1	13	175.2	165	71	17	5	56	9	90	3.48	+10	.251	.313	-31	0	0.7
1975	†Bos A	2	2	.500	40	2	0	0	0	15	3	27	72.2	69	31	5	0	31	3	43	3.84	+6	.247	.321	+84	0	0.3
1976	Cal A	7	8	.467	43	0	0	0	0	6	3	27	79.1	80	42	7	5	31	8	43	4.42	-24	.264	.338		0	-1.8
1977	Cal A	0	1	.000	13	0	0	0	0	2	1	7	21	22	8	3	0	3	2	15	3.00	+31	.272	.291		0	0.1
1977	Bal A	6	3	.667	36	0	0	0	0	3	6	21	39.2	49	19	2	1	15	4	20	3.63	+6	.308	.363		0	0.0
1977	Year	6	4	.600	49	0	0	0	0	5	7	28	60.2	71	27	5	1	18	6	35	3.41	+13	.296	.340		0	0.1

Year	Tm Lg	W	L	Pct	G	GS	CG	ShO	QS	SV	BS	QR	IP	H	R	HR	HB	BB	IB	SO	ERA	AERA	OAV	OOB	Sup	DL	PW
1978	Bos A	4	4	.500	37	1	0	0	0	7	3	27	77.1	71	30	5	4	32	5	42	3.03	+36	.246	.327	+118	0	1.0
1979	Bos A	10	6	.625	53	1	0	0	0	13	4	38	89	85	33	6	3	21	6	67	3.03	+47	.254	.300	+287	0	2.6
1980	Bos A	7	7	.500	43	7	1	0	4	3	4	21	132.2	127	67	17	5	44	7	63	4.14	+3	.251	.316	-19	0	0.1
1981	Sea A	4	6	.400	39	0	0	0	0	5	3	22	53.2	71	33	4	0	15	5	27	5.53	-30	.324	.361		0	-1.5
Total	13	108	117	.480	519	189	62	10	118	58	28	217	1875	1901	827	157	54	558	75	987	3.62	+3	.266	.321	-11	0	1.6
Team	5	30	29	.508	206	29	9	0	16	41	15	126	547.1	517	232	50	17	184	30	305	3.55	+16	.250	.315	-4		4.7
/60G	1	9	8	.508	60	8	3	0	5	12	4	37	159.1	151	68	15	5	54	9	89	3.55	+16	.250	.315	-4		1.4

DREISEWERD, CLEM Clemens Johann "Steamboat" B1.24.1916 Old Monroe MO D9.11.2001 Ocean Springs MS BL/TL/6'1.5"/195 d8.29 Mil 1945

Year	Tm Lg	W	L	Pct	G	GS	CG	ShO	QS	SV	BS	QR	IP	H	R	HR	HB	BB	IB	SO	ERA	AERA	OAV	OOB	Sup	DL	PW
1944	Bos A	2	4	.333	7	7	3	0		0			48.2	52	25	2	0	9		9	4.07	-16	.268	.300	-5	0	-0.4
1945	Bos A	0	1	.000	2	2	0	0		0			9.2	13	5	0	1	2		3	4.66	-27	.325	.372	-50	0	-0.2
1946	†Bos A	4	1	.800	20	1	0	0		0			47.1	50	22	3	0	15		19	4.18	-12	.276	.332	+110	0	-0.2
1948	StL A	0	2	.000	13	0	0	0		1			22.1	28	15	6	0	8		6	5.64	-19	.318	.375		0	-0.3
1948	NY N	0	0	+	4	0	0	0		1			12.2	17	8	3	0	5		2	5.68	-31	.321	.379		0	0.0
1948	Major	0	2	.000	17	0	0	0		2			34	45	23	9	0	13		8	5.66	-23	.319	.377		0	-0.3
Total	4	6	8	.429	46	10	3	0		2			140.2	160	75	14	1	39		39	4.54	-18	.288	.336	-7	0	-1.1
Team	3	6	6	.500	29	10	3	0		0			105.2	115	52	5	1	26		31	4.17	-16	.277	.321	-2		-0.8

DUBUC, JEAN Jean Joseph Octave Arthur "Chauncey" B9.15.1888 St.Johnsbury VT D8.28.1958 Fort Myers FL BR/TR/5'10.5"/185 d6.25 C2 Col Notre Dame

Year	Tm Lg	W	L	Pct	G	GS	CG	ShO	QS	SV	BS	QR	IP	H	R	HR	HB	BB	IB	SO	ERA	AERA	OAV	OOB	Sup	DL	PW
1918	†Bos A	0	1	.000	2	1	1	0		0			10.2	11	5	1	0	5		1	4.22	-36	.268	.348	-16		-0.1
Total	9	84	76	.525	256	150	101	12		13			1444.1	1290	672	19	47	577		438	3.04	-4	.245	.325	+13		1.5

DULIBA, BOB Robert John "Ach" B1.9.1935 Glen Lyon PA BR/TR/5'10"/(175–185) d8.11

Year	Tm Lg	W	L	Pct	G	GS	CG	ShO	QS	SV	BS	QR	IP	H	R	HR	HB	BB	IB	SO	ERA	AERA	OAV	OOB	Sup	DL	PW
1965	Bos A	4	2	.667	39	0	0	0	0	1		26	64.1	60	31	6	0	22	7	27	3.78	-1	.248	.308		0	-0.1
Total	7	17	12	.586	176	0	0	0	0	14		121	257	257	112	25	1	96	15	129	3.47	+8	.268	.332		72	0.3

DUMONT, GEORGE George Henry "Pea Soup" B11.13.1895 Minneapolis MN D10.13.1956 Minneapolis MN BR/TR/5'11"/163 d9.14

Year	Tm Lg	W	L	Pct	G	GS	CG	ShO	QS	SV	BS	QR	IP	H	R	HR	HB	BB	IB	SO	ERA	AERA	OAV	OOB	Sup	DL	PW
1919	Bos A	0	4	.000	13	2	0	0		0			35.1	45	21	1	1	19		12	4.33	-30	.326	.411	-48		-0.6
Total	5	10	23	.303	77	35	14	4		3			347	294	151	4	10	130		128	2.85	-4	.230	.306	-26		-1.8

DURHAM, ED Edward Fant "Bull" B8.17.1907 Chester SC D4.27.1976 Chester SC BL/TR/5'11"/170 d4.19

Year	Tm Lg	W	L	Pct	G	GS	CG	ShO	QS	SV	BS	QR	IP	H	R	HR	HB	BB	IB	SO	ERA	AERA	OAV	OOB	Sup	DL	PW
1929	Bos A	1	0	1.000	14	1	0	0		0			22.1	34	24	2	0	14		6	9.27	-54	.374	.457	-61		-0.5
1930	Bos A	4	15	.211	33	12	6	1		1			140	144	81	9	2	43		28	4.69	-2	.270	.326	-46		-0.4
1931	Bos A	8	10	.444	38	15	7	2		0			165.1	175	91	9	4	50		53	4.25	+1	.266	.322	-36		-0.6
1932	Bos A	6	13	.316	34	22	4	0		0			175.1	187	90	13	4	49		52	3.80	+18	.274	.327	-29		0.9
1933	Chi A	10	6	.625	24	21	6	0		0			138.2	137	74	12	5	46		65	4.48	-5	.256	.320	+18		0.0
Total	5	29	44	.397	143	71	23	3		1			641.2	677	360	45	15	202		204	4.45	-1	.271	.329	-21		-0.6
Team	4	19	38	.333	119	50	17	3		1			503	540	286	33	10	156		139	4.44	+0	.275	.331	-36		-0.6
/180I	1	7	14	.333	43	18	6	1		0			180	193	102	12	4	56		50	4.44	+0	.275	.331	-36		-0.2

EARLEY, ARNOLD Arnold Carl B6.4.1933 Lincoln Park MI D9.29.1999 Flint MI BL/TL/6'1"/(195–200) d9.27

Year	Tm Lg	W	L	Pct	G	GS	CG	ShO	QS	SV	BS	QR	IP	H	R	HR	HB	BB	IB	SO	ERA	AERA	OAV	OOB	Sup	DL	PW
1960	Bos A	0	1	.000	2	0	0	0	0	0		0	4	9	8	1	0	4	0	5	15.75	-74	.429	.520		0	-0.8
1961	Bos A	2	4	.333	33	0	0	0	0	7		22	49.2	42	31	3	0	34	3	44	3.99	+5	.226	.345		0	-0.3
1962	Bos A	4	5	.444	38	3	0	0	1	5		18	68.1	76	53	8	1	46	1	59	5.80	-29	.281	.384	-42	0	-1.8
1963	Bos A	3	7	.300	53	4	0	0	0	1		35	115.2	124	73	13	8	43	8	97	4.75	-20	.270	.342	+12	0	-1.1
1964	Bos A	1	1	.500	25	3	1	0	2	1		18	50.1	51	17	3	1	18	0	45	2.68	+44	.266	.332	+23	63	0.4
1965	Bos A	0	1	.000	57	0	0	0	0	0		40	74.1	79	42	5	3	29	8	47	3.63	+3	.271	.338		0	-0.1
1966	Chi N	2	1	.667	13	0	0	0	0	0		10	17.2	14	11	1	0	9	0	12	3.57	+3	.226	.319		0	-0.2
1967	Hou N	0	0	+	2	0	0	0	0	0		0	1.1	5	5	1	0	1	0	1	27.00	-88	.625	.667		0	-0.2
Total	8	12	20	.375	223	10	1	0	3	14		143	381.1	400	240	35	13	184	20	310	4.48	-13	.269	.352	-2	63	-4.1
Team	6	10	19	.345	208	10	1	0	3	14		133	362.1	381	224	33	13	174	20	297	4.45	-12	.268	.351	-1	63	-3.7
/60G	2	3	5	.345	60	3	0	0	1	4		38	104.2	110	65	10	4	50	6	86	4.44	-12	.268	.351	-1	18	-1.1

ECKERSLEY, DENNIS Dennis Lee B10.3.1954 Oakland CA BR/TR/6'2"/(175–195) [CleA72 3/50] d4.12 HF2004

Year	Tm Lg	W	L	Pct	G	GS	CG	ShO	QS	SV	BS	QR	IP	H	R	HR	HB	BB	IB	SO	ERA	AERA	OAV	OOB	Sup	DL	PW
1978	Bos A	20	8	.714	35	35	16	3	25	0	0	0	268.1	258	99	30	7	71	8	162	2.99	+38	.251	.302	+11	0	3.1
1979	Bos A	17	10	.630	33	33	17	2	24	0	0	0	246.2	234	89	29	6	59	4	150	2.99	+49	.250	.297	+5	0	4.0
1980	Bos A	12	14	.462	30	30	8	0	15	0	0	0	197.2	188	101	25	2	44	7	121	4.28	+0	.248	.289	-13	0	0.0
1981	Bos A	9	8	.529	23	23	8	2	12	0	0	0	154	160	82	9	3	35	2	79	4.27	-8	.267	.308	+11	0	-0.6
1982	Bos A★	13	13	.500	33	33	11	3	20	0	0	0	224.1	228	101	31	2	43	3	127	3.73	+17	.261	.296	-21	0	1.5
1983	Bos A	9	13	.409	28	28	2	0	15	0	0	0	176.1	223	119	27	6	39	4	77	5.61	-22	.303	.341	-22	0	-2.3
1984	Bos A	4	4	.500	9	9	2	0	4	0	0	0	64.2	71	38	10	1	13	2	33	5.01	-16	.284	.318	+19	0	-0.4
1998	†Bos A	4	1	.800	50	0	0	0	0	1	3	33	39.2	46	21	6	2	8	3	22	4.76	-1	.291	.331		53	0.1
Total	24	197	171	.535	1071	361	100	20	220	390	71	554	3285.2	3076	1382	347	75	738	91	2401	3.50	+17	.246	.290	-4	150	30.5
Team	8	88	71	.553	241	191	64	10	115	1	3	33	1371.2	1408	650	167	29	312	33	771	3.92	+9	.264	.306	-4	53	5.4
/180I	1	12	9	.553	32	25	8	1	15	0	0	4	180	185	85	22	4	41	4	101	3.92	+9	.264	.306	-4	7	0.7

EHMKE, HOWARD Howard Jonathan "Bob" B4.24.1894 Silver Creek NY D3.17.1959 Philadelphia PA BR/TR/6'3"/190 d4.12 Mil 1918

Year	Tm Lg	W	L	Pct	G	GS	CG	ShO	QS	SV	BS	QR	IP	H	R	HR	HB	BB	IB	SO	ERA	AERA	OAV	OOB	Sup	DL	PW
1923	Bos A	20	17	.541	43	39	28	2		3			316.2	318	155	12	20	119		121	3.78	+9	.272	.349	-11		1.9
1924	Bos A	19	17	.528	45	36	26	4		4			**315**	324	139	9	11	81		119	3.46	+26	.265	.316	-6		3.4
1925	Bos A	9	20	.310	34	31	**22**	0		1			260.2	285	141	8	11	85		95	3.73	+22	.285	.348	-39		1.7
1926	Bos A	3	10	.231	14	14	7	1		0			97.1	115	69	3	4	45		38	5.46	-25	.303	.382	+3		-1.7
Total	15	166	166	.500	427	338	199	20		14			2820.2	2873	1424	103	137	1042		1030	3.75	+4	.271	.343	-6		8.5
Team	4	51	64	.443	136	120	83	7		8			989.2	1042	504	32	46	330		373	3.83	+12	.276	.342	-15		5.3
/180I	1	9	12	.443	25	22	15	1		1			180	190	92	6	8	60		68	3.83	+12	.276	.342	-15		1.0

EIBEL, HACK Henry Hack B12.6.1893 Brooklyn NY D10.16.1945 Macon GA BL/TL/5'11"/220 d6.13.1912▲

Year	Tm Lg	W	L	Pct	G	GS	CG	ShO	QS	SV	BS	QR	IP	H	R	HR	HB	BB	IB	SO	ERA	AERA	OAV	OOB	Sup	DL	PW
1920	Bos A	0	0	+	3	0	0	0		0			10.1	10	4	0	0	3		5	3.48	+5	.270	.325			0.0

ELLSWORTH, DICK Richard Clark B3.22.1940 Lusk WY BL/TL/6'4"/(180–200) d6.22 s-Steve Col Fresno (CA) City

Year	Tm Lg	W	L	Pct	G	GS	CG	ShO	QS	SV	BS	QR	IP	H	R	HR	HB	BB	IB	SO	ERA	AERA	OAV	OOB	Sup	DL	PW
1968	Bos A	16	7	.696	31	28	10	1	16	0		2	196	196	74	16	7	37	3	106	3.03	+4	.260	.300	+29	0	-0.2
1969	Bos A	0	0	+	2	2	0	0	1	0	0	0	12	16	5	1	0	4	0	4	3.75	+2	.320	.370	-19	0	0.0
Total	13	115	137	.456	407	310	87	9	165	5	2	73	2155.2	2274	1033	194	45	595	71	1140	3.72	+0	.272	.322	-4	0	-2.7
Team	2	16	7	.696	33	30	10	1	17	0	0	2	208	212	79	17	7	41	3	110	3.07	+4	.264	.304	+26		-0.2
/180I	2	14	6	.696	29	26	9	1	15	0	0	2	180	183	68	15	6	35	3	95	3.07	+4	.264	.304	+26		-0.2

ELLSWORTH, STEVE Steven Clark B7.30.1960 Chicago IL BR/TR/6'8"/220 [BosA81 S1/9] d4.7 f-Dick Col Cal St.–Northridge

Year	Tm Lg	W	L	Pct	G	GS	CG	ShO	QS	SV	BS	QR	IP	H	R	HR	HB	BB	IB	SO	ERA	AERA	OAV	OOB	Sup	DL	PW
1988	Bos A	1	6	.143	8	7	0	0	3	0	0	1	36	47	29	7	1	16	1	16	6.75	-39	.315	.383	+17	0	-1.6

EMBREE, ALAN Alan Duane B1.23.1970 The Dalles OR BL/TL/6'2"/(185–190) [CleA89 5/125] d9.15 [DL 1993 Cle A 124]

Year	Tm Lg	W	L	Pct	G	GS	CG	ShO	QS	SV	BS	QR	IP	H	R	HR	HB	BB	IB	SO	ERA	AERA	OAV	OOB	Sup	DL	PW
2002	Bos A	1	2	.333	32	0	0	0	0	2	3	24	33.1	24	12	4	1	11	1	43	2.97	+51	.203	.273		15	0.5
2003	†Bos A	4	1	.800	65	0	0	0	0	1	1	47	55	49	26	5	0	16	3	45	4.25	+10	.241	.294		20	0.3
2004	†Bos A	2	2	.500	71	0	0	0	0	0	1	50	52.1	49	28	7	1	11	1	37	4.13	+18	.244	.284		0	0.3
2005	Bos A	1	4	.200	43	0	0	0	0	1	2	27	37.2	42	33	8	1	11	2	30	7.65	-41	.284	.333		0	-1.4
Total	13	34	36	.486	708	4	0	0	0	8	20	495	619.2	590	345	79	17	232	23	571	4.58	-4	.252	.319	-13	231	-0.5
Team	4	8	9	.471	211	0	0	0	0	4	7	148	178.1	164	99	24	3	49	7	155	4.69	-1	.245	.296		35	-0.3
/60G	1	2	3	.471	60	0	0	0	0	1	2	42	50.2	47	28	7	1	14	2	44	4.70	-1	.245	.296		10	-0.1

ERDOS, TODD Todd Michael B11.21.1973 Washington PA BR/TR/6'1"/(190–204) [SDN92 9/253] d6.8

Year	Tm Lg	W	L	Pct	G	GS	CG	ShO	QS	SV	BS	QR	IP	H	R	HR	HB	BB	IB	SO	ERA	AERA	OAV	OOB	Sup	DL	PW
2001	Bos A	0	0	+	10	0	0	0	0	0	0	5	16.1	15	9	2	3	8	1	7	4.96	-11	.263	.366		0	0.0
Total	5	2	0	1.000	63	0	0	0	0	2	1	34	93.2	105	62	12	12	45	3	58	5.57	-20	.283	.372		0	-0.8

ESHELMAN, VAUGHN Vaughn Michael B5.22.1969 Philadelphia PA BL/TL/6'3"/(210–215) [BalA91 4/108] d5.2 Col Houston [DL 1998 TB A 181]

Year	Tm Lg	W	L	Pct	G	GS	CG	ShO	QS	SV	BS	QR	IP	H	R	HR	HB	BB	IB	SO	ERA	AERA	OAV	OOB	Sup	DL	PW
1995	Bos A	6	3	.667	23	14	0	0	5	0	0	8	81.2	86	47	3	1	36	0	41	4.85	+0	.272	.346	+7	52	0.0
1996	Bos A	6	3	.667	39	10	0	0	3	0	0	18	87.2	112	79	13	2	58	4	59	7.08	-28	.311	.405	+27	26	-1.6
1997	Bos A	3	3	.500	21	6	0	0	2	0	1	6	42.2	58	32	3	2	17	5	18	6.33	-26	.330	.391	+18	0	-0.9
Total	3	15	9	.625	83	30	0	0	10	0	1	32	212	256	158	19	5	111	9	118	6.07	-19	.300	.380	+16	259	-2.5
/60G	2	11	7	.625	60	22	0	0	7	0	1	23	153.1	185	114	14	4	80	7	85	6.07	-19	.300	.380	-16	187	-1.8

Year	Tm Lg	W	L	Pct	G	GS	CG	ShO	QS	SV	BS	QR	IP	H	R	HR	HB	BB	IB	SO	ERA	AERA	OAV	OOB	Sup	DL	PW
EVANS, BILL William Lawrence B3.25.1919 Quanah TX D11.30.1983 Grand Junction CO BR/TR/6'2"/180 d4.21																											
1949	Chi A	0	1	.000	4	0	0	0		0			6.1	6	6	0	0	8		1	7.11	-41	.261	.452		0	-0.3
1951	Bos A	0	0	+	9	0	0	0		0			15.1	15	8	0	0	8		3	4.11	+9	.268	.359		0	-0.1
Total	2	0	1	.000	13	0	0	0		0			21.2	21	14	0	0	16		4	4.98	-12	.266	.389		0	-0.4
FARR, STEVE Steven Michael B12.12.1956 LaPlata MD BR/TR/5'11"/(190–206) d5.16 Col American																											
1994	Bos A	1	0	1.000	11	0	0	0	0	0	1	5	13	24	9	2	0	3	0	8	6.23	-19	.407	.435		9	-0.1
Total	11	48	45	.516	509	28	1	1	11	132	38	352	824.1	751	326	70	32	334	47	668	3.25	+28	.244	.322	-30	88	12.4
FASSERO, JEFF Jeffrey Joseph B1.5.1963 Springfield IL BL/TL/6'1"/(195–200) [StLN84 22/554] d5.4 Col U. of Mississippi																											
2000	Bos A	8	8	.500	38	23	0	0	7	0	0	11	130	153	72	16	1	50	2	97	4.78	+5	.296	.358	-6	15	0.5
Total	16	121	124	.494	720	242	17	2	117	25	24	332	2033.2	2083	1042	214	37	724	50	1643	4.11	+7	.264	.327	+2	45	4.5
/180I	1	11	11	.500	53	32	0	0	10	0	0	15	180	212	100	22	1	69	3	134	4.78	+5	.296	.358	+30	21	0.7
FERGUSON, ALEX James Alexander B2.16.1897 Montclair NJ D4.26.1976 Sepulveda CA BR/TR/6'0"/180 d8.16 Mil 1918																											
1918	NY A	0	0	+	1	0	0	0		0			1.2	2	0	0	0	2		1	0.00	-100	.333	.500			0.0
1921	NY A	3	1	.750	17	4	1	0		1			56.1	64	40	4	4	27		9	5.91	-28	.296	.385	+18		-0.6
1922	Bos A	9	16	.360	39	27	10	1		2			198.1	201	108	5	6	62		44	4.31	-5	.265	.326	-31		-1.0
1923	Bos A	9	13	.409	34	27	11	0		0			198.1	229	115	5	9	67		72	4.04	+2	.297	.360	-23		-0.6
1924	Bos A	14	17	.452	41	32	15	0		2			237.2	259	115	6	6	108		78	3.79	+15	.286	.366	-22		1.4
1925	Bos A	0	2	.000	5	4	0	0		1			15.2	22	22	6	1	5		5	10.91	-58	.314	.368	-12		-1.1
1925	NY A	4	2	.667	21	6	0	0		1			54.1	83	57	3	2	42		20	7.79	-45	.358	.460	+35		-2.1
1925	†Was A	5	1	.833	7	6	3	0		0			55.1	52	22	2	2	23		24	3.25	+30	.256	.338	+26		0.3
1925	Year	9	5	.643	33	16	3	0		2			125.1	157	101	11	5	70		49	6.18	-31	.311	.400	+20		-2.9
1926	Was A	3	4	.429	19	4	0	0		1			47.2	69	51	4	3	18		16	7.74	-50	.343	.405	+36		-2.8
1927	Phi N	8	16	.333	31	31	16	0		0			227	280	132	15	6	65		73	4.84	-15	.313	.363	-15		-1.8
1928	Phi N	5	10	.333	34	19	5	1		2			134.2	168	91	14	6	52		51	5.88	-27	.315	.382	+18		-2.2
1929	Phi N	1	2	.333	5	4	1	0		0			12.2	19	18	2	0	10		3	12.08	-57	.345	.446	-50		-1.4
1929	Bro N	0	1	.000	3	2	0	0		0			2	7	7	2	0	1		1	22.50	-79	.583	.615	+89		-0.7
1929	Year	1	3	.250	8	6	1	0		0			14.2	26	25	4	0	11		4	13.50	-62	.388	.474	-9		-2.1
Total	10	61	85	.418	257	166	62	2		10			1241.2	1455	778	68	45	482		397	4.93	-15	.299	.368	-10		-12.6
Team	4	32	48	.400	119	90	36	1		5			650	711	360	22	22	242		199	4.20	+0	.284	.352	-25		-1.3
/180I	1	9	13	.400	33	25	10	0		1			180	197	100	6	6	67		55	4.20	+0	.284	.352	-25		-0.4
FERRELL, WES Wesley Cheek B2.2.1908 Greensboro NC D12.9.1976 Sarasota FL BR/TR/6'2"/195 d9.9 b–Rick▲																											
1934	Bos A	14	5	.737	26	23	17	3		1			181	205	87	4	0	49		67	3.63	+32	.282	.327	+6		2.8
1935	Bos A	**25**	14	.641	41	**38**	**31**	3		0			**322.1**	336	149	16	3	108		110	3.52	+35	.267	.326	+1		**6.8**
1936	Bos A	20	15	.571	39	**38**	**28**	3		0			**301**	330	160	11	6	119		106	4.19	+27	.274	.343	-11		4.4
1937	Bos A	3	6	.333	12	11	5	0		0			73.1	111	66	14	1	34		31	7.61	-38	.348	.412	+34		-1.4
Total	15	193	128	.601	374	323	227	17		13			2623	2845	1382	132	23	1040		985	4.04	+17	.275	.343	+2	0	31.1
Team	4	62	40	.608	118	110	81	9		1			877.2	982	462	45	10	310		314	4.11	+20	.280	.340	+1		12.6
/180I	1	13	8	.608	24	23	17	2		0			180	201	95	9	2	64		64	4.11	+20	.280	.340	+1		2.6
FERRISS, DAVE David Meadow "Boo" B12.5.1921 Shaw MS BL/TR/6'2"/208 d4.29 C5 Col Mississippi St.																											
1945	Bos A✱	21	10	.677	35	31	26	5		2			264.2	263	101	6	7	85		94	2.96	+15	.264	.327	+18	0	3.0
1946	†Bos A☆	25	6	**.806**	40	35	26	6		3			274	274	109	14	3	71		106	3.25	+13	.259	.308	+44	0	1.8
1947	Bos A	12	11	.522	33	28	14	1		0			218.1	241	106	14	7	92		64	4.04	-4	.287	.362	+13	0	0.5
1948	Bos A	7	3	.700	31	9	1	0		3			115.1	127	71	7	7	61		30	5.23	-16	.286	.381	+35	0	-0.6
1949	Bos A	0	0	+	4	0	0	0		0			6.2	7	3	1	1	4		1	4.05	+8	.292	.414		73	0.1
1950	Bos A	0	0	+	1	0	0	0		0			1	2	2	0	0	1		1	18.00	-73	.500	.600		0	-0.1
Total	6	65	30	.684	144	103	67	12		8			880	914	392	42	25	314		296	3.64	+3	.272	.338	+26	73	4.7
/180I	1	13	6	.684	29	21	14	2	0	2	0	0	180	187	80	9	5	64		61	3.64	+3	.272	.338	-74	15	1.0
FINCH, JOEL Joel D B8.20.1956 South Bend IN BR/TR/6'2"/175 [BosA74 9/212] d6.12																											
1979	Bos A	0	3	.000	15	7	0	0	2	0	0	5	57.1	65	31	5	1	25	3	25	4.87	-8	.289	.361	-21	0	0.0
FINE, TOMMY Thomas Morgan B10.10.1914 Cleburne TX D1.10.2005 Little Elm TX BB/TR/6'0"/180 d4.26 Col Baylor																											
1947	Bos A	1	2	.333	9	7	1	0		0			36	41	24	0	1	19		10	5.50	-29	.285	.372	+24	0	-0.3
1950	StL A	0	1	.000	14	0	0	0		0			36.2	53	38	6	0	25		6	8.10	-39	.342	.433		0	-0.4
Total	2	1	3	.250	23	7	1	0		0			72.2	94	62	6	1	44		16	6.81	-35	.314	.404	+24	0	-0.7
FINNVOLD, GAR Anders Gar B3.11.1968 Boynton Beach FL BR/TR/6'5"/195 [BosA90 6/173] d5.10 Col Florida St.																											
1994	Bos A	0	4	.000	8	8	0	0	2	0	0	0	36.1	45	27	4	3	15	0	17	5.94	-15	.304	.377	-22	48	-0.4
FISCHER, HANK Henry William "Bulldog" B1.11.1940 Yonkers NY BR/TR/6'0"/(185–190) d4.16 Col Seton Hall																											
1966	Bos A	2	3	.400	6	5	1	0	2	0		1	31	35	12	4	1	11	1	26	2.90	+31	.287	.351	-54	0	0.5
1967	Bos A	1	2	.333	9	2	1	0	1	1		7	26.2	24	15	3	1	8	0	18	2.36	+48	.229	.289	+37	73	0.0
Total	6	30	39	.435	168	77	14	5	35	7		59	546.2	587	310	60	17	174	17	369	4.23	-16	.275	.332	+4	73	-6.5
Team	2	3	5	.375	15	7	2	0	3	1		8	57.2	59	27	7	2	19	1	44	2.65	+38	.260	.323	-28	73	0.5
FLEMING, BILL Leslie Fletchard B7.31.1913 Rowland CA D6.4.2006 Reno NV BR/TR/6'0"/190 d8.21 Mil 1945 Col St. Marys (CA)																											
1940	Bos A	1	2	.333	10	6	1	0		0			46.1	53	27	4	2	20		24	4.86	-7	.290	.366	-6		-0.3
1941	Bos A	1	1	.500	16	1	0	0		1			41.1	32	21	4	0	24		20	3.92	+6	.212	.320	+25	0	0.1
Total	6	16	21	.432	123	40	14	3		3			442	443	220	27	10	193		167	3.79	-6	.260	.339	-6	0	-1.0
Team	2	2	3	.400	26	7	1	0		1			87.2	85	48	8	2	44		44	4.41	-2	.254	.345	-2		-0.2
FLORIE, BRYCE Bryce Bettencourt B5.21.1970 Charleston SC BR/TR/5'11"/(190–195) [SDN88 5/110] d7.17																											
1999	Bos A	2	0	1.000	14	2	0	0	0	0	0	6	30	33	19	2	1	15	3	25	4.80	+4	.282	.366	+40	0	0.0
2000	Bos A	0	4	.000	29	0	0	0	0	1	1	18	49.1	57	30	5	1	19	6	34	4.56	+10	.294	.355		91	0.2
2001	Bos A	0	1	.000	7	0	0	0	0	0	0	3	8.2	12	11	1	0	7	3	7	11.42	-61	.316	.422		87	-0.6
Total	8	20	24	.455	261	29	0	0	10	2	8	147	493.2	500	285	46	20	243	30	395	4.47	+4	.265	.352	-15	254	-0.2
Team	3	2	5	.286	50	2	0	0	0	1	1	27	88	102	60	8	2	41	12	66	5.32	-7	.292	.366	+40	178	-0.4
/60G	4	2	6	.286	60	2	0	0	0	1	1	32	105.2	122	72	10	2	49	14	79	5.31	-7	.292	.366	+40	214	-0.5
FLOWERS, BEN Bennett B6.15.1927 Wilson NC BR/TR/6'4"/195 d9.29																											
1951	Bos A	0	0	+	1	0	0	0		0			3	2	0	0	0	1		2	0.00	-100	.200	.273		0	0.0
1953	Bos A	1	4	.200	32	6	1	1		3			79.1	87	39	6	1	24		36	3.86	+9	.280	.333	-26	0	0.2
1955	Det A	0	0	+	4	0	0	0		0			6	5	4	1	0	2	0	2	6.00	-36	.238	.292		0	-0.1
1955	StL N	1	0	1.000	4	4	0	0		0			27.1	27	12	1	0	12	0	19	3.62	+12	.255	.328	+4	0	0.0
1955	Major	1	0	1.000	8	4	0	0		0			33	32	16	2	0	14	0	21	4.05	+3	.252	.322	+4	0	-0.1
1956	StL N	1	1	.500	3	3	0	0		0			11.2	15	9	1	0	5	1	5	6.94	-46	.341	.392	+47	0	-0.5
1956	Phi N	0	2	.000	32	0	0	0		0			41	54	29	9	1	10	1	22	5.71	-35	.331	.369		0	-0.4
1956	Year	1	3	.250	35	3	0	0		0			52.2	69	38	10	1	15	2	27	5.98	-38	.333	.374	+49	0	-0.9
Total	4	3	7	.300	76	13	1	1		3			168.1	190	93	18	2	54	2	86	4.49	-10	.290	.343	+0	0	-0.8
Team	2	1	4	.200	33	6	1	1		3			82.1	89	39	6	1	25		38	3.72	+13	.277	.331	-26		0.2
FOREMAN, HAPPY August G. B7.20.1897 Memphis TN D2.13.1953 New York NY BL/TL/5'7"/160 d9.3																											
1924	Chi A	0	0	+	3	0	0	0		0			4	7	3	0	0	4		1	2.25	+83	.467	.579			0.0
1926	Bos A	0	0	+	3	0	0	0		0			7.1	3	3	0	0	5		3	3.68	+11	.130	.286			0.0
Total	2	0	0	+	6	0	0	0		0			11.1	10	6	0	0	9		4	3.18	+29	.263	.404			0.0
FOREMAN, FRANK Francis Isaiah "Monkey" B5.1.1863 Baltimore MD D11.19.1957 Baltimore MD BL/TL/6'0"/160 d5.15 b–Brownie																											
1901	Bos A	0	1	.000	1	1	1	0		0			8	8	9	1	2	2		1	9.00	-61	.258	.343	-23		-0.4
Total	11	96	93	.508	229	205	169	7		4			1721.2	1857	1186	47	142	659		586	3.97	+0	.268	.344	-3		0.8
FORNIELES, MIKE Jose Miguel (Torres) B1.18.1932 Havana, Cuba D2.11.1998 St.Petersburg FL BR/TR/5'11"/(155–172) d9.2																											
1952	Was A	2	2	.500	4	2	2	1		0			26.1	13	4	1	0	11		12	1.37	+160	.143	.235	-14	0	0.9
1953	Chi A	8	7	.533	39	16	5	0		3			153	160	68	8	2	61		72	3.59	+12	.270	.340	+21	0	0.5

Year	Tm Lg	W	L	Pct	G	GS	CG	ShO	QS	SV	BS	QR	IP	H	R	HR	HB	BB	IB	SO	ERA	AERA	OAV	OOB	Sup	DL	PW
1954	Chi A	1	2	.333	15	6	0	0		1			42	41	24	4	0	14		18	4.29	-13	.252	.309	+46	0	-0.2
1955	Chi A	6	3	.667	26	9	2	0		2			86.1	84	37	12	2	29	3	23	3.86	+2	.255	.317	+15	0	0.0
1956	Chi A	0	1	.000	6	0	0	0		0			15.2	22	9	1	0	6	1	6	4.60	-11	.306	.354		0	0.0
1956	Bal A	4	7	.364	30	11	1	1		1			111	109	59	7	0	25	2	53	3.97	-1	.266	.306	-42	0	-0.3
1956	Year	4	8	.333	36	11	1	1		1			126.2	131	68	8	0	31	3	59	4.05	-3	.272	.313	-43	0	-0.3
1957	Bal A	2	6	.250	15	4	1	1	3	0		6	57	57	30	4	0	17	2	43	4.26	-16	.257	.308	-19	0	-0.5
1957	Bos A	8	7	.533	25	18	7	1	15	2		58	125.1	136	61	7	3	38	3	64	3.52	+13	.271	.324	+23	0	0.2
1957	Year	10	13	.435	40	22	8	2	18	2		64	182.1	193	91	11	3	55	5	107	3.75	+3	.267	.319	+18	0	-0.3
1958	Bos A	4	6	.400	37	7	1	0	15	1		58	110.2	123	62	10	6	33	0	49	4.96	-19	.284	.339	-10	0	-0.7
1959	Bos A	5	3	.625	46	0	0	0	15	11		58	82	77	29	6	1	29	3	54	3.07	+32	.254	.318		0	1.1
1960	Bos A	10	5	.667	**70**	0	0	0	0	**14**		51	109	86	38	6	6	49	7	64	2.64	+53	.219	.312		0	2.6
1961	Bos A★	9	8	.529	57	2	1	0	1	15		35	119.1	121	65	18	2	54	7	70	4.68	-11	.265	.341	-26	0	-0.5
1962	Bos A	3	6	.333	42	1	0	0	0	5		25	82.1	96	57	14	8	37	4	36	5.36	-23	.303	.385	-100	0	-1.3
1963	Bos A	0	0	+	9	0	0	0	0	0		6	14	16	10	0	0	5	0	5	6.43	-41	.286	.339		0	-0.1
1963	Min A	1	1	.500	11	0	0	0	0	0		6	22.2	24	14	0	2	13	0	7	4.76	-24	.273	.371		0	-0.2
1963	Year	1	1	.500	20	0	0	0	0	0		12	36.2	40	24	0	2	18	0	12	5.40	-32	.278	.359		0	-0.3
Total	12	63	64	.496	432	76	20	4	49	55		303	1156.2	1165	567	98	32	421	32	576	3.96	+0	.263	.329	+4	0	1.5
Team	7	39	35	.527	286	28	9	1	46	48		291	642.2	655	322	61	26	245	24	342	4.08	+0	.266	.336	+7		1.3
/60G	1	8	7	.527	60	6	2	0	10	10		61	134.2	137	68	13	5	51	5	72	4.08	+0	.266	.336	+7		0.3
FORTUNE, GARY Garrett Reese B10.11.1894 High Point NC D9.23.1955 Washington DC BB/TR/5'11.5"/176 d10.5																											
1916	Phi N	0	1	.000	1	1	0	0		0			5	2	2	0	0	4		3	3.60	-26	.118	.286	-72		-0.1
1918	Phi N	0	2	.000	5	2	1	0		0			31	41	30	2	1	19		10	8.13	-63	.333	.427	+14		-0.8
1920	Bos A	0	2	.000	14	3	1	0		0			41.2	46	32	0	0	23		10	5.83	-37	.282	.371	-6		-0.6
Total	3	0	5	.000	20	6	2	0		0			77.2	89	64	2	1	46		23	6.61	-49	.294	.389	-11		-1.5
FOSSAS, TONY Emilio Antonio (Morejon) B9.23.1957 Havana, Cuba BL/TL/6'0"/(187–198) [TexA79 12/303] d5.15 Col South Florida																											
1988	Tex A	0	0	+	5	0	0	0	0	0	0	2	5.2	11	3	0	0	2	0	0	4.76	-14	.423	.464		0	0.0
1989	Mil A	2	2	.500	51	0	0	0	0	1	2	33	61	57	27	3	1	22	7	42	3.54	+9	.256	.321		0	0.2
1990	Mil A	2	3	.400	32	0	0	0	0	0	2	19	29.1	44	23	5	0	10	2	24	6.44	-40	.331	.375		0	-1.2
1991	Bos A	3	2	.600	64	0	0	0	0	1	1	47	57	49	27	3	3	28	9	29	3.47	+25	.236	.335		0	0.4
1992	Bos A	1	2	.333	60	0	0	0	0	2	1	43	29.2	31	9	1	1	14	3	19	2.43	+75	.279	.365		0	0.6
1993	Bos A	1	1	.500	71	0	0	0	0	0	2	51	40	38	28	4	2	15	4	39	5.17	-10	.242	.314		0	-0.1
1994	Bos A	2	0	1.000	44	0	0	0	0	1	0	33	34	35	18	6	1	15	1	31	4.76	+6	.263	.342		0	0.1
1995	StL N	3	0	1.000	58	0	0	0	0	0	0	47	36.2	28	6	1	1	10	3	40	1.47	+191	.214	.273		0	0.8
1996	†StL N	0	4	.000	65	0	0	0	0	2	5	46	47	43	19	7	0	21	3	36	2.68	+58	.231	.308		0	0.5
1997	StL N	2	7	.222	71	0	0	0	0	0	1	50	51.2	62	32	7	1	26	3	41	3.83	+9	.298	.377		0	-0.1
1998	Sea A	0	3	.000	23	0	0	0	0	0	1	12	11.1	19	11	1	0	6	0	10	8.74	-46	.404	.463		0	-0.8
1998	Chi N	0	0	+	8	0	0	0	0	0	0	3	4	8	4	0	0	6	0	6	9.00	-51	.421	.560		0	-0.1
1998	Tex A	1	0	1.000	10	0	0	0	0	0	0	10	7.1	3	0	0	0	4	0	7	0.00	-100	.120	.241		0	0.4
1998	Major	1	3	.250	41	0	0	0	0	0	1	25	22	30	15	1	0	16	0	23	5.96	-64	.330	.426		0	-0.5
1999	NY A	0	0	+	5	0	0	0	0	0	0	2	1	6	4	1	0	1	1	0	36.00	-87	.667	.700		0	-0.2
Total	12	17	24	.415	567	0	0	0	0	7	15	398	415.2	434	211	39	10	180	36	324	3.90	+10	.269	.344		0	0.5
Team	4	7	5	.583	239	0	0	0	0	4	4	174	160.2	153	82	14	7	72	17	118	3.98	+14	.251	.337			1.0
/60G	1	2	1	.583	60	0	0	0	0	1	1	44	40.1	38	21	4	2	18	4	30	3.98	+14	.251	.337			0.3
FOSSUM, CASEY Casey Paul B1.6.1978 Cherry Hill NJ BL/TL/6'1"/160 [BosA99 1/48] d7.28 Col Texas A&M																											
2001	Bos A	3	2	.600	13	7	0	0	0	0	0	6	44.1	44	26	4	6	20	1	26	4.87	-9	.259	.355	+19	0	-0.2
2002	Bos A	5	4	.556	43	12	0	0	6	1	0	24	106.2	113	56	12	4	30	0	101	3.46	+29	.268	.320	-3	0	0.5
2003	Bos A	6	5	.545	19	14	0	0	3	1	0	4	79	82	55	9	4	34	0	63	5.47	-15	.270	.348	+37	39	-0.9
2004	Ari N	4	15	.211	27	27	0	0	10	0	0	0	142	171	111	31	10	63	5	117	6.65	-31	.302	.379	-35	40	-3.3
2005	TB A	8	12	.400	36	25	0	0	10	0	1	5	162.2	170	100	21	18	60	3	128	4.92	-11	.266	.343	-13	0	-1.1
2006	TB A	6	6	.500	25	25	0	0	10	0	0	0	130	136	89	18	12	63	3	88	5.33	-13	.265	.356	+20	15	-0.9
Total	6	32	44	.421	163	110	0	0	39	2	1	39	664.2	716	437	95	54	270	12	523	5.20	-13	.274	.351	-1	94	-5.9
Team	3	14	11	.560	75	33	0	0	9	2	0	34	230	239	137	25	14	84	1	190	4.42	+2	.267	.337	+19	39	-0.6
/180I	2	11	9	.560	59	26	0	0	7	2	0	27	180	187	107	20	11	66	1	149	4.42	+2	.267	.337	+19	31	-0.5
FOSTER, RUBE George B1.5.1888 Lehigh OK D3.1.1976 Bokoshe OK BR/TR/5'7.5"/170 d4.10																											
1913	Bos A	3	3	.500	19	8	4	1		0			68.1	64	35	1	4	28		36	3.16	-7	.252	.336	-12		-0.3
1914	Bos A	14	8	.636	32	27	17	5		0			211.2	164	68	2	7	52		89	1.70	+58	.218	.274	-11		2.0
1915	†Bos A	19	8	.704	37	33	21	5		1			255.1	217	83	3	10	86		82	2.11	+31	.237	.310	+5		2.9
1916	†Bos A	14	7	.667	33	19	9	3		2			182.1	173	73	0	4	86		53	3.06	-10	.263	.352	-2		-0.4
1917	Bos A	8	7	.533	17	16	9	1		0			124.2	108	43	0	4	53		34	2.53	+2	.243	.329	+10		0.5
Total	5	58	33	.637	138	103	60	15		3			842.1	726	302	6	29	305		294	2.36	+16	.240	.316	-1		4.7
/180I	1	12	7	.637	29	22	13	3	0	1	0	0	180	155	65	1	6	65		63	2.36	+16	.240	.316	-79		1.0
FOULKE, KEITH Keith Charles B10.19.1972 San Diego CA BR/TR/6'0"/(195–210) [SFN94 9/256] d5.21 Col Lewis–Clark St.																											
2004	†Bos A	5	3	.625	72	0	0	0	0	32	7	58	83	63	22	8	6	15	5	79	2.17	+125	.206	.254		0	3.8
2005	Bos A	5	5	.500	43	0	0	0	0	15	4	30	45.2	53	30	8	5	18	1	34	5.91	-23	.288	.365		58	-1.1
2006	Bos A	3	1	.750	44	0	0	0	0	0	0	30	49.2	52	24	9	2	7	0	36	4.35	+7	.271	.298		67	0.1
Total	10	41	34	.547	588	8	0	0	2	190	35	448	755.2	624	286	87	43	181	22	695	3.30	+42	.223	.279	-30	156	15.9
Team	3	13	9	.591	159	0	0	0	0	47	11	118	178.1	168	76	25	13	40	6	149	3.73	+27	.246	.297		125	2.8
/60G	1	5	3	.591	60	0	0	0	0	18	4	45	67.1	63	29	9	5	15	2	56	3.73	+27	.246	.297		47	1.1
FOX, CHAD Chad Douglas B9.3.1970 Coronado CA BR/TR/6'3"/(175–210) [CinN92 23/633] d7.13 Col Tarleton St. [DL 2000 Mil N 181]																											
2003	Bos A	1	2	.333	17	0	0	0	0	3	2	11	18	19	10	2	1	17	2	19	4.50	+4	.264	.407		62	0.0
Total	8	10	11	.476	214	0	0	0	0	6	9	156	224.1	193	96	21	9	128	12	261	3.57	+20	.231	.336		955	1.8
FOXX, JIMMIE James Emory "Beast","Double X" B10.22.1907 Sudlersville MD D7.21.1967 Miami FL BR/TR/6'0"/195 d5.1.1925 C1 HF1951▲																											
1939	Bos A☆	0	0	+	1	0	0	0		0			1	0	0	0	0	0		1	0.00	-100	.000	.000			0.0
Total	2	1	0	1.000	10	2	0	0		0			23.2	13	4	0	1	14		11	1.52	+154	.165	.298	-23	0	0.4
FRANCIS, RAY Ray James B3.8.1893 Sherman TX D7.6.1934 Atlanta GA BL/TL/6'1.5"/182 d4.18																											
1925	Bos A	0	2	.000	6	4	0	0		0			28	44	29	3	1	13		4	7.71	-41	.373	.439	-21		-0.5
Total	3	12	28	.300	82	36	15	2		3			337	409	220	12	12	110		96	4.65	-16	.310	.368	-14		-3.3
FREEMAN, HERSH Hershell Baskin "Buster" B7.1.1928 Gadsden AL D1.17.2004 Orlando FL BR/TR/6'3"/(220–228) d9.10 Col Alabama																											
1952	Bos A	1	0	1.000	4	1	1	0		0			13.2	13	5	1	1	5		5	3.29	+20	.260	.339	-34	0	0.2
1953	Bos A	1	4	.200	18	2	0	0		0			39	50	31	2	0	17		15	5.54	-24	.316	.383	-79	0	-0.9
1955	Bos A	0	0	+	2	0	0	0		0			1.2	1	0	0	0	1	1	1	0.00	-100	.200	.333		0	0.0
Total	6	30	16	.652	204	3	1	0	0	37		66	359	387	176	25	7	109	22	158	3.74	+10	.281	.334	-64	0	2.2
Team	3	2	4	.333	24	3	1	0		0			54.1	64	36	3	1	23	1	21	4.80	-14	.300	.371	-64		-0.7
FROHWIRTH, TODD Todd Gerard B9.28.1962 Milwaukee WI BR/TR/6'4"/(190–205) [PhiN84 13/335] d8.10 Col Northwest Missouri																											
1994	Bos A	0	3	.000	22	0	0	0	0	1	0	12	26.2	40	36	3	2	17	2	13	10.80	-53	.339	.431		0	-1.6
Total	9	20	19	.513	284	0	0	0	0	11	11	197	417.2	389	190	23	13	172	25	259	3.60	+15	.250	.328		0	1.7
FUHR, OSCAR Oscar Lawrence B8.22.1893 Defiance MO D3.27.1975 Dallas TX BL/TL/6'0.5"/176 d4.19																											
1921	Chi N	0	0	+	1	0	0	0		0			4	11	9	1	0	0		2	9.00	-58	.500	.500			-0.2
1924	Bos A	3	6	.333	23	10	4	1		0			80.1	100	71	1	5	39		30	5.94	-26	.310	.392	+33		-1.6
1925	Bos A	0	6	.000	39	5	0	0		0			91.1	138	83	7	3	30		27	6.60	-31	.364	.415	+29		-1.0
Total	3	3	12	.200	63	15	4	1		0			175.2	249	163	9	8	69		59	6.35	-30	.344	.407	+31		-2.8
Team	2	3	12	.200	62	15	4	1		0			171.2	238	154	8	8	69		57	6.29	-29	.339	.404	+32		-2.6
/60G	2	3	12	.200	60	15	4	1		0			166	230	149	8	8	67		55	6.30	-29	.339	.404	+32		-2.5

Year	Tm Lg	W	L	Pct	G	GS	CG	ShO	QS	SV	BS	QR	IP	H	R	HR	HB	BB	IB	SO	ERA	AERA	OAV	OOB	Sup	DL	PW
FULLERTON, CURT Curtis Hooper B9.13.1898 Ellsworth ME D1.9.1975 Winthrop MA BL/TR/6'0"/162 d4.14																											
1921	Bos A	0	1	.000	4	1	1	0		0			15.1	22	17	3	1	10		4	8.80	-52	.355	.452	+18		-0.5
1922	Bos A	1	4	.200	31	3	0	0		0			64.1	70	40	4	5	35		17	5.46	-25	.290	.391	+3		-0.3
1923	Bos A	2	15	.118	37	15	6	0		1			143.1	167	108	9	6	71		37	5.09	-19	.300	.385	-49		-1.7
1924	Bos A	7	12	.368	33	20	9	0		2			152	166	93	1	6	73		33	4.32	+1	.283	.368	-23		-0.5
1925	Bos A	0	3	.000	4	2	0	0		0			22.2	22	11	1	2	9		3	3.18	+43	.259	.344	-54		0.4
1933	Bos A	0	2	.000	6	2	2	0		0			25.1	36	24	1	1	13		10	8.53	-49	.364	.442	-61		-0.6
Total	6	10	37	.213	115	43	18	0		3			423	483	293	19	21	211		104	5.11	-17	.296	.384	-32		-3.2
/180I	3	4	16	.213	49	18	8	0	0	1	0	0	180	206	125	8	9	90		44	5.11	-17	.296	.384	-71		-1.4
GABBARD, KASON Kason Ronald B4.8.1982 Oxford OH BL/TL/6'3"/200 [BosA00 29/872] d7.22 Col Indian River (FL) CC																											
2006	Bos A	1	3	.250	7	4	0	0	1	0	0	2	25.2	24	11	0	0	16	0	15	3.51	+33	.255	.364	-55	0	0.4
GALE, RICH Richard Blackwell B1.19.1954 Littleton NH BR/TR/6'7"/225 [KCA75 5/105] d4.30 C2 Col New Hampshire																											
1984	Bos A	2	3	.400	13	4	0	0	0	0	0	5	43.2	57	27	6	1	18	0	28	5.56	-24	.315	.380	+29	0	-0.5
Total	7	55	56	.495	195	144	21	5	69	2	2	30	970	997	544	82	18	457	28	518	4.54	-14	.269	.349	+6	0	-6.2
GALEHOUSE, DENNY Dennis Ward B12.7.1911 Marshallville OH D10.12.1998 Doylestown OH BR/TR/6'1"/195 d4.30 Def 1944																											
1939	Bos A	9	10	.474	30	18	6	1		0			146.2	160	84	6	1	52		68	4.54	+4	.276	.337	-23		0.1
1940	Bos A	6	6	.500	25	20	5	0		0			120	155	77	10	0	41		53	5.18	-13	.313	.366	+9		-1.1
1947	Bos A	11	7	.611	21	21	11	3		0			149	150	60	7	0	34		38	3.32	+17	.260	.301	+17	0	0.6
1948	Bos A	8	8	.500	27	15	6	1		3			137.1	152	68	10	2	46		38	4.00	+10	.282	.341	-5	0	0.5
1949	Bos A	0	0	+	2	0	0	0		0			2	4	3	1	0	3		0	13.50	-68	.400	.538		0	-0.1
Total	15	109	118	.480	375	258	100	17		13			2004	2148	999	104	18	735		851	3.97	+5	.275	.338	-5	0	1.8
Team	5	34	31	.523	105	74	28	5		3			555	621	292	34	3	176		197	4.25	+3	.282	.336	+1		0.0
/180I	2	11	10	.523	34	24	9	2		1			180	201	95	11	1	57		64	4.25	+3	.282	.336	+1		0.0
GALLAGHER, ED Edward Michael "Lefty" B11.28.1910 Dorchester MA D12.22.1981 Hyannis MA BB/TL/6'2"/197 d7.8 Col Boston College																											
1932	Bos A	0	3	.000	9	3	0	0		0			23.2	30	36	3	0	28		6	12.55	-64	.323	.479	-62		-1.9
GARCES, RICH Richard Aron (Mendoza) "El Guapo" B5.18.1971 Maracay, Aragua, Venez. BR/TR/6'0"/(215–255) d9.18																											
1990	Min A	0	0	+	5	0	0	0	0	2	0	4	5.2	4	2	0	0	4	0	1	1.59	+162	.200	.333		0	0.1
1993	Min A	0	0	+	3	0	0	0	0	0	0	3	4	4	2	0	0	2	0	3	0.00	-100	.250	.333		0	0.0
1995	Chi N	0	0	+	7	0	0	0	0	0	0	6	11	11	6	0	0	3	0	6	3.27	+27	.256	.304		0	0.0
1995	Fla N	0	2	.000	11	0	0	0	0	0	1	6	13.1	14	9	1	0	8	2	16	5.40	-20	.264	.361		0	-0.2
1995	Year	0	2	.000	18	0	0	0	0	0	1	12	24.1	25	15	1	0	11	2	22	4.44	-4	.260	.336		0	-0.2
1996	Bos A	3	2	.600	37	0	0	0	0	0	2	20	44	42	26	5	0	33	5	55	4.91	+4	.251	.366		63	0.2
1997	Bos A	0	1	.000	12	0	0	0	0	0	2	8	13.2	14	9	2	1	9	0	12	4.61	+1	.255	.364		46	0.0
1998	Bos A	1	1	.500	30	0	0	0	0	1	2	21	46	36	19	6	2	27	3	34	3.33	+42	.213	.327		95	0.3
1999	†Bos A	5	1	.833	30	0	0	0	0	2	1	25	40.2	25	9	1	0	18	1	33	1.55	+222	.171	.262		0	2.0
2000	Bos A	8	1	.889	64	0	0	0	0	1	4	50	74.2	64	28	7	1	23	5	69	3.25	+54	.229	.286		0	1.5
2001	Bos A	6	1	.857	62	0	0	0	0	1	1	44	67	55	32	6	4	25	1	51	3.90	+14	.219	.299		16	0.4
2002	Bos A	0	1	.000	26	0	0	0	0	0	0	18	21.1	21	20	4	3	12	2	16	7.59	-41	.273	.379		23	-0.3
Total	10	23	10	.697	287	0	0	0	0	7	13	205	341.1	290	162	32	11	164	19	296	3.74	+27	.227	.317		243	4.0
Team	7	23	8	.742	261	0	0	0	0	5	12	186	307.1	257	143	31	11	147	17	270	3.78	+27	.225	.315		243	4.1
/60G	2	5	2	.742	60	0	0	0	0	1	3	43	70.2	59	33	7	3	34	4	62	3.78	+27	.225	.315		56	0.9
GARDINER, MIKE Michael James B10.19.1965 Sarnia ON, Can. BB/TR/6'0"/(185–200) [SeaA87 18/449] d9.8 Col Indiana St.																											
1990	Sea A	0	2	.000	5	3	0	0	0	0	0	1	12.2	22	17	1	2	5	0	6	10.66	-63	.379	.439	-8	0	-1.2
1991	Bos A	9	10	.474	22	22	0	0	8	0	0	0	130	140	79	18	0	47	2	91	4.85	-11	.274	.333	+3	18	-1.0
1992	Bos A	4	10	.286	28	18	0	0	7	0	0	6	130.2	126	78	12	2	58	2	79	4.75	-11	.253	.330	-30	0	-0.6
1993	Mon N	2	3	.400	24	2	0	0	0	0	1	14	38	40	28	3	1	19	2	21	5.21	-20	.268	.349	+40	0	-0.6
1993	Det A	0	0	+	10	0	0	0	0	0	1	7	11.1	12	5	0	0	7	1	4	3.97	+10	.279	.380		0	0.0
1993	Major	2	3	.400	34	2	0	0	0	0	2	21	49	52	33	3	1	26	3	25	4.93	-13	.271	.356	+40	0	-0.6
1994	Det A	2	2	.500	38	1	0	0	0	5	1	28	58.2	53	35	10	0	23	5	31	4.14	+19	.233	.302	+68	0	0.1
1995	Det A	0	0	+	9	0	0	0	0	0	1	2	12.1	27	20	5	0	2	1	7	14.59	-67	.458	.460		105	-0.6
Total	6	17	27	.386	136	46	0	0	15	5	4	58	393.2	420	262	49	5	161	13	239	5.21	-16	.272	.339	-9	123	-3.9
Team	2	13	20	.394	50	40	0	0	15	0	0	6	260.2	266	157	30	2	105	4	170	4.80	-11	.264	.331	-12	18	-1.6
/180I	1	9	14	.394	35	28	0	0	10	0	0	4	180	184	108	21	1	73	3	117	4.80	-11	.264	.331	-12	12	-1.1
GARDNER, WES Wesley Brian B4.29.1961 Benton AR BR/TR/6'4"/(195–205) [NYN82 22/551] d7.29 Col Central Arkansas																											
1984	NY N	1	1	.500	21	0	0	0	0	1	2	14	25.1	34	19	0	0	8	2	19	6.39	-44	.321	.365		0	-0.6
1985	NY N	0	2	.000	9	0	0	0	0	0	0	8	12	18	14	1	0	8	2	11	5.25	-33	.375	.456		0	-0.8
1986	Bos A	0	0	+	1	0	0	0	0	0	0	0	1	1	1	0	0	0	0	1	9.00	-53	.333	.250		175	0.0
1987	Bos A	3	6	.333	49	1	0	0	0	10	2	25	89.2	98	55	17	2	42	7	70	5.42	-16	.279	.358	-20	0	-0.8
1988	†Bos A	8	6	.571	36	18	1	0	9	2	0	12	149	119	61	17	3	64	2	106	3.50	+18	.220	.302	-2	15	1.0
1989	Bos A	3	7	.300	22	16	0	0	3	0	0	5	86	97	64	10	1	47	7	81	5.97	-31	.287	.372	+16	57	-1.7
1990	Bos A	3	7	.300	34	9	0	0	3	0	2	15	77.1	77	43	6	2	35	0	58	4.89	-16	.259	.339	-26	30	-0.6
1991	SD N	0	1	.000	14	0	0	0	0	1	0	7	20.1	27	16	1	0	12	1	9	7.08	-46	.310	.394		0	-0.4
1991	KC A	0	0	+	3	0	0	0	0	0	0	3	5.2	5	4	0	0	2	0	3	1.59	+161	.208	.269		0	0.0
1991	Major	0	1	.000	17	0	0	0	0	1	0	10	25	32	20	1	0	14	1	12	5.88	-1	.288	.368		0	-0.4
Total	8	18	30	.375	189	44	1	0	15	14	6	89	466.1	476	277	52	8	218	21	358	4.90	-15	.265	.344	-1	277	-3.9
Team	5	17	26	.395	142	44	1	0	15	12	4	57	403	392	224	50	8	188	16	316	4.73	-11	.256	.337	-1	277	-2.1
/60G	2	7	11	.395	60	19	0	0	6	5	2	24	170.1	166	95	21	3	79	7	134	4.73	-11	.256	.337	-1	117	-0.9
GARMAN, MIKE Michael Douglas B9.16.1949 Caldwell ID BR/TR/6'3"/(198–215) [BosA67 1/3] d9.22																											
1969	Bos A	1	0	1.000	2	2	0	0	1	0	0	0	12.1	13	6	0	0	10	0	10	4.38	-13	.277	.404	+16	0	0.0
1971	Bos A	1	1	.500	3	3	0	0	2	0	0	0	18.2	15	8	3	1	9	1	6	3.86	-3	.217	.313	+4	0	0.0
1972	Bos A	0	1	.000	3	1	0	0	0	0	0	2	3.1	4	4	1	0	2	0	1	10.80	-70	.286	.375	-18	0	-0.5
1973	Bos A	0	0	+	12	0	0	0	0	0	0	5	22	32	15	1	0	15	3	9	5.32	-24	.352	.439		0	-0.2
Total	9	22	27	.449	303	8	0	0	3	42	22	197	433.2	411	198	34	9	202	58	213	3.63	+3	.254	.337	-17	0	1.1
Team	4	2	2	.500	20	6	0	0	3	0	0	7	56.1	64	33	5	1	36	4	26	4.95	-23	.290	.388	+4		-0.7
GARRISON, CLIFF Clifford William B8.13.1906 Bellemont OK D8.25.1994 Woodland CA BR/TR/6'0"/180 d4.16																											
1928	Bos A	0	0	+	6	0	0	0		0			16	22	15	2	0	6		0	7.88	-48	.361	.418			-0.3
GASTON, MILT Nathaniel Milton B1.27.1896 Ridgefield Park NJ D4.26.1996 Barnstable MA BR/TR (BB 1933)/6'1"/185 d4.20 b–Alex																											
1929	Bos A	12	19	.387	39	28	20	1		2			243.2	265	121	15	3	81		83	3.73	+15	.289	.348	-24		1.6
1930	Bos A	13	20	.394	38	34	20	2		2			273	272	138	15	0	98		99	3.92	+17	.259	.323	-19		1.8
1931	Bos A	2	13	.133	23	18	4	0		0			119	137	76	4	0	41		33	4.46	-4	.291	.348	-40		-0.8
Total	11	97	164	.372	355	269	127	10		8			2105	2338	1277	114	24	836		615	4.55	-3	.287	.355	-15		-4.1
Team	3	27	52	.342	100	80	44	3		4			635.2	674	335	34	3	220		215	3.95	+12	.276	.337	-25		2.6
/180I	1	8	15	.342	28	23	12	1		1			180	191	95	10	1	62		61	3.95	+12	.276	.337	-25		0.7
GIBSON, NORWOOD Norwood Ringold "Gibby" B3.11.1877 Peoria IL D7.7.1959 Peoria IL BR/TR/5'10"/165 d4.29 Col Notre Dame																											
1903	Bos A	13	9	.591	24	21	17	2		0			183.1	166	95	2	7	65		76	3.19	-5	.241	.313	-4		-0.1
1904	Bos A	17	14	.548	33	32	29	1		0			273	216	111	8	4	81		112	2.21	+21	.219	.281	-9		0.0
1905	Bos A	4	7	.364	23	17	9	0		0			134	118	77	9	5	55		67	3.69	-27	.238	.321	-3		-1.6
1906	Bos A	0	2	.000	5	2	1	0		0			18.2	25	21	2	0	7		3	5.30	-48	.325	.381	-87		-0.7
Total	4	34	32	.515	85	72	56	3		0			609	525	304	21	16	208		258	2.93	-5	.233	.303	-8		-2.4
/180I	1	10	9	.515	25	21	17	1	0	0	0	0	180	155	90	6	5	61		76	2.93	-5	.233	.303	-73		-0.7
GILLESPIE, BOB Robert William "Bunch" B10.8.1919 Columbus OH D11.4.2001 Winston–Salem NC BR/TR/6'4"/187 d5.11																											
1950	Bos A	0	0	+	1	0	0	0		0			1.1	2	3	1	0	4		0	20.25	-76	.333	.600		0	-0.1
Total	4	5	13	.278	58	23	2	0		0			202.1	223	127	8	2	102		59	5.07	-24	.286	.369	-22	0	-2.4

Year	Tm Lg	W	L	Pct	G	GS	CG	ShO	QS	SV	BS	QR	IP	H	R	HR	HB	BB	IB	SO	ERA	AERA	OAV	OOB	Sup	DL	PW
GLAZE, RALPH Daniel Ralph B3.13.1881 Denver CO D10.31.1968 Atascadero CA BR/TR/5'9"/165 d6.1 Col Dartmouth																											
1906	Bos A	4	6	.400	19	10	7	0		0			123	110	58	4	5	32		56	3.59	-23	.242	.299	+7		-0.6
1907	Bos A	9	13	.409	32	21	11	1		0			182.1	150	75	4	4	48		68	2.32	+11	.227	.283	-3		0.1
1908	Bos A	2	2	.500	10	3	2	0		0			34.2	43	24	1	0	5		13	3.38	-27	.253	.274	+11		-0.7
Total	3	15	21	.417	61	34	20	1		0			340	303	157	9	9	85		137	2.89	-9	.236	.288	+2		-1.2
/180I	2	8	11	.417	32	18	11	1	0	0	0	0	180	160	83	5	5	45		73	2.89	-9	.236	.288	-46		-0.6
GOMES, WAYNE Wayne Maurice B1.15.1973 Hampton VA BR/TR/6'2"/(220–227) [PhiN93 1/4] d6.13 Col Old Dominion																											
2002	Bos A	1	2	.333	20	0	0	0	0	1	0	14	21.1	20	11	2	3	12	2	15	4.64	-4	.241	.357		0	0.0
Total	6	30	23	.566	321	0	0	0	0	29	21	212	368	373	201	33	13	191	17	284	4.60	-4	.265	.356		66	-1.0
GONZALES, JOE Joe Madrid "Smokey" B3.19.1915 San Francisco CA D11.16.1996 Torrance CA BR/TR/5'9"/175 d8.25 Col USC																											
1937	Bos A	1	2	.333	8	2	2	0		0			31	37	16	1	0	11		11	4.35	+9	.291	.348	-27		0.0
GONZALEZ, JEREMI Geremis Segundo (Acosta) B1.8.1975 Maracaibo, Zulia, Venezuela BR/TR/6'2"/(180–220) d5.27 [DL 2000 Chi N 186]																											
2005	†Bos A	2	1	.667	28	3	0	0	0	0	0	16	56	64	39	7	2	16	2	28	6.11	-26	.288	.336	+9	0	-0.4
Total	6	30	35	.462	131	83	4	2	39	0	1	29	572.2	588	340	73	24	238	15	354	4.93	-9	.267	.341	-9	251	-2.5
GORDON, TOM Thomas B11.18.1967 Sebring FL BR/TR/5'9"/(160–195) [KCA86 6/157] d9.8 [DL 2000 Bos A 181]																											
1996	Bos A	12	9	.571	34	34	4	1	18	0	0	0	215.2	249	143	28	4	105	5	171	5.59	-9	.284	.359	+30	0	-0.6
1997	Bos A	6	10	.375	42	25	2	1	14	11	2	12	182.2	155	85	10	3	78	1	159	3.74	+24	.226	.306	-4	0	1.5
1998	†Bos A★	7	4	.636	73	0	0	0	0	**46**	1	59	79.1	55	24	2	0	25	1	78	2.72	+74	.191	.254		0	3.5
1999	†Bos A	0	2	.000	21	0	0	0	0	11	2	16	17.2	17	11	2	1	12	2	24	5.60	-11	.246	.366		129	-0.1
Total	18	130	119	.522	809	203	18	4	110	150	48	454	2036.2	1815	972	166	36	944	56	1870	3.91	+15	.238	.322	+3	490	18.6
Team	4	25	25	.500	170	59	6	2	32	68	5	87	495.1	476	263	42	8	220	9	432	4.45	+9	.248	.325	+16	129	4.3
/60G	1	9	9	.500	60	21	2	1	11	24	2	31	174.2	168	93	15	3	78	3	152	4.46	+9	.248	.325	+16	46	1.5
GRAY, DAVE David Alexander B1.7.1943 Ogden UT BR/TR/6'1"/195 d6.14 Col Weber St.																											
1964	Bos A	0	0	+	9	1	0	0	0	0		3	13	18	20	3	0	20	0	17	9.00	-57	.321	.494	+38	0	-0.4
GRAY, JEFF Jeffrey Edward B4.10.1963 Richmond VA BR/TR/6'1"/(185–190) d6.21 Col Florida St. [DL 1992 Bos A 182]																											
1988	Cin N	0	0	+	5	0	0	0	0	0	0	2	9.1	12	4	0	0	4	2	5	3.86	-7	.333	.381		0	0.0
1990	†Bos A	2	4	.333	41	0	0	0	0	9	3	28	50.2	53	27	3	1	15	3	50	4.44	-8	.268	.321		0	-0.2
1991	Bos A	2	3	.400	50	0	0	0	0	1	3	39	61.2	39	17	7	1	10	4	41	2.34	+85	.181	.219		70	1.0
Total	3	4	7	.364	96	0	0	0	0	10	6	69	121.2	104	48	10	2	29	9	96	3.33	+25	.231	.278		252	0.8
Team	2	4	7	.364	91	0	0	0	0	10	6	67	112.1	92	44	10	2	25	7	91	3.28	+29	.223	.269		70	0.8
/60G	1	3	5	.364	60	0	0	0	0	7	4	44	74	61	29	7	1	16	5	60	3.29	+29	.223	.269		46	0.5
GREGG, VEAN Sylveanus Augustus B4.13.1885 Chehalis WA D7.29.1964 Aberdeen WA BR/TL/6'1"/185 d4.12 b–Dave Col South Dakota St.																											
1914	Bos A	3	4	.429	12	9	4	0		0			68.1	71	39	0	0	37		24	3.95	-32	.283	.375	+17		-0.9
1915	Bos A	4	2	.667	18	9	3	1		3			75	71	37	2	5	32		43	3.36	-17	.260	.348	+37		-0.2
1916	Bos A	2	5	.286	21	7	3	0		0			77.2	71	30	0	3	30		41	3.01	-8	.259	.339	-6		-0.2
Total	8	92	63	.594	239	161	105	14		12			1393	1240	547	17	51	552		720	2.70	+17	.248	.329	-3		7.2
Team	3	9	11	.450	51	25	10	1		3			221	213	106	2	8	99		108	3.42	-20	.267	.354	+18		-1.3
/180I	2	7	9	.450	42	20	8	1		2			180	173	86	2	7	81		88	3.42	-20	.267	.354	+18		-1.1
GRIFFIN, MARTY Martin John B9.2.1901 San Francisco CA D11.19.1951 Los Angeles CA BR/TR/6'2"/200 d7.25																											
1928	Bos A	0	3	.000	11	3	0	0		0			37.2	42	21	0	0	17		9	5.02	-18	.300	.376	-73		-0.1
GRILLI, GUIDO Guido John B1.9.1939 Memphis TN BL/TL/6'0"/188 d4.12 Col Memphis																											
1966	Bos A	0	1	.000	6	0	0	0	0	0		5	4.2	5	6	1	0	9	0	4	7.71	-51	.278	.519		0	-0.4
GRISSOM, MARV Marvin Edward B3.31.1918 Los Molinos CA D9.19.2005 Red Bluff CA BR/TR/6'3"/(195–205) d9.10 C15 b–Lee																											
1953	Bos A	2	6	.250	13	11	1	1		0			59.1	61	34	5	1	30		31	4.70	-11	.266	.354	+9	0	-0.6
Total	10	47	45	.511	356	52	12	3	0	58		76	810	771	358	65	28	343	21	459	3.41	+15	.254	.334	+5	36	3.9
GROSS, KIP Kip Lee B8.24.1964 Scottsbluff NE BR/TR/6'2"/(190–195) [NYN86 4/102] d4.21 Col Nebraska																											
1999	Bos A	0	2	.000	11	1	0	0	0	0	1	7	12.2	15	11	3	3	8	2	9	7.82	-36	.294	.413	+68	18	-0.4
Total	6	7	8	.467	73	12	1	0	5	0	1	44	147.2	168	80	14	3	66	5	81	3.90	+0	.289	.362	+30	18	-0.9
GROVE, LEFTY Robert Moses B3.6.1900 Lonaconing MD D5.22.1975 Norwalk OH BL/TL/6'3"/190 d4.14 HF1947																											
1925	Phi A	10	12	.455	45	18	5	0		1			197	207	120	11	5	131		**116**	4.75	-2	.278	.390	-9		-0.5
1926	Phi A	13	13	.500	45	33	20	1		6			258	227	97	6	6	101		**194**	**2.51**	+66	.244	.322	-4		3.7
1927	Phi A	20	13	.606	51	28	14	1		9			262.1	251	116	6	2	79		**174**	3.19	+34	.252	.309	+10		3.0
1928	Phi A	**24**	8	.750	39	31	24	4		4			261.2	228	93	10	1	64		**183**	2.58	+56	.229	.277	+10		**4.7**
1929	†Phi A	20	6	**.769**	42	**37**	19	2		4			275.1	278	104	8	3	81		**170**	**2.81**	+51	.262	.316	+39		3.6
1930	†Phi A	**28**	5	**.848**	**50**	32	22	2		**9**			291	273	101	8	5	60		**209**	**2.54**	+84	**.247**	**.288**	+25		**6.9**
1931	†Phi A	**31**	4	**.886**	41	30	**27**	0		5			288.2	249	84	10	1	62		**175**	**2.06**	+118	.229	**.271**	+3		**8.2**
1932	Phi A	25	10	.714	44	30	**27**	0		7			291.2	269	101	13	1	79		188	**2.84**	+59	.241	**.292**	+15		**5.9**
1933	Phi A★	**24**	8	**.750**	45	28	**21**	2		6			275.1	280	113	12	4	83		114	3.20	+34	.261	.316	+9		3.1
1934	Bos A	8	8	.500	22	12	5	0		0			109.1	149	84	5	1	32		43	6.50	-26	.320	.365	-12		-1.9
1935	Bos A☆	20	12	.625	35	30	23	2		1			273	269	105	6	3	65		121	**2.70**	+76	.257	.302	-24		5.5
1936	Bos A★	17	12	.586	35	30	22	0		2			253.1	237	90	14	4	65		130	**2.81**	+89	.246	**.297**	-22		**6.6**
1937	Bos A☆	17	9	.654	32	32	21	3		0			262	269	101	9	1	83		153	3.02	+57	.261	.317	-8		3.9
1938	Bos A★	14	4	.778	24	21	12	1		1			163.2	169	65	8	1	52		99	**3.08**	+60	.263	.319	+10		3.0
1939	Bos A☆	15	4	**.789**	23	23	17	2		0			191	180	63	8	1	58		81	**2.54**	+86	.249	.305	-4		3.7
1940	Bos A	7	6	.538	22	21	9	1		0			153.1	159	73	20	1	50		62	3.99	+13	.269	.328	-4		0.5
1941	Bos A	7	7	.500	21	21	10	0		0			134	155	84	8	2	42		54	4.37	-5	.287	.340	+25	0	-0.8
Total	17	300	141	.680	616	457	298	35		55			3940.2	3849	1594	162	42	1187		2266	3.06	+48	.255	.311	+4	0	59.1
Team	8	105	62	.629	214	190	119	9		4			1539.2	1587	665	78	14	447		743	3.34	+43	.264	.317	-6		20.5
/180I	1	12	7	.629	25	22	14	1		0			180	186	78	9	2	52		87	3.34	+43	.264	.317	-6		2.4
GRUNDT, KEN Kenneth Allan B8.26.1969 Melrose Park IL BL/TL/6'4"/195 [SFN91 53/1354] d8.8 Col Missouri Southern																											
1996	Bos A	0	0	+	1	0	0	0	0	0	0	0	0.1	1	1	0	0	0	0	0	27.00	-81	.500	.500		0	0.0
1997	Bos A	0	0	+	2	0	0	0	0	0	0	1	3	5	3	0	0	0	0	0	9.00	-48	.357	.357		0	-0.1
Total	2	0	0	+	3	0	0	0	0	0	0	1	3.1	6	4	0	0	0	0	0	10.80	-56	.375	.375		0	-0.1
GUMPERT, RANDY Randall Pennington B1.23.1918 Monocacy PA BR/TR/6'3"/205 d6.13 Mil 1943–45 C1																											
1952	Bos A	1	0	1.000	10	1	0	0		1			19.2	15	11	1	1	5		6	4.12	-4	.205	.266	-34	0	-0.1
Total	10	51	59	.464	261	113	47	6		7			1052.2	1099	548	92	16	346		352	4.17	-2	.268	.328	-4	0	-1.6
GUNDERSON, ERIC Eric Andrew B3.29.1966 Portland OR BR/TL/6'0"/(175–195) [SFN87 2/48] d4.11 Col Portland St.																											
1995	Bos A	2	1	.667	19	0	0	0	0	0	0	13	12.1	13	7	0	2	9	1	9	5.11	-5	.295	.429		0	0.0
1996	Bos A	0	1	.000	28	0	0	0	0	0	0	14	17.1	21	17	5	2	8	2	7	8.31	-39	.300	.378		0	-0.3
Total	10	8	11	.421	254	5	0	0	1	2	8	158	229	274	140	29	10	84	18	137	4.95	-7	.299	.359	-40	169	-1.8
Team	2	2	2	.500	47	0	0	0	0	0	0	27	29.2	34	24	5	4	17	3	16	6.98	-28	.298	.399			-0.3
/60G	3	3	3	.500	60	0	0	0	0	0	0	34	38	43	31	6	5	22	4	20	6.95	-28	.298	.399			-0.4
GUTHRIE, MARK Mark Andrew B9.22.1965 Buffalo NY BR/TL/6'4"/(196–215) [MinA87 7/165] d7.25 Col Louisiana St.																											
1999	Bos A	1	1	.500	46	0	0	0	0	2	0	27	46.1	50	32	9	2	20	3	36	5.83	-14	.275	.348		20	-0.2
Total	15	51	54	.486	765	43	3	1	19	14	21	494	978.2	989	489	101	22	381	53	778	4.05	+6	.266	.335	-6	169	2.7
/60G	1	1	1	.500	60	0	0	0	0	3	0	35	60.1	65	42	12	3	26	4	47	5.84	-14	.275	.348		26	-0.3
HAGEMAN, CASEY Kurt Moritz B5.12.1887 Mt.Oliver PA D4.1.1964 New Bedford PA BL/TR/5'10.5"/186 d9.18 Col Geneva																											
1911	Bos A	0	2	.000	2	2	2	0		0			17	16	8	2	1	5		8	2.12	+55	.262	.328	-67		0.1
1912	Bos A	0	0	+	2	1	0	0		0			1.1	5	5	0	0	3		1	27.00	-87	.500	.615	+74		-0.1
Total	3	3	7	.300	32	11	4	0		1			120.1	108	63	2	9	40		47	3.07	-7	.243	.318	-14		0.2
Team	2	0	2	.000	4	3	2	0		0			18.1	21	13	2	1	8		9	3.93	-16	.296	.375	-20		0.0

Year	Tm Lg	W	L	Pct	G	GS	CG	ShO	QS	SV	BS	QR	IP	H	R	HR	HB	BB	IB	SO	ERA	AERA	OAV	OOB	Sup	DL	PW
HALAMA, JOHN John Thadeuz B2.22.1972 Brooklyn NY BL/TL/6'5"/(200–215) [HouN94 23/640] d4.2 Col St. Francis (NY)																											
2005	Bos A	1	1	.500	30	1	0	0	0	0	0	16	43.2	56	33	5	7	9	3	26	6.18	-27	.299	.353	+2	0	-0.4
Total	9	56	48	.538	262	119	2	2	40	0	1	95	911	1048	531	113	37	277	18	492	4.65	-2	.290	.343	+11	0	-1.3
HALL, CHARLEY Charles Louis "Sea Lion" (b Carlos Luis Hall) B7.27.1884 Ventura CA D12.6.1943 Ventura CA BL/TR/6'1"/187 d7.12																											
1906	Cin N	4	8	.333	14	9	9	1		1			95	86	56	1	8	50		49	3.32	-17	.258	.368	-6		-1.1
1907	Cin N	4	2	.667	11	8	5	0		0			68	51	22	0	4	43		25	2.51	+3	.226	.359	+10		0.3
1909	Bos A	6	4	.600	11	7	3	0		0			59.2	59	24	0	3	17		27	2.56	-2	.271	.332	+9		-0.2
1910	Bos A	12	9	.571	35	16	13	0		2			188.2	142	68	6	9	73		95	1.91	+34	.207	.292	+0		1.6
1911	Bos A	8	7	.533	32	10	6	0		**4**			146.1	149	79	3	5	72		83	3.75	-13	.279	.370	+34		-0.5
1912	†Bos A	15	8	.652	34	20	9	2		2			191	178	85	3	4	70		83	3.02	+13	.257	.329	+20		1.4
1913	Bos A	5	4	.556	35	4	2	0		2			105	97	67	1	5	46		48	3.43	-14	.238	.322	-24		-0.8
1916	StL N	0	4	.000	10	5	2	0		1			42.2	45	27	1	0	14		15	5.48	-52	.280	.337	-32		-1.1
1918	Det A	0	1	.000	6	1	0	0		0			13.1	14	10	1	0	6		2	6.75	-61	.269	.345	-100		-0.4
Total	9	54	47	.535	188	80	49	3		12			909.2	821	438	16	38	391		427	3.09	-5	.248	.334	+7		-0.8
Team	5	46	32	.590	147	57	33	2		10			690.2	625	323	13	26	278		336	2.89	+4	.246	.327	+12		1.5
/180I	1	12	8	.590	38	15	9	1		3			180	163	84	3	7	72		88	2.89	+4	.246	.327	+12		0.4
HAMMOND, CHRIS Christopher Andrew B1.21.1966 Atlanta GA BL/TL/6'1"/(190–210) [CinN86*6/148] d7.16 b–Steve Col Alabama–Birmingham																											
1997	Bos A	3	4	.429	29	8	0	0	2	1	1	14	65.1	81	45	5	2	27	4	48	5.92	-21	.310	.375	+21	93	-0.7
Total	14	66	62	.516	441	136	5	3	61	3	13	225	1123.2	1163	572	105	31	387	32	712	4.14	+1	.269	.332	-7	316	0.6
HANCOCK, JOSH Joshua Morgan B4.11.1978 Cleveland MS BR/TR/6'3"/(205–217) [BosA98 5/145] d9.10 Col Auburn																											
2002	Bos A	0	1	.000	3	1	0	0	0	0	0	2	7.1	5	3	1	0	2	0	6	3.68	+22	.200	.259	-59	0	0.1
Total	5	9	6	.600	94	12	0	0	6	1	2	57	165	161	88	28	2	54	4	101	4.25	+2	.252	.310	+16	151	-0.3
HANEY, CHRIS Christopher Deane B11.16.1968 Baltimore MD BL/TL/6'3"/(185–210) [MonN90 2/51] d6.21 f–Larry Col North Carolina–Charlotte																											
2002	Bos A	0	0	+	24	0	0	0	0	1	0	16	30	32	14	2	4	10	2	15	4.20	+7	.274	.343		0	0.1
Total	11	38	52	.422	196	125	8	4	50	1	1	47	824.2	924	510	94	31	286	10	442	5.07	-9	.284	.344	-14	228	-5.3
HANSACK, DEVERN Devern M. B2.5.1978 Pearl Lagoon, Nicaragua BR/TR/6'2"/180 d9.23																											
2006	Bos A	1	1	.500	2	2	1	1	0	0	0	0	10	6	3	2	0	1	0	8	2.70	+73	.171	.194	+21	0	0.4
HANSEN, CRAIG Craig R. B11.15.1983 Glen Cove NY BR/TR/6'6"/185 [BosA05 1/26] d9.19 Col St. John's																											
2005	Bos A	0	0	+	4	0	0	0	0	0	1	3	3	6	2	1	0	1	0	3	6.00	-24	.429	.438		0	0.0
2006	Bos A	2	2	.500	38	0	0	0	0	0	2	24	38	46	32	5	4	15	0	30	6.63	-30	.305	.376		0	-0.8
Total	2	2	2	.500	42	0	0	0	0	0	3	27	41	52	34	6	4	16	0	33	6.59	-29	.315	.381		0	-0.8
/60G	3	3	3	.500	60	0	0	0	0	0	4	39	58.2	74	49	9	6	23	0	47	6.57	-29	.315	.381			-1.1
HANSON, ERIK Erik Brian B5.18.1965 Kinnelon NJ BR/TR/6'6"/(205–215) [SeaA86 2/36] d9.5 Col Wake Forest																											
1995	†Bos A☆	15	5	.750	29	29	1	1	15	0	0	0	186.2	187	94	17	1	59	0	139	4.24	+15	.258	.311	+8	0	1.2
Total	11	89	84	.514	245	238	26	5	144	0	0	3	1555.1	1604	776	139	29	504	23	1175	4.15	+5	.267	.325	-7	306	4.4
/180I	1	14	5	.750	28	28	1	1	14	0		0	180	180	91	16	1	57	0	134	4.24	+15	.258	.311	+4		1.2
HARIKKALA, TIM Timothy Allan B7.15.1971 W.Palm Beach FL BR/TR/6'2"/185 [SeaA92 34/950] d5.27 Col Florida Atlantic																											
1999	Bos A	1	1	.500	7	0	0	0	0	0	0	4	13	15	9	0	1	6	1	7	6.23	-20	.306	.393		0	-0.2
Total	5	7	8	.467	72	1	0	0	0	0	7	43	96	97	64	15	3	36	6	46	5.91	-19	.264	.333	-63	0	-1.0
HARPER, HARRY Harry Clayton B4.24.1895 Hackensack NJ D4.23.1963 New York NY BL/TL/6'2"/165 d6.27																											
1920	Bos A	5	14	.263	27	22	11	1		0			162.2	163	73	9	2	66		71	3.04	+20	.275	.349	-42		0.4
Total	10	57	76	.429	219	171	66	12		5			1256	1100	531	26	40	582		623	2.87	+5	.244	.335	-12		-1.7
/180I	1	6	15	.263	30	24	12	1		0			180	180	81	10	2	73		79	3.04	+20	.275	.349	-36		0.4
HARRIS, GREG Greg Allen B11.2.1955 Lynwood CA BB/TR (TB 1995p)/6'0"/(165–175) d5.20 Col Long Beach (CA) City																											
1981	NY N	3	5	.375	16	14	0	0	5	1	0	2	68.2	65	36	8	2	28	2	54	4.46	-21	.245	.321	+8	0	-0.6
1982	Cin N	2	6	.250	34	10	1	0	4	1	0	18	91.1	96	56	12	2	37	1	67	4.83	-24	.274	.344	-16	0	-1.0
1983	Cin N	0	0	+	1	0	0	0	0	0	0	0	1	2	3	0	1	3	2	1	27.00	-86	.500	.750		0	-0.1
1984	Mon N	0	1	.000	15	0	0	0	0	2	0	13	17.2	10	4	0	2	7	1	15	2.04	+70	.172	.284		0	0.2
1984	†SD N	2	1	.667	19	1	0	0	0	1	0	13	36.2	28	14	3	2	18	0	30	2.70	+33	.209	.306	+72	0	0.4
1984	Year	2	2	.500	34	1	0	0	0	3	0	26	54.1	38	18	3	4	25	1	45	2.48	+43	.198	.299	+74	0	0.6
1985	Tex A	5	4	.556	58	0	0	0	0	11	4	48	113	74	35	7	5	43	3	111	2.47	+73	.186	.273		0	2.0
1986	Tex A	10	8	.556	73	0	0	0	0	20	11	54	111.1	103	40	12	1	42	6	95	2.83	+53	.251	.318		0	3.2
1987	Tex A	5	10	.333	42	19	0	0	7	0	4	12	140.2	157	92	18	4	56	3	106	4.86	-7	.281	.349	+24	0	-0.7
1988	Phi N	4	6	.400	66	1	0	0	0	1	1	54	107	80	34	7	4	52	14	71	2.36	+53	.209	.309	-2	0	1.3
1989	Phi N	2	2	.500	44	0	0	0	0	1	0	31	75.1	64	34	7	2	43	7	51	3.58	+0	.234	.340		0	0.1
1989	Bos A	2	2	.500	15	0	0	0	0	0	1	11	28	21	12	1	0	15	2	25	2.57	+60	.208	.308		0	0.4
1989	Major	4	4	.500	59	0	0	0	0	1	1	42	103	85	46	8	2	58	9	76	3.31	+16	.227	.331		0	0.5
1990	†Bos A	13	9	.591	34	30	1	0	12	0	0	3	184.1	186	90	13	6	77	7	117	4.00	+2	.265	.338	-1	0	0.4
1991	Bos A	11	12	.478	53	21	1	0	10	2	3	24	173	157	79	13	5	69	5	127	3.85	+12	.243	.318	-21	0	1.3
1992	Bos A	4	9	.308	70	2	1	0	1	4	6	52	107.2	82	38	6	4	60	11	73	2.51	+70	.215	.324	-68	0	2.1
1993	Bos A	6	7	.462	**80**	0	0	0	0	8	10	55	112.1	95	55	7	10	60	14	103	3.77	+23	.232	.341		0	1.1
1994	Bos A	3	4	.429	35	0	0	0	0	2	4	21	45.2	60	44	8	1	23	6	44	8.28	-39	.321	.396		0	-1.9
1994	NY A	0	1	.000	3	0	0	0	0	0	1	1	5	4	5	1	2	3	1	4	5.40	-15	.222	.375		0	-0.2
1994	Year	3	5	.375	38	0	0	0	0	2	5	22	50.2	64	49	9	3	26	7	48	7.99	-37	.312	.394		0	-2.1
1995	Mon N	2	3	.400	45	0	0	0	0	0	1	30	48.1	45	18	6	1	16	1	47	2.61	+65	.245	.308		0	0.7
Total	15	74	90	.451	703	98	4	0	39	54	46	442	1467	1329	689	129	54	652	86	1141	3.69	+13	.243	.327	-2	0	8.7
Team	6	39	43	.476	287	53	3	0	23	16	24	166	651	601	318	48	26	304	45	489	3.91	+11	.248	.334	-11		3.4
/60G	1	8	9	.476	60	11	1	0	5	3	5	35	136	126	66	10	5	64	9	102	3.92	+11	.248	.334	-11		0.7
HARRIS, JOE Joseph White B2.1.1882 Melrose MA D4.12.1966 Melrose MA BR/TR/6'1"/198 d9.22																											
1905	Bos A	1	2	.333	3	3	3	0		0			23	16	6	0	0	8		14	2.35	+15	.198	.270	-48		0.1
1906	Bos A	2	21	.087	30	24	20	1		2			235	211	130	5	7	67		99	3.52	-22	.243	.303	-56		-2.0
1907	Bos A	0	7	.000	12	5	3	0		0			59	57	28	0	1	13		24	3.05	-16	.256	.300	-42		-0.3
Total	3	3	30	.091	45	32	26	1		2			317	284	164	5	8	88		137	3.35	-19	.242	.300	-53		-2.2
/180I	2	2	17	.091	26	18	15	1	0	1	0	0	180	161	93	3	5	50		78	3.35	-19	.242	.300	-73		-1.2
HARRIS, MICKEY Maurice Charles B1.30.1917 New York NY D4.15.1971 Farmington MI BL/TL/6'0"/(185–195) d4.23 Mil 1942–45																											
1940	Bos A	4	2	.667	13	9	3	0		0			68.1	83	40	8	2	26		36	5.00	-10	.292	.356	+19		0.0
1941	Bos A	8	14	.364	35	22	11	1		1			194	189	86	6	2	86		111	3.25	+28	.250	.328	+14	0	2.0
1946	†Bos A☆	17	9	.654	34	30	15	0		0			222.2	236	105	18	3	76		131	3.64	+1	.268	.329	+21	0	0.2
1947	Bos A	5	4	.556	15	6	1	0		0			51.2	42	20	3	0	23		35	2.44	+59	.225	.310	-5	0	1.4
1948	Bos A	7	10	.412	20	17	6	1		0			113.2	120	73	10	1	59		42	5.30	-17	.273	.360	-6	0	-1.5
1949	Bos A	2	3	.400	7	6	2	0		0			37.2	53	26	3	1	20		14	5.02	-13	.323	.400	+13	0	-0.5
1949	Was A	2	12	.143	23	19	4	0		0			129	151	82	8	0	55		54	5.16	-18	.292	.360	-31	0	-1.0
1949	Year	4	15	.211	30	25	6	0		0			166.2	204	108	11	1	75		68	5.13	-17	.299	.369	-21	0	-1.5
1950	Was A	5	9	.357	**53**	0	0	0		**15**			98	93	56	9	1	46		41	4.78	-6	.247	.330		0	-0.2
1951	Was A	6	8	.429	41	0	0	0		4			87.1	87	45	6	1	43		47	3.81	+7	.260	.347		0	0.2
1952	Was A	0	0	+	1	0	0	0		0			1	1	1	1	0	0		0	9.00	-60	.250	.250		0	0.0
1952	Cle A	3	0	1.000	29	0	0	0		1			46.2	42	26	6	1	21		23	4.63	-28	.249	.335		0	-0.4
1952	Year	3	0	1.000	30	0	0	0		1			47.2	43	27	7	1	21		23	4.72	-29	.249	.333		0	-0.4
Total	9	59	71	.454	271	109	42	2		21			1050	1097	560	78	12	455		534	4.18	-2	.267	.342	+4	0	0.2
Team	6	43	42	.506	124	90	38	2		1			688	723	350	48	9	290		369	3.92	+4	.267	.340	+12		1.6
/180I	2	11	11	.506	32	24	10	1		0			180	189	92	13	2	76		97	3.92	+4	.267	.340	+12		0.4
HARRIS, REGGIE Reginald Allen B8.12.1968 Waynesboro VA BR/TR/6'1"/(180–217) [BosA87 1/26] d7.4																											
1996	Bos A	0	0	+	4	0	0	0	0	0	1	1	4.1	7	6	2	1	5	0	4	12.46	-59	.389	.542		0	-0.1
Total	6	2	3	.400	86	1	0	0	1	0	1	51	121	106	67	10	10	81	3	95	4.91	-16	.238	.361	-3	85	-0.5

Year	Tm Lg	W	L	Pct	G	GS	CG	ShO	QS	SV	BS	QR	IP	H	R	HR	HB	BB	IB	SO	ERA	AERA	OAV	OOB	Sup	DL	PW
HARRIS, BILL William Milton B6.23.1900 Wylie TX D8.21.1965 Charlotte NC BR/TR/6'1"/180 d4.22																											
1938	Bos A	5	5	.500	13	11	5	1		1			80.1	83	39	5	1	21		26	4.03	+22	.268	.316	+15		0.9
Total	7	24	22	.522	121	36	13	2		8			433.2	467	221	17	12	109		149	3.92	+1	.276	.324	+2		1.5
HARRISS, SLIM William Jennings Bryan B12.11.1896 Brownwood TX D9.19.1963 Temple TX BR/TR/6'6"/180 d4.19 Col Howard Payne																											
1926	Bos A	6	10	.375	21	18	6	1		0			113	135	66	0	2	33		34	4.46	-9	.311	.362	-16		-0.6
1927	Bos A	14	21	.400	44	27	11	1		1			217.2	253	127	8	9	66		77	4.18	+1	.298	.355	-25		-0.7
1928	Bos A	8	11	.421	27	15	4	1		1			128.1	141	74	5	2	33		37	4.63	-11	.287	.335	-36		-1.1
Total	9	95	135	.413	349	228	89	7		16			1750.1	1963	1006	75	41	630		644	4.25	+0	.290	.354	-16		-3.2
Team	3	28	42	.400	92	60	21	3		2			459	529	267	13	13	132		148	4.37	-5	.298	.351	-25		-2.4
/180I	1	11	16	.400	36	24	8	1		1			180	207	105	5	5	52		58	4.37	-5	.298	.351	-25		-0.9
HARSHMAN, JACK John Elvin B7.12.1927 San Diego CA BL/TL/6'2"/(185–190) d9.16.1948																											
1959	Bos A	2	3	.400	8	2	0	0	1	0		3	24.2	29	19	2	0	10	0	14	6.57	-38	.284	.348	-46	0	-1.1
Total	8	69	65	.515	217	155	61	12	66	7		34	1169.1	1025	508	96	22	539	17	741	3.50	+9	.235	.320	-2	86	7.0
HARTENSTEIN, CHUCK Charles Oscar "Twiggy" B5.26.1942 Seguin TX BR/TR/5'11"/165 d9.11.1965 C4 Col Texas																											
1970	Bos A	0	3	.000	17	0	0	0	0	1	2	10	19	21	17	6	1	12	5	12	8.05	-51	.288	.395		0	-1.1
Total	6	17	19	.472	187	0	0	0	0	23	7	114	297	317	157	34	9	89	21	135	4.52	-19	.280	.335		0	-2.4
HARTLEY, MIKE Michael Edward B8.31.1961 Hawthorne CA BR/TR/6'1"/(185–197) d9.10 Col Grossmont (CA) JC																											
1995	Bos A	0	0	+	5	0	0	0	0	0	0	3	7	8	7	1	2	2	0	2	9.00	-46	.308	.375		0	-0.1
Total	6	19	13	.594	202	6	1	1	4	4	10	132	318.2	287	142	28	19	139	19	259	3.70	+5	.241	.328	-18	37	0.8
HARTMAN, CHARLIE Charles Otto B8.10.1888 Los Angeles CA D10.22.1960 Los Angeles CA TL d6.24																											
1908	Bos A	0	0	+	1	0	0	0		0			2	1	1	0	0	2		1	4.50	-45	.143	.333			0.0
HARVILLE, CHAD Chad Ashley B9.16.1976 Selmer TN BR/TR/5'9"/(180–186) [OakA97 2/63] d6.23 Col Memphis																											
2005	Bos A	0	1	.000	8	0	0	0	0	0	0	5	7	7	5	1	1	3	0	3	6.43	-29	.269	.367		0	-0.1
Total	6	4	9	.308	175	0	0	0	0	2	6	117	181	188	115	26	8	103	7	147	5.22	-14	.269	.367		94	-1.2
HASH, HERB Herbert Howard B2.13.1911 Woolwine VA BR/TR/6'1"/180 d4.19 Col Richmond																											
1940	Bos A	7	7	.500	34	12	3	1		3			120	123	68	11	5	84		36	4.95	-9	.266	.385	+3		-0.4
1941	Bos A	1	0	1.000	4	0	0	0		1			8.1	7	5	1	0	7		3	5.40	-23	.226	.368		67	-0.1
Total	2	8	7	.533	38	12	3	1		4			128.1	130	73	12	5	91		39	4.98	-10	.264	.384	+3	67	-0.5
/180I	3	11	10	.533	53	17	4	1	0	6	0	0	180	182	102	17	7	128		55	4.98	-10	.264	.384	+44	94	-0.7
HASSLER, ANDY Andrew Earl B10.18.1951 Texas City TX BL/TL/6'5"/(215–220) [AnaA69 25/579] d5.30																											
1978	Bos A	2	1	.667	13	2	0	0	0	1	0	9	30	38	13	0	0	13	2	23	3.00	+37	.302	.367	+42	0	0.3
1979	Bos A	1	2	.333	8	0	0	0	0	0	0	4	15.1	23	17	0	1	7	0	7	8.80	-49	.365	.431		0	-1.2
Total	14	44	71	.383	387	112	26	5	57	29	10	193	1123.1	1125	562	67	32	520	49	630	3.83	-2	.264	.346	+0	62	-3.2
Team	2	3	3	.500	21	2	0	0	0	1	0	13	45.1	61	30	0	1	20	2	30	4.96	-15	.323	.389	+42		-0.9
HAUSMANN, CLEM Clemens Raymond B8.17.1919 Houston TX D8.29.1972 Baytown TX BR/TR/5'9"/165 d4.28																											
1944	Bos A	4	7	.364	32	12	3	0		2			137	139	55	6	3	69		43	3.42	-1	.266	.355	-26	0	-0.1
1945	Bos A	5	7	.417	31	13	4	2		2			125	131	77	5	2	60		30	5.04	-32	.270	.352	-35	0	-2.1
1949	Phi A	0	0	+	1	0	0	0		0			1	0	1	0	0	2		0	9.00	-54	.000	.500		0	0.0
Total	3	9	14	.391	64	25	7	2		4			263	270	133	11	5	131		73	4.21	-19	.267	.354	-31	0	-2.2
Team	2	9	14	.391	63	25	7	2		4			262	270	132	11	5	129		73	4.19	-19	.268	.354	-31		-2.2
/180I	1	6	10	.391	43	17	5	1		3			180	185	91	8	3	89		50	4.19	-19	.268	.354	-31		-1.5
HEFFNER, BOB Robert Frederic B9.13.1938 Allentown PA BR/TR/6'4"/(198–210) d6.19																											
1963	Bos A	4	9	.308	20	19	3	1	11	0		1	124.2	131	61	15	2	36	1	77	4.26	-11	.267	.318	-26	0	-0.6
1964	Bos A	7	9	.438	55	10	1	1	2	6		33	158.2	152	81	20	3	44	6	112	4.08	-6	.251	.305	+13	0	-0.4
1965	Bos A	0	2	.000	27	1	0	0	0	0		15	49	59	42	9	1	18	1	42	7.16	-48	.304	.364	+88	0	-0.9
1966	Cle A	0	1	.000	5	1	0	0	0	0		4	13	12	6	1	0	3	0	7	3.46	-1	.240	.283	-49	0	0.0
1968	Cal A	0	0	+	7	0	0	0	0	0		4	8	6	2	0	0	6	1	3	2.25	+30	.240	.375		0	0.1
Total	5	11	21	.344	114	31	4	2	13	6		57	353.1	360	192	45	6	107	9	241	4.51	-16	.264	.319	-10	0	-1.8
Team	3	11	20	.355	102	30	4	2	13	6		49	332.1	342	184	44	6	98	8	231	4.60	-17	.265	.319	-9		-1.9
/180I	2	6	11	.355	55	16	2	1	7	3		27	180	185	100	24	3	53	4	125	4.60	-17	.265	.319	-9		-1.0
HEFLIN, RANDY Randolph Rutherford B9.11.1918 Fredericksburg VA D8.17.1999 Fredericksburg VA BL/TR/6'0"/185 d6.9																											
1945	Bos A	4	10	.286	20	14	6	2		0			102	102	52	3	4	61		39	4.06	-16	.272	.380	-27	0	-1.2
1946	Bos A	0	1	.000	5	1	0	0		0			14.2	16	5	0	1	12		6	2.45	+49	.296	.433	+110	0	0.2
Total	2	4	11	.267	25	15	6	2		0			116.2	118	57	3	5	73		45	3.86	-11	.275	.387	-17	0	-1.0
HEIMACH, FRED Frederick Amos "Lefty" B1.27.1901 Camden NJ D6.1.1973 Ft.Myers FL BL/TL/6'0"/175 d10.1																											
1926	Bos A	2	9	.182	20	13	6	0		0			102	119	72	5	0	42		17	5.65	-28	.303	.370	-12		-1.1
Total	13	62	69	.473	296	127	56	5		7			1288.2	1510	755	64	27	360		334	4.46	-10	.296	.346	-4		-2.7
HENRY, BUTCH Floyd Bluford B10.7.1968 ElPaso TX BL/TL/6'1"/(195–205) [CinN87 15/388] d4.9 [DL 1996 Bos A 182]																											
1997	Bos A	7	3	.700	36	5	0	0	2	6	2	20	84.1	89	36	6	0	19	2	51	3.52	+32	.277	.315	-25	49	1.3
1998	Bos A	0	0	+	2	2	0	0	0	0	0	0	9	8	4	2	1	3	0	6	4.00	+18	.235	.316	+38	174	0.1
Total	7	33	33	.500	148	91	4	2	39	7	2	39	621	677	289	61	9	149	15	345	3.83	+9	.280	.322	-7	578	3.3
Team	2	7	3	.700	38	7	0	0	2	6	2	20	93.1	97	40	8	1	22	2	57	3.57	+31	.273	.315	-7	223	1.4
HENRY, JIM James Francis B6.26.1910 Danville VA D8.15.1976 Memphis TN BR/TR/6'2"/175 d4.23																											
1936	Bos A	5	1	.833	21	8	2	0		0			76.1	75	43	10	2	40		36	4.60	+16	.255	.348	+8		0.3
1937	Bos A	1	0	1.000	3	2	1	0		0			15.1	15	9	2	0	11		8	5.28	-10	.263	.382	+1		-0.1
1939	Phi N	0	1	.000	9	1	0	0		1			23	24	13	3	1	8		7	5.09	-21	.276	.344	+118		-0.2
Total	3	6	2	.750	33	11	3	0		1			114.2	114	65	15	3	59		51	4.79	+4	.260	.352	+17		0.0
Team	2	6	1	.857	24	10	3	0		0			91.2	90	52	12	2	51		44	4.71	+11	.256	.354	+7		0.2
HENRY, BILL William Rodman B10.15.1927 Alice TX BL/TL/6'2"/(175–195) d4.17 Col Houston																											
1952	Bos A	5	4	.556	13	10	5	0		0			76.2	75	40	7	2	36		23	3.87	+2	.254	.339	+20	0	0.1
1953	Bos A	5	5	.500	21	12	4	1		1			85.2	86	39	4	4	33		56	3.26	+29	.260	.334	-5	0	0.7
1954	Bos A	3	7	.300	24	13	3	1		0			95.2	104	56	9	1	49		38	4.52	-9	.270	.351	-4	0	-0.6
1955	Bos A	2	4	.333	17	7	0	0		0			59.2	56	28	7	0	21	2	23	3.32	+29	.247	.306	+12	0	0.3
Total	16	46	50	.479	527	44	12	2	0	90	0	400	913	842	386	89	25	296	43	621	3.26	+19	.244	.306	+6	0	7.2
Team	4	15	20	.429	75	42	12	2		1			317.2	321	163	27	7	139	2	140	3.80	+9	.259	.335	+4		0.5
/180I	2	8	11	.429	42	24	7	1		1			180	182	92	15	4	79	1	79	3.80	+9	.259	.335	+4		0.3
HERMANSON, DUSTIN Dustin Michael B12.21.1972 Springfield OH BR/TR/6'3"/(195–205) [SDN94 1/3] d5.8 Col Kent St.																											
2002	Bos A	1	1	.500	12	1	0	0	0	0	1	3	22	35	19	3	0	7	0	13	7.77	-42	.354	.393	+148	139	-0.6
Total	12	73	78	.483	357	180	4	2	95	56	17	116	1283	1285	675	160	32	460	32	874	4.21	+4	.263	.328	-4	342	2.2
HERNANDEZ, RAMON Ramon (Gonzalez) B8.31.1940 Carolina, PR BB/TL/5'9"/(165–170) d4.11																											
1977	Bos A	0	1	.000	12	0	0	0	0	1	0	6	12.2	14	10	2	1	7	1	8	5.68	-21	.280	.379		0	-0.2
Total	9	23	15	.605	337	0	0	0	0	46	11	238	430.1	399	158	23	14	135	42	255	3.03	+15	.245	.307		0	4.7
HERRIN, TOM Thomas Edward B9.12.1929 Shreveport LA D11.29.1999 Homer LA BR/TR/6'3"/190 d4.13 Col Louisiana Tech																											
1954	Bos A	1	2	.333	14	1	0	0		0			28.1	34	23	2	0	22		8	7.31	-44	.315	.424	-100	0	-0.7
HESKETH, JOE Joseph Thomas B2.15.1959 Lackawanna NY BL/TL/6'2"/(170–173) [MonN80 2/50] d8.7																											
1984	Mon N	2	2	.500	11	5	1	1	4	1	0	5	45	38	12	2	0	15	3	32	1.80	+92	.233	.294	-3	0	0.7
1985	Mon N	10	5	.667	25	25	2	1	16	0	0	0	155.1	125	52	10	0	45	2	113	2.49	+38	.222	.279	-6	44	1.3
1986	Mon N	6	5	.545	15	15	0	0	8	0	0	0	82.2	92	46	11	2	31	4	67	5.01	-25	.283	.347	-6	94	-1.3
1987	Mon N	0	0	+	18	0	0	0	0	1	0	12	28.2	23	12	2	2	15	3	31	3.14	+36	.211	.317		0	0.1
1988	Mon N	4	3	.571	60	0	0	0	0	9	2	43	72.2	63	30	1	0	35	9	64	2.85	+28	.242	.328		0	0.7
1989	Mon N	6	4	.600	43	0	0	0	0	3	1	27	48.1	54	34	5	0	26	6	44	5.77	-38	.292	.376		21	-2.3
1990	Mon N	1	0	1.000	2	0	0	0	0	0	0	2	3	2	0	0	0	2	1	3	0.00	-100	.200	.333		0	0.3

Year	Tm Lg	W	L	Pct	G	GS	CG	ShO	QS	SV	BS	QR	IP	H	R	HR	HB	BB	IB	SO	ERA	AERA	OAV	OOB	Sup	DL	PW
1990	Atl N	0	2	.000	31	0	0	0	0	5	4	21	31	30	23	5	1	12	0	21	5.81	-31	.248	.319		0	-0.6
1990	Year	1	2	.333	33	0	0	0	0	5	4	23	34	32	23	5	1	14	1	24	5.29	-24	.244	.320		0	-0.3
1990	Bos A	0	4	.000	12	2	0	0	0	0	0	4	25.2	37	12	2	0	11	1	26	3.51	+17	.333	.393	-89	0	0.2
1990	Major	1	6	.143	45	2	0	0	0	5	4	27	59	69	35	7	1	25	2	50	4.53	-14	.285	.353	-89	0	-0.1
1991	Bos A	12	4	.750	39	17	0	0	11	0	0	17	153.1	142	59	19	0	53	3	104	3.29	+32	.250	.313	+3	0	1.8
1992	Bos A	8	9	.471	30	25	1	0	11	1	0	3	148.2	162	84	15	2	58	9	104	4.36	-2	.276	.339	-7	0	-0.2
1993	Bos A	3	4	.429	28	5	0	0	1	1	0	15	53.1	62	35	4	0	29	4	34	5.06	-8	.294	.376	-20	45	-0.3
1994	Bos A	8	5	.615	25	20	0	0	8	0	0	3	114	117	70	9	2	46	3	83	4.26	+18	.267	.334	-1	0	0.4
Total	11	60	47	.561	339	114	4	2	59	21	7	152	961.2	947	469	85	9	378	48	726	3.78	+8	.259	.328	-4	204	0.8
Team	5	31	26	.544	134	69	1	0	31	2	0	42	495	520	260	49	4	197	20	351	4.04	+11	.272	.338	-6	45	1.9
/180I	2	11	9	.544	49	25	0	0	11	1	0	15	180	189	95	18	1	72	7	128	4.04	+11	.272	.338	-6	16	0.7
HETZEL, ERIC Eric Paul B9.25.1963 Crowley LA BR/TR/6'3"/(175–180) [BosA85 S1/1] d7.1 Col Louisiana St.																											
1989	Bos A	2	3	.400	12	11	0	0	1	0	0	0	50.1	61	39	7	2	28	1	33	6.26	-34	.296	.382	+32	21	-1.0
1990	Bos A	1	4	.200	9	8	0	0	3	0	0	0	35	39	28	3	1	21	0	20	5.91	-31	.281	.377	-28	0	-1.0
Total	2	3	7	.300	21	19	0	0	4	0	0	0	85.1	100	67	10	3	49	1	53	6.12	-33	.290	.380	+7	21	-2.0
HEVING, JOE Joseph William B9.2.1900 Covington KY D4.11.1970 Covington KY BR/TR/6'1"/185 d4.29 b–Johnnie																											
1938	Bos A	8	1	.889	16	11	7	1		2			82	94	35	5	1	22		34	3.73	+32	.283	.330	+35		1.2
1939	Bos A	11	3	.786	46	5	1	0		7			107	124	65	8	2	34		43	3.70	+28	.295	.350	+16		0.6
1940	Bos A	12	7	.632	39	7	4	0		3			119	129	63	7	3	42		55	4.01	+12	.272	.335	+79		0.6
Total	13	76	48	.613	430	40	17	3		63			1038.2	1136	559	64	24	380		429	3.90	+8	.279	.344	+20	0	1.7
Team	3	31	11	.738	101	23	12	1		12			308	347	163	20	6	98		132	3.83	+23	.283	.339	+44		2.4
/180I	2	18	6	.738	59	13	7	1		7			180	203	95	12	4	57		77	3.83	+23	.283	.339	+44		1.4
HILLMAN, DAVE Darius Dutton B9.14.1927 Dungannon VA BR/TR/5'11"/168 d4.30																											
1960	Bos A	0	3	.000	16	3	0	0	0	0		8	36.2	41	27	6	0	12	1	14	5.65	-28	.281	.333	-20	58	-0.5
1961	Bos A	3	2	.600	28	1	0	0	1	0		18	78	70	26	8	0	23	0	39	2.77	+51	.242	.296	-58	0	0.6
Total	8	21	37	.362	188	64	8	1	75	3		132	624	639	305	71	3	185	10	296	3.87	+3	.264	.315	-14	58	0.3
Team	2	3	5	.375	44	4	0	0	1	0		26	114.2	111	53	14	0	35	1	53	3.69	+12	.255	.309	-29	58	0.1
/60G	3	4	7	.375	60	5	0	0	1	0		35	156.1	151	72	19	0	48	1	72	3.69	+12	.255	.309	-29	79	0.1
HINRICHS, PAUL Paul Edwin "Herky" B8.31.1925 Marengo IA BR/TR/6'0"/180 d5.16 Col Concordia (TX)																											
1951	Bos A	0	0	+	4	0	0	0		0			3.1	7	8	1	0	4		1	21.60	-79	.412	.524		0	-0.3
HISNER, HARLEY Harley Parnell B11.6.1926 Maples IN BR/TR/6'1"/185 d9.30																											
1951	Bos A	0	1	.000	1	1	0	0		0			6	7	3	0	0	4		3	4.50	-1	.292	.393	-100	0	0.0
HOCKETTE, GEORGE George Edward "Lefty" B4.7.1908 Perth MS D1.20.1974 Plantation FL BL/TL/6'0"/174 d9.17																											
1934	Bos A	2	1	.667	3	3	3	2		0			27.1	22	5	3	0	6		14	1.65	+192	.218	.262	-28		1.0
1935	Bos A	2	3	.400	23	4	0	0		0			61	83	43	6	1	12		11	5.16	-8	.329	.362	-9		-0.1
Total	2	4	4	.500	26	7	3	2		0			88.1	105	48	9	1	18		25	4.08	+17	.297	.333	-17		0.9
HOEFT, BILLY William Frederick B5.17.1932 Oshkosh WI BL/TL/6'3"/(177–205) d4.18																											
1959	Bos A	0	3	.000	5	3	0	0	0	0		2	17.2	22	12	1	1	8	1	8	5.60	-28	.319	.383	-20	0	-0.4
Total	15	97	101	.490	505	200	75	17	100	33		195	1847.1	1820	883	173	36	685	45	1140	3.94	-2	.259	.325	+0	77	1.3
HOLCOMBE, KEN Kenneth Edward B8.23.1918 Burnsville NC BR/TR/5'11.5"/169 d4.27																											
1953	Bos A	1	0	1.000	3	0	0	0		1			6	9	4	0	0	3		1	6.00	-30	.333	.400		0	-0.2
Total	6	18	32	.360	99	48	18	2		2			375	377	196	25	3	170		118	3.98	+1	.265	.345	-23	0	-0.3
HOLTZ, MIKE Michael James B10.10.1972 Arlington VA BL/TL/5'9"/(175–188) [CalA94 17/461] d7.11 Col Clemson																											
2006	Bos A	0	0	+	3	0	0	0	0	0	0	1	1.2	3	3	0	1	4	0	2	16.20	-71	.429	.667		30	-0.1
Total	8	16	20	.444	353	0	0	0	0	3	12	238	240	245	146	25	15	131	17	223	4.76	-1	.266	.362		65	-0.0
HOUSE, TOM Thomas Ross B4.29.1947 Seattle WA BL/TL/5'11"/(175–190) [AtlN67 S3/48] d6.23 C8 Col USC																											
1976	Bos A	1	3	.250	36	0	0	0	0	4	2	25	43.2	39	22	4	2	19	4	27	4.33	-10	.241	.324		20	-0.1
1977	Bos A	1	0	1.000	8	0	0	0	0	0	0	5	7.2	15	11	0	0	6	0	6	12.91	-65	.405	.488		0	-0.7
Total	8	29	23	.558	289	21	4	0	9	33	13	187	536	516	258	49	20	182	33	261	3.79	+3	.256	.320	-6	43	1.1
Team	2	2	3	.400	44	0	0	0	0	4	2	30	51.1	54	33	4	2	25	4	33	5.61	-29	.271	.355		20	-0.8
/60G	3	3	4	.400	60	0	0	0	0	5	3	41	70	74	45	5	3	34	5	45	5.61	-29	.271	.355		27	-1.1
HOWARD, CHRIS Christian B11.18.1965 Lynn MA BR/TL/6'0"/185 d9.21 Col Miami [DL 1996 Tex A 182]																											
1993	Chi A	1	0	1.000	3	0	0	0	0	0	0	2	2.1	2	0	0	0	3	1	1	0.00	-100	.286	.500		0	0.2
1994	Bos A	1	0	1.000	37	0	0	0	0	1	1	25	39.2	35	17	5	0	12	4	22	3.63	+39	.233	.287		0	0.3
1995	Tex A	0	0	+	4	0	0	0	0	0	0	3	4	3	0	0	0	1	0	2	0.00	-100	.231	.267		0	0.1
Total	3	2	0	1.000	44	0	0	0	0	1	1	30	46	40	17	5	0	16	5	25	3.13	+59	.235	.296		182	0.6
HOWE, LES Lester Curtis "Lucky" B8.24.1895 Brooklyn NY D7.16.1976 Woodmere NY BR/TR/5'11.5"/170 d8.18																											
1923	Bos A	1	0	1.000	12	2	0	0		0			30	23	10	0	1	7		7	2.40	+71	.211	.265	+11		0.2
1924	Bos A	1	0	1.000	4	0	0	0		0			7.1	11	6	1	1	2		3	7.36	-41	.423	.483			-0.2
Total	2	2	0	1.000	16	2	0	0		0			37.1	34	16	1	2	9		10	3.38	+23	.252	.308	+11		0.0
HOWRY, BOB Bobby Dean B8.4.1973 Phoenix AZ BL/TR/6'5"/(215–220) [SFN94 5/144] d6.21 Col McNeese St.																											
2002	Bos A	1	3	.250	20	0	0	0	0	0	1	13	18	22	15	2	2	4	2	14	5.00	-10	.306	.350		0	-0.5
2003	Bos A	0	0	+	4	0	0	0	0	0	1	1	4.1	11	6	1	0	3	1	4	12.46	-63	.478	.519		38	-0.2
Total	9	29	31	.483	518	0	0	0	0	57	29	388	537	468	229	59	23	185	26	462	3.52	+31	.236	.305		38	7.4
Team	2	1	3	.250	24	0	0	0	0	0	2	14	22.1	33	21	3	2	7	3	18	6.45	-30	.347	.393		38	-0.7
HOY, PETER Peter Alexander B6.29.1966 Brockville ON, Can. BL/TR/6'7"/220 [BosA88 33/849] d4.11 Col LeMoyne (NY)																											
1992	Bos A	0	0	+	5	0	0	0	0	0	1	2	3.2	8	3	0	0	2	1	2	7.36	-42	.471	.526		0	0.0
HOYT, WAITE Waite Charles "Schoolboy" B9.9.1899 Brooklyn NY D8.25.1984 Cincinnati OH BR/TR/6'0"/180 d7.24 HF1969																											
1919	Bos A	4	6	.400	13	11	6	1		0			105.1	99	42	1	0	22		28	3.25	-7	.262	.303	-17		-0.3
1920	Bos A	6	6	.500	22	11	6	2		1			121.1	123	72	2	1	47		45	4.38	-17	.270	.339	+3		-1.3
Total	21	237	182	.566	674	425	226	26		52			3762.1	4037	1780	154	49	1003		1206	3.59	+12	.276	.325	+4		15.7
Team	2	10	12	.455	35	22	12	3		1			226.2	222	114	3	1	69		73	3.85	-13	.266	.323	-7		-1.6
/180I	2	8	10	.455	28	17	10	2		1			180	176	91	2	1	55		58	3.85	-13	.266	.323	-7		-1.3
HUDSON, JOE Joseph Paul B9.29.1970 Philadelphia PA BR/TR/6'1"/(175–180) [BosA92 27/758] d6.10 Col West Virginia																											
1995	†Bos A	0	1	.000	39	0	0	0	0	1	3	25	46	53	21	2	2	23	1	29	4.11	+18	.301	.386		0	0.2
1996	Bos A	3	5	.375	36	0	0	0	0	1	4	25	45	57	35	4	0	32	4	19	5.40	-6	.318	.418		0	-0.5
1997	Bos A	3	1	.750	26	0	0	0	0	0	0	15	35.2	39	16	1	4	14	2	14	3.53	+32	.289	.373		0	0.4
1998	Mil N	0	0	+	1	0	0	0	0	0	0	0	0.1	2	6	0	0	4	1	0	162.00	-97	1.000	.857		0	-0.2
Total	4	6	7	.462	102	0	0	0	0	2	7	65	127	151	78	7	6	73	8	62	4.82	+1	.307	.400		0	-0.1
Team	3	6	7	.462	101	0	0	0	0	2	7	65	126.2	149	72	7	6	69	7	62	4.41	+11	.304	.394			0.1
/60G	2	4	4	.462	60	0	0	0	0	1	4	39	75.1	89	43	4	4	41	4	37	4.40	+11	.304	.394			0.1
HUDSON, SID Sidney Charles B1.3.1915 Coalfield TN BR/TR/6'4"/180 d4.18 Mil 1943–45 C14																											
1952	Bos A	7	9	.438	21	18	7	0		0			134.1	145	64	9	7	36		50	3.62	+9	.276	.330	-11	0	0.5
1953	Bos A	6	9	.400	30	17	4	0		2			156	164	65	13	4	49		60	3.52	+20	.269	.327	-20	0	1.0
1954	Bos A	3	4	.429	33	5	0	0		5			71.1	83	43	5	2	30		27	4.42	-7	.296	.363	-23	0	-0.4
Total	12	104	152	.406	380	279	123	11		13			2181	2384	1212	136	48	835		734	4.28	-5	.278	.345	-15	0	-4.7
Team	3	16	22	.421	84	40	11	0		7			361.2	392	172	27	13	115		137	3.73	+10	.277	.335	-16		1.1
/180I	1	8	11	.421	42	20	5	0		3			180	195	86	13	6	57		68	3.73	+10	.277	.335	-16		0.5
HUGHES, ED Edward J. B10.5.1880 Chicago IL D10.14.1927 McHenry IL BR/TR/6'1"/180 d8.29.1902 b–Tom																											
1905	Bos A	3	2	.600	6	4	2	0		0			33.1	38	27	0	1	9		8	4.59	-41	.288	.338	+44		-1.2
1906	Bos A	0	0	+	2	0	0	0		0			10	15	7	0	0	3		3	5.40	-49	.349	.391			-0.2
Total	2	3	2	.600	8	4	2	0		0			43.1	53	34	0	1	12		11	4.78	-43	.303	.351	+44		-1.4

Year	Tm Lg	W	L	Pct	G	GS	CG	ShO	QS	SV	BS	QR	IP	H	R	HR	HB	BB	IB	SO	ERA	AERA	OAV	OOB	Sup	DL	PW
HUGHES, TOM Thomas James "Long Tom" B11.29.1878 Chicago IL D2.8.1956 Chicago IL BR/TR/6'1"/175 d9.7 b–Ed																											
1902	Bos A	3	3	.500	9	8	4	0		0			49.1	51	31	0	1	24		15	3.28	+9	.267	.352	+36		0.2
1903	†Bos A	20	7	.741	33	31	25	5		0			244.2	232	95	5	9	60		112	2.57	+18	.249	.301	+32		1.9
Total	13	132	174	.431	399	313	227	25		15			2644	2610	1292	52	102	853		1368	3.09	-7	.260	.324	-1		-6.4
Team	2	23	10	.697	42	39	29	5		0			294	283	126	5	10	84		127	2.69	+16	.252	.310	+33		2.1
/180I	1	14	6	.697	26	24	18	3		0			180	173	77	3	6	51		78	2.69	+16	.252	.310	+33		1.3
HUGHSON, TEX Cecil Carlton B2.9.1916 Buda TX D8.6.1993 San Marcos TX BR/TR/6'3"/198 d4.16 Mil 1944–45 Col Texas																											
1941	Bos A	5	3	.625	12	8	4	0		0			61	70	30	3	1	13		22	4.13	+1	.289	.328	-14	0	0.1
1942	Bos A☆	**22**	6	.786	38	30	**22**	4		4			**281**	258	92	10	1	75		**113**	2.59	+44	.245	.296	+23	0	3.7
1943	Bos A★	12	15	.444	35	32	**20**	4		2			266	242	87	23	2	73		114	2.64	+26	.247	.300	-15	0	1.6
1944	Bos A★	18	5	**.783**	28	23	19	2		5			203.1	172	57	4	2	41		112	2.26	+51	.225	**.267**	+40	0	3.1
1946	†Bos A	20	11	.645	39	35	21	6		3			278	252	89	15	2	51		172	2.75	+33	.238	.274	-10	0	3.0
1947	Bos A	12	11	.522	29	26	13	3		0			189.1	173	86	17	2	71		119	3.33	+17	.244	.314	-5	0	0.3
1948	Bos A	3	1	.750	15	0	0	0		0			19.1	21	14	0	0	7		6	5.12	-14	.276	.337		0	-0.5
1949	Bos A	4	2	.667	29	2	0	0		3			77.2	82	49	5	1	41		35	5.33	-18	.268	.356	+13	0	-0.9
Total	8	96	54	.640	225	156	99	19		17			1375.2	1270	504	77	11	372		693	2.94	+25	.245	.297	+3	0	10.4
/180I	1	13	7	.640	29	20	13	2	0	2	0	0	180	166	66	10	1	49		91	2.94	+25	.245	.297	-87		1.4
HUMPHREY, BILL Byron William B6.17.1911 Vienna MO D2.13.1992 Springfield MO BR/TR/6'0"/180 d4.24																											
1938	Bos A	0	0	+	2	0	0	0		0			2	5	2	0	0	1		0	9.00	-45	.500	.545			0.0
HUNT, BEN Benjamin Franklin "High Pockets" B11.10.1888 Eufaula OK D9.27.1927 Greybull WY BL/TL/6'5"/190 d8.24																											
1910	Bos A	2	3	.400	7	7	3	0		0			46.2	45	22	4	0	20		19	4.05	-37	.266	.344	+5		-0.7
1913	StL N	0	1	.000	2	1	0	0		0			8	6	5	0	1	9		6	3.38	-4	.240	.457	-77		-0.1
Total	2	2	4	.333	9	8	3	0		0			54.2	51	27	4	1	29		25	3.95	-33	.263	.362	-7		-0.8
HURD, TOM Thomas Carr "Whitey" B5.27.1924 Danville VA D9.5.1982 Waterloo IA BR/TR/5'9"/155 d7.30																											
1954	Bos A	2	0	1.000	16	0	0	0		1			29.2	21	11	2	0	12		14	3.03	+35	.198	.277		0	0.3
1955	Bos A	8	6	.571	43	0	0	0		5			80.2	72	32	7	1	38	10	48	3.01	+42	.242	.326		0	1.6
1956	Bos A	3	4	.429	40	0	0	0		5			76	84	52	5	3	47	2	34	5.33	-13	.289	.386		0	-0.4
Total	3	13	10	.565	99	0	0	0		11			186.1	177	95	14	4	97	12	96	3.96	+11	.255	.345		0	1.5
/60G	2	8	6	.565	60	0	0	0	0	7	0	0	113	107	58	8	2	59	0	58	3.96	+11	.255	.345			0.9
HURST, BRUCE Bruce Vee B3.24.1958 St.George UT BL/TL/6'3"/(185–220) [BosA76 1/22] d4.12																											
1980	Bos A	2	2	.500	12	7	0	0	1	0	0	2	30.2	39	33	4	2	16	0	16	9.10	-53	.307	.388	+44	0	-1.7
1981	Bos A	2	0	1.000	5	5	0	0	1	0	0	0	23	23	11	1	1	12	2	11	4.30	-9	.258	.346	+15	0	0.0
1982	Bos A	3	7	.300	28	19	0	0	6	0	0	4	117	161	87	16	3	40	2	53	5.77	-24	.333	.383	-5	0	-1.4
1983	Bos A	12	12	.500	33	32	6	2	16	0	0	1	211.1	241	102	22	3	62	5	115	4.09	+8	.290	.340	-7	0	1.0
1984	Bos A	12	12	.500	33	33	9	2	18	0	0	0	218	232	106	25	6	88	3	136	3.92	+7	.271	.341	+4	0	0.8
1985	Bos A	11	13	.458	35	31	6	1	15	0	3	0	229.1	243	123	31	3	70	4	189	4.51	-4	.273	.327	+26	0	-0.3
1986	†Bos A	13	8	.619	25	25	11	4	16	0	0	0	174.1	169	63	18	3	50	2	167	2.99	+40	.256	.310	-9	45	2.7
1987	Bos A☆	15	13	.536	33	33	15	3	18	0	0	0	238.2	239	124	35	1	76	5	190	4.41	+4	.262	.317	-4	0	0.6
1988	†Bos A	18	6	.750	33	32	7	1	20	0	0	0	216.2	222	98	21	2	65	1	166	3.66	+13	.264	.316	+33	16	1.1
1989	SD N	15	11	.577	33	33	**10**	2	26	0	0	0	244.2	214	84	16	0	66	7	179	2.69	+31	.237	.288	-6	0	2.2
1990	SD N	11	9	.550	33	33	9	0	22	0	0	0	223.2	188	85	21	1	63	5	162	3.14	+22	.228	.284	-11	0	1.4
1991	SD N	15	8	.652	31	31	4	0	23	0	0	0	221.2	201	89	17	3	59	3	141	3.29	+16	.241	.292	+3	0	1.2
1992	SD N	14	9	.609	32	32	6	4	22	0	0	0	217.1	223	96	22	0	51	3	131	3.85	-7	.267	.308	+9	0	-0.2
1993	SD N	0	1	.000	2	2	0	0	0	0	0	0	4.1	9	7	0	0	3	0	3	12.46	-67	.409	.480	+20	101	-0.7
1993	Col N	0	1	.000	3	3	0	0	0	0	0	0	8.2	6	5	1	0	3	0	6	5.19	-8	.194	.265	+7	42	0.0
1993	Year	0	2	.000	5	5	0	0	0	0	0	0	13	15	12	1	0	6	0	9	7.62	-40	.283	.356	+10	0	-0.7
1994	Tex A	2	1	.667	8	8	0	0	1	0	0	0	38	53	30	8	0	16	0	24	7.11	-32	.342	.394	+52	0	-0.5
Total	15	145	113	.562	379	359	83	23	205	0	3	7	2417.1	2463	1143	258	28	740	42	1689	3.92	+4	.265	.319	+6	204	6.2
Team	9	88	73	.547	237	217	54	13	111	0	3	7	1459	1569	747	173	24	479	24	1043	4.23	+2	.276	.332	+8	61	2.8
/180I	1	11	9	.547	29	27	7	2	14	0	0	1	180	194	92	21	3	59	3	129	4.23	+2	.276	.332	+8	8	0.3
HUSTING, BERT Berthold Juneau "Pete" B3.6.1878 Fond Du Lac WI D9.3.1948 Milwaukee WI BR/TR/5'10.5"/185 d8.16 Col Wisconsin–Madison																											
1902	Bos A	0	1	.000	1	1	1	0		0			8	15	15	0	0	8		4	9.00	-60	.395	.500	-20		-0.5
Total	3	23	21	.523	69	54	37	1		1			437.1	499	297	14	23	199		122	4.16	-13	.285	.366	+26		-2.4
IRVINE, DARYL Daryl Keith B11.15.1964 Harrisonburg VA BR/TR/6'3"/195 [BosA85*S1/20] d4.28 Col Ferrum																											
1990	Bos A	1	1	.500	11	0	0	0	0	0	0	6	17.1	15	10	0	0	10	3	9	4.67	-12	.246	.338		0	-0.1
1991	Bos A	0	0	+	9	0	0	0	0	0	0	3	18	25	13	2	2	9	1	8	6.00	-28	.321	.404		67	-0.1
1992	Bos A	3	4	.429	21	0	0	0	0	0	3	12	28	31	20	1	2	14	2	10	6.11	-30	.287	.370		0	-0.9
Total	3	4	5	.444	41	0	0	0	0	0	3	21	63.1	71	43	3	4	33	6	27	5.68	-26	.287	.372		67	-1.1
/60G	4	6	7	.444	60	0	0	0	0	0	4	31	92.2	104	63	4	6	48	9	40	5.69	-26	.287	.372		98	-1.6
JACOBSON, BEANY Albert Leonard (b Albin Leonard Jacobson) B6.5.1881 Port Washington WI D1.31.1933 Decatur IL BL/TL/6'0"/170 d4.30																											
1907	Bos A	0	0	+	2	1	0	0		0			2	2	3	0	0	3		1	9.00	-71	.250	.455	-48		-0.1
Total	4	22	46	.324	88	70	53	1		0			612.1	618	317	11	12	148		195	3.19	-18	.264	.311	-22		-5.4
JAMERSON, LEFTY Charles Dewey "Charlie" B1.26.1900 Enfield IL D8.4.1980 Mocksville NC BL/TL/6'1"/195 d8.16 Col Arkansas																											
1924	Bos A	0	0	+	1	0	0	0		0			1	1	2	0	0	3		0	18.00	-76	.250	.571			-0.1
JAMES, BILL William Henry "Big Bill" B1.20.1887 Detroit MI D5.25.1942 Venice CA BB/TR/6'4"/195 d6.12																											
1919	Bos A	3	5	.375	13	7	4	0		0			72.2	74	42	2	3	39		12	4.09	-26	.280	.379	+0		-1.0
Total	8	64	71	.474	203	146	68	9		4			1179.2	1110	559	16	48	578		408	3.20	-12	.258	.352	-1		-5.3
JARVIS, KEVIN Kevin Thomas B8.1.1969 Lexington KY BL/TR/6'2"/200 [CinN91 21/561] d4.6 Col Wake Forest																											
2006	Bos A	0	1	.000	4	3	0	0	0	0	0	1	16.2	22	12	1	1	6	1	7	4.86	-4	.324	.382	+1	0	-0.1
Total	12	34	49	.410	187	118	4	3	40	1	1	38	780.2	937	568	149	23	262	23	453	6.03	-26	.297	.353	+7	323	-11.6
JARVIS, RAY Raymond Arnold B5.10.1946 Providence RI BR/TR/6'2"/(185–198) [BosA65 11/370] d4.15																											
1969	Bos A	5	6	.455	29	12	2	0	6	1	0	12	100.1	105	59	8	3	43	1	36	4.75	-20	.274	.349	+10	21	-1.1
1970	Bos A	0	1	.000	15	0	0	0	0	0	1	8	16	17	12	1	2	14	1	8	3.94	+1	.274	.418		0	-0.1
Total	2	5	7	.417	44	12	2	0	6	1	1	20	116.1	122	71	9	5	57	2	44	4.64	-17	.274	.359	+10	21	-1.2
/60G	3	7	10	.417	60	16	3	0	8	1	1	27	158.2	166	97	12	7	78	3	60	4.64	-17	.274	.359	+50	29	-1.6
JENKINS, FERGIE Ferguson Arthur B12.13.1942 Chatham ON, Can. BR/TR/6'5"/(195–210) d9.10 C2 HF1991																											
1976	Bos A	12	11	.522	30	29	12	2	19	0	0	1	209	201	85	20	5	43	6	142	3.27	+19	.253	.292	-3	0	1.5
1977	Bos A	10	10	.500	28	28	11	1	15	0	0	0	193	190	91	30	0	36	2	105	3.68	+22	.257	.290	+3	0	1.3
Total	19	284	226	.557	664	594	267	49	391	7	2	48	4500.2	4142	1853	484	84	997	11	3192	3.34	+15	.243	.287	+1	0	30.4
Team	2	22	21	.512	58	57	23	3	34	0	0	1	402	391	176	50	5	79	8	247	3.47	+20	.255	.291	+0		2.8
/180I	1	10	9	.512	26	26	10	1	15	0	0	0	180	175	79	22	2	35	4	111	3.47	+20	.255	.291	+0		1.3
JOHNSON, RANKIN Adam Rankin Sr. "Tex" B2.4.1888 Burnet TX D7.2.1972 Williamsport PA BR/TR/6'1.5"/185 d4.20 s–Rankin																											
1914	Bos A	3	9	.250	16	13	4	2		0			99.1	92	41	2	3	34		24	3.08	-13	.265	.336	-48		-0.5
Total	3	22	30	.423	72	53	31	6		2			450	401	182	12	9	151		169	2.92	-7	.248	.315	-17		-1.9
JOHNSON, EARL Earl Douglas "Lefty" B4.2.1919 Redmond WA D12.3.1994 Seattle WA BL/TL/6'3"/190 d7.20 Mil 1942–45 b–Chet Col St. Marys (CA)																											
1940	Bos A	6	2	.750	17	10	2	0		0			70.1	69	33	0	2	39		26	4.09	+10	.260	.359	+7		0.2
1941	Bos A	4	5	.444	17	12	4	0		0			93.2	90	57	4	3	51		46	4.52	-8	.247	.344	+25	0	-0.1
1946	†Bos A	5	4	.556	29	5	0	0		3			80	78	39	5	2	39		40	3.71	-1	.250	.337	-39	0	0.1
1947	Bos A	12	11	.522	45	17	6	3		8			142.1	129	63	7	2	62		65	2.97	+31	.246	.328	-32	0	1.9
1948	Bos A	10	4	.714	35	3	1	0		5			91.1	98	49	7	0	42		45	4.53	-3	.276	.353	+37	0	-0.3
1949	Bos A	3	6	.333	19	3	0	0		0			49.1	65	45	1	4	29		20	7.48	-42	.327	.422	-25	0	-2.6
1950	Bos A	0	0	+	11	0	0	0		0			13.2	18	11	0	1	8		6	7.24	-32	.333	.429		0	-0.1
1951	Det A	0	0	+	6	0	0	0		1			5.2	9	5	0	0	2		2	6.35	-34	.375	.423		0	-0.1

Year	Tm Lg	W	L	Pct	G	GS	CG	ShO	QS	SV	BS	QR	IP	H	R	HR	HB	BB	IB	SO	ERA	AERA	OAV	OOB	Sup	DL	PW
Total	8	40	32	.556	179	50	13	3		17			546.1	556	302	24	14	272		250	4.30	-4	.265	.353	-5	0	-1.0
Team	7	40	32	.556	173	50	13	3		16			540.2	547	297	24	14	270		248	4.28	-3	.264	.352	-7		-0.9
/180I	2	13	11	.556	58	17	4	1		5			180	182	99	8	5	90		83	4.28	-3	.264	.352	-7		-0.3
JOHNSON, HANK Henry Ward B5.21.1906 Bradenton FL D8.20.1982 Bradenton FL BR/TR (BB 1933)/5'11.5"/175 d4.17																											
1933	Bos A	8	6	.571	25	21	7	0		1			155.1	156	84	13	3	74		65	4.06	+8	.263	.348	-7		0.7
1934	Bos A	6	8	.429	31	14	7	1		1			124.1	162	95	12	5	53		66	5.36	-10	.316	.385	-8		-0.9
1935	Bos A	2	1	.667	13	2	0	0		1			31	41	21	3	0	14		14	5.52	-14	.331	.399	+19		-0.3
Total	12	63	56	.529	249	116	45	4		11			1066.1	1107	665	89	32	567		568	4.75	-12	.268	.361	+16		-5.8
Team	3	16	15	.516	69	37	14	1		3			310.2	359	200	28	8	141		145	4.72	-3	.292	.368	-6		-0.5
/180I	2	9	9	.516	40	21	8	1		2			180	208	116	16	5	82		84	4.72	-3	.292	.368	-6		-0.3
JOHNSON, JASON Jason Michael B10.27.1973 Santa Barbara CA BR/TR/6'6"/(215–235) d8.27																											
2006	Bos A	0	4	.000	6	6	0	0	1	0	0	0	29.1	41	26	3	2	13	0	18	7.36	-37	.331	.397	-16	0	-1.0
Total	10	55	98	.359	239	219	6	1	100	0	0	8	1327.2	1489	812	176	55	486	22	790	4.99	-10	.283	.348	-8	146	-8.9
JOHNSON, JOHN HENRY John Henry B8.21.1956 Houston TX BL/TL/6'2"/(185–210) [SFN74 15/355] d4.10																											
1983	Bos A	3	2	.600	34	1	0	0	0	1	1	21	53.1	58	28	3	1	20	4	51	3.71	+18	.283	.342	-79	0	0.2
1984	Bos A	1	2	.333	30	3	0	0	1	1	0	17	63.2	64	26	7	0	27	1	57	3.53	+19	.260	.333	-35	15	0.3
Total	8	26	33	.441	214	61	9	2	27	9	5	105	602.2	585	294	60	5	250	21	407	3.90	+3	.256	.328	-12	31	1.4
Team	2	4	4	.500	64	4	0	0	1	2	1	38	117	122	54	10	1	47	5	108	3.62	+19	.271	.337	-46	15	0.5
/60G	2	4	4	.500	60	4	0	0	1	2	1	36	109.2	114	51	9	1	44	5	101	3.62	+19	.271	.337	-46	14	0.5
JOHNSON, VIC Victor Oscar B8.3.1920 Eau Claire WI D5.10.2005 Eau Claire WI BR/TL/6'0"/160 d5.3																											
1944	Bos A	0	3	.000	7	5	0	0		0			27.1	42	22	0	0	15		7	6.26	-46	.362	.435	+23	0	-1.0
1945	Bos A	6	4	.600	26	9	4	1		2			85.1	90	41	4	2	46		21	4.01	-15	.276	.369	+0	0	-0.6
1946	Cle A	0	1	.000	9	1	0	0		0			13.2	20	14	1	0	8		3	9.22	-64	.357	.438	-48	0	-0.6
Total	3	6	8	.429	42	15	4	1		2			126.1	152	77	5	2	69		31	5.06	-33	.305	.392	+5	0	-2.2
Team	2	6	7	.462	33	14	4	1		2			112.2	132	63	4	2	61		28	4.55	-25	.299	.386	+8		-1.6
JOHNSTON, JOEL Joel Raymond B3.8.1967 West Chester PA BR/TR/6'4"/(220–234) [KCA88 3/75] d9.5 Col Penn St.																											
1995	Bos A	0	1	.000	4	0	0	0	0	0	0	2	4	2	5	1	1	3	0	4	11.25	-57	.143	.333		0	-0.5
Total	5	3	5	.375	59	0	0	0	0	2	1	40	85.2	66	42	10	3	37	8	61	4.31	-4	.212	.302		0	0.1
JONES, BOBBY Robert Mitchell B4.11.1972 Orange NJ BR/TL/6'0"/(170–185) [MilA91 44/1140] d5.18 Col Chipola (FL) JC [DL 2001 NY N 190]																											
2004	Bos A	0	1	.000	3	0	0	0	0	0	0	1	3.1	3	2	1	0	8	1	3	5.40	-10	.273	.579		0	0.0
Total	6	14	21	.400	99	47	1	0	10	0	0	31	324.2	366	227	45	16	195	4	229	5.77	-9	.288	.386	-6	190	-1.7
JONES, SAM Samuel Pond "Sad Sam" B7.26.1892 Woodsfield OH D7.6.1966 Barnesville OH BR/TR/6'0"/170 d6.13																											
1916	Bos A	0	1	.000	12	0	0	0		1			27	25	14	0	0	10		7	3.67	-24	.272	.343			-0.1
1917	Bos A	0	1	.000	9	1	0	0		1			16.1	15	9	1	0	6		5	4.41	-41	.259	.328	-44		-0.3
1918	†Bos A	16	5	**.762**	24	21	16	5		0			184	151	66	1	8	70		44	2.25	+19	.230	.312	+14		1.0
1919	Bos A	12	20	.375	35	31	21	5		1			245	258	120	4	7	95		67	3.75	-19	.278	.350	+3		-2.2
1920	Bos A	13	16	.448	37	33	21	3		0			274	302	143	9	4	79		86	3.94	-7	.288	.340	-12		-0.9
1921	Bos A	23	16	.590	40	38	25	0		1			298.2	318	122	1	6	78		98	3.22	+31	.279	.329	-21		4.3
Total	22	229	217	.513	647	487	250	36		31			3883	4084	2008	152	69	1396		1223	3.84	+4	.274	.339	+0		7.2
Team	6	64	59	.520	157	124	83	13		4			1045	1069	474	16	25	338		307	3.39	+2	.272	.334	-7		1.8
/180I	1	11	10	.520	27	21	14	2		1			180	184	82	3	4	58		53	3.39	+2	.272	.334	-7		0.3
JONES, RICK Thomas Fredrick B4.16.1955 Jacksonville FL BL/TL/6'5"/(180–200) [BosA73 5/113] d4.18																											
1976	Bos A	5	3	.625	24	14	1	0	6	0	0	8	104.1	133	48	6	1	26	1	45	3.36	+15	.311	.348	+13	0	0.3
1977	Sea A	1	4	.200	10	10	0	0	1	0	0	0	42.1	47	25	10	0	37	2	16	5.10	-19	.283	.414	-2	62	-0.4
1978	Sea A	0	2	.000	3	2	0	0	0	0	0	1	12.1	17	8	1	0	7	0	11	5.84	-34	.315	.393	-53	0	-0.3
Total	3	6	9	.400	37	26	1	0	7	0	0	9	159	197	81	17	1	70	3	72	4.02	-1	.304	.370	+2	62	-0.4
JONES, TODD Todd Barton Givin B4.24.1968 Marietta GA BL/TR/6'3"/(200–230) [HouN89 1/27] d7.7 Col Jacksonville St.																											
2003	†Bos A	2	1	.667	26	0	0	0	0	0	0	16	29.1	32	19	2	0	13	2	31	5.52	-16	.269	.338		0	-0.2
Total	14	53	58	.477	874	1	0	0	0	263	66	641	969	958	459	85	34	402	53	821	3.91	+13	.261	.336	-4	65	9.0
JUDD, OSCAR Thomas William Oscar "Ossie" B2.14.1908 London ON, Can. D12.27.1995 Ingersoll ON, Can. BL/TL/6'0.5"/180 d4.16																											
1941	Bos A	0	0	+	7	0	0	0		1			12.1	15	12	1	0	10		5	8.76	-52	.300	.417		0	-0.1
1942	Bos A	8	10	.444	31	19	11	0		2			150.1	135	72	3	2	90		70	3.89	-4	.239	.346	+33	0	0.4
1943	Bos A☆	11	6	.647	23	20	8	1		0			155.1	131	58	2	3	69		53	2.90	+14	.230	.317	-11	0	1.1
1944	Bos A	1	1	.500	9	6	1	0		0			30	30	16	1	0	15		9	3.60	-6	.261	.346	+88	0	-0.1
1945	Bos A	0	1	.000	2	1	0	0		0			6.1	10	8	1	0	3		5	8.53	-60	.333	.394	-50	0	-0.5
1945	Phi N	5	4	.556	23	9	3	1		2			82.2	80	47	3	1	40		36	3.81	+1	.254	.340	-36	0	0.2
1945	Major	5	5	.500	25	10	3	1		2			88	90	55	4	1	43		41	4.15	-3	.261	.344	-37	0	-0.3
1946	Phi N	11	12	.478	30	24	12	1		2			173.1	169	86	6	1	90		65	3.53	-3	.260	.350	-5	0	0.5
1947	Phi N	4	15	.211	32	19	8	1		0			146.2	155	86	6	3	69		54	4.60	-13	.279	.361	-27	0	-0.8
1948	Phi N	0	2	.000	4	1	0	0		0			14.1	19	14	1	0	11		7	6.91	-43	.317	.423	-10	0	-0.6
Total	8	40	51	.440	161	99	43	4		7			771.1	744	399	24	10	397		304	3.90	-7	.256	.347	-2	0	0.1
Team	5	20	18	.526	72	46	20	1		3			354.1	321	166	8	5	187		142	3.68	-4	.241	.338	+19		0.8
/180I	3	10	9	.526	37	23	10	1		2			180	163	84	4	3	95		72	3.68	-4	.241	.338	+19		0.4
KALLIO, RUDY Rudolph B12.14.1892 Portland OR D4.6.1979 Newport OR BR/TR/5'10"/160 d4.25																											
1925	Bos A	1	4	.200	7	4	0	0		0			18.2	28	18	0	1	9		2	7.71	-41	.364	.437	-3		-0.9
Total	3	9	17	.346	49	27	10	2		1			222.1	234	124	0	3	93		75	4.17	-31	.277	.351	+11		-3.5
KARGER, ED Edwin "Loose" B5.6.1883 San Angelo TX D9.9.1957 Delta CO BL/TL/5'11"/185 d4.15																											
1906	Pit N	2	3	.400	6	2	0	0		0			28	21	11	0	2	9		8	1.93	+39	.204	.281	-5		0.3
1906	StL N	5	16	.238	25	20	17	0		1			191.2	193	85	0	7	43		73	2.72	-3	.271	.319	-27		0.0
1906	Year	7	19	.269	31	22	17	0		1			219.2	214	96	0	9	52		81	2.62	+0	.263	.314	-25		0.3
1907	StL N	15	19	.441	39	32	29	6		1			314	257	102	2	10	65		137	2.04	+23	.223	.270	-35		2.4
1908	StL N	4	9	.308	22	15	9	1		0			141.1	148	77	1	2	50		34	3.06	-23	.260	.322	-30		-0.8
1909	Cin N	1	3	.250	9	5	1	0		0			34.1	26	22	0	2	30		8	4.46	-42	.217	.382	+56		-0.5
1909	Bos A	5	2	.714	12	6	3	0		0			68	71	29	0	3	22		17	3.18	-21	.273	.337	+32		-0.4
1909	Major	6	5	.545	21	11	4	0		0			102	97	51	0	5	52		25	3.61	-28	.255	.352	+43		-0.9
1910	Bos A	11	7	.611	27	25	16	1		1			183.1	162	75	5	5	53		81	3.19	-20	.230	.289	+42		-0.1
1911	Bos A	5	8	.385	25	18	6	1		0			131	134	70	4	4	42		57	3.37	-3	.272	.334	+9		0.4
Total	6	48	67	.417	165	123	81	9		3			1091.2	1012	471	12	35	314		415	2.79	-6	.246	.305	-1		1.3
Team	3	21	17	.553	64	49	25	2		1			382.1	367	174	9	12	117		155	3.25	-14	.252	.313	+29		-0.1
/180I	1	10	8	.553	30	23	12	1		0			180	173	82	4	6	55		73	3.25	-14	.252	.313	+29		-0.0
KARL, ANDY Anton Andrew B4.8.1914 Mt.Vernon NY D4.8.1989 LaJolla CA BR/TR/6'1.5"/175 d4.24 Col Manhattan																											
1943	Bos A	1	1	.500	11	0	0	0		1			26	31	11	0	0	13		6	3.46	-4	.310	.389		0	0.1
Total	5	18	23	.439	191	4	1	0		26			422.2	451	200	16	5	130		107	3.51	+4	.279	.334	-25	0	-0.3
KARR, BENN Benjamin Joyce "Baldy" B11.28.1893 Mt.Pleasant MS D12.8.1968 Memphis TN BL/TR/6'0"/175 d4.20																											
1920	Bos A	3	8	.273	26	2	0	0		1			91.2	109	55	3	1	24		21	4.81	-24	.304	.349	-46		-0.7
1921	Bos A	8	7	.533	26	7	5	0		0			117.2	123	53	8	1	38		37	3.67	+15	.283	.342	-4		1.0
1922	Bos A	5	12	.294	41	13	7	0		1			183.1	212	115	10	5	45		41	4.47	-8	.302	.348	+7		-1.0
1925	Cle A	11	12	.478	32	24	12	1		0			197.2	248	127	8	6	80		41	4.78	-8	.317	.385	-2		-0.4
1926	Cle A	5	6	.455	30	7	4	0		1			113.1	137	72	9	6	41		23	5.00	-19	.291	.355	+19		-0.7
1927	Cle A	3	3	.500	22	5	1	0		2			76.2	92	49	5	1	32		17	5.05	-17	.315	.385	-13		-0.3
Total	6	35	48	.422	177	58	29	1		5			780.1	921	471	43	20	260		180	4.60	-10	.303	.362	+1		-2.1
Team	3	16	27	.372	93	22	12	0		2			392.2	444	223	21	7	107		99	4.31	-6	.297	.346	-1		-0.7
/180I	1	7	12	.372	43	10	6	0		1			180	204	102	10	3	49		45	4.31	-6	.297	.346	-1		-0.3

Year	Tm Lg	W	L	Pct	G	GS	CG	ShO	QS	SV	BS	QR	IP	H	R	HR	HB	BB	IB	SO	ERA	AERA	OAV	OOB	Sup	DL	PW
KELLETT, AL Alfred Henry B10.30.1901 Red Bank NJ D7.14.1960 New York NY BR/TR/6'3"/200 d6.29 Col Columbia																											
1924	Bos A	0	0	+	1	0	0	0		0			0	0	2	0	0	2		0	(2)	-100	+	1.000			-0.2
Total	2	0	1	.000	6	0	0	0		0			10	11	11	0	0	10		1	8.10	-49	.282	.429			-0.4
KELLUM, WIN Winford Ansley B4.11.1876 Waterford ON, Can. D8.10.1951 Big Rapids MI BB/TL/5'10"/190 d4.26																											
1901	Bos A	2	3	.400	6	6	5	0		0			48	61	42	3	3	7		8	6.38	-45	.305	.338	+24		-1.0
Total	3	20	16	.556	48	37	32	2		2			346.2	337	170	5	14	63		97	3.19	-5	.255	.297	+33		0.3
KELLY, ED Edward Leo B12.10.1888 Pawtucket RI D11.4.1928 Red Lodge MT BR/TR/5'11.5"/173 d4.14																											
1914	Bos A	0	0	+	3	0	0	0		0			2.1	1	1	0	0	1		4	0.00	-100	.100	.182			0.0
KEMMERER, RUSS Russell Paul "Rusty","Dutch" B11.1.1931 Pittsburgh PA BR/TR/6'3"/(200–210) d6.27 Col Pittsburgh																											
1954	Bos A	5	3	.625	19	9	2	1		0			75.1	71	35	4	2	41		37	3.82	+8	.257	.352	-21	0	0.3
1955	Bos A	1	1	.500	7	2	0	0		0			17.1	18	14	3	0	15	1	13	7.27	-41	.269	.402	+45	0	-0.5
1957	Bos A	0	0	+	1	0	0	0	0	0		1	4	5	2	0	0	2	1	1	4.50	-11	.333	.389		0	0.0
Total	9	43	59	.422	302	109	24	2	120	8		171	1066.2	1144	588	103	17	389	21	505	4.46	-14	.277	.339	-3	0	-6.5
Team	3	6	4	.600	27	11	2	1	0	0		1	96.2	94	51	7	2	58	2	51	4.47	-7	.263	.363	-9		-0.2
KENNEDY, BILL William Aulton "Lefty" B3.14.1921 Carnesville GA D4.9.1983 Seattle WA BL/TL/6'2"/(195–210) d4.26																											
1953	Bos A	0	0	+	16	0	0	0		2			24.1	24	13	2	1	17		14	3.70	+14	.255	.375		0	0.1
Total	8	15	28	.349	172	45	6	0	0	11		4	464.2	497	284	34	12	289	1	256	4.73	-8	.275	.379	-2	0	-2.2
KIECKER, DANA Dana Ervin B2.25.1961 Sleepy Eye MN BR/TR/6'3"/(180–195) [BosA83 8/203] d4.12 Col St. Cloud St.																											
1990	†Bos A	8	9	.471	32	25	0	0	13	0	0	2	152	145	74	7	9	54	2	93	3.97	+3	.253	.325	-6	0	0.3
1991	Bos A	2	3	.400	18	5	0	0	0	0	0	9	40.1	56	34	6	2	23	4	21	7.36	-41	.344	.429	+35	55	-1.2
Total	2	10	12	.455	50	30	0	0	13	0	0	11	192.1	201	108	13	11	77	6	114	4.68	-11	.273	.349	+1	55	-0.9
/180I	2	9	11	.455	47	28	0	0	12	0	0	10	180	188	101	12	10	72	6	107	4.68	-11	.273	.349	-5	51	-0.8
KIEFER, JOE Joseph William "Harlem Joe","Smoke" B7.19.1899 W.Leyden NY D7.5.1975 Utica NY BR/TR/5'11"/190 d10.1																											
1920	Chi A	0	1	.000	2	1	0	0		0			4.2	7	8	0	1	5		1	15.43	-76	.333	.481	+48		-0.8
1925	Bos A	0	2	.000	2	2	0	0		0			15	20	12	0	1	9		4	6.00	-24	.351	.448	-54		-0.3
1926	Bos A	0	2	.000	11	1	0	0		0			30	29	19	2	2	16		4	4.80	-15	.266	.370	-59		-0.1
Total	3	0	5	.000	15	4	0	0		0			49.2	56	39	2	4	30		9	6.16	-32	.299	.407	-30		-1.2
Team	2	0	4	.000	13	3	0	0		0			45	49	31	2	3	25		8	5.20	-19	.295	.397	-56		-0.4
KIELY, LEO Leo Patrick "Kiki" B11.30.1929 Hoboken NJ D1.18.1984 Montclair NJ BL/TL/6'2"/(180–185) d6.27 Mil 1952–53																											
1951	Bos A	7	7	.500	17	16	4	0		0			113.1	106	48	9	2	39		46	3.34	+34	.251	.317	-25	0	1.4
1954	Bos A	5	8	.385	28	19	4	1		0			131	153	74	12	1	58		59	3.50	+17	.295	.365	-9	0	0.2
1955	Bos A	3	3	.500	33	4	0	0		6			90	91	31	5	0	37	5	36	2.80	+53	.269	.341	-7	0	1.1
1956	Bos A	2	2	.500	23	0	0	0		3			31.1	47	25	1	2	14	5	9	5.17	-11	.362	.429		0	-0.5
1958	Bos A	5	2	.714	47	0	0	0	0	12		61	81	77	31	3	2	18	3	26	3.00	+34	.254	.299		0	0.9
1959	Bos A	3	3	.500	41	0	0	0	0	7		62	55.2	67	26	8	1	18	3	30	4.20	-3	.299	.352		0	0.0
1960	KC A	1	2	.333	20	0	0	0	0	1		14	20.2	21	4	1	1	5	0	6	1.74	+129	.266	.318		0	0.9
Total	7	26	27	.491	209	39	8	1	0	29		137	523	562	239	39	9	189	16	212	3.37	+25	.279	.342	-14	0	4.0
Team	6	25	25	.500	189	39	8	1	0	28		123	502.1	541	235	38	8	184	16	206	3.44	+23	.279	.343	-15		3.1
/60G	2	8	8	.500	60	12	3	0	0	9		39	159.1	172	75	12	3	58	5	65	3.44	+23	.279	.343	-15		1.0
KILLILAY, JACK John William B5.24.1887 Leavenworth KS D10.21.1968 Tulsa OK BR/TR/5'11"/165 d5.13																											
1911	Bos A	4	2	.667	14	7	1	0		0			61	65	26	0	10	36		28	3.54	-7	.302	.425	+16		-0.1
KIM, BYUNG-HYUN Byung-Hyun B1.19.1979 Kwangju, South Korea BR/TR/5'11"/(175–180) d5.29																											
2003	†Bos A	8	5	.615	49	5	0	0	3	16	3	31	79.1	70	38	6	8	18	3	69	3.18	+47	.230	.288	+82	0	1.8
2004	Bos A	2	1	.667	7	3	0	0	0	0	0	3	17.1	17	15	1	2	7	1	6	6.23	-22	.258	.338	+20	25	-0.4
Total	8	44	52	.458	366	65	0	0	29	86	24	232	722.2	650	361	74	64	308	32	699	4.15	+13	.241	.330	-6	123	7.6
Team	2	10	6	.625	56	8	0	0	3	16	3	34	96.2	87	53	7	10	25	4	75	3.72	+26	.235	.298	+59	25	1.4
/60G	2	11	6	.625	60	9	0	0	3	17	3	36	103.2	93	57	8	11	27	4	80	3.72	+26	.235	.298	+59	27	1.5
KIM, SUN-WOO Sun-Woo B9.4.1977 Inchon, South Korea BR/TR/6'2"/(180–190) d6.15																											
2001	Bos A	0	2	.000	20	2	0	0	1	0	0	10	41.2	54	27	1	4	21	5	27	5.83	-24	.312	.399	-6	0	-0.3
2002	Bos A	2	0	1.000	15	2	0	0	1	0	0	9	29	34	24	5	1	7	0	18	7.45	-40	.288	.328	+45	0	-0.5
Total	6	13	13	.500	118	38	1	1	10	0	0	44	337	396	211	44	27	127	20	211	5.31	-15	.295	.365	+9	35	-1.7
Team	2	2	2	.500	35	4	0	0	2	0	0	19	70.2	88	51	6	5	28	5	45	6.50	-31	.302	.371	+20		-0.8
KINDER, ELLIS Ellis Raymond "Old Folks" B7.26.1914 Atkins AR D10.16.1968 Jackson TN BR/TR/6'0"/(185–195) d4.30																											
1946	StL A	3	3	.500	33	7	1	0		1			86.2	78	35	8	0	36		59	3.32	+12	.241	.318	-5	0	0.1
1947	StL A	8	15	.348	34	26	10	2		1			194.1	201	105	11	0	82		110	4.49	-14	.264	.336	-33	0	-1.7
1948	Bos A	10	7	.588	28	22	10	1		0			178	183	84	10	2	63		53	3.74	+17	.266	.330	+22	0	0.4
1949	Bos A	23	6	**.793**	43	30	19	0		4			252	251	103	21	2	99		138	3.36	+30	.260	.330	+34	0	2.2
1950	Bos A	14	12	.538	48	23	11	1		9			207	212	105	23	1	78		95	4.26	+15	.263	.328	+36	0	1.4
1951	Bos A	11	2	.846	**63**	2	1	0		**14**			127	108	42	8	0	46		84	2.55	+75	.230	.298	+49	0	2.5
1952	Bos A	5	6	.455	23	10	4	0		4			97.2	85	33	11	1	28		50	2.58	+53	.234	.290	-47	105	1.1
1953	Bos A	10	6	.625	**69**	0	0	0		**27**			107	84	30	8	2	38		39	1.85	+127	.215	.288		0	**5.2**
1954	Bos A	8	8	.500	48	2	0	0		15			107	106	47	7	0	36		67	3.62	+14	.260	.318	+72	0	1.0
1955	Bos A	5	5	.500	43	0	0	0		18			66.2	57	22	4	1	15	4	31	2.84	+51	.229	.274		0	2.1
1956	StL N	2	0	1.000	22	0	0	0		6			25.2	23	11	3	0	9	3	4	3.51	+8	.245	.305		0	0.0
1956	Chi A	3	1	.750	29	0	0	0		3			29.2	33	10	2	0	8	0	19	2.73	+50	.277	.318		0	0.6
1956	Major	5	1	.833	51	0	0	0		9			54	56	21	5	0	17	3	23	3.09	+31	.263	.312		0	0.6
1957	Chi A	0	0	+	1	0	0	0	0	0		1	1	0	0	0	0	1	1	0	0.00	-100	.000	.250		0	0.0
Total	12	102	71	.590	484	122	56	10	0	102		1	1479.2	1421	627	116	9	539	8	749	3.43	+25	.252	.318	+12	105	14.9
Team	8	86	52	.623	365	89	45	2		91			1142.1	1086	466	92	9	403	4	557	3.28	+34	.250	.315	+24	105	15.9
/180I	1	14	8	.623	58	14	7	0		14			180	171	73	14	1	64	1	88	3.28	+34	.250	.315	+24	17	2.5
KINNEY, WALT Walter William B9.9.1893 Denison TX D7.1.1971 Escondido CA BL/TL/6'2"/186 d7.26																											
1918	Bos A	0	0	+	5	0	0	0		0			15	5	3	0	2	8		4	1.80	+49	.106	.263			0.0
Total	4	11	20	.355	63	30	18	1		2			290.2	274	164	10	11	136		129	3.59	-1	.254	.343	-10		0.4
KISON, BRUCE Bruce Eugene B2.18.1950 Pasco WA BR/TR/6'4"/(170–180) [PitN68 14/309] d7.4 C8																											
1985	Bos A	5	3	.625	22	9	0	0	3	1	1	9	92	98	43	9	1	32	4	56	4.11	+5	.274	.332	+12	22	0.4
Total	15	115	88	.567	380	246	36	8	137	12	9	88	1809.2	1693	839	150	68	662	58	1073	3.66	+3	.248	.319	+13	413	2.9
KLINE, BOB Robert George "Junior" B12.9.1909 Enterprise OH D3.16.1987 Westerville OH BR/TR/6'3"/200 d9.17																											
1930	Bos A	0	0	+	1	0	0	0		0			1	1	0	0	0	0		0	0.00	-100	.333	.333			0.0
1931	Bos A	5	5	.500	28	10	3	0		0			98	110	54	3	3	35		25	4.41	-2	.298	.364	+2		0.3
1932	Bos A	11	13	.458	47	19	4	1		2			172	203	117	10	1	76		31	5.28	-15	.294	.365	-22		-1.7
1933	Bos A	7	8	.467	46	8	1	0		4			127	127	70	5	6	67		16	4.54	-3	.265	.362	+4		0.1
1934	Phi A	6	2	.750	20	0	0	0		1			39.2	50	34	6	0	13		14	6.35	-31	.314	.366			-1.5
1934	Was A	1	0	1.000	6	0	0	0		0			4	10	8	0	1	4		1	15.75	-73	.500	.600			-0.9
1934	Year	7	2	.778	26	0	0	0		1			43.2	60	42	6	1	17		15	7.21	-39	.335	.396			-2.4
Total	5	30	28	.517	148	37	8	1		7			441.2	501	283	24	11	195		87	5.05	-13	.291	.367	-10		-3.7
Team	4	23	26	.469	122	37	8	1		6			398	441	241	18	10	178		72	4.82	-8	.286	.364	-10		-1.3
/180I	2	10	12	.469	55	17	4	0		3			180	199	109	8	5	81		33	4.82	-8	.286	.364	-10		-0.6
KLINE, RON Ronald Lee B3.9.1932 Callery PA D6.22.2002 Callery PA BR/TR/6'3"/(190–210) d4.21 Mil 1953–54																											
1969	Bos A	0	1	.000	16	0	0	0	0	1	1	10	17	24	11	4	0	17	3	7	4.76	-20	.329	.451		0	-0.1
Total	17	114	144	.442	736	203	44	8	156	108	5	392	2078	2113	991	217	33	731	1	989	3.75	+1	.266	.329	-19	0	2.5
KLINGER, BOB Robert Harold B6.4.1908 Allenton MO D8.19.1977 Villa Ridge MO BR/TR/6'0"/180 d4.19 Mil 1944–45																											
1946	†Bos A	3	2	.600	28	1	0	0		**9**			57	49	16	1	1	25		16	2.37	+55	.238	.323	-53	0	1.1
1947	Bos A	1	1	.500	28	0	0	0		5			42	42	20	5	1	24		12	3.86	+1	.253	.351		0	-0.1

RED SOX PITCHERS

Year	Tm Lg	W	L	Pct	G	GS	CG	ShO	QS	SV	BS	QR	IP	H	R	HR	HB	BB	IB	SO	ERA	AERA	OAV	OOB	Sup	DL	PW
Total	8	66	61	.520	265	130	48	7		23			1089.2	1153	525	46	20	358		357	3.68	+0	.271	.331	+10	0	-0.7
Team	2	4	3	.571	56	1	0	0		14			99	91	36	6	2	49		28	3.00	+25	.245	.336	-53		1.0
/60G	2	4	3	.571	60	1	0	0		15			106	98	39	6	2	53		30	3.00	+25	.245	.336	-53		1.1
KNACKERT, BRENT Brent Bradley B8.1.1969 Los Angeles CA BR/TR/6'3"/(185–195) [ChiA87 2/37] d4.10																											
1996	Bos A	0	1	.000	8	0	0	0	0	0	0	5	10	16	12	1	0	7	1	5	9.00	-43	.356	.434		0	-0.3
Total	2	1	2	.333	32	2	0	0	0	0	0	14	47.1	66	40	6	2	28	3	33	7.04	-40	.322	.403	-43	0	-0.8
KOLSTAD, HAL Harold Everette B6.1.1935 Rice Lake WI BR/TR/5'9"/190 d4.22 Col San Jose St.																											
1962	Bos A	0	2	.000	27	2	0	0	1	2		15	61.1	65	44	11	2	35	1	36	5.43	-24	.269	.363	-3	0	-0.6
1963	Bos A	0	2	.000	7	0	0	0	0	0		2	11	16	16	4	2	6	0	6	13.09	-71	.340	.436		0	-1.6
Total	2	0	4	.000	34	2	0	0	1	2		17	72.1	81	60	15	4	41	1	42	6.59	-38	.280	.375	-3	0	-2.2
KOONCE, CAL Calvin Lee B11.18.1940 Fayetteville NC D10.28.1993 Winston–Salem NC BR/TR/6'1"/(185–195) d4.14 Col Campbell																											
1970	Bos A	3	4	.429	23	8	1	0	6	2	2	10	76.1	64	32	7	3	29	3	37	3.54	+13	.231	.309	+6	0	0.5
1971	Bos A	0	1	.000	13	1	0	0	0	0	1	8	21	22	16	3	0	11	0	9	5.57	-33	.278	.367	+141	0	-0.2
Total	10	47	49	.490	334	90	9	3	47	24	7	172	971	972	464	85	25	368	57	504	3.78	-2	.264	.333	-5	0	-0.5
Team	2	3	5	.375	36	9	1	0	6	2	3	18	97.1	86	48	10	3	40	3	46	3.98	-1	.242	.322	+21		0.3
KRAMER, JACK John Henry B1.5.1918 New Orleans LA D5.18.1995 Metairie LA BR/TR/6'2"/190 d4.25 Def 1942																											
1948	Bos A	18	5	**.783**	29	29	14	2		0			205	233	104	12	0	64		72	4.35	+1	.284	.336	+52	0	0.1
1949	Bos A	6	8	.429	21	18	7	2		1			111.2	126	70	8	1	49		24	5.16	-15	.286	.358	+17	0	-0.8
Total	12	95	103	.480	322	215	88	14		7			1637.1	1761	895	92	10	682		613	4.24	-4	.276	.347	+7	0	-3.8
Team	2	24	13	.649	50	47	21	4		1			316.2	359	174	20	1	113		96	4.63	-5	.285	.344	+39		-0.7
/180I	1	14	7	.649	28	27	12	2		1			180	204	99	11	1	64		55	4.63	-5	.285	.344	+39		-0.4
KRAUSSE, LEW Lewis Bernard Jr. B4.25.1943 Media PA BR/TR/5'11"/(185–186) d6.16 f–Lew																											
1972	Bos A	1	3	.250	24	7	0	0	3	1	0	7	60.2	74	48	9	3	28	2	35	6.38	-49	.308	.387	-6	0	-1.4
Total	12	68	91	.428	321	167	21	5	92	21	1	105	1283.2	1205	635	137	35	493	62	721	4.00	-15	.248	.320	-9	0	-9.0
KREUGER, RICK Richard Allen B11.3.1948 Grand Rapids MI BR/TL/6'2"/185 d9.6 Col Michigan St.																											
1975	Bos A	0	0	+	2	0	0	0	0	0	0	1	4	3	2	0	0	1	0	1	4.50	-10	.200	.250		0	0.0
1976	Bos A	2	1	.667	8	4	1	0	2	0	0	4	31	31	14	3	0	16	0	12	4.06	-4	.272	.359	+30	0	0.1
1977	Bos A	0	1	.000	1	0	0	0	0	0	0	0	0	2	2	0	0	0	0	0	(2)	-100	1.000	1.000		0	-0.2
1978	Cle A	0	0	+	6	0	0	0	0	0	0	4	9.1	6	4	1	0	3	0	7	3.86	-2	.194	.243		0	0.0
Total	4	2	2	.500	17	4	1	0	2	0	0	9	44.1	42	22	4	0	20	0	20	4.47	-13	.259	.333	+30	0	-0.1
Team	3	2	2	.500	11	4	1	0	2	0	0	5	35	36	18	3	0	17	0	13	4.63	-16	.275	.356	+30		-0.1
KROH, RUBE Floyd Myron B8.25.1886 Friendship NY D3.17.1944 New Orleans LA BL/TL/6'2"/186 d9.30																											
1906	Bos A	1	0	1.000	1	1	1	1		0			9	2	0	0	0	4		5	0.00	-100	.074	.194	-48		0.3
1907	Bos A	1	4	.200	7	5	1	0		0			34.1	33	13	0	2	8		8	2.62	-2	.256	.309	-48		0.1
Total	6	14	9	.609	36	25	13	3		0			216.1	182	65	3	5	67		92	2.29	+15	.232	.296	-6		1.6
Team	2	2	4	.333	8	6	2	1		0			43.1	35	13	0	2	12		13	2.08	+26	.224	.288	-48		0.4
LACY, KERRY Kerry Ardeen B8.7.1972 Chattanooga TN BR/TR/6'2"/215 [TexA91 15/404] d8.16 Col Chattanooga St. (TN) CC [DL 1998 Bos A 181]																											
1996	Bos A	2	0	1.000	11	0	0	0	0	0	2	6	10.2	15	5	2	1	8	0	9	3.38	+51	.333	.444		0	0.3
1997	Bos A	1	1	.500	33	0	0	0	0	3	0	19	45.2	60	34	7	0	22	4	18	6.11	-24	.314	.381		0	-0.4
Total	2	3	1	.750	44	0	0	0	0	3	2	25	56.1	75	39	9	1	30	4	27	5.59	-15	.318	.394		181	-0.1
/60G	3	4	1	.750	60	0	0	0	0	4	3	34	76.2	102	53	12	1	41	5	37	5.60	-15	.318	.394		247	-0.1
LAKE, EDDIE Edward Erving "Sparky" B3.18.1916 Antioch CA D6.7.1995 Castro Valley CA BR/TR/5'7"/160 d9.26.1939▲																											
1944	Bos A	0	0	+	6	0	0	0		0			19.1	20	13	2	3	11		7	4.19	-19	.278	.395		0	-0.1
LAMABE, JACK John Alexander B10.3.1936 Farmingdale NY BR/TR/6'1"/(193–205) d4.17 Col Vermont																											
1962	Pit N	3	1	.750	46	0	0	0	0	2		35	78	70	35	4	0	40	8	56	2.88	+36	.238	.329		0	0.3
1963	Bos A	7	4	.636	65	2	0	0	1	6		45	151.1	139	63	8	4	46	11	93	3.15	+20	.247	.306	-18	0	0.6
1964	Bos A	9	13	.409	39	25	3	0	11	1		6	177.1	235	123	25	2	57	5	109	5.89	-35	.318	.367	+6	0	-4.0
1965	Bos A	0	3	.000	14	0	0	0	0	0		6	25.1	34	24	5	3	14	2	17	8.17	-54	.340	.432		0	-1.2
1965	Hou N	0	2	.000	3	2	0	0	0	0		1	12.2	17	9	3	0	3	1	6	4.26	-21	.315	.351	-48	0	-0.3
1965	Major	0	5	.000	17	2	0	0	0	0		7	37	51	33	8	3	17	3	23	6.87	-43	.331	.406	-48	0	-1.5
1966	Chi A	7	9	.438	34	17	3	2	6	0		14	121.1	116	55	9	1	35	1	67	3.93	-19	.251	.304	+16	0	-1.2
1967	Chi A	1	0	1.000	3	0	0	0	0	0		2	5	7	2	0	0	1	1	3	1.80	+72	.318	.348		0	0.1
1967	NY N	0	3	.000	16	2	0	0	1	1		10	31.2	24	15	4	0	8	1	23	3.98	-15	.200	.248	-48	0	-0.2
1967	†StL N	3	4	.429	23	1	1	1	1	4		15	47.2	43	16	2	0	10	3	30	2.83	+16	.244	.282	+60	0	0.5
1967	Year	3	7	.300	39	3	1	1	2	5		27	79.1	67	31	6	0	18	4	53	3.29	+1	.226	.268	-12	0	0.3
1967	Major	4	7	.364	42	3	1	1	2	5		27	83	74	33	6	0	19	5	56	3.20	+8	.233	.274	-12	0	0.4
1968	Chi N	3	2	.600	42	0	0	0	0	1		27	60.2	68	33	7	1	24	7	30	4.30	-27	.289	.350		0	-0.6
Total	7	33	41	.446	285	49	7	3	20	15		161	711	753	375	67	11	238	40	434	4.24	-15	.272	.330	+4	0	-6.0
Team	3	16	20	.444	118	27	3	0	12	7		57	354	408	210	38	9	117	18	219	4.88	-22	.291	.347	+4		-4.6
/60G	2	8	10	.444	60	14	2	0	6	4		29	180	207	107	19	5	59	9	111	4.88	-22	.291	.347	+4		-2.3
LAMP, DENNIS Dennis Patrick B9.23.1952 Los Angeles CA BR/TR/6'3"/(180–215) [ChiN71 3/62] d8.21																											
1988	Bos A	7	6	.538	46	0	0	0	0	0	1	33	82.2	92	39	3	2	19	3	49	3.48	+19	.284	.326		18	0.6
1989	Bos A	4	2	.667	42	0	0	0	0	2	1	31	112.1	96	37	4	0	27	6	61	2.32	+77	.235	.280		0	1.1
1990	†Bos A	3	5	.375	47	1	0	0	0	0	2	25	105.2	114	61	10	3	30	8	49	4.68	-13	.279	.330	-56	0	-0.4
1991	Bos A	6	3	.667	51	0	0	0	0	0	0	30	92	100	54	8	3	31	7	57	4.70	-8	.275	.335		0	-0.4
Total	16	96	96	.500	639	163	21	7	74	35	24	317	1830.2	1975	915	122	35	549	86	857	3.93	+4	.278	.331	-6	18	2.1
Team	4	20	16	.556	186	1	0	0	0	2	4	119	392.2	402	191	25	8	107	24	216	3.76	+11	.267	.317	-56	18	0.9
/60G	1	6	5	.556	60	0	0	0	0	1	1	38	126.2	130	62	8	3	35	8	70	3.76	+11	.267	.317		6	0.3
LANDIS, BILL William Henry B10.8.1942 Hanford CA BL/TL/6'2"/(175–180) d9.28 Mil 1968 Col West Hills (CA) JC																											
1963	KC A	0	0	+	1	0	0	0	0	0		1	1.2	0	0	0	0	1	0	3	0.00	-100	.000	.167		0	0.0
1967	Bos A	1	0	1.000	18	1	0	0	0	0		11	25.2	24	16	6	0	11	3	23	5.26	-34	.253	.330	+25	0	-0.3
1968	Bos A	3	3	.500	38	1	0	0	0	3		27	60	48	22	4	2	30	2	59	3.15	+0	.223	.320	-45	0	0.0
1969	Bos A	5	5	.500	45	5	0	0	3	1	1	23	82.1	82	53	7	3	49	3	50	5.25	-27	.269	.370	-49	0	-1.3
Total	4	9	8	.529	102	7	0	0	3	4	1	62	169.2	154	91	17	5	91	8	135	4.46	-21	.248	.345	-36	0	-1.6
Team	3	9	8	.529	101	7	0	0	3	4	1	61	168	154	91	17	5	90	8	132	4.50	-21	.250	.347	-38		-1.6
/60G	2	5	5	.529	60	4	0	0	2	2	1	36	99.2	91	54	10	3	53	5	78	4.51	-21	.250	.347	-38		-1.0
LAROSE, JOHN Henry John B10.25.1951 Pawtucket RI BL/TL/6'1"/185 [BosA70 S1/14] d9.20																											
1978	Bos A	0	0	+	1	0	0	0	0	0	0	0	2	3	5	1	0	3	1	0	22.50	-82	.375	.545		0	-0.2
LEE, SANG-HOON Sang-Hoon B3.11.1971 Seoul, South Korea BL/TL/6'1"/190 d6.29																											
2000	Bos A	0	0	+	9	0	0	0	0	0	0	6	11.2	11	4	2	2	4	0	6	3.09	+63	.262	.347		0	0.1
LEE, BILL William Francis "Spaceman" B12.28.1946 Burbank CA BL/TL/6'3"/(190–206) [BosA68 22/507] d6.25 Mil 1970 Col USC																											
1969	Bos A	1	3	.250	20	1	0	0	0	0	1	11	52	56	27	9	2	28	0	45	4.50	-15	.281	.372	-54	0	-0.3
1970	Bos A	2	2	.500	11	5	0	0	2	1	0	4	37	48	20	3	0	14	1	19	4.62	-14	.320	.378	-11	0	-0.3
1971	Bos A	9	2	.818	47	3	0	0	0	2	2	32	102	102	35	7	1	46	7	74	2.74	+36	.256	.333	+12	0	1.2
1972	Bos A	7	4	.636	47	0	0	0	0	5	2	32	84.1	75	31	5	1	32	8	43	3.20	+1	.248	.320		0	0.6
1973	Bos A☆	17	11	.607	38	33	18	1	26	1	0	5	284.2	275	100	20	5	76	2	120	2.75	+46	.257	.307	-13	0	3.6
1974	Bos A	17	15	.531	38	37	16	1	25	0	0	1	282.1	320	123	25	4	67	0	95	3.51	+10	.290	.331	-3	0	1.2
1975	†Bos A	17	9	.654	41	34	17	4	19	0	0	3	260	274	123	20	3	69	1	78	3.95	+3	.273	.319	+5	0	0.6
1976	Bos A	5	7	.417	24	14	1	0	6	3	0	8	96	124	68	13	3	28	1	29	5.63	-31	.307	.354	+2	52	-1.9
1977	Bos A	9	5	.643	27	16	4	0	8	1	0	4	128	155	67	14	0	29	1	31	4.43	+1	.306	.341	+1	0	0.2
1978	Bos A	10	10	.500	28	24	8	1	15	0	0	3	177	198	89	20	2	59	2	44	3.46	+19	.285	.340	-2	0	0.8
1979	Mon N	16	10	.615	33	33	6	3	22	0	0	0	222	230	91	20	1	46	1	59	3.04	+22	.265	.302	+0	0	1.9
1980	Mon N	4	6	.400	24	18	2	0	7	0	0	5	118	156	71	13	3	22	1	34	4.96	-27	.319	.349	+20	59	-1.2

Year	Tm Lg	W	L	Pct	G	GS	CG	ShO	QS	SV	BS	QR	IP	H	R	HR	HB	BB	IB	SO	ERA	AERA	OAV	OOB	Sup	DL	PW
1981	†Mon N	5	6	.455	31	7	0	0	6	6	0	20	88.2	90	33	6	2	14	2	34	2.94	+21	.265	.297	-14	0	1.3
1982	Mon N	0	0	+	7	0	0	0	0	0	0	4	12.1	19	7	1	0	1	0	8	4.38	-16	.352	.357		0	0.0
Total	14	119	90	.569	416	225	72	10	136	19	5	132	1944.1	2122	885	176	27	531	27	713	3.62	+8	.280	.327	+0	111	7.7
Team	10	94	68	.580	321	167	64	7	101	13	5	103	1503.1	1627	683	136	21	448	23	578	3.64	+9	.279	.330	-3	52	5.7
/180I	1	11	8	.580	38	20	8	1	12	2	1	12	180	195	82	16	3	54	3	69	3.64	+9	.279	.330	-3	6	0.7
LEFEBVRE, BILL Wilfred Henry "Lefty" B11.11.1915 Natick RI BL/TL/5'11.5"/180 d6.10 Mil 1945 Col Holy Cross▲																											
1938	Bos A	0	0	+	1	0	0	0		0			4	8	6	2	1	0		0	13.50	-63	.400	.429			0.0
1939	Bos A	1	1	.500	5	3	0	0		0			26.1	35	17	2	0	14		8	5.81	-19	.333	.412	+18		-0.1
Total	4	5	5	.500	36	10	3	0		3			132.1	162	89	10	2	51		36	5.03	-29	.306	.369	+19	0	-0.6
Team	2	1	1	.500	6	3	0	0		0			30.1	43	23	4	1	14		8	6.82	-30	.344	.414	+18		-0.1
LEHENY, REGIS Regis Francis B1.5.1908 Pittsburgh PA D11.2.1976 Pittsburgh PA BL/TL/6'0.5"/180 d5.21																											
1932	Bos A	0	0	+	2	0	0	0		0			2.2	5	5	0	0	3		1	16.88	-73	.417	.533			-0.1
LEISTER, JOHN John William B1.3.1961 San Antonio TX BR/TR/6'2"/(200–215) [BosA84*S3/52] d5.28 Col Michigan St.																											
1987	Bos A	0	2	.000	8	6	0	0	1	0	0	1	30.1	49	31	9	0	12	1	16	9.20	-50	.368	.418	+40	0	-0.8
1990	Bos A	0	0	+	2	1	0	0	0	0	0	0	5.2	7	5	0	0	4	0	3	4.76	-14	.304	.393	+11	0	-0.1
Total	2	0	2	.000	10	7	0	0	1	0	0	1	36	56	36	9	0	16	1	19	8.50	-47	.359	.414	+36	0	-0.9
LEONARD, DUTCH Hubert Benjamin B4.16.1892 Birmingham OH D7.11.1952 Fresno CA BL/TL/5'10.5"/185 d4.12 Mil 1918 Col St. Marys (CA)																											
1913	Bos A	14	17	.452	42	28	14	3		1			259.1	245	108	0	4	94		144	2.39	+23	.255	.324	+20		1.2
1914	Bos A	19	5	.792	36	25	17	7		3			224.2	139	34	3	8	60		176	**0.96**	+180	**.180**	**.246**	+15		4.8
1915	†Bos A	15	7	.682	32	21	10	2		0			183.1	130	57	3	14	67		116	2.36	+18	**.208**	.299	+5		1.7
1916	†Bos A	18	12	.600	48	34	17	6		6			274	244	87	6	8	66		144	2.36	+17	.247	.300	-10		1.4
1917	Bos A	16	17	.485	37	36	26	4		1			294.1	257	88	4	5	72		144	2.17	+19	.236	.286	-17		0.8
1918	Bos A	8	6	.571	16	16	12	3		0			125.2	119	51	0	2	53		47	2.72	-1	.254	.332	+33		-0.2
1919	Det A	14	13	.519	29	28	18	4		0			217.1	212	89	7	7	65		102	2.77	+15	.254	.313	-6		0.4
1920	Det A	10	17	.370	28	27	10	3		0			191.1	192	107	8	8	63		76	4.33	-14	.271	.338	-36		-0.7
1921	Det A	11	13	.458	36	32	16	1		1			245	273	125	15	10	63		120	3.75	+14	.286	.336	+1		0.8
1924	Det A	3	2	.600	9	7	3	0		1			51.1	68	32	1	1	18		26	4.56	-10	.327	.383	+8		-0.3
1925	Det A	11	4	.733	18	18	9	0		0			125.2	143	73	7	1	43		65	4.51	-5	.289	.347	+35		-0.4
Total	11	139	113	.552	331	272	152	33		13			2192	2022	851	54	68	664		1160	2.76	+15	.249	.312	+2		9.5
Team	6	90	64	.584	211	160	96	25		11			1361.1	1134	425	16	41	412		771	2.13	+29	.231	.296	+4		9.7
/180I	1	12	8	.584	28	21	13	3		1			180	150	56	2	5	54		102	2.13	+29	.231	.296	+4		1.3
LEROY, LOUIS Louis Paul "Chief" B2.18.1879 Omro WI D10.10.1944 Shawano WI BR/TR/5'10"/180 d9.22																											
1910	Bos A	0	0	+	1	0	0	0		0			4	7	9	1	0	2		3	11.25	-77	.389	.450			-0.2
Total	3	3	1	.750	15	5	3	0		1			72.2	66	42	3	3	15		39	3.22	-9	.244	.292	+36		-0.3
LESKANIC, CURTIS Curtis John B4.2.1968 Homestead PA BR/TR/6'0"/(180–196) [CleA89 8/203] d6.27 Col Louisiana St. [DL 2002 Mil N 183]																											
2004	†Bos A	3	2	.600	32	0	0	0	0	2	1	26	27.2	24	11	3	1	16	3	22	3.58	+36	.247	.353		23	0.7
Total	11	50	34	.595	603	11	0	0	2	55	31	408	712.2	678	365	80	17	362	23	641	4.36	+16	.253	.343	-21	264	6.0
LESTER, JON Jonathan Tyler B1.7.1984 Tacoma WA BL/TL/6'2"/190 [BosA02 2/57] d6.10																											
2006	Bos A	7	2	.778	15	15	0	0	5	0	0	0	81.1	91	43	7	5	43	1	60	4.76	-2	.294	.381	+21	39	0.0
LEWIS, TED Edward Morgan "Parson" B12.25.1872 Machynlleth, Wales D5.23.1936 Durham NH BR/TR/5'10.5"/158 d7.6 Col Williams																											
1901	Bos A	16	17	.485	39	34	31	1		1			316.1	299	172	14	8	91		103	3.53	+0	.247	.304	+5		0.0
Total	6	94	64	.595	183	153	136	7		4			1405	1379	753	57	39	511		378	3.53	+13	.255	.324	+6		5.8
/180I	1	9	10	.485	22	19	18	1		1			180	170	98	8	5	52		59	3.53	+0	.247	.304	-40		0.0
LILLIQUIST, DEREK Derek Jansen B2.20.1966 Winter Park FL BL/TL/6'0"/(195–214) [AtlN87 1/6] d4.13 Col Georgia																											
1995	Bos A	2	1	.667	28	0	0	0	0	0	3	15	23	27	17	7	0	9	2	9	6.26	-22	.303	.356		0	-0.4
Total	8	25	34	.424	262	52	1	1	23	17	15	144	483.2	532	245	59	9	134	25	261	4.13	-3	.283	.330	-17	0	0.4
LISENBEE, HOD Horace Milton B9.23.1898 Clarksville TN D11.14.1987 Clarksville TN BR/TR/5'11"/170 d4.23 Col Rhodes																											
1927	Was A	18	9	.667	39	34	17	0		0			242	221	114	6	3	78		105	3.57	+14	.245	.307	+5		0.7
1928	Was A	2	6	.250	16	9	3	0		0			77	102	58	4	5	32		13	6.08	-34	.326	.397	-9		-1.5
1929	Bos A	0	0	+	5	0	0	0		0			8.2	10	5	1	0	4		2	5.19	-18	.294	.368			0.0
1930	Bos A	10	17	.370	37	31	15	0		0			237.1	254	130	20	5	86		47	4.40	+5	.280	.346	-25		0.6
1931	Bos A	5	12	.294	41	17	6	0		0			164.2	190	108	13	3	49		42	5.19	-17	.281	.332	-11		-1.4
1932	Bos A	0	4	.000	19	6	3	0		0			73.1	87	55	9	1	25		13	5.65	-20	.296	.353	-40		-0.6
1936	Phi A	1	7	.125	19	7	4	0		0			85.2	115	69	9	0	24		17	6.20	-18	.322	.365	-38		-0.9
1945	Cin N	1	3	.250	31	3	0	0		1			80.1	97	56	12	2	16		14	5.49	-32	.294	.330	+58	0	-1.1
Total	8	37	58	.389	207	107	48	4		1			969	1076	595	74	19	314		253	4.81	-10	.282	.340	-12	0	-4.2
Team	4	15	33	.313	102	54	24	0		0			484	541	298	43	9	164		104	4.87	-8	.283	.343	-22		-1.4
/180I	1	6	12	.313	38	20	9	0		0			180	201	111	16	3	61		39	4.87	-8	.283	.343	-22		-0.5
LITTLEFIELD, DICK Richard Bernard B3.18.1926 Detroit MI D11.20.1997 Detroit MI BL/TL/6'0"/180 d7.7																											
1950	Bos A	2	2	.500	15	2	0	0		1			23.1	27	25	7	1	24		13	9.26	-47	.297	.448	-54	0	-1.5
Total	9	33	54	.379	243	83	16	2	0	9		30	761.2	750	461	92	12	413	18	495	4.71	-14	.260	.353	-23	0	-7.5
LOCKWOOD, SKIP Claude Edward B8.17.1946 Boston MA BR/TR/6'0"/(180–200) d4.23.1965▲																											
1980	Bos A	3	1	.750	24	1	0	0	0	2	1	14	45.2	61	31	4	0	17	3	11	5.32	-20	.321	.371	-16	0	-0.5
Total	12	57	97	.370	420	106	16	5	58	68	23	226	1236	1130	539	98	33	490	62	829	3.55	+0	.246	.320	-22	103	2.7
LOLLAR, TIM William Timothy B3.17.1956 Poplar Bluff MO BL/TL/6'3"/(195–204) [NYA78 4/104] d6.28 Col Arkansas																											
1985	Bos A	5	5	.500	16	10	1	0	4	1	0	3	67	57	37	9	1	40	0	44	4.57	-6	.230	.338	+3	0	-0.3
1986	Bos A	2	0	1.000	32	1	0	0	1	0	1	15	43	51	35	7	3	34	3	28	6.91	-39	.304	.421	+159	0	-0.5
Total	7	47	52	.475	199	131	9	4	67	4	1	40	906	841	459	93	17	480	21	600	4.27	-14	.249	.343	+0	0	-2.9
Team	2	7	5	.583	48	11	1	0	5	1	1	18	110	108	72	16	4	74	3	72	5.48	-22	.260	.373	+17		-0.8
/60G	3	9	6	.583	60	14	1	0	6	1	1	23	137.2	135	90	20	5	93	4	90	5.48	-22	.260	.373	+17		-1.0
LONBORG, JIM James Reynold B4.16.1942 Santa Maria CA BR/TR/6'5"/(195–210) d4.23 Col Stanford																											
1965	Bos A	9	17	.346	32	31	7	1	16	0		1	185.1	193	112	20	3	65	3	113	4.47	-17	.262	.323	+12	0	-2.1
1966	Bos A	10	10	.500	45	23	3	1	12	2		13	181.2	173	86	18	7	55	5	131	3.86	-2	.249	.308	+17	0	-0.2
1967	†Bos A☆	**22**	9	.710	39	**39**	15	2	22	0		0	273.1	228	102	23	19	83	5	**246**	3.16	+10	.225	.294	+10	0	1.0
1968	Bos A	6	10	.375	23	17	4	1	10	0		3	113.1	89	57	11	11	59	3	73	4.29	-26	.216	.327	+4	46	-1.4
1969	Bos A	7	11	.389	29	23	4	0	11	0	1	3	143.2	148	78	15	7	65	3	100	4.51	-15	.270	.354	-14	0	-1.1
1970	Bos A	4	1	.800	9	4	0	0	3	0	0	4	34	33	12	3	0	9	0	21	3.18	+25	.260	.304	-11	55	0.8
1971	Bos A	10	7	.588	27	26	5	1	14	0	0	1	167.2	167	86	15	14	67	6	100	4.13	-10	.259	.341	+29	0	-0.7
1972	Mil A	14	12	.538	33	30	11	2	23	1	0	3	223	197	75	17	11	76	11	143	2.83	+8	.238	.309	+8	0	0.7
1973	Phi N	13	16	.448	38	30	6	0	13	0	1	5	199.1	218	124	25	9	80	7	106	4.88	-22	.279	.350	-1	0	-3.2
1974	Phi N	17	13	.567	39	39	16	3	28	0	0	0	283	280	113	22	6	70	11	121	3.21	+18	.261	.308	-1	0	1.1
1975	Phi N	8	6	.571	27	26	6	2	14	0	0	1	159.1	161	84	12	5	45	7	72	4.12	-9	.257	.310	+11	0	-0.9
1976	†Phi N	18	10	.643	33	32	8	1	20	1	0	1	222	210	85	18	5	50	4	118	3.08	+16	.249	.292	+6	0	1.4
1977	†Phi N	11	4	.733	25	25	4	1	16	0	0	0	157.2	157	77	15	5	50	5	76	4.11	-2	.261	.321	+21	49	-0.3
1978	Phi N	8	10	.444	22	22	1	0	10	0	0	0	113.2	132	69	16	2	45	1	48	5.23	-31	.293	.359	+5	0	-2.6
1979	Phi N	0	1	.000	4	1	0	0	0	0	0	1	7.1	14	10	3	1	4	0	7	11.05	-65	.389	.463	-54	0	-0.7
Total	15	157	137	.534	425	368	90	15	212	4	2	36	2464.1	2400	1170	233	105	823	71	1475	3.86	-5	.255	.320	+8	150	-8.2
Team	7	68	65	.511	204	163	38	6	88	2	1	25	1099	1031	533	105	61	403	25	784	3.94	-8	.247	.320	+10	101	-3.7
/180I	1	11	11	.511	33	27	6	1	14	0	0	4	180	169	87	17	10	66	4	128	3.94	-8	.247	.320	+10	17	-0.6
LOONEY, BRIAN Brian James B9.26.1969 New Haven CT BL/TL/5'10"/(175–185) [MonN91 10/269] d9.26 Col Boston College																											
1993	Mon N	0	0	+	3	1	0	0	0	0	0	1	6	8	2	0	0	2	0	7	3.00	+39	.308	.357	+8	0	0.0
1994	Mon N	0	0	+	1	0	0	0	0	0	0	0	2	4	5	1	1	0	0	2	22.50	-81	.400	.455		0	-0.2
1995	Bos A	0	1	.000	3	1	0	0	0	0	0	0	4.2	12	9	1	0	4	1	2	17.36	-72	.545	.571	-43	0	-0.9
Total	3	0	1	.000	7	2	0	0	0	0	0	1	12.2	24	16	2	1	6	1	11	11.37	-61	.414	.463	-18	0	-1.1

Year	Tm Lg	W	L	Pct	G	GS	CG	ShO	QS	SV	BS	QR	IP	H	R	HR	HB	BB	IB	SO	ERA	AERA	OAV	OOB	Sup	DL	PW
LOPEZ, JAVIER Javier Alfonso B6.11.1977 San Juan, PR BL/TL/6'4"/(200–220) [AriN98 4/133] d4.1 Col Virginia																											
2006	Bos A	1	0	1.000	27	0	0	0	0	1	0	20	16.2	13	10	1	2	10	1	11	2.70	+73	.232	.362		0	0.1
Total	4	7	4	.636	198	0	0	0	0	4	4	145	132	142	89	9	10	59	10	83	5.66	-16	.277	.363		0	-1.1
LOWE, DEREK Derek Christopher B6.1.1973 Dearborn MI BR/TR/6'6"/(170–210) [SeaA91 8/214] d4.26																											
1997	Sea A	2	4	.333	12	9	0	0	2	0	0	2	53	59	43	11	2	20	2	39	6.96	-35	.282	.349	+15	0	-1.3
1997	Bos A	0	2	.000	8	0	0	0	0	0	2	6	16	15	6	0	2	3	1	13	3.38	+38	.268	.323		0	0.3
1997	Year	2	6	.250	20	9	0	0	2	0	2	8	69	74	49	11	4	23	3	52	6.13	-26	.279	.344	+14	0	-1.0
1998	†Bos A	3	9	.250	63	10	0	0	4	4	5	38	123	126	65	5	4	42	5	77	4.02	+17	.267	.329	-35	0	0.7
1999	†Bos A	6	3	.667	74	0	0	0	0	15	5	57	109.1	84	35	7	4	25	1	80	2.63	+89	.208	.260		0	2.6
2000	Bos A★	4	4	.500	74	0	0	0	0	**42**	5	58	91.1	90	27	6	2	22	5	79	2.56	+96	.257	.304		0	3.9
2001	Bos A	5	10	.333	67	3	0	0	1	24	6	41	91.2	103	39	7	5	29	9	82	3.53	+26	.283	.343	+4	0	1.9
2002	Bos A★	21	8	.724	32	32	1	1	24	0	0	0	219.2	166	65	12	12	48	0	127	2.58	+73	.211	.266	+23	0	**6.2**
2003	†Bos A	17	7	.708	33	33	1	0	17	0	0	0	203.1	216	113	17	11	72	4	110	4.47	+4	.272	.339	+28	0	0.5
2004	†Bos A	14	12	.538	33	33	0	0	12	0	0	0	182.2	224	138	15	8	71	2	105	5.42	-10	.299	.365	+17	0	-1.6
2005	LA N	12	15	.444	35	**35**	2	2	23	0	0	0	222	223	113	28	5	55	1	146	3.61	+15	.260	.307	+1	0	0.9
2006	†LA N	**16**	8	.667	35	34	1	0	20	0	0	1	218	221	97	14	5	55	2	123	3.63	+21	.262	.310	+0	0	1.9
Total	10	100	82	.549	466	189	5	3	103	85	23	203	1530	1527	741	122	60	442	32	981	3.81	+20	.259	.316	+10	0	16.0
Team	8	70	55	.560	384	111	2	1	58	85	23	200	1037	1024	488	69	48	312	27	673	3.72	+27	.258	.318	+17		14.5
/60G	1	11	9	.560	60	17	0	0	9	13	4	31	162	160	76	11	8	49	4	105	3.72	+27	.258	.318	+17		2.3
LUCEY, JOE Joseph Earl "Scootch" B3.27.1897 Holyoke MA D7.30.1980 Holyoke MA BR/TR/6'0"/168 d7.6.1920 Col Catholic America																											
1925	Bos A	0	1	.000	7	2	0	0		0			11	18	20	0	0	14		2	9.00	-50	.360	.500	+2		-0.6
LUCIER, LOU Louis Joseph B3.23.1918 Northbridge MA BR/TR/5'8"/160 d4.23																											
1943	Bos A	3	4	.429	16	9	3	0		0			74	94	35	1	2	33		23	3.89	-15	.322	.394	-1	0	-0.2
1944	Bos A	0	0	+	3	0	0	0		0			5.1	7	3	0	0	7		2	5.06	-33	.292	.452		0	-0.1
1944	Phi N	0	0	+	1	0	0	0		0			2	3	3	0	0	2		1	13.50	-73	.333	.455		0	-0.1
1944	Major	0	0	+	4	0	0	0		0			7	10	6	0	0	9		3	7.36	-44	.303	.452		0	-0.2
1945	Phi N	0	1	.000	13	0	0	0		1			20.1	14	9	1	0	5		5	2.21	+73	.194	.247		0	0.2
Total	3	3	5	.375	33	9	3	0		1			101.2	118	50	2	2	47		31	3.81	-10	.297	.374	-1	0	-0.2
Team	2	3	4	.429	19	9	3	0		0			79.1	101	38	1	2	40		25	3.97	-16	.320	.399	-1		-0.3
LUNDGREN, DEL Ebin Delmar B9.21.1899 Lindsborg KS D10.19.1984 Lindsborg KS BR/TR/5'8"/160 d4.27																											
1924	Pit N	0	1	.000	8	1	0	0		0			16.2	25	13	0	1	3		4	6.48	-41	.403	.439	-56		-0.3
1926	Bos A	0	2	.000	18	2	0	0		0			31	35	28	2	3	28		11	7.55	-46	.307	.455	-38		-0.6
1927	Bos A	5	12	.294	30	17	5	2		0			136.1	160	100	7	4	87		39	6.27	-33	.302	.405	-9		-2.8
Total	3	5	15	.250	56	20	5	2		0			184	220	141	9	8	118		54	6.51	-36	.312	.416	-14		-3.7
Team	2	5	14	.263	48	19	5	2		0			167.1	195	128	9	7	115		50	6.51	-36	.303	.414	-12		-3.4
/180I	2	5	15	.263	52	20	5	2		0			180	210	138	10	8	124		54	6.51	-36	.303	.414	-12		-3.7
LYLE, SPARKY Albert Walter B7.22.1944 DuBois PA BL/TL/6'1"/(182–198) d7.4																											
1967	Bos A	1	2	.333	27	0	0	0	0	5		25	43.1	33	13	3	2	14	1	42	2.28	+53	.213	.283		0	0.5
1968	Bos A	6	1	.857	49	0	0	0	0	11		35	65.2	67	25	6	0	14	2	52	2.74	+15	.261	.298		0	0.2
1969	Bos A	8	3	.727	71	0	0	0	0	17	9	49	102.2	91	33	8	1	48	4	93	2.54	+50	.240	.323		0	2.0
1970	Bos A	1	7	.125	63	0	0	0	0	20	10	43	67.1	62	37	5	1	34	5	51	3.88	+3	.244	.334		0	-0.3
1971	Bos A	6	4	.600	50	0	0	0	0	16	4	36	52.1	41	16	5	0	23	2	37	2.75	+35	.228	.311		0	1.5
Total	16	99	76	.566	899	0	0	0	0	238	86	648	1390.1	1292	519	84	14	481	81	873	2.88	+28	.251	.313		0	19.4
Team	5	22	17	.564	260	0	0	0	0	69	23	188	331.1	294	124	27	4	133	14	275	2.85	+28	.240	.314			3.9
/60G	1	5	4	.564	60	0	0	0	0	16	5	43	76.1	68	29	6	1	31	3	63	2.86	+28	.240	.314			0.9
LYON, BRANDON Brandon James B8.10.1979 Salt Lake City UT BR/TR/6'1"/(175–190) [TorA99 14/433] d8.4 Col Dixie (UT) JC [DL 2003 Pit N 7, 2004 Ari N 183]																											
2003	Bos A	4	6	.400	49	0	0	0	0	9	3	30	59	73	33	6	2	19	5	50	4.12	+13	.296	.346		32	0.4
Total	5	12	20	.375	175	21	0	0	9	23	12	101	282.2	326	168	39	7	85	16	178	4.87	-5	.288	.337	-20	314	-0.6
/60G	1	5	7	.400	60	0	0	0	0	11	4	37	72.1	89	40	7	2	23	6	61	4.11	+13	.296	.346		39	0.5
MACFAYDEN, DANNY Daniel Knowles "Deacon Danny" B6.10.1905 N.Truro MA D8.26.1972 Brunswick ME BR/TR/5'11"/170 d8.25																											
1926	Bos A	0	1	.000	3	1	1	0		0			13	10	7	0	0	7		1	4.85	-16	.217	.321	-79		0.0
1927	Bos A	5	8	.385	34	16	6	1		2			160.1	176	88	9	6	59		42	4.27	-1	.294	.363	-21		0.4
1928	Bos A	9	15	.375	33	28	9	0		0			195	215	123	12	7	78		61	4.75	-13	.289	.361	-13		-1.7
1929	Bos A	10	18	.357	32	27	14	0		0			221	225	108	8	5	81		61	3.62	+18	.271	.340	-26		1.5
1930	Bos A	11	14	.440	36	33	18	1		2			269.1	293	141	9	6	93		76	4.21	+9	.281	.343	-14		0.8
1931	Bos A	16	12	.571	35	32	17	2		0			230.2	263	121	4	7	79		74	4.02	+7	.281	.341	-4		0.3
1932	Bos A	1	10	.091	12	11	6	0		0			77.2	91	55	3	1	33		29	5.10	-12	.289	.358	-52		-0.8
1932	NY A	7	5	.583	17	15	9	0		1			121.1	137	69	11	2	37		33	3.93	+4	.281	.334	+38		-0.4
1932	Year	8	15	.348	29	26	15	0		1			199	228	124	14	3	70		62	4.39	-3	.284	.344	-2		-1.2
1933	NY A	3	2	.600	25	6	2	0		0			90.1	120	62	8	2	37		28	5.88	-34	.319	.383	+31		-1.3
1934	NY A	4	3	.571	22	11	4	0		0			96	110	57	5	2	31		41	4.50	-10	.288	.345	+48		-0.6
1935	Cin N	1	2	.333	7	4	1	0		0			36	39	22	1	0	13		13	4.75	-16	.281	.342	-25		-0.2
1935	Bos N	5	13	.278	28	20	7	1		0			151.2	200	96	8	5	34		46	5.10	-26	.314	.354	-9		-2.1
1935	Year	6	15	.286	35	24	8	1		0			187.2	239	118	9	5	47		59	5.04	-24	.308	.352	-12		-2.3
1936	Bos N	17	13	.567	37	31	21	2		0			266.2	268	97	5	5	66		86	2.87	+34	.259	.307	-25		2.8
1937	Bos N	14	14	.500	32	32	16	2		0			246	250	96	5	2	60		70	2.93	+23	.268	.313	-8		1.7
1938	Bos N	14	9	.609	29	29	19	5		0			219.2	208	82	6	5	64		58	2.95	+16	.247	.304	-17		0.9
1939	Bos N	8	14	.364	33	28	8	0		2			191.2	221	100	11	4	59		46	3.90	-5	.291	.345	-4		-0.6
1940	Pit N	5	4	.556	35	8	0	0		2			91.1	112	47	5	4	27		24	3.55	+7	.302	.356	+8		0.0
1941	Was A	0	1	.000	5	0	0	0		0			7	12	9	1	0	5		3	10.29	-61	.375	.459		0	-0.5
1943	Bos N	2	1	.667	10	1	0	0		0			21.1	31	14	1	1	9		5	5.91	-42	.344	.410	-25	0	-0.6
Total	17	132	159	.454	465	333	158	18		9			2706	2981	1394	112	64	872		797	3.96	+1	.281	.340	-10	0	-0.4
Team	7	52	78	.400	185	148	71	4		4			1167	1273	643	45	32	430		344	4.23	+3	.282	.349	-18		0.5
/180I	1	8	12	.400	29	23	11	1		1			180	196	99	7	5	66		53	4.23	+3	.282	.349	-18		0.1
MACLEOD, BILLY William Daniel B5.13.1942 Gloucester MA BL/TL/6'2"/185 d9.13																											
1962	Bos A	0	1	.000	2	0	0	0	0	0		1	1.2	4	1	0	0	1	0	2	5.40	-24	.444	.500		0	0.0
MACWHORTER, KEITH Keith B12.30.1955 Worcester MA BR/TR/6'4"/185 [LAN76 15/355] d5.10 Col Bryant																											
1980	Bos A	0	3	.000	14	2	0	0	1	0	0	9	42.1	46	27	3	2	18	3	21	5.53	-23	.280	.357	-58	0	-0.3
MADDUX, MIKE Michael Ausley B8.27.1961 Dayton OH BL/TR/6'2"/(180–190) [PhiN82 5/119] d6.3 C3 b–Greg Col Texas–El Paso																											
1995	†Bos A	4	1	.800	36	4	0	0	1	1	0	19	89.2	86	40	5	2	15	3	65	3.61	+35	.247	.281	+39	0	0.6
1996	Bos A	3	2	.600	23	7	0	0	4	0	0	5	64.1	76	37	12	5	27	2	32	4.48	+14	.295	.370	-1	88	0.3
Total	15	39	37	.513	472	48	2	1	16	20	15	295	861.2	873	428	67	32	284	40	564	4.05	+2	.265	.326	+5	273	0.2
Team	2	7	3	.700	59	11	0	0	5	1	0	24	154	162	77	17	7	42	5	97	3.97	+25	.267	.320	+14	88	0.9
/60G	2	7	3	.700	60	11	0	0	5	1	0	24	156.2	165	78	17	7	43	5	99	3.97	+25	.267	.320	+14	89	0.9
MAGRINI, PETE Peter Alexander B6.8.1942 San Francisco CA BR/TR/6'0"/195 d4.13 Col Santa Clara																											
1966	Bos A	0	1	.000	3	1	0	0	0	0		0	7.1	8	9	0	1	8	0	3	9.82	-61	.308	.459	-77	0	-0.6
MAHAY, RON Ronald Matthew B6.28.1971 Crestwood IL BL/TL/6'2"/(185–190) [BosA91 18/486] d5.21.1995 Col South Suburban (IL) JC																											
1997	Bos A	3	0	1.000	28	0	0	0	0	0	2	23	25	19	7	3	0	11	0	22	2.52	+85	.204	.288		0	0.6
1998	Bos A	1	1	.500	29	0	0	0	0	1	1	18	26	26	16	2	2	15	1	14	3.46	+37	.263	.358		0	0.1
Total	10	16	10	.615	301	3	0	0	0	3	9	208	352	331	182	50	4	170	18	299	4.12	+14	.246	.330	-14	36	1.6
Team	2	4	1	.800	57	0	0	0	0	1	3	41	51	45	23	5	2	26	1	36	3.00	+56	.234	.326			0.7
/60G	2	4	1	.800	60	0	0	0	0	1	3	43	53.2	47	24	5	2	27	1	38	3.00	+56	.234	.326			0.7
MAHOMES, PAT Patrick Lavon B8.9.1970 Bryan TX BR/TR/6'4"/(175–212) [MinA88 6/155] d4.12																											
1996	Bos A	2	0	1.000	11	0	0	0	0	2	0	7	12.1	9	8	3	0	6	0	6	5.84	-13	.209	.306		0	-0.1

Year	Tm Lg	W	L	Pct	G	GS	CG	ShO	QS	SV	BS	QR	IP	H	R	HR	HB	BB	IB	SO	ERA	AERA	OAV	OOB	Sup	DL	PW
1997	Bos A	1	0	1.000	10	0	0	0	0	0	0	4	10	15	10	2	2	10	1	5	8.10	-43	.366	.500		0	-0.3
Total	11	42	39	.519	308	63	0	0	14	5	8	151	709	738	461	116	11	392	25	452	5.47	-16	.272	.363	+4	17	-6.3
Team	2	3	0	1.000	21	0	0	0	0	2	0	11	22.1	24	18	5	2	16	1	11	6.85	-28	.286	.408			-0.4
MAHONEY, CHRIS Christopher John B6.11.1885 Milton MA D7.15.1954 Visalia CA BR/TR/5'9"/160 d7.12 Col Fordham																											
1910	Bos A	0	1	.000	2	1	0	0		1			11	16	11	1	0	5		6	3.27	-22	.327	.389	+31		-0.3
MALASKA, MARK Dennis Mark B1.17.1978 Youngstown OH BL/TL/6'3"/(190–210) [TBA00 8/226] d7.17 Col Akron																											
2003	TB A	2	1	.667	22	0	0	0	0	0	3	17	16	13	7	0	1	12	3	17	2.81	+63	.232	.377		0	0.4
2004	Bos A	1	1	.500	19	0	0	0	0	0	0	10	20	21	11	2	1	12	1	12	4.50	+9	.266	.370		0	0.1
Total	2	3	2	.600	41	0	0	0	0	0	3	27	36	34	18	2	2	24	4	29	3.75	+27	.252	.373		0	0.5
MALOY, PAUL Paul Augustus "Biff" B6.4.1892 Bascom OH D3.18.1976 Sandusky OH BR/TR/5'11"/185 d7.11																											
1913	Bos A	0	0	+	2	0	0	0		0			2	2	2	0	2	1		0	9.00	-67	.286	.500			-0.1
MANTEI, MATT Matthew Bruce B7.7.1973 Tampa FL BR/TR/6'1"/(181–200) [SeaA91 25/656] d6.18 [DL 1997 Fla N 181]																											
2005	Bos A	1	0	1.000	34	0	0	0	0	0	0	23	26.1	23	20	1	5	24	1	22	6.49	-30	.240	.416		93	-0.3
Total	10	14	18	.438	315	0	0	0	0	93	19	231	322.2	249	154	30	23	200	9	396	4.07	+10	.213	.337		948	3.5
MANZANILLO, JOSIAS Josias (Adams) B10.16.1967 San Pedro de Macoris, D.R. BR/TR/6'0"/(190–205) d10.5 b–Ravelo																											
1991	Bos A	0	0	+	1	0	0	0	0	0	0	0	1	2	2	0	0	3	0	1	18.00	-76	.400	.625		0	-0.1
Total	11	13	15	.464	267	1	0	0	0	6	17	176	342	330	198	46	18	153	20	300	4.71	-7	.255	.338	-15	240	-3.7
MARCHILDON, PHIL Philip Joseph "Babe" B10.25.1913 Penetanguishene ON, Can. D1.10.1997 Toronto ON, Can. BR/TR/5'11"/175 d9.22 Mil 1943–45																											
1950	Bos A	0	0	+	1	0	0	0		0			1.1	1	1	0	0	2		0	6.75	-27	.200	.429		0	0.0
Total	9	68	75	.476	185	162	82	6		2			1214.1	1084	605	81	23	684		481	3.93	+0	.240	.342	-3	0	-2.3
MARCUM, JOHNNY John Alfred "Footsie" B9.9.1909 Campbellsburg KY D9.10.1984 Louisville KY BL/TR/5'11"/197 d9.7																											
1933	Phi A	3	2	.600	5	5	4	2		0			37	28	12	0	0	20		14	1.95	+120	.200	.300	+15		1.1
1934	Phi A	14	11	.560	37	31	17	2		0			232	257	131	13	4	88		92	4.50	-3	.280	.346	+16		0.2
1935	Phi A	17	12	.586	39	27	19	2		3			242.2	256	125	9	2	83		99	4.08	+11	.268	.328	+16		2.1
1936	Bos A	8	13	.381	31	23	9	1		1			174	194	100	14	0	52		57	4.81	+10	.281	.332	-22		1.2
1937	Bos A	13	11	.542	37	23	9	1		3			183.2	230	104	17	2	47		59	4.85	-2	.306	.348	-5		0.7
1938	Bos A	5	6	.455	15	11	7	0		0			92.1	113	49	11	0	25		25	4.09	+20	.298	.342	-14		0.7
1939	StL A	2	5	.286	12	6	2	0		0			47.2	66	43	12	1	10		14	7.74	-37	.332	.367	-34		-1.2
1939	Chi A	3	3	.500	19	6	2	0		0			90	125	66	15	0	19		32	6.00	-21	.326	.357	+40		-0.5
1939	Year	5	8	.385	31	12	4	0		0			137.2	191	109	27	1	29		46	6.60	-28	.328	.361	+3		-1.7
Total	7	65	63	.508	195	132	69	8		7			1099.1	1269	630	91	9	344		392	4.66	+1	.287	.340	+1		4.3
Team	3	26	30	.464	83	57	25	2		4			450	537	253	42	2	124		141	4.68	+7	.295	.341	-14		2.6
/180I	1	10	12	.464	33	23	10	1		2			180	215	101	17	1	50		56	4.68	+7	.295	.341	-14		1.0
MARICHAL, JUAN Juan Antonio (Sanchez) "Manito" B10.20.1937 Laguna Verde, D.R. BR/TR/6'0"/185 d7.19 HF1983																											
1974	Bos A	5	1	.833	11	9	0	0	3	0	0	2	57.1	61	32	3	2	14	1	21	4.87	-21	.270	.317	+38	58	-0.5
Total	16	243	142	.631	471	457	244	52	326	2	0	11	3507	3153	1329	320	40	709	82	2303	2.89	+22	.237	.277	+16	58	27.7
MARTINEZ, ANASTACIO Anastacio Euclides B11.3.1978 Santa Cruz de Villomello, D.R. BR/TR/6'2"/180 d5.22																											
2004	Bos A	2	1	.667	11	0	0	0	0	0	0	6	10.2	13	10	2	1	6	0	5	8.44	-42	.289	.385		0	-0.6
MARTINEZ, PEDRO Pedro Jaime (b Pedro Jaime (Martinez)) B10.25.1971 Manoguayabo, D.R. BR/TR/5'11"/(150–180) d9.24 b–Ramon																											
1992	LA N	0	1	.000	2	1	0	0	1	0	0	1	8	6	2	0	0	1	0	8	2.25	+54	.200	.226	-74	0	0.1
1993	LA N	10	5	.667	65	2	0	0	0	2	1	48	107	76	34	5	4	57	4	119	2.61	+48	.201	.309	+5	0	2.0
1994	Mon N	11	5	.688	24	23	1	1	14	1	0	1	144.2	115	58	11	11	45	3	142	3.42	+24	.220	.294	-1	0	1.3
1995	Mon N	14	10	.583	30	30	2	2	18	0	0	0	194.2	158	79	21	11	66	1	174	3.51	+22	.227	.302	-4	0	1.7
1996	Mon N★	13	10	.565	33	33	4	1	18	0	0	0	216.2	189	100	19	3	70	3	222	3.70	+17	.232	.294	+5	0	1.0
1997	Mon N★	17	8	.680	31	31	**13**	4	25	0	0	0	241.1	158	65	16	9	67	5	305	**1.90**	+120	**.184**	**.249**	-21	0	**5.8**
1998	†Bos A☆	19	7	.731	33	33	3	2	25	0	0	0	233.2	188	82	26	8	67	3	251	2.89	+64	.217	.278	+0	0	4.6
1999	†Bos A★	**23**	4	**.852**	31	29	5	1	24	0	0	2	213.1	160	56	9	9	37	1	**313**	**2.07**	+141	**.205**	**.248**	+3	15	**8.1**
2000	Bos A✷	18	6	.750	29	29	7	0	25	0	0	0	217	128	44	17	14	32	0	**284**	**1.74**	+188	**.167**	**.213**	-16	16	**8.4**
2001	Bos A	7	3	.700	18	18	1	0	13	0	0	0	116.2	84	33	5	6	25	0	163	2.39	+86	.199	.253	-15	90	2.1
2002	Bos A☆	20	4	**.833**	30	30	2	0	21	0	0	0	199.1	144	62	13	15	40	1	**239**	**2.26**	+98	**.198**	**.254**	+21	0	5.2
2003	†Bos A	14	4	.778	29	29	3	0	21	0	0	0	186.2	147	52	7	9	47	0	206	**2.22**	+110	**.215**	**.272**	+2	26	4.4
2004	†Bos A	16	9	.640	33	33	1	1	22	0	0	0	217	193	99	26	16	61	0	227	3.90	+25	.238	.301	-9	0	2.6
2005	NY N✷	15	8	.652	31	31	4	1	23	0	0	0	217	159	69	19	4	47	3	208	2.82	+47	.204	**.252**	-1	0	2.9
2006	NY N✷	9	8	.529	23	23	0	0	13	0	0	0	132.2	108	72	19	10	39	2	137	4.48	-2	.220	.289	-12	60	-0.3
Total	15	206	92	.691	442	375	46	17	263	3	1	52	2645.2	2013	907	213	129	701	26	2998	2.81	+60	.209	.270	-3	207	49.9
Team	7	117	37	.760	203	201	22	4	151	0	0	2	1383.2	1044	428	103	77	309	5	1683	2.52	+89	.206	.261	-1	147	35.4
/180I	1	15	5	.760	26	26	3	1	20	0	0	0	180	136	56	13	10	40	1	219	2.52	+89	.206	.261	-1	19	4.6
MARTINEZ, RAMON Ramon Jaime (b Ramon Jaime (Martinez)) B3.22.1968 Santo Domingo, D.R. BR/TR/6'4"/(166–186) d8.13 b–Pedro																											
1999	†Bos A	2	1	.667	4	4	0	0	2	0	0	0	20.2	14	8	2	2	8	0	15	3.05	+63	.192	.286	+22	150	0.6
2000	Bos A	10	8	.556	27	27	0	0	7	0	0	0	127.2	143	94	16	9	67	3	89	6.13	-18	.283	.372	+9	31	-1.7
Total	14	135	88	.605	301	297	37	20	176	0	0	4	1895.2	1691	880	170	66	795	41	1427	3.67	+6	.239	.319	+10	389	4.1
Team	2	12	9	.571	31	31	0	0	9	0		0	148.1	157	102	18	11	75	3	104	5.70	-12	.272	.361	+11	181	-1.1
/180I	2	15	11	.571	38	38	0	0	11	0		0	180	191	124	22	13	91	4	126	5.70	-12	.272	.361	+11	220	-1.3
MASTERSON, WALT Walter Edward B6.22.1920 Philadelphia PA BR/TR/6'2"/(180–189) d5.8 Mil 1943–45																											
1949	Bos A	3	4	.429	18	5	1	0		4			55	58	30	2	0	35		19	4.25	+2	.283	.387	+48	0	-0.1
1950	Bos A	8	6	.571	33	15	6	0		1			129.1	145	91	15	1	82		60	5.64	-13	.287	.387	+18	0	-1.2
1951	Bos A	3	0	1.000	30	1	0	0		2			59.1	53	24	1	0	32		39	3.34	+34	.228	.322	+0	0	0.3
1952	Bos A	1	1	.500	5	1	0	0		0			9.1	18	12	1	0	11		3	11.57	-66	.400	.518	-78	0	-1.2
Total	14	78	100	.438	399	184	70	15		20			1649.2	1613	888	101	28	886	1	815	4.15	-4	.258	.353	-8	0	-5.1
Team	4	15	11	.577	86	22	7	0		7			253	274	157	19	1	160		121	5.02	-7	.278	.379	+20		-2.2
/60G	3	10	8	.577	60	15	5	0		5			176.2	191	110	13	1	112		84	5.01	-7	.278	.379	+20		-1.5
MATTHEWS, WILLIAM William Calvin B1.12.1878 Mahanoy City PA D1.23.1946 Mt.Carbon PA TR d8.28																											
1909	Bos A	0	0	+	5	1	0	0		0			16.2	16	8	1	0	10		6	3.24	-23	.271	.377	+13		-0.2
MAYS, CARL Carl William "Sub" B11.12.1891 Liberty KY D4.4.1971 ElCajon CA BL/TR/5'11.5"/195 d4.15																											
1915	Bos A	6	5	.545	38	6	2	0		**7**			131.2	119	54	0	5	21		65	2.60	+7	.244	.282	+18		0.4
1916	†Bos A	18	13	.581	44	24	14	2		3			245	208	79	3	9	74		76	2.39	+16	.234	.299	-3		2.8
1917	Bos A	22	9	.710	35	33	27	2		0			289	230	81	1	14	74		91	1.74	+48	.221	.282	+8		4.0
1918	†Bos A	21	13	.618	35	33	**30**	0		0			293.1	230	94	2	11	81		114	2.21	+21	.221	.284	+19		3.7
1919	Bos A	5	11	.313	21	16	14	2		2			146	131	57	2	5	40		53	2.47	+23	.247	.306	-22		0.6
1919	NY A	9	3	.750	13	13	12	1		0			120	96	34	3	5	37		54	1.65	+93	.216	.283	+28		2.3
1919	Year	14	14	.500	34	29	26	3		2			266	227	91	5	10	77		107	2.10	+48	.233	.295	+1		2.9
1920	NY A	26	11	.703	45	37	26	0		2			312	310	127	13	7	84		92	3.06	+25	.263	.316	+33		3.5
1921	†NY A	**27**	9	**.750**	**49**	38	30	1		**7**			**336.2**	332	145	11	9	76		70	3.05	+39	.257	.303	+52		5.4
1922	†NY A	13	14	.481	34	29	21	1		2			240	257	111	12	7	50		41	3.60	+11	.285	.327	+10		1.5
1923	NY A	5	2	.714	23	7	2	0		0			81.1	119	59	8	4	32		16	6.20	-36	.357	.420	+38		-1.2
1924	Cin N	20	9	.690	37	27	15	2		0			226	238	97	3	4	36		63	3.15	+20	.270	.302	+7		3.0
1925	Cin N	3	5	.375	12	5	3	0		2			51.2	60	22	0	2	13		10	3.31	+24	.294	.342	-34		0.9
1926	Cin N	19	12	.613	39	33	**24**	3		1			281	286	112	3	4	53		58	3.14	+18	.269	.306	+14		2.9
1927	Cin N	3	7	.300	14	9	6	0		0			82	89	39	1	1	10		17	3.51	+8	.276	.300	-48		1.0
1928	Cin N	4	1	.800	14	6	4	1		1			62.2	67	33	3	0	22		10	3.88	+2	.275	.335	+19		0.1
1929	NY N	7	2	.778	37	8	1	0		4			123	140	67	8	2	31		32	4.32	+6	.287	.333	+19		0.8
Total	15	208	126	.623	490	324	231	29		31			3021.1	2912	1211	73	89	734		862	2.92	+19	.257	.307	+17		31.7
Team	5	72	51	.585	173	112	87	6		12			1105	918	365	8	44	290		399	2.21	+24	.230	.290	+5		11.5
/180I	1	12	8	.585	28	18	14	1		2			180	150	59	1	7	47		65	2.21	+24	.230	.290	+5		1.9

Year	Tm Lg	W	L	Pct	G	GS	CG	ShO	QS	SV	BS	QR	IP	H	R	HR	HB	BB	IB	SO	ERA	AERA	OAV	OOB	Sup	DL	PW
MCCABE, DICK Richard James B2.21.1896 Mamaroneck NY D4.11.1950 Buffalo NY BR/TR/5'10.5"/159 d5.30																											
1918	Bos A	0	1	.000	3	1	0	0		0			9.2	13	4	0	0	2		3	2.79	-4	.351	.385	-100		0.0
1922	Chi A	1	0	1.000	3	0	0	0		0			3.1	4	2	0	0	0		1	5.40	-25	.308	.308			-0.1
Total	2	1	1	.500	6	1	0	0		0			13	17	6	0	0	2		4	3.46	-12	.340	.365	-100		-0.1
MCCALL, WINDY John William B7.18.1925 San Francisco CA BL/TL/6'0"/180 d4.25 Col San Francisco																											
1948	Bos A	0	1	.000	1	1	0	0		0			1.1	6	3	1	0	1		0	20.25	-78	.600	.636	-18	0	-0.3
1949	Bos A	0	0	+	5	0	0	0		0			9.1	13	12	2	0	10		8	11.57	-62	.333	.469		0	-0.3
Total	7	11	15	.423	134	15	4	0	0	12		1	253.2	249	134	26	11	103	11	144	4.22	-6	.257	.334	-12	0	-0.1
Team	2	0	1	.000	6	1	0	0		0			10.2	19	15	3	0	11		8	12.66	-66	.388	.500	-18		-0.6
MCCARTHY, TOM Thomas Michael B6.18.1961 Lundstahl, West Germany BR/TR/6'0"/180 [BosA79 7/182] d7.5																											
1985	Bos A	0	0	+	3	0	0	0	0	0	0	1	5	7	6	1	0	4	0	2	10.80	-60	.350	.440		0	-0.2
Total	3	3	2	.600	40	0	0	0	0	1	0	25	84.2	88	40	9	4	26	0	34	3.61	+8	.272	.330		0	0.5
MCDERMOTT, MICKEY Maurice Joseph "Maury" B8.29.1929 Poughkeepsie NY D8.7.2003 Phoenix AZ BL/TL/6'2"/(170–190) d4.24 C1▲																											
1948	Bos A	0	0	+	7	0	0	0		0			23.1	16	18	2	1	35		17	6.17	-29	.208	.460		0	-0.1
1949	Bos A	5	4	.556	12	12	6	2		0			80	63	37	5	3	52		50	4.05	+8	.220	.345	+20	0	0.5
1950	Bos A	7	3	.700	38	15	4	0		5			130	119	80	8	2	124		96	5.19	-6	.249	.406	+35	0	0.4
1951	Bos A	8	8	.500	34	19	9	1		3			172	141	72	9	5	92		127	3.35	+33	.226	.330	-5	0	2.0
1952	Bos A	10	9	.526	30	21	7	2		0			162	139	70	14	3	92		117	3.72	+6	.234	.340	-5	0	0.9
1953	Bos A	18	10	.643	32	30	8	4		0			206.1	169	82	9	2	109		92	3.01	+40	.224	.323	-8	0	4.1
1954	Was A	7	15	.318	30	26	11	1		1			196.1	172	95	8	3	110		95	3.44	+3	.239	.339	-7	0	0.2
1955	Was A	10	10	.500	31	20	8	1		1			156	140	75	9	9	100	2	78	3.75	+2	.243	.361	-4	0	1.0
1956	†NY A	2	6	.250	23	9	1	0		0			87	85	46	10	0	47	2	38	4.24	-9	.261	.350	-8	0	-0.1
1957	KC A	1	4	.200	29	4	0	0	0	0		17	69	68	47	9	0	50	2	29	5.48	-28	.266	.382	+41	0	0.0
1958	Det A	0	0	+	2	0	0	0	0	0		1	2	6	4	0	0	2	0	0	9.00	-55	.500	.571		0	-0.1
1961	StL N	1	0	1.000	19	0	0	0	0	4		15	27	29	17	3	0	15	2	15	3.67	+20	.271	.358		0	-0.1
1961	KC A	0	0	+	4	0	0	0	0	0		0	5.2	14	12	0	0	10	0	3	14.29	-71	.452	.585		0	-0.3
1961	Major	1	0	1.000	23	0	0	0	0	4		15	32	43	29	3	0	25	2	18	5.51	+4	.312	.415		0	-0.4
Total	12	69	69	.500	291	156	54	11	0	14		33	1316.2	1161	655	86	28	838	8	757	3.91	+5	.240	.354	+2	0	8.4
Team	6	48	34	.585	153	97	34	9		8			773.2	647	359	47	16	504		499	3.80	+14	.230	.350	+3		7.8
/180I	1	11	8	.585	36	23	8	2		2			180	151	84	11	4	117		116	3.80	+14	.230	.350	+3		1.8
MCDILL, ALLEN Allen Gabriel B8.23.1971 Greenville MS BL/TL/6'0"/(155–170) [NYN92 20/553] d5.15 Col Arkansas Tech																											
1997	KC A	0	0	+	3	0	0	0	0	0	0	1	4	3	6	1	1	8	0	2	13.50	-65	.214	.522		0	-0.2
1998	KC A	0	0	+	7	0	0	0	0	0	0	3	6	9	7	3	0	2	0	3	10.50	-54	.333	.379		0	-0.2
2000	Det A	0	0	+	13	0	0	0	0	0	0	6	10	13	9	2	1	1	0	7	7.20	-32	.317	.349		0	-0.1
2001	Bos A	0	0	+	15	0	0	0	0	0	1	9	14.2	13	9	2	1	7	1	16	5.52	-20	.236	.328		0	-0.1
Total	4	0	0	+	38	0	0	0	0	0	1	19	34.2	38	31	8	3	18	1	28	7.79	-40	.277	.371		0	-0.6
MCDONALD, JIM Jimmie Le Roy "Hot Rod" B5.17.1927 Grants Pass OR BR/TR (BB 1950–51)/5'10.5"/(185–192) d7.27																											
1950	Bos A	1	0	1.000	9	0	0	0		0			19	23	9	1	1	10		5	3.79	+29	.329	.420		0	0.2
Total	9	24	27	.471	136	55	15	3	0	1		16	468	489	262	24	8	231	2	158	4.27	-11	.273	.357	+9	60	-2.8
MCGLOTHEN, LYNN Lynn Everatt B3.27.1950 Monroe LA D8.14.1984 Dubach LA BL/TR/6'2"/(182–215) [BosA68 3/60] d6.25																											
1972	Bos A	8	7	.533	22	22	4	1	13	0	0	0	145	135	66	9	7	59	1	112	3.41	-5	.247	.326	+6	0	-0.1
1973	Bos A	1	2	.333	6	3	0	0	0	0	1	0	23	39	23	6	1	8	0	16	8.22	-51	.386	.429	+33	0	-1.1
Total	11	86	93	.480	318	201	41	13	112	2	6	71	1497.2	1553	735	127	25	572	63	939	3.98	-5	.270	.336	-7	42	-3.0
Team	2	9	9	.500	28	25	4	1	13	0	1	0	168	174	89	15	8	67	1	128	4.07	-18	.269	.342	+9		-1.2
/180I	2	10	10	.500	30	27	4	1	14	0	1	0	180	186	95	16	9	72	1	137	4.07	-18	.269	.342	+9		-1.3
MCGRAW, BOB Robert Emmett B4.10.1895 LaVeta CO D6.2.1978 Boise ID BR/TR/6'2"/160 d9.25 Mil 1918–19 Col Georgetown																											
1919	Bos A	0	2	.000	10	1	0	0		0			26.2	33	23	0	3	17		6	6.75	-55	.347	.461	+82		-0.9
Total	9	26	38	.406	168	47	17	1		6			579.1	675	393	31	11	265		164	5.00	-19	.303	.380	+1		-6.9
MCHALE, MARTY Martin Joseph B10.30.1886 Stoneham MA D5.7.1979 Hempstead NY BR/TR/5'11.5"/174 d9.28 Col Maine																											
1910	Bos A	0	2	.000	2	2	1	0		0			13.2	15	8	0	1	6		14	4.61	-45	.259	.338	+5		-0.4
1911	Bos A	0	0	+	4	1	0	0		0			9.1	19	12	1	1	3		3	9.64	-66	.475	.523	+98		-0.3
1916	Bos A	0	1	.000	2	1	0	0		0			6	7	7	0	1	4		1	3.00	-8	.280	.400	-100		-0.3
Total	6	11	30	.268	64	44	23	1		1			358.1	381	182	7	8	81		131	3.57	-20	.276	.320	-19		-3.1
Team	3	0	3	.000	8	4	1	0		0			29	41	27	1	3	13		18	5.90	-52	.333	.410	+2		-1.0
MCKAIN, ARCHIE Archie Richard "Happy" B5.12.1911 Delphos KS D5.21.1985 Salina KS BB/TL (BL 1941, 43)/5'10"/175 d4.25																											
1937	Bos A	8	8	.500	36	18	3	0		2			137	152	84	7	0	64		66	4.66	+2	.273	.348	-3		0.2
1938	Bos A	5	4	.556	37	5	1	0		6			99.2	119	60	6	2	44		27	4.52	+9	.297	.369	-4		0.2
1939	Det A	5	6	.455	32	11	4	1		4			129.2	120	66	6	0	54		49	3.68	+33	.247	.322	-10		1.5
1940	†Det A	5	0	1.000	27	0	0	0		3			51	48	18	2	0	25		24	2.82	+68	.247	.333			1.1
1941	Det A	2	1	.667	15	0	0	0		0			43	58	24	3	0	11		14	5.02	-10	.330	.369		0	0.0
1941	StL A	0	1	.000	8	0	0	0		1			10	16	9	2	1	4		2	8.10	-47	.364	.429		0	-0.4
1941	Year	2	2	.500	23	0	0	0		1			53	74	33	5	1	15		16	5.60	-20	.336	.381		0	-0.4
1943	StL A	1	1	.500	10	0	0	0		0			16	16	9	0	0	6		6	3.94	-16	.242	.306		0	-0.2
Total	6	26	21	.553	165	34	8	1		16			486.1	529	270	26	3	208		188	4.26	+12	.275	.347	-4	0	2.4
Team	2	13	12	.520	73	23	4	0		8			236.2	271	144	13	2	108		93	4.60	+5	.283	.357	-3		0.4
/180I	2	10	9	.520	56	17	3	0		6			180	206	110	10	2	82		71	4.60	+5	.283	.357	-3		0.3
MCLAUGHLIN, JUD Justin Theodore B3.24.1912 Brighton MA D9.27.1964 Cambridge MA BL/TL/5'11"/155 d6.23 Col Boston College																											
1931	Bos A	0	0	+	9	0	0	0		0			12	23	16	1	0	8		3	12.00	-64	.397	.470			-0.4
1932	Bos A	0	0	+	1	0	0	0		0			3	5	5	0	0	4		0	15.00	-70	.385	.529			-0.1
1933	Bos A	0	0	+	6	0	0	0		0			8.2	14	7	1	0	5		1	6.23	-30	.359	.432			-0.1
Total	3	0	0	+	16	0	0	0		0			23.2	42	28	2	0	17		4	10.27	-58	.382	.465			-0.6
MCMAHON, DON Donald John B1.4.1930 Brooklyn NY D7.22.1987 Los Angeles CA BR/TR/6'2"/(213–225) d6.30 C11																											
1966	Bos A	8	7	.533	49	0	0	0	0	9		39	78	65	29	7	3	38	8	57	2.65	+43	.232	.326		0	1.7
1967	Bos A	1	2	.333	11	0	0	0	0	2		7	17.2	14	8	3	0	13	0	10	3.57	-2	.215	.346		0	-0.1
Total	18	90	68	.570	874	2	0	0	1	153	17	816	1310.2	1054	482	104	34	579	84	1003	2.96	+19	.221	.308	-32	23	10.9
Team	2	9	9	.500	60	0	0	0	0	11		46	95.2	79	37	10	3	51	8	67	2.82	+33	.229	.330			1.6
/60G	2	9	9	.500	60	0	0	0	0	11		46	95.2	79	37	10	3	51	8	67	2.82	+33	.229	.330			1.6
MCMAHON, DOC Henry John B12.19.1886 Woburn MA D12.11.1929 Woburn MA TR d10.6 Col Holy Cross																											
1908	Bos A	1	0	1.000	1	1	1	0		0			9	14	3	0	0	0		3	3.00	-18	.350	.350	+206		0.0
MCNAUGHTON, GORDON Gordon Joseph B7.31.1910 Chicago IL D8.6.1942 Chicago IL BR/TR/6'1"/190 d8.13 Col Loyola–Chicago																											
1932	Bos A	0	1	.000	6	2	0	0		0			21	21	15	1	3	22		6	6.43	-30	.259	.434	+33		-0.1
MELENDEZ, JOSE Jose Luis (Garcia) B9.2.1965 Naguabo, PR BR/TR/6'2"/(175–190) d9.11																											
1993	Bos A	2	1	.667	9	0	0	0	0	0	1	6	16	10	4	2	0	5	3	14	2.25	+106	.179	.238		147	0.7
1994	Bos A	0	1	.000	10	0	0	0	0	0	0	5	16.1	20	11	3	2	8	2	9	6.06	-17	.323	.417		0	-0.1
Total	5	16	14	.533	109	12	0	0	5	3	4	70	220.2	197	90	27	7	60	15	172	3.47	+12	.241	.294	-24	147	2.0
Team	2	2	2	.500	19	0	0	0	0	0	1	11	32.1	30	15	5	2	13	5	23	4.18	+16	.254	.333		147	0.6
MENDOZA, RAMIRO Ramiro B6.15.1972 Los Santos, Pan BR/TR/6'2"/(154–195) d5.25																											
2003	Bos A	3	5	.375	37	5	0	0	0	0	1	19	66.2	98	51	10	5	20	4	36	6.75	-31	.349	.397	+31	53	-1.3
2004	†Bos A	2	1	.667	27	0	0	0	0	0	0	20	30.2	25	12	3	1	7	1	13	3.52	+39	.225	.277		98	0.4
Total	10	59	40	.596	342	62	2	2	25	16	16	196	797	891	412	82	35	181	23	463	4.30	+6	.283	.326	+20	263	2.9
Team	2	5	6	.455	64	5	0	0	0	0	1	39	97.1	123	63	13	6	27	5	49	5.73	-17	.314	.364	+31	151	-0.9
/60G	2	5	6	.455	60	5	0	0	0	0	1	37	91.1	115	59	12	6	25	5	46	5.73	-17	.314	.364	+31	142	-0.8

Year	Tm Lg	W	L	Pct	G	GS	CG	ShO	QS	SV	BS	QR	IP	H	R	HR	HB	BB	IB	SO	ERA	AERA	OAV	OOB	Sup	DL	PW
MEOLA, MIKE Emile Michael B10.19.1905 New York NY D9.1.1976 Fair Lawn NJ BR/TR/5'11"/175 d4.24																											
1933	Bos A	0	0	+	3	0	0	0		0			2.1	5	6	0	0	2		1	23.14	-81	.417	.500			-0.2
1936	StL A	0	1	.000	9	0	0	0		0			19.1	29	20	0	1	13		6	9.31	-42	.358	.453			-0.2
1936	Bos A	0	2	.000	6	3	1	0		1			21.1	29	17	0	1	10		8	5.48	-3	.326	.400	-50		-0.1
1936	Year	0	3	.000	15	3	1	0		1			40.2	58	37	0	2	23		14	7.30	-27	.341	.426	-51		-0.3
Total	2	0	3	.000	18	3	1	0		1			43	63	43	0	2	25		15	8.16	-35	.346	.431	-50		-0.5
Team	2	0	2	.000	9	3	1	0		1			23.2	34	23	0	1	12		9	7.23	-28	.337	.412	-50		-0.3
MERCKER, KENT Kent Franklin B2.1.1968 Indianapolis IN BL/TL/6'2"/(175–205) [AtlN86 1/5] d9.22																											
1999	†Bos A	2	0	1.000	5	5	0	0	2	0	0	0	25.2	23	12	0	1	13	0	17	3.51	+42	.235	.327	-18	16	0.3
Total	17	73	67	.521	677	150	2	1	59	25	26	366	1311.2	1294	671	153	32	599	46	911	4.16	+4	.259	.340	+2	350	0.4
MEREDITH, CLA Olise Cla B6.4.1983 Richmond VA BR/TR/6'0"/180 [BosA04 6/185] d5.8 Col Virginia Commonwealth																											
2005	Bos A	0	0	+	3	0	0	0	0	0	0	0	2.1	6	7	1	1	4	0	0	27.00	-83	.462	.611		0	-0.2
Total	2	5	1	.833	48	0	0	0	0	0	2	39	53	36	13	4	3	10	3	37	2.21	+89	.190	.243		0	1.8
MERENA, SPIKE John Joseph B11.18.1909 Paterson NJ D3.9.1977 Bridgeport CT BL/TL/6'0"/185 d9.16																											
1934	Bos A	1	2	.333	4	3	2	1		0			24.2	20	8	2	1	16		7	2.92	+65	.222	.346	-40		0.5
MEYER, RUSS Russell Charles "Rowdy","The Mad Monk" B10.25.1923 Peru IL D11.16.1998 Oglesby IL BB/TR/6'1"/(175–185) d9.13 C1																											
1957	Bos A	0	0	+	2	1	0	0	0	0		1	5	10	5	0	0	3	0	1	5.40	-26	.417	.464	-10	0	0.0
Total	13	94	73	.563	319	219	65	13	0	5		13	1531.1	1606	761	136	15	541	10	672	3.99	-1	.271	.333	+16	92	-2.6
MICHAELS, JOHN John Joseph B7.10.1907 Bridgeport CT D11.18.1996 Sebring FL BL/TL/5'10.5"/154 d4.16 gs–Jason																											
1932	Bos A	1	6	.143	28	8	2	0		0			80.2	101	59	4	3	27		16	5.13	-12	.304	.362	-29		-0.6
MIDKIFF, DICK Richard B9.28.1914 Gonzales TX D10.30.1956 Temple TX BR/TR/6'2"/185 d4.24 Col Texas																											
1938	Bos A	1	1	.500	13	2	0	0		0			35.1	43	30	5	0	21		10	5.09	-3	.305	.395	+7		-0.2
MILLER, WADE Wade T. B9.13.1976 Reading PA BR/TR/6'2"/(185–220) [HouN96 20/594] d7.7 Col Alvernia																											
2005	Bos A	4	4	.500	16	16	0	0	5	0	0	0	91	96	53	8	3	47	0	64	4.95	-8	.267	.354	+2	90	-0.2
Total	8	62	45	.579	148	144	5	1	80	0	0	2	880.2	814	427	103	27	371	15	743	4.00	+13	.246	.325	+3	387	5.8
MILLS, DICK Richard Alan B1.29.1945 Boston MA BR/TR/6'3"/199 [BosA66 S3/54] d9.7																											
1970	Bos A	0	0	+	2	0	0	0	0	0	0	1	3.2	6	4	0	1	3	0	3	2.45	+62	.353	.476		0	0.0
MINARCIN, RUDY Rudolph Anthony "Buster" B3.25.1930 N.Vandergrift PA BR/TR/6'0"/195 d4.11																											
1955	Cin N	5	9	.357	41	12	3	1		1			115.2	116	73	17	3	51	7	45	4.90	-14	.261	.339	+0	0	-0.9
1956	Bos A	1	0	1.000	3	1	0	0		0			9.2	9	4	2	1	8	0	5	2.79	+65	.250	.400	-4	0	0.2
1957	Bos A	0	0	+	26	0	0	0	0	2		17	44.2	44	30	5	1	30	4	20	4.43	-10	.267	.375		0	-0.2
Total	3	6	9	.400	70	13	3	1	0	3		17	170	169	107	24	5	89	11	70	4.66	-10	.262	.352	+1	0	-0.9
Team	2	1	0	1.000	29	1	0	0	0	2		17	54.1	53	34	7	2	38	4	25	4.14	-1	.264	.380	-4		0.0
MINCHEY, NATE Nathan Derek B8.31.1969 Austin TX BR/TR/6'8"/225 [MonN87 2/36] d9.12																											
1993	Bos A	1	2	.333	5	5	1	0	3	0	0	0	33	35	16	5	0	8	2	18	3.55	+31	.265	.307	+3	0	0.2
1994	Bos A	2	3	.400	6	5	0	0	1	0	0	0	23	44	26	1	0	14	2	15	8.61	-41	.427	.483	-42	0	-1.5
1996	Bos A	0	2	.000	2	2	0	0	0	0	0	0	6	16	11	1	0	5	0	4	15.00	-66	.533	.583	-9	94	-0.9
1997	Col N	0	0	+	2	0	0	0	0	0	0	0	2	5	3	0	0	1	0	1	13.50	-62	.556	.600		0	-0.1
Total	4	3	7	.300	15	12	1	0	4	0	0	0	64	100	56	7	0	28	4	38	6.75	-28	.365	.418	-18	94	-2.3
Team	3	3	7	.300	13	12	1	0	4	0	0	0	62	95	53	7	0	27	4	37	6.53	-26	.358	.412	-18	94	-2.2
MITCHELL, CHARLIE Charles Ross B6.24.1962 Dickson TN BR/TR/6'3"/170 [BosA82*4/95] d8.9 b–John Col Columbia St. (TN) CC																											
1984	Bos A	0	0	+	10	0	0	0	0	0	0	8	16.1	14	7	1	2	6	3	7	2.76	+53	.226	.314		0	0.1
1985	Bos A	0	0	+	2	0	0	0	0	0	1	1	1.2	5	3	1	0	0	0	2	16.20	-73	.500	.500		0	-0.1
Total	2	0	0	+	12	0	0	0	0	0	1	9	18	19	10	2	2	6	3	9	4.00	+5	.264	.338		0	0.0
MITCHELL, FRED Frederick Francis (b Frederick Francis Yapp) B6.5.1878 Cambridge MA D10.13.1970 Newton MA BR/TR/5'9.5"/185 d4.27 M7/C3▲																											
1901	Bos A	6	6	.500	17	13	10	0		0			108.2	115	67	2	11	51		34	3.81	-7	.268	.360	-4		-0.4
1902	Bos A	0	1	.000	1	0	0	0		0			4	8	5	1	0	5		2	11.25	-68	.421	.542			-0.4
Total	5	31	50	.383	97	86	71	2		1			718.1	806	470	16	53	303		216	4.10	-22	.286	.366	+3		-6.7
Team	2	6	7	.462	18	13	10	0		0			112.2	123	72	3	11	56		36	4.07	-13	.275	.368	-4		-0.8
MOFORD, HERB Herbert B8.6.1928 Brooksville KY D12.3.2005 Cincinnati OH BR/TR/6'1"/(170–175) d4.12																											
1959	Bos A	0	2	.000	4	2	0	0	0	0		1	8.2	10	11	3	0	6	0	7	11.42	-64	.286	.390	-2	0	-1.1
Total	4	5	13	.278	50	14	6	0	8	3		11	157.1	143	94	21	10	64	9	78	5.03	-19	.244	.327	-24	0	-1.9
MOLYNEAUX, VINCE Vincent Leo B8.17.1888 Lewiston NY D5.4.1950 Stamford CT BR/TR/6'0"/180 d7.5 Col Villanova																											
1917	StL A	0	0	+	7	0	0	0		0			22	18	15	0	0	20		4	4.91	-47	.237	.396			-0.3
1918	Bos A	1	0	1.000	6	0	0	0		0			10.2	3	4	0	0	8		1	3.38	-20	.086	.256			-0.1
Total	2	1	0	1.000	13	0	0	0		0			32.2	21	19	0	0	28		5	4.41	-40	.189	.353			-0.4
MONBOUQUETTE, BILL William Charles B8.11.1936 Medford MA BR/TR/5'11"/(190–195) d7.18 C3																											
1958	Bos A	3	4	.429	10	8	3	0	14	0		13	54.1	52	25	4	0	20	4	30	3.31	+21	.251	.313	-2	0	0.3
1959	Bos A	7	7	.500	34	17	4	0	14	0		13	151.2	165	86	15	3	33	1	87	4.15	-2	.285	.323	-4	0	-0.9
1960	Bos A★	14	11	.560	35	30	12	3	18	0		3	215	217	91	18	2	68	9	134	3.64	+11	.263	.319	-9	0	0.9
1961	Bos A	14	14	.500	32	32	12	1	22	0		0	236.1	233	106	24	0	100	1	161	3.39	+23	.254	.326	-12	0	1.9
1962	Bos A☆	15	13	.536	35	35	11	4	22	0		0	235.1	227	100	22	3	65	1	153	3.33	+24	.251	.302	-9	0	1.6
1963	Bos A☆	20	10	.667	37	36	13	1	20	0		0	266.2	258	119	31	0	42	6	174	3.81	-1	.250	.279	+19	0	-0.2
1964	Bos A	13	14	.481	36	35	7	5	21	1		1	234	258	114	34	1	40	4	120	4.04	-5	.277	.306	-5	0	-0.6
1965	Bos A	10	18	.357	35	35	10	2	20	0		0	228.2	239	114	32	1	40	5	110	3.70	+1	.269	.299	-8	0	-0.4
1966	Det A	7	8	.467	30	14	2	1	5	0		9	102.2	120	60	14	3	22	4	61	4.73	-26	.293	.330	+7	0	-1.9
1967	Det A	0	0	+	2	0	0	0	0	0		2	2	1	0	0	0	0	0	2	0.00	-100	.143	.143		0	0.0
1967	NY A	6	5	.545	33	10	2	1	9	1		15	133.1	122	39	6	4	17	7	53	2.36	+32	.246	.274	-14	0	1.0
1967	Year	6	5	.545	35	10	2	1	9	1		17	135.1	123	39	6	4	17	7	55	2.33	+34	.245	.273	-14	0	1.0
1968	NY A	5	7	.417	17	11	2	0	6	0		3	89.1	92	47	7	3	13	2	32	4.43	-34	.264	.293	-2	0	-1.7
1968	SF N	0	1	.000	7	0	0	0	0	1		5	12	11	9	4	0	2	0	5	3.75	-22	.239	.265		0	-0.3
1968	Major	5	8	.385	24	11	2	0	6	1		8	101	103	56	11	3	15	2	37	4.35	-33	.261	.289	-2	0	-2.0
Total	11	114	112	.504	343	263	78	18	171	3		64	1961.1	1995	910	211	20	462	44	1122	3.68	+4	.263	.305	-3	0	-0.3
Team	8	96	91	.513	254	228	72	16	151	1		30	1622	1649	755	180	10	408	31	969	3.69	+7	.262	.307	-4		2.6
/180I	1	11	10	.513	28	25	8	2	17	0		3	180	183	84	20	1	45	3	108	3.69	+7	.262	.307	-4		0.3
MOORE, WILCY William Wilcy "Cy" B5.20.1897 Bonita TX D3.29.1963 Hollis OK BR/TR/6'0"/195 d4.14																											
1927	†NY A	19	7	.731	50	12	6	1		**13**			213	185	68	3	1	59		75	**2.28**	+69	**.234**	**.289**	+19		4.5
1928	NY A	4	4	.500	35	2	0	0		2			60.1	71	44	4	0	31		18	4.18	-10	.286	.366	+103		-0.9
1929	NY A	6	4	.600	41	0	0	0		8			61	64	36	4	0	19		21	4.13	-7	.268	.322			-0.6
1931	Bos A	11	13	.458	53	15	8	1		**10**			185.1	195	88	7	1	55		37	3.88	+11	.269	.322	-36		1.3
1932	Bos A	4	10	.286	37	2	0	0		4			84.1	98	59	5	1	42		28	5.23	-14	.284	.363	-72		-1.1
1932	†NY A	2	0	1.000	10	1	0	0		4			25	27	8	1	0	6		8	2.52	+62	.273	.314	-16		0.4
1932	Year	6	10	.375	47	3	0	0		8			109.1	125	67	6	1	48		36	4.61	-5	.282	.353	-55		-0.7
1933	NY A	5	6	.455	35	0	0	0		8			62	92	53	1	0	20		17	5.52	-30	.333	.378			-2.9
Total	6	51	44	.537	261	32	14	2		49			691	732	356	25	3	232		204	3.70	+10	.269	.327	-9		0.7
Team	2	15	23	.395	90	17	8	1		14			269.2	293	147	12	2	97		65	4.31	+1	.274	.336	-40		0.2
/60G	1	10	15	.395	60	11	5	1		9			179.2	195	98	8	1	65		43	4.31	+1	.274	.336	-40		0.1
MOREHEAD, DAVE David Michael "Moe" B9.5.1942 San Diego CA BR/TR/6'1"/(180–200) d4.13																											
1963	Bos A	10	13	.435	29	29	6	1	14	0		0	174.2	137	82	20	0	99	2	136	3.81	-1	.211	.316	-11	0	-0.4
1964	Bos A	8	15	.348	32	30	3	1	15	0		2	166.2	156	101	14	4	112	2	139	4.97	-22	.248	.358	-14	0	-2.6
1965	Bos A	10	18	.357	34	33	5	2	17	0		0	192.2	157	103	18	3	113	1	163	4.06	-8	.217	.325	-20	0	-1.1
1966	Bos A	1	2	.333	12	5	0	0	0	0		5	28	31	17	7	0	7	0	20	5.46	-30	.274	.317	+20	16	-0.3

Year	Tm Lg	W	L	Pct	G	GS	CG	ShO	QS	SV	BS	QR	IP	H	R	HR	HB	BB	IB	SO	ERA	AERA	OAV	OOB	Sup	DL	PW
1967	†Bos A	5	4	.556	10	9	1	1	3	0		1	47.2	48	24	0	2	22	0	40	4.34	-20	.264	.348	+11	0	-0.7
1968	Bos A	1	4	.200	11	9	3	1	5	0		1	55	52	17	3	2	20	0	28	2.45	+29	.249	.320	-2	0	0.3
1969	KC A	2	3	.400	21	2	0	0	0	0	0	14	33	28	22	7	0	28	1	32	5.73	-35	.239	.384	-76	36	-0.9
1970	KC A	3	5	.375	28	17	1	0	9	1	0	8	121.2	121	64	9	1	62	3	69	3.62	+3	.261	.347	+0	0	-0.2
Total	8	40	64	.385	177	134	19	6	63	1	0	31	819.1	730	430	78	12	463	9	627	4.15	-10	.237	.336	-10	52	-5.9
Team	6	35	56	.385	128	115	18	6	54	0		9	664.2	581	344	62	11	373	5	526	4.17	-11	.232	.332	-11	16	-4.8
/180I	2	9	15	.385	35	31	5	2	15	0		2	180	157	93	17	3	101	1	142	4.17	-11	.232	.332	-11	4	-1.3
MORET, ROGER Rogelio (Torres) B9.16.1949 Guayama, PR BB/TL/6'4"/(160–175) d9.13																											
1970	Bos A	1	0	1.000	3	1	0	0	0	0	0	2	8.1	7	3	0	0	4	0	2	3.24	+23	.226	.314	-11	0	0.1
1971	Bos A	4	3	.571	13	7	4	1	5	0	0	4	71	50	24	5	2	40	4	47	2.92	+28	.205	.321	+3	0	0.5
1972	Bos A	0	0	+	3	0	0	0	0	0	0	3	5	5	3	0	0	6	0	4	3.60	-10	.263	.440		0	0.0
1973	Bos A	13	2	.867	30	15	5	2	8	3	1	10	156.1	138	60	19	3	67	2	90	3.17	+27	.238	.318	+20	21	1.4
1974	Bos A	9	10	.474	31	21	10	1	12	2	0	8	173.1	158	79	15	2	79	4	111	3.74	+3	.243	.323	-13	0	0.1
1975	†Bos A	14	3	.824	36	16	4	1	11	1	0	13	145	132	60	8	2	76	6	80	3.60	+13	.248	.341	+29	0	0.9
1976	Atl N	3	5	.375	27	12	1	0	4	1	2	11	77.1	84	44	7	1	27	2	30	5.00	-24	.280	.339	+18	57	-0.9
1977	Tex A	3	3	.500	18	8	0	0	4	4	0	6	72.1	59	41	6	0	38	2	39	3.73	+9	.220	.313	-1	81	-0.1
1978	Tex A	0	1	.000	7	2	0	0	1	1	0	3	14.2	23	8	1	1	2	0	5	4.91	-24	.390	.413	-64	126	-0.1
Total	9	47	27	.635	168	82	24	5	45	12	3	60	723.1	656	322	61	11	339	20	408	3.66	+8	.245	.329	+7	285	1.9
Team	6	41	18	.695	116	60	23	5	36	6	1	40	559	490	229	47	9	272	16	334	3.43	+15	.238	.327	+8	21	3.0
/180I	2	13	6	.695	37	19	7	2	12	2	0	13	180	158	74	15	3	88	5	108	3.43	+15	.238	.327	+8	7	1.0
MORGAN, CY Harry Richard B11.10.1878 Pomeroy OH D6.28.1962 Wheeling WV BR/TR/6'0"/175 d9.18																											
1907	Bos A	6	6	.500	16	13	9	2		0			114.1	77	35	1	3	34		50	1.97	+31	.193	.262	-39		0.4
1908	Bos A	14	13	.519	30	26	17	2		1			205	166	78	7	10	90		99	2.46	+0	.226	.319	-6		-0.1
1909	Bos A	2	6	.250	12	10	5	0		1			64.2	52	19	0	6	31		30	2.37	+6	.240	.350	-32		0.3
Total	10	78	78	.500	210	172	107	15		3			1445.1	1180	586	18	95	578		667	2.51	+5	.229	.318	+5		-0.4
Team	3	22	25	.468	58	49	31	4		2			384	295	132	8	19	155		179	2.30	+9	.218	.308	-20		0.6
/180I	1	10	12	.468	27	23	15	2		1			180	138	62	4	9	73		84	2.30	+9	.218	.308	-20		0.3
MORRIS, ED Walter Edward "Big Ed" B12.7.1899 Foshee AL D3.3.1932 Century FL BR/TR/6'2"/185 d8.5																											
1922	Chi N	0	0	+	5	0	0	0		0			12	22	17	1	0	6		5	8.25	-49	.386	.444			-0.3
1928	Bos A	19	15	.559	47	29	20	0		5			257.2	255	118	7	5	80		104	3.53	+17	.264	.323	-5		1.5
1929	Bos A	14	14	.500	33	26	17	2		1			208.1	227	118	7	2	95		73	4.45	-4	.282	.360	-19		-0.1
1930	Bos A	4	9	.308	18	9	3	0		0			65.1	67	42	1	0	38		28	4.13	+12	.260	.355	-65		0.2
1931	Bos A	5	7	.417	37	14	3	0		0			130.2	131	80	4	5	74		46	4.75	-9	.260	.361	-17		-0.7
Total	5	42	45	.483	140	78	43	2		6			674	702	375	20	12	293		256	4.19	+1	.271	.348	-19		0.6
Team	4	42	45	.483	135	78	43	2		6			662	680	358	19	12	287		251	4.12	+3	.268	.346	-19		0.9
/180I	1	11	12	.483	37	21	12	1		2			180	185	97	5	3	78		68	4.12	+3	.268	.346	-19		0.2
MORRISSEY, FRANK Michael Joseph "Deacon" B5.5.1876 Baltimore MD D2.22.1939 Baltimore MD TR/5'4"/140 d7.13																											
1901	Bos A	0	0	+	1	0	0	0		0			4.1	5	1	0	2	2		1	2.08	+70	.278	.409			0.0
Total	2	1	3	.250	6	5	5	0		0			44.1	45	17	0	4	10		14	2.23	+25	.262	.317	-35		0.1
MORTON, KEVIN Kevin Joseph B8.3.1968 Norwalk CT BR/TL/6'2"/185 [BosA89 1/29] d7.5 Col Seton Hall																											
1991	Bos A	6	5	.545	16	15	1	0	7	0	0	0	86.1	93	49	9	1	40	2	45	4.59	-6	.284	.356	+27	0	-0.2
MOSELEY, EARL Earl Victor "Vic" B9.7.1887 Middleburg OH D7.1.1963 Alliance OH BR/TR/5'9.5"/168 d6.17																											
1913	Bos A	8	5	.615	24	15	7	3		0			120.2	105	56	1	0	49		62	3.13	-6	.248	.326	-11		-0.4
Total	4	49	48	.505	136	100	65	12		3			855.2	775	367	13	6	340		469	3.01	-6	.247	.322	-1		-3.3
/180I	1	12	7	.615	36	22	10	4		0			180	157	84	1	0	73		92	3.13	-6	.248	.326	+33		-0.6
MOSER, WALTER Walter Fredrick B2.27.1881 Concord NC D12.10.1946 Philadelphia PA BR/TR/5'9"/170 d9.3																											
1906	Phi N	0	4	.000	6	4	4	0		0			42.2	49	35	0	1	15		17	3.59	-27	.295	.357	-86		-0.9
1911	Bos A	0	1	.000	6	3	1	0		0			24.2	37	28	0	1	11		11	4.01	-18	.366	.434	+32		-0.4
1911	StL A	0	2	.000	2	2	0	0		0			3.1	11	12	0	0	4		2	21.60	-84	.478	.556	-47		-1.0
1911	Year	0	3	.000	8	5	1	0		0			28	48	40	0	1	15		13	6.11	-46	.387	.457	+1		-1.4
Total	2	0	7	.000	14	9	5	0		0			70.2	97	75	0	2	30		30	4.58	-37	.334	.401	-30		-2.3
MOYER, JAMIE Jamie B11.18.1962 Sellersville PA BL/TL/6'0"/(170–180) [ChiN84 6/135] d6.16 Col St. Josephs (PA)																											
1996	Bos A	7	1	.875	23	10	0	0	3	0	0	8	90	111	50	14	1	27	2	50	4.50	+13	.300	.347	+29	0	0.5
Total	20	216	166	.565	571	518	30	9	284	0	2	31	3351	3455	1678	414	112	946	59	1992	4.17	+7	.266	.320	+2	168	11.1
MUELLER, GORDIE Joseph Gordon B12.10.1922 Baltimore MD D9.7.2006 Baltimore MD BR/TR/6'4"/200 d4.19 Col Loyola–Maryland																											
1950	Bos A	0	0	+	8	0	0	0		0			7	11	8	1	0	13		1	10.29	-52	.344	.533		0	-0.2
MUFFETT, BILLY Billy Arnold "Muff" B9.21.1930 Hammond IN BR/TR/6'1"/(186–198) d8.3 C18																											
1957	StL N	3	2	.600	23	0	0	0	2	8		38	44	35	11	1	0	13	4	21	2.25	+76	.222	.279		0	1.2
1958	StL N	4	6	.400	35	6	1	0	2	5		38	84	107	52	11	5	42	9	41	4.93	-16	.316	.397	-9	0	-0.9
1959	SF N	0	0	+	5	0	0	0	0	0		2	6.2	11	6	2	0	3	1	3	5.40	-29	.407	.467		0	-0.1
1960	Bos A	6	4	.600	23	14	4	1	12	0		6	125	116	53	6	5	36	2	75	3.24	+25	.242	.299	-33	0	0.9
1961	Bos A	3	11	.214	38	11	2	0	6	2		16	112.2	130	87	18	2	36	2	47	5.67	-27	.291	.344	-38	0	-2.1
1962	Bos A	0	0	+	1	1	0	0	0	0		0	4	8	4	0	0	2	0	1	9.00	-54	.471	.500	+30	0	-0.1
Total	6	16	23	.410	125	32	7	1	22	15		100	376.1	407	213	38	12	132	18	188	4.33	-6	.277	.339	-28	0	-1.1
Team	3	9	15	.375	62	26	6	1	18	2		22	241.2	254	144	24	7	74	4	123	4.47	-8	.269	.324	-33		-1.3
/180I	2	7	11	.375	46	19	4	1	13	1		16	180	189	107	18	5	55	3	92	4.47	-8	.269	.324	-33		-1.0
MULLIGAN, JOE Joseph Ignatius "Big Joe" B7.31.1913 Weymouth MA D6.5.1986 W.Roxbury MA BR/TR/6'4"/210 d6.28 Col Holy Cross																											
1934	Bos A	1	0	1.000	14	2	1	0		0			44.2	46	21	1	2	27		13	3.63	+32	.279	.387	+90		0.1
MULRONEY, FRANK Francis Joseph B4.8.1903 Mallard IA D11.11.1985 Aberdeen WA BR/TR/6'0"/170 d4.15 Col Iowa																											
1930	Bos A	0	1	.000	2	0	0	0		0			3	3	2	0	0	0		2	3.00	+54	.273	.273			0.0
MURPHY, JOHNNY John Joseph "Grandma" "Fireman","Fordham Johnny" B7.14.1908 New York NY D1.14.1970 New York NY BR/TR/6'2"/190 d5.19 Def 1944–45 Col Fordham																											
1947	Bos A	0	0	+	32	0	0	0		3			54.2	41	17	1	0	28		9	2.80	+39	.206	.304		0	0.5
Total	13	93	53	.637	415	40	17	0		107			1045	985	464	52	5	444		378	3.50	+17	.249	.326	+23	0	10.5
MURPHY, ROB Robert Albert B5.26.1960 Miami FL BL/TL/6'2"/(200–215) [CinN81*S1/3] d9.13 Col Florida																											
1989	Bos A	5	7	.417	74	0	0	0	0	9	7	52	105	97	38	7	1	41	8	107	2.74	+50	.251	.323		0	1.8
1990	†Bos A	0	6	.000	68	0	0	0	0	7	3	37	57	85	46	10	1	32	3	54	6.32	-35	.348	.420		0	-1.6
Total	11	32	38	.457	597	0	0	0	0	30	25	413	623.1	598	277	54	5	247	41	520	3.64	+9	.254	.324		19	2.1
Team	2	5	13	.278	142	0	0	0	0	16	10	89	162	182	84	17	2	73	11	161	4.00	+3	.289	.361			0.2
/60G	1	2	5	.278	60	0	0	0	0	7	4	38	68.1	77	35	7	1	31	5	68	4.01	+3	.289	.361			0.1
MURPHY, TOM Thomas Andrew B12.30.1945 Cleveland OH BR/TR/6'3"/(185–205) [AnaA67*S1/6] d6.13 Col Ohio U.																											
1976	Bos A	4	5	.444	37	0	0	0	0	8	5	21	81	91	43	5	2	25	11	32	3.44	+13	.290	.343		0	0.1
1977	Bos A	0	1	.000	16	0	0	0	0	0	0	6	30.2	44	25	6	0	12	0	13	6.75	-33	.338	.392		0	-0.3
Total	12	68	101	.402	439	147	22	3	79	59	29	190	1444	1425	664	123	63	493	73	621	3.78	-6	.263	.329	-11	20	-0.3
Team	2	4	6	.400	53	0	0	0	0	8	5	27	111.2	135	68	11	2	37	11	45	4.35	-7	.304	.357			-0.2
/60G	2	5	7	.400	60	0	0	0	0	9	6	31	126.1	153	77	12	2	42	12	51	4.36	-7	.304	.357			-0.2
MURPHY, WALTER Walter Joseph B9.27.1907 New York NY D3.23.1976 Houston TX BR/TR/6'1.5"/180 d4.19																											
1931	Bos A	0	0	+	2	0	0	0		0			2	4	2	0	0	1		0	9.00	-52	.444	.500			0.0
MURRAY, GEORGE George King "Smiler" B9.23.1898 Charlotte NC D10.18.1955 Memphis TN BR/TR/6'2"/200 d5.8 Col North Carolina St.																											
1922	NY A	3	2	.600	22	2	0	0		0			56.2	53	27	0	1	26		14	3.97	+1	.255	.340	-15		0.2
1923	Bos A	7	11	.389	39	18	5	0		0			177.2	190	111	9	7	87		40	4.91	-16	.291	.380	-31		-1.3
1924	Bos A	2	9	.182	28	7	0	0		0			80.1	97	68	6	7	32		27	6.72	-35	.307	.383	-45		-2.2
1926	Was A	6	3	.667	12	12	5	0		0			81.1	89	56	1	6	37		28	5.64	-31	.287	.374	+40		-1.6

Year	Tm Lg	W	L	Pct	G	GS	CG	ShO	QS	SV	BS	QR	IP	H	R	HR	HB	BB	IB	SO	ERA	AERA	OAV	OOB	Sup	DL	PW
1927	Was A	1	1	.500	7	3	0	0		0			18	18	18	1	2	15		5	7.00	-42	.265	.412	+30		-0.6
1933	Chi A	0	0	+	2	0	0	0		0			2.1	3	2	0	0	2		0	7.71	-45	.375	.500			0.0
Total	6	19	26	.422	110	42	10	0		0			416.1	450	282	17	23	199		114	5.38	-24	.288	.376	-10		-5.5
Team	2	9	20	.310	67	25	5	0		0			258	287	179	15	14	119		67	5.48	-23	.296	.381	-35		-3.5
/180I	1	6	14	.310	47	17	3	0		0			180	200	125	10	10	83		47	5.48	-23	.296	.381	-35		-2.4
MURRAY, MATT Matthew Michael B9.26.1970 Boston MA BL/TR/6'6"/235 [AtlN88 2/41] d8.12 [DL 1993 Atl N 97]																											
1995	Bos A	0	1	.000	2	1	0	0	0	0	0	0	3.1	11	10	1	0	3	0	1	18.90	-74	.524	.583	-23	0	-0.9
Total	1	0	3	.000	6	2	0	0	0	0	0	1	14	21	18	4	1	8	0	4	9.64	-54	.350	.435	-18	97	-1.2
MUSSER, PAUL Paul B6.24.1889 Millheim PA D7.7.1973 State College PA BR/TR/6'0"/175 d6.6 Mil 1918–19 Col Susquehanna																											
1912	Was A	0	0	+	7	2	0	0		2			20.2	16	7	0	2	16		10	2.61	+28	.225	.382	+44		0.0
1919	Bos A	0	2	.000	5	4	1	0		0			19.2	26	16	0	0	8		14	4.12	-27	.342	.405	+23		-0.6
Total	2	0	2	.000	12	6	1	0		2			40.1	42	23	0	2	24		24	3.35	-5	.286	.393	+27		-0.6
MUSTAIKIS, ALEX Alexander Dominick B3.26.1909 Chelsea MA D1.17.1970 Scranton PA BR/TR/6'3"/180 d7.7																											
1940	Bos A	0	1	.000	6	1	0	0		0			15	15	18	1	0	15		6	9.00	-50	.254	.405	-22		-0.3
MYERS, ELMER Elmer Glenn B3.2.1894 York Springs PA D7.29.1976 Collingswood NJ BR/TR/6'2"/185 d10.6 Mil 1918																											
1920	Bos A	9	1	.900	12	10	9	1		0			97	90	30	1	2	24		34	2.13	+71	.249	.299	+42		1.8
1921	Bos A	8	12	.400	30	20	11	0		0			172	217	107	11	10	53		40	4.87	-13	.315	.373	-6		-1.4
1922	Bos A	0	1	.000	3	1	0	0		0			5.2	10	11	1	2	3		1	17.47	-76	.370	.469	-59		-1.0
Total	8	55	72	.433	185	127	78	8		7			1102	1148	625	30	51	440		428	4.06	-20	.275	.352	-6		-9.4
Team	3	17	14	.548	45	31	20	1		0			274.2	317	148	13	14	80		75	4.16	-3	.294	.351	+8		-0.6
/180I	2	11	9	.548	29	20	13	1		0			180	208	97	9	9	52		49	4.16	-3	.294	.351	+8		-0.4
MYERS, MIKE Michael Stanley B6.26.1969 Cook Co. IL BL/TL/6'4"/(197–220) [SFN90 4/122] d4.25 Col Iowa St. [DL 1994 Fla N 60]																											
2004	†Bos A	1	0	1.000	25	0	0	0	0	0	0	17	15	16	7	2	0	6	1	9	4.20	+16	.267	.333		0	0.1
2005	†Bos A	3	1	.750	65	0	0	0	0	0	1	50	37.1	30	14	3	2	13	2	21	3.13	+45	.224	.300		0	0.6
Total	12	21	24	.467	811	0	0	0	0	14	24	587	487.1	466	245	52	40	233	31	402	4.23	+14	.254	.349		60	2.3
Team	2	4	1	.800	90	0	0	0	0	0	1	67	52.1	46	21	5	2	19	3	30	3.44	+35	.237	.310			0.7
/60G	1	3	1	.800	60	0	0	0	0	0	1	45	35	31	14	3	1	13	2	20	3.43	+35	.237	.310			0.5
NABHOLZ, CHRIS Christopher William B1.5.1967 Harrisburg PA BL/TL/6'5"/(210–215) [MonN88 2/49] d6.11 Col Towson																											
1994	Bos A	3	4	.429	8	8	0	0	2	0	0	0	42	44	32	5	2	29	1	23	6.64	-24	.282	.399	-29	0	-0.8
Total	6	37	35	.514	141	100	4	2	50	0	0	29	611.2	542	289	41	20	278	15	405	3.94	-3	.240	.327	+1	154	-0.0
NAGLE, JUDGE Walter Harold "Lucky" B3.10.1880 Santa Rosa CA D5.26.1971 Santa Rosa CA BR/TR/6'0"/176 d4.26																											
1911	Pit N	4	2	.667	8	3	1	0		1			27.1	33	16	3	1	6		11	3.62	-5	.324	.367	-27		-0.3
1911	Bos A	1	1	.500	5	1	0	0		0			27	27	12	2	0	6		12	3.33	-2	.262	.303	+10		-0.1
1911	Major	5	3	.625	13	4	1	0		1			54	60	28	5	1	12		23	3.48	-4	.293	.335	-18		-0.4
Total	1	5	3	.625	13	4	1	0		1			54.1	60	28	5	1	12		23	3.48	-3	.293	.335	-18		-0.4
NAGY, MIKE Michael Timothy B3.25.1948 Bronx NY BR/TR/6'3"/(195–200) d4.21																											
1969	Bos A	12	2	.857	33	28	7	1	14	0	0	4	196.2	183	84	10	11	106	3	84	3.11	+23	.245	.347	+28	0	0.6
1970	Bos A	6	5	.545	23	20	4	0	8	0	0	2	128.2	138	71	16	2	64	2	56	4.48	-11	.275	.358	+14	0	-0.3
1971	Bos A	1	3	.250	12	7	0	0	3	0	1	3	38	46	29	4	0	20	1	9	6.63	-44	.315	.395	-11	0	-1.1
1972	Bos A	0	0	+	1	0	0	0	0	0	0	0	2	3	2	0	1	0	0	2	9.00	-64	.375	.400		0	-0.1
1973	StL N	0	2	.000	9	7	0	0	2	0	0	2	40.2	44	21	4	1	15	2	14	4.20	-13	.282	.345	-14	0	-0.2
1974	Hou N	1	1	.500	9	0	0	0	0	0	0	4	12.2	17	13	3	1	5	0	5	8.53	-59	.309	.371		0	-1.0
Total	6	20	13	.606	87	62	11	1	27	0	1	15	418.2	431	220	37	16	210	8	170	4.15	-8	.267	.356	+15	0	-2.1
Team	4	19	10	.655	69	55	11	1	25	0	1	9	365.1	370	186	30	14	190	6	151	3.99	-3	.264	.356	+18		-0.9
/180I	2	9	5	.655	34	27	5	0	12	0	0	4	180	182	92	15	7	94	3	74	3.99	-3	.264	.356	+18		-0.4
NEAL, BLAINE Blaine B4.6.1978 Marlton NJ BL/TR/6'5"/(205–250) [FlaN96 4/104] d9.3																											
2005	Bos A	0	1	.000	8	0	0	0	0	0	0	3	8	15	9	2	0	3	0	3	9.00	-50	.429	.462		0	-0.4
Total	5	5	4	.556	113	0	0	0	0	0	4	62	124	161	74	13	3	51	8	93	5.08	-19	.319	.379		84	-1.0
NELSON, JOE Joseph George B10.25.1974 Alameda CA BR/TR/6'2"/(185–210) [AtlN96 4/122] d6.13 Col San Francisco																											
2004	Bos A	0	0	+	3	0	0	0	0	0	0	1	2.2	4	5	0	2	3	0	5	16.88	-71	.364	.563		0	-0.1
Total	3	1	1	.500	48	0	0	0	0	9	1	33	49.1	48	36	6	4	29	4	49	6.39	-27	.257	.365		110	-0.2
NEUBAUER, HAL Harold Charles B5.13.1902 Hoboken NJ D9.9.1949 Providence RI BR/TR/6'0.5"/185 d6.12 Col Brown																											
1925	Bos A	1	0	1.000	7	0	0	0		0			10.1	17	18	2	0	11		4	12.19	-63	.378	.500			-0.7
NEWHAUSER, DON Donald Louis B11.7.1947 Miami FL BR/TR/6'4"/(195–200) [BosA67*2/24] d6.15 Col Broward (FL) CC																											
1972	Bos A	4	2	.667	31	0	0	0	0	4	1	23	37	30	11	2	2	25	5	27	2.43	+33	.226	.354		0	0.6
1973	Bos A	0	0	+	9	0	0	0	0	1	0	7	12	9	2	0	1	13	2	8	0.00	-100	.205	.390		49	0.2
1974	Bos A	0	1	.000	2	0	0	0	0	0	0	0	3.2	5	4	0	0	4	1	2	9.82	-61	.357	.474		0	-0.4
Total	3	4	3	.571	42	0	0	0	0	5	1	30	52.2	44	17	2	3	42	8	37	2.39	+45	.230	.372		49	0.4
/60G	4	6	4	.571	60	0	0	0	0	7	1	43	75.1	63	24	3	4	60	11	53	2.39	+45	.230	.372		70	0.6
NEWSOM, BOBO Louis Norman "Buck" B8.11.1907 Hartsville SC D12.7.1962 Orlando FL BR/TR/6'2"/(195–220) d9.11																											
1937	Bos A	13	10	.565	30	27	14	1		0			207.2	193	114	14	3	119		127	4.46	+6	.243	.344	-18		0.8
Total	20	211	222	.487	600	483	246	31		21			3759.1	3769	1908	206	61	1732		2082	3.98	+7	.261	.342	-11	0	5.3
/180I	1	11	9	.565	26	23	12	1		0			180	167	99	12	3	103		110	4.46	+6	.243	.344	-29		0.7
NEWSOME, DICK Heber Hampton B12.13.1909 Ahoskie NC D12.15.1965 Ahoskie NC BR/TR/6'0"/185 d4.25 Col Wake Forest																											
1941	Bos A	19	10	.655	36	29	17	2		0			213.2	235	115	13	7	79		58	4.13	+1	.277	.344	+12	0	0.5
1942	Bos A	8	10	.444	24	23	11	0		0			158	174	98	11	0	67		40	5.01	-26	.278	.348	+5	0	-1.9
1943	Bos A	8	13	.381	25	22	8	2		0			154.1	166	83	8	5	68		40	4.49	-26	.274	.352	-10	0	-2.5
Total	3	35	33	.515	85	74	36	4		0			526	575	296	32	12	214		138	4.50	-16	.276	.347	+4	0	-3.9
/180I	1	12	11	.515	29	25	12	1	0	0	0	0	180	197	101	11	4	73		47	4.50	-16	.276	.347	-64		-1.3
NICHOLS, CHET Chester Raymond Jr. B2.22.1931 Pawtucket RI D3.27.1995 Lincoln RI BB/TL/6'1.5"/(170–195) d4.19 Mil 1952–53 f–Chet																											
1951	Bos N	11	8	.579	33	19	12	3		2			156	142	61	4	1	69		71	**2.88**	+27	.246	.327	-8	0	1.4
1954	Mil N	9	11	.450	35	20	5	1		1			122.1	132	68	5	4	65		55	4.41	-16	.286	.376	+9	0	-1.7
1955	Mil N	9	8	.529	34	21	6	0		1			144	139	79	20	1	67	6	44	4.00	-6	.253	.334	+23	0	-0.9
1956	Mil N	0	1	.000	2	0	0	0		0			4	9	3	1	0	3	1	2	6.75	-49	.563	.632		0	-0.3
1960	Bos A	0	2	.000	6	1	0	0	0	0		4	12.2	12	6	0	0	4	0	11	4.26	-5	.240	.296	-78	0	0.0
1961	Bos A	3	2	.600	26	2	0	0	0	3		20	51.2	40	12	3	0	26	1	20	2.09	+99	.221	.317	-58	31	1.4
1962	Bos A	1	1	.500	29	1	0	0	0	3		20	57	61	25	3	0	22	1	33	3.00	+38	.276	.339	+95	0	0.3
1963	Bos A	1	3	.250	21	7	0	0	1	0		9	52.2	61	30	8	0	24	0	27	4.78	-21	.298	.365	+1	0	-0.4
1964	Cin N	0	0	+	3	0	0	0	0	0		1	3	4	2	1	0	0	0	3	6.00	-40	.308	.308		0	0.0
Total	9	34	36	.486	189	71	23	4	1	10		54	603.1	600	286	45	6	280	9	266	3.64	+5	.264	.344	+4	31	-0.2
Team	4	5	8	.385	82	11	0	0	1	6		53	174	174	73	14	0	76	2	91	3.36	+20	.265	.338	-8	31	1.3
/60G	3	4	6	.385	60	8	0	0	1	4		39	127.1	127	53	10	0	56	1	67	3.36	+20	.265	.338	-8	23	1.0
NIPPER, AL Albert Samuel B4.2.1959 San Diego CA BR/TR/6'0"/(188–195) [BosA80 8/206] d9.6 C5 Col Truman St.																											
1983	Bos A	1	1	.500	3	2	1	0	2	0	0	1	16	17	4	0	1	7	0	5	2.25	+95	.293	.373	-59	0	0.4
1984	Bos A	11	6	.647	29	24	6	0	12	0	0	3	182.2	183	86	18	7	52	1	84	3.89	+8	.257	.313	+12	0	0.8
1985	Bos A	9	12	.429	25	25	5	0	12	0	0	0	162	157	83	14	9	82	3	85	4.06	+6	.256	.350	-14	7	0.5
1986	†Bos A	10	12	.455	26	26	3	0	8	0	0	0	159	186	108	24	4	47	2	79	5.38	-22	.290	.340	+5	37	-2.4
1987	Bos A	11	12	.478	30	30	6	0	14	0	0	0	174	196	115	30	7	62	1	89	5.43	-16	.284	.345	+11	24	-1.8
1988	Chi N	2	4	.333	22	12	0	0	7	1	0	9	80	72	37	9	3	34	2	27	3.04	+20	.238	.321	+2	47	0.0
1990	Cle A	2	3	.400	9	5	0	0	1	0	0	1	24	35	19	2	2	19	0	12	6.75	-42	.354	.448	-8	0	-1.3
Total	7	46	50	.479	144	124	21	0	56	1	0	14	797.2	846	452	97	33	303	9	381	4.52	-6	.271	.339	+2	115	-3.8
Team	5	42	43	.494	113	107	21	0	48	0	0	4	693.2	739	396	86	28	250	7	342	4.62	-6	.272	.337	+3	68	-2.5
/180I	1	11	11	.494	29	28	5	0	12	0	0	1	180	192	103	22	7	65	2	89	4.62	-6	.272	.337	+3	18	-0.6

Year	Tm Lg	W	L	Pct	G	GS	CG	ShO	QS	SV	BS	QR	IP	H	R	HR	HB	BB	IB	SO	ERA	AERA	OAV	OOB	Sup	DL	PW
NIPPERT, MERLIN Merlin Lee B9.1.1938 Mangum OK BR/TR/6'1"/175 d9.12 Col Oklahoma St.																											
1962	Bos A	0	0	+	4	0	0	0	0	0		2	6	4	3	1	0	4	1	3	4.50	-8	.200	.320		0	0.0
NIXON, WILLARD Willard Lee B6.17.1928 Taylorsville GA D12.10.2000 Rome GA BL/TR/6'2"/195 d7.7 Col Auburn																											
1950	Bos A	8	6	.571	22	15	2	0		2			101.1	126	75	7	2	58		57	6.04	-19	.310	.398	+3	0	-1.6
1951	Bos A	7	4	.636	33	14	2	1		1			125	136	79	12	7	56		70	4.90	-9	.285	.368	+29	0	-0.3
1952	Bos A	5	4	.556	23	13	5	0		0			103.2	115	64	12	4	61		50	4.86	-19	.290	.390	+28	0	-0.7
1953	Bos A	4	8	.333	23	15	5	1		0			116.2	114	57	6	1	59		57	3.93	+7	.254	.343	-1	0	0.4
1954	Bos A	11	12	.478	31	30	8	2		0			199.2	182	102	16	9	87		102	4.06	+1	.248	.333	-12	0	0.8
1955	Bos A	12	10	.545	31	31	7	3		0			208	207	102	10	3	85	2	95	4.07	+5	.259	.330	-16	0	1.3
1956	Bos A	9	8	.529	23	22	9	1		0			145.1	142	79	9	8	57	2	74	4.21	+10	.255	.331	+6	0	0.6
1957	Bos A	12	13	.480	29	29	11	1	19	0		0	191	207	86	10	7	56	3	96	3.68	+8	.280	.335	+14	0	1.3
1958	Bos A	1	7	.125	10	8	2	0	17	0		0	43.1	48	30	7	0	11	0	15	6.02	-33	.281	.324	-27	77	-1.2
Total	9	69	72	.489	225	177	51	9	36	3		0	1234	1277	674	89	41	530	7	616	4.39	-3	.270	.348	+1	77	0.6
/180I	1	10	11	.489	33	26	7	1	0	0	0	0	180	186	98	13	6	77	0	90	4.39	-3	.270	.348	-85	11	0.1
NOMO, HIDEO Hideo B8.31.1968 Osaka, Japan BR/TR/6'2"/(200–235) d5.2																											
2001	Bos A	13	10	.565	33	33	2	2	16	0	0	0	198	171	105	26	3	96	2	**220**	4.50	-1	.231	.320	+8	0	0.1
Total	11	123	109	.530	320	318	16	9	177	0	0	2	1972	1758	984	248	38	904	31	1915	4.21	-1	.239	.324	+1	99	-0.9
/180I	1	12	9	.565	30	30	2	2	15	0		0	180	155	95	24	3	87	2	200	4.50	-1	.231	.320	-2		0.1
NOURSE, CHET Chester Linwood B8.7.1887 Ipswich MA D4.20.1958 Clearwater FL BR/TR/6'3"/185 d7.27 Col Brown																											
1909	Bos A	0	0	+	3	0	0	0		0			5	5	5	0	0	5		3	7.20	-65	.263	.417			-0.2
OBERLIN, FRANK Frank Rufus "Flossie" B3.29.1876 Elsie MI D1.6.1952 Ashley IN BR/TR/6'1"/165 d9.20																											
1906	Bos A	1	3	.250	4	4	4	0		0			34	38	20	0	2	13		13	3.18	-13	.286	.358	-21		-0.3
1907	Bos A	1	5	.167	12	4	2	0		0			46	48	31	2	2	24		18	4.30	-40	.271	.365	-80		-1.1
1907	Was A	2	6	.250	11	8	3	0		0			48.2	57	38	0	2	12		18	4.62	-48	.294	.341	-13		-2.1
1907	Year	3	11	.214	23	12	5	0		0			94.2	105	69	2	4	36		36	4.47	-44	.283	.353	-37		-3.2
1909	Was A	1	4	.200	9	4	1	0		0			41	41	22	1	6	16		13	3.73	-35	.266	.358	-35		-0.7
1910	Was A	0	6	.000	8	6	6	0		0			57.1	52	32	0	2	23		18	2.98	-16	.259	.341	-55		-0.7
Total	4	5	24	.172	44	26	16	0		0			227	236	143	3	14	88		80	3.77	-33	.275	.352	-38		-4.9
Team	2	2	8	.200	16	8	6	0		0			80	86	51	2	4	37		31	3.82	-31	.277	.362	-50		-1.4
O'BRIEN, BUCK Thomas Joseph B5.9.1882 Brockton MA D7.25.1959 Boston MA BR/TR/5'10"/188 d9.9																											
1911	Bos A	5	1	.833	6	5	5	2		0			47.2	30	9	0	1	21		31	0.38	+768	.180	.275	-34		1.7
1912	†Bos A	20	13	.606	37	34	25	2		0			275.2	237	107	3	10	90		115	2.58	+32	.237	.306	-9		2.1
1913	Bos A	4	9	.308	15	12	6	0		0			90.1	103	42	0	0	35		54	3.69	-20	.307	.373	-1		-0.5
1913	Chi A	0	2	.000	6	3	0	0		0			18.1	21	14	0	0	13		4	3.93	-26	.323	.436	-24		-0.4
1913	Year	4	11	.267	21	15	6	0		0			108.2	124	56	0	0	48		58	3.73	-21	.310	.384	-6		-0.9
Total	3	29	25	.537	64	54	36	4		0			432	391	172	3	11	159		204	2.63	+25	.250	.323	-11		2.9
Team	3	29	23	.558	58	51	36	4		0			413.2	370	158	3	11	146		200	2.57	+28	.246	.317	-10		3.3
/180I	1	13	10	.558	25	22	16	2		0			180	161	69	1	5	64		87	2.57	+28	.246	.317	-10		1.4
O'DOUL, LEFTY Francis Joseph B3.4.1897 San Francisco CA D12.7.1969 San Francisco CA BL/TL/6'0"/180 d4.29▲																											
1919	NY A	0	0	+	3	0	0	0		0			5	7	6	0	0	4		2	3.60	-11	.304	.407			-0.1
1920	NY A	0	0	+	2	0	0	0		0			3.2	4	2	0	1	2		2	4.91	-22	.286	.412			0.0
1922	NY A	0	0	+	6	0	0	0		0			16	24	13	0	0	12		5	3.38	+19	.353	.450			0.0
1923	Bos A	1	1	.500	23	1	0	0		0			53	69	50	2	4	31		10	5.43	-24	.337	.433	+21		-0.7
Total	4	1	1	.500	34	1	0	0		0			77.2	104	71	2	5	49		19	4.87	-17	.335	.434	+21		-0.8
OHKA, TOMO Tomokazu B3.18.1976 Kyoto, Japan BR/TR (BB 2005p)/6'1"/(179–200) d7.19																											
1999	Bos A	1	2	.333	8	2	0	0	0	0	0	5	13	21	12	2	0	6	0	8	6.23	-20	.362	.415	+12	0	-0.5
2000	Bos A	3	6	.333	13	12	0	0	6	0	0	0	69.1	70	25	7	2	26	0	40	3.12	+61	.263	.331	-50	0	1.7
2001	Bos A	2	5	.286	12	11	0	0	2	0	0	0	52.1	69	40	7	2	19	0	37	6.19	-28	.317	.375	-7	0	-1.2
Total	8	48	58	.453	174	162	5	1	82	0	0	7	943	1037	482	112	30	261	25	538	4.04	+10	.280	.330	-8	172	3.1
Team	3	6	13	.316	33	25	0	0	8	0	0	5	134.2	160	77	16	4	51	0	85	4.61	+4	.295	.358	-26		0.0
/180I	4	8	17	.316	44	33	0	0	11	0	0	7	180	214	103	21	5	68	0	114	4.61	+4	.295	.358	-26		0.0
OJEDA, BOB Robert Michael B12.17.1957 Los Angeles CA BL/TL/6'1"/(185–195) d7.13 Col Sequoias (CA) [JC]																											
1980	Bos A	1	1	.500	7	7	0	0	1	0	0	0	26	39	20	2	0	14	1	12	6.92	-38	.361	.434	+5	0	-0.4
1981	Bos A	6	2	.750	10	10	2	0	7	0	0	0	66.1	50	25	6	2	25	2	28	3.12	+26	.212	.292	+19	0	0.7
1982	Bos A	4	6	.400	22	14	0	0	3	0	0	5	78.1	95	53	13	1	29	0	52	5.63	-23	.296	.355	-3	21	-1.2
1983	Bos A	12	7	.632	29	28	5	0	17	0	0	1	173.2	173	85	15	3	73	2	94	4.04	+9	.265	.336	+4	0	0.7
1984	Bos A	12	12	.500	33	32	8	0	17	0	0	1	216.2	211	106	17	2	96	2	137	3.99	+5	.259	.336	+0	16	0.7
1985	Bos A	9	11	.450	39	22	5	0	13	1	0	13	157.2	166	74	11	2	48	9	102	4.00	+8	.273	.327	-20	0	0.8
1986	†NY N	18	5	**.783**	32	30	7	2	21	0	0	2	217.1	185	72	15	2	52	3	148	2.57	+40	.230	.278	+20	0	2.3
1987	NY N	3	5	.375	10	7	0	0	3	0	0	3	46.1	45	23	5	0	10	1	21	3.88	-1	.253	.291	+18	113	-0.1
1988	NY N	10	13	.435	29	29	5	5	19	0	0	0	190.1	158	74	6	4	33	2	133	2.88	+13	.225	.261	-19	0	1.0
1989	NY N	13	11	.542	31	31	5	2	19	0	0	0	192	179	83	16	2	78	5	95	3.47	-5	.245	.317	+12	0	-0.6
1990	NY N	7	6	.538	38	12	0	0	5	0	2	23	118	123	53	10	2	40	4	62	3.66	+3	.272	.332	+8	0	0.3
1991	LA N	12	9	.571	31	31	2	1	23	0	0	0	189.1	181	78	15	3	70	9	120	3.18	+13	.257	.323	-5	0	1.1
1992	LA N	6	9	.400	29	29	2	1	14	0	0	0	166.1	169	80	8	1	81	8	94	3.63	-4	.268	.349	-3	0	-0.4
1993	Cle A	2	1	.667	9	7	0	0	3	0	0	2	43	48	22	5	0	21	0	27	4.40	+0	.289	.363	+5	124	0.1
1994	NY A	0	0	+	2	2	0	0	0	0	0	0	3	11	8	1	0	6	0	3	24.00	-81	.611	.680	+20	0	-0.3
Total	15	115	98	.540	351	291	41	16	165	1	2	50	1884.1	1833	856	145	24	676	48	1128	3.65	+4	.257	.321	+1	274	4.7
Team	6	44	39	.530	140	113	20	0	58	1	0	20	718.2	734	363	64	10	285	16	425	4.21	+1	.268	.336	-1	37	1.3
/180I	2	11	10	.530	35	28	5	0	15	0	0	5	180	184	91	16	3	71	4	106	4.21	+1	.268	.336	-1	9	0.3
OLIVER, DARREN Darren Christopher B10.6.1970 Rio Linda CA BR/TL/6'2"/(170–220) [TexA88 3/63] d9.1 f–Bob																											
2002	Bos A	4	5	.444	14	9	1	1	3	0	0	4	58	70	30	7	6	27	0	32	4.66	-4	.317	.401	-15	0	0.0
Total	13	91	80	.532	351	228	11	4	94	2	1	87	1488	1661	894	185	77	603	27	894	4.98	-4	.285	.357	+7	235	-2.3
OLMSTED, HANK Henry Theodore B1.12.1879 Sac Bay MI D1.6.1969 Bradenton FL BR/TR/5'8.5"/147 d7.15 Col Notre Dame																											
1905	Bos A	1	2	.333	3	3	3	0		0			25	18	10	0	0	12		6	3.24	-17	.205	.300	-74		-0.1
OLSON, TED Theodore Otto B8.27.1912 Quincy MA D12.9.1980 Weymouth MA BR/TR/6'2.5"/185 d6.21 Col Dartmouth																											
1936	Bos A	1	1	.500	5	3	1	0		0			18.1	24	16	3	0	8		5	7.36	-28	.324	.390	-34		-0.3
1937	Bos A	0	0	+	11	0	0	0		0			32.1	42	28	4	0	15		11	7.24	-34	.318	.388			-0.3
1938	Bos A	0	0	+	2	0	0	0		0			7	9	5	0	0	2		2	6.43	-23	.310	.355			-0.1
Total	3	1	1	.500	18	3	1	0		0			57.2	75	49	7	0	25		18	7.18	-31	.319	.385	-34		-0.7
O'NEILL, EMMETT Robert Emmett "Pinky" B1.13.1918 San Mateo CA D10.11.1993 Sparks NV BR/TR/6'2.5"/180 d8.3 Col St. Marys (CA)																											
1943	Bos A	1	4	.200	11	5	1	0		0			57.2	56	31	3	1	46		20	4.53	-27	.256	.387	-49	0	-0.5
1944	Bos A	6	11	.353	28	22	8	1		0			151.2	154	88	6	2	89		68	4.63	-27	.265	.365	+9	0	-2.2
1945	Bos A	8	11	.421	24	22	10	1		0			141.2	134	87	5	5	117		55	5.15	-34	.258	.399	+7	0	-2.7
1946	Chi N	0	0	+	1	0	0	0		0			1	0	0	0	0	3		1	0.00	-100	.000	.500		0	0.0
1946	Chi A	0	0	+	2	0	0	0		0			3.2	4	2	0	0	5		0	0.00	-100	.333	.529		0	0.0
1946	Major	0	0	+	3	0	0	0		0			4	4	2	0	0	8		1	0.00	-100	.267	.522		0	0.0
Total	4	15	26	.366	66	49	19	2		0			355.2	348	208	14	8	260		144	4.76	-29	.261	.385	+3	0	-5.4
Team	3	15	26	.366	63	49	19	2		0			351	344	206	14	8	252		143	4.82	-30	.261	.383	+2		-5.4
/180I	2	8	13	.366	32	25	10	1		0			180	176	106	7	4	129		73	4.82	-30	.261	.383	+2		-2.8
ONTIVEROS, STEVE Steven B3.5.1961 Tularosa NM BR/TR/6'0"/(180–190) [OakA82 2/54] d6.14 Col Michigan [DL 1991 Phi N 182, 1997 Ana A 181]																											
2000	Bos A	1	1	.500	3	1	0	0	0	0	0	2	5.1	9	6	1	0	4	0	1	10.13	-50	.375	.464	-63	0	-0.5
Total	10	34	31	.523	207	73	6	2	34	19	7	88	661.2	622	308	60	17	207	13	382	3.67	+14	.248	.307	+12	886	2.5

Year	Tm Lg	W	L	Pct	G	GS	CG	ShO	QS	SV	BS	QR	IP	H	R	HR	HB	BB	IB	SO	ERA	AERA	OAV	OOB	Sup	DL	PW
OSINSKI, DAN Daniel B11.17.1933 Chicago IL BR/TR/6'2"/(190–200) d4.11																											
1966	Bos A	4	3	.571	44	1	0	0	0	2		28	67.1	68	33	8	1	28	6	44	3.61	+5	.274	.349	-54	0	0.1
1967	†Bos A	3	1	.750	34	0	0	0	0	2		25	63.2	61	19	5	0	14	2	38	2.54	+37	.243	.283		0	0.6
Total	8	29	28	.509	324	21	5	2	9	18	3	196	589.2	556	256	47	6	264	39	400	3.34	+7	.250	.330	-4	0	1.2
Team	2	7	4	.636	78	1	0	0	0	4		53	131	129	52	13	1	42	8	82	3.09	+18	.259	.317	-54		0.7
/60G	2	5	3	.636	60	1	0	0	0	3		41	100.2	99	40	10	1	32	6	63	3.09	+18	.259	.317	-54		0.5
OSTERMUELLER, FRITZ Frederick Raymond B9.15.1907 Quincy IL D12.17.1957 Quincy IL BL/TL/5'11"/175 d4.21 Mil 1945																											
1934	Bos A	10	13	.435	33	23	10	0		3			198.2	200	93	7	1	99		75	3.49	+38	.262	.348	-28		2.7
1935	Bos A	7	8	.467	22	19	10	0		1			137.2	135	67	0	3	78		41	3.92	+21	.257	.356	-20		1.4
1936	Bos A	10	16	.385	43	23	7	1		2			180.2	210	115	8	3	84		90	4.88	+9	.288	.364	-9		0.9
1937	Bos A	3	7	.300	25	7	2	0		1			86.2	101	64	2	1	44		29	4.98	-5	.286	.367	+8		-0.3
1938	Bos A	13	5	.722	31	18	10	1		2			176.2	199	98	15	3	58		46	4.58	+8	.275	.331	+27		0.9
1939	Bos A	11	7	.611	34	20	8	0		4			159.1	173	86	6	2	58		61	4.24	+12	.277	.341	+22		0.7
1940	Bos A	5	9	.357	31	16	5	0		0			143.2	166	86	7	0	70		80	4.95	-9	.284	.361	+0		-0.2
1941	StL A	0	3	.000	15	2	0	0		0			46	45	26	3	0	23		20	4.50	-4	.257	.343	+21	0	0.0
1942	StL A	3	1	.750	10	4	2	0		0			43.2	46	22	4	0	17		21	3.71	+0	.266	.332	+44	0	-0.1
1943	StL A	0	2	.000	11	3	0	0		0			28.2	36	16	1	0	13		4	5.02	-34	.321	.392	-41	0	-0.3
1943	Bro N	1	1	.500	7	1	0	0		0			27.1	21	11	0	0	12		15	3.29	+2	.212	.297	-49	0	-0.1
1943	Major	1	3	.250	18	4	0	0		0			55	57	27	1	0	25		19	4.18	-16	.270	.347	-43	0	-0.4
1944	Bro N	2	1	.667	10	4	3	0		1			41.2	46	17	3	0	12		17	3.24	+10	.267	.315	-6	0	0.1
1944	Pit N	11	7	.611	28	24	14	1		1			204.2	201	79	7	1	65		80	2.73	+36	.260	.318	+2	0	1.9
1944	Year	13	8	.619	38	28	17	1		2			246.1	247	96	10	1	77		97	2.81	+31	.261	.317	+1	0	2.0
1945	Pit N	5	4	.556	14	11	4	1		0			80.2	74	45	6	2	37		29	4.57	-14	.236	.321	+11	0	-0.2
1946	Pit N	13	10	.565	27	25	16	2		0			193.1	193	70	5	3	56		57	2.84	+24	.263	.318	-6	0	2.5
1947	Pit N	12	10	.545	26	24	12	3		0			183	181	94	18	1	68		66	3.84	+10	.254	.320	+24	0	0.5
1948	Pit N	8	11	.421	23	22	10	2		0			134.1	143	73	13	1	41		43	4.42	-8	.262	.315	-20	0	-0.7
Total	15	114	115	.498	390	246	113	11		15			2066.2	2170	1062	105	21	835		774	3.99	+9	.268	.337	+0	0	9.7
Team	7	59	65	.476	219	126	52	2		13			1083.1	1184	609	45	13	491		422	4.38	+11	.275	.351	-2		6.1
/180I	1	10	11	.476	36	21	9	0		2			180	197	101	7	2	82		70	4.38	+11	.275	.351	-2		1.0
PALM, MIKE Richard Paul B2.13.1925 Boston MA BR/TR/6'3.5"/190 d7.11																											
1948	Bos A	0	0	+	3	0	0	0		0			3	6	2	0	0	5		1	6.00	-27	.400	.550		0	-0.1
PAPAI, AL Alfred Thomas B5.7.1917 Divernon IL D9.7.1995 Springfield IL BR/TR/6'3"/185 d4.24																											
1950	Bos A	4	2	.667	16	3	2	0		2			50.2	61	41	5	0	28		19	6.75	-27	.293	.377	-32	0	-1.0
Total	4	9	14	.391	88	18	8	0		4			239.2	281	171	17	1	138	2	70	5.37	-16	.291	.380	-18	0	-2.3
PAPE, LARRY Laurence Albert B7.21.1883 Norwood OH D7.21.1918 Swissvale PA BR/TR/5'11"/175 d7.6																											
1909	Bos A	2	0	1.000	11	3	2	1		2			57.1	46	17	0	5	12		18	2.04	+23	.221	.280	+3		0.0
1911	Bos A	10	8	.556	27	19	10	1		0			176.1	167	68	3	4	63		49	2.45	+34	.264	.335	-26		1.8
1912	Bos A	1	1	.500	13	2	1	0		1			48.2	74	36	0	2	16		17	4.99	-32	.366	.418	-2		-0.3
Total	3	13	9	.591	51	24	13	2		3			282.1	287	121	3	11	91		84	2.81	+12	.275	.340	-20		1.5
/180I	2	8	6	.591	33	15	8	1	0	2	0	0	180	183	77	2	7	58		54	2.81	+12	.275	.340	-49		1.0
PAPELBON, JONATHAN Jonathan Robert B11.23.1980 Baton Rouge LA BR/TR/6'4"/230 [BosA03 4/114] d7.31 Col Mississippi St.																											
2005	†Bos A	3	1	.750	17	3	0	0	0	0	1	10	34	33	11	4	3	17	2	34	2.65	+72	.260	.361	+29	0	0.7
2006	Bos A☆	4	2	.667	59	0	0	0	0	35	6	53	68.1	40	8	3	1	13	2	75	0.92	+407	.167	.211		0	4.6
Total	2	7	3	.700	76	3	0	0	0	35	7	63	102.1	73	19	7	4	30	4	109	1.50	+210	.199	.266	+29	0	5.3
/60G	2	6	2	.700	60	2	0	0	0	28	6	50	80.2	58	15	6	3	24	3	86	1.50	+210	.199	.266	+2		4.2
PARNELL, MEL Melvin Lloyd "Dusty" B6.13.1922 New Orleans LA BL/TL/6'0"/180 d4.20 [DL 1957 Bos A 86]																											
1947	Bos A	2	3	.400	15	5	1	0		0			50.2	60	41	1	1	27		23	6.39	-39	.296	.381	+5	0	-1.4
1948	Bos A	15	8	.652	35	27	16	1		0			212	205	87	7	4	90		77	3.14	+40	.252	.330	+6	0	2.2
1949	Bos A★	**25**	7	.781	39	33	**27**	4		2			**295.1**	258	102	8	5	134		122	2.77	+57	.237	.324	+23	0	5.2
1950	Bos A	18	10	.643	40	31	21	2		3			249	244	116	17	7	106		93	3.61	+36	.259	.338	+19	0	3.1
1951	Bos A★	18	11	.621	36	29	11	3		2			221	229	99	11	0	77		77	3.26	+37	.272	.333	-1	0	**3.3**
1952	Bos A	12	12	.500	33	29	15	3		2			214	207	94	13	5	89		107	3.62	+9	.255	.332	-5	0	0.6
1953	Bos A	21	8	.724	38	34	12	5		0			241	217	98	15	4	116		136	3.06	+37	.239	.328	-7	0	3.2
1954	Bos A	3	7	.300	19	15	4	1		0			92.1	104	45	7	1	35		38	3.70	+11	.287	.349	-7	47	0.2
1955	Bos A	2	3	.400	13	9	0	0		1			46	62	44	12	1	25	1	18	7.83	-45	.318	.395	+40	0	-1.4
1956	Bos A	7	6	.538	21	20	6	1		0			131.1	129	71	13	0	59	2	41	3.77	+23	.256	.333	-5	30	0.5
Total	10	123	75	.621	289	232	113	20		10			1752.2	1715	797	104	28	758	3	732	3.50	+25	.257	.335	+6	163	15.5
/180I	1	13	8	.621	30	24	12	2	0	1	0	0	180	176	82	11	3	78	0	75	3.50	+25	.257	.335	-89	17	1.6
PARTENHEIMER, STAN Stanwood Wendell "Party" B10.21.1922 Chicopee Falls MA D1.28.1989 Wilson NC BR/TL/5'11"/175 d5.27 f-Steve Col Wooster																											
1944	Bos A	0	0	+	1	1	0	0		0			1	3	2	0	0	2		0	18.00	-81	.500	.625	-51	0	-0.1
Total	2	0	0	+	9	3	0	0		0			14.1	15	11	2	0	18		6	6.91	-46	.278	.458	+29	0	-0.3
PATTEN, CASE Case Lyman "Casey" B5.7.1874 Westport NY D5.31.1935 Rochester NY BB/TL/6'0"/175 d5.4																											
1908	Bos A	0	1	.000	1	1	0	0		0			3	8	5	0	0	1		0	15.00	-84	.533	.563	+39		-0.5
Total	8	106	128	.453	270	238	206	17		4			2062.1	2154	1079	40	74	557		757	3.36	-12	.270	.323	-10		-13.5
PATTIN, MARTY Martin William B4.6.1943 Charleston IL BR/TR/5'11"/180 [AnaA65 7/127] d5.14 C1 Col Eastern Illinois																											
1972	Bos A	17	13	.567	38	35	13	4	22	0	1	2	253	232	102	19	9	65	3	168	3.24	+0	.243	.295	+6	0	0.2
1973	Bos A	15	15	.500	34	30	11	2	17	1	0	2	219.1	238	112	31	8	69	7	119	4.31	-7	.277	.335	+23	0	-0.6
Total	13	114	109	.511	475	224	64	14	143	25	7	159	2038.2	1933	905	209	45	603	75	1179	3.62	+2	.250	.306	+1	20	2.3
Team	2	32	28	.533	72	65	24	6	39	1	1	4	472.1	470	214	50	17	134	10	287	3.73	-3	.259	.314	+14		-0.4
/180I	1	12	11	.533	27	25	9	2	15	0	0	2	180	179	82	19	6	51	4	109	3.73	-3	.259	.314	+14		-0.2
PAULEY, DAVID David Wayne B6.17.1983 Longmont CO BR/TR/6'2"/185 [SDN01 8/240] d5.31																											
2006	Bos A	0	2	.000	3	3	0	0	1	0	0	0	16	31	14	1	2	6	1	10	7.88	-41	.419	.476	+1	34	-0.5
PAXTON, MIKE Michael De Wayne B9.3.1953 Memphis TN BR/TR/5'11"/190 [BosA75 23/538] d5.25 Col Memphis																											
1977	Bos A	10	5	.667	29	12	2	1	5	0	1	12	108	134	53	7	3	25	2	58	3.83	+17	.311	.350	+27	0	0.7
Total	4	30	24	.556	99	63	10	3	30	1	4	20	466.1	536	271	38	13	146	9	230	4.71	-12	.289	.342	+16	0	-2.2
PENA, ALEJANDRO Alejandro (Vasquez) B6.25.1959 Cambiaso, D.R. BR/TR/6'1"/(190–228) d8.13 [DL 1993 Pit N 182]																											
1995	Bos A	1	1	.500	17	0	0	0	0	0	0	9	24.1	33	23	5	0	12	2	25	7.40	-34	.314	.385		0	-0.5
Total	15	56	52	.519	503	72	12	7	43	74	19	324	1057.2	959	427	75	13	331	62	839	3.11	+18	.240	.299	-8	647	7.0
PENA, JESUS Jesus B3.8.1975 Santo Domingo, D.R. BL/TL/6'0"/170 d8.7																											
2000	Bos A	0	0	+	2	0	0	0	0	0	0	2	3	3	1	1	0	3	0	1	3.00	+67	.273	.429		0	0.0
Total	2	2	1	.667	48	0	0	0	0	1	1	29	46.2	49	34	10	2	42	5	40	5.21	-4	.269	.408		0	-0.3
PENA, JUAN Juan Francisco B6.27.1977 Santo Domingo, D.R. BR/TR/6'5"/215 [BosA95 27/746] d5.8 Col Miami-Dade Wolfson (FL) CC [DL 2000 Bos A 181, 2001 Bos A 57]																											
1999	Bos A	2	0	1.000	2	2	0	0	2	0	0	0	13	9	1	0	0	3	0	15	0.69	+620	.196	.245	+3	63	1.0
PENNINGTON, BRAD Brad Lee B4.14.1969 Salem IN BL/TL/6'5"/(205–215) [BalA89 12/297] d4.17 Col Vincennes (IN) JC																											
1996	Bos A	0	2	.000	14	0	0	0	0	0	0	9	13	6	5	1	0	15	1	13	2.77	+84	.140	.356		0	0.4
Total	5	3	6	.333	79	0	0	0	0	4	5	42	75.2	67	64	12	3	89	2	83	7.02	-33	.239	.423		25	-1.9
PENNOCK, HERB Herbert Jefferis "The Knight of Kennett Square" B2.10.1894 Kennett Square PA D1.30.1948 New York NY BB/TL/6'0"/160 d5.14 Mil 1918 C4 HF1948																											
1915	Bos A	0	0	+	5	1	0	0		0			14	23	16	0	0	10		7	9.64	-71	.390	.478	+162		-0.5
1916	Bos A	0	2	.000	9	2	0	0		1			26.2	23	11	0	1	8		12	3.04	-9	.245	.311	-73		-0.1
1917	Bos A	5	5	.500	24	5	4	1		1			100.2	90	49	2	3	23		35	3.31	-22	.243	.292	+17		-0.7
1919	Bos A	16	8	.667	32	26	16	5		0			219	223	78	2	3	48		70	2.71	+11	.274	.316	+20		1.0
1920	Bos A	16	13	.552	37	31	19	4		2			242.1	244	108	9	4	61		68	3.68	-1	.264	.312	-3		0.6

Year	Tm Lg	W	L	Pct	G	GS	CG	ShO	QS	SV	BS	QR	IP	H	R	HR	HB	BB	IB	SO	ERA	AERA	OAV	OOB	Sup	DL	PW
1921	Bos A	13	14	.481	32	31	15	1		0			222.2	268	121	7	2	59		91	4.04	+5	.307	.352	-21		0.5
1922	Bos A	10	17	.370	32	26	15	1		1			202	230	108	7	1	74		59	4.32	-5	.297	.359	-28		-0.5
1934	Bos A	2	0	1.000	30	2	1	0		1			62	68	31	2	0	16		16	3.05	+58	.276	.321	+63		0.3
Total	22	241	162	.598	617	419	247	35		33			3571.2	3900	1699	128	36	916		1227	3.60	+6	.282	.328	+13		7.3
Team	8	62	59	.512	201	124	70	12		6			1089.1	1169	522	29	14	299		358	3.67	-1	.281	.331	-6		0.6
/180I	1	10	10	.512	33	20	12	2		1			180	193	86	5	2	49		59	3.67	-1	.281	.331	-6		0.1
PERISHO, MATT Matthew Alan B6.8.1975 Burlington IA BL/TL/6'0"/(175–205) [AnaA93 3/75] d5.27																											
2005	Bos A	0	0	+	1	0	0	0	0	0	0	0	0	1	1	0	0	0	0	0	(1)	-100	1.000	1.000		0	-0.1
Total	8	11	17	.393	177	28	0	0	7	0	5	93	276	346	221	42	18	162	7	202	6.39	-27	.309	.401	-11	20	-4.4
PERSON, ROBERT Robert Alan B10.6.1969 Lowell MA BR/TR/6'0"/(180–195) [CleA89 25/645] d9.18 Col Seminole St. (OK) JC																											
2003	Bos A	0	0	+	7	0	0	0	0	1	0	3	11.2	11	10	0	1	8	0	10	7.71	-40	.250	.364		157	-0.2
Total	9	51	42	.548	206	135	4	2	63	9	2	43	897.1	813	496	129	35	438	12	773	4.64	-6	.242	.332	-1	337	-3.7
PERTICA, BILL William Andrew B8.17.1898 Santa Barbara CA D12.28.1967 Los Angeles CA BR/TR/5'9"/165 d8.7																											
1918	Bos A	0	0	+	1	0	0	0		0			3	3	1	0	0	0		1	3.00	-11	.273	.273			0.0
Total	4	22	18	.550	74	47	17	2		2			331	370	201	14	14	138		98	4.27	-13	.291	.367	+12		-3.2
PETERS, GARY Gary Charles B4.21.1937 Grove City PA BL/TL/6'2"/(190–200) d9.10 Col Grove City																											
1970	Bos A	16	11	.593	34	34	10	4	19	0	0	0	221.2	221	114	20	7	83	2	155	4.06	-2	.257	.325	+22	0	0.5
1971	Bos A	14	11	.560	34	32	9	1	17	1	0	2	214	241	111	25	6	70	3	100	4.37	-15	.288	.346	+12	0	-0.8
1972	Bos A	3	3	.500	33	4	0	0	2	1	1	17	85.1	91	48	10	3	38	8	67	4.32	-25	.279	.356	+30	0	-0.7
Total	14	124	103	.546	359	286	79	23	188	5	1	49	2081	1894	847	157	62	706	53	1420	3.25	+6	.243	.309	+7	0	12.7
Team	3	33	25	.569	101	70	19	5	38	2	1	19	521	553	273	55	16	191	13	322	4.23	-11	.273	.339	+18		-1.0
/180I	1	11	9	.569	35	24	7	2	13	1	0	7	180	191	94	19	6	66	4	111	4.23	-11	.273	.339	+18		-0.3
PETRY, DAN Daniel Joseph B11.13.1958 Palo Alto CA BR/TR/6'4"/(180–215) [DetA76 4/74] d7.8																											
1991	Bos A	0	0	+	13	0	0	0	0	1	0	8	22.1	21	17	3	1	12	2	12	4.43	-2	.250	.347		0	-0.1
Total	13	125	104	.546	370	300	52	11	164	1	0	48	2080.1	1984	1025	218	47	852	74	1063	3.95	+3	.253	.328	+5	139	3.4
PHILLIPS, ED Norman Edwin B9.20.1944 Ardmore OK BR/TR/6'1"/190 [BosA66 16/304] d4.9 Col Colby																											
1970	Bos A	0	2	.000	18	0	0	0	0	0	0	11	23.2	29	14	4	2	10	1	23	5.32	-25	.312	.387		0	-0.3
PICHARDO, HIPOLITO Hipolito Antonio (Balbina) B8.22.1969 Jicome Esperanza, D.R. BR/TR/6'1"/(160–195) d4.21 [DL 1999 KC A 182]																											
2000	Bos A	6	3	.667	38	1	0	0	0	1	1	27	65	63	29	1	3	26	2	37	3.46	+45	.260	.337	-25	0	1.2
2001	Bos A	2	1	.667	30	0	0	0	0	0	3	19	34.2	42	23	3	5	10	3	17	4.93	-10	.300	.363		58	-0.2
Total	10	50	44	.532	350	68	3	1	30	20	11	190	769.2	838	425	54	35	287	36	394	4.44	+5	.279	.346	-6	410	2.1
Team	2	8	4	.667	68	1	0	0	0	1	4	46	99.2	105	52	4	8	36	5	54	3.97	+21	.275	.347	-25	58	1.0
/60G	2	7	4	.667	60	1	0	0	0	1	4	41	88	93	46	4	7	32	4	48	3.97	+21	.275	.347	-25	51	0.9
PIERCE, JEFF Jeffrey Charles B6.7.1969 Poughkeepsie NY BR/TR/6'1"/185 d4.26 Col North Carolina St.																											
1995	Bos A	0	3	.000	12	0	0	0	0	0	1	7	15	16	12	0	0	14	4	12	6.60	-26	.286	.423		0	-0.5
PIERCY, BILL William Benton "Wild Bill" B5.2.1896 ElMonte CA D8.28.1951 Long Beach CA BR/TR/6'1"/185 d10.3																											
1917	NY A	0	1	.000	1	1	1	0		0			9	9	3	0	0	2		4	3.00	-10	.257	.297	-73		0.0
1921	†NY A	5	4	.556	14	10	5	1		0			81.2	82	40	4	7	28		35	2.98	+42	.263	.337	-3		0.9
1922	Bos A	3	9	.250	29	12	7	1		0			121.1	140	77	2	6	62		24	4.67	-12	.304	.394	-41		-0.8
1923	Bos A	8	17	.320	30	24	11	0		0			187.1	193	105	5	14	73		51	3.41	+21	.277	.357	-26		0.8
1924	Bos A	5	7	.417	23	18	3	0		0			121	156	87	4	10	66		20	5.95	-27	.335	.429	+8		-1.5
1926	Chi N	6	5	.545	19	5	1	0		0			90.1	96	52	1	6	37		31	4.48	-14	.280	.360	+26		-0.5
Total	6	27	43	.386	116	70	28	2		0			610.2	676	364	16	43	268		165	4.26	-3	.292	.376	-12		-1.1
Team	3	16	33	.327	82	54	21	1		0			429.2	489	269	11	30	201		95	4.48	-7	.301	.389	-18		-1.5
/180I	1	7	14	.327	34	23	9	0		0			180	205	113	5	13	84		40	4.48	-7	.301	.389	-18		-0.6
PIPGRAS, GEORGE George William B12.20.1899 Ida Grove IA D10.19.1986 Gainesville FL BR/TR/6'1.5"/185 d6.9 U9 b–Ed																											
1933	Bos A	9	8	.529	22	17	9	2		1			128.1	140	65	5	2	45		56	4.07	+8	.276	.337	+2		0.5
1934	Bos A	0	0	+	2	1	0	0		0			3.1	4	3	1	0	3		0	8.10	-41	.308	.438	+9		0.0
1935	Bos A	0	1	.000	5	1	0	0		0			5	9	9	3	1	5		2	14.40	-67	.391	.517	-63		-0.8
Total	11	102	73	.583	276	189	93	16		12			1488.1	1529	801	66	33	598		714	4.09	-2	.266	.339	+27		-3.2
Team	3	9	9	.500	29	19	9	2		1			136.2	153	77	9	3	53		58	4.54	-3	.282	.348	-1		-0.3
/180I	4	12	12	.500	38	25	12	3		1			180	202	101	12	4	70		76	4.54	-3	.282	.348	-1		-0.4
PIZARRO, JUAN Juan Ramon (Cordova) B2.7.1937 Santurce, PR BL/TL/5'11"/(170–197) d5.4																											
1968	Bos A	6	8	.429	19	12	6	0	9	2		4	107.2	97	46	15	0	44	4	84	3.59	-12	.242	.315	-3	0	-0.3
1969	Bos A	0	1	.000	6	0	0	0	0	2	0	4	9	14	7	2	0	6	0	4	6.00	-36	.359	.444		0	-0.3
Total	18	131	105	.555	488	245	79	17	175	28	4	206	2034.1	1807	890	201	41	888	67	1522	3.43	+4	.237	.319	+5	52	4.4
Team	2	6	9	.400	25	12	6	0	9	4	0	8	116.2	111	53	17	0	50	4	88	3.78	-15	.252	.327	-3		-0.6
PLYMPTON, JEFF Jeffrey Hunter B11.24.1965 Framingham MA BR/TR/6'2"/205 [BosA87 10/266] d6.15 Col Maine																											
1991	Bos A	0	0	+	4	0	0	0	0	0	0	4	5.1	5	0	0	0	4	0	2	0.00	-100	.263	.375		0	0.1
POINDEXTER, JENNINGS Chester Jennings "Jinx" B9.30.1910 Pauls Valley OK D3.3.1983 Norman OK BL/TL/5'10"/165 d9.15																											
1936	Bos A	0	2	.000	3	3	0	0		0			10.2	13	11	0	0	16		2	6.75	-21	.302	.492	-56		-0.4
Total	2	0	2	.000	14	4	0	0		0			41	42	30	0	0	31		14	4.83	-10	.264	.384	-24		-0.5
POLE, DICK Richard Henry B10.13.1950 Trout Creek MI BR/TR/6'3"/(195–200) d8.3 C18																											
1973	Bos A	3	2	.600	12	7	0	0	0	0	0	4	54.2	70	35	4	0	18	0	24	5.60	-28	.318	.370	+55	0	-0.7
1974	Bos A	1	1	.500	15	2	0	0	0	1	0	10	45	55	28	6	1	13	0	32	4.20	-8	.304	.352	+60	0	-0.2
1975	†Bos A	4	6	.400	18	11	2	1	4	0	0	5	89.2	102	46	11	2	32	4	42	4.42	-8	.290	.349	-21	62	-0.2
1976	Bos A	6	5	.545	31	15	1	0	8	0	0	8	120.2	131	62	8	2	48	3	49	4.33	-10	.279	.346	-17	0	-0.4
1977	Sea A	7	12	.368	25	24	3	0	8	0	0	0	122.1	127	76	16	6	57	2	51	5.15	-19	.270	.353	-20	26	-1.8
1978	Sea A	4	11	.267	21	18	2	0	5	0	1	1	98.2	122	82	16	3	41	3	41	6.48	-41	.306	.371	+3	0	-3.8
Total	6	25	37	.403	122	77	8	1	25	1	1	28	531	607	329	61	14	209	12	239	5.05	-21	.290	.356	-6	88	-7.1
Team	4	14	14	.500	76	35	3	1	12	1	0	27	310	358	171	29	5	111	7	147	4.56	-13	.293	.352	+1	62	-1.5
/180I	2	8	8	.500	44	20	2	1	7	1	0	16	180	208	99	17	3	64	4	85	4.56	-13	.293	.352	+1	36	-0.9
PORTERFIELD, BOB Erwin Coolidge B8.10.1923 Newport VA D4.28.1980 Sealy TX BR/TR/6'0"/(187–190) d8.8																											
1956	Bos A	3	12	.200	25	18	4	1		0			126	127	82	21	1	64	4	53	5.14	-10	.260	.347	-17	0	-0.4
1957	Bos A	4	4	.500	28	9	3	1	5	1		13	102.1	107	54	8	1	30	2	28	4.05	-1	.272	.324	-8	0	-0.1
1958	Bos A	0	0	+	2	0	0	0	3	0		11	4	3	2	1	0	0	0	1	4.50	-11	.214	.214		0	0.0
Total	12	87	97	.473	318	193	92	23	14	8		159	1567.2	1571	732	113	14	552	20	572	3.79	+2	.263	.326	-4	42	4.2
Team	3	7	16	.304	55	27	7	2	8	1		24	232.1	237	138	30	2	94	6	82	4.65	-7	.265	.335	-14		-0.5
/180I	2	5	12	.304	43	21	5	2	6	1		19	180	184	107	23	2	73	5	64	4.65	-7	.265	.335	-14		-0.4
PORTUGAL, MARK Mark Steven B10.30.1962 Los Angeles CA BR/TR/6'0"/(170–215) d8.14																											
1999	Bos A	7	12	.368	31	27	1	0	11	0	0	3	150.1	179	100	28	4	41	1	79	5.51	-10	.292	.337	-8	0	-0.7
Total	15	109	95	.534	346	283	16	4	150	5	4	38	1826.1	1813	896	209	36	607	27	1134	4.03	+0	.261	.321	+4	392	2.3
/180I	1	8	14	.368	37	32	1	0	13	0	0	4	180	214	120	34	5	49	1	95	5.51	-10	.292	.337	+10		-0.8
POTTER, NELS Nelson Thomas "Nellie" B8.23.1911 Mt.Morris IL D9.30.1990 Mt.Morris IL BL/TR/5'11"/180 d4.25 Col Manchester																											
1941	Bos A	2	0	1.000	10	0	0	0		0			20	21	10	0	0	16		6	4.50	-7	.284	.411		0	0.0
Total	12	92	97	.487	349	177	89	6		22			1686	1721	843	123	21	582		747	3.99	-1	.265	.328	-1	0	2.2
PRENTISS, GEORGE George Pepper (aka George Pepper Wilson in 1901) B6.10.1876 Wilmington DE D9.8.1902 Wilmington DE BB/TR/5'11"/175 d9.23																											
1901	Bos A	1	0	1.000	2	1	1	0		0			10	7	4	0	0	6		0	1.80	+96	.194	.310	+34		0.2
1902	Bos A	2	2	.500	7	4	3	0		0			41	55	31	0	0	10		9	5.27	-32	.322	.359	+36		-0.5
1902	Bal A	0	1	.000	2	2	0	0		0			6.2	14	10	1	0	5		1	10.80	-65	.424	.500	+24		-0.6
1902	Year	2	3	.400	9	6	3	0		0			47.2	69	41	1	0	15		10	6.04	-40	.338	.384	+33		-1.1
Total	2	3	3	.500	11	7	4	0		0			57.2	76	45	1	0	21		10	5.31	-32	.317	.372	+33		-0.9
Team	2	3	2	.600	9	5	4	0		0			51	62	35	0	0	16		9	4.59	-22	.300	.350	+36		-0.3

Year	Tm Lg	W	L	Pct	G	GS	CG	ShO	QS	SV	BS	QR	IP	H	R	HR	HB	BB	IB	SO	ERA	AERA	OAV	OOB	Sup	DL	PW
PRICE, JOE Joseph Walter B11.29.1956 Inglewood CA BR/TL/6'4"/(210–220) [CinN77 4/102] d6.14 Col Oklahoma																											
1989	Bos A	2	5	.286	31	5	0	0	0	0	1	19	70.1	71	35	8	0	30	3	52	4.35	-5	.262	.332	-21	0	-0.1
Total	11	45	49	.479	372	84	10	1	40	13	13	198	906	839	408	95	9	337	41	657	3.65	+2	.246	.313	-8	161	0.3
PRUIETT, TEX Charles Le Roy B4.10.1883 Osgood IN D3.6.1953 Ventura CA BL/TR/5'8"/176 d4.26																											
1907	Bos A	3	11	.214	35	17	6	2		3			173.2	166	77	1	8	59		54	3.11	-17	.254	.323	-41		-0.6
1908	Bos A	1	7	.125	13	6	1	1		2			58.2	55	26	1	2	21		28	1.99	+23	.275	.350	-68		-0.1
Total	2	4	18	.182	48	23	7	3		5			232.1	221	103	2	10	80		82	2.83	-10	.259	.329	-48		-0.7
/180I	2	3	14	.182	37	18	5	2	0	4	0	0	180	171	80	2	8	62		64	2.83	-10	.259	.329	-60		-0.5
PULSIPHER, BILL William Thomas B10.9.1973 Fort Benning GA BL/TL/6'3"/(200–228) [NYN91 2/66] d6.17 [DL 1997 NY N 32]																											
2001	Bos A	0	0	+	23	0	0	0	0	0	0	16	22	25	15	3	2	14	0	16	5.32	-17	.294	.402		0	-0.1
Total	6	13	19	.406	106	46	2	0	17	0	1	38	327	361	199	44	11	141	7	202	5.15	-17	.284	.357	-5	133	-2.7
QUANTRILL, PAUL Paul John B11.3.1968 London ON, Can. BL/TR/6'1"/(175–200) [BosA89 6/163] d7.20 Col Wisconsin–Madison																											
1992	Bos A	2	3	.400	27	0	0	0	0	1	4	21	49.1	55	18	1	1	15	5	24	2.19	+94	.288	.340		0	0.8
1993	Bos A	6	12	.333	49	14	1	1	6	1	1	24	138	151	73	13	2	44	14	66	3.91	+18	.279	.334	-32	0	0.9
1994	Bos A	1	1	.500	17	0	0	0	0	0	2	8	23	25	10	4	2	5	1	15	3.52	+43	.278	.323		0	0.3
Total	14	68	78	.466	841	64	1	1	22	21	46	567	1255.2	1442	601	112	45	336	68	725	3.83	+18	.292	.339	-17	71	9.5
Team	3	9	16	.360	93	14	1	1	6	2	7	53	210.1	231	101	18	5	64	20	105	3.47	+32	.281	.334	-32		2.0
/60G	2	6	10	.360	60	9	1	1	4	1	5	34	135.2	149	65	12	3	41	13	68	3.47	+32	.281	.334	-32		1.3
QUINN, FRANK Frank William B11.27.1927 Springfield MA D1.11.1993 Boynton Beach FL BR/TR/6'2"/180 d5.29 Col Yale																											
1949	Bos A	0	0	+	8	0	0	0		0			22	18	7	2	1	9		4	2.86	+52	.222	.308		0	0.1
1950	Bos A	0	0	+	1	0	0	0		0			2	2	2	0	0	1		0	9.00	-46	.250	.333		0	0.0
Total	2	0	0	+	9	0	0	0		0			24	20	9	2	1	10		4	3.38	+31	.225	.310		0	0.1
QUINN, JACK John Picus (b John Quinn Picus) B7.5.1883 Janesville PA D4.17.1946 Pottsville PA BR/TR/6'0"/196 d4.15																											
1922	Bos A	13	16	.448	40	32	16	4		0			256	263	119	9	3	59		67	3.48	+18	.267	.311	-1		1.4
1923	Bos A	13	17	.433	42	28	16	1		7			243	302	125	6	6	53		71	3.89	+6	.316	.356	-25		1.0
1924	Bos A	12	13	.480	44	25	13	2		7			228.2	241	109	10	12	52		64	3.27	+34	.273	.322	-18		2.2
1925	Bos A	7	8	.467	19	15	8	0		0			105	140	68	3	3	26		24	4.37	+4	.315	.357	-11		0.0
Total	23	247	218	.531	756	443	243	28		57			3920.1	4238	1837	102	91	860		1329	3.29	+13	.280	.323	-5		19.4
Team	4	45	54	.455	145	100	53	7		14			832.2	946	421	28	24	190		226	3.65	+16	.289	.333	-13		4.6
/180I	1	10	12	.455	31	22	11	2		3			180	204	91	6	5	41		49	3.65	+16	.289	.333	-13		1.0
RADATZ, DICK Richard Raymond "The Monster" B4.2.1937 Detroit MI D3.16.2005 Easton MA BR/TR/6'5"/(230–235) d4.10 Col Michigan St.																											
1962	Bos A	9	6	.600	**62**	0	0	0	0	**24**		50	124.2	95	32	9	4	40	2	144	2.24	+84	.211	.278		0	**3.9**
1963	Bos A★	15	6	.714	66	0	0	0	0	25		51	132.1	94	31	9	5	51	13	162	1.97	+92	.201	.285		0	**5.0**
1964	Bos A★	16	9	.640	79	0	0	0	0	**29**		60	157	103	44	13	7	58	9	181	2.29	+68	.186	.269		0	4.9
1965	Bos A	9	11	.450	63	0	0	0	0	22		43	124.1	104	57	11	5	53	11	121	3.91	-5	.227	.312		0	0.1
1966	Bos A	0	2	.000	16	0	0	0	0	4		11	19	24	10	3	0	11	2	19	4.74	-20	.304	.389		0	-0.2
1966	Cle A	0	3	.000	39	0	0	0	0	10		24	56.2	49	33	6	3	34	6	49	4.61	-25	.233	.344		0	-0.8
1966	Year	0	5	.000	55	0	0	0	0	14		35	75.2	73	43	9	3	45	8	68	4.64	-24	.253	.356		0	-1.0
1967	Cle A	0	0	+	3	0	0	0	0	0		2	3	5	2	1	0	2	0	1	6.00	-46	.357	.438		0	0.0
1967	Chi N	1	0	1.000	20	0	0	0	0	5		11	23.1	12	21	4	5	24	2	18	6.56	-46	.154	.380		0	-0.8
1967	Major	1	0	1.000	23	0	0	0	0	5		13	26	17	23	5	5	26	2	19	6.49	-46	.185	.387		0	-0.8
1969	Det A	2	2	.500	11	0	0	0	0	0	1	9	18.2	14	8	3	0	5	0	18	3.38	+12	.212	.268		0	0.1
1969	Mon N	0	4	.000	22	0	0	0	0	3	1	13	34.2	32	22	6	1	18	1	32	5.71	-35	.244	.340		0	-0.8
1969	Major	2	6	.250	33	0	0	0	0	3	2	22	52	46	30	9	1	23	1	50	4.89	-19	.234	.317		0	-0.7
Total	7	52	43	.547	381	0	0	0	0	122	2	274	693.2	532	260	65	30	296	46	745	3.13	+22	.212	.300		0	11.4
Team	5	49	34	.590	286	0	0	0	0	104		215	557.1	420	174	45	21	213	37	627	2.65	+46	.209	.289			13.7
/60G	1	10	7	.590	60	0	0	0	0	22		45	117	88	37	9	4	79	8	132	2.65	+46	.209	.289			2.9
RAINEY, CHUCK Charles David B7.14.1954 San Diego CA BR/TR/5'11"/195 [BosA74*1/19] d4.8 Col San Diego Mesa (CA) JC																											
1979	Bos A	8	5	.615	20	16	4	1	9	1	0	4	103.2	97	47	7	3	41	1	41	3.82	+17	.250	.325	-3	22	0.9
1980	Bos A	8	3	.727	16	13	2	1	6	0	0	0	87	92	49	7	2	41	3	43	4.86	-12	.273	.353	+13	94	-0.5
1981	Bos A	0	1	.000	11	2	0	0	1	0	0	8	40	39	21	2	0	13	1	20	2.70	+45	.252	.306	+3	0	0.1
1982	Bos A	7	5	.583	27	25	3	3	6	0	0	1	129	146	75	14	2	63	2	57	5.02	-13	.294	.373	+3	0	-0.6
1983	Chi N	14	13	.519	34	34	1	1	14	0	0	0	191	219	109	17	3	74	3	84	4.48	-15	.295	.358	+4	0	-1.7
1984	Chi N	5	7	.417	17	16	0	0	6	0	0	1	88.1	102	55	4	2	38	1	45	4.28	-9	.290	.361	+5	0	-1.0
1984	Oak A	1	1	.500	16	0	0	0	0	1	1	7	30.2	43	27	2	0	17	4	10	6.75	-44	.333	.403		0	-0.7
1984	Major	6	8	.429	33	16	0	0	6	1	1	8	118	145	82	6	2	55	5	55	4.92	-18	.301	.373	+5	0	-1.7
Total	6	43	35	.551	141	106	10	6	42	2	1	21	669.2	738	383	53	12	287	15	300	4.50	-9	.284	.355	+4	116	-3.5
Team	4	23	14	.622	74	56	9	5	22	1	0	13	359.2	374	192	30	7	158	7	161	4.38	-1	.272	.347	+4	116	-0.1
/180I	2	12	7	.622	37	28	5	3	11	1	0	7	180	187	96	15	4	79	4	81	4.38	-1	.272	.347	+4	58	-0.1
RAPP, PAT Patrick Leland B7.13.1967 Jennings LA BR/TR/6'3"/(195–230) [SFN89 15/388] d7.10 Col Southern Mississippi																											
1999	†Bos A	6	7	.462	37	26	0	0	12	0	0	9	146.1	147	78	13	7	69	1	90	4.12	+21	.263	.351	+5	0	0.9
Total	10	70	91	.435	259	239	9	5	113	0	0	13	1387.1	1468	790	133	49	683	32	825	4.68	-4	.276	.361	-1	17	-4.3
/180I	1	7	9	.462	46	32	0	0	15	0	0	11	180	181	96	16	9	85	1	111	4.12	+21	.263	.351	+29		1.1
REARDON, JEFF Jeffrey James B10.1.1955 Dalton MA BR/TR/6'1"/(190–205) d8.25 Col Massachusetts																											
1990	†Bos A	5	3	.625	47	0	0	0	0	21	7	35	51.1	39	19	5	1	19	4	33	3.16	+30	.206	.282		44	1.1
1991	Bos A★	1	4	.200	57	0	0	0	0	40	9	41	59.1	54	21	9	1	16	3	44	3.03	+43	.236	.286		0	1.6
1992	Bos A	2	2	.500	46	0	0	0	0	27	8	31	42.1	53	20	6	1	7	0	32	4.25	+0	.308	.335		0	0.2
Total	16	73	77	.487	880	0	0	0	0	367	10	651	1132.1	1000	426	109	27	358	65	877	3.16	+22	.236	.297		44	13.9
Team	3	8	9	.471	150	0	0	0	0	88	24	107	153	146	60	20	3	42	7	109	3.41	+24	.247	.299		44	2.9
/60G	1	3	4	.471	60	0	0	0	0	35	10	43	61.1	58	24	8	1	17	3	44	3.40	+24	.247	.299		18	1.2
REED, JERRY Jerry Maxwell B10.8.1955 Bryson City NC BR/TR/6'1"/190 [PhiN77 22/559] d9.11 Col Western Carolina																											
1990	Bos A	2	1	.667	29	0	0	0	0	2	1	18	45	55	27	1	0	16	2	17	4.80	-15	.302	.353		0	-0.2
Total	9	20	19	.513	238	12	0	0	2	18	10	154	479.1	477	238	47	10	172	25	248	3.94	+7	.261	.325	+2	89	1.0
REMLINGER, MIKE Michael John B3.23.1966 Middletown NY BL/TL/6'1"/(195–215) [SFN87 1/16] d6.15 Col Dartmouth																											
2005	Bos A	0	0	+	8	0	0	0	0	0	0	5	6.2	15	14	2	0	5	0	5	14.85	-69	.417	.488		0	-0.4
Total	14	53	55	.491	639	59	4	2	23	20	25	430	879	784	412	103	30	430	38	854	3.90	+10	.239	.331	-2	128	5.2
REMMERSWAAL, WIN Wilhelmus Abraham B3.8.1954 The Hague, Netherlands BR/TR/6'2"/160 d8.3																											
1979	Bos A	1	0	1.000	8	0	0	0	0	0	0	3	20.1	26	16	1	1	12	1	16	7.08	-37	.317	.402		0	-0.3
1980	Bos A	2	1	.667	14	0	0	0	0	0	0	9	35.1	39	18	4	0	9	1	20	4.58	-7	.295	.338		0	-0.1
Total	2	3	1	.750	22	0	0	0	0	0	0	12	55.2	65	34	5	1	21	2	36	5.50	-21	.304	.364		0	-0.4
RENKO, STEVE Steven B12.10.1944 Kansas City KS BR/TR/6'5"/(220–240) [NYN65 16/620] d6.27 Col Kansas																											
1979	Bos A	11	9	.550	27	27	4	1	14	0	0	0	171	174	86	22	2	53	1	99	4.11	+8	.260	.315	+9	0	0.6
1980	Bos A	9	9	.500	32	23	1	0	13	0	0	7	165.1	180	86	17	1	56	4	90	4.19	+2	.281	.337	-8	0	0.0
Total	15	134	146	.479	451	365	57	9	196	6	3	65	2494	2438	1233	248	22	1010	86	1455	3.99	-2	.256	.327	-4	54	0.3
Team	2	20	18	.526	59	50	5	1	27	0	0	7	336.1	354	172	39	3	109	5	189	4.15	+5	.270	.326	+1		0.6
/180I	1	11	10	.526	32	27	3	1	14	0	0	4	180	189	92	21	2	58	3	101	4.15	+5	.270	.326	+1		0.3
REYES, CARLOS Carlos Alberto B4.4.1969 Miami FL BB/TR/6'1"/190 d4.7 Col Florida Southern																											
1998	Bos A	1	1	.500	24	0	0	0	0	0	0	18	38.1	35	15	2	1	14	2	23	3.52	+34	.246	.316		0	0.3
Total	8	20	36	.357	293	29	0	0	7	4	6	175	558	576	309	86	17	220	21	360	4.66	-2	.267	.337	-31	48	-0.8
RHODES, GORDON John Gordon "Dusty" B8.11.1907 Winnemucca NV D3.22.1960 Long Beach CA BR/TR/6'0"/187 d4.29																											
1929	NY A	0	4	.000	10	4	0	0		0			42.2	57	32	3	2	16		13	4.85	-20	.333	.397	-18		-0.5
1930	NY A	0	0	+	3	0	0	0		0			2	3	3	0	0	4		1	9.00	-52	.500	.700			-0.1
1931	NY A	6	3	.667	18	11	4	0		0			87	82	49	3	0	52		36	3.41	+16	.235	.334	+47		0.1

Year	Tm Lg	W	L	Pct	G	GS	CG	ShO	QS	SV	BS	QR	IP	H	R	HR	HB	BB	IB	SO	ERA	AERA	OAV	OOB	Sup	DL	PW
1932	NY A	1	2	.333	10	2	1	0		0			24	25	22	0	0	21		15	7.88	-48	.275	.411	+130		-0.9
1932	Bos A	1	8	.111	12	11	4	0		0			79.1	79	46	5	0	31		22	5.11	-12	.261	.329	-55		-0.4
1932	Year	2	10	.167	22	13	5	0		0			103.1	104	68	5	0	52		37	5.75	-24	.264	.350	-28		-1.3
1933	Bos A	12	15	.444	34	29	14	0		0			232	242	126	13	1	93		85	4.03	+9	.265	.334	+14		1.2
1934	Bos A	12	12	.500	44	31	10	0		2			219	247	133	10	4	98		79	4.56	+5	.285	.360	+3		0.2
1935	Bos A	2	10	.167	34	19	1	0		2			146.1	195	103	14	1	60		44	5.41	-12	.324	.387	-17		-1.1
1936	Phi A	9	20	.310	35	28	13	1		1			216.1	266	162	26	2	102		61	5.74	-11	.304	.378	-32		-2.0
Total	8	43	74	.368	200	135	47	1		5			1048.2	1196	676	74	10	477		356	4.85	-5	.286	.361	-5		-3.5
Team	4	27	45	.375	124	90	29	0		4			676.2	763	408	42	6	282		230	4.63	+0	.284	.354	-5		-0.1
/180I	1	7	12	.375	33	24	8	0		1			180	203	109	11	2	75		61	4.63	+0	.284	.354	-5		-0.0
RICH, WOODY Woodrow Earl B3.9.1916 Morganton NC D4.18.1983 Morganton NC BL/TR/6'2"/185 d4.22 Mil 1945																											
1939	Bos A	4	3	.571	21	12	3	0		1			77	78	46	2	5	35		24	4.91	-4	.264	.352	+38		0.1
1940	Bos A	1	0	1.000	3	1	1	0		0			11.2	9	3	2	0	1		8	0.77	+483	.214	.233	-22		0.2
1941	Bos A	0	0	+	2	1	0	0		0			3.2	8	7	1	0	2		4	17.18	-76	.421	.476	+66	0	-0.2
1944	Bos N	1	1	.500	7	2	1	0		0			25	32	17	3	3	12		6	5.76	-34	.327	.416	+10	0	-0.4
Total	4	6	4	.600	33	16	5	0		1			117.1	127	73	8	8	50		42	5.06	-11	.280	.361	+35	0	-0.3
Team	3	5	3	.625	26	14	4	0		1			92.1	95	56	5	5	38		36	4.87	-4	.267	.346	+36		0.1
RIPLEY, ALLEN Allen Stevens B10.18.1952 Norwood MA BR/TR/6'3"/(180–200) d4.10 f–Walt																											
1978	Bos A	2	5	.286	15	11	1	0	7	0	0	2	73	92	49	10	3	22	2	26	5.55	-26	.311	.362	-17	0	-0.9
1979	Bos A	3	1	.750	16	3	0	0	1	1	1	4	64.2	77	42	9	3	25	5	34	5.15	-14	.295	.362	+9	0	-0.4
Total	5	23	27	.460	101	67	4	0	36	1	2	17	463.2	521	256	46	15	148	21	229	4.52	-16	.289	.345	-11	20	-3.7
Team	2	5	6	.455	31	14	1	0	8	1	1	6	137.2	169	91	19	6	47	7	60	5.36	-20	.303	.362	-11		-1.3
/180I	3	7	8	.455	41	18	1	0	10	1	1	8	180	221	119	25	8	61	9	78	5.36	-20	.303	.362	-11		-1.7
RIPLEY, WALT Walter Franklin B11.26.1916 Worcester MA D10.7.1990 Attleboro MA BR/TR/6'0"/168 d8.17 s–Allen																											
1935	Bos A	0	0	+	2	0	0	0		0			4	7	4	0	0	3		0	9.00	-47	.412	.500			-0.1
RISKE, DAVID David Richard B10.23.1976 Renton WA BR/TR/6'2"/(175–195) [CleA96 56/1560] d8.14 Col Green River (WA) CC [DL 2000 Cle A 17]																											
2006	Bos A	0	1	.000	8	0	0	0	0	0	0	4	9.2	8	4	2	2	3	0	5	3.72	+25	.222	.317		47	0.1
Total	7	18	14	.563	328	0	0	0	0	16	14	227	361.1	305	155	50	18	152	15	346	3.59	+23	.229	.314		108	2.6
RITCHIE, JAY Jay Seay B11.20.1936 Salisbury NC BR/TR/6'4"/(175–190) d8.4																											
1964	Bos A	1	1	.500	21	0	0	0	0	0		16	46	43	21	4	0	14	2	35	2.74	+41	.249	.303		0	0.1
1965	Bos A	1	2	.333	44	0	0	0	0	2		27	71	83	30	3	1	26	5	55	3.17	+18	.302	.361		0	0.2
1966	Atl N	0	1	.000	22	0	0	0	0	4		15	35.1	32	17	3	0	12	4	33	4.08	-11	.241	.303		0	0.0
1967	Atl N	4	6	.400	52	0	0	0	0	2		33	82.1	75	32	6	4	29	11	57	3.17	+5	.245	.317		0	0.4
1968	Cin N	2	3	.400	28	2	0	0	0	0		17	56.2	68	32	7	1	13	2	32	4.61	-31	.293	.332	-45	0	-0.9
Total	5	8	13	.381	167	2	0	0	0	8		108	291.1	301	132	23	6	94	24	212	3.49	+1	.269	.327	-45	0	-0.2
Team	2	2	3	.400	65	0	0	0	0	2		43	117	126	51	7	1	40	7	90	3.00	+26	.281	.339			0.3
/60G	2	2	3	.400	60	0	0	0	0	2		40	108	116	47	6	1	37	6	83	3.00	+26	.281	.339			0.3
ROBINSON, JACK John Edward B2.20.1921 Orange NJ D3.2.2000 Ormond Beach FL BR/TR/6'0"/175 d5.4																											
1949	Bos A	0	0	+	3	0	0	0		0			4	4	1	0	1	1		1	2.25	+94	.267	.353		0	0.1
ROCHFORD, MIKE Michael Joseph B3.14.1963 Methuen MA BL/TL/6'4"/205 [BosA82*1/17] d9.3 Col Santa Fe (FL) CC																											
1988	Bos A	0	0	+	2	0	0	0	0	0	0	1	2.1	4	0	0	0	1	0	1	0.00	-100	.364	.417		0	0.1
1989	Bos A	0	0	+	4	0	0	0	0	0	0	3	4	4	7	1	0	4	1	1	6.75	-39	.267	.400		0	-0.1
1990	Bos A	0	1	.000	2	1	0	0	0	0	0	0	4	10	10	1	0	4	0	0	18.00	-77	.526	.583	+56	0	-1.0
Total	3	0	1	.000	8	1	0	0	0	0	0	4	10.1	18	17	2	0	9	1	2	9.58	-57	.400	.482	+56	0	-1.0
RODRIGUEZ, FRANK Francisco B12.11.1972 Brooklyn NY BR/TR/6'0"/(195–210) [BosA90 2/41] d4.26																											
1995	Bos A	0	2	.000	9	2	0	0	0	0	0	2	15.1	21	19	3	0	10	1	14	10.57	-54	.323	.413	+101	0	-0.9
Total	7	29	39	.426	184	82	3	0	37	5	3	62	654	737	444	76	21	282	17	371	5.53	-12	.286	.358	+1	61	-4.4
ROGERS, LEE Lee Otis "Buck" B10.8.1913 Tuscaloosa AL D11.23.1995 Little Rock AR BR/TL/5'11"/170 d4.27 Col Alabama																											
1938	Bos A	1	1	.500	14	2	0	0		0			27.2	32	24	4	0	18		7	6.51	-24	.302	.403	-20		-0.3
1938	Bro N	0	2	.000	12	2	0	0		0			23.2	23	16	0	1	10		11	5.70	-32	.256	.337	-46		-0.2
1938	Major	1	3	.250	26	4	0	0		0			50	55	40	4	1	28		18	6.14	-28	.281	.373	-33		-0.5
Total	1	1	3	.250	26	4	0	0		0			51.1	55	40	4	1	28		18	6.14	-27	.281	.373	-32		-0.5
ROGGENBURK, GARRY Garry Earl B4.16.1940 Cleveland OH BR/TL/6'6"/(195–200) d4.20 Col Dayton [DL 1964 Min A 161]																											
1966	Bos A	0	0	+	1	0	0	0	0	0		0	0.1	1	0	0	0	1	0	0	0.00	-100	.500	.667		0	0.0
1968	Bos A	0	0	+	4	0	0	0	0	0		4	8.1	9	2	0	0	3	0	4	2.16	+46	.257	.316		65	0.0
1969	Bos A	0	1	.000	7	0	0	0	0	0	0	2	9.2	13	9	1	1	5	0	8	8.38	-54	.342	.432		0	-0.4
Total	5	6	9	.400	79	6	1	0	1	7	1	51	126	132	67	15	7	64	5	56	3.64	-1	.272	.362	-10	226	-0.8
Team	3	0	1	.000	12	0	0	0	0	0	0	6	18.1	23	11	1	1	9	0	12	5.40	-35	.307	.388		65	-0.4
ROHR, BILLY William Joseph B7.1.1945 San Diego CA BL/TL/6'3"/170 d4.14																											
1967	Bos A	2	3	.400	10	8	2	1	3	0		0	42.1	43	27	4	2	22	2	16	5.10	-32	.256	.349	+3	0	-0.9
1968	Cle A	1	0	1.000	17	0	0	0	0	1		10	18.1	18	16	5	0	10	2	5	6.87	-57	.265	.354		0	-0.5
Total	2	3	3	.500	27	8	2	1	3	1		10	60.2	61	43	9	2	32	4	21	5.64	-41	.258	.351	+3	0	-1.4
ROMO, VICENTE Vicente (Navarro) "Huevo" B4.12.1943 Santa Rosalia, Baja California, Mexico BR/TR/6'1"/(180–195) d4.11 b–Enrique																											
1969	Bos A	7	9	.438	52	11	4	1	6	11	2	28	127.1	116	51	14	1	50	6	89	3.18	+20	.247	.319	-10	0	1.2
1970	Bos A	7	3	.700	48	10	0	0	2	6	1	28	108	115	51	14	0	43	6	71	4.08	-2	.273	.338	+21	0	0.2
Total	8	32	33	.492	335	32	4	1	10	52	14	222	645.2	569	269	61	8	280	48	416	3.36	+6	.239	.318	+3	56	2.5
Team	2	14	12	.538	100	21	4	1	8	17	3	56	235.1	231	102	28	1	93	12	160	3.59	+8	.259	.328	+5		1.4
/60G	1	8	7	.538	60	13	2	1	5	10	2	34	141.1	139	61	17	1	56	7	96	3.59	+8	.259	.328	+5		0.8
ROSE, BRIAN Brian Leonard B2.13.1976 New Bedford MA BR/TR/6'3"/(212–220) [BosA94 3/75] d7.25																											
1997	Bos A	0	0	+	1	1	0	0	0	0	0	0	3	5	4	0	0	2	0	3	12.00	-61	.357	.438	-1	0	-0.1
1998	Bos A	1	4	.200	8	8	0	0	2	0	0	0	37.2	43	32	9	2	14	0	18	6.93	-32	.285	.351	+18	138	-1.0
1999	Bos A	7	6	.538	22	18	0	0	7	0	0	2	98	112	59	19	2	29	2	51	4.87	+2	.280	.332	-17	0	0.2
2000	Bos A	3	5	.375	15	12	0	0	3	0	0	3	53	58	37	11	3	21	3	24	6.11	-18	.274	.345	-13	0	-0.7
2000	Col N	4	5	.444	12	12	0	0	5	0	0	0	63.2	72	41	10	3	30	6	40	5.51	+5	.281	.361	-21	0	0.0
2000	Major	7	10	.412	27	24	0	0	8	0	0	3	116	130	78	21	6	51	9	64	5.79	-5	.278	.353	-17	0	-0.7
2001	NY N	0	1	.000	3	0	0	0	0	0	0	2	8.2	10	4	3	0	2	1	4	4.15	-3	.286	.324		0	0.0
2001	TB A	0	2	.000	7	3	0	0	0	0	0	3	20.1	31	20	4	0	12	0	11	8.85	-49	.356	.426	-18	0	-0.7
2001	Major	0	3	.000	10	3	0	0	0	0	0	5	28	41	24	7	0	14	1	15	7.45	-35	.336	.399	-18	0	-0.7
Total	5	15	23	.395	68	54	0	0	17	0	0	10	284.1	331	197	56	10	110	12	151	5.86	-13	.287	.352	-12	138	-2.3
Team	4	11	15	.423	46	39	0	0	12	0	0	5	191.2	218	132	39	7	66	5	96	5.73	-14	.281	.341	-8	138	-1.6
/180I	4	10	14	.423	43	37	0	0	11	0	0	5	180	205	124	37	7	62	5	90	5.73	-14	.281	.341	-8	130	-1.5
ROSS, BUSTER Chester Franklin B3.11.1903 Kuttawa KY D4.24.1982 Mayfield KY BL/TL/6'1"/195 d6.15																											
1924	Bos A	4	3	.571	30	2	1	1		1			93.1	109	49	3	0	30		16	3.47	+26	.307	.361	+45		0.4
1925	Bos A	3	8	.273	33	8	0	0		0			94.1	119	86	9	5	40		15	6.20	-27	.313	.386	-10		-1.9
1926	Bos A	0	1	.000	1	0	0	0		0			2.2	5	7	0	0	4		0	16.88	-76	.385	.529			-0.6
Total	3	7	12	.368	64	10	1	1		1			190.1	233	142	12	5	74		31	5.01	-11	.311	.377	+2		-2.1
/60G	3	7	11	.368	60	9	1	1	0	1	0	0	178.1	218	133	11	5	69		29	5.02	-11	.311	.377	-4		-2.0
RUFFING, RED Charles Herbert B5.3.1905 Granville IL D2.17.1986 Mayfield Hts. OH BR/TR/6'1.5"/205 d5.31 Mil 1943–44 C1 HF1967▲																											
1924	Bos A	0	0	+	8	2	0	0		0			23	29	17	0	3	9		10	6.65	-34	.333	.414	+35		-0.2
1925	Bos A	9	18	.333	37	27	13	3		1			217.1	253	135	10	2	75		64	5.01	-9	.299	.357	-12		-0.5
1926	Bos A	6	15	.286	37	22	6	0		2			166	169	96	4	5	68		58	4.39	-7	.274	.351	-31		-0.8
1927	Bos A	5	13	.278	26	18	10	0		2			158.1	160	94	7	4	87		77	4.66	-9	.277	.375	-28		-0.4
1928	Bos A	10	25	.286	42	34	**25**	1		2			289.1	303	147	8	10	96		118	3.89	+6	.275	.339	-29		1.8

Year	Tm Lg	W	L	Pct	G	GS	CG	ShO	QS	SV	BS	QR	IP	H	R	HR	HB	BB	IB	SO	ERA	AERA	OAV	OOB	Sup	DL	PW
1929	Bos A	9	22	.290	35	32	18	1		1			244.1	280	162	17	2	118		109	4.86	-12	.297	.376	-24		-1.1
1930	Bos A	0	3	.000	4	3	1	0		0			24	32	19	1	1	6		14	6.38	-28	.323	.368	-44		-0.4
Total	22	273	225	.548	624	538	335	45		16			4344	4284	2115	254	58	1541		1987	3.80	+9	.258	.323	+12	138	31.4
Team	7	39	96	.289	189	138	73	5		8			1122.1	1226	670	47	27	459		450	4.61	-8	.287	.360	-24		-1.6
/180I	1	6	15	.289	30	22	12	1		1			180	197	107	8	4	74		72	4.61	-8	.287	.360	-24		-0.3
RUPE, RYAN Ryan Kittman B3.31.1975 Houston TX BR/TR/6'5"/230 [TBA98 6/192] d5.5 Col Texas A&M																											
2003	Bos A	1	1	.500	4	1	0	0	1	0	1	1	10	13	9	4	0	1	0	7	6.30	-26	.302	.318	-21	0	-0.4
Total	5	24	38	.387	89	84	2	0	35	0	2	1	476.2	514	336	81	42	162	5	355	5.85	-19	.275	.343	-12	117	-6.1
RUSSELL, ALLAN Allan "Rubberarm" B7.31.1893 Baltimore MD D10.20.1972 Baltimore MD BB/TR/5'11"/165 d9.13 b–Lefty																											
1919	Bos A	10	4	.714	21	11	9	1		4			121.1	105	38	1	1	39		63	2.52	+20	.246	.310	+32		0.8
1920	Bos A	5	6	.455	16	10	7	0		1			107.2	100	44	3	3	38		53	3.01	+21	.251	.321	-2		0.5
1921	Bos A	6	11	.353	39	14	7	0		3			173	204	92	10	9	77		60	4.11	+3	.303	.382	-25		-0.3
1922	Bos A	6	7	.462	34	11	1	0		2			125.2	152	81	6	5	57		34	5.01	-18	.314	.392	-49		-1.3
Total	11	70	76	.479	345	112	54	5		42			1394.1	1382	693	58	44	610		603	3.52	-1	.269	.351	-20		-2.4
Team	4	27	28	.491	110	46	24	1		10			527.2	561	255	20	18	211		210	3.74	+2	.283	.357	-12		-0.3
/180I	1	9	10	.491	38	16	8	0		3			180	191	87	7	6	72		72	3.74	+2	.283	.357	-12		-0.1
RUSSELL, JACK Jack Erwin B10.24.1905 Paris TX D11.3.1990 Clearwater FL BR/TR/6'1.5"/178 d5.5																											
1926	Bos A	0	5	.000	36	5	1	0		0			98	94	40	2	1	24		17	3.58	+14	.268	.316	-13		0.6
1927	Bos A	4	9	.308	34	15	4	1		0			147	172	80	5	5	40		25	4.10	+3	.298	.348	-6		-0.1
1928	Bos A	11	14	.440	32	26	10	2		0			201.1	233	102	6	4	41		27	3.84	+7	.294	.332	-22		0.6
1929	Bos A	6	18	.250	35	32	13	0		0			227.1	263	132	12	3	40		37	3.92	+9	.290	.322	-24		0.1
1930	Bos A	9	20	.310	35	30	15	0		0			229.2	302	162	11	3	53		35	5.45	-15	.321	.359	-28		-2.4
1931	Bos A	10	18	.357	36	31	13	0		0			232	298	145	7	2	65		45	5.16	-17	.310	.355	-22		-1.7
1932	Bos A	1	7	.125	11	6	1	0		0			39.2	61	35	2	0	15		7	6.81	-34	.343	.394	-43		-1.6
1932	Cle A	5	7	.417	18	11	6	0		1			113	146	67	5	1	27		27	4.70	+1	.310	.349	-13		0.4
1932	Year	6	14	.300	29	17	7	0		1			152.2	207	102	7	1	42		34	5.25	-11	.319	.361	-24		-1.2
1933	†Was A	12	6	.667	50	3	2	0		**13**			124	119	45	3	1	32		28	2.69	+56	.255	.305	+22		3.1
1934	Was A☆	5	10	.333	**54**	9	3	0		**7**			157.2	179	86	6	2	56		38	4.17	+4	.287	.348	-1		0.5
1935	Was A	4	9	.308	43	7	2	0		3			126	170	88	10	2	37		30	5.71	-24	.324	.371	+21		-1.6
1936	Was A	3	2	.600	18	5	1	0		3			49.2	66	46	3	0	25		6	6.34	-25	.317	.391	+81		-1.2
1936	Bos A	0	3	.000	23	2	0	0		0			40	57	27	2	0	16		9	5.62	-6	.345	.403	-92		0.1
1936	Year	3	5	.375	41	7	1	0		3			89.2	123	73	5	0	41		15	6.02	-17	.330	.396	+25		-1.1
1937	Det A	2	5	.286	25	0	0	0		4			40.1	63	35	4	1	20		10	7.59	-38	.362	.431			-1.8
1938	†Chi N	6	1	.857	42	0	0	0		3			102.1	100	43	1	1	30		29	3.34	+15	.258	.313			0.7
1939	Chi N	4	3	.571	39	0	0	0		3			68.2	78	32	3	0	24		32	3.67	+7	.282	.339			0.1
1940	StL N	3	4	.429	26	0	0	0		1			54	53	22	1	0	26		16	2.50	+60	.252	.335			0.7
Total	15	85	141	.376	557	182	71	3		38			2050.2	2454	1187	83	26	571		418	4.46	-3	.299	.346	-15		-3.5
Team	8	41	94	.304	242	147	57	3		0			1215	1480	723	47	18	294		202	4.58	-5	.304	.345	-24		-4.4
/180I	1	6	14	.304	36	22	8	0		0			180	219	107	7	3	44		30	4.58	-5	.304	.345	-24		-0.7
RUSSELL, JEFF Jeffrey Lee B9.2.1961 Cincinnati OH BR/TR/6'3"/(195–210) [CinN79 5/126] d8.13																											
1993	Bos A	1	4	.200	51	0	0	0	0	33	4	40	46.2	39	16	1	1	14	1	45	2.70	+72	.231	.287		30	1.9
1994	Bos A	0	5	.000	29	0	0	0	0	12	3	20	28	30	17	3	1	13	2	18	5.14	-2	.270	.346		0	0.0
Total	14	56	73	.434	589	79	11	2	46	186	45	366	1099.2	1065	525	100	28	415	43	693	3.75	+12	.255	.323	-19	204	8.9
Team	2	1	9	.100	80	0	0	0	0	45	7	60	74.2	69	33	4	2	27	3	63	3.62	+32	.246	.311		30	1.9
/60G	2	1	7	.100	60	0	0	0	0	34	5	45	56	52	25	3	2	20	2	47	3.62	+32	.246	.311		23	1.4
RUTH, BABE George Herman "The Bambino","The Sultan of Swat" B2.6.1895 Baltimore MD D8.16.1948 New York NY BL/TL/6'2"/215 d7.11 C1 HF1936▲																											
1914	Bos A	2	1	.667	4	3	1	0		0			23	21	12	1	0	7		3	3.91	-31	.236	.292	+53		-0.3
1915	†Bos A	18	8	.692	32	28	16	1		0			217.2	166	80	3	6	85		112	2.44	+14	.212	.294	+37		2.8
1916	†Bos A	23	12	.657	44	**41**	23	0		1			323.2	230	83	0	8	118		170	**1.75**	+58	**.201**	.280	+8		**5.7**
1917	Bos A	24	13	.649	41	38	**35**	6		2			326.1	244	93	2	11	108		128	2.01	+28	.211	.284	+3		4.9
1918	†Bos A	13	7	.650	20	19	18	1		0			166.1	125	51	1	2	49		40	2.22	+21	.214	.277	+12		2.9
1919	Bos A	9	5	.643	17	15	12	0		1			133.1	148	59	2	2	58		30	2.97	+2	.290	.365	-1		1.4
1920	NY A	1	0	1.000	1	1	0	0		0			4	3	4	0	0	2		0	4.50	-15	.200	.294	+191		-0.1
1921	†NY A	2	0	1.000	2	1	0	0		0			9	14	10	1	0	9		2	9.00	-53	.350	.469	+156		-0.6
1930	NY A	1	0	1.000	1	1	1	0		0			9	11	3	0	0	2		3	3.00	+43	.306	.342	+80		0.3
1933	NY A★	1	0	1.000	1	1	1	0		0			9	12	5	0	0	3		0	5.00	-22	.308	.357	+31		0.0
Total	10	94	46	.671	163	148	107	17		4			1221.1	974	400	10	29	441		488	2.28	+22	.221	.297	+17		17.0
Team	6	89	46	.659	158	144	105	8		4			1190.1	934	378	9	29	425		483	2.19	+25	.219	.294	+13		17.4
/180I	1	13	7	.659	24	22	16	1		1			180	141	57	1	4	64		73	2.19	+25	.219	.294	+13		2.6
RYAN, JACK Jack "Gulfport" B9.19.1884 Lawrenceville IL D10.16.1949 Handsboro MS BR/TR/5'10"/165 d7.2																											
1908	Cle A	1	1	.500	8	1	1	0		1			35.2	27	12	3	1	2		7	2.27	+5	.220	.238	+43		0.1
1909	Bos A	3	3	.500	13	8	2	0		0			59.1	64	34	0	4	20		24	3.34	-25	.288	.358	-8		-0.7
1911	Bro N	0	1	.000	3	1	0	0		0			6	9	7	1	1	4		1	3.00	+11	.375	.483	-32		-0.2
Total	3	4	5	.444	24	10	3	0		1			101	100	53	4	6	26		32	2.94	-15	.271	.329	-5		-0.8
RYAN, KEN Kenneth Frederick B10.24.1968 Pawtucket RI BR/TR/6'3"/(200–230) d8.31																											
1992	Bos A	0	0	+	7	0	0	0	0	1	0	6	7	4	5	2	0	5	0	5	6.43	-34	.174	.310		0	-0.1
1993	Bos A	7	2	.778	47	0	0	0	0	1	3	32	50	43	23	2	3	29	5	49	3.60	+29	.235	.342		0	0.9
1994	Bos A	2	3	.400	42	0	0	0	0	13	3	34	48	46	14	1	1	17	3	32	2.44	+107	.256	.323		0	1.8
1995	Bos A	0	4	.000	28	0	0	0	0	7	3	19	32.2	34	20	4	1	24	6	34	4.96	-2	.268	.388		0	-0.1
1996	Phi N	3	5	.375	62	0	0	0	0	8	5	48	89	71	32	4	1	45	8	70	2.43	+78	.223	.321		0	1.5
1997	Phi N	1	0	1.000	22	0	0	0	0	0	0	13	20.2	31	23	5	2	13	1	10	9.58	-56	.344	.430		123	-0.6
1998	Phi N	0	0	+	17	1	0	0	0	0	0	11	22.2	21	12	1	1	20	1	16	4.37	-1	.253	.396	+92	122	0.0
1999	Phi N	1	2	.333	15	0	0	0	0	0	0	10	15.2	16	11	2	0	11	2	9	6.32	-26	.267	.380		0	-0.4
Total	8	14	16	.467	240	1	0	0	0	30	14	173	285.2	266	140	21	9	164	26	225	3.91	+17	.250	.352	+92	245	3.0
Team	4	9	9	.500	124	0	0	0	0	22	9	91	137.2	127	62	9	5	75	14	120	3.66	+31	.248	.346			2.5
/60G	2	4	4	.500	60	0	0	0	0	11	4	44	66.2	61	30	4	2	36	7	58	3.66	+31	.248	.346			1.2
RYBA, MIKE Dominic Joseph B6.9.1903 DeLancey PA D12.13.1971 Brookline Station MO BR/TR/5'11.5"/195 d9.22 C4 Col St. Francis (PA)																											
1935	StL N	1	1	.500	2	1	1	0		0			16	15	6	0	0	1		6	3.38	+21	.242	.254	-38		0.3
1936	StL N	5	1	.833	14	0	0	0		0			45	55	33	3	2	16		25	5.40	-27	.294	.356			-1.0
1937	StL N	9	6	.600	38	8	5	0		0			135	152	76	8	2	40		57	4.13	-4	.284	.336	+19		0.1
1938	StL N	1	1	.500	3	0	0	0		0			5	8	3	0	0	1		0	5.40	-27	.348	.375			-0.1
1941	Bos A	7	3	.700	40	3	0	0		6			121	143	72	14	0	42		54	4.46	-7	.297	.353	+66	0	-0.2
1942	Bos A	3	3	.500	18	0	0	0		3			44.1	49	25	5	1	13		16	3.86	-3	.278	.332		0	-0.2
1943	Bos A	7	5	.583	40	8	4	1		2			143.2	142	57	4	0	57		50	3.26	+2	.262	.333	+30	0	0.1
1944	Bos A	12	7	.632	42	7	2	0		2			138	119	57	7	0	39		50	3.33	+2	.233	.287	+16	0	0.3
1945	Bos A	7	6	.538	34	9	4	1		2			123	122	45	5	2	33		44	2.49	+37	.259	.310	+6	0	1.2
1946	†Bos A	0	1	.000	9	0	0	0		1			12.2	12	7	1	0	5		5	3.55	+3	.261	.333		0	0.0
Total	10	52	34	.605	240	36	16	2		16			783.2	817	381	47	7	247		307	3.66	+0	.269	.326	+18	0	0.5
Team	6	36	25	.590	183	27	10	2		16			582.2	587	263	36	3	189		219	3.41	+5	.264	.322	+22		1.2
/180I	2	11	8	.590	57	8	3	1		5			180	181	81	11	1	58		68	3.41	+5	.264	.322	+22		0.4
SABERHAGEN, BRET Bret William B4.11.1964 Chicago Heights IL BR/TR/6'1"/(160–200) [KCA82 19/480] d4.4 [DL 1996 Col N 182, 2000 Bos A 181]																											
1997	Bos A	0	1	.000	6	6	0	0	0	0	0	0	26	30	20	5	2	10	0	14	6.58	-29	.288	.353	+15	143	-0.3
1998	†Bos A	15	8	.652	31	31	0	0	18	0	0	0	175	181	82	22	6	29	1	100	3.96	+19	.264	.299	+0	0	1.7
1999	†Bos A	10	6	.625	22	22	0	0	10	0	0	0	119	122	43	11	2	11	0	81	2.95	+69	.265	.284	-1	63	3.2
2001	Bos A	1	2	.333	3	3	0	0	1	0	0	0	15	19	11	3	1	0	0	10	6.00	-26	.302	.313	+4	178	-0.4

Red Sox Pitchers

Year	Tm Lg	W	L	Pct	G	GS	CG	ShO	QS	SV	BS	QR	IP	H	R	HR	HB	BB	IB	SO	ERA	AERA	OAV	OOB	Sup	DL	PW
Total	16	167	117	.588	399	371	76	16	237	1	1	20	2562.2	2452	1036	218	59	471	34	1715	3.34	+26	.252	.289	-1	1016	27.9
Team	4	26	17	.605	62	62	0	0	29	0		0	335	352	156	41	11	50	1	205	3.90	+23	.268	.299	+1	384	4.2
/180I	2	14	9	.605	33	33	0	0	16	0		0	180	189	84	22	6	27	1	110	3.90	+23	.268	.299	+1	206	2.3
SADOWSKI, BOB Robert B2.19.1938 Pittsburgh PA BR/TR/6'2"/(188–195) d6.19 b–Ed b–Ted																											
1966	Bos A	1	1	.500	11	5	0	0	3	0		3	33.1	41	26	4	1	9	1	11	5.40	-30	.311	.354	+2	0	-0.5
Total	4	20	27	.426	115	54	13	1	31	8		38	439.2	416	209	41	16	130	17	257	3.87	-10	.250	.309	+7	0	-2.1
SAMBITO, JOE Joseph Charles B6.28.1952 Brooklyn NY BL/TL/6'1"/(185–190) [HouN73 17/404] d7.20 Col Adelphi [DL 1983 Hou N 182]																											
1986	†Bos A	2	0	1.000	53	0	0	0	0	12	0	33	44.2	54	26	4	2	16	3	30	4.84	-13	.298	.362		0	-0.2
1987	Bos A	2	6	.250	47	0	0	0	0	0	4	29	37.2	46	29	8	0	16	3	35	6.93	-34	.301	.367		0	-1.5
Total	11	37	38	.493	461	5	1	1	2	84	27	346	629	562	241	48	10	195	32	489	3.03	+16	.241	.300	-19	372	7.9
Team	2	4	6	.400	100	0	0	0	0	12	4	62	82.1	100	55	12	2	32	6	65	5.79	-25	.299	.364			-1.7
/60G	1	2	4	.400	60	0	0	0	0	7	2	37	49.1	60	33	7	1	19	4	39	5.80	-25	.299	.364			-1.0
SANDERS, KEN Kenneth George "Daffy" B7.8.1941 St.Louis MO BR/TR/5'11"/(170–185) d8.6																											
1966	Bos A	3	6	.333	24	0	0	0	0	2		15	47.1	36	22	2	2	28	9	33	3.80	+0	.214	.332		0	0.1
Total	10	29	45	.392	408	1	0	0	0	86	20	300	656.2	564	240	50	17	258	67	360	2.97	+19	.235	.312	+26	22	6.6
SANTANA, MARINO Marino (Castro) B5.10.1972 San Jose de los Llanos, D.R. BR/TR/6'1"/175 d9.4																											
1999	Bos A	0	0	+	3	0	0	0	0	0	0	2	4	8	7	3	0	3	0	4	15.75	-68	.444	.500		69	-0.2
Total	2	0	0	+	10	0	0	0	0	0	0	6	11.1	17	10	4	1	11	2	14	7.94	-39	.362	.483		69	-0.2
SANTIAGO, JOSE Jose Rafael (Alfonso) B8.15.1940 Juana Diaz, PR BR/TR/6'2"/(185–192) d9.9																											
1963	KC A	1	0	1.000	4	0	0	0	0	0		2	7	8	7	4	0	2	0	6	9.00	-57	.276	.323		0	-0.4
1964	KC A	0	6	.000	34	8	0	0	0	0		19	83.2	84	53	9	4	35	1	64	4.73	-19	.258	.336	+2	0	-0.9
1965	KC A	0	0	+	4	0	0	0	0	0		2	5	8	5	1	0	4	2	8	9.00	-61	.364	.462		0	-0.1
1966	Bos A	12	13	.480	35	28	7	1	17	2		6	172	155	87	17	2	58	0	119	3.66	+4	.238	.300	-6	0	0.0
1967	†Bos A	12	4	.750	50	11	2	0	6	5		25	145.1	138	61	15	2	47	3	109	3.59	-3	.251	.312	+57	0	0.3
1968	Bos A✱	9	4	.692	18	18	7	2	14	0		0	124	96	34	9	3	42	0	86	2.25	+40	.215	.286	+0	70	1.5
1969	Bos A	0	0	+	10	0	0	0	0	0	0	6	7.2	11	5	2	0	4	0	4	3.52	+9	.324	.395		134	0.0
1970	Bos A	0	2	.000	8	0	0	0	0	1	0	2	11.1	18	13	0	0	8	1	8	10.32	-61	.353	.441		22	-1.1
Total	8	34	29	.540	163	65	16	3	37	8	0	62	556	518	265	57	11	200	7	404	3.74	-4	.246	.313	+7	226	-0.7
Team	5	33	23	.589	121	57	16	3	37	8	0	39	460.1	418	200	43	7	159	4	326	3.42	+3	.241	.306	+8	226	0.7
/180I	2	13	9	.589	47	22	6	1	14	3	0	15	180	163	78	17	3	62	2	127	3.42	+3	.241	.306	+8	88	0.3
SAUERBECK, SCOTT Scott William B11.9.1971 Cincinnati OH BR/TL/6'3"/(190–200) [NYN94 23/624] d4.5 Col Miami–Ohio																											
2003	†Bos A	0	1	.000	26	0	0	0	0	0	1	15	16.2	17	14	1	4	18	3	18	6.48	-28	.266	.448		0	-0.2
Total	7	20	17	.541	471	0	0	0	0	5	17	336	386.1	344	183	31	24	243	31	389	3.82	+16	.242	.360		31	3.0
SAYLES, BILL William Nisbeth B7.27.1917 Portland OR D11.20.1996 Lincoln City OR BR/TR/6'2"/175 d7.17 Mil 1944–45 Col Oregon																											
1939	Bos A	0	0	+	5	0	0	0		0			14	14	13	1	0	13		9	7.07	-33	.264	.409			-0.2
Total	2	1	3	.250	28	3	1	0		0			78.2	87	56	2	0	46		52	5.61	-35	.279	.372	-22	0	-0.9
SCARBOROUGH, RAY Ray Wilson (b Rae Wilson Scarborough) B7.23.1917 Mt.Gilead NC D7.1.1982 Mount Olive NC BR/TR/6'0"/(178–185) d6.26 Mil 1943–45 C1 Col Wake Forest																											
1951	Bos A	12	9	.571	37	22	8	0		0			184	201	106	21	14	61		71	5.09	-12	.275	.342	+20	0	-1.0
1952	Bos A	1	5	.167	28	8	1	1		4			76.2	79	47	8	4	35		29	4.81	-18	.266	.351	-34	0	-0.6
Total	10	80	85	.485	318	168	59	9		14			1428.2	1487	755	89	44	611		564	4.13	-3	.267	.344	-4	0	-2.0
Team	2	13	14	.481	65	30	9	1		4			260.2	280	153	29	18	96		100	5.01	-14	.272	.345	+6		-1.6
/180I	1	9	10	.481	45	21	6	1		3			180	193	106	20	12	66		69	5.01	-14	.272	.345	+6		-1.1
SCHANZ, CHARLEY Charles Murrell B6.8.1919 Anacortes WA D5.28.1992 Sacramento CA BR/TR/6'3.5"/215 d4.20																											
1950	Bos A	3	2	.600	14	0	0	0		0			22.2	25	21	3	1	24		14	8.34	-41	.281	.439		0	-1.4
Total	5	28	43	.394	155	72	23	2		14			626.2	658	369	29	24	332		243	4.34	-14	.275	.369	-18	0	-5.8
SCHILLING, CURT Curtis Montague B11.14.1966 Anchorage AK BR/TR/6'4"/(205–235) [BosA86*2/39] d9.7 Col Yavapai (AZ) JC																											
2004	†Bos A✱	**21**	6	**.778**	32	32	3	0	23	0	0	0	226.2	206	84	23	5	35	0	203	3.26	+50	.239	.271	+33	0	4.5
2005	Bos A	8	8	.500	32	11	0	0	3	9	2	13	93.1	121	59	12	3	22	0	87	5.69	-20	.314	.352	+37	90	-1.6
2006	Bos A	15	7	.682	31	31	0	0	19	0	0	0	204	220	90	28	3	28	1	183	3.97	+18	.276	.303	+3	0	1.8
Total	19	207	138	.600	545	412	82	19	285	22	12	92	3110	2833	1250	326	50	688	42	3015	3.44	+27	.242	.285	-2	386	30.5
Team	3	44	21	.677	95	74	3	0	45	9	2	13	524	547	233	63	11	85	1	473	3.97	+19	.268	.299	+21	90	4.7
/180I	1	15	7	.677	33	25	1	0	15	3	1	4	180	188	80	22	4	29	0	162	3.97	+19	.268	.299	+21	31	1.6
SCHIRALDI, CALVIN Calvin Drew B6.16.1962 Houston TX BR/TR/6'4"/(200–216) [NYN83 1/27] d9.1 Col Texas																											
1984	NY N	0	2	.000	5	3	0	0	0	0	0	2	17.1	20	13	3	0	10	0	16	5.71	-37	.286	.375	-18	0	-0.5
1985	NY N	2	1	.667	10	4	0	0	0	0	2	2	26.1	43	27	4	3	11	0	21	8.89	-61	.368	.435	+20	15	-1.5
1986	†Bos A	4	2	.667	25	0	0	0	0	9	3	22	51	36	8	5	1	15	2	55	1.41	+198	.201	.265		0	2.3
1987	Bos A	8	5	.615	62	1	0	0	1	6	4	39	83.2	75	45	15	1	40	5	93	4.41	+4	.240	.326	-80	0	0.2
1988	Chi N	9	13	.409	29	27	2	1	14	1	0	1	166.1	166	87	13	2	63	7	140	4.38	-17	.257	.323	+5	30	-1.8
1989	Chi N	3	6	.333	54	0	0	0	0	4	4	38	78.2	60	34	7	1	50	2	54	3.78	+0	.209	.326		0	0.0
1989	SD N	3	1	.750	5	4	0	0	2	0	0	1	21.1	12	6	1	0	13	0	17	2.53	+39	.162	.287	+26	0	0.6
1989	Year	6	7	.462	59	4	0	0	2	4	4	39	100	72	40	8	1	63	2	71	3.51	+6	.199	.319	+19	0	0.6
1990	SD N	3	8	.273	42	8	0	0	3	1	1	21	104	105	59	11	1	60	6	74	4.41	-13	.264	.360	-15	0	-0.6
1991	Tex A	0	1	.000	3	0	0	0	0	0	0	0	4.2	5	6	3	0	5	0	1	11.57	-65	.263	.417		0	-0.6
Total	8	32	39	.451	235	47	2	1	20	21	14	126	553.1	522	285	62	9	267	22	471	4.28	-9	.248	.334	-4	45	-1.9
Team	2	12	7	.632	87	1	0	0	1	15	7	61	134.2	111	53	20	2	55	7	148	3.27	+35	.226	.304	-80		2.5
/60G	1	8	5	.632	60	1	0	0	1	10	5	42	93	77	37	14	1	38	5	102	3.27	+35	.226	.304	-80		1.7
SCHLITZER, BIFF Victor Joseph B12.4.1884 Rochester NY D1.4.1948 Wellesley Hills MA BR/TR/5'11"/175 d4.17 Col Dayton																											
1909	Bos A	4	4	.500	13	8	5	0		1			69.2	68	34	0	1	17		23	3.49	-28	.234	.279	+9		-0.7
Total	3	10	15	.400	44	29	16	2		1			217.1	198	107	4	6	71		87	3.60	-29	.239	.303	-12		-2.4
SCHMITZ, JOHNNY John Albert "Bear Tracks" B11.27.1920 Wausau WI BR/TL/6'0"/(168–170) d9.6 Mil 1943–45																											
1956	Bos A	0	0	+	2	0	0	0		0			4.1	5	2	0	0	4	0	0	0.00	-100	.278	.409		0	0.1
Total	13	93	114	.449	366	235	86	16		19			1812.2	1766	841	97	35	757	5	746	3.55	+7	.258	.335	-9	0	6.0
SCHOUREK, PETE Peter Alan B5.10.1969 Austin TX BL/TL/6'5"/(195–220) [NYN87 2/56] d4.9																											
1998	†Bos A	1	3	.250	10	8	0	0	4	0	0	2	44	45	21	7	1	14	1	36	4.30	+10	.273	.328	-9	0	0.2
2000	Bos A	3	10	.231	21	21	0	0	7	0	0	0	107.1	116	67	17	3	38	2	63	5.11	-2	.278	.341	-20	53	0.0
2001	Bos A	1	5	.167	33	0	0	0	0	0	1	19	30.1	35	19	4	1	15	3	20	4.45	+0	.292	.375		18	-0.2
Total	11	66	77	.462	288	176	3	1	74	2	3	71	1149	1198	642	140	39	420	36	813	4.59	-9	.270	.335	-5	264	-5.1
Team	3	5	18	.217	64	29	0	0	11	0	1	21	181.2	196	107	28	5	67	6	119	4.81	+1	.279	.344	-17	71	0.0
/60G	3	5	17	.217	60	27	0	0	10	0	1	20	170.1	184	100	26	5	63	6	112	4.80	+1	.279	.344	-17	67	0.0
SCHROLL, AL Albert Bringhurst "Bull" B3.22.1932 New Orleans LA D11.30.1999 Alexandria LA BR/TR/6'2"/210 d4.20 Col Tulane																											
1958	Bos A	0	0	+	5	0	0	0	2	0		10	10	6	5	1	0	4	0	7	4.50	-11	.176	.263		0	0.0
1959	Phi N	1	1	.500	3	0	0	0	0	0		1	9.1	12	9	1	0	6	0	4	8.68	-53	.353	.439		0	-0.7
1959	Bos A	1	4	.200	14	5	1	0	2	0		10	46	47	29	3	1	22	1	26	4.70	-14	.269	.350	-30	0	-0.4
1959	Major	2	5	.286	17	5	1	0	2	0		11	55	59	38	4	1	28	1	30	5.37	-21	.282	.365	-30	0	-1.1
1960	Chi N	0	0	+	2	0	0	0	0	0		0	2.2	3	3	1	0	5	0	2	10.13	-63	.273	.500		0	0.0
1961	Min A	4	4	.500	11	8	2	0	4	0		1	50	53	36	5	2	27	1	24	5.22	-19	.266	.360	+4	0	-0.7
Total	4	6	9	.400	35	13	3	0	8	0		22	118	121	82	11	3	64	2	63	5.34	-23	.267	.359	-8	0	-1.8
Team	2	1	4	.200	19	5	1	0	4	0		20	56	53	34	4	1	26	1	33	4.66	-13	.254	.336	-30		-0.4
SCHWALL, DON Donald Bernard B3.2.1936 Wilkes–Barre PA BR/TR/6'6"/(196–200) d5.21 Col Oklahoma																											
1961	Bos A★	15	7	.682	25	25	10	2	17	0		0	178.2	167	76	8	6	110	1	91	3.22	+29	.255	.366	+21	0	1.9
1962	Bos A	9	15	.375	33	32	5	1	12	0		0	182.1	180	118	18	10	121	1	89	4.94	-16	.260	.377	+5	0	-2.3
1963	Pit N	6	12	.333	33	24	3	2	12	0		7	167.2	158	72	13	6	74	13	86	3.33	-1	.255	.338	-13	0	0.1
1964	Pit N	4	3	.571	15	9	0	0	4	0		4	49.2	53	28	1	0	15	1	36	4.35	-19	.269	.321	+36	0	-0.5

Year	Tm Lg	W	L	Pct	G	GS	CG	ShO	QS	SV	BS	QR	IP	H	R	HR	HB	BB	IB	SO	ERA	AERA	OAV	OOB	Sup	DL	PW
1965	Pit N	9	6	.600	43	1	0	0	0	4		28	77	77	37	5	2	30	4	55	2.92	+20	.269	.341	-25	0	0.3
1966	Pit N	3	2	.600	11	4	0	0	3	0		5	41.2	31	13	3	1	21	2	24	2.16	+65	.209	.312	-14	0	0.7
1966	Atl N	3	3	.500	11	8	0	0	3	0		1	45.1	44	23	2	2	19	2	27	4.37	-17	.256	.333	+6	0	-0.5
1966	Year	6	5	.545	22	12	0	0	6	0		6	87	75	36	5	3	40	4	51	3.31	+9	.234	.323	+0	0	0.2
1967	Atl N	0	0	+	1	0	0	0	0	0		1	0.2	0	0	0	0	1	1	0	0.00	-100	.000	.500		0	0.0
Total	7	49	48	.505	172	103	18	5	51	4		46	743	710	367	50	27	391	25	408	3.72	+2	.257	.352	+8	0	-0.3
Team	2	24	22	.522	58	57	15	3	29	0		0	361	347	194	26	16	231	2	180	4.09	+1	.258	.372	+12		-0.4
/180I	1	12	11	.522	29	28	7	1	14	0		0	180	173	97	13	8	115	1	90	4.09	+1	.258	.372	+12		-0.2
SEANEZ, RUDY Rudy Caballero B10.20.1968 Brawley CA BR/TR/5'10"/(170–205) [CleA86 4/83] d9.7 [DL 1992 LA N 182, 1993 Col N 102]																											
2003	Bos A	0	1	.000	9	0	0	0	0	0	1	4	8.2	11	7	2	0	6	1	9	6.23	-25	.297	.386		0	-0.2
2006	Bos A	2	1	.667	41	0	0	0	0	0	1	28	46.2	51	28	6	1	26	1	48	4.82	-3	.271	.361		0	-0.1
Total	15	30	23	.566	429	0	0	0	0	11	24	293	446.2	399	228	46	10	233	21	471	4.21	+1	.237	.330		676	0.9
Team	2	2	2	.500	50	0	0	0	0	0	2	32	55.1	62	35	8	1	32	2	57	5.04	-7	.276	.365			-0.3
/60G	2	2	2	.500	60	0	0	0	0	0	2	38	66.1	74	42	10	1	38	2	68	5.05	-7	.276	.365			-0.4
SEAVER, TOM George Thomas "Tom Terrific" B11.17.1944 Fresno CA BR/TR/6'1"/(195–210) d4.13 HF1992 Col USC																											
1986	Bos A	5	7	.417	16	16	1	0	9	0	0	0	104.1	114	46	8	2	29	1	72	3.80	+11	.278	.326	-12	0	0.6
Total	20	311	205	.603	656	647	231	61	476	1	1	6	4783	3971	1674	380	76	1390	11	3640	2.86	+28	.226	.283	-4	51	49.5
SEGUI, DIEGO Diego Pablo (Gonzalez) B8.17.1937 Holguin, Cuba BR/TR/6'0"/(180–190) d4.12 s–David																											
1974	Bos A	6	8	.429	58	0	0	0	0	10	6	39	108	106	54	9	1	49	10	76	4.00	-4	.257	.334		0	-0.4
1975	†Bos A	2	5	.286	33	1	1	0	1	6	1	20	71	71	41	10	0	43	3	45	4.82	-16	.270	.373	-100	0	-0.6
Total	15	92	111	.453	639	171	28	7	82	71	18	331	1807.2	1656	867	185	18	786	86	1298	3.81	-4	.243	.322	-8	0	-2.5
Team	2	8	13	.381	91	1	1	0	1	16	7	59	179	177	95	19	1	92	13	121	4.32	-9	.262	.349	-100		-1.0
/60G	1	5	9	.381	60	1	1	0	1	11	5	39	118	117	63	13	1	61	9	80	4.32	-9	.262	.349	-100		-0.7
SEIBEL, PHIL Philip Matthew B1.28.1979 Louisville KY BL/TL/6'1"/195 [MonN00 8/225] d4.15 Col Texas																											
2004	Bos A	0	0	+	2	0	0	0	0	0	0	1	3.2	0	0	0	1	5	0	1	0.00	-100	.000	.333		0	0.1
SELE, AARON Aaron Helmer B6.25.1970 Golden Valley MN BR/TR/6'5"/(215–230) [BosA91 1/23] d6.23 Col Washington St.																											
1993	Bos A	7	2	.778	18	18	0	0	12	0	0	0	111.2	100	42	5	7	48	2	93	2.74	+69	.237	.322	-6	0	1.4
1994	Bos A	8	7	.533	22	22	2	0	12	0	0	0	143.1	140	68	13	9	60	2	105	3.83	+32	.261	.342	-6	0	1.6
1995	Bos A	3	1	.750	6	6	0	0	2	0	0	0	32.1	32	14	3	3	14	0	21	3.06	+59	.252	.338	+2	131	0.6
1996	Bos A	7	11	.389	29	29	1	0	12	0	0	0	157.1	192	110	14	8	67	2	137	5.32	-4	.303	.373	+0	18	-0.5
1997	Bos A	13	12	.520	33	33	1	0	17	0	0	0	177.1	196	115	25	15	80	4	122	5.38	-13	.279	.361	+0	0	-1.6
Total	14	145	110	.569	370	352	15	9	168	0	1	11	2099.1	2335	1174	220	110	777	37	1378	4.59	+2	.283	.349	+9	243	-0.6
Team	5	38	33	.535	108	108	4	0	55	0		0	622	660	349	60	42	269	10	478	4.41	+10	.273	.352	-2	149	1.5
/180I	1	11	10	.535	31	31	1	0	16	0		0	180	191	101	17	12	78	3	138	4.41	+10	.273	.352	-2	43	0.4
SELLERS, JEFF Jeffrey Doyle B5.11.1964 Compton CA BR/TR/6'1"/(175–195) [BosA82 8/202] d9.15																											
1985	Bos A	2	0	1.000	4	4	1	0	2	0	0	0	22.1	24	10	1	0	7	1	6	3.63	+19	.273	.323	+21	0	0.1
1986	Bos A	3	7	.300	14	13	1	0	7	0	0	1	82	90	56	13	3	40	1	51	4.94	-15	.282	.365	-10	0	-1.0
1987	Bos A	7	8	.467	25	22	4	2	9	0	0	0	139.2	161	85	10	3	61	0	99	5.28	-13	.298	.368	+0	0	-0.8
1988	Bos A	1	7	.125	18	12	1	0	5	0	0	3	85.2	89	49	9	3	56	3	70	4.83	-15	.268	.379	-32	63	-0.5
Total	4	13	22	.371	61	51	7	2	23	0	0	4	329.2	364	200	33	9	164	5	226	4.97	-12	.285	.367	-8	63	-2.2
/180I	2	7	12	.371	33	28	4	1	13	0	0	2	180	199	109	18	5	90	3	123	4.97	-12	.285	.367	-50	34	-1.2
SETTLEMIRE, MERLE Edgar Merle "Lefty" B1.19.1903 Santa Fe OH D6.12.1988 Russells Point OH BL/TL/5'9"/156 d4.13																											
1928	Bos A	0	6	.000	30	9	0	0		0			82.1	116	62	2	6	34		12	5.47	-25	.345	.415	-22		-0.8
SHEA, JOHN John Michael Joseph "Lefty" B12.27.1904 Everett MA D11.30.1956 Malden MA BL/TL/5'10.5"/171 d6.30 Col Boston College																											
1928	Bos A	0	0	+	1	0	0	0		0			1	1	2	0	0	1		0	18.00	-77	.250	.400			-0.1
SHELDON, ROLLIE Roland Frank B12.17.1936 Putnam CT BR/TR/6'4"/(190–201) d4.23 Col Connecticut																											
1966	Bos A	1	6	.143	23	10	1	0	5	0		7	79.2	106	49	15	2	23	4	38	4.97	-23	.320	.367	-24	0	-0.8
Total	5	38	36	.514	160	101	17	4	54	2		36	724.2	741	358	87	14	207	17	371	4.09	-11	.266	.317	+2	0	-4.4
SHEPHERD, KEITH Keith Wayne B1.21.1968 Wabash IN BR/TR/6'2"/(197–215) [PitN86 11/264] d9.6																											
1995	Bos A	0	0	+	2	0	0	0	0	0	0	0	1	4	4	0	0	2	0	0	36.00	-86	.571	.667		35	-0.1
Total	4	2	5	.286	41	1	0	0	0	3	5	21	63	80	57	10	1	30	2	34	6.71	-34	.315	.383	+13	35	-1.3
SHIELDS, BEN Benjamin Cowan "Big Ben","Lefty" B6.17.1903 Huntersville NC D1.24.1982 Woodruff SC BR/TL (BB 1930–31)/6'1.5"/195 d4.17																											
1930	Bos A	0	0	+	3	0	0	0		0			10	16	11	0	0	6		1	9.00	-49	.400	.478			-0.2
Total	4	4	0	1.000	13	2	2	0		0			41.1	55	39	3	2	27		9	8.27	-47	.335	.435	+28		-1.4
SHIELL, JASON Jason Alexander B10.19.1976 Savannah GA BR/TR/6'0"/180 [AtlN95 48/1328] d9.8 [DL 2004 Bos A 183]																											
2002	SD N	0	0	+	3	0	0	0	0	0	0	0	1.1	7	4	0	0	3	0	1	27.00	-86	.700	.769		0	-0.2
2003	Bos A	2	0	1.000	17	0	0	0	0	1	1	9	23.1	23	13	4	2	17	2	23	4.63	+1	.253	.382		0	0.0
2006	Atl N	0	2	.000	4	3	0	0	0	0	0	0	15.2	23	15	5	1	9	1	14	8.62	-47	.343	.423	-32	0	-0.6
Total	3	2	2	.500	24	3	0	0	0	1	1	9	40.1	53	32	9	3	29	3	38	6.92	-34	.315	.423	-32	183	-0.8
SHORE, ERNIE Ernest Grady B3.24.1891 East Bend NC D9.24.1980 Winston–Salem NC BR/TR/6'4"/220 d6.20 Mil 1918 Col Guilford																											
1912	NY N	0	0	+	1	0	0	0		1			1	8	10	1	0	1		1	27.00	-87	.667	.692			-0.6
1914	Bos A	10	5	.667	20	16	10	1		1			139.2	103	45	1	5	34		51	2.00	+35	.204	.261	-12		0.9
1915	†Bos A	19	8	.704	38	32	17	4		0			247	207	75	3	4	66		102	1.64	+69	.228	.283	-10		2.8
1916	†Bos A	16	10	.615	38	28	10	3		1			225.2	221	83	1	4	49		62	2.63	+5	.259	.302	-5		0.1
1917	Bos A	13	10	.565	29	27	14	1		1			226.2	201	76	1	12	55		57	2.22	+16	.240	.297	-6		0.8
1919	NY A	5	8	.385	20	13	3	0		0			95	105	50	4	1	44		24	4.17	-23	.288	.366	-30		-1.2
1920	NY A	2	2	.500	14	5	2	0		1			44.1	61	31	1	1	21		12	4.87	-22	.333	.405	+12		-0.4
Total	7	65	43	.602	160	121	56	9		5			979.1	906	370	12	27	270		309	2.47	+13	.247	.304	-9		2.4
Team	4	58	33	.637	125	103	51	9		3			839	732	279	6	25	204		272	2.12	+28	.236	.288	-8		4.6
/180I	1	12	7	.637	27	22	11	2		1			180	157	60	1	5	44		58	2.12	+28	.236	.288	-8		1.0
SHORT, BILL William Ross B11.27.1937 Kingston NY BL/TL/5'9"/(170–180) d4.23																											
1966	Bos A	0	0	+	8	0	0	0	0	0		5	8.1	10	6	1	0	2	0	2	4.32	-12	.294	.333		0	0.0
Total	6	5	11	.313	73	16	3	1	7	2	0	38	131.1	130	75	8	3	64	2	71	4.73	-28	.262	.346	-15	0	-1.7
SHOUSE, BRIAN Brian Douglas B9.26.1968 Effingham IL BL/TL/5'11"/(175–190) [PitN90 13/349] d7.31 Col Bradley [DL 1999 Ari N 16]																											
1998	Bos A	0	1	.000	7	0	0	0	0	0	0	3	8	9	5	2	0	4	0	5	5.63	-16	.281	.361		0	-0.1
Total	7	6	7	.462	280	0	0	0	0	3	5	191	223.2	224	110	21	16	83	19	151	3.98	+19	.261	.335		86	1.1
SIEBERT, SONNY Wilfred Charles B1.14.1937 St.Marys MO BR/TR/6'3"/(190–205) d4.26 C2 Col Missouri																											
1964	Cle A	7	9	.438	41	14	3	1	8	3		20	156	142	61	15	2	57	4	144	3.23	+11	.243	.310	-15	0	1.2
1965	Cle A	16	8	.667	39	27	4	1	17	1		11	188.2	139	58	14	5	46	2	191	2.43	+43	.206	**.259**	+2	0	2.7
1966	Cle A★	16	8	**.667**	34	32	11	1	24	1		2	241	193	89	25	6	62	3	163	2.80	+23	.221	.276	+11	0	1.3
1967	Cle A	10	12	.455	34	26	7	1	16	4		5	185.1	136	59	17	6	54	2	136	2.38	+37	.202	.266	-20	0	2.2
1968	Cle A	12	10	.545	31	30	8	4	20	0		1	206	145	76	12	8	88	10	146	2.97	+0	.198	.288	+13	0	0.4
1969	Cle A	0	1	.000	2	2	0	0	1	0	0	0	14	10	5	1	0	8	0	6	3.21	+18	.196	.305	-65	0	0.1
1969	Bos A	14	10	.583	43	22	2	0	11	5	3	17	163.1	151	93	21	4	68	1	127	3.80	+1	.245	.321	+9	0	-0.6
1969	Year	14	11	.560	45	24	2	0	12	5	3	17	177.1	161	98	22	4	76	1	133	3.76	+2	.241	.320	+3	0	-0.5
1970	Bos A	15	8	.652	33	33	7	2	21	0	0	0	222.2	207	98	29	6	60	2	142	3.44	+16	.248	.302	+2	0	1.1
1971	Bos A☆	16	10	.615	32	32	12	4	23	0	0	0	235.1	220	84	20	3	60	5	131	2.91	+28	.245	.292	+3	0	3.3
1972	Bos A	12	12	.500	32	30	7	3	17	0	0	1	196.1	204	105	17	7	59	4	123	3.80	-15	.264	.321	+29	0	-1.2
1973	Bos A	0	1	.000	2	0	0	0	0	0	1	0	2.1	5	2	1	0	1	0	5	7.71	-48	.417	.462		0	-0.2
1973	Tex A	7	11	.389	25	20	1	1	11	2	0	3	119.2	120	68	11	3	37	1	76	3.99	-6	.258	.314	-4	0	-0.8
1973	Year	7	12	.368	27	20	1	1	11	2	1	3	122	125	70	12	3	38	1	81	4.06	-7	.262	.318	-4	0	-1.0
1974	StL N	8	8	.500	28	20	5	3	12	0	0	5	133.2	150	66	8	3	51	14	68	3.84	-6	.288	.353	-2	23	-0.7
1975	SD N	3	2	.600	6	6	0	0	2	0	0	0	26.2	37	15	2	1	10	4	10	4.39	-20	.330	.387	-20	0	-0.2

Year	Tm Lg	W	L	Pct	G	GS	CG	ShO	QS	SV	BS	QR	IP	H	R	HR	HB	BB	IB	SO	ERA	AERA	OAV	OOB	Sup	DL	PW
1975	Oak A	4	4	.500	17	13	0	0	0	0	0	3	61	60	28	4	0	31	3	44	3.69	-1	.252	.335	-3	40	-0.1
1975	Major	7	6	.538	23	19	0	0	2	0	0	3	87	97	43	6	1	41	7	54	3.90	-7	.277	.351	-8	40	-0.3
Total	12	140	114	.551	399	307	67	21	183	16	4	68	2152	1919	907	197	54	692	55	1512	3.21	+10	.238	.301	+3	63	8.5
Team	5	57	41	.582	142	117	28	9	72	5	4	18	820	787	382	88	20	248	12	528	3.46	+7	.251	.308	+11		2.4
/180I	1	13	9	.582	31	26	6	2	16	1	1	4	180	173	84	19	4	54	3	116	3.46	+7	.251	.308	+11		0.5
SIMMONS, PAT Patrick Clement (b Patrick Clement Simoni) B11.29.1908 Watervliet NY D7.3.1968 Albany NY BR/TR/5'11"/172 d4.18																											
1928	Bos A	0	2	.000	31	3	0	0		1			69	69	38	4	1	38		16	4.04	+2	.271	.367	-18		-0.1
1929	Bos A	0	0	+	2	0	0	0		1			7	6	0	0	0	3		2	0.00	-100	.231	.310			0.1
Total	2	0	2	.000	33	3	0	0		2			76	75	38	4	1	41		18	3.67	+12	.267	.362	-18		0.0
SISLER, DAVE David Michael B10.16.1931 St.Louis MO BR/TR/6'4"/(190–200) d4.21 b–Dick f–George Col Princeton																											
1956	Bos A	9	8	.529	39	14	3	0		3			142.1	120	81	13	7	72	2	93	4.62	+0	.227	.326	-17	0	-0.1
1957	Bos A	7	8	.467	22	19	5	0	19	1		5	122.1	135	68	15	2	61	1	55	4.71	-15	.280	.361	+4	0	-0.9
1958	Bos A	8	9	.471	30	25	4	1	19	0		5	149.1	157	94	22	1	79	2	71	4.94	-19	.276	.361	+2	0	-1.5
1959	Bos A	0	0	+	3	0	0	0	19	0		5	6.2	9	5	3	0	1	0	3	6.75	-40	.310	.333		0	-0.1
1959	Det A	1	3	.250	32	0	0	0	0	7		22	51.2	46	28	4	1	36	1	29	4.01	+1	.242	.362		0	-0.1
1959	Year	1	3	.250	35	0	0	0	19	7		27	58.1	55	33	7	1	37	1	32	4.32	-6	.251	.359		0	-0.2
1960	Det A	7	5	.583	41	0	0	0	0	6		28	80	56	23	3	2	45	1	47	2.47	+60	.199	.311		0	2.2
1961	Was A	2	8	.200	45	1	0	0	0	11		30	60.1	55	34	6	3	48	5	30	4.18	-4	.251	.390	-78	0	-0.3
1962	Cin N	4	3	.571	35	0	0	0	0	1		26	43.2	44	19	4	0	26	3	27	3.92	+3	.270	.370		0	0.2
Total	7	38	44	.463	247	59	12	1	57	29		121	656.1	622	352	70	16	368	15	355	4.33	-5	.253	.351	-4	0	-0.6
Team	4	24	25	.490	94	58	12	1	57	4		15	420.2	421	248	53	10	213	5	222	4.79	-12	.262	.349	-2		-2.6
/180I	2	10	11	.490	40	25	5	0	24	2		6	180	180	106	23	4	91	2	95	4.79	-12	.262	.349	-2		-1.1
SKOK, CRAIG Craig Richard B9.1.1947 Dobbs Ferry NY BR/TL/6'0"/(175–190) d5.4 Col Florida St.																											
1973	Bos A	0	1	.000	11	0	0	0	0	1	0	4	28.2	35	22	2	0	11	2	22	6.28	-36	.304	.357		0	-0.4
Total	4	4	7	.364	107	0	0	0	0	5	4	77	150	170	93	19	3	58	12	85	4.86	-17	.289	.352		0	-1.3
SLAYTON, STEVE Foster Herbert B4.26.1902 Barre VT D12.20.1984 Manchester NH BR/TR/6'0"/163 d7.21 Col New Hampshire																											
1928	Bos A	0	0	+	3	0	0	0		0			7	6	3	0	0	3		2	3.86	+7	.240	.321			0.0
SLOCUMB, HEATHCLIFF Heath B6.7.1966 Jamaica NY BR/TR/6'3"/(210–220) d4.11																											
1996	Bos A	5	5	.500	75	0	0	0	0	31	8	60	83.1	68	31	2	3	55	5	88	3.02	+69	.222	.343		0	3.3
1997	Bos A	0	5	.000	49	0	0	0	0	17	5	31	46.2	58	32	4	3	34	4	36	5.79	-20	.312	.422		0	-0.8
Total	10	28	37	.431	548	0	0	0	0	98	31	382	631	636	320	38	21	358	40	513	4.08	+9	.263	.360		23	4.5
Team	2	5	10	.333	124	0	0	0	0	48	13	91	130	126	63	6	6	89	9	124	4.02	+23	.256	.373			2.5
/60G	1	2	5	.333	60	0	0	0	0	23	6	44	63	61	30	3	3	43	4	60	4.01	+23	.256	.373			1.2
SMITH, CHARLIE Charles Edwin B4.20.1880 Cleveland OH D1.3.1929 Wickliffe OH BR/TR/6'1"/185 d8.6 b–Fred																											
1909	Bos A	3	0	1.000	3	3	2	0		0			25	23	6	2	1	2		11	2.16	+16	.237	.260	+60		0.3
1910	Bos A	11	6	.647	24	18	11	0		1			156.1	141	57	4	2	35		53	2.30	+11	.248	.294	-1		0.1
1911	Bos A	0	0	+	1	1	0	0		0			2	2	3	1	0	1		0	9.00	-64	.250	.333	-34		0.0
Total	10	66	87	.431	212	148	87	10		3			1349.1	1309	587	22	29	353		570	2.81	-6	.259	.311	-16		-3.5
Team	3	14	6	.700	28	22	13	0		1			183.1	166	66	7	3	38		64	2.36	+8	.246	.290	+6		0.4
/180I	3	14	6	.700	27	22	13	0		1			180	163	65	7	3	37		63	2.36	+8	.246	.290	+6		0.4
SMITH, DAN Daniel Charles B9.15.1975 Flemington NJ BR/TR/6'3"/210 [TexA93 7/199] d6.8 [DL 2004 Mon N 183]																											
2000	Bos A	0	0	+	2	0	0	0	0	0	0	1	3.1	2	3	0	0	3	0	1	8.10	-38	.250	.357		0	-0.1
Total	4	7	12	.368	87	17	0	0	5	2	2	45	177.1	182	108	29	7	81	2	142	5.23	-15	.270	.351	+6	278	-2.0
SMITH, DOUG Douglass Weldon B5.25.1892 Millers Falls MA D9.18.1973 Greenfield MA BL/TL/5'10"/168 d7.10																											
1912	Bos A	0	0	+	1	0	0	0		0			3	4	1	0	0	0		1	3.00	+13	.364	.364			0.0
SMITH, EDDIE Edgar B12.14.1913 Mansfield NJ D1.2.1994 Willingboro NJ BB/TL/5'10"/174 d9.20 Mil 1944–45																											
1947	Bos A	1	3	.250	8	3	0	0		0			17	18	14	3	0	18		15	7.41	-48	.269	.424	+67	0	-1.1
Total	10	73	113	.392	282	197	91	8		12			1595.2	1554	816	106	33	739		694	3.82	+8	.256	.340	-23	0	4.4
SMITH, FRANK Frank Elmer "Nig","Piano Mover" (b Frank Elmer Schmidt) B10.28.1879 Pittsburgh PA D11.3.1952 Pittsburgh PA BR/TR/5'10.5"/194 d4.22 Col Grove City																											
1910	Bos A	1	2	.333	4	3	2	0		0			28	22	19	0	1	11		8	4.82	-47	.234	.321	-21		-0.6
1911	Bos A	0	0	+	1	1	0	0		0			2.1	6	4	0	0	3		1	15.43	-79	.500	.600	+208		-0.1
Total	11	139	111	.556	354	255	184	27		6			2273	1975	891	27	41	676		1051	2.59	-1	.237	.297	+9		6.6
Team	2	1	2	.333	5	4	2	0		0			30.1	28	23	0	1	14		9	5.64	-54	.264	.355	+36		-0.7
SMITH, GEORGE George Shelby B10.27.1901 Louisville KY D5.26.1981 Richmond VA BR/TR/6'1"/175 d4.21																											
1930	Bos A	1	2	.333	27	2	0	0		0			73.2	92	62	7	1	49		21	6.60	-30	.317	.418	+3		-0.6
Total	5	10	8	.556	132	7	1	0		3			330.2	354	225	17	5	218		135	5.28	-19	.283	.392	+2		-2.0
SMITH, LEE Lee Arthur B12.4.1957 Shreveport LA BR/TR/6'6"/(220–269) [ChiN75 2/28] d9.1																											
1988	†Bos A	4	5	.444	64	0	0	0	0	29	8	50	83.2	72	34	7	1	37	6	96	2.80	+48	.225	.306		0	1.5
1989	Bos A	6	1	.857	64	0	0	0	0	25	5	48	70.2	53	30	6	0	33	6	96	3.57	+15	.209	.299		0	0.7
1990	Bos A	2	1	.667	11	0	0	0	0	4	1	8	14.1	13	4	0	0	9	2	17	1.88	+118	.236	.344		0	0.7
Total	18	71	92	.436	1022	6	0	0	3	478	10	764	1289.1	1133	475	89	10	486	10	1251	3.03	+33	.237	.306	-25	35	22.9
Team	3	12	7	.632	139	0	0	0	0	58	14	106	168.2	138	68	13	1	79	14	209	3.04	+35	.219	.307			2.9
/60G	1	5	3	.632	60	0	0	0	0	25	6	46	72.2	60	29	6	0	34	6	90	3.05	+35	.219	.307			1.3
SMITH, PETE Peter Luke B3.19.1940 Natick MA BR/TR/6'2"/190 d9.13 Mil 1963 Col Colgate [DL 1964 Bos A 134]																											
1962	Bos A	0	1	.000	1	1	0	0	0	0		0	3.2	7	8	3	0	2	0	1	19.64	-79	.438	.474	+30	0	-0.8
1963	Bos A	0	0	+	6	1	0	0	1	0		4	15	11	6	2	0	6	2	6	3.60	+5	.212	.293	+17	0	0.0
Total	2	0	1	.000	7	2	0	0	1	0		4	18.2	18	14	5	0	8	2	7	6.75	-43	.265	.338	+27	134	-0.8
SMITH, BOB Robert Gilchrist B2.1.1931 Woodsville NH BR/TL/6'1.5"/(190–195) d4.29																											
1955	Bos A	0	0	+	1	0	0	0		0			1.2	1	0	0	0	1	0	1	0.00	-100	.200	.333		0	0.0
Total	4	4	9	.308	91	8	2	0	15	2		129	166.2	174	102	15	4	83	12	93	4.05	-5	.267	.353	-5	30	-1.6
SMITH, BOB Robert Walkup "Riverboat" B5.13.1927 Clarence MO D6.23.2003 Clarence MO BR/TL (BB 1959)/6'0"/180 d4.22 Col Missouri																											
1958	Bos A	4	3	.571	17	7	1	0	3	0		8	66.2	61	32	4	0	45	2	43	3.78	+6	.248	.362	+9	0	0.1
1959	Chi N	0	0	+	1	0	0	0	0	0		0	0.2	5	6	0	0	2	1	0	81.00	-95	.833	.875		0	-0.2
1959	Cle A	0	1	.000	12	3	0	0	0	0		6	29.1	31	19	2	0	12	0	17	5.22	-29	.282	.341	+12	0	-0.3
1959	Major	0	1	.000	13	3	0	0	0	0		6	29	36	25	2	0	14	1	17	6.90	-30	.310	.373	+12	0	-0.5
Total	2	4	4	.500	30	10	1	0	3	0		14	96.2	97	57	6	0	59	3	60	4.75	-18	.268	.365	+10	0	-0.4
SMITH, ZANE Zane William B12.28.1960 Madison WI BL/TL/6'2"/(195–207) [AtlN82 3/63] d9.10 Col Indiana St.																											
1995	†Bos A	8	8	.500	24	21	0	0	8	0	0	2	110.2	144	78	7	1	23	1	47	5.61	-13	.316	.347	+11	38	-1.2
Total	13	100	115	.465	360	291	35	16	169	3	1	48	1919.1	1980	933	122	31	583	55	1011	3.74	+6	.271	.326	-6	277	3.0
SMITHSON, MIKE Billy Mike B1.21.1955 Centerville TN BL/TR/6'8"/(200–215) [BosA76 5/118] d8.27 Col Tennessee																											
1988	†Bos A	9	6	.600	31	18	1	0	6	0	0	8	126.2	149	87	25	6	37	1	73	5.97	-31	.292	.345	+25	0	-2.4
1989	Bos A	7	14	.333	40	19	1	1	9	2	1	11	143.2	170	84	21	10	35	5	61	4.95	-17	.297	.343	+8	0	-1.4
Total	8	76	86	.469	240	204	41	6	99	2	1	19	1356.1	1473	745	168	73	383	25	731	4.58	-7	.277	.331	-2	28	-4.6
Team	2	16	20	.444	71	37	2	1	15	2	1	19	270.1	319	171	46	16	72	6	134	5.43	-24	.295	.344	+16		-3.8
/180I	1	11	13	.444	47	25	1	1	10	1	1	13	180	212	114	31	11	48	4	89	5.43	-24	.295	.344	+16		-2.5
SNYDER, KYLE Kyle Ehren B9.9.1977 Houston TX BB/TR/6'8"/(215–220) [KCA99 1/7] d5.1 Col North Carolina [DL 2004 KC A 183]																											
2003	KC A	1	6	.143	15	15	0	0	6	0	0	0	85.1	94	52	11	2	21	3	39	5.17	-7	.283	.321	-37	74	-0.2
2005	KC A	1	3	.250	13	3	0	0	0	0	0	7	36	55	29	3	1	10	1	19	6.75	-35	.353	.391	-1	64	-0.9
2006	KC A	0	0	+	1	1	0	0	0	0	0	0	2	10	9	1	0	1	0	2	22.50	-79	.556	.579	+221	0	-0.2
2006	Bos A	4	5	.444	16	10	0	0	1	0	0	3	58.1	77	42	11	2	19	3	55	6.02	-22	.314	.366	-27	0	-1.1
2006	Year	4	5	.444	17	11	0	0	1	0	0	3	60.1	87	51	12	2	20	3	57	6.56	-29	.331	.380	-5	0	-1.3
Total	3	6	14	.300	45	29	0	0	7	0	0	10	181.2	236	132	26	5	51	7	115	5.94	-21	.314	.356	-21	321	-2.4

Year	Tm Lg	W	L	Pct	G	GS	CG	ShO	QS	SV	BS	QR	IP	H	R	HR	HB	BB	IB	SO	ERA	AERA	OAV	OOB	Sup	DL	PW
SOMMERS, RUDY Rudolph B10.30.1886 Cincinnati OH D3.18.1949 Louisville KY BB/TL/5'11"/165 d9.8																											
1926	Bos A	0	0	+	2	0	0	0		0			2	3	3	0	0	3		0	13.50	-70	.333	.500			-0.1
1927	Bos A	0	0	+	7	0	0	0		0			14	18	15	2	0	14		2	8.36	-49	.353	.492			-0.2
Total	4	2	8	.200	33	8	2	0		2			101	113	73	4	3	53		44	4.81	-36	.294	.384	-11		-1.4
Team	2	0	0	+	9	0	0	0		0			16	21	18	2	0	17		2	9.00	-53	.350	.494			-0.3
SOTHORON, ALLEN Allen Sutton B4.27.1893 Bradford OH D6.17.1939 St.Louis MO BB/TR (BR 1924–26)/5'11"/182 d9.17 M1/C4 Col Juniata																											
1921	Bos A	0	2	.000	2	2	0	0		0			6	15	10	0	0	5		2	13.50	-69	.455	.526	-61		-0.9
Total	11	91	99	.479	264	193	102	17		9			1582.1	1583	786	34	54	596		576	3.31	+5	.264	.336	+2		-0.8
SPANSWICK, BILL William Henry B7.8.1938 Springfield MA BL/TL/6'3"/195 d4.18 Col Holy Cross																											
1964	Bos A	2	3	.400	29	7	0	0	1	0		13	65.1	75	51	9	3	44	1	55	6.89	-44	.306	.412	+28	0	-1.2
SPARKS, TULLY Thomas Frank B12.12.1874 Etna GA D7.15.1937 Anniston AL BR/TR/5'10"/160 d9.15 Col Beloit																											
1902	Bos A	7	9	.438	17	15	15	1		0			142.2	151	83	4	7	40		37	3.47	+3	.272	.329	-33		-0.1
Total	12	121	137	.469	314	270	203	19		8			2343.2	2250	1067	33	87	630		780	2.82	+4	.254	.310	-10		-2.2
/180I	1	9	11	.438	21	19	19	1		0			180	191	105	5	9	50		47	3.47	+3	.272	.329	-15		-0.1
SPRING, JACK Jack Russell B3.11.1933 Spokane WA BR/TL/6'1"/(167–182) d4.16 Col Washington St.																											
1957	Bos A	0	0	+	1	0	0	0	0	0		1	1	0	0	0	0	0	0	2	0.00	-100	.000	.000		0	0.0
Total	8	12	5	.706	155	5	0	0	4	8		101	186	195	106	21	5	78	18	86	4.26	-10	.273	.346	+67	0	-0.7
SPROWL, BOBBY Robert John B4.14.1956 Sandusky OH BL/TL/6'2"/190 [BosA77 2/39] d9.5 Col Alabama																											
1978	Bos A	0	2	.000	3	3	0	0	1	0	0	0	12.2	12	10	3	0	10	0	10	6.39	-36	.245	.373	-27	0	-0.4
Total	4	0	3	.000	22	4	0	0	2	0	0	9	46.1	54	30	4	0	27	1	34	5.44	-35	.292	.379	+1	0	-0.8
STALLARD, TRACY Evan Tracy B8.31.1937 Coeburn VA BR/TR/6'5"/(204–205) d9.24																											
1960	Bos A	0	0	+	4	0	0	0	0	0		4	4	0	0	0	0	2	0	6	0.00	-100	.000	.133		0	0.1
1961	Bos A	2	7	.222	43	14	1	0	5	2		17	132.2	110	75	15	1	96	2	109	4.88	-15	.229	.354	-9	0	-0.8
1962	Bos A	0	0	+	1	0	0	0	0	0		1	1	0	0	0	0	0	0	0	0.00	-100	.000	.000		0	0.0
Total	7	30	57	.345	183	104	21	3	53	4		46	764.2	716	398	92	16	343	19	477	4.17	-10	.248	.329	-8	0	-5.6
Team	3	2	7	.222	48	14	1	0	5	2		22	137.2	110	75	15	1	98	2	115	4.71	-12	.229	.348	-9		-0.7
/60G	4	3	9	.222	60	18	1	0	6	3		28	172	138	94	19	1	123	3	144	4.71	-12	.229	.348	-9		-0.9
STANGE, LEE Albert Lee B10.27.1936 Chicago IL BR/TR/5'10"/(168–175) d4.15 C12 Col Drake																											
1961	Min A	1	0	1.000	7	0	0	0	0	0		5	12.1	15	6	1	0	10	1	10	2.92	+45	.294	.410		0	0.1
1962	Min A	4	3	.571	44	6	1	0	1	3		28	95	98	57	14	1	39	3	70	4.45	-8	.271	.342	+60	0	-0.5
1963	Min A	12	5	.706	32	20	7	2	16	0		8	164.2	145	53	21	0	43	1	100	2.62	+39	.233	.283	+30	0	1.8
1964	Min A	3	6	.333	14	11	2	0	7	0		1	79.2	78	45	13	0	19	3	54	4.74	-25	.255	.297	+33	0	-1.0
1964	Cle A	4	8	.333	23	14	0	0	7	0		3	91.2	98	47	14	1	31	4	78	4.12	-13	.270	.329	-5	0	-0.8
1964	Year	7	14	.333	37	25	2	0	14	0		4	171.1	176	92	27	1	50	7	132	4.41	-19	.263	.314	+12	0	-1.8
1965	Cle A	8	4	.667	41	12	4	2	6	0		18	132	122	50	13	1	26	6	80	3.34	+4	.247	.284	-1	0	0.4
1966	Cle A	1	0	1.000	8	2	1	0	1	0		2	16	17	5	1	1	3	0	8	2.81	+22	.279	.318	-36	0	0.1
1966	Bos A	7	9	.438	28	19	8	2	13	0		4	153.1	140	65	17	1	43	9	77	3.35	+14	.246	.296	-24	0	0.3
1966	Year	8	9	.471	36	21	9	2	14	0		6	169.1	157	70	18	2	46	9	85	3.30	+14	.249	.298	-25	0	0.4
1967	†Bos A	8	10	.444	35	24	6	2	18	1		8	181.2	171	64	14	2	32	7	101	2.77	+26	.246	.281	-1	0	0.9
1968	Bos A	5	5	.500	50	2	1	0	0	12		37	103	89	54	10	1	25	5	53	3.93	-20	.237	.280	-17	0	-1.3
1969	Bos A	6	9	.400	41	15	2	0	7	3	1	18	137	137	70	14	6	56	8	59	3.68	+4	.256	.332	-4	0	-0.3
1970	Bos A	2	2	.500	20	0	0	0	0	2	0	12	27.1	34	24	5	2	12	3	14	5.60	-29	.301	.369		0	-1.0
1970	Chi A	1	0	1.000	16	0	0	0	0	0	1	10	22.1	28	13	5	0	5	1	14	5.24	-26	.295	.330		0	-0.2
1970	Year	3	2	.600	36	0	0	0	0	2	1	22	49.2	62	37	10	2	17	4	28	5.44	-28	.298	.352		0	-1.2
Total	10	62	61	.504	359	125	32	8	76	21	2	154	1216	1172	553	142	16	344	51	718	3.56	+2	.252	.304	+5	0	-1.5
Team	5	28	35	.444	174	60	17	4	38	18	1	79	602.1	571	277	60	12	168	32	304	3.45	+5	.250	.301	-10		-1.4
/180I	1	8	10	.444	52	18	5	1	11	5	0	24	180	171	83	18	4	50	10	91	3.45	+5	.250	.301	-10		-0.4
STANIFER, ROB Robert Wayne B3.10.1972 Easley SC BR/TR/6'3"/205 [FlaN94 12/320] d5.3 Col Anderson																											
2000	Bos A	0	0	+	8	0	0	0	0	0	0	5	13	22	19	3	0	4	1	3	7.62	-34	.355	.394		0	-0.3
Total	3	3	6	.333	82	0	0	0	0	2	3	52	106	119	75	17	3	42	3	61	5.43	-23	.282	.349		0	-1.4
STANLEY, BOB Robert William B11.10.1954 Portland ME BR/TR/6'4"/(205–225) [BosA74*S1/7] d4.16																											
1977	Bos A	8	7	.533	41	13	3	1	6	3	2	18	151	176	74	10	3	43	5	44	3.99	+12	.294	.343	+3	0	0.8
1978	Bos A	15	2	.882	52	3	0	0	3	10	5	36	141.2	142	50	5	1	34	5	38	2.60	+58	.266	.308	+89	0	2.8
1979	Bos A★	16	12	.571	40	30	9	4	17	1	0	7	216.2	250	110	14	4	44	4	56	3.99	+12	.294	.330	-5	0	1.1
1980	Bos A	10	8	.556	52	17	5	1	8	14	3	28	175	186	75	11	7	52	8	71	3.39	+26	.278	.335	+5	0	1.8
1981	Bos A	10	8	.556	35	1	0	0	1	0	3	16	98.2	110	46	3	6	38	4	28	3.83	+2	.294	.365	-54	0	0.5
1982	Bos A	12	7	.632	48	0	0	0	0	14	2	34	168.1	161	60	11	4	50	6	83	3.10	+40	.255	.312		0	3.1
1983	Bos A★	8	10	.444	64	0	0	0	0	33	14	49	145.1	145	56	7	3	38	12	65	2.85	+54	.266	.315		0	3.4
1984	Bos A	9	10	.474	57	0	0	0	0	22	5	37	106.2	113	57	9	2	23	9	52	3.54	+19	.267	.307		0	0.8
1985	Bos A	6	6	.500	48	0	0	0	0	10	8	33	87.2	76	30	7	2	30	10	46	2.87	+50	.237	.303		0	2.0
1986	†Bos A	6	6	.500	66	1	0	0	0	16	5	43	82.1	109	48	9	0	22	8	54	4.37	-4	.322	.360	+8	0	-0.5
1987	Bos A	4	15	.211	34	20	4	1	9	0	2	8	152.2	198	96	17	1	42	7	67	5.01	-9	.321	.363	-15	18	-0.9
1988	†Bos A	6	4	.600	57	0	0	0	0	5	6	40	101.2	90	41	6	7	29	7	57	3.19	+30	.242	.304		38	0.9
1989	Bos A	5	2	.714	43	0	0	0	0	4	0	27	79.1	102	54	4	1	26	2	32	4.88	-16	.321	.366		0	-0.7
Total	13	115	97	.542	637	85	21	7	44	132	55	376	1707	1858	797	113	41	471	87	693	3.64	+18	.282	.331	+1	56	15.1
/60G	1	11	9	.542	60	8	2	1	4	12	5	35	160.2	175	75	11	4	44	8	65	3.64	+18	.282	.331	-90	5	1.4
STANTON, MIKE William Michael B6.2.1967 Houston TX BL/TL/6'1"/(190–215) [AtlN87 13/324] d8.24 Col Southwestern (TX)																											
1995	†Bos A	1	0	1.000	22	0	0	0	0	0	1	18	21	17	9	3	0	8	0	10	3.00	+62	.224	.298		0	0.2
1996	Bos A	4	3	.571	59	0	0	0	0	1	4	38	56.1	58	24	9	0	23	4	46	3.83	+33	.275	.343		0	1.0
2005	Bos A	0	0	+	1	0	0	0	0	0	0	1	1	1	0	0	0	0	0	1	0.00	-100	.333	.333		0	0.0
Total	18	67	60	.528	1109	1	0	0	0	84	56	779	1056.1	1011	484	87	28	402	74	855	3.81	+15	.254	.324	+18	206	5.9
Team	3	5	3	.625	82	0	0	0	0	1	5	57	78.1	76	33	12	0	31	4	57	3.56	+41	.262	.331			1.2
/60G	2	4	2	.625	60	0	0	0	0	1	4	42	57.1	56	24	9	0	23	3	42	3.56	+41	.262	.331			0.9
STEELE, ELMER Elmer Rae B5.17.1886 Poughkeepsie NY D3.9.1966 Rhinebeck NY BB/TR/5'11"/200 d9.12																											
1907	Bos A	0	1	.000	4	1	0	0		0			11.1	11	7	0	0	1		10	1.59	+62	.256	.273	-100		-0.1
1908	Bos A	5	7	.417	16	13	9	1		0			118	85	34	1	3	13		37	1.83	+34	.209	.239	-23		0.4
1909	Bos A	4	4	.500	16	8	2	0		1			75.2	75	37	1	1	15		32	2.85	-12	.255	.294	+48		-0.3
1910	Pit N	0	3	.000	3	3	2	0		0			24	19	9	0	0	3		7	2.25	+38	.221	.247	-68		0.2
1911	Pit N	9	9	.500	31	16	7	2		2			166	153	65	5	4	31		52	2.60	+32	.256	.297	+42		1.4
1911	Bro N	0	0	+	5	2	0	0		0			23	24	10	0	0	5		9	3.13	+7	.258	.296	+46		0.0
1911	Year	9	9	.500	36	18	7	2		2			189	177	75	5	4	36		61	2.67	+28	.257	.297	+43		1.4
Total	5	18	24	.429	75	43	20	3		3			418	367	162	7	8	68		147	2.41	+22	.241	.278	+14		1.6
Team	3	9	12	.429	36	22	11	1		1			205	171	78	2	4	29		79	2.20	+13	.230	.263	-1		0.0
/180I	3	8	11	.429	32	19	10	1		1			180	150	68	2	4	25		69	2.20	+13	.230	.263	-1		0.0
STEPHENSON, JERRY Jerry Joseph B10.6.1943 Detroit MI BL/TR/6'2"/(175–200) d4.14 f–Joe																											
1963	Bos A	0	0	+	1	1	0	0	0	0		0	2.1	5	2	0	0	2	0	3	7.71	-51	.556	.538	+41	0	-0.1
1965	Bos A	1	5	.167	15	8	0	0	2	0		4	52	62	41	7	1	33	0	49	6.23	-40	.287	.382	-26	0	-1.3
1966	Bos A	2	5	.286	15	11	1	0	4	0		1	66.1	68	51	6	1	44	1	50	5.83	-35	.264	.370	+12	47	-1.5
1967	†Bos A	3	1	.750	8	6	0	0	2	1		2	39.2	32	18	4	1	16	2	24	3.86	-10	.227	.308	-8	0	-0.1
1968	Bos A	2	8	.200	23	7	2	0	1	0		7	68.2	81	51	4	2	42	3	51	5.64	-44	.295	.387	-13	0	-2.4
1969	Sea A	0	0	+	2	0	0	0	0	0	0	1	2.2	6	4	0	1	3	0	1	10.13	-64	.429	.556		0	-0.1
1970	LA N	0	0	+	3	0	0	0	0	0	0	1	6.2	11	7	0	0	5	0	6	9.45	-59	.379	.471		0	-0.2
Total	7	8	19	.296	67	33	3	0	9	1	0	16	238.1	265	174	21	6	145	6	184	5.70	-38	.281	.377	-4	47	-5.7
Team	5	8	19	.296	62	33	3	0	9	1		14	229	248	163	21	5	137	6	177	5.54	-36	.276	.371	-5	47	-5.4
/180I	4	6	15	.296	49	26	2	0	7	1		11	180	195	128	17	4	108	5	139	5.54	-36	.276	.371	-5	37	-4.2

Year	Tm Lg	W	L	Pct	G	GS	CG	ShO	QS	SV	BS	QR	IP	H	R	HR	HB	BB	IB	SO	ERA	AERA	OAV	OOB	Sup	DL	PW
STEWART, SAMMY Samuel Lee B10.28.1954 Asheville NC BR/TR/6'3"/(207–219) d9.1 Col Montreat																											
1986	Bos A	4	1	.800	27	0	0	0	0	0	0	14	63.2	64	33	7	0	48	2	47	4.38	-4	.266	.381		35	-0.1
Total	10	59	48	.551	359	25	4	1	10	45	18	222	956.2	863	421	77	16	502	43	586	3.59	+11	.245	.338	-8	79	4.3
STIGMAN, DICK Richard Lewis B1.24.1936 Nimrod MN BR/TL/6'3"/200 d4.22																											
1966	Bos A	2	1	.667	34	10	1	1	4	0		12	81	85	51	15	1	46	5	65	5.44	-30	.268	.361	-21	0	-0.7
Total	7	46	54	.460	235	119	30	5	57	16		74	922.2	819	442	133	8	406	22	755	4.03	-7	.237	.316	-3	56	-2.2
STIMSON, CARL Carl Remus B7.18.1894 Hamburg IA D11.9.1936 Omaha NE BB/TR/6'5"/190 d6.6																											
1923	Bos A	0	0	+	2	0	0	0		0			4	12	10	0	1	5		1	22.50	-82	.750	.818			-0.3
STOBBS, CHUCK Charles Klein B7.2.1929 Wheeling WV BL/TL/6'1"/(185–205) d9.15																											
1947	Bos A	0	1	.000	4	1	0	0		0			9	10	6	0	0	10		5	6.00	-35	.294	.455	-32	0	-0.2
1948	Bos A	0	0	+	6	0	0	0		0			7	9	5	0	0	7		4	6.43	-32	.321	.457		0	-0.1
1949	Bos A	11	6	.647	26	19	10	0		0			152	145	72	10	2	75		70	4.03	+8	.254	.343	+24	0	0.6
1950	Bos A	12	7	.632	32	21	6	0		1			169.1	158	104	17	5	88		78	5.10	-4	.250	.346	+51	0	0.0
1951	Bos A	10	9	.526	34	25	6	0		0			170	180	100	16	5	74		75	4.76	-6	.271	.349	+11	0	-0.7
Total	15	107	130	.451	459	238	65	7	58	19		172	1920.1	2003	1030	184	35	735	30	897	4.29	-5	.269	.336	-1	0	-5.1
Team	5	33	23	.589	102	66	22	0		1			507.1	502	287	43	12	254		232	4.70	-3	.260	.350	+27		-0.4
/180I	2	12	8	.589	36	23	8	0		0			180	178	102	15	4	90		82	4.70	-3	.260	.350	+27		-0.1
STONE, DEAN Darrah Dean B9.1.1930 Moline IL BL/TL/6'4"/(195–205) d9.13																											
1957	Bos A	1	3	.250	17	8	0	0	1	1		4	51.1	56	42	5	0	35	0	32	5.08	-22	.284	.386	+1	0	-0.8
Total	8	29	39	.426	215	85	19	5	3	12		50	686	705	402	47	13	373	14	380	4.47	-14	.269	.360	+0	0	-5.1
STURDIVANT, TOM Thomas Virgil "Snake" B4.28.1930 Gordon KS BL/TR/6'1"/(170–186) d4.14																											
1960	Bos A	3	3	.500	40	3	0	0	1	1		18	101.1	106	58	16	2	45	5	67	4.97	-19	.279	.353	-6	0	-0.5
Total	10	59	51	.536	335	101	22	7	104	17		143	1137	1029	521	107	34	449	37	704	3.74	+2	.244	.319	+5	30	2.5
/60G	2	5	5	.500	60	5	0	0	2	2		27	152	159	87	24	3	68	8	101	4.97	-19	.279	.353	+41		-0.8
SUCHECKI, JIM James Joseph B8.25.1926 Chicago IL D7.20.2000 Crofton MD BR/TR/5'11"/185 d5.20																											
1950	Bos A	0	0	+	4	0	0	0		0			4	3	2	0	0	4		3	4.50	+9	.231	.412		0	0.0
Total	3	0	6	.000	38	6	0	0		0			103.2	130	73	9	2	50		56	5.38	-19	.300	.374	-26	0	-0.9
SULLIVAN, FRANK Franklin Leal B1.23.1930 Hollywood CA BR/TR/6'6.5"/(210–215) d7.31																											
1953	Bos A	1	1	.500	14	0	0	0		0			25.2	24	16	3	1	11		17	5.61	-25	.264	.350		0	-0.2
1954	Bos A	15	12	.556	36	26	11	3		1			206.1	185	81	19	6	66		124	3.14	+31	.240	.304	+6	0	2.5
1955	Bos A★	**18**	13	.581	35	**35**	16	3		0			**260**	235	103	23	7	100	5	129	2.91	+47	.241	.313	+1	0	3.4
1956	Bos A☆	14	7	.667	34	33	12	1		0			242	253	112	22	8	82	6	116	3.42	+35	.268	.330	+7	0	1.6
1957	Bos A	14	11	.560	31	30	14	3	55	0		7	240.2	206	76	16	7	48	4	127	2.73	+46	.230	**.273**	-14	0	**3.5**
1958	Bos A	13	9	.591	32	29	10	2	54	3		7	199.1	216	91	12	3	49	0	103	3.57	+12	.278	.322	+4	0	0.8
1959	Bos A	9	11	.450	30	26	5	2	54	1		7	177.2	172	86	17	7	67	2	107	3.95	+3	.258	.331	-6	0	0.1
1960	Bos A	6	16	.273	40	22	4	0	7	1		14	153.2	164	94	12	6	52	6	98	5.10	-21	.269	.331	-8	0	-2.2
1961	Phi N	3	16	.158	49	18	1	1	7	6		22	159.1	161	93	19	5	55	5	114	4.29	-5	.262	.326	-30	0	-0.7
1962	Phi N	0	2	.000	19	0	0	0	0	0		9	23	38	21	2	2	12	2	12	6.26	-38	.396	.460		0	-0.6
1962	Min A	4	1	.800	21	0	0	0	0	5		13	33.1	33	17	3	0	13	0	10	3.24	+26	.258	.324		0	0.2
1962	Major	4	3	.571	40	0	0	0	0	5		22	56	71	38	5	2	25	2	22	4.47	-0	.317	.384		0	-0.4
1963	Min A	0	1	.000	10	0	0	0	0	1		6	11	15	7	1	0	4	1	2	5.73	-36	.349	.404		0	-0.2
Total	11	97	100	.492	351	219	73	15	177	18		85	1732	1702	797	149	52	559	31	959	3.60	+16	.257	.319	-3	0	8.2
Team	8	90	80	.529	252	201	72	14	170	6		35	1505.1	1455	659	124	45	475	23	821	3.47	+20	.254	.314	-1		9.5
/180I	1	11	10	.529	30	24	9	2	20	1		4	180	174	79	15	5	57	3	98	3.47	+20	.254	.314	-1		1.1
SUPPAN, JEFF Jeffrey Scot B1.2.1975 Oklahoma City OK BR/TR/6'2"/(203–220) [BosA93 2/49] d7.17																											
1995	Bos A	1	2	.333	8	3	0	0	1	0	0	5	22.2	29	15	4	0	5	1	19	5.96	-18	.312	.343	-11	0	-0.2
1996	Bos A	1	1	.500	8	4	0	0	0	0	0	3	22.2	29	19	3	1	13	0	13	7.54	-32	.330	.406	+23	36	-0.4
1997	Bos A	7	3	.700	23	22	0	0	9	0	0	0	112.1	140	75	12	4	36	1	67	5.69	-18	.305	.358	+18	0	-1.0
2003	Bos A	3	4	.429	11	10	0	0	4	0	0	1	63	70	41	12	2	20	0	32	5.57	-16	.281	.335	+11	0	-0.5
Total	12	106	101	.512	317	301	15	5	149	0	0	12	1864.2	2029	1042	247	66	612	29	1048	4.60	+2	.278	.337	-2	36	2.1
Team	4	12	10	.545	50	39	0	0	14	0	0	9	220.2	268	150	31	7	74	2	131	5.87	-20	.301	.355	+14	36	-2.1
/180I	3	10	8	.545	41	32	0	0	11	0	0	7	180	219	122	25	6	60	2	107	5.87	-20	.301	.355	+14	29	-1.7
SUSCE, GEORGE George Daniel B9.13.1931 Pittsburgh PA BR/TR/6'1"/(180–190) d4.15 f–George																											
1955	Bos A	9	7	.563	29	15	6	1		1			144.1	123	54	12	8	49	4	60	3.06	+40	.232	.305	-20	0	1.8
1956	Bos A	2	4	.333	21	6	0	0		0			69.2	71	54	14	4	44	1	26	6.20	-26	.262	.371	+3	0	-0.7
1957	Bos A	7	3	.700	29	5	0	0	3	1		15	88.1	93	45	6	3	41	5	40	4.28	-7	.274	.354	-15	0	-0.3
1958	Bos A	0	0	+	2	0	0	0	3	0		15	2	6	4	1	0	1	0	0	18.00	-78	.600	.583		0	-0.1
1958	Det A	4	3	.571	27	10	2	0	6	1		15	90.2	90	45	7	3	26	1	42	3.67	+10	.259	.312	-11	0	0.0
1958	Year	4	3	.571	29	10	2	0	9	1		30	92.2	96	49	8	3	27	1	42	3.98	+1	.269	.321	-11	0	-0.1
1959	Det A	0	0	+	9	0	0	0	6	0		15	14.2	24	22	4	2	9	0	9	12.89	-68	.358	.449		0	-0.6
Total	5	22	17	.564	117	36	8	1	18	3		60	409.2	407	224	44	20	170	11	177	4.42	-5	.260	.337	-12	0	0.1
Team	4	18	14	.563	81	26	6	1	6	2		30	304.1	293	157	33	15	135	10	126	4.23	+1	.255	.338	-14		0.7
/180I	2	11	8	.562	48	15	4	1	4	1		18	180	173	93	20	9	80	6	75	4.23	+1	.255	.338	-14		0.4
SWINDELL, GREG Forest Gregory B1.2.1965 Fort Worth TX BR/TL/6'3"/(225–239) [CleA86 1/2] d8.21 Col Texas																											
1998	†Bos A	2	3	.400	29	0	0	0	0	0	1	19	24	25	13	3	0	13	1	18	3.38	+40	.278	.369		0	0.4
Total	17	123	122	.502	664	269	40	12	157	7	18	278	2233.1	2313	1053	262	21	501	34	1542	3.86	+7	.268	.308	+1	284	7.0
SWORMSTEDT, LEN Leonard Brodbeck B10.6.1878 Cincinnati OH D7.19.1964 Salem MA BR/TR/5'11.5"/165 d9.29																											
1901	Cin N	2	1	.667	3	3	3	0		0			26	19	8	2	2	5		13	1.73	+85	.202	.257	-48		0.3
1902	Cin N	0	2	.000	2	2	2	0		0			18	22	11	1	0	5		3	4.00	-25	.301	.346	-55		-0.2
1906	Bos A	1	1	.500	3	2	2	0		0			21	17	6	0	1	0		6	1.29	+114	.224	.234	-21		0.2
Total	3	3	4	.429	8	7	7	0		0			65	58	25	3	3	10		22	2.22	+36	.239	.277	-43		0.3
TANANA, FRANK Frank Daryl B7.3.1953 Detroit MI BL/TL/6'3"/(185–200) [CalA71 1/13] d9.9																											
1981	Bos A	4	10	.286	24	23	5	2	12	0	0	1	141.1	142	70	17	4	43	4	78	4.01	-2	.265	.322	-3	0	0.0
Total	21	240	236	.504	638	616	143	34	380	1	1	16	4188.1	4063	1910	448	129	1255	11	2773	3.66	+6	.254	.312	+1	57	12.8
/180I	1	5	13	.286	31	29	6	3	15	0	0	1	180	181	89	22	5	55	5	99	4.01	-2	.265	.322	+24		0.0
TANNEHILL, JESSE Jesse Niles "Powder" B7.14.1874 Dayton KY D9.22.1956 Dayton KY BB/TL (BL 1903)/5'8"/150 d6.17 C1 b–Lee▲																											
1904	Bos A	21	11	.656	33	31	30	4		0			281.2	256	89	5	13	33		116	2.04	+31	.243	.275	+10		2.8
1905	Bos A	22	9	.710	37	32	27	6		0			271.2	238	91	7	13	59		113	2.48	+9	.237	.288	+22		1.9
1906	Bos A	13	11	.542	27	26	18	2		0			196.1	207	91	9	10	39		82	3.16	-13	.274	.318	+13		-0.3
1907	Bos A	6	7	.462	18	16	10	2		1			131	131	59	3	5	20		29	2.47	+4	.263	.298	-3		0.1
1908	Bos A	0	0	+	1	1	0	0		0			5	4	2	0	0	3		2	3.60	-32	.200	.304	+11		0.0
Total	15	197	117	.627	359	321	264	34		7			2759.1	2794	1199	40	130	478		944	2.80	+14	.263	.303	+9		20.2
Team	5	62	38	.620	116	106	85	14		1			885.2	836	332	24	41	154		342	2.50	+7	.251	.292	+12		4.5
/180I	1	13	8	.620	24	22	17	3		0			180	170	67	5	8	31		70	2.50	+7	.251	.292	+12		0.9
TATUM, KEN Kenneth Ray B4.25.1944 Alexandria LA BR/TR/6'2"/(200–205) d5.28 Col Mississippi St.																											
1969	Cal A	7	2	.778	45	0	0	0	0	22	1	42	86.1	51	13	1	4	39	5	65	1.36	+158	.172	.276		0	4.1
1970	Cal A	7	4	.636	62	0	0	0	0	17	8	42	88.2	68	35	12	5	26	5	50	2.94	+23	.208	.274		0	1.0
1971	Bos A	2	4	.333	36	1	0	0	0	9	3	23	53.2	50	27	3	8	25	7	21	4.19	-11	.255	.358	-28	29	-0.1
1972	Bos A	0	2	.000	22	0	0	0	0	4	2	16	29.1	32	12	3	2	15	3	15	3.07	+6	.283	.377		40	0.0
1973	Bos A	0	0	+	1	0	0	0	0	0	0	0	4	6	4	2	0	3	0	0	9.00	-55	.462	.529		0	-0.1
1974	Chi A	0	0	+	10	1	0	0	0	0	0	6	20.2	23	12	3	0	9	0	5	4.79	-22	.274	.340	+159	0	-0.1
Total	6	16	12	.571	176	2	0	0	0	52	14	129	282.2	230	103	24	19	117	20	156	2.93	+22	.224	.311	+74	69	4.8
Team	3	2	6	.250	59	1	0	0	0	13	5	39	87	88	43	8	10	43	10	36	4.03	-11	.273	.372	-28	69	-0.2
/60G	3	2	6	.250	60	1	0	0	0	13	5	40	88.1	89	44	8	10	44	10	37	4.04	-11	.273	.372	-28	70	-0.2

Year	Tm Lg	W	L	Pct	G	GS	CG	ShO	QS	SV	BS	QR	IP	H	R	HR	HB	BB	IB	SO	ERA	AERA	OAV	OOB	Sup	DL	PW
TAVAREZ, JULIAN Julian (Carmen) B5.22.1973 Santiago, D.R. BL/TR/6'2"/(165–195) d8.7																											
2006	Bos A	5	4	.556	58	6	1	0	2	1	2	30	98.2	110	54	10	6	44	3	56	4.47	+5	.293	.374	+14	0	0.1
Total	14	77	59	.566	700	85	2	0	34	22	24	437	1180	1282	650	93	84	457	62	682	4.34	+2	.282	.356	+6	80	0.3
/60G	1	5	4	.556	60	6	1	0	2	1	2	31	102	114	56	10	6	46	3	58	4.47	+5	.293	.374	+18		0.1
TAYLOR, HARRY James Harry B5.20.1919 E.Glenn IN D11.5.2000 Terre Haute IN BR/TR/6'1"/(175–190) d9.22																											
1946	Bro N	0	0	+	4	0	0	0		1			4.2	5	2	0	0	1		6	3.86	-12	.313	.353		0	0.0
1947	†Bro N	10	5	.667	33	20	10	2		1			162	130	63	10	5	83		58	3.11	+33	**.225**	.327	+12	0	1.4
1948	Bro N	2	7	.222	17	13	2	0		0			80.2	90	55	8	3	61		32	5.36	-25	.288	.408	+30	0	-1.0
1950	Bos A	2	0	1.000	3	2	2	1		0			19	13	3	0	0	8		8	1.42	+245	.197	.284	-8	0	0.7
1951	Bos A	4	9	.308	31	8	1	0		2			81.1	100	59	6	1	42		22	5.75	-22	.307	.388	+12	0	-1.8
1952	Bos A	1	0	1.000	2	1	1	0		0			10	6	2	1	1	6		1	1.80	+119	.176	.317	+144	0	0.2
Total	6	19	21	.475	90	44	16	3		4			357.2	344	184	25	10	201		127	4.10	+2	.258	.359	+18	0	-0.5
Team	3	7	9	.438	36	11	4	1		2			110.1	119	64	7	2	56		31	4.65	-3	.279	.366	+20		-0.9
TAYLOR, SCOTT Rodney Scott B8.2.1967 Defiance OH BL/TL/6'1"/(190–195) [BosA88 28/719] d9.17 Col Bowling Green																											
1992	Bos A	1	1	.500	4	1	0	0	0	0	0	2	14.2	13	8	4	0	4	0	7	4.91	-13	.245	.298	-36	0	-0.1
1993	Bos A	0	1	.000	16	0	0	0	0	0	0	8	11	14	10	1	1	12	3	8	8.18	-43	.311	.466		0	-0.3
Total	2	1	2	.333	20	1	0	0	0	0	0	10	25.2	27	18	5	1	16	3	15	6.31	-30	.276	.383	-36	0	-0.4
TERRY, YANK Lancelot Yank B2.11.1911 Bedford IN D11.4.1979 Bloomington IN BR/TR/6'1"/180 d8.3																											
1940	Bos A	1	0	1.000	4	1	0	0		0			19.1	24	19	2	0	11		9	8.84	-49	.304	.389	+134		-0.4
1942	Bos A	6	5	.545	20	11	3	0		1			85	82	48	5	2	43		37	3.92	-5	.248	.339	+25	0	-0.6
1943	Bos A	7	9	.438	30	22	7	0		1			163.2	147	70	8	1	63		63	3.52	-6	.242	.314	-3	0	-0.6
1944	Bos A	6	10	.375	27	17	3	0		0			132.2	142	72	10	3	65		30	4.21	-19	.276	.361	+14	0	-1.2
1945	Bos A	0	4	.000	12	4	1	0		0			56.2	68	29	8	0	14		28	4.13	-18	.296	.336	-31	0	-0.4
Total	5	20	28	.417	93	55	14	0		2			457.1	463	238	33	6	196		167	4.09	-15	.263	.339	+9	0	-3.2
/180I	2	8	11	.417	37	22	6	0	0	1	0	0	180	182	94	13	2	77		66	4.09	-15	.263	.339	-57		-1.3
THIELMAN, JAKE John Peter B5.20.1879 St.Cloud MN D1.28.1928 Minneapolis MN BR/TR/5'11"/175 d4.23 b-Henry Col Manhattan																											
1908	Bos A	0	0	+	1	0	0	0		0			0.2	3	4	1	0	0		0	40.50	-94	.600	.600			-0.1
Total	4	30	28	.517	65	56	49	3		0			475.1	483	234	9	23	107		158	3.16	-14	.267	.316	+0		-1.1
THOMAS, TOMMY Alphonse B12.23.1899 Baltimore MD D4.27.1988 Dallastown PA BR/TR/5'10"/175 d4.17 Col CC of Baltimore (MD)																											
1937	Bos A	0	2	.000	9	0	0	0		0			11	16	6	2	1	4		4	4.09	+16	.340	.404			0.1
Total	12	117	128	.478	398	267	128	15		12			2176.1	2341	1185	144	24	712		736	4.11	+4	.275	.333	-5		3.9
THOMAS, BLAINE Blaine M. "Baldy" B8.1888 Glendora CA D8.21.1915 Payson AZ BR/TR/5'10"/165 d8.25																											
1911	Bos A	0	0	+	2	2	0	0		0			4.2	3	2	0	1	7		0	0.00	-100	.273	.579	-1		0.1
THORMAHLEN, HANK Herbert Ehler "Lefty" B7.5.1896 Jersey City NJ D2.6.1955 Los Angeles CA BL/TL/6'0"/180 d9.29																											
1921	Bos A	1	7	.125	23	9	3	0		0			96.1	101	56	3	6	34		17	4.48	-6	.277	.349	-43		-0.3
Total	6	29	28	.509	104	64	27	4		2			565	550	267	19	21	203		148	3.33	+5	.261	.332	-2		0.1
TIANT, LUIS Luis Clemente (Vega) B11.23.1940 Marianao, Cuba BR/TR/5'11"/(180–205) d7.19																											
1964	Cle A	10	4	.714	19	16	9	3	12	1		3	127	94	41	13	2	47	2	105	2.83	+27	.207	.283	+16	0	1.2
1965	Cle A	11	11	.500	41	30	10	2	16	1		9	196.1	166	88	20	3	66	3	152	3.53	-1	.228	.293	+15	0	-0.3
1966	Cle A	12	11	.522	46	16	7	0	9	8		24	155	121	50	16	2	50	4	145	2.79	+23	.213	.279	-12	0	1.8
1967	Cle A	12	9	.571	33	29	9	1	22	2		3	213.2	177	76	24	1	67	2	219	2.74	+19	.221	.282	+9	0	1.7
1968	Cle A★	21	9	.700	34	32	19	0	27	0		1	258.1	152	53	16	4	73	4	264	**1.60**	+85	**.168**	.233	-4	0	**4.4**
1969	Cle A	9	20	.310	38	37	9	1	25	0	0	1	249.2	229	123	37	8	129	11	156	3.71	+2	.246	.340	-14	0	0.6
1970	†Min A	7	3	.700	18	17	2	1	5	0	0	0	92.2	84	36	12	2	41	0	50	3.40	+9	.246	.328	+32	63	1.2
1971	Bos A	1	7	.125	21	10	1	0	3	0	0	8	72.1	73	42	8	1	32	1	59	4.85	-23	.259	.333	-13	0	-0.9
1972	Bos A	15	6	.714	43	19	12	6	14	3	4	16	179	128	45	7	0	65	5	123	**1.91**	+70	.202	.275	+14	0	2.9
1973	Bos A	20	13	.606	35	35	23	0	25	0	0	0	272	217	105	32	7	78	3	206	3.34	+21	.219	**.278**	-11	0	2.6
1974	Bos A★	22	13	.629	38	38	25	0	28	0	0	0	311.1	281	106	21	4	82	3	176	2.92	+32	.241	.291	-5	0	3.5
1975	†Bos A	18	14	.563	35	35	18	2	22	0	0	0	260	262	126	25	4	72	0	142	4.02	+1	.264	.315	+4	0	0.1
1976	Bos A★	21	12	.636	38	38	19	3	26	0	0	0	279	274	107	25	3	64	2	131	3.06	+27	.260	.303	+9	0	2.7
1977	Bos A	12	8	.600	32	32	3	3	14	0	0	0	188.2	210	98	26	2	51	3	124	4.53	-1	.279	.325	+17	0	0.0
1978	Bos A	13	8	.619	32	31	12	5	17	0	0	1	212.1	185	80	26	5	57	4	114	3.31	+25	.234	.289	+5	13	1.9
1979	NY A	13	8	.619	30	30	5	1	17	0	0	0	195.2	190	94	22	0	53	1	104	3.91	+5	.251	.299	+17	0	0.4
1980	NY A	8	9	.471	25	25	3	0	10	0	0	0	136.1	139	79	10	1	50	3	84	4.89	-19	.265	.326	+8	22	-1.3
1981	Pit N	2	5	.286	9	9	1	0	4	0	0	0	57.1	54	31	3	0	19	2	32	3.92	-7	.243	.303	-16	0	-0.3
1982	Cal A	2	2	.500	6	5	0	0	2	0	0	0	29.2	39	20	3	0	8	0	30	5.76	-29	.310	.351	+20	0	-0.6
Total	19	229	172	.571	573	484	187	49	298	15	4	66	3486.1	3075	1400	346	49	1104	53	2416	3.30	+14	.236	.297	+5	98	21.6
Team	8	122	81	.601	274	238	113	19	149	3	4	25	1774.2	1630	709	170	26	501	21	1075	3.36	+17	.245	.298	+3	13	12.8
/180I	1	12	8	.601	28	24	11	2	15	0	0	3	180	165	72	17	3	51	2	109	3.36	+17	.245	.298	+3	1	1.3
TIMLIN, MIKE Michael August B3.10.1966 Midland TX BR/TR/6'4"/(205–210) [TorA87 5/127] d4.8 Col Southwestern (TX)																											
2003	†Bos A	6	4	.600	72	0	0	0	0	2	4	53	83.2	77	37	11	4	9	3	65	3.55	+31	.239	.268		0	1.1
2004	†Bos A	5	4	.556	76	0	0	0	0	1	3	48	76.1	75	35	8	5	19	3	56	4.13	+18	.257	.312		0	0.8
2005	†Bos A	7	3	.700	**81**	0	0	0	0	13	7	60	80.1	86	23	2	2	20	5	59	2.24	+103	.277	.319		0	2.6
2006	Bos A	6	6	.500	68	0	0	0	0	9	8	50	64	78	33	7	2	16	4	30	4.36	+7	.305	.349		18	0.4
Total	16	69	68	.504	961	4	0	0	1	139	79	688	1099.2	1062	478	102	43	343	65	809	3.55	+28	.255	.316	-64	207	15.7
Team	4	24	17	.585	297	0	0	0	0	25	22	211	304.1	316	128	28	13	64	15	210	3.52	+33	.268	.310		18	4.9
/60G	1	5	3	.585	60	0	0	0	0	5	4	43	61.1	64	26	6	3	13	3	42	3.53	+33	.268	.310		4	1.0
TOLAR, KEVIN Kevin Anthony B1.28.1971 Panama City FL BR/TL/6'3"/(225–230) [ChiA89 9/225] d9.11																											
2003	Bos A	0	0	+	6	0	0	0	0	0	0	5	4	5	5	1	0	2	0	3	9.00	-48	.313	.389		0	-0.1
Total	3	0	0	+	20	0	0	0	0	0	0	14	17.2	13	14	1	0	16	1	17	6.62	-31	.203	.363		0	-0.2
TORREZ, MIKE Michael Augustine B8.28.1946 Topeka KS BR/TR/6'5"/210 d9.10																											
1978	Bos A	16	13	.552	36	36	15	2	21	0	0	0	250	272	122	19	3	99	10	120	3.96	+4	.281	.347	+16	0	0.4
1979	Bos A	16	13	.552	36	36	12	1	18	0	0	0	252.1	254	144	20	5	121	8	125	4.49	-1	.264	.346	+23	0	-0.3
1980	Bos A	9	16	.360	36	32	6	1	14	0	0	2	207.1	256	124	18	1	75	10	97	5.08	-16	.313	.367	+3	0	-1.6
1981	Bos A	10	3	.769	22	22	2	0	9	0	0	0	127.1	130	61	10	0	51	2	54	3.68	+7	.267	.336	+21	0	0.2
1982	Bos A	9	9	.500	31	31	1	0	13	0	0	0	175.2	196	107	20	6	74	1	84	5.23	-17	.282	.353	+20	0	-1.4
Total	18	185	160	.536	494	458	117	15	245	0	0	20	3043.2	3043	1501	223	59	1371	84	1404	3.96	-2	.264	.343	+8	0	-2.2
Team	5	60	54	.526	161	157	36	4	75	0	0	2	1012.2	1108	558	87	15	420	31	480	4.51	-6	.282	.351	+16		-2.7
/180I	1	11	10	.526	29	28	6	1	13	0	0	0	180	197	99	15	3	75	6	85	4.51	-6	.282	.351	+16		-0.5
TRAUTWEIN, JOHN John Howard B8.7.1962 Lafayette Hill PA BR/TR/6'3"/195 d4.7 Col Northwestern																											
1988	Bos A	0	1	.000	9	0	0	0	0	0	0	4	16	26	17	2	1	9	0	8	9.00	-54	.382	.462		0	-0.5
TRIMBLE, JOE Joseph Gerard B10.12.1930 Providence RI BR/TR/6'1"/190 d4.29																											
1955	Bos A	0	0	+	2	0	0	0		0			2	0	0	0	0	3	0	1	0.00	-100	.000	.375		0	0.1
Total	2	0	2	.000	7	4	0	0	1	0		0	21.2	23	19	7	1	16	1	10	7.48	-49	.274	.396	+16	108	-0.7
TRLICEK, RICK Richard Alan B4.26.1969 Houston TX BR/TR/6'2"/200 [PhiN87 4/104] d4.8																											
1992	Tor A	0	0	+	2	0	0	0	0	0	0	1	1.2	2	2	0	0	2	0	1	10.80	-62	.286	.444		0	-0.1
1993	LA N	1	2	.333	41	0	0	0	0	1	0	28	64	59	32	3	2	21	4	41	4.08	-5	.244	.309		0	0.0
1994	Bos A	1	1	.500	12	1	0	0	0	0	1	5	22.1	32	21	5	0	16	2	7	8.06	-37	.330	.425	-64	0	-0.5
1996	NY N	0	1	.000	5	0	0	0	0	0	0	3	5.1	3	2	0	1	3	1	3	3.38	+19	.214	.389		0	0.1
1997	Bos A	3	4	.429	18	0	0	0	0	0	0	12	23.1	26	14	2	1	18	4	10	4.63	+1	.289	.409		0	-0.1
1997	NY N	0	0	+	9	0	0	0	0	0	1	5	9	10	9	2	0	5	0	4	8.00	-50	.303	.395		109	-0.2
1997	Major	3	4	.429	27	0	0	0	0	0	1	17	32	36	23	4	1	23	4	14	5.57	-13	.293	.405		109	-0.3
Total	5	5	8	.385	87	1	0	0	0	1	2	54	125.2	132	80	12	4	65	11	66	5.23	-19	.273	.363	-64	109	-0.8
Team	2	4	5	.444	30	1	0	0	0	0	1	17	45.2	58	35	7	1	34	6	17	6.31	-23	.310	.417	-64		-0.6

Year	Tm Lg	W	L	Pct	G	GS	CG	ShO	QS	SV	BS	QR	IP	H	R	HR	HB	BB	IB	SO	ERA	AERA	OAV	OOB	Sup	DL	PW
TROUT, DIZZY Paul Howard B6.29.1915 Sandcut IN D2.28.1972 Harvey IL BR/TR/6'2.5"/195 d4.25 s–Steve																										
1952	Bos A	9	8	.529	26	17	2	0		1			133.2	133	62	3	3	68		57	3.64	+8	.263	.354	-5	0	0.4
Total	15	170	161	.514	521	322	158	28	0	35		1	2725.2	2641	1166	112	34	1046	0	1256	3.23	+24	.255	.325	-4	0	29.7
/180I	1	12	11	.529	35	23	3	0		1			180	179	83	4	4	92		77	3.64	+8	.263	.354	+28		0.5
TRUJILLO, MIKE Michael Andrew B1.12.1960 Denver CO BR/TR/6'1"/180 [ChiA82 7/172] d4.14 Col Northern Colorado																										
1985	Bos A	4	4	.500	27	7	1	0	3	1	0	12	84	112	55	7	3	23	1	19	4.82	-11	.320	.365	+20	0	-0.5
1986	Bos A	0	0	+	3	0	0	0	0	0	0	2	5.2	7	6	0	0	6	2	4	9.53	-56	.304	.448		0	-0.1
1986	Sea A	3	2	.600	11	4	1	1	2	1	0	5	41.1	32	11	5	0	15	1	19	2.40	+78	.215	.285	-20	0	1.1
1986	Year	3	2	.600	14	4	1	1	2	1	0	7	47	39	17	5	0	21	3	23	3.26	+31	.227	.309	-20	0	1.0
1987	Sea A	4	4	.500	28	7	0	0	0	1	1	13	65.2	70	46	12	2	26	0	36	6.17	-23	.277	.346	-4	0	-0.9
1988	Det A	0	0	+	6	0	0	0	0	0	0	3	12.1	11	7	2	0	5	2	5	5.11	-25	.234	.308		0	-0.1
1989	Det A	1	2	.333	8	4	1	0	1	0	0	1	25.2	35	17	3	0	13	0	13	5.96	-36	.333	.397	+30	0	-0.5
Total	5	12	12	.500	83	22	3	1	6	3	1	36	234.2	267	142	29	5	88	6	96	5.02	-14	.288	.350	+7	0	-1.0
Team	2	4	4	.500	30	7	1	0	3	1	0	14	89.2	119	61	7	3	29	3	23	5.12	-16	.319	.371	+20		-0.6
TUDOR, JOHN John Thomas B2.2.1954 Schenectady NY BL/TL/6'0"/185 [BosA76*S3/57] d8.16 Col Georgia Southern																										
1979	Bos A	1	2	.333	6	6	1	0	2	0	0	0	28	39	23	2	0	9	1	11	6.43	-31	.345	.384	-15	0	-0.5
1980	Bos A	8	5	.615	16	13	5	0	10	0	0	2	92.1	81	35	4	3	31	1	45	3.02	+41	.238	.304	-2	0	1.7
1981	Bos A	4	3	.571	18	11	2	0	5	1	0	6	78.2	74	44	11	3	28	1	44	4.58	-14	.252	.319	+17	0	-0.4
1982	Bos A	13	10	.565	32	30	6	1	19	0	0	1	195.2	215	90	20	8	59	3	146	3.63	+20	.280	.336	-6	0	1.6
1983	Bos A	13	12	.520	34	34	7	2	16	0	0	0	242	236	122	32	4	81	3	136	4.09	+7	.255	.316	-16	0	0.7
1984	Pit N	12	11	.522	32	32	6	1	20	0	0	0	212	200	81	19	1	56	2	117	3.27	+11	.248	.295	-18	0	1.4
1985	†StL N	21	8	.724	36	36	14	0	27	0	0	0	275	209	68	14	5	49	4	169	1.93	+85	.209	**.249**	+10	0	5.6
1986	StL N	13	7	.650	30	30	3	0	22	0	0	0	219	197	81	22	1	53	5	107	2.92	+27	.244	.289	-6	20	1.6
1987	†StL N	10	2	.833	16	16	0	0	7	0	0	0	96	100	43	11	1	32	1	54	3.84	+9	.272	.331	+7	101	0.6
1988	StL N	6	5	.545	21	21	4	1	17	0	0	0	145.1	131	44	5	1	31	7	55	2.29	+54	.247	.287	-9	21	1.4
1988	†LA N	4	3	.571	9	9	1	0	5	0	0	0	52.1	58	16	5	0	10	0	32	2.41	+39	.284	.318	-6	0	0.7
1988	Year	10	8	.556	30	30	5	1	22	0	0	0	197.2	189	60	10	1	41	7	87	2.32	+50	.257	.295	-8	0	2.1
1989	LA N	0	0	+	6	3	0	0	0	0	0	3	14.1	17	5	1	0	6	0	9	3.14	+9	.309	.377	-14	141	0.0
1990	StL N	12	4	.750	25	22	1	1	17	0	0	3	146.1	120	48	10	2	30	4	63	2.40	+61	.225	.268	+10	22	2.5
Total	12	117	72	.619	281	263	50	16	167	1	0	15	1797	1677	700	156	29	475	32	988	3.12	+25	.248	.299	-4	305	16.9
Team	5	39	32	.549	106	94	21	3	52	1	0	9	636.2	645	314	69	18	208	9	382	3.96	+9	.264	.324	-7		3.1
/180I	1	11	9	.549	30	27	6	1	15	0	0	3	180	182	89	20	5	59	3	108	3.96	+9	.264	.324	-7		0.9
TURLEY, BOB Robert Lee "Bullet Bob" B9.19.1930 Troy IL BR/TR/6'2"/(214–218) d9.29 Mil 1952–53 C1																										
1963	Bos A	1	4	.200	11	7	0	0	1	0		3	41.1	42	28	6	1	28	0	35	6.10	-38	.256	.366	-23	0	-1.0
Total	12	101	85	.543	310	237	78	24	178	12		75	1712.2	1366	753	140	56	1068	21	1265	3.64	+1	.220	.337	+9	33	1.4
URBINA, UGUETH Ugueth Urtain (Villarreal) B2.15.1974 Caracas, Distrito Capital, Venez. BR/TR/6'2"/(185–205) d5.9																										
2001	Bos A	0	1	.000	19	0	0	0	0	9	1	14	20	16	5	1	0	3	0	32	2.25	+97	.219	.250		0	0.6
2002	Bos A★	1	6	.143	61	0	0	0	0	40	6	47	60	44	21	8	0	20	5	71	3.00	+49	.202	.266		0	2.0
Total	11	44	49	.473	583	21	0	0	8	237	48	425	697.1	539	289	86	6	307	30	814	3.45	+27	.210	.294	-23	145	12.0
Team	2	1	7	.125	80	0	0	0	0	49	7	61	80	60	26	9	0	23	5	103	2.81	+59	.206	.262			2.6
/60G	2	1	5	.125	60	0	0	0	0	37	5	46	60	45	20	7	0	17	4	77	2.81	+59	.206	.262			1.9
VALDEZ, CARLOS Carlos Luis (Lorenzo) B12.26.1971 Nizao Bani, D.R. BR/TR/5'11"/(175–191) d7.18																										
1998	Bos A	1	0	1.000	4	0	0	0	0	0	0	3	3.1	1	0	0	0	5	0	4	0.00	-100	.100	.375		0	0.3
Total	2	1	1	.500	15	0	0	0	0	0	0	11	18	20	10	1	1	13	1	11	5.00	-15	.290	.400		0	0.1
VALDEZ, SERGIO Sergio Sanchez (b Sergio Sanchez (Valdez)) B9.7.1964 Elias Pina, D.R. BR/TR/6'1"/190 d9.10 [DL 1996 SF N 182]																										
1994	Bos A	0	1	.000	12	1	0	0	0	0	0	5	14.1	25	14	4	0	8	1	4	8.16	-38	.391	.458	-27	0	-0.2
Total	8	12	20	.375	116	31	1	0	11	0	1	59	302.2	332	194	46	5	109	11	190	5.06	-22	.279	.340	-2	182	-4.2
VAN BUREN, JERMAINE Jermaine Russell B7.2.1980 Laurel MS BR/TR/6'1"/220 [ColN98 2/60] d8.31																										
2005	Chi N	0	2	.000	6	0	0	0	0	0	0	5	6	2	2	0	0	9	2	3	3.00	+46	.118	.423		0	0.2
2006	Bos A	1	0	1.000	10	0	0	0	0	0	0	6	13	14	17	1	0	15	1	8	11.77	-60	.292	.453		0	-0.6
Total	2	1	2	.333	16	0	0	0	0	0	0	11	19	16	19	1	0	24	3	11	9.00	-49	.246	.444		0	-0.4
VANDENBERG, HY Harold Harris B3.17.1906 Abilene KS D7.31.1994 Bloomington MN BR/TR/6'4"/220 d6.8																										
1935	Bos A	0	0	+	3	0	0	0		0			5.1	15	12	1	0	4		2	20.25	-77	.500	.559			-0.3
Total	7	15	10	.600	90	22	7	1		5			291.2	304	166	17	6	128		120	4.32	-15	.271	.349	+26	0	-1.2
VAN DYKE, BEN Benjamin Harrison B8.15.1888 Clintonville PA D10.22.1973 Sarasota FL BR/TL/6'1"/150 d5.11																										
1909	Phi N	0	0	+	2	0	0	0		0			7.1	7	3	0	0	4		5	3.68	-29	.269	.367			-0.1
1912	Bos A	0	0	+	3	1	0	0		0			14.1	13	10	0	1	7		8	3.14	+8	.245	.344	+225		-0.1
Total	2	0	0	+	5	1	0	0		0			21.2	20	13	0	1	11		13	3.32	-6	.253	.352	+225		-0.2
VAN EGMOND, TIM Timothy Layne B5.31.1969 Shreveport LA BR/TR/6'2"/(180–185) [BosA91 17/460] d6.26 Col Jacksonville St.																										
1994	Bos A	2	3	.400	7	7	1	0	3	0	0	0	38.1	38	27	7	0	21	3	22	6.34	-20	.255	.341	-11	0	-0.5
1995	Bos A	0	1	.000	4	1	0	0	0	0	0	2	6.2	9	7	2	0	6	0	5	9.45	-49	.310	.429	-43	15	-0.4
1996	Mil A	3	5	.375	12	9	0	0	3	0	0	2	54.2	58	35	6	1	23	2	33	5.27	-1	.274	.343	-41	0	-0.1
Total	3	5	9	.357	23	17	1	0	6	0	0	4	99.2	105	69	15	1	50	5	60	5.96	-14	.269	.349	-29	15	-1.0
Team	2	2	4	.333	11	8	1	0	3	0	0	2	45	47	34	9	0	27	3	27	6.80	-26	.264	.356	-15	15	-0.9
VEALE, BOB Robert Andrew B10.28.1935 Birmingham AL BB/TL/6'6"/(210–226) d4.16 Col Benedictine																										
1972	Bos A	2	0	1.000	6	0	0	0	0	2	0	6	8	2	0	0	0	3	0	10	0.00	-100	.083	.185		0	0.7
1973	Bos A	2	3	.400	32	0	0	0	0	11	4	24	36.1	37	16	2	0	12	2	25	3.47	+16	.268	.327		0	0.4
1974	Bos A	0	1	.000	18	0	0	0	0	2	2	10	13	15	8	2	0	4	1	16	5.54	-31	.283	.328		0	-0.2
Total	13	120	95	.558	397	255	78	20	169	21	6	94	1926	1684	755	91	29	858	62	1703	3.07	+13	.236	.319	+0	0	7.2
Team	3	4	4	.500	56	0	0	0	0	15	6	40	57.1	54	24	4	0	19	3	51	3.45	+12	.251	.311			0.9
/60G	3	4	4	.500	60	0	0	0	0	16	6	43	61.1	58	26	4	0	20	3	55	3.46	+12	.251	.311			1.0
VERAS, DARIO Dario Antonio B3.13.1973 Santiago, D.R. BR/TR/6'2"/155 d7.31																										
1998	Bos A	0	1	.000	7	0	0	0	0	0	0	3	8	12	9	0	1	7	0	2	10.13	-53	.343	.465		0	-0.5
Total	3	5	3	.625	53	0	0	0	0	0	1	37	61.2	64	37	8	4	29	7	46	4.67	-13	.268	.355		91	-0.5
VIOLA, FRANK Frank John B4.19.1960 Hempstead NY BL/TL/6'4"/(195–210) [MinA81 2/37] d6.6 Col St. Johns																										
1992	Bos A	13	12	.520	35	35	6	1	23	0	0	0	238	214	99	13	7	89	4	121	3.44	+24	.242	.313	-25	0	2.4
1993	Bos A	11	8	.579	29	29	2	1	16	0	0	0	183.2	180	76	12	6	72	5	91	3.14	+48	.259	.331	-13	0	2.6
1994	Bos A	1	1	.500	6	6	0	0	2	0	0	0	31	34	17	2	0	17	0	9	4.65	+9	.296	.381	-6	100	0.1
Total	15	176	150	.540	421	420	74	16	253	0	0	1	2836.1	2827	1303	294	48	864	39	1844	3.73	+13	.260	.316	-8	110	15.7
Team	3	25	21	.543	70	70	8	2	41	0		0	452.2	428	192	27	13	178	9	221	3.40	+31	.253	.325	-18	100	5.1
/180I	1	10	8	.543	28	28	3	1	16	0		0	180	170	76	11	5	71	4	88	3.40	+31	.253	.325	-18	40	2.0
VOLZ, JAKE Jacob Phillip "Silent Jake" B4.4.1878 San Antonio TX D8.11.1962 San Antonio TX BR/TR/5'10"/175 d9.28																										
1901	Bos A	1	0	1.000	1	1	1	0		0			7	6	9	2	0	9		5	9.00	-61	.231	.429	+91		-0.4
Total	3	2	4	.333	11	7	2	0		0			38.1	34	29	3	3	29		12	6.10	-56	.241	.382	-11		-1.8
WADE, JAKE Jacob Fields "Whistling Jake" B4.1.1912 Morehead City NC D2.1.2006 Wildwood NC BL/TL/6'2"/175 d4.22 Mil 1945 b–Ben Col North Carolina St.																										
1939	Bos A	1	4	.200	20	6	1	0		0			47.2	68	34	1	0	37		21	6.23	-24	.358	.463	-19		-0.7
Total	8	27	40	.403	171	71	20	3		3			668.1	690	421	42	9	440		291	5.00	-16	.269	.378	-11	0	-4.7
WAGNER, CHARLIE Charles Thomas "Broadway" B12.3.1912 Reading PA D8.31.2006 Reading PA BR/TR/5'11"/170 d4.19 Mil 1943–45 C1																										
1938	Bos A	1	3	.250	13	6	1	0		0			36.2	47	36	5	1	24		14	8.35	-41	.309	.407	+13		-1.1
1939	Bos A	3	1	.750	9	5	0	0		0			38.1	49	19	3	0	14		13	4.23	+12	.320	.377	+23		0.1
1940	Bos A	1	0	1.000	12	1	0	0		0			29.1	45	22	5	0	8		13	5.52	-19	.344	.381	+134		-0.2
1941	Bos A	12	8	.600	29	25	12	3		0			187.1	175	76	14	1	85		51	3.07	+36	.245	.326	+20	0	2.0
1942	Bos A	14	11	.560	29	26	17	2		0			205.1	184	87	5	5	95		52	3.29	+13	.247	.336	-2	0	0.6

Year	Tm Lg	W	L	Pct	G	GS	CG	ShO	QS	SV	BS	QR	IP	H	R	HR	HB	BB	IB	SO	ERA	AERA	OAV	OOB	Sup	DL	PW
1946	Bos A	1	0	1.000	8	4	0	0		0			30.2	32	21	6	0	19		14	5.87	-38	.276	.378	+87	0	-0.4
Total	6	32	23	.582	100	67	30	5		0			527.2	532	261	38	7	245		157	3.91	+4	.264	.346	+17	0	1.0
/180I	2	11	8	.582	34	23	10	2	0	0	0	0	180	181	89	13	2	84		54	3.91	+4	.264	.346	-60		0.3
WAGNER, GARY Gary Edward B6.28.1940 Bridgeport IL BR/TR/6'4"/(190–200) d4.18 Col Eastern Illinois																											
1969	Bos A	1	3	.250	6	1	0	0	0	0	0	2	16.1	18	11	1	0	15	0	9	6.06	-37	.300	.440	-100	0	-0.7
1970	Bos A	3	1	.750	38	0	0	0	0	7	1	30	40.1	36	21	3	2	19	1	20	3.35	+19	.232	.320		0	0.1
Total	6	15	19	.441	162	4	0	0	0	22	2	116	267.1	250	130	14	9	126	16	174	3.70	-7	.253	.340	-30	0	-1.9
Team	2	4	4	.500	44	1	0	0	0	7	1	32	56.2	54	32	4	2	34	1	29	4.13	-5	.251	.356	-100		-0.6
/60G	3	5	5	.500	60	1	0	0	0	10	1	44	77.1	74	44	5	3	46	1	40	4.13	-5	.251	.356	-100		-0.8
WAKEFIELD, TIM Timothy Stephen B8.2.1966 Melbourne FL BR/TR/6'2"/(195–215) [PitN88 8/200] d7.31 Col Florida Tech																											
1992	†Pit N	8	1	.889	13	13	4	1	10	0	0	0	92	76	26	3	1	35	1	51	2.15	+61	.232	.305	+6	0	1.2
1993	Pit N	6	11	.353	24	20	3	2	10	0	0	3	128.1	145	83	14	9	75	2	59	5.61	-27	.291	.389	-14	0	-2.3
1995	†Bos A	16	8	.667	27	27	6	1	18	0	0	0	195.1	163	76	22	9	68	0	119	2.95	+65	.227	.300	-8	0	4.2
1996	Bos A	14	13	.519	32	32	6	0	15	0	0	0	211.2	238	151	38	12	90	0	140	5.14	-1	.280	.353	-10	0	-0.8
1997	Bos A	12	15	.444	35	29	4	2	15	0	0	4	201.1	193	109	24	16	87	5	151	4.25	+10	.256	.343	-4	21	0.7
1998	†Bos A	17	8	.680	36	33	2	0	16	0	0	2	216	211	123	30	14	79	1	146	4.58	+3	.252	.324	+29	0	0.1
1999	†Bos A	6	11	.353	49	17	0	0	6	15	3	24	140	146	93	19	5	72	2	104	5.08	-2	.266	.352	-12	0	-0.5
2000	Bos A	6	10	.375	51	17	0	0	6	0	1	25	159.1	170	107	31	4	65	3	102	5.48	-8	.272	.340	+18	0	-0.8
2001	Bos A	9	12	.429	45	17	0	0	12	3	2	22	168.2	156	84	13	18	73	5	148	3.90	+14	.248	.339	-9	0	1.0
2002	Bos A	11	5	.688	45	15	0	0	11	3	2	24	163.1	121	57	15	9	51	2	134	2.81	+59	.204	.276	+10	0	2.6
2003	†Bos A	11	7	.611	35	33	0	0	18	1	0	2	202.1	193	106	23	12	71	0	169	4.09	+14	.246	.317	+10	0	0.8
2004	†Bos A	12	10	.545	32	30	0	0	15	0	0	2	188.1	197	121	29	16	63	3	116	4.87	+0	.264	.333	+9	0	-0.2
2005	†Bos A	16	12	.571	33	33	3	0	18	0	0	0	225.1	210	113	35	11	68	4	151	4.15	+9	.245	.307	-2	0	1.0
2006	Bos A	7	11	.389	23	23	1	0	13	0	0	0	140	135	80	19	10	51	0	90	4.63	+1	.248	.322	-6	57	-0.1
Total	14	151	134	.530	480	339	29	6	183	22	8	108	2432	2354	1329	315	146	948	28	1680	4.30	+8	.253	.329	+2	78	6.9
Team	12	137	122	.529	443	306	22	3	163	22	8	105	2211.2	2133	1220	298	136	838	25	1570	4.31	+10	.251	.326	+3	78	8.0
/180I	1	11	10	.529	36	25	2	0	13	2	1	9	180	174	99	24	11	68	2	128	4.31	+10	.251	.326	+3	6	0.7
WALBERG, RUBE George Elvin B7.27.1896 Pine City MN D10.27.1978 Tempe AZ BL/TL/6'1.5"/190 d4.29																											
1934	Bos A	6	7	.462	30	10	2	0		1			104.2	118	62	5	1	41		38	4.04	+19	.284	.350	-2		0.6
1935	Bos A	5	9	.357	44	10	4	0		3			142.2	152	71	10	2	54		44	3.91	+21	.273	.340	-36		1.0
1936	Bos A	5	4	.556	24	9	5	0		0			100.1	98	53	7	1	36		49	4.40	+21	.257	.323	-28		0.7
1937	Bos A	5	7	.417	32	11	3	0		1			104.2	143	72	7	3	46		46	5.59	-15	.332	.400	-15		-1.0
Total	15	155	141	.524	544	306	139	15		32			2644	2795	1423	163	27	1031		1085	4.16	+7	.273	.341	-1		7.6
Team	4	21	27	.438	130	40	14	0		5			452.1	511	258	29	7	177		177	4.44	+10	.286	.353	-20		1.3
/180I	2	8	11	.438	52	16	6	0		2			180	203	103	12	3	70		70	4.44	+10	.286	.353	-20		0.5
WALL, MURRAY Murray Wesley B9.19.1926 Dallas TX D10.8.1971 Lone Oak TX BR/TR/6'3"/(185–205) d7.4 Col Texas																											
1950	Bos N	0	0	+	1	0	0	0		0			4	6	5	0	0	2		2	9.00	-57	.333	.400		0	-0.1
1957	Bos A	3	0	1.000	11	0	0	0	0	1		60	24.1	21	11	3	0	2	0	13	3.33	+20	.233	.247		0	0.3
1958	Bos A	8	9	.471	52	1	0	0	0	10		59	114.1	109	51	14	5	33	4	53	3.62	+11	.255	.313	-33	0	0.8
1959	Bos A	1	4	.200	15	0	0	0	0	3		59	31.2	31	21	5	0	15	2	8	5.40	-25	.267	.348		0	-0.8
1959	Was A	0	0	+	1	0	0	0	0	0		1	1.1	3	1	1	0	0	0	0	6.75	-42	.600	.600		0	0.0
1959	Bos A	1	1	.500	11	0	0	0	0	0		59	17.1	26	11	2	1	11	4	6	5.71	-29	.371	.458		0	-0.3
1959	Year	2	5	.286	27	0	0	0	0	3		119	50.1	60	33	8	1	26	6	14	5.54	-27	.314	.395		0	-1.1
Total	4	13	14	.481	91	1	0	0	0	14		238	193	196	100	25	6	63	10	82	4.20	-4	.270	.330	-33	0	-0.1
Team	4	13	14	.481	89	1	0	0	0	14		237	187.2	187	94	24	6	61	10	80	4.08	-1	.266	.326	-33		0.0
/60G	3	9	9	.481	60	1	0	0	0	9		160	126.2	126	63	16	4	41	7	54	4.07	-1	.266	.326	-33		0.0
WASDIN, JOHN John Truman B8.5.1972 Fort Belvoir VA BR/TR/6'2"/(190–196) [OakA93 1/25] d8.24 Col Florida St.																											
1995	Oak A	1	1	.500	5	2	0	0	1	0	0	2	17.1	14	9	4	1	3	0	6	4.67	-3	.215	.261	-7	0	0.0
1996	Oak A	8	7	.533	25	21	1	0	8	0	1	0	131.1	145	96	24	4	50	5	75	5.96	-17	.283	.348	+4	0	-1.5
1997	Bos A	4	6	.400	53	7	0	0	1	0	2	29	124.2	121	68	18	3	38	4	84	4.40	+6	.251	.306	-18	0	0.1
1998	†Bos A	6	4	.600	47	8	0	0	2	0	1	25	96	111	57	14	2	27	8	59	5.25	-10	.288	.333	-4	0	-0.3
1999	†Bos A	8	3	.727	45	0	0	0	0	2	3	29	74.1	66	38	14	0	18	0	57	4.12	+21	.236	.280		19	0.9
2000	Bos A	1	3	.250	25	1	0	0	0	1	1	13	44.2	48	25	8	2	15	1	36	5.04	+0	.273	.328	-25	0	0.0
2000	Col N	0	3	.000	14	3	1	0	2	0	0	4	35.2	42	23	6	3	9	2	35	5.80	+0	.302	.353	-63	0	0.0
2000	Major	1	6	.143	39	4	1	0	2	1	1	17	79	90	48	14	5	24	3	71	5.38	+0	.286	.339	-54	0	0.0
2001	Col N	2	1	.667	18	0	0	0	0	0	3	12	24.1	32	19	7	1	8	2	17	7.03	-24	.320	.373		0	-0.3
2001	Bal A	1	1	.500	26	0	0	0	0	0	2	15	49.2	54	25	4	5	16	4	47	4.17	+3	.277	.341		0	0.0
2001	Major	3	2	.600	44	0	0	0	0	0	5	27	73	86	44	11	6	24	6	64	5.11	-6	.292	.352		0	-0.3
2003	Tor A	0	1	.000	3	2	0	0	0	0	0	0	5	16	13	2	0	4	0	5	23.40	-80	.533	.571	-13	0	-1.3
2004	Tex A	2	4	.333	15	10	0	0	4	0	0	2	65	83	52	18	3	23	2	36	6.78	-27	.305	.363	+16	0	-1.0
2005	Tex A	3	2	.600	31	6	0	0	2	4	2	17	75.2	77	37	9	1	20	2	44	4.28	+6	.261	.308	+8	0	0.1
2006	Tex A	2	2	.500	9	5	0	0	1	0	0	3	30	33	19	6	4	13	0	16	5.10	-8	.266	.355	+29	19	-0.2
Total	11	38	38	.500	316	65	2	0	21	7	15	151	773.2	842	481	134	29	244	30	517	5.26	-8	.276	.331	+0	38	-3.5
Team	4	19	16	.543	170	16	0	0	3	3	7	96	339.2	346	188	54	7	98	13	236	4.66	+3	.262	.312	-11	19	0.7
/60G	1	7	6	.543	60	6	0	0	1	1	2	34	120	122	66	19	2	35	5	83	4.66	+3	.262	.312	-11	7	0.2
WASLEWSKI, GARY Gary Lee B7.21.1941 Meriden CT BR/TR/6'4"/(190–195) d6.11 Col Connecticut																											
1967	†Bos A	2	2	.500	12	8	0	0	3	0		4	42	34	18	3	1	20	2	20	3.21	+8	.225	.314	-6	0	0.0
1968	Bos A	4	7	.364	34	11	2	0	7	2		13	105.1	108	50	9	6	40	9	59	3.67	-14	.269	.341	-17	0	-0.8
Total	6	11	26	.297	152	42	5	1	20	5	1	79	410.1	368	184	32	21	197	31	229	3.44	+1	.243	.336	-23	57	-0.5
Team	2	6	9	.400	46	19	2	0	10	2		17	147.1	142	68	12	7	60	11	79	3.54	-8	.257	.333	-12		-0.8
/180I	2	7	11	.400	56	23	2	0	12	2		21	180	173	83	15	9	73	13	97	3.54	-8	.257	.333	-12		-1.0
WEAVER, MONTE Montie Morton "Prof" B6.15.1906 Helton NC D6.14.1994 Orlando FL BL/TR/6'0"/170 d9.20 Col Emory & Henry																											
1939	Bos A	1	0	1.000	9	1	1	0		1			20.1	26	15	0	1	13		6	6.64	-29	.321	.421	+49		-0.3
Total	9	71	50	.587	201	135	57	2		4			1052	1137	591	62	5	435		297	4.36	+1	.276	.345	+8		0.1
WEILAND, BOB Robert George "Lefty" B12.14.1905 Chicago IL D11.9.1988 Chicago IL BL/TL/6'4"/215 d9.30 b–Ed																											
1928	Chi A	1	0	1.000	1	1	1	1		0			9	7	0	0	1	5		9	0.00	-100	.212	.333	-79		0.5
1929	Chi A	2	4	.333	15	9	1	0		1			62	62	42	3	3	43		25	5.81	-26	.268	.390	+1		-0.8
1930	Chi A	0	4	.000	14	3	0	0		0			32.2	38	31	1	2	21		15	6.61	-30	.297	.404	-57		-0.9
1931	Chi A	2	7	.222	15	8	3	0		0			75	75	55	3	4	46		38	5.16	-17	.259	.368	-8		-0.7
1932	Bos A	6	16	.273	43	27	7	0		1			195.2	231	125	11	6	97		63	4.51	+0	.295	.377	-25		-0.2
1933	Bos A	8	14	.364	39	27	12	0		3			216.1	197	107	19	5	100		97	3.87	+13	.244	.331	-35		0.7
1934	Bos A	1	5	.167	11	7	2	0		0			55.2	63	41	4	0	27		29	5.50	-13	.293	.372	-12		-0.5
1934	Cle A	1	5	.167	16	7	2	0		0			70	71	41	5	0	30		42	4.11	+11	.262	.336	-43		0.1
1934	Year	2	10	.167	27	14	4	0		0			125.2	134	82	9	0	57		71	4.73	-1	.276	.352	-27		-0.4
1935	StL A	0	2	.000	14	4	0	0		0			32	39	35	6	1	31		11	9.56	-50	.298	.436	+0		-0.8
1937	StL N	15	14	.517	41	**34**	21	2		0			264.1	283	127	14	5	94		105	3.54	+12	.276	.339	+6		1.1
1938	StL N	16	11	.593	35	29	11	1		1			228.1	248	118	14	4	67		117	3.59	+10	.272	.324	+12		0.3
1939	StL N	10	12	.455	32	23	6	3		1			146.1	146	69	4	6	50		63	3.57	+15	.264	.331	+3		0.5
1940	StL N	0	0	+	1	0	0	0		0			1	3	3	1	0	0		0	27.00	-85	.600	.600			-0.1
Total	12	62	94	.397	277	179	66	7		7			1388.1	1463	794	85	37	611		614	4.24	+0	.272	.350	-10		-0.8
Team	3	15	35	.300	93	61	21	0		4			467.2	491	273	34	11	224		189	4.33	+3	.272	.356	-28		0.0
/180I	1	6	13	.300	36	23	8	0		2			180	189	105	13	4	86		73	4.33	+3	.272	.356	-28		0.0
WELCH, JOHNNY John Vernon B12.2.1906 Washington DC D9.2.1940 St.Louis MO BL/TR/6'3"/184 d5.22																											
1926	Chi N	0	0	+	3	0	0	0		0			4.1	5	2	0	0	1		0	2.08	+85	.357	.400			0.1
1927	Chi N	0	0	+	1	0	0	0		0			1	0	1	0	0	3		1	9.00	-57	.000	.500			0.0

Year	Tm Lg	W	L	Pct	G	GS	CG	ShO	QS	SV	BS	QR	IP	H	R	HR	HB	BB	IB	SO	ERA	AERA	OAV	OOB	Sup	DL	PW
1928	Chi N	0	0	+	3	0	0	0		0			4	13	7	0	0	0		2	15.75	-76	.591	.591			-0.2
1931	Chi N	2	1	.667	8	3	1	0		0			33.2	39	16	2	1	10		7	3.74	+3	.291	.345	+48		0.2
1932	Bos A	4	6	.400	20	8	3	1		0			72.1	93	46	3	3	38		26	5.23	-14	.312	.395	-34		-0.3
1933	Bos A	4	9	.308	47	7	1	0		3			129	142	81	6	2	67		68	4.60	-5	.283	.370	-3		-0.5
1934	Bos A	13	15	.464	41	22	8	1		0			206.1	223	112	14	8	76		91	4.49	+7	.274	.342	+10		1.1
1935	Bos A	10	9	.526	31	19	10	1		2			143	155	82	4	4	53		48	4.47	+6	.273	.339	-4		0.6
1936	Bos A	2	1	.667	9	3	1	0		0			32.2	43	24	4	0	8		9	5.51	-4	.305	.342	+27		0.0
1936	Pit N	0	0	+	9	1	0	0		1			22	22	12	3	0	6		5	4.50	-10	.265	.315	+46		0.0
1936	Major	2	1	.667	18	4	1	0		1			54	65	36	7	0	14		14	5.10	-6	.290	.332	+32		0.0
Total	9	35	41	.461	172	63	24	3		6			648.1	735	383	36	18	262		257	4.66	-1	.285	.355	+3		1.0
Team	5	33	40	.452	148	59	23	3		5			583.1	656	345	31	17	242		242	4.66	+1	.282	.355	-1		0.9
/180I	2	10	12	.452	46	18	7	1		2			180	202	106	10	5	75		75	4.66	+1	.282	.355	-1		0.3
WELLS, DAVID David Lee "Boomer" B5.20.1963 Torrance CA BL/TL/6'4"/(225–250) [TorA82 2/30] d6.30																											
2005	†Bos A	15	7	.682	30	30	2	0	17	0	0	0	184	220	95	21	9	21	0	107	4.45	+2	.296	.321	+34	22	0.2
2006	Bos A	2	3	.400	8	8	0	0	4	0	0	0	47	64	30	10	0	8	0	24	4.98	-6	.327	.351	+13	117	-0.3
Total	20	230	148	.608	631	460	54	12	261	13	13	118	3281.2	3434	1605	385	80	677	60	2119	4.07	+10	.269	.308	+11	331	14.5
Team	2	17	10	.630	38	38	2	0	21	0		0	231	284	125	31	9	29	0	131	4.56	+0	.302	.327	+30	139	-0.1
/180I	2	13	8	.630	30	30	2	0	16	0		0	180	221	97	24	7	23	0	102	4.56	+0	.302	.327	+30	108	-0.1
WELZER, TONY Anton Frank B4.5.1899 , Germany D3.18.1971 Milwaukee WI BR/TR/5'11"/160 d4.13																											
1926	Bos A	4	3	.571	39	5	1	1		0			139	167	88	5	3	53		29	4.86	-16	.308	.373	-17		-0.2
1927	Bos A	6	11	.353	37	19	8	0		1			171.2	214	109	10	4	71		56	4.72	-11	.318	.386	-21		-1.0
Total	2	10	14	.417	76	24	9	1		1			310.2	381	197	15	7	124		85	4.78	-13	.313	.380	-19		-1.2
/180I	1	6	8	.417	44	14	5	1	0	1	0	0	180	221	114	9	4	72		49	4.78	-13	.313	.380	-53		-0.7
WENZ, FRED Frederick Charles "Fireball" B8.26.1941 Bound Brook NJ BR/TR/6'3"/(214–215) d6.4																											
1968	Bos A	0	0	+	1	0	0	0	0	0		1	1	0	0	0	0	2	0	3	0.00	-100	.000	.400		0	0.0
1969	Bos A	1	0	1.000	8	0	0	0	0	0	0	5	11	9	7	7	0	10	3	11	5.73	-33	.225	.380		0	-0.1
Total	3	3	0	1.000	31	0	0	0	0	1	0	21	42.1	36	23	9	1	25	3	38	4.68	-15	.229	.333		0	-0.3
Team	2	1	0	1.000	9	0	0	0	0	0	0	6	12	9	7	7	0	12	3	14	5.25	-28	.225	.382			-0.1
WERLE, BILL William George "Bugs" B12.21.1920 Oakland CA BL/TL/6'2.5"/(182–192) d4.22 C1 Col California																											
1953	Bos A	0	1	.000	5	0	0	0		0			11.2	7	3	1	0	1		4	1.54	+173	.179	.200		0	0.3
1954	Bos A	0	1	.000	14	0	0	0		0			24.2	41	13	5	2	10		14	4.38	-6	.376	.434		0	0.0
Total	6	29	39	.426	185	60	18	2		15			665.1	770	390	81	23	194		283	4.69	-10	.291	.345	-8	65	-2.1
Team	2	0	2	.000	19	0	0	0		0			36.1	48	16	6	2	11		18	3.47	+20	.324	.377			0.3
WEST, DAVID David Lee B9.1.1964 Memphis TN BL/TL/6'6"/(207–255) [NYN83 4/84] d9.24																											
1998	Bos A	0	0	+	6	0	0	0	0	0	0	1	2	7	6	1	0	7	0	4	27.00	-82	.538	.700		0	-0.2
Total	10	31	38	.449	204	78	2	0	31	3	9	76	569.1	525	321	65	16	311	10	437	4.66	-11	.244	.341	-10	373	-2.5
WHITE, MATT Matthew Joseph B8.19.1977 Pittsfield MA BR/TL/6'0"/(180–205) [CleA98 15/453] d5.27 Col Clemson																											
2003	Bos A	0	1	.000	3	0	0	0	0	0	0	0	3.2	10	11	1	0	3	0	0	27.00	-83	.526	.565		57	-1.3
2003	Sea A	0	0	+	3	0	0	0	0	0	0	1	2	3	3	2	0	2	0	0	13.50	-68	.375	.500		0	-0.1
2003	Year	0	1	.000	6	0	0	0	0	0	0	1	5.2	13	14	3	0	5	0	0	22.24	-80	.481	.545		0	-1.4
2005	Was N	0	1	.000	1	1	0	0	0	0	0	0	4	4	4	0	1	3	0	3	9.00	-54	.267	.400	-100	0	-0.4
Total	2	0	2	.000	7	1	0	0	0	0	0	1	9.2	17	18	3	1	8	0	3	16.76	-74	.405	.491	-100	57	-1.8
WIDMAR, AL Albert Joseph B3.20.1925 Cleveland OH D10.15.2005 Tulsa OK BR/TR/6'3"/185 d4.25 C17																											
1947	Bos A	0	0	+	2	0	0	0		0			1.1	1	2	1	0	2		1	13.50	-71	.200	.429		0	-0.1
Total	5	13	30	.302	114	42	12	1		5			388.1	461	244	41	5	176		143	5.21	-10	.294	.367	-20	0	-1.7
WIGHT, BILL William Robert "Lefty" B4.12.1922 Rio Vista CA BL/TL/6'1"/(180–190) d4.17																											
1951	Bos A	7	7	.500	34	17	4	2		0			118.1	128	77	5	0	63		38	5.10	-12	.282	.369	-5	0	-1.2
1952	Bos A	2	1	.667	10	2	0	0		0			24.1	14	11	3	1	14		5	2.96	+33	.169	.296	+22	0	0.2
Total	12	77	99	.438	347	198	66	15	12	8		27	1563	1656	791	74	14	714	7	574	3.95	+3	.277	.354	-16	0	-0.2
Team	2	9	8	.529	44	19	4	2		0			142.2	142	88	8	1	77		43	4.73	-8	.264	.357	-2		-1.0
/180I	3	11	10	.529	56	24	5	3		0			180	179	111	10	1	97		54	4.73	-8	.264	.357	-2		-1.3
WILLIAMS, DAVE David Owen B2.7.1881 Scranton PA D4.25.1918 Hot Springs AR BR/TL/5'11.5"/167 d7.2																											
1902	Bos A	0	0	+	3	0	0	0		0			18.2	22	18	0	1	11		7	5.30	-33	.293	.391			-0.2
WILLIAMS, STAN Stanley Wilson B9.14.1936 Enfield NH BR/TR/6'5"/(200–230) d5.17 C14																											
1972	Bos A	0	0	+	3	0	0	0	0	0	0	2	4.1	5	3	0	0	1	0	3	6.23	-48	.294	.333		0	-0.1
Total	14	109	94	.537	482	208	42	11	128	43	13	215	1764.1	1527	785	160	71	748	62	1305	3.48	+8	.232	.315	+1	0	4.3
WILLIAMSON, SCOTT Scott Ryan B2.17.1976 Fort Polk LA BR/TR/6'0"/(180–185) [CinN97 9/278] d4.5 Col Oklahoma St.																											
2003	†Bos A	0	1	.000	24	0	0	0	0	0	2	17	20.1	20	15	1	0	9	2	21	6.20	-25	.253	.326		0	-0.1
2004	Bos A	0	1	.000	28	0	0	0	0	1	1	23	28.2	11	6	0	3	18	1	28	1.26	+289	.115	.267		93	0.5
Total	8	27	28	.491	328	10	0	0	6	55	21	231	425	314	172	34	14	236	26	494	3.32	+37	.206	.316	-23	467	8.1
Team	2	0	2	.000	52	0	0	0	0	1	3	40	49	31	21	1	3	27	3	49	3.31	+45	.177	.292		93	0.4
/60G	2	0	2	.000	60	0	0	0	0	1	3	46	56.2	36	24	1	3	31	3	57	3.30	+45	.177	.292		107	0.5
WILLOUGHBY, JIM James Arthur B1.31.1949 Salinas CA BR/TR/6'2"/(180–205) [SFN67 11/218] d9.5																											
1971	SF N	0	1	.000	2	1	0	0	0	0	0	0	4	8	4	0	0	1	0	3	9.00	-62	.400	.429	-22	0	-0.4
1972	SF N	6	4	.600	11	11	7	0	10	0	0	0	87.2	72	25	8	2	14	4	40	2.36	+48	.222	.257	-4	0	1.4
1973	SF N	4	5	.444	39	12	1	1	4	1	0	19	123	138	74	21	3	37	4	60	4.68	-18	.295	.347	+5	0	-0.7
1974	SF N	1	4	.200	18	4	0	0	1	0	0	10	40.2	51	27	7	0	9	1	12	4.65	-18	.304	.339	-31	0	-0.5
1975	†Bos A	5	2	.714	24	0	0	0	0	8	1	17	48.1	46	25	6	2	16	3	29	3.54	+15	.247	.311		0	0.2
1976	Bos A	3	12	.200	54	0	0	0	0	10	3	40	99	94	38	4	8	31	12	37	2.82	+38	.256	.324		0	1.7
1977	Bos A	6	2	.750	31	0	0	0	0	2	2	16	54.2	54	32	5	2	18	3	33	4.94	-9	.258	.320		68	-0.3
1978	Chi A	1	6	.143	59	0	0	0	0	13	2	38	93.1	95	41	6	4	19	2	36	3.86	-1	.275	.319		0	0.2
Total	8	26	36	.419	238	28	8	1	15	34	8	140	550.2	558	266	57	21	145	29	250	3.79	+2	.267	.319	-8	68	1.6
Team	3	14	16	.467	109	0	0	0	0	20	6	73	202	194	95	15	12	65	18	99	3.56	+15	.255	.320		68	1.6
/60G	2	8	9	.467	60	0	0	0	0	11	3	40	111.1	107	52	8	7	36	10	54	3.56	+15	.255	.320		37	0.9
WILLS, TED Theodore Carl B2.9.1934 Fresno CA BL/TL/6'2"/(190–200) d5.24 Col Cal St.–Fresno																											
1959	Bos A	2	6	.250	9	8	2	0	5	0		0	56.1	68	35	9	1	24	2	24	5.27	-23	.302	.369	-35	0	-0.7
1960	Bos A	1	1	.500	15	0	0	0	0	1		6	30.1	38	26	4	3	16	1	28	7.42	-45	.317	.404		0	-0.6
1961	Bos A	3	2	.600	17	0	0	0	0	0		10	19.2	24	17	2	0	19	0	11	5.95	-30	.304	.434		0	-0.9
1962	Bos A	0	0	+	1	0	0	0	0	0		0	0	2	1	0	0	1	0	0	(1)	-100	1.000	1.000		0	-0.1
1962	Cin N	0	2	.000	26	5	0	0	1	3		15	61	61	36	12	5	23	0	58	5.31	-24	.266	.346	+48	0	-0.2
1962	Major	0	2	.000	27	5	0	0	1	3		15	61	63	37	12	5	24	0	58	5.46	-24	.273	.354	+48	0	-0.3
1965	Chi A	2	0	1.000	15	0	0	0	0	1		10	19	17	8	2	1	14	2	12	2.84	+12	.258	.386		0	0.1
Total	5	8	11	.421	83	13	2	0	6	5		41	186.1	210	123	29	10	97	5	133	5.51	-28	.291	.380	-1	0	-2.4
Team	4	6	9	.400	42	8	2	0	5	1		16	106.1	132	79	15	4	60	3	63	6.09	-33	.310	.396	-35		-2.3
/60G	6	9	13	.400	60	11	3	0	7	1		23	152	189	113	21	6	86	4	90	6.09	-33	.310	.396	-35		-3.3
WILSON, DUANE Duane Lewis B6.29.1934 Wichita KS BL/TL/6'1"/185 d7.3																											
1958	Bos A	0	0	+	2	2	0	0	1	0		0	6.1	10	5	0	0	7	1	3	5.68	-30	.400	.515	+12	0	-0.1
WILSON, JIM James Alger B2.20.1922 San Diego CA D9.2.1986 Newport Beach CA BR/TR/6'1.5"/(195–200) d4.18 Col San Diego St.																											
1945	Bos A	6	8	.429	23	21	8	2		0			144.1	121	61	7	1	88		50	3.30	+3	.228	.339	-11	0	0.2
1946	Bos A	0	0	+	1	0	0	0		0			0.2	2	2	1	0	0		0	27.00	-86	.500	.500		0	-0.1
Total	12	86	89	.491	257	217	75	19	58	2		10	1539	1479	743	151	29	608	27	692	4.01	-7	.254	.326	+8	0	-3.2
Team	2	6	8	.429	24	21	8	2		0			145	123	63	8	1	88		50	3.41	+0	.230	.340	-11		0.1
/180I	2	7	10	.429	30	26	10	2		0			180	153	78	10	1	109		62	3.41	+0	.230	.340	-11		0.1

Year	Tm Lg	W	L	Pct	G	GS	CG	ShO	QS	SV	BS	QR	IP	H	R	HR	HB	BB	IB	SO	ERA	AERA	OAV	OOB	Sup	DL	PW
WILSON, JACK John Francis "Black Jack" B4.12.1912 Portland OR D4.19.1995 Edmonds WA BR/TR/5'11"/210 d9.9 Col Portland																											
1934	Phi A	0	1	.000	2	2	1	0		0			9	15	12	1	0	9		2	12.00	-63	.405	.522	+19		-0.6
1935	Bos A	3	4	.429	23	6	2	0		1			64	72	35	0	2	36		19	4.22	+12	.290	.385	-30		0.6
1936	Bos A	6	8	.429	43	9	2	0		3			136.1	152	83	4	1	86		74	4.42	+20	.284	.384	-37		0.8
1937	Bos A	16	10	.615	51	21	14	1		7			221.1	209	111	13	3	119		137	3.70	+28	.248	.343	+18		2.1
1938	Bos A	15	15	.500	37	27	11	3		1			194.2	200	108	16	2	91		96	4.30	+15	.262	.342	-19		1.6
1939	Bos A	11	11	.500	36	22	6	0		2			177.1	198	109	10	1	75		80	4.67	+1	.281	.351	+3		-0.4
1940	Bos A	12	6	.667	41	16	9	0		5			157.2	170	104	17	3	87		102	5.08	-11	.270	.362	+44		-1.0
1941	Bos A	4	13	.235	27	12	4	1		1			116.1	140	82	7	5	70		55	5.03	-17	.300	.397	-10	0	-1.7
1942	Was A	1	4	.200	12	6	1	0		0			42	57	34	2	1	23		18	6.64	-45	.322	.403	+25	0	-1.4
1942	Det A	0	0	+	9	0	0	0		0			13	20	8	3	0	5		7	4.85	-19	.351	.403		0	-0.1
1942	Year	1	4	.200	21	6	1	0		0			55	77	42	5	1	28		25	6.22	-40	.329	.403	+22	0	-1.5
Total	9	68	72	.486	281	121	50	5		20			1131.2	1233	686	73	18	601		590	4.59	+2	.276	.364	+0	0	-0.1
Team	7	67	67	.500	258	113	48	5		20			1067.2	1141	632	67	17	564		563	4.44	+7	.272	.361	+0		2.0
/180I	1	11	11	.500	43	19	8	1		3			180	192	107	11	3	95		95	4.44	+7	.272	.361	+0		0.3
WILSON, JOHN John Samuel B4.25.1903 Coal City AL D8.27.1980 Chattanooga TN BR/TR/6'2"/164 d5.9																											
1927	Bos A	0	2	.000	5	2	2	0		0			25.1	31	19	1	0	13		8	3.55	+19	.326	.407	-70		-0.2
1928	Bos A	0	0	+	2	0	0	0		0			5	6	5	0	0	6		1	9.00	-54	.333	.500			-0.1
Total	2	0	2	.000	7	2	2	0		0			30.1	37	24	1	0	19		9	4.45	-6	.327	.424	-70		-0.3
WILSON, EARL Robert Earl (Name Changed From Wilson, Earl Lawrence) B10.2.1934 Ponchatoula LA D4.23.2005 Southfield MI BR/TR/6'3"/(214–220) d7.28																											
1959	Bos A	1	1	.500	9	4	0	0	0	0		4	23.2	21	17	2	0	31	0	17	6.08	-33	.241	.441	+101	0	-0.2
1960	Bos A	3	2	.600	13	9	2	0	4	0		0	65	61	36	4	0	48	1	40	4.71	-14	.247	.367	+9	0	-0.3
1962	Bos A	12	8	.600	31	28	4	1	15	0		1	191.1	163	86	21	6	111	2	137	3.90	+6	.231	.338	+7	0	1.0
1963	Bos A	11	16	.407	37	34	6	3	18	0		3	210.2	184	99	18	1	105	4	123	3.76	+1	.234	.323	-11	0	0.5
1964	Bos A	11	12	.478	33	31	5	0	15	0		1	202.1	213	121	37	2	73	3	166	4.49	-14	.269	.328	+17	0	-0.9
1965	Bos A	13	14	.481	36	36	8	1	21	0		0	230.2	221	119	27	4	77	4	164	3.98	-6	.250	.311	+8	0	0.2
1966	Bos A	5	5	.500	15	14	5	1	7	0		1	100.2	88	45	14	2	36	2	67	3.84	-1	.235	.303	+6	0	0.5
1966	Det A	13	6	.684	23	23	8	2	18	0		0	163.1	126	49	16	4	38	1	133	2.59	+34	.213	.265	+23	0	3.2
1966	Year	18	11	.621	38	37	13	3	25	0		1	264	214	94	30	6	74	3	200	3.07	+17	.222	.280	+16	0	3.7
1967	Det A	**22**	11	.667	39	38	12	0	28	0		1	264	216	103	34	3	92	7	184	3.27	+0	.224	.291	+26	0	1.0
1968	†Det A	13	12	.520	34	33	10	3	18	0		1	224.1	192	77	20	0	65	4	168	2.85	+6	.231	.287	-4	0	1.7
1969	Det A	12	10	.545	35	35	5	1	21	0	0	0	214.2	209	93	23	4	69	4	150	3.31	+14	.256	.315	+1	0	0.9
1970	Det A	4	6	.400	18	16	4	1	8	0	0	1	96	87	53	15	2	32	1	74	4.41	-14	.238	.303	-7	0	-0.5
1970	SD N	1	6	.143	15	9	0	0	4	0	0	4	65	82	36	5	2	19	2	29	4.85	-17	.309	.356	-1	0	-0.5
1970	Major	5	12	.294	33	25	4	1	12	0	0	5	161	169	89	20	4	51	3	103	4.58	-15	.268	.326	-5	0	-1.0
Total	11	121	109	.526	338	310	69	13	177	0	0	17	2051.2	1863	934	236	30	796	35	1452	3.69	-1	.242	.313	+8	0	6.6
Team	7	56	58	.491	174	156	30	6	80	0		10	1024.1	951	523	123	15	481	16	714	4.10	-5	.245	.328	+8		0.8
/180I	1	10	10	.491	31	27	5	1	14	0		2	180	167	92	22	3	85	3	125	4.10	-5	.245	.328	+8		0.1
WILTSE, HAL Harold James "Whitey" B8.6.1903 Clay City IL D11.2.1983 Bunkie LA BL/TL/5'9"/168 d4.13																											
1926	Bos A	8	15	.348	37	29	9	1		0			196.1	201	112	6	6	99		59	4.22	-3	.273	.363	-21		-0.9
1927	Bos A	10	18	.357	36	29	13	1		1			219	276	146	5	4	76		47	5.10	-17	.321	.379	-28		-2.2
1928	Bos A	0	2	.000	2	2	1	0		0			12	16	12	1	3	1		5	9.00	-54	.314	.364	-38		-0.7
1928	StL A	2	5	.286	26	5	0	0		0			72	93	49	4	3	35		23	5.25	-20	.316	.395	-7		-0.6
1928	Year	2	7	.222	28	7	1	0		0			84	109	61	5	6	36		28	5.79	-28	.316	.390	-16		-1.3
1931	Phi N	0	0	+	1	0	0	0		0			1	3	1	0	0	0		0	9.00	-53	.600	.600			0.0
Total	4	20	40	.333	102	65	23	2		1			500.1	589	320	16	16	211		134	4.87	-15	.303	.375	-24		-4.4
Team	3	18	35	.340	75	60	23	2		1			427.1	493	270	12	13	176		111	4.80	-14	.299	.371	-25		-3.8
/180I	1	8	15	.340	32	25	10	1		0			180	208	114	5	5	74		47	4.80	-14	.299	.371	-25		-1.6
WINGFIELD, TED Frederick Davis B8.7.1899 Bedford VA D7.18.1975 Johnson City TN BR/TR/5'11"/168 d9.23																											
1923	Was A	0	0	+	1	0	0	0		0			1	0	0	0	0	0		1	0.00	-100	.000	.000			0.0
1924	Was A	0	0	+	4	0	0	0		0			7	9	2	0	0	4		2	2.57	+57	.300	.382			0.0
1924	Bos A	0	2	.000	4	3	2	0		0			25.2	23	12	0	0	8		4	2.45	+78	.240	.298	-36		0.3
1924	Year	0	2	.000	8	3	2	0		0			32.2	32	14	0	0	12		6	2.48	+73	.254	.319	-35		0.3
1925	Bos A	12	19	.387	41	27	18	2		2			254.1	267	149	11	8	92		30	3.96	+15	.278	.346	-23		1.8
1926	Bos A	11	16	.407	43	20	9	1		3			190.2	220	119	11	2	50		30	4.44	-8	.298	.344	-36		-1.4
1927	Bos A	1	7	.125	20	8	2	0		0			74.2	105	60	2	3	27		1	5.06	-17	.357	.417	-43		-0.8
Total	5	24	44	.353	113	58	31	3		5			553.1	624	342	24	13	181		68	4.18	+3	.294	.353	-30		-0.1
Team	4	24	44	.353	108	58	31	3		5			545.1	615	340	24	13	177		65	4.21	+3	.295	.353	-31		-0.1
/180I	1	8	15	.353	36	19	10	1		2			180	203	112	8	4	58		21	4.21	+3	.295	.353	-31		-0.0
WINN, GEORGE George Benjamin "Breezy","Lefty" B10.26.1897 Perry GA D11.1.1969 Roberta GA BL/TL/5'11"/170 d4.29 Col Mercer																											
1919	Bos A	0	0	+	3	0	0	0		0			4.2	6	4	0	0	1		0	7.71	-61	.353	.389			-0.1
Total	3	1	2	.333	12	3	1	0		0			40.1	50	24	2	0	7		7	4.69	-17	.309	.337	-22		-0.2
WINTER, GEORGE George Lovington "Sassafras" B4.27.1878 New Providence PA D5.26.1951 Franklin Lakes NJ BR/TR/5'8"/155 d6.15 Col Gettysburg																											
1901	Bos A	16	12	.571	28	28	26	1		0			241	234	127	4	4	66		63	2.80	+26	.252	.304	+1		1.0
1902	Bos A	11	9	.550	20	20	18	0		0			168.1	149	77	2	7	53		51	2.99	+19	.238	.305	-16		1.0
1903	Bos A	9	8	.529	24	19	14	0		0			178.1	182	92	4	7	37		64	3.08	-1	.263	.307	+17		-0.8
1904	Bos A	8	4	.667	20	16	12	1		0			135.2	126	47	4	6	27		31	2.32	+15	.247	.293	+33		0.2
1905	Bos A	16	17	.485	35	27	24	2		0			264.1	249	118	5	5	54		119	2.96	-9	.251	.293	+0		-0.7
1906	Bos A	6	18	.250	29	22	18	1		2			207.2	215	118	8	5	38		72	4.12	-33	.270	.308	-6		-2.8
1907	Bos A	12	15	.444	35	27	21	4		1			256.2	198	91	2	3	61		88	2.07	+24	.215	.267	-10		1.4
1908	Bos A	4	14	.222	22	17	8	0		0			147.2	150	71	3	4	34		55	3.05	-19	.274	.321	-28		-1.2
1908	†Det A	1	5	.167	7	6	5	0		1			56.1	49	19	0	3	7		25	1.60	+51	.240	.276	-43		0.3
1908	Year	5	19	.208	29	23	13	0		1			204	199	90	3	7	41		80	2.65	-7	.265	.309	-32		-0.9
Total	8	83	102	.449	220	182	146	9		4			1656	1552	760	32	44	377		568	2.87	+1	.250	.297	-3		-1.6
Team	8	82	97	.458	213	176	141	9		3			1599.2	1503	741	32	41	370		543	2.91	+0	.250	.298	-2		-1.9
/180I	1	9	11	.458	24	20	16	1		0			180	169	83	4	5	42		61	2.91	+0	.250	.298	-2		-0.2
WINTERS, CLARENCE Clarence John B9.7.1898 Detroit MI D6.29.1945 Detroit MI TR d8.28																											
1924	Bos A	0	1	.000	4	2	0	0		0			7	22	16	0	0	4		3	20.57	-79	.512	.553	+45		-1.1
WISE, RICK Richard Charles B9.13.1945 Jackson MI BR/TR/6'2"/(195–200) d4.18																											
1974	Bos A	3	4	.429	9	9	1	0	3	0	0	0	49	47	23	2	1	16	1	25	3.86	+0	.251	.308	-3	25	0.0
1975	†Bos A	19	12	.613	35	35	17	1	21	0	0	0	255.1	262	126	34	4	72	1	141	3.95	+3	.263	.313	+17	0	0.2
1976	Bos A	14	11	.560	34	34	11	4	20	0	0	0	224.1	218	100	18	2	48	1	93	3.53	+10	.255	.294	-3	0	1.0
1977	Bos A	11	5	.688	26	20	4	2	11	0	0	3	128.1	151	68	19	4	28	1	85	4.77	-6	.291	.332	+7	0	-0.1
Total	18	188	181	.509	506	455	138	30	280	0	0	37	3127.1	3227	1455	261	44	804	83	1647	3.69	+1	.267	.313	-6	51	3.1
Team	4	47	32	.595	104	98	33	7	55	0	0	3	657	678	317	73	11	164	4	344	3.96	+3	.265	.310	+6	25	1.1
/180I	1	13	9	.595	28	27	9	2	15	0	0	1	180	186	87	20	3	45	1	94	3.96	+3	.265	.310	+6	7	0.3
WITTIG, JOHNNIE John Carl "Hans" B6.16.1914 Baltimore MD D2.24.1999 Nassawadox VA BR/TR/6'0"/180 d8.4 Def 1944–45																											
1949	Bos A	0	0	+	1	0	0	0		0			2	2	2	0	0	2		0	9.00	-52	.286	.444		0	0.0
Total	5	10	25	.286	84	39	7	1		4			307.1	344	181	23	2	163		121	4.89	-27	.286	.372	-24	0	-4.8
WOLCOTT, BOB Robert William B9.8.1973 Huntington Beach CA BR/TR/6'0"/(190–195) [SeaA92 2/52] d8.18																											
1999	Bos A	0	0	+	4	0	0	0	0	0	0	2	6.2	8	6	1	1	3	0	2	8.10	-38	.333	.414		0	-0.1
Total	5	16	21	.432	66	58	1	0	18	0	0	4	325.2	391	223	62	15	113	8	178	5.86	-19	.298	.359	+10	0	-3.4
WOLTER, HARRY Harry Meiggs B7.11.1884 Monterey CA D7.6.1970 Palo Alto CA BL/TR/5'10"/175 d5.14 Col Santa Clara▲																											
1907	Pit N	0	0	+	1	0	0	0		0			2	3	2	0	0	2		0	4.50	-46	.333	.455			-0.1

Year	Tm Lg	W	L	Pct	G	GS	CG	ShO	QS	SV	BS	QR	IP	H	R	HR	HB	BB	IB	SO	ERA	AERA	OAV	OOB	Sup	DL	PW
1907	StL N	0	2	.000	3	3	1	0		0			23	27	13	1	2	18		8	4.30	-42	.318	.448	+4		-0.2
1907	Year	0	2	.000	4	3	1	0		0			25	30	15	1	2	20		8	4.32	-42	.319	.448	+5		-0.3
1909	Bos A	4	4	.500	11	6	0	0		0			59	66	33	0	4	30		21	3.51	-29	.303	.397	-6		-0.8
Total	2	4	6	.400	15	9	1	0		0			84	96	48	1	6	50		29	3.75	-33	.308	.413	-3		-1.1
WOOD, JOE Joe "Smoky Joe" (b Howard Ellsworth Wood) B10.25.1889 Kansas City MO D7.27.1985 West Haven CT BR/TR/5'11"/180 d8.24 s–Joe▲																											
1908	Bos A	1	1	.500	6	2	1	1		0			22.2	14	12	0	1	16		11	2.38	+3	.161	.298	+25		-0.2
1909	Bos A	11	7	.611	24	19	13	4		0			160.2	121	51	1	6	43		88	2.18	+14	.209	.270	-7		0.5
1910	Bos A	12	13	.480	35	17	14	3		0			196.2	155	81	3	10	56		145	1.69	+51	.220	.287	-7		1.9
1911	Bos A	23	17	.575	44	33	25	5		3			275.2	226	113	2	11	76		231	2.02	+62	.223	.284	+5		**5.7**
1912	†Bos A	**34**	5	**.872**	43	38	**35**	0		1			344	267	104	2	12	82		258	1.91	+78	.216	.272	+22		7.6
1913	Bos A	11	5	.688	23	18	12	1		2			145.2	120	54	0	8	61		123	2.29	+29	.232	.323	+48		1.8
1914	Bos A	10	3	.769	18	14	11	1		0			113.1	94	38	1	0	34		67	2.62	+3	.229	.288	+10		0.4
1915	Bos A	15	5	**.750**	25	16	10	3		2			157.1	120	32	1	1	44		63	**1.49**	+87	.216	.275	+16		3.9
1917	Cle A	0	1	.000	5	1	0	0		1			15.2	17	7	0	0	7		2	3.45	-18	.309	.387	-24		-0.1
1919	Cle A	0	0	+	1	0	0	0		1			0.2	0	0	0	0	0		0	0.00	-100	.000	.000			0.1
1920	†Cle A	0	0	+	1	0	0	0		0			2	4	5	0	0	2		1	22.50	-83	.444	.545			-0.2
Total	11	117	57	.672	225	158	121	28		10			1434.1	1138	497	10	49	421		989	2.03	+46	.220	.285	+14		21.4
Team	8	117	56	.676	218	157	121	18		8			1416	1117	485	10	49	412		986	1.99	+49	.219	.284	+13		21.6
/180I	1	15	7	.676	28	20	15	2		1			180	142	62	1	6	52		125	1.99	+49	.219	.284	+13		2.7
WOOD, JOE Joe Frank B5.20.1916 Shohola PA D10.10.2002 Old Saybrook CT BR/TR/6'0"/190 d5.1 f–Joe Col Yale																											
1944	Bos A	0	1	.000	3	1	0	0		0			9.2	13	9	0	0	3		5	6.52	-48	.317	.364	-75	0	-0.4
WOOD, WILBUR Wilbur Forrester B10.22.1941 Cambridge MA BR/TL/6'0"/(180–200) d6.30																											
1961	Bos A	0	0	+	6	1	0	0	0	0		3	13	14	8	2	0	7	0	7	5.54	-25	.269	.350	+70	0	-0.1
1962	Bos A	0	0	+	1	1	0	0	1	0		0	7.2	6	3	0	0	3	0	3	3.52	+17	.214	.290	-35	0	0.0
1963	Bos A	0	5	.000	25	6	0	0	1	0		17	64.2	67	35	10	3	13	1	28	3.76	+1	.270	.311	-22	0	-0.3
1964	Bos A	0	0	+	4	0	0	0	0	0		1	5.2	13	11	1	0	3	2	5	17.47	-78	.433	.485		0	-0.4
Total	17	164	156	.512	651	297	114	24	188	57	13	263	2684	2582	1130	209	63	724	71	1411	3.24	+12	.254	.306	-1	167	14.6
Team	4	0	5	.000	36	8	0	0	2	0		21	91	100	57	13	3	26	3	43	4.85	-20	.279	.330	-12		-0.8
WOODARD, STEVE Steven Larry B5.15.1975 Hartselle AL BL/TR/6'4"/(217–236) [MilA94 5/123] d7.28																											
2003	Bos A	1	0	1.000	7	0	0	0	0	0	0	1	17.2	23	10	3	1	5	2	12	5.09	-8	.311	.358		0	0.0
Total	7	32	36	.471	162	94	3	0	39	0	1	43	667.1	782	397	90	31	149	20	464	4.94	-7	.292	.335	-10	81	-2.0
WOODS, PINKY George Rowland B5.22.1915 Waterbury CT D10.29.1982 Los Angeles CA BR/TR/6'5"/225 d6.20 Col Holy Cross																											
1943	Bos A	5	6	.455	23	12	2	0		1			100.2	109	61	6	1	55		32	4.92	-33	.284	.375	+2	0	-1.9
1944	Bos A	4	8	.333	38	20	5	1		0			170.2	171	73	4	6	88		56	3.27	+4	.266	.360	-12	0	0.0
1945	Bos A	4	7	.364	24	12	3	0		2			107.1	108	56	3	1	63		36	4.19	-19	.268	.368	+0	0	-0.7
Total	3	13	21	.382	85	44	10	1		3			378.2	388	190	13	8	206		124	3.97	-15	.272	.366	-5	0	-2.6
/180I	1	6	10	.382	40	21	5	0	0	1	0	0	180	184	90	6	4	98		59	3.97	-15	.272	.366	-55		-1.2
WOODS, JOHN John Fulton "Abe" B1.18.1898 Princeton WV D10.4.1946 Norfolk VA BR/TR/6'0"/175 d9.16 Col West Virginia																											
1924	Bos A	0	0	+	1	0	0	0		0			1	0	0	0	0	3		0	0.00	-100	.000	.500			0.0
WOODWARD, ROB Robert John B9.28.1962 Hanover NH BR/TR/6'3"/(185–212) [BosA81 3/70] d9.5																											
1985	Bos A	1	0	1.000	5	2	0	0	2	0	0	3	26.2	17	8	0	2	9	0	16	1.69	+156	.168	.250	+58	0	0.3
1986	Bos A	2	3	.400	9	6	0	0	2	0	0	1	35.2	46	26	4	1	11	0	14	5.30	-21	.313	.360	-21	0	-0.6
1987	Bos A	1	1	.500	9	6	0	0	3	0	0	0	37	53	33	6	1	15	0	15	7.05	-35	.338	.394	+26	0	-0.5
1988	Bos A	0	0	+	1	0	0	0	0	0	0	0	0.2	2	1	0	0	1	0	0	13.50	-69	.500	.600		0	0.0
Total	4	4	4	.500	24	14	0	0	7	0	0	4	100	118	68	10	4	36	0	45	5.04	-13	.289	.349	+12	0	-0.8
WORKMAN, HOGE Harry Hallworth B9.25.1899 Huntington WV D5.20.1972 Ft.Myers FL BR/TR/5'11"/170 d6.27 Col Ohio St.																											
1924	Bos A	0	0	+	11	0	0	0		0			18	25	19	2	2	11		7	8.50	-49	.325	.422			-0.4
WORTHINGTON, AL Allan Fulton "Red" B2.5.1929 Birmingham AL BR/TR/6'2"/205 d7.6 C2 Col Alabama																											
1960	Bos A	0	1	.000	6	0	0	0	0	0		2	11.2	17	12	1	0	11	3	7	7.71	-48	.340	.459		0	-0.4
Total	14	75	82	.478	602	69	11	3	18	110	1	426	1246.2	1130	546	105	27	527	61	834	3.39	+10	.243	.320	+0	0	8.0
WRIGHT, JIM James Clifton B12.21.1950 Reed City MI BR/TR/6'1"/165 [BosA69 4/83] d4.15																											
1978	Bos A	8	4	.667	24	16	5	3	10	0	0	4	116	122	51	8	7	24	2	56	3.57	+15	.276	.321	-14	0	0.6
1979	Bos A	1	0	1.000	11	1	0	0	1	0	0	3	23	19	13	5	3	7	1	15	5.09	-12	.226	.302	-19	102	-0.1
Total	2	9	4	.692	35	17	5	3	11	0	0	7	139	141	64	13	10	31	3	71	3.82	+9	.268	.318	-15	102	0.5
/180I	3	12	5	.692	45	22	6	4	14	0	0	9	180	183	83	17	13	40	4	92	3.82	+9	.268	.318	+10	132	0.6
WYATT, JOHN John Thomas B4.19.1935 Chicago IL D4.6.1998 Omaha NE BR/TR/5'11.5"/(195–205) d9.8																											
1966	Bos A	3	4	.429	42	0	0	0	0	8		27	71.2	59	27	3	4	27	3	63	3.14	+21	.229	.308		0	0.4
1967	†Bos A	10	7	.588	60	0	0	0	0	20		50	93.1	71	30	6	2	39	5	68	2.60	+34	.217	.303		0	1.9
1968	Bos A	1	2	.333	8	0	0	0	0	0		4	10.2	9	7	2	1	6	0	11	4.22	-25	.231	.348		0	-0.4
Total	9	42	44	.488	435	9	0	0	4	103	0	300	687.1	600	290	72	23	346	39	540	3.47	+8	.237	.331	+1	0	2.6
Team	3	14	13	.519	110	0	0	0	0	28		81	175.2	139	64	11	7	72	8	142	2.92	+23	.223	.308			1.9
/60G	2	8	7	.519	60	0	0	0	0	15		44	95.2	76	35	6	4	39	4	77	2.92	+23	.223	.308			1.0
WYCKOFF, WELDON John Weldon B2.19.1892 Williamsport PA D5.8.1961 Sheboygan Falls WI BR/TR/6'1"/175 d4.19 Col Bucknell																											
1916	Bos A	0	0	+	8	0	0	0		1			22.2	19	13	0	0	18		18	4.76	-42	.232	.370			-0.3
1917	Bos A	0	0	+	1	0	0	0		0			5	4	3	0	1	4		1	1.80	+43	.222	.391			0.0
1918	Bos A	0	0	+	1	0	0	0		0			2	4	1	0	0	1		2	0.00	-100	.400	.455			0.0
Total	6	23	34	.404	109	63	36	1		3			573.2	494	298	5	14	357		299	3.55	-21	.242	.358	+3		-5.1
Team	3	0	0	+	10	0	0	0		1			29.2	27	17	0	1	23		21	3.94	-31	.245	.381			-0.3
YOUNG, CY Denton True "Cyclone" B3.29.1867 Gilmore OH D11.4.1955 Newcomerstown OH BR/TR/6'2"/210 d8.6 M1 HF1937																											
1890	Cle N	9	7	.563	17	16	16	0		0			147.2	145	87	6	8	30		39	3.47	+3	.249	.295	-22		-0.3
1891	Cle N	27	22	.551	55	46	43	0		2			423.2	431	244	4	10	140		147	2.85	+22	.254	.314	+4		2.3
1892	†Cle N	**36**	12	**.750**	53	49	48	0		0			453	363	158	8	9	118		168	**1.93**	+76	.211	**.266**	+8		**6.4**
1893	Cle N	34	16	.680	53	46	42	1		1			422.2	442	230	10	10	103		102	3.36	+45	.261	**.307**	+2		6.5
1894	Cle N	26	21	.553	52	47	44	2		1			408.2	488	265	19	5	106		108	3.94	+39	.293	.337	-8		5.0
1895	†Cle N	**35**	10	.778	47	40	36	0		0			369.2	363	177	10	8	75		121	3.26	+53	.253	**.294**	-16		6.9
1896	†Cle N	28	15	.651	51	46	42	0		**3**			414.1	477	214	7	11	62		**140**	3.24	+40	.286	.316	-4		**5.7**
1897	Cle N	21	19	.525	46	38	35	2		0			335.2	391	189	7	9	49		88	3.78	+19	.289	.318	-11		2.3
1898	Cle N	25	13	.658	46	41	40	1		0			377.2	387	167	6	9	41		101	2.53	+43	.263	.287	+0		4.4
1899	StL N	26	16	.619	44	42	**40**	4		1			369.1	368	173	10	6	44		111	2.58	+54	.260	**.285**	+1		**5.1**
1900	StL N	19	19	.500	41	35	32	0		0			321.1	337	144	7	3	36		115	3.00	+21	.269	.291	-14		2.6
1901	Bos A	**33**	10	.767	43	41	38	0		0			371.1	324	112	6	7	37		**158**	**1.62**	+117	**.232**	**.256**	+10		**7.9**
1902	Bos A	**32**	11	.744	**45**	**43**	**41**	3		0			**384.2**	350	136	6	13	53		160	2.15	+66	.243	.276	+7		**6.0**
1903	†Bos A	**28**	9	**.757**	40	35	**34**	0		**2**			**341.2**	294	115	6	9	37		176	2.08	+46	.232	.259	+36		**4.8**
1904	Bos A	26	16	.619	43	41	40	0		1			380	327	104	6	4	29		200	1.97	+36	.233	**.251**	-6		3.8
1905	Bos A	18	19	.486	38	33	31	4		0			320.2	248	99	3	8	30		210	1.82	+48	.215	**.241**	-23		2.7
1906	Bos A	13	21	.382	39	34	28	0		2			287.2	288	137	3	8	25		140	3.19	-14	.263	.285	-26		-1.9
1907	Bos A	21	15	.583	43	37	33	6		2			343.1	286	101	3	7	51		147	1.99	+29	.229	**.263**	-14		2.4
1908	Bos A	21	11	.656	36	33	30	3		2			299	230	68	1	1	37		150	1.26	+95	.213	.240	+10		4.1
1909	Cle A	19	15	.559	35	34	30	3		0			294.1	267	110	4	8	59		109	2.26	+13	.250	.294	+10		0.9
1910	Cle A	7	10	.412	21	20	14	1		0			163.1	149	62	0	4	27		58	2.53	+2	.252	.289	-26		0.2
1911	Cle A	3	4	.429	7	7	4	0		0			46.1	54	28	2	1	13		20	3.88	-12	.298	.349	-40		-0.5
1911	Bos N	4	5	.444	11	11	8	2		0			80	83	47	4	3	15		35	3.71	+3	.268	.308	-34		-0.3
1911	Major	7	9	.438	18	18	12	2		0			126	137	75	6	4	28		55	3.78	-3	.279	.323	-36		-0.8
Total	22	511	316	.618	906	815	749	76		17			7356	7092	3167	138	161	1217		2803	2.63	+38	.252	.287	-3		77.0

Year	Tm	Lg	W	L	Pct	G	GS	CG	ShO	QS	SV	BS	QR	IP	H	R	HR	HB	BB	IB	SO	ERA	AERA	OAV	OOB	Sup	DL	PW
Team	8		192	112	.632	327	297	275	16		9			2728.1	2347	872	34	57	299		1341	2.00	+47	.233	.259	+0		29.8
/180I	1		13	7	.632	22	20	18	1		1			180	155	58	2	4	20		88	2.00	+47	.233	.259	+0		2.0

YOUNG, MATT Matthew John B8.9.1958 Pasadena CA BL/TL/6'3"/(205–210) [SeaA80 2/32] d4.6 Col UCLA [DL 1988 Oak A 182]

Year	Tm	Lg	W	L	Pct	G	GS	CG	ShO	QS	SV	BS	QR	IP	H	R	HR	HB	BB	IB	SO	ERA	AERA	OAV	OOB	Sup	DL	PW
1991	Bos	A	3	7	.300	19	16	0	0	6	0	0	2	88.2	92	55	4	2	53	2	69	5.18	-16	.266	.365	-17	57	-0.7
1992	Bos	A	0	4	.000	28	8	1	0	1	0	0	15	70.2	69	42	7	3	42	2	57	4.58	-7	.257	.360	-27	16	-0.2
Total	10		55	95	.367	333	163	20	5	70	25	17	113	1189.2	1207	661	99	37	565	28	857	4.40	-5	.265	.348	-12	351	-3.8
Team	2		3	11	.214	47	24	1	0	7	0	0	17	159.1	161	97	11	5	95	4	126	4.91	-13	.262	.363	-20	73	-0.9
/180I	2		3	12	.214	53	27	1	0	8	0	0	19	180	182	110	12	6	107	5	142	4.91	-13	.262	.363	-20	82	-1.0

YOUNG, TIM Timothy R. B10.15.1973 Gulfport MS BL/TL/5'9"/170 [MonN96 19/550] d9.5 Col Alabama

Year	Tm	Lg	W	L	Pct	G	GS	CG	ShO	QS	SV	BS	QR	IP	H	R	HR	HB	BB	IB	SO	ERA	AERA	OAV	OOB	Sup	DL	PW
1998	Mon	N	0	0	+	10	0	0	0	0	0	0	6	6	6	4	0	0	4	0	7	6.00	-30	.250	.357			0.0
2000	Bos	A	0	0	+	8	0	0	0	0	0	0	5	7	7	5	3	1	2	0	6	6.43	-22	.269	.345			0.0
Total	2		0	0	+	18	0	0	0	0	0	0	11	13	13	9	3	1	6	0	13	6.23	-26	.260	.351			0.0

ZAHNISER, PAUL Paul Vernon B9.6.1896 Sac City IA D9.26.1964 Klamath Falls OR BR/TR/5'10.5"/170 d5.18

Year	Tm	Lg	W	L	Pct	G	GS	CG	ShO	QS	SV	BS	QR	IP	H	R	HR	HB	BB	IB	SO	ERA	AERA	OAV	OOB	Sup	DL	PW
1923	Was	A	9	10	.474	33	21	10	1				0	177	201	103	7	3	76		52	3.86	-3	.291	.364	+21		-0.8
1924	Was	A	5	7	.417	24	14	5	1				0	92	98	52	2	4	49		28	4.40	-8	.283	.378	-10		-0.6
1925	Bos	A	5	12	.294	37	21	7	1				1	176.2	232	124	6	1	89		30	5.15	-12	.327	.403	-37		-1.3
1926	Bos	A	6	18	.250	30	24	7	1				0	172	213	106	5	3	69		35	4.97	-18	.321	.387	-41		-1.7
1929	Cin	N	0	0	+	1	0	0	0				0	1	2	3	1	0	1		0	27.00	-83	.400	.500			-0.1
Total	5		25	47	.347	125	80	29	4				1	618.2	746	388	21	11	284		145	4.66	-12	.309	.384	-20		-4.5
Team	2		11	30	.268	67	45	14	2				1	348.2	445	230	11	4	158		65	5.06	-15	.324	.395	-39		-3.0
/180I	1		6	15	.268	35	23	7	1				1	180	230	119	6	2	82		34	5.06	-15	.324	.395	-39		-1.5

ZEISER, MATT Mathias John B9.25.1888 Chicago IL D6.10.1942 Chicago IL BR/TR/5'10"/170 d4.27

Year	Tm	Lg	W	L	Pct	G	GS	CG	ShO	QS	SV	BS	QR	IP	H	R	HR	HB	BB	IB	SO	ERA	AERA	OAV	OOB	Sup	DL	PW
1914	Bos	A	0	0	+	2	0	0	0				0	10	9	4	0	1	8		0	1.80	+50	.281	.439			0.0

ZUBER, BILL William Henry "Goober" B3.26.1913 Middle Amana IA D11.2.1982 Cedar Rapids IA BR/TR/6'2"/195 d9.16

Year	Tm	Lg	W	L	Pct	G	GS	CG	ShO	QS	SV	BS	QR	IP	H	R	HR	HB	BB	IB	SO	ERA	AERA	OAV	OOB	Sup	DL	PW
1946	†Bos	A	5	1	.833	15	7	2	1				0	56.2	37	20	4	0	39		29	2.54	+44	.187	.321	+50	0	0.5
1947	Bos	A	1	0	1.000	20	1	0	0				0	50.2	60	32	4	0	31		23	5.33	-27	.311	.406	+14	0	-0.4
Total	11		43	42	.506	224	65	23	3				6	786	767	418	35	4	468		383	4.28	-13	.260	.362	+3	0	-4.7
Team	2		6	1	.857	35	8	2	1				0	107.1	97	52	8	0	70		52	3.86	-2	.248	.362	+46		0.1

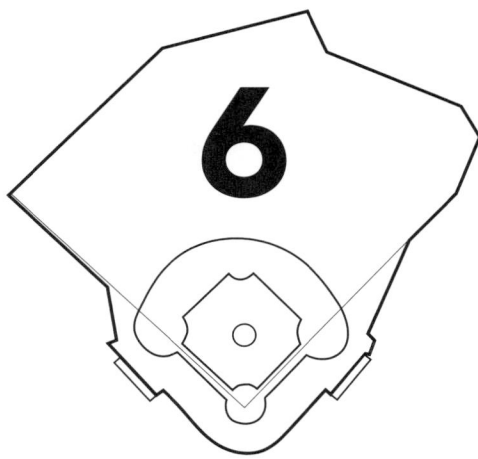

RED SOX MANAGERS AND COACHES

Managing a baseball team in Boston has never been easy. From the first professional league in 1871, the National Association, Boston had a strong leader in the legendary Harry Wright. Thirty years later Boston had a new franchise but an experienced leader in Jimmy Collins. Collins had been a star third baseman for the National League's Boston Beaneaters when he jumped at the chance to get away from the spendthrift club and join the new major league enterprise starting up at the Huntington Avenue Grounds. Collins was named manager of the Red Sox and led them to their first championship in the inaugural World Series in 1903. He managed the franchise's first 831 games, winning 455 times and twice taking the pennant. Collins established a level of excellence that his successors have had a hard time living up to.

Bill Carrigan won more world championships—his consecutive World Series victories are still the club's gold standard—and he won more games than Collins (489–455). Joe Cronin later amassed 1,071 wins and Pinky Higgins took over second place with 560. Several managers surpassed Collins' career winning percentage of .548 with the club: Jake Stahl (.621), Joe McCarthy (.606), Steve O'Neill (.602), Grady Little (.580), Fred Lake (.579), Don Zimmer (.575), Terry Francona (.574), and Kevin Kennedy (.559). Collins, however, spent more time managing the Red Sox than any of those eight. Collins had one of the great pitchers of all-time at his disposal, Cy Young, and he had the first third baseman to be elected to the National Baseball Hall of Fame in himself. Not every Red Sox manager has been so blessed with talent. Plus the fan base and media, though rabid, had not reached the fever pitch they would attain in future generations.

This section lists all 44 managers in franchise history: from Rudy York, who managed and lost his only game in 1959, to Cronin, who managed 1,987 games for the Red Sox. Cronin and Collins are the only men with protracted terms managing the Red Sox who eventually reached the Hall of Fame. But the reasons for their enshrinement in Cooperstown were for their deeds with bat and glove as opposed to what they did as managers with the club. Ed Barrow, Lou Boudreau, Frank Chance, Hugh Duffy, Bucky Harris, Billy Herman, Joe McCarthy, and Cy Young all reached the Hall of Fame for their feats beyond the Boston dugout. Barrow managed the Red Sox to the 1918 world championship, but he was elected to the Hall of Fame because of what he did putting together the Yankees—purging the Red Sox when he could—to give McCarthy the wherewithal to win seven world championships. Chance had one of the greatest records in history with the Cubs of the dead ball era, but his 61–91 mark with the 1923 Red Sox was the only last-place finish of his 11-year managing career; he died the following year. Boudreau's first great moment as a manager was beating the Red Sox with two home runs in the 1948 one-game playoff at Fenway Park (McCarthy was in the home dugout). Duffy and Herman made the Hall of Fame as players. Harris entered Cooperstown for what he did running other clubs, not the .500 Red Sox of 1934.

Cy Young started the 1907 season as manager, going 2–0 with himself on the mound and 1–3 the rest of the time. He didn't enjoy the job, and quickly stopped. Many is the manager who has the decision to move on made for him.

Managers sometimes miss games for suspension, illness, or personal reasons. A coach will take over for a day or two, but it is still the manager's team. Thus the record is reflected here as belonging to the manager and not the fill-in coach. When a long absence occurs, however, it is a different matter. Using the measuring stick of 30 consecutive games makes a coach the de facto skipper and thus his record is listed in this section.

Dismissal is separate all together. Interim managers are certainly running the show, even if they are keeping the bench warm until the new manager is located, signed, and delivered. A few interim managers have done so well they have been kept on for the next season and beyond. "Morgan Magic" in 1988 began as a fill-in gig and turned into a successful 563-game managing career for Joe Morgan.

The coaches follow the managers in this section just as they do in the dugout. Everyone who has been on the coaching staff is listed chronologically, as opposed to the managers, who are listed alphabetically in this section.

In this section, player/managers are designated with the years they both played and managed in bold. As many of them eventually shifted to managing only, this is important to note. Joe Cronin's career as a player/manager was successful, but he had his best season in 1946, the year after he hung up his spikes. Lou Boudreau in 1952 was Boston's last manager with the power to insert his name into the lineup.

Each manager's birth date is given. If the birth date is all that is listed in the first line besides his name, it signifies that he was a major league player. If his full name, nickname, birth date and place, and death date and place are listed, it means that the manager never played in the major leagues. The position is given, such as C for catcher Kevin Kennedy. In the cases of George Huff and Ed Barrow, *DNP* is added to show that they did not play in the minor leagues either. A manager's full career as a major league skipper is included, with stops before and after Boston recorded through 2006.

The **Finish** column indicates how the team fared under the manager in an 8-team league (1901–60), 10-team league (1961–68), 6-team division (1969–76),

7-team division (1977–93), and 5-team division (1994–present). A *t* in that column indicates a tie in the standings. In the case of multiple managers, the finish of each manager is given. In Del Baker's entry, for example, 8-8-7 in this column indicates that the club was in eighth place when he took over, was still eight when he was replaced, and finished the year in seventh. Baker's place in this group is indicated in the **Mgr/Yr** column, with ²/₃ signifying his stint was sandwiched between two other managers in 1960. Letters *e, c,* and *w* are listed next to teams for years after 1969 signifying East, Central, and West Divisions, respectively.

Symbols after the finish show if a team that finished first won one or more postseason series. A solid star ★ indicates the team won the World Series. A solid diamond ◆ means the team won the LSC but lost the World Series (1969–present). A hollow star ☆ indicates the team won the Division Series but lost the LCS (1995–present). A cross ✚ indicates a wild card team. A solid triangle ▲ shows that the team was tied at the end of the regular season for first place and played a one-game playoff.

The plus minus column (+/–) indicates how many games the team won compared to how many the team was projected to win based on its run production. So Jimy Williams' 4.1 in 2001 means that the Red Sox won 4 games more than they should have based on their runs produced and runs allowed. A rating below zero indicates a disappointing performance. For example, Williams' replacement in 2001, Joe Kerrigan, had a mark of –5.2, meaning the team should have won 5 more games during his 43 games as manager.

On the career line, the manager's lifetime seasons as a manager along with won-lost record and winning percentage are added under *Total*. A manager's record for the Red Sox portion of his career is listed as *Team*. If he did not manage a team other than the Red Sox, then his Boston numbers are merely listed as Total. If he managed just one year, there is no career line.

A manager's stops with other teams are listed only if he managed at least 30 percent of his games with the Red Sox. Therefore, only the Red Sox portion of the year-by-year record is listed for Del Baker, Lou Boudreau, Hugh Duffy, Bucky Harris, Ralph Houk, Joe McCarthy, John McNamara, Steve O'Neill, and Dick Williams.

Red Sox Manager Register

Year	Tm/Lg	W	L	Pct	Finish	Mgr/Yr	+/-
Baker, Del	B5.3.1892						
1960	Bos A	2	5	.286	8–8–7	2/3	-1.0
Total	9	419	360	.538			4.7
Barrow, Ed	Edward Grant "Cousin Ed"			B5.10.1868 Springfield, IL		D12.15.1953	
	Port Chester, NY (DNP)						
1903	Det A	65	71	.478	5		-6.0
1904	Det A	32	46	.410	7–7	1/2	0.1
1918	Bos A	75	51	.595	1★		1.2
1919	Bos A	66	71	.482	6		-3.8
1920	Bos A	72	81	.471	5		0.4
Total	5	310	320	.492			-8.1
Team	3	213	203	.512			-2.2
Barry, Jack	B4.26.1887						
1917	Bos A	90	62	.592	2		2.2
Boudreau, Lou	B7.17.1917						
1952	Bos A	76	78	.494	6		-2.0
1953	Bos A	84	69	.549	4		5.0
1954	Bos A	69	85	.448	4		-5.2
Total	16	1162	1224	.487			-6.9
Team	3	229	232	.497			-2.2
Carrigan, Bill	B10.22.1883						
1913	Bos A	40	30	.571	5–4	2/2	4.0
1914	Bos A	91	62	.595	2		5.5
1915	Bos A	101	50	.669	1★		6.9
1916	Bos A	91	63	.591	1★		5.8
1927	Bos A	51	103	.331	8		-0.7
1928	Bos A	57	96	.373	8		-1.2
1929	Bos A	58	96	.377	8		0.7
Total	7	489	500	.494			21.0
Chance, Frank	B9.9.1876						
1923	Bos A	61	91	.401	8		7.4
Total	11	946	648	.593			20.4
Collins, Jimmy	B1.16.1870						
1901	Bos A	79	57	.581	2		-3.4
1902	Bos A	77	60	.562	3		2.2
1903	Bos A	91	47	.659	1★		1.1
1904	Bos A	95	59	.617	1		1.7
1905	Bos A	78	74	.513	4		0.5
1906	Bos A	35	79	.307	8–8	1/2	-2.3
Total	6	455	376	.548			-0.3
Collins, Shano	B12.4.1885						
1931	Bos A	62	90	.408	6		3.2
1932	Bos A	11	44	.200	8–8	1/2	-4.4
Total	2	73	134	.353			-1.2
Cronin, Joe	B10.12.1906						
1933	Was A	99	53	.651	1		5.4
1934	Was A	66	86	.434	7		-2.7
1935	Bos A	78	75	.510	4		2.9
1936	Bos A	74	80	.481	6		-4.0
1937	Bos A	80	72	.526	5		-0.3
1938	Bos A	88	61	.591	2		-0.1
1939	Bos A	89	62	.589	2		4.9
1940	Bos A	82	72	.532	4t		0.8
1941	Bos A	84	70	.545	2		-3.7
1942	Bos A	93	59	.612	2		0.2
1943	Bos A	68	84	.447	7		-3.2
1944	Bos A	77	77	.500	4		-6.3
1945	Bos A	71	83	.461	7		1.9
1946	Bos A	104	50	.675	1		7.1
1947	Bos A	83	71	.539	3		0.9
Total	15	1236	1055	.540			3.7
Team	13	1071	916	.539			1.1
Donovan, Patsy	B3.16.1865						
1910	Bos A	81	72	.529	4		-3.9
1911	Bos A	78	75	.510	5		-2.3
Total	11	684	879	.438			6.8
Team	2	159	147	.520			-6.2
Duffy, Hugh	B11.26.1866						
1921	Bos A	75	79	.487	5		0.8
1922	Bos A	61	93	.396	8		1.2
Total	8	535	671	.444			-22.7
Team	2	136	172	.442			2.0
Fohl, Lee	B11.28.1876						
1924	Bos A	67	87	.435	7		-3.2
1925	Bos A	47	105	.309	8		-2.5
1926	Bos A	46	107	.301	8		-3.3
Total	11	713	792	.474			-5.6
Team	3	160	299	.349			-9.0
Francona, Terry	B4.22.1959						
1997	Phi N e	68	94	.420	5		3.9
1998	Phi N e	75	87	.463	3		3.3
1999	Phi N e	77	85	.475	3		-3.5
2000	Phi N e	65	97	.401	5		-4.1
2004	Bos A e	98	64	.605	2★❖		0.3
2005	Bos A e	95	67	.586	2❖		4.3
2006	Bos A e	86	76	.531	3		5.5
Total	7	564	570	.497			9.7
Team	3	279	207	.574			10.1

Year	Tm/Lg	W	L	Pct	Finish	Mgr/Yr	+/-
Harris, Bucky	B11.8.1896						
1934	Bos A	76	76	.500	4		-4.2
Total	29	2157	2218	.493			-32.5
Herman, Billy	B7.7.1909						
1947	Pit N	61	92	.399	8–7t	1/2	-8.7
1964	Bos A	2	0	1.000	8–8	2/2	1.1
1965	Bos A	62	100	.383	9		-6.8
1966	Bos A	64	82	.438	9–9	1/2	-2.0
Total	4	189	274	.408			-16.4
Team	3	128	182	.413			-7.7
Higgins, Pinky	B5.27.1909						
1955	Bos A	84	70	.545	4		-3.2
1956	Bos A	84	70	.545	4		4.2
1957	Bos A	82	72	.532	3		-0.3
1958	Bos A	79	75	.513	3		1.4
1959	Bos A	31	42	.425	8–8	1/3	-6.9
1960	Bos A	48	57	.457	8–7	3/3	3.3
1961	Bos A	76	86	.469	6		1.2
1962	Bos A	76	84	.475	8		0.9
Total	8	560	556	.502			0.6
Hobson, Butch	B8.17.1951						
1992	Bos A	73	89	.451	7		-0.5
1993	Bos A e	80	82	.494	5		0.2
1994	Bos A e	54	61	.470	4		3.0
Total	3	207	232	.472			2.7
Houk, Ralph	B8.9.1919						
1982	Bos A e	89	73	.549	3		4.0
1983	Bos A e	78	84	.481	6		2.0
1984	Bos A e	86	76	.531	4		0.6
Total	20	1619	1531	.514			29.0
Team	3	253	233	.521			6.6
Huff, George	George A. "Gee"			B6.11.1872 Champaign, IL		D10.1.1936	
	Champaign, IL (DNP)						
1907	Bos A	2	6	.250	4t–6–7	2/4	-1.4
Johnson, Darrell	B8.25.1928						
1974	Bos A e	84	78	.519	3		-0.6
1975	Bos A e	95	65	.594	1◆		6.5
1976	Bos A e	41	45	.477	5–3	1/2	-5.1
1977	Sea A w	64	98	.395	6		5.9
1978	Sea A w	56	104	.350	7		-2.1
1979	Sea A w	67	95	.414	6		-3.4
1980	Sea A w	39	65	.375	6–7	1/2	-1.0
1982	Tex A w	26	40	.394	6–6	2/2	-0.2
Total	8	472	590	.444			0.1
Team	3	220	188	.539			0.8
Jurges, Billy	B5.9.1908						
1959	Bos A	44	36	.550	8–5	3/3	2.5
1960	Bos A	15	27	.357	8–7	1/3	-2.9
Total	2	59	63	.484			-0.4
Kasko, Eddie	B6.27.1932						
1970	Bos A e	87	75	.537	3		-0.3
1971	Bos A e	85	77	.525	3		1.5
1972	Bos A e	85	70	.548	2		5.4
1973	Bos A e	88	73	.547	2–2	1/2	-1.8
Total	4	345	295	.539			4.8
Kennedy, Kevin	Kevin Curtis			B9.26.1954 Los Angeles, CA		BR/TR/6'3"/220(C)	
1993	Tex A w	86	76	.531	2		-3.1
1994	Tex A w	52	62	.456	1		2.4
1995	Bos A e	86	58	.597	1		5.3
1996	Bos A e	85	77	.525	3		3.4
Total	4	309	273	.531			8.1
Team	2	171	135	.559			8.7
Kerrigan, Joe	B1.30.1954						
2001	Bos A e	17	26	.395	2–2	2/2	-5.2
Lake, Fred	B10.16.1866						
1908	Bos A	22	17	.564	6–5	2/2	1.0
1909	Bos A	88	63	.583	3		6.8
1910	Bos N	53	100	.346	8		-1.1
Total	3	163	180	.475			6.8
Team	2	110	80	.579			7.8
Little, Grady	William Grady			B3.3.1950 Abilene, TX		BR/TR/5'11"/190(C)	
2002	Bos A e	93	69	.574	2		-7.0
2003	Bos A e	95	67	.586	2☆❖		0.2
2006	LA N w	88	74	.543	1		0.4
Total	3	276	210	.568			-6.4
Team	2	188	136	.580			-6.8
McCarthy, Joe	Joseph Vincent "Marse Joe"			B4.21.1887 Philadelphia, PA			
	D1.13.1978 Buffalo, NY BR/TR/5'8.5"/190(2B)						
1948	Bos A	96	59	.619	2▲		1.2
1949	Bos A	96	58	.623	2		-2.6
1950	Bos A	31	28	.525	4–3	1/2	-5.9
Total	24	2125	1333	.615			-23.6
Team	3	223	145	.606			-7.3
McGuire, Deacon	B11.18.1863						
1898	Was N	21	47	.309	10–11–11	3/4	-3.3
1907	Bos A	45	61	.425	8–7	4/4	-0.4
1908	Bos A	53	62	.461	6–5	1/2	-8.8
1909	Cle A	14	25	.359	4–6	2/2	-4.3

Year	Tm/Lg	W	L	Pct	Finish	Mgr/Yr	+/-
1910	Cle A	71	81	.467	5		7.0
1911	Cle A	6	11	.353	7–3	1/2	-2.3
Total	6	210	287	.423			-12.2
Team	2	98	123	.443			-9.2
McManus, Marty	B3.14.1900						
1932	Bos A	32	67	.323	8–8	2/2	4.2
1933	Bos A	63	86	.423	7		-5.9
Total	2	95	153	.383			-1.7
McNamara, John	John Francis		B6.4.1932 Sacramento, CA		BR/TR/5'10"/175(C)		
1985	Bos A e	81	81	.500	5		-7.9
1986	Bos A e	95	66	.590	1♦		4.8
1987	Bos A e	78	84	.481	5		-4.6
1988	Bos A e	43	42	.506	4–1	1/2	-5.9
Total	19	1168	1247	.484			5.5
Team	4	297	273	.521			-13.6
Morgan, Joe	B11.19.1930						
1988	Bos A e	46	31	.597	4–1	2/2	1.7
1989	Bos A e	83	79	.512	3		-1.8
1990	Bos A e	88	74	.543	1		3.4
1991	Bos A e	84	78	.519	2t		1.1
Total	4	301	262	.535			4.3
O'Neill, Steve	B7.6.1891						
1950	Bos A	63	32	.663	4–3	2/2	3.5
1951	Bos A	87	67	.565	3		2.5
Total	14	1040	821	.559			22.2
Team	2	150	99	.602			6.0
Pesky, Johnny	B9.27.1919						
1963	Bos A	76	85	.472	7		-0.6
1964	Bos A	70	90	.438	8–8	1/2	0.3
1980	Bos A e	1	4	.200	3–4	2/2	-1.5
Total	3	147	179	.451			-1.8
Popowski, Eddie	Edward Joseph		B8.20.1913 Sayreville, NJ		D12.4.2001		
	Sayreville, NJ BR/TR/5'4.5"/145(2B)						
1969	Bos A e	5	4	.556	3–3	2/2	0.5
1973	Bos A e	1	0	1.000	2–2	2/2	0.4
Total	2	6	4	.600			0.9
Runnels, Pete	B1.28.1928						
1966	Bos A	8	8	.500	9–9	2/2	0.8
Stahl, Chick	B1.10.1873						
1906	Bos A	14	26	.350	8–8	2/2	0.9
Stahl, Jake	B4.13.1879						
1905	Was A	64	87	.424	7		-4.6
1906	Was A	55	95	.367	7		-4.4
1912	Bos A	105	47	.691	1★		3.1
1913	Bos A	39	41	.488	5–4	1/2	-2.2
Total	4	263	270	.493			-8.0
Team	2	144	88	.621			0.9

Year	Tm/Lg	W	L	Pct	Finish	Mgr/Yr	+/-
Unglaub, Bob	B7.31.1881						
1907	Bos A	9	20	.310	6–8–7	3/4	-3.4
Wagner, Heinie	B9.23.1880						
1930	Bos A	52	102	.338	8		-5.1
Williams, Jimy	B10.4.1943						
1986	Tor A e	86	76	.531	4		-2.4
1987	Tor A e	96	66	.593	2		-3.7
1988	Tor A e	87	75	.537	3t		-2.3
1989	Tor A e	12	24	.333	6–1	1/2	-7.8
1997	Bos A e	78	84	.481	4		-2.4
1998	Bos A e	92	70	.568	2❖		-3.0
1999	Bos A e	94	68	.580	2☆❖		1.6
2000	Bos A e	85	77	.525	2		-0.6
2001	Bos A e	65	53	.551	2–2	1/2	4.1
2002	Hou N c	84	78	.519	2		-2.4
2003	Hou N c	87	75	.537	2		-6.7
2004	Hou N c	44	44	.500	5–2☆❖	1/2	-5.6
Total	12	910	790	.535			-31.5
Team	5	414	352	.540			-0.3
Williams, Dick	B5.7.1929						
1967	Bos A	92	70	.568	1		-0.3
1968	Bos A	86	76	.531	4		4.7
1969	Bos A e	82	71	.536	3–3	1/2	4.8
Total	21	1571	1451	.520			8.0
Team	3	260	217	.545			9.2
York, Rudy	B8.17.1913						
1959	Bos A	0	1	.000	8–8–5	2/3	-0.5
Young, Cy	B3.29.1867						
1907	Bos A	3	3	.500	4t–7	1/4	0.4
Zimmer, Don	B1.17.1931						
1972	SD N w	54	88	.380	4–6	2/2	1.0
1973	SD N w	60	102	.370	6		2.4
1976	Bos A e	42	34	.553	5–3	2/2	1.3
1977	Bos A e	97	64	.602	2t		2.4
1978	Bos A e	99	64	.607	2▲		3.5
1979	Bos A e	91	69	.569	3		-1.5
1980	Bos A e	82	73	.529	3–4	1/2	5.4
1981–1	Tex A w	33	22	.600	2		-2.2
1981–2	Tex A w	24	26	.480	3		-2.2
1982	Tex A w	38	58	.396	6–6	1/2	-0.2
1988	Chi N e	77	85	.475	4		-0.5
1989	Chi N e	93	69	.574	1		3.7
1990	Chi N e	77	85	.475	4t		4.4
1991	Chi N e	18	19	.486	4–4	1/3	0.4
1999	NY A e	21	15	.583	1–1	1/2	-0.6
Total	14	906	873	.509			17.4
Team	5	411	304	.575			11.1

Since baseball was first played it has been apparent that every team needs a leader. Given the permutations that can be made in creating a lineup, a manager is required to lay down the law, if not fill out the lineup card. As the responsibility and accountability of managers increased, managers coerced others to act as assistants and instructors, delegating responsibility to them for the perceived greater good of the team. It has not always been good for the manager.

The history of the game is filled with stories of old friends asked to help out as coaches and turning into adversaries, speaking poorly of the manager in front of the front office or players. While these machinations may lead to the manager's dismissal, it can often lead to the end of employment for the coach. Other times, the front office has asked for a sacrifice from the manager, a coach to be thrown to the masses in place of the manager's head. Some managers comply with the request, some resign. In either case, coaches in this section will be fitted with a minus sign if they left during the course of a season. Likewise, a plus sign is placed next to a coach's name if he was added to the staff after the season began. Coaches with +/- next to their name both came and went during the same season.

Coaches, like many others in the game, have become more specialized over the years. Where teams once had one or two coaches to help out with the pitchers or base-coaching duties, now most teams have six coaches on a major league staff. A bench coach is the latest power coaching spot, a sounding board for in-game decisions and a devil's advocate.

Coaching is still good work, if you can find it. Seven Red Sox coaches have made the ultimate step from the coaching box to the manager's chair: Heinie Wagner, Steve O'Neill, Billy Herman, Pete Runnels, Don Zimmer, Joe Morgan, and Joe Kerrigan. Those men are not fitted with minus signs because they remained on the coaching staff, even if their promotion came with its own office and their new position stenciled on the door.

Red Sox Coach Roster

1916
Heinie Wagner

1917
Heinie Wagner

1918
Heinie Wagner

1919
Heinie Wagner

1921
Jimmy Burke

1922
Jimmy Burke

1923
Jimmy Burke
Jack Ryan

1924
Lefty Leifield
Jack Ryan

1925
Lefty Leifield
Jack Ryan

1926
Bob Coleman
Lefty Leifield
Jack Ryan

1927
Jack Ryan
Heinie Wagner

1928
Heinie Wagner

1929
Heinie Wagner

1930
Jack McCallister

1931
Rudy Hulswitt

1932
Hugh Duffy
Rudy Hulswitt
Hank Patterson +/-

1933
Tom Daly
Rudy Hulswitt

1934
Tom Daly
Bibb Falk
Jack Onslow

1935
Tom Daly
Al Schacht

1936
Tom Daly
Herb Pennock
Al Schacht

1937
Tom Daly
Bing Miller
Herb Pennock

1938
Tom Daly
Herb Pennock

1939
Tom Daly
Herb Pennock

1940
Moe Berg
Tom Daly
Frank Shellenback

1941
Moe Berg
Tom Daly
Frank Shellenback

1942
Tom Daly
Frank Shellenback
Larry Woodall

1943
Tom Daly
Frank Shellenback
Larry Woodall

1944
Bill Burwell
Tom Daly
Frank Shellenback
Larry Woodall

1945
Del Baker
Tom Daly
Larry Woodall

1946
Del Baker
Tom Carey
Tom Daly
Larry Woodall

1947
Del Baker
Tom Carey
Paul Schreiber
Larry Woodall

1948
Del Baker
Earle Combs
Paul Schreiber
Larry Woodall

1949
Earle Combs
Kiki Cuyler
Paul Schreiber
Johnny Schulte

1950
Earle Combs
Steve O'Neill
Paul Schreiber
Johnny Schulte
George Susce +

1951
Earle Combs
Eddie Mayo
Paul Schreiber
George Susce

1952
Earle Combs
Bill McKechnie
Ski Melillo
Paul Schreiber
George Susce

1953
Del Baker
Bill McKechnie
Ski Melillo
Paul Schreiber
George Susce

1954
Del Baker
Buster Mills
Paul Schreiber
George Susce

1955
Del Baker
Jack Burns
Dave Ferriss
Mickey Owen
Paul Schreiber

1956
Del Baker
Jack Burns
Dave Ferriss
Mickey Owen
Paul Schreiber

1957
Del Baker
Jack Burns
Dave Ferriss
Paul Schreiber

1958
Del Baker
Jack Burns
Dave Ferriss
Paul Schreiber

1959
Del Baker
Jack Burns
Dave Ferriss
Rudy York

1960
Del Baker
Billy Herman
Sal Maglie
Rudy York

1961
Billy Herman
Sal Maglie
Len Okrie
Rudy York

1962
Billy Herman
Sal Maglie
Len Okrie
Rudy York

1963
Fritz Dorish
Billy Herman
Al Lakeman
Harry Malmberg

1964
Billy Herman
Al Lakeman
Harry Malmberg
Bob Turley

1965
Mace Brown
Billy Gardner
Len Okrie
Pete Runnels

1966
Billy Gardner
Sal Maglie
Len Okrie
Pete Runnels

1967
Bobby Doerr
Al Lakeman
Sal Maglie
Eddie Popowski

1968
Bobby Doerr
Darrell Johnson
Al Lakeman
Eddie Popowski

1969
Bobby Doerr
Darrell Johnson
Al Lakeman -
Eddie Popowski
Lee Stange +

1970
Doug Camilli
Don Lenhardt
Eddie Popowski
George Thomas -
Charley Wagner

1971
Doug Camilli
Harvey Haddix
Don Lenhardt
Eddie Popowski

1972
Doug Camilli
Don Lenhardt
Eddie Popowski
Lee Stange

1973
Doug Camilli
Don Lenhardt
Eddie Popowski
Lee Stange

1974
Don Bryant
Eddie Popowski
Lee Stange
Don Zimmer

1975
Don Bryant
Johnny Pesky
Eddie Popowski
Stan Williams
Don Zimmer

1976
Don Bryant
Johnny Pesky
Eddie Popowski
Stan Williams
Don Zimmer

1977
Walt Hriniak
Al Jackson
Johnny Pesky
Eddie Yost

1978
Walt Hriniak
Al Jackson
Johnny Pesky
Eddie Yost

1979
Walt Hriniak
Al Jackson
Johnny Pesky
Eddie Yost

1980
Tommy Harper
Walt Hriniak
Johnny Pesky
Johnny Podres
Eddie Yost

1981
Tommy Harper
Walt Hriniak
Johnny Pesky
Lee Stange
Eddie Yost

1982
Tommy Harper
Walt Hriniak
Johnny Pesky
Lee Stange
Eddie Yost

1983
Tommy Harper
Walt Hriniak
Johnny Pesky
Lee Stange
Eddie Yost

1984
Tommy Harper
Walt Hriniak
Johnny Pesky
Lee Stange
Eddie Yost

1985
Bill Fischer
Walt Hriniak
Rene Lachemann
Joe Morgan
Tony Torchia

1986
Bill Fischer
Walt Hriniak
Rene Lachemann
Joe Morgan

1987
Bill Fischer
Walt Hriniak
Joe Morgan
Rac Slider

1988
Al Bumbry
Bill Fischer
Walt Hriniak
Jerry McNertney +
Joe Morgan
Rac Slider

1989
Dick Berardino
Al Bumbry
Bill Fischer
Richie Hebner
Rac Slider

1990
Dick Berardino
Al Bumbry
Bill Fischer
Richie Hebner
Rac Slider

1991
Dick Berardino
Al Bumbry
Bill Fischer
Richie Hebner
John McLaren

1992
Gary Allenson
Al Bumbry
Rick Burleson
Rich Gale
Don Zimmer

1993
Gary Allenson
Al Bumbry
Rick Burleson
Mike Easler
Rich Gale

1994
Gary Allenson
Mike Easler -
Jim Rice +
Mike Roarke

John Wathan
Frank White

1995
John Cumberland -
Tim Johnson
Al Nipper +
Dave Oliver
Jim Rice
Herm Starrette
Frank White

1996
Dave Carlucci -
Sammy Ellis +
Tim Johnson
Al Nipper -
Dave Oliver
Jim Rice
Herm Starrette +
Frank White

1997
Dave Jauss
Joe Kerrigan
Wendell Kim
Grady Little
Jim Rice
Herm Starrette

1998
Dave Jauss
Joe Kerrigan
Wendell Kim
Grady Little
Dick Pole
Jim Rice

1999
John Cumberland
Dave Jauss

Joe Kerrigan
Wendell Kim
Grady Little
Jim Rice

2000
Buddy Bailey
John Cumberland
Tommy Harper
Joe Kerrigan
Wendell Kim
Jim Rice

2001
John Cumberland -
Rick Down
Tommy Harper
Joe Kerrigan
Gene Lamont
Nelson Norman
Ralph Treuel +

2002
Tony Cloninger
Mike Cubbage
Dwight Evans
Tommy Harper
Bob Kipper
Mike Stanley

2003
Tony Cloninger -
Mike Cubbage
Glenn Gregson +/-
Ron Jackson
Jerry Narron
Euclides Rojas
Dave Wallace +
Dallas Williams

2004
Ron Jackson
Lynn Jones
Brad Mills
Euclides Rojas
Dale Sveum
Dave Wallace

2005
Bill Haselman
Ron Jackson
Lynn Jones
Brad Mills
Dale Sveum
Dave Wallace

2006
DeMarlo Hale
Bill Haselman
Ron Jackson
Brad Mills
Al Nipper
Dave Wallace

2007
Luis Alicea
John Farrell
DeMarlo Hale *
Dave Magadan
Brad Mills *
Gary Tuck

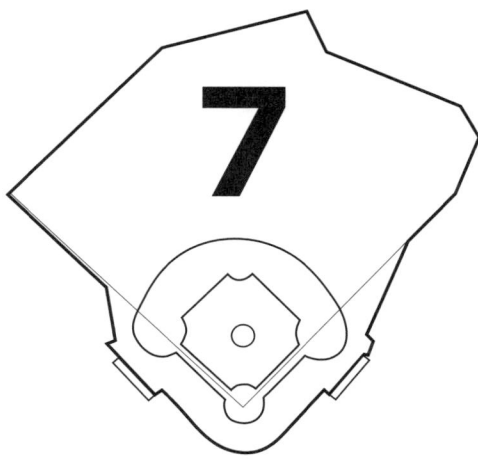

RED SOX EXECUTIVES AND BROADCASTERS

Red Sox Ownership History

When Ban Johnson hatched his original plan for the American League to emerge as a major league in 1901, the plan did not call for a franchise in Boston. Johnson was originally hoping that the National League would accept its new competition with semi-open arms and, as a result, did not place teams in some major cities in order to hold off on declaring total war against the senior circuit. The National League, however, was not receptive to Johnson's plan, and told him exactly where he could go. Underestimating Johnson's resolve and backing, the NL announced that it would support an alternative new major league, the American Association, and that the new league would launch baseball teams in many of the same cities that the American League was fielding teams, plus Boston. Johnson, in response, decided to take the American League instead to Boston to compete directly against the Boston National League team already there. A franchise that was originally destined for Buffalo thus ended up in Beantown.

The team that would eventually be known as the Boston Red Sox thus came into existence not because of the desire of a city to host another baseball team or the desire of a businessman to own a team, but as a strategic move by a new league jockeying for position. As a result, the early owners of the Red Sox were, at best, forced to run the team under Johnson's thumb and at worst, as no more than tools for Johnson. This unhealthy ownership situation's consequences would reverberate for over a century, long after Johnson and the other principals involved in the situation were dead.

The first official owner of the Red Sox was Charles Somers. In reality, Somers was Ban Johnson's—and thus the American League's—bank. Somers financed much of the growth that enabled the American League to become a major league. When Johnson decided that the American League should have a franchise in Boston, he turned to Somers to finance it. Somers already owned the league's Cleveland franchise and had also financed the Chicago and Philadelphia entries in the American League. Somers' bank accounts were still flush, however, thanks to all the money he had made in coal mining, and so he willingly coughed up the money to own the new Boston team, too.

When the American League began operating as a major league, it didn't matter much who the individual owners were, since Ban Johnson more or less ran every team. He decided where and how baseball talent would be distributed through the league. So Boston, an important front in the battle against the National League, was able to stock up on talent. Johnson's first order of business for his new Boston club was to send Connie Mack to Boston to sign star third baseman Jimmie Collins away from Boston's National League team.

Once the new Boston team was successfully established, Johnson immediately began seeking a new owner to replace Somers, who had no interest in holding on to his ownership of the Boston franchise one minute longer than the league required. It did not take long to arrange the sale of the Boston franchise to another Johnson confidante, Milwaukee lawyer Henry Killilea. Killilea sold his Milwaukee franchise, which would move to St. Louis and become the Browns the following season, in order to pick

up the Boston franchise. Killilea's term of ownership eventually turned sour for all concerned, and Boston's 1903 World Series victory gave him the opportunity to sell out to a local owner at a substantial profit. Killilea received many offers for the team, the most promising of which came from local politician John "Honey Fitz" Fitzgerald. Fitzgerald would later be elected mayor of Boston and a congressman, and his grandson would become president of the United States, but Johnson preferred that the team be sold to a local owner he could easily control. That scotched Killilea's deal with Fitzgerald and instead engineered the sale of the ball club to John Irving Taylor, a young, directionless playboy whose father, *Boston Globe* publisher General Charles Taylor, supplied the money necessary to purchase the team.

Johnson was indeed able to continue to control the Sox through Taylor, but Taylor proved incompetent at running the team and ended up giving away talent in bushels. Taylor's most lasting contributions to Boston baseball history—the Red Sox nickname and the push to build Fenway Park—are indeed meritorious, but in no way make up for one of the most ineffectual ownership stints in the history of major league baseball. So when, in 1911, Taylor decided he'd rather be the landlord of a baseball team, than the owner of a baseball team, Johnson stepped in and arranged for Taylor to sell half the club to Senators manager James McAleer and Robert McCoy, the American League secretary. This pair was backed by money from Johnson himself, though the exact arrangement involved is unknown. Taylor stayed with the club and supervised the construction of the ballpark, but despite his continued partial ownership, he no longer had any role in running the ballclub itself.

McAleer, however, quickly fell into disfavor with Ban Johnson. So while McAleer accompanied John McGraw and many other baseball dignitaries on a world baseball tour during the 1913–14 off-season, Johnson sold McAleer's stake in the team to businessman Joseph Lannin, who later in 1914 bought out John I. Taylor's remaining share of the Red Sox. Lannin, however, grew frustrated with Ban Johnson and the politics of major league baseball after only a few years at the helm. He decided to sell the club and go back to being a fan. Without Johnson's approval or authorization, Lannin sold the Red Sox to the highest bidders, Harry Frazee and Hugh Ward, who paid $675,000 for the ballclub in December 1916. Johnson maneuvered every which way to scuttle the deal, but he was unsuccessful.

Frazee, meanwhile, looked at the purchase as an expansion to his entertainment holdings. He had no idea that he was joining a rather exclusive club with a unique power structure, and that his entry into the American League without a "permission slip" from Ban Johnson would earn Johnson's permanent enmity.

Frazee's entrance into the league would hasten the split of the American League into pro-Johnson and anti-Johnson camps, and that split would eventually drive both Frazee and Johnson out of baseball.

The American League Schism

Frazee and Johnson's relationship was relatively peaceful during Frazee's first year as an owner, but in 1918, with Johnson ready to give up the baseball season because of the war, Frazee did an end run around Johnson to save the season and successfully convinced government officials that baseball was too important to the morale of the country to let it shut down completely. Frazee was furious at what he saw as Johnson's incompetence at dealing with the situation, while Johnson bristled at what he saw as an attack on his authority by Frazee. After the 1918 season, Frazee and New York Giants owner Harry Hempstead proposed that former President William Taft become the leader of major league baseball. Johnson proceeded to threaten to terminate the Red Sox franchise as a result of the rampant gambling that existed at Fenway Park, a problem that Johnson had known about for 20 years. Neither side was willing to back down. In 1919 Johnson tried to block the Red Sox from trading Carl Mays to the Yankees, and the case went to a New York court, where Johnson lost. Frazee, with the help of the Yankees and White Sox ownership, tried to oust Johnson during the off-season. Though weakened, Johnson still had the votes of the other five teams in the league.

Meanwhile, Frazee sold Babe Ruth to the Yankees for $100,000 (plus additional financial considerations from New York). The sale was certainly controversial, but opinion at the time was divided in almost all circles. Despite Ruth's record-setting 1919 season, many felt the problems caused by his constant misbehavior outweighed anything he could do on the field. Despite many stories written since then, Frazee's sale of Ruth was not a result of Frazee needing money; it was a judgment call which, in retrospect, was a misjudgment of epic proportions. Frazee's plan was to use the cash he got to rebuild the Red Sox, but he could never buy enough talent to equal what Ruth became.

After the Black Sox Scandal broke, Frazee and his allies again proposed hiring a commissioner. This time the idea was approved, and Judge Kenesaw Mountain Landis began his reign. As a result, Johnson's power was greatly diminished, but he was still president of the American League, and he still wanted Frazee out. Frazee's deal making wasn't helping; though most of Frazee's trades and sales seemed reasonable when they were made, few turned out very well, and the Red Sox became mediocre, though not terrible. Since Frazee had never made any attempt to win the support of the

Boston press, the combination of frustration over the team's mediocrity and anger from Johnson's allies lead to such a relentless pounding of the owner by the media that several years later Frazee finally decided to sell off the team. Frazee is still vilified by the press in the Hub.

Veteran baseball man Bob Quinn bought out Frazee with the hope of restoring the Red Sox. Those hopes quickly fell apart, however, when soon after the purchase Quinn's main financial backer, Palmer Winslow, fell ill and died. As a result, the franchise went through the least successful stretch in its history, one which included six straight last-place finishes from 1925 to 1930. The one highlight for the Red Sox under Quinn's ownership was outfielder Earl Webb's improbable (he never had more than 30 doubles in any other season) 67 doubles in 1930 to set a still-standing major league record. Quinn finally conceded defeat and sold the team to Tom Yawkey in 1933.

Tom Yawkey was no baseball man, but he had grown up around the game, as his adoptive father once owned the Detroit Tigers. Yawkey was soon to turn 30 and gain control of the extraordinarily large fortune he had inherited from that father. He decided he wanted to own a baseball team. He approached future Hall of Famer Eddie Collins, a fellow Irving School alumnus, about that possibility. Collins spread the word about Yawkey's interest and eventually Bob Quinn approached him about buying the Red Sox. Yawkey's trust purchased the team in February and two months later, when Yawkey turned 30, he officially took over. Eddie Collins happily agreed to join the Red Sox as the general manager, and he would stay with the franchise for the rest of his life.

Having purchased an awful team, Yawkey spent a lot of money on talent from other clubs during his early years as owner. The Red Sox improved, but they did not start winning pennants, so Yawkey shifted his spending toward the farm system by the end of the 1930s. No one ever doubted Yawkey's desire to win the World Series, but his Red Sox never reached that pinnacle during his more than 40 years of ownership. Yawkey made sure his teams had stars, and he often coddled those stars, but the rest of the team was rarely talented or well treated. As the years went on without any championships, Yawkey became less interested in the team. Whether he was behind the often racist tendencies of the franchise or just didn't interfere with them is unknown, but the damage they did during his ownership is the same either way. Only after Yawkey hired Dick O'Connell, someone who did not come from the world of baseball men and cronies that had made the organization its own territory for decades, did the Red Sox stop repeating the same mistakes over and over. As general manager, O'Connell made the club win with a young cast that was fun to watch. Boston won two pennants in an eight-season span, a level of success not seen—or repeated as yet—since before Frazee sold the Babe.

Can't Anyone Here Own This Team?

Tom Yawkey's ownership came to an end when he died of cancer on July 9, 1976, leading to almost two decades of unsettled and sometime embarrassing ownership controversies. Yawkey's will put the club's fate into the hands of his wife, Jean Yawkey and two other trustees, James Curran and Joseph LaCour. As expected, the club was quickly put up for sale. A controversial deal was made to sell the club to an ownership syndicate headed by Haywood Sullivan and Buddy LeRoux. This sale agreement was controversial for two reasons. First, the A-T-O Inc, which had once been known as the Automatic Sprinkler Corp. of America but was now the conglomerate parent company of Rawlings Sporting Goods, had made a higher bid that was ignored in favor of the syndicate's offer. A-T-O sued the Yawkey Trust, arguing that, as a charitable operation, the Trust was legally bound to accept the highest offer. Another bidding group led by former Red Sox center fielder Dom DiMaggio also loudly complained that the bidding had been rigged. The second area of controversy was that Sullivan and LeRoux's ownership group was extremely undercapitalized; their offer was made with the help of a bank loan whose conditions sharply limited the amount beyond the sale price that the syndicate could invest in the Red Sox. Sullivan and LeRoux reportedly put up only $200,000 of their own money to make the deal. As a result, the American League rejected the purchase agreement, 11–3. Bud Selig, then head of the American League Finance Committee, justified the vote thusly: "This isn't Cleveland, it's Boston, the flagship of the American League. This is the most important franchise in the American League, and we can't afford to let it be underfinanced or second-rate."

By the time the sale agreement was rejected by the league, however, Sullivan and LeRoux had already burrowed inside the organization. Sullivan replaced Dick O'Connell as the team's new general manager and LeRoux was appointed as vice president. The sale agreement was quickly rewritten without the bank loan in order to earn the American League's approval. The deal was saved by Jean Yawkey, who financed much of the purchase herself through various financial mechanisms and was added to the new ownership structure as a third general partner.

During the first few years of the new ownership, Jean Yawkey stayed in the background, letting Sullivan and LeRoux call the shots. After Sullivan made a series of egregious errors that resulted in the exits of Red Sox stars Fred Lynn, Rick Burleson, and Carlton Fisk in the 1980–81 off-season, Yawkey lured John Harrington, the

team's former controller, back to the Red Sox in order to represent her interests in the ballclub and the Yawkey Trust on an everyday basis.

Publicly, it appeared that the Red Sox ownership situation had stabilized, but the reality was very different. Sullivan and Yawkey were both determined to invest as much as the team needed to win a championship, while LeRoux and his allies among the limited partners wanted to focus solely on the bottom line of dollars and cents. Since Yawkey and Sullivan controlled two of the three general partnership shares, they simply didn't need LeRoux's support to create Red Sox policy. So LeRoux was left without any influence on the path of the organization. LeRoux looked into selling his shares to local businessman David Mugar, but instead he moved to overthrow Sullivan and Yawkey in a coup attempt that fell on a night at Fenway Park that would live in infamy.

It was June 6, 1983, Tony Conigliaro Night at Fenway Park. It was not, however, an occasion to celebrate. Conigliaro lay bedridden in a nearby hospital, unable to pay for his medical treatment. The Red Sox organization hoped that, by honoring Conigliaro and his 1967 team on that night, they could aid Conigliaro both financially and spiritually. Unfortunately, Conigliaro's situation became a secondary matter when LeRoux called for a press conference to announce that he and the club's limited partners had voted to oust Yawkey and Harrington from their positions running the Red Sox. LeRoux, a la Al Haig, pronounced himself to be in total control. LeRoux also announced the re-hiring of Dick O'Connell as general manager. After LeRoux ended his press conference, Haywood Sullivan and John Harrington held a press conference of their own and declared that Leroux had no authority to make any changes and that Sullivan and Yawkey were still general partners. The night ended with no one sure who was in control of the Red Sox.

Sullivan and Yawkey were able to obtain an injunction against LeRoux the following day, and later in the year, the courts confirmed that two was indeed still more than one. LeRoux simply didn't have the power to overrule his fellow general partners and the limited partners had no say in the matter. So LeRoux and his limited partner allies were forced to sell their stakes before the end of the year. LeRoux, however, maintained his general partnership and continued tangling with Sullivan and Yawkey in and out of court until he finally sold out to Jean Yawkey two years later.

Once LeRoux sold out to Jean Yawkey, however, Haywood Sullivan found himself in a similar position to the one LeRoux had held. Yawkey no longer needed Sullivan's support to make ownership level decisions, and so Sullivan's influence in the organization was sharply reduced. After Jean Yawkey died on February 26, 1992, John Harrington assumed control of the Red Sox as the representative and head of the Jean Yawkey Trust. Almost everyone expected Harrington to quickly sell the team, including Sullivan, who by now was backed by a richer group of investors than had been in his corner in 1977.

Harrington, however, defied expectations and put off selling the club for almost a decade. A frustrated Sullivan sold his share to the Yawkey Trust in late 1993 for $12 million. Harrington, meanwhile, established a much higher profile than anyone had expected, becoming a favored advisor of Bud Selig, now the acting commissioner of Major League Baseball.

Harrington argued that his job was to sell the Red Sox for the highest price possible in order to enrich the Trust and facilitate its charitable endeavors. He argued that until the economics of MLB stabilized and the plans for a new stadium were finalized he could not obtain that price. Harrington's attempts to build a new Fenway Park went nowhere, but on October 9, 2000, Harrington finally put the Red Sox up for sale. There was no shortage of potential buyers.

Cable television magnate Charles Dolan made a strong offer. Lawyer Miles Prentice, who had previously bid on the Royals, kept himself in the bidding until the end. Local officials and the area press pushed the bid of local businessmen Joe O'Donnell and Steve Karp. In the end, though, the Red Sox were sold to a group headed by Marlins owner John Henry and former Padres owner Tom Werner. The selection of the Henry/Werner group, which didn't even get together until just before the final bids were due, was extremely controversial in Boston. There were strong suspicions that Bud Selig had interfered with the process in order to ensure that the new owners would be supportive of the commissioner's policies.

In order for Henry to buy the Red Sox, MLB itself purchased the Montreal Expos to free Expos owner Jeffrey Loria to buy the Marlins from Henry, who obviously wouldn't be allowed to own two teams at once, unlike the first Red Sox owner, Charles Somers. The attorney general of Massachusetts launched an investigation of the sale and eventually pushed the Henry group into giving $20 million dollars extra to charity.

Whatever the truth, the sale went through on February 27, 2002. At first, suspicious of the deal and upset that O'Donnell and Karp did not win the bidding, Henry's group was greeted warily. Once Henry and Larry Lucchino announced that the team would stay in Fenway Park for the foreseeable future, the community warmed up significantly to the new owners. And the club's 2004 world championship didn't exactly hurt their reputation in town either. John Henry has reinvented the Red Sox organization by turning it into perhaps the most progressive and methodical in baseball, and no Red Sox owner has ever been more respected by the team's fans.

Red Sox Owners

Name	Partners	Term Began	Term Ended	Reason For Exit	Notes	Purchase Price	Post-Sale
Charles W. Somers		1901	August 10, 1901	Had only invested in club at request of Ban Johnson	Owner of Cleveland franchise		Somers owned the Cleveland franchise until he ran into financial difficulties in 1916 and was forced to sell the team
Henry J. Killilea	Matthew Killilea (died July 1902)	August 10, 1901	April 18, 1904	Ban Johnson wanted local ownership	Had owned Milwaukee AL franchise; Purchase not announced until January 28, 1902	$45,000 for 56 percent of team	$45,000 for 56 percent of team
John I. Taylor		April 18, 1904	September 15, 1911	Sold half of club to finance Fenway	John Irving's Father, General Charles Taylor, publisher of Boston Globe, supplied the money for the purchase	$145,000	Continued to own part of Red Sox until bought out by Lannin in 1914
James R. McAleer	Robert McCoy	September 15, 1911	December 9, 1913	Ban Johson sold it out from under McAleer	Had been Senators manager	$150,000 for 50 percent of team	
Joseph J. Lannin		December 9, 1913	December 12, 1916	Frustrated with baseball poltics	Had been minority owner of Braves	$200,000; later bought out Taylor's share and Fenway	
Harry Frazee	Hugh Ward, G.M. Anderson	December 12, 1916	August 1, 1923	War with Ban Johnson limited his options, and Boston press was uniformly hostile		$675,000	
Bob Quinn	Palmer Winslow	August 1, 1923	February 25, 1933	Disastrous term as owner	Palmer Winslow, the largest investor in Quinn's ownership group, died soon after the purchase, greatly limiting how much Quinn could invest in the ball club.	$1.5 million	
Tom Yawkey		February 25, 1933	July 9, 1976	Death		$1.2 million	
Jean Yawkey (Tom Yawkey Estate)	James Curran, Joseph LaCour.	July 10, 1976	May 22, 1978				
Jean Yawkey (JRY Corp), Haywood Sullivan, Buddy LeRoux	Rodgers Badgett was largest limited partner	May 23, 1978	1980			$20.5 million	
Jean Yawkey (Jean R. Yawkey Trust), Buddy LeRoux, Haywood Sullivan	Rodgers Badgett was largest limited partner through December 4, 1985	1981	March 30, 1987	LeRoux 's coup attempt failed when Superior Court Chief Justice James P. Lynch ruled that it was invalid on August 9, 1983, and after many lawsuits, he finally agreed to be bought out	John Harrington hired to work for Red Sox and Yawkey Trust February 1, 1981		
Jean Yawkey (Jean R. Yawkey Trust)	Haywood Sullivan (Once Yawkey bought out LeRoux's share of the general partnership, Sullivan's 1/3 was no longer meaningful)	March 31, 1987	Febuary 26, 1992	Jean Yawkey's death			
John Harrington (representing Jean R. Yawkey Trust)	Haywood Sullivan (through November 23, 1993)	Febuary 27, 1992	Febuary 26, 2002				John Harrington remains in charge of the Yawkey Trust
John W. Henry	Tom Werner, Larry Lucchino	Febuary 27, 2002			Henry was owner of Marlins when he bought Red Sox	$700 million for Red Sox and 80 percent of NESN; $20 million more was promised to charities after negotiations with attorney general	

Red Sox General Managers

There was no such thing as a "general manager" during the early days of major league baseball. Between the 1870s and 1920s owners ran most aspects of their teams' business, including decisions about player personnel. Few owners of the time were willing to leave their teams' fortunes in the hands of "baseball people," as most owners do today. Besides, the purchase of a team in those days was also a purchase of membership into baseball aristocracy. Baseball teams weren't just an investment for their owners; they were businesses to run. And so almost every club owner had the ultimate responsibility to make the final decisions on major baseball-related issues, regardless of their personal level of expertise. Some proved to be quite adept at this baseball business; others should've asked for help.

At the beginning of the 20th century, a few on-field managers gained major influence over player personnel decisions. In most cases, these managers became so important to their franchises that they were awarded partial ownership. But owners still ran most baseball clubs, especially on clubs that switched managers often. Red Sox manager Ed Barrow made Babe Ruth into an everyday player—with input and help from outfielder Harry Hooper—and led the Red Sox to the 1918 world championship. But Barrow left the franchise only a few years later as a result of Red Sox owner Harry Frazee's player sales and trades. Barrow headed in the same direction that Frazee had sent many Red Sox players, to the New York Yankees. Yankees owner Jacob Ruppert brought Barrow in to oversee the team's front office. Though his new title with the Yankees was business manager, his role with the team was what today is usually referred to as general manager. Barrow thus effectively became baseball's first general manager, and as such put together the first Yankees dynasty. Meanwhile, no one was minding the store in Boston.

Up to the time of Frazee, Red Sox owners kept control of the team's operations themselves while accepting varying levels of manager input. When Frazee was finally forced to sell out to Bob Quinn, the new ownership group was unable to achieve anything with the Red Sox. Quinn sold out to Tom Yawkey at the beginning of 1933. Yawkey immediately brought in the first Red Sox general manager, future Hall of Famer Eddie Collins. Though the Red Sox would not win a World Series under Collins, he helped turn the Red Sox from a totally moribund franchise into a frequent contender, first by using Yawkey's money to buy players from other teams and then by more wisely putting those funds to use in the farm system.

Collins' health started to decline sharply in the mid-1940s. The Hall of Fame second baseman slowly ceded his power over player personnel to Red Sox field manager Joe Cronin, who was officially appointed general manager at the end of the 1947 season. Cronin kept the job until he was elected president of the American League in January 1959, but little good can be said about his reign as Red Sox GM. Cronin is almost certainly the person most responsible for the franchise's failure to integrate at the same speed as most other major league teams. In fact, the Red Sox were the last team to put an African American in a major league uniform and it happened only after Cronin's move to the AL presidency. The personnel Cronin hired would taint the Red Sox organization with racism until the 1990s. Cronin's successor in Boston, Bucky Harris, though a Hall of Fame manager, proved so inept in personnel matters that he lasted less than two years on the job.

Officially, Dick O'Connell replaced Harris as the GM in the fall of 1960. But while O'Connell ran the front office, he did not have final say over most player personnel matters. Pinky Higgins' ascension from manager to general manager after the 1962 season changed O'Connell's job title to put him in charge of the club's business operations. Higgins was fired after three more disastrous Red Sox seasons went by. Tom Yawkey searched for the perfect GM outside the organization with no success, and he begrudgingly gave O'Connell not only the position of general manager but its power as well. It turned out to be the most important hire Yawkey ever made.

O'Connell quickly remade both the major league team and the entire organization. O'Connell changed the racial makeup of the team drastically; while African Americans players still faced obstacles from elements within the organization and the city, the barriers that had completely blocked them from careers with the Sox were removed. O'Connell's hiring of tough rookie manager Dick Williams paid quick dividends. Williams led the Red Sox to the "Impossible Dream" pennant of 1967, a season that started the Red Sox on a revival in the city that's still going strong today. Carl Yastrzemski became arguable the most popular player in Red Sox history. Iconic players such as Carlton Fisk, Dwight Evans, Jim Rice, and Fred Lynn made huge impacts.

After Tom Yawkey died, however, and a long ownership dispute ensued, O'Connell was replaced by part-owner Haywood Sullivan. (O'Connell agreed to return as part of an attempted ownership coup by part-owner Buddy LeRoux six years later, but the coup failed.) Sullivan stayed on for seven years and eventually replaced himself with Lou Gorman in 1984; Sullivan stayed on as the team's chief operating officer and remained co-owner. His stint is primarily remembered for his failure to send contract offers to Red Sox

stars Rick Burleson, Fred Lynn, and Carlton Fisk by the official deadline in November 1980 and the club's subsequent loss of all three players, as well as the questionable use of a second-round pick in the 1982 amateur draft on his son, catcher Marc Sullivan, who turned out to be a .186 hitter for the big club. Gorman lasted an up-and-down decade as GM before being promoted out of the job in 1994. Gorman is often derided for his unfathomable trade of Jeff Bagwell for Larry Andersen (Gorman would later defend the trade by arguing "Who knew?"), but he also made trades that turned out much better for the Sox such as his swindle of Lee Smith from the Cubs for Calvin Schiraldi and Al Nipper.

Red Sox chairman John Harrington appointed rising star Dan Duquette as the new general manager in 1994. Duquette had helped put together the excellent Expos team whose title would be stolen by the strike, and he emphasized a strong farm system in his early years in Boston. In the later years of his administration, however, he neglected developing players as he seemed to grow more desperate in attempts to acquire veterans from other clubs to be the last piece of the puzzle. Duquette's term was probably best known for his stormy relationship with the media and the departures of Roger Clemens and Mo Vaughn. Both Duquette and John Harrington were poor at building personal relationships both within and outside the organization. Much of the Boston media was merciless in their criticism of the two men as a result, both fairly and unfairly. One thing Duquette does deserve praise for is his finishing of the job Dick O'Connell started. Under Duquette, the final elements of the pervasive racism that had undermined the franchise for years, creating situations like the legal battles over Tommy Harper's firing in the 1980s, were put out to pasture.

After Harrington finally engineered the $700 million sale of the Red Sox and most of NESN from the Yawkey Trust to John Henry, Tom Werner, Larry Lucchino, and associated investors, the new owners wasted little time in firing Duquette. Mike Port stayed on as the temporary GM for a year. Billy Beane was hired for the position, but Beane quickly changed his mind and decided to stay near his family in Oakland. After a long, fruitless search for another experienced GM, the Red Sox went in-house and hired the youngest general manger in baseball history, Theo Epstein, 28. Epstein helped engineer Boston's 2004 world championship, their first since 1918, and after a brief resignation during the winter of 2005–06, the result of a power struggle with team president Larry Lucchino, he is secure today in his position as general manager, even as the millions of eyes in Red Sox nation watch his every move.

Here with, a list of Red Sox General Managers in chronological order and information about their terms in the postion:

Eddie Collins
Edward Trowbridge Collins Sr. (Cocky)
Vice President/General Manager
Record: 1210–1078
Started 2/25/1933
Left 9/29/1947
Reason for Leaving: Switched to advisory position
    because of declining health

Joe Cronin
Joseph Edward Cronin
Vice President/General Manager
Record: 1006–842
Started 9/29/1947
Left 1/14/1959
Reason for Leaving: Elected President of American League

Bucky Harris
Stanley Raymond Harris
Executive Vice President/General Manager
Started 1/15/1959
Left 9/27/1960
Reason for Leaving: Fired

Dick O'Connell
Richard Henry O'Connell
Executive Vice President/General Manager 216–252
Started 9/27/1960
Left 10/6/1962
Reason for Leaving: Higgins promoted to GM; O'Connell
    continued to run the business side

Mike Higgins
Michael Franklin Higgins (Pinky)
Executive Vice President/General Manager
Record: 282–350
Started 10/6/1962
Left 9/16/1965
Reason for Leaving: Fired

Dick O'Connell
Richard Henry O'Connell
General Manager
Record: 1046–90
Started 9/16/1965
Left 10/24/1977
Reason for Leaving: Fired by new ownership
TSN Executive of the Year: 1967, 1975

Haywood Sullivan
Haywood Cooper Sullivan
Executive Vice President/General Manager
Record: 499–416
Started 10/24/1977
Left 2/1/1984
Reason for Leaving: Remained in charge of operations

Lou Gorman

James Lou Gorman

Vice President/Director of Baseball Operations through
6/5/1984; Vice President/ General Manager through
10/16/1987; Senior Vice President/General Manager

Record: 837–782

Started 2/1/1984

Left 1/26/1994

Reason for Leaving: Promoted

Dan Duquette

Daniel F. Duquette

Executive Vice President/General Manager

Record: 656–574

Started 1/26/1994

Left 2/28/2002

Reason for Leaving: Fired by new ownership
1992

Mike Port

Michael D. Port

Vice President of Baseball Operations/Interim General
Manager

Record: 93–69

Started 2/28/2002

Left 11/25/2002

Reason for Leaving: Remained in front office

Theo Epstein

Theo Nathan Epstein

Senior Vice President/General Manager 288–198

Started 11/25/2002

Left 10/31/2005

Reason for Leaving: Contract expired; declined extension

Larry Lucchino

Larry Lucchino

President/CEO

Started 11/1/2005

Left 1/24/2006

Reason for Leaving: Remained in charge of operations

Theo Epstein

Theo Nathan Epstein

Executive Vice President/General Manager 86–76

Started 1/24/2006

Remains in Position

Hubcasting: The Red Sox on Radio and Television

Showing a devotion perhaps matched, but not bettered, by fans of other clubs, Red Sox Nation, from Dorchester to Orono and all points east (and west), can now follow its team by radio, television, satellite, and the Internet. But like all other "original 16" teams of the early and mid 20th century, the Red Sox began their romance with broadcasting long ago, back on the AM dial.

Ironically, the Red Sox began their time on radio on a string of stations called the Yankee Network (perish the thought). The name, of course, referred more to northeasterners' adopted persona as "Yanks" than to the hated New York Americans. Starting in 1925, the Yankee Network broadcast home games of both the Red Sox and the National League Braves, who shared Boston with the Carmines before leaving for Milwaukee in 1953.

While Gus Rooney is credited with the first Red Sox (and Braves) broadcasts in 1925, over WNAC (now known as WRKO), Fred Hoey is remembered as the club's first full-time voice. Hoey had worked as a sportswriter since 1909, at the now defunct *Journal*, *Post*, and *American*, later becoming the Braves' official scorer. He was deemed a natural for the radio waves.

Starting in 1933, WNAC broadcast all Red Sox home games. Each broadcast in this era began 15 minutes before game time, when pregame host Jerry O'Leary greeted listeners with his signature, "It's a beauuuuuuuuutiful day for the ball game!" A popular local advertising man, O'Leary held his position on the broadcasts from 1930 through the early 1960s.

By 1936 the Yankee Network's broadcasts of Red Sox games reached 10 stations. (Eventually more than 20 stations were part of the Yankee Network.) General Mills was the main sponsor, as indeed they were for most major league teams' radio broadcasts at that time. Socony Vacuums also bought ad time on the Yankee Network.

Hoey was selected for the national broadcasts of the 1933 World Series, but the opportunity turned out to be a curse. Apparently intoxicated, he had to be taken off the air during Game 1. Sponsors canned Hoey in 1936 because he was not "chatty" enough, but public outcry forced the sponsors to re-hire him. Hoey proudly went out, of his own accord, two years later. By that time WAAB had taken over the radio broadcasts, but the games went back on WNAC in 1942 and continued there until 1946. The 64-year-old Hoey died in his suburban home on November 17, 1949, by accidental asphyxiation.

When Hoey left the broadcasts, Bronx-born Frankie Frisch took over. Frisch, however, left in mid-season 1940 to manage the Pittsburgh Pirates. Jim Britt jumped into the void, having cut his teeth on football at Notre Dame and baseball in Buffalo.

Britt was an immediate hit for his erudite and accurate reporting. His signature sign-off, "Remember, if you can't play a sport, be one, will you?" was recalled fondly in Boston for many years.

During 1943–45, when Britt served in the military, his sidekick, Tom Hussey, replaced him on both Sox and Braves broadcasts. George Hartrick briefly became the new number two man. Longtime Hub radio and TV personality Leo Egan also helped out on the broadcasts in both the late 1930s and late 1940s.

When Britt returned, the broadcasting world had changed. WHDH had bought the exclusive rights to Red Sox radio in 1946, and the next season, the Red Sox and Braves began telecasting on WBZ and WNAC. Britt, Hussey, and former pitcher Bump Hadley manned the mikes on both radio and TV.

Despite his obvious talent as an announcer, Britt had his problems. Some fans thought he was pompous. Occasionally he had a drink too many, and he was pulled over more than once by the police.

In addition, he made what was, in retrospect, a poor career decision. Hoey, Britt, and company had been re-creating road games off ticker-tape since the 1930s, but only in 1951 did the Red Sox elect to cover road games live (after most clubs had already done so). Britt decided instead to stay in Boston, eschewing travel, and cover Braves games exclusively.

The Braves moved to Milwaukee in 1953, costing Britt his chance at big-league play-by-play. His decision opened the door for Curt Gowdy's ascension into Red Sox annals. Britt died in California, at age 70, in 1981, forgotten less than three decades after his days of glory.

Curt and Murph

Curt Gowdy, heretofore a football announcer, had spent 1949 and 1950 describing Yankees games. When he came to Boston in 1951, Gowdy became an immediate favorite of Red Sox fans listening over WHDH and a network that topped 50 stations. His first sidekick, Bob Delaney, a self-described salesman who apparently didn't even *like* baseball, was *not* an immediate favorite. He left following the 1953 campaign. Hussey was the third man in the booth through 1954, by which time Bob Murphy had joined Gowdy.

The late Murphy is best remembered for broadcasting the New York Mets for their first 42 seasons, but he cut his teeth at Fenway Park. While the teams he and Gowdy announced weren't great (1954–59), the mix of Gowdy's rough-hewn, Wyoming-bred, often excitable style and the more precise, somewhat scholarly, but friendly demeanor of the Oklahoma-raised Murphy proved memorable.

Beginning in 1955, the BoSox went with a two-man booth. But after Gowdy missed much of 1957 with a back problem, the team brought in a third member, Bill Crowley, who stuck around through 1960, when he became the team's public relations director.

Art Gleeson joined the booth in 1960, taking over for Murphy, who moved to the Orioles. A more significant find came aboard the following season when 37-year-old Ned Martin filled Crowley's post. Philadelphia raised and most recently the voice of Detroit's Class AAA club in Charleston, West Virginia, Martin was relaxed and knowledgeable, perfect for Boston's fanatical and well-informed fan base.

By this time the Red Sox were on WHDH's radio and television frequencies. After showing all 77 Hose home games between 1949 and 1953, the team settled into a pattern of telecasting between 51 and 56 contests a year, mixing home and road, through 1971.

Gowdy left in 1966 for NBC. He would broadcast *Game of the Week* as well as continue his football work, which had taken off with ABC and the infant American Football League. Martin slid into the number one seat on Red Sox radio, where he would remain through 1978. He also was the lead announcer on televised games through 1971 and, accepting a lesser role following two decades on the job, on over-the-air broadcasts from 1979 to 1987.

In 1965 the Red Sox booth welcomed their second ex-player, former pitcher Mel Parnell. He remained for four years. In 1966 Ken Coleman came on board, beginning a career in Boston nearly as long and memorable as that of Ned Martin.

The enthusiastic Coleman, born in suburban Quincy in 1925, was a Red Sox fan from birth. After 10 years of telecasting the Cleveland Indians, he came back home and almost immediately was thrown into the cauldron of 1967, Boston's "Impossible Dream" season, their first pennant of the TV age, and their first appearance in the World Series since 1946.

Martin, Coleman, and Parnell became, for that summer, the soundtrack of life in New England. And they helped revitalize the game in Boston, raising fans' expectations that the team would contend every year. And from 1967 on, the Red Sox have been a very good club, indeed contending almost every year...with enough pathos thrown in to make a memorable Greek tragedy.

During the late 1960s and early 1970s, Coleman and Martin were baseball in Boston, joined by Johnny Pesky. When Coleman was let go prior to 1975, veteran Jim Woods joined Martin on the radio; WSBK, the new TV rightsholder, wanted a new broadcasting team: Dick Stockton and Ken Harrelson. Stockton, a generalist who would seemingly do any sporting event, seemed little more than a rehash of the more baseball-minded Martin. An outspoken former Boston slugger, Harrelson

was initially a disaster. Nonetheless, he hung around doing television games until 1981.

From 1972 to 1974 the club's TV games were shown on WBZ, but the following season the rights went to WSBK, which held them until 1995. From 1975 on, the Sox showed an increasing number of games over the tube, reaching 100 for the first time in 1982. TV-38 also provided sound and pictures to cities and outpost throughout New England a few times per week, with games sometimes available from two stations in the same market on Sunday afternoons.

In 1983, however, cable TV made its first appearance at Fenway, as NESN (New England Sports Network) began its run with 87 games described by Kent Derdivanis and former BoSox second sacker Mike Andrews. The Red Sox co-founded the network, showing foresight in their aim to control content and advertising revenue. The team provided NESN at least half and, eventually, nearly all of the team's games. WSBK joined the cable game as well, following in the footsteps of independent stations in Chicago and Atlanta by using sports coverage to become a would-be "superstation" in the 1980s. TV-38 enabled Red Sox broadcasts to penetrate into the New York market, but the venture did not last.

For the 2003 season NESN was granted rights to show 120 Red Sox games, and from that point, over-the-air coverage slowly petered out. By 2006 the *only* way to watch the team was on cable, except for nationally televised games. The club's popularity has the Red Sox scheduled for 10 appearances on Fox's national broadcast of Saturday afternoon games in 2007.

Unclear Signal on Radio

On radio, however, things have been a bit more muddied. WHDH held the rights through 1975, when WMEX won them. The station changed its call letters to WITS in 1979, at which point Martin and sidekick Jim Woods were canned for not being enthusiastic enough about the constant commercials they were being asked to read during the games.

By 1983 Red Sox stock had fallen some, and the best radio deal available was on WPLM-FM. By 1989, however, the team attracted enough interest to score an AM deal, with WRKO. In 1995 the rights were taken over by WEEI—by this time an all-sports station—and the two stations split the team's contests.

A returning Ken Coleman worked on WITS in 1980–82 with young Jon Miller, who would go on to greater glory in Baltimore and ESPN. Former Red Sox backup catcher Bob Montgomery joined Boston's TV team in 1982, following Harrelson's move to the Chicago White Sox. Montgomery started with Martin and later teamed with Sean McDonough, forming a genuine on-air rapport.

When Miller departed following the 1982 campaign, Joe Castiglione replaced him on radio. In the last 25 years, Castiglione—like Coleman, experienced in Indians games, but born and bred in New England—has worked his way into local fans' hearts. He is as much a part of the team as David Ortiz or Curt Schilling. And in 2004 he had the distinction of being the first announcer in franchise history to proclaim that the Red Sox had just won the world championship.

Coleman retired in 1989, and Castiglione remained the number two man under Bob Starr with the move to WRKO. But from 1993 on, Castiglione has been the top dog, mostly working with former Astros and Expos radio man Jerry Trupiano. The latter, a workmanlike veteran, was let go following last season in favor of Dave O'Brien and Glenn Geffner.

Castiglione's effect hasn't been limited to his work on the radio. Don Orsillo, a Red Sox television broadcaster since 2001, took classes at Northeastern University from Castiglione. Orsillo replaced the popular Sean McDonough, who did over-the-air telecasts from 1988 through 2004 on WSBK, WABU, and WFXT. McDonough, son of the late Boston newspaper columnist Will McDonough, a powerful figure in Boston, found himself on the wrong end of the franchise's increasing focus on cable broadcasts.

McDonough and Orsillo tell a tale about the current state of broadcasting: They are nearly interchangeable in tone and style, sporting the typical television "announcer voices" so prevalent these days. Before choosing Orsillo in 2001, NESN went through several different voices (Derdivanis, Martin, Bob Kurtz), but since 1988, have had just one analyst: former Boston second baseman Jerry Remy. If Orsillo is competent and anodyne, Remy is Back Bay and down to earth. He is immensely popular in New England, an ex-jock who knows how to break down the game.

NESN has grown from a simple cable TV network into a major player. The Red Sox own 80 percent of the network (the NHL's Bruins own the rest), giving the ball club complete control over editorial content. Yet Remy, because of his authority and popularity, is critical of Red Sox misplays without reprimand.

Bilingual BoSox

For the last 20 years the Red Sox have made it possible for fans speaking Spanish to hear games on the radio. Bobby Serrano and Hector Martinez did the honors through the 1998 campaign (joined for 1993 by former Boston pitcher Mike Fornieles). The games initially aired on WRCA, then WROL and WLYN through 2002.

J.P. Villaman, known as "Papa Oso," took over the color duties for Martinez in 1999, and when Serrano left

following the 2001 campaign, Luis Tiant Jr. and Juan Baez entered the booth. Baez departed after the one year in favor of Uri Berenguer, who has become a respected play-by-play man. Tiant departed after 2004. But the big change came as a result of tragedy.

Villaman, returning from a Red Sox series at Yankee Stadium, was killed in a road accident on May 29, 2005. Bill Kulik, who has built the Spanish Beisbol Network into a growing concern both in Boston and Philadelphia, joined Berenguer in the booth before Juan Oscar Baez was hired. The games have been back on WROL since 2003.

With Fenway Park regularly sold out and road games featuring thousands of fans in all manner of Red Sox regalia, the club has a financial concern—if not a regional responsibility—to feed the insatiable appetite for baseball demanded by Red Sox Nation. The radio network stretches to 65 different stations and there indeed parts of New England where Red Sox games can be found on three or more places on the dial, even in Spanish on the 5 stations that carry the club en español. While there's no chance of the team's radio chain being renamed the Yankee Network anytime soon, the Boston club's radio and TV operations are on an equal footing with their rivals in the Bronx. Not to mention anyone else in the game.

1926
Radio: Gus Rooney (WNAC)

1927
Radio: Fred Hoey, Gerry Harrison (WNAC)

1928
Radio: Fred Hoey (WNAC)

1929
Radio: Fred Hoey (WNAC)

1930
Radio: Fred Hoey (WNAC)

1931
Radio: Fred Hoey (WNAC)

1932
Radio: Fred Hoey (WNAC)

1933
Radio: Fred Hoey (WNAC)

1934
Radio: Fred Hoey (WNAC)

1935
Radio: Fred Hoey (WNAC)

1936
Radio: Fred Hoey (WNAC)

1937
Radio: Fred Hoey (WAAB)

1938
Radio: Fred Hoey (WAAB)

1939
Radio: Frankie Frisch, Leo Egan (WAAB)

1940
Radio: Jim Britt (WAAB)

1941
Radio: Jim Britt (WAAB)

1942
Radio: Jim Britt-Tom Hussey (WAAB-WNAC)

1943
Radio: Tom Hussey, Jim Hartrick (WNAC)

1944
Radio: Tom Hussey, Jim Hartrick (WNAC)

1945
Radio: Tom Hussey, Jim Hartrick (WNAC)

1946
Radio: Jim Britt, Tom Hussey (WNAC)

1947
Radio: Jim Britt, Tom Hussey, Leo Egan (WHDH)
TV: Jim Britt, Tom Hussey (WBZ/WNAC)

1948
Radio: Jim Britt, Tom Hussey, Leo Egan (WHDH)
TV: Jim Britt, Tom Hussey, Bump Hadley (WBZ/WNAC)

1949
Radio: Jim Britt, Tom Hussey, Leo Egan (WHDH)
TV: Jim Britt, Tom Hussey, Bump Hadley (WBZ/WNAC)

1950
Radio: Jim Britt, Tom Hussey, Leo Egan (WHDH)
TV: Jim Britt, Tom Hussey, Bump Hadley (WBZ/WNAC)

1951
Radio: Curt Gowdy, Bob Delaney, Tom Hussey (WHDH)
TV: Curt Gowdy, Bob Delaney, Tom Hussey (WBZ/WNAC)

1952
Radio: Curt Gowdy, Bob Delaney, Tom Hussey (WHDH)
TV: Curt Gowdy, Bob Delaney, Tom Hussey (WBZ/WNAC)

1953
Radio: Curt Gowdy, Bob Delaney, Tom Hussey (WHDH)
TV: Curt Gowdy, Bob Delaney, Tom Hussey (WBZ/WNAC)

1954
Radio: Curt Gowdy, Bob Murphy, Tom Hussey (WHDH)
TV: Curt Gowdy, Bob Murphy (WBZ/WNAC)

1955
Radio: Curt Gowdy, Bob Murphy (WHDH)
TV: Curt Gowdy, Bob Murphy (WBZ/WNAC)

1956
Radio: Curt Gowdy, Bob Murphy (WHDH)
TV: Curt Gowdy, Bob Murphy (WBZ)

1957
Radio: Curt Gowdy, Bob Murphy (WHDH)
TV: Curt Gowdy, Bob Murphy, Don Gillis (WBZ)

1958
Radio: Curt Gowdy, Bob Murphy, Bill Crowley (WHDH)
TV: Curt Gowdy, Bob Murphy, Bill Crowley (WHDH)

1959
Radio: Curt Gowdy, Bob Murphy, Bill Crowley (WHDH)
TV: Curt Gowdy, Bob Murphy (WHDH)

1960
Radio: Curt Gowdy, Bob Murphy, Art Gleeson (WHDH)
TV: Curt Gowdy, Bob Murphy, Art Gleeson (WHDH)

1961
Radio: Curt Gowdy, Art Gleeson, Ned Martin (WHDH)
TV: Curt Gowdy, Art Gleeson, Ned Martin (WHDH)

1962
Radio: Curt Gowdy, Art Gleeson, Ned Martin (WHDH)
TV: Curt Gowdy, Art Gleeson, Ned Martin (WHDH)

1963
Radio: Curt Gowdy, Art Gleeson, Ned Martin (WHDH)
TV: Curt Gowdy, Art Gleeson, Ned Martin (WHDH)

1964
Radio: Curt Gowdy, Art Gleeson, Ned Martin (WHDH)
TV: Curt Gowdy, Art Gleeson, Ned Martin (WHDH)

1965
Radio: Curt Gowdy, Ned Martin, Mel Parnell (WHDH)
TV: Curt Gowdy, Ned Martin, Mel Parnell (WHDH)

1966
Radio: Ned Martin, Ken Coleman, Mel Parnell (WHDH)
TV: Ned Martin, Ken Coleman, Mel Parnell (WHDH)

1967
Radio: Ned Martin, Ken Coleman, Mel Parnell (WHDH)
TV: Ned Martin, Ken Coleman, Mel Parnell (WHDH)

1968
Radio: Ned Martin, Ken Coleman, Mel Parnell (WHDH)
TV: Ned Martin, Ken Coleman, Mel Parnell (WHDH)

1969
Radio: Ned Martin, Ken Coleman, Johnny Pesky (WHDH)
TV: Ned Martin, Ken Coleman, Johnny Pesky (WHDH)

1970
Radio: Ned Martin, Ken Coleman, Johnny Pesky (WHDH)
TV: Ned Martin, Ken Coleman, Johnny Pesky (WHDH)

1971
Radio: Ned Martin, Ken Coleman, Johnny Pesky (WHDH)
TV: Ned Martin, Ken Coleman, Johnny Pesky (WHDH)

1972
Radio: Ned Martin, John MaClean-Dave Martin (WHDH)
TV: Ken Coleman, Johnny Pesky (WBZ)

1973
Radio: Ned Martin, Dave Martin (WHDH)
TV: Ken Coleman, Johnny Pesky (WBZ)

1974
Radio: Ned Martin, Jim Woods (WHDH)
TV: Ken Coleman, Johnny Pesky (WBZ)

1975
Radio: Ned Martin, Jim Woods, Al Walker (WHDH)
TV: Dick Stockton, Ken Harrelson (WSBK)

1976
Radio: Ned Martin, Jim Woods (WMEX)
TV: Dick Stockton, Ken Harrelson (WSBK)

1977
Radio: Ned Martin, Jim Woods (WMEX)
TV: Dick Stockton, Ken Harrelson (WSBK)

1978
Radio: Ned Martin, Jim Woods (WMEX)
TV: Dick Stockton, Ken Harrelson (WSBK)

1979
Radio: Ken Coleman, Rico Petrocelli (WITS)
TV: Ned Martin, Ken Harrelson (WSBK)

1980
Radio: Ken Coleman, Jon Miller (WITS)
TV: Ned Martin, Ken Harrelson (WSBK)

1981
Radio: Ken Coleman, Jon Miller (WITS)
TV: Ned Martin, Ken Harrelson (WSBK)

1982
Radio: Ken Coleman, Jon Miller (WITS)
TV: Ned Martin, Bob Montgomery (WSBK)

1983
Radio: Ken Coleman, Joe Castiglione (WPLM-FM/WHDH)
TV: Ned Martin, Bob Montgomery (WSBK)

1984
Radio: Ken Coleman, Joe Castiglione (WPLM-FM)
TV: Ned Martin, Bob Montgomery (WSBK)
Cable: Kent Derdivanis, Mike Andrews (NESN)

1985
Radio: Ken Coleman, Joe Castiglione (WPLM-FM)
TV: Ned Martin, Bob Montgomery (WSBK)
Cable: Ned Martin, Bob Montgomery (NESN)

1986
Radio: Ken Coleman, Joe Castiglione (WPLM-FM)
TV: Ned Martin, Bob Montgomery (WSBK)
Cable: Ned Martin, Bob Montgomery (NESN)

1987
Radio: Ken Coleman, Joe Castiglione (WPLM-FM)
TV: Ned Martin, Bob Montgomery (WSBK)
Cable: Ned Martin, Bob Montgomery (NESN)

1988
Radio: Ken Coleman, Joe Castiglione (WPLM-FM)
TV: Sean McDonough, Bob Montgomery (WSBK)
Cable: Ned Martin, Jerry Remy (NESN)
Spanish Radio: Bobby Serrano, Hector Martinez (WRCA)

1989
Radio: Ken Coleman, Joe Castiglione (WPLM-FM)
TV: Sean McDonough, Bob Montgomery (WSBK)
Cable: Ned Martin, Jerry Remy (NESN)
Spanish Radio: Bobby Serrano, Hector Martinez (WRCA)

1990
Radio: Joe Castiglione, Bob Starr (WRKO)
TV: Sean McDonough, Bob Montgomery (WSBK)
Cable: Ned Martin, Jerry Remy (NESN)
Spanish Radio: Bobby Serrano, Hector Martinez (WRCA)

1991
Radio: Joe Castiglione, Bob Starr (WRKO)
TV: Sean McDonough, Bob Montgomery (WSBK)
Cable: Ned Martin, Jerry Remy (NESN)
Spanish Radio: Bobby Serrano, Hector Martinez (WROL)

1992
Radio: Joe Castiglione, Bob Starr (WRKO)
TV: Sean McDonough, Bob Montgomery (WSBK)

Cable: Ned Martin, Jerry Remy (NESN)
Spanish Radio: Bobby Serrano, Hector Martinez (WROL)

1993
Radio: Joe Castiglione, Jerry Trupiano (WRKO)
TV: Sean McDonough, Bob Montgomery (WSBK)
Cable: Bob Kurtz, Jerry Remy (NESN)
Spanish Radio: Bobby Serrano, Hector Martinez (WROL)

1994
Radio: Joe Castiglione, Jerry Trupiano (WRKO)
TV: Sean McDonough, Bob Montgomery (WSBK)
Cable: Bob Kurtz, Jerry Remy (NESN)
Spanish Radio: Bobby Serrano, Hector Martinez (WROL)

1995
Radio: Joe Castiglione, Jerry Trupiano (WEEI)
TV: Sean McDonough, Bob Montgomery (WSBK)
Cable: Bob Kurtz, Jerry Remy (NESN)
Spanish Radio: Bobby Serrano, Hector Martinez (WROL)

1996
Radio: Joe Castiglione, Jerry Trupiano (WEEI)
TV: Sean McDonough, Jerry Remy (WABU)
Cable: Bob Kurtz, Jerry Remy (NESN)
Spanish Radio: Bobby Serrano, Hector Martinez (WROL)

1997
Radio: Joe Castiglione, Jerry Trupiano (WEEI)
TV: Sean McDonough, Jerry Remy (WABU)

Cable: Bob Kurtz, Jerry Remy (NESN)
Spanish Radio: Bobby Serrano, Hector Martinez (WROL)

1998
Radio: Joe Castiglione, Jerry Trupiano (WEEI)
TV: Sean McDonough, Jerry Remy (WABU)
Cable: Bob Kurtz, Jerry Remy (NESN)
Spanish Radio: Bobby Serrano, Hector Martinez (WRCA)

1999
Radio: Joe Castiglione, Jerry Trupiano (WEEI)
TV: Sean McDonough, Jerry Remy (WFXT)
Cable: Bob Kurtz, Jerry Remy (NESN)
Spanish Radio: Bobby Serrano, J.P. Villaman (WRCA)

2000
Radio: Joe Castiglione, Jerry Trupiano (WEEI)
TV: Sean McDonough, Jerry Remy (WFXT)
Cable: Bob Kurtz, Jerry Remy, Bob Rodgers (NESN)
Spanish Radio: Bobby Serrano, J.P. Villaman (WRCA)

2001
Radio: Joe Castiglione, Jerry Trupiano (WEEI)
TV: Sean McDonough, Jerry Remy (WFXT)
Cable: Don Orsillo, Jerry Remy (NESN)
Spanish Radio: Bobby Serrano, J.P. Villaman (WLYN)

2002
Radio: Joe Castiglione, Jerry Trupiano (WEEI)
TV: Sean McDonough, Jerry Remy (WSBK/WBZ)

Cable: Don Orsillo, Jerry Remy (NESN)
Spanish Radio: J.P. Villaman, Luis Tiant, Juan Baez (WLYN)

2003
Radio: Joe Castiglione, Jerry Trupiano (WEEI)
TV: Sean McDonough, Jerry Remy (WABU)
Cable: Don Orsillo, Jerry Remy (NESN)
Spanish Radio: J.P. Villaman, Luis Tiant, Uri Berenguer (WROL)

2004
Radio: Joe Castiglione, Jerry Trupiano (WEEI)
TV: Sean McDonough, Jerry Remy (WSBK)
Cable: Don Orsillo, Jerry Remy (NESN)
Spanish Radio: J.P. Villaman, Luis Tiant, Uri Berenguer, Bill Kulik (WROL)

2005
Radio: Joe Castiglione, Jerry Trupiano (WEEI)
TV: Don Orsillo, Jerry Remy (WSBK)
Cable: Don Orsillo, Jerry Remy (NESN)
Spanish Radio: J.P. Villaman-Juan Oscar Baez, Uri Berenguer, Bill Kulik (WROL)

2006
Radio: Joe Castiglione, Jerry Trupiano (WEEI)
Cable: Don Orsillo, Jerry Remy (NESN)
Spanish Radio: Uri Berenguer, Juan Oscar Baez (WROL)

2007
Radio: Joe Castiglione, Dave O'Brien, Glenn Geffner (WRKO/WEEI)
Cable: Don Orsillo, Jerry Remy (NESN)
Spanish Radio: Uri Berenguer, Juan Oscar Baez (WROL)

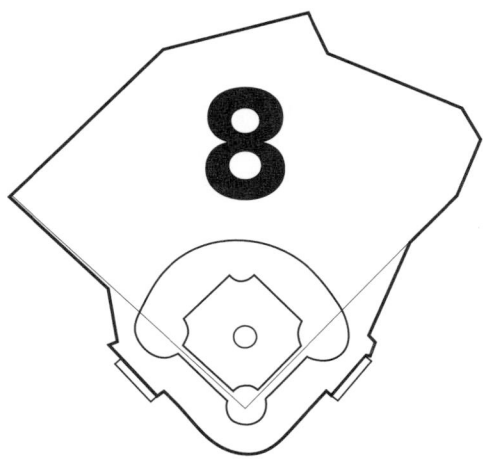

THE HISTORICAL RECORD

The emergence of the American League is one of the most significant events in the history of American sport. Ban Johnson's bold venture succeeded in challenging the established National Leagues after three other leagues had failed in the 19th century. The AL was the Hatfield to the NL's McCoy in the first two-plus seasons of their shared existence; they formed a cautious alliance when it became apparent that their continued war would do nothing but harm both their enterprises. The World Series as we know it today was the offspring of this union. The leagues jointly tried everything possible to squeeze out the Federal League in 1914–15. The American League has survived two world wars, the Black Sox Scandal, the shifting of established franchises to new markets, its first expansion in its 60th year, "the Year of the Pitcher," the designated hitter, crippling strikes, the loss of importance of league identity, stagnant television ratings, and the ongoing cloud of steroids. The last 105 years have seen plenty, but the game remains strong.

The American League has seen dynasties in Boston, Philadelphia, Oakland, and New York (no matter your definition or counting procedure, the Yankees have had multiple eras of dominance). Despite talk of market disparity, two-time world champions over the past 20 years in the AL include "small-market" Toronto and Minnesota. Long-thirsty AL franchises in Chicago and Anaheim (now the Los Angeles Angels of Anaheim, their fourth different city designation since their birth in 1961) have raised World Series trophies in the past five years. Yet no drought ended more spectacularly than the one finally vanquished by the Red Sox in 2004.

The Historical Record tracks everything that has happened in the AL during the regular season from its inception through 2006. At the top of each Historical Record page are the final standings for the league for a given season, along with team batting, baserunning, pitching, and fielding statistics. The wild card team for every season since 1995 is listed in **bold**.

Below the standings and team statistics are individual league-leaders in 35 categories of batting, pitching, and fielding stats. Each category lists the top five players (unless multiple tied players would lengthen the list past the top five). Among the batting and pitching leaders, the minimums for qualifying as a league leader for any average or rate statistics are normally the same as qualifying for the batting or ERA titles. However, the minimum for qualifying as a league leader in Base Runners per 9 Innings was deliberately set low enough to include relief pitchers (60 innings pitched). This was in contrast to other pitching leaders like Opponents' Average and Opponents OBP, for which relief pitchers would typically not qualify. The relief pitching categories (starting with Games and ending with Relief Ranking) have been grouped together for ease of comparison.

The lists below show all abbreviations used in the Historical Record section. Those that have not been defined elsewhere are explained here. Further information about the statistics, formulas, and computations shown in the Historical Record section can be found in the Glossary at the end of the encyclopedia. When reading the explanations below, keep in mind that the Red Sox played a handful of home games at spacious Braves Field in 1916 and 1939–42.

W: Wins

L: Losses

T: Ties. Ties occur only if the game has completed five or more full innings, the game was tied after the last full inning, and no further runs have scored unless the home team goes ahead in the bottom of the current inning.

PCT: Winning Percentage. Calculated by dividing the number of wins by the number of wins and losses.

GB: Games Behind. The number of games each club finished behind first place.

R: Runs

OR: Opponent Runs

HR: Home Runs

AVG: Batting Average. Hits divided by at-bats.

OBP: On-Base Percentage. Hits plus walks plus hit by pitch divided by at-bats plus walks plus hit by pitch plus sacrifice flies.

SLG: Slugging Average. Total bases divided by at-bats.

OPS: On-Base Plus Slugging Average. This figure is multiplied by 1000, so .400 plus .500 is 900.

AOPS: On-Base Plus Slugging Average. On-base percentage and slugging average are added and normalized for the context of the offensive level of the league and the team's home park and converted to a scale in which 100 is average. It is expressed here as the number above or below average, so 116 is written as +16 and 84 is written as -16.

PF: Hitters' Park Factor. This measures how the team's home park affects offense; it is used to adjust the team's raw offensive performance to account for the team's home park. This also includes a correction for not having to face your own pitchers; it is used in AOPS and ABR.

SB: Stolen Bases

CG. Complete Games

HR: Home Runs Allowed

BB. Bases on Balls Allowed

SO: Strikeouts

BR/9: Baserunners Allowed Per 9 Innings

ERA: Earned Run Average. Calculated by dividing earned runs by innings pitched and multiplying by 9.

AERA: Adjusted Earned Run Average. Calculated by normalizing ERA for the context of offensive level of the league and the team's home park and converting to a scale in which 100 is average. It is expressed here as the number above or below average, so 110 is written as +10 and 90 is written as -10.

OAV: Opponents' Batting Average. Hits allowed divided by opponent at-bats.

OOB: Opponents' On-Base Percentage. Hits plus walks plus hit by pitch divided by at-bats plus walks plus hit by pitch plus sacrifice flies.

FW: Fielding Wins. Number of wins the team achieved through its fielding compared to the average team in context of the league offensive level and the team's home park.

PW: Pitching Wins. Number of wins the team achieved through its pitching compared to the average team in context of the league offensive level and the team's home park.

BW: Batting Wins. Number of wins the team achieved through its hitting compared to the average team in context of the league offensive level and the team's home park.

BSW: Basestealing Wins. Number of wins the team achieved through its basestealing compared to the average team in context of the league offensive level and the team's home park.

DIF: Differential. Measures the difference between how many games the team was projected to win based on its hitting, pitching, fielding, and baserunning, and how many games the team actually won. It is measured the same way as teams measure how many games they are behind in the standings.

LEADERBOARDS

Not shown among team statistics.

Batter-Fielder Wins. The sum of a player's batting wins, basestealing wins, and fielding wins, this figure indicates how many games the player won or lost for his team compared to the average player.

Adjusted Batter Runs. Batter runs are adjusted to the home park and the league average offensive level but ignoring the offensive contributions of pitchers.

Hits

Doubles

Triples

Total Bases. Calculated by adding singles plus 2x doubles plus 3x triples plus 4x home runs.

Runs Batted In

Stolen Bases

Basestealing Runs. The number of runs added by a team's basestealing attempts.

Fielding Runs Infield and Outfield. Measures how the difference between how many games the players saves or loses for his team in the field compared to an average fielder. The formula takes into account putouts, assists, double plays, and errors. Defensive innings are based on play-by-play from 1969 forward; they are estimated for previous years.

Wins

Fewest Bases on Balls Per Game

Games

Saves. The save became an official statistic in 1969. Saves are calculated based on the official definition of saves at the time. Saves before 1969 are based on how many times a relief pitcher finished a victory for his team without getting a win.

Base Runners Per 9 Innings

Adjusted Relief Runs. How many runs the pitcher allowed to score compared to the average pitcher in the context of the league offensive level and the pitcher's home park(s). Relief pitchers are those who average less than 3 innings per appearance.

Relief Ranking. Calculated by putting Adjusted Relief Runs into context by the importance of the relief innings pitched; takes into account the number of saves and decisions assigned to the pitcher.

Innings Pitched

Adjusted Starter Runs. How many runs the pitcher allowed to score compared to the average pitcher in the context of the league offensive level and the pitcher's home park(s). Starting pitchers are those who average at least 3 innings per appearance.

Pitcher Wins. Individual pitcher wins are calculated by adding up pitching, batting, fielding, and basestealing wins; this is different from team pitching wins.

1901 AMERICAN LEAGUE

TEAM	W	L	T	PCT	GB	R	OR	HR	AVG	OBP	SLG	OPS	AOPS	PF	SB	CG	HR	BB	SO	BR/9	ERA	AERA	OAV	OOB	FW	PW	BW	BSW	DIF
Chi	83	53	1	.610		**819**	631	32	.276	.350	.370	720	+8	97	**280**	110	27	312	394	11.9	**2.98**	+17	.263	.315	.9	**6.4**	**5.8**		1.9
Bos	79	57	2	.581	4	759	**608**	37	.278	.330	.381	711	+4	98	157	123	33	294	**396**	11.2	3.04	+16	**.251**	**.301**	1.6	6.1	1.8		1.5
Det	74	61	1	.548	8.5	741	694	29	.279	.340	.370	710	-2	105	204	118	22	313	350	12.8	3.30	+16	.280	.330	-3.3	6.1	-1.4		5.1
Phi	74	62	1	.544	9	805	760	35	.289	.337	.395	732	+3	104	173	**124**	**20**	374	350	13.3	4.00	-6	.280	.339	1.4	-2.8	1.1		6.3
Bal	68	65	2	.511	13.5	760	750	24	**.294**	**.353**	**.397**	**750**	**+8**	104	207	115	21	344	271	13.3	3.73	+4	.282	.338	-2.9	1.4	4.2		-1.2
Was	61	72	5	.459	20.5	682	771	33	.269	.326	.364	690	-3	99	127	118	51	**284**	308	13.3	4.09	-11	.291	.339	**2.4**	-5.2	-1.2		-1.5
Cle	54	82	2	.397	29	666	831	12	.271	.313	.348	661	-8	96	125	122	22	464	334	14.5	4.12	-14	.286	.358	2.1	-7.0	-5.1		-4.0
Mil	48	89	2	.350	35.5	641	828	26	.261	.314	.345	659	-9	95	176	107	32	395	376	13.6	4.06	-11	.283	.344	-1.8	-5.9	-4.2		-8.6
Total	549					5873		228	.277	.333	.371	704			1449	937		2780	2736	13.0	3.66		.277	.333					

Batter-Fielder Wins		Batting Average		On-Base Percentage		Slugging Average		On-Base Plus Slugging		Adjusted OPS		Adjusted Batter Runs	
Lajoie-Phi	**8.1**	Lajoie-Phi	.426	Lajoie-Phi	.463	Lajoie-Phi	.643	Lajoie-Phi	1106	Lajoie-Phi	196	Lajoie-Phi	69.2
Collins-Bos	**4.2**	Freeman-Bos	.339	Freeman-Bos	.400	Freeman-Bos	.520	Freeman-Bos	920	Freeman-Bos	157	Freeman-Bos	37.0
Freeman-Bos	**2.7**	Collins-Bos	.332	Stahl-Bos	.377	Collins-Bos	.495	Collins-Bos	869	Collins-Bos	142	Collins-Bos	31.2
Parent-Bos	**1.4**	Parent-Bos	.306	Collins-Bos	.375	Stahl-Bos	.439	Stahl-Bos	816	Stahl-Bos	128	Stahl-Bos	20.1

Runs		Hits		Doubles		Triples		Home Runs		Total Bases		Runs Batted In	
Lajoie-Phi	145	Lajoie-Phi	232	Lajoie-Phi	48	Williams-Bal	21	Lajoie-Phi	14	Lajoie-Phi	350	Lajoie-Phi	125
Collins-Bos	108	Collins-Bos	187	Collins-Bos	42	Keister-Bal	21	Freeman-Bos	12	Collins-Bos	279	Freeman-Bos	114
Stahl-Bos	105	Freeman-Bos	166	Parent-Bos	23	Stahl-Bos	16	Stahl-Bos	6	Freeman-Bos	255	Collins-Bos	94
Dowd-Bos	104	Dowd-Bos	159	Freeman-Bos	23	Collins-Bos	16	Collins-Bos	6	Stahl-Bos	226	Stahl-Bos	72

Stolen Bases		Base Stealing Runs		Fielding Runs-Infield		Fielding Runs-Outfield		Wins		Winning Pct.		Complete Games	
Isbell-Chi	52			Clingman-Was	22.1	Seymour-Bal	13.9	Young-Bos	33	Griffith-Chi	.774	McGinnity-Bal	39
Dowd-Bos	33			Collins-Bos	12.8	Dowd-Bos	1.3	Winter-Bos	16	Young-Bos	.767	Young-Bos	38
Stahl-Bos	29			Ferris-Bos	7.4			Lewis-Bos	16	Winter-Bos	.571	Lewis-Bos	31
Collins-Bos	19			Dowd-Bos	.1			Mitchell-Bos	6	Lewis-Bos	.485	Winter-Bos	26

Strikeouts		Fewest BB/Game		Games		Saves		Base Runners/9		Adjusted Relief Runs		Relief Ranking	
Young-Bos	158	Young-Bos	.90	McGinnity-Bal	48	Hoffer-Cle	3	Young-Bos	8.92				
Lewis-Bos	103	Winter-Bos	2.46	Young-Bos	43	Lewis-Bos	1	Lewis-Bos	11.32				
Winter-Bos	63	Lewis-Bos	2.59	Lewis-Bos	39			Winter-Bos	11.35				
Mitchell-Bos	34			Winter-Bos	28			Cuppy-Bos	12.25				

Innings Pitched		Opponents' Avg.		Opponents' OBP		Earned Run Average		Adjusted ERA		Adjusted Starter Runs		Pitcher Wins	
McGinnity-Bal	382.0	Young-Bos	.232	Young-Bos	.256	Young-Bos	1.62	Young-Bos	217	Young-Bos	77.0	Young-Bos	7.9
Young-Bos	371.1	Lewis-Bos	.247	Lewis-Bos	.304	Winter-Bos	2.80	Winter-Bos	126	Winter-Bos	14.5	Winter-Bos	1.0
Lewis-Bos	316.1	Winter-Bos	.252	Winter-Bos	.304	Lewis-Bos	3.53	Lewis-Bos	100	Lewis-Bos	4.0	Prentiss-Bos	.2
Winter-Bos	241.0									Prentiss-Bos	1.6		

1902 AMERICAN LEAGUE

TEAM	W	L	T	PCT	GB	R	OR	HR	AVG	OBP	SLG	OPS	AOPS	PF	SB	CG	HR	BB	SO	BR/9	ERA	AERA	OAV	OOB	FW	PW	BW	BSW	DIF
Phi	83	53	1	.610		**775**	636	38	.287	.340	.389	729	+4	104	201	114	33	368	**455**	12.7	3.29	+11	.273	.334	1.4	4.6	2.2		6.8
StL	78	58	4	.574	5	619	607	29	.265	.323	.353	676	-6	99	137	120	36	343	348	12.0	3.34	+6	.266	.321	1.5	2.5	-2.7		8.6
Bos	77	60	1	.562	6.5	664	**600**	42	.278	.322	.383	705	-2	103	132	123	27	431	431	**11.5**	**3.02**	+18	**.258**	**.311**	7.1		-2.1		1.5
Chi	74	60	4	.552	8	675	602	14	.268	.332	.335	667	-5	96	**265**	116	30	331	346	12.1	3.41	-1	.269	.323	**2.3**	-.5	-1.3		6.5
Cle	69	67	1	.507	14	686	667	33	**.289**	.336	.389	725	**+11**	96	140	116	26	411	361	12.4	3.28	+5	.260	.327	.3	2.0	**6.9**		-8.3
Was	61	75	2	.449	22	707	790	**47**	.283	.335	**.395**	730	+7	101	121	**130**	56	**312**	300	13.2	4.36	-15	.291	.341	-1.3	-8.1	4.4		-2.0
Det	52	83	2	.385	30.5	566	657	22	.251	.312	.320	632	-21	102	130	116	**20**	370	245	12.7	3.56	+2	.274	.333	-2.5	.9	-11.6		-2.4
Bal	50	88	3	.362	34	715	848	33	.277	**.342**	.385	727	+3	104	189	119	30	354	258	14.3	4.33	-13	.309	.360	-3.5	-6.9	1.8		-10.4
Total	553					5407		258	.275	.331	.369	700			1315	954		2815	2744	12.6	3.57		.275	.331					

Batter-Fielder Wins		Batting Average		On-Base Percentage		Slugging Average		On-Base Plus Slugging		Adjusted OPS		Adjusted Batter Runs	
Lajoie-Phi-Cle	**5.6**	Delahanty-Was	.376	Delahanty-Was	.453	Delahanty-Was	.590	Delahanty-Was	1043	Delahanty-Was	186	Delahanty-Was	57.7
Collins-Bos	**2.1**	Dougherty-Bos	.342	Dougherty-Bos	.407	Freeman-Bos	.502	Freeman-Bos	854	Freeman-Bos	131	Freeman-Bos	20.9
Criger-Bos	**1.7**	Stahl-Bos	.323	Stahl-Bos	.375	Collins-Bos	.459	Collins-Bos	820	Collins-Bos	123	Dougherty-Bos	13.9
Freeman-Bos	**1.2**	Collins-Bos	.322	Collins-Bos	.360	Stahl-Bos	.421	Dougherty-Bos	805	Dougherty-Bos	120	2 players tied	11.5

Runs		Hits		Doubles		Triples		Home Runs		Total Bases		Runs Batted In	
Hartsel-Phi	109	Hickman-Bos-Cle	193	Delahanty-Was	43	Williams-Bal	21	Seybold-Phi	16	Hickman-Bos-Cle	288	Freeman-Bos	121
Fultz-Phi	109	Freeman-Bos	174	Davis-Phi	43	Freeman-Bos	19	Freeman-Bos	11	Freeman-Bos	283	Ferris-Bos	63
Stahl-Bos	92	Stahl-Bos	164	Freeman-Bos	38	Ferris-Bos	14	Ferris-Bos	8	Stahl-Bos	214	Parent-Bos	62
Parent-Bos	91	Parent-Bos	156	Parent-Bos	31	Stahl-Bos	11	2 players tied	6	Parent-Bos	212	Collins-Bos	61

Stolen Bases		Base Stealing Runs		Fielding Runs-Infield		Fielding Runs-Outfield		Wins		Winning Pct.		Complete Games	
Hartsel-Phi	47			Ferris-Bos	23.8	Selbach-Bal	10.4	Young-Bos	32	Bernhard-Phi-Cle	.783	Young-Bos	41
Stahl-Bos	24			Collins-Bos	8.3			Dinneen-Bos	21	Young-Bos	.744	Dinneen-Bos	39
Dougherty-Bos	20			Parent-Bos	.0			Winter-Bos	11	Dinneen-Bos	.500	Winter-Bos	18
Collins-Bos	18							Sparks-Bos	7			Sparks-Bos	15

Strikeouts		Fewest BB/Game		Games		Saves		Base Runners/9		Adjusted Relief Runs		Relief Ranking	
Waddell-Phi	210	Orth-Was	1.11	Young-Bos	45	Powell-StL	2	Bernhard-Phi-Cle	8.68				
Young-Bos	160	Young-Bos	1.24	Dinneen-Bos	42	Altrock-Bos	1	Young-Bos	9.73				
Dinneen-Bos	136	Dinneen-Bos	2.40	Winter-Bos	20			Dinneen-Bos	11.03				
Winter-Bos	51	Sparks-Bos	2.52	Sparks-Bos	17			Winter-Bos	11.17				

Innings Pitched		Opponents' Avg.		Opponents' OBP		Earned Run Average		Adjusted ERA		Adjusted Starter Runs		Pitcher Wins	
Young-Bos	384.2	Bernhard-Phi-Cle	.216	Bernhard-Phi-Cle	.254	Siever-Det	1.91	Siever-Det	191	Young-Bos	59.4	Young-Bos	6.0
Dinneen-Bos	371.1	Winter-Bos	.238	Young-Bos	.276	Young-Bos	2.15	Young-Bos	166	Dinneen-Bos	33.1	Dinneen-Bos	2.3
Winter-Bos	168.1	Young-Bos	.243	Dinneen-Bos	.302	Dinneen-Bos	2.93	Dinneen-Bos	122	Winter-Bos	12.1	Winter-Bos	1.0
Sparks-Bos	142.2	Dinneen-Bos	.249	Winter-Bos	.305	Winter-Bos	2.99	Winter-Bos	119	Altrock-Bos	.6		

1903 AMERICAN LEAGUE

TEAM	W	L	T	PCT	GB	R	OR	HR	AVG	OBP	SLG	OPS	AOPS	PF	SB	CG	HR	BB	SO	BR/9	ERA	AERA	OAV	OOB	FW	PW	BW	BSW	DIF
Bos	91	47	3	.659		708	504	48	.272	.313	.392	705	+11	105	141	123	23	269	579	10.4	2.57	+18	.242	.288	2.3	6.5	5.7		7.5
Phi	75	60	2	.556	14.5	597	519	32	.264	.309	.363	672	+2	105	157	112	20	271	728	11.3	2.98	+3	.246	.305	3.2	1.0	1.3		1.9
Cle	77	63	0	.550	15	639	579	31	.265	.308	.373	681	+12	98	175	125	16	271	521	10.6	2.73	+5	.247	.293	-3.2	1.9	6.5		1.8
NY	72	62	2	.537	17	579	573	18	.249	.309	.330	639	-8	106	160	111	19	245	463	10.9	3.08	+1	.255	.299	.0	.5	-3.7		8.2
Det	65	71	1	.478	25	567	539	12	.268	.318	.351	669	+10	97	128	123	19	336	554	11.5	2.75	+6	.256	.310	-.9	2.2	5.7		-10.0
StL	65	74	0	.468	26.5	500	525	12	.244	.290	.317	607	-10	97	101	124	26	237	511	11.0	2.77	+5	.260	.300	.2	2.0	-5.6		-1.0
Chi	60	77	1	.438	30.5	516	613	14	.247	.301	.314	615	-6	96	180	114	23	287	391	11.5	3.02	-7	.260	.309	-1.8	-3.1	-2.2		-1.4
Was	43	94	3	.314	47.5	437	691	17	.231	.277	.311	588	-20	102	131	122	38	306	452	12.4	3.82	-18	.277	.325	.8	-9.2	-11.3		-5.7
Total	554					4543		184	.255	.303	.344	648			1173	954		2266	4199	11.2	2.96		.255	.303					

Batter-Fielder Wins		Batting Average		On-Base Percentage		Slugging Average		On-Base Plus Slugging		Adjusted OPS		Adjusted Batter Runs	
Lajoie-Cle	**8.1**	Lajoie-Cle	.344	Barrett-Det	.407	Lajoie-Cle	.518	Lajoie-Cle	896	Lajoie-Cle	170	Lajoie-Cle	40.6
Collins-Bos	**2.9**	Dougherty-Bos	.331	Dougherty-Bos	.372	Freeman-Bos	.496	Freeman-Bos	823	Freeman-Bos	137	Freeman-Bos	23.4
Parent-Bos	**2.6**	Parent-Bos	.304	Collins-Bos	.329	Collins-Bos	.448	Dougherty-Bos	796	Dougherty-Bos	131	Dougherty-Bos	21.8
2 players tied	**1.8**	Collins-Bos	.296	Freeman-Bos	.328	Parent-Bos	.441	Collins-Bos	777	Collins-Bos	125	Collins-Bos	14.5

Runs		Hits		Doubles		Triples		Home Runs		Total Bases		Runs Batted In	
Dougherty-Bos	107	Dougherty-Bos	195	Seybold-Phi	45	Crawford-Det	25	Freeman-Bos	13	Freeman-Bos	281	Freeman-Bos	104
Collins-Bos	88	Parent-Bos	170	Freeman-Bos	39	Freeman-Bos	20	Ferris-Bos	9	Dougherty-Bos	250	Parent-Bos	80
Parent-Bos	83	Freeman-Bos	163	Collins-Bos	33	Parent-Bos	17	Collins-Bos	5	Parent-Bos	247	Collins-Bos	72
Freeman-Bos	74	Collins-Bos	160	Parent-Bos	31	Collins-Bos	17	2 players tied	4	Collins-Bos	242	Ferris-Bos	66

Stolen Bases		Base Stealing Runs		Fielding Runs-Infield		Fielding Runs-Outfield		Wins		Winning Pct.		Complete Games	
Bay-Cle	45			Lajoie-Cle	39.1	Lush-Det	12.8	Young-Bos	28	Young-Bos	.757	3 players tied	34
Dougherty-Bos	35			Ferris-Bos	14.3	Dougherty-Bos	3.6	Dinneen-Bos	21	Hughes-Bos	.741	Young-Bos	34
Parent-Bos	24			Collins-Bos	10.3			Hughes-Bos	20	Dinneen-Bos	.618	Dinneen-Bos	32
Collins-Bos	23			Parent-Bos	7.6			Gibson-Bos	13			Hughes-Bos	25

Strikeouts		Fewest BB/Game		Games		Saves		Base Runners/9		Adjusted Relief Runs		Relief Ranking	
Waddell-Phi	302	Young-Bos	.97	Plank-Phi	43	5 players tied	2	Joss-Cle	8.82				
Young-Bos	176	Winter-Bos	1.87	Young-Bos	40	Young-Bos	2	Young-Bos	8.96				
Dinneen-Bos	148	Dinneen-Bos	1.99	Dinneen-Bos	37	Dinneen-Bos	2	Dinneen-Bos	9.78				
Hughes-Bos	112	Hughes-Bos	2.21	Hughes-Bos	33			Hughes-Bos	11.07				

Innings Pitched		Opponents' Avg.		Opponents' OBP		Earned Run Average		Adjusted ERA		Adjusted Starter Runs		Pitcher Wins	
Young-Bos	341.2	Moore-Cle	.217	Joss-Cle	.256	Moore-Cle	1.74	Moore-Cle	164	Young-Bos	34.0	Young-Bos	4.8
Dinneen-Bos	299.0	Dinneen-Bos	.230	Young-Bos	.259	Young-Bos	2.08	Young-Bos	146	Dinneen-Bos	27.8	Dinneen-Bos	2.9
Hughes-Bos	244.2	Young-Bos	.232	Dinneen-Bos	.276	Dinneen-Bos	2.26	Dinneen-Bos	134	Hughes-Bos	13.4	Hughes-Bos	1.9
Gibson-Bos	183.1	Gibson-Bos	.241	Hughes-Bos	.302	Hughes-Bos	2.57	Hughes-Bos	118				

1904 AMERICAN LEAGUE

TEAM	W	L	T	PCT	GB	R	OR	HR	AVG	OBP	SLG	OPS	AOPS	PF	SB	CG	HR	BB	SO	BR/9	ERA	AERA	OAV	OOB	FW	PW	BW	BSW	DIF
Bos	95	59	3	.617		608	466	26	.247	.301	.340	641	+2	106	101	148	31	233	612	9.4	2.12	+26	.233	.270	1.6	9.4	1.0		6.0
NY	92	59	4	.609	1.5	598	526	27	.259	.308	.347	655	+7	105	163	123	29	311	684	10.0	2.57	+6	.232	.282	-.8	2.3	4.6		10.4
Chi	89	65	2	.578	6	600	482	14	.242	.300	.316	616	+4	96	216	134	13	303	550	9.8	2.30	+7	.229	.279	1.7	2.7	3.2		4.4
Cle	86	65	3	.570	7.5	647	482	27	.260	.308	.354	662	+16	99	178	141	10	285	627	10.6	2.22	+14	.249	.294	.4	5.4	9.6		-4.9
Phi	81	70	4	.536	12.5	557	482	31	.249	.298	.336	634	+1	105	137	136	13	366	887	10.4	2.35	+14	.230	.291	.8	5.4	.1		-.8
StL	65	87	4	.428	29	481	604	10	.239	.291	.294	585	-4	94	150	135	25	333	577	11.0	2.83	-12	.251	.303	-.2	-6.5	-2.1		-2.2
Det	62	90	10	.408	32	505	627	11	.231	.282	.292	574	-10	97	112	143	16	433	556	11.6	2.77	-8	.250	.314	.0	-4.0	-6.8		-3.2
Was	38	113	6	.252	55.5	437	743	10	.227	.275	.288	563	-16	98	150	137	19	347	533	12.5	3.62	-27	.279	.330	-3.1	-15.9	-9.8		-8.6
Total	626					4433		156	.244	.295	.321	616			1207	097		2611	5026	10.7	2.60		.244	.295					

Batter-Fielder Wins		Batting Average		On-Base Percentage		Slugging Average		On-Base Plus Slugging		Adjusted OPS		Adjusted Batter Runs	
Lajoie-Cle	**7.4**	Lajoie-Cle	.376	Lajoie-Cle	.413	Lajoie-Cle	.546	Lajoie-Cle	959	Lajoie-Cle	204	Lajoie-Cle	64.3
Criger-Bos	**2.3**	Parent-Bos	.291	Stahl-Bos	.366	Stahl-Bos	.416	Stahl-Bos	782	Stahl-Bos	139	Stahl-Bos	27.8
Collins-Bos	**1.7**	Stahl-Bos	.290	Parent-Bos	.330	Freeman-Bos	.412	Freeman-Bos	741	Freeman-Bos	127	Freeman-Bos	16.4
Parent-Bos	**.9**	Freeman-Bos	.280	Freeman-Bos	.329	Parent-Bos	.389	Parent-Bos	719	Parent-Bos	120	Parent-Bos	12.4

Runs		Hits		Doubles		Triples		Home Runs		Total Bases		Runs Batted In	
Dougherty-Bos-NY	113	Lajoie-Cle	208	Lajoie-Cle	49	3 players tied	19	Davis-Phi	10	Lajoie-Cle	302	Lajoie-Cle	102
Parent-Bos	85	Parent-Bos	172	Collins-Bos	33	Stahl-Bos	19	Freeman-Bos	7	Freeman-Bos	246	Freeman-Bos	84
Collins-Bos	85	Collins-Bos	171	Stahl-Bos	27	Freeman-Bos	19	Parent-Bos	6	Stahl-Bos	244	Parent-Bos	77
Stahl-Bos	83	Stahl-Bos	170	Ferris-Bos	23	Collins-Bos	13	3 players tied	3	Collins-Bos	239	2 players tied	67

Stolen Bases		Base Stealing Runs		Fielding Runs-Infield		Fielding Runs-Outfield		Wins		Winning Pct.		Complete Games	
Flick-Cle	38			Tannehill-Chi	27.3	McIntyre-Det	12.4	Chesbro-NY	41	Chesbro-NY	.774	Chesbro-NY	48
Bay-Cle	38			Collins-Bos	5.2			Young-Bos	26	Tannehill-Bos	.656	Young-Bos	40
Parent-Bos	20							Dinneen-Bos	23	Dinneen-Bos	.622	Dinneen-Bos	37
Collins-Bos	19							Tannehill-Bos	21	Young-Bos	.619	Tannehill-Bos	30

Strikeouts		Fewest BB/Game		Games		Saves		Base Runners/9		Adjusted Relief Runs		Relief Ranking	
Waddell-Phi	349	Young-Bos	.69	Chesbro-NY	55	Patten-Was	3	Young-Bos	8.53				
Young-Bos	200	Tannehill-Bos	1.05	Young-Bos	43	Young-Bos	1	Dinneen-Bos	9.33				
Dinneen-Bos	153	Dinneen-Bos	1.69	Dinneen-Bos	37			Tannehill-Bos	9.65				
Tannehill-Bos	116	Gibson-Bos	2.67	2 players tied	33			Gibson-Bos	9.92				

Innings Pitched		Opponents' Avg.		Opponents' OBP		Earned Run Average		Adjusted ERA		Adjusted Starter Runs		Pitcher Wins	
Chesbro-NY	454.2	Chesbro-NY	.208	Young-Bos	.251	Joss-Cle	1.59	Waddell-Phi	165	Chesbro-NY	41.2	Chesbro-NY	6.1
Young-Bos	380.0	Gibson-Bos	.219	Dinneen-Bos	.268	Young-Bos	1.97	Young-Bos	136	Young-Bos	33.4	Young-Bos	3.8
Dinneen-Bos	335.2	Dinneen-Bos	.230	Tannehill-Bos	.275	Tannehill-Bos	2.04	Tannehill-Bos	131	Tannehill-Bos	19.4	Tannehill-Bos	2.8
Tannehill-Bos	281.2	Young-Bos	.233	Gibson-Bos	.281	Dinneen-Bos	2.20	Dinneen-Bos	122	Dinneen-Bos	17.3	Dinneen-Bos	1.7

1905 AMERICAN LEAGUE

TEAM	W	L	T	PCT	GB	R	OR	HR	AVG	OBP	SLG	OPS	AOPS	PF	SB	CG	HR	BB	SO	BR/9	ERA	AERA	OAV	OOB	FW	PW	BW	BSW	DIF
Phi	92	56	4	.622		623	488	24	.255	.310	.338	648	+9	102	190	117	21	409	895	10.5	2.19	+21	.227	.294	.3	7.5	5.9		4.3
Chi	92	60	6	.605	2	612	451	11	.237	.305	.304	609	+3	96	194	131	11	329	613	9.6	1.99	+24	.226	.277	4.1	8.6	3.1		.2
Det	79	74	1	.516	15.5	512	604	13	.243	.302	.311	613	-1	101	129	124	11	474	578	11.7	2.83	-4	.246	.318	.4	-2.0	-.3		4.4
Bos	78	74	1	.513	16	579	565	29	.234	.305	.311	616	+0	101	131	124	33	292	652	10.2	2.84	-5	.238	.286	-1.6	-2.2	.8		5.1
Cle	76	78	1	.494	19	564	587	18	.255	.301	.334	635	+6	101	188	140	23	334	555	10.9	2.85	-8	.245	.299	2.8	-3.5	2.6		-2.9
NY	71	78	3	.477	21.5	586	621	23	.248	.307	.319	626	-7	111	200	88	26	396	642	11.1	2.93	+0	.246	.307	-1.5	-.2	-3.8		2.1
Was	64	87	3	.424	29.5	559	623	22	.224	.274	.302	576	-8	96	169	118	12	385	539	11.2	2.87	-8	.247	.308	-3.0	-4.0	-5.7		1.1
StL	54	99	3	.353	40.5	512	608	16	.232	.288	.289	577	-7	95	144	134	19	389	633	11.0	2.74	-7	.243	.304	-1.3	-3.7	-4.1		-13.4
Total	617					4547		156	.241	.299	.314	613			1345	976		3008	5107	10.8	2.65		.241	.299					

Batter-Fielder Wins		Batting Average		On-Base Percentage		Slugging Average		On-Base Plus Slugging		Adjusted OPS		Adjusted Batter Runs	
Davis-Chi	4.4	Flick-Cle	.308	Hartsel-Phi	.409	Flick-Cle	.462	Flick-Cle	845	Flick-Cle	165	Flick-Cle	37.7
Collins-Bos	2.2	Collins-Bos	.276	Selbach-Bos	.355	Collins-Bos	.370	Collins-Bos	700	Collins-Bos	120	Selbach-Bos	12.7
Criger-Bos	1.7	Stahl-Bos	.258	Burkett-Bos	.339	Ferris-Bos	.361	Selbach-Bos	697	Selbach-Bos	120	Collins-Bos	11.7
Ferris-Bos	.9	Burkett-Bos	.257	Stahl-Bos	.332	Burkett-Bos	.344	Burkett-Bos	682	Burkett-Bos	115	Burkett-Bos	10.8

Runs		Hits		Doubles		Triples		Home Runs		Total Bases		Runs Batted In	
Davis-Phi	93	Stone-StL	187	Davis-Phi	47	Flick-Cle	18	Davis-Phi	8	Stone-StL	259	Davis-Phi	83
Burkett-Bos	78	Burkett-Bos	147	Collins-Bos	26	Ferris-Bos	16	Ferris-Bos	6	Burkett-Bos	197	Collins-Bos	65
Collins-Bos	66	Parent-Bos	141	Ferris-Bos	24	Burkett-Bos	13	4 players tied	4	Ferris-Bos	189	Ferris-Bos	59
Stahl-Bos	61	Collins-Bos	140	Freeman-Bos	20	Freeman-Bos	8			Collins-Bos	188	Freeman-Bos	49

Stolen Bases		Base Stealing Runs		Fielding Runs-Infield		Fielding Runs-Outfield		Wins		Winning Pct.		Complete Games	
Hoffman-Phi	46			Cassidy-Was	34.8	McIntyre-Det	17.8	Waddell-Phi	27	Waddell-Phi	.730	3 players tied	35
Parent-Bos	25			Ferris-Bos	14.6			Tannehill-Bos	22	Tannehill-Bos	.710	Young-Bos	31
Stahl-Bos	18			Collins-Bos	5.2			Young-Bos	18	Young-Bos	.486	Tannehill-Bos	27
Collins-Bos	18							Winter-Bos	16	Winter-Bos	.485	Winter-Bos	24

Strikeouts		Fewest BB/Game		Games		Saves		Base Runners/9		Adjusted Relief Runs		Relief Ranking	
Waddell-Phi	287	Young-Bos	.84	Waddell-Phi	46	Buchanan-StL	2	Young-Bos	8.03				
Young-Bos	210	Winter-Bos	1.84	Young-Bos	38	Dinneen-Bos	1	Tannehill-Bos	10.27				
Winter-Bos	119	Dinneen-Bos	1.85	Tannehill-Bos	37			Winter-Bos	10.49				
Tannehill-Bos	113	Tannehill-Bos	1.95	Winter-Bos	35			Dinneen-Bos	10.79				

Innings Pitched		Opponents' Avg.		Opponents' OBP		Earned Run Average		Adjusted ERA		Adjusted Starter Runs		Pitcher Wins	
Mullin-Det	347.2	Waddell-Phi	.200	Young-Bos	.241	Waddell-Phi	1.48	Waddell-Phi	179	Waddell-Phi	40.1	Waddell-Phi	4.5
Young-Bos	320.2	Young-Bos	.216	Tannehill-Bos	.289	Young-Bos	1.82	Young-Bos	147	Young-Bos	25.4	Young-Bos	2.7
Tannehill-Bos	271.2	Tannehill-Bos	.238	Winter-Bos	.293	Tannehill-Bos	2.48	Tannehill-Bos	108	Tannehill-Bos	9.1	Tannehill-Bos	1.9
Winter-Bos	264.1	Winter-Bos	.251	Dinneen-Bos	.299	Winter-Bos	2.96	Winter-Bos	91	Harris-Bos	1.6	Harris-Bos	.1

1906 AMERICAN LEAGUE

TEAM	W	L	T	PCT	GB	R	OR	HR	AVG	OBP	SLG	OPS	AOPS	PF	SB	CG	HR	BB	SO	BR/9	ERA	AERA	OAV	OOB	FW	PW	BW	BSW	DIF
Chi	93	58	3	.616		570	460	7	.230	.301	.286	587	-9	97	216	117	11	255	543	9.8	2.13	+19	.239	.280	1.8	7.3	-3.4		11.8
NY	90	61	4	.596	3	640	543	17	.266	.316	.339	655	-2	21	192	99	21	351	605	10.8	2.78	+7	.246	.301	.1	2.7	-.1		11.7
Cle	89	64	4	.582	5	663	481	12	.279	.325	.357	682	+21	99	203	133	16	365	530	10.3	2.09	+25	.232	.289	3.8	9.6	13.6		-14.5
Phi	78	67	4	.538	12	561	539	32	.247	.308	.330	638	+2	103	165	107	9	425	749	11.0	2.60	+5	.236	.305	-.2	1.8	1.9		2.1
StL	76	73	5	.510	16	560	499	20	.247	.304	.312	616	+2	96	221	133	14	314	558	10.0	2.23	+16	.230	.284	-1.1	6.2	2.0		-5.5
Det	71	78	2	.477	21	518	598	10	.242	.295	.306	601	-9	103	206	128	14	389	469	12.4	3.06	-10	.272	.330	.4	-4.6	-5.6		6.3
Was	55	95	1	.367	37.5	519	665	26	.238	.289	.309	598	-3	95	233	115	15	451	558	12.4	3.25	-19	.265	.331	-.8	-10.2	-2.3		-6.7
Bos	49	105	1	.318	45.5	463	706	13	.237	.284	.304	588	-11	100	99	124	37	285	549	11.0	3.41	-19	.262	.306	-3.9	-11.3	-7.5		-5.3
Total	613					4494		137	.249	.303	.318	621			1535	956		2835	4561	11.0	2.69		.249	.303					

Batter-Fielder Wins		Batting Average		On-Base Percentage		Slugging Average		On-Base Plus Slugging		Adjusted OPS		Adjusted Batter Runs	
Lajoie-Cle	7.6	Stone-StL	.358	Stone-StL	.417	Stone-StL	.501	Stone-StL	918	Stone-StL	195	Stone-StL	63.3
Stahl-Bos	1.8	Grimshaw-Bos	.290	Stahl-Bos	.346	Grimshaw-Bos	.383	Stahl-Bos	713	Stahl-Bos	123	Stahl-Bos	16.9
Grimshaw-Bos	.7	Stahl-Bos	.286	Parent-Bos	.277	Stahl-Bos	.366	Ferris-Bos	622	Ferris-Bos	94	Grimshaw-Bos	10.3
2 players tied	.5	Freeman-Bos	.250	Ferris-Bos	.262	Ferris-Bos	.360	Parent-Bos	574	Parent-Bos	80	Tannehill-Bos	5.9

Runs		Hits		Doubles		Triples		Home Runs		Total Bases		Runs Batted In	
Flick-Cle	98	Lajoie-Cle	214	Lajoie-Cle	48	Flick-Cle	22	Davis-Phi	12	Stone-StL	291	Davis-Phi	96
Parent-Bos	67	Stahl-Bos	170	Ferris-Bos	25	Ferris-Bos	13	Stahl-Bos	4	Stahl-Bos	218	Stahl-Bos	51
Stahl-Bos	63	Parent-Bos	141	Stahl-Bos	24	Grimshaw-Bos	12	Ferris-Bos	2	Parent-Bos	178	Parent-Bos	49
Ferris-Bos	47	Grimshaw-Bos	124	Freeman-Bos	18	Parent-Bos	10			Ferris-Bos	178	Grimshaw-Bos	48

Stolen Bases		Base Stealing Runs		Fielding Runs-Infield		Fielding Runs-Outfield		Wins		Winning Pct.		Complete Games	
Flick-Cle	39			Tannehill-Chi	32.4	Niles-StL	13.7	Orth-NY	27	Plank-Phi	.760	Orth-NY	36
Anderson-Was	39			Ferris-Bos	7.9	Stahl-Bos	6.5	Young-Bos	13			Young-Bos	28
Parent-Bos	16			Freeman-Bos	3.3	Freeman-Bos	.7	Tannehill-Bos	13			Dinneen-Bos	22
Stahl-Bos	13							Dinneen-Bos	8			Harris-Bos	20

Strikeouts		Fewest BB/Game		Games		Saves		Base Runners/9		Adjusted Relief Runs		Relief Ranking	
Waddell-Phi	196	Young-Bos	.78	Chesbro-NY	49	Hess-Cle	3	White-Chi	8.33				
Young-Bos	140	Winter-Bos	1.65	Young-Bos	39	Bender-Phi	3	Young-Bos	10.04				
Harris-Bos	99	Tannehill-Bos	1.79	Harris-Bos	30	3 players tied	2	Glaze-Bos	10.76				
Tannehill-Bos	82	Dinneen-Bos	2.14	Winter-Bos	29			Dinneen-Bos	10.78				

Innings Pitched		Opponents' Avg.		Opponents' OBP		Earned Run Average		Adjusted ERA		Adjusted Starter Runs		Pitcher Wins	
Orth-NY	338.2	Pelty-StL	.206	White-Chi	.249	White-Chi	1.52	White-Chi	167	Rhoads-Cle	28.5	White-Chi	3.9
Young-Bos	287.2	Harris-Bos	.243	Young-Bos	.285	Dinneen-Bos	2.92	Dinneen-Bos	94	Kroh-Bos	2.7	Kroh-Bos	.3
Harris-Bos	235.0	Dinneen-Bos	.255	Dinneen-Bos	.300	Tannehill-Bos	3.16	Tannehill-Bos	87	Swormstedt-Bos	2.6	Swormstedt-Bos	.2
Dinneen-Bos	218.2	Young-Bos	.264	Harris-Bos	.303	Young-Bos	3.19	Young-Bos	86				

1907 AMERICAN LEAGUE

TEAM	W	L	T	PCT	GB	R	OR	HR	AVG	OBP	SLG	OPS	AOPS	PF	SB	CG	HR	BB	SO	BR/9	ERA	AERA	OAV	OOB	FW	PW	BW	BSW	DIF
Det	92	58	3	.613		693	531	11	.266	.313	.335	648	+8	104	196	120	8	380	512	11.2	2.33	+12	.251	.309	1.0	4.3	4.4		7.3
Phi	88	57	5	.607	1.5	584	511	22	.255	.311	.329	640	+6	102	137	106	13	378	789	10.3	2.35	+11	.226	.290	.4	4.1	4.7		6.3
Chi	87	64	6	.576	5.5	588	474	5	.238	.302	.283	585	-5	97	175	112	13	305	604	10.3	2.22	+8	.245	.290	3.4	3.1	-1.8		6.8
Cle	85	67	6	.559	8	531	525	11	.241	.295	.310	605	-3	101	193	127	8	362	513	10.8	2.26	+11	.244	.300	1.3	4.0	-1.8		5.5
NY	70	78	4	.473	21	605	667	15	.249	.299	.315	614	-7	108	206	93	13	428	511	12.3	3.03	-8	.262	.325	-4.4	-3.5	-4.6		8.5
StL	69	83	3	.454	24	541	555	10	.253	.308	.313	621	+3	100	144	129	17	352	463	10.8	2.61	-4	.245	.300	.8	-1.8	2.1		-8.1
Bos	59	90	6	.396	32.5	466	558	18	.234	.281	.292	573	-11	99	125	100	22	337	517	10.2	2.45	+5	.236	.288	.2	2.0	-8.2		-9.5
Was	49	102	3	.325	43.5	506	693	12	.243	.304	.299	603	+5	92	223	106	10	344	570	11.8	3.11	-22	.268	.320	-2.4	-12.3	4.1		-15.9
Total	617					4514		104	.247	.302	.309	611			1399	893		2886	4479	10.9	2.54		.247	.302					

Batter-Fielder Wins		Batting Average		On-Base Percentage		Slugging Average		On-Base Plus Slugging		Adjusted OPS		Adjusted Batter Runs	
Lajoie-Cle	7.0	Cobb-Det	.350	Hartsel-Phi	.405	Cobb-Det	.468	Cobb-Det	848	Cobb-Det	164	Cobb-Det	40.4
Shaw-Bos	1.0	Parent-Bos	.276	Sullivan-Bos	.315	Parent-Bos	.355	Unglaub-Bos	622	Unglaub-Bos	99	Parent-Bos	7.1
Parent-Bos	.6	Unglaub-Bos	.254	Unglaub-Bos	.284	Unglaub-Bos	.338	Sullivan-Bos	598	Sullivan-Bos	92	Chadbourne-Bos	1.5
2 players tied	.0	Sullivan-Bos	.245	Ferris-Bos	.254	Ferris-Bos	.314	Ferris-Bos	568	Ferris-Bos	82	Tannehill-Bos	1.4

Runs		Hits		Doubles		Triples		Home Runs		Total Bases		Runs Batted In	
Crawford-Det	102	Cobb-Det	212	Davis-Phi	35	Flick-Cle	18	Davis-Phi	8	Cobb-Det	283	Cobb-Det	119
Sullivan-Bos	73	Unglaub-Bos	138	Ferris-Bos	25	Unglaub-Bos	13	Ferris-Bos	4	Unglaub-Bos	184	Unglaub-Bos	62
Barrett-Bos	52	Sullivan-Bos	135	Parent-Bos	19	Barrett-Bos	6	Wagner-Bos	2	Ferris-Bos	176	Ferris-Bos	60
Parent-Bos	51	Ferris-Bos	135	Sullivan-Bos	18	Parent-Bos	5			Sullivan-Bos	156	Grimshaw-Bos	33

Stolen Bases		Base Stealing Runs		Fielding Runs-Infield		Fielding Runs-Outfield		Wins		Winning Pct.		Complete Games	
Cobb-Det	53			Lajoie-Cle	44.9	D.Jones-Det	12.8	White-Chi	27	Donovan-Det	.862	Walsh-Chi	37
Wagner-Bos	20			Ferris-Bos	7.6	Parent-Bos	2.4	Joss-Cle	27	Young-Bos	.583	Young-Bos	33
Sullivan-Bos	16							Young-Bos	21			Winter-Bos	21
Unglaub-Bos	14							Winter-Bos	12			Glaze-Bos	11

Strikeouts		Fewest BB/Game		Games		Saves		Base Runners/9		Adjusted Relief Runs		Relief Ranking	
Waddell-Phi	232	White-Chi	1.18	Walsh-Chi	56	3 players tied	4	Young-Bos	9.02				
Young-Bos	147	Young-Bos	1.34	Young-Bos	43	Pruiett-Bos	3	Winter-Bos	9.19				
Winter-Bos	88	Winter-Bos	2.14	Winter-Bos	35	Young-Bos	2	Glaze-Bos	9.97				
Glaze-Bos	68	Glaze-Bos	2.37	Pruiett-Bos	35	2 players tied	1	Tannehill-Bos	10.72				

Innings Pitched		Opponents' Avg.		Opponents' OBP		Earned Run Average		Adjusted ERA		Adjusted Starter Runs		Pitcher Wins	
Walsh-Chi	422.1	Dygert-Phi	.214	Young-Bos	.263	Walsh-Chi	1.60	Walsh-Chi	150	Walsh-Chi	32.8	Walsh-Chi	4.6
Young-Bos	343.1	Winter-Bos	.216	Winter-Bos	.267	Young-Bos	1.99	Young-Bos	129	Young-Bos	24.9	Young-Bos	2.4
Winter-Bos	256.2	Glaze-Bos	.227	Glaze-Bos	.283	Winter-Bos	2.07	Winter-Bos	124	Winter-Bos	12.3	Winter-Bos	1.4
Glaze-Bos	182.1	Young-Bos	.229	Pruiett-Bos	.324	Glaze-Bos	2.32	Glaze-Bos	111	Glaze-Bos	2.7	Glaze-Bos	.1

1908 AMERICAN LEAGUE

TEAM	W	L	T	PCT	GB	R	OR	HR	AVG	OBP	SLG	OPS	AOPS	PF	SB	CG	HR	BB	SO	BR/9	ERA	AERA	OAV	OOB	FW	PW	BW	BSW	DIF
Det	90	63	1	.588		647	547	19	.263	.312	.347	659	+15	104	165	119	12	318	553	11.1	2.40	+0	.255	.306	-2.1	.2	8.8		6.6
Cle	90	64	3	.584	0.5	569	459	18	.239	.297	.309	606	+3	100	177	108	16	328	548	9.7	2.02	+18	.229	.280	1.6	6.4	1.7		3.3
Chi	88	64	4	.579	1.5	537	470	3	.224	.298	.271	569	-9	98	209	107	11	284	623	9.4	2.22	+4	.225	.269	3.2	1.6	-3.1		10.3
StL	83	69	3	.546	6.5	544	483	20	.245	.296	.310	606	+2	101	126	107	7	387	607	10.3	2.15	+11	.230	.294	2.7	4.1	1.3		-1.1
Bos	75	79	1	.487	15.5	564	513	14	.245	.291	.312	607	+0	103	156	102	18	364	624	10.5	2.28	+8	.238	.295	-1.4	3.0	-.9		-2.6
Phi	68	85	4	.444	22	486	562	21	.223	.281	.292	573	-14	107	116	102	16	410	741	10.6	2.56	+0	.235	.298	.6	-.5	-8.4		-.2
Was	67	85	3	.441	22.5	479	539	8	.235	.293	.296	589	+6	92	170	106	16	348	649	10.5	2.34	-3	.241	.294	.1	-1.5	3.4		-11.0
NY	51	103	1	.331	39.5	460	713	13	.236	.284	.291	574	-9	101	231	90	26	458	585	12.0	3.16	-22	.252	.322	-4.1	-11.6	-5.8		-4.4
Total	622					4286		116	.239	.294	.304	598			1350	841		2897	4930	10.5	2.39		.239	.294					

Batter-Fielder Wins		Batting Average		On-Base Percentage		Slugging Average		On-Base Plus Slugging		Adjusted OPS		Adjusted Batter Runs	
Lajoie-Cle	8.0	Cobb-Det	.324	Gessler-Bos	.394	Cobb-Det	.475	Cobb-Det	842	Cobb-Det	166	Cobb-Det	40.0
Wagner-Bos	3.2	Gessler-Bos	.308	McConnell-Bos	.343	Gessler-Bos	.423	Gessler-Bos	817	Gessler-Bos	161	Gessler-Bos	31.0
Gessler-Bos	2.4	McConnell-Bos	.279	Lord-Bos	.297	Cravath-Bos	.383	McConnell-Bos	678	McConnell-Bos	117	Cravath-Bos	11.9
Cravath-Bos	.8	Lord-Bos	.259	Wagner-Bos	.288	McConnell-Bos	.335	Lord-Bos	614	Lord-Bos	97	McConnell-Bos	10.2

Runs		Hits		Doubles		Triples		Home Runs		Total Bases		Runs Batted In	
McIntyre-Det	105	Cobb-Det	188	Cobb-Det	36	Cobb-Det	20	Crawford-Det	7	Cobb-Det	276	Cobb-Det	108
McConnell-Bos	77	Lord-Bos	145	Lord-Bos	15	Gessler-Bos	14	Gessler-Bos	3	Gessler-Bos	184	Gessler-Bos	63
Wagner-Bos	62	McConnell-Bos	140	Gessler-Bos	13	Cravath-Bos	11	3 players tied	2	Lord-Bos	178	Wagner-Bos	46
Lord-Bos	61	Gessler-Bos	134	Wagner-Bos	11	Thoney-Bos	9			McConnell-Bos	168	McConnell-Bos	43

Stolen Bases		Base Stealing Runs		Fielding Runs-Infield		Fielding Runs-Outfield		Wins		Winning Pct.		Complete Games	
Dougherty-Chi	47			Lajoie-Cle	46.8	McIntyre-Det	16.4	Walsh-Chi	40	Walsh-Chi	.727	Walsh-Chi	42
McConnell-Bos	31			Wagner-Bos	32.4	Thoney-Bos	3.9	Young-Bos	21	Young-Bos	.656	Young-Bos	30
Lord-Bos	23							Morgan-Bos	14			Morgan-Bos	17
Wagner-Bos	20							Cicotte-Bos	11			Cicotte-Bos	17

Strikeouts		Fewest BB/Game		Games		Saves		Base Runners/9		Adjusted Relief Runs		Relief Ranking	
Walsh-Chi	269	Joss-Cle	.83	Walsh-Chi	66	Walsh-Chi	6	Joss-Cle	7.31				
Young-Bos	150	Young-Bos	1.11	Cicotte-Bos	39	Young-Bos	2	Steele-Bos	7.70				
Morgan-Bos	99	Cicotte-Bos	2.56	Young-Bos	36	Pruiett-Bos	2	Young-Bos	8.07				
Cicotte-Bos	95	Burchell-Bos	3.26	Burchell-Bos	31	Cicotte-Bos	2	Arellanes-Bos	9.23				

Innings Pitched		Opponents' Avg.		Opponents' OBP		Earned Run Average		Adjusted ERA		Adjusted Starter Runs		Pitcher Wins	
Walsh-Chi	464.0	Joss-Cle	.197	Joss-Cle	.218	Joss-Cle	1.16	Joss-Cle	205	Walsh-Chi	42.7	Walsh-Chi	6.8
Young-Bos	299.0	Young-Bos	.213	Young-Bos	.240	Young-Bos	1.26	Young-Bos	194	Young-Bos	36.4	Young-Bos	4.1
Cicotte-Bos	207.1	Morgan-Bos	.226	Cicotte-Bos	.318	Cicotte-Bos	2.43	Cicotte-Bos	101	Steele-Bos	8.4	Cicotte-Bos	.5
Morgan-Bos	205.0	Burchell-Bos	.247	Morgan-Bos	.319	Morgan-Bos	2.46	Morgan-Bos	100	Arellanes-Bos	4.6	Steele-Bos	.4

1909 AMERICAN LEAGUE

TEAM	W	L	T	PCT	GB	R	OR	HR	AVG	OBP	SLG	OPS	AOPS	PF	SB	CG	HR	BB	SO	BR/9	ERA	AERA	OAV	OOB	FW	PW	BW	BSW	DIF
Det	98	54	6	.645		666	493	19	.267	.325	.342	667	+13	104	280	117	16	359	528	10.6	2.26	+11	.238	.293	.4	4.4	8.5		8.7
Phi	95	58	0	.621	3.5	605	411	21	.256	.321	.343	664	+15	102	201	110	9	386	728	9.9	1.93	+24	.217	.282	1.8	8.4	9.1		-.8
Bos	88	63	1	.583	9.5	601	549	20	.263	.321	.333	654	+12	102	215	75	18	384	555	10.9	2.59	-4	.243	.303	-1.3	-1.7	6.8		8.7
Chi	78	74	7	.513	20	492	464	4	.221	.291	.275	566	-11	96	211	115	8	340	669	9.9	2.05	+14	.229	.283	2.4	5.3	-5.8		.0
NY	74	77	2	.490	23.5	589	587	16	.248	.313	.311	624	+3	101	187	94	21	422	597	11.4	2.65	-5	.248	.316	-3.6	-2.4	2.4		2.1
Cle	71	82	2	.464	27.5	493	532	10	.241	.288	.313	601	-8	104	173	110	9	348	568	10.6	2.40	+6	.250	.307	-.0	2.3	-5.7		-2.0
StL	61	89	4	.407	36	441	575	10	.232	.287	.279	566	-9	93	136	105	16	383	620	11.4	2.88	-16	.261	.319	.5	-8.4	-5.5		-.6
Was	42	110	4	.276	56	380	656	9	.223	.276	.275	551	-16	-95	136	99	12	424	653	11.6	3.04	-20	.248	.312	-.0	-11.1	-10.0		-12.8
Total	620					4267		109	.244	.303	.309	612			1539	825		3046	4918	10.8	2.47		.244	.303					

Batter-Fielder Wins		Batting Average		On-Base Percentage		Slugging Average		On-Base Plus Slugging		Adjusted OPS		Adjusted Batter Runs	
Cobb-Det	6.0	Cobb-Det	.377	Cobb-Det	.431	Cobb-Det	.517	Cobb-Det	947	Cobb-Det	190	Cobb-Det	59.2
Speaker-Bos	4.6	Lord-Bos	.315	Stahl-Bos	.377	Speaker-Bos	.443	Stahl-Bos	812	Stahl-Bos	153	Speaker-Bos	29.8
Carrigan-Bos	1.9	Speaker-Bos	.309	Speaker-Bos	.362	Stahl-Bos	.434	Speaker-Bos	805	Speaker-Bos	151	Stahl-Bos	27.2
Wagner-Bos	1.7	Carrigan-Bos	.296	Lord-Bos	.349	Carrigan-Bos	.368	Lord-Bos	712	Lord-Bos	122	Lord-Bos	11.8

Runs		Hits		Doubles		Triples		Home Runs		Total Bases		Runs Batted In	
Cobb-Det	116	Cobb-Det	216	Crawford-Det	35	Baker-Phi	19	Cobb-Det	9	Cobb-Det	296	Cobb-Det	107
Lord-Bos	89	Speaker-Bos	168	Speaker-Bos	26	Speaker-Bos	13	Speaker-Bos	7	Speaker-Bos	241	Speaker-Bos	77
Speaker-Bos	73	Lord-Bos	168	Stahl-Bos	19	Stahl-Bos	12	Stahl-Bos	6	Lord-Bos	194	Stahl-Bos	60
Niles-Bos	65	Niles-Bos	134	Wagner-Bos	16	McConnell-Bos	8	2 players tied	2	Stahl-Bos	189	Wagner-Bos	49

Stolen Bases		Base Stealing Runs		Fielding Runs-Infield		Fielding Runs-Outfield		Wins		Winning Pct.		Complete Games	
Cobb-Det	76			Lajoie-Cle	23.3	Speaker-Bos	18.5	Mullin-Det	29	Mullin-Det	.784	Smith-Chi	37
Lord-Bos	36			McConnell-Bos	10.5	Niles-Bos	2.3	Arellanes-Bos	16	Arellanes-Bos	.571	Arellanes-Bos	17
Speaker-Bos	35			Wagner-Bos	9.8			Cicotte-Bos	14			Wood-Bos	13
Niles-Bos	27							Wood-Bos	11			Cicotte-Bos	10

Strikeouts		Fewest BB/Game		Games		Saves		Base Runners/9		Adjusted Relief Runs		Relief Ranking	
Smith-Chi	177	Joss-Cle	1.15	Smith-Chi	51	Arellanes-Bos	8	Walsh-Chi	8.60				
Wood-Bos	88	Arellanes-Bos	1.68	Arellanes-Bos	45	Pape-Bos	2	Arellanes-Bos	9.36				
Cicotte-Bos	82	Wood-Bos	2.41	Cicotte-Bos	27	Steele-Bos	1	Wood-Bos	9.52				
Arellanes-Bos	82	Cicotte-Bos	3.10	Wood-Bos	24	Cicotte-Bos	1	Cicotte-Bos	9.65				

Innings Pitched		Opponents' Avg.		Opponents' OBP		Earned Run Average		Adjusted ERA		Adjusted Starter Runs		Pitcher Wins	
Smith-Chi	365.0	Morgan-Bos-Phi	.202	Walsh-Chi	.253	Krause-Phi	1.39	Krause-Phi	172	Walsh-Chi	24.9	Walsh-Chi	4.1
Arellanes-Bos	230.2	Cicotte-Bos	.207	Wood-Bos	.270	Cicotte-Bos	1.94	Cicotte-Bos	128	Arellanes-Bos	7.3	Smith-Chi	4.1
Cicotte-Bos	162.1	Wood-Bos	.209	Arellanes-Bos	.270	Wood-Bos	2.18	Wood-Bos	114	Wood-Bos	6.7	Cicotte-Bos	.9
Wood-Bos	160.2	Arellanes-Bos	.229	Cicotte-Bos	.280	Arellanes-Bos	2.18	Cicotte-Bos	114	Cicotte-Bos	4.9	Arellanes-Bos	.8

1910 AMERICAN LEAGUE

TEAM	W	L	T	PCT	GB	R	OR	HR	AVG	OBP	SLG	OPS	AOPS	PF	SB	CG	HR	BB	SO	BR/9	ERA	AERA	OAV	OOB	FW	PW	BW	BSW	DIF
Phi	102	48	5	.680		674	442	19	.266	.326	.355	681	+20	99	207	123	8	450	789	10.2	1.79	+33	.221	.292	3.9	10.8	12.3		.0
NY	88	63	5	.583	14.5	626	557	20	.248	.320	.322	642	+1	106	288	110	16	364	654	10.7	2.61	+2	.243	.300	.2	.6	1.2		10.5
Det	86	68	1	.558	18	679	584	28	.261	.329	.344	673	+10	107	249	108	34	460	532	11.6	2.82	-7	.248	.319	-.0	-2.9	6.3		5.6
Bos	81	72	5	.529	22.5	641	564	43	.259	.323	.351	674	+14	102	194	100	30	414	670	10.7	2.45	+4	.235	.297	-1.1	1.6	8.7		-4.6
Cle	71	81	9	.467	32	548	593	9	.244	.296	.308	604	+3	101	189	92	18	488	617	11.9	2.68	-6	.261	.319	-.6	-5.4	-5.1		2.2
Chi	68	85	3	.444	35.5	457	479	7	.211	.275	.261	536	-24	-96	183	103	16	381	785	9.8	2.03	+18	.222	.281	-1.7	6.6	-15.1		1.8
Was	66	85	6	.437	36.5	501	551	9	.236	.309	.289	598	-2	95	192	119	19	375	674	10.8	2.46	+1	.244	.304	1.8	.6	-.4		-11.4
StL	47	107	4	.305	57	451	743	12	.218	.281	.274	555	-16	-94	169	101	14	532	557	12.6	3.09	-20	.265	.341	-6.3	-10.8	-10.0		-2.9
Total	628					4577		147	.243	.308	.313	621			1671	856		3464	5278	11.0	2.52		.243	.308					

Batter-Fielder Wins		Batting Average		On-Base Percentage		Slugging Average		On-Base Plus Slugging		Adjusted OPS		Adjusted Batter Runs	
Lajoie-Cle	8.9	Cobb-Det	.383	Cobb-Det	.456	Cobb-Det	.551	Cobb-Det	1008	Cobb-Det	202	Lajoie-Cle	69.3
Speaker-Bos	4.8	Speaker-Bos	.340	Speaker-Bos	.404	Speaker-Bos	.468	Speaker-Bos	873	Speaker-Bos	169	Speaker-Bos	42.5
Lewis-Bos	1.9	Gardner-Bos	.283	Hooper-Bos	.346	Stahl-Bos	.424	Stahl-Bos	758	Stahl-Bos	134	Stahl-Bos	18.3
2 players tied	.9	Lewis-Bos	.283	Wagner-Bos	.335	Lewis-Bos	.407	Lewis-Bos	734	Lewis-Bos	127	Lewis-Bos	14.7

Runs		Hits		Doubles		Triples		Home Runs		Total Bases		Runs Batted In	
Cobb-Det	106	Lajoie-Cle	227	Lajoie-Cle	51	Crawford-Det	19	Stahl-Bos	10	Lajoie-Cle	304	Crawford-Det	120
Speaker-Bos	92	Speaker-Bos	183	Lewis-Bos	29	Stahl-Bos	16	Lewis-Bos	8	Speaker-Bos	252	Stahl-Bos	77
Hooper-Bos	81	Hooper-Bos	156	Wagner-Bos	26	Speaker-Bos	14	Speaker-Bos	7	Stahl-Bos	225	Lewis-Bos	68
Stahl-Bos	68	Lewis-Bos	153	Speaker-Bos	20	3 players tied	10	Carrigan-Bos	3	Lewis-Bos	220	Speaker-Bos	65

Stolen Bases		Base Stealing Runs		Fielding Runs-Infield		Fielding Runs-Outfield		Wins		Winning Pct.		Complete Games	
Collins-Phi	81			McBride-Was	32.8	Lewis-Bos	11.5	Coombs-Phi	31	Bender-Phi	.821	Johnson-Was	38
Hooper-Bos	40					Hooper-Bos	8.8	Cicotte-Bos	15	Cicotte-Bos	.577	Cicotte-Bos	20
Speaker-Bos	35					Speaker-Bos	8.6	Collins-Bos	13			Collins-Bos	18
Wagner-Bos	26							2 players tied	12			Karger-Bos	16

Strikeouts		Fewest BB/Game		Games		Saves		Base Runners/9		Adjusted Relief Runs		Relief Ranking	
Johnson-Was	313	Walsh-Chi	1.49	3 players tied	45	Walsh-Chi	5	Walsh-Chi	7.47				
Wood-Bos	145	Young-Cle	1.49	Cicotte-Bos	36	Hall-Bos	2	Collins-Bos	9.09				
Collins-Bos	109	Collins-Bos	1.51	3 players tied	35	4 players tied	1	Wood-Bos	10.11				
Cicotte-Bos	104	Wood-Bos	2.56					C.Smith-Bos	10.25				

Innings Pitched		Opponents' Avg.		Opponents' OBP		Earned Run Average		Adjusted ERA		Adjusted Starter Runs		Pitcher Wins	
Johnson-Was	370.0	Walsh-Chi	.187	Walsh-Chi	.226	Walsh-Chi	1.27	Walsh-Chi	189	Coombs-Phi	46.6	Walsh-Chi	6.3
Cicotte-Bos	250.0	Hall-Bos	.207	Collins-Bos	.264	Collins-Bos	1.62	Collins-Bos	158	Collins-Bos	21.8	Collins-Bos	1.9
Collins-Bos	244.2	Wood-Bos	.220	Wood-Bos	.287	Wood-Bos	1.69	Wood-Bos	151	Hall-Bos	9.8	Wood-Bos	1.9
Wood-Bos	196.2	Collins-Bos	.229	Karger-Bos	.289	Hall-Bos	1.91	Hall-Bos	134	Wood-Bos	9.1	Hall-Bos	1.6

1911 AMERICAN LEAGUE

TEAM	W	L	T	PCT	GB	R	OR	HR	AVG	OBP	SLG	OPS	AOPS	PF	SB	CG	HR	BB	SO	BR/9	ERA	AERA	OAV	OOB	FW	PW	BW	BSW	DIF
Phi	101	50	1	.669		861	602	**35**	.296	.357	.398	755	+19	98	226	97	**17**	487	739	12.5	3.01	+5	.264	.338	**4.9**	2.2	**12.2**		6.3
Det	89	65	0	.578	13.5	831	777	30	.292	.355	.388	743	+8	105	**276**	**108**	28	460	538	13.3	3.73	-7	.283	.348	-.9	-4.2	5.2		12.0
Cle	80	73	3	.523	22	693	712	20	.282	.333	.369	702	+1	101	209	93	**17**	552	675	12.9	3.36	+1	.267	.345	.3	.7	-.7		3.2
Chi	77	74	3	.510	24	718	624	20	.269	.325	.350	675	-3	97	201	85	22	**384**	**752**	11.5	2.97	+8	**.255**	**.310**	3.4	3.8	-2.8		-2.9
Bos	78	75	0	.510	24	680	643	**35**	.275	.350	.363	713	+6	99	190	87	21	473	711	12.2	**2.74**	**+19**	.262	.332	-1.4	**7.9**	4.8		-9.8
NY	76	76	1	.500	25.5	684	723	25	.272	.344	.362	706	-3	107	269	90	26	406	667	12.3	3.54	+1	.270	.329	-1.7	.9	-2.1		2.9
Was	64	90	0	.416	38.5	624	765	16	.258	.330	.320	650	-11	98	215	106	39	410	628	12.8	3.52	-7	.277	.334	-.0	-3.7	-6.2		-3.0
StL	45	107	0	.296	56.5	567	812	17	.239	.307	.311	618	-19	-96	125	92	28	463	383	13.4	3.86	-13	.278	.342	-3.8	-7.2	-11.9		-8.1
Total	614					5658		198	.273	.338	.358	696			1711	758		3635	5093	12.6	3.34		.273	.338					

Batter-Fielder Wins	Batting Average	On-Base Percentage	Slugging Average	On-Base Plus Slugging	Adjusted OPS	Adjusted Batter Runs
Cobb-Det 6.6	Cobb-Det .420	Jackson-Cle .468	Cobb-Det .621	Cobb-Det 1088	Cobb-Det 193	Cobb-Det 71.7
Gardner-Bos 3.3	Speaker-Bos .334	Speaker-Bos .418	Speaker-Bos .502	Speaker-Bos 920	Speaker-Bos 158	Speaker-Bos 40.5
Speaker-Bos 3.3	Hooper-Bos .311	Hooper-Bos .399	D.Lewis-Bos .437	Hooper-Bos 794	Hooper-Bos 123	Hooper-Bos 19.7
Hooper-Bos 1.8	D.Lewis-Bos .307	Gardner-Bos .373	Hooper-Bos .395	D.Lewis-Bos 792	D.Lewis-Bos 122	D.Lewis-Bos 12.7

Runs	Hits	Doubles	Triples	Home Runs	Total Bases	Runs Batted In
Cobb-Det 147	Cobb-Det 248	Cobb-Det 47	Cobb-Det 24	Baker-Phi 11	Cobb-Det 367	Cobb-Det 127
Hooper-Bos 93	Speaker-Bos 167	Speaker-Bos 34	Speaker-Bos 13	Speaker-Bos 8	Speaker-Bos 251	D.Lewis-Bos 86
Speaker-Bos 88	Hooper-Bos 163	D.Lewis-Bos 32	Wagner-Bos 8	D.Lewis-Bos 7	Hooper-Bos 207	Speaker-Bos 70
Gardner-Bos 80	D.Lewis-Bos 144	Yerkes-Bos 24	Gardner-Bos 8	2 players tied 4	D.Lewis-Bos 205	Yerkes-Bos 57

Stolen Bases	Base Stealing Runs	Fielding Runs-Infield	Fielding Runs-Outfield	Wins	Winning Pct.	Complete Games
Cobb-Det 83		Tannehill-Chi 36.3	Hogan-Phi-StL 12.6	Coombs-Phi 28	Bender-Phi .773	Johnson-Was 36
Hooper-Bos 38		Gardner-Bos 22.7	Hooper-Bos 5.8	Wood-Bos 23	Wood-Bos .575	Wood-Bos 25
Gardner-Bos 27			D.Lewis-Bos 4.7	Collins-Bos 11		Cicotte-Bos 16
Speaker-Bos 25			Speaker-Bos 2.8	Cicotte-Bos 11		Collins-Bos 14

Strikeouts	Fewest BB/Game	Games	Saves	Base Runners/9	Adjusted Relief Runs	Relief Ranking
Walsh-Chi 255	White-Chi 1.47	Walsh-Chi 56	3 players tied 4	Gregg-Cle 9.86		
Wood-Bos 231	Collins-Bos 2.03	Wood-Bos 44	Hall-Bos 4	Wood-Bos 10.22		
Cicotte-Bos 106	Wood-Bos 2.48	Cicotte-Bos 35	Wood-Bos 3	Collins-Bos 10.73		
Collins-Bos 86	Cicotte-Bos 2.99	Hall-Bos 32	Collins-Bos 1	Pape-Bos 11.94		

Innings Pitched	Opponents' Avg.	Opponents' OBP	Earned Run Average	Adjusted ERA	Adjusted Starter Runs	Pitcher Wins
Walsh-Chi 368.2	Gregg-Cle .205	Walsh-Chi .280	Gregg-Cle 1.80	Gregg-Cle 189	Johnson-Was 43.1	Wood-Bos 5.7
Wood-Bos 275.2	Wood-Bos .223	Wood-Bos .284	Wood-Bos 2.02	Wood-Bos 162	Wood-Bos 33.7	Collins-Bos 2.0
Cicotte-Bos 220.0	Collins-Bos .256	Collins-Bos .302	Collins-Bos 2.40	Collins-Bos 136	Collins-Bos 19.2	Pape-Bos 1.8
Collins-Bos 194.2	Pape-Bos .264	Pape-Bos .335	Pape-Bos 2.45	Pape-Bos 134	Pape-Bos 18.7	O'Brien-Bos 1.7

1912 AMERICAN LEAGUE

TEAM	W	L	T	PCT	GB	R	OR	HR	AVG	OBP	SLG	OPS	AOPS	PF	SB	CG	HR	BB	SO	BR/9	ERA	AERA	OAV	OOB	FW	PW	BW	BSW	DIF
Bos	105	47	2	.691		**799**	544	29	.277	**.355**	**.380**	735	+10	105	185	**108**	18	385	712	**11.0**	2.76	+24	.248	**.306**	2.4	10.1	7.3		9.2
Was	91	61	2	.599	14	699	581	20	.256	.324	.341	665	-6	101	273	98	24	525	**828**	11.8	2.82	+25	**.242**	.320	.7	**10.4**	-3.6		7.6
Phi	90	62	1	.592	15	779	658	22	**.282**	.349	.377	726	**+17**	96	258	95	**12**	518	601	12.3	3.32	-7	.258	.336	**2.5**	-3.3	**11.1**		3.7
Chi	78	76	4	.506	28	639	648	17	.255	.317	.329	646	-7	97	213	85	26	426	698	11.8	3.06	+5	.264	.322	1.5	2.7	-5.0		1.8
Cle	75	78	2	.490	30.5	677	681	12	.273	.333	.353	686	-2	103	194	94	15	523	622	12.9	3.30	+4	.272	.346	1.4	2.0	-1.5		-3.4
Det	69	84	1	.451	36.5	720	777	19	.268	.343	.349	692	+6	97	**277**	107	16	521	512	13.3	3.77	-13	.277	.350	-1.7	-7.2	5.1		-3.7
StL	53	101	3	.344	53	552	764	19	.248	.315	.320	635	-10	96	176	85	17	442	547	12.7	3.71	-10	.277	.341	-1.6	-5.5	-6.7		-10.3
NY	50	102	1	.329	55	630	842	18	.259	.329	.334	663	-10	106	247	105	28	436	637	13.0	4.13	-12	.282	.344	-4.4	-6.6	-7.0		-8.0
Total	619					5495		156	.265	.333	.348	681			1823	777		3776	5157	12.3	3.34		.265	.333					

Batter-Fielder Wins	Batting Average	On-Base Percentage	Slugging Average	On-Base Plus Slugging	Adjusted OPS	Adjusted Batter Runs
Speaker-Bos 7.2	Cobb-Det .409	Speaker-Bos .464	Cobb-Det .584	Cobb-Det 1040	Cobb-Det 203	Cobb-Det 71.5
Gardner-Bos 2.2	Speaker-Bos .383	Gardner-Bos .383	Speaker-Bos .567	Speaker-Bos 1031	Speaker-Bos 185	Speaker-Bos 68.2
Cady-Bos 1.2	Gardner-Bos .315	Wagner-Bos .358	Gardner-Bos .449	Gardner-Bos 832	Gardner-Bos 131	Gardner-Bos 20.0
2 players tied .6	Stahl-Bos .301	Lewis-Bos .346	Stahl-Bos .429	Lewis-Bos 754	Lewis-Bos 110	Wood-Bos 10.8

Runs	Hits	Doubles	Triples	Home Runs	Total Bases	Runs Batted In
Collins-Phi 137	Jackson-Cle 226	Speaker-Bos 53	Jackson-Cle 26	Baker-Phi 10	Jackson-Cle 331	Baker-Phi 130
Speaker-Bos 136	Cobb-Det 226	Lewis-Bos 36	Gardner-Bos 18	Speaker-Bos 10	Speaker-Bos 329	Lewis-Bos 109
Hooper-Bos 98	Speaker-Bos 222	Wagner-Bos 25	Speaker-Bos 12	Lewis-Bos 6	Lewis-Bos 237	Speaker-Bos 90
Gardner-Bos 88	Lewis-Bos 165	Gardner-Bos 24	Hooper-Bos 12	2 players tied 3	Gardner-Bos 232	Gardner-Bos 86

Stolen Bases	Base Stealing Runs	Fielding Runs-Infield	Fielding Runs-Outfield	Wins	Winning Pct.	Complete Games
Milan-Was 88		McBride-Was 27.8	Speaker-Bos 16.3	Wood-Bos 34	Wood-Bos .872	Wood-Bos 35
Speaker-Bos 52			Lewis-Bos 6.1	O'Brien-Bos 20	Bedient-Bos .690	O'Brien-Bos 25
Hooper-Bos 29			Hooper-Bos 1.2	Bedient-Bos 20	Hall-Bos .652	Bedient-Bos 19
Gardner-Bos 25				Hall-Bos 15	O'Brien-Bos .606	Collins-Bos 17

Strikeouts	Fewest BB/Game	Games	Saves	Base Runners/9	Adjusted Relief Runs	Relief Ranking
Johnson-Was 303	Bender-Phi 1.74	Walsh-Chi 62	Walsh-Chi 10	Johnson-Was 8.56		
Wood-Bos 258	Collins-Bos 1.90	Wood-Bos 43	Hall-Bos 2	Wood-Bos 9.44		
Bedient-Bos 122	Bedient-Bos 2.14	Bedient-Bos 41	Bedient-Bos 2	Bedient-Bos 10.29		
O'Brien-Bos 115	Wood-Bos 2.15	O'Brien-Bos 37	2 players tied 1	Collins-Bos 10.66		

Innings Pitched	Opponents' Avg.	Opponents' OBP	Earned Run Average	Adjusted ERA	Adjusted Starter Runs	Pitcher Wins
Walsh-Chi 393.0	Johnson-Was .196	Johnson-Was .248	Johnson-Was 1.39	Johnson-Was 241	Johnson-Was 77.1	Johnson-Was 10.6
Wood-Bos 344.0	Wood-Bos .216	Wood-Bos .272	Wood-Bos 1.91	Wood-Bos 179	Wood-Bos 53.1	Wood-Bos 7.6
O'Brien-Bos 275.2	O'Brien-Bos .237	Bedient-Bos .288	Collins-Bos 2.53	Collins-Bos 135	O'Brien-Bos 23.7	O'Brien-Bos 2.1
Bedient-Bos 231.0	Bedient-Bos .240	Collins-Bos .297	O'Brien-Bos 2.58	O'Brien-Bos 133	Collins-Bos 22.3	Collins-Bos 2.1

1913 AMERICAN LEAGUE

TEAM	W	L	T	PCT	GB	R	OR	HR	AVG	OBP	SLG	OPS	AOPS	PF	SB	CG	HR	BB	SO	BR/9	ERA	AERA	OAV	OOB	FW	PW	BW	BSW	DIF
Phi	96	57	0	.627		794	592	33	.280	.356	.375	731	+24	98	221	69	24	532	630	11.8	3.19	-13	.243	.321	3.3	-7.3	16.7		6.9
Was	90	64	1	.584	6.5	596	562	19	.252	.317	.326	643	-7	102	287	78	35	465	758	11.0	2.73	+8	.233	.306	.4	3.6	-5.3		14.3
Cle	86	66	3	.566	9.5	633	536	16	.268	.331	.348	679	+2	103	191	93	19	502	689	11.8	2.54	+19	.251	.324	1.6	7.6	1.4		-.5
Bos	79	71	1	.527	15.5	631	610	17	.268	.336	.364	700	+9	103	189	83	6	442	710	11.9	2.94	+0	.262	.325	1.4	-.3	5.4		-2.5
Chi	78	74	1	.513	17.5	488	498	24	.236	.299	.311	610	-14	99	156	84	10	438	602	11.0	2.33	+25	.239	.305	.5	9.5	-9.8		1.8
Det	66	87	0	.431	30	625	716	24	.265	.336	.355	691	+11	99	218	90	13	504	468	12.6	3.38	-14	.267	.339	-2.5	-7.6	6.8		-7.2
NY	57	94	2	.377	38	529	668	8	.237	.320	.292	612	-15	99	203	75	31	455	530	12.2	3.27	-9	.262	.330	-1.9	-4.4	-8.0		-4.2
StL	57	96	2	.373	39	528	642	18	.237	.306	.312	618	-10	97	209	104	21	454	476	12.2	3.06	-4	.269	.335	-2.2	-2.3	-7.0		-7.9
Total	614					4824		159	.256	.325	.336	661			1674	676		3792	4863	11.8	2.93		.256	.325					

Batter-Fielder Wins		Batting Average		On-Base Percentage		Slugging Average		On-Base Plus Slugging		Adjusted OPS		Adjusted Batter Runs	
Collins-Phi	7.0	Cobb-Det	.390	Cobb-Det	.467	Jackson-Cle	.551	Jackson-Cle	1011	Cobb-Det	196	Jackson-Cle	63.4
Speaker-Bos	6.5	Speaker-Bos	.363	Speaker-Bos	.441	Speaker-Bos	.533	Speaker-Bos	974	Speaker-Bos	180	Speaker-Bos	53.6
Hooper-Bos	1.4	Lewis-Bos	.298	Engle-Bos	.363	Hooper-Bos	.399	Hooper-Bos	759	Hooper-Bos	119	Hooper-Bos	14.0
Lewis-Bos	1.1	Engle-Bos	.289	Hooper-Bos	.359	Lewis-Bos	.397	Engle-Bos	747	Engle-Bos	116	Engle-Bos	9.9

Runs		Hits		Doubles		Triples		Home Runs		Total Bases		Runs Batted In	
Collins-Phi	125	Jackson-Cle	197	Jackson-Cle	39	Crawford-Det	23	Baker-Phi	12	Crawford-Det	298	Baker-Phi	117
Hooper-Bos	100	Speaker-Bos	189	Speaker-Bos	35	Speaker-Bos	22	Hooper-Bos	4	Speaker-Bos	277	Lewis-Bos	90
Speaker-Bos	94	Hooper-Bos	169	Lewis-Bos	31	3 players tied	12	Speaker-Bos	3	Hooper-Bos	234	Speaker-Bos	71
Engle-Bos	75	Lewis-Bos	164	2 players tied	29			Janvrin-Bos	3	Lewis-Bos	219	Gardner-Bos	63

Stolen Bases		Base Stealing Runs		Fielding Runs-Infield		Fielding Runs-Outfield		Wins		Winning Pct.		Complete Games	
Milan-Was	75			Weaver-Chi	35.5	Speaker-Bos	18.6	Johnson-Was	36	Johnson-Was	.837	Johnson-Was	29
Speaker-Bos	46					Lewis-Bos	11.2	Collins-Bos	19	Collins-Bos	.704	Collins-Bos	19
Engle-Bos	28					Hooper-Bos	7.7	Bedient-Bos	15	Bedient-Bos	.517	Bedient-Bos	15
Hooper-Bos	26					Engle-Bos	1.2	Leonard-Bos	14			Leonard-Bos	14

Strikeouts		Fewest BB/Game		Games		Saves		Base Runners/9		Adjusted Relief Runs		Relief Ranking	
Johnson-Was	243	Johnson-Was	.99	Russell-Chi	52	Bender-Phi	13	Johnson-Was	7.26				
Leonard-Bos	144	Collins-Bos	1.35	Bedient-Bos	43	Bedient-Bos	5	Collins-Bos	10.25				
Wood-Bos	123	Bedient-Bos	2.33	Leonard-Bos	42	Wood-Bos	2	Bedient-Bos	11.40				
Bedient-Bos	122	Leonard-Bos	3.26	Hall-Bos	35	Hall-Bos	2	Moseley-Bos	11.49				

Innings Pitched		Opponents' Avg.		Opponents' OBP		Earned Run Average		Adjusted ERA		Adjusted Starter Runs		Pitcher Wins	
Johnson-Was	346.0	Johnson-Was	.190	Johnson-Was	.220	Johnson-Was	1.14	Johnson-Was	258	Johnson-Was	69.8	Johnson-Was	10.9
Leonard-Bos	259.1	Leonard-Bos	.255	Collins-Bos	.294	Wood-Bos	2.29	Leonard-Bos	123	Collins-Bos	12.5	Wood-Bos	1.8
Bedient-Bos	259.0	Bedient-Bos	.263	Bedient-Bos	.314	Leonard-Bos	2.39	Collins-Bos	112	Leonard-Bos	10.8	Collins-Bos	1.3
Collins-Bos	246.2	Collins-Bos	.264	Leonard-Bos	.324	Collins-Bos	2.63	Bedient-Bos	106	Wood-Bos	9.4	Leonard-Bos	1.2

1914 AMERICAN LEAGUE

TEAM	W	L	T	PCT	GB	R	OR	HR	AVG	OBP	SLG	OPS	AOPS	PF	SB	CG	HR	BB	SO	BR/9	ERA	AERA	OAV	OOB	FW	PW	BW	BSW	DIF
Phi	99	53	6	.651		749	529	29	.272	.348	.352	700	+23	96	231	89	18	521	720	11.6	2.78	-6	.249	.322	3.5	-3.2	15.7	-.0	7.1
Bos	91	62	6	.595	8.5	589	564	18	.250	.320	.338	658	+5	100	177	88	18	393	602	10.3	2.36	+14	.236	.295	1.8	5.6	3.1	-1.0	4.9
Was	81	73	4	.526	19	572	519	18	.244	.313	.320	633	-7	104	220	75	20	520	784	11.0	2.54	+11	.233	.311	1.0	4.4	-4.4	.6	2.4
Det	80	73	4	.523	19.5	615	618	25	.258	.336	.344	680	+9	103	211	81	17	498	567	11.8	2.86	-2	.249	.322	-1.1	-1.1	6.4	.8	-1.6
StL	71	82	6	.464	28.5	523	615	17	.243	.306	.319	625	-1	96	233	81	20	540	553	12.1	2.85	-5	.251	.327	-2.7	-2.5	-2.1	-.0	2.0
NY	70	84	3	.455	30	537	550	12	.229	.315	.287	602	-12	100	251	98	30	390	563	10.9	2.81	-2	.250	.308	1.9	-1.1	-6.3	.3	-1.7
Chi	70	84	3	.455	30	487	560	19	.239	.302	.311	613	-8	99	167	74	15	401	660	10.5	2.48	+8	.239	.298	-1.9	3.4	-6.1	-.2	-2.3
Cle	51	102	4	.333	48.5	538	709	10	.245	.310	.312	622	-10	104	167	69	10	666	688	13.4	3.21	-10	.267	.357	-1.9	-5.9	-6.6	-.4	-10.7
Total	631					4610		148	.248	.319	.323	642			1657	655		3929	5137	11.5	2.73		.248	.319					

Batter-Fielder Wins		Batting Average		On-Base Percentage		Slugging Average		On-Base Plus Slugging		Adjusted OPS		Adjusted Batter Runs	
Speaker-Bos	7.3	Cobb-Det	.368	Collins-Phi	.452	Cobb-Det	.513	Speaker-Bos	926	Collins-Phi	179	Collins-Phi	57.6
Carrigan-Bos	2.1	Speaker-Bos	.338	Speaker-Bos	.423	Speaker-Bos	.503	Lewis-Bos	755	Speaker-Bos	178	Speaker-Bos	56.7
Hooper-Bos	.9	Lewis-Bos	.278	Lewis-Bos	.357	Lewis-Bos	.398	Hooper-Bos	700	Lewis-Bos	127	Lewis-Bos	17.7
Cady-Bos	.4	Gardner-Bos	.259	Hooper-Bos	.336	Gardner-Bos	.385	Gardner-Bos	688	Hooper-Bos	110	Hoblitzel-Bos	9.7

Runs		Hits		Doubles		Triples		Home Runs		Total Bases		Runs Batted In	
Collins-Phi	122	Speaker-Bos	193	Speaker-Bos	46	Crawford-Det	26	Baker-Phi	9	Speaker-Bos	287	Crawford-Det	104
Speaker-Bos	101	Gardner-Bos	143	Lewis-Bos	37	Gardner-Bos	19	Speaker-Bos	4	Gardner-Bos	213	Speaker-Bos	90
Hooper-Bos	85	Lewis-Bos	142	Hooper-Bos	23	Speaker-Bos	18	Gardner-Bos	3	Lewis-Bos	203	Lewis-Bos	79
Scott-Bos	66	Hooper-Bos	137	Gardner-Bos	23	Hooper-Bos	15	2 players tied	2	Hooper-Bos	193	Gardner-Bos	68

Stolen Bases		Base Stealing Runs		Fielding Runs-Infield		Fielding Runs-Outfield		Wins		Winning Pct.		Complete Games	
Maisel-NY	74	Maisel-NY	10.3	Bush-Det	31.8	Speaker-Bos	23.0	Johnson-Was	28	Bender-Phi	.850	Johnson-Was	33
Speaker-Bos	42	Wood-Bos	.2			Hooper-Bos	9.9	Collins-Bos	20	Leonard-Bos	.792	Leonard-Bos	17
Janvrin-Bos	29	Thomas-Bos	.2					Leonard-Bos	19	Collins-Bos	.606	Foster-Bos	17
Lewis-Bos	22	Foster-Bos	.2					Foster-Bos	14			Collins-Bos	16

Strikeouts		Fewest BB/Game		Games		Saves		Base Runners/9		Adjusted Relief Runs		Relief Ranking	
Johnson-Was	225	McHale-NY	1.55	Johnson-Was	51	4 players tied	4	Leonard-Bos	8.29				
Leonard-Bos	176	Collins-Bos	1.85	Bedient-Bos	42	Leonard-Bos	3	Shore-Bos	9.15				
Foster-Bos	89	Foster-Bos	2.21	Collins-Bos	39	Bedient-Bos	2	Foster-Bos	9.48				
Collins-Bos	72	Bedient-Bos	2.28	Leonard-Bos	36	Shore-Bos	1	Wood-Bos	10.16				

Innings Pitched		Opponents' Avg.		Opponents' OBP		Earned Run Average		Adjusted ERA		Adjusted Starter Runs		Pitcher Wins	
Johnson-Was	371.2	Leonard-Bos	.180	Leonard-Bos	.246	Leonard-Bos	.96	Leonard-Bos	279	Johnson-Was	45.3	Johnson-Was	7.2
Collins-Bos	272.1	Foster-Bos	.218	Foster-Bos	.274	Foster-Bos	1.70	Foster-Bos	158	Leonard-Bos	43.3	Leonard-Bos	4.8
Leonard-Bos	224.2	Collins-Bos	.258	Collins-Bos	.298	Shore-Bos	2.00	Collins-Bos	107	Foster-Bos	18.5	Foster-Bos	2.0
Foster-Bos	211.2	Bedient-Bos	.281	Bedient-Bos	.331	Collins-Bos	2.51	Bedient-Bos	75	Shore-Bos	9.8	Shore-Bos	.9

179

1915 AMERICAN LEAGUE

TEAM	W	L	T	PCT	GB	R	OR	HR	AVG	OBP	SLG	OPS	AOPS	PF	SB	CG	HR	BB	SO	BR/9	ERA	AERA	OAV	OOB	FW	PW	BW	BSW	DIF
Bos	101	50	4	.669		669	499	14	.260	.336	.339	675	+10	97	118	81	18	446	634	10.7	2.39	+16	.231	.300	2.5	6.6	7.3	-.9	10.1
Det	100	54	2	.649	2.5	778	597	23	.268	.357	.358	715	+14	105	241	86	14	492	550	11.5	2.86	+6	.243	.316	.5	2.5	10.4	.9	8.7
Chi	93	61	1	.604	9.5	717	509	25	.258	.345	.348	693	+10	103	233	91	14	350	635	10.4	2.43	+22	.241	.294	2.7	8.8	6.6	-.7	-1.4
Was	85	68	2	.556	17	569	491	12	.244	.312	.312	624	-10	102	186	87	12	455	715	10.7	2.31	+29	.232	.302	2.2	10.7	-6.9	1.1	1.4
NY	69	83	2	.454	32.5	584	588	31	.233	.317	.305	622	-9	100	198	101	41	517	559	12.0	3.06	-4	.254	.329	2.9	-2.1	-4.7	.4	-3.5
StL	63	91	5	.409	39.5	522	680	19	.246	.315	.315	630	-2	96	202	76	21	612	566	12.4	3.04	-6	.249	.338	-4.3	-3.4	-2.4	-.6	-3.2
Cle	57	95	2	.375	44.5	539	670	20	.240	.312	.317	629	-9	102	138	62	18	518	610	12.0	3.13	-3	.256	.329	-1.2	-1.4	-5.8	-.5	-10.1
Phi	43	109	2	.283	58.5	545	889	16	.237	.304	.311	615	-8	97	127	78	22	827	588	15.0	4.29	-32	.278	.388	-5.0	-22.0	-5.9	.4	-.4
Total	621					4923		160	.248	.325	.326	651			1443	662		4217	4857	11.8	2.93		.248	.325					

Batter-Fielder Wins		Batting Average		On-Base Percentage		Slugging Average		On-Base Plus Slugging		Adjusted OPS		Adjusted Batter Runs	
E.Collins-Chi	6.6	Cobb-Det	.369	Cobb-Det	.486	Fournier-Chi	.491	Cobb-Det	973	Cobb-Det	182	Cobb-Det	66.6
Speaker-Bos	3.6	Speaker-Bos	.322	Speaker-Bos	.416	Speaker-Bos	.411	Speaker-Bos	827	Speaker-Bos	152	Speaker-Bos	39.2
Cady-Bos	1.2	Lewis-Bos	.291	Lewis-Bos	.348	Hoblitzel-Bos	.396	Lewis-Bos	731	Lewis-Bos	122	Ruth-Bos	15.6
Gainer-Bos	1.1	Hoblitzel-Bos	.283	Hooper-Bos	.342	Lewis-Bos	.382	Hooper-Bos	669	Hooper-Bos	103	Lewis-Bos	14.3

Runs		Hits		Doubles		Triples		Home Runs		Total Bases		Runs Batted In	
Cobb-Det	144	Cobb-Det	208	Veach-Det	40	Crawford-Det	19	Roth-Chi-Cle	7	Cobb-Det	274	Veach-Det	112
Speaker-Bos	108	Speaker-Bos	176	Lewis-Bos	31	Hooper-Det	13	Ruth-Bos	4	Speaker-Bos	225	Crawford-Det	112
Hooper-Bos	90	Lewis-Bos	162	Speaker-Bos	25	Speaker-Bos	12	3 players tied	2	Lewis-Bos	213	Lewis-Bos	76
Lewis-Bos	69	Hooper-Bos	133	Hooper-Bos	20	Hoblitzel-Bos	12			Hooper-Bos	185	Speaker-Bos	69

Stolen Bases		Base Stealing Runs		Fielding Runs-Infield		Fielding Runs-Outfield		Wins		Winning Pct.		Complete Games	
Cobb-Det	96	Cobb-Det	7.8	Boone-NY	20.5	Strunk-Phi	11.1	Johnson-Was	27	Wood-Bos	.750	Johnson-Was	35
Speaker-Bos	29	Gainer-Bos	.8			Hooper-Bos	8.7	Shore-Bos	19	Shore-Bos	.704	Foster-Bos	21
Hooper-Bos	22	Lewis-Bos	.6			Speaker-Bos	7.8	Foster-Bos	19	Foster-Bos	.704	Shore-Bos	17
Lewis-Bos	14	Wagner-Bos	.4					Ruth-Bos	18	Ruth-Bos	.692	Ruth-Bos	16

Strikeouts		Fewest BB/Game		Games		Saves		Base Runners/9		Adjusted Relief Runs		Relief Ranking	
Johnson-Was	203	Johnson-Was	1.50	Faber-Chi	50	Mays-Bos	7	Johnson-Was	8.90				
Leonard-Bos	116	Shore-Bos	2.40	Coveleski-Det	50	Gregg-Bos	3	Wood-Bos	9.44				
Ruth-Bos	112	Wood-Bos	2.52	Shore-Bos	38	Wood-Bos	2	Mays-Bos	9.91				
Shore-Bos	102	Foster-Bos	3.03	Mays-Bos	38	Collins-Bos	2	Shore-Bos	10.09				

Innings Pitched		Opponents' Avg.		Opponents' OBP		Earned Run Average		Adjusted ERA		Adjusted Starter Runs		Pitcher Wins	
Johnson-Was	336.2	Leonard-Bos	.208	Johnson-Was	.260	Wood-Bos	1.49	Johnson-Was	191	Johnson-Was	51.1	Johnson-Was	7.4
Foster-Bos	255.1	Ruth-Bos	.212	Wood-Bos	.275	Shore-Bos	1.64	Wood-Bos	186	Shore-Bos	27.2	Wood-Bos	3.9
Shore-Bos	247.0	Wood-Bos	.216	Shore-Bos	.283	Foster-Bos	2.11	Shore-Bos	169	Wood-Bos	24.9	Foster-Bos	2.9
Ruth-Bos	217.2	Shore-Bos	.228	Ruth-Bos	.294	Leonard-Bos	2.36	Foster-Bos	131	Foster-Bos	18.8	2 players tied	2.8

1916 AMERICAN LEAGUE

TEAM	W	L	T	PCT	GB	R	OR	HR	AVG	OBP	SLG	OPS	AOPS	PF	SB	CG	HR	BB	SO	BR/9	ERA	AERA	OAV	OOB	FW	PW	BW	BSW	DIF
Bos	91	63	2	.591		550	480	14	.248	.317	.318	635	-3	100	129	76	10	463	584	11.0	2.48	+12	.239	.307	3.0	5.0	-2.4		8.4
Chi	89	65	1	.578	2	601	497	17	.251	.319	.339	658	+3	101	197	73	14	405	644	10.3	2.36	+17	.236	.296	1.5	7.0	1.0		2.5
Det	87	67	4	.565	4	670	595	17	.264	.337	.350	687	+9	104	190	81	12	578	531	12.1	2.97	-4	.248	.333	1.1	-2.0	6.2		4.6
NY	80	74	2	.519	11	577	561	35	.246	.318	.326	644	-2	102	179	84	37	476	616	11.2	2.77	+4	.244	.314	.7	1.9	-1.8		2.2
StL	79	75	4	.513	12	588	545	14	.245	.331	.307	638	+3	95	234	74	15	478	505	11.3	2.58	+6	.248	.316	-.9	3.0	3.9		-3.9
Cle	77	77	3	.500	14	630	602	16	.250	.324	.331	655	-3	106	160	65	16	467	537	12.0	2.90	+3	.264	.328	.0	1.7	-1.3		-.3
Was	76	77	6	.497	14.5	536	543	12	.242	.320	.306	626	-5	99	185	85	14	490	706	11.3	2.67	+4	.244	.314	.2	2.0	-2.7		-.0
Phi	36	117	1	.235	54.5	447	776	19	.242	.303	.313	616	-9	95	151	94	26	715	575	13.8	3.92	-27	.267	.364	-5.5	-17.6	-4.4		-13.0
Total	625					4599		144	.248	.321	.324	645			1425	632		4072	4698	11.6	2.82		.248	.321					

Batter-Fielder Wins		Batting Average		On-Base Percentage		Slugging Average		On-Base Plus Slugging		Adjusted OPS		Adjusted Batter Runs	
Speaker-Cle	5.7	Speaker-Cle	.386	Speaker-Cle	.470	Speaker-Cle	.502	Speaker-Cle	972	Speaker-Cle	181	Speaker-Cle	59.5
Hooper-Bos	1.1	Gardner-Bos	.308	Gardner-Bos	.372	Walker-Bos	.394	Gardner-Bos	759	Gardner-Bos	128	Gardner-Bos	16.5
Thomas-Bos	1.1	Hooper-Bos	.271	Hooper-Bos	.361	Gardner-Bos	.387	Hooper-Bos	711	Hooper-Bos	113	Ruth-Bos	13.1
2 players tied	.9	Lewis-Bos	.268	Hoblitzel-Bos	.338	Hooper-Bos	.350	Walker-Bos	697	Walker-Bos	109	Hooper-Bos	11.0

Runs		Hits		Doubles		Triples		Home Runs		Total Bases		Runs Batted In	
Cobb-Det	113	Speaker-Cle	211	Speaker-Cle	41	Jackson-Chi	21	Pipp-NY	12	Jackson-Chi	293	Pratt-StL	103
Hooper-Bos	75	Hooper-Bos	156	Graney-Cle	41	Walker-Bos	11	Walker-Bos	3	Hooper-Bos	201	Gardner-Bos	62
Walker-Bos	68	Gardner-Bos	152	Walker-Bos	29	Hooper-Bos	11	Ruth-Bos	3	Lewis-Bos	193	Lewis-Bos	56
Hoblitzel-Bos	57	Lewis-Bos	151	Lewis-Bos	29	Gardner-Bos	7	Gainer-Bos	3	Gardner-Bos	191	Walker-Bos	46

Stolen Bases		Base Stealing Runs		Fielding Runs-Infield		Fielding Runs-Outfield		Wins		Winning Pct.		Complete Games	
Cobb-Det	68	Cobb-Det	6.6	Lajoie-Phi	26.7	Milan-Was	14.1	Johnson-Was	25	Cicotte-Chi	.682	Johnson-Was	36
Hooper-Bos	27	Hooper-Bos	2.1	Scott-Bos	5.3	Hooper-Bos	5.2	Ruth-Bos	23	Ruth-Bos	.657	Ruth-Bos	23
Lewis-Bos	16							Mays-Bos	18	Shore-Bos	.615	Leonard-Bos	17
Walker-Bos	14							Leonard-Bos	18	Leonard-Bos	.600	Mays-Bos	14

Strikeouts		Fewest BB/Game		Games		Saves		Base Runners/9		Adjusted Relief Runs		Relief Ranking	
Johnson-Was	228	Russell-Chi	1.43	Davenport-StL	59	Shawkey-NY	8	Russell-Chi	8.51				
Ruth-Bos	170	Shore-Bos	1.95	Leonard-Bos	48	Leonard-Bos	6	Ruth-Bos	9.90				
Leonard-Bos	144	Leonard-Bos	2.17	Ruth-Bos	44	Mays-Bos	3	Leonard-Bos	10.45				
Mays-Bos	76	Mays-Bos	2.72	Mays-Bos	44	Foster-Bos	2	Mays-Bos	10.69				

Innings Pitched		Opponents' Avg.		Opponents' OBP		Earned Run Average		Adjusted ERA		Adjusted Starter Runs		Pitcher Wins	
Johnson-Was	369.2	Ruth-Bos	.201	Russell-Chi	.254	Ruth-Bos	1.75	Ruth-Bos	158	Ruth-Bos	35.1	Ruth-Bos	5.7
Ruth-Bos	323.2	Mays-Bos	.234	Ruth-Bos	.280	Leonard-Bos	2.36	Leonard-Bos	117	Leonard-Bos	13.3	Mays-Bos	2.8
Leonard-Bos	274.0	Leonard-Bos	.247	Mays-Bos	.299	Mays-Bos	2.39	Mays-Bos	116	Mays-Bos	11.1	Leonard-Bos	1.4
Mays-Bos	245.0	Shore-Bos	.259	Leonard-Bos	.300	Shore-Bos	2.63	Shore-Bos	105	Shore-Bos	2.8	Shore-Bos	.0

1917 AMERICAN LEAGUE

TEAM	W	L	T	PCT	GB	R	OR	HR	AVG	OBP	SLG	OPS	AOPS	PF	SB	CG	HR	BB	SO	BR/9	ERA	AERA	OAV	OOB	FW	PW	BW	BSW	DIF
Chi	100	54	2	.649		655	463	18	.253	.329	.326	655	+3	102	219	78	10	413	517	10.6	2.16	+23	.238	.298	2.3	8.5	2.4		9.8
Bos	90	62	5	.592	9	555	455	14	.246	.314	.319	633	+0	99	105	115	12	413	509	10.5	2.20	+17	.231	.295	3.9	6.9	-.3		3.5
Cle	88	66	2	.571	12	584	543	13	.245	.324	.322	646	-4	107	210	73	17	438	451	11.1	2.52	+12	.247	.310	-.5	5.0	-1.8		8.3
Det	78	75	1	.510	21.5	639	577	25	.259	.328	.344	672	+11	100	163	78	12	504	516	11.4	2.56	+3	.240	.316	-.1	1.4	7.2		-7.1
Was	74	79	4	.484	25.5	544	566	4	.241	.313	.304	617	-5	99	166	84	12	537	637	11.4	2.75	-5	.239	.316	-1.0	-2.2	-3.1		3.9
NY	71	82	2	.464	28.5	524	558	27	.239	.310	.308	618	-7	101	136	87	28	427	571	11.1	2.66	+1	.252	.314	.6	.3	-4.3		-2.1
StL	57	97	1	.370	43	510	687	15	.246	.305	.315	620	-2	96	157	66	19	537	429	12.3	3.20	-19	.257	.332	-3.4	-11.0	-2.2		-3.3
Phi	55	98	1	.359	44.5	529	691	17	.254	.316	.323	639	+1	99	112	80	23	562	516	12.5	3.27	-16	.261	.338	-1.4	-8.6	.7		-12.3
Total	622					4540		133	.248	.318	.320	638			1268	661		3831	4146	11.4	2.66		.248	.318					

Batter-Fielder Wins	Batting Average	On-Base Percentage	Slugging Average	On-Base Plus Slugging	Adjusted OPS	Adjusted Batter Runs
Cobb-Det 7.4	Cobb-Det .383	Cobb-Det .444	Cobb-Det .570	Cobb-Det 1014	Cobb-Det 210	Cobb-Det 75.9
Lewis-Bos 1.4	Lewis-Bos .302	Hooper-Bos .355	Lewis-Bos .392	Lewis-Bos 735	Lewis-Bos 125	Ruth-Bos 16.7
Thomas-Bos .9	Gardner-Bos .265	Lewis-Bos .342	Walker-Bos .359	Hooper-Bos 704	Hooper-Bos 116	Lewis-Bos 14.4
Gainer-Bos .8	Hoblitzel-Bos .257	Gardner-Bos .341	Hooper-Bos .349	Gardner-Bos 686	Gardner-Bos 110	Hooper-Bos 13.0

Runs	Hits	Doubles	Triples	Home Runs	Total Bases	Runs Batted In
Bush-Det 112	Cobb-Det 225	Cobb-Det 44	Cobb-Det 24	Pipp-NY 9	Cobb-Det 335	Veach-Det 103
Hooper-Bos 89	Lewis-Bos 167	Lewis-Bos 29	Hooper-Bos 11	Hooper-Bos 3	Lewis-Bos 217	Lewis-Bos 65
Lewis-Bos 55	Hooper-Bos 143	Scott-Bos 24	Lewis-Bos 9	4 players tied 2	Hooper-Bos 195	Gardner-Bos 61
Gardner-Bos 53	Gardner-Bos 133	Gardner-Bos 23			Gardner-Bos 173	Scott-Bos 50

Stolen Bases	Base Stealing Runs	Fielding Runs-Infield	Fielding Runs-Outfield	Wins	Winning Pct.	Complete Games
Cobb-Det 55		Chapman-Cle 23.6	Felsch-Chi 14.6	Cicotte-Chi 28	Russell-Chi .750	Ruth-Bos 35
Hooper-Bos 21		Scott-Bos 8.4	Lewis-Bos 4.9	Ruth-Bos 24	Mays-Bos .710	Mays-Bos 27
Gardner-Bos 16			Walker-Bos 3.8	Mays-Bos 22	Ruth-Bos .649	Leonard-Bos 26
3 players tied 12				Leonard-Bos 16	Leonard-Bos .485	Shore-Bos 14

Strikeouts	Fewest BB/Game	Games	Saves	Base Runners/9	Adjusted Relief Runs	Relief Ranking
Johnson-Was 188	Russell-Chi 1.52	Danforth-Chi 50	Danforth-Chi 9	Cicotte-Chi 8.28		
Leonard-Bos 144	Shore-Bos 2.18	Ruth-Bos 41	Ruth-Bos 2	Mays-Bos 9.90		
Ruth-Bos 128	Leonard-Bos 2.20	Leonard-Bos 37		Ruth-Bos 10.01		
Mays-Bos 91	Mays-Bos 2.30	Mays-Bos 35		Leonard-Bos 10.21		

Innings Pitched	Opponents' Avg.	Opponents' OBP	Earned Run Average	Adjusted ERA	Adjusted Starter Runs	Pitcher Wins
Cicotte-Chi 346.2	Coveleski-Cle .194	Cicotte-Chi .248	Cicotte-Chi 1.53	Cicotte-Chi 173	Cicotte-Chi 44.8	Cicotte-Chi 5.7
Ruth-Bos 326.1	Ruth-Bos .211	Mays-Bos .282	Mays-Bos 1.74	Mays-Bos 148	Mays-Bos 24.7	Ruth-Bos 4.9
Leonard-Bos 294.1	Mays-Bos .221	Ruth-Bos .284	Ruth-Bos 2.01	Ruth-Bos 128	Ruth-Bos 22.2	Mays-Bos 4.0
Mays-Bos 289.0	Leonard-Bos .236	Leonard-Bos .286	Leonard-Bos 2.17	Leonard-Bos 119	Leonard-Bos 15.8	2 players tied .8

1918 AMERICAN LEAGUE

TEAM	W	L	T	PCT	GB	R	OR	HR	AVG	OBP	SLG	OPS	AOPS	PF	SB	CG	HR	BB	SO	BR/9	ERA	AERA	OAV	OOB	FW	PW	BW	BSW	DIF
Bos	75	51	0	.595		474	380	15	.249	.322	.327	649	+3	98	110	105	9	380	392	10.8	2.31	+16	.231	.302	2.5	5.5	1.7		2.4
Cle	73	54	2	.575	2.5	504	447	9	.260	.344	.341	685	+2	98	171	78	9	343	364	11.5	2.64	+14	.262	.319	-.7	4.7	2.6		2.9
Was	72	56	2	.563	4	461	412	4	.256	.318	.315	633	-2	98	137	75	10	395	505	10.6	2.14	+27	.231	.298	-1.8	9.0	-1.6		2.3
NY	60	63	3	.488	13.5	493	475	20	.257	.320	.330	650	-1	102	92	59	25	463	370	12.5	3.00	-6	.261	.340	1.9	-2.6	-.9		.0
StL	58	64	1	.475	15	426	448	5	.259	.331	.320	651	+5	97	119	67	11	402	346	11.5	2.75	-1	.246	.319	-.2	-.2	3.1		-5.7
Chi	57	67	0	.460	17	457	446	8	.256	.322	.321	643	-5	101	119	76	9	300	349	11.3	2.73	+0	.261	.314	1.2	-.3	-1.2		-4.7
Det	55	71	2	.437	20	476	538	13	.249	.325	.318	643	+4	96	123	74	10	437	374	12.4	3.40	-22	.263	.335	-1.1	-11.6	2.0		2.7
Phi	52	76	2	.406	24	412	538	22	.243	.303	.308	611	-12	101	83	80	13	486	277	12.7	3.22	-9	.266	.348	-1.9	-4.1	-7.4		1.4
Total	508					3703		96	.254	.323	.322	646			974	614		3206	2977	11.7	2.77		.254	.323					

Batter-Fielder Wins	Batting Average	On-Base Percentage	Slugging Average	On-Base Plus Slugging	Adjusted OPS	Adjusted Batter Runs
T.Cobb-Det 4.3	T.Cobb-Det .382	T.Cobb-Det .440	Ruth-Bos .555	T.Cobb-Det 955	T.Cobb-Det 196	T.Cobb-Det 47.7
Ruth-Bos 2.7	Ruth-Bos .300	Hooper-Bos .391	Hooper-Bos .405	Hooper-Bos 796	Hooper-Bos 142	Ruth-Bos 37.5
Hooper-Bos 2.2	Hooper-Bos .289	Shean-Bos .331	Strunk-Bos .344	Strunk-Bos 660	Strunk-Bos 101	Hooper-Bos 27.3
Thomas-Bos .3	McInnis-Bos .272	Strunk-Bos .316	McInnis-Bos .322	Shean-Bos 646	Shean-Bos 97	Mays-Bos 9.3

Runs	Hits	Doubles	Triples	Home Runs	Total Bases	Runs Batted In
Chapman-Cle 84	Burns-Phi 178	Speaker-Cle 33	T.Cobb-Det 14	Walker-Phi 11	Burns-Phi 236	Veach-Det 78
Hooper-Bos 81	Hooper-Bos 137	Ruth-Bos 26	Hooper-Bos 13	Ruth-Bos 11	Hooper-Bos 192	Ruth-Bos 66
Shean-Bos 58	McInnis-Bos 115	Hooper-Bos 26	Ruth-Bos 11	3 players tied 1	Ruth-Bos 176	McInnis-Bos 56
2 players tied 50	Shean-Bos 112	Strunk-Bos 18	Strunk-Bos 9		Strunk-Bos 142	Hooper-Bos 44

Stolen Bases	Base Stealing Runs	Fielding Runs-Infield	Fielding Runs-Outfield	Wins	Winning Pct.	Complete Games
Sisler-StL 45		Peckinpaugh-NY 22.1	S.Collins-Chi 11.9	Johnson-Was 23	Jones-Bos .762	Perry-Phi 30
Hooper-Bos 24		Scott-Bos 20.8		Mays-Bos 21	Mays-Bos .618	Mays-Bos 30
Strunk-Bos 20		McInnis-Bos 5.4		Jones-Bos 16	Bush-Bos .500	Bush-Bos 26
2 players tied 11				Bush-Bos 15		Ruth-Bos 18

Strikeouts	Fewest BB/Game	Games	Saves	Base Runners/9	Adjusted Relief Runs	Relief Ranking
Johnson-Was 162	Cicotte-Chi 1.35	Mogridge-NY 45	Mogridge-NY 7	Johnson-Was 8.81	Houck-StL 3.2	Houck-StL 2.6
Bush-Bos 125	Mays-Bos 2.49	Bagby-Cle 45	Bush-Bos 2	Ruth-Bos 9.52		
Mays-Bos 114	Ruth-Bos 2.65	Bush-Bos 36		Mays-Bos 9.88		
Leonard-Bos 47	Bush-Bos 3.00	Mays-Bos 35		Bush-Bos 11.06		

Innings Pitched	Opponents' Avg.	Opponents' OBP	Earned Run Average	Adjusted ERA	Adjusted Starter Runs	Pitcher Wins
Perry-Phi 332.1	Sothoron-StL .205	Johnson-Was .260	Johnson-Was 1.27	Johnson-Was 214	Johnson-Was 51.4	Johnson-Was 7.6
Mays-Bos 293.1	Ruth-Bos .214	Ruth-Bos .277	Bush-Bos 2.11	Bush-Bos 127	Bush-Bos 16.5	Mays-Bos 3.7
Bush-Bos 272.2	Mays-Bos .221	Mays-Bos .284	Mays-Bos 2.21	Mays-Bos 121	Mays-Bos 16.3	Ruth-Bos 2.9
Jones-Bos 184.0	Jones-Bos .230	Bush-Bos .307	Ruth-Bos 2.22	Ruth-Bos 121	Ruth-Bos 10.1	Bush-Bos 2.8

1919 AMERICAN LEAGUE

TEAM	W	L	T	PCT	GB	R	OR	HR	AVG	OBP	SLG	OPS	AOPS	PF	SB	CG	HR	BB	SO	BR/9	ERA	AERA	OAV	OOB	FW	PW	BW	BSW	DIF
Chi	88	52	0	.629		667	534	25	.287	.351	.380	731	+11	100	150	88	24	342	468	11.5	3.04	+5	.262	.315	1.6	2.0	7.1		7.2
Cle	84	55	0	.604	3.5	636	537	24	.278	.354	.381	735	+7	106	117	79	19	362	432	11.8	2.94	+14	.264	.321	-.0	5.3	4.7		4.5
NY	80	59	2	.576	7.5	578	506	45	.267	.326	.356	682	-4	101	101	85	47	433	500	11.3	2.82	+13	.240	.309	.7	5.7	-2.6		6.8
Det	80	60	0	.571	8	618	578	23	.283	.346	.381	727	+13	98	121	85	35	436	428	12.4	3.30	-3	.266	.333	-.2	-1.5	8.0		3.7
StL	67	72	1	.482	20.5	533	567	31	.264	.335	.355	681	-5	103	74	78	35	421	415	12.3	3.13	+6	.263	.328	-.8	2.4	-3.9		-.2
Bos	66	71	1	.482	20.5	564	552	33	.261	.336	.344	680	+3	94	108	89	16	421	381	12.5	3.31	-9	.275	.341	3.8	-4.6	2.6		-4.3
Was	56	84	2	.400	32	533	570	24	.260	.325	.339	664	-7	99	142	68	20	451	536	12.3	3.01	+6	.259	.328	-1.4	2.9	-4.6		-10.9
Phi	36	104	0	.257	52	457	742	35	.244	.300	.334	634	-18	-101	103	72	44	503	417	13.8	4.26	-20	.292	.364	-3.5	-11.6	-12.4		-6.5
Total	560					4586		240	.268	.333	.359	692			916	644		3369	3577	12.2	3.22		.268	.333					

Batter-Fielder Wins		Batting Average		On-Base Percentage		Slugging Average		On-Base Plus Slugging		Adjusted OPS		Adjusted Batter Runs	
Ruth-Bos	7.3	Cobb-Det	.384	Ruth-Bos	.456	Ruth-Bos	.657	Ruth-Bos	1114	Ruth-Bos	224	Ruth-Bos	76.3
Schang-Bos	3.1	Ruth-Bos	.322	Hooper-Bos	.374	Schang-Bos	.373	Hooper-Bos	734	Hooper-Bos	113	Schang-Bos	22.7
Hooper-Bos	1.2	Schang-Bos	.306	McInnis-Bos	.341	McInnis-Bos	.361	McInnis-Bos	702	McInnis-Bos	103	Hooper-Bos	12.7
McNally-Bos	.5	McInnis-Bos	.305	Vitt-Bos	.309	Hooper-Bos	.360	Scott-Bos	621	Scott-Bos	79	Wilhoit-Bos	1.5

Runs		Hits		Doubles		Triples		Home Runs		Total Bases		Runs Batted In	
Ruth-Bos	103	Veach-Det	191	Veach-Det	45	Veach-Det	17	Ruth-Bos	29	Ruth-Bos	284	Ruth-Bos	114
Hooper-Bos	76	Cobb-Det	191	Ruth-Bos	34	Ruth-Bos	12	Hooper-Bos	3	Hooper-Bos	177	McInnis-Bos	58
Vitt-Bos	64	Scott-Bos	141	Hooper-Bos	25	Hooper-Bos	6	McInnis-Bos	1	Scott-Bos	160	Schang-Bos	55
Schang-Bos	43	Ruth-Bos	139	Scott-Bos	19	McInnis-Bos	5			McInnis-Bos	159	Hooper-Bos	49

Stolen Bases		Base Stealing Runs		Fielding Runs-Infield		Fielding Runs-Outfield		Wins		Winning Pct.		Complete Games	
E.Collins-Chi	33			Peckinpaugh-NY	25.5	Felsch-Chi	17.4	Cicotte-Chi	29	Cicotte-Chi	.806	Cicotte-Chi	30
Hooper-Bos	23			Vitt-Bos	17.9	Ruth-Bos	9.3	Pennock-Bos	16	Pennock-Bos	.667	Jones-Bos	21
Schang-Bos	15			Scott-Bos	10.5	Hooper-Bos	6.1	Jones-Bos	12			Pennock-Bos	16
Vitt-Bos	9			McInnis-Bos	2.8			Ruth-Bos	9			Ruth-Bos	12

Strikeouts		Fewest BB/Game		Games		Saves		Base Runners/9		Adjusted Relief Runs		Relief Ranking	
Johnson-Was	147	Cicotte-Chi	1.44	Shaw-Was	45	3 players tied	5	Cicotte-Chi	9.01	Phillips-Cle	1.1	Phillips-Cle	.9
Pennock-Bos	70	Pennock-Bos	1.97	Jones-Bos	35	Ruth-Bos	1	Hoyt-Bos	10.34				
Jones-Bos	67	Jones-Bos	3.49	Pennock-Bos	32	Jones-Bos	1	Pennock-Bos	11.26				
Ruth-Bos	30			Ruth-Bos	17			Jones-Bos	13.22				

Innings Pitched		Opponents' Avg.		Opponents' OBP		Earned Run Average		Adjusted ERA		Adjusted Starter Runs		Pitcher Wins	
Shaw-Was	306.2	Johnson-Was	.219	Johnson-Was	.259	Johnson-Was	1.49	Johnson-Was	215	Johnson-Was	52.4	Johnson-Was	6.7
Cicotte-Chi	306.2	Pennock-Bos	.274	Pennock-Bos	.316	Pennock-Bos	2.71	Pennock-Bos	111	Pennock-Bos	9.2	Ruth-Bos	1.4
Jones-Bos	245.0	Jones-Bos	.278	Jones-Bos	.350	Ruth-Bos	2.97	Jones-Bos	81			Pennock-Bos	1.0
Pennock-Bos	219.0					Jones-Bos	3.75						

1920 AMERICAN LEAGUE

TEAM	W	L	T	PCT	GB	R	OR	HR	AVG	OBP	SLG	OPS	AOPS	PF	SB	CG	HR	BB	SO	BR/9	ERA	AERA	OAV	OOB	FW	PW	BW	BSW	DIF
Cle	98	56	0	.636		857	642	35	.303	.376	.417	793	+13	103	73	94	31	401	466	12.3	3.41	+11	.276	.331	2.1	5.6	10.1	-.5	3.7
Chi	96	58	0	.623	2	794	665	37	.295	.357	.402	759	+7	100	109	45	405	438	12.3	3.59	+5	.280	.335	1.2	2.3	4.8	.0	10.7
NY	95	59	0	.617	3	838	629	115	.280	.350	.426	776	+7	104	64	88	48	420	480	12.3	3.32	+15	.270	.328	1.4	7.3	4.6	-.4	5.2
StL	76	77	1	.497	21.5	797	766	50	.308	.363	.419	782	+10	103	121	84	53	578	444	13.7	4.03	-3	.283	.359	-1.2	-2.1	6.8	.9	-4.8
Bos	72	81	1	.471	25.5	650	698	22	.269	.342	.350	692	-7	96	98	92	39	461	481	12.7	3.82	-5	.279	.339	2.2	-3.0	-4.0	-.6	-.9
Was	68	84	1	.447	29	723	802	36	.291	.351	.386	737	+4	97	160	81	51	520	418	13.7	4.17	-11	.288	.357	-1.3	-6.9	2.4	.5	-2.8
Det	61	93	1	.396	37	652	833	30	.270	.334	.359	693	-9	98	76	74	46	561	483	13.7	4.04	-8	.284	.359	-.9	-5.0	-6.3	.3	-4.0
Phi	48	106	2	.312	50	558	834	44	.252	.305	.338	643	-26	-101	50	79	56	461	423	13.8	3.93	+2	.302	.362	-3.3	1.1	-19.1	-.2	-7.5
Total	617					5869		369	.284	.347	.387	735			751	701		3807	3633	13.1	3.79		.284	.347					

Batter-Fielder Wins		Batting Average		On-Base Percentage		Slugging Average		On-Base Plus Slugging		Adjusted OPS		Adjusted Batter Runs	
Ruth-NY	9.3	Sisler-StL	.407	Ruth-NY	.532	Ruth-NY	.847	Ruth-NY	1379	Ruth-NY	252	Ruth-NY	110.5
Hooper-Bos	2.7	Hendryx-Bos	.328	Hooper-Bos	.411	Hooper-Bos	.470	Hooper-Bos	881	Hooper-Bos	139	Hooper-Bos	32.9
Schang-Bos	1.8	Hooper-Bos	.312	Menosky-Bos	.383	Schang-Bos	.450	Menosky-Bos	776	Menosky-Bos	110	Schang-Bos	23.1
Foster-Bos	.2	Schang-Bos	.305	McInnis-Bos	.321	Hendryx-Bos	.413	McInnis-Bos	677	McInnis-Bos	83	Hendryx-Bos	13.0

Runs		Hits		Doubles		Triples		Home Runs		Total Bases		Runs Batted In	
Ruth-NY	158	Sisler-StL	257	Speaker-Cle	50	Jackson-Chi	20	Ruth-NY	54	Sisler-StL	399	Ruth-NY	137
Hooper-Bos	91	Hooper-Bos	167	Schang-Bos	30	Hooper-Bos	17	Hooper-Bos	7	Hooper-Bos	252	Hendryx-Bos	73
Menosky-Bos	80	McInnis-Bos	166	Hooper-Bos	30	Scott-Bos	12	Scott-Bos	4	Scott-Bos	210	McInnis-Bos	71
Schang-Bos	58	Menosky-Bos	158	Menosky-Bos	24	Menosky-Bos	9	Schang-Bos	4	Menosky-Bos	209	Menosky-Bos	64

Stolen Bases		Base Stealing Runs		Fielding Runs-Infield		Fielding Runs-Outfield		Wins		Winning Pct.		Complete Games	
Rice-Was	63	Rice-Was	3.4	Ward-NY	16.5	Rice-Was	17.0	Bagby-Cle	31	Bagby-Cle	.721	Bagby-Cle	30
Menosky-Bos	23	Foster-Bos	.8	Scott-Bos	14.1	Hooper-Bos	5.3	Pennock-Bos	16	Pennock-Bos	.552	Jones-Bos	21
Hooper-Bos	16	Paschal-Bos	.2	Foster-Bos	8.5			Bush-Bos	15	Bush-Bos	.500	Pennock-Bos	19
McNally-Bos	13	Devine-Bos	.2					Jones-Bos	13			Bush-Bos	18

Strikeouts		Fewest BB/Game		Games		Saves		Base Runners/9		Adjusted Relief Runs		Relief Ranking	
Coveleski-Cle	133	Quinn-NY	1.71	Bagby-Cle	48	Shocker-StL	5	Coveleski-Cle	10.09				
Bush-Bos	88	Pennock-Bos	2.27	Pennock-Bos	37	Kerr-Chi	5	Pennock-Bos	11.48				
Jones-Bos	86	Jones-Bos	2.59	Jones-Bos	37	Pennock-Bos	2	Russell-Bos	11.79				
Harper-Bos	71	Bush-Bos	3.47	Bush-Bos	35	4 players tied	1	Jones-Bos	12.65				

Innings Pitched		Opponents' Avg.		Opponents' OBP		Earned Run Average		Adjusted ERA		Adjusted Starter Runs		Pitcher Wins	
Bagby-Cle	339.2	Coveleski-Cle	.243	Coveleski-Cle	.285	Shawkey-NY	2.45	Shawkey-NY	155	Coveleski-Cle	44.4	Coveleski-Cle	5.5
Jones-Bos	274.0	Pennock-Bos	.264	Pennock-Bos	.312	Harper-Bos	3.04	Harper-Bos	119	Harper-Bos	7.6	Pennock-Bos	.6
Bush-Bos	243.2	Harper-Bos	.275	Jones-Bos	.340	Jones-Bos	3.68	Jones-Bos	99	Russell-Bos	7.1	Russell-Bos	.5
Pennock-Bos	242.1	Jones-Bos	.288	Harper-Bos	.349	Jones-Bos	3.94	Jones-Bos	92	Pennock-Bos	2.7	Harper-Bos	.4

1921 AMERICAN LEAGUE

TEAM	W	L	T	PCT	GB	R	OR	HR	AVG	OBP	SLG	OPS	AOPS	PF	SB	CG	HR	BB	SO	BR/9	ERA	AERA	OAV	OOB	FW	PW	BW	BSW	DIF
NY	98	55	0	.641		**948**	708	**134**	.300	.375	**.464**	**839**	+16	102	89	**92**	51	470	**481**	13.1	**3.82**	+11	**.277**	**.342**	-.3	**5.9**	11.8	.2	3.9
Cle	94	60	0	.610	4.5	925	712	42	.308	.383	.430	813	+11	102	51	81	**43**	**431**	475	**13.0**	3.90	+9	.288	.344	.8	5.1	10.0	.2	.8
StL	81	73	0	.526	17.5	835	845	67	.304	.357	.425	782	-2	106	91	77	71	556	477	13.9	4.61	-3	.288	.360	-.3	-2.0	-2.0	.0	8.2
Was	80	73	1	.523	18	704	738	42	.277	.342	.383	725	-5	95	**112**	80	51	442	452	13.3	3.97	+4	.291	.349	-.9	2.2	-4.5	**.7**	6.1
Bos	75	79	0	.487	23.5	668	**696**	17	.277	.335	.361	696	-16	-97	83	88	53	452	446	13.3	3.98	+6	.291	.352	**3.5**	3.6	-10.9	.1	1.8
Det	71	82	1	.464	27	883	852	58	**.316**	**.385**	.433	818	+15	99	95	73	71	495	452	14.2	4.40	-3	.297	.361	-.8	-1.9	**12.2**	-.5	-14.6
Chi	62	92	0	.403	36.5	683	858	35	.283	.343	.379	722	-10	99	94	84	52	549	392	14.4	4.94	-14	.303	.372	1.0	-10.2	-7.4	-.6	2.2
Phi	53	100	2	.346	45	657	894	82	.274	.331	.389	720	-12	-101	69	75	85	548	431	14.3	4.61	-3	.300	.367	-3.1	-2.2	-9.9	.1	-8.4
Total	616					6303		477	.292	.357	.408	765			684	650		3943	3606	13.7	4.28		.292	.357					

Batter-Fielder Wins		Batting Average		On-Base Percentage		Slugging Average		On-Base Plus Slugging		Adjusted OPS		Adjusted Batter Runs	
Ruth-NY	**9.4**	Heilmann-Det	.394	Ruth-NY	.512	Ruth-NY	.846	Ruth-NY	1359	Ruth-NY	236	Ruth-NY	117.7
Scott-Bos	**1.9**	Pratt-Bos	.324	Menosky-Bos	.388	Pratt-Bos	.461	Pratt-Bos	839	Pratt-Bos	116	Pratt-Bos	12.4
Pratt-Bos	**1.4**	McInnis-Bos	.307	Pratt-Bos	.378	Collins-Bos	.406	Menosky-Bos	766	Menosky-Bos	99	Jones-Bos	5.1
		Leibold-Bos	.306	Foster-Bos	.371	McInnis-Bos	.394	Leibold-Bos	751	Leibold-Bos	94	Pennock-Bos	2.6

Runs		Hits		Doubles		Triples		Home Runs		Total Bases		Runs Batted In	
Ruth-NY	177	Heilmann-Det	237	Speaker-Cle	52	3 players tied	18	Ruth-NY	59	Ruth-NY	457	Ruth-NY	171
Leibold-Bos	88	McInnis-Bos	179	Pratt-Bos	36	Collins-Bos	12	Pratt-Bos	5	Pratt-Bos	240	Pratt-Bos	102
Pratt-Bos	80	Pratt-Bos	169	McInnis-Bos	31	Pratt-Bos	10	Collins-Bos	4	McInnis-Bos	230	McInnis-Bos	76
Menosky-Bos	77	Collins-Bos	155	Collins-Bos	29	McInnis-Bos	10	Menosky-Bos	3	Collins-Bos	220	Collins-Bos	69

Stolen Bases		Base Stealing Runs		Fielding Runs-Infield		Fielding Runs-Outfield		Wins		Winning Pct.		Complete Games	
Sisler-StL	35	Sisler-StL	3.8	Scott-Bos	41.2	Veach-Det	12.9	Shocker-StL	27	Mays-NY	.750	Faber-Chi	32
Collins-Bos	15	Walters-Bos	.7	McInnis-Bos	4.3	Collins-Bos	3.7	Mays-NY	27	Bush-Bos	.640	Jones-Bos	25
Leibold-Bos	13	Menosky-Bos	.5	Collins-Bos	.3			Jones-Bos	23	Jones-Bos	.590	Bush-Bos	21
Foster-Bos	13	Collins-Bos	.5	Pratt-Bos	.1			Bush-Bos	16			Pennock-Bos	15

Strikeouts		Fewest BB/Game		Games		Saves		Base Runners/9		Adjusted Relief Runs		Relief Ranking	
Johnson-Was	143	Hasty-Phi	2.01	Mays-NY	49	Middleton-Det	7	Faber-Chi	10.53				
Jones-Bos	98	Jones-Bos	2.35	Jones-Bos	40	Mays-NY	7	Jones-Bos	12.11				
Bush-Bos	96	Pennock-Bos	2.38	Russell-Bos	39	Russell-Bos	3	Bush-Bos	12.14				
Pennock-Bos	91	Myers-Bos	2.77	Bush-Bos	37	3 players tied	1	Karr-Bos	12.39				

Innings Pitched		Opponents' Avg.		Opponents' OBP		Earned Run Average		Adjusted ERA		Adjusted Starter Runs		Pitcher Wins	
Mays-NY	336.2	Faber-Chi	.242	Faber-Chi	.297	Faber-Chi	2.48	Faber-Chi	171	Faber-Chi	64.1	Faber-Chi	6.8
Jones-Bos	298.2	Bush-Bos	.260	Jones-Bos	.329	Jones-Bos	3.22	Jones-Bos	131	Jones-Bos	34.3	Jones-Bos	4.3
Bush-Bos	254.1	Jones-Bos	.279	Bush-Bos	.330	Bush-Bos	3.50	Bush-Bos	121	Bush-Bos	22.1	Bush-Bos	2.8
Pennock-Bos	222.2	Russell-Bos	.303	Pennock-Bos	.352	Pennock-Bos	4.04	Pennock-Bos	105	Karr-Bos	8.4	Karr-Bos	1.0

1922 AMERICAN LEAGUE

TEAM	W	L	T	PCT	GB	R	OR	HR	AVG	OBP	SLG	OPS	AOPS	PF	SB	CG	HR	BB	SO	BR/9	ERA	AERA	OAV	OOB	FW	PW	BW	BSW	DIF
NY	94	60	0	.610		758	**618**	95	.287	.353	.412	765	+3	102	62	**100**	73	423	458	**11.9**	3.39	+18	**.268**	**.325**	2.0	8.9	1.7	-.3	4.6
StL	93	61	0	.604	1	**867**	643	98	**.313**	**.372**	**.455**	**827**	+17	104	136	79	71	419	**534**	12.1	**3.38**	+22	**.268**	.327	-.5	**10.9**	**12.4**	**.7**	-7.5
Det	79	75	1	.513	15	828	791	54	.306	**.372**	.415	787	+15	97	78	67	62	473	461	13.7	4.27	-9	.288	.354	.2	-6.5	11.8	-.0	-3.4
Cle	78	76	1	.506	16	768	817	32	.292	.364	.398	762	+4	101	90	76	58	464	489	13.7	4.59	-13	.296	.356	-.5	-9.0	4.2	.4	5.9
Chi	77	77	1	.500	17	691	691	45	.289	.343	.373	716	-8	100	109	86	57	529	484	13.0	3.94	+3	.278	.346	**2.2**	1.5	-4.8	-.0	1.1
Was	69	85	0	.448	25	650	706	45	.268	.334	.367	701	-7	95	97	84	49	500	422	13.4	3.81	+1	.286	.354	-.2	.6	-5.1	.3	-3.6
Phi	65	89	1	.422	29	705	830	**111**	.270	.331	.402	733	-6	103	60	73	107	469	373	13.7	4.59	-8	.297	.357	-1.2	-5.0	-5.3	-.6	.2
Bos	61	93	1	.396	33	598	769	45	.263	.316	.357	673	-18	-99	64	71	**48**	503	359	13.5	4.30	-5	.287	.354	-1.8	-3.0	-14.2	-.4	3.4
Total	618					5865		525	.285	.348	.398	746			696	636		3780	3580	13.1	4.03		.285	.348					

Batter-Fielder Wins		Batting Average		On-Base Percentage		Slugging Average		On-Base Plus Slugging		Adjusted OPS		Adjusted Batter Runs	
Sisler-StL	**6.3**	Sisler-StL	.420	Speaker-Cle	.474	Ruth-NY	.672	Ruth-NY	1106	Ruth-NY	181	Sisler-StL	60.0
Harris-Bos	**.6**	Harris-Bos	.316	Pratt-Bos	.361	Harris-Bos	.478	Pratt-Bos	788	Pratt-Bos	106	Harris-Bos	10.3
Lynch-Bos	**.0**	Burns-Bos	.306	Burns-Bos	.341	Burns-Bos	.446	Burns-Bos	787	Burns-Bos	104	Pratt-Bos	5.6
		Pratt-Bos	.301	S.Collins-Bos	.289	Pratt-Bos	.427	S.Collins-Bos	647	S.Collins-Bos	68	2 players tied	1.5

Runs		Hits		Doubles		Triples		Home Runs		Total Bases		Runs Batted In	
Sisler-StL	134	Sisler-StL	246	Speaker-Cle	48	Sisler-StL	18	Williams-StL	39	Williams-StL	367	Williams-StL	155
Pratt-Bos	73	Pratt-Bos	183	Pratt-Bos	44	Harris-Bos	9	Burns-Bos	12	Pratt-Bos	259	Pratt-Bos	86
Burns-Bos	71	Burns-Bos	171	Burns-Bos	32	Pratt-Bos	7	Pratt-Bos	6	Burns-Bos	249	Burns-Bos	73
Menosky-Bos	61	Harris-Bos	129	Harris-Bos	30	S.Collins-Bos	6	Harris-Bos	6	Harris-Bos	195	Harris-Bos	54

Stolen Bases		Base Stealing Runs		Fielding Runs-Infield		Fielding Runs-Outfield		Wins		Winning Pct.		Complete Games	
Sisler-StL	51	Sisler-StL	4.6	Harris-Was	31.2	Veach-Det	9.7	Rommel-Phi	27	Bush-NY	.788	Faber-Chi	31
Menosky-Bos	9	Burns-Bos	1.1	Harris-Bos	1.9	Menosky-Bos	5.6	R.Collins-Bos	14			Quinn-Bos	16
Burns-Bos	8	3 players tied	.2			Harris-Bos	4.0	Quinn-Bos	13			Pennock-Bos	15
2 players tied	7							Pennock-Bos	10			R.Collins-Bos	15

Strikeouts		Fewest BB/Game		Games		Saves		Base Runners/9		Adjusted Relief Runs		Relief Ranking	
Shocker-StL	149	Shocker-StL	1.47	Rommel-Phi	51	Jones-NY	8	Faber-Chi	10.82	Murray-NY	1.2	Murray-NY	1.0
R.Collins-Bos	69	Quinn-Bos	2.07	Karr-Bos	41	Russell-Bos	2	Quinn-Bos	11.43				
Quinn-Bos	67	Karr-Bos	2.21	Quinn-Bos	40	Ferguson-Bos	2	Ferguson-Bos	12.21				
Pennock-Bos	59	Ferguson-Bos	2.81	Ferguson-Bos	39	3 players tied	1	Karr-Bos	12.86				

Innings Pitched		Opponents' Avg.		Opponents' OBP		Earned Run Average		Adjusted ERA		Adjusted Starter Runs		Pitcher Wins	
Faber-Chi	352.0	Davis-StL	.250	Faber-Chi	.299	Faber-Chi	2.81	Faber-Chi	144	Faber-Chi	46.6	Shocker-StL	4.9
Quinn-Bos	256.0	Ferguson-Bos	.265	Quinn-Bos	.311	Quinn-Bos	3.48	Quinn-Bos	118	Quinn-Bos	16.0	Quinn-Bos	1.4
R.Collins-Bos	210.2	Quinn-Bos	.267	Ferguson-Bos	.326	R.Collins-Bos	3.76	R.Collins-Bos	109	R.Collins-Bos	8.7	R.Collins-Bos	.6
Pennock-Bos	202.0	R.Collins-Bos	.274	Karr-Bos	.348	Ferguson-Bos	4.31	2 players tied	95				

1923 AMERICAN LEAGUE

TEAM	W	L	T	PCT	GB	R	OR	HR	AVG	OBP	SLG	OPS	AOPS	PF	SB	CG	HR	BB	SO	BR/9	ERA	AERA	OAV	OOB	FW	PW	BW	BSW	DIF
NY	98	54	0	.645		823	**622**	105	.291	.357	**.422**	779	+8	102	69	**101**	68	491	**506**	**12.3**	3.62	+9	**.263**	.330	3.3	4.7	5.5	-.5	8.9
Det	83	71	1	.539	16	831	741	41	.300	.377	.401	778	+13	98	87	61	58	447	447	13.1	4.09	-6	.283	.345	.0	-3.4	10.7	.3	-1.7
Cle	82	71	0	.536	16.5	**888**	746	59	**.301**	**.381**	.420	**801**	**+17**	100	79	77	**36**	465	407	13.2	3.91	+1	.285	.346	-1.7	.4	**13.8**	-.4	-6.7
Was	75	78	2	.490	23.5	720	747	26	.274	.346	.367	713	-2	95	102	71	56	563	474	14.0	3.98	-5	.291	.364	-.9	-3.1	-1.2	.5	3.2
StL	74	78	2	.487	24	688	720	82	.281	.339	.398	737	-6	106	64	83	59	528	488	13.2	3.93	+6	.275	.348	1.4	3.4	-5.3	.1	-1.6
Phi	69	83	1	.454	29	661	761	53	.271	.333	.370	703	-11	101	72	65	68	550	400	13.5	4.08	+1	.280	.352	-1.4	.0	-8.2	.0	2.5
Chi	69	85	2	.448	30	692	741	42	.279	.350	.373	723	-3	99	**191**	74	49	534	467	13.4	4.05	-2	.283	.353	1.1	-1.3	-1.5	**.7**	-7.0
Bos	61	91	2	.401	37	584	809	34	.261	.318	.351	669	-19	101	79	77	48	520	412	13.9	4.20	-2	.294	.366	-2.0	-1.5	-14.2	-.8	3.4
Total	616					5887		442	.282	.351	.388	739			743	609		4100	3601	13.3	3.98		.282	.351					

Batter-Fielder Wins		Batting Average		On-Base Percentage		Slugging Average		On-Base Plus Slugging		Adjusted OPS		Adjusted Batter Runs	
Ruth-NY	**10.1**	Heilmann-Det	.403	Ruth-NY	.545	Ruth-NY	.764	Ruth-NY	1309	Ruth-NY	238	Ruth-NY	119.2
Harris-Bos	**1.7**	Harris-Bos	.335	Harris-Bos	.406	Harris-Bos	.520	Harris-Bos	925	Harris-Bos	142	Harris-Bos	28.6
Burns-Bos	**.8**	Burns-Bos	.328	Burns-Bos	.386	Burns-Bos	.470	Burns-Bos	856	Burns-Bos	124	Burns-Bos	19.8
Picinich-Bos	**.5**	Reichle-Bos	.258	McMillan-Bos	.299	Shanks-Bos	.336	McMillan-Bos	625	McMillan-Bos	64	Picinich-Bos	3.6

Runs		Hits		Doubles		Triples		Home Runs		Total Bases		Runs Batted In	
Ruth-NY	151	Jamieson-Cle	222	Speaker-Cle	59	Rice-Was	18	Ruth-NY	41	Ruth-NY	399	Ruth-NY	131
Burns-Bos	91	Burns-Bos	181	Burns-Bos	47	Goslin-Was	18	Harris-Bos	13	Burns-Bos	259	Burns-Bos	82
Harris-Bos	82	Harris-Bos	162	Harris-Bos	28	Harris-Bos	11	Burns-Bos	7	Harris-Bos	251	Harris-Bos	76
Collins-Bos	41	Shanks-Bos	118	McMillan-Bos	24	4 players tied	5	Shanks-Bos	3	Shanks-Bos	156	Shanks-Bos	57

Stolen Bases		Base Stealing Runs		Fielding Runs-Infield		Fielding Runs-Outfield		Wins		Winning Pct.		Complete Games	
Collins-Chi	48	Mostil-Chi	3.4	Peckinpaugh-Was	21.8	Mostil-Chi	16.0	Uhle-Cle	26	Pennock-NY	.760	Uhle-Cle	29
McMillan-Bos	13	McMillan-Bos	1.1	McMillan-Bos	3.1	Shanks-Bos	.3	Ehmke-Bos	20	Ehmke-Bos	.541	Ehmke-Bos	28
Burns-Bos	9	DeVormer-Bos	.7					Quinn-Bos	13			Quinn-Bos	16
		Harris-Bos	.5					Ferguson-Bos	9			2 players tied	11

Strikeouts		Fewest BB/Game		Games		Saves		Base Runners/9		Adjusted Relief Runs		Relief Ranking	
Johnson-Was	130	Shocker-StL	1.59	Rommel-Phi	56	Russell-Was	9	Shocker-StL	11.16				
Ehmke-Bos	121	Quinn-Bos	1.96	Quinn-Bos	43	Quinn-Bos	7	Ehmke-Bos	12.99				
Ferguson-Bos	72	Ferguson-Bos	3.04	Quinn-Bos	42	Ehmke-Bos	3	Quinn-Bos	13.37				
Quinn-Bos	71	Ehmke-Bos	3.38	Murray-Bos	39	Fullerton-Bos	1	Piercy-Bos	13.45				

Innings Pitched		Opponents' Avg.		Opponents' OBP		Earned Run Average		Adjusted ERA		Adjusted Starter Runs		Pitcher Wins	
Uhle-Cle	357.2	Shawkey-NY	.246	Shocker-StL	.306	Coveleski-Cle	2.76	Coveleski-Cle	143	Vangilder-StL	27.8	Uhle-Cle	3.4
Ehmke-Bos	316.2	Ehmke-Bos	.272	Ehmke-Bos	.349	Piercy-Bos	3.41	Piercy-Bos	120	Ehmke-Bos	16.3	Ehmke-Bos	1.9
Quinn-Bos	243.0	Piercy-Bos	.277	Quinn-Bos	.356	Ehmke-Bos	3.78	Ehmke-Bos	109	Quinn-Bos	8.7	Quinn-Bos	1.0
Ferguson-Bos	198.1	Murray-Bos	.291	Piercy-Bos	.357	Quinn-Bos	3.89	Quinn-Bos	106	Piercy-Bos	8.2	Piercy-Bos	.8

1924 AMERICAN LEAGUE

TEAM	W	L	T	PCT	GB	R	OR	HR	AVG	OBP	SLG	OPS	AOPS	PF	SB	CG	HR	BB	SO	BR/9	ERA	AERA	OAV	OOB	FW	PW	BW	BSW	DIF
Was	92	62	2	.597		755	**613**	22	.294	.361	.387	748	+1	97	116	74	**34**	505	469	**12.2**	3.34	+21	**.259**	.330	1.3	**10.6**	1.3	.1	1.6
NY	89	63	1	.586	2	798	667	98	.289	.352	**.426**	**778**	+6	98	76	59	62	**487**	487	13.4	3.86	+8	.284	.353	**2.0**	4.2	2.5	-.2	4.4
Det	86	68	2	.558	6	**849**	796	35	**.298**	**.373**	.404	777	**+8**	98	100	60	55	**467**	441	13.5	4.19	-2	.293	.354	.4	-1.1	**6.7**	.0	3.0
StL	74	78	1	.487	17	769	807	67	.295	.356	.408	764	-4	106	85	66	68	517	386	13.8	4.57	-1	.289	.358	.3	-.8	-3.3	-.5	2.4
Phi	71	81	0	.467	20	685	778	63	.281	.334	.389	723	-10	101	77	68	43	597	371	14.4	4.39	-2	.292	.368	-.5	-1.4	-8.1	-.2	4.2
Cle	67	86	0	.438	24.5	755	814	41	.296	.361	.399	760	+0	101	85	**87**	43	503	315	14.3	4.40	-3	.300	.365	-1.0	-1.9	.0	**.4**	-7.1
Bos	67	87	3	.435	25	735	806	30	.277	.356	.374	730	-6	100	78	73	43	523	414	13.9	4.35	-1.0	.290	.359	-1.0	.2	-3.8	.1	-5.5
Chi	66	87	1	.431	25.5	793	858	41	.288	.365	.382	747	+1	97	**137**	76	52	512	360	14.3	4.74	-13	.305	.368	-2.4	-9.3	1.9	.3	-1.1
Total	617					6139		397	.290	.357	.397	754			747	580		4146	3243	13.7	4.23		.290	.357					

Batter-Fielder Wins		Batting Average		On-Base Percentage		Slugging Average		On-Base Plus Slugging		Adjusted OPS		Adjusted Batter Runs	
Ruth-NY	**8.4**	Ruth-NY	.378	Ruth-NY	.513	Ruth-NY	.739	Ruth-NY	1252	Ruth-NY	221	Ruth-NY	104.0
Harris-Bos	**1.2**	Boone-Bos	.337	Harris-Bos	.406	Boone-Bos	.497	Boone-Bos	901	Boone-Bos	131	Boone-Bos	23.0
Shanks-Bos	**.5**	Flagstead-Bos	.307	Boone-Bos	.404	Harris-Bos	.430	Harris-Bos	835	Harris-Bos	115	Harris-Bos	15.0
Clark-Bos	**.4**	Harris-Bos	.301	Flagstead-Bos	.401	Veach-Bos	.426	Flagstead-Bos	823	Flagstead-Bos	112	Flagstead-Bos	13.6

Runs		Hits		Doubles		Triples		Home Runs		Total Bases		Runs Batted In	
Ruth-NY	143	Rice-Was	216	J.Sewell-Cle	45	Pipp-NY	19	Ruth-NY	46	Ruth-NY	391	Goslin-Was	129
Flagstead-Bos	106	Wambsganss-Bos	174	Heilmann-Det	45	Veach-Bos	9	Boone-Bos	13	Boone-Bos	242	Veach-Bos	99
Wambsganss-Bos	93	Flagstead-Bos	172	Wambsganss-Bos	41	Harris-Bos	9	Veach-Bos	5	Flagstead-Bos	236	Boone-Bos	98
Harris-Bos	82	Boone-Bos	164	Harris-Bos	36	Flagstead-Bos	7	Flagstead-Bos	5	Wambsganss-Bos	225	Harris-Bos	77

Stolen Bases		Base Stealing Runs		Fielding Runs-Infield		Fielding Runs-Outfield		Wins		Winning Pct.		Complete Games	
Collins-Chi	42	Collins-Chi	3.3	J.Sewell-Cle	21.8	Hooper-Chi	10.4	Johnson-Was	23	Johnson-Was	.767	Thurston-Chi	28
Wambsganss-Bos	14	Harris-Bos	1.0	Wambsganss-Bos		Harris-Bos	.0	Ehmke-Bos	19	Ehmke-Bos	.528	Ehmke-Bos	26
Ezzell-Bos	12	Ezzell-Bos	.9	13.0				Ferguson-Bos	14			Ferguson-Bos	15
Flagstead-Bos	10	Picinich-Bos	.8	Harris-Bos	5.2			Quinn-Bos	12			Quinn-Bos	13

Strikeouts		Fewest BB/Game		Games		Saves		Base Runners/9		Adjusted Relief Runs		Relief Ranking	
Johnson-Was	158	Smith-Cle	1.53	Marberry-Was	50	Marberry-Was	15	Johnson-Was	10.37	Speece-Was	4.0	Speece-Was	2.0
Ehmke-Bos	119	Quinn-Bos	2.05	Ehmke-Bos	45	Quinn-Bos	7	Ehmke-Bos	11.89				
Ferguson-Bos	78	Ehmke-Bos	2.31	Quinn-Bos	44	Ehmke-Bos	4	Quinn-Bos	12.00				
Quinn-Bos	64	Ferguson-Bos	4.09	Ferguson-Bos	41	2 players tied	2	Ross-Bos	13.40				

Innings Pitched		Opponents' Avg.		Opponents' OBP		Earned Run Average		Adjusted ERA		Adjusted Starter Runs		Pitcher Wins	
Ehmke-Bos	315.0	Johnson-Was	.224	Johnson-Was	.284	Johnson-Was	2.72	Baumgartner-Phi	149	Johnson-Was	43.8	Johnson-Was	4.9
Ferguson-Bos	237.2	Ehmke-Bos	.265	Ehmke-Bos	.316	Quinn-Bos	3.27	Quinn-Bos	134	Ehmke-Bos	33.3	Ehmke-Bos	3.4
Quinn-Bos	228.2	Quinn-Bos	.273	Quinn-Bos	.322	Ehmke-Bos	3.46	Ehmke-Bos	126	Quinn-Bos	23.2	Quinn-Bos	2.2
Fullerton-Bos	152.0	Ferguson-Bos	.286	Ferguson-Bos	.366	Ferguson-Bos	3.79	Ferguson-Bos	115	Ferguson-Bos	16.8	Ferguson-Bos	1.4

1925 AMERICAN LEAGUE

TEAM	W	L	T	PCT	GB	R	OR	HR	AVG	OBP	SLG	OPS	AOPS	PF	SB	CG	HR	BB	SO	BR/9	ERA	AERA	OAV	OOB	FW	PW	BW	BSW	DIF
Was	96	55	1	.636		829	670	56	.303	.373	.411	784	+6	98	**135**	69	49	543	463	13.3	3.70	+14	.278	.351	1.8	7.6	5.1	.4	5.7
Phi	88	64	1	.579	8.5	831	713	76	**.307**	.364	.434	798	+1	107	67	61	60	544	**495**	13.3	3.87	+20	**.276**	**.347**	-.6	**10.5**	.0	.0	2.1
StL	82	71	1	.536	15	900	906	**110**	.298	.360	**.439**	799	+3	105	85	67	99	675	419	15.0	4.92	-5	.298	.380	-1.4	-3.4	1.0	-.3	9.6
Det	81	73	2	.526	16.5	**903**	829	50	.302	**.379**	.413	792	**+9**	99	97	66	70	556	419	14.2	4.61	-6	.296	.366	1.9	-4.4	**7.2**	**.5**	-1.2
Chi	79	75	0	.513	18.5	811	770	38	.284	.370	.385	755	+2	95	131	71	69	**489**	374	13.6	4.29	-3	.295	.356	.2	-2.1	4.0	.4	-4.1
Cle	70	84	1	.455	27.5	782	817	52	.297	.361	.399	760	-3	101	90	**93**	**41**	493	345	14.0	4.49	-2	.296	.359	-.4	-.8	-1.7	-.0	-4.0
NY	69	85	2	.448	28.5	706	774	**110**	.275	.336	.410	746	-4	98	69	80	78	505	492	13.6	4.33	-2	.289	.353	**2.7**	-1.0	-4.8	-.4	-4.5
Bos	47	105	0	.309	49.5	639	922	41	.266	.336	.364	700	-17	-100	42	68	67	510	310	14.7	4.97	-8	.308	.374	-4.2	-5.6	-12.2	-.4	-6.6
Total	616					6401		533	.292	.360	.408	768			716	575		4315	3317	14.0	4.39		.292	.360					

Batter-Fielder Wins		Batting Average		On-Base Percentage		Slugging Average		On-Base Plus Slugging		Adjusted OPS		Adjusted Batter Runs	
Speaker-Cle	**4.3**	Heilmann-Det	.393	Speaker-Cle	.479	Williams-StL	.613	Cobb-Det	1066	Cobb-Det	171	Heilmann-Det	55.5
Prothro-Bos	**.3**	Boone-Bos	.330	Boone-Bos	.406	Boone-Bos	.479	Boone-Bos	885	Boone-Bos	124	Boone-Bos	18.9
Herrera-Bos	**.3**	Vache-Bos	.313	Flagstead-Bos	.356	Vache-Bos	.464	Todt-Bos	782	Todt-Bos	97	Vache-Bos	5.0
2 players tied	**.1**	Prothro-Bos	.313	Todt-Bos	.343	Todt-Bos	.439	Flagstead-Bos	741	Flagstead-Bos	88	Rothrock-Bos	1.5

Runs		Hits		Doubles		Triples		Home Runs		Total Bases		Runs Batted In	
Mostil-Chi	135	Simmons-Phi	253	McManus-StL	44	Goslin-Was	20	Meusel-NY	33	Simmons-Phi	392	Meusel-NY	138
Flagstead-Bos	84	Flagstead-Bos	160	Flagstead-Bos	38	Todt-Bos	13	Todt-Bos	11	Todt-Bos	239	Todt-Bos	75
Boone-Bos	79	Boone-Bos	157	Boone-Bos	34	Vache-Bos	7	Boone-Bos	9	Boone-Bos	228	Boone-Bos	68
Todt-Bos	62	Todt-Bos	151	Todt-Bos	29	Boone-Bos	7	Boone-Bos	6	Flagstead-Bos	220	Flagstead-Bos	61

Stolen Bases		Base Stealing Runs		Fielding Runs-Infield		Fielding Runs-Outfield		Wins		Winning Pct.		Complete Games	
Mostil-Chi	43	Goslin-Was	3.1	J.Sewell-Cle	15.8	Goslin-Was	14.3	Rommel-Phi	21	Coveleski-Was	.800	Smith-Cle	22
Prothro-Bos	9	Picinich-Bos	.4	Wambsganss-Bos	8.4	Flagstead-Bos	14.0	Lyons-Chi	21			Ehmke-Bos	22
Ezzell-Bos	9	Rosenthal-Bos	.2	Todt-Bos	2.6			Wingfield-Bos	12			Wingfield-Bos	18
Flagstead-Bos	5	Herrera-Bos	.2					2 players tied	9			Ruffing-Bos	13

Strikeouts		Fewest BB/Game		Games		Saves		Base Runners/9		Adjusted Relief Runs		Relief Ranking	
Grove-Phi	116	Smith-Cle	1.82	Marberry-Was	55	Marberry-Was	15	Pennock-NY	11.05	Marberry-Was	5.2	Marberry-Was	8.9
Ehmke-Bos	95	Ehmke-Bos	2.93	Wingfield-Bos	41	Wingfield-Bos	2	Wingfield-Bos	12.99				
Ruffing-Bos	64	Ruffing-Bos	3.11	Fuhr-Bos	39	4 players tied	1	Ehmke-Bos	13.15				
2 players tied	30	Wingfield-Bos	3.26	2 players tied	37			Ruffing-Bos	13.67				

Innings Pitched		Opponents' Avg.		Opponents' OBP		Earned Run Average		Adjusted ERA		Adjusted Starter Runs		Pitcher Wins	
Pennock-NY	277.0	Johnson-Was	.250	Pennock-NY	.303	Coveleski-Was	2.84	Coveleski-Was	149	Coveleski-Was	40.9	Johnson-Was	4.6
Ehmke-Bos	260.2	Wingfield-Bos	.278	Wingfield-Bos	.346	Ehmke-Bos	3.73	Ehmke-Bos	122	Ehmke-Bos	20.9	Wingfield-Bos	1.8
Wingfield-Bos	254.1	Ehmke-Bos	.285	Ehmke-Bos	.348	Wingfield-Bos	3.96	Wingfield-Bos	115	Wingfield-Bos	12.8	Ehmke-Bos	1.7
Ruffing-Bos	217.1	Ruffing-Bos	.299	Ruffing-Bos	.357	Ruffing-Bos	5.01	Ruffing-Bos	91	Fullerton-Bos	3.0	Fullerton-Bos	.4

1926 AMERICAN LEAGUE

TEAM	W	L	T	PCT	GB	R	OR	HR	AVG	OBP	SLG	OPS	AOPS	PF	SB	CG	HR	BB	SO	BR/9	ERA	AERA	OAV	OOB	FW	PW	BW	BSW	DIF
NY	91	63	1	.591		**847**	713	121	.289	**.369**	.437	806	+19	98	79	63	56	478	486	12.8	3.86	+0	.274	.337	-1.1	-.0	**13.4**	-.0	1.9
Cle	88	66	0	.571	3	738	612	27	.289	.349	.386	735	-8	88	**96**	49	**450**	381	12.5	3.40	+19	.271	.334	1.1	9.7	-1.8	**.8**	1.3
Phi	83	67	0	.553	6	677	**570**	61	.269	.341	.383	724	-10	106	56	62	**38**	451	**571**	12.3	**3.00**	+39	**.268**	**.331**	.9	**16.3**	-7.3	.0	-1.9
Was	81	69	2	.540	8	802	761	43	**.292**	.364	.401	765	+9	98	117	65	45	566	418	14.0	4.34	-11	.287	.361	.2	-7.2	6.4	-.2	6.8
Chi	81	72	2	.529	9.5	730	665	32	.289	.361	.390	751	+6	101	**123**	85	47	506	458	12.7	3.74	-8	.271	.336	1.6	1.6	5.6	-.4	-4.7
Det	79	75	0	.513	12	793	830	36	.291	.367	.398	765	+5	101	88	57	58	555	469	14.0	4.41	-8	.292	.363	.0	-5.1	4.2	-.1	3.0
StL	62	92	1	.403	29	682	845	72	.276	.335	.394	729	-8	105	64	64	86	502	337	14.7	4.66	-8	.297	.379	-2.6	-5.3	-7.1	-.5	.5
Bos	46	107	1	.301	44.5	562	835	32	.256	.321	.343	664	-18	-97	52	53	45	546	336	13.9	4.72	-14	.294	.365	-.2	-9.6	-13.6	-.1	-7.1
Total	616					5831		424	.281	.351	.392	743			667	545		4206	3456	13.3	4.02		.281	.351					

Batter-Fielder Wins		Batting Average		On-Base Percentage		Slugging Average		On-Base Plus Slugging		Adjusted OPS		Adjusted Batter Runs	
Ruth-NY	**8.5**	Manush-Det	.378	Ruth-NY	.516	Ruth-NY	.737	Ruth-NY	1253	Ruth-NY	228	Ruth-NY	102.8
Rigney-Bos	**4.3**	Flagstead-Bos	.299	Rigney-Bos	.395	Flagstead-Bos	.429	Rigney-Bos	772	Rigney-Bos	105	Rigney-Bos	10.0
Regan-Bos	**.3**	Rigney-Bos	.270	Haney-Bos	.330	Rigney-Bos	.377	Todt-Bos	669	Todt-Bos	76	Flagstead-Bos	5.6
Flagstead-Bos	**.2**	Rosenthal-Bos	.267	Todt-Bos	.306	Rosenthal-Bos	.372	Haney-Bos	613	Haney-Bos	63	Welzer-Bos	2.4

Runs		Hits		Doubles		Triples		Home Runs		Total Bases		Runs Batted In	
Ruth-NY	139	Rice-Was	216	Burns-Cle	64	Gehrig-NY	20	Ruth-NY	47	Ruth-NY	365	Ruth-NY	146
Rigney-Bos	71	Burns-Cle	216	Rigney-Bos	32	Todt-Bos	12	Todt-Bos	7	Todt-Bos	217	Todt-Bos	69
Flagstead-Bos	65	Todt-Bos	153	Flagstead-Bos	31	Haney-Bos	7	3 players tied	4	Rigney-Bos	198	Rigney-Bos	53
Todt-Bos	56	Rigney-Bos	142	Regan-Bos	7	Flagstead-Bos	7			Flagstead-Bos	178	Haney-Bos	52

Stolen Bases		Base Stealing Runs		Fielding Runs-Infield		Fielding Runs-Outfield		Wins		Winning Pct.		Complete Games	
Mostil-Chi	35	Mostil-Chi	2.8	Rigney-Bos	21.1	Goslin-Was	14.1	Uhle-Cle	27	Uhle-Cle	.711	Uhle-Cle	32
Haney-Bos	13	Haney-Bos	.8	Regan-Bos	15.7			Wingfield-Bos	11			Wingfield-Bos	9
Rigney-Bos	6	Gaston-Bos	.7	Todt-Bos	10.0			Wiltse-Bos	8			Wiltse-Bos	9
Regan-Bos	6	Rosenthal-Bos	.5	Haney-Bos	7.6			2 players tied	6			Zahniser-Bos	7

Strikeouts		Fewest BB/Game		Games		Saves		Base Runners/9		Adjusted Relief Runs		Relief Ranking	
Grove-Phi	194	Pennock-NY	1.45	Marberry-Was	64	Marberry-Was	22	Russell-Bos	10.93	Pate-Phi	19.6	Marberry-Was	21.2
Wiltse-Bos	59	Wingfield-Bos	2.36	Wingfield-Bos	43	Wingfield-Bos	3	Wingfield-Bos	12.84	Russell-Bos	7.6	Russell-Bos	3.8
Ruffing-Bos	58	Zahniser-Bos	3.61	Welzer-Bos	39	Ruffing-Bos	2	Ruffing-Bos	13.12				
Zahniser-Bos	35	Ruffing-Bos	3.69	2 players tied	37			Wiltse-Bos	14.03				

Innings Pitched		Opponents' Avg.		Opponents' OBP		Earned Run Average		Adjusted ERA		Adjusted Starter Runs		Pitcher Wins	
Uhle-Cle	318.1	Thomas-Chi	.244	Pennock-NY	.313	Grove-Phi	2.51	Grove-Phi	166	Uhle-Cle	44.6	Uhle-Cle	5.4
Wiltse-Bos	196.1	Grove-Phi	.244	Wingfield-Bos	.344	Wiltse-Bos	4.22	Wiltse-Bos	96			Russell-Bos	.6
Wingfield-Bos	190.2	Wiltse-Bos	.273	Ruffing-Bos	.351	Ruffing-Bos	4.39	Ruffing-Bos	93			3 players tied	.0
Zahniser-Bos	172.0	Ruffing-Bos	.274	Wiltse-Bos	.363	Wingfield-Bos	4.44	Wingfield-Bos	92				

1927 AMERICAN LEAGUE

TEAM	W	L	T	PCT	GB	R	OR	HR	AVG	OBP	SLG	OPS	AOPS	PF	SB	CG	HR	BB	SO	BR/9	ERA	AERA	OAV	OOB	FW	PW	BW	BSW	DIF
NY	110	44	1	.714		975	599	158	.307	.383	.489	872	+35	97	90	82	42	409	431	11.9	3.20	+20	.267	.323	.7	10.2	25.5	-.2	-3.1
Phi	91	63	1	.591	19	841	726	56	.303	.372	.414	786	+3	106	101	65	65	442	553	12.6	3.97	+7	.278	.338	1.0	4.2	3.3	.0	5.4
Was	85	69	3	.552	25	782	730	29	.287	.351	.386	737	-3	99	133	62	53	491	497	12.6	3.97	+2	.269	.335	.8	1.3	-1.7	1.1	6.4
Det	82	71	3	.536	27.5	845	805	51	.289	.363	.409	772	+5	101	139	75	52	577	421	14.0	4.14	+2	.290	.364	.1	.9	3.3	.5	.7
Chi	70	83	0	.458	39.5	662	708	36	.278	.344	.378	722	-6	98	89	85	55	440	365	12.7	3.91	+3	.283	.342	1.6	1.9	-3.3	-.6	-6.0
Cle	66	87	0	.431	43.5	668	766	26	.283	.337	.379	716	-10	101	65	72	37	508	366	13.9	4.27	-2	.295	.361	.2	-1.0	-6.9	-1.0	-1.7
StL	59	94	2	.386	50.5	724	904	55	.276	.338	.380	718	-12	103	90	80	79	604	385	14.7	4.95	-12	.304	.378	-2.5	-8.3	-8.6	-.2	2.1
Bos	51	103	0	.331	59	597	856	28	.259	.320	.357	677	-18	-98	81	63	56	558	381	14.5	4.72	-11	.305	.376	-1.4	-7.2	-13.2	.3	-4.5
Total	619					6094		439	.285	.351	.399	751			788	584		4029	3399	13.4	4.14		.285	.351					

Batter-Fielder Wins		Batting Average		On-Base Percentage		Slugging Average		On-Base Plus Slugging		Adjusted OPS		Adjusted Batter Runs	
Ruth-NY	**8.8**	Heilmann-Det	.398	Ruth-NY	.486	Ruth-NY	.772	Ruth-NY	1258	Ruth-NY	229	Gehrig-NY	108.8
Rogell-Bos	**.8**	Tobin-Bos	.310	Flagstead-Bos	.374	Regan-Bos	.408	Flagstead-Bos	775	Flagstead-Bos	103	MacFayden-Bos	4.4
Flagstead-Bos	**.4**	Flagstead-Bos	.285	Regan-Bos	.315	Shaner-Bos	.406	Regan-Bos	723	Regan-Bos	88	Flagstead-Bos	3.8
Haney-Bos	**.3**	Hartley-Bos	.275	Todt-Bos	.280	Flagstead-Bos	.401	Todt-Bos	617	Todt-Bos	61	Haney-Bos	3.4

Runs		Hits		Doubles		Triples		Home Runs		Total Bases		Runs Batted In	
Ruth-NY	158	Combs-NY	231	Gehrig-NY	52	Combs-NY	23	Ruth-NY	60	Gehrig-NY	447	Gehrig-NY	175
Flagstead-Bos	63	Flagstead-Bos	133	Regan-Bos	37	Regan-Bos	10	Todt-Bos	6	Regan-Bos	191	Flagstead-Bos	69
Rothrock-Bos	61	Regan-Bos	128	Shaner-Bos	33	3 players tied	8	Flagstead-Bos	4	Flagstead-Bos	187	Regan-Bos	66
Todt-Bos	55	Todt-Bos	122	Flagstead-Bos	26			2 players tied	3	Todt-Bos	174	Todt-Bos	52

Stolen Bases		Base Stealing Runs		Fielding Runs-Infield		Fielding Runs-Outfield		Wins		Winning Pct.		Complete Games	
Sisler-StL	27	Sisler-StL	3.5	Gehringer-Det	17.1	Falk-Chi	18.1	Lyons-Chi	22	Hoyt-NY	.759	Lyons-Chi	30
Flagstead-Bos	12	Flagstead-Bos	1.9	Todt-Bos	8.3	Flagstead-Bos	3.9	Hoyt-NY	22			Wiltse-Bos	13
Shaner-Bos	11	Shaner-Bos	1.0	Rothrock-Bos	3.7			Harriss-Bos	14			Harriss-Bos	11
Regan-Bos	10	Todt-Bos	.6	Shaner-Bos	.7			Wiltse-Bos	10			Ruffing-Bos	10

Strikeouts		Fewest BB/Game		Games		Saves		Base Runners/9		Adjusted Relief Runs		Relief Ranking	
Grove-Phi	174	Quinn-Phi	1.65	Braxton-Was	58	Moore-NY	13	Moore-NY	10.35	Braxton-Was	18.7	Braxton-Was	24.1
Ruffing-Bos	77	Harriss-Bos	2.73	Harriss-Bos	44	Braxton-Was	13	Russell-Bos	13.29				
Harriss-Bos	77	Wiltse-Bos	3.12	Welzer-Bos	37	Ruffing-Bos	2	MacFayden-Bos	13.53				
Welzer-Bos	56	MacFayden-Bos	3.31	Wiltse-Bos	36	MacFayden-Bos	2	Harriss-Bos	13.56				

Innings Pitched		Opponents' Avg.		Opponents' OBP		Earned Run Average		Adjusted ERA		Adjusted Starter Runs		Pitcher Wins	
Thomas-Chi	307.2	Moore-NY	.234	Moore-NY	.289	Moore-NY	2.28	Moore-NY	169	Thomas-Chi	42.0	Lyons-Chi	4.7
Lyons-Chi	307.2	Ruffing-Bos	.277	Braxton-Was	.289	Harriss-Bos	4.18	Harriss-Bos	101	Bradley-Bos	3.0	MacFayden-Bos	.4
Wiltse-Bos	219.0	MacFayden-Bos	.294	Harriss-Bos	.355	MacFayden-Bos	4.27	MacFayden-Bos	99	Bennett-Bos	2.1	Bradley-Bos	.3
Harriss-Bos	217.2	Harriss-Bos	.298	MacFayden-Bos	.363	Ruffing-Bos	4.66	Ruffing-Bos	90	Russell-Bos	1.9	Bennett-Bos	.0

1928 AMERICAN LEAGUE

TEAM	W	L	T	PCT	GB	R	OR	HR	AVG	OBP	SLG	OPS	AOPS	PF	SB	CG	HR	BB	SO	BR/9	ERA	AERA	OAV	OOB	FW	PW	BW	BSW	DIF
NY	101	53	0	.656		894	685	133	.296	.365	.450	815	+24	97	51	82	59	452	487	12.7	3.74	+1	.276	.335	-.0	.3	17.1	-.4	7.1
Phi	98	55	0	.641	2.5	829	615	89	.295	.363	.436	799	+12	103	59	81	66	454	607	11.8	3.36	+19	.259	.318	.6	9.5	9.4	-.3	2.3
StL	82	72	0	.532	19	772	742	63	.274	.346	.393	739	-3	103	78	80	93	454	456	12.8	4.17	+1	.282	.340	.2	.3	-1.8	.4	5.9
Was	75	79	1	.487	26	718	705	40	.284	.346	.393	739	+1	99	108	77	40	462	462	12.5	3.88	+3	.272	.335	1.0	1.8	.5	.4	-5.7
Chi	72	82	1	.468	29	656	725	24	.270	.334	.358	692	-12	99	144	88	66	501	418	13.4	3.98	+2	.287	.352	.5	.8	-8.0	.4	1.4
Det	68	86	0	.442	33	744	804	62	.279	.340	.401	741	-1	102	113	65	58	567	451	13.7	4.32	-5	.281	.355	-1.5	-3.2	-1.5	-.0	-2.8
Cle	62	92	1	.403	39	674	830	34	.285	.335	.382	717	-7	101	71	52	51	416	416	14.2	4.47	-7	.303	.368	-1.6	-4.9	-5.4	-.4	-2.7
Bos	57	96	1	.373	43.5	589	770	38	.264	.319	.361	680	-14	-98	97	70	49	452	407	13.2	4.39	-7	.288	.349	.9	-4.3	-10.4	.0	-5.8
Total	617					5876		483	.281	.344	.397	741			700	614		3827	3704	13.0	4.04		.281	.344					

Batter-Fielder Wins		Batting Average		On-Base Percentage		Slugging Average		On-Base Plus Slugging		Adjusted OPS		Adjusted Batter Runs	
Ruth-NY	**7.1**	Goslin-Was	.379	Gehrig-NY	.467	Ruth-NY	.709	Ruth-NY	1172	Ruth-NY	211	Ruth-NY	92.1
Myer-Bos	**2.0**	Myer-Bos	.313	Myer-Bos	.379	Taitt-Bos	.434	Taitt-Bos	784	Taitt-Bos	107	Ruffing-Bos	13.0
Regan-Bos	**.1**	K.Williams-Bos	.303	Flagstead-Bos	.366	K.Williams-Bos	.413	K.Williams-Bos	769	Myer-Bos	104	Myer-Bos	5.2
		Taitt-Bos	.299	K.Williams-Bos	.356	Todt-Bos	.406	Myer-Bos	769	K.Williams-Bos	103	Flagstead-Bos	3.4

Runs		Hits		Doubles		Triples		Home Runs		Total Bases		Runs Batted In	
Ruth-NY	163	Manush-StL	241	Manush-StL	47	Combs-NY	21	Ruth-NY	54	Ruth-NY	380	Ruth-NY	142
Flagstead-Bos	84	Myer-Bos	168	Gehrig-NY	47	Taitt-Bos	14	Todt-Bos	12	Todt-Bos	219	Gehrig-NY	142
Myer-Bos	78	Flagstead-Bos	148	Flagstead-Bos	41	Todt-Bos	8	K.Williams-Bos	8	Taitt-Bos	209	Regan-Bos	75
Todt-Bos	61	Taitt-Bos	144	Todt-Bos	31	2 players tied	6	Regan-Bos	7	Myer-Bos	209	Todt-Bos	73

Stolen Bases		Base Stealing Runs		Fielding Runs-Infield		Fielding Runs-Outfield		Wins		Winning Pct.		Complete Games	
Myer-Bos	30	Rice-Was	2.5	Gerber-StL-Bos	25.7	Jamieson-Cle	15.9	Pipgras-NY	24	Crowder-StL	.808	Ruffing-Bos	25
Taitt-Bos	13	Goslin-Was	2.5	Regan-Bos	15.1	Taitt-Bos	6.0	Grove-Phi	24	Morris-Bos	.559	Morris-Bos	20
Rothrock-Bos	12	Myer-Bos	1.0	Myer-Bos	6.1	Flagstead-Bos	1.7	Morris-Bos	19			Russell-Bos	10
Flagstead-Bos	12	Taitt-Bos	.8	Todt-Bos	2.7	Rogell-Bos	.0	Russell-Bos	11			MacFayden-Bos	9

Strikeouts		Fewest BB/Game		Games		Saves		Base Runners/9		Adjusted Relief Runs		Relief Ranking	
Grove-Phi	183	Rommel-Phi	1.35	Marberry-Was	48	Hoyt-NY	8	Braxton-Was	9.32				
Ruffing-Bos	118	Russell-Bos	1.83	Morris-Bos	47	Morris-Bos	5	Morris-Bos	11.88				
Morris-Bos	104	Morris-Bos	2.79	Ruffing-Bos	42	Ruffing-Bos	2	Harriss-Bos	12.34				
MacFayden-Bos	61	Ruffing-Bos	2.99	MacFayden-Bos	33	4 players tied	1	Russell-Bos	12.43				

Innings Pitched		Opponents' Avg.		Opponents' OBP		Earned Run Average		Adjusted ERA		Adjusted Starter Runs		Pitcher Wins	
Pipgras-NY	300.2	Braxton-Was	.222	Braxton-Was	.267	Braxton-Was	2.51	Braxton-Was	159	Grove-Phi	40.7	Grove-Phi	4.7
Ruffing-Bos	289.1	Morris-Bos	.264	Morris-Bos	.323	Morris-Bos	3.53	Morris-Bos	116	Morris-Bos	16.2	Ruffing-Bos	1.8
Morris-Bos	257.2	Ruffing-Bos	.275	Russell-Bos	.332	Russell-Bos	3.84	Russell-Bos	107	Ruffing-Bos	6.4	Morris-Bos	1.5
Russell-Bos	201.1	MacFayden-Bos	.289	Ruffing-Bos	.339	Ruffing-Bos	3.89	Ruffing-Bos	106	Russell-Bos	5.1	Russell-Bos	.6

1929 AMERICAN LEAGUE

TEAM	W	L	T	PCT	GB	R	OR	HR	AVG	OBP	SLG	OPS	AOPS	PF	SB	CG	HR	BB	SO	BR/9	ERA	AERA	OAV	OOB	FW	PW	BW	BSW	DIF
Phi	104	46	1	.693		901	615	122	.296	.365	.451	816	+11	104	63	70	73	487	573	12.4	3.44	+23	.264	.329	2.6	11.2	7.9	.4	6.8
NY	88	66	0	.571	18	899	775	142	.295	.364	.450	814	+23	104	52	64	83	484	484	13.1	4.19	-8	.278	.341	.8	-5.4	16.4	-.1	-.7
Cle	81	71	0	.533	24	717	736	62	.294	.354	.417	771	+0	104	75	80	56	488	389	13.9	4.05	+9	.295	.357	-.6	5.1	.0	-.9	1.4
StL	79	73	2	.520	26	733	713	46	.276	.352	.381	733	-9	104	70	83	100	462	415	12.8	4.08	+8	.279	.340	2.2	4.6	-5.5	.3	1.3
Was	71	81	1	.467	34	730	776	48	.276	.347	.375	722	-10	101	89	62	48	496	494	12.9	4.34	-2	.276	.342	-.3	-1.5	-5.8	.3	2.3
Det	70	84	1	.455	36	926	928	110	.299	.360	.453	813	+14	100	95	82	73	646	467	15.0	4.96	-14	.301	.377	-3.0	-9.8	10.2	-.0	-4.3
Chi	59	93	0	.388	46	627	792	37	.268	.325	.363	688	-17	100	109	78	78	505	328	13.4	4.41	-3	.284	.351	.0	-2.1	-12.4	.5	-3.2
Bos	58	96	1	.377	48	605	803	28	.267	.325	.365	690	-15	98	86	84	78	496	416	13.6	4.43	-4	.291	.355	-1.6	-2.4	-10.9	-.5	-3.6
Total	613					6138		595	.284	.349	.407	757			639	603		4065	3566	13.4	4.24		.284	.349					

Batter-Fielder Wins		Batting Average		On-Base Percentage		Slugging Average		On-Base Plus Slugging		Adjusted OPS		Adjusted Batter Runs	
Ruth-NY	5.4	Fonseca-Cle	.369	Foxx-Phi	.463	Ruth-NY	.697	Ruth-NY	1128	Ruth-NY	199	Ruth-NY	72.3
Williams-Bos	.7	Rothrock-Bos	.300	Rothrock-Bos	.361	Scarritt-Bos	.411	Rothrock-Bos	769	Rothrock-Bos	100	Williams-Bos	9.9
Heving-Bos	.4	Scarritt-Bos	.294	Reeves-Bos	.343	Rothrock-Bos	.408	Scarritt-Bos	749	Scarritt-Bos	94	Morris-Bos	2.4
B.Barrett-Bos	.2	Regan-Bos	.288	Scarritt-Bos	.337	Regan-Bos	.407	Todt-Bos	698	Todt-Bos	80	Bayne-Bos	2.2

Runs		Hits		Doubles		Triples		Home Runs		Total Bases		Runs Batted In	
Gehringer-Det	131	Gehringer-Det	215	3 players tied	45	Gehringer-Det	19	Ruth-NY	46	Simmons-Phi	373	Simmons-Phi	157
Rothrock-Bos	70	Alexander-Det	215	Todt-Bos	38	Scarritt-Bos	17	Rothrock-Bos	6	Scarritt-Bos	222	Scarritt-Bos	71
Scarritt-Bos	69	Scarritt-Bos	159	Regan-Bos	27	Todt-Bos	10	Todt-Bos	4	Todt-Bos	210	Todt-Bos	64
Reeves-Bos	66	Rothrock-Bos	142	Scarritt-Bos	26	2 players tied	7	Williams-Bos	3	Rothrock-Bos	193	Rothrock-Bos	59

Stolen Bases		Base Stealing Runs		Fielding Runs-Infield		Fielding Runs-Outfield		Wins		Winning Pct.		Complete Games	
Gehringer-Det	27	Gehringer-Det	2.4	Melillo-StL	20.4	Simmons-Phi	19.6	Earnshaw-Phi	24	Grove-Phi	.769	Thomas-Chi	24
Rothrock-Bos	24	Rothrock-Bos	.7	Reeves-Bos	4.9	Rothrock-Bos	2.6	Morris-Bos	14			M.Gaston-Bos	20
Scarritt-Bos	13	Rhyne-Bos	.5	Todt-Bos	2.5			M.Gaston-Bos	12			Ruffing-Bos	18
2 players tied	7	B.Barrett-Bos	.3					MacFayden-Bos	10			Morris-Bos	17

Strikeouts		Fewest BB/Game		Games		Saves		Base Runners/9		Adjusted Relief Runs		Relief Ranking	
Grove-Phi	170	Russell-Bos	1.58	Marberry-Was	49	Marberry-Was	11	Marberry-Was	11.07				
Ruffing-Bos	109	M.Gaston-Bos	2.99	M.Gaston-Bos	39	M.Gaston-Bos	2	Russell-Bos	12.11				
M.Gaston-Bos	83	MacFayden-Bos	3.30	Russell-Bos	35	5 players tied	1	MacFayden-Bos	12.67				
Morris-Bos	73	Morris-Bos	4.10	Ruffing-Bos	35			M.Gaston-Bos	12.89				

Innings Pitched		Opponents' Avg.		Opponents' OBP		Earned Run Average		Adjusted ERA		Adjusted Starter Runs		Pitcher Wins	
Gray-StL	305.0	Earnshaw-Phi	.241	Marberry-Was	.308	Grove-Phi	2.81	Grove-Phi	150	Grove-Phi	42.6	Marberry-Was	4.0
Ruffing-Bos	244.1	MacFayden-Bos	.271	Russell-Bos	.322	MacFayden-Bos	3.62	MacFayden-Bos	118	MacFayden-Bos	15.0	M.Gaston-Bos	1.6
M.Gaston-Bos	243.2	Morris-Bos	.282	MacFayden-Bos	.340	M.Gaston-Bos	3.73	M.Gaston-Bos	114	M.Gaston-Bos	14.4	MacFayden-Bos	1.5
Russell-Bos	227.1	M.Gaston-Bos	.289	M.Gaston-Bos	.348	Russell-Bos	3.92	Russell-Bos	109	Russell-Bos	3.1	2 players tied	.1

1930 AMERICAN LEAGUE

TEAM	W	L	T	PCT	GB	R	OR	HR	AVG	OBP	SLG	OPS	AOPS	PF	SB	CG	HR	BB	SO	BR/9	ERA	AERA	OAV	OOB	FW	PW	BW	BSW	DIF
Phi	102	52	0	.662		951	751	125	.294	.369	.452	821	+8	104	48	72	84	488	672	12.9	4.28	+9	.274	.337	3.0	5.2	6.0	.0	10.7
Was	94	60	0	.610	8	892	689	57	.302	.364	.426	795	+6	100	101	78	52	504	504	12.5	3.96	+16	.264	.332	2.3	8.8	5.0	.0	.9
NY	86	68	0	.558	16	1062	898	152	.309	.384	.488	872	+31	96	91	65	93	524	572	13.9	4.88	-12	.287	.352	-.7	-8.9	23.4	.0	-4.9
Cle	81	73	0	.526	21	890	915	72	.304	.364	.431	795	+2	104	51	68	85	528	442	14.6	4.88	-1	.305	.368	-2.5	-.8	2.4	-.3	5.2
Det	75	79	0	.487	27	783	833	82	.284	.344	.421	765	-4	102	91	68	86	524	574	14.0	4.70	-4	.286	.359	.2	1.2	-3.1	-.0	-.2
StL	64	90	0	.416	38	751	886	75	.268	.333	.391	724	-15	103	93	68	124	449	470	13.9	5.07	-4	.300	.356	.4	-2.6	-10.9	-.2	.3
Chi	62	92	0	.403	40	729	884	63	.276	.328	.391	719	-11	94	74	63	74	407	471	13.6	4.71	-2	.300	.352	-2.4	-1.4	-8.3	.4	-3.3
Bos	52	102	0	.338	50	612	814	47	.264	.313	.365	678	-21	96	42	78	75	488	356	13.4	4.68	-2	.286	.348	-.0	-1.1	-15.6	-.0	-8.2
Total	616					6670		673	.288	.351	.421	772			598	560		3958	4081	13.6	4.65		.288	.351					

Batter-Fielder Wins		Batting Average		On-Base Percentage		Slugging Average		On-Base Plus Slugging		Adjusted OPS		Adjusted Batter Runs	
Gehrig-NY	7.7	Simmons-Phi	.381	Ruth-NY	.493	Ruth-NY	.732	Ruth-NY	1225	Ruth-NY	216	Ruth-NY	100.0
Berry-Bos	1.0	Webb-Bos	.323	Webb-Bos	.385	Webb-Bos	.523	Webb-Bos	908	Webb-Bos	133	Webb-Bos	22.3
Webb-Bos	.7	Oliver-Bos	.293	Oliver-Bos	.339	Todt-Bos	.439	Regan-Bos	696	Oliver-Bos	78	Morris-Bos	2.1
		Scarritt-Bos	.289	Regan-Bos	.303	Regan-Bos	.393	Oliver-Bos	690	Regan-Bos	78	Smith-Bos	1.9

Runs		Hits		Doubles		Triples		Home Runs		Total Bases		Runs Batted In	
Simmons-Phi	152	Hodapp-Cle	225	Hodapp-Cle	51	Combs-NY	22	Ruth-NY	49	Gehrig-NY	419	Gehrig-NY	174
Oliver-Bos	86	Oliver-Bos	189	Regan-Bos	35	Regan-Bos	10	Webb-Bos	16	Webb-Bos	235	Webb-Bos	66
Webb-Bos	61	Webb-Bos	145	Oliver-Bos	34	Scarritt-Bos	8	Todt-Bos	11	Oliver-Bos	227	Todt-Bos	62
Regan-Bos	54	Regan-Bos	135	Webb-Bos	30	2 players tied	6	Berry-Bos	6	Regan-Bos	199	Regan-Bos	53

Stolen Bases		Base Stealing Runs		Fielding Runs-Infield		Fielding Runs-Outfield		Wins		Winning Pct.		Complete Games	
McManus-Det	23	Lary-NY	2.4	Cronin-Was	26.5	Haas-Phi	7.4	Grove-Phi	28	Grove-Phi	.848	Lyons-Chi	29
Reeves-Bos	6	Reeves-Bos	.6	Rhyne-Bos	2.8	Oliver-Bos	6.0	Gaston-Bos	13			Gaston-Bos	20
Oliver-Bos	6	Todt-Bos	.5	Todt-Bos	1.9			MacFayden-Bos	11			MacFayden-Bos	18
Sweeney-Bos	5	2 players tied	.4					Lisenbee-Bos	10			2 players tied	15

Strikeouts		Fewest BB/Game		Games		Saves		Base Runners/9		Adjusted Relief Runs		Relief Ranking	
Grove-Phi	209	Pennock-NY	1.15	Grove-Phi	50	Grove-Phi	9	Grove-Phi	10.45	Quinn-Phi	2.4	Quinn-Phi	4.2
Gaston-Bos	99	Russell-Bos	2.08	Gaston-Bos	38	MacFayden-Bos	2	Durham-Bos	12.15				
MacFayden-Bos	76	MacFayden-Bos	3.11	Lisenbee-Bos	37	Gaston-Bos	2	Gaston-Bos	12.20				
Lisenbee-Bos	47	Gaston-Bos	3.23	MacFayden-Bos	36	Durham-Bos	1	Lisenbee-Bos	13.08				

Innings Pitched		Opponents' Avg.		Opponents' OBP		Earned Run Average		Adjusted ERA		Adjusted Starter Runs		Pitcher Wins	
Lyons-Chi	297.2	Grove-Phi	.247	Grove-Phi	.288	Grove-Phi	2.54	Grove-Phi	184	Grove-Phi	65.8	Grove-Phi	6.9
Gaston-Bos	273.0	Hadley-Was	.247	Gaston-Bos	.323	Gaston-Bos	3.92	Gaston-Bos	117	Gaston-Bos	20.4	Gaston-Bos	1.8
MacFayden-Bos	269.1	Gaston-Bos	.259	MacFayden-Bos	.343	MacFayden-Bos	4.21	MacFayden-Bos	109	MacFayden-Bos	13.6	MacFayden-Bos	.8
Lisenbee-Bos	237.1	Lisenbee-Bos	.280	Lisenbee-Bos	.346	Lisenbee-Bos	4.40	Lisenbee-Bos	105	Lisenbee-Bos	7.0	Lisenbee-Bos	.6

1931 AMERICAN LEAGUE

TEAM	W	L	T	PCT	GB	R	OR	HR	AVG	OBP	SLG	OPS	AOPS	PF	SB	CG	HR	BB	SO	BR/9	ERA	AERA	OAV	OOB	FW	PW	BW	BSW	DIF
Phi	107	45	1	.704		858	**626**	118	.287	.355	.435	790	+7	106	25	**97**	73	457	574	**11.9**	**3.47**	+30	.256	.316	3.2	**14.2**	4.2	-.0	9.5
NY	94	59	2	.614	13.5	**1067**	760	155	.297	.383	.457	840	+35	94	**138**	78	67	543	686	12.9	4.20	-6	.263	.332	1.7	-3.8	26.5	.9	-7.8
Was	92	62	2	.597	16	843	690	49	.285	.345	.400	745	+0	101	72	60	73	498	582	12.6	3.76	+14	.264	.327	3.3	7.7	.2	-.4	4.2
Cle	78	76	1	.506	30	885	833	71	.296	.363	.419	782	+5	106	63	76	64	561	470	14.4	4.63	+0	.286	.355	-2.0	-.2	4.5	-.4	-.8
StL	63	91	0	.409	45	721	870	76	.271	.333	.390	723	-8	104	73	65	84	**448**	436	13.8	4.76	-3	.293	.348	-2.1	-1.6	-6.1	-.9	-3.3
Bos	62	90	1	.408	45	625	800	37	.262	.315	.349	664	-15	-95	42	61	**54**	473	365	13.5	4.60	-6	.285	.344	.4	-4.2	-11.1	-.3	1.2
Det	61	93	0	.396	47	651	836	43	.268	.330	.371	701	-13	103	117	86	79	597	511	14.1	4.59	+0	.282	.355	-1.4	-.0	-9.6	-.2	-5.1
Chi	56	97	3	.366	51.5	704	939	27	.260	.323	.343	666	-14	-94	94	54	82	588	421	14.5	5.04	-15	.287	.358	-2.7	-11.6	-10.3	.9	3.3
Total	618					6354		576	.278	.344	.396	740			624	577		4165	4045	13.5	4.38		.278	.344					

Batter-Fielder Wins		Batting Average		On-Base Percentage		Slugging Average		On-Base Plus Slugging		Adjusted OPS		Adjusted Batter Runs	
Ruth-NY	**8.1**	Simmons-Phi	.390	Ruth-NY	.495	Ruth-NY	.700	Ruth-NY	1195	Ruth-NY	223	Ruth-NY	104.4
Webb-Bos	**3.0**	Webb-Bos	.333	Webb-Bos	.404	Webb-Bos	.528	Webb-Bos	932	Webb-Bos	151	Webb-Bos	47.0
Rhyne-Bos	**1.6**	Sweeney-Bos	.295	Rothrock-Bos	.343	Pickering-Bos	.393	Rothrock-Bos	726	Rothrock-Bos	96	Kline-Bos	2.7
Berry-Bos	**.4**	Berry-Bos	.283	Rhyne-Bos	.341	Berry-Bos	.389	Sweeney-Bos	696	Sweeney-Bos	87	Brillheart-Bos	1.7

Runs		Hits		Doubles		Triples		Home Runs		Total Bases		Runs Batted In	
Gehrig-NY	163	Gehrig-NY	211	Webb-Bos	67	Johnson-Det	19	Ruth-NY	46	Gehrig-NY	410	Gehrig-NY	184
Webb-Bos	96	Webb-Bos	196	Oliver-Bos	35	Oliver-Bos	5	Gehrig-NY	46	Webb-Bos	311	Webb-Bos	103
Rothrock-Bos	81	Oliver-Bos	162	Rhyne-Bos	34	VanCamp-Bos	4	Webb-Bos	14	Oliver-Bos	207	Oliver-Bos	70
Rhyne-Bos	75	Rhyne-Bos	154	Rothrock-Bos	32	Pickering-Bos	4	Pickering-Bos	9	Rhyne-Bos	194	Sweeney-Bos	58

Stolen Bases		Base Stealing Runs		Fielding Runs-Infield		Fielding Runs-Outfield		Wins		Winning Pct.		Complete Games	
Chapman-NY	61	Chapman-NY	5.4	Melillo-StL	35.3	West-Was	13.6	Grove-Phi	31	Grove-Phi	.886	Grove-Phi	27
Rothrock-Bos	13	Berry-Bos	.9	Rhyne-Bos	18.0	Oliver-Bos	5.8	MacFayden-Bos	16	MacFayden-Bos	.571	Ferrell-Cle	27
Sweeney-Bos	5	Rothrock-Bos	.4	Sweeney-Bos	8.4			Moore-Bos	11			MacFayden-Bos	17
2 players tied	4	2 players tied	.2	Miller-Bos	2.4			Russell-Bos	10			Russell-Bos	13

Strikeouts		Fewest BB/Game		Games		Saves		Base Runners/9		Adjusted Relief Runs		Relief Ranking	
Grove-Phi	175	Pennock-NY	1.43	Hadley-Was	55	Moore-Bos	10	Grove-Phi	9.73	Kimsey-StL	.7	Kimsey-StL	.8
MacFayden-Bos	74	Russell-Bos	2.52	Moore-Bos	53			Moore-Bos	12.19				
Durham-Bos	53	Moore-Bos	2.67	Lisenbee-Bos	41			Durham-Bos	12.47				
Morris-Bos	46	Lisenbee-Bos	2.68	Durham-Bos	38			Lisenbee-Bos	13.23				

Innings Pitched		Opponents' Avg.		Opponents' OBP		Earned Run Average		Adjusted ERA		Adjusted Starter Runs		Pitcher Wins	
Walberg-Phi	291.0	Hadley-Was	.218	Grove-Phi	.271	Grove-Phi	2.06	Grove-Phi	218	Grove-Phi	73.9	Grove-Phi	8.2
Russell-Bos	232.0	Durham-Bos	.266	Moore-Bos	.322	Moore-Bos	3.88	Moore-Bos	111	Moore-Bos	10.4	Moore-Bos	1.3
MacFayden-Bos	230.2	Moore-Bos	.269	Durham-Bos	.322	MacFayden-Bos	4.02	MacFayden-Bos	107	MacFayden-Bos	6.1	MacFayden-Bos	.3
Moore-Bos	185.1	2 players tied	.281	Lisenbee-Bos	.332	Durham-Bos	4.25	Durham-Bos	101	Durham-Bos	.4	Kline-Bos	.3

1932 AMERICAN LEAGUE

TEAM	W	L	T	PCT	GB	R	OR	HR	AVG	OBP	SLG	OPS	AOPS	PF	SB	CG	HR	BB	SO	BR/9	ERA	AERA	OAV	OOB	FW	PW	BW	BSW	DIF
NY	107	47	2	.695		**1002**	724	160	.286	**.376**	.454	**830**	+28	95	77	**96**	93	561	**780**	12.8	3.98	+2	**.260**	.331	.2	1.6	**21.5**	-.3	7.1
Phi	94	60	0	.610	13	981	752	**172**	.290	.366	**.457**	823	+15	106	38	95	112	595	595	13.0	4.45	+2	.271	.336	**3.8**	1.0	11.0	.3	.9
Was	93	61	0	.604	14	840	**716**	61	.284	.347	.408	755	+2	99	70	66	73	526	437	13.0	4.16	+4	.271	.337	**3.8**	2.3	1.6	.2	8.2
Cle	87	65	1	.572	19	845	747	78	.285	.357	.413	770	-1	107	52	94	70	**446**	**446**	12.8	4.12	**+15**	.273	**.329**	-.2	**8.3**	-.6	-.4	3.8
Det	76	75	2	.503	29.5	799	787	80	.273	.335	.401	736	-8	104	**103**	67	89	592	521	13.5	4.30	+9	.269	.346	.0	5.4	-6.1	**.8**	.4
StL	63	91	0	.409	44	736	898	67	.276	.339	.388	727	-11	106	69	63	103	574	496	14.3	5.01	-3	.290	.359	.0	-2.0	-8.1	-.4	-3.5
Chi	49	102	1	.325	56.5	667	987	36	.267	.327	.360	687	-10	-94	89	50	88	580	379	14.4	4.82	-10	.287	.359	-4.6	-7.1	-7.2	.2	-7.7
Bos	43	111	0	.279	64	566	915	53	.251	.314	.351	665	-20	-97	46	42	79	612	365	14.6	5.02	-10	.289	.364	-2.6	-7.3	-14.6	-.3	-9.2
Total	615					6436		707	.277	.346	.404	750			544	573		4402	4012	13.6	4.48		.277	.346					

Batter-Fielder Wins		Batting Average		On-Base Percentage		Slugging Average		On-Base Plus Slugging		Adjusted OPS		Adjusted Batter Runs	
Foxx-Phi	**6.7**	Alexander-Det-Bos	.367	Ruth-NY	.489	Foxx-Phi	.749	Foxx-Phi	1218	Ruth-NY	206	Foxx-Phi	91.5
Spognardi-Bos	**.3**	Oliver-Bos	.264	Olson-Bos	.347	McManus-Bos	.374	Pickering-Bos	677	Pickering-Bos	77	Welch-Bos	1.8
Storie-Bos	**.0**	Pickering-Bos	.260	Pickering-Bos	.320	Pickering-Bos	.357	Olson-Bos	660	Olson-Bos	74	McNaughton-Bos	.4
		Olson-Bos	.248	Oliver-Bos	.305	Oliver-Bos	.327	Oliver-Bos	632	Oliver-Bos	66	Spognardi-Bos	.0

Runs		Hits		Doubles		Triples		Home Runs		Total Bases		Runs Batted In	
Foxx-Phi	151	Simmons-Phi	216	McNair-Phi	47	Cronin-Was	18	Foxx-Phi	58	Foxx-Phi	438	Foxx-Phi	169
Olson-Bos	58	Oliver-Bos	120	Pickering-Bos	28	Olson-Bos	6	McManus-Bos	5	Pickering-Bos	163	Pickering-Bos	40
Pickering-Bos	47	Pickering-Bos	119	Oliver-Bos	23	4 players tied	5	Pickering-Bos	2	Oliver-Bos	149	Oliver-Bos	37
2 players tied	39	Olson-Bos	100	McManus-Bos	21			2 players tied	1	Olson-Bos	126	Warstler-Bos	34

Stolen Bases		Base Stealing Runs		Fielding Runs-Infield		Fielding Runs-Outfield		Wins		Winning Pct.		Complete Games	
Chapman-NY	38	Walker-Det	4.5	Warstler-Bos	22.8	Vosmik-Cle	18.9	Crowder-Was	26	Allen-NY	.810	Grove-Phi	27
Warstler-Bos	9					Oliver-Bos	2.8	Kline-Bos	11			Weiland-Bos	7
Rhyne-Bos	3							Weiland-Bos	6			Kline-Bos	4
Pickering-Bos	3							Durham-Bos	6			Durham-Bos	4

Strikeouts		Fewest BB/Game		Games		Saves		Base Runners/9		Adjusted Relief Runs		Relief Ranking	
Ruffing-NY	190	Brown-Cle	1.71	Marberry-Was	54	Marberry-Was	13	Grove-Phi	10.77	Kimsey-StL-Chi	7.7	Kimsey-StL-Chi	7.2
Weiland-Bos	63	Durham-Bos	2.52	Kline-Bos	47	Kline-Bos	2	Durham-Bos	12.32				
Durham-Bos	52	Kline-Bos	3.98	Weiland-Bos	43	Weiland-Bos	1	Lisenbee-Bos	13.87				
Kline-Bos	31	Weiland-Bos	4.46	Durham-Bos	34			Michaels-Bos	14.62				

Innings Pitched		Opponents' Avg.		Opponents' OBP		Earned Run Average		Adjusted ERA		Adjusted Starter Runs		Pitcher Wins	
Crowder-Was	327.0	Ruffing-NY	.226	Grove-Phi	.292	Grove-Phi	2.84	Grove-Phi	159	Grove-Phi	54.0	Grove-Phi	5.9
Weiland-Bos	195.2	Durham-Bos	.274	Durham-Bos	.327	Durham-Bos	3.80	Durham-Bos	118	Durham-Bos	13.2	Durham-Bos	.9
Durham-Bos	175.1	Kline-Bos	.294	Kline-Bos	.365	Weiland-Bos	4.51	Weiland-Bos	100				
Kline-Bos	172.0	Weiland-Bos	.295	Weiland-Bos	.377	Kline-Bos	5.28	Kline-Bos	85				

188

1933 AMERICAN LEAGUE

TEAM	W	L	T	PCT	GB	R	OR	HR	AVG	OBP	SLG	OPS	AOPS	PF	SB	CG	HR	BB	SO	BR/9	ERA	AERA	OAV	OOB	FW	PW	BW	BSW	DIF
Was	99	53	1	.651		850	665	60	.287	.353	.402	755	+7	99	65	68	64	452	447	12.2	3.82	+9	.263	.322	2.6	5.4	5.2	.0	9.7
NY	91	59	2	.607	7	927	768	144	.283	.369	.440	809	+29	94	76	66	612	711	13.6	4.36	-11	.267	.344	.4	-7.6	20.4	.0	2.8
Phi	79	72	1	.523	19.5	875	853	139	.285	.362	.440	802	+18	101	34	69	77	644	423	14.6	4.81	-11	.283	.361	-1.9	-7.4	12.4	.0	.4
Cle	75	76	0	.497	23.5	654	669	50	.261	.321	.360	681	-18	-105	36	74	60	465	437	12.4	3.71	+20	.264	.325	.9	10.1	-12.9	-.2	1.5
Det	75	79	1	.487	25	722	733	57	.269	.329	.380	709	-8	102	68	69	84	561	575	12.9	3.95	+9	.263	.335	-.2	5.3	-6.4	.0	-.8
Chi	67	83	1	.447	31	683	814	43	.272	.342	.360	702	-4	96	43	53	85	519	423	13.5	4.45	-5	.277	.343	-1.0	-3.1	-1.9	-.3	-1.7
Bos	63	86	0	.423	34.5	700	758	50	.271	.339	.377	716	-3	99	58	60	75	591	467	13.6	4.35	+1	.271	.348	-2.2	.4	-1.7	.4	-8.3
StL	55	96	2	.364	43.5	669	820	64	.253	.322	.360	682	-19	-106	72	55	96	531	426	14.0	4.82	-3	.289	.354	1.5	-2.2	-13.4	-.0	-6.3
Total	608					6080		607	.273	.342	.390	732			452	518		4375	3909	13.3	4.28		.273	.342					

Batter-Fielder Wins		Batting Average		On-Base Percentage		Slugging Average		On-Base Plus Slugging		Adjusted OPS		Adjusted Batter Runs	
Foxx-Phi	**6.9**	Foxx-Phi	.356	Cochrane-Phi	.459	Foxx-Phi	.703	Foxx-Phi	1153	Foxx-Phi	199	Foxx-Phi	82.4
R.Johnson-Bos	**1.1**	R.Johnson-Bos	.313	R.Johnson-Bos	.387	R.Johnson-Bos	.466	R.Johnson-Bos	853	R.Johnson-Bos	126	R.Johnson-Bos	19.2
Hodapp-Bos	**1.1**	Hodapp-Bos	.312	Cooke-Bos	.386	Cooke-Bos	.447	Cooke-Bos	833	Cooke-Bos	121	Cooke-Bos	16.1
McManus-Bos	**.8**	Cooke-Bos	.293			Jolley-Bos	.445					McManus-Bos	5.8

Runs		Hits		Doubles		Triples		Home Runs		Total Bases		Runs Batted In	
Gehrig	138	Manush-Was	221	Cronin-Was	45	Manush-Was	17	Foxx-Phi	48	Foxx-Phi	403	Foxx-Phi	163
R.Johnson-Bos	88	R.Johnson-Bos	151	Cooke-Bos	35	Cooke-Bos	10	R.Johnson-Bos	10	R.Johnson-Bos	225	R.Johnson-Bos	95
Cooke-Bos	86	Cooke-Bos	133	Jolley-Bos	32	R.Johnson-Bos	7	Jolley-Bos	9	Cooke-Bos	203	Jolley-Bos	65
Hodapp-Bos	55	Hodapp-Bos	129	2 players tied	30	Hodapp-Bos	5	2 players tied	5	Jolley-Bos	183	2 players tied	54

Stolen Bases		Base Stealing Runs		Fielding Runs-Infield		Fielding Runs-Outfield		Wins		Winning Pct.		Complete Games	
Chapman-NY	27	Walker-Det	2.6	Melillo-StL	22.3	Chapman-NY	14.1	Grove-Phi	24	Grove-Phi	.750	Grove-Phi	21
R.Johnson-Bos	13	Stumpf-Bos	.9			R.Johnson-Bos	.8	Crowder-Was	24			Rhodes-Bos	14
Cooke-Bos	7	McManus-Bos	.7					Rhodes-Bos	12			Weiland-Bos	12
Stumpf-Bos	4	Almada-Bos	.3					3 players tied	8			H.Johnson-Bos	7

Strikeouts		Fewest BB/Game		Games		Saves		Base Runners/9		Adjusted Relief Runs		Relief Ranking	
Gomez-NY	163	Brown-Cle	1.65	Crowder-Was	52	Russell-Was	13	Heving-Chi	10.83	Russell-Was	19.6	Russell-Was	30.3
Weiland-Bos	97	Rhodes-Bos	3.61	Welch-Bos	47	Kline-Bos	4	Weiland-Bos	12.56	Kline-Bos	.2	Kline-Bos	.2
Rhodes-Bos	85	Weiland-Bos	4.16	Kline-Bos	46	Welch-Bos	3	Rhodes-Bos	13.03				
Welch-Bos	68	H.Johnson-Bos	4.29	Weiland-Bos	39	Weiland-Bos	3	H.Johnson-Bos	13.50				

Innings Pitched		Opponents' Avg.		Opponents' OBP		Earned Run Average		Adjusted ERA		Adjusted Starter Runs		Pitcher Wins	
Hadley-StL	316.2	Bridges-Det	.226	Marberry-Det	.302	Pearson-Cle	2.33	Harder-Cle	151	Harder-Cle	35.1	Harder-Cle	4.4
Rhodes-Bos	232.0	Weiland-Bos	.244	Weiland-Bos	.331	Weiland-Bos	3.87	Weiland-Bos	113	Weiland-Bos	13.2	Rhodes-Bos	1.2
Weiland-Bos	216.1	H.Johnson-Bos	.263	Rhodes-Bos	.334	Rhodes-Bos	4.03	Rhodes-Bos	109	Rhodes-Bos	7.4	Weiland-Bos	.7
H.Johnson-Bos	155.1	Rhodes-Bos	.265	H.Johnson-Bos	.348	H.Johnson-Bos	4.06	H.Johnson-Bos	108	H.Johnson-Bos	4.9	H.Johnson-Bos	.7

1934 AMERICAN LEAGUE

TEAM	W	L	T	PCT	GB	R	OR	HR	AVG	OBP	SLG	OPS	AOPS	PF	SB	CG	HR	BB	SO	BR/9	ERA	AERA	OAV	OOB	FW	PW	BW	BSW	DIF
Det	101	53	0	.656		958	708	74	.300	.376	.424	800	+13	100	125	74	86	488	640	12.9	4.06	+8	.273	.335	1.2	4.8	10.9	.6	6.5
NY	94	60	0	.610	7	842	669	135	.278	.364	.419	783	+17	93	71	83	71	542	656	12.4	3.76	+13	.254	.324	1.3	-.9	12.4	-.1	-1.4
Cle	85	69	0	.552	16	814	763	100	.287	.353	.423	776	+5	102	52	72	70	509	554	13.7	4.28	+6	.275	.349	.4	3.7	3.3	-.1	.6
Bos	76	76	1	.500	24	820	775	51	.274	.350	.383	733	-10	107	116	68	70	543	538	13.8	4.32	+11	.283	.351	-.5	6.3	-7.2	.7	.6
Phi	68	82	3	.453	31	764	838	144	.280	.343	.425	768	+8	96	57	68	84	480	480	14.4	5.01	-13	.264	.363	-9.0	-4.3	-.1	-1.2
StL	67	85	2	.441	33	674	800	62	.268	.335	.373	708	-18	108	43	50	94	632	499	14.3	4.49	+11	.283	.361	-.4	6.3	-13.0	-.2	-1.7
Was	66	86	3	.434	34	729	806	51	.278	.348	.382	730	-1	96	47	61	74	503	499	13.9	4.68	-8	.291	.355	1.0	-5.3	-.6	-.5	-4.7
Chi	53	99	1	.349	47	704	946	71	.263	.336	.363	699	-16	103	36	72	139	628	506	14.9	5.41	-12	.292	.367	-1.6	-8.9	-11.1	-.3	-1.1
Total	615					6305		688	.279	.351	.399	750			547	548		4611	4285	13.8	4.50		.279	.351					

Batter-Fielder Wins		Batting Average		On-Base Percentage		Slugging Average		On-Base Plus Slugging		Adjusted OPS		Adjusted Batter Runs	
Gehrig-NY	**7.9**	Gehrig-NY	.363	Gehrig-NY	.465	Gehrig-NY	.706	Gehrig-NY	1172	Gehrig-NY	213	Gehrig-NY	100.4
Werber-Bos	**3.9**	Werber-Bos	.321	Werber-Bos	.397	Werber-Bos	.472	Werber-Bos	868	Werber-Bos	115	Werber-Bos	15.1
R.Ferrell-Bos	**1.1**	R.Johnson-Bos	.320	R.Ferrell-Bos	.390	R.Johnson-Bos	.467	R.Johnson-Bos	846	R.Johnson-Bos	110	W.Ferrell-Bos	8.1
Bishop-Bos	**.9**	Reynolds-Bos	.303	R.Johnson-Bos	.379	Solters-Bos	.447	R.Ferrell-Bos	779	R.Ferrell-Bos	95	R.Johnson-Bos	8.0

Runs		Hits		Doubles		Triples		Home Runs		Total Bases		Runs Batted In	
Gehringer-Det	134	Gehringer-Det	214	Greenberg-Det	63	Chapman-NY	13	Gehrig-NY	49	Gehrig-NY	409	Gehrig-NY	165
Werber-Bos	129	Werber-Bos	200	R.Johnson-Bos	43	Werber-Bos	10	Werber-Bos	11	Werber-Bos	294	R.Johnson-Bos	119
Morgan-Bos	95	R.Johnson-Bos	182	Werber-Bos	41	R.Johnson-Bos	10	Solters-Bos	7	R.Johnson-Bos	266	Reynolds-Bos	86
R.Johnson-Bos	85	Morgan-Bos	141	R.Ferrell-Bos	29	Reynolds-Bos	9	R.Johnson-Bos	7	Morgan-Bos	186	Morgan-Bos	79

Stolen Bases		Base Stealing Runs		Fielding Runs-Infield		Fielding Runs-Outfield		Wins		Winning Pct.		Complete Games	
Werber-Bos	40	White-Det	4.1	Hale-Cle	25.9	Johnson-Phi	8.6	Gomez-NY	26	Gomez-NY	.839	Gomez-NY	25
R.Johnson-Bos	11	Werber-Bos	3.5	Werber-Bos	17.1			W.Ferrell-Bos	14			W.Ferrell-Bos	17
Cissell-Bos	11	Morgan-Bos	1.2					Welch-Bos	13			Rhodes-Bos	10
Solters-Bos	9	Cissell-Bos	1.0					Rhodes-Bos	12			Ostermueller-Bos	10

Strikeouts		Fewest BB/Game		Games		Saves		Base Runners/9		Adjusted Relief Runs		Relief Ranking	
Gomez-NY	158	W.Ferrell-Bos	2.44	Russell-Was	54	Russell-Was	7	Gomez-NY	10.19	Pennock-Bos	8.9	Bean-Cle	4.5
Welch-Bos	91	Welch-Bos	3.32	Rhodes-Bos	44	Ostermueller-Bos	3	Pennock-Bos	12.19			Pennock-Bos	4.5
Rhodes-Bos	79	Rhodes-Bos	4.03	Welch-Bos	41	Rhodes-Bos	2	W.Ferrell-Bos	12.63				
Ostermueller-Bos	75	Ostermueller-Bos	4.48	Ostermueller-Bos	33			Welch-Bos	13.39				

Innings Pitched		Opponents' Avg.		Opponents' OBP		Earned Run Average		Adjusted ERA		Adjusted Starter Runs		Pitcher Wins	
Gomez-NY	281.2	Gomez-NY	.215	Gomez-NY	.282	Gomez-NY	2.33	Harder-Cle	174	Gomez-NY	59.3	Harder-Cle	5.7
Rhodes-Bos	219.0	Ostermueller-Bos	.262	W.Ferrell-Bos	.327	Ostermueller-Bos	3.49	Gomez-NY	174	Ostermueller-Bos	26.5	W.Ferrell-Bos	2.8
Welch-Bos	206.1	Welch-Bos	.274	Welch-Bos	.342	W.Ferrell-Bos	3.63	Ostermueller-Bos	138	W.Ferrell-Bos	22.0	Ostermueller-Bos	2.7
Ostermueller-Bos	198.2	W.Ferrell-Bos	.282	Ostermueller-Bos	.348	Welch-Bos	4.49	W.Ferrell-Bos	132	Welch-Bos	10.7	Welch-Bos	1.1

1935 AMERICAN LEAGUE

TEAM	W	L	T	PCT	GB	R	OR	HR	AVG	OBP	SLG	OPS	AOPS	PF	SB	CG	HR	BB	SO	BR/9	ERA	AERA	OAV	OOB	FW	PW	BW	BSW	DIF
Det	93	58	1	.616		**919**	665	106	**.290**	**.366**	**.435**	**801**	+16	97	70	**87**	78	522	584	13.1	3.82	+9	.271	.339	**2.3**	5.3	**12.1**	.1	-2.3
NY	89	60	0	.597	3	818	**632**	104	.280	.358	.416	774	+11	94	68	76	91	516	**594**	**12.2**	**3.60**	+12	**.251**	**.321**	.8	6.7	8.3	.0	-1.4
Cle	82	71	3	.536	12	776	739	93	.284	.341	.421	762	+0	102	63	67	68	**457**	498	12.9	4.15	+8	.278	.335	-.3	5.1	-1.0	-.4	2.1
Bos	78	75	1	.510	16	718	732	69	.276	.353	.392	745	-8	107	91	82	**67**	520	470	13.5	4.05	**+17**	.280	.346	-1.4	**9.4**	-5.3	.0	-1.2
Chi	74	78	1	.487	19.5	738	750	74	.275	.348	.382	730	-8	103	46	80	105	574	436	13.5	4.38	+6	.272	.346	1.3	3.3	-5.4	.1	-1.3
Was	67	86	1	.438	27	823	903	32	.285	.357	.381	738	-1	97	54	67	89	613	456	15.1	5.25	-18	.302	.374	-.0	-13.7	.5	.0	3.7
StL	65	87	3	.428	28.5	718	930	73	.270	.344	.384	728	-10	105	45	42	92	641	435	15.2	5.26	-9	.297	.371	-.9	-6.3	-7.4	**.2**	3.4
Phi	58	91	0	.389	34	710	869	**112**	.279	.341	.406	747	-1	99	43	58	73	704	469	15.0	5.12	-11	.285	.372	-1.4	-7.8	-1.8	-.2	-5.3
Total	611					6220		663	.280	.351	.402	753			480	559		4547	3942	13.8	4.46		.280	.351					

Batter-Fielder Wins		Batting Average		On-Base Percentage		Slugging Average		On-Base Plus Slugging		Adjusted OPS		Adjusted Batter Runs	
Foxx-Phi	**5.9**	Myer-Was	.349	Gehrig-NY	.466	Foxx-Phi	.636	Foxx-Phi	1096	Foxx-Phi	182	Gehrig-NY	71.7
R.Ferrell-Bos	**2.1**	R.Johnson-Bos	.315	R.Johnson-Bos	.398	Cronin-Bos	.460	Cronin-Bos	830	Cronin-Bos	106	W.Ferrell-Bos	20.4
Werber-Bos	**1.8**	Cooke-Bos	.306	R.Ferrell-Bos	.388	Cooke-Bos	.439	R.Johnson-Bos	822	R.Johnson-Bos	105	R.Johnson-Bos	7.1
Berg-Bos	**.0**	R.Ferrell-Bos	.301	Cronin-Bos	.370	Werber-Bos	.424	R.Ferrell-Bos	801	R.Ferrell-Bos	100	Cooke-Bos	5.5

Runs		Hits		Doubles		Triples		Home Runs		Total Bases		Runs Batted In	
Gehrig-NY	125	Vosmik-Cle	216	Vosmik-Cle	47	Vosmik-Cle	20	Greenberg-Det	36	Greenberg-Det	389	Greenberg-Det	170
Almada-Bos	85	Almada-Bos	176	Cronin-Bos	37	Cronin-Bos	14	Foxx-Phi	36	Cronin-Bos	256	Cronin-Bos	95
Werber-Bos	84	R.Johnson-Bos	174	R.Ferrell-Bos	34	R.Johnson-Bos	9	Werber-Bos	14	R.Johnson-Bos	234	R.Johnson-Bos	66
Dahlgren-Bos	77	Cronin-Bos	164	R.Johnson-Bos	33	Almada-Bos	9	2 players tied	9	Almada-Bos	230	Dahlgren-Bos	63

Stolen Bases		Base Stealing Runs		Fielding Runs-Infield		Fielding Runs-Outfield		Wins		Winning Pct.		Complete Games	
Werber-Bos	29	Lary-Was-StL	4.8	Appling-Chi	24.9	Solters-Bos-StL	13.5	W.Ferrell-Bos	25	Auker-Det	.720	W.Ferrell-Bos	31
Almada-Bos	20	Werber-Bos	3.9	Werber-Bos	13.6	R.Johnson-Bos	1.9	Grove-Bos	20	W.Ferrell-Bos	.641	Grove-Bos	23
R.Johnson-Bos	11	Almada-Bos	1.3	Almada-Bos	.0			Welch-Bos	10	Grove-Bos	.625	Welch-Bos	10
2 players tied	6	Reynolds-Bos	.5					Ostermueller-Bos	7			Ostermueller-Bos	10

Strikeouts		Fewest BB/Game		Games		Saves		Base Runners/9		Adjusted Relief Runs		Relief Ranking	
Bridges-Det	163	Harder-Cle	1.66	VanAtta-NY-StL	58	Knott-StL	7	Grove-Bos	11.11	L.Brown-Cle	13.7	L.Brown-Cle	16.2
Grove-Bos	121	Grove-Bos	2.14	Walberg-Bos	44	Walberg-Bos	3	W.Ferrell-Bos	12.48	Wilson-Bos	3.7	Wilson-Bos	3.8
W.Ferrell-Bos	110	W.Ferrell-Bos	3.02	W.Ferrell-Bos	41	Welch-Bos	2	Walberg-Bos	13.12				
Welch-Bos	48			Grove-Bos	35	Rhodes-Bos	2	Welch-Bos	13.34				

Innings Pitched		Opponents' Avg.		Opponents' OBP		Earned Run Average		Adjusted ERA		Adjusted Starter Runs		Pitcher Wins	
W.Ferrell-Bos	322.1	Allen-NY	.238	Rowe-Det	.301	Grove-Bos	2.70	Grove-Bos	176	Grove-Bos	55.0	W.Ferrell-Bos	6.8
Grove-Bos	273.0	Grove-Bos	.257	Grove-Bos	.302	W.Ferrell-Bos	3.52	W.Ferrell-Bos	135	W.Ferrell-Bos	41.2	Grove-Bos	5.5
Rhodes-Bos	146.1	W.Ferrell-Bos	.267	W.Ferrell-Bos	.326	Ostermueller-Bos	3.92			Ostermueller-Bos	13.4	Ostermueller-Bos	1.4
Welch-Bos	143.0					Welch-Bos	4.47			Walberg-Bos	13.3	Walberg-Bos	1.0

1936 AMERICAN LEAGUE

TEAM	W	L	T	PCT	GB	R	OR	HR	AVG	OBP	SLG	OPS	AOPS	PF	SB	CG	HR	BB	SO	BR/9	ERA	AERA	OAV	OOB	FW	PW	BW	BSW	DIF
NY	102	51	2	.667		**1065**	731	182	.300	**.381**	**.483**	864	+24	97	77	77	84	663	**624**	13.8	**4.17**	+12	**.271**	.351	.8	7.2	**17.9**	.1	-.5
Det	83	71	0	.539	19.5	921	871	94	.300	.371	.438	808	+6	100	73	76	100	562	526	14.2	5.00	-1	.289	.358	**1.3**	-.6	5.1	-.2	.4
Chi	81	70	2	.536	20	920	873	60	.292	.374	.397	771	-6	104	66	**80**	104	578	414	14.5	5.06	+3	.293	.363	.4	1.8	-3.4	.2	6.6
Was	82	71	0	.536	20	889	799	62	.295	.365	.414	779	+5	94	**104**	78	**73**	588	462	14.0	4.58	+4	.279	.353	-.4	2.7	3.7	**.6**	-1.1
Cle	80	74	3	.519	22.5	921	862	123	**.304**	.364	.461	825	+9	101	66	74	**73**	607	619	14.5	4.83	+4	.289	.362	.0	2.8	5.6	-.5	5.0
Bos	74	80	1	.481	28.5	775	764	86	.276	.349	.400	749	-14	106	55	78	78	**552**	584	**13.6**	4.39	**+21**	.277	**.346**	.7	**11.8**	-10.2	-.4	-4.9
StL	57	95	3	.375	44.5	804	1064	79	.279	.356	.403	759	-9	103	62	54	115	609	399	16.0	6.24	-14	.314	.385	-.6	-10.8	-6.4	.5	-1.6
Phi	53	100	1	.346	49	714	1045	72	.269	.336	.376	712	-16	-98	59	68	131	696	405	15.7	6.08	-16	.300	.381	-1.9	-12.7	-12.5	-.3	3.9
Total	618					7009		758	.289	.363	.421	784			562	585		4855	4033	14.6	5.04		.289	.363					

Batter-Fielder Wins		Batting Average		On-Base Percentage		Slugging Average		On-Base Plus Slugging		Adjusted OPS		Adjusted Batter Runs	
Gehrig-NY	**6.6**	Appling-Chi	.388	Gehrig-NY	.478	Gehrig-NY	.696	Gehrig-NY	1174	Gehrig-NY	193	Gehrig-NY	90.9
Foxx-Bos	**3.3**	Foxx-Bos	.338	Foxx-Bos	.440	Foxx-Bos	.631	Foxx-Bos	1071	Foxx-Bos	153	Foxx-Bos	49.2
R.Ferrell-Bos	**2.0**	R.Ferrell-Bos	.312	R.Ferrell-Bos	.406	R.Ferrell-Bos	.461	R.Ferrell-Bos	867	R.Ferrell-Bos	108	W.Ferrell-Bos	11.5
		Cramer-Bos	.292	Werber-Bos	.382	Werber-Bos	.407	Werber-Bos	790	Werber-Bos	90	R.Ferrell-Bos	6.6

Runs		Hits		Doubles		Triples		Home Runs		Total Bases		Runs Batted In	
Gehrig-NY	167	Averill-Cle	232	Gehringer-Det	60	3 players tied	15	Gehrig-NY	49	Trosky-Cle	405	Trosky-Cle	162
Foxx-Bos	130	Foxx-Bos	198	McNair-Bos	36	Kroner-Bos	8	Foxx-Bos	41	Foxx-Bos	369	Foxx-Bos	143
Cramer-Bos	99	Cramer-Bos	188	Foxx-Bos	32	Foxx-Bos	8	Werber-Bos	10	Cramer-Bos	233	McNair-Bos	74
Werber-Bos	89	Werber-Bos	147	Cramer-Bos	31	Cramer-Bos	7	R.Ferrell-Bos	8	Werber-Bos	218	Werber-Bos	67

Stolen Bases		Base Stealing Runs		Fielding Runs-Infield		Fielding Runs-Outfield		Wins		Winning Pct.		Complete Games	
Lary-StL	37	Lary-StL	5.0	Hale-Cle	16.7	Solters-StL	12.5	Bridges-Det	23	Pearson-NY	.731	W.Ferrell-Bos	28
Werber-Bos	23	Foxx-Bos	1.5	Foxx-Bos	2.3	Cramer-Bos	11.4	W.Ferrell-Bos	20	Grove-Bos	.586	Grove-Bos	22
Foxx-Bos	13	Werber-Bos	.5			Werber-Bos	1.3	Grove-Bos	17	W.Ferrell-Bos	.571	Marcum-Bos	9
2 players tied	4	Dahlgren-Bos	.0					Ostermueller-Bos	10			Ostermueller-Bos	7

Strikeouts		Fewest BB/Game		Games		Saves		Base Runners/9		Adjusted Relief Runs		Relief Ranking	
Bridges-Det	175	Lyons-Chi	2.23	VanAtta-StL	52	Malone-NY	9	Grove-Bos	10.87	Brown-Chi	2.9	Brown-Chi	2.9
Grove-Bos	130	Grove-Bos	2.31	Wilson-Bos	43	Wilson-Bos	3	Walberg-Bos	12.11				
W.Ferrell-Bos	106	Marcum-Bos	2.69	Ostermueller-Bos	43	Ostermueller-Bos	2	Marcum-Bos	12.72				
Ostermueller-Bos	90	W.Ferrell-Bos	3.56	W.Ferrell-Bos	39	Grove-Bos	2	W.Ferrell-Bos	13.60				

Innings Pitched		Opponents' Avg.		Opponents' OBP		Earned Run Average		Adjusted ERA		Adjusted Starter Runs		Pitcher Wins	
W.Ferrell-Bos	301.0	Pearson-NY	.233	Grove-Bos	.297	Grove-Bos	2.81	Grove-Bos	189	Grove-Bos	67.0	Grove-Bos	6.6
Grove-Bos	253.1	Grove-Bos	.246	Marcum-Bos	.332	W.Ferrell-Bos	4.19	W.Ferrell-Bos	127	W.Ferrell-Bos	35.7	W.Ferrell-Bos	4.4
Ostermueller-Bos	180.2	W.Ferrell-Bos	.274	W.Ferrell-Bos	.343	Marcum-Bos	4.81	Marcum-Bos	110	Marcum-Bos	11.8	Marcum-Bos	1.2
Marcum-Bos	174.0	Marcum-Bos	.281	Ostermueller-Bos	.364	Ostermueller-Bos	4.88	Ostermueller-Bos	109	Walberg-Bos	10.9	Ostermueller-Bos	.9

1937 AMERICAN LEAGUE

TEAM	W	L	T	PCT	GB	R	OR	HR	AVG	OBP	SLG	OPS	AOPS	PF	SB	CG	HR	BB	SO	BR/9	ERA	AERA	OAV	OOB	FW	PW	BW	BSW	DIF
NY	102	52	3	.662		979	671	174	.283	.369	.456	825	+13	101	60	82	92	506	652	12.5	3.65	+22	.261	.325	.2	11.7	9.8	.0	3.2
Det	89	65	1	.578	13	935	841	150	.292	.370	.452	822	+11	102	89	70	102	635	485	14.2	4.87	-4	.279	.357	1.4	-2.8	8.2	.3	4.9
Chi	86	68	0	.558	16	780	730	67	.280	.350	.400	750	-5	100	70	70	115	532	533	13.2	4.17	+10	.273	.341	-.2	6.0	-3.5	.3	6.5
Cle	83	71	2	.539	19	817	768	103	.280	.352	.423	775	+0	101	78	64	61	566	630	14.0	4.39	+5	.285	.356	.8	3.0	.0	-.2	2.4
Bos	80	72	2	.526	21	821	775	100	.281	.357	.411	768	-4	104	79	74	92	597	682	14.0	4.48	+6	.279	.352	-.4	3.6	-2.8	-.4	4.1
Was	73	80	5	.477	28.5	757	841	47	.279	.351	.379	730	-6	96	61	75	96	671	524	14.1	4.58	-3	.275	.357	.3	-2.2	-4.0	.0	2.5
Phi	54	97	3	.358	46.5	699	854	94	.267	.341	.397	738	-7	98	95	65	105	613	469	14.3	4.85	-3	.281	.358	-1.7	-1.8	-4.8	.3	-13.5
StL	46	108	2	.299	56	715	1023	71	.285	.348	.399	747	-7	101	30	55	143	653	468	16.2	6.00	-20	.315	.390	-.0	-15.6	-4.6	-.3	-10.4
Total	622					6503		806	.281	.355	.415	770			562	555		4773	4443	14.1	4.62		.281	.355					

Batter-Fielder Wins		Batting Average		On-Base Percentage		Slugging Average		On-Base Plus Slugging		Adjusted OPS		Adjusted Batter Runs	
Clift-StL	7.4	Gehringer-Det	.371	Gehrig-NY	.473	DiMaggio-NY	.673	Gehrig-NY	1116	Gehrig-NY	177	Gehrig-NY	74.1
Foxx-Bos	1.8	Cronin-Bos	.307	Cronin-Bos	.402	Foxx-Bos	.538	Foxx-Bos	929	Foxx-Bos	127	Foxx-Bos	23.3
Cronin-Bos	1.2	Cramer-Bos	.305	Foxx-Bos	.392	Cronin-Bos	.486	Cronin-Bos	887	Cronin-Bos	118	Cronin-Bos	18.3
Peacock-Bos	.0	Higgins-Bos	.302	Higgins-Bos	.385	McNair-Bos	.453	Higgins-Bos	809	Higgins-Bos	100	Marcum-Bos	5.3

Runs		Hits		Doubles		Triples		Home Runs		Total Bases		Runs Batted In	
DiMaggio-NY	151	Bell-StL	218	Bell-StL	51	Walker-Chi	16	DiMaggio-NY	46	DiMaggio-NY	418	Greenberg-Det	183
Foxx-Bos	111	Cronin-Bos	175	Cronin-Bos	40	Kreevich-Chi	16	Foxx-Bos	36	Foxx-Bos	306	Foxx-Bos	127
Cronin-Bos	102	Higgins-Bos	172	Higgins-Bos	33	Cramer-Bos	11	Cronin-Bos	18	Cronin-Bos	277	Cronin-Bos	110
Cramer-Bos	90	Cramer-Bos	171	McNair-Bos	29	Mills-Bos	8	McNair-Bos	12	Higgins-Bos	242	Higgins-Bos	106

Stolen Bases		Base Stealing Runs		Fielding Runs-Infield		Fielding Runs-Outfield		Wins		Winning Pct.		Complete Games	
Chapman-Was-Bos	35	Chapman-Was-Bos	3.5	Clift-StL	41.3	Johnson-Phi	9.6	Gomez-NY	21	Allen-Cle	.938	W.Ferrell-Bos-Was	26
Werber-Phi	35	Dallessandro-Bos	.0	Foxx-Bos	11.4	Cramer-Bos	2.2	Grove-Bos	17	Grove-Bos	.654	Grove-Bos	21
Mills-Bos	11	Cronin-Bos	.0					Wilson-Bos	16	Wilson-Bos	.615	Wilson-Bos	14
2 players tied	10							Marcum-Bos	13			Marcum-Bos	9

Strikeouts		Fewest BB/Game		Games		Saves		Base Runners/9		Adjusted Relief Runs		Relief Ranking	
Gomez-NY	194	Stratton-Chi	2.02	Brown-Chi	53	Brown-Chi	18	Stratton-Chi	9.89	Brown-Chi	12.0	Brown-Chi	20.0
Grove-Bos	153	Marcum-Bos	2.30	Wilson-Bos	51	Wilson-Bos	7	Grove-Bos	12.13				
Wilson-Bos	137	Grove-Bos	2.85	Marcum-Bos	37	Marcum-Bos	3	Wilson-Bos	13.46				
McKain-Bos	66	Wilson-Bos	4.84	McKain-Bos	36	McKain-Bos	2	Marcum-Bos	13.67				

Innings Pitched		Opponents' Avg.		Opponents' OBP		Earned Run Average		Adjusted ERA		Adjusted Starter Runs		Pitcher Wins	
W.Ferrell-Bos-Was	281.0	Gomez-NY	.223	Stratton-Chi	.280	Gomez-NY	2.33	Stratton-Chi	191	Gomez-NY	66.9	Gomez-NY	6.8
Grove-Bos	262.0	Wilson-Bos	.248	Grove-Bos	.317	Grove-Bos	3.02	Gomez-NY	191	Grove-Bos	48.5	Grove-Bos	3.9
Wilson-Bos	221.1	Grove-Bos	.261	Wilson-Bos	.343	Wilson-Bos	3.70	Grove-Bos	157	Wilson-Bos	21.9	Wilson-Bos	2.1
Marcum-Bos	183.2	Marcum-Bos	.306	Marcum-Bos	.348	Marcum-Bos	4.85	Wilson-Bos	128	Gonzales-Bos	1.8	Marcum-Bos	.7

1938 AMERICAN LEAGUE

TEAM	W	L	T	PCT	GB	R	OR	HR	AVG	OBP	SLG	OPS	AOPS	PF	SB	CG	HR	BB	SO	BR/9	ERA	AERA	OAV	OOB	FW	PW	BW	BSW	DIF
NY	99	53	5	.651		966	710	174	.274	.366	.446	812	+11	100	91	91	85	566	567	13.1	3.91	+16	.268	.339	.5	9.1	7.8	.8	4.8
Bos	88	61	1	.591	9.5	902	751	98	.299	.378	.434	812	+5	105	55	67	102	528	484	13.8	4.46	+11	.281	.349	-1.1	6.1	4.6	-.6	4.6
Cle	86	66	1	.566	13	847	782	113	.281	.350	.434	784	+4	98	83	68	100	681	717	14.1	4.60	+1	.268	.355	1.2	.6	2.3	.5	5.4
Det	84	70	1	.545	16	862	795	137	.272	.359	.411	770	-6	106	76	75	110	608	435	14.4	4.79	+4	.287	.361	1.6	2.8	-4.2	.1	6.6
Was	75	76	1	.497	23.5	814	873	85	.293	.362	.416	778	+8	93	65	59	92	615	515	14.3	4.94	-3	.276	.358	-.5	-6.1	6.7	.0	-.6
Chi	65	83	1	.439	32	709	752	67	.277	.343	.383	726	-14	102	56	83	101	550	432	13.8	4.36	+12	.279	.350	-1.6	6.9	-9.9	-.2	-4.2
StL	55	97	4	.362	44	755	962	92	.281	.355	.397	752	-5	100	51	71	132	737	632	15.7	5.80	-14	.295	.382	1.8	-10.8	-3.1	-.3	-8.5
Phi	53	99	2	.349	46	726	956	98	.270	.348	.396	744	-5	97	65	56	142	599	473	14.9	5.48	-12	.292	.365	-1.8	-8.5	-3.4	-.4	-8.9
Total	613					6581		864	.281	.358	.415	773			542	570		4924	4255	14.3	4.79		.281	.358					

Batter-Fielder Wins		Batting Average		On-Base Percentage		Slugging Average		On-Base Plus Slugging		Adjusted OPS		Adjusted Batter Runs	
Foxx-Bos	5.8	Foxx-Bos	.349	Foxx-Bos	.462	Foxx-Bos	.704	Foxx-Bos	1166	Foxx-Bos	180	Foxx-Bos	71.9
Cronin-Bos	4.4	Chapman-Bos	.340	Cronin-Bos	.428	Cronin-Bos	.536	Cronin-Bos	964	Cronin-Bos	134	Cronin-Bos	31.8
Chapman-Bos	1.6	Cronin-Bos	.325	Chapman-Bos	.418	Chapman-Bos	.494	Chapman-Bos	912	Chapman-Bos	122	Chapman-Bos	18.6
Desautels-Bos	.7	Vosmik-Bos	.324	Higgins-Bos	.388	Vosmik-Bos	.446	Vosmik-Bos	830	Vosmik-Bos	103	Dickman-Bos	3.8

Runs		Hits		Doubles		Triples		Home Runs		Total Bases		Runs Batted In	
Greenberg-Det	144	Vosmik-Bos	201	Cronin-Bos	51	Heath-Cle	18	Greenberg-Det	58	Foxx-Bos	398	Foxx-Bos	175
Foxx-Bos	139	Cramer-Bos	198	Chapman-Bos	40	Foxx-Bos	9	Foxx-Bos	50	Cronin-Bos	284	Higgins-Bos	106
Vosmik-Bos	121	Foxx-Bos	197	Vosmik-Bos	37	Cramer-Bos	8	Cronin-Bos	17	Vosmik-Bos	277	Cronin-Bos	94
Cramer-Bos	116	Cronin-Bos	172	Cramer-Bos	36	Chapman-Bos	8	Vosmik-Bos	9	Cramer-Bos	250	Vosmik-Bos	86

Stolen Bases		Base Stealing Runs		Fielding Runs-Infield		Fielding Runs-Outfield		Wins		Winning Pct.		Complete Games	
Crosetti-NY	27	Lary-Cle	3.0	Gordon-NY	20.5	Johnson-Phi	9.6	Ruffing-NY	21	Ruffing-NY	.750	Newsom-StL	31
Chapman-Bos	13	Nonnenkamp-Bos	1.0	Doerr-Bos	9.0	Cramer-Bos	5.5	Wilson-Bos	15	Bagby-Bos	.577	Grove-Bos	12
Higgins-Bos	10	Chapman-Bos	.8	Foxx-Bos	7.4	Chapman-Bos	5.4	Bagby-Bos	15	Wilson-Bos	.500	Wilson-Bos	11
Cronin-Bos	7	Peacock-Bos	.5	Cronin-Bos	7.3	Vosmik-Bos	3.5	Grove-Bos	14			2 players tied	10

Strikeouts		Fewest BB/Game		Games		Saves		Base Runners/9		Adjusted Relief Runs		Relief Ranking	
Feller-Cle	240	Leonard-Was	2.14	Humphries-Cle	45	Murphy-NY	11	Leonard-Was	11.32	Murphy-NY	4.9	Murphy-NY	6.1
Grove-Bos	99	Grove-Bos	2.86	Bagby-Bos	43	McKain-Bos	6	Harris-Bos	11.76	McKain-Bos	3.5	McKain-Bos	3.3
Wilson-Bos	96	Ostermueller-Bos	2.95	Wilson-Bos	37	Ostermueller-Bos	2	Grove-Bos	12.21				
Bagby-Bos	73	Bagby-Bos	4.08	McKain-Bos	37	Bagby-Bos	2	Ostermueller-Bos	13.25				

Innings Pitched		Opponents' Avg.		Opponents' OBP		Earned Run Average		Adjusted ERA		Adjusted Starter Runs		Pitcher Wins	
Newsom-StL	329.2	Feller-Cle	.220	Leonard-Was	.305	Grove-Bos	3.08	Grove-Bos	160	Ruffing-NY	37.1	Ruffing-NY	4.5
Bagby-Bos	198.2	Wilson-Bos	.262	Grove-Bos	.319	Bagby-Bos	4.21	Bagby-Bos	117	Grove-Bos	32.5	Grove-Bos	3.0
Wilson-Bos	194.2	Grove-Bos	.263	Ostermueller-Bos	.331	Wilson-Bos	4.30	Wilson-Bos	115	Bagby-Bos	14.2	Wilson-Bos	1.6
Ostermueller-Bos	176.2	Ostermueller-Bos	.275	Wilson-Bos	.342	Ostermueller-Bos	4.58	Ostermueller-Bos	108	Wilson-Bos	12.9	Bagby-Bos	1.6

1939 AMERICAN LEAGUE

TEAM	W	L	T	PCT	GB	R	OR	HR	AVG	OBP	SLG	OPS	AOPS	PF	SB	CG	HR	BB	SO	BR/9	ERA	AERA	OAV	OOB	FW	PW	BW	BSW	DIF
NY	106	45	1	.702		967	556	166	.287	.374	.451	825	+19	98	72	87	85	567	565	11.9	3.31	+32	.241	.319	2.9	15.3	14.0	.2	-1.9
Bos	89	62	1	.589	17	890	795	124	.291	.363	.436	799	+6	104	42	52	77	543	539	14.0	4.56	+4	.287	.355	.0	2.3	4.5	-.7	7.2
Cle	87	67	0	.565	20.5	797	700	85	.280	.350	.413	763	+5	97	72	69	75	602	614	13.3	4.08	+8	.267	.344	.2	4.7	3.0	-.1	2.1
Chi	85	69	1	.552	22.5	755	737	64	.275	.349	.374	723	-11	99	62	99	454	535	12.7	4.31	+10	.275	.333	1.0	5.8	-7.6	.3	8.6
Det	81	73	1	.526	26.5	849	762	124	.279	.356	.426	782	-1	108	88	64	104	574	633	13.3	4.29	+14	.268	.341	-.6	7.9	-1.3	.5	-2.4
Was	65	87	1	.428	41.5	702	797	44	.278	.346	.379	725	-2	93	94	72	75	602	521	13.6	4.60	-6	.271	.348	-1.1	-3.8	-.6	.3	-5.7
Phi	55	97	1	.362	51.5	711	1022	98	.271	.336	.400	736	-4	98	60	50	148	579	397	15.3	5.79	-19	.307	.375	-1.4	-14.7	-3.6	.0	-1.4
StL	43	111	2	.279	64.5	733	1035	91	.268	.339	.381	720	-12	102	48	56	133	739	516	16.4	6.01	-19	.310	.393	-.6	-15.3	-8.8	-.4	-8.8
Total	615					6404		796	.279	.352	.407	759			589	512		4660	4320	13.8	4.62		.279	.352					

Batter-Fielder Wins		Batting Average		On-Base Percentage		Slugging Average		On-Base Plus Slugging		Adjusted OPS		Adjusted Batter Runs	
DiMaggio-NY	5.5	DiMaggio-NY	.381	Foxx-Bos	.464	Foxx-Bos	.694	Foxx-Bos	1158	DiMaggio-NY	185	Foxx-Bos	62.0
Foxx-Bos	5.2	Foxx-Bos	.360	Williams-Bos	.436	Williams-Bos	.609	Williams-Bos	1045	Foxx-Bos	185	Williams-Bos	52.7
Williams-Bos	4.1	Williams-Bos	.327	Cronin-Bos	.407	Cronin-Bos	.492	Cronin-Bos	899	Williams-Bos	158	Cronin-Bos	21.5
Cronin-Bos	3.2	Doerr-Bos	.318	Doerr-Bos	.365	Doerr-Bos	.448	Doerr-Bos	813	Cronin-Bos	124	Bagby-Bos	2.6

Runs		Hits		Doubles		Triples		Home Runs		Total Bases		Runs Batted In	
Rolfe-NY	139	Rolfe-NY	213	Rolfe-NY	46	Lewis-Was	16	Foxx-Bos	35	Williams-Bos	344	Williams-Bos	145
Williams-Bos	131	Williams-Bos	185	Williams-Bos	44	Williams-Bos	11	Williams-Bos	31	Foxx-Bos	324	Cronin-Bos	107
Foxx-Bos	130	Cramer-Bos	183	Tabor-Bos	33	Foxx-Bos	10	Cronin-Bos	19	Tabor-Bos	258	Foxx-Bos	105
Cramer-Bos	110	Foxx-Bos	168	Cronin-Bos	33	Tabor-Bos	8	Tabor-Bos	14	Cronin-Bos	256	Tabor-Bos	95

Stolen Bases		Base Stealing Runs		Fielding Runs-Infield		Fielding Runs-Outfield		Wins		Winning Pct.		Complete Games	
Case-Was	51	Case-Was	5.3	Doerr-Bos	26.5	Johnson-Phi	9.7	Feller-Cle	24	Grove-Bos	.789	Newsom-StL-Det	24
Tabor-Bos	16	Desautels-Bos	.3	Foxx-Bos	7.6	Williams-Bos	1.3	Grove-Bos	15			Feller-Cle	24
Cronin-Bos	6	Williams-Bos	.0	Tabor-Bos	4.4			3 players tied	11			Grove-Bos	17
2 players tied	4	Tabor-Bos	.0	Cronin-Bos	3.8							Ostermueller-Bos	8

Strikeouts		Fewest BB/Game		Games		Saves		Base Runners/9		Adjusted Relief Runs		Relief Ranking	
Feller-Cle	246	Lyons-Chi	1.36	Brown-Chi	61	Murphy-NY	19	Lyons-Chi	9.85	Brown-Chi	10.5	Brown-Chi	20.4
Grove-Bos	81	Grove-Bos	2.73	Dickman-Bos	48	Heving-Bos	7	Grove-Bos	11.26	Heving-Bos	6.1	Heving-Bos	8.1
Wilson-Bos	80	Ostermueller-Bos	3.28	Heving-Bos	46	Dickman-Bos	5	Galehouse-Bos	13.07	Dickman-Bos	1.5	Dickman-Bos	1.5
Galehouse-Bos	68	Wilson-Bos	3.81	Wilson-Bos	36	Ostermueller-Bos	4	Ostermueller-Bos	13.16				

Innings Pitched		Opponents' Avg.		Opponents' OBP		Earned Run Average		Adjusted ERA		Adjusted Starter Runs		Pitcher Wins	
Feller-Cle	296.2	Feller-Cle	.210	Lyons-Chi	.276	Grove-Bos	2.54	Grove-Bos	186	Feller-Cle	54.2	Feller-Cle	6.0
Grove-Bos	191.0	Grove-Bos	.249	Grove-Bos	.305	Ostermueller-Bos	4.24	Ostermueller-Bos	112	Grove-Bos	45.2	Grove-Bos	3.7
Wilson-Bos	177.1	Ostermueller-Bos	.277	Ostermueller-Bos	.341	Wilson-Bos	4.67	Wilson-Bos	101	Ostermueller-Bos	9.0	Ostermueller-Bos	.7
Ostermueller-Bos	159.1	Wilson-Bos	.281	Wilson-Bos	.351					Galehouse-Bos	3.8	Heving-Bos	.6

1940 AMERICAN LEAGUE

TEAM	W	L	T	PCT	GB	R	OR	HR	AVG	OBP	SLG	OPS	AOPS	PF	SB	CG	HR	BB	SO	BR/9	ERA	AERA	OAV	OOB	FW	PW	BW	BSW	DIF
Det	90	64	1	.584		888	717	134	.286	.366	.442	808	+5	110	66	59	102	570	752	13.2	4.01	+19	.266	.338	-.7	9.9	4.7	.2	-1.2
Cle	89	65	1	.578	1	710	637	101	.265	.332	.398	730	-2	97	53	72	86	512	686	12.2	3.63	+16	.254	.324	1.7	8.8	-2.1	.0	3.5
NY	88	66	1	.571	2	817	671	155	.259	.344	.418	762	+7	96	59	76	119	511	559	12.6	3.89	+4	.261	.328	1.6	2.3	5.5	.1	1.6
Chi	82	72	1	.532	8	735	672	73	.278	.340	.387	727	-7	101	52	83	111	480	574	11.9	3.74	+18	.250	.313	-.2	9.9	-5.1	-.8	1.2
Bos	82	72	0	.532	8	872	825	145	.286	.356	.449	805	+10	104	55	51	124	625	613	14.5	4.89	-8	.284	.359	.4	-5.5	7.2	-.3	3.2
StL	67	87	2	.435	23	757	882	118	.263	.333	.401	734	-6	102	51	64	113	646	439	14.8	5.12	-11	.290	.367	1.3	-7.5	-4.7	-.1	1.0
Was	64	90	0	.416	26	665	811	52	.271	.331	.374	705	-5	94	74	93	118	618	618	14.2	4.60	-9	.281	.359	-.7	-6.3	-3.9	.8	-2.9
Phi	54	100	0	.351	36	703	932	105	.262	.334	.387	721	-5	98	48	72	135	534	488	14.0	5.22	-15	.283	.348	-3.1	-10.8	-3.8	.0	-5.4
Total	619					6147		883	.271	.342	.407	750			478	551		4496	4729	13.4	4.38		.271	.342					

Batter-Fielder Wins		Batting Average		On-Base Percentage		Slugging Average		On-Base Plus Slugging		Adjusted OPS		Adjusted Batter Runs	
DiMaggio-NY	4.5	DiMaggio-NY	.352	Williams-Bos	.442	Greenberg-Det	.670	Greenberg-Det	1103	DiMaggio-NY	176	Greenberg-Det	57.4
Greenberg-Det	4.5	Williams-Bos	.344	Foxx-Bos	.412	Williams-Bos	.594	Williams-Bos	1036	Williams-Bos	159	Williams-Bos	53.1
Williams-Bos	4.0	Finney-Bos	.320	Cronin-Bos	.380	Foxx-Bos	.581	Foxx-Bos	993	Foxx-Bos	148	Foxx-Bos	39.2
Doerr-Bos	3.1	Cramer-Bos	.303	Finney-Bos	.360	Tabor-Bos	.510	Cronin-Bos	882	Cronin-Bos	122	Cronin-Bos	18.5

Runs		Hits		Doubles		Triples		Home Runs		Total Bases		Runs Batted In	
Williams-Bos	134	3 players tied	200	Greenberg-Det	50	McCosky-Det	19	Greenberg-Det	41	Greenberg-Det	384	Greenberg-Det	150
Foxx-Bos	106	Cramer-Bos	200	Williams-Bos	43	Finney-Bos	15	Foxx-Bos	36	Williams-Bos	333	Foxx-Bos	119
Cronin-Bos	104	Williams-Bos	193	Doerr-Bos	37	Williams-Bos	14	Cronin-Bos	24	Foxx-Bos	299	Williams-Bos	113
Cramer-Bos	94	Doerr-Bos	173	Cramer-Bos	35	Cramer-Bos	12	Williams-Bos	23	Doerr-Bos	296	Cronin-Bos	111

Stolen Bases		Base Stealing Runs		Fielding Runs-Infield		Fielding Runs-Outfield		Wins		Winning Pct.		Complete Games	
Case-Was	35	Case-Was	4.2	Heffner-StL	15.7	Kreevich-Chi	6.9	Feller-Cle	27	Rowe-Det	.842	Feller-Cle	31
Tabor-Bos	14	Doerr-Bos	.5	Doerr-Bos	13.4	DiMaggio-Bos	5.6	Wilson-Bos	12			Wilson-Bos	9
Doerr-Bos	10	Finney-Bos	.4	Foxx-Bos	7.8	Finney-Bos	3.3	Heving-Bos	12			Grove-Bos	9
2 players tied	7			Tabor-Bos	3.0			Bagby-Bos	10			Bagby-Bos	6

Strikeouts		Fewest BB/Game		Games		Saves		Base Runners/9		Adjusted Relief Runs		Relief Ranking	
Feller-Cle	261	Lyons-Chi	1.79	Feller-Cle	43	Benton-Det	17	Bonham-NY	8.70	Eisenstat-Cle	10.6	Brown-Chi	10.3
Wilson-Bos	102	Bagby-Bos	4.09	Wilson-Bos	41	Wilson-Bos	5	Grove-Bos	12.33				
Ostermueller-Bos	80	Wilson-Bos	4.97	Heving-Bos	39	3 players tied	3	Heving-Bos	13.16				
Grove-Bos	62			Bagby-Bos	36			Johnson-Bos	14.08				

Innings Pitched		Opponents' Avg.		Opponents' OBP		Earned Run Average		Adjusted ERA		Adjusted Starter Runs		Pitcher Wins	
Feller-Cle	320.1	Feller-Cle	.210	Feller-Cle	.285	Feller-Cle	2.61	Newsom-Det	168	Feller-Cle	61.5	Feller-Cle	6.8
Bagby-Bos	182.2	Wilson-Bos	.270	Wilson-Bos	.362	Bagby-Bos	4.73	Bagby-Bos	95	Grove-Bos	9.2	Heving-Bos	.6
Wilson-Bos	157.2	Bagby-Bos	.296	Bagby-Bos	.368	Wilson-Bos	5.08	Wilson-Bos	89	Heving-Bos	4.3	Grove-Bos	.5
Grove-Bos	153.1									Johnson-Bos	4.1	2 players tied	.2

1941 AMERICAN LEAGUE

TEAM	W	L	T	PCT	GB	R	OR	HR	AVG	OBP	SLG	OPS	AOPS	PF	SB	CG	HR	BB	SO	BR/9	ERA	AERA	OAV	OOB	FW	PW	BW	BSW	DIF
NY	101	53	2	.656		830	631	151	.269	.346	.419	765	+11	99	51	75	81	598	589	12.4	3.53	+12	.248	.325	.5	6.4	7.3	.1	9.7
Bos	84	70	1	.545	17	865	750	124	.283	.366	.430	796	+15	102	67	70	88	611	574	13.7	4.19	+0	.270	.347	.0	-.3	11.7	-.2	-4.3
Chi	77	77	2	.500	24	638	649	47	.255	.322	.343	665	-16	-99	91	106	89	521	564	12.1	3.52	+16	.252	.320	-.3	8.9	-11.8	.2	3.0
Det	75	79	1	.487	26	686	743	81	.263	.340	.375	715	-13	110	43	52	80	645	697	13.4	4.18	+9	.260	.341	-.7	5.0	-8.9	.1	2.5
Cle	75	79	1	.487	26	677	668	103	.256	.323	.393	716	+1	95	63	68	71	660	617	13.4	3.90	+1	.259	.344	.7	.7	-.8	-.2	-3.4
Was	70	84	2	.455	31	728	798	52	.272	.331	.376	707	-1	95	79	69	69	603	544	13.9	4.35	-7	.279	.353	-.7	-4.7	-2.4	.6	.3
StL	70	84	3	.455	31	765	823	91	.266	.360	.390	750	+3	103	50	65	120	549	454	13.8	4.72	-9	.283	.350	1.3	-6.0	3.4	-.2	-5.5
Phi	64	90	0	.416	37	713	840	85	.268	.340	.387	727	+2	98	27	64	136	557	386	13.8	4.83	-13	.279	.348	-1.6	-9.4	.9	-.6	-2.3
Total	622					5902		734	.266	.341	.389	730			471	569		4744	4425	13.3	4.15		.266	.341					

Batter-Fielder Wins		Batting Average		On-Base Percentage		Slugging Average		On-Base Plus Slugging		Adjusted OPS		Adjusted Batter Runs	
Williams-Bos	8.5	Williams-Bos	.406	Williams-Bos	.553	Williams-Bos	.735	Williams-Bos	1287	Williams-Bos	232	Williams-Bos	101.7
Cronin-Bos	3.5	Cronin-Bos	.311	Foxx-Bos	.412	Cronin-Bos	.508	Foxx-Bos	917	Foxx-Bos	138	Cronin-Bos	30.0
Foxx-Bos	2.3	Foxx-Bos	.300	Cronin-Bos	.406	Foxx-Bos	.505	Cronin-Bos	914	Cronin-Bos	137	Foxx-Bos	29.6
DiMaggio-Bos	1.0	Finney-Bos	.288	DiMaggio-Bos	.385	Doerr-Bos	.450	DiMaggio-Bos	792	DiMaggio-Bos	107	DiMaggio-Bos	9.7

Runs		Hits		Doubles		Triples		Home Runs		Total Bases		Runs Batted In	
Williams-Bos	135	Travis-Was	218	Boudreau-Cle	45	Heath-Cle	20	Williams-Bos	37	DiMaggio-NY	348	DiMaggio-Bos	125
DiMaggio-Bos	117	Williams-Bos	185	Cronin-Bos	38	Finney-Bos	10	Foxx-Bos	19	Williams-Bos	335	Williams-Bos	120
Cronin-Bos	98	DiMaggio-Bos	165	DiMaggio-Bos	37	Foxx-Bos	8	3 players tied	16	Cronin-Bos	263	Foxx-Bos	105
Foxx-Bos	87	Cronin-Bos	161	Williams-Bos	33					Foxx-Bos	246	Tabor-Bos	101

Stolen Bases		Base Stealing Runs		Fielding Runs-Infield		Fielding Runs-Outfield		Wins		Winning Pct.		Complete Games	
Case-Was	33	Case-Was	4.1	Bloodworth-Was	27.2	Case-Was	11.7	Feller-Cle	25	Gomez-NY	.750	Lee-Chi	30
Tabor-Bos	17	Fox-Bos	1.3	Foxx-Bos	7.6	S.Chapman-Phi	11.7	D.Newsome-Bos	19	D.Newsome-Bos	.655	D.Newsome-Bos	17
DiMaggio-Bos	13	S.Newsome-Bos	.8	Tabor-Bos	.3	DiMaggio-Bos	3.6	Wagner-Bos	12			Wagner-Bos	12
S.Newsome-Bos	10	DiMaggio-Bos	.8					Dobson-Bos	12			Harris-Bos	11

Strikeouts		Fewest BB/Game		Games		Saves		Base Runners/9		Adjusted Relief Runs		Relief Ranking	
Feller-Cle	260	Lyons-Chi	1.78	Feller-Cle	44	Murphy-NY	15	Humphries-Chi	10.55	Murphy-NY	17.5	Murphy-NY	30.1
Harris-Bos	111	D.Newsome-Bos	3.33	Ryba-Bos	40	Ryba-Bos	6	Hughson-Bos	12.39				
Dobson-Bos	69	Harris-Bos	3.99	D.Newsome-Bos	36			Wagner-Bos	12.54				
D.Newsome-Bos	58	Wagner-Bos	4.08	Harris-Bos	35			Harris-Bos	12.85				

Innings Pitched		Opponents' Avg.		Opponents' OBP		Earned Run Average		Adjusted ERA		Adjusted Starter Runs		Pitcher Wins	
Feller-Cle	343.0	Benton-Det	.221	Lee-Chi	.293	Lee-Chi	2.37	Lee-Chi	173	Lee-Chi	56.1	Lee-Chi	6.5
D.Newsome-Bos	213.2	Wagner-Bos	.245	Wagner-Bos	.326	Wagner-Bos	3.07	Wagner-Bos	136	Wagner-Bos	22.3	Harris-Bos	2.0
Harris-Bos	194.0	Harris-Bos	.250	Harris-Bos	.328	Harris-Bos	3.25	Harris-Bos	128	Harris-Bos	18.2	Wagner-Bos	2.0
Wagner-Bos	187.1	D.Newsome-Bos	.277	D.Newsome-Bos	.344	D.Newsome-Bos	4.13	D.Newsome-Bos	101	Hughson-Bos	1.5	D.Newsome-Bos	.5

1942 AMERICAN LEAGUE

TEAM	W	L	T	PCT	GB	R	OR	HR	AVG	OBP	SLG	OPS	AOPS	PF	SB	CG	HR	BB	SO	BR/9	ERA	AERA	OAV	OOB	FW	PW	BW	BSW	DIF
NY	103	51	0	.669		801	507	108	.269	.346	.394	740	+18	98	69	88	71	431	558	11.2	2.91	+18	.244	.304	2.0	8.9	12.5	.6	1.9
Bos	93	59	0	.612	9	761	594	103	.276	.352	.403	755	+16	103	68	84	65	553	500	12.1	3.44	+8	.247	.322	1.0	4.3	11.2	-.4	.9
StL	82	69	0	.543	19.5	730	637	98	.259	.338	.385	723	+9	102	37	68	63	505	488	12.7	3.59	+3	.262	.330	.4	1.7	6.0	-.3	-1.4
Cle	75	79	2	.487	28	590	659	50	.253	.320	.345	665	+0	94	69	61	61	560	448	12.4	3.59	-4	.254	.327	1.0	-2.5	-.7	-.9	1.1
Det	73	81	2	.474	30	589	587	76	.246	.314	.348	658	-15	100	39	65	50	598	671	12.5	3.13	+26	.248	.326	-.8	12.1	-10.6	-.3	-4.5
Chi	66	82	0	.446	34	538	609	25	.246	.316	.318	634	-13	98	114	86	74	473	432	12.3	3.58	+0	.258	.325	-.1	.3	-7.7	.3	-.9
Was	62	89	0	.411	39.5	653	817	40	.258	.333	.341	674	-2	99	98	68	50	558	496	13.8	4.58	-20	.263	.349	-2.7	-14.2	-.7	1.4	2.7
Phi	55	99	0	.357	48	549	801	33	.249	.309	.325	634	-14	-99	44	67	89	639	546	13.5	4.45	-15	.263	.344	-.6	-10.1	-10.3	-.4	-.6
Total	611					5211		533	.257	.329	.357	686			538	587		4317	4139	12.6	3.66		.257	.329					

Batter-Fielder Wins		Batting Average		On-Base Percentage		Slugging Average		On-Base Plus Slugging		Adjusted OPS		Adjusted Batter Runs	
Williams-Bos	8.5	Williams-Bos	.356	Williams-Bos	.499	Williams-Bos	.648	Williams-Bos	1147	Williams-Bos	214	Williams-Bos	89.9
Pesky-Bos	4.5	Pesky-Bos	.331	Pesky-Bos	.375	Doerr-Bos	.455	Doerr-Bos	824	Doerr-Bos	127	Doerr-Bos	19.7
Doerr-Bos	4.1	Doerr-Bos	.290	Doerr-Bos	.369	DiMaggio-Bos	.437	DiMaggio-Bos	801	DiMaggio-Bos	121	DiMaggio-Bos	17.3
DiMaggio-Bos	2.7	DiMaggio-Bos	.286	DiMaggio-Bos	.364	Pesky-Bos	.416	Pesky-Bos	791	Pesky-Bos	118	Pesky-Bos	14.1

Runs		Hits		Doubles		Triples		Home Runs		Total Bases		Runs Batted In	
Williams-Bos	141	Pesky-Bos	205	Kolloway-Chi	40	Spence-Was	15	Williams-Bos	36	Williams-Bos	338	Williams-Bos	137
DiMaggio-Bos	110	Williams-Bos	186	DiMaggio-Bos	36	Pesky-Bos	9	Doerr-Bos	15	DiMaggio-Bos	272	Doerr-Bos	102
Pesky-Bos	105	DiMaggio-Bos	178	Doerr-Bos	35	DiMaggio-Bos	8	DiMaggio-Bos	14	Pesky-Bos	258	Tabor-Bos	75
Doerr-Bos	71	Doerr-Bos	158	Williams-Bos	34	2 players tied	7	Tabor-Bos	12	Doerr-Bos	248	Lupien-Bos	70

Stolen Bases		Base Stealing Runs		Fielding Runs-Infield		Fielding Runs-Outfield		Wins		Winning Pct.		Complete Games	
Case-Was	44	Case-Was	7.6	Rizzuto-NY	30.0	DiMaggio-Bos	13.1	Hughson-Bos	22	Bonham-NY	.808	Bonham-NY	22
DiMaggio-Bos	16	Conroy-Bos	.4	Pesky-Bos	19.6	Williams-Bos	4.2	Wagner-Bos	14	Hughson-Bos	.786	Hughson-Bos	22
Pesky-Bos	12	Campbell-Bos	.2	Doerr-Bos	12.0			Dobson-Bos	11			Wagner-Bos	17
Lupien-Bos	10	Pesky-Bos	.2					Brown-Bos	9			2 players tied	11

Strikeouts		Fewest BB/Game		Games		Saves		Base Runners/9		Adjusted Relief Runs		Relief Ranking	
Newsom-Was	113	Bonham-NY	.96	Haynes-Chi	40	Murphy-NY	11	Bonham-NY	8.92	Ferrick-Cle	14.5	Haynes-Chi	13.3
Hughson-Bos	113	Hughson-Bos	2.40	Hughson-Bos	38	Brown-Bos	6	Butland-Bos	9.78	Brown-Bos	1.7	Brown-Bos	3.3
Dobson-Bos	72	Dobson-Bos	3.35	Brown-Bos	34	Hughson-Bos	4	Hughson-Bos	10.70				
Judd-Bos	70	D.Newsome-Bos	3.82	Judd-Bos	31	Ryba-Bos	3	Dobson-Bos	11.09				

Innings Pitched		Opponents' Avg.		Opponents' OBP		Earned Run Average		Adjusted ERA		Adjusted Starter Runs		Pitcher Wins	
Hughson-Bos	281.0	Newhouser-Det	.207	Bonham-NY	.259	Lyons-Chi	2.10	Lyons-Chi	172	Hughson-Bos	35.0	Lyons-Chi	3.8
Wagner-Bos	205.1	Dobson-Bos	.231	Hughson-Bos	.296	Hughson-Bos	2.59	Hughson-Bos	144	Butland-Bos	15.0	Hughson-Bos	3.7
Dobson-Bos	182.2	Hughson-Bos	.245	Dobson-Bos	.303	Wagner-Bos	3.29	Wagner-Bos	113	Dobson-Bos	10.1	Butland-Bos	1.0
D.Newsome-Bos	158.0	Wagner-Bos	.247	Wagner-Bos	.336	Dobson-Bos	3.30	Dobson-Bos	113	Wagner-Bos	9.3	Dobson-Bos	1.0

1943 AMERICAN LEAGUE

TEAM	W	L	T	PCT	GB	R	OR	HR	AVG	OBP	SLG	OPS	AOPS	PF	SB	CG	HR	BB	SO	BR/9	ERA	AERA	OAV	OOB	FW	PW	BW	BSW	DIF
NY	98	56	1	.636		**669**	542	100	.256	**.337**	**.376**	713	+14	101	46	**83**	60	489	653	11.0	2.93	+10	**.234**	.301	.2	5.1	**10.1**	-.9	6.5
Was	84	69	0	.549	13.5	666	595	47	.254	.336	.347	683	+10	96	142	61	48	540	495	12.0	3.18	+1	.246	.318	-1.0	.3	8.0	**1.6**	-1.4
Cle	82	71	0	.536	15.5	600	577	55	.255	.329	.350	679	+12	94	47	64	52	606	585	11.9	3.15	-1	.239	.322	.3	-.8	8.2	-.8	-1.4
Chi	82	72	1	.532	16	573	594	33	.247	.322	.320	642	-6	100	70	54	501	476	12.1	3.20	-.0	.255	.324	-.2	2.3	-3.6	1.1	5.3
Det	78	76	1	.506	20	632	560	77	**.261**	.324	.359	683	-2	108	40	67	51	549	**706**	11.4	3.00	+17	**.234**	.308	-.7	8.2	-1.7	-.4	-4.4
StL	72	80	1	.474	25	596	604	78	.245	.322	.349	671	+0	102	37	64	74	**488**	572	12.4	3.41	-3	.263	.327	**.6**	-1.4	.3	-.5	-3.0
Bos	68	84	3	.447	29	568	607	57	.244	.308	.332	640	-8	102	86	62	61	615	513	12.6	3.45	-4	.257	.336	**.6**	-2.4	-6.3	.0	-.0
Phi	49	105	1	.318	49	497	717	26	.232	.294	.297	591	-22	100	55	73	73	536	503	12.9	4.05	-16	.265	.336	.1	-10.6	-15.3	-.0	-2.2
Total	617					4796		473	.249	.322	.341	663			626	544		4324	4503	12.0	3.30		.249	.322					

Batter-Fielder Wins		Batting Average		On-Base Percentage		Slugging Average		On-Base Plus Slugging		Adjusted OPS		Adjusted Batter Runs	
Boudreau-Cle	**6.8**	Appling-Chi	.328	Appling-Chi	.419	York-Det	.527	Keller-NY	922	Keller-NY	167	Keller-NY	45.1
Doerr-Bos	**3.2**	Fox-Bos	.288	Doerr-Bos	.339	Doerr-Bos	.412	Doerr-Bos	751	Doerr-Bos	117	Doerr-Bos	12.4
Cronin-Bos	**.8**	Doerr-Bos	.270	Fox-Bos	.337	Tabor-Bos	.374	Fox-Bos	703	Fox-Bos	104	Cronin-Bos	7.3
Culberson-Bos	**.6**	S.Newsome-Bos	.265	Lupien-Bos	.317	Fox-Bos	.366	Tabor-Bos	674	Tabor-Bos	95	Partee-Bos	4.0

Runs		Hits		Doubles		Triples		Home Runs		Total Bases		Runs Batted In	
Case-Was	102	Wakefield-Det	200	Wakefield-Det	38	Moses-Chi	12	York-Det	34	York-Det	301	York-Det	118
Doerr-Bos	78	Doerr-Bos	163	Doerr-Bos	32	Lindell-NY	12	Doerr-Bos	16	Doerr-Bos	249	Tabor-Bos	85
Lupien-Bos	65	Lupien-Bos	155	Tabor-Bos	26	Lupien-Bos	9	Tabor-Bos	13	Lupien-Bos	206	Doerr-Bos	75
Tabor-Bos	57	Fox-Bos	141	Fox-Bos	24	Culberson-Bos	6	2 players tied	5	Tabor-Bos	201	Lupien-Bos	47

Stolen Bases		Base Stealing Runs		Fielding Runs-Infield		Fielding Runs-Outfield		Wins		Winning Pct.		Complete Games	
Case-Was	61	Case-Was	8.5	Boudreau-Cle	25.1	Tucker-Chi	9.2	Trout-Det	20	Chandler-NY	.833	Chandler-NY	20
Fox-Bos	22	Culberson-Bos	3.1	Doerr-Bos	9.4			Chandler-NY	20			Hughson-Bos	20
Lupien-Bos	16	Fox-Bos	2.0	S.Newsome-Bos	8.5			Hughson-Bos	12			Dobson-Bos	9
Culberson-Bos	14	2 players tied	.4	Lupien-Bos	2.7			Judd-Bos	11			2 players tied	8

Strikeouts		Fewest BB/Game		Games		Saves		Base Runners/9		Adjusted Relief Runs		Relief Ranking	
Reynolds-Cle	151	Leonard-Was	1.88	Brown-Bos	49	Maltzberger-Chi	14	Chandler-NY	9.07	Brown-Bos	11.6	Caster-StL	18.0
Hughson-Bos	114	Hughson-Bos	2.47	Ryba-Bos	40	Brown-Bos	9	Hughson-Bos	10.73			Brown-Bos	15.9
Terry-Bos	63	Dobson-Bos	3.12	Hughson-Bos	35	Ryba-Bos	2	Dobson-Bos	11.01				
Dobson-Bos	63	Terry-Bos	3.46	Terry-Bos	30	Hughson-Bos	2	Terry-Bos	11.60				

Innings Pitched		Opponents' Avg.		Opponents' OBP		Earned Run Average		Adjusted ERA		Adjusted Starter Runs		Pitcher Wins	
Bagby-Cle	273.0	Reynolds-Cle	.202	Chandler-NY	.261	Chandler-NY	1.64	Chandler-NY	197	Chandler-NY	42.1	Chandler-NY	5.3
Hughson-Bos	266.0	Judd-Bos	.230	Hughson-Bos	.300	Hughson-Bos	2.64	Hughson-Bos	125	Hughson-Bos	19.6	Hughson-Bos	1.6
Dobson-Bos	164.1	Dobson-Bos	.239	Dobson-Bos	.305	Judd-Bos	2.90	Judd-Bos	114	Judd-Bos	6.0	Brown-Bos	1.6
Terry-Bos	163.2	Terry-Bos	.242	Terry-Bos	.314	Dobson-Bos	3.12	Dobson-Bos	106	Dobson-Bos	3.6	Judd-Bos	1.1

1944 AMERICAN LEAGUE

TEAM	W	L	T	PCT	GB	R	OR	HR	AVG	OBP	SLG	OPS	AOPS	PF	SB	CG	HR	BB	SO	BR/9	ERA	AERA	OAV	OOB	FW	PW	BW	BSW	DIF
StL	89	65	0	.578		684	587	72	.252	.323	.352	675	-6	106	44	71	58	469	**581**	12.1	3.17	+14	.259	.320	.5	6.6	-3.9	-.2	9.0
Det	88	66	2	.571	1	658	581	60	.263	.332	.354	686	-3	100	61	**87**	39	452	568	11.9	**3.09**	**+16**	.257	.318	-.5	**7.6**	-1.3	-.6	5.8
NY	83	71	0	.539	6	674	617	**96**	.264	.333	**.387**	720	+8	103	91	78	82	532	529	12.3	3.39	+3	.257	.326	**1.3**	1.6	5.4	**.9**	-3.2
Bos	77	77	2	.500	12	**739**	676	69	**.270**	**.336**	.380	716	**+12**	99	60	58	66	592	524	13.0	3.82	-11	.263	.339	.6	-6.9	**9.0**	-.1	-2.6
Phi	72	82	1	.468	17	525	594	36	.257	.314	.327	641	-9	99	42	72	58	390	534	11.4	3.26	+7	**.252**	**.307**	.2	3.7	-7.4	-.1	-1.3
Cle	72	82	1	.468	17	643	677	70	.266	.331	.372	703	+11	96	48	48	40	621	524	13.2	3.65	-10	.265	.344	.9	-6.1	8.2	-.4	-7.6
Chi	71	83	0	.461	18	543	662	23	.247	.307	.320	627	-14	99	66	64	68	420	481	12.0	3.58	-4	.264	.320	-.2	-2.4	-9.7	-.2	6.5
Was	64	90	0	.416	25	592	664	33	.261	.324	.330	654	-3	96	**127**	83	48	475	503	12.4	3.49	-7	.264	.327	-2.3	-4.0	-1.6	.7	-5.9
Total	619					5058		459	.260	.325	.353	678			539	561		3951	4244	12.3	3.43		.260	.325					

Batter-Fielder Wins		Batting Average		On-Base Percentage		Slugging Average		On-Base Plus Slugging		Adjusted OPS		Adjusted Batter Runs	
Boudreau-Cle	**7.5**	Boudreau-Cle	.327	B.Johnson-Bos	.431	Doerr-Bos	.528	B.Johnson-Bos	959	B.Johnson-Bos	175	B.Johnson-Bos	56.6
B.Johnson-Bos	**5.3**	Doerr-Bos	.325	Doerr-Bos	.399	B.Johnson-Bos	.528	Doerr-Bos	927	Doerr-Bos	166	Doerr-Bos	39.9
Doerr-Bos	**5.1**	B.Johnson-Bos	.324	Fox-Bos	.354	Tabor-Bos	.445	Tabor-Bos	779	Tabor-Bos	123	Fox-Bos	13.3
Tabor-Bos	**1.7**	Fox-Bos	.315	Tabor-Bos	.334	Fox-Bos	.419	Fox-Bos	773	Fox-Bos	122	Tabor-Bos	11.4

Runs		Hits		Doubles		Triples		Home Runs		Total Bases		Runs Batted In	
Stirnweiss-NY	125	Stirnweiss-NY	205	Boudreau-Cle	45	Stirnweiss-NY	16	Etten-NY	22	Lindell-NY	297	Stephens-StL	109
B.Johnson-Bos	106	B.Johnson-Bos	170	B.Johnson-Bos	40	Lindell-NY	16	B.Johnson-Bos	17	B.Johnson-Bos	277	B.Johnson-Bos	106
Doerr-Bos	95	Fox-Bos	156	Fox-Bos	37	Doerr-Bos	10	Doerr-Bos	15	Doerr-Bos	247	Doerr-Bos	81
Metkovich-Bos	94	2 players tied	152	Doerr-Bos	29	2 players tied	8	Tabor-Bos	13	Metkovich-Bos	223	Tabor-Bos	72

Stolen Bases		Base Stealing Runs		Fielding Runs-Infield		Fielding Runs-Outfield		Wins		Winning Pct.		Complete Games	
Stirnweiss-NY	55	Stirnweiss-NY	8.3	Mayo-Det	33.5	Spence-Was	15.4	Newhouser-Det	29	Hughson-Bos	.783	Trout-Det	33
Metkovich-Bos	13	Metkovich-Bos	1.5	Newsome-Bos	8.8	B.Johnson-Bos	5.2	Hughson-Bos	18			Hughson-Bos	19
Fox-Bos	10	McBride-Bos	.9	Tabor-Bos	3.8			Ryba-Bos	12			Bowman-Bos	10
Culberson-Bos	6	Fox-Bos	.5	Doerr-Bos	2.3			Bowman-Bos	12			O'Neill-Bos	8

Strikeouts		Fewest BB/Game		Games		Saves		Base Runners/9		Adjusted Relief Runs		Relief Ranking	
Newhouser-Det	187	Harris-Phi	1.34	Heving-Cle	63	3 players tied	12	Berry-Phi	8.33	Berry-Phi	17.2	Berry-Phi	29.2
Hughson-Bos	112	Hughson-Bos	1.81	Ryba-Bos	42	Barrett-Bos	8	Hughson-Bos	9.52				
O'Neill-Bos	68	Bowman-Bos	3.42	Woods-Bos	38	Hughson-Bos	5	Ryba-Bos	10.30				
Woods-Bos	56	Woods-Bos	4.64	Barrett-Bos	38	2 players tied	2	Bowman-Bos	12.89				

Innings Pitched		Opponents' Avg.		Opponents' OBP		Earned Run Average		Adjusted ERA		Adjusted Starter Runs		Pitcher Wins	
Trout-Det	352.1	Gromek-Cle	.219	Hughson-Bos	.267	Trout-Det	2.12	Trout-Det	168	Trout-Det	53.1	Trout-Det	8.2
Hughson-Bos	203.1	Hughson-Bos	.225	Bowman-Bos	.336	Hughson-Bos	2.26	Hughson-Bos	151	Hughson-Bos	26.6	Hughson-Bos	3.1
Woods-Bos	170.2	Woods-Bos	.266	Woods-Bos	.360	Woods-Bos	3.27	Woods-Bos	104	Ryba-Bos	1.7	Ryba-Bos	.3
Bowman-Bos	168.1	Bowman-Bos	.269			Bowman-Bos	4.81	Bowman-Bos	71	Hausmann-Bos	1.7	Woods-Bos	.0

1945 AMERICAN LEAGUE

TEAM	W	L	T	PCT	GB	R	OR	HR	AVG	OBP	SLG	OPS	AOPS	PF	SB	CG	HR	BB	SO	BR/9	ERA	AERA	OAV	OOB	FW	PW	BW	BSW	DIF
Det	88	65	2	.575		633	565	77	.256	.324	.361	685	-2	106	60	78	48	538	588	12.1	2.99	+18	.250	.322	.4	8.4	-1.7	-.2	4.7
Was	87	67	2	.565	1.5	622	562	27	.258	.330	.334	664	+7	92	110	82	42	440	550	11.2	2.92	+6	.242	.301	-1.0	3.2	5.0	.5	2.2
StL	81	70	3	.536	6	597	548	63	.249	.316	.341	657	-9	105	25	91	59	506	570	11.8	3.14	+12	.249	.316	1.2	5.9	-6.0	-.1	4.6
NY	81	71	0	.533	6.5	676	606	93	.259	.343	.373	716	+8	105	64	78	66	485	474	11.8	3.45	+0	.250	.316	-.7	.1	6.3	.3	-1.0
Cle	73	72	2	.503	11	557	548	65	.255	.326	.359	685	+9	96	19	76	39	501	497	12.4	3.31	-2	.257	.328	1.7	-1.0	5.4	-.3	-5.3
Chi	71	78	1	.477	15	596	633	22	.262	.326	.337	663	+1	97	78	84	63	448	486	12.7	3.69	-10	.270	.332	-1.1	-6.0	.2	.2	3.2
Bos	71	83	3	.461	17.5	599	674	50	.260	.330	.346	676	+0	102	72	71	58	656	490	13.4	3.80	-10	.264	.348	-.1	-6.4	.0	.2	.3
Phi	52	98	3	.347	34.5	494	638	33	.245	.306	.316	622	-14	100	25	65	55	571	531	12.9	3.62	-5	.262	.337	-.3	-3.1	-10.3	-.7	-8.7
Total	612					4774		430	.255	.325	.346	671			453	625		4145	4186	12.3	3.36		.255	.325					

Batter-Fielder Wins		Batting Average		On-Base Percentage		Slugging Average		On-Base Plus Slugging		Adjusted OPS		Adjusted Batter Runs	
Stirnweiss-NY	7.2	Stirnweiss-NY	.309	Lake-Bos	.412	Stirnweiss-NY	.476	Stirnweiss-NY	862	Stirnweiss-NY	143	Stirnweiss-NY	33.9
Lake-Bos	6.5	Newsome-Bos	.290	B.Johnson-Bos	.358	Lake-Bos	.425	Lake-Bos	822	Lake-Bos	136	Lake-Bos	28.6
Newsome-Bos	2.3	B.Johnson-Bos	.280	Metkovich-Chi	.331	B.Johnson-Bos	.410	B.Johnson-Bos	783	B.Johnson-Bos	124	B.Johnson-Bos	16.1
B.Johnson-Bos	1.2	Lake-Bos	.279	Newsome-Bos	.322	Newsome-Bos	.370	Newsome-Bos	692	Newsome-Bos	98	Ferriss-Bos	11.1

Runs		Hits		Doubles		Triples		Home Runs		Total Bases		Runs Batted In	
Stirnweiss-NY	107	Stirnweiss-NY	195	Moses-Chi	35	Stirnweiss-NY	22	Stephens-StL	24	Stirnweiss-NY	301	Etten-NY	111
Lake-Bos	81	B.Johnson-Bos	148	Newsome-Bos	30	McBride-Bos	7	B.Johnson-Bos	12	B.Johnson-Bos	225	B.Johnson-Bos	74
B.Johnson-Bos	71	Metkovich-Bos	140	Lake-Bos	27	B.Johnson-Bos	7	Lake-Bos	11	Lake-Bos	194	Metkovich-Bos	62
Metkovich-Bos	65	Lake-Bos	132	B.Johnson-Bos	27	Culberson-Bos	6	Culberson-Bos	6	Metkovich-Bos	187	Lake-Bos	51

Stolen Bases		Base Stealing Runs		Fielding Runs-Infield		Fielding Runs-Outfield		Wins		Winning Pct.		Complete Games	
Stirnweiss-NY	33	Dickshot-Chi	2.9	Stirnweiss-NY	25.2	Cullenbine-Cle-Det	9.1	Newhouser-Det	25	Newhouser-Det	.735	Newhouser-Det	29
Metkovich-Bos	19	Metkovich-Bos	2.1	Lake-Bos	23.7	B.Johnson-Bos	3.5	Ferriss-Bos	21	Ferriss-Bos	.677	Ferriss-Bos	26
B.Steiner-Bos	10	Camilli-Bos	.4	Newsome-Bos	16.2			O'Neill-Bos	8			O'Neill-Bos	10
Lake-Bos	9	Newsome-Bos	.3					Ryba-Bos	7			Wilson-Bos	8

Strikeouts		Fewest BB/Game		Games		Saves		Base Runners/9		Adjusted Relief Runs		Relief Ranking	
Newhouser-Det	212	Bonham-NY	1.10	Berry-Phi	52	Turner-NY	10	Wolff-Was	9.14	Berry-Phi	15.0	Berry-Phi	16.8
Ferriss-Bos	94	Ferriss-Bos	2.89	Barrett-Bos	37	Barrett-Bos	3	Barrett-Bos	11.09	Barrett-Bos	6.9	Barrett-Bos	5.6
O'Neill-Bos	55			Ferriss-Bos	35			Ryba-Bos	11.49				
Wilson-Bos	50			Ryba-Bos	34			Clark-Bos	11.63				

Innings Pitched		Opponents' Avg.		Opponents' OBP		Earned Run Average		Adjusted ERA		Adjusted Starter Runs		Pitcher Wins	
Newhouser-Det	313.1	Newhouser-Det	.211	Wolff-Was	.258	Newhouser-Det	1.81	Newhouser-Det	194	Newhouser-Det	58.4	Newhouser-Det	7.6
Ferriss-Bos	264.2	Ferriss-Bos	.264	Ferriss-Bos	.327	Ferriss-Bos	2.96	Ferriss-Bos	115	Ferriss-Bos	12.5	Ferriss-Bos	3.0
Wilson-Bos	144.1					O'Neill-Bos	5.15			Ryba-Bos	9.8	Ryba-Bos	1.2
O'Neill-Bos	141.2									Clark-Bos	2.6	Barrett-Bos	.6

1946 AMERICAN LEAGUE

TEAM	W	L	T	PCT	GB	R	OR	HR	AVG	OBP	SLG	OPS	AOPS	PF	SB	CG	HR	BB	SO	BR/9	ERA	AERA	OAV	OOB	FW	PW	BW	BSW	DIF
Bos	104	50	2	.675		792	594	109	.271	.356	.402	758	+13	106	45	79	89	501	667	12.1	3.38	+8	.254	.319	1.5	4.4	10.5	.0	10.6
Det	92	62	1	.597	12	704	567	108	.258	.330	.374	711	+0	106	65	94	97	497	896	11.5	3.22	+14	.241	.307	.5	6.8	.4	.4	6.9
NY	87	67	0	.565	17	684	547	136	.248	.334	.387	721	+7	101	48	68	66	552	653	11.9	3.13	+10	.243	.319	.7	5.1	4.9	.2	-.9
Was	76	78	1	.494	28	608	706	60	.260	.327	.366	693	+6	94	51	71	81	547	537	13.1	3.74	-11	.269	.339	-2.8	-6.7	4.4	-.2	4.4
Chi	74	80	1	.481	30	562	595	37	.257	.333	.333	656	-6	94	78	62	80	508	550	12.1	3.10	+10	.255	.323	-.7	5.2	-4.6	-.1	-2.8
Cle	68	86	2	.442	36	537	638	79	.245	.313	.356	669	-1	94	57	63	84	649	789	12.6	3.62	-9	.245	.331	1.0	-5.3	-1.0	-.1	-3.5
StL	66	88	2	.429	38	621	710	84	.251	.313	.356	669	-11	105	23	73	73	573	574	13.3	3.95	-6	.272	.343	.3	-3.4	-8.6	-.3	1.0
Phi	49	105	1	.318	55	529	680	40	.253	.318	.338	656	-9	99	39	61	83	577	562	13.2	3.90	-9	.264	.340	-.2	-5.4	-7.0	.2	-15.5
Total	621					5037		653	.256	.328	.364	692			406	561		4404	5228	12.5	3.50		.256	.328					

Batter-Fielder Wins		Batting Average		On-Base Percentage		Slugging Average		On-Base Plus Slugging		Adjusted OPS		Adjusted Batter Runs	
Williams-Bos	8.1	Vernon-Was	.353	Williams-Bos	.497	Williams-Bos	.667	Williams-Bos	1164	Williams-Bos	211	Williams-Bos	88.3
Doerr-Bos	4.8	Williams-Bos	.342	Pesky-Bos	.401	Doerr-Bos	.453	Pesky-Bos	827	Pesky-Bos	124	Pesky-Bos	23.4
Pesky-Bos	4.6	Pesky-Bos	.335	DiMaggio-Bos	.393	York-Bos	.437	DiMaggio-Bos	820	DiMaggio-Bos	122	DiMaggio-Bos	17.7
2 players tied	1.7	DiMaggio-Bos	.316	York-Bos	.371	2 players tied	.427	York-Bos	808	York-Bos	118	York-Bos	16.2

Runs		Hits		Doubles		Triples		Home Runs		Total Bases		Runs Batted In	
Williams-Bos	142	Pesky-Bos	208	Vernon-Was	51	Edwards-Cle	16	Greenberg-Det	44	Williams-Bos	343	Greenberg-Det	127
Pesky-Bos	115	Williams-Bos	176	Pesky-Bos	43	Doerr-Bos	9	Williams-Bos	38	Pesky-Bos	265	Williams-Bos	123
Doerr-Bos	95	DiMaggio-Bos	169	Williams-Bos	37	Williams-Bos	8	Doerr-Bos	18	Doerr-Bos	264	York-Bos	119
DiMaggio-Bos	85	York-Bos	160	Doerr-Bos	34	DiMaggio-Bos	7	York-Bos	17	York-Bos	253	Doerr-Bos	116

Stolen Bases		Base Stealing Runs		Fielding Runs-Infield		Fielding Runs-Outfield		Wins		Winning Pct.		Complete Games	
Case-Cle	28	Case-Cle	2.3	Doerr-Bos	27.3	Zarilla-StL	9.6	Newhouser-Det	26	Ferriss-Bos	.806	Feller-Cle	36
DiMaggio-Bos	10	Metkovich-Bos	.7	Pesky-Bos	12.3	Williams-Bos	2.4	Feller-Cle	26	Harris-Bos	.654	Ferriss-Bos	26
Pesky-Bos	9	H.Wagner-Bos	.3	York-Bos	5.9	DiMaggio-Bos	2.3	Ferriss-Bos	25	Hughson-Bos	.645	Hughson-Bos	21
Metkovich-Bos	8	Pellagrini-Bos	.2					Hughson-Bos	20			Harris-Bos	15

Strikeouts		Fewest BB/Game		Games		Saves		Base Runners/9		Adjusted Relief Runs		Relief Ranking	
Feller-Cle	348	Hughson-Bos	1.65	Feller-Cle	48	Klinger-Bos	9	Ruffing-NY	8.85	Caldwell-Chi	12.9	Caldwell-Chi	24.4
Hughson-Bos	172	Ferriss-Bos	2.33	Ferriss-Bos	40	Johnson-Bos	3	Hughson-Bos	9.87	Klinger-Bos	8.3	Klinger-Bos	9.5
Harris-Bos	131	Harris-Bos	3.07	Hughson-Bos	39	Hughson-Bos	3	Ferriss-Bos	11.43				
Ferriss-Bos	106	Dobson-Bos	3.67	Harris-Bos	34	Ferriss-Bos	3	Dobson-Bos	11.72				

Innings Pitched		Opponents' Avg.		Opponents' OBP		Earned Run Average		Adjusted ERA		Adjusted Starter Runs		Pitcher Wins	
Feller-Cle	371.1	Newhouser-Det	.201	Newhouser-Det	.269	Newhouser-Det	1.94	Newhouser-Det	189	Newhouser-Det	51.1	Newhouser-Det	6.4
Hughson-Bos	278.0	Dobson-Bos	.234	Hughson-Bos	.274	Hughson-Bos	2.75	Hughson-Bos	133	Hughson-Bos	30.0	Hughson-Bos	3.0
Ferriss-Bos	274.0	Hughson-Bos	.238	Ferriss-Bos	.308	Dobson-Bos	3.24	Dobson-Bos	113	Ferriss-Bos	13.3	Ferriss-Bos	1.8
Harris-Bos	222.2	Ferriss-Bos	.259	Dobson-Bos	.309	Ferriss-Bos	3.25	Ferriss-Bos	113	Dobson-Bos	5.8	Klinger-Bos	1.1

1947 AMERICAN LEAGUE

TEAM	W	L	T	PCT	GB	R	OR	HR	AVG	OBP	SLG	OPS	AOPS	PF	SB	CG	HR	BB	SO	BR/9	ERA	AERA	OAV	OOB	FW	PW	BW	BSW	DIF
NY	97	57	1	.630		794	568	115	.271	.349	.407	756	+17	99	27	73	95	628	691	12.2	3.39	+4	.238	.323	1.5	2.4	12.2	.2	3.7
Det	85	69	4	.552	12	714	642	103	.258	.353	.377	730	+6	103	52	77	79	531	648	12.4	3.57	+6	.258	.326	-1.0	3.1	6.3	-.7	.2
Bos	83	71	3	.539	14	720	669	103	.265	.349	.382	731	+2	107	41	64	84	575	586	12.8	3.81	+2	.261	.335	-.0	1.1	2.2	.0	2.6
Cle	80	74	3	.519	17	687	588	112	.259	.324	.385	709	+6	99	29	55	94	628	590	12.2	3.44	+1	.240	.325	1.9	.7	2.7	-.3	-2.5
Phi	78	76	2	.506	19	633	614	61	.252	.333	.349	682	-6	102	37	70	85	597	493	12.3	3.51	+9	.247	.326	-.4	4.7	-3.6	.0	.3
Chi	70	84	1	.455	27	553	661	53	.256	.321	.342	663	-7	96	91	47	76	603	522	13.0	3.64	+0	.261	.339	-1.2	.3	-5.1	.4	-1.5
Was	64	90	0	.416	33	496	675	42	.241	.313	.321	634	-16	-97	53	67	63	579	551	13.2	3.97	-6	.267	.342	-.5	-3.8	-11.1	-.2	2.7
StL	59	95	0	.383	38	564	744	90	.241	.320	.350	670	-10	102	69	50	103	604	552	13.4	4.33	-10	.272	.348	.0	-6.7	-7.0	.2	-4.4
Total	623					5161		679	.256	.333	.364	698			399	503		4745	4633	12.7	3.71		.256	.333					

Batter-Fielder Wins		Batting Average		On-Base Percentage		Slugging Average		On-Base Plus Slugging		Adjusted OPS		Adjusted Batter Runs	
Williams-Bos	7.2	Williams-Bos	.343	Williams-Bos	.499	Williams-Bos	.634	Williams-Bos	1133	Williams-Bos	199	Williams-Bos	82.7
Doerr-Bos	3.3	Pesky-Bos	.324	Pesky-Bos	.393	Mele-Bos	.448	Mele-Bos	805	Mele-Bos	114	Pesky-Bos	11.4
DiMaggio-Bos	1.8	Mele-Bos	.302	DiMaggio-Bos	.376	Doerr-Bos	.426	Pesky-Bos	785	Pesky-Bos	110	Mele-Bos	7.0
Pesky-Bos	.9	DiMaggio-Bos	.283	Mele-Bos	.356	Pesky-Bos	.392	DiMaggio-Bos	766	DiMaggio-Bos	105	Ferriss-Bos	6.7

Runs		Hits		Doubles		Triples		Home Runs		Total Bases		Runs Batted In	
Williams-Bos	125	Pesky-Bos	207	Boudreau-Cle	45	Henrich-NY	13	Williams-Bos	32	Williams-Bos	335	Williams-Bos	114
Pesky-Bos	106	Williams-Bos	181	Williams-Bos	40	Doerr-Bos	10	Doerr-Bos	17	Pesky-Bos	250	Doerr-Bos	95
Doerr-Bos	79	Doerr-Bos	145	Pesky-Bos	27	Williams-Bos	9	Mele-Bos	12	Doerr-Bos	239	Mele-Bos	73
DiMaggio-Bos	75	DiMaggio-Bos	145	Doerr-Bos	23	2 players tied	8	Mele-Bos	8	Mele-Bos	203	DiMaggio-Bos	71

Stolen Bases		Base Stealing Runs		Fielding Runs-Infield		Fielding Runs-Outfield		Wins		Winning Pct.		Complete Games	
Dillinger-StL	34	Dillinger-StL	2.9	Doerr-Bos	25.2	DiMaggio-Bos	15.0	Feller-Cle	20	Reynolds-NY	.704	Newhouser-Det	24
Pesky-Bos	12	Moses-Bos	.7			Williams-Bos	1.1	Dobson-Bos	18	Dobson-Bos	.692	Dobson-Bos	15
DiMaggio-Bos	10	Gutteridge-Bos	.3					3 players tied	12			Ferriss-Bos	14
3 players tied	3	DiMaggio-Bos	.1									Hughson-Bos	13

Strikeouts		Fewest BB/Game		Games		Saves		Base Runners/9		Adjusted Relief Runs		Relief Ranking	
Feller-Cle	196	Galehouse-StL-Bos	2.48	Klieman-Cle	58	Page-NY	17	Chandler-NY	9.91	Page-NY	18.1	Page-NY	30.3
Hughson-Bos	119	Dobson-Bos	2.87	Johnson-Bos	45	Klieman-Cle	17	Dobson-Bos	10.90	Murphy-Bos	7.3	Murphy-Bos	3.6
Dobson-Bos	110	Hughson-Bos	3.38	Dorish-Bos	41	Johnson-Bos	8	Hughson-Bos	11.69				
Johnson-Bos	65	Ferriss-Bos	3.79	2 players tied	33	Klinger-Bos	5	Johnson-Bos	12.20				

Innings Pitched		Opponents' Avg.		Opponents' OBP		Earned Run Average		Adjusted ERA		Adjusted Starter Runs		Pitcher Wins	
Feller-Cle	299.0	Shea-NY	.200	Dobson-Bos	.299	Haynes-Chi	2.42	Haynes-Chi	151	Feller-Cle	28.7	Newhouser-Det	3.7
Dobson-Bos	228.2	Dobson-Bos	.238	Hughson-Bos	.314	Dobson-Bos	2.95	Dobson-Bos	132	Dobson-Bos	23.1	Hutchinson-Det	3.7
Ferriss-Bos	218.1	Hughson-Bos	.244	Ferriss-Bos	.362	Hughson-Bos	3.33	Hughson-Bos	117	Johnson-Bos	9.8	Dobson-Bos	2.6
Hughson-Bos	189.1	Ferriss-Bos	.287			Ferriss-Bos	4.04	Ferriss-Bos	96	Hughson-Bos	8.5	Johnson-Bos	1.9

1948 AMERICAN LEAGUE

TEAM	W	L	T	PCT	GB	R	OR	HR	AVG	OBP	SLG	OPS	AOPS	PF	SB	CG	HR	BB	SO	BR/9	ERA	AERA	OAV	OOB	FW	PW	BW	BSW	DIF
Cle	97	58	1	.626		840	568	155	.282	.360	.431	791	+19	97	54	66	82	625	593	12.1	3.22	+26	.239	.323	1.4	13.4	13.2	-.1	-8.3
Bos	96	59	0	.619	1	907	720	121	.274	.374	.409	783	+9	105	38	70	83	592	513	13.4	4.26	+3	.270	.345	1.2	1.9	7.9	.4	7.0
NY	94	60	0	.610	2.5	857	633	139	.278	.356	.432	788	+16	99	24	62	94	641	654	12.9	3.75	+9	.250	.336	.9	5.1	10.4	-.1	.6
Phi	84	70	0	.545	12.5	729	735	68	.260	.353	.362	715	-4	100	40	74	86	638	486	13.9	4.43	-3	.275	.355	1.3	-1.9	-1.8	.0	9.4
Det	78	76	0	.506	18.5	700	726	78	.267	.353	.375	728	-4	103	22	60	92	589	678	12.9	4.15	+5	.259	.335	.9	-3.2	-1.9	-.1	1.0
StL	59	94	2	.386	37	671	849	63	.271	.345	.378	723	-4	103	63	35	103	737	531	14.9	5.01	-9	.281	.371	-1.6	-6.3	-3.8	.0	-5.9
Was	56	97	1	.366	40	578	796	31	.244	.322	.331	653	-19	-97	76	42	81	734	446	14.4	4.65	-7	.273	.364	-.9	-4.5	-13.6	.3	-1.8
Chi	51	101	2	.336	44.5	559	814	55	.251	.329	.331	660	-16	-97	46	35	89	673	403	14.4	4.89	-13	.280	.365	-1.2	-9.2	-11.4	-.3	-2.8
Total	618					5841		710	.266	.349	.382	731			363	444		5229	4304	13.6	4.29		.266	.349					

Batter-Fielder Wins		Batting Average		On-Base Percentage		Slugging Average		On-Base Plus Slugging		Adjusted OPS		Adjusted Batter Runs	
Boudreau-Cle	7.1	Williams-Bos	.369	Williams-Bos	.497	Williams-Bos	.615	Williams-Bos	1112	Williams-Bos	185	Williams-Bos	71.5
Williams-Bos	5.9	Goodman-Bos	.310	Goodman-Bos	.414	Doerr-Bos	.505	Doerr-Bos	891	Doerr-Bos	129	Doerr-Bos	21.5
Doerr-Bos	3.7	DiMaggio-Bos	.285	Pesky-Bos	.394	Stephens-Bos	.471	Stephens-Bos	821	Stephens-Bos	112	Goodman-Bos	10.0
Stephens-Bos	2.5	Doerr-Bos	.285	Doerr-Bos	.386	DiMaggio-Bos	.401	Goodman-Bos	801	Goodman-Bos	108	Stephens-Bos	7.2

Runs		Hits		Doubles		Triples		Home Runs		Total Bases		Runs Batted In	
Henrich-NY	138	Dillinger-StL	207	Williams-Bos	44	Henrich-NY	14	DiMaggio-NY	39	DiMaggio-NY	355	DiMaggio-NY	155
DiMaggio-Bos	127	Williams-Bos	188	DiMaggio-Bos	40	Stephens-Bos	8	Stephens-Bos	29	Williams-Bos	313	Stephens-Bos	137
Williams-Bos	124	DiMaggio-Bos	185	Goodman-Bos	27	Pesky-Bos	6	Doerr-Bos	27	Stephens-Bos	299	Williams-Bos	127
Pesky-Bos	124	Stephens-Bos	171	2 players tied	26	Doerr-Bos	6	Williams-Bos	25	Doerr-Bos	266	Doerr-Bos	111

Stolen Bases		Base Stealing Runs		Fielding Runs-Infield		Fielding Runs-Outfield		Wins		Winning Pct.		Complete Games	
Dillinger-StL	28	Dillinger-StL	2.3	Priddy-StL	22.5	Coan-Was	11.9	Newhouser-Det	21	Kramer-Bos	.783	Lemon-Cle	20
DiMaggio-Bos	10	DiMaggio-Bos	1.5	Doerr-Bos	9.4	DiMaggio-Bos	8.7	Kramer-Bos	18	Parnell-Bos	.652	Parnell-Bos	16
3 players tied	5	Moses-Bos	1.1	Stephens-Bos	9.0			Dobson-Bos	16	Dobson-Bos	.615	Dobson-Bos	16
		Williams-Bos	.9	Pesky-Bos	6.8			Parnell-Bos	15			Kramer-Bos	14

Strikeouts		Fewest BB/Game		Games		Saves		Base Runners/9		Adjusted Relief Runs		Relief Ranking	
Feller-Cle	164	Hutchinson-Det	1.95	Page-NY	55	Christopher-Cle	17	Paige-Cle	10.40	Klieman-Cle	13.6	Christopher-Cle	11.6
Dobson-Bos	116	Kramer-Bos	2.81	Dobson-Bos	38	Johnson-Bos	5	Dobson-Bos	12.11				
Parnell-Bos	77	Kinder-Bos	3.19	Parnell-Bos	35	Galehouse-Bos	3	Kinder-Bos	12.54				
Kramer-Bos	72	Dobson-Bos	3.38	Johnson-Bos	35	Ferriss-Bos	3	Parnell-Bos	12.69				

Innings Pitched		Opponents' Avg.		Opponents' OBP		Earned Run Average		Adjusted ERA		Adjusted Starter Runs		Pitcher Wins	
Lemon-Cle	293.2	Shea-NY	.208	Hutchinson-Det	.297	Bearden-Cle	2.43	Bearden-Cle	167	Bearden-Cle	42.9	Lemon-Cle	6.6
Dobson-Bos	245.1	Parnell-Bos	.252	Dobson-Bos	.320	Parnell-Bos	3.14	Parnell-Bos	140	Parnell-Bos	26.4	Parnell-Bos	2.2
Parnell-Bos	212.0	Dobson-Bos	.253	Kinder-Bos	.330	Dobson-Bos	3.56	Dobson-Bos	123	Dobson-Bos	18.7	Dobson-Bos	1.8
Kramer-Bos	205.0	Kinder-Bos	.266	Parnell-Bos	.330	Kinder-Bos	3.74	Kinder-Bos	117	Kinder-Bos	11.5	Galehouse-Bos	.5

1949 AMERICAN LEAGUE

TEAM	W	L	T	PCT	GB	R	OR	HR	AVG	OBP	SLG	OPS	AOPS	PF	SB	CG	HR	BB	SO	BR/9	ERA	AERA	OAV	OOB	FW	PW	BW	BSW	DIF
NY	97	57	1	.630		829	637	115	.269	.362	.400	762	+8	100	58	59	98	812	671	13.6	3.69	+10	.242	.351	.0	5.4	5.7	.5	8.3
Bos	96	58	1	.623	1	896	667	131	.282	.381	.420	801	+11	107	43	84	82	661	598	13.5	3.97	+10	.262	.347	1.1	5.5	9.1	.4	2.9
Cle	89	65	0	.578	8	675	574	112	.260	.339	.384	723	-1	98	44	65	82	611	594	12.4	3.36	+19	.247	.329	2.1	10.0	-2.0	-.0	2.1
Det	87	67	1	.565	10	751	655	88	.267	.361	.378	739	+2	100	39	70	102	628	631	12.8	3.77	+10	.254	.335	.4	5.9	1.8	-.7	2.5
Phi	81	73	0	.526	16	726	725	82	.260	.361	.369	730	+4	97	36	85	105	758	490	14.1	4.23	-3	.263	.360	-.1	-1.8	3.3	.2	2.5
Chi	63	91	0	.409	34	648	737	43	.257	.347	.347	694	-7	97	62	57	108	693	502	13.7	4.30	-3	.264	.353	-.2	-1.8	-4.5	-.3	-7.2
StL	53	101	1	.344	44	667	913	117	.254	.339	.377	716	-8	104	38	43	113	685	432	15.4	5.21	-13	.294	.377	-1.6	-9.1	-6.6	-.2	-6.4
Was	50	104	0	.325	47	584	868	81	.254	.333	.356	689	-10	98	46	44	79	779	451	15.0	5.10	-16	.276	.373	-1.4	-12.1	-8.0	.2	-5.7
Total	618					5776		769	.263	.353	.379	732			366	507		5627	4369	13.8	4.20		.263	.353					

Batter-Fielder Wins		Batting Average		On-Base Percentage		Slugging Average		On-Base Plus Slugging		Adjusted OPS		Adjusted Batter Runs	
Williams-Bos	6.4	Kell-Det	.343	Williams-Bos	.490	Williams-Bos	.650	Williams-Bos	1141	Williams-Bos	187	Williams-Bos	79.9
Doerr-Bos	5.1	Williams-Bos	.343	Pesky-Bos	.408	Stephens-Bos	.539	Stephens-Bos	930	Stephens-Bos	135	Stephens-Bos	29.6
Stephens-Bos	3.9	Doerr-Bos	.309	DiMaggio-Bos	.404	Doerr-Bos	.497	Doerr-Bos	890	Doerr-Bos	126	Doerr-Bos	19.2
Pesky-Bos	2.5	DiMaggio-Bos	.307	Doerr-Bos	.393	DiMaggio-Bos	.420	DiMaggio-Bos	824	DiMaggio-Bos	110	DiMaggio-Bos	12.3

Runs		Hits		Doubles		Triples		Home Runs		Total Bases		Runs Batted In	
Williams-Bos	150	Mitchell-Cle	203	Williams-Bos	39	Mitchell-Cle	23	Williams-Bos	43	Williams-Bos	368	Williams-Bos	159
DiMaggio-Bos	126	Williams-Bos	194	DiMaggio-Bos	34	Doerr-Bos	9	Stephens-Bos	39	Stephens-Bos	329	Stephens-Bos	159
Stephens-Bos	113	DiMaggio-Bos	186	Stephens-Bos	31	Pesky-Bos	7	Doerr-Bos	18	Doerr-Bos	269	Doerr-Bos	109
Pesky-Bos	111	Pesky-Bos	185	Doerr-Bos	30	DiMaggio-Bos	5	DiMaggio-Bos	8	DiMaggio-Bos	254	Pesky-Bos	69

Stolen Bases		Base Stealing Runs		Fielding Runs-Infield		Fielding Runs-Outfield		Wins		Winning Pct.		Complete Games	
Dillinger-StL	20	Rizzuto-NY	1.9	Doerr-Bos	27.1	Valo-Phi	9.4	Parnell-Bos	25	Kinder-Bos	.793	Parnell-Bos	27
DiMaggio-Bos	9	Tebbetts-Bos	1.4	Pesky-Bos	18.9	DiMaggio-Bos	5.8	Kinder-Bos	23	Parnell-Bos	.781	Kinder-Bos	19
Tebbetts-Bos	8	Goodman-Bos	.4	Stephens-Bos	2.0			Dobson-Bos	14			Dobson-Bos	12
Pesky-Bos	8	Pesky-Bos	.4					Stobbs-Bos	11			Stobbs-Bos	10

Strikeouts		Fewest BB/Game		Games		Saves		Base Runners/9		Adjusted Relief Runs		Relief Ranking	
Trucks-Det	153	Hutchinson-Det	2.48	Page-NY	60	Page-NY	27	Hutchinson-Det	10.49	Page-NY	22.7	Page-NY	41.9
Kinder-Bos	138	Kinder-Bos	3.54	Kinder-Bos	43	Kinder-Bos	4	Parnell-Bos	12.10				
Parnell-Bos	122	Parnell-Bos	4.08	Parnell-Bos	39	Hughson-Bos	3	Kinder-Bos	12.57				
Dobson-Bos	87	Dobson-Bos	4.11	Dobson-Bos	33	2 players tied	2	Stobbs-Bos	13.14				

Innings Pitched		Opponents' Avg.		Opponents' OBP		Earned Run Average		Adjusted ERA		Adjusted Starter Runs		Pitcher Wins	
Parnell-Bos	295.1	Byrne-NY	.183	Hutchinson-Det	.290	Garcia-Cle	2.36	Garcia-Cle	169	Parnell-Bos	49.2	Lemon-Cle	5.6
Kinder-Bos	252.0	Parnell-Bos	.237	Parnell-Bos	.324	Parnell-Bos	2.77	Parnell-Bos	157	Kinder-Bos	27.1	Parnell-Bos	5.2
Dobson-Bos	212.2	Kinder-Bos	.260	Kinder-Bos	.330	Kinder-Bos	3.36	Kinder-Bos	130	Dobson-Bos	10.2	Kinder-Bos	2.2
Stobbs-Bos	152.0	Dobson-Bos	.269	Dobson-Bos	.348	Dobson-Bos	3.85	Dobson-Bos	113	Stobbs-Bos	6.6	Dobson-Bos	.9

1950 AMERICAN LEAGUE

TEAM	W	L	T	PCT	GB	R	OR	HR	AVG	OBP	SLG	OPS	AOPS	PF	SB	CG	HR	BB	SO	BR/9	ERA	AERA	OAV	OOB	FW	PW	BW	BSW	DIF
NY	98	56	1	.636		914	691	159	.282	.367	.441	808	+16	97	41	66	118	708	712	13.5	4.15	+3	.255	.348	1.3	2.2	11.0	.1	6.4
Det	95	59	3	.617	3	837	713	114	.282	.369	.417	786	+4	103	23	72	141	553	576	13.0	4.12	+14	.267	.339	1.3	8.1	3.6	-.6	5.7
Bos	94	60	0	.610	4	1027	804	161	.302	.385	.464	849	+12	110	32	66	121	748	630	14.4	4.88	+0	.270	.364	1.7	.2	9.5	.3	5.4
Cle	92	62	1	.597	6	806	654	164	.269	.358	.422	780	+9	97	40	69	120	647	674	12.8	3.75	+15	.248	.333	.7	8.8	6.4	-.0	-.8
Was	67	87	1	.435	31	690	813	76	.260	.347	.360	707	-9	95	42	59	99	648	486	14.2	4.66	-4	.278	.359	-1.4	-2.3	-5.8	-.2	-.7
Chi	60	94	2	.390	38	625	749	93	.260	.333	.364	697	-14	-97	19	62	107	734	566	14.0	4.41	+2	.263	.356	.2	1.1	-10.6	-.1	-7.6
StL	58	96	0	.377	40	684	916	106	.246	.337	.370	707	-16	-104	39	56	129	651	448	15.2	5.20	-5	.295	.372	-3.1	-3.3	-11.7	-.2	-.7
Phi	52	102	0	.338	46	670	913	100	.261	.349	.378	727	-6	98	42	50	138	729	466	15.3	5.49	-17	.287	.376	-.8	-13.2	-4.1	.2	-7.1
Total	620					6253		973	.271	.356	.402	759			278	500		5418	4558	14.0	4.58		.271	.356					

Batter-Fielder Wins		Batting Average		On-Base Percentage		Slugging Average		On-Base Plus Slugging		Adjusted OPS		Adjusted Batter Runs	
Rizzuto-NY	4.0	Goodman-Bos	.354	Doby-Cle	.442	DiMaggio-NY	.585	Doby-Cle	986	Doby-Cle	156	Doby-Cle	46.9
Rosen-Cle	4.0	DiMaggio-Bos	.328	Pesky-Bos	.437	Dropo-Bos	.583	Dropo-Bos	961	Dropo-Bos	130	Williams-Bos	34.1
Doerr-Bos	2.4	Zarilla-Bos	.325	Goodman-Bos	.427	Doerr-Bos	.519	Zarilla-Bos	915	Zarilla-Bos	122	Dropo-Bos	21.7
Pesky-Bos	2.3	Dropo-Bos	.322	Zarilla-Bos	.423	Stephens-Bos	.511	Doerr-Bos	886	Goodman-Bos	115	Zarilla-Bos	18.0

Runs		Hits		Doubles		Triples		Home Runs		Total Bases		Runs Batted In	
DiMaggio-Bos	131	Kell-Det	218	Kell-Det	56	3 players tied	11	Rosen-Cle	37	Dropo-Bos	326	Stephens-Bos	144
Stephens-Bos	125	DiMaggio-Bos	193	Stephens-Bos	34	Doerr-Bos	11	Dropo-Bos	34	Stephens-Bos	321	Dropo-Bos	144
Pesky-Bos	112	Stephens-Bos	185	Zarilla-Bos	32	DiMaggio-Bos	11	Stephens-Bos	30	Doerr-Bos	304	Doerr-Bos	120
Doerr-Bos	103	Dropo-Bos	180	DiMaggio-Bos	30	Zarilla-Bos	10	Williams-Bos	28	DiMaggio-Bos	266	Williams-Bos	97

Stolen Bases		Base Stealing Runs		Fielding Runs-Infield		Fielding Runs-Outfield		Wins		Winning Pct.		Complete Games	
DiMaggio-Bos	15	DiMaggio-Bos	1.9	Priddy-Det	27.9	Woodling-NY	12.4	B.Lemon-Cle	23	Raschi-NY	.724	B.Lemon-Cle	22
Williams-Bos	3	Williams-Bos	.7	Pesky-Bos	16.4	DiMaggio-Bos	3.3	Parnell-Bos	18	Parnell-Bos	.643	Garver-StL	22
Doerr-Bos	3	3 players tied	.2	Doerr-Bos	9.4			Dobson-Bos	15	Dobson-Bos	.600	Parnell-Bos	21
				Stephens-Bos	1.0			Kinder-Bos	14			Dobson-Bos	12

Strikeouts		Fewest BB/Game		Games		Saves		Base Runners/9		Adjusted Relief Runs		Relief Ranking	
B.Lemon-Cle	170	Hutchinson-Det	1.86	Harris-Was	53	Harris-Was	15	Gromek-Cle	10.56	Judson-Chi	7.8	Ferrick-StL-NY	10.6
McDermott-Bos	96	Kinder-Bos	3.39	Kinder-Bos	48	Kinder-Bos	9	Kinder-Bos	12.65				
Kinder-Bos	95	Dobson-Bos	3.53	Parnell-Bos	40	McDermott-Bos	5	Parnell-Bos	12.90				
Parnell-Bos	93	Parnell-Bos	3.83	Dobson-Bos	39	Dobson-Bos	4	Dobson-Bos	12.98				

Innings Pitched		Opponents' Avg.		Opponents' OBP		Earned Run Average		Adjusted ERA		Adjusted Starter Runs		Pitcher Wins	
B.Lemon-Cle	288.0	Wynn-Cle	.212	Wynn-Cle	.305	Wynn-Cle	3.20	Garver-StL	146	Garver-StL	39.1	Garver-StL	4.9
Parnell-Bos	249.0	Stobbs-Bos	.250	Kinder-Bos	.328	Parnell-Bos	3.61	Parnell-Bos	136	Parnell-Bos	30.1	Parnell-Bos	3.1
Kinder-Bos	207.0	Parnell-Bos	.259	Parnell-Bos	.338	Dobson-Bos	4.18	Dobson-Bos	117	Dobson-Bos	16.0	Dobson-Bos	1.9
Dobson-Bos	206.2	Kinder-Bos	.263	Dobson-Bos	.343	Kinder-Bos	4.26	Kinder-Bos	115	Kinder-Bos	14.4	Kinder-Bos	1.4

1951 AMERICAN LEAGUE

TEAM	W	L	T	PCT	GB	R	OR	HR	AVG	OBP	SLG	OPS	AOPS	PF	SB	CG	HR	BB	SO	BR/9	ERA	AERA	OAV	OOB	FW	PW	BW	BSW	DIF
NY	98	56	0	.636		798	621	140	.269	.349	.408	757	+13	96	78	66	92	562	664	12.4	3.56	+7	.250	.328	.3	4.3	8.9	.6	6.9
Cle	93	61	1	.604	5	696	594	140	.256	.336	.389	725	+6	94	52	76	85	577	642	12.2	3.38	+12	.245	.323	.9	6.7	4.0	.1	4.2
Bos	87	67	0	.565	11	804	725	127	.266	.358	.392	750	-2	110	20	46	99	599	658	13.2	4.14	+8	.264	.342	.5	4.5	-.4	-.0	5.5
Chi	81	73	1	.526	17	714	644	86	.270	.349	.385	734	+5	98	99	74	109	549	572	12.2	3.50	+15	.252	.323	.0	8.5	3.7	-.0	-8.1
Det	73	81	0	.474	25	685	741	104	.265	.338	.380	718	-1	100	37	51	103	602	597	13.2	4.29	-3	.262	.342	-.7	-1.8	-1.8	-.2	.4
Phi	70	84	0	.455	28	736	745	102	.262	.349	.386	735	+1	102	47	52	109	569	437	13.4	4.47	-4	.272	.347	.8	-2.7	1.8	.0	-6.9
Was	62	92	0	.403	36	672	764	54	.263	.336	.355	691	-7	98	45	58	110	630	475	13.7	4.49	-9	.269	.348	-.5	-5.8	-4.7	-.0	-3.9
StL	52	102	0	.338	46	611	882	86	.247	.317	.357	674	-16	103	35	56	132	801	550	15.5	5.18	-15	.282	.379	-1.2	-11.0	-12.0	-.4	-.4
Total	617					5716		839	.262	.342	.381	723			413	479		4889	4595	13.2	4.12		.262	.342					

Batter-Fielder Wins		Batting Average		On-Base Percentage		Slugging Average		On-Base Plus Slugging		Adjusted OPS		Adjusted Batter Runs	
Fain-Phi	**4.3**	Fain-Phi	.344	Williams-Bos	.464	Williams-Bos	.556	Williams-Bos	1019	Doby-Cle	163	Williams-Bos	52.1
Joost-Phi	**4.3**	Williams-Bos	.318	Pesky-Bos	.417	Doerr-Bos	.448	Pesky-Bos	815	Williams-Bos	159	Pesky-Bos	11.2
Williams-Bos	**4.1**	Pesky-Bos	.313	Goodman-Bos	.388	DiMaggio-Bos	.418	DiMaggio-Bos	788	Pesky-Bos	110	Stephens-Bos	9.8
2 players tied	**2.0**	Goodman-Bos	.297	DiMaggio-Bos	.370	Pesky-Bos	.398	Goodman-Bos	761	DiMaggio-Bos	103	Doerr-Bos	7.5

Runs		Hits		Doubles		Triples		Home Runs		Total Bases		Runs Batted In	
DiMaggio-Bos	113	Kell-Det	191	3 players tied	36	Minoso-Cle-Chi	14	Zernial-Chi-Phi	33	Williams-Bos	295	Zernial-Chi-Phi	129
Williams-Bos	109	DiMaggio-Bos	189	Goodman-Bos	34	Pesky-Bos	6	Williams-Bos	30	DiMaggio-Bos	267	Williams-Bos	126
Pesky-Bos	93	Williams-Bos	169	DiMaggio-Bos	34	3 players tied	4	Vollmer-Bos	22	Goodman-Bos	204	Vollmer-Bos	85
Goodman-Bos	92	Goodman-Bos	162	Williams-Bos	28			Stephens-Bos	17	Pesky-Bos	191	Stephens-Bos	78

Stolen Bases		Base Stealing Runs		Fielding Runs-Infield		Fielding Runs-Outfield		Wins		Winning Pct.		Complete Games	
Minoso-Cle-Chi	31	Minoso-Cle-Chi	3.3	Fain-Phi	16.2	Coan-Was	18.4	Feller-Cle	22	Feller-Cle	.733	Garver-StL	24
Goodman-Bos	7	Hatfield-Bos	.2	Stephens-Bos	11.8	Goodman-Bos	3.2	Parnell-Bos	18	Parnell-Bos	.621	Parnell-Bos	11
DiMaggio-Bos	4	Boudreau-Bos	.2	Doerr-Bos	6.4	Williams-Bos	1.6	Scarborough-Bos	12			McDermott-Bos	9
2 players tied	2	Goodman-Bos	.1	Pesky-Bos	2.3			Kinder-Bos	11			Scarborough-Bos	8

Strikeouts		Fewest BB/Game		Games		Saves		Base Runners/9		Adjusted Relief Runs		Relief Ranking	
Raschi-NY	164	Hutchinson-Det	1.29	Kinder-Bos	63	Kinder-Bos	14	Aloma-Chi	10.13	Kinder-Bos	24.3	Kinder-Bos	28.4
McDermott-Bos	127	Scarborough-Bos	2.98	Scarborough-Bos	37	McDermott-Bos	3	Kinder-Bos	10.91	Masterson-Bos	7.2	Masterson-Bos	3.8
Kinder-Bos	84	Parnell-Bos	3.14	Parnell-Bos	36	3 players tied	2	Kiely-Bos	11.67				
Parnell-Bos	77	Stobbs-Bos	3.92					McDermott-Bos	12.45				

Innings Pitched		Opponents' Avg.		Opponents' OBP		Earned Run Average		Adjusted ERA		Adjusted Starter Runs		Pitcher Wins	
Wynn-Cle	274.1	Reynolds-NY	.213	Lopat-NY	.298	Rogovin-Det-Chi	2.78	Rogovin-Det-Chi	146	Rogovin-Det-Chi	29.7	Lopat-NY	3.3
Parnell-Bos	221.0	McDermott-Bos	.226	McDermott-Bos	.330	Parnell-Bos	3.26	Parnell-Bos	137	Parnell-Bos	23.7	Parnell-Bos	3.3
Scarborough-Bos	184.0	Stobbs-Bos	.271	Parnell-Bos	.333	McDermott-Bos	3.35	McDermott-Bos	133	McDermott-Bos	19.7	Kinder-Bos	2.5
McDermott-Bos	172.0	Parnell-Bos	.272	Scarborough-Bos	.342	Stobbs-Bos	4.76	Stobbs-Bos	94	Kiely-Bos	12.8	McDermott-Bos	2.0

1952 AMERICAN LEAGUE

TEAM	W	L	T	PCT	GB	R	OR	HR	AVG	OBP	SLG	OPS	AOPS	PF	SB	CG	HR	BB	SO	BR/9	ERA	AERA	OAV	OOB	FW	PW	BW	BSW	DIF
NY	95	59	0	.617		727	557	129	.267	.341	.403	744	+21	94	52	72	94	581	666	12.1	3.14	+6	.243	.324	.8	3.2	14.1	.0	-.2
Cle	93	61	1	.604	2	763	606	148	.262	.342	.404	746	+22	94	46	80	94	556	671	11.9	3.32	+1	.241	.316	.7	4.3	15.3	.0	1.2
Chi	81	73	2	.526	14	610	568	80	.252	.327	.348	675	-7	101	61	53	86	578	774	11.7	3.25	+12	.238	.316	1.1	6.5	-4.3	.4	.2
Phi	79	75	1	.513	16	664	723	89	.253	.343	.359	702	-4	106	52	73	113	526	562	12.8	4.15	-5	.263	.333	.0	-2.9	-1.1	-.0	6.0
Was	78	76	3	.506	17	598	608	50	.239	.317	.326	643	-12	97	48	75	78	577	574	12.7	3.37	+5	.258	.332	.6	3.1	-8.1	.2	5.2
Bos	76	78	0	.494	19	668	658	113	.255	.328	.377	705	-4	108	59	53	107	623	624	13.1	3.80	+4	.256	.340	-.3	2.0	-3.2	.0	.5
StL	64	90	1	.416	31	604	733	82	.250	.317	.352	669	-8	100	48	48	111	588	581	13.0	4.12	-5	.260	.339	-.8	-3.1	-5.8	-.1	-3.1
Det	50	104	2	.325	45	557	738	103	.243	.318	.352	670	-8	101	27	51	111	591	702	13.0	4.25	-10	.262	.338	-.6	-6.8	-6.1	-.4	-13.1
Total	621					5191		794	.253	.330	.365	695			375	505		4630	5154	12.5	3.67		.253	.330					

Batter-Fielder Wins		Batting Average		On-Base Percentage		Slugging Average		On-Base Plus Slugging		Adjusted OPS		Adjusted Batter Runs	
Fain-Phi	**4.5**	Fain-Phi	.327	Fain-Phi	.438	Doby-Cle	.541	Mantle-NY	924	Doby-Cle	166	Mantle-NY	48.4
Goodman-Bos	**3.4**	Goodman-Bos	.306	DiMaggio-Bos	.371	Goodman-Bos	.394	Doby-Cle	924	Mantle-NY	166	Vollmer-Bos	8.6
Lepcio-Bos	**.8**	DiMaggio-Bos	.294	Goodman-Bos	.370	DiMaggio-Bos	.377	Goodman-Bos	764	Goodman-Bos	104	Goodman-Bos	4.4
2 players tied	**.5**							DiMaggio-Bos	747	DiMaggio-Bos	100	McDermott-Bos	2.4

Runs		Hits		Doubles		Triples		Home Runs		Total Bases		Runs Batted In	
Doby-Cle	104	Fox-Chi	192	Fain-Phi	43	Avila-Cle	11	Doby-Cle	32	Rosen-Cle	297	Rosen-Cle	105
DiMaggio-Bos	81	Goodman-Bos	157	Goodman-Bos	27	Vollmer-Bos	4	Gernert-Bos	19	Goodman-Bos	202	Gernert-Bos	67
Goodman-Bos	79	DiMaggio-Bos	143	3 players tied	20	Throneberry-Bos	3	Vollmer-Bos	11	DiMaggio-Bos	183	Goodman-Bos	56
Gernert-Bos	58	White-Bos	107			Goodman-Bos	3	White-Bos	10	Gernert-Bos	170	Vollmer-Bos	50

Stolen Bases		Base Stealing Runs		Fielding Runs-Infield		Fielding Runs-Outfield		Wins		Winning Pct.		Complete Games	
Minoso-Chi	22	Jensen-NY-Was	1.9	Goodman-Bos	23.0	Philley-Phi	6.9	Shantz-Phi	24	Shantz-Phi	.774	Lemon-Cle	28
Throneberry-Bos	16	Throneberry-Bos	1.1					Parnell-Bos	12			Parnell-Bos	15
Goodman-Bos	8	Goodman-Bos	1.1					McDermott-Bos	10			McDermott-Bos	7
DiMaggio-Bos	6	Gernert-Bos	.5									2 players tied	5

Strikeouts		Fewest BB/Game		Games		Saves		Base Runners/9		Adjusted Relief Runs		Relief Ranking	
Reynolds-NY	160	Shantz-Phi	2.03	Kennedy-Chi	47	Dorish-Chi	11	Shantz-Phi	9.56	Dorish-Chi	11.9	Dorish-Chi	17.3
McDermott-Bos	117	Parnell-Bos	3.74	Delock-Bos	39	Benton-Bos	6	Kinder-Bos	10.51				
Parnell-Bos	107	McDermott-Bos	5.11	Parnell-Bos	33	Delock-Bos	5	Parnell-Bos	12.66				
2 players tied	50			McDermott-Bos	30	Kinder-Bos	4	Brodowski-Bos	12.87				

Innings Pitched		Opponents' Avg.		Opponents' OBP		Earned Run Average		Adjusted ERA		Adjusted Starter Runs		Pitcher Wins	
Lemon-Cle	309.2	Lemon-Cle	.208	Shantz-Phi	.272	Reynolds-NY	2.06	Reynolds-NY	161	Shantz-Phi	42.7	Shantz-Phi	5.1
Parnell-Bos	214.0	McDermott-Bos	.234	Parnell-Bos	.332	Parnell-Bos	3.62	Parnell-Bos	109	Kinder-Bos	13.2	Benton-Bos	1.2
McDermott-Bos	162.0	Parnell-Bos	.255	McDermott-Bos	.340	McDermott-Bos	3.72	McDermott-Bos	106	Parnell-Bos	8.6	Kinder-Bos	1.1
Brodowski-Bos	114.2									McDermott-Bos	6.1	McDermott-Bos	.9

1953 AMERICAN LEAGUE

TEAM	W	L	T	PCT	GB	R	OR	HR	AVG	OBP	SLG	OPS	AOPS	PF	SB	CG	HR	BB	SO	BR/9	ERA	AERA	OAV	OOB	FW	PW	BW	BSW	DIF
NY	99	52	0	.656		801	547	139	.273	.359	.417	776	+20	97	34	50	94	500	604	12.1	3.20	+15	.251	.321	.3	8.0	14.4	-.4	1.1
Cle	92	62	1	.597	8.5	770	627	160	.270	.349	.410	759	+14	97	33	81	92	519	586	12.2	3.64	+3	.253	.325	.4	1.7	9.8	.1	2.9
Chi	89	65	2	.578	11.5	716	592	74	.258	.341	.364	705	-7	103	73	57	113	583	714	12.2	3.41	+18	.246	.324	.6	9.5	-3.7	.1	5.5
Bos	84	69	0	.549	16	656	632	101	.264	.332	.384	716	-6	105	33	41	92	584	642	12.7	3.58	+18	.254	.331	-.9	9.1	-4.3	-.4	3.9
Was	76	76	0	.500	23.5	687	614	69	.263	.343	.368	711	+0	98	65	76	112	478	515	12.2	3.66	+6	.258	.324	.7	3.6	1.2	.6	-6.1
Det	60	94	4	.390	40.5	695	923	108	.266	.331	.387	718	+0	99	30	50	154	585	645	14.4	5.25	-23	.291	.363	.1	-18.3	-.1	-.2	1.5
Phi	59	95	3	.383	41.5	632	799	116	.256	.321	.372	693	-11	104	41	51	121	594	566	13.6	4.67	-8	.271	.349	-.0	-5.6	-8.7	.5	-4.2
StL	54	100	0	.351	46.5	555	778	112	.249	.317	.363	680	-13	102	17	28	101	626	639	13.8	4.48	-6	.273	.351	-1.0	-4.0	-9.6	-.4	-8.0
Total	618					5512		879	.262	.337	.383	720			326	434		4469	4911	12.9	3.99		.262	.337					

Batter-Fielder Wins		Batting Average		On-Base Percentage		Slugging Average		On-Base Plus Slugging		Adjusted OPS		Adjusted Batter Runs	
Rosen-Cle	7.4	Vernon-Was	.337	Woodling-NY	.429	Rosen-Cle	.613	Rosen-Cle	1034	Rosen-Cle	181	Rosen-Cle	68.0
Williams-Bos	1.7	Goodman-Bos	.313	Goodman-Bos	.384	Kell-Bos	.483	Kell-Bos	866	Kell-Bos	126	Williams-Bos	20.9
Goodman-Bos	1.3	Kell-Bos	.307	Kell-Bos	.383	White-Bos	.435	Goodman-Bos	793	Goodman-Bos	108	Kell-Bos	18.3
White-Bos	1.3	Umphlett-Bos	.283	Gernert-Bos	.371	Gernert-Bos	.415	Gernert-Bos	786	Gernert-Bos	106	Goodman-Bos	8.2

Runs		Hits		Doubles		Triples		Home Runs		Total Bases		Runs Batted In	
Rosen-Cle	115	Kuenn-Det	209	Vernon-Was	43	Rivera-Chi	16	Rosen-Cle	43	Rosen-Cle	367	Rosen-Cle	145
Piersall-Bos	76	Goodman-Bos	161	Kell-Bos	41	Piersall-Bos	9	Gernert-Bos	21	Kell-Bos	222	Kell-Bos	73
Goodman-Bos	73	Piersall-Bos	159	White-Bos	34	Umphlett-Bos	5	Williams-Bos	13	Goodman-Bos	210	Gernert-Bos	71
Gernert-Bos	73	Kell-Bos	141	Goodman-Bos	33	Goodman-Bos	5	White-Bos	13	2 players tied	207	White-Bos	64

Stolen Bases		Base Stealing Runs		Fielding Runs-Infield		Fielding Runs-Outfield		Wins		Winning Pct.		Complete Games	
Minoso-Chi	25	Michaels-Phi	1.5	Strickland-Cle	21.0	Busby-Was	12.9	Porterfield-Was	22	Lopat-NY	.800	Porterfield-Was	24
Piersall-Bos	11	Coan-Was	1.5	Bolling-Bos	4.6	Piersall-Bos	10.9	Parnell-Bos	21	Parnell-Bos	.724	Parnell-Bos	12
Kell-Bos	5	Kell-Bos	.4					McDermott-Bos	18	McDermott-Bos	.643	McDermott-Bos	8
Umphlett-Bos	4	2 players tied	.2					Brown-Bos	11			Brown-Bos	6

Strikeouts		Fewest BB/Game		Games		Saves		Base Runners/9		Adjusted Relief Runs		Relief Ranking	
Pierce-Chi	186	Lopat-NY	1.61	Kinder-Bos	69	Kinder-Bos	27	Raschi-NY	10.24	Kinder-Bos	24.7	Kinder-Bos	47.3
Parnell-Bos	136	Hudson-Bos	2.83	Parnell-Bos	38	Flowers-Bos	3	Kinder-Bos	10.43	Flowers-Bos	3.1	Flowers-Bos	2.0
McDermott-Bos	92	Brown-Bos	3.08	McDermott-Bos	32	Kennedy-Bos	2	McDermott-Bos	12.21				
Brown-Bos	62	Parnell-Bos	4.33	Flowers-Bos	32	Hudson-Bos	2	Hudson-Bos	12.52				

Innings Pitched		Opponents' Avg.		Opponents' OBP		Earned Run Average		Adjusted ERA		Adjusted Starter Runs		Pitcher Wins	
B.Lemon-Cle	286.2	Pierce-Chi	.218	Raschi-NY	.283	Lopat-NY	2.42	Lopat-NY	152	Pierce-Chi	37.8	Kinder-Bos	5.2
Parnell-Bos	241.0	McDermott-Bos	.224	McDermott-Bos	.323	McDermott-Bos	3.01	McDermott-Bos	140	Parnell-Bos	27.8	McDermott-Bos	4.1
McDermott-Bos	206.1	Parnell-Bos	.239	Brown-Bos	.327	Parnell-Bos	3.06	Parnell-Bos	137	McDermott-Bos	25.2	Parnell-Bos	3.2
Brown-Bos	166.1	2 players tied	.269	Hudson-Bos	.327	Hudson-Bos	3.52	Hudson-Bos	120	Hudson-Bos	13.6	Hudson-Bos	1.0

1954 AMERICAN LEAGUE

TEAM	W	L	T	PCT	GB	R	OR	HR	AVG	OBP	SLG	OPS	AOPS	PF	SB	CG	HR	BB	SO	BR/9	ERA	AERA	OAV	OOB	FW	PW	BW	BSW	DIF
Cle	111	43	2	.721		746	504	156	.262	.341	.403	744	+8	102	30	77	89	486	678	10.9	2.78	+32	.232	.297	.7	14.7	6.7	-.2	12.1
NY	103	51	1	.669	8	805	563	133	.268	.348	.408	756	+18	97	34	51	86	552	655	12.2	3.26	+5	.251	.325	.8	3.0	13.5	-.4	9.1
Chi	94	60	1	.610	17	711	521	94	.267	.347	.379	726	+3	103	98	60	94	517	701	11.6	3.05	+22	.244	.312	1.8	10.8	3.1	.4	.9
Bos	69	85	2	.448	42	700	728	123	.266	.345	.395	740	-2	111	51	41	118	612	707	13.3	4.01	+2	.265	.341	-2.0	1.4	.3	.4	-8.2
Det	68	86	1	.442	43	584	664	90	.258	.324	.367	689	-3	98	48	58	138	506	603	12.5	3.81	-3	.261	.328	.6	-1.9	-2.6	-.2	-4.9
Was	66	88	1	.429	45	632	680	81	.246	.325	.355	680	-3	95	37	69	79	573	562	13.0	3.84	-7	.265	.338	.2	-4.8	-1.2	.4	-5.6
Bal	54	100	0	.351	57	483	668	52	.251	.313	.338	651	-9	-93	30	58	78	688	668	13.0	3.88	-8	.250	.338	-.4	-4.9	-6.6	-.1	-11.0
Phi	51	103	2	.331	60	542	875	94	.236	.305	.342	647	-17	-100	30	49	141	685	555	14.7	5.18	-25	.285	.366	-1.6	-19.1	-12.5	-.1	7.3
Total	621					5203		823	.257	.331	.373	704			358	463		4619	5129	12.6	3.72		.257	.331					

Batter-Fielder Wins		Batting Average		On-Base Percentage		Slugging Average		On-Base Plus Slugging		Adjusted OPS		Adjusted Batter Runs	
Williams-Bos	5.1	Avila-Cle	.341	Williams-Bos	.513	Minoso-Chi	.535	Williams-Bos	1148	Williams-Bos	193	Williams-Bos	60.7
Bolling-Bos	1.1	Goodman-Bos	.303	Goodman-Bos	.370	Jensen-Bos	.472	Jensen-Bos	831	Jensen-Bos	115	Jensen-Bos	12.3
Goodman-Bos	.7	Piersall-Bos	.285	Jensen-Bos	.359	White-Bos	.426	Goodman-Bos	746	Goodman-Bos	95	Nixon-Bos	4.9
Lepcio-Bos	.7	White-Bos	.282	Piersall-Bos	.338	Piersall-Bos	.395	2 players tied	732	2 players tied	90	Brewer-Bos	2.4

Runs		Hits		Doubles		Triples		Home Runs		Total Bases		Runs Batted In	
Mantle-NY	129	Kuenn-Det	201	Vernon-Was	33	Minoso-Chi	18	Doby-Cle	32	Minoso-Chi	304	Doby-Cle	126
Williams-Bos	93	Fox-Chi	201	White-Bos	25	Agganis-Bos	8	Williams-Bos	29	Jensen-Bos	274	Jensen-Bos	117
Jensen-Bos	92	Jensen-Bos	160	Jensen-Bos	25	Jensen-Bos	7	Jensen-Bos	25	Williams-Bos	245	Williams-Bos	89
Piersall-Bos	77	Goodman-Bos	148	Goodman-Bos	25	2 players tied	4	White-Bos	14	White-Bos	210	White-Bos	75

Stolen Bases		Base Stealing Runs		Fielding Runs-Infield		Fielding Runs-Outfield		Wins		Winning Pct.		Complete Games	
Jensen-Bos	22	Busby-Was	3.0	Coleman-NY	14.6	Diering-Bal	9.8	Wynn-Cle	23	Consuegra-Chi	.842	Porterfield-Was	21
Agganis-Bos	6	Jensen-Bos	2.4	Bolling-Bos	9.1			Lemon-Cle	23	Sullivan-Bos	.556	Lemon-Cle	21
Piersall-Bos	5	Piersall-Bos	.8	Lepcio-Bos	7.9			Sullivan-Bos	15			Sullivan-Bos	11
		Maxwell-Bos	.7	Goodman-Bos	6.1			Nixon-Bos	11			Nixon-Bos	8

Strikeouts		Fewest BB/Game		Games		Saves		Base Runners/9		Adjusted Relief Runs		Relief Ranking	
Turley-Bal	185	Lopat-NY	1.75	Dixon-Was-Phi	54	Sain-NY	22	Mossi-Cle	9.29	Mossi-Cle	18.6	Mossi-Cle	15.8
Sullivan-Bos	124	Sullivan-Bos	2.88	Kinder-Bos	48	Kinder-Bos	15	Sullivan-Bos	11.21	Kinder-Bos	6.4	Kinder-Bos	10.6
Nixon-Bos	102	Nixon-Bos	3.92	Brown-Bos	40	Hudson-Bos	5	Kinder-Bos	11.94				
Brewer-Bos	69	Brewer-Bos	5.26	Sullivan-Bos	36	2 players tied	1	Nixon-Bos	12.53				

Innings Pitched		Opponents' Avg.		Opponents' OBP		Earned Run Average		Adjusted ERA		Adjusted Starter Runs		Pitcher Wins	
Wynn-Cle	270.2	Turley-Bal	.203	Garcia-Cle	.282	Garcia-Cle	2.64	Garcia-Cle	139	Garcia-Cle	31.0	Gromek-Det	3.7
Sullivan-Bos	206.1	Sullivan-Bos	.240	Sullivan-Bos	.304	Sullivan-Bos	3.14	Sullivan-Bos	131	Sullivan-Bos	21.0	Lemon-Cle	3.7
Nixon-Bos	199.2	Nixon-Bos	.248	Nixon-Bos	.333	Nixon-Bos	4.06	Nixon-Bos	101	Parnell-Bos	3.4	Sullivan-Bos	2.5
Brewer-Bos	162.2	Brewer-Bos	.249	Brewer-Bos	.355	Brewer-Bos	4.65	Brewer-Bos	88	Kemmerer-Bos	3.0	Kinder-Bos	1.0

1955 AMERICAN LEAGUE

TEAM	W	L	T	PCT	GB	R	OR	HR	AVG	OBP	SLG	OPS	AOPS	PF	SB	CG	HR	BB	SO	BR/9	ERA	AERA	OAV	OOB	FW	PW	BW	BSW	DIF
NY	96	58	0	.623		762	569	175	.260	.340	**.418**	758	+12	98	55	52	108	688	731	12.3	**3.23**	+16	**.232**	.326	.5	8.2	**8.2**	.5	1.6
Cle	93	61	0	.604	3	698	601	148	.257	.349	.394	743	+2	104	28	45	111	558	877	12.1	3.39	+18	.245	.319	1.7	9.2	3.6	.0	1.5
Chi	91	63	1	.591	5	725	**557**	116	**.268**	.344	.388	732	+0	103	**69**	55	111	**497**	720	**11.9**	3.37	+17	.251	**.317**	1.5	8.9	1.2	.1	2.2
Bos	84	70	0	.545	12	755	652	137	.264	**.351**	.402	753	+0	109	43	44	128	582	674	12.7	3.72	+15	.253	.329	.0	8.1	1.8	**.6**	-3.5
Det	79	75	0	.513	17	**775**	658	130	.266	.345	.394	739	+7	98	41	**66**	126	517	629	12.6	3.79	+1	.261	.328	-.2	.8	6.6	.3	-5.6
KC	63	91	1	.409	33	638	911	121	.261	.322	.382	704	-6	101	22	29	175	707	572	14.6	5.35	-22	.278	.363	-.5	-17.2	-5.1	-.6	9.5
Bal	57	97	2	.370	39	540	754	54	.240	.314	.320	634	-17	-93	34	35	103	625	595	13.4	4.21	-9	.266	.344	-1.7	-6.4	-12.3	-.7	1.1
Was	53	101	0	.344	43	598	789	80	.248	.322	.351	673	-8	95	25	37	**99**	634	607	14.2	4.62	-17	.279	.359	-1.0	-12.4	-5.6	-.4	-4.5
Total	618					5491		961	.258	.336	.381	717			317	363		4808	5405	13.0	3.96		.258	.336					

Batter-Fielder Wins		Batting Average		On-Base Percentage		Slugging Average		On-Base Plus Slugging		Adjusted OPS		Adjusted Batter Runs	
Mantle-NY	5.5	Kaline-Det	.340	Mantle-NY	.431	Mantle-NY	.611	Mantle-NY	1042	Mantle-NY	181	Mantle-NY	62.2
Williams-Bos	4.3	Goodman-Bos	.294	Goodman-Bos	.394	Jensen-Bos	.479	Jensen-Bos	848	Jensen-Bos	118	Williams-Bos	52.2
Jensen-Bos	.6	Piersall-Bos	.283	Jensen-Bos	.369	Zauchin-Bos	.430	Piersall-Bos	792	Piersall-Bos	104	Jensen-Bos	15.2
Stephens-Bos	.4	Klaus-Bos	.283	Piersall-Bos	.364	Piersall-Bos	.427	Zauchin-Bos	765	Zauchin-Bos	97	Nixon-Bos	4.9

Runs		Hits		Doubles		Triples		Home Runs		Total Bases		Runs Batted In	
Smith-Cle	123	Kaline-Det	200	Kuenn-Det	38	Mantle-NY	11	Mantle-NY	37	Kaline-Det	321	Boone-Det	116
Goodman-Bos	100	Goodman-Bos	176	Goodman-Bos	31	Carey-NY	11	Williams-Bos	28	Jensen-Bos	275	Jensen-Bos	116
Jensen-Bos	95	Jensen-Bos	158	White-Bos	30	Jensen-Bos	6	Zauchin-Bos	27	Williams-Bos	225	Zauchin-Bos	93
Klaus-Bos	83	Klaus-Bos	153	Jensen-Bos	27	Piersall-Bos	5	Jensen-Bos	26	Piersall-Bos	220	Williams-Bos	83

Stolen Bases		Base Stealing Runs		Fielding Runs-Infield		Fielding Runs-Outfield		Wins		Winning Pct.		Complete Games	
Rivera-Chi	25	Torgeson-Det	2.0	Fox-Chi	31.1	Rivera-Chi	11.4	3 players tied	18	Byrne-NY	.762	Ford-NY	18
Jensen-Bos	16	Klaus-Bos	1.3	Hatton-Bos	4.1	Stephens-Bos	2.7	F.Sullivan-Bos	18	F.Sullivan-Bos	.581	F.Sullivan-Bos	16
Piersall-Bos	6	Jensen-Bos	1.1	Zauchin-Bos	.0	Piersall-Bos	.5	Nixon-Bos	12			Brewer-Bos	9
Klaus-Bos	6	Piersall-Bos	1.0					Brewer-Bos	11			Nixon-Bos	7

Strikeouts		Fewest BB/Game		Games		Saves		Base Runners/9		Adjusted Relief Runs		Relief Ranking	
Score-Cle	245	Gromek-Det	1.84	Narleski-Cle	60	Narleski-Cle	19	Kinder-Bos	9.85	Consuegra-Chi	17.5	Kinder-Bos	21.0
F.Sullivan-Bos	129	F.Sullivan-Bos	3.46	Kinder-Bos	43	Kinder-Bos	18	Susce-Bos	11.22	Kiely-Bos	14.1	Hurd-Bos	17.1
Nixon-Bos	95	Nixon-Bos	3.68	Hurd-Bos	43	Kiely-Bos	6	F.Sullivan-Bos	11.84	Kinder-Bos	10.7	Kiely-Bos	10.6
Brewer-Bos	91	Brewer-Bos	4.06	F.Sullivan-Bos	35	Hurd-Bos	5	Hurd-Bos	12.38	Hurd-Bos	10.1		

Innings Pitched		Opponents' Avg.		Opponents' OBP		Earned Run Average		Adjusted ERA		Adjusted Starter Runs		Pitcher Wins	
F.Sullivan-Bos	260.0	Turley-NY	.193	Pierce-Chi	.277	Pierce-Chi	1.97	Pierce-Chi	201	Pierce-Chi	44.7	Pierce-Chi	5.3
Nixon-Bos	208.0	F.Sullivan-Bos	.241	F.Sullivan-Bos	.313	F.Sullivan-Bos	2.91	F.Sullivan-Bos	148	F.Sullivan-Bos	33.9	F.Sullivan-Bos	3.4
Brewer-Bos	192.2	Nixon-Bos	.259	Nixon-Bos	.330	Nixon-Bos	4.07	Nixon-Bos	105	Susce-Bos	19.0	Kinder-Bos	2.1
Susce-Bos	144.1	Brewer-Bos	.263	Brewer-Bos	.344	Brewer-Bos	4.20	Brewer-Bos	102	Delock-Bos	8.4	Susce-Bos	1.8

1956 AMERICAN LEAGUE

TEAM	W	L	T	PCT	GB	R	OR	HR	AVG	OBP	SLG	OPS	AOPS	PF	SB	CG	HR	BB	SO	BR/9	ERA	AERA	OAV	OOB	FW	PW	BW	BSW	DIF
NY	97	57	0	.630		**857**	631	190	.270	.347	**.434**	781	+15	97	51	50	114	652	732	12.9	3.63	+7	.249	.335	.6	3.9	**10.3**	-.0	5.3
Cle	88	66	1	.571	9	712	**581**	153	.244	.335	.381	716	-8	102	40	65	116	564	845	**11.9**	**3.32**	+27	**.238**	**.314**	1.0	**13.1**	-4.8	-.0	1.7
Chi	85	69	0	.552	12	776	634	128	.267	.349	.397	746	+1	101	**70**	65	118	**524**	722	12.3	3.73	+10	.255	.324	**1.3**	5.8	2.0	**.5**	-1.6
Bos	84	70	1	.545	13	780	751	139	.275	**.362**	.419	781	+0	112	28	50	130	668	712	13.3	4.17	+11	.254	.340	-1.2	6.3	1.4	.1	.4
Det	82	72	1	.532	15	**775**	699	150	**.279**	.356	.420	776	+10	100	43	62	140	655	788	13.4	4.06	+1	.264	.348	.4	.9	8.0	-.1	-4.5
Bal	69	85	0	.448	28	571	705	91	.244	.320	.350	670	-11	-92	39	38	**99**	547	715	12.8	4.20	-7	.263	.334	.5	-4.4	-7.6	-.4	4.0
Was	59	95	1	.383	38	652	924	112	.250	.314	.377	718	-5	100	36	171	663	663	13.6	5.33	-19	.287	.373	-1.3	-14.4	-2.6	-.2	.6
KC	52	102	0	.338	45	619	831	112	.252	.315	.370	685	-14	100	40	30	187	679	636	14.1	4.86	-11	.271	.357	-1.1	-7.6	-11.1	-.0	-5.2
Total	618					5756		1075	.260	.341	.394	735			348	398		5019	5813	13.2	4.16		.260	.341					

Batter-Fielder Wins		Batting Average		On-Base Percentage		Slugging Average		On-Base Plus Slugging		Adjusted OPS		Adjusted Batter Runs	
Mantle-NY	8.1	Mantle-NY	.353	Williams-Bos	.479	Mantle-NY	.705	Mantle-NY	1169	Mantle-NY	213	Mantle-NY	90.0
Williams-Bos	2.9	Williams-Bos	.345	Jensen-Bos	.405	Williams-Bos	.605	Williams-Bos	1084	Williams-Bos	164	Williams-Bos	43.6
Jensen-Bos	1.1	Jensen-Bos	.315	Klaus-Bos	.378	Vernon-Bos	.511	Jensen-Bos	901	Jensen-Bos	123	Jensen-Bos	20.4
Gernert-Bos	.9	Vernon-Bos	.310	Piersall-Bos	.350	Jensen-Bos	.497	Piersall-Bos	799	Piersall-Bos	99	Vernon-Bos	16.4

Runs		Hits		Doubles		Triples		Home Runs		Total Bases		Runs Batted In	
Mantle-NY	132	Kuenn-Det	196	Piersall-Bos	40	4 players tied	11	Mantle-NY	52	Mantle-NY	376	Mantle-NY	130
Piersall-Bos	91	Jensen-Bos	182	Klaus-Bos	29	Jensen-Bos	11	Williams-Bos	24	Jensen-Bos	287	Jensen-Bos	97
Klaus-Bos	91	Piersall-Bos	176	Williams-Bos	28	Goodman-Bos	8	Jensen-Bos	20	Piersall-Bos	270	Piersall-Bos	87
Jensen-Bos	80	Klaus-Bos	141	Vernon-Bos	28	Piersall-Bos	5	Gernert-Bos	16	Williams-Bos	242	Vernon-Bos	84

Stolen Bases		Base Stealing Runs		Fielding Runs-Infield		Fielding Runs-Outfield		Wins		Winning Pct.		Complete Games	
Aparicio-Chi	21	Aparicio-Chi	3.2	McDougald-NY	8.8	Kaline-Det	12.2	Lary-Det	21	Ford-NY	.760	Pierce-Chi	21
Jensen-Bos	11	Jensen-Bos	1.4	DeMaestri-KC	8.8	Piersall-Bos	7.3	Brewer-Bos	19	Brewer-Bos	.679	Lemon-Cle	21
Piersall-Bos	7	Buddin-Bos	.4	Buddin-Bos	6.9	Stephens-Bos	3.5	Sullivan-Bos	14			Brewer-Bos	15
2 players tied	2			Gernert-Bos	4.9			Delock-Bos	13			Sullivan-Bos	12

Strikeouts		Fewest BB/Game		Games		Saves		Base Runners/9		Adjusted Relief Runs		Relief Ranking	
Score-Cle	263	Stobbs-Was	2.03	Zuverink-Bal	62	Zuverink-Bal	16	Score-Cle	10.58	Narleski-Cle	17.7	Narleski-Cle	16.1
Brewer-Bos	127	Sullivan-Bos	3.05	Delock-Bos	48	Delock-Bos	9	Brewer-Bos	11.68	Delock-Bos	7.1	Delock-Bos	11.1
Sullivan-Bos	116	Brewer-Bos	4.13	Hurd-Bos	40	Hurd-Bos	5	Sisler-Bos	12.58				
Delock-Bos	105			Sisler-Bos	39	2 players tied	3	Sullivan-Bos	12.76				

Innings Pitched		Opponents' Avg.		Opponents' OBP		Earned Run Average		Adjusted ERA		Adjusted Starter Runs		Pitcher Wins	
Lary-Det	294.0	Score-Cle	.186	Donovan-Chi	.290	Ford-NY	2.47	Score-Cle	166	Wynn-Cle	46.3	Wynn-Cle	5.1
Brewer-Bos	244.1	Brewer-Bos	.220	Score-Cle	.290	Sullivan-Bos	3.42	Sullivan-Bos	135	Brewer-Bos	30.2	Brewer-Bos	3.9
Sullivan-Bos	242.0	Sullivan-Bos	.268	Brewer-Bos	.307	Brewer-Bos	3.50	Brewer-Bos	132	Sullivan-Bos	27.0	Sullivan-Bos	1.6
Nixon-Bos	145.1			Sullivan-Bos	.330					Parnell-Bos	8.4	Delock-Bos	.9

1957 AMERICAN LEAGUE

TEAM	W	L	T	PCT	GB	R	OR	HR	AVG	OBP	SLG	OPS	AOPS	PF	SB	CG	HR	BB	SO	BR/9	ERA	AERA	OAV	OOB	FW	PW	BW	BSW	DIF
NY	98	56	0	.636		723	534	145	.268	.339	.409	748	+12	98	49	41	110	580	810	11.7	3.00	+20	.234	.315	.2	9.9	9.0	.0	1.8
Chi	90	64	1	.584	8	707	566	106	.260	.345	.375	720	+2	101	109	59	124	470	665	11.6	3.35	+12	.248	.311	1.1	6.4	3.9	.9	.6
Bos	82	72	0	.532	16	721	668	153	.262	.341	.405	746	+4	106	29	55	116	498	692	12.6	3.88	+3	.264	.329	-1.2	1.7	4.1	.2	.2
Det	78	76	0	.506	20	614	614	116	.257	.323	.378	701	-5	103	36	52	147	505	756	11.9	3.56	+8	.250	.318	.3	4.8	-3.5	-.6	.0
Bal	76	76	2	.500	21	597	588	87	.252	.318	.353	671	-5	94	57	44	95	493	767	11.5	3.46	+4	.243	.310	.8	2.2	-3.0	.3	-.3
Cle	76	77	0	.497	21.5	682	722	140	.252	.329	.382	711	+1	99	40	46	130	618	807	13.3	4.06	-8	.261	.340	-1.4	-5.6	1.9	-.5	5.1
KC	59	94	1	.386	38.5	563	710	166	.244	.295	.394	689	-9	102	35	26	153	565	626	12.7	4.19	-6	.260	.333	.1	-3.5	-7.5	.1	-6.7
Was	55	99	0	.357	43	603	808	111	.244	.316	.363	679	-8	99	13	31	149	580	691	13.7	4.85	-20	.278	.349	-.0	-14.7	-5.0	-.7	-1.6
Total	616					5210		1024	.255	.326	.382	708			368	354		4309	5814	12.4	3.79		.255	.326					

Batter-Fielder Wins		Batting Average		On-Base Percentage		Slugging Average		On-Base Plus Slugging		Adjusted OPS		Adjusted Batter Runs	
Mantle-NY	8.0	Williams-Bos	.388	Williams-Bos	.526	Williams-Bos	.731	Williams-Bos	1257	Williams-Bos	227	Mantle-NY	94.0
Williams-Bos	7.3	Malzone-Bos	.292	Jensen-Bos	.367	Jensen-Bos	.469	Jensen-Bos	836	Jensen-Bos	121	Williams-Bos	84.3
Klaus-Bos	2.3	Jensen-Bos	.281	Piersall-Bos	.331	Malzone-Bos	.427	Malzone-Bos	751	Malzone-Bos	98	Jensen-Bos	17.2
Malzone-Bos	1.8	Piersall-Bos	.261	Klaus-Bos	.326	Piersall-Bos	.415	Piersall-Bos	746	Piersall-Bos	98	Nixon-Bos	4.6

Runs		Hits		Doubles		Triples		Home Runs		Total Bases		Runs Batted In	
Mantle-NY	121	Fox-Chi	196	Minoso-Chi	36	3 players tied	9	Sievers-Was	42	Sievers-Was	331	Sievers-Was	114
Piersall-Bos	103	Malzone-Bos	185	Gardner-Bal	36	Piersall-Bos	5	Williams-Bos	38	Williams-Bos	307	Malzone-Bos	103
Williams-Bos	96	Williams-Bos	163	Malzone-Bos	31	Malzone-Bos	5	Jensen-Bos	23	Malzone-Bos	271	Jensen-Bos	103
2 players tied	82	Piersall-Bos	159	Jensen-Bos	29	3 players tied	4	Piersall-Bos	19	Jensen-Bos	255	Williams-Bos	87

Stolen Bases		Base Stealing Runs		Fielding Runs-Infield		Fielding Runs-Outfield		Wins		Winning Pct.		Complete Games	
Aparicio-Chi	28	Aparicio-Chi	3.4	Bridges-Was	27.7	Maxwell-Det	10.1	Pierce-Chi	20	Sturdivant-NY	.727	Pierce-Chi	16
Piersall-Bos	14	Piersall-Bos	1.0	Malzone-Bos	21.0	Piersall-Bos	2.3	Bunning-Det	20	Donovan-Chi	.727	Donovan-Chi	16
Jensen-Bos	8	Klaus-Bos	.4	Klaus-Bos	21.0	Jensen-Bos	1.1	Brewer-Bos	16	Brewer-Bos	.552	Brewer-Bos	15
2 players tied	2	Mauch-Bos	.2	Vernon-Bos	2.8			F.Sullivan-Bos	14			F.Sullivan-Bos	14

Strikeouts		Fewest BB/Game		Games		Saves		Base Runners/9		Adjusted Relief Runs		Relief Ranking	
Wynn-Cle	184	F.Sullivan-Bos	1.80	Zuverink-Bal	56	Grim-NY	19	O'Dell-Bal	9.68	Staley-Chi	19.4	Zuverink-Bal	19.1
Brewer-Bos	128	Nixon-Bos	2.64	Delock-Bos	49	Delock-Bos	11	F.Sullivan-Bos	9.76	Delock-Bos	3.7	Delock-Bos	6.9
F.Sullivan-Bos	127	Brewer-Bos	3.51	Brewer-Bos	32	Minarcin-Bos	2	Porterfield-Bos	12.14				
Nixon-Bos	96			F.Sullivan-Bos	31			Delock-Bos	12.26				

Innings Pitched		Opponents' Avg.		Opponents' OBP		Earned Run Average		Adjusted ERA		Adjusted Starter Runs		Pitcher Wins	
Bunning-Det	267.1	Turley-NY	.194	F.Sullivan-Bos	.273	Shantz-NY	2.45	Shantz-NY	147	F.Sullivan-Bos	34.5	F.Sullivan-Bos	3.5
F.Sullivan-Bos	240.2	F.Sullivan-Bos	.230	Brewer-Bos	.324	F.Sullivan-Bos	2.73	F.Sullivan-Bos	146	Nixon-Bos	7.0	Nixon-Bos	1.3
Brewer-Bos	238.1	Brewer-Bos	.250	Nixon-Bos	.335	Nixon-Bos	3.68	Nixon-Bos	108	Brewer-Bos	4.2	Brewer-Bos	.6
Nixon-Bos	191.0	Nixon-Bos	.280			Brewer-Bos	3.85	Brewer-Bos	103	Baumann-Bos	.6	Delock-Bos	.6

1958 AMERICAN LEAGUE

TEAM	W	L	T	PCT	GB	R	OR	HR	AVG	OBP	SLG	OPS	AOPS	PF	SB	CG	HR	BB	SO	BR/9	ERA	AERA	OAV	OOB	FW	PW	BW	BSW	DIF
NY	92	62	1	.597		759	577	164	.268	.336	.416	752	+16	96	48	53	116	557	796	11.8	3.22	+10	.235	.313	-.1	5.3	12.1	.2	-2.4
Chi	82	72	1	.532	10	634	615	101	.257	.327	.367	694	-1	98	101	55	152	515	751	11.8	3.61	+1	.250	.317	.7	.5	-.1	1.4	2.5
Bos	79	75	1	.513	13	697	691	155	.256	.338	.400	738	+2	107	29	44	121	521	695	12.7	3.92	+2	.264	.332	-1.1	1.3	2.9	-.2	-1.3
Cle	77	76	0	.503	14.5	694	635	161	.258	.325	.403	728	+8	98	50	51	123	604	766	12.5	3.73	-2	.249	.328	-1.5	-1.3	5.8	-.4	-2.0
Det	77	77	0	.500	15	659	606	109	.266	.326	.389	715	-5	104	48	59	133	437	797	11.9	3.59	+12	.252	.314	1.1	6.4	-2.5	-.2	-5.2
Bal	74	79	1	.484	17.5	521	575	108	.241	.308	.350	658	-9	95	33	55	106	403	749	11.3	3.40	+6	.249	.306	.6	3.3	-5.7	-.3	-.5
KC	73	81	2	.474	19	642	713	138	.247	.307	.381	688	-8	102	22	42	150	467	721	12.2	4.15	-6	.252	.323	.1	-3.7	-5.6	-.6	5.8
Was	61	93	0	.396	31	553	747	121	.240	.307	.357	664	-10	98	22	28	156	558	762	13.3	4.53	-16	.272	.341	.5	-11.2	-7.3	-.8	2.8
Total	619					5159		1057	.254	.322	.383	705			353	387		4062	6037	12.2	3.77		.254	.322					

Batter-Fielder Wins		Batting Average		On-Base Percentage		Slugging Average		On-Base Plus Slugging		Adjusted OPS		Adjusted Batter Runs	
Mantle-NY	5.5	Williams-Bos	.328	Williams-Bos	.458	Colavito-Cle	.620	Williams-Bos	1042	Mantle-NY	189	Mantle-NY	71.2
Runnels-Bos	4.1	Runnels-Bos	.322	Runnels-Bos	.416	Williams-Bos	.584	Jensen-Bos	931	Williams-Bos	174	Williams-Bos	48.3
Jensen-Bos	3.1	Malzone-Bos	.295	Jensen-Bos	.396	Jensen-Bos	.535	Runnels-Bos	854	Jensen-Bos	144	Jensen-Bos	37.1
Williams-Bos	2.8	Jensen-Bos	.286	Buddin-Bos	.349	Runnels-Bos	.438	Gernert-Bos	755	Runnels-Bos	127	Runnels-Bos	26.6

Runs		Hits		Doubles		Triples		Home Runs		Total Bases		Runs Batted In	
Mantle-NY	127	Fox-Chi	187	Kuenn-Det	39	Power-KC-Cle	10	Mantle-NY	42	Mantle-NY	307	Jensen-Bos	122
Runnels-Bos	103	Malzone-Bos	185	Runnels-Bos	32	Runnels-Bos	5	Jensen-Bos	35	Jensen-Bos	293	Malzone-Bos	87
Jensen-Bos	83	Runnels-Bos	183	Jensen-Bos	31	Piersall-Bos	5	Williams-Bos	26	Malzone-Bos	264	Williams-Bos	85
Williams-Bos	81	Jensen-Bos	157	Malzone-Bos	30	2 players tied	3	Gernert-Bos	20	Runnels-Bos	249	Gernert-Bos	69

Stolen Bases		Base Stealing Runs		Fielding Runs-Infield		Fielding Runs-Outfield		Wins		Winning Pct.		Complete Games	
Aparicio-Chi	29	Aparicio-Chi	4.3	Kubek-NY	21.2	Kaline-Det	20.4	Turley-NY	21	Turley-NY	.750	3 players tied	19
Piersall-Bos	12	Piersall-Bos	1.9	Buddin-Bos	18.5	Piersall-Bos	3.3	Delock-Bos	14			Sullivan-Bos	10
Jensen-Bos	9	Jensen-Bos	.6	Malzone-Bos	16.5	Stephens-Bos	.1	Sullivan-Bos	13			Brewer-Bos	10
Gernert-Bos	2	Gernert-Bos	.4	Runnels-Bos	8.3			Brewer-Bos	12			Delock-Bos	9

Strikeouts		Fewest BB/Game		Games		Saves		Base Runners/9		Adjusted Relief Runs		Relief Ranking	
Wynn-Chi	179	Donovan-Chi	1.92	Clevenger-Was	55	Duren-NY	20	Wilhelm-Cle-Bal	9.76	Hyde-Was	21.3	Hyde-Was	32.6
Brewer-Bos	124	Sullivan-Bos	2.21	Wall-Bos	52	Kiely-Bos	12	Kiely-Bos	10.78	Kiely-Bos	8.5	Kiely-Bos	9.5
Sullivan-Bos	103	Delock-Bos	3.15	Kiely-Bos	47	Wall-Bos	10	Wall-Bos	11.57	Wall-Bos	5.4	Wall-Bos	8.3
Delock-Bos	82	Brewer-Bos	3.68	Fornieles-Bos	37	Sullivan-Bos	3	Delock-Bos	11.87				

Innings Pitched		Opponents' Avg.		Opponents' OBP		Earned Run Average		Adjusted ERA		Adjusted Starter Runs		Pitcher Wins	
Lary-Det	260.1	Turley-NY	.206	Ford-NY	.276	Ford-NY	2.01	Ford-NY	176	Ford-NY	37.4	Ford-NY	3.9
Brewer-Bos	227.1	Delock-Bos	.252	Delock-Bos	.314	Delock-Bos	3.38	Delock-Bos	119	Delock-Bos	11.8	Delock-Bos	1.1
Sullivan-Bos	199.1	Brewer-Bos	.259	Sullivan-Bos	.322	Sullivan-Bos	3.57	Sullivan-Bos	112	Sullivan-Bos	9.1	Kiely-Bos	.9
Delock-Bos	160.0	Sullivan-Bos	.278	Brewer-Bos	.333	Brewer-Bos	3.72	Brewer-Bos	108	Monbouquette-Bos	3.1	2 players tied	.8

1959 AMERICAN LEAGUE

TEAM	W	L	T	PCT	GB	R	OR	HR	AVG	OBP	SLG	OPS	AOPS	PF	SB	CG	HR	BB	SO	BR/9	ERA	AERA	OAV	OOB	FW	PW	BW	BSW	DIF
Chi	94	60	2	.610		669	588	97	.250	.327	.364	691	-4	99	113	44	129	525	761	11.7	3.29	+14	.242	.311	.6	7.7	-1.0	.5	9.2
Cle	89	65	0	.578	5	745	646	167	.263	.321	.408	729	+9	96	33	58	148	635	799	12.3	3.75	-2	.239	.323	.7	-1.0	6.0	-.6	7.0
NY	79	75	1	.513	15	687	647	153	.260	.319	.402	721	+7	97	45	38	120	594	836	12.2	3.60	+1	.244	.322	.5	.7	4.2	.0	-3.5
Det	76	78	0	.494	18	713	732	160	.258	.335	.400	735	+2	105	34	53	177	432	829	11.9	4.20	-3	.254	.315	.9	-2.0	2.0	-.0	-2.0
Bos	75	79	0	.487	19	726	696	125	.256	.335	.385	720	-2	105	68	38	135	589	724	13.2	4.17	-3	.266	.341	.5	-1.6	.9	.5	-2.3
Bal	74	80	1	.481	20	551	621	109	.238	.310	.345	655	-13	98	36	45	111	476	735	11.5	3.56	+6	.246	.311	-.4	3.5	-8.6	-.1	2.5
KC	66	88	0	.429	28	681	760	117	.263	.326	.390	716	+0	102	34	44	148	492	703	13.4	4.35	-8	.274	.338	-1.2	-5.2	.4	-.2	-4.8
Was	63	91	0	.409	31	619	701	163	.237	.308	.379	687	-7	100	51	46	123	467	694	12.3	4.01	-2	.259	.321	-1.4	-1.4	-4.3	-.2	-6.7
Total	618					5391		1091	.253	.323	.384	707			414	366		4210	6081	12.3	3.86		.253	.323					

Batter-Fielder Wins		Batting Average		On-Base Percentage		Slugging Average		On-Base Plus Slugging		Adjusted OPS		Adjusted Batter Runs	
Runnels-Bos	**3.9**	Kuenn-Det	.353	Yost-Det	.435	Kaline-Det	.530	Kaline-Det	940	Mantle-NY	152	Mantle-NY	40.7
Jensen-Bos	**3.3**	Runnels-Bos	.314	Runnels-Bos	.415	Jensen-Bos	.492	Jensen-Bos	863	Jensen-Bos	131	Runnels-Bos	25.3
Malzone-Bos	**1.2**	Malzone-Bos	.280	Jensen-Bos	.372	Malzone-Bos	.437	Runnels-Bos	841	Runnels-Bos	126	Jensen-Bos	25.2
Gernert-Bos	**.8**	Jensen-Bos	.277	Buddin-Bos	.366	Runnels-Bos	.427	Malzone-Bos	760	Malzone-Bos	103	Williams-Bos	7.2

Runs		Hits		Doubles		Triples		Home Runs		Total Bases		Runs Batted In	
Yost-Det	115	Kuenn-Det	198	Kuenn-Det	42	Allison-Was	9	Killebrew-Was	42	Colavito-Cle	301	Jensen-Bos	112
Jensen-Bos	101	Runnels-Bos	176	Malzone-Bos	34	Runnels-Bos	6	Colavito-Cle	42	Malzone-Bos	264	Malzone-Bos	92
Runnels-Bos	95	Malzone-Bos	169	Runnels-Bos	33	Keough-Bos	5	Jensen-Bos	28	Jensen-Bos	263	Runnels-Bos	57
Malzone-Bos	90	Jensen-Bos	148	Jensen-Bos	31	3 players tied	4	Malzone-Bos	19	Runnels-Bos	239	Buddin-Bos	53

Stolen Bases		Base Stealing Runs		Fielding Runs-Infield		Fielding Runs-Outfield		Wins		Winning Pct.		Complete Games	
Aparicio-Chi	56	Aparicio-Chi	7.8	Gardner-Bal	21.8	Jensen-Bos	10.5	Wynn-Chi	22	Shaw-Chi	.750	Pascual-Was	17
Jensen-Bos	20	Jensen-Bos	2.7	Malzone-Bos	9.7	Gernert-Bos	.7	Casale-Bos	13			Brewer-Bos	11
Geiger-Bos	9	Malzone-Bos	1.3	Runnels-Bos	9.0			Delock-Bos	11			Casale-Bos	9
3 players tied	6	Buddin-Bos	1.0	Gernert-Bos	5.0			Brewer-Bos	10			F.Sullivan-Bos	5

Strikeouts		Fewest BB/Game		Games		Saves		Base Runners/9		Adjusted Relief Runs		Relief Ranking	
Bunning-Det	201	Brown-Bal	1.76	Staley-Chi	67	Lown-Chi	15	Shantz-NY	9.22	Staley-Chi	17.2	Duren-NY	23.7
Brewer-Bos	121	F.Sullivan-Bos	3.39	Fornieles-Bos	46	Fornieles-Bos	11	Fornieles-Bos	11.74	Fornieles-Bos	9.3	Fornieles-Bos	11.0
F.Sullivan-Bos	107	Brewer-Bos	3.68	Kiely-Bos	41	Kiely-Bos	7	Monbouquette-Bos	11.93	Kiely-Bos	.3	Kiely-Bos	.4
Casale-Bos	93	Casale-Bos	4.46	Brewer-Bos	36	Brewer-Bos	2	Delock-Bos	12.33				

Innings Pitched		Opponents' Avg.		Opponents' OBP		Earned Run Average		Adjusted ERA		Adjusted Starter Runs		Pitcher Wins	
Wynn-Chi	255.2	Score-Cle	.210	Ditmar-NY	.268	Wilhelm-Bal	2.19	Wilhelm-Bal	173	Wilhelm-Bal	39.8	Pascual-Was	4.7
Brewer-Bos	215.1	Casale-Bos	.238	Casale-Bos	.329	Brewer-Bos	3.76	Brewer-Bos	108	Delock-Bos	13.8	Delock-Bos	1.2
Casale-Bos	179.2	F.Sullivan-Bos	.258	F.Sullivan-Bos	.331	F.Sullivan-Bos	3.95	F.Sullivan-Bos	103	Brewer-Bos	8.1	Fornieles-Bos	1.1
F.Sullivan-Bos	177.2	Brewer-Bos	.265	Brewer-Bos	.336	Casale-Bos	4.31	Casale-Bos	94	F.Sullivan-Bos	2.0	Chittum-Bos	.7

1960 AMERICAN LEAGUE

TEAM	W	L	T	PCT	GB	R	OR	HR	AVG	OBP	SLG	OPS	AOPS	PF	SB	CG	HR	BB	SO	BR/9	ERA	AERA	OAV	OOB	FW	PW	BW	BSW	DIF
NY	97	57	1	.630		746	627	193	.260	.329	.426	755	+15	94	37	38	123	609	712	12.0	3.52	+2	.238	.320	.2	1.1	10.7	-.1	8.1
Bal	89	65	0	.578	8	682	606	123	.253	.332	.377	709	-1	99	37	48	117	552	785	11.8	3.52	+8	.241	.317	1.4	4.6	.2	-.1	6.0
Chi	87	67	0	.565	10	741	617	112	.270	.345	.396	741	+7	99	122	42	127	533	695	12.3	3.60	+5	.258	.326	1.4	2.8	6.8	.9	-1.8
Cle	76	78	0	.494	21	667	693	127	.267	.325	.388	713	+1	97	58	32	161	636	771	12.8	3.95	-5	.252	.334	.2	-3.4	.9	.3	1.1
Was	73	81	0	.474	24	672	696	147	.244	.324	.384	708	-2	99	52	34	130	538	775	12.6	3.77	+3	.260	.329	-2.1	1.8	-1.2	-.5	-1.9
Det	71	83	0	.461	26	633	644	150	.239	.324	.375	699	-7	103	66	40	141	474	824	11.9	3.64	+9	.251	.316	-.5	5.0	-5.0	.2	-5.7
Bos	65	89	0	.422	32	658	775	124	.261	.333	.389	722	-4	100	34	34	120	580	767	13.6	4.62	-13	.273	.346	-.6	-8.5	-.5	-.3	-2.0
KC	58	96	1	.377	39	615	756	110	.249	.316	.366	682	-11	101	16	44	160	525	664	13.1	4.38	-9	.271	.339	.3	-6.0	-7.5	-.1	-5.7
Total	617					5414		1086	.255	.328	.388	716			422	312		4447	5993	12.5	3.87		.255	.328					

Batter-Fielder Wins		Batting Average		On-Base Percentage		Slugging Average		On-Base Plus Slugging		Adjusted OPS		Adjusted Batter Runs	
Aparicio-Chi	**3.9**	Runnels-Bos	.320	Yost-Det	.414	Maris-NY	.581	Mantle-NY	957	Mantle-NY	166	Mantle-NY	51.4
Runnels-Bos	**3.5**	Wertz-Bos	.282	Runnels-Bos	.401	Wertz-Bos	.460	Wertz-Bos	796	Runnels-Bos	112	Williams-Bos	41.7
Williams-Bos	**3.4**	Malzone-Bos	.271	Buddin-Bos	.338	Malzone-Bos	.398	Runnels-Bos	795	Wertz-Bos	110	Runnels-Bos	13.4
Geiger-Bos	**1.1**	Buddin-Bos	.245	Wertz-Bos	.335	Runnels-Bos	.394	Malzone-Bos	711	Malzone-Bos	89	Geiger-Bos	8.7

Runs		Hits		Doubles		Triples		Home Runs		Total Bases		Runs Batted In	
Mantle-NY	119	Minoso-Chi	184	Francona-Cle	36	Fox-Chi	10	Mantle-NY	40	Mantle-NY	294	Maris-NY	112
Runnels-Bos	80	Runnels-Bos	169	Malzone-Bos	30	Clinton-Bos	5	Williams-Bos	29	Malzone-Bos	237	Wertz-Bos	103
Buddin-Bos	62	Malzone-Bos	161	Runnels-Bos	29	Buddin-Bos	5	Wertz-Bos	19	Runnels-Bos	208	Malzone-Bos	79
Malzone-Bos	60	Wertz-Bos	125	Wertz-Bos	22	2 players tied	3	Malzone-Bos	14	Wertz-Bos	204	Williams-Bos	72

Stolen Bases		Base Stealing Runs		Fielding Runs-Infield		Fielding Runs-Outfield		Wins		Winning Pct.		Complete Games	
Aparicio-Chi	51	Aparicio-Chi	8.4	Aparicio-Chi	33.5	Piersall-Cle	8.6	Perry-Cle	18	Perry-Cle	.643	Lary-Det	15
Runnels-Bos	5	Runnels-Bos	.4	Runnels-Bos	14.1			Estrada-Bal	18			Monbouquette-Bos	12
Clinton-Bos	4	Buddin-Bos	.2	Malzone-Bos	12.5			Monbouquette-Bos	14			Brewer-Bos	8
Buddin-Bos	4			Wertz-Bos	2.8			2 players tied	10			4 players tied	4

Strikeouts		Fewest BB/Game		Games		Saves		Base Runners/9		Adjusted Relief Runs		Relief Ranking	
Bunning-Det	201	Brown-Bal	1.25	Fornieles-Bos	70	Klippstein-Cle	14	Staley-Chi	9.52	Staley-Chi	15.4	Staley-Chi	28.2
Monbouquette-Bos	134	Monbouquette-Bos	2.85	F.Sullivan-Bos	40	Fornieles-Bos	14	Muffett-Bos	11.30	Fornieles-Bos	15.2	Fornieles-Bos	23.1
F.Sullivan-Bos	98	Brewer-Bos	3.47	Sturdivant-Bos	40	Borland-Bos	3	Fornieles-Bos	11.64				
Muffett-Bos	75			Monbouquette-Bos	35			Monbouquette-Bos	12.01				

Innings Pitched		Opponents' Avg.		Opponents' OBP		Earned Run Average		Adjusted ERA		Adjusted Starter Runs		Pitcher Wins	
Lary-Det	274.1	Estrada-Bal	.218	Brown-Bal	.283	Baumann-Chi	2.67	Bunning-Det	142	Bunning-Det	30.6	Staley-Chi	3.2
Monbouquette-Bos	215.0	Monbouquette-Bos	.263	Monbouquette-Bos	.319	Monbouquette-Bos	3.64	Monbouquette-Bos	111	Monbouquette-Bos	11.5	Fornieles-Bos	2.6
Brewer-Bos	186.2	Brewer-Bos	.301	Brewer-Bos	.364	Brewer-Bos	4.82	Brewer-Bos	84	Muffett-Bos	9.3	Monbouquette-Bos	.9
F.Sullivan-Bos	153.2											Muffett-Bos	.9

163g

1961 AMERICAN LEAGUE

TEAM	W	L	T	PCT	GB	R	OR	HR	AVG	OBP	SLG	OPS	AOPS	PF	SB	CG	HR	BB	SO	BR/9	ERA	AERA	OAV	OOB	FW	PW	BW	BSW	DIF
NY	109	53	1	.673		827	612	**240**	.263	.330	**.442**	**772**	**+18**	95	28	47	137	542	866	**11.5**	3.46	+7	.239	.311	**1.6**	4.5	**12.3**	-.2	9.8
Det	101	61	1	.623	8	**841**	671	180	**.266**	**.347**	.421	768	+8	103	98	**62**	170	**469**	836	11.7	3.55	+16	.252	.311	.3	8.7	7.2	**.7**	3.0
Bal	95	67	1	.586	14	691	**588**	149	.254	.326	.390	716	+1	97	39	54	**109**	617	926	**11.5**	**3.22**	**+20**	**.227**	**.308**	1.4	**10.7**	1.0	-.4	1.3
Chi	86	76	1	.531	23	765	726	138	.265	.335	.395	730	+3	98	**100**	39	158	498	814	12.4	4.06	-3	.268	.326	1.4	-2.3	2.8	.6	2.5
Cle	78	83	0	.484	30.5	737	752	150	**.266**	.326	.406	732	+4	97	34	35	178	599	801	12.8	4.15	-5	.258	.331	.6	-3.4	3.0	.2	-2.9
Bos	76	86	1	.469	33	729	792	112	.254	.334	.374	708	-6	102	56	35	167	679	831	13.5	4.29	-3	.266	.345	.4	-1.9	-3.6	-.2	.2
Min	70	90	1	.438	38	707	778	167	.250	.326	.397	723	-6	106	47	49	163	570	914	12.8	4.28	-1	.256	.329	-1.4	-.6	-4.3	-.7	-3.0
LA	70	91	1	.435	38.5	744	784	189	.245	.331	.398	729	-9	111	37	25	180	713	**973**	13.4	4.31	+5	.254	.341	-2.4	2.8	-6.0	-.4	-4.4
Was	61	100	0	.379	47.5	618	776	119	.244	.315	.367	682	-11	99	81	39	131	586	666	12.8	4.23	-5	.260	.333	-.4	-3.4	-7.3	-.0	-8.3
KC	61	100	1	.379	47.5	683	863	90	.247	.320	.354	674	-16	102	58	32	141	629	703	14.0	4.74	-12	.275	.351	-1.4	-8.4	-10.1	.3	.2
Total	811					7342		1534	.256	.329	.395	724			578	417		5902	8330	12.6	4.02		.256	.329					

Batter-Fielder Wins		Batting Average		On-Base Percentage		Slugging Average		On-Base Plus Slugging		Adjusted OPS		Adjusted Batter Runs	
Cash-Det	**7.6**	Cash-Det	.361	Cash-Det	.487	Mantle-NY	.687	Cash-Det	1148	Mantle-NY	210	Mantle-NY	85.6
Buddin-Bos	**1.6**	Malzone-Bos	.266	Jensen-Bos	.350	Geiger-Bos	.407	Geiger-Bos	756	Geiger-Bos	99	Runnels-Bos	9.9
Schilling-Bos	**.9**	Yastrzemski-Bos	.266	Geiger-Bos	.349	Yastrzemski-Bos	.396	Jensen-Bos	742	Jensen-Bos	96	Buddin-Bos	8.8
Green-Bos	**.8**	Jensen-Bos	.263	Schilling-Bos	.340	Jensen-Bos	.392	Yastrzemski-Bos	721	Yastrzemski-Bos	90	Green-Bos	5.2

Runs		Hits		Doubles		Triples		Home Runs		Total Bases		Runs Batted In	
Maris-NY	132	Cash-Det	193	Kaline-Det	41	Wood-Det	14	Maris-NY	61	Maris-NY	366	Maris-NY	142
Mantle-NY	132	Schilling-Bos	167	Yastrzemski-Bos	31	Yastrzemski-Bos	6	Geiger-Bos	18	Yastrzemski-Bos	231	Malzone-Bos	87
Schilling-Bos	87	Malzone-Bos	157	Schilling-Bos	25	Geiger-Bos	6	Pagliaroni-Bos	16	Malzone-Bos	228	Yastrzemski-Bos	80
Geiger-Bos	82	Yastrzemski-Bos	155	Buddin-Bos	22	Malzone-Bos	4	Malzone-Bos	14	Schilling-Bos	211	Jensen-Bos	66

Stolen Bases		Base Stealing Runs		Fielding Runs-Infield		Fielding Runs-Outfield		Wins		Winning Pct.		Complete Games	
Aparicio-Chi	53	Aparicio-Chi	7.1	Boyer-NY	28.5	Kaline-Det	13.5	Ford-NY	25	Ford-NY	.862	Lary-Det	22
Geiger-Bos	16	Geiger-Bos	2.1	Schilling-Bos	14.6	Jensen-Bos	6.7	Schwall-Bos	15	Schwall-Bos	.682	Monbouquette-Bos	12
Jensen-Bos	9	Runnels-Bos	.8	Malzone-Bos	1.1	Geiger-Bos	2.8	Monbouquette-Bos	14			Schwall-Bos	10
Schilling-Bos	7	3 players tied	.2	Runnels-Bos	.4			Conley-Bos	11			Conley-Bos	6

Strikeouts		Fewest BB/Game		Games		Saves		Base Runners/9		Adjusted Relief Runs		Relief Ranking	
Pascual-Min	221	Mossi-Det	1.76	Arroyo-NY	65	Arroyo-NY	29	Donovan-Was	9.39	Arroyo-NY	20.7	Arroyo-NY	41.5
Monbouquette-Bos	161	Conley-Bos	2.93	Fornieles-Bos	57	Fornieles-Bos	15	Hillman-Bos	10.73	Hillman-Bos	12.4	Hillman-Bos	7.2
Conley-Bos	113	Monbouquette-Bos	3.81	Stallard-Bos	43	Earley-Bos	7	Monbouquette-Bos	12.68				
Stallard-Bos	109	Schwall-Bos	5.54	Muffett-Bos	38	Nichols-Bos	3	Fornieles-Bos	13.35				

Innings Pitched		Opponents' Avg.		Opponents' OBP		Earned Run Average		Adjusted ERA		Adjusted Starter Runs		Pitcher Wins	
Ford-NY	283.0	Estrada-Bal	.207	Donovan-Was	.267	Donovan-Was	2.40	Donovan-Was	167	Hoeft-Bal	28.2	Arroyo-NY	4.4
Monbouquette-Bos	236.1	Monbouquette-Bos	.254	Monbouquette-Bos	.326	Schwall-Bos	3.22	Schwall-Bos	129	Monbouquette-Bos	18.3	Schwall-Bos	1.9
Conley-Bos	199.2	Schwall-Bos	.255	Conley-Bos	.343	Monbouquette-Bos	3.39	Monbouquette-Bos	123	Schwall-Bos	17.1	Monbouquette-Bos	1.9
Schwall-Bos	178.2	Conley-Bos	.287	Schwall-Bos	.366	Conley-Bos	4.91	Conley-Bos	85	Brewer-Bos	2.3	Nichols-Bos	1.4

160g Yaz played every game in LF (AL Record)

1962 AMERICAN LEAGUE

TEAM	W	L	T	PCT	GB	R	OR	HR	AVG	OBP	SLG	OPS	AOPS	PF	SB	CG	HR	BB	SO	BR/9	ERA	AERA	OAV	OOB	FW	PW	BW	BSW	DIF
NY	96	66	0	.593		**817**	680	199	**.267**	.337	**.426**	**763**	**+15**	97	42	33	146	499	838	**11.6**	3.70	+1	**.247**	**.310**	.4	.8	**11.7**	-.3	2.5
Min	91	71	1	.562	5	798	713	185	.260	**.338**	.412	750	+4	104	33	**53**	166	**493**	**948**	11.9	3.89	+5	.253	.317	.5	3.0	3.9	-.2	2.8
LA	86	76	0	.531	10	718	706	137	.250	.325	.380	705	-1	97	46	23	**118**	616	858	12.8	3.70	+4	.253	.330	-2.2	2.7	.1	-.1	4.5
Det	85	76	0	.528	10.5	758	692	**209**	.248	.330	.411	741	+1	104	69	46	169	503	873	12.4	3.81	**+7**	.259	.321	-1.1	**4.1**	1.5	.6	-.6
Chi	85	77	0	.525	11	707	**658**	92	.257	.334	.372	706	-4	100	76	50	123	537	821	12.0	3.73	+5	.251	.317	**1.6**	2.9	-.7	.0	.1
Cle	80	82	0	.494	16	682	745	180	.245	.312	.388	700	-3	97	35	45	174	594	780	12.7	4.14	-6	.258	.331	-.1	-4.4	-2.7	-.0	6.2
Bal	77	85	0	.475	19	652	680	156	.248	.314	.387	701	+0	94	45	32	147	549	898	12.0	**3.69**	+0	.249	.318	.9	.1	.2	-.3	-4.9
Bos	76	84	0	.475	19	707	756	146	.258	.324	.403	727	-2	103	39	34	159	632	923	13.1	4.22	-2	.258	.337	.3	-1.4	-1.2	-.5	-1.1
KC	72	90	0	.444	24	745	837	116	.263	.332	.386	718	-5	105	76	32	199	655	825	13.5	4.79	-12	.263	.343	.3	-8.5	-3.1	**.7**	1.7
Was	60	101	1	.373	35.5	599	716	132	.250	.308	.373	681	-10	99	**99**	38	151	593	771	12.5	4.04	+0	.256	.328	-.1	-.1	-8.0	.0	-12.3
Total	809					7183		1552	.255	.325	.394	719			560	386		5671	8535	12.4	3.97		.255	.325					

Batter-Fielder Wins		Batting Average		On-Base Percentage		Slugging Average		On-Base Plus Slugging		Adjusted OPS		Adjusted Batter Runs	
Mantle-NY	**5.0**	Runnels-Bos	.326	Mantle-NY	.486	Mantle-NY	.605	Mantle-NY	1091	Mantle-NY	198	Mantle-NY	62.9
Bressoud-Bos	**3.7**	Yastrzemski-Bos	.296	Runnels-Bos	.408	Yastrzemski-Bos	.469	Runnels-Bos	863	Runnels-Bos	129	Runnels-Bos	27.0
Yastrzemski-Bos	**1.7**	Malzone-Bos	.283	Yastrzemski-Bos	.363	Runnels-Bos	.456	Yastrzemski-Bos	832	Yastrzemski-Bos	118	Yastrzemski-Bos	17.7
Runnels-Bos	**1.3**	Bressoud-Bos	.277	Geiger-Bos	.344	Bressoud-Bos	.444	Bressoud-Bos	773	Bressoud-Bos	103	Clinton-Bos	16.2

Runs		Hits		Doubles		Triples		Home Runs		Total Bases		Runs Batted In	
Pearson-LA	115	Richardson-NY	209	Robinson-Chi	45	Cimoli-KC	15	Killebrew-Min	48	Colavito-Det	309	Killebrew-Min	126
Yastrzemski-Bos	99	Yastrzemski-Bos	191	Yastrzemski-Bos	43	Clinton-Bos	10	Malzone-Bos	21	Yastrzemski-Bos	303	Malzone-Bos	95
Runnels-Bos	80	Runnels-Bos	183	Bressoud-Bos	40	Bressoud-Bos	9	Yastrzemski-Bos	19	Bressoud-Bos	266	Yastrzemski-Bos	94
Bressoud-Bos	79	Malzone-Bos	175	Runnels-Bos	33	Yastrzemski-Bos	6	Clinton-Bos	18	Malzone-Bos	264	Clinton-Bos	75

Stolen Bases		Base Stealing Runs		Fielding Runs-Infield		Fielding Runs-Outfield		Wins		Winning Pct.		Complete Games	
Aparicio-Chi	31	Wood-Det	4.2	Versalles-Min	34.9	Colavito-Det	12.4	Terry-NY	23	Herbert-Chi	.690	Pascual-Min	18
Geiger-Bos	18	Schilling-Bos	.2	Bressoud-Bos	22.7	Yastrzemski-Bos	8.4	Monbouquette-Bos	15	Monbouquette-Bos	.536	Monbouquette-Bos	11
Yastrzemski-Bos	7	Green-Bos	.2	Malzone-Bos	7.6			Conley-Bos	15	Conley-Bos	.517	Conley-Bos	9
2 players tied	3	2 players tied	.1	Schilling-Bos	6.8			Wilson-Bos	12			Schwall-Bos	5

Strikeouts		Fewest BB/Game		Games		Saves		Base Runners/9		Adjusted Relief Runs		Relief Ranking	
Pascual-Min	206	Donovan-Cle	1.69	Radatz-Bos	62	Radatz-Bos	24	Hall-Bal	9.20	Radatz-Bos	26.4	Radatz-Bos	39.8
Monbouquette-Bos	153	Monbouquette-Bos	2.49	Fornieles-Bos	42	Fornieles-Bos	5	Radatz-Bos	10.03	Nichols-Bos	5.3	Nichols-Bos	2.6
Radatz-Bos	144	Conley-Bos	2.53	Earley-Bos	38	Earley-Bos	5	Monbouquette-Bos	11.28				
Wilson-Bos	137	Wilson-Bos	5.22	Monbouquette-Bos	35	Nichols-Bos	3	Conley-Bos	11.58				

Innings Pitched		Opponents' Avg.		Opponents' OBP		Earned Run Average		Adjusted ERA		Adjusted Starter Runs		Pitcher Wins	
Terry-NY	298.2	Aguirre-Det	.205	Aguirre-Det	.267	Aguirre-Det	2.21	Aguirre-Det	184	Aguirre-Det	40.6	Radatz-Bos	3.9
Conley-Bos	241.2	Wilson-Bos	.231	Monbouquette-Bos	.302	Monbouquette-Bos	3.33	Monbouquette-Bos	124	Monbouquette-Bos	19.1	Monbouquette-Bos	1.6
Monbouquette-Bos	235.1	Monbouquette-Bos	.251	Conley-Bos	.308	Wilson-Bos	3.90	Wilson-Bos	106	Wilson-Bos	7.6	Wilson-Bos	1.0
Wilson-Bos	191.1	Conley-Bos	.256	Wilson-Bos	.338	Conley-Bos	3.95	Conley-Bos	105	Conley-Bos	5.9	Conley-Bos	1.0

1963 AMERICAN LEAGUE

TEAM	W	L	T	PCT	GB	R	OR	HR	AVG	OBP	SLG	OPS	AOPS	PF	SB	CG	HR	BB	SO	BR/9	ERA	AERA	OAV	OOB	FW	PW	BW	BSW	DIF
NY	104	57	0	.646		714	547	188	.252	.309	.403	712	+5	99	42	**59**	115	476	965	**10.8**	3.07	+14	**.232**	**.295**	1.4	7.7	3.3	-.3	11.5
Chi	94	68	0	.580	10.5	683	**544**	114	.250	.323	.365	688	+1	98	64	49	**100**	**440**	932	10.9	**2.97**	**+18**	.239	.297	.3	**9.5**	1.8	.1	1.4
Min	91	70	0	.565	13	**767**	602	**225**	**.255**	.325	**.430**	**755**	**+15**	102	32	58	162	459	941	11.2	3.28	+11	.242	.302	-.5	6.1	**10.8**	-.0	-5.8
Bal	86	76	0	.531	18.5	644	621	146	.249	.310	.380	690	+3	96	**97**	35	137	507	913	11.7	3.45	+1	.248	.314	**2.1**	.4	1.9	**.7**	-.0
Det	79	83	0	.488	25.5	700	703	148	.252	**.327**	.382	709	+2	103	73	42	195	477	930	11.9	3.90	-4	.253	.315	1.3	-2.6	2.2	.2	-3.1
Cle	79	83	0	.488	25.5	635	702	169	.239	.301	.381	682	-3	99	59	40	176	478	**1018**	11.6	3.79	-5	.249	.309	-.4	-2.9	-2.1	-.3	3.7
Bos	76	85	0	.472	28	666	704	171	.252	.312	.400	712	+2	103	27	29	152	539	1009	12.0	3.97	-5	.248	.316	-.0	-3.0	1.3	-.3	-2.4
KC	73	89	0	.451	31.5	615	704	95	.247	.313	.353	666	-12	106	47	35	156	540	887	12.4	3.92	+0	.256	.324	.5	-.3	-7.7	-.2	-.3
LA	70	91	0	.435	34	597	660	95	.250	.309	.354	663	-3	94	43	30	120	578	889	12.0	3.52	-3	.242	.318	-1.6	-1.8	-1.7	-.4	-5.0
Was	56	106	0	.346	48.5	578	812	138	.227	.293	.351	644	-14	100	68	29	176	537	744	12.8	4.42	-16	.266	.331	-2.6	-11.7	-10.1	.2	-.9
Total	808					6599		1489	.247	.312	.380	692			552	406		5031	9228	11.7	3.63		.247	.312					

Batter-Fielder Wins		Batting Average		On-Base Percentage		Slugging Average		On-Base Plus Slugging		Adjusted OPS		Adjusted Batter Runs	
Yastrzemski-Bos	**4.2**	Yastrzemski-Bos	.321	Yastrzemski-Bos	.418	Killebrew-Min	.555	Allison-Min	911	Allison-Min	150	Yastrzemski-Bos	40.7
Stuart-Bos	**1.5**	Malzone-Bos	.291	Bressoud-Bos	.329	Stuart-Bos	.521	Yastrzemski-Bos	894	Yastrzemski-Bos	145	Stuart-Bos	17.4
Geiger-Bos	**1.0**	Stuart-Bos	.261	Malzone-Bos	.327	Yastrzemski-Bos	.475	Stuart-Bos	833	Stuart-Bos	125	Bressoud-Bos	8.7
Mantilla-Bos	**.9**	Bressoud-Bos	.260	Stuart-Bos	.312	Bressoud-Bos	.451	Bressoud-Bos	780	Bressoud-Bos	113	Mantilla-Bos	8.0

Runs		Hits		Doubles		Triples		Home Runs		Total Bases		Runs Batted In	
Allison-Min	99	Yastrzemski-Bos	183	Yastrzemski-Bos	40	Versalles-Min	13	Killebrew-Min	45	Stuart-Bos	319	Stuart-Bos	118
Yastrzemski-Bos	91	Malzone-Bos	169	Stuart-Bos	25	Clinton-Bos	7	Stuart-Bos	42	Yastrzemski-Bos	271	Clinton-Bos	77
Stuart-Bos	81	Stuart-Bos	160	Schilling-Bos	25	Bressoud-Bos	6	Clinton-Bos	22	Malzone-Bos	243	Malzone-Bos	71
Clinton-Bos	71	Schilling-Bos	135	Malzone-Bos	25	Geiger-Bos	5	Bressoud-Bos	20	Clinton-Bos	233	Yastrzemski-Bos	68

Stolen Bases		Base Stealing Runs		Fielding Runs-Infield		Fielding Runs-Outfield		Wins		Winning Pct.		Complete Games	
Aparicio-Bal	40	Aparicio-Bal	6.7	Hansen-Chi	27.5	Hall-Min	10.5	Ford-NY	24	Ford-NY	.774	Terry-NY	18
Geiger-Bos	9	Geiger-Bos	.6	Stuart-Bos	6.5	Yastrzemski-Bos	8.8	Monbouquette-Bos	20	Radatz-Bos	.714	Pascual-Min	18
Yastrzemski-Bos	8	Mejias-Bos	.5	Malzone-Bos	2.7	Clinton-Bos	6.7	Radatz-Bos	15	Monbouquette-Bos	.667	Monbouquette-Bos	13
Mejias-Bos	4	2 players tied	.0					Wilson-Bos	11			2 players tied	6

Strikeouts		Fewest BB/Game		Games		Saves		Base Runners/9		Adjusted Relief Runs		Relief Ranking	
Pascual-Min	202	Donovan-Cle	1.22	S.Miller-Bal	71	S.Miller-Bal	27	Dailey-Min	8.20	Radatz-Bos	26.0	Radatz-Bos	48.1
Monbouquette-Bos	174	Monbouquette-Bos	1.42	Radatz-Bos	66	Radatz-Bos	25	Monbouquette-Bos	10.13	Lamabe-Bos	8.2	Lamabe-Bos	6.1
Radatz-Bos	162	Wilson-Bos	4.49	Lamabe-Bos	65	Lamabe-Bos	6	Radatz-Bos	10.20				
Morehead-Bos	136	Morehead-Bos	5.10	Earley-Bos	53	Earley-Bos	1	Lamabe-Bos	11.24				

Innings Pitched		Opponents' Avg.		Opponents' OBP		Earned Run Average		Adjusted ERA		Adjusted Starter Runs		Pitcher Wins	
Ford-NY	269.1	Downing-NY	.184	Terry-NY	.271	Peters-Chi	2.33	Peters-Chi	150	Peters-Chi	33.6	Radatz-Bos	5.0
Monbouquette-Bos	266.2	Morehead-Bos	.211	Monbouquette-Bos	.279	Wilson-Bos	3.76	Wilson-Bos	101	Monbouquette-Bos	1.5	Lamabe-Bos	.6
Wilson-Bos	210.2	Wilson-Bos	.234	Morehead-Bos	.316	Morehead-Bos	3.81	Morehead-Bos	99			Wilson-Bos	.5
Morehead-Bos	174.2	Monbouquette-Bos	.250	Wilson-Bos	.323	Monbouquette-Bos	3.81	Monbouquette-Bos	99			Smith-Bos	.0

1964 AMERICAN LEAGUE

TEAM	W	L	T	PCT	GB	R	OR	HR	AVG	OBP	SLG	OPS	AOPS	PF	SB	CG	HR	BB	SO	BR/9	ERA	AERA	OAV	OOB	FW	PW	BW	BSW	DIF
NY	99	63	2	.611		730	577	162	.253	.317	.387	704	+0	102	54	46	129	504	989	11.0	3.15	+15	.234	.299	1.1	8.2	.1	**.5**	8.1
Chi	98	64	0	.605	1	642	**501**	106	.247	.320	.353	673	-3	97	75	44	124	**401**	955	**10.1**	**2.72**	**+27**	**.226**	**.282**	.2	**13.1**	-1.6	.2	5.0
Bal	97	65	1	.599	2	679	567	162	.248	.316	.387	703	+1	100	78	44	129	456	939	11.0	3.16	+13	.239	.300	**1.9**	7.2	2.1	.3	4.6
Det	85	77	1	.525	14	699	678	157	.253	.319	.395	714	+2	102	60	35	164	536	993	12.0	3.84	-5	.244	.316	1.0	-3.0	2.4	.3	3.4
LA	82	80	0	.506	17	544	551	102	.242	.304	.344	648	-5	90	49	30	**100**	530	965	11.5	2.91	+13	.236	.309	-.7	7.0	-3.3	-.5	-1.6
Min	79	83	1	.488	20	**737**	678	**221**	.252	**.322**	**.427**	**749**	**+13**	101	46	**47**	181	545	1099	11.8	3.58	+0	.243	.312	-1.1	.1	**9.9**	.0	-11.0
Cle	79	83	2	.488	20	689	693	164	.247	.312	.380	692	-1	99	**79**	37	154	565	**1162**	12.3	3.75	-4	.255	.324	.6	-2.6	-.3	-.1	.5
Bos	72	90	0	.444	27	688	793	186	**.258**	**.322**	.416	738	+6	105	18	21	178	571	1094	13.1	4.50	-14	.266	.336	-.7	-10.0	4.7	-.4	-2.7
Was	62	100	0	.383	37	578	733	125	.231	.299	.348	647	-14	100	47	27	172	505	794	12.2	3.98	-7	.259	.322	-.0	-4.6	-9.7	-.1	-4.5
KC	57	105	1	.352	42	621	836	166	.239	.311	.379	690	-5	103	34	18	220	614	966	13.5	4.71	-19	.269	.344	-1.9	-14.3	-3.4	-.1	-4.3
Total	814					6607		1551	.247	.315	.382	696			540	349		5227	9956	11.8	3.63		.247	.315					

Batter-Fielder Wins		Batting Average		On-Base Percentage		Slugging Average		On-Base Plus Slugging		Adjusted OPS		Adjusted Batter Runs	
Fregosi-LA	**5.6**	Oliva-Min	.323	Mantle-NY	.423	Powell-Bal	.606	Mantle-NY	1015	Mantle-NY	177	Mantle-NY	52.9
Yastrzemski-Bos	**3.5**	Bressoud-Bos	.293	Yastrzemski-Bos	.374	Stuart-Bos	.491	Bressoud-Bos	828	Bressoud-Bos	123	Mantilla-Bos	23.6
Bressoud-Bos	**2.7**	Yastrzemski-Bos	.289	Bressoud-Bos	.372	Bressoud-Bos	.456	Yastrzemski-Bos	825	Yastrzemski-Bos	122	Bressoud-Bos	21.0
Mantilla-Bos	**2.3**	Stuart-Bos	.279	Stuart-Bos	.320	Yastrzemski-Bos	.451	Stuart-Bos	811	Stuart-Bos	117	Yastrzemski-Bos	19.3

Runs		Hits		Doubles		Triples		Home Runs		Total Bases		Runs Batted In	
Oliva-Min	109	Oliva-Min	217	Oliva-Min	43	Versalles-Min	10	Killebrew-Min	49	Oliva-Min	374	B.Robinson-Bal	118
Bressoud-Bos	86	Stuart-Bos	168	Bressoud-Bos	41	Rollins-Min	10	Stuart-Bos	33	Stuart-Bos	296	Stuart-Bos	114
Yastrzemski-Bos	77	Bressoud-Bos	166	Yastrzemski-Bos	29	Yastrzemski-Bos	9	Mantilla-Bos	30	Bressoud-Bos	258	Yastrzemski-Bos	67
Stuart-Bos	73	Yastrzemski-Bos	164	Stuart-Bos	27	Jones-Bos	4	Conigliaro-Bos	24	Yastrzemski-Bos	256	Mantilla-Bos	64

Stolen Bases		Base Stealing Runs		Fielding Runs-Infield		Fielding Runs-Outfield		Wins		Winning Pct.		Complete Games	
Aparicio-Bal	57	Aparicio-Bal	6.6	Knoop-LA	37.9	Yastrzemski-Bos	19.5	Peters-Chi	20	Bunker-Bal	.792	Chance-LA	15
Yastrzemski-Bos	6	Jones-Bos	.3	Malzone-Bos	5.9			Chance-LA	20	Radatz-Bos	.640	Monbouquette-Bos	7
Jones-Bos	6							Radatz-Bos	16			Wilson-Bos	5
Conigliaro-Bos	2							Monbouquette-Bos	13			3 players tied	3

Strikeouts		Fewest BB/Game		Games		Saves		Base Runners/9		Adjusted Relief Runs		Relief Ranking	
Downing-NY	217	Monbouquette-Bos	1.54	Wyatt-KC	81	Radatz-Bos	29	Hall-Bal	7.60	B.Lee-LA	27.9	Radatz-Bos	46.7
Radatz-Bos	181	Lamabe-Bos	2.89	Radatz-Bos	79	Heffner-Bos	6	Radatz-Bos	9.63	Radatz-Bos	25.9		
Wilson-Bos	166	Wilson-Bos	3.25	Heffner-Bos	55	3 players tied	1	Heffner-Bos	11.29				
Morehead-Bos	139	Morehead-Bos	6.05	Lamabe-Bos	39			Monbouquette-Bos	11.50				

Innings Pitched		Opponents' Avg.		Opponents' OBP		Earned Run Average		Adjusted ERA		Adjusted Starter Runs		Pitcher Wins	
Chance-LA	278.1	Horlen-Chi	.190	Horlen-Chi	.248	Chance-LA	1.65	Chance-LA	199	Chance-LA	57.7	Chance-LA	5.6
Monbouquette-Bos	234.0	Morehead-Bos	.248	Monbouquette-Bos	.306	Monbouquette-Bos	4.04	Monbouquette-Bos	96			Radatz-Bos	4.9
Wilson-Bos	202.1	Wilson-Bos	.269	Wilson-Bos	.328	Wilson-Bos	4.49	Wilson-Bos	86			Earley-Bos	.4
Lamabe-Bos	177.1	Monbouquette-Bos	.277	Morehead-Bos	.358	Morehead-Bos	4.97	Morehead-Bos	78			Ritchie-Bos	.1

1965 AMERICAN LEAGUE

TEAM	W	L	T	PCT	GB	R	OR	HR	AVG	OBP	SLG	OPS	AOPS	PF	SB	CG	HR	BB	SO	BR/9	ERA	AERA	OAV	OOB	FW	PW	BW	BSW	DIF
Min	102	60	0	.630		774	600	150	.254	.324	.399	723	+7	104	92	32	166	503	934	11.2	3.14	+13	.235	.301	-2.3	7.0	6.0	.6	9.6
Chi	95	67	0	.586	7	647	555	125	.246	.315	.364	679	+5	94	50	21	122	460	946	10.6	2.99	+7	.231	.292	.6	3.7	4.6	-.4	5.6
Bal	94	68	0	.580	8	641	578	125	.238	.307	.363	670	-6	102	67	32	120	510	939	11.0	2.98	+16	.233	.300	.6	8.4	-3.4	.0	7.3
Det	89	73	0	.549	13	680	602	162	.238	.312	.374	686	+0	101	57	45	137	509	1069	11.4	3.35	+4	.237	.306	1.3	2.1	.4	-.5	4.7
Cle	87	75	0	.537	15	663	613	156	.250	.315	.379	694	+2	101	109	41	129	500	1156	11.0	3.30	+6	.232	.298	1.4	2.2	.5	-1.3	
NY	77	85	0	.475	25	611	604	149	.235	.299	.364	663	-5	99	35	41	126	511	1001	11.6	3.28	+4	.245	.311	-.0	2.1	-4.3	-.2	-1.6
Cal	75	87	0	.463	27	527	569	92	.239	.297	.341	638	-11	99	107	39	91	563	847	11.5	3.17	+7	.237	.312	.8	3.9	-7.5	.0	-3.4
Was	70	92	0	.432	32	591	721	136	.228	.304	.350	654	-7	99	30	21	160	633	867	12.8	3.93	-12	.254	.334	-.4	-7.7	-4.4	-.3	1.6
Bos	62	100	0	.383	40	669	791	165	.251	.327	.400	727	+7	106	47	33	158	543	993	12.6	4.24	-12	.260	.327	-1.6	-8.1	6.1	-.1	-15.2
KC	59	103	0	.364	43	585	755	110	.240	.309	.358	667	-3	99	110	18	161	574	882	12.6	4.24	-18	.256	.329	-.2	-12.6	-2.0	.3	-7.5
Total	810					6388		1370	.242	.311	.369	680			704	323		5306	9634	11.6	3.46		.242	.311					

Batter-Fielder Wins		Batting Average		On-Base Percentage		Slugging Average		On-Base Plus Slugging		Adjusted OPS		Adjusted Batter Runs	
Buford-Chi	5.3	Oliva-Min	.321	Yastrzemski-Bos	.395	Yastrzemski-Bos	.536	Yastrzemski-Bos	932	Yastrzemski-Bos	154	Yastrzemski-Bos	38.1
Yastrzemski-Bos	3.5	Yastrzemski-Bos	.312	Mantilla-Bos	.374	Conigliaro-Bos	.512	Conigliaro-Bos	850	Conigliaro-Bos	131	Conigliaro-Bos	19.9
Conigliaro-Bos	2.1	Mantilla-Bos	.275	Thomas-Bos	.361	Thomas-Bos	.464	Thomas-Bos	826	Thomas-Bos	126	Thomas-Bos	19.3
Petrocelli-Bos	1.6	Thomas-Bos	.271	Conigliaro-Bos	.338	Mantilla-Bos	.416	Mantilla-Bos	790	Mantilla-Bos	118	Mantilla-Bos	15.6

Runs		Hits		Doubles		Triples		Home Runs		Total Bases		Runs Batted In	
Versalles-Min	126	Oliva-Min	185	Versalles-Min	45	Versalles-Min	12	Conigliaro-Bos	32	Versalles-Min	308	Colavito-Cle	108
Conigliaro-Bos	82	Yastrzemski-Bos	154	Yastrzemski-Bos	45	Campaneris-KC	12	Thomas-Bos	22	Conigliaro-Bos	267	Mantilla-Bos	92
Yastrzemski-Bos	78	Mantilla-Bos	147	Thomas-Bos	27	Green-Bos	6	Yastrzemski-Bos	20	Yastrzemski-Bos	265	Conigliaro-Bos	82
Thomas-Bos	74	Thomas-Bos	141	Green-Bos	24	2 players tied	5	Mantilla-Bos	18	Thomas-Bos	242	Thomas-Bos	75

Stolen Bases		Base Stealing Runs		Fielding Runs-Infield		Fielding Runs-Outfield		Wins		Winning Pct.		Complete Games	
Campaneris-KC	51	Campaneris-KC	4.6	Knoop-Cal	22.9	Conigliaro-Bos	9.0	Grant-Min	21	Grant-Min	.750	Stottlemyre-NY	18
Jones-Bos	8	Jones-Bos	1.4	Thomas-Bos	4.2	Yastrzemski-Bos	2.8	Wilson-Bos	13			Monbouquette-Bos	10
Green-Bos	8	Green-Bos	1.1					Morehead-Bos	10			Wilson-Bos	8
2 players tied	7	Geiger-Bos	.7					Monbouquette-Bos	10			Lonborg-Bos	7

Strikeouts		Fewest BB/Game		Games		Saves		Base Runners/9		Adjusted Relief Runs		Relief Ranking	
McDowell-Cle	325	Terry-Cle	1.25	Fisher-Chi	82	Kline-Was	29	Wilhelm-Chi	7.63	Wilhelm-Chi	23.3	S.Miller-Bal	44.3
Wilson-Bos	164	Monbouquette-Bos	1.57	Radatz-Bos	63	Radatz-Bos	22	Monbouquette-Bos	11.02	Ritchie-Bos	3.7	Ritchie-Bos	1.9
Morehead-Bos	163	Wilson-Bos	3.00	Earley-Bos	57	Ritchie-Bos	2	Duliba-Bos	11.47	Radatz-Bos	.0	Radatz-Bos	.0
Radatz-Bos	121	Lonborg-Bos	3.16	Ritchie-Bos	44	Duliba-Bos	1	Radatz-Bos	11.73				

Innings Pitched		Opponents' Avg.		Opponents' OBP		Earned Run Average		Adjusted ERA		Adjusted Starter Runs		Pitcher Wins	
Stottlemyre-NY	291.0	McDowell-Cle	.185	Siebert-Cle	.259	McDowell-Cle	2.18	McDowell-Cle	160	McDowell-Cle	37.5	S.Miller-Bal	4.9
Wilson-Bos	230.2	Morehead-Bos	.217	Fisher-Chi	.259	Monbouquette-Bos	3.70	Monbouquette-Bos	101			Ritchie-Bos	.2
Monbouquette-Bos	228.2	Wilson-Bos	.250	Monbouquette-Bos	.299	Wilson-Bos	3.98	Wilson-Bos	94			Wilson-Bos	.2
Morehead-Bos	192.2	Lonborg-Bos	.262	Wilson-Bos	.311	Morehead-Bos	4.06	Morehead-Bos	92			Radatz-Bos	.0

1966 AMERICAN LEAGUE

TEAM	W	L	T	PCT	GB	R	OR	HR	AVG	OBP	SLG	OPS	AOPS	PF	SB	CG	HR	BB	SO	BR/9	ERA	AERA	OAV	OOB	FW	PW	BW	BSW	DIF
Bal	97	63	0	.606		755	601	175	.258	.324	.409	733	+18	98	55	23	127	514	1070	11.1	3.32	+0	.233	.301	1.3	.2	14.0	-.4	1.9
Min	89	73	0	.549	9	663	581	144	.249	.316	.382	698	+0	106	67	52	139	392	1015	10.4	3.13	+15	.232	.286	.0	7.6	1.2	-.0	-.8
Det	88	74	0	.543	10	719	698	179	.251	.321	.406	727	+11	102	41	36	185	520	1026	11.9	3.85	-10	.247	.315	1.1	-6.3	9.5	-.4	3.2
Chi	83	79	1	.512	15	574	517	87	.231	.297	.331	628	-8	93	153	38	101	403	896	10.2	2.68	+18	.226	.282	-1.1	9.2	-4.8	.6	-1.9
Cle	81	81	0	.500	17	574	586	155	.237	.297	.360	657	-6	100	53	49	129	489	1111	11.0	3.23	+7	.232	.297	.0	3.8	-4.4	-.4	1.0
Cal	80	82	0	.494	18	604	643	122	.232	.303	.354	657	-2	97	80	31	136	511	836	11.8	3.56	-6	.251	.317	.2	-3.7	-1.5	-.2	4.1
KC	74	86	0	.463	23	564	648	70	.236	.294	.337	631	-10	97	132	19	106	630	854	12.3	3.56	-4	.241	.323	-.0	-2.7	-7.3	1.2	2.9
Was	71	88	0	.447	25.5	557	659	126	.234	.295	.355	650	-7	99	53	25	154	448	866	11.1	3.70	-7	.242	.302	-.3	-4.1	-4.9	-.2	1.0
Bos	72	90	0	.444	26	655	731	145	.240	.310	.376	686	-7	110	35	32	164	577	977	12.4	3.92	-3	.253	.325	-.9	-1.7	-3.9	-.2	-2.3
NY	70	89	1	.440	26.5	611	612	162	.235	.299	.374	673	+3	96	49	29	124	443	842	11.3	3.41	-3	.248	.306	-.3	-1.6	1.7	.0	-9.4
Total	806					6276		1365	.240	.306	.369	674			718	334		4927	9493	11.3	3.44		.240	.306					

Batter-Fielder Wins		Batting Average		On-Base Percentage		Slugging Average		On-Base Plus Slugging		Adjusted OPS		Adjusted Batter Runs	
F.Robinson-Bal	6.3	F.Robinson-Bal	.316	F.Robinson-Bal	.410	F.Robinson-Bal	.637	F.Robinson-Bal	1047	F.Robinson-Bal	200	F.Robinson-Bal	78.0
Yastrzemski-Bos	1.7	Yastrzemski-Bos	.278	Yastrzemski-Bos	.368	Conigliaro-Bos	.487	Conigliaro-Bos	817	Conigliaro-Bos	120	Yastrzemski-Bos	16.8
Foy-Bos	1.6	Conigliaro-Bos	.265	Foy-Bos	.364	Scott-Bos	.433	Yastrzemski-Bos	799	Yastrzemski-Bos	117	Conigliaro-Bos	14.3
Petrocelli-Bos	.6	Foy-Bos	.262	Conigliaro-Bos	.330	Yastrzemski-Bos	.431	Foy-Bos	778	Foy-Bos	112	Foy-Bos	12.2

Runs		Hits		Doubles		Triples		Home Runs		Total Bases		Runs Batted In	
F.Robinson-Bal	122	Oliva-Min	191	Yastrzemski-Bos	39	Knoop-Cal	11	F.Robinson-Bal	49	F.Robinson-Bal	367	F.Robinson-Bal	122
Foy-Bos	97	Yastrzemski-Bos	165	Conigliaro-Bos	26	Foy-Bos	8	Conigliaro-Bos	28	Conigliaro-Bos	272	Conigliaro-Bos	93
Yastrzemski-Bos	81	Conigliaro-Bos	148	Foy-Bos	23	Scott-Bos	7	Scott-Bos	27	Scott-Bos	260	Scott-Bos	90
Conigliaro-Bos	77	Scott-Bos	147	Petrocelli-Bos	20	Conigliaro-Bos	7	Petrocelli-Bos	18	Yastrzemski-Bos	256	Yastrzemski-Bos	80

Stolen Bases		Base Stealing Runs		Fielding Runs-Infield		Fielding Runs-Outfield		Wins		Winning Pct.		Complete Games	
Campaneris-KC	52	Campaneris-KC	7.9	Knoop-Cal	21.8	Northrup-Det	10.1	Kaat-Min	25	Siebert-Cle	.667	Kaat-Min	19
Yastrzemski-Bos	8	G.Smith-Bos	.9	Petrocelli-Bos	4.9	Yastrzemski-Bos	9.7	Santiago-Bos	12			Santiago-Bos	7
G.Smith-Bos	4	Scott-Bos	.9	Foy-Bos	3.6			Lonborg-Bos	10			Brandon-Bos	5
Scott-Bos	4	3 players tied	.2	G.Smith-Bos	1.8			Brandon-Bos	8			Lonborg-Bos	3

Strikeouts		Fewest BB/Game		Games		Saves		Base Runners/9		Adjusted Relief Runs		Relief Ranking	
McDowell-Cle	225	Kaat-Min	1.62	Fisher-Chi-Bal	67	Aker-KC	32	Wilhelm-Chi	7.52	Aker-KC	18.6	Aker-KC	28.2
Lonborg-Bos	131	Lonborg-Bos	2.72	Lonborg-Bos	45	4 players tied	2	Santiago-Bos	11.25	Osinski-Bos	.5	Osinski-Bos	.5
Santiago-Bos	119	Santiago-Bos	3.03	Osinski-Bos	44			Brandon-Bos	11.59				
Brandon-Bos	101			Brandon-Bos	40			Lonborg-Bos	11.64				

Innings Pitched		Opponents' Avg.		Opponents' OBP		Earned Run Average		Adjusted ERA		Adjusted Starter Runs		Pitcher Wins	
Kaat-Min	304.2	McDowell-Cle	.188	Peters-Chi	.260	Peters-Chi	1.98	Peters-Chi	160	Peters-Chi	28.9	Peters-Chi	4.0
Lonborg-Bos	181.2	Santiago-Bos	.238	Santiago-Bos	.300	Santiago-Bos	3.66	Santiago-Bos	104	Brandon-Bos	6.5	Brandon-Bos	.8
Santiago-Bos	172.0	Lonborg-Bos	.249	Lonborg-Bos	.308	Lonborg-Bos	3.86	Lonborg-Bos	99	Bennett-Bos	4.6	Fischer-Bos	.5
Brandon-Bos	157.2									Fischer-Bos	2.6	Bennett-Bos	.4

1967 AMERICAN LEAGUE

TEAM	W	L	T	PCT	GB	R	OR	HR	AVG	OBP	SLG	OPS	AOPS	PF	SB	CG	HR	BB	SO	BR/9	ERA	AERA	OAV	OOB	FW	PW	BW	BSW	DIF
Bos	92	70	0	.568		**722**	614	**158**	**.255**	.321	**.395**	**716**	+9	108	68	41	142	477	1010	11.3	3.36	+4	.239	.304	-.6	2.1	7.3	-.5	2.7
Min	91	71	2	.562	1	671	590	131	.240	.309	.369	678	-2	108	55	**58**	115	**396**	1089	10.9	3.14	+10	.243	.296	.1	5.4	-.4	.0	4.8
Det	91	71	1	.562	1	683	587	152	.243	**.325**	.376	701	**+11**	103	37	46	151	472	1038	10.8	3.32	-2	.230	.295	.0	-1.0	**9.3**	.3	1.4
Chi	89	73	0	.549	3	531	**491**	89	.225	.291	.320	611	-10	96	124	36	**87**	465	927	**10.4**	**2.45**	**+27**	**.219**	**.287**	-.3	**12.4**	-6.8	.0	2.8
Cal	84	77	0	.522	7.5	567	587	114	.238	.301	.349	650	+2	96	40	19	118	525	892	11.4	3.19	-2	.237	.308	**1.3**	-.9	.8	-.3	2.6
Was	76	85	0	.472	15.5	550	637	115	.223	.288	.326	614	-9	96	53	24	113	495	878	11.4	3.38	-7	.242	.307	-.8	-4.1	-6.8	.0	7.1
Bal	76	85	0	.472	15.5	654	592	138	.240	.310	.372	682	+9	99	54	29	116	566	1034	11.2	3.32	-5	.228	.304	.5	-3.1	6.7	.0	-8.7
Cle	75	87	0	.463	17	559	613	131	.235	.293	.359	652	-3	101	53	49	120	559	**1189**	11.3	3.25	+1	.231	.305	1.0	.3	-2.2	-1.0	-4.1
NY	72	90	1	.444	20	522	621	100	.225	.296	.317	613	-10	96	63	37	110	480	898	11.5	3.24	-3	.249	.310	-1.3	-2.1	-6.1	.3	.2
KC	62	99	0	.385	29.5	533	660	69	.233	.296	.330	626	-6	97	**132**	26	125	558	990	11.7	3.68	-13	.238	.313	-.0	-8.8	-4.1	**1.0**	-6.6
Total	810					5992		1197	.236	.303	.351	654			679	365		4993	9945	11.2	3.23		.236	.303					

Batter-Fielder Wins	Batting Average	On-Base Percentage	Slugging Average	On-Base Plus Slugging	Adjusted OPS	Adjusted Batter Runs
Yastrzemski-Bos 6.9	Yastrzemski-Bos .326	Yastrzemski-Bos .418	Yastrzemski-Bos .622	Yastrzemski-Bos 1040	F.Robinson-Bal 189	Yastrzemski-Bos 67.2
Petrocelli-Bos 2.6	Scott-Bos .303	Scott-Bos .373	Scott-Bos .465	Scott-Bos 839	Yastrzemski-Bos 189	Scott-Bos 26.7
Conigliaro-Bos 1.3	Andrews-Bos .263	Andrews-Bos .346	Petrocelli-Bos .420	Petrocelli-Bos 750	Scott-Bos 136	Conigliaro-Bos 16.7
Andrews-Bos 1.1	Petrocelli-Bos .259	Petrocelli-Bos .330	Smith-Bos .389	Smith-Bos 704	Petrocelli-Bos 112	Petrocelli-Bos 7.9

Runs	Hits	Doubles	Triples	Home Runs	Total Bases	Runs Batted In
Yastrzemski-Bos 112	Yastrzemski-Bos 189	Oliva-Min 34	Blair-Bal 12	Killebrew-Min 44	Yastrzemski-Bos 360	Yastrzemski-Bos 121
Andrews-Bos 79	Scott-Bos 171	Yastrzemski-Bos 31	Scott-Bos 7	Yastrzemski-Bos 44	Scott-Bos 263	Scott-Bos 82
Smith-Bos 78	Smith-Bos 139	Smith-Bos 24	Smith-Bos 6	Conigliaro-Bos 20	Smith-Bos 220	Conigliaro-Bos 67
Scott-Bos 74	Andrews-Bos 130	Petrocelli-Bos 24	Conigliaro-Bos 5	Scott-Bos 19	Petrocelli-Bos 206	Petrocelli-Bos 66

Stolen Bases	Base Stealing Runs	Fielding Runs-Infield	Fielding Runs-Outfield	Wins	Winning Pct.	Complete Games
Campaneris-KC 55	Campaneris-KC 6.5	B.Robinson-Bal 32.1	Blair-Bal 9.1	Wilson-Det 22	Horlen-Chi .731	Chance-Min 18
Smith-Bos 16	Smith-Bos 1.4	Petrocelli-Bos 5.3	Yastrzemski-Bos 6.3	Lonborg-Bos 22	Lonborg-Bos .710	Lonborg-Bos 15
Yastrzemski-Bos 10	Ryan-Bos .4		Smith-Bos .3	Santiago-Bos 12		Stange-Bos 6
Scott-Bos 10				Wyatt-Bos 10		Bennett-Bos 4

Strikeouts	Fewest BB/Game	Games	Saves	Base Runners/9	Adjusted Relief Runs	Relief Ranking
Lonborg-Bos 246	Merritt-Min 1.19	Locker-Chi 77	Rojas-Cal 27	Horlen-Chi 8.72	Wilhelm-Chi 16.1	Wilhelm-Chi 22.4
Santiago-Bos 109	Stange-Bos 1.59	Wyatt-Bos 60	Wyatt-Bos 20	Stange-Bos 10.16	Wyatt-Bos 8.6	Wyatt-Bos 17.3
Stange-Bos 101	Lonborg-Bos 2.73	Santiago-Bos 50	Santiago-Bos 5	Osinski-Bos 10.60	Osinski-Bos 6.7	Osinski-Bos 4.2
Brandon-Bos 96		2 players tied 39	Lyle-Bos 5	Wyatt-Bos 10.80	Santiago-Bos .2	Santiago-Bos .2

Innings Pitched	Opponents' Avg.	Opponents' OBP	Earned Run Average	Adjusted ERA	Adjusted Starter Runs	Pitcher Wins
Chance-Min 283.2	Peters-Chi .199	Horlen-Chi .253	Horlen-Chi 2.06	Horlen-Chi 151	Horlen-Chi 33.5	Horlen-Chi 3.8
Lonborg-Bos 273.1	Lonborg-Bos .225	Stange-Bos .281	Stange-Bos 2.77	Stange-Bos 126	Stange-Bos 12.9	Wyatt-Bos 1.9
Stange-Bos 181.2	Stange-Bos .246	Lonborg-Bos .294	Lonborg-Bos 3.16	Lonborg-Bos 110	Lonborg-Bos 11.7	Lonborg-Bos 1.0
Brandon-Bos 157.2					Waslewski-Bos .7	Stange-Bos .9

1968 AMERICAN LEAGUE

TEAM	W	L	T	PCT	GB	R	OR	HR	AVG	OBP	SLG	OPS	AOPS	PF	SB	CG	HR	BB	SO	BR/9	ERA	AERA	OAV	OOB	FW	PW	BW	BSW	DIF
Det	103	59	2	.636		**671**	**492**	**185**	.235	.307	**.385**	**692**	**+13**	103	26	**59**	129	486	1115	**10.3**	2.71	+11	.217	**.284**	**2.0**	5.6	**9.6**	-.7	5.4
Bal	91	71	0	.562	12	579	497	133	.225	.304	.352	656	+5	100	78	53	101	502	1044	**10.3**	**2.66**	+10	.212	.285	1.0	4.9	5.3	.5	-1.8
Cle	86	75	1	.534	16.5	516	504	75	.234	.293	.327	620	-4	98	115	48	98	540	**1157**	**10.3**	**2.66**	**+12**	**.206**	.285	.6	**5.8**	-2.9	.3	1.6
Bos	86	76	0	.531	17	614	611	125	.236	**.313**	.352	665	+2	106	76	55	115	523	972	11.7	3.33	-5	.241	.312	.6	-3.1	3.6	-.7	4.7
NY	83	79	2	.512	20	536	531	109	.214	.292	.318	610	-6	97	90	45	99	424	831	10.8	2.79	+4	.240	.297	.0	2.3	-3.6	.0	3.2
Oak	82	80	1	.506	21	569	544	94	**.240**	.304	.343	647	+7	96	**147**	45	124	505	997	10.9	2.94	-4	.227	.295	-.4	-2.4	5.0	**1.1**	-2.3
Min	79	83	0	.488	24	562	546	105	.237	.299	.350	649	-2	106	98	46	**92**	**414**	996	10.5	2.89	+7	.229	.288	-2.0	3.3	-1.1	.2	-2.4
Cal	67	95	0	.414	36	498	615	83	.227	.291	.318	609	-6	97	62	29	131	519	869	11.2	3.43	-15	.233	.303	-.2	-9.6	-4.2	-.6	.7
Chi	67	95	0	.414	36	463	527	71	.228	.284	.311	595	-14	101	90	20	97	451	834	11.1	2.75	+10	.236	.301	-.8	5.2	-10.4	.0	-8.0
Was	65	96	0	.404	37.5	524	665	124	.224	.287	.336	623	-2	97	29	26	118	517	826	12.3	3.64	-20	.258	.325	-.7	-13.5	-1.9	-.2	.8
Total	812					5532		1104	.230	.297	.339	637			811	426		4881	9641	10.9	2.98		.230	.297					

Batter-Fielder Wins	Batting Average	On-Base Percentage	Slugging Average	On-Base Plus Slugging	Adjusted OPS	Adjusted Batter Runs
Yastrzemski-Bos 6.3	Yastrzemski-Bos .301	Yastrzemski-Bos .426	F.Howard-Was .552	Yastrzemski-Bos 922	F.Howard-Was 173	Yastrzemski-Bos 53.1
Andrews-Bos 3.3	Harrelson-Bos .275	Andrews-Bos .368	Harrelson-Bos .518	Harrelson-Bos 874	Yastrzemski-Bos 169	Harrelson-Bos 34.8
Harrelson-Bos 3.1	Andrews-Bos .271	Harrelson-Bos .356	Yastrzemski-Bos .495	Smith-Bos 772	Harrelson-Bos 154	Smith-Bos 19.4
Petrocelli-Bos 2.1	Smith-Bos .265	Smith-Bos .342	Smith-Bos .430	Andrews-Bos 723	Smith-Bos 126	Andrews-Bos 12.9

Runs	Hits	Doubles	Triples	Home Runs	Total Bases	Runs Batted In
McAuliffe-Det 95	Campaneris-Oak 177	Smith-Bos 37	Fregosi-Cal 13	F.Howard-Was 44	F.Howard-Was 330	Harrelson-Bos 109
Yastrzemski-Bos 90	Yastrzemski-Bos 162	Yastrzemski-Bos 32	Smith-Bos 5	Harrelson-Bos 35	Harrelson-Bos 277	Yastrzemski-Bos 74
Harrelson-Bos 79	Smith-Bos 148	Andrews-Bos 22	Harrelson-Bos 4	Yastrzemski-Bos 23	Yastrzemski-Bos 267	Smith-Bos 69
Smith-Bos 78	Harrelson-Bos 147	Foy-Bos 18	3 players tied 2	Smith-Bos 15	Smith-Bos 240	Foy-Bos 60

Stolen Bases	Base Stealing Runs	Fielding Runs-Infield	Fielding Runs-Outfield	Wins	Winning Pct.	Complete Games
Campaneris-Oak 62	Campaneris-Oak 5.9	Clarke-NY 29.0	Yastrzemski-Bos 11.2	McLain-Det 31	McLain-Det .838	McLain-Det 28
Foy-Bos 26	Foy-Bos 2.9	Petrocelli-Bos 11.4	Harrelson-Bos 4.3	Ellsworth-Bos 16	Culp-Bos .727	Culp-Bos 11
Smith-Bos 22	Yastrzemski-Bos .8	Andrews-Bos 6.1	Smith-Bos 1.9	Culp-Bos 16	Ellsworth-Bos .696	Ellsworth-Bos 10
Yastrzemski-Bos 13	Thomas-Bos .2	Foy-Bos 2.5		Bell-Bos 11		Bell-Bos 9

Strikeouts	Fewest BB/Game	Games	Saves	Base Runners/9	Adjusted Relief Runs	Relief Ranking
McDowell-Cle 283	Peterson-NY 1.23	Wood-Chi 88	Worthington-Min 18	McNally-Bal 7.91	Wood-Chi 20.0	Wood-Chi 32.9
Culp-Bos 190	Ellsworth-Bos 1.70	Stange-Bos 50	Stange-Bos 12	Stange-Bos 10.05	Lyle-Bos 1.9	Lyle-Bos 2.6
Ellsworth-Bos 106	Bell-Bos 3.07	Lyle-Bos 49	Lyle-Bos 11	Santiago-Bos 10.23	Landis-Bos .8	Landis-Bos .8
Bell-Bos 103	Culp-Bos 3.41	Landis-Bos 38	Landis-Bos 3	Culp-Bos 10.69		

Innings Pitched	Opponents' Avg.	Opponents' OBP	Earned Run Average	Adjusted ERA	Adjusted Starter Runs	Pitcher Wins
McLain-Det 336.0	Tiant-Cle .168	McNally-Bal .232	Tiant-Cle 1.60	Tiant-Cle 185	Tiant-Cle 39.7	Tiant-Cle 4.4
Culp-Bos 216.1	Culp-Bos .210	Culp-Bos .291	Culp-Bos 2.91	Culp-Bos 108	Santiago-Bos 12.3	McLain-Det 4.4
Bell-Bos 199.1	Bell-Bos .239	Ellsworth-Bos .300	Ellsworth-Bos 3.03	Ellsworth-Bos 104	Culp-Bos 5.8	Santiago-Bos 1.5
Ellsworth-Bos 196.0	Ellsworth-Bos .260	Bell-Bos .306	Bell-Bos 3.12	Bell-Bos 101	Morehead-Bos 4.1	Culp-Bos .4

1969 AMERICAN LEAGUE

TEAM	W	L	T	PCT	GB	R	OR	HR	AVG	OBP	SLG	OPS	AOPS	PF	SB	CG	HR	BB	SO	BR/9	ERA	AERA	OAV	OOB	FW	PW	BW	BSW	DIF
East																													
Bal	109	53	0	.673		779	**517**	175	.265	**.343**	.414	757	+17	101	82	50	**117**	498	897	**10.5**	**2.83**	**+27**	**.223**	.290	**2.2**	**13.1**	**13.7**	-.0	-1.0
Det	90	72	0	.556	19	701	601	182	.242	.316	.387	703	-1	104	35	**55**	128	586	**1032**	11.6	3.31	+13	.232	.310	.5	7.2	-1.0	-.5	2.7
Bos	87	75	0	.537	22	743	736	**197**	.251	.333	**.415**	748	+10	105	41	30	155	685	935	13.2	3.92	-3	.256	.341	-1.0	-1.7	8.2	-1.0	1.5
Was	86	76	0	.531	23	694	644	148	.251	.330	.378	708	+10	95	52	28	135	656	835	12.4	3.49	+0	.244	.328	-.0	.2	7.8	-.6	-2.4
NY	80	81	1	.497	28.5	562	587	94	.235	.308	.344	652	-9	97	119	53	118	522	801	11.2	3.23	+9	.236	.304	.5	4.9	-5.6	-.2	-.1
Cle	62	99	0	.385	46.5	573	717	119	.237	.307	.345	652	-15	103	85	35	134	681	1000	12.9	3.94	-4	.248	.335	-.4	-2.3	-10.0	.4	-6.2
West																													
Min	97	65	0	.599		**790**	618	163	**.268**	.340	.408	748	+13	103	115	41	119	524	906	11.7	3.24	+12	.246	.313	-.6	6.9	10.5	-.1	-.7
Oak	88	74	0	.543	9	740	678	148	.249	.329	.376	705	+8	96	100	42	163	586	887	12.0	3.71	-7	.245	.320	.2	-5.0	6.4	.6	4.8
Cal	71	91	1	.438	26	528	652	88	.230	.300	.319	619	-17	-96	54	25	126	517	885	11.7	3.54	-1	.242	.313	.2	-.8	-12.5	-.5	3.5
KC	69	93	1	.426	28	586	688	98	.240	.309	.338	647	-14	101	129	42	136	560	894	11.9	3.72	-1	.246	.316	-1.0	-.4	-9.9	-.2	-.9
Chi	68	94	0	.420	29	625	723	112	.247	.320	.357	677	-8	105	54	29	146	564	810	12.9	4.21	-9	.267	.337	1.0	-5.8	-5.6	.2	-2.8
Sea	64	98	1	.395	33	639	799	125	.234	.316	.346	662	-8	99	**167**	21	172	653	963	13.5	4.35	-16	.264	.343	-1.5	-12.1	-5.1	**1.4**	.3
Total	973					7960		1649	.246	.321	.369	690			1033	451		7032	0845	12.1	3.62		.246	.321					

Batter-Fielder Wins — Petrocelli-Bos 7.6; Andrews-Bos 3.0; Yastrzemski-Bos 2.7; Smith-Bos 1.9

Batting Average — Carew-Min .332; Smith-Bos .309; Petrocelli-Bos .297; Andrews-Bos .293

On-Base Percentage — Killebrew-Min .427; Petrocelli-Bos .403; Andrews-Bos .390; Smith-Bos .368

Slugging Average — Jackson-Oak .608; Petrocelli-Bos .589; Smith-Bos .527; Yastrzemski-Bos .507

On-Base Plus Slugging — Jackson-Oak 1018; Petrocelli-Bos 992; Smith-Bos 895; Yastrzemski-Bos 870

Adjusted OPS — Jackson-Oak 189; Petrocelli-Bos 168; Smith-Bos 142; Yastrzemski-Bos 135

Adjusted Batter Runs — Jackson-Oak 69.6; Petrocelli-Bos 50.9; Smith-Bos 29.7; Yastrzemski-Bos 29.1

Runs — Jackson-Oak 123; Yastrzemski-Bos 96; Petrocelli-Bos 92; Smith-Bos 87

Hits — Oliva-Min 197; Smith-Bos 168; Petrocelli-Bos 159; Yastrzemski-Bos 154

Doubles — Oliva-Min 39; Petrocelli-Bos 32; Smith-Bos 29; Yastrzemski-Bos 28

Triples — Unser-Was 8; Smith-Bos 7; Scott-Bos 5; O'Brien-Bos 5

Home Runs — Killebrew-Min 49; Yastrzemski-Bos 40; Petrocelli-Bos 40; Smith-Bos 25

Total Bases — Howard-Was 340; Petrocelli-Bos 315; Yastrzemski-Bos 306; Smith-Bos 286

Runs Batted In — Killebrew-Min 140; Yastrzemski-Bos 111; Petrocelli-Bos 97; Smith-Bos 93

Stolen Bases — Harper-Sea 73; Yastrzemski-Bos 15; Smith-Bos 7; Scott-Bos 4

Base Stealing Runs — Campaneris-Oak 10.8; Yastrzemski-Bos .9; Nagy-Bos .2; Landis-Bos .2

Fielding Runs-Infield — Knoop-Cal-Chi 32.5; Aparicio-Chi 32.5; Petrocelli-Bos 6.3

Fielding Runs-Outfield — Blair-Bal 11.7; Yastrzemski-Bos 3.3

Wins — McLain-Det 24; Culp-Bos 17; Nagy-Bos 12; Lyle-Bos 8

Winning Pct. — Palmer-Bal .800; Culp-Bos .680

Complete Games — Stottlemyre-NY 24; Culp-Bos 9; Nagy-Bos 7; Lonborg-Bos 4

Strikeouts — McDowell-Cle 279; Culp-Bos 172; Lonborg-Bos 100; Lyle-Bos 93

Fewest BB/Game — Peterson-NY 1.42; Culp-Bos 3.13; Nagy-Bos 4.85

Games — Wood-Chi 76; Lyle-Bos 71; Landis-Bos 45; Stange-Bos 41

Saves — Perranoski-Min 31; Lyle-Bos 17; Stange-Bos 3; 3 players tied 1

Base Runners/9 — Hall-Bal 8.09; Culp-Bos 11.10; Lyle-Bos 12.27; Stange-Bos 13.07

Adjusted Relief Runs — K.Tatum-Cal 22.2; Lyle-Bos 14.0

Relief Ranking — Perranoski-Min 40.7; Lyle-Bos 18.7

Innings Pitched — McLain-Det 325.0; Culp-Bos 227.0; Nagy-Bos 196.2; Lonborg-Bos 143.2

Opponents' Avg. — Messersmith-Cal .190; Culp-Bos .231; Nagy-Bos .245

Opponents' OBP — Cuellar-Bal .260; Bosman-Was .260; Culp-Bos .299; Nagy-Bos .347

Earned Run Average — Bosman-Was 2.19; Nagy-Bos 3.11; Culp-Bos 3.81

Adjusted ERA — Bosman-Was 160; Nagy-Bos 123; Culp-Bos 100

Adjusted Starter Runs — McLain-Det 37.2; Nagy-Bos 12.3; Culp-Bos 3.4

Pitcher Wins — Perranoski-Min 4.3; Lyle-Bos 2.0; Nagy-Bos .6; Culp-Bos .4

1970 AMERICAN LEAGUE

TEAM	W	L	T	PCT	GB	R	OR	HR	AVG	OBP	SLG	OPS	AOPS	PF	SB	CG	HR	BB	SO	BR/9	ERA	AERA	OAV	OOB	FW	PW	BW	BSW	DIF
East																													
Bal	108	54	0	.667		**792**	**574**	179	.257	**.344**	.401	745	+10	102	84	60	139	469	941	**11.0**	3.15	**+17**	.240	**.300**	1.1	9.1	9.5	.6	6.7
NY	93	69	1	.574	15	680	612	111	.251	.324	.365	689	+0	96	105	36	**130**	**451**	777	11.4	3.24	+10	.249	.306	.4	5.8	1.2	.3	4.3
Bos	87	75	0	.537	21	786	722	**203**	.262	.335	**.428**	**763**	+9	101	50	38	156	594	1003	12.6	3.87	+3	.251	.327	-1.2	1.8	7.5	-.6	-1.5
Det	79	83	0	.488	29	666	731	148	.238	.322	.374	696	-3	101	29	33	153	623	1045	13.1	4.09	-8	.260	.336	.2	-5.4	-.9	-.4	4.5
Cle	76	86	0	.469	32	649	675	183	.249	.314	.394	708	-4	105	25	34	163	689	**1076**	12.8	3.91	+2	.247	.335	.2	1.6	-3.1	-.7	-2.9
Was	70	92	0	.432	38	626	689	138	.238	.321	.358	679	-3	96	72	60	139	611	823	12.6	3.80	-5	.252	.328	1.1	-3.3	-.6	.2	-8.4
West																													
Min	98	64	0	.605		744	605	153	**.262**	.327	.403	730	+5	97	57	26	130	486	940	11.5	3.23	+14	.244	.308	.7	7.9	.4	-.6	4.9
Oak	89	73	0	.549	9	678	593	171	.249	.325	.392	717	+7	97	**131**	33	134	542	858	11.4	3.30	+7	**.234**	.307	-.3	3.9	5.4	.6	-1.6
Cal	86	76	0	.531	12	631	630	114	.251	.309	.363	672	-6	97	69	21	154	559	922	11.6	3.48	+4	.237	.312	.5	-2.4	.7	**.7**	6.5
Mil	65	97	1	.401	33	613	751	126	.242	.319	.358	677	-7	100	91	31	146	587	895	12.6	4.21	-10	.255	.330	.0	-7.1	-4.3	-.6	-4.2
KC	65	97	0	.401	33	611	705	97	.244	.309	.348	657	-13	100	97	30	138	641	915	12.4	3.78	-1	.247	.328	-.9	-.8	-9.6	.4	-5.0
Chi	56	106	0	.346	42	633	822	123	.253	.315	.362	677	-10	104	53	20	164	556	762	13.6	4.54	-15	.280	.347	-1.7	-10.5	-7.6	.0	-5.3
Total	973					8109		1746	.250	.322	.379	701			863	382		6808	0957	12.2	3.71		.250	.322					

Batter-Fielder Wins — Harper-Mil 5.6; Yastrzemski-Bos 5.5; Petrocelli-Bos 2.7; Smith-Bos 2.4

Batting Average — Johnson-Cal .329; Yastrzemski-Bos .329; Smith-Bos .303; Scott-Bos .296

On-Base Percentage — Yastrzemski-Bos .452; Smith-Bos .361; Scott-Bos .355; Andrews-Bos .344

Slugging Average — Yastrzemski-Bos .592; T.Conigliaro-Bos .498; Smith-Bos .497; Petrocelli-Bos .473

On-Base Plus Slugging — Yastrzemski-Bos 1044; Smith-Bos 858; T.Conigliaro-Bos 822; Scott-Bos 821

Adjusted OPS — Yastrzemski-Bos 174; Smith-Bos 126; Scott-Bos 118; T.Conigliaro-Bos 117

Adjusted Batter Runs — Yastrzemski-Bos 64.5; Smith-Bos 20.5; Scott-Bos 11.3; Petrocelli-Bos 10.8

Runs — Yastrzemski-Bos 125; Smith-Bos 109; Andrews-Bos 91; T.Conigliaro-Bos 89

Hits — Oliva-Min 204; Yastrzemski-Bos 186; Smith-Bos 176; Petrocelli-Bos 152

Doubles — 3 players tied 36; Smith-Bos 32; Petrocelli-Bos 31; Yastrzemski-Bos 29

Triples — Tovar-Min 13; Smith-Bos 7; Scott-Bos 5; 2 players tied 3

Home Runs — Howard-Was 44; Yastrzemski-Bos 40; T.Conigliaro-Bos 36; Petrocelli-Bos 29

Total Bases — Yastrzemski-Bos 335; Smith-Bos 288; T.Conigliaro-Bos 279; Petrocelli-Bos 276

Runs Batted In — Howard-Was 126; T.Conigliaro-Bos 116; Petrocelli-Bos 103; Yastrzemski-Bos 102

Stolen Bases — Campaneris-Oak 42; Yastrzemski-Bos 23; Smith-Bos 10; 2 players tied 4

Base Stealing Runs — Otis-KC 6.6; Yastrzemski-Bos .5; Pavletich-Bos .2; T.Conigliaro-Bos .2

Fielding Runs-Infield — Brinkman-Was 31.4

Fielding Runs-Outfield — Oliva-Min 13.3; Smith-Bos 6.8; B.Conigliaro-Bos 1.6

Wins — 3 players tied 24; Culp-Bos 17; Peters-Bos 16; Siebert-Bos 15

Winning Pct. — Cuellar-Bal .750; Siebert-Bos .652; Peters-Bos .593; Culp-Bos .548

Complete Games — Cuellar-Bal 21; Culp-Bos 15; Peters-Bos 10; Siebert-Bos 7

Strikeouts — McDowell-Cle 304; Culp-Bos 197; Peters-Bos 155; Brett-Bos 155

Fewest BB/Game — Peterson-NY 1.38; Siebert-Bos 2.43; Culp-Bos 3.26; Brett-Bos 3.37

Games — Wood-Chi 77; Lyle-Bos 63; Romo-Bos 48; Brett-Bos 41

Saves — Perranoski-Min 34; Lyle-Bos 20; Wagner-Bos 7; Romo-Bos 6

Base Runners/9 — Hall-Bal 8.36; Siebert-Bos 11.03; Culp-Bos 11.21; Koonce-Bos 11.32

Adjusted Relief Runs — Grant-Oak 25.6; Romo-Bos 1.1

Relief Ranking — McDaniel-NY 32.4; Romo-Bos 1.1

Innings Pitched — Palmer-Bal 305.0; McDowell-Cle 305.0; Culp-Bos 251.1; Siebert-Bos 222.2

Opponents' Avg. — Messersmith-Cal .205; Culp-Bos .224; Siebert-Bos .248; Peters-Bos .257

Opponents' OBP — Peterson-NY .279; Culp-Bos .299; Siebert-Bos .302; Peters-Bos .325

Earned Run Average — Segui-Oak 2.56; Culp-Bos 3.04; Siebert-Bos 3.44; Peters-Bos 4.06

Adjusted ERA — Segui-Oak 138; Culp-Bos 131; Siebert-Bos 116; Peters-Bos 98

Adjusted Starter Runs — Palmer-Bal 35.0; Culp-Bos 22.1; Siebert-Bos 12.7; Koonce-Bos 4.6

Pitcher Wins — McDaniel-NY 3.5; Culp-Bos 2.2; Siebert-Bos 1.1; Lonborg-Bos .8

1971 AMERICAN LEAGUE

TEAM	W	L	T	PCT	GB	R	OR	HR	AVG	OBP	SLG	OPS	AOPS	PF	SB	CG	HR	BB	SO	BR/9	ERA	AERA	OAV	OOB	FW	PW	BW	BSW	DIF
East																													
Bal	101	57	0	.639		**742**	**530**	158	**.261**	**.347**	.398	**745**	**+17**	101	66	**71**	125	**416**	793	**10.8**	**2.99**	**+14**	.239	**.295**	.7	7.1	**14.2**	.1	-.0
Det	91	71	0	.562	12	701	645	**179**	.254	.325	**.405**	730	+8	104	35	53	126	609	**1000**	12.3	3.63	+0	.247	.325	**1.2**	-.3	6.2	-.7	3.6
Bos	85	77	0	.525	18	691	667	161	.252	.322	.397	719	+2	107	51	44	136	535	871	12.5	3.80	-2	.259	.327	.6	-1.4	2.6	-.0	2.3
NY	82	80	0	.506	21	648	641	97	.254	.328	.360	688	+7	95	75	67	126	423	707	11.3	3.43	-4	.252	.306	.1	-2.8	5.8	-.3	-1.8
Was	63	96	0	.396	38.5	537	660	86	.230	.307	.326	633	-10	95	68	30	132	554	762	12.5	3.70	-9	.258	.331	-1.0	-5.7	-6.6	-.0	-3.2
Cle	60	102	0	.370	43	543	747	109	.238	.300	.342	642	-20	110	57	21	154	770	937	13.6	4.28	-10	.252	.348	.6	-6.3	-14.1	.0	-1.2
West																													
Oak	101	60	0	.627		691	564	160	.252	.321	.384	705	+8	98	80	57	131	501	999	**10.8**	3.05	+9	**.228**	.296	.5	4.9	5.8	-.0	9.3
KC	85	76	0	.528	16	603	566	80	.250	.313	.353	666	-4	99	**130**	34	**84**	496	775	11.6	3.25	+6	.247	.314	-.4	3.2	-2.5	**1.4**	2.7
Chi	79	83	0	.488	22.5	617	597	138	.250	.325	.373	698	+1	103	83	46	100	468	976	11.4	3.12	**+14**	.247	.307	-1.9	**7.3**	1.7	-.4	-8.7
Cal	76	86	0	.469	25.5	511	576	96	.231	.290	.329	619	-13	-93	72	39	101	607	904	11.5	3.10	+5	.230	.310	-.2	2.7	-10.2	.4	2.3
Min	74	86	0	.463	26.5	654	670	116	.260	.323	.372	695	+0	103	66	43	139	529	895	12.4	3.81	-7	.257	.326	.4	-4.6	1.0	-.0	-2.7
Mil	69	92	0	.429	32	534	609	104	.229	.304	.329	633	-14	99	82	32	130	569	795	12.1	3.38	+3	.247	.321	-.7	1.7	-9.1	-.0	-3.3
Total	966					7472		1484	.247	.317	.364	681			865	537		6477	0414	11.9	3.46		.247	.317					

Batter-Fielder Wins		Batting Average		On-Base Percentage		Slugging Average		On-Base Plus Slugging		Adjusted OPS		Adjusted Batter Runs	
Nettles-Cle	**5.9**	Oliva-Min	.337	Murcer-NY	.427	Oliva-Min	.546	Murcer-NY	969	Murcer-NY	182	Murcer-NY	60.5
Smith-Bos	**2.6**	Smith-Bos	.283	Yastrzemski-Bos	.381	Smith-Bos	.489	Smith-Bos	840	Smith-Bos	127	Smith-Bos	22.2
Petrocelli-Bos	**1.7**	Scott-Bos	.263	Petrocelli-Bos	.354	Petrocelli-Bos	.461	Petrocelli-Bos	815	Petrocelli-Bos	122	Petrocelli-Bos	17.6
Yastrzemski-Bos	**1.6**	Yastrzemski-Bos	.254	Smith-Bos	.352	Scott-Bos	.441	Yastrzemski-Bos	772	Yastrzemski-Bos	112	Yastrzemski-Bos	13.0

Runs		Hits		Doubles		Triples		Home Runs		Total Bases		Runs Batted In	
Buford-Bal	99	Tovar-Min	204	Smith-Bos	33	Patek-KC	11	Melton-Chi	33	Smith-Bos	302	Killebrew-Min	119
Smith-Bos	85	Smith-Bos	175	Conigliaro-Bos	26	Kennedy-Bos	5	Smith-Bos	30	Petrocelli-Bos	255	Smith-Bos	96
Petrocelli-Bos	82	Scott-Bos	141	Petrocelli-Bos	24	Scott-Bos	4	Petrocelli-Bos	28	Scott-Bos	237	Petrocelli-Bos	89
Yastrzemski-Bos	75	Petrocelli-Bos	139	2 players tied	23	Petrocelli-Bos	4	Scott-Bos	24	Yastrzemski-Bos	199	Scott-Bos	78

Stolen Bases		Base Stealing Runs		Fielding Runs-Infield		Fielding Runs-Outfield		Wins		Winning Pct.		Complete Games	
Otis-KC	52	Otis-KC	8.6	Nettles-Cle	46.1	Tovar-Min	14.1	Lolich-Det	25	McNally-Bal	.808	Lolich-Det	29
Smith-Bos	11	Smith-Bos	1.4	Griffin-Bos	6.3	Yastrzemski-Bos	10.7	Siebert-Bos	16	Siebert-Bos	.615	Siebert-Bos	12
Griffin-Bos	11	Griffin-Bos	.7			Smith-Bos	7.1	Peters-Bos	14			Culp-Bos	12
Yastrzemski-Bos	8	2 players tied	.4					Culp-Bos	14			Peters-Bos	9

Strikeouts		Fewest BB/Game		Games		Saves		Base Runners/9		Adjusted Relief Runs		Relief Ranking	
Lolich-Det	308	Peterson-NY	1.38	Sanders-Mil	83	Sanders-Mil	31	Blue-Oak	8.68	Sanders-Mil	22.9	Sanders-Mil	40.5
Culp-Bos	151	Siebert-Bos	2.29	Bolin-Bos	52	Lyle-Bos	16	Siebert-Bos	10.82	Lee-Bos	9.9	Lee-Bos	10.0
Siebert-Bos	131	Culp-Bos	2.49	Lyle-Bos	50	Tatum-Bos	9	Culp-Bos	11.44				
2 players tied	100	Peters-Bos	2.94	Lee-Bos	47	Bolin-Bos	6	Moret-Bos	11.66				

Innings Pitched		Opponents' Avg.		Opponents' OBP		Earned Run Average		Adjusted ERA		Adjusted Starter Runs		Pitcher Wins	
Lolich-Det	376.0	Blue-Oak	.189	Blue-Oak	.251	Blue-Oak	1.82	Wood-Chi	186	Wood-Chi	55.1	Wood-Chi	5.7
Culp-Bos	242.1	Siebert-Bos	.245	Siebert-Bos	.292	Siebert-Bos	2.91	Siebert-Bos	128	Siebert-Bos	19.3	Siebert-Bos	3.3
Siebert-Bos	235.1	Culp-Bos	.253	Culp-Bos	.305	Culp-Bos	3.60	Culp-Bos	103	Moret-Bos	6.4	Lyle-Bos	1.5
Peters-Bos	214.0	Lonborg-Bos	.259	Lonborg-Bos	.341	Lonborg-Bos	4.13	Lonborg-Bos	90	Curtis-Bos	2.0	Lee-Bos	1.2

1972 AMERICAN LEAGUE

TEAM	W	L	T	PCT	GB	R	OR	HR	AVG	OBP	SLG	OPS	AOPS	PF	SB	CG	HR	BB	SO	BR/9	ERA	AERA	OAV	OOB	FW	PW	BW	BSW	DIF
East																													
Det	86	70	0	.551		558	514	122	.237	.305	.356	661	-1	104	17	46	101	465	952	11.2	2.96	+7	.236	.304	**1.9**	3.4	-.2	-.4	3.3
Bos	85	70	0	.548	0.5	**640**	620	124	.248	.318	**.376**	**694**	+7	106	66	48	101	512	918	12.1	3.47	-7	.251	.321	-.0	-4.0	5.8	**.5**	5.3
Bal	80	74	0	.519	5	519	**430**	100	.229	.302	.339	641	-7	104	78	**62**	**85**	**395**	788	**10.0**	**2.53**	**+23**	.224	**.282**	1.6	**9.8**	-3.5	.4	-5.2
NY	79	76	0	.510	6.5	557	527	103	.249	.316	.357	673	+9	98	71	35	87	419	625	11.5	3.05	-2	.252	.310	-.3	-1.1	6.8	.1	-4.0
Cle	72	84	0	.462	14	472	519	91	.234	.293	.330	623	-12	104	49	47	123	534	846	11.5	2.92	+11	.237	.311	.8	5.6	-8.2	-.9	-3.3
Mil	65	91	0	.417	21	493	595	88	.235	.302	.328	630	-4	98	64	37	116	486	740	11.7	3.45	-12	.247	.312	-.5	-7.0	-3.1	-.7	-1.7
West																													
Oak	93	62	0	.600		604	457	**134**	.240	.306	.366	672	**+11**	95	87	42	96	418	862	10.2	2.58	+10	.226	.284	-.0	5.1	7.5	.2	2.7
Chi	87	67	0	.565	5.5	566	538	108	.238	.310	.346	656	+0	102	100	36	94	431	936	11.2	3.12	+0	.245	.305	-.4	-.1	.3	**.5**	9.7
Min	77	77	0	.500	15.5	537	535	93	.244	.310	.344	654	-4	105	53	37	105	444	838	10.7	2.84	+13	.230	.294	-1.8	6.1	-2.0	-.3	-2.0
KC	76	78	0	.494	16.5	580	545	78	**.255**	**.327**	.353	680	+10	100	85	44	**85**	405	801	11.3	3.24	-6	.251	.307	.7	-3.6	**8.1**	.4	-6.5
Cal	75	80	0	.484	18	454	533	78	.242	.293	.330	623	-4	95	57	57	90	620	**1000**	11.5	3.06	-4	**.222**	.310	.8	-2.5	-3.8	.0	2.9
Tex	54	100	0	.351	38.5	461	628	56	.217	.290	.290	580	-18	-97	**126**	11	92	613	868	12.6	3.53	-14	.246	.329	-2.2	-8.5	-11.5	.2	-1.0
Total	929					6441		1175	.239	.306	.343	649			853	502		5742	0174	11.3	3.06		.239	.306					

Batter-Fielder Wins		Batting Average		On-Base Percentage		Slugging Average		On-Base Plus Slugging		Adjusted OPS		Adjusted Batter Runs	
D.Allen-Chi	**5.8**	Carew-Min	.318	D.Allen-Chi	.420	D.Allen-Chi	.603	D.Allen-Chi	1023	D.Allen-Chi	198	D.Allen-Chi	65.1
Fisk-Bos	**5.1**	Fisk-Bos	.293	Fisk-Bos	.370	Fisk-Bos	.538	Fisk-Bos	909	Fisk-Bos	159	Fisk-Bos	32.9
Smith-Bos	**2.3**	Smith-Bos	.270	Smith-Bos	.365	Smith-Bos	.475	Smith-Bos	840	Smith-Bos	141	Smith-Bos	25.5
Yastrzemski-Bos	**1.1**	Yastrzemski-Bos	.264	Yastrzemski-Bos	.357	Yastrzemski-Bos	.391	Yastrzemski-Bos	748	Yastrzemski-Bos	117	Yastrzemski-Bos	12.5

Runs		Hits		Doubles		Triples		Home Runs		Total Bases		Runs Batted In	
Murcer-NY	102	Rudi-Oak	181	Piniella-KC	33	Rudi-Oak	9	D.Allen-Chi	37	Murcer-NY	314	D.Allen-Chi	113
Harper-Bos	92	Harper-Bos	141	Harper-Bos	29	Fisk-Bos	9	Fisk-Bos	22	Fisk-Bos	246	Petrocelli-Bos	75
Smith-Bos	75	Fisk-Bos	134	Fisk-Bos	28	Smith-Bos	4	Smith-Bos	21	Smith-Bos	222	Smith-Bos	74
Fisk-Bos	74	Smith-Bos	126	Aparicio-Bos	26	Aparicio-Bos	3	Petrocelli-Bos	15	Harper-Bos	216	Yastrzemski-Bos	68

Stolen Bases		Base Stealing Runs		Fielding Runs-Infield		Fielding Runs-Outfield		Wins		Winning Pct.		Complete Games	
Campaneris-Oak	52	Campaneris-Oak	6.5	Patek-KC	37.7	Berry-Cal	8.0	Wood-Chi	24	Hunter-Oak	.750	Perry-Cle	29
Harper-Bos	25	Harper-Bos	3.0	Petrocelli-Bos	5.3	Smith-Bos	.1	Perry-Cle	24	Tiant-Bos	.714	Pattin-Bos	13
Smith-Bos	15	Smith-Bos	1.9					Pattin-Bos	17	Pattin-Bos	.567	Tiant-Bos	12
Griffin-Bos	9	Griffin-Bos	1.3					Tiant-Bos	15			Curtis-Bos	8

Strikeouts		Fewest BB/Game		Games		Saves		Base Runners/9		Adjusted Relief Runs		Relief Ranking	
Ryan-Cal	329	Peterson-NY	1.58	Lindblad-Tex	66	Lyle-NY	35	Nelson-KC	7.89	Lyle-NY	13.6	Lyle-NY	25.9
Pattin-Bos	168	Pattin-Bos	2.31	Lee-Bos	47	Lee-Bos	5	Tiant-Bos	9.70	Lee-Bos	1.8	Lee-Bos	2.4
Tiant-Bos	123	Siebert-Bos	2.70	Tiant-Bos	43	Bolin-Bos	5	Pattin-Bos	10.89				
Siebert-Bos	123	Curtis-Bos	2.92	Pattin-Bos	38	2 players tied	4	Lee-Bos	11.53				

Innings Pitched		Opponents' Avg.		Opponents' OBP		Earned Run Average		Adjusted ERA		Adjusted Starter Runs		Pitcher Wins	
Wood-Chi	376.2	Ryan-Cal	.171	Nelson-KC	.234	Tiant-Bos	1.91	Perry-Cle	170	Perry-Cle	49.2	Perry-Cle	6.8
Pattin-Bos	253.0	Tiant-Bos	.202	Tiant-Bos	.275	Pattin-Bos	3.24	Tiant-Bos	170	Tiant-Bos	24.6	Tiant-Bos	2.9
Siebert-Bos	196.1	Pattin-Bos	.243	Pattin-Bos	.295	Curtis-Bos	3.73	Pattin-Bos	100	Pattin-Bos	1.2	Veale-Bos	.7
Tiant-Bos	179.0	Siebert-Bos	.264	Siebert-Bos	.321	Siebert-Bos	3.80	Curtis-Bos	87			2 players tied	.6

1973 AMERICAN LEAGUE

TEAM	W	L	T	PCT	GB	R	OR	HR	AVG	OBP	SLG	OPS	AOPS	PF	SB	CG	HR	BB	SO	BR/9	ERA	AERA	OAV	OOB	FW	PW	BW	BSW	DIF
East																													
Bal	97	65	0	.599		754	**561**	119	.266	**.345**	.389	734	+5	101	**146**	67	124	475	715	**11.0**	**3.07**	**+23**	**.240**	**.302**	1.3	**11.9**	6.0	**1.0**	-4.2
Bos	89	73	0	.549	8	738	647	147	.267	.338	**.401**	**739**	+1	106	114	67	158	499	808	12.2	3.65	+10	.259	.323	.8	5.8	1.7	.9	-1.3
Det	85	77	0	.525	12	642	674	157	.254	.320	.390	710	-7	107	28	39	154	493	911	12.4	3.90	+5	.265	.326	**1.7**	3.0	-5.2	-.4	5.0
NY	80	82	0	.494	17	641	610	131	.261	.322	.378	700	-1	98	47	47	109	**457**	708	11.7	3.34	+11	.254	.313	-.8	6.0	-1.0	-.5	-4.7
Mil	74	88	0	.457	23	708	731	145	.253	.325	.388	713	+1	99	110	50	119	623	671	13.2	3.98	-5	.265	.340	-.2	-3.0	1.1	.0	-5.1
Cle	71	91	0	.438	26	680	826	**158**	.256	.315	.387	702	-5	102	60	55	172	602	883	13.4	4.58	-14	.271	.343	.2	-10.2	-4.5	-1.1	5.7
West																													
Oak	94	68	0	.580		**758**	615	147	.260	.333	.389	722	**+8**	96	128	46	143	494	797	11.3	3.29	+8	.241	.305	.3	4.8	**6.4**	.8	.7
KC	88	74	0	.543	6	755	752	114	.261	.339	.381	720	-5	108	105	40	114	617	790	13.5	4.19	-2	.273	.346	-1.4	-1.3	-1.8	-.1	11.7
Min	81	81	0	.500	13	738	692	120	**.270**	.342	.393	735	+2	104	87	48	115	519	879	12.4	3.77	+5	.259	.324	.2	3.1	2.7	.3	-6.2
Cal	79	83	0	.488	15	629	657	93	.253	.318	.348	666	-7	93	59	**72**	**104**	614	**1010**	12.4	3.53	+1	.246	.324	-.8	.8	-4.4	-.3	2.7
Chi	77	85	0	.475	17	652	705	111	.256	.324	.372	696	-7	104	83	48	110	574	848	13.0	3.86	+2	.266	.336	-.1	1.3	-5.2	-.7	.7
Tex	57	105	0	.352	37	619	844	110	.255	.318	.361	679	-6	96	91	35	130	680	831	14.1	4.64	-19	.273	.353	-1.1	-14.6	-4.3	.0	-4.1
Total	972					8314		1552	.259	.328	.381	710			1058	614		6647	9851	12.5	3.82		.259	.328					

Batter-Fielder Wins		Batting Average		On-Base Percentage		Slugging Average		On-Base Plus Slugging		Adjusted OPS		Adjusted Batter Runs	
Carew-Min	**5.8**	Carew-Min	.350	Mayberry-KC	.417	Jackson-Oak	.531	Jackson-Oak	914	Jackson-Oak	164	Jackson-Oak	46.9
Smith-Bos	**3.0**	Yastrzemski-Bos	.296	Yastrzemski-Bos	.407	Yastrzemski-Bos	.463	Yastrzemski-Bos	870	Yastrzemski-Bos	137	Yastrzemski-Bos	31.7
Fisk-Bos	**1.9**	Cepeda-Bos	.289	Harper-Bos	.351	Cepeda-Bos	.444	Cepeda-Bos	793	Cepeda-Bos	116	Smith-Bos	28.6
Yastrzemski-Bos	**1.8**	Harper-Bos	.281	Cepeda-Bos	.350	Fisk-Bos	.441	Harper-Bos	774	Harper-Bos	110	Cepeda-Bos	11.4

Runs		Hits		Doubles		Triples		Home Runs		Total Bases		Runs Batted In	
Jackson-Oak	99	Carew-Min	203	Garcia-Mil	32	Carew-Min	11	Jackson-Oak	32	3 players tied	295	Jackson-Oak	117
Harper-Bos	92	Yastrzemski-Bos	160	Bando-Oak	32	Bumbry-Bal	11	Fisk-Bos	26	Yastrzemski-Bos	250	Yastrzemski-Bos	95
Yastrzemski-Bos	82	Harper-Bos	159	Yastrzemski-Bos	25	Miller-Bos	7	Smith-Bos	21	Cepeda-Bos	244	Cepeda-Bos	86
Smith-Bos	79	Cepeda-Bos	159	Cepeda-Bos	25	Griffin-Bos	5	Cepeda-Bos	20	Harper-Bos	239	2 players tied	71

Stolen Bases		Base Stealing Runs		Fielding Runs-Infield		Fielding Runs-Outfield		Wins		Winning Pct.		Complete Games	
Harper-Bos	54	Harper-Bos	7.0	Patek-KC	39.8	North-Oak	15.4	Wood-Chi	24	Hunter-Oak	.808	Perry-Cle	29
Aparicio-Bos	13	Aparicio-Bos	2.5			Harper-Bos	1.0	Tiant-Bos	20	Lee-Bos	.607	Tiant-Bos	23
Miller-Bos	12	Evans-Bos	1.1					Lee-Bos	17	Tiant-Bos	.606	Lee-Bos	18
Yastrzemski-Bos	9	Fisk-Bos	.8					Pattin-Bos	15	Pattin-Bos	.500	Pattin-Bos	11

Strikeouts		Fewest BB/Game		Games		Saves		Base Runners/9		Adjusted Relief Runs		Relief Ranking	
Ryan-Cal	383	Kaat-Min-Chi	1.73	Hiller-Det	65	Hiller-Det	38	Jackson-Bal	8.74	Hiller-Det	34.8	Hiller-Det	61.1
Tiant-Bos	206	Lee-Bos	2.40	Bolin-Bos	39	Bolin-Bos	15	Tiant-Bos	9.99				
Lee-Bos	120	Tiant-Bos	2.58	Lee-Bos	38	Veale-Bos	11	Lee-Bos	11.26				
Pattin-Bos	119	Pattin-Bos	2.83	2 players tied	35	Moret-Bos	3	Moret-Bos	11.97				

Innings Pitched		Opponents' Avg.		Opponents' OBP		Earned Run Average		Adjusted ERA		Adjusted Starter Runs		Pitcher Wins	
Wood-Chi	359.1	Bibby-Tex	.192	Tiant-Bos	.278	Palmer-Bal	2.40	Blyleven-Min	158	Blyleven-Min	48.2	Hiller-Det	6.7
Lee-Bos	284.2	Tiant-Bos	.219	Lee-Bos	.307	Lee-Bos	2.75	Lee-Bos	146	Lee-Bos	36.7	Lee-Bos	3.6
Tiant-Bos	272.0	Lee-Bos	.257	Curtis-Bos	.330	Tiant-Bos	3.34	Tiant-Bos	121	Tiant-Bos	22.6	Tiant-Bos	2.6
Curtis-Bos	221.1	Curtis-Bos	.264	Pattin-Bos	.335	Curtis-Bos	3.58	Curtis-Bos	113	Moret-Bos	14.6	Bolin-Bos	1.6

1974 AMERICAN LEAGUE

TEAM	W	L	T	PCT	GB	R	OR	HR	AVG	OBP	SLG	OPS	AOPS	PF	SB	CG	HR	BB	SO	BR/9	ERA	AERA	OAV	OOB	FW	PW	BW	BSW	DIF
East																													
Bal	91	71	0	.562		659	612	116	.256	.322	.370	692	+1	98	145	57	101	480	701	11.6	3.27	+6	.253	.314	1.0	3.7	1.7	**1.2**	2.5
NY	89	73	0	.549	2	671	623	101	.263	.324	.368	692	+0	99	53	53	104	528	829	12.1	3.31	+7	.256	.323	.2	4.0	.8	-.2	3.1
Bos	84	78	0	.519	7	**696**	661	109	.264	.333	.377	710	-3	107	104	**71**	126	463	751	12.1	3.72	+3	.262	.320	.0	1.9	-.5	.3	1.3
Cle	77	85	0	.475	14	662	694	131	.255	.311	.370	681	-4	99	79	45	138	479	650	12.0	3.80	-4	.260	.320	-.0	-2.8	-3.6	-.7	3.1
Mil	76	86	0	.469	15	647	660	120	.244	.309	.369	678	-6	100	106	43	126	493	621	12.3	3.76	-3	.266	.326	**1.1**	-2.1	-4.2	-.4	.6
Det	72	90	0	.444	19	620	768	131	.247	.303	.366	669	-11	104	67	54	148	621	869	13.0	4.16	-8	.262	.338	-.7	-5.4	-9.3	.0	6.4
West																													
Oak	90	72	0	.556		689	**551**	132	.247	.321	.373	694	+5	94	**164**	49	**90**	**430**	755	**11.1**	**2.95**	**+13**	**.246**	**.302**	.3	**7.0**	4.4	.4	-3.0
Tex	84	76	1	.525	5	690	698	99	**.272**	**.336**	.377	713	**+8**	98	113	62	126	449	871	12.0	3.82	-6	.260	.318	-1.1	-4.1	**6.1**	-.4	3.4
Min	82	80	1	.506	8	673	669	111	**.272**	**.336**	.378	714	+2	103	74	43	115	513	934	12.3	3.64	+2	.260	.325	-.3	1.5	2.1	.0	-2.3
Chi	80	80	3	.500	9	684	721	**135**	.268	.330	**.389**	**719**	+3	103	64	55	103	548	826	12.7	3.94	-5	.263	.332	-.0	-3.1	3.3	-.5	.3
KC	77	85	0	.475	13	667	662	89	.259	.327	.364	691	-6	106	146	54	91	482	731	12.2	3.51	+9	.263	.322	-.4	4.9	-3.9	.6	-5.2
Cal	68	94	1	.420	22	618	657	95	.254	.321	.356	677	+0	95	119	64	101	649	**986**	12.7	3.52	-2	.248	.332	-.0	-.9	.4	-.2	-12.3
Total	973					7976		1369	.258	.323	.371	694			1234	650		6135	9524	12.2	3.62		.258	.323					

Batter-Fielder Wins		Batting Average		On-Base Percentage		Slugging Average		On-Base Plus Slugging		Adjusted OPS		Adjusted Batter Runs	
Carew-Min	**6.9**	Carew-Min	.364	Carew-Min	.433	D.Allen-Chi	.563	D.Allen-Chi	938	Jackson-Oak	170	Burroughs-Tex	50.0
Fisk-Bos	**2.3**	Yastrzemski-Bos	.301	Yastrzemski-Bos	.414	Yastrzemski-Bos	.445	Yastrzemski-Bos	859	Yastrzemski-Bos	139	Yastrzemski-Bos	32.7
Yastrzemski-Bos	**1.5**	Evans-Bos	.281	Petrocelli-Bos	.336	Evans-Bos	.421	Petrocelli-Bos	757	Petrocelli-Bos	110	Fisk-Bos	13.8
Evans-Bos	**1.1**	Petrocelli-Bos	.267	Evans-Bos	.335	Petrocelli-Bos	.421	Evans-Bos	756	Evans-Bos	110	Carbo-Bos	9.4

Runs		Hits		Doubles		Triples		Home Runs		Total Bases		Runs Batted In	
Yastrzemski-Bos	93	Carew-Min	218	Rudi-Oak	39	Rivers-Cal	11	D.Allen-Chi	32	Rudi-Oak	287	Burroughs-Tex	118
Harper-Bos	66	Yastrzemski-Bos	155	Yastrzemski-Bos	25	Evans-Bos	8	Yastrzemski-Bos	15	Yastrzemski-Bos	229	Yastrzemski-Bos	79
Evans-Bos	60	Evans-Bos	130	Cooper-Bos	24	Griffin-Bos	4	Petrocelli-Bos	15	Evans-Bos	195	Petrocelli-Bos	76
Beniquez-Bos	60	Petrocelli-Bos	121	Petrocelli-Bos	23	2 players tied	3	Carbo-Bos	12	Petrocelli-Bos	191	Evans-Bos	70

Stolen Bases		Base Stealing Runs		Fielding Runs-Infield		Fielding Runs-Outfield		Wins		Winning Pct.		Complete Games	
North-Oak	54	Jackson-Oak	3.8	Nettles-NY	20.3	Evans-Bos	11.6	Jenkins-Tex	25	Cuellar-Bal	.688	Jenkins-Tex	29
Harper-Bos	28	Miller-Bos	2.2					Hunter-Oak	25	Tiant-Bos	.629	Tiant-Bos	25
Beniquez-Bos	19	Harper-Bos	2.0					Tiant-Bos	22	Lee-Bos	.531	Lee-Bos	16
Miller-Bos	13	Fisk-Bos	.8					Lee-Bos	17			2 players tied	10

Strikeouts		Fewest BB/Game		Games		Saves		Base Runners/9		Adjusted Relief Runs		Relief Ranking	
Ryan-Cal	367	Jenkins-Tex	1.23	Fingers-Oak	76	Forster-Chi	24	Hunter-Oak	8.99	Murphy-Mil	24.2	Murphy-Mil	44.3
Tiant-Bos	176	Lee-Bos	2.14	Segui-Bos	58	Segui-Bos	10	Tiant-Bos	10.61				
Moret-Bos	111	Tiant-Bos	2.37	Cleveland-Bos	41	Drago-Bos	3	Drago-Bos	11.58				
Cleveland-Bos	103	Cleveland-Bos	2.81	2 players tied	38	2 players tied	2	Moret-Bos	12.41				

Innings Pitched		Opponents' Avg.		Opponents' OBP		Earned Run Average		Adjusted ERA		Adjusted Starter Runs		Pitcher Wins	
Ryan-Cal	332.2	Ryan-Cal	.190	Hunter-Oak	.258	Hunter-Oak	2.49	G.Perry-Cle	145	G.Perry-Cle	41.9	Murphy-Mil	5.0
Tiant-Bos	311.1	Tiant-Bos	.241	Tiant-Bos	.291	Tiant-Bos	2.92	Tiant-Bos	132	Tiant-Bos	32.4	Tiant-Bos	3.5
Lee-Bos	282.1	Moret-Bos	.243	Drago-Bos	.313	Drago-Bos	3.48	Drago-Bos	110	Lee-Bos	9.2	Lee-Bos	1.2
Cleveland-Bos	221.1	Drago-Bos	.251	Moret-Bos	.323	Lee-Bos	3.51	Lee-Bos	110	Drago-Bos	8.3	Drago-Bos	.7

1975 AMERICAN LEAGUE

TEAM	W	L	T	PCT	GB	R	OR	HR	AVG	OBP	SLG	OPS	AOPS	PF	SB	CG	HR	BB	SO	BR/9	ERA	AERA	OAV	OOB	FW	PW	BW	BSW	DIF
East																													
Bos	95	65	0	.594		**796**	709	134	**.275**	**.344**	**.417**	**761**	+5	108	66	62	145	**490**	720	12.4	3.98	+2	.265	.325	.9	1.1	**5.1**	-.7	8.6
Bal	90	69	0	.566	4.5	682	**553**	124	.252	.326	.373	699	+3	94	104	**70**	110	500	717	**11.1**	**3.17**	+12	.242	**.306**	**2.6**	6.4	2.9	.3	-1.7
NY	83	77	0	.519	12	681	588	110	.264	.325	.382	707	+0	99	102	**70**	104	502	809	11.7	3.29	**+13**	.249	.314	1.1	**6.8**	.4	.0	-5.4
Cle	79	80	0	.497	15.5	688	703	**153**	.261	.327	.392	719	+2	100	106	37	136	599	800	12.7	3.84	-1	.258	.333	1.1	-.7	1.4	-.9	-1.4
Mil	68	94	0	.420	28	675	792	146	.250	.320	.389	709	-1	101	65	36	133	624	643	13.7	4.34	-11	.271	.348	-1.4	-7.9	-.5	-.9	-2.3
Det	57	102	0	.358	37.5	570	786	125	.249	.301	.366	667	-16	-104	63	52	137	533	787	13.3	4.27	-6	.275	.340	-1.1	-3.7	-12.7	-.7	-4.3
West																													
Oak	98	64	0	.605		758	606	151	.254	.333	.391	724	**+6**	98	183	36	**102**	523	784	11.4	3.27	+11	**.236**	**.306**	.7	6.3	**5.1**	**1.1**	3.7
KC	91	71	0	.562	7	710	649	118	.261	.333	.394	727	+2	103	155	52	108	498	815	12.0	3.47	+11	.258	.320	.0	6.2	2.5	.7	.5
Tex	79	83	0	.488	19	714	733	134	.256	.330	.371	701	-1	99	102	60	123	518	792	12.4	3.86	-3	.261	.327	-2.0	-1.6	-.2	.0	1.8
Min	76	83	0	.478	20.5	724	736	121	.271	.341	.386	727	+4	101	81	57	137	617	846	12.9	4.05	-6	.257	.335	-.9	-3.7	4.1	.0	-3.0
Chi	75	86	0	.466	22.5	655	703	94	.255	.331	.358	689	-6	101	101	34	107	655	799	13.5	3.93	-1	.268	.347	.9	-.8	-3.3	.2	-2.5
Cal	72	89	0	.447	25.5	628	723	55	.246	.322	.328	650	-10	-93	**220**	59	123	613	**975**	12.6	3.89	-8	.253	.330	-1.6	-5.5	-5.8	1.0	3.5
Total	963					8281		1465	.258	.328	.379	707			1348	625		6672	9487	12.5	3.78		.258	.328					

Batter-Fielder Wins		Batting Average		On-Base Percentage		Slugging Average		On-Base Plus Slugging		Adjusted OPS		Adjusted Batter Runs	
Harrah-Tex	**6.9**	Carew-Min	.359	Carew-Min	.421	Lynn-Bos	.566	Lynn-Bos	967	Mayberry-KC	167	Mayberry-KC	55.3
Lynn-Bos	**4.1**	Lynn-Bos	.331	Lynn-Bos	.401	Rice-Bos	.491	Rice-Bos	841	Lynn-Bos	159	Lynn-Bos	42.2
Fisk-Bos	**2.4**	Rice-Bos	.309	Yastrzemski-Bos	.371	Yastrzemski-Bos	.405	Yastrzemski-Bos	776	Rice-Bos	126	Carbo-Bos	21.4
Evans-Bos	**2.3**	Yastrzemski-Bos	.269	Rice-Bos	.350	Burleson-Bos	.329	Burleson-Bos	634	Yastrzemski-Bos	110	Rice-Bos	18.0

Runs		Hits		Doubles		Triples		Home Runs		Total Bases		Runs Batted In	
Lynn-Bos	103	Brett-KC	195	Lynn-Bos	47	Rivers-Cal	13	Scott-Mil	36	Scott-Mil	318	Scott-Mil	109
Rice-Bos	92	Lynn-Bos	175	Yastrzemski-Bos	30	Brett-KC	13	Jackson-Oak	36	Lynn-Bos	299	Lynn-Bos	105
Yastrzemski-Bos	91	Rice-Bos	174	Rice-Bos	29	Lynn-Bos	7	Rice-Bos	22	Rice-Bos	277	Rice-Bos	102
Burleson-Bos	66	2 players tied	146	Burleson-Bos	25	2 players tied	6	Lynn-Bos	21	Yastrzemski-Bos	220	Burleson-Bos	62

Stolen Bases		Base Stealing Runs		Fielding Runs-Infield		Fielding Runs-Outfield		Wins		Winning Pct.		Complete Games	
Rivers-Cal	70	Rivers-Cal	10.5	Belanger-Bal	29.5	Evans-Bos	18.7	Palmer-Bal	23	Torrez-Bal	.690	Hunter-NY	30
Rice-Bos	10	Rice-Bos	.5	Burleson-Bos	1.8	Lynn-Bos	2.4	Hunter-NY	23	Lee-Bos	.654	Tiant-Bos	18
Lynn-Bos	10	Lynn-Bos	.5					Wise-Bos	19	Wise-Bos	.613	Wise-Bos	17
2 players tied	8	Yastrzemski-Bos	.4					Tiant-Bos	18	Tiant-Bos	.563	Lee-Bos	17

Strikeouts		Fewest BB/Game		Games		Saves		Base Runners/9		Adjusted Relief Runs		Relief Ranking	
Tanana-Cal	269	Jenkins-Tex	1.87	Fingers-Oak	75	Gossage-Chi	26	Hunter-NY	9.22	Gossage-Chi	31.4	Gossage-Chi	46.9
Tiant-Bos	142	Lee-Bos	2.39	Lee-Bos	41	Drago-Bos	15	Tiant-Bos	11.70	Drago-Bos	3.2	Drago-Bos	3.1
Wise-Bos	141	Tiant-Bos	2.49	Drago-Bos	40	Willoughby-Bos	8	Wise-Bos	11.91				
Moret-Bos	80	Wise-Bos	2.54	Moret-Bos	36	Segui-Bos	6	Lee-Bos	11.98				

Innings Pitched		Opponents' Avg.		Opponents' OBP		Earned Run Average		Adjusted ERA		Adjusted Starter Runs		Pitcher Wins	
Hunter-NY	328.0	Hunter-NY	.208	Hunter-NY	.261	Palmer-Bal	2.09	Palmer-Bal	170	Palmer-Bal	53.0	Palmer-Bal	5.7
Tiant-Bos	260.0	Wise-Bos	.263	Wise-Bos	.313	Lee-Bos	3.95	Lee-Bos	103	Moret-Bos	8.9	Moret-Bos	.9
Lee-Bos	260.0	Cleveland-Bos	.263	Tiant-Bos	.315	Wise-Bos	3.95	Wise-Bos	103	Lee-Bos	4.9	Lee-Bos	.6
Wise-Bos	255.1	Tiant-Bos	.264	Cleveland-Bos	.317	Tiant-Bos	4.02	Tiant-Bos	101	Tiant-Bos	2.8	Drago-Bos	.3

1976 AMERICAN LEAGUE

TEAM	W	L	T	PCT	GB	R	OR	HR	AVG	OBP	SLG	OPS	AOPS	PF	SB	CG	HR	BB	SO	BR/9	ERA	AERA	OAV	OOB	FW	PW	BW	BSW	DIF
East																													
NY	97	62	0	.610		730	**575**	120	.269	.328	.389	717	**+10**	100	163	62	97	448	674	**10.9**	**3.19**	+7	**.241**	**.298**	.9	3.9	**7.3**	.8	4.6
Bal	88	74	0	.543	10.5	619	598	119	.243	.310	.358	668	+1	95	150	59	**80**	489	678	11.7	3.32	-1	.255	.315	**1.5**	-.4	.2	.7	5.1
Bos	83	79	0	.512	15.5	716	660	**134**	.263	.324	**.402**	**726**	+0	112	95	49	109	**409**	673	12.0	3.52	**+10**	.267	.318	.2	**5.5**	.5	-1.0	-3.2
Cle	81	78	0	.509	16	615	615	85	.263	.321	.359	680	+0	99	75	30	**80**	533	928	12.1	3.47	+1	.255	.324	1.2	.7	.0	-1.5	1.0
Det	74	87	0	.460	24	609	709	101	.257	.315	.365	680	-5	104	107	55	101	550	738	12.6	3.87	-4	.263	.331	-1.4	-2.3	-3.6	-.3	1.2
Mil	66	95	0	.410	32	570	655	88	.246	.311	.340	651	-7	98	62	45	99	567	677	12.6	3.64	-4	.260	.331	-.5	-2.2	-5.2	-1.5	-5.1
West																													
KC	90	72	0	.556		713	611	65	.269	.327	.371	698	+3	101	218	41	83	493	735	11.5	3.21	+9	.247	.309	.3	5.1	3.6	.6	-.6
Oak	87	74	0	.540	2.5	686	598	113	.246	.323	.361	684	+4	96	**341**	39	96	415	711	11.5	3.26	+3	.255	.308	-.0	1.9	4.5	**2.8**	-2.6
Min	85	77	0	.525	5	**743**	704	81	**.274**	**.341**	.375	716	+8	102	146	29	89	610	762	12.8	3.69	-3	.259	.335	-1.6	-2.1	7.0	.0	.7
Tex	76	86	0	.469	14	616	652	80	.250	.321	.341	662	-8	102	87	63	106	461	773	12.0	3.45	+4	.262	.320	-.7	2.2	-4.6	-.3	-1.7
Cal	76	86	0	.469	14	550	631	63	.235	.306	.318	624	-12	-94	126	**64**	95	553	**992**	11.7	3.36	+0	**.241**	.313	-.3	-.2	-7.3	-.6	3.5
Chi	64	97	0	.398	25.5	586	745	73	.255	.314	.349	663	-7	101	120	54	87	600	802	13.0	4.25	-16	.266	.338	.7	-11.6	-4.5	.2	-1.5
Total	967					7753		1122	.256	.320	.361	681			1690	590		6128	9143	12.0	3.52		.256	.320					

Batter-Fielder Wins		Batting Average		On-Base Percentage		Slugging Average		On-Base Plus Slugging		Adjusted OPS		Adjusted Batter Runs	
Grich-Bal	**4.8**	Brett-KC	.333	McRae-KC	.407	R.Jackson-Bal	.502	McRae-KC	868	R.Jackson-Bal	157	McRae-KC	39.5
Fisk-Bos	**3.3**	Lynn-Bos	.314	Lynn-Bos	.367	Rice-Bos	.482	Lynn-Bos	835	Lynn-Bos	130	Lynn-Bos	19.7
Burleson-Bos	**2.9**	Burleson-Bos	.291	Burleson-Bos	.365	Lynn-Bos	.467	Rice-Bos	797	Rice-Bos	119	Yastrzemski-Bos	14.3
Lynn-Bos	**2.1**	Rice-Bos	.282	Yastrzemski-Bos	.357	Yastrzemski-Bos	.432	Yastrzemski-Bos	790	Yastrzemski-Bos	118	Rice-Bos	10.6

Runs		Hits		Doubles		Triples		Home Runs		Total Bases		Runs Batted In	
White-NY	104	Brett-KC	215	Otis-KC	40	Brett-KC	14	Nettles-NY	32	Brett-KC	298	L.May-Bal	109
Lynn-Bos	76	Rice-Bos	164	Evans-Bos	34	Rice-Bos	8	Rice-Bos	25	Rice-Bos	280	Yastrzemski-Bos	102
Fisk-Bos	76	Lynn-Bos	159	Lynn-Bos	32	Lynn-Bos	8	Yastrzemski-Bos	21	Lynn-Bos	237	Rice-Bos	85
2 players tied	75	Burleson-Bos	157	Burleson-Bos	27	Cooper-Bos	6	2 players tied	17	Yastrzemski-Bos	236	Cooper-Bos	78

Stolen Bases		Base Stealing Runs		Fielding Runs-Infield		Fielding Runs-Outfield		Wins		Winning Pct.		Complete Games	
North-Oak	75	Campaneris-Oak	7.7	Remy-Cal	19.2	Beniquez-Tex	12.9	Palmer-Bal	22	Campbell-Min	.773	Fidrych-Det	24
Lynn-Bos	14	Cooper-Bos	1.2	Burleson-Bos	2.9	Evans-Bos	7.2	Tiant-Bos	21	Tiant-Bos	.636	Tiant-Bos	19
Burleson-Bos	14	Fisk-Bos	.9			Lynn-Bos	3.5	Wise-Bos	14			Jenkins-Bos	12
Fisk-Bos	12	3 players tied	.0					Jenkins-Bos	12			Wise-Bos	11

Strikeouts		Fewest BB/Game		Games		Saves		Base Runners/9		Adjusted Relief Runs		Relief Ranking	
Ryan-Cal	327	Bird-KC	1.41	Campbell-Min	78	Lyle-NY	23	Tanana-Cal	9.18	Littell-KC	17.4	Hiller-Det	29.5
Jenkins-Bos	142	Jenkins-Bos	1.85	Willoughby-Bos	54	Willoughby-Bos	10	Jenkins-Bos	10.72	Willoughby-Bos	9.8	Willoughby-Bos	15.6
Tiant-Bos	131	Wise-Bos	1.93	Cleveland-Bos	41	House-Bos	4	Wise-Bos	10.75				
Wise-Bos	93	Tiant-Bos	2.06	Tiant-Bos	38	Lee-Bos	3	Tiant-Bos	11.00				

Innings Pitched		Opponents' Avg.		Opponents' OBP		Earned Run Average		Adjusted ERA		Adjusted Starter Runs		Pitcher Wins	
Palmer-Bal	315.0	Ryan-Cal	.195	Tanana-Cal	.261	Fidrych-Det	2.34	Fidrych-Det	159	Fidrych-Det	36.1	Fidrych-Det	4.5
Tiant-Bos	279.0	Cleveland-Bos	.246	Jenkins-Bos	.292	Tiant-Bos	3.06	Tiant-Bos	127	Tiant-Bos	24.2	Tiant-Bos	2.7
Wise-Bos	224.1	Jenkins-Bos	.253	Wise-Bos	.294	Cleveland-Bos	3.07	Cleveland-Bos	127	Jenkins-Bos	14.0	Willoughby-Bos	1.7
Jenkins-Bos	209.0	Wise-Bos	.255	Tiant-Bos	.303	Jenkins-Bos	3.27	Jenkins-Bos	119	Cleveland-Bos	11.6	Jenkins-Bos	1.5

1977 AMERICAN LEAGUE

TEAM	W	L	T	PCT	GB	R	OR	HR	AVG	OBP	SLG	OPS	AOPS	PF	SB	CG	HR	BB	SO	BR/9	ERA	AERA	OAV	OOB	FW	PW	BW	BSW	DIF
East																													
NY	100	62	0	.617		831	**651**	184	.281	.344	.444	788	**+14**	99	93	52	139	486	758	11.8	3.61	+10	.254	**.315**	.6	5.7	**11.0**	.1	1.6
Bal	97	64	0	.602	2.5	719	653	148	.261	.329	.393	722	+2	94	90	**65**	124	494	737	12.0	3.74	+2	.260	.322	**2.0**	1.4	2.0	.2	10.9
Bos	97	64	0	.602	2.5	859	712	**213**	.281	.345	**.465**	**810**	+6	111	66	40	158	**378**	758	12.3	4.11	+9	.278	.325	.5	5.2	5.6	-.2	5.4
Det	74	88	0	.457	26	714	751	166	.264	.318	.410	728	-8	105	60	44	162	470	784	12.5	4.13	+4	.271	.327	.0	2.6	-6.3	-.3	-3.1
Cle	71	90	0	.441	28.5	676	739	100	.269	.334	.380	714	-3	97	87	45	136	550	876	12.5	4.10	-3	.261	.329	.7	-1.9	-1.2	-1.1	-6.0
Mil	67	95	0	.414	33	639	765	125	.258	.314	.389	703	-10	100	85	38	136	566	719	13.0	4.32	-5	.268	.337	.2	-3.6	-7.5	-.5	-2.7
Tor	54	107	0	.335	45.5	605	822	100	.252	.316	.365	681	-16	-101	65	40	152	623	771	13.7	4.57	-7	.278	.350	-1.2	-5.1	-11.4	-.5	-8.3
West																													
KC	102	60	0	.630		822	**651**	146	.277	.340	.436	776	+9	101	170	41	**110**	499	850	11.8	**3.52**	**+14**	**.251**	**.315**	.3	**8.1**	7.5	.7	4.3
Tex	94	68	0	.580	8	767	657	135	.270	.342	.405	747	+2	101	154	49	134	471	864	**11.7**	3.56	**+14**	.255	**.315**	1.5	8.0	2.8	.4	.3
Chi	90	72	0	.556	12	844	771	192	.278	.344	.444	788	+13	100	42	34	136	516	842	13.2	4.25	-4	.277	.339	-.9	-2.9	10.7	-.6	2.6
Min	84	77	0	.522	17.5	**867**	776	123	**.282**	**.348**	.417	765	+8	99	105	35	151	507	737	13.0	4.36	-9	.278	.340	-.0	-6.3	8.1	.0	1.6
Cal	74	88	0	.457	28	675	695	131	.255	.324	.386	710	-4	97	159	53	136	572	**965**	12.5	3.72	+5	.256	.330	-.2	3.3	-2.2	.4	-8.3
Sea	64	98	0	.395	38	624	855	133	.256	.312	.381	693	-12	100	110	18	194	578	785	13.5	4.83	-14	.272	.344	-.2	-10.8	-9.0	.1	3.0
Oak	63	98	0	.391	38.5	605	749	117	.240	.308	.352	660	-20	-99	**176**	32	145	560	788	12.8	4.04	+0	.265	.333	-2.7	-.3	-14.1	**.8**	-1.2
Total	1131					10247		2013	.266	.330	.405	735			1462	586		7270	1234	12.6	4.06		.266	.330					

Batter-Fielder Wins		Batting Average		On-Base Percentage		Slugging Average		On-Base Plus Slugging		Adjusted OPS		Adjusted Batter Runs	
Carew-Min	**6.5**	Carew-Min	.388	Carew-Min	.449	Rice-Bos	.593	Carew-Min	1019	Carew-Min	178	Carew-Min	69.3
Fisk-Bos	**4.6**	Rice-Bos	.320	Fisk-Bos	.402	Fisk-Bos	.521	Rice-Bos	969	Rice-Bos	144	Rice-Bos	37.2
Rice-Bos	**3.0**	Fisk-Bos	.315	Rice-Bos	.376	Yastrzemski-Bos	.505	Fisk-Bos	922	Fisk-Bos	136	Fisk-Bos	29.2
Yastrzemski-Bos	2.6	Yastrzemski-Bos	.296	Yastrzemski-Bos	.372	Scott-Bos	.500	Yastrzemski-Bos	877	Yastrzemski-Bos	124	Yastrzemski-Bos	20.0

Runs		Hits		Doubles		Triples		Home Runs		Total Bases		Runs Batted In	
Carew-Min	128	Carew-Min	239	McRae-KC	54	Carew-Min	16	Rice-Bos	39	Rice-Bos	382	Hisle-Min	119
Fisk-Bos	106	Rice-Bos	206	Burleson-Bos	36	Rice-Bos	15	Scott-Bos	33	Scott-Bos	292	Rice-Bos	114
Rice-Bos	104	Burleson-Bos	194	Hobson-Bos	33	Burleson-Bos	7	Hobson-Bos	30	Hobson-Bos	290	Hobson-Bos	112
Scott-Bos	103	Fisk-Bos	169	2 players tied	29	Doyle-Bos	6	Yastrzemski-Bos	28	Yastrzemski-Bos	282	2 players tied	102

Stolen Bases		Base Stealing Runs		Fielding Runs-Infield		Fielding Runs-Outfield		Wins		Winning Pct.		Complete Games	
Patek-KC	53	Page-Oak	7.5	Campaneris-Tex	26.1	Lemon-Chi	23.1	3 players tied	20	Splittorff-KC	.727	Ryan-Cal	22
Burleson-Bos	13	Yastrzemski-Bos	2.1	Burleson-Bos	20.1	Yastrzemski-Bos	9.7	Campbell-Bos	13			Palmer-Bal	22
Yastrzemski-Bos	11	Miller-Bos	.7					Tiant-Bos	12			Jenkins-Bos	11
Miller-Bos	11	Evans-Bos	.2					2 players tied	11			Cleveland-Bos	9

Strikeouts		Fewest BB/Game		Games		Saves		Base Runners/9		Adjusted Relief Runs		Relief Ranking	
Ryan-Cal	341	Rozema-Det	1.40	Lyle-NY	72	Campbell-Bos	31	Foucault-Det	9.81	Lyle-NY	26.2	Campbell-Bos	42.7
Tiant-Bos	124	Jenkins-Bos	1.68	Campbell-Bos	69	Stanley-Bos	3	Aase-Bos	10.23	Campbell-Bos	22.3		
Campbell-Bos	114	Cleveland-Bos	2.03	Stanley-Bos	41	Willoughby-Bos	2	Jenkins-Bos	10.54				
Jenkins-Bos	105	Tiant-Bos	2.43	Cleveland-Bos	36	Cleveland-Bos	2	Campbell-Bos	11.38				

Innings Pitched		Opponents' Avg.		Opponents' OBP		Earned Run Average		Adjusted ERA		Adjusted Starter Runs		Pitcher Wins	
Palmer-Bal	319.0	Ryan-Cal	.193	Eckersley-Cle	.276	Tanana-Cal	2.54	Tanana-Cal	155	Tanana-Cal	41.8	Campbell-Bos	4.5
Jenkins-Bos	193.0	Jenkins-Bos	.257	Jenkins-Bos	.290	Jenkins-Bos	3.68	Jenkins-Bos	122	Jenkins-Bos	13.2	Jenkins-Bos	1.3
Cleveland-Bos	190.1	Tiant-Bos	.279	Cleveland-Bos	.320	Cleveland-Bos	4.26	Cleveland-Bos	105	Aase-Bos	12.1	Aase-Bos	1.0
Tiant-Bos	188.2	Cleveland-Bos	.281	Tiant-Bos	.325	Tiant-Bos	4.53	Tiant-Bos	99	Stanley-Bos	6.8	Stanley-Bos	.8

1978 AMERICAN LEAGUE

TEAM	W	L	T	PCT	GB	R	OR	HR	AVG	OBP	SLG	OPS	AOPS	PF	SB	CG	HR	BB	SO	BR/9	ERA	AERA	OAV	OOB	FW	PW	BW	BSW	DIF
East																													
NY	100	63	0	.613		735	**582**	125	.267	.329	.388	717	+3	98	98	39	111	478	817	**11.3**	**3.18**	+15	**.243**	**.306**	1.5	8.0	2.7	.6	5.6
Bos	99	64	0	.607	1	796	657	172	.267	.336	.424	760	+1	110	74	57	137	464	706	12.4	3.54	**+16**	.270	.327	-.3	**8.8**	2.4	-.3	7.0
Mil	93	69	0	.574	6.5	**804**	650	**173**	**.276**	**.339**	**.432**	**771**	**+14**	101	95	62	109	**398**	577	11.8	3.65	+4	.262	.313	-.6	2.1	**11.4**	.1	-1.0
Bal	90	71	0	.559	9	659	633	154	.258	.326	.396	722	+8	94	75	**65**	107	509	754	11.7	3.56	-1	.251	.316	**1.6**	-.8	6.5	-.6	2.8
Det	86	76	0	.531	13.5	714	653	129	.271	**.339**	.392	731	+2	103	90	60	135	503	684	12.2	3.64	+7	.263	.325	1.2	3.9	2.3	.6	-3.0
Cle	69	90	0	.434	29	639	694	106	.261	.323	.379	702	-2	99	64	36	**100**	568	739	12.7	3.97	-5	.261	.332	.8	-3.2	-1.5	-.9	-5.6
Tor	59	102	0	.366	40	590	775	98	.250	.308	.359	667	-15	102	28	35	149	614	758	13.6	4.54	-13	.279	.351	.4	-9.3	-11.1	-1.3	-.2
West																													
KC	92	70	0	.568		743	634	98	.268	.329	.399	728	+1	103	**216**	53	108	478	657	11.6	3.44	+11	.251	.313	-.6	6.1	1.6	**1.8**	2.1
Tex	87	75	0	.537	5	692	632	132	.253	.332	.381	713	-1	101	196	54	108	421	776	11.6	3.36	+11	.259	.312	-.8	6.4	.8	1.0	-1.5
Cal	87	75	0	.537	5	691	666	108	.259	.330	.370	700	-1	97	86	44	125	599	**892**	12.4	3.65	-1	.253	.327	.2	-.5	.9	-.6	6.0
Min	73	89	0	.451	19	666	678	82	.267	**.339**	.375	714	-1	103	99	48	102	520	703	12.5	3.69	+4	.266	.330	-.4	2.2	.5	.1	-10.4
Chi	71	90	0	.441	20.5	634	731	106	.264	.317	.379	696	-6	101	83	38	128	586	710	12.8	4.21	-10	.259	.334	-.0	-6.8	-4.6	-.7	2.7
Oak	69	93	0	.426	23	532	690	100	.245	.303	.351	654	-13	-95	144	26	106	582	750	12.6	3.62	+1	.259	.330	-2.3	.4	-9.7	-1.0	.6
Sea	56	104	0	.350	35	614	834	97	.248	.314	.359	673	-11	100	123	28	155	567	630	13.6	4.67	-18	.280	.348	-.2	-13.4	-7.5	1.0	-3.9
Total	1131					9509		1680	.261	.326	.385	711			1471	645		7287	0153	12.4	3.76		.261	.326					

Batter-Fielder Wins		Batting Average		On-Base Percentage		Slugging Average		On-Base Plus Slugging		Adjusted OPS		Adjusted Batter Runs	
Smalley-Min	**5.1**	Carew-Min	.333	Carew-Min	.411	Rice-Bos	.600	Rice-Bos	970	Singleton-Bal	154	Rice-Bos	44.5
Rice-Bos	**4.2**	Rice-Bos	.315	Lynn-Bos	.380	Lynn-Bos	.492	Lynn-Bos	872	Rice-Bos	153	Lynn-Bos	24.4
Fisk-Bos	**3.9**	Lynn-Bos	.298	Rice-Bos	.370	Fisk-Bos	.475	Fisk-Bos	841	Lynn-Bos	131	Fisk-Bos	19.4
Lynn-Bos	**1.6**	Fisk-Bos	.284	Yastrzemski-Bos	.367	Evans-Bos	.449	Yastrzemski-Bos	790	Fisk-Bos	123	Yastrzemski-Bos	10.2

Runs		Hits		Doubles		Triples		Home Runs		Total Bases		Runs Batted In	
LeFlore-Det	126	Rice-Bos	213	Brett-KC	45	Rice-Bos	15	Rice-Bos	46	Rice-Bos	406	Rice-Bos	139
Rice-Bos	121	Remy-Bos	162	Fisk-Bos	39	Remy-Bos	6	Evans-Bos	24	Fisk-Bos	271	Fisk-Bos	88
Fisk-Bos	94	Fisk-Bos	162	Lynn-Bos	33	Fisk-Bos	5	Lynn-Bos	22	Lynn-Bos	266	Lynn-Bos	82
Remy-Bos	87	Lynn-Bos	161	Burleson-Bos	32	Burleson-Bos	5	Fisk-Bos	20	Evans-Bos	223	Yastrzemski-Bos	81

Stolen Bases		Base Stealing Runs		Fielding Runs-Infield		Fielding Runs-Outfield		Wins		Winning Pct.		Complete Games	
LeFlore-Det	68	Cruz-Sea	9.5	Belanger-Bal	30.3	Bosetti-Tor	14.4	Guidry-NY	25	Guidry-NY	.893	Caldwell-Mil	23
Remy-Bos	30	Remy-Bos	2.0	Burleson-Bos	19.5	Rice-Bos	3.5	Eckersley-Bos	20	Stanley-Bos	.882	Eckersley-Bos	16
Evans-Bos	8	Fisk-Bos	.8	Remy-Bos	.7	Evans-Bos	1.2	Torrez-Bos	16	Eckersley-Bos	.714	Torrez-Bos	15
Burleson-Bos	8	Hobson-Bos	.2					Stanley-Bos	15	Torrez-Bos	.552	Tiant-Bos	12

Strikeouts		Fewest BB/Game		Games		Saves		Base Runners/9		Adjusted Relief Runs		Relief Ranking	
Ryan-Cal	260	Jenkins-Tex	1.48	Lacey-Oak	74	Gossage-NY	27	Guidry-NY	8.55	Gossage-NY	22.1	Gossage-NY	41.1
Eckersley-Bos	162	Eckersley-Bos	2.38	Stanley-Bos	52	Stanley-Bos	10	Tiant-Bos	10.47	Stanley-Bos	20.5	Stanley-Bos	25.4
Torrez-Bos	120	Tiant-Bos	2.42	Drago-Bos	37	Drago-Bos	7	Stanley-Bos	11.24	Drago-Bos	8.4	Drago-Bos	9.6
Tiant-Bos	114	Lee-Bos	3.00	Torrez-Bos	36	2 players tied	4	Eckersley-Bos	11.27				

Innings Pitched		Opponents' Avg.		Opponents' OBP		Earned Run Average		Adjusted ERA		Adjusted Starter Runs		Pitcher Wins	
Palmer-Bal	296.0	Guidry-NY	.193	Guidry-NY	.249	Guidry-NY	1.74	Guidry-NY	210	Guidry-NY	59.6	Guidry-NY	6.4
Eckersley-Bos	268.1	Tiant-Bos	.234	Tiant-Bos	.289	Eckersley-Bos	2.99	Eckersley-Bos	138	Eckersley-Bos	31.9	Eckersley-Bos	3.1
Torrez-Bos	250.0	Eckersley-Bos	.251	Eckersley-Bos	.302	Tiant-Bos	3.31	Tiant-Bos	125	Tiant-Bos	21.1	Stanley-Bos	2.8
Tiant-Bos	212.1	Torrez-Bos	.281	Lee-Bos	.340	Lee-Bos	3.46	Lee-Bos	119	Lee-Bos	7.2	Tiant-Bos	1.9

1979 AMERICAN LEAGUE

TEAM	W	L	T	PCT	GB	R	OR	HR	AVG	OBP	SLG	OPS	AOPS	PF	SB	CG	HR	BB	SO	BR/9	ERA	AERA	OAV	OOB	FW	PW	BW	BSW	DIF
East																													
Bal	102	57	0	.642		757	**582**	181	.261	.336	.419	755	+6	97	99	52	133	467	786	**11.0**	**3.26**	**+24**	**.241**	**.301**	.8	**12.6**	5.5	.2	3.5
Mil	95	66	0	.590	8	807	722	185	.280	.345	.448	793	**+12**	100	100	**61**	162	**381**	580	12.3	4.03	+4	.279	.324	.7	2.4	9.4	.0	1.9
Bos	91	69	0	.569	11.5	841	711	**194**	**.283**	.344	**.456**	**800**	+8	106	60	47	133	463	731	12.5	4.03	+10	.270	.328	-.2	6.1	6.5	-.5	-1.0
NY	89	71	0	.556	13.5	734	672	150	.266	.328	.406	734	-1	98	65	43	123	455	731	12.0	3.83	+7	.268	.323	1.0	4.4	-1.1	-.5	5.2
Det	85	76	0	.528	18	770	738	164	.269	.339	.415	754	-1	103	176	25	167	547	802	12.8	4.27	+2	.265	.335	**1.1**	1.0	-.0	.6	1.9
Cle	81	80	0	.503	22	760	805	138	.258	.340	.384	724	-5	100	143	28	138	570	781	13.2	4.57	-6	.272	.339	.3	-4.4	-2.1	-.3	7.0
Tor	53	109	0	.327	50.5	613	862	95	.251	.311	.363	674	-20	-101	75	44	165	594	613	13.8	4.82	-9	.281	.353	-1.0	-6.5	-14.6	-.6	-5.2
West																													
Cal	88	74	0	.543		**866**	768	164	.282	**.351**	.429	780	**+12**	97	100	46	131	573	**820**	13.0	4.34	-6	.267	.336	.3	-4.3	**10.7**	.0	.2
KC	85	77	0	.525	3	851	816	116	.282	.343	.422	765	+3	102	**207**	42	165	536	640	12.7	4.45	-4	.267	.331	-.3	-3.0	3.1	**1.6**	2.6
Tex	83	79	0	.512	5	750	698	140	.278	.334	.409	743	+0	99	79	26	135	532	773	12.1	3.86	+7	.253	.321	.6	4.3	.5	-.3	-3.1
Min	82	80	0	.506	6	764	725	112	.278	.341	.402	743	-4	104	66	31	128	452	721	12.8	4.13	+6	.285	.338	.4	3.8	-2.4	-.4	-.4
Chi	73	87	0	.456	14	730	748	127	.275	.333	.410	743	-1	100	97	28	**114**	618	675	12.9	4.10	+4	.256	.334	-1.9	2.1	-.5	-.3	-6.5
Sea	67	95	0	.414	21	711	820	132	.269	.331	.404	735	-5	102	126	37	165	571	736	13.6	4.58	-5	.281	.348	.0	-3.2	-3.3	.7	-8.2
Oak	54	108	0	.333	34	573	860	108	.239	.302	.346	648	-22	-95	104	41	147	654	726	14.5	4.75	-15	.288	.363	-1.9	-11.4	-16.3	-.4	2.9
Total	1128					10527		2006	.270	.334	.408	743			1497	551		7413	0115	12.8	4.22		.270	.334					

Batter-Fielder Wins		Batting Average		On-Base Percentage		Slugging Average		On-Base Plus Slugging		Adjusted OPS		Adjusted Batter Runs	
Smalley-Min	**5.6**	Lynn-Bos	.333	Lynn-Bos	.423	Lynn-Bos	.637	Lynn-Bos	1059	Lynn-Bos	173	Lynn-Bos	57.1
Lynn-Bos	**5.3**	Rice-Bos	.325	Rice-Bos	.381	Rice-Bos	.596	Rice-Bos	977	Rice-Bos	152	Rice-Bos	44.0
Rice-Bos	**3.1**	Burleson-Bos	.278	Evans-Bos	.364	Hobson-Bos	.496	Evans-Bos	820	Evans-Bos	114	Watson-Bos	20.2
Burleson-Bos	**2.8**	Evans-Bos	.274	Yastrzemski-Bos	.346	Evans-Bos	.456	Yastrzemski-Bos	796	Yastrzemski-Bos	108	Evans-Bos	10.7

Runs		Hits		Doubles		Triples		Home Runs		Total Bases		Runs Batted In	
Baylor-Cal	120	Brett-KC	212	Lemon-Chi	44	Brett-KC	20	Thomas-Mil	45	Rice-Bos	369	Baylor-Cal	139
Rice-Bos	117	Rice-Bos	201	Cooper-Mil	44	Hobson-Bos	7	Rice-Bos	39	Lynn-Bos	338	Rice-Bos	130
Lynn-Bos	116	Lynn-Bos	177	Lynn-Bos	42	Rice-Bos	6	Lynn-Bos	39	Hobson-Bos	262	Lynn-Bos	122
Burleson-Bos	93	Burleson-Bos	174	Rice-Bos	39	Burleson-Bos	5	Hobson-Bos	28	Yastrzemski-Bos	233	Hobson-Bos	93

Stolen Bases		Base Stealing Runs		Fielding Runs-Infield		Fielding Runs-Outfield		Wins		Winning Pct.		Complete Games	
Wilson-KC	83	Wilson-KC	14.1	Smalley-Min	32.6	Wilson-KC	13.1	Flanagan-Bal	23	Caldwell-Mil	.727	D.Martinez-Bal	18
Remy-Bos	14	Fisk-Bos	.7	Burleson-Bos	30.2	Evans-Bos	4.5	Eckersley-Bos	17	Eckersley-Bos	.630	Eckersley-Bos	17
Rice-Bos	9	Rice-Bos	.6					Torrez-Bos	16	Stanley-Bos	.571	Torrez-Bos	12
Burleson-Bos	9	Dwyer-Bos	.3					Stanley-Bos	16	Torrez-Bos	.552	Stanley-Bos	9

Strikeouts		Fewest BB/Game		Games		Saves		Base Runners/9		Adjusted Relief Runs		Relief Ranking	
Ryan-Cal	223	McGregor-Bal	1.19	Marshall-Min	90	Marshall-Min	32	McGregor-Bal	9.79	Kern-Tex	38.7	Kern-Tex	61.5
Eckersley-Bos	150	Stanley-Bos	1.83	Drago-Bos	53	Drago-Bos	13	Eckersley-Bos	10.91	Burgmeier-Bos	15.2	Drago-Bos	26.2
Torrez-Bos	125	Eckersley-Bos	2.15	Burgmeier-Bos	44	Campbell-Bos	9	Drago-Bos	11.02	Drago-Bos	13.5	Burgmeier-Bos	9.2
Renko-Bos	99	Renko-Bos	2.79	Campbell-Bos	41	Burgmeier-Bos	4	Burgmeier-Bos	11.06	Campbell-Bos	1.4	Campbell-Bos	2.1

Innings Pitched		Opponents' Avg.		Opponents' OBP		Earned Run Average		Adjusted ERA		Adjusted Starter Runs		Pitcher Wins	
D.Martinez-Bal	292.1	Ryan-Cal	.212	McGregor-Bal	.273	Guidry-NY	2.78	Eckersley-Bos	149	Eckersley-Bos	38.9	Kern-Tex	6.3
Torrez-Bos	252.1	Eckersley-Bos	.250	Eckersley-Bos	.297	Eckersley-Bos	2.99	Stanley-Bos	112	Stanley-Bos	9.2	Eckersley-Bos	4.0
Eckersley-Bos	246.2	Renko-Bos	.260	Renko-Bos	.315	Stanley-Bos	3.99	Renko-Bos	109	Rainey-Bos	7.7	Drago-Bos	2.6
Stanley-Bos	216.2	Torrez-Bos	.264	Stanley-Bos	.330	Renko-Bos	4.11	Torrez-Bos	99	Renko-Bos	6.5	Stanley-Bos	1.1

1980 AMERICAN LEAGUE

TEAM	W	L	T	PCT	GB	R	OR	HR	AVG	OBP	SLG	OPS	AOPS	PF	SB	CG	HR	BB	SO	BR/9	ERA	AERA	OAV	OOB	FW	PW	BW	BSW	DIF
East																													
NY	103	59	0	.636		820	662	189	.267	.343	.425	768	+11	99	86	29	**102**	463	845	11.8	3.58	+10	.259	.316	.0	6.1	9.4	.3	6.3
Bal	100	62	0	.617	3	805	**640**	156	.273	.342	.413	755	+8	99	111	42	134	507	789	12.1	3.64	+9	.261	.323	**2.4**	5.2	6.7	.7	3.9
Mil	86	76	0	.531	17	811	682	**203**	.275	.329	**.448**	**777**	**+14**	98	131	48	137	**420**	575	12.3	3.71	+5	.273	.323	-.5	3.3	**10.0**	.6	-8.3
Bos	83	77	0	.519	19	757	767	162	.283	.340	.436	776	+5	105	79	30	129	481	696	12.9	4.38	-3	.279	.337	-.7	-1.8	4.7	-.2	1.1
Det	84	78	1	.519	19	**830**	757	143	.273	.348	.409	757	+4	103	75	40	152	558	741	12.8	4.25	-3	.267	.334	.3	-2.1	4.6	-1.0	1.2
Cle	79	81	0	.494	23	738	807	89	.277	**.350**	.381	731	-1	101	118	35	137	552	843	13.3	4.68	-12	.275	.341	1.8	-8.6	1.9	.3	3.7
Tor	67	95	0	.414	36	624	762	126	.251	.309	.383	692	-15	104	67	39	135	635	705	13.4	4.19	+3	.274	.348	.3	1.8	-12.0	-1.3	-2.8
West																													
KC	97	65	0	.599		809	694	115	**.286**	.345	.413	758	+5	102	**185**	37	129	465	614	12.2	3.83	+6	.267	.323	-.2	3.4	5.0	**2.2**	5.5
Oak	83	79	0	.512	14	686	642	137	.259	.322	.385	707	-1	94	175	**94**	142	521	769	**11.6**	**3.46**	+10	**.244**	**.310**	.5	5.9	-1.2	.6	-3.8
Min	77	84	0	.478	19.5	670	724	99	.265	.319	.381	700	-15	107	62	35	120	468	744	12.4	3.93	**+11**	.272	.328	-.6	**6.4**	-11.1	-.5	2.4
Tex	76	85	2	.472	20.5	756	752	124	.284	.339	.405	744	+6	97	91	35	119	519	**890**	13.1	4.02	-4	.277	.339	-.5	-2.4	5.2	-.0	-6.8
Chi	70	90	2	.438	26	587	722	91	.259	.311	.370	681	-14	-100	68	32	108	563	724	12.8	3.92	+3	.263	.333	-1.9	2.1	-10.4	-.7	.9
Cal	65	95	0	.406	31	698	797	106	.265	.332	.378	710	-5	99	91	22	141	529	725	13.3	4.52	-13	.278	.342	.1	-9.2	-2.2	-.5	-3.2
Sea	59	103	1	.364	38	610	793	104	.248	.308	.356	664	-20	-102	116	31	159	540	703	13.2	4.38	-5	.278	.341	-.6	-3.5	-14.8	.0	-3.2
Total	1132					10201		1844	.269	.331	.399	731			1455	549		7221	0363	12.7	4.03		.269	.331					

Batter-Fielder Wins		Batting Average		On-Base Percentage		Slugging Average		On-Base Plus Slugging		Adjusted OPS		Adjusted Batter Runs	
G.Brett-KC	**6.5**	G.Brett-KC	.390	G.Brett-KC	.454	G.Brett-KC	.664	G.Brett-KC	1118	G.Brett-KC	201	G.Brett-KC	64.0
Burleson-Bos	**3.7**	Rice-Bos	.294	Evans-Bos	.358	Rice-Bos	.504	Evans-Bos	842	Evans-Bos	123	Lynn-Bos	18.8
Lynn-Bos	**2.3**	Fisk-Bos	.289	Fisk-Bos	.353	Evans-Bos	.484	Rice-Bos	840	Rice-Bos	121	Evans-Bos	16.0
Stapleton-Bos	**2.2**	Burleson-Bos	.278	Burleson-Bos	.341	2 players tied	.467	Fisk-Bos	819	Fisk-Bos	117	Rice-Bos	12.4

Runs		Hits		Doubles		Triples		Home Runs		Total Bases		Runs Batted In	
Wilson-KC	133	Wilson-KC	230	Yount-Mil	49	Wilson-KC	15	Oglivie-Mil	41	Cooper-Mil	335	Cooper-Mil	122
Burleson-Bos	89	Burleson-Bos	179	Evans-Bos	37	Griffin-Tor	15	Jackson-NY	41	Perez-Bos	273	Perez-Bos	105
Rice-Bos	81	Perez-Bos	161	Stapleton-Bos	33	Rice-Bos	6	Perez-Bos	25	Rice-Bos	254	Rice-Bos	86
2 players tied	73	Rice-Bos	148	Lynn-Bos	32	2 players tied	5	Rice-Bos	24	Burleson-Bos	236	Fisk-Bos	62

Stolen Bases		Base Stealing Runs		Fielding Runs-Infield		Fielding Runs-Outfield		Wins		Winning Pct.		Complete Games	
Henderson-Oak	100	Wilson-KC	13.9	Burleson-Bos	31.2	Wilson-KC	13.9	Stone-Bal	25	Stone-Bal	.781	Langford-Oak	28
Remy-Bos	14	Lynn-Bos	2.6			Henderson-Oak	13.9	Eckersley-Bos	12			Eckersley-Bos	8
Lynn-Bos	12	Remy-Bos	1.0			Lynn-Bos	2.3	Stanley-Bos	10			Torrez-Bos	6
Burleson-Bos	12	2 players tied	.7					2 players tied	9			2 players tied	5

Strikeouts		Fewest BB/Game		Games		Saves		Base Runners/9		Adjusted Relief Runs		Relief Ranking	
Barker-Cle	187	Matlack-Tex	1.84	Quisenberry-KC	75	Quisenberry-KC	33	May-NY	9.39	Corbett-Min	34.8	Corbett-Min	45.2
Eckersley-Bos	121	Eckersley-Bos	2.00	Burgmeier-Bos	62	Gossage-NY	33	Burgmeier-Bos	9.91	Burgmeier-Bos	21.0	Burgmeier-Bos	28.5
Torrez-Bos	97	Stanley-Bos	2.67	Stanley-Bos	52	Burgmeier-Bos	24	Eckersley-Bos	10.65				
Renko-Bos	90	Renko-Bos	3.05	Drago-Bos	43	Stanley-Bos	14	Tudor-Bos	11.21				

Innings Pitched		Opponents' Avg.		Opponents' OBP		Earned Run Average		Adjusted ERA		Adjusted Starter Runs		Pitcher Wins	
Langford-Oak	290.0	Norris-Oak	.209	May-NY	.268	May-NY	2.46	May-NY	161	Norris-Oak	43.8	Corbett-Min	4.8
Torrez-Bos	207.1	Eckersley-Bos	.248	Eckersley-Bos	.289	Stanley-Bos	3.39	Stanley-Bos	126	Stanley-Bos	14.8	Norris-Oak	4.8
Eckersley-Bos	197.2	Stanley-Bos	.278	Stanley-Bos	.335	Renko-Bos	4.19	Renko-Bos	102	Tudor-Bos	11.6	Burgmeier-Bos	3.1
Stanley-Bos	175.0	Renko-Bos	.281	Renko-Bos	.337	Eckersley-Bos	4.28	Eckersley-Bos	100	Crawford-Bos	2.3	Stanley-Bos	1.8

1981 AMERICAN LEAGUE

TEAM	W	L	T	PCT	GB	R	OR	HR	AVG	OBP	SLG	OPS	AOPS	PF	SB	CG	HR	BB	SO	BR/9	ERA	AERA	OAV	OOB	FW	PW	BW	BSW	DIF
EastSplit Season: First-half Winner NY (34-22); Second-half Winner MIL (31-22)																													
Mil	62	47	0	.569		493	459	96	.257	.313	.391	704	+6	96	39	25	83	347	489	12.3	3.70	-1	.260	.326	.8	-.6	2.8	-.4	3.9
Bal	59	46	0	.562	1	429	437	88	.251	.329	.379	708	+4	100	41	16	64	287	606	**10.7**	**2.90**	**+25**	**.235**	**.293**	.7	**8.0**	3.7	-.0	-6.8
NY	59	48	0	.551	2	421	**343**	100	.252	.325	.391	716	+6	99	47	33	83	373	476	11.5	3.53	+7	.236	.310	**1.0**	2.7	-.2	-.0	2.0
Det	60	49	0	.550	2	427	404	65	.256	.331	.368	699	-3	104	61	19	90	354	536	12.4	3.81	+3	.262	.328	-.4	1.2	3.7	-.5	1.0
Bos	59	49	0	.546	2.5	**519**	481	90	**.275**	**.340**	**.399**	**739**	+5	107	32	33	67	311	569	12.7	3.88	-5	.274	.330	-.4	-2.1	-.9	1.3	2.6
Cle	52	51	0	.505	7	431	442	39	.263	.327	.351	678	-4	99	**119**	20	72	377	451	12.5	3.81	+4	.252	.326	-1.3	1.5	-13.0	-.6	-2.6
Tor	37	69	0	.349	23.5	329	466	61	.226	.286	.330	616	-27	-106	66														
WestSplit Season: First-half Winner OAK (37-23); Second-half Winner KC (30-23)																													
Oak	64	45	0	.587		458	403	**104**	.247	.312	.379	691	+2	96	98	23	67	322	488	11.4	3.40	+2	.243	.308	.7	.8	2.9	-.5	.5
Tex	57	48	0	.543	5	452	389	49	.270	.326	.369	695	+5	95	46	20	73	336	529	12.0	3.47	+4	.252	.319	-.3	1.6	4.9	.4	-5.6
Chi	54	52	0	.509	8.5	476	423	76	.272	.335	.387	722	**+10**	99	86	24	75	**273**	404	11.7	3.56	+1	.260	.313	.5	.5	1.8	.3	-4.6
KC	50	53	0	.485	11	397	405	61	.267	.325	.383	708	+3	100	100	27	81	323	426	12.1	3.70	-1	.261	.321	-.9	-.3	2.3	-.3	-4.9
Cal	51	59	0	.464	13.5	476	453	97	.256	.330	.380	710	+3	101	44	10	76	360	478	12.8	4.23	-8	.271	.334	-.3	-3.9	-4.0	.5	-2.8
Sea	44	65	1	.404	20	426	521	89	.251	.314	.368	682	-8	105	100	13	79	376	500	13.0	3.98	-1	.272	.338	-.6	-.3	-11.5	-.3	-.8
Min	41	68	1	.376	23	378	486	47	.240	.293	.338	631	-24	106	34	**334**		4761	**6905**	12.1	3.66		.256	.321					
Total	750					6112		1062	.256	.321	.373	693			913	549		7221	0363	12.7	4.03		.269	.331					

Batter-Fielder Wins		Batting Average		On-Base Percentage		Slugging Average		On-Base Plus Slugging		Adjusted OPS		Adjusted Batter Runs	
Grich-Cal	**5.2**	Lansford-Bos	.336	Hargrove-Cle	.424	Grich-Cal	.543	Evans-Bos	937	Grich-Cal	162	Evans-Bos	35.1
Evans-Bos	**3.6**	Remy-Bos	.307	Evans-Bos	.415	Evans-Bos	.522	Lansford-Bos	828	Evans-Bos	159	Lansford-Bos	16.5
Lansford-Bos	**1.3**	Evans-Bos	.296	Lansford-Bos	.389	Rice-Bos	.441	Rice-Bos	775	Lansford-Bos	130	Rice-Bos	8.3
Rice-Bos	**.1**	Miller-Bos	.291	Remy-Bos	.368	Lansford-Bos	.439	Stapleton-Bos	747	Rice-Bos	116	Stapleton-Bos	2.7

Runs		Hits		Doubles		Triples		Home Runs		Total Bases		Runs Batted In	
Henderson-Oak	89	Henderson-Oak	135	Cooper-Mil	35	Castino-Min	9	4 players tied	22	Evans-Bos	215	Murray-Bal	78
Evans-Bos	84	Lansford-Bos	134	Lansford-Bos	23	Evans-Bos	4	Evans-Bos	22	Rice-Bos	199	Evans-Bos	71
Lansford-Bos	61	Rice-Bos	128	Evans-Bos	19	Perez-Bos	3	Rice-Bos	17	Lansford-Bos	175	Rice-Bos	62
Remy-Bos	55	Evans-Bos	122	Rice-Bos	18	Lansford-Bos	3	Stapleton-Bos	10	Stapleton-Bos	150	Yastrzemski-Bos	53

Stolen Bases		Base Stealing Runs		Fielding Runs-Infield		Fielding Runs-Outfield		Wins		Winning Pct.		Complete Games	
Henderson-Oak	56	Cruz-Sea	6.7	Bell-Tex	34.3	Wilson-KC	17.6	4 players tied	14	Vuckovich-Mil	.778	Langford-Oak	18
Lansford-Bos	15	Remy-Bos	1.3	Hoffman-Bos	2.8	Evans-Bos	6.1	Torrez-Bos	10			Eckersley-Bos	8
Remy-Bos	9							Stanley-Bos	10			Tanana-Bos	5
2 players tied	3							Eckersley-Bos	9			3 players tied	2

Strikeouts		Fewest BB/Game		Games		Saves		Base Runners/9		Adjusted Relief Runs		Relief Ranking	
Barker-Cle	127	Honeycutt-Tex	1.20	Corbett-Min	54	Fingers-Mil	28	Fingers-Mil	7.96	Fingers-Mil	22.6	Fingers-Mil	41.4
Clear-Bos	82	Eckersley-Bos	2.05	Stanley-Bos	35	Clear-Bos	9	Ojeda-Bos	10.45	Burgmeier-Bos	6.0	Burgmeier-Bos	9.5
Eckersley-Bos	79	Tanana-Bos	2.74	Clear-Bos	34	Campbell-Bos	7	Eckersley-Bos	11.57	Campbell-Bos	2.3	Stanley-Bos	2.9
Tanana-Bos	78	Torrez-Bos	3.60	Burgmeier-Bos	32	Burgmeier-Bos	6	Tudor-Bos	12.01	Stanley-Bos	1.8	Campbell-Bos	1.6

Innings Pitched		Opponents' Avg.		Opponents' OBP		Earned Run Average		Adjusted ERA		Adjusted Starter Runs		Pitcher Wins	
Leonard-KC	201.2	McCatty-Oak	.211	Guidry-NY	.256	McCatty-Oak	2.33	Stewart-Bal	157	McCatty-Oak	27.1	Fingers-Mil	4.6
Eckersley-Bos	154.0	Tanana-Bos	.265	Eckersley-Bos	.308	Torrez-Bos	3.68	Torrez-Bos	107	Ojeda-Bos	6.0	Burgmeier-Bos	1.1
Tanana-Bos	141.1	Eckersley-Bos	.267	Tanana-Bos	.322	Tanana-Bos	4.01	Tanana-Bos	98	Torrez-Bos	2.6	Ojeda-Bos	.7
Torrez-Bos	127.1	Torrez-Bos	.267	Torrez-Bos	.336	Eckersley-Bos	4.27	Eckersley-Bos	92	Rainey-Bos	2.1	2 players tied	.5

1982 AMERICAN LEAGUE

TEAM	W	L	T	PCT	GB	R	OR	HR	AVG	OBP	SLG	OPS	AOPS	PF	SB	CG	HR	BB	SO	BR/9	ERA	AERA	OAV	OOB	FW	PW	BW	BSW	DIF
East																													
Mil	95	67	1	.586		**891**	717	**216**	.279	.335	**.455**	**790**	**+20**	95	84	34	152	511	717	12.5	3.98	-4	.270	.330	.1	-2.6	**15.4**	-.2	1.3
Bal	94	68	1	.580	1	774	687	179	.266	.341	.419	760	+8	99	49	38	147	488	719	**12.0**	3.99	+2	.257	**.317**	**1.4**	1.1	7.7	-.5	3.3
Bos	89	73	0	.549	6	753	713	136	.274	.340	.407	747	-2	106	42	23	155	478	816	12.8	4.03	+8	.276	.334	.3	4.7	-.2	-.6	3.8
Det	83	79	0	.512	12	729	685	177	.266	.324	.418	742	+1	101	93	**45**	172	554	740	12.1	**3.80**	+7	**.251**	.321	.5	4.5	.9	-.5	-3.4
NY	79	83	0	.488	16	709	716	161	.256	.328	.398	726	-1	99	69	24	113	491	939	12.2	3.99	+1	.264	.323	-.0	.5	.5	-.3	-2.6
Tor	78	84	0	.481	17	651	701	106	.262	.314	.383	697	-17	109	118	41	147	493	776	12.1	3.95	**+14**	.257	.319	-.5	**8.0**	-12.4	-.4	2.3
Cle	78	84	0	.481	17	683	748	109	.262	.341	.373	714	-4	101	151	31	122	589	882	12.5	4.11	+1	.257	.327	.2	.6	-1.5	.7	-3.0
West																													
Cal	93	69	0	.574		814	**670**	186	.274	**.347**	.433	780	+12	101	55	40	124	482	728	**12.0**	3.82	+7	.259	.321	1.0	4.3	10.4	-.8	-2.9
KC	90	72	0	.556	3	784	717	132	**.285**	.337	.428	765	+7	101	133	16	163	471	650	12.2	4.08	+0	.262	.320	-.0	-.1	6.2	1.0	1.9
Chi	87	75	0	.537	6	786	710	136	.273	.337	.413	750	+4	101	136	30	**99**	**460**	753	12.4	3.87	+5	.270	.326	-1.5	3.2	4.0	.8	-.5
Sea	76	86	0	.469	17	651	712	130	.254	.311	.381	692	-14	104	131	23	173	547	**1002**	12.2	3.88	+10	.256	.324	-.7	6.2	-10.7	-.2	.4
Oak	68	94	0	.420	25	691	819	149	.236	.309	.367	676	-12	-97	**232**	42	177	648	697	13.5	4.54	-13	.268	.343	-1.8	-10.0	-8.7	**1.9**	5.6
Tex	64	98	0	.395	29	590	749	115	.249	.308	.359	667	-14	-96	63	32	128	483	690	13.1	4.28	-9	.280	.339	.3	-6.8	-10.5	-.4	.4
Min	60	102	0	.370	33	657	819	148	.257	.316	.396	712	-9	103	38	26	208	643	812	13.4	4.72	-10	.269	.344	1.0	-7.0	-6.7	-.5	-7.8
Total	1135					10163		2080	.264	.328	.402	730			1394	445		7338	0921	12.5	4.07		.264	.328					

Batter-Fielder Wins		Batting Average		On-Base Percentage		Slugging Average		On-Base Plus Slugging		Adjusted OPS		Adjusted Batter Runs	
Yount-Mil	**7.1**	Wilson-KC	.332	Evans-Bos	.402	Yount-Mil	.578	Yount-Mil	957	Yount-Mil	168	Yount-Mil	58.1
Evans-Bos	**3.2**	Rice-Bos	.309	Rice-Bos	.375	Evans-Bos	.534	Evans-Bos	936	Evans-Bos	146	Evans-Bos	42.4
Boggs-Bos	**2.9**	Lansford-Bos	.301	Lansford-Bos	.359	Rice-Bos	.494	Rice-Bos	868	Rice-Bos	129	Rice-Bos	23.0
Rice-Bos	**1.0**	Evans-Bos	.292	Yastrzemski-Bos	.358	Lansford-Bos	.444	Lansford-Bos	803	Lansford-Bos	114	Boggs-Bos	13.5

Runs		Hits		Doubles		Triples		Home Runs		Total Bases		Runs Batted In	
Molitor-Mil	136	Yount-Mil	210	Yount-Mil	46	Wilson-KC	15	Thomas-Mil	39	Yount-Mil	367	McRae-KC	133
Evans-Bos	122	Remy-Bos	178	McRae-KC	46	Evans-Bos	7	R.Jackson-Cal	39	Evans-Bos	325	Evans-Bos	98
Remy-Bos	89	Evans-Bos	178	Evans-Bos	37	Rice-Bos	5	Evans-Bos	32	Rice-Bos	283	Rice-Bos	97
Rice-Bos	86	Rice-Bos	177	2 players tied	28	Lansford-Bos	4	Rice-Bos	24	2 players tied	214	Yastrzemski-Bos	72

Stolen Bases		Base Stealing Runs		Fielding Runs-Infield		Fielding Runs-Outfield		Wins		Winning Pct.		Complete Games	
Henderson-Oak	130	Henderson-Oak	13.9	Bell-Tex	37.7	Brunansky-Min	11.3	Hoyt-Chi	19	Vuckovich-Mil	.750	Stieb-Tor	19
Remy-Bos	16	Lansford-Bos	.6	Hoffman-Bos	16.0			Clear-Bos	14	Palmer-Bal	.750	Eckersley-Bos	11
Lansford-Bos	9	Remy-Bos	.4	Stapleton-Bos	5.2			Tudor-Bos	13			Tudor-Bos	6
2 players tied	5	2 players tied	.2					Eckersley-Bos	13			Rainey-Bos	3

Strikeouts		Fewest BB/Game		Games		Saves		Base Runners/9		Adjusted Relief Runs		Relief Ranking	
Bannister-Sea	209	John-NY-Cal	1.58	VandeBerg-Sea	78	Quisenberry-KC	35	Gossage-NY	8.81	Stanley-Bos	23.5	Spillner-Cle	42.0
Tudor-Bos	146	Eckersley-Bos	1.73	Clear-Bos	55	Stanley-Bos	14	Burgmeier-Bos	10.73	Burgmeier-Bos	21.4	Clear-Bos	29.0
Eckersley-Bos	127	Stanley-Bos	2.67	Stanley-Bos	48	Clear-Bos	14	Aponte-Bos	10.91	Clear-Bos	14.5	Stanley-Bos	28.1
Clear-Bos	109	Tudor-Bos	2.71	2 players tied	40	Aponte-Bos	3	Eckersley-Bos	10.95	Aponte-Bos	11.2	Burgmeier-Bos	14.1

Innings Pitched		Opponents' Avg.		Opponents' OBP		Earned Run Average		Adjusted ERA		Adjusted Starter Runs		Pitcher Wins	
Stieb-Tor	288.1	Sutcliffe-Cle	.226	Palmer-Bal	.286	Sutcliffe-Cle	2.96	Sutcliffe-Cle	140	Stieb-Tor	36.2	3 players tied	4.2
Eckersley-Bos	224.1	Stanley-Bos	.255	Eckersley-Bos	.296	Stanley-Bos	3.10	Stanley-Bos	140	Eckersley-Bos	14.9	Stanley-Bos	3.1
Tudor-Bos	195.2	Eckersley-Bos	.261	Stanley-Bos	.312	Tudor-Bos	3.63	Tudor-Bos	120	Tudor-Bos	13.2	Clear-Bos	3.0
Torrez-Bos	175.2	Tudor-Bos	.280	Tudor-Bos	.336	Eckersley-Bos	3.73	Eckersley-Bos	117			2 players tied	1.6

1983 AMERICAN LEAGUE

TEAM	W	L	T	PCT	GB	R	OR	HR	AVG	OBP	SLG	OPS	AOPS	PF	SB	CG	HR	BB	SO	BR/9	ERA	AERA	OAV	OOB	FW	PW	BW	BSW	DIF
East																													
Bal	98	64	0	.605		799	652	**168**	.269	**.340**	.421	761	+9	99	61	36	130	452	774	11.9	3.63	+10	.261	.316	.5	6.0	8.5	-.3	2.3
Det	92	70	0	.568	6	789	679	156	.274	.335	.427	762	+10	98	93	42	170	522	875	11.6	3.80	+3	**.242**	.309	.3	2.2	8.6	-.3	.2
NY	91	71	0	.562	7	770	703	153	.273	.337	.416	753	+9	97	84	**47**	116	455	892	11.9	3.86	+2	.260	.315	-.5	1.3	7.7	-.1	1.6
Tor	89	73	0	.549	9	795	726	167	**.277**	.338	**.436**	**774**	+4	107	131	43	145	517	835	12.4	4.12	+5	.259	.325	.9	3.2	3.7	-.1	.4
Mil	87	75	0	.537	11	764	708	132	**.277**	.333	.418	751	**+13**	93	101	35	133	491	689	12.6	4.02	-6	.270	.329	**1.0**	-4.3	**10.0**	-.0	-.6
Bos	78	84	0	.481	20	724	775	142	.270	.335	.409	744	-3	108	30	29	158	493	767	13.0	4.34	+1	.279	.337	.0	.6	-1.7	-.7	-1.2
Cle	70	92	0	.432	28	704	785	86	.265	.338	.369	707	-10	104	109	34	120	529	794	13.1	4.43	-4	.275	.339	.5	-2.6	-4.8	-.6	-3.5
West																													
Chi	99	63	0	.611		**800**	650	157	.262	.329	.413	742	-1	104	165	35	128	**447**	877	**11.4**	3.67	+15	.248	**.307**	.6	8.4	-.4	1.4	8.1
KC	79	83	1	.488	20	696	767	109	.271	.320	.397	717	-5	101	182	19	133	471	593	12.7	4.25	-4	.274	.330	-1.9	-2.5	-3.9	**1.9**	4.4
Tex	77	85	1	.475	22	639	**609**	106	.255	.310	.366	676	-14	-99	119	43	**97**	471	826	11.7	**3.31**	**+22**	.252	.313	**1.0**	**11.9**	-10.4	-.0	-6.5
Oak	74	88	0	.457	25	708	782	121	.262	.326	.381	707	-1	95	**235**	22	135	626	719	13.1	4.34	-11	.263	.337	-1.5	-8.0	.4	1.2	.9
Cal	70	92	0	.432	29	722	779	154	.260	.322	.393	715	-4	100	41	39	130	496	668	13.2	4.31	-6	.284	.341	-1.3	-4.6	-2.8	-1.0	-1.3
Min	70	92	0	.432	29	709	822	141	.261	.319	.401	720	-7	104	44	20	163	580	748	13.6	4.66	-9	.280	.348	.5	-6.0	-5.1	-.5	.0
Sea	60	102	0	.370	39	558	740	111	.240	.301	.360	661	-22	-104	144	25	145	544	**910**	12.9	4.12	+4	.268	.337	-.3	2.3	-15.9	-.1	-7.0
Total	1135					10177		1903	.266	.328	.401	728			1539	469		7094	0967	12.5	4.06		.266	.328					

Batter-Fielder Wins		Batting Average		On-Base Percentage		Slugging Average		On-Base Plus Slugging		Adjusted OPS		Adjusted Batter Runs	
Ripken-Bal	**7.0**	Boggs-Bos	.361	Boggs-Bos	.444	Brett-KC	.563	Brett-KC	947	Murray-Bal	157	Murray-Bal	47.6
Boggs-Bos	**4.4**	Rice-Bos	.305	Rice-Bos	.361	Rice-Bos	.550	Boggs-Bos	931	Boggs-Bos	146	Boggs-Bos	43.2
Rice-Bos	**3.3**	Remy-Bos	.275	Evans-Bos	.338	Boggs-Bos	.486	Rice-Bos	911	Rice-Bos	137	Rice-Bos	30.9
Jurak-Bos	**.4**	Hoffman-Bos	.260	Remy-Bos	.320	Armas-Bos	.453	Evans-Bos	774	Evans-Bos	104	Nichols-Bos	3.9

Runs		Hits		Doubles		Triples		Home Runs		Total Bases		Runs Batted In	
Ripken-Bal	121	Ripken-Bal	211	Ripken-Bal	47	Yount-Mil	10	Rice-Bos	39	Rice-Bos	344	Cooper-Mil	126
Boggs-Bos	100	Boggs-Bos	210	Boggs-Bos	44	Boggs-Bos	7	Armas-Bos	36	Boggs-Bos	283	Rice-Bos	126
Rice-Bos	90	Rice-Bos	191	Rice-Bos	34	Remy-Bos	5	Evans-Bos	22	Armas-Bos	260	Armas-Bos	107
Armas-Bos	77	Remy-Bos	163	Stapleton-Bos	31	2 players tied	4	2 players tied	10	Evans-Bos	205	Boggs-Bos	74

Stolen Bases		Base Stealing Runs		Fielding Runs-Infield		Fielding Runs-Outfield		Wins		Winning Pct.		Complete Games	
Henderson-Oak	108	Henderson-Oak	17.1	T.Cruz-Sea-Bal	24.2	Ward-Min	18.5	Hoyt-Chi	24	Dotson-Chi	.759	Guidry-NY	21
Remy-Bos	11	Remy-Bos	1.4	Boggs-Bos	4.2	Rice-Bos	9.7	Tudor-Bos	13			Tudor-Bos	7
Nichols-Bos	7	Evans-Bos	.7					Ojeda-Bos	12			Hurst-Bos	6
3 players tied	3							Hurst-Bos	12			2 players tied	5

Strikeouts		Fewest BB/Game		Games		Saves		Base Runners/9		Adjusted Relief Runs		Relief Ranking	
Morris-Det	232	Hoyt-Chi	1.07	Quisenberry-KC	69	Quisenberry-KC	45	Quisenberry-KC	8.35	Quisenberry-KC	32.7	Quisenberry-KC	38.4
Tudor-Bos	136	Eckersley-Bos	1.99	Stanley-Bos	64	Stanley-Bos	33	Stanley-Bos	11.52	Stanley-Bos	21.1	Stanley-Bos	33.2
Hurst-Bos	115	Hurst-Bos	2.64	Clear-Bos	48	Clear-Bos	4	Boyd-Bos	11.58	Aponte-Bos	4.8	Aponte-Bos	6.7
Ojeda-Bos	94	Tudor-Bos	3.01	3 players tied	34	Aponte-Bos	3	Tudor-Bos	11.94				

Innings Pitched		Opponents' Avg.		Opponents' OBP		Earned Run Average		Adjusted ERA		Adjusted Starter Runs		Pitcher Wins	
Morris-Det	293.2	Boddicker-Bal	.216	Hoyt-Chi	.260	Honeycutt-Tex	2.42	Honeycutt-Tex	167	Stieb-Tor	37.1	Quisenberry-KC	4.0
Tudor-Bos	242.0	Tudor-Bos	.255	Tudor-Bos	.316	Ojeda-Bos	4.04	Ojeda-Bos	109	Boyd-Bos	8.8	Stanley-Bos	3.4
Hurst-Bos	211.1	Ojeda-Bos	.265	Ojeda-Bos	.336	Hurst-Bos	4.09	Hurst-Bos	107	Hurst-Bos	8.6	Hurst-Bos	1.0
Eckersley-Bos	176.1	Hurst-Bos	.290	Hurst-Bos	.340	Tudor-Bos	4.09	Tudor-Bos	107	Tudor-Bos	7.6	Boyd-Bos	.9

1984 AMERICAN LEAGUE

TEAM	W	L	T	PCT	GB	R	OR	HR	AVG	OBP	SLG	OPS	AOPS	PF	SB	CG	HR	BB	SO	BR/9	ERA	AERA	OAV	OOB	FW	PW	BW	BSW	DIF
East																													
Det	104	58	0	.642		**829**	**643**	**187**	.271	**.342**	.432	774	**+13**	100	106	19	130	489	914	**11.5**	**3.49**	**+13**	**.246**	**.308**	.3	**7.6**	**10.7**	-.2	4.6
Tor	89	73	1	.549	15	750	696	143	.273	.331	.421	752	+2	104	**193**	34	140	528	875	12.3	3.86	+7	.257	.323	.6	4.2	2.1	**1.7**	-.6
NY	87	75	0	.537	17	758	679	130	.276	.339	.404	743	+9	97	62	15	**120**	518	**992**	12.4	3.78	+1	.264	.325	-.5	.9	7.7	-.2	-1.9
Bos	86	76	0	.531	18	810	764	181	**.283**	.341	**.441**	**782**	+10	105	38	40	141	517	927	12.9	4.18	+0	.270	.332	-.6	.3	7.3	-.2	-1.8
Bal	85	77	0	.525	19	681	667	160	.252	.328	.391	719	+0	98	51	**48**	137	512	714	12.1	3.71	+5	.256	.320	.5	3.2	1.0	-.3	-.4
Cle	75	87	1	.463	29	761	766	123	.265	.335	.384	719	-4	102	126	21	141	545	803	12.8	4.26	-3	.269	.332	-.7	-2.2	-1.1	-.1	-1.9
Mil	67	94	0	.416	36.5	641	734	96	.262	.317	.370	687	-8	97	52	13	137	480	785	12.8	4.06	-4	.274	.331	-.3	-2.8	-5.4	-1.1	-3.9
West																													
KC	84	78	0	.519		673	686	117	.268	.317	.399	716	-4	101	106	18	136	**433**	724	11.8	3.92	+3	.258	.312	.0	1.9	-3.3	-.1	4.4
Cal	81	81	0	.500	3	696	697	150	.249	.319	.381	700	-7	100	80	36	143	474	754	12.5	3.96	+1	.271	.328	.2	.5	-4.6	-.2	4.1
Min	81	81	0	.500	3	673	675	114	.265	.318	.385	703	-12	105	39	32	159	463	713	12.1	3.85	+10	.260	.319	**.7**	5.7	-7.8	-.4	1.8
Oak	77	85	0	.475	7	738	796	158	.259	.327	.404	731	+7	94	145	15	155	592	695	13.7	4.48	-16	.278	.348	-.8	-12.1	6.8	.8	1.2
Sea	74	88	0	.457	10	682	774	129	.258	.324	.384	708	-4	99	116	26	138	619	972	13.5	4.31	-7	.270	.345	.2	-4.7	-2.7	.2	.0
Chi	74	88	0	.457	10	679	736	172	.247	.314	.395	709	-10	105	109	43	155	483	840	12.0	4.13	+1	.256	.317	.6	.6	-7.1	.5	-1.5
Tex	69	92	0	.429	14.5	656	714	120	.261	.313	.377	690	-13	104	81	38	148	518	863	12.5	3.91	+7	.260	.325	-.4	3.9	-10.2	-.2	-4.7
Total	1134					10027		1980	.264	.326	.398	724			1304	398		7171	1571	12.5	3.99		.264	.326					

Batter-Fielder Wins		Batting Average		On-Base Percentage		Slugging Average		On-Base Plus Slugging		Adjusted OPS		Adjusted Batter Runs	
Ripken-Bal	**9.4**	Mattingly-NY	.343	Murray-Bal	.410	Baines-Chi	.541	Evans-Bos	920	Mattingly-NY	158	Murray-Bal	50.3
Boggs-Bos	**4.4**	Boggs-Bos	.325	Boggs-Bos	.407	Evans-Bos	.532	Easler-Bos	892	Evans-Bos	145	Evans-Bos	41.5
Evans-Bos	**2.9**	Easler-Bos	.313	Evans-Bos	.388	Armas-Bos	.531	Armas-Bos	831	Easler-Bos	137	Easler-Bos	30.8
Easler-Bos	**2.8**	Barrett-Bos	.303	Easler-Bos	.376	Easler-Bos	.516	Boggs-Bos	823	Boggs-Bos	123	Boggs-Bos	24.2

Runs		Hits		Doubles		Triples		Home Runs		Total Bases		Runs Batted In	
Evans-Bos	121	Mattingly-NY	207	Mattingly-NY	44	Moseby-Tor	15	Armas-Bos	43	Armas-Bos	339	Armas-Bos	123
Boggs-Bos	109	Boggs-Bos	203	Evans-Bos	37	Collins-Tor	15	Evans-Bos	32	Evans-Bos	335	Rice-Bos	122
Armas-Bos	107	Easler-Bos	188	Easler-Bos	31	Evans-Bos	8	Rice-Bos	28	Easler-Bos	310	Evans-Bos	104
Rice-Bos	98	Evans-Bos	186	Boggs-Bos	31	Rice-Bos	7	Easler-Bos	27	Rice-Bos	307	Easler-Bos	91

Stolen Bases		Base Stealing Runs		Fielding Runs-Infield		Fielding Runs-Outfield		Wins		Winning Pct.		Complete Games	
Henderson-Oak	66	Wilson-KC	8.6	Ripken-Bal	39.3	Vukovich-Cle	18.8	Boddicker-Bal	20	Alexander-Tor	.739	Hough-Tex	17
Gutierrez-Bos	12	Gutierrez-Bos	.9	Boggs-Bos	22.3	Rice-Bos	3.8	Ojeda-Bos	12			Boyd-Bos	10
Barrett-Bos	5	Rice-Bos	.9	Buckner-Bos	5.5			Hurst-Bos	12			Hurst-Bos	9
2 players tied	4	Evans-Bos	.3	Barrett-Bos	.4			Boyd-Bos	12			Ojeda-Bos	8

Strikeouts		Fewest BB/Game		Games		Saves		Base Runners/9		Adjusted Relief Runs		Relief Ranking	
Langston-Sea	204	Hoyt-Chi	1.64	Hernandez-Det	80	Quisenberry-KC	44	Hernandez-Det	8.72	Hernandez-Det	33.8	Hernandez-Det	41.3
Ojeda-Bos	137	Boyd-Bos	2.41	Stanley-Bos	57	Stanley-Bos	22	Stanley-Bos	11.64	Johnson-Bos	5.5	Stanley-Bos	7.1
Hurst-Bos	136	Nipper-Bos	2.56	Clear-Bos	47	Clear-Bos	8	Eckersley-Bos	11.83	Crawford-Bos	3.6	Johnson-Bos	2.8
Boyd-Bos	134	Hurst-Bos	3.63	Crawford-Bos	35	2 players tied	1	Boyd-Bos	11.88	Stanley-Bos	3.6	Crawford-Bos	2.7

Innings Pitched		Opponents' Avg.		Opponents' OBP		Earned Run Average		Adjusted ERA		Adjusted Starter Runs		Pitcher Wins	
Stieb-Tor	267.0	Stieb-Tor	.221	Black-KC	.283	Boddicker-Bal	2.79	Stieb-Tor	146	Stieb-Tor	39.9	Hernandez-Det	4.3
Hurst-Bos	218.0	Nipper-Bos	.257	Nipper-Bos	.313	Nipper-Bos	3.89	Nipper-Bos	108	Nipper-Bos	7.6	Stanley-Bos	.8
Ojeda-Bos	216.2	Ojeda-Bos	.259	Boyd-Bos	.314	Hurst-Bos	3.92	Hurst-Bos	107	Hurst-Bos	7.3	Nipper-Bos	.8
Boyd-Bos	197.2	Boyd-Bos	.269	Ojeda-Bos	.336	Ojeda-Bos	3.99	Ojeda-Bos	105	Ojeda-Bos	6.2	Hurst-Bos	.8

1985 AMERICAN LEAGUE

TEAM	W	L	T	PCT	GB	R	OR	HR	AVG	OBP	SLG	OPS	AOPS	PF	SB	CG	HR	BB	SO	BR/9	ERA	AERA	OAV	OOB	FW	PW	BW	BSW	DIF
East																													
Tor	99	62	0	.615		759	**588**	158	.269	.331	.425	756	+2	103	144	18	147	484	823	**11.3**	**3.31**	**+28**	.243	**.306**	.2	**14.5**	2.2	.0	1.6
NY	97	64	0	.602	2	**839**	660	176	.267	.344	.425	769	**+11**	98	**155**	25	157	518	907	11.9	3.69	+10	.251	.316	.2	5.8	**9.9**	**1.1**	-.5
Det	84	77	0	.522	15	729	688	202	.253	.318	.424	742	+1	100	75	31	141	556	943	11.7	3.78	+9	**.240**	.311	-.8	5.2	.9	-.3	-1.5
Bal	83	78	0	.516	16	818	764	**214**	.263	.336	**.430**	766	+10	98	69	32	160	568	793	13.1	4.38	-7	.270	.338	-.0	-5.0	8.1	-.5	-.0
Bos	81	81	1	.500	18.5	800	720	162	**.282**	**.347**	.429	**776**	+6	104	66	35	130	540	913	12.7	4.06	+6	.265	.331	-.8	4.0	6.2	.0	-9.4
Mil	71	90	0	.441	28	690	802	101	.263	.319	.379	698	-10	100	69	34	175	499	777	12.8	4.39	-4	.271	.331	-.7	-3.1	-6.9	-.2	1.4
Cle	60	102	0	.370	39.5	729	861	116	.265	.324	.385	709	-7	100	132	24	170	547	702	13.6	4.91	-15	.281	.346	-.6	-11.7	-4.1	-.1	-4.5
West																													
KC	91	71	0	.562		687	639	154	.252	.313	.401	714	-7	101	128	27	**103**	463	846	11.9	3.49	+20	.257	.315	.1	11.0	-5.3	.6	3.6
Cal	90	72	0	.556	1	732	703	153	.251	.333	.386	719	-4	100	106	22	171	514	767	12.3	3.91	+5	.263	.326	1.0	3.5	-1.6	.0	6.1
Chi	85	77	1	.525	6	736	720	146	.253	.315	.392	707	-12	105	108	20	161	569	**1023**	12.5	4.07	+7	.256	.327	**1.1**	4.3	-8.4	-.1	7.2
Min	77	85	0	.475	14	705	782	141	.264	.326	.407	733	-7	106	68	**41**	164	**462**	767	12.4	4.48	-1	.268	.326	.5	-.8	-4.3	-.5	1.0
Oak	77	85	0	.475	14	757	787	155	.264	.325	.401	726	+4	93	117	10	172	607	785	12.9	4.41	-12	.259	.331	-.6	-9.1	3.6	.0	2.1
Sea	74	88	0	.457	17	719	818	171	.255	.326	.412	738	-1	101	94	23	154	637	868	13.4	4.68	-10	.265	.343	.4	-6.9	.2	.3	-1.0
Tex	62	99	0	.385	28.5	617	785	129	.253	.322	.381	703	-10	102	130	18	173	501	863	12.9	4.56	-7	.269	.331	.5	-4.5	-6.9	-.3	-7.2
Total 1132						10317		2178	.261	.327	.406	733			1461	360		7465	1777	12.5	4.15		.261	.327					

Batter-Fielder Wins		Batting Average		On-Base Percentage		Slugging Average		On-Base Plus Slugging		Adjusted OPS		Adjusted Batter Runs	
Henderson-NY	**6.9**	Boggs-Bos	.368	Boggs-Bos	.450	Brett-KC	.585	Brett-KC	1022	Brett-KC	177	Brett-KC	64.4
Boggs-Bos	**5.6**	Buckner-Bos	.299	Evans-Bos	.378	Rice-Bos	.487	Boggs-Bos	928	Boggs-Bos	148	Boggs-Bos	50.6
Gedman-Bos	**3.5**	Gedman-Bos	.295	Gedman-Bos	.362	Gedman-Bos	.484	Gedman-Bos	846	Gedman-Bos	124	Evans-Bos	23.4
Buckner-Bos	**2.2**	Rice-Bos	.291	Rice-Bos	.349	Boggs-Bos	.478	Rice-Bos	836	2 players tied	122	Gedman-Bos	16.9

Runs		Hits		Doubles		Triples		Home Runs		Total Bases		Runs Batted In	
Henderson-NY	146	Boggs-Bos	240	Mattingly-NY	48	Wilson-KC	21	Evans-Det	40	Mattingly-NY	370	Mattingly-NY	145
Evans-Bos	110	Buckner-Bos	201	Buckner-Bos	46	Gedman-Bos	5	Evans-Bos	29	Boggs-Bos	312	Buckner-Bos	110
Boggs-Bos	107	Evans-Bos	162	Boggs-Bos	42	Armas-Bos	5	Rice-Bos	27	Buckner-Bos	301	Rice-Bos	103
Buckner-Bos	89	Rice-Bos	159	Gedman-Bos	30	Easler-Bos	4	Armas-Bos	23	Evans-Bos	280	Gedman-Bos	80

Stolen Bases		Base Stealing Runs		Fielding Runs-Infield		Fielding Runs-Outfield		Wins		Winning Pct.		Complete Games	
Henderson-NY	80	Henderson-NY	14.1	Buckner-Bos	25.4	Barfield-Tor	15.1	Guidry-NY	22	Guidry-NY	.786	Blyleven-Cle-Min	24
Buckner-Bos	18	Buckner-Bos	2.6	Barrett-Bos	16.3			Boyd-Bos	15	Boyd-Bos	.536	Boyd-Bos	13
Lyons-Bos	12	Gutierrez-Bos	1.5	Boggs-Bos	9.4			Hurst-Bos	11			Hurst-Bos	6
Gutierrez-Bos	10	Evans-Bos	.8					2 players tied	9			2 players tied	5

Strikeouts		Fewest BB/Game		Games		Saves		Base Runners/9		Adjusted Relief Runs		Relief Ranking	
Blyleven-Cle-Min	206	Haas-Mil	1.39	Quisenberry-KC	84	Quisenberry-KC	37	Ontiveros-Oak	7.96	James-Chi	24.8	Moore-Cal	47.1
Hurst-Bos	189	Boyd-Bos	2.21	Stanley-Bos	48	Crawford-Bos	12	Stanley-Bos	11.09	Stanley-Bos	13.8	Stanley-Bos	20.0
Boyd-Bos	154	Hurst-Bos	2.75	Crawford-Bos	44	Stanley-Bos	10	Clemens-Bos	11.26	Clear-Bos	3.2	Crawford-Bos	4.0
Ojeda-Bos	102	Nipper-Bos	4.56	Clear-Bos	41	Clear-Bos	3	Boyd-Bos	11.37	Crawford-Bos	3.0	Clear-Bos	2.4

Innings Pitched		Opponents' Avg.		Opponents' OBP		Earned Run Average		Adjusted ERA		Adjusted Starter Runs		Pitcher Wins	
Blyleven-Cle-Min	293.2	Stieb-Tor	.213	Saberhagen-KC	.271	Stieb-Tor	2.48	Stieb-Tor	171	Stieb-Tor	47.1	Stieb-Tor	4.9
Boyd-Bos	272.1	Nipper-Bos	.256	Boyd-Bos	.306	Boyd-Bos	3.70	Boyd-Bos	117	Boyd-Bos	20.2	Boyd-Bos	2.1
Hurst-Bos	229.1	Boyd-Bos	.261	Hurst-Bos	.327	Nipper-Bos	4.06	Nipper-Bos	106	Clemens-Bos	11.3	Stanley-Bos	2.0
Nipper-Bos	162.0	Hurst-Bos	.273	Nipper-Bos	.350	Hurst-Bos	4.51	Hurst-Bos	96	Ojeda-Bos	6.5	Clemens-Bos	1.3

1986 AMERICAN LEAGUE

TEAM	W	L	T	PCT	GB	R	OR	HR	AVG	OBP	SLG	OPS	AOPS	PF	SB	CG	HR	BB	SO	BR/9	ERA	AERA	OAV	OOB	FW	PW	BW	BSW	DIF
East																													
Bos	95	66	0	.590		794	696	144	.271	.346	.415	761	+5	101	41	36	167	**474**	1033	12.4	3.93	+7	.266	.325	-.2	4.0	6.1	-.7	5.2
NY	90	72	0	.556	5.5	797	738	188	.271	**.347**	**.430**	**777**	**+11**	99	139	13	175	492	878	12.3	4.11	+0	.263	.323	.0	.3	**9.6**	**1.0**	-1.9
Det	87	75	0	.537	8.5	798	714	**198**	.263	.338	.424	762	+6	100	138	33	183	571	880	12.3	4.02	+3	.251	.323	1.1	2.2	5.0	.6	-2.9
Tor	86	76	1	.531	9.5	809	733	181	.269	.329	.427	756	+1	103	110	16	164	487	1002	12.2	4.08	+4	.261	.322	**1.7**	2.6	.9	.0	-.0
Cle	84	78	1	.519	11.5	**831**	841	157	**.284**	.337	**.430**	767	+9	99	**141**	31	167	605	744	13.7	4.58	-9	.273	.346	-1.7	-6.3	6.6	.8	3.7
Mil	77	84	0	.478	18	667	734	127	.255	.321	.385	706	-12	103	100	29	158	494	952	12.6	4.01	+8	.267	.328	-1.2	5.1	-8.1	.0	.5
Bal	73	89	0	.451	22.5	708	760	169	.258	.327	.395	722	-4	99	64	17	177	535	954	12.6	4.30	-3	.263	.328	-.5	-2.3	-2.0	-.2	-3.1
West																													
Cal	92	70	0	.568		786	684	167	.255	.338	.404	742	+2	99	109	29	153	478	955	**11.5**	3.84	+7	.248	**.309**	1.2	4.6	3.0	.5	1.6
Tex	87	75	0	.537	5	771	743	184	.267	.331	.428	759	+2	103	103	15	145	736	**1059**	13.2	4.11	+5	.249	.340	.3	3.2	1.4	-1.1	2.2
KC	76	86	0	.469	16	654	**673**	137	.252	.313	.390	703	-12	102	97	24	**121**	479	888	12.1	**3.82**	**+12**	.258	.319	.2	**6.8**	-9.1	.0	-3.0
Oak	76	86	0	.469	16	731	760	163	.252	.322	.390	712	+0	93	139	22	166	667	937	12.8	4.31	-10	**.247**	.330	-.5	-7.1	.3	.5	1.8
Chi	72	90	0	.444	20	644	699	121	.247	.310	.363	673	-21	-104	115	18	143	561	895	12.2	3.93	+10	.251	.323	.6	6.1	-14.8	.2	-1.0
Min	71	91	0	.438	21	741	839	196	.261	.325	.428	753	+0	103	81	**39**	200	503	937	13.4	4.77	-9	.281	.342	.5	-6.6	-.2	-.8	-3.0
Sea	67	95	0	.414	25	718	835	158	.253	.326	.399	725	-5	101	93	33	171	585	944	13.9	4.65	-8	.283	.353	-1.7	-6.1	-3.6	-1.0	-1.6
Total 1134						10449		2290	.262	.330	.408	737			1470	355		7667	3058	12.7	4.18		.262	.330					

Batter-Fielder Wins		Batting Average		On-Base Percentage		Slugging Average		On-Base Plus Slugging		Adjusted OPS		Adjusted Batter Runs	
Boggs-Bos	**5.4**	Boggs-Bos	.357	Boggs-Bos	.453	Mattingly-NY	.573	Mattingly-NY	967	Mattingly-NY	162	Mattingly-NY	58.2
Rice-Bos	**3.3**	Rice-Bos	.324	Rice-Bos	.384	Rice-Bos	.490	Boggs-Bos	939	Boggs-Bos	155	Boggs-Bos	53.5
Gedman-Bos	**2.3**	Barrett-Bos	.286	Evans-Bos	.376	Boggs-Bos	.486	Rice-Bos	874	Rice-Bos	136	Rice-Bos	33.1
Evans-Bos	**1.8**	Buckner-Bos	.267	Barrett-Bos	.353	Evans-Bos	.476	Evans-Bos	853	Evans-Bos	130	Evans-Bos	26.3

Runs		Hits		Doubles		Triples		Home Runs		Total Bases		Runs Batted In	
Henderson-NY	130	Mattingly-NY	238	Mattingly-NY	53	Butler-Cle	14	Barfield-Tor	40	Mattingly-NY	388	Carter-Cle	121
Boggs-Bos	107	Boggs-Bos	207	Boggs-Bos	47	Barrett-Bos	4	Baylor-Bos	31	Rice-Bos	303	Rice-Bos	110
Rice-Bos	98	Rice-Bos	200	3 players tied	39	Armas-Bos	4	Evans-Bos	26	Boggs-Bos	282	Buckner-Bos	102
Barrett-Bos	94	Barrett-Bos	179					Rice-Bos	20	Buckner-Bos	265	Evans-Bos	97

Stolen Bases		Base Stealing Runs		Fielding Runs-Infield		Fielding Runs-Outfield		Wins		Winning Pct.		Complete Games	
Henderson-NY	87	Henderson-NY	12.8	Owen-Sea-Bos	35.8	Barfield-Tor	16.0	Clemens-Bos	24	Clemens-Bos	.857	Candiotti-Cle	17
Barrett-Bos	15	Barrett-Bos	.9	Buckner-Bos	19.5	Rice-Bos	8.4	Boyd-Bos	16	Boyd-Bos	.615	Hurst-Bos	11
Buckner-Bos	6	Romine-Bos	.4	Boggs-Bos	5.9	Evans-Bos	.3	Hurst-Bos	13			Clemens-Bos	10
2 players tied	3	Romero-Bos	.4					Nipper-Bos	10			Boyd-Bos	10

Strikeouts		Fewest BB/Game		Games		Saves		Base Runners/9		Adjusted Relief Runs		Relief Ranking	
Langston-Sea	245	Guidry-NY	1.78	Williams-Tex	80	Righetti-NY	46	Clemens-Bos	8.86	Eichhorn-Tor	43.9	Eichhorn-Tor	55.7
Clemens-Bos	238	Boyd-Bos	1.89	Stanley-Bos	66	Stanley-Bos	16	Boyd-Bos	11.30	Crawford-Bos	1.2	Crawford-Bos	.6
Hurst-Bos	167	Clemens-Bos	2.37	Sambito-Bos	53	Sambito-Bos	12	Hurst-Bos	11.46				
Boyd-Bos	129	Hurst-Bos	2.58	Crawford-Bos	40	Schiraldi-Bos	9	Nipper-Bos	13.42				

Innings Pitched		Opponents' Avg.		Opponents' OBP		Earned Run Average		Adjusted ERA		Adjusted Starter Runs		Pitcher Wins	
Blyleven-Min	271.2	Clemens-Bos	.195	Clemens-Bos	.252	Clemens-Bos	2.48	Clemens-Bos	169	Clemens-Bos	48.8	Eichhorn-Tor	5.8
Clemens-Bos	254.0	Hurst-Bos	.256	Boyd-Bos	.302	Hurst-Bos	2.99	Hurst-Bos	140	Hurst-Bos	24.0	Clemens-Bos	5.1
Boyd-Bos	214.1	Boyd-Bos	.265	Hurst-Bos	.310	Boyd-Bos	3.78	Boyd-Bos	111	Boyd-Bos	10.6	Hurst-Bos	2.7
Hurst-Bos	174.1											Schiraldi-Bos	2.3

1987 AMERICAN LEAGUE

TEAM	W	L	T	PCT	GB	R	OR	HR	AVG	OBP	SLG	OPS	AOPS	PF	SB	CG	HR	BB	SO	BR/9	ERA	AERA	OAV	OOB	FW	PW	BW	BSW	DIF
East																													
Det	98	64	0	.605		**896**	735	**225**	.272	.349	**.451**	**800**	**+14**	96	106	33	180	563	976	12.5	4.02	+6	.256	.325	.1	3.6	**12.5**	-.2	1.0
Tor	96	66	0	.593	2	845	**655**	215	.269	.336	.446	782	+3	102	126	18	158	567	1064	**11.8**	**3.74**	**+21**	**.244**	**.316**	.8	**11.7**	2.2	.2	.1
Mil	91	71	0	.562	7	862	817	163	.276	.346	.428	774	+1	103	**176**	28	169	529	1039	12.9	4.62	-1	.271	.333	-1.3	-.5	1.4	**.5**	9.9
NY	89	73	0	.549	9	788	758	196	.262	.336	.418	754	-1	99	105	19	179	542	900	12.8	4.36	+1	.266	.332	1.3	1.0	.0	.0	5.6
Bos	78	84	0	.481	20	842	825	174	**.278**	**.352**	.430	782	+3	103	77	**47**	190	517	1034	13.4	4.77	-5	.282	.344	.8	-3.2	3.8	-.7	-3.7
Bal	67	95	0	.414	31	729	880	211	.258	.322	.418	740	-4	98	69	17	226	547	870	13.3	5.01	-12	.276	.341	.8	-9.0	-3.1	-.9	-1.9
Cle	61	101	0	.377	37	742	957	187	.263	.324	.422	746	-5	101	140	24	219	606	849	14.1	5.28	-14	.278	.351	-1.8	-10.8	-4.1	.4	-3.7
West																													
Min	85	77	0	.525		786	806	196	.261	.328	.430	758	-5	104	113	16	210	564	990	13.1	4.63	+0	.266	.337	**1.6**	.0	-3.4	-.6	6.4
KC	83	79	0	.512	2	715	691	168	.262	.328	.412	740	-9	103	125	44	**128**	548	923	12.7	3.86	+19	.261	.330	-.5	10.6	-5.9	.4	-2.6
Oak	81	81	0	.500	4	806	789	199	.260	.333	.428	761	+7	94	140	18	176	531	1042	12.5	4.32	-4	.258	.324	-1.1	-2.9	5.7	.1	-1.8
Sea	78	84	0	.481	7	760	801	161	.272	.335	.428	763	-5	105	174	39	199	**497**	919	12.8	4.49	+5	.272	.332	.1	3.4	-2.9	**.5**	-4.2
Chi	77	85	0	.475	8	748	746	173	.258	.319	.415	734	-10	103	138	29	189	537	792	12.5	4.30	+7	.259	.327	.5	4.7	-7.3	.4	-2.2
Tex	75	87	0	.463	10	823	849	194	.266	.333	.430	763	-1	101	120	20	199	760	**1103**	13.7	4.63	-3	.253	.347	-1.7	-2.0	.4	-.6	-2.1
Cal	75	87	0	.463	10	770	803	172	.252	.326	.401	727	-6	97	125	20	212	504	941	12.5	4.38	-1	.264	.327	.4	-1.0	-3.8	.4	-1.9
Total	1134					11112		2634	.265	.333	.425	759			1734	372		7812	3442	12.9	4.46		.265	.333					

Batter-Fielder Wins		Batting Average		On-Base Percentage		Slugging Average		On-Base Plus Slugging		Adjusted OPS		Adjusted Batter Runs	
Boggs-Bos	**6.5**	Boggs-Bos	.363	Boggs-Bos	.461	McGwire-Oak	.618	Boggs-Bos	1049	Boggs-Bos	172	Boggs-Bos	64.5
Barrett-Bos	**3.0**	Evans-Bos	.305	Evans-Bos	.417	Boggs-Bos	.588	Evans-Bos	986	Evans-Bos	155	Evans-Bos	48.0
Evans-Bos	**2.8**	Barrett-Bos	.293	Barrett-Bos	.351	Evans-Bos	.569	Burks-Bos	765	Burks-Bos	97	Greenwell-Bos	27.3
Greenwell-Bos	**2.2**	Burks-Bos	.272	Owen-Bos	.337	Burks-Bos	.441	Barrett-Bos	701	Barrett-Bos	85	Horn-Bos	8.8

Runs		Hits		Doubles		Triples		Home Runs		Total Bases		Runs Batted In	
Molitor-Mil	114	Seitzer-KC	207	Molitor-Mil	41	Wilson-KC	15	McGwire-Oak	49	Bell-Tor	369	Bell-Tor	134
Evans-Bos	109	Puckett-Min	207	Boggs-Bos	40	Owen-Bos	7	Evans-Bos	34	Boggs-Bos	324	Evans-Bos	123
Boggs-Bos	108	Boggs-Bos	200	Evans-Bos	37	Greenwell-Bos	6	Boggs-Bos	24	Evans-Bos	308	Greenwell-Bos	89
Burks-Bos	94	Evans-Bos	165	Greenwell-Bos	31	Boggs-Bos	6	Burks-Bos	20	Burks-Bos	246	Boggs-Bos	89

Stolen Bases		Base Stealing Runs		Fielding Runs-Infield		Fielding Runs-Outfield		Wins		Winning Pct.		Complete Games	
Reynolds-Sea	60	Wilson-KC	9.1	Barrett-Bos	32.6	White-Cal	17.6	Stewart-Oak	20	Clemens-Bos	.690	Clemens-Bos	18
Burks-Bos	27	Burks-Bos	3.8	Boggs-Bos	8.2	Burks-Bos	6.9	Clemens-Bos	20	Hurst-Bos	.536	Hurst-Bos	15
Barrett-Bos	15	Barrett-Bos	2.6					Hurst-Bos	15			Nipper-Bos	6
Owen-Bos	11							Nipper-Bos	11			3 players tied	4

Strikeouts		Fewest BB/Game		Games		Saves		Base Runners/9		Adjusted Relief Runs		Relief Ranking	
Langston-Sea	262	Long-Chi	1.49	Eichhorn-Tor	89	Henke-Tor	34	Henke-Tor	8.33	Henke-Tor	21.6	Henke-Tor	29.2
Clemens-Bos	256	Clemens-Bos	2.65	Schiraldi-Bos	62	Gardner-Bos	10	Clemens-Bos	10.86	Schiraldi-Bos	1.2	Schiraldi-Bos	1.8
Hurst-Bos	190	Hurst-Bos	2.87	Gardner-Bos	49	Schiraldi-Bos	6	Hurst-Bos	11.92	Bolton-Bos	1.0	Bolton-Bos	.5
Sellers-Bos	99	Nipper-Bos	3.21	Sambito-Bos	47			Schiraldi-Bos	12.48				

Innings Pitched		Opponents' Avg.		Opponents' OBP		Earned Run Average		Adjusted ERA		Adjusted Starter Runs		Pitcher Wins	
Hough-Tex	285.1	Key-Tor	.221	Key-Tor	.272	Key-Tor	2.76	Key-Tor	164	Clemens-Bos	49.2	Viola-Min	4.5
Clemens-Bos	281.2	Clemens-Bos	.235	Clemens-Bos	.295	Clemens-Bos	2.97	Clemens-Bos	154	Hurst-Bos	5.2	Clemens-Bos	4.5
Hurst-Bos	238.2	Hurst-Bos	.262	Hurst-Bos	.317	Hurst-Bos	4.41	Hurst-Bos	104			Hurst-Bos	.6
Nipper-Bos	174.0	Nipper-Bos	.284	Nipper-Bos	.345	Nipper-Bos	5.43	Nipper-Bos	84			Schiraldi-Bos	.2

1988 AMERICAN LEAGUE

TEAM	W	L	T	PCT	GB	R	OR	HR	AVG	OBP	SLG	OPS	AOPS	PF	SB	CG	HR	BB	SO	BR/9	ERA	AERA	OAV	OOB	FW	PW	BW	BSW	DIF
East																													
Bos	89	73	0	.549		**813**	689	124	**.283**	**.357**	.420	**777**	**+12**	105	65	26	143	493	**1085**	12.3	3.97	+4	.259	.322	1.6	2.3	**10.9**	-.5	-6.4
Det	88	74	0	.543	1	703	658	143	.250	.324	.378	702	-1	97	87	34	150	497	890	11.8	3.71	+3	.248	.312	.6	2.1	.3	-.3	4.2
Tor	87	75	0	.537	2	763	680	**158**	.268	.332	.419	751	+8	101	107	16	143	528	904	12.4	3.80	+4	.256	.326	.6	2.6	6.3	.5	-3.9
Mil	87	75	0	.537	2	682	**616**	113	.257	.314	.375	689	-9	101	**159**	30	125	**437**	832	**11.2**	3.45	**+16**	.248	**.303**	-.0	**8.9**	-6.6	1.0	2.7
NY	85	76	0	.528	3.5	772	748	148	.263	.333	.395	728	+3	100	146	16	157	487	861	12.7	4.26	-7	.267	.328	-.9	-4.9	4.0	**1.2**	5.0
Cle	78	84	0	.481	11	666	731	134	.261	.314	.387	701	-8	103	97	35	120	442	812	12.4	4.16	-1	.270	.326	-.3	-.5	-5.8	-.3	3.8
Bal	54	107	0	.335	34.5	550	789	137	.238	.305	.359	664	-13	-98	69	20	153	523	709	13.2	4.54	-13	.274	.340	.0	-9.8	-9.2	-.7	-6.8
West																													
Oak	104	58	0	.642		800	620	156	.263	.336	.399	735	+8	97	129	22	116	553	983	11.8	**3.44**	+10	.247	.316	.9	6.3	7.7	.2	7.9
Min	91	71	0	.562	13	759	672	151	.274	.340	**.421**	761	+9	103	107	18	146	453	897	12.3	3.93	+4	.266	.325	**2.1**	2.3	7.4	-.6	-1.2
KC	84	77	0	.522	19.5	704	648	121	.259	.321	.391	712	-3	101	137	29	**102**	465	886	12.1	3.65	+9	.258	.318	-.3	5.5	-1.8	.5	-.3
Cal	75	87	0	.463	29	714	771	124	.261	.321	.385	706	-1	98	86	26	135	568	817	13.1	4.32	-10	.270	.338	-.9	-7.4	-.2	-.6	3.0
Chi	71	90	0	.441	32.5	631	757	132	.244	.303	.370	673	-13	100	98	11	138	533	754	12.7	4.12	-3	.266	.331	-2.1	-2.0	-9.6	-.2	4.3
Tex	70	91	0	.435	33.5	637	735	112	.252	.320	.368	688	-10	103	130	**41**	129	654	912	12.6	4.05	+1	**.244**	.329	-.7	.7	-6.8	.2	-4.0
Sea	68	93	0	.422	35.5	664	744	148	.257	.317	.398	715	-5	105	95	28	144	558	981	12.5	4.15	+1	.256	.327	-.2	.3	-3.7	-.7	-8.2
Total	1131					9858		1901	.259	.324	.391	715			1512	352		7191	2323	12.4	3.97		.259	.324					

Batter-Fielder Wins		Batting Average		On-Base Percentage		Slugging Average		On-Base Plus Slugging		Adjusted OPS		Adjusted Batter Runs	
Boggs-Bos	**6.4**	Boggs-Bos	.366	Boggs-Bos	.476	Canseco-Oak	.569	Boggs-Bos	965	Canseco-Oak	171	Boggs-Bos	62.2
Greenwell-Bos	**4.7**	Greenwell-Bos	.325	Greenwell-Bos	.416	Greenwell-Bos	.531	Greenwell-Bos	946	Boggs-Bos	165	Greenwell-Bos	49.1
Burks-Bos	**2.7**	Burks-Bos	.294	Evans-Bos	.375	Boggs-Bos	.490	Evans-Bos	861	Greenwell-Bos	157	Evans-Bos	27.2
Reed-Bos	**2.0**	Evans-Bos	.293	Burks-Bos	.367	Evans-Bos	.487	Burks-Bos	848	Evans-Bos	134	Burks-Bos	23.4

Runs		Hits		Doubles		Triples		Home Runs		Total Bases		Runs Batted In	
Boggs-Bos	128	Puckett-Min	234	Boggs-Bos	45	3 players tied	11	Canseco-Oak	42	Puckett-Min	358	Canseco-Oak	124
Evans-Bos	96	Boggs-Bos	214	Greenwell-Bos	39	Greenwell-Bos	8	Greenwell-Bos	22	Greenwell-Bos	313	Greenwell-Bos	119
Burks-Bos	93	Greenwell-Bos	192	Burks-Bos	37	Evans-Bos	7	Evans-Bos	21	Boggs-Bos	286	Evans-Bos	111
Greenwell-Bos	86	Barrett-Bos	173	Evans-Bos	31	Boggs-Bos	6	Burks-Bos	18	Evans-Bos	272	Burks-Bos	92

Stolen Bases		Base Stealing Runs		Fielding Runs-Infield		Fielding Runs-Outfield		Wins		Winning Pct.		Complete Games	
Henderson-NY	93	Henderson-NY	15.9	Guillen-Chi	40.8	Barfield-Tor	13.1	Viola-Min	24	Viola-Min	.774	Stewart-Oak	14
Burks-Bos	25	Burks-Bos	2.3	Reed-Bos	7.9	Burks-Bos	2.7	Hurst-Bos	18	Hurst-Bos	.750	Clemens-Bos	14
Greenwell-Bos	16	Evans-Bos	.8	Barrett-Bos	5.4	Greenwell-Bos	2.6	Clemens-Bos	18	Clemens-Bos	.600	Hurst-Bos	7
Barrett-Bos	7	Greenwell-Bos	.7	Boggs-Bos	2.7			2 players tied	9				

Strikeouts		Fewest BB/Game		Games		Saves		Base Runners/9		Adjusted Relief Runs		Relief Ranking	
Clemens-Bos	291	Anderson-Min	1.65	Crim-Mil	70	Eckersley-Oak	45	Eckersley-Oak	7.93	Henneman-Det	19.7	Henneman-Det	37.7
Hurst-Bos	166	Clemens-Bos	2.11	Smith-Bos	64	Smith-Bos	29	Clemens-Bos	9.72	Stanley-Bos	9.5	Smith-Bos	15.1
Gardner-Bos	106	Hurst-Bos	2.70	Stanley-Bos	57	Stanley-Bos	5	Smith-Bos	11.15	Smith-Bos	9.5	Stanley-Bos	9.3
Smith-Bos	96			Lamp-Bos	46	Gardner-Bos	2	Gardner-Bos	11.23	Lamp-Bos	4.0	Lamp-Bos	5.6

Innings Pitched		Opponents' Avg.		Opponents' OBP		Earned Run Average		Adjusted ERA		Adjusted Starter Runs		Pitcher Wins	
Stewart-Oak	275.2	Robinson-Det	.197	Higuera-Mil	.263	Anderson-Min	2.45	Anderson-Min	167	Higuera-Mil	40.2	Viola-Min	4.7
Clemens-Bos	264.0	Clemens-Bos	.220	Clemens-Bos	.270	Higuera-Mil	2.45	Clemens-Bos	141	Clemens-Bos	34.3	Clemens-Bos	3.7
Hurst-Bos	216.2	Hurst-Bos	.264	Hurst-Bos	.316	Clemens-Bos	2.93	Hurst-Bos	113	Gardner-Bos	11.1	Smith-Bos	1.5
Gardner-Bos	149.0					Hurst-Bos	3.66			Hurst-Bos	10.2	Hurst-Bos	1.1

1989 AMERICAN LEAGUE

TEAM	W	L	T	PCT	GB	R	OR	HR	AVG	OBP	SLG	OPS	AOPS	PF	SB	CG	HR	BB	SO	BR/9	ERA	AERA	OAV	OOB	FW	PW	BW	BSW	DIF
East																													
Tor	89	73	0	.549		731	651	142	.260	.323	.398	721	+3	99	144	12	99	478	849	11.8	3.58	+6	.255	.317	-.1	3.5	3.0	.4	1.3
Bal	87	75	0	.537	2	708	686	129	.252	.326	.379	705	+1	97	118	16	134	486	676	12.6	4.00	-5	.272	.331	**2.3**	-3.2	1.3	.0	5.5
Bos	83	79	0	.512	6	**774**	735	108	**.277**	**.351**	**.403**	**754**	**+5**	106	56	14	131	548	1054	12.5	4.01	+2	.261	.328	-.1	1.5	**6.4**	-.7	-5.1
Mil	81	81	0	.500	8	707	679	126	.259	.318	.382	700	-3	99	**165**	16	129	457	812	12.2	3.80	+1	.265	.321	-1.8	.8	-1.9	.8	2.1
NY	74	87	0	.460	14.5	698	792	130	.269	.331	.391	722	+4	99	137	15	150	521	787	13.4	4.50	-14	.281	.344	.1	-10.0	3.1	.2	.0
Cle	73	89	0	.451	16	604	654	127	.245	.310	.365	675	-12	102	74	23	107	**452**	844	11.8	3.65	+9	.257	.313	.4	5.2	-8.8	-.9	-4.0
Det	59	103	0	.364	30	617	816	116	.242	.318	.351	669	-10	98	103	24	150	652	831	13.9	4.53	-16	.274	.352	-.3	-11.6	-6.3	-.2	-3.6
West																													
Oak	99	63	0	.611		712	**576**	127	.261	.331	.381	712	+3	97	157	17	103	510	930	**11.3**	**3.09**	**+20**	**.238**	**.305**	-.2	**10.4**	3.6	.8	3.4
KC	92	70	0	.568	7	690	635	101	.261	.329	.373	702	-3	100	154	27	**86**	455	978	11.7	3.55	+9	.257	.314	.7	5.3	-.9	**.9**	5.0
Cal	91	71	0	.562	8	669	578	**145**	.256	.311	.386	697	-3	98	89	**32**	113	465	897	11.6	3.28	+16	.253	.312	1.7	9.1	-3.3	-.0	2.5
Tex	83	79	0	.512	16	695	714	122	.263	.326	.394	720	+0	102	101	26	119	654	**1112**	12.4	3.91	+2	.239	.324	-.6	1.1	.5	-.2	1.2
Min	80	82	0	.494	19	740	738	117	.276	.334	.402	736	-1	107	111	19	139	500	851	12.8	4.28	-3	.269	.332	1.1	-2.1	.8	-.0	-.7
Sea	73	89	0	.451	26	694	728	134	.257	.320	.384	704	-5	103	81	15	114	560	897	12.7	4.00	+1	.259	.330	-1.1	.5	-3.8	-.8	-2.9
Chi	69	92	0	.429	29.5	693	750	94	.271	.328	.383	711	+2	98	97	9	144	539	778	12.9	4.23	-9	.269	.335	-1.6	-6.4	1.7	-.4	-4.8
Total	1133					9732		1718	.261	.326	.384	709			1587	265		7277	2296	12.4	3.88		.261	.326					

Batter-Fielder Wins		Batting Average		On-Base Percentage		Slugging Average		On-Base Plus Slugging		Adjusted OPS		Adjusted Batter Runs	
R.Henderson-NY-Oak	4.6	Puckett-Min	.339	Boggs-Bos	.430	Sierra-Tex	.543	McGriff-Tor	924	McGriff-Tor	161	McGriff-Tor	50.1
Boggs-Bos	**4.3**	Boggs-Bos	.330	Evans-Bos	.397	Esasky-Bos	.500	Boggs-Bos	879	Boggs-Bos	140	Boggs-Bos	41.3
Evans-Bos	**2.3**	Greenwell-Bos	.308	Reed-Bos	.376	Evans-Bos	.463	Evans-Bos	861	Evans-Bos	135	Evans-Bos	28.4
Reed-Bos	**2.1**	Reed-Bos	.288	Greenwell-Bos	.370	Boggs-Bos	.449	Esasky-Bos	855	Esasky-Bos	130	Esasky-Bos	22.1

Runs		Hits		Doubles		Triples		Home Runs		Total Bases		Runs Batted In	
R.Henderson-NY-Oak	113	Puckett-Min	215	Boggs-Bos	51	Sierra-Tex	14	McGriff-Tor	36	Sierra-Tex	344	Sierra-Tex	119
Boggs-Bos	113	Boggs-Bos	205	Reed-Bos	42	Boggs-Bos	7	Esasky-Bos	30	Esasky-Bos	282	Esasky-Bos	108
Greenwell-Bos	87	Greenwell-Bos	178	Greenwell-Bos	36	Burks-Bos	6	Evans-Bos	20	Boggs-Bos	279	Evans-Bos	100
Evans-Bos	82	Esasky-Bos	156	Evans-Bos	27	Esasky-Bos	5	Greenwell-Bos	14	Greenwell-Bos	256	Greenwell-Bos	95

Stolen Bases		Base Stealing Runs		Fielding Runs-Infield		Fielding Runs-Outfield		Wins		Winning Pct.		Complete Games	
R.Henderson-NY-Oak	77	R.Henderson-NY-Oak	12.0	Reynolds-Sea	24.6	Snyder-Cle	12.9	Saberhagen-KC	23	Saberhagen-KC	.793	Saberhagen-KC	12
Burks-Bos	21	Burks-Bos	2.9	Boggs-Bos	3.1			Clemens-Bos	17	Clemens-Bos	.607	Clemens-Bos	8
Greenwell-Bos	13	Greenwell-Bos	1.1	Reed-Bos	2.5			Boddicker-Bos	15	Boddicker-Bos	.577	Boddicker-Bos	3
2 players tied	4	Kutcher-Bos	.7					Dopson-Bos	12			Dopson-Bos	2

Strikeouts		Fewest BB/Game		Games		Saves		Base Runners/9		Adjusted Relief Runs		Relief Ranking	
Ryan-Tex	301	Key-Tor	1.13	Crim-Mil	76	Russell-Tex	38	Saberhagen-KC	8.71	Montgomery-KC	25.5	Montgomery-KC	33.7
Clemens-Bos	230	Boddicker-Bos	3.02	Murphy-Bos	74	Smith-Bos	25	Lamp-Bos	9.85	Lamp-Bos	19.4	Murphy-Bos	16.9
Boddicker-Bos	145	Clemens-Bos	3.30	Smith-Bos	64	Murphy-Bos	9	Smith-Bos	10.95	Murphy-Bos	14.4	Lamp-Bos	9.9
Murphy-Bos	107	Dopson-Bos	3.67	Stanley-Bos	43	Stanley-Bos	4	Clemens-Bos	11.23	Smith-Bos	4.8	Smith-Bos	7.2

Innings Pitched		Opponents' Avg.		Opponents' OBP		Earned Run Average		Adjusted ERA		Adjusted Starter Runs		Pitcher Wins	
Saberhagen-KC	262.1	Ryan-Tex	.187	Saberhagen-KC	.251	Saberhagen-KC	2.16	Saberhagen-KC	179	Saberhagen-KC	48.4	Saberhagen-KC	5.3
Clemens-Bos	253.1	Clemens-Bos	.231	Clemens-Bos	.305	Clemens-Bos	3.13	Clemens-Bos	132	Clemens-Bos	25.7	Clemens-Bos	2.7
Boddicker-Bos	211.2	Dopson-Bos	.257	Dopson-Bos	.328	Dopson-Bos	3.99	Dopson-Bos	103	Boddicker-Bos	4.8	Murphy-Bos	1.8
Dopson-Bos	169.1	Boddicker-Bos	.267	Boddicker-Bos	.330	Boddicker-Bos	4.00	Boddicker-Bos	103	Dopson-Bos	2.6	Lamp-Bos	1.1

1990 AMERICAN LEAGUE

TEAM	W	L	T	PCT	GB	R	OR	HR	AVG	OBP	SLG	OPS	AOPS	PF	SB	CG	HR	BB	SO	BR/9	ERA	AERA	OAV	OOB	FW	PW	BW	BSW	DIF
East																													
Bos	88	74	0	.543		699	664	106	**.272**	**.344**	.395	739	+1	105	53	15	**92**	519	997	12.5	3.72	+10	.261	.327	-.2	5.7	2.4	-1.1	.2
Tor	86	76	0	.531	2	**767**	661	167	.265	.328	**.419**	**747**	+5	102	111	6	143	**445**	892	11.9	3.84	+3	.260	.317	**2.0**	1.8	3.9	.2	-2.9
Det	79	83	0	.488	9	750	754	**172**	.259	.337	.409	746	**+7**	101	82	15	154	661	856	13.3	4.39	-10	.259	.341	-.7	-6.6	5.5	-.6	.4
Cle	77	85	0	.475	11	732	737	110	.267	.324	.391	715	-1	100	107	12	163	518	860	12.9	4.26	-8	.270	.334	.2	-5.4	-.6	.0	1.7
Bal	76	85	0	.472	11.5	669	698	132	.245	.330	.370	700	-2	97	94	10	161	537	776	12.5	4.04	-6	.264	.328	1.6	-3.9	-.2	-.2	-1.8
Mil	74	88	0	.457	14	732	760	128	.256	.320	.384	704	-4	100	**164**	23	121	469	771	12.9	4.08	-5	.275	.331	-1.8	-3.4	-2.3	.7	-.2
NY	67	95	0	.414	21	603	749	147	.241	.300	.366	666	-16	-101	119	15	144	618	909	12.9	4.21	-5	.261	.336	-.4	-3.7	-12.1	.6	1.6
West																													
Oak	103	59	0	.636		733	**570**	164	.254	.336	.391	727	**+7**	96	141	18	123	494	831	**11.2**	**3.18**	**+17**	**.238**	**.302**	**2.0**	**9.5**	**5.9**	**.8**	3.9
Chi	94	68	0	.580	9	682	633	106	.258	.320	.379	699	-3	98	140	17	106	548	914	11.8	3.61	+6	.244	.316	-.3	3.8	-2.4	-.5	12.5
Tex	83	79	0	.512	20	676	696	110	.259	.331	.376	707	-3	100	115	**25**	113	623	997	12.5	3.83	+2	.248	.327	-.8	1.5	-1.3	.5	2.1
Cal	80	82	0	.494	23	690	706	147	.260	.329	.391	720	+3	98	69	21	106	544	944	12.8	3.79	+1	.267	.334	-1.4	.6	2.1	-.4	-2.0
Sea	77	85	0	.475	26	640	680	107	.259	.333	.373	706	-4	101	105	21	120	606	**1064**	12.3	3.69	+7	.243	.321	-.6	4.5	-1.4	.0	-6.5
KC	75	86	0	.466	27.5	707	709	100	.267	.328	.395	723	+2	99	107	18	116	560	1006	13.0	3.93	-2	.264	.334	-.2	-1.3	2.5	-.2	-6.3
Min	74	88	0	.457	29	666	729	100	.265	.324	.385	709	-9	106	96	13	134	489	872	12.7	4.12	+1	.273	.332	1.1	.4	-5.8	-.1	-2.6
Total	1133					9746		1796	.259	.327	.388	715			1503	229		7631	2689	12.5	3.91		.259	.327					

Batter-Fielder Wins		Batting Average		On-Base Percentage		Slugging Average		On-Base Plus Slugging		Adjusted OPS		Adjusted Batter Runs	
R.Henderson-Oak	**7.7**	Brett-KC	.329	R.Henderson-Oak	.439	Fielder-Det	.592	R.Henderson-Oak	1016	R.Henderson-Oak	189	R.Henderson-Oak	64.2
J.Reed-Bos	**2.3**	Boggs-Bos	.302	Boggs-Bos	.386	Burks-Bos	.486	Burks-Bos	835	Burks-Bos	125	Boggs-Bos	20.5
Pena-Bos	**.8**	Greenwell-Bos	.297	J.Reed-Bos	.371	Brunansky-Bos	.438	Boggs-Bos	804	Boggs-Bos	120	Burks-Bos	18.3
3 players tied	**.6**	Burks-Bos	.296	Greenwell-Bos	.367	Greenwell-Bos	.434	Greenwell-Bos	801	Greenwell-Bos	118	Greenwell-Bos	15.4

Runs		Hits		Doubles		Triples		Home Runs		Total Bases		Runs Batted In	
R.Henderson-Oak	119	Palmeiro-Tex	191	Brett-KC	45	Fernandez-Tor	17	Fielder-Det	51	Fielder-Det	339	Fielder-Det	132
Burks-Bos	89	Boggs-Bos	187	J.Reed-Bos	45	Burks-Bos	8	Burks-Bos	21	Burks-Bos	286	Burks-Bos	89
Boggs-Bos	89	Greenwell-Bos	181	Boggs-Bos	44	Greenwell-Bos	6	Brunansky-Bos	15	Greenwell-Bos	265	Greenwell-Bos	73
Greenwell-Bos	71	Burks-Bos	174	Burks-Bos	33	2 players tied	5	Greenwell-Bos	14	Boggs-Bos	259	Brunansky-Bos	71

Stolen Bases		Base Stealing Runs		Fielding Runs-Infield		Fielding Runs-Outfield		Wins		Winning Pct.		Complete Games	
R.Henderson-Oak	65	R.Henderson-Oak	10.8	Espinoza-NY	22.9	Orsulak-Bal	8.9	Welch-Oak	27	Welch-Oak	.818	Stewart-Oak	11
Burks-Bos	9	Romine-Bos	.9	Quintana-Bos	13.2	Brunansky-Bos	3.9	Clemens-Bos	21	Clemens-Bos	.778	Morris-Det	11
Pena-Bos	8	Barrett-Bos	.9	J.Reed-Bos	7.4			Boddicker-Bos	17	Boddicker-Bos	.680	Clemens-Bos	7
Greenwell-Bos	8			Rivera-Bos	5.0			Harris-Bos	13			Boddicker-Bos	4

Strikeouts		Fewest BB/Game		Games		Saves		Base Runners/9		Adjusted Relief Runs		Relief Ranking	
Ryan-Tex	232	Anderson-Min	1.86	Thigpen-Chi	77	Thigpen-Chi	57	Eckersley-Oak	5.52	Farr-KC	26.9	Eckersley-Oak	44.7
Clemens-Bos	209	Clemens-Bos	2.13	Murphy-Bos	68	Reardon-Bos	21	Clemens-Bos	10.01				
Boddicker-Bos	143	Boddicker-Bos	2.72	Reardon-Bos	47	Gray-Bos	9	Boddicker-Bos	12.00				
Harris-Bos	117	Harris-Bos	3.76	Lamp-Bos	47	Murphy-Bos	7	Bolton-Bos	12.11				

Innings Pitched		Opponents' Avg.		Opponents' OBP		Earned Run Average		Adjusted ERA		Adjusted Starter Runs		Pitcher Wins	
Stewart-Oak	267.0	Ryan-Tex	.188	Ryan-Tex	.267	Clemens-Bos	1.93	Clemens-Bos	212	Clemens-Bos	50.6	Clemens-Bos	6.2
Clemens-Bos	228.1	Clemens-Bos	.228	Clemens-Bos	.278	Boddicker-Bos	3.36	Boddicker-Bos	122	Boddicker-Bos	19.1	Boddicker-Bos	2.0
Boddicker-Bos	228.0	Boddicker-Bos	.258	Boddicker-Bos	.319	Harris-Bos	4.00	Harris-Bos	102	Bolton-Bos	10.8	Bolton-Bos	1.3
Harris-Bos	184.1	Harris-Bos	.265	Harris-Bos	.338					Dopson-Bos	2.8	Reardon-Bos	1.1

1991 AMERICAN LEAGUE

TEAM	W	L	T	PCT	GB	R	OR	HR	AVG	OBP	SLG	OPS	AOPS	PF	SB	CG	HR	BB	SO	BR/9	ERA	AERA	OAV	OOB	FW	PW	BW	BSW	DIF
East																													
Tor	91	71	0	.562		684	**622**	133	.257	.322	.400	722	-6	104	148	10	121	523	971	**11.5**	**3.50**	**+20**	**.238**	**.307**	-.6	**11.3**	-3.3	**1.0**	1.6
Det	84	78	0	.519	7	817	794	**209**	.247	.333	.416	749	+4	102	109	18	148	593	739	13.6	4.51	-7	.280	.348	.7	-5.3	3.7	.4	3.5
Bos	84	78	0	.519	7	731	712	126	.269	.340	.401	741	-1	106	59	15	147	530	999	12.3	4.01	+8	.257	.323	.0	4.7	.7	-.5	-1.9
Mil	83	79	0	.512	8	799	744	116	.271	.336	.396	732	+4	98	106	23	147	527	859	12.7	4.14	-4	.266	.332	-.0	-2.6	3.6	-.4	1.5
NY	71	91	0	.438	20	674	777	147	.256	.316	.387	703	-8	101	109	3	152	506	936	12.8	4.42	-6	.271	.334	-.9	-4.1	-5.4	.7	-.2
Bal	67	95	0	.414	24	686	796	170	.254	.319	.401	720	+2	96	50	8	147	504	868	12.8	4.59	-14	.273	.333	**1.4**	-10.4	.9	-.5	-5.4
Cle	57	105	0	.352	34	576	759	79	.254	.313	.350	663	-18	101	84	22	110	**441**	862	12.7	4.23	-2	.276	.329	-1.8	-1.0	-12.7	-.6	-7.9
West																													
Min	95	67	0	.586		776	652	140	**.280**	**.344**	.420	764	+5	105	107	21	139	488	876	11.9	3.69	+16	.255	.317	1.2	8.9	4.5	-.4	-.2
Chi	87	75	0	.537	8	758	681	139	.262	.336	.391	727	+2	98	134	**28**	154	601	923	11.8	3.79	+5	.239	.315	.0	3.4	2.5	-.0	.0
Tex	85	77	0	.525	10	**829**	814	177	.270	.341	**.424**	**765**	**+12**	98	102	9	151	662	**1022**	13.3	4.47	-9	.262	.341	-1.0	-7.0	**10.1**	.0	1.8
Oak	84	78	0	.519	11	760	776	159	.248	.331	.389	720	+3	95	**151**	14	155	655	892	13.3	4.57	-16	.260	.342	.5	-12.4	4.0	.7	10.2
Sea	83	79	0	.512	12	702	674	126	.255	.328	.383	711	-4	100	97	10	136	628	1003	12.7	3.79	+9	.253	.332	.3	5.6	-2.2	.2	-1.9
KC	82	80	0	.506	13	727	722	117	.264	.328	.394	722	-2	101	119	17	**105**	529	1004	12.6	3.92	+6	.261	.327	-.5	3.5	-1.0	-.2	-.8
Cal	81	81	0	.500	14	653	649	115	.255	.314	.374	688	-11	100	94	18	141	543	990	12.1	3.69	+12	.250	.321	.8	6.8	-8.2	-.3	.9
Total	1134					10172		1953	.260	.329	.395	724			1469	216		7730	2944	12.6	4.09		.260	.329					

Batter-Fielder Wins		Batting Average		On-Base Percentage		Slugging Average		On-Base Plus Slugging		Adjusted OPS		Adjusted Batter Runs	
C.Ripken-Bal	**8.5**	Franco-Tex	.341	Thomas-Chi	.453	Tartabull-KC	.593	Thomas-Chi	1006	Thomas-Chi	181	Thomas-Chi	71.1
Boggs-Bos	**3.8**	Boggs-Bos	.332	Boggs-Bos	.421	Clark-Bos	.466	Boggs-Bos	881	Boggs-Bos	137	Boggs-Bos	33.3
Plantier-Bos	**1.6**	Greenwell-Bos	.300	Quintana-Bos	.375	Boggs-Bos	.460	Clark-Bos	840	Clark-Bos	125	Clark-Bos	19.1
2 players tied	**1.4**	Quintana-Bos	.295	Clark-Bos	.374	Burks-Bos	.422	Quintana-Bos	787	Quintana-Bos	112	Plantier-Bos	15.4

Runs		Hits		Doubles		Triples		Home Runs		Total Bases		Runs Batted In	
Molitor-Mil	133	Molitor-Mil	216	Palmeiro-Tex	49	Molitor-Mil	13	Fielder-Det	44	C.Ripken-Bal	368	Fielder-Det	133
Boggs-Bos	93	Boggs-Bos	181	Reed-Bos	42	Johnson-Chi	13	Canseco-Oak	44	Boggs-Bos	251	Clark-Bos	87
Reed-Bos	87	Reed-Bos	175	Boggs-Bos	42	Greenwell-Bos	6	Clark-Bos	28	Reed-Bos	236	Greenwell-Bos	83
Greenwell-Bos	76	Greenwell-Bos	163	Burks-Bos	33	2 players tied	3	Brunansky-Bos	16	Greenwell-Bos	228	Quintana-Bos	71

Stolen Bases		Base Stealing Runs		Fielding Runs-Infield		Fielding Runs-Outfield		Wins		Winning Pct.		Complete Games	
R.Henderson-Oak	58	Alomar-Tor	7.8	Sojo-Cal	26.6	Orsulak-Bal	17.2	Gullickson-Det	20	Erickson-Min	.714	McDowell-Chi	15
Greenwell-Bos	15	Greenwell-Bos	1.5	Reed-Bos	10.8	Brunansky-Bos	.4	Erickson-Min	20	Clemens-Bos	.643	Clemens-Bos	13
Lyons-Bos	10	Lyons-Bos	1.1	Quintana-Bos	8.9			Clemens-Bos	18			Morton-Bos	1
Pena-Bos	8	Pena-Bos	.7	Rivera-Bos	7.4			Hesketh-Bos	12			Harris-Bos	1

Strikeouts		Fewest BB/Game		Games		Saves		Base Runners/9		Adjusted Relief Runs		Relief Ranking	
Clemens-Bos	241	Swindell-Cle	1.17	D.Ward-Tor	81	Harvey-Cal	46	Gray-Bos	7.30	Frohwirth-Bal	22.0	Harvey-Cal	32.8
Harris-Bos	127	Clemens-Bos	2.16	Fossas-Bos	64	Reardon-Bos	40	Clemens-Bos	9.59	Gray-Bos	13.3	Reardon-Bos	16.1
Hesketh-Bos	104	Harris-Bos	3.59	Reardon-Bos	57	Harris-Bos	2	Hesketh-Bos	11.45	Reardon-Bos	8.6	Gray-Bos	10.0
Gardiner-Bos	91			Harris-Bos	53	2 players tied	1	Darwin-Bos	11.91	Fossas-Bos	4.0	Fossas-Bos	3.3

Innings Pitched		Opponents' Avg.		Opponents' OBP		Earned Run Average		Adjusted ERA		Adjusted Starter Runs		Pitcher Wins	
Clemens-Bos	271.1	Ryan-Tex	.172	Ryan-Tex	.263	Clemens-Bos	2.62	Clemens-Bos	165	Clemens-Bos	46.5	Clemens-Bos	4.7
Harris-Bos	173.0	Clemens-Bos	.221	Clemens-Bos	.270	Harris-Bos	3.85	Harris-Bos	113	Hesketh-Bos	18.1	Hesketh-Bos	1.8
Hesketh-Bos	153.1	Harris-Bos	.243	Harris-Bos	.318					Harris-Bos	10.0	Reardon-Bos	1.6
Gardiner-Bos	130.0											Harris-Bos	1.3

1992 AMERICAN LEAGUE

TEAM	W	L	T	PCT	GB	R	OR	HR	AVG	OBP	SLG	OPS	AOPS	PF	SB	CG	HR	BB	SO	BR/9	ERA	AERA	OAV	OOB	FW	PW	BW	BSW	DIF
East																													
Tor	96	66	0	.593		780	682	163	.263	.333	**.414**	**747**	+3	105	129	18	124	541	954	12.1	3.91	+5	.248	.318	1.4	3.0	2.7	1.0	6.9
Mil	92	70	0	.568	4	740	**604**	82	.268	.330	.375	705	-2	99	**256**	19	127	**435**	793	**11.3**	**3.43**	+13	**.246**	**.305**	**1.6**	7.2	-.1	**1.1**	1.2
Bal	89	73	0	.549	7	705	656	148	.259	.340	.398	738	+3	103	89	20	124	518	846	12.1	3.79	+7	.256	.322	1.4	4.4	3.3	-.2	-.8
NY	76	86	0	.469	20	733	746	163	.261	.328	.406	734	+4	100	78	20	129	612	851	13.0	4.21	-6	.263	.338	.2	-4.3	3.7	-.1	-4.5
Cle	76	86	0	.469	20	674	746	127	.266	.323	.383	706	-2	99	144	13	159	566	890	12.9	4.11	-4	.268	.336	-1.3	-3.0	-1.9	.3	.9
Det	75	87	0	.463	21	**791**	794	**182**	.256	.337	.407	744	+6	101	66	10	155	564	693	13.3	4.60	-13	.277	.343	.1	-9.8	5.5	-.6	-1.2
Bos	73	89	0	.451	23	599	669	84	.246	.321	.347	668	-19	107	44	22	107	535	943	12.3	3.58	**+18**	.255	.323	-1.2	**10.0**	-12.7	-1.3	-2.9
West																													
Oak	96	66	0	.593		745	672	142	.258	**.346**	.386	732	**+10**	95	143	8	129	601	843	12.7	3.73	+1	.256	.331	-.4	.7	**9.5**	.6	4.6
Min	90	72	0	.556	6	747	653	104	**.277**	.341	.391	732	+1	104	123	16	121	479	923	11.8	3.70	+10	.254	.316	1.3	5.9	1.9	-.4	.3
Chi	86	76	0	.531	10	738	690	110	.261	.336	.383	719	+2	99	160	21	123	550	810	12.3	3.82	+1	.252	.323	-.6	.9	2.6	1.0	1.0
Tex	77	85	0	.475	19	682	753	159	.250	.321	.393	714	+2	97	81	19	113	598	**1034**	13.0	4.09	-7	.264	.337	-2.0	-4.6	1.7	-.3	1.2
KC	72	90	0	.444	24	610	667	75	.256	.315	.364	679	-13	103	131	9	**106**	512	834	12.3	3.81	+7	.259	.323	-.2	4.2	-9.6	-.1	-3.3
Cal	72	90	0	.444	24	579	671	88	.243	.301	.338	639	-22	101	160	**26**	130	532	888	12.6	3.84	+4	.264	.331	-.9	2.7	-16.7	-.5	6.4
Sea	64	98	0	.395	32	679	799	149	.263	.323	.402	725	+1	101	100	21	129	661	894	13.6	4.55	-12	.266	.348	.3	-8.9	.5	-.2	-8.8
Total	1134					9802		1776	.259	.328	.385	713			1704	242		7704	2196	12.5	3.94		.259	.328					

Batter-Fielder Wins		Batting Average		On-Base Percentage		Slugging Average		On-Base Plus Slugging		Adjusted OPS		Adjusted Batter Runs	
Ventura-Chi	**5.1**	E.Martinez-Sea	.343	Thomas-Chi	.439	McGwire-Oak	.585	Thomas-Chi	975	McGwire-Oak	178	Thomas-Chi	66.4
Reed-Bos	**1.6**	Brunansky-Bos	.266	Brunansky-Bos	.354	Brunansky-Bos	.445	Brunansky-Bos	799	Brunansky-Bos	115	Brunansky-Bos	10.9
Valentin-Bos	**1.3**	Boggs-Bos	.259	Boggs-Bos	.353	Boggs-Bos	.358	Boggs-Bos	711	Boggs-Bos	94	Wedge-Bos	3.1
Naehring-Bos	**.7**	Reed-Bos	.247	Reed-Bos	.321	Reed-Bos	.316	Reed-Bos	638	Reed-Bos	74	Valentin-Bos	2.8

Runs		Hits		Doubles		Triples		Home Runs		Total Bases		Runs Batted In	
Phillips-Det	114	Puckett-Min	210	Thomas-Chi	46	Johnson-Chi	12	Gonzalez-Tex	43	Puckett-Min	313	Fielder-Det	124
Reed-Bos	64	Reed-Bos	136	E.Martinez-Sea	46	Boggs-Bos	4	Brunansky-Bos	15	Brunansky-Bos	204	Brunansky-Bos	74
Boggs-Bos	62	Boggs-Bos	133	Brunansky-Bos	31	Burks-Bos	3	Vaughn-Bos	13	Boggs-Bos	184	Vaughn-Bos	57
Brunansky-Bos	47	Brunansky-Bos	122	Reed-Bos	27	Brunansky-Bos	3	Burks-Bos	8	Reed-Bos	174	Boggs-Bos	50

Stolen Bases		Base Stealing Runs		Fielding Runs-Infield		Fielding Runs-Outfield		Wins		Winning Pct.		Complete Games	
Lofton-Cle	66	Lofton-Cle	10.3	Reed-Bos	30.4	Raines-Chi	9.6	Morris-Tor	21	Mussina-Bal	.783	McDowell-Chi	13
Reed-Bos	7	Burks-Bos	.4	Cooper-Bos	5.8	Zupcic-Bos	.9	Brown-Tex	21	Clemens-Bos	.621	Clemens-Bos	11
Winningham-Bos	6	Valentin-Bos	.2					Clemens-Bos	18			Viola-Bos	6
Burks-Bos	5							Viola-Bos	13			Darwin-Bos	2

Strikeouts		Fewest BB/Game		Games		Saves		Base Runners/9		Adjusted Relief Runs		Relief Ranking	
Johnson-Sea	241	Bosio-Mil	1.71	Rogers-Tex	81	Eckersley-Oak	51	Eckersley-Oak	8.32	D.Ward-Tor	22.0	Eckersley-Oak	35.7
Clemens-Bos	208	Clemens-Bos	2.26	Harris-Bos	70	Reardon-Bos	27	Clemens-Bos	10.00	Harris-Bos	17.9	Harris-Bos	20.5
Darwin-Bos	124	Viola-Bos	3.37	Fossas-Bos	60	Harris-Bos	4	Viola-Bos	11.72				
Viola-Bos	121			Darwin-Bos	51	Darwin-Bos	3	Darwin-Bos	12.11				

Innings Pitched		Opponents' Avg.		Opponents' OBP		Earned Run Average		Adjusted ERA		Adjusted Starter Runs		Pitcher Wins	
Brown-Tex	265.2	Johnson-Sea	.206	Mussina-Bal	278	Clemens-Bos	2.41	Clemens-Bos	177	Clemens-Bos	45.1	Clemens-Bos	5.3
Clemens-Bos	246.2	Clemens-Bos	.224	Clemens-Bos	.278	Viola-Bos	3.44	Viola-Bos	124	Viola-Bos	22.0	Viola-Bos	2.4
Viola-Bos	238.0	Viola-Bos	.242	Viola-Bos	.313					Darwin-Bos	7.0	Harris-Bos	2.1
Darwin-Bos	161.1									Dopson-Bos	.6	Quantrill-Bos	.8

1993 AMERICAN LEAGUE

TEAM	W	L	T	PCT	GB	R	OR	HR	AVG	OBP	SLG	OPS	AOPS	PF	SB	CG	HR	BB	SO	BR/9	ERA	AERA	OAV	OOB	FW	PW	BW	BSW	DIF
East																													
Tor	95	67	0	.586		847	742	159	**.279**	.350	**.436**	786	+8	102	**170**	11	134	620	1023	13.1	4.21	+4	.261	.336	.5	2.4	7.1	**1.7**	2.3
NY	88	74	0	.543	7	821	761	178	**.279**	.353	.435	788	**+13**	97	39	11	170	552	899	12.8	4.35	-4	.266	.333	.6	-2.8	11.7	-.6	-1.8
Bal	85	77	0	.525	10	786	745	157	.267	.346	.413	759	-2	105	73	21	153	579	900	12.8	4.31	+5	.261	.333	.9	2.9	.2	-.5	.6
Det	85	77	0	.525	10	**899**	837	178	.275	**.362**	.434	**796**	**+13**	100	104	11	188	542	828	13.4	4.65	-7	.276	.342	-1.0	-4.8	**12.0**	-.2	-2.0
Bos	80	82	0	.494	15	686	698	114	.264	.330	.395	725	-12	106	73	9	127	552	997	**12.3**	3.77	**+22**	**.252**	**.322**	-.4	**12.5**	-8.0	.0	-5.1
Cle	76	86	0	.469	19	790	813	141	.275	.335	.409	744	-1	100	159	7	182	591	888	13.8	4.58	-5	.281	.351	-1.9	-3.2	-.9	1.3	-.3
Mil	69	93	0	.426	26	733	792	125	.258	.328	.378	706	-10	99	138	**26**	153	522	810	13.0	4.45	-3	.271	.336	-.9	-2.3	-7.1	-.4	-1.2
West																													
Chi	94	68	0	.580		776	**664**	162	.265	.338	.411	749	+2	98	106	16	125	566	974	12.4	**3.70**	+14	.255	.328	.2	8.1	1.9	.0	2.8
Tex	86	76	0	.531	8	835	751	**181**	.267	.329	.431	760	+5	97	113	20	144	562	957	13.0	4.28	-2	.267	.337	-1.0	-1.6	3.9	-.2	3.8
KC	84	78	0	.519	10	675	694	125	.263	.320	.397	717	-15	107	100	16	**105**	571	985	12.4	4.04	+14	.254	.327	1.0	8.2	-10.9	-.6	5.3
Sea	82	80	0	.506	12	734	731	161	.260	.339	.406	745	-3	102	91	22	135	605	**1083**	13.0	4.20	+6	.259	.337	**1.5**	3.9	-1.2	-.6	-2.5
Cal	71	91	0	.438	23	684	770	114	.260	.331	.380	711	-12	103	169	**26**	153	550	843	13.1	4.34	+4	.270	.339	-.3	2.7	-8.3	-.0	-4.1
Min	71	91	0	.438	23	693	830	121	.264	.327	.385	712	-10	101	83	5	148	**514**	901	13.4	4.71	-7	.283	.344	.9	-4.8	-7.7	-.4	2.0
Oak	68	94	0	.420	26	715	846	158	.254	.330	.394	724	-1	95	131	8	157	680	864	14.1	4.90	-16	.276	.356	.2	-12.7	-.3	.5	-.7
Total	1134					10674		2074	.267	.337	.408	745			1549	209		8006	2952	13.0	4.32		.267	.337					

Batter-Fielder Wins		Batting Average		On-Base Percentage		Slugging Average		On-Base Plus Slugging		Adjusted OPS		Adjusted Batter Runs	
Olerud-Tor	**5.7**	Olerud-Tor	.363	Olerud-Tor	.473	Gonzalez-Tex	.632	Olerud-Tor	1072	Olerud-Tor	184	Olerud-Tor	75.0
Valentin-Bos	**2.9**	Greenwell-Bos	.315	Vaughn-Bos	.390	Vaughn-Bos	.525	Vaughn-Bos	915	Vaughn-Bos	136	Vaughn-Bos	29.6
Fletcher-Bos	**1.6**	Vaughn-Bos	.297	Greenwell-Bos	.379	Greenwell-Bos	.480	Greenwell-Bos	859	Greenwell-Bos	122	Greenwell-Bos	17.6
Greenwell-Bos	**1.0**	Hatcher-Bos	.287	Cooper-Bos	.355	Valentin-Bos	.447	Valentin-Bos	793	Valentin-Bos	105	Valentin-Bos	4.2

Runs		Hits		Doubles		Triples		Home Runs		Total Bases		Runs Batted In	
Palmeiro-Tex	124	Molitor-Tor	211	Olerud-Tor	54	Johnson-Chi	14	Gonzalez-Tex	46	Griffey-Sea	359	Belle-Cle	129
Vaughn-Bos	86	Greenwell-Bos	170	Valentin-Bos	40	Greenwell-Bos	6	Vaughn-Bos	29	Vaughn-Bos	283	Vaughn-Bos	101
Fletcher-Bos	81	Vaughn-Bos	160	Greenwell-Bos	38	Fletcher-Bos	5	Greenwell-Bos	13	Greenwell-Bos	259	Greenwell-Bos	72
Greenwell-Bos	77	Cooper-Bos	147	Vaughn-Bos	34	3 players tied	3	Dawson-Bos	13	2 players tied	209	Dawson-Bos	67

Stolen Bases		Base Stealing Runs		Fielding Runs-Infield		Fielding Runs-Outfield		Wins		Winning Pct.		Complete Games	
Lofton-Cle	70	Lofton-Cle	10.5	Gallego-NY	26.2	Kirby-Cle	14.1	McDowell-Chi	22	Key-NY	.750	Finley-Cal	13
Fletcher-Bos	16	Fletcher-Bos	2.5	Valentin-Bos	16.4			Darwin-Bos	15	Darwin-Bos	.577	Viola-Bos	2
Hatcher-Bos	14	McNeely-Bos	1.3	Fletcher-Bos	13.3			Viola-Bos	11			Darwin-Bos	2
McNeely-Bos	6	Hatcher-Bos	.6					Clemens-Bos	11			Clemens-Bos	2

Strikeouts		Fewest BB/Game		Games		Saves		Base Runners/9		Adjusted Relief Runs		Relief Ranking	
Johnson-Sea	308	Key-NY	1.64	Harris-Bos	80	D.Ward-Tor	45	Montgomery-KC	9.27	Montgomery-KC	22.1	Montgomery-KC	44.2
Clemens-Bos	160	Darwin-Bos	1.92	Fossas-Bos	71	Montgomery-KC	45	Darwin-Bos	9.73	Harris-Bos	9.5	Harris-Bos	11.1
Darwin-Bos	130	Clemens-Bos	3.15	Russell-Bos	51	Russell-Bos	33	Clemens-Bos	11.88	Quantrill-Bos	8.4	Quantrill-Bos	9.9
Harris-Bos	103	Viola-Bos	3.53	Quantrill-Bos	49	Harris-Bos	8	Bankhead-Bos	12.31	Bankhead-Bos	7.8	Bankhead-Bos	3.9

Innings Pitched		Opponents' Avg.		Opponents' OBP		Earned Run Average		Adjusted ERA		Adjusted Starter Runs		Pitcher Wins	
Eldred-Mil	258.0	Johnson-Sea	.203	Darwin-Bos	.272	Appier-KC	2.56	Appier-KC	180	Appier-KC	50.6	Appier-KC	5.1
Darwin-Bos	229.1	Darwin-Bos	.230	Clemens-Bos	.315	Viola-Bos	3.14	Viola-Bos	148	Darwin-Bos	33.4	Darwin-Bos	3.5
Clemens-Bos	191.2	Clemens-Bos	.244	Viola-Bos	.331	Darwin-Bos	3.26	Darwin-Bos	142	Viola-Bos	27.3	Viola-Bos	2.6
Viola-Bos	183.2	Viola-Bos	.259			Clemens-Bos	4.46	Clemens-Bos	104	Sele-Bos	20.6	Russell-Bos	1.9

1994 AMERICAN LEAGUE

TEAM	W	L	T	PCT	GB	R	OR	HR	AVG	OBP	SLG	OPS	AOPS	PF	SB	CG	HR	BB	SO	BR/9	ERA	AERA	OAV	OOB	FW	PW	BW	BSW	DIF
East																													
NY	70	43	0	.619		670	534	139	**.290**	**.374**	.462	**836**	**+18**	97	55	8	120	398	656	12.9	4.34	+6	.267	.335	.1	2.8	**11.8**	-.6	-.6
Bal	63	49	0	.563	6.5	589	**497**	139	.272	.349	.438	787	-4	106	69	13	131	**351**	666	12.5	4.31	+17	.263	.327	**1.5**	7.2	-1.8	**.6**	-.4
Tor	55	60	0	.478	16	566	579	115	.269	.336	.424	760	-7	101	79	13	127	482	**832**	13.8	4.70	+4	.266	.348	.2	1.8	-3.5	.3	-1.2
Bos	54	61	0	.470	17	552	621	120	.263	.334	.421	755	-11	105	81	6	120	450	729	13.9	4.93	+2	.276	.351	.2	1.0	-5.8	.0	1.1
Det	53	62	0	.461	18	652	671	161	.265	.352	.454	806	+5	101	46	15	148	449	560	14.3	5.38	-9	.282	.356	.1	-4.7	3.2	-.6	-2.6
Central																													
Chi	67	46	0	.593		633	498	121	.287	.366	.444	810	+9	99	77	13	115	377	754	**12.1**	**3.96**	+18	**.250**	**.317**	.2	7.8	5.8	.2	-3.5
Cle	66	47	0	.584	1	**679**	562	**167**	**.290**	.351	**.484**	835	+11	101	131	**17**	**94**	404	666	13.6	4.36	+9	.275	.346	-.4	4.1	6.3	**.6**	-1.1
KC	64	51	0	.557	4	574	532	100	.269	.335	.419	754	-11	105	**140**	5	95	392	717	12.6	4.23	**+19**	.260	.328	.2	**7.9**	-6.1	.4	4.0
Min	53	60	0	.469	14	594	688	103	.276	.340	.427	767	-5	101	94	6	153	388	602	14.5	5.68	-13	.299	.361	.4	-7.6	-2.1	.5	5.3
Mil	53	62	0	.461	15	547	586	99	.263	.335	.408	743	-14	105	59	11	127	421	577	13.2	4.62	+10	.269	.340	-.0	4.5	-7.3	-.5	-1.2
West																													
Tex	52	62	0	.456		613	697	124	.280	.353	.436	789	+1	101	82	10	157	394	683	14.1	5.45	-11	.288	.351	-1.4	-6.5	1.1	.0	1.6
Oak	51	63	0	.447	1	549	589	113	.260	.330	.399	729	-6	92	91	12	128	510	732	13.7	4.80	-7	.257	.347	-.3	-3.5	-2.5	.0	.2
Sea	49	63	0	.438	2	569	616	153	.269	.335	.451	786	-2	102	48	13	109	486	763	14.3	4.99	-1	.274	.357	-.8	-.7	-1.4	-.2	-3.9
Cal	47	68	0	.409	5.5	543	660	120	.264	.334	.409	743	-12	102	65	11	150	436	682	14.3	5.42	-9	.287	.360	.5	-5.3	-6.0	-.9	1.2
Total	797					8330		1774	.273	.345	.434	779			1117	153		5938	9619	13.5	4.80		.273	.345					

Batter-Fielder Wins		Batting Average		On-Base Percentage		Slugging Average		On-Base Plus Slugging		Adjusted OPS		Adjusted Batter Runs	
Thomas-Chi	**5.2**	O'Neill-NY	.359	Thomas-Chi	.487	Thomas-Chi	.729	Thomas-Chi	1217	Thomas-Chi	212	Thomas-Chi	75.4
Valentin-Bos	**2.2**	Valentin-Bos	.316	Vaughn-Bos	.408	Vaughn-Bos	.576	Vaughn-Bos	984	Vaughn-Bos	144	Vaughn-Bos	27.4
Vaughn-Bos	**1.1**	Vaughn-Bos	.310	Valentin-Bos	.400	Valentin-Bos	.505	Valentin-Bos	905	Valentin-Bos	127	Valentin-Bos	13.8
Cooper-Bos	**.6**	Cooper-Bos	.282	Nixon-Bos	.360	2 players tied	.453	Greenwell-Bos	800	Greenwell-Bos	101	Greenwell-Bos	1.0

Runs		Hits		Doubles		Triples		Home Runs		Total Bases		Runs Batted In	
Thomas-Chi	106	Lofton-Cle	160	Knoblauch-Min	45	L.Johnson-Chi	14	Griffey-Sea	40	Belle-Cle	294	Puckett-Min	112
Vaughn-Bos	65	Vaughn-Bos	122	Valentin-Bos	26	Cooper-Bos	4	Vaughn-Bos	26	Vaughn-Bos	227	Vaughn-Bos	82
Nixon-Bos	60	Nixon-Bos	109	Vaughn-Bos	25	Valentin-Bos	2	Dawson-Bos	16	Cooper-Bos	167	Cooper-Bos	53
Greenwell-Bos	60	Cooper-Bos	104	Greenwell-Bos	25	Berryhill-Bos	2	Cooper-Bos	13	Valentin-Bos	152	Valentin-Bos	49

Stolen Bases		Base Stealing Runs		Fielding Runs-Infield		Fielding Runs-Outfield		Wins		Winning Pct.		Complete Games	
Lofton-Cle	60	Lofton-Cle	9.0	Valentin-Mil	21.3	Edmonds-Cal	8.3	Key-NY	17	Bere-Chi	.857	Johnson-Sea	9
Nixon-Bos	42	Nixon-Bos	5.7	Cooper-Bos	10.1	Greenwell-Bos	.2	Clemens-Bos	9			Clemens-Bos	3
Tinsley-Bos	13	Tinsley-Bos	2.9	Naehring-Bos	4.5			Sele-Bos	8			Sele-Bos	2
Fletcher-Bos	8	Fletcher-Bos	1.4	Valentin-Bos	3.7			Hesketh-Bos	8			VanEgmond-Bos	1

Strikeouts		Fewest BB/Game		Games		Saves		Base Runners/9		Adjusted Relief Runs		Relief Ranking	
Johnson-Sea	204	Gubicza-KC	1.80	Wickman-NY	53	L.Smith-Bal	33	Ontiveros-Oak	9.75	Eichhorn-Bal	21.2	Eichhorn-Bal	30.1
Clemens-Bos	168	Hesketh-Bos	3.63	Fossas-Bos	44	Ryan-Bos	13	Clemens-Bos	10.49	Ryan-Bos	13.4	Ryan-Bos	19.6
Sele-Bos	105	Clemens-Bos	3.74	Ryan-Bos	42	4 players tied	1	Hesketh-Bos	13.03	Howard-Bos	6.2	Howard-Bos	3.1
Hesketh-Bos	83	Sele-Bos	3.77	Howard-Bos	37			Sele-Bos	13.12	Bankhead-Bos	1.9	Bankhead-Bos	2.3

Innings Pitched		Opponents' Avg.		Opponents' OBP		Earned Run Average		Adjusted ERA		Adjusted Starter Runs		Pitcher Wins	
Finley-Cal	183.1	Clemens-Bos	.203	Ontiveros-Oak	.271	Ontiveros-Oak	2.65	Clemens-Bos	177	Cone-KC	38.7	Cone-KC	4.3
Clemens-Bos	170.2	Sele-Bos	.261	Clemens-Bos	.288	Clemens-Bos	2.85	Sele-Bos	132	Clemens-Bos	38.5	Clemens-Bos	3.2
Sele-Bos	143.1	Hesketh-Bos	.267	Hesketh-Bos	.334	Sele-Bos	3.83	Hesketh-Bos	118	Sele-Bos	17.9	Ryan-Bos	1.8
Hesketh-Bos	114.0			Sele-Bos	.342	Hesketh-Bos	4.26			Hesketh-Bos	4.7	Sele-Bos	1.6

1995 AMERICAN LEAGUE

TEAM	W	L	T	PCT	GB	R	OR	HR	AVG	OBP	SLG	OPS	AOPS	PF	SB	CG	HR	BB	SO	BR/9	ERA	AERA	OAV	OOB	FW	PW	BW	BSW	DIF
East																													
Bos	86	58	0	.597		791	698	175	.280	.357	.455	812	+6	103	99	7	**127**	476	888	12.9	4.39	+10	.268	.334	-1.2	6.0	5.2	-.0	4.1
NY	79	65	1	.549	7	749	688	122	.276	.357	.420	777	+2	99	50	18	159	535	908	13.0	4.56	+1	.261	.334	**1.4**	.8	3.6	-.5	1.7
Bal	71	73	0	.493	15	704	640	173	.262	.342	.428	770	-3	102	92	**19**	149	523	930	12.3	4.31	+11	**.245**	.322	**1.4**	6.0	-1.6	-.2	-6.6
Det	60	84	0	.417	26	654	844	159	.247	.327	.404	731	-11	100	73	5	170	536	729	14.8	5.49	-12	.296	.365	-.4	-8.9	-7.5	-.3	5.2
Tor	56	88	0	.389	30	642	777	140	.260	.328	.409	737	-10	100	75	16	145	654	894	14.2	4.88	-3	.267	.356	.0	-1.8	-6.7	**.4**	-8.1
Central																													
Cle	100	44	0	.694		**840**	**607**	**207**	**.291**	**.361**	**.479**	**840**	**+14**	102	**132**	10	135	**445**	926	**12.1**	**3.83**	**+23**	.255	**.320**	-.2	**12.0**	**10.1**	**.4**	5.7
KC	70	74	0	.486	30	629	691	119	.260	.328	.396	724	-15	102	120	11	142	503	763	13.0	4.49	+7	.268	.338	.4	4.0	-9.8	.2	3.1
Chi	68	76	1	.472	32	755	758	146	.280	.354	.431	785	+7	96	110	12	164	617	892	14.2	4.85	-8	.275	.356	-.5	-5.4	6.1	**.4**	-4.6
Mil	65	79	0	.451	35	740	747	128	.266	.336	.409	745	-12	106	105	7	146	603	699	14.3	4.82	+4	.280	.360	-.4	2.3	-8.4	.3	-.8
Min	56	88	0	.389	44	703	889	120	.279	.346	.419	765	-3	101	105	7	210	533	790	14.3	5.76	-17	.287	.356	-.1	-12.4	-1.4	-.3	-1.8
West																													
Sea	79	66	0	.545		796	708	182	.276	.350	.448	798	+5	101	110	9	149	591	**1068**	13.8	4.50	+6	.268	.347	-.3	3.6	3.6	**.4**	-.7
Cal	78	67	0	.538	1	801	697	186	.277	.352	.448	800	+7	99	58	8	163	486	901	12.9	4.52	+4	.265	.333	.2	2.5	5.5	-.7	-2.1
Tex	74	70	0	.514	4.5	691	720	138	.265	.338	.410	748	-10	103	90	14	152	514	838	13.6	4.66	+4	.278	.346	.0	2.3	-6.1	-.3	6.1
Oak	67	77	0	.465	11.5	730	761	169	.264	.341	.420	761	+2	95	112	8	153	556	890	13.6	4.93	-8	.269	.347	-.2	-5.6	2.0	.3	-1.4
Total	1010					10225		2164	.270	.344	.427	771			1331	151		7572	2116	13.5	4.71		.270	.344					

Batter-Fielder Wins		Batting Average		On-Base Percentage		Slugging Average		On-Base Plus Slugging		Adjusted OPS		Adjusted Batter Runs	
E.Martinez-Sea	**5.8**	E.Martinez-Sea	.356	E.Martinez-Sea	.479	Belle-Cle	.690	E.Martinez-Sea	1107	E.Martinez-Sea	184	E.Martinez-Sea	73.4
Valentin-Bos	**4.6**	Naehring-Bos	.307	Naehring-Bos	.415	Vaughn-Bos	.575	Vaughn-Bos	963	Vaughn-Bos	143	Vaughn-Bos	34.8
Naehring-Bos	**2.3**	Canseco-Bos	.306	Valentin-Bos	.399	Canseco-Bos	.556	Canseco-Bos	933	Valentin-Bos	137	Valentin-Bos	31.0
Vaughn-Bos	**1.9**	Vaughn-Bos	.300	Vaughn-Bos	.388	Valentin-Bos	.533	Valentin-Bos	931	Canseco-Bos	136	Canseco-Bos	21.0

Runs		Hits		Doubles		Triples		Home Runs		Total Bases		Runs Batted In	
E.Martinez-Sea	121	Johnson-Chi	186	E.Martinez-Sea	52	Lofton-Cle	13	Belle-Cle	50	Belle-Cle	377	Belle-Cle	126
Belle-Cle	121	Vaughn-Bos	165	Belle-Cle	52	O'Leary-Bos	6	Vaughn-Bos	39	Vaughn-Bos	316	Vaughn-Bos	126
Valentin-Bos	108	Valentin-Bos	155	Valentin-Bos	37	Greenwell-Bos	4	Valentin-Bos	27	Valentin-Bos	277	Valentin-Bos	102
Vaughn-Bos	98	Greenwell-Bos	143	O'Leary-Bos	31	3 players tied	3	Canseco-Bos	24	Greenwell-Bos	221	Canseco-Bos	81

Stolen Bases		Base Stealing Runs		Fielding Runs-Infield		Fielding Runs-Outfield		Wins		Winning Pct.		Complete Games	
Lofton-Cle	54	Johnson-Chi	6.7	Fryman-Det	27.3	Cordova-Min	13.8	Mussina-Bal	19	Johnson-Sea	.900	McDowell-NY	8
Valentin-Bos	20	Valentin-Bos	2.7	Alicea-Bos	14.9			Wakefield-Bos	16	Hanson-Bos	.750	Wakefield-Bos	6
Tinsley-Bos	18	Hosey-Bos	1.3	Naehring-Bos	6.8			Hanson-Bos	15	Wakefield-Bos	.667	Hanson-Bos	1
Alicea-Bos	13	Tinsley-Bos	1.2	Valentin-Bos	6.2			Clemens-Bos	10				

Strikeouts		Fewest BB/Game		Games		Saves		Base Runners/9		Adjusted Relief Runs		Relief Ranking	
Johnson-Sea	294	Mussina-Bal	2.03	Orosco-Bal	65	Mesa-Cle	46	Percival-Cal	7.78	Mesa-Cle	25.5	Mesa-Cle	44.5
Hanson-Bos	139	Hanson-Bos	2.84	Belinda-Bos	63	Belinda-Bos	10	Maddux-Bos	10.34	Belinda-Bos	13.9	Belinda-Bos	19.8
Clemens-Bos	132	Wakefield-Bos	3.13	Cormier-Bos	48	Ryan-Bos	7	Belinda-Bos	10.72	Maddux-Bos	11.9	Cormier-Bos	8.1
Wakefield-Bos	119			Hudson-Bos	39	3 players tied	1	Wakefield-Bos	11.06	Cormier-Bos	8.6	Maddux-Bos	6.2

Innings Pitched		Opponents' Avg.		Opponents' OBP		Earned Run Average		Adjusted ERA		Adjusted Starter Runs		Pitcher Wins	
Cone-Tor-NY	229.1	Johnson-Sea	.201	Johnson-Sea	.266	Johnson-Sea	2.48	Johnson-Sea	193	Johnson-Sea	53.9	Johnson-Sea	4.6
Wakefield-Bos	195.1	Wakefield-Bos	.227	Wakefield-Bos	.300	Wakefield-Bos	2.95	Wakefield-Bos	165	Wakefield-Bos	37.9	Wakefield-Bos	4.2
Hanson-Bos	186.2	Hanson-Bos	.258	Hanson-Bos	.311	Hanson-Bos	4.24	Hanson-Bos	115	Hanson-Bos	13.7	Belinda-Bos	1.8
Clemens-Bos	140.0									Clemens-Bos	11.0	Hanson-Bos	1.2

1996 AMERICAN LEAGUE

TEAM	W	L	T	PCT	GB	R	OR	HR	AVG	OBP	SLG	OPS	AOPS	PF	SB	CG	HR	BB	SO	BR/9	ERA	AERA	OAV	OOB	FW	PW	BW	BSW	DIF
East																													
NY	92	70	0	.568		871	787	162	.288	.360	.436	796	+0	100	96	6	**143**	610	1139	13.3	4.65	+6	**.265**	.341	1.2	4.4	1.7	-.2	3.9
Bal	88	74	1	.543	4	949	903	**257**	.274	.350	.472	822	+6	99	76	13	209	597	1047	13.7	5.14	-4	.280	.349	.9	-3.0	5.2	-.4	4.2
Bos	85	77	0	.525	7	928	921	209	.283	.359	.457	816	+2	102	91	17	185	722	**1165**	14.7	4.98	+2	.279	.360	-1.2	1.5	2.9	-.2	1.0
Tor	74	88	0	.457	18	766	809	177	.259	.331	.420	751	-11	-99	116	**19**	187	610	1033	13.2	4.57	+10	.266	.340	.2	6.4	-8.8	.5	-5.2
Det	53	109	0	.327	39	783	1103	204	.256	.323	.420	743	-14	-100	87	10	241	784	957	16.1	6.38	-20	.296	.384	-1.4	-18.4	-11.6	-.5	3.8
Central																													
Cle	99	62	0	.615		952	**769**	218	**.293**	**.369**	.475	844	+11	100	160	13	173	484	1033	**12.7**	**4.34**	**+13**	.271	**.331**	-.7	8.2	10.6	**1.0**	-.6
Chi	85	77	0	.525	14.5	898	794	195	.281	.360	.447	807	+7	96	105	7	174	616	1039	13.4	4.52	+5	.270	.343	.2	3.6	6.9	.2	-7.0
Mil	80	82	0	.494	19.5	894	899	178	.279	.353	.441	794	-5	104	101	6	213	635	846	14.1	5.14	+1	.278	.354	-1.2	.7	-3.1	-.2	2.7
Min	78	84	0	.481	21.5	877	900	118	.288	.357	.425	782	-5	102	143	13	233	581	959	13.6	5.28	-3	.277	.346	1.1	-2.1	-2.5	.5	-.0
KC	75	86	0	.466	24	746	786	123	.267	.332	.398	730	-17	-100	**195**	17	176	**460**	926	12.9	4.55	+10	.277	.335	.0	6.8	-12.6	.5	-.4
West																													
Tex	90	72	1	.556		928	799	221	.284	.358	.469	827	+1	106	83	**19**	168	582	976	13.6	4.65	**+13**	.278	.347	**1.5**	**8.4**	1.2	.2	-2.2
Sea	85	76	0	.528	4.5	**993**	895	245	.287	.366	**.484**	**850**	**+12**	100	90	4	216	605	1000	14.0	5.21	-5	.279	.353	.1	-3.6	**10.9**	-.0	-2.9
Oak	78	84	0	.481	12	861	900	243	.265	.344	.452	796	+0	99	58	7	205	644	884	14.4	5.20	-4	.287	.362	.6	-3.5	.2	-.5	.3
Cal	70	91	0	.435	19.5	762	943	192	.276	.339	.431	770	-8	101	53	12	219	662	1052	14.3	5.30	-5	.275	.357	-.9	-3.6	-6.9	-.8	1.8
Total	1133					12208		2742	.277	.350	.445	795			1454	163		8592	4056	13.9	4.99		.277	.350					

Batter-Fielder Wins		Batting Average		On-Base Percentage		Slugging Average		On-Base Plus Slugging		Adjusted OPS		Adjusted Batter Runs	
Alomar-Bal	**6.1**	Rodriguez-Sea	.358	McGwire-Oak	.467	McGwire-Oak	.730	McGwire-Oak	1198	McGwire-Oak	199	F.Thomas-Chi	71.5
Vaughn-Bos	**2.3**	Vaughn-Bos	.326	Vaughn-Bos	.420	Vaughn-Bos	.583	Vaughn-Bos	1003	Vaughn-Bos	149	Vaughn-Bos	50.2
Canseco-Bos	**1.9**	Valentin-Bos	.296	Valentin-Bos	.374	Valentin-Bos	.436	Valentin-Bos	811	Valentin-Bos	103	Canseco-Bos	25.7
3 players tied	**1.7**	O'Leary-Bos	.260	O'Leary-Bos	.327	O'Leary-Bos	.427	O'Leary-Bos	753	O'Leary-Bos	87	Jefferson-Bos	23.8

Runs		Hits		Doubles		Triples		Home Runs		Total Bases		Runs Batted In	
Rodriguez-Sea	141	Molitor-Min	225	Rodriguez-Sea	54	Knoblauch-Min	14	McGwire-Oak	52	Rodriguez-Sea	379	Belle-Cle	148
Vaughn-Bos	118	Vaughn-Bos	207	Jefferson-Bos	30	O'Leary-Bos	5	Vaughn-Bos	44	Vaughn-Bos	370	Vaughn-Bos	143
Valentin-Bos	84	Valentin-Bos	156	Vaughn-Bos	29	Jefferson-Bos	4	Canseco-Bos	28	Valentin-Bos	230	Canseco-Bos	82
Naehring-Bos	77	Jefferson-Bos	134	Valentin-Bos	29	2 players tied	3	Stanley-Bos	24	Jefferson-Bos	229	O'Leary-Bos	81

Stolen Bases		Base Stealing Runs		Fielding Runs-Infield		Fielding Runs-Outfield		Wins		Winning Pct.		Complete Games	
Lofton-Cle	75	Lofton-Cle	10.6	Gonzalez-Tor	28.4	Becker-Min	17.2	Pettitte-NY	21	Nagy-Cle	.773	Hentgen-Tor	10
Frye-Bos	18	Frye-Bos	2.6	Naehring-Bos	7.9			Wakefield-Bos	14			Wakefield-Bos	6
Valentin-Bos	9	Garciaparra-Bos	1.1	Valentin-Bos	6.4			Gordon-Bos	12			Clemens-Bos	6
Cuyler-Bos	7	Greenwell-Bos	.9					Clemens-Bos	10			Gordon-Bos	4

Strikeouts		Fewest BB/Game		Games		Saves		Base Runners/9		Adjusted Relief Runs		Relief Ranking	
Clemens-Bos	257	Haney-KC	2.01	Myers-Det	83	Wetteland-NY	43	Percival-Cal	8.64	M.Rivera-NY	35.3	Hernandez-Chi	54.7
Gordon-Bos	171	Wakefield-Bos	3.83	Guardado-Min	83	Slocumb-Bos	31	Clemens-Bos	12.09	Slocumb-Bos	19.2	Slocumb-Bos	34.3
Wakefield-Bos	140	Clemens-Bos	3.93	Slocumb-Bos	75	Belinda-Bos	2	Slocumb-Bos	13.61	Maddux-Bos	4.1	Maddux-Bos	2.9
Sele-Bos	137	Gordon-Bos	4.38	Eshelman-Bos	39	Hudson-Bos	1	Wakefield-Bos	14.46				

Innings Pitched		Opponents' Avg.		Opponents' OBP		Earned Run Average		Adjusted ERA		Adjusted Starter Runs		Pitcher Wins	
Hentgen-Tor	265.2	Guzman-Tor	.228	Guzman-Tor	.289	Guzman-Tor	2.93	Guzman-Tor	171	Hentgen-Tor	52.7	Hentgen-Tor	5.2
Clemens-Bos	242.2	Clemens-Bos	.237	Clemens-Bos	.317	Clemens-Bos	3.63	Clemens-Bos	140	Clemens-Bos	41.1	Clemens-Bos	3.3
Gordon-Bos	215.2	Wakefield-Bos	.280	Wakefield-Bos	.353	Wakefield-Bos	5.14	Wakefield-Bos	99			Slocumb-Bos	3.3
Wakefield-Bos	211.2	Gordon-Bos	.284	Gordon-Bos	.359	Gordon-Bos	5.59	Gordon-Bos	91			2 players tied	.3

1997 AMERICAN LEAGUE

TEAM	W	L	T	PCT	GB	R	OR	HR	AVG	OBP	SLG	OPS	AOPS	PF	SB	CG	HR	BB	SO	BR/9	ERA	AERA	OAV	OOB	FW	PW	BW	BSW	DIF
East																													
Bal	98	64	0	.605		812	**681**	196	.268	.341	.429	770	+3	97	63	8	164	563	1139	**12.3**	3.91	+13	**.253**	**.323**	.8	7.9	2.9	-.0	5.4
NY	96	66	0	.593	2	891	688	161	.287	**.362**	.436	798	+8	99	99	11	**144**	532	1165	12.5	**3.84**	+16	.260	.327	.5	9.7	8.9	-.4	-3.7
Det	79	83	0	.488	19	784	790	176	.258	.332	.415	747	-6	100	**161**	13	178	552	982	12.9	4.56	+1	.266	.334	**1.1**	.8	-4.2	.4	-.1
Bos	78	84	0	.481	20	851	857	185	**.291**	.352	.463	815	+9	102	68	7	149	611	987	13.9	4.85	-4	.277	.351	-1.3	-3.0	7.7	-.7	-5.7
Tor	76	86	0	.469	22	654	694	147	.244	.310	.389	699	-19	-100	134	**19**	167	497	1150	12.4	3.92	**+17**	.263	.326	1.0	**10.1**	-14.8	.6	-1.9
Central																													
Cle	86	75	0	.534		868	815	220	.286	.358	.467	825	+9	104	118	4	181	575	1036	13.6	4.73	-1	.276	.347	.3	-.5	8.2	-.0	-2.5
Chi	80	81	0	.497	6	779	833	158	.273	.341	.417	758	+0	97	106	6	175	575	961	13.4	4.73	-7	.271	.340	-.9	-5.1	1.0	-.0	4.6
Mil	78	83	0	.484	8	681	742	135	.260	.325	.398	723	-13	101	103	6	177	542	1016	12.7	4.22	+10	.261	.333	-.5	6.0	-9.6	-.2	1.9
Min	68	94	0	.420	18.5	772	861	132	.270	.333	.409	742	-9	102	151	10	187	**495**	908	13.3	5.00	-7	.283	.342	.6	-4.9	-6.6	**.9**	-3.0
KC	67	94	0	.416	19	747	820	158	.264	.333	.407	740	-11	103	130	11	186	531	961	13.2	4.70	+1	.274	.340	**1.1**	.6	-8.0	.0	-7.3
West																													
Sea	90	72	0	.556		**925**	833	**264**	.280	.355	**.485**	**840**	**+17**	100	89	9	192	598	**1207**	13.5	4.78	-5	.267	.342	-.8	-3.9	**13.9**	.0	-.3
Ana	84	78	0	.519	6	829	794	161	.272	.346	.416	762	-2	100	126	9	202	605	1050	13.4	4.52	+2	.269	.343	-.6	1.3	-.6	-.2	3.1
Tex	77	85	0	.475	13	807	823	187	.274	.334	.438	772	-6	107	72	8	169	541	925	13.7	4.69	+3	.283	.347	-.5	2.3	-5.1	-.2	-.4
Oak	65	97	0	.401	25	764	946	197	.260	.339	.423	762	-2	100	71	2	197	642	953	15.2	5.48	-16	.301	.372	-.6	-13.5	-1.1	-.2	-.6
Total	1132					11164		2477	.271	.340	.428	768			1491	123		7859	4440	13.3	4.56		.271	.340					

Batter-Fielder Wins		Batting Average		On-Base Percentage		Slugging Average		On-Base Plus Slugging		Adjusted OPS		Adjusted Batter Runs	
Griffey-Sea	**6.0**	F.Thomas-Chi	.347	F.Thomas-Chi	.456	Griffey-Sea	.646	F.Thomas-Chi	1067	F.Thomas-Chi	183	F.Thomas-Chi	71.9
Valentin-Bos	**4.0**	Jefferson-Bos	.319	E.Martinez-Sea	.456	Vaughn-Bos	.560	Vaughn-Bos	980	Vaughn-Bos	150	Vaughn-Bos	42.4
Garciaparra-Bos	**3.4**	Vaughn-Bos	.315	Vaughn-Bos	.420	Garciaparra-Bos	.534	Garciaparra-Bos	875	Valentin-Bos	123	Valentin-Bos	20.4
Vaughn-Bos	**2.3**	O'Leary-Bos	.309	Valentin-Bos	.372	Valentin-Bos	.499	Valentin-Bos	871	Garciaparra-Bos	122	Garciaparra-Bos	19.2

Runs		Hits		Doubles		Triples		Home Runs		Total Bases		Runs Batted In	
Griffey-Sea	125	Garciaparra-Bos	209	Valentin-Bos	47	Garciaparra-Bos	11	Griffey-Sea	56	Griffey-Sea	393	Griffey-Sea	147
Garciaparra-Bos	122	Valentin-Bos	176	Garciaparra-Bos	44	Valentin-Bos	5	Vaughn-Bos	35	Garciaparra-Bos	365	Garciaparra-Bos	98
Valentin-Bos	95	Vaughn-Bos	166	Frye-Bos	36	O'Leary-Bos	4	Garciaparra-Bos	30	Vaughn-Bos	295	Vaughn-Bos	96
Vaughn-Bos	91	Cordero-Bos	160	Bragg-Bos	35	Cordero-Bos	3	2 players tied	18	Valentin-Bos	287	O'Leary-Bos	80

Stolen Bases		Base Stealing Runs		Fielding Runs-Infield		Fielding Runs-Outfield		Wins		Winning Pct.		Complete Games	
Hunter-Det	74	Knoblauch-Min	10.1	Cirillo-Mil	24.0	Cameron-Chi	13.0	Clemens-Tor	21	Johnson-Sea	.833	Hentgen-Tor	9
Garciaparra-Bos	22	Garciaparra-Bos	1.7	Valentin-Bos	17.7	Bragg-Bos	5.9	Sele-Bos	13			Clemens-Tor	9
Frye-Bos	19	Frye-Bos	1.4	Garciaparra-Bos	3.4			Wakefield-Bos	12			Wakefield-Bos	4
Bragg-Bos	10	Coleman-Bos	.2					4 players tied	7			Gordon-Bos	2

Strikeouts		Fewest BB/Game		Games		Saves		Base Runners/9		Adjusted Relief Runs		Relief Ranking	
Clemens-Tor	292	Burkett-Tex	1.43	Myers-Det	88	Myers-Bal	45	Jones-Mil	8.29	Quantrill-Tor	23.9	Jones-Mil	46.0
Gordon-Bos	159	Gordon-Bos	3.84	Wasdin-Bos	53	Gordon-Bos	11	Henry-Bos	11.53	Henry-Bos	10.5	Henry-Bos	12.5
Wakefield-Bos	151	Wakefield-Bos	3.89	Corsi-Bos	52	Henry-Bos	6	Gordon-Bos	11.63	Corsi-Bos	6.8	Corsi-Bos	8.9
Sele-Bos	122	Sele-Bos	4.06	Gordon-Bos	42	Lacy-Bos	3	Wasdin-Bos	11.70	Wasdin-Bos	2.9	Wasdin-Bos	2.1

Innings Pitched		Opponents' Avg.		Opponents' OBP		Earned Run Average		Adjusted ERA		Adjusted Starter Runs		Pitcher Wins	
Hentgen-Tor	264.0	Johnson-Sea	.194	Clemens-Tor	.273	Clemens-Tor	2.05	Clemens-Tor	224	Clemens-Tor	74.8	Clemens-Tor	7.9
Clemens-Tor	264.0	Gordon-Bos	.226	Gordon-Bos	.306	Gordon-Bos	3.74	Gordon-Bos	124	Gordon-Bos	17.3	Gordon-Bos	1.5
Wakefield-Bos	201.1	Wakefield-Bos	.256	Wakefield-Bos	.343	Wakefield-Bos	4.25	Wakefield-Bos	110	Wakefield-Bos	6.7	Henry-Bos	1.3
Gordon-Bos	182.2	Sele-Bos	.279	Sele-Bos	.361	Sele-Bos	5.38	Sele-Bos	87			Corsi-Bos	.9

1998 AMERICAN LEAGUE

TEAM	W	L	T	PCT	GB	R	OR	HR	AVG	OBP	SLG	OPS	AOPS	PF	SB	CG	HR	BB	SO	BR/9	ERA	AERA	OAV	OOB	FW	PW	BW	BSW	DIF
East																													
NY	114	48	0	.704		**965**	**656**	207	.288	**.364**	.460	**824**	**+18**	96	153	**22**	**156**	466	1080	**11.7**	**3.82**	**+14**	**.247**	**.312**	.9	**9.0**	**15.7**	**.4**	7.0
Bos	92	70	0	.568	22	876	729	205	.280	.348	.463	811	+7	102	72	5	168	504	1025	12.3	4.18	+13	.255	.321	.5	8.0	5.7	-.5	-2.6
Tor	88	74	1	.543	26	816	768	221	.266	.340	.448	788	+3	100	**184**	10	169	587	1154	12.7	4.28	+9	.256	.329	-.6	5.7	2.6	**.4**	-1.1
Bal	79	83	0	.488	35	817	785	214	.273	.347	.447	794	+7	98	86	16	169	535	1065	13.1	4.74	-4	.272	.338	**1.8**	-3.0	5.9	-.5	-6.2
TB	63	99	0	.389	51	620	751	111	.261	.321	.385	706	-19	-103	120	7	171	643	1008	13.4	4.35	+10	.261	.345	1.1	6.4	-14.8	-.6	-10.1
Central																													
Cle	89	73	0	.549		850	779	198	.272	.347	.448	795	+1	104	143	9	171	563	1037	13.5	4.44	+7	.274	.344	.2	4.9	2.3	.2	.4
Chi	80	82	1	.494	9	861	931	198	.271	.339	.444	783	+4	98	127	8	211	580	911	13.8	5.22	-12	.278	.348	-1.4	-10.0	2.9	**.4**	7.0
KC	72	89	0	.447	16.5	714	899	134	.263	.324	.399	723	-16	-104	135	6	196	568	999	13.9	5.15	-6	.281	.350	-.7	-4.3	-12.1	**.4**	8.1
Min	70	92	0	.432	19	734	818	115	.266	.328	.389	717	-16	-103	112	7	180	**457**	952	13.2	4.75	+1	.284	.338	.3	.6	-12.2	-.1	.4
Det	65	97	0	.401	24	722	863	165	.264	.323	.415	738	-11	101	122	9	185	595	947	13.6	4.93	-4	.277	.348	-.0	-2.7	-8.4	-.2	-4.6
West																													
Tex	88	74	0	.543		940	871	201	**.289**	.357	.462	819	+5	106	82	10	164	519	994	13.8	4.99	-2	.285	.346	-.4	-1.5	5.3	-.5	4.1
Ana	85	77	0	.525	3	787	783	147	.272	.335	.415	750	-8	102	93	3	164	630	1091	13.5	4.49	+6	.267	.344	.4	3.7	-5.4	-.2	5.5
Sea	76	85	0	.472	11.5	859	855	**234**	.276	.345	**.468**	813	+8	101	115	17	196	528	**1156**	13.4	4.93	-5	.273	.340	-.7	-3.9	6.7	**.4**	-7.1
Oak	74	88	0	.457	14	804	866	149	.257	.338	.397	735	-8	99	131	12	179	529	922	13.4	4.81	-4	.276	.342	-1.5	-2.8	-5.1	**.4**	2.0
Total	1134					11365		2499	.271	.340	.432	771			1675	141		7704	4341	13.2	4.65		.271	.340					

Batter-Fielder Wins		Batting Average		On-Base Percentage		Slugging Average		On-Base Plus Slugging		Adjusted OPS		Adjusted Batter Runs	
Belle-Chi	**5.8**	Williams-NY	.339	Martinez-Sea	.429	Belle-Chi	.655	Belle-Chi	1055	Belle-Chi	173	Belle-Chi	66.9
Garciaparra-Bos	**3.0**	Vaughn-Bos	.337	Vaughn-Bos	.402	Vaughn-Bos	.591	Vaughn-Bos	993	Vaughn-Bos	151	Vaughn-Bos	46.0
Vaughn-Bos	**2.7**	Garciaparra-Bos	.323	Garciaparra-Bos	.362	Garciaparra-Bos	.584	Garciaparra-Bos	946	Garciaparra-Bos	139	Garciaparra-Bos	31.9
2 players tied	**1.8**	O'Leary-Bos	.270	Lewis-Bos	.352	O'Leary-Bos	.468	2 players tied	782	Valentin-Bos	100	Jefferson-Bos	8.2

Runs		Hits		Doubles		Triples		Home Runs		Total Bases		Runs Batted In	
Jeter-NY	127	Rodriguez-Sea	213	Gonzalez-Tex	50	Offerman-KC	13	Griffey-Sea	56	Belle-Chi	399	Gonzalez-Tex	157
Valentin-Bos	113	Vaughn-Bos	205	Valentin-Bos	44	O'Leary-Bos	8	Vaughn-Bos	40	Vaughn-Bos	360	Garciaparra-Bos	122
Garciaparra-Bos	111	Garciaparra-Bos	195	Garciaparra-Bos	37	Garciaparra-Bos	8	Garciaparra-Bos	35	Garciaparra-Bos	353	Vaughn-Bos	115
Vaughn-Bos	107	O'Leary-Bos	165	O'Leary-Bos	36	2 players tied	4	2 players tied	23	O'Leary-Bos	286	O'Leary-Bos	83

Stolen Bases		Base Stealing Runs		Fielding Runs-Infield		Fielding Runs-Outfield		Wins		Winning Pct.		Complete Games	
Henderson-Oak	66	Henderson-Oak	10.0	Easley-Det	25.7	Lawton-Min	14.3	3 players tied	20	Wells-NY	.818	Erickson-Bal	11
Lewis-Bos	29	Lewis-Bos	2.2	Valentin-Bos	18.2	Lewis-Bos	2.3	Martinez-Bos	19	Martinez-Bos	.731	Martinez-Bos	3
Garciaparra-Bos	12	Sadler-Bos	.9	Benjamin-Bos	4.0	O'Leary-Bos	1.1	Wakefield-Bos	17	Wakefield-Bos	.680	Wakefield-Bos	2
2 players tied	5	Benjamin-Bos	.7					Saberhagen-Bos	15	Saberhagen-Bos	.652		

Strikeouts		Fewest BB/Game		Games		Saves		Base Runners/9		Adjusted Relief Runs		Relief Ranking	
Clemens-Tor	271	Wells-NY	1.22	Runyan-Det	88	Gordon-Bos	46	Jackson-Cle	8.44	Jackson-Cle	22.8	Gordon-Bos	36.8
Martinez-Bos	251	Saberhagen-Bos	1.49	Gordon-Bos	73	Lowe-Bos	4	Gordon-Bos	9.08	Gordon-Bos	18.4	Corsi-Bos	9.8
Wakefield-Bos	146	Martinez-Bos	2.58	Lowe-Bos	63	4 players tied	1	Martinez-Bos	10.13	Corsi-Bos	14.4	Lowe-Bos	6.7
Saberhagen-Bos	100	Wakefield-Bos	3.29	Corsi-Bos	59			Saberhagen-Bos	11.11	Lowe-Bos	7.2		

Innings Pitched		Opponents' Avg.		Opponents' OBP		Earned Run Average		Adjusted ERA		Adjusted Starter Runs		Pitcher Wins	
Erickson-Bal	251.1	Clemens-Tor	.197	Wells-NY	.265	Clemens-Tor	2.65	Clemens-Tor	176	Clemens-Tor	51.5	Clemens-Tor	5.2
Martinez-Bos	233.2	Martinez-Bos	.217	Martinez-Bos	.278	Martinez-Bos	2.89	Martinez-Bos	164	Martinez-Bos	46.9	Martinez-Bos	4.6
Wakefield-Bos	216.0	Wakefield-Bos	.252	Saberhagen-Bos	.299	Saberhagen-Bos	3.96	Saberhagen-Bos	119	Saberhagen-Bos	15.6	Gordon-Bos	3.5
Saberhagen-Bos	175.0	Saberhagen-Bos	.264	Wakefield-Bos	.324	Wakefield-Bos	4.58	Wakefield-Bos	103	Schourek-Bos	2.9	Saberhagen-Bos	1.7

1999 AMERICAN LEAGUE

TEAM	W	L	T	PCT	GB	R	OR	HR	AVG	OBP	SLG	OPS	AOPS	PF	SB	CG	HR	BB	SO	BR/9	ERA	AERA	OAV	OOB	FW	PW	BW	BSW	DIF
East																													
NY	98	64	0	.605		900	731	193	.282	.366	.453	819	**+10**	99	104	6	**158**	581	1111	12.8	4.13	+14	.255	.330	.2	8.8	**9.1**	-.3	-.8
Bos	94	68	0	.580	4	836	**718**	176	.278	.350	.448	798	-1	103	67	6	160	**469**	**1131**	**12.0**	**4.00**	**+24**	**.253**	**.315**	-.6	**14.0**	.0	-.4	.1
Tor	84	78	0	.519	14	883	862	212	.280	.352	.457	809	+3	102	119	14	191	575	1009	13.8	4.92	+0	.280	.349	.4	-.2	3.2	.3	-.8
Bal	78	84	0	.481	20	851	815	203	.279	.353	.447	800	+7	97	107	**17**	198	647	982	13.6	4.77	-2	.269	.348	**1.3**	-1.2	6.0	.1	-9.2
TB	69	93	0	.426	29	772	913	145	.274	.343	.411	754	-9	102	73	6	172	695	1055	14.9	5.06	-2	.286	.370	-1.1	-1.5	-7.1	-.6	-1.7
Central																													
Cle	97	65	0	.599		**1009**	860	209	.289	**.373**	.467	**840**	+7	105	**147**	3	197	634	1120	13.6	4.89	+4	.268	.346	.4	2.6	7.9	**.9**	4.2
Chi	75	86	1	.466	21.5	777	870	162	.277	.337	.429	766	-8	102	110	6	210	596	968	14.2	4.92	+0	.282	.353	-1.1	.0	-6.0	.1	1.4
Det	69	92	0	.429	27.5	747	882	212	.261	.326	.443	769	-7	102	108	4	209	583	976	13.8	5.17	-4	.276	.349	.4	-2.8	-6.6	-.6	-1.9
KC	64	97	0	.398	32.5	856	921	151	.282	.348	.433	781	-6	104	127	11	202	643	831	14.7	5.35	-5	.288	.365	-.6	-3.9	-4.0	.8	-8.8
Min	63	97	1	.394	33	686	845	105	.264	.328	.384	712	-23	-105	118	13	208	487	927	13.3	5.00	+3	.283	.341	1.1	2.2	-17.1	-.0	-3.2
West																													
Tex	95	67	0	.586		945	859	230	**.293**	.361	**.479**	**840**	+6	106	111	6	186	509	979	13.6	5.07	+2	.286	.346	-.2	1.2	5.4	.0	7.6
Oak	87	75	0	.537	8	893	846	235	.259	.355	.446	801	+6	97	70	6	160	569	967	13.5	4.69	+1	.274	.344	-.4	.4	6.0	-.3	.4
Sea	79	83	0	.488	16	859	905	**244**	.269	.343	.455	798	+3	99	130	7	191	684	980	14.9	5.24	-9	.287	.368	.0	-6.9	2.0	.7	2.2
Ana	70	92	0	.432	25	711	826	158	.256	.322	.395	717	-18	-100	71	4	177	624	877	13.5	4.79	+2	.269	.346	.4	1.2	-14.2	-.5	2.0
Total	1132					11725		2635	.275	.347	.439	786			1462	109		8296	3913	13.7	4.86		.275	.347					

Batter-Fielder Wins
R.Alomar-Cle 5.1
Garciaparra-Bos **4.7**
Varitek-Bos 1.7
Daubach-Bos .6

Batting Average
Garciaparra-Bos .357
Offerman-Bos .294
Stanley-Bos .281
O'Leary-Bos .280

On-Base Percentage
Martinez-Sea .447
Garciaparra-Bos .418
Stanley-Bos .393
Offerman-Bos .391

Slugging Average
M.Ramirez-Cle .663
Garciaparra-Bos .603
O'Leary-Bos .495
Varitek-Bos .482

On-Base Plus Slugging
M.Ramirez-Cle 1105
Garciaparra-Bos 1022
Stanley-Bos 859
O'Leary-Bos 838

Adjusted OPS
M.Ramirez-Cle 170
Garciaparra-Bos 152
Stanley-Bos 115
2 players tied 108

Adjusted Batter Runs
M.Ramirez-Cle 59.1
Garciaparra-Bos 43.3
Daubach-Bos 14.6
Stanley-Bos 12.5

Runs
R.Alomar-Cle 138
Offerman-Bos 107
Garciaparra-Bos 103
O'Leary-Bos 84

Hits
Jeter-NY 219
Garciaparra-Bos 190
Offerman-Bos 172
O'Leary-Bos 167

Doubles
Green-Tor 45
Garciaparra-Bos 42
Varitek-Bos 39
Offerman-Bos 37

Triples
Offerman-Bos 11
Lewis-Bos 6
Nixon-Bos 5
2 players tied 4

Home Runs
Griffey-Sea 48
O'Leary-Bos 28
Garciaparra-Bos 27
Daubach-Bos 21

Total Bases
Green-Tor 361
Garciaparra-Bos 321
O'Leary-Bos 295
Offerman-Bos 255

Runs Batted In
M.Ramirez-Cle 165
Garciaparra-Bos 104
O'Leary-Bos 103
Varitek-Bos 76

Stolen Bases
Hunter-Det-Sea 44
Offerman-Bos 18
Lewis-Bos 16
Garciaparra-Bos 14

Base Stealing Runs
Hunter-Det-Sea 6.9
Garciaparra-Bos 2.0
Buford-Bos 1.3
Nixon-Bos .3

Fielding Runs-Infield
Bordick-Bal 35.1
Valentin-Bos 12.4

Fielding Runs-Outfield
Dye-KC 14.3
Lewis-Bos .8
O'Leary-Bos .5

Wins
P.Martinez-Bos 23
Saberhagen-Bos 10
Wasdin-Bos 8
4 players tied 7

Winning Pct.
P.Martinez-Bos .852

Complete Games
D.Wells-Tor 7
P.Martinez-Bos 5
Portugal-Bos 1

Strikeouts
P.Martinez-Bos 313
Wakefield-Bos 104
Rapp-Bos 90
Saberhagen-Bos 81

Fewest BB/Game
Heredia-Oak 1.53
P.Martinez-Bos 1.56

Games
Wells-Min 76
Groom-Oak 76
Lowe-Bos 74
Cormier-Bos 60

Saves
Rivera-NY 45
Wakefield-Bos 15
Lowe-Bos 15
Gordon-Bos 11

Base Runners/9
Zimmerman-Tex 7.70
P.Martinez-Bos 8.69
Lowe-Bos 9.30
Wasdin-Bos 10.17

Adjusted Relief Runs
Foulke-Chi 31.7
Lowe-Bos 28.3
Wasdin-Bos 7.1
Cormier-Bos 6.8

Relief Ranking
Rivera-NY 46.2
Lowe-Bos 27.9
Wasdin-Bos 9.8
Cormier-Bos 3.4

Innings Pitched
D.Wells-Tor 231.2
P.Martinez-Bos 213.1
Portugal-Bos 150.1
Rapp-Bos 146.1

Opponents' Avg.
P.Martinez-Bos .205

Opponents' OBP
P.Martinez-Bos .248

Earned Run Average
P.Martinez-Bos 2.07

Adjusted ERA
P.Martinez-Bos 241

Adjusted Starter Runs
P.Martinez-Bos 67.2
Saberhagen-Bos 26.7
Rapp-Bos 12.6
Pena-Bos 6.1

Pitcher Wins
P.Martinez-Bos 8.1
Saberhagen-Bos 3.2
Lowe-Bos 2.6
Garces-Bos 2.0

2000 AMERICAN LEAGUE

TEAM	W	L	T	PCT	GB	R	OR	HR	AVG	OBP	SLG	OPS	AOPS	PF	SB	CG	HR	BB	SO	BR/9	ERA	AERA	OAV	OOB	FW	PW	BW	BSW	DIF
East																													
NY	87	74	0	.540		871	814	205	.277	.354	.450	804	+3	99	99	9	177	577	1040	13.2	4.76	+0	.263	.336	.2	.0	3.7	-.0	2.6
Bos	85	77	0	.525	2.5	792	**745**	167	.267	.341	.423	764	-11	103	43	7	173	498	1121	**12.3**	**4.23**	**+18**	**.257**	**.322**	.2	**11.3**	-7.5	-.6	.6
Tor	83	79	0	.512	4.5	861	908	**244**	.275	.341	.469	810	+0	103	89	**15**	195	560	978	14.0	5.14	-2	.285	.354	.7	-1.6	-.7	.2	3.4
Bal	74	88	0	.457	13.5	794	913	184	.272	.341	.435	776	+0	95	**126**	14	202	665	1017	14.1	5.37	-13	.275	.352	-.2	-10.4	.4	-.0	3.2
TB	69	92	0	.429	18	733	842	162	.257	.329	.399	728	-15	-99	90	10	198	533	955	13.5	4.86	+1	.277	.345	-.4	.4	-11.9	-.2	.6
Central																													
Chi	95	67	0	.586		**978**	839	216	.286	.356	.470	826	+3	104	119	5	195	614	1037	13.5	4.66	+8	.270	.346	-1.2	5.6	3.4	.5	5.7
Cle	90	72	0	.556	5	950	816	221	**.288**	**.367**	.470	**837**	+6	104	113	6	173	666	**1213**	13.8	4.84	+3	.270	.350	**2.4**	2.4	**6.6**	.7	-3.0
Det	79	83	0	.488	16	823	827	177	.275	.343	.438	781	-3	99	83	6	177	**496**	978	13.3	4.71	+4	.280	.340	.5	2.7	-2.0	-.0	-3.1
KC	77	85	0	.475	18	879	930	150	**.288**	.348	.425	773	-10	106	121	10	239	693	927	14.5	5.48	-5	.282	.362	.6	-3.7	-7.4	**.8**	5.7
Min	69	93	0	.426	26	748	880	116	.270	.337	.407	744	-18	107	90	6	212	516	1042	13.7	5.14	+2	.287	.347	.6	1.5	-13.5	-.2	-.5
West																													
Oak	91	70	0	.565		947	813	239	.270	.360	.458	818	**+7**	99	40	7	**158**	615	963	13.8	4.58	+6	.274	.348	-1.3	3.9	6.5	-.2	1.5
Sea	91	71	0	.562	0.5	907	780	198	.269	.361	.442	803	+4	98	122	4	167	634	998	13.2	4.49	+7	.262	.339	.8	4.7	5.1	.1	-.7
Ana	82	80	0	.506	9.5	864	869	236	.280	.352	**.472**	824	+4	103	93	5	228	662	846	13.9	5.00	+3	.273	.351	-1.2	2.1	3.1	-.3	-2.6
Tex	71	91	0	.438	20.5	848	974	173	.283	.352	.446	798	+0	101	69	3	202	661	918	15.2	5.52	-8	.294	.369	-1.3	-6.1	.0	-.6	-2.0
Total	1132					11995		2688	.276	.349	.443	792			1297	107		8390	4033	13.7	4.91		.276	.349					

Batter-Fielder Wins
A.Rodriguez-Sea 6.6
Garciaparra-Bos 5.0
Everett-Bos 2.2
Burkhart-Bos .3

Batting Average
Garciaparra-Bos .372
Everett-Bos .300
Nixon-Bos .276
O'Leary-Bos .261

On-Base Percentage
J.Giambi-Oak .476
Garciaparra-Bos .434
Everett-Bos .373
Nixon-Bos .368

Slugging Average
M.Ramirez-Cle .697
Garciaparra-Bos .599
Everett-Bos .587
Nixon-Bos .461

On-Base Plus Slugging
M.Ramirez-Cle 1154
Garciaparra-Bos 1033
Everett-Bos 959
Nixon-Bos 830

Adjusted OPS
J.Giambi-Oak 185
Garciaparra-Bos 155
Everett-Bos 135
Nixon-Bos 106

Adjusted Batter Runs
Delgado-Tor 76.7
Garciaparra-Bos 47.5
Everett-Bos 25.5
2 players tied 5.0

Runs
Damon-KC 136
Garciaparra-Bos 104
Everett-Bos 82
Offerman-Bos 73

Hits
Erstad-Ana 240
Garciaparra-Bos 197
Everett-Bos 149
O'Leary-Bos 134

Doubles
Delgado-Tor 57
Garciaparra-Bos 51
Everett-Bos 32
Daubach-Bos 32

Triples
Guzman-Min 20
Nixon-Bos 8
O'Leary-Bos 4
Everett-Bos 4

Home Runs
Glaus-Ana 47
Everett-Bos 34
Garciaparra-Bos 21
Daubach-Bos 21

Total Bases
Delgado-Tor 378
Garciaparra-Bos 317
Everett-Bos 291
Daubach-Bos 222

Runs Batted In
Martinez-Sea 145
Everett-Bos 108
Garciaparra-Bos 96
Daubach-Bos 76

Stolen Bases
Damon-KC 46
Everett-Bos 11
Lewis-Bos 10
Nixon-Bos 8

Base Stealing Runs
R.Alomar-Cle 7.2
Nixon-Bos 1.4
Everett-Bos 1.0
Lewis-Bos .5

Fielding Runs-Infield
Velarde-Oak 22.0
Offerman-Bos 6.1

Fielding Runs-Outfield
Martinez-TB-Tx-Tor 11.5
Nixon-Bos 1.4

Wins
D.Wells-Tor 20
Hudson-Oak 20
P.Martinez-Bos 18
R.Martinez-Bos 10

Winning Pct.
Hudson-Oak .769
P.Martinez-Bos .750

Complete Games
D.Wells-Tor 9
P.Martinez-Bos 7

Strikeouts
P.Martinez-Bos 284
Wakefield-Bos 102
Fassero-Bos 97
R.Martinez-Bos 89

Fewest BB/Game
D.Wells-Tor 1.21
P.Martinez-Bos 1.33

Games
Wunsch-Chi 83
Lowe-Bos 74
Garces-Bos 64
Cormier-Bos 64

Saves
LJones-Det 42
Lowe-Bos 42
4 players tied 1

Base Runners/9
P.Martinez-Bos 7.22
Garces-Bos 10.61
Lowe-Bos 11.23
Arrojo-Bos 11.73

Adjusted Relief Runs
Lowe-Bos 25.0
Garces-Bos 15.0
Pichardo-Bos 10.2
Cormier-Bos 2.2

Relief Ranking
Lowe-Bos 41.3
Garces-Bos 16.6
Pichardo-Bos 13.1
Cormier-Bos 1.7

Innings Pitched
Mussina-Bal 237.2
P.Martinez-Bos 217.0
Wakefield-Bos 159.1
Fassero-Bos 130.0

Opponents' Avg.
P.Martinez-Bos .167

Opponents' OBP
P.Martinez-Bos .213

Earned Run Average
P.Martinez-Bos 1.74

Adjusted ERA
P.Martinez-Bos 288

Adjusted Starter Runs
P.Martinez-Bos 78.3
Ohka-Bos 14.9
Fassero-Bos 4.9
Crawford-Bos 3.7

Pitcher Wins
P.Martinez-Bos 8.4
Lowe-Bos 3.9
Ohka-Bos 1.7
Garces-Bos 1.5

2001 AMERICAN LEAGUE

TEAM	W	L	T	PCT	GB	R	OR	HR	AVG	OBP	SLG	OPS	AOPS	PF	SB	CG	HR	BB	SO	BR/9	ERA	AERA	OAV	OOB	FW	PW	BW	BSW	DIF
East																													
NY	95	65	1	.594		804	713	203	.267	.334	.435	769	+0	101	161	7	158	465	**1266**	12.1	4.02	+10	.257	.318	.3	6.4	.4	.8	7.2
Bos	82	79	0	.509	13.5	772	745	198	.266	.334	.439	773	+2	100	46	3	**146**	544	1259	12.7	4.15	+7	.254	.329	.0	4.4	1.8	-1.1	-3.7
Tor	80	82	0	.494	16	767	753	195	.263	.325	.430	755	-5	102	156	7	165	490	1041	13.0	4.28	+7	.275	.339	1.0	4.5	-4.0	.6	-3.1
Bal	63	98	1	.391	32.5	687	829	136	.248	.319	.380	699	-11	-95	133	10	194	528	938	13.2	4.67	-8	.269	.337	-.6	-5.8	-8.3	.2	-2.9
TB	62	100	0	.383	34	672	887	121	.258	.320	.388	708	-13	-98	115	1	207	569	1030	13.6	4.94	-9	.273	.345	-1.4	-6.6	-9.6	-.2	-1.2
Central																													
Cle	91	71	0	.562		897	821	212	.278	.350	.458	808	+7	104	79	3	148	573	1218	13.3	4.64	-1	.270	.341	.4	-.9	6.2	-.6	4.8
Min	85	77	0	.525	6	771	766	164	.272	.337	.433	770	-4	106	146	12	192	445	965	12.5	4.51	+3	.268	.325	.4	2.3	-2.4	.0	3.7
Chi	83	79	0	.512	8	798	795	214	.268	.334	.451	785	-1	106	123	8	181	500	921	12.9	4.55	+2	.266	.334	-.2	1.4	-.6	-.3	1.7
Det	66	96	0	.407	25	724	876	139	.260	.320	.409	729	-7	98	133	**16**	180	553	859	14.2	5.01	-12	.288	.357	-1.0	-9.1	-5.3	-.1	.4
KC	65	97	0	.401	26	729	858	152	.266	.318	.409	727	-18	110	100	5	209	576	911	13.6	4.87	+2	.276	.348	-.2	1.1	-14.1	-.2	-2.7
West																													
Sea	116	46	0	.716		**927**	**627**	169	**.288**	**.360**	.445	805	**+17**	95	**174**	8	160	465	1051	**11.2**	**3.54**	+20	**.236**	**.301**	**1.8**	11.7	**15.7**	**1.4**	4.4
Oak	102	60	0	.630	14	884	645	199	.264	.345	.439	784	+4	101	68	13	153	**440**	1117	11.5	3.59	**+27**	.249	.308	-.6	**14.8**	5.5	-.4	1.8
Ana	75	87	0	.463	41	691	730	158	.261	.327	.405	732	-10	102	116	6	168	525	947	12.8	4.20	+11	.263	.331	.7	6.5	-7.0	-.2	-6.0
Tex	73	89	0	.451	43	890	968	**246**	.275	.344	**.471**	**815**	+9	103	97	4	222	596	951	14.6	5.71	-17	.293	.362	.0	-13.6	7.9	.0	-2.4
Total	1133					11013		2506	.267	.334	.428	762			1647	103		7269	4474	12.9	4.47		.267	.334					

Batter-Fielder Wins		Batting Average		On-Base Percentage		Slugging Average		On-Base Plus Slugging		Adjusted OPS		Adjusted Batter Runs	
A.Rodriguez-Tex	**6.9**	Suzuki-Sea	.350	J.Giambi-Oak	.477	J.Giambi-Oak	.660	J.Giambi-Oak	1137	J.Giambi-Oak	196	J.Giambi-Oak	84.2
Ramirez-Bos	**3.8**	Ramirez-Bos	.306	Ramirez-Bos	.405	Ramirez-Bos	.609	Ramirez-Bos	1014	Ramirez-Bos	162	Ramirez-Bos	50.0
Varitek-Bos	**1.9**	Nixon-Bos	.280	Nixon-Bos	.376	Nixon-Bos	.505	Nixon-Bos	881	Nixon-Bos	130	Nixon-Bos	25.5
Nixon-Bos	**1.6**	Offerman-Bos	.267	Offerman-Bos	.342	Offerman-Bos	.374	Offerman-Bos	716	Offerman-Bos	89	Daubach-Bos	14.5

Runs		Hits		Doubles		Triples		Home Runs		Total Bases		Runs Batted In	
A.Rodriguez-Tex	133	Suzuki-Sea	242	J.Giambi-Oak	47	Guzman-Min	14	A.Rodriguez-Tex	52	A.Rodriguez-Tex	393	Boone-Sea	141
Nixon-Bos	100	Ramirez-Bos	162	Ramirez-Bos	33	O'Leary-Bos	6	Ramirez-Bos	41	Ramirez-Bos	322	Ramirez-Bos	125
Ramirez-Bos	93	Nixon-Bos	150	Nixon-Bos	31	Nixon-Bos	4	Nixon-Bos	27	Nixon-Bos	270	Nixon-Bos	88
Offerman-Bos	76	Offerman-Bos	140	Bichette-Bos	30	Everett-Bos	4	Daubach-Bos	22	Daubach-Bos	207	Daubach-Bos	71

Stolen Bases		Base Stealing Runs		Fielding Runs-Infield		Fielding Runs-Outfield		Wins		Winning Pct.		Complete Games	
Suzuki-Sea	56	Suzuki-Sea	7.4	Gonzalez-Tor	33.3	Hunter-Min	18.6	Mulder-Oak	21	Clemens-NY	.870	Sparks-Det	8
Everett-Bos	9	Everett-Bos	1.3	Offerman-Bos	2.8			Nomo-Bos	13			Nomo-Bos	2
Nixon-Bos	7	Offerman-Bos	.4					F.Castillo-Bos	10			Martinez-Bos	1
2 players tied	5	2 players tied	.2					2 players tied	9				

Strikeouts		Fewest BB/Game		Games		Saves		Base Runners/9		Adjusted Relief Runs		Relief Ranking	
Nomo-Bos	220	Radke-Min	1.04	Quantrill-Tor	80	M.Rivera-NY	50	Rhodes-Sea	7.81	Foulke-Chi	21.0	Foulke-Chi	42.0
Martinez-Bos	163	Wakefield-Bos	3.90	Beck-Bos	68	Lowe-Bos	24	Martinez-Bos	8.87	Arrojo-Bos	11.2	Lowe-Bos	18.7
Wakefield-Bos	148	Nomo-Bos	4.36	Lowe-Bos	67	Urbina-Bos	9	Garces-Bos	11.28	Lowe-Bos	9.7	Arrojo-Bos	9.7
Cone-Bos	115			Garces-Bos	62	Beck-Bos	6	F.Castillo-Bos	11.72	Garces-Bos	4.1	Beck-Bos	4.2

Innings Pitched		Opponents' Avg.		Opponents' OBP		Earned Run Average		Adjusted ERA		Adjusted Starter Runs		Pitcher Wins	
Garcia-Sea	238.2	Garcia-Sea	.225	Mussina-NY	.274	Garcia-Sea	3.05	Mays-Min	148	Mays-Min	37.6	Mays-Min	4.4
Nomo-Bos	198.0	Nomo-Bos	.231	Nomo-Bos	.320	Wakefield-Bos	3.90	Wakefield-Bos	114	Martinez-Bos	27.4	Martinez-Bos	2.1
Wakefield-Bos	168.2	Wakefield-Bos	.248	Wakefield-Bos	.339	Nomo-Bos	4.50	Nomo-Bos	99	Wakefield-Bos	8.8	Lowe-Bos	1.9
F.Castillo-Bos	136.2									F.Castillo-Bos	2.9	2 players tied	1.0

2002 AMERICAN LEAGUE

TEAM	W	L	T	PCT	GB	R	OR	HR	AVG	OBP	SLG	OPS	AOPS	PF	SB	CG	HR	BB	SO	BR/9	ERA	AERA	OAV	OOB	FW	PW	BW	BSW	DIF
East																													
NY	103	58	0	.640		**897**	697	223	.275	**.354**	**.455**	**809**	**+14**	99	100	9	144	**403**	1135	11.7	3.87	+12	.256	.309	-1.2	7.2	**12.7**	.4	3.4
Bos	93	69	0	.574	10.5	859	665	177	.277	.345	.444	789	+6	102	80	5	146	430	**1157**	**11.5**	3.75	+19	**.246**	**.308**	.2	11.0	6.1	.3	-5.5
Tor	78	84	0	.481	25.5	813	828	187	.261	.327	.430	757	-5	104	71	6	177	590	991	13.5	4.80	-4	.269	.344	.0	-2.8	-2.8	.4	2.2
Bal	67	95	0	.414	36.5	667	773	165	.246	.309	.403	712	-7	95	110	8	208	549	967	13.0	4.46	-3	.266	.336	.9	-2.0	-5.9	.2	-7.2
TB	55	106	0	.342	48	673	918	133	.253	.314	.390	704	-12	-98	102	**12**	215	620	925	14.3	5.29	-15	.279	.357	-1.2	-11.8	-9.4	.2	-3.3
Central																													
Min	94	67	0	.584		768	712	167	.272	.332	.437	769	-1	103	79	8	184	439	1026	12.1	4.12	+8	.261	.318	**1.9**	5.2	.0	-.9	7.3
Chi	81	81	0	.500	13.5	856	798	217	.268	.338	.449	787	+3	104	75	7	190	528	945	12.7	4.53	-1	.260	.330	.6	-.5	3.0	.1	-3.2
Cle	74	88	0	.457	20.5	739	837	192	.249	.321	.412	733	-9	102	52	9	142	603	1058	13.7	4.91	-10	.274	.348	-.4	-7.3	-6.2	-.7	7.5
KC	62	100	0	.383	32.5	737	891	140	.256	.323	.398	721	-19	113	**140**	**12**	212	572	909	13.8	5.21	-4	.281	.349	-1.4	-3.2	-14.1	.3	-.6
Det	55	106	0	.342	39	575	864	124	.248	.300	.379	679	-18	-96	65	11	163	463	794	13.5	4.92	-11	.285	.343	-2.1	-8.5	-13.6	-.6	-.8
West																													
Oak	103	59	0	.636		800	654	205	.261	.339	.432	771	+4	99	46	9	**135**	474	1021	11.9	**3.68**	**+22**	.252	.315	.3	**12.3**	3.9	-.2	5.6
Ana	99	63	0	.611	4	851	**644**	152	**.282**	.341	.433	774	+6	98	117	7	169	509	999	11.8	3.69	+21	.247	.314	1.2	12.2	5.6	.3	-1.3
Sea	93	69	0	.574	10	814	699	152	.275	.350	.419	769	+8	97	137	8	178	441	1063	11.9	4.07	+6	.257	.315	1.1	3.7	7.5	**.5**	-.8
Tex	72	90	0	.444	31	843	882	**230**	.269	.338	**.455**	793	+6	103	62	4	194	669	1030	14.2	5.15	-7	.272	.355	.5	-5.4	5.1	-.3	-8.9
Total	1132					10892		2464	.264	.331	.424	755			1236	115		7290	4020	12.8	4.46		.264	.331					

Batter-Fielder Wins		Batting Average		On-Base Percentage		Slugging Average		On-Base Plus Slugging		Adjusted OPS		Adjusted Batter Runs	
A.Rodriguez-Tex	**7.4**	Ramirez-Bos	.349	Ramirez-Bos	.450	Thome-Cle	.677	Thome-Cle	1122	Thome-Cle	190	Thome-Cle	68.3
Garciaparra-Bos	**5.4**	Garciaparra-Bos	.310	Damon-Bos	.356	Ramirez-Bos	.647	Ramirez-Bos	1097	Ramirez-Bos	184	Ramirez-Bos	56.6
Ramirez-Bos	**4.6**	Hillenbrand-Bos	.293	Garciaparra-Bos	.352	Garciaparra-Bos	.528	Garciaparra-Bos	880	Garciaparra-Bos	129	Garciaparra-Bos	26.2
Varitek-Bos	**1.3**	Damon-Bos	.286	Daubach-Bos	.348	Nixon-Bos	.470	Daubach-Bos	812	Daubach-Bos	112	Floyd-Bos	11.1

Runs		Hits		Doubles		Triples		Home Runs		Total Bases		Runs Batted In	
Soriano-NY	128	Soriano-NY	209	Anderson-Ana	56	Damon-Bos	11	A.Rodriguez-Tex	57	A.Rodriguez-Tex	389	A.Rodriguez-Tex	142
Damon-Bos	118	Garciaparra-Bos	197	Garciaparra-Bos	56	Garciaparra-Bos	5	Ramirez-Bos	33	Garciaparra-Bos	335	Garciaparra-Bos	120
Garciaparra-Bos	101	Hillenbrand-Bos	186	Hillenbrand-Bos	43	Hillenbrand-Bos	4	Nixon-Bos	24	Hillenbrand-Bos	291	Ramirez-Bos	107
Hillenbrand-Bos	94	Damon-Bos	178	Nixon-Bos	36	2 players tied	3	Garciaparra-Bos	24	Ramirez-Bos	282	Nixon-Bos	94

Stolen Bases		Base Stealing Runs		Fielding Runs-Infield		Fielding Runs-Outfield		Wins		Winning Pct.		Complete Games	
Soriano-NY	41	Jeter-NY	6.0	Bordick-Bal	26.2	Erstad-Ana	19.4	Zito-Oak	23	Martinez-Bos	.833	Byrd-KC	7
Damon-Bos	31	Damon-Bos	4.7	Garciaparra-Bos	18.8			Lowe-Bos	21	Lowe-Bos	.724	Martinez-Bos	2
Henderson-Bos	8	Baerga-Bos	1.3	R.Sanchez-Bos	4.4			Martinez-Bos	20			3 players tied	1
Baerga-Bos	6	Henderson-Bos	1.1	Hillenbrand-Bos	4.0			Burkett-Bos	13				

Strikeouts		Fewest BB/Game		Games		Saves		Base Runners/9		Adjusted Relief Runs		Relief Ranking	
Martinez-Bos	239	Reed-Min	1.24	Koch-Oak	84	Guardado-Min	45	Rhodes-Sea	7.49	Romero-Min	23.8	Percival-Ana	32.9
Wakefield-Bos	134	Martinez-Bos	1.81	Urbina-Bos	61	Urbina-Bos	40	Martinez-Bos	8.98	Urbina-Bos	10.3	Urbina-Bos	20.6
Lowe-Bos	127	Lowe-Bos	1.97	Wakefield-Bos	45	Wakefield-Bos	3	Lowe-Bos	9.26	Fossum-Bos	7.1	Fossum-Bos	5.5
Burkett-Bos	124	Burkett-Bos	2.60	Fossum-Bos	43	Embree-Bos	2	Urbina-Bos	9.60				

Innings Pitched		Opponents' Avg.		Opponents' OBP		Earned Run Average		Adjusted ERA		Adjusted Starter Runs		Pitcher Wins	
Halladay-Tor	239.1	Martinez-Bos	.198	Martinez-Bos	.254	Martinez-Bos	2.26	Martinez-Bos	198	Lowe-Bos	48.2	Lowe-Bos	6.2
Lowe-Bos	219.2	Wakefield-Bos	.204	Lowe-Bos	.266	Lowe-Bos	2.58	Lowe-Bos	173	Martinez-Bos	45.9	Martinez-Bos	5.2
Martinez-Bos	199.1	Lowe-Bos	.211	Wakefield-Bos	.276	Wakefield-Bos	2.81	Wakefield-Bos	159	Wakefield-Bos	29.8	Wakefield-Bos	2.6
Burkett-Bos	173.0	Castillo-Bos	.274	Castillo-Bos	.337	Burkett-Bos	4.53	Burkett-Bos	99	Burkett-Bos	.4	Urbina-Bos	2.0

2003 AMERICAN LEAGUE

TEAM	W	L	T	PCT	GB	R	OR	HR	AVG	OBP	SLG	OPS	AOPS	PF	SB	CG	HR	BB	SO	BR/9	ERA	AERA	OAV	OOB	FW	PW	BW	BSW	DIF
East																													
NY	101	61	1	.623		877	716	230	.271	.356	.453	809	+13	99	98	8	145	375	1119	11.9	4.02	+9	.265	.314	-.4	5.9	12.3	.3	1.9
Bos	95	67	0	.586	6	961	809	238	.289	.360	.491	851	+17	104	88	5	153	488	1141	12.7	4.48	+4	.263	.327	-.4	2.7	15.1	.0	-3.4
Tor	86	76	0	.531	15	894	826	190	.279	.349	.455	804	+6	104	37	14	184	485	984	13.2	4.69	+1	.276	.337	-.7	.8	6.1	-.7	-.5
Bal	71	91	1	.438	30	743	820	152	.268	.323	.405	728	-8	99	89	9	198	526	981	13.6	4.76	-3	.278	.346	.0	-2.5	-6.6	.0	-1.0
TB	63	99	0	.389	38	715	852	137	.265	.320	.404	724	-8	98	142	7	196	639	877	13.7	4.93	-7	.264	.347	.1	-5.3	-6.4	1.0	-7.5
Central																													
Min	90	72	0	.556		801	758	155	.277	.341	.431	772	-2	104	94	7	187	402	997	12.2	4.41	+2	.268	.319	1.0	1.3	.0	-.1	6.8
Chi	86	76	0	.531	4	791	715	220	.263	.331	.446	777	-1	104	77	12	162	518	1056	12.2	4.17	+10	.253	.321	.7	6.3	-.6	.0	-1.5
KC	83	79	0	.512	7	836	867	162	.274	.336	.427	763	-6	107	120	7	190	566	865	13.8	5.05	-5	.279	.348	-.1	-3.4	-4.2	.5	9.3
Cle	68	94	0	.420	22	699	778	158	.254	.316	.401	717	-12	100	86	5	179	501	943	12.6	4.21	+5	.264	.329	-1.2	3.4	-9.0	-.8	-5.5
Det	43	119	0	.265	47	591	928	153	.240	.300	.375	675	-19	-96	98	3	195	557	764	13.9	5.30	-17	.286	.352	-1.8	-14.6	-15.4	-.6	-5.5
West																													
Oak	96	66	0	.593		768	643	176	.254	.327	.417	744	-5	101	48	16	140	499	1018	11.8	3.63	+26	.246	.314	-.0	14.4	-3.5	-.0	4.3
Sea	93	69	0	.574	3	795	637	139	.271	.344	.410	754	+3	95	108	8	173	466	1001	11.6	3.76	+15	.247	.311	2.3	9.1	4.2	.4	-4.0
Ana	77	85	0	.475	19	736	743	150	.268	.330	.413	743	-1	96	129	5	190	486	980	12.6	4.28	+2	.261	.327	.0	1.5	-.6	.0	-5.0
Tex	71	91	0	.438	25	826	969	239	.266	.330	.454	784	-3	107	65	4	208	603	1009	14.4	5.67	-12	.288	.360	.6	-9.9	-1.9	-.0	1.2
Total	1135					11033		2499	.267	.333	.428	761			1279	110		7111	3735	12.9	4.52		.267	.333					

Batter-Fielder Wins		Batting Average		On-Base Percentage		Slugging Average		On-Base Plus Slugging		Adjusted OPS		Adjusted Batter Runs	
Rodriguez-Tex	**6.7**	Mueller-Bos	.326	Ramirez-Bos	.427	Rodriguez-Tex	.600	Delgado-Tor	1019	Delgado-Tor	160	Delgado-Tor	55.6
Ramirez-Bos	**4.1**	Ramirez-Bos	.325	Mueller-Bos	.398	Ortiz-Bos	.592	Ramirez-Bos	1014	Ramirez-Bos	158	Ramirez-Bos	52.6
Garciaparra-Bos	**3.7**	Nixon-Bos	.306	Nixon-Bos	.396	Ramirez-Bos	.587	Nixon-Bos	975	Nixon-Bos	147	Mueller-Bos	32.3
Mueller-Bos	**3.1**	Garciaparra-Bos	.301	Ortiz-Bos	.369	Nixon-Bos	.578	Ortiz-Bos	961	Ortiz-Bos	142	Nixon-Bos	31.2

Runs		Hits		Doubles		Triples		Home Runs		Total Bases		Runs Batted In	
Rodriguez-Tex	124	Wells-Tor	215	Wells-Tor	49	Guzman-Min	14	Rodriguez-Tex	47	Wells-Tor	373	Delgado-Tor	145
Garciaparra-Bos	120	Garciaparra-Bos	198	Anderson-Ana	49	Garciaparra-Bos	13	Ramirez-Bos	37	Garciaparra-Bos	345	Garciaparra-Bos	105
Ramirez-Bos	117	Ramirez-Bos	185	Mueller-Bos	45	Nixon-Bos	6	Ortiz-Bos	31	Ramirez-Bos	334	Ramirez-Bos	104
Damon-Bos	103	Mueller-Bos	171	Ortiz-Bos	39	Damon-Bos	6	2 players tied	28	Mueller-Bos	283	Ortiz-Bos	101

Stolen Bases		Base Stealing Runs		Fielding Runs-Infield		Fielding Runs-Outfield		Wins		Winning Pct.		Complete Games	
Crawford-TB	55	Crawford-TB	8.6	Hudson-Tor	44.6	Cameron-Sea	16.2	Halladay-Tor	22	Halladay-Tor	.759	3 players tied	9
Damon-Bos	30	Damon-Bos	4.5	Garciaparra-Bos	6.6			Lowe-Bos	17	Lowe-Bos	.708	Martinez-Bos	3
Garciaparra-Bos	19	Garciaparra-Bos	2.4	Mueller-Bos	.6			Martinez-Bos	14			Lowe-Bos	1
Jackson-Bos	16	Jackson-Bos	.7					Burkett-Bos	12			Burkett-Bos	1

Strikeouts		Fewest BB/Game		Games		Saves		Base Runners/9		Adjusted Relief Runs		Relief Ranking	
Loaiza-Chi	207	Wells-NY	.85	Miller-Tor	79	Foulke-Oak	43	Foulke-Oak	8.72	Marte-Chi	25.9	Foulke-Oak	48.0
Martinez-Bos	206	Martinez-Bos	2.27	Timlin-Bos	72	Kim-Bos	16	Timlin-Bos	9.68	Timlin-Bos	9.8	Kim-Bos	17.9
Wakefield-Bos	169	Burkett-Bos	2.33	Embree-Bos	65	Lyon-Bos	9	Martinez-Bos	9.79	Kim-Bos	9.6	Timlin-Bos	11.0
Lowe-Bos	110	Wakefield-Bos	3.16	2 players tied	49	Fox-Bos	3	Kim-Bos	10.89	Embree-Bos	3.6	Lyon-Bos	3.8

Innings Pitched		Opponents' Avg.		Opponents' OBP		Earned Run Average		Adjusted ERA		Adjusted Starter Runs		Pitcher Wins	
Halladay-Tor	266.0	Martinez-Bos	.215	Martinez-Bos	.272	Martinez-Bos	2.22	Martinez-Bos	210	Martinez-Bos	48.8	Loaiza-Chi	5.5
Lowe-Bos	203.1	Wakefield-Bos	.246	Wakefield-Bos	.317	Wakefield-Bos	4.09	Wakefield-Bos	114	Wakefield-Bos	10.6	Martinez-Bos	4.4
Wakefield-Bos	202.1	Lowe-Bos	.272	Burkett-Bos	.330	Lowe-Bos	4.47	Lowe-Bos	104	Lowe-Bos	3.6	Kim-Bos	1.8
Martinez-Bos	186.2	Burkett-Bos	.281	Lowe-Bos	.339	Burkett-Bos	5.15	Burkett-Bos	90			Timlin-Bos	1.1

2004 AMERICAN LEAGUE

TEAM	W	L	T	PCT	GB	R	OR	HR	AVG	OBP	SLG	OPS	AOPS	PF	SB	CG	HR	BB	SO	BR/9	ERA	AERA	OAV	OOB	FW	PW	BW	BSW	DIF
East																													
NY	101	61	0	.623		897	808	242	.268	.353	.458	811	+9	100	84	1	182	445	1058	12.7	4.69	-2	.271	.328	.6	-1.5	8.8	.2	12.0
Bos	98	64	0	.605	3	949	768	222	.282	.360	.472	832	+9	106	68	4	159	447	1132	12.2	4.18	+17	.255	.318	-.5	10.1	8.5	-.1	-1.0
Bal	78	84	0	.481	23	842	830	169	.281	.345	.432	777	+2	99	101	8	159	687	1090	13.8	4.70	-1	.264	.348	-.0	-.7	2.8	.2	-5.4
TB	70	91	0	.435	30.5	714	842	145	.258	.320	.405	725	-10	98	132	3	192	580	923	13.5	4.81	-3	.265	.342	-.6	-2.2	-7.7	.8	-.8
Tor	67	94	0	.416	33.5	719	823	145	.260	.328	.403	731	-16	106	58	6	181	608	956	13.8	4.91	+0	.273	.348	1.0	-.3	-11.0	-.3	-2.9
Central																													
Min	92	70	0	.568		780	715	191	.266	.332	.431	763	-5	103	116	4	167	431	1123	12.2	4.03	+15	.267	.323	.5	9.2	-3.9	.3	4.9
Chi	83	79	0	.512	9	865	831	242	.268	.333	.457	790	+0	103	78	8	224	527	1013	13.1	4.91	-4	.272	.338	.5	-3.2	.0	-.6	5.2
Cle	80	82	0	.494	12	858	857	184	.276	.351	.444	795	+10	96	94	8	201	579	1115	13.5	4.81	-10	.271	.342	.2	-7.7	9.3	-.4	-2.3
Det	72	90	0	.444	20	827	844	201	.272	.337	.449	786	+7	96	86	7	190	530	995	13.3	4.93	-9	.275	.340	-2.0	-7.1	5.2	-.4	-4.7
KC	58	104	0	.358	34	720	905	150	.259	.322	.397	719	-14	-100	67	6	208	518	887	14.0	5.15	-10	.290	.352	-1.3	-7.4	-10.2	-.7	-3.5
West																													
Ana	92	70	0	.568		836	734	162	.282	.341	.429	770	+3	96	143	2	170	502	1164	12.5	4.28	+4	.263	.326	1.1	2.8	2.9	.9	3.2
Oak	91	71	0	.562	1	793	742	189	.270	.343	.433	776	+2	99	47	10	164	544	1034	12.7	4.17	+11	.262	.332	1.1	6.9	2.5	-.2	-.3
Tex	89	73	0	.549	3	860	794	227	.266	.329	.457	786	-2	104	69	5	182	547	979	13.5	4.53	+9	.273	.344	-.5	5.7	-1.0	-.2	4.1
Sea	63	99	0	.389	29	698	823	136	.270	.331	.396	727	-6	95	110	7	212	575	1036	13.2	4.76	-6	.265	.338	.4	-4.7	-4.7	.4	-9.4
Total	1133					11358		2605	.270	.338	.433	771			1253	79		7520	4505	13.1	4.63		.270	.338					

Batter-Fielder Wins		Batting Average		On-Base Percentage		Slugging Average		On-Base Plus Slugging		Adjusted OPS		Adjusted Batter Runs	
Tejada-Bal	**6.6**	Suzuki-Sea	.372	Mora-Bal	.419	Ramirez-Bos	.613	Ramirez-Bos	1009	Hafner-Cle	162	Guerrero-Ana	54.3
Varitek-Bos	**3.2**	Ramirez-Bos	.308	Ramirez-Bos	.397	Ortiz-Bos	.603	Ortiz-Bos	983	Ramirez-Bos	150	Ramirez-Bos	43.7
Ortiz-Bos	**2.7**	Damon-Bos	.304	Varitek-Bos	.390	Varitek-Bos	.482	Varitek-Bos	872	Ortiz-Bos	143	Ortiz-Bos	37.8
Ramirez-Bos	**2.5**	Ortiz-Bos	.301	Millar-Bos	.383	Damon-Bos	.477	2 players tied	857	Varitek-Bos	118	Damon-Bos	15.3

Runs		Hits		Doubles		Triples		Home Runs		Total Bases		Runs Batted In	
Guerrero-Ana	124	Suzuki-Sea	262	Roberts-Bal	50	Crawford-TB	19	Ramirez-Bos	43	Guerrero-Ana	366	Tejada-Bal	150
Damon-Bos	123	Damon-Bos	189	Ortiz-Bos	47	Damon-Bos	6	Ortiz-Bos	41	Ortiz-Bos	351	Ortiz-Bos	139
Ramirez-Bos	108	Ramirez-Bos	175	Ramirez-Bos	44	3 players tied	3	Damon-Bos	20	Ramirez-Bos	348	Ramirez-Bos	130
Ortiz-Bos	94	Ortiz-Bos	175	Bellhorn-Bos	37			2 players tied	18	Damon-Bos	296	Damon-Bos	94

Stolen Bases		Base Stealing Runs		Fielding Runs-Infield		Fielding Runs-Outfield		Wins		Winning Pct.		Complete Games	
Crawford-TB	59	Crawford-TB	7.7	Hudson-Tor	33.2	Baldelli-TB	10.0	Schilling-Bos	21	Schilling-Bos	.778	3 players tied	5
Damon-Bos	19	Damon-Bos	1.4					P.Martinez-Bos	16	P.Martinez-Bos	.640	Schilling-Bos	3
Varitek-Bos	10	Varitek-Bos	1.1					Lowe-Bos	14			P.Martinez-Bos	1
2 players tied	6	Bellhorn-Bos	1.0					Wakefield-Bos	12				

Strikeouts		Fewest BB/Game		Games		Saves		Base Runners/9		Adjusted Relief Runs		Relief Ranking	
Santana-Min	265	Lieber-NY	.92	Quantrill-NY	86	Rivera-NY	53	Gordon-NY	8.03	Gordon-NY	24.3	Rivera-NY	47.4
P.Martinez-Bos	227	Schilling-Bos	1.39	Timlin-Bos	76	Foulke-Bos	32	Foulke-Bos	9.11	Nathan-Min	24.3	Foulke-Bos	38.7
Schilling-Bos	203	Arroyo-Bos	2.37	Foulke-Bos	72	Williamson-Bos	1	Schilling-Bos	9.77	Foulke-Bos	24.1	Timlin-Bos	8.8
Arroyo-Bos	142	P.Martinez-Bos	2.53	Embree-Bos	71	Timlin-Bos	1	P.Martinez-Bos	11.20	Timlin-Bos	8.1		

Innings Pitched		Opponents' Avg.		Opponents' OBP		Earned Run Average		Adjusted ERA		Adjusted Starter Runs		Pitcher Wins	
Buehrle-Chi	245.1	Santana-Min	.192	Santana-Min	.249	Santana-Min	2.61	Santana-Min	178	Santana-Min	51.9	Santana-Min	5.6
Schilling-Bos	226.2	P.Martinez-Bos	.238	Schilling-Bos	.271	Schilling-Bos	3.26	Schilling-Bos	150	Schilling-Bos	42.7	Schilling-Bos	4.5
P.Martinez-Bos	217.0	Schilling-Bos	.239	P.Martinez-Bos	.301	P.Martinez-Bos	3.90	P.Martinez-Bos	125	P.Martinez-Bos	25.8	Foulke-Bos	3.8
Wakefield-Bos	188.1	Arroyo-Bos	.249	Arroyo-Bos	.314	Arroyo-Bos	4.03	Arroyo-Bos	121	Arroyo-Bos	12.7	P.Martinez-Bos	2.6

2005 AMERICAN LEAGUE

TEAM	W	L	T	PCT	GB	R	OR	HR	AVG	OBP	SLG	OPS	AOPS	PF	SB	CG	HR	BB	SO	BR/9	ERA	AERA	OAV	OOB	FW	PW	BW	BSW	DIF
East																													
NY	95	67	0	.586		886	789	229	.276	.355	.450	805	**+14**	99	84	8	164	463	985	12.8	4.52	-5	.269	.332	.5	-3.6	**11.9**	.3	4.9
Bos	95	67	0	.586		**910**	805	199	**.281**	**.357**	.454	**811**	+9	104	45	6	164	440	959	13.1	4.74	-4	.276	.335	-.4	-3.1	9.8	-.0	7.8
Tor	80	82	0	.494	15	775	705	136	.265	.331	.407	738	-10	105	72	**9**	185	444	958	12.4	4.06	+13	.264	.324	.5	7.6	-5.9	-.2	-3.0
Bal	74	88	0	.457	21	729	800	189	.269	.327	.434	761	+1	100	83	2	180	580	1052	13.2	4.56	-4	.263	.336	-.3	-2.6	.9	-.1	-4.8
TB	67	95	0	.414	28	750	936	157	.274	.329	.425	754	+1	98	151	1	194	615	949	14.2	5.39	-19	.280	.355	-1.5	-15.1	.9	**.9**	.8
Central																													
Chi	99	63	0	.611		741	645	200	.262	.322	.425	747	-7	104	137	**9**	167	459	1040	11.6	**3.61**	**+25**	.249	.310	.6	**13.7**	-4.8	.0	8.4
Cle	93	69	0	.574	6	790	**642**	207	.271	.334	.453	787	+11	97	62	6	157	413	1050	**11.3**	**3.61**	+15	.247	**.302**	-.2	8.9	9.2	-.5	-5.3
Min	83	79	0	.512	16	688	662	134	.259	.323	.391	714	-12	102	102	**9**	169	**348**	965	11.4	3.71	+18	.261	.307	.0	10.3	-8.9	.0	.5
Det	71	91	0	.438	28	723	787	168	.272	.321	.428	749	-1	98	66	7	193	461	907	12.6	4.51	-5	.272	.330	-.5	-3.8	-.8	-.1	-4.8
KC	56	106	0	.346	43	701	935	126	.263	.320	.396	716	-8	97	53	4	178	580	924	14.6	5.49	-20	.291	.362	-1.6	-16.9	-5.2	-.6	-.7
West																													
LA	95	67	0	.586		761	643	147	.270	.325	.409	734	-3	97	**161**	7	158	443	**1126**	11.7	3.68	+16	.254	.312	1.1	9.5	-2.5	.8	5.1
Oak	88	74	0	.543	7	772	658	155	.262	.330	.407	737	-4	99	31	**9**	**154**	504	1075	11.7	3.69	+19	**.241**	.311	1.0	10.5	-2.1	-.7	-1.7
Tex	79	83	0	.488	16	865	858	**260**	.267	.329	**.468**	797	+6	103	67	2	159	522	932	13.6	4.96	-8	.279	.343	-.4	-6.2	4.9	.3	-.6
Sea	69	93	0	.426	26	699	751	130	.256	.317	.391	708	-6	93	102	6	179	496	892	12.8	4.49	-7	.268	.332	**1.2**	-5.2	-4.2	-.0	-3.7
Total	1134					10790		2437	.268	.330	.424	755			1216	85		6768	3814	12.6	4.35		.268	.330					

Batter-Fielder Wins		Batting Average		On-Base Percentage		Slugging Average		On-Base Plus Slugging		Adjusted OPS		Adjusted Batter Runs	
A.Rodriguez-NY	**6.0**	M.Young-Tex	.331	Giambi-NY	.440	A.Rodriguez-NY	.610	A.Rodriguez-NY	1031	A.Rodriguez-NY	171	A.Rodriguez-NY	65.5
Ortiz-Bos	**4.2**	Damon-Bos	.316	Ortiz-Bos	.397	Ortiz-Bos	.604	Ortiz-Bos	1001	Ortiz-Bos	156	Ortiz-Bos	51.1
M.Ramirez-Bos	**3.5**	Ortiz-Bos	.300	M.Ramirez-Bos	.388	M.Ramirez-Bos	.594	M.Ramirez-Bos	982	M.Ramirez-Bos	151	M.Ramirez-Bos	41.7
Damon-Bos	**1.9**	Mueller-Bos	.295	Mueller-Bos	.369	Varitek-Bos	.489	Varitek-Bos	856	Varitek-Bos	120	Varitek-Bos	15.2
Runs		**Hits**		**Doubles**		**Triples**		**Home Runs**		**Total Bases**		**Runs Batted In**	
A.Rodriguez-NY	124	M.Young-Tex	221	Tejada-Bal	50	Crawford-TB	15	A.Rodriguez-NY	48	Teixeira-Tex	370	Ortiz-Bos	148
Ortiz-Bos	119	Damon-Bos	197	Ortiz-Bos	40	Damon-Bos	6	Ortiz-Bos	47	Ortiz-Bos	363	M.Ramirez-Bos	144
Damon-Bos	117	Ortiz-Bos	180	Renteria-Bos	36	Renteria-Bos	4	M.Ramirez-Bos	45	M.Ramirez-Bos	329	Damon-Bos	75
M.Ramirez-Bos	112	Renteria-Bos	172	Damon-Bos	35	Mueller-Bos	3	Varitek-Bos	22	Damon-Bos	274	2 players tied	70
Stolen Bases		**Base Stealing Runs**		**Fielding Runs-Infield**		**Fielding Runs-Outfield**		**Wins**		**Winning Pct.**		**Complete Games**	
Figgins-LA	62	Figgins-Ala	7.7	Hudson-Tor	28.3	Suzuki-Sea	12.8	Colon-Ala	21	Lee-Cle	.783	Halladay-Tor	5
Damon-Bos	18	Damon-Bos	3.6	Millar-Bos	10.1	Nixon-Bos	7.6	Wakefield-Bos	16	Wells-Bos	.682	Wakefield-Bos	3
Renteria-Bos	9	Renteria-Bos	.6			Damon-Bos	4.4	Wells-Bos	15	Wakefield-Bos	.571	Wells-Bos	2
3 players tied	2	2 players tied	.4			M.Ramirez-Bos	.0	Arroyo-Bos	14			Clement-Bos	1
Strikeouts		**Fewest BB/Game**		**Games**		**Saves**		**Base Runners/9**		**Adjusted Relief Runs**		**Relief Ranking**	
Santana-Min	238	Silva-Min	.43	Timlin-Bos	81	Wickman-Cle	45	Howry-Cle	8.01	Rivera-NY	23.5	Rivera-NY	47.1
Wakefield-Bos	151	Wells-Bos	1.03	Myers-Bos	65	Rodriguez-LA	45	Wakefield-Bos	11.54	Timlin-Bos	19.0	Timlin-Bos	26.7
Clement-Bos	146	Arroyo-Bos	2.37	Foulke-Bos	43	Foulke-Bos	15	Timlin-Bos	12.10				
Wells-Bos	107	Wakefield-Bos	2.72	Arroyo-Bos	35	Timlin-Bos	13	Wells-Bos	12.23				
Innings Pitched		**Opponents' Avg.**		**Opponents' OBP**		**Earned Run Average**		**Adjusted ERA**		**Adjusted Starter Runs**		**Pitcher Wins**	
Buehrle-Chi	236.2	Santana-Min	.210	Santana-Min	.250	Millwood-Cle	2.86	Santana-Min	152	Santana-Min	40.4	Rivera-NY	4.9
Wakefield-Bos	225.1	Wakefield-Bos	.245	Wakefield-Bos	.307	Wakefield-Bos	4.15	Wakefield-Bos	109	Wakefield-Bos	8.5	Timlin-Bos	2.6
Arroyo-Bos	205.1	Clement-Bos	.260	Wells-Bos	.321	Wells-Bos	4.45	Wells-Bos	102	Wells-Bos	2.8	Wakefield-Bos	1.0
Clement-Bos	191.0	Arroyo-Bos	.266	Arroyo-Bos	.322	Arroyo-Bos	4.51	Arroyo-Bos	101	Clement-Bos	.1	Papelbon-Bos	.7

2006 AMERICAN LEAGUE

TEAM	W	L	T	PCT	GB	R	OR	HR	AVG	OBP	SLG	OPS	AOPS	PF	SB	CG	HR	BB	SO	BR/9	ERA	AERA	OAV	OOB	FW	PW	BW	BSW	DIF
East																													
NY	97	65	0	.599		**930**	767	210	.285	**.363**	.461	**824**	**+12**	100	139	5	170	496	1019	12.6	4.41	+3	.262	.326	-.4	1.8	**11.2**	**1.0**	2.4
Tor	87	75	0	.537	10	809	754	199	.284	.348	.463	811	+4	104	65	6	185	504	1076	12.7	4.37	+8	.262	.328	-.0	5.2	3.8	-.4	-2.5
Bos	86	76	0	.531	11	820	825	192	.269	.351	.435	786	+0	102	51	3	181	509	1070	13.4	4.83	-3	.278	.343	**2.4**	-2.4	1.8	-.4	3.6
Bal	70	92	0	.432	27	768	899	164	.277	.339	.424	763	-1	97	121	5	216	613	1016	14.2	5.35	-16	.284	.357	-.3	-12.6	-.0	.7	1.2
TB	61	101	0	.377	36	689	856	190	.255	.314	.420	734	-11	-99	134	3	180	606	979	14.4	4.96	-6	.286	.358	-1.3	-4.4	-9.3	.4	-5.4
Central																													
Min	96	66	0	.593		801	683	143	**.287**	.347	.425	772	-1	100	101	1	182	**356**	**1164**	**11.8**	3.95	+15	.267	**.312**	1.1	9.2	-.2	.0	4.9
Det	95	67	0	.586	1	822	**675**	203	.274	.329	.449	778	+1	98	60	3	160	489	1003	12.2	**3.84**	**+17**	.257	.321	-.6	**9.8**	-.0	-.8	5.6
Chi	90	72	0	.556	6	868	794	**236**	.280	.342	**.464**	806	+4	102	93	5	200	433	1012	12.6	4.61	+1	.271	.326	.6	.9	3.3	-.3	4.5
Cle	78	84	0	.481	18	870	782	196	.280	.349	.457	806	**+12**	96	55	**13**	166	429	948	13.0	4.41	-2	.282	.335	-1.4	-1.5	9.7	-.3	-9.5
KC	62	100	0	.383	34	757	971	124	.271	.332	.411	743	-7	98	65	3	213	637	904	14.8	5.65	-17	.292	.367	.0	-14.2	-4.8	-.5	.5
West																													
Oak	93	69	0	.574		771	727	175	.260	.340	.412	752	-4	98	61	5	162	529	1003	13.1	4.21	+8	.272	.338	1.1	4.9	-1.9	-.1	8.0
LA	89	73	0	.549	4	766	732	159	.274	.334	.425	759	-1	96	**148**	5	**158**	471	**1164**	12.0	4.04	+10	**.254**	.316	-1.9	6.3	-.9	.6	3.9
Tex	80	82	0	.494	13	835	784	183	.278	.338	.446	784	+1	100	53	3	162	496	972	13.3	4.60	+2	.278	.341	.0	1.1	1.4	-.4	-3.2
Sea	78	84	0	.481	15	756	792	172	.272	.325	.424	749	-2	94	106	6	183	560	1067	13.1	4.60	-4	.267	.337	.8	-3.1	-2.1	.3	1.2
Total	1134					11262		2546	.275	.339	.437	776			1252	66		7128	4397	13.1	4.56		.275	.339					

Batter-Fielder Wins		Batting Average		On-Base Percentage		Slugging Average		On-Base Plus Slugging		Adjusted OPS		Adjusted Batter Runs	
Hafner-Cle	**5.4**	Mauer-Min	.347	Hafner-Cle	.439	Hafner-Cle	.659	Hafner-Cle	1097	Hafner-Cle	187	Hafner-Cle	64.2
Ortiz-Bos	**4.5**	Ramirez-Bos	.321	Ramirez-Bos	.439	Ortiz-Bos	.636	Ramirez-Bos	1058	Ramirez-Bos	168	Ortiz-Bos	55.9
Ramirez-Bos	**3.2**	Ortiz-Bos	.287	Ortiz-Bos	.413	Ramirez-Bos	.619	Ortiz-Bos	1049	Ortiz-Bos	163	Ramirez-Bos	50.4
Lowell-Bos	**2.5**	Loretta-Bos	.285	Youkilis-Bos	.381	Lowell-Bos	.475	Lowell-Bos	814	Youkilis-Bos	109	Youkilis-Bos	12.0
Runs		**Hits**		**Doubles**		**Triples**		**Home Runs**		**Total Bases**		**Runs Batted In**	
Sizemore-Cle	134	Suzuki-Sea	224	Sizemore-Cle	53	Crawford-TB	16	Ortiz-Bos	54	Ortiz-Bos	355	Ortiz-Bos	137
Ortiz-Bos	115	Loretta-Bos	181	Lowell-Bos	47	7 players tied	2	Ramirez-Bos	35	Ramirez-Bos	278	Ramirez-Bos	102
Youkilis-Bos	100	Lowell-Bos	163	Youkilis-Bos	42			Lowell-Bos	20	Lowell-Bos	272	Lowell-Bos	80
2 players tied	79	Ortiz-Bos	160	Loretta-Bos	33			Youkilis-Bos	13	Youkilis-Bos	244	Youkilis-Bos	72
Stolen Bases		**Base Stealing Runs**		**Fielding Runs-Infield**		**Fielding Runs-Outfield**		**Wins**		**Winning Pct.**		**Complete Games**	
Crawford-TB	58	Crawford-TB	9.6	Inge-Det	24.7	Markakis-Bal	8.3	Wang-NY	19	Halladay-Tor	.762	Sabathia-Cle	6
Crisp-Bos	22	Crisp-Bos	3.4	Lowell-Bos	20.8	Nixon-Bos	1.8	Santana-Min	19	Schilling-Bos	.682	Wakefield-Bos	1
Harris-Bos	6	Cora-Bos	.6	Youkilis-Bos	2.2			Beckett-Bos	16	Beckett-Bos	.593	Tavarez-Bos	1
Cora-Bos	6	Loretta-Bos	.5	Loretta-Bos	1.3			Schilling-Bos	15			Hansack-Bos	1
Strikeouts		**Fewest BB/Game**		**Games**		**Saves**		**Base Runners/9**		**Adjusted Relief Runs**		**Relief Ranking**	
Santana-Min	245	Schilling-Bos	1.24	Proctor-NY	83	Rodriguez-LA	47	Papelbon-Bos	7.11	Papelbon-Bos	27.6	Papelbon-Bos	47.1
Schilling-Bos	183	Beckett-Bos	3.25	Timlin-Bos	68	Papelbon-Bos	35	Schilling-Bos	11.07	Timlin-Bos	2.2	Timlin-Bos	4.3
Beckett-Bos	158			Papelbon-Bos	59	Timlin-Bos	9	Beckett-Bos	12.09	Tavarez-Bos	1.4	Tavarez-Bos	1.2
Wakefield-Bos	90			Tavarez-Bos	58	2 players tied	1	Wakefield-Bos	12.60				
Innings Pitched		**Opponents' Avg.**		**Opponents' OBP**		**Earned Run Average**		**Adjusted ERA**		**Adjusted Starter Runs**		**Pitcher Wins**	
Santana-Min	233.2	Santana-Min	.216	Santana-Min	.258	Santana-Min	2.77	Santana-Min	165	Santana-Min	45.9	3 players tied	4.6
Beckett-Bos	204.2	Beckett-Bos	.245	Schilling-Bos	.303	Schilling-Bos	3.97	Schilling-Bos	118	Schilling-Bos	18.3	Papelbon-Bos	4.6
Schilling-Bos	204.0	Schilling-Bos	.276	Beckett-Bos	.317	Beckett-Bos	5.01	Beckett-Bos	93	Gabbard-Bos	3.1	Schilling-Bos	1.8
Wakefield-Bos	140.0									Hansack-Bos	2.2	3 players tied	.4

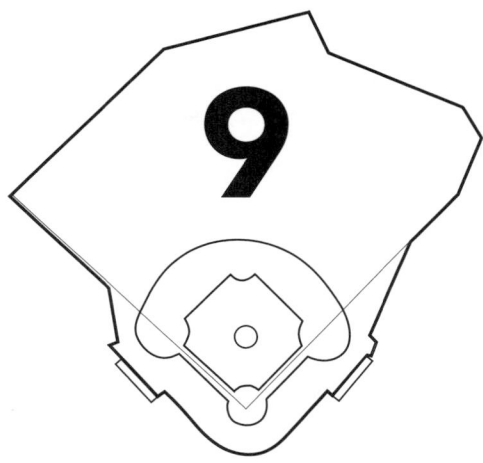

POSTSEASON

When the first postseason game was played in the 20th century, the Red Sox were there. In fact, the Red Sox hosted it. Postseason games had been played in the 19th century between the National League and American Association as far back as 1884—another New England team, the NL's Providence Grays, beat the AA New York Mets in that first series—but the first modern World Series was a landmark event in the game's history. A bitter feud between AL and NL had threatened the prosperity of both leagues and peace had reluctantly been established in 1903. This set the stage for Pittsburgh Pirates owner Barney Dreyfuss to challenge Henry Killilea's Boston club to a best-of-nine series. (Though dubbed the World's Series and featuring a city spelled "Pittsburg," for continuity's sake this book will move forward in time and attach the "h" to one name and drop "s" from another. Likewise, the Boston nine will be called the Red Sox even though the club went by any number of names—Americans and Pilgrims among the most popular—during the early years of the club's existence.)

Cy Young pitched the first World Series game and helped sell tickets, literally, when he wasn't pitching at Huntington Avenue Grounds. The man really could do it all. And the Red Sox could do no wrong in October, winning 5 of the first 15 World Series. It started with the defeat of the Pirates from the established league even after losing three of the first four games. The Red Sox won a thriller in 1912 against the New York Giants, the same club that had stood up the AL and Boston in 1904, refusing to play that year's World Series. The Red Sox

marched through successive championships in 1915 and 1916 against Philadelphia and Brooklyn, respectively. The 1918 world championship seemed to be as much about the Great War as it was about Babe Ruth and the Red Sox. The season was truncated by the war, the players and owners battled about the World Series pot, and offense appeared to be another rationed wartime commodity. The Red Sox scored nine times over six games and won anyway, but it would be their last such win for a very long time.

Over the ensuing 86 years the Red Sox endured every seeming postseason hardship imaginable. Four times they lost the seventh game of the World Series, twice to the St. Louis Cardinals, and once each to the Cincinnati Reds and New York Mets. New postseason potholes emerged that Dreyfuss and Killea had never dreamed of when they had initiated this challenge. Expansion created larger leagues and resulted in a divisional format, East and West, in 1969. The Red Sox were in the AL East, naturally, along with foes such as the New York Yankees (originally the Baltimore Orioles) and the Baltimore Orioles (originally the Milwaukee Brewers and then the St. Louis Browns). Yes, a lot had changed since 1903.

The division champion in each league played one another in a best-of-five League Championship Series for the pennant and a World Series berth. The Red Sox took their first AL East title in 1975. Boston knocked off the dynastic Oakland A's, the first team other than the Yankees to reach the postseason five straight seasons.

They then lost to the Reds in an epic World Series that is far more famous today than any of the first five Red Sox world championships. The 1978 season, like the 1948 campaign, ended in a tie for first place, necessitating a one-game playoff. Though considered part of the regular season, both playoffs—especially the bitter 1978 defeat at the hands of the Yankees at Fenway Park—are touchstone moments for Red Sox fans not even alive for either game.

The 1986 postseason brought one of the most exhilarating comebacks in franchise history, followed by perhaps the club's most excruciating collapse. The 1988 and 1990 division champion Red Sox did not win a game in either ALCS, extended to a best-of-seven affair since 1985. Eagerness to copy the lucrative playoff formats in other sports led to another postseason tier: the Division Series. Three divisions were created in each league, with the Red Sox, Yankees, Orioles, Blue Jays, and Tigers (Detroit would be sent to the Central Division in favor of the expansion Tampa Bay Devil Rays in 1998). The inclusion of a wild card meant that for the first time a team could go to the postseason without finishing first. The new alignment kicked off in 1994, the year the postseason was cancelled because of the baseball strike.

The Red Sox were on the field for the first Division Series on October 3, 1995—the shortsighted and short-lived entity known as "The Baseball Network" broadcast all the games at the same time, thus keeping fans in other markets from watching—and Boston was summarily bounced by Cleveland. The Indians won again in the 1998 Division Series, Boston's first appearance as a wild card. Pedro Martinez ended the club's losing streak of 13 consecutive postseason games that dated back to the 1986 World Series. The next year he ended a string of five successive postseason series losses, although an old foe eliminated Boston in a new way. The wild card enabled both the Yankees and Red Sox to face each other in the ALCS and New York won the pennant in Fenway Park. The Yankees ended Boston's season in the ALCS again in 2003, a bitter conclusion after the Red Sox had rallied from two games to none to beat Oakland in the Division Series. The 2004 postseason would reverse Boston's fortune.

The Red Sox, once again the AL's wild card, swept the Anaheim Angels in the Division Series. The Yankees won the first three games of the ALCS, but the Red Sox stormed back and took the last four in dramatic fashion, the first team in postseason history to stage such a rally. Boston then slew the Cardinals in the World Series and took home the club's first world championship since 1918. The encore was brief as the Chicago White Sox knocked off the Red Sox in the 2005 Division Series.

This section chronicles every postseason game in franchise history. It includes a lead-in about the teams that year or in that particular series, a summary of each game in the series, and cumulative statistics for the Red Sox. It likewise includes the one-game playoffs in 1948 and 1978, even though those are considered regular-season games. Boxscores of these games are included. The information used here was obtained free of charge from and is copyrighted by Retrosheet. Interested parties may contact Retrosheet at *www.retrosheet.org*.

In 1949, a year after Babe Ruth's death, an award was given to the best player in the World Series as chosen several weeks after the fact by the New York chapter of the Baseball Writers Association. (Ruth had set postseason records for pitching excellence with Boston before he started launching long balls for the club's chief rival.) The *Sport* Magazine Most Valuable Player Award was given out at the World Series, along with a new car, starting in 1955. The MVP came to be voted on by the writers and executives present during the World Series; it remains an official award long after the magazine's end. Both awards are noted below, even if the recipient is a member of the opposing team. Nothing is listed if the Red Sox did not reach that round of postseason play. The ALCS began recognizing an MVP starting in 1980. The Division Series does not yet have an official MVP.

Year	ALCS MVP	World Series MVP	Babe Ruth Award
1967	Not Played	Bob Gibson, St. Louis	Lou Brock, St. Louis
1975	None Given	Pete Rose, Cincinnati	Luis Tiant, Red Sox
1986	Marty Barrett, Red Sox	Ray Knight, New York Mets	Ray Knight, New York Mets
1988	Dennis Eckersley, Oakland		
1990	Dave Stewart, Oakland		
1999	Orlando Hernandez, New York Yankees		
2003	Mariano Rivera, New York Yankees		
2004	David Ortiz, Red Sox	Manny Ramirez, Red Sox	Keith Foulke

RED SOX IN OCTOBER

1903	World Series	Boston (AL) 5, Pittsburgh 3 (NL)
1912	World Series	Boston 5 (AL), New York 3 (NL)
1915	World Series	Boston 4 (AL), Philadelphia 1 (NL)
1916	World Series	Boston 4 (AL), Brooklyn 1 (NL)
1918	World Series	Boston 4 (AL), Chicago 2 (NL)
1946	World Series	St. Louis 4 (NL), Boston 3 (AL)
1948	AL Playoff Game	Cleveland defeats Boston
1967	World Series	St. Louis 4 (NL), Boston 3 (AL)
1975	AL Championship Series	Boston 3 (AL), Oakland 0
	World Series	Cincinnati 4 (NL), Boston 3 (AL)
1978	AL Playoff Game	New York defeats Boston
1986	AL Championship Series	Boston 4 (E), California 3 (W)
	World Series	New York 4 (NL), Boston 3 (AL)

1988	AL Championship Series	Oakland 4 (W), Boston 0 (E)
1990	AL Championship Series	Oakland 4 (W), Boston 0 (E)
1995	AL Division Series	Cleveland 3 (C), Boston 0 (WC)
1998	AL Division Series	Cleveland 3 (C), Boston 1 (WC)
1999	AL Division Series	Boston 3 (WC), Cleveland 2 (C)
	AL Championship Series	New York 4 (E), Boston 1 (WC)
2003	AL Division Series	Boston 3 (WC), Oakland 2 (W)
	AL Championship Series	New York 4 (E), Boston 3 (WC)
2004	AL Division Series	Boston 3 (WC), Anaheim 2 (W)
	AL Championship Series	Boston 4 (WC), New York 3 (E)
	World Series	Boston 4 (AL), St. Louis 0 (NL)
2005	AL Division Series	Chicago 3 (C), Boston 0 (WC)

(E) East Division champions; (W) West Division Champions;
(C) Central Division champions; (WC) AL wild card

☒ ☒ ☒

1903 World Series, Boston Red Sox vs. Pittsburgh Pirates

The American League and National League still didn't like each other, but after two years of raids to drive each other out of business, the leagues decided they had to live together or risk dying separately. They made no provisions for playing one another, however. By the end of summer, the two leagues had runaway winners and Barney Dreyfuss of Pittsburgh and Henry Killilea of Boston agreed to play a best-of-nine postseason series. Such "world series" had occurred in the 19th century between the NL and the American Association, but nothing with the kind of excitement this caused.

Huntington Avenue Grounds was crammed on October 1 to see Cy Young, who had led the AL in wins in each season of its brief existence and who that year had passed Pud Galvin's all-time mark of 361 wins. Boston also had Bill Dinneen, a 21-game winner, who had failed to complete just two games but had finished two other wins for teammates. The Pirates, however, limped into the first "modern" postseason. Honus Wagner injured his right leg and backup Otto Krueger was out after a

beaning. Staff ace Sam Leever, with the highest winning percentage and lowest ERA in the NL, had a bad shoulder, and Ed Donheny was hospitalized with a mental disorder, never to pitch again. Player-manager Fred Clarke relied on one man, Deacon Phillippe.

No other pitcher has ever started more often in a World Series than Phillippe in 1903, who started five times and won three before losing his last two. Dinneen won three games as well, including deciding Game 8 for Boston. Cy Young won the other two. The Pirates still made more money—$1,316 per man—because owner Barney Dreyfuss gave his share to the players.

The Red Sox could have been the first repeat World Series champion in 1904, but it was not to be. New York Giants owner John T. Brush and manager John McGraw declined to play the 1904 World Series. McGraw had a simmering feud with AL president Ban Johnson following his 1902 attempt to sink the original AL Baltimore Orioles, who survived McGraw's managerial machinations and moved to New York to become the Highlanders (later the Yankees). Boston's pennant would have to suffice in 1904, but the club would get a long overdue shot at McGraw's Giants in 1912.

BOS (AL)

PLAYER, POS	G	AB	R	H	2B	3B	HR	RBI	BB	SO	SB	AVG	OBP
J.Collins, 3b	8	36	5	9	1	2	0	1	1	1	3	.250	.270
P.Dougherty, of	8	34	3	8	0	2	2	5	2	6	0	.235	.278
C.Stahl, of	8	33	6	10	1	3	0	3	1	2	2	.303	.324
B.Freeman, of	8	32	6	9	0	3	0	4	2	2	0	.281	.324
F.Parent, ss	8	32	8	9	0	3	0	4	1	1	0	.281	.314
H.Ferris, 2b	8	31	3	9	0	1	0	5	0	6	0	.290	.290
C.LaChance, 1b	8	27	5	6	2	1	0	4	3	2	0	.222	.300
L.Criger, c	8	26	1	6	0	0	0	4	2	3	0	.231	.286
C.Young, p	4	15	1	2	0	1	0	3	0	3	0	.133	.133
B.Dinneen, p	4	12	1	3	0	0	0	0	2	2	0	.250	.357
D.Farrell, ph	2	2	0	0	0	0	0	1	0	0	0	.000	.000
J.O'Brien, ph	2	2	0	0	0	0	0	0	0	1	0	.000	.000
TOTALS		**282**	**39**	**71**	**4**	**16**	**2**	**34**	**14**	**29**	**5**	**.252**	**.293**

PITCHER	W	L	ERA	G	GS	SV	IP	H	BB	SO
B.Dinneen	3	1	2.06	4	4	0	35.0	29	8	28
C.Young	2	1	1.85	4	3	0	34.0	31	4	17
T.Hughes	0	1	9.00	1	1	0	2.0	4	2	0
TOTALS	**5**	**3**	**2.15**	**9**	**8**	**0**	**71.0**	**64**	**14**	**45**

PIT (NL)

PLAYER, POS	G	AB	R	H	2B	3B	HR	RBI	BB	SO	SB	AVG	OBP
G.Beaumont, of	8	34	6	9	0	1	0	1	2	4	2	.265	.306
F.Clarke, of	8	34	3	9	2	1	0	2	1	5	1	.265	.286
T.Leach, 3b	8	33	3	9	0	4	0	7	1	4	1	.273	.294
J.Sebring, of	8	30	3	11	0	1	1	3	1	4	0	.367	.387
K.Bransfield, 1b	8	29	5	6	0	2	0	1	1	6	1	.207	.233
C.Ritchey, 2b	8	27	2	3	1	0	0	2	4	7	1	.111	.226
H.Wagner, ss	8	27	2	6	1	0	0	3	3	4	3	.222	.300
E.Phelps, c	8	26	1	6	2	0	0	1	1	6	0	.231	.259
D.Phillippe, p	5	18	1	4	0	0	0	1	0	3	0	.222	.222
S.Leever, p	2	4	0	0	0	0	0	0	0	0	0	.000	.000
H.Smith, c	1	3	0	0	0	0	0	0	0	0	0	.000	.000
B.Kennedy, p	1	2	0	1	1	0	0	0	0	0	0	.500	.500
B.Veil, p	1	2	0	0	0	0	0	0	0	2	0	.000	.000
G.Thompson, p	1	1	0	0	0	0	0	0	0	0	0	.000	.000
TOTALS		**270**	**24**	**64**	**7**	**9**	**1**	**21**	**14**	**45**	**9**	**.237**	**.277**

PITCHER	W	L	ERA	G	GS	SV	IP	H	BB	SO
D.Phillippe	3	2	2.86	5	5	0	44.0	38	3	22
S.Leever	0	2	5.40	2	2	0	10.0	13	3	2
B.Kennedy	0	1	5.14	1	1	0	7.0	11	3	3
B.Veil	0	0	1.29	1	0	0	7.0	6	5	1
G.Thompson	0	0	4.50	1	0	0	2.0	3	0	1
TOTALS	**3**	**5**	**3.34**	**10**	**8**	**0**	**70.0**	**71**	**14**	**29**

1903 WORLD SERIES - BOS(AL) DEFEATS PIT(NL), 5 GAMES TO 3

GAME 1, OCT. 1					
PIT	401	100	100	7	12	2
BOS	000	000	201	3	6	4

PITCHERS: PHILLIPPE VS YOUNG
ATTENDANCE: 16,242

GAME 2, OCT. 2					
PIT	000	000	000	0	3	2
BOS	200	001	00X	3	9	0

PITCHERS: LEEVER, Veil(2) VS DINNEEN
ATTENDANCE: 9,415

GAME 3, OCT. 3					
PIT	012	000	010	4	7	0
BOS	000	100	010	2	4	2

PITCHERS: PHILLIPPE VS HUGHES, Young(3)
ATTENDANCE: 18,801

GAME 4, OCT. 6					
BOS	000	010	003	4	9	1
PIT	100	010	30X	5	12	1

PITCHERS: DINNEEN VS PHILLIPPE
ATTENDANCE: 7,600

GAME 5, OCT. 7					
BOS	000	006	410	11	14	2
PIT	000	000	020	2	6	4

PITCHERS: YOUNG VS KENNEDY, Thompson(8)
ATTENDANCE: 12,322

GAME 6, OCT. 8					
BOS	003	020	100	6	10	1
PIT	000	000	300	3	10	3

PITCHERS: DINNEEN VS LEEVER
ATTENDANCE: 11,556

GAME 7, OCT. 10					
BOS	200	202	010	7	11	4
PIT	000	101	001	3	10	3

PITCHERS: YOUNG VS PHILLIPPE
ATTENDANCE: 17,038

GAME 8, OCT. 13					
PIT	000	000	000	0	4	3
BOS	000	201	00X	3	8	0

PITCHERS: PHILLIPPE VS DINNEEN
ATTENDANCE: 7,4553

Game 1. Some writers found it ironic that this "world" championship should cover only seven states in one country, but Boston couldn't get enough of it. More than 16,000 squeezed into every corner of Huntington Avenue Grounds for Game 1. Young threw the first pitch and took the first loss. After the first two Pirates were retired, Tommy Leach tripled into the overflow crowd for the first hit, then scored the first run on Wagner's single. Pittsburgh scored three more before Boston even batted, as Jimmy Sebring hit the first homer and Phillippe recorded the first win.

Game 2. Boston returned the favor and roughed up Pittsburgh's starter in the first inning. Patsy Dougherty homered to lead off the game and added another in the sixth, the last home run hit in the World Series until 1908! Leever's shoulder clearly wasn't right, as he lasted just an inning while Dinneen tossed a three-hitter and fanned 11.

Game 3. Clarke went with Phillippe again, and he was even better the second time around. Young pitched just as well, but he didn't enter the game until starter Long Tom Hughes was chased in the third inning.

Game 4. The first modern World Series game in Pittsburgh featured another win by Deacon Phillippe after a day off and a rainout made it possible for him to make his third start in six days. Phillippe showed signs of weakness, though, allowing three runs and five hits in the ninth before retiring the final two batters with the bases full to give the Pirates a 3-games-to-1 lead.

Game 5. With Boston unable to afford another loss, Game 5 went into the sixth inning scoreless. Clarke set the stage for a six-run inning by dropping a fly ball as he tried to avoid a collision with Wagner. Two batters later, Wagner made the first of his two errors in the inning as Young and Dougherty collected back-to-back triples to cash in on Pittsburgh's largesse. Boston followed with four more in the seventh for the first double-digit score in the World Series.

Game 6. Leever even bettered his second start, not allowing a hit to the first eight batters, but Dinneen's two-out single started a three-run rally. Boston had six runs before Pittsburgh scored three times in the seventh. Dinneen pitched out of a bases-loaded jam to even the Series.

Game 7. A postponement for cold weather allowed Phillippe to start a fourth time, but Young survived 10 hits and four errors to pull out the win. Catcher Lou Criger drove in three runs as Boston left Pittsburgh with its first lead of the Series.

Game 8. Another rainout stretched the World Series to nearly its second week, but Boston put an end to it. Phillippe's durability was admirable, and he had his best outing since Game 3, though he labored under the workload as Dinneen thrived, winning his third game in four tries by shutting out the Pirates on four hits. Wagner, who batted .222 with one extra-base hit, struck out to give Boston the new century's first world championship.

1912 World Series, Boston Red Sox vs. New York Giants

The American League had changed a lot since the Red Sox won the first World Series in 1903. The Detroit Tigers and Philadelphia Athletics had won three pennants apiece, while the Red Sox had used nine different managers—including interims—and had touched bottom before resurfacing. Their last pennant had been in 1904 when the Giants refused to play in a World Series. The Giants changed their tune and played the Series against Philadelphia in 1905, becoming the first NL team to win one, and New York lost the 1911 rematch with the A's. While the Giants had breakneck speed, superb hitting, and solid defense, John McGraw's biggest weapon in 1912 was the same one he'd had when he'd spurned the Red Sox in 1904: Christy Mathewson. The Sox countered with Smoky Joe Wood, winner of 16 straight during the year and 34 overall. Their "Million Dollar Outfield"—Duffy Lewis, Tris Speaker, and Harry Hooper—didn't hurt.

Luck was with the Red Sox in this one. Although New York outscored Boston by six runs, outhit them by 50 points, and received three stellar starts from Matty, they blew two late leads in a game that wound up as a tie. In the finale, two balls in the last inning that should have been caught set the stage for the first "walkoff" world championship—some 90 years before that term entered the lexicon.

BOS (AL)

PLAYER, POS	G	AB	R	H	2B	3B	HR	RBI	BB	SO	SB	AVG	OBP
D.Lewis, of	8	32	4	5	3	0	0	1	2	2	0	.156	.206
J.Stahl, 1b	8	32	3	9	2	0	0	2	0	6	2	.281	.281
S.Yerkes, 2b	8	32	3	8	0	2	0	4	2	3	0	.250	.294
H.Hooper, of	8	31	3	9	2	1	0	2	4	4	2	.290	.371
T.Speaker, of	8	30	4	9	1	2	0	2	4	2	1	.300	.382
H.Wagner, ss	8	30	1	5	1	0	0	3	6	1	0	.167	.242
L.Gardner, 3b	8	28	4	5	2	1	1	5	2	5	0	.179	.250
H.Cady, c	7	22	1	3	0	0	0	1	0	3	0	.136	.136
B.Carrigan, c	2	7	0	0	0	0	0	0	0	0	0	.000	.000
J.Wood, p	4	7	1	2	0	0	0	1	1	0	0	.286	.375
H.Bedient, p	4	6	0	0	0	0	0	0	0	0	0	.000	.000
R.Collins, p	2	5	0	0	0	0	0	0	0	2	0	.000	.000
C.Hall, p	2	4	0	3	0	0	0	0	1	0	0	.750	.800
C.Engle, ph	3	3	1	1	1	0	0	2	0	0	0	.333	.333
B.O'Brien, p	2	2	0	0	0	0	0	0	0	2	0	.000	.000
N.Ball, ph	1	1	0	0	0	0	0	0	0	1	0	.000	.000
O.Henriksen, ph	2	1	0	1	1	0	0	1	0	0	0	1.000	1.000
TOTALS		273	25	60	14	6	1	21	19	36	6	.220	.272

PITCHER	W	L	ERA	G	GS	SV	IP	H	BB	SO
J.Wood	3	1	3.68	4	3	0	22.0	27	3	21
H.Bedient	1	0	0.50	4	2	0	18.0	10	7	7
R.Collins	0	0	1.26	2	1	0	14.1	14	0	6
C.Hall	0	0	3.38	2	0	0	10.2	11	9	1
B.O'Brien	0	2	5.00	2	2	0	9.0	12	3	4
TOTALS	4	3	2.55	14	8	0	74.0	74	22	39

NY (NL)

PLAYER, POS	G	AB	R	H	2B	3B	HR	RBI	BB	SO	SB	AVG	OBP
L.Doyle, 2b	8	33	5	8	1	0	1	2	3	2	2	.242	.306
F.Merkle, 1b	8	33	5	9	2	1	0	3	0	7	1	.273	.273
F.Snodgrass, of	8	33	2	7	2	0	0	2	2	5	1	.212	.257
R.Murray, of	8	31	5	10	4	1	0	4	2	2	0	.323	.364
B.Herzog, 3b	8	30	6	12	4	1	0	5	1	3	2	.400	.441
A.Fletcher, ss	8	28	1	5	1	0	0	3	1	4	1	.179	.207
C.Meyers, c	8	28	2	10	0	1	0	3	2	3	1	.357	.400
J.Devore, of	7	24	4	6	0	0	0	0	7	5	4	.250	.419
C.Mathewson, p	3	12	0	2	0	0	0	0	0	4	0	.167	.167
J.Tesreau, p	3	8	0	3	0	0	0	2	1	3	0	.375	.444
B.Becker, of	2	4	1	0	0	0	0	0	2	0	0	.000	.333
R.Marquard, p	2	4	0	0	0	0	0	0	1	0	0	.000	.200
M.McCormick, ph	5	4	0	1	0	0	0	1	0	0	0	.250	.250
D.Crandall, p	1	1	0	0	0	0	0	0	0	1	0	.000	.000
A.Wilson, c	2	1	0	1	0	0	0	0	0	0	0	1.000	1.000
T.Shafer, ss	3	0	0	0	0	0	0	0	0	0	0	.000	.000
TOTALS		274	31	74	14	4	1	25	22	39	12	.270	.330

PITCHER	W	L	ERA	G	GS	SV	IP	H	BB	SO
C.Mathewson	0	2	1.26	3	3	0	28.2	23	5	10
J.Tesreau	1	2	3.13	3	3	0	23.0	19	11	15
R.Marquard	2	0	0.50	2	2	0	18.0	14	2	9
R.Ames	0	0	4.50	1	0	0	2.0	3	1	0
D.Crandall	0	0	0.00	1	0	0	2.0	1	0	2
TOTALS	3	4	1.71	10	8	0	73.2	60	19	36

1912 WORLD SERIES - BOS(AL) DEFEATS NY (NL), 4 GAMES TO 3 (1 TIE GAME)

GAME 1, OCT. 8				
BOS	000 001 300	4	6	1
NY	002 000 001	3	8	1

PITCHERS: WOOD VS TESREAU, Crandall(8)
ATTENDANCE: 35,730

GAME 2, OCT. 9				
NY	010 100 030 10	6	11	5
BOS	300 010 010 10	6	10	1

PITCHERS: Mathewson VS Collins, Hall(8), Bedient(11)
ATTENDANCE: 30,148

GAME 3, OCT. 10				
NY	010 010 000	2	7	1
BOS	000 000 001	1	7	0

PITCHERS: MARQUARD VS O'BRIEN, Bedient(9)
ATTENDANCE: 34,624

GAME 4, OCT. 11				
BOS	010 100 001	3	8	1
NY	000 000 100	1	9	1

PITCHERS: WOOD VS TESREAU, Ames(8)
ATTENDANCE: 36,502

GAME 5, OCT. 12				
NY	000 000 100	1	3	1
BOS	002 000 00X	2	5	1

PITCHERS: MATHEWSON VS BEDIENT
ATTENDANCE: 34,683

GAME 6, OCT. 14				
BOS	020 000 000	2	7	2
NY	500 000 00X	5	11	2

PITCHERS: O'BRIEN, Collins(2) VS MARQUARD
ATTENDANCE: 30,622

GAME 7, OCT. 15				
NY	610 002 101	11	16	4
BOS	010 000 210	4	9	3

PITCHERS: TESREAU VS WOOD, Hall(2)
ATTENDANCE: 32,694

GAME 8, OCT. 16				
NY	001 000 000 1	2	9	2
BOS	000 000 100 2	3	8	5

PITCHERS: MATHEWSON VS Bedient, WOOD(8)
ATTENDANCE: 17,034

Game 1. McGraw started his third-best pitcher, Jeff Tesreau, in the opener. Tesreau kept the Red Sox off the scoreboard for five innings and owned a 2–1 lead in the seventh with two outs and two on. Hooper doubled down the first-base line to tie the game, and Steve Yerkes followed with a two-run single. Smoky Joe was in a similar situation in the ninth, except that the tying run was on third and the go-ahead run on second with one out. Wood fanned Art Fletcher and pitcher Doc Crandall, a .313 hitter in 1912, to end the game.

Game 2. The Big Six went 11 innings and allowed just two earned runs. Unfortunately for Mathewson, the Giants made five errors that led to four unearned runs, including the tying runs in the eighth and 10th. With Boston trailing, 6–5, Speaker would have been out on his inside-the-park homer try if catcher Art Wilson, who'd just entered the game, had handled the throw. The game was called by darkness an inning later.

Game 3. Rube Marquard topped Buck O'Brien as the Giants evened the Series. The Red Sox had the tying and winning runs in scoring position in the bottom of the ninth, but Hick Cady's line drive was caught to end the game.

Game 4. Smoky Joe defeated Tesreau for the second time in the World Series. New York nearly tied it in the seventh when Moose McCormick bowled over Cady at the plate, but the catcher held the ball and Wood held the Giants the rest of the way.

Game 5. Mathewson was again undone by his defense. Boston reached him for back-to-back triples by Hooper and Yerkes, but second baseman Larry Doyle's error brought in a second run. After the Giants scored an unearned run in the seventh, Hugh Bedient retired Mathewson and set down New York in order the rest of the way.

Game 6. Manager Jake Stahl gambled and sent out O'Brien, a 20-game winner, hoping to pull out the win and the world championship. If not, he had a fully rested Wood to pitch in Boston. Part A of the plan failed as New York scored five times in the first inning to knock out O'Brien.

Game 7. Part B of Stahl's plan failed as 22-year-old ace Smoky Joe had some jitters and was hammered for six first-inning runs. Tesreau, one of five Giants with at least two hits, allowed four meaningless runs as the Giants romped and tied the Series.

Game 8. A Wednesday afternoon brought out the smallest crowd by far in the Series—just 17,034 at Fenway—for deciding Game 8. Boston's Bedient allowed a third-inning run on Red Murray's double and got help from right fielder Hooper, whose spectacular catch saved a home run by Doyle. Mathewson held the lead until two outs in the seventh. Olaf Henricksen, in his only at bat, ripped a two-out double to tie the game. Wood, who'd been knocked out in the first inning the previous day, came on in relief. Fred Merkle's single in the 10th brought in the go-ahead run to set up one of the most exciting finishes in World Series history. Fred Snodgrass dropped an easy fly ball to put Clyde Engle on second with none out in the bottom of the inning. Snodgrass then made a remarkable catch on Hooper for the first out, with Engle taking third. Yerkes walked, setting up a force with Speaker coming up. Speaker, a .383 hitter that year, lifted a catchable foul pop that neither Mathewson nor Merkle pursued as catcher Chief Meyers came a long way and just missed it. Speaker then singled to tie the game, followed by Larry Gardner's long fly that plated the winning run. Though there were plenty of culprits, "Snodgrass' Muff" became the rallying cry for those in the search for a scapegoat.

⊗ ⊗ ⊗

1915 World Series, Boston Red Sox vs. Philadelphia Phillies

For the second straight year, Boston beat Philadelphia. This time, though, it was the Red Sox and Phillies, as opposed to the Braves and Athletics. After four pennants in five seasons, the Athletics had given up. With the Phillies and the Federal League making life unprofitable for his club, A's owner Connie Mack sold or traded off his top assets. The Phillies, meanwhile, took their first pennant under rookie manager Pat Moran. It helped that Grover Cleveland Alexander captured the pitching Triple Crown, a remarkable feat given that he pitched in the Baker Bowl.

Bill Carrigan, Boston's second-year manager, guided the Red Sox to 101 wins, just enough to fend off Ty Cobb and the Tigers. Boston had the top four pitchers in the league in winning percentage—with the youngest, 20-year-old Babe Ruth, not even rating a start in the World Series. It wasn't necessary.

Although Boston scored just two more runs than Philadelphia, 12–10, six of Philadelphia's eight regulars batted below .200. The Red Sox committed more errors than the Phils, but their defense shined otherwise, especially in the outfield. Duffy Lewis, Tris Speaker, and Harry Hooper caused plenty of trouble with their bats, too, hitting .363 as a group. Location was a crucial factor. The Red Sox moved over to massive Braves Field, which

not only held more paying customers but also helped to contain Phillies' slugger Gavvy Cravath, whose 24 homers were the most to date in the century. Philadelphia owner Bill Baker, to his everlasting regret, gave up yet more real estate in his compact park by putting extra seats right in the spot that Hooper favored most.

BOS (AL)

PLAYER, POS	G	AB	R	H	2B	3B	HR	RBI	BB	SO	SB	AVG	OBP
H.Hooper, of	5	20	4	7	0	0	2	3	2	4	0	.350	.409
D.Lewis, of	5	18	1	8	1	0	1	5	1	4	0	.444	.474
E.Scott, ss	5	18	0	1	0	0	0	0	0	3	0	.056	.056
J.Barry, 2b	5	17	1	3	0	0	0	1	1	2	0	.176	.222
L.Gardner, 3b	5	17	2	4	0	1	0	0	1	0	0	.235	.278
T.Speaker, of	5	17	2	5	0	1	0	0	4	1	0	.294	.429
D.Hoblitzel, 1b	5	16	1	5	0	0	0	1	0	1	1	.313	.313
R.Foster, p	2	8	0	4	1	0	0	1	0	2	0	.500	.500
H.Cady, c	4	6	0	2	0	0	0	0	1	2	0	.333	.429
E.Shore, p	2	5	0	1	0	0	0	0	0	3	0	.200	.200
P.Thomas, c	2	5	0	1	0	0	0	0	0	0	0	.200	.200
D.Gainer, 1b	1	3	1	1	0	0	0	0	0	0	0	.333	.333
D.Leonard, p	1	3	0	0	0	0	0	0	0	2	0	.000	.000
B.Carrigan, c	1	2	0	0	0	0	0	0	1	1	0	.000	.333
O.Henriksen, ph	2	2	0	0	0	0	0	0	0	0	0	.000	.000
H.Janvrin, ss	1	1	0	0	0	0	0	0	0	0	0	.000	.000
B.Ruth, ph	1	1	0	0	0	0	0	0	0	0	0	.000	.000
TOTALS		**159**	**12**	**42**	**2**	**2**	**3**	**11**	**11**	**25**	**1**	**.264**	**.316**

PITCHER	W	L	ERA	G	GS	SV	IP	H	BB	SO
R.Foster	2	0	2.00	2	2	0	18.0	12	2	13
E.Shore	1	1	2.12	2	2	0	17.0	12	8	6
D.Leonard	1	0	1.00	1	1	0	9.0	3	0	6
TOTALS	**4**	**1**	**1.84**	**5**	**5**	**0**	**44.0**	**27**	**10**	**25**

PHI (NL)

PLAYER, POS	G	AB	R	H	2B	3B	HR	RBI	BB	SO	SB	AVG	OBP
D.Paskert, of	5	19	2	3	0	0	0	0	1	2	0	.158	.200
D.Bancroft, ss	5	17	2	5	0	0	0	1	2	2	0	.294	.368
M.Stock, 3b	5	17	1	2	1	0	0	0	1	0	0	.118	.167
E.Burns, c	5	16	1	3	0	0	0	0	1	2	0	.188	.235
G.Cravath, of	5	16	2	2	1	1	0	1	2	6	0	.125	.222
F.Luderus, 1b	5	16	1	7	2	0	1	6	1	4	0	.438	.471
B.Niehoff, 2b	5	16	1	1	0	0	0	0	1	5	0	.063	.118
P.Whitted, of-1b	5	15	0	1	0	0	0	1	1	0	1	.067	.125
P.Alexander, p	2	5	0	1	0	0	0	0	0	1	0	.200	.200
E.Mayer, p	2	4	0	0	0	0	0	0	0	0	0	.000	.000
G.Chalmers, p	1	3	0	1	0	0	0	0	0	1	0	.333	.333
E.Rixey, p	1	2	0	1	0	0	0	0	0	0	0	.500	.500
B.Byrne, ph	1	1	0	0	0	0	0	0	0	0	0	.000	.000
B.Killefer, ph	1	1	0	0	0	0	0	0	0	0	0	.000	.000
B.Becker, of	2	0	0	0	0	0	0	0	0	0	0	.000	.000
O.Dugey, pr	2	0	0	0	0	0	0	0	0	0	1	.000	.000
TOTALS		**148**	**10**	**27**	**4**	**1**	**1**	**9**	**10**	**25**	**2**	**.182**	**.244**

PITCHER	W	L	ERA	G	GS	SV	IP	H	BB	SO
P.Alexander	1	1	1.53	2	2	0	17.2	14	4	10
E.Mayer	0	1	2.38	2	2	0	11.1	16	2	7
G.Chalmers	0	1	2.25	1	1	0	8.0	8	3	6
E.Rixey	0	1	4.05	1	0	0	6.2	4	2	2
TOTALS	**1**	**4**	**2.27**	**6**	**5**	**0**	**43.2**	**42**	**11**	**25**

1915 WORLD SERIES - BOS(AL) DEFEATS PHI(NL), 4 GAMES TO 1

GAME 1, OCT. 8						
BOS	000	000	010	1	8	1
PHI	000	100	02X	3	5	1

PITCHERS: SHORE VS ALEXANDER
ATTENDANCE: 19,343

GAME 2, OCT. 9						
BOS	100	000	001	2	10	0
PHI	000	010	000	1	3	1

PITCHERS: FOSTER VS MAYER
ATTENDANCE: 20,306

GAME 3, OCT. 11						
PHI	001	000	000	1	3	0
BOS	000	100	001	2	6	1

PITCHERS: ALEXANDER VS LEONARD
ATTENDANCE: 42,300

GAME 4, OCT. 12						
PHI	000	000	010	1	7	0
BOS	001	001	00X	2	8	1

PITCHERS: CHALMERS VS SHORE
ATTENDANCE: 41,096

GAME 5, OCT. 13						
BOS	011	000	021	5	10	1
PHI	200	200	000	4	9	1

PITCHERS: FOSTER VS Mayer, RIXEY(3)
ATTENDANCE: 20,306

Game 1. Alexander thrived at soggy Baker Bowl. Although Lewis tied the game with a single in the top of the eighth, the Phillies scored twice in the bottom of the inning without hitting a ball out of the infield. Ruth, his eyes on the short right-field fence, grounded out in the ninth in his first World Series at-bat and only appearance in this Series.

Game 2. Woodrow Wilson, the first U.S. President to attend a World Series game, watched Rube Foster rap out as many hits as he allowed. The pitcher's third hit brought in the go-ahead run with two outs in the top of the ninth; Foster then set down the side in order to nail down the victory.

Game 3. A record crowd of 42,300 greeted the Red Sox at Braves Field. The two-month-old structure, erected because of 1914's "Miracle" Braves, suited the Red Sox just fine. Dutch Leonard became the second Boston pitcher in as many games to throw a three-hitter and win, 2–1, on a run in the ninth. Lewis, who made a brilliant catch on Cravath's blast to save two runs earlier, singled in Hooper to end the game after Alexander, who'd walked Speaker intentionally earlier in the inning, left first base open.

Game 4. The Red Sox scored two runs and won their third straight game. This time Ernie Shore mastered the Phillies. Hooper and Lewis drove in the Boston runs. Cravath got his only extra-base hit of the Series, a triple, and scored on a hit by Fred Luderas, the most productive Phillies' hitter against Boston. Foster retired Possum Whitted with the tying run on second.

Game 5. All four World Series home runs came in one afternoon, mostly thanks to the Baker Bowl's temporary

seats in center and the bounce rule. The Phillies scored as many runs in the first inning as they did in their trip to Boston. With Erskine Mayer pitching instead of the ailing Alexander, the Sox tied it in the third on Hooper's drive that bounced into the extra seats (a home run under the rules of the day). After Luderas actually cleared the wall for Philadelphia, Lewis tied the score in the eighth on a two-run bounce blast into the temporary stands off Eppa Rixey. Boston broke the tie with a Hooper hopper in the ninth. A bouncer ended the Series, as Foster got Bill Killefer to ground to shortstop Everett Scott to capture the third crown for the Red Sox.

1916 World Series, Boston Red Sox vs. Brooklyn Dodgers

The Red Sox, fresh off a world championship, dispatched their best player for a large cash sum. Babe Ruth? No. The 21-year-old was already the league's top southpaw and his hitting prowess—his three home runs and .419 slugging were unsurpassed by any Red Sox regular—no longer needed quantifying with the term "for a pitcher." It was Tris Speaker whom the Red Sox had to live without due to a salary dispute. Tilly Walker, purchased from the St. Louis Browns for far less than the $55,000 Boston received from Cleveland for "Spoke," brought the "Million Dollar Outfield" down a few zeroes. The Red Sox won 10 fewer games than in 1915, but they took the AL pennant by a similar margin anyway.

Brooklyn was a feel-good story. The franchise hadn't won an NL pennant since the turn of the century and had a losing record every year from 1904–14. Wilbert Robinson had renovated the club, now called the Robins in his honor, after leaving the Giants in a clash with old friend John McGraw. Former Giants pitcher Rube Marquard was the biggest name on Uncle Robby's staff. Zack Wheat, Jake Daubert, and young Casey Stengel cobbled together enough runs to beat out the Phillies for the pennant.

The Red Sox, playing in their third World Series in five seasons, were adept at pushing across extra runs or getting crucial outs late in close games. Robinson's strategy was to throw southpaws at Boston, so he kept 25-game winner Jake Pfeffer in the bullpen until Game 5. Brooklyn held left-handed-swinging Larry Gardner to a .176 average, but he hit Boston's only two home runs (both against southpaws) and drove in six; Harry Hooper, another lefty, hit .333 and scored six runs. Righty-swinging Duffy Lewis, as he'd shown in the 1915 Series, was able to hit everyone. Babe Ruth hardly let anyone score, and the Red Sox became the first team to win four World Series.

BOS (AL)

PLAYER, POS	G	AB	R	H	2B	3B	HR	RBI	BB	SO	SB	AVG	OBP
H.Janvrin, 2b	5	23	2	5	3	0	0	1	0	6	0	.217	.217
H.Hooper, of	5	21	6	7	1	1	0	1	3	1	1	.333	.417
L.Gardner, 3b	5	17	2	3	0	0	2	6	0	2	0	.176	.176
D.Hoblitzel, 1b	5	17	3	4	1	1	0	2	6	0	0	.235	.435
D.Lewis, of	5	17	3	6	2	1	0	1	2	1	0	.353	.421
E.Scott, ss	5	16	1	2	0	1	0	1	1	1	0	.125	.176
T.Walker, of	3	11	3	3	0	1	0	1	1	2	0	.273	.333
E.Shore, p	2	7	0	0	0	0	0	0	0	2	0	.000	.000
C.Shorten, of	2	7	0	4	0	0	0	2	0	1	0	.571	.571
P.Thomas, c	3	7	0	1	0	1	0	0	0	1	0	.143	.143
B.Ruth, p	1	5	0	0	0	0	0	1	0	2	0	.000	.000
H.Cady, c	2	4	1	1	0	0	0	0	3	0	0	.250	.571
B.Carrigan, c	1	3	0	2	0	0	0	1	0	1	0	.667	.667
D.Leonard, p	1	3	0	0	0	0	0	0	1	3	0	.000	.250
J.Walsh, of	1	3	0	0	0	0	0	0	0	0	0	.000	.000
R.Foster, p	1	1	0	0	0	0	0	0	0	0	0	.000	.000
D.Gainer, ph	1	1	0	1	0	0	0	1	0	0	0	1.000	1.000
C.Mays, p	2	1	0	0	0	0	0	0	0	1	0	.000	.000
O.Henriksen, ph	1	0	1	0	0	0	0	0	1	0	0	.000	1.000
M.McNally, pr	1	0	1	0	0	0	0	0	0	0	0	.000	.000
TOTALS		164	21	39	7	6	2	18	18	25	1	.238	.313

PITCHER	W	L	ERA	G	GS	SV	IP	H	BB	SO
E.Shore	2	0	1.53	2	2	0	17.2	12	4	9
B.Ruth	1	0	0.64	1	1	0	14.0	6	3	4
D.Leonard	1	0	1.00	1	1	0	9.0	5	4	3
C.Mays	0	1	5.06	1	1	1	5.1	8	3	2
R.Foster	0	0	0.00	1	0	0	3.0	3	0	1
TOTALS	4	1	1.47	7	5	1	49.0	34	14	19

BRO (NL)

PLAYER, POS	G	AB	R	H	2B	3B	HR	RBI	BB	SO	SB	AVG	OBP
H.Myers, of	5	22	2	4	0	0	1	3	0	3	0	.182	.182
G.Cutshaw, 2b	5	19	2	2	1	0	0	2	1	1	0	.105	.150
Z.Wheat, of	5	19	2	4	0	1	0	1	2	2	1	.211	.286
J.Daubert, 1b	4	17	1	3	0	1	0	0	2	3	0	.176	.263
M.Mowrey, 3b	5	17	2	3	0	0	0	1	3	2	0	.176	.300
I.Olson, ss	5	16	1	4	0	1	0	2	2	2	0	.250	.333
C.Stengel, of	4	11	2	4	0	0	0	0	1	0	0	.364	.364
J.Johnston, of	3	10	1	3	0	1	0	0	1	0	0	.300	.364
C.Meyers, c	3	10	0	2	0	1	0	0	1	0	0	.200	.273
O.Miller, c	2	8	0	1	0	0	0	0	0	1	0	.125	.125
S.Smith, p	1	5	0	1	1	0	0	0	0	0	0	.200	.200
F.Merkle, 1b	3	4	0	1	0	0	0	1	2	0	0	.250	.500
J.Pfeffer, p	4	4	0	1	0	0	0	0	0	2	0	.250	.250
J.Coombs, p	1	3	0	1	0	0	0	1	0	0	0	.333	.333
R.Marquard, p	2	3	0	0	0	0	0	0	0	1	0	.000	.000
G.Getz, ph	1	1	0	0	0	0	0	0	0	0	0	.000	.000
O.O'Mara, ph	1	1	0	0	0	0	0	0	0	1	0	.000	.000
TOTALS		170	13	34	2	5	1	11	14	19	1	.200	.269

PITCHER	W	L	ERA	G	GS	SV	IP	H	BB	SO
S.Smith	0	1	1.35	1	1	0	13.1	7	6	2
R.Marquard	0	2	5.73	2	2	0	11.0	12	6	9
J.Pfeffer	0	1	1.69	3	1	1	10.2	7	4	5
J.Coombs	1	0	4.26	1	1	0	6.1	7	1	1
L.Cheney	0	0	3.00	1	0	0	3.0	4	1	5
N.Rucker	0	0	0.00	1	0	0	2.0	1	0	3
W.Dell	0	0	0.00	1	0	0	1.0	1	0	0
TOTALS	1	4	2.85	10	5	1	47.1	39	18	25

1916 WORLD SERIES - BOS(AL) DEFEATS BRO(NL), 4 GAMES TO 1

GAME 1, OCT. 7					
BRO	000 100 004	5	10	4	
BOS	001 010 31X	6	8	1	

PITCHERS: MARQUARD, Pfeffer(8) VS SHORE, Mays(9)

ATTENDANCE: 36,117

GAME 2, OCT. 9					
BRO	100 000 000000 00	1	6	2	
BOS	001 000 000000 01	2	7	1	

PITCHERS: SMITH VS RUTH

ATTENDANCE: 41,373

GAME 3, OCT. 10					
BOS	000 002 100	3	7	1	
BRO	001 120 00X	4	10	0	

PITCHERS: MAYS, Foster(6) VS COOMBS, Pfeffer(7)

ATTENDANCE: 21,087

GAME 4, OCT. 11					
BOS	030 110 100	6	10	1	
BRO	200 000 000	2	5	4	

PITCHERS: LEONARD VS MARQUARD, Cheney(5), Rucker(8)

ATTENDANCE: 21,662

GAME 5, OCT. 12					
BRO	010 000 000	1	3	3	
BOS	012 010 00X	4	7	2	

PITCHERS: PFEFFER, Dell(8) VS SHORE

ATTENDANCE: 42,620

Game 1. The Red Sox had this game going away, until the ninth inning. With Boston up, 6–1, Brooklyn sent nine to the plate, scoring four times, and had the bases loaded with the tying run at third. Carl Mays, brought in to replace Shore, got Daubert to hit a grounder in the hole that shortstop Everett Scott snagged and threw to first just in time for the final out.

Game 2. Ruth's first start in a World Series game was memorable, to say the least. Hy Myers hit an inside-the-park home run off Ruth in the first inning, but Ruth tied the game in the third with a groundout that plated Scott. Then…nothing. Cavernous Braves Field, serving as home to the Red Sox for the second consecutive October because it could hold the biggest crowd in World Series history (47,373), lived up to its reputation as a pitcher's haven as Ruth and Sherry Smith exchanged goose eggs in the fading light. Some players felt the game should have been called, but it went on into the 14th when Boston's Dick Hoblitzell walked for the fourth time and was sacrificed to second. Del Gainer, batting for Larry Gardner (0-for-5) singled to left, bringing home pinch runner Mike McNally. The consecutive scoreless inning streak Ruth started that day would stretch to 29 2/3 innings yet would one day be broken; his 14 innings in one World Series game, though, should stand forever.

Game 3. The World Series debut of Ebbets Field came one day after the longest Series game in history (Game 3 in 2005 would tie it for innings, though Game 2 in 1916 was played in just 2:32). Brooklyn was ready, scoring for the first time in 16 innings on George Cutshaw's single in the third. The lead was 4–0 when the Sox rallied to cut it to a run off Jack Coombs. Jeff Pfeffer came on in relief and retired the last eight.

Game 4. Brooklyn scored twice in the first inning of Game 4, but Dutch Leonard controlled the game from that point with help from Boston's bats. Gardner gave the Red Sox the lead with his second home run in as many days, an inside-the-park shot to left-center. Manager Bill Carrigan, inserting himself in the lineup as catcher for the last time in his career, singled in the fourth run.

Game 5. Shore was masterful, hurling a three-hitter with the only run scoring on a passed ball. Boston got that run back when Lewis scored on a short fly. The Red Sox took the lead on an error and added to it on run-scoring hits by Chick Shorten and Hal Janvrin. Boston made a couple of outstanding plays behind Shore, but the World Series ended on a routine popup to Scott.

1918 World Series, Boston Red Sox vs. Chicago Cubs

Baseball had to rush to complete the schedule to beat a Labor Day deadline imposed by the nervous owners, who were losing money. As a result, the regular season finished on September 2, with the World Series beginning three days later.

Both teams were missing key players who had enlisted in the Army to fight in World War I. The Cubs lost star hurler Grover Cleveland Alexander, who signed up after pitching in only three games in 1918, while the Sox were without outfielder Duffy Lewis and player-manager Jack Barry for the entire season.

The Series almost didn't get finished. The players threatened a strike before the fifth game, demanding a larger share of the ticket receipts, though they backed off their threat after listening to an ardent plea from AL president Ban Johnson.

Perhaps the players were really just tired of not hitting the ball. This would be the last fall classic where neither team hit a home run, and Boston's nine total runs and .186 team batting average remain the lowest ever by a winning team.

BOS (AL)

PLAYER, POS	G	AB	R	H	2B	3B	HR	RBI	BB	SO	SB	AVG	OBP
A.Strunk, of	6	23	1	4	1	1	0	0	0	5	0	.174	.174
H.Hooper, of	6	20	0	4	0	0	0	0	2	2	0	.200	.273
S.McInnis, 1b	6	20	2	5	0	0	0	1	1	1	0	.250	.286
E.Scott, ss	6	20	0	2	0	0	0	1	1	1	0	.100	.143
G.Whiteman, of	6	20	2	5	0	1	0	1	2	1	1	.250	.318
D.Shean, 2b	6	19	2	4	1	0	0	0	4	3	1	.211	.348
F.Thomas, 3b	6	17	0	2	0	0	0	0	1	2	0	.118	.167
S.Agnew, c	4	9	0	0	0	0	0	0	0	0	0	.000	.000
W.Schang, c	5	9	1	4	0	0	0	1	2	3	1	.444	.545
C.Mays, p	2	5	1	1	0	0	0	0	1	0	0	.200	.333
B.Ruth, p-of	3	5	0	1	0	1	0	2	0	2	0	.200	.200
J.Bush, p	2	2	0	0	0	0	0	0	1	0	0	.000	.333
J.Dubuc, ph	1	1	0	0	0	0	0	0	0	1	0	.000	.000
S.Jones, p	1	1	0	0	0	0	0	0	0	1	0	.000	.500
H.Miller, ph	1	1	0	0	0	0	0	0	0	0	0	.000	.000
TOTALS		172	9	32	2	3	0	6	16	21	3	.186	.259

PITCHER	W	L	ERA	G	GS	SV	IP	H	BB	SO
C.Mays	2	0	1.00	2	2	0	18.0	10	3	5
B.Ruth	2	0	1.06	2	2	0	17.0	13	7	4
J.Bush	0	1	3.00	2	1	0	9.0	7	3	0
S.Jones	0	1	3.00	1	1	0	9.0	7	5	5
TOTALS	4	2	1.70	7	6	1	53.0	37	18	14

CHI (NL)

PLAYER, POS	G	AB	R	H	2B	3B	HR	RBI	BB	SO	SB	AVG	OBP
L.Mann, of	6	22	0	5	2	0	0	2	0	0	0	.227	.227
C.Hollocher, ss	6	21	2	4	0	1	0	1	1	1	1	.190	.227
D.Paskert, of	6	21	0	4	1	0	0	2	2	2	0	.190	.261
M.Flack, of	6	19	2	5	1	0	0	0	4	1	1	.263	.391
F.Merkle, 1b	6	18	1	5	0	0	0	1	4	3	0	.278	.409
C.Pick, 2b	6	18	2	7	1	0	0	0	1	1	1	.389	.421
C.Deal, 3b	6	17	0	3	0	0	0	0	0	1	0	.176	.176
B.Killefer, c	6	17	2	2	1	0	0	2	2	0	0	.118	.211
H.Vaughn, p	3	10	0	0	0	0	0	0	0	5	0	.000	.000
L.Tyler, p	3	5	0	1	0	0	0	2	2	0	0	.200	.429
B.O'Farrell, c	3	3	0	0	0	0	0	0	0	0	0	.000	.000
T.Barber, ph	3	2	0	0	0	0	0	0	0	0	0	.000	.000
C.Hendrix, p	2	1	0	1	0	0	0	0	0	0	0	1.000	1.000
B.McCabe, ph	3	1	1	0	0	0	0	0	0	0	0	.000	.000
C.Wortman, 2b	1	1	0	0	0	0	0	0	0	0	0	.000	.000
R.Zeider, 3b	2	0	0	0	0	0	0	0	2	0	0	.000	1.000
TOTALS		176	10	37	5	1	0	10	18	14	3	.210	.291

PITCHER	W	L	ERA	G	GS	SV	IP	H	BB	SO
H.Vaughn	1	2	1.00	3	3	0	27.0	17	5	17
L.Tyler	1	1	1.17	3	3	0	23.0	14	11	4
P.Douglas	0	1	0.00	1	0	0	1.0	1	0	0
C.Hendrix	0	0	0.00	1	0	0	1.0	0	0	0
TOTALS	2	4	1.04	8	6	0	52.0	32	16	21

1918 WORLD SERIES - BOS(AL) DEFEATS CHI(NL), 4 GAMES TO 2

GAME 1, SEPT. 5

BOS	000	100	000		1	5	0
CHI	000	000	000		0	6	0

PITCHERS: RUTH VS VAUGHN
ATTENDANCE: 19,274

GAME 2, SEPT. 6

BOS	000	000	001		1	6	1
CHI	030	000	00X		3	7	1

PITCHERS: BUSH VS TYLER
ATTENDANCE: 20,040

GAME 3, SEPT. 7

BOS	000	200	000		2	7	0
CHI	000	010	000		1	7	1

PITCHERS: MAYS VS VAUGHN
ATTENDANCE: 27,054

GAME 4, SEPT. 9

CHI	000	000	020		2	7	1
BOS	000	200	01X		3	4	0

PITCHERS: Tyler, DOUGLAS(8) VS RUTH, Bush(9)
ATTENDANCE: 22,183

GAME 5, SEPT. 10

CHI	001	000	002		3	7	0
BOS	000	000	000		0	5	0

PITCHERS: VAUGHN VS JONES
ATTENDANCE: 24,694

GAME 6, SEPT. 11

CHI	000	100	000		1	3	2
BOS	002	000	00X		2	5	0

PITCHERS: TYLER, Hendrix(8) VS MAYS
ATTENDANCE: 15,238

Game 1. Babe Ruth, who began playing the outfield regularly this season, started for the Sox and was masterful, allowing only six hits and a walk. The Cubs' best chance to score came in the first when they loaded the bases with two outs, but Ruth got Charlie Pick to fly to left to end the threat.

Game 2. The three runs the Cubs scored in the bottom of the second were the most scored in any single inning in the series. They might have scored more, but pitcher Lefty Tyler was thrown out at second trying to advance after his two-run single, and Max Flack was gunned down trying to steal for the third out.

Game 3. The Sox singled Hippo Vaughn to death in the fourth for their only runs of the game. Other than that inning, Boston only got one runner as far as third the rest of the way. The game ended when Pick was thrown out at the plate trying to score from second on a passed ball.

Game 4. After batting Ruth ninth in the opening game, the Sox moved the Bambino up to sixth in the batting order, still the only time a pitcher has hit anywhere other than ninth in a World Series. The switch paid dividends as Babe tripled in two runs in the fourth inning. The Cubs snapped Ruth's 29 2/3-inning postseason scoreless streak with two runs in the eighth to tie it, but Boston came right back with the winning tally in the bottom of the inning as catcher Bill Killefer's passed ball led to an unearned run.

Game 5. Vaughn came back on only two days rest and hurled a gem as Boston managed to get only two runners as far as second base. Dode Paskert's two-run double in the ninth gave the Cubs a couple of key insurance runs.

Game 6. Boston scored its only two runs in the third on a two-out error by right fielder Flack. The Cubs got one of them back in the top of the next inning when Flack, who led off with a single, scored on a safety by Fred Merkle. Chicago would get only one more runner the entire game (a sixth-inning walk), handing the Sox had their fourth championship in seven years—and their last for 86 more.

1946 World Series, Boston Red Sox vs. St. Louis Cardinals

It was a long time coming for Boston. The Red Sox won 100 games for the first time since Babe Ruth was in his first full year as a pitcher and since Tris Speaker centered the "Million Dollar Outfield." Since buying the dilapidated franchise in 1933, Tom Yawkey had spent freely to build the Red Sox into a championship-caliber club. Ted Williams, Bobby Doerr, and Dom DiMaggio—cornerstones of the 1946 team—never played a game for another team (a total of 5,556 games). Manager Joe Cronin, now retired as a player, had been brought over for $225,000 at the height of the Depression. He had the respect of a clubhouse full of veterans, not just of the game, but of World War II.

The Cardinals knew plenty about success. St. Louis was at the tail end of a run like Boston had enjoyed in the days of Ruth and Speaker. Since 1926, the Cardinals had won eight pennants and five world championships. With Hall of Famers Red Schoendienst, Enos Slaughter, and Stan Musial, plus former MVP Marty Marion and four-time All-Star Terry Moore in the lineup, the Cards had plenty of offense as well as the lowest ERA in baseball. The only thing for certain was that one team would capture its sixth world championship.

It was not a World Series to remember for Musial and Williams, but it would be the last for both and the only for Teddy Ballgame. Johnny Pesky's hesitation on a Game 7 relay, captured on film, would be fodder for Red Sox angst over the next six decades as Enos "Country" Slaughter's daring dash on the play defined his career.

STL (NL)

PLAYER, POS	G	AB	R	H	2B	3B	HR	RBI	BB	SO	SB	AVG	OBP
R.Schoendienst, 2b	7	30	3	7	1	0	0	1	0	2	1	.233	.233
W.Kurowski, 3b	7	27	5	8	3	0	0	2	0	3	0	.296	.296
T.Moore, of	7	27	1	4	0	0	0	2	2	6	0	.148	.207
S.Musial, 1b	7	27	3	6	4	1	0	4	4	2	1	.222	.323
E.Slaughter, of	7	25	5	8	1	1	1	2	4	3	1	.320	.414
M.Marion, ss	7	24	1	6	2	0	0	4	1	1	0	.250	.280
J.Garagiola, c	5	19	2	6	2	0	0	4	0	3	0	.316	.316
H.Walker, of	7	17	3	7	2	0	0	6	4	2	0	.412	.524
H.Brecheen, p	3	8	2	1	0	0	0	1	0	1	0	.125	.125
D.Rice, c	3	6	2	3	1	0	0	0	2	0	0	.500	.625
M.Dickson, p	2	5	1	2	2	0	0	1	0	1	0	.400	.400
E.Dusak, of	4	4	0	1	1	0	0	0	2	2	0	.250	.500
R.Munger, p	1	4	0	1	0	0	0	0	0	2	0	.250	.250
H.Pollet, p	2	4	0	0	0	0	0	0	0	1	0	.000	.000
A.Brazle, p	1	2	0	0	0	0	0	0	0	0	0	.000	.000
D.Sisler, ph	2	2	0	0	0	0	0	0	0	0	0	.000	.000
N.Jones, ph	1	1	0	0	0	0	0	0	0	1	0	.000	.000
TOTALS		232	28	60	19	2	1	27	19	30	3	.259	.320

PITCHER	W	L	ERA	G	GS	SV	IP	H	BB	SO
H.Brecheen	3	0	0.45	3	2	0	20.0	14	5	11
M.Dickson	0	1	3.86	2	2	0	14.0	11	4	7
H.Pollet	0	1	3.48	2	2	0	10.1	12	4	3
R.Munger	1	0	1.00	1	1	0	9.0	9	3	2
A.Brazle	0	1	5.40	1	0	0	6.2	7	6	4
J.Beazley	0	0	0.00	1	0	0	1.0	1	0	1
T.Wilks	0	0	0.00	1	0	0	1.0	2	0	0
TOTALS	4	3	2.32	11	7	0	62.0	56	22	28

BOS (AL)

PLAYER, POS	G	AB	R	H	2B	3B	HR	RBI	BB	SO	SB	AVG	OBP
J.Pesky, ss	7	30	2	7	0	0	0	0	1	3	1	.233	.258
D.DiMaggio, of	7	27	2	7	3	0	0	3	2	2	0	.259	.310
T.Williams, of	7	25	2	5	0	0	0	1	5	5	0	.200	.333
P.Higgins, 3b	7	24	1	5	1	0	0	2	2	0	0	.208	.269
R.York, 1b	7	23	6	6	1	1	2	5	6	4	0	.261	.414
B.Doerr, 2b	6	22	1	9	1	0	1	3	2	2	0	.409	.458
H.Wagner, c	5	13	0	0	0	0	0	0	0	1	0	.000	.000
T.McBride, of	5	12	0	2	0	0	0	1	0	1	0	.167	.167
W.Moses, of	4	12	1	5	0	0	0	0	1	2	0	.417	.462
R.Partee, c	5	10	1	1	0	0	0	1	1	2	0	.100	.182
L.Culberson, of	5	9	1	2	0	0	1	1	1	2	1	.222	.300
D.Ferriss, p	2	6	0	0	0	0	0	0	0	1	0	.000	.000
D.Gutteridge, 2b	3	5	1	2	0	0	0	1	0	0	0	.400	.400
J.Dobson, p	3	3	0	0	0	0	0	0	0	2	0	.000	.000
M.Harris, p	2	3	0	1	0	0	0	0	0	1	0	.333	.333
T.Hughson, p	3	3	0	1	0	0	0	0	1	0	0	.333	.500
C.Metkovich, ph	2	2	1	1	1	0	0	0	0	0	0	.500	.500
R.Russell, 3b	2	2	1	2	0	0	0	0	0	0	0	1.000	1.000
J.Bagby, p	1	1	0	0	0	0	0	0	0	0	0	.000	.000
E.Johnson, p	3	1	0	0	0	0	0	0	0	0	0	.000	.000
P.Campbell, pr	1	0	0	0	0	0	0	0	0	0	0	.000	.000
TOTALS		233	20	56	7	1	4	18	22	28	2	.240	.309

PITCHER	W	L	ERA	G	GS	SV	IP	H	BB	SO
T.Hughson	0	1	3.14	3	2	0	14.1	14	3	8
D.Ferriss	1	0	2.03	2	2	0	13.1	13	2	4
J.Dobson	1	0	0.00	3	1	0	12.2	4	3	10
M.Harris	0	2	3.72	2	2	0	9.2	11	4	5
E.Johnson	1	0	2.70	3	0	0	3.1	1	2	1
J.Bagby	0	0	3.00	1	0	0	3.0	6	1	1
B.Zuber	0	0	4.50	1	0	0	2.0	3	1	1
M.Brown	0	0	27.00	1	0	0	1.0	4	1	0
B.Klinger	0	1	13.50	1	0	0	0.2	2	1	0
M.Ryba	0	0	13.50	1	0	0	0.2	2	1	0
C.Dreisewerd	0	0	0.00	1	0	0	0.1	0	0	0
TOTALS	3	4	2.95	19	7	0	61.0	60	19	30

1946 WORLD SERIES - STL(NL) DEFEATS BOS(AL), 4 GAMES TO 3

GAME 1, OCT. 6						
BOS	010	000	001	1	3	9	2
STL	000	001	010	0	2	7	0

PITCHERS: Hughson, JOHNSON(9) VS POLLET
ATTENDANCE: 36,218

GAME 2, OCT. 7						
BOS	000	000	000	0	4	1
STL	001	020	00X	3	6	0

PITCHERS: HARRIS, Dobson(8) VS BRECHEEN
ATTENDANCE: 35,815

GAME 3, OCT. 9						
STL	000	000	000	0	6	1
BOS	300	000	01X	4	8	0

PITCHERS: DICKSON, Wilks(8) VS FERRISS
ATTENDANCE: 34,500

GAME 4, OCT. 10						
STL	033	010	104	12	20	1
BOS	000	100	020	3	9	4

PITCHERS: MUNGER VS HUGHSON, Bagby(3), Zuber(6), Brown(8), Ryba(9), Dreisewerd(9)
ATTENDANCE: 35,645

GAME 5, OCT. 11						
STL	010	000	002	3	4	1
BOS	110	001	30X	6	11	3

PITCHERS: Pollet, BRAZLE(1), Beazley(8) VS DOBSON
ATTENDANCE: 35,982

GAME 6, OCT. 13						
BOS	000	000	100	1	7	0
STL	003	000	01X	4	8	0

PITCHERS: HARRIS, Hughson(3), Johnson(8) VS BRECHEEN
ATTENDANCE: 35,768

GAME 7, OCT. 15

BOS	100	000	020		3	8	0
STL	010	020	01X		4	9	1

PITCHERS: Ferriss, Dobson(5), KLINGER(8), Johnson(8)
VS Dickson, BRECHEEN(8)

ATTENDANCE: 36,143

Game 1. The Sox had wrapped up their pennant in mid-September, but the Cardinals were forced into the first playoff in major league history, sweeping the best-of-three series from the Dodgers. Howie Pollett, who tossed a complete game in the playoff opener against Brooklyn, was superb against Boston until the final two innings of Game 1 when he allowed a game-tying, two-out single by Tom McBride in the ninth and a go-ahead home run to Rudy York an inning later.

Game 2. Harry "The Cat" Brecheen tossed a four-hit shutout to even the World Series as he retired the last 14 Red Sox in order. Brecheen's bunt was mishandled by Boston's Mickey Harris to set up a two-run fifth inning.

Game 3. Dave "Boo" Ferriss was brilliant, tossing a six-hitter as the Series shifted to Fenway and the Red Sox reacted right away to the friendly surroundings. With two outs and a base open in the first, Murry Dickson walked Williams intentionally and York followed with a three-run homer. York also scored the game's only other run in the eighth.

Game 4. The Cardinals pounded six Sox pitchers in a 20-hit barrage as Slaughter, Whitey Kurowski, and Joe Garagiola (Nos. 4–5–6 in the order) had four hits apiece for the Cards. It made for a long day for Boston, but it allowed George Munger to go all the way for St. Louis to even the Series.

Game 5. The Splendid Splinter drove in his only run of the Series as more obscure figures like Don Gutteridge, Leon Culberson, Pinky Higgins, and Roy Partee also drove in runs to help Boston pull away. Joe Dobson went all the way as the Red Sox left Fenway Park needing one win for the championship.

Game 6. Needing to win to stay alive, St. Louis scored three times in the third inning to knock out Mickey Harris. Boston again had no luck with "The Cat," who tossed a seven-hitter to even the Series for the third time.

Game 7. After alternating wins for the first six games, Game 7 broke the pattern. Starter Dickson snapped a fifth-inning tie with an RBI-double and Red Schoendienst singled him in for a 3–1 lead. Dickson was chased after the first two batters reached in the top of the eighth, with Brecheen coming in and getting the next two outs. DiMaggio then doubled tie the game. With Slaughter on first and two down in the bottom of the eighth, Walker's hit off Bob Klinger scored Slaughter on Pesky's infamous relay. Brecheen permitted two hits to start the ninth, then retired the next three for his third win of the Series and the sixth championship for the Redbirds.

One-Game Playoff, Boston Red Sox vs. Cleveland Indians, October 4, 1948

Although it has the look and feel of a postseason game and is the potential carrier for even more angst than a single postseason game because a loss immediately ends the season without any bunting displayed over the first row boxes, be warned: *a one-game playoff is not a postseason game.* It is an extra game played to settle a regular-season tie in the standings at the conclusion of the season, and so is considered an extension of the regular season.

The Red Sox hosted the first one-game playoff in history. The Cardinals and Dodgers had played a best-of-three series in 1946, won by St. Louis. Disparity between the two leagues was deemed quite proper six decades back and this was one of the biggest differences. Of course, it didn't come up much, but when it finally did, "one and done" was a tough way to go. The best-of-three playoff went the way of the dodo when the League Championship Series was added to MLB's calendar in 1969.

In 1948 all that the Indians and Red Sox really shared was that they weren't in this position very often. While Boston had won a pennant in 1946 before losing to the Cardinals (who'd fought their way through the best-of-three with Brooklyn), the Red Sox hadn't been to another World Series since 1918. The Indians hadn't been to a World Series since 1920, when former Red Sox great Tris Speaker led the Tribe to its first world championship.

Both the Indians and Red Sox bulged with talent in 1948. The rosters of both clubs were loaded with major league veterans as well as military veterans. These were intense men, with future Hall of Famers on each roster: Ted Williams and Bobby Doerr for Boston; Bob Feller, Bob Lemon, and Larry Doby in Cleveland. Both managers were of Cooperstown caliber as well. Joe McCarthy, winner of nine pennants and seven world

championships, was in his first year managing the Red Sox, while player-manager Lou Boudreau, 30 years younger than McCarthy, was managing for the first time.

Despite his lack of experience, Boudreau made the right move and McCarthy didn't. Boudreau went with Gene Bearden, an overworked rookie knuckleballer with a metal plate in his head (he was wounded when his ship went down in the Pacific in 1943). McCarthy decided against going with his hard-throwing youngster, Mel Parnell, who was rested and ready to go. Ellis Kinder was even more rested. Both had won their last starts as the Red Sox finished with a four-game winning streak to force the playoff. Instead, McCarthy chose a 36-year-old former Indians and Browns pitcher whose last win had been three weeks earlier: Denny Galehouse. The name can still be repeated with anger by many Red Sox fans.

The coin flip by AL president Will Harridge had been won by Boston 10 days earlier, so Fenway filled for the contest on Monday afternoon, October 4. Galehouse retired the first two batters before Boudreau homered into the screen in left. Vern Stephens singled in Johnny Pesky in the bottom of the inning to quickly tie it.

Galehouse got through three innings, but that's all he had in him. Boudreau singled off him to start the fourth, Joe Gordon singled, and Ken Keltner followed

with a three-run homer. Kinder came in but wasn't so great, either. He allowed another run in that inning before hurling the last six innings, allowing eight hits. Boudreau rapped out another single and home run, capping off an MVP season with a four-hit day and his only pennant as a manager.

Doerr hit a two-run homer to make it 6–3 after an error prolonged the sixth inning, but Kinder couldn't keep it close. McCarthy stuck with the veteran, eschewing both a call to the bullpen and pinch hitters.

Bearden won his 20th game of the year and his sixth win in 16 games as the Indians moved on to play the Braves in the World Series. He picked up a victory and got the final outs in relief in Boston one week later to clinch Cleveland's second—and last—world championship. If the Red Sox had won the playoff, it would have been the only Boston vs. Boston World Series.

As frustrating as it was for the Red Sox, the finish in 1949—losing a one-game lead with two play against the Yankees—would leave them with consecutive 96-win seasons that both ended 1-game out. And Galehouse? The man who'd won the first World Series game in St. Louis Browns history called it quits after two bad outings in '49.

CLEVELAND INDIANS 8, BOSTON RED SOX 3
Game played on Monday, October 4, 1948 at Fenway Park (D)

CLEVELAND INDIANS

	AB	R	H	RBI	BB	PO	A
Mitchell lf	5	0	1	0	0	0	0
Clark 1b	2	0	0	0	0	5	0
Robinson 1b	2	1	1	0	0	9	0
Boudreau ss	4	3	4	2	1	3	5
Gordon 2b	4	1	1	0	1	2	3
Keltner 3b	5	1	3	3	0	0	6
Doby cf	5	1	2	0	0	1	0
Kennedy rf	2	0	0	0	0	0	0
Hegan c	3	1	0	1	1	6	1
Bearden p	3	0	1	0	1	0	2
TOTALS	**35**	**8**	**13**	**7**	**4**	**27**	**17**

FIELDING
DP: 3. Hegan-Boudreau, Gordon-Boudreau-Robinson, Bearden-Gordon-Robinson
E: Gordon

BATTING
2B: Doby 2 (23); Keltner (24)
HR: Boudreau 2 (18); Keltner (31).
SH: Kennedy 2 (3), Robinson (9)
Team LOB: 7

BOSTON RED SOX

	AB	R	H	RBI	BB	PO	A
DiMaggio cf	4	0	0	0	0	3	0
Pesky 3b	4	1	1	0	0	3	4
Williams lf	4	1	1	0	0	3	0
Stephens ss	4	0	1	1	0	2	4
Doerr 2b	4	1	1	2	0	5	2
Spence rf	1	0	0	0	2	1	0
Hitchcock ph	0	0	0	0	1	0	0
Wright pr	0	0	0	0	0	0	0
Goodman 1b	3	0	0	0	1	7	1
Tebbetts c	4	0	1	0	0	3	1
Galehouse p	0	0	0	0	1	0	1
Kinder p	2	0	0	0	0	0	1

FIELDING
DP: 2. Stephens-Doerr-Goodman 2
E: Williams

BATTING -
2B: Pesky (26)
HR: Doerr (27)
Team LOB: 5

CLE A	1	0	0	4	1	0	0	1	1	-	8	13	1
BOS A	1	0	0	0	0	2	0	0	0	-	3	5	1

CLEVELAND INDIANS	IP	H	R	ER	BB	SO	HR
Bearden W(20–7)	9	5	3	3	5	6	1
Totals	9	5	3	3	5	6	1

BOSTON RED SOX	IP	H	R	ER	BB	SO	HR
Galehouse L(8–8)	3	5	4	4	1	2	
Kinder	6	8	4	3	3	2	1
Totals	9	13	8	7	4	3	3

Umpires: Bill McGowan, Bill Summers, Eddie Rommel, Charlie Berry
Time of Game: 2:24
Attendance: 33,957

Galehouse pitched to 3 batters in 4th inning
WP: Kinder (2)

1967 World Series, Boston Red Sox vs. St. Louis Cardinals

After so little had happened to the Red Sox in the two decades after 1946, so much occurred in 1967. Dick Williams was hired as a rookie manager; beloved local boy Tony Conigliaro was hit in the eye with a pitch in a horrifying scene; Jim Lonborg emerged as the league's best pitcher; and in the midst of one of the tightest pennant races in history, Carl Yastrzemski won the Triple Crown by going 7–for–8 to beat the Twins in the do-or-die final two games of the season. It was dubbed, fittingly enough, "The Impossible Dream."

The Cardinals' dreams seemed a little clearer. After enduring their own down period between their triumph over the Red Sox in the 1946 World Series and their beating the Yankees in 1964, the Cardinals had re-emerged as one of the game's top teams. Among all the pitchers dominating the game in 1967, fearsome Bob Gibson stood out even after missing more than two months with a broken leg. Lou Brock, Curt Flood, Roger Maris, Orlando Cepeda, and Tim McCarver gave the club a lethal combination of speed, power, and tenacity.

The teams were well matched from the opening pitch. With Gibson and Lonborg pitching one day apart and dominating opponents, the teams split the two games that neither ace pitched. When the two aces finally met in Game 7, Lonborg was spent and Boston's dream ended abruptly, unforgettable but still unfulfilled.

STL (NL)

PLAYER, POS	G	AB	R	H	2B	3B	HR	RBI	BB	SO	SB	AVG	OBP
L.Brock, of	7	29	8	12	2	1	1	3	2	3	7	.414	.452
O.Cepeda, 1b	7	29	1	3	2	0	0	1	0	4	0	.103	.103
C.Flood, of	7	28	2	5	1	0	0	3	3	3	0	.179	.258
R.Maris, of	7	26	3	10	1	0	1	7	3	1	0	.385	.448
J.Javier, 2b	7	25	2	9	3	0	1	4	0	6	0	.360	.360
T.McCarver, c	7	24	3	3	1	0	0	2	2	2	0	.125	.192
M.Shannon, 3b	7	24	3	5	1	0	1	2	1	4	0	.208	.240
D.Maxvill, ss	7	19	1	3	0	1	0	1	4	1	0	.158	.304
B.Gibson, p	3	11	1	1	0	0	1	1	1	2	0	.091	.167
N.Briles, p	2	3	0	0	0	0	0	0	0	0	0	.000	.000
D.Hughes, p	2	3	0	0	0	0	0	0	0	3	0	.000	.000
D.Ricketts, ph	3	3	0	0	0	0	0	0	0	0	0	.000	.000
B.Tolan, ph	3	2	1	0	0	0	0	0	1	1	0	.000	.333
S.Carlton, p	1	1	0	0	0	0	0	0	0	0	0	.000	.000
P.Gagliano, ph	1	1	0	0	0	0	0	0	0	0	0	.000	.000
E.Spiezio, ph	1	1	0	0	0	0	0	0	0	0	0	.000	.000
E.Bressoud, ss	2	0	0	0	0	0	0	0	0	0	0	.000	.000
TOTALS		229	25	51	11	2	5	24	17	30	7	.223	.276

PITCHER	W	L	ERA	G	GS	SV	IP	H	BB	SO
B.Gibson	3	0	1.00	3	3	0	27.0	14	5	26
N.Briles	1	0	1.64	2	1	0	11.0	7	1	4
D.Hughes	0	1	5.00	2	2	0	9.0	9	3	7
S.Carlton	0	1	0.00	1	1	0	6.0	3	2	5
J.Lamabe	0	1	6.75	3	0	0	2.2	5	0	4
R.Washburn	0	0	0.00	2	0	0	2.1	1	1	2
R.Willis	0	0	27.00	3	0	0	1.0	2	4	1
H.Woodeshick	0	0	0.00	1	0	0	1.0	1	0	0
J.Hoerner	0	0	40.50	3	0	0	0.2	4	1	0
L.Jaster	0	0	0.00	1	0	0	0.1	2	0	0
TOTALS	4	3	2.66	20	7	0	61.0	48	17	49

BOS (AL)

PLAYER, POS	G	AB	R	H	2B	3B	HR	RBI	BB	SO	SB	AVG	OBP
G.Scott, 1b	7	26	3	6	1	1	0	0	3	6	0	.231	.310
C.Yastrzemski, of	7	25	4	10	2	0	3	5	4	1	0	.400	.483
R.Smith, of	7	24	3	6	1	0	2	3	2	2	0	.250	.308
R.Petrocelli, ss	7	20	3	4	1	0	2	3	3	8	0	.200	.304
E.Howard, c	7	18	0	2	0	0	0	1	1	2	0	.111	.158
D.Jones, 3b	6	18	2	7	0	0	0	1	1	3	0	.389	.421
J.Adair, 2b	5	16	0	2	0	0	0	1	0	3	1	.125	.125
J.Foy, 3b	6	15	2	2	1	0	0	1	1	5	0	.133	.188
M.Andrews, 2b	5	13	2	4	0	0	0	1	0	1	0	.308	.308
K.Harrelson, of	4	13	0	1	0	0	0	1	1	3	0	.077	.143
J.Tartabull, of	7	13	1	2	0	0	0	0	1	2	0	.154	.214
J.Lonborg, p	3	9	0	0	0	0	0	0	0	7	0	.000	.000
N.Siebern, of	3	3	0	1	0	0	0	1	0	0	0	.333	.333
R.Gibson, c	2	2	0	0	0	0	0	0	0	2	0	.000	.000
M.Ryan, c	1	2	0	0	0	0	0	0	0	1	0	.000	.000
J.Santiago, p	3	2	1	1	0	0	1	1	0	1	0	.500	.500
G.Thomas, of	2	2	0	0	0	0	0	0	0	1	0	.000	.000
G.Waslewski, p	2	1	0	0	0	0	0	0	0	1	0	.000	.000
TOTALS		222	21	48	6	1	8	19	17	49	1	.216	.278

PITCHER	W	L	ERA	G	GS	SV	IP	H	BB	SO
J.Lonborg	2	1	2.63	3	3	0	24.0	14	2	11
J.Santiago	0	2	5.59	3	2	0	9.2	16	3	6
G.Waslewski	0	0	2.16	2	1	0	8.1	4	2	7
G.Bell	0	1	5.06	3	1	1	5.1	8	1	1
J.Wyatt	1	0	4.91	2	0	0	3.2	1	3	1
D.Morehead	0	0	0.00	2	0	0	3.1	0	4	3
L.Stange	0	0	0.00	1	0	0	2.0	3	0	0
J.Stephenson	0	0	9.00	1	0	0	2.0	3	1	0
K.Brett	0	0	0.00	2	0	0	1.1	0	1	1
D.Osinski	0	0	6.75	2	0	0	1.1	2	0	0
TOTALS	3	4	3.39	21	7	1	61.0	51	17	30

1967 WORLD SERIES - STL(NL) DEFEATS BOS(AL), 4 GAMES TO 3

GAME 1, OCT. 4

STL	001	000	100	2	10	0
BOS	001	000	000	1	6	0

PITCHERS: GIBSON VS SANTIAGO, Wyatt(8)

ATTENDANCE: 34,796

GAME 2, OCT. 5

STL	000	000	000	0	1	1
BOS	000	101	30X	5	9	0

PITCHERS: HUGHES, Willis(6), Hoerner(7), Lamabe(7) VS LONBORG

ATTENDANCE: 35,188

GAME 3, OCT. 7

BOS	000	001	100	2	7	1
STL	120	001	01X	5	10	0

PITCHERS: BELL, Waslewski(3), Stange(6), Osinski(8) VS BRILES

ATTENDANCE: 54,575

GAME 4, OCT. 8

BOS	000	000	000	0	5	0
STL	402	000	00X	6	9	0

PITCHERS: SANTIAGO, Bell(1), Stephenson(3), Morehead(5), Brett(8) VS GIBSON

ATTENDANCE: 54,575

GAME 5, OCT. 9

BOS	001	000	002	3	6	1
STL	000	000	001	1	3	2

PITCHERS: LONBORG VS CARLTON, Washburn(7), Willis(9), Lamabe(9)

ATTENDANCE: 54,575

GAME 6, OCT. 11

STL	002	000	200	4	8	0
BOS	010	300	40X	8	12	1

PITCHERS: Hughes, Willis(4), Briles(5), LAMABE(7), Hoerner(7), Jaster(7), Washburn(7), Woodeshick(8) VS Waslewski, WYATT(6), Bell(8)

ATTENDANCE: 35,188

GAME 7, OCT. 12

STL	002	023	000	7	10	1
BOS	000	010	010	2	3	1

PITCHERS: GIBSON VS LONBORG, Santiago(7), Morehead(9), Osinski(9), Brett(9)

ATTENDANCE: 35,188

Game 1. With Lonborg resting after clinching the pennant on the final day, Jose Santiago drew the assignment of facing Gibson in Game 1. Santiago was splendid on the mound and with the bat, as he homered in the same inning he allowed the Cardinals a run. Maris drove in Brock for the second time on the day with a groundout in the seventh, and Gibson made it stand up.

Game 2. Trailing one game to none at home, the Red Sox needed perfection...and they came close. Lonborg retired the first 19 batters before he walked Flood in the seventh. He still had a no-hitter intact with two outs in the eighth until Julian Javier doubled to the left-field corner. Lonborg finished with the fourth one-hitter in Series history as Yaz hit two homers and drove in four.

Game 3. The first World Series game at new Busch Stadium belonged to the home team. Brock began the game with a triple and, by the time he batted again in the third, Sox starter Gary Bell was gone, thanks to Mike Shannon's two-run homer in the second. After Boston inched closer on an RBI-single by Dalton Jones and a homer by Reggie Smith, St. Louis used speed to tack on two runs on Brock's bunt, a wild pickoff, and a single in the sixth; followed by an infield hit by Maris and a double by Cepeda in the eighth.

Game 4. With Gibson pitching, the Cardinals wanted it to be over quickly. It was. St. Louis scored four times in the first, knocking out Santiago and bringing in the previous day's failed starter, Bell. Jerry Stephenson allowed two more St. Louis runs in the third inning before Ken Brett, 19, mopped up and became the youngest pitcher to appear in a World Series. Maris and McCarver each knocked in two runs as Gibson mowed down Boston with a five-hit shutout.

Game 5. Facing elimination, Lonborg wasn't as sharp as in Game 2, but he was close enough. With a 1–0 lead to work with, he held the Cardinals to just two hits over eight innings, walking none. Elston Howard's bases-loaded single in the ninth brought in two runs—one on an error—and Lonborg allowed his first hit in five innings in the ninth. Maris connected on a two-out home run to spoil the shutout, but not the day.

Game 6. Back at Fenway, the Red Sox became the first team in World Series history to hit three home runs in one inning: Yastrzemski, Smith, and Rico Petrocelli in the fourth. The Cards rallied to tie the game in the seventh on Brock's two-run homer to the bleachers in center. Boston wasted no time in retaking the lead as Joe Foy, Mike Andrews, Jerry Adair, and Smith all rapped run-scoring singles in the home seventh and St. Louis became the first team to use eight pitchers in one Series game. The Red Sox used three, with John Wyatt getting the win and Bell pitching the final two frames to knot the Series.

Game 7. Gibson pitched Game 7 on three days' rest; with Lonborg sallying forth on only two. As he'd done in 1964, the awesome Gibson completed three games, but he added a new twist with a home run for his third win. Brock stole three more bases to give him a record seven steals, and unlikely slugger Javier hit a three-run blast over the Green Monster in the sixth against Lonborg to put the world championship on ice.

Ⓧ Ⓧ Ⓧ

1975 American League Championship Series, Boston Red Sox vs. Oakland A's

In 1975 the Red Sox held off the Orioles, winners of five of the first six AL East Division titles, to earn their first trip to the League Championship Series. While Boston had holdovers Carl Yastrzemski and Rico Petrocelli from the 1967 "Impossible Dream" club, the lineup also featured talented youngsters Rick Burleson, Cecil Cooper, Dwight Evans, and Carlton Fisk. Two rookies were at the heart of the lineup: Fred Lynn and Jim Rice. While Lynn became the first player to win the Rookie of the Year and MVP Awards the same year, Rice was hit with a pitch on the wrist in late September and missed the entire postseason.

For youngsters who did not know what it was like when the Yankees won every year, there was the Oakland A's. The brash and mustachioed club with the colorful uniforms won its fifth straight AL West title after vanquishing different NL teams in the World Series for the past three years. After Catfish Hunter became the first of many A's to fly the coop, Oakland wasn't as dominant in 1975, but they still won more games than anyone in the league.

The Oakland juggernaut, whose origins dated back to the mid-1960s in Kansas City, sputtered and died over a weekend in 1975. The A's used a two-man starting

staff in the ALCS—Ken Holtzman and Vida Blue—and neither looked good. Oakland's once infallible bullpen added fire to the mix as five Sox regulars hit .364 or better. Reggie Jackson and Sal Bando valiantly tried to rally

the troops, batting .458 between them, but no one was able to drive them in. Each scored just once as Boston pitchers allowed just five others to touch home plate in the sweep.

BOS (E)

PLAYER, POS	G	AB	R	H	2B	3B	HR	RBI	BB	SO	SB	AVG	OBP
J.Beniquez, dh	3	12	2	3	0	0	0	1	0	1	2	.250	.250
C.Fisk, c	3	12	4	5	1	0	0	2	0	2	1	.417	.417
R.Petrocelli, 3b	3	12	1	2	0	0	1	2	0	3	0	.167	.167
D.Doyle, 2b	3	11	3	3	0	0	0	2	0	1	0	.273	.273
F.Lynn, of	3	11	1	4	1	0	0	3	0	0	0	.364	.364
C.Yastrzemski, of	3	11	4	5	1	0	1	2	1	1	1	.455	.500
C.Cooper, 1b	3	10	0	4	2	0	0	1	0	2	0	.400	.400
D.Evans, of	3	10	1	1	1	0	0	0	1	2	0	.100	.182
R.Burleson, ss	3	9	2	4	2	0	0	1	1	0	0	.444	.500
TOTALS		**98**	**18**	**31**	**8**	**0**	**2**	**14**	**3**	**12**	**3**	**.316**	**.337**

PITCHER	W	L	ERA	G	GS	SV	IP	H	BB	SO
L.Tiant	1	0	0.00	1	1	0	9.0	3	3	8
R.Wise	1	0	2.45	1	1	0	7.1	6	3	2
R.Cleveland	0	0	5.40	1	1	0	5.0	7	1	2
D.Drago	0	0	0.00	2	0	2	4.2	2	1	2
R.Moret	1	0	0.00	1	0	0	1.0	1	1	0
TOTALS	**3**	**0**	**1.67**	**6**	**3**	**2**	**27.0**	**19**	**9**	**14**

OAK (W)

PLAYER, POS	G	AB	R	H	2B	3B	HR	RBI	BB	SO	SB	AVG	OBP
S.Bando, 3b	3	12	1	6	2	0	0	2	0	3	0	.500	.500
R.Jackson, of	3	12	1	5	0	0	1	3	0	2	0	.417	.417
J.Rudi, 1b-of	3	12	1	3	2	0	0	0	0	1	0	.250	.250
C.Washington, of-dh	3	12	1	3	1	0	0	1	0	2	0	.250	.250
B.Campaneris, ss	3	11	1	0	0	0	0	0	1	1	0	.000	.083
B.North, of	3	10	0	0	0	0	0	1	2	0	0	.000	.167
G.Tenace, c-1b	3	9	0	0	0	0	0	0	3	2	0	.000	.250
B.Williams, dh	3	8	0	0	0	0	0	0	1	1	0	.000	.111
P.Garner, 2b	3	5	0	0	0	0	0	0	0	1	0	.000	.000
J.Holt, 1b	3	3	0	1	1	0	0	0	0	0	0	.333	.333
R.Fosse, c	1	2	0	0	0	0	0	0	0	1	0	.000	.000
C.Tovar, 2b	2	2	2	1	0	0	0	0	1	0	0	.500	.667
T.Harper, ph	1	0	0	0	0	0	0	0	1	0	0	.000	1.000
D.Hopkins, dh	1	0	0	0	0	0	0	0	0	0	0	.000	.000
T.Martinez, 2b	3	0	0	0	0	0	0	0	0	0	0	.000	.000
TOTALS		**98**	**7**	**19**	**6**	**0**	**1**	**7**	**9**	**14**	**0**	**.194**	**.262**

PITCHER	W	L	ERA	G	GS	SV	IP	H	BB	SO
K.Holtzman	0	2	4.09	2	2	0	11.0	12	1	7
P.Lindblad	0	0	0.00	2	0	0	4.2	5	1	0
R.Fingers	0	1	6.75	1	0	0	4.0	5	1	3
V.Blue	0	0	9.00	1	1	0	3.0	6	0	2
G.Abbott	0	0	0.00	1	0	0	1.0	0	0	0
J.Todd	0	0	9.00	3	0	0	1.0	3	0	0
D.Bosman	0	0	0.00	1	0	0	0.1	0	0	0
TOTALS	**0**	**3**	**4.32**	**11**	**3**	**0**	**25.0**	**31**	**3**	**12**

1975 CHAMPIONSHIP SERIES - BOS(E) DEFEATS OAK(W), 3 GAMES TO 0

GAME 1, OCT. 4						
OAK	000	000	010	1	3	4
BOS	200	000	50X	7	8	3

PITCHERS: HOLTZMAN, Todd(7), Lindblad(7), Bosman(7), Abbott(8) VS TIANT

ATTENDANCE: 35,578

GAME 2, OCT. 5						
OAK	200	100	000	3	10	0
BOS	000	301	11X	6	12	0

PITCHERS: Blue, Todd(4), FINGERS(5) VS Cleveland, MORET(6), Drago(7)

ATTENDANCE: 35,578

GAME 3, OCT. 7						
BOS	000	130	010	5	11	1
OAK	000	001	020	3	6	2

PITCHERS: WISE, Drago(8) VS HOLTZMAN, Todd(5), Lindblad(5)

ATTENDANCE: 49,358

Game 1. After the first two Red Sox were retired in the first inning, Oakland made three consecutive errors to plate two runs. The A's settled down and so did Boston's Luis Tiant, who did not allow a hit until Joe Rudi singled to start the fifth. With the score still 2–0 in the seventh, five hits, two Juan Beniquez steals, and another key Oakland error made it 7–0. An unearned run by Oakland in the eighth ended the shutout, but Tiant finished with a three-hitter.

Game 2. Oakland looked a bit more like the team of postseason veterans than the green-and-gold butterfingers of Game 1. Jackson still had his swagger, launching a two-run home run off Reggie Cleveland in the first inning. Oakland added a run in the top of the fourth to

make it 3–0, but then the Red Sox showed their mettle. Yastrzemski hit a two-run homer as the Red Sox rallied to tie it in the bottom of the inning. Fisk, Petrocelli, and Lynn each knocked in runs during a four-inning bashing of Rollie Fingers.

Game 3. Holtzman, making his second start, was solid the first time through the order until a two-out error in the fourth set up Boston's first run. Left-handed hitters Denny Doyle and Yaz got two-out hits in the fifth to chase the southpaw before Fisk then singled in a run and another scored on a wild pitch. Rick Wise ran into trouble in the eighth, but Dick Drago got out of the jam with a double play before he retired the side in the ninth to end Oakland's reign.

※

1975 World Series, Boston Red Sox vs. Cincinnati Reds

At a time when so much was happening in America, when some thought baseball was fit only to entertain the older generation, and enlightened others considered the

game too slow, a World Series for the ages was played. The Red Sox and Reds had never met in three-quarters of a century of shared existence but, from the moment Luis Tiant twirled and threw the first pitch, there was something special about this 11-day contest. After Tiant's masterful first game, five of the next six games were decided

by one run, with four won in the final inning. Three days of rain in Boston made it seem like Game 6 would never come; when it did, it seemed like it would never end.

Bernie Carbo became a New England folk hero, Dwight Evans gave birth to a Homeric legend with his game-saving play, and Carlton Fisk's waving arms turned millions into cheerleaders at home with the archetypal "reaction shot." And when Pete Rose flopped into third base after Joe Morgan's deciding hit a night later, it was as if the dirt from his dive had spilled out onto the living room floor. Every moment seemed like life and death, with every batter, pitcher, pinch hitter and pinch runner a character in a television mini-series. The Reds carried off the championship banner as the Red Sox were carried off on their shields—and people who thought they no longer needed to worry about a passé game now counted the days until spring when it would start all over again.

CIN (NL)

PLAYER, POS	G	AB	R	H	2B	3B	HR	RBI	BB	SO	SB	AVG	OBP
J.Bench, c	7	29	5	6	2	0	1	4	2	4	0	.207	.258
G.Foster, of	7	29	1	8	1	0	0	2	1	1	1	.276	.300
D.Concepcion, ss	7	28	3	5	1	0	1	4	0	1	3	.179	.200
T.Perez, 1b	7	28	4	5	0	0	3	7	3	9	1	.179	.258
J.Morgan, 2b	7	27	4	7	1	0	0	3	5	1	2	.259	.375
P.Rose, 3b	7	27	3	10	1	1	0	2	5	1	0	.370	.469
K.Griffey, of	7	26	4	7	3	1	0	4	4	2	2	.269	.367
C.Geronimo, of	7	25	3	7	0	1	2	3	3	5	0	.280	.357
D.Gullett, p	3	7	1	2	0	0	0	0	0	2	0	.286	.286
M.Rettenmund, ph	3	3	0	0	0	0	0	0	0	1	0	.000	.000
J.Billingham, p	3	2	0	0	0	0	0	0	0	1	0	.000	.000
D.Chaney, ph	2	2	0	0	0	0	0	0	0	1	0	.000	.000
T.Crowley, ph	2	2	0	1	0	0	0	0	0	1	0	.500	.500
D.Driessen, ph	2	2	0	0	0	0	0	0	0	0	0	.000	.000
E.Armbrister, ph	4	1	1	0	0	0	0	0	2	0	0	.000	.667
P.Borbon, p	3	1	0	0	0	0	0	0	0	0	0	.000	.000
P.Darcy, p	2	1	0	0	0	0	0	0	0	1	0	.000	.000
R.Eastwick, p	5	1	0	0	0	0	0	0	0	0	0	.000	.000
W.McEnaney, p	5	1	0	1	0	0	0	0	0	0	0	1.000	1.000
G.Nolan, p	2	1	0	0	0	0	0	0	0	0	0	.000	.000
F.Norman, p	2	1	0	0	0	0	0	0	0	0	0	.000	.000
TOTALS		**244**	**29**	**59**	**9**	**3**	**7**	**29**	**25**	**30**	**9**	**.242**	**.316**

PITCHER	W	L	ERA	G	GS	SV	IP	H	BB	SO
D.Gullett	1	1	4.34	3	3	0	18.2	19	10	15
J.Billingham	0	0	1.00	3	1	0	9.0	8	5	7
R.Eastwick	2	0	2.25	5	0	1	8.0	6	3	4
W.McEnaney	0	0	2.70	5	0	1	6.2	3	2	5
G.Nolan	0	0	6.00	2	2	0	6.0	6	1	2
C.Carroll	1	0	3.18	5	0	0	5.2	4	2	3
P.Darcy	0	1	4.50	2	0	0	4.0	3	2	1
F.Norman	0	1	9.00	2	1	0	4.0	8	3	2
P.Borbon	0	0	6.00	3	0	0	3.0	3	2	1
TOTALS	**4**	**3**	**3.88**	**30**	**7**	**2**	**65.0**	**60**	**30**	**40**

BOS (AL)

PLAYER, POS	G	AB	R	H	2B	3B	HR	RBI	BB	SO	SB	AVG	OBP
D.Doyle, 2b	7	30	3	8	1	1	0	0	2	1	0	.267	.313
C.Yastrzemski, 1b-of	7	29	7	9	0	0	0	4	4	1	0	.310	.394
R.Petrocelli, 3b	7	26	3	8	1	0	0	4	3	6	0	.308	.379
C.Fisk, c	7	25	5	6	0	0	2	4	7	7	0	.240	.406
F.Lynn, of	7	25	3	7	1	0	1	5	3	5	0	.280	.357
R.Burleson, ss	7	24	1	7	1	0	0	2	4	2	0	.292	.393
D.Evans, of	7	24	3	7	1	1	1	5	3	4	0	.292	.370
C.Cooper, 1b	5	19	0	1	1	0	0	1	0	3	0	.053	.053
J.Beniquez, of	3	8	0	1	0	0	0	1	1	1	0	.125	.222
L.Tiant, p	3	8	2	2	0	0	0	0	2	4	0	.250	.400
B.Carbo, of	4	7	3	3	1	0	2	4	1	1	0	.429	.500
B.Lee, p	2	6	0	1	0	0	0	0	0	3	0	.167	.167
R.Cleveland, p	3	2	0	0	0	0	0	0	0	2	0	.000	.000
R.Miller, of	3	2	0	0	0	0	0	0	0	0	0	.000	.000
R.Wise, p	2	2	0	0	0	0	0	0	0	0	0	.000	.000
D.Griffin, ph	1	1	0	0	0	0	0	0	0	0	0	.000	.000
B.Montgomery, ph	1	1	0	0	0	0	0	0	0	0	0	.000	.000
TOTALS		**239**	**30**	**60**	**7**	**2**	**6**	**30**	**30**	**40**	**0**	**.251**	**.337**

PITCHER	W	L	ERA	G	GS	SV	IP	H	BB	SO
L.Tiant	2	0	3.60	3	3	0	25.0	25	8	12
B.Lee	0	0	3.14	2	2	0	14.1	12	3	7
R.Cleveland	0	1	6.75	3	1	0	6.2	7	3	5
J.Willoughby	0	1	0.00	3	0	0	6.1	3	0	2
R.Wise	1	0	8.44	2	1	0	5.1	6	2	2
D.Drago	0	1	2.25	4	0	0	4.0	3	1	1
R.Moret	0	0	0.00	3	0	0	1.2	2	3	1
J.Burton	0	1	9.00	2	0	0	1.0	1	3	0
D.Segui	0	0	0.00	1	0	0	1.0	0	0	0
D.Pole	0	0	INF	1	0	0	0.0	0	2	0
TOTALS	**3**	**4**	**3.86**	**22**	**7**	**0**	**65.1**	**59**	**25**	**30**

1975 WORLD SERIES - CIN(NL) DEFEATS BOS(AL), 4 GAMES TO 3

GAME 1, OCT. 11

| CIN | 000 | 000 | 000 | | 0 | 5 | 0 |
| BOS | 000 | 000 | 60X | | 6 | 12 | 0 |

PITCHERS: GULLETT, Carroll(7), McEnaney(7) VS TIANT

ATTENDANCE: 35,205

GAME 2, OCT. 12

| CIN | 000 | 100 | 002 | | 3 | 7 | 1 |
| BOS | 100 | 001 | 000 | | 2 | 7 | 0 |

PITCHERS: Billingham, Borbon(6), McEnaney(7), EASTWICK(8) VS Lee, DRAGO(9)

ATTENDANCE: 35,205

GAME 3, OCT. 14

| BOS | 010 | 001 | 102 | 0 | 5 | 10 | 2 |
| CIN | 000 | 230 | 000 | 1 | 6 | 7 | 0 |

PITCHERS: Wise, Burton(5), Cleveland(7), WILLOUGHBY(7), Moret(10) VS Nolan, Darcy(5), Carroll(7), McEnaney(7), EASTWICK(9)

ATTENDANCE: 55,392

GAME 4, OCT. 15

| BOS | 000 | 500 | 000 | | 5 | 11 | 1 |
| CIN | 200 | 200 | 000 | | 4 | 9 | 1 |

PITCHERS: TIANT VS NORMAN, Borbon(4), Carroll(5), Eastwick(7)

ATTENDANCE: 55,667

GAME 5, OCT. 16

| BOS | 100 | 000 | 001 | | 2 | 5 | 0 |
| CIN | 000 | 113 | 01X | | 6 | 8 | 0 |

PITCHERS: CLEVELAND, Willoughby(6), Pole(8), Segui(8) VS GULLETT, Eastwick(9)

ATTENDANCE: 56,393

GAME 6, OCT. 21

| CIN | 000 | 030 | 210000 | | 6 | 14 | 0 |
| BOS | 300 | 000 | 030001 | | 7 | 10 | 1 |

PITCHERS: Nolan, Norman(3), Billingham(3), Carroll(5), Borbon(6), Eastwick(8), McEnaney(9), DARCY(10) VS Tiant, Moret(8), Drago(9), WISE(12)

ATTENDANCE: 35,205

GAME 7, OCT. 22

| CIN | 000 | 002 | 101 | | 4 | 9 | 0 |
| BOS | 003 | 000 | 000 | | 3 | 5 | 2 |

PITCHERS: Gullett, Billingham(5), CARROLL(7), McEnaney(9) VS Lee, Moret(7), Willoughby(7), BURTON(9), Cleveland(9)

ATTENDANCE: 35,205

Game 1. Don Gullett and Tiant locked in a scoreless duel until the seventh inning. Yastrzemski's diving catch helped derail a Reds rally in the top of the inning; in the home seventh Tiant singled to start a six-run rally as Boston batted around. Tiant finished with a five-hit shutout, the first complete game in the Series since 1971.

Game 2. Petrocelli broke a 1–1 tie with a run-scoring single in the sixth as Boston's Bill Lee pitched into the ninth before being removed for Dick Drago after a leadoff double. Drago got the next two outs before Dave Concepcion tied the game and Ken Griffey doubled him home to let Cincinnati escape Fenway with the Series tied.

Game 3. In Game 3 it was the Red Sox who rallied late. The Reds led 5–1 after five innings at Riverfront Stadium on home runs by Johnny Bench, Dave Concepcion, and Cesar Geronimo. Carbo's pinch-hit homer pulled Boston closer in the seventh, and Fisk's two-run homer off Rawly Eastwick tied the game in the ninth. Nonetheless, it took a bunt to really make things interesting. With Geronimo on first in the 10th, Ed Armbrister (who had one sacrifice all year) bunted in front of the plate, then froze. Fisk pushed the rookie out of the way and then threw the ball into center field, moving runners to second and third. Despite a long protest that the batter should have been ruled out for interference, the call stood. Roger Moret came in and walked Rose intentionally and caught Merv Rettenmund looking before Joe Morgan ended the saga with a drive over Lynn's head.

Game 4. The Red Sox scored five times in the fourth, with a two-run triple by Dewey Evans igniting the inning. Tiant, who singled and scored in the rally, allowed Cincy to surge with two outs in the bottom of the inning to cut the lead to 5–4. The Reds put the tying run on base in all but one of the last five innings, but Tiant extracted himself each time, the last on an over-the-shoulder catch by Lynn with two on in the ninth.

Game 5. The Reds trailed early before pulling ahead in the middle innings, with Tony Perez's three-run blast off Reggie Cleveland the deciding factor. Gullett was working on a two-hitter until two outs in the ninth when he surrendered three straight hits before Eastwick got the final out.

Game 6. In the beginning, Game 6 looked like a laugher for the Red Sox. Lynn launched a three-run homer into the right-center bleachers in the first inning though Tiant, making his third start thanks to the rainouts, labored despite the early lead. Ken Griffey's two-run triple and Johnny Bench's single tied the game in the fifth. George Foster doubled in the go-ahead runs in the seventh and, when Geronimo homered in the top of the eighth, the sportswriters started tallying votes for the Series MVP. Eastwick, the leading candidate for the award, came in to pitch in the eighth with the tying run at the plate. Carbo made the already-written ledes irrelevant as he created a tumult with his three-run, pinch-hit homer to center field. Boston loaded the bases in the ninth before Foster threw out Denny Doyle, who had tagged up on a short fly. Two innings later, a long fly off the bat of Griffey was snagged by Evans after a long run and turned into another stunning double play. Rookie Pat Darcy, in his third inning (the longest stint of any of the eight pitchers used by Captain Hook, Sparky Anderson), threw a sinker to Fisk, who blasted it down the left-field line, waving his arms to keep it fair in the famous shot. When the fly ball struck the foul pole, the excitement at Fenway reached a new fever pitch, and the Series was tied.

Game 7. By Game 7, it was obvious that leads didn't mean much in this World Series. With the Red Sox up, 3–0, in the third inning of the deciding game—courtesy of two bases-loaded walks by Gullett—the two teams had already combined to blow eight leads (five by Boston). Bill Lee nearly got through the sixth without allowing a run, but an errant throw allowed Perez to bat. Lee threw his signature blooper pitch, but Perez crushed it to make the score 3–2. Rose singled in the tying run off Roger Moret in the seventh. With two outs in the ninth, Morgan, who'd been moved up in the lineup by Anderson, blooped a single to center off Jim Burton. Finally, Will McEnaney induced Yaz to fly to center for Cincinnati's first world championship since 1940.

❉ ❉ ❉

One-Game Playoff, Boston Red Sox vs. New York Yankees, October 2, 1978

In their 75 seasons of shared existence, the Yankees and Red Sox have finished one-two in the standings seven times. Boston won the first time, in 1904, but the Yankees had triumphed the next six times: five between 1938 and 1949, and again in 1977. However, 1978 looked like it was going to be different. The Red Sox broke out to a huge lead and were up by 14 games over the Yankees on July 19, with Milwaukee and Baltimore ahead of New York. Jim Rice pummeled the ball, new acquisitions Dennis Eckersley and Mike Torrez pitched with urgency, and the heroes of the 1975 pennant winners—Luis Tiant, Fred Lynn, Rick Burleson, Carlton Fisk, and Carl Yastrzemski—were all still going strong. Then things started going very wrong in Boston.

At the same time, a sour season started to change in New York. Billy Martin, with two pennants and a world championship in just two full years with the Yankees, was under extreme pressure. On one side was Reggie Jackson,

whom Martin had tried to fight in the dugout at Fenway Park during a nationally televised game in 1977. Jackson missed signs at key times and had been suspended by the manager for insubordination. On the other side was meddlesome owner George Steinbrenner, with his frequent public decrees and blustery threats. Martin told them both off. "The two of them deserve each other," he said. "One's a born liar, the other's convicted." (Steinbrenner had been convicted for illegal donations to President Nixon's 1972 re-election campaign.) Martin resigned the next day.

Bob Lemon, who'd been fired by the White Sox, took over. A Hall of Fame pitcher who was as calm as Martin was explosive, the Yankees went 48–20 after he took the reins. New York lopped 10 games off Boston's lead in six weeks, coming into Boston in early September and dismembering the hometown team in a four-game sweep known as the "Boston Massacre." Boston went 1–8 at this crucial point and was trailing New York by 3½ games before the Sox suddenly resumed being the team that had flattened opponents earlier in the year. They finished the year 11–2, tying the Yankees on the last day of the season.

Thirty years almost to the day from the first one-game playoff in history, also played in Boston, Fenway filled on a Monday afternoon for the showdown between these intense rivals. Ron Guidry, 24–3 on the year, was on the hill for New York, while Red Sox manager Don Zimmer went with 16-game winner Mike Torrez, who had clinched the world championship for the Yankees the previous fall.

Local hero Yaz gave Boston the early lead by pulling a ball inside the right-field foul pole in the second inning. Torrez, meanwhile, allowed only two hits through six innings. In the bottom of the sixth the Red Sox added a run when Rice singled in Burleson for his 139th RBI and a 2–0 lead.

Torrez retired Graig Nettles to open the seventh, but Chris Chambliss and Roy White followed with singles. Rookie second baseman Brian Doyle, subbing for injured Willie Randolph, was pinch hit for by Jim Spencer. He flied out to left and up came ninth-place hitter Bucky Dent. People in New York screamed at their TVs and radios that the Yankees had to pinch hit for

Dent, but Lemon could not because the Yankees' only available infielder, Fred Stanley, had to go in to play second base for Doyle.

Dent's famous fly ball landed in the net atop the Green Monster, whereas at just about any other stadium in the league—especially Yankee Stadium—it would have harmlessly landed in Yastrzemski's glove. Torrez then walked Mickey Rivers; Bob Stanley replaced him and Rivers stole second. Thurman Munson doubled to right-center to make it 4–2. Jackson's long home run leading off the eighth against Stanley ran the score to 5–2.

Again, just when it looked like things were all over for the Red Sox, they rallied. Jerry Remy doubled in the eighth, Yaz singled him in, Fisk singled, and Lynn followed with a base hit that made it a one-run game with only one out. Ferocious stopper Rich Gossage, who had entered in the seventh inning and retired Bob Bailey (in his last career at bat) and Burleson with a runner on second, again excelled under pressure. Butch Hobson flied out to right, and George Scott struck out to end the inning.

The Yankees were retired in the ninth—Dent struck out against Andy Hassler—and everyone took a deep breath as the players readied for the bottom of the ninth. Dwight Evans flied out as a pinch hitter, but Burleson walked. Then Remy hit a line drive into the bright sun in right. Lou Piniella didn't see it until the ball landed, and he desperately stuck out his glove. If Piniella had been left-handed (like Reggie Jackson) or unlucky (like the Red Sox) it probably would have gotten by him and tied the game. Instead, the ball bounced right into his glove, Piniella fired it in, and Burleson had to hold up at second. Had he gotten to third, a long fly like the one Rice then hit to Piniella would have tied the game. Burleson moved to third, but there were two outs. Next came Yaz, Boston's last hope.

Distressingly for the Hub faithful, their iconic figure popped up a rising fastball to Nettles, providing the denouement as the hated Yankees won their third straight AL East title. Boston had won 99 games, enough to win any other division in baseball with relative ease that year. Those old enough to remember Denny Galehouse and the 1948 one-game playoff with Cleveland could now carry Bucky Dent's name around for another quarter century.

NEW YORK YANKEES 5, BOSTON RED SOX 4
Game Played on Monday, October 2, 1978 (D) at Fenway Park

NEW YORK YANKEES

	AB	R	H	RBI	BB	SO	PO	A
Rivers cf	2	1	1	0	2	0	2	0
Blair ph,cf	1	0	1	0	0	0	0	0
Munson c	5	0	1	1	0	3	7	1
Piniella rf	4	0	1	0	0	0	4	0
Jackson dh	4	1	1	1	0	0	0	0
Nettles 3b	4	0	0	0	0	1	1	3
Chambliss 1b	4	1	1	0	0	0	8	0
White lf	3	1	1	0	1	1	4	0
Thomasson lf	0	0	0	0	0	0	1	0
Doyle 2b	2	0	0	0	0	0	0	0
Spencer ph	1	0	0	0	0	0	0	0
Stanley 2b	1	0	0	0	0	0	0	0
Dent ss	4	1	1	3	0	1	0	2
Guidry p	0	0	0	0	0	0	0	1
Gossage p	0	0	0	0	0	0	0	0
TOTALS	35	5	8	5	3	6	27	7

BOSTON RED SOX

	AB	R	H	RBI	BB	SO	PO	A
Burleson ss	4	1	1	0	1	1	4	2
Remy 2b	4	1	2	0	0	0	2	5
Rice rf	5	0	1	1	0	1	4	0
Yastrzemski lf	5	2	2	2	0	1	2	0
Fisk c	3	0	1	0	1	0	5	1
Lynn cf	4	0	1	1	0	0	1	0
Hobson dh	4	0	1	0	0	1	0	0
Scott 1b	4	0	2	0	0	2	8	0
Brohamer 3b	1	0	0	0	0	0	1	1
Bailey ph	1	0	0	0	0	1	0	0
Duffy 3b	0	0	0	0	0	0	0	0
Evans ph	1	0	0	0	0	0	0	0
Torrez p	0	0	0	0	0	0	0	0
Stanley p	0	0	0	0	0	0	0	0
Hassler p	0	0	0	0	0	0	0	0
Drago p	0	0	0	0	0	0	0	0
TOTALS	36	4	11	4	2	7	27	9

FIELDING
PB: Munson (8).

BATTING
2B: Rivers (25,off Torrez); Munson (27,off Stanley).
HR: Dent (5,7th inning off Torrez 2 on 2 out); Jackson (27,8th inning off Stanley 0 on 0 out).
Team LOB: 6.
BASERUNNING
SB: Rivers 2 (25,2nd base off Torrez/Fisk,2nd base off Stanley/Fisk).

BATTING
2B: Scott (16,off Guidry); Burleson (32,off Guidry); Remy (24,off Gossage).
HR: Yastrzemski (17,2nd inning off Guidry 0 on 0 out).
SH: Brohamer (4,off Guidry); Remy (14,off Guidry).
IBB: Fisk (6,by Guidry).
Team LOB: 9

NY A	0	0	0	0	0	0	4	1	0	-	5	8	0
BOS A	0	1	0	0	0	1	0	2	0	-	4	11	0

NEW YORK YANKEES	IP	H	R	ER	BB	SO	HR
Guidry W(25-3)	6.1	6	2	2	1	5	1
Gossage SV(27)	2.2	5	2	2	1	2	0
Totals	9	11	4	4	2	7	1

IBB: Guidry (1,Fisk).

BOSTON RED SOX	IP	H	R	ER	BB	SO	HR
Torrez L(16-13)	6.2	5	4	4	3	4	1
Stanley	0.1	2	1	1	0	0	1
Hassler	1.2	1	0	0	0	2	0
Drago	0.1	0	0	0	0	0	0
Totals	9	8	5	5	3	6	2

Stanley faced 1 batter in the 8th inning
Umpires: Don Denkinger, Jim Evans, Al Clark, Steve Palermo   Time of Game: 2:52   Attendance: 32,925

Ⓧ Ⓧ Ⓧ

1986 American League Championship Series, Boston Red Sox vs. California Angels

A dozen seasons after the 1975 World Series, a lot had happened to the Red Sox. However, there had been no more October thrills despite three of the best seasons in a row the club had experienced since Ted Williams came home from one war and before he left for the next: 287 wins and 580 home runs, with 6.7 million people cramming into Fenway Park. Yet the bitter aftertaste of the 1977, 1978, and 1979 seasons was a one-game playoff and Bucky (expletive deleted) Dent. By 1986 the Red Sox still had Dwight Evans and Jim Rice, mainstays of the 1975 team (though Rice was hurt for the '75 postseason). The '86 Red Sox had a core of solid young players as well: Wade Boggs, who earned his third batting title, second baseman Marty Barrett, and catcher Rich Gedman, plus two key acquisitions in Dave Henderson and Don Baylor.

First baseman Bill Buckner was the toughest hitter in the league to strike out, and his 102 RBIs were second only to Rice on the Sox. The bullpen was strong, and Roger Clemens had quickly grown into the league's best pitcher, becoming the first to ever strike out 20 in a game along the way to winning 20 more than he lost.

The Angels didn't have the level of baggage the Red Sox carried, but they did have plenty of talent. California took its third AL West title in eight seasons in 1986, but it still stuck in their craw how they'd won the first two and dropped the last three to Milwaukee in the 1982 ALCS. Manager Gene Mauch had moved on to director of player personal before he returned to the dugout in 1985. At age 60, the combative Mauch had won more than 1,800 games, but no pennants. California's crew of veterans—Bob Boone, Bobby Grich, Doug DeCinces, Reggie Jackson, Brian Downing, Don Sutton, and Donnie Moore, plus young first baseman Wally Joyner—very badly wanted their grizzled skipper to see his first World Series. One side had to give.

BOS (E)

PLAYER, POS	G	AB	R	H	2B	3B	HR	RBI	BB	SO	SB	AVG	OBP
J.Rice, of	7	31	8	5	1	0	2	6	1	8	0	.161	.188
M.Barrett, 2b	7	30	4	11	2	0	0	5	2	2	0	.367	.406
W.Boggs, 3b	7	30	3	7	1	1	0	2	4	1	0	.233	.324
B.Buckner, 1b	7	28	3	6	1	0	0	3	0	2	0	.214	.214
D.Evans, of	7	28	2	6	1	0	1	4	3	3	0	.214	.290
R.Gedman, c	7	28	4	10	1	0	1	6	0	4	0	.357	.357
D.Baylor, dh	7	26	6	9	3	0	1	2	4	5	0	.346	.433
S.Owen, ss	7	21	5	9	0	1	0	3	2	2	1	.429	.478
T.Armas, of	5	16	1	2	1	0	0	0	0	2	0	.125	.125
D.Henderson, of	5	9	3	1	0	0	1	4	2	2	0	.111	.273
D.Stapleton, 1b	4	3	2	2	0	0	0	0	1	0	0	.667	.750
M.Greenwell, ph	2	2	0	1	0	0	0	0	0	0	0	.500	.500
E.Romero, ss	1	2	0	0	0	0	0	0	0	0	0	.000	.000
TOTALS		254	41	69	11	2	6	35	19	31	1	.272	.330

PITCHER	W	L	ERA	G	GS	SV	IP	H	BB	SO
R.Clemens	1	1	4.37	3	3	0	22.2	22	7	17
B.Hurst	1	0	2.40	2	2	0	15.0	18	1	8
O.Can Boyd	1	1	4.61	2	2	0	13.2	17	3	8
C.Schiraldi	0	1	1.50	4	0	0	6.0	5	3	9
B.Stanley	0	0	4.76	3	0	0	5.2	7	3	1
S.Crawford	1	0	0.00	1	0	0	1.2	1	2	1
J.Sambito	0	0	0.00	3	0	0	0.2	1	1	0
TOTALS	4	3	3.58	18	7	1	65.1	71	20	44

CAL (W)

PLAYER, POS	G	AB	R	H	2B	3B	HR	RBI	BB	SO	SB	AVG	OBP
D.DeCinces, 3b	7	32	2	9	3	0	1	3	0	2	0	.281	.281
D.Schofield, ss	7	30	4	9	1	0	1	2	1	5	1	.300	.323
B.Downing, of	7	27	2	6	0	0	1	7	4	5	0	.222	.333
R.Jackson, dh	6	26	2	5	2	0	0	2	2	7	0	.192	.250
G.Pettis, of	7	26	4	9	1	0	1	4	3	5	0	.346	.414
B.Grich, 2b-1b	6	24	1	5	0	0	1	3	0	8	0	.208	.208
B.Boone, c	7	22	4	10	0	0	1	2	1	3	0	.455	.478
R.Jones, of	6	17	4	3	1	0	0	2	5	2	0	.176	.364
R.Wilfong, 2b	4	13	1	4	1	0	0	2	0	2	0	.308	.308
G.Hendrick, of-1b	3	12	0	1	0	0	0	0	0	2	0	.083	.083
R.Burleson, 2b-dh	4	11	0	3	0	0	0	0	0	0	0	.273	.273
W.Joyner, 1b	3	11	3	5	2	0	1	2	2	0	0	.455	.538
J.Narron, c	4	2	1	1	0	0	0	0	1	1	0	.500	.667
D.White, of	4	2	2	1	0	0	0	0	0	1	0	.500	.500
J.Howell, ph	2	1	0	0	0	0	0	0	1	1	0	.000	.500
TOTALS		256	30	71	11	0	7	29	20	44	1	.277	.338

PITCHER	W	L	ERA	G	GS	SV	IP	H	BB	SO
M.Witt	1	0	2.55	2	2	0	17.2	13	2	8
J.Candelaria	1	1	0.84	2	2	0	10.2	11	6	7
D.Sutton	0	0	1.86	2	1	0	9.2	6	1	4
K.McCaskill	0	2	7.71	2	2	0	9.1	16	5	7
D.Corbett	1	0	5.40	3	0	0	6.2	9	2	2
D.Moore	0	1	7.20	3	0	1	5.0	8	2	0
G.Lucas	0	0	11.57	4	0	0	2.1	3	1	2
C.Finley	0	0	0.00	2	0	0	2.0	1	0	1
V.Ruhle	0	0	13.50	1	0	0	0.2	2	0	0
TOTALS	3	4	3.94	22	7	1	64.0	69	19	31

1986 CHAMPIONSHIP SERIES - BOS(E) DEFEATS CAL(W), 4 GAMES TO 3

GAME 1, OCT. 7					
CAL	041 000 030	8	11	0
BOS	000 001 000	1	5	1

PITCHERS: WITT VS CLEMENS, Sambito(8), Stanley(8)

ATTENDANCE: 32,993

GAME 2, OCT. 8					
CAL	000 110 000	2	11	3
BOS	110 010 33X	9	13	2

PITCHERS: McCASKILL, Lucas(8), Corbett(8) VS HURST

ATTENDANCE: 32,786

GAME 3, OCT. 10					
BOS	010 000 020	3	9	1
CAL	000 001 31X	5	8	0

PITCHERS: BOYD, Sambito(7), Schiraldi(8) VS CANDE-LARIA, Moore(8)

ATTENDANCE: 64,206

GAME 4, OCT. 11						
BOS	000 001 020	00	3	6	1
CAL	000 000 003	01	4	11	2

PITCHERS: Clemens, SCHIRALDI(9) VS Sutton, Lucas(7), Ruhle(7), Finley(8), CORBETT(8)

ATTENDANCE: 64,223

GAME 5, OCT. 12						
BOS	020 000 004	01	7	12	0
CAL	001 002 201	00	6	13	0

PITCHERS: Hurst, Stanley(7), Sambito(9), CRAW-FORD(9), Schiraldi(11) VS Witt, Lucas(9), MOORE(9), Finley(11)

ATTENDANCE: 64,223

GAME 6, OCT. 14					
CAL	200 000 110	4	11	1
BOS	205 010 20X	10	16	1

PITCHERS: McCASKILL, Lucas(3), Corbett(4), Finley(7) VS BOYD, Stanley(8)

ATTENDANCE: 32,998

GAME 7, OCT. 15					
CAL	000 000 010	1	6	2
BOS	030 400 10X	8	8	1

PITCHERS: CANDELARIA, Sutton(4), Moore(8) VS CLEMENS, Schiraldi(8)

ATTENDANCE: 33,001

Game 1. The first October appearance for Roger Clemens went badly as Mike Witt tossed a five-hitter while Clemens was victimized by the big inning. He retired the first two batters in the second, but then five straight Angels reached base and four scored.

Game 2. The Red Sox took a 3–2 lead in the fifth inning on a double by Evans. Boston maintained its lead when Grich was thrown out at the plate trying to score the next inning. Three errors in the seventh blew the game open before Rice's first postseason homer capped the scoring an inning later. Bruce Hurst's 11-hit complete game wasn't pretty, but it gave Boston a tie as it headed to California.

Game 3. Mauch was ejected for arguing when the umpires reversed a safe call on Joyner at the plate. Unlikely sluggers Dick Schofield and Gary Pettis homered in the seventh as the Angels snapped a 1–1 tie in the game and the series.

Game 4. Clemens was fashioning a 3–0 shutout in the ninth inning when DeCinces led off with a home run. After two singles, Calvin Schiraldi came in and allowed a double and an intentional walk before fanning Bobby Grich for the second out. Schiraldi then drilled Downing to plate the tying run. After Schiraldi issued another intentional pass to face Grich in the 11th, the veteran singled in the winning run to put the Angels one game away from the World Series.

Game 5. From Rich Gedman's home run in the second inning to the first out of the ninth, nothing went Boston's way. Grich's long fly bounced off the glove of Henderson, playing for the first time in the ALCS, and landed in the stands for a two-run homer. Bob Stanley replaced Hurst, allowing Rob Wilfong to double in a run before Downing brought in the fifth run. Witt dodged trouble until Baylor's two-run homer in the ninth suddenly made it a 5–4 game. Witt got the next batter, but Mauch summoned southpaw Gary Lucas, who plunked Gedman. Moore entered the game, and Dave Henderson then entered the scrolls of Boston immortals with his dramatic home run. The Angels tied it in the ninth, but DeCinces flew out to short right and Grich lined out to pitcher Steve Crawford. Henderson nailed Moore again in the 11th, this time for a sac fly that plated the go-ahead run before Schiraldi set down the Angels in order. Stunned California prepared for its return to Fenway.

Game 6. The Angels got off to a fast start with successive run-scoring doubles by Jackson and DeCinces off Oil Can Boyd but, when the Red Sox tied the score without getting a hit in the bottom of the inning, it seemed inevitable that Boston would prevail. The inevitable happened in the third inning when the Red Sox produced four straight hits to knock out Kirk McCaskill. Boston rolled on to even the series.

Game 7. Clemens, starting his third game of the LCS, collected his first postseason win. Boggs made it 3–0 on a two-run single in the second inning, and Rice's three-run homer chased John Candelaria in the fourth. Schiraldi blew the shutout, but the lead was plenty safe as the Red Sox came back from the dead to bury the Angels.

Ⓜ

1986 World Series, Boston Red Sox vs. New York Mets

The Mets and Red Sox had more in common than one might have thought as the two emerged on the other side of epic League Championship Series. It had been a while since either franchise had been in this position, as nine AL teams had reached the postseason since the Red Sox in 1975, and 10 NL teams had seen October's glow since the Mets in 1973. The teams had two of the brightest young pitchers in the game in Roger Clemens and Dwight Gooden, who'd started against each other

in the All-Star Game. Boston GM Lou Gorman, who'd been hired away from the Mets, had been responsible for keeping manager Davey Johnson in that organization in the early 1980s. Gorman had also worked out a trade between the clubs the previous winter that netted the Mets starter Bob Ojeda for reliever Calvin Schiraldi and other prospects. Despite enjoying a common dislike for the Yankees, the two clubs' passionate fan bases quickly elevated this confrontation into a border war.

The Red Sox won the early battles in Shea Stadium, winning twice before the Mets reversed the tide in the first two games at Fenway. When Bruce Hurst beat New York for the second time in Game 5, Boston regained the advantage. Game 6 rivaled the classic sixth game between the Red Sox and Reds in 1975, only this time it was Boston that was utterly devastated as a star first baseman's career was tarnished beyond recognition and the Series was inconceivably tied.

NY (NL)

PLAYER, POS	G	AB	R	H	2B	3B	HR	RBI	BB	SO	SB	AVG	OBP
G.Carter, c	7	29	4	8	2	0	2	9	0	4	0	.276	.276
L.Dykstra, of	7	27	4	8	0	0	2	3	2	7	0	.296	.345
K.Hernandez, 1b	7	26	1	6	0	0	0	4	5	1	0	.231	.355
M.Wilson, of	7	26	3	7	1	0	0	1	0	6	3	.269	.296
D.Strawberry, of	7	24	4	5	1	0	1	4	4	6	3	.208	.321
R.Knight, 3b	6	23	4	9	1	0	1	5	2	2	0	.391	.440
R.Santana, ss	7	20	3	5	0	0	0	2	2	5	0	.250	.318
W.Backman, 2b	6	18	4	6	0	0	0	1	3	2	1	.333	.429
D.Heep, dh-of	5	11	0	1	0	0	0	2	1	1	0	.091	.167
T.Teufel, 2b	3	9	1	4	1	0	1	1	1	2	0	.444	.500
K.Mitchell, of-dh	5	8	1	2	0	0	0	0	0	3	0	.250	.250
H.Johnson, 3b-ss	2	5	0	0	0	0	0	0	0	2	0	.000	.000
L.Mazzilli, of	4	5	2	2	0	0	0	0	0	0	0	.400	.400
R.Darling, p	3	3	0	0	0	0	0	0	0	1	0	.000	.000
D.Gooden, p	2	2	1	1	0	0	0	0	0	0	0	.500	.500
B.Ojeda, p	2	2	0	0	0	0	0	0	0	1	0	.000	.000
K.Elster, ss	1	1	0	0	0	0	0	0	0	0	0	.000	.000
J.Orosco, p	4	1	0	1	0	0	0	1	0	0	0	1.000	1.000
TOTALS		240	32	65	6	0	7	29	21	43	7	.271	.332

PITCHER	W	L	ERA	G	GS	SV	IP	H	BB	SO
R.Darling	1	1	1.53	3	3	0	17.2	13	10	12
B.Ojeda	1	0	2.08	2	2	0	13.0	13	5	9
D.Gooden	0	2	8.00	2	2	0	9.0	17	4	9
R.McDowell	1	0	4.91	5	0	0	7.1	10	6	2
S.Fernandez	0	0	1.35	2	0	0	6.2	6	1	10
J.Orosco	0	0	0.00	4	0	2	5.2	2	0	6
R.Aguilera	1	0	12.00	2	0	0	3.0	8	1	4
D.Sisk	0	0	0.00	1	0	0	0.2	0	1	1
TOTALS	4	3	3.29	22	7	2	63.0	69	28	53

BOS (AL)

PLAYER, POS	G	AB	R	H	2B	3B	HR	RBI	BB	SO	SB	AVG	OBP
B.Buckner, 1b	7	32	2	6	0	0	0	1	0	3	0	.188	.188
W.Boggs, 3b	7	31	3	9	3	0	0	3	4	2	0	.290	.371
M.Barrett, 2b	7	30	1	13	2	0	0	4	5	2	0	.433	.514
R.Gedman, c	7	30	1	6	1	0	1	1	0	10	0	.200	.200
J.Rice, of	7	27	6	9	1	1	0	6	9	9	0	.333	.455
D.Evans, of	7	26	4	8	2	0	2	9	4	3	0	.308	.400
D.Henderson, of	7	25	6	10	1	1	2	5	2	6	0	.400	.448
S.Owen, ss	7	20	2	6	0	0	0	2	5	6	0	.300	.440
D.Baylor, dh	4	11	1	2	1	0	0	1	1	3	0	.182	.250
R.Clemens, p	2	4	1	0	0	0	0	0	0	1	0	.000	.000
M.Greenwell, ph	4	3	0	0	0	0	0	0	1	2	0	.000	.250
B.Hurst, p	3	3	0	0	0	0	0	0	0	3	0	.000	.000
T.Armas, ph	1	1	0	0	0	0	0	0	0	1	0	.000	.000
S.Crawford, p	3	1	0	0	0	0	0	0	0	0	0	.000	.000
E.Romero, ss	3	1	0	0	0	0	0	0	0	0	0	.000	.000
C.Schiraldi, p	3	1	0	0	0	0	0	0	0	1	0	.000	.000
B.Stanley, p	5	1	0	0	0	0	0	0	0	1	0	.000	.000
D.Stapleton, 1b	3	1	0	0	0	0	0	0	0	0	0	.000	.000
TOTALS		248	27	69	11	2	5	26	28	53	0	.278	.357

PITCHER	W	L	ERA	G	GS	SV	IP	H	BB	SO
B.Hurst	2	0	1.96	3	3	0	23.0	18	6	17
R.Clemens	0	0	3.18	2	2	0	11.1	9	6	11
O.Can Boyd	0	1	7.71	1	1	0	7.0	9	1	3
A.Nipper	0	1	7.11	2	1	0	6.1	10	2	2
B.Stanley	0	0	0.00	5	0	1	6.1	5	1	4
S.Crawford	1	0	6.23	3	0	0	4.1	5	0	4
C.Schiraldi	0	2	13.50	3	0	1	4.0	7	3	2
J.Sambito	0	0	27.00	2	0	0	0.1	2	2	0
TOTALS	3	4	4.31	21	7	2	62.2	65	21	43

1986 WORLD SERIES - NY (NL) DEFEATS BOS(AL), 4 GAMES TO 3

GAME 1, OCT. 18

```
BOS   000  000  100        1   5   0
NY    000  000  000        0   4   1
```
PITCHERS: HURST, Schiraldi(9) VS DARLING, McDowell(8)
ATTENDANCE: 55,076

GAME 2, OCT. 19

```
BOS   003  120  201        9   18   0
NY    002  010  000        3   8    1
```
PITCHERS: Clemens, CRAWFORD(5), Stanley(7) VS GOODEN, Aguilera(6), Orosco(7), Fernandez(9), Sisk(9)
ATTENDANCE: 55,063

GAME 3, OCT. 21

```
NY    400  000  210        7   13   0
BOS   001  000  000        1   5    0
```
PITCHERS: OJEDA, McDowell(8) VS BOYD, Sambito(8), Stanley(8)
ATTENDANCE: 33,595

GAME 4, OCT. 22

```
NY    000  300  210        6   12   0
BOS   000  000  020        2   7    1
```
PITCHERS: DARLING, McDowell(7), Orosco(8) VS NIPPER, Crawford(7), Stanley(9)
ATTENDANCE: 33,920

GAME 5, OCT. 23

```
NY    000  000  011        2   10   1
BOS   011  020  00X        4   12   0
```
PITCHERS: GOODEN, Fernandez(5) VS HURST
ATTENDANCE: 34,010

GAME 6, OCT. 25

```
BOS   110  000  100  2      5   13   3
NY    000  020  010  3      6   8    2
```
PITCHERS: Clemens, SCHIRALDI(8), Stanley(10) VS Ojeda, McDowell(7), Orosco(8), AGUILERA(9)
ATTENDANCE: 55,078

GAME 7, OCT. 27

```
BOS   030  000  020        5   9   0
NY    000  003  32X        8   10  0
```
PITCHERS: Hurst, SCHIRALDI(7), Sambito(7), Stanley(7), Nipper(8), Crawford(8) VS Darling, Fernandez(4), McDOWELL(8), Orosco(8)
ATTENDANCE: 55,032

Game 1. The Mets and Red Sox remained scoreless through six frames on a bitterly cold night at Shea. A leadoff walk put Rice on first, then Ron Darling's wild pitch moved him to second before a routine grounder went through second baseman Tim Teufel's legs and Rice beat the throw to the plate. Hurst allowed four hits and four walks through eight innings, but no runs. Schiraldi finished off his former teammates in the ninth.

Game 2. When the ballyhooed duel between "The Rocket" and "Dr. K" devolved into a slugfest, Boston manager John McNamara moved to keep the Mets from answering back. With two runners on, Gary Carter up, and Boston leading 6–2 in the fifth, McNamara replaced Clemens with Steve Crawford. Carter singled in a run, but Crawford escaped further damage and Boston rolled. Dave Henderson, Dwight Evans, and Wade Boggs each drove in two runs.

Game 3. With the Mets down two games to none, Len Dykstra homered, Carter poked a long run-scoring double, the Red Sox botched a rundown, and Danny Heep, the first designated hitter in Mets history, singled in two runs—and that was just the first inning. Ojeda stifled the Red Sox in his return to Boston as New York won handily.

Game 4. Carter homered twice and doubled as the Mets evened the Series. Darling pitching seven shutout innings; the Red Sox managed only one futile threat in the eighth. With Al Nipper ineffective, like Oil Can Boyd the night before, it was clear that Boston's second-line pitching couldn't cut it.

Game 5. Hurst earned Boston its first victory at Fenway in a World Series game since Carlton's Fisk famous home run in 1975, going the distance. Meanwhile Gooden, pitching on three-day's rest, was knocked out in the fifth after allowing a dozen base runners.

Game 6. Clemens was up by a run when McNamara removed him after seven innings. Reliever Schiraldi's bounced throw on a bunt set up the tying run in the eighth. Dave Henderson homered and Marty Barrett knocked in an insurance run in the 10th inning for Boston. Schiraldi retired the first two Mets in the bottom of the inning before allowing three straights hits. With Bob Stanley pitching, Boston still needed just one strike for the championship when Stanley's inside pitch eluded catcher Gedman to tie the game. When Mookie Wilson's routine grounder rolled between first baseman Buckner's aging legs to win the game, it evened the Series and spawned yet another sad saga in BoSox history.

Game 7. A day of rain enabled the Red Sox to bring back Hurst on three day's rest. The southpaw allowed only one hit through five innings as the Sox scored three times in the second on consecutive home runs by Evans and Gedman and an RBI-single by Boggs—the first earned runs in the World Series against Darling. While Sid Fernandez held Boston hitless, the Mets rallied against Hurst. Keith Hernandez lined a two-run single; the tying run scored on a unconventional fielder's choice. Ray Knight, the Series MVP, broke the tie with a home run. The Mets added two more runs, but Evans doubled in a pair in the eighth to make it a one-run game with none out. Jesse Orosco retired the last six Boston batters—and singled in a run, to boot—to give the Mets the world championship.

⚾ ⚾ ⚾

1988 American League Championship Series, Boston Red Sox vs. Oakland Athletics

The Red Sox seemed stuck in the malaise that had engulfed them since the devastating loss in the 1986 World Series. By mid-July the team was in fourth place and nine games out when manager John McNamara was finally let go. Longtime minor league manager Joe Morgan took over as manager in Beantown while the club considered more prominent replacements. The Red Sox reeled off 12 victories in a row and won 24 straight at Fenway Park (five of those of McNamara's account). "Morgan Magic" consumed Boston and "Walpole Joe" was anointed full-time skipper. The Red Sox played nearly .600 ball after the change and squeaked past the ancient Tigers by a game for the American League East crown.

Oakland had changed a lot since they'd met Boston in the 1975 ALCS. That team had been at the end of its run, soon to lose its best players to newfound free agency. They'd lost 108 games in a season, been sold, thrived and then died under "Billyball" before rebuilding under cerebral skipper Tony La Russa. The Athletics—no longer the just the A's—won 104 games, the most by the franchise since Connie Mack's last pennant in Philadelphia in 1931. Oakland had the first 40–40 player—a base-stealing, homer-hitting Jose Canseco—who was paired with a quieter "Bash Brother," Mark McGwire. The pitching, with 21-game winner Dave Stewart and 45-save closer Dennis Eckersley, was the best in the league.

The ALCS was about as one-sided in 1988 as it had been in 1975, only with Oakland paddling Boston this time. Former Red Sox stars hurt the Olde Town Team: Dave Henderson and Carney Lansford combined to bat .333 with several key hits, while Eckersley, a 20-game winner in Boston, shut down his former club in each game.

OAK (W)

PLAYER, POS	G	AB	R	H	2B	3B	HR	RBI	BB	SO	SB	AVG	OBP
C.Lansford, 3b	4	17	4	5	1	0	1	2	0	2	0	.294	.294
J.Canseco, of	4	16	4	5	1	0	3	4	1	2	1	.313	.353
D.Henderson, of	4	16	2	6	1	0	1	4	1	7	0	.375	.412
M.McGwire, 1b	4	15	4	5	0	0	1	3	1	5	0	.333	.375
W.Weiss, ss	4	15	2	5	2	0	0	2	0	4	0	.333	.333
M.Gallego, 2b	4	12	1	1	0	0	0	0	0	3	0	.083	.083
D.Parker, dh-of	3	12	1	3	1	0	0	0	0	4	0	.250	.250
R.Hassey, c	4	8	2	4	1	0	1	3	1	1	0	.500	.556
T.Phillips, of-2b	2	7	0	2	1	0	0	0	1	3	0	.286	.375
D.Baylor, dh	2	6	0	0	0	0	0	0	1	2	0	.000	.143
L.Polonia, of	3	5	0	2	0	0	0	0	0	1	0	.400	.500
S.Javier, of	2	4	0	2	0	0	0	1	1	0	0	.500	.600
T.Steinbach, c	2	4	0	1	0	0	0	0	2	0	0	.250	.500
TOTALS		137	20	41	8	0	7	20	10	35	1	.299	.347

PITCHER	W	L	ERA	G	GS	SV	IP	H	BB	SO
D.Stewart	1	0	1.35	2	2	0	13.1	9	6	11
S.Davis	0	0	0.00	1	1	0	6.1	2	5	4
D.Eckersley	0	0	0.00	4	0	4	6.0	1	2	5
G.Nelson	2	0	0.00	2	0	0	4.2	5	1	0
R.Honeycutt	1	0	0.00	3	0	0	2.0	0	2	0
B.Welch	0	0	27.00	1	1	0	1.2	6	2	0
C.Young	0	0	0.00	1	0	0	1.1	1	0	2
G.Cadaret	0	0	27.00	1	0	0	0.1	1	0	0
E.Plunk	0	0	0.00	1	0	0	0.1	1	0	1
TOTALS	4	0	2.00	16	4	4	36.0	26	18	23

BOS (E)

PLAYER, POS	G	AB	R	H	2B	3B	HR	RBI	BB	SO	SB	AVG	OBP
E.Burks, of	4	17	2	4	1	0	0	0	0	3	0	.235	.235
M.Barrett, 2b	4	15	2	1	0	0	0	0	1	0	0	.067	.125
R.Gedman, c	4	14	1	5	0	0	1	1	2	1	0	.357	.438
M.Greenwell, of	4	14	2	3	1	0	1	3	3	0	0	.214	.353
W.Boggs, 3b	4	13	2	5	0	0	0	3	3	4	0	.385	.500
J.Rice, dh	4	13	0	2	0	0	0	1	2	4	0	.154	.267
D.Evans, of	4	12	1	2	1	0	0	1	3	5	0	.167	.333
T.Benzinger, 1b	4	11	0	1	0	0	0	0	1	3	0	.091	.167
J.Reed, ss	4	11	1	3	1	0	0	0	2	1	0	.273	.385
L.Parrish, 1b	4	6	0	0	0	0	0	0	0	2	0	.000	.000
S.Owen, dh	1	0	0	0	0	0	0	0	1	0	0	.000	1.000
E.Romero, pr	1	0	0	0	0	0	0	0	0	0	0	.000	.000
K.Romine, pr	2	0	1	0	0	0	0	0	0	0	0	.000	.000
TOTALS		126	11	26	4	0	2	10	18	23	0	.206	.310

PITCHER	W	L	ERA	G	GS	SV	IP	H	BB	SO
B.Hurst	0	2	2.77	2	2	0	13.0	10	5	12
R.Clemens	0	0	3.86	1	1	0	7.0	6	0	8
W.Gardner	0	0	5.79	1	0	0	4.2	6	2	8
L.Smith	0	1	8.10	2	0	0	3.1	6	1	4
M.Boddicker	0	1	20.25	1	1	0	2.2	8	1	2
M.Smithson	0	0	0.00	1	0	0	2.1	3	0	1
B.Stanley	0	0	9.00	2	0	0	1.0	2	1	0
TOTALS	0	4	5.29	10	4	0	34.0	41	10	35

1988 CHAMPIONSHIP SERIES - OAK(W) DEFEATS BOS(E), 4 GAMES TO 0

GAME 1, OCT. 5

```
OAK   000   100   010      2   6   0
BOS   000   000   100      1   6   0
```

PITCHERS: Stewart, HONEYCUTT(7), Eckersley(8) VS HURST

ATTENDANCE: 34,104

GAME 2, OCT. 6

```
OAK   000   000   301      4   10   1
BOS   000   000   002   100   3   4   1
```

PITCHERS: Davis, Cadaret(7), NELSON(7), Eckersley(9) VS Clemens, Stanley(8), SMITH(8)

ATTENDANCE: 34,605

GAME 3, OCT. 8

```
BOS   320   000   100      6   12   0
OAK   042   010   12X      10   15   1
```

PITCHERS: BODDICKER, Gardner(3), Stanley(8) VS Welch, NELSON(2), Young(6), Plunk(7), Honeycutt(7), Eckersley(8)

ATTENDANCE: 49,261

GAME 4, OCT. 9

```
BOS   000   001   000      1   4   0
OAK   101   000   02X      4   10   1
```

PITCHERS: HURST, Smithson(5), Smith(7) VS STEWART, Honeycutt(8), Eckersley(9)

ATTENDANCE: 49,406

Game 1. Bruce Hurst and Dave Stewart performed as advertised. Canseco homered off Hurst in the fourth inning, and the Red Sox nicked Oakland for their only run in the seventh. The next inning, though, old friends Lansford and Henderson put together the go-ahead rally. Eckersley pitched the last two innings, allowing only a two-out double to Jody Reed (the only hit he allowed in four appearances).

Game 2. Pitching dominated the first six innings. Boston scored the first run of the game on a two-out error by Henderson in the sixth. Ellis Burks followed with a single to make it 2–0, but the lead lasted only two batters as Henderson singled off Roger Clemens to start the seventh and Canseco followed with a home run. Lansford later singled and scored when McGwire, batting seventh despite his 32 home runs, singled to give Oakland the lead. Storm Davis, with just two hits allowed (and five walks), left after striking out Reed to start the seventh. Lefty Greg Cadaret came in to face Rich Gedman, who homered to tie the game. Walt Weiss singled in the go-ahead run off Lee Smith in the ninth, then Eck set down the Sox in order.

Game 3. Mike Greenwell doubled in two runs and homered his first two times up to chase Bob Welch, but Mike Boddicker was just as shaky for Boston. McGwire and Lansford homered in the bottom of the second as Oakland cut the lead to 5–4. Ron Hassey homered the next inning to give the Athletics the lead, before Henderson added a two-run homer in the eighth to give Oakland a comfortable lead.

Game 4. Canseco hit his third homer of the series in the first to get Oakland moving. After Henderson doubled in a run in third, neither team scored again until the Sox managed a run off Stewart in the sixth. The Athletics scored twice in eighth against Smith as the series became a tale of two closers: Smith had an 8.10 ERA and a loss; Eckersley allowed three baserunners in six innings (none going past second base), saved all four games, and became the first reliever to earn the MVP in an LCS.

1990 American League Championship Series, Boston Red Sox vs. Oakland Athletics

Since the Red Sox and Athletics had met in the 1988 ALCS, Oakland had dominated the AL. Although shocked by Los Angeles in the 1988 World Series, Oakland had come back stronger in 1989 and swept San Francisco in the earthquake-interrupted fall classic.

The Red Sox lost a little of the "Morgan Magic" as they slid to third in 1989, but it returned in 1990. Boston's 88 wins, however, were 15 fewer than Oakland's. The season's final weeks provided that same feeling that had emerged during the summer of 1988 when Morgan took over the club and the Sox just couldn't lose at Fenway. Jeff Stone's first hit of the year won a crucial game the final weekend and Tom Brunansky's sliding grab on the

last play of the season had overshadowed the questions heading into the ALCS. Despite the league's highest average, how would the Red Sox match up against Oakland's power? (The trio of Jose Canseco, Mark McGwire, and AL MVP-to-be Rickey Henderson had two fewer home runs than the whole Boston club, 106–104.) Could Roger Clemens put together a top-notch postseason? (In three career postseason series he'd won once as the Sox had lost four of his other five starts.) These answers would come swiftly.

The Athletics were more dominant in the 1990 ALCS than two years earlier, as the Red Sox scored just once each game while the Athletics touched home 20 times. Boston's bullpen was needed plenty but couldn't get key outs and, while Clemens did have a good Game 1, his ejection in the clincher was an embarrassing conclusion to a thrilling year.

OAK (W)

PLAYER, POS	G	AB	R	H	2B	3B	HR	RBI	BB	SO	SB	AVG	OBP
R.Henderson, of	4	17	1	5	0	0	0	3	1	2	2	.294	.333
C.Lansford, 3b	4	16	2	7	1	0	0	2	0	1	0	.438	.438
H.Baines, dh	4	14	2	5	1	0	0	3	2	1	1	.357	.438
M.McGwire, 1b	4	13	2	2	0	0	0	2	3	3	0	.154	.313
J.Canseco, of	4	11	3	2	0	0	0	1	5	5	2	.182	.438
T.Steinbach, c	3	11	2	5	0	0	0	1	1	2	0	.455	.500
M.Gallego, ss-2b	4	10	1	4	1	0	0	2	1	1	0	.400	.455
W.McGee, of-dh	3	9	3	2	1	0	0	0	1	2	2	.222	.300
W.Randolph, 2b	4	8	1	3	0	0	0	3	1	0	0	.375	.444
W.Weiss, ss	2	7	2	0	0	0	0	0	2	2	0	.000	.222
D.Henderson, of	2	6	0	1	0	0	0	1	0	2	1	.167	.250
R.Hassey, c-dh	2	3	0	1	0	0	0	0	2	0	0	.333	.600
D.Jennings, of	1	1	0	0	0	0	0	0	0	0	0	.000	.000
J.Quirk, ph	1	1	0	1	0	0	0	0	0	0	0	1.000	1.000
L.Blankenship, dh	3	0	1	0	0	0	0	0	0	0	1	.000	.000
TOTALS		127	20	38	4	0	0	18	19	21	9	.299	.404

PITCHER	W	L	ERA	G	GS	SV	IP	H	BB	SO
D.Stewart	2	0	1.13	2	2	0	16.0	8	2	4
B.Welch	1	0	1.23	1	1	0	7.1	6	3	4
M.Moore	1	0	1.50	1	1	0	6.0	4	1	5
D.Eckersley	0	0	0.00	3	0	2	3.1	2	0	3
R.Honeycutt	0	0	0.00	3	0	1	1.2	0	0	0
G.Nelson	0	0	0.00	1	0	0	1.2	3	0	0
TOTALS	4	0	1.00	11	4	3	36.0	23	6	16

BOS (E)

PLAYER, POS	G	AB	R	H	2B	3B	HR	RBI	BB	SO	SB	AVG	OBP
W.Boggs, 3b	4	16	1	7	1	0	1	1	1	3	0	.438	.438
E.Burks, of	4	15	1	4	2	0	0	0	1	1	1	.267	.313
J.Reed, 2b-ss	4	15	0	2	0	0	0	1	0	2	0	.133	.133
M.Greenwell, of	4	14	1	0	0	0	0	0	2	2	0	.000	.125
T.Pena, c	4	14	0	3	0	0	0	0	0	0	0	.214	.214
D.Evans, dh	4	13	0	3	1	0	0	0	1	3	0	.231	.286
C.Quintana, 1b	4	13	0	0	0	0	0	1	1	0	0	.000	.071
T.Brunansky, of	4	12	0	1	0	0	0	1	1	3	0	.083	.154
L.Rivera, ss	4	9	1	2	1	0	0	0	0	2	0	.222	.222
M.Marshall, ph	3	3	0	1	0	0	0	0	0	0	0	.333	.333
D.Heep, ph	2	2	0	0	0	0	0	0	0	0	0	.000	.000
M.Barrett, 2b	3	0	0	0	0	0	0	0	0	0	0	.000	.000
R.Kutcher, pr	2	0	0	0	0	0	0	0	0	0	0	.000	.000
TOTALS		126	4	23	5	0	1	4	6	16	1	.183	.220

PITCHER	W	L	ERA	G	GS	SV	IP	H	BB	SO
M.Boddicker	0	1	2.25	1	1	0	8.0	6	3	7
R.Clemens	0	1	3.52	2	2	0	7.2	7	5	4
D.Kiecker	0	0	1.59	1	1	0	5.2	6	1	2
J.Gray	0	0	2.70	2	0	0	3.1	4	1	2
L.Andersen	0	1	6.00	3	0	0	3.0	3	3	3
T.Bolton	0	0	0.00	2	0	0	3.0	2	2	3
J.Reardon	0	0	9.00	1	0	0	2.0	3	1	0
R.Murphy	0	0	13.50	1	0	0	0.2	2	1	0
G.Harris	0	1	27.00	1	0	0	0.1	3	0	0
D.Lamp	0	0	108.00	1	0	0	0.1	2	2	0
TOTALS	0	4	4.50	15	4	0	34.0	38	19	21

1990 CHAMPIONSHIP SERIES - OAK(W) DEFEATS BOS(E), 4 GAMES TO 0

GAME 1, OCT. 6

OAK	000	000	117	9	13	0
BOS	000	100	000	1	5	1

PITCHERS: STEWART, Eckersley(9) VS Clemens, ANDERSEN(7), Bolton(8), Gray(8), Lamp(9), Murphy(9)

ATTENDANCE: 35,192

GAME 2, OCT. 7

OAK	000	100	102	4	13	1
BOS	001	000	000	1	6	1

PITCHERS: WELCH, Honeycutt(8), Eckersley(8) VS Kiecker, HARRIS(6), Andersen(7), Reardon(8)

ATTENDANCE: 35,070

GAME 3, OCT. 9

BOS	010	000	000	1	8	3
OAK	000	202	00X	4	6	0

PITCHERS: BODDICKER VS MOORE, Nelson(7), Honeycutt(8), Eckersley(9)

ATTENDANCE: 49,026

GAME 4, OCT. 10

BOS	000	000	001	1	4	1
OAK	030	000	00X	3	6	0

PITCHERS: CLEMENS, Bolton(2), Gray(5), Andersen(8) VS STEWART, Honeycutt(9)

ATTENDANCE: 49,052

Game 1. Clemens gave the Red Sox six shutout innings. Larry Andersen came in to protect the 1-0 lead that had stood since Wade Boggs' fourth-inning homer, the only home run by either team in the series. Oakland tied it in the seventh on a sac fly by Henderson and took the lead when Carney Lansford singled in a run in the eighth. Things turned ugly in the ninth as the Athletics scored seven times on five hits (two by Henderson), two stolen bases, a passed ball, and an error.

Game 2. Boston led on a Carlos Quintana sacrifice fly in the third inning against Bob Welch. Red Sox rookie Dana Kiecker came out after five innings with the game tied, 1–1. Harold Baines drove in the first three runs for Oakland, with Mark McGwire knocking in the last run in the ninth and Dennis Eckersley recording the final four outs.

Game 3. The Sox scored first for the third straight game, but it didn't end any better in Oakland than it had in Boston. Willie Randolph and Dave Henderson RBIs gave the Athletics the lead in the fourth inning; two unearned runs scored in the sixth inning. Oakland used four pitchers to secure the win while Mike Boddicker went all the way for Boston.

Game 4. In the most bizarre moment of the series, Clemens was ejected in the second inning. Umpire Terry Cooney tossed Clemens as he stood on the mound in the stretch position, cursing the umpire because of a tight strike zone. Tom Bolton, summoned with two on and two out in a 1–0 game, surrendered a double to ninth-place hitter Mike Gallego to make it 3–0. Series MVP Dave Stewart defeated Boston for the third time in four ALCS starts, while Eck notched his sixth save in seven appearances against the Sox in the 1988 and 1990 postseasons.

ℋ ℋ ℋ

1995 American League Division Series, Boston Red Sox vs. Cleveland Indians

After the strike wiped out the 1994 postseason, baseball's return in the spring transmitted more anger than appreciation in many major league cities. So what better way to bring the game back to two old-time hotbeds than by reawakening a couple of franchises?

The Red Sox hadn't won more than 80 games since Joe Morgan was dispatched after the 1991 season. His replacement, Butch Hobson, fared badly and faded away during the strike, replaced by Kevin Kennedy. Boston got great mileage out of retreads Jose Canseco, Erik Hanson,

and Tim Wakefield, plus great production out of shortstop John Valentin and an MVP season from Mo Vaughn (though the vote seemed skewed against the Indians' surly Albert Belle) as the Sox held off the Yankees.

Cleveland had waited since 1954 for a return to the postseason, and the Indians had been in position for the wild card when the 1994 season ended abruptly. The Tribe didn't mess around in 1995. The Indians had great numbers for a reduced 144-game season: 100 wins, 46 saves by Jose Mesa, plus an unprecedented 50 home runs and 50 doubles by Belle. Second-year Jacobs Field set a city attendance record and was second in the AL with 2.8 million; Boston was fourth at 2.1 million. Cleveland was primed for October baseball.

CLE (C)

PLAYER, POS	G	AB	R	H	2B	3B	HR	RBI	BB	SO	SB	AVG	OBP
C.Baerga, 2b	3	14	2	4	1	0	0	1	0	1	0	.286	.286
K.Lofton, of	3	13	1	2	0	0	0	0	1	3	0	.154	.214
E.Murray, dh	3	13	5	5	0	1	1	3	2	1	0	.385	.467
J.Thome, 3b	3	13	1	2	0	0	1	3	1	6	0	.154	.214
M.Ramirez, of	3	12	1	0	0	0	0	0	1	2	0	.000	.077
O.Vizquel, ss	3	12	2	2	1	0	0	4	2	2	1	.167	.286
S.Alomar, c	3	11	1	2	1	0	0	1	0	1	0	.182	.182
A.Belle, of	3	11	3	3	1	0	1	3	4	3	0	.273	.467
P.Sorrento, 1b	3	10	2	3	0	0	0	1	2	3	0	.300	.417
T.Pena, c	2	2	1	1	0	0	1	1	0	0	0	.500	.500
A.Espinoza, 3b	1	1	0	0	0	0	0	0	0	0	0	.000	.000
W.Kirby, of	3	1	0	1	0	0	0	0	0	0	0	1.000	1.000
H.Perry, ph	1	1	0	0	0	0	0	0	0	0	0	.000	.000
TOTALS		114	17	25	4	1	4	17	13	22	1	.219	.321

PITCHER	W	L	ERA	G	GS	SV	IP	H	BB	SO
O.Hershiser	1	0	0.00	1	1	0	7.1	3	2	7
C.Nagy	1	0	1.29	1	1	0	7.0	4	5	6
D.Martinez	0	0	3.00	1	1	0	6.0	5	0	2
J.Tavarez	0	0	6.75	3	0	0	2.2	5	0	3
J.Mesa	0	0	0.00	2	0	0	2.0	0	2	0
P.Assenmacher	0	0	0.00	3	0	0	1.2	0	0	3
J.Poole	0	0	5.40	1	0	0	1.2	2	1	2
K.Hill	1	0	0.00	1	0	0	1.1	1	1	0
E.Plunk	0	0	0.00	1	0	0	1.1	1	1	1
TOTALS	3	0	1.74	14	3	0	31.0	21	11	26

BOS (E)

PLAYER, POS	G	AB	R	H	2B	3B	HR	RBI	BB	SO	SB	AVG	OBP
M.Greenwell, of	3	15	0	3	0	0	0	0	0	1	0	.200	.200
M.Vaughn, 1b	3	14	0	0	0	0	0	0	1	7	0	.000	.067
J.Canseco, dh-of	3	13	0	0	0	0	0	0	2	2	0	.000	.133
T.Naehring, 3b	3	13	2	4	0	0	1	1	0	1	0	.308	.308
D.Hosey, of	3	12	1	0	0	0	0	0	2	3	1	.000	.143
J.Valentin, ss	3	12	1	3	1	0	1	2	3	1	0	.250	.400
L.Alicea, 2b	3	10	1	6	1	0	1	1	2	2	1	.600	.667
M.Macfarlane, c	3	9	0	3	0	0	0	1	0	3	0	.333	.333
L.Tinsley, of	1	5	0	0	0	0	0	0	1	2	0	.000	.167
R.Jefferson, dh	1	4	1	1	0	0	0	0	0	1	0	.250	.250
W.McGee, of	2	4	0	1	0	0	0	1	0	2	0	.250	.250
B.Haselman, c	1	2	0	0	0	0	0	0	0	0	0	.000	.000
M.Stairs, ph	1	1	0	0	0	0	0	0	0	1	0	.000	.000
TOTALS		114	6	21	2	0	3	6	11	26	2	.184	.256

PITCHER	W	L	ERA	G	GS	SV	IP	H	BB	SO
E.Hanson	0	1	4.50	1	1	0	8.0	4	4	5
R.Clemens	0	0	3.86	1	1	0	7.0	5	1	5
T.Wakefield	0	1	11.81	1	1	0	5.1	5	5	4
M.Maddux	0	0	0.00	2	0	0	3.0	2	1	1
M.Stanton	0	0	0.00	1	0	0	2.1	1	0	4
Z.Smith	0	1	6.75	1	0	0	1.1	1	0	0
J.Hudson	0	0	0.00	1	0	0	1.0	2	1	0
R.Aguilera	0	0	13.50	1	0	0	0.2	3	0	1
R.Cormier	0	0	13.50	2	0	0	0.2	2	1	2
S.Belinda	0	0	0.00	1	0	0	0.1	0	0	0
TOTALS	0	3	5.16	12	3	0	29.2	25	13	22

1995 DIVISION SERIES - CLE(C) DEFEATS BOS(E), 3 GAMES TO 0

GAME 1, OCT. 3								
BOS	002	000	010	010	0	4	11	2
CLE	000	003	000	010	1	5	10	2

PITCHERS: Clemens, Cormier(8), Belinda(8), Stanton(8), Aguilera(11), Maddux(11), SMITH(12) VS Martinez, Tavarez(7), Assenmacher(8), Plunk(8), Mesa(10), Poole(11), HILL(12)

ATTENDANCE: 44,218

GAME 2, OCT. 4						
BOS	000	000	000	0	3	1
CLE	000	020	02X	4	4	2

PITCHERS: HANSON VS HERSHISER, Tavarez(8), Assenmacher(8), Mesa(9)

ATTENDANCE: 44,264

GAME 3, OCT. 6						
CLE	021	005	000	8	11	2
BOS	000	100	010	2	7	1

PITCHERS: NAGY, Tavarez(8), Assenmacher(9) VS WAKEFIELD, Cormier(6), Maddux(6), Hudson(9)

ATTENDANCE: 34,211

Game 1. The first postseason game in Cleveland in 41 years was also the first Division Series in major league history. (The four different Division Series games were broadcast simultaneously on the "The Baseball Network.") Two rain delays totaling almost an hour added to the drama and the lateness of the game as it dragged deep into the night. The Red Sox tied it in the eighth on Luis Alicea's home run, just before the second rain delay. Tim Naehring homered for Boston in the top of the 11th, but Belle led off the bottom of the inning with a home run. Former Boston catcher Tony Pena, who didn't enter the game until the 11th inning, homered off Zane Smith to end the 13-inning marathon in its fifth hour.

Game 2. After both teams used seven pitchers the previous night, the hitters helped out by getting just seven hits combined as Game 2 was completed in nearly half the time of the opener. One of those hits was Omar Vizquel's two-run double in the fifth off Hanson to break up a scoreless game. Eddie Murray added a two-run home run in the eighth in support of Orel Hershiser.

Game 3. Wakefield's knuckleball wasn't at its best as the teams moved to Fenway Park. He allowed five walks and five hits, including Jim Thome's two-run homer to open the second inning. The Tribe plated five runs in the sixth to knock out both Wakefield and the Sox as Charles Nagy got the win to end Cleveland's two-generation postseason drought.

1998 American League Division Series, Boston Red Sox vs. Cleveland Indians

Since the Indians and Red Sox had last met in the Division Series, the teams had drawn closer in talent. The Indians had lost Albert Belle to free agency and Dennis Martinez and Eddie Murray had retired. Yet the Tribe had won two pennants in three seasons because they had Manny Ramirez and Omar Vizquel, while Jim Thome had switched corners on the diamond. The Red Sox had a new ace, Pedro Martinez, a more reliable bullpen, a star shortstop in Nomar Garciaparra, and production galore from college buddies Mo Vaughn and John Valentin.

Boston won a game this time—its first postseason win after 13 consecutive losses dating back 13 seasons—but it wasn't much consolation. Cleveland had home-field advantage over wild-card Boston, even though the Sox won three more games than the Indians, as Boston finished 22 games behind a Yankees club that broke Cleveland's 1954 AL record of 111 wins.

The Red Sox outhit the Indians and outscored them 20–18, but Cleveland came from behind in all three wins. Valentin batted .467, Vaughn .412, and Garciaparra .333, accounting for all five home runs and 18 of Boston's 19 RBIs. Four other Sox regulars were missing in action, however, batting .111 or lower and scoring once among them.

CLE (C)

PLAYER, POS	G	AB	R	H	2B	3B	HR	RBI	BB	SO	SB	AVG	OBP
D.Justice, of-dh	4	16	2	5	4	0	1	6	0	1	0	.313	.313
K.Lofton, of	4	16	5	6	1	0	2	4	1	1	2	.375	.412
J.Thome, 1b-dh	4	15	2	2	0	0	2	2	2	5	0	.133	.235
O.Vizquel, ss	4	15	1	1	0	0	0	0	1	0	0	.067	.125
M.Ramirez, of	4	14	2	5	2	0	2	3	1	4	0	.357	.400
S.Alomar, c	4	13	2	3	3	0	0	2	1	4	0	.231	.286
T.Fryman, 3b	4	13	1	2	1	0	0	0	3	4	1	.154	.313
J.Cora, 2b	4	10	2	0	0	0	0	0	3	2	0	.000	.231
B.Giles, of-dh	3	10	1	2	1	0	0	0	1	4	0	.200	.273
R.Sexson, 1b	3	2	0	0	0	0	0	0	0	2	0	.000	.500
E.Wilson, 2b	1	2	0	0	0	0	0	0	0	0	0	.000	.000
TOTALS		126	18	26	12	0	7	17	15	26	3	.206	.306

PITCHER	W	L	ERA	G	GS	SV	IP	H	BB	SO
C.Nagy	1	0	1.13	1	1	0	8.0	4	0	3
B.Colon	0	0	1.59	1	1	0	5.2	5	3	3
D.Burba	1	0	5.06	1	0	0	5.1	4	2	4
J.Wright	0	1	12.46	1	1	0	4.1	7	2	6
M.Jackson	0	0	4.50	3	0	3	4.0	3	1	1
P.Shuey	0	0	0.00	3	0	0	3.0	3	1	4
D.Jones	0	0	6.75	1	0	0	2.2	3	1	1
P.Assenmacher	0	0	0.00	3	0	0	1.0	2	0	2
J.Poole	0	0	0.00	2	0	0	1.0	1	1	2
S.Reed	1	0	40.50	2	0	0	0.2	1	1	1
D.Gooden	0	0	54.00	1	0	0	0.1	1	2	1
TOTALS	3	1	5.00	19	4	3	36.0	34	14	28

BOS (E)

PLAYER, POS	G	AB	R	H	2B	3B	HR	RBI	BB	SO	SB	AVG	OBP
M.Vaughn, 1b	4	17	3	7	2	0	2	7	1	5	0	.412	.444
T.O'Leary, of	4	16	0	1	0	0	0	0	1	4	0	.063	.118
N.Garciaparra, ss	4	15	4	5	1	0	3	11	1	0	0	.333	.375
M.Stanley, dh	4	15	1	4	0	0	0	0	2	5	0	.267	.353
J.Valentin, 3b	4	15	5	7	1	0	0	0	3	1	0	.467	.556
D.Lewis, of	4	14	4	5	2	0	0	1	1	3	1	.357	.400
D.Bragg, of	3	12	0	1	0	0	0	0	0	5	0	.083	.083
M.Benjamin, 2b-1b	4	11	1	1	0	0	0	0	1	3	0	.091	.167
S.Hatteberg, c	3	9	0	1	0	0	0	0	3	1	0	.111	.333
J.Varitek, c	1	4	0	1	0	0	0	1	0	1	0	.250	.250
M.Cummings, ph	3	3	0	0	0	0	0	0	0	0	0	.000	.000
T.Nixon, of	2	3	0	1	0	0	0	0	1	0	0	.333	.500
D.Buford, of-dh	3	1	2	0	0	0	0	0	0	0	0	.000	.000
D.Sadler, 2b	3	0	0	0	0	0	0	0	0	0	0	.000	.000
TOTALS		135	20	34	6	0	5	19	14	28	1	.252	.331

PITCHER	W	L	ERA	G	GS	SV	IP	H	BB	SO
P.Martinez	1	0	3.86	1	1	0	7.0	6	0	8
B.Saberhagen	0	1	3.86	1	1	0	7.0	4	1	7
P.Schourek	0	0	0.00	1	1	0	5.1	2	4	1
D.Lowe	0	0	2.08	2	0	0	4.1	3	1	2
J.Corsi	0	0	0.00	2	0	0	3.0	1	1	2
T.Gordon	0	1	9.00	2	0	0	3.0	4	4	1
J.Wasdin	0	0	10.80	1	0	0	1.2	2	1	2
G.Swindell	0	0	0.00	1	0	0	1.1	0	1	1
T.Wakefield	0	1	33.75	1	1	0	1.1	3	2	1
D.Eckersley	0	0	9.00	1	0	0	1.0	1	0	1
TOTALS	1	3	4.63	13	4	0	35.0	26	15	26

1998 DIVISION SERIES - CLE(C) DEFEATS BOS(E), 3 GAMES TO 1

GAME 1, SEPT.T 2

BOS	300	032	030	11	12	0
CLE	000	002	100	3	7	0

PITCHERS: MARTINEZ, Corsi(8) VS WRIGHT, Jones(5), Reed(8), Assenmacher(8), Poole(8), Shuey(8), Assenmacher(9)

ATTENDANCE: 45,185

GAME 2, SEPT.T 3

BOS	201	002	000	5	10	0
CLE	151	001	01X	9	9	1

PITCHERS: WAKEFIELD, Wasdin(2), Lowe(4), Swindell(6), Gordon(8) VS Gooden, BURBA(1), Shuey(6), Assenmacher(8), Jackson(8)

ATTENDANCE: 45,229

GAME 3, OCT. 2

CLE	000	011	101	4	5	0
BOS	000	100	002	3	6	0

PITCHERS: NAGY, Jackson(9) VS SABERHAGEN, Corsi(8), Eckersley(9)

ATTENDANCE: 33,114

GAME 4, OCT. 3

CLE	000	000	020	2	5	0
BOS	000	100	000	1	6	0

PITCHERS: Colon, Poole(6), REED(7), Shuey(8), Jackson(9) VS Schourek, Lowe(6), GORDON(8)

ATTENDANCE: 33,537

Game 1. The Red Sox took quick action. Mo Vaughn launched a three-run homer before Martinez even threw a pitch. Boston had an 8–0 lead—on Garciaparra's homer and Vaughn's second blast of the day—before Cleveland scored. Vaughn doubled in two runs in the eighth for a seven-RBI day for Boston's first postseason win since Game 5 of the 1986 World Series.

Game 2. Cleveland starter Dwight Gooden and manager Mike Hargrove were ejected for arguing balls and strikes in the first inning. The Red Sox had a 2–0 lead and 17-game winner Wakefield on the mound, but his knuckleball proved very hittable and he was gone by the second inning. His replacement, John Wasdin, didn't help, surrendering a three-run homer to the first batter, David Justice. Dave Burba, Gooden's replacement, faltered in the sixth, but the Indians escaped with the lead and tacked on a run in the bottom of the inning on an RBI-double by Ramirez.

Game 3. Boston took a 1–0 lead on a groundout in the fourth inning, the only run Nagy allowed in eight innings. Cleveland scored single runs in four of the last five innings on homers by Thome, Kenny Lofton, and two by Ramirez. Vaughn launched his last home run in a Boston uniform with one on in the ninth before Michael Jackson retired the next two batters for the Tribe.

Game 4. Boston scored first for the fourth straight game when Garciaparra smacked a fourth-inning home run off Bartolo Colon. Journeyman Pete Schourek started because Boston manager Jimy Williams wanted to have Martinez on regular rest for a potential Game 5. Schourek pitched shutout ball into the sixth inning, then Derek Lowe retired the next five batters and Tom Gordon, who'd broken the major league mark with 44 consecutive saves, came in to begin the eighth. Justice lined a two-run double to give Cleveland the lead, then the Indians survived a jam in the eighth and Jackson retired the Sox in order in the ninth to clinch the series.

ⓧ ⓧ ⓧ

1999 American League Division Series, Boston Red Sox vs. Cleveland Indians

Since the 1986 ALCS, the Red Sox had lost five straight postseason series, including two Division Series to Cleveland. The third time proved to be the charm.

The Indians, champions of the AL Central for the fifth straight year, won 97 games and finished with an enormous 21½-game lead. They seemed more focused on the Yankees, whom they had met the past two post-seasons and who were again laying waste to Texas just as the Red Sox-Indians ALDS got interesting.

After Cleveland won the first two games at The Jake, a seismic shift occurred during Boston's six-run, seventh inning in Game 3 at Fenway. From the bottom of the seventh onward, the Red Sox outscored the Indians, 41–18 the rest of the series, including the biggest post-season output in baseball history in Game 4 that evened

the series. When it was over, the Red Sox had won the ALDS with a sorry 6.02 ERA, but Cleveland's was even more bloated at 9.63. John Valentin, the only regular who played in the two previous Division Series losses to Cleveland, batted .500 and drove in 12 runs. As a result, the Indians fired manager Mike Hargrove, who took a team that had gone four decades without finishing first to five straight division titles.

BOS (E)

PLAYER, POS	G	AB	R	H	2B	3B	HR	RBI	BB	SO	SB	AVG	OBP
J.Valentin, 3b	5	22	6	7	2	0	3	12	0	4	0	.318	.318
J.Varitek, c	5	21	7	5	3	0	1	3	0	4	0	.238	.238
T.O'Leary, of	5	20	4	4	0	0	2	7	2	3	0	.200	.273
M.Stanley, 1b	5	20	4	10	2	1	0	2	2	3	0	.500	.545
J.Offerman, 2b	5	18	4	7	1	0	1	6	7	0	0	.389	.560
B.Daubach, dh-1b	4	16	3	4	2	0	1	3	0	7	0	.250	.250
D.Lewis, of	4	16	5	6	1	0	0	2	0	2	1	.375	.375
T.Nixon, of	5	14	5	3	3	0	0	6	4	5	0	.214	.389
N.Garciaparra, ss	5	12	6	5	2	0	2	4	3	3	0	.417	.533
L.Merloni, ss	3	6	1	2	0	0	0	1	1	1	0	.333	.429
B.Huskey, dh	2	5	0	1	0	0	0	0	0	1	0	.200	.200
D.Buford, of	1	3	0	0	0	0	0	0	0	1	0	.000	.000
D.Sadler, 3b-dh	2	2	1	1	0	0	0	0	0	1	0	.500	.500
S.Hatteberg, c	1	1	1	1	0	0	0	1	0	0	0	1.000	1.000
TOTALS		**176**	**47**	**56**	**17**	**1**	**10**	**47**	**19**	**35**	**1**	**.318**	**.394**

PITCHER	W	L	ERA	G	GS	SV	IP	H	BB	SO
P.Martinez	1	0	0.00	2	1	0	10.0	3	4	11
D.Lowe	1	1	4.32	3	0	0	8.1	6	1	7
R.Martinez	0	0	3.18	1	1	0	5.2	5	3	6
R.Cormier	0	0	0.00	2	0	0	4.0	2	1	4
B.Saberhagen	0	1	27.00	2	2	0	3.2	9	4	2
R.Garces	1	0	3.86	2	0	0	2.1	2	3	2
R.Beck	0	0	0.00	2	0	0	2.0	2	0	2
T.Gordon	0	0	4.50	2	0	0	2.0	1	1	3
T.Wakefield	0	0	13.50	2	0	0	2.0	3	4	4
K.Mercker	0	0	10.80	1	1	0	1.2	3	3	1
J.Wasdin	0	0	27.00	2	0	0	1.2	2	4	1
TOTALS	**3**	**2**	**6.02**	**21**	**5**	**0**	**43.1**	**38**	**28**	**43**

CLE (C)

PLAYER, POS	G	AB	R	H	2B	3B	HR	RBI	BB	SO	SB	AVG	OBP
O.Vizquel, ss	5	21	3	5	1	1	0	3	2	3	0	.238	.304
R.Alomar, 2b	5	19	4	7	0	0	0	3	2	3	2	.368	.429
M.Ramirez, of	5	18	5	1	1	0	0	1	4	8	0	.056	.227
J.Thome, 1b	5	17	7	6	0	0	4	10	4	5	0	.353	.476
K.Lofton, of	5	16	5	2	1	0	0	1	5	6	2	.125	.333
T.Fryman, 3b	5	15	2	4	0	0	1	4	3	2	1	.267	.400
S.Alomar, c	5	14	1	2	0	0	0	1	2	6	0	.143	.250
H.Baines, dh	4	14	1	5	0	0	1	4	2	1	0	.357	.438
W.Cordero, dh-of	3	9	3	5	0	0	1	2	1	2	0	.556	.600
D.Justice, of	3	8	0	0	0	0	0	1	2	2	0	.000	.200
R.Sexson, 1b-of	3	6	1	1	0	0	0	1	1	3	0	.167	.286
D.Roberts, of	2	3	0	0	0	0	0	0	0	2	0	.000	.000
E.Wilson, 2b	3	2	0	0	0	0	0	0	0	0	0	.000	.000
E.Diaz, c	2	1	0	0	0	0	0	0	0	0	0	.000	.000
TOTALS		**163**	**32**	**38**	**7**	**1**	**7**	**31**	**28**	**43**	**5**	**.233**	**.351**

PITCHER	W	L	ERA	G	GS	SV	IP	H	BB	SO
C.Nagy	1	0	7.20	2	2	0	10.0	11	2	6
B.Colon	0	1	9.00	2	2	0	9.0	11	4	12
S.DePaula	0	0	1.80	3	0	0	5.0	2	3	5
D.Burba	0	0	0.00	1	1	0	4.0	1	1	0
P.Shuey	1	1	11.25	3	0	0	4.0	4	4	5
S.Karsay	0	1	9.00	2	0	0	3.0	5	1	3
S.Reed	0	0	30.86	2	0	0	2.1	9	1	1
M.Jackson	0	0	4.50	2	0	0	2.0	2	3	2
J.Wright	0	1	22.50	1	0	0	2.0	4	1	1
P.Assenmacher	0	0	27.00	1	0	0	1.0	5	0	0
R.Rincon	0	0	40.50	1	0	0	0.2	2	1	1
TOTALS	**2**	**3**	**9.63**	**20**	**5**	**0**	**43.0**	**56**	**19**	**35**

1999 DIVISION SERIES - BOS(E) DEFEATS CLE(C), 3 GAMES TO 2

GAME 1, OCT. 6

BOS	010	100	000	2	5	1
CLE	000	002	001	3	6	1

PITCHERS: P.Martinez, LOWE(5), Cormier(9), Garces(9) VS Colon, SHUEY(9)

ATTENDANCE: 45,182

GAME 2, OCT. 7

BOS	001	000	000	1	6	0
CLE	006	500	00X	11	8	0

PITCHERS: SABERHAGEN, Wasdin(3), Wakefield(5), Gordon(7), Beck(8) VS NAGY, Karsay(8), Jackson(9)

ATTENDANCE: 45,184

GAME 3, OCT. 9

CLE	000	101	100	3	9	1
BOS	000	021	60X	9	11	2

PITCHERS: Burba, WRIGHT((5), Rincon(7), DePaula(7), Reed(8) VS R.Martinez, LOWE(6), Beck(9)

ATTENDANCE: 33,539

GAME 4, OCT. 10

CLE	110	040	001	7	8	0
BOS	253	530	32X	23	24	0

PITCHERS: COLON, Karsay(2), Reed(4), DePaula(5), Assenmacher(7), Shuey(8) VS Mercker, GARCES(2), Wakefield(5), Wasdin(5), Cormier(5), Gordon(9)

ATTENDANCE: 33,898

GAME 5, OCT. 11

BOS	205	100	301	12	10	0
CLE	323	000	000	8	7	1

PITCHERS: Saberhagen, Lowe(2), P.MARTINEZ(4) VS Nagy, DePaula(4), SHUEY(7), Jackson(9)

ATTENDANCE: 45,114

Game 1. Pedro Martinez was forced to leave the game after four innings with a strained back as the Sox held a 2–0 lead. Valentin's sixth-inning throwing error put a runner on base for Jim Thome, who launched a home run off Derek Lowe to tie the game. Travis Fryman drove in the decisive run of the opener in the bottom of the ninth with a single.

Game 2. Bret Saberhagen was knocked out in the third inning in a drubbing that cried out for the 10-run rule (though it wouldn't be the last game in the series that could have used the "mercy rule"). Boston actually held a brief lead in the third before the Indians went ahead on a two-run triple by Omar Vizquel, then salted the game away on a three-run homer by Harold Baines.

Cleveland scored five times off John Wasdin the next inning, capped by Thome's grand slam.

Game 3. The Red Sox and Indians jockeyed back and forth through the first six innings. The Indians tied the game in the top of the seventh and had a chance to get out of a jam in the bottom of the inning. Valentin, whose poor throw had allowed Cleveland to tie the game, laced a two-out double to plate two runs. Brian Daubach followed with a three-run homer, Lou Merloni collected an RBI-single, and there would be no sweep.

Game 4. Boston put together the greatest postseason scoring display with a 23–7 Sunday night win that saw the Sox outscore 19 NFL teams that played earlier that

day. It was also more runs than the Red Sox had scored in any of the four previous postseason *series* they'd played since 1986. Cleveland's first-inning lead lasted two batters. Valentin homered with one aboard, starting a night in which he drove in seven and clubbed two homers. Trot Nixon and Jose Offerman each had five RBIs, Mike Stanley collected five hits, and Jason Varitek scored five runs. Boston scored in every inning except the sixth. Even with the one-sided laugher, both teams used six pitchers.

Game 5. Despite the change in venue to Cleveland, the offensive barrage continued. Again, neither starter lasted long, but the Red Sox had a secret weapon: Pedro Martinez. After leaving Game 1 due to back problems, Martinez came out of the bullpen in the fourth and tossed six innings of no-hit relief in one of the most masterful October performances ever seen. Rookie Sean DePaula pitched three shutout innings for the Indians to maintain an 8–8 tie, but the Red Sox surged ahead after Paul Shuey replaced him. Troy O'Leary's three-run blast in the seventh—his grand slam in the third had erased a 5–2 deficit—propelled the Sox into the lead for good. O'Leary's .200 batting average in the series was the lowest of any of the seven players who started all five games.

1999 American League Championship Series, Boston Red Sox vs. New York Yankees

The Red Sox and Yankees took their 96-year-old rivalry into mid-October for the first time. Not that the fierce hatred between the clubs' passionate fans hadn't engendered nasty thoughts about the other through many a long winter. The creation of the wild card had made it possible for the East Division rivals to meet in a postseason series separate from the regular season. In 1999, the Yankees steamrolled Texas and the Red Sox rose from the dead to win three straight against Cleveland after being down two games to none.

The results of this first postseason meeting only fed the angst that had been gnawing at Boston fans since the Sox sold a certain prized slugger to New York during the winter of 1920. The Yankees rallied late to win each of the first two games in the Bronx. The three at Fenway Park were one-sided. Boston's 13-spot in Game 3 gave some pleasure to the Fenway faithful by paddling their once-beloved Roger Clemens. Outside that 21-hit barrage, however, Yankees pitching limited Boston to just eight runs in the other four games.

The Yankees scored 15 of their 23 from the seventh inning on, while the Red Sox did not score against five New York relievers not named Irabu. The Red Sox also set an LCS mark with 10 errors. Boston's only consolation was dealing the Yanks their lone blemish on an otherwise perfect October where they swept the Rangers and the Braves. Fans on both sides of the rivalry will attest, however, that there can be no moral victories between the Bombers and the Carmines.

NY (E)

PLAYER, POS	G	AB	R	H	2B	3B	HR	RBI	BB	SO	SB	AVG	OBP
P.O'Neill, of	5	21	2	6	0	0	0	1	1	5	0	.286	.318
D.Jeter, ss	5	20	3	7	1	0	1	3	2	3	0	.350	.409
B.Williams, of	5	20	3	5	1	0	1	2	2	5	1	.250	.318
T.Martinez, 1b	5	19	3	5	1	0	1	3	2	4	0	.263	.333
S.Brosius, 3b	5	18	3	4	0	1	2	3	1	4	0	.222	.263
C.Knoblauch, 2b	5	18	3	6	1	0	0	1	3	0	1	.333	.429
C.Davis, dh	5	11	0	1	0	0	0	1	3	4	0	.091	.286
J.Posada, c	3	10	1	1	0	0	1	2	1	2	0	.100	.182
S.Spencer, of	3	9	1	1	0	0	0	0	1	6	0	.111	.200
J.Girardi, c	3	8	0	2	0	0	0	0	0	2	0	.250	.250
R.Ledee, of	3	8	2	2	0	0	1	4	1	4	0	.250	.333
C.Curtis, of-dh	3	6	1	0	0	0	0	0	0	2	1	.000	.000
D.Strawberry, dh	3	6	1	2	0	0	1	1	1	2	0	.333	.429
C.Bellinger, dh-ss	3	1	0	0	0	0	0	0	0	1	0	.000	.000
L.Sojo, 2b	2	1	0	0	0	0	0	0	0	0	0	.000	.000
TOTALS		**176**	**23**	**42**	**4**	**1**	**8**	**21**	**18**	**44**	**3**	**.239**	**.313**

PITCHER	W	L	ERA	G	GS	SV	IP	H	BB	SO
O.Hernandez	1	0	1.80	2	2	0	15.0	12	6	13
A.Pettitte	1	0	2.45	1	1	0	7.1	8	1	5
D.Cone	1	0	2.57	1	1	0	7.0	7	3	9
H.Irabu	0	0	13.50	1	0	0	4.2	13	0	3
M.Rivera	1	0	0.00	3	0	2	4.2	5	0	3
R.Mendoza	0	0	0.00	2	0	1	2.1	0	0	2
R.Clemens	0	1	22.50	1	1	0	2.0	6	2	2
A.Watson	0	0	0.00	3	0	0	1.0	2	2	1
J.Nelson	0	0	0.00	2	0	0	0.2	0	0	0
M.Stanton	0	0	0.00	3	0	0	0.1	1	1	0
TOTALS	**4**	**1**	**3.80**	**19**	**5**	**3**	**45.0**	**54**	**15**	**38**

BOS (E)

PLAYER, POS	G	AB	R	H	2B	3B	HR	RBI	BB	SO	SB	AVG	OBP
J.Offerman, 2b	5	24	4	11	0	1	0	2	1	3	1	.458	.480
J.Valentin, 3b	5	23	3	8	2	0	1	5	2	4	0	.348	.400
N.Garciaparra, ss	5	20	2	8	2	0	2	5	2	2	1	.400	.455
T.O'Leary, of	5	20	2	7	3	0	0	1	2	5	0	.350	.409
J.Varitek, c	5	20	1	4	1	1	1	1	1	4	0	.200	.238
M.Stanley, 1b	5	18	1	4	0	0	0	1	2	4	0	.222	.300
B.Daubach, dh-1b	5	17	2	3	1	0	1	3	1	4	0	.176	.222
D.Lewis, of	5	17	2	2	1	0	0	1	1	3	1	.118	.167
T.Nixon, of	5	14	2	4	2	0	0	1	5	0	0	.286	.333
D.Buford, of	4	5	1	2	0	0	0	0	0	2	1	.400	.400
B.Huskey, dh	4	5	1	1	1	0	0	0	1	1	0	.200	.333
S.Hatteberg, c	3	1	0	0	0	0	0	0	1	0	0	.000	.000
L.Merloni, ph	1	0	0	0	0	0	0	0	1	0	0	.000	1.000
D.Sadler, of-dh	2	0	0	0	0	0	0	0	0	0	0	.000	.000
TOTALS		**184**	**21**	**54**	**13**	**2**	**5**	**19**	**15**	**38**	**4**	**.293**	**.350**

PITCHER	W	L	ERA	G	GS	SV	IP	H	BB	SO
K.Mercker	0	1	4.70	2	2	0	7.2	12	4	5
P.Martinez	1	0	0.00	1	1	0	7.0	2	1	12
R.Martinez	0	1	4.05	1	1	0	6.2	6	3	5
D.Lowe	0	0	1.42	3	0	0	6.1	6	2	7
B.Saberhagen	0	1	1.50	1	1	0	6.0	5	1	5
R.Cormier	0	0	0.00	4	0	0	3.2	3	4	4
R.Garces	0	0	12.00	2	0	0	3.0	3	1	2
T.Gordon	0	0	13.50	3	0	0	2.0	3	1	3
P.Rapp	0	0	0.00	1	0	0	1.0	0	1	1
R.Beck	0	1	27.00	2	0	0	0.2	2	0	1
TOTALS	**1**	**4**	**3.68**	**20**	**5**	**0**	**44.0**	**42**	**18**	**44**

1999 CHAMPIONSHIP SERIES - NY (E) DEFEATS BOS(E), 4 GAMES TO 1

GAME 1, OCT. 13						
BOS	210 000 000 0		3	8	2
NY	020 000 100 1		4	10	1

PITCHERS: Mercker, Garces(5), Lowe(7), Cormier(9), BECK(10) VS Hernandez, RIVERA(9)

ATTENDANCE: 57,181

GAME 2, OCT. 14					
BOS	000 020 000	2	10	0
NY	000 100 20X	3	7	0

PITCHERS: R.MARTINEZ, Gordon(7), Cormier(7) VS CONE, Stanton(8), Nelson(8), Watson(8), Mendoza(8), Rivera(9)

ATTENDANCE: 57,180

GAME 3, OCT. 16					
NY	000 000 010	1	3	3
BOS	222 021 40X	13	21	1

PITCHERS: CLEMENS, Irabu(3), Stanton(7), Watson(8) VS P.MARTINEZ, Gordon(8), Rapp(9)

ATTENDANCE: 33,190

GAME 4, OCT. 17					
NY	010 200 006	9	11	0
BOS	011 000 000	2	10	3

PITCHERS: PETTITTE, Rivera(8) VS SABERHAGEN, Lowe(7), Cormier(8), Garces(8), Beck(9)

ATTENDANCE: 33,586

GAME 5, OCT. 18					
NY	200 000 202	6	11	1
BOS	000 000 010	1	5	2

PITCHERS: HERNANDEZ, Stanton(8), Nelson(8), Watson(8), Mendoza(8) VS MERCKER, Lowe(4), Cormier(7), Gordon(9)

ATTENDANCE: 33,589

Game 1. The Sox took an early 3–0 lead after two against Orlando Hernandez but did not score again. Kent Mercker gave two runs back on a homer to ninth-place hitter Scott Brosius in the bottom of the second. Brosius put an even bigger hurt on the Red Sox when he slammed into catcher Jason Varitek and dislodged the ball for the tying run in the seventh. Bernie Williams homered off Rod Beck in the 10th for the 'W'.

Game 2. Boston sent Martinez to the mound; unfortunately for Boston, it was brother Ramon and not super-star Pedro. Ramon did hold a lead in the seventh until Chuck Knoblauch's two-out double tied the game. Paul O'Neill singled off Tom Gordon for the lead. After David Cone threw seven innings, the Yankees used four pitchers to piece together a scoreless eighth. Mariano Rivera allowed a pair of two-out hits in the ninth, but he ended the game by fanning Damon Buford.

Game 3. Clemens, who'd left Boston for Toronto as a free agent and then complained enough to get traded to the Yankees in 1999, was howled at during his long walk to the dugout when Yankees skipper Joe Torre replaced him in the third inning. Irabu, high-priced import relegated to mop-up duty, absorbed 13 hits; starting with a home run to the first batter he faced, Brian Daubach. After the Yankees had replaced veterans with younger players and the game was an official laugher at 13–0, Torre finally removed Irabu. Nomar Garciaparra had four hits and John Valentin drove in five runs, giving him 12 in eight October games. Pedro Martinez was superb.

Game 4. Two BoSox errors led to two unearned runs in the fourth to give the Yankees the lead. The score remained 3–2 into the eighth when a tag on a double play was missed by Chuck Knoblauch and by umpire Tim Tschida. The field was littered with debris from the fans in reaction to the call. The Yankees punished this boorish behavior with six runs the following inning, capped by Ricky Ledee's grand slam.

Game 5. ALCS MVP Orlando Hernandez left in the eighth having thrown 14 consecutive scoreless innings after a tough beginning in Game 1. The Yankees scored all the runs they would need, two batters into Game 5 on Derek Jeter's two-run homer. New York added a pair of tallies in both the seventh and the ninth to clinch the pennant.

2003 American League Division Series, Boston Red Sox vs. Oakland Athletics

The 2003 Red Sox snuck past Seattle to win the wild card, 100 years after Boston won the first modern World Series. What was most noteworthy about the season, though, was the coupling of David Ortiz and Manny Ramirez. Ortiz, coming off the best season of his career, was non-tendered by the Twins and signed with Boston a month later, making the Sox an offensive juggernaut. Besides his intimidating presence in the lineup, Ortiz was also the youngest regular on the veteran club that included a revamped infield of Kevin Millar, Todd Walker, and Bill Mueller: Boston hit 61 more home runs and scored 102 more runs than in 2002.

Something was happening in Oakland, too. The Athletics had been in the postseason every year since the Red Sox had last appeared. According to the best-selling book *Moneyball*, it didn't much matter who managed the club. Oakland GM Billy Beane let three-time AL West champion manager Art Howe take a higher-paying gig, replacing him with coach Ken Macha, who won the team's fourth straight divisional title.

Oakland wins in the first two Division Series games did not translate in the east, where less-than athletic baserunning kept the Red Sox alive in Game 3. Oakland had the lead again the next day when Boston made another come-back. A cross-country flight home didn't alter the results, as Oakland was dispatched in the first round in October for the fourth consecutive year. If the postseason truly was so many parts luck, as some quoted in *Moneyball* claimed, then Oakland's seemed to be all bad.

BOS (E)

PLAYER, POS	G	AB	R	H	2B	3B	HR	RBI	BB	SO	SB	AVG	OBP
K.Millar, 1b	5	21	0	5	0	0	0	0	2	4	0	.238	.304
D.Ortiz, dh	5	21	0	2	1	0	0	2	0	7	0	.095	.174
N.Garciaparra, ss	5	20	2	6	1	0	0	3	3	1	0	.300	.391
M.Ramirez, of	5	20	2	4	0	0	1	3	3	7	0	.200	.304
J.Damon, of	5	19	2	6	2	0	1	3	2	1	2	.316	.381
B.Mueller, 3b	5	19	0	2	1	0	0	0	3	4	0	.105	.227
T.Walker, 2b	5	16	4	5	0	0	3	4	0	1	0	.313	.313
J.Varitek, c	5	14	4	4	0	0	2	2	2	2	0	.286	.375
T.Nixon, of	4	10	1	2	0	0	1	2	1	3	0	.200	.273
G.Kapler, of	4	9	0	0	0	0	0	0	0	3	0	.000	.000
D.Jackson, 2b	4	5	0	0	0	0	0	0	0	2	0	.000	.000
D.Mirabelli, c	2	4	2	2	1	0	0	0	0	2	0	.500	.500
A.Brown, of	4	2	0	0	0	0	0	0	0	0	0	.000	.000
D.McCarty, ph	1	0	0	0	0	0	0	0	0	0	0	.000	.000
TOTALS		**180**	**17**	**38**	**6**	**0**	**8**	**16**	**18**	**39**	**3**	**.211**	**.290**

PITCHER	W	L	ERA	G	GS	SV	IP	H	BB	SO
P.Martinez	1	0	3.86	2	2	0	14.0	13	5	9
D.Lowe	0	1	0.93	3	1	1	9.2	7	7	6
T.Wakefield	0	1	3.52	2	1	0	7.2	7	3	7
J.Burkett	0	0	6.75	1	1	0	5.1	9	2	1
S.Williamson	2	0	0.00	5	0	0	5.0	2	3	8
M.Timlin	0	0	0.00	3	0	0	4.1	0	0	5
A.Embree	0	0	0.00	3	0	0	2.0	1	0	0
B.Kim	0	0	13.50	1	0	0	0.2	0	1	1
TOTALS	**3**	**2**	**2.77**	**20**	**5**	**1**	**48.2**	**38**	**21**	**37**

OAK (W)

PLAYER, POS	G	AB	R	H	2B	3B	HR	RBI	BB	SO	SB	AVG	OBP
M.Tejada, ss	5	23	0	2	1	0	0	2	0	4	0	.087	.087
E.Chavez, 3b	5	22	1	1	1	0	0	0	1	3	1	.045	.087
E.Durazo, dh	5	21	3	5	2	0	0	3	3	4	0	.238	.333
M.Ellis, 2b	5	17	2	2	0	0	0	0	4	7	0	.118	.286
S.Hatteberg, 1b	5	17	3	3	0	0	0	0	5	3	0	.176	.364
R.Hernandez, c	4	15	1	3	0	0	0	2	2	1	0	.200	.294
E.Byrnes, of	5	13	2	6	1	0	0	2	0	5	1	.462	.462
J.Dye, of	4	13	2	3	0	0	1	3	0	2	0	.231	.231
J.Guillen, of	4	11	1	5	1	0	0	1	3	2	0	.455	.571
T.Long, of	4	8	0	2	0	0	0	0	1	3	0	.250	.333
C.Singleton, of	2	7	2	2	2	0	0	0	1	1	1	.286	.375
W.McMillon, of	3	6	0	1	0	0	0	1	1	1	0	.167	.286
A.Melhuse, c	2	5	1	3	0	1	0	1	0	1	0	.600	.600
F.Menechino, 2b	1	0	0	0	0	0	0	0	0	0	0	.000	.000
TOTALS		**178**	**18**	**38**	**8**	**1**	**1**	**15**	**21**	**37**	**3**	**.213**	**.310**

PITCHER	W	L	ERA	G	GS	SV	IP	H	BB	SO
B.Zito	1	1	3.46	2	2	0	13.0	9	4	13
T.Lilly	0	0	0.00	2	1	0	9.0	7	2	7
T.Hudson	0	0	3.52	2	2	0	7.2	10	1	6
K.Foulke	0	1	3.60	3	0	0	5.0	4	2	3
R.Rincon	0	0	4.50	4	0	0	4.0	4	1	3
S.Sparks	0	0	4.50	1	0	0	4.0	2	3	1
C.Bradford	0	0	0.00	4	0	0	3.2	4	2	5
R.Harden	1	1	13.50	2	0	0	1.1	2	2	1
J.Mecir	0	0	0.00	1	0	0	0.2	1	1	0
TOTALS	**2**	**3**	**2.98**	**21**	**5**	**0**	**48.1**	**38**	**18**	**39**

2003 DIVISION SERIES - BOS(E) DEFEATS OAK(W), 3 GAMES TO 2

GAME 1, OCT. 1

BOS	100	010	200000	4	12	2
OAK	003	000	001001	5	8	0

PITCHERS: Martinez, Timlin(8), Kim(9), Embree(9), Williamson(10), LOWE(11) VS Hudson, Rincon(7), Bradford(8), Foulke(9), HARDEN(12)

ATTENDANCE: 50,606

GAME 2, OCT. 2

BOS	001	000	000	1	6	1
OAK	050	000	00X	5	6	0

PITCHERS: WAKEFIELD, Embree(7), Williamson(8) VS ZITO, Bradford(8), Foulke(9)

ATTENDANCE: 36,305

GAME 3, OCT. 4

OAK	000	001	000 00	1	6	4
BOS	010	000	000 02	3	7	2

PITCHERS: Lilly, Bradford(8), Rincon(9), Mecir(10), HARDEN(11) VS Lowe, Timlin(8), WILLIAMSON(11)

ATTENDANCE: 35,460

GAME 4, OCT. 5

OAK	010	003	000	4	11	1
BOS	002	001	02X	5	7	0

PITCHERS: Hudson, Sparks(2), Rincon(6), FOULKE(8) VS Burkett, Wakefield(6), WILLIAMSON(8)

ATTENDANCE: 35,048

GAME 5, OCT. 6

BOS	000	004	000	4	6	0
OAK	000	101	010	3	7	0

PITCHERS: MARTINEZ, Embree(8), Timlin(8), Williamson(9), Lowe(9) VS ZITO, Lilly(7), Bradford(9), Rincon(9)

ATTENDANCE: 49,397

Game 1. Exactly 100 years from the start of the modern World Series, Boston and Oakland opened the Division Series. Cy Young lost that first game in 1903, but three-time Cy Young Award winner Pedro Martinez had the lead after seven. Oakland tied it in the ninth on Erubiel Durazo's two-out single against Byung-Hyun Kim. With the game still tied in the 12th, Derek Lowe issued an intentional walk (his third walk in the inning), and Oakland catcher Ramon Hernandez shocked everyone with a bunt to push in the winning run.

Game 2. Oakland scored five times in the second on just two hits—an RBI-single by Ramon Hernandez and a two-run double by Eric Byrnes—against Tim Wakefield. Barry Zito stymied the Red Sox on five hits over seven innings as Oakland racked up its 10th consecutive postseason win over Boston, dating back to 1988.

Game 3. The Athletics could have completed a sweep if not for a series of brain cramps at Fenway Park. Oakland third baseman Eric Chavez was called for obstruction as Boston scored in the second inning. An obstruction call against Bill Mueller of the Sox was reversed in their favor when Miguel Tejada stopped running and was tagged out at home in the sixth inning. Earlier in the inning, Byrnes jarred the ball loose in a collision with catcher Jason Varitek, but he never touched home plate and Varitek tagged him out as he limped toward the dugout. The game was still tied at 1–1 when Trot Nixon homered against Rich Harden in the 11th. It was Boston's first postseason win against Oakland since 1975.

Game 4. Oakland again had Boston on the ropes. The Athletics scored three times against tired starter John Burkett in the sixth inning, with Jermaine Dye's homer snapping a brief tie. The Athletics, forced to go to the bullpen early when Tim Hudson left with an injury after one inning, faltered in the eighth when David Ortiz laced a two-out double against Keith Foulke to bring in the go-ahead runs. Scott Williamson retired all six hitters he faced to force Game 5.

Game 5. At home now, Oakland took the early lead against Martinez. Varitek tied it with a leadoff homer in the sixth, and Manny Ramirez blasted a three-run shot against Barry Zito. Lowe didn't make any new friends in Oakland with a gesture to the home team's bench after getting the last two batters looking with the tying and winning runs on base in the ninth. Nonetheless, the Sox survived three elimination games, a horrifying collision between Johnny Damon and Damian Jackson, and the AL's best pitching staff to reach the LCS.

2003 American League Championship Series, Boston Red Sox vs. New York Yankees

This was the series that cemented the Yankees-Red Sox rivalry as the greatest in all of team sports. Neither team had more than a one-game lead in the LCS, and New York scored only one more run than Boston over the course of the series. It took an epic home run in the bottom of the 11th inning of the seventh game to decide the pennant winner. What the distraught citizens of Red Sox Nation could not know, of course, was that 2003's bitter disappointment was merely a cruel prelude to the glorious October of 2004.

NY (E)

PLAYER, POS	G	AB	R	H	2B	3B	HR	RBI	BB	SO	SB	AVG	OBP
D.Jeter, ss	7	30	3	7	2	0	1	2	2	4	1	.233	.281
A.Soriano, 2b	7	30	0	4	1	0	0	3	1	11	2	.133	.161
J.Posada, c	7	27	5	8	4	0	1	6	3	4	0	.296	.367
J.Giambi, dh	7	26	4	6	0	0	3	3	4	7	0	.231	.333
N.Johnson, 1b	7	26	4	6	1	0	1	3	2	4	0	.231	.286
H.Matsui, of	7	26	3	8	3	0	0	4	1	3	0	.308	.333
B.Williams, of	7	26	5	5	1	0	0	2	4	3	0	.192	.300
A.Boone, 3b	7	17	2	3	0	0	1	2	1	6	1	.176	.222
K.Garcia, of	5	16	1	4	0	0	0	3	2	4	0	.250	.333
E.Wilson, 3b	2	7	0	1	0	0	0	0	0	1	0	.143	.143
D.Dellucci, of	3	3	1	1	0	0	0	0	0	1	1	.333	.333
J.Rivera, of	2	2	0	0	0	0	0	0	0	1	0	.000	.000
R.Sierra, of	3	2	1	1	0	0	1	1	1	0	0	.500	.667
TOTALS		**238**	**30**	**54**	**12**	**0**	**8**	**29**	**21**	**49**	**5**	**.227**	**.300**

PITCHER	W	L	ERA	G	GS	SV	IP	H	BB	SO
M.Mussina	0	2	4.11	3	2	0	15.1	16	4	17
A.Pettitte	1	0	4.63	2	2	0	11.2	17	4	10
R.Clemens	1	0	5.00	2	2	0	9.0	11	2	8
M.Rivera	1	0	1.13	4	0	2	8.0	5	0	6
D.Wells	1	0	2.35	2	1	0	7.2	5	2	5
J.Contreras	0	1	5.79	4	0	0	4.2	6	2	7
J.Nelson	0	0	6.00	4	0	0	3.0	4	0	3
F.Heredia	0	0	3.38	5	0	0	2.2	0	3	3
G.White	0	0	4.50	2	0	0	2.0	4	0	1
TOTALS	**4**	**3**	**3.94**	**28**	**7**	**2**	**64.0**	**68**	**17**	**60**

BOS (E)

PLAYER, POS	G	AB	R	H	2B	3B	HR	RBI	BB	SO	SB	AVG	OBP
N.Garciaparra, ss	7	29	2	7	0	1	0	1	2	8	0	.241	.290
K.Millar, 1b	7	29	3	7	0	0	1	3	1	9	0	.241	.267
M.Ramirez, of	7	29	6	9	1	0	2	4	1	4	0	.310	.333
B.Mueller, 3b	7	27	1	6	2	0	0	0	2	7	0	.222	.276
T.Walker, 2b	7	27	5	10	1	1	2	2	1	2	0	.370	.393
D.Ortiz, dh	7	26	4	7	1	0	2	6	3	8	0	.269	.345
T.Nixon, of	7	24	3	8	1	0	3	5	3	7	1	.333	.407
J.Damon, of	5	20	1	4	1	0	0	1	3	3	1	.200	.304
J.Varitek, c	6	20	4	6	2	0	2	3	1	5	0	.300	.333
G.Kapler, of	3	8	0	1	0	0	0	0	0	3	0	.125	.125
D.Mirabelli, c	3	7	0	2	0	0	0	0	0	2	0	.286	.286
D.Jackson, 2b	5	3	0	1	0	0	0	1	0	1	0	.333	.333
D.McCarty, ph	1	1	0	0	0	0	0	0	0	1	0	.000	.000
TOTALS		**250**	**29**	**68**	**9**	**2**	**12**	**26**	**17**	**60**	**2**	**.272**	**.326**

PITCHER	W	L	ERA	G	GS	SV	IP	H	BB	SO
P.Martinez	0	1	5.65	2	2	0	14.1	16	2	14
D.Lowe	0	2	6.43	2	2	0	14.0	14	7	5
T.Wakefield	2	1	2.57	3	2	0	14.0	8	6	10
M.Timlin	0	0	0.00	5	0	0	5.1	1	2	6
A.Embree	1	0	0.00	5	0	0	4.2	3	0	1
J.Burkett	0	0	7.36	1	1	0	3.2	7	0	1
B.Arroyo	0	0	2.70	3	0	0	3.1	2	2	5
S.Williamson	0	0	3.00	3	0	3	3.0	1	0	6
T.Jones	0	0	0.00	1	0	0	0.1	1	1	1
S.Sauerbeck	0	0	0.00	1	0	0	0.1	1	1	0
TOTALS	**3**	**4**	**4.00**	**26**	**7**	**3**	**63.0**	**54**	**21**	**49**

2003 CHAMPIONSHIP SERIES - NY (E) DEFEATS BOS(E), 4 GAMES TO 3

GAME 1, OCT. 8

| BOS | 000 | 220 | 100 | 5 | 13 | 0 |
| NY | 000 | 000 | 200 | 2 | 3 | 0 |

PITCHERS: WAKEFIELD, Embree(7), Timlin(8), Williamson(9) VS MUSSINA, Heredia(6), Nelson(7), White(7), Contreras(9)

ATTENDANCE: 56,281

GAME 2, OCT. 9

| BOS | 010 | 001 | 000 | 2 | 10 | 1 |
| NY | 021 | 000 | 20X | 6 | 8 | 0 |

PITCHERS: LOWE, Sauerbeck(7), Arroyo(8) VS PETTITTE, Contreras(7), Rivera(9)

ATTENDANCE: 56,295

GAME 3, OCT. 11

| NY | 011 | 200 | 000 | 4 | 7 | 0 |
| BOS | 200 | 100 | 000 | 3 | 6 | 0 |

PITCHERS: CLEMENS, Heredia(7), Contreras(7), Rivera(8) VS MARTINEZ, Timlin(8), Embree(9)

ATTENDANCE: 34,209

GAME 4, OCT. 13

| NY | 000 | 010 | 001 | 2 | 6 | 1 |
| BOS | 000 | 110 | 10X | 3 | 6 | 0 |

PITCHERS: MUSSINA, Heredia(7), Nelson(8) VS WAKEFIELD, Timlin(8), Williamson(9)

ATTENDANCE: 34,599

GAME 5, OCT. 14

| NY | 030 | 000 | 010 | 4 | 7 | 1 |
| BOS | 000 | 100 | 010 | 2 | 6 | 1 |

PITCHERS: WELLS, Rivera(8) VS LOWE, Embree(8), Arroyo(9)

ATTENDANCE: 34,619

GAME 6, OCT. 15

| BOS | 004 | 000 | 302 | 9 | 16 | 1 |
| NY | 100 | 410 | 000 | 6 | 12 | 2 |

PITCHERS: Burkett, Arroyo(4), Jones(6), EMBREE(6), Timlin(8), Williamson(9) VS Pettitte, CONTRERAS(6), Heredia(7), Nelson(8), White(9)

ATTENDANCE: 56,277

GAME 7, OCT. 16

| BOS | 030 | 100 | 010 | 00 | 5 | 11 | 0 |
| NY | 000 | 010 | 130 | 01 | 6 | 11 | 1 |

PITCHERS: Martinez, Embree(8), Timlin(8), WAKEFIELD(9) VS Clemens, Mussina(4), Heredia(7), Nelson(7), Wells(7), RIVERA(8)

ATTENDANCE: 56,279

Game 1. Knuckleballer Tim Wakefield baffled the Yankees, giving up only two hits in six innings and enabling Boston to jump out to a 5–0 lead. David Ortiz, Manny Ramirez, and Todd Walker all homered off Yankees starter Mike Mussina.

Game 2. Boston got three hits and a walk in the top of the first yet failed to score thanks to a double play as Bill Mueller struck out and Gabe Kapler was caught stealing. That meant Nick Johnson's two-run homer in the bottom of the second gave the Yankees the lead for good.

Game 3. Tempers flared in the fourth inning when Boston ace Pedro Martinez hit a batter. Roger Clemens retaliated by throwing one up and in to Ramirez as both benches emptied. A 13-minute delay featured 72-year-old Yankees bench coach Don Zimmer charging like an enraged bull at Martinez, who easily stepped out of the way and sent Zimmer sprawling to the ground. Later in the game, a Red Sox employee got in a fight with New York reliever Jeff Nelson and backup outfielder Karim Garcia in the visiting bullpen.

Game 4. The game was delayed a day by rain, giving tempers a chance to calm down. When it was back to baseball, the Red Sox evened the series as Wakefield again stymied Yankees hitters, this time giving up just one run in seven innings. Scott Williamson struck out the side in the ninth for the save, despite allowing a solo home run to Ruben Sierra.

Game 5. Three runs in the second, all scoring on two-out singles, were enough for the Yankees, who got splendid pitching from David Wells. Mariano Rivera came into the game in the eighth and gave up a leadoff triple to Todd Walker, who then scored on a groundout. Rivera threw a perfect ninth to close out the victory.

Game 6. Neither starter was effective, with New York's Andy Pettitte lasting only five and Boston's John Burkett failing to make it out of the fourth. Boston won because its quintet of relievers (five hits and one run in 5 1/3 innings) were better than New York's foursome, who were racked for eight hits and five runs in four innings.

Game 7. Boston fans were certainly feeling confident with Martinez on the mound holding a 4–0 lead. However, Martinez ran out of gas in the eighth after Boston manager Grady Little failed to relieve him to the howls of millions of armchair managers. The valiant Red Sox ace then allowed the three tying runs on a pair of doubles by Hideki Matsui and Jorge Posada. Neither team had a legitimate chance to score for the next two and a half innings until Aaron Boone, who had entered the game in the eighth, came to bat in the bottom of the 11th. Boone (facing Wakefield, who had taken the mound in the 10th) lofted a home run down the left-field line to propel the Yankees into the World Series, Red Sox Nation into a frenzy of self-flagellation, and Grady Little into looking for another job.

⚾ ⚾ ⚾

2004 American League Division Series, Boston Red Sox vs. Anaheim Angels

The 2004 Red Sox had hit the skids when Jason Varitek hit back. From the time he punched Yankees superstar Alex Rodriguez on July 24 at Fenway Park—in a game the Red Sox rallied to win in the bottom of the ninth against peerless closer Mariano Rivera—Boston went 46–20. The Sox became the game's best offensive team while shutting out more opponents and allowing fewer hits, home runs, and baserunners than any club in the league. A deadline deal dispatched unhappy shortstop Nomar Garciaparra, whose range was dramatically diminished, and brought shortstop Orlando Cabrera and two others—Dave Roberts and Doug Mientkiewicz—with specific skills that would be needed at crucial moments in October.

The Angels ended Oakland's four-year run in the postseason. Vladimir Guerrero smashed six home runs in the final six games to help the Angels dethrone the Athletics in the West on the penultimate day of the season. Yet the Angels were a team of contradictions. They had just two complete games all year while making the fewest relief appearances of any major league team by far. They struck out more than any AL team, both at the plate and on the mound. When opponents did put the ball in play, the Angels committed the fewest errors in the league despite having two outfielders playing the infield—Darin Erstad and Chone Figgins—and a center fielder in Garrett Anderson who'd been a corner outfielder for four seasons. The Angels stole the most bases in the majors and tied the Red Sox for highest batting average, yet they walked fewer times than any AL team.

The Red Sox dominated the first two games of the Division Series in Anaheim and Boston held a seemingly secure 6–1 lead in the seventh inning of Game 3. Yet the Red Sox had seen how quickly a series could turn around after their rousing Division Series comeback against the Athletics the previous autumn. The call went out for "Big Papi"—certainly not for the last time—to rescue "the Idiots" from their own undoing. Big Papi didn't disappoint.

BOS (E)

PLAYER, POS	G	AB	R	H	2B	3B	HR	RBI	BB	SO	SB	AVG	OBP
J.Damon, of	3	15	4	7	1	0	0	0	1	2	3	.467	.500
O.Cabrera, ss	3	13	1	2	1	0	0	3	2	2	0	.154	.267
M.Ramirez, of	3	13	3	5	2	0	1	7	1	4	0	.385	.429
B.Mueller, 3b	3	12	3	4	0	0	0	0	1	1	0	.333	.385
J.Varitek, c	3	12	3	2	0	0	1	2	2	5	0	.167	.286
M.Bellhorn, 2b	3	11	2	1	0	0	0	0	5	4	0	.091	.375
D.Ortiz, dh	3	11	4	6	2	0	1	4	5	2	0	.545	.688
K.Millar, 1b	3	10	2	3	0	0	1	4	1	1	0	.300	.364
T.Nixon, of	2	8	0	2	0	0	0	2	2	1	0	.250	.400
G.Kapler, of	2	5	2	1	0	0	0	0	0	0	0	.200	.200
D.Mientkiewicz, 1b	3	4	0	2	0	0	0	1	0	0	0	.500	.500
K.Youkilis, 3b	1	2	0	0	0	0	0	0	0	1	0	.000	.000
P.Reese, 2b	3	0	1	0	0	0	0	0	0	0	0	.000	.000
D.Roberts, ph	1	0	0	0	0	0	0	0	0	0	0	.000	.000
TOTALS		116	25	35	6	0	4	23	20	23	3	.302	.409

PITCHER	W	L	ERA	G	GS	SV	IP	H	BB	SO
P.Martinez	1	0	3.86	1	1	0	7.0	6	2	6
C.Schilling	1	0	2.70	1	1	0	6.2	9	2	4
B.Arroyo	0	0	3.00	1	1	0	6.0	3	2	7
K.Foulke	0	0	0.00	2	0	1	3.0	2	1	5
M.Timlin	0	0	9.00	3	0	0	3.0	3	1	5
A.Embree	0	0	0.00	2	0	0	1.0	0	1	0
D.Lowe	1	0	0.00	1	0	0	1.0	1	1	0
M.Myers	0	0	27.00	2	0	0	0.1	0	1	1
TOTALS	3	0	3.54	13	3	1	28.0	24	11	28

ANA (W)

PLAYER, POS	G	AB	R	H	2B	3B	HR	RBI	BB	SO	SB	AVG	OBP
C.Figgins, 2b-3b	3	14	0	2	0	0	0	0	0	5	1	.143	.143
G.Anderson, of	3	13	1	2	0	0	0	0	0	3	0	.154	.154
D.Eckstein, ss	3	12	2	4	0	0	0	0	0	1	0	.333	.333
V.Guerrero, of	3	12	1	2	0	0	1	6	2	4	0	.167	.286
T.Glaus, dh	3	11	3	4	2	0	2	3	2	4	0	.364	.462
J.Da Vanon, of	3	10	1	2	0	0	0	0	2	1	0	.200	.333
D.Erstad, 1b	3	10	2	5	1	0	1	2	3	1	0	.500	.615
D.McPherson, 3b	3	9	0	1	0	0	0	1	0	4	0	.111	.111
B.Molina, c	3	6	0	1	0	0	0	0	0	2	0	.167	.167
J.Molina, c	2	3	2	1	0	0	0	0	2	0	0	.333	.600
A.Amezaga, 2b	2	2	0	0	0	0	0	0	0	2	0	.000	.000
C.Pride, ph	2	2	0	0	0	0	0	0	0	1	0	.000	.000
C.Kotchman, ph	2	1	0	0	0	0	0	0	0	0	0	.000	.000
A.Riggs, of	2	1	0	0	0	0	0	0	0	0	0	.000	.000
TOTALS		106	12	24	3	0	4	12	11	28	1	.226	.311

PITCHER	W	L	ERA	G	GS	SV	IP	H	BB	SO
B.Colon	0	0	4.50	1	1	0	6.0	7	3	3
F.Rodriguez	0	2	3.86	2	0	0	4.2	4	3	5
B.Donnelly	0	0	10.80	2	0	0	3.1	3	2	5
K.Escobar	0	0	8.10	1	1	0	3.1	5	5	4
J.Washburn	0	1	10.80	2	1	0	3.1	6	3	3
S.Shields	0	0	6.00	2	0	0	3.0	5	2	3
K.Gregg	0	0	0.00	1	0	0	2.0	3	1	0
D.Ortiz	0	0	4.50	1	0	0	2.0	2	1	0
TOTALS	0	3	6.18	12	3	0	27.2	35	20	23

2004 DIVISION SERIES - BOS(E) DEFEATS ANA(W), 3 GAMES TO 0

GAME 1, OCT. 5

BOS	100	700	010		9	11	1
ANA	000	000	200		3	9	1

PITCHERS: SCHILLING, Embree(7), Timlin(8) VS WASHBURN, Shields(4), Gregg(6), Ortiz(8)

ATTENDANCE: 44,608

GAME 2, OCT. 6

BOS	010	002	104		8	12	0
ANA	010	020	000		3	7	0

PITCHERS: MARTINEZ, Timlin(8), Myers(8), Foulke(8) VS Colon, RODRIGUEZ(7), Donnelly(9)

ATTENDANCE: 45,118

GAME 3, OCT. 8

ANA	000	100	500	0	6	8	2
BOS	002	310	000	2	8	12	0

PITCHERS: Escobar, Shields(4), Donnelly(5), RODRIGUEZ(8), Washburn(10) VS Arroyo, Myers(7), Timlin(7), Embree(7), Foulke(8), LOWE(10)

ATTENDANCE: 35,547

Game 1. Although Boston had the better record, Anaheim received home-field advantage as a division winner. From the outset, though, the Sox were the superior team. Ortiz singled in Manny Ramirez in the first inning. The two sluggers both started and finished a seven-run explosion in the fourth inning. Ortiz walked leading off and Kevin Millar promptly homered. A two-run error made it 5–0, and Ramirez turned the lights out early with a three-run homer as Curt Schilling cruised to the win.

Game 2. Guerrero singled in two runs off Pedro Martinez in the fifth; Manny Ramirez homered against Bartolo Colon with one on to tie it in the sixth. Ramirez lifted a sacrifice fly against Francisco Rodriguez to give the Red Sox a 4–3 lead in the seventh. After three Boston pitchers maneuvered out of trouble in the eighth, the Sox blew the game open with a two-out, bases-clearing double by Cabrera in the ninth.

Game 3. Boston was preparing to celebrate a Division Series sweep as they led by five runs in the seventh inning of Game 3. Bronson Arroyo, sharp through six innings, was removed after a leadoff walk. A base on balls by Mike Myers brought in Mike Timlin, who filled the bases but got two outs. A walk to Erstad forced in a run; more importantly, it brought up Guerrero. The feared slugger, with one hit in the series at that point, quickly deposited a grand slam into the bullpen in right field to tie the game. The game remained tied until the 10th, when lefty Jarrod Washburn was summoned with first base open and two outs to face Ortiz. "Big Papi" promptly hit the first series-ending home run in Red Sox history as a Friday night celebration erupted at Fenway.

2004 American League Championship Series, Boston Red Sox vs. New York Yankees

After so many bitter disappointments over 86 years, Boston finally ended New York's domination just when it looked like the Red Sox didn't stand a chance. The Yankees had an invincible three-games-to-none lead in the series and were coming off a 19–8 shellacking that left Boston's pitching staff as dented as the Green Monster. From that point on, a new band of Red Sox emerged—although they looked just like the same

"Idiots," as they had dubbed themselves, who'd thrilled Boston fans all year.

After the ninth inning of Game 4 and the most famous stolen base in franchise history, the Red Sox outscored the Yankees, 22–9, and outhit them, 40–26. Since Jack Chesbro's wild pitch assured the 1904 pennant for Boston against New York, each do-or-die meeting in this rivalry had gone only one way for a century. Unbelievably, that was reversed in the next three days.

When it was over, there were piles of "Idiots" hugging on the field in the Bronx and pandemonium in New England and all points in Red Sox Nation. Babe who?

BOS (E)

PLAYER, POS	G	AB	R	H	2B	3B	HR	RBI	BB	SO	SB	AVG	OBP
J.Damon, of	7	35	5	6	0	0	2	7	2	8	2	.171	.216
D.Ortiz, dh	7	31	6	12	0	1	3	11	4	7	0	.387	.457
B.Mueller, 3b	7	30	4	8	1	0	0	1	2	1	0	.267	.313
M.Ramirez, of	7	30	3	9	1	0	0	0	5	4	0	.300	.400
O.Cabrera, ss	7	29	5	11	2	0	0	5	3	5	1	.379	.438
T.Nixon, of	7	29	4	6	1	0	1	3	0	5	0	.207	.207
J.Varitek, c	7	28	5	9	1	0	2	7	2	6	0	.321	.367
M.Bellhorn, 2b	7	26	3	5	2	0	2	4	5	11	0	.192	.323
K.Millar, 1b	7	24	4	6	3	0	0	2	5	4	0	.250	.379
D.Mientkiewicz, 1b	4	4	0	2	1	0	0	0	0	1	0	.500	.500
G.Kapler, of	2	3	0	1	0	0	0	0	0	0	0	.333	.333
D.Mirabelli, c	1	1	0	0	0	0	0	0	0	0	0	.000	.000
P.Reese, 2b	3	1	0	0	0	0	0	0	0	1	0	.000	.000
D.Roberts, ph	2	0	2	0	0	0	0	0	0	0	1	.000	.000
TOTALS		271	41	75	12	1	10	40	28	53	4	.277	.347

PITCHER	W	L	ERA	G	GS	SV	IP	H	BB	SO
P.Martinez	0	1	6.23	3	2	0	13.0	14	9	14
D.Lowe	1	0	3.18	2	2	0	11.1	7	1	6
C.Schilling	1	1	6.30	2	2	0	10.0	10	2	5
T.Wakefield	1	0	8.59	3	0	0	7.1	9	3	6
K.Foulke	0	0	0.00	5	0	1	6.0	1	6	6
M.Timlin	0	0	4.76	5	0	0	5.2	10	5	2
A.Embree	0	0	3.86	6	0	0	4.2	9	1	3
B.Arroyo	0	0	15.75	3	1	0	4.0	8	2	3
C.Leskanic	1	0	10.13	3	0	0	2.2	3	3	2
M.Myers	0	0	7.71	3	0	0	2.1	5	1	4
R.Mendoza	0	1	4.50	2	0	0	2.0	2	0	1
TOTALS	4	3	5.87	37	7	1	69.0	78	33	51

NY (E)

PLAYER, POS	G	AB	R	H	2B	3B	HR	RBI	BB	SO	SB	AVG	OBP
B.Williams, of	7	36	4	11	3	0	2	10	0	5	0	.306	.306
H.Matsui, of	7	34	9	14	6	1	2	10	2	4	0	.412	.444
A.Rodriguez, 3b	7	31	8	8	2	0	2	5	4	6	0	.258	.343
D.Jeter, ss	7	30	5	6	1	0	0	5	6	2	1	.200	.333
G.Sheffield, of	7	30	7	10	3	0	1	5	6	8	0	.333	.438
J.Posada, c	7	27	4	7	1	0	0	2	7	1	0	.259	.417
M.Cairo, 2b	7	25	4	7	3	0	0	4	2	4	1	.280	.333
T.Clark, 1b	5	21	0	3	1	0	0	1	0	9	0	.143	.143
R.Sierra, dh	5	21	1	7	1	1	0	2	3	8	0	.333	.417
J.Olerud, 1b	4	12	1	2	0	0	1	2	1	1	0	.167	.231
K.Lofton, dh	3	10	1	3	0	0	1	2	2	3	1	.300	.417
B.Crosby, of	1	0	1	0	0	0	0	0	0	0	0	.000	.000
TOTALS		277	45	78	21	2	9	44	33	51	3	.282	.371

PITCHER	W	L	ERA	G	GS	SV	IP	H	BB	SO
J.Lieber	1	1	3.14	2	2	0	14.1	12	1	5
M.Mussina	1	0	4.26	2	2	0	12.2	16	2	15
M.Rivera	0	0	1.29	5	0	2	7.0	6	2	6
T.Gordon	0	0	8.10	6	0	0	6.2	10	2	3
E.Loaiza	0	1	1.42	2	0	0	6.1	5	3	5
J.Vazquez	1	0	9.95	2	0	0	6.1	9	7	6
O.Hernandez	0	0	5.40	1	1	0	5.0	3	5	6
K.Brown	0	1	21.60	2	2	0	3.1	9	4	2
P.Quantrill	0	1	5.40	4	0	0	3.1	8	0	2
T.Sturtze	0	0	2.70	4	0	0	3.1	2	2	2
F.Heredia	0	0	0.00	3	0	0	1.1	1	0	1
TOTALS	3	4	5.17	33	7	2	69.2	75	28	53

2004 CHAMPIONSHIP SERIES - BOS(E) DEFEATS NY (E), 4 GAMES TO 3

GAME 1, OCT. 12

BOS	000	000	520	7	10	0
NY	204	002	02X	10	14	0

PITCHERS: SCHILLING, Leskanic(4), Mendoza(5), Wakefield(6), Embree(7), Timlin(8), Foulke(8) VS MUSSINA, Sturtze(7), Gordon(8), Rivera(8)

ATTENDANCE: 56,135

GAME 2, OCT. 13

BOS	000	000	010	1	5	0
NY	100	002	00X	3	7	0

PITCHERS: MARTINEZ, Timlin(7), Embree(7), Foulke(8) VS LIEBER, Gordon(8), Rivera(8)

ATTENDANCE: 56,136

GAME 3, OCT. 1

NY	303	520	402	19	22	1
BOS	042	000	200	8	15	0

PITCHERS: Brown, Vazquez(3), Quantrill(7), Gordon(9) VS Arroyo, MENDOZA(3), Leskanic(4), Wakefield(4), Embree(7), Myers(8)

ATTENDANCE: 35,126

GAME 4, OCT. 1

NY	002	002	000	000	4	12	1
BOS	000	030	001	002	6	8	0

PITCHERS: Hernandez, Sturtze(6), Rivera(8), Gordon(10), QUANTRILL(12) VS Lowe, Timlin(6), Foulke(7), Embree(10), Myers(11), LESKANIC(11)

ATTENDANCE: 34,826

GAME 5, OCT. 1

NY	010	003	000	000	00	4	12	1
BOS	200	000	020	000	01	5	13	1

PITCHERS: Mussina, Sturtze(7), Gordon(7), Rivera(8), Heredia(10), Quantrill(10), LOAIZA(11) VS Martinez, Timlin(7), Foulke(8), Arroyo(10), Myers(11), Embree(11), WAKEFIELD(12)

ATTENDANCE: 35,120

GAME 6, OCT. 1

BOS	000	400	000	4	11	0
NY	000	000	110	2	6	0

PITCHERS: SCHILLING, Arroyo(8), Foulke(9) VS LIEBER, Heredia(8), Quantrill(8), Sturtze(9)

ATTENDANCE: 56,128

GAME 7, OCT. 2

BOS	240	200	011	10	13	0
NY	001	000	200	3	5	1

PITCHERS: LOWE, Martinez(7), Timlin(8), Embree(9) VS BROWN, Vazquez(2), Loaiza(4), Heredia(7), Gordon(8), Rivera(9)

ATTENDANCE: 56,129

Game 1. The Red Sox fell behind 8–0 as the Yankees pounded injured Curt Schilling. Mike Mussina retired 19 straight Sox, but Boston exploded for five runs with two outs in the seventh—including a two-run homer by Jason Varitek off Tanyon Sturtze. The Red Sox scored twice more in the eighth on a David Ortiz drive that bounced off Hideki Matsui's glove and brought in two runs to cut it to 8–7. Mariano Rivera came in to get the last out, then pitched through trouble in the ninth. A two-run double by Bernie Williams provided a cushion as the Yankees took the opener.

Game 2. Pedro Martinez allowed a run-scoring single to Gary Sheffield in the first inning and a two-run homer to John Olerud in the sixth, but the Yankees' Jon Lieber allowed just three hits in seven innings. The only run charged to Lieber came on a groundout in the eighth.

Game 3. After a rainout, the Yankees had their hitting shoes on. They scored three times in the first inning, but the Red Sox tied it in the second and went ahead on Derek Jeter's error. Their lead lasted only one batter. Alex Rodriguez homered, starting a Yankees barrage that saw them score 15 more times against a half-dozen pitchers. A-Rod, Sheffield, Matsui, and Williams accounted for 16 hits, 15 runs (including a run by a pinch runner), and 15 RBIs. The Red Sox couldn't keep up the pace, although the teams combined for 37 hits (22 by New York). It was the highest-scoring postseason game in Yankees history and the most runs in a game in a best-of-seven series. So far, the Yankees had held the lead after 48 of the 52 half-innings played.

Game 4. The Red Sox batted in the ninth inning of Game 4 down by one run, trailing the Yankees three games to none, and facing the most successful reliever in postseason history. Rivera's leadoff walk to Kevin Millar, though, spurred hope. Pinch runner Dave Roberts stole second base by an eyelash and scored the tying run on Bill Mueller's single. Ortiz popped up with the bases loaded in the ninth, but his two-run homer in the 12th won the game as Boston avoided the sweep.

Game 5. Ortiz came through again at two crucial junctures. "Big Papi" homered off Tom Gordon in the eighth, then Varitek tied the game with a sac fly off Rivera later in the inning. Some six innings and many breathless

moments later, Ortiz singled in Johnny Damon as the Bombers left 18 runners on base and missed their second chance to close out the series. Despite three passed balls in the 13th inning with flutterballer Wakefield on the mound, no Yankees scored.

Game 6. Now the Red Sox had to get their mojo working in the Bronx. Schilling pitched despite a ruptured ankle tendon that bloodied his sock, yet the tenacious right-hander stymied the Yankees. Boston scored all of its runs in the third inning, three of them coming on Mark Bellhorn's home run that was originally ruled to be in play; the umpires changed the call after they huddled and agreed that the ball had hit a fan in the stands on the fly. The umpires reversed another call in the eighth inning when Rodriguez slapped the ball out of Bronson Arroyo's hand near first base. These reversals netted the Red Sox two runs, took away one from the Yankees, and set up a Game 7 showdown.

Game 7. The Yankees were forced to start ailing Kevin Brown, 39, and the Red Sox took advantage by commencing to take BP at the Stadium. Series MVP David Ortiz hit his third homer in four games to help the Sox go ahead before Damon hit a grand slam in the second to knock out Brown. He later added another homer, finishing the game with six RBIs. Derek Lowe was outstanding and the Red Sox became the first team ever to rally from three games down in postseason history.

✺

2004 World Series, Boston Red Sox vs. St. Louis Cardinals

No team in major league history had ever come back from three-games-to-none to win an October series. For the Red Sox to really end this infernal "Curse of the Bambino," however, they had to win a world championship after 86 years of waiting.

Just as it had turned to gold for the third postseason meeting between the Red Sox and the Yankees, Red Sox Nation needed a similar reversal against the Cardinals, who had knocked off the Sox in seven games in both the

1946 and 1967 World Series. The 2004 Cardinals were a potent club who'd barely survived their own seven-game LCS against division rival Houston. Even with the Yankees slain, no one in Boston dared take a 105-win team lightly.

In the end, though, the fall classic was a laugher after the first game. Boston held the St. Louis to a .190 batting average, scored twice as many runs, and limited Scott Rolen, Jim Edmonds, and Reggie Sanders to a combined 1-for-39. The Redbirds scored just three runs over the final three games. The dream was no longer impossible; the fabled "curse" was finally kicked.

BOS (AL)

PLAYER, POS	G	AB	R	H	2B	3B	HR	RBI	BB	SO	SB	AVG	OBP
J.Damon, of	4	21	4	6	2	1	1	2	0	1	0	.286	.286
O.Cabrera, ss	4	17	3	4	1	0	0	3	3	1	0	.235	.350
M.Ramirez, of	4	17	2	7	0	0	1	4	3	3	0	.412	.500
B.Mueller, 3b	4	14	3	6	2	0	0	2	4	0	0	.429	.556
T.Nixon, of	4	14	1	5	3	0	0	3	1	1	0	.357	.400
D.Ortiz, 1b-dh	4	13	3	4	1	0	1	4	4	1	0	.308	.471
J.Varitek, c	4	13	2	2	0	1	0	2	1	4	0	.154	.214
M.Bellhorn, 2b	4	10	3	3	1	0	1	4	5	2	0	.300	.533
K.Millar, 1b	4	8	2	1	1	0	0	0	2	2	0	.125	.300
D.Mirabelli, c	1	3	1	1	0	0	0	0	0	0	0	.333	.333
G.Kapler, of	4	2	0	0	0	0	0	0	0	1	0	.000	.000
D.Lowe, p	1	2	0	0	0	0	0	0	0	1	0	.000	.000
P.Martinez, p	1	2	0	0	0	0	0	0	1	2	0	.000	.333
D.Mientkiewicz, 1b	4	1	0	0	0	0	0	0	0	0	0	.000	.000
P.Reese, 2b	4	1	0	0	0	0	0	0	0	0	0	.000	.000
TOTALS		**138**	**24**	**39**	**11**	**2**	**4**	**24**	**24**	**20**	**0**	**.283**	**.404**

PITCHER	W	L	ERA	G	GS	SV	IP	H	BB	SO
D.Lowe	1	0	0.00	1	1	0	7.0	3	1	4
P.Martinez	1	0	0.00	1	1	0	7.0	3	2	6
C.Schilling	1	0	0.00	1	1	0	6.0	4	1	4
K.Foulke	1	0	1.80	4	0	1	5.0	4	1	8
T.Wakefield	0	0	12.27	1	1	0	3.2	3	5	2
M.Timlin	0	0	6.00	3	0	0	3.0	2	1	0
B.Arroyo	0	0	6.75	2	0	0	2.2	4	1	4
A.Embree	0	0	0.00	3	0	0	1.2	1	0	4
TOTALS	**4**	**0**	**2.50**	**16**	**4**	**1**	**36.0**	**24**	**12**	**32**

STL (NL)

PLAYER, POS	G	AB	R	H	2B	3B	HR	RBI	BB	SO	SB	AVG	OBP
J.Edmonds, of	4	15	2	1	0	0	0	0	1	6	0	.067	.125
A.Pujols, 1b	4	15	1	5	2	0	0	0	1	3	0	.333	.375
E.Renteria, ss	4	15	2	5	3	0	0	1	2	2	0	.333	.412
S.Rolen, 3b	4	15	0	0	0	0	0	1	1	1	0	.000	.063
L.Walker, of	4	14	2	5	2	0	2	3	2	2	0	.357	.438
T.Womack, 2b	4	11	1	2	0	0	0	0	1	2	0	.182	.250
R.Sanders, of-dh	4	9	1	0	0	0	0	0	4	5	1	.000	.308
M.Matheny, c	4	8	0	2	0	0	0	2	0	3	0	.250	.250
M.Anderson, 2b-dh	4	6	0	1	1	0	0	0	0	1	0	.167	.167
R.Cedeno, of	3	4	1	1	0	0	0	0	0	0	2	.250	.250
J.Mabry, of	2	4	0	0	0	0	0	0	0	2	0	.000	.000
S.Taguchi, of	2	4	1	1	0	0	0	1	0	2	0	.250	.250
Y.Molina, c	3	3	0	0	0	0	0	0	0	1	0	.000	.000
H.Luna, 2b	1	1	0	0	0	0	0	0	0	1	0	.000	.000
J.Marquis, p	3	1	1	0	0	0	0	0	0	0	0	.000	.000
J.Suppan, p	1	1	0	1	0	0	0	0	0	0	0	1.000	1.000
TOTALS		126	12	24	8	0	2	8	12	32	1	.190	.266

PITCHER	W	L	ERA	G	GS	SV	IP	H	BB	SO
J.Marquis	0	1	3.86	2	1	0	7.0	6	7	4
D.Haren	0	0	0.00	2	0	0	4.2	4	3	2
J.Suppan	0	1	7.71	1	1	0	4.2	8	1	4
M.Morris	0	1	8.31	1	1	0	4.1	4	4	3
R.King	0	0	0.00	3	0	0	2.2	1	1	1
W.Williams	0	0	27.00	1	1	0	2.1	8	3	1
J.Isringhausen	0	0	0.00	1	0	0	2.0	1	1	2
J.Tavarez	0	1	4.50	2	0	0	2.0	1	0	1
C.Eldred	0	0	10.80	2	0	0	1.2	4	0	2
K.Calero	0	0	13.50	2	0	0	1.1	2	4	0
A.Reyes	0	0	0.00	2	0	0	1.1	0	0	0
TOTALS	0	4	6.09	19	4	0	34.0	39	24	20

2004 WORLD SERIES - BOS(AL) DEFEATS STL(NL), 4 GAMES TO 0

GAME 1, OCT. 23

STL	011	302	020	9	11	1
BOS	403	000	22X	11	13	4

PITCHERS: Williams, Haren(3), Calero(7), King(7), Eldred(7), TAVAREZ(8) VS Wakefield, Arroyo(4), Timlin(7), Embree(8), FOULKE(8)

ATTENDANCE: 35,035

GAME 2, OCT. 24

STL	000	100	010	2	5	0
BOS	200	202	00X	6	8	4

PITCHERS: MORRIS, Eldred(5), King(6), Marquis(7), Reyes(8) VS SCHILLING, Embree(7), Timlin(8), Foulke(8)

ATTENDANCE: 35,001

GAME 3, OCT. 26

BOS	100	120	000	4	9	0
STL	000	000	001	1	4	0

PITCHERS: MARTINEZ, Timlin(8), Foulke(9) VS SUPPAN, Reyes(5), Calero(6), King(7), Tavarez(9)

ATTENDANCE: 52,015

GAME 4, OCT. 27

BOS	102	000	000	3	9	0
STL	000	000	000	0	4	0

PITCHERS: LOWE, Arroyo(8), Embree(8), Foulke(9) VS MARQUIS, Haren(7), Isringhausen(8)

ATTENDANCE: 52,037

Game 1. The Red Sox delighted the Fenway faithful by scoring four times in the first, three on a homer by David Ortiz. After St. Louis cut it to 4–2, Boston added three more in the third. The Cardinals scored three times in the fourth on just one hit, as Tim Wakefield departed after five walks and a hit batsman. Doubles by Edgar Renteria and Larry Walker tied the game in the fifth against Bronson Arroyo. Manny Ramirez and Ortiz gave Boston the lead in the seventh, but errors by Ramirez on consecutive plays enabled the Cardinals to tie the game again. Once more the Red Sox took the lead as Mark Bellhorn rung the right-field foul pole with a runner on in the eighth. Despite two blown leads, four errors, and innumerable moments of angst for Red Sox fans, Boston prevailed in the opener as Keith Foulke retired St. Louis in the ninth.

Game 2. The Game 2 drama was all in a sock. As in Game 6 of the ALCS, fresh stitches held together Schilling's ruptured tendon sheath on his right ankle. TV cameras focused on the few inches of bloody sock visible. The Cardinals, meanwhile, scored just once in six innings against the wounded veteran. Jason Varitek's two-run triple gave Boston the lead in the first inning, Bellhorn added a two-run double in the fourth, and Orlando Cabrera knocked in two more in the sixth.

Game 3. The first World Series game in St. Louis in 17 years featured the usual sea of red, this time spilt between Redbirds and Red Sox fans. Pedro Martinez pitched brilliantly in what would be his last start in a Boston uniform. The Cardinals should have tied the game in the third inning, but a grounder with a runner on third turned into a DP when first baseman Ortiz saw Cardinals pitcher Jeff Suppan hesitate and gunned him out trying to get back to the base. Manny Ramirez drove in two runs and gunned down another at the plate. St. Louis broke up the shutout on Walker's home run in the ninth: that was Walker's and the Cards' second and final home run of the Series.

Game 4. A full lunar eclipse seemed just one of many signs that 86 years of frustration were nearing an end. Johnny Damon led off with a home run. Trot Nixon doubled three times and knocked in two as, for the second straight night, the Sox limited the Cards to four hits. St. Louis had stranded baserunners in each of the last five innings as Derek Lowe picked up his third series-clinching victory of 2004. Foulke closed it out in the ninth by retiring Edgar Renteria, whose single had ended the 1997 World Series. Exactly 18 years after losing Game 7 in 1986 to the Mets, the Red Sox finally proclaimed themselves as world champions.

2005 American League Division Series, Boston Red Sox vs. Chicago White Sox

A magical run to a long overdue world championship switched Sox in 2005. The White Sox allowed 13½ games to fall off what seemed like an insurmountable lead in the AL Central, regrouping in the final week just as it looked like they were spent. But Chicago unexpectedly swept the hard-charging Indians at Jacobs Field on the final weekend; in doing so, they helped the Red Sox claim the AL wild card.

The Red Sox had planned on beating out the Yankees for the AL East title. Boston trailed New York by one game heading into the season-ending series at Fenway Park. However, the rivals split their first two games, allowing the Yankees to clinch their eighth straight AL East title. The next day, though, as the Yankees started Jaret Wright instead of Mike Mussina, Curt Schilling captured and the Red Sox cruised to the wild card while simultaneously helping the Angels gain home-field advantage against New York in the Division Series. Although it quickly became apparent the Sox-on-Sox Division Series belonged to the Pale Hose, New York's extra game in Anaheim (courtesy of Boston) did the Yankees in.

The 2005 Division Series marked the first time the Red Sox had been swept in nine postseason series dating back to 1995. Boston ended with an ERA of 7.56, while Chicago's starters pitched well enough and its bullpen allowed just four hits and no runs. It was tough to live with in Boston, but Red Sox fans could certainly sympathize with a team that was finally on the way to its first world championship since World War I.

CHI (C)

PLAYER, POS	G	AB	R	H	2B	3B	HR	RBI	BB	SO	SB	AVG	OBP
T.Iguchi, 2b	3	12	1	3	0	0	1	4	0	3	0	.250	.250
P.Konerko, 1b	3	12	3	3	0	0	2	4	0	1	0	.250	.250
C.Everett, dh	3	11	2	3	0	0	0	0	0	0	0	.273	.273
S.Podsednik, of	3	11	3	3	1	0	1	4	1	1	1	.273	.333
J.Dye, of	3	10	1	2	0	0	0	1	2	0	0	.200	.273
A.Rowand, of	3	10	3	4	2	0	0	2	1	1	1	.400	.455
J.Uribe, ss	3	10	4	4	1	0	1	4	0	2	0	.400	.400
J.Crede, 3b	3	9	2	1	0	0	0	1	1	1	0	.111	.200
A.Pierzynski, c	3	9	5	4	2	0	2	4	1	0	1	.444	.500
G.Blum, 1b	1	1	0	0	0	0	0	0	0	0	0	.000	.000
W.Harris, 2b	1	1	0	1	0	0	0	1	0	0	0	1.000	1.000
T.Perez, of	1	1	0	0	0	0	0	0	0	0	0	.000	.000
TOTALS		97	24	28	6	0	7	24	5	11	3	**.289**	**.355**

PITCHER	W	L	ERA	G	GS	SV	IP	H	BB	SO
J.Contreras	1	0	2.35	1	1	0	7.2	8	0	6
M.Buehrle	1	0	5.14	1	1	0	7.0	8	1	2
F.Garcia	1	0	5.40	1	1	0	5.0	5	4	1
O.Hernandez	0	0	0.00	1	0	0	3.0	1	0	4
B.Jenks	0	0	0.00	2	0	2	3.0	1	1	1
C.Politte	0	0	0.00	1	0	0	1.0	1	0	0
N.Cotts	0	0	0.00	1	0	0	0.1	0	0	0
D.Marte	0	0	INF	1	0	0	0.0	1	2	0
TOTALS	3	0	3.00	9	3	2	27.0	25	8	14

BOS (E)

PLAYER, POS	G	AB	R	H	2B	3B	HR	RBI	BB	SO	SB	AVG	OBP
J.Damon, of	3	13	2	3	1	0	0	0	1	4	0	.231	.286
E.Renteria, ss	3	13	1	3	2	0	0	1	0	1	0	.231	.286
T.Graffanino, 2b	3	12	0	3	2	0	0	0	0	0	0	.250	.250
D.Ortiz, dh	3	12	2	4	2	0	1	1	0	3	0	.333	.333
B.Mueller, 3b	3	11	0	0	0	0	0	1	2	0	.000	.083
T.Nixon, of	3	11	1	3	0	0	0	1	1	1	0	.273	.333
M.Ramirez, of	3	10	2	3	0	0	2	4	2	0	0	.300	.417
J.Varitek, c	3	10	1	3	0	0	0	1	0	2	0	.300	.300
J.Olerud, 1b	3	7	0	2	1	0	0	0	2	0	0	.286	.444
K.Millar, 1b	2	3	0	1	1	0	0	1	0	1	0	.333	.333
D.Mirabelli, c	1	2	0	0	0	0	0	0	0	0	0	.000	.000
A.Cora, ss	1	0	0	0	0	0	0	0	0	0	0	.000	.000
A.Hyzdu, of	1	0	0	0	0	0	0	0	0	0	0	.000	.000
A.Machado, ph	1	0	0	0	0	0	0	0	0	0	0	.000	.000
TOTALS		104	9	25	9	0	3	8	8	14	0	**.240**	**.295**

PITCHER	W	L	ERA	G	GS	SV	IP	H	BB	SO
D.Wells	0	1	2.70	1	1	0	6.2	7	0	2
T.Wakefield	0	1	6.75	1	1	0	5.1	6	1	4
J.Papelbon	0	0	0.00	2	0	0	4.0	2	0	2
M.Clement	0	1	21.60	1	1	0	3.1	7	0	0
J.Gonzalez	0	0	15.43	1	0	0	2.1	2	1	0
C.Bradford	0	0	0.00	2	0	0	1.1	1	0	1
B.Arroyo	0	0	18.00	1	0	0	1.0	2	2	1
M.Timlin	0	0	9.00	1	0	0	1.0	1	0	1
M.Myers	0	0	INF	1	0	0	0.0	0	1	0
TOTALS	0	3	7.56	11	3	0	25.0	28	5	11

2005 DIVISION SERIES - CHI(C) DEFEATS BOS(E), 3 GAMES TO 0

GAME 1, OCT. 4

BOS	000	200	000	2	9	0
CHI	501	204	02X	14	11	1

PITCHERS: CLEMENT, Bradford(4), Gonzalez(5), Arroyo(8) VS CONTRERAS, Cotts(8), Politte(9)

ATTENDANCE: 40,717

GAME 2, OCT. 5

BOS	202	000	000	4	9	1
CHI	000	050	00X	5	9	0

PITCHERS: WELLS, Papelbon(7) VS BUEHRLE, Jenks(8)

ATTENDANCE: 40,799

GAME 3, OCT. 7

CHI	002	002	001	5	8	0
BOS	000	201	000	3	7	1

PITCHERS: GARCIA, Marte(6), Hernandez(6), Jenks(9) VS WAKEFIELD, Bradford(6), Myers(6), Papelbon(6), Timlin(9)

ATTENDANCE: 35,496

Game 1. The White Sox pounded Matt Clement, who hit two of the first three batters he faced and allowed three straight two-out hits, the last a three-run homer by A.J. Pierzynski. Paul Konerko homered off Clement in the third, then Jose Uribe took him deep in the fourth before he was finally yanked. Scott Podsednik and Pierzynski (again) homered before Chicago emptied its bench. Jose Contreras threw strikes and was never in trouble.

Game 2. The Red Sox hit Mark Buehrle early. Manny Ramirez singled in two runs in the first and Boston scored twice on three hits in the third. Buehrle, the league's most durable starter, allowed only two hits over

his last four innings. Chicago only scored against David Wells in the fifth inning, but it was enough. After Aaron Rowand and Joe Crede singled in runs, Wells induced Uribe to hit into what looked like an inning-ending double play. Like Boston's chances, however, the grounder went through second baseman Tony Graffanino's legs. Tadahito Iguchi then homered to give the White Sox the lead. Bobby Jenks pitched the final two innings for Chicago.

Game 3. After the White Sox took an early lead, David Ortiz and Ramirez hit consecutive home runs off Freddy Garcia in the fourth inning to tie the game. Paul Konerko's two-run homer in the sixth chased Tim Wakefield and gave the White Sox the lead. Ramirez homered again leading off the sixth then Boston loaded the bases with none out. Orlando Hernandez entered for his first work of the series and retired Jason Varitek, Graffanino, and Johnny Damon to keep the tying run from scoring. In a brilliant performance, "El Duque" allowed but one batter to reach base in three innings. Chicago added an insurance run on a squeeze play in the ninth, then Jenks finished off Boston for Chicago's first postseason series win since 1917.

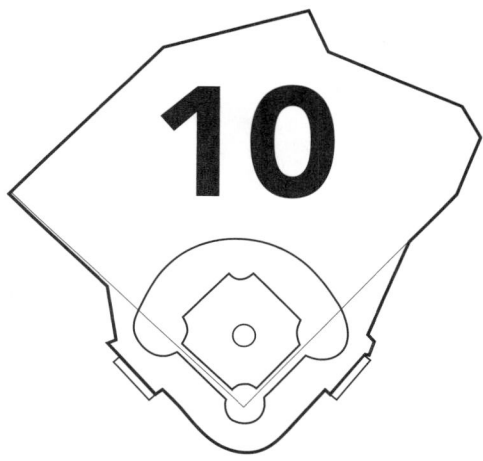

RED SOX AND THE ALL-STAR GAME

The first All-Star pitch in history landed in a Red Sox mitt. Rick Ferrell started behind the plate in the first All-Star at Comiskey Park on July 6, 1933. He stayed in the whole game, as did everyone in the American League starting lineup except for aging icon Babe Ruth in right field and starting pitcher Lefty Gomez. The next year Ferrell did not start and did not play. That was the first of 36 times in Red Sox All-Star history that a player has made the trip and gotten a great seat for the game. Seventy-three years later Red Sox outfielder Manny Ramirez opted not to participate without even giving a questionable excuse. How things have changed.

In the 1950 All-Star Game at Comiskey, Ted Williams broke his elbow slamming into the wall to rob Ralph Kiner of a hit in the first inning. He stayed in the game through the eighth inning, but he wound up missing regular-season games until September. That's a worst-case scenario, but it illustrates how important All-Star Games were long before there was any "incentive" like home-field advantage in the World Series for the winning league or the cash bonuses that many modern contracts have for making the All-Star roster. Whether the player actually goes to the game appears irrelevant for the bonus.

Ted Williams was one of the great All-Star performers in history. He relished the game and enjoyed it whole-heartedly, as the whole country clearly saw in newsreel footage as he hopped around the bases after his two-out, three-run homer in the bottom of the ninth won the 1941 game in Detroit. All-Star MVPs were first given out in 1962, after Williams' retirement, or he surely would have earned a couple. There are three Red Sox who have earned the prize for All-Star excellence: Carl Yastrzemski (1970), Roger Clemens (1986), and Pedro Martinez (1999).

The Red Sox who played in the 17 All-Star Games with Williams, the teammates who played in the 18 contests with Yastrzemski, and those All-Star Sox who came before and after the Splendid Splinter and Yaz are listed in the Red Sox All-Star roster. Positions are given for where they played in the game, like Jimmie Foxx filling in at third base in the 1936 All-Star Game (a position he played just seven times in six years in Boston), or the many Red Sox who served as pinch hitters in the All-Star Game. **DNP** signifies the player was chosen but did not play, **injured** means he was chosen but could not play due to injury, and **replacement** signifies he was named to the team after another player was injured.

A statistics section gives the year-by-year and career All-Star numbers for players chosen from the Red Sox. Also included is a summary of the three All-Star Games played at Fenway Park.

A category often overlooked is the record of managers who represented the league because they won the previous year's pennant, as has long been the custom for choosing managers for the game. (Joe Cronin was given a chance to manage the American League in 1940 after Joe McCarthy had managed the previous four years; the result was the first All-Star shutout.) The five Red Sox managers who've guided the American League are listed below along with information about the games, including a note of how many of his own players the manager took with him.

Manager	Year	Result	Site	Red Sox on Team
Joe Cronin	1940	L, 4–0	St. Louis	4
Joe Cronin	1947	W, 2–1	Chicago (Wrigley)	8
Dick Williams	1968	L, 1–0	Houston	4
Darrell Johnson	1976	L, 7–1	Philadelphia	2
John McNamara	1987	L, 2–0	Oakland	3
Terry Francona	2005	W, 7–5	Detroit	5

Red Sox Selected to the All-Star Game

1933
Rick Ferrell, c

1934
Rick Ferrell, c (dnp)

1935
Joe Cronin, ss
Rick Ferrell, c (dnp)
Lefty Grove, p (dnp)

1936
Rick Ferrell, c
Jimmie Foxx, 3b
Lefty Grove, p

1937
Doc Cramer, of (dnp)
Joe Cronin, ss
Jimmie Foxx, ph
Lefty Grove, p (dnp)

1938
Doc Cramer, of
Joe Cronin, ss
Jimmie Foxx, 1b
Lefty Grove, p

1939
Doc Cramer, of
Joe Cronin, ss
Jimmie Foxx, 1b (dnp)
Lefty Grove, p (dnp)

1940
Doc Cramer, of (dnp)
Lou Finney, of
Jimmie Foxx, 1b
Ted Williams, of

1941
Joe Cronin, ss
Dom DiMaggio, of
Bobby Doerr, 2b
Jimmie Foxx, 1b
Ted Williams, of

1942
Dom DiMaggio, of (dnp)
Bobby Doerr, 2b (dnp)
Tex Hughson, p (dnp)
Ted Williams, of

1943
Bobby Doerr, 2b
Tex Hughson, p
Oscar Judd, p (dnp)

1944
Bobby Doerr, 2b
Pete Fox, of (dnp)
 (replacement)
Tex Hughson, p
Bob Johnson, of

1945 (no game)
Dave Ferriss, p
Bob Johnson, of

1946
Dom DiMaggio, of
Bobby Doerr, 2b
Dave Ferriss, p (dnp)
Mickey Harris, p (dnp)
Johnny Pesky, ss
Hal Wagner, c
Ted Williams, of
Rudy York, 1b

1947
Bobby Doerr, 2b
Ted Williams, of

1948
Joe Dobson, p (dnp)
 (replacement)
Bobby Doerr, 2b
Vern Stephens, ss
Birdie Tebbetts, c
Ted Williams, ph

1949
Dom DiMaggio, of
Billy Goodman, 1b
Mel Parnell, p
Vern Stephens, ss
Birdie Tebbetts, c
Ted Williams, of

1950
Dom DiMaggio, of
Bobby Doerr, 2b
Walt Dropo, 1b
Vern Stephens, ss (dnp)
Ted Williams, of

1951
Dom DiMaggio, of
Bobby Doerr, 2b
Mel Parnell, p
Vern Stephens, ph
Ted Williams, of

1952
Dom DiMaggio, of
George Kell, 3b (injured)

1953
Billy Goodman, 2b
George Kell, ph
Sammy White, c (dnp)
Ted Williams, of (honorary)

1954
Jim Piersall, of
Ted Williams, of

1955
Jackie Jensen, ph
Frank Sullivan, p
Ted Williams, of

1956
Tom Brewer, p
Jim Piersall, of
Frank Sullivan, p (dnp)
Mickey Vernon, 1b
Ted Williams, of

1957
Frank Malzone, 3b
Ted Williams, of

1958
Jackie Jensen, of
Frank Malzone, 3b
Ted Williams, of

1959
Game 1
Frank Malzone, 3b
Pete Runnels, ph
Ted Williams, of
Game 2
Frank Malzone, 3b
Pete Runnels, 1b
Ted Williams, of

1960
Game 1
Frank Malzone, 3b
Bill Monbouquette, p
Pete Runnels, 2b
Ted Williams, ph
Game 2
Frank Malzone, 3b
Bill Monbouquette, p (dnp)
Pete Runnels, 2b
Ted Williams, ph

1961
Game 1
Mike Fornieles, p
Game 2
Don Schwall, p

1962
Game 1
Bill Monbouquette, p (dnp)
Game 2
Pete Runnels, ph (added)

1963
Frank Malzone, 3b
Bill Monbouquette, p (dnp)
 (replacement)
Dick Radatz, p
Carl Yastrzemski, of

1964
Eddie Bressoud, ss (dnp)
 (replacement)
Frank Malzone, 3b (dnp)
Dick Radatz, p

1965
Felix Mantilla, 2b
Carl Yastrzemski, of (injured)

1966
George Scott, 1b
Carl Yastrzemski, of (dnp)

1967
Tony Conigliaro, of
Jim Lonborg, p (dnp)
Rico Petrocelli, ss
Carl Yastrzemski, of

1968
Gary Bell, p (dnp)
 (replacement)
Ken Harrelson, ph
Jose Santiago, p (injured)
Carl Yastrzemski, of

1969
Mike Andrews, 2b
 (replacement)
Ray Culp, p
Rico Petrocelli, ss
Reggie Smith, of
Carl Yastrzemski, of

1970
Jerry Moses, c (dnp)
Carl Yastrzemski, of

1971
Luis Aparicio, ss
Sonny Siebert, p (dnp)
Carl Yastrzemski, of

1972
Luis Aparicio, ss (injured)
Carlton Fisk, c
Reggie Smith, ph
 (replacement)
Carl Yastrzemski, of

1973
Carlton Fisk, c
Bill Lee, p (dnp)
Carl Yastrzemski, 1b (injured)

1974
Carlton Fisk, c (injured)
Luis Tiant, p
Carl Yastrzemski, 1b

1975
Fred Lynn, of
Carl Yastrzemski, ph

1976
Carlton Fisk, c
Fred Lynn, of
Luis Tiant, p
Carl Yastrzemski, of

1977
Rick Burleson, ss
Bill Campbell, p
Carlton Fisk, c
Fred Lynn, of
Jim Rice, of
George Scott, 1b
Carl Yastrzemski, of

1978
Rick Burleson, ss (injured)
Dwight Evans, of
 (replacement)
Carlton Fisk, c
Fred Lynn, of
Jerry Remy, 2b (dnp)
 (replacement)
Jim Rice, of
Carl Yastrzemski, of (injured)

1979
Rick Burleson, ss
Fred Lynn, of
Jim Rice, of
Bob Stanley, p
Carl Yastrzemski, 1b

1980
Tom Burgmeier, p (dnp)
Carlton Fisk, c
Fred Lynn, of
Jim Rice, of (injured)

1981
Dwight Evans, of

1982
Mark Clear, p (dnp)
Dennis Eckersley, p
Carl Yastrzemski, ph

1983
Jim Rice, of
Bob Stanley, p
Carl Yastrzemski, ph

1984
Tony Armas, of (dnp)
Jim Rice, of

1985
Wade Boggs, 3b
Rich Gedman, c (replacement)
Jim Rice, of

1986
Wade Boggs, 3b
Roger Clemens, p
Rich Gedman, c
Jim Rice, ph

1987
Wade Boggs, 3b
Dwight Evans, of
Bruce Hurst, p (dnp)

1988
Wade Boggs, 3b
Roger Clemens, p
Mike Greenwell, of

1989
Wade Boggs, 3b
Mike Greenwell, of

1990
Wade Boggs, 3b
Ellis Burks, of (injured)
Roger Clemens, p (dnp)

1991
Wade Boggs, 3b
Roger Clemens, p
Jeff Reardon, p

1992
Wade Boggs, 3b
Roger Clemens, p

1993
Scott Cooper, 3b

1994
Scott Cooper, 3b

1995
Erik Hanson, p (dnp)
Mo Vaughn, 1b

1996
Mo Vaughn, 1b

1997
Nomar Garciaparra, ss

1998
Tom Gordon, p
Pedro Martinez, p (dnp)
Mo Vaughn, 1b (injured)

1999
Nomar Garciaparra, ss
Pedro Martinez, p
Jose Offerman, 2b

2000
Carl Everett, of
Nomar Garciaparra, ss
Derek Lowe, p
Pedro Martinez, p (injured)

2001
Manny Ramirez, of

2002
Johnny Damon, of
Nomar Garciaparra, ss
Shea Hillenbrand, 3b
Derek Lowe, p
Pedro Martinez, p (injured)
Manny Ramirez, of
Ugueth Urbina, p
 (replacement)

2003
Nomar Garciaparra, ss
Manny Ramirez, of (injured)
Jason Varitek, c (dnp)

2004
David Ortiz, 1b
Manny Ramirez, of
Curt Schilling, p (injured)

2005
Matt Clement, p
 (replacement)
Johnny Damon, of
David Ortiz, dh
Manny Ramirez, of
Jason Varitek, c

2006
Mark Loretta, 2b
David Ortiz, 1b
Jonathan Papelbon, p
Manny Ramirez, of (declined)

Red Sox All-Star Register

YEAR	POS	AVG	AB	R	H	2B	3B	HR	RBI	BB	SO	SB
MIKE ANDREWS												
1969	2b	.000	1	0	0	0	0	0	0	0	0	0
LUIS APARICIO												
1971	ss	.333	3	1	1	0	0	0	0	0	0	0
1972	ss	(injured)										
TONY ARMAS												
1984	of	(dnp)										
WADE BOGGS												
1985	3b	.000	0	0	0	0	0	0	0	1	0	0
1986	3b	.333	3	0	1	0	0	0	0	0	0	0
1987	3b	.000	3	0	0	0	0	0	0	0	0	0
1988	3b	.333	3	0	1	0	0	0	0	0	0	0
1989	3b	.333	3	1	1	0	0	1	1	0	0	0
1990	3b	1.000	2	0	2	0	0	0	0	1	0	0
1991	3b	.500	2	1	1	0	0	0	0	1	0	0
1992	3b	.333	3	1	1	0	0	0	0	0	1	0
Total	8	.368	19	3	7	0	0	1	1	3	1	0
EDDIE BRESSOUD												
1964	ss	(dnp)										
ELLIS BURKS												
1990	of (injured)												
RICK BURLESON												
1977	ss	.000	2	0	0	0	0	0	0	0	0	0
1978	ss	(injured)										
1979	ss	.000	2	1	0	0	0	0	0	0	1	0
Total	2	.000	4	1	0	0	0	0	0	0	1	0
TONY CONIGLIARO												
1967	of	.000	6	0	0	0	0	0	0	0	2	0
SCOTT COOPER												
1993	3b	.000	2	0	0	0	0	0	0	0	1	0
1994	3b	.500	2	1	1	1	0	0	1	0	0	0
Total	2	.250	4	1	1	1	0	0	1	0	1	0
DOC CRAMER												
1937	of	(dnp)										
1938	of	.000	2	0	0	0	0	0	0	0	0	0
1939	of	.250	4	0	1	0	0	0	0	0	1	0
1940	of	(dnp)										
Total	2	.167	6	0	1	0	0	0	0	0	1	0
JOE CRONIN												
1935	ss	.000	4	0	0	0	0	0	1	0	1	0
1937	ss	.250	4	1	1	1	0	0	0	0	0	0
1938	ss	.667	3	0	2	1	0	0	1	1	0	0
1939	ss	.250	4	0	1	0	0	0	0	0	1	0
1941	ss	.000	2	0	0	0	0	0	0	0	1	0
Total	5	.235	17	1	4	2	0	0	2	1	3	0
JOHNNY DAMON												
2002	of	.333	3	1	1	0	0	0	0	0	1	1
2005	of	.500	2	1	1	0	0	0	0	0	0	0
Total	2	.400	5	2	2	0	0	0	0	0	1	1
DOM DIMAGGIO												
1941	of	1.000	1	0	1	0	0	0	1	0	0	0
1942	of	(dnp)										
1946	of	.500	2	0	1	0	0	0	0	0	0	0
1949	of	.400	5	2	2	1	0	0	1	0	1	0
1950	of	.000	2	0	0	0	0	0	0	0	0	0
1951	of	.200	5	0	1	0	0	0	0	0	2	0
1952	of	.500	2	0	1	1	0	0	0	1	1	0
Total	6	.353	17	2	6	2	0	0	2	1	4	0
BOBBY DOERR												
1941	2b	.000	3	0	0	0	0	0	0	0	1	0
1942	2b	(dnp)										
1943	2b	.500	4	1	2	0	0	1	3	0	0	0
1944	2b	.000	3	0	0	0	0	0	0	0	1	0
1946	2b	.000	2	0	0	0	0	0	0	0	0	0
1947	2b	.500	2	1	1	0	0	0	0	0	0	1
1948	2b	.000	2	0	0	0	0	0	0	0	1	0
1950	2b	.000	3	0	0	0	0	0	0	0	0	0
1951	2b	1.000	1	0	1	0	0	0	0	1	0	0
Total	8	.200	20	2	4	0	0	1	3	1	3	1
WALT DROPO												
1950	1b	.333	3	0	1	0	1	0	0	0	0	0
DWIGHT EVANS												
1978	of	.000	1	0	0	0	0	0	0	0	1	0
1981	of	.500	2	1	1	0	0	0	0	1	0	0
1987	of	1.000	2	0	2	0	0	0	0	1	0	0
Total	3	.600	5	1	3	0	0	0	0	2	1	0
CARL EVERETT												
2000	of	.000	2	0	0	0	0	0	1	1	0	0
RICK FERRELL												
1933	c	.000	3	0	0	0	0	0	0	0	0	0
1934	c	(dnp)										
1935	c	(dnp)										
1936	c	.000	2	0	0	0	0	0	0	0	2	0
Total	2	.000	5	0	0	0	0	0	0	0	2	0
LOU FINNEY												
1940	of	.000	0	0	0	0	0	0	0	1	0	0
CARLTON FISK												
1972	c	.500	2	1	1	0	0	0	0	0	1	0
1973	c	.000	2	0	0	0	0	0	0	0	0	0
1974	c	(injured)										
1976	c	.000	1	0	0	0	0	0	0	0	0	0
1977	c	.000	2	0	0	0	0	0	0	0	1	0
1978	c	.000	2	0	0	0	0	0	1	0	0	0
1980	c	.000	2	0	0	0	0	0	0	0	2	0
Total	6	.091	11	1	1	0	0	0	1	0	4	0
PETE FOX												
1944	of	(dnp)										
JIMMIE FOXX												
1936	3b	.500	2	1	1	0	0	0	0	0	1	0
1937	ph	.000	1	0	0	0	0	0	0	0	0	0
1938	1b	.250	4	0	1	0	0	0	0	0	1	0
1939	1b	(dnp)										
1940	1b	.000	3	0	0	0	0	0	0	0	1	0
1941	1b	.000	1	0	0	0	0	0	0	0	1	0
Total	5	.182	11	1	2	0	0	0	0	0	4	0
NOMAR GARCIAPARRA												
1997	ss	.000	1	0	0	0	0	0	0	0	0	0
1999	ss	.000	2	0	0	0	0	0	0	0	0	0
2000	ss	.500	2	1	1	0	0	0	0	0	0	0
2002	ss	.000	1	0	0	0	0	0	0	0	0	0
2003	ss	.000	1	0	0	0	0	0	0	0	0	0
Total	5	.143	7	1	1	0	0	0	0	0	0	0
RICH GEDMAN												
1985	c	.000	1	0	0	0	0	0	0	0	1	0
1986	c	.000	0	0	0	0	0	0	0	0	0	0
Total	2	.000	1	0	0	0	0	0	0	0	1	0
BILLY GOODMAN												
1949	1b	.000	0	0	0	0	0	0	0	0	0	0
1953	2b	.000	2	0	0	0	0	0	0	1	0	0
Total	2	.000	2	0	0	0	0	0	0	1	0	0
MIKE GREENWELL												
1988	of	.000	1	0	0	0	0	0	0	0	0	0
1989	of	.000	0	0	0	0	0	0	0	0	0	0
Total	2	.000	1	0	0	0	0	0	0	0	0	0
KEN HARRELSON												
1968	ph	.000	1	0	0	0	0	0	0	0	0	0
SHEA HILLENBRAND												
2002	3b	.000	2	0	0	0	0	0	0	0	1	0
JACKIE JENSEN												
1955	ph	.000	1	0	0	0	0	0	0	0	0	0
1958	of	.000	4	0	0	0	0	0	1	0	1	0
Total	2	.000	5	0	0	0	0	0	1	0	1	0
BOB JOHNSON												
1944	of	.000	3	0	0	0	0	0	0	1	1	0
1945	of(no game)												
GEORGE KELL												
1952	3b(injured)												
1953	ph	.000	1	0	0	0	0	0	0	0	0	0
MARK LORETTA												
2006	2b	.000	2	0	0	0	0	0	0	0	0	0
FRED LYNN												
1975	of	.000	2	0	0	0	0	0	0	0	1	0
1976	of	.333	3	1	1	0	0	1	1	0	1	0
1977	of	.000	1	1	0	0	0	0	0	1	0	0
1978	of	.250	4	0	1	0	0	0	0	0	1	0
1979	of	1.000	1	1	1	0	0	1	2	0	0	0
1980	of	.333	3	0	1	0	0	1	2	0	1	0
Total	6	.286	14	4	4	0	0	3	5	1	4	0
FRANK MALZONE												
1957	3b	.000	2	0	0	0	0	0	0	0	0	0
1958	3b	.250	4	1	1	0	0	0	0	0	1	0
1959-1	3b	.000	2	0	0	0	0	0	0	0	0	0
1959-2	3b	.250	4	1	1	0	0	1	1	0	0	0
1960-1	3b	.000	3	0	0	0	0	0	0	0	0	0
1960-2	3b	.000	2	0	0	0	0	0	0	1	0	0
1963	3b	.333	3	1	1	0	0	0	1	0	0	0
1964	3b	(dnp)										
Total	7	.150	20	3	3	0	0	1	2	1	1	0
FELIX MANTILLA												
1965	2b	.000	2	0	0	0	0	0	0	0	0	0
JERRY MOSES												
1970	c	(dnp)										
JOSE OFFERMAN												
1999	2b	.000	1	0	0	0	0	0	0	0	0	0
DAVID ORTIZ												
2004	1b	1.000	1	2	1	0	0	1	2	2	0	0
2005	dh	.667	3	0	2	0	0	1	0	0	0	0
2006	1b	.000	2	0	0	0	0	0	0	0	1	0
Total	3	.500	6	2	3	0	0	1	3	2	1	0
JOHNNY PESKY												
1946	ss	.000	2	0	0	0	0	0	0	0	0	0
RICO PETROCELLI												
1967	ss	.000	1	0	0	0	0	0	0	0	0	0
1969	ss	.333	3	0	1	1	0	0	0	0	1	0
Total	2	.250	4	0	1	1	0	0	0	0	1	0
JIM PIERSALL												
1954	of	.000	0	0	0	0	0	0	0	0	0	0
1956	of	.000	1	0	0	0	0	0	0	0	0	0
Total	2	.000	1	0	0	0	0	0	0	0	0	0
MANNY RAMIREZ												
2001	of	.000	1	0	0	0	0	0	0	0	1	0
2002	of	1.000	2	0	2	0	0	0	1	0	0	0
2003	of (injured)												
2004	of	.500	2	1	1	0	0	1	2	0	0	0
2005	of	.000	2	0	0	0	0	0	0	0	1	0
2006	of(declined)												
Total	4	.429	7	1	3	0	0	1	3	0	2	0
JERRY REMY												
1978	2b	(dnp)										

YEAR	POS	AVG	AB	R	H	2B	3B	HR	RBI	BB	SO	SB
JIM RICE												
1977	of	.500	2	0	1	0	0	0	0	0	0	0
1978	of	.000	4	0	0	0	0	0	0	0	2	0
1979	of	.200	5	0	1	1	0	0	0	0	2	0
1980	of (injured)											
1983	of	.500	4	1	2	0	0	1	1	0	0	0
1984	of	.000	1	0	0	0	0	0	0	0	1	0
1985	of	.000	3	0	0	0	0	0	0	1	2	0
1986	ph	.000	1	0	0	0	0	0	0	0	1	0
Total	7	.200	20	1	4	1	0	1	1	1	8	0
PETE RUNNELS												
1959–1	ph	.000	0	0	0	0	0	0	0	0	0	0
1959–2	1b	.000	3	0	0	0	0	0	0	1	2	0
1960–1	2b	.000	1	0	0	0	0	0	0	1	0	0
1960–2	2b	.000	2	0	0	0	0	0	0	1	1	0
1962–2	ph	1.000	1	1	1	0	0	1	1	0	0	0
Total	5	.143	7	1	1	0	0	1	1	3	3	0
GEORGE SCOTT												
1966	1b	.000	2	0	0	0	0	0	0	0	0	0
1977	1b	.500	2	1	1	0	0	1	2	0	0	0
Total	2	.250	4	1	1	0	0	1	2	0	0	0
REGGIE SMITH												
1969	of	.000	2	1	0	0	0	0	0	0	0	0
1972	ph	.000	1	0	0	0	0	0	0	0	1	0
Total	2	.000	3	1	0	0	0	0	0	0	1	0
VERN STEPHENS												
1948	ss	.500	2	0	1	0	0	0	0	0	1	0
1949	ss	.000	2	0	0	0	0	0	0	0	1	0
1950	ss	(dnp)										
1951	ph	.000	1	0	0	0	0	0	0	0	1	0
Total	3	.200	5	0	1	0	0	0	0	0	3	0
BIRDIE TEBBETTS												
1948	c	.000	1	1	0	0	0	0	0	2	1	0
1949	c	1.000	2	0	2	1	0	0	1	0	0	0
Total	2	.667	3	1	2	1	0	0	1	2	1	0
JASON VARITEK												
2003	c	(dnp)										
2005	c	1.000	1	1	1	0	0	0	0	1	0	0
MO VAUGHN												
1995	1b	.000	2	0	0	0	0	0	0	0	2	0
1996	1b	.333	3	0	1	1	0	0	0	0	0	0
1998	1b(injured)											
Total	2	.200	5	0	1	1	0	0	0	0	2	0
MICKEY VERNON												
1956	1b	.000	2	0	0	0	0	0	0	0	0	0

YEAR	POS	AVG	AB	R	H	2B	3B	HR	RBI	BB	SO	SB
HAL WAGNER												
1946	c	.000	1	0	0	0	0	0	0	0	0	0
SAMMY WHITE												
1953	c	(dnp)										
TED WILLIAMS												
1940	of	.000	2	0	0	0	0	0	0	1	0	0
1941	of	.500	4	1	2	1	0	1	4	1	1	0
1942	of	.250	4	0	1	0	0	0	0	0	0	0
1946	of	1.000	4	4	4	0	0	2	5	1	0	0
1947	of	.500	4	0	2	1	0	0	0	0	1	0
1948	ph	.000	0	0	0	0	0	0	0	1	0	0
1949	of	.000	2	1	0	0	0	0	0	2	1	0
1950	of	.250	4	0	1	0	0	0	1	1	1	0
1951	of	.333	3	0	1	0	1	0	0	1	1	0
1953	of(honorary)											
1954	of	.000	2	0	0	0	0	0	0	1	2	0
1955	of	.333	3	1	1	0	0	0	1	1	0	0
1956	of	.250	4	1	1	0	0	1	2	0	1	0
1957	of	.000	3	1	0	0	0	0	0	1	0	0
1958	of	.000	2	0	0	0	0	0	0	0	1	0
1959–1	ph	.000	0	0	0	0	0	0	0	1	0	0
1959–2	of	.000	3	0	0	0	0	0	0	0	1	0
1960–1	ph	.000	1	0	0	0	0	0	0	0	0	0
1960–2	ph	1.000	1	0	1	0	0	0	0	0	0	0
Total	18	.304	46	10	14	2	1	4	12	11	10	0
CARL YASTRZEMSKI												
1963	of	.000	2	0	0	0	0	0	0	0	1	0
1965	of (injured)											
1966	of (dnp)											
1967	of	.750	4	0	3	1	0	0	0	2	1	0
1968	of	.000	4	0	0	0	0	0	0	0	2	0
1969	of	.000	1	0	0	0	0	0	0	0	0	0
1970	of	.667	6	1	4	1	0	0	1	0	0	0
1971	of	.000	3	0	0	0	0	0	0	0	0	0
1972	of	.000	3	0	0	0	0	0	0	0	1	0
1973	1b(injured)											
1974	1b	.000	1	0	0	0	0	0	0	1	0	0
1975	ph	1.000	1	1	1	0	0	1	3	0	0	0
1976	of	.000	2	0	0	0	0	0	0	0	0	0
1977	of	.000	2	0	0	0	0	0	0	0	1	0
1978	of (injured)											
1979	1b	.667	3	0	2	0	0	0	1	0	0	0
1982	ph	.000	1	0	0	0	0	0	0	0	1	0
1983	ph	.000	1	0	0	0	0	0	0	0	1	0
Total	14	.294	34	2	10	2	0	1	5	4	8	0
RUDY YORK												
1946	1b	.500	2	0	1	0	0	0	0	0	0	0

YEAR	W	L	ERA	GS	SV	IP	H	R	ER	HR	BB	SO
GARY BELL												
1968	(dnp)											
TOM BREWER												
1956	0	0	13.50	0	0	2.0	4	3	3	0	1	2
TOM BURGMEIER												
1980	(dnp)											
BILL CAMPBELL												
1977	0	0	0.00	0	0	1.0	0	0	0	0	1	2
MARK CLEAR												
1982	(dnp)											
ROGER CLEMENS												
1986	1	0	0.00	1	0	3.0	0	0	0	0	0	2
1988	0	0	0.00	0	0	1.0	0	0	0	0	0	1
1990	(dnp)											
1991	0	0	9.00	0	0	1.0	1	1	1	0	0	0
1992	0	0	0.00	0	0	1.0	2	0	0	0	0	0
Total (4)	1		1.50	1	0	6.0	3	1	1	1	0	3
MATT CLEMENT												
2005	0	0	0.00	0	0	1.0	0	0	0	0	1	1
RAY CULP												
1969	0	0	0.00	0	0	1.0	0	0	0	0	0	2
JOE DOBSON												
1948	(dnp)											
DENNIS ECKERSLEY												
1982	0	1	9.00	1	0	3.0	2	3	3	0	2	1
DAVE FERRISS												
1945	(no game)											
1946	(dnp)											
MIKE FORNIELES												
1961–1	0	0	27.00	0	0	0.1	2	1	1	0	0	0
TOM GORDON												
1998	0	0	9.00	0	0	1.0	3	2	1	0	1	0
LEFTY GROVE												
1935	(dnp)											
1936	0	1	6.00	1	0	3.0	3	2	2	0	2	2
1937	(dnp)											
1938	0	0	0.00	0	0	2.0	4	2	0	0	0	3
1939	(dnp)											
Total (2)	0		3.60	1	0	5.0	7	4	2	0	2	5
ERIK HANSON												
1995	(dnp)											

YEAR	W	L	ERA	GS	SV	IP	H	R	ER	HR	BB	SO
MICKEY HARRIS												
1946	(dnp)											
TEX HUGHSON												
1942	(dnp)											
1943	0	0	6.00	0	1	3.0	5	2	2	0	0	2
1944	0	1	16.20	0	0	1.2	5	4	3	0	1	2
Total (2)	0	1	9.64	0	1	4.2	10	6	5	0	1	4
BRUCE HURST												
1987	(dnp)											
OSCAR JUDD												
1943	(dnp)											
BILL LEE												
1973	(dnp)											
JIM LONBORG												
1967	(dnp)											
DEREK LOWE												
2000	0	0	0.00	0	0	1.0	0	0	0	0	0	0
2002	0	0	4.50	1	0	2.0	2	1	1	0	0	0
Total (2)	0	0	3.00	1	0	3.0	2	1	1	0	0	0
PEDRO MARTINEZ												
1998	(dnp)											
1999	1	0	0.00	1	0	2.0	0	0	0	0	0	5
2000	(injured)											
2002	(injured)											
BILL MONBOUQUETTE												
1960–1	0	1	18.00	1	0	2.0	5	4	4	0	0	2
1960–2	(dnp)											
1962–1	(dnp)											
1963	(dnp)											
JONATHAN PAPELBON												
2006	0	0	0.00	0	0	0.0	0	0	0	0	0	0
MEL PARNELL												
1949	0	0	27.00	1	0	1.0	3	3	3	0	1	1
1951	0	0	9.00	0	0	1.0	3	1	1	0	0	1
Total (2)	0	0	18.00	1	0	2.0	6	4	4	0	1	2
DICK RADATZ												
1963	0	0	4.50	0	0	2.0	2	1	1	0	0	5
1964	0	1	13.50	0	0	2.2	2	4	4	0	2	5
Total (2)	0	1	9.64	0	0	4.2	4	5	5	0	2	10
JEFF REARDON												
1991	0	0	0.00	0	0	0.2	1	0	0	0	0	0

YEAR	W	L	ERA	GS	SV	IP	H	R	ER	HR	BB	SO
JOSE SANTIAGO												
1968 (injured)												
CURT SCHILLING												
2004 (injured)												
DON SCHWALL												
1961–2	0		0	3.00	0	0	3.0	5	1	1	0	1	2
SONNY SIEBERT												
1971 (dnp)												
BOB STANLEY												
1979	0	0	4.50	0	0	2.0	1	1	1	0	0	0

YEAR	W	L	ERA	GS	SV	IP	H	R	ER	HR	BB	SO
1983	0	0	0.00	0	0	2.0	2	0	0	0	0	0
Total	2	0	0	2.25	0	4.0	3	1	1	0	0	0
FRANK SULLIVAN												
1955	0	1	2.70	0	0	3.1	4	1	1	0	1	4
1956 (dnp)												
LUIS TIANT												
1974	0	1	9.00	0	0	2.0	4	3	2	0	1	0
1976	0	0	0.00	0	0	2.0	1	0	0	0	0	1
Total	2	0	1	4.50	0	0	4.0	5	3	2	0	1	1
UGUETH URBINA												
2002	0	0	0.00	0	0	1.0	0	0	0	0	0	1

1946 All-Star Game

AL 12, NL 0
Managers: Steve O'Neill (AL), Charlie Grimm (NL)

World War II travel restrictions had forced the cancellation of the 1945 All-Star Game, the only year since 1933 that the game has not been played. The American League dumped two years' worth of offense on Fenway Park. Bob Feller, Hal Newhouser, and Jack Kramer held the National League to just 3 singles and a walk while fanning 10. Ted Williams outhit the senior circuit himself.

Williams had four hits and a walk and knocked in five runs. He scored four times, the first on a home run by Charlie Keller off Claude Passeau in the opening inning to start the barrage. He homered to center field against Kirby Higbe in the fourth. The score was 9–0 when Williams came up with two men on in the eighth against Rip Sewell, whose super-slow "eephus" pitch had kept National Leaguers off stride the first three months of the season. Not Teddy Ballgame, not on this day. He ripped the pitch into the right-field bullpen, the first time anyone had homered off the pitch all year.

It was a red-letter Red Sox day. The first three batters in Detroit manager Steve O'Neill's All-Star lineup were Red Sox: Dom DiMaggio, Johnny Pesky, and Williams. Bobby Doerr started and hit fifth. In all, eight Red Sox were picked for the team, the most in club history. And why not? The Red Sox were playing .700 ball and had a 7 ½-game lead in the standings. It all made for a lot of happy Fenway faces.

AMERICAN LEAGUE 12, NATIONAL LEAGUE 0
PLAYED ON TUESDAY, JULY 9, 1946 (D) AT FENWAY PARK

```
NL  0 0 0   0 0 0   0 0 0  -  0  3  0
AL  2 0 0   1 3 0   2 4 x  - 12 14  1
```

BATTING

National League	AB	R	H	RBI	BB	SO	PO	A
Schoendienst 2b	2	0	0	0	0	0	0	2
Gustine ph,2b	1	0	0	0	1	1	1	1
Musial lf	2	0	0	0	0	0	0	0
Ennis ph,lf	2	0	0	0	0	2	0	0
Hopp cf	2	0	1	0	0	0	0	0
Lowrey ph,cf	2	0	1	0	0	0	3	0
Walker rf	3	0	0	0	0	0	1	0
Slaughter rf	1	0	0	0	0	0	0	0
Kurowski 3b	3	0	0	0	0	2	2	1
Verban ph	1	0	0	0	0	0	0	0
Mize 1b	1	0	0	0	0	0	7	0
McCormick ph,1b	1	0	0	0	0	0	1	1
Cavarretta ph,1b	1	0	0	0	0	1	1	0
Cooper c	1	0	1	0	0	0	0	0
Masi c	2	0	0	0	0	0	4	1
Marion ss	3	0	0	0	0	2	4	6
Passeau p	1	0	0	0	0	1	0	1
Higbe p	1	0	0	0	0	1	0	0
Blackwell p	0	0	0	0	0	0	0	0
Lamanno ph	1	0	0	0	0	0	0	0
Sewell p	0	0	0	0	0	0	0	0
Totals	**31**	**0**	**3**	**0**	**1**	**10**	**24**	**13**

American League	AB	R	H	RBI	BB	SO	PO	A
DiMaggio cf	2	0	1	0	0	0	1	0
Spence cf	0	1	0	0	1	0	1	0
Chapman cf	2	0	1	0	0	1	1	0
Pesky ss	2	0	0	0	0	0	1	0
Stephens ss	3	1	2	2	0	0	0	4
Williams lf	4	4	4	5	1	0	1	0
Keller rf	4	2	1	2	1	1	1	0
Doerr 2b	2	0	0	0	0	0	1	1
Gordon 2b	2	0	1	2	0	0	1	1
Vernon 1b	2	0	0	0	0	0	2	1
York 1b	2	0	1	0	0	0	5	0
Keltner 3b	0	0	0	0	1	0	0	0
Stirnweiss 3b	3	1	1	0	0	1	0	0
Hayes c	1	0	0	0	0	0	3	0
Rosar c	2	1	1	0	0	0	5	0
Wagner c	1	0	0	0	0	0	4	0
Feller p	0	0	0	0	0	0	0	0
Appling ph	1	0	0	0	0	0	0	0
Newhouser p	1	1	1	0	0	0	1	0
Dickey ph	1	0	0	0	0	1	0	0
Kramer p	1	1	1	0	0	0	0	0
Totals	**36**	**12**	**14**	**12**	**4**	**3**	**27**	**7**

FIELDING
DP: 2. Marion-Mize, Schoendienst-Marion-Mize

FIELDING
E: Pesky (1)

BATTING
2B: Stephens (1,off Higbe); Gordon (1,off Blackwell)

HR: Keller (1, 1st inning off Passeau 1 on 2 out); Williams 2 (2, 4th inning off Higbe 0 on 0 out, 8th inning off Sewell 2 on 2 out)

IBB: Spence (1, by Higbe)

Team LOB: 4

PITCHING

National League	IP	H	R	ER	BB	SO	HR
Passeau L (0–1)	3	2	2	2	2	0	1
Higbe	1.1	5	4	4	1	2	1
Blackwell	2.2	3	2	2	1	1	0
Sewell	1	4	4	4	0	0	1
Totals	8	14	12	12	4	3	3

WP: Blackwell (1).
IBB: Higbe (1,Spence).

American League	IP	H	R	ER	BB	SO	HR
Feller W (1–0)	3	2	0	0	0	3	0
Newhouser	3	1	0	0	0	4	0
Kramer SV (1)	3	0	0	0	1	3	0
Totals	9	3	0	0	1	10	0

Umpires: Bill Summers, Dusty Boggess, Eddie Rommel, Larry Goetz
Time of Game: 2:19
Attendance: 34,906

1961 All-Star Game

AL 1, NL 1
Managers: Paul Richards (AL), Danny Murtaugh (NL)

Two All-Star Games were held between 1959 and 1962 to raise money for the players' pension fund. It was for a good cause, but it did not always inspire thrilling baseball with two breaks in the season instead of one.

Unlike the first All-Star Game in 1961, with the National League rallying to win in the bottom of the 10th, the second game at Fenway Park ended in a tie. If a tie is like kissing your sister, a tie in an exhibition game had to be like kissing the sister with the garlic breath.

It started out with the promise of excitement as Rocky Colavito homered in the first inning for the

American League against Bob Purkey. The lead held until Red Sox rookie Don Schwall allowed Bill White's single to tie the game in the sixth. The inning had been prolonged when sure-handed shortstop Luis Aparicio couldn't make a play on a slow grounder. Schwall, Boston's lone representative and the eventual AL Rookie of the Year, permitted five hits in his three innings. AL starter Jim Bunning and Camilo Pasqual each threw three no-hit innings before and after the rook.

After nine innings had been completed, the rain that had been falling since the eighth turned heavy and the field was cleared. Thirty minutes later both leagues and everyone else were sent home. The tie was at least caused by weather, unlike the stalemate in 2002 in a retractable-roof stadium the result of both teams using up all their pitchers and then calling it a night with no winner.

AMERICAN LEAGUE 1, NATIONAL LEAGUE 1
PLAYED ON MONDAY, JULY 31, 1961 (D) AT FENWAY PARK

```
NL  0 0 0   0 0 1   0 0 0 - 1 5 1
AL  1 0 0   0 0 0   0 0 0 - 1 4 0
```

BATTING

National League	AB	R	H	RBI	BB	SO	PO	A
Wills ss	2	0	1	0	0	0	1	1
Aaron rf	2	0	0	0	0	1	0	0
Miller p	0	0	0	0	0	0	0	0
Mathews 3b	3	1	0	0	1	1	0	2
Mays cf	3	0	1	0	1	0	1	0
Cepeda lf	3	0	0	0	0	0	0	0
Clemente rf	2	0	0	0	0	0	0	0
Kasko ss	1	0	1	0	0	0	2	4
Banks ph,ss	1	0	0	0	0	1	0	0
White 1b	4	0	2	1	0	0	11	1
Bolling 2b	4	0	0	0	0	0	3	2
Burgess c	1	0	0	0	0	1	2	0
Roseboro c	3	0	0	0	0	3	6	0
Purkey p	0	0	0	0	0	0	0	1
Stuart ph	1	0	0	0	0	0	0	0
Mahaffey p	0	0	0	0	0	0	0	0
Musial ph	1	0	0	0	0	1	0	0
Koufax p	0	0	0	0	0	0	0	0
Altman ph,rf	1	0	0	0	0	0	0	0
Totals	32	1	5	1	2	7	27	11

FIELDING
DP: 2. Bolling-Kasko-White, White-Kasko-Bolling
E: Bolling (1)
PB: Burgess (1)
BATTING
2B: White (1, off Schwall)
HBP: Cepeda (1, by Schwall)
Team LOB: 7

American League	AB	R	H	RBI	BB	SO	PO	A
Cash 1b	4	0	0	0	0	1	11	0
Colavito lf	4	1	1	1	0	0	3	0
Kaline rf	4	0	2	0	0	0	1	0
Mantle cf	3	0	0	0	1	2	2	0
Romano c	1	0	0	0	0	0	1	0
Maris ph	1	0	0	0	0	0	0	0
Howard c	2	0	0	0	0	1	6	0
Aparicio ss	2	0	0	0	1	1	1	3
Sievers ph	1	0	0	0	0	1	0	0
Temple 2b	2	0	0	0	1	1	2	3
Robinson 3b	3	0	1	0	0	1	0	3
Bunning p	1	0	0	0	0	0	0	0
Schwall p	1	0	0	0	0	0	0	0
Pascual p	1	0	0	0	0	0	0	0
Totals	30	1	4	1	3	8	27	9

BATTING
HR: Colavito (1, 1st inning off Purkey 0 on 1 out)
Team LOB: 5

BASERUNNING
SB: Kaline (1, 2nd base off Miller/Roseboro)

PITCHING

National League	IP	H	R	ER	BB	SO	HR
Purkey	2	1	1	1	2	2	1
Mahaffey	2	0	0	0	1	0	0
Koufax	2	2	0	0	0	1	0
Miller	3	1	0	0	0	5	0
Totals	9	4	1	1	3	8	1

American League	IP	H	R	ER	BB	SO	HR
Bunning	3	0	0	0	0	1	0
Schwall	3	5	1	1	1	2	0
Pascual	3	0	0	0	1	4	0
Totals	9	5	1	1	2	7	0

HBP: Schwall (1, Cepeda).
Umpires: Larry Napp, Frank Secory, Red Flaherty, Ed Sudol, Al Smith, Chris Pelekoudas
Time of Game: 2:27
Attendance: 31,851

1999 All-Star Game

AL 4, NL 1
Managers: Joe Torre (AL), Bruce Bochy (NL)

The greatest players of the 20th century were announced and paraded on the field—several in uniform for the game—but all bowed to Ted Williams and gathered around. Unlike the stiff ceremony on Major League Baseball and the network's timetable, the Splendid Splinter was driven to the mound and lingered while All-Stars and Hall of Famers alike pressed near him. Like children around Santa Claus, even the most jaded of the crew seemed to genuinely hope the "greatest hitter who ever lived" might recognize him. Williams had thrown out the first pitch in the 1953 All-Star Game, just after he returned from active pilot duty and survived being shot down in Korea; 46 years later he still had everyone's attention and still made a decent pitch.

Not one to be upstaged, especially at his home park, Pedro Martinez burned through the National League lineup. He fanned Barry Larkin, Larry Walker, and Sammy Sosa. With a lead to start the second inning—Jim Thome and Cal Ripken singled in runs off future Red Sox ace and raconteur Curt Schilling—Martinez wasn't slowing down. He struck out Mark McGwire, the first time a pitcher began an All-Star Game by striking out the first four (just as he'd broken new ground by fanning the first three). A Roberto Alomar error put Jeff Bagwell on first, but Martinez struck out Matt Williams while Ivan Rodriguez threw out Bagwell trying to steal second. He'd already tied the AL record for All-Star strikeouts and many watching wished the catcher's throw hadn't been true so Martinez could have gone for six. (He may have been throwing a little too nasty as Martinez was forced to miss two starts after his All-Star Game MVP performance.)

Larkin singled in a run off David Cone to make it 2–1 in the third. The AL scored twice in the fourth, but the highlight was Derek Jeter imitating the batter's box mannerisms of Nomar Garciaparra, whom he replaced at shortstop. Jeter struck out, one of a record 22 K's between the All-Stars (the AL had 12). It turned out to be a pitcher's night on an evening that honored "the greatest hitter who ever lived."

AMERICAN LEAGUE 4, NATIONAL LEAGUE 1
PLAYED ON TUESDAY, JULY 13, 1999 (N) AT FENWAY PARK

```
NL  0 0 1   0 0 0   0 0 0 - 1 7 1
AL  2 0 0   2 0 0   0 0 x - 4 6 2
```

BATTING

National League	AB	R	H	RBI	BB	SO	PO	A
Larkin ss	3	0	1	1	0	1	1	1
A. Gonzalez ph,ss	1	0	0	0	0	0	1	0
Walker rf	2	0	0	0	0	1	1	0
L. Gonzalez lf	2	0	1	0	0	0	0	0
Sosa cf	3	0	0	0	0	2	1	0
Guerrero rf	1	0	0	0	0	0	1	0
McGwire 1b	2	0	0	0	1	2	3	0
Casey 1b	1	0	0	0	0	0	4	0
Williams 3b	3	0	1	0	0	1	1	0
Sprague 3b	1	0	0	0	0	0	0	0
Bagwell dh	3	0	1	0	0	2	0	0
Sheffield ph,dh	1	0	0	0	0	0	0	0
Piazza c	2	0	1	0	0	1	6	0
Lieberthal c	1	0	0	0	0	0	1	0
Nilsson c	1	0	0	0	0	1	3	0
Burnitz lf,rf	2	1	1	0	0	0	0	0
Jordan cf	1	0	1	0	1	0	0	0
Bell 2b	1	0	0	0	1	1	0	1
Kent 2b	1	0	0	0	1	0	1	2
Schilling p	0	0	0	0	0	0	0	0
Johnson p	0	0	0	0	0	0	0	0
Bottenfield p	0	0	0	0	0	0	0	0
Lima p	0	0	0	0	0	0	0	0
Millwood p	0	0	0	0	0	0	0	1
Ashby p	0	0	0	0	0	0	0	0
Hampton p	0	0	0	0	0	0	0	0
Hoffman p	0	0	0	0	0	0	0	0
Wagner p	0	0	0	0	0	0	0	0
Totals	**32**	**1**	**7**	**1**	**4**	**12**	**24**	**5**

FIELDING
E: Williams (1)

BATTING
2B: Burnitz (1, off Cone); L. Gonzalez (1, off Mussina)   **Team LOB:** 8

BASERUNNING
CS: Williams (1,2nd base by Martinez/Rodriguez); Jordan (1,2nd base by Zimmerman/Ausmus)

American League	AB	R	H	RBI	BB	SO	PO	A
Lofton lf,cf	3	1	1	0	0	1	0	0
Williams cf	1	0	0	0	0	1	0	0
Garciaparra ss	2	0	0	0	0	0	0	0
Jeter ss	1	0	0	0	0	1	1	0
Vizquel ss	1	0	0	0	0	0	1	4
Griffey cf	2	0	0	0	0	1	0	0
Surhoff lf	2	0	0	0	0	0	0	0
Ramirez rf	1	1	0	0	1	1	0	0
Green rf	1	0	1	0	0	0	0	0
Ordonez rf	1	0	0	0	0	0	0	0
Thome 1b	2	1	1	1	1	0	4	0
Coomer 1b	1	0	0	0	0	0	4	0
Ripken 3b	1	1	1	1	0	0	0	0
Fernandez 3b	2	0	0	0	0	1	0	2
Palmeiro dh	2	0	1	1	0	0	0	0
Baines ph,dh	1	0	1	0	0	0	0	0
Jaha ph,dh	1	0	0	0	0	1	0	0
Rodriguez c	2	0	0	0	0	1	10	1
Ausmus c	1	0	0	0	0	0	2	1
Alomar 2b	2	0	0	1	0	1	2	2
Offerman ph,2b	1	0	0	0	0	0	3	0
Martinez p	0	0	0	0	0	0	0	0
Cone p	0	0	0	0	0	0	0	0
Mussina p	0	0	0	0	0	0	0	0
Rosado p	0	0	0	0	0	0	0	0
Zimmerman p	0	0	0	0	0	0	0	0
Hernandez p	0	0	0	0	0	0	0	0
Wetteland p	0	0	0	0	0	0	0	1
Totals	**31**	**4**	**6**	**4**	**2**	**10**	**27**	**12**

FIELDING
DP: 3. Rodriguez-Alomar, Fernandez-Alomar-Thome, Wetteland-Vizquel-Coomer
E: Alomar (1), Offerman (1)

BATTING
HBP: Ripken (1, by Bottenfield)   **Team LOB:** 6

BASERUNNING
SB: Lofton (1, 2nd base off Schilling/Piazza)

PITCHING

National League	IP	H	R	ER	BB	SO	HR
Schilling L(0-1)	2	3	2	2	1	3	0
Johnson	1	0	0	0	0	1	0
Bottenfield	1	1	2	2	1	2	0
Lima	1	1	0	0	0	1	0
Millwood	1	1	0	0	0	1	0
Ashby	0.1	0	0	0	0	0	0
Hampton	0.2	0	0	0	0	0	0
Hoffman	0.1	0	0	0	0	0	0
Wagner	0.2	0	0	0	0	2	0
Totals	**8**	**6**	**4**	**4**	**2**	**10**	**0**

HBP: Bottenfield (1, Ripken).

American League	IP	H	R	ER	BB	SO	HR
Martinez W(1-0)	2	0	0	0	0	5	0
Cone	2	4	1	1	1	3	0
Mussina	1	1	0	0	1	2	0
Rosado	1	1	0	0	0	1	0
Zimmerman	1	0	0	0	2	0	0
Hernandez	1	0	0	0	0	0	0
Wetteland SV(1)	1	1	0	0	0	1	0
Totals	**9**	**7**	**1**	**1**	**4**	**12**	**0**

Umpires: Jim Evans, Terry Tata, Dale Ford, Angel Hernandez, Mark Johnson, Larry Vanover
Time of Game: 2:53   **Attendance:** 34,187

Use of boxscores copyright © 1996–2006 by Retrosheet. All Rights Reserved.

The Sporting News All-Stars

Almost a decade before baseball's All-Star Game was born, *The Sporting News* was selecting its own such team at the end of every major league season. From 1925 through 1960, *The Sporting News* named one All Star team covering both major leagues. Since 1961, the first year the major leagues expanded, *The Sporting News* has named one All-Star team for each league. The composition of the All-Star teams have varied little over the years, though the number of pitchers selected has fluctuated back and forth and a slot for a designated hitter was added to the American League All-Star team in 1974. The first list features every Red Sox *Sporting News* All-Star and the years selected. (No Red Sox was chosen until the 14th season of selections.) The second list is a ranking of how many times each Red Sox has been honored (with the career total in brackets including years outside Boston).

1938
1B Jimmie Foxx
SS Joe Cronin

1939
1B Jimmie Foxx
SS Joe Cronin
OF Ted Williams

1940
OF Ted Williams

1941
OF Ted Williams

1942
SS Johnny Pesky
OF Ted Williams
P   Tex Hughson

1944
2B Bobby Doerr

1945
P   Dave Ferriss

1946
OF Ted Williams

1947
OF Ted Williams

1948
C   Birdie Tebbetts
OF Ted Williams

1949
OF Ted Williams
P   Mel Parnell
P   Ellis Kinder

1950
1B Walt Dropo

1951
OF Ted Williams

1952
3B George Kell

1955
OF Ted Williams

1956
OF Ted Williams

1957
OF Ted Williams

1958
OF Ted Williams

1963
3B Frank Malzone
OF Carl Yastrzemski

1964
1B Dick Stuart

1965
OF Carl Yastrzemski

1967
OF Carl Yastrzemski
P   Jim Lonborg

1968
OF Ken Harrelson

1969
SS Rico Petrocelli

1970
OF Reggie Smith

1972
C   Carlton Fisk
SS Luis Aparicio

1975
OF Jim Rice
OF Fred Lynn

1977
C   Carlton Fisk
SS Rick Burleson
OF Jim Rice

1978
OF Jim Rice
OF Fred Lynn

1979
OF Jim Rice
OF Fred Lynn

1982
OF Dwight Evans

1983
3B Wade Boggs
OF Jim Rice1984
OF Tony Armas
OF Dwight Evans

1985
3B Wade Boggs

1986
3B Wade Boggs
OF Jim Rice
C   Rich Gedman
DH Don Baylor
RHP Roger Clemens

1987
3B Wade Boggs
OF Dwight Evans
RHP Roger Clemens

1988
3B Wade Boggs
OF Mike Greenwell

1990
OF Ellis Burks

1991
3B Wade Boggs
RHP Roger Clemens

1995
1B Mo Vaughn

1997
SS Nomar Garciaparra

1998
RHP Pedro Martinez

1999
SS Nomar Garciaparra
RHP Pedro Martinez

2000
RHP Pedro Martinez

2001
OF Manny Ramirez

2002
DH Manny Ramirez
RHP Derek Lowe

2003
3B Bill Mueller

2004
OF Manny Ramirez
DH David Ortiz

2005
C   Jason Varitek
OF Johnny Damon
OF Manny Ramirez
DH David Ortiz

2006
OF Manny Ramirez
DH David Ortiz

Red Sox *Sporting News* All-Stars Ranked by Times Selected

Ted Williams	13	Joe Cronin	2 [7]	Ellis Burks	1 [2]	Tex Hughson	1	Reggie Smith	1
Wade Boggs	6 [7]	Jimmie Foxx	2 [5]	Rick Burleson	1 [2]	Ellis Kinder	1	Dick Stuart	1
Jim Rice	6	Carlton Fisk	2 [4]	Johnny Damon	1	Jim Lonborg	1	Birdie Tebbetts	1
Manny Ramirez	5 [7]	Dwight Evans	2	Bobby Doerr	1	Derek Lowe	1	Jason Varitek	1
Roger Clemens	3 (5)	Nomar Garciaparra	2	Walt Dropo	1	Frank Malzone	1	Mo Vaughn	1
Fred Lynn	3	George Kell	1 [6]	Dave Ferriss	1	Bill Mueller	1		
Pedro Martinez	3	Luis Aparicio	1 [5]	Rich Gedman	1	Mel Parnell	1		
David Ortiz	3	Don Baylor	1 [3]	Mike Greenwell	1	Johnny Pesky	1		
Carl Yastrzemski	3	Tony Armas	1 [2]	Ken Harrelson	1	Rico Petrocelli	1		

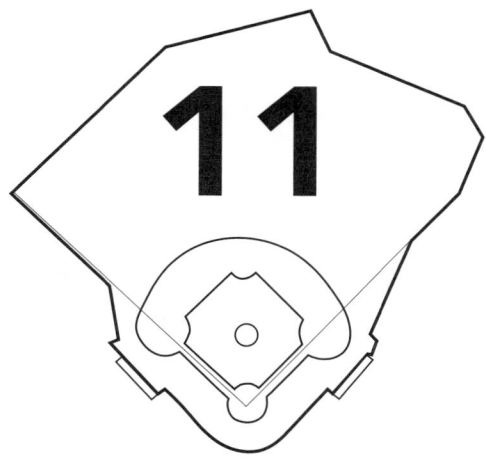

RED SOX ALL-TIME TEAM AND LEADERS

The Red Sox have many measuring sticks for greatness: Cy Young, Tris Speaker, Babe Ruth, Jimmie Foxx, Ted Williams, Carl Yastrzemski, Jim Rice, Dwight Evans, Wade Boggs, Roger Clemens, Nomar Garciaparra, Pedro Martinez, Manny Ramirez...the list goes on and on. Where do these men rank in terms of the greatest Red Sox ever? That's a fun question. One answer can be found in the All-Time Team section. Chosen by a group vote by the editors of this book and *The ESPN Baseball Encyclopedia*, the first and second teams take into account career Red Sox numbers, Beantown longevity, and good old-fashioned opinion.

The Leaders section that follows the All-Time Team is based strictly on fact. It looks at numbers two ways: for a year and for a career. The first part of this section catalogs numbers compiled over a full Red Sox career, taking into account the long tenures of Williams and Evans, Rice and Ramirez. Yaz's prolonged career—all 23 years with the Red Sox—places him in the all-time top 10 in major league history for games, at bats, hits, doubles, plate appearances, extra base hits, total bases, and walks. So who do you think heads many of the offensive categories in this section?

The single-season numbers, however, are a mix of the fluky and the consistent. The same names recur at the top of many categories with the occasional short-timer cracking the list. Williams owns the first 11 spots on the walk percentage list, but only one hitter has come within a dozen doubles of obscure Earl Webb's 1931 mark of 67. David Ortiz toppled Foxx's 1938 single-season home run mark in 2006, but no Red Sox slugger has ever come close to the 175 RBIs forged by "Double X" in 1938. Need proof that Tim Wakefield has

been in Boston a long time? Look at all the career pitching categories with Wakefield's name ahead of Cy Young's. The single-season section has a few varied names—Dutch Leonard's miniscule 0.96 ERA in 1914—but most of the lists are dominated by the likes of Young and Martinez. Red Sox as of 2006 are listed in bold.

While the aforementioned Young and Martinez mastered their day, the differences between the dead ball and the modern eras are so great, that several categories in this section are additionally grouped by the period in which they played. Those eras for the Red Sox are broken down into six significant periods since the founding of the American League and the Red Sox in 1901.

- The 1901–20 era, covering the dead ball period and World War I, the banning of the spitball, the dominance of the Red Sox, and the scandal of the Black Sox. It ends when offensive numbers start to jump.

- The next period, 1921–42, takes the major leagues through the time when offense dominated the game until World War II created severe player shortages.

- The third era, 1943–60, begins with the peak war years and continues through baseball's integration, and includes the first relocation of franchises since the early 1900s. This period culminates the same year as Ted Williams' brilliant career, truly the end of an era.

- The 1961–72 era features expansion of the leagues as well as the strike zone (plus the latter's reversion), the 162-game schedule, the collapse of offense, and the onset of divisional play.

- The 1973–87 period begins with a singular change to the rules in the American League, the designated hitter, and features the heyday of multipurpose stadiums, indoor baseball arriving in the AL, and the proliferation of artificial turf. More people come to the games and witness more offense, but the first prolonged strike splits the 1981 season in two.

- The current era of 1988 to present features a new explosion of offense, smaller ballparks, bigger crowds, more expansion, the wild card, and inter-league play.

Players are only eligible to be listed in one era each, regardless of whether their careers spanned two or more eras. They are placed in the era in which they played the most games or pitched the most innings. Their lifetime totals, however, are used to rank them in the era they played the most.

- **Plate Appearances** count every time a batter completes an at bat, including hits, outs, walks, sacrifices, hit-by-pitches, reaching on errors, etc.

- **Strikeout Percentage** divides strikeouts by at bats to indicate what percentage of the time a batter strikes out.

- **At Bats per Strikeout** indicates how infrequently a batter strikes out.

- **Relative Batting Average** is a player's batting average compared to the league's batting average (where the latter is 1.0).

- **Home Runs per 500 At Bats** is derived by dividing home runs by games played and multiplied by 150. While the regular season has been 162 games since 1961, for most of baseball history the schedule has been 154 games or less.

- **Runs/150 Games** and **RBI 150/Games** show a player's typical production in a full season.

- **Total Chances** consists of putouts plus assists plus errors.

- **Relief Wins** and **Relief Losses** are decisions for pitchers who did not start the game.

- **Blown Saves** and **Save Percentage** are from 1969 to the present only.

- **Player Overall Wins:** Player Overall Wins measures how many wins a player was worth to his team overall above or below that of an average player. It is determined by adding together a player's batting wins, fielding wins, baserunning wins, and pitching wins.

- **Adjusted Reliever Runs:** How many runs a reliever has saved or cost his team compared to an average reliever, adjusted for league and park.

- **Relief Ranking:** Ranking that takes into account the higher value of innings pitched by relievers in addition to their overall runs allowed compared to average.

The minimums for Single-Season Leaders include:

- Starting Pitchers (for rate statistics): 1 inning pitched per scheduled game;
- Relief Pitchers (for rate statistics): 0.5 innings pitched per scheduled game;
- Pitcher Winning Percentage: 15 wins;
- Save Percentage: 20 saves;
- Batters (for rate statistics): 3.1 plate appearances per scheduled game;
- Pinch-Hit Batting Average: 30 at bats;
- Pitcher Batting Average: 20 hits (it does not count Red Sox pitcher's batting stats since 1973 because of the designated hitter rule);
- Stolen Base Percentage: 20 steals
- Fielding Statistics: 0.66 games played per scheduled game.
- Catcher Fielding Statistics: 0.5 games played per scheduled game.

The minimum for Career Leaders include:

- Starting Pitchers (for rate statistics): 400 innings
- Relief Pitchers (for rate statistics): 200 innings
- Save Percentage: 25 saves;
- Batters (for rate statistics): 400 games;
- Pinch-Hit Batting Average: 15 pinch hits;
- Pitcher Batting Average: 20 hits;
- Stolen Base Percentage: 40 steals.

Following the career and single-season leaders is a chart of the annual Red Sox leaders in many categories. Also included are attendance, record, manager, among other team results.

Red Sox All-Time Team

First Team

Catcher

Carlton Fisk - After sporadic appearances with the Red Sox starting in 1969, the native New Englander established himself as a major league regular in 1972 with one of the greatest seasons any major league catcher has ever had. That year he won the Rookie of the Year Award unanimously and finished fourth in the MVP race

while also winning a Gold Glove. Pudge, as Red Sox fans affectionately called him, continued to star for the Red Sox until he was traded after the 1980 season. He ended his Red Sox career with a batting average of .284, an on-base percentage of .356, and a slugging average of .481. He is best remembered, of course, for a single moment: his home run that ended unforgettable Game 6 of the 1975 World Series. He is also known for having caught more games in his career than any other major league player. But Fisk was more than a record and a home run; he's one of the top five catchers of all time, and most of his great years were achieved playing for the Red Sox.

First Base

Jimmie Foxx - Foxx was already a huge star when the Red Sox acquired him from the Philadelphia Athletics after the 1935 season. The slugger did not have his greatest seasons with the Red Sox, but he still clubbed 222 home runs and slugged .605 for the Red Sox in his 8 seasons with Boston. Foxx won the MVP and set the franchise single-season home run record in 1938 with 50, a mark that stood until 2006. Overall, Foxx was probably the second greatest first baseman of all time, behind only Lou Gehrig, so it is no surprise that even the back half of his career earns him the title of the Boston's best first baseman of all time.

Second Base

Bobby Doerr - Doerr's election to the Baseball Hall of Fame was somewhat controversial, but there's no doubt that he's the greatest second baseman the Red Sox have ever had. He spent all 14 seasons of his major league career with the Red Sox, posting a .288 batting average, a .362 on-base percentage, and a .461 slugging average in 1,865 games. He was regarded by many as the best defensive second baseman of his era and was an All-Star nine times. His best season came in 1944, when he slugged .528 and *The Sporting News* selected him as its AL Player of the Year

Shortstop

Nomar Garciaparra - The number of babies born in Boston named Nomar may have decreased sharply over the past few years, but Nomar Garciaparra is still remembered fondly by Red Sox fans for his achievements in a Boston uniform. Until injuries got the better of him in 2004, Garciaparra was an elite shortstop He was often mentioned along with Derek Jeter and Alex Rodriguez as the greatest trio of shortstops any league has ever featured at the same time. Garciaparra was an athletic albeit unorthodox defensive shortstop, but it was his offensive game that made him a star. Nomar batted over .300 in every Red Sox season during which he had at least 100 at bats. For his Red Sox career, his

batting average was .323 and he slugged .550. No Red Sox middle infielder has ever come close to Nomar in terms of offensive production.

Third Base

Wade Boggs - Boggs was the on-base king of the baseball world during the 1980s, posting an OBP of .443 for the decade, 40 points higher than any other player. He also averaged more than 40 doubles a year during his 10 full seasons with the Red Sox. Boggs was renowned for his superstitions, but no Red Sox hitter except perhaps Ted Williams ever turned hitting into as much of a science. Boggs and Williams went about things differently, but both were tops in their field at Fenway.

Left Field

Ted Williams - He wanted to be known as the greatest hitter who ever lived, and while not everyone agrees that he achieved that, he's the only other player in the conversation besides Babe Ruth and Barry Bonds. He's clearly the best player Boston has ever had.

Center Field

Tris Speaker - After Teddy Ballgame and the Babe (when he wasn't pitching), Tris Speaker was the third-greatest everyday player in Red Sox history. Speaker hit for a .337 average while playing for the Red Sox during the dead ball era, and his prowess in center field was legendary. Among players the Sox have traded, sold, or allowed to leave as free agents, no one other than Ruth produced more after they were no longer Sox, though Boston at least got to benefit from Spoke's greatest seasons.

Right Field

Dwight Evans - Evans spent all but one year of his career with the Red Sox, but in some ways he had two separate careers with Boston. In the 1970s Evans was valued primarily for his defense in Fenway's tough right field. In 1980 and 1981, though, Evans started really contributing with his bat, and while his defense slipped sharply as he aged, he remained an offensive force for the rest of his career. When he left Boston as a free agent after the 1990 season after 19 years with the team, he had a .272 average as a Red Sox, with a .369 on-base percentage and a .473 slugging average. Evans' set of skills was far less showy than those of his teammate in the outfield Jim Rice, but in the end he provided just as much value to the Red Sox as Rice did.

Designated Hitter

Manny Ramirez - Since coming to the Red Sox as a free agent in 2001, Ramirez has established himself as the best hitter the Red Sox have had since Ted Williams. No one thinks of Manny as a student of the game like Williams was, but his approach at the plate is one Williams no

doubt would have admired. Year in and year out, Manny's name finishes near or at the top in many statistical categories. He has been among the top five players in the league in on-base plus slugging in all six seasons he has played for the Sox. He won the batting title in 2002, led the league in on-base percentage in 2002, 2003, and 2006, and topped the league in slugging average in 2004. He finished among the top 10 in MVP voting each of his first 5 years with the Red Sox, and in the top 20 in 2006. Manny's fielding in left field is, at best, an adventure, and occasionally turns into a horror flick, hence his tap on the shoulder as the DH here.

Starting Pitchers

Roger Clemens - He had more than the twilight of his career ahead of him when he left the Red Sox as a free agent after the 1996 season, but Roger Clemens still achieved more in a Red Sox uniform than he did pitching anywhere else. Clemens won three Cy Young Awards in Boston, and deserved to win more. He won the American League MVP Award in 1986, something no other starting pitcher has done since 1971. He led the league in ERA four times and seven times was among the top five. He led the league in strikeouts five times. He was among the league's top 10 in innings in 9 of his 11 full seasons with the Red Sox.

Cy Young - The man who would come to define pitching greatness for future generations pitched for the Red Sox for nine seasons, during which he threw 2,728 $\frac{1}{3}$ innings and posted a 2.00 ERA, 47 percent better than an average pitcher of the time. Young's longevity and durability led to 511 career wins and several more records that will never be broken, but his ability to control the strike zone has never been equaled or surpassed, either. He led the American League in strikeout-to-walk ratio 5 of the 8 seasons he spent with the Red Sox. He and Clemens share the franchise mark with 192 wins.

Pedro Martinez - In his early years with the Red Sox, Martinez pitched with a combination of power and command that was as dominating as any pitcher has ever been. His ERA for the six seasons with the Red Sox was 2.50, an astonishing 89 percent better than the average ERA achieved by his peers. Martinez was unanimously awarded the Cy Young in 1999 and 2000; only two other pitchers, Greg Maddux and Sandy Koufax, have ever been recognized similarly.

Lefty Grove - When the greatest left-handed pitcher in baseball history is your number four starter, that's some rotation. The Red Sox had Lefty Grove for the downside of his career, but that was still 1,539 $\frac{2}{3}$ innings for Boston, with an adjusted ERA 44 percent better than that of the average pitcher.

Relief Pitchers

Ellis Kinder - Kinder pitched for the Red Sox from 1948 to 1956, appearing in 356 games, 276 of them in relief. Most relievers of the time were failed starters. Kinder was not that, but he was far more effective coming in from the bullpen. His best season came in 1955, when he pitched 107 innings in 69 relief appearances while posting a tiny 1.85 ERA. He threw 1,142 $\frac{1}{3}$ innings overall for the Red Sox in his career while managing a 3.28 ERA.

Dick Radatz - "The Monster" was one of only a few relief pitchers to be widely recognized before the save became an official statistic in 1969. Radatz came up to the big leagues for Boston in 1962, and proceeded to strike out 144 batters in 124 $\frac{2}{3}$ innings, all in relief, while having a 2.24 ERA. His pitching earned him third place in Rookie of the Year balloting. He proceeded to pitch just as effectively in 1963 and 1964. Writers made him the first relief pitcher to ever finish among the top 10 in MVP voting in two consecutive years. While he was never as dominant as he was those three years, Radatz dominated hitters as few had done before and in the process became a prototype of sorts for the modern closer.

Joe Wood - Wood was a fine starter for the Red Sox from 1908 to 1915, but 56 of his appearances came in relief, so he qualifies as a reliever on this team. Even when Wood started, Smoky Joe did not throw the huge innings totals that most starters of his era did; he threw over 200 innings only twice in his career, although one of those seasons was his monster 34-win (including 16 in a row), 258-strikeout 1912 season, which he capped off with 3 wins in the World Series. His smoking fastball—hence the name—enabled him to strike out more batters per inning than virtually any other pitcher of his era. He finished his Boston career with a 1.99 ERA and 986 strikeouts over 1,418 innings and became an outfielder in Cleveland after his arm gave out.

Second Team

Catcher

Jason Varitek - Aside from Carlton Fisk, the Red Sox do not have a rich history of catchers. Varitek, who was acquired from Seattle along with Derek Lowe for Heathcliff Slocumb, has established himself over the last decade head and shoulders above anyone not called Pudge. Varitek is not the type of player who gets a lot of black ink in the *Baseball Encyclopedia*, and the only awards he has won were the 2005 Gold Glove and Silver Slugger, but Boston's captain is above average at almost every part of his job.

First Base

Mo Vaughn - It took Mo Vaughn three seasons to establish himself as a major leaguer, but once he did he proved

to be Boston's most powerful first baseman since Jimmie Foxx. In his six years as a Red Sox regular, from 1993 to 1998, Vaughn blasted 213 home runs, the sixth-highest total of any American League player during those years; he drove in 663 runs, the fifth-highest total. His on-base percentage in those six years was .405, and his slugging percentage .569, while his adjusted on-base plus slugging was 47 percent above average; only Frank Thomas, Ken Griffey Jr., and Albert Belle created more runs in the AL during this period. The less said about his defense the better, but Mo was an offensive force to be reckoned with.

Second Base
Jody Reed - Reed is not the type of player who makes All-Time All-Star teams, but second base has historically been a weak spot for the Red Sox. For four of his five years as a regular for Boston, Reed was a solid hitting regular who played above average defense, especially at second base. He ended his Red Sox career with a .358 on-base percentage and, while no power hitter, he was able to take enough advantage of the Green Monster to hit 40 doubles three years in a row.

Shortstop
Joe Cronin - The Red Sox have a long history of very good shortstops, and a good argument can be made for many other shortstops, including Rico Petrocelli, Johnny Pesky, Rick Burleson, and John Valentin, earning this honor. But Cronin had the greatest non-Red Sox career of all these players, and that gives him the edge. Cronin spent the last 11 years of his playing career as player/manager for the Red Sox; he spent another 15 years with the franchise, managing through 1947 and then becoming general manager. Cronin's defense was never as sharp with the Red Sox as it had been in the first half of his career with the Senators, but his bat was just as potent. Only seven major leaguers created more runs than Cronin from 1938 to 1941.

Third Base
Jimmy Collins - Collins was the first Boston Red Sox. When Ban Johnson decided that his American League needed a team in Boston in 1901, he sent Connie Mack to Beantown to lure Collins, from the Boston's National League club. With the Braves, Collins had been best known for his defense, but during his six years with the Red Sox he excelled with his stick too. During his six years as the Red Sox regular third baseman and manager, he created 385 runs (fourth-best in the league) and led Boston to two AL championships and a victory in the first-ever World Series.

Left Field
Carl Yastrzemski - Only Ted Williams could push Yaz to second team in any Red Sox classification. Despite playing much of his best baseball during an era when the rules favored pitchers, Yaz is the all-time leader among Red Sox in runs, hits, singles, doubles, total bases, and RBI, and is second to Williams in home runs. Many of Yaz's accomplishments are due to his great longevity—he has 3,262 more at bats with the Red Sox than any other player—but his eight-year peak, from 1963 to 1970, is one of the 15 greatest eight-year peaks of all time. During this eight-year stretch, he led the league in batting average three times, in on-base percentage five times, and in slugging average three times. In 1967 he became the 14th—and last—hitter in modern baseball history to win the Triple Crown. After slugging over .500 four times through 1970, he only did so once during the last 13 years of his career. But he was able to stay a decent player long enough to accumulate 3,419 hits, the sixth-highest total in baseball history.

Center Field
Fred Lynn - Fred Lynn couldn't have had a better beginning in 1975 as he became the first player to ever win the Rookie of the Year and MVP in the same season. Lynn led the AL that year in runs, doubles, and slugging percentage, and he was honored for his fielding prowess with a Gold Glove. Lynn could not maintain that level of excellence, partially because his aggressive style of play led to frequent injuries. In 1979, however, he topped his rookie performance with the best offensive year of his career, leading the league in batting average, on-base percentage, and batting average. The next year he earned his fourth Gold Glove as a Red Sox centerfielder, but that turned out to be his last year with the Sox. His six seasons of sometimes brilliant play, during which his on-base percentage was .383 and his slugging average .520, earn him the spot as the franchise's second-best center fielder in a close call over Reggie Smith.

Right Field
Harry Hooper - Though he was enshrined in the Hall of Fame in 1981, Hooper is probably the least-known everyday player on these teams. Once upon a time, however, he was a member of Boston's "Million Dollar Outfield" along with Tris Speaker and Duffy Lewis. Hooper is also the only player in franchise history to have been a member of four world championship teams. Hooper's strengths were his defensive play and his on-base skills. The leadoff hitter for most of his time with the Red Sox, he posted a .363 OBP in the 1910s for Boston (the 16th-highest mark in the American League of players with more than 2,500 plate appearances in that span). He still holds the Red Sox records as the all-time triples leader with 130 and steals king with 300.

279

Designated Hitter

Jim Rice - Rice can't beat out Ted Williams and Yaz for the left field spots, so he takes the second DH spot. Rice spent all 16 seasons of his career with the Sox, and he was a major offensive contributor from 1975 through 1986. He simply terrorized American League pitchers from 1977 to 1979 with a slugging percentage of .596, the highest of any player in baseball. Over the course of those three years, he created almost 100 runs more than any other AL player and was 1978 AL MVP. No Red Sox other than Williams and Foxx has ever been as devastating a hitter as Rice was in those three seasons.

Really
Yaz
67-70
way
better!

Honorable Mention

David Ortiz - David Ortiz is the kind of player that exceptions are made for. If you are reading this book, you already have a good idea what David Ortiz has done since joining the Red Sox in 2003. He hasn't yet played enough years for the Sox to earn a regular spot on this team, but all the dramatic hits Ortiz has provided during the last four seasons saves him a place here.

Starting Pitchers

Babe Ruth - The decision to turn Babe Ruth into an everyday pitcher was not as obvious a decision as it seems in retrospect. The Babe was an outstanding pitcher. In his six years on the mound for the Red Sox, he threw 1,190 1/3 innings with an ERA of only 2.19, 25 percent better than the league average. The Red Sox won an overwhelming percentage of games he pitched, giving him an 89-46 win-loss record for Boston. He anchored the 1916 and 1918 world championship clubs, throwing 29 2/3 consecutive shutout innings in the World Series. If it wasn't for the devastating effect World War I had on baseball rosters, the Red Sox might never have given Ruth a chance to play every day when he wasn't pitching. It's hard to say whether Ruth would have made the Hall of Fame as a pitcher, but he was certainly off to a good start when his career took him in another direction.

Wes Ferrell - Arguable the greatest hitting pitcher of all time except for the Babe, Ferrell could pitch a little too. In his four years with the Red Sox in the mid-1930s, he posted an ERA 21 percent better than league average pitching while throwing 877 2/3 innings. At the plate, he hit .308 with a .384 on-base percentage and a .490 slugging average, producing offense at a rate higher than the average hitter even in that era of inflated offense. Nobody has come along since with similar two-way skills.

Mel Parnell - Unlike every other starter on these teams, Mel Parnell spent his entire careers with the Red Sox. He wasn't a dominating force on the mound, but he was club's ace from 1948 to 1953, posting a 109–53 record in those years. Overall, he threw 1752 1/3 innings in his

career, with an ERA of 3.50, 25 percent better than league average pitching.

Luis Tiant - After being the best AL pitcher not named Denny McLain in 1968, Tiant was released twice in 1971 before he was picked up by the Red Sox. He wasn't that good in Boston, either, but the Red Sox gave him another chance the next year and he reverted to his old form. El Tiante spent six more seasons in Boston, throwing 1,774 2/3 innings to trail only Roger Clemens, Cy Young, and Tim Wakefield in team annals. His effervescent Tiant had a 122–81 record and a 3.36 ERA in Boston, plus starts in all three wins by the Red Sox in the 1975 World Series.

Relief Pitchers

Bob Stanley - Stanley is the only pitcher on these teams besides Mel Parnell to spend his entire career with the Red Sox. Though not appreciated much by fans—he was one strike away from ending the 1986 World Series only to be undone by a catchable wild pitch and a trickling grounder—Stanley was a solid reliever for almost his entire career. Part of the problem was that Stanley's role on the staff shifted often between starter, swingman, long reliever, short reliever, set-up man, and closer. His flexibility was extremely useful to the Sox. He finished his career 1,707 innings pitched, a very high total for someone who made more than 85 percent of his appearances out of the bullpen, and a career ERA of 3.64.

Carl Mays - No pitcher was ever surrounded by more controversies than Carl Mays, and those controversies have kept him out of the Hall of Fame, but there's no doubt Mays was one of the best pitchers of his generation. Mays came up with the Red Sox in 1915, appearing in 173 career games for the Red Sox, 61 of which came in relief (earning him an assignment to the bullpen on this team). He pitched a total of 1,105 innings for Boston while posting an adjusted ERA 24 percent better than average.

Derek Lowe - Few players have achieved so many highs and lows as Derek Lowe did during his Red Sox career. Lowe was generally quite effective during his 1999–2001 stint into the bullpen, but he was terrific in his first year as a starter in 2002. He threw the first no-hitter at Fenway in 37 years, won 21 games, and wound up third in the Cy Young voting. His last two years as a starter in Boston were disappointing, and he left as a free agent after not receiving a significant offer from Boston, but not before he managed to go out on a high note by playing a key role in Boston's 2004 world championship. He earned his spot on this team with his years in the bullpen. He wasn't the most dominant closer in baseball, but he made himself one of the more valuable ones by throwing 292 1/3 innings over three years, with 81 saves in 98 opportunities.

Career Leaders

Games

1	Carl Yastrzemski	3308
2	Dwight Evans	2505
3	Ted Williams	2292
4	Jim Rice	2089
5	Bobby Doerr	1865
6	Harry Hooper	1647
7	Wade Boggs	1625
8	Rico Petrocelli	1553
9	Dom DiMaggio	1399
10	Frank Malzone	1359
11	Mike Greenwell	1269
12	George Scott	1192
13	Duffy Lewis	1184
14	Billy Goodman	1177
15	Joe Cronin	1134
16	Larry Gardner	1123
17	Rick Miller	1101
18	Everett Scott	1096
19	Carlton Fisk	1078
20	**Jason Varitek**	**1068**
21	Tris Speaker	1065
22	Mo Vaughn	1046
23	Jackie Jensen	1039
24	Rick Burleson	1031
25	Johnny Pesky	1029
26	Reggie Smith	1014
27	Hobe Ferris	991
	John Valentin	991
29	Freddy Parent	986
30	**Trot Nixon**	**982**
31	Sammy White	981
32	Nomar Garciaparra	966
	Heinie Wagner	966
34	Troy O'Leary	962
35	Jim Piersall	931
36	Marty Barrett	929
37	Rich Gedman	906
38	Phil Todt	895
39	Jimmie Foxx	887
40	**Manny Ramirez**	**850**
41	Fred Lynn	828
42	Buck Freeman	820
43	Jim Tabor	806
44	Tony Conigliaro	802
45	Ira Flagstead	789
46	Chick Stahl	781
47	Jimmy Collins	741
48	Ellis Burks	733
49	Pete Runnels	732
50	Doc Cramer	722

At Bats

1	Carl Yastrzemski	11988
2	Dwight Evans	8726
3	Jim Rice	8225
4	Ted Williams	7706
5	Bobby Doerr	7093
6	Harry Hooper	6270
7	Wade Boggs	6213
8	Dom DiMaggio	5640
9	Rico Petrocelli	5390
10	Frank Malzone	5273
11	Mike Greenwell	4623
12	Billy Goodman	4399
13	Duffy Lewis	4325
14	George Scott	4234
15	Johnny Pesky	4085
16	Rick Burleson	4064
17	Nomar Garciaparra	3968
18	Tris Speaker	3935
19	Larry Gardner	3919
20	Joe Cronin	3892
21	Everett Scott	3887
22	Carlton Fisk	3860
23	Jackie Jensen	3857
24	Freddy Parent	3846
25	Mo Vaughn	3828
26	Reggie Smith	3780
27	John Valentin	3709
28	Hobe Ferris	3689
29	**Jason Varitek**	**3543**
30	Troy O'Leary	3456
31	Jim Piersall	3369
32	Marty Barrett	3362
33	Sammy White	3342
34	Jimmie Foxx	3288
35	**Trot Nixon**	**3285**
36	Heinie Wagner	3277
37	Phil Todt	3218
38	Doc Cramer	3111
39	**Manny Ramirez**	**3105**
40	Buck Freeman	3077
41	Jim Tabor	3074
42	Fred Lynn	3062
43	Chick Stahl	3004
44	Jimmy Collins	2972
45	Tony Conigliaro	2955
46	Ira Flagstead	2941
47	Rich Gedman	2856
48	Ellis Burks	2827
49	Jerry Remy	2809
50	Jody Reed	2658

Runs by era

1988–2006		
1	Nomar Garciaparra	709
2	Mike Greenwell	657
3	Mo Vaughn	628
4	John Valentin	596
5	**Manny Ramirez**	**593**
6	**Trot Nixon**	**547**
7	Troy O'Leary	490
1973–87		
1	Dwight Evans	1435
2	Jim Rice	1249
3	Wade Boggs	1067
4	Carlton Fisk	627
5	Fred Lynn	523
6	Rick Burleson	514
7	Marty Barrett	417
1961–72		
1	Carl Yastrzemski	1816
2	Rico Petrocelli	653
3	Frank Malzone	641
4	Reggie Smith	592
5	George Scott	527
6	Tony Conigliaro	441
7	Mike Andrews	327
1943–60		
1	Ted Williams	1798
2	Bobby Doerr	1094
3	Dom DiMaggio	1046
4	Johnny Pesky	776
5	Billy Goodman	688
6	Jackie Jensen	597
7	Jim Piersall	502
1921–42		
1	Jimmie Foxx	721
2	Joe Cronin	645
3	Doc Cramer	509
4	Ira Flagstead	466
5	Jim Tabor	393
6	Billy Werber	366
7	Phil Todt	349
1901–20		
1	Harry Hooper	988
2	Tris Speaker	704
3	Freddy Parent	519
4	Duffy Lewis	500
5	Larry Gardner	496
6	Chick Stahl	464
7	Jimmy Collins	448

Hits

1	Carl Yastrzemski	3419
2	Ted Williams	2654
3	Jim Rice	2452
4	Dwight Evans	2373
5	Wade Boggs	2098
6	Bobby Doerr	2042
7	Harry Hooper	1707
8	Dom DiMaggio	1680
9	Frank Malzone	1454
10	Mike Greenwell	1400
11	Rico Petrocelli	1352
12	Billy Goodman	1344
13	Tris Speaker	1327
14	Nomar Garciaparra	1281
15	Johnny Pesky	1277
16	Duffy Lewis	1248
17	Joe Cronin	1168
18	Mo Vaughn	1165
19	Rick Burleson	1114
20	Larry Gardner	1106
21	Carlton Fisk	1097
22	Jackie Jensen	1089
23	George Scott	1088
24	Reggie Smith	1064
25	Jimmie Foxx	1051
	Freddy Parent	1051
27	John Valentin	1043
28	**Manny Ramirez**	**980**
29	Everett Scott	956
30	Troy O'Leary	954
31	**Jason Varitek**	**952**
32	Fred Lynn	944
33	Doc Cramer	940
34	Marty Barrett	935
35	Jim Piersall	919
36	**Trot Nixon**	**912**
37	Jimmy Collins	881
	Sammy White	881
39	Buck Freeman	879
40	Hobe Ferris	876
41	Chick Stahl	871
42	Ira Flagstead	867
43	Jim Tabor	838
44	Phil Todt	832
45	Pete Runnels	825
46	Heinie Wagner	822
47	Jerry Remy	802
48	Ellis Burks	791
49	Tony Conigliaro	790
50	Jody Reed	743

Doubles

1	Carl Yastrzemski	646
2	Ted Williams	525
3	Dwight Evans	474
4	Wade Boggs	422
5	Bobby Doerr	381
6	Jim Rice	373
7	Dom DiMaggio	308
8	Nomar Garciaparra	279
9	Mike Greenwell	275
10	Joe Cronin	270
11	John Valentin	266
12	Duffy Lewis	254
13	Billy Goodman	248
14	Harry Hooper	246
15	Tris Speaker	241
16	Rico Petrocelli	237
17	Frank Malzone	234
18	**Jason Varitek**	**231**
19	Fred Lynn	217
20	Troy O'Leary	209
21	Carlton Fisk	207
22	**Trot Nixon**	**204**
	Reggie Smith	204
24	Rick Burleson	203
25	**Manny Ramirez**	**201**
26	Mo Vaughn	199
27	Ira Flagstead	196
	Johnny Pesky	196
29	Jackie Jensen	187
30	Jimmie Foxx	181
31	Jody Reed	180
32	Jimmy Collins	171
33	Phil Todt	169
34	Rich Gedman	164
35	Marty Barrett	162
	Jim Tabor	162
	Sammy White	162
38	Ellis Burks	160
39	Buck Freeman	158
	Jim Piersall	158
	George Scott	158
42	Freddy Parent	156
43	**David Ortiz**	**155**
44	Larry Gardner	151
45	Bill Regan	150
46	Hobe Ferris	148
47	Pete Runnels	147
48	Doc Cramer	146
49	Everett Scott	141
50	Johnny Damon	136

Plate Appearances

1	Carl Yastrzemski	13991
2	Dwight Evans	10240
3	Ted Williams	9791
4	Jim Rice	9058
5	Bobby Doerr	8028
6	Harry Hooper	7330
7	Wade Boggs	7323
8	Dom DiMaggio	6478
9	Rico Petrocelli	6170
10	Frank Malzone	5702
11	Mike Greenwell	5166
12	Billy Goodman	5064
13	Duffy Lewis	4884
14	Johnny Pesky	4760
15	George Scott	4740
16	Joe Cronin	4584
17	Tris Speaker	4551
18	Jackie Jensen	4518
19	Larry Gardner	4511
20	Rick Burleson	4491
21	Mo Vaughn	4452
22	Carlton Fisk	4353
23	Nomar Garciaparra	4345
24	John Valentin	4269
25	Everett Scott	4266
26	Reggie Smith	4264
27	Freddy Parent	4240
28	**Jason Varitek**	**4040**
29	Jimmie Foxx	3934
30	Hobe Ferris	3927
31	**Trot Nixon**	**3829**
32	Marty Barrett	3816
33	Jim Piersall	3815
34	Troy O'Leary	3788
35	Heinie Wagner	3714
36	**Manny Ramirez**	**3688**
37	Sammy White	3617
38	Phil Todt	3558
39	Fred Lynn	3513
40	Chick Stahl	3407
41	Doc Cramer	3400
42	Ira Flagstead	3396
43	Buck Freeman	3385
44	Jim Tabor	3351
45	Tony Conigliaro	3299
46	Jimmy Collins	3224
47	Ellis Burks	3132
48	Rich Gedman	3129
49	Jerry Remy	3118
50	Jody Reed	3067

Runs

1	Carl Yastrzemski	1816
2	Ted Williams	1798
3	Dwight Evans	1435
4	Jim Rice	1249
5	Bobby Doerr	1094
6	Wade Boggs	1067
7	Dom DiMaggio	1046
8	Harry Hooper	988
9	Johnny Pesky	776
10	Jimmie Foxx	721
11	Nomar Garciaparra	709
12	Tris Speaker	704
13	Billy Goodman	688
14	Mike Greenwell	657
15	Rico Petrocelli	653
16	Joe Cronin	645
17	Frank Malzone	641
18	Mo Vaughn	628
19	Carlton Fisk	627
20	Jackie Jensen	597
21	John Valentin	596
22	**Manny Ramirez**	**593**
23	Reggie Smith	592
24	**Trot Nixon**	**547**
25	George Scott	527
26	Fred Lynn	523
27	Freddy Parent	519
28	Rick Burleson	514
29	Doc Cramer	509
30	Jim Piersall	502
31	Duffy Lewis	500
32	Larry Gardner	496
33	Troy O'Leary	490
34	**Jason Varitek**	**479**
35	Ira Flagstead	466
36	Chick Stahl	464
37	Johnny Damon	461
38	Vern Stephens	449
39	Jimmy Collins	448
40	Ellis Burks	446
41	Tony Conigliaro	441
42	Marty Barrett	417
43	**David Ortiz**	**407**
	Pete Runnels	407
45	Buck Freeman	403
46	Heinie Wagner	398
47	Jim Tabor	393
48	Jerry Remy	385
49	Hobe Ferris	383
50	Rick Miller	374

Runs/150 Games by era

1988–2006		
1	Johnny Damon	115.8
2	Nomar Garciaparra	110.1
3	**Manny Ramirez**	**104.6**
4	**David Ortiz**	**103.8**
5	Jose Offerman	95.2
6	Ellis Burks	91.3
7	John Valentin	90.2
1973–87		
1	Wade Boggs	98.5
2	Fred Lynn	94.7
3	Tommy Harper	91.7
4	Jim Rice	89.7
5	Carlton Fisk	87.2
6	Dwight Evans	85.9
7	Jerry Remy	81.3
1961–72		
1	Reggie Smith	87.6
2	Mike Andrews	86.7
3	Tony Conigliaro	82.5
4	Carl Yastrzemski	82.3
5	Joe Foy	80.7
6	Gary Geiger	73.1
7	Frank Malzone	70.8
1943–60		
1	Ted Williams	117.7
2	Johnny Pesky	113.1
3	Dom DiMaggio	112.2
4	Vern Stephens	102.0
5	Bobby Doerr	88.0
6	Billy Goodman	87.7
7	Jackie Jensen	86.2
1921–42		
1	Jimmie Foxx	121.9
2	Doc Cramer	105.7
3	Billy Werber	103.8
4	Roy Johnson	91.2
5	Ira Flagstead	88.6
6	Joe Cronin	85.3
7	Dusty Cooke	85.0
1901–20		
1	Tris Speaker	99.2
2	Jimmy Collins	90.7
3	Harry Hooper	90.0
4	Chick Stahl	89.1
5	Freddy Parent	79.0
6	Buck Freeman	73.7
7	Clyde Engle	69.7

Hits by era

1988–2006		
1	Mike Greenwell	1400
2	Nomar Garciaparra	1281
3	Mo Vaughn	1165
4	John Valentin	1043
5	**Manny Ramirez**	**980**
6	Troy O'Leary	954
7	**Jason Varitek**	**952**
1973–87		
1	Jim Rice	2452
2	Dwight Evans	2373
3	Wade Boggs	2098
4	Rick Burleson	1114
5	Carlton Fisk	1097
6	Fred Lynn	944
7	Marty Barrett	935
1961–72		
1	Carl Yastrzemski	3419
2	Frank Malzone	1454
3	Rico Petrocelli	1352
4	George Scott	1088
5	Reggie Smith	1064
6	Tony Conigliaro	790
7	Mike Andrews	563
1943–60		
1	Ted Williams	2654
2	Bobby Doerr	2042
3	Dom DiMaggio	1680
4	Billy Goodman	1344
5	Johnny Pesky	1277
6	Jackie Jensen	1089
7	Jim Piersall	919
1921–42		
1	Joe Cronin	1168
2	Jimmie Foxx	1051
3	Doc Cramer	940
4	Ira Flagstead	867
5	Jim Tabor	838
6	Phil Todt	832
7	Roy Johnson	611
	Bill Regan	611
1901–20		
1	Harry Hooper	1707
2	Tris Speaker	1327
3	Duffy Lewis	1248
4	Larry Gardner	1106
5	Freddy Parent	1051
6	Everett Scott	956
7	Jimmy Collins	881

Doubles by era

1988–2006		
1	Nomar Garciaparra	279
2	Mike Greenwell	275
3	John Valentin	266
4	**Jason Varitek**	**231**
5	Troy O'Leary	209
6	**Trot Nixon**	**204**
7	**Manny Ramirez**	**201**
1973–87		
1	Dwight Evans	474
2	Wade Boggs	422
3	Jim Rice	373
4	Fred Lynn	217
5	Carlton Fisk	207
6	Rick Burleson	203
7	Rich Gedman	164
1961–72		
1	Carl Yastrzemski	646
2	Rico Petrocelli	237
3	Frank Malzone	234
4	Reggie Smith	204
5	George Scott	158
6	Tony Conigliaro	121
7	Eddie Bressoud	115
1943–60		
1	Ted Williams	525
2	Bobby Doerr	381
3	Dom DiMaggio	308
4	Billy Goodman	248
5	Johnny Pesky	196
6	Jackie Jensen	187
7	Sammy White	162
1921–42		
1	Joe Cronin	270
2	Ira Flagstead	196
3	Jimmie Foxx	181
4	Phil Todt	169
5	Jim Tabor	162
6	Bill Regan	150
7	Doc Cramer	146
1901–20		
1	Duffy Lewis	254
2	Harry Hooper	246
3	Tris Speaker	241
4	Jimmy Collins	171
5	Buck Freeman	158
6	Freddy Parent	156
7	Larry Gardner	151

Triples

1	Harry Hooper	130
2	Tris Speaker	106
3	Buck Freeman	90
4	Bobby Doerr	89
5	Larry Gardner	87
6	Jim Rice	79
7	Hobe Ferris	77
8	Dwight Evans	72
9	Ted Williams	71
10	Jimmy Collins	65
11	Freddy Parent	63
12	Duffy Lewis	62
	Chick Stahl	62
14	Carl Yastrzemski	59
15	Dom DiMaggio	57
16	Phil Todt	56
17	Nomar Garciaparra	50
	Jake Stahl	50
19	Wade Boggs	47
	Heinie Wagner	47
21	Johnny Pesky	46
22	Jimmie Foxx	45
23	Doc Cramer	44
	Joe Cronin	44
25	Everett Scott	41
26	Mike Greenwell	38
	George Scott	38
28	Lou Finney	37
	Troy O'Leary	37
30	Bill Regan	36
31	Billy Goodman	34
32	Lou Criger	33
	Carlton Fisk	33
	Reggie Smith	33
35	Ira Flagstead	32
	Jim Piersall	32
37	Joe Harris	30
	Roy Johnson	30
	Babe Ruth	30
40	Shano Collins	29
	Johnny Damon	29
	Fred Lynn	29
43	Jackie Jensen	28
	Trot Nixon	**28**
45	Ellis Burks	27
	Jim Tabor	27
47	Lou Clinton	26
	Jack Rothrock	26
49	3 players tied	25

Home Runs

1	Ted Williams	521
2	Carl Yastrzemski	452
3	Jim Rice	382
4	Dwight Evans	379
5	**Manny Ramirez**	**234**
6	Mo Vaughn	230
7	Bobby Doerr	223
8	Jimmie Foxx	222
9	Rico Petrocelli	210
10	Nomar Garciaparra	178
11	**David Ortiz**	**173**
12	Jackie Jensen	170
13	Tony Conigliaro	162
	Carlton Fisk	162
15	George Scott	154
16	Reggie Smith	149
17	**Trot Nixon**	**133**
18	Frank Malzone	131
	Jason Varitek	**131**
20	Mike Greenwell	130
21	Fred Lynn	124
22	Vern Stephens	122
23	John Valentin	121
24	Joe Cronin	119
25	Troy O'Leary	117
26	Tony Armas	113
27	Dick Gernert	101
28	Ellis Burks	94
	Butch Hobson	94
30	Jim Tabor	90
31	Dom DiMaggio	87
32	Brian Daubach	86
33	Wade Boggs	85
34	Rich Gedman	83
35	Dick Stuart	75
36	Mike Stanley	73
37	Gary Geiger	71
38	Jim Piersall	66
39	Sammy White	63
40	Eddie Bressoud	57
41	Tom Brunansky	56
	Johnny Damon	56
43	Felix Mantilla	54
44	Ted Lepcio	53
45	Jose Canseco	52
	Kevin Millar	52
	Phil Todt	52
48	Walt Dropo	51
49	Reggie Jefferson	50
50	4 players tied	49

Home Runs/500 at bats

1	**David Ortiz**	**39.5**
2	**Manny Ramirez**	**37.7**
3	Ted Williams	33.8
4	Jimmie Foxx	33.8
5	Mo Vaughn	30.0
6	Tony Armas	27.9
7	Tony Conigliaro	27.4
8	Mike Stanley	25.6
9	Vern Stephens	24.0
10	Brian Daubach	23.9
11	Jim Rice	23.2
12	Nomar Garciaparra	22.4
13	Dick Gernert	22.4
14	Jackie Jensen	22.0
15	Dwight Evans	21.7
16	Butch Hobson	21.1
17	Carlton Fisk	21.0
18	Fred Lynn	20.2
19	**Trot Nixon**	**20.2**
20	Reggie Smith	19.7
21	Rico Petrocelli	19.5
22	Carl Yastrzemski	18.9
23	**Jason Varitek**	**18.5**
24	George Scott	18.2
25	Tom Brunansky	18.0
26	Reggie Jefferson	17.9
27	Gary Geiger	17.7
28	Kevin Millar	17.3
29	Lou Clinton	17.2
30	Troy O'Leary	16.9
31	Ellis Burks	16.6
32	Ted Lepcio	16.3
33	John Valentin	16.3
34	Bobby Doerr	15.7
35	Joe Cronin	15.3
36	Bob Tillman	15.2
37	Cecil Cooper	15.0
38	Jim Tabor	14.6
39	Eddie Bressoud	14.6
40	Rich Gedman	14.5
41	Bill Mueller	14.2
42	Mike Greenwell	14.1
43	Joe Foy	13.5
44	Tim Naehring	13.1
45	Scott Hatteberg	13.0
46	Frank Malzone	12.4
47	Bill Buckner	11.6
48	Tommy Harper	11.5
49	Johnny Damon	11.3
50	Mike Andrews	11.2

Extra Base Hits

1	Carl Yastrzemski	1157
2	Ted Williams	1117
3	Dwight Evans	925
4	Jim Rice	834
5	Bobby Doerr	693
6	Wade Boggs	554
7	Nomar Garciaparra	507
8	Rico Petrocelli	469
9	Dom DiMaggio	452
10	Jimmie Foxx	448
11	Mike Greenwell	443
12	**Manny Ramirez**	**440**
13	Mo Vaughn	439
14	Joe Cronin	433
15	Harry Hooper	406
16	John Valentin	404
17	Carlton Fisk	402
18	Frank Malzone	386
	Reggie Smith	386
	Tris Speaker	386
21	Jackie Jensen	385
22	**Jason Varitek**	**372**
23	Fred Lynn	370
24	**Trot Nixon**	**365**
25	Troy O'Leary	363
26	George Scott	350
27	Duffy Lewis	343
28	**David Ortiz**	**336**
29	Tony Conigliaro	306
30	Buck Freeman	296
	Billy Goodman	296
32	Ellis Burks	281
33	Jim Tabor	279
34	Phil Todt	277
35	Vern Stephens	266
36	Rick Burleson	262
37	Jimmy Collins	261
38	Hobe Ferris	259
	Rich Gedman	259
40	Jim Piersall	256
41	Ira Flagstead	255
	Johnny Pesky	255
43	Larry Gardner	254
44	Sammy White	245
45	Freddy Parent	238
46	Johnny Damon	221
	Brian Daubach	221
48	Tony Armas	219
49	Butch Hobson	211
50	Dick Gernert	205

Runs Batted In

1	Carl Yastrzemski	1844
2	Ted Williams	1839
3	Jim Rice	1451
4	Dwight Evans	1346
5	Bobby Doerr	1247
6	Jimmie Foxx	788
7	Rico Petrocelli	773
8	Mo Vaughn	752
9	Joe Cronin	737
10	Jackie Jensen	733
11	Mike Greenwell	726
12	Frank Malzone	716
13	**Manny Ramirez**	**712**
14	Nomar Garciaparra	690
15	Wade Boggs	687
16	Duffy Lewis	629
17	Dom DiMaggio	618
18	Carlton Fisk	568
19	George Scott	562
	Vern Stephens	562
21	**Jason Varitek**	**543**
22	Tris Speaker	542
23	Reggie Smith	536
24	John Valentin	528
25	**David Ortiz**	**525**
26	**Trot Nixon**	**523**
27	Fred Lynn	521
28	Jim Tabor	517
29	Troy O'Leary	516
30	Buck Freeman	504
31	Tony Conigliaro	501
32	Harry Hooper	497
33	Larry Gardner	481
34	Billy Goodman	464
35	Hobe Ferris	418
36	Phil Todt	409
37	Sammy White	404
38	Ellis Burks	388
39	Freddy Parent	386
40	Jimmy Collins	385
41	Dick Gernert	377
42	Jim Piersall	366
43	Johnny Pesky	361
44	Rick Burleson	360
45	Butch Hobson	358
46	Rich Gedman	356
47	Tony Armas	352
48	Everett Scott	346
49	Heinie Wagner	341
50	Chick Stahl	339

Triples by era

1988–2006		
1	Nomar Garciaparra	50
2	Mike Greenwell	38
3	Troy O'Leary	37
4	Johnny Damon	29
5	**Trot Nixon**	**28**
6	Ellis Burks	27
7	Jose Offerman	17
	John Valentin	17
1973–87		
1	Jim Rice	79
2	Dwight Evans	72
3	Wade Boggs	47
4	Carlton Fisk	33
5	Fred Lynn	29
6	Rick Miller	23
7	Rick Burleson	21
1961–72		
1	Carl Yastrzemski	59
2	George Scott	38
3	Reggie Smith	33
4	Lou Clinton	26
5	Tony Conigliaro	23
	Gary Geiger	23
7	Rico Petrocelli	22
1943–60		
1	Bobby Doerr	89
2	Ted Williams	71
3	Dom DiMaggio	57
4	Johnny Pesky	46
5	Billy Goodman	34
6	Jim Piersall	32
7	Jackie Jensen	28
1921–42		
1	Phil Todt	56
2	Jimmie Foxx	45
3	Doc Cramer	44
	Joe Cronin	44
5	Lou Finney	37
6	Bill Regan	36
7	Ira Flagstead	32
1901–20		
1	Harry Hooper	130
2	Tris Speaker	106
3	Buck Freeman	90
4	Larry Gardner	87
5	Hobe Ferris	77
6	Jimmy Collins	65
7	Freddy Parent	63

Home Runs by era

1988–2006		
1	**Manny Ramirez**	**234**
2	Mo Vaughn	230
3	Nomar Garciaparra	178
4	**David Ortiz**	**173**
5	**Trot Nixon**	**133**
6	**Jason Varitek**	**131**
7	Mike Greenwell	130
1973–87		
1	Jim Rice	382
2	Dwight Evans	379
3	Carlton Fisk	162
4	Fred Lynn	124
5	Tony Armas	113
6	Butch Hobson	94
7	Wade Boggs	85
1961–72		
1	Carl Yastrzemski	452
2	Rico Petrocelli	210
3	Tony Conigliaro	162
4	George Scott	154
5	Reggie Smith	149
6	Frank Malzone	131
7	Dick Stuart	75
1943–60		
1	Ted Williams	521
2	Bobby Doerr	223
3	Jackie Jensen	170
4	Vern Stephens	122
5	Dick Gernert	101
6	Dom DiMaggio	87
7	Jim Piersall	66
1921–42		
1	Jimmie Foxx	222
2	Joe Cronin	119
3	Jim Tabor	90
4	Phil Todt	52
5	Billy Werber	38
6	Earl Webb	35
7	Roy Johnson	31
1901–20		
1	Babe Ruth	49
2	Buck Freeman	48
3	Tris Speaker	39
4	Hobe Ferris	34
5	Harry Hooper	30
6	Duffy Lewis	27
7	Jimmy Collins	25

Home Runs/500 at bats by era

1988–2006		
1	**David Ortiz**	**39.5**
2	**Manny Ramirez**	**37.7**
3	Mo Vaughn	30.0
4	Mike Stanley	25.6
5	Brian Daubach	23.9
6	Nomar Garciaparra	22.4
7	**Trot Nixon**	**20.2**
1973–87		
1	Tony Armas	27.9
2	Jim Rice	23.2
3	Dwight Evans	21.7
4	Butch Hobson	21.1
5	Carlton Fisk	21.0
6	Fred Lynn	20.2
7	Cecil Cooper	15.0
1961–72		
1	Tony Conigliaro	27.4
2	Reggie Smith	19.7
3	Rico Petrocelli	19.5
4	Carl Yastrzemski	18.9
5	George Scott	18.2
6	Gary Geiger	17.7
7	Lou Clinton	17.2
1943–60		
1	Ted Williams	33.8
2	Vern Stephens	24.0
3	Dick Gernert	22.4
4	Jackie Jensen	22.0
5	Ted Lepcio	16.3
6	Bobby Doerr	15.7
7	Jim Piersall	9.8
1921–42		
1	Jimmie Foxx	33.8
2	Joe Cronin	15.3
3	Jim Tabor	14.6
4	Billy Werber	9.3
5	Joe Harris	8.2
6	Phil Todt	8.1
7	Roy Johnson	7.9
1901–20		
1	Buck Freeman	7.8
2	Jake Stahl	6.4
3	Tris Speaker	5.0
4	Hobe Ferris	4.6
5	Jimmy Collins	4.2
6	Duffy Lewis	3.1
7	Chick Stahl	2.8

Total Bases

1	Carl Yastrzemski	5539
2	Ted Williams	4884
3	Jim Rice	4129
4	Dwight Evans	4128
5	Bobby Doerr	3270
6	Wade Boggs	2869
7	Dom DiMaggio	2363
8	Harry Hooper	2303
9	Rico Petrocelli	2263
10	Nomar Garciaparra	2194
11	Mike Greenwell	2141
12	Frank Malzone	2123
13	Mo Vaughn	2074
14	Jimmie Foxx	1988
15	Tris Speaker	1897
16	**Manny Ramirez**	**1893**
17	Joe Cronin	1883
18	Carlton Fisk	1856
19	Jackie Jensen	1842
20	George Scott	1784
21	Reggie Smith	1781
22	Duffy Lewis	1707
23	John Valentin	1706
24	Billy Goodman	1702
25	Johnny Pesky	1604
26	**Jason Varitek**	**1596**
27	Fred Lynn	1591
28	Troy O'Leary	1588
29	**Trot Nixon**	**1571**
30	Larry Gardner	1479
31	Rick Burleson	1473
32	Tony Conigliaro	1443
33	Freddy Parent	1390
34	Buck Freeman	1361
35	Jim Piersall	1339
36	**David Ortiz**	**1334**
37	Jim Tabor	1324
38	Ellis Burks	1287
39	Hobe Ferris	1280
40	Sammy White	1272
41	Phil Todt	1269
42	Jimmy Collins	1257
43	Vern Stephens	1251
44	Ira Flagstead	1208
45	Everett Scott	1200
46	Rich Gedman	1178
47	Doc Cramer	1177
48	Chick Stahl	1168
49	Marty Barrett	1166
50	Pete Runnels	1101

Runs Batted In by era

1988–2006		
1	Mo Vaughn	752
2	Mike Greenwell	726
3	**Manny Ramirez**	**712**
4	Nomar Garciaparra	690
5	**Jason Varitek**	**543**
6	John Valentin	528
7	**David Ortiz**	**525**
1973–87		
1	Jim Rice	1451
2	Dwight Evans	1346
3	Wade Boggs	687
4	Carlton Fisk	568
5	Fred Lynn	521
6	Rick Burleson	360
7	Butch Hobson	358
1961–72		
1	Carl Yastrzemski	1844
2	Rico Petrocelli	773
3	Frank Malzone	716
4	George Scott	562
5	Reggie Smith	536
6	Tony Conigliaro	501
7	Gary Geiger	246
1943–60		
1	Ted Williams	1839
2	Bobby Doerr	1247
3	Jackie Jensen	733
4	Dom DiMaggio	618
5	Vern Stephens	562
6	Billy Goodman	464
7	Sammy White	404
1921–42		
1	Jimmie Foxx	788
2	Joe Cronin	737
3	Jim Tabor	517
4	Phil Todt	409
5	Roy Johnson	327
6	Ira Flagstead	299
7	Bill Regan	282
1901–20		
1	Duffy Lewis	629
2	Tris Speaker	542
3	Buck Freeman	504
4	Harry Hooper	497
5	Larry Gardner	481
6	Hobe Ferris	418
7	Freddy Parent	386

Walks

1	Ted Williams	2021
2	Carl Yastrzemski	1845
3	Dwight Evans	1337
4	Wade Boggs	1004
5	Harry Hooper	826
6	Bobby Doerr	809
7	Dom DiMaggio	750
8	Jim Rice	670
9	Rico Petrocelli	661
10	Jimmie Foxx	624
11	Joe Cronin	585
	Jackie Jensen	585
13	Johnny Pesky	581
14	Billy Goodman	561
15	Mo Vaughn	519
16	**Manny Ramirez**	**513**
17	Mike Greenwell	460
18	Tris Speaker	459
19	**Trot Nixon**	**454**
20	John Valentin	441
21	Reggie Smith	425
22	George Scott	418
23	**Jason Varitek**	**406**
24	Carlton Fisk	389
25	Larry Gardner	388
26	Fred Lynn	382
27	Pete Runnels	378
28	Don Buddin	373
29	**David Ortiz**	**354**
30	Jim Piersall	338
31	Dick Gernert	336
32	Ira Flagstead	335
33	Frank Malzone	327
34	Vern Stephens	320
35	Jody Reed	319
36	Rick Burleson	310
	Heinie Wagner	310
38	Marty Barrett	304
39	Duffy Lewis	303
40	Rick Miller	302
41	Mike Andrews	295
42	Chick Stahl	280
43	Nomar Garciaparra	279
44	Troy O'Leary	276
45	Rick Ferrell	269
46	Billy Werber	268
47	Tony Conigliaro	264
48	Johnny Damon	262
49	Jose Offerman	260
50	Ellis Burks	254

Walk Percentage (BB/PA)

1	Ted Williams	20.64
2	Jimmie Foxx	15.86
3	Don Buddin	14.59
4	**Manny Ramirez**	**13.91**
5	**David Ortiz**	**13.74**
6	Wade Boggs	13.71
7	Carl Yastrzemski	13.19
8	Dwight Evans	13.06
9	Jackie Jensen	12.95
10	Rick Ferrell	12.82
11	Dick Gernert	12.79
12	Joe Cronin	12.76
13	Pete Runnels	12.58
14	Johnny Pesky	12.21
15	Mike Andrews	11.96
16	**Trot Nixon**	**11.86**
17	Mo Vaughn	11.66
18	Dom DiMaggio	11.58
19	Billy Werber	11.28
20	Harry Hooper	11.27
21	Vern Stephens	11.14
22	Billy Goodman	11.08
23	Tim Naehring	10.92
24	Gary Geiger	10.88
25	Fred Lynn	10.87
26	Rico Petrocelli	10.71
27	Jody Reed	10.40
28	John Valentin	10.33
29	Gene Stephens	10.31
30	Roy Johnson	10.31
31	Rick Miller	10.29
32	Tris Speaker	10.09
33	Bobby Doerr	10.08
34	**Jason Varitek**	**10.05**
35	Reggie Smith	9.97
36	Ira Flagstead	9.86
37	Brian Daubach	9.54
38	Johnny Damon	9.42
39	Bob Tillman	9.26
40	Clyde Engle	9.21
41	Ted Lepcio	9.11
42	Eddie Bressoud	9.10
43	Bill Carrigan	9.05
44	Carlton Fisk	8.94
45	Mike Greenwell	8.90
46	Jim Piersall	8.86
47	George Scott	8.82
48	Larry Gardner	8.60
49	Heinie Wagner	8.35
50	Chick Stahl	8.22

Strikeouts

1	Dwight Evans	1643
2	Jim Rice	1423
3	Carl Yastrzemski	1393
4	Mo Vaughn	954
5	Rico Petrocelli	926
6	George Scott	850
7	**Jason Varitek**	**780**
8	Ted Williams	709
9	**Manny Ramirez**	**671**
10	**Trot Nixon**	**621**
11	Bobby Doerr	608
12	Carlton Fisk	588
13	Tony Conigliaro	577
14	Dom DiMaggio	571
15	Jimmie Foxx	568
16	Troy O'Leary	562
17	Reggie Smith	498
18	Butch Hobson	495
19	John Valentin	487
20	Brian Daubach	477
21	Wade Boggs	470
22	Ellis Burks	458
23	**David Ortiz**	**457**
24	Tony Armas	454
25	Rich Gedman	448
26	Jackie Jensen	425
27	Frank Malzone	423
28	Dick Gernert	420
29	Joe Cronin	408
30	Nomar Garciaparra	406
31	Fred Lynn	394
32	Eddie Bressoud	387
33	Rick Miller	373
34	Don Buddin	371
35	Mike Greenwell	364
36	Rick Burleson	360
37	Sammy White	356
38	Ted Lepcio	350
39	Gary Geiger	325
	Bob Tillman	325
41	Tom Brunansky	321
42	Jim Piersall	317
43	Tim Naehring	312
44	Lou Clinton	306
45	Jim Tabor	305
46	Reggie Jefferson	300
47	Luis Rivera	296
48	Mike Stanley	293
49	Mark Bellhorn	286
50	Johnny Damon	284

At Bats per Strikeout

1	Stuffy McInnis	40.9
2	Lou Finney	32.2
3	Tom Oliver	31.7
4	Doc Cramer	31.4
5	Johnny Peacock	27.0
6	Rick Ferrell	23.9
7	Skeeter Newsome	23.0
8	Johnny Pesky	21.6
9	Joe Harris	19.5
10	Everett Scott	18.3
11	Billy Goodman	18.0
12	Ira Flagstead	17.5
13	Bill Buckner	17.3
14	Marty Barrett	16.3
15	Hal Rhyne	16.1
16	Phil Todt	15.5
17	Dick Hoblitzel	15.3
18	Shano Collins	14.0
19	Roy Johnson	13.3
20	Billy Werber	13.3
21	Wade Boggs	13.2
22	Birdie Tebbetts	12.8
23	Mike Greenwell	12.7
24	Dave Stapleton	12.5

Strikeout Percentage

1	Brian Daubach	26.47
2	Mo Vaughn	24.92
3	Tony Armas	22.44
4	Butch Hobson	22.20
5	**Jason Varitek**	**22.02**
6	**Manny Ramirez**	**21.61**
7	Ted Lepcio	21.58
8	Reggie Jefferson	21.46
9	Lou Clinton	21.44
10	**David Ortiz**	**20.88**
11	Tom Brunansky	20.64
12	Mike Stanley	20.56
13	Bob Tillman	20.10
14	George Scott	20.08
15	Eddie Bressoud	19.77
16	Luis Rivera	19.72
17	Tony Conigliaro	19.53
18	**Trot Nixon**	**18.90**
19	Dwight Evans	18.83
20	Dick Gernert	18.63
21	Kevin Millar	18.19
22	Gary Allenson	17.72
23	Gene Stephens	17.55
24	Don Buddin	17.45

Batting Average

1	Ted Williams	.344
2	Wade Boggs	.338
3	Tris Speaker	.337
4	Nomar Garciaparra	.323
5	Pete Runnels	.320
6	Jimmie Foxx	.320
7	Reggie Jefferson	.316
8	**Manny Ramirez**	**.316**
9	Joe Harris	.315
10	Roy Johnson	.313
11	Johnny Pesky	.313
12	Fred Lynn	.308
13	Billy Goodman	.306
14	Mo Vaughn	.304
15	Bill Mueller	.303
16	Mike Greenwell	.303
17	Doc Cramer	.302
18	Rick Ferrell	.302
19	Lou Finney	.301
20	Joe Cronin	.300
21	Jim Rice	.298
22	Dom DiMaggio	.298
23	Jimmy Collins	.296
24	Stuffy McInnis	.296
25	Johnny Damon	.295
26	Ira Flagstead	.295
27	**David Ortiz**	**.294**
28	Chick Stahl	.290
29	Pete Fox	.289
30	Duffy Lewis	.289
31	Bobby Doerr	.288
32	Birdie Tebbetts	.287
33	Mike Menosky	.286
34	Buck Freeman	.286
35	Jerry Remy	.286
36	Carl Yastrzemski	.285
37	Carlton Fisk	.284
38	Dusty Cooke	.284
39	Cecil Cooper	.283
40	Vern Stephens	.283
41	Jackie Jensen	.282
42	Larry Gardner	.282
43	Kevin Millar	.282
44	Tim Naehring	.282
45	Reggie Smith	.281
46	John Valentin	.281
47	Billy Werber	.281
48	Ellis Burks	.280
49	Jody Reed	.280
50	Bill Buckner	.279

Batting Average by era

1988–2006

1	Nomar Garciaparra	.323
2	Reggie Jefferson	.316
3	**Manny Ramirez**	**.316**
4	Mo Vaughn	.304
5	Bill Mueller	.303
6	Mike Greenwell	.303
7	Johnny Damon	.295

1973–87

1	Wade Boggs	.338
2	Fred Lynn	.308
3	Jim Rice	.298
4	Jerry Remy	.286
5	Carlton Fisk	.284
6	Cecil Cooper	.283
7	Bill Buckner	.279

1961–72

1	Carl Yastrzemski	.285
2	Reggie Smith	.281
3	Frank Malzone	.276
4	Eddie Bressoud	.270
5	Mike Andrews	.268
6	Russ Nixon	.268
7	Tony Conigliaro	.267

1943–60

1	Ted Williams	.344
2	Pete Runnels	.320
3	Johnny Pesky	.313
4	Billy Goodman	.306
5	Dom DiMaggio	.298
6	Pete Fox	.289
7	Bobby Doerr	.288

1921–42

1	Jimmie Foxx	.320
2	Joe Harris	.315
3	Roy Johnson	.313
4	Doc Cramer	.302
5	Rick Ferrell	.302
6	Lou Finney	.301
7	Joe Cronin	.300

1901–20

1	Tris Speaker	.337
2	Jimmy Collins	.296
3	Stuffy McInnis	.296
4	Chick Stahl	.290
5	Duffy Lewis	.289
6	Buck Freeman	.286
7	Larry Gardner	.282

On-Base Percentage

1	Ted Williams	.482
2	Jimmie Foxx	.429
3	Wade Boggs	.428
4	**Manny Ramirez**	**.416**
5	Tris Speaker	.414
6	Pete Runnels	.408
7	Johnny Pesky	.401
8	Joe Cronin	.394
	Rick Ferrell	.394
	Mo Vaughn	.394
11	Joe Harris	.393
12	Dusty Cooke	.392
13	**David Ortiz**	**.391**
14	Billy Goodman	.386
	Roy Johnson	.386
16	Dom DiMaggio	.383
17	Fred Lynn	.382
	Mike Stanley	.382
19	Carl Yastrzemski	.379
20	Bill Mueller	.378
21	Jackie Jensen	.375
22	Ira Flagstead	.374
23	Nomar Garciaparra	.370
24	Dwight Evans	.369
	Mike Menosky	.369
26	Mike Greenwell	.368
27	Birdie Tebbetts	.367
	Billy Werber	.367
29	**Trot Nixon**	**.366**
30	Tim Naehring	.365
31	Vern Stephens	.364
32	Reggie Jefferson	.363
33	Johnny Damon	.362
	Bobby Doerr	.362
	Harry Hooper	.362
	Kevin Millar	.362
37	John Valentin	.361
38	Mike Andrews	.360
39	Jose Offerman	.359
40	Don Buddin	.358
	Jody Reed	.358
42	Scott Hatteberg	.357
	Chick Stahl	.357
44	Carlton Fisk	.356
45	Reggie Smith	.355
46	Dick Gernert	.352
	Jim Rice	.352
48	Lou Finney	.351
49	3 players tied	.350

Slugging Average

1	Ted Williams	.634
2	**Manny Ramirez**	**.610**
3	**David Ortiz**	**.609**
4	Jimmie Foxx	.605
5	Nomar Garciaparra	.553
6	Mo Vaughn	.542
7	Fred Lynn	.520
8	Reggie Jefferson	.505
9	Jim Rice	.502
10	Vern Stephens	.492
11	Brian Daubach	.488
12	Tony Conigliaro	.488
13	Joe Cronin	.484
14	Mike Stanley	.483
15	Tris Speaker	.482
16	Carlton Fisk	.481
17	Tony Armas	.480
18	**Trot Nixon**	**.478**
19	Jackie Jensen	.478
20	Joe Harris	.475
21	Bill Mueller	.474
22	Dwight Evans	.473
23	Reggie Smith	.471
24	Mike Greenwell	.463
25	Carl Yastrzemski	.462
26	Wade Boggs	.462
27	Bobby Doerr	.461
28	John Valentin	.460
29	Troy O'Leary	.459
30	Roy Johnson	.458
31	Ellis Burks	.455
32	Kevin Millar	.451
33	**Jason Varitek**	**.450**
34	Cecil Cooper	.447
35	Buck Freeman	.442
36	Johnny Damon	.441
37	Lou Clinton	.440
38	Butch Hobson	.439
39	Dick Gernert	.436
40	Eddie Bressoud	.435
41	Jim Tabor	.431
42	Tom Brunansky	.430
43	Pete Runnels	.427
44	Billy Werber	.425
45	Jimmy Collins	.423
46	Dusty Cooke	.422
47	Gary Geiger	.422
48	George Scott	.421
49	Tim Naehring	.420
50	Rico Petrocelli	.420

On-Base plus Slugging

1	Ted Williams	1116
2	Jimmie Foxx	1034
3	**Manny Ramirez**	**1026**
4	**David Ortiz**	**1000**
5	Mo Vaughn	936
6	Nomar Garciaparra	923
7	Fred Lynn	902
8	Tris Speaker	896
9	Wade Boggs	890
10	Joe Cronin	878
11	Joe Harris	868
	Reggie Jefferson	868
13	Mike Stanley	865
14	Vern Stephens	856
15	Jim Rice	854
16	Jackie Jensen	853
17	Bill Mueller	852
18	Roy Johnson	844
	Trot Nixon	**844**
20	Dwight Evans	842
21	Carl Yastrzemski	841
22	Carlton Fisk	837
23	Pete Runnels	835
24	Mike Greenwell	831
25	Brian Daubach	829
26	Reggie Smith	826
27	Bobby Doerr	823
28	John Valentin	821
29	Tony Conigliaro	819
30	Dusty Cooke	814
31	Kevin Millar	813
32	Rick Ferrell	804
33	Johnny Damon	803
34	Dom DiMaggio	802
35	**Jason Varitek**	**798**
36	Ellis Burks	796
37	Johnny Pesky	794
38	Billy Werber	792
39	Troy O'Leary	790
40	Dick Gernert	788
41	Ira Flagstead	785
42	Tim Naehring	785
43	Buck Freeman	781
44	Billy Goodman	773
45	Eddie Bressoud	772
46	Cecil Cooper	771
	Scott Hatteberg	771
48	Jake Stahl	769
49	Tony Armas	768
50	Lou Finney	762

Adjusted OPS

1	Ted Williams	186
2	Tris Speaker	165
3	**Manny Ramirez**	**161**
4	Jimmie Foxx	154
5	**David Ortiz**	**152**
6	Wade Boggs	140
7	Fred Lynn	139
8	Mo Vaughn	138
9	Jake Stahl	134
10	Nomar Garciaparra	133
11	Buck Freeman	128
	Reggie Smith	128
	Carl Yastrzemski	128
14	Dwight Evans	126
	Jim Rice	126
16	Carlton Fisk	125
	Joe Harris	125
18	Jimmy Collins	123
	Pete Runnels	123
20	Jackie Jensen	122
21	Tony Conigliaro	121
	Joe Cronin	121
	Chick Stahl	121
24	Mike Greenwell	119
	Reggie Jefferson	119
	Bill Mueller	119
27	Duffy Lewis	118
28	Mike Stanley	117
29	**Trot Nixon**	**116**
	Vern Stephens	116
31	Larry Gardner	115
	Harry Hooper	115
	Roy Johnson	115
34	Bobby Doerr	114
35	Ellis Burks	113
36	Cecil Cooper	111
37	Brian Daubach	110
38	Dom DiMaggio	109
	Dick Hoblitzel	109
	John Valentin	109
41	Mike Andrews	108
	Eddie Bressoud	108
	Kevin Millar	108
	Johnny Pesky	108
	Rico Petrocelli	108
46	Johnny Damon	107
47	Dusty Cooke	106
	Joe Foy	106
	Dick Gernert	106
50	2 players tied	104

Games

First Base
1 George Scott — 988
2 Mo Vaughn — 928
3 Phil Todt — 852
4 Jimmie Foxx — 807
5 Carl Yastrzemski — 765

Second Base
1 Bobby Doerr — 1852
2 Hobe Ferris — 985
3 Marty Barrett — 906
4 Jerry Remy — 685
5 Doug Griffin — 603

Shortstop
1 Everett Scott — 1093
2 Rick Burleson — 1004
3 Nomar Garciaparra — 956
4 Freddy Parent — 909
5 Joe Cronin — 897

Third Base
1 Wade Boggs — 1520
2 Frank Malzone — 1335
3 Larry Gardner — 929
4 Jim Tabor — 789
5 Jimmy Collins — 735

Outfield
1 Ted Williams — 2151
2 Dwight Evans — 2079
3 Carl Yastrzemski — 2076
4 Harry Hooper — 1637
5 Jim Rice — 1543
6 Dom DiMaggio — 1373
7 Duffy Lewis — 1165
8 Mike Greenwell — 1164
9 Tris Speaker — 1053
10 Jackie Jensen — 1026

Catcher
1 Jason Varitek — 1017
2 Carlton Fisk — 990
3 Sammy White — 967
4 Rich Gedman — 857
5 Bill Carrigan — 649

Pitcher
1 Bob Stanley — 637
2 Tim Wakefield — 443
3 Derek Lowe — 384
4 Roger Clemens — 383
5 Ellis Kinder — 365

Fielding Average

First Base
1 Stuffy McInnis — .996
2 Pete Runnels — .995
3 Carl Yastrzemski — .994
4 Phil Todt — .992
5 Jimmie Foxx — .991

Second Base
1 Marty Barrett — .986
2 Chuck Schilling — .985
3 Jody Reed — .984
4 Jerry Remy — .982
5 Doug Griffin — .981

Shortstop
1 John Valentin — .972
2 Vern Stephens — .971
3 Rick Burleson — .970
4 Rico Petrocelli — .969
5 Nomar Garciaparra — .969

Third Base
1 Rico Petrocelli — .970
2 Johnny Pesky — .963
3 Wade Boggs — .959
4 Frank Malzone — .956
5 Larry Gardner — .940

Outfield
1 Darren Lewis — .992
2 Johnny Damon — .991
3 Jim Piersall — .989
4 Gary Geiger — .988
5 Fred Lynn — .987
6 Dwight Evans — .987
7 Tom Oliver — .986
8 Ellis Burks — .986
9 Troy O'Leary — .985
10 Rick Miller — .984

Catcher
1 Tony Pena — .994
2 Jason Varitek — .993
3 Bob Tillman — .988
4 Rich Ferrell — .987
5 Sammy White — .985

Pitcher
1 Charlie Wagner — .992
2 Bill Monbouquette — .985
3 Joe Dobson — .980
4 Frank Sullivan — .979
5 Dave Ferriss — .979

Total Chances/Game (Infield)

First Base
1 Candy LaChance — 11.38
2 Stuffy McInnis — 11.35
3 Phil Todt — 11.00
4 Jake Stahl — 10.97
5 Dick Hoblitzel — 10.53
6 Dick Gernert — 9.70
7 Jimmie Foxx — 9.68
8 George Scott — 9.37
9 Bill Buckner — 9.27
10 Carl Yastrzemski — 9.17

Second Base
1 Bill Regan — 5.93
2 Bobby Doerr — 5.86
3 Hobe Ferris — 5.83
4 Billy Goodman — 5.46
5 Jody Reed — 5.21
6 Mike Andrews — 5.04
7 Chuck Schilling — 5.03
8 Jerry Remy — 5.00
9 Marty Barrett — 4.98
10 Doug Griffin — 4.90

Shortstop
1 Heinie Wagner — 6.03
2 Freddy Parent — 5.74
3 Everett Scott — 5.41
4 Johnny Pesky — 5.30
5 Rick Burleson — 5.22
6 Joe Cronin — 5.22
7 Hal Rhyne — 5.08
8 Vern Stephens — 5.06
9 Don Buddin — 5.03
10 Rico Petrocelli — 4.76

Third Base
1 Jimmy Collins — 3.71
2 Jim Tabor — 3.43
3 Johnny Pesky — 3.41
4 Larry Gardner — 3.25
5 Frank Malzone — 3.21
6 Joe Foy — 3.10
7 Butch Hobson — 2.89
8 Rico Petrocelli — 2.89
9 Wade Boggs — 2.83

Assists (Infield)

First Base
1 Jimmie Foxx — 614
2 Phil Todt — 610
3 George Scott — 590
4 Mo Vaughn — 544
5 Carl Yastrzemski — 512
6 Bill Buckner — 501
7 Dick Gernert — 384
8 Stuffy McInnis — 346
9 Carlos Quintana — 259
10 Billy Goodman — 240

Second Base
1 Bobby Doerr — 5710
2 Hobe Ferris — 3064
3 Marty Barrett — 2627
4 Jerry Remy — 1988
5 Bill Regan — 1978
6 Billy Goodman — 1635
7 Jody Reed — 1541
8 Doug Griffin — 1518
9 Mike Andrews — 1422
10 Chuck Schilling — 1366

Shortstop
1 Everett Scott — 3394
2 Rick Burleson — 3247
3 Freddy Parent — 2975
4 Nomar Garciaparra — 2721
5 Joe Cronin — 2691
6 Heinie Wagner — 2585
7 Rico Petrocelli — 2283
8 Don Buddin — 1877
9 Johnny Pesky — 1709
10 John Valentin — 1659

Third Base
1 Wade Boggs — 2956
2 Frank Malzone — 2824
3 Larry Gardner — 1823
4 Jim Tabor — 1662
5 Jimmy Collins — 1573
6 Rico Petrocelli — 1453
7 Butch Hobson — 1042
8 Johnny Pesky — 978
9 Billy Werber — 811
10 Joe Foy — 796

Assists/Game (Infield)

First Base
1 Bill Buckner — 1.00
2 Jimmie Foxx — 0.77
3 Phil Todt — 0.72
4 Dick Gernert — 0.71
5 Stuffy McInnis — 0.68
6 Carl Yastrzemski — 0.67
7 George Scott — 0.60
8 Mo Vaughn — 0.59
9 Pete Runnels — 0.52
10 Dick Hoblitzel — 0.51

Second Base
1 Bill Regan — 3.40
2 Hobe Ferris — 3.12
3 Jody Reed — 3.11
4 Bobby Doerr — 3.09
5 Jerry Remy — 2.91
6 Marty Barrett — 2.90
7 Billy Goodman — 2.84
8 Chuck Schilling — 2.73
9 Mike Andrews — 2.59
10 Doug Griffin — 2.52

Shortstop
1 Freddy Parent — 3.28
2 Rick Burleson — 3.24
3 Heinie Wagner — 3.22
4 Vern Stephens — 3.20
5 Johnny Pesky — 3.12
6 Everett Scott — 3.11
7 Joe Cronin — 3.01
8 John Valentin — 2.99
9 Don Buddin — 2.97
10 Rico Petrocelli — 2.95
11 Hal Rhyne — 2.95

Third Base
1 Jimmy Collins — 2.15
2 Johnny Pesky — 2.15
3 Frank Malzone — 2.12
4 Jim Tabor — 2.11
5 Rico Petrocelli — 2.00
6 Joe Foy — 1.98
7 Larry Gardner — 1.97
8 Wade Boggs — 1.95
9 Butch Hobson — 1.84

Double Plays

First Base
1 George Scott — 815
2 Mo Vaughn — 785
3 Jimmie Foxx — 707
4 Phil Todt — 680
5 Carl Yastrzemski — 610

Second Base
1 Bobby Doerr — 1507
2 Marty Barrett — 578
3 Jerry Remy — 466
4 Billy Goodman — 443
5 Bill Regan — 387

Shortstop
1 Rick Burleson — 699
2 Joe Cronin — 565
3 Nomar Garciaparra — 534
4 Don Buddin — 438
5 Everett Scott — 437

Third Base
1 Wade Boggs — 299
2 Frank Malzone — 286
3 Jim Tabor — 153
4 Rico Petrocelli — 150
5 Johnny Pesky — 121

Outfield
1 Tris Speaker — 64
2 Harry Hooper — 56
3 Dwight Evans — 40
4 Duffy Lewis — 35
5 Dom DiMaggio — 32
6 Ted Williams — 30
Carl Yastrzemski — 30
8 Ira Flagstead — 28
9 Chick Stahl — 20
10 Jim Rice — 19

Catcher
1 Sammy White — 79
2 Bill Carrigan — 66
3 Lou Criger — 62
4 Carlton Fisk — 61
5 Rich Gedman — 51

Pitcher
1 Bob Stanley — 38
2 Frank Sullivan — 30
3 Willard Nixon — 27
Mel Parnell — 27
5 Tom Brewer — 22

Putouts (Outfield)

Outfield
1 Dwight Evans — 4255
2 Ted Williams — 4158
3 Carl Yastrzemski — 3941
4 Dom DiMaggio — 3859
5 Jim Rice — 3103
6 Harry Hooper — 2757
7 Tris Speaker — 2562
8 Reggie Smith — 2332
9 Jim Piersall — 2239
10 Fred Lynn — 2213
11 Duffy Lewis — 2174
12 Mike Greenwell — 2091
13 Jackie Jensen — 2032
14 Ira Flagstead — 1978
15 Doc Cramer — 1914
16 Rick Miller — 1785
17 Trot Nixon — 1763
18 Troy O'Leary — 1694
19 Ellis Burks — 1662
20 Chick Stahl — 1542
21 Johnny Damon — 1457
22 Tom Oliver — 1425
23 Tony Conigliaro — 1328
24 Gary Geiger — 1177
25 Tony Armas — 1075
26 Manny Ramirez — 1031
27 Roy Johnson — 974
28 Darren Lewis — 945
29 Mike Menosky — 902
30 Tom Brunansky — 807
Pete Fox — 807
32 Buck Freeman — 782
33 Lou Clinton — 758
Shano Collins — 758
35 Leon Culberson — 734
36 Darren Bragg — 719
37 Dusty Cooke — 715
38 Gene Stephens — 692
39 Tommy Harper — 677
40 Jack Rothrock — 639
41 Catfish Metkovich — 637
42 Mel Almada — 605
43 Joe Vosmik — 598
44 Lou Finney — 583
45 Russ Scarritt — 579
46 Bob Johnson — 566
47 Earl Webb — 544
48 Patsy Dougherty — 524
49 Al Zarilla — 517
50 Kip Selbach — 485

Putouts/Game (Outfield)

Outfield
1 Tom Oliver — 2.83
2 Dom DiMaggio — 2.82
3 Fred Lynn — 2.73
4 Doc Cramer — 2.67
5 Ira Flagstead — 2.59
6 Jim Piersall — 2.55
7 Johnny Damon — 2.47
8 Tris Speaker — 2.44
9 Ellis Burks — 2.38
10 Reggie Smith — 2.38
11 Gary Geiger — 2.18
12 Dwight Evans — 2.05
13 Rick Miller — 2.02
14 Jim Rice — 2.02
15 Jackie Jensen — 1.99
16 Chick Stahl — 1.99
17 Ted Williams — 1.94
18 Carl Yastrzemski — 1.90
19 Duffy Lewis — 1.87
20 Trot Nixon — 1.87
21 Troy O'Leary — 1.82
22 Mike Greenwell — 1.80
23 Tony Conigliaro — 1.74
24 Harry Hooper — 1.69
25 Manny Ramirez — 1.58
26 Buck Freeman — 1.40
27 Gene Stephens — 1.27

Fielding Runs
1 Bobby Doerr — 178
2 Rick Burleson — 103
3 Tris Speaker — 102
4 Lou Criger — 100
5 Everett Scott — 89
6 Frank Malzone — 82
John Valentin — 82
8 Carl Yastrzemski — 80
9 Hobe Ferris — 76
10 Wade Boggs — 65
11 Tony Pena — 62
Johnny Pesky — 62
Jody Reed — 62
14 Carlton Fisk — 59
Harry Hooper — 59
16 Bill Buckner — 53
17 Marty Barrett — 49
18 Dom DiMaggio — 46
19 Skeeter Newsome — 44
20 Jimmie Foxx — 41
21 Jimmy Collins — 37
Ted Lepcio — 37
23 Wally Gerber — 32
24 Rick Ferrell — 30
25 Pete Runnels — 28
Vern Stephens — 28
Phil Todt — 28
28 Duffy Lewis — 27
29 Eddie Lake — 26
30 Dwight Evans — 25
Ira Flagstead — 25
32 Scott Fletcher — 24
Hal Rhyne — 24
Jason Varitek — 24
35 Roxy Walters — 23
36 Tom Oliver — 22
Pokey Reese — 22
38 Mike Lowell — 21
Tim Naehring — 21
Jim Piersall — 21
Bill Wambsganss — 21
Rabbit Warstler — 21
43 Topper Rigney — 20
44 Kevin Millar — 19
Carlos Quintana — 19
Reggie Smith — 19
47 Lou Clinton — 18
Fred Hatfield — 18
Chuck Schilling — 18
50 2 players tied — 17

Fielding Wins
1 Bobby Doerr — 17.4
2 Tris Speaker — 10.6
3 Lou Criger — 10.5
4 Rick Burleson — 10.5
5 Everett Scott — 9.4
6 Frank Malzone — 8.4
7 Carl Yastrzemski — 8.2
8 Hobe Ferris — 7.9
9 John Valentin — 7.7
10 Wade Boggs — 6.4
11 Tony Pena — 6.3
12 Jody Reed — 6.3
13 Harry Hooper — 6.2
14 Johnny Pesky — 6.1
15 Carlton Fisk — 6.0
16 Bill Buckner — 5.2
17 Marty Barrett — 4.9
18 Skeeter Newsome — 4.6
19 Dom DiMaggio — 4.5
20 Ted Lepcio — 3.8
21 Jimmy Collins — 3.8
22 Jimmie Foxx — 3.7
23 Wally Gerber — 3.1
24 Duffy Lewis — 2.9
25 Pete Runnels — 2.8
26 Eddie Lake — 2.8
27 Rick Ferrell — 2.8
28 Vern Stephens — 2.7
29 Phil Todt — 2.7
30 Dwight Evans — 2.5
31 Ira Flagstead — 2.4
32 Scott Fletcher — 2.3
33 Roxy Walters — 2.3
34 Jason Varitek — 2.3
35 Hal Rhyne — 2.2
36 Jim Piersall — 2.1
37 Pokey Reese — 2.1
38 Tom Oliver — 2.0
39 Reggie Smith — 2.0
40 Tim Naehring — 2.0
41 Mike Lowell — 2.0
42 Bill Wambsganss — 2.0
43 Rabbit Warstler — 2.0
44 Topper Rigney — 1.9
45 Carlos Quintana — 1.9
46 Chuck Schilling — 1.9
47 Lou Clinton — 1.8
48 Rico Petrocelli — 1.8
49 Kevin Millar — 1.8
50 Fred Hatfield — 1.8

284

Stolen Bases

1	Harry Hooper	300
2	Tris Speaker	267
3	Carl Yastrzemski	168
4	Heinie Wagner	141
5	Larry Gardner	134
6	Freddy Parent	129
7	Tommy Harper	107
	Billy Werber	107
9	Chick Stahl	105
10	Jimmy Collins	102
	Duffy Lewis	102
12	Dom DiMaggio	100
13	Johnny Damon	98
	Jerry Remy	98
15	Ellis Burks	95
	Jackie Jensen	95
17	Nomar Garciaparra	84
	Reggie Smith	84
19	Clyde Engle	80
	Mike Greenwell	80
21	Harry Lord	77
22	Dwight Evans	76
23	Hobe Ferris	72
24	Rick Burleson	67
25	Patsy Dougherty	65
	Jake Stahl	65
27	Jim Tabor	64
28	Rick Miller	63
29	Hal Janvrin	62
30	Carlton Fisk	61
	Amby McConnell	61
	Everett Scott	61
33	Darren Lewis	60
34	Buck Freeman	59
35	Jim Piersall	58
	Jim Rice	58
37	Marty Barrett	57
	Gary Geiger	57
	Jack Rothrock	57
40	Bobby Doerr	54
41	Ira Flagstead	51
	Pete Fox	51
43	Roy Johnson	48
	Johnny Pesky	48
45	Mike Menosky	47
	John Valentin	47
47	Dick Hoblitzel	46
48	Fred Lynn	43
49	Otis Nixon	42
50	Catfish Metkovich	41

Stolen Base Average

1	Johnny Damon	82.4
2	Otis Nixon	80.8
3	Tommy Harper	76.4
4	Nomar Garciaparra	75.0
5	Marty Barrett	73.1
6	Billy Werber	72.8
7	Catfish Metkovich	71.9
8	Jackie Jensen	70.9
9	Gary Geiger	70.4
10	Jeff Frye	70.2
11	Carlton Fisk	70.1
12	Ben Chapman	69.0
13	Jerry Remy	68.5
14	Ellis Burks	68.3
15	Pete Fox	68.0
16	Jim Piersall	65.9
17	Darren Lewis	65.2
18	Mike Greenwell	65.0
19	Jack Rothrock	63.3
20	Fred Lynn	63.2
21	Jim Rice	63.0
22	Dom DiMaggio	61.7
23	Reggie Smith	61.3
24	Roy Johnson	60.8

Base Stealing Wins

1	Johnny Damon	1.4
2	Tommy Harper	1.3
3	Billy Werber	0.9
4	Nomar Garciaparra	0.8
5	Jackie Jensen	0.7
6	Jerry Remy	0.6
7	Ellis Burks	0.5
8	Otis Nixon	0.5
9	Marty Barrett	0.5
10	Carlton Fisk	0.4
11	Gary Geiger	0.4
12	Scott Fletcher	0.4
13	Catfish Metkovich	0.4
14	**Coco Crisp**	**0.3**
15	Pete Fox	0.3
16	Leon Culberson	0.3
17	Jeff Frye	0.3
18	Mike Greenwell	0.2
19	Lee Tinsley	0.2
20	Jim Piersall	0.2
21	Ben Chapman	0.2
22	Luis Aparicio	0.2
23	Carl Everett	0.2
24	Jackie Gutierrez	0.2

Pitcher Batting Average by era

1988–2006

1973–87

1961–72

1	Gary Peters	.250
2	Earl Wilson	.202
3	Sonny Siebert	.199
4	Jim Lonborg	.155

1943–60

1	Mickey McDermott	.281
2	Dave Ferriss	.250
3	Willard Nixon	.242
4	Tom Brewer	.207
5	Mel Parnell	.198
6	Joe Dobson	.164
7	Ellis Kinder	.150

1921–42

1	Wes Ferrell	.308
2	Red Ruffing	.269
3	Ted Wingfield	.237
4	Fritz Ostermueller	.233
5	Johnny Marcum	.218
6	Jack Wilson	.204
7	Johnny Welch	.202

1901–20

1	Babe Ruth	.299
2	Joe Bush	.286
3	Joe Wood	.244
4	Carl Mays	.243
5	Jesse Tannehill	.225
6	Cy Young	.219
7	Rube Foster	.215

Pitcher Batting Runs

1	Babe Ruth	73
2	Wes Ferrell	45
3	Joe Wood	32
4	Earl Wilson	29
5	Dave Ferriss	23
	Carl Mays	23
7	Mickey McDermott	20
8	Red Ruffing	18
9	Willard Nixon	17
10	Jesse Tannehill	16
11	Joe Bush	15
	Gary Peters	15
13	Sonny Siebert	14
14	Cy Young	13
15	Rube Foster	9
	Mickey Harris	9
	Tom Hughes	9
18	Ken Brett	8
19	Gene Conley	7
	Charley Hall	7
	Sam Jones	7
22	Jerry Casale	6
	Ray Collins	6
	Fritz Ostermueller	6
	Herb Pennock	6
26	Johnny Marcum	5
27	Billy Muffett	4
	Jose Santiago	4
29	Frank Baumann	3
	Gary Bell	3
	Dennis Bennett	3
	Dick Newsome	3
	Bob Porterfield	3
34	Bucky Brandon	2
	Eddie Cicotte	2
	Ken Tatum	2
	Ted Wills	2
	Ted Wingfield	2
39	Many players tied	1

Adjusted Batting Runs

1	Ted Williams	1067
2	Carl Yastrzemski	508
3	Wade Boggs	406
4	Dwight Evans	338
5	Tris Speaker	326
6	**Manny Ramirez**	**296**
7	Jimmie Foxx	280
8	Jim Rice	279
9	Mo Vaughn	227
10	Nomar Garciaparra	187
11	**David Ortiz**	**173**
12	Fred Lynn	168
13	Babe Ruth	160
14	Reggie Smith	142
15	Harry Hooper	137
16	Joe Cronin	135
17	Bobby Doerr	133
18	Mike Greenwell	129
19	Carlton Fisk	125
	Jackie Jensen	125
21	Buck Freeman	103
22	Pete Runnels	102
23	Dom DiMaggio	93
24	**Trot Nixon**	**88**
25	Duffy Lewis	83
	Chick Stahl	83
27	Jimmy Collins	80
28	Tony Conigliaro	78
29	Bob Johnson	73
	Johnny Pesky	73
31	Earl Webb	71
32	Larry Gardner	68
33	Rico Petrocelli	64
34	Jake Stahl	62
35	John Valentin	58
36	Joe Harris	54
37	Vern Stephens	52
38	Wally Schang	50
39	Roy Johnson	48
	Felix Mantilla	48
41	Ellis Burks	47
	Jose Canseco	47
43	Bill Mueller	46
44	Bernie Carbo	45
	Wes Ferrell	45
	Mike Stanley	45
47	Ike Boone	42
	Doc Gessler	42
49	Patsy Dougherty	40
50	Reggie Jefferson	38

Adjusted Batting Wins

1	Ted Williams	103.0
2	Carl Yastrzemski	52.3
3	Wade Boggs	39.9
4	Tris Speaker	34.0
5	Dwight Evans	33.8
6	Jim Rice	27.8
7	**Manny Ramirez**	**27.8**
8	Jimmie Foxx	25.4
9	Mo Vaughn	21.3
10	Nomar Garciaparra	17.4
11	Babe Ruth	16.9
12	Fred Lynn	16.8
13	**David Ortiz**	**16.2**
14	Reggie Smith	15.2
15	Harry Hooper	14.5
16	Bobby Doerr	13.0
17	Carlton Fisk	12.8
18	Joe Cronin	12.7
19	Mike Greenwell	12.5
20	Jackie Jensen	12.5
21	Buck Freeman	10.5
22	Pete Runnels	10.2
23	Dom DiMaggio	9.2
24	Duffy Lewis	8.8
25	Chick Stahl	8.5
26	**Trot Nixon**	**8.3**
27	Tony Conigliaro	8.2
28	Jimmy Collins	8.1
29	Bob Johnson	7.6
30	Johnny Pesky	7.2
31	Larry Gardner	7.2
32	Rico Petrocelli	6.8
33	Jake Stahl	6.7
34	Earl Webb	6.5
35	John Valentin	5.4
36	Joe Harris	5.1
37	Wally Schang	5.1
38	Vern Stephens	5.0
39	Felix Mantilla	5.0
40	Doc Gessler	4.8
41	Ellis Burks	4.7
42	Bernie Carbo	4.6
43	Roy Johnson	4.5
44	Bill Mueller	4.4
45	Jose Canseco	4.3
46	Mike Stanley	4.2
47	Wes Ferrell	4.1
48	Patsy Dougherty	4.0
49	Ike Boone	3.9
50	Mike Andrews	3.7

Batter-Fielder Wins by era

1988–2006

1	Nomar Garciaparra	25.1
2	**Manny Ramirez**	**21.7**
3	John Valentin	17.6
4	**David Ortiz**	**13.3**
5	**Jason Varitek**	**10.4**
6	Jody Reed	9.7
7	Mo Vaughn	9.3
8	Mike Greenwell	7.2
9	Johnny Damon	4.3
10	Bill Mueller	4.0
	Trot Nixon	**4.0**
12	Tim Naehring	3.7
13	Jose Canseco	3.4
14	Ellis Burks	2.7

1973–87

1	Wade Boggs	43.9
2	Dwight Evans	24.0
3	Carlton Fisk	23.9
4	Jim Rice	18.4
5	Fred Lynn	15.6
6	Rick Burleson	13.5
7	Marty Barrett	3.7
8	Bernie Carbo	3.5
9	Mike Easler	1.9
10	Bob Watson	1.7
11	Rich Gedman	1.3

1961–72

1	Carl Yastrzemski	42.7
2	Rico Petrocelli	15.6
3	Reggie Smith	13.6
4	Eddie Bressoud	7.0
5	Mike Andrews	5.2
6	Felix Mantilla	3.4
7	Ken Harrelson	2.3
8	Tony Conigliaro	2.2
9	Jim Pagliaroni	1.8
	Dick Stuart	1.8
11	Joe Foy	1.6
12	Frank Malzone	1.0

1943–60

1	Ted Williams	86.5
2	Bobby Doerr	40.3
3	Johnny Pesky	16.5
4	Pete Runnels	13.4
5	Vern Stephens	10.5
6	Dom DiMaggio	10.1
7	Jackie Jensen	8.7
8	Eddie Lake	6.7
9	Bob Johnson	6.5
10	Don Buddin	5.7
11	Billy Goodman	3.2
12	Ted Lepcio	3.0
13	Skeeter Newsome	2.9
14	Hal Wagner	1.1

1921–42

1	Jimmie Foxx	22.3
2	Joe Cronin	15.3
3	Rick Ferrell	6.9
4	Topper Rigney	3.9
5	Earl Webb	3.5
6	Joe Harris	3.4
	Buddy Myer	3.4
8	Billy Werber	2.5
9	Ben Chapman	2.2
10	Dale Alexander	1.6
11	Johnny Hodapp	1.1
	Marty McManus	1.1
13	Ira Flagstead	1.0

1901–20

1	Tris Speaker	37.1
2	Jimmy Collins	13.4
3	Harry Hooper	10.9
4	Babe Ruth	10.0
5	Lou Criger	8.8
6	Larry Gardner	5.4
7	Duffy Lewis	5.1
8	Wally Schang	4.9
9	Bill Carrigan	4.6
10	Buck Freeman	4.2
11	Jake Stahl	3.6
12	Doc Gessler	3.3
13	Pinch Thomas	2.3
14	Heinie Wagner	1.9

Batter-Fielder Wins

1	Ted Williams	86.5
2	Wade Boggs	43.9
3	Carl Yastrzemski	42.7
4	Bobby Doerr	40.3
5	Tris Speaker	37.1
6	Nomar Garciaparra	25.1
7	Dwight Evans	24.0
8	Carlton Fisk	23.9
9	Jimmie Foxx	22.3
10	**Manny Ramirez**	**21.7**
11	Jim Rice	18.4
12	John Valentin	17.6
13	Johnny Pesky	16.5
14	Fred Lynn	15.6
	Rico Petrocelli	15.6
16	Joe Cronin	15.3
17	Reggie Smith	13.6
18	Rick Burleson	13.5
19	Jimmy Collins	13.4
	Pete Runnels	13.4
21	**David Ortiz**	**13.3**
22	Harry Hooper	10.9
23	Vern Stephens	10.5
24	**Jason Varitek**	**10.4**
25	Dom DiMaggio	10.1
26	Babe Ruth	10.0
27	Jody Reed	9.7
28	Mo Vaughn	9.3
29	Lou Criger	8.8
30	Jackie Jensen	8.7
31	Mike Greenwell	7.2
32	Eddie Bressoud	7.0
33	Rick Ferrell	6.9
34	Eddie Lake	6.7
35	Bob Johnson	6.5
36	Don Buddin	5.7
37	Larry Gardner	5.4
38	Mike Andrews	5.2
39	Duffy Lewis	5.1
40	Wally Schang	4.9
41	Bill Carrigan	4.6
42	Johnny Damon	4.3
43	Buck Freeman	4.2
44	Bill Mueller	4.0
	Trot Nixon	**4.0**
46	Topper Rigney	3.9
47	Marty Barrett	3.7
	Tim Naehring	3.7
49	Jake Stahl	3.6
50	2 players tied	3.5

Pinch Hits

1	Dalton Jones	55
2	Rick Miller	50
3	Russ Nixon	43
4	Ted Williams	33
5	Olaf Henricksen	29
	Joe Cronin	29
7	Jack Rothrock	27
8	Gene Stephens	25
	Jason Varitek	**25**
10	3 players tied	23

Pinch Hit Average

1	Phil Gagliano	.354
2	Jack Rothrock	.310
3	Ted Williams	.305
4	Russ Nixon	.305
5	Vic Wertz	.302
6	Lou Finney	.299
7	Ted Williams	.297
8	Joe Cronin	.290
9	Rick Miller	.286
10	**Jason Varitek**	**.284**

Pinch Hit Home Runs

1	Ted Williams	7
2	Joe Cronin	5
3	Del Wilber	4
4	Bernie Carbo	3
	Rich Gedman	3
	Scott Hatteberg	3
	Charlie Maxwell	3
	Stan Spence	3
	Clyde Vollmer	3

Wins

1	Roger Clemens	192
	Cy Young	192
3	**Tim Wakefield**	**137**
4	Mel Parnell	123
5	Luis Tiant	122
6	Pedro Martinez	117
	Joe Wood	117
8	Bob Stanley	115
9	Joe Dobson	106
10	Lefty Grove	105
11	Tex Hughson	96
	Bill Monbouquette	96
13	Bill Lee	94
14	Tom Brewer	91
15	Dutch Leonard	90
	Frank Sullivan	90
17	Babe Ruth	89
18	Dennis Eckersley	88
	Bruce Hurst	88
20	Ellis Kinder	86
21	Bill Dinneen	85
22	Ray Collins	84
23	Ike Delock	83
24	George Winter	82
25	Carl Mays	72
26	Ray Culp	71
27	Derek Lowe	70
28	Willard Nixon	69
29	Jim Lonborg	68
30	Jack Wilson	67
31	Dave Ferriss	65
32	Sam Jones	64
33	Wes Ferrell	62
	Herb Pennock	62
	Jesse Tannehill	62
36	Oil Can Boyd	60
	Mike Torrez	60
38	Fritz Ostermueller	59
39	Rube Foster	58
	Ernie Shore	58
41	Sonny Siebert	57
42	Earl Wilson	56
43	Eddie Cicotte	52
	Danny MacFayden	52
45	Howard Ehmke	51
46	Dick Radatz	49
47	Mickey McDermott	48
48	Rick Wise	47
49	3 players tied	46

Wins by era

1988–2006

1	Roger Clemens	192
2	**Tim Wakefield**	**137**
3	Pedro Martinez	117
4	Derek Lowe	70
5	**Curt Schilling**	**44**
6	Mike Boddicker	39
	Greg Harris	39

1973–87

1	Luis Tiant	122
2	Bob Stanley	115
3	Bill Lee	94
4	Dennis Eckersley	88
	Bruce Hurst	88
6	Oil Can Boyd	60
	Mike Torrez	60

1961–72

1	Bill Monbouquette	96
2	Ray Culp	71
3	Jim Lonborg	68
4	Sonny Siebert	57
5	Earl Wilson	56
6	Dick Radatz	49
7	Dave Morehead	35

1943–60

1	Mel Parnell	123
2	Joe Dobson	106
3	Tex Hughson	96
4	Tom Brewer	91
5	Frank Sullivan	90
6	Ellis Kinder	86
7	Ike Delock	83

1921–42

1	Lefty Grove	105
2	Jack Wilson	67
3	Wes Ferrell	62
4	Fritz Ostermueller	59
5	Danny MacFayden	52
6	Howard Ehmke	51
7	Jack Quinn	45

1901–20

1	Cy Young	192
2	Joe Wood	117
3	Dutch Leonard	90
4	Babe Ruth	89
5	Bill Dinneen	85
6	Ray Collins	84
7	George Winter	82

Winning Percentage

1	Pedro Martinez	.760
2	Roger Moret	.695
3	Dave Ferriss	.684
4	**Curt Schilling**	**.677**
5	Joe Wood	.676
6	Babe Ruth	.659
7	Tex Hughson	.640
8	Mike Boddicker	.639
9	Rube Foster	.637
	Ernie Shore	.637
11	Tom Burgmeier	.636
12	Roger Clemens	.634
13	Cy Young	.632
14	Lefty Grove	.629
15	Ellis Kinder	.623
16	Mel Parnell	.621
17	Jesse Tannehill	.620
18	Wes Ferrell	.608
19	Mark Clear	.603
20	Luis Tiant	.601
21	Joe Dobson	.596
22	Rick Wise	.595
23	Dick Radatz	.590
24	Charley Hall	.590
25	Jose Santiago	.589
	Chuck Stobbs	.589
27	Carl Mays	.585
	Mickey McDermott	.585
29	Dutch Leonard	.584
30	Charlie Wagner	.582
31	Sonny Siebert	.582
32	Bill Lee	.580
33	Ray Collins	.575
34	Gary Peters	.569
35	Derek Lowe	.560
36	Bronson Arroyo	.558
37	Buck O'Brien	.558
38	Earl Johnson	.556
39	Dennis Eckersley	.553
40	Hugh Bedient	.551
41	Ray Culp	.550
42	John Tudor	.549
43	Bruce Hurst	.547
44	Joe Hesketh	.544
45	Frank Viola	.543
46	Bob Stanley	.542
47	Joe Bush	.541
48	Ike Delock	.535
49	Aaron Sele	.535
50	Marty Pattin	.533

Games Started by era

1988–2006

1	Roger Clemens	382
2	**Tim Wakefield**	**306**
3	Pedro Martinez	201
4	Derek Lowe	111
5	Aaron Sele	108
6	John Dopson	85
7	Mike Boddicker	82

1973–87

1	Luis Tiant	238
2	Bruce Hurst	217
3	Dennis Eckersley	191
4	Bill Lee	167
5	Mike Torrez	157
6	Oil Can Boyd	145
7	Bob Ojeda	113

1961–72

1	Bill Monbouquette	228
2	Jim Lonborg	163
3	Earl Wilson	156
4	Ray Culp	155
5	Sonny Siebert	117
6	Dave Morehead	115
7	Gene Conley	72

1943–60

1	Mel Parnell	232
2	Tom Brewer	217
3	Joe Dobson	202
4	Frank Sullivan	201
5	Willard Nixon	177
6	Tex Hughson	156
7	Ike Delock	142

1921–42

1	Lefty Grove	190
2	Danny MacFayden	148
3	Jack Russell	147
4	Red Ruffing	138
5	Fritz Ostermueller	126
6	Howard Ehmke	120
7	Jack Wilson	113

1901–20

1	Cy Young	297
2	George Winter	176
3	Bill Dinneen	174
4	Dutch Leonard	160
5	Joe Wood	157
6	Ray Collins	151
7	Babe Ruth	144

Complete Games by era

1988–2006

1	Roger Clemens	100
2	Pedro Martinez	22
	Tim Wakefield	**22**
4	Mike Boddicker	8
	Frank Viola	8
6	Tom Gordon	6
7	Danny Darwin	4
	Aaron Sele	4

1973–87

1	Luis Tiant	113
2	Dennis Eckersley	64
	Bill Lee	64
4	Bruce Hurst	54
5	Oil Can Boyd	39
6	Mike Torrez	36
7	Rick Wise	33

1961–72

1	Bill Monbouquette	72
2	Ray Culp	51
3	Jim Lonborg	38
4	Earl Wilson	30
5	Sonny Siebert	28
6	Marty Pattin	24
7	Gary Peters	19

1943–60

1	Mel Parnell	113
2	Tex Hughson	99
3	Joe Dobson	90
4	Tom Brewer	75
5	Frank Sullivan	72
6	Dave Ferriss	67
7	Willard Nixon	51

1921–42

1	Lefty Grove	119
2	Howard Ehmke	83
3	Wes Ferrell	81
4	Red Ruffing	73
5	Danny MacFayden	71
6	Jack Russell	57
7	Jack Quinn	53

1901–20

1	Cy Young	275
2	Bill Dinneen	156
3	George Winter	141
4	Joe Wood	121
5	Babe Ruth	105
6	Dutch Leonard	96
7	Ray Collins	90

Saves

1	Bob Stanley	132
2	Dick Radatz	104
3	Ellis Kinder	91
4	Jeff Reardon	88
5	Derek Lowe	85
6	Sparky Lyle	69
7	Tom Gordon	68
8	Lee Smith	58
9	Bill Campbell	51
10	Ugueth Urbina	49
11	Mike Fornieles	48
	Heathcliff Slocumb	48
13	**Keith Foulke**	**47**
14	Jeff Russell	45
15	Dick Drago	41
16	Tom Burgmeier	40
17	Mark Clear	38
18	**Jonathan Papelbon**	**35**
19	Ike Delock	31
20	Bobby Bolin	28
	Leo Kiely	28
	John Wyatt	28
23	**Mike Timlin**	**25**
24	Ken Ryan	22
	Tim Wakefield	**22**
26	Jim Willoughby	20
	Jack Wilson	20
28	Lee Stange	18
29	Steve Crawford	17
	Tex Hughson	17
	Vicente Romo	17
32	Mace Brown	16
	Greg Harris	16
	Earl Johnson	16
	Byung-Hyun Kim	16
	Rob Murphy	16
	Diego Segui	16
38	Calvin Schiraldi	15
	Bob Veale	15
40	Arnold Earley	14
	Bob Klinger	14
	Wilcy Moore	14
	Jack Quinn	14
	Murray Wall	14
45	Bill Lee	13
	Fritz Ostermueller	13
	Ken Tatum	13
48	5 players tied	12

Losses

1	**Tim Wakefield**	**122**
2	Cy Young	112
3	Roger Clemens	111
4	Bob Stanley	97
	George Winter	97
6	Red Ruffing	96
7	Jack Russell	94
8	Bill Monbouquette	91
9	Bill Dinneen	85
10	Tom Brewer	82
11	Luis Tiant	81
12	Frank Sullivan	80
13	Danny MacFayden	78
14	Mel Parnell	75
15	Bruce Hurst	73
16	Ike Delock	72
	Joe Dobson	72
	Willard Nixon	72
19	Dennis Eckersley	71
20	Bill Lee	68
21	Jack Wilson	67
22	Jim Lonborg	65
	Fritz Ostermueller	65
24	Howard Ehmke	64
	Dutch Leonard	64
26	Ray Collins	62
	Lefty Grove	62
28	Sam Jones	59
	Herb Pennock	59
30	Ray Culp	58
	Earl Wilson	58
32	Oil Can Boyd	56
	Dave Morehead	56
	Joe Wood	56
35	Derek Lowe	55
36	Tex Hughson	54
	Jack Quinn	54
	Mike Torrez	54
39	Milt Gaston	52
	Ellis Kinder	52
41	Carl Mays	51
42	Alex Ferguson	48
43	Eddie Cicotte	46
	Babe Ruth	46
45	Ed Morris	45
	Gordon Rhodes	45
47	Ted Wingfield	44
48	Greg Harris	43
	Al Nipper	43
50	Mickey Harris	42

Games Started

1	Roger Clemens	382
2	**Tim Wakefield**	**306**
3	Cy Young	297
4	Luis Tiant	238
5	Mel Parnell	232
6	Bill Monbouquette	228
7	Tom Brewer	217
	Bruce Hurst	217
9	Joe Dobson	202
10	Pedro Martinez	201
	Frank Sullivan	201
12	Dennis Eckersley	191
13	Lefty Grove	190
14	Willard Nixon	177
15	George Winter	176
16	Bill Dinneen	174
17	Bill Lee	167
18	Jim Lonborg	163
19	Dutch Leonard	160
20	Mike Torrez	157
	Joe Wood	157
22	Tex Hughson	156
	Earl Wilson	156
24	Ray Culp	155
25	Ray Collins	151
26	Danny MacFayden	148
27	Jack Russell	147
28	Oil Can Boyd	145
29	Babe Ruth	144
30	Ike Delock	142
31	Red Ruffing	138
32	Fritz Ostermueller	126
33	Sam Jones	124
	Herb Pennock	124
35	Howard Ehmke	120
36	Sonny Siebert	117
37	Dave Morehead	115
38	Bob Ojeda	113
	Jack Wilson	113
40	Carl Mays	112
41	Derek Lowe	111
42	Wes Ferrell	110
43	Aaron Sele	108
44	Al Nipper	107
45	Jesse Tannehill	106
46	Dave Ferriss	103
	Rube Foster	103
	Ernie Shore	103
49	Eddie Cicotte	102
50	Jack Quinn	100

Complete Games

1	Cy Young	275
2	Bill Dinneen	156
3	George Winter	141
4	Joe Wood	121
5	Lefty Grove	119
6	Mel Parnell	113
	Luis Tiant	113
8	Babe Ruth	105
9	Roger Clemens	100
10	Tex Hughson	99
11	Dutch Leonard	96
12	Ray Collins	90
	Joe Dobson	90
14	Carl Mays	87
15	Jesse Tannehill	85
16	Howard Ehmke	83
	Sam Jones	83
18	Wes Ferrell	81
19	Tom Brewer	75
20	Red Ruffing	73
21	Bill Monbouquette	72
	Frank Sullivan	72
23	Danny MacFayden	71
24	Herb Pennock	70
25	Dave Ferriss	67
26	Joe Bush	65
	Eddie Cicotte	65
28	Dennis Eckersley	64
	Bill Lee	64
30	Rube Foster	60
31	Jack Russell	57
32	Norwood Gibson	56
33	Bruce Hurst	54
34	Jack Quinn	53
35	Fritz Ostermueller	52
36	Ray Culp	51
	Willard Nixon	51
	Ernie Shore	51
39	Jack Wilson	48
40	Ellis Kinder	45
41	Milt Gaston	44
42	Ed Morris	43
43	Hugh Bedient	41
44	Oil Can Boyd	39
45	Mickey Harris	38
	Jim Lonborg	38
47	Alex Ferguson	36
	Dick Newsome	36
	Buck O'Brien	36
	Mike Torrez	36

Shutouts

1	Dutch Leonard	25
2	Mel Parnell	20
3	Ray Collins	19
	Tex Hughson	19
	Luis Tiant	19
6	Joe Wood	18
7	Joe Dobson	17
8	Bill Dinneen	16
	Bill Monbouquette	16
	Cy Young	16
11	Rube Foster	15
12	Frank Sullivan	14
	Jesse Tannehill	14
14	Tom Brewer	13
	Ray Culp	13
	Bruce Hurst	13
	Sam Jones	13
18	Dave Ferriss	12
	Herb Pennock	12
20	Joe Bush	10
	Roger Clemens	10
	Dennis Eckersley	10
23	Wes Ferrell	9
	Lefty Grove	9
	Mickey McDermott	9
	Willard Nixon	9
	Ernie Shore	9
	Sonny Siebert	9
	George Winter	9
30	Babe Ruth	8
31	Eddie Cicotte	7
	John Curtis	7
	Howard Ehmke	7
	Bill Lee	7
	Jack Quinn	7
	Bob Stanley	7
	Rick Wise	7
38	Oil Can Boyd	6
	Ike Delock	6
	Jim Lonborg	6
	Carl Mays	6
	Dave Morehead	6
	Marty Pattin	6
	Earl Wilson	6
45	Many players tied	5

Saves by era

1988–2006

1	Jeff Reardon	88
2	Derek Lowe	85
3	Tom Gordon	68
4	Lee Smith	58
5	Ugueth Urbina	49
6	Heathcliff Slocumb	48
7	**Keith Foulke**	**47**

1973–87

1	Bob Stanley	132
2	Bill Campbell	51
3	Dick Drago	41
4	Tom Burgmeier	40
5	Mark Clear	38
6	Jim Willoughby	20
7	Steve Crawford	17

1961–72

1	Dick Radatz	104
2	Sparky Lyle	69
3	Bobby Bolin	28
	John Wyatt	28
5	Lee Stange	18
6	Vicente Romo	17
7	Arnold Earley	14

1943–60

1	Ellis Kinder	91
2	Mike Fornieles	48
3	Ike Delock	31
4	Leo Kiely	28
5	Tex Hughson	17
6	Mace Brown	16
	Earl Johnson	16

1921–42

1	Jack Wilson	20
2	Wilcy Moore	14
	Jack Quinn	14
4	Fritz Ostermueller	13
5	Joe Heving	12
6	Allan Russell	10
7	Emerson Dickman	8
	Howard Ehmke	8
	Red Ruffing	8

1901–20

1	Carl Mays	12
2	Dutch Leonard	11
3	Charley Hall	10
4	Hugh Bedient	9
	Cy Young	9
6	Joe Wood	8
7	Herb Pennock	6

Save percentage

1	Tom Gordon	93.15
2	Ugueth Urbina	87.50
3	Jeff Russell	86.54
4	**Jonathan Papelbon**	**83.33**
5	**Keith Foulke**	**81.03**
6	Lee Smith	80.56
7	Tom Burgmeier	80.00
8	Derek Lowe	78.70
9	Heathcliff Slocumb	78.69
10	Jeff Reardon	78.57
11	Bobby Bolin	75.68
12	Dick Drago	73.21
13	Bob Stanley	70.59
14	Mark Clear	65.52
15	Bill Campbell	62.96
16	**Mike Timlin**	**53.19**

Blown saves

1	Bob Stanley	55
2	Bill Campbell	30
3	Greg Harris	24
	Jeff Reardon	24
5	Derek Lowe	23
	Sparky Lyle	23
7	**Mike Timlin**	**22**
8	Mark Clear	20
9	Dick Drago	15
10	Lee Smith	14
11	Jim Corsi	13
	Heathcliff Slocumb	13
13	Rich Garces	12
14	Steve Crawford	11
	Keith Foulke	**11**
16	Tom Burgmeier	10
	Rob Murphy	10
18	Rod Beck	9
	Bobby Bolin	9
	Ken Ryan	9
21	**Tim Wakefield**	**8**
22	Many players tied	7

Innings Pitched by era

1988–2006		
1	Roger Clemens	2776.0
2	**Tim Wakefield**	**2211.2**
3	Pedro Martinez	1383.2
4	Derek Lowe	1037.0
5	Greg Harris	651.0
6	Aaron Sele	622.0
7	Danny Darwin	534.1
1973–87		
1	Luis Tiant	1774.2
2	Bob Stanley	1707.0
3	Bill Lee	1503.1
4	Bruce Hurst	1459.0
5	Dennis Eckersley	1371.2
6	Oil Can Boyd	1016.2
7	Mike Torrez	1012.2
1961–72		
1	Bill Monbouquette	1622.0
2	Jim Lonborg	1099.0
3	Ray Culp	1092.1
4	Earl Wilson	1024.1
5	Sonny Siebert	820.0
6	Dave Morehead	664.2
7	Lee Stange	602.1
1943–60		
1	Mel Parnell	1752.2
2	Joe Dobson	1544.0
3	Tom Brewer	1509.1
4	Frank Sullivan	1505.1
5	Tex Hughson	1375.2
6	Willard Nixon	1234.0
7	Ike Delock	1207.2
1921–42		
1	Lefty Grove	1539.2
2	Jack Russell	1215.0
3	Danny MacFayden	1167.0
4	Red Ruffing	1122.1
5	Fritz Ostermueller	1083.1
6	Jack Wilson	1067.2
7	Howard Ehmke	989.2
1901–20		
1	Cy Young	2728.1
2	George Winter	1599.2
3	Bill Dinneen	1501.0
4	Joe Wood	1416.0
5	Dutch Leonard	1361.1
6	Ray Collins	1336.0
7	Babe Ruth	1190.1

Fewest Hits/9 innings by era

1988–2006		
1	Pedro Martinez	6.79
2	Roger Clemens	7.65
3	Greg Harris	8.31
4	Frank Viola	8.51
5	Tom Gordon	8.65
6	**Tim Wakefield**	**8.68**
7	Wes Gardner	8.75
1973–87		
1	Roger Moret	7.89
2	Mark Clear	7.96
3	Luis Tiant	8.27
4	Dick Drago	8.50
5	Fergie Jenkins	8.75
6	Tom Burgmeier	8.96
7	John Tudor	9.12
1961–72		
1	Dick Radatz	6.78
2	Dave Morehead	7.87
3	Ray Culp	7.89
4	Jose Santiago	8.17
5	Earl Wilson	8.36
6	Jim Lonborg	8.44
7	Lee Stange	8.53
1943–60		
1	Mickey McDermott	7.53
2	Tex Hughson	8.31
3	Joe Dobson	8.53
4	Ellis Kinder	8.56
5	Frank Sullivan	8.70
6	Mel Parnell	8.81
7	Tom Brewer	8.81
1921–42		
1	Charlie Wagner	9.07
2	Ed Morris	9.24
3	Lefty Grove	9.28
4	Howard Ehmke	9.48
5	Milt Gaston	9.54
6	Allan Russell	9.57
7	Jack Wilson	9.62
1901–20		
1	Babe Ruth	7.06
2	Joe Wood	7.10
3	Carl Mays	7.48
4	Dutch Leonard	7.50
5	Cy Young	7.74
6	Rube Foster	7.76
7	Norwood Gibson	7.76

Home Runs Allowed by era

1988–2006		
1	**Tim Wakefield**	**298**
2	Roger Clemens	194
3	Pedro Martinez	103
4	Danny Darwin	70
5	Derek Lowe	69
6	**Curt Schilling**	**63**
7	Aaron Sele	60
1973–87		
1	Bruce Hurst	173
2	Luis Tiant	170
3	Dennis Eckersley	167
4	Bill Lee	136
5	Oil Can Boyd	126
6	Bob Stanley	113
7	Mike Torrez	87
1961–72		
1	Bill Monbouquette	180
2	Earl Wilson	123
3	Jim Lonborg	105
4	Ray Culp	103
5	Sonny Siebert	88
6	Gene Conley	65
7	Dave Morehead	62
1943–60		
1	Ike Delock	135
2	Tom Brewer	126
3	Frank Sullivan	124
4	Mel Parnell	104
5	Ellis Kinder	92
6	Willard Nixon	89
7	Joe Dobson	88
1921–42		
1	Lefty Grove	78
2	Jack Wilson	67
3	Red Ruffing	47
	Jack Russell	47
5	Wes Ferrell	45
	Danny MacFayden	45
	Fritz Ostermueller	45
1901–20		
1	Bill Dinneen	39
2	Cy Young	34
3	George Winter	32
4	Herb Pennock	29
5	Jesse Tannehill	24
6	Norwood Gibson	21
7	Joe Bush	16
	Sam Jones	16
	Dutch Leonard	16

Fewest Walks/9 innings

1988–2006		
1	**Curt Schilling**	**1.46**
2	Pedro Martinez	2.01
3	Bronson Arroyo	2.35
4	Danny Darwin	2.37
5	Derek Lowe	2.71
6	Roger Clemens	2.78
7	Mike Boddicker	2.83
1973–87		
1	Fergie Jenkins	1.77
2	Dennis Eckersley	2.05
3	Tom Burgmeier	2.15
4	Rick Wise	2.25
5	Oil Can Boyd	2.29
6	Bob Stanley	2.48
7	Luis Tiant	2.54
1961–72		
1	Bill Monbouquette	2.26
2	Lee Stange	2.51
3	Marty Pattin	2.55
4	Sonny Siebert	2.72
5	Gene Conley	2.88
6	Jose Santiago	3.11
7	Gary Peters	3.30
1943–60		
1	Tex Hughson	2.43
2	Frank Sullivan	2.84
3	Denny Galehouse	2.85
4	Ellis Kinder	3.18
5	Dave Ferriss	3.21
6	Leo Kiely	3.30
7	Mike Fornieles	3.43
1921–42		
1	Jack Quinn	2.05
2	Jack Russell	2.18
3	Johnny Marcum	2.48
4	Lefty Grove	2.61
5	Ted Wingfield	2.92
6	Howard Ehmke	3.00
7	Milt Gaston	3.11
1901–20		
1	Cy Young	0.99
2	Jesse Tannehill	1.56
3	Ray Collins	1.81
4	Bill Dinneen	2.03
5	George Winter	2.08
6	Ernie Shore	2.19
7	Hugh Bedient	2.25

Innings Pitched

1	Roger Clemens	2776.0
2	Cy Young	2728.1
3	**Tim Wakefield**	**2211.2**
4	Luis Tiant	1774.2
5	Mel Parnell	1752.2
6	Bob Stanley	1707.0
7	Bill Monbouquette	1622.0
8	George Winter	1599.2
9	Joe Dobson	1544.0
10	Lefty Grove	1539.2
11	Tom Brewer	1509.1
12	Frank Sullivan	1505.1
13	Bill Lee	1503.1
14	Bill Dinneen	1501.0
15	Bruce Hurst	1459.0
16	Joe Wood	1416.0
17	Pedro Martinez	1383.2
18	Tex Hughson	1375.2
19	Dennis Eckersley	1371.2
20	Dutch Leonard	1361.1
21	Ray Collins	1336.0
22	Willard Nixon	1234.0
23	Jack Russell	1215.0
24	Ike Delock	1207.2
25	Babe Ruth	1190.1
26	Danny MacFayden	1167.0
27	Ellis Kinder	1142.1
28	Red Ruffing	1122.1
29	Carl Mays	1105.0
30	Jim Lonborg	1099.0
31	Ray Culp	1092.1
32	Herb Pennock	1089.1
33	Fritz Ostermueller	1083.1
34	Jack Wilson	1067.2
35	Sam Jones	1045.0
36	Derek Lowe	1037.0
37	Earl Wilson	1024.1
38	Oil Can Boyd	1016.2
39	Mike Torrez	1012.2
40	Howard Ehmke	989.2
41	Eddie Cicotte	885.2
	Jesse Tannehill	885.2
43	Dave Ferriss	880.0
44	Wes Ferrell	877.2
45	Rube Foster	842.1
46	Ernie Shore	839.0
47	Jack Quinn	832.2
48	Sonny Siebert	820.0
49	Joe Bush	779.2
50	Mickey McDermott	773.2

Fewest Hits/9 innings

1	Dick Radatz	6.78
2	Pedro Martinez	6.79
3	Babe Ruth	7.06
4	Joe Wood	7.10
5	Carl Mays	7.48
6	Dutch Leonard	7.50
7	Mickey McDermott	7.53
8	Roger Clemens	7.65
9	Cy Young	7.74
10	Rube Foster	7.76
11	Norwood Gibson	7.76
12	Ernie Shore	7.85
13	Dave Morehead	7.87
14	Roger Moret	7.89
15	Ray Culp	7.89
16	Mark Clear	7.96
17	Buck O'Brien	8.05
18	Charley Hall	8.14
19	Jose Santiago	8.17
20	Bill Dinneen	8.23
21	Luis Tiant	8.27
22	Tex Hughson	8.31
23	Greg Harris	8.31
24	Eddie Cicotte	8.35
25	Earl Wilson	8.36
26	Ray Collins	8.39
27	Jim Lonborg	8.44
28	George Winter	8.46
29	Jesse Tannehill	8.50
30	Dick Drago	8.50
31	Frank Viola	8.51
32	Lee Stange	8.53
33	Joe Dobson	8.53
34	Ellis Kinder	8.56
35	Sonny Siebert	8.64
36	Tom Gordon	8.65
37	**Tim Wakefield**	**8.68**
38	Frank Sullivan	8.70
39	Hugh Bedient	8.74
40	Fergie Jenkins	8.75
41	Wes Gardner	8.75
42	Mel Parnell	8.81
43	Tom Brewer	8.81
44	Bronson Arroyo	8.84
45	Danny Darwin	8.88
46	Derek Lowe	8.89
47	Chuck Stobbs	8.91
48	Marty Pattin	8.96
49	Tom Burgmeier	8.96
50	Mike Boddicker	8.97

Home Runs Allowed

1	**Tim Wakefield**	**298**
2	Roger Clemens	194
3	Bill Monbouquette	180
4	Bruce Hurst	173
5	Luis Tiant	170
6	Dennis Eckersley	167
7	Bill Lee	136
8	Ike Delock	135
9	Oil Can Boyd	126
	Tom Brewer	126
11	Frank Sullivan	124
12	Earl Wilson	123
13	Bob Stanley	113
14	Jim Lonborg	105
15	Mel Parnell	104
16	Ray Culp	103
	Pedro Martinez	103
18	Ellis Kinder	92
19	Willard Nixon	89
20	Joe Dobson	88
	Sonny Siebert	88
22	Mike Torrez	87
23	Al Nipper	86
24	Lefty Grove	78
25	Tex Hughson	77
26	Rick Wise	73
27	Danny Darwin	70
28	Derek Lowe	69
	John Tudor	69
30	Reggie Cleveland	67
	Jack Wilson	67
32	Gene Conley	65
33	Bob Ojeda	64
34	**Curt Schilling**	**63**
35	Dave Morehead	62
36	Mike Fornieles	61
37	Aaron Sele	60
	Lee Stange	60
39	Gary Peters	55
40	John Wasdin	54
41	Dave Sisler	53
42	Dick Drago	50
	Wes Gardner	50
	Fergie Jenkins	50
	Marty Pattin	50
46	John Dopson	49
	Joe Hesketh	49
48	Greg Harris	48
	Mickey Harris	48
50	4 players tied	47

Walks

1	Roger Clemens	856
2	**Tim Wakefield**	**838**
3	Mel Parnell	758
4	Tom Brewer	669
5	Joe Dobson	604
6	Jack Wilson	564
7	Willard Nixon	530
8	Ike Delock	514
9	Mickey McDermott	504
10	Luis Tiant	501
11	Fritz Ostermueller	491
12	Earl Wilson	481
13	Bruce Hurst	479
14	Frank Sullivan	475
15	Bob Stanley	471
16	Red Ruffing	459
17	Bill Lee	448
18	Lefty Grove	447
19	Danny MacFayden	430
20	Babe Ruth	425
21	Mike Torrez	420
22	Dutch Leonard	412
	Joe Wood	412
24	Bill Monbouquette	408
25	Ray Culp	404
26	Ellis Kinder	403
	Jim Lonborg	403
28	Dave Morehead	373
29	Tex Hughson	372
30	George Winter	370
31	Bill Dinneen	338
	Sam Jones	338
33	Howard Ehmke	330
34	Dave Ferriss	314
35	Dennis Eckersley	312
	Derek Lowe	312
37	Wes Ferrell	310
38	Pedro Martinez	309
39	Rube Foster	305
40	Greg Harris	304
41	Mark Clear	300
42	Herb Pennock	299
	Cy Young	299
44	Jack Russell	294
45	Mickey Harris	290
	Carl Mays	290
47	Eddie Cicotte	289
48	Ed Morris	287
49	Bob Ojeda	285
50	2 players tied	282

Strikeouts

1	Roger Clemens	2590
2	Pedro Martinez	1683
3	**Tim Wakefield**	**1570**
4	Cy Young	1341
5	Luis Tiant	1075
6	Bruce Hurst	1043
7	Joe Wood	986
8	Bill Monbouquette	969
9	Frank Sullivan	821
10	Ray Culp	794
11	Jim Lonborg	784
12	Dennis Eckersley	771
	Dutch Leonard	771
14	Lefty Grove	743
15	Tom Brewer	733
16	Mel Parnell	732
17	Earl Wilson	714
18	Tex Hughson	693
	Bob Stanley	693
20	Joe Dobson	690
21	Derek Lowe	673
22	Ike Delock	661
23	Dick Radatz	627
24	Willard Nixon	616
25	Bill Dinneen	602
26	Bill Lee	578
27	Oil Can Boyd	571
28	Jack Wilson	563
29	Ellis Kinder	557
30	George Winter	543
31	Sonny Siebert	528
32	Dave Morehead	526
33	Ray Collins	511
34	Mickey McDermott	499
35	Greg Harris	489
36	Babe Ruth	483
37	Mike Torrez	480
38	Aaron Sele	478
39	**Curt Schilling**	**473**
40	Red Ruffing	450
41	Tom Gordon	432
42	Bob Ojeda	425
43	Fritz Ostermueller	422
44	Eddie Cicotte	407
45	Mark Clear	403
46	Carl Mays	399
47	John Tudor	382
48	Howard Ehmke	373
49	Mickey Harris	369
50	Herb Pennock	358

Strikeouts/9 innings

1 Pedro Martinez 10.95
2 Dick Radatz 10.13
3 Mark Clear 9.06
4 Roger Clemens 8.40
5 Curt Schilling 8.12
6 Tom Gordon 7.85
7 Dave Morehead 7.12
8 Wes Gardner 7.06
9 Aaron Sele 6.92
10 Greg Harris 6.76
11 Ray Culp 6.54
12 Bruce Hurst 6.43
13 Jim Lonborg 6.42
14 Tim Wakefield 6.39
15 Joe Hesketh 6.38
16 Jose Santiago 6.37
17 Earl Wilson 6.27
18 Joe Wood 6.27
19 Danny Darwin 5.90
20 Mike Boddicker 5.86
21 Derek Lowe 5.84
22 Mickey McDermott 5.80
23 Sonny Siebert 5.80
24 Bronson Arroyo 5.74
25 Gary Peters 5.56
26 Fergie Jenkins 5.53
27 Marty Pattin 5.47
28 Luis Tiant 5.45
29 John Tudor 5.40
30 Roger Moret 5.38
31 Bill Monbouquette 5.38
32 Bob Ojeda 5.32
33 Dutch Leonard 5.10
34 Dennis Eckersley 5.06
35 John Curtis 5.06
36 Oil Can Boyd 5.05
37 Dick Drago 5.02
38 Ike Delock 4.93
39 Frank Sullivan 4.91
40 Gene Conley 4.87
41 Mickey Harris 4.83
42 Mike Fornieles 4.79
43 Tom Burgmeier 4.75
44 Dave Sisler 4.75
45 Jack Wilson 4.75
46 Rick Wise 4.71
47 John Dopson 4.60
48 Lee Stange 4.54
49 Tex Hughson 4.53
50 Willard Nixon 4.49

Earned Run Average

1 Joe Wood 1.99
2 Cy Young 2.00
3 Ernie Shore 2.12
4 Dutch Leonard 2.13
5 Babe Ruth 2.19
6 Carl Mays 2.21
7 Rube Foster 2.36
8 Jesse Tannehill 2.50
9 Ray Collins 2.51
10 Pedro Martinez 2.52
11 Buck O'Brien 2.57
12 Dick Radatz 2.65
13 Eddie Cicotte 2.69
14 Tom Burgmeier 2.72
15 Bill Dinneen 2.81
16 Charley Hall 2.89
17 George Winter 2.91
18 Norwood Gibson 2.93
19 Tex Hughson 2.94
20 Hugh Bedient 3.05
21 Roger Clemens 3.06
22 Joe Bush 3.27
23 Ellis Kinder 3.28
24 Lefty Grove 3.34
25 Luis Tiant 3.36
26 Sam Jones 3.39
27 Frank Viola 3.40
28 Jose Santiago 3.42
29 Roger Moret 3.43
30 Leo Kiely 3.44
31 Lee Stange 3.45
32 Sonny Siebert 3.46
33 Fergie Jenkins 3.47
   Frank Sullivan 3.47
35 Mike Boddicker 3.49
36 Ray Culp 3.50
   Mel Parnell 3.50
38 Dick Drago 3.55
39 Joe Dobson 3.57
40 Dave Ferriss 3.64
   Bill Lee 3.64
   Bob Stanley 3.64
43 John Curtis 3.65
   Jack Quinn 3.65
45 Herb Pennock 3.67
46 Bill Monbouquette 3.69
47 Derek Lowe 3.72
48 Marty Pattin 3.73
49 Allan Russell 3.74
50 Mickey McDermott 3.80

Opponent Batting Average

1 Pedro Martinez .206
2 Dick Radatz .209
3 Babe Ruth .219
  Joe Wood .219
5 Roger Clemens .229
6 Carl Mays .230
  Mickey McDermott .230
8 Dutch Leonard .231
9 Dave Morehead .232
10 Norwood Gibson .233
   Cy Young .233
12 Ray Culp .234
13 Ernie Shore .236
14 Roger Moret .238
15 Mark Clear .239
16 Rube Foster .240
17 Jose Santiago .241
18 Bill Dinneen .244
19 Tex Hughson .245
   Luis Tiant .245
   Earl Wilson .245
22 Charley Hall .246
   Buck O'Brien .246
24 Jim Lonborg .247
25 Tom Gordon .248
   Greg Harris .248
27 Dick Drago .250
   Ellis Kinder .250
   Lee Stange .250
   George Winter .250
31 Eddie Cicotte .251
   Joe Dobson .251
   Sonny Siebert .251
   Jesse Tannehill .251
   Tim Wakefield .251
36 Frank Viola .253
37 Bronson Arroyo .254
   Ray Collins .254
   Frank Sullivan .254
40 Fergie Jenkins .255
41 Danny Darwin .256
   Wes Gardner .256
43 Tom Brewer .257
   Mel Parnell .257
45 Derek Lowe .258
46 Marty Pattin .259
47 Hugh Bedient .260
   Ike Delock .260
   Chuck Stobbs .260
50 Mike Boddicker .261

Opponent On-Base Pct.

1 Cy Young .259
2 Pedro Martinez .261
3 Joe Wood .284
4 Ernie Shore .288
5 Dick Radatz .289
6 Bill Dinneen .290
   Carl Mays .290
8 Roger Clemens .291
   Fergie Jenkins .291
10 Jesse Tannehill .292
11 Ray Collins .294
   Babe Ruth .294
13 Dutch Leonard .296
14 Tex Hughson .297
15 Luis Tiant .298
   George Winter .298
17 Curt Schilling .299
18 Lee Stange .301
19 Norwood Gibson .303
20 Danny Darwin .305
21 Dennis Eckersley .306
   Jose Santiago .306
23 Ray Culp .307
   Bill Monbouquette .307
25 Sonny Siebert .308
26 Hugh Bedient .310
   Rick Wise .310
28 Tom Burgmeier .312
29 Oil Can Boyd .314
   Marty Pattin .314
   Frank Sullivan .314
32 Bronson Arroyo .315
   Dick Drago .315
   Ellis Kinder .315
35 Rube Foster .316
36 Lefty Grove .317
   Buck O'Brien .317
38 Eddie Cicotte .318
   Derek Lowe .318
40 Jim Lonborg .320
41 Reggie Cleveland .321
42 Joe Dobson .322
43 Mike Boddicker .323
44 John Tudor .324
45 Tom Gordon .325
   Frank Viola .325
47 Tim Wakefield .326
48 Charley Hall .327
   Roger Moret .327
50 Earl Wilson .328

Adjusted Pitching Runs

1 Roger Clemens 410
2 Pedro Martinez 340
3 Cy Young 275
4 Lefty Grove 237
5 Bret Saberhagen 216
6 Tom Gordon 207
7 Jeff Gray 194
8 Butch Henry 193
9 Mel Parnell 147
10 Joe Wood 139
11 Ellis Kinder 132
12 Luis Tiant 121
13 Tex Hughson 112
14 Frank Sullivan 109
15 Derek Lowe 108
16 Bob Stanley 104
17 Dutch Leonard 94
18 Joe Dobson 86
19 Curt Schilling 83
20 Wes Ferrell 78
21 Dick Radatz 77
22 Babe Ruth 71
23 Ray Collins 65
24 Tom Burgmeier 62
25 Carl Mays 60
26 Dennis Eckersley 57
27 Howard Ehmke 55
28 Fritz Ostermueller 52
29 Curt Schilling 51
   Frank Viola 51
31 Bill Lee 50
32 Jack Quinn 49
33 Ernie Shore 48
34 Mickey McDermott 47
35 Bill Monbouquette 45
36 Bill Dinneen 41
37 Mike Timlin 39
38 Mike Boddicker 38
39 Leo Kiely 35
   Jonathan Papelbon 35
41 Dick Drago 34
   Rich Garces 34
   Buck O'Brien 34
44 Roger Moret 33
45 Rube Foster 32
46 Danny Darwin 28
   Milt Gaston 28
48 Greg Harris 27
   Fergie Jenkins 27
50 Sparky Lyle 26

Games

1 Bob Stanley 637
2 Tim Wakefield 443
3 Derek Lowe 384
4 Roger Clemens 383
5 Ellis Kinder 365
6 Cy Young 327
7 Ike Delock 322
8 Bill Lee 321
9 Mike Timlin 297
10 Mel Parnell 289
11 Greg Harris 287
12 Mike Fornieles 286
   Dick Radatz 286
14 Luis Tiant 274
15 Rich Garces 261
16 Sparky Lyle 260
17 Joe Dobson 259
18 Jack Wilson 258
19 Bill Monbouquette 254
20 Frank Sullivan 252
21 Jack Russell 242
22 Tom Brewer 241
   Dennis Eckersley 241
24 Tony Fossas 239
25 Bruce Hurst 237
26 Mark Clear 225
   Tex Hughson 225
   Willard Nixon 225
29 Fritz Ostermueller 219
30 Joe Wood 218
31 Lefty Grove 214
32 Tom Burgmeier 213
   George Winter 213
34 Alan Embree 211
   Dutch Leonard 211
36 Arnold Earley 208
37 Dick Drago 206
38 Jim Lonborg 204
39 Pedro Martinez 203
40 Herb Pennock 201
41 Ray Collins 199
42 Bill Campbell 192
43 Leo Kiely 189
   Red Ruffing 189
45 Dennis Lamp 186
46 Danny MacFayden 185
47 Bill Dinneen 180
48 Lee Stange 174
   Earl Wilson 174
50 3 players tied 173

Relief Wins

1 Bob Stanley 85
2 Dick Radatz 49
3 Ellis Kinder 39
4 Mark Clear 35
5 Ike Delock 34
6 Mike Fornieles 31
7 Bill Campbell 28
8 Mike Ryba 26
   Mike Ryba 26
   Jack Wilson 26
11 Mike Timlin 24
   Earl Johnson 24
13 Rich Garces 23
14 Dick Drago 22
   Sparky Lyle 22
16 Tom Burgmeier 21
   Charley Hall 21
18 Greg A. Harris 20
   Dennis Lamp 20
20 Joe Heving 19
21 Mace Brown 18
   Bill Lee 18
   John Wasdin 18
24 Derek Lowe 17

Relief Losses

1 Bob Stanley 61
2 Dick Radatz 34
3 Ellis Kinder 29
4 Mark Clear 23
   Mike Fornieles 23
   Greg A. Harris 23
7 Derek Lowe 21
8 Bill Campbell 19
9 Mike Ryba 17
   Dick Drago 17
   Sparky Lyle 17
   Mike Timlin 17
   Mike Ryba 17
   Jack Wilson 17
15 Ike Delock 16
   Dennis Lamp 16
   Jim Willoughby 16
18 Arnold Earley 14
   Ben Karr 14
20 Rob Murphy 13
   Tim Wakefield 13
   John Wyatt 13
   Earl Johnson 13
24 2 players tied 12

Relief Games

1 Bob Stanley 552
2 Mike Timlin 297
3 Dick Radatz 286
4 Ellis Kinder 276
5 Derek Lowe 273
6 Rich Garces 261
7 Sparky Lyle 260
8 Mike Fornieles 258
9 Tony Fossas 239
10 Greg Harris 234
11 Mark Clear 225
12 Tom Burgmeier 212
13 Alan Embree 211
14 Arnold Earley 198
15 Bill Campbell 192
16 Dennis Lamp 185
17 Ike Delock 180
18 Dick Drago 177
19 Rheal Cormier 160
20 Keith Foulke 159
21 Steve Crawford 157
22 Bill Lee 154
   John Wasdin 154
24 2 players tied 150

Relief Innings Pitched

1 Bob Stanley 1159.0
2 Dick Radatz 557.1
3 Ellis Kinder 498.2
4 Mike Fornieles 466.2
5 Tom Burgmeier 401.1
6 Mark Clear 400.1
7 Mike Ryba 397.2
   Mike Ryba 397.2
9 Dennis Lamp 387.2
10 Ike Delock 367.1
   Derek Lowe 367.1
12 Dick Drago 352.1
13 Greg A. Harris 338.0
14 Bill Campbell 335.0
15 Sparky Lyle 331.1
16 Jack Wilson 324.1
17 Bill Lee 319.2
18 Rich Garces 307.1
19 Arnold Earley 304.1
   Mike Timlin 304.1
21 Steve Crawford 297.2
22 Charley Hall 290.2
23 Tim Wakefield 265.1
24 Earl Johnson 256.2

Adjusted Reliever Runs

1 Bob Stanley 117
2 Ellis Kinder 94
3 Derek Lowe 73
4 Dick Radatz 71
5 Tom Burgmeier 66
6 Ike Delock 42
7 Mike Timlin 38
8 Dick Drago 38
9 Jack Wilson 35
10 Rich Garces 34
11 Jonathan Papelbon 31
12 Joe Heving 31
13 Tim Wakefield 28
14 Sparky Lyle 28
15 Greg A. Harris 27
16 Joe Wood 26
17 Bill Campbell 25
18 Earl Johnson 25
19 Luis Aponte 23
20 Charley Hall 23
21 Jim Corsi 22
22 Rheal Cormier 22
23 Chet Nichols 20
24 Leo Kiely 20

Relief Ranking

1 Bob Stanley 158
2 Ellis Kinder 149
3 Dick Radatz 121
4 Derek Lowe 87
5 Ike Delock 67
6 Tom Burgmeier 66
7 Jonathan Papelbon 53
8 Dick Drago 51
9 Mike Timlin 50
10 Bill Campbell 46
11 Joe Heving 44
12 Rich Garces 42
13 Jack Wilson 41
14 Joe Wood 40
15 Sparky Lyle 39
16 Earl Johnson 37
17 Lee Smith 32
18 Tom Gordon 31
19 Greg A. Harris 28
20 Mace Brown 27
21 Tim Wakefield 27
22 Ken Ryan 27
23 Keith Foulke 26
24 Ugueth Urbina 26

Adjusted Earned Run Average

1 Pedro Martinez 189
2 Tom Burgmeier 157
3 Joe Wood 149
4 Cy Young 147
5 Dick Radatz 146
6 Roger Clemens 145
7 Lefty Grove 143
8 Ellis Kinder 134
9 Frank Viola 131
10 Dutch Leonard 129
11 Buck O'Brien 128
   Ernie Shore 128
13 Derek Lowe 127
14 Tex Hughson 125
   Mel Parnell 125
   Babe Ruth 125
17 Carl Mays 124
18 Leo Kiely 123
19 Wes Ferrell 120
   Fergie Jenkins 120
   Frank Sullivan 120
22 Curt Schilling 119
23 Mike Boddicker 118
   Bob Stanley 118
25 Luis Tiant 117
26 Dick Drago 116
   Rube Foster 116
   Jack Quinn 116
29 Ray Collins 115
   Joe Dobson 115
   Roger Moret 115
32 Mickey McDermott 114
33 Bronson Arroyo 112
   Howard Ehmke 112
   Milt Gaston 112
36 Greg Harris 111
   Joe Hesketh 111
   Fritz Ostermueller 111
39 Danny Darwin 110
   Aaron Sele 110
   Tim Wakefield 110
   Rube Walberg 110
43 Dennis Eckersley 109
   Tom Gordon 109
   Bill Lee 109
   John Tudor 109
47 Many players tied 107

Adjusted ERA by era

1988–2006

1	Pedro Martinez	189
2	Roger Clemens	145
3	Frank Viola	131
4	Derek Lowe	127
5	**Curt Schilling**	**119**
6	Mike Boddicker	118
7	Bronson Arroyo	112

1973–87

1	Tom Burgmeier	157
2	Fergie Jenkins	120
3	Bob Stanley	118
4	Luis Tiant	117
5	Dick Drago	116
6	Roger Moret	115
7	Dennis Eckersley	109
	Bill Lee	109
	John Tudor	109

1961–72

1	Dick Radatz	146
2	Bill Monbouquette	107
	Sonny Siebert	107
4	Lee Stange	105
5	Ray Culp	104
6	Jose Santiago	103
7	Marty Pattin	97

1943–60

1	Ellis Kinder	134
2	Tex Hughson	125
	Mel Parnell	125
4	Leo Kiely	123
5	Frank Sullivan	120
6	Joe Dobson	115
7	Mickey McDermott	114

1921–42

1	Lefty Grove	143
2	Wes Ferrell	120
3	Jack Quinn	116
4	Howard Ehmke	112
	Milt Gaston	112
6	Fritz Ostermueller	111
7	Rube Walberg	110

1901–20

1	Joe Wood	149
2	Cy Young	147
3	Dutch Leonard	129
4	Buck O'Brien	128
	Ernie Shore	128
6	Babe Ruth	125
7	Carl Mays	124

Pitcher Wins

1	Roger Clemens	42.0
2	Pedro Martinez	35.4
3	Cy Young	29.8
4	Joe Wood	21.6
5	Lefty Grove	20.5
6	Babe Ruth	17.4
7	Ellis Kinder	15.9
8	Mel Parnell	15.5
9	Bob Stanley	15.1
10	Derek Lowe	14.5
11	Dick Radatz	13.7
12	Luis Tiant	12.8
13	Wes Ferrell	12.6
14	Carl Mays	11.5
15	Tex Hughson	10.4
16	Dutch Leonard	9.7
17	Frank Sullivan	9.5
18	Joe Dobson	8.4
19	**Tim Wakefield**	**8.0**
20	Mickey McDermott	7.8
21	Tom Burgmeier	6.7
22	Ray Collins	6.5
23	Fritz Ostermueller	6.1
24	Bill Lee	5.7
25	Dennis Eckersley	5.4
26	Howard Ehmke	5.3
	Jonathan Papelbon	**5.3**
28	Frank Viola	5.1
29	Bill Campbell	5.0
30	**Mike Timlin**	**4.9**
31	Dick Drago	4.7
	Dave Ferriss	4.7
	Rube Foster	4.7
	Curt Schilling	**4.7**
35	Jack Quinn	4.6
	Ernie Shore	4.6
37	Jesse Tannehill	4.5
38	Tom Gordon	4.3
39	Mike Boddicker	4.2
	Bret Saberhagen	4.2
41	Rich Garces	4.1
42	Joe Bush	4.0
43	Sparky Lyle	3.9
44	Tom Brewer	3.6
45	Greg Harris	3.4
46	Buck O'Brien	3.3
47	Leo Kiely	3.1
	John Tudor	3.1
49	Roger Moret	3.0
50	2 players tied	2.9

Pitcher Wins by era

1988–2006

1	Roger Clemens	42.0
2	Pedro Martinez	35.4
3	Derek Lowe	14.5
4	**Tim Wakefield**	**8.0**
5	**Jonathan Papelbon**	**5.3**
6	Frank Viola	5.1
7	**Mike Timlin**	**4.9**

1973–87

1	Bob Stanley	15.1
2	Luis Tiant	12.8
3	Tom Burgmeier	6.7
4	Bill Lee	5.7
5	Dennis Eckersley	5.4
6	Bill Campbell	5.0
7	Dick Drago	4.7

1961–72

1	Dick Radatz	13.7
2	Sparky Lyle	3.9
3	Bill Monbouquette	2.6
4	Sonny Siebert	2.4
5	Bobby Bolin	2.0
6	John Wyatt	1.9
7	Don McMahon	1.6

1943–60

1	Ellis Kinder	15.9
2	Mel Parnell	15.5
3	Tex Hughson	10.4
4	Frank Sullivan	9.5
5	Joe Dobson	8.4
6	Mickey McDermott	7.8
7	Dave Ferriss	4.7

1921–42

1	Lefty Grove	20.5
2	Wes Ferrell	12.6
3	Fritz Ostermueller	6.1
4	Howard Ehmke	5.3
5	Jack Quinn	4.6
6	Milt Gaston	2.6
	Johnny Marcum	2.6

1901–20

1	Cy Young	29.8
2	Joe Wood	21.6
3	Babe Ruth	17.4
4	Carl Mays	11.5
5	Dutch Leonard	9.7
6	Ray Collins	6.5
7	Rube Foster	4.7

Player Overall Wins by era

1988–2006

1	Roger Clemens	42.0
2	Pedro Martinez	35.4
3	Nomar Garciaparra	25.1
4	**Manny Ramirez**	**21.7**
5	John Valentin	17.6
6	Derek Lowe	14.5
7	**David Ortiz**	**13.3**
8	**Jason Varitek**	**10.4**
9	Jody Reed	9.7
10	Mo Vaughn	9.3
11	**Tim Wakefield**	**8.0**
12	Mike Greenwell	7.2
13	**Jonathan Papelbon**	**5.3**
14	Frank Viola	5.1

1973–87

1	Wade Boggs	43.9
2	Dwight Evans	24.0
3	Carlton Fisk	23.9
4	Jim Rice	18.4
5	Fred Lynn	15.6
6	Bob Stanley	15.1
7	Rick Burleson	13.5
8	Luis Tiant	12.8
9	Tom Burgmeier	6.7
10	Bill Lee	5.7
11	Dennis Eckersley	5.4
12	Bill Campbell	5.0
13	Dick Drago	4.7
14	Marty Barrett	3.7

1961–72

1	Carl Yastrzemski	42.7
2	Rico Petrocelli	15.6
3	Dick Radatz	13.7
4	Reggie Smith	13.6
5	Eddie Bressoud	7.0
6	Mike Andrews	5.2
7	Sparky Lyle	3.9
8	Felix Mantilla	3.4
9	Bill Monbouquette	2.6
10	Sonny Siebert	2.4
11	Ken Harrelson	2.3
12	Tony Conigliaro	2.2
13	Bobby Bolin	2.0
14	John Wyatt	1.9

1943–60

1	Ted Williams	86.5
2	Bobby Doerr	40.3
3	Johnny Pesky	16.5
4	Ellis Kinder	15.9
5	Mel Parnell	15.5
6	Pete Runnels	13.4
7	Vern Stephens	10.5
8	Tex Hughson	10.4
9	Dom DiMaggio	10.1
10	Frank Sullivan	9.5
11	Jackie Jensen	8.7
12	Joe Dobson	8.4
13	Mickey McDermott	7.8
14	Eddie Lake	6.6

1921–42

1	Jimmie Foxx	22.3
2	Lefty Grove	20.5
3	Joe Cronin	15.3
4	Wes Ferrell	12.6
5	Rick Ferrell	6.9
6	Fritz Ostermueller	6.1
7	Howard Ehmke	5.3
8	Jack Quinn	4.6
9	Topper Rigney	3.9
10	Earl Webb	3.5
11	Joe Harris	3.4
	Buddy Myer	3.4
13	Milt Gaston	2.6
	Johnny Marcum	2.6

1901–20

1	Tris Speaker	37.1
2	Cy Young	29.8
3	Babe Ruth	27.4
4	Joe Wood	21.6
5	Jimmy Collins	13.4
6	Carl Mays	11.5
7	Harry Hooper	10.9
8	Dutch Leonard	9.7
9	Lou Criger	8.8
10	Ray Collins	6.5
11	Larry Gardner	5.4
12	Duffy Lewis	5.0
13	Wally Schang	4.9
14	Rube Foster	4.7

Player Overall Wins

1	Ted Williams	86.5
2	Wade Boggs	43.9
3	Carl Yastrzemski	42.7
4	Roger Clemens	42.0
5	Bobby Doerr	40.3
6	Tris Speaker	37.1
7	Pedro Martinez	35.4
8	Cy Young	29.8
9	Babe Ruth	27.4
10	Nomar Garciaparra	25.1
11	Dwight Evans	24.0
12	Carlton Fisk	23.9
13	Jimmie Foxx	22.3
14	**Manny Ramirez**	**21.7**
15	Joe Wood	21.6
16	Lefty Grove	20.5
17	Jim Rice	18.4
18	John Valentin	17.6
19	Johnny Pesky	16.5
20	Ellis Kinder	15.9
21	Fred Lynn	15.6
	Rico Petrocelli	15.6
23	Mel Parnell	15.5
24	Joe Cronin	15.3
25	Bob Stanley	15.1
26	Derek Lowe	14.5
27	Dick Radatz	13.7
28	Reggie Smith	13.6
29	Rick Burleson	13.5
30	Jimmy Collins	13.4
	Pete Runnels	13.4
32	**David Ortiz**	**13.3**
33	Luis Tiant	12.8
34	Wes Ferrell	12.6
35	Carl Mays	11.5
36	Harry Hooper	10.9
37	Vern Stephens	10.5
38	Tex Hughson	10.4
	Jason Varitek	**10.4**
40	Dom DiMaggio	10.1
41	Dutch Leonard	9.7
	Jody Reed	9.7
43	Frank Sullivan	9.5
44	Mo Vaughn	9.3
45	Lou Criger	8.8
46	Jackie Jensen	8.7
47	Joe Dobson	8.4
48	**Tim Wakefield**	**8.0**
49	Mickey McDermott	7.8
50	Mike Greenwell	7.2
51	Eddie Bressoud	7.0
52	Rick Ferrell	6.9
53	Tom Burgmeier	6.7
54	Eddie Lake	6.6
55	Ray Collins	6.5
	Bob Johnson	6.5
57	Fritz Ostermueller	6.1
58	Bill Lee	5.7
	Don Buddin	5.7
60	Dennis Eckersley	5.4
	Larry Gardner	5.4
62	Howard Ehmke	5.3
	Jonathan Papelbon	**5.3**
64	Mike Andrews	5.2
65	Frank Viola	5.1
66	Bill Campbell	5.0
	Duffy Lewis	5.0
68	**Mike Timlin**	**4.9**
	Wally Schang	4.9
70	Dick Drago	4.7
	Dave Ferriss	4.7
	Rube Foster	4.7
	Curt Schilling	**4.7**
74	Jack Quinn	4.6
	Ernie Shore	4.6
	Jesse Tannehill	4.6
	Bill Carrigan	4.6
78	Jesse Tannehill	4.6
79	Tom Gordon	4.3
	Johnny Damon	4.3
81	Mike Boddicker	4.2
	Bret Saberhagen	4.2
	Buck Freeman	4.2
84	Rich Garces	4.1
85	Joe Bush	4.0
	Bill Mueller	4.0
	Trot Nixon	**4.0**
88	Sparky Lyle	3.9
	Topper Rigney	3.9
90	Marty Barrett	3.7
	Tim Naehring	3.7
92	Tom Brewer	3.6
	Jake Stahl	3.6
94	Bernie Carbo	3.5
	Earl Webb	3.5
96	Greg Harris	3.4
	Jose Canseco	3.4
	Joe Harris	3.4
	Felix Mantilla	3.4
	Buddy Myer	3.4
101	Buck O'Brien	3.3
	Doc Gessler	3.3
103	Billy Goodman	3.2
104	Leo Kiely	3.1
	John Tudor	3.1
106	Roger Moret	3.0
	Ted Lepcio	3.0
108	Jeff Reardon	2.9
	Lee Smith	2.9
	Skeeter Newsome	2.9
111	**Keith Foulke**	**2.8**
	Bruce Hurst	2.8
	Fergie Jenkins	2.8
114	Ellis Burks	2.7
115	Mace Brown	2.6
	Danny Darwin	2.6
	Milt Gaston	2.6
	Johnny Marcum	2.6
	Bill Monbouquette	2.6
	Ugueth Urbina	2.6
121	Ken Ryan	2.5
	Calvin Schiraldi	2.5
	Heathcliff Slocumb	2.5
	Mike Lowell	**2.5**
	Billy Werber	2.5
126	Joe Heving	2.4
	Sonny Siebert	2.4
128	Ken Harrelson	2.3
	Pinch Thomas	2.3
130	Bill Dinneen	2.2
	Ben Chapman	2.2
	Tony Conigliaro	2.2
133	Tom Hughes	2.1
134	Bobby Bolin	2.0
	Paul Quantrill	2.0
	Jack Wilson	2.0
137	Luis Aponte	1.9
	Jim Corsi	1.9
	Joe Hesketh	1.9
	Jeff Russell	1.9
	John Wyatt	1.9
	Mike Easler	1.9
	Scott Fletcher	1.9
	Heinie Wagner	1.9
145	Sam Jones	1.8
	Patsy Dougherty	1.8
	Jim Pagliaroni	1.8
	Dick Stuart	1.8
149	Luis Alicea	1.7
	Hick Cady	1.7
	Bob Watson	1.7
152	Mark Clear	1.6
	Mickey Harris	1.6
	Don McMahon	1.6
	Jim Willoughby	1.6
	Dale Alexander	1.6
	Joe Foy	1.6
	Reggie Jefferson	1.6
159	Charley Hall	1.5
	Tom Hurd	1.5
	Larry Pape	1.5
	Aaron Sele	1.5
	Jeff Frye	1.5
	Del Gainer	1.5
165	Rod Beck	1.4
	Stan Belinda	1.4
	Oil Can Boyd	1.4
	Butch Henry	1.4
	Byung-Hyun Kim	1.4
	Vicente Romo	1.4
	Kevin Millar	1.4
	Chick Stahl	1.4
173	Eddie Cicotte	1.3
	Rheal Cormier	1.3
	Mike Fornieles	1.3
	Chet Nichols	1.3
	Bob Ojeda	1.3
	Rube Walberg	1.3
	Carl Everett	1.3
	Rich Gedman	1.3
	Ossee Schreckengost	1.3
182	Mike Stanton	1.2
	Mark Bellhorn	1.2
184	Sid Hudson	1.1
	Rick Wise	1.1
	Nick Esasky	1.1
	Johnny Hodapp	1.1
	Marty McManus	1.1
	Freddy Parent	1.1
	Hal Wagner	1.1
191	Many players tied	1.0

Plate Appearances

1	Wade Boggs, 1985	758
2	Dom DiMaggio, 1948	756
3	Mo Vaughn, 1996	752
4	Jim Rice, 1978	746
5	Dwight Evans, 1985	744
6	Wade Boggs, 1989	742
7	Chuck Schilling, 1961	738
	Dwight Evans, 1984	738
9	Nomar Garciaparra, 1997	734
10	Bill Wambsganss, 1924	731
11	Ted Williams, 1949	730
12	Dwight Evans, 1982	727
13	Wade Boggs, 1984	726
14	Rick Burleson, 1977	721
15	Johnny Pesky, 1947	719
	Carl Yastrzemski, 1962	719
	Wade Boggs, 1988	719
	Nomar Garciaparra, 2003	719
19	Dom DiMaggio, 1951	718
	Rick Burleson, 1980	718
	Bill Buckner, 1985	718
22	Doc Cramer, 1938	717
23	Billy Werber, 1934	716
	Vern Stephens, 1948	716
	Jerry Remy, 1982	716
26	Billy Goodman, 1955	715
27	Doc Cramer, 1936	713
	Johnny Pesky, 1949	713
	Marty Barrett, 1986	713
	Wade Boggs, 1990	713
	David Ortiz, 2005	**713**
32	Doc Cramer, 1940	712
33	Vern Stephens, 1949	711
34	Jim Rice, 1977	710
35	Jim Rice, 1984	708
36	Carl Yastrzemski, 1969	707
37	Dom DiMaggio, 1949	706
38	Johnny Pesky, 1946	703
	Mark Loretta, 2006	**703**
40	Dom DiMaggio, 1942	702
	Johnny Damon, 2002	702
	Johnny Damon, 2004	702
43	Tom Oliver, 1930	700
44	Carl Yastrzemski, 1970	697
45	Jody Reed, 1991	696
46	Many players tied	693

Single-Season Leaders

At Bats

1	Nomar Garciaparra, 1997	684
2	Jim Rice, 1978	677
3	Bill Buckner, 1985	673
4	Rick Burleson, 1977	663
5	Doc Cramer, 1940	661
6	Doc Cramer, 1938	658
	Nomar Garciaparra, 2003	658
8	Jim Rice, 1984	657
9	Wade Boggs, 1985	653
10	Dom DiMaggio, 1948	648
11	Tom Oliver, 1930	646
	Chuck Schilling, 1961	646
	Carl Yastrzemski, 1962	646
14	Jim Rice, 1977	644
	Rick Burleson, 1980	644
16	Doc Cramer, 1936	643
17	Dom DiMaggio, 1951	639
	Tony Armas, 1984	639
19	Johnny Pesky, 1947	638
20	Bill Wambsganss, 1924	636
	Jerry Remy, 1982	636
22	Vern Stephens, 1948	635
	Mo Vaughn, 1996	635
	Nomar Garciaparra, 2002	635
	Mark Loretta, 2006	**635**
26	Frank Malzone, 1957	634
	Shea Hillenbrand, 2002	634
28	Jimmy Collins, 1904	631
29	Dwight Evans, 1984	630
30	Bill Buckner, 1986	629
31	Vern Stephens, 1950	628
32	Frank Malzone, 1958	627
	Rick Burleson, 1979	627
34	Rick Burleson, 1978	626
	Jim Rice, 1983	626
36	Wade Boggs, 1984	625
	Marty Barrett, 1986	625
38	Johnny Damon, 2005	624
39	Billy Werber, 1934	623
	Johnny Damon, 2002	623
	Edgar Renteria, 2005	623
42	Dom DiMaggio, 1942	622
43	Joe Vosmik, 1938	621
	Johnny Pesky, 1946	621
	Wade Boggs, 1989	621
	Johnny Damon, 2004	621
47	Johnny Pesky, 1942	620
48	Frank Malzone, 1962	619
	Jim Rice, 1979	619
	Wade Boggs, 1990	619

Runs

1	Ted Williams, 1949	150
2	Ted Williams, 1946	142
3	Ted Williams, 1942	141
4	Jimmie Foxx, 1938	139
5	Tris Speaker, 1912	136
6	Ted Williams, 1941	135
7	Ted Williams, 1940	134
8	Ted Williams, 1939	131
	Dom DiMaggio, 1950	131
10	Jimmie Foxx, 1936	130
	Jimmie Foxx, 1939	130
12	Billy Werber, 1934	129
13	Wade Boggs, 1988	128
14	Dom DiMaggio, 1948	127
15	Dom DiMaggio, 1949	126
16	Ted Williams, 1947	125
	Vern Stephens, 1950	125
	Carl Yastrzemski, 1970	125
19	Ted Williams, 1948	124
	Johnny Pesky, 1948	124
21	Johnny Damon, 2004	123
22	Dwight Evans, 1982	122
	Nomar Garciaparra, 1997	122
24	Joe Vosmik, 1938	121
	Jim Rice, 1978	121
	Dwight Evans, 1984	121
27	Nomar Garciaparra, 2003	120
28	**David Ortiz, 2005**	**119**
29	Mo Vaughn, 1996	118
	Johnny Damon, 2002	118
31	Dom DiMaggio, 1941	117
	Jim Rice, 1979	117
	Manny Ramirez, 2003	**117**
	Johnny Damon, 2005	117
35	Doc Cramer, 1938	116
	Fred Lynn, 1979	116
37	Johnny Pesky, 1946	115
	David Ortiz, 2006	**115**
39	Vern Stephens, 1948	114
40	Vern Stephens, 1949	113
	Dom DiMaggio, 1951	113
	Wade Boggs, 1989	113
	John Valentin, 1998	113
44	Johnny Pesky, 1950	112
	Carl Yastrzemski, 1967	112
	Manny Ramirez, 2005	**112**
47	Jimmie Foxx, 1937	111
	Johnny Pesky, 1949	111
	Nomar Garciaparra, 1998	111
50	3 players tied	110

Runs by era

1988–2006		
1	Wade Boggs, 1988	128
2	Johnny Damon, 2004	123
3	Nomar Garciaparra, 1997	122
4	Nomar Garciaparra, 2003	120
5	**David Ortiz, 2005**	**119**
6	Mo Vaughn, 1996	118
	Johnny Damon, 2002	118
1973–87		
1	Dwight Evans, 1982	122
2	Jim Rice, 1978	121
	Dwight Evans, 1984	121
4	Jim Rice, 1979	117
5	Fred Lynn, 1979	116
6	Dwight Evans, 1985	110
7	Wade Boggs, 1984	109
	Dwight Evans, 1987	109
1961–72		
1	Carl Yastrzemski, 1970	125
2	Carl Yastrzemski, 1967	112
3	Reggie Smith, 1970	109
4	Carl Yastrzemski, 1962	99
5	Joe Foy, 1966	97
6	Carl Yastrzemski, 1969	96
7	Rico Petrocelli, 1969	92
	Tommy Harper, 1972	92
1943–60		
1	Ted Williams, 1949	150
2	Ted Williams, 1946	142
3	Dom DiMaggio, 1950	131
4	Dom DiMaggio, 1948	127
5	Dom DiMaggio, 1949	126
6	Ted Williams, 1947	125
	Vern Stephens, 1950	125
1921–42		
1	Ted Williams, 1942	141
2	Jimmie Foxx, 1938	139
3	Ted Williams, 1941	135
4	Ted Williams, 1940	134
5	Ted Williams, 1939	131
6	Jimmie Foxx, 1936	130
	Jimmie Foxx, 1939	130
1901–20		
1	Tris Speaker, 1912	136
2	Jimmy Collins, 1901	108
	Tris Speaker, 1915	108
4	Patsy Dougherty, 1903	107
5	Chick Stahl, 1901	105
6	Tommy Dowd, 1901	104
7	Babe Ruth, 1919	103

Hits

1	Wade Boggs, 1985	240
2	Tris Speaker, 1912	222
3	Wade Boggs, 1988	214
4	Jim Rice, 1978	213
5	Wade Boggs, 1983	210
6	Nomar Garciaparra, 1997	209
7	Johnny Pesky, 1946	208
8	Johnny Pesky, 1947	207
	Wade Boggs, 1986	207
	Mo Vaughn, 1996	207
11	Jim Rice, 1977	206
12	Johnny Pesky, 1942	205
	Wade Boggs, 1989	205
	Mo Vaughn, 1998	205
15	Wade Boggs, 1984	203
16	Joe Vosmik, 1938	201
	Jim Rice, 1979	201
	Bill Buckner, 1985	201
19	Billy Werber, 1934	200
	Doc Cramer, 1940	200
	Jim Rice, 1986	200
	Wade Boggs, 1987	200
23	Jimmie Foxx, 1936	198
	Doc Cramer, 1938	198
	Nomar Garciaparra, 2003	198
26	Jimmie Foxx, 1938	197
	Nomar Garciaparra, 2000	197
	Nomar Garciaparra, 2002	197
	Johnny Damon, 2005	197
30	Earl Webb, 1931	196
31	Patsy Dougherty, 1903	195
	Nomar Garciaparra, 1998	195
33	Ted Williams, 1949	194
	Rick Burleson, 1977	194
35	Tris Speaker, 1914	193
	Ted Williams, 1940	193
	Dom DiMaggio, 1950	193
38	Mike Greenwell, 1988	192
39	Carl Yastrzemski, 1962	191
	Jim Rice, 1983	191
41	Nomar Garciaparra, 1999	190
42	Tris Speaker, 1913	189
	Tom Oliver, 1930	189
	Dom DiMaggio, 1951	189
	Carl Yastrzemski, 1967	189
	Johnny Damon, 2004	189
47	Doc Cramer, 1936	188
	Ted Williams, 1948	188
	Mike Easler, 1984	188
50	2 players tied	187

Hits by era

1988–2006		
1	Wade Boggs, 1988	214
2	Nomar Garciaparra, 1997	209
3	Mo Vaughn, 1996	207
4	Wade Boggs, 1989	205
	Mo Vaughn, 1998	205
6	Nomar Garciaparra, 2003	198
7	3 players tied	197
1973–87		
1	Wade Boggs, 1985	240
2	Jim Rice, 1978	213
3	Wade Boggs, 1983	210
4	Wade Boggs, 1986	207
5	Jim Rice, 1977	206
6	Wade Boggs, 1984	203
7	Jim Rice, 1979	201
	Bill Buckner, 1985	201
1961–72		
1	Carl Yastrzemski, 1962	191
2	Carl Yastrzemski, 1967	189
3	Carl Yastrzemski, 1970	186
4	Pete Runnels, 1962	183
	Carl Yastrzemski, 1963	183
6	Reggie Smith, 1970	176
7	Frank Malzone, 1962	175
	Reggie Smith, 1971	175
1943–60		
1	Johnny Pesky, 1946	208
2	Johnny Pesky, 1947	207
3	Ted Williams, 1949	194
4	Dom DiMaggio, 1950	193
5	Dom DiMaggio, 1951	189
6	Ted Williams, 1948	188
7	Dom DiMaggio, 1949	186
1921–42		
1	Johnny Pesky, 1942	205
2	Joe Vosmik, 1938	201
3	Billy Werber, 1934	200
	Doc Cramer, 1940	200
5	Jimmie Foxx, 1936	198
	Doc Cramer, 1938	198
7	Jimmie Foxx, 1938	197
1901–20		
1	Tris Speaker, 1912	222
2	Patsy Dougherty, 1903	195
3	Tris Speaker, 1914	193
4	Tris Speaker, 1913	189
5	Jimmy Collins, 1901	187
6	Tris Speaker, 1910	183
7	Tris Speaker, 1915	176

Doubles

1	Earl Webb, 1931	67
2	Nomar Garciaparra, 2002	56
3	Tris Speaker, 1912	53
4	Joe Cronin, 1938	51
	Wade Boggs, 1989	51
	Nomar Garciaparra, 2000	51
7	George Burns, 1923	47
	Fred Lynn, 1975	47
	Wade Boggs, 1986	47
	John Valentin, 1997	47
	David Ortiz, 2004	**47**
	Mike Lowell, 2006	**47**
13	Tris Speaker, 1914	46
	Bill Buckner, 1985	46
15	Carl Yastrzemski, 1965	45
	Wade Boggs, 1988	45
	Jody Reed, 1990	45
	Bill Mueller, 2003	45
19	Del Pratt, 1922	44
	Ted Williams, 1939	44
	Ted Williams, 1948	44
	Wade Boggs, 1983	44
	Wade Boggs, 1990	44
	Nomar Garciaparra, 1997	44
	John Valentin, 1998	44
	Manny Ramirez, 2004	**44**
27	Roy Johnson, 1934	43
	Ted Williams, 1940	43
	Johnny Pesky, 1946	43
	Carl Yastrzemski, 1962	43
	Shea Hillenbrand, 2002	43
32	Jimmy Collins, 1901	42
	Fred Lynn, 1979	42
	Wade Boggs, 1985	42
	Jody Reed, 1989	42
	Wade Boggs, 1991	42
	Jody Reed, 1991	42
	Nomar Garciaparra, 1999	42
	Kevin Youkilis, 2006	**42**
40	Bill Wambsganss, 1924	41
	Ira Flagstead, 1928	41
	Billy Werber, 1934	41
	George Kell, 1953	41
	Eddie Bressoud, 1964	41
45	Many players tied	40

Doubles by era

1988–2006		
1	Nomar Garciaparra, 2002	56
2	Wade Boggs, 1989	51
	Nomar Garciaparra, 2000	51
4	John Valentin, 1997	47
	David Ortiz, 2004	**47**
	Mike Lowell, 2006	**47**
7	Wade Boggs, 1988	45
	Jody Reed, 1990	45
	Bill Mueller, 2003	45
1973–87		
1	Fred Lynn, 1975	47
	Wade Boggs, 1986	47
3	Bill Buckner, 1985	46
4	Wade Boggs, 1983	44
5	Fred Lynn, 1979	42
	Wade Boggs, 1985	42
7	Wade Boggs, 1987	40
1961–72		
1	Carl Yastrzemski, 1965	45
2	Carl Yastrzemski, 1962	43
3	Eddie Bressoud, 1964	41
4	Eddie Bressoud, 1962	40
	Carl Yastrzemski, 1963	40
6	Carl Yastrzemski, 1966	39
7	Reggie Smith, 1968	37
1943–60		
1	Ted Williams, 1948	44
2	Johnny Pesky, 1946	43
3	George Kell, 1953	41
4	Bob Johnson, 1944	40
	Ted Williams, 1947	40
	Dom DiMaggio, 1948	40
	Jim Piersall, 1956	40
1921–42		
1	Earl Webb, 1931	67
2	Joe Cronin, 1938	51
3	George Burns, 1923	47
4	Del Pratt, 1922	44
	Ted Williams, 1939	44
6	Roy Johnson, 1934	43
	Ted Williams, 1940	43
1901–20		
1	Tris Speaker, 1912	53
2	Tris Speaker, 1914	46
3	Jimmy Collins, 1901	42
4	Buck Freeman, 1903	39
5	Buck Freeman, 1902	38
6	Duffy Lewis, 1914	37
7	Duffy Lewis, 1912	36

Triples

1	Tris Speaker, 1913	22
2	Buck Freeman, 1903	20
3	Buck Freeman, 1902	19
	Buck Freeman, 1904	19
	Chick Stahl, 1904	19
	Larry Gardner, 1914	19
7	Larry Gardner, 1912	18
	Tris Speaker, 1914	18
9	Freddy Parent, 1903	17
	Jimmy Collins, 1903	17
	Harry Hooper, 1920	17
	Russ Scarritt, 1929	17
13	Jimmy Collins, 1901	16
	Chick Stahl, 1901	16
	Hobe Ferris, 1905	16
	Jake Stahl, 1910	16
17	Buck Freeman, 1901	15
	Hobe Ferris, 1901	15
	Harry Hooper, 1914	15
	Lou Finney, 1940	15
	Jim Rice, 1977	15
	Jim Rice, 1978	15
23	Hobe Ferris, 1902	14
	Doc Gessler, 1908	14
	Tris Speaker, 1910	14
	Doug Taitt, 1928	14
	Joe Cronin, 1935	14
	Ted Williams, 1940	14
29	Jimmy Collins, 1904	13
	Jesse Burkett, 1905	13
	Hobe Ferris, 1906	13
	Bob Unglaub, 1907	13
	Tris Speaker, 1909	13
	Tris Speaker, 1911	13
	Harry Hooper, 1915	13
	Harry Hooper, 1918	13
	Phil Todt, 1925	13
	Nomar Garciaparra, 2003	13
39	Many players tied	12

Triples by era

1988–2006		
1	Nomar Garciaparra, 2003	13
2	Nomar Garciaparra, 1997	11
	Jose Offerman, 1999	11
	Johnny Damon, 2002	11
5	Mike Greenwell, 1988	8
	Ellis Burks, 1990	8
	Nomar Garciaparra, 1998	8
	Troy O'Leary, 1998	8
	Trot Nixon, 2000	**8**
1973–87		
1	Jim Rice, 1977	15
	Jim Rice, 1978	15
3	Dwight Evans, 1974	8
	Fred Lynn, 1976	8
	Jim Rice, 1976	8
	Dwight Evans, 1984	8
1961–72		
1	Lou Clinton, 1962	10
2	Eddie Bressoud, 1962	9
	Carl Yastrzemski, 1964	9
	Carlton Fisk, 1972	9
5	Joe Foy, 1966	8
6	Lou Clinton, 1963	7
	Tony Conigliaro, 1966	7
	George Scott, 1966	7
	George Scott, 1967	7
	Reggie Smith, 1969	7
	Reggie Smith, 1970	7
1943–60		
1	Dom DiMaggio, 1950	11
	Bobby Doerr, 1950	11
	Jackie Jensen, 1956	11
4	Bobby Doerr, 1944	10
	Bobby Doerr, 1947	10
	Al Zarilla, 1950	10
7	Tony Lupien, 1943	9
	Bobby Doerr, 1946	9
	Ted Williams, 1947	9
	Bobby Doerr, 1949	9
	Jim Piersall, 1953	9
1921–42		
1	Russ Scarritt, 1929	17
2	Lou Finney, 1940	15
3	Doug Taitt, 1928	14
	Joe Cronin, 1935	14
	Ted Williams, 1940	14
6	Phil Todt, 1925	13
7	Shano Collins, 1921	12
	Phil Todt, 1926	12
	Doc Cramer, 1940	12
1901–20		
1	Tris Speaker, 1913	22
2	Buck Freeman, 1903	20
3	Buck Freeman, 1902	19
	Buck Freeman, 1904	19
	Chick Stahl, 1904	19
	Larry Gardner, 1914	19
7	Larry Gardner, 1912	18
	Tris Speaker, 1914	18

Home Runs

1	**David Ortiz, 2006**	**54**
2	Jimmie Foxx, 1938	50
3	**David Ortiz, 2005**	**47**
4	Jim Rice, 1978	46
5	**Manny Ramirez, 2005**	**45**
6	Carl Yastrzemski, 1967	44
	Mo Vaughn, 1996	44
8	Ted Williams, 1949	43
	Tony Armas, 1984	43
	Manny Ramirez, 2004	**43**
11	Dick Stuart, 1963	42
12	Jimmie Foxx, 1936	41
	Manny Ramirez, 2001	**41**
	David Ortiz, 2004	**41**
15	Rico Petrocelli, 1969	40
	Carl Yastrzemski, 1969	40
	Carl Yastrzemski, 1970	40
	Mo Vaughn, 1998	40
19	Vern Stephens, 1949	39
	Jim Rice, 1977	39
	Fred Lynn, 1979	39
	Jim Rice, 1979	39
	Jim Rice, 1983	39
	Mo Vaughn, 1995	39
25	Ted Williams, 1946	38
	Ted Williams, 1957	38
27	Ted Williams, 1941	37
	Manny Ramirez, 2003	**37**
29	Jimmie Foxx, 1937	36
	Jimmie Foxx, 1940	36
	Ted Williams, 1942	36
	Tony Conigliaro, 1970	36
	Tony Armas, 1983	36
34	Jimmie Foxx, 1939	35
	Jackie Jensen, 1958	35
	Ken Harrelson, 1968	35
	Mo Vaughn, 1997	35
	Nomar Garciaparra, 1998	35
	Manny Ramirez, 2006	**35**
40	Walt Dropo, 1950	34
	Dwight Evans, 1987	34
	Carl Everett, 2000	34
43	Dick Stuart, 1964	33
	George Scott, 1977	33
	Manny Ramirez, 2002	**33**
46	Ted Williams, 1947	32
	Tony Conigliaro, 1965	32
	Dwight Evans, 1982	32
	Dwight Evans, 1984	32
50	3 players tied	31

Home Runs by era

1988–2006		
1	**David Ortiz, 2006**	**54**
2	**David Ortiz, 2005**	**47**
3	**Manny Ramirez, 2005**	**45**
4	Mo Vaughn, 1996	44
5	**Manny Ramirez, 2004**	**43**
6	**Manny Ramirez, 2001**	**41**
	David Ortiz, 2004	**41**
1973–87		
1	Jim Rice, 1978	46
2	Tony Armas, 1984	43
3	Jim Rice, 1977	39
	Fred Lynn, 1979	39
	Jim Rice, 1979	39
	Jim Rice, 1983	39
7	Tony Armas, 1983	36
1961–72		
1	Carl Yastrzemski, 1967	44
2	Dick Stuart, 1963	42
3	Rico Petrocelli, 1969	40
	Carl Yastrzemski, 1969	40
	Carl Yastrzemski, 1970	40
6	Tony Conigliaro, 1970	36
7	Ken Harrelson, 1968	35
1943–60		
1	Ted Williams, 1949	43
2	Vern Stephens, 1949	39
3	Ted Williams, 1946	38
	Ted Williams, 1957	38
5	Jackie Jensen, 1958	35
6	Walt Dropo, 1950	34
7	Ted Williams, 1947	32
1921–42		
1	Jimmie Foxx, 1938	50
2	Jimmie Foxx, 1936	41
3	Ted Williams, 1941	37
4	Jimmie Foxx, 1937	36
	Jimmie Foxx, 1940	36
	Ted Williams, 1942	36
7	Jimmie Foxx, 1939	35
1901–20		
1	Babe Ruth, 1919	29
2	Buck Freeman, 1903	13
3	Buck Freeman, 1901	12
4	Buck Freeman, 1902	11
	Babe Ruth, 1918	11
6	Jake Stahl, 1910	10
	Tris Speaker, 1912	10

Home Runs/500 at bats by era

1988–2006		
1	**David Ortiz, 2006**	**48.4**
2	**Manny Ramirez, 2005**	**40.6**
3	**David Ortiz, 2005**	**39.1**
4	**Manny Ramirez, 2006**	**39.0**
5	**Manny Ramirez, 2001**	**38.8**
6	**Manny Ramirez, 2004**	**37.9**
7	**Manny Ramirez, 2002**	**37.8**
1973–87		
1	Fred Lynn, 1979	36.7
2	Jim Rice, 1978	34.0
3	Tony Armas, 1984	33.6
4	Jim Rice, 1979	31.5
5	Dwight Evans, 1987	31.4
6	Tony Armas, 1983	31.4
7	Jim Rice, 1983	31.2
1961–72		
1	Carl Yastrzemski, 1967	38.0
2	Rico Petrocelli, 1969	37.4
3	Carl Yastrzemski, 1970	35.3
4	Dick Stuart, 1963	34.3
5	Carl Yastrzemski, 1969	33.2
6	Ken Harrelson, 1968	32.7
7	Tony Conigliaro, 1970	32.1
1943–60		
1	Ted Williams, 1957	45.2
2	Ted Williams, 1949	38.0
3	Ted Williams, 1954	37.6
4	Ted Williams, 1946	37.0
5	Vern Stephens, 1949	32.0
6	Jackie Jensen, 1958	31.9
7	Ted Williams, 1958	31.6
1921–42		
1	Jimmie Foxx, 1938	44.2
2	Ted Williams, 1941	40.6
3	Jimmie Foxx, 1939	37.5
4	Jimmie Foxx, 1936	35.0
5	Jimmie Foxx, 1940	35.0
6	Ted Williams, 1942	34.5
7	Jimmie Foxx, 1937	31.6
1901–20		
1	Babe Ruth, 1919	33.6
2	Buck Freeman, 1901	12.2
3	Buck Freeman, 1903	11.5
4	Buck Freeman, 1902	9.8
5	Jake Stahl, 1910	9.4
6	Tris Speaker, 1912	8.6
7	Hobe Ferris, 1903	8.6

Total Bases

1	Jim Rice, 1978	406
2	Jimmie Foxx, 1938	398
3	Jim Rice, 1977	382
4	Mo Vaughn, 1996	370
5	Jimmie Foxx, 1936	369
	Jim Rice, 1979	369
7	Ted Williams, 1949	368
8	Nomar Garciaparra, 1997	365
9	**David Ortiz, 2005**	**363**
10	Carl Yastrzemski, 1967	360
	Mo Vaughn, 1998	360
12	**David Ortiz, 2006**	**355**
13	Nomar Garciaparra, 1998	353
14	**David Ortiz, 2004**	**351**
15	**Manny Ramirez, 2004**	**348**
16	Nomar Garciaparra, 2003	345
17	Ted Williams, 1939	344
	Jim Rice, 1983	344
19	Ted Williams, 1946	343
20	Tony Armas, 1984	339
21	Ted Williams, 1942	338
	Fred Lynn, 1979	338
23	Ted Williams, 1941	335
	Ted Williams, 1947	335
	Carl Yastrzemski, 1970	335
	Dwight Evans, 1984	335
	Nomar Garciaparra, 2002	335
28	**Manny Ramirez, 2003**	**334**
29	Ted Williams, 1940	333
30	Tris Speaker, 1912	329
	Vern Stephens, 1949	329
	Manny Ramirez, 2005	**329**
33	Walt Dropo, 1950	326
34	Dwight Evans, 1982	325
35	Jimmie Foxx, 1939	324
	Wade Boggs, 1987	324
37	**Manny Ramirez, 2001**	**322**
38	Vern Stephens, 1950	321
	Nomar Garciaparra, 1999	321
40	Dick Stuart, 1963	319
41	Nomar Garciaparra, 2000	317
42	Mo Vaughn, 1995	316
43	Rico Petrocelli, 1969	315
44	Ted Williams, 1948	313
	Mike Greenwell, 1988	313
46	Wade Boggs, 1985	312
47	Earl Webb, 1931	311
48	Mike Easler, 1984	310
49	Dwight Evans, 1987	308
50	2 players tied	307

Runs Batted In by era

1988–2006		
1	**David Ortiz, 2005**	**148**
2	**Manny Ramirez, 2005**	**144**
3	Mo Vaughn, 1996	143
4	**David Ortiz, 2004**	**139**
5	**David Ortiz, 2006**	**137**
6	**Manny Ramirez, 2004**	**130**
7	Mo Vaughn, 1995	126
1973–87		
1	Jim Rice, 1978	139
2	Jim Rice, 1979	130
3	Jim Rice, 1983	126
4	Tony Armas, 1984	123
	Dwight Evans, 1987	123
6	Fred Lynn, 1979	122
	Jim Rice, 1984	122
1961–72		
1	Carl Yastrzemski, 1967	121
2	Dick Stuart, 1963	118
3	Tony Conigliaro, 1970	116
4	Dick Stuart, 1964	114
5	Carl Yastrzemski, 1969	111
6	Ken Harrelson, 1968	109
7	Rico Petrocelli, 1970	103
1943–60		
1	Ted Williams, 1949	159
	Vern Stephens, 1949	159
3	Walt Dropo, 1950	144
	Vern Stephens, 1950	144
5	Vern Stephens, 1948	137
6	Ted Williams, 1948	127
7	Ted Williams, 1951	126
1921–42		
1	Jimmie Foxx, 1938	175
2	Ted Williams, 1939	145
3	Jimmie Foxx, 1936	143
4	Ted Williams, 1942	137
5	Jimmie Foxx, 1937	127
6	Ted Williams, 1941	120
7	Roy Johnson, 1934	119
	Jimmie Foxx, 1940	119
1901–20		
1	Buck Freeman, 1902	121
2	Buck Freeman, 1901	114
	Babe Ruth, 1919	114
4	Duffy Lewis, 1912	109
5	Buck Freeman, 1903	104
6	Jimmy Collins, 1901	94
7	3 players tied	90

Walk Percentage (BB/PA)

1	Ted Williams, 1954	25.86
2	Ted Williams, 1941	24.26
3	Ted Williams, 1947	23.38
4	Ted Williams, 1946	23.21
5	Ted Williams, 1949	22.19
6	Ted Williams, 1957	21.79
7	Ted Williams, 1942	21.61
8	Ted Williams, 1951	21.33
9	Ted Williams, 1956	20.28
10	Ted Williams, 1948	19.75
11	Ted Williams, 1958	18.96
12	Babe Ruth, 1919	18.63
13	Carl Yastrzemski, 1970	18.36
14	Eddie Lake, 1945	18.09
15	Carl Yastrzemski, 1968	17.92
16	**Manny Ramirez, 2006**	**17.92**
17	Wade Boggs, 1988	17.39
18	Jimmie Foxx, 1938	17.37
19	**David Ortiz, 2006**	**17.35**
20	Stan Spence, 1948	17.19
21	Johnny Pesky, 1950	17.19
22	Carl Yastrzemski, 1971	17.10
23	Dwight Evans, 1981	16.87
24	Carl Yastrzemski, 1974	16.43
25	Jack Clark, 1991	16.41
26	Topper Rigney, 1926	16.39
27	Jimmie Foxx, 1940	16.34
28	Dwight Evans, 1987	16.13
29	Carl Yastrzemski, 1973	16.10
30	Jimmie Foxx, 1941	15.98
31	Jimmie Foxx, 1939	15.81
32	Ted Williams, 1939	15.81
33	Wade Boggs, 1987	15.74
34	Dwight Evans, 1989	15.71
35	Don Buddin, 1959	15.62
36	Dwight Evans, 1982	15.41
37	Dwight Evans, 1985	15.32
38	Rico Petrocelli, 1969	15.24
39	Bob Johnson, 1944	15.18
40	Dwight Evans, 1986	15.16
41	Jimmie Foxx, 1936	15.15
	Wade Boggs, 1986	15.15
43	Jackie Jensen, 1958	15.11
44	Dick Gernert, 1953	14.92
45	Tim Naehring, 1995	14.81
46	Jimmie Foxx, 1937	14.71
47	Johnny Pesky, 1951	14.66
48	Johnny Pesky, 1948	14.62
49	Gary Geiger, 1961	14.52
50	Ted Williams, 1940	14.52

Home Runs/500 at bats

1	**David Ortiz, 2006**	**48.4**
2	Ted Williams, 1957	45.2
3	Jimmie Foxx, 1938	44.2
4	**Manny Ramirez, 2005**	**40.6**
5	Ted Williams, 1941	40.6
6	**David Ortiz, 2005**	**39.1**
7	**Manny Ramirez, 2006**	**39.0**
8	**Manny Ramirez, 2001**	**38.8**
9	Carl Yastrzemski, 1967	38.0
10	Ted Williams, 1949	38.0
11	**Manny Ramirez, 2004**	**37.9**
12	**Manny Ramirez, 2002**	**37.8**
13	Ted Williams, 1954	37.6
14	Jimmie Foxx, 1939	37.5
15	Rico Petrocelli, 1969	37.4
16	Ted Williams, 1946	37.0
17	Fred Lynn, 1979	36.7
18	Mo Vaughn, 1995	35.5
19	Carl Yastrzemski, 1970	35.3
20	**David Ortiz, 2004**	**35.2**
21	Jimmie Foxx, 1936	35.0
22	Jimmie Foxx, 1940	35.0
23	Mo Vaughn, 1996	34.6
24	**David Ortiz, 2003**	**34.6**
25	Ted Williams, 1942	34.5
26	Dick Stuart, 1963	34.3
27	Carl Everett, 2000	34.3
28	Jim Rice, 1978	34.0
29	Tony Armas, 1984	33.6
30	Babe Ruth, 1919	33.6
31	Mo Vaughn, 1997	33.2
32	Carl Yastrzemski, 1969	33.2
33	Mo Vaughn, 1994	33.0
34	Mo Vaughn, 1998	32.8
35	Ken Harrelson, 1968	32.7
36	**Manny Ramirez, 2003**	**32.5**
37	Tony Conigliaro, 1970	32.1
38	Vern Stephens, 1949	32.0
39	Jackie Jensen, 1958	31.9
40	**Trot Nixon, 2003**	**31.7**
41	Jimmie Foxx, 1937	31.6
42	Ted Williams, 1958	31.6
43	Jim Rice, 1979	31.5
44	Dwight Evans, 1987	31.4
45	Tony Armas, 1983	31.4
46	Jim Rice, 1983	31.2
47	Tony Conigliaro, 1965	30.7
48	Walt Dropo, 1950	30.4
49	Ted Williams, 1947	30.3
	Jose Canseco, 1995	30.3

Extra Base Hits

1	Jimmie Foxx, 1938	92
2	**David Ortiz, 2004**	**91**
3	**David Ortiz, 2005**	**88**
4	**Manny Ramirez, 2004**	**87**
5	Ted Williams, 1939	86
	Jim Rice, 1978	86
7	Ted Williams, 1949	85
	Nomar Garciaparra, 1997	85
	Nomar Garciaparra, 2002	85
	David Ortiz, 2006	**85**
11	Earl Webb, 1931	84
	Jim Rice, 1979	84
13	Ted Williams, 1946	83
	Jim Rice, 1977	83
15	Fred Lynn, 1979	82
16	Jimmie Foxx, 1936	81
	Ted Williams, 1947	81
18	Ted Williams, 1940	80
	Nomar Garciaparra, 1998	80
20	Carl Yastrzemski, 1967	79
21	Nomar Garciaparra, 2003	78
22	Tony Armas, 1984	77
	Dwight Evans, 1984	77
24	Jimmie Foxx, 1939	76
	Dwight Evans, 1982	76
	Manny Ramirez, 2001	**76**
	Manny Ramirez, 2005	**76**
28	Tris Speaker, 1912	75
	Babe Ruth, 1919	75
	Ted Williams, 1942	75
	Fred Lynn, 1975	75
	Nomar Garciaparra, 2000	75
33	Rico Petrocelli, 1969	74
	Jim Rice, 1983	74
	Mo Vaughn, 1996	74
	Manny Ramirez, 2003	**74**
37	Joe Cronin, 1938	73
	Ted Williams, 1941	73
	Dwight Evans, 1987	73
	Mo Vaughn, 1998	73
	Nomar Garciaparra, 1999	73
42	Buck Freeman, 1903	72
	Ted Williams, 1948	72
	Vern Stephens, 1949	72
	David Ortiz, 2003	**72**
46	Dick Stuart, 1963	71
47	Many players tied	70

Runs Batted In

1	Jimmie Foxx, 1938	175
2	Ted Williams, 1949	159
	Vern Stephens, 1949	159
4	**David Ortiz, 2005**	**148**
5	Ted Williams, 1939	145
6	Walt Dropo, 1950	144
	Vern Stephens, 1950	144
	Manny Ramirez, 2005	**144**
9	Jimmie Foxx, 1936	143
	Mo Vaughn, 1996	143
11	Jim Rice, 1978	139
	David Ortiz, 2004	**139**
13	Ted Williams, 1942	137
	Vern Stephens, 1948	137
	David Ortiz, 2006	**137**
16	Jim Rice, 1979	130
	Manny Ramirez, 2004	**130**
18	Jimmie Foxx, 1937	127
	Ted Williams, 1948	127
20	Ted Williams, 1951	126
	Jim Rice, 1983	126
	Mo Vaughn, 1995	126
23	**Manny Ramirez, 2001**	**125**
24	Ted Williams, 1946	123
	Tony Armas, 1984	123
	Dwight Evans, 1987	123
27	Jackie Jensen, 1958	122
	Fred Lynn, 1979	122
	Jim Rice, 1984	122
	Nomar Garciaparra, 1998	122
31	Buck Freeman, 1902	121
	Carl Yastrzemski, 1967	121
33	Ted Williams, 1941	120
	Bobby Doerr, 1950	120
	Nomar Garciaparra, 2002	120
36	Roy Johnson, 1934	119
	Jimmie Foxx, 1940	119
	Rudy York, 1946	119
	Mike Greenwell, 1988	119
40	Dick Stuart, 1963	118
41	Jackie Jensen, 1954	117
42	Bobby Doerr, 1946	116
	Jackie Jensen, 1955	116
	Tony Conigliaro, 1970	116
45	Mo Vaughn, 1998	115
46	Buck Freeman, 1901	114
	Babe Ruth, 1919	114
	Ted Williams, 1947	114
	Dick Stuart, 1964	114
	Jim Rice, 1977	114

Walks

1	Ted Williams, 1947	162
	Ted Williams, 1949	162
3	Ted Williams, 1946	156
4	Ted Williams, 1941	147
5	Ted Williams, 1942	145
6	Ted Williams, 1951	144
7	Ted Williams, 1954	136
8	Carl Yastrzemski, 1970	128
9	Ted Williams, 1948	126
10	Wade Boggs, 1988	125
11	Jimmie Foxx, 1938	119
	Ted Williams, 1957	119
	Carl Yastrzemski, 1968	119
	David Ortiz, 2006	**119**
15	Dwight Evans, 1985	114
16	Dwight Evans, 1982	112
17	Topper Rigney, 1926	108
18	Ted Williams, 1939	107
	Wade Boggs, 1989	107
20	Eddie Lake, 1945	106
	Carl Yastrzemski, 1971	106
	Dwight Evans, 1987	106
23	Jimmie Foxx, 1936	105
	Carl Yastrzemski, 1973	105
	Wade Boggs, 1986	105
	Wade Boggs, 1987	105
27	Johnny Pesky, 1950	104
	Carl Yastrzemski, 1974	104
29	Ted Williams, 1956	102
	David Ortiz, 2005	**102**
31	Babe Ruth, 1919	101
	Jimmie Foxx, 1940	101
	Dom DiMaggio, 1948	101
	Vern Stephens, 1949	101
	Carl Yastrzemski, 1969	101
36	Johnny Pesky, 1949	100
	Manny Ramirez, 2006	**100**
38	Jimmie Foxx, 1937	99
	Johnny Pesky, 1948	99
	Billy Goodman, 1955	99
	Jackie Jensen, 1958	99
	Dwight Evans, 1989	99
43	Ted Williams, 1958	98
	Rico Petrocelli, 1969	98
45	Dwight Evans, 1986	97
	Manny Ramirez, 2003	**97**
47	Many players tied	96

Strikeouts

1	Mark Bellhorn, 2004	177
2	Butch Hobson, 1977	162
3	Tony Armas, 1984	156
4	Mo Vaughn, 1996	154
	Mo Vaughn, 1997	154
6	George Scott, 1966	152
7	Mo Vaughn, 1995	150
8	**Manny Ramirez, 2001**	**147**
9	Dick Stuart, 1963	144
	Mo Vaughn, 1998	144
11	Mike Easler, 1984	134
12	Jack Clark, 1991	133
	David Ortiz, 2004	**133**
14	Tony Armas, 1983	131
15	Dick Stuart, 1964	130
	Mo Vaughn, 1993	130
	Brian Daubach, 2000	130
18	Mike Easler, 1985	129
19	Jim Rice, 1978	126
	Brian Daubach, 2002	126
	Jason Varitek, 2004	**126**
22	Dwight Evans, 1982	125
23	**Manny Ramirez, 2004**	**124**
	David Ortiz, 2005	**124**
25	Jim Rice, 1976	123
26	Jim Rice, 1975	122
	Butch Hobson, 1978	122
	Wil Cordero, 1997	122
29	Jim Rice, 1977	120
	Kevin Youkilis, 2006	**120**
31	Jimmie Foxx, 1936	119
	George Scott, 1967	119
	Dwight Evans, 1978	119
	Manny Ramirez, 2005	**119**
35	Eddie Bressoud, 1962	118
	Lou Clinton, 1963	118
37	Dwight Evans, 1986	117
	Nick Esasky, 1989	117
	Jason Varitek, 2005	**117**
	David Ortiz, 2006	**117**
41	Tony Conigliaro, 1965	116
42	Dwight Evans, 1984	115
43	Carl Everett, 2000	113
	Trot Nixon, 2001	**113**
45	Tony Conigliaro, 1966	112
	George Scott, 1977	112
	Mo Vaughn, 1994	112
48	Tony Conigliaro, 1969	111
	Don Baylor, 1986	111
50	**Trot Nixon, 2002**	**109**

Strikeout Percentage

1988–2006

1	Mark Bellhorn, 2004	33.84
2	Mo Vaughn, 1997	29.22
3	Mo Vaughn, 1994	28.43
4	Brian Daubach, 2002	28.38
5	**Manny Ramirez, 2001**	**27.79**
6	Jack Clark, 1991	27.65
7	Mo Vaughn, 1995	27.27

1973–87

1	Butch Hobson, 1977	27.32
2	Tony Armas, 1984	24.41
3	Dwight Evans, 1978	23.94
4	Butch Hobson, 1978	23.83
5	Tony Armas, 1983	22.82
6	Mike Easler, 1985	22.71
7	Mike Easler, 1984	22.30

1961–72

1	George Scott, 1966	25.29
2	Dick Stuart, 1963	23.53
3	Tony Conigliaro, 1965	22.26
4	Tony Conigliaro, 1969	21.94
5	Dick Stuart, 1964	21.56
6	Lou Clinton, 1963	21.07
7	George Scott, 1967	21.06

1943–60

1	Norm Zauchin, 1955	22.01
2	Don Buddin, 1958	21.33
3	Don Buddin, 1959	20.41
4	Dick Gernert, 1958	18.10
5	Dick Gernert, 1953	16.60
6	Rudy York, 1946	16.06
7	Don Buddin, 1960	13.79

1921–42

1	Jimmie Foxx, 1941	21.15
2	Jimmie Foxx, 1936	20.34
3	Jimmie Foxx, 1940	16.89
4	Jimmie Foxx, 1937	16.87
5	Dusty Cooke, 1933	15.64
6	Urbane Pickering, 1932	15.54
7	Jimmie Foxx, 1939	15.42

1901–20

1	Babe Ruth, 1919	13.43
2	Duffy Lewis, 1915	11.31
3	Hal Janvrin, 1914	10.16
4	Duffy Lewis, 1913	9.98
5	Duffy Lewis, 1916	9.95
6	Mike Menosky, 1920	9.77
7	Duffy Lewis, 1917	9.76

Batting Average by era

1988–2006

1	Nomar Garciaparra, 2000	.372
2	Wade Boggs, 1988	.366
3	Nomar Garciaparra, 1999	.357
4	**Manny Ramirez, 2002**	**.349**
5	Mo Vaughn, 1998	.337
6	Wade Boggs, 1991	.332
7	Wade Boggs, 1989	.330

1973–87

1	Wade Boggs, 1985	.368
2	Wade Boggs, 1987	.363
3	Wade Boggs, 1983	.361
4	Wade Boggs, 1986	.357
5	Carney Lansford, 1981	.336
6	Fred Lynn, 1979	.333
7	Fred Lynn, 1975	.331

1961–72

1	Carl Yastrzemski, 1970	.329
2	Carl Yastrzemski, 1967	.326
3	Pete Runnels, 1962	.326
4	Carl Yastrzemski, 1963	.321
5	Carl Yastrzemski, 1965	.312
6	Reggie Smith, 1969	.309
7	Reggie Smith, 1970	.303

1943–60

1	Ted Williams, 1957	.388
2	Ted Williams, 1948	.369
3	Billy Goodman, 1950	.354
4	Ted Williams, 1956	.345
5	Ted Williams, 1954	.345
6	Ted Williams, 1947	.343
7	Ted Williams, 1949	.343

1921–42

1	Ted Williams, 1941	.406
2	Jimmie Foxx, 1939	.360
3	Ted Williams, 1942	.356
4	Jimmie Foxx, 1938	.349
5	Ted Williams, 1940	.344
6	Ben Chapman, 1938	.340
7	Jimmie Foxx, 1936	.338

1901–20

1	Tris Speaker, 1912	.383
2	Tris Speaker, 1913	.363
3	Patsy Dougherty, 1902	.342
4	Tris Speaker, 1910	.340
5	Buck Freeman, 1901	.339
6	Tris Speaker, 1914	.338
7	Tris Speaker, 1911	.334

On-Base Percentage by era

1988–2006

1	Wade Boggs, 1988	.480
2	**Manny Ramirez, 2002**	**.451**
3	**Manny Ramirez, 2006**	**.445**
4	Nomar Garciaparra, 2000	.439
5	Wade Boggs, 1989	.434
6	**Manny Ramirez, 2003**	**.430**
7	Wade Boggs, 1991	.425

1973–87

1	Wade Boggs, 1987	.467
2	Wade Boggs, 1986	.455
3	Wade Boggs, 1985	.452
4	Wade Boggs, 1983	.449
5	Fred Lynn, 1979	.426
6	Dwight Evans, 1987	.422
7	Carl Yastrzemski, 1974	.421

1961–72

1	Carl Yastrzemski, 1970	.453
2	Carl Yastrzemski, 1968	.429
3	Carl Yastrzemski, 1967	.421
4	Carl Yastrzemski, 1963	.419
5	Pete Runnels, 1962	.411
6	Rico Petrocelli, 1969	.407
7	Carl Yastrzemski, 1965	.398

1943–60

1	Ted Williams, 1957	.528
2	Ted Williams, 1954	.516
3	Ted Williams, 1947	.499
4	Ted Williams, 1946	.497
5	Ted Williams, 1948	.497
6	Ted Williams, 1949	.490
7	Ted Williams, 1956	.479

1921–42

1	Ted Williams, 1941	.553
2	Ted Williams, 1942	.499
3	Jimmie Foxx, 1939	.464
4	Jimmie Foxx, 1938	.462
5	Ted Williams, 1940	.442
6	Jimmie Foxx, 1936	.440
7	Ted Williams, 1939	.436

1901–20

1	Tris Speaker, 1912	.464
2	Babe Ruth, 1919	.456
3	Tris Speaker, 1913	.441
4	Tris Speaker, 1914	.423
5	Tris Speaker, 1911	.418
6	Tris Speaker, 1915	.416
7	Harry Hooper, 1920	.411

Slugging Average by era

1988–2006

1	**Manny Ramirez, 2002**	**.647**
2	**David Ortiz, 2006**	**.636**
3	**Manny Ramirez, 2006**	**.619**
4	**Manny Ramirez, 2004**	**.613**
5	**Manny Ramirez, 2001**	**.609**
6	**David Ortiz, 2005**	**.604**
7	Nomar Garciaparra, 1999	.603

1973–87

1	Fred Lynn, 1979	.637
2	Jim Rice, 1978	.600
3	Jim Rice, 1979	.596
4	Jim Rice, 1977	.593
5	Wade Boggs, 1987	.588
6	Dwight Evans, 1987	.569
7	Fred Lynn, 1975	.566

1961–72

1	Carl Yastrzemski, 1967	.622
2	Carl Yastrzemski, 1970	.592
3	Rico Petrocelli, 1969	.589
4	Carlton Fisk, 1972	.538
5	Carl Yastrzemski, 1965	.536
6	Reggie Smith, 1969	.527
7	Dick Stuart, 1963	.521

1943–60

1	Ted Williams, 1957	.731
2	Ted Williams, 1946	.667
3	Ted Williams, 1949	.650
4	Ted Williams, 1954	.635
5	Ted Williams, 1947	.634
6	Ted Williams, 1948	.615
7	Ted Williams, 1956	.605

1921–42

1	Ted Williams, 1941	.735
2	Jimmie Foxx, 1938	.704
3	Jimmie Foxx, 1939	.694
4	Ted Williams, 1942	.648
5	Jimmie Foxx, 1936	.631
6	Ted Williams, 1939	.609
7	Ted Williams, 1940	.594

1901–20

1	Babe Ruth, 1919	.657
2	Tris Speaker, 1912	.567
3	Tris Speaker, 1913	.533
4	Buck Freeman, 1901	.520
5	Tris Speaker, 1914	.503
6	Tris Speaker, 1911	.502
7	Buck Freeman, 1902	.502

On-Base plus Slugging by era

1988–2006

1	**Manny Ramirez, 2002**	**1097**
2	**Manny Ramirez, 2006**	**1058**
3	**David Ortiz, 2006**	**1049**
4	Nomar Garciaparra, 2000	1033
5	Nomar Garciaparra, 1999	1022
6	**Manny Ramirez, 2003**	**1014**
7	**Manny Ramirez, 2001**	**1014**

1973–87

1	Fred Lynn, 1979	1059
2	Wade Boggs, 1987	1049
3	Dwight Evans, 1987	986
4	Jim Rice, 1979	977
5	Jim Rice, 1978	970
6	Jim Rice, 1977	969
7	Fred Lynn, 1975	967

1961–72

1	Carl Yastrzemski, 1970	1044
2	Carl Yastrzemski, 1967	1040
3	Rico Petrocelli, 1969	992
4	Carl Yastrzemski, 1965	932
5	Carl Yastrzemski, 1968	922
6	Carlton Fisk, 1972	909
7	Reggie Smith, 1969	895

1943–60

1	Ted Williams, 1957	1257
2	Ted Williams, 1946	1164
3	Ted Williams, 1954	1148
4	Ted Williams, 1949	1141
5	Ted Williams, 1947	1133
6	Ted Williams, 1948	1112
7	Ted Williams, 1956	1084

1921–42

1	Ted Williams, 1941	1287
2	Jimmie Foxx, 1938	1166
3	Jimmie Foxx, 1939	1158
4	Ted Williams, 1942	1147
5	Jimmie Foxx, 1936	1071
6	Ted Williams, 1939	1045
7	Ted Williams, 1940	1036

1901–20

1	Babe Ruth, 1919	1114
2	Tris Speaker, 1912	1031
3	Tris Speaker, 1913	974
4	Tris Speaker, 1914	926
5	Buck Freeman, 1901	920
6	Tris Speaker, 1911	920
7	Harry Hooper, 1920	881

Batting Average

1	Ted Williams, 1941	.406
2	Ted Williams, 1957	.388
3	Tris Speaker, 1912	.383
4	Nomar Garciaparra, 2000	.372
5	Ted Williams, 1948	.369
6	Wade Boggs, 1985	.368
7	Wade Boggs, 1988	.366
8	Tris Speaker, 1913	.363
9	Wade Boggs, 1987	.363
10	Wade Boggs, 1983	.361
11	Jimmie Foxx, 1939	.360
12	Nomar Garciaparra, 1999	.357
13	Wade Boggs, 1986	.357
14	Ted Williams, 1942	.356
15	Billy Goodman, 1950	.354
16	Jimmie Foxx, 1938	.349
17	**Manny Ramirez, 2002**	**.349**
18	Ted Williams, 1956	.345
19	Ted Williams, 1954	.345
20	Ted Williams, 1940	.344
21	Ted Williams, 1947	.343
22	Ted Williams, 1949	.343
23	Patsy Dougherty, 1902	.342
24	Ted Williams, 1946	.342
25	Tris Speaker, 1910	.340
26	Ben Chapman, 1938	.340
27	Buck Freeman, 1901	.339
28	Jimmie Foxx, 1936	.338
29	Tris Speaker, 1914	.338
30	Ike Boone, 1924	.337
31	Mo Vaughn, 1998	.337
32	Carney Lansford, 1981	.336
33	Joe Harris, 1923	.335
34	Johnny Pesky, 1946	.335
35	Tris Speaker, 1911	.334
36	Fred Lynn, 1979	.333
37	Earl Webb, 1931	.333
38	Jimmy Collins, 1901	.332
39	Wade Boggs, 1991	.332
40	Fred Lynn, 1975	.331
41	Johnny Pesky, 1942	.331
42	Patsy Dougherty, 1903	.331
43	Wade Boggs, 1989	.330
44	Ike Boone, 1925	.330
45	Carl Yastrzemski, 1970	.329
46	George Burns, 1923	.328
47	Ted Williams, 1958	.328
48	Dom DiMaggio, 1950	.328
49	Ted Williams, 1939	.327
50	Carl Yastrzemski, 1967	.326

On-Base Percentage

1	Ted Williams, 1941	.553
2	Ted Williams, 1957	.526
3	Ted Williams, 1954	.513
4	Ted Williams, 1942	.499
5	Ted Williams, 1947	.499
6	Ted Williams, 1946	.497
7	Ted Williams, 1948	.497
8	Ted Williams, 1949	.490
9	Ted Williams, 1956	.479
10	Wade Boggs, 1988	.476
11	Jimmie Foxx, 1939	.464
12	Tris Speaker, 1912	.464
13	Ted Williams, 1951	.464
14	Jimmie Foxx, 1938	.462
15	Wade Boggs, 1987	.461
16	Ted Williams, 1958	.458
17	Babe Ruth, 1919	.456
18	Wade Boggs, 1986	.453
19	Carl Yastrzemski, 1970	.452
20	Wade Boggs, 1985	.450
21	**Manny Ramirez, 2002**	**.450**
22	Wade Boggs, 1983	.444
23	Ted Williams, 1940	.442
24	Tris Speaker, 1913	.441
25	Jimmie Foxx, 1936	.440
26	**Manny Ramirez, 2006**	**.439**
27	Johnny Pesky, 1950	.437
28	Ted Williams, 1939	.436
29	Nomar Garciaparra, 2000	.434
30	Bob Johnson, 1944	.431
31	Wade Boggs, 1989	.430
32	Joe Cronin, 1938	.428
33	**Manny Ramirez, 2003**	**.427**
34	Billy Goodman, 1950	.427
35	Carl Yastrzemski, 1968	.426
36	Tris Speaker, 1914	.423
37	Al Zarilla, 1950	.423
38	Fred Lynn, 1979	.423
39	Wade Boggs, 1991	.421
40	Mo Vaughn, 1997	.420
41	Mo Vaughn, 1996	.420
42	Nomar Garciaparra, 1999	.418
43	Ben Chapman, 1938	.418
44	Carl Yastrzemski, 1963	.418
45	Carl Yastrzemski, 1967	.418
46	Tris Speaker, 1911	.418
47	Dwight Evans, 1987	.417
48	Johnny Pesky, 1951	.417
49	Tris Speaker, 1915	.416
50	Pete Runnels, 1958	.416

Slugging Average

1	Ted Williams, 1941	.735
2	Ted Williams, 1957	.731
3	Jimmie Foxx, 1938	.704
4	Jimmie Foxx, 1939	.694
5	Ted Williams, 1946	.667
6	Babe Ruth, 1919	.657
7	Ted Williams, 1949	.650
8	Ted Williams, 1942	.648
9	**Manny Ramirez, 2002**	**.647**
10	Fred Lynn, 1979	.637
11	**David Ortiz, 2006**	**.636**
12	Ted Williams, 1954	.635
13	Ted Williams, 1947	.634
14	Jimmie Foxx, 1936	.631
15	Carl Yastrzemski, 1967	.622
16	**Manny Ramirez, 2006**	**.619**
17	Ted Williams, 1948	.615
18	**Manny Ramirez, 2004**	**.613**
19	Ted Williams, 1939	.609
20	**Manny Ramirez, 2001**	**.609**
21	Ted Williams, 1956	.605
22	**David Ortiz, 2005**	**.604**
23	Nomar Garciaparra, 1999	.603
24	**David Ortiz, 2004**	**.603**
25	Jim Rice, 1978	.600
26	Nomar Garciaparra, 2000	.599
27	Jim Rice, 1979	.596
28	**Manny Ramirez, 2005**	**.594**
29	Ted Williams, 1940	.594
30	Jim Rice, 1977	.593
31	Carl Yastrzemski, 1970	.592
32	**David Ortiz, 2003**	**.592**
33	Mo Vaughn, 1998	.591
34	Rico Petrocelli, 1969	.589
35	Wade Boggs, 1987	.588
36	**Manny Ramirez, 2003**	**.587**
37	Carl Everett, 2000	.587
38	Nomar Garciaparra, 1998	.584
39	Ted Williams, 1958	.584
40	Walt Dropo, 1950	.583
41	Mo Vaughn, 1996	.583
42	Jimmie Foxx, 1940	.581
43	**Trot Nixon, 2003**	**.578**
44	Mo Vaughn, 1994	.576
45	Mo Vaughn, 1995	.575
46	Dwight Evans, 1987	.569
47	Tris Speaker, 1912	.567
48	Fred Lynn, 1975	.566
49	Mo Vaughn, 1997	.560
50	2 players tied	.556

On-Base plus Slugging

1	Ted Williams, 1941	1287
2	Ted Williams, 1957	1257
3	Jimmie Foxx, 1938	1166
4	Ted Williams, 1946	1164
5	Jimmie Foxx, 1939	1158
6	Ted Williams, 1954	1148
7	Ted Williams, 1942	1147
8	Ted Williams, 1949	1141
9	Ted Williams, 1947	1133
10	Babe Ruth, 1919	1114
11	Ted Williams, 1948	1112
12	**Manny Ramirez, 2002**	**1097**
13	Ted Williams, 1956	1084
14	Jimmie Foxx, 1936	1071
15	Fred Lynn, 1979	1059
16	**Manny Ramirez, 2006**	**1058**
17	Wade Boggs, 1987	1049
18	**David Ortiz, 2006**	**1049**
19	Ted Williams, 1939	1045
20	Carl Yastrzemski, 1970	1044
21	Ted Williams, 1958	1042
22	Carl Yastrzemski, 1967	1040
23	Ted Williams, 1940	1036
24	Nomar Garciaparra, 2000	1033
25	Tris Speaker, 1912	1031
26	Nomar Garciaparra, 1999	1022
27	Ted Williams, 1951	1019
28	**Manny Ramirez, 2003**	**1014**
29	**Manny Ramirez, 2001**	**1014**
30	**Manny Ramirez, 2004**	**1009**
31	Mo Vaughn, 1996	1003
32	**David Ortiz, 2005**	**1001**
33	Mo Vaughn, 1998	993
34	Jimmie Foxx, 1940	993
35	Rico Petrocelli, 1969	992
36	Dwight Evans, 1987	986
37	Mo Vaughn, 1994	984
38	**David Ortiz, 2004**	**983**
39	**Manny Ramirez, 2005**	**982**
40	Mo Vaughn, 1997	980
41	Jim Rice, 1979	977
42	**Trot Nixon, 2003**	**975**
43	Tris Speaker, 1913	974
44	Jim Rice, 1978	970
45	Jim Rice, 1977	969
46	Fred Lynn, 1975	967
47	Wade Boggs, 1988	965
48	Joe Cronin, 1938	964
49	Mo Vaughn, 1995	963
50	**David Ortiz, 2003**	**961**

Adjusted OPS

1	Ted Williams, 1941	232
2	Ted Williams, 1957	227
3	Babe Ruth, 1919	224
4	Ted Williams, 1942	214
5	Ted Williams, 1946	211
6	Ted Williams, 1947	199
7	Ted Williams, 1954	193
8	Carl Yastrzemski, 1967	189
9	Ted Williams, 1949	187
10	Ted Williams, 1948	185
11	Jimmie Foxx, 1939	185
12	Tris Speaker, 1912	185
13	**Manny Ramirez, 2002**	**184**
14	Tris Speaker, 1913	180
15	Jimmie Foxx, 1938	180
16	Tris Speaker, 1914	178
17	Bob Johnson, 1944	175
18	Carl Yastrzemski, 1970	174
19	Ted Williams, 1958	174
20	Fred Lynn, 1979	173
21	Wade Boggs, 1987	172
22	Tris Speaker, 1910	169
23	Carl Yastrzemski, 1968	169
24	**Manny Ramirez, 2006**	**168**
25	Rico Petrocelli, 1969	168
26	Bobby Doerr, 1944	166
27	Wade Boggs, 1988	165
28	Ted Williams, 1956	164
29	**David Ortiz, 2006**	**163**
30	**Manny Ramirez, 2001**	**162**
31	Doc Gessler, 1908	161
32	Ted Williams, 1940	159
33	Ted Williams, 1951	159
34	Dwight Evans, 1981	159
35	Fred Lynn, 1975	159
36	Carlton Fisk, 1972	159
37	Ted Williams, 1939	158
38	**Manny Ramirez, 2003**	**158**
39	Tris Speaker, 1911	158
40	Mike Greenwell, 1988	157
41	Buck Freeman, 1901	157
42	**David Ortiz, 2005**	**156**
43	Wade Boggs, 1986	155
44	Nomar Garciaparra, 2000	155
45	Dwight Evans, 1987	155
46	Ken Harrelson, 1968	154
47	Carl Yastrzemski, 1965	154
48	Jim Rice, 1978	153
49	Jake Stahl, 1909	153
50	Jimmie Foxx, 1936	153

Adjusted Batting Wins

1	Ted Williams, 1941	9.5
2	Ted Williams, 1942	8.9
3	Ted Williams, 1946	8.9
4	Ted Williams, 1957	8.4
5	Ted Williams, 1947	8.3
6	Babe Ruth, 1919	7.7
7	Ted Williams, 1949	7.6
8	Carl Yastrzemski, 1967	7.2
9	Ted Williams, 1948	6.7
10	Tris Speaker, 1912	6.6
11	Carl Yastrzemski, 1970	6.6
12	Jimmie Foxx, 1938	6.4
13	Tris Speaker, 1914	6.1
14	Wade Boggs, 1988	6.1
15	Ted Williams, 1954	6.1
16	Wade Boggs, 1987	6.1
17	Carl Yastrzemski, 1968	5.9
18	Bob Johnson, 1944	5.8
19	Tris Speaker, 1913	5.6
20	Jimmie Foxx, 1939	5.6
21	Fred Lynn, 1979	5.5
22	**Manny Ramirez, 2002**	**5.4**
23	Rico Petrocelli, 1969	5.2
24	Wade Boggs, 1986	5.2
25	**David Ortiz, 2006**	**5.2**
26	Ted Williams, 1955	5.1
27	Ted Williams, 1951	5.0
28	**Manny Ramirez, 2003**	**5.0**
29	Wade Boggs, 1985	5.0
30	Ted Williams, 1940	4.9
31	Mike Greenwell, 1988	4.9
32	Ted Williams, 1958	4.9
33	**David Ortiz, 2005**	**4.9**
34	Ted Williams, 1939	4.8
35	**Manny Ramirez, 2001**	**4.7**
36	Tris Speaker, 1910	4.7
37	**Manny Ramirez, 2006**	**4.6**
38	Jim Rice, 1978	4.6
39	Dwight Evans, 1987	4.5
40	Mo Vaughn, 1996	4.5
41	Earl Webb, 1931	4.3
42	Mo Vaughn, 1998	4.3
43	Jimmie Foxx, 1936	4.3
44	Nomar Garciaparra, 2000	4.2
45	Carl Yastrzemski, 1963	4.2
46	Ted Williams, 1956	4.2
47	Jim Rice, 1979	4.2
48	Wade Boggs, 1983	4.2
49	Fred Lynn, 1975	4.2
50	Dwight Evans, 1984	4.2

Stolen Base Average

1	**Coco Crisp, 2006**	**84.6**
2	Johnny Damon, 2002	83.8
3	Johnny Damon, 2003	83.3
4	Ellis Burks, 1987	81.8
5	Ellis Burks, 1989	80.8
	Otis Nixon, 1994	80.8
7	Billy Werber, 1935	80.6
8	Jackie Jensen, 1959	80.0
	John Valentin, 1995	80.0
10	Tommy Harper, 1973	79.4
11	Tommy Harper, 1972	78.1
12	Joe Foy, 1968	76.5
13	Jackie Jensen, 1954	75.9
14	Ellis Burks, 1988	73.5
15	Pete Fox, 1943	73.3
16	Billy Werber, 1934	72.7
17	Harry Hooper, 1916	71.1
18	Nomar Garciaparra, 1997	71.0
19	Darren Lewis, 1998	70.7
20	Tommy Harper, 1974	70.0
21	Jerry Remy, 1978	69.8
22	Mel Almada, 1935	69.0
23	Buddy Myer, 1928	65.2
24	Jack Rothrock, 1929	64.9

Base Stealing Wins

1	Tommy Harper, 1973	0.7
2	Otis Nixon, 1994	0.5
3	Johnny Damon, 2002	0.5
4	Johnny Damon, 2003	0.4
5	Billy Werber, 1935	0.4
6	Ellis Burks, 1987	0.4
7	Tommy Harper, 1972	0.3
8	Joe Foy, 1968	0.3
9	Billy Werber, 1934	0.3
10	**Coco Crisp, 2006**	**0.3**
11	Ellis Burks, 1989	0.3
12	Jackie Jensen, 1959	0.3
13	Jackie Jensen, 1954	0.2
14	John Valentin, 1995	0.2
15	Ellis Burks, 1988	0.2
16	Harry Hooper, 1916	0.2
17	Pete Fox, 1943	0.2
18	Jerry Remy, 1978	0.2
19	Tommy Harper, 1974	0.2
20	Darren Lewis, 1998	0.2

Pitcher Batting Runs

1	Wes Ferrell, 1935	20.2
2	Babe Ruth, 1917	16.5
3	Babe Ruth, 1915	15.0
4	Babe Ruth, 1916	13.0
5	Red Ruffing, 1928	12.4
6	Babe Ruth, 1918	11.8
7	Cy Young, 1903	11.7
8	Wes Ferrell, 1936	11.3
9	Dave Ferriss, 1945	10.6
10	Joe Wood, 1912	10.1
11	Sonny Siebert, 1971	9.4
12	Carl Mays, 1918	9.3
13	Earl Wilson, 1965	8.5
14	Joe Wood, 1911	8.3
15	Gary Peters, 1971	8.2
16	Earl Wilson, 1964	8.1
17	Wes Ferrell, 1934	7.9
18	Rube Foster, 1915	7.1
19	Carl Mays, 1916	6.8
20	Joe Bush, 1921	6.8
21	Mickey McDermott, 1953	6.8
22	Dave Ferriss, 1947	6.7
23	Lloyd Brown, 1933	6.5
24	Tom Hughes, 1903	6.3
25	Ed Karger, 1910	6.2
26	Gary Peters, 1970	6.2
27	Joe Bush, 1918	6.1
28	Jesse Tannehill, 1905	6.1
29	Carl Mays, 1917	6.0
30	Jesse Tannehill, 1906	5.9
31	Red Ruffing, 1929	5.5
32	Sonny Siebert, 1972	5.5
33	Sam Jones, 1921	5.0
34	Earl Wilson, 1963	5.0
35	Dutch Leonard, 1915	5.0
36	Gordon Rhodes, 1933	5.0
37	Charley Hall, 1912	4.9
38	Johnny Marcum, 1937	4.8
39	Willard Nixon, 1954	4.8
40	Hal Brown, 1953	4.8
41	Willard Nixon, 1955	4.8
42	Willard Nixon, 1957	4.6
43	Joe Wood, 1910	4.6
44	Herb Pennock, 1920	4.4
45	Norwood Gibson, 1903	4.3
46	Tom Brewer, 1956	4.2
47	Mel Parnell, 1951	3.8
48	Gene Conley, 1961	3.8
49	Gene Conley, 1962	3.6
50	Mickey Harris, 1946	3.4

Total Chances/Game (Infield)

First Base

1	Phil Todt, 1926	12.36
2	Stuffy McInnis, 1918	12.19
3	Candy LaChance, 1902	11.72
4	Bob Unglaub, 1907	11.58
5	Stuffy McInnis, 1920	11.38
6	Dick Hoblitzel, 1917	11.36
7	Myron Grimshaw, 1906	11.32
8	Jake Stahl, 1909	11.29
9	Candy LaChance, 1904	11.24
10	Stuffy McInnis, 1919	11.23

Second Base

1	Bill Regan, 1926	6.41
2	Bill Wambsganss, 1924	6.37
3	Hobe Ferris, 1901	6.30
4	Bobby Doerr, 1939	6.24
5	Billy Goodman, 1952	6.21
6	Bobby Doerr, 1949	6.12
7	Bill Regan, 1930	6.11
8	Hobe Ferris, 1907	6.09
9	Bobby Doerr, 1946	6.07
10	Hobe Ferris, 1902	6.06

Shortstop

1	Heinie Wagner, 1907	6.61
2	Heinie Wagner, 1908	6.56
3	Rabbit Warstler, 1932	6.24
4	Everett Scott, 1921	6.06
5	Freddy Parent, 1902	6.06
6	Heinie Wagner, 1909	6.06
7	Heinie Wagner, 1913	5.97
8	Eddie Lake, 1945	5.88
9	Freddy Parent, 1906	5.87
10	Freddy Parent, 1903	5.82

Third Base

1	Jimmy Collins, 1901	4.21
2	Jimmy Collins, 1902	3.90
3	Billy Werber, 1935	3.78
4	Billy Werber, 1934	3.75
5	Ossie Vitt, 1919	3.70
6	Jim Tabor, 1940	3.69
7	Johnny Pesky, 1950	3.69
8	Billy Klaus, 1956	3.61
9	Johnny Pesky, 1949	3.60

Assists/Game (Infield)

First Base

1	Bill Buckner, 1986	1.14
2	Bill Buckner, 1985	1.14
3	Carlos Quintana, 1990	0.93
4	Jimmie Foxx, 1941	0.90
5	Dick Stuart, 1963	0.86
6	Bill Buckner, 1984	0.85
7	Phil Todt, 1926	0.82
8	Dick Gernert, 1958	0.82
9	Phil Todt, 1927	0.81
10	Joe Harris, 1924	0.80

Second Base

1	Bill Regan, 1926	3.69
2	Bill Regan, 1930	3.46
3	Hobe Ferris, 1902	3.44
4	Bill Regan, 1928	3.42
5	Bobby Doerr, 1939	3.42
6	Jody Reed, 1992	3.32
7	Billy Goodman, 1952	3.30
8	Bill Regan, 1927	3.28
9	Hobe Ferris, 1901	3.26
10	Luis Alicea, 1995	3.25

Shortstop

1	Heinie Wagner, 1908	3.72
2	Freddy Parent, 1902	3.57
3	Heinie Wagner, 1907	3.55
4	Billy Klaus, 1957	3.53
5	Eddie Lake, 1945	3.53
6	Rabbit Warstler, 1932	3.49
7	Vern Stephens, 1948	3.48
8	Milt Bolling, 1954	3.46
9	Everett Scott, 1921	3.43
10	Rick Burleson, 1979	3.42

Third Base

1	Billy Werber, 1934	2.48
2	Frank Malzone, 1958	2.44
3	Frank Malzone, 1957	2.42
4	Wade Boggs, 1983	2.41
5	Jimmy Collins, 1902	2.38
6	Jimmy Collins, 1901	2.38
7	Fred Haney, 1926	2.35
8	Frank Malzone, 1959	2.32
9	Ossie Vitt, 1919	2.32
10	Jim Tabor, 1939	2.28

Stolen Bases

1	Tommy Harper, 1973	54
2	Tris Speaker, 1912	52
3	Tris Speaker, 1913	46
4	Tris Speaker, 1914	42
	Otis Nixon, 1994	42
6	Harry Hooper, 1910	40
	Billy Werber, 1934	40
8	Harry Hooper, 1911	38
9	Harry Lord, 1909	36
10	Patsy Dougherty, 1903	35
	Tris Speaker, 1909	35
	Tris Speaker, 1910	35
13	Tommy Dowd, 1901	33
14	Amby McConnell, 1908	31
	Johnny Damon, 2002	31
16	Buddy Myer, 1928	30
	Jerry Remy, 1978	30
	Johnny Damon, 2003	30
19	Chick Stahl, 1901	29
	Harry Hooper, 1912	29
	Hal Janvrin, 1914	29
	Tris Speaker, 1915	29
	Billy Werber, 1935	29
	Darren Lewis, 1998	29
25	Clyde Engle, 1913	28
	Tommy Harper, 1974	28
27	Harry Niles, 1909	27
	Larry Gardner, 1911	27
	Harry Hooper, 1916	27
	Ellis Burks, 1987	27
31	Amby McConnell, 1909	26
	Heinie Wagner, 1910	26
	Harry Hooper, 1913	26
	Joe Foy, 1968	26
35	Freddy Parent, 1905	25
	Tris Speaker, 1911	25
	Larry Gardner, 1912	25
	Tommy Harper, 1972	25
	Ellis Burks, 1988	25
40	Chick Stahl, 1902	24
	Freddy Parent, 1903	24
	Clyde Engle, 1911	24
	Harry Hooper, 1918	24
	Jack Rothrock, 1929	24
45	Jimmy Collins, 1903	23
	Harry Lord, 1908	23
	Harry Hooper, 1919	23
	Mike Menosky, 1920	23
	Billy Werber, 1936	23
	Carl Yastrzemski, 1970	23

Pitcher Batting Average by era

1988–2006

1973–87

1961–72

1	Gary Peters, 1971	.271
2	Sonny Siebert, 1971	.266
3	Gary Peters, 1970	.244
4	Sonny Siebert, 1972	.236
5	Gary Bell, 1968	.220
6	Gene Conley, 1961	.219
7	Earl Wilson, 1963	.208

1943–60

1	Mel Parnell, 1951	.309
2	Mickey McDermott, 1953	.301
3	Tom Brewer, 1956	.298
4	Willard Nixon, 1957	.293
5	Hal Brown, 1953	.293
6	Dave Ferriss, 1947	.273
	Mickey McDermott, 1951	.273

1921–42

1	Wes Ferrell, 1935	.347
2	Joe Bush, 1921	.325
3	Red Ruffing, 1928	.314
4	Red Ruffing, 1929	.307
5	Danny MacFayden, 1927	.283
6	Wes Ferrell, 1934	.282
7	Lloyd Brown, 1933	.281

1901–20

1	Babe Ruth, 1917	.325
2	Cy Young, 1903	.321
3	Babe Ruth, 1915	.315
4	Ed Karger, 1910	.294
5	Joe Wood, 1912	.290
6	Carl Mays, 1918	.288
7	Tom Hughes, 1903	.280

Fielding Average

First Base

1	Stuffy McInnis, 1921	.999
2	Phil Todt, 1928	.997
3	Carl Yastrzemski, 1975	.996
4	Stuffy McInnis, 1920	.996
5	Nick Esasky, 1989	.996

Second Base

1	**Mark Loretta, 2006**	**.994**
2	Bobby Doerr, 1948	.993
3	Chuck Schilling, 1961	.991
4	Marty Barrett, 1988	.990
5	Bobby Doerr, 1943	.990

Shortstop

1	**Alex Gonzalez, 2006**	**.985**
2	Vern Stephens, 1950	.981
3	Rico Petrocelli, 1969	.981
4	Rick Burleson, 1978	.981
5	Rick Burleson, 1979	.980

Third Base

1	**Mike Lowell, 2006**	**.987**
2	Rico Petrocelli, 1971	.976
3	Grady Hatton, 1955	.976
4	Johnny Pesky, 1950	.974
5	Bill Mueller, 2005	.972

Outfield (250 chances accepted)

1	Ken Harrelson, 1968	1.000
	Carl Yastrzemski, 1977	1.000
3	Johnny Damon, 2003	.997
4	Johnny Damon, 2002	.997
5	**Trot Nixon, 2005**	**.996**
6	Babe Ruth, 1919	.996
7	Darren Bragg, 1998	.996
8	**Trot Nixon, 2006**	**.995**
9	Ted Williams, 1957	.995
10	Dwight Evans, 1973	.995

Catcher

1	Pete Daley, 1957	1.000
	Rick Cerone, 1988	1.000
3	**Jason Varitek, 2004**	**.998**
4	**Jason Varitek, 2002**	**.996**
5	Damon Berryhill, 1994	.995

Pitcher (90 chances accepted)

1	Carl Mays, 1917	.993
2	Jesse Tannehill, 1904	.991
3	Jack Quinn, 1922	.990
4	Babe Ruth, 1917	.984
5	Ted Wingfield, 1925	.983

Assists (Infield)

First Base

1	Bill Buckner, 1985	184
2	Bill Buckner, 1986	157
3	Carlos Quintana, 1990	137
4	Dick Stuart, 1963	134
5	Phil Todt, 1926	126
6	Tony Lupien, 1943	118
7	Jimmie Foxx, 1938	116
	Rudy York, 1946	116
9	George Scott, 1977	115
10	Phil Todt, 1927	112
	Jimmie Foxx, 1941	112
	George Scott, 1966	112

Second Base

1	Bill Wambsganss, 1924	494
2	Bobby Doerr, 1943	490
3	Del Pratt, 1922	484
4	Bobby Doerr, 1946	483
5	Bobby Doerr, 1940	480
6	Marty Barrett, 1985	479
7	Jody Reed, 1992	472
8	Bill Regan, 1928	469
9	Bobby Doerr, 1947	466
10	Hobe Ferris, 1902	461

Shortstop

1	Heinie Wagner, 1908	569
2	Vern Stephens, 1948	540
3	Everett Scott, 1921	528
	Rick Burleson, 1980	528
5	Rick Burleson, 1979	523
6	Vern Stephens, 1949	508
7	Hal Rhyne, 1931	502
8	Rick Burleson, 1975	498
9	Everett Scott, 1920	496
10	Freddy Parent, 1904	493

Third Base

1	Frank Malzone, 1958	378
2	Frank Malzone, 1957	370
3	Wade Boggs, 1983	368
4	Frank Malzone, 1959	357
5	Jim Tabor, 1939	338
6	Wade Boggs, 1985	335
7	Rico Petrocelli, 1971	334
8	Johnny Pesky, 1949	333
9	Wade Boggs, 1984	330
10	Jimmy Collins, 1901	328

Double Plays

First Base

1	Rudy York, 1946	154
2	Jimmie Foxx, 1938	153
3	George Scott, 1977	150
	Tony Perez, 1980	150
5	Tony Lupien, 1943	149

Second Base

1	Bobby Doerr, 1949	134
2	Bobby Doerr, 1943	132
3	Bobby Doerr, 1950	130
4	Bobby Doerr, 1946	129
5	Chuck Schilling, 1961	121

Shortstop

1	Rick Burleson, 1980	147
2	Vern Stephens, 1949	128
3	Vern Stephens, 1950	115
4	Vern Stephens, 1948	113
	Nomar Garciaparra, 1997	113

Third Base

1	Johnny Pesky, 1949	48
2	Frank Malzone, 1961	45
3	Frank Malzone, 1959	40
	Wade Boggs, 1983	40
5	**Mike Lowell, 2006**	**39**

Outfield

1	Tris Speaker, 1909	12
	Tris Speaker, 1914	12
3	Chick Stahl, 1906	9
	Duffy Lewis, 1910	9
	Tris Speaker, 1912	9
	Nemo Leibold, 1921	9
7	6 players tied	8

Catcher

1	Muddy Ruel, 1922	17
2	Wally Schang, 1919	15
	Roxy Walters, 1920	15
	Tony Pena, 1991	15
5	7 players tied	13

Pitcher

1	Dave Ferriss, 1945	10
2	Howard Ehmke, 1923	8
	Bob Stanley, 1980	8
4	Joe Bush, 1920	7
	Bob Weiland, 1932	7
	Tex Hughson, 1942	7
	Tom Brewer, 1958	7

Putouts (Outfield)

Outfield

1	Dom DiMaggio, 1948	503
2	Tom Oliver, 1930	477
3	Jim Piersall, 1956	455
4	Doc Cramer, 1936	443
5	Dom DiMaggio, 1942	439
6	Tom Oliver, 1931	433
7	Ira Flagstead, 1925	429
8	Jim Piersall, 1955	425
9	Tris Speaker, 1914	423
10	Dom DiMaggio, 1949	420
11	Doc Cramer, 1938	417
12	Dom DiMaggio, 1947	413
13	Fred Lynn, 1978	408
14	Fred Lynn, 1975	404
15	Jim Piersall, 1957	397
16	Johnny Damon, 2005	394
17	Dom DiMaggio, 1946	390
	Dom DiMaggio, 1950	390
	Reggie Smith, 1968	390
20	Dom DiMaggio, 1941	386
	Reggie Smith, 1971	386
22	Tom Umphlett, 1953	382
	Darren Lewis, 1998	382
24	Fred Lynn, 1979	381
25	Tris Speaker, 1915	378
26	Dom DiMaggio, 1951	376
27	Tris Speaker, 1913	374
	Ira Flagstead, 1924	374
29	Tris Speaker, 1912	372
	Carl Yastrzemski, 1964	372
31	Ellis Burks, 1988	370
32	Fred Lynn, 1976	367
33	Doc Cramer, 1937	365
	Darren Bragg, 1997	365
35	Johnny Damon, 2003	362
36	Reggie Smith, 1970	361
37	Doc Cramer, 1939	356
38	Jim Piersall, 1953	352
	Johnny Damon, 2002	352
40	Johnny Damon, 2004	349
41	Ted Williams, 1947	347
42	Ira Flagstead, 1928	346
	Dwight Evans, 1982	346
44	Chick Stahl, 1906	344
45	Jack Rothrock, 1929	342
46	Jim Rice, 1983	339
47	Tris Speaker, 1910	337
	Mel Almada, 1935	337
	Ted Williams, 1949	337
50	Jim Rice, 1984	336

Fielding Runs

First Base

1	Bill Buckner, 1985	25
2	Bill Buckner, 1986	19
3	Carlos Quintana, 1990	13
4	Jimmie Foxx, 1937	11
5	Kevin Millar, 2005	10

Second Base

1	Marty Barrett, 1987	33
2	Jody Reed, 1992	30
3	Bobby Doerr, 1946	27
4	Bobby Doerr, 1949	27
5	Bobby Doerr, 1939	26

Shortstop

1	Everett Scott, 1921	41
2	Heinie Wagner, 1908	32
3	Rick Burleson, 1980	31
4	Rick Burleson, 1979	30
5	Eddie Lake, 1945	24

Third Base

1	Wade Boggs, 1984	22
2	Billy Werber, 1934	22
3	Frank Malzone, 1957	21
4	**Mike Lowell, 2006**	**21**
5	Johnny Pesky, 1949	19

Outfield

1	Tris Speaker, 1914	23
2	Carl Yastrzemski, 1964	19
3	Dwight Evans, 1975	19
4	Tris Speaker, 1913	19
5	Tris Speaker, 1909	18
6	Tris Speaker, 1912	16
7	Dom DiMaggio, 1947	15
8	Ira Flagstead, 1923	14
9	Ira Flagstead, 1925	14
10	Dom DiMaggio, 1942	13

Catcher

1	Lou Criger, 1903	23
2	Tony Pena, 1993	20
3	Lou Criger, 1901	20
4	Carlton Fisk, 1976	19
5	Tony Pena, 1992	19

Pitcher

1	Carl Mays, 1918	9
2	Carl Mays, 1916	9
3	Carl Mays, 1917	8
4	Joe Wood, 1912	7
5	Ted Wingfield, 1925	7

Relative Batting Average

1	Ted Williams, 1957	1.476
2	Ted Williams, 1941	1.472
3	Wade Boggs, 1988	1.413
4	Wade Boggs, 1985	1.407
5	Tris Speaker, 1912	1.406
6	Tris Speaker, 1913	1.374
7	Wade Boggs, 1987	1.370
8	Wade Boggs, 1986	1.365
9	Tris Speaker, 1910	1.361
10	Wade Boggs, 1983	1.359
11	Ted Williams, 1948	1.353
12	Nomar Garciaparra, 2000	1.348
13	Carl Yastrzemski, 1967	1.343
14	Ted Williams, 1942	1.341
15	**Manny Ramirez, 2002**	**1.320**
16	Tris Speaker, 1914	1.318
17	Carney Lansford, 1981	1.311
18	Ted Williams, 1947	1.306
19	Ted Williams, 1946	1.299
20	Ted Williams, 1954	1.299
21	Nomar Garciaparra, 1999	1.299
22	Ted Williams, 1956	1.291
23	Fred Lynn, 1975	1.285
24	Carl Yastrzemski, 1970	1.274
25	Wade Boggs, 1991	1.274
26	Johnny Pesky, 1946	1.271
27	Billy Goodman, 1950	1.270
28	Wade Boggs, 1989	1.266
29	Ted Williams, 1949	1.266
30	Carl Yastrzemski, 1968	1.263
31	Tris Speaker, 1915	1.261
32	Carl Yastrzemski, 1963	1.258
33	Patsy Dougherty, 1903	1.257
34	Ted Williams, 1958	1.256
35	Jimmie Foxx, 1939	1.256
36	Mike Greenwell, 1988	1.255
37	Doc Gessler, 1908	1.254
38	Harry Lord, 1909	1.245
39	George Scott, 1967	1.245
40	Johnny Pesky, 1942	1.244
41	Carl Yastrzemski, 1965	1.243
42	Mo Vaughn, 1998	1.238
43	Pete Runnels, 1962	1.238
44	Jim Rice, 1986	1.238
45	Fred Lynn, 1979	1.236
46	Johnny Pesky, 1947	1.236
47	Ted Williams, 1940	1.232
48	Wade Boggs, 1984	1.232
49	Pete Runnels, 1958	1.232
50	Fred Lynn, 1976	1.225

Putouts/Game (Outfield)

Outfield

1	Dom DiMaggio, 1948	3.25
2	Tom Oliver, 1930	3.10
3	Dom DiMaggio, 1947	3.08
4	Ira Flagstead, 1925	2.98
5	Jim Piersall, 1956	2.94
6	Tom Oliver, 1931	2.93
7	Dom DiMaggio, 1949	2.92
8	Dom DiMaggio, 1942	2.91
9	Jim Piersall, 1955	2.89
10	Doc Cramer, 1936	2.88
11	Fred Lynn, 1976	2.87
12	Tom Oliver, 1932	2.83
13	Doc Cramer, 1938	2.82
14	Tony Armas, 1983	2.81
15	Tom Umphlett, 1953	2.81
16	Fred Lynn, 1975	2.81
17	Dom DiMaggio, 1950	2.79
18	Dom DiMaggio, 1946	2.75
19	Fred Lynn, 1980	2.75
20	Doc Cramer, 1937	2.74
21	Fred Lynn, 1978	2.74
22	Tris Speaker, 1914	2.71
23	Tris Speaker, 1913	2.69
24	Dom DiMaggio, 1941	2.68
25	Johnny Damon, 2005	2.68
26	Jack Rothrock, 1929	2.67
27	Fred Lynn, 1979	2.66
28	Fred Lynn, 1977	2.66
29	Doc Cramer, 1939	2.64
30	Jim Piersall, 1957	2.63
31	Tony Armas, 1984	2.61
32	Ellis Burks, 1988	2.61
33	Ira Flagstead, 1924	2.60
34	Dom DiMaggio, 1951	2.58
35	Ira Flagstead, 1928	2.56
36	Ira Flagstead, 1927	2.53
37	Tris Speaker, 1915	2.52
38	Reggie Smith, 1968	2.52
39	Johnny Damon, 2003	2.51
40	Carl Yastrzemski, 1964	2.51
41	Darren Lewis, 1998	2.51
42	Jim Piersall, 1958	2.51
43	Reggie Smith, 1970	2.49
44	Otis Nixon, 1994	2.47
45	Dom DiMaggio, 1952	2.46
46	Dwight Evans, 1975	2.44
47	Darren Bragg, 1997	2.43
48	Tris Speaker, 1912	2.43
49	Reggie Smith, 1971	2.43
50	Ellis Burks, 1987	2.42

Fielding Average

First Base

1	Stuffy McInnis, 1921	.999
2	Phil Todt, 1928	.997
3	Carl Yastrzemski, 1975	.996
4	Stuffy McInnis, 1920	.996
5	Nick Esasky, 1989	.996

Second Base

1	**Mark Loretta, 2006**	**.994**
2	Bobby Doerr, 1948	.993
3	Chuck Schilling, 1961	.991
4	Marty Barrett, 1988	.990
5	Bobby Doerr, 1943	.990

Shortstop

1	**Alex Gonzalez, 2006**	**.985**
2	Vern Stephens, 1950	.981
3	Rico Petrocelli, 1969	.981
4	Rick Burleson, 1978	.981
5	Rick Burleson, 1979	.980

Third Base

1	**Mike Lowell, 2006**	**.987**
2	Rico Petrocelli, 1971	.976
3	Grady Hatton, 1955	.976
4	Johnny Pesky, 1950	.974
5	Bill Mueller, 2005	.972

Outfield (250 chances accepted)

1	Ken Harrelson, 1968	1.000
	Carl Yastrzemski, 1977	1.000
3	Johnny Damon, 2003	.997
4	Johnny Damon, 2002	.997
5	**Trot Nixon, 2005**	**.996**
6	Babe Ruth, 1919	.996
7	Darren Bragg, 1998	.996
8	**Trot Nixon, 2006**	**.995**
9	Ted Williams, 1957	.995
10	Dwight Evans, 1973	.995

Catcher

1	Pete Daley, 1957	1.000
	Rick Cerone, 1988	1.000
3	**Jason Varitek, 2004**	**.998**
4	**Jason Varitek, 2002**	**.996**
5	Damon Berryhill, 1994	.995

Pitcher (90 chances accepted)

1	Carl Mays, 1917	.993
2	Jesse Tannehill, 1904	.991
3	Jack Quinn, 1922	.990
4	Babe Ruth, 1917	.984
5	Ted Wingfield, 1925	.983

Batter-Fielder Wins by era

1988–2006

1	Wade Boggs, 1988	6.4
2	Nomar Garciaparra, 2002	5.4
3	Nomar Garciaparra, 2000	5.0
4	Mike Greenwell, 1988	4.7
	Nomar Garciaparra, 1999	4.7
6	John Valentin, 1995	4.6
	Manny Ramirez, 2002	**4.6**
8	**David Ortiz, 2006**	**4.5**
9	Wade Boggs, 1989	4.3
10	**David Ortiz, 2005**	**4.2**
11	**Manny Ramirez, 2003**	**4.1**
12	John Valentin, 1997	4.0
13	Wade Boggs, 1991	3.8
	Manny Ramirez, 2001	**3.8**

1973–87

1	Wade Boggs, 1987	6.5
2	Wade Boggs, 1985	5.6
3	Wade Boggs, 1986	5.4
4	Fred Lynn, 1979	5.3
5	Carlton Fisk, 1977	4.6
6	Wade Boggs, 1983	4.4
	Wade Boggs, 1984	4.4
8	Jim Rice, 1978	4.2
9	Fred Lynn, 1975	4.1
10	Carlton Fisk, 1978	3.9
11	Rick Burleson, 1980	3.7
12	Dwight Evans, 1981	3.6
13	Rich Gedman, 1985	3.5
14	Carlton Fisk, 1976	3.3
	Jim Rice, 1983	3.3
	Jim Rice, 1986	3.3

1961–72

1	Rico Petrocelli, 1969	7.6
2	Carl Yastrzemski, 1967	6.9
3	Carl Yastrzemski, 1968	6.3
4	Carl Yastrzemski, 1970	5.5
5	Carlton Fisk, 1972	5.1
6	Carl Yastrzemski, 1963	4.2
7	Eddie Bressoud, 1962	3.7
8	Carl Yastrzemski, 1964	3.5
	Carl Yastrzemski, 1965	3.5
10	Mike Andrews, 1968	3.3
11	Ken Harrelson, 1968	3.1

1943–60

1	Ted Williams, 1946	8.1
2	Ted Williams, 1957	7.3
3	Ted Williams, 1947	7.2
4	Eddie Lake, 1945	6.5
5	Ted Williams, 1949	6.4
6	Ted Williams, 1948	5.9
7	Bob Johnson, 1944	5.3
8	Bobby Doerr, 1944	5.1
	Bobby Doerr, 1949	5.1
	Ted Williams, 1954	5.1
11	Bobby Doerr, 1946	4.8
12	Johnny Pesky, 1946	4.6
13	Ted Williams, 1955	4.3
14	Ted Williams, 1951	4.1
	Pete Runnels, 1958	4.1

1921–42

1	Ted Williams, 1941	8.5
	Ted Williams, 1942	8.5
3	Jimmie Foxx, 1938	5.8
4	Jimmie Foxx, 1939	5.2
5	Johnny Pesky, 1942	4.5
6	Joe Cronin, 1938	4.4
7	Topper Rigney, 1926	4.3
8	Ted Williams, 1939	4.1
	Bobby Doerr, 1942	4.1
10	Ted Williams, 1940	4.0
11	Billy Werber, 1934	3.9
12	Joe Cronin, 1941	3.5
13	Jimmie Foxx, 1936	3.3
14	Joe Cronin, 1939	3.2

1901–20

1	Tris Speaker, 1914	7.3
	Babe Ruth, 1919	7.3
3	Tris Speaker, 1912	7.2
4	Tris Speaker, 1913	6.5
5	Tris Speaker, 1910	4.8
6	Tris Speaker, 1909	4.6
7	Jimmy Collins, 1901	4.2
8	Tris Speaker, 1915	3.6
9	Tris Speaker, 1911	3.3
	Larry Gardner, 1911	3.3
11	Heinie Wagner, 1908	3.2
12	Wally Schang, 1919	3.1
13	Jimmy Collins, 1903	2.9

Batter-Fielder Wins

1	Ted Williams, 1941	8.5
	Ted Williams, 1942	8.5
3	Ted Williams, 1946	8.1
4	Rico Petrocelli, 1969	7.6
5	Tris Speaker, 1914	7.3
	Babe Ruth, 1919	7.3
	Ted Williams, 1957	7.3
8	Tris Speaker, 1912	7.2
	Ted Williams, 1947	7.2
10	Carl Yastrzemski, 1967	6.9
11	Tris Speaker, 1913	6.5
	Eddie Lake, 1945	6.5
	Wade Boggs, 1987	6.5
14	Ted Williams, 1949	6.4
	Wade Boggs, 1988	6.4
16	Carl Yastrzemski, 1968	6.3
17	Ted Williams, 1948	5.9
18	Jimmie Foxx, 1938	5.8
19	Wade Boggs, 1985	5.6
20	Carl Yastrzemski, 1970	5.5
21	Wade Boggs, 1986	5.4
	Nomar Garciaparra, 2002	5.4
23	Bob Johnson, 1944	5.3
	Fred Lynn, 1979	5.3
25	Jimmie Foxx, 1939	5.2
26	Bobby Doerr, 1944	5.1
	Bobby Doerr, 1949	5.1
	Ted Williams, 1954	5.1
	Carlton Fisk, 1972	5.1
30	Nomar Garciaparra, 2000	5.0
31	Tris Speaker, 1910	4.8
	Bobby Doerr, 1946	4.8
33	Mike Greenwell, 1988	4.7
	Nomar Garciaparra, 1999	4.7
35	Tris Speaker, 1909	4.6
	Johnny Pesky, 1946	4.6
	Carlton Fisk, 1977	4.6
	John Valentin, 1995	4.6
	Manny Ramirez, 2002	**4.6**
40	Johnny Pesky, 1942	4.5
	David Ortiz, 2006	**4.5**
42	Joe Cronin, 1938	4.4
	Wade Boggs, 1983	4.4
	Wade Boggs, 1984	4.4
45	Topper Rigney, 1926	4.3
	Ted Williams, 1955	4.3
	Wade Boggs, 1989	4.3
48	4 players tied	4.2

Pinch Hits

1	Joe Cronin, 1943	18
2	Rick Miller, 1983	17
3	Dick Williams, 1963	16
4	Lenny Green, 1966	15
5	Rick Miller, 1984	14
6	Bing Miller, 1935	13
	Lou Finney, 1939	13
	Dalton Jones, 1966	13
	Dalton Jones, 1967	13
10	Charlie Maxwell, 1954	12

Pinch Hit Average

1	Vic Wertz, 1960	.556
2	Bernie Carbo, 1974	.500
	Doug Griffin, 1975	.500
4	Rick Miller, 1983	.486
5	Ted Williams, 1959	.458
6	Mike Stanley, 1997	.450
7	Joe Cronin, 1943	.429
8	Tony Horton, 1967	.429
9	Russ Nixon, 1961	.421
10	Gary Geiger, 1960	.417

Pinch Hit Home Runs

1	Joe Cronin, 1943	5
2	Del Wilber, 1953	4
3	Charlie Maxwell, 1951	3
	Ted Williams, 1957	3
5	Many players tied	2

Wins

1	Joe Wood, 1912	34
2	Cy Young, 1901	33
3	Cy Young, 1902	32
4	Cy Young, 1903	28
5	Cy Young, 1904	26
6	Wes Ferrell, 1935	25
	Dave Ferriss, 1946	25
	Mel Parnell, 1949	25
9	Babe Ruth, 1917	24
	Roger Clemens, 1986	24
11	Bill Dinneen, 1904	23
	Joe Wood, 1911	23
	Babe Ruth, 1916	23
	Sam Jones, 1921	23
	Ellis Kinder, 1949	23
	Pedro Martinez, 1999	23
17	Jesse Tannehill, 1905	22
	Carl Mays, 1917	22
	Tex Hughson, 1942	22
	Jim Lonborg, 1967	22
	Luis Tiant, 1974	22
22	Bill Dinneen, 1902	21
	Bill Dinneen, 1903	21
	Jesse Tannehill, 1904	21
	Cy Young, 1907	21
	Cy Young, 1908	21
	Carl Mays, 1918	21
	Dave Ferriss, 1945	21
	Mel Parnell, 1953	21
	Luis Tiant, 1976	21
	Roger Clemens, 1990	21
	Derek Lowe, 2002	21
	Curt Schilling, 2004	**21**
34	Tom Hughes, 1903	20
	Hugh Bedient, 1912	20
	Buck O'Brien, 1912	20
	Ray Collins, 1914	20
	Howard Ehmke, 1923	20
	Lefty Grove, 1935	20
	Wes Ferrell, 1936	20
	Tex Hughson, 1946	20
	Bill Monbouquette, 1963	20
	Luis Tiant, 1973	20
	Dennis Eckersley, 1978	20
	Roger Clemens, 1987	20
	Pedro Martinez, 2002	20
47	Many players tied	19

Wins by era

1988–2006		
1	Pedro Martinez, 1999	23
2	Roger Clemens, 1990	21
	Derek Lowe, 2002	21
	Curt Schilling, 2004	**21**
5	Pedro Martinez, 2002	20
6	Pedro Martinez, 1998	19
7	5 players tied	18
1973–87		
1	Roger Clemens, 1986	24
2	Luis Tiant, 1974	22
3	Luis Tiant, 1976	21
4	Luis Tiant, 1973	20
	Dennis Eckersley, 1978	20
	Roger Clemens, 1987	20
7	Rick Wise, 1975	19
1961–72		
1	Jim Lonborg, 1967	22
2	Bill Monbouquette, 1963	20
3	Ray Culp, 1969	17
	Ray Culp, 1970	17
	Marty Pattin, 1972	17
6	Dick Radatz, 1964	16
	Ray Culp, 1968	16
	Dick Ellsworth, 1968	16
	Gary Peters, 1970	16
	Sonny Siebert, 1971	16
1943–60		
1	Dave Ferriss, 1946	25
	Mel Parnell, 1949	25
3	Ellis Kinder, 1949	23
4	Dave Ferriss, 1945	21
	Mel Parnell, 1953	21
6	Tex Hughson, 1946	20
7	Tom Brewer, 1956	19
1921–42		
1	Wes Ferrell, 1935	25
2	Sam Jones, 1921	23
3	Tex Hughson, 1942	22
4	Howard Ehmke, 1923	20
	Lefty Grove, 1935	20
	Wes Ferrell, 1936	20
7	3 players tied	19
1901–20		
1	Joe Wood, 1912	34
2	Cy Young, 1901	33
3	Cy Young, 1902	32
4	Cy Young, 1903	28
5	Cy Young, 1904	26
6	Babe Ruth, 1917	24
7	Bill Dinneen, 1904	23
	Joe Wood, 1911	23
	Babe Ruth, 1916	23

Losses

1	Red Ruffing, 1928	25
2	Red Ruffing, 1929	22
3	Bill Dinneen, 1902	21
	Cy Young, 1906	21
	Joe Harris, 1906	21
	Slim Harriss, 1927	21
7	Sam Jones, 1919	20
	Howard Ehmke, 1925	20
	Milt Gaston, 1930	20
	Jack Russell, 1930	20
11	Cy Young, 1905	19
	Bill Dinneen, 1906	19
	Ted Wingfield, 1925	19
	Milt Gaston, 1929	19
15	George Winter, 1906	18
	Red Ruffing, 1925	18
	Paul Zahniser, 1926	18
	Hal Wiltse, 1927	18
	Danny Mac Fayden, 1929	18
	Jack Russell, 1929	18
	Jack Russell, 1931	18
	Bill Monbouquette, 1965	18
	Dave Morehead, 1965	18
24	Ted Lewis, 1901	17
	George Winter, 1905	17
	Joe Wood, 1911	17
	Dutch Leonard, 1913	17
	Dutch Leonard, 1917	17
	Herb Pennock, 1922	17
	Bill Piercy, 1923	17
	Howard Ehmke, 1923	17
	Jack Quinn, 1923	17
	Howard Ehmke, 1924	17
	Alex Ferguson, 1924	17
	Hod Lisenbee, 1930	17
	Jim Lonborg, 1965	17
37	Cy Young, 1904	16
	Sam Jones, 1920	16
	Sam Jones, 1921	16
	Jack Quinn, 1922	16
	Alex Ferguson, 1922	16
	Ted Wingfield, 1926	16
	Bob Weiland, 1932	16
	Fritz Ostermueller, 1936	16
	Jim Bagby, 1940	16
	Frank Sullivan, 1960	16
	Earl Wilson, 1963	16
	Ray Culp, 1971	16
	Mike Torrez, 1980	16
50	Many players tied	15

Winning Percentage

1	Bob Stanley, 1978	.882
2	Joe Wood, 1912	.872
3	Roger Clemens, 1986	.857
4	Pedro Martinez, 1999	.852
5	Pedro Martinez, 2002	.833
6	Dave Ferriss, 1946	.806
7	Ellis Kinder, 1949	.793
8	Dutch Leonard, 1914	.792
9	Lefty Grove, 1939	.789
10	Tex Hughson, 1942	.786
11	Tex Hughson, 1944	.783
	Jack Kramer, 1948	.783
13	Mel Parnell, 1949	.781
14	Roger Clemens, 1990	.778
	Curt Schilling, 2004	**.778**
16	Cy Young, 1901	.767
17	Sam Jones, 1918	.762
18	Cy Young, 1903	.757
19	Joe Wood, 1915	.750
	Bruce Hurst, 1988	.750
	Erik Hanson, 1995	.750
	Pedro Martinez, 2000	.750
23	Cy Young, 1902	.744
24	Tom Hughes, 1903	.741
25	Pedro Martinez, 1998	.731
26	Ray Culp, 1968	.727
27	Mel Parnell, 1953	.724
	Derek Lowe, 2002	.724
29	Dick Radatz, 1963	.714
	Luis Tiant, 1972	.714
	Dennis Eckersley, 1978	.714
32	Jesse Tannehill, 1905	.710
	Carl Mays, 1917	.710
	Jim Lonborg, 1967	.710
35	Derek Lowe, 2003	.708
36	Ray Collins, 1913	.704
	Ernie Shore, 1915	.704
	Rube Foster, 1915	.704
39	Dick Ellsworth, 1968	.696
40	Babe Ruth, 1915	.692
	Joe Dobson, 1947	.692
42	Hugh Bedient, 1912	.690
	Roger Clemens, 1987	.690
44	Dutch Leonard, 1915	.682
	Don Schwall, 1961	.682
	David Wells, 2005	.682
	Curt Schilling, 2006	**.682**
48	Ray Culp, 1969	.680
	Mike Boddicker, 1990	.680
	Tim Wakefield, 1998	**.680**

Games

1	**Mike Timlin, 2005**	**81**
2	Greg Harris, 1993	80
3	Dick Radatz, 1964	79
4	**Mike Timlin, 2004**	**76**
5	Heathcliff Slocumb, 1996	75
6	Rob Murphy, 1989	74
	Derek Lowe, 1999	74
	Derek Lowe, 2000	74
9	Tom Gordon, 1998	73
10	**Mike Timlin, 2003**	**72**
	Keith Foulke, 2004	**72**
12	Sparky Lyle, 1969	71
	Alan Embree, 2004	71
14	Mike Fornieles, 1960	70
	Greg Harris, 1992	70
16	Ellis Kinder, 1953	69
	Bill Campbell, 1977	69
18	Rob Murphy, 1990	68
	Rod Beck, 2001	68
	Mike Timlin, 2006	**68**
21	Derek Lowe, 2001	67
22	Dick Radatz, 1963	66
	Bob Stanley, 1986	66
24	Jack Lamabe, 1963	65
	Alan Embree, 2003	65
26	Bob Stanley, 1983	64
	Lee Smith, 1988	64
	Lee Smith, 1989	64
	Tony Fossas, 1991	64
	Rheal Cormier, 2000	64
	Rich Garces, 2000	64
32	Ellis Kinder, 1951	63
	Dick Radatz, 1965	63
	Sparky Lyle, 1970	63
	Stan Belinda, 1995	63
	Derek Lowe, 1998	63
37	Dick Radatz, 1962	62
	Tom Burgmeier, 1980	62
	Calvin Schiraldi, 1987	62
	Rich Garces, 2001	62
41	Ugueth Urbina, 2002	61
42	John Wyatt, 1967	60
	Rheal Cormier, 1999	60
44	Jim Corsi, 1998	59
	Jonathan Papelbon, 2006	**59**
46	Diego Segui, 1974	58
	Julian Tavarez, 2006	**58**
48	5 players tied	57

Games by era

1988–2006		
1	**Mike Timlin, 2005**	**81**
2	Greg Harris, 1993	80
3	**Mike Timlin, 2004**	**76**
4	Heathcliff Slocumb, 1996	75
5	Rob Murphy, 1989	74
	Derek Lowe, 1999	74
	Derek Lowe, 2000	74
1973–87		
1	Bill Campbell, 1977	69
2	Bob Stanley, 1986	66
3	Bob Stanley, 1983	64
4	Tom Burgmeier, 1980	62
	Calvin Schiraldi, 1987	62
6	Diego Segui, 1974	58
7	Bob Stanley, 1984	57
1961–72		
1	Dick Radatz, 1964	79
2	Sparky Lyle, 1969	71
3	Dick Radatz, 1963	66
4	Jack Lamabe, 1963	65
5	Dick Radatz, 1965	63
	Sparky Lyle, 1970	63
7	Dick Radatz, 1962	62
1943–60		
1	Mike Fornieles, 1960	70
2	Ellis Kinder, 1953	69
3	Ellis Kinder, 1951	63
4	Murray Wall, 1958	52
5	Mace Brown, 1943	49
	Ike Delock, 1957	49
7	Ellis Kinder, 1950	48
	Ellis Kinder, 1954	48
	Ike Delock, 1956	48
1921–42		
1	Wilcy Moore, 1931	53
2	Jack Wilson, 1937	51
3	Emerson Dickman, 1939	48
4	Ed Morris, 1928	47
	Bob Kline, 1932	47
	Johnny Welch, 1933	47
7	Bob Kline, 1933	46
	Joe Heving, 1939	46
1901–20		
1	Dutch Leonard, 1916	48
2	Cy Young, 1902	45
	Frank Arellanes, 1909	45
4	Joe Wood, 1911	44
	Babe Ruth, 1916	44
	Carl Mays, 1916	44
7	5 players tied	43

Games Started

1	Cy Young, 1902	43
2	Bill Dinneen, 1902	42
3	Cy Young, 1901	41
	Cy Young, 1904	41
	Babe Ruth, 1916	41
6	Howard Ehmke, 1923	39
	Jim Lonborg, 1967	39
8	Joe Wood, 1912	38
	Babe Ruth, 1917	38
	Sam Jones, 1921	38
	Wes Ferrell, 1935	38
	Wes Ferrell, 1936	38
	Luis Tiant, 1974	38
	Luis Tiant, 1976	38
15	Bill Dinneen, 1904	37
	Cy Young, 1907	37
	Bill Lee, 1974	37
18	Dutch Leonard, 1917	36
	Howard Ehmke, 1924	36
	Bill Monbouquette, 1963	36
	Earl Wilson, 1965	36
	Mike Torrez, 1978	36
	Mike Torrez, 1979	36
	Roger Clemens, 1987	36
25	Cy Young, 1903	35
	Tex Hughson, 1946	35
	Dave Ferriss, 1946	35
	Frank Sullivan, 1955	35
	Bill Monbouquette, 1962	35
	Bill Monbouquette, 1964	35
	Bill Monbouquette, 1965	35
	Ray Culp, 1971	35
	Marty Pattin, 1972	35
	Luis Tiant, 1973	35
	Luis Tiant, 1975	35
	Rick Wise, 1975	35
	Dennis Eckersley, 1978	35
	Oil Can Boyd, 1985	35
	Roger Clemens, 1988	35
	Roger Clemens, 1989	35
	Roger Clemens, 1991	35
	Frank Viola, 1992	35
43	Many players tied	34

Games Started by era

1988–2006		
1	Roger Clemens, 1988	35
	Roger Clemens, 1989	35
	Roger Clemens, 1991	35
	Frank Viola, 1992	35
5	Mike Boddicker, 1989	34
	Mike Boddicker, 1990	34
	Danny Darwin, 1993	34
	Roger Clemens, 1996	34
	Tom Gordon, 1996	34
1973–87		
1	Luis Tiant, 1974	38
	Luis Tiant, 1976	38
3	Bill Lee, 1974	37
4	Mike Torrez, 1978	36
	Mike Torrez, 1979	36
	Roger Clemens, 1987	36
7	Luis Tiant, 1973	35
	Luis Tiant, 1975	35
	Rick Wise, 1975	35
	Dennis Eckersley, 1978	35
	Oil Can Boyd, 1985	35
1961–72		
1	Jim Lonborg, 1967	39
2	Bill Monbouquette, 1963	36
	Earl Wilson, 1965	36
4	Bill Monbouquette, 1962	35
	Bill Monbouquette, 1964	35
	Bill Monbouquette, 1965	35
	Ray Culp, 1971	35
	Marty Pattin, 1972	35
1943–60		
1	Tex Hughson, 1946	35
	Dave Ferriss, 1946	35
	Frank Sullivan, 1955	35
4	Mel Parnell, 1953	34
5	Mel Parnell, 1949	33
	Frank Sullivan, 1956	33
7	6 players tied	32
1921–42		
1	Howard Ehmke, 1923	39
2	Sam Jones, 1921	38
	Wes Ferrell, 1935	38
	Wes Ferrell, 1936	38
5	Howard Ehmke, 1924	36
6	Red Ruffing, 1928	34
	Milt Gaston, 1930	34
1901–20		
1	Cy Young, 1902	43
2	Bill Dinneen, 1902	42
3	Cy Young, 1901	41
	Cy Young, 1904	41
	Babe Ruth, 1916	41
6	Joe Wood, 1912	38
	Babe Ruth, 1917	38

Home Runs Allowed by era

1988–2006		
1	**Tim Wakefield, 1996**	**38**
2	**Josh Beckett, 2006**	**36**
3	**Tim Wakefield, 2005**	**35**
4	Danny Darwin, 1993	31
	Tim Wakefield, 2000	**31**
6	**Tim Wakefield, 1998**	**30**
7	**Tim Wakefield, 2004**	**29**
1973–87		
1	Bruce Hurst, 1987	35
2	Rick Wise, 1975	34
3	Luis Tiant, 1973	32
	John Tudor, 1983	32
	Oil Can Boyd, 1986	32
6	3 players tied	31
1961–72		
1	Earl Wilson, 1964	37
2	Bill Monbouquette, 1964	34
3	Gene Conley, 1961	33
4	Bill Monbouquette, 1965	32
5	Bill Monbouquette, 1963	31
6	Sonny Siebert, 1970	29
7	Gene Conley, 1962	28
1943–60		
1	Tom Brewer, 1957	24
2	Tex Hughson, 1943	23
	Ellis Kinder, 1950	23
	Frank Sullivan, 1955	23
5	Frank Sullivan, 1956	22
	Dave Sisler, 1958	22
7	6 players tied	21
1921–42		
1	Hod Lisenbee, 1930	20
	Lefty Grove, 1940	20
3	Bob Weiland, 1933	19
4	Red Ruffing, 1929	17
	Johnny Marcum, 1937	17
	Jack Wilson, 1940	17
7	Wes Ferrell, 1935	16
	Jack Wilson, 1938	16
1901–20		
1	Ted Lewis, 1901	14
2	Bill Dinneen, 1902	9
	Norwood Gibson, 1905	9
	Jesse Tannehill, 1906	9
	Harry Harper, 1920	9
	Herb Pennock, 1920	9
	Sam Jones, 1920	9

Complete Games by era

1988–2006		
1	Roger Clemens, 1988	14
2	Roger Clemens, 1991	13
3	Roger Clemens, 1992	11
4	Roger Clemens, 1989	8
5	Bruce Hurst, 1988	7
	Roger Clemens, 1990	7
	Pedro Martinez, 2000	7
1973–87		
1	Luis Tiant, 1974	25
2	Luis Tiant, 1973	23
3	Luis Tiant, 1976	19
4	Bill Lee, 1973	18
	Luis Tiant, 1975	18
	Roger Clemens, 1987	18
7	Bill Lee, 1975	17
	Rick Wise, 1975	17
	Dennis Eckersley, 1979	17
1961–72		
1	Jim Lonborg, 1967	15
	Ray Culp, 1970	15
3	Bill Monbouquette, 1963	13
	Marty Pattin, 1972	13
1943–60		
1	Mel Parnell, 1949	27
2	Dave Ferriss, 1945	26
	Dave Ferriss, 1946	26
4	Tex Hughson, 1946	21
	Mel Parnell, 1950	21
6	Tex Hughson, 1943	20
7	Tex Hughson, 1944	19
	Ellis Kinder, 1949	19
1921–42		
1	Wes Ferrell, 1935	31
2	Howard Ehmke, 1923	28
	Wes Ferrell, 1936	28
4	Howard Ehmke, 1924	26
5	Sam Jones, 1921	25
	Red Ruffing, 1928	25
7	Lefty Grove, 1935	23
1901–20		
1	Cy Young, 1902	41
2	Cy Young, 1904	40
3	Bill Dinneen, 1902	39
4	Cy Young, 1901	38
5	Bill Dinneen, 1904	37
6	Joe Wood, 1912	35
	Babe Ruth, 1917	35

Shutouts

1	Cy Young, 1904	10
	Joe Wood, 1912	10
3	Babe Ruth, 1916	9
4	Carl Mays, 1918	8
	Roger Clemens, 1988	8
6	Cy Young, 1903	7
	Dutch Leonard, 1914	7
	Joe Bush, 1918	7
	Luis Tiant, 1974	7
	Roger Clemens, 1987	7
11	Bill Dinneen, 1903	6
	Jesse Tannehill, 1905	6
	Cy Young, 1907	6
	Ray Collins, 1914	6
	Dutch Leonard, 1916	6
	Babe Ruth, 1917	6
	Lefty Grove, 1936	6
	Tex Hughson, 1946	6
	Dave Ferriss, 1946	6
	Ellis Kinder, 1949	6
	Ray Culp, 1968	6
	Luis Tiant, 1972	6
23	Cy Young, 1901	5
	Tom Hughes, 1903	5
	Bill Dinneen, 1904	5
	Joe Wood, 1911	5
	Rube Foster, 1914	5
	Rube Foster, 1915	5
	Sam Jones, 1918	5
	Herb Pennock, 1919	5
	Sam Jones, 1919	5
	Sam Jones, 1921	5
	Dave Ferriss, 1945	5
	Joe Dobson, 1948	5
	Mel Parnell, 1953	5
	Bill Monbouquette, 1964	5
	Luis Tiant, 1978	5
	Bob Ojeda, 1984	5
	Roger Clemens, 1992	5
40	Many players tied	4

Saves

1	Tom Gordon, 1998	46
2	Derek Lowe, 2000	42
3	Jeff Reardon, 1991	40
	Ugueth Urbina, 2002	40
5	**Jonathan Papelbon, 2006**	**35**
6	Bob Stanley, 1983	33
	Jeff Russell, 1993	33
8	**Keith Foulke, 2004**	**32**
9	Bill Campbell, 1977	31
	Heathcliff Slocumb, 1996	31
11	Dick Radatz, 1964	29
	Lee Smith, 1988	29
13	Ellis Kinder, 1953	27
	Jeff Reardon, 1992	27
15	Dick Radatz, 1963	25
	Lee Smith, 1989	25
17	Dick Radatz, 1962	24
	Tom Burgmeier, 1980	24
	Derek Lowe, 2001	24
20	Dick Radatz, 1965	22
	Bob Stanley, 1984	22
22	Jeff Reardon, 1990	21
23	John Wyatt, 1967	20
	Sparky Lyle, 1970	20
25	Ellis Kinder, 1955	18
26	Sparky Lyle, 1969	17
27	Sparky Lyle, 1971	16
	Bob Stanley, 1986	16
	Byung-Hyun Kim, 2003	16
30	Ellis Kinder, 1954	15
	Mike Fornieles, 1961	15
	Bobby Bolin, 1973	15
	Dick Drago, 1975	15
	Derek Lowe, 1999	15
	Tim Wakefield, 1999	**15**
	Keith Foulke, 2005	**15**
37	Ellis Kinder, 1951	14
	Mike Fornieles, 1960	14
	Bob Stanley, 1980	14
	Mark Clear, 1982	14
	Bob Stanley, 1982	14
42	Dick Drago, 1979	13
	Ken Ryan, 1994	13
	Mike Timlin, 2005	**13**

Save percentage

1	Tom Gordon, 1998	97.9
2	Tom Burgmeier, 1980	92.3
3	Derek Lowe, 2000	89.4
4	Jeff Russell, 1993	89.2
5	Ugueth Urbina, 2002	87.0
6	**Jonathan Papelbon, 2006**	**85.4**
7	Byung-Hyun Kim, 2003	84.2
8	Dick Drago, 1975	83.3
	Lee Smith, 1989	83.3
	Tim Wakefield, 1999	**83.3**
11	**Keith Foulke, 2004**	**82.1**
12	Jeff Reardon, 1991	81.6
13	Bob Stanley, 1984	81.5
14	Sparky Lyle, 1971	80.0
	Derek Lowe, 2001	80.0
16	Heathcliff Slocumb, 1996	79.5
17	**Keith Foulke, 2005**	**78.9**
18	Lee Smith, 1988	78.4
19	Jeff Reardon, 1992	77.1
20	Bob Stanley, 1986	76.2
21	Bobby Bolin, 1973	75.0
	Jeff Reardon, 1990	75.0
	Derek Lowe, 1999	75.0
24	Bill Campbell, 1977	73.8

Blown saves

1	Bob Stanley, 1983	14
2	Bill Campbell, 1977	11
	Bill Campbell, 1978	11
4	Sparky Lyle, 1970	10
	Greg Harris, 1993	10
6	Sparky Lyle, 1969	9
	Mark Clear, 1982	9
	Jeff Reardon, 1991	9
9	Bill Campbell, 1979	8
	Bob Stanley, 1985	8
	Lee Smith, 1988	8
	Jeff Reardon, 1992	8
	Heathcliff Slocumb, 1996	8
	Mike Timlin, 2006	**8**
15	Rob Murphy, 1989	7
	Jeff Reardon, 1990	7
	Jim Corsi, 1997	7
	Keith Foulke, 2004	**7**
	Mike Timlin, 2005	**7**
20	Many players tied	6

Fewest HR Allowed/ 9 innings by era

1988–2006		
1	Roger Clemens, 1990	0.28
2	Pedro Martinez, 2003	0.34
3	Pedro Martinez, 1999	0.38
4	Roger Clemens, 1992	0.40
5	Frank Viola, 1992	0.49
6	Derek Lowe, 2002	0.49
7	Tom Gordon, 1997	0.49
1973–87		
1	Reggie Cleveland, 1976	0.16
2	Dennis Eckersley, 1981	0.53
3	Bob Stanley, 1980	0.57
4	Bob Stanley, 1979	0.58
5	Bob Stanley, 1982	0.59
6	Luis Tiant, 1974	0.61
7	Roger Clemens, 1987	0.61
1961–72		
1	Gary Bell, 1968	0.32
2	Luis Tiant, 1972	0.35
3	Don Schwall, 1961	0.40
4	Mike Nagy, 1969	0.46
5	Marty Pattin, 1972	0.68
6	Lee Stange, 1967	0.69
7	Dick Ellsworth, 1968	0.73
1943–60		
1	Oscar Judd, 1943	0.12
2	Tex Hughson, 1944	0.18
3	Dave Ferriss, 1945	0.20
4	Pinky Woods, 1944	0.21
5	Joe Dobson, 1943	0.22
6	Mel Parnell, 1949	0.24
7	Mel Parnell, 1948	0.30
1921–42		
1	Sam Jones, 1921	0.03
2	Danny Mac Fayden, 1931	0.16
3	Rip Collins, 1922	0.17
4	Lefty Grove, 1935	0.20
5	Wes Ferrell, 1934	0.20
6	Hal Wiltse, 1927	0.21
7	Red Ruffing, 1926	0.22
1901–20		
1	Babe Ruth, 1916	0.00
2	Dutch Leonard, 1913	0.00
3	Hugh Bedient, 1913	0.00
4	Eddie Cicotte, 1908	0.00
5	Rube Foster, 1916	0.00
6	Cy Young, 1908	0.03
7	Carl Mays, 1917	0.03

Innings Pitched by era

1988–2006		
1	Roger Clemens, 1991	271.1
2	Roger Clemens, 1988	264.0
3	Roger Clemens, 1989	253.1
4	Roger Clemens, 1992	246.2
5	Roger Clemens, 1996	242.2
6	Frank Viola, 1992	238.0
7	Pedro Martinez, 1998	233.2
1973–87		
1	Luis Tiant, 1974	311.1
2	Bill Lee, 1973	284.2
3	Bill Lee, 1974	282.1
4	Roger Clemens, 1987	281.2
5	Luis Tiant, 1976	279.0
6	Oil Can Boyd, 1985	272.1
7	Luis Tiant, 1973	272.0
1961–72		
1	Jim Lonborg, 1967	273.1
2	Bill Monbouquette, 1963	266.2
3	Marty Pattin, 1972	253.0
4	Ray Culp, 1970	251.1
5	Ray Culp, 1971	242.1
6	Gene Conley, 1962	241.2
7	Bill Monbouquette, 1961	236.1
1943–60		
1	Mel Parnell, 1949	295.1
2	Tex Hughson, 1946	278.0
3	Dave Ferriss, 1946	274.0
4	Tex Hughson, 1943	266.0
5	Dave Ferriss, 1945	264.2
6	Frank Sullivan, 1955	260.0
7	Ellis Kinder, 1949	252.0
1921–42		
1	Wes Ferrell, 1935	322.1
2	Howard Ehmke, 1923	316.2
3	Howard Ehmke, 1924	315.0
4	Wes Ferrell, 1936	301.0
5	Sam Jones, 1921	298.2
6	Red Ruffing, 1928	289.1
7	Tex Hughson, 1942	281.0
1901–20		
1	Cy Young, 1902	384.2
2	Cy Young, 1904	380.0
3	Cy Young, 1901	371.1
	Bill Dinneen, 1902	371.1
5	Joe Wood, 1912	344.0
6	Cy Young, 1907	343.1
7	Cy Young, 1903	341.2

Fewest Hits/9 innings by era

1988–2006		
1	Pedro Martinez, 2000	5.31
2	Pedro Martinez, 2002	6.50
3	Roger Clemens, 1994	6.54
4	**Tim Wakefield, 2002**	**6.67**
5	Pedro Martinez, 1999	6.75
6	Derek Lowe, 2002	6.80
7	Pedro Martinez, 2003	7.09
1973–87		
1	Roger Clemens, 1986	6.34
2	Luis Tiant, 1973	7.18
3	Luis Tiant, 1978	7.84
4	Roger Clemens, 1987	7.92
5	Luis Tiant, 1974	8.12
6	Roger Moret, 1974	8.20
7	Reggie Cleveland, 1976	8.42
1961–72		
1	Luis Tiant, 1972	6.44
2	Ray Culp, 1968	6.91
3	Dave Morehead, 1963	7.06
4	Dave Morehead, 1965	7.33
5	Jim Lonborg, 1967	7.51
6	Ray Culp, 1970	7.56
7	Earl Wilson, 1962	7.67
1943–60		
1	Tom Brewer, 1956	7.37
2	Mickey McDermott, 1953	7.37
3	Mickey McDermott, 1951	7.38
4	Oscar Judd, 1943	7.59
5	Tex Hughson, 1944	7.61
6	Frank Sullivan, 1957	7.70
7	Mickey McDermott, 1952	7.72
1921–42		
1	Joe Dobson, 1942	7.64
2	Charlie Wagner, 1942	8.06
3	Bob Weiland, 1933	8.20
4	Tex Hughson, 1942	8.26
5	Charlie Wagner, 1941	8.41
6	Lefty Grove, 1936	8.42
7	Lefty Grove, 1939	8.48
1901–20		
1	Dutch Leonard, 1914	5.57
2	Dutch Leonard, 1915	6.38
3	Babe Ruth, 1916	6.40
4	Eddie Cicotte, 1909	6.49
5	Babe Ruth, 1917	6.73
6	Babe Ruth, 1918	6.76
7	Charley Hall, 1910	6.77

Saves by era

1988–2006		
1	Tom Gordon, 1998	46
2	Derek Lowe, 2000	42
3	Jeff Reardon, 1991	40
	Ugueth Urbina, 2002	40
5	**Jonathan Papelbon, 2006**	**35**
6	Jeff Russell, 1993	33
7	**Keith Foulke, 2004**	**32**
1973–87		
1	Bob Stanley, 1983	33
2	Bill Campbell, 1977	31
3	Tom Burgmeier, 1980	24
4	Bob Stanley, 1984	22
5	Bob Stanley, 1986	16
1961–72		
1	Dick Radatz, 1964	29
2	Dick Radatz, 1963	25
3	Dick Radatz, 1962	24
4	Dick Radatz, 1965	22
5	John Wyatt, 1967	20
	Sparky Lyle, 1970	20
7	Sparky Lyle, 1969	17
1943–60		
1	Ellis Kinder, 1953	27
2	Ellis Kinder, 1955	18
3	Ellis Kinder, 1954	15
4	Ellis Kinder, 1951	14
	Mike Fornieles, 1960	14
6	Leo Kiely, 1958	12
7	Ike Delock, 1957	11
	Mike Fornieles, 1959	11
1921–42		
1	Wilcy Moore, 1931	10
2	Jack Quinn, 1923	7
	Jack Quinn, 1924	7
	Jack Wilson, 1937	7
	Joe Heving, 1939	7
6	Archie McKain, 1938	6
	Mike Ryba, 1941	6
	Mace Brown, 1942	6
1901–20		
1	Frank Arellanes, 1909	8
2	Carl Mays, 1915	7
3	Dutch Leonard, 1916	6
4	Hugh Bedient, 1913	5
5	Charley Hall, 1911	4
6	Tex Pruiett, 1907	3
	Joe Wood, 1911	3
	Dutch Leonard, 1914	3
	Carl Mays, 1916	3

Home Runs Allowed

1	**Tim Wakefield, 1996**	**38**
2	Earl Wilson, 1964	37
3	**Josh Beckett, 2006**	**36**
4	Bruce Hurst, 1987	35
	Tim Wakefield, 2005	**35**
6	Bill Monbouquette, 1964	34
	Rick Wise, 1975	34
8	Gene Conley, 1961	33
9	Bill Monbouquette, 1965	32
	Luis Tiant, 1973	32
	John Tudor, 1983	32
	Oil Can Boyd, 1986	32
13	Bill Monbouquette, 1963	31
	Marty Pattin, 1973	31
	Dennis Eckersley, 1982	31
	Bruce Hurst, 1985	31
	Danny Darwin, 1993	31
	Tim Wakefield, 2000	**31**
19	Fergie Jenkins, 1977	30
	Dennis Eckersley, 1978	30
	Al Nipper, 1987	30
	Tim Wakefield, 1998	**30**
23	Sonny Siebert, 1970	29
	Dennis Eckersley, 1979	29
	Tim Wakefield, 2004	**29**
26	Gene Conley, 1962	28
	Tom Gordon, 1996	28
	Mark Portugal, 1999	28
	Curt Schilling, 2006	**28**
30	Earl Wilson, 1965	27
	Dennis Eckersley, 1983	27
32	Luis Tiant, 1977	26
	Luis Tiant, 1978	26
	Oil Can Boyd, 1985	26
	Pedro Martinez, 1998	26
	Hideo Nomo, 2001	26
	Pedro Martinez, 2004	26
38	Jack Lamabe, 1964	25
	Ray Culp, 1969	25
	Gary Peters, 1971	25
	Reggie Cleveland, 1974	25
	Bill Lee, 1974	25
	Luis Tiant, 1975	25
	Luis Tiant, 1976	25
	Dennis Eckersley, 1980	25
	Bruce Hurst, 1984	25
	Oil Can Boyd, 1988	25
	Mike Smithson, 1988	25
	Aaron Sele, 1997	25
	John Burkett, 2002	25

Innings Pitched

1	Cy Young, 1902	384.2
2	Cy Young, 1904	380.0
3	Cy Young, 1901	371.1
	Bill Dinneen, 1902	371.1
5	Joe Wood, 1912	344.0
6	Cy Young, 1907	343.1
7	Cy Young, 1903	341.2
8	Bill Dinneen, 1904	335.2
9	Babe Ruth, 1917	326.1
10	Babe Ruth, 1916	323.2
11	Wes Ferrell, 1935	322.1
12	Cy Young, 1905	320.2
13	Howard Ehmke, 1923	316.2
14	Ted Lewis, 1901	316.1
15	Howard Ehmke, 1924	315.0
16	Luis Tiant, 1974	311.1
17	Wes Ferrell, 1936	301.0
18	Bill Dinneen, 1903	299.0
	Cy Young, 1908	299.0
20	Sam Jones, 1921	298.2
21	Mel Parnell, 1949	295.1
22	Dutch Leonard, 1917	294.1
23	Carl Mays, 1918	293.1
24	Red Ruffing, 1928	289.1
25	Carl Mays, 1917	289.0
26	Cy Young, 1906	287.2
27	Bill Lee, 1973	284.2
28	Bill Lee, 1974	282.1
29	Jesse Tannehill, 1904	281.2
	Roger Clemens, 1987	281.2
31	Tex Hughson, 1942	281.0
32	Luis Tiant, 1976	279.0
33	Tex Hughson, 1946	278.0
34	Joe Wood, 1911	275.2
	Buck O'Brien, 1912	275.2
36	Dutch Leonard, 1916	274.0
	Sam Jones, 1920	274.0
	Dave Ferriss, 1946	274.0
39	Jim Lonborg, 1967	273.1
40	Norwood Gibson, 1904	273.0
	Milt Gaston, 1930	273.0
	Lefty Grove, 1935	273.0
43	Joe Bush, 1918	272.2
44	Ray Collins, 1914	272.1
	Oil Can Boyd, 1985	272.1
46	Luis Tiant, 1973	272.0
47	Jesse Tannehill, 1905	271.2
48	Roger Clemens, 1991	271.1
49	Danny Mac Fayden, 1930	269.1
50	Dennis Eckersley, 1978	268.1

Fewest Hits/9 innings

1	Pedro Martinez, 2000	5.31
2	Dutch Leonard, 1914	5.57
3	Roger Clemens, 1986	6.34
4	Dutch Leonard, 1915	6.38
5	Babe Ruth, 1916	6.40
6	Luis Tiant, 1972	6.44
7	Eddie Cicotte, 1909	6.49
8	Pedro Martinez, 2002	6.50
9	Roger Clemens, 1994	6.54
10	**Tim Wakefield, 2002**	**6.67**
11	Babe Ruth, 1917	6.73
12	Pedro Martinez, 1999	6.75
13	Babe Ruth, 1918	6.76
14	Charley Hall, 1910	6.77
15	Joe Wood, 1909	6.78
16	Derek Lowe, 2002	6.80
17	Babe Ruth, 1915	6.86
18	Joe Wood, 1915	6.86
19	Ray Culp, 1968	6.91
20	Cy Young, 1908	6.92
21	George Winter, 1907	6.94
22	Cy Young, 1905	6.96
23	Rube Foster, 1914	6.97
24	Joe Wood, 1912	6.99
25	Carl Mays, 1918	7.06
26	Dave Morehead, 1963	7.06
27	Pedro Martinez, 2003	7.09
28	Joe Wood, 1910	7.09
29	Norwood Gibson, 1904	7.12
30	Carl Mays, 1917	7.16
31	Luis Tiant, 1973	7.18
32	Pedro Martinez, 1998	7.24
33	Roger Clemens, 1991	7.26
34	Cy Morgan, 1908	7.29
35	Dave Morehead, 1965	7.33
36	Tom Brewer, 1956	7.37
37	Mickey McDermott, 1953	7.37
38	Mickey McDermott, 1951	7.38
39	Joe Wood, 1911	7.38
40	Sam Jones, 1918	7.39
41	Roger Clemens, 1988	7.40
42	Ralph Glaze, 1907	7.40
43	Roger Clemens, 1992	7.41
44	Frank Arellanes, 1909	7.49
45	Cy Young, 1907	7.50
46	Jim Lonborg, 1967	7.51
47	**Tim Wakefield, 1995**	**7.51**
48	Ray Collins, 1910	7.54
49	Ernie Shore, 1915	7.54
50	Ray Culp, 1970	7.56

Walks

1	Mel Parnell, 1949	134
2	Mickey McDermott, 1950	124
3	Don Schwall, 1962	121
	Mike Torrez, 1979	121
5	Howard Ehmke, 1923	119
	Wes Ferrell, 1936	119
	Jack Wilson, 1937	119
8	Babe Ruth, 1916	118
	Red Ruffing, 1929	118
10	Emmett O'Neill, 1945	117
11	Mel Parnell, 1953	116
12	Dave Morehead, 1965	113
13	Tom Brewer, 1956	112
	Dave Morehead, 1964	112
15	Earl Wilson, 1962	111
16	Don Schwall, 1961	110
17	Mickey McDermott, 1953	109
18	Babe Ruth, 1917	108
	Alex Ferguson, 1924	108
	Wes Ferrell, 1935	108
21	Mel Parnell, 1950	106
	Mike Nagy, 1969	106
	Roger Clemens, 1996	106
24	Earl Wilson, 1963	105
	Tom Gordon, 1996	105
26	Rip Collins, 1922	103
27	Bob Weiland, 1933	100
	Frank Sullivan, 1955	100
	Bill Monbouquette, 1961	100
30	Bill Dinneen, 1902	99
	Hal Wiltse, 1926	99
	Fritz Ostermueller, 1934	99
	Ellis Kinder, 1949	99
	Dave Morehead, 1963	99
	Mike Torrez, 1978	99
36	Milt Gaston, 1930	98
	Gordon Rhodes, 1934	98
38	Bob Weiland, 1932	97
	Joe Dobson, 1949	97
40	Red Ruffing, 1928	96
	Tracy Stallard, 1961	96
	Bob Ojeda, 1984	96
	Hideo Nomo, 2001	96
44	Sam Jones, 1919	95
	Ed Morris, 1929	95
	Charlie Wagner, 1942	95
	Tom Brewer, 1954	95
48	Dutch Leonard, 1913	94
	Joe Bush, 1920	94
50	Many players tied	93

Fewest Walks/9 innings

1	Cy Young, 1904	0.69
2	Cy Young, 1906	0.78
3	Cy Young, 1905	0.84
4	Cy Young, 1901	0.90
5	Cy Young, 1903	0.97
6	David Wells, 2005	1.03
7	Jesse Tannehill, 1904	1.05
8	Cy Young, 1908	1.11
9	**Curt Schilling, 2006**	**1.24**
10	Cy Young, 1902	1.24
11	Pedro Martinez, 2000	1.33
12	Cy Young, 1907	1.34
13	Ray Collins, 1913	1.35
14	**Curt Schilling, 2004**	**1.39**
15	Bill Monbouquette, 1963	1.42
16	Bret Saberhagen, 1998	1.49
17	Ray Collins, 1910	1.51
18	Bill Monbouquette, 1964	1.54
19	Pedro Martinez, 1999	1.56
20	Bill Monbouquette, 1965	1.57
21	Jack Russell, 1929	1.58
22	Lee Stange, 1967	1.59
23	George Winter, 1906	1.65
24	Tex Hughson, 1946	1.65
25	Frank Arellanes, 1909	1.68
26	Fergie Jenkins, 1977	1.68
27	Bill Dinneen, 1904	1.69
28	Dick Ellsworth, 1968	1.70
29	Dennis Eckersley, 1982	1.73
30	Jesse Tannehill, 1906	1.79
31	Frank Sullivan, 1957	1.80
32	Pedro Martinez, 2002	1.81
33	Tex Hughson, 1944	1.81
34	Bob Stanley, 1979	1.83
35	Jack Russell, 1928	1.83
36	George Winter, 1905	1.84
37	Bill Dinneen, 1905	1.85
38	Ray Collins, 1914	1.85
39	Fergie Jenkins, 1976	1.85
40	George Winter, 1903	1.87
41	Oil Can Boyd, 1986	1.89
42	Ray Collins, 1912	1.90
43	Danny Darwin, 1993	1.92
44	Rick Wise, 1976	1.93
45	Ernie Shore, 1916	1.95
46	Jesse Tannehill, 1905	1.95
47	Jack Quinn, 1923	1.96
48	Derek Lowe, 2002	1.97
49	Herb Pennock, 1919	1.97
50	Bill Dinneen, 1903	1.99

Strikeouts

1	Pedro Martinez, 1999	313
2	Roger Clemens, 1988	291
3	Pedro Martinez, 2000	284
4	Joe Wood, 1912	258
5	Roger Clemens, 1996	257
6	Roger Clemens, 1987	256
7	Pedro Martinez, 1998	251
8	Jim Lonborg, 1967	246
9	Roger Clemens, 1991	241
10	Pedro Martinez, 2002	239
11	Roger Clemens, 1986	238
12	Joe Wood, 1911	231
13	Roger Clemens, 1989	230
14	Pedro Martinez, 2004	227
15	Hideo Nomo, 2001	220
16	Cy Young, 1905	210
17	Roger Clemens, 1990	209
18	Roger Clemens, 1992	208
19	Luis Tiant, 1973	206
	Pedro Martinez, 2003	206
21	**Curt Schilling, 2004**	**203**
22	Cy Young, 1904	200
23	Ray Culp, 1970	197
24	Ray Culp, 1968	190
	Bruce Hurst, 1987	190
26	Bruce Hurst, 1985	189
27	**Curt Schilling, 2006**	**183**
28	Dick Radatz, 1964	181
29	Cy Young, 1903	176
	Dutch Leonard, 1914	176
	Luis Tiant, 1974	176
32	Bill Monbouquette, 1963	174
33	Tex Hughson, 1946	172
	Ray Culp, 1969	172
35	Tom Gordon, 1996	171
36	Babe Ruth, 1916	170
37	**Tim Wakefield, 2003**	**169**
38	Marty Pattin, 1972	168
	Roger Clemens, 1994	168
40	Bruce Hurst, 1986	167
41	Earl Wilson, 1964	166
	Bruce Hurst, 1988	166
43	Earl Wilson, 1965	164
44	Dave Morehead, 1965	163
	Pedro Martinez, 2001	163
46	Dick Radatz, 1963	162
	Dennis Eckersley, 1978	162
48	Bill Monbouquette, 1961	161
49	Cy Young, 1902	160
	Roger Clemens, 1993	160

Strikeouts/9 innings

1	Pedro Martinez, 1999	13.20
2	Pedro Martinez, 2000	11.78
3	Pedro Martinez, 2002	10.79
4	Hideo Nomo, 2001	10.00
5	Pedro Martinez, 2003	9.93
6	Roger Clemens, 1988	9.92
7	Pedro Martinez, 1998	9.67
8	Roger Clemens, 1996	9.53
9	Pedro Martinez, 2004	9.41
10	Roger Clemens, 1994	8.86
11	Bruce Hurst, 1986	8.62
12	Roger Clemens, 1986	8.43
13	Roger Clemens, 1990	8.24
14	Roger Clemens, 1987	8.18
15	Roger Clemens, 1989	8.17
16	Jim Lonborg, 1967	8.10
17	**Curt Schilling, 2006**	**8.07**
18	**Curt Schilling, 2004**	**8.06**
19	Roger Clemens, 1991	7.99
20	Ray Culp, 1968	7.90
21	**Tim Wakefield, 2001**	**7.90**
22	Tom Gordon, 1997	7.83
23	Dave Morehead, 1965	7.61
24	Roger Clemens, 1992	7.59
25	Joe Wood, 1911	7.54
26	**Tim Wakefield, 2003**	**7.52**
27	Roger Clemens, 1993	7.51
28	Dave Morehead, 1964	7.51
29	Bruce Hurst, 1985	7.42
30	Earl Wilson, 1964	7.38
31	**Tim Wakefield, 2002**	**7.38**
32	Bruce Hurst, 1987	7.16
33	Bronson Arroyo, 2004	7.15
34	Tom Gordon, 1996	7.14
35	Ray Culp, 1970	7.05
36	Dutch Leonard, 1914	7.05
37	Dave Morehead, 1963	7.01
38	**Josh Beckett, 2006**	**6.95**
39	Bruce Hurst, 1988	6.90
40	**Matt Clement, 2005**	**6.88**
41	Ray Culp, 1969	6.82
42	Luis Tiant, 1973	6.82
43	**Tim Wakefield, 1997**	**6.75**
44	Joe Wood, 1912	6.75
45	John Tudor, 1982	6.72
46	Erik Hanson, 1995	6.70
47	Mickey McDermott, 1951	6.65
48	Joe Wood, 1910	6.64
49	Greg Harris, 1991	6.61
50	Aaron Sele, 1994	6.59

Earned Run Average

1	Dutch Leonard, 1914	0.96
2	Cy Young, 1908	1.26
3	Joe Wood, 1915	1.49
4	Ray Collins, 1910	1.62
5	Cy Young, 1901	1.62
6	Ernie Shore, 1915	1.64
7	Joe Wood, 1910	1.69
8	Rube Foster, 1914	1.70
9	Pedro Martinez, 2000	1.74
10	Carl Mays, 1917	1.74
11	Babe Ruth, 1916	1.75
12	Cy Young, 1905	1.82
13	Charley Hall, 1910	1.91
14	Joe Wood, 1912	1.91
15	Luis Tiant, 1972	1.91
16	Roger Clemens, 1990	1.93
17	Eddie Cicotte, 1909	1.94
18	Cy Young, 1904	1.97
19	Cy Young, 1907	1.99
20	Babe Ruth, 1917	2.01
21	Joe Wood, 1911	2.02
22	Jesse Tannehill, 1904	2.04
23	Pedro Martinez, 1997	2.07
24	George Winter, 1907	2.07
25	Cy Young, 1903	2.08
26	Joe Bush, 1918	2.11
27	Rube Foster, 1915	2.11
28	Cy Young, 1902	2.15
29	Dutch Leonard, 1917	2.17
30	Joe Wood, 1909	2.18
31	Frank Arellanes, 1909	2.18
32	Bill Dinneen, 1904	2.20
33	Norwood Gibson, 1904	2.21
34	Carl Mays, 1918	2.21
35	Pedro Martinez, 2003	2.22
36	Babe Ruth, 1918	2.22
37	Ernie Shore, 1917	2.22
38	Sam Jones, 1918	2.25
39	Tex Hughson, 1944	2.26
40	Bill Dinneen, 1903	2.26
	Pedro Martinez, 2002	2.26
42	Charlie Smith, 1910	2.30
43	Ralph Glaze, 1907	2.32
44	Dutch Leonard, 1915	2.36
45	Dutch Leonard, 1916	2.36
46	Carl Mays, 1916	2.39
47	Dutch Leonard, 1913	2.39
48	Ray Collins, 1911	2.40
49	Roger Clemens, 1992	2.41
50	Eddie Cicotte, 1908	2.43

Earned Run Average by era

1988–2006

1	Pedro Martinez, 2000	1.74
2	Roger Clemens, 1990	1.93
3	Pedro Martinez, 1999	2.07
4	Pedro Martinez, 2003	2.22
5	Pedro Martinez, 2002	2.26
6	Roger Clemens, 1992	2.41
7	Derek Lowe, 2002	2.58

1973–87

1	Roger Clemens, 1986	2.48
2	Bill Lee, 1973	2.75
3	Luis Tiant, 1974	2.92
4	Roger Clemens, 1987	2.97
5	Dennis Eckersley, 1978	2.99
6	Dennis Eckersley, 1979	2.99
7	Bruce Hurst, 1986	2.99

1961–72

1	Luis Tiant, 1972	1.91
2	Lee Stange, 1967	2.77
3	Sonny Siebert, 1971	2.91
4	Ray Culp, 1968	2.91
5	Dick Ellsworth, 1968	3.03
6	Ray Culp, 1970	3.04
7	Mike Nagy, 1969	3.11

1943–60

1	Tex Hughson, 1944	2.26
2	Tex Hughson, 1943	2.64
3	Frank Sullivan, 1957	2.73
4	Tex Hughson, 1946	2.75
5	Mel Parnell, 1949	2.77
6	Oscar Judd, 1943	2.90
7	Frank Sullivan, 1955	2.91

1921–42

1	Lefty Grove, 1939	2.54
2	Tex Hughson, 1942	2.59
3	Lefty Grove, 1935	2.70
4	Lefty Grove, 1936	2.81
5	Lefty Grove, 1937	3.02
6	Charlie Wagner, 1941	3.07
7	Lefty Grove, 1938	3.08

1901–20

1	Dutch Leonard, 1914	0.96
2	Cy Young, 1908	1.26
3	Joe Wood, 1915	1.49
4	Ray Collins, 1910	1.62
5	Cy Young, 1901	1.62
6	Ernie Shore, 1915	1.64
7	Joe Wood, 1910	1.69

Adjusted Earned Run Average

1	Pedro Martinez, 2000	288
2	Dutch Leonard, 1914	280
3	Pedro Martinez, 1999	241
4	Cy Young, 1901	217
5	Roger Clemens, 1990	212
6	Pedro Martinez, 2003	210
7	Pedro Martinez, 2002	198
8	Cy Young, 1908	195
9	Lefty Grove, 1936	189
10	Joe Wood, 1915	187
11	Lefty Grove, 1939	186
12	Joe Wood, 1912	178
13	Roger Clemens, 1994	177
14	Roger Clemens, 1992	177
15	Lefty Grove, 1935	176
16	Derek Lowe, 2002	173
17	Luis Tiant, 1972	170
18	Roger Clemens, 1986	169
19	Ernie Shore, 1915	169
20	Cy Young, 1902	166
21	Roger Clemens, 1991	165
22	**Tim Wakefield, 1995**	**165**
23	Pedro Martinez, 1998	164
24	Joe Wood, 1911	162
25	Lefty Grove, 1938	160
26	**Tim Wakefield, 2002**	**159**
27	Rube Foster, 1914	158
28	Babe Ruth, 1916	158
29	Ray Collins, 1910	158
30	Mel Parnell, 1949	157
31	Lefty Grove, 1937	157
32	Roger Clemens, 1987	154
33	Joe Wood, 1910	151
34	Tex Hughson, 1944	151
35	**Curt Schilling, 2004**	**150**
36	Dennis Eckersley, 1979	149
37	Carl Mays, 1917	148
38	Cy Young, 1905	148
39	Frank Viola, 1993	148
40	Frank Sullivan, 1955	148
41	Bill Lee, 1973	146
42	Frank Sullivan, 1957	146
43	Cy Young, 1903	146
44	Tex Hughson, 1942	144
45	Danny Darwin, 1993	142
46	Roger Clemens, 1988	141
47	Bob Stanley, 1982	140
48	Bruce Hurst, 1986	140
49	Roger Clemens, 1996	140
50	Mel Parnell, 1948	140

Adjusted Pitching Wins

1	Pedro Martinez, 2000	8.2
2	Pedro Martinez, 1999	7.9
3	Cy Young, 1901	7.9
4	Lefty Grove, 1936	6.8
5	Roger Clemens, 1990	6.1
6	Cy Young, 1902	6.0
7	Derek Lowe, 2002	6.0
8	Lefty Grove, 1935	6.0
9	Joe Wood, 1912	5.9
10	Roger Clemens, 1992	5.3
11	Pedro Martinez, 2002	5.2
12	Roger Clemens, 1986	5.2
13	Dutch Leonard, 1914	5.1
14	Mel Parnell, 1949	5.1
15	Pedro Martinez, 1998	4.8
16	Roger Clemens, 1991	4.7
17	**Curt Schilling, 2004**	**4.7**
18	Roger Clemens, 1987	4.7
19	Joe Wood, 1911	4.6
20	Pedro Martinez, 2003	4.5
21	Wes Ferrell, 1935	4.4
22	Lefty Grove, 1937	4.3
23	Cy Young, 1908	4.3
24	**Tim Wakefield, 1995**	**4.2**
25	Lefty Grove, 1939	4.1
26	Babe Ruth, 1916	4.0
27	Dennis Eckersley, 1979	4.0
28	Sam Jones, 1921	3.9
29	Cy Young, 1904	3.9
30	Frank Sullivan, 1955	3.9
31	Roger Clemens, 1988	3.7
32	Cy Young, 1903	3.7
33	Frank Sullivan, 1957	3.6
34	Bill Lee, 1973	3.6
35	Luis Tiant, 1974	3.6
36	Tex Hughson, 1942	3.5
37	Wes Ferrell, 1936	3.5
38	Danny Darwin, 1993	3.5
39	Howard Ehmke, 1924	3.4
40	Tex Hughson, 1946	3.4
41	Roger Clemens, 1996	3.4
42	Joe Wood, 1915	3.3
43	Bill Dinneen, 1902	3.3
44	Dennis Eckersley, 1978	3.3
45	Luis Tiant, 1972	3.2
46	Tex Hughson, 1944	3.2
47	Bret Saberhagen, 1999	3.2
48	Roger Clemens, 1994	3.2
49	Mickey McDermott, 1953	3.2
50	Lefty Grove, 1938	3.2

Opponent Batting Average

1	Pedro Martinez, 2000	.167
2	Dutch Leonard, 1914	.180
3	Roger Clemens, 1986	.195
4	Pedro Martinez, 2002	.198
5	Babe Ruth, 1916	.201
6	Luis Tiant, 1972	.202
7	Roger Clemens, 1994	.203
8	**Tim Wakefield, 2002**	**.204**
9	Pedro Martinez, 1999	.205
10	Charley Hall, 1910	.207
11	Eddie Cicotte, 1909	.207
12	Dutch Leonard, 1915	.208
13	Joe Wood, 1909	.209
14	Ray Culp, 1968	.210
15	Babe Ruth, 1917	.211
16	Derek Lowe, 2002	.211
17	Dave Morehead, 1963	.211
18	Babe Ruth, 1915	.212
19	Cy Young, 1908	.213
20	Babe Ruth, 1918	.214
21	Pedro Martinez, 2003	.215
22	George Winter, 1907	.215
23	Cy Young, 1905	.215
24	Joe Wood, 1915	.216
25	Joe Wood, 1912	.216
26	Pedro Martinez, 1998	.217
27	Dave Morehead, 1965	.217
28	Rube Foster, 1914	.218
29	Norwood Gibson, 1904	.219
30	Luis Tiant, 1973	.219
31	Joe Wood, 1910	.220
32	Roger Clemens, 1988	.220
33	Tom Brewer, 1956	.220
34	Carl Mays, 1918	.221
35	Roger Clemens, 1991	.221
36	Carl Mays, 1917	.221
37	Joe Wood, 1911	.223
38	Mickey McDermott, 1953	.224
39	Roger Clemens, 1992	.224
40	Ray Culp, 1970	.224
41	Jim Lonborg, 1967	.225
42	Tex Hughson, 1944	.225
43	Tom Gordon, 1997	.226
44	Mickey McDermott, 1951	.226
45	Cy Morgan, 1908	.226
46	Ralph Glaze, 1907	.227
47	**Tim Wakefield, 1995**	**.227**
48	Roger Clemens, 1990	.228
49	Ernie Shore, 1915	.228
50	Frank Arellanes, 1909	.229

Opponent On-Base Pct.

1	Pedro Martinez, 2000	.214
2	Cy Young, 1908	.240
3	Cy Young, 1905	.241
4	Dutch Leonard, 1914	.246
5	Pedro Martinez, 1999	.249
6	Cy Young, 1904	.251
7	Roger Clemens, 1986	.253
8	Pedro Martinez, 2002	.255
9	Cy Young, 1901	.256
10	Cy Young, 1903	.259
11	Cy Young, 1907	.263
12	Ray Collins, 1910	.264
13	George Winter, 1907	.267
14	Tex Hughson, 1944	.267
15	Derek Lowe, 2002	.267
16	Bill Dinneen, 1904	.268
17	Frank Arellanes, 1909	.270
	Joe Wood, 1909	.270
19	Roger Clemens, 1988	.270
20	Joe Wood, 1912	.272
21	Roger Clemens, 1991	.272
22	**Curt Schilling, 2004**	**.273**
23	Pedro Martinez, 2003	.274
24	Tex Hughson, 1946	.274
25	Rube Foster, 1914	.274
26	Danny Darwin, 1993	.274
27	Frank Sullivan, 1957	.275
28	Jesse Tannehill, 1904	.275
29	Joe Wood, 1915	.275
30	Bill Dinneen, 1903	.276
31	Cy Young, 1902	.276
32	Luis Tiant, 1972	.277
33	Babe Ruth, 1918	.277
34	**Tim Wakefield, 2002**	**.278**
35	Bill Monbouquette, 1963	.280
36	Roger Clemens, 1990	.280
37	Eddie Cicotte, 1909	.280
38	Pedro Martinez, 1998	.280
39	Babe Ruth, 1916	.280
40	Roger Clemens, 1992	.280
41	Norwood Gibson, 1904	.281
42	Luis Tiant, 1973	.281
43	Lee Stange, 1967	.282
44	Carl Mays, 1917	.282
45	Ralph Glaze, 1907	.283
46	Ernie Shore, 1915	.283
47	Carl Mays, 1918	.284
48	Joe Wood, 1911	.284
49	Babe Ruth, 1917	.284
50	Cy Young, 1906	.285

Relief Wins

1	Dick Radatz, 1964	16
2	Dick Radatz, 1963	15
3	Mark Clear, 1982	14
4	Bill Campbell, 1977	13
	Bob Stanley, 1978	13
6	Bob Stanley, 1982	12
7	Joe Heving, 1939	11
	Ike Delock, 1956	11
9	Ellis Kinder, 1951	10
	Ellis Kinder, 1953	10
	Mike Fornieles, 1960	10
	John Wyatt, 1967	10
	Dick Drago, 1979	10
	Bob Stanley, 1981	10
15	Mace Brown, 1942	9
	Ike Delock, 1957	9
	Dick Radatz, 1962	9
	Dick Radatz, 1965	9
	Bob Stanley, 1984	9
	Earl Johnson, 1948	9
	Mike Ryba, 1944	9
22	Many players tied	8

Relief Losses

1	Jim Willoughby, 1976	12
2	Dick Radatz, 1965	11
3	Bob Stanley, 1983	10
	Bob Stanley, 1984	10
	Derek Lowe, 2001	10
6	Dick Radatz, 1964	9
	Bill Campbell, 1977	9
	Mark Clear, 1982	9
9	Ellis Kinder, 1954	8
	Murray Wall, 1958	8
	Diego Segui, 1974	8
	Greg Harris, 1992	8
13	Mike Fornieles, 1961	7
	Don McMahon, 1966	7
	John Wyatt, 1967	7
	Vicente Romo, 1969	7
	Sparky Lyle, 1970	7
	Bob Stanley, 1981	7
	Bob Stanley, 1982	7
	Rob Murphy, 1989	7
	Greg Harris, 1993	7
22	Many players tied	6

Relief Games

1	**Mike Timlin, 2005**	**81**
2	Greg Harris, 1993	80
3	Dick Radatz, 1964	79
4	**Mike Timlin, 2004**	**76**
5	Heathcliff Slocumb, 1996	75
6	Rob Murphy, 1989	74
	Derek Lowe, 1999	74
	Derek Lowe, 2000	74
9	Tom Gordon, 1998	73
10	**Mike Timlin, 2003**	**72**
	Keith Foulke, 2004	**72**
12	Sparky Lyle, 1969	71
	Alan Embree, 2004	71
14	Mike Fornieles, 1960	70
15	Ellis Kinder, 1953	69
	Bill Campbell, 1977	69
17	Rob Murphy, 1990	68
	Greg Harris, 1992	68
	Rod Beck, 2001	68
	Mike Timlin, 2006	**68**
21	Dick Radatz, 1963	66
22	Bob Stanley, 1986	65
	Alan Embree, 2003	65
24	Many players tied	64

Relief Innings Pitched

1	Bob Stanley, 1982	168.1
2	Dick Radatz, 1964	157.0
3	Bob Stanley, 1983	145.1
4	Bill Campbell, 1977	140.0
5	Jack Lamabe, 1963	139.1
6	Dick Radatz, 1963	132.1
7	Dick Radatz, 1962	124.2
8	Dick Radatz, 1965	124.1
9	Bob Stanley, 1978	120.2
10	Ellis Kinder, 1951	113.2
11	Dennis Lamp, 1989	112.1
	Greg Harris, 1993	112.1
13	Murray Wall, 1958	111.1
14	Emerson Dickman, 1939	109.2
15	Derek Lowe, 1999	109.1
16	Mike Fornieles, 1960	109.0
17	Diego Segui, 1974	108.0
18	Ellis Kinder, 1953	107.0
19	Bob Stanley, 1984	106.2
20	Mike Ryba, 1941	105.2
21	Mike Fornieles, 1961	105.0
	Mark Clear, 1982	105.0
	Rob Murphy, 1989	105.0
24	Sparky Lyle, 1969	102.2

Adjusted Reliever Runs

1	Derek Lowe, 1999	27.9
2	**Jonathan Papelbon, 2006**	**27.8**
3	Ellis Kinder, 1951	27.1
4	Ellis Kinder, 1953	26.6
5	Dick Radatz, 1964	25.6
6	Dick Radatz, 1962	25.2
7	Dick Radatz, 1963	24.6
8	Derek Lowe, 2000	24.5
9	**Keith Foulke, 2004**	**23.8**
10	Tom Burgmeier, 1980	23.6
11	Bob Stanley, 1983	23.2
12	Earl Johnson, 1948	22.8
13	Tom Burgmeier, 1982	22.1
14	Bob Stanley, 1982	22.0
15	Bill Campbell, 1977	21.6
16	Dennis Lamp, 1989	21.1
17	Bob Stanley, 1980	19.8
18	**Mike Timlin, 2005**	**19.7**
19	Heathcliff Slocumb, 1996	18.8
20	Tom Gordon, 1998	17.4
21	Bob Stanley, 1978	16.7
22	Mike Fornieles, 1960	16.3
23	Tom Burgmeier, 1979	16.0
24	Charley Hall, 1912	15.9

Relief Ranking

1	Ellis Kinder, 1953	50.9
2	**Jonathan Papelbon, 2006**	**47.5**
3	Dick Radatz, 1964	45.2
4	Dick Radatz, 1963	44.8
5	Bill Campbell, 1977	41.4
6	Derek Lowe, 2000	40.3
7	**Keith Foulke, 2004**	**38.2**
8	Dick Radatz, 1962	38.0
9	Bob Stanley, 1983	36.5
10	Tom Gordon, 1998	34.8
11	Earl Johnson, 1948	34.7
12	Heathcliff Slocumb, 1996	33.6
13	Tom Burgmeier, 1980	32.1
14	Ellis Kinder, 1951	31.1
15	Mark Clear, 1982	29.7
16	**Mike Timlin, 2005**	**27.7**
17	Derek Lowe, 1999	27.5
18	Bob Stanley, 1982	26.4
19	Dick Drago, 1979	25.8
20	Bob Stanley, 1980	25.1
21	Mike Fornieles, 1960	24.5
22	Calvin Schiraldi, 1986	22.1
23	Bob Stanley, 1978	21.8
24	Rich Garces, 1999	21.5

Pitcher Wins

1	Pedro Martinez, 2000	8.4
2	Pedro Martinez, 1999	8.1
3	Cy Young, 1901	7.9
4	Joe Wood, 1912	7.6
5	Wes Ferrell, 1935	6.8
6	Lefty Grove, 1936	6.6
7	Roger Clemens, 1990	6.2
	Derek Lowe, 2002	6.2
9	Cy Young, 1902	6.0
10	Joe Wood, 1911	5.7
	Babe Ruth, 1916	5.7
12	Lefty Grove, 1935	5.5
13	Roger Clemens, 1992	5.3
14	Mel Parnell, 1949	5.2
	Ellis Kinder, 1953	5.2
	Pedro Martinez, 2002	5.2
17	Roger Clemens, 1986	5.1
18	Dick Radatz, 1963	5.0
19	Babe Ruth, 1917	4.9
	Dick Radatz, 1964	4.9
21	Cy Young, 1903	4.8
	Dutch Leonard, 1914	4.8
23	Roger Clemens, 1991	4.7
24	Pedro Martinez, 1998	4.6
	Jonathan Papelbon, 2006	**4.6**
26	Bill Campbell, 1977	4.5
	Roger Clemens, 1987	4.5
	Curt Schilling, 2004	**4.5**
29	Wes Ferrell, 1936	4.4
	Pedro Martinez, 2003	4.4
31	Sam Jones, 1921	4.3
32	**Tim Wakefield, 1995**	**4.2**
33	Cy Young, 1908	4.1
	Mickey McDermott, 1953	4.1
35	Carl Mays, 1917	4.0
	Dennis Eckersley, 1979	4.0
37	Joe Wood, 1915	3.9
	Lefty Grove, 1937	3.9
	Tom Brewer, 1956	3.9
	Dick Radatz, 1962	3.9
	Derek Lowe, 2000	3.9
42	Cy Young, 1904	3.8
	Keith Foulke, 2004	**3.8**
44	Carl Mays, 1918	3.7
	Lefty Grove, 1939	3.7
	Tex Hughson, 1942	3.7
	Roger Clemens, 1988	3.7
48	Bill Lee, 1973	3.6
49	4 players tied	3.5

Pitcher Wins by era

1988–2006

1	Pedro Martinez, 2000	8.4
2	Pedro Martinez, 1999	8.1
3	Roger Clemens, 1990	6.2
	Derek Lowe, 2002	6.2
5	Roger Clemens, 1992	5.3
6	Pedro Martinez, 2002	5.2
7	Roger Clemens, 1991	4.7
8	Pedro Martinez, 1998	4.6
	Jonathan Papelbon, 2006	**4.6**
10	**Curt Schilling, 2004**	**4.5**
11	Pedro Martinez, 2003	4.4
12	**Tim Wakefield, 1995**	**4.2**
13	Derek Lowe, 2000	3.9
14	**Keith Foulke, 2004**	**3.8**

1973–87

1	Roger Clemens, 1986	5.1
2	Bill Campbell, 1977	4.5
	Roger Clemens, 1987	4.5
4	Dennis Eckersley, 1979	4.0
5	Bill Lee, 1973	3.6
6	Luis Tiant, 1974	3.5
7	Bob Stanley, 1983	3.4
8	Dennis Eckersley, 1978	3.1
	Tom Burgmeier, 1980	3.1
	Bob Stanley, 1982	3.1
11	Mark Clear, 1982	3.0
12	Bob Stanley, 1978	2.8
13	Luis Tiant, 1976	2.7
	Bruce Hurst, 1986	2.7

1961–72

1	Dick Radatz, 1963	5.0
2	Dick Radatz, 1964	4.9
3	Dick Radatz, 1962	3.9
4	Sonny Siebert, 1971	3.3
5	Luis Tiant, 1972	2.9

1943–60

1	Mel Parnell, 1949	5.2
	Ellis Kinder, 1953	5.2
3	Mickey McDermott, 1953	4.1
4	Tom Brewer, 1956	3.9
5	Frank Sullivan, 1957	3.5
6	Frank Sullivan, 1955	3.4
7	Mel Parnell, 1951	3.3
8	Mel Parnell, 1953	3.2
9	Tex Hughson, 1944	3.1
	Mel Parnell, 1950	3.1
11	Dave Ferriss, 1945	3.0
	Tex Hughson, 1946	3.0
13	Joe Dobson, 1947	2.6
	Mike Fornieles, 1960	2.6

1921–42

1	Wes Ferrell, 1935	6.8
2	Lefty Grove, 1936	6.6
3	Lefty Grove, 1935	5.5
4	Wes Ferrell, 1936	4.4
5	Sam Jones, 1921	4.3
6	Lefty Grove, 1937	3.9
7	Lefty Grove, 1939	3.7
	Tex Hughson, 1942	3.7
9	Howard Ehmke, 1924	3.4
10	Lefty Grove, 1938	3.0
11	Joe Bush, 1921	2.8
	Wes Ferrell, 1934	2.8
13	Fritz Ostermueller, 1934	2.7

1901–20

1	Cy Young, 1901	7.9
2	Joe Wood, 1912	7.6
3	Cy Young, 1902	6.0
4	Joe Wood, 1911	5.7
	Babe Ruth, 1916	5.7
6	Babe Ruth, 1917	4.9
7	Cy Young, 1903	4.8
	Dutch Leonard, 1914	4.8
9	Cy Young, 1908	4.1
10	Carl Mays, 1917	4.0
11	Joe Wood, 1915	3.9
12	Cy Young, 1904	3.8
13	Carl Mays, 1918	3.7
14	Bill Dinneen, 1903	2.9
	Rube Foster, 1915	2.9
	Babe Ruth, 1918	2.9

Player Overall Wins by era

1988–2006

1	Pedro Martinez, 2000	8.4
2	Pedro Martinez, 1999	8.1
3	Wade Boggs, 1988	6.4
4	Roger Clemens, 1990	6.2
	Derek Lowe, 2002	6.2
6	Nomar Garciaparra, 2002	5.4
7	Roger Clemens, 1992	5.3
8	Pedro Martinez, 2002	5.2
9	Nomar Garciaparra, 2000	5.0
10	Roger Clemens, 1991	4.7
	Mike Greenwell, 1988	4.7
	Nomar Garciaparra, 1999	4.7
13	Pedro Martinez, 1998	4.6
	Jonathan Papelbon, 2006	**4.6**
	John Valentin, 1995	4.6
	Manny Ramirez, 2002	**4.6**

1973–87

1	Wade Boggs, 1987	6.5
2	Wade Boggs, 1985	5.6
3	Wade Boggs, 1986	5.4
4	Fred Lynn, 1979	5.3
5	Roger Clemens, 1986	5.1
6	Carlton Fisk, 1977	4.6
7	Bill Campbell, 1977	4.5
	Roger Clemens, 1987	4.5
9	Wade Boggs, 1983	4.4
	Wade Boggs, 1984	4.4
11	Jim Rice, 1978	4.2
12	Fred Lynn, 1975	4.1
13	Dennis Eckersley, 1979	4.0
14	Carlton Fisk, 1978	3.9

1961–72

1	Rico Petrocelli, 1969	7.6
2	Carl Yastrzemski, 1967	6.9
3	Carl Yastrzemski, 1968	6.3
4	Carl Yastrzemski, 1970	5.5
5	Carlton Fisk, 1972	5.1
6	Dick Radatz, 1963	5.0
7	Dick Radatz, 1964	4.9
8	Carl Yastrzemski, 1963	4.2
9	Dick Radatz, 1962	3.9
10	Eddie Bressoud, 1962	3.7
11	Carl Yastrzemski, 1964	3.5
	Carl Yastrzemski, 1965	3.5
13	Sonny Siebert, 1971	3.3
	Mike Andrews, 1968	3.3

1943–60

1	Ted Williams, 1946	8.1
2	Ted Williams, 1957	7.3
3	Ted Williams, 1947	7.2
4	Eddie Lake, 1945	6.5
5	Ted Williams, 1949	6.4
6	Ted Williams, 1948	5.9
7	Bob Johnson, 1944	5.3
8	Mel Parnell, 1949	5.2
	Ellis Kinder, 1953	5.2
10	Bobby Doerr, 1944	5.1
	Bobby Doerr, 1949	5.1
	Ted Williams, 1954	5.1
13	Bobby Doerr, 1946	4.8
14	Johnny Pesky, 1946	4.6

1921–42

1	Ted Williams, 1941	8.5
	Ted Williams, 1942	8.5
3	Wes Ferrell, 1935	6.8
4	Lefty Grove, 1936	6.6
5	Jimmie Foxx, 1938	5.8
6	Lefty Grove, 1935	5.5
7	Jimmie Foxx, 1939	5.2
8	Johnny Pesky, 1942	4.5
9	Wes Ferrell, 1936	4.4
	Joe Cronin, 1938	4.4
11	Sam Jones, 1921	4.3
	Topper Rigney, 1926	4.3
13	Ted Williams, 1939	4.1
	Bobby Doerr, 1942	4.1

1901–20

1	Babe Ruth, 1919	8.7
2	Cy Young, 1901	7.9
3	Joe Wood, 1912	7.6
4	Tris Speaker, 1914	7.3
5	Tris Speaker, 1912	7.2
6	Tris Speaker, 1913	6.5
7	Cy Young, 1902	6.0
8	Joe Wood, 1911	5.7
	Babe Ruth, 1916	5.7
10	Babe Ruth, 1918	5.6
11	Babe Ruth, 1917	4.9
12	Cy Young, 1903	4.8
	Dutch Leonard, 1914	4.8
	Tris Speaker, 1910	4.8

Player Overall Wins

1	Babe Ruth, 1919	8.7
2	Ted Williams, 1941	8.5
	Ted Williams, 1942	8.5
4	Pedro Martinez, 2000	8.4
5	Pedro Martinez, 1999	8.1
	Ted Williams, 1946	8.1
7	Cy Young, 1901	7.9
8	Joe Wood, 1912	7.6
	Rico Petrocelli, 1969	7.6
10	Tris Speaker, 1914	7.3
	Ted Williams, 1957	7.3
12	Tris Speaker, 1912	7.2
	Ted Williams, 1947	7.2
14	Carl Yastrzemski, 1967	6.9
15	Wes Ferrell, 1935	6.8
16	Lefty Grove, 1936	6.6
17	Tris Speaker, 1913	6.5
	Eddie Lake, 1945	6.5
	Wade Boggs, 1987	6.5
20	Ted Williams, 1949	6.4
	Wade Boggs, 1988	6.4
22	Carl Yastrzemski, 1968	6.3
23	Roger Clemens, 1990	6.2
	Derek Lowe, 2002	6.2
25	Cy Young, 1902	6.0
26	Ted Williams, 1948	5.9
27	Jimmie Foxx, 1938	5.8
28	Joe Wood, 1911	5.7
	Babe Ruth, 1916	5.7
30	Babe Ruth, 1918	5.6
	Wade Boggs, 1985	5.6
32	Lefty Grove, 1935	5.5
	Carl Yastrzemski, 1970	5.5
34	Wade Boggs, 1986	5.4
	Nomar Garciaparra, 2002	5.4
36	Roger Clemens, 1992	5.3
	Bob Johnson, 1944	5.3
	Fred Lynn, 1979	5.3
39	Mel Parnell, 1949	5.2
	Ellis Kinder, 1953	5.2
	Pedro Martinez, 2002	5.2
	Jimmie Foxx, 1939	5.2
43	Roger Clemens, 1986	5.1
	Bobby Doerr, 1944	5.1
	Bobby Doerr, 1949	5.1
	Ted Williams, 1954	5.1
	Carlton Fisk, 1972	5.1
48	Dick Radatz, 1963	5.0
	Nomar Garciaparra, 2000	5.0
50	Babe Ruth, 1917	4.9
	Dick Radatz, 1964	4.9
52	Cy Young, 1903	4.8
	Dutch Leonard, 1914	4.8
	Tris Speaker, 1910	4.8
	Bobby Doerr, 1946	4.8
56	Roger Clemens, 1991	4.7
	Mike Greenwell, 1988	4.7
	Nomar Garciaparra, 1999	4.7
59	Pedro Martinez, 1998	4.6
	Jonathan Papelbon, 2006	**4.6**
	Tris Speaker, 1909	4.6
	Johnny Pesky, 1946	4.6
	Carlton Fisk, 1977	4.6
	John Valentin, 1995	4.6
	Manny Ramirez, 2002	**4.6**
66	Bill Campbell, 1977	4.5
	Roger Clemens, 1987	4.5
	Curt Schilling, 2004	**4.5**
	Johnny Pesky, 1942	4.5
	David Ortiz, 2006	**4.5**
71	Wes Ferrell, 1936	4.4
	Pedro Martinez, 2003	4.4
	Joe Cronin, 1938	4.4
	Wade Boggs, 1983	4.4
	Wade Boggs, 1984	4.4
76	Sam Jones, 1921	4.3
	Topper Rigney, 1926	4.3
	Ted Williams, 1955	4.3
	Wade Boggs, 1989	4.3
80	**Tim Wakefield, 1995**	**4.2**
	Jimmy Collins, 1901	4.2
	Carl Yastrzemski, 1963	4.2
	Jim Rice, 1978	4.2
	David Ortiz, 2005	**4.2**
85	Cy Young, 1908	4.1
	Mickey McDermott, 1953	4.1
	Ted Williams, 1939	4.1
	Bobby Doerr, 1942	4.1
	Ted Williams, 1951	4.1
	Pete Runnels, 1958	4.1
	Fred Lynn, 1975	4.1
	Manny Ramirez, 2003	**4.1**
93	Carl Mays, 1917	4.0
	Dennis Eckersley, 1979	4.0
	Ted Williams, 1940	4.0
	John Valentin, 1997	4.0
97	Many players tied	3.9

RED SOX ALL-TIME TEAM AND LEADERS

Year	FIN	W-L	R-OR	HR-OHR	Manager	ATT	AVG		OBP		SLG		Year
1901	2	79–57	759–608	37–33	J.Collins	289,448	Freeman	.339	Freeman	.400	Freeman	.520	1901
1902	3	77–60	664–600	42–27	J.Collins	348,567	Dougherty	.342	Dougherty	.407	Freeman	.502	1902
1903	**1**	91–47	708–504	48–23	J.Collins	379,338	Dougherty	.331	Dougherty	.372	Freeman	.496	1903
1904	1s	95–59	608–466	26–31	J.Collins	623,295	Parent	.291	Stahl	.366	Stahl	.416	1904
1905	4	78–74	579–565	29–33	J.Collins	468,828	J.Collins	.276	Selbach	.355	J.Collins	.370	1905
1906	8	49–105	463–706	13–37	J.Collins/Stahl	410,209	Grimshaw	.290	Stahl	.346	Grimshaw	.383	1906
1907	7	59–90	466–558	18–22	Young/Huff/Unglaub/McGuire	436,777	Parent	.276	Sullivan	.315	Parent	.355	1907
1908	5	75–79	564–513	14–18	McGuire/Lake	473,048	Gessler	.308	**Gessler**	**.394**	Gessler	.423	1908
1909	3	88–63	601–549	20–18	Lake	668,965	Lord	.315	Stahl	.377	Speaker	.443	1909
1910	4	81–72	641–564	43–30	Donovan	584,619	Speaker	.340	Speaker	.404	Speaker	.468	1910
1911	4t	78–75	680–643	35–21	Donovan	503,961	Speaker	.334	Speaker	.418	Speaker	.502	1911
1912	**1**	105–47	799–544	29–18	Stahl	597,096	Speaker	.383	**Speaker**	**.464**	Speaker	.567	1912
1913	4	79–71	631–610	17–6	Stahl/Carrigan	437,194	Speaker	.363	Speaker	.441	Speaker	.533	1913
1914	2	91–62	589–510	18–18	Carrigan	481,359	Speaker	.338	Speaker	.423	Speaker	.503	1914
1915	**1**	101–50	669–499	14–18	Carrigan	539,885	Speaker	.322	Speaker	.416	Speaker	.411	1915
1916	**1**	91–63	550–480	14–10	Carrigan	496,397	Gardner	.308	Gardner	.372	Walker	.394	1916
1917	2	90–62	555–455	14–12	Barry	387,856	Lewis	.302	Hooper	.355	Lewis	.392	1917
1918	**1**	75–51	474–380	15–9	Barrow	249,513	Ruth	.300	Hooper	.391	**Ruth**	**.555**	1918
1919	5t	66–71	564–552	33–16	Barrow	417,291	Ruth	.322	**Ruth**	**.456**	**Ruth**	**.657**	1919
1920	5	72–81	650–698	22–39	Barrow	402,445	Hendryx	.328	Hooper	.411	Hooper	.470	1920
1921	5	75–79	668–696	17–53	Duffy	279,273	Pratt	.324	Menosky	.388	Pratt	.461	1921
1922	8	61–93	598–769	45–48	Duffy	259,184	Harris	.316	Pratt	.361	Harris	.478	1922
1923	8	61–91	584–809	34–48	Chance	229,688	Harris	.335	Harris	.406	Harris	.520	1923
1924	7	67–87	735–806	30–43	Fohl	448,556	Boone	.337	Harris	.406	Boone	.497	1924
1925	8	47–105	639–922	41–67	Fohl	267,782	Boone	.330	Boone	.406	Boone	.479	1925
1926	8	46–107	562–835	32–45	Fohl	285,155	Flagstead	.299	Rigney	.395	Flagstead	.429	1926
1927	8	51–103	597–856	28–56	Carrigan	305,275	Tobin	.310	Flagstead	.374	Regan	.408	1927
1928	8	57–96	589–770	38–49	Carrigan	396,920	Myer	.313	Myer	.379	Taitt	.434	1928
1929	8	58–96	605–803	28–78	Carrigan	394,620	Rothrock	.300	Rothrock	.361	Scarritt	.411	1929
1930	8	52–102	612–814	47–75	Wagner	444,045	Webb	.323	Webb	.385	Webb	.523	1930
1931	6	62–90	625–800	37–54	S.Collins	350,975	Webb	.333	Webb	.404	Webb	.528	1931
1932	8	43–111	566–915	53–79	S.Collins/McManus	182,150	Oliver	.264	Olson	.347	McManus	.374	1932
1933	7	63–86	700–758	50–75	McManus	268,715	R.Johnson	.313	R.Johnson	.387	R.Johnson	.466	1933
1934	4	76–76	820–775	51–70	Harris	610,640	Werber	.321	Werber	.397	Werber	.472	1934
1935	4	78–75	718–732	69–67	Cronin	558,568	R.Johnson	.315	R.Johnson	.398	Cronin	.460	1935
1936	6	74–80	775–764	86–78	Cronin	626,895	Foxx	.338	Foxx	.440	Foxx	.631	1936
1937	5	80–72	821–775	100–92	Cronin	559,659	Cronin	.307	Cronin	.402	Foxx	.538	1937
1938	2	88–61	902–751	98–102	Cronin	646,459	**Foxx**	**.349**	**Foxx**	**.462**	**Foxx**	**.704**	1938
1939	2	89–62	890–795	124–77	Cronin	573,070	Foxx	.360	**Foxx**	**.464**	**Foxx**	**.694**	1939
1940	4t	82–72	872–825	145–124	Cronin	716,234	Williams	.344	**Williams**	**.442**	Williams	.594	1940
1941	2	84–70	865–750	124–88	Cronin	718,497	**Williams**	**.406**	**Williams**	**.553**	**Williams**	**.735**	1941
1942	2	93–59	761–594	103–65	Cronin	730,340	**Williams**	**.356**	**Williams**	**.499**	**Williams**	**.648**	1942
1943	7	68–84	563–607	57–61	Cronin	358,275	Fox	.288	Doerr	.339	Doerr	.412	1943
1944	4	77–77	739–676	69–66	Cronin	506,975	Doerr	.325	**B.Johnson**	**.431**	**Doerr/B.Johnson**	**.528**	1944
1945	7	71–83	599–674	50–58	Cronin	603,794	Newsome	.290	**Lake**	**.412**	B.Johnson	.425	1945
1946	1s	104–50	792–594	109–89	Cronin	1,416,944	Williams	.342	**Williams**	**.497**	**Williams**	**.667**	1946
1947	3	83–71	720–669	103–84	Cronin	1,427,315	**Williams**	**.343**	**Williams**	**.499**	**Williams**	**.634**	1947
1948	2p	96–59	907–720	121–83	McCarthy	1,558,798	**Williams**	**.369**	**Williams**	**.497**	**Williams**	**.615**	1948
1949	2	96–58	896–667	131–82	McCarthy	1,596,650	**Williams**	**.343**	**Williams**	**.490**	**Williams**	**.650**	1949
1950	3	94–60	1027–804	161–121	McCarthy/O'Neill	1,344,080	**Goodman**	**.354**	Pesky	.437	Dropo	.583	1950
1951	3	87–67	804–725	127–99	O'Neill	1,312,282	Williams	.318	**Williams**	**.464**	**Williams**	**.556**	1951
1952	6	76–78	668–658	113–107	Boudreau	1,115,750	Goodman	.306	DiMaggio	.371	Goodman	.394	1952
1953	4	84–69	656–632	101–92	Boudreau	1,026,133	Goodman	.313	Goodman	.384	Kell	.483	1953
1954	4	69–85	700–728	123–118	Boudreau	931,127	Goodman	.303	**Williams**	**.513**	Jensen	.472	1954
1955	4	84–70	755–652	137–128	Higgins	1,203,200	Goodman	.294	Goodman	.394	Jensen	.479	1955
1956	4	84–70	780–751	139–130	Higgins	1,137,158	Williams	.345	**Williams**	**.479**	Williams	.605	1956
1957	3	82–72	721–668	153–116	Higgins	1,181,087	**Williams**	**.388**	**Williams**	**.526**	**Williams**	**.731**	1957
1958	3	79–75	697–691	155–121	Higgins	1,077,047	**Williams**	**.328**	**Williams**	**.458**	Williams	.584	1958
1959	5	75–79	726–696	125–135	Higgins/York/Jurges	984,102	Runnels	.314	Runnels	.415	Jensen	.492	1959
1960	7	65–89	658–775	124–127	Jurges/Baker/Higgins	1,129,866	**Runnels**	**.320**	Runnels	.401	Wertz	.460	1960
1961	6#	76–86	729–792	112–167	Higgins	850,589	Malzone/Yastrzemski	.266	Jensen	.350	Geiger	.407	1961
1962	7t	76–84	707–756	146–159	Higgins	733,080	**Runnels**	**.326**	Runnels	.408	Yastrzemski	.469	1962
1963	7	76–85	666–704	171–152	Pesky	942,642	**Yastrzemski**	**.321**	**Yastrzemski**	**.418**	Stuart	.521	1963
1964	8	72–90	688–793	186–178	Pesky/Herman	883,276	Bressoud	.293	Yastrzemski	.374	Stuart	.491	1964
1965	9	62–100	669–791	165–158	Herman	652,201	Yastrzemski	.312	**Yastrzemski**	**.395**	**Yastrzemski**	**.536**	1965
1966	9	72–90	655–731	145–164	Herman/Runnels	811,172	Yastrzemski	.278	Yastrzemski	.368	Conigliaro	.487	1966
1967	1s	92–70	722–614	158–142	D.Williams	1,727,832	**Yastrzemski**	**.326**	**Yastrzemski**	**.418**	**Yastrzemski**	**.622**	1967
1968	4	86–76	614–611	125–115	D.Williams	1,940,788	**Yastrzemski**	**.301**	**Yastrzemski**	**.426**	Harrelson	.518	1968
1969	3E#	87–75	743–736	197–155	D.Williams/Popowski	1,833,246	Smith	.309	Petrocelli	.403	Petrocelli	.589	1969
1970	3E	87–75	786–722	203–156	Kasko	1,595,278	**Yastrzemski**	**.329**	**Yastrzemski**	**.452**	**Yastrzemski**	**.592**	1970
1971	3E	85–77	691–667	161–136	Kasko	1,678,732	Smith	.283	Yastrzemski	.381	Smith	.489	1971
1972	2E	85–70	640–620	124–101	Kasko	1,441,718	Fisk	.293	Fisk	.370	Fisk	.538	1972
1973	2E	89–73	738–647	147–158	Kasko/Popowski	1,481,002	Yastrzemski	.296	Yastrzemski	.407	Yastrzemski	.463	1973
1974	3E	84–78	696–661	109–126	D.Johnson	1,556,411	Yastrzemski	.301	Yastrzemski	.414	Yastrzemski	.445	1974
1975	1Es	95–65	796–709	134–145	D.Johnson	1,748,587	Lynn	.331	Lynn	.401	**Lynn**	**.566**	1975
1976	3E	83–79	716–660	134–109	D.Johnson/Zimmer	1,895,846	Lynn	.314	Lynn	.367	Rice	.482	1976
1977	2Et#	97–64	859–712	213–158	Zimmer	2,074,549	Rice	.320	Fisk	.402	**Rice**	**.593**	1977
1978	2Ep	99–64	796–657	172–137	Zimmer	2,320,643	Rice	.315	Lynn	.380	**Rice**	**.600**	1978
1979	3E	91–69	841–711	194–133	Zimmer	2,353,114	**Lynn**	**.333**	**Lynn**	**.423**	**Lynn**	**.637**	1979
1980	4Et	83–77	757–767	162–129	Zimmer/Pesky	1,956,092	Rice	.294	Evans	.358	Rice	.504	1980
1981	5E+	59–49	519–481	90–67	Houk	1,060,379	**Lansford**	**.336**	Evans	.415	Evans	.522	1981
1982	3E	89–73	753–713	136–155	Houk	1,950,124	Rice	.309	**Evans**	**.402**	Evans	.534	1982
1983	6E	78–84	724–775	142–158	Houk	1,782,285	**Boggs**	**.361**	**Boggs**	**.444**	Rice	.550	1983
1984	4E	86–76	810–764	181–141	Houk	1,661,618	Boggs	.325	Boggs	.407	Evans	.532	1984
1985	5E	81–81	800–720	162–130	McNamara	1,786,633	**Boggs**	**.368**	**Boggs**	**.450**	Rice	.487	1985
1986	1Es	95–66	794–696	144–167	McNamara	2,147,641	**Boggs**	**.357**	**Boggs**	**.453**	Rice	.490	1986
1987	5E	78–84	842–825	174–190	McNamara	2,231,551	**Boggs**	**.363**	**Boggs**	**.461**	Boggs	.588	1987
1988	1Ec	89–73	813–689	124–143	McNamara/Morgan	2,464,851	**Boggs**	**.366**	**Boggs**	**.476**	Greenwell	.531	1988
1989	3E	83–79	774–735	108–131	Morgan	2,510,012	Boggs	.330	**Boggs**	**.430**	Esasky	.500	1989
1990	1Ec	88–74	699–664	106–92	Morgan	2,528,986	Boggs	.302	Boggs	.386	Burks	.486	1990
1991	2Et	84–78	731–712	126–147	Morgan	2,562,435	Boggs	.332	Boggs	.421	Clark	.466	1991
1992	7E	73–89	599–669	84–107	Hobson	2,468,574	Brunansky	.266	Brunansky	.354	Brunansky	.445	1992
1993	5E#	80–82	686–698	114–127	Hobson	2,422,021	Greenwell	.315	Vaughn	.390	Vaughn	.525	1993
1994	4E	54–61	552–621	120–120	Hobson	1,775,818	Valentin	.316	Vaughn	.408	Vaughn	.576	1994
1995	1Ed	86–58	791–698	175–127	Kennedy	2,164,410	Naehring	.307	Naehring	.415	Vaughn	.575	1995
1996	3E	85–77	928–921	209–185	Kennedy	2,315,231	Vaughn	.326	Vaughn	.420	Vaughn	.583	1996
1997	4E	78–84	851–857	185–149	J.Williams	2,226,136	Jefferson	.319	Vaughn	.420	Vaughn	.560	1997
1998	2Ed	92–70	876–729	205–168	J.Williams	2,343,947	Vaughn	.337	Vaughn	.402	Vaughn	.591	1998
1999	2Ec	94–68	836–718	176–160	J.Williams	2,446,162	**Garciaparra**	**.357**	Garciaparra	.418	Garciaparra	.603	1999
2000	2E	85–77	792–745	167–173	J.Williams	2,586,032	**Garciaparra**	**.372**	Garciaparra	.434	Garciaparra	.599	2000
2001	2E	82–79	772–745	198–146	J.Williams/Kerrigan	2,625,333	Ramirez	.306	Ramirez	.405	Ramirez	.609	2001
2002	2E	93–69	859–665	177–146	Little	2,650,063	**Ramirez**	**.349**	**Ramirez**	**.450**	Ramirez	.647	2002
2003	2Ec	95–67	961–809	238–153	Little	2,724,165	**Mueller**	**.326**	**Ramirez**	**.427**	Ortiz	.592	2003
2004	**2E**	98–64	949–768	222–159	Francona	2,837,304	Ramirez	.308	Ramirez	.397	**Ramirez**	**.613**	2004
2005	2Ed	95–67	910–805	199–164	Francona	2,847,888	Damon	.316	Ortiz	.397	Ortiz	.604	2005
2006	3E	86–76	820–825	192–181	Francona	2,930,588	Ramirez	.321	**Ramirez**	**.439**	Ortiz	.636	2006

t = Tie, p = Played in one-game playoff, d = played in Division Series, c = Played in League Championship Series, E = Played in AL East, s = World Series champion, + = 1981 split strike season,
* = team won World Series, or player led or tied for league lead, **Bold** = team won World Series

Year	AOPS		HR		RBI		Runs		Hits		Doubles		Year
1901	Freeman	157	Freeman	12	Freeman	114	J.Collins	108	J.Collins	187	J.Collins	42	1901
1902	Freeman	131	Freeman	11	Freeman	121	Stahl	92	Freeman	174	Freeman	38	1902
1903	Freeman	137	Freeman	13	Freeman	104	Dougherty	107	Dougherty	195	Freeman	39	1903
1904	Stahl	139	Freeman	7	Freeman	84	Parent/J.Collins	85	Parent	172	J.Collins	33	1904
1905	J.Collins/Selbach	120	Ferris	6	J.Collins	65	Burkett	78	Burkett	147	J.Collins	26	1905
1906	Stahl	123	Stahl	4	Stahl	51	Parent	67	Stahl	170	Ferris	25	1906
1907	Unglaub	99	Ferris	4	Ferris	62	Sullivan	73	Unglaub	138	Ferris	25	1907
1908	Gessler	161	Gessler	3	Gessler	63	McConnell	77	Lord	145	Lord	15	1908
1909	Stahl	153	Speaker	7	Speaker	77	Lord	89	Speaker/Lord	168	Speaker	26	1909
1910	Speaker	169	Stahl	10	Stahl	77	Speaker	92	Speaker	183	Lewis	29	1910
1911	Speaker	158	Speaker	8	D.Lewis	86	Hooper	93	Speaker	167	Speaker	34	1911
1912	Speaker	185	Speaker	10	Lewis	109	Speaker	136	Speaker	222	Speaker	53	1912
1913	Speaker	180	Hooper	4	Lewis	90	Hooper	100	Speaker	189	Speaker	35	1913
1914	Speaker	178	Speaker	4	Speaker	90	Speaker	101	Speaker	193	Speaker	46	1914
1915	Speaker	152	Ruth	4	Lewis	76	Speaker	108	Speaker	176	Lewis	31	1915
1916	Gardner	128	Walker/Ruth/Gainer	3	Gardner	62	Hooper	75	Hooper	156	Walker/Lewis	29	1916
1917	Lewis	125	Hooper	3	Lewis	65	Hooper	89	Lewis	167	Lewis	29	1917
1918	Hooper	142	Ruth	11	Ruth	66	Hooper	81	Hooper	137	Ruth/Hooper	26	1918
1919	Ruth	224	Ruth	29	Ruth	114	Ruth	103	Scott	141	Ruth	34	1919
1920	Hooper	139	Hooper	7	Hendryx	73	Hooper	91	Hooper	167	Schang/Hooper	30	1920
1921	Pratt	116	Pratt	5	Pratt	102	Leibold	88	McInnis	179	Pratt	36	1921
1922	Pratt	106	Burns	12	Pratt	86	Pratt	73	Pratt	183	Pratt	44	1922
1923	Harris	142	Harris	13	Burns	82	Burns	91	Burns	181	Burns	47	1923
1924	Boone	131	Boone	13	Veach	99	Flagstead	106	Wambsganss	174	Wambsganss	41	1924
1925	Boone	124	Todt	11	Todt	75	Flagstead	84	Flagstead	160	Flagstead	38	1925
1926	Rigney	105	Todt	7	Todt	69	Rigney	71	Todt	153	Rigney	32	1926
1927	Flagstead	103	Todt	6	Flagstead	69	Flagstead	63	Flagstead	133	Regan	37	1927
1928	Taitt	107	Todt	12	Regan	75	Flagstead	84	Myer	168	Flagstead	41	1928
1929	Rothrock	100	Rothrock	6	Scarritt	71	Rothrock	70	Scarritt	159	Todt	38	1929
1930	Webb	133	Webb	16	Webb	66	Oliver	86	Oliver	189	Regan	35	1930
1931	Webb	151	Webb	14	Webb	103	Webb	96	Webb	196	Webb	67	1931
1932	Pickering	77	McManus	5	Pickering	40	Olson	58	Oliver	120	Pickering	28	1932
1933	R.Johnson	126	R.Johnson	10	R.Johnson	95	R.Johnson	88	R.Johnson	151	Cooke	35	1933
1934	Werber	115	Werber	11	R.Johnson	119	Werber	129	Werber	200	R.Johnson	43	1934
1935	Cronin	106	Werber	14	Cronin	95	Almada	85	Almada	176	Cronin	37	1935
1936	Foxx	153	Foxx	41	Foxx	143	Foxx	130	Foxx	198	McNair	36	1936
1937	Foxx	127	Foxx	36	Foxx	127	Foxx	111	Cronin	175	Cronin	40	1937
1938	Foxx	180	Foxx	50	Foxx	175	Foxx	139	Vosmik	201	Cronin	51	1938
1939	Foxx	185	Foxx	35	Williams	145	Williams	131	Williams	185	Williams	44	1939
1940	Williams	159	Foxx	36	Foxx	119	Williams	134	Cramer	200	Williams	43	1940
1941	Williams	232	Williams	37	Williams	120	Williams	135	Williams	185	Cronin	38	1941
1942	Williams	214	Williams	36	Williams	137	Williams	141	Pesky	205	DiMaggio	36	1942
1943	Doerr	117	Doerr	16	Tabor	85	Doerr	78	Doerr	163	Doerr	32	1943
1944	B.Johnson	175	B.Johnson	17	B.Johnson	106	B.Johnson	106	B.Johnson	170	B.Johnson	40	1944
1945	Lake	136	B.Johnson	12	B.Johnson	74	Lake	81	B.Johnson	148	Newsome	30	1945
1946	Williams	211	Williams	38	Williams	123	Williams	142	Pesky	208	Pesky	43	1946
1947	Williams	199	Williams	32	Williams	114	Williams	125	Pesky	207	Williams	40	1947
1948	Williams	185	Stephens	29	Stephens	137	DiMaggio	127	Williams	188	Williams	44	1948
1949	Williams	187	Williams	43	Williams/Stephens	159	Williams	150	Williams	194	Williams	39	1949
1950	Dropo	130	Dropo	34	Stephens/Dropo	144	DiMaggio	131	DiMaggio	193	Stephens	34	1950
1951	Williams	159	Williams	30	Williams	126	DiMaggio	113	DiMaggio	189	Goodman/DiMaggio	34	1951
1952	Goodman	104	Gernert	19	Gernert	67	DiMaggio	81	Goodman	157	Goodman	27	1952
1953	Kell	126	Gernert	21	Kell	73	Piersall	76	Goodman	161	Kell	41	1953
1954	Williams	193	Williams	29	Jensen	117	Williams	93	Jensen	160	White/Jensen/Goodman	25	1954
1955	Jensen	118	Williams	28	Jensen	116	Goodman	100	Goodman	176	Goodman	31	1955
1956	Williams	164	Williams	24	Jensen	97	Piersall/Klaus	91	Jensen	182	Piersall	40	1956
1957	Williams	227	Williams	38	Malzone/Jensen	103	Piersall	103	Malzone	185	Malzone	31	1957
1958	Williams	174	Jensen	35	Jensen	122	Runnels	103	Malzone	185	Runnels	32	1958
1959	Jensen	131	Jensen	28	Jensen	112	Jensen	101	Runnels	176	Malzone	34	1959
1960	Runnels	112	Williams	29	Wertz	103	Runnels	80	Runnels	169	Malzone	30	1960
1961	Geiger	99	Geiger	18	Malzone	87	Schilling	87	Schilling	167	Yastrzemski	31	1961
1962	Runnels	129	Malzone	21	Malzone	95	Yastrzemski	99	Yastrzemski	191	Yastrzemski	43	1962
1963	Yastrzemski	145	Stuart	42	Stuart	118	Yastrzemski	91	Yastrzemski	183	Yastrzemski	40	1963
1964	Bressoud	123	Stuart	33	Stuart	114	Bressoud	86	Stuart	168	Bressoud	41	1964
1965	Yastrzemski	154	Conigliaro	32	Mantilla	92	Conigliaro	82	Yastrzemski	154	Yastrzemski	45	1965
1966	Conigliaro	120	Conigliaro	28	Conigliaro	93	Foy	97	Yastrzemski	165	Yastrzemski	39	1966
1967	Yastrzemski	189	Yastrzemski	44	Yastrzemski	121	Yastrzemski	112	Yastrzemski	189	Yastrzemski	31	1967
1968	Yastrzemski	169	Harrelson	35	Harrelson	109	Yastrzemski	90	Yastrzemski	162	Smith	37	1968
1969	Petrocelli	168	Yastrzemski/Petrocelli	40	Yastrzemski	111	Yastrzemski	96	Smith	168	Petrocelli	32	1969
1970	Yastrzemski	174	Yastrzemski	40	T.Conigliaro	116	Yastrzemski	125	Yastrzemski	186	Smith	32	1970
1971	Smith	127	Smith	30	Smith	96	Smith	85	Smith	175	Smith	33	1971
1972	Fisk	159	Fisk	22	Petrocelli	75	Harper	92	Harper	141	Harper	29	1972
1973	Yastrzemski	137	Fisk	26	Yastrzemski	95	Harper	92	Yastrzemski	160	Yastrzemski/Cepeda	25	1973
1974	Yastrzemski	139	Yastrzemski/Petrocelli	15	Yastrzemski	79	Yastrzemski	93	Yastrzemski	155	Yastrzemski	25	1974
1975	Lynn	159	Rice	22	Lynn	105	Lynn	103	Lynn	175	Lynn	47	1975
1976	Lynn	130	Rice	25	Yastrzemski	102	Lynn/Fisk	76	Rice	164	Evans	34	1976
1977	Rice	144	Rice	39	Rice	114	Fisk	106	Rice	206	Burleson	36	1977
1978	Rice	153	Rice	46	Rice	139	Rice	121	Rice	213	Fisk	39	1978
1979	Lynn	173	Rice/Lynn	39	Rice	130	Rice	117	Rice	201	Lynn	42	1979
1980	Evans	123	Perez	25	Perez	105	Burleson	89	Burleson	179	Evans	37	1980
1981	Evans	159	Evans	22	Evans	71	Evans	84	Lansford	134	Lansford	23	1981
1982	Evans	146	Evans	32	Evans	98	Evans	122	Remy/Evans	178	Evans	37	1982
1983	Boggs	146	Rice	39	Rice	126	Boggs	100	Boggs	210	Boggs	44	1983
1984	Evans	145	Armas	43	Armas	123	Evans	121	Boggs	203	Evans	37	1984
1985	Boggs	148	Evans	29	Buckner	110	Evans	110	Boggs	240	Buckner	46	1985
1986	Boggs	155	Baylor	31	Rice	110	Boggs	107	Boggs	207	Boggs	47	1986
1987	Boggs	172	Evans	34	Evans	123	Boggs	108	Boggs	200	Boggs	40	1987
1988	Boggs	165	Greenwell	22	Greenwell	119	Boggs	128	Boggs	214	Boggs	45	1988
1989	Boggs	140	Esasky	30	Esasky	108	Boggs	113	Boggs	205	Boggs	51	1989
1990	Burks	125	Burks	21	Burks	89	Burks/Boggs	89	Boggs	187	J.Reed	45	1990
1991	Boggs	137	Clark	28	Clark	87	Boggs	93	Boggs	181	Reed/Boggs	42	1991
1992	Brunansky	115	Brunansky	15	Brunansky	74	Reed	64	Reed	136	Brunansky	31	1992
1993	Vaughn	136	Vaughn	29	Vaughn	101	Vaughn	86	Greenwell	170	Valentin	40	1993
1994	Vaughn	144	Vaughn	26	Vaughn	82	Vaughn	65	Vaughn	122	Valentin	26	1994
1995	Vaughn	143	Vaughn	39	Vaughn	126	Valentin	108	Vaughn	165	Valentin	37	1995
1996	Vaughn	149	Vaughn	44	Vaughn	143	Valentin	118	Vaughn	207	Jefferson	30	1996
1997	Vaughn	150	Vaughn	35	Garciaparra	98	Garciaparra	122	Garciaparra	209	Valentin	47	1997
1998	Vaughn	151	Vaughn	40	Garciaparra	122	Valentin	113	Vaughn	205	Valentin	44	1998
1999	Garciaparra	152	O'Leary	28	Garciaparra	104	Offerman	107	Garciaparra	190	Garciaparra	42	1999
2000	Garciaparra	155	Everett	34	Everett	108	Garciaparra	104	Garciaparra	197	Garciaparra	51	2000
2001	Ramirez	162	Ramirez	41	Ramirez	125	Nixon	100	Ramirez	162	Ramirez	33	2001
2002	Ramirez	184	Ramirez	33	Garciaparra	120	Damon	118	Garciaparra	197	Garciaparra	56	2002
2003	Ramirez	158	Ramirez	37	Garciaparra	105	Garciaparra	120	Garciaparra	198	Mueller	45	2003
2004	Ramirez	150	Ramirez	43	Ortiz	139	Damon	123	Damon	189	Ortiz	47	2004
2005	Ortiz	156	Ortiz	47	Ortiz	148	Ortiz	119	Damon	197	Ortiz	40	2005
2006	Ramirez	168	Ortiz	54	Ortiz	137	Ortiz	115	Loretta	181	Lowell	47	2006

= In 1961 the American League expanded from 8 to 10 teams. In 1969 it expanded to 12 teams and split into 6-team divisions. In 1977 the league expanded to 14 teams, with 7 teams in each division. In 1994 the league split into two 5-team divisions (including the AL East) and one 4-team division.

Year	Triples		SB		BFW		ERA		AERA		IP		Year
1901	Stahl/J.Collins	16	Dowd	33	J.Collins	4.2	**Young**	**1.62**	**Young**	**217**	Young	371.1	1901
1902	Freeman	19	Stahl	24	J.Collins	2.1	Young	2.15	Young	166	**Young**	**384.2**	1902
1903	Freeman	20	Dougherty	35	J.Collins	2.9	Young	2.08	Young	146	**Young**	**341.2**	1903
1904	**Stahl/Freeman**	**19**	Parent	20	Criger	2.3	Young	1.97	Young	136	Young	380	1904
1905	Ferris	16	Parent	25	J.Collins	2.2	Young	1.82	Young	147	Young	320.2	1905
1906	Ferris	13	Parent	16	Stahl	1.8	Dinneen	2.92	Dinneen	94	Young	287.2	1906
1907	Unglaub	13	Wagner	20	Shaw	1	Young	1.99	Young	129	Young	343.1	1907
1908	Gessler	14	McConnell	31	Wagner	3.2	Young	1.26	Young	194	Young	299	1908
1909	Speaker	13	Lord	36	Speaker	4.6	Cicotte	1.94	Cicotte	128	Arellanes	230.2	1909
1910	Stahl	16	Hooper	40	Speaker	4.8	Ra.Collins	1.62	Ra.Collins	158	Cicotte	250	1910
1911	Speaker	13	Hooper	38	Gardner/Speaker	3.3	Wood	2.02	Wood	162	Wood	275.2	1911
1912	Gardner	18	Speaker	52	**Speaker**	**7.2**	Wood	1.91	Wood	179	Wood	344	1912
1913	Speaker	22	Speaker	46	Speaker	6.5	Wood	2.29	Leonard	123	Leonard	259.1	1913
1914	Gardner	19	Speaker	42	**Speaker**	**7.3**	**Leonard**	**.96**	**Leonard**	**279**	Ra.Collins	272.1	1914
1915	Hooper	13	Speaker	29	Speaker	3.6	**Wood**	**1.49**	Wood	186	Foster	255.1	1915
1916	Walker/Hooper	11	Hooper	27	Hooper/Thomas	1.1	**Ruth**	**1.75**	**Ruth**	**158**	Ruth	323.2	1916
1917	Hooper	11	Hooper	21	Lewis	1.4	Mays	1.74	Mays	148	Ruth	326.1	1917
1918	Hooper	13	Hooper	24	Ruth	2.7	Bush	2.11	Bush	127	Mays	293.1	1918
1919	Ruth	12	Hooper	23	**Ruth**	**7.3**	Pennock	2.71	Pennock	111	Jones	245	1919
1920	Hooper	17	Menosky	23	Hooper	2.7	Harper	3.04	Harper	119	Jones	274	1920
1921	S.Collins	12	S.Collins	15	Scott	1.9	Jones	3.22	Jones	131	Jones	298.2	1921
1922	Harris	9	Menosky	9	Harris	0.6	Quinn	3.48	Quinn	118	Quinn	256	1922
1923	Harris	11	McMillan	13	Harris	1.7	Piercy	3.41	Piercy	120	Ehmke	316.2	1923
1924	Veach/Harris	9	Wambsganss	14	Harris	1.2	Quinn	3.27	Quinn	134	**Ehmke**	**315.0**	1924
1925	Todt	13	Prothro/Ezzell	9	Prothro/Herrera	0.3	Ehmke	3.73	Ehmke	122	Ehmke	260.2	1925
1926	Todt	12	Haney	13	Rigney	4.3	Wiltse	4.22	Wiltse	96	Wiltse	196.1	1926
1927	Regan	10	Flagstead	12	Rogell	0.8	Harriss	4.18	Harriss	101	Wiltse	219	1927
1928	Taitt	14	**Myer**	**30**	Myer	2	Morris	3.53	Morris	116	Ruffing	289.1	1928
1929	Scarritt	17	Rothrock	24	K.Williams	0.7	MacFayden	3.62	MacFayden	118	Ruffing	244.1	1929
1930	Regan	10	Reeves/Oliver	6	Berry	1	Gaston	3.92	Gaston	117	Gaston	273	1930
1931	Oliver	5	Rothrock	13	Webb	3	Moore	3.88	Moore	111	Russell	232	1931
1932	Olson	6	Warstler	9	Spognardi	0.3	Durham	3.8	Durham	118	Weiland	195.2	1932
1933	Cooke	10	R.Johnson	13	R.Johnson/Hodapp	1.1	Weiland	3.87	Weiland	113	Rhodes	232	1933
1934	Werber/R.Johnson	10	**Werber**	**40**	Werber	3.9	Ostermueller	3.49	Ostermueller	138	Rhodes	219	1934
1935	Cronin	14	**Werber**	**29**	R.Ferrell	2.1	**Grove**	**2.70**	**Grove**	**176**	**W.Ferrell**	**322.1**	1935
1936	Kroner/Foxx	8	Werber	23	Foxx	3.3	**Grove**	**2.81**	**Grove**	**189**	**W.Ferrell**	**301.0**	1936
1937	Cramer	11	Mills	11	Foxx	1.8	Grove	3.02	Grove	157	Grove	262	1937
1938	Foxx	9	Chapman	13	**Foxx**	**5.8**	**Grove**	**3.08**	**Grove**	**160**	Bagby	198.2	1938
1939	Williams	11	Tabor	16	Foxx	5.2	**Grove**	**2.54**	**Grove**	**186**	Grove	191	1939
1940	Finney	15	Tabor	14	Williams	4	Bagby	4.73	Bagby	95	Bagby	182.2	1940
1941	Finney	10	Tabor	17	**Williams**	**8.5**	Wagner	3.07	Wagner	136	D.Newsome	213.2	1941
1942	Pesky	9	DiMaggio	16	**Williams**	**8.5**	Hughson	2.59	Hughson	144	**Hughson**	**281.0**	1942
1943	Lupien	9	Fox	22	Doerr	3.2	Hughson	2.64	Hughson	125	Hughson	266	1943
1944	Doerr	10	Metkovich	13	B.Johnson	5.3	Hughson	2.26	Hughson	151	Hughson	203.1	1944
1945	McBride/B.Johnson	7	Metkovich	19	Lake	6.5	Ferriss	2.96	Ferriss	115	Ferriss	264.2	1945
1946	Doerr	9	DiMaggio	10	**Williams**	**8.1**	Hughson	2.75	Hughson	133	Hughson	278	1946
1947	Doerr	10	Pesky	12	**Williams**	**7.2**	Dobson	2.95	Dobson	132	Dobson	228.2	1947
1948	Stephens	8	DiMaggio	10	Williams	5.9	Parnell	3.14	Parnell	140	Dobson	245.1	1948
1949	Doerr	9	DiMaggio	9	**Williams**	**6.4**	Parnell	2.77	Parnell	157	**Parnell**	**295.1**	1949
1950	**Doerr/DiMaggio**	**11**	**DiMaggio**	**15**	Doerr	2.4	Parnell	3.61	Parnell	136	Parnell	249	1950
1951	Pesky	6	Goodman	7	Williams	4.1	Parnell	3.26	Parnell	137	Parnell	221	1951
1952	Vollmer	4	Throneberry	16	Goodman	3.4	Parnell	3.62	Parnell	109	Parnell	214	1952
1953	Piersall	9	Piersall	11	Williams	1.7	McDermott	3.01	McDermott	140	Parnell	241	1953
1954	Agganis	8	**Jensen**	**22**	**Williams**	**5.1**	F.Sullivan	3.14	F.Sullivan	131	F.Sullivan	206.1	1954
1955	Jensen	6	Jensen	16	Williams	4.3	F.Sullivan	2.91	F.Sullivan	148	**F.Sullivan**	**260.0**	1955
1956	**Jensen**	**11**	Jensen	11	Williams	2.9	F.Sullivan	3.42	F.Sullivan	135	Brewer	244.1	1956
1957	Piersall/Malzone	5	Piersall	14	Williams	7.3	F.Sullivan	2.73	F.Sullivan	146	F.Sullivan	240.2	1957
1958	Runnels/Piersall	5	Piersall	12	Runnels	4.1	Delock	3.38	Delock	119	Brewer	227.1	1958
1959	Runnels	6	Jensen	20	**Runnels**	**3.9**	Brewer	3.76	Brewer	108	Brewer	215.1	1959
1960	Clinton/Buddin	5	Runnels	5	Runnels	3.5	Monbouquette	3.64	Monbouquette	111	Monbouquette	215	1960
1961	Yastrzemski/Geiger	6	Geiger	16	Buddin	1.6	Schwall	3.22	Schwall	129	Monbouquette	236.1	1961
1962	Clinton	10	Geiger	18	Bressoud	3.7	Monbouquette	3.33	Monbouquette	124	Conley	241.2	1962
1963	Clinton	7	Geiger	9	**Yastrzemski**	**4.2**	Wilson	3.76	Wilson	101	Monbouquette	266.2	1963
1964	Yastrzemski	9	Yastrzemski/Jones	6	Yastrzemski	3.5	Monbouquette	4.04	Monbouquette	96	Monbouquette	234	1964
1965	Green	6	Jones/Green	8	Yastrzemski	3.5	Monbouquette	3.7	Monbouquette	101	Wilson	230.2	1965
1966	Foy	8	Yastrzemski	8	Yastrzemski	1.7	Santiago	3.66	Santiago	104	Lonborg	181.2	1966
1967	Scott	7	Smith	16	**Yastrzemski**	**6.9**	Stange	2.77	Stange	126	Lonborg	273.1	1967
1968	Smith	5	Foy	26	**Yastrzemski**	**6.3**	Culp	2.91	Culp	108	Culp	216.1	1968
1969	Smith	7	Yastrzemski	15	**Petrocelli**	**7.6**	Nagy	3.11	Nagy	123	Culp	227	1969
1970	Smith	7	Yastrzemski	23	Yastrzemski	5.5	Culp	3.04	Culp	131	Culp	251.1	1970
1971	Kennedy	5	Smith/Griffin	11	Smith	2.6	Siebert	2.91	Siebert	128	Culp	242.1	1971
1972	**Fisk**	**9**	Harper	25	Fisk	5.1	**Tiant**	**1.91**	**Tiant**	**170**	Pattin	253	1972
1973	Miller	7	**Harper**	**54**	Smith	3	Lee	2.75	Lee	146	Lee	284.2	1973
1974	Evans	8	Harper	28	Fisk	2.3	Tiant	2.92	Tiant	132	Tiant	311.1	1974
1975	Lynn	7	Rice/Lynn	10	Lynn	4.1	Lee/Wise	3.95	Lee/Wise	103	Tiant/Lee	260	1975
1976	Rice/Lynn	8	Lynn/Burleson	14	Fisk	3.3	Tiant	3.06	Tiant/Cleveland	127	Tiant	279	1976
1977	Rice	15	Burleson	13	Fisk	4.6	Jenkins	3.68	Jenkins	122	Jenkins	193	1977
1978	**Rice**	**15**	Remy	30	Rice	4.2	Eckersley	2.99	Eckersley	138	Eckersley	268.1	1978
1979	Hobson	7	Remy	14	Lynn	5.3	Eckersley	2.99	**Eckersley**	**149**	Torrez	252.1	1979
1980	Rice	6	Remy	14	Burleson	3.7	Stanley	3.39	Stanley	126	Torrez	207.1	1980
1981	Evans	4	Lansford	15	Evans	3.6	Torrez	3.68	Torrez	107	Eckersley	154	1981
1982	Evans	7	Remy	16	Evans	3.2	Stanley	3.1	**Stanley**	**140**	Eckersley	224.1	1982
1983	Boggs	7	Remy	11	Boggs	4.4	Ojeda	4.04	Ojeda	109	Tudor	242	1983
1984	Evans	8	Gutierrez	12	Boggs	4.4	Nipper	3.89	Nipper	108	Hurst	218	1984
1985	Gedman/Armas	5	Buckner	18	Boggs	5.6	Boyd	3.7	Boyd	117	Boyd	272.1	1985
1986	Barrett/Armas	4	Barrett	15	**Boggs**	**5.4**	**Clemens**	**2.48**	**Clemens**	**169**	Clemens	254	1986
1987	Owen	7	Burks	27	**Boggs**	**6.5**	Clemens	2.97	Clemens	154	Clemens	281.2	1987
1988	Greenwell	8	Burks	25	**Boggs**	**6.4**	Clemens	2.93	Clemens	141	Clemens	264	1988
1989	Boggs	7	Burks	21	Boggs	4.3	Clemens	3.13	Clemens	132	Clemens	253.1	1989
1990	Burks	8	Burks	9	J.Reed	2.3	**Clemens**	**1.93**	**Clemens**	**212**	Clemens	228.1	1990
1991	Greenwell	6	Greenwell	15	Boggs	3.8	**Clemens**	**2.62**	**Clemens**	**165**	**Clemens**	**271.1**	1991
1992	Boggs	4	Reed	7	Reed	1.6	**Clemens**	**2.41**	**Clemens**	**177**	Clemens	246.2	1992
1993	Greenwell	6	Fletcher	16	Valentin	2.9	Viola	3.14	Viola	148	Darwin	229.1	1993
1994	Cooper	4	Nixon	42	Valentin	2.2	Clemens	2.85	**Clemens**	**177**	Clemens	170.2	1994
1995	O'Leary	6	Valentin	20	Valentin	4.6	Wakefield	2.95	Wakefield	165	Wakefield	195.1	1995
1996	O'Leary	5	Frye	18	Vaughn	2.3	Clemens	3.63	Clemens	140	Clemens	242.2	1996
1997	**Garciaparra**	**11**	Garciaparra	22	Valentin	4	Gordon	3.74	Gordon	124	Wakefield	201.1	1997
1998	O'Leary/Garciaparra	8	Lewis	29	Garciaparra	3	P.Martinez	2.89	P.Martinez	164	P.Martinez	233.2	1998
1999	**Offerman**	**11**	Offerman	18	Garciaparra	4.7	**P.Martinez**	**2.07**	**P.Martinez**	**241**	P.Martinez	213.1	1999
2000	Nixon	8	Everett	11	Garciaparra	5	**P.Martinez**	**1.74**	**P.Martinez**	**288**	P.Martinez	217	2000
2001	O'Leary	6	Everett	9	Ramirez	3.8	Wakefield	3.9	Wakefield	114	Nomo	198	2001
2002	**Damon**	**11**	Damon	31	Garciaparra	5.4	**P.Martinez**	**2.26**	**P.Martinez**	**198**	Lowe	219.2	2002
2003	Garciaparra	13	Damon	30	Ramirez	4.1	**P.Martinez**	**2.22**	**P.Martinez**	**210**	Lowe	203.1	2003
2004	Damon	6	Damon	19	Varitek	3.2	Schilling	3.26	Schilling	150	Schilling	226.2	2004
2005	Damon	6	Damon	18	Ortiz	4.2	Wakefield	4.15	Wakefield	109	Wakefield	225.1	2005
2006	7 players tied	2	Crisp	22	Ortiz	4.5	Schilling	3.97	Schilling	118	Beckett	204.2	2006

+ = In 1981, the American League played a split season due to a strike. Boston finished in fifth place with a 30–26 record in the first half, and in a tie for second place with a 29-23 record in the second half.

Year	Strikeouts		OAVG		BR/9		Wins		GP		Saves		PW		Year
1901	**Young**	**158**	**Young**	**.232**	**Young**	**8.92**	**Young**	**33**	Young	43	Lewis	1	**Young**	**7.9**	1901
1902	Young	160	Winter	.238	Young	9.73	**Young**	**32**	**Young**	**45**	Altrock	1	**Young**	**6.0**	1902
1903	Young	176	Dinneen	.230	Young	8.96	**Young**	**28**	Young	40	**Young/Dinneen**	**2**	**Young**	**4.8**	1903
1904	Young	200	Gibson	.219	**Young**	**8.53**	Young	26	Young	43	Young	1	Young	3.8	1904
1905	Young	210	Young	.216	**Young**	**8.03**	Tannehill	22	Young	38	Dinneen	1	Young	2.7	1905
1906	Young	140	Harris	.243	Young	10.04	Young/Tannehill	13	Young	39	Young/Harris/Winter	2	Kroh	0.3	1906
1907	Young	147	Winter	.216	**Young**	**9.02**	Young	21	Young	43	Pruiett	3	Young	2.4	1907
1908	Young	150	Young	.213	Steele	7.7	Young	21	Cicotte	39	Young/Pruiett/Cicotte	2	Young	4.1	1908
1909	Wood	88	Cicotte	.207	Arellanes	9.36	Arellanes	16	Arellanes	45	**Arellanes**	**8**	Cicotte	0.9	1909
1910	Wood	145	Hall	.207	Ra.Collins	9.09	Cicotte	15	Cicotte	36	Hall	2	Ra.Collins/Wood	1.9	1910
1911	Wood	231	Wood	.223	Wood	10.22	Wood	23	Wood	44	**Hall**	**4**	**Wood**	**5.7**	1911
1912	Wood	258	Wood	.216	Wood	9.44	**Wood**	**34**	Wood	43	Hall/Bedient	2	Wood	7.6	1912
1913	Leonard	144	Leonard	.255	Ra.Collins	10.25	Ra.Collins	19	Bedient	43	Bedient	5	Wood	1.8	1913
1914	Leonard	176	**Leonard**	**.180**	**Leonard**	**8.29**	Ra.Collins	20	Bedient	42	Leonard	3	Leonard	4.8	1914
1915	Leonard	116	**Leonard**	**.208**	Wood	9.44	Shore/Foster	19	Shore/Mays	38	**Mays**	**7**	Wood	3.9	1915
1916	Ruth	170	**Ruth**	**.201**	Ruth	9.9	Ruth	23	Leonard	48	Leonard	6	**Ruth**	**5.7**	1916
1917	Leonard	144	Ruth	.211	Mays	9.9	Ruth	24	Ruth	41	Ruth	2	Ruth	4.9	1917
1918	Bush	125	Ruth	.214	Ruth	9.52	Mays	21	Bush	36	Bush	2	Mays	3.7	1918
1919	Pennock	70	Pennock	.274	Hoyt	10.34	Pennock	16	Jones	35	Ruth/Jones	1	Ruth	1.4	1919
1920	Bush	88	Pennock	.264	Pennock	11.48	Pennock	16	Pennock/Jones	37	Pennock	2	Pennock	0.6	1920
1921	Jones	98	Bush	.260	Jones	12.11	Jones	23	Jones	40	Russell	3	Jones	4.3	1921
1922	Ri.Collins	69	Ferguson	.265	Quinn	11.43	Ri.Collins	14	Karr	41	Russell/Ferguson	2	Quinn	1.4	1922
1923	Ehmke	121	Ehmke	.272	Ehmke	12.99	Ehmke	20	Ehmke	43	Quinn	7	Ehmke	1.9	1923
1924	Ehmke	119	Ehmke	.265	Ehmke	11.89	Ehmke	19	Ehmke	45	Quinn	7	Ehmke	3.4	1924
1925	Ehmke	95	Wingfield	.278	Wingfield	12.99	Wingfield	12	Wingfield	41	Wingfield	2	Wingfield	1.8	1925
1926	Wiltse	59	Wiltse	.273	**Russell**	**10.93**	Wingfield	11	Wingfield	43	Wingfield	3	Russell	0.6	1926
1927	Ruffing/Harriss	77	Ruffing	.277	Russell	13.29	Harriss	14	Harriss	44	Ruffing/MacFayden	2	MacFayden	0.4	1927
1928	Ruffing	118	Morris	.264	Morris	11.88	Morris	19	Morris	47	Morris	5	Ruffing	1.8	1928
1929	Ruffing	109	MacFayden	.271	Russell	12.11	Morris	14	M.Gaston	39	M.Gaston	2	M.Gaston	1.6	1929
1930	Gaston	99	Gaston	.259	Durham	12.15	Gaston	13	Gaston	38	MacFayden/Gaston	2	Gaston	1.8	1930
1931	MacFayden	74	Durham	.266	Moore	12.19	MacFayden	16	Moore	53	**Moore**	**10**	Moore	1.3	1931
1932	Weiland	63	Durham	.274	Durham	12.32	Kline	11	Kline	47	Kline	2	Durham	0.9	1932
1933	Weiland	97	Weiland	.244	Weiland	12.56	Rhodes	12	Welch	47	Kline	4	Rhodes	1.2	1933
1934	Welch	91	Ostermueller	.262	Pennock	12.19	W.Ferrell	14	Rhodes	44	Ostermueller	3	W.Ferrell	2.8	1934
1935	Grove	121	Grove	.257	**Grove**	**11.11**	**W.Ferrell**	**25**	Walberg	44	Walberg	3	**W.Ferrell**	**6.8**	1935
1936	Grove	130	Grove	.246	**Grove**	**10.87**	W.Ferrell	20	Wilson/Ostermueller	43	Wilson	3	**Grove**	**6.6**	1936
1937	Grove	153	Wilson	.248	Grove	12.13	Grove	17	Wilson	51	Wilson	7	Grove	3.9	1937
1938	Grove	99	Wilson	.262	Harris	11.76	Wilson/Bagby	15	Bagby	43	McKain	6	Grove	3	1938
1939	Grove	81	Grove	.249	Grove	11.26	Grove	15	Dickman	48	Heving	7	Grove	3.7	1939
1940	Wilson	102	Wilson	.270	Grove	12.33	Wilson/Heving	12	Wilson	41	Wilson	5	Heving	0.6	1940
1941	Harris	111	Wagner	.245	Hughson	12.39	D.Newsome	19	Ryba	40	Ryba	6	Harris/Wagner	2	1941
1942	**Hughson**	**113**	Dobson	.231	Butland	9.78	**Hughson**	**22**	Hughson	38	Brown	6	Hughson	3.7	1942
1943	Hughson	114	Judd	.230	Hughson	10.73	Hughson	12	**Brown**	**49**	Brown	9	Hughson/Brown	1.6	1943
1944	Hughson	112	Hughson	.225	Hughson	9.52	Hughson	18	Ryba	42	Barrett	8	Hughson	3.1	1944
1945	Ferriss	94	Ferriss	.264	Barrett	11.09	Ferriss	21	Barrett	37	Barrett	3	Ferriss	3	1945
1946	Hughson	172	Dobson	.234	Hughson	9.87	Ferriss	25	Ferriss	40	**Klinger**	**9**	Hughson	3	1946
1947	Hughson	119	Dobson	.238	Dobson	10.9	Dobson	18	Johnson	45	Johnson	8	Dobson	2.6	1947
1948	Dobson	116	Parnell	.252	Dobson	12.11	Kramer	18	Dobson	38	Johnson	5	Parnell	2.2	1948
1949	Kinder	138	Parnell	.237	Parnell	12.1	**Parnell**	**25**	Kinder	43	Kinder	4	Parnell	5.2	1949
1950	McDermott	96	Stobbs	.250	Kinder	12.65	Parnell	18	Kinder	48	Kinder	9	Parnell	3.1	1950
1951	McDermott	127	McDermott	.226	Kinder	10.91	Parnell	18	**Kinder**	**63**	**Kinder**	**14**	**Parnell**	**3.3**	1951
1952	McDermott	117	McDermott	.234	Kinder	10.51	Parnell	12	Delock	39	Benton	6	Benton	1.2	1952
1953	Parnell	136	McDermott	.224	Kinder	10.43	Parnell	21	**Kinder**	**69**	**Kinder**	**27**	**Kinder**	**5.2**	1953
1954	F.Sullivan	124	F.Sullivan	.240	F.Sullivan	11.21	F.Sullivan	15	Kinder	48	Kinder	15	F.Sullivan	2.5	1954
1955	F.Sullivan	129	F.Sullivan	.241	**Kinder**	**9.85**	**F.Sullivan**	**18**	Kinder/Hurd	43	Kinder	18	F.Sullivan	3.4	1955
1956	Brewer	127	Brewer	.220	Brewer	11.68	Brewer	19	Delock	48	Delock	9	Brewer	3.9	1956
1957	Brewer	128	F.Sullivan	.230	F.Sullivan	9.76	Brewer	16	Delock	49	Delock	11	**F.Sullivan**	**3.5**	1957
1958	Brewer	124	Delock	.252	Kiely	10.78	Delock	14	Wall	52	Kiely	12	Delock	1.1	1958
1959	Brewer	121	Casale	.238	Fornieles	11.74	Casale	13	Fornieles	46	Fornieles	11	Delock	1.2	1959
1960	Monbouquette	134	Monbouquette	.263	Muffett	11.3	Monbouquette	14	**Fornieles**	**70**	**Fornieles**	**14**	Fornieles	2.6	1960
1961	Monbouquette	161	Monbouquette	.254	Hillman	10.73	Schwall	15	Fornieles	57	Fornieles	15	Schwall/Monbouquette	1.9	1961
1962	Monbouquette	153	Wilson	.231	Radatz	10.03	Monbouquette/Conley	15	**Radatz**	**62**	**Radatz**	**24**	**Radatz**	**3.9**	1962
1963	Monbouquette	174	Morehead	.211	Monbouquette	10.13	Monbouquette	20	Radatz	66	**Radatz**	**25**	**Radatz**	**5.0**	1963
1964	Radatz	181	Morehead	.248	Radatz	9.63	Radatz	16	**Radatz**	**79**	**Radatz**	**29**	Radatz	4.9	1964
1965	Wilson	164	Morehead	.217	Monbouquette	11.02	Wilson	13	Radatz	63	Radatz	22	Ritchie/Wilson	0.2	1965
1966	Lonborg	131	Santiago	.238	Santiago	11.25	Santiago	12	Lonborg	45	4 players tied	2	Brandon	0.8	1966
1967	**Lonborg**	**246**	Lonborg	.225	Stange	10.16	**Lonborg**	**22**	Wyatt	60	Wyatt	20	Wyatt	1.9	1967
1968	Culp	190	Culp	.210	Stange	10.05	Ellsworth/Culp	16	Stange	50	Stange	12	Santiago	1.5	1968
1969	Culp	172	Culp	.231	Culp	11.1	Culp	17	Lyle	71	Lyle	17	Lyle	2	1969
1970	Culp	197	Culp	.224	Siebert	11.03	Culp	17	Lyle	63	Lyle	20	Culp	2.2	1970
1971	Culp	151	Siebert	.245	Siebert	10.82	Siebert	16	Bolin	52	Lyle	16	Siebert	3.3	1971
1972	Pattin	168	Tiant	.202	Tiant	9.7	Pattin	17	Lee	47	Lee/Bolin	5	Tiant	2.9	1972
1973	Tiant	206	Tiant	.219	Tiant	9.99	Tiant	20	Bolin	39	Bolin	15	Lee	3.6	1973
1974	Tiant	176	Tiant	.241	Tiant	10.61	Tiant	22	Segui	58	Segui	10	Tiant	3.5	1974
1975	Tiant	142	Wise/Cleveland	.263	Tiant	11.7	Wise	19	Lee	41	Drago	15	Moret	0.9	1975
1976	Jenkins	142	Cleveland	.246	Jenkins	10.72	Tiant	21	Willoughby	54	Willoughby	10	Tiant	2.7	1976
1977	Tiant	124	Jenkins	.257	Aase	10.23	Campbell	13	Campbell	69	**Campbell**	**31**	**Campbell**	**4.5**	1977
1978	Eckersley	162	Tiant	.234	Tiant	10.47	Eckersley	20	Stanley	52	Stanley	10	Eckersley	3.1	1978
1979	Eckersley	150	Eckersley	.250	Eckersley	10.91	Eckersley	17	Drago	53	Drago	13	Eckersley	4	1979
1980	Eckersley	121	Eckersley	.248	Burgmeier	9.91	Eckersley	12	Burgmeier	62	Burgmeier	24	Burgmeier	3.1	1980
1981	Clear	82	Tanana	.265	Ojeda	10.45	Torrez/Stanley	10	Stanley	35	Clear	9	Burgmeier	1.1	1981
1982	Tudor	146	Stanley	.255	Burgmeier	10.73	Clear	14	Clear	55	Stanley/Clear	14	Stanley	3.1	1982
1983	Tudor	136	Tudor	.255	Stanley	11.52	Tudor	13	Stanley	64	Stanley	33	Stanley	3.4	1983
1984	Ojeda	137	Nipper	.257	Stanley	11.64	Ojeda/Hurst/Boyd	12	Stanley	57	Stanley	22	Stanley/Nipper/Hurst	0.8	1984
1985	Hurst	189	Nipper	.256	Stanley	11.09	Boyd	15	Stanley	48	Crawford	12	Boyd	2.1	1985
1986	Clemens	238	**Clemens**	**.195**	**Clemens**	**8.86**	**Clemens**	**24**	Stanley	66	Stanley	16	Clemens	5.1	1986
1987	Clemens	256	Clemens	.235	Clemens	10.86	**Clemens**	**20**	Schiraldi	62	Gardner	10	**Clemens**	**4.5**	1987
1988	**Clemens**	**291**	Clemens	.220	Clemens	9.72	Hurst/Clemens	18	Smith	64	Smith	29	Clemens	3.7	1988
1989	Clemens	230	Clemens	.231	Lamp	9.85	Clemens	17	Murphy	74	Smith	25	Clemens	2.7	1989
1990	Clemens	209	Clemens	.228	Clemens	10.01	Clemens	21	Murphy	68	Reardon	21	**Clemens**	**6.2**	1990
1991	**Clemens**	**241**	Clemens	.221	**Gray**	**7.30**	Clemens	18	Fossas	64	Reardon	40	**Clemens**	**4.7**	1991
1992	Clemens	208	Clemens	.224	Clemens	10	Clemens	18	Harris	70	Reardon	27	**Clemens**	**5.3**	1992
1993	Clemens	160	Darwin	.230	Darwin	9.73	Darwin	15	**Harris**	**80**	Russell	33	Darwin	3.5	1993
1994	Clemens	168	**Clemens**	**.203**	Clemens	10.49	Clemens	9	Fossas	44	Ryan	13	Clemens	3.2	1994
1995	Hanson	139	Wakefield	.227	Maddux	10.34	Wakefield	16	Belinda	63	Belinda	10	Wakefield	4.2	1995
1996	**Clemens**	**257**	Clemens	.237	Clemens	12.09	Wakefield	14	Slocumb	75	Slocumb	31	Clemens/Slocumb	3.3	1996
1997	Gordon	159	Gordon	.226	Henry	11.53	Sele	13	Wasdin	53	Gordon	11	Gordon	1.5	1997
1998	P.Martinez	251	P.Martinez	.217	Gordon	9.08	P.Martinez	19	Gordon	73	**Gordon**	**46**	P.Martinez	4.6	1998
1999	**P.Martinez**	**313**	**P.Martinez**	**.205**	P.Martinez	8.69	**P.Martinez**	**23**	Lowe	74	Wakefield/Lowe	15	**P.Martinez**	**8.1**	1999
2000	**P.Martinez**	**284**	**P.Martinez**	**.167**	**P.Martinez**	**7.22**	P.Martinez	18	Lowe	74	**Lowe**	**42**	**P.Martinez**	**8.4**	2000
2001	**Nomo**	**220**	Nomo	.231	P.Martinez	8.87	Nomo	13	Beck	68	Lowe	24	Martinez	2.1	2001
2002	**P.Martinez**	**239**	**P.Martinez**	**.198**	P.Martinez	8.98	Lowe	21	Urbina	61	Urbina	40	**Lowe**	**6.2**	2002
2003	P.Martinez	206	**P.Martinez**	**.215**	Timlin	9.68	Lowe	17	Timlin	72	Kim	16	P.Martinez	4.4	2003
2004	P.Martinez	227	P.Martinez	.238	Foulke	9.11	**Schilling**	**21**	Timlin	76	Foulke	32	Schilling	4.5	2004
2005	Wakefield	151	Wakefield	.245	Wakefield	11.54	Wakefield	16	**Timlin**	**81**	Foulke	15	Timlin	2.6	2005
2006	Schilling	183	Beckett	.245	**Papelbon**	**7.11**	Beckett	16	Timlin	68	Papelbon	35	**Papelbon**	**4.6**	2006

Bold indicates player led the American League in that category.

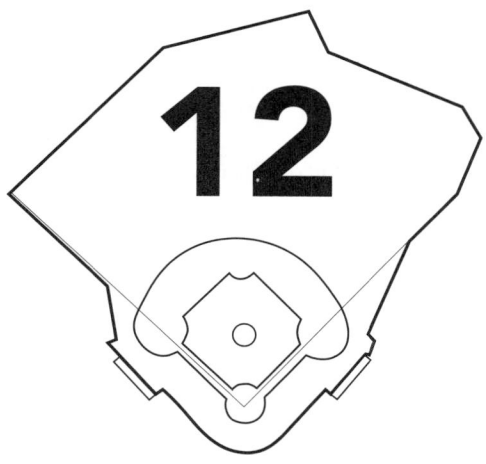

RED SOX ROSTERS

One of the main purposes of this book is to provide information and statistics for everyone whose ever played for the Red Sox. The 855 Red Sox who appear in the Player Register and the 705 who appear in the Pitcher Register are listed by the years they appeared in games for the club. Likewise, the Managers Register traces the 44 managers in franchise history, giving the details of their records in a given year, the place they finished in, and how they fared compared to projections for runs scored and allowed. The Rosters section has a simpler purpose: who was on the team.

Who played where and how often, however, is a little more complicated. Scan through this section and you'll find the answers to dozens of trivia questions. Who got most of the playing time in left field when Ted Williams served as a pilot in World War II (Bob Johnson) and Korea (Hoot Evers)? Which four future Hall of Famers spent the 1980 season with the Red Sox? (Dennis Eckersley, Carlton Fisk, Tony Perez, and Carl Yastrzemski)? And then there are facts that are just hard to fathom when players from different eras are compared straight up: Six pitchers were used all season to help the Red Sox claim the first world championship in 1903; the 2003 Red Sox used 26 pitchers.

These rosters provide much more complete information than typical rosters do about how each team was put together and how players were utilized in a given season. This is especially true in the past two decades, when teams have become much more reluctant to let young pitchers learn the ropes or to let struggling players work their way out of slumps. The increasing frequency of serious injuries has also resulted in less stable lineups. The enormous amount of money at stake is also

a major factor in the decreasing amount of patience exhibited by teams at every level. Big league teams, managers, and players have lived under the microscope of the media throughout baseball history, but now that media microscope broadcasts high definition, full-color video accompanied by unabashedly critical commentary, 24-7. This intense pressure has resulted in numerous lineups and fewer "set" positions than in the past. This roster-coding scheme may seem complex, but it gives a much more detailed understanding of whatever team is being examined.

Simpler rosters that showed pitching staffs composed simply of *SPs* and *RPs* would be far less useful than rosters showing that many pitchers spent part of the season in the rotation as well as the bullpen. Rosters that showed position players only by their primary positions, or that labeled all reserves simply as utility players, would also omit much useful information. The most common combination codes are, not surprisingly, *RS* and *SR*, followed by several codes for utility players. Two-position combination codes normally show up only a few times for each team.

From top to bottom, rosters list starting pitchers first, then relief pitchers, then regular position players, and then reserves. Non-playing managers are shown last.

Pitchers. There are more than just starters and relievers. The versatile pitcher who fills several roles is listed by the role he occupied most. Pitcher codes are:

SP – starting pitcher;
RP – relief pitcher;
SR – starter-reliever;
RS – reliever-starter;
CL – closer.

Pitchers are assigned codes according to the following rules:

If a starting pitcher has 0–9 games in relief, he is labeled as *SP*.

If a pitcher has 10 or more games in relief, and if at least one third of his appearances are games started, then he is labeled as *SR*.

If the pitcher has started at least 5 games and has 10 or more games in relief, he is labeled as *RS*—provided he started less than one third of the time.

If a relief pitcher has from 0–4 games started, he is labeled as *RP*.

If a relief pitcher's saves total is equal to at least one third of his relief appearances, then he is labeled as *CL*.

Position Players. All position players are listed by the position they played most, even if that position was "utility." Position players who played in fewer than 60 percent of their team's games are marked by a dash after their position code.

Regular players are always listed in the order shown below. If a player appeared in at least 75 percent of his team's games at one position, he is shown as the regular with the following codes:

C – catcher
1B – first base (*1* when combined with other positions)
2B – second base (*2* when combined)
3B – third base (*3* when combined)
SS – shortstop (*S* when combined)
LF– left fielder (*L* when combined)
CF– center fielder (*M* when combined)
RF – right fielder (*R* when combined)
DH – designated hitter (*D* when combined)

If no one played at least 75 percent of a team's games at one position, the regular shown will be the player who played the most games at that position—unless a player happened to have played the most games at two positions. If so, that player will be shown where he played the most, and the player with the second-most games at the other position will be shown as the regular.

In the overwhelming majority of circumstances, the regular at each position will have the standard position code or a combination code that starts with the first letter of that position (e.g., *3S* for third base/shortstop; *L1* for left field/first base). However, when a team has several players shifting among different positions during the season, the regular shown at a particular position might not have the expected code. (This usually happens on bad teams that have no set lineup; see the 1923 Red Sox.)

In these rare circumstances, the "regular" third baseman might be someone who played only 40 games there, but who still played third more than anyone else on that team who wasn't a regular at another position. For example, in 1918 Fred Thomas played only 41 games at third base for the pennant-winning Red Sox, but that was still more than anyone else, so Thomas is shown as the regular.

Aside from the position codes shown above, four other codes are used for players who have played less than 75 percent of their games at one position. Details on these codes are found below:

OF – outfield (*O* when used in combination);
IF – infield (*I* when used in combination);
UT – utility player (*U* when used in combination);
P – Pitcher (when used in combination with position codes).

Combination Position Codes. Most of the rules in this section apply only to a small fraction of the players and pitchers listed in the team rosters. Most of the remaining players are shown with two-position codes. But these exceptions require some explanation.

If a player played between 50 percent and 75 percent of his games at one position, his primary position will be signified by the *first* letter of the above codes. (Exception: To avoid confusion with catcher, we have revived the old newspaper box score code *M*—for "middle outfielder"—to indicate center field.)

Players with at least half their games at one position, but less than three quarters of their games at that position, are also given a secondary position code. The secondary code assigned depends on how many games they played at other positions, of course, as well as the number of other positions they played. The rules for secondary position codes are:

If a player played at least 25 percent of his other games at a position other than his primary position, the secondary position will be shown as the second letter of his position code.

If the player did not play 25 percent of his other games at any single position, but he did play at least 25 percent of his additional (i.e., non-primary position) games in the infield, the second letter of his position code will be *I*.

If the player did not play 25 percent of his other games at a single position, but he did play at least 25 percent of his additional games in the outfield, the second letter of his position code will be *O*. In 1987 Red Sox rookie Todd Benzinger played 14 games in left field, 5 in center, and 47 in right field. Thus he qualifies for an *RO* code, with 50–75 percent of his games in right, less than 25 percent at any other position, but a total of 19 games in left and center. The result of his outfield dexterity? He spent most of his career as a first baseman.

If a player's games are scattered among so many positions that none of these conditions apply, his secondary code will be *U*.

If the player's secondary position was pitcher and he pitched in at least 10 games, his second letter will be *P*. Only a few position players since 1901—the most famous being Babe Ruth, of course—have pitched in 10 games in one year while also playing in half their team's games.

Utility Codes. No two-letter coding scheme can account for all the ways that managers can use players during a season. Therefore, a few utility codes are used to cover versatile players who didn't play 50 percent of their games at any position. (Of course, complete data on games at position for every player can be found in the Player Register.) Utility codes indicating specific positions are used only for catchers. Otherwise, utility codes are assigned by the following rules:

If the player played all three outfield positions but never played the infield, he will be labeled *UO* (utility outfielder). Wily Mo Pena was a designated hitter 5 times for the Red Sox in 2006; the other 76 games he spent in the outfield. Including games where he switched positions during the contest (versatile players will do that), it broke down to 18 games in left field, 27 in center, and 39 in right. Since Pena did not have 50 percent of his games at any one position, yet he played all three outfield positions, he is labeled *UO*.

If the player played two outfield positions but never played the infield, he will be labeled *OF* (outfield).

If the player played three or four infield positions but never played the outfield, he will be labeled as *UI* (utility infielder).

If the player played two infield positions but never played the outfield, he will be labeled as *IF* (infielder).

If the player played two or more outfield positions as well as at least one infield position, and he played more games in the outfield than in the infield, he will be labeled as *OI* (outfielder-infielder).

If the player played two or more infield positions and at least one outfield position, and he played more games in the infield than in the outfield, he will be labeled as *IO* (infielder-outfielder).

If a player's first or second position (in terms of number of games) is catcher, but he played less than 50 percent of his games

there or at any other position, he will be labeled as *IC* (infielder/catcher) or *OC* (outfielder/catcher) depending on whether he played primarily in the infield or the outfield. If he played more games at catcher than elsewhere, and he did not play another defensive position in most of his other games (i.e., he was a DH or a pinch hitter), he will be labeled as *UC* (utility catcher).

If a player doesn't fit into any of these categories, he will be labeled as *UT* (utility).

Managers. Managers are indicated by the code *M*; see the Manager Register introduction for an explanation of who qualifies as a manager. If a team had multiple managers in a season, the order in which these managers served is shown by the number after the *M* (i.e., the first manager will be *M1*, the second *M2*, etc.). Managers' names are italicized in the rosters. Player/managers are shown with standard position code(s) and located as a player; their italicization indicates managerial status. Non-playing managers are shown at the end of the team roster.

1901

SP C Young
SP T Lewis
SP G Winter
SP F Mitchell
SP N Cuppy
SP W Kellum
SP- G Prentiss
SP- B Beville
SP- F Foreman
SP- J Volz
SP- F Morrissey
C O Schreckengost
1B B Freeman
2B H Ferris
SS F Parent
3B J Collins
LF T Dowd
CF C Stahl
RF C Hemphill
C- L Criger
3B- H Gleason
CF- C Jones
1U- L McLean
C- J Slattery

1902

SP C Young
SP B Dinneen
SP G Winter
SP T Sparks
SP T Hughes
SP- G Prentiss
SP- D Adkins
SP- N Altrock
SP- D Williams
SP- P Deininger
SP- B Husting
SP- F Mitchell
C L Criger
1B C LaChance
2B H Ferris
SS F Parent
3B J Collins
LF P Dougherty
CF C Stahl
RF B Freeman
UT- H Gleason
LF- C Hickman
C- J Warner
2B- G Wilson

1903

SP C Young
SP B Dinneen
SP T Hughes
SP N Gibson
SP G Winter
SP- N Altrock
C L Criger
1B C LaChance
2B H Ferris
SS F Parent
3B J Collins
LF P Dougherty
CF- C Stahl
RF B Freeman
MU J O'Brien
C- D Farrell
U1- H Gleason
C- A Smith
CU- J Stahl
C- G Stone

1904

SP C Young
SP B Dinneen
SP J Tannehill
SP N Gibson
SP G Winter
C L Criger
1B C LaChance
2B H Ferris
SS F Parent
3B J Collins
LF K Selbach
CF C Stahl
RF B Freeman
C- T Doran
LF- P Dougherty
C- D Farrell
OI- B O'Neill
UI- B Unglaub

1905

SP C Young
SP J Tannehill
SP G Winter
SP B Dinneen
SP N Gibson
SP- E Barry
SP- E Hughes
SP- H Olmsted
SP- J Harris
C L Criger
1B- M Grimshaw
2B H Ferris
SS F Parent
3B J Collins
LF J Burkett
CF C Stahl
RF K Selbach
1R B Freeman
C- C Armbruster
UC- T Doran
C- D Farrell
OI- J Godwin
1B- C LaChance
C- A McGovern
C- F Owens
RU- P Rising
UI- B Unglaub

1906

SP C Young
SP J Harris
SP B Dinneen
SP G Winter
SP J Tannehill
SP R Glaze
SP- F Oberlin
SP- L Swormstedt
SP- E Barry
SP- N Gibson
SP- E Hughes
SP- R Kroh
C- C Armbruster
1B M Grimshaw
2B H Ferris
SS F Parent
3B- R Morgan
LF J Hoey
CF C Stahl
RF- J Hayden
R1 B Freeman
C- B Carrigan
2B- C Chadbourne
3B- J Collins
C- L Criger
C- T Doran
UT- J Godwin
C- C Graham
C- B Peterson
LF- K Selbach
2B- H Wagner

1907

SP C Young
SP G Winter
SR R Glaze
SR T Pruiett
SP J Tannehill
SP C Morgan
SP J Harris
SP- F Oberlin
SP- R Kroh
SP- B Dinneen
SP- E Barry
SP- E Steele
SP- F Burchell
SP- B Jacobson
C- L Criger
1B B Unglaub
2B H Ferris
SS H Wagner
3B J Knight
LF J Barrett
CF D Sullivan
RF B Congalton
UT F Parent
C- C Armbruster
LF- C Chadbourne
3B- J Collins
RF- B Freeman
UT- M Grimshaw
OF- J Hoey
3B- H Lord
3B- D McGuire
C- B Peterson
C- A Shaw
RU- T Speaker
LU- G Whiteman
M2 G Huff

1908

SP C Young
SR E Cicotte
SP C Morgan
SR F Burchell
SP G Winter
SP E Steele
SP F Arellanes
SP T Pruiett
SP- R Glaze
SP- J Wood
SP- K Brady
SP- D McMahon
SP- J Tannehill
SP- C Patten
SP- C Hartman
SP- J Thielman
C- L Criger
1B- J Stahl
2B A McConnell
SS H Wagner
3B H Lord
LF J Thoney
CF D Sullivan
RF D Gessler
LU G Cravath
MU-J Barrett
LF- W Carlisle
C- B Carrigan
C- P Donahue
3B- L Gardner
RF- J Hoey
UT- F LaPorte
CU- E McFarland
C- D McGuire
CF- J McHale
IF- H Niles
C- H Ostdiek
CF- T Speaker
1B- B Unglaub
M2 F Lake

1909

SR F Arellanes
SR E Cicotte
SP J Wood
SP C Chech
SP E Steele
SP R Collins
SP B Schlitzer
SP E Karger
SP C Morgan
SP C Hall
SP J Ryan
SP L Pape
SP F Burchell
SP- C Smith
SP- W Matthews
SP- F Anderson
SP- J Chesbro
SP- C Nourse
C B Carrigan
1B J Stahl
2B A McConnell
SS H Wagner
3B H Lord
LO H Niles
CF T Speaker
RF D Gessler
1U- B Danzig
C- P Donahue
2S- C French
IF- L Gardner
LF- H Hooper
LR- P Howard
CU- B Madden
C- T Spencer
LF- J Thoney
IP- H Wolter
UP- S Yerkes
M F Lake

1910

SP E Cicotte
SP R Collins
SR J Wood
SR C Hall
SP E Karger
SP C Smith
SP F Arellanes
SP- B Hunt
SP- F Smith
SP- M McHale
SP- C Mahoney
SP- F Barberich
SP- L LeRoy
C B Carrigan
1B J Stahl
2B L Gardner
SS H Wagner
3B- H Lord
LF D Lewis
CF T Speaker
RF H Hooper
UT C Engle
1U- H Bradley
CU- P Donahue
2B- C French
SS- E Hearne
C- R Kleinow
SS- D Lerchen
C- B Madden
2B- A McConnell
UT- D Moskiman
RU- H Myers
RU- H Niles
CF- R Pond
3B- B Purtell
M P Donovan

1911

SR J Wood
SR E Cicotte
SP R Collins
SP L Pape
SP E Karger
SP J Killilay
SP B O'Brien
SP- J Nagle
SP- W Moser
SP- C Hageman
SP- J Bushelman
SP- M McHale
SP- B Thomas
SP- C Smith
SP- F Smith
RS C Hall
C- B Carrigan
UT C Engle
2S- H Wagner
SS S Yerkes
32 L Gardner
LF D Lewis
CF T Speaker
RF H Hooper
1C R Williams
1B- T Baker
1B- H Bradley
SS- S Carlstrom
SS- J Giannini
1B- H Gunning
RU- O Henriksen
31- H Janvrin
C- R Kleinow
2B- J Lewis
2U- W Lonergan
C- B Madden
1B- H Myers
C- L Nunamaker
3U- B Purtell
UO- J Riggert
CF- J Thoney
C- T Tonneman
OF- L Wilson
M P Donovan

1912

SP J Wood
SP B O'Brien
SR H Bedient
SP R Collins
SR C Hall
SP- E Cicotte
SP- B Van Dyke
SP- J Bushelman
SP- D Smith
SP- C Hageman
RP L Pape
C- B Carrigan
1B J Stahl
2B S Yerkes
SS H Wagner
3B L Gardner
LF D Lewis
CF T Speaker
RF H Hooper
2B- N Ball
1B- H Bradley
C- H Cady
IO- C Engle
OF- O Henriksen
SU- M Krug
C- L Nunamaker
CU- P Thomas

1913

SR H Bedient
SR D Leonard
SP R Collins
SP J Wood
SP E Moseley
SP B O'Brien
SR R Foster
SP F Anderson
SP- P Maloy
SP- E Chaney
RP C Hall
C- B Carrigan
1B C Engle
2B S Yerkes
SS H Wagner
3B L Gardner
LF D Lewis
CF T Speaker
RF H Hooper
UI- N Ball
C- H Cady
OF- O Henriksen
SI- H Janvrin
1B- B Mundy
C- L Nunamaker
RL- W Rehg
UC- W Snell
CF- J Stahl
C- P Thomas

1914

SP R Collins
SR D Leonard
SP R Foster
SR H Bedient
SP E Shore
SP J Wood
SP R Johnson
SP V Gregg
SP- B Ruth
SP- G Cooper
SP- M Zeiser
SP- E Kelly
RS F Coumbe
C- B Carrigan
1B- D Hoblitzel
2B- S Yerkes
SS E Scott
3B L Gardner
LF D Lewis
CF T Speaker
RF H Hooper
UI H Janvrin
C- H Cady
IO- C Engle
IO- D Gainer
UO- O Henriksen
CU- L Nunamaker
C- L Pratt
OF- W Rehg
23- B Swanson
C- P Thomas
1B- S Wilson

1915

SP R Foster
SP E Shore
SP B Ruth
SR D Leonard
SP J Wood
SR R Collins
SP V Gregg
SP- H Pennock
SP- R Comstock
SP- G Cooper
RS C Mays
C- P Thomas
1B D Hoblitzel
2B- H Wagner
SS E Scott
3B L Gardner
LF D Lewis
CF T Speaker
RF H Hooper
SI H Janvrin
2B- J Barry
C- H Cady
C- B Carrigan
1U- D Gainer
C- R Haley
UO- O Henriksen
3B- M McNally
US- W Rehg
2U- B Rodgers
MU-C Shorten

1916

SP B Ruth
SR D Leonard
SR C Mays
SR E Shore
SR R Foster
SP- H Pennock
SP- W Wyckoff
SP- M McHale
RS V Gregg
RP- S Jones
C P Thomas
1B D Hoblitzel
2B J Barry
SS E Scott
3B L Gardner
LF D Lewis
CF T Walker
RF H Hooper
S2 H Janvrin
C- S Agnew
C- H Cady
C- B Carrigan
1B- D Gainer
3B- R Haley
UO- O Henriksen
IO- M McNally
UO- C Shorten
3I- H Wagner
OI- J Walsh

1917

SP B Ruth
SP D Leonard
SP C Mays
SP E Shore
SP R Foster
SP- S Jones
SP- W Wyckoff
RS H Pennock
RP- L Bader
C- S Agnew
1B D Hoblitzel
2B J Barry
SS E Scott
3B L Gardner
LF D Lewis
CF T Walker
RF H Hooper
C- H Cady
2B- J Cooney
1B- D Gainer
3B- O Henriksen
2U- H Janvrin
C- W Mayer
UI- M McNally
UO- C Shorten
C- P Thomas
CF- J Walsh

1918

SP C Mays
SP J Bush
SP S Jones
SP D Leonard
SP- L Bader
SP- W Kinney
SP- V Molyneaux
SP- J Dubuc
SP- D McCabe
SP- B Pertica
SP- W Wyckoff
C- S Agnew
1B S McInnis
2B D Shean
SS E Scott
3B- F Thomas
LF- G Whiteman
CF A Strunk
RF H Hooper
Lp B Ruth
CU W Schang
3B- W Barbare
3B- R Bluhm
3B- G Cochran
3B- J Coffey
S3- E Gonzalez
1B- D Hoblitzel
C- W Mayer
LF- H Miller
3B- J Stansbury
2U- F Truesdale
23- H Wagner
M E Barrow

1919

SP S Jones
SP H Pennock
SP C Mays
SR A Russell
SP W Hoyt
SP R Caldwell
SP B James
SP- B McGraw
SP- P Musser
SP- J Bush
SP- G Winn
RP- G Dumont
C W Schang
1B S McInnis
2B- R Shannon
SS E Scott
3B O Vitt
Lp B Ruth
CF- B Roth
RF H Hooper
2B- J Barry
UT- D Gainer
LU- F Gilhooley
MU-B Lamar
UI- M McNally
C- N McNeil
2B- D Shean
CF- A Strunk
C- R Walters
RF- J Wilhoit
M E Barrow

1920

SP S Jones
SP J Bush
SP H Pennock
SP H Harper
SR W Hoyt
SP A Russell
SP E Myers
SP- H Deviney
RP B Karr
RP- G Fortune
C- R Walters
1B S McInnis
2B M McNally
SS E Scott
3B E Foster
LF M Menosky
CF T Hendryx
RF H Hooper
CM W Schang
UO- G Bailey
2B- C Brady
CU- E Chaplin
CU- M Devine
OP- H Eibel
1B- R Grimes
IO- H Hiller
LF- H Hunter
RM- G Orme
RF- B Paschal

CU- P Smith
RF- J Statz
3U- O Vitt
M E Barrow

1921
SP S Jones
SP J Bush
SP H Pennock
SR A Russell
SR E Myers
SR H Thormahlen
SP- C Fullerton
SP- A Sothoron
SP- S Dodge
RS B Karr
C M Ruel
1B S McInnis
2B D Pratt
SS E Scott
3B E Foster
LF M Menosky
CF N Leibold
RM S Collins
UC- E Chaplin
RF- T Hendryx
RF- H Hiller
UO- E Neitzke
RF- J Perrin
UT- P Pittinger
UR- S Vick
3B- O Vitt
C- R Walters
M H Duffy

1922
SP J Quinn
SP R Collins
SP H Pennock
SR A Ferguson
SR B Piercy
SP- E Myers
SP- S Dodge
RS B Karr
RS A Russell
RP C Fullerton
C M Ruel
1B G Burns
2B D Pratt
SS- J Mitchell
3B- J Dugan
LU M Menosky
CF- N Leibold
OI S Collins
LU J Harris
C- E Chaplin
3B- C Fewster
3U- E Foster
C- W Lynch
SS- C Maynard
CF- E Miller
S3- F O'Rourke
3S- P Pittinger
CF- D Reichle
RF- E Smith
C- R Walters
M H Duffy

1923
SP H Ehmke
SR J Quinn
SP A Ferguson
SP B Piercy
SR G Murray
SR C Fullerton
SP- C Blethen
SP- C Stimson
SP- D Black
RP L O'Doul
RP- L Howe
C- V Picinich
1B G Burns
2S- C Fewster
SS- J Mitchell
32 H Shanks
LF J Harris
MU D Reichle
RF I Flagstead
MR S Collins
32 N McMillan
CF- I Boone
CU- A DeVormer
RF- J Donahue
2B- F Fuller
CF- N Leibold

UO- M Menosky
2U- P Pittinger
U3- C Skinner
C- R Walters
M F Chance

1924
SP H Ehmke
SP A Ferguson
SR J Quinn
SR C Fullerton
SP B Piercy
SR O Fuhr
SP- T Wingfield
SP- R Ruffing
SP- L Howe
SP- C Winters
SP- L Jamerson
SP- A Kellett
RP B Ross
RS G Murray
RP- H Workman
C S O'Neill
1B J Harris
2B B Wambsganss
SS- D Lee
3B D Clark
LF B Veach
CF I Flagstead
RF I Boone
OI- S Collins
U3- J Connolly
3U- H Ezzell
SS- C Geygan
CU- J Heving
C- V Picinich
S3- H Shanks
UT- P Todt
LF- D Williams
M L Fohl

1925
SP H Ehmke
SR T Wingfield
SR R Ruffing
SR P Zahniser
SP J Quinn
SP- B Francis
SP- C Fullerton
SP- R Kallio
SP- A Ferguson
SP- J Kiefer
SP- J Lucey
SP- H Neubauer
SP- B Adams
RS B Ross
RS O Fuhr
C- V Picinich
1B P Todt
2B B Wambsganss
SS- D Lee
3B D Prothro
OF R Carlyle
CF I Flagstead
RF I Boone
OF T Vache
C- J Bischoff
MU- S Collins
SS- B Connolly
3B- H Ezzell
SS- C Geygan
SS- T Gross
1B- J Harris
2B- M Herrera
C- J Heving
LF- T Jenkins
2B- B Rogell
RL- S Rosenthal
SS- J Rothrock
C- A Stokes
LF- B Veach
SS- H Welch
LU- D Williams
M L Fohl

1926
SP H Wiltse
SR T Wingfield
SP P Zahniser
SR R Ruffing
SP S Harriss
SP F Heimach
SP H Ehmke
SP- D Mac Fayden

SP- H Foreman
SP- B Ross
SP- R Sommers
RS T Welzer
RS J Russell
RP- D Lundgren
RP- J Kiefer
C A Gaston
1B P Todt
2B B Regan
SS T Rigney
3B F Haney
OF S Rosenthal
CF I Flagstead
MR B Jacobson
C- J Bischoff
OF- F Bratschi
RF- R Carlyle
LU- H Fitzgerald
3B- B Fowler
3B- C Geygan
2I- M Herrera
LU- S Langford
LF- S Langford
SS- D Lee
IF- E McCann
C- B Moore
UL- J Rothrock
LU- W Shaner
C- A Stokes
RF- J Tobin
M L Fohl

1927
SP H Wiltse
SR S Harriss
SR T Welzer
SP R Ruffing
SR J Russell
SR D Lundgren
SR T Wingfield
SP- J Wilson
SP- H Bradley
SP- B Sommers
SP- F Bennett
SP- B Cremins
SP- F Bushey
C G Hartley
1B P Todt
2B B Regan
SS B Myer
3U- B Rogell
LO W Shaner
CF I Flagstead
RF J Tobin
RL C Carlyle
UI J Rothrock
1B- R Carlyle
UR- E Eggert
ML- J Freeman
3U- F Haney
C- F Hofmann
LF- B Jacobson
S3- M Karow
C- B Moore
3U- T Rigney
3U- R Rollings
UO- A Tarbert
SS- P Wanninger
UL- F Welch
M B Carrigan

1928
SP R Ruffing
SR E Morris
SP J Russell
SP D Mac Fayden
SR S Harriss
SP M Griffin
SP- C Garrison
SP- H Wiltse
SP- S Slayton
SP- J Wilson
SP- J Shea
SP- F Bennett
RS M Settlemire
RP P Simmons
RS H Bradley
C- F Hofmann
1B P Todt
2B B Regan
SS W Gerber
3B B Myer
LF K Williams
CF I Flagstead

RF D Taitt
SU B Rogell
UT J Rothrock
C- C Asbjornson
C- C Berry
C- J Heving
C- P Hinson
MR- G Loepp
SU- F Moncewicz
UT- R Rollings
UO- C Sumner
RF- A Tarbert
OF- D Williams
M B Carrigan

1929
SR M Gaston
SP R Ruffing
SP J Russell
SP D Mac Fayden
SP E Morris
SP- H Lisenbee
SP- P Simmons
SP- H Bradley
RS B Bayne
RP E Carroll
RP- R Dobens
RP- E Durham
C- C Berry
1B P Todt
2B B Regan
SS H Rhyne
3B B Reeves
LF R Scarritt
CF J Rothrock
3U- B Barrett
RU E Bigelow
S2 B Narleski
C- C Asbjornson
RF B Barrett
MU- J Cicero
C- E Connolly
LF- I Flagstead
C- A Gaston
IF- W Gerber
2B- G Gillis
CU- J Heving
LR- J Ryan
1U- J Standaert
OF- D Taitt
OI- K Williams
M B Carrigan

1930
SP M Gaston
SP D Mac Fayden
SP H Lisenbee
SP J Russell
SR E Durham
SP E Morris
SP- R Ruffing
SP- B Shields
RS B Bayne
SP- F Mulroney
SP- B Kline
RP G Smith
RP- F Bushey
C- C Berry
1B P Todt
2B B Regan
SS H Rhyne
3U O Miller
LF R Scarritt
CF T Oliver
RF E Webb
OF C Durst
RF- B Barrett
OI- J Cicero
C- E Connolly
LF- J Galvin
C- J Heving
UI- B Narleski
3I- B Reeves
OI- J Rothrock
U3- C Small
1U- B Sweeney
SS- R Warstler
RF- T Winsett
M H Wagner

1931
SP J Russell
SP D Mac Fayden
SR E Durham
SR H Lisenbee
SR E Morris

SP M Gaston
SR B Kline
SP- J McLaughlin
SP- W Murphy
RS W Moore
RP- J Brillheart
C C Berry
1B B Sweeney
2S- R Warstler
SS H Rhyne
3U O Miller
LI J Rothrock
CF T Oliver
RF E Webb
3U U Pickering
LU A Van Camp
C- E Connolly
U1- P Creeden
OF- J Lucas
2B- O Marquardt
2B- B Marshall
32- M McManus
3B- B McWilliams
2B- M Olson
2B- B Reeves
C- M Ruel
LU- G Rye
LF- R Scarritt
1B- J Smith
C- H Storie
LF- G Stumpf
U2- T Winsett
M S Collins

1932
SR B Weiland
SR E Durham
SP B Kline
SP I Andrews
SP G Rhodes
SP D Mac Fayden
SR J Welch
SP- P Appleton
SP- J Russell
SP- E Gallagher
SP- G McNaughton
SP- P Donohue
SP- J McLaughlin
SP- R Leheny
RP W Moore
RS J Michaels
RS H Lisenbee
RS L Boerner
C- B Tate
1B D Alexander
2B M Olson
SS R Warstler
3B U Pickering
LF S Jolley
CF T Oliver
RO R Johnson
OI J Watwood
C- C Berry
C- E Connolly
LF- J Lucas
23 M McManus
2B- O Smith
C- H Patterson
1U- J Reder
SS- H Rhyne
LF- J Rothrock
2I- A Spognardi
C- H Storie
UO- G Stumpf
1U- A Van Camp
RF- E Webb
M1 S Collins

1933
SP G Rhodes
SR B Weiland
SR L Brown
SP H Johnson
SR I Andrews
SR G Pipgras
SP- C Fullerton
SP- J McLaughlin
SP- M Meola
RS J Welch
RS B Kline
C R Ferrell
1B D Alexander
2B J Hodapp
SS R Warstler
3I M McManus
LU S Jolley
ML D Cooke

RO R Johnson
S3 B Werber
LM- M Almada
OF- B Fothergill
UI- B Friberg
CU- J Gooch
1B- J Judge
UC- L Legett
3B- G Mulleavy
2B- F Muller
CF T Oliver
U3- M Olson
1O- B Seeds
C- M Shea
UO- G Stumpf
3B- B Walters
OF- J Watwood
OF- T Winsett

1934
SR G Rhodes
SR J Welch
SP F Ostermueller
SP W Ferrell
SR H Johnson
SR L Grove
SP B Weiland
SP- G Hockette
SP- S Merena
SP- G Pipgras
RS R Walberg
RP H Pennock
RP- J Mulligan
C R Ferrell
1B E Morgan
2B B Cissell
SS L Lary
3B B Werber
LF R Johnson
C- G Hinkle
U3 J Judge
UI- R Kellett
C- L Legett
23- F Muller
2B- A Niemiec
UM- B Seeds
3B- B Walters
M B Harris

1935
SP W Ferrell
SP L Grove
SR G Rhodes
SR J Welch
SP F Ostermueller
SP- S Bowers
SP- J Cascarella
SP- G Pipgras
SP- H Vandenberg
SP- W Ripley
RS R Walberg
RS J Wilson
RP G Hockette
RP- H Johnson
C R Ferrell
1B B Dahlgren
2B S Melillo
SS J Cronin
3B B Werber
LF R Johnson
CF M Almada
UO D Cooke
C- M Berg
2U- M Bishop
C- G Dickey
2B- D Farrell
3B- J Kroner
OF- B Miller
RF- C Reynolds
OF- M Solters
UI- D Williams

1936
SP W Ferrell
SP L Grove
SR F Ostermueller

SR F Ostermueller
SP J Henry
SP- J Welch
SP- M Meola
SP- J Cascarella
SP- J Poindexter
SP- S Bowers
SP- E Dickman
RS J Wilson
RP- J Russell
C R Ferrell
1B J Foxx
2B S Melillo
S2 E McNair
3L B Werber
LF- H Manush
CF D Cramer
RU D Cooke
RU M Almada
C- M Berg
S3- J Cronin
1B- B Dahlgren
C- G Dickey
RL- F Gaffke
IO- J Kroner
OF- B Miller

1937
SR L Grove
SR J Wilson
SR B Newsom
SR J Marcum
SR A McKain
SR R Walberg
SP W Ferrell
SP- J Gonzales
SP- J Henry
SP- T Thomas
RS F Ostermueller
RP- T Olson
C G Desautels
1B J Foxx
2B E McNair
SS J Cronin
3B P Higgins
LF B Mills
CF D Cramer
RF B Chapman
RU- M Almada
C- M Berg
C- S Bowers
UO- D Dallessandro
LF- B Daughters
2B- B Doerr
C- R Ferrell
RL- F Gaffke
2U- S Melillo
C- J Peacock

1938
SR J Bagby
SR J Wilson
SR F Ostermueller
SP L Grove
SR E Dickman
SP J Marcum
SP J Heving
SP B Harris
SP- C Wagner
SP- A Baker
SP- T Olson
SP- B Lefebvre
SP- B Humphrey
RS A McKain
RP- D Midkiff
RP- L Rogers
C G Desautels
1B J Foxx
2B B Doerr
SS J Cronin
3B P Higgins
LF J Vosmik
CF D Cramer
RF B Chapman
CU- M Berg
OC- F Gaffke
UI- E McNair
OI- R Nonnenkamp
C- J Peacock
3U- J Tabor

1939
SP L Grove
SR J Wilson

SR F Ostermueller
SP E Auker
SR D Galehouse
SP J Bagby
SP W Rich
SP- C Wagner
SP- B Lefebvre
SP- M Weaver
RP B Sayles
RP E Dickman
RS J Heving
RS J Wade
C J Peacock
1B J Foxx
2B B Doerr
SS J Cronin
3B J Tabor
LF J Vosmik
CF D Cramer
RF T Williams
UT L Finney
C- M Berg
S3- B Berger
2U- T Carey
C- G Desautels
1B- F Gaffke
UO- R Nonnenkamp

1940
SR J Bagby
SR J Wilson
SP L Grove
SR F Ostermueller
SR H Hash
SP D Galehouse
SP E Johnson
SP M Harris
SP- B Fleming
SP- B Butland
SP- Y Terry
SP- A Mustaikis
SP- W Rich
RS J Heving
RS E Dickman
RP- C Wagner
C- G Desautels
1C J Foxx
2B B Doerr
SS J Cronin
3B J Tabor
LF T Williams
MO D DiMaggio
MO D Cramer
R1 L Finney
UI- T Carey
3B- C Gelbert
C- J Glenn
1B- T Lupien
1B- R Nonnenkamp
IF- M Owen
C- J Peacock
OF- S Spence

1941
SP D Newsome
SR M Harris
SP C Wagner
SP L Grove
SP J Dobson
SR J Wilson
SP E Johnson
SP T Hughson
SP- E Dickman
SP- O Judd
SP- H Hash
SP- W Rich
RP M Ryba
RP- B Fleming
RP- N Potter
C F Pytlak
1B J Foxx
2B B Doerr
SS J Cronin
3B J Tabor
LF T Williams
CF D DiMaggio
RU L Finney
LF- P Campbell
UI- T Carey
1B- A Flair
RU- P Fox
3U- O Hale
SU S Newsome
C- J Peacock
OI- S Spence

1942
SP T Hughson
SP C Wagner
SP J Dobson
SP D Newsome
SR O Judd
SR B Butland
SP Y Terry
SP K Chase
RP M Brown
RP M Ryba
C- B Conroy
1B T Lupien
2B B Doerr
SS J Pesky
3B J Tabor
LF T Williams
CF D DiMaggio
RF L Finney
US- P Campbell
2B- T Carey
UI- J Cronin
RF- P Fox
1B- J Foxx
CF- A Gilbert
UI- S Newsome
C- J Peacock

1943
SP T Hughson
SP Y Terry
SP J Dobson
SP O Judd
SP D Newsome
SR P Woods
SP L Lucier
SP E O'Neill
SP- K Chase
RS M Ryba
RP M Brown
RP- A Karl
C   R Partee
1B T Lupien
2B B Doerr
SS S Newsome
3B J Tabor
ML- L Culberson
MR- C Metkovich
RF P Fox
LF- B Barna
C- B Conroy
US- J Cronin
C- D Doyle
LU- F Garrison
SS- E Lake
LU- J Lazor
CF- T McBride
MU- D Miles
CU- J Peacock
LF- A Simmons

1944
SP T Hughson
SR P Woods
SP J Bowman
SP E O'Neill
SR C Hausmann
SR Y Terry
SP R Cecil
SP C Dreisewerd
SP- O Judd
SP- V Johnson
SP- J Wood
SP- L Lucier
SP- S Partenheimer
RS M Ryba
RP F Barrett
C- R Partee
1B- L Finney
2B B Doerr
SS S Newsome
3B J Tabor
LF B Johnson
M1 C Metkovich
RF P Fox
32- J Bucher
C- B Conroy
1U- J Cronin
CF- L Culberson
RF- F Garrison
SU- E Lake
OC- J Lazor
OI- T McBride
CU- J Peacock
C- H Wagner

1945
SP D Ferriss
SP J Wilson
SP E O'Neill
SR C Hausmann
SR P Woods
SR R Heflin
SR V Johnson
SP O Clark
SP Y Terry
SP- R Cecil
SP- J Bowman
SP- C Dreiseward
SP- O Judd
RS M Ryba
RP F Barrett
C- B Garbark
1O C Metkovich
2S S Newsome
SS E Lake
3B- J Tobin
LF B Johnson
CF L Culberson
RU J Lazor
MO T McBride
3U- J Bucher
1B- D Camilli
U3- L Christopher
3B- J Cronin
CF- L Finney
RF- P Fox
C- B Holm
3B- T LaForest
3U- N Polly
CU- F Pytlak
2B- B Steiner
C- R Steiner
C- F Walters

1946
SP T Hughson
SP D Ferriss
SP M Harris
SP J Dobson
SR J Bagby
SP B Zuber
SP- C Wagner
SP- B Butland
SP- R Heflin
SP- M Ryba
SP- M Deutsch
SP- J Wilson
RS E Johnson
RP B Klinger
RP C Dreisewerd
RP- M Brown
C   H Wagner
1B R York
2B B Doerr
SS J Pesky
3B R Russell
LF T Williams
CF D DiMaggio
RF- C Metkovich
3B- E Andres
UC- P Campbell
2B- T Carey
OI- L Culberson
MU- A Gilbert
IF- D Gutteridge
3B- P Higgins
OF- J Lazor
RU- T McBride
C- E McGah
RF- W Moses
C- R Partee
3S- E Pellagrini
C- F Pytlak
U3- B Steiner
M   J Cronin

1947
SP J Dobson
SP D Ferriss
SP T Hughson
SR E Johnson
SP D Galehouse
SP M Harris
SP- T Fine
SP- E Smith
SP- C Deal
SP- C Stobbs
SP- B Butland
SP- A Widmar
RS H Dorish
RP J Murphy
RP B Zuber
RS M Parnell
RP- B Klinger
C- B Tebbetts
1B J Jones
2B B Doerr
SS J Pesky
3B- S Hayes
LF T Williams
CF D DiMaggio
RO S Mele
C- L Aulds
C- M Batts
3B- M Combs
OI- L Culberson
U3- B Goodman
IF- D Gutteridge
C- F Hayes
RU- T McBride
C- E McGah
RU- W Moses
C- R Partee
3S- E Pellagrini
3U- R Russell
3B- S Shofner
C- H Wagner
1B- R York
M   J Cronin

1948
SP J Dobson
SP M Parnell
SP J Kramer
SP E Kinder
SR D Galehouse
SP M Harris
SP- M McDermott
SP- H Dorish
SP- E Caldwell
SP- C Stobbs
SP- C Deal
SP- M Palm
SP- W McCall
RS D Ferriss
RP E Johnson
RP- T Hughson
C   B Tebbetts
1B B Goodman
2B B Doerr
SS V Stephens
3B J Pesky
LF T Williams
CF D DiMaggio
RF A Zarilla
IO B Goodman
C- M Batts
C- M Combs
UR- F Hatfield
3U- K Keltner
U3- C Maxwell
UO- T O'Brien
U3- J Piersall
C- B Rosar
C- B Scherbarth
UI- L Stringer
UO- C Vollmer
OF- T Wright
M1 J McCarthy
M2 S O'Neill

1949
SP M Parnell
SR E Kinder
SP J Dobson
SP C Stobbs
SP J Kramer
SP M McDermott
SP- M Harris
SP- F Quinn
SP- W McCall
SP- H Dorish
SP- D Ferriss
SP- J Robinson
SP- J Wittig
SP- D Galehouse
RP T Hughson
RS W Masterson
RP E Johnson
C   B Tebbetts
1B B Goodman
2B B Doerr
SS V Stephens
3B J Pesky
LF T Williams
CF D DiMaggio
RF C Vollmer
UT B Goodman
C- M Batts
SU- L Boudreau
RF- B DiPietro
C- A Evans
M   Guerra
3U- F Hatfield
IF- M Hoderlein
OF- C Maxwell
RU- S Mele
RU- T O'Brien
OF- S Spence
UR- L Stringer
LF- T Wright
M   J McCarthy

1950
SP M Parnell
SR E Kinder
SR J Dobson
SR C Stobbs
SR M McDermott
SR W Masterson
SP W Nixon
SP H Taylor
SP- J McDonald
SP- G Mueller
SP- J Atkins
SP- J Suchecki
SP- F Quinn
SP- D Ferriss
SP- B Gillespie
SP- P Marchildon
RP A Papai
RP- D Littlefield
RP- C Schanz
RP- E Johnson
C- B Tebbetts
1B W Dropo
2B B Doerr
SS V Stephens
3B J Pesky
LF- T Williams
CF D DiMaggio
RF A Zarilla
IO B Goodman
C- M Batts
C- M Combs
UR- F Hatfield
3U- C Maxwell
UO- T O'Brien
U3- J Piersall
C- B Rosar
C- B Scherbarth
UI- L Stringer
UO- C Vollmer
OF- T Wright
M1 J McCarthy
M2 S O'Neill

1951
SP M Parnell
SR R Scarborough
SR M McDermott
SP C Stobbs
SR W Nixon
SR B Wight
SP L Kiely
SP- B Evans
SP- H Hisner
SP- P Hinrichs
SP- B Flowers
RP E Kinder
RS H Taylor
RP W Masterson
C- L Moss
1B W Dropo
2B B Doerr
SS J Pesky
3B V Stephens
LF T Williams
CF D DiMaggio
RF C Vollmer
IF- F Baker
IF- B Consolo
3B- D DiMaggio
2S- T Lepcio
SS- J Lipon
2B- J Merson
C- L Moss
UT B Goodman
SU- A Richter
C- A Robinson
C- B Rosar
RU- T Wright
1B- N Zauchin
M   S O'Neill

1952
SP M Parnell
SP M McDermott
SP H Brown
SR S Hudson
SP W Nixon
SP B Henry
SP D Trout
SP S Hudson
SP D Brodowski
SR W Nixon
SR E Kinder
SP- R Gumpert
SP- H Freeman
SP- H Taylor
SP- J Atkins
SP- J McDonald
RS I Delock
RS R Scarborough
RP- A Benton
RP- R Brickner
C   S White
1B D Gernert
2U B Goodman
SS- J Lipon
3B- G Hatton
LF T Williams
MR J Jensen
RU J Piersall
2I B Goodman
UO K Olson
US- S Mele
1R- S Mele
1B- G Morton
C- M Owen
C- D Wilber
M   L Boudreau

1953
SP M Parnell
SP M McDermott
SP H Brown
SR S Hudson
SP W Nixon
SP B Henry
SP M Werle
SP- K Holcombe
CL E Kinder
RS B Flowers
RP I Delock
RP- H Freeman
RP- B Kennedy
RP- F Sullivan
C   S White
1B D Gernert
2B B Goodman
SS M Bolling
3B G Kell
LF H Evers
CF T Umphlett
RF J Piersall
IF- F Baker
IF- B Consolo
3B- D DiMaggio
2S- T Lepcio
SS- J Lipon
2B- J Merson
C- G Niarhos
LF- K Olson
SS- A Richter
LF- G Stephens
CF- C Vollmer
IC- D Wilber
LU- T Williams
UO- A Zarilla
M   L Boudreau

1954
SR F Sullivan
SP W Nixon
SP T Brewer
SP L Kiely
SR B Henry
SP M Parnell
SR R Kemmerer
SR T Clevenger
SP- J Dobson
RP E Kinder
RS H Brown
RS S Hudson
RP- T Hurd
RP- T Herrin
RP- B Werle
C   S White
1B H Agganis
2I T Lepcio
SS M Bolling
3B H Hatton
LF T Williams
MR J Jensen
RU J Piersall
2I B Goodman
UO K Olson
IF- F Baker
SI- B Consolo
US- H Evers
US- D Gernert
3B- G Kell
UT- D Lenhardt
UO- C Maxwell
1R- S Mele
1B- G Morton
C- M Owen
C- D Wilber
M   L Boudreau

1955
SP F Sullivan
SP W Nixon
SP T Brewer
SR I Delock
SR G Susce
SR B Henry
SP M Parnell
SP- F Baumann
SP- R Kemmerer
SP- H Brown
SP- J Trimble
SP- H Freeman
SP- B Smith
RP L Kiely
RP T Hurd
CL E Kinder
RP- D Brodowski
C   S White
1U D Gernert
2B- T Lepcio
3U- F Malzone
OF- S Mele
UO- K Olson
C- J Pagliaroni
C- H Sullivan
LU- F Throneberry
M   P Higgins

1956
SP T Brewer
SP F Sullivan
SP W Nixon
SR D Sisler
SP M Parnell
SP B Porterfield
SP- F Baumann
SP- R Minarcin
SP- J Schmitz
RS I Delock
RP T Hurd
RS G Susce
RP L Kiely
RP- H Dorish
C   S White
1B M Vernon
2B B Goodman
SS D Buddin
3B B Klaus
LF T Williams
CF J Piersall
RF J Jensen
UT D Gernert
LU G Stephens
SI- M Bolling
2U- B Consolo
C- P Daley
2B- G Hatton
RF- M Keough
23- T Lepcio
3B- F Malzone
2B- G Mauch
UO- F Throneberry
1U- N Zauchin
M   P Higgins

1957
SP F Sullivan
SP T Brewer
SP W Nixon
SP M Fornieles
SP D Sisler
SP D Stone
SP- F Baumann
SP- R Meyer
SP- R Kemmerer
SP- J Spring
RP I Delock
RS B Porterfield
RS G Susce
RP R Minarcin
RP- B Chakales
RP- M Wall
C   S White
1U D Gernert
21 P Runnels
SS D Buddin
3B F Malzone
LO- G Stephens
ML G Geiger
RF J Jensen
MU M Keough
1U V Wertz
LU T Williams
2U- B Avila
UO- J Busby
U2- B Consolo
C- P Daley
C- D Gile
2B- P Green
UM- T Lepcio
SS- J Mahoney
CF- J Mallett
UM- H Plews
LU- B Renna
CU- H Sullivan
M1 P Higgins
M2 R York
M3 B Jurges

1958
SP T Brewer
SP F Sullivan
SR I Delock
SP D Sisler
SR B Smith
SP T Bowsfield
SP B Monbouquette
SP F Baumann
SP- W Nixon
SP- A Schroll
SP- D Wilson
SP- B Porterfield
SP- J Casale
SP- G Susce
RP M Wall
RS M Fornieles
RP L Kiely
RP- B Byerly
C   S White
1B D Gernert
2B B Goodman
SS D Buddin
3B F Malzone
LF T Williams
CF J Piersall
RF J Jensen
LU G Stephens
2B- K Aspromonte
C- L Berberet
UI- B Consolo
C- P Daley
OI- M Keough
U1- B Klaus
U1- B Renna
M   P Higgins

1959
SP T Brewer
SP J Casale
SP F Sullivan
SR B Monbouquette
SR I Delock
SR F Baumann
SP T Wills
SP- A Schroll
SP- J Harshman
SP- E Wilson
SP- B Hoeft
SP- T Bowsfield
SP- H Moford
SP- D Sisler
RP M Fornieles
RP L Kiely
RP- M Wall
RP- N Chittum
RP- M Wall
C   S White
1U D Gernert
21 P Runnels
SS D Buddin
3B F Malzone
LO- G Stephens
ML G Geiger
RF J Jensen
MU M Keough
1U V Wertz
LU T Williams
2U- B Avila
UO- J Busby
U2- B Consolo
C- P Daley
C- D Gile
2B- P Green
UM- T Mahoney
CF- J Mallett
UM- H Sullivan
LU- B Renna
CU- H Sullivan
M1 B Jurges
M2 D Baker
M3 P Higgins

1960
SP B Monbouquette
SP T Brewer
SR F Sullivan
SP I Delock
SP B Muffett
SR J Casale
SP E Wilson
SP- C Nichols
SP- A Worthington
SP- N Chittum
SP- A Earley
SP- T Stallard
RP M Fornieles
RP T Sturdivant
RP T Borland
RP- D Hillman
RP- T Wills
RP- T Bowsfield
C- R Nixon
1B V Wertz
2B P Runnels
SS D Buddin
3B F Malzone
LF T Williams
CF W Tasby
RF L Stringer
2S P Green
1U- R Boone
LF- J Busby
2B- M Coughtry
RF- G Geiger
C1- D Gile
LO- C Hardy
1B- M Jackson
MU- M Keough
CU- J Pagliaroni
UC- R Repulski
C- E Sadowski
LO- G Stephens
C- H Sullivan
OI- B Thomson
UL- R Webster
M1 B Jurges
M2 D Baker
M3 P Higgins

1961
SP B Monbouquette
SP G Conley
SP D Schwall
SP I Delock
SP G Cisco
SP- T Brewer
SP- W Wood
SP- T Borland
RS T Stallard

RP M Fornieles
RS B Muffett
RP D Hillman
RP A Earley
RP C Nichols
RP- T Wills
C J Pagliaroni
1B P Runnels
2B C Schilling
SS D Buddin
3B F Malzone
LF C Yastrzemski
CF G Geiger
RF J Jensen
RF- L Clinton
1B- D Gile
UC- J Ginsberg
SU- P Green
UO- C Hardy
UI- B Harrell
C- R Nixon
US- A Repulski
1B V Wertz
M P Higgins

1962
SP G Conley
SP B Monbouquette
SP E Wilson
SP D Schwall
SP I Delock
SR G Cisco
SP- W Wood
SP- M Nippert
SP- B Muffett
SP- B Mac Leod
SP- P Smith
SP- T Stallard
SP- T Wills
CL D Radatz
RP M Fornieles
RP A Earley
RP H Kolstad
RP C Nichols
C- J Pagliaroni
1B P Runnels
2B C Schilling
SS E Bressoud
3B F Malzone
LF C Yastrzemski
CF G Geiger
RM C Hardy
RF L Clinton
2U- B Gardner
1B- D Gile
IF- P Green
CU- R Nixon
UC- D Philley
C- B Tillman
M P Higgins

1963
SP B Monbouquette
SP E Wilson
SP D Morehead
SP B Heffner
SP- G Conley
SP- B Turley
SP- I Delock
SP- P Smith
SP- M Fornieles
SP- H Kolstad
SP- J Stephenson
RP J Lamabe
CL D Radatz
RP A Earley
RS W Wood
RS C Nichols
C- B Tillman
1B D Stuart
2B C Schilling
SS E Bressoud
3B F Malzone
LF C Yastrzemski
MU G Geiger
RF L Clinton
MU R Mejias
C R Nixon
2U- B Gardner
OF- J Gosger
IO- F Mantilla
SS- R Petrocelli
IO- D Williams
M J Pesky

1964
SP B Monbouquette
SP E Wilson
SR J Lamabe
SR D Morehead
SR E Connolly
SP- D Gray
SP- W Wood
CL D Radatz
RS B Heffner
RS P Charton
RS B Spanswick
RP A Earley
RP- J Ritchie
C B Tillman
1B D Stuart
2U D Jones
SS E Bressoud
3B F Malzone
LU T Conigliaro
CF C Yastrzemski
RF L Thomas
UT F Mantilla
RF- L Clinton
RU- G Geiger
UT- B Guindon
LU- T Horton
UO- R Mejias
CU- R Nixon
C- M Ryan
2B- C Schilling
UT- A Smith
UT- D Williams
M1 J Pesky
M2 Herman

1965
SP E Wilson
SP B Monbouquette
SP D Morehead
SP J Lonborg
SR D Bennett
SP J Stephenson
CL D Radatz
RP A Earley
RP J Ritchie
RP B Duliba
RP B Heffner
RP- J Lamabe
C B Tillman
1B L Thomas
2B F Mantilla
SS R Petrocelli
3B F Malzone
LF C Yastrzemski
MU L Green
RF T Conigliaro
SS E Bressoud
3U D Jones
UO- G Geiger
CF- J Gosger
1U- T Horton
2B- J Moses
CU- R Nixon
C- M Ryan
2U- C Schilling
2B- R Schlesinger
M Herman

1966
SR J Lonborg
SP J Santiago
SR B Brandon
SP L Stange
SP E Wilson
SR R Sheldon
SP D Bennett
SP J Stephenson
SP- B Sadowski
SP- H Fischer
SP- D Morehead
SP- B Short
SP- P Magrini
SP- G Grilli
SP- G Roggenburk
RP D McMahon
RS D Stigman
RP J Wyatt
RP D Osinski
RP K Sanders
RP- D Radatz
C M Ryan
1B G Scott
2B G Smith
SS R Petrocelli
3B J Foy

LF C Yastrzemski
CF- D Demeter
RF T Conigliaro
2U D Jones
U2- J Christopher
MU- J Gosger
OF- L Green
1B- T Horton
UI- E Kasko
CF- R Smith
MU- J Tartabull
UT- G Thomas
C- B Tillman
M1 Herman
M2 P Runnels

1967
SP J Lonborg
SR L Stange
SP G Bell
SR B Brandon
SP D Bennett
SP- D Morehead
SP- B Rohr
SP- G Waslewski
SP- J Stephenson
SP- H Fischer
SP- K Brett
RS J Santiago
RP J Wyatt
RP D Osinski
RP- S Lyle
RP- B Landis
RP- G Cisco
RP- D McMahon
C- M Ryan
1B G Scott
2B M Andrews
SS R Petrocelli
3B J Foy
LF C Yastrzemski
CF R Smith
RF- T Conigliaro
UO J Tartabull
UI- J Adair
OI- D Demeter
C- R Gibson
RF- K Harrelson
UM-T Horton
C- E Howard
UI- D Jones
RF- J Landis
IF- K Poulsen
UT- N Siebern
OI- G Thomas
C- B Tillman
M D Williams

1968
SP R Culp
SP G Bell
SP D Ellsworth
SP J Santiago
SP J Lonborg
SP J Pizarro
SP D Morehead
SP- B Brandon
SP- J Wyatt
SP- G Roggenburk
SP- F Wenz
RP L Stange
RS G Waslewski
RP S Lyle
RS J Stephenson
RP B Landis
C- R Gibson
1B G Scott
2B M Andrews
SS R Petrocelli
3B J Foy
LF C Yastrzemski
CF R Smith
RF K Harrelson
1I D Jones
SI- J Adair
SS- L Alvarado
C- E Howard
RF- J Lahoud
C- J Moses
CU- G Oliver
OF- F Robinson
UT- N Siebern
UO- J Tartabull
UO- G Thomas
M D Williams

1969
SP R Culp
SP M Nagy
SR S Siebert
SP J Lonborg
SR L Stange
SR R Jarvis
SP- K Brett
SP- G Wagner
SP- D Ellsworth
SP- M Garman
SP- J Pizarro
SP- F Wenz
SP- G Roggenburk
RS V Romo
RP S Lyle
RS B Landis
RP B Lee
RP- R Kline
RP- J Santiago
C- R Gibson
1U D Jones
2B M Andrews
SS R Petrocelli
31 G Scott
LF C Yastrzemski
CF R Smith
RF T Conigliaro
OI J Lahoud
3I S O'Brien
SS- L Alvarado
C- J Azcue
MO-B Conigliaro
CU- C Fisk
1B- K Harrelson
OI- D Lock
CU- J Moses
1B- T Muser
C- T Satriano
UT- D Schofield
UT- G Thomas
M1 D Williams
M2 E Popowski

1970
SP R Culp
SP S Siebert
SP G Peters
SR K Brett
SP M Nagy
SP C Koonce
SP- B Lee
SP- J Lonborg
SP- J Santiago
SP- B Bolin
SP- R Moret
SP- D Mills
SP- J Curtis
RS V Romo
RP S Lyle
RP- G Wagner
RP- L Stange
RP- E Phillips
RP- C Hartenstein
RP- R Jarvis
C- J Moses
1L C Yastrzemski
2B M Andrews
SS R Petrocelli
31 G Scott
LO B Conigliaro
CF R Smith
RF T Conigliaro
IF- L Alvarado
UT- M Derrick
3U- C Fanzone
UT- M Fiore
3B- J Kennedy
LR- J Lahoud
UI- T Matchick
C- B Montgomery
1C- D Pavletich
C- T Satriano
UI- D Schofield
LU- G Thomas
M E Kasko

1971
SP R Culp
SP S Siebert
SP G Peters
SP J Lonborg
SP L Tiant
SP R Moret
DH O Cepeda
CF R Smith

SP- M Garman
RP B Lee
RP B Bolin
RP S Lyle
RP K Tatum
RP K Brett
RP- C Koonce
C- D Josephson
1B G Scott
2B D Griffin
SS L Aparicio
3B R Petrocelli
LF C Yastrzemski
CF R Conigliaro
MR R Smith
RU J Lahoud
SS- J Beniquez
1B- C Cooper
U1- M Fiore
C- C Fisk
UT- P Gagliano
2B- R Hunter
2S- J Kennedy
UO- R Miller
C- B Montgomery
LU- B Oglivie
CU- D Pavletich
OF- G Thomas
M E Kasko

1972
SP M Pattin
SP S Siebert
SR L Tiant
SP J Curtis
SP L McGlothen
SP R Culp
SP- B Veale
SP- R Moret
SP- S Williams
SP- M Garman
SP- M Nagy
RP B Lee
RP G Peters
RS L Krausse
RP- D Newhauser
RP- B Bolin
RP- K Tatum
C C Fisk
1B- D Cater
2B D Griffin
SS L Aparicio
3B R Petrocelli
L1 C Yastrzemski
CF T Harper
RF R Smith
OF B Oglivie
SS- J Beniquez
UT- B Burda
UM-C Cooper
C- V Correll
LF- D Evans
UT- P Gagliano
LF- B Gallagher
1U- D Josephson
UI- J Kennedy
LU- A Kosco
ML- R Miller
C- B Montgomery
M E Kasko

1973
SP B Lee
SP L Tiant
SP J Curtis
SP M Pattin
SR R Moret
SP D Pole
SP R Culp
SP- L McGlothen
SP- D Newhauser
SP- K Tatum
SP- S Siebert
CL B Bolin
CL- B Veale
RP- C Skok
RP- M Garman
C C Fisk
1U C Yastrzemski
2B D Griffin
SS L Aparicio
3B R Petrocelli
LF T Harper
UO R Miller
RF D Evans
DH O Cepeda
CF R Smith

13- D Cater
1B- C Cooper
S2- M Guerrero
IF- B Hunter
IF- J Kennedy
C- B Montgomery
OF- B Oglivie
M1 E Kasko
M2 E Popowski

1974
SP L Tiant
SP B Lee
SR R Cleveland
SR D Drago
SR R Moret
SP J Marichal
SP R Wise
SP- S Barr
SP- L Clemons
SP- D Newhauser
RP D Segui
RP- D Pole
RP- B Veale
C- B Montgomery
1L C Yastrzemski
2B- D Griffin
SS- M Guerrero
3B R Petrocelli
OF B Darwin
CF J Beniquez
RF D Evans
LD T Harper
SS R Burleson
MU R Miller
1D C Cooper
23 D McAuliffe
C- T Blackwell
UT- D Cater
C- B Didier
C- C Fisk
2B- C Goggin
3B- T Hughes
HU- D Johnson
23- J Kennedy
UO- F Lynn
CU- T McCarver
DU- J Rice

1975
SP B Lee
SP L Tiant
SP R Wise
SR R Cleveland
SR R Moret
SP D Pole
SP- S Barr
SP- R Kreuger
CL D Drago
RP D Segui
RP J Willoughby
RP J Burton
C- C Fisk
1B C Yastrzemski
2B D Griffin
SS R Burleson
3B R Petrocelli
OF B Carbo
CF F Lynn
RF D Evans
LD J Rice
D1 C Cooper
2B- K Andrew
OI- J Beniquez
C- T Blackwell
DU- T Conigliaro
2B- S Dillard
2B- D Doyle
3I- B Heise
3U- B Hobson
2B- B Hunter
1D- D Johnson
3B- D McAuliffe
CU- T McCarver
C- A Merchant
UO- R Miller
C- B Montgomery

1976
SP L Tiant
SP R Wise
SP F Jenkins
SR R Cleveland
SR D Pole
SR J Jones
SR B Lee
SP- R Kreuger

RP J Willoughby
RP T Murphy
RP- T House
C C Fisk
1B- E Kasko
3B- B Hobson
LD J Rice
CF F Lynn
RF D Evans
1D C Cooper
UO R Miller
1U- J Baker
DH- B Carbo
OF- B Darwin
UI- S Dillard
2B- D Griffin
3S- B Heise
D1- D Johnson
CU- A Merchant
C- B Montgomery
3B- R Petrocelli
C- E Whitt
M2 D Zimmer

1977
SP F Jenkins
SP R Cleveland
SP L Tiant
SR B Lee
SP R Wise
SP D Aase
SP- T House
SP- J Burton
SP- R Kreuger
CL B Campbell
RS B Stanley
RP J Willoughby
RP- T Murphy
RP- R Hernandez
C C Fisk
1B G Scott
2B D Doyle
3B B Hobson
LF C Yastrzemski
CF F Lynn
RM- R Miller
DO J Rice
2B- R Aviles
2L- B Bailey
1U- J Baker
LM-S Bowen
RU- B Carbo
UO- D Coleman
DH- T Cox
DR- B Darwin
C- B Diaz
2U- S Dillard
RU- D Evans
2U- D Griffin
DU- T Helms
C- B Montgomery
M D Zimmer

1978
SP D Eckersley
SP M Torrez
SP L Tiant
SP B Lee
SP J Wright
SP- A Ripley
SP- B Sprowl
SP- J LaRose
SP- R Cleveland
RP B Stanley
RP D Drago
RP T Burgmeier
RP B Campbell
RP- A Hassler
C C Fisk
1B G Scott
2B J Remy
SS R Burleson
3B B Hobson
OI C Yastrzemski
CF F Lynn
RF D Evans
LD J Rice
DH- B Bailey
MU-S Bowen
IF- J Brohamer
OF- B Carbo
UI- F Duffy
UO- G Hancock

1C- F Kendall
C- B Montgomery
M D Zimmer

1979
SP M Torrez
SP D Eckersley
SR B Stanley
SP S Renko
SP C Rainey
SP J Finch
SP- J Tudor
SP- W Remmerswaal
SP- A Hassler
RP D Drago
RP T Burgmeier
RP A Ripley
RP B Campbell
RP- J Wright
C G Allenson
1D- B Watson
2B- J Remy
SS R Burleson
3B B Hobson
LF J Rice
CF F Lynn
RF D Evans
UT C Yastrzemski
23- J Brohamer
2U- F Duffy
UT- J Dwyer
UC- C Fisk
C- B Montgomery
C- M O'Berry
2S- J Papi
UO- T Poquette
1B- G Scott
2B- T Sizemore
2I- L Wolfe
M D Zimmer

1980
SP M Torrez
SP D Eckersley
SS R Burleson
SP J Tudor
SP C Rainey
SP- S Crawford
SP- B Hurst
SP- B Ojeda
SP- J Billingham
SP- L Aponte
RS B Stanley
RS D Drago
CL T Burgmeier
RS P Lockwood
RP- K Mac Whorter
RP- B Campbell
RP- W Remmerswaal
C C Fisk
1B T Perez
2B D Stapleton
SS R Burleson
3B G Hoffman
LF J Rice
CF F Lynn
RF D Evans
OI C Yastrzemski
CU- G Allenson
MO-S Bowen
3U- J Brohamer
OI- J Dwyer
UC- R Gedman
UO- G Hancock
3D- B Hobson
CF- R Nichols
3B- S Papi
CU- D Rader
2B- J Remy
2B- T Sizemore
SS- J Valdez
2D- C Walker
3B- L Wolfe
M1 D Zimmer
M2 J Pesky

1981
SP D Eckersley
SP F Tanana
SP M Torrez
SP J Tudor
SP B Ojeda
SP S Crawford
SP C Rainey
SP- B Hurst

SP- L Aponte
RP B Stanley
RP M Clear
RP T Burgmeier
RP B Campbell
C- R Gedman
1D T Perez
2B J Remy
SS G Hoffman
3B C Lansford
LF J Rice
CF R Miller
RF D Evans
D1 C Yastrzemski
UI D Stapleton
C- G Allenson
OF- G Hancock
C- J Lickert
MU- R Nichols
LU- T Poquette
UT- J Rudi
C- D Schmidt
SS- J Valdez
2B- C Walker
M R Houk

1982
SP D Eckersley
SP J Tudor
SP M Torrez
SP C Rainey
SP B Hurst
SP B Ojeda
SP B Denman
SP- S Crawford
SP- O Boyd
SP- M Brown
RP B Stanley
RP M Clear
RP T Burgmeier
RP L Aponte
C- G Allenson
1I D Stapleton
2B J Remy
SS G Hoffman
3B C Lansford
LF J Rice
CF R Miller
RF D Evans
DH Yastrzemski
IO W Boggs
2B- M Barrett
C- R Gedman
RU- G Hancock
3B- E Jurak
C- R LaFrancois
ML- R Nichols
DU- T Perez
C- M Sullivan
SS- J Valdez
M R Houk

1983
SP J Tudor
SP B Hurst
SP D Eckersley
SP B Ojeda
SP M Brown
SP O Boyd
SP- A Nipper
CL B Stanley
RP M Clear
RS D Bird
RP L Aponte
RP J Johnson
C- G Allenson
1B D Stapleton
2B J Remy
SS G Hoffman
3B W Boggs
LF J Rice
CF T Armas
RF D Evans
DH C Yastrzemski
OI R Miller
OI R Nichols
2U- M Barrett
C- R Gedman
OF- L Graham
SS- J Gutierrez
S1- E Jurak
C- J Newman
2B- J Valdez
LF- C Walker
M R Houk

1984
SP B Hurst
SP B Ojeda
SP O Boyd
SP A Nipper
SP R Clemens
SP M Brown
SP D Eckersley
SP- R Gale
SP- J Dorsey
CL B Stanley
RP M Clear
RP J Johnson
RP S Crawford
RP- C Mitchell
C R Gedman
1B B Buckner
2B M Barrett
SS J Gutierrez
3B W Boggs
LF J Rice
CF T Armas
RF D Evans
DH M Easler
C- G Allenson
SS- G Hoffman
UI- E Jurak
OI- R Miller
C- J Newman
UO- R Nichols
2B- J Remy
1B- D Stapleton
C- M Sullivan
US- C Walker
M R Houk

1985
SP O Boyd
SP B Hurst
SP A Nipper
SP B Ojeda
SP R Clemens
SR B Kison
SP T Lollar
SP- R Woodward
SP- J Sellers
SP- J Dorsey
SP- T McCarthy
SP- M Brown
SP- C Mitchell
RP S Crawford
RP B Stanley
RS M Trujillo
RP M Clear
C R Gedman
1B B Buckner
2B M Barrett
SS J Gutierrez
3B W Boggs
LF J Rice
CF S Lyons
RF D Evans
DH M Easler
MU T Armas
LF- M Greenwell
SS- G Hoffman
IO- E Jurak
UO- R Miller
OI- R Nichols
LR- K Romine
CU- D Sax
IF- D Stapleton
C- M Sullivan
M J McNamara

1986
SP R Clemens
SP O Boyd
SP B Hurst
SP A Nipper
SP T Seaver
SP J Sellers
SP M Brown
SP- R Woodward
SP- M Trujillo
SP- W Gardner
RP B Stanley
RP S Stewart
RP S Crawford
CL C Schiraldi
RP J Sambito
RP- T Lollar
C R Gedman
1B B Buckner
2B M Barrett
SS E Romero

3B W Boggs
LF J Rice
CF T Armas
RF D Evans
DH D Baylor
1B- P Dodson
OF- M Greenwell
CF- D Henderson
SS- G Hoffman
CF- S Lyons
SS- S Owen
SS- R Quinones
CF- K Romine
C1- D Sax
OI- M Stenhouse
C- M Sullivan
MU- L Tarver
M J McNamara

1987
SP R Clemens
SP B Hurst
SP A Nipper
SR B Stanley
SP J Sellers
SP- O Boyd
SP- R Woodward
SP- J Leister
RP W Gardner
RP C Schiraldi
RP S Crawford
RP T Bolton
RP- J Sambito
C- M Sullivan
1R D Evans
2B M Barrett
SS S Owen
3B W Boggs
LF J Rice
CF E Burks
LU M Greenwell
DH D Baylor
RO- T Benzinger
1B- B Buckner
1B- P Dodson
C- R Gedman
UO- D Henderson
SS- G Hoffman
DH- S Horn
C- J Marzano
UI- J Reed
UI- E Romero
UO- K Romine
C- D Sax
C- D Sheaffer
M J McNamara

1988
SP R Clemens
SP B Hurst
SR W Gardner
SP O Boyd
SP M Smithson
SP M Boddicker
SP J Sellers
SP- S Ellsworth
SP- J Trautwein
SP- S Curry
SP- M Rochford
SP- Z Crouch
SP- R Woodward
CL L Smith
RP B Stanley
RP D Lamp
RP- T Bolton
C- R Gedman
1R T Benzinger
2B M Barrett
SS J Reed
3B W Boggs
LF M Greenwell
CF E Burks
R1 D Evans
DH J Rice
RM- B Anderson
C- R Cerone
1B- P Dodson
DU- S Horn
OI- R Kutcher
C- J Marzano
SS- S Owen
1D- L Parrish
RU- C Quintana
UI- E Romero
RU- K Romine
M1 J McNamara
M2 J Morgan

1989
SP R Clemens
SP M Boddicker
SP J Dopson
SR M Smithson
SP W Gardner
SP O Boyd
SP E Hetzel
SP- T Bolton
SP- M Rochford
RP D Lamp
RP R Murphy
CL L Smith
RP B Stanley
RS J Clark
RP- G Harris
C R Cerone
1B N Esasky
2B- M Barrett
SS- L Rivera
3B W Boggs
LF M Greenwell
CF E Burks
RF T Brunansky
DH J Clark
IO- M Brumley
3B- S Cooper
UT- W Housie
UT- S Lyons
UT- M Marshall
C- J Marzano
SS- L Rivera
3B W Boggs
LF M Greenwell
CF E Burks
C- R Gedman
OI- D Heep
UT- R Kutcher
1U- R Lancellotti
UT- M Marshall
C- J Marzano
SS- T Naehring
2B- J Pankovits
UT- P Plantier
UT- R Robidoux
UO- K Romine
U1- J Stone
M J Morgan

1990
SP M Boddicker
SP R Clemens
SP G Harris
SP D Kiecker
SP T Bolton
SP- E Hetzel
SP- J Dopson
SP- J Leister
SP- M Rochford
RP D Lamp
RS W Gardner
CL J Reardon
RP R Murphy
RP J Gray
RP- J Reed
RP- J Hesketh
RP- L Andersen
CL- L Smith
RP- D Irvine
C T Pena
1B C Quintana
2B J Reed
SS L Rivera
3B W Boggs
LF M Greenwell
CF E Burks
RF T Brunansky
DH D Evans
2B- M Barrett
1U- B Buckner
CF- S Cooper
C- R Gedman
OI- D Heep
UT- R Kutcher
1U- R Lancellotti
UT- M Marshall
C- J Marzano
SS- T Naehring
2B- J Pankovits
UT- P Plantier
UT- R Robidoux
UO- K Romine
U1- J Stone
M J Morgan

1991
SP R Clemens
SR G Harris
SR J Hesketh
SP M Gardiner
SP T Bolton
SP M Young
SP K Morton
SP D Darwin
SP- J Irvine
SP- J Plympton
SP- J Dopson

SP- J Manzanillo
CL J Reardon
RP D Lamp
RP J Gray
RP T Fossas
RS- D Kiecker
RP- D Petry
C T Pena
1B C Quintana
2B J Reed
SS L Rivera
3B W Boggs
LF M Greenwell
CF E Burks
RF T Brunansky
DH J Clark
IO- M Brumley
3B- S Cooper
UT- W Housie
UT- S Lyons
UT- M Marshall
C- J Marzano
SS- T Naehring
RL- P Plantier
UO- K Romine
1U- M Vaughn
H- E Wedge
UO- B Zupcic
M J Morgan

1992
SP R Clemens
SP F Viola
SP J Hesketh
SP J Dopson
SR M Gardiner
SP- S Taylor
SP- K Ryan
SP- J Hoy
RS D Darwin
RP G Harris
RS M Young
CL J Reardon
RP P Quantrill
RP- T Fossas
RP- T Bolton
RP- D Irvine
C T Pena
1B M Vaughn
2B J Reed
SS L Rivera
3B W Boggs
LF- B Hatcher
ML B Zupcic
RU T Brunansky
DH- J Clark
13 S Cooper
OF H Winningham
RU P Plantier
2U- T Barrett
3B- M Brumley
CF- E Burks
C- J Flaherty
LF- M Greenwell
UT- S Lyons
C- J Marzano
IO- T Naehring
SS- J Valentin
DU- E Wedge
M B Hobson

1993
SP D Darwin
SP R Clemens
SP F Viola
SP J Dopson
SP A Sele
SP- N Minchey
SP- J Melendez
RS P Quantrill
RP G Harris
CL J Russell
RP S Bankhead
RS J Hesketh
RP K Ryan
RP- T Fossas
RP- C Bailey
RP- S Taylor
C T Pena
1B M Vaughn
2B S Fletcher
SS J Valentin
3B S Cooper
LF M Greenwell
CF B Hatcher
UO B Zupcic
DH A Dawson

1R C Quintana
LU- G Blosser
RU- J Byrd
RD- J Calderon
RF- R Deer
C- J Flaherty
UT- S Lyons
MU-J McNeely
C- B Melvin
UI- T Naehring
3D- L Ortiz
2S- J Richardson
UI- E Riles
UI- L Rivera
M B Hobson

1994
SP R Clemens
SP A Sele
SP J Hesketh
SP D Darwin
SP C Nabholz
SP T Van Egmond
SP G Finnvold
SP- F Viola
SP- N Minchey
SP- C Bailey
RP K Ryan
RP G Harris
RP C Howard
CL J Russell
RP S Bankhead
RP T Fossas
RP- T Frohwirth
RP- R Trlicek
RP- J Melendez
RP- S Farr
C D Berryhill
1B M Vaughn
2B- S Fletcher
SS J Valentin
3B S Cooper
LF M Greenwell
CF O Nixon
RL- T Brunansky
DH A Dawson
2I T Naehring
OF- G Blosser
RU- W Chamberlain
RF- B Hatcher
UI- G Litton
H- L Ortiz
S2- C Rodriguez
C- R Rowland
3B- S Royer
UO L Tinsley
OF- A Tomberlin
C- D Valle
H- E Wedge
LD- B Zupcic
M B Hobson

1995
SP T Wakefield
SP E Hanson
SP R Clemens
SP Z Smith
SP V Eshelman
SP- A Sele
SP- J Suppan
SP- F Rodriguez
SP- T Van Egmond
SP- M Hartley
SP- B Looney
3D- J Johnston
SP- M Murray
SP- B Bark
SP- K Shepherd
RS R Cormier
RP M Maddux
RP S Belinda
CL R Aguilera
RP J Hudson
RP- K Ryan
RP- A Pena
RP- D Lilliquist
RP- M Stanton
RP- J Pierce
C M Macfarlane
1B M Vaughn
2B L Alicea
SS J Valentin
3B T Naehring
LF M Greenwell

CF L Tinsley
RF T O'Leary
DH J Canseco
UI- J Bell
RD- W Chamberlain
3I- C Donnels
C- B Haselman
DR- D Hollins
CF- D Hosey
OF- C James
DU- R Jefferson
RM- W McGee
CF- K Rhodes
2S- C Rodriguez
SU- S Rodriguez
C- R Rowland
UI- T Shumpert
OF- M Stairs
RF- M Whiten
M K Kennedy

1996
SP R Clemens
SP T Gordon
SP T Wakefield
SP A Sele
SR J Moyer
SP J Suppan
SP- B Knackert
SP- J Doherty
SP- N Minchey
SP- R Harris
SP- K Grundt
CL H Slocumb
RP- J Hudson
RP- R Garces
RP- S Belinda
RP- E Gunderson
RP- P Mahomes
RP- B Pennington
RP- K Lacy
C M Stanley
1B M Vaughn
2B J Frye
SS J Valentin
3B T Naehring
LF- M Greenwell
CF- L Tinsley
RL T O'Leary
DH- J Canseco
UT R Jefferson
UI- E Beltre
CF- D Bragg
IF- P Clark
CF- A Cole
2U- W Cordero
MR- M Cuyler
CO- A Delgado
SS- N Garciaparra
C- B Haselman
C- S Hatteberg
ML- D Hosey
RU- J Malave
IF- J Manto
3B- J Manto
C- W McKeel
RF- K Mitchell
RF- T Nixon
RF- R Pemberton
RF- G Pirkl
IF- A Pozo
SS- T Rodriguez
IO- B Selby
3B- J Tatum
M K Kennedy

1997
SP T Wakefield
SR T Gordon
SP A Sele
SP J Suppan
SP S Avery
SP- B Saberhagen
SP- D Lowe
SP- T Borland
SP- K Grundt
SP- B Rose
RS J Wasdin
RS B Henry
RS C Hammond

CL H Slocumb
RP J Corsi
RP K Lacy
RS- V Eshelman
RP- M Brandenburg
RP- J Hudson
RP- R Mahay
RP- R Garces
RP- P Mahomes
C S Hatteberg
1B M Vaughn
2U J Frye
SS N Garciaparra
3B- T Naehring
LF W Cordero
CF D Bragg
RF T O'Leary
DH R Jefferson
D1- S Stanley
23 J Valentin
UI- M Benjamin
CF- M Coleman
C- B Haselman
MU-S Mack
LF- J Malave
C- W McKeel
RF- R Pemberton
3B- A Pozo
3B- C Pride
MU-J Tavarez
C- J Varitek
M J Williams

1998
SP P Martinez
SP T Wakefield
SP B Saberhagen
SR S Avery
SP- P Schourek
SP- B Rose
SP- J Cho
SP- B Barkley
SP- B Henry
SP- B Checo
SP- B Shouse
SP- D Veras
SP- C Valdez
SP- D West
RS D Lowe
CL T Gordon
RS J Wasdin
RP J Corsi
RP- R Garces
RP- D Eckersley
RP- C Reyes
RP- R Mahay
RP- G Swindell
C S Hatteberg
1B M Vaughn
2I M Benjamin
SS N Garciaparra
3B J Valentin
LF T O'Leary
MR D Lewis
RF D Bragg
DH- R Jefferson
UT- B Ashley
CF- D Buford
UT- M Cummings
2D- K Johns
2B- M Lemke
DH- J Leyritz
UT- O Merced
2B- L Merloni
DR- K Mitchell
OF- T Nixon
IC- M Romero
2B- D Sadler
IF- C Snopek
D1- S Stanley
C- J Varitek
M J Williams

1999
SP P Martinez
SR T Wakefield
SP M Portugal
SR P Rapp
SP B Saberhagen
SP B Rose
SP J Cho
SP- K Mercker
SP- R Martinez
SP- T Harikkala
SP- T Ohka
SP- J Pena

SP- B Wolcott	SP- J Pena	RP R Beck	RP- R Garces	2B T Walker	RO G Kapler	RF T Nixon	3B M Lowell
SP- M Santana	RS T Wakefield	RP R Garces	RP- B Howry	SS N Garciaparra	DH D Ortiz	DH D Ortiz	LF M Ramirez
SP- K Bullinger	CL D Lowe	RP- S Kim	C J Varitek	3B B Mueller	H- E Burks	2I- A Cora	CF C Crisp
RP D Lowe	RP R Garces	RP- H Pichardo	1B- T Clark	LF M Ramirez	SS- O Cabrera	RF- J Cruz	RF T Nixon
RP J Wasdin	RP R Cormier	RP- P Schourek	2B R Sanchez	CF J Damon	SO- C Crespo	2B- T Graffanino	DH D Ortiz
RP R Cormier	RP H Pichardo	CL- U Urbina	SS N Garciaparra	RF T Nixon	UT- B Daubach	RM- G Kapler	C- J Bard
RP- M Guthrie	RP B Florie	RP- B Pulsipher	3B S Hillenbrand	D1 D Ortiz	1U- A Dominique	UO- A Hyzdu	SI- A Cora
RP- R Garces	RP- J Wasdin	RP- T Erdos	LU- R Henderson	UT D Jackson	SS- N Garciaparra	UT- A Machado	MO-W Harris
RP- B Florie	RP- R Beck	RP- A McDill	CF J Damon	1B- A Abad	2S- R Gutierrez	1B- D McCarty	OI- E Hinske
CL- T Gordon	C J Varitek	C- S Hatteberg	RF T Nixon	ML- A Brown	LU- A Hyzdu	C- D Mirabelli	C- K Huckaby
RP- J Corsi	1D- M Stanley	1B B Daubach	LD M Ramirez	3L- L Collier	C- S Martinez	RM- J Payton	RL- G Kapler
RP- R Beck	21 J Offerman	21 J Offerman	UT B Daubach	DU- J Giambi	1U- D McCarty	1U- R Petagine	C- J Lopez
RP- K Gross	SS N Garciaparra	S2 M Lansing	LF- B Agbayani	CD- B Haselman	1B- D Mientkiewicz	SS- H Ramirez	C- C Miller
C J Varitek	3I M Alexander	3B S Hillenbrand	31- S Andrews	31- S Hillenbrand	C- D Mirabelli	C- K Shoppach	C- D Mirabelli
1B M Stanley	LF T O'Leary	LR T O'Leary	IF- C Baerga	OI- G Kapler	RF- T Nixon	UO- A Stern	ML- D Mohr
2B J Offerman	CF C Everett	CF C Everett	C- K Brown	OI- D McCarty	UO- D Roberts	UI- R Vazquez	UO- D Murphy
SS N Garciaparra	RF T Nixon	RM T Nixon	UT- J Diaz	IO- L Merloni	3B- E Snyder	C- S Wooten	2B- D Pedroia
3B J Valentin	1D B Daubach	DL M Ramirez	OF- C Floyd	C- D Mirabelli	3B- K Youkilis	3I- K Youkilis	1B- C Pena
LF T O'Leary	UO- D Lewis	OF D Bichette	2B- L Merloni	UI- F Sanchez	*M T Francona*	*M T Francona*	UO- W Pena
MR D Lewis	3B- S Berry	OI- I Alcantara	C- D Mirabelli	*M G Little*			1U- J Snow
RF T Nixon	DH- D Bichette	D1- N Garciaparra	UT- B Nelson		**2005**	**2006**	CF- A Stern
DU- R Jefferson	1B- R Brogna	SS- N Garciaparra	1D- J Offerman	**2004**	SP T Wakefield	SP J Beckett	*M T Francona*
1D B Daubach	DH- M Burkhart	SS- C Grebeck	IF- F Sanchez	SP C Schilling	SP B Arroyo	SP C Schilling	
CF- D Buford	OF- M Cummings	C- M Jensen	*M G Little*	SP P Martinez	SP M Clement	SP T Wakefield	**2007***
LM- M Coleman	2B- J Frye	UO- D Lewis		SP T Wakefield	SP D Wells	SP J Lester	SP J Beckett
2U- C Fonville	H- G Gaetti	SS- J Lofton	**2003**	SP D Lowe	SR C Schilling	SP M Clement	SP C Schilling
2U- J Frye	OF- B Gilkey	SS- L Merloni	SP D Lowe	SP B Arroyo	SP W Miller	SP K Snyder	SP T Wakefield
C- C Gubanich	CU- S Hatteberg	C- D Mirabelli	SP T Wakefield	SP- B Kim	SP- L Dinardo	SP- D Wells	SP D Matsuzaka
C- S Hatteberg	2B- M Lansing	C- J Oliver	SP P Martinez	SP- P Astacio	SP- B Neal	SP- L Dinardo	SP J Tavarez
DH- B Huskey	3B- L Merloni	1U- C Pickering	SP J Burkett	SP- J Brown	SP- C Harville	SP- J Johnson	RP J Papelbon
C- S Lomasney	LF- C Pride	2U- A Santos	SP C Fossum	SP- J Anderson	SP- M Remlinger	SP- K Gabbard	RP M Timlin
SI- L Merloni	UT- D Sadler	IO- C Stynes	SP J Suppan	SP- A Alvarez	SP- C Hansen	SP- K Jarvis	RP B Donnelly
OF- J Nunnally	SS- A Sheets	SS- J Valentin	SP- B Arroyo	SP- P Seibel	SP- A Alvarez	SP- D Pauley	RP J Piniero
UT- D Sadler	3B- E Sprague	C- J Varitek	SP- S Woodard	SP- B Jones	SP- C Meredith	SP- D Hansack	RP J Romero
3B- W Veras	3B- J Valentin	*M1 J Williams*	SP- R Person	SP- J Nelson	SP- S Cassidy	SP- D Riske	RP J Lopez
C- L Webster	3B- W Veras	*M2 J Kerrigan*	SP- B Chen	SP- F Castillo	SP- M Stanton	SP- M Burns	RP K Snyder
M J Williams	*M J Williams*		SP- R Nixon	CL K Foulke	SP- M Perisho	SP- A Alvarez	C J Varitek
		2002	SP- R Seanez	RP M Timlin	RP M Timlin	SP- M Holtz	1B K Youkilis
2000	**2001**	SP D Lowe	SP- H Almonte	RP A Embree	CL K Foulke	CL J Papelbon	2B D Pedroia
SP P Martinez	SP H Nomo	SP P Martinez	SP- B Howry	RP- R Mendoza	RP J Gonzalez	RS J Tavarez	SS J Lugo
SR J Fassero	SR T Wakefield	SP J Burkett	SP- K Tolar	RP- S Williamson	RP- J Halama	RP M Timlin	3B M Lowell
SP R Martinez	SP F Castillo	SR F Castillo	SP- M White	RP- C Leskanic	RP- A Embree	RP M Delcarmen	LF M Ramirez
SP P Schourek	SP D Cone	SP D Oliver	RS B Kim	RP- L Dinardo	RP- M Myers	RP K Foulke	CF C Crisp
SP R Arrojo	SP P Martinez	SP- J Hancock	RP M Timlin	RP- T Adams	RP- J Papelbon	RP- R Seanez	RF J Drew
SP T Ohka	SP T Ohka	RS T Wakefield	RP B Lyon	RP- M Malaska	RP- K Foulke	RP- C Hansen	DH D Ortiz
SP B Rose	SP- C Fossum	RS C Fossum	RS R Mendoza	RP- M Myers	RP- C Bradford	RP- B Corey	C- D Mirabelli
SP- P Crawford	SP- C Crawford	CL U Urbina	RP A Embree	RP- A Martinez	C J Varitek	RP- J Lopez	S2- A Cora
SP- R Stanifer	SP- B Saberhagen	RS R Arrojo	RP- T Jones	C J Varitek	1B K Millar	RP- J Van Buren	IO- E Hinske
SP- S Lee	SP- W Banks	RP- W Banks	RP- J Shiell	1B K Millar	2B- M Bellhorn	RP- C Breslow	MR- W Pena
SP- T Young	SP- B Florie	RP- A Embree	RP- C Fox	2B M Bellhorn	SS E Renteria	C J Varitek	
SP- H Carrasco	SP- C Castillo	RP- C Haney	RP- S Williamson	S2- P Reese	3B B Mueller	1B K Youkilis	**Through April*
SP- R Croushore	CL D Lowe	RP- S Kim	RP- S Sauerbeck	3B B Mueller	LF M Ramirez	2B M Loretta	*of 2007*
SP- S Ontiveros	RS R Arrojo	RP- W Gomes	C J Varitek	LF M Ramirez	CF J Damon	SS A Gonzalez	
SP- D Smith		RP- D Hermanson	1U K Millar	CF J Damon			

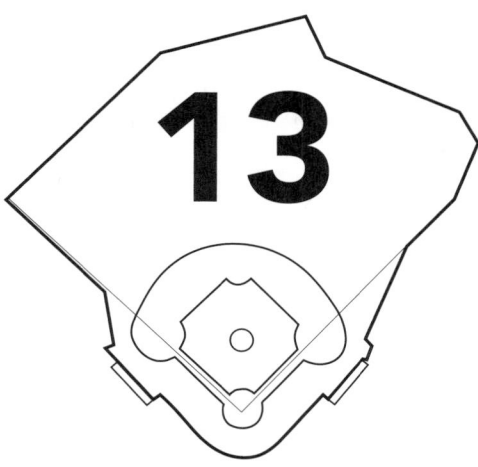

RED SOX MINOR LEAGUE SYSTEM

From Ted Williams to Carlton Fisk to Jonathan Papelbon, the Red Sox have enjoyed the benefits of great homegrown players. Finding and nurturing talent, though, can be a risky proposition. Plenty of hot prospects have turned to dust upon their promotion to the big leagues, or faded away before they ever got close. The minor leagues have long been the proving ground of whether a prospect is a building block for the future, trade bait, or an expendable commodity. Most minor leaguers invariably fall into the latter category.

The structure of the minor leagues has changed greatly since the practice of farm clubs became widespread in the 1930s. The Red Sox have changed affiliates many times over and leagues have come and gone and merged. The Red Sox started with two minor league teams in 1932: Hazleton, Pennsylvania, and Wilmington, North Carolina. They dropped both the following year and wound up with a single club in Reading, Pennsylvania. By 1937 the Red Sox had 11 clubs, yet by the middle of World War II they were down to 3. The high-water mark for Boston farm clubs was 13 in 1948. Fifteen years later they were down to five clubs. The Red Sox held steady with five clubs from 1973 to 1988, when they added a rookie team in Arizona. The club has had a rookie team in Florida in the Gulf Coast League every year since 1989. The team has also had many affiliates in the Dominican Summer League and Venezuelan Summer League in recent years. Many of these players are signed at age 16 and play on their home soil; if they make the grade they can obtain a visa and play on U.S. soil. But it is still a long way from the minor leagues to Boston.

Since 1963 the minor leagues have been divided into three major classes: A, AA, and AAA. Currently there are only two official levels of Class A: short season A and full season A. Virtually every major league team, however, still effectively promotes players through three levels of Class A baseball: short season A, full season A, and A+ (usually referred to as high A). Boston's Class A clubs in 2007 include Lowell in the New York-Penn League (short season, beginning in June), Greenville in the South Atlantic League (long season, opening in April), and, as of 2007, a new affiliate in Lancaster of the California League (A+, or where the top prospects generally wind up at some point in their development).

But if this were 1962 or earlier, it's likely that those three teams would be distributed in leagues whose level of baseball was classified by letters of the alphabet other than A. In 1963, after a decade during which the minor leagues shrunk dramatically as a result of the rising popularity of watching television instead of seeing prospects in person, the structure of the minor leagues was overhauled. In most cases, Class D baseball leagues turned into short season Class A leagues, Class C baseball leagues became full season Class A or Low A leagues, and Class B teams emerged as Class A+ or high A leagues. But not all leagues emerged from the transition in the same slot they were in before; the Florida State League, for example, transformed from a Class D league into a high A league. That is the reason the charts in this section have been broken down into groups through 1962 and from 1963 to present.

The current structure for minor league clubs differs in other ways from how it was in the first half of the 20th century. What was considered Class AA before World War II has been the equivalent of Class AAA baseball since 1946. During its 10 years of existence, A1 was considered higher than A yet lower than AA. A1 was, however, equivalent to what the Class AA level is today. That's a mouthful of the alphabet, but it can be summarized somewhat simply:

A (1902–11) = AA (1912–45) = AAA (1946–present)

A1 (1936–45) = AA (1946–present)

A (1912–62) = AA (1963–present)

Class B, C, D (through 1962) = Class A (1963–present)

Rookie Leagues were a new classification as of 1963. While some Class D leagues may have been essentially for players just starting professional baseball, the Rookie Leagues started in 1963 were new in that they were designed for this specific purpose. Today, the Appalachian League and the Pioneer League are considered more advanced Rookie Leagues than the Gulf Coast League and Arizona League, both of which play their games at spring training complexes and do not try to attract fans to their games.

And there were always plenty of leagues. Below are our abbreviations for minor leagues affiliated by the major leagues.

AFL - Alabama Florida League
APL - Appalachian League
AASN - American Association
AML - Arizona Mexico League
AML - Arkansas-Missouri League
ARL - Arkansas State League
ASL - Alabama State League
ATL - Arizona Texas League
AZL - Arizona League
BIS - Bi-State League
BL - Border League
BRL - Blue Ridge League
BSL - Big State League
CAL Canadian American League
CCL - Cape Breton Colliery League
CCR - Cocoa Rookie League
CL - California League
CNL - Colonial League
CPL - Coastal Plain League
CRL - Carolina League
CSL - Cotton States League
CTA - Central Association
CTL - Central League
CTSL - Connecticut State League
DL - Dixie League
DSL - Dominican Summer League
EDL - East Dixie League
EL - Eastern League
ESL - Eastern Shore League
ETL - East Texas League
EVL - Evangeline League
FSL - Florida State League
FWL - Far West League
GAL - Georgia Alabama League
GCL - Gulf Coast League
GFL - Georgia Florida League
GSL - Georgia State League
GSL - Gulf States League
III - Three I League
IL - International League
ISL - Illinois State League
ITL - Interstate League
KIT - Kentucky-Illinois-Tennessee League
KOM - Kansas-Oklahoma-Missouri League
LHL - Longhorn League
LSL - Lone Star League
MAL - Middle Atlantic League
MOL - Mississippi-Ohio Valley League

MSL - Michigan State League
MTL - Mountain State League
MWL - Midwest League
NAL - North Atlantic League
NAR - Northeast Arkansas League
NCL - North Carolina State League
NEL - New England League
NEN - Northeastern League
NNL - Northwestern League
NRL - Northern League
NSL - Nebraska State League
NWL - Northwest League
NYP - New York-Penn League
OIL - Ohio-Indiana League
OSL - Ohio State League
PCL - Pacific Coast League
PML - Piedmont League
PNL - Pioneer League
PONY - Pennsylvania-Ohio-New York League
PSA - Pennsylvania State Association
PVL - Provincial League
QPL - Quebec Provincial League
RGV - Rio Grande Valley League
SA - Southern Association
SAL - South Atlantic League
SEL - Southeastern League
SIL - Southwest International League
SL - Southern League
SML - Sophomore League
SRL - Sarasota Rookie League
SSL - Sooner State League
SUNS - Sunset League
SWL - Southwestern League
THL - Tar Heel League
TL - Texas League
TML - West Texas-New Mexico League
TPL - Twin Ports League
TRL - Tri-State League
TSL - Tobacco State League
TVL Texas Valley League
VL - Virginia League
VSL - Venezuelan Summer League
WA - Western Association
WCL - Western Carolina League
WDL - West Dixie League
WIL - Western International League
WL - Western League
WSL - Wisconsin State League

	Class AAA	Class AA	Class A	Class A	Class A	Class A	Rookie	Venezuela	Dominican
2007	Pawtucket (IL)	Portland, ME (EL)	Lancaster, CA (CL)	Greenville, SC (SAL)	Lowell (NYP)		GCL		DSL
2006	Pawtucket (IL)	Portland, ME (EL)	Wilmington, NC (CRL)	Greenville, SC (SAL)	Lowell (NYP)		GCL		DSL
2005	Pawtucket (IL)	Portland, ME (EL)	Wilmington, NC (CRL)	Greenville, SC (SAL)	Lowell (NYP)		GCL	$VSL	DSL
2004	Pawtucket (IL)	Portland, ME (EL)	Augusta, GA (SAL)	Sarasota (FSL)	Lowell (NYP)		GCL	VSL	DSL
2003	Pawtucket (IL)	Portland, ME (EL)	Augusta, GA (SAL)	Sarasota (FSL)	Lowell (NYP)		GCL		DSL (2)
2002	Pawtucket (IL)	Trenton (EL)	Augusta, GA (SAL)	Sarasota (FSL)	Lowell (NYP)		GCL		DSL
2001	Pawtucket (IL)	Trenton (EL)	Augusta, GA (SAL)	Sarasota (FSL)	Lowell (NYP)		GCL		DSL (2)
2000	Pawtucket (IL)	Trenton (EL)	Augusta, GA (SAL)	Sarasota (FSL)	Lowell (NYP)		GCL		DSL
1999	Pawtucket (IL)	Trenton (EL)	Augusta, GA (SAL)	Sarasota (FSL)	Lowell (NYP)		GCL		DSL
1998	Pawtucket (IL)	Trenton (EL)	Michigan (MWL)	Sarasota (FSL)	Lowell (NYP)		GCL		DSL
1997	Pawtucket (IL)	Trenton (EL)	Michigan (MWL)	Sarasota (FSL)	Lowell (NYP)		GCL		DSL
1996	Pawtucket (IL)	Trenton (EL)	Michigan (MWL)	Sarasota (FSL)	Lowell (NYP)		GCL		$DSL
1995	Pawtucket (IL)	Trenton (EL)	Michigan (MWL)	Sarasota (FSL)	Utica (NYP)		GCL		
1994	Pawtucket (IL)	New Britain (EL)	Lynchburg, VA (CRL)	Sarasota (FSL)	Utica (NYP)		GCL		
1993	Pawtucket (IL)	New Britain (EL)	Lynchburg, VA (CRL)	Ft. Lauderdale (FSL)	Utica (NYP)		GCL		
1992	Pawtucket (IL)	New Britain (EL)	Lynchburg, VA (CRL)	Winter Haven (FSL)	Elmira, NY (NYP)		GCL		
1991	Pawtucket (IL)	New Britain (EL)	Lynchburg, VA (CRL)	Winter Haven (FSL)	Elmira, NY (NYP)		GCL		
1990	Pawtucket (IL)	New Britain (EL)	Lynchburg, VA (CRL)	Winter Haven (FSL)	Elmira, NY (NYP)		GCL		$DSL
1989	Pawtucket (IL)	New Britain (EL)	Lynchburg, VA (CRL)	Winter Haven (FSL)	Elmira, NY (NYP)		GCL		$DSL
1988	Pawtucket (IL)	New Britain (EL)	Lynchburg, VA (CRL)	Winter Haven (FSL)	Elmira, NY (NYP)		AZL		
1987	Pawtucket (IL)	New Britain (EL)	Greensboro (SAL)	Winter Haven (FSL)	Elmira, NY (NYP)				
1986	Pawtucket (IL)	New Britain (EL)	Greensboro (SAL)	Winter Haven (FSL)	Elmira, NY (NYP)				
1985	Pawtucket (IL)	New Britain (EL)	Greensboro (SAL)	Winter Haven (FSL)	Elmira, NY (NYP)				
1984	Pawtucket (IL)	New Britain (EL)	Winston-Salem (CRL)	Winter Haven (FSL)	Elmira, NY (NYP)				
1983	Pawtucket (IL)	Bristol, CT (EL)	Winston-Salem (CRL)	Winter Haven (FSL)	Elmira, NY (NYP)				
1982	Pawtucket (IL)	Bristol, CT (EL)	Winston-Salem (CRL)	Winter Haven (FSL)	Elmira, NY (NYP)				
1981	Pawtucket (IL)	Bristol, CT (EL)	Winston-Salem (CRL)	Winter Haven (FSL)	Elmira, NY (NYP)				
1980	Pawtucket (IL)	Bristol, CT (EL)	Winston-Salem (CRL)	Winter Haven (FSL)	Elmira, NY (NYP)				
1979	Pawtucket (IL)	Bristol, CT (EL)	Winston-Salem (CRL)	Winter Haven (FSL)	Elmira, NY (NYP)				
1978	Pawtucket (IL)	Bristol, CT (EL)	Winston-Salem (CRL)	Winter Haven (FSL)	Elmira, NY (NYP)				
1977	Pawtucket (IL)	Bristol, CT (EL)	Winston-Salem (CRL)	Winter Haven (FSL)	Elmira, NY (NYP)				
1976	Pawtucket (IL)	Bristol, CT (EL)	Winston-Salem (CRL)	Winter Haven (FSL)	Elmira, NY (NYP)				
1975	Pawtucket (IL)	Bristol, CT (EL)	Winston-Salem (CRL)	Winter Haven (FSL)	Elmira, NY (NYP)				
1974	Pawtucket (IL)	Bristol, CT (EL)	Winston-Salem (CRL)	Winter Haven (FSL)	Elmira, NY (NYP)				
1973	Pawtucket (IL)	Bristol, CT (EL)	Winston-Salem (CRL)	Winter Haven (FSL)	Elmira, NY (NYP)				
1972	Louisville (IL)	Pawtucket (EL)	Winston-Salem (CRL)	Winter Haven (FSL)	Williamsport (NYP)	Greenville, SC (WCL)			
1971	Louisville (IL)	Pawtucket (EL)	Winston-Salem (CRL)	Winter Haven (FSL)	Williamsport (NYP)	Greenville, SC (WCL)			
1970	Louisville (IL)	Pawtucket (EL)	Winston-Salem (CRL)	Winter Haven (FSL)	Jamestown, NY (NYP)	Greenville, SC (WCL)			
1969	Louisville (IL)	Pittsfield (EL)	Winston-Salem (CRL)	Winter Haven (FSL)	Jamestown, NY (NYP)	Greenville, SC (WCL)			
1968	Louisville (IL)	Pittsfield (EL)	Winston-Salem (CRL)	Waterloo, IA (MWL)	Jamestown, NY (NYP)	Greenville, SC (WCL)			
1967	Toronto (IL)	Pittsfield (EL)	Winston-Salem (CRL)	Waterloo, IA (MWL)		Greenville, SC (WCL)			
1966	Toronto (IL)	Pittsfield (EL)	Winston-Salem (CRL)	Waterloo, IA (MWL)	Oneonta, NY (NYP)	Covington, VA (APL)			
1965	Toronto (IL)	Pittsfield (EL)	Winston-Salem (CRL)	Waterloo, IA (MWL)	Wellsville, NY (NYP)	Harlan, KY (APL)			
1964	Seattle (PCL)	Reading (EL)	Winston-Salem (CRL)	Waterloo, IA (MWL)	Wellsville, NY (NYP)	Statesville, GA (SAL)			
1963	Seattle (PCL)	Reading (EL)	Winston-Salem (CRL)	Waterloo, IA (MWL)	Wellsville, NY (NYP)				

Before 1963	Secondary Team	Third Team	Fourth Team

Class AAA
Seattle 1961–62 (PCL)
Minneapolis 1937–38, 1958–60 (AASN)
^San Francisco 1956–57 (PCL)
Louisville 1939–55 (AASN) — Toronto 1947 (IL)

Class AA
Memphis 1958 (AASN)
Oklahoma City 1956–57 (TL)
Birmingham 1948–52 (SA)
New Orleans 1946–47 (SA)
San Diego 1936–37(PCL)
Syracuse 1934–36 (IL)

Class A
York, PA 1962 (EL)
Johnstown, PA 1961 (EL)
Allentown 1959–60 (EL)
Albany 1952–54, 1956–57(EL)
Montgomery 1955 (SAL)
*Little Rock 1936–40 (SA) — Hazleton, PA 1937–38 (NYP)
Scranton 1939–51 (EL)
Elmira, NY 1936 (NYP)
Knoxville 1935 (SA)
Reading, PA 1933–34 (NYP)

Class B
Winston-Salem 1961–62 (CRL)
Raleigh 1958–60 (CRL)
Greensboro 1941–42, 1953–57 (CRL)
Roanoke 1943–53 (PML) — Lynn, MA 1946–48 (NEL)
Rocky Mount, NC 1936–40 (PML)
Charlotte 1935 (PML)
Columbia-Asheville 1934 (PML)
#Hazleton, PA 1933 (NYP)
Wilmington, NC 1932 (PML)

Class C
Pocatello, ID 1962 (PNL)
San Jose 1947–55 (CL) — Auburn, NY 1948 (NYP)
Oneonta, NY 1941–42, 1946–51 (NYP) — Canton, OH 1936–42 (OSL)
Clarksdale, MS 1938–39 (CSL)
Brockville, Ontario 1937 (CAL)
Joplin, MO 1934 (WL)

Class D
Waterloo, IA 1958–62 (MWL) — Olean, NY 1961–62 (NYP) — Alpine, TX 1959–61 (SML)
Corning, NY 1954–60 (NYP) — Lafayette, IN 1956–57 (MWL) — Lexington, NE 1956–58 (NSL) — &Bluefield, WV 1954–55 (APL)
Salisbury, NC 1953 (THL)
High Point-Thomasville, NC 1951–52 (NCL)
Kinston, NC 1950 (CPL) — Marion, OH 1949–50 (OIL)
Hornell, Ontario 1949 (PONY) — Oroville, CA 1948 (FWL) — Valley, AL 1948–49 (GAL) — %Wellsville, NY 1947–48 (PONY)

Before 1963	Secondary Team	Third Team	Fourth Team
Milford, DE 1946–48 (ESL)	Geneva, AL 1946 (ASL)	New Iberia, LA 1946 (EVL)	Tarboro, NC 1946 (CPL)
Middletown, OH 1944 (OSL)			
Danville-Schofield, VA 1939–42 (BIS)	Owensboro, KY 1941–42 (KIT)		
Crookston, MN 1938 (NRL)	Elizabethton, TN 1937–40 (APL)	Centreville, MD 1937, 1939–41 (ESL)	Moultrie, GA 1937 (GFL)
Mansfield, OH 1937 (OSL)			
Eau Claire, WI 1936 (NRL)	McKeesport, PA 1936 (PSA)		

$ Co-op team operated with one or more other major league clubs.

(2)   Franchise had two teams in the same league.

^   The Pacific Coast League was considered an "open" league in 1952–57 because it had aspirations of becoming a third major league. It didn't, but of the eight cities that hosted PCL teams in the years before the Giants and Dodgers moved west, five became the home of major league teams by 1969 (Los Angeles, Oakland, San Diego, San Francisco, and Seattle).

*   Listed as A1.

Hazleton was a Red Sox Class A team in 1937–38, and a Class B team in 1932. It was a member of the New York-Penn League in both instances.

&   In the 1950s the Red Sox had no more than three Class D teams at any time. Bluefield is listed as a fourth team in 1954–55 because of the overlap of the other teams in the chain during that period.

     Pawtucket was in the Eastern League from 1970–73 as a Class AA franchise. The Rhode Island team transferred to Class AAA when it became Boston's top affiliate in 1974.

     Wellsville was a member of the Pennsylvania-Ohio-New York League in 1947–48 in Class D. When the Red Sox returned to the Pennsylvania town in 1963, it was a member of the New York-Penn League and represented the Red Sox in Class A.

     Greenville was a member of the Western Carolina League in 1967–71 in Class A. When Greenville rejoined the Red Sox as an affiliate in 2005, it was still in Class A, but it was as a member of the South Atlantic League.

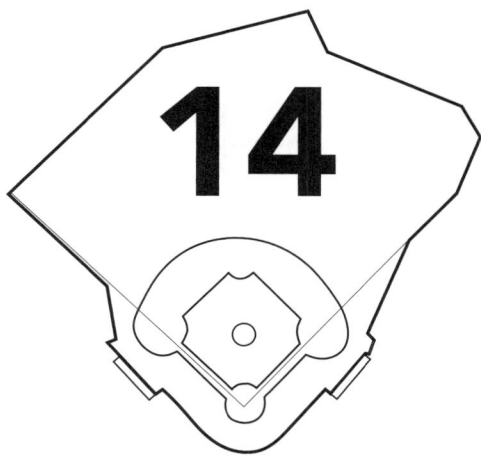

RED SOX YEAR-BY-YEAR DRAFT PICKS

The majority of baseball's talent base makes the jump from amateur to professional through the annual amateur draft. Most drafted players, however, do not reach the major leagues. First-round picks are more likely than not to make it to the big leagues, yet even a large number of those players fail to make a significant impact. The long-term result of each team's annual draft varies enormously. A draft originally viewed as average could end up producing several stars, no major leaguers whatsoever, or six or seven major leaguers of marginal quality.

Held annually since 1965, the draft is all about projection. Fingers are crossed that a player a team wants is available when their turn comes up—picks are made in reverse order of finish by the major league team with compensation picks added in the first three rounds for lost free agents—and that the player selected will turn out to be worthy of the pick. Boston's top draft picks in 1983 were Ellis Burks and Roger Clemens, with Burks the first pick in January and Clemens the club's top pick in June (There was more than one draft per year through 1986.). Even though no other Boston 1983 draftee made an impact for the Red Sox at the major league level, few teams will ever produce a draft class as valuable as those two players alone.

Boston's 1999 draft picks, on the other hand, produced no one who would have a major league impact for the Red Sox. But since the club eventually used Casey Fossum as the primary prospect in a deal for Curt Schilling, the ultimate mission of producing wins at the big league level was still ultimately accomplished. Sometimes a solid return on paper can turn out to be nothing special. Boston's 1997 draft, for example, featured nine future major leaguers, including David Eckstein. Yet no one from that draft class ever had a significant positive impact on the team. The organization gave up on Eckstein too quickly and released him; he's since been the starting shortstop on two world champion clubs.

Organizations put enormous effort into preparing for each year's draft, but ultimately the best any front office can do is make educated guesses and hope that the franchise can coax the best out of the players the team ends up with. Sometimes the can't-miss first pick of the draft is going to permanently stall in Class A, while the 1,027th pick is destined for the Hall of Fame.

In the years before the draft was instituted, the wealthiest teams could stockpile players while everyone else scrambled for talent. Misspent bonus money and arcane rules that actually hindered player development led to the adoption of the amateur free-agent draft in 1965 (the name was changed to first-year player draft in 1998). It was quite similar to the National Football League's system for talent distribution inaugurated almost 30 years earlier.

Major League Baseball has conducted an amateur draft every June for more than four decades, but it no longer holds a draft at any other time in the year. Three separate drafts were originally scheduled each year. A January draft, held annually until 1986, was designed for junior college players and others who no longer attended college. An August draft featured players who participated in amateur summer leagues, but it was eliminated after two years.

Today, the 50-round draft is open only for players who are residents of the United States, Canada, or a U.S. territory such as Puerto Rico. These players must have graduated high school or attend a junior or community

college. Those attending four-year colleges are only eligible for the draft after their junior year or their 21st birthdays. Any team can sign residents of other countries as free agents after their 16th birthday.

The list that follows includes every Red Sox player drafted, the round they were taken, the position they played at the time of selection, and the high school or college they attended. The high school city or town, along with the state, is given when it is not included in the school's name.

As for the years of the draft, *Reg* stands for the Regular rounds of the draft held in June and in January, *Sec* stands for the Secondary phase of the draft (reserved for players who'd once been drafted but hadn't signed; it was eliminated in 1987), and *Legion* is for the draft held only in August 1965–66. Players are listed in bold if the Red Sox signed them after the draft and they reached the major leagues. Players who did not sign with the Red Sox during the signing period following the draft but reached the majors after a later draft are listed in italics.

1965 June (Reg)
1. **Billy Conigliaro, OF, Swampscott HS (MA)**
2. John Hetrick, OF, Hershey HS (PA)
3. **Ken Poulsen, 3B-OF, Birmingham HS (Van Nuys, CA)**
4. Fred Marden, P, Brandeis University
5. **Amos Otis, SS, Williamson HS (Mobile, AL)**
6. Jim L. Thomas, P, Cal State Sacramento
7. **Jim Hutto, 3B-P, Pensacola HS (FL)**
8. Doug Shores, C, Northeast HS (Greensboro, NC)
9. Ron Shotts, 3B, Chaffey HS (Ontario, CA)
10. Tony Ciarpelli, P, West Genesee HS (Camillus, NY)
11. Dennis Best, OF, Gillespie HS (IL)
12. Manuel Washington, SS, Paragould HS (AR)
13. Michael Weber, P, Greenville HS (Pocahontas, IL)
14. Wayne Fuzzard, P, McCarthy HS (Fort Pierce, FL)
15. Bill Farmer, P, Choctaw HS (OK)
16. Reid Braden, 1B, Cerritos College (CA)
17. Brian Edgerly, OF, Colgate University
18. **Ray Jarvis, P, Hope HS (Providence, RI)**
19. John Iannelli, P, East Boston HS (MA)
20. William Barkley, SS, Sam Houston State University

1965 August (Legion)
1. Mike McCall, SS, Greenville HS (SC)

1966 January (Reg)
1. Jim Rife, C, Lebanon Valley College (PA)
2. **Mark Schaeffer, P, Cleveland HS (Canoga Park, CA)**
3. Donald Fox, P, Colley HS (Detroit, MI)
4. Donald Peters, P, Tusculum College (TN)

1966 January (Sec)
1. **Dick Baney, P, Anaheim HS (CA)**
2. Daniel Rudanovich, OF, University of Missouri
3. Kenneth Hall, P, Nassau Community College (NY)
4. *Jophrey Brown, P, Grambling State University (LA)*

1966 June (Reg)
1. **Ken Brett, P-OF, El Segundo HS (CA)**
2. Joseph McCullough, IF, Dickinson HS (Jersey City, NJ)
3. Rick Hoban, P, West HS (Cleveland, OH)
4. *Skip Jutze, C, Central Connecticut State University*
5. Wayne McGhee, P, Fresno State
6. **Mike Nagy, P, St. Helena HS (Bronx, NY)**
7. Daniel Smith, SS, Red Lion HS (Windsor, PA)
8. Roger McComas, P, Odessa, TX
9. Ernie Aguirre, C, Bakersfield HS (CA)
10. Nicholas Deflorio, SS, Carey HS (Franklin Square, NY)
11. William Hathaway, P, Palm Springs HS (CA)
12. Thomas Stephenson, P, Anaheim, CA
13. Richard Guy, 3B, Jemison HS (AL)
14. Harry Greenfield, OF, Husson College
15. Bernard Burns, OF, Indiana University of Pennsylvania
16. **Ed Phillips, P, Colby College**
17. Dennis Udy, P, University of Utah
18. William O'Neill, C, Windsor Locks HS (CT)
19. John Frye, OF, Michigan State University
20. Bernard Linn, P, Grossmont HS (El Cajon, CA)
21. Eugene Collins, P, Choctawhatchee HS (Fort Walton Beach, FL)
22. James Chenevert, OF, Redemptorist HS (Baton Rouge, LA)
23. Jack Fulmer, 3B, Arkansas State University
24. James Whinery, 3B, Thomas Downey HS (Modesto, CA)
25. Steve Egan, C, Pittsburg State University (KS)
26. Richard Goedert, 1B, Mira Costa College (CA)
27. Otis Griggs, C, Andalusia HS (AL)
28. Louis Inman, 3B, Mississippi Valley State University

1966 June (Sec)
1. Donald Cook, P, Long Island University
2. Jim Rife, C, Lebanon Valley College (PA)
3. **Dick Mills, P, Parsons College (IA)**
4. George Girard, P, Marblehead, MA

1967 January (Reg)
1. **Carlton Fisk, C, Charlestown, NH**
2. **Don Newhauser, P, Broward Community College (FL)**
3. *Craig Skok, P, Broward Community College (FL)*

1967 January (Sec)
1. Harold Harris, SS, Hewitt-Trussville HS (Birmingham, AL)
2. Michael Koritko, IF-OF, Stratford, CT
3. Bob Bryant, P, USC
4. Jack Fulmer, 3B, Arkansas State University
5. *Geoff Zahn, P, University of Michigan*
6. Charles Kline, P, Michigan State University
7. *Bill Zepp, P, University of Michigan*

1967 June (Reg)
1. **Mike Garman, P, Caldwell HS (ID)**
2. Danny Graham, SS, Bishop Montgomery HS (Torrance, CA)
3. Christopher Cross, C, Englewood HS (Jacksonville, FL)
4. Dudley Mitchell, OF-1B, Thomas Jefferson HS (Denver, CO)
5. Michael Witt, OF, McLane HS (Fresno, CA)
6. Samuel Phillips, P, Eastern Hills HS (Fort Worth, TX)
7. Alan Wolfenbarger, SS, Rutledge HS (TN)
8. Steven Salata, C-OF, Trinity Pawling Prep HS (Pawling, NY)
9. Cal Meier, SS, Grossmont Community College (CA)
10. Mark Kleibl, 3B, Norland HS (Miami, FL)
11. Ronald Sheppard, 3B, Altus HS (OK)
12. John Newton, SS, Manteca HS (CA)
13. Lawrence Bellm, P, University of Southern Illinois-Edwardsville
14. James Thurston, 3B-SS, Central HS (Little Rock, AR)
15. James Powers, C, St. Bernard HS (Waterford, CT)
16. Michael Spellman, P, St. Bernard HS (Waterford, CT)
17. Michael James, OF-SS, McKinney HS (TX)
18. Tommy Harmon, C, Eastern Hills HS (Fort Worth, TX)
19. Walter Povlick, P, East Central HS (Tulsa, OK)

1967 June (Sec)
1. Kris Krebs, SS, Manatee Community College (FL)
2. Ray Henningsen, 2B, Santa Clara University
3. Rod Austin, OF, Santa Clara University
4. John Clifton, P, Chapman University (CA)
5. Neil Rivenburg, OF, Southern Oregon State University
6. Stephen Eagan, C, Pittsburg State University (KS)

1968 January (Reg)
1. Walter Ransom, SS, South Gate, CA
2. Thomas Combs, OF, America River (Fla.) Community College
3. Ronald Falls, P, Grossmont Community College (CA)
4. Mickey Whitson, P, Gulf Coast Community College

1968 January (Sec)
1. Douglas Sandstedt, P, Omaha, NE
2. Wendell Franke, IF, Mesa Community College
3. John Walker, C, Sacramento City College
4. Thomas Skendarian, OF, Brown University
5. Gerald Burton, OF, St. Louis Community College at Meramec
6. Larry Gonsalves, P, Fresno State
7. David Brown, OF, University of Texas

1968 June (Reg)
1. Tom Maggard, OF-C, John Glenn HS (Norwalk, CA)
2. Curtis Suchan, IF-OF, Jesuit HS (Tampa, FL)
3. **Lynn McGlothen, P, Grambling HS (Simsboro, LA)**
4. Allen Collins, C, Glendora HS (Glendora, CA)

5. Manny Crespo, SS, Miami Senior HS (Miami, FL)
6. **Cecil Cooper, 1B, Brenham HS (Brenham, TX)**
7. Harold Kurtzman, IF, University of California (Beverly Hills, CA)
8. Roy Handel, C, Columbus HS (Columbus, GA)
9. Edward Baird, P, University of Connecticut
10. Michael O'Banion, C, Dos Palos HS (Dos Palos, CA)
11. **Ben Oglivie, IF-OF, Roosevelt HS (Bronx, NY)**
12. Robert Overmiller, 3B, Red Lion HS (Sexton, PA)
13. Frank Mannerino, OF, Oak Lawn Community HS (Oak Lawn, IL)
14. Terry Williams, P, Davenport West HS (Davenport, IA)
15. Thomas King, P, Acton-Boxboro HS (West Acton, MA)
16. William Brown, IF, Fresno State
17. Michael Collins, P, West Covina HS (West Covina, CA)
18. Lonnie Keeter, IF, David Douglas HS (Portland, OR)
19. Curtis Jordan, C, Middle Georgia College
20. Donald Grate, SS, Harvard University
21. Frank Addonizo, C, St. John's University (NY)
22. **Bill Lee, P, USC**
23. John Moss, IF, University of Alabama
24. Doug Miller, C-OF, Klamath Union HS (Klamath Falls, OR)
25. Robert Hoepfinger, OF, Timon HS (Buffalo, NY)
26. William Croken, C, Malden HS (Malden, MA)
27. Roger Ward, P, Chaminade HS (Fort Lauderdale, FL)
28. Felix Skalski, 3B, Kalamazoo Valley Community College
29. Thomas Walsh, P, Tilton-Northfield HS (Tilton, NH)
30. Blaine Young, P, Bishop Stang HS (Fairhaven, MA)
31. Michael Neal, P, Shasta College (CA)
32. Michael Harvison, IF, Polytechnical HS (Fort Worth, TX)
33. Richard Perry, C-1B, St. Johnsville HS (St. Johnsville, NY)
34. George Reebe, OF, Natick HS (Natick, MA)
35. Jeff Guenther, P, Katella HS (Anaheim, CA)
36. Michael Comuso, P, Lawrence Central HS (Lawrence, MA)

1968 June (Sec)
1. **John Curtis, P, Clemson University**
2. Ronald Soucie, P, Husson College (ME)
3. Richard Wicks, P, McNeese State University (LA)
4. Allen Truskowski, P, St. Clair County Community College (MI)
5. Nicholas Furlong, P, University of Notre Dame

1969 January (Reg)
1. William Norton, 1B, Merrimack College (MA)
2. Richard Licini, 1B, University of Notre Dame
3. *John Grubb, OF, Manatee Community College (FL)*
4. William Hamilton, C, Broward Community College (FL)

1969 January (Sec)
1. Gary Myers, OF, College of San Mateo (CA)
2. Kenneth Rutkowski, C-P, SUNY-Buffalo
3. John Zbercot, C, St. Claire Shores, MI
4. Ronald Garlin, OF, Miramar Isles, FL
5. Wayne Milan, P, Broward Community College (FL)
6. John Stephens, OF, Gulf Coast Community College (FL)
7. Gerald Daughtry, C, Blinn College (TX)

1969 June (Reg)
1. Noel Jenks, OF, University of Minnesota
2. **Rick Miller, OF, Michigan State University**
3. **Buddy Hunter, IF-OF, Pershing College (NE)**
4. **Jim Wright, P, Coopersville HS (MI)**
5. **Dwight Evans, 3B-OF, Chatsworth HS (Northridge, CA)**
6. Michael Cummings, SS, Grambling State University (LA)
7. **Steve Barr, P, Carson HS (Torrance, CA)**

8. Eric Brown, C, Morristown East HS
(Morristown, TN)
9. Robert Kerr, P, Arvada HS (CO)
10. William Hernandez, OF-C, George Washington HS
(New York, NY)
11. Clark Adkins, OF, Ray HS (Corpus Christi, TX)
12. Lindsay Graham, P, Dulaney HS (Timonium, MD)
13. Vaughan Sykes, P, Mebane, NC
14. Greg McCollum, 1B, Meadowdale HS
(Lynwood, WA)
15. David Klastava, P-IF, Scotch Plains HS (NJ)
16. James Torres, OF, Arlington Heights HS
(Fort Worth, TX)
17. Donald Small, 1B-P, Southwestern HS
(DeLeon Springs, FL)
18. **Dave Coleman, IF-OF, Stebbins HS
(Dayton, OH)**
19. Perry Renfro, P, Butler HS (Huntsville, AL)
20. Larry Smith, OF, Tennessee Tech University
21. Thomas Kramer, C, Dieruff HS (Allentown, PA)
22. Fernando Santiago, 1B, Monroe HS (Bronx, NY)
23. Scott Sholbe, SS, Grand Junction HS (CO)
24. Donald Rhoden, SS, Franklin County HS
(Winchester, TN)
25. James Bryant, P, Columbia State Community
College (TN)

1969 June (Sec)
1. William Ward, P, Southern Tech Institute
2. Phillip Corddry, P, University of Maryland
3. John Fletcher, C, Mississippi State University
4. David Allen, P, Westark Community College (AR)

1970 June (Reg)
1. John Klitsner, 1B, Birmingham HS (Encino, CA)
2. Wayne Milam, P, Broward Community College (FL)
3. Steve Miller, C, University of Virginia
4. Larry Patton, OF-P, Columbia State Community
College (TN)
5. James Paul, P, Henry Ford CC (MI)
6. Shawn Harris, P, Johnson and Wales Community
College (MA)
7. James Jackson, P, Fullerton College (CA)

1970 January (Sec)
1. **Rick Burleson, SS, Warren HS
(South Gate, CA)**
2. Robert Perkins, P, Manatee Community College
3. Harry Chapman, P, Sarasota HS (FL)
4. Edgar Bellamy, 2B, Fort Cobb HS (OK)
5. Donald Rhoton, P, Columbia State Community
College (TN)

1970 June (Reg)
1. Jimmy Hacker, 3B, Temple HS (TX)
2. Fred Wegner, OF, Fresno HS (CA)
3. John Schmidt, 3B-P, Lutheran HS (Denver, CO)
4. Charles Ross, P, Wilson HS (Long Beach, CA)
5. Donald Dudley, P, St. Joseph Central HS
(St. Joseph, MO)
6. Tom Jones, P, Carson-Newman College
7. Jerry Spencer, P, Southwest Texas State University
8. Keith Durant, OF-P, Rippowam HS (Stamford, CT)
9. Kenneth Watkins, P, Southwest Missouri State
University
10. Michael Mooney, C, Cardinal Dougherty HS
(Buffalo, NY)
11. Ramsey Koschak, OF, Central HS (San Angelo, TX)
12. John Binks, P, Forest Park HS (Beaumont, TX)
13. **Tim Blackwell, 3B-C, Crawford HS
(San Diego, CA)**
14. Leo Veleas, OF, University of New Haven
15. Peter Peckham, P, Mount Pleasant HS
(Providence, RI)
16. Anthony McLin, OF, Stillman College (AL)
17. William Kouns, P, William Carey College (MS)
18. Jack Wick, SS, San Pedro HS (CA)
19. Bruce Kombrinck, P, Gulf Coast Community
College (FL)
20. Robert Caballero, OF, Loyola University (LA)
21. Kenneth Kollmyer, OF, Hoover HS (San Diego, CA)
22. Karl King, P-OF, Ansonia HS (CT)
23. Chad Nielsen, 1B, Ogden HS (UT)
24. Jerry Dewitt, P-OF, El Dorado HS (Orange, CA)
25. Dave Barton, 1B, Costa Mesa HS (Santa Ana, CA)
26. Richard Nichols, 2B, Florida State University
27. George Maldonado, OF, University of
Nevada-Reno
28. James Duckhorn, OF, Reedley Junior College (CA)
29. John Sinclair, P, Husson College (ME)
30. Frank Johnstone, P, Alvin HS (TX)

1970 June (Sec)
1. **John Larose, P, Cumberland HS (RI)**
2. Dave Elmendorf, OF, Texas A&M University
3. Larry O'Brien, 1B-OF, Long Beach City College
4. Alan Jackson, P, Northeastern University
5. Charles Bates, 3B-SS, Los Angeles Community
College

1971 January (Reg)
1. Howard Echots, 3B, Columbia State Community
College (TN)

2. Craig Kimball, OF, San Francisco, CA
3. Dwayne Mayberry, OF, San Francisco, CA
4. *Eric Rasmussen, P, Indian Hills Community
College (IA)*
5. Michael Averil, OF, Fullerton College (CA)
6. Elliott Jones, P, Vanderbilt University
7. Dale Bjerke, P, St. Clair County Community
College (MI)

1971 January (Sec)
1. *Jim Otten, P, Mesa Community College (AZ)*
2. Steve Foran, P, University of Denver
3. *John Tamargo, OF, Miami-Dade Community
College*
4. *Roy Smalley, SS, Los Angeles, CA*
5. Steve Boryczewski, C, Seton Hall University

1971 June (Reg)
1. **Jim Rice, OF, Hannah HS (Anderson, SC)**
2. Milt Jefferson, 3B, Manual Arts HS
(Los Angeles, CA)
3. James Vosk, P, Middletown HS (Red Bank, NJ)
4. Tom Pokarski, P, Northview HS (Covina, CA)
5. Tom Cassell, SS, Mansfield College (PA)
6. Terry Stokes, SS, University of Pittsburgh
7. Paul Flanagan, OF, Columbus HS (Dorchester, MA)
8. James Snypes, IF-OF, University of South Alabama
9. **Bill Moran, P, Louisburg College (NC)**
10. Michael Sherwood, SS, Bella Vista HS
(Fair Oaks, CA)
11. Paul Smith, C-OF, South HS (Framingham, MA)
12. David Sauve, 2B, University of Maryland
13. Clyde Zimmerman, SS, Southern Columbia HS
(Catawissa, PA)
14. James Barrineau, P, South Boston HS (MA)
15. Thomas Cason, P, Jacksonville State University
16. Chester Lucas, OF, Citronelle HS (AL)
17. Richard Wehner, P, St. Clement HS (Detroit, MI)
18. Stephen Chapman, P, University of Minnesota
19. Kelly Jones, P, Boise HS (ID)
20. Kenneth Nicar, C, Sam Houston HS (Houston, TX)
21. Jerry Stamps, C, Jess Lanier HS (Bessemer, AL)
22. John Seymour, C-3B, St. Lawrence University
23. Ken Inglis, P, Montclair State University
24. Richard Seid, C, Oak Park HS (MI)
25. **Mark Bomback, P, Durfee HS (Fall River, MA)**
26. **Jack Baker, 1B, Auburn University**
27. Ronnie Goodman, OF, Port Jefferson HS
(Mount Sinai, NY)
28. Steve Kooshkalis, P, Peabody HS (MA)

1971 June (Secondary Active)
1. Lynn McKinney, P, Rio Hondo Junior College (CA)
2. Earl Nance, P, Auburn University
3. Henry Baker, 3B, Southern University (LA)

1971 June (Secondary Delayed)
1. **Jim Burton, P, University of Michigan**
2. Ed Scruggs, P, Lynchburg College (VA)
3. Kurt Lohrke, SS, Santa Clara University
4. *Duane Kuiper, SS, Southern Illinois University*
5. Mike Hansen, P, Arizona State University
6. Steve Prestridge, P, Delta State University (MS)
7. Bill Todd, P, University of Missouri

1972 January (Reg)
1. Cliff Holland, P, Canada College (CA)
2. Jimmie Williams, P, Indian Hills Community
College (IA)
3. Harold Stutte, P, Contra Costa Junior College (CA)
4. John Webb, IF, Seminole Community College (FL)

1972 January (Sec)
1. Ken Daughty, OF-IF, Lamar Community
College (CO)
2. Joe Burgess, P, Eastern Oklahoma State
Community College
3. Larry Meekins, P, Louisburg College (NC)
4. Ralph Darin, P, Central Michigan University
5. *Roy Smalley, SS, Los Angeles Community College*

1972 June (Reg)
1. Joel Bishop, SS, McClatchy HS (Sacramento, CA)
2. **Steve Dillard, SS, University of Mississippi**
3. Randy Markley, OF, Lynwood HS (Long Beach, CA)
4. Ronnie Sims, P, Dorman HS (Una, SC)
5. William Fewox, P, Truman HS (Kansas City, MO)
6. **Don Aase, P, Savanna HS (Anaheim, CA)**
7. Steven Samuelson, P, College of St. Thomas (MN)
8. Mark Jones, IF, Arlington Heights HS
(Fort Worth, TX)
9. Ludwig Benedetti, SS, Long Island University
10. **Andy Merchant, OF, Auburn University**
11. Steve Tarbell, P, Upland HS (CA)
12. *Donnie Moore, OF-P, Monterey HS (Lubbock, TX)*
13. Joseph Spaulding, OF, Connors State College (OK)
14. William Bohne, SS, Blinn College (TX)
15. **Ernie Whitt, C, Macomb County Community
College (MI)**
16. Ray Boneschans, P, Oak Ridge HS (Orlando, FL)
17. Albert Ryan, 2B, University of South Alabama
18. Robert Leonard, 3B, Panola College (TX)
19. Herb Loveless, P, Ionia HS (MI)
20. David Chapman, IF, Compton HS (CA)

21. Richard Marshall, P, South Park HS
(Beaumont, TX)
22. Barry Sbragia, P, Washington State University

1972 June (Sec)
1. Brad Hanson, SS, Valencia Community
College (CA)

1973 January (Reg)
1. Lloyd Thompson, 3B, Blinn College (TX)
2. William Daves, C, Motlow State Community
College (TN)
3. Brian McCune, P, Eastern Illinois University
4. Larry Howser, SS-2B, Manatee Community
College (FL)
5. Ted Updike, 1B, San Diego Mesa College

1973 January (Sec)
1. Mike Payne, P, Delta State University (MS)
2. *Bob Pate, 3B-OF, San Diego Mesa College*
3. Michael Hill, P, Three Rivers Community
College (MO)
4. Kevin Stephenson, P, Seminole Community
College (FL)
5. Greg McCollum, 1B, University of Puget Sound
6. Mark Kilmurray, SS, University of New Haven
7. Tom Farias, P, American International
College (MA)
8. Glen Smith, SS-3B, Bordentown, NJ

1973 June (Reg)
1. **Ted Cox, SS, Midwest City HS (OK)**
2. **Fred Lynn, OF, USC**
3. Charles Meyers, 2B, Oklahoma State University
4. Curran Percival, P, Chapman University (CA)
5. **Rick Jones, P, Forrest HS (Jacksonville, FL)**
6. Glenn Bannister, OF, University of Oklahoma
7. William St. Claire, P, Springfield Tech HS (MA)
8. **Butch Hobson, 3B, University of Alabama**
9. Rick Berg, OF, Apple Valley HS (Apple Valley, CA)
10. Roswell Brayton, P, Harvard University
11. Chris Dilorenzo, P, West Rome HS (GA)
12. Barrett Jackson, OF-1B, Piscataway HS
(Plainfield, NJ)
13. Jack Medick, C, University of Nebraska
14. James Lease, P, William Carey College (MS)
15. Carmen Coppoi, P, Claymont HS (DE)
16. Lanny Phillips, 3B-OF, University of Oklahoma
17. James Bodinski, OF, North Attleboro HS (MA)
18. Mike Cunico, SS, Pueblo HS Central (CO)
19. Michael Bennett, OF, Western Illinois University
20. Collin Youtz, P, Lebanon HS (PA)
21. Greg Eastin, P, Ridge HS (Basking Ridge, NJ)
22. Larry Morello, OF, Lafayette HS (Brooklyn, NY)

1974 January (Reg)
1. **Chuck Rainey, P, San Diego Mesa College**
2. Ralph Russo, 1B, Quinnipiac College (CT)
3. Stephen Kotenda, 2B, Stetson University (FL)
4. James Wargo, SS, Gulf Coast Community
College (FL)
5. Brad Liedtke, OF-P, Fullerton College (CA)

1974 January (Sec)
1. **Bob Stanley, P, Kearny HS (NJ)**
2. **Steven Burke, P, Merritt College (CA)**
3. Greg Kane, C, Yavapai Community College (AZ)

1974 June (Reg)
1. Eddie Ford, SS, University of South Carolina
2. Jimmy Schankle, C, Lubbock HS (TX)
3. Ronny Patrick, C, Castlewood HS (VA)
4. Charles Reilly, 2B, Adelphi University (NY)
5. Craig Brooks, OF, Richmond HS (CA)
6. Robert Klass, P, Southern Illinois University
7. **Sam Bowen, 2B, Valdosta State
University (GA)**
8. Paul McClure, IF, University of Wyoming
9. **Joel Finch, P, Washington HS
(South Bend, IN)**
10. Lee Roy Russell, P, Bibb County HS (Brent, AL)
11. Charles Pinkney, OF, Kingsborough Community
College (NY)
12. John Tagharino, P, Tampa HS Catholic (FL)
13. Michael Wholey, P, Lakes HS (Tacoma, WA)
14. Mark Barr, P, USC
15. Burke Suter, P, High Point, NC
16. Jeff Hardy, SS, Gulf Coast Community College (FL)
17. Jackie Snell, P, George C. Wallace Community
College (AL)
18. Jerome Register, OF, Valdosta State
University (GA)

1974 June (Sec)
1. Marvin Townsend, SS, Campbell University (NC)
2. David Koza, P, Eastern Oklahoma State
Community College

1975 January (Reg)
1. Walter Bigos, P, Cerritos College (CA)
2. Tim Vranich, SS, St. Petersburg College (FL)
3. Edward Nuss, P, Valencia Community College (CA)
4. James McKenzie, P, Solano Community
College (CA)
5. David Isaacson, P, College of the Redwoods (CA)

1975 January (Sec)
1. Ken Huizenga, OF, USC
2. Jerry Ennis, SS, Bakersfield Junior College
3. Chris Gandy, OF, Sacramento City College
4. Jerry Stamps, C-1B, University of South Alabama
5. Mike Morrissey, P, Schenectady, NY

1975 June (Reg)
1. Otis Foster, 1B, High Point, NC
2. **Dave Schmidt, C, Mission Viejo HS (CA)**
3. **Ed Jurak, SS, San Pedro HS (CA)**
4. Michael Moore, P, Oak Park HS (Kansas City, MO)
5. Larry Hyman, 3B, Irwin County HS (Mystic, GA)
6. **Mike Howard, P, South Portland HS (ME)**
7. *Larry Littleton, OF, University of Georgia*
8. Bob Hampton, OF, Stanford University
9. *Dave Stegman, OF, University of Arizona*
10. **Dave Stapleton, 2B, University of South Alabama**
11. Gary Purcell, OF, University of New Orleans
12. Carlton Steele, OF, Westfield State College (MA)
13. Breen Newcomer, P, University of Oklahoma
14. Phllip Welch, P, Providence College
15. Richard Waller, P, Montclair State University
16. David Schoppee, P, Deering HS (Portland, ME)
17. Richard McAlister, C, Louisiana Tech University
18. Happy Vincent, 3B, Palm Springs HS (CA)
19. Thomas Streightiff, OF, Juniata College (PA)
20. Larry Ennis, OF, Farleigh Dickinson (NJ)
21. Timothy Clemmons, OF, Southeastern HS (Chillicothe, OH)
22. **Mike O'Berry, C, University of South Alabama**
23. Mike Paxton, P-IF, Memphis State University
24. Peter Khoury, OF, Durfee HS (Fall River, MA)

1975 June (Sec)
1. Ronald Evans, 3B, North Carolina State University

1976 January (Reg)
1. Nate Puryear, P, Stillman College (AL)
2. **Dennis Burtt, P, Santa Ana College**
3. Steven Schneck, P, Kalamazoo Valley Community College
4. Gary Hoyle, C, Broward Community College (FL)
5. Roscoe Alburtis, 1B, Blinn College (TX)
6. Jeffrey Spahr, P, Gulf Coast Community College (FL)
7. **Terry Leach, P, Auburn University**
8. Russell Cain, C, George C. Wallace Community College (AL)

1976 January (Sec)
1. David Tyler, 3B, Vanderbilt University
2. Greg Jemison, OF, Seton Hall University
3. **John Tudor, P, Georgia Southern University**
4. Bruce Poole, P, University of South Alabama

1976 June (Reg)
1. **Bruce Hurst, P, Dixie HS (St. George, UT)**
2. **Glenn Hoffman, SS, Savanna HS (Anaheim, CA)**
3. Mark Twogood, OF, Loara HS (Anaheim, CA)
4. Larry Jones, P, Florida State University
5. **Mike Smithson, P, University of Tennessee**
6. Ron Kovach, P, Grand Junction HS (CO)
7. **Wade Boggs, SS, Plant HS (Tampa, FL)**
8. Ronald Harrington, C, William Carey College (MS)
9. **Gary Allenson, C, Arizona State University**
10. Danny Parks, P, Memphis State University
11. David Denton, 2B, UNLV
12. **Reid Nichols, 2B, Ocala Forest HS (Ocala, FL)**
13. John Edwards, C, University of LaVerne (CA)
14. Larry Edwards, P, Bishop Walsh HS (Lavale, MD)
15. Dan Swanson, P, Aragon HS (San Mateo, CA)
16. Byron Ormsby, SS, University of Arkansas
17. Jack Sauer, P, Northwestern Business Junior College (CA)
18. Glenn Fisher, SS, Mansfield College (PA)
19. John Kidd, 3B, SUNY-Buffalo
20. Mike Ongarato, OF, Cal Poly San Luis Obispo
21. Frederick Opper, 1B, Mount St. Michael's HS (Mount Vernon, NY)
22. **Chico Walker, 2B, Tilden Tech HS (Chicago, IL)**
23. Peter Reilly, C, Trinity HS (Manchester, NH)
24. Jerome King, P, San Diego HS (CA)
25. Randy Lamprecht, C, Rice University
26. John Faccinto, 3B, Gorman HS (Las Vegas, NV)

1976 June (Sec)
1. Steve Miller, P, Lower Columbia Community College

1977 January (Reg)
1. Marcus Bell, P, Cleveland State Community College
2. Carl Pankratz, P, Temple Junior College (TX)
3. John Morgan, 3B, Chelmsford, MA
4. Rodney Feight, P, Indian River Community College (FL)
5. Stephen Annarummo, OF, Community College of Rhode Island
6. Ron Koenigsfeld, SS, Indian Hills Community College (IA)

1977 January (Sec)
1. **Jim Wilson, 3B, Cerritos College (CA)**

1977 June (Reg)
1. Andrew Madden, P, New Hartford HS (NY)
2. **Bobby Sprowl, P, University of Alabama**
3. Scott Sullivan, OF, Cupertino HS (Los Gatos, CA)
4. Erwin Bryant, SS, Columbia State Community College (TN)
5. Mark Baum, P, Northland HS (Columbus, OH)
6. Scott Burk, P, Oklahoma State University
7. Richard Parr, OF, Greenville College (IL)
8. **Roger Lafrancois, OF, University of Oklahoma**
9. Charles Thompson, P, DeKalb Junior College (GA)
10. **Steve Shields, P, Hokes Bluff HS (Gadsden, AL)**
11. Bill Swiacki, P, Amherst College
12. Frank Gill, 2B, Fairfield University (CT)
13. Richard Colbert, C, Joliet Catholic HS (Joliet, IL)
14. Barry Butera, SS-3B, Tulane University
15. Alvin Hulbert, P, Westboro HS (MA)
16. Mark Saunders, P, Allderdice HS (Pittsburgh, PA)
17. *Gary Redus, SS-OF, Athens State College (AL)*
18. Bruce Alexander, P, Kokomo HS (IN)
19. Rosaire Viens, P, Sacred Heart University (CT)
20. Eli Roberson, OF, Robert E. Lee HS (Baytown, TX)
21. Russell Laribee, OF, University of Connecticut
22. *Gerry Davis, OF, Ewing HS (Trenton, NJ)*
23. Richard Nesloney, P, Lamar University (TX)
24. Mark Kaeterle, SS, Vocational HS (New Bedford, MA)
25. **Pete Ladd, P, University of Massachusetts**
26. **Lee Graham, OF, Lake Weir HS (Belleview, FL)**

1977 June (Sec)
1. Stephen Collins, P, Fresno State
2. Ronald Lee, SS, Blinn College (TX)

1978 January (Reg)
1. Bruce Kastelic, SS, Ranger College (TX)
2. *Matt Young, P, Pasadena City College*
3. Milton Ondracek, P, San Jacinto College (TX)
4. Daniel Weppner, P, Palm Beach College (FL)
5. Howard Brodsky, C, Miami North Beach HS (Miami, FL)
6. James Funderburk, P, Orange Coast College (CA)

1978 January (Sec)
1. **Brian Denman, 1B-P, Richfield, MA**
2. Mark Paradise, P, Marblehead HS (MA)

1978 June (Reg)
4. Edward Connors, P, North Bergen HS (NJ)
5. Del Bender, OF-IF, Mississippi State University
6. Steve Schaefer, P, Alhambra HS (CA)
7. Ken Hagemann, 1B, Tottenville HS (Staten Island, NY)
8. Ken Young, OF, University of New Haven
9. Russ Quetti, SS, University of Maine
10. Donald Hayford, P, Lakeland HS (FL)
11. Craig Vandersteen, P, Grand Ledge HS (MI)
12. James Fabiano, SS, Westwood, ME
13. **John Lickert, C, Langley HS (Pittsburgh, PA)**
14. Licyd Bessard, OF, Abbeville HS (LA)
15. Robert Parker, OF, William Carey College (MS)
16. Mark Mitchell, P, North Hills HS (Pittsburgh, PA)
17. Steve Reish, P, Union City HS (IN)
18. Gary Givens, P, Georgia Southern University
19. Harold Nataupsky, C, Marblehead HS (MA)
20. Keith Pecka, OF, Kankakee Community College (IL)

1978 June (Sec)
1. *Marty Barrett, IF, Mesa Community College (AZ)*

1979 January (Reg)
1. Kevin Kane, P, Cuesta College (CA)
2. Michael Dolinar, SS, Bakersfield Junior College
3. Harley Woody, P, Columbia State Community College (TN)
4. Michael Burton, P, Mobile, AL
5. Kenneth Cox, 1B, Columbia State Community College (TN)
6. Lee Pruitt, OF-C, Westark Community College (AR)
7. Scott Gering, P-OF, St. Johns River Community College (FL)
8. Timothy Wadsworth, C-1B, Pensacola, FL

1979 January (Sec)

1979 June (Reg)
2. **Marc Sullivan, C, University of Florida**
3. John Ackley, OF, Mahopac HS (Carmel, NY)
4. Gib Seibert, P, Sahuaro HS (Tueson, AZ)
5. Jim Watkins, OF, University of Florida
6. Rick Thompson, SS, Glen Oaks HS (Canton, OH)
7. **Tom McCarthy, P, Plymouth Carver HS (Plymouth, MA)**
8. Steven True, P, Marlow HS (OK)
9. Charles Sandberg, 1B, University of Florida
10. Jerry Miklosi, SS, Western Michigan University
11. *Tommy Dunbar, OF, Middle Georgia College*
12. Ronnie Perry, SS, Holy Cross College
13. Glen Kuin, P, Sauguoit HS (NY)

14. Mickey Meister, P, Redwood HS (San Rafael, CA)
15. Reggie Whittemore, OF, David Lipscomb College (TN)
16. Mark Sewald, P, Bishop Montgomery HS (Carson, CA)
17. John Leonard, P, Connellsville HS (Dawson, PA)
18. Eddie Lee, OF, University of South Alabama
19. Bob Birrell, P, Brandeis University
20. Jay Fredlund, OF, Lafayette University
21. David Holt, OF, Fresno State
22. Glenn Eddins, 3B, David Lipscomb College (TN)

1979 June (Sec)
1. **Marty Barrett, 2B, Arizona State University**
2. Jeems Teller, OF, Sacramento City College

1980 January (Reg)
1. *Ray Krawczyk, P, Golden West College (CA)*
2. Michael Rosales, P, Lamar Community College (CO)
3. Brice Cote, P, Mercer County Community College (NJ)
4. Wallace Dulling, P, Columbia State Community College (TN)
5. David Frank, SS-2B, Solano Community College (CA)
6. Nathan Banes, P, St. Johns River Community College (FL)
7. **Glenn Davis, 1B-OF, Middle Georgia College**

1980 January (Sec)
1. Juan Bustabad, SS, Miami-Dade Community College
2. Guy Burgess, P, Palm Beach College

1980 June (Reg)
2. **Mike Brown, P, Clemson University**
3. Mitch Johnson, P, Donegal HS (Mt. Joy, PA)
4. Jeff Hall, C, Rochester Institute of Technology
5. Ronnie Hill, P, Dixie HS (Bloomington, UT)
6. **Pat Dodson, 1B, UCLA**
7. Mark Margis, P, Culver City HS (CA)
8. **Al Nipper, P, Northeast Missouri State University**
9. Michael Bryant, OF, University of Lowell
10. Brian Zell, OF, Cal Poly Pomona University
11. Timothy Duncan, SS, Christian Brothers University (TN)
12. *Dave Magadan, 3B, Jesuit HS (Tampa, FL)*
13. Simon Glenn, OF, Texas A&M University
14. Mark Weinbrecht, P, Clairemont HS (San Diego, CA)
15. Tyrone Herman, P, Minnesota State Mankato University
16. **Oil Can Boyd, P, Jackson State University**
17. Marcus Handley, P, Larue County HS (Hodgenville, KY)
18. Robert Sandling, OF, Crete-Monee HS (Park Forest, IL)
19. Al Bowlin, P, Grace Davis HS (Modesto, CA)
20. **Tom Bolton, P, Antioch HS (Brentwood, TN)**
21. Parker Wilson, 3B, Livingston University
22. George Mecerod, P, Adelphi University (NY)
23. Bobby Falls, 2B, West Mecklenburg HS (Charlotte, NC)
24. Mike Ciampa, OF, Westfield State College (MA)
25. Jeff Hunter, 3B, University of Nebraska
26. William Lowry, P, Santa Ynez HS (Goleta, CA)
27. George Greco, P, Iona College (NY)

1980 June (Sec)
1. Clem Freeman, P, Manatee Community College (FL)
2. Steve Garrett, P, Chabot College (CA)

1981 January (Reg)
1. **Danny Sheaffer, C, Harrisburg Area Community College (PA)**
2. Joe Artstrom, OF, Miami-Dade New World Center Community College
3. David Scheller, P, Lewis and Clark Community College (IL)
4. Robyn Lynch, 1B, Garden City Community College (KS)
5. Joey Farrill, P, Gulf Coast Community College (FL)
6. Robert Meyer, P, Golden West College (CA)
7. John Wallace, OF, Fresno City College
8. John Sorensen, P, Joliet Junior College (IL)
9. Steven Seaman, SS, Beaver County Community College (PA)
10. Mark Wenzel, P, Fresno City College

1981 January (Sec)
1. Dave Malpeso, C, Miami-Dade Community College
2. Michael Jefferson, OF, Contra Costa Junior College (CA)

1981 June (Reg)
1. **Steve Lyons, SS-OF, Oregon State University**
1. Kevin Burrell, OF, Poway HS (CA)
2. Chris Howard, 2B, Boone HS (Orlando, FL)
3. **Rob Woodward, P, Lebanon HS (NH)**
4. **Todd Benzinger, 1B, New Richmond HS (Cincinnati, OH)**

5. Peter Gonzales, OF, San Leandro HS (CA)
6. Kevin Chaton, P, University of Kansas
7. Kevin Fowler, SS, Donar HS (Stillwater, OK)
8. John Key, P, Central HS (Muskogee, OK)
9. Charles Fisher, OF, Jacksonville State University
10. Craig Walck, 3B, Ursinus Junior College (PA)
11. Peter Mancini, 2B, Memorial HS (West New York, NJ)
12. Chuck Davis, P, Jacksonville State University
13. Pat Castiglia, 1B, Eckerd College (FL)
14. Willie Weston, P, Mississippi Valley State University
15. Kevin Johnston, OF, Logan HS (LaCrosse, WI)
16. Troy Howerton, P, Arkansas City HS (KS)
17. Bruce Lockhart, P, Brunswick HS (ME)
18. Jeff Achilles, P, University of Houston
19. Bill Carpenter, SS, Brandeis University
20. Darryl Menard, P, Clearlake HS (Seabrook, TX)
21. Brian Smith, P, South HS (Weymouth, MA)

1981 June (Sec)
1. **Steve Ellsworth, P, Cal State Northridge**
2. Tony Beal, P, Seminole Community College (FL)

1982 January (Reg)
1. **Mike Rochford, P, Santa Fe Community College**
2. Curt Kindred, P, Fullerton College (CA)
3. Scott Skripko, P, Middle Georgia College
4. **Charles Mitchell, P, Columbia State Community College (TN)**
5. John Roth, OF, Cypress College (CA)
6. Mike Gildehaus, P, Jefferson Junior College (NY)
7. Ted Langdon, P, Brevard College (NC)
8. Irving Weston, OF, Kingsborough Community College (NY)
9. Kevin Smith, P, Seminole Community College (FL)
10. Gregory Haynes, 1B-C, Jackson State Community College (TN)

1982 January (Sec)
1. Jose Rodiles, P, Seminole Junior College (OK)

1982 June (Reg)
1. **Sam Horn, 1B, Morse HS (San Diego, CA)**
1. Rob Parkins, P, Cerritos HS (CA)
1. Jeff Ledbetter, 1B-OF, Florida State University
2. **Kevin Romine, OF, Arizona State University**
2. Steve Jongewaard, SS, Fountain Valley HS (CA)
3. **Mike Greenwell, 3B, North Fort Myers HS (FL)**
4. Tim Gordon, 3B, University of Maryland
5. Gary Miller-Jones, 2B, University of South Alabama
6. Sam Nattile, 3B, University of Central Florida
7. Jay Grate, P-SS, East Noble HS (Avila, IN)
8. **Jeff Sellers, P, Paramount HS (Long Beach, CA)**
9. Fred Carter, OF, Millwood HS (Oklahoma City, OK)
10. Dave Oliva, OF, Santa Clara University
11. Don O'Toole, P, Moore Catholic HS (Staten island, NY)
12. Rob Geels, C, Fresno State
13. Mike Mesh, SS, Southern Illinois University
14. Scott Diez, P, Miami Dade South Community College
15. Tom Bonk, 1B, La Salle
16. Brustor Minor, P, Columbus, MS
17. Ed Mondelli, P, Neshamini HS (Hulmeville, PA)
18. Billy Joe Richardson, C, Southern Illinois University
19. Scott Gay, P, Milford HS (NH)

1982 June (Sec)

1983 January (Reg)
1. **Ellis Burks, OF, Ranger College (TX)**
2. Michael Kane, 3B, Truman Junior College (IL)
3. Roy Hall, 2B-3B, Columbia State College (TN)
4. Richard Winfield, C, Truman Junior College (IL)
5. *Eric Hetzel, P, Eastern Oklahoma State Community College*
6. Michael Adams, P, Garden City Community College (NY)
7. Terry Seik, 3B, Las Vegas, NV
8. Kevin Camilli, OF, Polk Community College (FL)
9. Laverne Jackson, OF, Bethune, SC
10. Craig Gutman, P, El Camino College (CA)

1983 January (Sec)
1. Richard Helzer, P, Marin Community College (CA)

1983 June (Reg)
1. **Roger Clemens, P, University of Texas**
2. **Mike Brumley, SS, University of Texas**
3. John Toale, 3B, Taravella HS (Coral Springs, FL)
4. Paul Thoutsis, OF, Holy Name HS (Worcester, MA)
5. Tony Latham, OF, University of Virginia
6. Gary Tremblay, OF, Coastal Carolina University (SC)
7. **John Mitchell, P, Overton HS (Nashville, TN)**
8. **Dana Kiecker, P, St. Cloud State University (MN)**
9. Chris Cannizzaro, 2B, San Diego State University

10. Alvin Hamilton, 2B, Southwest Missouri State University
11. Steve Beer, P, Loara HS (Anaheim, CA)
12. *Kirt Manwaring, C, Horsehead Central HS (Horsehead, NY)*
13. Ray Revak, P, Key West HS (FL)
14. Billy Sheeks, P, Christian Brothers HS (Memphis, TN)
15. Michael Dalton, P, De Anza Junior College (CA)
16. Jim Hines, P, Crane Hill, AL
17. Demarlo Hale, 1B, Southern University (LA)
18. Blane Lockley, OF, Franklin HS (Baldwin, LA)
19. John Sanderski, P, St. Johns HS (Oxford, MA)

1983 June (Sec)
1. *Randy Byers, OF, Paris Junior College (TX)*

1984 January (Reg)
1. **Greg Mayberry, P, Ferrum College (VA)**
2. Mark Winner, P, Taft Junior College CA)
3. *Daryl Irvine, P, Ferrum College (VA)*
4. Paul Slifko, P, DeKalb Junior College (GA)
5. Charles Bell, OF, Nashville, TN
6. Pat Hewes, C, Bakersfield Junior College
7. Tary Scott, 1B, Walters State Community College (TN)
8. Jimmy Hitt, P, Chipola Junior College (FL)
9. George Creekmore, P, College of the Sequoias (CA)

1984 January (Sec)
1. **Dan Gakeler, 1B, Mercer County Community College (NJ)**
2. Larry Herrel, P, Tulsa, OK
3. **John Leister, P, Michigan State University**

1984 June (Reg)
1. **John Marzano, C, Temple University**
2. Scott Wade, OF, Oklahoma State University
3. Brock Knight, P, American Fork HS (UT)
4. *Sean Berry, SS, West Torrance HS (CA)*
5. Steve Boyd, OF, Southern Illinois University
6. Larry Schwartz, P, Seton Hall University
7. **Steve Curry, P, Manatee Community College (FL)**
8. **Jody Reed, SS, Florida State University**
9. Tony Defrancesco, C, Seton Hall University
10. Odie Abril, P, Colton HS (CA)
11. Michael Fenn, P, David Lipscomb College (TN)
12. Brad Powell, P, University of North Carolina
13. **Zachary Crouch, P, Cordova HS (Sacramento, CA)**
14. Mickey Pina, OF, Bridgewater HS (MA)
15. *Derek Lilliquist, P, Sarasota HS (FL)*
16. Scott Jordan, OF, Georgia Tech
17. Terry Griffin, P, Florrist HS (Jacksonville, FL)
18. Brian Nichols, C, El Cerrito HS (Richmond, CA)
19. Larry Riddle, P, University of Texas-El Paso
20. *Jack McDowell, P, Notre Dame HS (Van Nuys, CA)*
21. Mike Goff, 2B, University of Alabama-Birmingham
22. Dan Sullivan, 1B, UCLA
23. Tim Weinfurtner, P, Palmetto HS (Miami, FL)
24. Joe Stephenson, P, Sonoma State University (CA)

1984 June (Sec)
1. Chris Moritz, SS, San Jacinto College (TX)

1985 January (Reg)
1. Tim Speakman, C, Fullerton College (CA)
2. Rod Simon, P, Central Arizona College
3. Oscar Murphy, P, Columbia State College (TN)
4. Greg Bochesa, C, Los Angeles Harbor Community College
5. Ricky Carriger, P, Northeastern Oklahoma A&M University
6. Steven Meyer, P, Westark Community College (AR)
7. Dell Carter, OF, Kings River Junior College (CA)
8. Tom Kane, P, Manatee Community College (FL)
9. Steve Mrowka, 3B, Polk Community College (FL)
10. Tim Good, C, Angelina College (TX)
11. Kevin Edwards, SS, Westark Community College (AR)

1985 January (Sec)
1. **Daryl Irvine, P, Ferrum College (VA)**
2. Ken Morris, P, Angelina College (TX)

1985 June (Reg)
1. Dan Gabriele, P, Western HS (Walled Lake, MI)
2. *Lance Blankenship, 3B, University of California*
3. *Tino Martinez, 1B, Jefferson HS (Tampa, FL)*
4. Don McGowan, P, Central Missouri State University
5. Mike Clarkin, P, University of Minnesota
6. **Todd Pratt, OF, Hilltop HS (Chula Vista, CA)**
7. Gary Gouldrup, 3B, Oliver Ames HS (North Easton, MA)
8. Scott Middaugh, P, Patrick Henry HS (San Diego, CA)
9. Jim Orsag, 1B, University of Illinois
10. **Brady Anderson, OF, University of California-Irvine**
11. Chris Bayer, P, Pace University (NY)
12. Greg Lotzar, OF, Central Michigan University

13. Mike Bianco, C, Seminole HS (FL)
14. Mike Carista, P, Saugus, MA
15. Derek Livernois, P, Lyman HS (Altamonte Springs, FL)
16. Ron Stephens, SS, Linsly Institute (Wheeling, WV)
17. James Boehne, P, Louisiana Tech University
18. Kerman Williams, P, Vanguard HS (Ocala, FL)
19. Gregg Magistri, P, Louisiana Tech University
20. Billy Plante, 3B, Virginia Tech
21. James Cox, P, Harrisburg, OH
22. Tom Hostetler, P, East Mississippi Junior College
23. Cliff Suggs, P, Cooper HS (Abilene, TX)
24. Erik Laseke, 2B, Columbia State Community College (TN)
25. John Abbott, P, Visalia, CA
26. *Ed Sprague, OF, St. Mary's HS (Stockton, CA)*
27. Grady Hall, P, Northwestern University

1985 June (Sec)
1. **Eric Hetzel, P, Louisiana State University**
2. Bill Zupka, P, Queensborough Community College (NY)

1986 January (Reg)
1. *Alan Mills, P, Polk Community College (FL)*
2. **Curt Schilling, P, Yavapai Community College (AZ)**
3. Scott Boggs, IF, Columbia State Community College (TN)
4. William Rawdon, P, Columbia State Community College (TN)
5. Michael Whiting, P, Eastern Utah Community College
6. Michael Leland, C, San Joaquin Delta College (CA)
7. Thomas McGee, OF, San Jacinto College (TX)
8. Glen O'Donnell, IF, Quinsigamond Community College (MA)
9. Charlie Holmes, P, Mount San Antonio College (CA)
10. Andres Cruz, OF, Laredo Junior College (TX)
11. Lem Pilkinton, C, Columbia State Community College (TN)
12. Kendrick Bourne, OF, Chaffey College (CA)

1986 January (Sec)
1. Ray Revak, P, Key West, FL
2. Mike Bianco, OF, Indian River Community College (FL)

1986 June (Reg)
1. Greg McMurtry, OF, Brockton HS (MA)
2. Paul Williams, C, Smiley HS (Houston, TX)
3. **Scott Cooper, 3B-P, Pattonville HS (St. Louis, MO)**
4. Charles Wacha, P, Columbus College (OH)
5. Steve Bast, P, USC
6. Bart Haley, P, Grand Canyon University (AZ)
7. **Mike Garcia, P, North HS (Moreno Valley, CA)**
8. David Milstien, SS, Simi Valley HS (CA)
9. Joe Kelly, P, Notre Dame HS (Whitesboro, NY)
10. Jim Morrison, P, Anna-Jonesboro HS (IL)
11. Terry Marrs, OF, Lake Worth HS (FL)
12. David Walters, P, Campbell University (NC)
13. Joe Marchese, 2B, Minnesota State Mankato University
14. Anthony Hill, OF, University of Rhode Island
15. Brian Warfel, P, Labette Community College (KS)
16. Steven Tucker, P, Riverview HS (Sarasota, FL)
17. Tony Kounas, C, San Gorgonio HS (Highland, CA)
18. Ron Warren, P, Troy State University (AL)
19. Tim Buheller, OF, Virginia Tech
20. Mike Baker, 2B, University of Nevada-Reno
21. Tom Sepela, P, John A. Logan College (IL)
22. Stu Weidie, OF, University of New Orleans
23. Chris Hanks, OF, Roaring Forks HS (Carbondale, CO)

1986 June (Sec)
1. Ed Banasiak, P, County College of Morris (NJ)

1987 June (Reg)
1. Reggie Harris, P, Waynesboro HS (VA)
1. **Bob Zupcic, OF, Oral Roberts University (OK)**
2. Paul Brown, P, University of Hawaii
3. Craig Wilson, C, Cerritos College (CA)
4. Scott Powers, SS, Brandeis University
5. Steve Michael, OF, Emporia State University (KS)
6. Ronnie Richardson, P, Lee HS (Columbus, MS)
7. Scott Vonderlieth, P, Mission Bay HS (San Diego, CA)
8. **James Byrd, SS, Seminole Junior College (OK)**
9. **Mike Kelly, OF, University of South Florida**
10. **Jeff Plympton, P, University of Maine**
11. **Phil Plantier, 3B, Poway HS (CA)**
12. Pedro Matilla, C, Southridge HS (Miami, FL)
13. Peter Estrada, P, Irvington HS (NJ)
14. Sam Melton, 3B, Columbia State Community College (TN)
15. *Desi Wilson, 1B, Glen Cove HS (NY)*
16. Larry Scannell, OF, Lewis University (IL)
17. Vince Degifico, 1B, University of Southern Maine
18. Stewart Lee, 3B, Jacksonville State University

19. Scott Thompson, OF, Westminster HS (MD)
20. Kevin Digiacomo, C, Ithaca HS (NY)
21. James Wray, P, Troy State University (AL)
22. Anthony Mosley, P, Fort Meade HS (PA)
23. Richard Santiago, P, Palm Bay HS (FL)
24. Pat Pesavento, SS, University of Notre Dame
25. *Jay Owens, OF, Glen Este HS (Cincinnati, OH)*
26. *Stan Spencer, P, Columbia River HS (Vancouver, WA)*
27. Greg McCollum, P, University of Illinois
28. Chris Hanks, OF, College of Southern Idaho
29. Don Redmond, OF, Guilford College (NC)
30. Jesse Cross, P, Middle Georgia College
31. Clint Creed, C, Triton HS (Dunn, NC)

1988 June (Reg)
1. Tom Fischer, P, University of Wisconsin
2. Andy Rush, P, Somerset HS (PA)
3. Mickey Rivers, OF, Bacone Junior College (OK)
4. Dan Kite, P, Louisiana State University
5. **John Valentin, SS, Seton Hall University**
6. Ed Riley, P, St. Peter-Marien HS (Worcester, MA)
7. Dave Owen, P, Carson-Newman College (TN)
8. **Tim Naehring, SS, University of Miami-Ohio**
9. Willie Tatum, 3B, University of the Pacific
10. Meredith Moore, OF, Nogales HS (La Puente, CA)
11. David Stuart, P, Indian River Community College (FL)
12. Alan Sanders, P, Lower Columbia Community College (WA)
13. Richard Witherspoon, OF, Nogales HS (La Puente, CA)
14. Garrett Jenkins, OF, Steubenville HS (OH)
15. Howard Landry, P, University of Southwest Louisiana
16. Bernie Dzafic, P, Lincoln Land Community College (IL)
17. Eric Slinkard, OF, Chula Vista HS (CA)
18. *Hilly Hathaway, P, Sandaiwood HS (Jacksonville, FL)*
19. Kevin Crowder, 2B-3B, Keene HS (NH)
20. Corey Powell, OF, Patrick Henry HS (San Diego, CA)
21. Gary Kinser, P, Columbia State Community College (TN)
22. Chris Whitehead, 3B, Middle Tennessee State University
23. Scott Bakkum, P, Aquinas HS (LaCrosse, WI)
24. Bernard Doyle, OF, North Newton HS (Morocco, IL)
25. **John Flaherty, C, George Washington University**
26. Joe Blasucci, SS, South Broward HS (Hollywood, FL)
27. Mark Mitchelson, P, Hillsborough Community College (FL)
28. **Scott Taylor, P, Bowling Green State University (OH)**
29. John Spencer, OF, University of Lowell
30. Andrew Flagler, 1B, Valencia Community College (CA)
31. Dan Robinson, 3B, San Jacinto College (TX)
32. Michael Rebhan, P, Lake City Community College (FL)
33. **Peter Hoy, P, LeMoyne College (NY)**
34. Barton Moore, 2B, Jefferson State College (AL)
35. Gary Posey, OF, Gulf Coast Community College (FL)
36. Jim Wiley, OF-P, Westark Community College (AR)
37. Steve Worrell, P, Lower Cape May Regional HS (Cape May, NJ)
38. Roger Luce, OF, San Jacinto College (TX)

1989 June (Reg)
1. **Greg Blosser, OF, Sarasota HS (FL)**
1. **Mo Vaughn, 1B, Seton Hall University**
1. **Kevin Morton, P, Seton Hall University**
2. **Jeff McNeely, OF, Spartanburg Methodist College**
3. **Eric Wedge, C, Wichita State University**
4. **Jeff Bagwell, 3B, University of Hartford**
5. Tim Mitchell, OF, Culver City HS (Los Angeles, CA)
6. **Paul Quantrill, P, University of Wisconsin**
7. Paul Anacki, P, Sandwich HS (MA)
8. Stoney Burke, C, Avon HS (Danville, IN)
9. Cedric Santiago, P, Yauco, PR
10. **Greg Hansell, P, Kennedy HS (La Palma, CA)**
11. Jason Friedman, OF-1B, Cypress College (CA)
12. Peter Janicki, P, El Dorado HS (Placentia, CA)
13. Chris Wimmer, 2B, East HS (Wichita, KS)
14. Fred Starks, P-OF, Rockledge HS (FL)
15. James Dennison, P, Jacksonville State University
16. Tim Graham, OF, Lancaster HS (OH)
17. Colin Dixon, 1B, Southeastern Louisiana University
18. Lawrence Grant, SS, Bailard HS (Seattle, WA)
19. H. B. Awkard, OF, Nelson County HS (Faber, VA)
20. Billy Wallace, P, Monroe Academy HS (Monroeville, AL)
21. Ernie Brown, P, Catonsville Community College (MD)

22. Brian Conroy, P, University of Massachusetts
23. Dom Desantis, P, Miami-Dade Community College
24. Troy Vann, OF, Community College of San Francisco
25. Terre Woods, C, Hinds Community College (MS)
26. Sean Darrock, P, Mission Bay HS (San Diego, CA)
27. Mark Williams, OF, Patrick Henry Junior College (AL)
28. Randy Brown, SS, San Jacinto College (TX)
29. Tracy Wildes, P, Sandalwood HS (Jacksonville, FL)
30. David Ring, P, Columbia Central HS (Columbia, TN)
31. Jerald Shelton, 3B, Shelton State Community College (AL)
32. Sean Hickman, P, Linn-Benton Community College (OR)
33. John Lammon, OF, Solano Community College (CA)
34. Bryan Niemeyer, OF, Minster HS (OH)
35. Michael Hickey, SS, Edmond Memorial HS (Edmond, OK)
36. Willie Dukes, OF, Mississippi Delta Junior College
37. Michael Canton, SS, San Augustine HS (TX)
38. Melvin Gonzales, P, Arecibo, PR
39. John Malzone, OF, North Adams State College
40. John Locker, P, University of Michigan
41. Roberto Santa, 1B, Arecibo, PR

1990 June (Reg)
2. **Frankie Rodriguez, P-SS, Eastern District HS (Brooklyn, NY)**
3. **Walt McKeel, OF, Greene Central HS (Snow Hill, NC)**
4. Greg Thomas, OF, Lake Brantley HS (Altamonte Springs, FL)
5. Tim Tackett, OF, Waverly HS (OH)
6. **Gar Finnvold, P, Florida State University**
7. Todd Miller, P, Temple University
8. Aaron Knieper, P, Nouvel Catholic HS (Saginaw, MI)
9. John Collett, P, Citrus Junior College (FL)
10. Rikchy Borrero, C, Hormigueros, PR
11. Terry Powers, P, Volunteer State Community College (TN)
12. David Schmidt, 2B, Southwestern Community College (NC)
13. Greg Graham, SS, University of Louisville
14. Quinn Feno, 1B-OF, New Bedford HS (MA)
15. Bruce Chick, OF, University of Georgia
16. **Erik Plantenberg, P, San Diego State University**
17. Evan Pratte, 2B-SS, Southwest Missouri State University
18. Robert Henkel, P, San Jacinto College (TX)
19. Brian Young, P, Ohio University
20. Mike Dekneef, SS, Lewis-Clark State College (ID)
21. Chad Trahan, P, Seminole Junior College (OK)
22. David Klvac, P, San Jacinto College (TX)
23. Ryan Maloney, P, Lancaster HS (OH)
24. Timothy Smith, P, Boston College
25. William Norris, 3B, Eckerd College (FL)
26. *Les Norman, OF, College of St. Francis (IL)*
27. Chris Davis, P, College of the Sequoias (CA)
28. John Crimmins, C, Norwood HS (MA)
29. Scott Bethea, SS, Louisiana State University
30. Jerry Burns, P, Napa Valley Junior College (CA)
31. Jeffrey Johnson, P, Fresno City College
32. Joseph Mondello, P, San Jacinto College (TX)
33. James Young, OF, Weaver HS (AL)
34. Nicolas Ortiz, 3B-SS, Cidra, PR
35. **Tim Davis, 2B, Southern Illinois University**
37. Greg Sorrell, 1B-OF, Poway HS (CA)

1991 June (Reg)
1. **Aaron Sele, P, Washington State University**
1. J. J. Johnson, OF, Pine Plains HS (NY)
1. **Scott Hatteberg, OF, Washington State University**
2. Terry Horn, P, Yukon HS (OK)
2. Chad Schoenvogel, P, Blinn College (TX)
3. Joe Caruso, P, Loyola Marymount University (CA)
4. Joe Ciccarella, 1B-P, Loyola Marymount University (CA)
5. Mark Carroll, OF, Holliston HS (MA)
6. Donny Jones, OF, Poway HS (CA)
7. Dan Collier, OF, Enterprise State Junior College (AL)
8. **Luis Ortiz, 3B, Union University (TN)**
9. Dan McDonald, 3B, Evans HS (Orlando, FL)
10. **Tony Rodriguez, SS, University of Charleston**
11. Jimmy Crowley, 3B, Clemson University
12. Craig Bush, P, Lancaster HS (OH)
13. John Eierman, OF, Rice University
14. Dana Levangie, C, American International College (MA)
15. **Cory Bailey, P, Southeastern Illinois College**
16. Tony Ferreira, 2B, Manatee Community College (FL)
17. **Tim VanEgmond, P, Jacksonville State University**

18. **Ron Mahay, OF, South Suburban College (IL)**
19. Brian Bright, OF, University of Massachusetts
20. Cesar Martinez, P, Chula Vista HS (San Diego, CA)
21. **Joel Bennett, P, East Stroudsburg College (PA)**
22. Jim Lentz, P, Columbia State Community College (TN)
23. Bryan Brown, OF, Tulane University
24. Ryan Beeney, SS, Newark HS (OH)
25. Melvin Walker, OF, McNair HS (Atlanta, GA)
26. Jesus Armendariz, P, Howard Junior College (TX)
27. Jake Austin, OF, Wake Forest University
28. Rafael Gutierrez, OF, Sandalwood HS (Jacksonville, FL)
29. Lance Davis, P, Mary Montgomery HS (Semmes, AL)
30. Chris Wiggs, SS, Santa Fe Catholic HS (Lakeland, FL)
31. Daren Hobson, P, Meridian College (MS)
32. Joshua Stough, P, Walker County HS (Jasper, AL)
33. Diogenes Baez, OF, Connors State Junior College (OK)
34. Kevin Becker, P, Hilliard HS (Galloway, OH)
35. Jerry Taylor, C-OF, Goliad HS (TX)
36. Richie Wyman, OF, Central Florida Community College
37. Ken Albarado, OF, Woodlawn HS (Baton Rouge, LA)
38. Steven Carver, SS, The Bolles School (Jacksonville, FL)
39. Chris Davis, P, Northwest Missouri State University

1992 June (Reg)
2. Tony Sheffield, OF, Tullahoma HS (TN)
3. Doug Hecker, 1B, University of Tennessee
4. **Joe Hamilton, 3B, Dighton-Rehobeth HS (MA)**
5. **Steve Rodriguez, 2B, Pepperdine University**
6. Derek Vinyard, P, San Diego State University
7. **Joey Depastino, P-OF, Riverview HS (Sarasota, FL)**
8. J. B. Bowles, 3B, Montgomery HS (Rockville, MD)
9. Todd Carey, SS, Brown University
10. Mark Senkowitz, C, Ohio Wesleyan University
11. Aaron Rounsifer, SS, Vista HS (CA)
12. Chad Amos, P, Ohio State University
13. **Bill Selby, SS, University of Southern Mississippi**
14. James Tyrell, P, Dutchess Community College (NY)
15. Gettys Glaze, P, The Citadel
16. Ricardo Gama, 2B, Southridge HS (Miami, FL)
17. Chris McCranie, SS, Colquitt County HS (Moultrie, GA)
18. Eric Norman, SS, Jones County HS (Haddock, GA)
19. Brent Hansen, P, University of California
20. Rob Berryman, P, Yorktown, VA
21. Leif McKinley, P, Chemeketa Community College (OR)
22. Jeff Martin, OF, Vanderbilt University
23. Wes Brooks, P, Belleville Area Junior College (IL)
24. Bob Juday, SS-2B, Michigan State University
25. Jeff Faino, P, Florida Tech College
26. Eric Cormier, P, Milford HS (MA)
27. **Joe Hudson, P, West Virginia University**
28. Rick Milligan, OF, San Joaquin Delta College (CA)
29. Ricky Craig, P, Webb City HS (Jasper, MO)
30. Scott Bakkum, P, University of Minnesota
31. Wilredo Rivera, OF, Vega Alta, PR
32. Randy Lawrence, P, Ferrum College (VA)
33. Ethan Faggett, OF, Dunbar HS (Burleson, TX)
34. Marcus Cuper, P, Voorhees HS (High Bridge, NJ)
35. Andrew Moore, 2B, Bridgewater College (VA)
36. **Lou Merloni, SS, Providence College**
37. Jason Smith, C, University of West Florida
38. T. J. O'Donnell, SS, Old Dominion University
39. Joe Barksdale, P, Southern Union State College (AL)
40. Steve McCollough, C, Eisenhower HS (Lawton, OK)
41. Reggie Hightower, OF, George C. Wallace Community College (AL)
42. Gresham Fortune, OF, East Central Junior College (MS)
43. **Kevin Gibbs, SS, St. John's HS (Davidsonville, MD)**
44. Eric Demoura, SS, Taunton HS (MA)
45. Chris Wagner, P, Santa Fe Community College
46. Allen Williams, 3B, University of Arkansas
47. Brian Johnson, 1B, Lee County HS (Albany, GA)
48. Lewis Spencer, SS, Hampton HS (VA)
49. Rico Wood, 2B, Southern Union State College (AL)
50. Michael Linenberger, OF, Mississippi Gulf Coast Junior College

1993 June (Reg)
1. **Trot Nixon, OF, New Hanover HS (Wilmington, NC)**
2. **Jeff Suppan, P, Crespi HS (Encino, CA)**
3. **Ryan McGuire, 1B, UCLA**
4. Shawn Senior, P, North Carolina State University
5. Kevin Clark, 3B, Cypress College (CA)

6. **Peter Munro, P, Cardoza HS (Bayside, NY)**
7. David Gibralter, 3B, Duncanville HS (TX)
8. *Sean DePaula, P, Cardinal Cushing Central HS (Derry, MA)*
9. Dean Peterson, P, Allegheny Community College (PA)
10. **Lou Merloni, SS, Providence College**
11. Kurt Bogott, P, St. Xavier College
12. Pat Murphy, 2B, University of South Alabama
13. Wilfredo Rivera, OF, Vega Alta, PR
14. David Smith, SS, LeMoyne College (NY)
15. Jacob Cook, P, Greenville HS (OH)
16. **Andy Abad, OF, Middle Georgia College**
17. Greg Patton, SS, George Washington University
18. *Keith McDonald, OF, Cypress College (CA)*
19. Courtney Arrolado, SS, Valhalla HS (El Cajon, CA)
20. Edward Westfall, P, Deltona HS (FL)
21. John Graham, OF, University of Massachusetts
22. Craig Phillip, P, Aurora University (IL)
23. Mark Ballard, P, University of Maine
24. Greg Kennedy, P, University of Southern Mississippi
25. **Shayne Bennett, P, College of DuPage (IL)**
26. Christian McCarter, OF, Northeast Louisiana University
27. Scotty Hartfield, OF, Hattiesburg HS (MS)
28. Steve Hayward, P, Seton Hall University
29. Jeff Belcher, OF, Calhoun Community College (AL)
30. Jim Larkin, 3B, Holy Cross College
31. Aaron Fuller, 2B, University of California
32. Nathan Tebbs, 2B, College of Southern Idaho
33. Ricky Rodriguez, SS, Miami Springs HS (Miami Springs, FL)
34. James Fernandes, P, Brandeis University
35. John Walker, 2B, Grand Rapids Community College
36. Gavin Jackson, SS, Chipola Junior College (FL)
37. Mark Dewalt, P, Upper Arlington HS (OH)
38. Wayne Slater, O.F, F. D. Roosevelt HS (Brooklyn, NY)
39. Tony Brannon, 2B, Johnstown-Monroe HS (OH)
40. Patrick McLendon, C, Lee HS (Baytown, TX)
41. *Daniel Ardoin, C, Texarkana College (TX)*
42. Chad Helmer, P, East Bay HS (Ruskin, FL)
43. Eric Ford, OF, Jacksonville State University
44. Kenneth Davis, P, Chipola Junior College (FL)
45. Joseph Hayward, OF, Boston College
46. Scott Brewer, P, Southern Union State College
47. Alphonso Johnson, SS, Hollandale Simmons HS (Hollandale, MS)
48. Ricky Joe Redd, OF, Mississippi State University (AL)
49. Michael Davis, P, Northwest Whitfield HS (Rocky Face, GA)
50. Chris Ciraulo, C, Cardinal Newman HS (Santa Rosa, CA)

1994 June (Reg)
1. **Nomar Garciaparra, SS, Georgia Tech**
3. **Brian Rose, P, Dartmouth HS (MA)**
4. Rob Welch, P, Twin Falls HS (ID)
5. **Brian Barkley, P, Midway HS (Waco, TX)**
6. Joe Mamott, SS, Canisius College (NY)
7. Denis McLaughlin, P, Old Dominion University
8. Chad Barnhardt, C, Lake Wales HS (FL)
9. Chris Allison, 2B, Bradley University (IL)
10. Damien Sapp, C, Pleasant Grove HS (UT)
11. **Donnie Sadler, SS, Valley Mills HS (TX)**
12. Antonio Santiago, P, Carolina, PR
13. **Carl Pavano, P, Southington HS (CT)**
14. Mike Jacobs, P, East Carolina University
15. Matt Bazzani, C, University of California-Santa Barbara
16. Chuck Malloy, P, St. Joseph's University (PA)
17. Robert Moore, P, University of Hawaii
18. **Michael Coleman, OF, Stratford HS (Nashville, TN)**
19. Tony Derosso, 1B, Colquitt County HS (Moultrie, GA)
20. Bartt Carney, OF, Indian Hills Community College (IA)
21. Chris Westcott, P, University of New Orleans
22. Shawn Rogers, P, University of Hawaii
23. Casey Child, OF, Mountain View HS (Orem, UT)
24. Robert Butler, P, Rend Lake Junior College
25. Marc Lewis, OF, Calhoun Community College (AL)
26. Jayson Black, P, Crestview HS (Convoy, OH)
27. Rawlin Goodwin, OF, Sulphur HS (LA)
28. Torrance Miller, OF, South Georgia Junior College
29. Nathan Barns, OF, Central HS (Rapid City, SD)
30. John McNeese, P, University of Mississippi
31. Dave Elliott, OF, Western Michigan University
32. Wayne Montgomery, P, Stratford Academy HS (Macon, GA)
33. John Raifstanger, 2B, Springfield College (MA)
34. *David Maurer, P, Howard Junior College (TX)*
35. Derrick Lewis, P, Lanier HS (Montgomery, AL)
36. Angel Diaz, OF, Lake Gibson HS (Lakeland, FL)
37. Jack Koch, P, Osceola HS (Kissimmee, FL)
38. Joe Robinson, SS, Indian Hills Community College (IA)

39. Tim Palmer, OF, Fresno City College
40. **Pat Daneker, P, Loyalsock Township HS (Williamsport, PA)**
41. Jessie Thompson, OF, Hinds Community College (MS)
42. Ken Arnold, 3B, Chipola Junior College (FL)
43. Dexter Battle, 1B, Hillsborough HS (Tampa, FL)
44. Mike Whitley, P, Southwest Missouri State University
45. Rene Justiniano, P, Triton Junior College (IL)
46. Chris Kurek, C, St. Bonaventure University (NY)
47. Jamey Price, P, University of Mississippi

1995 June (Reg)
1. Andy Yount, P, Kingwood HS (TX)
1. Corey Jenkins, OF, Dreher HS (Columbia, SC)
2. Jose Olmeda, SS, Fajardo, PR
3. Jay Yennaco, P, Pinkerton Academy HS (Windham, NH)
4. Mike Spinelli, P, Revere HS (MA)
5. **Steve Lomasney, C, Peabody HS (MA)**
6. **Matt Kinney, P, Bangor HS (ME)**
7. **Cole Liniak, SS, San Dieguito HS (Encinitas, CA)**
8. Luis Cardona, C, San Sebastian, PR
9. **Paxton Crawford, P, Carlsbad HS (Carlsbad, NM)**
10. Lakevie Austin, P, Emmanuel College (GA)
11. Jeff Sauve, P, Clemson University
12. **Jim Chamblee, SS, Odessa Junior College (TX)**
13. Andy Noffke, P, Ohio State University
14. Andrew Beinbrink, 3B, Scripps Ranch HS (San Diego, CA)
15. Kevan Cannon, P, Ohio State University
16. **Rontrez Johnson, OF, Marshall HS (TX)**
17. Bobby Rodgers, P, Wake Forest University
18. Felipe Roman, OF, Rio Piedras, PR
19. Ben Stallings, P, Apollo HS (Owensboro, KY)
20. Dwight Ferguson, OF, Miami-Dade Christian HS (Carol City, FL)
21. Curtis Romboli, P, Boston College
22. Pete Prodanov, 3B-OF, Oklahoma State University
23. Chuck Lopez, OF, Gahr HS (Cerritos, CA)
24. Chris Toomey, OF-P, Dana Hills HS (Dana Point, CA)
25. Scott Jones, P, University of Miami-Ohio
26. Moises Rojas, OF, Brito Miami Private School (FL)
27. **Juan Pena, P, Miami-Dade Wolfson Community College**
28. Kaleb Harp, OF, DeKalb HS (TX)
29. Bob Rauch, P-SS, Lamar University (TX)
30. Mark Varriano, OF, University of North Dakota
31. Cliff Brand, P, Central Gwinnett HS (Lawrenceville, GA)
32. Cordele Mincey, P, Dodge County HS (Milan, GA)
33. Matt Burch, P, Edison HS (Horseheads, NY)
34. Bart Vaughn, P, Mt. Dora Bible HS (Orlando, FL)
35. Nick Gruber, C, Haddon Township HS (Westmont, NJ)
36. Derrick Lewis, P, Central Alabama Community College
37. Angel Diaz, OF, Hillsborough Community College (FL)
38. Tim Boeth, SS, Leon HS (Tallahassee, FL)
39. Jason Wilson, P, South Broward HS (Hollywood, FL)
40. Jim Farrell, P, Kent State University
41. Brian Messer, P, Northwest HS (Shawnee, KS)
42. Juan Chaidez, C, Miami-Dade Christian HS (Hialeah, FL)
43. *Pat Burrell, 3B, Bellarmine College Preparatory HS (San Jose, CA)*
44. Bryan Wright, SS, Escambia HS (Pensacola, FL)
45. Kris Brown, OF, Central HS (Kalamazoo, MI)

1996 June (Reg)
1. Josh Garrett, P, South Spencer HS (Richland, IN)
1. **Chris Reitsma, P, Calgary Christian HS (Alberta)**
2. Gary LoCurto, 1B, University HS (San Diego, CA)
2. Jason Sekany, P, University of Virginia
3. **Demell Stenson, OF, LaGrange HS (GA)**
4. **John Barnes, OF, Grossmont Community College (CA)**
5. Bobby Brito, C, Cypress HS (CA)
6. Mike Perini, OF, Carlsbad HS (Carlsbad, NM)
7. Rob Ramsay, P, Washington State University
8. **Justin Duchscherer, P, Coronado HS (Lubbock, TX)**
9. Marcus Martinez, P, Monterey HS (Lubbock, TX)
10. **Shea Hillenbrand, SS, Mesa Community College (AZ)**
11. Brian Musgrave, P, Appalachian State University (NC)
12. Dion Ruecker, SS, Texas Tech
13. Skipp Benzing, P, Indian Hills Community College (IA)
14. Justin Lynch, P, Marina HS (Huntington Beach, CA)
15. Mark Robbins, 3B, Derry HS (KS)

16. Jeff Keaveney, 1B-OF, University of Southern Maine
17. Justin Crisafulli, P, Arizona Western Junior College
18. Mike McKinley, P, Scottsdale Community College
19. Mike Rupp, P, Monte Vista HS (Spring Valley, CA)
20. Chuck Beale, P, Stetson University
21. Javier Fuentes, SS-2B, Arizona State University
22. *Aaron Harang, P, Patrick Henry HS (San Diego, CA)*
23. Paul McCurtain, P, Mesa Community College (AZ)
24. Robert Brandt, P, A&M Consolidated HS (College Station, TX)
25. Dominic Barrett, OF, Trimble Tech HS (Fort Worth, TX)
26. Chris Thompson, P, Saint Leo College (FL)
27. Ryan Murray, P, Tampa Bay Tech HS (Tampa, FL)
28. Erik Metzger, C, Samford University (AL)
29. *Josh Stewart, P, Livingston Central HS (Ledbetter, KY)*
30. William Whitaker, P, First Coast HS (Jacksonville, FL)
31. Matt Frick, C, Yavapai Community College (AZ)
32. *Mike Bynum, P, Middleburg HS (FL)*
33. Adam Roller, P, Lakeland HS (FL)
34. Jaime Bonilla, P, Lake City Community College (FL)
35. Kasey Kuhlmeyer, P, San Pasqual HS (Escondido, CA)
36. Ken Sarna, SS, Durango HS (Las Vegas, NV)
37. Jeremy Swindell, P, Clear Lake HS (Houston, TX)
38. Travis McRoberts, SS, El Capitan HS (El Cajon, CA)
39. **Andre Thompson, OF, Delta State University (MS)**
40. Curtis Anthony, SS, Bishop Gorman HS (Las Vegas, NV)
42. Wesley Warren, OF, Arcadia HS (Scottsdale, AZ)
43. Jamaon Halbig, C, Southwestern Junior College (CA)
44. Bart Vaughn, P, Manatee Community College (FL)

1997 June (Reg)
1. John Curtice, P, Great Bridge HS (Chesapeake, VA)
1. Mark Fischer, OF, Georgia Tech
2. Aaron Capista, SS, Joliet Catholic HS (Joliet, IL)
2. Eric Glaser, P, Highlands HS (Fort Thomas, KY)
3. **Travis Harper, P, James Madison University (VA)**
4. **Ramon Santos, SS, Miguel Melendez HS (Cayey, PR)**
5. Greg Miller, P, Aurora HS (West Aurora, IL)
6. Kris Wilken, OF, Eldorado HS (Albuquerque, NM)
7. Jeff Taglienti, P, Tufts University
8. Andrew Hazlett, P, University of Portland (OR)
9. *Justin Wayne, P, Punahou HS (Honolulu, HI)*
10. **Marty McCleary, P, Mount Vernon Nazarene College (OH)**
11. Tom Miller, P, Ohio University
12. Billy Rich, OF, University of Connecticut
13. Charles Terni, SS, Montville HS (Uncasville, CT)
14. Chad Alevras, C, University of New Mexico
15. Rick O'Dette, P, St. Joseph's University (PA)
16. Jorge Deleon, 3B, University of South Florida
17. Kenny Rayborn, P, University of South Alabama
18. Danny Haas, P, University of Louisville
19. **David Eckstein, 2B, University of Florida**
20. Brian Partenheimer, P, Indiana University
21. Joe Thomas, P, Marietta College (OH)
22. Derek Rix, 1B, Florida Junior College
23. **Nate Bump, P, Penn State University**
24. Jason Fingers, P, Torrey Pines HS (San Diego, CA)
25. Chris Domurat, OF, Sandwich HS (Forestdale, MA)
26. Heath McMurray, P, Splendora HS (TX)
27. Justin Fry, P, Ohio State University
28. David Sticket, SS, Temple University (PA)
29. Ryan Yeager, SS, Port St. Joe HS (FL)
30. *Bret Prinz, P, Phoenix Junior College*
31. Matt Kamalsky, P, Somerset HS (PA)
32. Robert Hardy, P, Countryside HS (Clearwater, FL)
33. Patrick Santoro, SS, Fenwick HS (Elmwood Park, IL)
34. Layne Meyer, P, Polk Community College (FL)
35. Jason Berni, P, Rancho Bernardo HS (San Diego, CA)
36. Ryan Atkinson, P, Bellarmine College Preparatory HS (San Jose, CA)
37. Donovan Marbury, P, University of Southern Mississippi
38. *Dennis Tankersiey, P, St. Charles HS (MO)*
39. Shawn Weaver, P, Bald Eagle-Nittany HS (Loganton, PA)
40. Chad Zaucha, OF, Mount Pleasant HS (PA)
41. Matthew Slagter, P, Jefferson HS (Tampa, FL)
42. Scott Candelaria, SS, La Cueva HS (Albuquerque, NM)
43. Nicholas Gray, SS, Florida HS (Tallahassee, FL)
44. Todd Smith, 3B, Apopka HS (FL)
45. *Joseph Thurston, SS, Vallejo HS (CA)*

1998 June (Reg)
1. **Adam Everett, SS, University of South Carolina**

321

3. **Mike Maroth, P, University of Central Florida**
4. Jerome Gamble, P, Ben Russell HS (Alexander City, AL)
5. **Josh Hancock, P, Auburn University**
6. Richard Riccobono, P, Commack HS (NY)
7. Syketo Anderson, 2B, Prattville HS (AL)
8. Frederick Silverthorn, P, J. J. Pearce HS (Richardson, TX)
9. *Mark Teixeira, 3B, Mount St. Joseph HS (Severna Park, MD)*
10. Lenny Dinardo, P, Santa Fe HS (High Spring, FL)
11. Carlos Rodriguez, OF, University of Louisville
12. David Benham, C, Liberty University
13. *Mike Rabelo, C, Ridgewood HS (New Port Richey, FL)*
14. Matt Phillips, P, University of Delaware
15. Lance Surridge, P, University of North Carolina
16. Jason Norton, P, University of South Alabama
17. Benito Flores, P, Cal State Fullerton
18. Terrance Hill, P, Southern University (LA)
19. Shon Norris, P, University of North Carolina
20. Tony James, 2B, San Jose State University
21. Andrew Checketts, P, Oregon State University
22. Thomas Linarelli, P, University of Washington
23. Drew Larned, C, Fairfield University (CT)
24. Joseph Adeeb, P, Vanderbilt University
25. **John Hattig, IF, Southern HS (Piti, Guam)**
26. *Ben Kozlowski, P, Seminole HS (FL)*
27. James Gates, OF, Butler HS (Huntsville, AL)
28. Jason Blanton, P, Brevard Community College (FL)
29. Ryan Siebert, P, Germantown HS (Germantown, TN)
30. James Garcia, P, West Torrance HS (CA)
31. Robert Floyd, P, Satsuma HS (AL)
32. Richard Hart, 1B, Lubbock Christian HS (TX)
33. Heath Heiberger, P, Putnam County HS (Hennepin, IL)
34. Chadwick Johnson, C, Bradley University (IL)
35. Mark Younk, C , Texas HS (Wake Village, TX)
36. Tonayne Brown, OF, Lurleen B. Wallace Junior College (AL)
37. Anthony Caridi, C, Klein HS (Spring, TX)
38. **Dennis Tankersley, P, St. Louis Community College at Meramec**
39. Rob Shabansky, P, University of Arizona
40. Philip Ledesma, OF, Rider College (NJ)
41. Jason Fingers, P, Central Arizona College
42. Bryan Barnowski, DH, Southwick Tolland HS (Granville, MA)
43. Ronald Bohinski, SS, Lakeland HS (FL)
44. John Parrado, C, Miami Lakes HS (FL)
45. Jonathan Smithers, 3B, Florida College
46. Chris Hart, C, Clearwater HS (Palm Harbor, FL)
47. Richie Smith, 2B, Liberty County HS (Marianna, FL)
48. Darry Burgess, P, Alvin HS (TX)

1999 June (Reg)
1. Rick Asadoorian, OF, Whitinsville HS (Northbridge, MA)
1. Brad Baker, P, Pioneer Valley Regional School (Northfield, MA)
2. **Casey Fossum, P, Texas A&M University**
2. Mat Thompson, P, Timberline HS (Boise, ID)
3. Rich Rundles, P, Jefferson County HS (New Market, TN)
3. Antron Seiber, OF, Independence HS (LA)
4. Rory Shortell, P, Madison HS (Portland, OR)
5. Greg Montalbano, P, Northeastern University
6. Jon Kail, P, Baldwin HS (Pittsburgh, PA)
7. Rich Carroll, 1B, Venice HS (FL)
8. Andrew Heimbach, P, Mount Vernon Nazarene College (OH)
9. Richard Thoms, P, Mississippi State University
10. Brian Wiese, OF, Mississippi State University
11. Kregg Jarvais, C, University of Maine
12. **Lew Ford, CF, Dallas Baptist University**
13. Michael Dwyer, 1B, University of Richmond
14. B.J. Leach, P, Florida Southern College
15. Brian Wiley, P, The Citadel
16. Charlie Manning, P, Polk Community College (FL)
17. Hiram Duncan, 3B, Mississippi Gulf Coast Junior College
18. Jeff Waldron, C, Boston College
19. Jason Bottenfield, P, University of Texas-Pan American
20. Dan Generelli, P, Quinsigamond Community College (MA)
21. Jason Henderson, P, Bishop Hendricken HS (Warwick, RI)
22. Ellis Debrow, 1B, Woodham HS (Pensacola, FL)
23. Nicolas Puckett, P, Timberline HS (Boise, ID)
24. Rex Rundgren, IF, Mid Pacific Institute HS (Honolulu, HI)
25. Tim McCabe, SS, North Catholic HS (Wexford, PA)
26. **Marshall McDougall, IF, Florida State University**
27. *Mark Kiger, IF, Grossmont Community College (CA)*
28. Jonathan Anderson, SS, University of Illinois
29. Barton Hollis, P, Lawrence County HS (Moulton, AL)

30. Charlie Frasier, 3B, Santa Rosa Junior College (CA)
31. **Jaime Bubela, OF, Baylor University**
32. David Flournoy, OF, Deer Valley HS (Antioch, CA)
33. Perry Miley, CF, William Carey College (MS)
34. Dan Giese, P, University of San Diego
35. Ben Marbury, LF, Rockford, AL
36. John Brandon, OF, Panola Junior College (TX)
37. *Chris Mabeus, P, Eastern Arizona Junior College*
38. Jesse Cooksey, P, Port Neches-Groves HS (Port Arthur, TX)
39. Matthew Ames, 1B, Stanhope Elmore HS (Millbrook, AL)
40. Anthony Bass, LF, Booker T. Washington HS (Tulsa, OK)
41. Justin Smetana, P, Cardinal HS (Huntsburg, OH)
42. Bryan Rinehart, 2B, Southington HS (CT)
43. Ryan Coffin, P, Desert Vista HS (Phoenix, AZ)
44. James Lindsey, CF, Lee Davis HS (Mechanicsville, VA)
45. Brady Williams, IF, Pasco-Hernando Community College (FL)
46. Joe Kerrigan, SS, Temple University
47. James Burgess, OF, Durango HS (Las Vegas)
48. Joseph Kjose, P, Cochise County Community College (AZ)
49. Jordan Remy, 2B, Weston HS (MA)
50. Brian Buscher, 3B, Terry Parker HS (Jacksonville, FL)

2000 June (Reg)
1. Phil Dumatrait, P, Bakersfield Junior College
2. **Manny Delcarmen, P, West Roxbury HS (Hyde Park, MA)**
3. Matt Cooper, IF, Ripley HS (Stillwater, OK)
4. Charles Mims, P, Prattville HS (AL)
5. Brian Esposito, C-1B, University of Connecticut
6. Kenny Perez, IF, South Miami HS (Miami, FL)
7. Tony Fontana, P, Bowling Green State University (OH)
8. Brian Adams, P, Liberty University (VA)
9. Patrick Johnson, RF, William Carey College (MS)
10. Eric Doble, P, Arizona State University
11. **Freddy Sanchez, 2B, Oklahoma City University**
12. Shane Hall, P, Eastern Arizona Junior College
13. Miguel Quintana, IF, Florida International University
14. Ian Perio, P, University of San Francisco
15. Dustin Brisson, 1B, University of Central Florida
16. Josh Thigpen, P, Rogers HS (Killen, AL)
17. Chris Elmore, P, University of North Carolina
18. Haas Pratt, 3B, Rancho Bernardo HS (San Diego, CA)
19. Justin Sherrod, OF, Rollins College (FL)
20. Brian Bentley, P, University of Louisville
21. James Carroll, P, Mississippi State University
22. Felix Villegas, P, Muscatine Community College (IA)
23. Raul Nieves, IF, University of Mobile
24. Freddie Money, OF, Wallace Community College (AL)
25. Jon Guitterez, P, Central Arizona College
26. Marcellus Dawson , OF, Muscatine Community College (IA)
27. James Morrison, P, Beulah HS (Valley, AL)
28. Travis Kaats, CF, Desert Mountain HS (Scottsdale, AZ)
29. **Kason Gabbard, P, Royal Palm Beach HS (FL)**
30. Jeremy Terni, SS, Montville HS (Uncasville, CT)
31. Tommy Major, P, New London HS (CT)
32. Eric Rollins, P, Latta HS (Ada, OK)
33. Bart Braun, P, Vallejo HS (Vallejo, CA)
34. John Carreon, P, Arizona Western Junior College
35. Dusty Brown, OF, Bradshaw HS (Dewey, AZ)
36. Mike Guerrero, OF, South Mountain College (AZ)
37. Brett Bonvechio, 1B, Prospect HS (Santa Clara, CA)
38. Daniel Coffee, RF, Saint Bernard's HS (Old Lyme, CT)
39. Gabriel Roberti, P, West Hills HS (Lakeside, CA)
40. Brad Bettcher, P, Palo Verde HS (Tucson, AZ)
41. Ferrari Miller, CF, Castlemont HS (Oakland, CA)
42. Javi Herrera, C, Gulliver Prep HS (Miami, FL)
43. *Chris Duffy, OF, South Mountain College (AZ)*
44. Kevin Brown, IF, University of Miami (FL)
45. Nathan Goodrich, P, Mercyhurst College (PA)
46. Donald Benson, OF, Mt. San Jacinto Junior College (CA)

2001 June (Reg)
2. **Kelly Shoppach, C, Baylor University**
2. Matt Chico, P, Fallbrook HS (CA)
3. Jonathan Devries, C, Irvine HS (CA)
4. Stefan Bailie, IF, Washington State University
5. Eric West, IF, Southside HS (AL)
6. Justin James, P, Yukon HS (OK)
7. Rolando Viera, P, Cuba
8. **Kevin Youkilis, IF, University of Cincinnati**
9. Billy Simon, P, Wellington HS (FL)
10. Ben Crockett, P, Harvard University
11. Shane Rhodes, P, West Virginia University

12. Ryan Brunner, OF, University of Northern Iowa
13. Alec Porzel, SS, University of Notre Dame
14. Chris Farley, P, Mahar Regional HS (Orange, MA)
15. Ryan Carroll, P, Mississippi State University
16. Antonio Gonzalez, CF, Framingham HS (MA)
17. Michael Grant, P, Danville Area Community College (IL)
18. Brian Lane, P, University of Richmond
19. *Jeremy Brown, C, University of Alabama*
20. Devoris Williams, OF, Greensboro HS (AL)
21. Charles Weatherby, P, University of North Carolina-Wilmington
22. Gerald Rogers, P, Boston College
23. Pedro Suarez, P, Mount Miguel HS (Spring Valley, CA)
24. Jason Ramos, SS, G. Holmes Braddock Senior HS (Miami.)
25. Kris Coffey, OF, Dallas Baptist University
26. Kenneth Trapp, P, Dallas Baptist University
27. Bryan Kent, 3B, Southwest Texas State University
28. Steven Ponder, P, Texas A&M University
29. Mario Campos, OF, Trevecca Nazarene University (TN)
30. Richard Sander, P, Cal State San Bernardino University
31. Brett Rudrude, P, Cal State San Bernardino University
32. Kyle Jackson, P, Alvirne HS (Hudson, NH)
33. Christopher Honsa, P, Corona Del Sol HS (Chandler, AZ)
34. Eron Brown, 3B, Auburn HS (AL)
35. Koley Kolberg, P, Coppell HS (TX)
36. Adam Sabari, 1B, Cardinal Mooney HS (Sarasota, FL)
37. Emmanuel Lopez, 1B, Globe HS (AZ)
38. Jacob Almestica, P, Medardo Carazo HS (Trujillo Alto, PR)
39. Ricky Bauer, P, Mid Pacific Institute HS (Honolulu, HI)
40. Josh Bolen, OF, Illinois Central College
41. Bart Braun, P, Napa Valley Junior College (CA)
42. Tommy Major, P, Briarcliffe College (NY)
43. Tanner Wootan, 2B, Mountain View HS (Mesa, AZ)
44. Terrence Taylor, CF, Marin Community College (CA)
45. Brent Tarbett, OF, Community College of Southern Nevada
46. Chris Keeran, CF, Eastlake HS (Chula Vista, CA)
47. Donald Benson, OF, Mount San Antonio College (CA)

2002 June (Reg)
2. **Jon Lester, P, Bellarmine Prep HS (Puyallup, WA)**
3. Scott White, 3B, Walton HS (Marietta, GA)
4. Chris Smith, P, University of California-Riverside
5. Chad Spann, 3B, Southland Academy HS (Albany, GA)
6. Gary Browning, P, Wayne County HS (Jesup, GA)
7. Jason Neighborgal, P, Riverside HS (Hillsborough, NC)
8. Brandon Moss, 2B, Loganville HS (Monroe, GA)
9. Tyler Pelland, P, Mount Abraham HS (Bristol, VT)
10. Greg Stone, IF, Bacone Junior College (OK)
11. Michael Goss, OF, Jackson State University
12. Dustin Majewski, OF, University of Texas
13. Clay Stone, P, Ruston HS (LA)
14. Andy Priola, P, Faulkner University (AL)
15. Ian Cronkhite, OF, Westmoore HS (Moore, OK)
16. Peter Ciofrone, 2B, Smithtown HS (NY)
17. Arian Alcala, 3B, St Thomas, VI
18. Robert Smith, OF, Southeast Missouri State University
19. Tom MacLane, P, Florida Atlantic University
20. Luis Villarreal, P, Northwood University
21. Alberto Concepcion, C-3B, USC
22. John Anderson, P, Arkansas State University
23. Dave Pahucki, P, Siena College (NY)
24. Pat Boran, IF, Princeton University
25. Jim Buckley, C, Siena College (NY)
26. Adam Davis, P, Metter HS (Pulaski, GA)
27. Mike Armstrong, P, Chabot College (CA)
28. Mike Barclay, OF, University of South Florida
29. Matt Clarkson, C, Broken Arrow HS (Broken Arrow, OK)
30. Jonathan Williams, P, Opelika HS (AL)
31. Steven Boggs, CF, San Diego HS (San Diego)
32. Brock Hunton, P, Dublin Coffman HS (Dublin, OH)
33. Luke Taylor, P, Lowndes County HS (Valdosta, GA)
34. Mitchell Woolf, P, Madison HS (Rexburg, ID)
35. Jose Vaquedano, P, Vernon College (TX)
36. Don Powers, P, Shawnee HS (OK)
37. Ricardo Romero, P, Theodore Roosevelt HS (Los Angeles, CA)
38. Koley Kolberg, P, Navarro College (TX)
39. Tyler Jacobson, P, Auburn Riverside HS (Sumner, WA)
40. Dustin Roddy, C, Northeast Texas Community College

41. Matthew Inouye, C, Mid Pacific Institute HS (Honolulu, HI)
42. Rosalino Valenzuela, P, Marcos De Niza HS (Guadalupe, AZ)
43. Lance Schartz, C, Garden City Community College (NY)
44. David Baker, C, Rogers HS (Puyallup, WA)
45. *Brian Bannister, P, USC*
46. Douglas Harris, P, Lone Oak HS (Paducah, KY)
47. Anthony Bianucci, OF, Daytona Beach College
48. Sergio Roman, C, Allen County Community College (KS)
49. Robert Caruso, 1B, Chaminade Madonna HS (Hollywood, FL)
50. Seth Dhaenens, SS, Mountain Pointe HS (Chandler, AZ)

2003 June (Reg)

1. **David Murphy, OF, Baylor University**
1. **Matt Murton, OF, Georgia Tech**
2. **Abe Alvarez, P, Long Beach State University**
2. Mickey Hall, OF, Walton HS (Marietta, GA)
3. Beau Vaughn, P, Arizona State University
4. **Jonathan Papelbon, P, Mississippi State University**
5. Brian Marshall, P, Virginia Commonwealth University
6. Jessie Corn, P, Jacksonville State University
7. Jeremy West, C, Arizona State University
8. Lee Curtis, 2B, College of Charleston
9. John Wilson, P, Northeastern Junior College (CO)
10. Chris Durbin, OF, Baylor University
11. Barry Hertzler, P, Central Connecticut State University
12. Justin Sturge, P, Coastal Carolina University (SC)
13. Zach Basch, P, University of Nevada-Reno
14. Zach Borowiak, SS, Southeast Missouri State University
15. Chris Turner, OF, Texarkana College (TX)
16. Kevin Ool, P, Marist College (NY)
17. William Newton, P, Mountain View HS (Orem, UT)
18. Tom Cochran, P, Middle Georgia College
19. Jarrett Gardner, P, University of Arkansas
20. Josh Morris, OF, Cartersville HS (GA)
21. Mike Dennison, P, Wichita State University
22. Kala Kaaihue, C, Iolani HS (Kailua, HI)
23. David Coffey, OF, University of Georgia
24. Ignacio Suarez, SS, Southwest Texas State University
25. Drew Moffitt, OF, Wichita State University
26. Jason Ramos, SS, St. Petersburg College
27. Andrew Sharpe, SS, Los Angeles Pierce College
28. Davey Penny, P, East Carolina University (SC)
29. Doug Fink, P, Manatee Community College (FL)
30. **David Sanders, P, Wichita State University**
31. Greg Schilling, P, Taravella HS (Tamarac, FL)
32. Matt Pike, P, Centennial HS (Pueblo, CO)
33. Scooter Jordan, OF, Texas Tech
34. Arthur Santos, P, Florida International University
35. Erich Cloninger, P, Liberty University (VA)
36. Ben Sosebee, P, Truett-McConnell Community College (GA)
37. Chris Johnson, SS, Bishop Verot HS (Fort Myers, FL)
38. McBryde, OF, Palm Beach Gardens HS (North Palm Beach, FL)
39. Jeffrey Culpepper, OF, Gonzaga University (WA)
40. Michael Rutledge, SS, Cullman HS (AL)
41. Lance Shartz, C, Garden City Community College (NY)
42. Dallas Williams, OF, Pike HS (Indianapolis, IN)
43. Scott Thomas, Chaminade College Prep HS (St. Louis, MO)
44. Tom Caple, OF, University of San Diego
45. Terrence Cramer, P, Palm Beach College
46. Victor Rodriguez, C, Cape Coral HS (Cape Coral, FL)
47. A.J. Loyd, OF, Bishop Carroll HS (Wichita, KN)
48. Adam Davis, P, Middle Georgia College
49. Jason Smith, P, Bourne HS (Buzzards Bay, MA)
50. Mitch Stachowsky, C, College of Southern Idaho

2004 June (Reg)

2. **Dustin Pedroia, SS, Arizona State University**
3. Andrew Dobies, P, University of Virginia
4. Thomas Hottovy, P, Wichita State University
5. Ryan Schroyer, P, San Diego State University

6. **Cla Meredith, P, Virginia Commonwealth University**
7. Patrick Perry, C-1B, Northern Colorado
8. Kyle Bono, P, University of Central Florida
9. Matthew Vanderbosch, CF, Oral Roberts University (OK)
10. Steven Pearce, 1B, University of South Carolina
11. Ryan Phillips, P, Barton County Community College (KS)
12. Michael Rozier, P, Henry County HS (GA)
13. Matthew Ciaramella, CF, University of Utah
14. Robert Swindell, P, Charleston Southern University
15. Dustin Kelly, SS, Cuesta College (CA)
16. Matthew Clarkson, C, Arkansas-Fort Smith
17. Jeremy Haynes, OF, Madison County HS (FL)
18. Randall Beam, P, Florida Atlantic University
19. Logan Sorensen, 1B, Wichita State University
20. Brian Van Kirk, C, Westminster Academy (FL)
21. Charles Jeroloman, SS, Auburn University
22. John Burgess, 1B, Georgia State University
23. Matthew Goodson, P, University of Texas
24. Matthew Spencer, 1B, Morristown West HS (TN)
25. Michael Jones, OF, Arizona Western University
26. Jacob Renshaw, P, Ventura Community College (CA)
27. Justin Phillabaum, P-1B, Royal Palm Beach HS (FL)
28. Michael James, P, University of Connecticut
29. David Seccombe, P, UNLV
30. Andrew Ehrlich, P, Stanford University
31. Brendan Winn, RF, University of South Carolina
32. Bradley Herbert, P, East Providence HS (RI)
33. John Wells, P, Timbercreek HS (FL)
34. Andrew Pinckney, 3B, Emory University (GA)
35. Thomas Lanier, P, University of Georgia
36. Cooper Eddy, P, University of New Mexico
37. Glenn Swanson, P, University of California-Irvine
38. Colby Summer, P, University of Hawaii
39. Zak Farkes, SS, Harvard University
40. Nick Francona, P, Lawrenceville School (PA)
41. Steven Edlefsen, SS, Barton County Community College (KS)
42. Kyle Peter, CF, Archbishop O'Hara HS (MO)
43. Tyler Latham, P, Hewitt Trussville HS (AL)
44. Beau Mills, 3B, Golden West HS (CA)
45. Adam Campbell, 3B, University of British Columbia
46. Tom Caple, OF, University of San Diego
47. Jesse Easley, 1B, University of Florida
48. Felipe Garcia, C, Cal State Fullerton
49. Blake Tillett, P, Brandon HS (FL)
50. Raudel Alfonso, P, Hialeah Senior HS (FL)

2005 June (Reg)

1. Jacoby Ellsbury, CF, Oregon State University
1. **Craig Hansen, P, St John's University (NY)**
1. Clay Buchholz, P, Angelina College (TX)
1. Jed Lowrie, 2B, Stanford University
1. Michael Bowden, P, Waubonsie Valley HS (IL)
2. Jonathan Egan, C, Cross Creek HS (GA)
4. William Blue, P, Morro Bay HS (CA)
5. Reid Engel, CF, Lewis-Palmer HS (CO)
6. Jeffrey Corsaletti, CF, University of Florida
7. Yahmed Yema, RF, Florida International University
8. James Zink, P, Everett Community College (WA)
9. Mark Wagner, C, University of California-Irvine
10. Kevin Guyette, P, University of Arizona
11. Ismael Casillas, P, Benedictine College (KS)
12. Kyle Fernandes, P, Massasoit Community College (MA)
13. Jay Johnson, CF, Xavier University (OH)
14. Pedro Alvarez, SS, Horace Mann School (NY)
15. Patrick Thomas, P, Jeffersonville HS (IN)
16. Matthew Mercurio, 3B, Florida Southern College
17. Dominic Ramos, SS, Texas State University
18. Nick Criaris, C, St Peters Prep School (NJ)
19. James Baxter, P, Villanova University
20. Charles Blackmon, P, Young Harris College (GA)
21. Robert Johnson, P, Navarro College (TX)
22. Orvil Aviles, P, Fernando Callejo HS (Manati, PR)
23. Carl Lipsey, 2B, Jackson State University
24. James Twomley, P, University of Massachusetts
25. Ricardo Sanchez, C, Barry University (FL)
26. Kirby Yates, P, Kauai HS (HI)
27. Matthew Hancock, P, Oral Roberts University (OK)
28. Ryan Hinson, P, Northwestern HS (SC)
29. Christopher Jones, P, Indiana State University

30. Ryan Colvin, P, Carroll HS (TX)
31. Luis Exposito, C, Champagnat Catholic School (Hialeah, FL)
32. Jeffrey Natale, 2B, Trinity College (CT)
33. John Hester, C, Stanford University
34. Allan Dykstra, 1B, Rancho Bernardo HS (CA)
35. Jason Determann, P, Louisiana State University
36. Mark McClure, P, Hillsborough HS (FL)
37. Jason Schnitzer, P, Los Alamitos HS (CA)
38. Levi Tapia, C, Ralston Valley HS (CO)
39. Billy Bell, CF, Nicholls State University (LA)
40. Blake Maxwell, P, Methodist College (NC)
41. Edward Degerman, P, Rice University
42. Miguel Alicea, RF, Manuela Toro HS (Caguas, PR)
43. Jason Castro, C, Castro Valley HS (CA)
44. Christopher Garcia, 1B, Xaverian HS (Brooklyn, NY)
45. James Bamberg, C, Tallahassee Community College (FL)
46. Terry Large, P, University of Alabama
47. Alex Wolfe, C, Timpanogos HS (Payson, UT)
48. Matthew Sheely, CF, Palm Beach Gardens HS (FL)
49. Erik Turgeon, P, Dunedin HS (FL)
50. Colin Arnold, LF, Kings Academy (FL)

2006 June (Reg)

1. Jason Place, CF, Wren HS (SC)
1. Daniel Bard, P, University of North Carolina
1. Kristofer Johnson, P, Wichita State University
1. Caleb Clay, P, Cullman HS (AL)
2. Justin Masterson, P, San Diego State University
3. Aaron Bates, 1B, North Carolina State University
3. Bryson Cox, P, Rice University
4. Jonathan Still, C, North Carolina State University
5. Dustin Richardson, P, Texas Tech
6. Zachary Daeges, 3B, Creighton University (NE)
7. Kristopher Negron, SS, Cosumnes River College (CA)
8. Rafael Cabreja, CF, James Monroe HS (Bronx, NY)
9. Ryan Kalish, CF, Red Bank Catholic HS (NJ)
10. Kyle Snyder, P, Wellington Community HS (FL)
11. Brandon Belt, CF, Hudson HS (TX)
12. Ryan Khoury, SS, University of Utah
13. Jordan Craft, P, Dallas Baptist University
14. Matthew LaPorta, 1B, University of Florida
15. Jorge Jimenez, 3B, Porterville College (CA)
16. Tyler Weeden, C, Edmond Santa Fe HS (OK)
17. William Reddick, LF, Middle Georgia College
18. Lars Anderson, 1B, Jesuit HS (Fair Oaks, CA)
19. Richard Lentz, P, University of Washington
20. Kyle Gilligan, SS, Etobicoke Collegiate Institute HS (Toronto, Ontario)
21. Brian Steinocher, P, Stephen F Austin State University (TX)
22. Michael Christl, P, Bradley University (IL)
23. Paul Smyth, OF, San Diego State University
24. Robert Phares, P, Shelton State Community College (AL)
25. Sean Gleason, P, Lamar Community College (CO)
26. Chad Gross, 1B, Claremont HS (CA)
27. Charles New, P, Mercer University (GA)
28. Carmine Giardina, P, Durant HS (FL)
29. Devin Foreman, 1B, Hales Franciscan School (IL)
30. Donald Lawson, P, University of West Alabama
31. Logan Shafer, CF, Cuesta College (CA)
32. Mike Chambers, 2B, Franklin Pierce College (NH)
33. Jeffrey Rea, 2B, Mississippi State University
34. Bryan Morgado, P, Florida Christian School (Miami, FL)
35. Jeremy Rahman, CF, Hazelwood Central HS (MO)
36. Darren Blocker, 3B, Connors State College (OK)
37. Justin Marks, P, Owensboro Catholic HS (KY)
38. Travis Beazley, P, Randolph-Macon College (VA)
39. Jordan Abruzzo, C, University of San Diego
40. Corey Davisson, C, West HS (Fresno, CA)
41. Peter Tountas, SS, Jefferson College (MO)
42. Douglas Graybill, P, Sarasota HS (FL)
43. Jeffrey Vincent, CF, Niagara University (NY)
44. Andrew Leary, P, Sierra Vista HS (NV)
45. Jacob McCarter, P, University of Alabama
46. Junior Rodriguez, 3B, Coral Gables HS (FL)
47. Nicholas Hill, P, United States Military Academy (NY)
48. Josh Papelbon, P, University of North Florida
49. Patrick Thomas, P, Wabash Valley College (IL)
50. Darrell Fisherbaugh, P, University of Hawaii

Major League Players Developed By Red Sox Since 1975

From 1975–2006, Boston's player-development system has produced 237 big-leaguers, ranging from cuppa-java guys like Steve Lomasney and Jeff Plympton to stalwarts like Marty Barrett and Bruce Hurst. And, of course, Hub Heroes like Jim Lonborg, Tony Conigliaro, Jim Rice, Wade Boggs, and Roger Clemens.

Most players developed by an organization were originally drafted or signed by that organization and made their major league debut with that team. Some players, of course, will be traded to another club while still in the minors and later make their ML debut in another uniform (e.g., Jeff Bagwell and Curt Schilling, two especially painful mistakes). Note that an organization can "gain" or "lose" credit for a player if he was released before ever reaching the high minors (i.e., Double A).

This list shows all 237 players produced by the Red Sox' system since 1975, with their debut year and team (if not Boston). Their career games or innings pitched with Boston and with other teams are also shown through 2006.

Player/Debut (Team)	G/IP Bos/Other
Don Aase 1977	92/1014 ip
Andy Abad 2001 Oak	9/6 g
Gary Allenson 1979	402/14 g
Abe Alvarez 2004	10/0 ip
Luis Alvarado 1968	76/387 g
Brady Anderson 1988	41/1793 g
Luis Aponte 1980	169/50 ip
Ramon Aviles 1977	1/116 g
Jeff Bagwell 1991 Hou	0/2150 g
Cory Bailey 1993	19/185 ip
Jack Baker 1976	14/0 g
Brian Barkley 1998	11/0 ip
John Barnes 2000 Min	0/20 g
Marty Barrett 1982	929/12 g
Steve Barr 1974	16/67 ip
Juan Beniquez 1971	233/1328 g
Shayne Bennett 1997 Mon	0/124 ip
Todd Benzinger 1987	193/731 g
Rafael Betancourt 2003 Cle	0/227 ip
Tim Blackwell 1974	103/323 g
Tony Blanco 2005 Was	0/56 g
Greg Blosser 1993	22/0 g
Wade Boggs 1982	1625/848 g
Tom Bolton 1987	366/171 ip
Mark Bomback 1978 Mil	0/312 ip
Sam Bowen 1977	16/0 g
Oil Can Boyd 1982	1013/372 ip
Ken Brett 1967	239/1283 ip
Mike Brown 1982	237/15 ip
Mike Brumley 1987 ChiN	65/236 g
Ellis Burks 1987	733/1267 g
Morgan Burkhart 2000	36/6 g
Steve Burke 1977 Sea	0/64 ip
Rick Burleson 1974	1031/315 g
Dennis Burtt 1985 Min	0/30 ip
Jim Burton 1975	55/0 ip
Jim Byrd 1993	2/0 g
Jim Chamblee 2003 Cin	0/2 g
Robinson Checo 1997	20/15 ip
Jin Cho 1998	57/0 ip
Roger Clemens 1984	2771/2038 ip
Dave Coleman 1977	11/0 g
Michael Coleman 1997	10/12 g
Tony Conigliaro 1964	802/74 g
Cecil Cooper 1971	406/1490 g
Scott Cooper 1990	399/193 g
Jim Corsi 1988 Oak	147/331 ip
Ted Cox 1977	13/275 g
Paxton Crawford 2000	65/0 ip
Steve Crawford 1980	380/180 ip
Jack Cressend 2000 Min	0/159 ip
Zach Crouch 1988	1/0 ip
Steve Curry 1988	11/0 ip
Jack Curtis 1970	403/1234 ip
Mike Dalton 1991 Det	0/8 ip
Jorge De La Rosa 2004 Mil	0/142 ip
Manny Delcarmen 2005	62/0 ip
Alex Delgado 1996	26/0 g
Puchy Delgado 1977 Sea	0/13 g
Brian Denman 1982	49/0 ip
Joe Depastino 2003 NYN	0/2 g
Bo Diaz 1977	2/991 g
Steve Dillard 1975	124/314 g
Pat Dodson 1986	52/0 g
Melvin Dorta 2006 Was	0/15 g
Justin Duchscherer 2001 Tex	0/266 ip
David Eckstein 2001 Ana	0/848 g
Steve Ellsworth 1988	36/0 ip
Dwight Evans 1972	2505/101 g
Adam Everett 2001 Hou	0/583 g
Jared Fernandez 2001 Cin	0/107 ip
Joel Finch 1979	57/0 ip
Gar Finnvold 1994	36/0 ip
Carlton Fisk 1969	1078/1424 g
John Flaherty 1992	48/999 g
Don Florence 1995 NYN	0/12 ip
Lew Ford 2003 Min	0/439 g
Casey Fossum 2001	229/434 ip
Frank Francisco 2004 Tex	0/58 ip

Player/Debut (Team)	G/IP Bos/Other
Jim Fregosi 1961 LAA	0/1903 g
Kason Gabbard 2006	25/0 ip
Dan Gakeler 1991 Det	0/73 ip
Nomar Garciaparra 1996	966/227 g
Mike Garman 1969	55/375 ip
Rich Gedman 1980	906/127 g
Lee Graham 1983	5/0 g
Mike Greenwell 1985	1269/0 g
Jackie Gutierrez 1983	259/97 g
Josh Hancock 2002	7/157 ip
Craig Hansen 2005	41/0 ip
Devern Hansack 2006	10/0 ip
Greg Hansell 1995 LAN	0/136 ip
John Hattig 2006 Tor	0/13 g
Scott Hatteberg 1995	454/710 g
Eric Hetzel 1989	85/0 ip
Shea Hillenbrand 2001	344/526 g
Butch Hobson 1975	623/115 g
Glenn Hoffman 1980	678/88 g
Sam Horn 1987	103/286 g
Peter Hoy 1992	3/0 ip
Joe Hudson 1995	126/0 ip
Buddy Hunter 1971	22/0 g
Bruce Hurst 1980	1456/955 ip
Daryl Irvine 1990	63/0 ip
Rontrez Johnson 2003 KC	0/8 g
Rick Jones 1976	104/54 ip
Ed Jurak 1982	160/44 g
Dana Kiecker 1990	192/0 ip
Sun Kim 2001	70/264 ip
Matt Kinney 2000 Min	0/388 ip
Rick Kreuger 1975	35/9 ip
Peter Ladd 1979 Hou	0/285 ip
Roger LaFrancois 1982	8/0 g
Joe Lahoud 1968	254/537 g
John LaRose 1978	2/0 ip
Wil Ledezma 2003 Det	0/246 ip
Bill Lee 1969	1502/440 ip
Sang-Hoon Lee 2000	11/0 ip
John Leister 1987	35/0 ip
Jon Lester 2006	81/0 ip
John Lickert 1981	1/0 g
Cole Liniak 1999 ChiN	0/15 g
James Lofton 2001	8/0 g
Steve Lomasney 1999	1/0 g
Jim Lonborg 1965	1096/1363 ip
Sparky Lyle 1967	329/1055 ip
Fred Lynn 1974	828/1141 g
Steve Lyons 1985	328/625 g
Ron Mahay 1995	51/298 ip
Jose Malave 1996	45/0 g
Josias Manzanillo 1991	1/337 ip
Mike Maroth 2002 Det	0/800 ip
Anastacio Martinez 2004	10/0 ip
John Marzano 1987	169/132 g
Tom McCarthy 1985	5/79 ip
Lynn McGlothen 1972	168/1327 ip
Ryan McGuire 1997 Mon	0/368 g
Walt McKeel 1996	6/5 g
Marty McLeary 2004 SD	0/20 ip
Jeff McNeely 1993	21/0 g
Andy Merchant 1975	3/0 g
Cla Meredith 2005	2/50 ip
Lou Merloni 1998	273/152 g
Bart Miadich 2001 Ana	0/12 ip
Rick Miller 1971	1101/381 g
Steve Mintz 1995 SF	0/24 ip
Bobby Mitchell 1970 NYA	0/273 g
Charlie Mitchell 1984	17/0 ip
John Mitchell 1986 NYN	0/239 ip
Bob Montgomery 1970	387/0 g
Roger Moret 1970	558/163 ip
Kevin Morton 1991	86/0 ip
Jerry Moses 1965	155/231 g
Peter Munro 1999 Tor	0/313 ip
David Murphy 2006	20/0 g
Matt Murton 2005 ChiN	0/195 g
Tony Muser 1969	2/661 g
Tim Naehring 1990	547/0 g

Player/Debut (Team)	G/IP Bos/Other
Reid Nichols 1980	338/202 g
Al Nipper 1983	693/104 ip
Trot Nixon 1996	982/0 g
Mike O'Berry 1979	43/154 g
Ben Oglivie 1971	166/1588 g
Tomokazu Ohka 1999	134/806 ip
Bobby Ojeda 1980	716/1164 ip
Luis Ortiz 1993	16/44 g
Jon Papelbon 2005	102/0 ip
Carl Pavano 1998 Mon	0/1035 ip
Mike Paxton 1977	108/357 ip
Dustin Pedroia 2006	31/0 g
Juan Pena 1999	13/0 ip
Juan Perez 2006 Pit	0/3 ip
Rico Petrocelli 1963	1553/0 g
Erik Plantenberg 1993 Sea	0/41 ip
Phil Plantier 1990	175/435 g
Jeff Plympton 1991	5/0 ip
Dick Pole 1973	308/220 ip
Todd Pratt 1992 Phi	0/662 g
Paul Quantrill 1992	210/1041 ip
Carlos Quintana 1988	438/0 g
Rey Quinones 1986	62/389 g
Chuck Rainey 1979	359/309 ip
Hanley Ramirez 2005	2/158 g
Robert Ramsay 1999 Sea	0/68 ip
Jody Reed 1987	715/569 g
Chris Reitsma 2001 Cin	0/584 ip
Win Remmerswaal 1979	55/0 ip
Jim Rice 1974	2089/0 g
Allen Ripley 1978	137/324 ip
Mike Rochford 1988	10/0 ip
Frankie Rodriguez 1995	15/636 ip
Steve Rodriguez 1995	6/12 g
Tony Rodriguez 1996	27/0 g
Kevin Romine 1985	331/0 g
Victor Rosario 1990 Atl	0/9 g
Brian Rose 1997	191/91 ip
Ken Ryan 1992	137/146 ip
Donnie Sadler 1998	156/294 g
Anibal Sanchez 2006 Fla	0/114 ip
Freddy Sanchez 2002	32/298 g
Angel Santos 2001	9/32 g
Curt Schilling 1988 Bal	523/2579 ip
Dave Schmidt 1981	15/0 g
George Scott 1966	1192/842 g
Bill Selby 1996	40/162 g
Aaron Sele 1993	620/1475 ip
Jeff Sellers 1985	328/0 ip
Danny Sheaffer 1987	25/382 g
Steve Shields 1985 Atl	0/217 ip
Kelly Shoppach 2005	9/41 g
Craig Skok 1973	28/121 ip
Roger Slagle 1979 NYA	0/2 ip
Mike Smithson 1982 Tex	269/1085 ip
Reggie Smith 1966	1014/973 g
Bobby Sprowl 1978	12/33 ip
Bob Stanley 1977	1701/0 ip
Dave Stapleton 1980	582/0 g
Dernell Stenson 2003 Cin	0/37 g
Marc Sullivan 1982	137/0 g
Scott Taylor 1992	25/0 ip
John Tudor 1979	635/1159 ip
Julio Valdez 1980	65/0 g
John Valentin 1992	991/114 g
Tim VanEgmond 1994	44/54 ip
Mo Vaughn 1991	1046/466 g
Wilton Veras 1999	85/0 g
Chico Walker 1980	32/494 g
Eric Wedge 1991	30/9 g
Ernie Whitt 1976	8/1320 g
Dana Williams 1989	8/0 g
Bob Woodward 1985	98/0 ip
Wilbur Wood 1961	89/2588 ip
Jim Wright 1978	139/0 ip
Carl Yastrzemski 1961	3308/0 g
Kevin Youkilis 2004	263/0 g
Eddie Zambrano 1993 ChiN	0/75 g
Bob Zupcic 1991	287/32 g

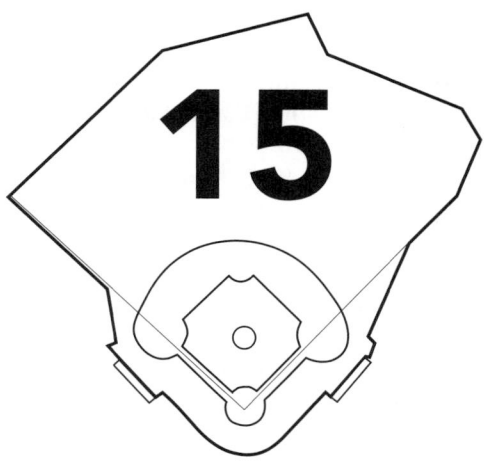

RED SOX TRANSACTIONS

The new Boston franchise in the American League was barely more than a rumor when the team executed its very first transaction on February 11, 1901, the signing of Jimmy Collins to a guaranteed one-year, $4,000 contract. The signing of Collins to play third base and manage the new team was more than just a simple acquisition. Collins was already the most popular baseball player in the city, having starred for Boston's National League franchise since 1895. His acquisition signaled the team's intentions to be a "major league" franchise in more than just a literal sense. The plan worked so well that Boston quickly became an American League city. The Braves, meanwhile, played second fiddle for the full half century of the shared run by old league and new in Beantown.

The Red Sox have made many transactions over the years, but few have had as positive an impact as their first one. It's clear that the Red Sox have exported far more talent than they have imported, although they have brought to the fold such luminaries as Cy Young, Lefty Grove, Jimmie Foxx, Joe Cronin, Dennis Eckersley, Pedro Martinez, and Curt Schilling.

Red Sox Nation has earned the right to be anxious when their hometown team announces its latest trade, especially when it involves giving up young talent. This section rates and analyzes the 10 best and worst deals the Red Sox have ever made, with the most prominent name(s) in italics. Following that is a log detailing the transactions the Red Sox have made involving major league players from the team's very first deal to their most recent one (as of March 2007). Abbreviations in this section include PTBNL (player to be named later) and UFC (undisclosed future considerations). An asterisk after a date means that it is approximate. The log presented here is by far the most comprehensive ever published. Credit for collecting the bulk of the information presented in the log belongs to Tom Ruane and all the other dedicated researchers at Retrosheet. The information used here was obtained free of charge from and is copyrighted by Retrosheet. Interested parties may contact Retrosheet at *www.retrosheet.org*. Those interested in finding out who the Red Sox got for Fred Lynn, George Scott, Tris Speaker, or Red Ruffing, read on.

Red Sox Best Trades

1. Carl Pavano and a player to be named later to Expos for *Pedro Martinez* (November 18, 1997); Montreal received Tony Armas (December 18, 1997)

After the 1996 season, longtime Red Sox ace Roger Clemens declared free agency and went looking for a new deal. Boston did not make a strong effort to re-sign the multiple Cy Young award winner. General manager Dan Duquette explained the team did not pursue Clemens because he was in "the twilight of his career." Clemens signed with the Toronto Blue Jays, and proceeded to win the Cy Young Award the following year (and three more times in the decade since then).

While Clemens prospered during the 1997 season, his old team did not. After winning at least 85 games in the two previous seasons, the Red Sox sank below .500.

The team's pitching staff, its worst in a decade, was the main culprit in the descent of the Sox. Duquette knew he needed an ace. And he knew where he could find one. Duquette's former employer, the Montreal Expos, had that year's National League Cy Young Award winner: Pedro Martinez. The 300-strikeout, 26-year-old ace was due for a big raise, and he would be eligible for free agency after the 1998 season. The always cash-strapped Expos knew they could no longer afford Pedro.

The Red Sox and the Yankees both pursued Pedro vigorously. Boston prevailed because of better pitching prospects to trade. The Expos received Carl Pavano, who would be named the ninth-best prospect in the game that winter by *Baseball America*; hard-throwing Tony Armas, the son of the former Red Sox center fielder, went to Montreal to complete the trade a month later.

The Red Sox quickly signed their new ace to a six-year, $69 million contract. Rarely has a baseball team spent its money so wisely. Pavano and Armas both turned out to be major league material, but Pedro won two Cy Youngs and helped lead the Sox to the promised land.

2. Heathcliff Slocumb to Mariners for *Derek Lowe* and *Jason Varitek* (July 31, 1997)

It was the middle of the summer of 1997, and the Red Sox were already out of the race. Not only were the pieces not coming together for the Sox, but the team clearly didn't have many of the pieces it needed. Red Sox catcher Mike Stanley had turned into a designated hitter. The weak starting rotation was led by Tom Gordon and Tim Wakefield, neither of whom could be considered an ace. Boston had signed Steve Avery the previous winter and expected him to strengthen the rotation; instead, he weakened it. Closer Heathcliff Slocumb was hearing the boos as he went through a season during which he was a better arsonist than fireman.

To the rescue came Mariners GM Woody Williams. The Mariners were strong contenders in the AL West in 1997, but their bullpen was the worst in baseball. Norm Charlton, the aged Mariners closer, was having a horrible season. Seattle came to Fenway just days before the trading deadline. Slocumb pitched a shutout inning against the Mariners in the second game of the series. Slocumb registered 95 mph on the radar gun, and the M's thought he could be the answer to their problems.

So Woodward inquired about Slocumb's availability. Duquette had a good idea of what he wanted: pitching and catching. Duquette remembered Jason Varitek from Georgia Tech, where he had played alongside Nomar Garciaparra, and the Cape Cod League. A Boston scout had also been following Derek Lowe's performances for Tacoma in the Pacific Coast League. Both Varitek and Lowe were prospects, but neither was a top prospect. Varitek had been a first-round draft pick, but he hadn't lived up to expectations in the minors.

Less than an hour before the trade deadline, and after Slocumb had blown a save and the game that night for the Red Sox, Duquette and Woodward agreed on the terms of the trade. Slocumb was indeed an improvement over Charlton and he helped the Mariners finish in first place. But Slocumb's 1998 season became a nightmare for Mariners fans, and his major league career would end just two years later Meanwhile, in exchange for Slocumb, the Red Sox acquired the player who would catch more games for the Red Sox than any player in franchise history, plus one of the few pitchers in major league history to win 20 games in one season and save 40 games in another. And, never to be forgotten in Boston, Lowe wound up winning the clinching games in the 2004 Division Series, League Championship Series, and World Series.

3. Gordon Rhodes, George Savino and $150,000 to Athletics for *Jimmie Foxx* and Johnny Marcum (December 10, 1935)

4. Bob Kline, Rabbit Warstler and $125,000 to Athletics in exchange for *Lefty Grove*, Rube Walberg, and Max Bishop (December 12, 1933).

Tom Yawkey became the owner of the Red Sox just in time for one of Connie Mack's periodical dismantlings of the Athletics. Yawkey was ready to spend as much money as was needed to return the Red Sox to respectability and Mack was set to once again tear down his team (and this time would never be able to build it back up). Yawkey's two best investments during these years were future Hall of Famers Lefty Grove and Jimmie Foxx. Grove, perhaps the best left-handed pitcher of all time, was no longer at his peak and had a horrendous first year with the Sox. The following season, however, he was able to regroup and make adjustments and it turned out that while he wasn't the same fireballer he'd been with Philadelphia, he still had plenty left in the tank. Foxx, who'd won the Triple Crown for the A's in 1933, didn't need to make any adjustments and quickly became the best hitter the Red Sox had ever had up to that point (Babe Ruth notwithstanding). Only Ted Williams has passed "Double X" since.

5. Lyn Lary and $250,000 to Senators for *Joe Cronin* (October 26, 1934)

Tom Yawkey found out everybody has a price, even for a family member. Clark Griffith at first declined to sell his son-in-law, Joe Cronin, Washington's hard-hitting shortstop and pennant-winning manager. Yawkey, however, raised his bid so high that Griffith was unable to

resist. So the Red Sox acquired a future Hall of Famer as both their shortstop and their manager. Cronin would remain with the organization as a player, manager, and general manager for a quarter of a century.

6. Al Nipper and Calvin Schiraldi to Cubs in exchange for *Lee Smith* (December 8, 1987)

Lou Gorman's finest hour as Red Sox general manager occurred when this deal fell into his lap and he pounced on it without a second thought. The Red Sox were more than happy to send the hard-throwing but erratic Schiraldi, who was never going to be able to live down his 1986 World Series failures as long as he remained in Boston, and Nipper, who was only a borderline major league pitcher, for one of the top relief pitchers in baseball history. Smith remained in Boston only until May 4, 1990, when he was traded to St. Louis for outfielder Tom Brunansky, but Smith was a significant upgrade over Schiraldi and helped lead the team to the 1988 AL East title.

7. Vean Gregg, Merlin Kopp, Pinch Thomas and $60,000 to Athletics for Amos Strunk, *Bullet Joe Bush,* and *Wally Schang* (December 14, 1917)

In one of Harry Frazee's first trades, the Sox picked up valuable Joe Bush and Wally Schang and gave up nothing of consequence. It would be a rare quality move of the Frazee era.

8. Del Pratt and Rip Collins to Tigers in for Carl Holling, *Howard Ehmke*, Danny Clark, Babe Herman, and $25,000 (October 30, 1922)

When you make a lot of deals, one of them might turn out all right. After sending Carl Mays, Babe Ruth, Waite Hoyt, Everett Scott, Sad Sam Jones, and the aforementioned Wally Schang and Bullet Joe Bush to the Yankees between July 1919 and July 1922, the Red Sox made a trade with another team. This deal with the Tigers netted $25,000 and gave them three seasons with an ace in Howard Ehmke. It also brought the club young Babe Herman, but it was several years before he rose to stardom with the Brooklyn Dodgers.

9. Rick Wise, Mike Paxton, Ted Cox, and Bo Diaz to Indians for *Dennis Eckersley* and Fred Kendall (March 30, 1978)

Ted Cox was a hot young prospect for the Red Sox, starting his major league career with a record six straight hits and batting .362 as a Boston call-up in September 1977, but his career fizzled after the deal to Cleveland. Dennis Eckersley, still just 22, won 20 games his first year in Boston and was still an effective starter for the Red Sox when Rick Wise was forced into retirement. His later

renaissance as a star reliever gives Eck the unique distinction of being part of one of the best *and* worst trades in club history.

10. Casey Fossum, Brandon Lyon, Jorge de la Rosa, and Michael Goss to Diamondbacks for *Curt Schilling* (November 28, 2003)

Coming off a bitter defeat to the Yankees in the 2003 ALCS, the Red Sox set their sights on Curt Schilling. Because of his no-trade clause with Arizona, Schilling could decline any deal and he publicly pondered whether he wanted to go to the Red Sox or to another suitor, namely the Yankees. Boston general manager Theo Epstein moved into Schilling's house just before Thanksgiving and filled Schilling with stats, projections, and New England lore even as his host stuffed him with turkey. By the end of the 72-hour window imposed by Major League Baseball, Schilling said yes to Epstein and the Diamondbacks said yes to the bevy of appetizing prospects—the Casey Fossum Special—that turned out to not be very filling in the long run.

Red Sox Worst Trades

1. *Babe Ruth* sold to Yankees for $100,000 (January 3, 1920)

There's no doubt that the sale of Babe Ruth is the worst "trade" in baseball history, but it certainly wasn't seen that way at the time. While it was clear that Ruth was a huge star and a major gate attraction, observers around the game were divided on what Ruth's future would bring. For one thing, Ruth's power was not appreciated by those devoted to the more "scientific" game that baseball was at the time. More importantly, though, Ruth's behavior was so out-of-control at times that there was doubt that any team could handle him. Harry Frazee, the Red Sox owner, felt that his team would be better off using the money from his friends on the Yankees to stock up on younger players. (There is no truth to the many stories that Yawkey was in financial trouble or needed the money to finance a Broadway production.) Frazee's plan turned out to be a mistake of epic proportions.

2. *Jeff Bagwell* to Astros for Larry Andersen (August 30, 1990)

"Who knew?" was Red Sox GM Lou Gorman's later defense for a trade that Red Sox fans will never forgive. It's certainly true that no one knew that Jeff Bagwell would become a major power hitter and a dominant player for a decade. But many people knew that Bagwell was a terrific hitter. Scouts started raving about his bat in spring training. Other teams were inquiring about

Bagwell's availability all season long, according to several reports in the *Boston Globe* that summer. And Bagwell had put up an incredible campaign for a 22-year-old player whose home ballpark strongly favored pitchers. At the time Gorman traded Bagwell, what Bagwell had achieved was very clear; his season-ending stats included a .333 season, a league-leading 34 doubles, and 74 walks, the fourth-highest total in the league. No New Britain Red Sox had ever put up those kinds of numbers at that age. In October Bill James and STATS Inc. would project Bagwell as the 1991 NL batting champion based on his 1990 Eastern League statistics. After Bagwell's stint in instructional league that fall, Astros player personnel director Bob Watson told Peter Gammons that Bagwell hit "like a right-handed Don Mattingly."

The Red Sox desperately needed to add a reliever to their bullpen. But it did not need to be Larry Andersen, who would become a free agent after only one month (plus a miserable 1990 ALCS for Boston) as a result of the collusion rulings. Gorman would later argue that Red Sox lawyers assured him that Andersen would not be awarded free agency, but in the summer months preceding the trade, various media outlets had repeatedly reported that free agency for players in Andersen's class was a very strong possibility. Once again, Gorman seemed unaware of what anybody who read the *Boston Globe* sports pages on a daily basis already knew.

3. *Tris Speaker* to Indians for Sad Sam Jones, Fred Thomas, and $55,000 (April 12, 1916)

The greatest everyday player in club history and the centerpiece of Boston's "Million Dollar Outfield" was sold after holding out for a bigger contract in the spring of 1916. Everyone in baseball was shocked by the deal, and Red Sox fans were incensed. Ban Johnson quietly arranged the deal before other teams knew that Speaker was on the market. It remains unclear whether Red Sox owner Joseph Lannin really wanted to trade Speaker or if Ban Johnson pushed him to make the deal. Unlike Boston's trades of other future Hall of Famers, the Red Sox did get to see the best of Speaker. Yet Spoke was such a great player that his career in Cleveland, where he eventually became player/manager and led the club to its first world championship, was only slightly inferior to the career he had in Boston. He is still the all-time major league record holder with 792 doubles (among his 3,514 hits) and was the best defensive center fielder in history, at least until Willie Mays.

4. *Red Ruffing* to Yankees for Cedric Durst and $50,000 (May 6, 1930)

From 1919 to 1930 the Red Sox traded an entire Hall of Fame pitching staff to the New York Yankees.

Combined, this series of trades was just as damaging to the Red Sox as the Ruth sale. Ruffing was the last and best of this pre-Yawkey Red Sox group that became Yankees. Ruffing had been rushed to the major leagues and was only marginally effective in his first five full seasons for the Red Sox, setting the club mark for losses with 25 in 1928, plus 22 more the next season. The Red Sox were actually more impressed with his bat than his arm and the team considered making him an outfielder despite the fact that an earlier foot injury had permanently limited his mobility. The Yankees and their manager Miller Huggins believed that Ruffing could be a far more successful pitcher once he gained more experience and got away from the awful Red Sox. The Yankees were easily able to pry Ruffing from the Sox early in the 1930 season. Ruffing went 15–5 the rest of the season and soon emerged as one of the leaders of the Yankees rotation for the next decade.

5. *Carl Mays* to Yankees for Allen Russell, Bob McGraw, and $40,000. (July 29, 1919)

Many years after his death, Carl Mays remains a controversial figure among baseball aficionados. Mays' numbers are comparable, and in many cases superior to, those of members of the Hall of Fame, yet he received scant support in Cooperstown. His questionable character and an unfortunate pitch made him a loathed figure by teammates, managers, and writers.

Boston's trade of Mays to the Yankees is in some ways more important than the Babe Ruth sale because of the controversy and enmity it created at the time. Mays started the controversy himself by walking out on the Red Sox after a rough start on July 13, 1919. Already agitated by personal issues, Mays had become overwhelmingly frustrated by the bad play of his teammates. He had pitched quite effectively that season, but the team had not played well offensively or defensively behind him and, as a result, the pitcher had only a 5–12 record. Mays declared that he would not pitch another game for the Red Sox. American League president Ban Johnson was offended by Mays' walkout and ordered that the pitcher be held accountable for his actions before any trade was made. The Red Sox, however, felt that trying to punish Mays was pointless; they simply wanted to deal the pitcher as soon as possible.

Half the league was interested in acquiring the temperamental star pitcher. The Yankees offered reliever Allan Russell, pitching prospect Bob McGraw, and $50,000. Red Sox owner Harry Frazee agreed to the deal. A furious Johnson ruled that the trade was invalid, but neither the Red Sox nor the Yankees paid attention to the league president's decree. He suspended Mays, but the Yankees went to court and won an injunction

preventing Johnson from enforcing the suspension. Several court battles later the Yankees emerged victorious. The battle led to an American League civil war, and that war would leave Johnson out of a job and the Red Sox franchise in ruins.

Mays pitched in the major leagues until the end of the decade. But accusations of throwing games, the death of Ray Chapman as a result of being hit in the head by a Mays pitch in 1920, and his walking out on the Red Sox permanently cast a cloud over his reputation. Meanwhile, the pitchers the Red Sox got in exchange for Mays never made much of an impact in the major leagues.

6. *Gavvy Cravath* to White Sox (February 16, 1909)

The worst of John Taylor's many bad moves, Gavvy Cravath would move on to Phillies a year later and become the greatest slugger before Babe Ruth, leading the league in home runs six times. The Red Sox did silence him in 1915, containing his mighty swing in cavernous Braves Field in the World Series.

7. *Dennis Eckersley* and Mike Brumley to Cubs for Bill Buckner (May 25, 1984)

Dennis Eckersley was a successful starter for the Cubs for two years before moving on to Oakland, where, after some initial struggles, he would become the most dominant closer in baseball history. Meanwhile, Bill Buckner had roughly 2,200 at-bats with the Sox, posting a .279 batting average along with a .315 on-base percentage and a .410 slugging percentage during his term as Boston's first baseman. A solid major leaguer on the downward swing of his career—as Eckersley also seemed to be—was forgivable; the grounder that eluded him in the 1986 World Series was not.

8. *Waite Hoyt*, Harry Harper, Wally Schang, and Mike McNally to Yankees for Muddy Ruel, Del Pratt, Sammy Vick, and Hank Thormahlen (December 15, 1920)

This trade looked reasonable at the time; it just didn't turn out that way in the long run. Waite Hoyt's two years in a Red Sox uniform had not been at all successful; his health was a huge question mark. Harry Harper and Wally Schang were veterans whose best years appeared to be behind them. Mike McNally was a poor-hitting

backup infielder. In return, Boston was getting at least two well-regarded players, Muddy Ruel and Del Pratt. Coming almost a year after the Ruth deal, this trade had the same bad Boston karma.

Hoyt got healthy and turned out to be far better than anyone expected. He spent a decade with the Yankees and continued pitching in the majors until 1938. He threw more than 3,700 innings in all, only 6 percent of them for the Red Sox. Schang's best years were indeed mostly behind him, but he was able to stay a productive major leaguer for the rest of the decade. Meanwhile, Pratt's defense went downhill faster than expected, while after only two years with the Red Sox Ruel forced Frazee into trading him for scraps by threatening to retire.

9. *Sparky Lyle* to Yankees for Danny Cater and a player to be named later (March 22, 1972); Boston Red Sox received Mario Guerrero (June 30, 1972)

Sparky Lyle went on to become the first reliever to win the AL Cy Young Award. That 1977 performance helped the Yankees edge the Red Sox for the division title. By then Danny Cater had retired and become famous for being traded for Sparky Lyle.

10. *Herb Pennock* to Yankees for Camp Skinner, Norm McMillan, George Murray, and $50,000 (January 30, 1923)

There are numerous other one-way deals in Red Sox history: Cecil Cooper (1976), Ben Oglivie (1973), Wilbur Wood (1964), George Stone (1904), and the 2006 panic move that sent Cla Meredith, Josh Bard, and cash to San Diego for personal catcher Doug Mirabelli. All are certainly bad moves, but a deal between the Yankees and Red Sox, especially one involving a future Hall of Famer, edges out the crowded field for the final spot in the top 10.

By 1923, owner Harry Frazee had resigned himself to letting someone else own the Red Sox and he sold off his players for cash and bodies in preparation. Herb Pennock had been both starting and relieving for the Red Sox since the team acquired him in 1915, but he was an average pitcher at best. Once he was traded to the Yankees, however, he instantly became an excellent pitcher. Pennock, however, owes his 240-win career more to New York's offense and his longevity than to his arm.

Best Red Sox Free Agent Signings

1. Cy Young on March 19, 1901

Cy Young was the second player and first pitcher the Red Sox signed, and he may rank as the best free agent pitcher in major league history.

2. David Ortiz on January 22, 2003

When the Red Sox signed Ortiz to a one-year, $1.25 million deal to replace Brian Daubach as their left-handed first baseman/designated hitter, they expected good things from a hitter they knew had a high ceiling. Ortiz, however, had struggled with injuries and the Twins did not offer him a contract after the 2002 season because they did not think he could stay healthy. "Big Papi" has surpassed all expectations.

3. Jimmy Collins on February 11, 1901

The first man the Red Sox ever signed, Jimmy Collins was already a star in Boston thanks to his play for the National League team in the city. His signing as third baseman and manager gave the American League club instant credibility. Collins persuaded other players to join the new team, and his presence made it easier to lure players from other cities. He led the Red Sox to two pennants and a victory in the first ever World Series.

4. Tim Wakefield on April 26, 1995

Six days after the Pirates released Tim Wakefield, the Red Sox signed the knuckleballer to a minor league contract. One month later he was back in the major leagues pitching effectively for the Red Sox. Eleven years later Wakefield is still there, having pitched more innings than any Red Sox pitcher other than Roger Clemens and Cy Young, and having established himself as the most versatile pitcher in club annals.

5. Bill Mueller on January 10, 2003

When Bill Mueller signed a two-year, $4.5 million contract with the Red Sox, it wasn't even a sure thing that he would be an everyday player for Boston. In the end, he was a lot more; Mueller won a batting championship with a career year in 2003 and helped lead Boston to a World Series victory in 2004.

Worst Red Sox Free Agent Signings

1. Matt Young on December 4, 1990

Red Sox ownership was unwilling to spend the cash necessary to sign premium free agents. In 1990, however, a Red Sox team desperate for pitching finally plunged into the market and came up with Matt Young, a pitcher who had just finished his first successful year as a starter in six years, and even then his record was 8–18. Ignoring Young's history of injuries and wildness, the Sox signed him to a three-year, $6.35 million deal. He never exceeded 100 innings in a season again and was out of baseball when his contract expired. His Red Sox career is best remembered for the unofficial no-hitter he threw—and lost—to the Indians on April 12, 2002.

2. Steve Avery on January 22, 1997

After losing Roger Clemens to free agency following the 1996 season, the Red Sox tried to fill the gap by signing Steve Avery to a complicated contract that assured him of at least $4.85 million for one season but could have potentially been worth $20 million for three. Avery was unable to even pitch as well as Clemens at his worst, posting a 5.64 ERA in his two awful years with the Sox.

3. Jose Offerman on November 16, 1998

After it was clear that Mo Vaughn was not returning to Boston in 1999, the Red Sox signed Jose Offerman to a four-year, $26 million contract. Offerman was a decent hitter for a middle infielder, but a poor fielder, and he wasn't a good enough hitter to justify a regular spot at another position. Red Sox GM Dan Duquette defended the signing at the time by explaining that Offerman would replace Vaughn's on-base percentage and add speed to the lineup, ignoring his many weaknesses and that Offerman was coming off a career season he was unlikely to repeat. He hit well in his first season in Boston, but that's the only positive thing to be said about Offerman's Sox stint.

4. Matt Clement on December 22, 2004

After losing Pedro Martinez and Derek Lowe to free agency, GM Theo Epstein signed Matt Clement to a three-year, $25 million contract. The Sox hoped the erratic but hard-throwing Clement could build on his solid 2004, which had been the best year of his career. Clement was only mediocre in his first year with the Sox, and injuries destroyed the rest of his Boston stay.

5. Danny Darwin on December 19, 1990

Two weeks after signing Matt Young, the Red Sox once again opened the checkbook for pitching by signing veteran Danny Darwin to a four-year, $11.8 million deal. Coming off a career year during in which he had posted a 2.21 ERA in 162 2/3 innings, the Red Sox intended to make the 35-year-old swingman a mainstay as a starter. Darwin stayed in the Red Sox rotation over a full season just once in his four years with the Sox, and his performance ranged from the terrific to the terrible.

Red Sox Transactions Register

February 11, 1901
Jimmie Collins signed as a free agent.

March 19, 1901
Cy Young signed as a free agent.

July 15, 1901*
Larry McLean released.

August 15, 1901
Nig Cuppy released.
Jack Slattery signed as a free agent.*

November 16, 1901
Traded Ossee Schreckengost to Indians for Candy LaChance.

March 13, 1902
Bert Husting signed as a free agent.

April 1902
Sold Fred Mitchell to Athletics.

April 29, 1902
Sold Bert Husting to Athletics.

June 1902
Sold George Prentiss to Orioles.

June 3, 1902
Sold Charlie Hickman to Indians.

July 1902
Purchased Tom Hughes from Orioles.

August 1902*
Tully Sparks signed as a free agent.

April 1903
Sold Nick Altrock to White Sox.

December 20, 1903
Traded Tom Hughes to Yankees for Jesse Tannehill.

January 16, 1904
Sold Jake Stahl and George Stone to Senators.

June 17, 1904
Traded Patsy Dougherty to Yankees for Bob Unglaub.

July 4, 1904
Traded Bill O'Neill to Senators for Kip Selbach.

December 26, 1904
Traded George Stone and cash to Browns for Jesse Burkett.

May 18, 1905
Lost Tom Doran to Tigers on waivers.

August 1905
Purchased John Godwin from Bloomington(III) for $750.
Purchased Ed Hughes from Davenport(III).

August 6, 1905
Purchased Joe Harris from Fall River (NEL).

August 8, 1905
Purchased Pop Rising from New London (CTSL) for $1,200.

November 1905
Ralph Glaze signed as a free agent.

February 1906
Yip Owens released.

May 20, 1907
Purchased Bunk Congalton from Indians.

June 7, 1907
Claimed Deacon McGuire from Yankees on waivers.
Traded Jimmy Collins to Athletics for John Knight.

June 15, 1907
Claimed Larry Schlafly from Senators on waivers.

June 18, 1907
Traded Larry Schlafly and Moose Grimshaw to Toronto (EL) for Jack Thoney.

June 22, 1907
Traded Bill Dinneen to Browns for Beany Jacobson and $1,000.

August 1, 1907
Purchased Cy Morgan from Browns.

August 10, 1907
Traded cash and a PTBNL to Baltimore (IL) for Fred Burchell; Baltimore (IL) received John Knight (December 28, 1907).

August 11, 1907
Sold Frank Oberlin to Senators.

September 1, 1907
Sold Charlie Armbruster to White Sox.

October 13, 1907
Received Frank LaPorte from Yankees as part of 3-team trade in which White Sox sent Jake Stahl to Yankees; and Red Sox sent Freddy Parent to White Sox.

November 5, 1907
Sold Hobe Ferris to Yankees.

January 2, 1908
Traded Al Shaw to White Sox for Ed McFarland.

May 31, 1908
Traded Jesse Tannehill to Senators for Casey Patten.

July 10, 1908
Purchased Jake Stahl from Yankees.
Sold Bob Unglaub to Senators.

July 20, 1908
Traded Tex Pruiett to Indians for Jake Thielman.

July 26, 1908
Lost George Winter to Tigers on waivers.

August 17, 1908
Traded Frank LaPorte to Yankees for Harry Niles.

August 28, 1908
Deacon McGuire released.

September 20, 1908
Sold Denny Sullivan to Indians.

November 9, 1908
Sold Chet Chadbourne to Indianapolis (AASN).
Sold Ralph Glaze to Indianapolis (AASN).

November 23, 1908
Harry Hooper signed as a non-drafted free agent.

December 12, 1908
Traded Lou Criger to Browns for Tubby Spencer.

February 16, 1909
Sold Gavvy Cravath to White Sox.
Traded Cy Young to Indians for Charlie Chech, Jack Ryan, and $12,500.

July 26, 1909
Traded Charlie Chech, Jack Ryan and cash to St Paul (AASN) in Exchange for Ed Karger and Charley Hall.

September 9, 1909
Traded Doc Gessler to Senators for Charlie Smith.

September 11, 1909
Claimed Jack Chesbro from Yankees on waivers.

January 18, 1910
Lost Harry Wolter to Yankees on waivers.

April 21, 1910
Sold Elmer Steele to Providence (EL).

May 10, 1910
Purchased Clyde Engle from Yankees.

May 19, 1910
Sold Charlie French to White Sox.

May 26, 1910
Purchased Red Kleinow from Yankees.

May 27, 1910
Sold Harry Niles to Indians.

June 10, 1910
Sold Pat Donahue to Athletics.

July 23, 1910
Purchased Walter Moser from Oakland (PCL).

August 9, 1910
Traded Harry Lord and Amby McConnell to White Sox for Frank Smith and Billy Purtell.

September 1, 1910

Major League Draft
Selected Hugh Bedient from Fall River (NEL).
Selected Jack Killilay from Spokane (NWL).
Selected Joe Riggert from Omaha (WL).

May 9, 1911
Sold Charlie Smith to Newark (EL).

May 11, 1911
Purchased Hap Myers from Browns.
Sold Frank Smith to Reds for $5,000 plus undisclosed sum to Browns for withdrawing waiver claim.

June 21, 1911
Purchased Judge Nagle from Pirates.

June 24, 1911
Lost Bunny Madden to Phillies on waivers.

August 5, 1911
Red Kleinow released.

September 1, 1911*
Sold Walter Moser to Browns.

January 5, 1912
Traded Hal Janvrin, Marty McHale, Walter Lonergan, Jack Thoney, Billy Purtell, and Hap Myers to Jersey City (IL) for Hick Cady.

February 6, 1912
Sold Jack Fournier to White Sox.

June 25, 1912
Purchased Neal Ball from Indians for $2,500.

July 9, 1912
Sold Eddie Cicotte to White Sox.

November 25, 1912
Sold Hugh Bradley to Jersey City (IL).

January 1913
Claimed Wally Rehg from Pirates on waivers.

July 2, 1913
Sold Buck O'Brien to White Sox for $5,000.

May 13, 1914
Sold Les Nunamaker to Yankees.

May 24, 1914
Claimed Del Gainer from Tigers on waivers.

May 27, 1914
Purchased Guy Cooper from Yankees.

July 9, 1914
Purchased Babe Ruth, Ernie Shore, and Ben Egan from Baltimore (IL) for more than $25,000.

July 16, 1914
Claimed Dick Hoblitzell from Reds on waivers.

July 28, 1914
Traded Rankin Johnson, Fritz Coumbe, and Ben Egan to Indians for Vean Gregg.

June 4, 1915
Purchased Bill Rodgers from Portland (PCL).

June 6, 1915
Claimed Herb Pennock from Athletics on waivers.

July 2, 1915
Purchased Jack Barry from Athletics.

July 8, 1915
Sold Bill Rodgers to Reds.

August 12, 1915
Sold Ralph Comstock to Reds.

December 16, 1915
Purchased Sam Agnew from Browns.

April 8, 1916
Purchased Tilly Walker from Browns.

April 12, 1916
Traded Tris Speaker to Indians for Sad Sam Jones, Fred Thomas, and $55,000.

May 1916
Sold Marty McHale to Indians.

September 2, 1916
Traded Richard Haley to Athletics for Jimmy Walsh.

February 24, 1917
Sold Smoky Joe Wood to Indians for $15,000.

December 14, 1917
Traded Vean Gregg, Merlin Kopp, Pinch Thomas, and $60,000 to Athletics for Amos Strunk, Bullet Joe Bush, and Wally Schang.

January 10, 1918
Traded Larry Gardner, Tilly Walker, and Hick Cady to Athletics in Exchange for Stuffy McInnis.

April 1, 1918
Traded Rube Foster to Reds for Dave Shean; Rube Foster refused to report to Reds and Red Sox sent cash (April 1918) to complete trade.

August 9, 1918
Purchased Jack Coffey from Tigers.

December 18, 1918
Traded Ernie Shore and Duffy Lewis to Yankees for Frank Gilhooley, Slim Love, Ray Caldwell, Roxy Walters, and $15,000.

January 1919
Sold Sam Agnew to Senators.
Sold Walter Barbare to Pirates.
Sold Dutch Leonard to Tigers.
Sold Fred Thomas to Athletics.

January 17, 1919
Traded Hal Janvrin and cash to Senators for Eddie Ainsmith and George Dumont.
Traded Eddie Ainsmith, Chick Shorten, and Slim Love to Tigers for Ossie Vitt.

February 28, 1919
Sold Wally Mayer to Browns for $5,000.

May 24, 1919
Purchased Bill James from Tigers.

June 13, 1919
Purchased Bill Lamar from Yankees.

June 27, 1919
Traded Amos Strunk and Jack Barry to Athletics for Braggo Roth and Red Shannon.

July 29, 1919
Traded Carl Mays to Yankees for Allen Russell, Bob McGraw, and $40,000.

August 18, 1919
Lost Bill James to White Sox on waivers.

January 1920
Purchased Tim Hendryx from Browns.

January 3, 1920
Sold Babe Ruth to Yankees for $100,000.

January 20, 1920
Traded Braggo Roth and Red Shannon to Senators for Mike Menosky, Harry Harper, and Eddie Foster.

March 1920
Sold Bill Lamar to Dodgers.

May 1920
Purchased Gene Bailey from Braves.

June 1920
Claimed Elmer Myers from Indians on waivers.

June 7, 1920
Claimed Jigger Statz from Giants on waivers.

December 15, 1920
Traded Waite Hoyt, Harry Harper, Wally Schang, and Mike McNally to Yankees for Muddy Ruel, Del Pratt, Sammy Vick, and Hank Thormahlen.

March 4, 1921
Traded Harry Hooper to White Sox for Shano Collins and Nemo Leibold.

May 20, 1921
Claimed Allen Sothoron from Browns on waivers.

June 1921*
Lost Allen Sothoron to Indians on waivers.

December 20, 1921
Traded Everett Scott, Bullet Joe Bush, and Sad Sam Jones to Yankees for Roger Peckinpaugh, Jack Quinn, Rip Collins, and Bill Piercy.

December 24, 1921
Traded Stuffy McInnis to Indians for George Burns, Joe Harris, and Elmer Smith.

January 10, 1922
Received Frank O'Rourke from Senators as part of 3-team trade in which Senators sent Jose Acosta and Bing Miller to Athletics; Athletics sent Joe Dugan to Red Sox; and Red Sox sent Roger Peckinpaugh to Senators.

February 24, 1922
Claimed Alex Ferguson from Yankees on waivers.

July 23, 1922
Traded Joe Dugan and Elmer Smith to Yankees for Chick Fewster, Elmer Miller, Johnny Mitchell, Lefty O'Doul, and $50,000.

August 15, 1922
Lost Eddie Foster to Browns on waivers.

October 24, 1922
Lost Frank O'Rourke to Tigers on waivers.

October 30, 1922
Traded Del Pratt and Rip Collins to Tigers for Carl Holling, Howard Ehmke, Danny Clark, Babe Herman, and $25,000.

January 3, 1923
Traded George Pipgras and Harvey Hendrick to Yankees for Al DeVormer and cash.

January 30, 1923
Traded Herb Pennock to Yankees for Camp Skinner, Norm McMillan, George Murray, and $50,000.

February 10, 1923
Traded Muddy Ruel and Allen Russell to Senators for Val Picinich, Howie Shanks, and Ed Goebel.

April 20, 1923
Purchased Ira Flagstead from Tigers.

May 26, 1923
Lost Nemo Leibold to Senators on waivers.

August 8, 1923
Traded $4,000 and 2 players to be named to Danville (III) for Red Ruffing.

November 1923
Sold Johnny Mitchell to Dodgers.

January 7, 1924
Traded George Burns, Roxy Walters, and Chick Fewster to Indians for Dan Boone, Steve O'Neill, Joe Connolly, and Bill Wambsganss.

January 12, 1924
Purchased Bobby Veach from Tigers.

April 14, 1924
Traded Norm McMillan to Browns for Homer Ezzell.

August 17, 1924
Traded Oscar Fuhr to San Antonio (Texas) for Clarence Winters.

September 10, 1924
Purchased Ted Wingfield from Senators.

December 10, 1924
Traded Howie Shanks to Yankees for Mike McNally.

December 11, 1924
Traded Mike McNally to Senators for Doc Prothro.

December 15, 1924
Lost Steve O'Neill to Yankees on waivers.

April 26, 1925
Traded Joe Harris to Senators for Paul Zahniser and Roy Carlyle.

May 5, 1925
Traded Bobby Veach and Alex Ferguson to Yankees for Ray Francis and $9,000.

July 10, 1925
Lost Jack Quinn to Athletics on waivers.

July 11, 1925
Purchased John Bischoff from White Sox.

December 9, 1925
Traded Tex Vache and Homer Ezzell to Tigers for Fred Haney.

December 12, 1925
Sold Bill Wambsganss to Athletics for $4,000.

February 10, 1926
Sold Val Picinich to Reds.

April 7, 1926
Purchased Topper Rigney from Tigers.

June 15, 1926
Lost Roy Carlyle to Yankees on waivers.
Traded Tom Jenkins and Howard Ehmke to Athletics for Fred Heimach, Slim Harriss, and Baby Doll Jacobson.

July 31, 1926
Jack Tobin signed as a free agent.

November 1926
Purchased Frank Welch from Athletics.

May 2, 1927
Traded Topper Rigney to Senators for Buddy Myer.

June 12, 1927
Sold Baby Doll Jacobson to Indians.

July 12, 1927
Sold Fred Haney to Cubs.

December 1927
Lost Grover Hartley to Indians on waivers.

December 15, 1927
Purchased Ken Williams from Browns for $10,000.

April 25, 1928
Traded Hal Wiltse to Browns for Wally Gerber.

September 1928*
Purchased Ed Durham from Mobile (SA).

October 3, 1928

Major League Draft

Selected Bob Barrett from Buffalo (IL).
Selected Jerry Standaert from Memphis (SA).

November 22, 1928
Purchased Bill Bayne from Indians.

December 15, 1928
Traded Buddy Myer to Senators for Milt Gaston, Hod Lisenbee, Bobby Reeves, Grant Gillis, and Elliott Bigelow.

May 23, 1929
Traded Doug Taitt to White Sox for Bill Barrett.

May 25, 1929
Lost Ira Flagstead to Senators on waivers.

October 7, 1929

Major League Draft

Selected Otto Miller from Milwaukee (AA).
Selected George Smith from Seattle (PCL).
Selected Bill Sweeney from Toronto (IL).

January 29, 1930
Sold Ken Williams to Yankees.

April 26, 1930
Traded Bill Barrett to Senators for Earl Webb.

May 6, 1930
Traded Red Ruffing to Yankees for Cedric Durst and $50,000.

September 30, 1930

Major League Draft

Selected Jim Brillheart from Minneapolis (AA).
Selected Wilcy Moore from St Paul (AA).

December 15, 1930
Purchased Muddy Ruel from Senators.

January 1931
Lost Johnnie Heving to Athletics on waivers.
Lost Bill Regan to Pirates on waivers.

February 3, 1931
Sold Phil Todt to Athletics.

August 31, 1931
Traded Muddy Ruel to Tigers for Marty McManus.

December 2, 1931
Traded Milt Gaston to White Sox for Bob Weiland.

April 29, 1932
Traded Charlie Berry and Jack Rothrock to White Sox for Bennie Tate, Smead Jolley, Johnny Watwood, and $7,500.

May 14, 1932
Pete Donohue released.

June 5, 1932
Traded Danny MacFayden to Yankees for Ivy Andrews, Hank Johnson, and $50,000.

June 10, 1932
Traded Jack Russell to Indians for Pete Appleton.

June 12, 1932
Traded Earl Webb to Tigers for Dale Alexander and Roy Johnson.

August 1, 1932
Traded Wilcy Moore to Yankees for Gordon Rhodes.

December 15, 1932
Traded Ed Durham and Hal Rhyne to White Sox for Johnny Hodapp, Greg Mulleavy, Bob Fothergill, and Bob Seeds.

January 7, 1933
Bernie Friberg signed as a free agent.
Traded Al Van Camp and cash to Louisville (AA) for Merv Shea.

April 13, 1933
Sold Greg Mulleavy to Buffalo (IL).

May 9, 1933
Traded Merv Shea and cash to Browns for Rick Ferrell and Lloyd Brown.

May 12, 1933
Purchased George Pipgras and Billy Werber from Yankees for $100,000.

June 17, 1933
Purchased Lou Legett from Albany (IL).

July 5, 1933*
Purchased Bucky Walters from Mission (PCL).

July 7, 1933
Bob Fothergill released.

July 27, 1933
Joe Judge signed as a free agent.

August 21, 1933
Curt Fullerton signed as a free agent.

October 2, 1933
Marty McManus released.

October 12, 1933
Traded Lloyd Brown to Indians for Bill Cissell.

October 30, 1933
Sold Johnny Hodapp to Cardinals.

October 31, 1933
Sold Tom Oliver to Baltimore (IL).

December 12, 1933
Traded Bob Kline, Rabbit Warstler, and $125,000 to Athletics for Lefty Grove, Rube Walberg, and Max Bishop.

December 14, 1933
Traded Ivy Andrews, Smead Jolley, and cash to Browns for Carl Reynolds.

January 13, 1934
Sold Curt Fullerton to Kansas City (AA).

January 20, 1934
Herb Pennock signed as a free agent.

May 14, 1934
Joe Judge released.

May 15, 1934
Traded Freddie Muller and $20,000 to Yankees for Lyn Lary.

May 25, 1934
Traded Bob Weiland, Bob Seeds, and $25,000 to Indians for Wes Ferrell and Dick Porter.

June 14, 1934
Sold Bucky Walters to Phillies.

October 26, 1934
Traded Lyn Lary and $225,000 to Senators for Joe Cronin.

November 22, 1934
Sold Ed Morgan to Cardinals.

January 14, 1935
Purchased Bing Miller from Athletics.

February 1, 1935
Traded Bill Cissell to Portland (PCL) for Jack Wilson.

April 16, 1935
Moe Berg signed as a free agent.

May 1, 1935
Purchased Dib Williams from Athletics.

May 27, 1935
Traded Moose Solters and cash to Browns for Ski Melillo.

June 2, 1935
George Pipgras released.

June 30, 1935
Purchased Joe Cascarella from Athletics.

October 1, 1935

Major League Draft

Selected Manny Salvo from Dodgers.

November 22, 1935
Purchased Bobby Doerr and George Myatt from Hollywood (PCL) for $75,000.

December 10, 1935
Traded Gordon Rhodes, George Savino, and $150,000 to Athletics Jimmie Foxx and Johnny Marcum.

December 17, 1935
Traded Carl Reynolds and Roy Johnson to Senators for Heinie Manush.

January 4, 1936
Traded Hank Johnson, Al Niemiec, and $75,000 to Athletics for Doc Cramer and Eric McNair.

May 13, 1936
Purchased Mike Meola from Browns.

June 4, 1936
Lost Johnny Welch to Pirates on waivers.

June 13, 1936
Traded Joe Cascarella to Senators for Jack Russell.

August 25, 1936
Returned George Myatt to San Diego (PCL).

September 8, 1936
Purchased Archie McKain from Indians.

September 27, 1936
Heinie Manush and Bing Miller released.

December 2, 1936
Johnny Peacock signed as a free agent.
Purchased Gene Desautels and Manny Salvo from San Diego (PCL).

December 9, 1936
Traded Billy Werber to Athletics for Pinky Higgins.

February 17, 1937
Sold Babe Dahlgren to Yankees.

March 20, 1937
Jack Russell released.

April 15, 1937
Sold John Kroner to Indians.

June 11, 1937
Traded Rick Ferrell, Wes Ferrell, and Mel Almada to Senators for Ben Chapman and Bobo Newsom.

July 16, 1937
Tommy Thomas signed as a free agent.

August 20, 1937
Sold Dusty Cooke to Reds.

October 4, 1937
Tommy Thomas and Rube Walberg released.

October 5, 1937

Major League Draft

Lost Joe Walsh to Braves.

December 2, 1937
Traded Bobo Newsom, Red Kress, and Buster Mills to Browns for Joe Vosmik.

December 3, 1937
Purchased Nig Lipscomb from Browns.

February 11, 1938
Pat Malone signed as a free agent.

April 16, 1938
Purchased Roy Parmelee from Cubs.

May 14, 1938
Bob Daughters released.

August 1, 1938
Sold Joe Gonzales to Indians.
Purchased Joe Heving from Indians.

August 2, 1938
Traded Johnny Marcum and $20,000 to Buffalo (IL) for Bill Harris.

August 12, 1938
Traded Lee Rogers to Dodgers for Johnnie Chambers.

October 4, 1938

Major League Draft

Lost Roy Parmelee to Athletics.

December 6, 1938
Purchased Chief Hogsett from Senators.
Traded Johnny Marcum to Browns for Tom Carey.

December 7, 1938
Purchased Phil Weintraub from Phillies.

December 15, 1938
Sold Bill Harris to Giants.
Traded Ben Chapman to Indians for Denny Galehouse and Tommy Irwin.
Traded Pinky Higgins and Archie McKain to Tigers for Elden Auker, Jake Wade, and Chet Morgan.

December 21, 1938
Traded Eric McNair to White Sox for Boze Berger.

February 18, 1939
Sold George Dickey to Oklahoma City (TL).

March 27, 1939
Purchased Monte Weaver from Senators.

May 8, 1939
Purchased Lou Finney from Athletics.

June 14, 1939
Purchased Roy Parmelee from Athletics.

June 15, 1939
Sold Bill Kerksieck to Phillies.

June 17, 1939
Received Fred Sington from Dodgers.

July 18, 1939
Sold Pee Wee Reese to Dodgers for $35,000 and 4 players.

August 12, 1939
Purchased Bill Butland from Minneapolis (AA).

September 6, 1939
Sold Jake Wade to Browns.

November 12, 1939
Purchased Dom DiMaggio from San Francisco (PCL).

December 8, 1939
Purchased Marv Owen from White Sox.

December 26, 1939
Sold Boze Berger to Dodgers.

January 31, 1940
Moe Berg released.

February 8, 1940
Sold Elden Auker to Browns.

February 12, 1940
Sold Joe Vosmik to Dodgers for $25,000.

April 14, 1940
Sold Ted Olson to Phillies.

April 25, 1940
Purchased Joe Glenn from Browns.

April 28, 1940
Sold Art Mahan to Phillies.

July 23, 1940
Larry Jansen granted free agency.

August 2, 1940
Sold Wes Flowers to Dodgers.

August 12, 1940
Purchased Bill Fleming from Hollywood (PCL).

August 18, 1940
Claimed Charlie Gelbert from Senators on waivers.

September 5, 1940
Received Skeeter Newsome from Phillies for UFC.
Traded Al Brazle to Cardinals for Mike Ryba.

September 11, 1940
Sold Red Nonnenkamp to Yankees.

October 1, 1940

Major League Draft

Selected Oscar Judd from Cardinals.

December 3, 1940
Sold Denny Galehouse and Fritz Ostermueller to Browns.

December 12, 1940
Purchased Pete Fox from Tigers.
Traded Doc Cramer to Senators for Gee Walker.
Traded Gene Desautels, Jim Bagby, and Gee Walker to Indians for Frankie Pytlak, Odell Hale, and Joe Dobson.

February 3, 1941
Sold Joe Heving to Indians.

March 22, 1941
Alex Mustaikis released.

April 1, 1941
Sold Al Flair to Baltimore (IL).

June 19, 1941
Lost Odell Hale to Giants on waivers.

June 30, 1941
Purchased Nels Potter from Athletics.

September 8, 1941
Purchased Eddie Pellagrini from San Diego (PCL).

September 30, 1941

Major League Draft

Selected Bill Conroy from Oakland (PCL).

December 10, 1941
Purchased Mace Brown from Dodgers.

December 13, 1941
Traded Stan Spence and Jack Wilson to Senators for Ken Chase and Johnny Welaj.

December 22, 1941
Sold Bill Fleming to Cubs.

January 14, 1942
Moe Berg released.

April 10, 1942
Emerson Dickman released.

June 1, 1942
Lost Jimmie Foxx to Cubs on waivers.

September 8, 1942
Purchased Eddie Lake from Cardinals.

November 2, 1942

Major League Draft

Selected Herb Bremer from Little Rock (SA).
Lost Eli Hodkey to Phillies.
Selected Don Lang from Yankees.
Lost Nels Potter to Browns.

July 6, 1943
Traded Dee Miles and cash to San Francisco (PCL) for George Metkovich.

September 28, 1943
Purchased Eddie Mayo from Athletics.

October 15, 1943
Al Simmons released.

November 1, 1943

Major League Draft

Selected Clem Hausmann from Yankees.
Lost Eddie Mayo to Tigers.

November 6, 1943

Minor League Draft

Selected Nick Polly from Reds.

December 4, 1943
Purchased Bob Johnson from Senators.

April 13, 1944
Lost Tony Lupien to Phillies on waivers.

May 7, 1944
Traded Ford Garrison to Athletics for Hal Wagner.

June 10, 1944
Traded Stan Partenheimer to Cardinals for Frank Barrett.

June 11, 1944
Sold Johnny Peacock to Phillies.

August 23, 1944
Purchased Clem Dreisewerd from Cardinals.

November 1, 1944

Major League Draft

Selected Loyd Christopher from Seattle (PCL).
Lost Vance Dinges to Phillies.
Selected Billy Holm from Cubs.

November 7, 1944

Minor League Draft

Selected Lindsay Deal from Atlanta (SA).

May 26, 1945
Lost Loyd Christopher to Cubs on waivers.

May 31, 1945
Lost Oscar Judd to Phillies on waivers.

July 27, 1945
Sold Lou Finney to Browns.

August 10, 1945*
Claimed Red Steiner from Indians on waivers.

December 12, 1945
Sold Skeeter Newsome to Phillies.
Traded Vic Johnson and cash to Indians for Jim Bagby.

December 18, 1945
Dolph Camilli released.

December 27, 1945
Bob Johnson released.

1946
Bud Sheely released.

January 3, 1946
Traded Eddie Lake to Tigers for Rudy York.

January 22, 1946
Sold Jim Tabor to Phillies.

March 1946
Sold Frank Barrett to Braves.

March 29, 1946
Herb Bremer, Pete Fox, and Bob Garbark released.
Lost Emmett O'Neill to Cubs on waivers.

May 9, 1946*
Bob Klinger signed as a free agent.

May 19, 1946
Purchased Pinky Higgins from Tigers.

June 6, 1946
Joe Cronin released.

June 18, 1946
Purchased Bill Zuber from Yankees.

July 1946
Traded Bill Howerton and Don Lang to Cardinals for Jim Gleeson.

July 23, 1946
Tom Carey released.
Purchased Wally Moses from White Sox.

August 5, 1946
Frankie Pytlak released.

October 29, 1946
Mace Brown and Mike Ryba released.

October 30, 1946
Charlie Wagner released.

November 1, 1946

Major League Draft

Lost Virgil Stallcup to Reds.

November 10, 1946

Minor League Draft

Lost Grady Wilson to Cardinals.

November 17, 1946

Minor League Draft

Lost Tom Poholsky to Cardinals.

December 17, 1946
Pinky Higgins released.

February 10, 1947
Sold Jim Bagby to Pirates.

March 1947*
Frankie Hayes signed as a free agent.

April 2, 1947
Sold George Metkovich to Indians.

April 15, 1947*
Johnny Murphy signed as a free agent.

May 14, 1947
Sold Tom McBride to Senators.

May 20, 1947
Traded Hal Wagner to Tigers for Birdie Tebbetts.

May 21, 1947
Frankie Hayes released.

June 1947
Dale Long signed as a free agent.

June 14, 1947
Traded Rudy York to White Sox for Jake Jones.

June 20, 1947
Purchased Denny Galehouse from Browns.

August 9, 1947
Traded Lum Harris, Jack Aragon, and Frank Genovese to Giants for Augie Bergamo, Ken Jungels, and Russ Rolandson.

September 24, 1947
Bob Klinger released.

September 25, 1947
Traded cash and 2 players to be named later to San Francisco (PCL) for Neill Sheridan; San Francisco (PCL) received Tommy Fine and Strick Shofner (October 22, 1947).

October 1947
Sold Paul Campbell to Tigers.

October 20, 1947
Johnny Murphy released.
Eddie Smith released.

November 10, 1947

Major League Draft

Lost Bill Kennedy to Indians.
Selected Babe Martin from Browns.
Selected Johnny Ostrowski from Cubs.

November 17, 1947
Traded Roy Partee, Jim Wilson, Al Widmar, Eddie Pellagrini, Pete Layden, Joe Ostrowski, and $310,000 to Browns for Vern Stephens and Jack Kramer.

November 18, 1947
Traded Sam Dente, Clem Dreisewerd, Bill Sommers, and $65,000 to Browns for Ellis Kinder and Billy Hitchcock.

December 10, 1947
Traded Al Kozar and Leon Culberson to Senators for Stan Spence.

January 20, 1948*
Purchased Tommy O'Brien from Cardinals.

March 26, 1948
Sold Don Gutteridge to Pirates.

May 15, 1948
Returned Johnny Ostrowski to Cubs.

July 26, 1948
Claimed Earl Caldwell from White Sox on waivers.

September 19, 1948
Purchased Lou Stringer from White Sox.

November 10, 1948

Major League Draft

Lost Irv Medlinger to Browns.

November 15, 1948
Wally Moses released.

November 24, 1948

Minor League Draft

Lost Jack Faszholz to Cardinals.
Lost Ray Jablonski to Cardinals.
Lost Dale Long to Tigers.

May 8, 1949
Traded Stan Spence and cash to Browns for Al Zarilla.

May 11, 1949
Denny Galehouse released.

May 17, 1949*
Traded Cot Deal to Cardinals for Charlie Harrington.

June 13, 1949
Traded Sam Mele and Mickey Harris to Senators for Walt Masterson.

September 20, 1949*
Traded John Hofmann and cash to Seattle (PCL) for Charley Schanz.

October 2, 1949
Sold Jim Davis to Seattle (PCL).

October 8, 1949
Traded Billy Hitchcock to Athletics for Buddy Rosar.

October 12, 1949
Purchased Bob Gillespie from White Sox.

October 13, 1949
Sold Windy McCall to Pirates.

November 17, 1949

Major League Draft

Lost Sid Schacht to Browns.
Lost George Strickland to Pirates.

December 1, 1949
Claimed Al Papai from Browns on waivers.

March 26, 1950
Sold Jack Kramer to Giants.

April 18, 1950
Ken Keltner signed as a free agent.

May 8, 1950
Traded Tommy O'Brien and Merl Combs to Senators for Clyde Vollmer.

May 9, 1950
Sold Fritz Dorish to Browns.

May 12, 1950
Lost Frank Quinn to Senators on waivers.

June 6, 1950
Ken Keltner released.

July 1950
Sold Babe Martin to Tigers.

July 2, 1950
Phil Marchildon signed as a free agent.

July 5, 1950
Lost Al Papai to Cardinals on waivers.
Lost Charley Schanz to Browns on waivers.

July 21, 1950
Phil Marchildon released.

September 10, 1950
Purchased Harry Taylor from Dodgers.

October 1, 1950*
Earl Johnson released.

October 9, 1950
Traded Mike Palm and cash to White Sox for Bill Evans.

November 16, 1950

Major League Draft

Lost Joe DeMaestri to White Sox.
Selected Paul Hinrichs from Yankees.

November 27, 1950
Lou Boudreau signed as a free agent.

December 4, 1950

Minor League Draft

Selected Ralph Brickner from Portsmouth (PML).

December 10, 1950
Traded Al Zarilla, Joe Dobson, and Dick Littlefield to White Sox for Bill Wight and Ray Scarborough.

December 13, 1950
Sold Birdie Tebbetts to Indians.

December 18, 1950
Purchased Mike Guerra from Athletics.

February 5, 1951
Claimed Al Evans from Senators on waivers.

May 7, 1951
Traded Mike Guerra to Senators for Len Okrie and $25,000.

May 17, 1951
Traded Jim Suchecki, Matt Batts, $100,000, and a PTNBL to Browns for Les Moss; Browns received Jim McDonald (July 18, 1951).

August 6, 1951
Claimed Aaron Robinson from Tigers on waivers.

October 23, 1951
Buddy Rosar released.

October 31, 1951
Lou Boudreau released.

November 13, 1951
Traded Mel Hoderlein and Chuck Stobbs to White Sox for Randy Gumpert and Don Lenhardt.

November 19, 1951

Major League Draft

Selected Hal Bevan from Pirates.
Lost George Wilson to White Sox.

November 28, 1951
Traded Les Moss and Tom Wright to Browns for Gus Niarhos and Ken Wood.

May 3, 1952
Lost Hal Bevan to Athletics on waivers.

May 12, 1952
Purchased Del Wilber from Phillies.

May 29, 1952
Purchased Windy McCall from Pirates.

June 3, 1952
Traded Bill Wight, Walt Dropo, Fred Hatfield, Johnny Pesky, and Don Lenhardt to Tigers for Dizzy Trout, George Kell, Johnny Lipon, and Hoot Evers.

June 9, 1952
Traded Ken Wood to Senators for Archie Wilson.

June 10, 1952
Traded Walt Masterson and Randy Gumpert to Senators for Sid Hudson.

June 25, 1952
Claimed Paul Lehner from Indians on waivers.

June 27, 1952
Purchased Al Benton from San Diego (PCL).

June 30, 1952
Claimed George Schmees from Browns on waivers.

July 5, 1952
Paul Lehner released.

July 24, 1952
Ken Holcombe signed as a free agent.

August 22, 1952
Sold Ray Scarborough to Yankees.

August 31, 1952
Purchased Al Zarilla from Browns.

October 2, 1952
Claimed Bill Werle from Cardinals on waivers.

October 15, 1952
Lou Boudreau released.

December 1, 1952

Major League Draft

Selected Jack Merson from Pirates.

February 9, 1953
Traded Vern Stephens to White Sox for Hal Brown, Bill Kennedy and Marv Grissom.

April 1, 1953*
Sold Windy McCall to San Francisco (PCL).

April 22, 1953
Sold Clyde Vollmer to Senators.

May 12, 1953
Purchased Floyd Baker from Senators.

July 1, 1953
Lost Marv Grissom to Giants on waivers.

September 8, 1953
Sold Johnny Lipon to Browns.

November 24, 1953
Dom DiMaggio released.

December 9, 1953
Traded Mickey McDermott and Tom Umphlett to Senators for Jackie Jensen.

December 13, 1953
Joe Dobson signed as a free agent.

February 26, 1954
Mickey Owen signed as a free agent.

May 12, 1954
Purchased Don Lenhardt from Orioles.

May 18, 1954
Lost Hoot Evers to Giants on waivers.

May 23, 1954
Traded George Kell to White Sox for Grady Hatton and $100,000.

July 15, 1954*
Sold Gus Niarhos to Phillies.

July 18, 1954
Lost Floyd Baker to Phillies on waivers.

July 25, 1954
Purchased Tom Hurd from White Sox.

July 29, 1954
Claimed Sam Mele from Orioles on waivers.

October 14, 1954
Purchased Owen Friend from Indians.

November 22, 1954

Major League Draft

Lost Ben Flowers to Tigers.
Selected Joe Trimble from Pirates.

December 14, 1954
Traded Del Wilber to Giants for Billy Klaus.

December 24, 1954
Sold Charlie Maxwell to Orioles.

January 11, 1955
Mickey Owen released.

March 29, 1955
Eddie Joost signed as a free agent.

April 7, 1955
Sid Hudson released.

May 10, 1955
Sold Hersh Freeman to Reds.

May 11, 1955
Sold Hal Brown to Oakland (PCL).
Returned Joe Trimble to Pirates.

June 12, 1955
Sold Owen Friend to Cubs.

June 23, 1955
Sold Sam Mele to Reds.

October 3, 1955
Eddie Joost released.

November 8, 1955
Traded Karl Olson, Dick Brodowski, Tex Clevenger, Neil Chrisley, and Al Curtis to Senators for Mickey Vernon, Bob Porterfield, Johnny Schmitz, and Tom Umphlett.

November 27, 1955

Minor League Draft

Lost Ed Mayer to Cardinals.

December 4, 1955
Lost Ellis Kinder to Cardinals on waivers.

February 8, 1956
Purchased Pumpsie Green from Stockton (CL).

March 12, 1956
Dizzy Trout released.

May 11, 1956
Sold Grady Hatton to Cardinals.

May 14, 1956
Sold Johnny Schmitz to Orioles.

June 4, 1956
Purchased Max Surkont from Cardinals.

June 25, 1956
Purchased Fritz Dorish from Orioles.

August 20, 1956
Sold Max Surkont to Giants.

September 9, 1956
Purchased Gene Mauch from Cubs.
Purchased Rudy Minarcin from Reds.

October 9, 1956
Fritz Dorish released.

December 3, 1956

Major League Draft

Lost Bob Smith to Cardinals.
Selected Jack Spring from Phillies.

January 1957
Traded Bill Henry to Cubs for Frank Kellert and cash.

March 14, 1957
Traded Eli Grba and Gordie Windhorn to Yankees for Bill Renna.

April 13, 1957
Claimed Russ Meyer from Reds on waivers.

April 29, 1957
Traded Milt Bolling, Russ Kemmerer, and Faye Throneberry to Senators for Bob Chakales and Dean Stone.

April 30, 1957
Purchased Karl Olson from Senators.
Traded Karl Olson to Tigers for Jack Phillips.

May 13, 1957
Russ Meyer released.

June 14, 1957
Traded Billy Goodman to Orioles for Mike Fornieles.

December 2, 1957

Major League Draft

Selected Chuck Churn from Pirates.

December 17, 1957
Gene Mauch released.

January 23, 1958
Traded Albie Pearson and Norm Zauchin to Senators for Pete Runnels.

January 29, 1958
Purchased Art Schult from Senators.
Lost Mickey Vernon to Indians on waivers.

March 26, 1958
Lost Chuck Churn to Indians on waivers.

May 1, 1958
Traded Ken Aspromonte to Senators for Lou Berberet.

May 7, 1958
Sold Bob Porterfield to Pirates.

May 12, 1958
Lost George Susce to Tigers on waivers.

June 24, 1958
Traded Jack Spring to Senators for Bud Byerly; Jack Spring returned to Red Sox (July 11, 1958); Red Sox sent Joe Albanese (July 11, 1958) to complete trade.

July 20, 1958*
Traded Jack Spring to Indians for Stu Locklin.

October 6, 1958
Sent Al Schroll to Phillies for UFC.

December 2, 1958
Traded Lou Berberet to Tigers for Herb Moford.
Traded Jim Piersall to Indians for Vic Wertz and Gary Geiger.

December 15, 1958
Traded Billy Klaus to Orioles for Jim Busby.

March 9, 1959
Traded Bob Smith to Cubs for Chuck Tanner.

March 15, 1959
Traded Dean Stone to Cardinals for Nelson Chittum.

April 10, 1959
Willard Nixon released.

May 2, 1959
Traded Dave Sisler and Ted Lepcio to Tigers for Billy Hoeft.

May 7, 1959
Al Schroll returned from Phillies.

May 21, 1959
Claimed Bobby Avila from Orioles on waivers.

June 11, 1959
Traded Billy Consolo and Murray Wall to Senators for Herb Plews and Dick Hyde; Dick Hyde returned to Senators and Murray Wall returned to Red Sox (June 14, 1959).

June 15, 1959
Traded Billy Hoeft to Orioles for Jack Harshman.

July 15, 1959*
Sold Art Schult to Cubs.

July 16, 1959
Jerry Zimmerman released.

July 21, 1959
Lost Bobby Avila to Braves on waivers.

July 26, 1959
Traded Bud Byerly to Giants for Billy Muffett and cash.

July 30, 1959
Lost Jack Harshman to Indians on waivers.

August 1, 1959
Sold Ken McBride to White Sox.

September 9, 1959
Sold Chuck Tanner to Indians.

November 3, 1959
Traded Frank Baumann to White Sox for Ron Jackson.

November 21, 1959
Traded Dick Gernert to Cubs for Jim Marshall and Dave Hillman.

December 1, 1959
Traded Al Schroll to Cubs for Bobby Thomson.

December 3, 1959
Traded Pete Daley to Athletics for Tom Sturdivant.

January 8, 1960
Traded Leo Kiely to Indians for Ray Webster.

March 16, 1960
Traded Sammy White and Jim Marshall to Indians for Russ Nixon; Sammy White refused to report to Indians; trade voided (March 25, 1960).

March 29, 1960
Traded Jim Marshall to Giants for Al Worthington.

April 26, 1960
Jim Busby released.

May 6, 1960
Traded Nelson Chittum to Dodgers for Rip Repulski.

May 17, 1960
Traded Ron Jackson to Braves for Ray Boone.

June 9, 1960
Traded Gene Stephens to Orioles for Willie Tasby.

June 13, 1960
Traded Marty Keough and Ted Bowsfield to Indians for Russ Nixon and Carroll Hardy.

July 1, 1960
Bobby Thomson released.

September 1, 1960
Sent Al Worthington to White Sox for UFC.

September 14, 1960
Ray Boone released.

November 28, 1960

Major League Draft

Selected Billy Harrell from Cardinals.

December 14, 1960

Expansion Draft

Lost Jerry Casale, Jim Fregosi, Fred Newman, and Ed Sadowski to Angels.
Lost Jim Mahoney, Tom Sturdivant, Haywood Sullivan, and Willie Tasby to Senators.

December 15, 1960
Traded Frank Sullivan to Phillies for Gene Conley.

May 17, 1961
Joe Ginsberg signed as a free agent.

June 15, 1961
Sold Sammy White to Braves.

June 26, 1961
Rip Repulski released.

September 8, 1961
Lost Vic Wertz to Tigers on waivers.

October 13, 1961
Sent Dave Hillman to Reds for UFC.

October 20, 1961
Tom Brewer and Joe Ginsberg released.

November 26, 1961
Traded Don Buddin to Astros for Eddie Bressoud.

November 27, 1961

Major League Draft

Lost Marlan Coughtry to Angels.

March 24, 1962
Traded Tom Borland to Astros for Dave Philley.

April 17, 1962
Dave Hillman returned from Reds.

April 26, 1962
Sold Dave Hillman to Mets.

May 8, 1962
Sold Ted Wills to Reds.

June 12, 1962
Traded Tom Umphlett and cash to Yankees for Billy Gardner.

August 14, 1962
Dave Philley released.

September 7, 1962
Lost Galen Cisco to Mets on waivers.

November 20, 1962
Traded Jim Pagliaroni and Don Schwall to Pirates for Dick Stuart and Jack Lamabe.

November 26, 1962
Traded Pete Runnels to Astros for Roman Mejias.

December 10, 1962
Traded Carroll Hardy to Astros for Dick Williams.

December 11, 1962
Traded Tracy Stallard, Pumpsie Green, and a PTNBL to Mets for Felix Mantilla; Mets received Al Moran (January 14, 1963).

March 1963*
Bob Heffner returned from Reds.

April 1963*
Purchased Bobby Smith from Cardinals.

June 9, 1963
Ike Delock released.

June 14, 1963
Sold Mike Fornieles to Twins.

July 24, 1963
Bob Turley signed as a free agent.

October 2, 1963
Billy Gardner released.

October 4, 1963
Chet Nichols released.

October 14, 1963
Bob Turley released.

December 2, 1963

First-Year Draft

Selected Billy Rohr from Pirates.
Selected Reggie Smith from Twins.
Lost Luke Walker to Pirates.

1964
Bobby Smith released.

April 25, 1964
Gene Conley released.

June 4, 1964
Traded Lou Clinton to Angels for Lee Thomas.

August 5, 1964
Al Smith signed as a free agent.

September 6, 1964
Sold Wilbur Wood to Pirates.

October 14, 1964
Al Smith and Dick Williams released.

November 29, 1964
Traded Dick Stuart to Phillies for Dennis Bennett.

November 30, 1964

Minor League Draft

Selected Gary Waslewski from Pirates.

March 30, 1965
Purchased Lenny Green from Orioles.

April 17, 1965*
Traded Hal Kolstad to Angels for Bob Duliba.

May 3, 1965
Claimed John Sanders from Athletics on waivers.

May 7, 1965
Lost Bill Schlesinger to Athletics on waivers.

September 14, 1965
Traded Jack Lamabe to Astros for Bucky Brandon.

October 4, 1965
Traded Bill Monbouquette to Tigers for George Smith, George Thomas, and a PTNBL; Red Sox received Jackie Moore (October 13, 1966).

October 15, 1965
Purchased Jose Santiago from Athletics.

November 29, 1965

Major League Draft

Lost Gary Geiger to Braves.
Lost Bob Heffner to Indians.
Selected Ken Sanders from Athletics.

November 30, 1965
Frank Malzone released.
Traded Eddie Bressoud to Mets for Joe Christopher.

December 15, 1965
Traded Lee Thomas, Arnold Earley, and a PTNBL to Braves for Bob Sadowski and Dan Osinski; Atlanta Braves received Jay Ritchie (January 11, 1966).

April 3, 1966
Traded Felix Mantilla to Astros for Eddie Kasko.

April 6, 1966
Traded Russ Nixon and Chuck Schilling to Twins for Dick Stigman and a PTNBL; Red Sox received Jose Calero (April 17, 1966).

May 1966
Ed Rakow signed as a free agent.

May 12, 1966
Traded Bob Duliba and Fred Holmes to Athletics for Syd O'Brien, Arlie Burge and Stan Bledsoe.

June 2, 1966
Traded Dick Radatz to Indians for Don McMahon and Lee Stange.

June 6, 1966
Galen Cisco signed as a free agent.

June 13, 1966
Traded Jim Gosger, Ken Sanders, and Guido Grilli to Athletics for John Wyatt, Rollie Sheldon, and Jose Tartabull.

June 14, 1966
Traded Earl Wilson and Joe Christopher to Tigers for Don Demeter and a PTNBL; Red Sox received Julio Navarro (June 21, 1966).

August 15, 1966
Purchased Bill Short from Orioles.
Traded cash and 2 players to be named later to Reds for Hank Fischer; Reds received Dick Stigman and Rollie Sheldon (December 15, 1966).

September 7, 1966
Purchased Garry Roggenburk from Twins.

October 17, 1966
Sold Bill Short to Pirates.

October 21, 1966
Lenny Green and Eddie Kasko released.

November 28, 1966

Major League Draft

Selected Bill Landis from Athletics.

November 29, 1966

Minor League Draft

Lost Ed Connolly to Indians.
Lost Amos Otis to Mets.
Lost Mike Page to Braves.

December 1966
Traded Julio Navarro and Ed Rakow to Braves for Chris Cannizzaro and John Herrnstein.

1967
Steve Blateric released.

June 2, 1967
Traded Don McMahon and Bob Snow to White Sox for Jerry Adair.

June 4, 1967
Traded Tony Horton and Don Demeter to Indians for Gary Bell.

June 24, 1967
Traded Dennis Bennett to Mets for Al Yates and cash.

July 15, 1967
Purchased Norm Siebern from Giants.

August 3, 1967
Traded Pete Magrini and a PTNBL to Yankees for Elston Howard; Yankees received Ron Klimkowski (August 8, 1967).

August 8, 1967
Sold Bob Tillman to Yankees.

August 22, 1967
Jim Landis signed as a free agent.

August 28, 1967
Ken Harrelson signed as a free agent.
Jim Landis released.

September 1, 1967
Pete Charton released.

November 28, 1967

Major League Draft

Selected George Spriggs from Pirates.

November 30, 1967
Traded Bill Schlesinger and cash to Cubs for Ray Culp.

December 15, 1967
Traded Mike Ryan and cash to Phillies for Dick Ellsworth and Gene Oliver.

February 21, 1968
Jackie Moore released.

April 3, 1968
Dan Osinski released.

April 5, 1968
Returned George Spriggs to Pirates.

April 8, 1968
Russ Nixon signed as a free agent.

April 26, 1968
Sold Billy Rohr to Indians.

May 17, 1968
Sold John Wyatt to Yankees.

June 1968
Purchased Bill Schlesinger from Cubs.

June 27, 1968
Sold Gene Oliver to Cubs.
Purchased Juan Pizarro from Pirates.

July 31, 1968
Purchased Floyd Robinson from Athletics.

August 7, 1968
Norm Siebern released.

August 14, 1968
Sold Galen Cisco to Royals.

October 15, 1968

Expansion Draft

Lost Joe Foy to Royals (4th pick).
Lost Dave Morehead to Royals (15th pick).
Lost Gary Bell to Pilots (21st pick).
Lost Dick Baney to Pilots (33rd pick).
Lost Bucky Brandon to Pilots (44th pick).
Lost Jerry Adair to Royals (51st pick).

October 29, 1968
Elston Howard and Floyd Robinson released.

December 2, 1968

Major League Draft

Lost Bobby Mitchell to Yankees.
Lost Russ Nixon to White Sox.

December 3, 1968
Traded Gary Waslewski to Cardinals for Dick Schofield.

March 11, 1969
Traded Mark Schaeffer to Astros for Hal King.

March 18, 1969
Purchased Bill Kelso from Reds.

March 29, 1969
Returned Bill Kelso to Reds.

April 17, 1969
Jerry Stephenson released.

April 19, 1969
Traded Ken Harrelson, Juan Pizarro, and Dick Ellsworth to Indians in exchange for Sonny Siebert, Joe Azcue, and Vicente Romo.

May 5, 1969
Traded Bill Schlesinger to Phillies for Don Lock.

May 7, 1969
Sold Jose Tartabull to Athletics.

June 15, 1969
Traded Joe Azcue to Angels for Tom Satriano.

June 23, 1969
Sold Garry Roggenburk to Pilots.

July 5, 1969
Purchased Ron Kline from Giants.

September 6, 1969
Traded Mike Jackson to Phillies for Gary Wagner.

November 25, 1969
Sold Fred Wenz to Phillies.

December 1, 1969

Major League Draft
Selected Mike Derrick from Tigers.
Lost Hal King to Braves.
Lost Ken Wright to Royals.

December 13, 1969
Traded Dalton Jones to Tigers for Tommy Matchick.
Traded Syd O'Brien and Billy Farmer to White Sox for Gary Peters and Don Pavletich; Billy Farmer refused to report to White Sox and Red Sox sent Gerry Janeski (March 9, 1970) to complete trade.

1970
Ron Kline released.

April 4, 1970
Sold Russ Gibson to Giants.

May 28, 1970
Traded Tommy Matchick to Royals for Mike Fiore.

June 8, 1970
Purchased Cal Koonce from Mets.

June 15, 1970
Purchased Ron Willis and Rip Williams from Cardinals.

June 26, 1970
Purchased John Kennedy from Brewers.

June 29, 1970
Sold Lee Stange to White Sox.

July 14, 1970
Received Chuck Hartenstein from Cardinals for UFC.

September 10, 1970
Traded a PTNBL to Brewers for Bobby Bolin; Brewers received Al Yates (October 6, 1970).

October 6, 1970*
Traded Bill Landis to Cardinals for Billy McCool.

October 11, 1970
Traded Tony Conigliaro, Ray Jarvis, and Jerry Moses to Angels for Ken Tatum, Jarvis Tatum, and Doug Griffin.

October 21, 1970
Traded Dick Schofield to Cardinals for Jim Campbell.

November 30, 1970

Major League Draft
Lost Cecil Cooper to Cardinals.

December 1, 1970
Traded Mike Andrews and Luis Alvarado to White Sox for Luis Aparicio.

December 3, 1970
Purchased Don Bryant from Astros.
Traded Carmen Fanzone to Cubs for Phil Gagliano.

December 31, 1970
Sold Chuck Hartenstein to White Sox.

February 19, 1971
Traded Billy McCool to Royals for Hawk Taylor.

March 31, 1971
Traded Vicente Romo and Tony Muser to White Sox for Duane Josephson and Danny Murphy.

April 5, 1971
Cecil Cooper returned from Cardinals.

April 7, 1971
Tom Satriano, Jarvis Tatum, and Gary Wagner released.

May 17, 1971
Luis Tiant signed as a free agent.

June 28, 1971
George Thomas released.

August 17, 1971
Cal Koonce released.

October 10, 1971
Traded Jim Lonborg, Ken Brett, Billy Conigliaro, Joe Lahoud, George Scott, and Don Pavletich to Brewers for Marty Pattin, Lew Krausse, Tommy Harper, and Pat Skrable.

November 29, 1971

Major League Draft
Selected Bob Gallagher from Dodgers.

March 20, 1972
Purchased Bobby Pfeil from Brewers.
Traded Mike Fiore to Cardinals for Bob Burda.

March 22, 1972
Traded Sparky Lyle to Yankees for Danny Cater and a player to be named later; Red Sox received Mario Guerrero (June 30, 1972).

June 13, 1972
Stan Williams signed as a free agent.

August 15, 1972
Traded Chris Coletta to Angels for Andy Kosco.

August 25, 1972
Bob Burda released.

September 2, 1972
Purchased Bob Veale from Pirates.

September 23, 1972
Stan Williams released.

September 24, 1972
Bob Burda signed as a free agent.

October 27, 1972
Bob Burda, Ray Culp, and Gary Peters released.

November 27, 1972

Major League Draft
Lost Bob Gallagher to Astros.

1973
Ray Culp signed as a free agent.

January 18, 1973
Orlando Cepeda signed as a free agent.

January 24, 1973
Traded Mike Nagy to Cardinals for a PTNBL; Red Sox received Lance Clemons (March 29, 1973).

March 27, 1973
Lew Krausse released.
Traded Phil Gagliano and Andy Kosco to Reds for Mel Behney.

May 4, 1973
Sent Sonny Siebert to Rangers for UFC.

October 23, 1973
Traded Ben Oglivie to Tigers for Dick McAuliffe.

October 24, 1973
Traded Marty Pattin to Royals for Dick Drago.

October 25, 1973
Ray Culp released.
Bob Veale released.

October 26, 1973
Traded Reggie Smith and Ken Tatum to Cardinals for Rick Wise and Bernie Carbo.

December 3, 1973

Major League Draft
Lost Bill Moran to White Sox.

December 7, 1973
Purchased Juan Marichal from Giants.
Traded Lynn McGlothen, John Curtis, and Mike Garman to Cardinals in exchange for Reggie Cleveland, Diego Segui, and Terry Hughes.

December 10, 1973
Sold Buddy Hunter to Royals.

1974
Bob Veale signed as a free agent.

March 26, 1974
Luis Aparicio, Bobby Bolin, and Orlando Cepeda released.
Traded Vic Correll to Braves for Chuck Goggin.

March 28, 1974
Purchased Bob Didier from Tigers.

July 1974
Dick Colpaert released.

September 1, 1974
Purchased Tim McCarver from Cardinals.

September 7, 1974
Purchased Deron Johnson from Brewers.

October 24, 1974
John Kennedy, Juan Marichal, Dick McAuliffe, and Bob Veale released.

October 25, 1974
Deron Johnson released.

December 2, 1974
Traded Tommy Harper to California Angels for Bob Heise.

December 9, 1974
Traded Bob Didier to Astros for Roe Skidmore.

March 5, 1975
Tony Conigliaro signed as a free agent.

March 29, 1975
Traded Danny Cater to Cardinals for Danny Godby.

April 4, 1975
Traded Mario Guerrero to Cardinals for a PTNBL; Red Sox received Jim Willoughby (July 4, 1975).

June 14, 1975
Traded cash and a PTNBL to California Angels for Denny Doyle; California Angels received Chuck Ross (March 5, 1976).

June 23, 1975
Tim McCarver released.

August 21, 1975
Dick McAuliffe signed as a free agent.

September 2, 1975
Tony Conigliaro released.

September 21, 1975
Traded cash and a PTNBL to White Sox for Deron Johnson; White Sox received Chuck Erickson (November 7, 1975).

October 24, 1975
Dick McAuliffe released.

November 17, 1975
Traded Juan Beniquez, Steve Barr, and a PTNBL to Rangers for Fergie Jenkins; Rangers received Craig Skok (December 12, 1975).

December 12, 1975
Traded Roger Moret to Braves for Tom House.

January 9, 1976
Sold Terry Hughes to Cardinals.

February 15, 1976
Gene Michael signed as a free agent.

March 3, 1976
Traded Dick Drago to Angels for John Balaz, Dick Sharon, and Dave Machemer.

April 7, 1976
Diego Segui released.

April 19, 1976
Sold Tim Blackwell to Phillies.

May 4, 1976
Gene Michael released.

June 3, 1976
Traded Bernie Carbo to Brewers for Tom Murphy and Bobby Darwin.

June 4, 1976
Deron Johnson released.

November 5, 1976

Expansion Draft
Lost Dick Pole to Mariners (7th pick).
Lost Rick Jones to Mariners (22nd pick).
Lost Ernie Whitt to Blue Jays (34th pick).
Lost Steve Burke to Mariners (44th pick).
Lost Puchy Delgado to Mariners (56th pick).

November 6, 1976
Bill Campbell signed as a free agent.

November 22, 1976
Darryl Cias signed as a free agent.

December 6, 1976
Sold Bob Heise to Royals.
Traded Cecil Cooper to Brewers for George Scott and Bernie Carbo.

January 4, 1977
Traded Dave Machemer to Angels for John Doherty.

March 26, 1977
Rico Petrocelli released.

April 5, 1977
Darryl Cias released.

April 7, 1977
Mark Bomback released.

May 28, 1977
Sold Tom House to Mariners.
Traded Bobby Darwin to Cubs for Ramon Hernandez.

June 21, 1977
Doug Griffin released.
Tommy Helms signed as a free agent.

July 27, 1977
Sold Tom Murphy to Blue Jays.

August 20, 1977
Ramon Hernandez released.

September 12, 1977
Keith MacWhorter signed as a free agent.

September 19, 1977
Traded Frank Newcomer and cash to Reds for Bob Bailey.

November 2, 1977
Rick Miller granted free agency.

November 23, 1977
Mike Torrez signed as a free agent.

November 30, 1977
Jack Brohamer signed as a free agent.

December 8, 1977
Traded Don Aase and cash to Angels for Jerry Remy.

December 9, 1977
Traded Jack Baker to Indians for Garry Hancock.

December 14, 1977
Traded Fergie Jenkins to Rangers for John Poloni and cash.

December 27, 1977
Dick Drago signed as a free agent.

January 30, 1978
Traded Steve Dillard to Tigers for Michael Burns, Frank Harris, and cash.

February 17, 1978
Tom Burgmeier signed as a free agent.

March 24, 1978
Traded Rick Kreuger to Indians for Frank Duffy.

March 25, 1978
Tommy Helms released.

March 28, 1978
Denny Doyle released.

March 29, 1978
Traded Jim Burton to Mets for Leo Foster.

March 30, 1978
Traded Rick Wise, Mike Paxton, Ted Cox, and Bo Diaz to Indians for Dennis Eckersley and Fred Kendall.

April 5, 1978
Sold Ramon Aviles to Phillies.
Sold Jim Willoughby to White Sox.

April 18, 1978
Sold Reggie Cleveland to Rangers.

June 15, 1978
Sold Bernie Carbo to Indians.

July 24, 1978
Purchased Andy Hassler from Royals.

September 21, 1978
Juan Agosto released.

October 27, 1978
Purchased Mike Easler from Pirates.

November 2, 1978
Fred Kendall and Luis Tiant granted free agency.

December 5, 1978
Minor League Draft
Lost Keith MacWhorter to Mariners.

December 7, 1978
Traded Bill Lee to Expos for Stan Papi.

January 19, 1979
Steve Renko signed as a free agent.

February 3, 1979
Traded Dave Coleman to Twins for Larry Wolfe.

March 15, 1979
Purchased Jim Dwyer from Giants.
Traded Mike Easler to Pirates for George Hill, Martin Rivas, and cash.

April 2, 1979
Keith MacWhorter returned from Mariners.

May 10, 1979
Luis Aponte released.

May 22, 1979
Frank Duffy released.

June 13, 1979
Traded Pete Ladd, cash, and a PTNBL to Astros for Bob Watson; Astros received Bobby Sprowl (June 19, 1979).
Traded George Scott to Royals for Tom Poquette.

June 15, 1979
Sold Andy Hassler to Mets.

August 17, 1979
Traded cash and a PTNBL to Cubs for Ted Sizemore; Cubs received Mike O'Berry (October 23, 1979).

November 1, 1979
Bob Montgomery and Bob Watson granted free agency.

November 16, 1979
Tony Perez signed as a free agent.

November 27, 1979
Skip Lockwood signed as a free agent.

February 28, 1980
Luis Aponte signed as a free agent.

March 30, 1980
Traded cash and a PTNBL to Phillies for Dave Rader; Phillies received Stan Papi (May 12, 1980).

April 6, 1980
Sold Allen Ripley to Giants.

May 12, 1980
Received Jack Billingham from Tigers for UFC.

May 30, 1980
Ted Sizemore released.

June 20, 1980
Sold Jack Brohamer to Indians.

June 21, 1980
Jack Billingham released.

October 22, 1980
Jim Dwyer granted free agency.

November 23, 1980
Dave Rader granted free agency.

December 10, 1980
Traded Rick Burleson and Butch Hobson to Angels for Carney Lansford, Rick Miller, and Mark Clear.

January 23, 1981
Traded Fred Lynn and Steve Renko to Angels for Frank Tanana, Jim Dorsey, and Joe Rudi.

February 12, 1981
Carlton Fisk granted free agency.

April 6, 1981
Skip Lockwood released.

April 8, 1981
Traded Dick Drago to Mariners for Manny Sarmiento.

August 12, 1981
Lost Tom Poquette to Rangers on waivers.

October 23, 1981
Sold Manny Sarmiento to Pirates.

November 13, 1981
Bill Campbell, Jerry Remy, Joe Rudi, and Frank Tanana granted free agency.

December 8, 1981
Jerry Remy signed as a free agent.

January 26, 1982
Purchased John Verhoeven from Twins.

February 25, 1982
Mark Fidrych signed as a free agent.

April 9, 1982
Traded Mike Smithson to Rangers for John Henry Johnson.

November 1, 1982
Tony Perez released.

November 10, 1982
Tom Burgmeier granted free agency.

December 6, 1982
Traded Carney Lansford, Garry Hancock, and Jerry King to Athletics for Tony Armas and Jeff Newman.

December 10, 1982
Traded Chuck Rainey to Cubs for Doug Bird.

January 13, 1983
Traded Mike Torrez to Mets for a PTNBL; Red Sox received Mike Davis (February 15, 1983).

January 17, 1983
Purchased Brian Kingman from Athletics.

March 25, 1983
Brian Kingman released.

October 20, 1983
Steve Shields granted free agency.

November 7, 1983
Doug Bird granted free agency.

December 6, 1983
Traded John Tudor to Pirates for Mike Easler.

February 20, 1984
Rich Gale signed as a free agent.

March 24, 1984
Traded Luis Aponte to Indians for Mike Poindexter and Paul Perry.

May 25, 1984
Traded Dennis Eckersley and Mike Brumley to Cubs for Bill Buckner.

October 15, 1984
Dennis Burtt and Chico Walker granted free agency.

November 8, 1984
Gary Allenson and Rich Gale granted free agency.

November 9, 1984
Purchased Ed Glynn from Mets.

December 3, 1984
Major League Draft
Selected Mike Trujillo from Giants.

January 14, 1985
Bruce Kison signed as a free agent.

January 23, 1985
Dave Sax signed as a free agent.

April 1, 1985
Jim Corsi signed as a free agent.
John Henry Johnson released.

April 4, 1985
Jeff Newman released.

May 1, 1985
Sent Ed Glynn to Expos for UFC.

July 11, 1985
Traded Reid Nichols to White Sox for Tim Lollar.

November 12, 1985
Bruce Kison and Rick Miller granted free agency.

November 13, 1985
Traded Tom McCarthy, Bob Ojeda, John Mitchell, and Chris Bayer to Mets for Calvin Schiraldi, Wes Gardner, John Christensen, and LaSchelle Tarver.

November 14, 1985
Jim Dorsey released.

December 10, 1985
Jerry Remy released.

December 11, 1985
Traded Mark Clear to Brewers for Ed Romero.

December 12, 1985
Traded Charlie Mitchell to Twins for Mike Stenhouse.

December 17, 1985
Traded Jackie Gutierrez to Orioles for Sammy Stewart.

January 31, 1986
Jim Corsi released.
Joe Sambito signed as a free agent.

March 19, 1986
Ed Jurak released.

March 28, 1986
Traded Mike Easler to Yankees for Don Baylor.

April 5, 1986
Jim Corsi signed as a free agent.

June 29, 1986
Traded Steve Lyons to White Sox for Tom Seaver.

August 19, 1986
Traded Rey Quinones, cash, and 3 players to be named later to Mariners for Spike Owen and Dave Henderson; Mariners received Mike Brown and Mike Trujillo (August 22, 1986) and John Christensen (September 25, 1986).

October 15, 1986
Mike Stenhouse granted free agency.

November 12, 1986
Tony Armas, Rich Gedman, Glenn Hoffman, Joe Sambito, Tom Seaver, Dave Stapleton, and Sammy Stewart granted free agency.

December 5, 1986
Joe Sambito signed as a free agent.

December 20, 1986
Glenn Hoffman signed as a free agent.

March 30, 1987
Tim Lollar released.

April 2, 1987
Jim Corsi released.

May 2, 1987
Rich Gedman signed as a free agent.

July 23, 1987
Bill Buckner released.

August 21, 1987
Traded Glenn Hoffman to Dodgers for a PTNBL; Red Sox received Billy Bartels (December 8, 1987).

September 1, 1987
Traded Don Baylor to Twins for a PTNBL; Red Sox received Enrique Rios (December 18, 1987).
Traded Dave Henderson to Giants for a PTNBL; Red Sox received Randy Kutcher (December 9, 1987).

November 9, 1987
Steve Crawford and Joe Sambito granted free agency.

December 7, 1987
Major League Draft
Selected John Trautwein from Expos.

December 8, 1987
Traded Al Nipper and Calvin Schiraldi to Cubs for Lee Smith.

December 14, 1987
Traded Marc Sullivan to Astros for Randy Randle.

January 5, 1988
Dennis Lamp signed as a free agent.

January 18, 1988
Mike Smithson signed as a free agent.

March 10, 1988
Glenn Hoffman signed as a free agent.

March 28, 1988
Todd Pratt returned from Indians.

April 15, 1988
Rick Cerone signed as a free agent.

July 16, 1988
Larry Parrish signed as a free agent.

July 29, 1988
Traded Brady Anderson and Curt Schilling to Orioles for Mike Boddicker.

August 31, 1988
Returned John Trautwein to Expos.
Traded Victor Rosario to Expos for John Trautwein.

October 15, 1988
Pat Dodson and Danny Sheaffer granted free agency.

October 28, 1988
Larry Parrish released.

November 4, 1988
Bruce Hurst, Dennis Lamp, and Mike Smithson granted free agency.

November 20, 1988
Dennis Lamp signed as a free agent.

December 8, 1988
Traded Spike Owen and Dan Gakeler to Expos for John Dopson and Luis Rivera.

December 13, 1988
Traded Todd Benzinger, Jeff Sellers, and a PTNBL to Reds for Nick Esasky and Rob Murphy; Reds received Luis Vasquez (January 12, 1989).

December 15, 1988
Glenn Hoffman released.

December 19, 1988
Mike Smithson signed as a free agent.

February 6, 1989
Danny Heep signed as a free agent.

May 5, 1989
Joe Price signed as a free agent.

May 17, 1989
Rick Lancellotti signed as a free agent.

June 26, 1989
Purchased Jeff Stone from Rangers.

August 2, 1989
Traded Dana Williams to White Sox for Ray Chadwick.

August 5, 1989
Ed Romero released.

August 7, 1989
Claimed Greg Harris from Phillies on waivers.

October 12, 1989
Jeff Stone released.

October 22, 1989
Mike Dalton granted free agency.

November 13, 1989
Jim Rice released.

November 27, 1989
Tony Pena signed as a free agent.

December 4–5, 1989
Major League Draft
Lost Reggie Harris to Athletics.
Lost Eddie Zambrano to Indians.

December 6, 1989
Dennis Lamp signed as a free agent.
Jeff Reardon signed as a free agent.

December 13, 1989
Billy Jo Robidoux signed as a free agent.
Jeff Stone signed as a free agent.

December 19, 1989
Rick Cerone released.

December 20, 1989
Sam Horn and Bob Stanley released.

February 5, 1990
Jim Pankovits signed as a free agent.

February 6, 1990
Mike Dalton signed as a free agent.

February 15, 1990
Bill Buckner signed as a free agent.
Greg Harris signed as a free agent.

April 7, 1990
Jeff Gray signed as a free agent.

May 3, 1990
Jerry Reed signed as a free agent.

May 4, 1990
Traded Lee Smith to Cardinals for Tom Brunansky.

June 5, 1990
Bill Buckner released.

June 8, 1990
Sent Rich Gedman to Astros for UFC.

July 27, 1990
Traded Greg Hansell, Ed Perozo, and a PTNBL to Mets for Mike Marshall; Mets received Paul Williams (November 19,1990).

July 31, 1990
Joe Hesketh signed as a free agent.

August 2, 1990
Purchased Wayne Housie from Salinas (California).

August 12, 1990
Jerry Reed released.

August 23, 1990
Cecilio Guante signed as a free agent.

August 30, 1990
Traded Jeff Bagwell to Astros for Larry Andersen.

October 5, 1990
Tom Brunansky granted free agency.

October 15, 1990
Mike Dalton and Rick Lancellotti granted free agency.

October 24, 1990
Dwight Evans released.

November 5, 1990
Mike Boddicker and Danny Heep granted free agency.

November 20, 1990
Jeff Stone released.

December 4, 1990
Billy Jo Robidoux released.
Matt Young signed as a free agent.

December 7, 1990
Larry Andersen granted free agency.

December 14, 1990
Marty Barrett released.

December 15, 1990
Jack Clark signed as a free agent.
Traded Wes Gardner to Padres for Steve Hendricks and Brad Hoyer.

December 19, 1990
Tom Brunansky signed as a free agent.
Danny Darwin signed as a free agent.

January 23, 1991
Mike Brumley signed as a free agent.
Tony Fossas signed as a free agent.

February 1, 1991
John Moses signed as a free agent.

February 7, 1991
Tom Barrett signed as a free agent.

April 1, 1991
John Moses released.
Traded Rob Murphy to Mariners for Mike Gardiner.

April 18, 1991
Steve Lyons signed as a free agent.

July 20, 1991
Mike Marshall released.

August 9, 1991
Kevin Romine released.

August 16, 1991
Traded a PTNBL to Braves for Dan Petry; Braves received Mickey Pina (November 13, 1991).

October 15, 1991
Tom Barrett and Todd Pratt granted free agency.

October 28, 1991
Joe Hesketh granted free agency.

November 1, 1991
Dan Petry granted free agency.

November 4, 1991
Dennis Lamp granted free agency.

November 5, 1991
Steve Lyons granted free agency.

December 19, 1991
Joe Hesketh signed as a free agent.

January 2, 1992
Frank Viola signed as a free agent.

January 17, 1992
Tom Barrett signed as a free agent.

January 29, 1992
Herm Winningham signed as a free agent.

March 24, 1992
Josias Manzanillo granted free agency.

April 16, 1992
Bob Geren signed as a free agent.

June 27, 1992
Purchased Steve Lyons from Expos.

July 9, 1992
Traded Tom Bolton to Reds for Billy Hatcher.

August 30, 1992
Traded Jeff Reardon to Braves for Nate Minchey and Sean Ross.

October 15, 1992
Tom Barrett, Bob Geren, and Wayne Housie granted free agency.

October 16, 1992
Mike Brumley granted free agency.

October 26, 1992
Wade Boggs granted free agency.

October 28, 1992
Tom Brunansky granted free agency.

November 2, 1992
Billy Hatcher granted free agency.

November 4, 1992
Steve Lyons granted free agency.

November 6, 1992
Herm Winningham granted free agency.

November 17, 1992

Expansion Draft

Lost Jody Reed to Rockies (13th pick).
Lost Eric Wedge to Rockies (48th pick).

November 27, 1992
Billy Hatcher signed as a free agent.

December 1, 1992
Scott Fletcher signed as a free agent.

December 7, 1992

Major League Draft

Lost Erik Plantenberg to Mariners.

December 8, 1992
Scott Bankhead signed as a free agent.
Traded Mike Gardiner and Terry Powers to Expos for Ivan Calderon.

December 9, 1992
Andre Dawson signed as a free agent.
Traded Phil Plantier to Padres for Jose Melendez.

December 11, 1992
Tony Fossas released.

December 14, 1992
Bob Melvin signed as a free agent.

December 19, 1992
Ellis Burks granted free agency.

January 18, 1993
Tony Fossas signed as a free agent.

March 1, 1993
Jeff Russell signed as a free agent.

March 24, 1993
John Marzano released.

March 30, 1993
Matt Young released.

April 2, 1993
Traded Daryl Irvine to Pirates for Jeff Richardson.

April 3, 1993
Ernie Riles signed as a free agent.

April 21, 1993
Steve Mintz signed as a free agent.

May 7, 1993
Steve Lyons signed as a free agent.

May 11, 1993
Franklin Stubbs signed as a free agent.

August 17, 1993
Ivan Calderon released.

August 21, 1993
Received Rob Deer from Tigers for UFC.

October 15, 1993
Steve Mintz, Jeff Richardson, and Franklin Stubbs granted free agency.

October 19, 1993
Tony Pena granted free agency.

October 25, 1993
Ernie Riles and Luis Rivera granted free agency.

October 29, 1993
John Dopson granted free agency.

November 1, 1993
Rob Deer granted free agency.

November 4, 1993
Steve Lyons granted free agency.

December 7, 1993
Otis Nixon signed as a free agent.

December 8, 1993
Carlos Rodriguez signed as a free agent.

December 16, 1993
Jose Munoz signed as a free agent.

December 20, 1993
Tony Fossas granted free agency.

December 30, 1993
Dave Valle signed as a free agent.

January 20, 1994
Tony Fossas signed as a free agent.
Chris Howard signed as a free agent.

February 1, 1994
Damon Berryhill signed as a free agent.

February 4, 1994
Andy Tomberlin signed as a free agent.

February 10, 1994
Sergio Valdez signed as a free agent.

February 18, 1994
Purchased Matt Stairs and Pete Young from Expos.

March 7, 1994
Pat Lennon signed as a free agent.

March 18, 1994
Claimed Jeff Pierce from Reds on waivers.

March 22, 1994
Traded a PTNBL to Mariners for Lee Tinsley; Mariners received Jim Smith (September 15, 1994).

March 23, 1994
Traded a PTNBL to Expos for Glenn Murray; Expos received Derek Vinyard (September 15, 1994).

March 29, 1994
Todd Frohwirth signed as a free agent.

March 30, 1994
Greg Litton signed as a free agent.

April 1, 1994
Claimed Ricky Trlicek from Dodgers on waivers.
Traded John Flaherty to Tigers for Rich Rowland.

April 9, 1994
Mario Diaz signed as a free agent.

April 12, 1994
Bob Melvin released.

May 2, 1994
Eric Wedge signed as a free agent.

May 5, 1994
Lost Bob Zupcic to White Sox on waivers.

May 25, 1994
Mario Diaz released.

May 26, 1994
Mike Sharperson signed as a free agent.

May 31, 1994
Traded Paul Quantrill and Billy Hatcher to Phillies for Wes Chamberlain and Mike Sullivan.

June 3, 1994
Traded Brian Conroy to Colorado Rockies for Keith Shepherd.

June 16, 1994
Traded Dave Valle to Brewers for Tom Brunansky.

June 27, 1994
Greg Harris released.

July 1, 1994
Traded Jeff Russell to Indians for Chris Nabholz and Steve Farr.

July 15, 1994
Claimed Stan Royer from Cardinals on waivers.

July 17, 1994
Mike Sharperson released.

September 1, 1994
Sold Scott Bankhead to Yankees.

October 6, 1994
Andy Tomberlin granted free agency.

October 14, 1994
Scott Fletcher and Greg Litton granted free agency.

October 15, 1994
Todd Frohwirth, Jose Melendez, Jose Munoz, and Sergio Valdez granted free agency.

October 17, 1994
Don Florence granted free agency.

October 20, 1994
Tom Brunansky and Frank Viola granted free agency.

October 21, 1994
Danny Darwin and Andre Dawson granted free agency.

October 24, 1994
Joe Hesketh granted free agency.

October 25, 1994
Steve Farr granted free agency.

October 31, 1994
Damon Berryhill granted free agency.

November 7, 1994
Juan Bell signed as a free agent.
Bill Haselman signed as a free agent.

November 9, 1994
Received Brian Looney from Expos for UFC.

November 17, 1994
Claimed Heath Haynes from Expos on waivers.

November 18, 1994
Claimed Bill Wertz from Indians on waivers.

December 5, 1994
Carlos Rodriguez and Ricky Trlicek released.

December 7, 1994
Traded Jeff McNeely and Nate Minchey to Cardinals for Luis Alicea.

December 9, 1994
Lost Heath Haynes to Athletics on waivers.
Traded Otis Nixon and Luis Ortiz to Rangers for Jose Canseco.

December 13, 1994
Received Terry Shumpert from Royals for UFC.

December 16, 1994
Joel Johnston signed as a free agent.

December 23, 1994
Tony Fossas and Chris Nabholz granted free agency.

January 9, 1995
Carlos Rodriguez signed as a free agent.

February 20, 1995
Mike Porzio signed as a free agent.

April 1, 1995
Mike Porzio released.

April 8, 1995
Mike Macfarlane signed as a free agent.

April 9, 1995
Stan Belinda signed as a free agent.
Reggie Jefferson signed as a free agent.
Traded Cory Bailey and Scott Cooper to Cardinals for Rheal Cormier and Mark Whiten.

April 11, 1995
Erik Hanson signed as a free agent.

April 14, 1995
Claimed Troy O'Leary from Brewers on waivers.

April 17, 1995
Mike Hartley signed as a free agent.

April 18, 1995
Zane Smith signed as a free agent.

April 22, 1995
Derek Lilliquist signed as a free agent.

April 23, 1995
Alejandro Pena signed as a free agent.

April 26, 1995
Tim Wakefield signed as a free agent.

May 1995
Wally Whitehurst signed as a free agent.

May 26, 1995
Claimed Tuffy Rhodes from Cubs on waivers.

May 30, 1995
Mike Maddux signed as a free agent.

June 4, 1995
Brian Bark signed as a free agent.

June 5, 1995
Keith Shepherd released.

June 6, 1995
Willie McGee signed as a free agent.

June 10, 1995
Received Chris Donnels from Astros for UFC.

June 13, 1995
Alejandro Pena released.

July 6, 1995
Traded Frankie Rodriguez and a PTNBL to Twins in exchange for Rick Aguilera; Twins received J. J. Johnson (October 11, 1995).

July 16, 1995
Derek Lilliquist released.

July 20, 1995
Pat Lennon released.

July 22, 1995
Joel Johnston released.

July 24, 1995
Traded Mark Whiten to Phillies for Dave Hollins.

July 26, 1995
Wally Whitehurst released.

July 31, 1995
Traded 2 players to be named later to Braves for Mike Stanton and a PTNBL; Braves received Mike Jacobs and Marc Lewis (August 31, 1995) and Red Sox received Matt Murray (August 31, 1995).

August 2, 1995
Bill Wertz released.

August 3, 1995
Mike Hartley released.

August 10, 1995
Claimed Eric Gunderson from Mariners on waivers.

August 14, 1995
Traded Wes Chamberlain to Royals for Chris James.

August 31, 1995
Claimed Dwayne Hosey from Royals on waivers.
Traded Chris Howard to Rangers for Jack Voigt.

September 8, 1995
Lost Steve Rodriguez to Tigers on waivers.

October 6, 1995
Claimed Brent Cookson from Royals on waivers.

October 9, 1995
Luis Aquino signed as a free agent.

October 12, 1995
Claimed J.J. Thobe from Expos on waivers.

October 13, 1995
Claimed Butch Henry from Expos on waivers.

October 14, 1995
Chris James and Matt Stairs granted free agency.

October 16, 1995
Alex Delgado, Tuffy Rhodes, Rich Rowland, and Jack Voigt granted free agency.

October 26, 1995
Chris Donnels released.

October 27, 1995
Luis Aquino released.

October 30, 1995
Jose Canseco granted free agency.

October 31, 1995
Rick Aguilera granted free agency.

November 1, 1995
Jim Tatum signed as a free agent.

November 3, 1995
Willie McGee granted free agency.

November 6, 1995
Mike Macfarlane and Mike Maddux granted free agency.

November 8, 1995
Brad Pennington signed as a free agent.

November 9, 1995
Ken Grundt signed as a free agent.

November 20, 1995
Ramon Caraballo signed as a free agent.

November 27, 1995
Brent Knackert signed as a free agent.

December 4, 1995
Major League Draft
Selected Joe Crawford from Mets.

December 6, 1995
Jose Canseco signed as a free agent.

December 12, 1995
Alex Delgado signed as a free agent.

December 13, 1995
Alan Zinter signed as a free agent.

December 14, 1995
Rich Garces signed as a free agent.
Mike Stanley signed as a free agent.

December 15, 1995
Mike Maddux signed as a free agent.

December 17, 1995
Nate Minchey signed as a free agent.

December 19, 1995
Juan Bell signed as a free agent.

December 20, 1995
Dave Hollins granted free agency.

December 21, 1995
Milt Cuyler signed as a free agent.
Tom Gordon signed as a free agent.

December 26, 1995
Chuck Ricci signed as a free agent.

1996
Phil Clark signed as a free agent.

January 2, 1996
Jamie Moyer signed as a free agent.

January 3, 1996
Tim VanEgmond signed as a free agent.

January 10, 1996
Traded Shayne Bennett, Rheal Cormier, and Ryan McGuire to Expos for Wil Cordero and Bryan Eversgerd.

January 22, 1996
Esteban Beltre signed as a free agent.
Alex Cole signed as a free agent.

January 29, 1996
Traded Glenn Murray, Ken Ryan, and Lee Tinsley to Phillies for Rick Holyfield, Heathcliff Slocumb and Larry Wimberly.

February 15, 1996
Felix Jose signed as a free agent.

February 27, 1996
Frank Bolick signed as a free agent.

March 8, 1996
Kevin Mitchell signed as a free agent.

March 19, 1996
Lost Luis Alicea to Cardinals on waivers.

March 25, 1996
Claimed John Doherty from Tigers on waivers.

March 26, 1996
Sold Joe Crawford to Mets.

April 18, 1996
Traded Bryan Eversgerd to Rangers for a PTNBL; Red Sox received Rudy Pemberton (April 24, 1996).

April 26, 1996
Adam Hyzdu signed as a free agent.

May 6, 1996
Joel Bennett released.

May 7, 1996
Reggie Harris signed as a free agent.
Jeff Manto signed as a free agent.

May 12, 1996
Felix Jose released.

May 17, 1996
Lost Brad Pennington to Angels on waivers.

June 5, 1996
Jeff Frye signed as a free agent.

June 6, 1996
Tim VanEgmond released.

June 8, 1996
Sold Jim Tatum to Padres.

June 9, 1996
Traded Scott Bakkum to Phillies for Lee Tinsley.

June 10, 1996
Tom McGraw signed as a free agent.

June 13, 1996
Esteban Beltre granted free agency.

July 23, 1996
Traded Jeff Manto to Mariners for Arquimedez Pozo.

July 28, 1996
Frank Bolick released.

July 30, 1996
Traded Jamie Moyer to Mariners for Darren Bragg.
Traded Kevin Mitchell to Reds for Roberto Mejia and Brad Tweedie.

July 31, 1996
Traded Mike Stanton and a PTNBL to Rangers for Mark Brandenburg and Kerry Lacy; Rangers received Dwayne Hosey (November 4, 1996).

August 1, 1996
Claimed Greg Pirkl from Mariners on waivers.

August 2, 1996
Sent Brent Cookson to Orioles for UFC.

August 26, 1996
Traded a PTNBL to Twins for Pat Mahomes; Minnesota Twins received Brian Looney (December 17, 1996).

August 29, 1996
Claimed Jeff Manto from Mariners on waivers.

October 7, 1996
Eric Gunderson released.

October 8, 1996
Claimed Bob Milacki from Mariners on waivers.

October 9, 1996
Claimed Mike Campbell from Cubs on waivers.

October 10, 1996
Milt Cuyler granted free agency.

October 11, 1996
Claimed Greg Hansell from Twins on waivers.

October 14, 1996
Claimed Ricky Trlicek from Mets on waivers.

October 15, 1996
Alex Cole, Alex Delgado, Ken Grundt, Brent Knackert, Tom McGraw, and Alan Zinter granted free agency.

October 18, 1996
Mike Greenwell granted free agency.

October 22, 1996
Bob Milacki released.

October 29, 1996
Sold Mike Campbell to Yokohama Bay Stars (JCL).

November 1, 1996
Mike Maddux granted free agency.

November 5, 1996
Sold Phil Clark to Kintetsu Buffaloes (JPL).

November 25, 1996
Sent Lee Tinsley to Mariners for UFC.
Traded a PTBNL to Marlins for Jesus Tavarez; Marlins received Robert Rodgers (December 10, 1996).

December 5, 1996
Reggie Harris released.

December 6, 1996
Robinson Checo signed as a free agent.

December 7, 1996
Mike Maddux signed as a free agent.

December 9, 1996
Bret Saberhagen signed as a free agent.

December 13, 1996
Tim Naehring signed as a free agent.

December 14, 1996
Shane Mack signed as a free agent.

December 17, 1996
Chris Hammond signed as a free agent.

December 20, 1996
Chris Donnels signed as a free agent.

December 27, 1996
Johnny Ruffin signed as a free agent.

January 22, 1997
Steve Avery signed as a free agent.

January 23, 1997
Ken Grundt signed as a free agent.

January 27, 1997
Traded Jose Canseco to Athletics for John Wasdin and cash.

January 31, 1997
Mike Benjamin signed as a free agent.

February 3, 1997
Jim Corsi signed as a free agent.
Roberto Mejia released.

February 8, 1997
Scott Leius signed as a free agent.

February 10, 1997
Gary Bennett signed as a free agent.

February 15, 1997
Mike Williams signed as a free agent.

March 6, 1997
Tim Spehr signed as a free agent.

March 14, 1997
Mike Williams released.

March 25, 1997
Purchased Carlos Valdez from Giants.

March 26, 1997
Chris Donnels, Greg Hansell, and Mike Maddux released.
Sold Tim Spehr to Royals.

March 29, 1997
Scott Leius released.

May 1, 1997
Sold Johnny Ruffin to Kintetsu Buffaloes (JPL).

May 8, 1997
Rusty Meacham signed as a free agent.

May 12, 1997
Traded Ricky Trlicek to Mets for Toby Borland.

June 18, 1997
Rudy Pemberton granted free agency.

June 27, 1997
Pat Mahomes released.

June 30, 1997
Pete Walker signed as a free agent.

July 31, 1997
Traded Heathcliff Slocumb to Mariners for Derek Lowe and Jason Varitek.

August 13, 1997
Traded Mike Stanley and Randy Brown to Yankees for Tony Armas and a PTBNL; Red Sox received Jim Mecir (September 29, 1997).

August 30, 1997
Curtis Pride signed as a free agent.

September 25, 1997
Claimed B.J. Waszgis from Orioles on waivers.

September 28, 1997
Wil Cordero released.

October 7, 1997
Jesus Tavarez granted free agency.

October 15, 1997
Lost Vaughn Eshelman to Athletics on waivers.

October 17, 1997
Toby Borland and Pete Walker granted free agency.

October 27, 1997
Mike Benjamin granted free agency.

October 28, 1997
Brian Shouse signed as a free agent.

October 29, 1997
Travis Harper granted free agency.

October 30, 1997
Chris Hammond granted free agency.

October 31, 1997
Bret Saberhagen granted free agency.

November 6, 1997
Traded Mark Brandenburg, Bill Haselman, and Aaron Sele to Rangers for Damon Buford and Jim Leyritz.

November 17, 1997
Bret Saberhagen signed as a free agent.

November 18, 1997
Traded Carl Pavano and a PTBNL to Expos for Pedro Martinez; Expos received Tony Armas (December 18, 1997).

November 21, 1997
Mike Benjamin signed as a free agent.

November 24, 1997
Purchased Jimmy Hurst from Tigers.

December 3, 1997
Jim Corsi signed as a free agent.

December 9, 1997
Dennis Eckersley signed as a free agent.

December 23, 1997
Darren Lewis signed as a free agent.

January 14, 1998
Pete Walker signed as a free agent.

January 28, 1998
Keith Mitchell signed as a free agent.

January 29, 1998
Carlos Valdez signed as a free agent.

March 19, 1998
Claimed Midre Cummings from Reds on waivers.

March 26, 1998
Mark Lemke signed as a free agent.

March 30, 1998
Billy Ashley signed as a free agent.
Traded Bo Dodson to Orioles for Keith Johns.

May 22, 1998
Steve Schrenk signed as a free agent.

June 18, 1998
Traded Mike Blais to Astros for David West.

June 20, 1998
Traded Ethan Faggett and Jim Leyritz to Padres for Carlos Reyes, Mandy Romero, and Dario Veras.

June 25, 1998
Brian Shouse released.

July 30, 1998
Traded Peter Munro and Jay Yennaco to Blue Jays for Mike Stanley.

July 31, 1998
Traded Joe Hudson to Brewers for Eddy Diaz.
Traded John Barnes, Matt Kinney, and Joe Thomas to Minnesota Twins for Orlando Merced and Greg Swindell.

August 6, 1998
Purchased Pete Schourek from Astros.

August 31, 1998
Traded Corey Jenkins to White Sox for Chris Snopek.

September 1, 1998
Orlando Merced released.

September 8, 1998
David West released.

October 15, 1998
Keith Johns and Steve Schrenk granted free agency.

October 16, 1998
Walt McKeel, Bill Selby, Pete Walker, and B.J. Waszgis granted free agency.

October 22, 1998
Butch Henry granted free agency.

October 23, 1998
Pete Schourek and Mo Vaughn granted free agency.

October 26, 1998
Mike Benjamin and Mark Lemke granted free agency.

October 27, 1998
Greg Swindell granted free agency.

October 28, 1998
Purchased Morgan Burkhart from Richmond (FL).

November 3, 1998

Granted Free Agency
Dennis Eckersley and Darren Lewis.

November 4, 1998
Creighton Gubanich signed as a free agent.

November 5, 1998
Darren Lewis signed as a free agent.

November 11, 1998
Traded a PTBNL to Diamondbacks for Bob Wolcott; Diamondbacks received Bart Miadich (December 15, 1998).

November 16, 1998
Raul Gonzalez signed as a free agent.
Jose Offerman signed as a free agent.

November 20, 1998
Purchased Tomo Ohka from Yokohama Bay
    Stars (JCL).
Carlos Valdez released.

November 23, 1998
Billy Ashley and Rich Garces released.

December 7, 1998
Lost Dario Veras to Royals on waivers.

December 10, 1998
Purchased Marino Santana from Tigers.

December 11, 1998
Mark Portugal signed as a free agent.

December 14, 1998
Israel Alcantara signed as a free agent.
Kirk Bullinger signed as a free agent.
Brad Clontz signed as a free agent.
Tim Harikkala signed as a free agent.
Carlos Reyes released.

December 16, 1998
Claimed Steve Connelly from Athletics on
    waivers.

December 18, 1998
Brian Daubach signed as a free agent.

December 19, 1998
Mark Guthrie signed as a free agent.

December 21, 1998
Darren Bragg, Robinson Checo, and Keith
    Mitchell granted free agency.

January 5, 1999
Rheal Cormier signed as a free agent.
Kip Gross signed as a free agent.

January 8, 1999
Lost Steve Connelly to Giants on waivers.

January 11, 1999
Pat Rapp signed as a free agent.

January 12, 1999
Pedro Valdes signed as a free agent.

February 3, 1999
Tim Young signed as a free agent.

February 4, 1999
Chad Fonville signed as a free agent.

February 28, 1999
Rich Garces signed as a free agent.

March 11, 1999
Ramon Martinez signed as a free agent.

March 25, 1999
Traded Pat Flury to Reds for Jon Nunnally.

March 30, 1999
Midre Cummings released.
Lost Ron Mahay to Athletics on waivers.

April 5, 1999
Pedro Valdes released.

April 6, 1999
Brad Clontz released.

April 22, 1999
Lost Jack Cressend to Twins on waivers.

May 31, 1999
Traded Brian Partenheimer to Marlins for
    Rob Stanifer.

June 22, 1999
Jim Corsi released.

July 21, 1999
Traded cash and a PTBNL to Devil Rays for
    Julio Santana; Devil Rays received Will
    Silverthorn (July 30, 1999).

July 26, 1999
Traded Robert Ramsay to Mariners for Butch
    Huskey.

July 28, 1999
Lenny Webster signed as a free agent.

July 31, 1999
Traded Mike Maroth to Tigers for Bryce
    Florie.
Traded Mandy Romero to Mets for a PTBNL;
    Red Sox received Kelly Ramos (November
    18, 1999).

August 4, 1999
Traded Jose Olmeda to Indians for Mike
    Matthews.

August 20, 1999
Lenny Webster released.

August 24, 1999
Traded Mike Matthews and David Benham
    to Cardinals for Kent Mercker.

August 31, 1999
Traded Mark Guthrie and a PTBNL to Cubs
    for Rod Beck; Cubs received Cole Liniak
    (September 1, 1999).

September 27, 1999
Mark Portugal released.

October 4, 1999
Kirk Bullinger, Kip Gross, and Tim Harikkala
    granted free agency.

October 15, 1999
Andy Abad, Israel Alcantara, Joe Depastino,
    Raul Gonzalez, and Creighton Gubanich
    granted free agency.

November 2, 1999
Pat Rapp granted free agency.

November 4, 1999
Reggie Jefferson granted free agency.

November 8, 1999
Kent Mercker granted free agency.

November 12, 1999
Traded Jon Nunnally to Mets for Jermaine
    Allensworth.

November 18, 1999
Rafael Betancourt, Marino Santana, and Bob
    Wolcott released.

November 22, 1999
Sold Lou Merloni to Yokohama Bay Stars
    (Japan Central).

December 12, 1999
Traded Damon Buford to Cubs for Manny
    Alexander.

December 13, 1999

Major League Draft
Lost Marty McLeary to Expos.
Lost Chris Reitsma to Devil Rays.

December 14, 1999
Traded Adam Everett and Greg Miller to
    Astros for Carl Everett.

December 16, 1999
Aaron Holbert signed as a free agent.

December 21, 1999
Shea Hillenbrand, Butch Huskey, and Julio
    Santana granted free agency.

December 22, 1999
Jeff Fassero signed as a free agent.

January 4, 2000
Israel Alcantara signed as a free agent.

January 19, 2000
Marty Cordova signed as a free agent.

January 23, 2000
Andy Sheets signed as a free agent.

January 29, 2000
Shea Hillenbrand signed as a free agent.

February 2, 2000
Julio Santana signed as a free agent.

February 11, 2000
Hipolito Pichardo signed as a free agent.

March 4, 2000
Juan Diaz signed as a free agent.

March 17, 2000
Marty McLeary returned from Expos.

March 26, 2000
Marty Cordova released.

March 28, 2000
Chris Reitsma returned from Devil Rays.

March 30, 2000
Claimed Nerio Rodriguez from Mets on waivers.

April 2, 2000
Gary Gaetti signed as a free agent.
Pete Schourek signed as a free agent.

April 5, 2000
Kevin Foster signed as a free agent.

April 26, 2000
Received Curtis Pride from Mets for UFC.

June 2, 2000
Dan Smith signed as a free agent.

June 15, 2000
Julio Santana released.

June 26, 2000
Carlos Castillo signed as a free agent.

June 30, 2000
Traded Cesar Saba and Dennis Tankersley to Padres for Ed Sprague.

July 4, 2000
Bernard Gilkey signed as a free agent.

July 8, 2000
Curtis Pride released.

July 23, 2000
Sean Berry signed as a free agent.

July 27, 2000
Traded Jeff Frye, Brian Rose, John Wasdin, and Jeff Taglienti to Rockies for Rolando Arrojo, Rich Croushore, Mike Lansing, and cash.

July 28, 2000
Lou Merloni signed as a free agent.

July 31, 2000
Mike Stanley released.

August 2, 2000
Traded Aaron Holbert to Marlins for a PTBNL; Red Sox received Nelson Lara (March 30, 2001).

August 3, 2000
Claimed Rico Brogna from Phillies on waivers.

August 10, 2000
Sean Berry released.

August 16, 2000
Lost David Eckstein to Angels on waivers.

August 23, 2000
Ed Sprague released.

August 31, 2000
Traded Hector De Los Santos to Twins for Midre Cummings.
Traded Chris Reitsma and John Curtice to Reds for Dante Bichette.

September 9, 2000
Traded Lewford to Twins for Hector Carrasco.

September 10, 2000
Steve Ontiveros signed as a free agent.

September 20, 2000
Traded a PTBNL to White Sox for Jesus Pena; White Sox received Mike Rupp (March 19, 2001).

October 13, 2000
Midre Cummings and Andy Sheets granted free agency.

October 15, 2000
Jared Fernandez and Nerio Rodriguez granted free agency.

October 18, 2000
Carlos Castillo, Kevin Foster, and Dan Smith granted free agency.

October 27, 2000
Carlos Castillo signed as a free agent.

November 1, 2000
Manny Alexander, Rico Brogna, Hector Carrasco, Rheal Cormier, Jeff Fassero, Bernard Gilkey, Tom Gordon, Ramon Martinez, Steve Ontiveros, Pete Schourek, and Tim Wakefield granted free agency.

November 16, 2000
Traded Michael Coleman and Donnie Sadler to Reds for Chris Stynes.

November 17, 2000
Rob Stanifer granted free agency.

December 7, 2000
Frank Castillo signed as a free agent.
Pete Schourek signed as a free agent.
Tim Wakefield signed as a free agent.

December 13, 2000
Rafael Betancourt signed as a free agent.

December 15, 2000
Hideo Nomo signed as a free agent.
Sold Tim Young to Hiroshima Toyo Carp (JCL).

December 18, 2000
Allen McDill signed as a free agent.

December 19, 2000
Manny Ramirez signed as a free agent.

December 21, 2000
Israel Alcantara granted free agency.

January 4, 2001
Brian Williams signed as a free agent.

January 5, 2001
Kent Mercker signed as a free agent.
Bryan Ward signed as a free agent.

January 11, 2001
Israel Alcantara signed as a free agent.
David Cone signed as a free agent.

January 18, 2001
Traded Rich Croushore to Mets for Frank Graham.

January 19, 2001
Craig Grebeck signed as a free agent.

January 22, 2001
Trever Miller signed as a free agent.

January 29, 2001
Todd Erdos signed as a free agent.
Gus Gandarillas signed as a free agent.

February 22, 2001
Purchased Jorge de la Rosa from Monterrey (ML).

March 28, 2001
Derrin Ebert signed as a free agent.
Kent Mercker released.

April 18, 2001
Bill Pulsipher signed as a free agent.

May 2, 2001
Marcus Jensen signed as a free agent.

May 16, 2001
Gus Gandarillas released.

June 1, 2001
Purchased James Lofton from Sonomo County (WL).

June 12, 2001
Traded Justin Duchscherer to Rangers for Doug Mirabelli.

June 15, 2001
Lost Marcus Jensen to Rangers on waivers.

June 19, 2001
Ken Hill signed as a free agent.

July 2, 2001
Joe Oliver signed as a free agent.

July 30, 2001
Bryce Florie released.

July 31, 2001
Traded Tomo Ohka and Rich Rundles to Expos for Ugueth Urbina.

August 3, 2001
Pete Schourek released.

August 18, 2001
Purchased Mike Rose from Diamondbacks.

August 19, 2001
Quilvio Veras signed as a free agent.

August 23, 2001
Willie Banks signed as a free agent.
Lost Bill Pulsipher to White Sox on waivers.

September 6, 2001
Claimed Calvin Pickering from Reds on waivers.

September 26, 2001
Carlos Castillo released.

October 9, 2001
Morgan Burkhart and Craig Grebeck released.

October 15, 2001
Rafael Betancourt, Jim Chamblee, Derrin Ebert, Ken Hill, James Lofton, Trever Miller, Jesus Pena, Quilvio Veras, and Bryan Ward granted free agency.

October 27, 2001
James Lofton signed as a free agent.

November 5, 2001
Rod Beck, Dante Bichette, Darren Lewis, Hideo Nomo, Troy O'Leary, Joe Oliver, Hipolito Pichardo, Bret Saberhagen, and John Valentin granted free agency.

November 6, 2001
David Cone granted free agency.

November 13, 2001
Rob Stanifer signed as a free agent.

November 16, 2001
Tim Young signed as a free agent.

November 20, 2001
Claimed Tony Clark from Tigers on waivers.

November 21, 2001
Michael Coleman signed as a free agent.

December 4, 2001
Claimed Jeff Wallace from Devil Rays on waivers.

December 12, 2001
Traded Carl Everett to Rangers for Darren Oliver.

December 15, 2001
Traded Rick Asadoorian, Luis Garcia, and Dustin Brisson to Cardinals for Dustin Hermanson.

December 18, 2001
Carlos Baerga signed as a free agent.

December 19, 2001
John Burkett signed as a free agent.
Bry Nelson signed as a free agent.
Traded Scott Hatteberg to Rockies for Pokey Reese.

December 21, 2001
Johnny Damon signed as a free agent.
Steve Lomasney signed as a free agent.

February 1, 2002
Rob Stanifer released.

February 5, 2002
Shane Andrews signed as a free agent.

February 12, 2002
Todd Erdos signed as a free agent.

February 13, 2002
Rickey Henderson signed as a free agent.

February 27, 2002
Rey Sanchez signed as a free agent.

March 30, 2002
Chris Haney signed as a free agent.

April 19, 2002
Kevin Brown signed as a free agent.

April 26, 2002
Acquired Andy Dominique from Phillies.
Mike Rose released.

April 27, 2002
Wayne Gomes signed as a free agent.

June 6, 2002
Chris Michalak signed as a free agent.

June 21, 2002
Purchased Rob Ryan from Athletics.

June 26, 2002
Traded Brad Baker and Dan Giese to Padres for Alan Embree and Andy Shibilo.

July 2, 2002
Darren Oliver released.

July 11, 2002
Michael Coleman released.

July 16, 2002
Claimed Warren Morris from Cardinals on waivers.

July 30, 2002
Traded Sun-Woo Kim and Seung Song to Expos for Cliff Floyd.

July 31, 2002
Traded Frank Francisco and Byeong Hak An to White Sox for Bob Howry.

August 1, 2002
Rich Garces released.

August 8, 2002
Sent Jose Offerman to Mariners for UFC.

August 9, 2002
Jason Boyd signed as a free agent.
Joe Nelson signed as a free agent.

August 26, 2002
Claimed Benny Agbayani from Rockies on waivers.

August 27, 2002
Joe Nelson released.

August 29, 2002
Chris Haney released.

September 3, 2002
Sold Tim Young to Indians.

September 30, 2002
Rob Ryan granted free agency.

October 2, 2002
Claimed Jason Shiell from Padres on waivers.

October 9, 2002
Claimed Brandon Lyon from Blue Jays on waivers.

October 14, 2002
Kevin Brown and Calvin Pickering granted free agency.

October 15, 2002
Jason Boyd, Paxton Crawford, Todd Erdos, Rontrez Johnson, James Lofton, Steve Lomasney, Chris Michalak, Warren Morris, and Bry Nelson granted free agency.

October 22, 2002
Hansel Izquierdo signed as a free agent.

October 28, 2002
Cliff Floyd and Ugueth Urbina granted free agency.

October 29, 2002
Carlos Baerga and Rickey Henderson granted free agency.

October 30, 2002
Tony Clark and Rey Sanchez granted free agency.

November 1, 2002
Dustin Hermanson granted free agency.

November 6, 2002
Chris Coste signed as a free agent.
James Lofton signed as a free agent.

November 8, 2002
Justin Kaye signed as a free agent.

November 18, 2002
Kevin Tolar signed as a free agent.

November 25, 2002
Steve Woodard signed as a free agent.

November 27, 2002
Claimed Ryan Rupe from Devil Rays on waivers.

December 6, 2002
Wayne Gomes released.

December 12, 2002
Traded 2 players to be named later to Reds for Todd Walker; Reds received Josh Thigpen and Tony Blanco (December 16, 2002).

December 15, 2002
Traded Joshua Hancock to Phillies for Jeremy Giambi.

December 16, 2002
Larry Sutton signed as a free agent.
Traded Luis Cruz to Padres for Cesar Crespo.

December 18, 2002
Damian Jackson signed as a free agent.

December 21, 2002
Brian Daubach granted free agency.

December 24, 2002
Chad Fox signed as a free agent.

December 31, 2002
Ramiro Mendoza signed as a free agent.

January 3, 2003
Andy Abad signed as a free agent.

January 6, 2003
Mike Timlin signed as a free agent.

January 10, 2003
Bill Mueller signed as a free agent.

January 17, 2003
Claimed Earl Snyder from Indians on waivers.

January 22, 2003
David Ortiz signed as a free agent.

January 23, 2003
Hector Almonte signed as a free agent.

February 4, 2003
Claimed Bronson Arroyo from Pirates on waivers.

February 15, 2003
Purchased Kevin Millar from Marlins.

February 22, 2003
Robert Person signed as a free agent.

February 25, 2003
Lost Dernell Stenson to Reds on waivers.

March 18, 2003
Traded Javier Lopez to Colorado Rockies for a PTNBL; Red Sox received Ryan Cameron (March 29, 2003).

March 21, 2003
Lou Collier signed as a free agent.

March 25, 2003
Juan Diaz released.
Lost Lou Merloni to Padres on waivers.

March 26, 2003
Returned Adrian Brown to Devil Rays.
Frank Castillo released.

March 28, 2003
Adrian Brown signed as a free agent.
Claimed Dicky Gonzalez from Expos on waivers.

March 31, 2003
James Lofton and Larry Sutton released.

April 11, 2003
Bill Haselman signed as a free agent.

April 15, 2003
Marty McLeary released.

April 17, 2003
Trace Coquillette signed as a free agent.

May 5, 2003
Hansel Izquierdo released.

May 6, 2003
Rudy Seanez signed as a free agent.

May 7, 2003
Claimed Bruce Chen from Astros on waivers.

May 29, 2003
Traded Shea Hillenbrand to Diamondbacks for Byung-Hyun Kim.

June 6, 2003
Traded Matt White to Mariners for Shelton Fulse.

June 12, 2003
Chad Mottola signed as a free agent.

June 22, 2003
Traded Angel Santos to Indians for Jamie Brown.

June 23, 2003
Kelly Dransfeldt signed as a free agent.

June 28, 2003
Purchased Gabe Kapler from Colorado Rockies.

July 2, 2003
Todd Jones signed as a free agent.
Justin Kaye released.

July 7, 2003
Hector Almonte granted free agency.

July 11, 2003
Claimed Bryan Hebson from Expos on waivers.

July 22, 2003
Traded Brandon Lyon and Anastacio Martinez to Pirates for Mike Gonzalez and Scott Sauerbeck.

July 29, 2003
Rudy Seanez released.

July 30, 2003
Chad Fox released.
Traded Phil Dumatrait to Reds for Scott Williamson.

July 31, 2003
Traded Mike Gonzalez, Freddy Sanchez, and cash to Pirates for Brandon Lyon, Jeff Suppan, and Anastacio Martinez.

August 4, 2003
Claimed Dave McCarty from Athletics on waivers.

August 28, 2003
Traded Rene Miniel to Padres for Lou Merloni.

October 3, 2003
Bruce Chen granted free agency.

October 8, 2003
Lou Collier granted free agency.

October 14, 2003
Steve Woodard granted free agency.

October 15, 2003
Trace Coquillette, Chris Coste, Kelly Dransfeldt, Dicky Gonzalez, Junior Herndon, and Chad Mottola granted free agency.

October 21, 2003
Ryan Rupe granted free agency.

October 23, 2003
Adrian Brown granted free agency.

October 24, 2003
Bob Howry released.

October 26, 2003
Robert Person and Todd Walker granted free agency.

October 27, 2003
Dave McCarty and Jeff Suppan granted free agency.

October 28, 2003
Mike Timlin granted free agency.

October 30, 2003
Bill Haselman and Todd Jones granted free agency.

November 10, 2003
Trace Coquillette signed as a free agent.
Adam Hyzdu signed as a free agent.

November 12, 2003
Bobby Jones signed as a free agent.

November 17, 2003
Andy Abad released.
Mike Timlin signed as a free agent.

November 18, 2003
Jeremy Giambi released.
Kevin Tolar released.

November 19, 2003
Tim Hamulack signed as a free agent.

November 20, 2003
Claimed Edwin Almonte from Mets on waivers.
Claimed Phil Seibel from Mets on waivers.

November 28, 2003
Traded Casey Fossum, Brandon Lyon, Jorge de la Rosa, and Michael Goss to Diamondbacks for Curt Schilling.

December 8, 2003
Claimed Mark Malaska from Devil Rays on waivers.

December 15, 2003

Major League Draft

Selected Colter Bean from Yankees.
Selected Lenny DiNardo from Mets.

December 16, 2003
Received Mark Bellhorn from Rockies for UFC.
Dave McCarty signed as a free agent.

December 20, 2003
Edwin Almonte granted free agency.

December 21, 2003
Damian Jackson, Gabe Kapler, Lou Merloni, Scott Sauerbeck, and Jason Shiell granted free agency.

December 22, 2003
Edwin Almonte signed as a free agent.
Gabe Kapler signed as a free agent.
Jason Shiell signed as a free agent.

December 23, 2003
Pokey Reese signed as a free agent.

January 5, 2004
Sent Melvin Dorta to Expos for UFC.

January 7, 2004
Keith Foulke signed as a free agent.

January 8, 2004
Claimed Michel Hernandez from Yankees on waivers.

January 14, 2004
Brian Daubach signed as a free agent.

January 16, 2004
Nick Bierbrodt signed as a free agent.

January 18, 2004
Ed Yarnall signed as a free agent.

January 21, 2004
Claimed Reynaldo Garcia from Rangers on waivers.

January 22, 2004
Lost Reynaldo Garcia to Rangers on waivers.

January 26, 2004
Paul Rigdon signed as a free agent.

February 3, 2004
Terry Shumpert signed as a free agent.

February 6, 2004
Ellis Burks signed as a free agent.

February 13, 2004
Tony Womack signed as a free agent.

February 14, 2004
Carlos Febles signed as a free agent.

February 20, 2004
Frank Castillo signed as a free agent.

March 8, 2004
George Lombard signed as a free agent.

March 18, 2004
Returned Colter Bean to Yankees.
Claimed Frank Brooks from Athletics on waivers.

March 20, 2004
Nick Bierbrodt granted free agency.

March 21, 2004
Traded Tony Womack to Cardinals for Matt Duff.

March 24, 2004
Lost Michel Hernandez to Phillies on waivers.

March 30, 2004
Joe Nelson signed as a free agent.

March 31, 2004
Returned Frank Brooks to Pirates.
Terry Shumpert released.

April 8, 2004
Claimed John Stephens from Orioles on waivers.

April 18, 2004
Received Scott Cassidy from Blue Jays for UFC.

April 19, 2004
Sent Ed Yarnall to Phillies for UFC.

April 21, 2004
Purchased Brad Thomas from Twins.

April 28, 2004
Raul Casanova signed as a free agent.

June 14, 2004
Purchased Matt Beech from Long Island (Atlantic).

June 22, 2004
Curt Leskanic signed as a free agent.

June 24, 2004
Sent Raul Casanova to Royals for UFC.

July 2, 2004
Purchased Brandon Puffer from Padres.
Traded Andrew Shipman to Cubs for Jimmy Anderson.

July 14, 2004
Pedro Astacio signed as a free agent.

July 21, 2004
Received Ricky Gutierrez from Cubs for UFC.

July 24, 2004
Traded John Hattig to Blue Jays for Terry Adams.

July 31, 2004
Traded Henri Stanley to Dodgers for Dave Roberts.
Traded Nomar Garciaparra and Matt Murton to Cubs as part of 4-team trade in which Cubs sent Brendan Harris, Alex Gonzalez, and Francis Beltran to Expos; Expos sent Orlando Cabrera to Red Sox; Minnesota Twins sent Doug Mientkiewicz to Red Sox; and Cubs sent Justin Jones to Minnesota Twins.

August 1, 2004
Jimmy Anderson released.

August 6, 2004
Claimed Mike Myers from Mariners on waivers.

August 18, 2004
Matt Beech released.

August 31, 2004
Purchased Sandy Martinez from Indians.

September 3, 2004
Claimed Tim Hummel from Reds on waivers.

September 22, 2004
Phil Seibel released.

October 4, 2004
Cesar Crespo, Brian Daubach, and Earl Snyder granted free agency.

October 5, 2004
Joe Nelson granted free agency.

October 8, 2004
Bobby Jones granted free agency.

October 11, 2004
Frank Castillo granted free agency.

October 12, 2004
Phil Seibel signed as a free agent.

October 15, 2004
Edwin Almonte, Jamie Brown, Scott Cassidy, Trace Coquillette, Andy Dominique, Matt Duff, Carlos Febles, Tim Hamulack, Bryan Hebson, George Lombard, Brandon Puffer, Jason Shiell, and Brad Thomas granted free agency.

October 28, 2004
Gabe Kapler granted free agency.

October 29, 2004
Terry Adams and Pedro Astacio granted free agency.

November 1, 2004
Orlando Cabrera, Curt Leskanic, Derek Lowe, Dave McCarty, Ramiro Mendoza, Doug Mirabelli, Mike Myers, Pokey Reese, Jason Varitek, and Scott Williamson granted free agency.

November 2, 2004
Ellis Burks and Pedro Martinez granted free agency.

November 5, 2004
Scott Cassidy signed as a free agent.

November 9, 2004
Ricky Gutierrez granted free agency.

November 10, 2004
Claimed Billy Traber from Indians on waivers.

November 18, 2004
Jason Kershner signed as a free agent.

November 19, 2004
Chip Ambres signed as a free agent.
Kris Wilson signed as a free agent.

November 29, 2004
Jamie Brown signed as a free agent.
Doug Mirabelli signed as a free agent.

December 8, 2004
Matt Mantei signed as a free agent.

December 13, 2004
Major League Draft
Selected Adam Stern from Braves.

December 14, 2004
Billy McMillon signed as a free agent.

December 15, 2004
Simon Pond signed as a free agent.

December 17, 2004
John Halama signed as a free agent.
David Wells signed as a free agent.

December 19, 2004
Edgar Renteria signed as a free agent.

December 20, 2004
Traded Dave Roberts to Padres for Jay Payton, Ramon Vazquez, David Pauley, and cash.

December 21, 2004
Lenny DiNardo signed as a free agent.

December 22, 2004
Matt Clement signed as a free agent.
Wade Miller signed as a free agent.

December 24, 2004
Jason Varitek signed as a free agent.

December 27, 2004
Mike Moriarty signed as a free agent.

January 3, 2005
George Lombard signed as a free agent.

January 4, 2005
Jamie Brown released.

January 7, 2005
Jack Cressend signed as a free agent.

January 10, 2005
Josias Manzanillo signed as a free agent.

January 11, 2005
Dave McCarty signed as a free agent.

January 13, 2005
Jason Childers signed as a free agent.
Shawn Wooten signed as a free agent.

January 17, 2005
Geremi Gonzalez signed as a free agent.

January 21, 2005
Luis Figueroa signed as a free agent.

January 27, 2005
Traded Doug Mientkiewicz and cash to Mets for Ian Bladergroen.

February 7, 2005
Dave Berg signed as a free agent.

February 11, 2005
Roberto Petagine signed as a free agent.

February 15, 2005
Received Alejandro Machado from Nationals for UFC.

March 22, 2005
Traded Adam Hyzdu to Padres for Blaine Neal.

March 26, 2005
Jared Sandberg signed as a free agent.

March 29, 2005
Anastacio Martinez released.
Traded Carlos De La Cruz and Kevin Ool to Cardinals for Mike Myers.

March 30, 2005
Charles Johnson released.
Traded Byung-Hyun Kim and cash to Rockies for Charles Johnson and Chris Narveson.

March 31, 2005
Jason Childers and Kris Wilson released.

April 13, 2005
Anastacio Martinez signed as a free agent.

April 16, 2005
John Stephens released.

April 18, 2005
Mike Moriarty released.

May 2, 2005
John Olerud signed as a free agent.

May 5, 2005
Sent Simon Pond to Orioles for UFC.

May 11, 2005
Lost Blaine Neal to Colorado Rockies on waivers.

May 19, 2005
Sold Jason Kershner to Padres.

May 27, 2005
Rich Garces signed as a free agent.

June 6, 2005
Jason Pearson signed as a free agent.

June 22, 2005
Sent Tim Hummel to Cardinals for UFC.

July 6, 2005
Purchased Jim Mann from Nashua (Atlantic).

July 7, 2005
Traded Ramon Vazquez to Indians for Alex Cora.

July 13, 2005
Traded Jay Payton and cash to Athletics for Chad Bradford.

July 15, 2005
Gabe Kapler signed as a free agent.

July 19, 2005
Alan Embree released.
Traded Scott Cassidy to Padres for Adam Hyzdu.
Traded Chip Ambres and Juan Cedeno to Royals for Tony Graffanino.

July 26, 2005
John Halama released.

July 30, 2005
Traded Kenny Perez and Kyle Bono to Diamondbacks for Jose Cruz and cash.

August 6, 2005
Matt Perisho signed as a free agent.

August 8, 2005
Lost Chris Narveson to Cardinals on waivers.

August 9, 2005
Ricky Bottalico signed as a free agent.
Lost Jose Cruz to Dodgers on waivers.
Traded Olivio Astacio to Cubs for Mike Remlinger and cash.

August 14, 2005
Jason Pearson released.

August 19, 2005
Mark Bellhorn released.

August 25, 2005
Ricky Bottalico released.

August 28, 2005
Mike Remlinger released.

August 29, 2005
Claimed Chad Harville from Astros on waivers.

August 31, 2005
Rich Garces released.

September 15, 2005
Matt Perisho released.

September 29, 2005
Traded Rhys Taylor and Yader Peralta to Nationals for Mike Stanton.

October 3, 2005
Shawn Wooten granted free agency.

October 12, 2005
Mike Stanton granted free agency.

October 13, 2005
Adam Hyzdu released.

October 14, 2005
Geremi Gonzalez granted free agency.

October 15, 2005
Dave Berg, Luis Figueroa, George Lombard, Jim Mann, Anastacio Martinez, Billy McMillon, Juan Perez, and Jared Sandberg granted free agency.

October 27, 2005
Kevin Millar and Bill Mueller granted free agency.

October 28, 2005
Johnny Damon and Tony Graffanino granted free agency.

October 31, 2005
Mike Myers granted free agency.

November 1, 2005
Matt Mantei granted free agency.

November 10, 2005
John Olerud granted free agency.

November 11, 2005
Luke Allen signed as a free agent.

November 18, 2005
Gabe Kapler released.

November 24, 2005
Traded Hanley Ramirez, Anibal Sanchez, Harvey Garcia, and Jesus Delgado to Marlins for Josh Beckett, Mike Lowell, and Guillermo Mota.

November 28, 2005
Mark Malaska released.

December 1, 2005
Purchased Jermaine Van Buren from Cubs.

December 7, 2005
Traded Doug Mirabelli to Padres for Mark Loretta.

December 8, 2005
Traded Edgar Renteria and cash to Braves for Andy Marte.

December 9, 2005
Devern Hansack signed as a free agent.

December 11, 2005
Ken Huckaby signed as a free agent.

December 20, 2005
Rudy Seanez signed as a free agent.

December 21, 2005
Chad Bradford and Wade Miller granted free agency.

December 29, 2005
Matt Ginter signed as a free agent.

January 3, 2006
John Flaherty signed as a free agent.

January 9, 2006
J.T. Snow signed as a free agent.

January 11, 2006
Tony Graffanino signed as a free agent.

January 18, 2006
Julian Tavarez signed as a free agent.

January 19, 2006
Willie Harris signed as a free agent.

January 23, 2006
Dustan Mohr signed as a free agent.

January 27, 2006
Traded Guillermo Mota, Andy Marte, Kelly Shoppach, and cash to Indians for Coco Crisp, David Riske and Josh Bard.

February 1, 2006
Craig Breslow signed as a free agent.
Mike Holtz signed as a free agent.
Gabe Kapler signed as a free agent.

February 6, 2006
Alex Gonzalez signed as a free agent.
Roberto Petagine released.

March 16, 2006
Javier Cardona signed as a free agent.

March 19, 2006
Juan Gonzalez signed as a free agent.

March 20, 2006
Traded Bronson Arroyo and cash to Reds for Wily Mo Pena.

March 24, 2006
Claimed Hee-Seop Choi from Dodgers on waivers.

March 28, 2006
Lost Tony Graffanino to Royals on waivers.

April 25, 2006
Corky Miller signed as a free agent.

May 1, 2006
Traded Cla Meredith, Josh Bard, and cash to Padres for Doug Mirabelli.

June 15, 2006
Traded David Riske to White Sox for Javier Lopez.

June 16, 2006
Claimed Kyle Snyder from Royals on waivers.

June 21, 2006
Received Jason Johnson from Indians for UFC.

June 26, 2006
Mike Holtz released.

June 27, 2006
J.T. Snow released.

July 2, 2006
Matt Ginter released.

July 30, 2006
Traded Luis Mendoza to Rangers for Bryan Corey.

August 4, 2006
Purchased Javy Lopez from Orioles for PTNBL and cash; Baltimore received Adam Stern (October 3, 2006).

August 17, 2006
Received Eric Hinske from Blue Jays for UFC.
Carlos Pena signed as a free agent.

August 28, 2006
Jason Johnson and Rudy Seanez released.
Traded Tim Bausher and cash to Reds for Mike Burns.

August 31, 2006
Received Kevin Jarvis from Diamondbacks for UFC.
Traded David Wells to Padres for a PTNBL; Red Sox received George Kotteras (September 5, 2006).

September 8, 2006
Javy Lopez released.

October 2, 2006
Willie Harris granted free agency.

October 3, 2006
Hee-Seop Choi granted free agency.

October 5, 2006
Corky Miller granted free agency.

October 9, 2006
Ken Huckaby and Alejandro Machado granted free agency.

October 10, 2006
Kevin Jarvis granted free agency.

October 13, 2006
Bryan Corey signed as free agent.
Carlos Pena granted free agency.

October 29, 2006
Trot Nixon and Gabe Kapler granted free agency.

October 30, 2006
Mark Loretta and Alex Gonzalez granted free agency.

November 10, 2006
Keith Foulke granted free agency.

November 30, 2006
Hideki Okajima signed as a free agent.

December 14, 2006
Daisuke Matsuzaka signed as a free agent.

December 15, 2006
Julio Lugo signed as a free agent.
Traded Phil Siebel to Angels for Brendan Donnelly.
J.C. Romero signed as free agent.

December 20, 2006
Travis Hughes signed as a free agent.
Alberto Castillo signed as a free agent.
Ed Rogers signed as a free agent.
Kerry Robinson signed as a free agent.

December 21, 2006
Adam Bernero signed as a free agent.

December 22, 2006
Runelvys Hernandez signed as a free agent.

January 4, 2007
Joel Pineiro signed as a free agent.

January 10, 2007
Jamal Strong signed as a free agent.

January 12, 2007
Alex Ochoa signed as a free agent.

January 13, 2007
Tike Redman signed as free agent.

January 24, 2007
Brendan Donnelly signed as a free agent.
Kevin Cash signed as a free agent.

January 26, 2007
J.D. Drew signed as a free agent.

February 14, 2007
Lost Lenny DiNardo to Athletics on waivers.

March 27, 2007
Traded Alberto Castillo to Orioles for Cory Keylor.

March 30, 2007
Alex Ochoa, Tike Redman, and Jamal Strong released.

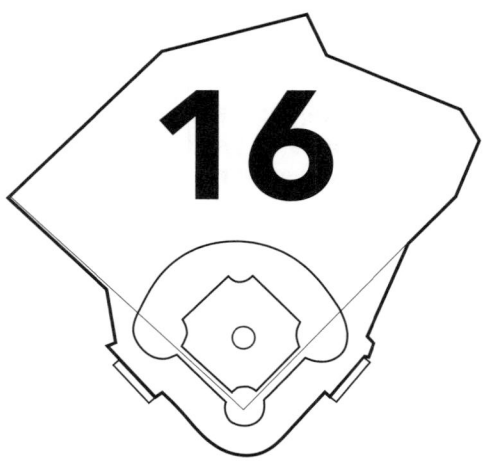

THE AWARDS

Long before fans thought of themselves as Red Sox Nation, the Boston faithful felt their heroes were getting jobbed in the awards voting. Ted Williams was Exhibit A, B, C, and D. Williams finished in the top 10 in the American League Most Valuable Player voting 12 times during the 15 seasons he played at least 100 games. He received at least 1 MVP vote every year that he played except for 1952, when he batted just 10 times. Yet Teddy Ballgame's results in the voting were baffling. He won the award twice, in 1946 and 1949, but he finished second four times: the year he hit .406, his two Triple Crown seasons a war apart, and his .388 season at age 39, the highest anyone had hit since he cracked .400. Each time Williams lost out in close votes to Yankees: Joe DiMaggio in 1941 and 1947, Joe Gordon in 1942, and Mickey Mantle in 1957.

That's not to say that the Red Sox have always been denied in the voting. In 1911 Detroit's Ty Cobb took the first league award decided by baseball writers, called the Chalmers Award (this came a year after Chalmers, an automobile manufacturer of the day, had decided to give a car to the leading hitter, resulting in both Cobb and Nap Lajoie receiving the prize after a bitter batting title dispute). The award was to go to the player deemed "most important and useful" to both his team and the league. Writers have since been trying to come to grips with the vagaries of such decrees.

Boston center fielder Tris Speaker, who finished a distant second in the AL voting in 1911, carried the vote the next year for the pennant-winning Red Sox. The Chalmers Award was given for the last time in 1914.

An MVP was awarded in the AL from 1922 to 1928—with several problematic restrictions—and it resumed on an annual basis in 1931. It has been awarded every year since in both leagues, even during strike seasons. The system originally allowed for one writer from each city to fill out a 10-place ballot. Since 1938 players have been awarded 14 points for a first-place vote. Three voters in each city were chosen to vote between 1938 and 1961, but that was reduced to the current number of two in '62. As for what defines an MVP, that remains an elusive question—Ted Williams certainly thought so—but a loose interpretation seemed to be similar to some people's definition of a work of art: You'd know one when you saw one.

It was more than a quarter century after Speaker, in 1938, that another Red Sox player captured the award: Jimmie Foxx. Williams followed with his two and Jackie Jensen captured the award in 1958, beating out Yankee Bob Turley. Williams' replacement in left field, Carl Yastrzemski, earned MVP for winning the Triple Crown and leading Boston to the pennant during the "Impossible Dream" season of 1967. When the Red Sox took another pennant in 1975, Fred Lynn became the first player in history named MVP and Rookie of the Year the same year. Jim Rice, who'd finished third to Lynn in the MVP voting as a rookie, captured the MVP with a dominant 1978 season. Roger Clemens became the only Red Sox pitcher to win the MVP in 1986, with Rice placing in the top four for the fifth time. Mo Vaughn won a controversial MVP vote for the division champs in 1995, but since then the Red Sox have been on the other end of a couple of contentious decisions.

While Nomar Garciaparra finished a distant second to Ranger Juan Gonzalez in 1998, Pedro Martinez and David Ortiz wound up second in ensuing seasons because some writers had problems voting for players at their positions. Martinez's 1999 season was legendary, allowing three runs a game below the league average, among numerous other feats. He received the most first-place votes for MVP that year. Two writers, however, did not think a pitcher should contend for MVP and left him off their ballots entirely. Martinez finished second to Texas catcher Ivan Rodriguez by a single vote. In 2004 David Ortiz's superb season fueled numerous discussions about whether a designated hitter should by MVP. Yankees third baseman Alex Rodriguez took the award in a tight race.

While the league MVP remains the game's most prestigious award, there are plenty of others that garner serious attention each year. The Cy Young Award, named for the Red Sox pitching great, has been given annually to the best pitcher since 1956 (and to the top hurler in each league since 1967). The award has gone to three Boston hurlers a total of six times: Clemens (3), Martinez (2), and Jim Lonborg (1). Since the Rookie of the Year was established in 1947 (and given in each league starting in 1949), five Red Sox have been honored, starting with Walt Dropo in 1950. The Manager of the Year Award, the fourth award voted on by the baseball writers, has gone to two Red Sox skippers since it was inaugurated in 1983: Jimy Williams and John McNamara.

The Red Sox have received 35 Gold Gloves for fielding excellence through 2006, with the hardware doled out to everyone from the great (Yaz) to the obscure (Doug Griffin) to the peculiar (Jimmy Piersall). Silver Sluggers have been awarded to the top hitters at each position since 1980. Dwight Evans and Carney Lansford became the first Red Sox to win the award in 1981, with Evans the first player in team history to take home a Silver Slugger and a Gold Glove the same year.

There are plenty of other awards. Many have long been distributed by a publication (*The Sporting News*) and one is even doled out by an antacid manufacturer (Rolaids). There are awards for perseverance and humanitarianism, a Red Sox Hall of Fame, and honors distributed at the local level. The section ends with retired uniform numbers, the greatest single honor the club can bestow on a player who has worn the uniform since 1931, the year the Red Sox started stitching numbers on their backs.

Finalists for the MVP, Cy Young, Rookie of the Year, and manager of the Year are listed by their places in the voting (with their place in parentheses). An asterisk is used when there is a tie in the voting. A number sign (#) indicates a unanimous winner. Red Sox finishing first in the baseball writer award lists are in bold. Years are skipped in these lists if no Red Sox player finishes in the top 10 for MVP and top 5 for the Cy Young, Rookie of the Year, or Manager of the Year. For MVP, Cy Young, and Manager of the Year awards there is also an alphabetical listing of every member of the Red Sox to garner significant support for each award, a list of the years they received that support, the place they finished in the voting, and a ranking of the players with the most seasons garnering such support. A number in brackets next to a player's name identifies the number of times he had a high finish in the voting in his career, including years with other teams. Since a player can only be considered for Rookie of the Year once, the top Red Sox vote getters are simply listed by year.

Most Valuable Player Award

Red Sox Top 10 Finishes by Year

Year	Players
2006	David Ortiz (3)
2005	David Ortiz (2), Manny Ramirez (4)
2004	Manny Ramirez (3), David Ortiz (4)
2003	David Ortiz (5), Manny Ramirez (6), Nomar Garciaparra (7)
2002	Manny Ramirez (9)
2001	Manny Ramirez (9)
2000	Pedro Martinez (5), Nomar Garciaparra (9)
1999	Pedro Martinez (2), Nomar Garciaparra (7)
1998	Nomar Garciaparra (2), Mo Vaughn (4*)
1997	Nomar Garciaparra (8)
1996	Mo Vaughn(5)
1995	**Mo Vaughn (1)**, John Valentin (9)
1991	Roger Clemens (10)
1990	Roger Clemens (3)
1988	Mike Greenwell (2), Wade Boggs (6), Dwight Evans (9)
1987	Dwight Evans (4), Wade Boggs (9)
1986	**Roger Clemens (1)**, Jim Rice (3), Wade Boggs (7)
1985	Wade Boggs (4)
1984	Tony Armas (7)
1983	Jim Rice (4)
1982	Dwight Evans (7)
1981	Dwight Evans (3), Carney Lansford (6)
1979	Fred Lynn (4), Dwight Evans (5)
1978	**Jim Rice (1)**, Carlton Fisk (9)
1977	Jim Rice (4), Carlton Fisk (8), Bill Campbell (10)
1975	**Fred Lynn (1)**, Jim Rice (3)
1972	Carlton Fisk (4), Luis Tiant (8)
1970	Carl Yastrzemski (4)
1969	Rico Petrocelli (7)
1968	Ken Harrelson (3), Carl Yastrzemski (9)
1967	**Carl Yastrzemski (1)**, Jim Lonborg (6), George Scott (10)

1965	Carl Yastrzemski (10)	Dave Ferriss	1945 (4), 1946 (7)
1964	Dick Radatz (9)	Carlton Fisk	1972 (4), 1977 (8), 1978 (9)
1963	Dick Radatz (5), Carl Yastrzemski (6)	Ira Flagstead	1925 (7)
1959	Jackie Jensen (10)	Jimmie Foxx	**1938 (1)**, 1939 (2), 1940 (6)

1958   **Jackie Jensen (1)**, Ted Williams (7), Pete Runnels (10)

1957   Ted Williams (2), Frank Malzone (7)

1956   Ted Williams (6)

1955   Ted Williams (4), Jackie Jensen (10)

1954   Ted Williams (10)

1953   Jimmy Piersall (9)

1951   Ellis Kinder (7)

1950   Walt Dropo (6)

1949   **Ted Williams (1)**, Mel Parnell (4), Ellis Kinder (5), Vern Stephens (7)

1948   Ted Williams (3), Vern Stephens (4)

1947   Ted Williams (2)

1946   **Ted Williams (1)**, Bobby Doerr (3), Johnny Pesky (4), Dave Ferriss (7), Dom DiMaggio (9)

1945   Dave Ferriss (4)

1944   Bobby Doerr (7), Bob Johnson (9)

1942   Ted Williams (2), Johnny Pesky (3), Tex Hughson (6)

1941   Ted Williams (2), Dick Newsome (9)

1940   Jimmie Foxx (6)

1939   Jimmie Foxx (2), Ted Williams (4)

1938   **Jimmie Foxx (1)**, Joe Cronin (7)

1937   Joe Cronin (7)

1935   Wes Ferrell (2)

1934   Wes Ferrell (8)

1931   Earl Webb (6)

1928   Buddy Myer (9)

1925   Ira Flagstead (7)

1923   George Burns (10)

1913   Tris Speaker (4)

1912   **Tris Speaker (1)**, Joe Wood (5), Heinie Wagner (10)

1911   Tris Speaker (6)

Red Sox Top 10 MVP Finishes by Player, Alphabetical

Tony Armas	1984 (7)
Wade Boggs	1985 (4), 1986 (7), 1987 (9), 1988 (6)
George Burns	1923 (10)
Bill Campbell	1977 (10)
Roger Clemens	**1986 (1)**, 1990 (3), 1991 (10)
Joe Cronin	1937 (7), 1938 (7)
Bobby Doerr	1944 (7), 1946 (3)
Walt Dropo	1950 (6)
Dwight Evans	1979 (5), 1981 (3), 1982 (7), 1987 (4), 1988 (9)
Wes Ferrell	1934 (8), 1935 (2)

Nomar Garciaparra	1997 (8), 1998 (2), 1999 (7), 2000 (9), 2003 (7)
Mike Greenwell	1988 (2)
Ken Harrelson	1968 (3)
Tex Hughson	1942 (6)
Jackie Jensen	1955 (10), **1958 (1)**, 1959 (10)
Bob Johnson	1944 (9)
Ellis Kinder	1949 (5), 1951 (7)
Carney Lansford	1981 (6)
Jim Lonborg	1967 (6)
Fred Lynn	**1975 (1)**, 1979 (4)
Frank Malzone	1957 (7)
Pedro Martinez	1999 (2), 2000 (5)
Buddy Myer	1928 (9)
Dick Newsome	1941 (9)
David Ortiz	2003 (5), 2004 (4), 2005 (2), 2006 (3)
Mel Parnell	1949 (4)
Johnny Pesky	1942 (3), 1946 (4)
Rico Petrocelli	1969 (7)
Jimmy Piersall	1953 (9)
Dick Radatz	1963 (5), 1964 (9)
Manny Ramirez	2001 (9), 2002 (9), 2003 (6), 2004 (3), 2005 (4)
Jim Rice	1975 (3), 1977 (4), **1978 (1)**, 1983 (4), 1986 (3)
Pete Runnels	1958 (10)
George Scott	1967 (10)
Tris Speaker	1911 (6), **1912 (1)**, 1913 (4)
Vern Stephens	1948 (4), 1949 (7)
Luis Tiant	1972 (8)
John Valentin	1995 (9)
Mo Vaughn	**1995 (1)**, 1996 (5), 1998 (4*)
Heinie Wagner	1912 (10)
Earl Webb	1931 (6)
Ted Williams	1939 (4), 1941 (2), 1942 (2), **1946 (1)**, 1947 (2), 1948 (3), **1949 (1)**, 1954 (10), 1955 (4), 1956 (6), 1957 (2), 1958 (7), 1956 (6), 1957 (2), 1958 (7)
Joe Wood	1912 (5)
Carl Yastrzemski	1963 (6), 1965 (10), **1967 (1)**, 1968 (9), 1970 (4)

Red Sox Top 10 MVP Finishes, Total

Ted Williams	12	Manny Ramirez	5 [8]
Dwight Evans	5	Nomar Garciaparra	5
Jim Rice	5	Carl Yastrzemski	5
Wade Boggs	4	David Ortiz	4
Roger Clemens	3 [6]	Jimmie Foxx	3 [6]

Carlton Fisk	3 [5]	Jackie Jensen	3
Tris Speaker	3	Mo Vaughn	3
Vern Stephens	2 [6]	Joe Cronin	2 [5]
Bobby Doerr	2	Wes Ferrell	2
Dave Ferriss	2	Ellis Kinder	2
Fred Lynn	2	Pedro Martinez	2
Johnny Pesky	2	Dick Radatz	2
Bob Johnson	1 [3]	Tony Armas	1 [2]
Bill Campbell	1 [2]	Buddy Myer	1 [2]
George Scott	1 [2]	Luis Tiant	1 [2]
George Burns	1	Walt Dropo	1
Ira Flagstead	1	Mike Greenwell	1
Ken Harrelson	1	Tex Hughson	1
Carney Lansford	1	Jim Lonborg	1
Frank Malzone	1	Dick Newsome	1
Mel Parnell	1	Rico Petrocelli	1
Jimmy Piersall	1	Pete Runnels	1
John Valentin	1	Heinie Wagner	1
Earl Webb	1	Joe Wood	1

Cy Young Award

Red Sox Top 5 Finishes by Year

2004	Curt Schilling (2), Pedro Martinez (4)
2003	Pedro Martinez (3)
2002	Pedro Martinez (2), Derek Lowe (3)
2000	**Pedro Martinez (1#)**
1999	**Pedro Martinez (1#)**
1998	Pedro Martinez (2)
1995	Tim Wakefield (3)
1992	Roger Clemens (3)
1991	**Roger Clemens (1)**
1990	Roger Clemens (2)
1987	**Roger Clemens (1)**
1986	**Roger Clemens (1#)**
1978	Dennis Eckersley (4)
1977	Bill Campbell (5)
1976	Luis Tiant (5)
1974	Luis Tiant (4*)
1967	**Jim Lonborg (1)**

Red Sox Top 5 Cy Young Finishes by Pitcher, Alphabetical

Bill Campbell	1977 (5)
Roger Clemens	**1986 (1#)**, **1987 (1)**, 1990 (2), **1991 (1)**, 1992 (3)
Dennis Eckersley	1978 (4)
Jim Lonborg	**1967 (1)**
Derek Lowe	2002 (3)

Pedro Martinez	1998 (2), **1999 (1#)**, **2000 (1#)**, 2002 (2), 2003 (3)
Curt Schilling	2004 (2)
Luis Tiant	1974 (4*), 1976 (5)
Tim Wakefield	1995 (3)

Red Sox Top 5 Cy Young Finishes, Total

Roger Clemens	5 [10]	Pedro Martinez	5 [6]
Luis Tiant	2	Dennis Eckersley	1 [4]
Curt Schilling	1 [4]	Bill Campbell	1
Jim Longborg	1	Derek Lowe	1
Tim Wakefield	1		

Rookie of the Year Award

Top 5 Red Sox Finishes By Year

2006	Jonathan Papelbon (2)
1999	Brian Daubach (4)
1997	**Nomar Garciaparra (1#)**
1988	Jody Reed (3)
1987	Mike Greenwell (2)
1982	Wade Boggs (3)
1981	Rich Gedman (2), Bob Ojeda (3)
1980	Dave Stapleton (2)
1975	**Fred Lynn (1)**, Jim Rice (2)
1974	Rick Burleson (4)
1972	**Carlton Fisk (1#)**
1971	Doug Griffin (4)
1969	Mike Nagy (2)
1967	Reggie Smith (2)
1966	George Scott (3)
1962	Dick Radatz (5)
1961	**Don Schwall (1)**, Chuck Schilling (4)
1957	Frank Malzone (2)
1955	Billy Klaus (2), Norm Zauchin (3)
1953	Tom Umphlett (2)
1952	Sammy White (3)
1950	**Walt Dropo (1)**
1948	Billy Goodman (5)

Manager of the Year Award

Red Sox Top 5 Finishes by Year

2004	Terry Francona (5)
2003	Grady Little (4)
2001	Jimy Williams (4)
1999	**Jimy Williams (1)**
1998	Jimy Williams (2)
1995	Kevin Kennedy (2)

1991	Joe Morgan (4*)	
1990	Joe Morgan (3)	
1988	Joe Morgan (2)	
1986	**John McNamara (1)**	

Red Sox Top 5 Finishes by Manager, Alphabetical

Terry Francona	2004 (5)
Kevin Kennedy	1995 (2)
Grady Little	2003 (4)
John McNamara	**1986 (1)**
Joe Morgan	1988 (2), 1990(3), 1991, (4*)
Jimy Williams	1998 (2), **1999 (1)**, 2001(4)

Red Sox Top 5 Finishes, Total

Joe Morgan	3
Jimy Williams	3
Grady Little	1 (2)
Terry Francona	1
Kevin Kennedy	1
John McNamara	1

Gold Glove Awards

Recognizing the underrated art of defense, the baseball glove and equipment manufacturer Rawlings began awarding Gold Gloves to the best fielders at each position on the diamond in 1957. The Red Sox have traditionally not been regarded as a great fielding team, but the Sox have won their share of Gold Gloves, especially the outfielders who patrol the treacherous acreage and wacky angles of Fenway Park. Below is a list of those award winners in alphabetical order and the years they won along with a ranking of which Boston fielders won the most Gold Gloves.

Red Sox Gold Glove Winners, Alphabetical

Mike Boddicker	P	1990
Ellis Burks	OF	1990
Rick Burleson	SS	1979
Dwight Evans	OF	1976, 1978, 1979, 1981–85
Carlton Fisk	C	1972
Doug Griffin	2B	1972
Fred Lynn	OF	1975, 1978–80
Jackie Jensen	OF	1959
Frank Malzone	3B	1957–59
Tony Pena	C	1991

Jimmy Piersall	OF	1958
George Scott	1B	1967–68, 1971
Reggie Smith	OF	1968
Jason Varitek	C	2005
Carl Yastrzemski	OF	1963, 1965, 1967–69, 1971, 1977

Red Sox Gold Gloves by Position and Times Won

Pitcher (1)	Mike Boddicker	1
Catcher (3)	Carlton Fisk	1
	Tony Pena	1
	Jason Varitek	1
First Base (3)	George Scott	3 (8)
Second Base (1)	Doug Griffin	1
Third Base (3)	Frank Malzone	3 (4)
Shortstop (1)	Rick Burleson	1
Outfield (23)	Dwight Evans	8
	Carl Yastrzemski	7
	Fred Lynn	4
	Jimmy Piersall	1 (2)
	Jackie Jensen	1
	Reggie Smith	1
	Ellis Burks	1

Silver Slugger Awards

In 1980 Hillerich & Bradsby, the manufacturers of the Louisville Slugger bat, created the Silver Slugger Awards to honor the best offensive player at each position each year. Below are lists of the Red Sox who have won the award and a ranking of which Red Sox players have won the most Silver Sluggers.

Red Sox Silver Slugger Winners, Alphabetical

Tony Armas	CF	1984
Don Baylor	DH	1986
Wade Boggs	3B	1983, 1986–89, 1991
Ellis Burks	CF	1990
Dwight Evans	RF	1981, 1987
Nomar Garciaparra	SS	1997
Mike Greenwell	LF	1987
Carney Lansford	3B	1981
Bill Mueller	3B	2003
David Ortiz	DH	2004–06
Manny Ramirez	LF	2001–06
Jim Rice	LF	1983–84
John Valentin	SS	1995
Mo Vaughn	1B	1995
Jason Varitek	C	2005

Red Sox Silver Sluggers by Times Won

Wade Boggs	6 (8)
Manny Ramirez	5 (9)
David Ortiz	3
Dwight Evans	2
Jim Rice	2
Tony Armas	1
Ellis Burks	1
Nomar Garciaparra	1
Mike Greenwell	1
Carney Lansford	1
Bill Mueller	1
Mo Vaughn	1
John Valentin	1
Jason Varitek	1

The Sporting News Awards

When the American League ceased giving out an official MVP Award after the 1929 season, the weekly newspaper *The Sporting News*, then known as "the Bible of Baseball," immediately stepped into the breach and started selecting its own Player of the Year in 1930. Over the years *The Sporting News* has added many other awards to its repertoire, including Pitcher of the Year, Rookie Player of the Year, Rookie Pitcher of the Year, Manager of the Year, Reliever of the Year, Comeback Player of the Year, and Executive of the Year. *The Sporting News* is no longer strongly tied to baseball, but most of these awards are still presented annually in some form. While voting totals for these awards have never been released to the public, the names of the winners provide an important thread into the history of baseball. The Red Sox have received their fair share.

AL Player of the Year

1978	Jim Rice
1975	Fred Lynn
1968	Ken Harrelson
1967	Carl Yastrzemski
1958	Jackie Jensen
1957	Ted Williams
1949	Ted Williams
1947	Ted Williams
1944	Bobby Doerr
1938	Jimmie Foxx

AL Pitcher of the Year

2000	Pedro Martinez
1999	Pedro Martinez
1991	Roger Clemens
1986	Roger Clemens
1967	Jim Lonborg
1949	Ellis Kinder

AL Rookie Player of the Year

1997	Nomar Garciaparra
1981	Rich Gedman
1975	Fred Lynn
1972	Carlton Fisk

AL Rookie Pitcher of the Year

1993	Aaron Sele
1969	Mike Nagy
1961	Don Scwhall

AL Manager of the Year

1999	Jimy Williams
1986	John McNamara
1967	Dick Williams

AL Comeback Player of the Year

1998	Bret Saberhagen
1995	Tim Wakefield
1972	Luis Tiant
1969	Tony Conigliaro
1968	Ken Harrelson

AL Fireman/Reliever of the Year

1998	Tom Gordon
1977	Bill Campbell
1964	Dick Radatz
1962	Dick Radatz
1960	Mike Fornieles

Major League Executive of the Year

1975	Dick O'Connell
1967	Dick O'Connell
1946	Tom Yawkey

Other National Awards

While the aforementioned awards are generally well known, they are not the end of the national honors in the game. The Rolaids Relief Award has been presented every year since 1976 to the top relief pitcher according to a Rolaids statistical formula. The Fred Hutchinson and Lou Gehrig Awards are given to major league baseball players who are outstanding citizens of the game and make significant contributions to their communities.

Not listed is the Tony Conigliaro Award, a prestigious tribute especially in New England because of the man it honors. It has been given annually since 1991, the year after Tony C. died in poor health at age 45. He was a native hero and the club's right-handed compliment to Carl Yastrzemski when he was hit by a pitch in the face in 1967, leading to eye problems that ended his career despite comebacks both valiant and heartbreaking. The award is given annually to a player who overcomes a life-threatening obstacle and provides inspiration to others. No Red Sox player has ever won the award, but 2006 Boston third baseman Mike Lowell, who overcame testicular cancer and started his rookie year for the Florida Marlins just three months after surgery, was the recipient in 1998.

Rolaids Relief Pitcher of the Year Award Winners

1998   Tom Gordon
1977   Bill Campbell

Fred Hutchinson Memorial Award Winners

2006   Mark Loretta
1994   Andre Dawson
1970   Tony Conigliaro
1967   Carl Yastrzemski

Lou Gehrig Memorial Award Winner

1980   Tony Perez

Boston Baseball Writers Awards

The Boston chapter of the Baseball Writers Association of America presents numerous awards to Red Sox and other major league personnel at its annual dinner each winter. The annual winners of three of those awards are listed below. The Tom Yawkey Award, handed out annually since 1938 but rechristened after the Red Sox owner's death in 1976, is awarded to the Boston MVP. Before 1953 members of the Boston Braves were also eligible for the award. The Jackie Jensen Spirit Award is given annually to a Red Sox player who plays with the effort and desire that Jackie Jensen personified when he played for the Red Sox in the 1950s. The BoSox Club Man of the Year Award is presented to an individual associated with the Red Sox who has made great contributions to both the club and the community.

Jackie Jensen Spirit Award Winners

2006   Mike Lowell, 3B
2005   Johnny Damon, CF
2004   Johnny Damon, CF
2003   Kevin Millar, 1B
2002   Tim Wakefield, P
2001   Brian Daubach, 1B–DH
2000   Pete Schourek, P
1999   Jason Varitek, C
1998   Bret Saberhagen, P
1997   Jeff Frye, 2B–3B
1996   Bill Haselman, C
1993   Andre Dawson, RF–DH
1992   Steve Palermo, Umpire
1991   Jeff Gray, P
1990   Tony Pena, C

Thomas A. Yawkey Red Sox Most Valuable Player Award

2006   David Ortiz, DH   3
2005   David Ortiz, DH
2004   David Ortiz, DH
2003   Jason Varitek, C
2002   Derek Lowe, P; Pedro Martinez, P   3
2001   Trot Nixon, OF
2000   Pedro Martinez, P
1999   Pedro Martinez, P
1998   Nomar Garciaparra, SS   2
1997   Nomar Garciaparra, SS
1996   Mo Vaughn, 1B   4
1995   Mo Vaughn, 1B
1994   Mo Vaughn, 1B
1993   Mo Vaughn, 1B
1992   Roger Clemens, P   4
1991   Roger Clemens, P
1990   Roger Clemens, P
1989   Nick Esasky, 1B
1988   Mike Greenwell, LF
1987   Dwight Evans, 1B–RF   4

1986	Roger Clemens, P
1985	Wade Boggs, 3B
1984	Dwight Evans, RF; Tony Armas, CF
1983	Jim Rice, LF 2
1982	Dwight Evans, RF
1981	Dwight Evans, RF
1980	Rick Burleson, SS
1979	Rick Burleson, SS
1978	Jim Rice, LF
1977	Carlton Fisk, C 2
1976	Carl Yastrzemski, 1B–LF 6
1975	Fred Lynn, CF
1974	Carl Yastrzemski,1B–LF
1973	Tommy Harper, LF
1972	Carlton Fisk, C
1971	Reggie Smith, OF
1970	Carl Yastrzemski, 1B–LF
1969	Rico Petrocelli, SS
1968	Ken Harrelson, CF
1967	Carl Yastrzemski, LF
1966	Tony Conigliaro, RF
1965	Carl Yastrzemski, LF
1964	Dick Radatz, P
1963	Carl Yastrzemski, LF
1962	Eddie Bressoud, SS
1961	Chuck Schilling, 2B
1960	Vic Wertz, 1B
1959	Frank Malzone, 3B 2
1958	Jackie Jensen, RF 2
1957	Frank Malzone, 3B
1956	Jimmy Piersall, CF
1955	Ted Williams, LF 4
1954	Jackie Jensen, OF
1953	Ellis Kinder, P
1951	Ellis Kinder, P
1950	Billy Goodman, INF-OF
1949	Ted Williams, LF
1946	Ted Williams, LF
1941	Ted Williams, LF
1938	Jimmie Foxx, 1B

BoSox Club Man of the Year Winners

2006	Gabe Kapler, OF
2005	Mike Timlin, P
2004	Jason Varitek, C
2003	Ron Jackson, Hitting Coach
2002	Carlos Baerga, DH-2B
2001	Ben Mondor, Pawtucket Executive
2000	John Harrington, CEO
1999	Trot Nixon, RF
1998	Tim Wakefield, P
1997	Wendell Kim, Third-Base Coach
1996	Heathcliff Slocumb, P

1995	Tim Naehring, 3B
1994	Ken Ryan, P
1993	Mo Vaughn, 1B
1992	Roger Clemens, P
1991	Tony Fossas, P
1990	Tony Pena, C
1989	Dennis Lamp, P
1988	Bill Fischer, Pitching Coach
1987	Bruce Hurst, P
1986	Marty Barrett, 2B
1985	Wade Boggs, 3B
1984	Mike Easler, DH
1983	Carl Yastrzemski, DH
1982	Bob Stanley, P
1981	Jerry Remy, 2B
1980	Steve Renko, P
1979	Tom Burgmeier, P
1978	Bill Campbell, P
1977	Butch Hobson, 3B
1976	Reggie Cleveland, P
1975	Denny Doyle, 2B
1974	Rick Miller, CF
1973	Tommy Harper, LF
1972	Bob Montgomery, C
1971	John Kennedy, 2B–SS
1970	Gerry Moses, C
1969	Lee Stange, P
1968	Mike Andrews, 2B
1967	Rico Petrocelli, SS

Red Sox Hall of Fame

The Red Sox Hall of Fame was created in 1995 in order to honor the careers of both on-field and off-field Red Sox personnel. Players are eligible for nomination to the Red Sox Hall of Fame if they spent at least three years with the club and have been retired for at least three years. Any player who fits that description and is inducted to the National Baseball Hall of Fame is automatically enshrined in the Red Sox Hall of Fame. There is a 15-member nominating committee consisting of club executives, broadcasters, active and retired members of the media, and other officials from local organizations.

Important moments in Red Sox history are also voted into the Red Sox Hall of Fame. A list of those moments is included below along with a list of everyone inducted into the Red Sox Hall of Fame through 2006.

Name, Position	Red Sox Years
Wade Boggs, 3B	1982–89
Dick Bresciani, Exe.	1972–Present
Rick Burleson, SS	1974–80
Bill Carrigan, C/Man.	1906, 1908–16, 1927–29
Ken Coleman, Broadcaster	1966–74, 1979–89

Eddie Collins, Exe.	1933–51
Jimmy Collins, 3B/Man.	1901–07
Tony Conigliaro, RF	1964–67, 1969–70, 1975
Joe Cronin, SS/Man./Exe.	1935–58
Bobby Doerr, 2B	1937–51
Dom DiMaggio, CF	1940–42, 1946–53
Dennis Eckersley, P	1978–84, 1998
Dwight Evans, RF	1972–90
Rick Ferrell, P	1933–37
Dave Ferriss, P	1945–50
Carlton Fisk, C	1969, 1971–80
Jimmie Foxx, 1B	1936–42
Larry Gardner, 3B	1908–17
Billy Goodman, INF-OF	1947–57
Lou Gorman, Exe.	1984–96
Curt Gowdy, Broadcaster	1951–65
Lefty Grove, P	1934–41
John Harrington, Exe.	1973–02
Harry Hooper, OF	1909–20
Tex Hughson, P	1941–44, 1946–49
Bruce Hurst, P	1980–88
Jackie Jensen, RF	1954–59, 1961
Ellis Kinder, P	1948–55
Duffy Lewis, OF	1910–17
Jim Lonborg, P	1965–71
Fred Lynn, CF	1974–80
Frank Malzone, 3B	1955–65
Ned Martin, Broadcaster	1961–92
Ben Mondor, Pawtucket Exe.	1977–Present
Bill Monbouquette, P	1958–65
Joe Morgan, Man./Coach/Scout	1971–Present
Dick O'Connell, Exe.	1949–77
Mel Parnell, P	1947–56
Johnny Pesky, SS-3B	1942,1946–52
Rico Petrocelli, SS-3B	1963, 1965–76
Dick Radatz, P	1962–66
Jerry Remy, 2B/Announcer	1977–84, 1988–Present
Jim Rice, LF	1974–89
Pete Runnels, 1B/2B	1958–62
Babe Ruth, P, LF	1914–19
George Scott, 1B	1966–71
Reggie Smith, CF/RF	1966–73
Tris Speaker, CF	1907–15
Bob Stanley, P	1977–89
Vern Stephens, SS	1948–52
Haywood Sullivan, Exe.	1966–93
Luis Tiant, P	1971–78
Dick Williams, Man.	1967–69
Ted Williams, LF	1939–60
Joe Wood, P	1908–15
Jean Yawkey, Owner	1976–92
Tom Yawkey, Owner	1933–76
Carl Yastrzemski, LF	1961–83
Cy Young, P	1901–06

Moments Inducted into the Red Sox Hall of Fame

- Dave Roberts steals second base against the Yankees in the ninth inning of Game 4 of the 2004 ALCS.
- Bernie Carbo pinch hits a three-run home run in the bottom of the eighth inning to tie Game 6 of the 1975 World Series.
- Earl Wilson throws a no-hitter against the Los Angeles Angels on June 26, 1962 at Fenway Park.
- Dave Henderson hits a two-run home run to put the Red Sox in the lead in the top of the ninth inning in Game 5 of the 1986 ALCS in Anaheim.
- Carlton Fisk hits a game-winning home run off the left-field foul pole against the Cincinnati Reds in the 12th inning of Game 6 of the 1975 World Series.
- Roger Clemens becomes the first pitcher to record 20 strikeouts in a single game against the Seattle Mariners on April 29, 1986.

Retired Uniform Numbers

Despite their long and spectacular history, the Red Sox have retired relatively few uniform numbers. The team has a policy of only retiring the numbers of players who were members of the Red Sox for at least a decade and have been inducted into the Baseball Hall of Fame. Joe Cronin's No. 4 and Ted Williams' No. 9 were the first numbers retired by the organization on May 29, 1984. Bobby Doerr followed in 1988, Carl Yastrzemski in 1989, and Carlton Fisk in 2000. The five uniform numbers retired by the Red Sox, along with Jackie Robinson's number retired in his honor by Major League Baseball in 1997, are posted on Fenway Park's right-field façade.

Red Sox Retired Uniform Numbers

1	Bobby Doerr
4	Joe Cronin
8	Carl Yastrzemski
9	Ted Williams
27	Carlton Fisk
42	Jackie Robinson

National Baseball Hall of Fame

Thirty-four former members of the Red Sox organization have been inducted into the National Baseball Hall of Fame since elections began in 1936. Four of those 34—Bobby Doerr, Ted Williams, Carl Yastrzemski, and owner Tom Yawkey—spent their entire careers with the Red Sox. Doerr, Williams, Yastrzemski, Wade Boggs, Joe Cronin, Rick Ferrell, Carlton Fisk, Jimmie Foxx, and Lefty Grove have been enshrined into the Hall of Fame with a Red Sox cap on their plaques. A total of 14 plaques in Cooperstown belong to men who spent at least 30 percent of their career with the Red Sox.

This section contains the vote totals of every Red Sox who has ever received at least one vote in Hall of Fame balloting. The Red Sox players, managers, and executives are listed in alphabetical order. After each name is the percentage of that individual's career spent with the Red Sox.

When the balloting was conducted by an organization other than the Baseball Writers Association of America, it is noted as the following:

V	Veteran's Election of 1936
O/T Com.	Old-Timers Committee, 1939 to 1949
Vet. Com.	Veterans Committee, 1953 to present.

Other abbreviations used include *N*, which indicates that the voting was conducted by the 1946 Nominating Committee vote, from which no one was directly elected, and *RO*, which indicates a run-off election. Run-offs were held twice during the 1960s after an initial round of balloting by the writers elected no one.

Red Sox in the Hall of Fame

Player	Boston Years	Position(s)	Inducted
Babe Ruth	1914–19	Pitcher/Outfield	1936
Tris Speaker	1907–15	Outfield	1937
Cy Young	1901–08	Pitcher	1937
Jimmy Collins	1901–07	Manager/Third Base	1945
Jesse Burkett	1905	Outfield	1946
Jack Chesbro	1909	Pitcher	1946
Lefty Grove	1934–41	Pitcher	1947
Herb Pennock	1915–17, 1919–22	Pitcher	1948
Jimmie Foxx	1936–42	First Base	1951
Ed Barrow	1918–20	Manager	1953
Al Simmons	1943	Outfield	1953
Joe Cronin	1935–47	Manager/Shortstop	1956
Joe McCarthy	1948–50	Manager	1957
Heinie Manush	1936	Outfield	1964
Ted Williams	1939–42, 1945–60	Outfield	1966
Red Ruffing	1924–30	Pitcher	1967
Waite Hoyt	1919–20	Pitcher	1969
Lou Boudreau	1951–54	Manager/Shortstop	1970
Harry Hooper	1909–20	Outfield	1971
Bucky Harris	1934	Manager	1975
Tom Yawkey	1933–76	Owner	1980
George Kell	1952–54	Third Base	1983
Juan Marichal	1974	Pitcher	1983
Luis Aparicio	1971–73	Shortstop	1984
Rick Ferrell	1933–37	Catcher	1984
Bobby Doerr	1937–44, 1946–51	Second Base	1986
Carl Yastrzemski	1961–83	Outfield/First Base	1989
Fergie Jenkins	1976–77	Pitcher	1991
Tom Seaver	1986	Pitcher	1992
Orlando Cepeda	1973	Designated Hitter	1999
Carlton Fisk	1969, 1971–80	Catcher	2000
Tony Perez	1980–82	First Base/DH	2000
Dennis Eckersley	1978–84, 1998	Pitcher	2004
Wade Boggs	1982–92	Third Base	2005

Note: Does not include coaches or members of the front office, except for Tom Yawkey.

RICK AGUILERA (4.1)
2006 ... 3

NICK ALTROCK (1.8)
1937 ... 3
1938 ... 7
1939 ... 6
1953 ... 1
1954 ... 2
1958 ... 20
1960 ... 18

LUIS APARICIO (14.1)
Inducted in 1984
1979 ... 120
1980 ... 124
1981 ... 48
1982 ... 174
1983 ... 252
1984 ... 341

BOB BAILEY (2.3)
1984 ... 1

ED BARROW (6.7)
Inducted in 1953
Executive
1953 Vet. Com.

JACK BARRY (26.1)
1938 ... 3
1939 ... 1

DON BAYLOR (11.7)
1994 ... 12
1995 ... 12

MOE BERG (22.3)
1958 ... 3
1960 ... 5

CHARLIE BERRY (51.6)
1955 ... 1
1958 ... 3

JACK BILLINGHAM (1.5)
1986 ... 1

MAX BISHOP (11.7)
1955 ... 1
1956 ... 1
1958 ... 4
1960 ... 5

WADE BOGGS (66.6)
Inducted in 2005
2005 ... 474

LOU BOUDREAU (5.2)
Inducted in 1970
1956 ... 2
1958 ... 64
1960 ... 35
1962 ... 12
1964 ... 68
1964 RO ... 43
1966 ... 115
1967 ... 143
1967 RO ... 68
1968 ... 146
1969 ... 218
1970 ... 232

BILL BUCKNER (20.9)
1996 ... 10

JESSE BURKETT (7.2)
Inducted in 1946
1936 V ... 1
1937 ... 1
1938 ... 2
1942 ... 4
1945 ... 2
1946 NOM ... 2
1946 O/T Com.

JOE BUSH (22.7)
1958 ... 5

BILL CAMPBELL (27.4)
1993 ... 1

BILL CARRIGAN (100.0)
1937 ... 5
1938 ... 4
1939 ... 2
1945 ... 3

ORLANDO CEPEDA (6.7)
Inducted in 1999
1980 ... 48
1981 ... 77
1982 ... 42
1983 ... 59
1984 ... 124
1985 ... 114
1986 ... 152
1987 ... 179
1988 ... 199
1989 ... 176
1990 ... 211
1991 ... 192

1992 ... 246
1993 ... 252
1994 ... 335
1999 Vet. Com.

BEN CHAPMAN (14.0)
1949 ... 1
1952 ... 1

JACK CHESBRO (0.3)
Inducted in 1946
1937 ... 1
1938 ... 2
1939 ... 6
1946 NOM ... 1
1946 O/T Com.

JACK CLARK (11.1)
1998 ... 7

JIMMY COLLINS (43.0)
Inducted in 1945
1936 V ... 8
1936 ... 58
1937 ... 66
1938 ... 79
1939 ... 72
1942 ... 68
1945 ... 121
1945 O/T Com.

SHANO COLLINS (25.8)
1937 ... 1

DOC CRAMER (32.2)
1956 ... 4
1958 ... 2
1960 ... 1
1962 ... 1
1964 ... 12

GAVY CRAVATH (7.7)
1937 ... 2
1938 ... 2
1939 ... 2
1946 NOM ... 1
1947 ... 2

LOU CRIGER (62.1)
1936 V ... 1
1936 ... 7
1937 ... 16
1938 ... 11
1939 ... 2
1946 NOM ... 6

JOE CRONIN (53.4)
Inducted in 1956
1947 ... 6
1948 ... 25
1949 ... 33
1949 RO ... 16
1950 ... 33
1951 ... 44
1952 ... 48
1953 ... 69
1954 ... 85
1955 ... 135
1956 ... 152

ANDRE DAWSON (7.5)
2002 ... 214
2003 ... 248
2004 ... 253
2005 ... 270
2006 ... 317

DOM DIMAGGIO (100.0)
1960 ... 4
1962 ... 2
1964 ... 12
1968 ... 8
1969 ... 13
1970 ... 15
1971 ... 15
1972 ... 36
1973 ... 43

BILL DINNEEN (46.0)
1938 ... 4
1939 ... 7
1942 ... 1
1945 ... 1
1946 NOM ... 1

BOBBY DOERR (100.0)
Inducted in 1986
1953 ... 2
1956 ... 5
1958 ... 25
1960 ... 15
1962 ... 10
1964 ... 24
1964 RO ... 5
1966 ... 30
1967 ... 35
1967 RO ... 15
1968 ... 48

1969 ... 62
1970 ... 75
1971 ... 78
1986 Vet. Com.

WALT DROPO (22.0)
1967 ... 1

JOE DUGAN (5.8)
1937 ... 1
1938 ... 1
1948 ... 3
1949 ... 2
1956 ... 1
1958 ... 5
1960 ... 8

DENNIS ECKERSLEY (22.5)
Inducted in 2004
2004 ... 421

HOWARD EHMKE (31.9)
1938 ... 1
1949 ... 1
1951 ... 1
1952 ... 1
1953 ... 3
1954 ... 4
1955 ... 8
1956 ... 8
1958 ... 7
1960 ... 12

DWIGHT EVANS (96.1)
1997 ... 28
1998 ... 49
1999 ... 18

RICK FERRELL (27.7)
Inducted in 1984
1956 ... 1
1958 ... 1
1960 ... 1
1984 Vet. Com.

WES FERRELL (34.3)
1948 ... 1
1949 ... 1
1956 ... 7
1960 ... 8
1962 ... 1

CARLTON FISK (43.1)
Inducted in 2000
1999 ... 330
2000 ... 397

EDDIE FOSTER (19.0)
1947 ... 2

JIMMIE FOXX (38.3)
Inducted in 1951
1936 ... 21
1946 NOM ... 26
1947 ... 10
1948 ... 50
1949 ... 85
1949 RO ... 89
1950 ... 103
1951 ... 179

GARY GAETTI (0.2)
2006 ... 4

MIKE GREENWELL (100.0)
2002 ... 2

MARV GRISSOM (3.7)
1966 ... 2

LEFTY GROVE (34.7)
Inducted in 1947
1936 ... 12
1945 ... 28
1946 NOM ... 71
1946 ... 61
1947 ... 123

BUCKY HARRIS (3.4)
Inducted in 1975
Manager
1938 ... 1
1939 ... 1
1948 ... 3
1949 ... 11
1950 ... 4
1951 ... 9
1952 ... 12
1953 ... 21
1958 ... 45
1960 ... 31
1975 Vet. Com.

GRADY HATTON (17.5)
1966 ... 4
1967 ... 1

TOMMY HELMS (1.5)
1983 ... 1

DAVE HENDERSON (7.2)
2000 ... 2

PINKY HIGGINS (19.8)
1950 ... 2
1951 ... 1
1958 ... 6
1960 ... 3

HARRY HOOPER (71.3)
Inducted in 1971
1937 ... 6
1938 ... 4
1939 ... 5
1948 ... 2
1950 ... 2
1951 ... 3
1971 Vet. Com.

ELSTON HOWARD (7.0)
1974 ... 19
1975 ... 23
1976 ... 55
1977 ... 43
1978 ... 41
1979 ... 30
1980 ... 29
1981 ... 83
1982 ... 40
1983 ... 32
1984 ... 45
1985 ... 54
1986 ... 51
1987 ... 44
1988 ... 53

WAITE HOYT (5.2)
Inducted in 1969
1939 ... 1
1942 ... 1
1946 NOM ... 1
1948 ... 7
1949 ... 7
1950 ... 11
1951 ... 13
1952 ... 12
1953 ... 14
1954 ... 14
1955 ... 33
1956 ... 37
1958 ... 37
1960 ... 29
1962 ... 18
1969 Vet. Com.

BRUCE HURST (62.5)
2000 ... 1

FERGIE JENKINS (8.7)
Inducted in 1991
1989 ... 234
1990 ... 296
1991 ... 334

JACKIE JENSEN (72.3)
1967 ... 3
1968 ... 3
1969 ... 1
1970 ... 2
1971 ... 1
1972 ... 1

BOB JOHNSON (15.4)
1948 ... 1
1956 ... 1

SAM JONES (24.3)
1939 ... 1
1955 ... 1
1956 ... 1

JOE JUDGE (2.1)
1937 ... 1
1938 ... 2
1949 ... 1
1955 ... 2
1956 ... 2
1958 ... 9
1960 ... 15

GEORGE KELL (13.1)
Inducted in 1983
1964 ... 33
1964 RO ... 8
1966 ... 29
1967 ... 40
1967 RO ... 11
1968 ... 47
1969 ... 60
1970 ... 90
1971 ... 105
1972 ... 115
1973 ... 114
1974 ... 94
1975 ... 114
1976 ... 129
1977 ... 141
1983 Vet. Com.

KEN KELTNER (0.9)
1958 ... 1
1960 ... 1

ELLIS KINDER (75.4)
1964 ... 3

CARNEY LANSFORD (12.4)
1998 ... 3

BILL LEE (77.2)
1988 ... 3

DUFFY LEWIS (81.2)
1937 ... 3
1938 ... 5
1939 ... 6
1945 ... 1
1951 ... 2
1952 ... 11
1953 ... 20
1954 ... 20
1955 ... 34

JIM LONBORG (48.0)
1985 ... 3
1986 ... 3

SPARKY LYLE (28.9)
1988 ... 56
1989 ... 25
1990 ... 25
1991 ... 15

FRED LYNN (42.1)
1996 ... 26
1997 ... 22

HEINIE MANUSH (4.1)
Inducted in 1964
1948 ... 1
1949 ... 1
1956 ... 13
1958 ... 22
1960 ... 20
1962 ... 15
1964 Vet. Com.

JUAN MARICHAL (2.3)
Inducted in 1983
1981 ... 233
1982 ... 305
1983 ... 313

CARL MAYS (35.3)
1958 ... 6

JOE MCCARTHY (12.5)
Inducted in 1957
Manager
1939 ... 3
1947 ... 2
1951 ... 1
1953 ... 1
1958 ... 2
1957 Vet. Com.

TIM MCCARVER (1.2)
1986 ... 16

WILLIE MCGEE (3.0)
2005 ... 26
2006 ... 12

STUFFY MCINNIS (25.2)
1937 ... 1
1938 ... 4
1939 ... 4
1948 ... 5
1949 ... 8
1950 ... 1
1951 ... 3

LARRY MCLEAN (1.0)
1937 ... 1

DON MCMAHON (6.9)
1980 ... 1

MARTY MCMANUS (11.8)
1958 ... 2
1960 ... 2

BING MILLER (5.9)
1958 ... 1
1960 ... 6

KEVIN MITCHELL (2.2)
2004 ... 2

WALLY MOSES (10.7)
1958 ... 1
1960 ... 1
1968 ... 4
1969 ... 4
1970 ... 5
1971 ... 7

BUDDY MYER (14.6)
1949 ... 1

BOBO NEWSOM (5.0)
1960 ... 6
1962 ... 3

1964 ... 17
1964 RO ... 1
1966 ... 25
1967 ... 19
1967 RO ... 6
1968 ... 22
1969 ... 32
1970 ... 12
1971 ... 17
1972 ... 31
1973 ... 33

LEFTY O'DOUL (3.7)
1948 ... 4
1949 ... 4
1950 ... 9
1951 ... 13
1952 ... 19
1953 ... 11
1956 ... 5
1958 ... 27
1960 ... 45
1962 ... 13

STEVE O'NEILL (6.7)
1948 ... 2
1949 ... 6
1950 ... 1
1951 ... 3
1952 ... 10
1953 ... 13
1958 ... 10

LARRY PARRISH (2.7)
1994 ... 2

TONY PENA (27.3)
2003 ... 2

HERB PENNOCK (32.6)
Inducted in 1948
1937 ... 15
1938 ... 37
1939 ... 40
1942 ... 72
1945 ... 45
1946 NOM ... 41
1946 ... 16
1947 ... 86
1948 ... 94

TONY PEREZ (10.9)
Inducted in 2000
1992 ... 215
1993 ... 233
1994 ... 263
1995 ... 259
1996 ... 309
1997 ... 312
1998 ... 321
1999 ... 302
2000 ... 385

JOHNNY PESKY (81.0)
1960 ... 1

RICO PETROCELLI (100.0)
1982 ... 3

BOB PORTERFIELD (17.3)
1966 ... 1

JACK QUINN (19.2)
1948 ... 2
1958 ... 9
1960 ... 2

JEFF REARDON (17.0)
2000 ... 24

JERRY REMY (61.5)
1990 ... 1

JIM RICE (100.0)
1995 ... 137
1996 ... 166
1997 ... 178
1998 ... 203
1999 ... 146
2000 ... 257
2001 ... 298
2002 ... 260
2003 ... 259
2004 ... 276
2005 ... 307
2006 ... 337

MUDDY RUEL (17.8)
1946 NOM ... 1
1950 ... 4
1951 ... 1
1952 ... 1
1953 ... 8
1954 ... 5
1955 ... 11
1956 ... 16
1958 ... 10
1960 ... 9

RED RUFFING (30.3)
Inducted in 1967
1948 ... 4
1949 ... 22
1949 RO ... 4
1950 ... 12
1951 ... 9
1952 ... 10
1953 ... 24
1954 ... 29
1955 ... 60
1956 ... 97
1958 ... 99
1960 ... 86
1962 ... 72
1964 ... 141
1964 RO ... 184
1966 ... 208
1967 ... 212
1967 RO ... 266

BABE RUTH (15.6)
Inducted in 1936
1936 ... 215

WALLY SCHANG (17.5)
1948 ... 1
1950 ... 1
1956 ... 1
1958 ... 8
1960 ... 11

EVERETT SCOTT (66.3)
1937 ... 2
1938 ... 2
1939 ... 1
1942 ... 1
1947 ... 1
1948 ... 3
1949 ... 3
1950 ... 3
1951 ... 2

1952 ... 4
1953 ... 5
1954 ... 4
1955 ... 8
1956 ... 1

GEORGE SCOTT (58.6)
1986 ... 1

TOM SEAVER (2.4)
Inducted in 1992
1992 ... 425

SONNY SIEBERT (35.6)
1981 ... 1

AL SIMMONS (1.8)
Inducted in 1953
1936 ... 4
1946 NOM ... 1
1947 ... 6
1948 ... 60
1949 ... 89
1949 RO ... 76
1950 ... 90
1951 ... 116
1952 ... 141
1953 ... 199

LEE SMITH (13.6)
2003 ... 210
2004 ... 185
2005 ... 200
2006 ... 234

REGGIE SMITH (51.0)
1988 ... 3

TULLY SPARKS (5.4)
1946 NOM ... 1

TRIS SPEAKER (38.2)
Inducted in 1937
1936 ... 133
1937 ... 165

BIRDIE TEBBETTS (36.1)
1958 ... 8
1960 ... 1

BOBBY THOMSON (2.2)
1966 ... 12
1967 ... 10
1967 RO ... 1
1968 ... 13
1969 ... 6
1970 ... 4
1971 ... 4
1972 ... 10
1973 ... 3
1974 ... 6
1975 ... 10
1976 ... 9
1977 ... 10
1978 ... 5
1979 ... 11

LUIS TIANT (47.8)
1988 ... 132
1989 ... 47
1990 ... 42
1991 ... 32
1992 ... 50
1993 ... 62
1994 ... 42
1995 ... 45
1996 ... 64

1997 ... 53
1998 ... 62
1999 ... 53
2000 ... 86
2001 ... 63
2002 ... 85

MIKE TORREZ (32.6)
1990 ... 1

DIZZY TROUT (5.0)
1964 ... 1

JOHN TUDOR (37.7)
1996 ... 2

BOBBY VEACH (7.9)
1937 ... 1

MICKEY VERNON (9.2)
1966 ... 20
1967 ... 14
1967 RO ... 2
1968 ... 22
1969 ... 21
1970 ... 10
1971 ... 12
1972 ... 12
1973 ... 23
1974 ... 27
1975 ... 22
1976 ... 52
1977 ... 52
1978 ... 66
1979 ... 88
1980 ... 96

FRANK VIOLA (16.6)
2002 ... 2

RUBE WALBERG (23.9)
1958 ... 1
1960 ... 1

BUCKY WALTERS (10.5)
1950 ... 4
1952 ... 3
1953 ... 10
1956 ... 5
1958 ... 33
1960 ... 19
1962 ... 5
1964 ... 35
1964 RO ... 8
1966 ... 56
1967 ... 65
1967 RO ... 24
1968 ... 67
1969 ... 20
1970 ... 29

BILL WAMBSGANSS (17.9)
1942 ... 1
1950 ... 1
1953 ... 1
1954 ... 4
1955 ... 5
1956 ... 1

BOB WATSON (4.6)
1990 ... 3

BILLY WERBER (40.8)
1949 ... 1
1950 ... 1
1952 ... 1
1958 ... 3

VIC WERTZ (17.4)
1970 ... 2
1971 ... 2
1972 ... 4
1973 ... 2
1974 ... 2
1975 ... 5
1976 ... 5
1977 ... 4
1978 ... 4

KEN WILLIAMS (14.8)
1956 ... 1
1958 ... 1

TED WILLIAMS (100.0)
Inducted in 1966
1966 ... 282

JIM WILSON (9.3)
1964 ... 2

JOE WOOD (32.6)
1937 ... 13
1938 ... 6
1939 ... 2
1942 ... 1
1946 NOM ... 5
1947 ... 29
1948 ... 5
1950 ... 1
1951 ... 5

WILBUR WOOD (5.5)
1984 ... 14
1985 ... 16
1986 ... 23
1987 ... 26
1988 ... 30
1989 ... 14

TOM YAWKEY (100.0)
Inducted in 1980
Executive
1980 Vet. Com.

CARL YASTRZEMSKI (100.0)
Inducted in 1989
1989 ... 423

RUDY YORK (12.6)
1962 ... 1
1964 ... 10

CY YOUNG (36.1)
Inducted in 1937
1936 V ... 32
1936 ... 111
1937 ... 153

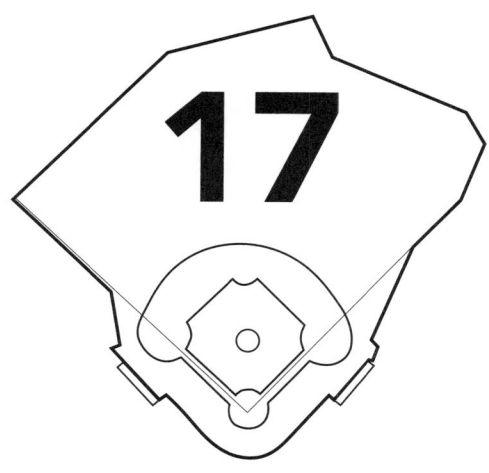

GREAT PERFORMANCES

While the Red Sox have not always known success as a team, the franchise has had many outstanding individual performers from Cy Young to Manny Ramirez. This chapter focuses on performances. Lists cover everything from league leaders to great games to remarkable moments, with breakdowns of selected events. The section culminates with a few extraordinary postseason performances, including one stretched out over three years by Babe Ruth the pitcher and another where John Valentin suddenly turned into Babe Ruth the hitter.

The section begins with lists of Red Sox who have finished at the top of American League statistical categories. These lists are set up by most recent seasons, so David Ortiz and his 2006 club-record 54 home runs, the most in the league since 2002, leads things off. Few franchises can boast a history with as many prodigious players as the Red Sox, as is well illustrated in the pages that follow. An asterisk signifies a tie for the league lead.

League Leaders

Red Sox American League Home Run Champions

Year	Player	Home Runs
2006	David Ortiz	54
1984	Tony Armas	43
1983	Jim Rice	39
1981	Dwight Evans	22
1978	Jim Rice	46
1977	Jim Rice	39
1967	Carl Yastrzemski	44
1965	Tony Conigliaro	32
1949	Ted Williams	43
1947	Ted Williams	32
1942	Ted Williams	36
1941	Ted Williams	37
1939	Jimmie Foxx	35
1919	Babe Ruth	29
1918	Babe Ruth	11
1912	Tris Speaker	10
1910	Jake Stahl	10
1903	Buck Freeman	13

Red Sox American League Batting Champions

Year	Player	Average
2003	Bill Mueller	.326
2002	Manny Ramirez	.349
2000	Nomar Garciaparra	.372
1999	Nomar Garciaparra	.357
1988	Wade Boggs	.366
1987	Wade Boggs	.363
1986	Wade Boggs	.357
1985	Wade Boggs	.368
1983	Wade Boggs	.361
1981	Carney Lansford	.336
1979	Fred Lynn	.333

1968	Carl Yastrzemski	.301
1967	Carl Yastrzemski	.326
1963	Carl Yastrzemski	.321
1962	Pete Runnels	.326
1960	Pete Runnels	.320
1958	Ted Williams	.328
1957	Ted Williams	.388
1950	Billy Goodman	.354
1948	Ted Williams	.369
1947	Ted Williams	.343
1942	Ted Williams	.356
1941	Ted Williams	.406
1938	Jimmie Foxx	.349
1932	Dale Alexander	.367

Red Sox American League Runs Leaders

1989	Wade Boggs	*113
1988	Wade Boggs	128
1984	Dwight Evans	121
1975	Fred Lynn	103
1974	Carl Yastrzemski	93
1970	Carl Yastrzemski	125
1967	Carl Yastrzemski	112
1951	Dom DiMaggio	113
1950	Dom DiMaggio	131
1949	Ted Williams	150
1947	Ted Williams	125
1946	Ted Williams	142
1942	Ted Williams	141
1941	Ted Williams	135
1940	Ted Williams	134
1919	Babe Ruth	103
1903	Patsy Dougherty	107

Red Sox American League RBI Leaders

2006	David Ortiz	137
2005	David Ortiz	148
1995	Mo Vaughn	126*
1984	Tony Armas	123
1983	Jim Rice	126*
1978	Jim Rice	139
1968	Ken Harrelson	109
1967	Carl Yastrzemski	121
1959	Jackie Jensen	112
1958	Jackie Jensen	122
1955	Jackie Jensen	116*
1950	Walt Dropo, Vern Stephens	155*
1949	Vern Stephens, Ted Williams	159*
1947	Ted Williams	114

1942	Ted Williams	137
1939	Ted Williams	145
1938	Jimmie Foxx	175

Red Sox American League Hits Leaders

1997	Nomar Garciaparra	209
1985	Wade Boggs	240
1978	Jim Rice	213
1967	Carl Yastrzemski	189
1947	Johnny Pesky	207
1946	Johnny Pesky	208
1940	Doc Cramer	200*
1938	Joe Vosmik	201
1914	Tris Speaker	193
1903	Patsy Dougherty	195

Red Sox American League Slugging Percentage Leaders

2004	Manny Ramirez	.613
1979	Fred Lynn	.637
1978	Jim Rice	.600
1977	Jim Rice	.593
1975	Fred Lynn	.566
1970	Carl Yastrzemski	.592
1967	Carl Yastrzemski	.622
1965	Carl Yastrzemski	.536
1957	Ted Williams	.731
1954	Ted Williams	.635
1951	Ted Williams	.556
1949	Ted Williams	.650
1948	Ted Williams	.615
1947	Ted Williams	.634
1946	Ted Williams	.667
1942	Ted Williams	.648
1941	Ted Williams	.735
1939	Jimmie Foxx	.694
1938	Jimmie Foxx	.704
1919	Babe Ruth	.657
1918	Babe Ruth	.555

Red Sox American League On-Base Percentage Leaders

2006	Manny Ramirez	.439
2003	Manny Ramirez	.427
2002	Manny Ramirez	.450
1989	Wade Boggs	.430
1988	Wade Boggs	.476
1987	Wade Boggs	.461
1986	Wade Boggs	.453

1985	Wade Boggs	.450
1983	Wade Boggs	.444
1982	Dwight Evans	.402
1979	Fred Lynn	.423
1970	Wade Boggs	.452
1968	Carl Yastrzemski	.426
1967	Carl Yastrzemski	.418
1965	Carl Yastrzemski	.395
1961	Carl Yastrzemski	.418
1958	Ted Williams	.458
1957	Ted Williams	.526
1956	Ted Williams	.479
1954	Ted Williams	.513
1951	Ted Williams	.464
1949	Ted Williams	.490
1948	Ted Williams	.497
1947	Ted Williams	.499
1946	Ted Williams	.497
1942	Ted Williams	.499
1941	Ted Williams	.553
1940	Ted Williams	.442
1939	Jimmie Foxx	.464
1938	Jimmie Foxx	.462
1919	Babe Ruth	.456
1912	Tris Speaker	.464
1908	Doc Gessler	.394

Red Sox American League Strikeout Leaders

Year	Player	Strikeouts
2002	Pedro Martinez	239
2001	Hideo Nomo	220
2000	Pedro Martinez	284
1999	Pedro Martinez	313
1996	Roger Clemens	257
1991	Roger Clemens	241
1988	Roger Clemens	291
1967	Jim Lonborg	246
1942	Tex Hughson	113
1901	Cy Young	158

Red Sox American League ERA Leaders

Year	Player	ERA
2003	Pedro Martinez	2.22
2002	Pedro Martinez	2.26
2000	Pedro Martinez	1.74
1999	Pedro Martinez	2.07
1992	Roger Clemens	2.41
1991	Roger Clemens	2.62
1990	Roger Clemens	1.93

1986	Roger Clemens	2.48
1972	Luis Tiant	1.91
1949	Mel Parnell	2.78
1939	Lefty Grove	2.54
1938	Lefty Grove	3.08
1936	Lefty Grove	2.81
1935	Lefty Grove	2.70
1916	Babe Ruth	1.75
1915	Joe Wood	1.49
1914	Dutch Leonard	0.96
1901	Cy Young	1.62

Red Sox American League Wins Leaders

2004	Curt Schilling	21
1999	Pedro Martinez	23
1987	Roger Clemens	*20
1986	Roger Clemens	24
1967	Jim Lonborg	*22
1955	Frank Sullivan	*18
1945	Mel Parnell	25
1942	Tex Hughson	22
1935	Wes Ferrell	25
1912	Joe Wood	34
1903	Cy Young	33
1902	Cy Young	32
1901	Cy Young	28

Red Sox American League Inning Leaders

1991	Roger Clemens	271.1
1955	Frank Sullivan	260
1949	Mel Parnell	295.1
1942	Tex Hughson	281
1936	Wes Ferrell	301
1935	Wes Ferrell	322.1
1924	Howard Ehmke	315
1903	Cy Young	341.2
1902	Cy Young	384.2

Red Sox American Triple Crown Winners

Batting

Year	Player	Average	Home Runs	RBI
1942	Ted Williams	.356	36	137
1947	Ted Williams	.343	32	114
1967	Carl Yastrzemski	.326	44	121

Pitching

Year	Player	Wins	Strikeouts	ERA
1901	Cy Young	33	158	1.62
1999	Pedro Martinez	23	313	1.90

The Summer of Love Those Red Sox

The Red Sox franchise was moribund in the mid-1960s. The team on the field had no spark once Ted Williams retired after the 1960 season. Most fans simply stopped coming to Fenway Park completely. The Sox were expected to struggle once again in 1967, but general manager Dick O'Connell brought in a demanding rookie manager, Dick Williams, and several new faces. It quickly became apparent that these were not the same old Sox.

Leading the charge toward the "Impossible Dream" was Ted Williams' successor in left field, Carl Yastrzemski. Yaz had the season of his life and won the Triple Crown, a feat no hitter has achieved since. The Red Sox fought off three teams in the final week of the season in the last true winner-take-all pennant race (baseball switched to multiple divisions after 1968, a season that was a runaway in both leagues). Yaz's September of '67 was about as productive as any month by any player under such pressurized circumstances. The last game of the year, on the first day of October, clinched the pennant and made the dream of the club's first pennant in 21 years a reality. Yaz's other months went all right, too.

Carl Yastrzemski, 1967

Month	G	AB	R	H	2B	3B	HR	RBI	BB	AVG	OBP
Apr.	14	61	8	18	3	2	2	9		.295	.348	.508
May	28	93	22	28	5	1	8	22		.301	.421	.634
June	28	97	15	37	7	0	8	22		.381	.478	.701
July	29	106	17	32	4	0	8	22		.302	.367	.566
Aug.	35	126	28	34	6	1	9	20		.270	.377	.548
Sep.	26	92	21	36	5	0	9	24		.391	.486	.739
Oct.	1	4	1	4	1	0	0	2		1.000	1.000	1.250
Total	**161**	**579**	**112**	**189**	**31**	**4**	**44**	**121**		**.326**	**.418**	**.622**

Highs and Lows

This portion covers many of the greatest—and a few of the worst—performances in a season, in a month, in a game, and in an inning by Red Sox hitters, pitchers, and fielders. It also includes marks set by the team as a whole. All seasonal records are based on the minimum number of plate appearances required for eligibility for the batting title and other rate-based awards.

Red Sox Single Season Highs, Individual Batters

Games Played	163	Jim Rice (1978)
Plate Appearances	758	Wade Boggs (1985)
At-Bats	684	Nomar Garciaparra (1997)

Bases On Balls	162	Ted Williams (1947, 1949)
Int. Bases On Balls	33	Ted Williams (1957)
Hit By Pitcher	35	Don Baylor (1986)
Hits	240	Wade Boggs (1985)
Games Hit In Safely	135	Wade Boggs (1985)
Singles	187	Wade Boggs (1985)
Doubles	67	Earl Webb (1931)
Triples	22	Tris Speaker (1913)
Home Runs	54	David Ortiz (2006)
Home Runs at Home	35	Jimmie Foxx (1938)
Home Runs on the Road	32	David Ortiz (2006)
Inside-the-Park HRs	8	Tris Speaker (1912)
Grand Slams	4	Babe Ruth (1919)
Pinch hits	18	Joe Cronin (1943)
Pinch-Hit HRs	5	Joe Cronin (1943)
Extra-Base Hits	92	Jimmie Foxx (1938)
Extra Bases	201	Jimmie Foxx (1938)
Total Bases	406	Jim Rice (1978)
Runs	150	Ted Williams (1949)
RBI	175	Jimmie Foxx (1938)
Stolen Bases	54	Tommy Harper (1973)
Caught Stealing	19	Mike Menosky (1920)
Batting Average	.406	Ted Williams (1941)
On-Base Percentage	.553	Ted Williams (1941)
Slugging Average	735	Ted Williams (1941)
Sacrifice flies	12	Jackie Jensen (1955, 1959)
		Jimmy Piersall (1956)
Sacrifice hits	35	Fred Parent (1905)
Ground into Double Plays	36	Jim Rice (1984)
Strikeouts	177	Mark Bellhorn (2004)

Red Sox Single-Season Lows, Individual Batters

Fewest Ground into Double Plays	1	Ellis Burks (1987)
Fewest Strikeouts	9	Stuffy McInnis (1921)

Red Sox Single-Month Highs, Individual Batters

Hits in a Month	53	Johnny Pesky (August 1946)
		Dom DiMaggio (August 1950)
HRs in a Month	14	Jackie Jensen (June 1958)
		David Ortiz (July 2006)

Red Sox Single-Game Highs, Individual Batters

Runs: 6
Johnny Pesky (May 8, 1946 vs. CHI-A)
Spike Owen (August 21, 1986 at CLE)

Hits: 6
Jimmy Piersall (June 10, 1953 at STL-A)

Doubles: 4
 Billy Werber (July 17, 1935 vs. CLE, Game 1)
 Al Zarilla (June 8, 1950 vs. STL-A)
 Orlando Cepeda (August. 8, 1973 at KC)
 Rick Miller (May 11, 1981 at TOR)

Triples: 3
 Patsy Dougherty (September 5, 1903 vs. PHI-A)

Total Bases: 16
 Fred Lynn (June 18, 1975 at DET)

RBI: 10
 Rudy York (July 27, 1946 at STL-A)
 Norm Zauchin (May 27, 1955 vs. WAS)
 Fred Lynn (June 18, 1975 at DET)
 Nomar Garciaparra (May 10, 1999 vs. SEA)

Walks: 6
 Jimmie Foxx (June 16, 1938 at STL-A)

Intentional Walks: 3
 Carl Yastrzemski (April 17, 1968 vs. CHI-A)
 Wade Boggs (April 10, 1990 vs. DET)

Most Strikeouts: 5
 Ray Jarvis (April 20, 1969 vs. CLE)
 Phil Plantier (October. 1, 1991 vs. DET)

Sacrifice Hits: 4
 Jack Barry (August 21, 1916 vs. CLE)

Stolen Bases: 4
 Jerry Remy (June 14, 1980 at CAL)

3-Home Run Games by Red Sox Batters

Jim Tabor (July 4, 1939 at PHI-A)
Ted Williams (July 14, 1946 vs. CLE, Game 1)
Bobby Doerr (June 8, 1950 vs. STL-A)
Clyde Vollmer (July 26, 1951 vs. CHI-A)
Norm Zauchin (May 27, 1955 vs. WAS)
Ted Williams (May 8, 1957 at CHI-A)
Ted Williams (June 13, 1957 at CLE)
Ken Harrelson (June 14, 1968 at CLE)
Joe Lahoud (June 11, 1969 at MIN)
Fred Lynn (June 18, 1975 at DET)
Carl Yastrzemski (May 19, 1976 at DET)
Jim Rice (August 29, 1977 vs. OAK)
Jim Rice (August 29, 1983 at TOR, Game 2)
Tom Brunansky (September 29, 1990 vs. TOR)
Jack Clark (July 31, 1991 vs. OAK, 14 innings)
John Valentin (June 2, 1995 vs. SEA)
Mo Vaughn (September 24, 1996 vs. BAL)
Mo Vaughn (May 30, 1997 vs. NY-AL)
Nomar Garciaparra (May 10, 1999 vs. SEA)
Trot Nixon (July 24, 1999 at DET)
Jason Varitek (May 20, 2001 at KC)

Nomar Garciaparra (July 23, 2002 vs. TB, Game 1)
Bill Mueller (July 29, 2003 at TEX)
Kevin Millar (July 23, 2004 vs. NY-A)

Other Red Sox Records, Individual Batters

Longest Hitting Streak: 34 Games
 Dom DiMaggio (1949)

Consecutive At-Bats Concluding With Hits: 12
 Mike Higgins (1938)

Consecutive Plate Appearances Reaching Base Safely:
 Ted Williams 16 (1957)

Ted Williams: The Last .400 Hitter

In all of baseball history, only 19 players have posted a batting average over .400 in a single season. Only eight players have achieved that level of performance since the beginning of the 20th century. Only one player has done so since Bill Terry hit .401 in 1930. That player, of course, is Ted Williams.

It was 1941, and World War II was already well underway in Europe. Most Americans, however, were still hoping that their country would stay out of the war, and their eyes were more focused on baseball than on what was happening abroad. It was only Ted Williams' third major league season. Williams had already had two superb seasons in 1939 and 1940, but he had not yet established himself yet as a great hitter in historical terms. In his rookie season he had hit .327, seventh-best in the league. In his sophomore season he had batted .344, third in the league. So while Williams had established himself as a possible contender for the batting title, few had any reason to expect a historic season from the Splendid Splinter.

The season started slowly for Williams. Hobbled by an ankle injury he suffered during spring training, Williams wasn't able to start successive games until later April. On the morning of May 3, Williams woke up with a .307 average, the lowest batting average he would have at any point during the season. Only then did Williams start rolling, getting a hit in 28 of his next 29 games and raising his average to .438 on June 5, the highest point his average reached that season. Williams' remarkable hitting, however, was overshadowed during the summer by Joe DiMaggio's hitting streak, which would total 56 games before ending in Cleveland on July 16.

It was around that point that Williams, again struggling through an injury and missing games, saw his average drop slightly below .400 again. After a period during which he started only 1 of 12 games and

377

missed 8 entirely, Williams was back in the lineup for good on July 22. He would not miss another game the rest of the season.

Once his average rose back to .400, it stayed above that mark—even rising to .414—before sliding down because of a 4-for-17 slump. On the next to last day of the season he went 1 for 4 to stand at .3996. Aware that Williams' average would be rounded up to .400, Red Sox manager Joe Cronin offered to rest his star for the season-ending doubleheader in Philadelphia to preserve his average. Williams famously refused the Sunday off and proceeded to go 4 for 5 in the first game and 2 for 3 in the second game, turning his final .406 average into one of baseball's iconic numbers. Years later, when referring to his status as baseball's last .400 hitter, he would proclaim, "If I had known people were going to make such a big deal about it, I would have done it more often."

Ted Williams, 1941 Month-By-Month

	AB	R	H	HR	RBI	BB	K	Mon Avg	Seas Avg
Apr.	18	3	7	1	5	1	1	0.389	0.389
May	101	29	44	6	22	22	3	0.436	0.429
June	94	33	35	8	29	30	5	0.372	0.404
July	63	20	27	6	19	16	5	0.429	0.409
Aug.	107	31	43	10	26	50	8	0.402	0.406
Sep.	73	19	29	6	19	26	5	0.397	0.406
Season	456	135	185	37	120	145	27	0.406	0.406

Ted Williams' Last Series vs. Athletics at Shibe Park

	AB	R	H	HR	RBI	BB	K	Seas Avg
Sept. 27, 1941	4	1	1	0	0	1	1	0.3996
Sept. 28, 1941								
Game 1	5	2	4	1	2	0	0	0.404
Game 2	3	0	2	0	0	0	0	0.406

More Highs and Lows

Red Sox Single-Season Highs, Individual Pitchers

Games	81	Mike Timlin (2005)
Starts	43	Cy Young (1902)
Complete Games	41	Cy Young (1902)
Innings Pitched	384.2	Cy Young (1902)
Wins	34	Joe Wood (1912)
Losses	25	Red Ruffing (1928)
Winning Percentage	.882	Bob Stanley, 15–2 (1978)
Shutouts	10	Cy Young (1904)
		Joe Wood (1912)
Saves	46	Tom Gordon (1998)
Strikeouts	313	Pedro Martinez (1999)
Strikeouts Per 9 IP	13.2	Pedro Martinez (1999)
Bases On Balls Allowed	134	Mel Parnell (1949)
Hit Batsmen	20	Howard Ehmke (1923)
		Bronson Arroyo (2004)
Hits Allowed	350	Cy Young (1902)
Home Runs Allowed	38	Tim Wakefield (1996)
Runs Allowed	172	Ted Lewis (1901)
Earned Runs Allowed	140	Wes Ferrell (1936)
Wild Pitches	21	Earl Wilson (1963)

Red Sox Single-Season Lows, Individual Pitchers

ERA	0.96	Dutch Leonard (1914)
Batting Average Against	.167	Pedro Martinez (2000)
On-Base Percentage Against	.213	Pedro Martinez (2000)

Other Red Sox Records, Individual Pitchers

Most Consecutive Scoreless Innings Pitched: 45.2
  Cy Young (1904)

Most Opening Day Starts: 8
  Roger Clemens (1988–94, 1996)

Red Sox Single-Game Highs, Individual Pitchers

Innings: 24
  Joe Harris (September 1, 1906 vs. PHI-A)

Strikeouts: 20
  Roger Clemens (Apr. 29, 1986 vs. SEA; Sept. 18, 1996 at DET)

Balks: 4
  John Dopson (June 13, 1989 vs. DET)

Walks: 11
  Ken Chase (May 9, 1943 vs. WAS, Game 2)
  Mickey McDermott (May 20, 1948 at CLE)

Home Runs Allowed: 6
  Tim Wakefield (August 8, 2004 at DET)

Red Sox Single-Inning Highs, Individual Pitchers

Strikeouts: 4
  Tim Wakefield (August 10, 1999 at KC, 9th)

Batters Faced: 16
Merle Adkins (July 8, 1902 vs. PHI-A, 6th)
Lefty O'Doul (July 7, 1923 vs. CLE, 6th)
Howard Ehmke (September 28, 1923 vs. NY-A, 6th)

Hits Allowed: 12
Merle Adkins (July 8, 1902 vs. PHI-A, 6th)

Runs Allowed: 13
Lefty O'Doul (July 7, 1923 at CLE, 6th)

Red Sox Single-Season Team Records

Most Players: 55 in 1996

Fewest Players: 18 in 1904

Most Games: 163 in 1961, 1978, 1985

Most Extra-Inning Games: 31 in 1943
(15 Won, 14 Lost, 2 Tied)

Most One-Run Games: 59 in 1943 (29–30), 1961 (33–26)

Most Games Won: 105 in 1912 (45 Lost, 2 Tied)

Most Games Lost: 111 in 1932 (43 Won)

Most Consecutive Games Won, Season: 15 in 1946

Most Consecutive Games Won, Home: 24 in 1988

Most Consecutive Games Lost, Season: 20 in 1906

Most Consecutive Years Postseason Appearances:
3 (2003–05)

Highest Team Winning Percentage: .691 in 1912
(Won 105, Lost 47)

Lowest Team Winning Percentage: .279 in 1932
(Won 43, Lost 111)

Other Red Sox Team Records

Longest Game: 6:35 (August 25, 2001)

Longest 9-Inning Game: 4:45 (August 18, 2006)

Longest Winning Streak: 15 Games (April 25–May 10, 1946)

Longest Losing Streak: 20 Games (May 1–24, 1906)

Most Wins in a Month: 25 (July 1948, out of 34 games)

Fewest Errors in a Season: 93 (1988)

Red Sox Single-Season Team Highs, Offense

Most Runs Scored	1,027	1950
Fewest Runs Scored	463	1906
Most Home Runs	238	2003
Most Home Runs, Home	124	1977
Most Home Runs, Road	127	2003

Bases on Balls	835	1949
Strikeouts	1,189	2004
Hit by Pitch	72	2002
Runs Batted In	974	1950
Batting Average	.302	1950
Highest Slugging Average	.491	2003
Grounded into Double Play	174	1990
Left on Base	1,308	1989
Shut Out	28	1906

Red Sox Single-Season Team Lows, Offense

Hit by Pitch	11	1934
Strikeouts	344	1921
Batting Average	.234	1905, 1907
Grounded into Double Play	94	1942
Slugging Average	.292	1907
Caught Stealing	12	2005
Shut Out	1	1995

Red Sox Single-Game Team Highs, Offense

Runs: 29 (vs. STL-A, June 8, 1950)

Hits: 28 (vs. STL-A, June 8, 1950; vs. FLA, June 27, 2003)

Singles: 24 (vs. DET, June 18, 1953)

Doubles: 12 (at DET, July 29, 1990)

Home Runs: 8 (vs. TOR, July 4, 1977)

Total Bases: 60 (vs. STL-A, June 8, 1950)

Pinch Hits: 4 (at NY-A, September 8, 1995)

Strikeouts: 19 (vs. CAL, August 12, 1974)

Bases on Balls: 15 (at WAS, July 7, 1949;
at CHI-A, May 7, 1992)

Grounded into Double Plays: 6 (vs. MIN, July 18, 1990)

Hit into Triple Plays: 2 (vs. MIN, July 17, 1990)

Red Sox Single-Inning Team Highs, Offense

Runs Scored: 17 (vs. DET, June 18, 1953, 7th inning)

Hits: 14 (vs. DET, June 18, 1953, 7th inning)

Doubles: 5 (at TOR, June 21, 1994, 1st inning;
at TOR, June 1, 2003, 3rd inning)

Triples: 4 (vs. DET, May 6, 1934, 4th inning)

Total Bases: 25 (at PHI, September 24, 1940,
6th inning, Game 1)

Red Sox Single-Season Team Highs, Pitching

Bases on Balls	748	(1950)
Complete Games	48	(1904)
ERA	5.02	(1932)
Home Runs Allowed	190	(1987)
Saves	53	(1998)
Shutouts	26	(1918)

Red Sox Single-Season Team Lows, Pitching

Home Runs Allowed	6	(1913)
Shutouts	3	(1923, 1932, 1994)
ERA	2.12	(1904)

Red Sox Single-Season Team Highs, Fielding

Errors	373	(1901)
Double Plays	207	(1949)
Triple Plays	3	(1924, 1979)
Passed Balls	35	(1998)

Red Sox Single-Season Team Lows, Fielding

Errors	66	(2006)
Double Plays	74	(1913)
Passed Balls	3	(1933, 1975)

Red Sox Single-Game Team Highs, Pitching

HRs Allowed: 7 (vs. NY-A, May 30, 1961; vs. BAL, May 17, 1967; at DET, August 8, 2004)

Strikeouts: 20 (vs. SEA, April 29, 1986; at DET, September 18, 1996)

Walks: 18 (at CLE, May 20, 1948)

Roger Clemens' 20-Strikeout Games

When the Seattle Mariners came to Boston to play the Red Sox for the last few days of April 1986, few people were paying attention. The Red Sox, after finishing fifth the previous season in the AL East, were not expected to contend in 1986. Their opponents had yet to achieve a

single .500 season since they began play in 1977. Roger Clemens, who was due to start against the Mariners on the night of April 29, had stormed through the Red Sox farm system and reached the majors as a much talked about prospect two years before, but a series of injuries had quieted the buzz around him. The buzz was a roar and Roger was the "Rocket" by the time he finished the year with a 24–4 record, 238 strikeouts, 2.48 ERA, and a .195 opponent batting average.

The April 29 game was not broadcast over the airwaves either on television or on AM radio; the game had been pushed over onto an FM station because the club's regular radio station was broadcasting the Celtics-Hawks NBA playoff game. Everyone's mind or body seemed to be at Boston Garden, or at least somewhere else. The Red Sox press box was barely occupied. The Fenway Park crowd numbered just 13,414 on a Tuesday night. And then Roger Clemens proceeded to become the first pitcher in baseball history to strike out 20 in a regulation game. Incredibly, he did it without walking a batter. Ten years later, on the last road trip of his final season with the Red Sox, Clemens repeated his feat, this time at Tiger Stadium. Again he walked none and again the crowd was sparse (8,779). It would be two more years before someone not named Clemens matched his record. Below is a list of his strikeout victims in both games listed by inning, with $ noting batters that went down looking.

April 29, 1986 vs. Seattle at Fenway Park

MARINERS 1ST: Spike Owen, Phil Bradley, Ken Phelps

MARINERS 2ND: Jim Presley, $Ivan Calderon

MARINERS 3RD: $Steve Henderson

MARINERS 4TH: Phil Bradley, Ken Phelps, $Gorman Thomas (after Don Baylor dropped a foul pop hit by Thomas on the previous pitch)

MARINERS 5TH: $Jim Presley, $Ivan Calderon, $Danny Tartabull

MARINERS 6TH: Steve Henderson, $Steve Yeager

MARINERS 7TH: Phil Bradley, Ken Phelps

MARINERS 8TH: Ivan Calderon, Steve Henderson

MARINERS 9TH: Spike Owen, $Phil Bradley (The last batter, Ken Phelps, grounded out.)

September 18, 1996 vs. Detroit at Tiger Stadium

TIGERS 1ST: Ruben Sierra, Tony Clark

TIGERS 2ND: Travis Fryman, $Melvin Nieves, Phil Nevin

TIGERS 3RD: Kimera Bartee, $Bobby Higginson

TIGERS 4TH: $Ruben Sierra, Tony Clark

TIGERS 5TH: $Travis Fryman, Melvin Nieves, Phil Nevin

TIGERS 6TH: Kimera Bartee, Bobby Higginson, $Alan Trammell

TIGERS 7TH: Tony Clark, Travis Fryman

TIGERS 8TH: $Brad Ausmus, Phil Hiatt

TIGERS 9TH: Travis Fryman (to end the game)

Other High Strikeout Games by Red Sox

17 Pedro Martinez (May 6, 2000 vs. TB)
17 Pedro Martinez (September 10, 1999 at NY-A)
17 Bill Monbouquette (May 12, 1961 at WAS)
16 Pedro Martinez (April 8, 2001 vs. TB)
16 Pedro Martinez (June 4, 1999 vs. ATL-N)
16 Roger Clemens (July 15, 1988 vs. KC, Game 1)
16 Roger Clemens (May 9, 1988 at KC)
15 Pedro Martinez (July 23, 2000 vs. CHI-A)
15 Pedro Martinez (May 12, 2000 at BAL)
15 Pedro Martinez (September 4, 1999 at SEA)
15 Pedro Martinez (August 24, 1999 at MIN)
15 Pedro Martinez (May 12, 1999 vs. SEA)
15 Pedro Martinez (May 7, 1999 at ANA)
15 Roger Clemens (July 9, 1988 at CHI-A, Game 2)
15 Roger Clemens (August 21, 1984 vs. KC)
15 Mickey McDermott (July 28, 1951 vs. CLE, 16 innings)
15 Joe Wood (July 7, 1911 at STL-A)

Red Sox Consecutive Games Played Streaks

Everett Scott played 1,307 consecutive games between 1916 and 1925. That remains the third longest such streak in baseball history, behind only Cal Ripken and Lou Gehrig's far more famous stints of durability. Scott played the first 832 games of that streak with the Red Sox, and thus is far and away the Red Sox record holder in this category. The other nine follow Scott.

GAMES	PLAYER	STREAK
832	Everett Scott	June 20, 1916–October 2, 1921
535	Buck Freeman	July 27, 1901–June 6, 1905
475	Frank Malzone	May 21, 1957–June 7, 1960
448	Candy LaChance	April 19, 1902–April 28, 1905
413	Freddy Parent	April 26, 1901–Sept. 25, 1903
408	Freddy Parent	May 23, 1904–Sept. 4, 1906
380	Dwight Evans	October 4, 1980–August 6, 1983
360	Vern Stephens	April 19, 1948–August 28, 1950
352	Bobby Doerr	July 19, 1942–August 22, 1944
350	Carl Yastrzemski	July 27, 1968–August 21, 1970

Unassisted Triple Plays

Unassisted triple plays are more of a freak occurrence than a great performance, but they are extraordinarily rare and do require heads up play. There have been only 12 unassisted triple plays in major league history and the Red Sox are one of only two teams to have done it twice (the Cleveland Indians are the other). Both were turned at Fenway Park.

John Valentin, SS - July 8, 1994 vs. SEA
Valentin caught a line drive hit by Marc Newfield, ran to his left, and stepped on second base to force out Mike Blowers. He tagged Keith Mitchell arriving from first base.

George Burns, 1B - September 14, 1923 vs. CLE
Burns caught a line drive hit by Frank Brower. He tagged Rube Lutzke off first base, ran to second base, and stepped on the bag before Riggs Stephenson could return. It was the first triple play unassisted turned by a first baseman in major league history.

Consecutive Game On-Base Streaks

Three of the longest consecutive game on-base streaks in baseball history belong to the Red Sox. Not surprisingly, Ted Williams, the player with the highest career on-base percentage in baseball history, had the longest such streak of any player in history. Williams reached base in 84 consecutive games in 1949. He also is third on the list with a 69-game streak he achieved in 1941. (Joe DiMaggio has the second longest on-base streak on the all-time list; he put together a 74-game on-base streak around his legendary 56 game hitting streak in 1941.) Wade Boggs' 57 game on-base streak in 1985 is tied for eighth all-time.

Ted Williams	84	July 1, 1949–September 27, 1949
Ted Williams	69	July 19–September 28, 1941
Wade Boggs	58	May 27–July 31, 1985

No-Hitters

No-hitters are always special. Even baseball fans whose preference is a slugfest over a pitcher's duels can't help but be drawn into the drama that always builds around a pitcher when it is late in the game and he has held the opposition hitless. The Red Sox have had their share of no-hitters over the years, including a perfect game by Cy Young and the only no-hitter in history with a relief pitcher, Ernie Shore, throwing all nine innings. Shore's game requires an explanation.

Babe Ruth started the first game of the double-header at Fenway Park against Washington on June 23, 1917. Yet after walking the first batter, Ruth argued with

umpire Brick Owens about how balls and strikes were being called, and took a swing at the ump to boot, earning an ejection (and later a suspension). Shore entered and put together the most spotless relief outing ever. The runner on first, Ray Morgan, was thrown out trying to steal, and Shore retired all 26 batters he faced. So it was a perfect game for Shore, but not for the Red Sox pitching staff (or even a complete game). For many years it was considered a perfect game, a ruling some 70 years after the fact by Major League Baseball struck it from perfection. It is considered an official no-hitter. The game was the only no-hitter Babe Ruth was involved in as a pitcher. It remains the only combined no-hitter in club history.

Cy Young threw the first no-hitter in franchise history and the only official perfect game. All Red Sox throwing a no-hitter follow, including a second for Boston in 1908 for Young, which was the third of his career because he had one earlier in the National League. Dutch Leonard is the only other Red Sox pitcher to twice toss no-hitters. A (2) or (3) after Young, Leonard, or Hideo Nomo indicates the no-hitter was the second or third no-hitter of the pitcher's career.

Official No-Hitters
(9 or More Innings) by Red Sox

Cy Young (2), vs. PHI-A, 3–0; May 5, 1904 (Perfect Game)
Jesse Tannehill, at CHI-A, 6–0; August 17, 1904
Bill Dinneen, vs. CHI-A, 2–0; September 27, 1905, Game 1
Cy Young (3), at NY-A, 8–0; June 30, 1908
Joe Wood, vs. STL-A, 5–0; July 29, 1911, Game 1
Rube Foster, vs. NY-A, 2–0; June 21, 1916
Dutch Leonard, vs. STL-A, 4–0; August 30, 1916
Ernie Shore, vs. WAS, 4–0; June 23, 1917, Game 1
Dutch Leonard (2), at DET, 5–0; June 3, 1918
Howard Ehmke, at PHI-A, 4–0; September 7, 1923
Mel Parnell, vs. CHI-A, 4–0; July 14, 1956
Earl Wilson, vs. LA-A, 2–0; June 26, 1962
Bill Monbouquette, at CHI-A, 1–0; August 1, 1962
Dave Morehead, vs. CLE, 2–0; September 16, 1965
Hideo Nomo (2), at BAL, 3–0; April 4, 2001
Derek Lowe, BOS vs. TB, 10–0; April 27, 2002

Official No-Hitters
(9 or More Innings) Against Red Sox

Dusty Rhoades, CLE vs. BOS, 2–1; September 18, 1908
Ed Walsh, CHI-A vs. BOS, 5–0; August 27, 1911
George Mogridge, NY-A at BOS, 2–1; April 24, 1917
Walter Johnson, WAS at BOS AL, 1–0; July 1, 1920
Ted Lyons, CHI at BOS AL, 6–0; August 21, 1926

Bobby Burke, WAS vs. BOS, 5–0; August 8, 1931
Allie Reynolds (2), NY-A vs. BOS AL, 8–0; September 28, 1951, Game 1
Jim Bunning, DET at BOS, 3–0; July 20, 1958, Game 1
Tom Phoebus, BAL vs. BOS, 6–0; April 27, 1968
Dave Righetti, NY-A vs. BOS, 4–0; July 4, 1983
Chris Bosio, SEA vs. BOS, 7–0; April 22, 1993

No-Hit Games
(Less Than 9 Innings) by Red Sox

Matt Young, 8 innings (loss) at CLE, 1–2; April 12, 1992, Game 1
Devern Hansack, 5 innings (rain), vs. BAL, 9–0; October 1, 2006

No-Hit Games
(Less Than 9 Innings) against Red Sox

Dean Chance, 5 innings (rain), MIN vs. BOS, 2–0; August 6, 1967

No-Hit Games Broken Up
in Extra Innings Against Red Sox

Bobo Newsom, STL-A vs. BOS, 1–2; September 18, 1934 (lost on 1 hit in 10th).

Postseason Performances

Babe Ruth's World Series Shutout Streak

Babe Ruth set numerous batting records in World Series play. Many of those marks have since been broken by future Yankees who played in more Series games than the Babe and never sat the bench waiting for their turn to pitch. In the 1916 and 1918 World Series, Ruth the Red Sox southpaw set a record for the most consecutive scoreless innings, 29 2/3, in World Series history. The mark would stand until Yankee Whitey Ford surpassed it in 1962 with 33 2/3 consecutive scoreless innings over 3 World Series. No one has come close to either pitcher's Series streak since then.

Ruth's brilliant pitching is also reflected in his career World Series ERA of 0.87, a Red Sox and American League record and the second-lowest Series ERA of all time for pitchers with at least 30 innings in the fall classic. Harry Brecheen's 0.83 World Series ERA set over the 1943, 1944, and 1946 for the St. Louis Cardinals is the lowest career mark.

Ruth's World Series pitching career comprises three World Series starts for the Red Sox. In his first World

Series start in Game 2 of the 1916 Series against Brooklyn, Ruth gave up a solo home run in the top of the first inning. But Ruth would drive in the tying run and throw 13 more innings without allowing another run that day at Braves Field. It remains the longest outing in postseason history; tough-luck loser Sherry Smith is second on the list for his 13 1/3 innings of work before a soft single snapped the tie.

	IP	H	R	ER	BB	SO	HR
Ruth W (1–0)	14	6	1	1	3	4	1

The streak would continue in the first game of the 1918 World Series pitting the Sox against the Chicago Cubs at Comiskey Park (like the Red Sox used Braves Field as home for the 1915 and 1916 World Series, the Cubs used the other league's park to fit in more paying customers). Ruth edged Hippo Vaughn in the 1–0 win.

	IP	H	R	ER	BB	SO	HR
Ruth W (1–0)	9	6	0	0	1	4	0

Ruth would further extend the streak in Game 4 of that World Series against the Cubs, this time at home in Fenway Park. But with two outs in the eighth, Ruth's streak ended when Bill Killefer scored on a ground out by Charlie Hollocher. The Cubs tied the game later in the inning and after Boston took the lead, Ruth moved to left field and watched Joe Bush saved it.

	IP	H	R	ER	BB	SO	HR
Ruth W (2–0)	8	7	2	2	6	0	0

Bernie Carbo: Hitting '75 in a Pinch

The 1975 World Series is best remembered for Carlton Fisk's game-winning home run off the foul pole at Fenway Park in the 12th inning of Game 6. The game would have been over hours earlier if not for spare outfielder Bernie Carbo. His three-run home run with two outs in the eighth inning off Cincinnati's Rawly Eastwick tied the game. His blast to center field also made Carbo just the second player to hit two pinch home runs in one World Series; he'd also hit one in Game 3 to spark a comeback in Cincinnati. The only other player to twice go deep as a World Series pinch hitter was Chuck Essegian of the 1959 Dodgers, and his second pinch-hit home run came in the ninth inning of the final game of the Series with the Dodgers already up, 8–3.

Carl Yastrzemski's Postseason Legacy

Carl Yastrzemski didn't make many appearances in the highlight films of the 1975 World Series, but the Red Sox hero did have a good Series at the plate. He went 9 for 29 and scored more runs than anyone in that classic fall

classic (7). Together with his 10 hits in 25 at-bats in the 1967 World Series, including the most home runs of anyone in that Series against St. Louis (3), Yaz was a lifetime .352 hitter in the World Series. That remains the highest career average of any Red Sox in World Series play. It is also the 12th highest of any player with at least 50 World Series plate appearances. Figure in his .455 batting average in his only ALCS in 1975 and Yaz's .369 postseason average comes out sixth all-time. Fred Lynn, whose 1975 Boston postseason average of .306 is half the .611 batting explosion for the Angels in the 1982 ALCS, is second all-time in postseason batting average at .407.

1999: No Power Shortage

On October 10, 1999 the Red Sox set numerous team postseason records as they romped to a 23–7 victory over the Cleveland Indians in Game 4 of the Division Series. It was a Sunday during football season and the Red Sox piled up the offense as if Fenway Park was still home to the AFL Patriots. But the Red Sox did it all with bats and shattered numerous marks.

Postseason Team Highs Set in Game 4

Runs	23
Hits	24
At-Bats	48
Total Bases	44
Margin of Victory	16 runs
Extra-Base Hits	12

Jason Varitek set a club postseason record by scoring 5 runs and John Valentin tied the major league mark with 7 RBIs in a postseason game. The Red Sox, who had lost the first two games in the Division Series, came back to win by scoring 44 games in the last 3 games. A brilliant relief outing by Pedro Martinez in Game 5 gave Boston its first postseason series triumph since the 1986 American League Championship Series.

The Red Sox moved on to face the Yankees in the 1999 ALCS, a match that the Sox would lose in 5 games. But in the one game Boston won, Pedro Martinez set a postseason Red Sox record for strikeouts with 12 whiffs in only 7 innings as Boston pounded Roger Clemens and won easily, 13–1. Pedro's dominance that day echoed his performance at Yankee Stadium a little more than one month earlier on September 10, 1999, when he became the only pitcher in baseball history to ever strike out 17 Yankees in a game. The usually dominant Yankees had only two baserunners: Chili Davis, whose second-inning home run was his club's only hit, and Chuck Knoblauch, who was hit by a pitch and thrown out stealing in the eighth.

David Ortiz and the 2004 Comeback

Decades of unsatisfying postseason endings turned around in three weeks that New England will never forget in 2004. Trailing three games to none in the 2004 ALCS and down by a score of 3–2 in the bottom of the ninth inning at Fenway Park, the Red Sox tied the game in the bottom of the ninth as Bill Mueller singled against Mariano Rivera to bring in pinch runner Dave Roberts, who had just stolen second base. The Red Sox won the game in the bottom of the 12th on a two-run homer by David Ortiz, the second in a series of record-breaking "walk-off" hits that Ortiz would have in the postseason. Boston became the first team in major league history, and only the third team in the history of North American sports (the other two occurred in the NHL), to rally from three games down to win a postseason series.

Ortiz started his game-ending mission in Game 3 of the Division Series with a home run in the bottom of the 10th inning off Jarrod Washburn to sweep the Angels. Even after his winning blast in Game 4 of the ALCS against the Yankees, the Red Sox were still down three games to one, so the following night Ortiz helped launch an eighth-inning comeback with a solo home run. Six innings later, Ortiz singled in the winning run in the 14th for his third such hit in 10 days. The rest of Boston's march to the pennant and world championship would occur in nine innings with the Red Sox in the field, but no one in Boston will ever forget Big Papi's place in all that, even if he was in the dugout as the designated hitter when the last outs were made.

"Walk-Off" Postseason Victories by the Red Sox

1912 World Series, Game 8: After New York Giant Fred Snodgrass' "muff" and a foul pop that fell untouched allowed Tris Speaker to tie the game in the bottom of the 10th, Steve Yerkes scored on a sacrifice fly by Larry Gardner to give the Red Sox a 3–2 victory in the deciding game and a world championship in their first season at Fenway Park.

1915 World Series, Game 3: Duffy Lewis singled in Harry Hooper with the winning run in the bottom of the ninth for a 2–1 victory over the Phillies.

1916 World Series, Game 2: Del Gainer pinch hit with one out in the bottom of the 14th inning and singled in Mike McNally to give the Red Sox a 2–1 victory over Brooklyn. Babe Ruth, who threw all 14 innings, earned the win.

1975 World Series, Game 6: Carlton Fisk led off the bottom of the 12th inning against Cincinnati's Pat Darcy with a home run off the left-field foul pole to force a seventh game of the World Series.

2003 ALDS, Game 3: Trot Nixon hit a two-run home run off Oakland pitcher Rich Harden and the Red Sox captured their first win on their way to taking the Division Series.

2004 ALDS, Game 3: After the Angels rallied to tie the game, David Ortiz blasted a two-run home run over the Green Monster in the 10th inning to sweep the Division Series.

2004 ALCS, Game 4: David Ortiz hit a two-run home run off Yankee Paul Quantrill into the right-field bullpen to give the Red Sox their first victory in the ALCS after trailing three games to none.

2004 ALCS, Game 5: The next night David Ortiz came up against Esteban Loaiza in the bottom of the 14th and singled in Johnny Damon with the winning run and spurring the Red Sox toward the greatest postseason series comeback in the game's history. The end of Boston's 86-year world championship drought could be directly traced to Big Papi's bat.

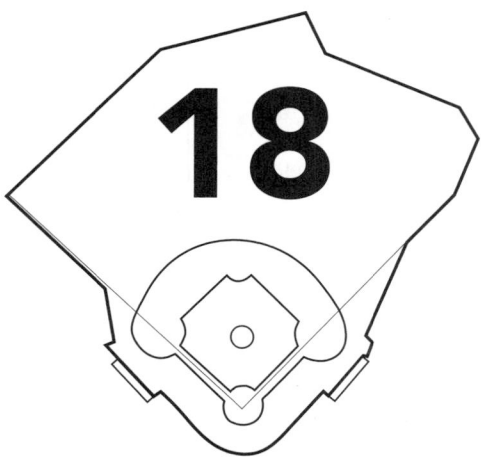

FENWAY PARK

This is not a history of the greatest games at Fenway, nor of the legendary players and clubs that have played there. Nor is it a chronicle of the Red Sox's best seasons. Those can be found elsewhere in this book. This is a look back at how the original Fenway Park evolved over three decades into the beloved institution of modern memory.

More than any other big-league ballpark built since 1901, Fenway Park epitomizes the twentieth century history of modern major league arenas. From the "parks" and "fields" of the early decades of the century, to the grand stadiums of the mid-twentieth century, to the multipurpose superstadia of the 1960s and 1970s, and finally, to the chic retro ballparks of the *fin de siecle*, the home of New England's Olde Towne team has always figured prominently.

Now, in what would be the dotage of most ballparks, Fenway has been extensively remodeled, heavily renovated, and completely re-thought. The result of the past five years of renovations is a ballpark that is beautiful as well as functional: a striking combination of old and new. Fenway Park entered the new century carrying the legitimate mantle of its storied past; that history is now overlaid by a thick veneer of consumer cosseting—designed to pleasantly but efficiently bleed the green from the wallets and purses of fans whose hearts bleed Sox' carmine.

Why has Fenway survived as the other classic fields have been abandoned, one-by-one? Several factors have kept it intact and vibrant. The most important were its intimate size, its location in a thriving neighborhood, a

relatively successful club over the years, and the current visionary Boston ownership. For, when we look back a century, the original Fenway Park was far different from the perception fans have of the grand dame today.

The ballpark in the Fens section of Boston opened during the great ballpark building boom of 1909–1915. That brief but frenzied epoch of construction both introduced the American public to modern sports venues and defined the National Pastime for more than half a century.

Though it is now completely forgotten, and though it was a huge improvement over its predecessor, Fenway started its existence as a pretty plain structure. Thirteen new ballparks were built in those seven historic years for the 16 American League and National League clubs, from Philadelphia's Shibe Park in 1909 to Boston's Braves Field in 1915.

Attendance at Fenway demonstrated that the new home of the Boston Americans was evolutionary, not revolutionary. In its inaugural season, Fenway saw a jump in its turnstile count, but that was mostly due to the Sox winning 105 games and capturing the AL pennant going away. When compared to the major league average, Boston attendance in the three years before Fenway was built was 45 percent higher; in the first three years at Fenway, the Bostons drew at a rate 53 percent above the norm.

In that revolutionary context, Fenway was perceived as rather ordinary for the time. It clearly wasn't regarded with the awe of palatial new parks like Shibe, Forbes, or Comiskey—or even of crosstown Braves

Field. All that remains of those fan palaces of yesteryear, however, are sepia memories and bronze markers, yet Fenway soldiers on in the middle of its tenth decade.

At 95 years old, Fenway is the oldest ballpark in use in the major leagues and the only one certain to see its centennial. While the 2006 bleacher expansion at Wrigley Field has made Chicago's North Side jewel much more likely to survive till 2014, it's still possible that a new owner could decide that the paucity of luxury boxes at the Friendly Confines will necessitate a new home for the Cubbies in the next six years.

The golden years of Fenway stand as a stark contrast to those of Tiger Stadium, Detroit's legendary greensward that coincidentally opened for business on the same day in 1912. While both ballparks housed a flagship franchise in the American League, and while both were witness to the glory years of some of the greatest hitters the game has ever seen, Tiger Stadium was abandoned after the 1999 season. It is now a dark, colossal hulk awaiting demolition, with some hope that the field and a portion of the grandstand can be preserved.

In a stroke of bad luck, the inaugural Opening Day of April 20 for those two parks coincided with the breaking news of the sinking of the *Titanic*, dampening the hoopla and diverting most of the attention from their debuts.

During the 1915 and 1916 World Series the Red Sox chose to play their home games at Braves Field because of its larger capacity and because the newer Braves Field (opened late in 1915) was then thought of as a state-of-the-art venue, even though Fenway was still brand-new. That was a curious reversal of circumstances, as the Miracle Braves played their 1914 World Series home games at Fenway rather than at their tiny, outmoded South End Grounds (capacity about 11,000). The NL Braves also played all their regular-season home games in 1914 and 1915 at Fenway before they moved into the grand new Braves Field on August 18, 1915.

Another turnaround from Fenway Park's origins typifies the evolution of ballparks in the past century:

the change from a solid *pitchers' park* to a historically good hitters' park. In its earliest configurations, Fenway was a great place to pitch, and Babe Ruth's dominance of AL hitters was partly due to his friendly home field. Fenway was also an absolute graveyard for the long ball, which simultaneously depressed the budding slugger's power numbers.

The context in which Ruth both pitched and hit in Fenway is so poorly understood today that few baseball fans and historians know that Ruth's league-leading totals of 11 home runs in 1918 and 29 home runs in 1919 with Boston are *not* out of context with his 54 home runs in 1920 with New York. Thus, if anyone had been analyzing the numbers, the seemingly apocalyptic 1920 season—at least to those diehard fans that decried the ascension of power-based game that The Sultan of Swat wrought—was actually foretold by Ruth's final seasons in Boston.

As if the enormity (in the true sense of the word, not the common usage of today) of the sale of The Bambino needed any more emphasis, the effect on Boston's attendance confirms the magnitude of Harry Frazee's historical miscalculation. For the franchise's first 19 seasons, the Red Sox drew above the big-league average. In 1920, however, crowds plummeted to only 69 percent of the major league norm, then remained below par for the next 14 years while Ruth's mighty Yankees prospered.

In the 1930s, Fenway became a hitter's park when its grand canyon of a center field was shortened by 79 feet. In the 1940s, it became an excellent hitter's park when the distances to right-center and right field were dramatically shortened. Since then, as Fenway's dimensions have held constant, the changes in the park's effect on scoring have mostly been due to changes in *other* AL parks (i.e., to the league offensive average).

The following table shows how different Fenway was when it was built and how it has changed over the years, how an ordinary ballpark a century ago has become the last surviving jewel in the American League's crown.

Fenway Park Vital Statistics

OP YR	CL YR	LFFL	LCF	CF	RCF	RFFL	Deepest	HP/BS	LF HT	LCF HT	CF HT	RCF HT	RF HT	CAPACITY
1912	1920	321		488		314		68	25					35,000
1921	1921	324		488		313.5		68	25	25				
1922	1925	324	360	488	374	313.5	550	68	25	25				
1926	1929	320.5		488		358.5	550	68	25	25				
1930	1930	320		468		358	550	68	25	25				
1931	1932	318		468		325	593	68	25	25				
1933	1933	320		468		358	593	68	25	25				
1934	1935	310	379	389		334	420	60	37	37	17			
1936	1937	310	379	389		332	420	60	37	37	17			
1938	1938	310	379	389		322	420	60	37	37	17			
1939	1939	310	379	389	405	332	420	60	37	37	17			
1940	1941	310	379	389	382	304	420	60	37	37	17	5.25	3'-5'	
1942	1942	310	379	389	381	302	420	60	37	37	17	5.25	3'-5'	
1943	1946	310	379	389	380	302	420	60	37	37	17	5.25	3'-5'	
1947	1947	310	379	389	380	302	420	60	37	37	17	5.25	3'-5'	35,500
1947	1948	310	379	389	380	302	420	60	37	37	17	5.25	3'-5'	
1949	1952	310	379	389	380	302	420	60	37	37	17	5.25	3'-5'	35,200
1953	1953	310	379	389	380	302	420	60	37	37	17	5.25	3'-5'	34,824
1954	1957	310	379	390	380	302	420	60	37	37	17	5.25	3'-5'	
1958	1960	310	379	390	380	302	420	60	37	37	17	5.25	3'-5'	34,819
1961	1964	310	379	390	380	302	420	60	37	37	17	5.25	3'-5'	33,357
1965	1967	310	379	390	380	302	420	60	37	37	17	5.25	3'-5'	33,524
1968	1970	310	379	390	380	302	420	60	37	37	17	5.25	3'-5'	33,375
1971	1975	310	379	390	380	302	420	60	37	37	17	5.25	3'-5'	33,379
1976	1976	310	379	390	380	302	420	60	37	37	17	5.25	3'-5'	33,437
1977	1977	310	379	390	380	302	420	60	37	37	17	5.25	3'-5'	33,513
1978	1978	310	379	390	380	302	420	60	37	37	17	5.25	3'-5'	33,502
1979	1979	310	379	390	380	302	420	60	37	37	17	5.25	3'-5'	33,538
1980	1982	310	379	390	380	302	420	60	37	37	17	5.25	3'-5'	33,536
1983	1984	310	379	390	380	302	420	60	37	37	17	5.25	3'-5'	33,465
1985	1988	310	379	390	380	302	420	60	37	37	17	5.25	3'-5'	33,583
1989	1989	310	379	390	380	302	420	60	37	37	17	5.25	3'-5'	34,182
1990	1990	310	379	390	380	302	420	60	37	37	17	5.25	3'-5'	34,171
1991	1991	310	379	390	380	302	420	60	37	37	17	5.25	3'-5'	34,142
1992	1993	310	379	390	380	302	420	60	37	37	17	5.25	3'-5'	33,925
1994	1996	310	379	390	380	302	420	60	37	37	17	5.25	3'-5'	33,871
1997	1997	310	379	390	380	302	420	60	37	37	17	5.25	3'-5'	
1998	1999	310	379	390	380	302	420	60	37	37	17	5.25	3'-5'	33,455/33,871
2000	2000	310	379	390	380	302	420	60	37	37	17	5.25	3'-5'	33,575/33,991
2001	2002	310	379	390	380	302	420	60	37	37	17	5.25	3'-5'	33,577/33,993
2003	2003	310	379	390	380	302	420	60	37	37	17	5.25	3'-5'	34,482/34,898
2004	2005	310	379	390	380	302	420	60	37	37	17	5.25	3'-5'	34,679/35,095
2006	2006	310	379	390	380	302	420	60	37	37	17	5.25	3'-5'	35,692/36,108
2007		310	379	390	380	302	420	60	37	37	17	5.25	3'-5'	35,920/36,336

Dimensions shown are for the left field and right field foul lines (LFFL/RFFL), left center and right center (LCF/RCF), center field (CF), and for the deepest part of the park (to the right of straightaway center). Also shown is the distance from home plate to the backstop (HP/BS) and the heights (HT) of the outfield walls. The height of the right field wall varies from a low of three feet at the foul pole.

The first year and last year of each particular configuration is shown. Note that, in 1947, there was a midseason change.

Capacity since 1998 is shown as (day/night) and does not include standing room.

Name Origin: At the time, Red Sox owner John Taylor explained to the press "It's in the Fenway section of Boston, isn't it? Then call it Fenway Park." However, his family's real estate business was named Fenway Realty, and that could have been a significant reason for giving the ballpark its name.

Home Teams: Boston Red Sox (1912–Present), Boston Braves (September 1914–July 1915; April 17 and 28, 1946, because of wet paint on seats at Braves Field)

Cost to Build: $650,000

Designed by: Osborn Engineering

Major Renovations: The wooden grandstands and left-field wall were replaced in 1934 by concrete structures, and left field was mostly leveled off. In 1936 a 23-foot screen was installed above the left field wall to prevent damage to property on adjoining Landsdowne Street from flying baseballs. In 1946 a small second deck was installed around the infield, and bullpens were moved in front of the bleachers in right field. The advertisements on the left-field wall were eliminated and the whole wall was painted green in 1947, the same year that lights were finally installed (on June 13). Luxury boxes were added in left and right fields in 1982, and an indoor structure of club seats was built above the infield grandstand in 1989. Seats were installed above the Green Monster and the screen was removed in 2003.

Location: Fenway neighborhood of Boston; north of the Back Bay Fens but just south of Kenmore Square and the Massachusetts Turnpike

Mass Transit Routes to Fenway: Subway/Trolley (Green Line to Kenmore Station), Bus (Routes 8, 8A, 57, 60, and 65 to Kenmore Square)

Altitude: 10 feet

Opening Capacity: 35,000

Current Capacity: 36,108 (35,692 for day games)

Opening Outfield Dimensions: 321/488/314

Current Outfield Dimensions: 310-379/390/380-302 (The park is 420 feet deep to the right of center field)

Opening Fence Heights: 37-37/17/5.25-3 (1940; full data not available for previous years. Left field was originally 25 feet tall before it was rebuilt to 37 feet in 1934.)

Current Fence Heights: 37-37/17/5.25-3

Opening Distance to Backstop: 68 feet

Current Distance to Backstop: 60 feet

Home Opener: April 20, 1912 (Red Sox 7, Yankees 6; games were scheduled for the two previous days but both were rained out.)

Fenway's Other Tenants: NFL Boston Redskins (1933–36), Boston Yanks (1944–48), Boston Patriots (1963–68), NCAA Football Boston College (1916–56, sporadically) Boston University (c. 1940–54); USA (United Soccer Association) Boston Rovers (1967); NASL (North American Soccer League) Boston Beacons (1968)

Other Events Hosted by Fenway: Beanpot Baseball Tournament (1990–Present), College Baseball, Cape Cod Baseball, High School Baseball, Political Rallies, Concerts (2003–Present)

Unique Features

Duffy's Cliff: Left Field used to have an incline of about 5 or 6 feet, so leftfielders running back on the ball would literally have to run uphill. Sox left fielder Duffy Lewis was considered the expert at playing the hill, so it was named after him.

Green Monster: The 37-foot wall in left field is known as the Green Monster. There was always a large wall in Fenway's left field, but the current wall wasn't built until 1934, and it didn't become the dominating feature of Fenway Park until it was painted all green in 1947.

Manual Scoreboard: Fenway has a large manual scoreboard on the left-field wall built in 1934. Personnel inside the Green Monster continually update it during games.

Pesky's Pole: The right-field foul pole is only 302 feet down the line, a very short distance for a home run to have to travel. But the wall quickly deepens as it moves away from the foul line, so there is only a very small area of the right-field wall where a shallow fly ball in fair territory can turn into a home run. Johnny Pesky hit only 17 home runs in his career, but he hit enough sneaky fly balls around the foul pole for homers to make teammate Mel Parnell dub it "Pesky's Pole." The name stuck, probably partly because Parnell later repeated the story as an announcer and Pesky remained part of the Red Sox organization in various capacities for most of the last half century. The pole was officially named for him in 2006.

The Red Seat: Ted Williams connected off Detroit's Fred Hutchinson for the longest home run ever hit into the Fenway bleachers on June 9, 1946. The 502-foot blast hit a man's straw hat on the fly. A seat has been painted red in the bleachers in that exact spot, even though at the time fans sat on a bench as opposed to individual seats.

Small Foul Territory: It has perhaps the smallest foul territory in the majors, just 60 feet behind home plate and almost none in right or left field

The Triangle: An area to the right of center field where the back of the bullpen meets the stands and the 17-foot high wall to form a triangle 420 feet from home plate.

Williamburg: The name given to the bullpens constructed in right field in 1940. The addition of those bullpens shortened the distance most fly balls had to travel to right field to turn into home runs by about 23 feet. The biggest beneficiary was Red Sox slugger Ted Williams who, maybe not totally coincidentally, had just joined the team the year before. Williams hit a significant number of home runs in his career that would not have been home runs in Fenway before the bullpens were installed.

❊ ❊ ❊

Average Ticket Price, 1950: $1.56
Average Ticket Price, 1960: $1.76
Average Ticket Price, 1970: $2.67
Average Ticket Price, 1980: $4.48
Average Ticket Price, 1991: $10.39
Average Ticket Price, 2002: $39.68
Average Ticket Price, 2006: $46.46

Recent Public Address Announcers: Sherm Feller (1967–93), Leslie Sterling (1994–96), Ed Brickley (1997–2002), Carl Beane (2003–Present)

World Series Hosted: 1912, 1914 (Boston Braves), 1918, 1946, 1967, 1975, 1986, and 2004

Playoff Games (and Type) Hosted: 1975 (LCS), 1986 (LCS), 1988 (LCS), 1990 (LCS), 1995 (DS), 1998 (DS), 1999 (DS, LCS), 2003 (DS, LCS), 2004 (DS, LCS), and 2005(DS)

Regular-Season One-Game Tiebreakers Hosted: 1948 and 1978

All-Star Games Hosted: 1946, 1961(Game 2), and 1999

Last Official No-Hitter Thrown: April 27, 2002 (Derek Lowe against the Devil Rays)

Most Runs in a Game, Home Team: 29 (June 8, 1950 vs. Browns)

Most Runs In A Game, Both Teams: 35 (May 31, 1970 vs. White Sox)

Home Runs by Red Sox Players: 5,361

Most Home Runs in by Individual Player, Career: 248 (Ted Williams)

Red Sox Fenway Record: 4,182–3,158 (7,369 games)

Animals in Play: May 17, 1947: A seagull drops a 3-pound fish on Browns pitcher Ellis Kinder; April 14, 1974: Willie Horton's popup over home plate strikes and kills a pigeon which lands at the feet of Red Sox catcher Bob Montgomery.

Longest Game by Innings: September 3–4, 1981 (Red Sox 8 Mariners 7 in 20 innings)

Largest Crowd, Regular Season: 47,627 (September 22, 1935 doubleheader vs. Yankees)

Largest Crowd, Regular Season (1946–2002): 36,388 (April 22, 1975 vs. Indians)

Largest Crowd, Regular Season (2003–Present): 36,920 (June 10, 2006 vs. Indians)

Smallest Crowd: 409 (September 29, 1965 vs. Angels)

Highest Seasonal Attendance: 2,930,588 (2006)

Lowest Seasonal Attendance: 182,150 (1932)

Fenway Park's Park Factors by Decade (How much Fenway Park increased or decreased run scoring when compared to the average AL park):

1912–19: -4.7 percent

1920–29: -1.7 percent

1930–39: +2.7 percent

1940–49: +7.1 percent

1950–59: +17.8 percent

1960–69: +13.0 percent

1970–79: +17.3 percent

1980–89: +9.3 percent

1990–99: +7.6 percent

2000–06: +4.3 percent

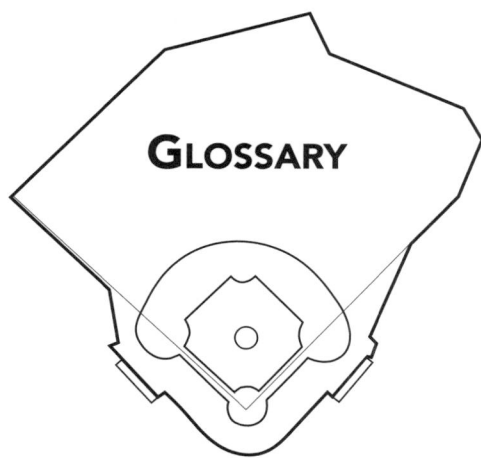

GLOSSARY

Average Value: The analytical statistics in this book almost always use the league average as a baseline. The use of this baseline, which in this book is always set to equal zero, enables readers to quickly see whether the performance being measured is above-average, below-average, and how much above or below. Above-average players are needed to win pennants; below-average players can only make limited contributions to their teams because their efforts, by definition, lead teams to losing. Examples: Zero (0) means average, *+10* would be 10 percent above average, and *-20* would be 20 percent below average. Note that, for batters, league averages do not include pitcher batting.

Basestealing Runs: The basic formula for BSR is (.22 times Stolen Bases) minus (.35 times Caught Stealings).

Basestealing Wins: Basestealing Runs divided by Runs per Win, which varies by year but is usually in the neighborhood of 10. The actual number is equal to 10 times the square root of the combined number of runs scored by both teams per inning, which is usually around 1.

Batter-Fielder Wins: The sum of a player's Batting Wins, Basestealing Wins, and Fielding Wins.

Batting Runs: The basic formula for BR is .33 times (BB plus HBP), plus (.47 times Hits), plus (.38 times Doubles), plus (.55 times Triples), plus (.93 times Home Runs), minus x times (At Bats -Hits), where x is a factor to make the league average come out at zero (normally around .25 to .30) .

Batting Wins: Batting Runs divided by Runs per Win, which varies by year but is usually about 10.

Blown Saves: The number of Save Opportunities not converted by the relief pitcher into Saves because he allowed the tying run to score. This statistic has only been compiled back to 1969, when the modern save was first defined.

Caught Stealing: This statistic is not available for any year prior to 1914 and is not always available for the years 1914–1951.

Differential: The measure of the difference between how many games the team was projected to win (based on its hitting, pitching, fielding, and baserunning performances), and how many games the team actually won. It is shown the same way as teams measure how many games they are behind in the standings.

Earned Run Average: The number of earned runs allowed per 9 innings pitched. The formula for its calculation is (Earned Runs times 9) divided by Innings Pitched. The formula for Adjusted ERA is (League ERA times Park Factor) divided by ERA.

Fielding Runs: Fielding Runs are an estimate of the number of runs saved by a fielder compared to an average player at his position. There is a different formula for every position.

Fielding Wins: Fielding Runs divided by Runs per Win.

Games Behind (or Ahead): The number of games one team is behind (or ahead) of another team in the standings. In this volume, it is usually used when referring to how far a team is out of first place or how far a team in first place is ahead of its rival or rivals. If the Red Sox are 83–66, the Yankees are 72–76, and the Devil Rays are 60–89, the Red Sox are 10½ games in front of the Yankees and 23 games ahead of the Devil Rays, the Yankees are 10½ games behind the Red Sox and 12½ games ahead of the Devil Rays, and the Devil Rays are 23 games behind the Red Sox and 12½ games behind the Yankees.

Normalizing: Most baseball statistics need to be placed in context to be properly understood. A .467 slugging average in Yankee Stadium in 1965 means something very different than a .467 slugging average in Fenway Park in 2005—the former is a far more impressive performance than the latter. By normalizing a statistic and setting the baseline to zero, readers can easily compare players across leagues and eras simply by comparing the percentage by which players over- or underperformed their peers.

On-Base Percentage: OBP is currently defined as (Hits plus Bases on Balls plus Hit-by-Pitches) divided by (At Bats plus Bases on Balls plus Hit-by-Pitches plus Sacrifice Flies). This volume uses that definition from 1954 on, but sacrifice fly data is not available in previous years, so it is not used in calculating the statistic in earlier years.

OPS: The sum of on-base percentage and slugging average was first introduced the 1984 book *The Hidden Game of Baseball*. Its popularity has increased greatly in recent years because it is easy to calculate when OBP and SLG are available and because it provides an easy-to-understand raw measurement of offensive production. Adjusted OPS measures the percentage by which a player's offensive production is better or worse than that of his peers. The formula for AOPS is 100 times (Player OBP divided by League OBP) plus (Player SLG divided by League SLG)) – 200. Thus a player with OBP and SLG equal to the league average will have a rating of 0 (100 x 2 – 200).

Park Factor: This measure of how the team's home park affects hitters and pitchers is used to adjust performance to take into account the context of the team's home park. Separate park factors are used for batting and pitching in order to adjust for the fact that pitchers and hitters never get to face their own teammates.

Pitching Runs: The number of runs a pitcher saves or allows compared to a league average pitcher. The basic formula for Pitching Runs is (League ERA times Innings Pitched) minus Earned Runs. The Pitching Runs calculations in this book include an additional factor that takes Unearned Runs into account.

Pitcher Wins: The total number of wins a pitcher is worth to his team compared to the average pitcher, including his pitching, his fielding, and his batting and basestealing (if any).

Pitching Wins: The wins a pitcher achieves for his team above and below that of a league average pitcher *while pitching*. It is calculated by dividing Adjusted Pitcher Runs by Runs per Win and then adjusting the result for the impact of his innings (since the innings of relief pitchers can have more impact on team wins and losses than the same number of innings from starters).

Positional Adjustment: Value in baseball is determined by the scarcity of talent: it is a lot harder to find a shortstop who can hit 20 home runs per year than a first baseman that can hit 20 homers. Therefore, when calculating the overall value of a player, he is compared to other players at his position.

Quality Relief: A QR is a relief appearance in which a pitcher allows less than one run for every two innings pitched. Inherited runners are counted only in excess of their expected rates of scoring, based on the bases occupied and number of outs, while runners left for the next pitcher are counted at the expected scoring rates, regardless of what actually happens. Note that the QR statistic was developed because the most commonly used stat to evaluate setup pitchers, the Hold, only applies when a reliever is brought into the game in a Save Situation. Thus, it inappropriately applies a measurement designed for closers to middle relievers, who don't get many chances to finish the game and earn the Save. For more information on the research behind QR, see *MapleStreetPress.com*.

Quality Starts: A QS is any start in which a pitcher throws at least six innings and does not allow more than three earned runs.

Run Support: Run support is calculated by adding up all the runs scored in a pitcher's starts, dividing that total by his games started, adjusting that result for the context of his league and home park, and then setting the baseline to zero. The reason to count all runs scored by a pitcher's team is that a pitcher's won-lost record can obviously be affected by runs scored long after he leaves the game. (Note that this definition is different than most published run support numbers, which simply take the number of runs scored by a pitcher's team while he was in the game and normalize to nine innings pitched.)

Save: The Save rule has been changed several times since it was first instituted in 1969. The current definition was adopted in 1975; it awards a Save if a relief pitcher finishes off a victory—and is not the winning pitcher—in three different situations:

1. He enters with a lead of no more than three runs and pitches at least one inning;
2. He enters with the tying run at-bat, on-base, or on-deck; or
3. He pitches at least three innings effectively.

For the years before the Save became an official statistic, the original 1969 rule was retroactively applied. That simpler and much easier standard awarded a Save to any pitcher who finished off a win and did not get credit for the victory.

Stolen Bases: The current definition of a Stolen Base has been used since 1955. Previously, the rules specifying when a Stolen Base was credited to a baserunner had been changed numerous times.

For more technical information on many of these statistics, see MapleStreetPress.com.

Contributors

GARY GILLETTE is co-editor and the creative force behind two groundbreaking sports encyclopedias: *The ESPN Baseball Encyclopedia*—now in its fourth edition—and the *ESPN Pro Football Encyclopedia*, first published in 2006. A nationally known baseball author and analyst and a frequent guest on sports talk radio shows, Gillette is president of 24-7 Baseball, L.L.C. and co-chair of the Society for American Baseball Research's Business of Baseball Committee.

Gillette's recent projects include editing *Tigers Corner 2007*, a new annual from Maple Street Press that was published in March. He is working on a new Tigers encyclopedia for Maple Street called *The Ultimate Tigers Companion* as well as on a history of big-league ballparks, entitled *Diamonds in the Grass*, that will be published by Sterling in 2008. Gillette was also a baseball columnist for *ESPN.com's* MLB Insider in 2005-06. He lives in Detroit with Vicki, his wife of 32 seasons, and their two children, Karolina and Kamil.

PETE PALMER co-authored *The Hidden Game of Baseball*, co-edited *Total Baseball* and *Who's Who in Baseball*, and is a contributor to *The Sporting News MLB Fact Book* and The *Sporting News Record Book*. Inventor of on-base plus slugging, now universally used as a good measure of batting strength, he also discovered the concept of 10 runs per win (i.e., an increase of 10 runs scored or a decrease of 10 runs allowed results is about one extra win). Palmer developed other seminal analytical concepts linear weights and player and pitcher wins. He was a member of the board of directors of Project Scoresheet, a grass roots organization set up to collect play-by-play information for current games, and is a contributor to Retrosheet.

Palmer has been a member of SABR since 1973 and was chairman of the Statistical Analysis Committee for 15 years (1974–88). He was given the Bob Davids Award, SABR's highest honor, in 1989. He was editor of the original *Barnes Official Encyclopedia of Baseball* from 1975–79; served as a consultant to Sports Information Center, the official statisticians for the American League from 1976–87; and introduced on-base percentage as an official AL stat in 1979. Palmer is the co-editor of *The ESPN Baseball Encyclopedia*, now in its fourth edition, and *The ESPN Pro Football Encyclopedia*, the second edition of which will be published in 2007. Palmer was lucky enough to attend Ted Williams' last game in Boston on September 28, 1960, and has been blessed by his marriage to Beth Statz, the grandniece of 1920 Red Sox outfielder Jigger Statz. They have three children: Emily, Daniel, and Stephen.

STUART SHEA is the editor of Maple Street Press' *Wrigley Season Ticket 2007* and an associate editor of *The ESPN Baseball Encyclopedia*, published by Sterling. He is the author of four books, including *Wrigley Field: The Unauthorized Biography* and the upcoming *Fab Four FAQ: Everything Left to Know About the Beatles ... and More!* For nearly 15 years, he has covered the Chicago Cubs for a variety of organizations, most recently for *MLB.com*.

MATTHEW SILVERMAN authored *Mets Essential* for Triumph Books in 2007 and is collaborating on of two forthcoming books. The first, with Jon Springer, is *Mets by the Numbers* from Skyhorse Publishing. The second, with Greg Spira, is Meet the Mets by Maple Street Press. He served as managing editor for the first edition of *The ESPN Pro Football Encyclopedia* and has been an associate editor for *The ESPN Baseball Encyclopedia* since 2004. As associate publisher at Total Sports Publishing, Silverman served as principal editor for *Baseball: The Biographical Encyclopedia* as well as the managing editor for the sixth and seventh editions of *Total Baseball* and the second edition of *Total Football*. He edited several other books, including *Total Packers, Total Cowboys, Total Super Bowl*, and two versions of *Total Mets*. Silverman attended the Ted Williams Baseball Camp for three summers as a youth, and later had the honor of editing Teddy Ballgame's final autobiography, *Ted Williams: My Life in Pictures*. He resides in High Falls, New York, with his wife, Debbie, daughter, Jan, and son, Tyler.

GREG SPIRA is a writer, editor, and researcher living in Kingston, New York. He has served as an associate editor on the first four editions of *The ESPN Baseball Encyclopedia*, *The ESPN Pro Football Encyclopedia*, and helped edit the seventh edition of *Total Baseball*. He co-edited the *USA Today Sports Weekly's Best Baseball Writing 2005* and has contributed to books such as *Baseball: The Biographical Encyclopedia, Baseball Prospectus, Total Basketball*, and *Wrigley Season Ticket 2007*. Spira will be co-editor for the upcoming book, *Meet the Mets*, by Maple Street Press. He has been a member of the Society for American Baseball Research for more than 15 years. As an Internet denizen for more than a decade, he has contributed to many web sites both editorially and conceptually. *BaseballBooks.net*, a web site he maintains, focuses on sports books. Spira grew up in Whitestone, New York, and was graduated with a degree in history from Harvard College. Born a Mets fan, he started rooting for the Red Sox as well on July 14, 1988.

DOUG WHITE is an associate editor of *The ESPN Baseball Encyclopedia* and has been writing about baseball since 1996. He has contributed to many publications, including *The Great American Baseball Stat Book, The Scouting Report*, and *The USA Today Baseball Weekly Insider*. A contributing editor to *Total Baseball Daily*, he now covers the Reds for *MLB.com*. He also writes for John Benson's annual *Rotisserie League Baseball* scouting book and *Rotisserie Baseball Annual*. White umpires college and semi-pro baseball. He and his wife, Anita, live in Muncie, Indiana, with their children Aaron, Sarah, and Katherine.